THE WINSTON CANADIAN DICTIONARY

REVISED

National Library of Canada Cataloguing in Publication

The Winston Canadian dictionary. — Rev. ed.

ISBN 0-7747-1576-6

1. English language—Dictionaries.

PE3235.W55 2003 423 C2003-903125-X

Revised edition of The Winston Canadian Dictionary developed by:
Adrianna Edwards and Ron Edwards
Focus Strategic Communications Incorporated

Nelson
1120 Birchmount Road
Toronto, Ontario M1K 5G4
1-800-668-0671
www.nelson.com

ISBN-13: 978-0-7747-1576-8
ISBN-10: 0-7747-1576-6

More than 2 million copies of the first edition sold.

Printed in Canada

3 4 5 07 06

CONTENTS

INTRODUCTORY MATTER

FOREWORD

In the *Winston Canadian Dictionary* some 38,550 terms have been selected and defined. Most of these are used in a meaningful context in order to help explain them.

In the main listings, the short hyphen is used to show the syllabification. The pronunciation follows in parentheses. It, too, divides the word into syllables by means of the short hyphen, but omits the hyphen under the accents. Example: pop-u-lar-i-ty (pop′u-lar′i-ti). The long hyphen is used to separate the parts of compound words. Examples: jack–rab-bit, cub-by–hole.

Such expressions as *Slang, Colloq., Archaic,* and *Poetic* will help the reader to grasp something of the distinction between literary prose composition and daily speech. With these aids, the reader can learn to understand the place and proper use of each form.

Many compound terms, following the trend of the modern press of Canada, are written solid, rather than hyphenated. Examples: eyetooth, radioactive, sagebrush, transcontinental, watermelon.

The dictionary can prove instrumental in improving enunciation. Using the simplified "Key to Pronunciation" provided on the page opposite, the reader can master the principles of articulate speech—accent, syllabification, and precision of consonant and vowel sounds (especially the long *a*'s, *e*'s, and *u*'s of the accented syllable).

A minimum number of diacritical marks has been employed in the "Key to Pronunciation." The breve [̮̇], the modified breve [̮], and the modified macron [̱], which are indicative of an unaccented vowel, have been omitted. The emphasis is on the pronunciation of the accented vowel in the assumption that the unaccented vowel will then offer little difficulty.

The dictionary should be an integral component of continuing language development. Kept close at hand in the classroom, office and home, it should provide a constant reference for ascertaining the spelling, pronunciation, and meaning of words, new and unusual or old and familiar.

KEY TO PRONUNCIATION

A. VOWELS

Symbol	Key Word
a	c*a*t
ā	*a*pe
ä	j*a*r, c*a*r
å	*a*sk, m*a*st
â	c*a*re
e	t*e*n
ē	*e*ve
ė	writ*e*r
i	*i*f, p*i*ty, b*e*gin, r*e*ly
ī	b*i*te
o	t*o*p
ō	n*o*
ô	d*o*g, *a*ll, *o*r
u	*u*p
ū	m*u*te
û	c*u*r, h*e*r
o͞o	f*oo*l
oo	b*oo*k, f*u*ll

B. DIPHTHONGS

oi	*oi*l
ou	*ou*t

C. (a) COMPOUND CONSONANT SOUNDS

ng	si*ng*
sh	*sh*e
ch	*ch*in
th	thin
th	this
hw	*wh*y
zh	azure
qu	kw, as in *qu*it
x	(1) ks, as in a*x*
	(2) gz, as in exit
	(3) ksh or sh, as in an*x*ious
	(4) zh, as in luxurious (*-gzh*)
	(5) z, as in xylophone (initial *x*)

(b) SINGLE CONSONANT SOUNDS

g	*g*et
j	*j*et
y	*y*et

Fourteen consonants have their ordinary English values: b, d, f, h, k, l, m, n, p, r, t, v, w, z.

N.B.: c, q, and x do not appear as sound symbols since *c* has always the sound of *k* or *s*; *qu* is always *kw*, there being no *q's* unaccompanied by *u's*; and initial *x* is sounded as *z*, otherwise as *ks*, *gz*, *ksh*, *sh*, or *zh*.

D. FOREIGN SOUNDS

ö	Fr. *feu*, Ger. sch*ö*n
ô̂	Fr. coq, Ger. d*o*ch
ü	Fr. l*ü*ne, Ger. f*ü*r
kh	Sc. lo*ch*, Ger. *ach*
ṅ	Fr. e*n*fa*n*t, no*m*
y'	Fr. Vers*ailles* (vâr´såy'˜)

USING THE PRONUNCIATION KEY

Key words illustrating the commoner sounds, especially of the vowels, are given at the bottom of each page. For pronunciation symbols other than these, the pronunciation key on p. v and the illustrations of sound symbols on pp. vi and vii of the introductory matter should be consulted.

The characteristic sound of a word of more than one syllable is largely determined by its accenting. The primary or heavy stress is marked [ʹ] and the secondary or light [ʹ]. Examples: avoirdupois (avʹėr-dū-poizʹ), civilization (sivʹi-li-zāʹshun), fortify (fôrʹti-fiʹ).

The other important step toward mastery of pronunciation is to note any long vowel(s) in a word. In the key, a long vowel is shown by a short line over it, called a macron [¯]. Examples: know (nō), duel (dūʹel), unscrupulous (un-skrōōʹpū-lus).

THE SYMBOLS ILLUSTRATED

a as in c*a*t, g*a*rret, c*a*nteen (short *a*).

ā as in p*a*le, *a*ge, prev*ai*l, w*ei*gh, st*ea*k, th*ey*, su*e*de (long *a*).

ä as in c*a*lm, f*a*ther (broad or Italian *a*).

â as in f*a*re, p*a*rent, th*e*re, *ai*r, h*ei*r (usually in an unaccented syllable before *r*).

å as in gr*a*ss, st*a*ff, p*a*th, d*a*nce (the softened flat *a*).

e as in *e*dge, *e*ffort, s*e*t (short *e*).

ē as in *e*ven, s*ei*ze, p*eo*ple, qu*ay*, t*ea*m, mach*i*ne, w*ei*rd (long *e*).

ė as in lat*e*r, beav*e*r, begg*a*r (slurred *e* before *r*).

i as in (1) h*i*m, m*y*th, *i*ll (short *i*).
(2) b*e*fall, b*e*come, r*e*ly, r*e*sume (the long *e* sound when shortened in an unaccented syllable).
(3) cop*y*, hon*ey*, bus*y*, fish*y* (final *y*).
(4) sav*a*ge, ad*a*ge, garb*a*ge, pref*a*ce, pal*a*ce, prel*a*te, clim*a*te (slurred *a* before a final consonant preceding silent *e*).
(5) lad*ie*s, hurr*ie*s, part*ie*s (in words that change *y* to *i* and add *es*).

ī as in m*i*le, *ai*sle, sen*i*le, *i*ce (long *i*).

o as in *o*dd, G*o*d, pr*o*p, b*o*x, b*o*ttom, l*o*g, h*o*t, d*o*ll (short o).

ō as in h*o*pe, f*oa*m, b*eau*, s*ew*, r*oa*d, *oh*, fl*ow*, d*oe* (long *o*).

ô as in h*o*rn, *o*rder, *o*rb, t*a*lk, h*au*l, br*oa*d, r*aw*, f*ough*t, *augh*t (intermediate *o*).

u as in c*u*p, h*o*ney, en*ou*gh, hicc*ou*gh (short *u*).

ū as in c*u*te, c*u*re, *u*nit, *yew*, *you*, f*ew*, f*eu*d, q*ueue*, b*eau*ty, adi*eu*, c*ue*, su*i*t (long *u*).

û as in b*u*rn, occ*u*r, f*u*r, w*o*rd, ref*e*r, l*ea*rn, m*i*rth, t*e*rm, th*i*rst, w*o*rm, m*y*rtle, h*u*rt (usually before an *r* in the same syllable).

ōō as in b*oo*t, n*oo*n, m*oo*d, m*o*ve, *oo*ze, tr*ou*pe, fr*ui*t, r*u*le, can*oe*, tr*ue*, s*ou*p, man*oeu*vre, rh*eu*matism (the long *oo* sound).

oo as in f*oo*t, p*u*t, p*u*ll, c*ou*ld, tearf*u*l, wolf, sh*ou*ld, l*oo*k, g*oo*d, b*u*ll (the short *oo* sound).

oi as in t*oi*l, f*oi*l, dec*oy*, ah*oy* (diphthong).

ou as in sh*ou*t, br*ow*, b*ou*gh (diphthong).

g as in *g*et, *g*old, *gh*ost (hard *g*).

j as in *j*oy, a*g*e, *g*em, e*dg*e, cor*di*al (soft *g*).

s as in *s*ing, cea*s*e.

y as in *y*et, *y*ear, *y*ou, on*i*on.

ng as in so*ng*, to*ng*ue, u*n*cle, fi*ng*er.

ch as in *ch*in, cat*ch*, ques*ti*on, righ*te*ous.

sh as in *sh*ow, *s*ure, ac*ti*on, ten*si*on, tena*ci*ous, o*ce*an, ma*ch*ine.

th as in *th*in, ba*th*, e*th*er (voiceless).

th as in *th*en, ba*the*, ei*th*er (voiced).

hw as in *wh*en, *wh*y, *wh*ere.

b, d, f, h, k, l, m, n, p, r, t, v, w, z (14 consonants) have their ordinary English values.

c, q, and x are not used as sound symbols. The *c* is equivalent to a *k* as in a*c*t, or an *s* as in *c*ede. The letter *q* in English is found only in combination with *u*, that is, as *qu*, and is usually pronounced *kw*, as in *qu*ick, re*qu*est, *qu*ite. Sometimes it is sounded *k*, as in li*q*uor, uni*q*ue. The letter x in sound is compound, being equivalent to
(1) *ks*, as in fi*x*, la*x*, e*x*cept
(2) *gz*, as in e*x*act, e*x*amine, e*x*ist
(3) *ksh* or *sh*, as in an*x*ious
(4) *zh*, as in lu*x*urious (-*gzh*)
(5) *z*, as in *x*ylem, *x*enon, an*xi*ety (usually *x* as the first letter of a word).

Sounds in Foreign Languages

kh for the German or Scottish *ch:* a*ch* (akh); lo*ch* (lokh).

ṅ for the French nasal: e*n*fa*n*t (äṅ′fäṅ′); bie*n* (byâṅ).

âṅ for the French sound in vois*in* (vwåzâṅ′); s*im*ple (sâṅpl′).

ö for the German umlauted *o* of *oe:* sch*ö*n (shön), G*oe*the (gö′t?); also final *eu* or before *s*, *x*, *z*, *t* in French words: f*eu* (fö), j*eu* (zhö), dans*eu*se (däṅ′söz′). Otherwise, French *eu* is like û: p*eu*r (pûr), dans*eu*r (däṅ′sûr′).

ü for the German umlauted *u:* f*ü*r (für), L*ü*beck (lü′bek), and for French *u:* l*u*ne (lün), d*u* (dü).

ô̂ for the short, open *o* of French co*q* (k ô̂ k) and German d*o*ch (d ô̂ kh), the *o* being pronounced more quickly than in English words like *dog*, *soft*.

y′ French Vers*aill*es (vâr′såy′′). The French *y′* is pronounced almost like *ye*, but does not make an extra syllable. Similarly, *r′*, *m′*, *l′* following a consonant are not sounded to make an extra syllable: *simple* (sâṅpl′).

In French, all full syllables are pronounced with nearly equal stress; but there is usually a rising inflection or slight stress on the last syllable, which has somewhat the effect of the English accent. In this book, French words are shown with a primary accent on the last syllable, representing this rising inflection or slight stress, and with secondary accents on all other full syllables.

SPELLING OF INFLECTED FORMS

A. Vagaries of English Spelling

1. *Doubling a Final Consonant*

One rule of spelling that governs over 2,000 common words, especially verb inflections, ought to be mastered by the reader:

Whenever one-syllable words, and words of more than one syllable that are accented on the last syllable, *end in a single consonant preceded by a single vowel*, they double the final consonant before adding a suffix beginning with a vowel; otherwise, no doubling takes place. (For application of this rule, *qu* is considered to be two consonants, *kw*.) Examples: *abet, abettor; bag, baggage; big, bigger; equal, equalled; equip, equipped; occur, occurred; pin, pinned; plot, plotting; prefer, preferring; rebel, rebellious; tub, tubby*.

Examples of words that do not double the final consonant because they do not conform to the rule: *pain, pained; pine, pined; benefit, benefited; merit, meritorious; profit, profiting*.

An exception is *chagrin, chagrined*.

The commonest exceptions concern words ending in *el* that do not conform to the rule. Examples: *apparelled, bevelled, cancelled, dialled, dishevelled, libelled, quarrelled, revelled, yodelled*. There is, however, a growing tendency to apply the rule fairly rigidly as is done in the U.S., with the result that sometimes the Canadian press spells these *appareled, beveled, canceled, dialed, disheveled, libeled, quarreled, reveled, yodeled*, though Canadian usage does not yet sanction so rigid an application of the rule as to permit such spellings as *kidnaped, marvelous, traveler*, and *worshiper*.

2. *Ei and Ie Words*

Usually when the *ei* or *ie* combination is sounded like long *e* the "lice" rule applies, that is, i after *l* and *e* after c. Examples: *believe, relieve, conceive, deceive*.

3. *Dropping Final (Silent) E*

Final *e* is usually dropped before suffixes beginning with a vowel, but retained before those beginning with a consonant. Examples: *coming, famous, desirable, forcible, grievous, guidance, tonal, tonic; apelike, awesome, careless, dukedom, hateful, movement, shapely*.

Exceptions:

(1) A few *-oe* endings: *canoeing, hoeing, shoeing, toeing*.

(2) A few that retain the *e* to prevent their being confused with words that look like them: *dyeing, singeing, tingeing*.

(3) Words ending in *-ce* and *-ge* that retain the *e* in order to make the *c* or *g* soft in sound: *advantageous, changeable, courageous, enforceable, manageable, noticeable, outrageous, peaceable, serviceable*.

(4) A few ending in *-ue: argument, duly, suing, truly, truism*.

(5) Some verbs ending in *ie* change the *ie* to *y* when the suffix begins with a vowel: *tie, tying; vie, vying*.

(6) Some words may either drop or retain the final *e: acknowledgment, acknowledgement; judgment, judgement; milage, mileage; salable, saleable*.

4. *Words Ending in C*

When a suffix beginning with a

vowel is added to words ending in *c*, a *k* is inserted to prevent a soft *s* sound: *picnicking, trafficked, mimicking, panicky, shellacked.*

Exceptions: Some one-syllable verbs ending in *c: arc, disc.*

5. *Final Y Preceded by a Consonant*

   (a) Words ending in a *y* preceded by a consonant usually change *y* to *i* before a suffix, unless the suffix begins with *i: busy, busily, business; dry, driest, drily or dryly; icy, icier, icily, iciness; pity, pitiable, pitiful, pitiless; crying, drying, flying, trying.*

Exceptions: A word ending in *y* preceded by a consonant, especially if a one-syllable word, may

(1) use either *y* or *i* for the comparative form of an adjective: *dryer, drier; spryer, sprier; shyer, shier;*

(2) retain *y* before *-ly* and *-ness: shyly, shyness; wryly, wryness; dryly, dryness; busyness;*

(3) use either *y* or *i* for the noun form: *flier; flyer;*

(4) arbitrarily retain the *y: ladyship, fairylike, babyish, busyness; Spys, Storeys;*

(5) use both adverbial forms: *dryly, drily; slyly, slily.*

(6) retain *y* in a possessive: *everybody's.*

   (b) Words ending in *y* preceded by a consonant usually change *y* to *i* before adding -*es* (i) to form plurals of nouns: *allies, ladies;* (ii) to form the third person singular: *cries, defies, marries, tries.*

6. *Final Y Preceded by a Vowel*

These words simply add *s* (a) to form plurals of nouns: *boys, chimneys, keys, valleys;* (b) to form the third person singular: *allays, buys, obeys, says.*

They also simply add suffixes: *joy, joyful, joyous; key, keyed, keying; gluey, glueyness; gay, gayest;* but *gaily* or *gayly; gaiety* or *gayety.*

Exceptions: *day, daily; lay, laid; say, said; slay, slain.*

7. *Words Ending in L*

A number of words which end in an *l* that in U.S. practice is doubled before a suffix, leave the *l* undoubled in Canada and Great Britain: *enrol, enrolment; fulfil, fulfilment; install, instalment; thraldom; skilful; wilful.*

8. *Sounding of a Retained Final Vowel*

Words ending in a vowel retain the vowel sound before a suffix beginning with a vowel *agree, agreeable; ski, skied; taxi, taxiing (taxying); weigh, weighing; bow, bowed; shampoo, shampooing; charivari, charivaried.*

If a verb ends in two vowels, the third person singular usually adds *s*, not *es: baas; boohoos; moos; hoodoos.*

If a word ends in two *ee*'s, the final *e* is dropped before a suffix beginning with *e: free, freed, freer, freest.*

B. Inflections: Their Spelling and Pronunciation

Plural of Nouns

1. Add *-s* (pronounced s) if the singular ends in the sound of *f, k, p, t,* or *th* as in *breath*—that is, any sound with which the sound of *s* readily combines; as, *puffs, rakes, tops, hopes, hats, births*. The sound

of *th* in a few such words changes in the plural to that of *th* as in *breathe*, and the *s* is pronounced z (see 2 *b* below); as, *baths, mouths*.

2. Add *-s* (pronounced z) if the singular ends:

   (a) In a vowel sound; as, *trees, laws*.

   (b) In the sound of *b, d, g, ng, l, m, n, r, v,* or *th* as in *breathe*—that is, any voiced consonant sound with which the sound of *z* readily combines; as, *cabs, odes, bags, tongs, bells, plumes, tins, fires, Slavs, tithes*.

3. Add *-es* (pronounced ez) if the singular ends in a sibilant, or hissing sound, whether voiced or unvoiced—that is, in the sound of *s, sh, ch, z, zh,* or *j*—and has no final silent *-e;* as, *dresses, marshes, matches, topazes*.

4. Add *-s* if the singular ends in a sibilant sound and has a final silent *-e*, the final *e* combining with the *s* to form an additional syllable (pronounced ez); as, *laces, moustaches, avalanches, breezes, garages, edges*.

Plurals formed according to the rules stated above are considered regular, and are not given in this dictionary unless required for some special reason.

The following classes of plurals are considered irregular, and are noted in this book:

5. Nouns ending in *-y* preceded by a consonant form the plural by changing the *y* to *i* and adding *-es* (the *-ies* being pronounced iz); as, *lady, ladies*. Nouns ending in *-y* preceded by a vowel add *-s* according to rule, but their plurals are usually given; as, *turkey, turkeys*.

6. Nouns ending in *-o* preceded by a vowel form the plural in *-os* (pronounced *?z*); as, *cameos, folios;* nouns ending in *-o* preceded by a consonant usually form the plural in -*oes;* as, *echoes, heroes, mosquitoes, mottoes, Negroes, potatoes, tomatoes*, etc.; but musical terms ending in *-o* add *-s* only, whether a vowel or a consonant precedes the 0; as, *sopranos, altos*.

7. A few nouns ending in the sound of *f* change the *f* to *v* and add *-es* (pronounced z); as, *loaf, loaves*.

8. A few plurals are formed in other ways than by the addition of *-s* or *-es*. Among these are *geese, mice, children, oxen, deer, sheep, dice;* foreign plurals, as *theses, alumni, alumnae, phenomena, cherubim;* and other scattered cases.

9. The plurals of symbols and abbreviations are usually formed by adding *'s:* a's, y's, +'s, –'s (pluses, minuses); 8's, 205's; if's, and's; but pp. (*pl.* of *p.* for *page);* ll. (*pl.* of *l.* for *line*); MSS. (*pl.* of *MS.* for *manuscript*).

Examples: (1) *But* me no *but's*. (2) His *U's* were like *V's*, and his 2's and *Q's* looked like *Z's*.

10. The plurals of proper names are usually formed by adding *s* or *es*, as required: (1) There are three Marys and two Jameses in our class. (2) The Joneses were visiting the McColls.

Third Person Singular of Verbs

The third person singular indicative of all regular and most irregular verbs is formed according to rules 1–4 for the plural of nouns; as, *gets, hears, wishes, rises*.

Principal Parts of Verbs

1. Regular verbs add *-ed* to the infinitive to form the past tense and past participle, and *-ing* to form the present participle. The *-ing* is always pronounced as an additional syllable.
2. If the infinitive ends in *-d* or *-t* that is not silent, the *-ed* is pronounced ed or id; as, *ended, heated.*
3. If the infinitive ends in the sound of *b, g, ng, j, l, m, n, r, v, z, zh,* or *th* as in *breathe*—that is, any voiced consonant except *d*—or in a vowel sound, the *-ed* is pronounced d; as, *hurled, hurrahed;* but note rules 5 and 6 below.
4. If the infinitive ends in the sound of *f, k, p, s, sh, ch, th,* as in *breath*—that is, any unvoiced consonant except *t*—the *-ed* is pronounced t; as, *amassed, attacked, marched;* but note 5 and 6 below.

Principal parts derived according to the rules stated above are considered regular, and are not given in this dictionary unless required for some special reason.

Principal parts formed according to the following rules are considered irregular, and are given in this book:

5. *(a)* Final *-e,* whether silent or not, is dropped before *-ed;* as, *agreed, judged.*

   (b) Final silent *-e* preceded by a consonant is usually dropped before *-ing;* as, *racing, judging.* In words where final silent *-e* is preceded by a consonant and *l* or *r,* those letters unite with *-ing* to form a single syllable; as, *cou-pling* from *couple.*

   (c) Final *-y* preceded by a consonant is changed to *i* before *-ed,* but is retained before *-ing;* as, *cried, crying; replied, replying.*

   (d) Final silent *-e* preceded by *i* is dropped and the *i* is changed to *y* before *-ing;* as, *dying, lying.*
6. Verbs of one syllable, and verbs of more than one syllable if accented on the last syllable, ending in a single consonant preceded by a single vowel, double the final consonant before *-ed* and *-ing;* as, *plan, planned, planning; prefer, preferred, preferring.*
7. A considerable number of verbs have entirely irregular parts; as, *buy, bought, buying; bear,* past tense *bore,* past participle *borne* or *born,* present participle *bearing.* A few are defective, as *can* (no infinitive form), past tense *could.* Many verbs, once regular, have been contracted and now appear to be irregular; as, *put, set,* past tense and past participle *put, set; read* (pronounced red), *kept, slept,* past tense and past participle of *read, keep, sleep.*

Comparison of Adjectives and Adverbs

1. Adjectives of one syllable are regularly compared by adding *-er* and *-est* to the positive degree to form, respectively,

the comparative and superlative; as, *old, older, oldest.*

2. Adjectives of more than two syllables are usually compared by using the words *more* and *most* with the positive; as, *beautiful, more beautiful, most beautiful.*

3. Adjectives of two syllables are compared by adding *-er, -est* (but see rule 5), if the resulting form is easily pronounced; as, *yellow, yellower, yellowest;* otherwise they are compared by the use of *more* and *most;* as, *spacious, more spacious, most spacious.* Usage varies according to individual taste; many adjectives can be compared in either way; as, *corrupt, corrupter* or *more corrupt,* etc.

4. Adverbs are usually compared by the use of *more* and *most,* though a few use *-er* and *-est;* as, *near, nearer, nearest; often, oftener, oftenest.* Some adverbs are not compared; as, *here, there, now, then.*

Comparatives and superlatives formed in accordance with the rules stated above are considered regular, and are not given in this dictionary unless required for some special reason.

The following cases of comparison are considered irregular, and are noted in this book:

5. A final silent *-e* is dropped before the endings *-er* and *-est;* as, *fine, finer, finest; noble, nobler, noblest.*

6. Adjectives of one syllable, and adjectives of more than one syllable if accented on the last syllable, ending in a single consonant preceded by a single vowel, double the final consonant before *-er* and *-est;* as, *big, bigger, biggest.*

7. Adjectives ending in *-y* change the *y* to *i* before *-er* and *-est;* as, *happy, happier, happiest.*

8. A number of the commoner adjectives, and a few adverbs, are entirely irregular; as, *good, better, best; bad, worse, worst; ill* (the adverb), *worse, worst; far, farther, farthest.*

9. Many adverbs which may also function as prepositions have an adjective function when compared, forming the comparative in *-er* and the superlative by adding *-most* to the positive or comparative; as, *in, inner, inmost* or *innermost.* Some adjectives have only the superlative; as, *topmost, uttermost.*

ABBREVIATIONS USED IN THIS BOOK

A.D. . . . . . anno Domini (*Latin* = in the year of our Lord); used in giving dates
adj. . . . . adjective
adv. . . . . adverb, adverbial
B.C. . . . . before Christ; used in giving dates
cap. . . . . capital
colloq. . . . . colloquial
comp. . . . . comparative
conj. . . . . conjunction
def. . . . . definition
esp. . . . . especially
etc. . . . et cetera (*Latin* = and others)
fem. . . . . feminine
indef. . . . . indefinite
interj. . . . . interjection
masc. . . . . masculine
n. . . . . noun
neut. . . . . neuter
pl. . . . . plural
p.p. . . . . participle, past
p.pr. . . . . participle, present
prep. . . . . preposition
pron. . . . . pronoun, pronominal
p.t. . . . . past tense
sing. . . . . singular
superl. . . . . superlative
syn. . . . . synonym(s)
U.S. . . . . United States
v.i. . . . . verb, intransitive
v.t. . . . . verb, transitive

A

[1]**A, a** (ā), *n.* [*pl.* A's, a's], **1,** the first letter of the alphabet; **2,** in *music,* the sixth note in the major scale of C:—A, *adj.* **1,** first in order or class; as, an *A* rating; **2,** having the form of an A; as, an *A* tent:—**A1** (ā′wun′), excellent; first-class.

[2]**a** (a; when stressed, ā), *adj.* or *indefinite article* one; any, as, *a* student was here; *a* student is studying in the library: used instead of *an* before words beginning with a consonant or a consonant sound, or with a sounded *h*; as, *a* student, *a* unit, *a* youth, *a* holiday, *a* hotel.

a- (a-), *prefix* meaning *in, on,* or *to*; as, *a*top, *a*blaze, etc.

aard-vark (ärd′värk′), *n.* an African animal that catches ants and termites with its long, sticky tongue.

ab- (ab-), *prefix* meaning *from, away from*; as, *ab*duct (to take or carry away).

a-back (a-bak′), *adv.* backward:—**taken aback,** surprised; disconcerted; as, she was *taken aback* by his pessimistic attitude.

ab-a-cus (ab′a-kus), *n.* [*pl.* abacuses (-kus-iz) or abaci (-sī)], a frame with beads or balls sliding on wires, used for thousands of years for counting or calculating: an early form of the modern calculator.

Abacus

a-ban-don (a-ban′dun), *v.t.* **1,** to give up entirely; as, to *abandon* a house, a ship, or work; **2,** to yield (oneself) without restraint; as, he *abandoned* himself to grief:—*n.* reckless enthusiasm; as, she danced with *abandon.*—*n.* **a-ban′don-ment.**—*adj.* **a-ban′ doned.**

a-base (a-bās′), *v.t.* [abased, abas-ing], to humble; as, he *abased* himself.—*n.* **a-base′ ment.**

a-bash (a-bash′), *v.t.* to embarrass; shame; disconcert; as, she was *abashed* at the rebuke.

a-bashed (a-basht′), *adj.* overcome with surprise or shame; confused; disconcerted.

a-bate (a-bāt), *v.i.* [abat-ed, abat-ing], to decrease; subside; as, the flood has *abated:*—*v.t.* **1,** to put an end to; as, *abate* a nuisance; **2,** to reduce, as a debt.—*n.* **a-bate′ment.**

a-bat-toir (ab′a-twôr′), *n.* a building where animals are killed for market. Also called *slaughterhouse.*

ab-bey (ab′i), *n.* [*pl.* abbeys], **1,** one or more buildings where men or women live a religious life apart from the world, governed by an [illegible] (for monks) or abbess (for nuns); [illegible] church that was once part of a monastery; as, Westminster *Abbey.*

ab-bre-vi-ate (a-brē′vi-āt′), *v.t.* [abbreviat-ed, abbreviat-ing], to shorten; esp., to shorten (a word) by writing only a part, as *Apr.* for *April.*—*n.* **ab-bre′vi-a′tion.**

ab-di-cate (ab′di-kāt′), *v.t.* [abdicat-ed, abdicat-ing], to give up, as kingly or queenly power; resign (a throne):—*v.t.* to give up sovereign power; as, the king *abdicated.*—*n.* **ab′di-ca′tion.**

ab-do-men (ab′dō-men; ab-dō′men), *n.* **1,** the large cavity of the body below the diaphragm, containing the digestive organs; **2,** in insects, the rear section of the body.—*adj.* **ab-dom′i-nal.**

ab-duct (ab-dukt′), *v.t.* to kidnap; to carry off a person by force or by a trick; as, to *abduct* a school mascot.—*n.* **ab-duc′tor.**—*n.* **ab-duc′tion.**

A-ben-aki (a′be-nak′ē), *n.* **1,** an Aboriginal people living mostly in southern Québec and Maine who speak an Algonquian language; **2,** the language of these people.

ab-er-ra-tion (ab′ėr-ā′shun), *n.* **1,** departure from what is right, true, proper, etc.; **2,** mental disorder; **3,** a deviation from the normal.

a-bet (a-bet′), *v.t.* [abet-ted, abet-ting], to encourage or aid, esp. in a crime; as, he aided and *abetted* the thief.—*n.* **a-bet′tor.**

a-bey-ance (a-bā′ans), *n.* a postponing of something; as, the project was left *in abeyance.*

ab-hor (ab-hôr′), *v.t.* [abhorred, abhorring], to shrink from with disgust; as, the humane girl *abhors* cruelty.—*adj.* **abhor′rent.**—*n.* **ab-hor′rence.**

a-bide (a-bid′), *v.i.* [*p.t.* and *p.p.* abode (a-bōd′) or abid-ed. *p.pr.* abid-ing], **1,** to live; dwell; **2,** to endure; as, great love *abides;*—**abide by,** to remain faithful to; accept or follow; as, to *abide by* a promise:—*v.t.* to put up with; as, I cannot *abide* him.

a-bil-i-ty (a-bil′i-ti), *n.* [*pl.* abilities], power to do something; as, *ability* to work; also, skill; talent; as, a man of *ability.*

ab-ject (ab′jekt; ab-jekt′), *adj.* **1,** degraded; craven; as, an *abject* coward; **2,** contemptible; as, *abject* submission; hopeless; as, *abject* poverty.—*adv.* **ab′ject-ly.**

a-blaze (a-blāz′), *adj.* **1,** on fire; as, the hut was *ablaze;* **2,** aglow; full of colour, as autumn woods; **3,** ardent; eager.

a-ble (ā′bl), *adj.* **1,** having power, skill, or means; as, she is ill and not *able* to go; is he *able* to drive a car?; they are not *able* to buy lunch; **2,** skillful; unusually clever; as, an *able* lawyer.—*adv.* **a′bly.**

ab-lu-tion (a-blū′shun; -blōō), *n.* a washing or cleansing of the body or part of the body; as, he performs his *ablutions* religiously.

ab-ne-ga-tion (ab′ne-gā′shun), *n.* denial, esp. self-denial; a renouncing of self.

ab-nor-mal (ab-nôr′mal), *adj.* differing from what is usual or expected; out of the ordinary; above or below the average; as, *abnormal* weather.—*adv.* **ab-nor′mal-ly.**

a-board (a-bōrd′), *adv.* on or into a ship, train, plane, etc.:—*prep.* on board of; in or into; as, to be, or go, *aboard* a ship.

a-bode (a-bōd′), *n.* a place of residence; home; as, this cottage is my *abode.*

a-bol-ish (a-bol′ish), *v.t.* to do away with; put an end to; as, to *abolish* slavery.

ab-o-li-tion (ab′o-lish′un), *n.* the destroying of, or doing away with, something; as, the *abolition* of a school's dress code.—*n.* **ab′o-li′tion-ist.**

a-bom-i-na-ble (a-bom′i-na-bl), *adj.* hateful; odious; as, he is a rude fellow with *abominable* manners.—*adv.* **a-bom′i-na-bly.**

a-bom-i-nate (a-bom′i-nāt′), *v.t.* [abominat-ed, abominat-ing], to detest; loathe.—*n.* **a-bom′i-na′tion.**

Ab-o-rig-i-ne or **ab-o-rig-i-ne** (ab′o-rij′i-nē′), *n.* **1,** one of a group of people who have lived in Australia for thousands of years; **2,** one of a group of people who were the earliest known inhabitants of an area, such as the Inuit of northern Canada.—*adj.* **Ab′o-rig′i-nal.**

a-bort (a-bôrt′) *v.t.* **1,** to end a pregnancy prematurely; to miscarry; **2,** to cause something to end prematurely; as, to *abort* the computer program; **3,** to cut short, cancel, or abandon; as, to *abort* the space mission; **4,** to fail to develop biologically.

abor-tion (a-bôr′shun), *n.* **1,** the intentional, premature termination of a pregnancy resulting in the expulsion of the fetus; **2,** anything that is arrested in development or that fails to mature completely; **3,** the failure of an operation; as, the mission was an *abortion;* **4,** something malformed or hideous; a monstrosity.—*n.* **a-bor′tion-ist.**

a-bor-tive (a-bôr′tiv), *adj.* **1,** fruitless; unsuccessful; as, an *abortive* attempt; **2,** imperfectly developed.

a-bound (a-bound′), *v.i.* **1,** to exist in great numbers or amount; as, deer *abound* in these hills; **2,** to be richly supplied; as, his speech *abounded* in wit.

a-bout (a-bout′), *adv.* **1,** around; on every side; near by; as, they stood *about;* **2,** in a reversed position; as, to face *about;* **3,** in rotation; as, turn *about* is fair play; **4,** in a state of action; as, he is up and *about;* **5,** on the point of; as, I am *about* to leave; **6,** approximately; nearly; as, *about* finished:—*prep.* **1,** concerning; relating to; as, a story *about* a bear; something wrong *about* the plan; **2,** on all sides of; near to; as, trees *about* the lake; **3,** on the person of; as, I haven't a loonie *about* me.

a-bove (a-buv′), *adv.* **1,** in a higher place; overhead; as, directly *above;* **2,** in heaven or in the sky; as, up *above;* **3,** before this; as, see page 6 *above:*—*prep.* **1,** over; higher than; **2,** superior to; as, to be *above* deceit; **3,** beyond; as, *above* reproach; **4,** in excess of; as, *above* 10 dollars:—*adj.* stated previously; as, the *above* objection.

a-bove-board (a-buv′bōrd′), *adv.* openly; without trickery; as, he acted *aboveboard:*—*adj.* honest; as, she was always *aboveboard* in her dealings.

ab-ra-sion (a-brā′zhun), *n.* **1,** the injury caused by rubbing or scraping; as, a skin *abrasion;* **2,** a wearing or rubbing away.—*v.* **ab-rade′.**

a-breast (a-brest′), *adj.* and *adv.* side by side; as, the three boys walked *abreast;* not behind; current; as, *abreast* of the times.

a-bridge (a-brij′), *v.t.* [abridged, abridging], **1,** to shorten; condense, as a book; **2,** to deprive of (a right, privilege, liberty, etc.).—*n.* **a-bridg′ment; a-bridge′ment.**

a-broad (a-brôd′), *adv.* **1,** far and wide; as, the news spread *abroad;* **2,** out of doors; as, to walk *abroad;* **3,** in, or to go to, a foreign country.

ab-ro-gate (ab′ro-gāt′), *v.t.* [abrogat-ed, abrogat-ing], to annul; abolish; repeal; as, to *abrogate* a law, rule, or custom.

ab-rupt (a-brupt′), *adj.* **1,** sudden; as, an *abrupt* turn; **2,** short or curt; as, an *abrupt* manner; **3,** steep, as a hill.

ab-scess (ab′ses), *n.* pus forming at a certain point, or focus, of infection; as, an *abscess* around a tooth.

ab-scond (ab-skond′), *v.i.* to flee secretly, esp. after some wrongdoing; as, she *absconded* with the stolen money.

ab-sence (ab′sens), *n.* **1,** a being away, or the period of being away; as, an *absence* of one week; **2,** lack; as, *absence* of heat.

ab-sent (ab′sent), *adj.* **1,** not present; missing; lacking; **2,** lost in thought; inattentive; as, an *absent* manner:—*v.t.* (ab-sent′), to withdraw (oneself).—*adv.* **ab′sent-ly.**

ab-sen-tee (ab′sen-tē′), *n.* one who is away from work, school, duty, etc.:—*adj.* away; as, *absentee* employee.

ab-sent–mind-ed (ab′sent–mīn′did), *adj.* lost in thought; hence, inattentive; forgetful.—*adv.* **ab′sent–mind′ed-ly.**

ab-so-lute (ab′so-lūt; -lōōt), *adj.* **1,** whole; complete; perfect; as, the *absolute* truth; **2,** having power or authority that is not restricted by laws or by a constitution; as, an *absolute* monarch; **3,** positive; certain; as, an *absolute* fact.—*adv.* **ab′so-lute-ly.**

absolute majority, elected by a majority of more than half of all voters.

absolute zero, the theoretically coldest temperature possible, characterized by a complete absence of heat; zero Kelvin or minus 273.15 degrees Celsius.

ab-solve (ab-solv′), *v.t.* [absolved, absolv-ing], **1,** to release or set free, as from a duty; **2,** to acquit; pronounce not guilty; as, a jury's verdict *absolved* him of guilt.—*n.* **ab′so-lu′tion** (ab′so-lū′shun).

ab-sorb (ab-sôrb′), *v.t.* **1,** to drink in; suck or swallow up; as, a sponge *absorbs* water; **2,** to interest deeply; take all of one's attention; as, baseball *absorbs* Jenna now.—*adj.* **ab-sorb′ent; ab-sorb′ing.**—*n.* **ab-sorp′tion** (ab-sôrp′shun).

ab-stain (ab-stān′), *v.i.* to refrain; keep away; as, to *abstain* from the use of tobacco.—*n.* **ab-stain′er; ab′sti-nence.**

ab-stract (ab′strakt), *n.* a summing up of the main points, as of a book or an argument:—*adj.* (ab′strakt; ab-strakt′), **1,** considered apart from actual facts or a real situation; as, *abstract* justice; **2,** withdrawn (in thought); as, she had an *abstract* air; **3,** in *grammar*, describing a noun that has a quality or characteristic but that does not name the person or thing that possesses it; thus, "strength" is an *abstract* noun, but a word like "wrestler," which names a person, is a *concrete* noun:—*v.t.* (ab-strakt′), **1,** to take away or draw out, esp. secretly or dishonestly; **2,** to make a summary of (a book).—*n.* **ab-strac′tion.**—*adv.* **ab-stract′ly.**

ab-stract-ed (ab-strak′tid), *adj.* absent-minded; lost in thought.

ab-struse (ab-stro͞os′), *adj.* hard to understand; as, philosophy deals with *abstruse* problems; hidden; concealed.

ab-surd (ab-sûrd′), *adj.* contrary to reason or sense; ridiculous; silly.—*n.* **ab-surd′-i-ty.**—*adv.* **ab-surd′ly.**

a-bun-dance (a-bun′dans), *n.* overflowing quantity or amount; great plenty; as, an *abundance* of food.—*adj.* **a-bun′dant.**—*adv.* **a-bun′dant-ly.**

a-buse (a-būz′), *v.t.* [abused, abus-ing], **1,** to use improperly; misuse; as, to *abuse* a privilege; to abuse drugs; **2,** to maltreat; as, to *abuse* animals; **3,** to use violent language to; as, he *abused* his men; **4,** to strain; overtax; as, to *abuse* one's health:—*n.* (a-bûs′), **1,** misuse, as of a privilege or drugs; **2,** cruel treatment, as of animals; **3,** violent language; **4,** a straining or overtaxing, as of one's health; **5,** a corrupt or wrong practice; as, political *abuses*.—*adj.* **a-bu′sive** (a-bū′siv).—*adv.* **a-bu′sive-ly.**

a-but (a-but′), *v.i.* [abut-ted, abut-ting], to join end to end; end against; followed by *on, upon, against*; as, the house *abuts* on the hill.

a-buzz (a-buz′), *adj.* **1,** filled with excited activity; as, *abuzz* with anticipation; **2,** filled with buzzing sounds.

a-byss (a-bis′), *n.* **1,** a deep chasm; **2,** anything bottomless or unbounded.—*adj.* **a-bys′mal** (a-biz′mal).

ac-a-de-mia (a′ka-dē′mē-a), *n.* the academic community, esp. universities as a group.

ac-a-dem-ic (a′ka-de′mik), *adj.* **1,** having to do with education; as, an *academic* career; **2,** having to do with an idea rather than a real issue; theoretical; as, an *academic* argument.

a-cad-e-my (a-kad′e-mi), *n.* [*pl.* academies], **1,** a university; **2,** a school for special study; as, a military *academy*; **3,** a group of writers, scientists, or scholars.—*adj.* **ac′a-dem′ic; ac′a-dem′i-cal.**

A-ca-di-a (a-kā′di-a), *n.* **1,** a former French colony, 1604–1713, in the Maritime provinces; **2,** the area in the Maritimes with French settlement and culture; **3,** the Maritime provinces, in general.—*adj.* and *n.* **A-ca′di-an.**

a cap-pel-la (ä′ ka-pe′la), *adj.* and *adv.* singing unaccompanied by musical instruments; as, The Nylons sing *a cappella*.

ac-cede (ak-sēd′), *v.i.* [acced-ed, acced-ing], **1,** to agree or yield, as to a request; **2,** to succeed, as to a throne.

ac-cel-er-ate (ak-sel′ėr-āt′), *v.t.* [accelerat-ed, accelerat-ing], **1,** to cause to move, act, or change more quickly; as, to *accelerate* an engine; **2,** to cause to come sooner; as, death was *accelerated* by grief.—*n.* **ac-cel′er-a′tion.**

ac-cel-er-at-or (ak-sel′ėr-āt′ėr), *n.* **1,** a device, like the foot pedal of a car, for increasing the speed of a machine; **2,** anything that speeds up a process or chemical reaction.

ac-cent (ak′sent), *n.* **1,** emphasis; stress; esp., the stress laid upon a syllable of a word or upon a note of music; **2,** any of several characters, as [′,′], used in writing and printing to show which syllable of a word is to be stressed; **3,** a special or peculiar method of pronouncing; as, to speak French with an English *accent*:—*v.t.* (ak-sent′; ak′sent), **1,** to utter with special stress, as a word; **2,** to mark with an *accent*; **3,** to emphasize; as, his remarks were *accented* by gestures.—*v.t.* **ac-cen′tu-ate′.**

ac-cept (ak-sept′), *v.t.* **1,** to take or receive, as a gift; consent to take, as an office; take with resignation, as one's fate; **2,** to agree to; as, I *accept* your terms; **3,** to recognize as true, as a creed; **4,** to admit (a person) to favour; as, the club *accepted* the stranger.—*n.* **accept′ance.**—*adv.* **ac-cept′a-bly.**

ac-cept-a-ble (ak-sept′a-bl), *adj.* good enough to be accepted; adequate; satisfactory; as, an *acceptable* average to her is at least a B.

ac-cess (ak′ses), *n.* **1,** admittance or approach to a person or place; also, a way or means of approach; as, a drawbridge gave *access* to the castle; **2,** an attack; fit; as, an *access* of coughing; an *access* of rage:—*v.t.* to gain entry to; get in to; as, to *access* the computer network by entering the correct password.

ac-ces-si-ble (ak-ses′i-bl), *adj.* **1,** easy to reach; as, the book was easily *accessible* because the shelf was low; **2,** open to influence; as, *accessible* to reason, pity, etc.; **3,** approachable; as, the mayor was *accessible* to every citizen.—*n.* **ac-ces′si-bil-i-ty.**

ac-ces-sion (ak-se′shun), *n.* the act of coming into an office, dignity, or estate; as, the *accession* of a queen; or one's *accession* to wealth or property.

ac-ces-sor-y (ak-ses′or-i; ak′), *adj.* **1,** contributing to an effect; **2,** helping another in crime:—*n.* **1,** an article that adds to the use or appearance of something else; as, jewellery and shoes are *accessories* for a dress; *accessories* for a car; **2,** a person who assists a criminal before or after a crime.

ac-ci-dent (ak′si-dent), *n.* **1,** an unexpected or unforeseen event, generally unfortunate; **2,** something done unintentionally; a mishap; **3,** chance; as, to lose or find something by *accident.*—*adj.* **ac′ci-den′tal.**—*adv.* **ac-ci-den′tal-ly.**

ac-claim (a-klām′), *v.t.* **1,** to applaud; **2,** to hail or proclaim by shouting; as, to *acclaim* a champion:—*n.* a shout of joy or praise.

ac-cla-ma-tion (ak′la-mā′shun), *n.* **1,** shout of approval, joy, etc.; **2,** approbation in any form; **3,** uncontested election, usually unanimous; as, elected by *acclamation.*

ac-cli-ma-tize (a-klī′ma-tīz′), *v.t.* [-tized (-tīzd), -tiz-ing], to get accustomed to a new climate (or conditions):—*v.i.* to become adapted (to); as, shorthorns became *acclimatized* to our winters.

ac-co-lade (a′kō-lād′; a′kō-läd′), *n.* **1,** a statement of praise; recognition of merit; an award; **2,** the ceremony conferring knighthood.

ac-com-mo-date (a-kom′o-dāt′), *v.t.* [accommodat-ed, accommodat-ing], **1,** to supply lodgings, food, etc.; as, this hotel can *accommodate* 100 guests; **2,** to oblige or help; as, he *accommodated* me by cashing a cheque; **3,** to fit or adapt; as, we *accommodated* ourselves to our new surroundings.—*adj.* **ac-com′mo-dat′ing.**

ac-com-mo-da-tion (a-kom′o-dā′shun), *n.* **1,** the act or process of adjusting or fitting something to something else; as, the *accommodation* of one's plans to those of others; the *accommodation* of the eye to distant objects; **2,** willingness to oblige; **3,** the thing furnished in order to oblige, as a loan of money; **4,** lodgings; as, hotel *accommodation.*

ac-com-pa-ny (a-kum′pa-ni), *v.t.* [accompanied, accompany-ing], **1,** to go with; escort; as, a guide *accompanied* the party; **2,** to supplement or join (with); as, she *accompanied* her words with a glance; **3,** in *music,* to follow (a singer or player) on an instrument.—*n.* **ac-com′pa-ni-ment.**

ac-com-plice (a-kom′plis; -kum′), *n.* an associate or companion in crime; as, two robbers were caught, but an *accomplice* escaped.

ac-com-plish (a-kom′plish; -kum′), *v.t.* **1,** to complete; finish, as a task; **2,** to carry out; fulfill; as, she *accomplished* her purpose.—*adj.* **ac-com′plished.**—*n.* **ac-com′plish-ment.**

ac-cord (a-kôrd′), *v.t.* to give; grant; as, to *accord* due praise:—*v.i.* to be in harmony; agree; as, your point of view *accords* with mine:—*n.* agreement; harmony; as, you and I are in *accord* on the way to solve the problem; the Meech Lake *Accord.*—*n.* **accord′ance;** as, I am acting *in accordance with* his wishes.—*prep.* **according to,** as stated by; on the authority of; as, *according to* the forecast, it will be sunny tomorrow.

ac-cord-ing-ly (a-kôr′ding-li), *adv.* **1,** in agreement with what might be expected; suitably; as, you are now grown and must act *accordingly;* **2,** consequently; therefore.

ac-cor-di-on (a-kôr′di-un), *n.* a portable musical instrument, consisting of bellows, metal reeds, and a keyboard, played by alternately extending the ends of the instrument and pushing them together, thus forcing air through the reeds:—*adj.* folded and creased like the bellows of an accordion; as, *accordion* pleats.

ACCORDION

ac-cost (a-kôst′), *v.t.* to speak to first; address; as, a mugger *accosted* me.

ac-count (a-kount′), *v.i.* **1,** to give a reckoning or make a report of money received and money spent; as, he *accounted* for all the money; **2,** to give an explanation or reason; as, I cannot *account* for his conduct:—*v.t.* to think of; consider as; as, although he failed, he was *accounted* a hero:—*n.* **1,** a record of business dealings involving money; a bill; as, an *account* with a computer store; **2,** any reckoning; as, he rendered an *account* of his expenses; **3,** a record or report, as of events; **4,** cause or explanation; as, give an *account* of your actions; **5,** importance; worth; as, of no *account;* **6, accounts,** financial records; bookkeeping records; as, his *accounts* are in order.

ac-count-a-ble (a-koun′ta-bl), *adj.* **1,** bound to give an explanation of one's conduct; responsible; answerable; as, the politician should be held *accountable* for her conduct; **2,** capable of being explained; as, his failure is *accountable* if you recall his lack of training.—*n.* **ac-count′a-bil′i-ty.**

ac-count-ant (a-koun′tant), *n.* one who is trained in keeping track of financial records.—*n.* **ac-count′an-cy.**

ac-cred-it (a-kred′it), *v.t.* **1,** to authorize; furnish with credentials; as, an *accredited* delegate; **2,** to attribute; ascribe; as, the discovery is *accredited to* Copernicus; he is *accredited with* saying that; **3,** to take as valid; as, an *accredited* story.—*n.* **ac-cred-i-ta′tion.**—*adj.* **ac-cred′it-ed.**

ac-crue (a-kro͞o′), *v.i.* grow; increase; be added; as, interest *accrued* on the loan; prestige *accrued* from his social contacts.

ac-cul-tur-ate (a-kul′che-rāt′), *v.t.* and *v.i.* to adapt an individual or a group to a culture; to assimilate a culture; to cause an individual or group to adapt or adopt another culture.

ac-cu-mu-late (a-kū′mū-lāt′), *v.t.* and *v.i.* [accumulat-ed, accumulat-ing], to collect; gather; pile up; as, to *accumulate* money in the bank; books *accumulate* on a table.—*n.* **ac-cu′mu-la′tion; ac-cu′mu-la′tor** (data storage location in a calculator or computer).—*adj.* **ac-cu′mu-la′tive.**

ac-cu-rate (ak′ū-rit), *adj.* free from error; as, an *accurate* list; precise; as, an *accurate* person.—*adv.* **ac′cu-rate-ly.**—*n.* **ac-cu-ra-cy.**

ac-cuse (a-kūz′), *v.t.* [accused, accus-ing], to charge with guilt; blame; as, to *accuse* a person of theft.—*n.* **ac′cu-sa′tion.**—*n.* **ac-cus′er.**—*adv.* **ac-cus′ing-ly.**

ac-cus-tom (a-kus′tum), *v.t.* to make used to something; to familiarize; as, to *accustom* oneself to new conditions.

ac-cus-tomed (a-kus′tumd), *adj.* **1,** according to custom or habit; usual; regular; as, to sit in your *accustomed* seat; **2,** used to; as, to be *accustomed* to her unusual habits.

ace (ās), *n.* **1,** a playing card or die with a single spot; **2,** one who excels in doing some particular thing; as, a football *ace*; an *ace* at computer games.

a-cer-bic (a-sėr′bik), *adj.* **1,** harsh or bitter mood or temper; as, an *acerbic* remark; **2,** a sour or bitter taste.

ache (āk), *n.* continuous pain, bodily or mental; as, a tooth*ache*; heart*ache*:—*v.i.* [ached, ach-ing], **1,** to suffer from, or throb with, pain; as, my head *aches*; **2,** to have a strong desire; to long for.

a-chieve (a-chēv′), *v.t.* [achieved, achiev-ing], **1,** to accomplish; as, he *achieved* his goal; **2,** to gain or get by effort; as, to *achieve* success.—*n.* **a-chieve′ment; a-chiev′er.**

A-chil-les heel or **Achilles′ heel,** *n.* a weak or vulnerable area; as, vanity is her *Achilles heel.*

ac-id (as′id), *adj.* **1,** sharp or biting to the taste, as vinegar; sour; **2,** sharp or bitter in manner; as, the critic's *acid* tone:—*n.* **1,** a sour substance, often liquid; **2,** in *chemistry,* that which combines with a base to form a salt.—*n.* **a-cid-i-ty.**

acid rain, rain or snow containing acid from the burning of fossil fuels such as coal and petroleum: it is harmful to plant and animal life.

acid test, a crucial or decisive test, esp. one that establishes the true worth of a person or thing.

ac-knowl-edge (ak-nol′ij), *v.t.* [acknowledged, acknowledg-ing], **1,** to admit as real or genuine; as, to *acknowledge* a fault or a signature; **2,** to respect; recognize; as, to *acknowledge* Dickens as a great novelist; **3,** to admit the receipt of; express thanks for; as, to *acknowledge* a letter or a gift.—*n.* **ac-knowl′edge-ment; ac-knowl′edg-ment.**

ac-me (ak′mi), *n.* the highest point; perfection; as, her dancing was the *acme* of grace.

ac-ne (ak′ni), *n.* a skin disease marked by eruption of pimples, due to a clogging of the oil glands.

a-corn (ā′kôrn; ā′kėrn), *n.* the fruit of the oak tree; a nut with its base set in a woody cup.

a-cous-tics (a-kous′tiks; a-ko͞os′tiks), *n.* **1,** the science that studies how sounds are made and how sound carries; **2,** the qualities of a place that make it easy or hard to hear sounds in it; as, excellent *acoustics* in the concert hall.—*adj.* **acoustic,** associated with the sense of hearing or with sound; as, the *acoustic* properties of a room; also, not electric; as, an *acoustic* guitar.

ac-quaint (a-kwānt′), *v.t.* to make aware of something; familiarize; as, I *acquainted* him with the contents of this letter.

ac-quaint-ance (a-kwān′tans), *n.* **1,** knowledge of a person or a thing gained by contact or experience; as, an *acquaintance* with a book and with its author; **2,** a person whom one knows slightly.—*n.* **ac-quaint′ance-ship.**

ac-qui-esce (ak′wi-es′), *v.i.* [acquiesced, acquiesc-ing], to agree in silence; submit or assent without objection; as, she *acquiesced* in her son's decision.—*adj.* **ac′-qui-es′cent.**—*n.* **ac′qui-es′cence.**

ac-quire (a-kwīr′), *v.t.* [acquired, acquir-ing], to gain or obtain, usually by one's own effort; as, she *acquired* speed in swimming; he *acquired* a name for honesty; they *acquired* a summer cottage.—*n.* **ac-qui-si′tion.**

ac-quis-i-tive (a-kwiz′i-tiv), *adj.* having a strong desire to get or gain property or money for oneself.

ac-quit (a-kwit′), *v.t.* [acquit-ted, acquitting], **1,** to free (a person) from an accusation or an obligation; to clear (of a charge); as, the court *acquitted* the prisoner; **2,** to discharge or carry out one's duty or obligations; as, all the members of the hockey team *acquitted* themselves well.—*n.* **ac-quit′tal.**

a-cre (ā′kėr), *n.* **1,** a measure of land area (4047 square metres); **2,** a piece of land; a field; **3,** acres, lands, or a landed estate; as, ancestral *acres.*—*n.* **a′cre-age** (ā′kėr-ij).

ac-rid (ak′rid), *adj.* **1,** bitter; sharp-tasting; pungent, as smoke; **2,** ill-tempered; bitter; harsh and sharp; as, his *acrid* retort stung her.—*adv.* **ac′rid-ly.**

ac-ri-mo-ny (ak′ri-mo-ni), *n.* harshness or bitterness of speech or temper; as, he spoke with *acrimony.*—*adj.* **ac-ri-mo′ni-ous,** extremely bitter in language or manner; as, an *acrimonious* debate.

ac-ro-bat (ak′rō-bat′), *n.* one who performs skilled or daring gymnastic feats, such as tumbling, vaulting, etc.—*adj.* **ac′ro-bat′ic.**

ac-ro-nym (ak′ro-nim), *n.* a word made from the first letters or syllables of a series of words; some are written as ordinary words, such as radar (*ra*dio *d*etection *a*nd *r*anging), and others are sets of initials, such as NATO (*N*orth *A*tlantic *T*reaty *O*rganization).

a-cross (a-kros′), *prep.* **1,** from one side to the other of; as, she swam *across* the stream; **2,** on the other side of; opposite side; as, she lives *across* the road:—*adv.* from one side to the other; as, to cut cloth straight *across*; to fly *across.*

a-cros-tic (a-kros′tik), *n.* a poem or puzzle in which the first, middle, or end letters of each line form a word, motto, or pattern.

a-cryl-ic (a-kri′lik), *n.* one of a group of artificial materials made mainly from petroleum, widely used in paints, fabrics, and other products.

act (akt), *n.* **1,** a deed; thing done; **2,** the process of doing; as, Maria is in the *act* of cleaning out her desk; **3,** a decree or law; as, an *act* of Parliament; **4,** one of the principal divisions of a play, a show, or an opera:—*v.t.* to perform or take the part of, as in a show, play, or movie:—*v.i.* **1,** to do something; as, you must *act* quickly; **2,** to behave; as, she *acts* unusually; **3,** to take a part in a movie or play; **4,** to produce an effect; as, the drug *acted* quickly.

act-ing (ak′ting), *adj.* performing the duties of another; as, the *acting* chairman:—*n.* **1,** the art of performing on the stage or screen; **2,** false or insincere behaviour; as, his enthusiasm was mere *acting.*

ac-tion (ak′shun), *n.* **1,** the doing of something; a deed; as, a kind *action*; **2,** the tendency to act; as, people of *action*; **3,** the effect of one body or substance upon another, as of sunlight on plants; **4,** a suit at law; **5,** the effective or acting part of a mechanism; as, the *action* of our piano needs repair; **6,** the progress of events, as in a movie; **7,** a battle; **8, actions,** conscious acts; conduct; behaviour; as, we judge a person by his or her *actions.*

ac-tive (ak′tiv), *adj.* **1,** given or inclined to action; brisk; lively; as, an *active* body does not always house an *active* mind; **2,** in action or operation; as, an *active* volcano; **3,** in *grammar,* using a verb to show the subject of the sentence doing or causing the action: opposite of passive.—*v.t.* **ac′ti-vate′.**

ac-tiv-i-ty (ak-tiv′i-ti), *n.* **1,** something that is done or to be done; as, to be involved in a science *activity*; **2,** the state of being active; action; as, physical *activities* such as swimming, inline skating, walking, tennis, etc.

ac-tor (ak′tėr), *n.* one who takes the part of a character in a play or movie; a theatrical or movie player.

ACTRA (ac′tra′) *abbrev.* short for *Alliance for Canadian Cinema, Television, and Radio Artists.*

ac-tu-al (ak′tū-al), *adj.* existing in fact; real: not imaginary.—*adv.* **ac′tu-al-ly.**

ac-tu-a-ry (ak′tū-er′i: ak′choo-ėr-i), *n.* an expert in calculating insurance risks, premiums, etc., and who works for insurance companies.

a-cu-men (a-kū′men), *n.* keenness; quickness of insight; as, she has business *acumen.*

ac-u-punc-ture (a′kū-pungk′chūr), *n.* a form of medical treatment first used in China, which eases pain and disease through the use of thin needles inserted at certain points in the body.

a-cute (a-kūt′), *adj.* **1,** sharp-pointed; not blunt; **2,** mentally quick; as, an *acute* person; sensitive; keen; as, an *acute* sense of smell; *acute* insight; **3,** severe; as, *acute* pain; **4,** critical; as, the *acute* stage in a fever; **5,** very important; serious; as, an *acute* shortage of food.—*adv.* **a-cute′ly.**—*n.* **a-cute′ness.**

ad (ad), *n.* Same as **advertisement.**

ad- (ad), *prefix* meaning *to, toward, near, next to*; as, *ad*join, *ad*mit, *ad*verb, etc.

A.D. (ā′dē′), *abbrev.* in dates, after the birth of Christ; as, 457 A.D.: short for *Anno Domini* ("in the year of our Lord"). Compare with *B.C.*

ad-age (ad′ij), *n.* a pointed and well-known saying; a proverb; as, "Waste not, want not" is an *adage.*

ad-a-mant (ad′a-mant; ad′a-mant′), *adj.* extremely hard; unyielding or inflexible; as, she was *adamant* about not going to the party.

Adam's apple, a bump in the front of the throat just below the chin, esp. in men.

a-dapt (a-dapt′), *v.i.* and *v.t.* to make suitable; change so as to fit new conditions; become adapted; as, many animals *adapt* to new or changing environments; to *adapt* a book to a movie; her eyes *adapted* themselves to the dark.—*adj.* **a-dapt′a-ble.**

a-dapt-a-tion (a′dap′tā′shun), *n.* **1,** the act of adapting, making fit, or adjusting; **2,** something made by adapting; as, a film *adaptation* of a novel; **3,** an adjustment by which an individual or species changes to fit a change in its environment.

a-dapt-er or **a-dapt-or** (a-dap′tėr), *n.* something that adapts one thing to another, makes equipment compatible, or expands capabilities; as, an *adapter* to connect a DVD player to a TV; an *adapter* to expand the capabilities of a computer.

add (ad), *v.t.* **1,** to join or unite into a whole; esp. to sum up (a set of numbers); **2,** to bring (additional items); to put with others; increase; as, to *add* books to a library; **3,** to go on to say.—*n.* **add′er.**

ad-den-dum (a-den′dum), *n.* [*pl.* -da], something to be added; an appendix; a supplement.

ad-der (ad′ėr), *n.* **1,** any of several harmless North American snakes; **2,** the poisonous viper of Europe.

ad-dict (a-dikt′), *v.t.* to devote or give (oneself) up to a habit (sometimes a bad one); as, he *addicts* himself to music, alcohol, etc:—*n.* (ad′ikt), one who is given over to a habit; as, a drug *addict.*—*n.* **ad-dic′tion.**—*adj.* **ad-dict′ed.**

ad-di-tion (a-dish′un), *n.* **1,** the act, process, or result of summing up numbers, or of adding or joining something to something else; **2,** a thing that is added or joined; as, an *addition* to a house.—*adj.* **ad-di′tion-al** (extra; as, *additional* information).—*adv.* **ad-di′tion-al-ly.**

ad-di-tive (ad′i-tiv), *n.* something that is added to another thing, often to improve or enhance it; as, *additives* are often added to food to preserve it.

ad-dress (a-dres′), *v.t.* **1,** to speak or write to; **2,** to direct, as a piece of correspondence; as, to *address* a letter, an e-mail; **3,** to apply or devote (oneself) to a duty, task, etc.:—*n.* **1,** a speech delivered or written; **2,** manners and bearing; **3,** tact; cleverness; **4,** (also, ad′res), the place to which one's mail is directed; the direction written on the letter or package; **5,** in *computing,* the codes in the memory of a computer that help it to find a piece of information; also, the letters and/or numbers representing a person's e-mail location; as, an e-mail *address.*

a-dept (a-dept′), *adj.* highly skilled:—*n.* (a-dept′; ad′ept), one who is fully proficient or skilled in an art; an expert; as, he is an *adept* at diving.

ad-e-quate (ad′e-kwit), *adj.* equal to requirement; enough to meet a certain need; as, his skill was *adequate* for the job.—*n.* **ad′e-qua-cy** (ad′e-kwa-si).—*adv.* **ad′e-quate-ly.**—*n.* **ad′e-quate-ness.**

ad-here (ad-hēr′), *v.i.* [adhered, adher-ing], **1,** to stick fast as if glued; as, candy *adheres* to paper; **2,** to be attached or devoted, as to a person, principle, or party; as, he *adhered* to his plans.—*n.* **ad-her′ence.**—*n.* and *adj.* **ad-her-ent.**

ad-he-sion (ad-hē′zhun), *n.* **1,** the state of sticking fast to something; **2,** continued allegiance, as to a cause or party; **3,** the sticking together, as in a wound, of tissues that normally are separated.

ad-he-sive (ad-hē′sive), *adj.* **1,** holding fast; **2,** sticky; made so as to stick; as, *adhesive* tape:—*n.* a substance used to stick things together, as paste, glue, tape, etc.—*n.* **ad-he′sive-ness.**

a-dieu (a-dū′; a′dyö′), *n.* [*pl.* adieus (a-dūz′), or adieux (a-dyö′)], a farewell:—*interj.* French for goodbye! farewell!

a-di-os (ad′ē-ōs or äd′ē-ōs′), *interj.* Spanish for goodbye! farewell!

ad-ja-cent (a-jā′sent), *adj.* **1,** near; adjoining; as, *adjacent* fields; **2,** in *geometry,* (two angles) with a common side between them.—*n.* **ad-ja′cen-cy.**

ad-jec-tive (aj′ik-tiv), *n.* a part of speech expressing quality or condition; a word used to limit or define a noun or pronoun; as, a *bad* law, a *wise* person; a *green* leaf.—*adj.* **ad′jec-ti′val** (aj′ik-tī′val).

ad-join-ing (a-join′ing), *adj.* being next to or near; as, the library *adjoining* the school.

ad-journ (a-jûrn′), *v.t.* to bring (a meeting) to a close; also, to put off to another time; as, to *adjourn* a debate:—*v.i.* to come to a close, or to cease business for a time; as, the court *adjourned.*—*n.* **ad-journ′ment.**

ad-junct (aj′ungkt), *n.* something added to another thing, but not essentially part of it; as, a lean-to is an *adjunct* of a house; a subordinate, auxiliary, or dependent addition.

ad-just (a-just′), *v.t.* **1,** to settle, as insurance claims, differences, disputes, etc.; **2,** to put in proper order or position; change; move; regulate; as, to *adjust* a car seat, eyeglasses, the speed on the VCR, a car engine, etc.—*adj.* **ad-just′a-ble.**—*n.* **ad-just′er.**—*n.* **ad-just′ment.**

ad–lib (ad′–lib′) *v.t.* and *v.i.* [–libbed (–libd), –lib-bing], **1,** *Colloq.* to improvise or speak lines not in the script (on the stage, television, etc.); **2,** the full form is *ad libitum,* in *music* abbreviated to *ad lib′*: opposite of *obbligato*:—*n.* something that is said in this way; as, a funny *ad-lib*:—*adj.* improvised; as, an *ad-lib* presentation.

ad-min-is-ter (ad-min′is-tėr), *v.t.* **1,** to manage or conduct; as, to *administer* the affairs of state; **2,** to supply or give, as justice or relief; **3,** to cause to take; as, he *administered* the oath; **4,** in law, to settle; as, to *administer* an estate:—*v.i.* **1,** to manage affairs; **2,** in law, to settle an estate.

ad-min-is-tra-tion (ad-min′is-trā′shun), *n.* **1,** the act of managing; management; as, his *administration* of the estate was honest; **2,** that part of a government that manages the affairs of a nation, state, city, etc.; the body of people who compose the government, or their term of office; as, the policies of the *administration* were severely criticized.—*adj.* **ad-min′is-tra′tive.**—*n.* **ad-min′is-tra′tor.**

ad-min-is-tra-tive as-sis-tant. Same as **secretary.**

ad-mi-ra-ble (ad′mi-ra-bl), *adj.* worthy of wonder and approval; excellent; as, *admirable* behaviour.—*adv.* **ad′mi-ra-bly.**

ad-mir-al (ad′mi-ral), *n.* the highest rank of officer in a navy; a flag officer; as, rear *admiral*; *Admiral* of the Fleet.—*n.* **ad′mi-ral-ty.**

ad-mi-ra-tion (ad′mi-rā′shun), *n.* **1,** wonder mingled with approval and gratification or delight; as, the listeners were filled with *admiration*; **2,** the object of these feelings; as, she was the *admiration* of her classmates.

ad-mire (ad-mīr′), *v.t.* [admired, admir-ing], **1,** to regard with wonder, approval, and delight; as, to *admire* the sunset; **2,** to esteem highly; as, Greta *admires* her teacher.—*n.* **ad-mir′er.**—*adv.* **ad-mir′ing-ly.**

ad-mis-si-ble (ad-mis′i-bl), *adj.* allowable; permissible; as, this form of argument is not *admissible.*—*adv.* **ad-mis′si-bly.**

ad-mis-sion (ad-mish′un), *n.* **1,** the power or permission to enter; as, *admission* is limited to certain days; **2,** the price paid for permission to enter; **3,** acknowledgment that something is true; as, he made full *admission* of his guilt; **4,** the act of allowing someone to enter a place; as, *admission* to York University.

ad-mit (ad-mit′), *v.t.* [admit-ted, admit-ting], **1,** to permit to enter; **2,** to allow as valid in argument; accept as true; as, I *admit* the justice of your viewpoint; **3,** to permit to have certain privileges; as, to *admit* to bail; **4,** to be capable of; allow; as, the words *admit* no other meaning.

ad-mit-tance (ad-mit′ans), *n.* the literal action of letting in, as distinguished from *admission*, which is the action of letting in together with granting the rights, privileges, society, etc., that belong to the place of admission.

ad-mon-ish (ad-mon′ish), *v.t.* **1,** to reprove gently; as, she *admonished* the noisy child; **2,** to urge; exhort; as, the teacher *admonished* the students to be patient.—*n.* **ad′mo-ni-′tion** (ad′mo-nish′un).

ad nau-se-am (ad nä′zē-am), *adv.* to a sickening or disgusting degree; as, she spoke about her trip *ad nauseam.*

a-do-be (a-dō′bi), *n.* **1,** unburnt brick dried in the sun, used in southwestern U.S. and Mexico; **2,** a structure made of such brick.

ad-o-les-cent (ad′ō-les′ent), *adj.* growing up; passing from childhood to adulthood; youthful:—*n.* a person past childhood, but not yet fully grown; a teenager.—*n.* **ad′o-les′cence.**

a-dopt (a-dopt′), *v.t.* **1,** to choose or take to be one's own; as, to *adopt* a child, or a plan; **2,** to use, approve, or accept; as, the boys *adopted* his idea; the school *adopted* the new program.—*n.* **a-dop′tion.**

a-dore (a-dōr′), *v.t.* [adored, ador-ing], **1,** to regard with warm admiration and affection; as, the mother *adores* her baby; **2,** to worship; as, to *adore* God.—*adj.* **a-dor′a-ble.**—*n.* **ad′o-ra′tion.**

a-dorn (a-dôrn′), *v.t.* to decorate; ornament; as, to *adorn* the room with flowers.—*n.* **a-dorn′ment.**

ad-ren-al-in (a-dren′a-lin), *n.* a stimulating hormone secreted by the adrenal glands.

a-drift (a-drift′), *adj.* and *adv.* floating at random; at the mercy of wind and tide; as, to cast a boat *adrift.*

a-droit (a-droit′), *adj.* clever; expert; skill-ful.—*adv.* **a-droit′ly.**—*n.* **a-droit′ness.**

ad-u-la-tion (ad′ū-lā′shun), *n.* servile praise or flattery.—*adj.* **ad′u-la-tor-y.**

a-dult (a-dult′; ad′ult), *adj.* grown to full size:—*n.* a full-grown animal or person.

a-dul-ter-y (a-dul′tė-ri), *n.* sexual intercourse with a person other than one's spouse.—*n.* **a-dul′ter-er, a-dul′ter-ess.**—*adj.* **a-dul′ter-ous.**

ad-vance (ad-våns′), *v.i.* [advanced, advanc-ing], **1,** to go forward; **2,** to rise in rank, price, etc.; as, he *advanced* to the presidency; the cost of food *advanced*:—*v.t.* **1,** to help forward; as, his money *advanced* the work; **2,** to promote; as, they *advanced* him to the principalship; **3,** to increase, as prices; **4,** to offer, as an opinion; **5,** to furnish (money) beforehand; as, he *advanced* me 20 dollars:—*n.* **1,** a moving forward; **2,** improvement; **3,** rise in rank or value; **4,** an approach, as to make someone's acquaintance, adjust a quarrel, etc.; as, he was the first to make *advances*; **5,** a loan or money paid before it is due; as, an *advance* that an author receives on a book:—*adj.* ahead of time; as, an *advance* warning.—*n.* **ad-vance′ment.**

ad-vanced (ad-vånst′), *adj.* far along in life or time, or far ahead of others in any course of action, outlook, or the like; as, a person of *advanced* ideas.

advance poll, **1,** an early poll for voters who cannot vote on election day; **2,** the number of votes cast in that poll.

ad-van-tage (ad-vån′tij), *n.* **1,** superiority in position, skill, etc.; **2,** benefit from favourable circumstances; a useful or helpful result; as, the *advantages* of foreign travel; to take *advantage* of the good weather.

ad-van-ta-geous (ad′van-tā′jus), *adj.* useful; favourable; profitable.—*adv.* **ad-van-ta′geous-ly.**

ad-vent (ad′vent), *n.* a coming; arrival; as, the *advent* of fall:—**Advent,** the period including the four Sundays before Christmas.

ad-ven-ture (ad-ven′tūr; -choor), *n.* **1,** a bold undertaking, involving risk and danger; as, the *adventures* of explorers; **2,** the encountering of new and exciting events; as, to crave *adventure*; **3,** an unusual or exciting experience; as, one's first hot air balloon ride is an *adventure*:—*v.t.* and *v.i.* [adventured, adventur-ing], to take a chance: venture.—*adj.* **ad-ven′tur-ous; ad-ven′ture-some.**—*n.* **ad-ven′tur-er.**

ad-verb (ad′vûrb), *n.* a word used: **1,** to modify a verb, telling the time, place, or manner of the action; as, you came *early*; he came *here* yesterday; I read *slowly*; **2,** to modify an adjective or another adverb, indicating degree; as, *very* pretty; *too* quickly.—*adj.* **ad-ver′bi-al.**

ad-ver-sar-y (ad′vėr-sa-ri; -ser′), *n.* [*pl.* adversaries], an enemy; opponent; antagonist.

ad-verse (ad′vûrs; ad-vûrs′), *adj.* **1,** opposed; not favourable or good; as, *adverse* winds; **2,** critical or disapproving; as, *adverse* reports.—*adv.* **ad′verse-ly** or **ad-verse′ly.**

ad-ver-si-ty (ad-vûr′si-ti), *n.* [*pl.* –ties], misfortune; lack of prosperity; hardship.

ad-ver-tise (ad′vėr-tiz′; ad′vėr-tiz′), *v.t.* [advertised, advertis-ing], to turn the attention of others to; announce, esp. by printed matter, radio, television, on the Internet, etc.; as, to *advertise* a sale; publish:—*v.i.* to give public notice, as by circular, newspaper, radio, television, etc.:—**advertise for,** to ask for by public notice.—*n.* **a′ver-tis′er.**

ad-ver-tise-ment (ad′vėr-tīz′ment or ad-vûr′tis-ment; -tiz-), *n.* a notice or public announcement, esp. about something wanted or offered for sale.—*n.* **ad′ver-tis-ing.**

ad-ver-to-ri-al (ad′vėr-tōr-ē-al), *n.* an advertisement for products or services that mimics real editorial reporting.

ad-vice (ad-vīs′), *n.* an opinion offered as a guide to someone's action; recommendation; counsel.—*adj.* **ad-vis-a-ble.**—*n.* **ad-vis′a-bil′i-ty.**

ad-vise (ad-vīz′), *v.t.* [advised, advis-ing], **1,** to give advice to; as, he *advised* me to go; **2,** to notify; as, she *advised* me of my promotion:—*v.i.* to get advice; consult; as, he *advised* with me about his plans.—*n.* **ad-vis′er; ad-vi′sor.**

ad-vis-ed-ly (ad-vī′zid-li), *adv.* deliberately; after careful thought; as, he chose *advisedly* to delay payment.

ad-vi-so-ry (ad-vī′zo-ri), *adj.* having power to give advice; as, an *advisory* board.

ad-vo-cate (ad′vō-kāt′; -kit), *n.* **1,** one who pleads the cause of another, esp. in a court of law; **2,** one who is in favour of something; as, an *advocate* for animal rights:—*v.t.* (ad′vō-kāt′), [advocat-ed, advocat-ing], to urge; as, he *advocated* mercy.—*n.* **ad′vo-ca-cy** (ad′vō-ka-si).

aer-i-al (âr′i-al), *adj.* **1,** living in the air, as do certain plants; also, produced in or from the air; as, *aerial* currents; *aerial* photographs; **2,** high; lofty; as, *aerial* towers; **3,** not real or substantial; imaginary; as, *aerial* flights of fancy:—*n.* in radio or television systems, one or more wires suspended in the air to receive or radiate energy; an antenna.

aero- (âr′ō), *prefix* meaning *air, oxygen, atmosphere, gas,* or *aviation*; as, *aero*space, *aero*bics, *aero*sol, *aero*nautics, etc.

aer-o-bat-ics (âr′ō-bat′iks), *n.* [*pl.* used as *sing.*], stunts, esp. in an airplane.

aer-o-bic (âr-ō′bik), *adj.* using or growing with oxygen; as, most plants are *aerobic*.

aerobic exercise or **aerobics**, exercise that strengthens the heart and lungs by increasing the efficiency of oxygen taken in by the body.

aer-o-dy-nam-ics (âr-ō-dī-nam′iks), *n.* the interaction between the air and solid bodies moving through it; the study of this; as, to use the principles of *aerodynamics* to design better airplanes.

aer-o-nau-tics (âr′ō-nô′tiks), *n.* [*pl.* used as *sing.*], the science of aviation, or of designing, manufacturing, and operating aircraft.—*adj.* **a′er-o-nau′tic; a′er-o-nau′ti-cal.**

aer-o-sol (âr′ō-säl′), *n.* **1,** minute liquid or solid particles held in gas, such as fog and smoke; **2,** a substance under pressure, sealed inside a container, that is released through a valve in a fine mist or foam, such as shaving cream, deodorant, hair spray, paint, etc.; also the container holding this substance:—*adj.* pertaining to this type of substance or the container; as, *aerosol* spray.

aer-o-space (âr′ō-spās′), *n.* all the area above the earth; the earth's atmosphere and the space beyond it.

aes-thet-ic or **es-thet-ic** (es-thet′ik), *adj.* **1,** having to do with beauty; **2,** sensitive to the beautiful in art or nature; having a cultivated, artistic taste.—*adj.* **aes-thet′-i-cal.**

aes-the-ti-cian or **es-the-ti-cian** (es-the-tish′an), *n.* **1,** a beautician; **2,** one who is devoted to the study of beauty in art or in nature.

a-far (a-fär′), *adv.* at, to, or from a distance; as, he went *afar* seeking work.

af-fa-ble (af′a-bl), *adj.* courteous; friendly.—*n.* **af′fa-bil′i-ty.**—*adv.* **af′fa-bly.**

af-fair (a-fâr′), *n.* **1,** concern; proceeding; matter; as, luncheon is a simple *affair;* **2,** that which is done, or is to be done; as, a hard *affair* to manage; **3,** affairs, business of any kind; as, *affairs* of state.

[1]af-fect (a-fekt′), *v.t.* to produce an effect upon; as, his tale *affected* me deeply.

[2]af-fect (a-fekt′), *v.t.* **1,** to pretend to do or to have; as, she *affected* a sympathy she did not feel; **2,** to show a liking for; as, he *affected* loud T-shirts.

af-fec-ta-tion (af′ek-tā′shun), *n.* the assuming of a manner merely to create an impression; also, an instance of this; as, *affectation* of wit, wealth, manners, etc.—*adj.* **af-fect′ed.**

af-fect-ing (a-fek′ting), *adj.* having power to excite the emotions; pathetic; as, the mother's grief was most *affecting.*

af-fec-tion (a-fek′shun), *n.* love; fondness; as, *affection* for animals.—*adj.* **af-fec′tion-ate.**—*adv.* **af-fec′tion-ate-ly.**

af-fi-da-vit (af′i-dā′vit), *n.* a sworn statement in writing, esp. one made before a court or notary public.

af-fil-i-ate (a-fil′i-āt′), *v.t.* [affiliat-ed, affiliat-ing], to join; as, to *affiliate* oneself with a certain set of people:—*v.i.* to become connected or associated; as, one company *affiliated* with the other:—*n.* (a-fil′ē-it) a person or thing that is affiliated; as, a TV station that is an *affiliate* of CBC.—*n.* **af-fil′i-a′tion.**

af-fin-i-ty (a-fin′i-ti), *n.* [*pl.* -ties], **1,** a close relationship; as, an *affinity* between two races of people, or between two languages; **2,** special attraction; as, the *affinity* of salt for water; **3,** a liking for a person; also, the person liked.

af-firm (a-fûrm′), *v.t.* and *v.i.* to declare solemnly, as to a court, but without taking oath; to declare vigorously and strongly; as, he *affirmed* his belief in my honesty.—*n.* **af′fir-ma′tion** (af′ėr-mā′shun).

af-firm-a-tive (a-fûr′ma-tiv), *n.* the side in a debate that defends a proposition; as, the *affirmative* won:—*adj.* **1,** answering, or consisting of, "yes"; as, an *affirmative* answer; **2,** supporting a proposition; as, the *affirmative* side.—*adv.* **af-firm′a-tive-ly.**

affirmative action, a policy, esp. in the U.S., to help advance women and minorities in education and employment.

af-fix (a-fiks′), *v.t.* to attach or add; as, I *affixed* the document to the e-mail:—*n.* (af′iks), a part added to a word, as a prefix like *ad-* or *un-*, or a suffix like *-able* or *-ness.*

af-flict (a-flikt′), *v.t.* to distress with pain or great trouble; make miserable.—*n.* **af-flic′tion.**

af-flu-ent (af′loo-ent), *adj.* having abundance; wealthy; rich; as, an *affluent* citizen; *affluent* times.—*n.* **af′flu-ence.**

af-ford (a-fōrd′), *v.t.* **1,** to supply; produce; yield; as, singing *affords* him pleasure; **2,** to bear the expense of; as, she can *afford* a car; **3,** to manage to give; spare; as, I can *afford* the time.

af-front (a-frunt′), *v.t.* to insult intentionally; as, the student *affronted* the teacher:—*n.* an insult; as, an *affront* to one's honour.

a-fi-cio-na-do (a′fish-a-nä′dō; a′fis-ya-nä′dō), *n.* someone who is an enthusiastic fan or devotee and knowledgeable about a particular pursuit or activity; as, an *aficionado* of hockey.

a-flame (a-flām′), *adj.* on fire; blazing; also, ardent; as, *aflame* with patriotism.

a-float (a-flōt′), *adj.* and *adv.* **1,** floating on water, as a vessel; on board ship, as the crew; **2,** awash; covered with water, as a deck; **3,** in circulation; commonly talked about; as, a rumour is *afloat.*

a-foot (a-foot′), *adj.* and *adv.* **1,** on foot; **2,** astir; as, a conspiracy was *afoot.*

a-fraid (a-frād′), *adj.* filled with fear; frightened; as, he was *afraid* of the dog.

a-fresh (a-fresh′), *adv.* again; anew; newly; over again; as, to start *afresh.*

Af-ri-can (af′ri-kan), *n.* a person who inhabits or originates from Africa:—*adj.* relating to the continent, the people, the language, or the culture of Africa.

aft (åft), *adj.* and *adv.* toward the stern of a ship; as, the *aft* cabin; to go *aft.*

af-ter (åf′tėr), *prep.* **1,** in succession to; as, B comes *after* A; **2,** later than; as, John arrived *after* Joan; **3,** in imitation of; in the manner of; as, a painting *after* Raphael; **4,** in pursuit of; as, she ran *after* the dog; **5,** by the name of; as, he is named *after* his father; **6,** in spite of; as, *after* all your help, she failed:—*conj.* following the time when; as, *after* they have dinner, they may go:—*adv.* afterward; as, she arrived shortly *after:*—*adj.* **1,** later; as, in *after* days; **2,** in the rear; as, the *after* deck.

after all, in spite of; nevertheless; as, she came *after all.*

af-ter-birth (åf′tėr-bûrth′), *n.* the placenta and fetal membranes discharged after birth.

af-ter-math (åf′tėr-math′), *n.* result; (bad) consequences; as, the *aftermath* of the war.

af-ter-noon (åf′tėr-nōōn′), *n.* the time between noon and evening:—*adj.* occurring in the afternoon (af′tėr-nōōn′).

af-ter-shave (åf′tėr-shāv′), *n.* a lotion, usually scented and astringent, that is applied to the face after shaving.

af-ter-shock (åf′tėr-shok′), *n.* **1,** a smaller tremor following the main shock of an earthquake; **2,** an after-effect.

af-ter-taste (åf′tėr-tāst′), *n.* **1,** the taste

that remains after eating or drinking; **2,** the persistent sensation or feeling that remains after an event; as, the *aftertaste* of defeat.

af-ter-thought (åf′tėr-thôt′), *n.* a second or later thought about something, esp. one that comes too late.

af-ter-ward (åf′tėr-wėrd) or **af-ter-wards** (åf′tėr-wėrdz), *adv.* at a later time.

af-ter-word (åf′tėr-wûrd′), *n.* an epilogue or concluding comment of a book.

a-gain (a-gen′; a-gān′), *adv.* **1,** a second time; once more; as, do it *again*; **2,** in return; as, give the book back *again*; **3,** further; on the other hand; as, then *again*, I need cash.

a-gainst (a-genst′; a-gānst′), *prep.* **1,** in contact with; near to; as, to lean *against* a tree; **2,** opposite to; facing; in the direction of; as, over *against* the wall; **3,** in opposition to; as, a law *against* speeding.

age (āj), *n.* **1,** a particular time or period in life; as, the *age* of six; the *age* of childhood; **2,** a period in history; as, the computer *age*; **3,** the latter part of life; as, the wisdom of *age*; **4,** *Colloq.* a long or weary time; as, it's *ages* since I saw you:—**of age,** legally old enough; 18 years old; as, he just came *of age*:—*v.i.* and *v.t.* [aged, ag-ing or age-ing], to grow old, or cause to grow old; as, to *age* cheese.

ag-ed (ā′jid), *adj.* **1,** old; far on in years; as, an *aged* man; **2,** (*ājd*), of the age of; as, a child *aged* three.

a-gen-cy (ā′jen-si), *n.* [*pl.* agencies], **1,** the business or place of business of one who acts for another; as, a ticket or real estate *agency*; **2,** help; active influence; as, crops grow through the *agency* of rain.

a-gen-da (a-jen′da), *n. pl.* **1,** the list of items on a program of business to be brought up or discussed at a meeting; **2,** *Colloq.* any plan of things to be done; as, what's on the *agenda* for this weekend?

a-gent (ā′jent), *n.* **1,** one who acts, esp. for another; as, an *agent* for a firm or author; **2,** an active power or cause; as, religion is an *agent* for good; **3,** something that produces a certain effect; as, yeast is an *agent* that causes dough to rise; **4,** a person who works for a government agency.

ag-gra-vate (ag′ra-vāt′), *v.t.* [aggravat-ed, aggravat-ing], **1,** to increase, as a burden; make worse; as, worry will only *aggravate* your illness; **2,** *Colloq.* to annoy; irritate; as, his boasting *aggravates* me.—*adj.* **ag′gra-vat′ing.**—*n.* **ag′gra-va′tion.**

ag-gre-gate (ag′re-gāt′), *v.t.* [aggregat-ed, aggregat-ing], to collect or bring together; gather into one whole or mass:—*n.* (ag′re-git), **1,** the entire number; total; **2,** a mass formed by the sticking together of similar particles:—*adj.* taken as a whole; as, the *aggregate* amount.—*n.* **ag′gre-ga′tion.**

ag-gres-sion (a-gresh′un), *n.* an unprovoked attack or assault.—*n.* **ag-gres′sor.**

ag-gres-sive (a-gres′iv), *adj.* **1,** energetic; pushing; competitive; as, an *aggressive* salesperson or athlete; **2,** first to attack or quarrel, esp. without a cause; as, an *aggressive* nation.—*adv.* **ag-gres′sive-ly.**—*n.* **ag-gres′sive-ness.**

ag-grieved (a-grēvd′), *adj.* having a grievance; having cause of grief or offence; as, he felt *aggrieved* at being left out.

a-ghast (a-gåst′), *adj.* struck with sudden surprise, horror, or terror; as, she stood *aghast* at the damage done by the tornado.

ag-ile (aj′il; aj′īl), *adj.* quick-moving; active; nimble; also, mentally quick; as, an *agile* mind.—*n.* **a-gil′i-ty** (a-jil′i-ti).

ag-i-tate (aj′i-tāte′), *v.t.* [agitat-ed, agitat-ing], **1,** to stir violently; as, the storm *agitates* the sea; **2,** to excite; disturb; as, losing her job *agitated* her; **3,** to discuss publicly; argue for; as, to *agitate* for the repeal of a law:—*v.i.* to stir up public interest; as, to *agitate* for shorter working hours.—*n.* **ag′i-ta′tion.**—*n.* **ag′i-ta′tor.**

a-glow (a-glō′), *adj.* bright; flushed; as, cheeks *aglow* with health.

ag-nos-tic (ag-nos′tik) *n.* and *adj.* one who holds that we cannot know whether there is a God or anything beyond physical life.

a-go (a-go′), *adj.* and *adv.* past; in past time; as, an hour *ago*; long *ago*.

ag-o-nize (ag′o-nīz′), *v.i.* [agonized, agoniz-ing], **1,** to suffer extreme pain, anguish, or grief; **2,** to make a great effort; struggle; as, to *agonize* over an essay:—*v.t.* to torment or torture.

ag-o-ny (ag′o-ni), *n.* [*pl.* agonies], **1,** intense suffering of body or mind; as, an earache is *agony*; she suffered *agonies* of remorse for her carelessness; **2,** the death struggle of a person, etc.

a-gree (a-grē′), *v.i.* [agreed, agree-ing], **1,** to consent; as, he *agreed* to the plan to go; **2,** to be in harmony; as, I *agree* with you:—**agree with, 1,** in *grammar*, to correspond with; as, the verb *agrees with* its subject in person and number; **2,** to suit physically; as, fruit *agrees with* me.

a-gree-a-ble (a-grē′a-bl), *adj.* **1,** ready or willing to agree; **2,** pleasant; as, an *agreeable* afternoon; having pleasing manners or personality; as, an *agreeable* companion.

a-gree-ment (a-grē′ment), *n.* **1,** harmony of opinions or feelings; **2,** in *grammar*, the correspondence of one word with another in gender, number, case, or person; **3,** a compact; contract; as, the *agreement* for the sale was drawn up and signed; a trade *agreement* between two countries.

ag-ri-cul-ture (ag′ri-kul′tûr), *n.* the cultivation of the soil; farming.—*adj.* **ag′ri-cul′tur-al.**—*n.* **ag′ri-cul′tur-ist; ag′ri-cul′tur-al-ist.**

a-gron-o-my (a-grän′o-mi), *n.* the branch of agriculture dealing with crop production and soil management; the management of farmland.—*n.* **a-gron′o-mist.**—*adj.* **ag′ron-o′mic.**—*adv.* **ag′ro-nom′i-cal-ly.**

a-ground (a-ground′), *adv.* and *adj.* stranded, as a ship on a shoal, reef, etc.; as, the boat ran *aground.*

a-head (a-hed′), *adv.* in front; forward; onward; advanced.

a-hoy (a-hoi′), *interj.* a call used in hailing a vessel; as, ship *ahoy*!

aid (ād), *n.* help; assistance; as, to come to someone's *aid*; also, something that is helpful; as, a hearing *aid:*—*v.t.* to help; as, to *aid* someone.

aide (ād′), *n.* an assistant; as, the prime minister's *aides.*

AIDS (āds), *n.* a serious disease that affects a person's immune system, making it difficult to fight off other diseases: short for *A*cquired *I*mmune *D*eficiency *S*yndrome.

ail (āl), *v.t.* to trouble with pain or discomfort; as, what *ails* the child?—*v.i.* to feel pain; be ill; as, they are all *ailing.*

ail-ment (āl′ment), *n.* sickness; illness.

aim (ām), *v.t.* to point at someone or something; as, to *aim* a camera; hence, to direct; as, the remark was *aimed* at you:—*v.i.* **1,** to point something; **2,** to direct one's efforts:—*n.* **1,** the pointing of something; **2,** a goal or purpose.

aim-less (ām′lis), *adj.* without a definite intention or purpose; as, an *aimless* stroll.

air (âr), *n.* **1,** a mixture of gases, consisting chiefly of oxygen and nitrogen, which surrounds the earth; the atmosphere; **2,** a light or fresh breeze; **3,** an appearance or manner; as, an *air* of dignity; **4,** a tune or melody; as, she hummed an *air*; **5,** airs, affected manners; as, she put on *airs:*—**on/off air,** that which is/is not being broadcast:—**up in the air,** not decided; uncertain; as, plans that are *up in the air:*—*v.t.* **1,** to expose to the *air*; ventilate; **2,** to make a public display of; as, he is always *airing* his views; **3,** to broadcast. Also, **air′ hock′ey; air′ mat′tress.**

air bag, a safety device consisting of a bag that inflates to restrain automotive passengers in the event of a collision.

air brake, 1, a brake operated by compressed air; **2,** the flaplike device used to slow the speed of aircraft.

air-borne (âr′bōrn′), *adj.* carried by, in, or on air; as, *airborne* planes, troops, bacteria.

air–con-di-tion (âr′–kon-dish′un), *v.t.* to provide desirable temperature, humidity, and purity by circulating treated air within a structure; to cool.—*adj.* **air′–con-di′tioned.**

air–con-di-tion-ing, a system of treating the air in a room, building, car, or other closed place, which makes the air cooler, drier, and cleaner.—**air′–con-di′tion-er.**

air-craft (âr′kråft′), *n.* [*pl.* aircraft], any type of machine for flying, as a helicopter, glider, or airplane.

aircraft carrier, a large warship with a long, flat deck that planes use to land and take off from.

air-fare (âr′fâr′), *n.* the cost for a flight on an airplane.

air force or **Air Force,** the branch of the military forces of a country that is responsible for military aircraft.

air-head (âr′hed′), *n.* **1,** an airbase established in captured enemy territory: compare to *beachhead;* **2,** *Slang* a mindless, flighty, or stupid person.

air-i-ness (âr′i-nis), *n.* **1,** openness to the air; as, the *airiness* of an apartment; **2,** delicacy; lightness; **3,** sprightliness; jauntiness; as, an *airiness* of manner.

air-lift (âr′lift′), *n.* an airplane service ferrying supplies and people over inaccessible territory:—*v.t.* to carry someone or something by this method; as, to *airlift* the injured person.

air-line (âr′līn′), *n.* **1,** a company that moves people and goods by aircraft; also, a system of air transport; **2,** the route used by the air system or company; **3,** the air hose used by an underwater diver:—*adj.* pertaining to air transport; as, the *airline* industry.—*n.* **air′lin′er.**

air-mail or **air–mail** (âr′māl), *n.* a system of sending mail by means of aircraft:—*v.t.* to send something this way:—*adj.* and *adv.* pertaining to something sent this way; as, an *airmail* letter; to send a package *airmail.*

air-plane (âr′plān′), *n.* a motor-driven aircraft, kept aloft by the force of the air upon its winglike planes.

air-play (âr′plā′), *n.* broadcasting of audio or audiovisual recordings over radio or television; as, her new CD is getting a lot of *airplay.*

air pocket, an air current or vacuum that causes an aircraft to lose altitude abruptly.

air-port (âr′pôrt′), *n.* a place with facilities for the departure, landing, loading, fuelling, or repairing of aircraft.

air pressure or **atmospheric pressure,** the pressure exerted on the earth's surface by the weight of the air above it, not felt by people because of the equal pressure on all sides.

air-ship (âr′ship′), *n.* a motor-driven aircraft that is lighter than air and which has propulsion and steering systems; a dirigible.

air-sick (âr′sik′), *adj.* nausea, dizziness, and associated illnesses caused by the motion of an aircraft.—*n.* **air′sick′ness.**

air-space (âr′spās′), *n.* the air or sky above a country, legally agreed among nations to be part of that country's territory.

air-speed (âr′spēd′), *n.* the speed of an aircraft relative to the air around it rather than to the ground.

air-strip (âr′strip′), *n.* a runway for the takeoff and landing of airplanes.

air-tight (âr′tīt′), *adj.* **1,** so tight that no air can get in or out; **2,** without flaw; as, he has an *airtight* alibi.

air time (âr′tīm′), *n.* **1,** the starting time of a radio or television program; as, 10 minutes to *airtime*; **2,** the amount of broadcasting time assigned to a program, commercial, etc.

air-waves (âr′wāvs′), *n. pl.* the medium used to broadcast radio and television signals.

air-y (âr′i), *adj.* [air-i-er, air-i-est], **1,** open to the air; breezy; **2,** of the air; as, *airy* spirits; **3,** delicate; light; as, *airy* fabric; **4,** happy; lighthearted.—*adv.* **air′i-ly.**

aisle (īl), *n.* a long, narrow passageway; as, an *aisle* in a theatre, in a store, on an airplane, etc.

a-jar (a-jär′), *adv.* and *adj.* slightly open.

a.k.a. or **AKA** (ā.′kā.′ā.′), *abbrev.* also known as; as, Wayne Gretzky, *a.k.a.* "The Great One."

a-kimbo (a-kim′bō), *adj.* and *adv.* with the hands supported on the hips and the elbows turned outward; bent; as, he stood with arms *akimbo.*

a-kin (a-kin′), *adj.* **1,** related by blood; **2,** of the same kind; near in nature or character; compatible; as, the two schemes are closely *akin.*

al-a-bas-ter (al′a-bås′tėr), *n.* a kind of stone, usually white, of fine texture, often carved into vases or ornaments:—*adj.* made of alabaster; white like alabaster.

a-lac-ri-ty (a-lak′ri-ti), *n.* eager readiness to do something; as, he accepted the invitation with *alacrity.*

a-larm (a-lärm′), *n.* **1,** a call to arms; hence, a warning of danger; as, he gave the *alarm;* **2,** the fear of danger; as, *alarm* seized the camp; **3,** a device to warn or awaken persons; as, a fire *alarm:*—*v.t.* to arouse to a sense of danger; startle; as, we were *alarmed* by the smell of smoke.—*adj.* **a-larm′ing.**—*adv.* **a-larm′ing-ly.**

alarm clock, a clock that can be set to ring, buzz, play music, or make a similar noise at a certain time, usually used to awaken a sleeping person.

a-larm-ist (a-lär′mist), *n.* one who exaggerates bad news or foretells calamities.

al-ba-tross (al′ba-trôs′), *n.* **1,** a very large web-footed sea bird, of southern waters, capable of remarkably long flights from land; **2,** something problematic or that causes deep concern.

al-be-it (ôl-bē′it), *conj.* although; even though; as, a light, *albeit* a faint one.

Al-ber-to-saur-us (al-bėrt′o-sôr′us), *n.* a dinosaur similar to Tyrannosaurus rex, the remains of which were first found in Alberta in the 1880s.

al-bi-no (al-bī′nō), *n.* a person or animal that lacks colouring in the skin, eyes, and hair.

al-bum (al′bum), *n.* **1,** a book with blank pages, in which to keep a collection of photographs, stamps, autographs, etc.; **2,** a long-playing record or tape.

al-che-my (al′ke-mi), *n.* an early form of chemistry of changing baser metals to gold; hence, any mysterious change.

al-co-hol (al′kō-hol′), *n.* a colourless liquid, made by the fermentation of grapes, grain, etc., and forming the intoxicating substance in all fermented and distilled liquors; also, various kinds of this substance used in medicine, as fuel, and for many other products.—*adj.* and *n.* **al′co-hol′ic.**—*n.* **al′co-hol-ism′.**

al-cove (al′kōv), *n.* a recess in a room, as for a window seat or bookcase; also, a very small room opening into a larger room.

al-der-man (ôl′dėr-man), *n.* [*pl.* aldermen], in some cities of Canada and the U.S., a member of the city's governing body representing a ward or district.

ale (āl), *n.* a fairly dark fermented liquor made from malt and hops; a type of beer.

a-lert (a-lûrt′), *adj.* **1,** watchful; wide-awake; as, an *alert* watchdog; **2,** nimble; active; quick to understand; as, an *alert* child:—*n.* warning of an attack, as from the air:—*v.t.* to warn of an attack:—**on the alert,** ready to act; on the lookout.—*adv.* **a-lert′ly.**—*n.* **a-lert′-ness.**

al-fal-fa (al-fal′fa), *n.* a kind of clover, having purple flowers and very deep roots, grown as food for cattle, horses, and people; as, *alfalfa* sprouts.

al-gae (al′jē), *n. pl.* [*sing.* alga (al′ga)], a group of flowerless, rootless, stemless, and leafless water plants, including the seaweeds.

al-ge-bra (al′je-bra), *n.* a branch of mathematics that represents unknown quantities by the use of letters and other symbols, instead of by numbers, as in arithmetic.

Al-gon-qui-an or **Al-gon-quin** (al-gông′kwē-in; al-gông′kwin), *adj.* the languages spoken by groups of Aboriginal peoples from Labrador to the Rockies, including Abenaki, Blackfoot, Cree, Malecite, Micmac, Ojibwa, and Ottawa; **2,** *n.* the Aboriginal people who speak these languages.

al-go-rithm (al′go-ri′*th*m), *n.* a step-by-step procedure, process, or set of rules for calculating or problem solving, esp. with a computer.

a-li-as (ā′li-as), *n.* an assumed name; as, the forger had two *aliases:*—*adv.* otherwise called; as, Max, *alias* Sam.

al-i-bi (al′i-bī′), *n.* [*pl.* alibis], **1,** the plea offered by a person accused of a crime, of having been elsewhere at the time the crime was committed; **2,** *Colloq.* an excuse.

al-ien (āl′yen; ā′li-en), *n.* **1,** a foreigner; a person who is not a citizen of the country in which he or she is living; **2,** a being from another planet:—*adj.* **1,** foreign; as, *alien* peoples; **2,** being from another planet; as, an *alien* flying object; **3,** strange; unnatural; as, language *alien* to these people.

al-ien-ate (āl′ye-nāte; ā′li-en-āt′), *v.t.* [alienat-ed, alienat-ing], to estrange (a person); cause (affection) to turn away; to separate; as, she was *alienated* from her brother; to *alienate* herself from the group.—*n.* **al′ien-a′tion** (āl′yen-ā-shun; ā′li-en-ā′shun).—*adj.* **al′ien-a-ble.**

a-light (a-līt′), *adj.* **1,** kindled and burning, as a fire; **2,** lighted up; excited; as, the child's face was *alight* with joy:—*v.i.* **1,** to come down, as from a horse or train; **2,** to descend and settle; to land, as an airplane.

a-lign (a-līn′), *v.t.* and *v.i.* **1,** to put or get into line; as, to *align* troops; the girls *aligned* quickly; **2,** to join or co-operate with; as, to *align* on foreign policy.

a-lign-ment (a-līn′ment), *n.* the act of arranging, or an arrangement, in a straight line; as, the *alignment* was good; the *alignment* of the car wheels; **2,** co-operation; as, the *alignment* between two nations.

a-like (a-līk′), *adj.* resembling one another; similar:—*adv.* in a similar manner.

al-i-men-ta-ry (al′i-men′ta-ri), *adj.* pertaining to food and nutrition:—**alimentary canal,** the digestive tract of the body, consisting of esophagus, stomach, and intestines, through which food passes.

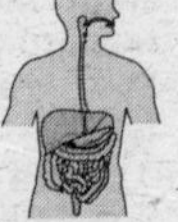
ALIMENTARY CANAL

al-i-mo-ny (al′i-mō′ni), *n.* money required by law to be paid to a former husband or wife after a divorce.

a-live (a-līv′), *adj.* **1,** having life; **2,** lively; animated; as, *alive* with excitement; **3,** attentive; sensitive; as, he is *alive* to his opportunities; **4,** full of living things; swarming; as, the stream is *alive* with fish.

al-ka-li (al′ka-lī′; al′ka-li), *n.* [*pl.* alkalis; -lies], a chemical substance, as soda or potash, that neutralizes acids and combines with them to form salts; a base.—*adj.* **al′ka-line.**

alkaline battery, a long-lasting dry cell with an alkaline electrolyte that is stronger and more durable than traditional batteries.

all (ôl), *adj.* **1,** the whole of; every bit of; as, *all* the world; **2,** every one of; as, *all* humans; **3,** as much as possible; as, with *all* speed; **4,** nothing but; as, *all* work and no play:—*n.* and *pron.* **1,** the whole number or quantity; as, *all* of us, or *all* of the money we have; **2,** one's entire possessions; as, he lost, or gave, his *all*:—*adv.* **1,** wholly; as, *all* wrong; **2,** exhausted; as, *all* in.

Al-lah (al′a; ål-lä′), *n.* the Muslim name of the Supreme Being or God.

al-lay (a-lā′), *v.t.* to quiet or calm; lessen; as, to *allay* your fears.

al-lege (a-lej′), *v.t.* [alleged, alleg-ing], **1,** to offer as an argument, plea, or excuse; as, she *alleged* illness for her failure to come; **2,** to assert; as, he *alleges* his innocence.—*adj.* **al-leged′.**—*adv.* **al-leg′ed-ly.**—*n.* **al′le-ga′tion.**

al-le-giance (a-lē′jens), *n.* **1,** the loyalty, faithfulness, or obligation of a person to his or her country; **2,** fidelity to a thing, cause, or person; as, we pledged *allegiance* to our new leader.

al-le-gor-y (al′e-gōr′i), *n.* [*pl.* allegories], a story, usually aiming to teach something, as Bunyan's *Pilgrim's Progress*, in which the characters stand for ideas or qualities, such as truth, loyalty, etc.—*adj.* **al′le-gor′i-cal** (al′e-gōr′i-kal).—*adv.* **al′le-gor′i-cal-ly.**

al-ler-gen (al′ėr-jen), *n.* a substance, such as pollen or ragweed, that causes an allergic reaction; as, peanuts are an increasingly common *allergen*.

al-ler-gy (al′ėr-ji), *n.* [*pl.* allergies], extreme sensitivity to certain things, as pollens, fruits, nuts, etc. Hives, asthma, and hay fever are common *allergies*.—*adj.* **al-ler-gic**.

al-le-vi-ate (a-lē′vi-āt′), *v.t.* [alleviat-ed, alleviat-ing], to lighten; lessen; make easier; as, a drug to *alleviate* pain.

al-ley (al′i), *n.* [*pl.* alleys], **1,** a narrow space between buildings; a back street in a city; **2,** a long, narrow enclosure for games; as, a bowling *alley*.—*n.* **al′ley-way′.**

al-li-ance (a-lī′ans), *n.* **1,** a union between or among nations, groups, or persons; as, an *alliance* by marriage; **2,** a group of persons, societies, or nations, united by treaty or agreement.

al-li-ga-tor (al′i-gā′tėr), *n.* a large, lizard-like, carnivorous reptile related to the crocodile, with a short, broad head and blunt snout.

all–in-clu-sive (ôl′–in-klōō′siv; ôl′–in-klū′siv), *n.* including everything; as, an *all-inclusive* vacation.

al-lit-er-a-tion (a-lit′ėr-ā′shun), *n.* the repetition of initial sounds in a phrase; as, the *t*eeming *t*rout *t*winkled below.

al-lo-cate (al′ō-kāt′), *v.t.* [-cat-ed, -cat-ing], to assign; allot; set apart; as, they *allocated* funds for the event.

al-lo-phone (a′lo-fōn′), *n.* **1,** a person whose mother tongue is neither English nor French; as, the *allophones* of Québec; **2,** in *linguistics*, one of two or more variations of the same phoneme or sound; as, the p's in "*p*ot" and "s*p*ot" are *allophones*.

al-lot (a-lot′), *v.t.* [allot-ted, allot-ting], to distribute (amounts or shares); assign; as, to *allot* a certain amount of time on a computer.—*n.* **al-lot′ment.**

al-low (a-lou′), *v.t.* **1,** to permit; as, smoking is not *allowed;* **2,** to concede; acknowledge, as a claim; **3,** to set apart; as, to *allow* 10 percent for breakage; **4,** to give; let someone have; as, he *allows* you too much money:—*v.i.* to make concession or provision; take into account; as, to *allow* for shrinking.—*adj.* **al-low′a-ble.**

al-low-ance (a-lou′ans), *n.* **1,** a quantity or sum allotted; as, a weekly *allowance;* **2,** an amount deducted or added; as, an *allowance* for cash; **3,** tolerance; as, to make *allowances* for small children because of their age.

al-loy (al′oi), *n.* **1,** any mixture of metals; as, steel is an *alloy* of iron and carbon; **2,** a baser metal used in mixture with a finer one; as, copper is often used as an *alloy* with gold; **3,** something that lowers or takes from the value or perfection of something; as, pleasure without *alloy:*—*v.t.* (a-loi′), **1,** to melt together (two or more metals); **2,** esp., to debase by mixture, as gold with copper; **3,** to lessen by mixing; as, hope *alloyed* with fear.

all–pur-pose (ôl′–pûr′pus), *adj.* suitable for many uses or purposes; as, *all-purpose* flour.

all right, *Colloq.* **1,** correct; satisfactory; **2,** yes; certainly.

all–round (ôl′–round′), *adj.* **1,** able to do many things; as, an *all-round* student; **2,** generally useful; as, an *all-round* tool.

al-lude (a-lūd′), *v.i.* [allud-ed, allud-ing], to refer indirectly or in passing; as, I *allude* to events familiar to you all.

al-lure (a-lūr′), *v.t.* [allured, allur-ing], to tempt by the offer of something desirable; entice; attract.—*adj.* **al-lur′ing.**

al-lu-sion (a-lū′zhun), *n.* **1,** a passing reference; as, do not make any *allusion* to his loss; **2,** a hint or reference, usually to something generally familiar, used by way of illustration; as, a literary *allusion.*

al-lu-vi-al (a-lū-vi-al), *adj.* composed of clay, mud, etc., deposited by running water; as, *alluvial* soil.

al-ly (a-lī′), *v.t.* [allied, ally-ing], to unite or bind, as by marriage, treaty, league, confederacy, or friendship:—*n.* (al′ī), [*pl.* allies (al′īz)], a nation, family, or the like, so united to another, esp. a nation that helps another in war:—**Allies, 1,** the countries allied against the Central Powers in World War I; **2,** the countries allied against the Axis Powers in World War II; as, Canada was one of the *Allies* in the two world wars.

al-ma ma-ter (al′ma mä′tėr), *n.* the school that one attended and from which one graduated.

al-ma-nac (ôl′ma-nak′), *n.* a yearb[illegible] or calendar of days, weeks, and mon[illegible]ten giving information about the we[illegible] sun, moon, stars, tides, festivals, etc.

al-might-y (ôl-mīt′i), *adj.* having unlimited power; all-powerful:—**the Almighty,** God; Supreme Being.

al-mond (ä′mund; am′und), *n.* **1,** the nutlike fruit of a small tree somewhat like the peach: it is eaten alone or used as a flavouring for candy and other foods; **2,** the tree itself.

al-most (ôl′mōst; ôl-mōst′), *adv.* nearly.

al-oe (al′ō), *n.* a succulent plant with thick, spiny leaves found chiefly in South Africa:—**aloe vera,** a type of aloe with medicinal properties, used in creams, deodorants, soaps, etc.

a-loft (a-loft′; a-lôft′), *adv.* **1,** on high; far above the earth; **2,** esp., at the masthead, high above the deck of a ship.

a-lo-ha (a-lō′hä), *interj.* hello or goodbye, esp. in Hawaii.

a-lone (a-lōn′), *adj.* and *adv.* **1,** by oneself; apart; as, he usually walks *alone;* the house stands *alone;* **2,** only; as, she *alone* knows it; **3,** without the aid of another; as, he did that job *alone:*—**let alone,** not to mention; as, to have a hard time with the first question, *let alone* the whole test.

a-long (a-long′), *prep.* by the length of; lengthwise of; as, *along* the shore:—*adv.* **1,** parallel; near; as, he ran *along* beside me; **2,** forward; as, to pass something *along.*

a-loof (a-lo͞of′), *adj.* not very friendly; removed or distant; as, the *aloof* girl was really very shy:—*adv.* apart; as, he stood *aloof* from the crowd.—*adv.* **a-loof′ly.**—*n.* **a-loof′ness.**

a-loud (a-loud′), *adv.* loudly; as, to call *aloud* for help; also, out loud, with a normal voice; as, he read *aloud.*

al-pac-a (al-pak′a), *n.* **1,** a domesticated sheeplike animal of the Andes, with fine long woolly hair; **2,** a thin cloth made from this hair.

al-pha (al′fa), *n.* **1,** the first letter in the Greek alphabet; **2,** the first in a series; **3,** the brightest star in a constellation:—*adj.* the highest ranked, most important, or dominant, esp. social animals; as, the *alpha* female of the pack.

al-pha-bet (al′fa-bet′), *n.* a set of letters used in writing a language; also, these letters arranged in a certain traditional order.—*adj.* **al′pha-bet′i-cal.**—*adv.* **al′pha-bet′i-cal-ly.**

al-pha-bet-ize (al′fa-be-tīz′), *v.t.* [-betized, -betiz-ing], to arrange, as a list of words, in alphabetical order.

al-read-y (ôl-red′i), *adv.* **1,** previously; before a particular time; beforehand; as, she has *already* left; **2,** so soon; as, are you leaving *already?*

al-so (ôl′sō), *adv.* in addition; besides; too.

al-so-ran (ôl′sō-ran′), *n.* **1,** a horse or dog that does not finish in the first three places in a race; **2,** someone who loses a competition; as, he was an *also-ran* in the election; **3,** someone who is unimportant or insignificant.

al-tar (ôl′tėr), *n.* **1,** any raised place or structure used as a centre for religious services.

al-ter (ôl′tėr), *v.t.* and *v.i.* to change; make or become different; as, she *altered* the dress; his manners *altered* for the better.—*adj.* **al′ter-a-ble.**—*n.* **al′ter-a′tion.**

al-ter-ca-tion (ôl′tėr-kā′shun; al′-), *n.* a quarrel or dispute; wrangle; as, the baseball pitcher had an *altercation* with the umpire.

alter ego, 1, a very close, intimate friend; **2,** another side of one's personality; a second self.

al-ter-nate (ôl′tėr-nit; al′-), *adj.* **1,** taking place by turns, first one and then the other; as, *alternate* chills and fever; **2,** every other (one) of a series; as, *alternate* months:—*n.* a substitute; as, an *alternate* on the school's hockey team:—*v.t.* (ôl′tėr-nāt′; al′-) [alternat-ed, alternat-ing], to cause to occur by turns; interchange; as, she *alternated* her questions between the boys and the girls:—*v.i.* to take place by turns; as, day *alternates* with night.—*adv.* **al′ter-nate-ly.**

alternating current (AC), an electric current that reverses its direction at regular intervals, used in houses and other buildings, whereas batteries use *direct current (DC)*.

al-ter-na-tion (ôl-tėr-nā′shun; al′-), *n.* a following in succession, one after the other; as, the *alternation* of day and night.

al-ter-na-tive (ôl-tûr′na-tiv; al-), *n.* **1,** a choice from among two or more things or courses of action; as, she had the *alternative* of going to a concert or to a movie; **2,** either of the two choices; as, she chose the second *alternative*, namely, the movie:—*adj.* giving the choice of two or more things, only one of which may be taken, done, etc.—*adv.* **al-ter′na-tive-ly.**

al-though (ôl-*th*ō′), *conj.* though; even if; in spite of.

al-ti-tude (al′ti-tūd′), *n.* **1,** height; height above sea level; as, the *altitude* of a mountain; **2,** a high place or region.

al-to (al′tō), *n.* [*pl.* altos], **1,** the part sung by the lowest female voice or highest male voice; **2,** a person with such a voice, the voice itself, or a musical instrument with the same range:—*adj.* relating to this type of voice or range; as, an *alto* saxophone.

al-to-geth-er (ôl′too-geth′ėr), *adv.* **1,** completely; wholly; entirely; as, to be closed down *altogether*; **2,** on the whole; in the main; as, *altogether*, the party was a success; **3,** with all included; counting all; as, *altogether*, that was a great show.

al-tru-ism (al′trōō-izm), *n.* unselfish regard for the interests of others.—*n.* **al′-tru-ist.**—*adj.* **al′tru-is′tic.**

a-lu-mi-num (a-lū′mi-num), *n.* a bluish-white, non-rusting, pliable, conductive metal, used where lightness and strength are needed, such as in wire, pots and pans, utensils, aircraft and car parts, and machinery.—*n.* **a-lu′mi-num foil′.**

a-lum-nus (a-lum′nus), *n.* [*pl.* alumni (a-lum′ni; a-lum′nē)], someone who has attended or graduated from a school, college, or university; **2,** someone who has worked for or been a member of an organization; as, a phone company *alumnus.*—*n.fem.* **a-lum′na** [*pl.* alumnae (a-lum′nē; a-lum′nī)].

always (ôl′wāz; ôl′wiz), *adv.* at all times.

Alz-hei-mer's disease (älts′hī′mėrz; alts′hī′ mėrz), *n.* a disease of the central nervous system that leads to severe mental degeneration and premature senility and death.

am (am), first person, *sing.*, present indicative, of *be*; as, I *am* tired.

AM or **am** (ā′em′), *abbrev.* short for *amplitude modulation*, one of the two main kinds of radio signals: the signal is sent out the same number of times per second, but the strength of the signal changes. See also *FM*.

A.M. or **a.m.** (ā′em′), *abbrev.* in the morning, between midnight and noon: short for *ante meridiem* (before noon). Compare *P.M.*

a-mal-ga-mate (a-mal′ga-māt′), *v.t.* [amalgamat-ed, amalgamat-ing], **1,** to alloy or mix (a metal) with mercury or with another metal; **2,** to mix to form a compound:—*v.i.* to mix or combine so as to become indistinguishable; unite; as, one solution may *amalgamate* with another.—*n.* **a-mal′ga-ma′tion.**

a-mass (a-mas′), *v.t.* to collect into a heap; gather; accumulate; as, he *amassed* great wealth.

am-a-teur (am′a-tūr′; am′a-tûr), *n.* **1,** one who engages in any art, study, or sport for pleasure, and not for money; as, a golf *amateur*; **2,** one whose work lacks professional finish:—*adj.* non-professional; as, *amateur* standing in athletics; *amateur* dramatics:—*adj.* of or by an amateur; as, an *amateur* photographer: opposite of *professional.*—*adj.* **am′a-teur′ish.**

a-maze (a-māz′), *v.t.* [amazed, amaz-ing], to overwhelm with astonishment; as, your news *amazes* me.—*n.* **a-maze′ment.**—*adj.* **a-maz′ing.**—*adv.* **a-maz′ing-ly.**

am-bas-sa-dor (am-bas′a-dėr), *n.* **1,** a government agent of highest rank representing his or her country's interests at a foreign capital; **2,** any representative or agent charged with a special mission.

am-ber (am′bėr), *n.* **1,** a yellowish hard

resin, or gum, capable of high polish, which is made into beads and other jewellery: a fossil from the resin of pine trees that grew millions of years ago; **2,** the reddish-yellow colour of amber:—*adj.* made of amber; also, amber-coloured.

am-bi-dex-trous (am′bi-deks′trus), *adj.* able to use both hands equally well.—*adv.* **am′bi-dex′trous-ly.**

am-big-u-ous (am-big′ū-us), *adj.* doubtful; having two or more possible meanings; as, *ambiguous* words; *ambiguous* actions.—*adv.* **am-big′u-ous-ly.**—*n.* **am′bi-gu′i-ty** (am′bi-gū′i-ti).

am-bi-tion (am-bish′un), *n.* **1,** an eager desire to gain or do something; as, she has an *ambition* to be a soccer player; **2,** the thing desired; as, he has attained his *ambition* to be a surgeon.

am-bi-tious (am-bish′us), *adj.* **1,** full of ambition; determined to succeed; as, *ambitious* students; **2,** eager; aspiring; as, *ambitious* for knowledge; **3,** requiring great skill or effort for success; as, they planned an *ambitious* program.

am-biv-a-lent (am-biv′a-lent), *adj.* **1,** having conflicted or opposite feelings, such as love and hate, at the same time; **2,** uncertain, indecisive; as, to be *ambivalent* about attending university.

am-ble (am′bl), *v.i.* [amb-led, am-bling], **1,** to walk at an easy pace; meander; **2,** of horses, to pace, or go at a gait in which the animal lifts the two feet on the same side together:—*n.* **1,** the ambling gait of a horse; **2,** any easy gait.—*n.* **am′bler.**

am-bu-lance (am′bū-lans), *n.* an enclosed, specially equipped vehicle for carrying the sick and wounded.

am-bush (am′boosh), *n.* **1,** a concealed station from which to attack the enemy unexpectedly; **2,** troops so attacking:—*v.t.* to waylay; attack from ambush.

a-me-lio-rate (a-mē′lē-o-rāt; a-mēl′yo-rāt), *v.t.* and *v.i.* to improve or make better; as, to *ameliorate* your grades in math.

a-men (ā′men′; ä′men′), *interj.* verily; so be it: a word used at the end of a prayer, blessing, etc., to express solemn assent or approval.—*n.* **a′men′.**

a-me-na-ble (a-mē′na-bl; a-men′a-bl), *adj.* **1,** easy to lead; ready to accept advice; **2,** liable; as, *amenable* to the law.—*adv.* **a-me′na-bly.**

a-mend (a-mend′), *v.t.* **1,** to change for the better; improve; correct; as, he tried to *amend* his faults; **2,** to change formally; as, to *amend* a law.—*n.* **a-mend′ment.**

a-mends (a-mendz′), *n. pl.* payment or reparation for loss or injury inflicted on someone else; as, he made *amends* for the results of his careless driving.

a-men-i-ty (a-men′i-ti; a-mēn′i-ti), [*pl.* amenities], **1,** pleasantness; **2,** *pl.* civilities; as, please observe the social *amenities.*

a-mi-a-ble (ā′mi-a-bl), *adj.* friendly; easy-going; kindly; as, an *amiable* disposition.—*adv.* **a′mi-a-bly.**—*n.* **a′mi-a-bil′i-ty.**

am-i-ca-ble (am′i-ka-bl), *adj.* friendly; peaceful; as, an *amicable* discussion.—*adv.* **am′i-ca-bly.**—*n.* **am′i-ca-bil′i-ty.**

a-mid or **a-midst** (a-mid′; a-midst′), *prep.* in the middle of; surrounded by; as, a treasure *amid* the rubble.

a-mi-no acid (a-mē′nō as′id), *n.* one of a group of organic compounds that are part of the structure of proteins and are essential to the workings of the human body.

a-miss (a-mis′), *adj.* wrong; faulty; as, something is *amiss:*—*adv.* wrongly; as, you take my words *amiss.*

am-i-ty (am′i-ti), *n.* [*pl.* amities], friendship; peaceful relations.

am-mo-ni-a (a-mō′ni-a; a-mōn′ya), *n.* **1,** a clear, strong-smelling gas, which is a mixture of nitrogen and hydrogen, and which is readily soluble in water; **2,** a solution of this gas in water, for household cleaning use.

am-mu-ni-tion (am′ū-nish′un), *n.* **1,** bullets, shells, bombs, missiles, and other such weapons that can be fired or launched against an enemy; **2,** facts or arguments that support a statement or point of view; as, *ammunition* for her side of the debate.

am-ne-si-a (am-nē′zhi-a), *n.* loss of memory.

am-nes-ty (am′nes-ti), *n.* **1,** a pardon or forgiveness, esp. for political offences; **2,** the period of time during which lawbreakers will be pardoned:—*v.t.* to grant a pardon.

a-moe-ba or **a-me-ba** (a-mē′ba), *n.* [*pl.* amoebas or amoebae (a-mē′bē)], an aquatic protozoan or microscopic water animal without definite shape: one of the simplest forms of life.

a-mong or **a-mongst** (a-mung′; a-mungst′), *prep.* **1,** in the group with; surrounded by; as, *among* friends; *among* all his wealth; **2,** by the united action of; as, *among* them all, they succeeded; **3,** in the time of; as, *among* the ancient Greeks; **4,** by distribution to; as, to divide the estate *among* the heirs.

am-o-rous (am′o-rus), *adj.* inclined to love; having to do with love; as, an *amorous* nature; *amorous* letters.

a-mount (a-mount′), *v.i.* **1,** to be equal or equivalent; as, his answer *amounted* to a threat; **2,** to add up; as, it *amounts* to 100; **3,** to develop into; become; as, to *amount* to something in life:—*n.* **1,** the total sum; as, the *amount* is 25 cents; **2,** a measure; quantity; as, an unusual *amount* of courage.

amp (amp), *n.* short for *ampere* and *amplifier.*

am-pere (am′pâr; am′pēr), *n.* a unit for measuring strength of electric current; viz., the amount sent by one volt through a resistance of one ohm.

am-per-sand (am′pėr-sand′), *n.* the character [&], denoting *and.*

am-phet-a-mine (am-fe′ta-mēn′), *n.* a highly addictive drug that stimulates the central nervous system.

am-phib-i-an (am-fib′i-an), *n.* **1,** a cold-blooded animal that can live both on land and in water; as, frogs are *amphibians;* **2,** an aircraft that can take off from, and alight upon, either land or water; **3,** a tank, truck, or other vehicle that can travel across land or water:—*adj.* able to live on land and in water.—*adj.* **am-phib′i-ous.**

am-phi-the-a-tre or **am-phi-the-a-ter** (am′fi-thē′a-tėr), *n.* **1,** an oval or circular building with rows of seats rising in a slope around a central space, or arena; **2,** anything resembling an amphitheatre in shape or purpose.

am-ple (am′pl), *adj.* **1,** full; of large size, extent, or volume; **2,** abundant.

am-pli-fi-er (am′pli-fī′ėr), *n.* a device for increasing the strength of an electronic signal; as, a stereo *amplifier.*

am-pli-fy (am′pli-fī′), *v.t.* [amplified, amplify-ing], to make larger, fuller, or louder; as, she *amplified* her statement.—*n.* **am′pli-fi-ca′tion.**

am-ply (am′pli), *adv.* fully; sufficiently.

am-pu-tate (am-pū-tāt′), *v.t.* [amputat-ed, amputat-ing], to cut off, as an arm or leg.—*n.* **am′pu-ta′tion.**

a-muse (a-mūz′), *v.t.* [amused, amus-ing], **1,** to entertain; as, to *amuse* children with toys; **2,** to cause to smile or laugh; as, the antics of the clown *amused* her.—*adj.* **a-mus′ing.**—*adv.* **a-mus′ing-ly.**

a-muse-ment (a-mūz′ment), *n.* **1,** that which entertains; a pastime; **2,** pleasant entertainment, esp. if it is amusing:—*adj.* having to do with amusement; entertaining; as, *amusement* park.

an (an; *unstressed,* un), *indefinite sing. article* a; any; each: used instead of *a* before a vowel sound or silent *h;* as, *an* ell, *an* hour; but *a* hotel, *a* yoke, *a* union.

an-a-bol-ic ste-roid, (a′na-bä′lik stâr′oid), *n.* a synthetic hormone sometimes illegally used by athletes to increase their size or strength temporarily; as, Ben Johnson was caught using *anabolic steroids.*

a-nach-ro-nism (a-nak′ro-nizm), *n.* an assigning of a person or an event to a period other (esp. earlier) than the correct one; as, having Sir John A. Macdonald talking on a cell phone would be an *anachronism.*

an-a-con-da (an′u-kon′du), *n.* a very large (up to 9 metres long), powerful, non-poisonous snake found in South America, which can coil around an animal and suffocate or crush it to death.

an-a-gram (an′a-gram′), *n.* a word or phrase obtained by changing the order of the letters of another word or phrase, as "live" from "evil":—**anagrams,** a game in which the players strive to form the largest number of words from any given letters.

an-a-logue computer or **analog computer** (an-a-läg), a non-digital computing machine; a device that operates in a continuous, variable circuit.

a-nal-o-gy (a-nal′o-ji), *n.* [*pl.* analogies], a partial agreement or likeness between two things somewhat different; as, the *analogy* between an eye and a camera.—*adj.* **a-nal′o-gous** (a-nal′o-gus).

an-a-lyze or **an-a-lyse** (an′a-līz′), *v.t.* [analysed, analys-ing], **1,** to separate or break down into parts or elements; as, to *analyze* a chemical compound; **2,** to examine critically; as, to *analyze* evidence, motives, character, etc.—*n.* **a-nal′y-sis; an′a-lyst.**—*adj.* **an-a-lyt′ic; an-a-lyt′i-cal.**

an-arch-y (an′är-ki), *n.* [*pl.* anarchies], **1,** the absence or lack of government; hence, a condition of general confusion and terror resulting from the overthrow or disregard of laws; **2,** any state of extreme disorder.—*n.* **an′arch-ist.**

a-nath-e-ma (a-nath′i-ma), *n.* **1,** a solemn curse and excommunication by the church; **2,** any curse; **3,** a thing or person greatly disliked.

a-nat-o-my (a-nat′o-mi), *n.* **1,** the science that studies the structure of the parts of plants and animals, and the relation of these parts to one another; **2,** the dissecting of a plant or animal to study its structure; **3,** the body or parts of a plant or animal.—*adj.* **an′a-tom′ical; an′a-tom′ic.**

an-ces-tor (an′ses′tėr), *n.* a person from whom one is descended.—*adj.* **an-ces′tral.**

an-ces-try (an′ses′tri), *n.* [*pl.* ancestries], the line of one's descent traced back through parents, grandparents, etc.; also, one's ancestors.

an-chor (ang′kėr), *n.* **1,** a heavy iron or steel implement that, when dropped, hooks into the ground and moors a ship or boat in a particular place; **2,** any similar thing to hold fast a movable object:—*v.t.* to make or hold fast, as a ship:—*v.i.* to lie secure in harbour; as, the ship *anchored* in the bay.—*n.* **an′chor-age; an′chor-per′son.**

an-cient (ān′shent), *adj.* **1,** of very great age; as, *ancient* rocks; **2,** pertaining to times long past; as, *ancient* history:—*n.* **1,** an aged person; **2,** one who lived in olden times:—**the ancients,** civilized peoples of times long past, as the early Romans, Greeks, Hebrews, Egyptians, etc:—**ancient history,** the history of people from the earliest known time to the fall of the Roman Empire.—*adv.* **an′cient-ly.**

an-cil-lar-y (an′si-lâ′ri), *adj.* not essential; supplementary; subordinate; as, *ancillary* reading material.

and (and), *co-ordinate conj.* a connective that joins expressions (words, phrases, or clauses) of equal grammatical value; as, Ivan *and* Maria are here; to have *and* to hold.

an-drog-y-nous (an-drä′ji-nus), *adj.* **1,** having characteristics of both male and female; **2,** being neither markedly male nor female in appearance.—*n.* **an-drog′y-ny.**

an-ec-dote (an′ik-dōt′), *n.* a brief story intended to amuse or instruct.

a-ne-mi-a or **a-nae-mi-a** (a-nē′mi-a), *n.* a diseased condition caused by loss of blood or by the lack of red corpuscles in the blood, making a person feel tired and weak.—*adj.* **a-ne′mic.**

an-es-the-si-a or **an-aes-the-si-a** (an-as-thē′zhi-a; an′es-thē′zha), *n.* a partial or complete loss of sensation, due to disease, inhaling of gas, hypnotism, etc.:—**general anesthesia,** the complete loss of sensation, resulting in total or partial unconsciousness:—**local anesthesia,** the loss of sensation in only a portion of the body.

an-es-thet-ic or **an-aes-thet-ic** (an′es-thet′ik), *adj.* causing loss of sensation:—*n.* a gas or drug that causes temporary loss of sensation in the body.

a-new (a-nū′), *adv.* a second time; over again.

an-gel (ān′jel), *n.* **1,** in some religions, a heavenly being or spirit, often pictured in human form, but with wings; **2,** a good, innocent, kind, or lovely person.—*adj.* **an-gel′ic** (an-jel′ik).

an-ger (ang′gėr), *n.* rage; a strong emotion aroused by a sense of injury or wrong:—*v.t.* to provoke to resentment; enrage.

an-gi-na (an-jī′na), *n.* **1,** angina pectoris; chest pains resulting from overexertion and a lack of oxygen to the heart; **2,** a disease characterized by suffocation and intense pain.

[1]**an-gle** (ang′gl), *n.* **1,** the figure formed at the point of intersection of two lines; **2,** the space between such lines; **3,** a corner; a sharp edge; **4,** a point of view; as, he sees it from all *angles*:—*v.t.* to move or hit something at an angle; as, to *angle* the ball or chair; **2,** to bias or skew something from a certain point of view; as, to *angle* an essay in some way:—*v.i.* to turn at an angle; as, the path *angled* to the left.

ANGLES: A, ACUTE ANGLE; B, RIGHT ANGLE; C, OBTUSE ANGLE.

[2]**an-gle** (ang′gl), *v.i.* [an-gled, an-gling], **1,** to fish with hook and line; **2,** to use tricks in obtaining something; as, to *angle* for a compliment.

an-gler (ang′glėr), *n.* one who fishes, esp. for pleasure.

An-gli-can-ism (ang′li-ka-nizm′), *n.* the Church of England, founded by Henry VIII during the Protestant Reformation of the early 16th century: an important religion in many countries of the Commonwealth and former British colonies.—*n.* and *adj.* **An′gli-can.**

An-gli-cize (ang′gli-sīz′), *v.t.* [Anglicized, Angliciz-ing], to make English in manners, customs, speech, etc.; as, we have *Anglicized* such a foreign word as *chauffeur.*

An-glo-phone or **an-glo-phone** (ang′glu-fōn′), *n.* a person whose first or native language is English.

Anglo–Saxon (ang′glo–sak′sun), *n.* **1,** a member of one of the tribes that came from what is now Germany and Scandinavia to invade England about 1500 years ago; **2,** the language of these people, the earliest form of what is now the English language.

an-gry (ang′gri), *adj.* **1,** feeling or showing wrath, rage, or resentment; as, an *angry* beast; an *angry* look; **2,** inflamed; red; as, an *angry*-looking wound.—*adv.* **an′gri-ly.**

an-guish (ang′gwish), *n.* extreme suffering, esp. of mind; as, a mother's *anguish* over the death of her child.

an-gu-lar (ang′gū-lėr), *adj.* **1,** having angles or points; sharp-cornered; as, *angular* figures; **2,** bony; ungainly; awkward; as, an *angular* youth.—*n.* **an′gu-lar′i-ty** (ang′gu-lar′i-ti).

an-i-mal (an′i-mal), *n.* **1,** a living being that can feel, move about of its own will, and has a nervous system and sense organs, such as a human, dog, sparrow, fish, snake, fly, etc.; **2,** any mammal other than a human, as a dog, monkey, etc:—*adj.* relating to animals; as, the *animal* kingdom; like or characteristic of an animal; as, animal spirits; sensual; bestial: opposite of *spiritual.*

an-i-mate (an′i-māt′), *v.t.* [animat-ed, animat-ing], to give life to; inspire with energy or activity; enliven; as, joy *animates* his face:—*adj.* (an′i-mit), endowed with life; as, biology deals with *animate* beings.—*adj.* **an′i-mat-ed, 1,** full of spirit and vigour; as, *animated* dialogue; **2,** taking on, through motion, the semblance of life; as, an *animated* cartoon.—*n.* **an′i-ma′tion.**

an-i-mos-i-ty (an′i-mos′i-ti), *n.* [*pl.* animosities], hostility; hatred; enmity.

an-kle (ang′kl), *n.* the joint connecting the foot with the leg.

an-nex (a-neks′; a′neks), *v.t.* to unite, as a smaller thing to a greater; as, to *annex* a province to a kingdom:—*n.* (an′eks), a building added to or adjoining another building.—*n.* **an′nex-a′tion.**

an-ni-hi-late (a-nī′i-lāt′), *v.t.* [annihilat-ed, annihilat-ing], to blot or wipe out of existence; destroy; as, the people of Pompeii were *annihilated* by the eruption of Vesuvius.—*n.* **an-ni′hi-la′tion.**

an-ni-ver-sa-ry (an′i-vûr′sa-ri), *n.* [*pl.* anniversaries], the yearly return of the date of an event; as, they celebrated their wedding *anniversary.*

an-no-tate (an′ō-tāt′), *v.t.* [annotat-ed, annotat-ing], to make notes upon, by way of comment or criticism; as, to *annotate* an essay.—*n.* **an′no-ta′tion.**

an-nounce (a-nouns′), *v.t.* [announced, announc-ing], **1,** to proclaim; make known formally or publicly; publish; as, she *announced* her daughter's engagement; **2,** to state formally the presence or approach of; as, the butler *announced* the guests; **3,** to introduce or tell about something on radio or television.—*n.* **an-nounce′ment.**

an-nounc-er (a-noun′sėr), *n.* **1,** one who announces something; **2,** a person on radio or television who introduces programs and performers, identifies the station, or reads the news.

an-noy (a-noi′), *v.t.* to disturb or trouble; irritate; as, a dog growls when it is *annoyed.*—*adj.* **an-noy′ing.**

an-noy-ance (a-noi′ans), *n.* **1,** the act of causing irritation; as, he finds pleasure in the *annoyance* of his friends; **2,** the sense of being annoyed; irritation; as, my *annoyance* over the delay was great; **3,** the thing or act that irritates; as, his tardiness was an *annoyance.*

an-nu-al (an′ū-al), *adj.* **1,** occurring once a year; yearly; as, an *annual* banquet; **2,** taking a year to complete; as, the *annual* rotation of the seasons; **3,** done, reckoned, or published yearly; as, *annual* dues; an *annual* report or newsletter; **4,** lasting but one year or season; as, an *annual* plant:—*n.* **1,** a publication appearing once a year; **2,** a plant living only one year or season.—*adv.* **an′nu-al-ly.**

an-nu-i-ty (a-nū′i-ti), *n.* [*pl.* annuities], **1,** a sum of money paid, as by an insurance company, for a specified period in regular instalments; **2,** the right to receive such instalments; as, he invested his money in an *annuity.*

an-nul (a-nul′), *v.t.* [annulled, annul-ling], to abolish or do away with, as a law, decree, or compact; as, the marriage has been *annulled.*—*n.* **an-nul′ment.**

anode (an′ōd), *n.* the positive pole or electrode of a battery, vacuum tube, etc. Compare **cathode.**

a-nom-a-ly (a-nom′a-li), *n.* [*pl.* anomalies], irregularity; anything that varies from the common rule, or is abnormal or peculiar; as, a winter thunderstorm is an *anomaly.*—*adj.* **a-nom′a-lous.**

a-non-y-mous (a-non′i-mus), *adj.* **1,** not known by name; as, an *anonymous* author; **2,** without the author's name; as, an *anonymous* poem; **3,** from or by a person who does not want to give his or her name; as, an *anonymous* donor.—*adv.* **a-non′-y-mous-ly.**—*n.* **an′o-nym′i-ty.**

a-no-rak (an′u-rak), *n.* a parka; a waterproof jacket with a hood, originally made from fur by the Inuit.

an-o-rex-i-a (an′u-rek′sē-yu), *n.* a disease that causes a person to lose all desire to eat because of a fear of becoming overweight. Also called *anorexia nervosa.*—*adj.* **an-o-rex′ic.**

an-oth-er (a-nu*th*′ėr), *pron.* **1,** one more of the same kind; as, I have one hat, but I need *another;* **2,** a different person or thing; as, in the dark I took her for *another:*—*adj.* **1,** additional; as, please give me *another* orange; **2,** different; as, choose *another* book if you don't like this one.

an-swer (ån′sėr), *n.* **1,** a response or reply, as to a letter; **2,** a reply to a charge; as, to say nothing in *answer* to an accusation; **3,** a solution, as of a mathematical problem:—*v.t.* **1,** to speak, write, or act in reply to; as, to *answer* the bell; to *answer* a letter; **2,** to reply to in defence; as, to *answer* a charge; **3,** to correspond to; as, he *answers* the description; **4,** to be sufficient for; as, this *answers* the purpose:—*v.i.* **1,** to speak, write, or act in reply; **2,** to be accountable; as, I cannot *answer* for this mixture.—*adj.* **an-swer-a-ble.**

ant (ant), *n.* a small insect, famed for its industry. Ants live in communities or colonies in holes that they burrow in wood or in the ground.

ant-ac-id (ant′a′sid; ant′a′sid), *n.* a substance that prevents or neutralizes acidity, esp. in the stomach:—*adj.* counteracting or neutralizing acid.

an-tag-o-nism (an-tag′o-nizm), *n.* dislike or opposition between two persons, forces, parties, etc.; hostility; hatred; as, their *antagonism* was of long standing.—*n.* **an-tag′o-nist.**—*adj.* **an-tag′o-nis′tic.**—*adv.* **an-tag′o-nis′ti-cal-ly.**

an-tag-o-nize (an-tag′o-niz′), *v.t.* [antagonized, antagoniz-ing], to make hostile; turn into an enemy; as, her rudeness *antagonizes* her associates.

Ant-arc-tic (ant-ärk′tik), *adj.* **1,** opposite to the North Pole, or Arctic regions; **2,** located in, or relating to, the South Pole:—*n.* **the Antarctic** (or **Antarctica**), the continent surrounding the South Pole:—**Antarctic Circle,** an imaginary circle parallel to the equator and distant 23° 30′ from the South Pole.—**Antarctic Ocean,** the South Polar ocean.

ant-eat-er (ant′ēt′ėr), *n.* an animal that feeds upon ants. It has a long, sticky tongue, with which it licks up the ants.

an-te-ced-ent (an′ti-sē′dent), *n.* **1,** someone or something that goes before or precedes; **2,** in *grammar*, a noun, pronoun, etc., later referred to by a pronoun; as, in the sentence "James played football until he hurt his leg," "James" is the *antecedent* of "he":—**antecedents,** the previous events or influences in a person's life; also, ancestry; as, his unfortunate *antecedents* account for his criminal traits.

an-te-lope (an′ti-lōp′), *n.* any of a large group of graceful, long-horned African or southern Asian animals, including the gazelle, eland, and kudu: they resemble deer, but are, in fact, related to goats and cows.

an-ten-na (an-ten′a), *n.* [*pl.* antennae (an-ten′ē)], **1,** one of the feelers that grows on the heads of insects, centipedes, lobsters, etc.; **2,** [*pl.* antennas], in radio and television, a metal wire or rod for sending and receiving electromagnetic messages.

an-them (an′them), *n.* **1,** a song of praise or triumph; as, the national *anthem* of Canada is "O Canada"; **2,** a piece of sacred music, often a Biblical passage set to music.

an-ther (an′thėr), *n.* in a flower, the part of the stamen that produces the pollen. (See *flower,* illustration.)

an-thol-o-gy (an-thol′o-ji), *n.* [*pl.* anthologies], a collection of choice poems or prose passages from a variety of authors.

an-thrax (an′thraks), *n.* an infectious and often fatal disease of cattle and sheep, and sometimes of humans.

an-thro-pol-o-gy (an′thrō-pol′o-ji), *n.* the science of humans and their origins, institutions, myths, etc.—*adj.* **an′thro-pol-o′gi-cal.**—*n.* **an′thro-pol′o-gist.**

an-ti- or **an-ti–** (an′ti-; an′ti– or an′tī-; an′tī–), *prefix* meaning *against, opposed to,* or *opposite of;* as, *anti*-aircraft, *anti*dote, *anti*freeze, *anti*-inflation, *anti*social, *anti*-war, etc.

an-ti-bal-lis-tic missile (an′ti-ba-lis′tik), *n.* a defensive guided missile designed to intercept and destroy incoming missiles in flight.

an-ti-bi-ot-ic (an′ti-bī-ot′ik), *n.* a chemical substance extracted from living organisms, like moulds and fungi, which is able to destroy other organisms, and is therefore useful in treatment of bacterial infection; as, penicillin is an *antibiotic*.

an-ti-bod-y (an′ti-bod′i), *n.* [*pl.* antibodies], proteins produced by the body to weaken or destroy foreign elements such as bacteria and toxins, making the body resistant to certain illnesses and diseases.

an-tic (an′tik) *n.* a comical trick or action; as, the *antics* of a puppy.

an-tic-i-pate (an-tis′i-pāt′), *v.t.* [anticipat-ed, anticipat-ing], **1,** to look forward to; expect; esp., to await with pleasure; as, to *anticipate* a party; **2,** to foresee (a command, need, wish, etc.) and do ahead of time what needs doing; as, they *anticipated* our hunger; **3,** to be before (another) in doing something; as, A *anticipated* B in the discovery.—*n.* **an-tic′i-pa′tion.**

an-ti-cli-max (an′ti-klī′maks), *n.* opposite of climax; descent from the sublime to the ridiculous, or from the important to the trivial and uninteresting; as, washing dishes after a party is an *anticlimax.*—*adj.* **an-ti-cli-mac′tic.**

an-ti-dote (an′ti-dōt′), *n.* **1,** a medicine that counteracts a poison; **2,** hence, a remedy; as, hard work served as an *antidote* to his troubles.

an-ti-freeze (an′ti-frēz′), *n.* a liquid, as alcohol or glycol, used in winter to prevent car engines and radiators from freezing up.

an-ti-his-ta-mine (an′ti-his′ta-mēn′; an′ti-his′ta-min′), *n.* a drug that is used to treat colds and allergies such as hay fever and asthma.

an-ti-ox-i-dant (an′ti-äk′si-dent), *n.* **1,** a substance such as vitamin C or E that protects the body's cells from the harmful effects of oxygen; **2,** anything that inhibits oxidation.

an-tip-a-thy (an-tip′a-thi), *n.* [*pl.* antipathies], a strong, instinctive hatred or dislike.—*adj.* **an′ti-pa-thet′ic.**

an-ti-per-spi-rant (an′ti-pûr′spi-rent), *n.* an astringent substance that stops or slows perspiration.

an-ti-quar-i-an (an′ti-kwâr′i-an) *adj.* relating to ancient times or to the relics and ruins of past peoples; as, *antiquarian* studies:—*n.* one who collects ancient relics, or who studies the customs, events, and records of past peoples.

an-ti-quat-ed (an′ti-kwāt′id), *adj.* old-fashioned; out of date; as, *antiquated* clothes; *antiquated* ideas.

an-tique (an-tēk′), *adj.* belonging to an earlier period of time; ancient; as, an *antique* vase:—*n.* something old; a relic of an earlier time than the present; something that is more than 50 (in Canada) or 100 years old; as, this chair is an *antique.*

an-tiq-ui-ty (an-tik′wi-ti), *n.* [*pl.* antiquities], **1,** the early ages, esp. before the Middle Ages; as, the pyramids are a relic of *antiquity*; **2,** great age; as, the *antiquity* of ruins; **3, antiquities,** relics that throw light upon ancient times; as, Chinese *antiquities* in a museum.

an-ti-sep-tic (an′ti-sep′tik), *adj.* preventing the growth of disease-causing micro-organisms; as, salt in water makes an *antiseptic* gargle:—*n.* an *antiseptic* substance, as hydrogen peroxide, alcohol, or iodine.

an-ti-so-cial (an′ti-sō′shal), *adj.* **1,** opposed to or against the interests of society, or of people and citizens as a whole; as, robbery and murder are *antisocial* acts; **2,** avoiding other people; not friendly.

an-ti-the-sis (an-tith′e-sis), *n.* [*pl.* antitheses (an-tith′e-sēz′)], **1,** the exact opposite; as, black is the *antithesis* of white; **2,** opposition; contrast; as, an *antithesis* of ideas; **3,** an expression that emphasizes contrast; as, "Give me liberty, or give me death," is an *antithesis.*

an-ti-tox-in (an′ti-tok′sin), *n.* **1,** a substance formed in the body of a person or animal to fight a disease or toxin; **2,** an antiserum containing the antitoxin of a particular disease, such as diphtheria, that helps the body to resist the effects of the germs.

an-ti-vi-rus (an′ti-vī′rus), *n.* in *computing,* a software program designed to detect, quarantine, and destroy computer viruses.

ant-ler (ant′lėr), *n.* the horn, or a branch of the horn, of a deer, moose, or elk.—*adj.* **ant′lered** (ant′lėrd).

an-to-nym (an′tō-nim), *n.* a word that has an opposite meaning of another word; as, "hot" is the *antonym* of "cold": opposite of *synonym.*

a-nus (ā′nus), *n.* in animals, the posterior opening of the digestive tract.

an-vil (an′vil), *n.* a block of iron on which metals are hammered and shaped.

anx-i-e-ty (ang-zī′e-ti), *n.* [*pl.* anxieties], **1,** mental uneasiness from fear of misfortune; as, their *anxiety* increased with the storm; **2,** eager desire tinged with fear; as, *anxiety* to make good.

anx-ious (angk′shus; ang′shus), *adj.* **1,** deeply concerned; greatly troubled or worried; uneasy; as, *anxious* about one's health; **2,** desirous; eager; as, *anxious* to please.—*adv.* **anx′ious-ly.**

an-y (en′i), *adj.* **1,** one of several, but no matter which; as, you may have *any* book here; **2,** some, used with a negative, or in a question; as, I haven't *any* time; **3,** every; as, I did what *any* person would do:—*pron.* some; as, give me some nails if you have *any*:—*adv.* to any extent; at all; in any degree; as, don't go *any* farther.

an-y-bod-y (en′i-bod′i; -bud′), *pron.* **1,** an ordinary person; any person of a group; as, *anybody* can do it if he or she tries; **2,** *Colloq.* someone of importance; as, is she *anybody*?

an-y-how (en′i-hou′), *adv.* **1,** in any way; hence, carelessly; in a haphazard way; as, she just does her work *anyhow*; **2,** at any rate; as, *anyhow*, you are here now.

an-y-more (en′i-mōr′; en′i-môr′), *adv.* at this time, now; as, she is not here *anymore.*

an-y-one (en′i-wun′), *pron.* any person; anybody; as, *anyone* can do that.

an-y-place (en′i-plās′), *adv.* to, in, or at any place; anywhere; as, to sit *anyplace.*

an-y-thing (en′i-thing′), *pron.* a thing of any sort whatever; as, *anything* can happen.

an-y-time (en′i-tīm′), *adv.* at any time; as, to leave *anytime.*

an-y-way (en′i-wā′), *adv.* **1,** in any manner; as, do it *anyway* you like; **2,** nevertheless; anyhow; as, I am tired, but I'm going *anyway.*

an-y-where (en′i-hwâr′), *adv.* in or at any place; as, put it *anywhere.*

a-or-ta (ā-ôr′ta), *n.* [*pl.* aortas], the large artery that carries blood away from the heart to branch arteries that supply the entire body.

a-part (a-pärt′), *adv.* **1,** separately in time or place; as, to live *apart*; to spread your arms *apart*; **2,** in, or into, pieces; as, it fell *apart*; he took the watch *apart*:—**apart from, 1,** separated from; as, she lives *apart from* her parents; **2,** not considering; leaving out of account; as, *apart from* the plot, the book interested me.

a-part-heid (a-pär′tīt′; a-pär′tāt′), *n.* racial separation, esp. as practised formerly by the government of South Africa.

a-part-ment (a-pärt′ment), *n.* a separate room, or suite of rooms, used to live in. Also **apartment building** and **apartment block.**

ap-a-thy (ap′a-thi), *n.* [*pl.* apathies], lack of feeling or interest; indifference; as, to arouse a person from *apathy.*—*adj.* **ap′a-thet′ic.**

ape (āp), *n.* **1,** a tailless animal, related to the monkey, like humans in structure and organs, as the gorilla, chimpanzee, orang-utan; **2,** a silly mimic:—*v.t.* [aped, ap-ing], to imitate; as, the boy *apes* his elders.

ap-er-ture (ap′ėr-tūr; -chėr), *n.* an opening; gap; hole; as, an *aperture* in a wall.

a-pex (ā′peks), *n.* [*pl.* apexes (ā′pek-sez) or apices (ā′pi-sēz′; ap′i-sēz′)], the peak or summit of something, as of a mountain, triangle, etc.

a-phid (ā′fid; af′id), *n.* a small insect that sucks the sap of plants.

a-pi-ar-y (ā′pi-ė-ri), *n.* [*pl.* apiaries], a place where bees are kept; also, a collection of beehives.

a-piece (a-pēs′), *adv.* for each one; as, the pencils cost 50 cents *apiece.*

a-poc-a-lypse (a-pä′ka-lips′), *n.* **1,** catastrophic destruction as the end of the world; Armageddon; **2,** revelation or prophecy:—**Apocalypse,** the last book of the New Testament of the Bible; the Book of Revelations.—*adj.* **apoc-a-lyp′tic.**

a-poc-ry-phal (a-päk′ri-fal), *adj.* of doubtful authority; uncertain or questionable authenticity; mythical; false or counterfeit; as, *apocryphal* rumours.

a-pol-o-gize (a-pol′o-jīz′), *v.i.* [apologized, apologiz-ing], **1,** to make an excuse; **2,** to express regret for a fault, wrong, etc.—*adj.* **a-pol′o-get′ic; a-pol′o-get′i-cal.**

a-pol-o-gy (a-pol′o-ji), *n.* [*pl.* apologies], **1,** an excuse or expression of regret for something one has said or done; as, she made an *apology* for being noisy; **2,** something spoken, written, or offered in defence; as, an *apology* for terrorism; **3,** a poor substitute; a makeshift; as, this drawing is only an *apology* for a map.

ap-o-plex-y (ap′o-plek′si), *n.* the sudden loss of consciousness, or of the power to feel or move; a stroke. It is usually caused by the breaking of a blood vessel in the brain.—*adj.* **ap′o-plec′tic.**

a-pos-tle (a-pos′l), *n.* **1,** one of the 12 men chosen by Jesus to teach his gospel to the world (Luke 6:13); also, a disciple, like Paul, given the same work to do; **2,** a pioneer missionary; as, Livingstone was the *apostle* to Africa; **3,** a leader of any reform; as, an *apostle* of antiracism.

ap-os-tol-ic (ap′os-tol′ik) or **ap-os-tol-i-cal** (-tol′i-kal), *adj.* **1,** relating to the 12 apostles of Christ, their times, doctrine, etc.; **2,** coming from the Pope; papal; as, an *apostolic* blessing.

a-pos-tro-phe (a-pos′tro-fi), *n.* **1,** a breaking off in a speech to address a person, usually absent or dead, or an abstract idea or imaginary object; **2,** a punctuation mark used to show various things: **a,** a contraction; as, *I'll* for *I will*; **b,** the omission of one or more letters from a word; as, *can't* for *cannot*; '98 for 1998; **c,** the possessive case of nouns; as, the *cat's* fur; *Ulysses'* shield; **d,** the plural of letters and figures, as *x's* and *v's*, *6's* and *7's*.—*v.t.* **a-pos′tro-phize′.**

ap-pall or **ap-pal** (a-pôl′), *v.t.* [appalled, appal-ling], to frighten; shock; dismay; as, danger of war *appalled* us.—*adj.* **ap-pal′ling.**

ap-pa-ra-tus (ap′a-rā′tus; ap′a-rat′us), *n.* [*pl.* apparatus or apparatuses], **1,** an outfit of tools, utensils, or instruments for any kind of work; as, laboratory *apparatus*; **2,** the set of organs that performs some natural process; as, the digestive *apparatus*.

ap-par-el (a-par′el), *n.* clothing; dress; as, children's *apparel*:—*v.t.* to clothe; fit out.

ap-par-ent (a-pâr′ent; a-par′ent), *adj.* **1,** open to view; easily seen; **2,** easily understood; evident; **3,** appearing or seeming, rather than true or real; as, his *apparent* remorse fooled us.—*adv.* **ap-par′ent-ly.**

ap-pa-ri-tion (ap′a-rish′un), *n.* something startling and unreal that suddenly appears; a ghost or spectre.

ap-peal (a-pēl′), *v.t.* to transfer or refer to a higher court or judge; as, to *appeal* a case:—*v.i.* **1,** to make an earnest request; as, he *appealed* for aid; **2,** to be of interest; make a favourable impression; as, good music *appeals* to me:—*n.* **1,** a call for aid or sympathy; **2,** interest; attraction; as, your proposal has no *appeal* for me; **3,** the transfer of a case from a lower to a higher court.—*adj.* **ap-peal′ing.**

ap-pear (a-pēr′), *v.i.* **1,** to come into sight; as, the moon *appeared*; **2,** to seem; as, he *appears* to be ill; **3,** to come before the public; as, the book *appeared* in June; this actor *appeared* in *Hamlet*; **4,** to come formally into a court of law.

ap-pear-ance (a-pēr′ans), *n.* **1,** the act of becoming visible; as, the *appearance* of the sun from behind a cloud; **2,** a look; bearing; as, Charles Dickens had a dignified *appearance*; **3,** outward show; as, an *appearance* of humility; **4,** the act of coming before the public or in court; as, an *appearance* in court.

ap-pease (a-pēz′), *v.t.* [appeased, appeasing], **1,** to quiet; pacify; as, to *appease* an angry person; **2,** to satisfy; as, to *appease* one's hunger or curiosity.

ap-pel-la-tion (ap′e-lā′shun), *n.* a name or title by which a person or thing is described or known; as, one *appellation* of England is "Albion."

ap-pend (a-pend′), *v.t.* **1,** to attach or affix, as a seal; **2,** to attach or add, as supplementary matter to a book.

ap-pend-age (a-pen′dij), *n.* something attached to a greater thing, and forming a part of it, as a leg to an animal's or person's body.

ap-pen-di-ci-tis (a-pen′di-sī′tis), *n.* an inflammation of the vermiform appendix: in serious cases, the appendix must be surgically removed in an operation called an *appendectomy*.

ap-pen-dix (a-pen′diks), *n.* [*pl.* appendixes (a-pen′dik-sez) or appendices (a-pen′di-sēz′)], **1,** that which is added to give further information; as, the *appendix* to a book; **2,** a wormlike sac situated near the entrance to the large intestine, in the lower right-hand side of the abdomen; called in full *vermiform appendix*.

ap-pe-tite (ap′e-tīt′), *n.* **1,** a physical craving for food; **2,** a strong and active desire; as, an *appetite* for books; an *appetite* for fighting.

ap-pe-tiz-er (ap′e-tīz′ėr), *n.* **1,** a food or drink served before a meal to stimulate the desire for food, such as shrimp, crackers and cheese, and vegetables with dip, etc.; **2,** anything that arouses interest in things to follow.—*adj.* **ap′pe-tiz′ing.**

ap-plaud (a-plôd′), *v.t.* **1,** to express approval of, esp. by a clapping of the hands; **2,** to commend; as, I *applaud* your stand in the matter:—*v.i.* to clap the hands, or otherwise show approval.

ap-plause (a-plôz′), *n.* an expression of approval, as by handclapping.

ap-ple (ap′l), *n.* **1,** the round, fleshy fruit grown on trees in temperate regions; as, the MacIntosh is Canada's most famous *apple;* **2,** the tree itself.

ap-pli-ance (a-plī′ans), *n.* an article or device for some special use or purpose, esp. around the house, such as a toaster, stove, microwave, dishwasher, etc.

ap-pli-ca-ble (ap′li-ka-bl), *adj.* suitable; fit; capable of being used or applied; as, this excuse is not *applicable* to your case.—*n.* **ap′pli-ca-bil′i-ty.**

ap-pli-ca-tion (ap′li-kā′shun), *n.* **1,** the act of putting on; as, the *application* of ice to a sprained ankle; **2,** the thing put on; as, cold *applications;* **3,** practical demonstration or use, as of a theory or law; **4,** close attention, as to work; **5,** a program that allows a computer to perform a certain operation; as, a word-processing application; **6,** a personal or written request, as for a job.—*n.* **ap′pli-cant; ap′pli-ca-tor.**

ap-ply (a-plī′), *v.t.* [applied, apply-ing], **1,** to bring into contact with something; lay on; as, to *apply* a bandage; to *apply* a coat of paint; **2,** to put into practice; as, to *apply* a rule; **3,** to devote to a particular purpose; as, *apply* yourself to study:—*v.i.* **1,** to ask; petition; request; as, *apply* early if you want a ticket; to *apply* for a job; to *apply* to the University of Toronto; **2,** to have some connection; as, this does not *apply* to you.

ap-point (a-point′), *v.t.* **1,** to name for an office; as, to *appoint* a chairman; **2,** to set; fix; as, to *appoint* a day for a game.—*adj.* **ap-poin′tive.**

ap-point-ee (a-poin′tē′), *n.* a person named to an office; as, political *appointees.*

ap-point-ment (a-point′ment), *n.* **1,** the act of naming or appointing to an office; **2,** the position or office so assigned; **3,** an engagement; mutual agreement to meet.

ap-por-tion (a-pōr′shun), *v.t.* to divide and distribute; allot; as, ample food was *apportioned* to the homeless people.—*n.* **ap-por′tion-ment.**

ap-po-si-tion (ap′ō-zish′un), *n.* **1,** the act of placing together; also, the condition of being in close contact; **2,** in *grammar,* the relation of a noun to another noun near which it is placed, as its equivalent, or as explanatory of it. In the expression "Crusoe spoke to Friday, his servant," "servant" is in *apposition* to "Friday."—*adj.* **ap′po-site; ap-pos′i-tive.**—*adv.* **ap-pos′i-tive-ly.**

ap-praise (a-prāz′), *v.t.* [appraised, apprais-ing], to estimate or fix the price or value of; as, to *appraise* a person's worth; to *appraise* land for taxation.—*n.* **ap-prais′al.**—*n.* **ap-prais′er.**

ap-pre-ci-a-ble (a-prē′shi-a-bl; a-prē′sha-bl), *adj.* capable of being estimated; perceptible; as, an *appreciable* gain.—*adv.* **ap-pre′ci-a-bly.**

ap-pre-ci-ate (a-prē′shi-āt′), *v.t.* [appreci-at-ed, appreciat-ing], **1,** to value justly; esteem; **2,** to have a cultivated understanding of; be sensitive to; as, to *appreciate* art:—*v.i.* to increase in price or value; as, real estate *appreciates* in boom times.—*n.* **ap-pre′ci-a′tion.**—*adj.* **ap-pre′ci-a′tive.**

ap-pre-hend (ap′ri-hend′), *v.t.* **1,** to lay hold of; seize; arrest; as, to *apprehend* a fugitive; **2,** to take mental hold of; as, I *apprehend* his meaning; **3,** to anticipate with fear; as, to *apprehend* danger:—*v.i.* to catch the meaning.—*n.* **ap′pre-hen′sion.**

ap-pre-hen-sive (ap′ri-hen′siv), *adj.* afraid; fearful, as of trouble; worried, as for someone's safety.—*adv.* **ap′pre-hen′sive-ly.**—*n.* **ap′pre-hen′sive-ness.**

ap-pren-tice (a-pren′tis), *n.* **1,** a person who is learning a trade or craft by practical experience under a skilled worker; formerly, one bound by an agreement to work for a definite length of time in return for the training; **2,** a novice, or one slightly skilled in anything:—*v.t.* [apprenticed, apprentic-ing], to put under a master for training in a trade.—*n.* **ap-pren′tice-ship.**

ap-prise (a-prīz′), *v.t.* [apprised, appris-ing], to give notice to; warn; inform; as, I *apprised* him of danger.

ap-proach (a-prōch′), *v.i.* to draw near; as, a stranger is *approaching:*—*v.t.* **1,** to come near to (a thing, place, or condition); as, to *approach* a school; to *approach* perfection; **2,** to present an idea or request; as, to *approach* a coach with an idea:—*n.* **1,** the act of drawing near; as, we noticed the *approach* of a car; **2,** the way by which one draws near; as, the *approach* to the city was lined with trees; **3,** in *golf,* a shot that aims to place the ball on the green.—*adj.* **approach′a-ble.**

ap-pro-ba-tion (ap′rō-bā′shun), *n.* the act of declaring something to be good; commendation; approval; as, the audience clapped in *approbation.*

ap-pro-pri-ate (a-prō′pri-āt′), *v.t.* [appro-priat-ed, appropriat-ing], **1,** to take and use for one's own; as, I *appropriated* your pen; **2,** to set apart for a particular purpose, often by legislative act; as, to *appropriate* money for roads:—*adj.* (a-prō′pri-it), fit; suitable; proper; as, an *appropriate* response to the question.—*adv.* **ap-pro′pri-ate-ly.**—*n.* **ap-pro′pri-ate-ness.**

ap-prov-al (a-prōōv′al), *n.* **1,** favourable opinion; the thinking well of a person or his act; as, your idea has my *approval;* **2,** permission or consent; as, parents' *approval* to go on the trip.

ap-prove (a-prōōv′), *v.i.* [approved, approv-ing], to express a favourable opinion; as, we *approve* of his friends:—*v.t.* to give permission or consent; accept; allow; as, to *approve* plans.—*adv.* **ap-prov′ing-ly.**

ap-prox-i-mate (a-prok′si-mit), *adj.* almost

equal; nearly correct; not exact but nearly so; as, an *approximate* price:—*v.t.* (a-prok′si-māt′), [approximat-ed, approximat-ing], to come close to; estimate; as, Vera's conduct *approximates* folly; to *approximate* the size of a room.—*adv.* **ap-prox′i-mate-ly.**—*n.* **ap-prox′i-ma′tion.**

a-pri-cot (ā′pri-kot′, ap-), *n.* **1,** an orange-coloured fruit of the plum family, similar to the peach in texture of skin and flesh; **2,** the tree itself.

A-pril (ā′pril), *n.* the fourth month of the year, between March and May (30 days):—**April Fools' Day,** a name for April 1, a day on which people often try to fool others with tricks and jokes.

a-pron (ā′prun), *n.* **1,** a garment, made of cloth or other material, worn in front to protect one's clothes or as part of a costume; **2,** the front part of an area or surface; as, the *apron* of a stage.

ap-ro-pos (ap′ro-pō′), *adv.* with reference (to); as, *apropos* of that remark, I have this to say:—*adj.* appropriate; fitting; suitable; as, an *apropos* remark.

apt (apt), *adj.* **1,** suitable; appropriate; as, an *apt* reply; **2,** inclined; likely; as, he is *apt* to be careless; **3,** quick to learn; as, an *apt* student.—*adv.* **apt′ly.**

ap-ti-tude (ap′ti-tūd′), *n.* **1,** natural ability; talent; as, *aptitude* for painting; **2,** ability or quickness to learn:—**aptitude test,** a test that shows which subjects or work people are best suited for or would excel in.

a-quar-i-um (a-kwâr′i-um), *n.* [*pl.* aquariums or aquaria (a-kwâr′i-a)], **1,** a tank, bowl, or artificial pond in which living water plants and water animals are kept; **2,** a building devoted to the care and exhibition of large collections of water plants and animals.

A-quar-i-us (a-kwâr′i-us), *n.* **1,** a central constellation, the Water Bearer; **2,** the eleventh sign of the zodiac [♒], which the sun enters about January 21.

a-quat-ic (a-kwat′ik; a-kwot′ik), *adj.* **1,** in or on water; as, *aquatic* sports; **2,** growing in water:—**aquatics,** sports that take place in the water.

aq-ue-duct (ak′we-dukt), *n.* **1,** a pipe or artificial channel for conducting water from a distance; **2,** a bridgelike structure that supports such a conduit.

a-que-ous (ā′kwi-us; ak′wi-us), *adj.* **1,** of the nature of water; watery; **2,** produced by water; as, *aqueous* rocks.

aq-ui-line (ak′wi-līn′; ak′wi-lin), *adj.* curved like an eagle's beak; as, an *aquiline* nose.

Ar-ab (âr′ab′), *n.* a member of a Semitic people who speak Arabic and who are located throughout the Middle East and North Africa:—*adj.* pertaining to Arabs.—*adj.* **Ar′a-bic.**

Arabic numerals (âr′u-bik), the signs commonly used to write numbers (1, 2, 3, 4, etc.), introduced to Europe by the Arabs.

ar-a-ble (ar′a-bl), *adj.* suitable for cultivation; tillable; as, *arable* land.

a-rach-nid (a-rak′nid), *n.* any of a group of insectlike land animals, such as a spider, scorpion, mite, or tick, having four pairs of legs: unlike insects, they do not have wings or antennae, and their bodies are divided into two main parts, not three.

ar-bi-ter (är′bi-tėr), *n.* **1,** a person chosen or appointed to settle a dispute; an umpire; an arbitrator; **2,** one who has full power to make decisions; as, one is the *arbiter* of one's own life.—*n.* **ar-bit′ra-ment.**

ar-bi-trar-y (ar′bi-trėr-i; -trer-i), *adj.* **1,** ruled only by one's own wishes or ideas in making decisions; despotic; as, an *arbitrary* ruler; **2,** based on one's own opinions and wishes, and not on any rule or law; as, an *arbitrary* decision.—*adv.* **ar′bi-trar-i-ly.**

ar-bi-trate (är′bi-trāt′), *v.t.* [arbitrat-ed, arbitrat-ing], **1,** to hear as a judge, and decide; settle a dispute; as, the father *arbitrated* the family differences; **2,** to refer (a dispute) to others for settlement; as, we decided to *arbitrate* the issue:—*v.t.* to act as arbiter or judge.—*n.* **ar′bi-tra′tion; ar′bi-tra′tor.**

ar-bo-re-al (är-bō′ri-al), *adj.* **1,** like trees; relating to trees; **2,** living in trees, as monkeys and squirrels.

ar-bour or **ar-bor** (är′bėr), *n.* **1,** a latticework bower of vines; as, a grape *arbour*; **2,** a shaded nook or walk.

arc (ärk), *n.* **1,** part of a curved line; esp. a part of the circumference of a circle; also, a curved line or path; **2,** in *electricity*, a short band of light, sometimes curved, formed when a powerful electric current passes across a space between two mints, generally of carbon, in a broken circuit:—*v.i.* [arced, arc-ing], to form an arc.

ar-cade (är-kād′), *n.* **1,** a row of arches supported by pillars; **2,** an arched gallery or passageway, often between buildings, esp. one lined with shops; **3,** a place where people pay to play different types of games, esp. electronic games. Also called *video arcade.*

ar-cane (är-kān′), *adj.* mysterious, esoteric, obscure; not widely understood; as, *arcane* technical details.

[1]arch (ärch), *n.* **1,** a structure of brick or masonry, the wedge-shaped parts of which follow a curved line, usually forming the top of a door, window, or gateway; **2,** an opening or passage covered by such a structure; an archway; **3,** anything

THE ARC DE TRIOMPHE

arch-shaped; as, the *arch* of the foot:—*v.t.* **1,** to cover with a curved or arched structure; **2,** to bend or curve; as, the cat *arched* its back:—*v.i.* to form an arch-shaped bend or curve; as, *arching* trees.—*n.* **arch′way.**

²arch (ärch), *adj.* **1,** mischievous; roguish; as, an *arch* look; **2,** chief; of the first rank; as, an *arch* villain: often used as a prefix, as in *arch*bishop, *arch*duke.—*adj.* **arch′ly.**—*n.* **arch′ness.**

ar-chae-ol-o-gy (är-ki-ol′o-ji), *n.* the scientific study of the human past from excavation of fossils, buildings, remains, etc.—*adj.* **ar-chae-ol-o′gi-cal.**—*n.* **ar-chae-ol′o-gist.**

ar-cha-ic (är-kā′ik), *adj.* old-fashioned; primitive; as, a phonograph is *archaic*; of words, no longer in common use; as, the word "methinks" is *archaic.*

arch-bish-op (ärch′bish′up), *n.* a bishop of highest rank, with authority over a group of dioceses.—*n.* **arch′bish′op-ric; arch′di′o-cese.**

arch-er (är′chėr), *n.* a person skilled in using the bow and arrow.

arch-er-y (är′chė-ri), *n.* **1,** the use, or skill in the use, of bow and arrow; **2,** a company of archers.

ar-che-type (är′ki-tīp′), *n.* **1,** the original model or prototype; **2,** a perfect example; an ideal; as, an *archetype* of business success; **3,** a recurring theme or symbol in literature or art.

ar-chi-pel-a-go (är′ki-pel′a-gō′), *n.* [*pl.* archipelagos or archipelagoes], a sea containing numerous islands: also, a group of islands.

ar-chi-tect (är′ki-tekt′), *n.* one who plans or designs buildings, bridges, etc., and superintends their construction; also, anyone who designs or develops something; as, an *architect* of the environmental program.

ar-chi-tec-ture (är′ki-tek′tūr; choor), *n.* **1,** the science and art of building for both use and beauty; **2,** the manner or style of building; as, the new building is an example of Gothic *architecture*; **3,** construction; shape; workmanship; as, the *architecture* of this library has many defects.—*adj.* **ar′chi-tec′tur-al.**

ar-chive (är′kīv), *n.* a record preserved as evidence:—**archives,** the place in which public records or historical documents are kept; such records.

Arc-tic (ärk′tik), *adj.* located in, or relating to, the region of the North Pole; northern; frigid:—**Arctic Circle,** an imaginary circle parallel to the equator at 66 1/3°N:—**Arctic Ocean,** the North Polar ocean.

arctic char or **Arctic char,** a fish of the trout family, found throughout the Arctic.

ar-dent (ärd′ent), *adj.* blazing; hence, passionate; eager; as, an *ardent* desire.

ar-dour or **ar-dor** (är′dėr), *n.* burning heat; hence, warmth of affection; eagerness.

ar-du-ous (är′dū-us; joo-), *adj.* **1,** steep; hard to climb; **2,** attended with great labour or exertion; difficult; as, an *arduous* task; **3,** strenuous; as, *arduous* efforts.

¹are (är), second person, singular and plural, present indicative, of *be.*

²are (ãr; är), *n.* in the metric system, a measure of surface, esp. of land; 100 square metres (119.6 square yards), abbreviated as "a"; as, 50 *a* of land.

a-re-a (âr′i-a), *n.* [*pl.* areas], **1,** any level, bounded surface; as, the *area* of a floor; the shaded *area* of a drawing; **2,** extent of surface, esp. of the earth's surface; as, the *area* of Canada; **3,** a region; as, a hilly *area*; **4,** scope; range; as, his activities covered a wide *area*; **5,** in *geometry,* the total surface of a plane or solid figure, calculated by multiplying length by width; as, the *area* of a square or of a cube.

area code, a combination of three numbers assigned to geographic areas, used to dial directly by telephone from one region to another, and sometimes within the same region, in Canada or the world, esp. when calling long distance.

a-re-na (a-rē′na), *n.* **1,** in ancient Rome, the enclosed space of an amphitheatre, in which fights between gladiators took place; **2,** a similar modern building for sports events, circuses, and shows; **3,** any place of contest or rivalry; as, the *arena* of politics.

ar-gue (är′gū), *v.i.* [argued, argu-ing], **1,** to give reasons for or against an opinion, measure, etc., try to prove or disprove something; as, to *argue* for a lower tariff; **2,** to debate; dispute:—*v.t.* to persuade by force of words; as, she *argued* the point endlessly; to quarrel; have a disagreement; as, they always *argue* in front of the children.

ar-gu-ment (är′gū-ment), *n.* **1,** a reason for or against a thing; as, I know of no *argument* against it; **2,** a discussion containing reasons for or against something; **3,** the subject, as of a speech or essay; also, an outline or summary, as of a book; **4,** a disagreement or quarrel.—*adj.* **ar′gu-men′ta-tive.**

a-ri-a (âr′i-a; ä′ri-a), *n.* **1,** an air or tune; **2,** an elaborate solo part in an opera, etc.

ar-id (ar′id), *adj.* dry; parched; as, an *arid* desert.—*n.* **a-rid′i-ty** (a-rid′i-ti).

A-ri-es (âr′ēz), *n.* **1,** a northern constellation, the Ram; **2,** the first sign of the zodiac [♈], which the sun enters about March 21.

a-rise (a-rīz′), *v.i.* [*p.t.* arose (a-rōz′), *p.p.* aris-en (a-riz′n), *p.pr.* aris-ing], **1,** to stand up; change to a standing position from one of sitting, kneeling, or lying; get up after sleep; **2,** to ascend; move upward; as, the sun *arose*; **3,** to spring up; begin; as, then a dispute *arose*.

ar-is-toc-ra-cy (ar′is-tok′ra-si), *n.* [*pl.* aristocracies], **1,** government by persons of the highest rank in a state; **2,** a state with such a government; **3,** the nobility or any group of people thought of as having great power, intelligence, or ability.—*n.* **ar-is-to-crat.**—*adj.* **ar-is-to-crat-ic.**

a-rith-me-tic (a-rith′me-tik), *n.* the science of numbers; the art of reckoning by the use of figures; the branch of mathematics that includes adding, subtracting, multiplying, and dividing.—*adj.* **ar′ith-met′i-cal.**

ark (ärk), *n.* **1,** a chest or oblong box containing the Covenant, or tables of the Law, in the Jewish Tabernacle (Exodus 25); **2,** a ship, such as the one in which Noah and his family remained during the Flood (Genesis 6).

[1]**arm** (ärm), *n.* **1,** one of the two upper limbs; esp., that part of the upper limb between shoulder and hand; **2,** the front or fore limb of any animal having a backbone; **3,** a part resembling, or corresponding to, an arm, as the side of a chair, an inlet of the sea, a branch of a tree, etc.

[2]**arm** (ärm), *n.* **1,** a weapon, such as a gun, knife, or bomb; as, the right to bear *arms*; **2,** a branch of the military service, as the infantry, navy, etc.; **3,** heraldic emblems or devices; as, the coat of *arms* of Canada:—*v.t.* **1,** to furnish with *arms*; **2,** to supply with anything that gives strength or power; as, to *arm* yourself with information:—*v.i.* to fit oneself with arms; take up arms.

ar-ma-da (är-mā′da; är-må′da), *n.* a fleet of armed vessels, aircraft, etc.

ar-ma-dil-lo (är′ma-dil′ō), *n.* [*pl.* armadillos], any of several South and Central American insect-eating burrowing animals having the head and body protected by an armour of bony plates. Some kinds, when attacked, curl up into a ball.

ar-ma-ment (ar′ma-ment), *n.* **1,** a nation's entire war equipment or military strength; also, equipment in guns and ammunition; **2,** the act of arming for war.

arm-chair (ärm′châr′; ärm′châr′), *n.* a chair with supports for the arms.

armed forces, the military force of a nation.

arm-ful (ärm′fool), *n.* [*pl.* armfuls], as much as one arm, or both, can hold.

arm-hole (ärm′hōl′), *n.* in a garment, an opening for the arm.

ar-mi-stice (är′mi-stis), *n.* a pause in war by agreement of both sides; a truce.

ar-mour or **armor** (är′mėr), *n.* **1,** a covering of metal, leather, etc., worn of old, to protect the body in battle or jousting; **2,** the steel plating of a warship; **3,** any protective covering, as the scales of a fish:—*v.t.* to furnish with a protective covering.—*adj.* **ar′moured; ar-mo′ri-al.**—*n.* **ar′mour-er; ar′mour-y.**

arm-pit (ärm′pit′), *n.* the pit or hollow beneath the arm where it joins the shoulder.

arm's length, **1,** without intimacy; at a distance to prevent or restrict familiarity; as, to keep business associates at *arm's length*; **2,** provision that parties to a transaction are on an equal footing; **3,** the length of an arm.

arms race, a competition between nations to develop and stockpile the most powerful weapons.

arm-twist-ing (ärm′-twis′ting), *n.* strong direct pressure to persuade others to support a certain course of action; forceful persuasion; as, despite a lot of *arm-twisting*, her parents would not let her go to the party.—*v.t.* **arm-twist.**

ar-my (är′mi), *n.* [*pl.* armies], **1,** a large body of soldiers trained and equipped for war; **2,** a great number or multitude; a host; as, an *army* of beetles; **3,** an organized body of persons engaged in furthering a common cause; as, an *army* of workers.

a-ro-ma (a-rō′ma), *n.* a pleasant smell or fragrance.—*adj.* **ar′o-mat′ic** (ar′ō-mat′ik).

aro-ma-ther-a-py (a-rō′ma-ther′a-pi), *n.* the art of using fragrant extracts and oils to affect the mood, relieve stress, and promote health.

a-rose (a-rōz′), *p.t.* of *arise*.

a-round (a-round′), *adv.* **1,** in a circle; as, to go *around* on a merry-go-round; **2,** on every side; round about; as, to rush *around*; **3,** near at hand; as, no one is around:—*prep.* **1,** circling or encircling; as, to walk *around* a tree; a belt *around* a waist; **2,** on all sides of; as, the air *around* us; **3,** somewhat near; approximately; as, a town is *around* 15 kilometres from here.

a-rouse (a-rouz′), *v.t.* [aroused, arous-ing], **1,** to waken; as, she sleeps soundly but is easily *aroused*; **2,** to stir to life; excite to activity; as, his anger is not easily *aroused*.

ar-raign (a-rān′), *v.t.* **1,** to summon (a prisoner) into court to answer a charge; accuse; **2,** to find fault with; call in question; as, I do not *arraign* his honesty.—*n.* **arraign′ment.**

ar-range (a-rānj′), *v.t.* [arranged, arranging], **1,** to put into suitable order; as, to *arrange* flowers or CDs; **2,** to adjust or settle, as a dispute; bring about, as an interview or compromise; **3,** to change to fit; adapt or adjust; as, to *arrange* music for the songs:—*v.i.* to make preparations in advance; as, I have *arranged* for the use of the hall.

ar-range-ment (a-rānj′ment), *n.* **1,** the act of arranging something, or the thing that is arranged; as, a flower *arrangement*; **2,** the act of arranging a piece of music, or a piece of music that has been arranged; **3,** plans or preparations; as, *arrangements* for a wedding.

ar-ray (a-rā′), *n.* **1,** orderly or formal arrangement; as, troops in battle *array*; **2,** a fine or imposing collection or display; as, an *array* of silver; an *array* of talent; **3,** clothing, especially fine clothing; as, the crowds were in holiday *array*; **4,** in *mathematics*, data arranged in rows and columns; **5,** in *computing*, similar items arranged consecutively in the memory:—*v.t.* **1,** to place or dispose in order; to marshal; as, to *array* troops in battle formation; **2,** to deck or dress; as, the guests were beautifully *arrayed*.

ar-rears (a-rērz′), *n.pl.* that which should be done or paid, but is still undone or unpaid; debts or unfinished work; as, *arrears* on your credit card statement:—**in arrears,** behind with what should have already been done or paid; as, her account was *in arrears*.—*n.* **ar-rear′age.**

ar-rest (a-rest′), *v.t.* **1,** to stop or check; as, to *arrest* a runaway horse; also, to attract and hold; as, bright colours *arrest* the eye; **2,** to seize and hold (a person) by legal authority; take prisoner:—*n.* **1,** the act of checking or stopping; as, the *arrest* of decay; **2,** the act of taking a person prisoner.

ar-riv-al (a-rīv′al), *n.* **1,** the act of coming to a place, or reaching a destination; as, her *arrival* was unexpected; **2,** a person arriving; as, a late *arrival*.

ar-rive (a-rīv′), *v.i.* [arrived, arriv-ing], **1,** to come to, or reach, a given place; **2,** to reach a result by a process of thought; as, to *arrive* at a conclusion.

ar-ro-gance (ar′ō-gans), *n.* a display of too great confidence in oneself or one's abilities; pride; conceit; extreme haughtiness; contempt of others.—*adj.* **ar′ro-gant.**

ar-row (ar′ō), *n.* **1,** a slender, pointed shaft, usually feathered and barbed, and made to be shot from a bow; **2,** something shaped like an arrow; **3,** a figure on maps, signboards, etc., to indicate direction.—*n.* **ar′row-head′.**

ar-se-nal (är′se-nal), *n.* a public building for storing, making, or repairing military equipment of all kinds.

ar-se-nic (är′se-nik; ärs′nik), *n.* a poisonous greyish-white chemical element:—*adj.* (är-sen′ik), containing arsenic.

ar-son (är′sn), *n.* the malicious or intentional act of setting fire to a building or other property, which is a criminal offence.—*n.* **ar′son-ist.**

art (ärt), *n.* **1,** skill acquired by study or practice; natural aptitude; knack; as, the *art* of sewing; **2,** the body of knowledge and experience related to a particular occupation or profession; as, the *art* of engineering; **3,** the study or creation of beautiful things; as in painting, drawing, sculpture, architecture, music, literature, and dancing: usually called *fine arts*; **4,** the work produced by painters, sculptors, musicians, etc.; **5, arts,** in universities, certain branches of learning such as literature, history, languages, philosophy, etc.; the humanities; **6,** craft; cunning; as, her *art* and wiles failed.

ar-ter-y (är′tė-ri), *n.* [*pl.* arteries], **1,** one of the tubes that carry blood from the heart to all parts of the body, as opposed to a *vein*, which carries blood back to the heart; **2,** any great channel or main thoroughfare.—*adj.* **ar-te′ri-al** (är-tē′ri-al).

ar-te-sian well (är-tē′zhan), a well made by boring into the ground deep enough to reach water, which, from internal pressure, will gush to the surface.

art-ful (ärt′fool), *adj.* **1,** skillful; clever; as, *artful* presentations; **2,** cunning; crafty; as, her *artful* ways displeased us; an *artful* computer hacker.

ar-thri-tis (är-thrī′tis), *n.* inflammation or disease of a joint (as in rheumatism).

ar-thro-pod (ar′thro-pod′), *n.* any spineless animal with jointed legs and segmented body, as crabs and lobsters, spiders, insects, arachnids, centipedes and millipedes, etc.

ar-ti-choke (är′ti-chōk′), *n.* a tall plant, the edible flower head of which is used as a vegetable; also, the vegetable.

ARTICHOKE

ar-ti-cle (är′ti-kl), *n.* **1,** a thing belonging to a particular class of things; as, an *article* of clothing; **2,** a single section of a written legal document, as a clause of a contract, treaty, creed, etc.; as, an *article* of law; **3,** a prose composition or story, complete in itself, in a newspaper, magazine, etc.; **4,** in *grammar*, any of the words *a*, *an*, or *the*, used before a noun:—*v.t.* [arti-cled, arti-cling], to bind by written agreement; as, he *articled* his son to a carpenter as an apprentice.

ar-tic-u-late (är-tik′ū-lāt′), *v.t.* [articulat-ed, articulat-ing], **1,** to unite by means of joints; form or fit; as, to *articulate* a program for the whole school; **2,** to utter in distinct syllables; as, do not mumble; *articulate* your words:—*v.i.* **1,** to utter distinct sounds; **2,** to be jointed, formed, or fitted:—*adj.* (är-tik′ū-lit), **1,** jointed, formed, or fitted; as, an *articulate* science program; **2,** spoken with distinctness; **3,** able to speak, or to express oneself, clearly and well.—*adv.* **ar-tic′u-late-ly.**—*n.* **ar-tic′u-la′tion.**

ar-ti-fact or **artefact** (är′ti-fakt′), *n.* a human-made object; something created by human beings for a particular purpose, such as a tool, ornament, or weapon.

ar-ti-fice (är′ti-fis), *n.* **1,** skill in invention or design; **2,** a ruse or trick.—*n.* **ar-ti′fi-cer.**

ar-ti-fi-cial (är′ti-fish′al), *adj.* **1,** not natural; made by people in imitation of nature; as, *artificial* teeth; *artificial* ice; *artificial* grass; **2,** affected; insincere; as, an *artificial* smile.—*adv.* **ar′ti-fi′cial-ly.**—*n.* **ar′ti-fi′ci-al′i-ty.**

artificial insemination, the introduction of sperm into the womb to cause fertilization of the eggs without sexual contact.

artificial intelligence, the capability of computers and other machines to simulate human thinking and reasoning, such as making use of previous information to recognize and solve a problem: artificial intelligence makes it possible for a computer to play chess; also, the branch of computer science pertaining to this.

artificial language, 1, an invented language developed for a special purpose such as computer programming; **2,** a deliberately fabricated language combining vocabulary and grammar, etc., from a number of languages; as, Esperanto is an *artificial language.*

artificial life, the study of synthetic systems that mimic natural ones, such as computer systems that simulate the behaviour of living things.

artificial respiration, the forcing of air into and out of the lungs of a person whose breathing has stopped.

ar-til-ler-y (är-til′ė-ri), *n.* **1,** in war, cannons, mounted guns, rockets, etc., together with their ammunition; **2,** that branch of an army that uses these arms.

ar-ti-san (är′ti-zan′; är′ti-zan), *n.* a person specially trained to work with his or her hands, as a bricklayer or carpenter.

art-ist (är′tist), *n.* **1,** a person who practises an art, such as painting, music, or literature; **2,** in any field, a person who shows creative power in his or her work; as, your cook is an *artist.*—*adj.* **ar-tis′tic.**—*adv.* **ar-tis′ti-cal-ly.**

art-ist-ry (är′tis-tri), *n.* beauty of workmanship or effect; also, artistic skill.

art-less (ärt′lis), *adj.* **1,** lacking skill or art; clumsy; **2,** free from deceit; natural; uncontrived; as, an *artless* walk or smile.—*adv.* **art′less-ly.**

art-work (ärt′wûrk′), *n.* **1,** illustrative material, such as photos or drawings, prepared for including in a book, magazine, etc.; **2,** works of art in aggregate.

as (az), *adv.* **1,** equally; similarly; to the same extent; as, paper plates will do *as* well; he swam just *as* far yesterday; **2,** thus; for example: used in introducing an example or illustrative quotations:—*conj.* **1,** because; as, he sat down, *as* he was tired; **2,** while; when; as, they fled *as* we approached; **3,** in the way that; as, we did *as* we were told:—*prep.* in the role of; as, he entered the contest *as* an amateur:—*relative pron.* that; which: used after *such, same,* etc.; as, send me such books *as* you have ready.

as-bes-tos (as-bes′tos; az-), *n.* a fibrous, unburnable mineral substance, formerly used in making fireproof materials, such as firefighters' uniforms, but now considered harmful: the substance has been linked to certain kinds of cancer.

as-cend (a-send′), *v.t.* and *v.i.* **1,** to climb or go up; also, to mount; as, to *ascend* the stairs; we watched the kite *ascend;* **2,** to move upward in rank or level; as, to *ascend* to presidency of the company.

as-cend-ant (a-sen′dant) or **as-cend-ent,** *adj.* **1,** rising; predominant; **2,** above the horizon.—*n.* **as-cend′an-cy; as-cend′en-cy.**

as-cen-sion (a-sen′shun), *n.* a moving upward; a rising.

as-cent (a-sent′), *n.* **1,** a rising; as, the *ascent* of an airplane; **2,** the act of climbing; as, the *ascent* of a mountain; **3,** an upward slope; **4,** the act of rising to a higher rank or level.

as-cer-tain (as′ėr-tān′), *v.t.* to find out definitely; discover; as, it is not so easy to *ascertain* truth.—*adj.* **as′cer-tain′a-ble.**—*n.* **as′cer-tain′ment.**

as-cet-ic (a-set′ik), *n.* one who renounces the comforts and pleasures of life and devotes oneself to religious duties; also, one who practises self-denial:—*adj.* self-denying; as, the monks lived *ascetic* lives.—*n.* **as-cet′i-cism.**

ASCII (as′kē′), *n.* in *computing,* American Standard Code for Information Interchange, a protocol for information exchange between different types of computers.

as-cribe (a-skrīb′), *v.t.* [ascribed, ascrib-ing], **1,** to regard or speak of (something) as caused by something else; attribute; as, she *ascribed* her success to hard work; **2,** to regard or speak of (something) as belonging to someone; attribute; as, the poem was *ascribed* to Burns; valour is *ascribed* to a hero.—*adj.* **as-crib′a-ble.**

¹ash (ash), *n.* a common timber and shade tree, or its tough, elastic wood, used for making furniture and baseball bats.

²ash (ash), *n.* **1,** what remains of a substance that has been burned; as, wood *ash;* coal *ash;* **2,** the colour of wood ashes; a whitish or brownish grey.—*adj.* **ash′en; ash′y.**

a-shamed (a-shāmd′), *adj.* **1,** feeling shame or regret; as, he was *ashamed* of his rude act; **2,** fearful of reproach or scorn; as, *ashamed* to beg.

a-shore (a-shōr′), *adv.* on shore; to the shore; as, a ship driven *ashore.*

A-sian (ā′zhen; ā′shen), *n.* a person who inhabits or originates from Asia:—*adj.* relating to the continent, the people, the language, or the culture of Asia.

a-side (a-sīd′), *adv.* **1,** on or to one side; as, to pull a curtain *aside;* **2,** away or apart; as, to set *aside* five dollars:—*n.* a remark in a low tone, intended not to be overheard.

as-i-nine (as′i-nīn′), *adj.* like an ass; hence, stupid; silly; as, an *asinine* remark.

ask (åsk), *v.t.* **1,** to seek an answer to; as, to *ask* a question; also, to put a question to; as, *ask* her how old she is; **2,** to beg or request; as, to *ask* a favour; **3,** to inquire about; as, to *ask* the way; **4,** to invite; as, I was *asked* to the party; **5,** to claim; demand; as, what price do you *ask*?—*v.i.* **1,** to make a request; as, to *ask* for money; **2,** to inquire; as, to *ask* for the manager.

a-skance (a-skans′), *adv.* with a sidelong glance; hence, with suspicion or distrust; as, to look *askance* at a newcomer.

a-skew (a-skū′), *adv.* and *adj.* awry; out of order; off the true or straight; as, the picture is hanging *askew.*

a-sleep (a-slēp′), *adj.* and *adv.* **1,** sleeping; **2,** numb; as, my foot is *asleep.*

asp (asp), *n.* a small poisonous snake of Africa, Europe, and Asia.

as-par-a-gus (a-spar′a-gus), *n.* the tender young stalks of a garden plant of the lily family, used as a vegetable; also, the plant.

as-par-tame (a′spär-tām′), *n.* a low-calorie artificial sweetener made from aspartic acid.

as-pect (as′pekt), *n.* **1,** appearance; look; as, the pirate's fierce *aspect;* **2,** a particular way that something can be looked at or thought of; as, a certain *aspect* of a plan; **3,** a side or part facing a given direction; as, the southern *aspect* of the fort.

as-pen (as′pen; ås′pen), *n.* a kind of poplar tree with leaves that tremble in the faintest breeze:—*adj.* relating to such a tree.

as-per-i-ty (as-per′i-ti), *n.* [*pl.* asperities], **1,** roughness of surface; unevenness; **2,** hence, harshness or sharpness of temper; as, he spoke with *asperity* of the trouble we had caused him.

as-perse (a-spûrs′), *v.t.* [aspersed, aspersing], to spread damaging or false reports about (a person or his or her character); to slander.—*n.* **as-per′sion.**

as-phalt (as′fôlt; as′falt), *n.* **1,** a dark-coloured, tarlike mineral substance; **2,** a preparation of this substance, used for paving, roofing, and cementing.

as-phyx-i-ate (as-fik′si-āt′), *v.t.* [asphyxiated, asphyxiat-ing], to cause unconsciousness or death to by cutting off the supply of air; to suffocate.—*n.* **as-phyx′i-a′tion.**

as-pic (as′pik), *n.* a clear meat jelly, served cold, and used as a garnish, or to make a mould of meat, fish, or vegetables.

as-pi-ra-tion (as′pi-rā′shun), *n.* **1,** the act of breathing; a breath; **2,** the strong desire to attain a high or noble goal; ambition; as, an *aspiration* to become an artist; **3,** the pronunciation of the letter *h* as in "horse."

as-pire (a-spīr′), *v.i.* [aspired, aspir-ing], to have an earnest desire to attain something great or noble; as, he *aspired* to fame as an artist.—*n.* **as-pir′ant.**

as-pi-rin (as′pi-rin), *n.* a drug, usually in the form of white tablets, used to reduce pain and fever.

ass (ås; as), *n.* **1,** the donkey (with longer ears and shorter mane than the horse); **2,** a vain, self-important, or silly person.

as-sail (a-sāl′), *v.t.* to fall upon or attack violently; also, to attack with words; as, they *assailed* him with threats and jeers.—*adj.* **as-sail′a-ble.**—*n.* **as-sail′ant.**

as-sas-sin (a-sas′in), *n.* a person who kills secretly or treacherously.

as-sas-si-nate (a-sas′i-nāt′), *v.t.* [assassinated, assassinat-ing], to kill by secret or treacherous means, esp. an important or famous person such as a political leader.—*n.* **as-sas′si-na′tion.**

as-sault (a-sôlt′), *n.* **1,** in *law,* a threat or attempt to hurt another person; **2,** a violent attack, by physical force, or by force of words; as, an *assault* on the enemy's camp; an *assault* on the character of an opponent:—*v.t.* to attack violently; assail.

as-say (a-sā′), *n.* **1,** the act or process of analyzing a metallic compound, ore, or alloy; esp., the testing of gold or silver coin or bullion to see if it is of standard purity; **2,** the substance tested:—*v.t.* **1,** to make a chemical analysis of; **2,** to test or examine.—*adj.* **as-say′a-ble.**—*n.* **as-say′er.**

as-sem-ble (a-sem′bl), *v.t.* [assem-bled assem-bling], **1,** to gather together into one place or mass; collect; as, he *assembled* the committee; **2,** to fit together, as parts of machinery:—*v.i.* to meet or come together; convene; as, the Senate *assembles* today.—*n.* **as-sem′blage.**

as-sem-bly (a-sem′bli), *n.* [*pl.* assemblies], **1,** a collection or company of persons brought together in one place and for a common object; a meeting; congregation; **2,** the fitting together of parts to make a complete machine; as, the *assembly* of a car:—**Assembly,** a body of lawmakers, as in some provinces or foreign countries:—**Legislative Assembly,** the one-chamber legislature in many provinces:—**National Assembly,** the one-chamber legislature in Québec.

assembly language, in *computing,* a low-level computer programming language that corresponds to binary machine language.

assembly line, a line of workers and equipment along which a product being put together, such as a car, is passed until it is completed.

as-sent (a-sent′), *v.i.* to agree; consent; express agreement; as, to *assent* to a request:—*n.* the act of agreeing; consent; as, do you *assent* to my plan?

as-sert (a-sûrt′), *v.t.* **1,** to state positively;

declare with assurance; affirm; as, let me *assert* my belief; **2,** to insist upon; as, to *assert* one's rights; make (oneself) felt; as, he invariably *asserts* himself.

as-ser-tion (a-sûr′shun), *n.* **1,** the act of declaring positively; **2,** a positive declaration or statement.

as-ser-tive (a-sûr′tiv), *adj.* **1,** inclined to make very positive statements; overconfident; as, an *assertive* person often takes charge; **2,** declarative; as, this is an *assertive* sentence.—*n.* **as-ser′tive-ness.**

as-sess (a-ses′), *v.t.* **1,** to fix or determine the amount of; as, to *assess* the damages; **2,** to fix or set (a tax), as on property; **3,** to value officially for the purpose of taxation; as, the property was *assessed* at $250,000; **4,** to charge a fee; as, to *assess* members $200 per year.—*adj.* **as-sess′a-ble.**—*n.* **as-sess′ment; as-ses′sor.**

as-set (as′et), *n.* **1,** anything of value that belongs to a business, a person, etc.; an advantage; as, integrity is a business *asset*; bank deposits are an *asset*; **2, assets,** all the property of a person, firm, or estate which may be used to pay debts and obligations.

as-sid-u-ous (a-sid′ū-us; -sij′oo-), *adj.* persistent; persevering; hardworking; as, Myra was an *assiduous* worker for peace.—*n.* **as′si-du′i-ty** (as′i-dū′i-ti).

as-sign (a-sīn′), *v.t.* **1,** to allot, as seats; **2,** to appoint, as to a duty; **3,** to give out, as lessons or homework; **4,** to settle definitely; as, to *assign* a time for a meeting; **5,** to transfer (property) to another.—*n.* **as-sign′ment.**

as-sim-i-late (a-sim′i-lāt′), *v.t.* [assimilat-ed, assimilat-ing], to absorb; make a part of oneself:—*v.i.* to be absorbed.

as-sim-i-la-tion (a-sim′i-lā′shun), *n.* **1,** a bringing into agreement; **2,** in *physiology*, the absorption of digested food, and its conversion into living tissue; metabolism; **3,** the adoption of a prevailing culture by a minority group.

as-sist (a-sist′), *v.t.* and *v.i.* to help; aid:—*n.* a play that helps another player to score in sports such as hockey, basketball, and soccer.—*n.* **as-sist′ance.**—*adj.* **as-sist′ed.**

as-sist-ant (a-sis′tant), *adj.* **1,** helping; lending aid; **2,** acting under another person of higher authority; as, an *assistant* editor:—*n.* a helper.

assisted suicide, suicide performed with the help of another, often a physician, usually when the subject is terminally ill and often unable to carry out the act himself or herself.

as-so-ci-ate (a-sō′shi-it; a-sō′si-it; -āt′), *n.* **1,** a companion; **2,** someone joined with another in an undertaking; partner, as in business; **3,** a member of a society or institution:—*adj.* **1,** joined with someone in interest or purpose; **2,** sharing office or authority; as, an *associate* judge; **3,** admitted to some but not all rights or privileges; as, an *associate* member of a club:—*v.t.* (a-sō′shi-āt′; a-sō′si-āt′) [associat-ed, associat-ing], to unite; combine; connect in thought; as, I *associate* green with grass:—*v.i.* to keep company; as, don't *associate* with evil persons.

as-so-ci-a-tion (a-sō′shi-ā′shun; a-sō′si-ā′shun), *n.* **1,** a joining together; **2,** fellowship; **3,** a body of persons organized for a common object; a corporation; **4,** a connection between related ideas.

as-so-nance (as′ō-nans), *n.* **1,** similarity of sound; **2,** a partial rhyme in which stressed words like *fate* and *take* have similar vowel, but unlike consonant, sounds.

as-sort (a-sôrt′), *v.t.* **1,** to separate into classes; sort; **2,** to agree; as, his actions *assort* well with his character.

as-sort-ed (a-sôr′tid), *adj.* of different kinds; various; as, *assorted* vegetables.

as-sort-ment (a-sôrt′ment), *n.* **1,** the act of separating and arranging; **2,** a collection of various kinds of things; as, an *assortment* of cheeses.

as-suage (a-swāj′), *v.t.* [assuaged, assuag-ing], to lessen; as, time *assuaged* her grief.

as-sume (a-sūm′), *v.t.* [assumed, assuming], **1,** to take upon oneself, undertake; as, to *assume* the leadership; to *assume* responsibility; **2,** to take for granted; suppose; as, to *assume* that something is true; **3,** to pretend; put on; as, he *assumed* an air of surprise; **4,** to undertake (an office or duty).—*n.* **as-sump′tion** (a-sump′shun).

as-sur-ance (a-shŏŏr′ans), *n.* **1,** a statement intended to give certainty or confidence; as, *assurances* of his safety came in every e-mail; **2,** certain proof; freedom from doubt; utmost certainty; as, *assurance* of success; **3,** self-reliance; self-confidence; as, frequent speaking in public gave him *assurance*; also called *self-assurance*; **4,** impudence; too much self-confidence; as, his *assurance* cost him his friends.

as-sure (a-shŏŏr′), *v.t.* [assured, assur-ing], **1,** to make certain; as, practice *assures* skill; to *assure* that the door is locked; **2,** to declare confidently (to); promise; as, he *assured* us she would come.—*adv.* **as-sur′ed-ly.**

as-ter (as′tėr), *n.* a leafy-stemmed plant related to the daisy, with white, pink, blue, or purple star-shaped flowers; also, the flower.

as-ter-isk (as′tėr-isk), *n.* the figure of a star [*], used in printing or writing as a reference mark, or to show an omission:—*v.t.* to mark with such a star.

a-stern (a-stûrn′), *adv.* **1,** at or toward the rear end of a ship; **2,** behind a ship.

as-ter-oid (as′tė-roid′), *n.* one of several

thousand small, rocky planets that orbit the sun.

asth-ma (az′ma; as′ma), *n.* a disease that causes a person to have difficulty in breathing.—*adj.* **asth-mat′ic.**

as-ton-ish (a-ston′ish), *v.t.* to strike with sudden wonder; surprise; amaze; astound.—*adj.* **as-ton′ish-ing.**—*n.* **as-ton′ish-ment.**

as-tound (a-stound′), *v.t.* to strike with amazement; shock; astonish.—*adj.* **as-tound′ing.**

as-tral (as′tral), *adj.* of, like, or from the stars; as, *astral* rays reach us from the constellation Orion.

a-stray (a-strā′), *adv.* out of the proper way or place; as, to go *astray*:—*adj.* wandering; confused.

a-stride (a-strīd′), *adv.* with one leg on each side:—*prep.* straddling.

as-trin-gent (a-strin′jent), *adj.* **1,** tending to pucker or wrinkle the skin, such as alum; styptic; as, an *astringent* cream; **2,** sharp or severe; as, *astringent* criticism:—*n.* a substance that contracts tissues.

as-trol-o-gy (a-strol′o-ji), *n.* the practice that claims to predict events by the position of the sun, moon, and planets and their influence on people's lives.—*adj.* **as′tro-log′i-cal** (as′tro-loj′i-kal).—*n.* **as-trol′o-ger.**

as-tro-naut (as′tro-nôt′), *n.* a person who is trained to pilot, navigate, and travel in a spacecraft to outer space.

as-tro-nom-i-cal (as′tro-näm′i-kl), *adj.* **1,** having to do with astronomy; **2,** very large, a great number; as, *astronomical* prices; an *astronomical* number of stars in the sky.

as-tron-o-my (as-tron′o-mi), *n.* the science of the nature and movements of stars, planets, etc.—*n.* **as-tron′o-mer.**

as-tro-phys-ics (as′trō-fiz′iks), *n.* the science that deals with the properties (physical, chemical, etc.) of celestial bodies.—*adj.* **as′tro-phys′i-cal.**

as-tute (as-tūt′), *adj.* shrewd; cunning; crafty; subtle.—*n.* **as-tute′ness.**

a-sy-lum (a-sī′lum), *n.* **1,** a place of refuge or security; a shelter; **2,** formerly, an institution for the care of the helpless or mentally ill: also called *insane asylum*; **3,** protection given to people who flee their own country and enter another.

a-sym-me-try (ā′si′me-tri), *n.* without balanced proportion or symmetry.—*adj.* **a-sym-met′ric; a-sym-met′ri-cal.**—*adv.* **a-sym-met′ri-cal-ly.**

at (at), *prep.* **1,** indicating nearness in place or time; as, to be *at* home *at* noon; **2,** indicating such conditions as occupation, cause, price, etc.; as, *at* play; *at* 50 cents; *at* will.

ate (āt), *p.t.* of *eat.*

a-the-ist (ā′thē-ist), *n.* one who disbelieves in, or denies, the existence of God or the Supreme Being.—*n.* **a′the-ism.**—*adj.* **a′the-is′tic.**

ath-lete (ath′lēt), *n.* a trained person who contends in sports or games of physical strength or endurance:—**athletics** (ath-let′iks), sports and games that require skill, speed, and strength.—*adj.* **ath-let′ic** (ath-let′ik).

athlete's foot, a contagious fungal infection of the feet that includes symptoms such as itching, flaking, and cracking of the skin, esp. between the toes.

athletic supporter, a jockstrap; a male undergarment that supports and protects the genitals during sports or other strenuous physical activity.

At-lan-tic (at-lan′tik), *n.* the ocean between the Americas and Europe and Africa:—*adj.* of, on, in, or near the Atlantic Ocean; as, the *Atlantic* coast:—**Atlantic provinces,** Nova Scotia, New Brunswick, Prince Edward Island, and Newfoundland. Compare *Maritime provinces.*

at-las (at′las), *n.* **1,** a bound volume of maps or charts:—**Atlas,** a god of the ancient Greeks who was thought to support the world on his shoulders.

ATM (ā′tē′em′), *abbrev.* short for *automated teller machine.*

at-mos-phere (at′mos-fēr′), *n.* **1,** the air that surrounds the earth; **2,** the air in any particular place; as, the damp *atmosphere* of a cellar; **3,** a surrounding or pervading influence; mood or feeling; as, an *atmosphere* of peace; **4,** the mass of air and gases that surrounds any star or planet.—*adj.* **at′mos-pher′ic** (at′mos-fer′ik).

at-oll (a-tol′; at′ol), *n.* a circular coral reef surrounding a lake or lagoon.

at-om (at′um), *n.* **1,** the smallest unit of an element, made up of protons, neutrons, electrons, and a nucleus; **2,** a minute quantity or particle.

ATOM

a-tom-ic (a-tom′ik), *adj.* **1,** having to do with atoms or using atomic energy; as, *atomic* research; an *atomic* submarine; **2,** relating to minute things or quantities:—**atomic bomb,** a highly destructive bomb, using the explosive energy stored in the smallest particles of matter:—**atomic theory,** the idea that elements consist of minute parts having all the properties of the elements.

atomic age, the era that began in 1945, which is characterized by the use of atomic energy.

atomic energy, the energy that exists within atoms: certain atoms can be made to release some of the energy very slowly, as in a nuclear reactor, or very quickly, as in an atomic bomb.

atomic number, the number of protons in the nucleus of an atom, which determines the position of the element in the periodic table.

at-om-iz-er (at′o-mī′zėr), *n.* a device for changing a liquid, esp. a medicine or perfume, into a fine spray.

a-tone (a-tōn′), *v.i.* [atoned, aton-ing], to do something to make up for some offence or wrong; as, Alexandra tried to *atone* for hurting Sonia's feelings by giving her a doll.—*n.* **a-tone′ment.**

a-top (a-top′), *adv.* at or to the top:—*prep.* on top of.

a-tri-um (ā′trē-um), *n.* **1,** a large central hall, often several stories high, lit from above by a skylight or opening; **2,** the central room in an ancient Roman house; **3,** an upper chamber of the heart.

a-tro-cious (a-trō′shus), *adj.* **1,** very cruel or horrible; as, *atrocious* crimes; **2,** very bad; of poor quality; as, an *atrocious* taste in clothes.—*adv.* **a-tro′cious-ly.**

a-troc-i-ty (a-tros′i-ti), *n.* [*pl.* atrocities], **1,** an outrageous or cruel deed; **2,** something ugly or very faulty; as, that hat is an *atrocity.*

at-ro-phy (at′ro-fi), *v.i.* [atrophied (at′-ro-fid), atrophy-ing], to waste or wither away, from lack of food or from disuse:—*n.* a wasting of the body, or any part of it, due to lack of food or to disuse.

at-tach (a-tach′), *v.t.* **1,** to fasten to or upon something; connect; as, to *attach* a cheque to a letter; **2,** to assign, as to a military company; appoint; **3,** to affix; as, to *attach* a document to an e-mail; **4,** to attribute; as, to *attach* importance to something; **5,** to bind by ties of affection or self-interest; **6,** to take by law:—*v.i.* to be fixed; adhere.

at-ta-ché (at′a-shā′; a-tash′ā), *n.* [*pl.* attachés], a member of a suite or staff; esp., a subordinate attached to the staff of a foreign minister or ambassador:—**attaché case,** a briefcase.

at-tach-ment (a-tach′ment), *n.* **1,** the act of fastening, or the thing fastened; **2,** affection; **3,** something extra that may be connected to something else; as, *attachments* for a vacuum cleaner; an *attachment* to the e-mail; **4,** legal seizure of goods or persons.

at-tack (a-tak′), *v.t.* **1,** to set upon with physical force, or with words; assail; as, to *attack* with sword or pen; **2,** to begin to have a harmful effect upon; as, worms are *attacking* our trees; **3,** to begin work on; as, to *attack* a problem; **4,** to criticize bitterly:—*v.i.* to make an assault:—*n.* **1,** an assault; onset; **2,** a bitter criticism; **3,** the first step of an undertaking; **4,** a seizure, as of illness; as, a coughing *attack.*

at-tain (a-tān′), *v.t.* **1,** to reach; arrive at; as, to *attain* the top of a hill; **2,** to achieve; gain; accomplish; as, to *attain* one's goal.—*n.* **at-tain′ment.**—*adj.* **at-tain′a-ble.**

at-tempt (a-tempt′), *v.t.* to make an effort to do; try; as, to *attempt* a flight, or to fly:—*n.* **1,** trial; effort; as, to make four *attempts* to land the jump; **2,** an attack; as, an *attempt* on a person's life.

at-tend (a-tend′), *v.t.* **1,** to wait upon; care for; **2,** to escort; accompany; **3,** to be present at; as, to *attend* a concert:—*v.i.* **1,** to give heed to; as, *attend* to my warning; **2,** to be in waiting, as a bridesmaid at a wedding; **3,** to look after something; as, to *attend* to business.—*n.* **at′tend-ee′.**

at-tend-ance (a-ten′dans), *n.* **1,** the fact of being present, as at school; **2,** the state of looking after or waiting upon some person or thing; as, the nurse is in *attendance*; **3,** the number of persons present; also, the record of this number; as, to take the *attendance.*

at-tend-ant (a-ten′dant), *adj.* accompanying or immediately following; as, illness *attendant* on overeating:—*n.* **1,** one who serves or waits upon another; a servant or companion; as, he dismissed his *attendants*; **2,** one who is frequently present, as at school.

at-ten-tion (a-ten′shun), *n.* **1,** the fixing of one's thoughts closely on something; concentration; **2,** a military position in which soldiers stand very straight, with their arms at their sides, feet together, and eyes straight ahead; **3,** an act of courtesy.

attention deficit disorder (ADD), a syndrome characterized by short attention span, impulsiveness, and often hyperactivity, resulting in learning and behavioural problems.

at-ten-tive (a-ten′tiv), *adj.* **1,** heedful; intent; as, an *attentive* student; **2,** polite; eager to offer courtesies.

at-ten-u-ate (a-ten′ū-āt′), *v.t.* **1,** to make thin or slender; **2,** to weaken, lessen, or reduce (in force or intensity).

at-test (a-test′), *v.t.* **1,** to bear witness to; affirm the truth of, esp. by signing one's name or by oath; **2,** to give proof of; as, your work *attests* your ability.

at-tic (at′ik), *n.* the space immediately beneath the roof of a house or other building; a garret.

at-tire (a-tīr′), *n.* clothes; finery:—*v.t.* [attired, attir-ing], to clothe; array.

at-ti-tude (at′i-tūd′), *n.* **1,** bodily position or pose; esp., position assumed to show feeling, purpose, mood, etc.; as, to take a threatening *attitude*; **2,** way of thinking or feeling; as, his *attitude* of indifference.

at-tor-ney (a-tûr′ni), *n.* [*pl.* attorneys], a lawyer; one legally appointed by another to act for that person in any legal matter:—

power of attorney, the right to act in another person's place, esp. in legal or business matters; also, the written statement.

At-tor-ney Gen-er-al, *n.* [*pl.* Attorneys General or Attorney Generals], the chief law officer of a state or nation: in Canada, the chief law officer of the country or of a province.

at-tract (a-trakt′), *v.t.* **1,** to draw to oneself by personal charm, or the like; as, he *attracts* friends easily; **2,** to cause to approach; as, a magnet *attracts* steel; **3,** to draw forth; win; as, intelligence *attracts* attention.—*adj.* **at-trac′tive.**

at-trac-tion (a-trak′shun), *n.* **1,** the power or act of drawing to or toward; **2,** the thing that attracts; as, intelligence has an *attraction* for all.

¹at-trib-ute (a-trib′ūt), *v.t.* [attribut-ed, attribut-ing], **1,** to consider (a quality) as belonging to a person or thing; as, we *attribute* grace to a dancer; **2,** to consider (a thing) as being caused by something else; as, I *attribute* Sylvie's popularity to her honesty.—*n.* **at′tri-bu′tion.**

²at-tri-bute (at′ri-būt′), *n.* **1,** a trait or characteristic, thought of as belonging to a person or thing; as, honesty is a good *attribute* to have; **2,** a symbol; as, the crown is an *attribute* of royalty.

at-trib-u-tive (a-trib′ū-tiv), *adj.* in *grammar*, an adjective that immediately precedes the noun it modifies; as, "red," in the expression "red bricks," is an *attributive* (or adherent) adjective.

at-tri-tion (a-trish′un), *n.* a wearing away or down; as, our forces shrank in a war of *attrition.*

at-tune (a-tūn′), *v.t.* [attuned, attun-ing], **1,** to put in tune; **2,** to bring into harmony; as, his spirit was *attuned* to nature.

au-burn (ô′bėrn), *adj.* reddish brown.

auc-tion (ôk′shun), *n.* a public sale of property to the highest bidder:—*v.t.* to sell to the highest bidder.—*n.* **auc′tion-eer′.**

au-da-cious (ô-dā′shus), *adj.* **1,** bold; daring; **2,** too bold; insolent; impudent.

au-dac-i-ty (ô-das′i-ti), *n.* [*pl.* audacities], **1,** rash boldness; **2,** impudence.

au-di-ble (ô′di-bl), *adj.* loud enough to be heard.—*adv.* **au′di-bly.**—*n.* **au′di-bil′i-ty.**

au-di-ence (ô′di-ens), *n.* **1,** a group of persons who listen to, watch, or read something, such as TV programs, movies, plays, concerts, magazines, books, or sports events; **2,** all the people who appreciate and support something; as, an *audience* for foreign films; **3,** a formal interview with a person of authority; as, an *audience* with the prime minister.

au-di-o (ô′di-ō′), *adj.* **1,** having to do with sound; **2,** having to do with sending and receiving sound by means of a TV, radio, etc; as, CD players are *audio* equipment; **3,** in television, the sound phase as distinct from the *video*, or picture, portion; **2,** relating to apparatus using audible frequencies; as, *audio* amplifier:—*n.* something that sends or receives sound.

au-di-o tape or **au-di-o–tape, 1,** a magnetic tape used to record and play back sound; **2,** a recording on such tape.

au-di-o-vis-u-al aids, films, slides, videotapes, recordings, and materials other than textbooks used in classroom teaching.

au-dit (ô′dit), *n.* an official examination of claims or accounts:—*v.t.* to examine and adjust, as accounts or claims.

au-di-tion (ô-dish′un), *n.* **1,** act or sense of hearing; **2,** a test hearing given a singer, musician, actor, etc.:—*v.t.* to give such a hearing:—*v.i.* to perform an audition.

au-di-tor (ô′di-tėr), *n.* **1,** a listener; **2,** a person appointed to examine and verify accounts and claims; **3,** someone who can attend a class at a university but not get credit for it.

au-di-tor-i-um (ô′di-tōr′i-um), [*pl.* auditoriums or auditoria], *n.* a building or room, designed for public gatherings; also, the part of a theatre, or the like, assigned to the audience.

au-di-tor-y (ô′di-tōr′i), *adj.* having to do with hearing or the organs of hearing; as, the *auditory* nerve.

aug-ment (ôg-ment′), *v.t.* to increase in size or extent; to make bigger; as, the general *augmented* his forces.—*n.* **aug′men-ta′tion** (ôg′men-tā′shun).

au-gust (ô-gust′), *adj.* **1,** majestic; having grandeur and dignity; **2,** of high rank; noble.

Au-gust (ô′gust), *n.* the eighth month of the year, between July and September (31 days).

auk (ôk), *n.* a kind of diving bird with small wings used as paddles, and a heavy body, found in cold northern waters.

aunt (ånt; änt), *n.* the sister of one's father or mother; also, an uncle's wife.

au-ra (ô′ra), *n.* **1,** an invisible emanation, as the aroma of flowers; **2,** a distinctive atmosphere about a person or thing; as, an *aura* of culture.

au re-voir (ō′ re-vwär′), *French*, goodbye; until I see you again.

au-ror-a bor-e-a-lis (ô-rō′ra bō′ri-ā′lis; bō′ri-al′is), a glow, or streamers of light, supposed to be of electrical origin, appearing in the northern sky at night, best seen in northern latitudes. Also called *northern lights*.

aus-pic-es (ôs′pi-siz), *n.pl.* **1,** omens or signs; **2,** protection; patronage; as, a play given under the *auspices* of the club.

aus-pi-cious (ôs-pish′us), *adj.* **1,** promising success or happiness; as, *auspicious* circumstances; **2,** successful; prosperous; as, an *auspicious* year.

aus-tere (ôs-tēr′), *adj.* **1,** rigidly strict in manner of living or thinking; **2,** severely simple; unadorned; as, an *austere* building.—*adv.* **aus-tere′ly.**—*n.* **aus-ter′i-ty.**

au-then-tic (ô-then′tik), *adj.* **1,** genuine; original; as, an *authentic* painting by Raphael; **2,** duly authorized; true; trustworthy; as, *authentic* information.—*n.* **au′then-tic′i-ty** (ô′then-tis′i-ti).

au-then-ti-cate (ô-then′ti-kāt′), *v.t.* [authenticat-ed, authenticat-ing], to establish as real or genuine, as the authorship of a book, a signature, etc.—*n.* **au-then′ti-ca′tion.**

au-thor (ô′thėr), *n.* **1,** one who composes or writes a book, articles, poems, etc.; **2,** a person who begins or originates anything; as, the *author* of the revolution.

au-thor-i-ta-tive (ô-thor′i-tā′tiv), *adj.* **1,** having acknowledged authority, entitled to obedience or acceptance; **2,** commanding in manner; imperative.

au-thor-i-ty (ô-thor′i-ti), *n.* [*pl.* authorities], **1,** the right to act or command; as, a general's *authority*; **2,** one whose knowledge or judgment on a subject is entitled to acceptance; an expert; as, Audubon is an *authority* on birds; also, a book, quotation, etc., cited in justification of a statement or action:—**authorities,** government officials; people who enforce the law.

au-thor-ize (ô′thėr-īz′), *v.t.* [authorized, authoriz-ing], **1,** to give (a person) the right to act; as, he is *authorized* to act for us; **2,** to approve officially or legally; allow; as, to *authorize* the purchase of supplies.—*n.* **au′thor-i-za′tion.**

au-tism (ä′tizm′), *n.* a mental disorder characterized by self-absorption and an inability to respond to outside stimuli.

au-to (ô′tō), *n.* [*pl.* autos], *abbrev.* short for automobile.

au-to- (ô′tō-), *prefix* meaning *for* or *by itself* or *oneself*; as, *auto*biography, *auto*matic, *auto*mobile, etc.

au-to-bi-og-ra-phy (ô′tō-bī-og′ra-fi; ô′-tō-bi-og′ra-fi), *n.* [*pl.* autobiographies], a life history of a person, written by himself or herself.—*n.* **au′to-bi-og′ra-pher.**—*adj.* **au′to-bi′o-graph′ic** (ô′tō-bī′o-graf′ik); **au′to-bi′o-graph′i-cal.**

au-to-crat (ô′tō-krat′), *n.* **1,** a ruler with unlimited power; **2,** a person who demands obedience to his or her will; as, the soccer coach was an *autocrat* during games.—*n.* **au-toc′ra-cy.**—*adj.* **au′to-crat′ic.**

au-to-graph (ô′tō-gråf), *n.* a person's own handwriting or signature, esp. a famous person:—*v.t.* to write one's signature in or on; as, to *autograph* a book or a photograph.

au-to-mate (ô′tō-māt), *v.t.* [automat-ed, auto- mat-ing], to operate or convert to automatic operation or automation:—*v.i.* to undergo automation.—*adj.* **au′to-mat-ed.**

automated teller machine, banking machines; computerized electronic machines that perform basic banking functions: abbreviated as *ATM*.

au-to-mat-ic (ô′tō-mat′ik), *adj.* **1,** designed to work without attention; as, an *automatic* garage-door opener; **2,** done unconsciously, without thinking; as, breathing is *automatic*:—*n.* any machine or device that is automatic.—*adv.* **au′to-mat′i-cal-ly.**

automatic pilot or **au-to-pil-ot** (ô′tō-pī′lut), *n.* **1,** a device that automatically steers an airplane, ship, car, or other vehicle; **2,** the state of performing activities without conscious thought or reflection; as, he is running on *automatic pilot*.

au-to-ma-tion (ô′tō-mā′shun), *n.* the use of self-operating machines or electronic devices to control processes of production, inspection, calculation, sorting, etc.

au-tom-a-ton (ô-tom′a-ton′; -tun), *n.* [*pl.* automata], a person or apparatus that is made to move or act like a human or animal, as a robot.

au-to-mo-bile (ô′to-mō-bēl′; ô′to-mō′bēl), *n.* a four-wheeled powered vehicle with an engine by which it is propelled, used mainly to carry passengers; a motor car:—*adj.* having to do with these vehicles.—*n.* **au′to-mo-bil′ist** (ô′to-mō-bēl′ist; ô′to-mō′bil-ist).

au-to-mo-tive (ô′to-mō′tiv), *adj.* pertaining to self-propelled vehicles; as, the *automotive* industries.

au-ton-o-my (ô-ton′o-mi), *n.* [*pl.* -mies (-miz)], the power or right of self-government.—*adj.* **au-ton′o-mous.**

au-top-sy (ô′top-si; ô′tup-si), *n.* [*pl.* autopsies], the medical examination and dissection of a dead body to find the cause of death, extent of disease, injury, etc.

au-tumn (ô′tum), *n.* the season following summer: also called *fall*:—*adj.* belonging to this season; as, *autumn* fruits.—*adj.* **au-tum′nal.**

autumnal equinox, the point at which the sun crosses the equator, around September 23, marking the beginning of autumn or fall in the Northern Hemisphere.

aux-il-ia-ry (ôg-zil′ya-ri), *adj.* helping; assisting; as, *auxiliary* forces:—*n.* [*pl.* auxiliaries], **1,** a helper; an ally; aid of any kind; **2,** in *grammar*, a verb, such as *be, have, may*, which helps to form the moods and tenses of other verbs; as, in "they have come," "have" is the *auxiliary*; **3, auxiliaries,** foreign troops in the service of a nation at war.

a-vail (a-vāl′), *v.i.* to be of use or value:—

v.t. to benefit; help; as, shouting did not *avail* us:—**avail oneself of,** to take advantage of; utilize:—*n.* use; means toward an end; as, crying was of no *avail*.

a-vail-a-ble (a-vāl′a-bl), *adj.* **1,** at hand; ready to be used; **2,** suitable for one's purpose.—*n.* **a-vail′a-bil′i-ty.**

av-a-lanche (av′a-lansh), *n.* **1,** a large mass of snow or earth sliding down a mountain; **2,** anything that overwhelms by speed and volume; as, an *avalanche* of words.

av-a-rice (av′a-ris), *n.* the passion for hoarding or acquiring wealth; greed.—*adj.* **av′a-ri′cious** (av′a-rish′us).

a-venge (a-venj′), *v.t.* [avenged, aveng-ing], **1,** to inflict just punishment in return for (a wrong or injury); as, to *avenge* an insult; **2,** to exact punishment on behalf of; as, to *avenge* someone's death.—*n.* **a-veng′er.**

av-e-nue (av′e-nū′), *n.* **1,** a wide road or street; **2,** a way of approach to a place or goal; as, an *avenue* to success.

av-er-age (av′ėr-ij), *n.* **1,** something of a usual character, midway between extremes, as between too much and too little, very good and very bad, etc.; obtained by dividing the sum of several quantities by the number of quantities; as, the *average* of 5, 8, and 14 is 9:—*adj.* **1,** arrived at by dividing the sum of several quantities by their number; as, the *average* height of the students; **2,** ordinary; usual:—*v.t.* [averaged, averag-ing], to find the average of (a series of numbers or the like):—*v.i.* to do, perform, or get as an average rate, sum, amount, etc.; as, the car *averaged* 80 kilometres per hour.

a-verse (a-vûrs′), *adj.* **1,** unwilling; reluctant; **2,** having a dislike; as, *averse* to hard work.—*n.* **a-ver′sion.**

a-vert (a-vûrt′), *v.t.* **1,** to turn aside, as one's eyes; **2,** to turn or ward off; **3,** to prevent; as, to *avert* a strike.

a-vi-ar-y (ā′vi-er′i), *n.* [*pl.* aviaries], a place for the keeping of birds.

a-vi-a-tion (ā′vi-ā′shun), *n.* the art, science, or business of building and flying airplanes or other aircraft.

a-vi-a-tor (ā′vi-ā′tėr), *n.* the pilot of an airplane.

av-id (av′id), *adj.* **1,** extremely eager; enthusiastic; as, an *avid* hockey player; **2,** greedy; as, *avid* for food.—*adv.* **av′id-ly.**—*n.* **a-vid′i-ty** (a-vid′i-ti).

av-o-ca-do (av′ō-kä′dō), *n.* a tropical pear-shaped American or West Indian fruit; the alligator pear.

av-o-ca-tion (av′ō-kā′shun), *n.* an activity other than one's occupation; hobby; as, the lawyer's *avocation* is playing the violin.

a-void (a-void′), *v.t.* to keep away from; shun.—*n.* **a-void′ance.**—*adj.* **a-void′a-ble.**

av-oir-du-pois (av′-ėr-dū-poiz′; av′ėr-du-poiz′), *n.* **1,** the common system of measuring weight, in pounds of 16 ounces each (.454 kilograms): used in Canada before the adoption of the metric system; **2,** *Colloq.* weight; heaviness.

a-vow (a-vou′), *v.t.* to declare openly; admit; as, to *avow* one's faults.—*n.* **a-vow′al.**—*adj.* **a-vowed′.**—*adv.* **a-vow′ed-ly.**

a-wait (a-wāt′), *v.t.* **1,** to wait for; expect; as, to *await* news; **2,** to be ready for; as, I *await* your commands; **3,** to be in store for; as, happiness *awaits* you.

a-wake (a-wāk′), *v.t.* [*p.t.* and *p.p.* awoke (a-wōk′) or awaked (a-wākt′), *p.pr.* awak-ing], **1,** to rouse from sleep; **2,** to rouse from inactivity; stimulate; as, to *awake* interest:—*v.i.* **1,** to cease to sleep; **2,** to rouse oneself; become alert:—*adj.* **1,** not asleep; **2,** fully aware; on the alert; as, she was *awake* to the danger.

a-wak-en (a-wāk′en), *v.t.* and *v.i.* to rouse from sleep or as if from sleep; awake.—*n.* and *adj.* **a-wak′en-ing.**

a-ward (a-wôrd′), *v.t.* **1,** to give or assign, as does a judge or jury, after careful consideration; as, to *award* the victim $10,000; **2,** to bestow, as a prize:—*n.* **1,** a careful and deliberate decision; **2,** that which is awarded.

a-ware (a-wâr′), *adj.* conscious; informed; knowing; as, he is well *aware* of his shortcomings.

a-wash (a-wosh′; a-wôsh′), *adj.* and *adv.* **1,** afloat; tossed about by water; **2,** washed over; covered with water.

a-way (a-wā′), *adv.* **1,** at or to a distance; off; aside; as, to be *away*; to look *away*; **2,** out of one's possession; as, to give *away*; **3,** in another place; absent; as, to go *away*; **4,** continuously; as, to work *away*; **5,** out of existence; as, to die *away*:—*adj.* **1,** at a distance; as, far *away* from the store; **2,** not present; absent; as, to be *away* on vacation; **3,** in an opponent's territory; as, *away* games.

awe (ô), *n.* wonder tinged with fear; reverence; as, to live in *awe* of nature:—*v.t.* [awed, aw-ing], to produce feelings of solemn respect or fear in; as, to be *awed* by the Rockies.

awe-some (ô′sum), *adj.* **1,** majestic; wonderful; extraordinary; as, an *awesome* aurora borealis; **2,** *Slang* great.—*n.* **awe′some-ness.**

aw-ful (ô′fool), *adj.* **1,** inspiring reverence or fear; **2,** appalling, as a calamity; **3,** extreme in any sense; very bad, great, ugly, etc.; as, *awful* language; an *awful* dress; an *awful* thirst.—*n.* **aw′ful-ness.**—*adv.* **aw′ful-ly.**

a-while (a-hwīl′), *adv.* for a short time; briefly.

awk-ward (ôk′wėrd), *adj.* **1,** unskillful; bungling; clumsy; as, an *awkward* worker; **2,** ungraceful; ungainly in action or form;

as, an
rassed; a ... rd skater; 3, ill at ease; embar-
difficult to ... els *awkward* in company; 4,
awkward situ... ith; embarrassing; as, an
n. **awk′ward-ne**... *adv.* **awk′ward-ly.**—

awn-ing (ôn′ing), *n.* ...
of canvas, stretched on ... like covering, as
above a window or door a... me and used
rain or sun. ... elter from

a-woke (a-wōk′), *p.t.* of *awake.*

a-wry (a-rī′), *adv.* and *adj.* **1,** turn... twisted to one side; out of the right lin... crooked; **2,** wrong; amiss; as, the plan went *awry.*

axe or **ax** (aks), *n.* a hewing or chopping tool, consisting of an iron head with a steel cutting edge, fixed to a handle.

ax-i-om (ak′si-um), *n.* a self-evident truth; a statement accepted without pr... f. An axiom of geometry is "The short... distance between two points is the ... ight line between them."—*adj.* **ax′i-o-ma**...

ax-is (ak′sis), *n.* [*pl.* axes (ak′sēz)], ... traight line, real or imaginary, about wh... body turns, or seems to turn; as, the eart... s.

ax-le (ak′sl), *n.* the bar on which ... wheel turns; also, the centre rod of a w... t revolves along with it.

a-za-le-a (a-zāl′ya), *n.* a shrub of the ... family, grown for its abundant an... ... flowers.

az-u... (ā′zhūr; azh′ėr), *adj.* sky blue:— clear b... sky; **2,** a sky-blue colour.

B

B, b (bē), *n.* [*pl.* B's, b's], **1,** the second letter of the alphabet, following A; **2,** the seventh tone in the major scale of C; **3,** the second-highest mark, grade, or level.

babble (bab′l), *v.i.* [bab-bled, bab-bling], **1,** to talk indistinctly or imperfectly; **2,** to talk childishly or foolishly; **3,** to chatter; also, to make a murmuring sound:—*v.t.* **1,** to utter indistinctly or imperfectly; as, he *babbled* his words; **2,** to blab (secrets):—*n.* **1,** foolish talk; **2,** a confused prattle or continuous murmuring.—*n.* **bab′bler.**

ba-boon (ba-bo͞on′), *n.* a kind of large, hairy monkey, usually with a short tail and a doglike face and found in Africa and Southeast Asia.

ba-by (bā′bi), *n.* [*pl.* babies], an infant; a young or small child:—*adj.* for a baby; as, a *baby* crib, *baby* toys:—*v.t.* [ba-bied, ba-by-ing], to treat like a baby; give special attention to; as, to *baby* a sore foot.—*adj.* **ba′by-ish.**

baby bonus, formerly, the Canadian monthly allowance paid to parents of minor children.

baby boom, the dramatic rise in the birthrate following the end of World War II into the 1960s.—*n.* **baby boomer.**

baby shower, a party held by the female friends and relatives of an expectant mother to give gifts, often of a particular kind, for the baby.

ba-by–sit (bā′bi–sit′), *v.t.* and *v.i.* [baby–sat, baby–sit-ting], to take care of a child or children while the parents are away from home, usually for a short period of time.—*n.* **ba′by–sit′ter.**

bac-ca-lau-re-ate (ba′ka-lär′ē-it), *n.* a bachelor's degree; the first degree granted by most postsecondary educational institutions.

bach-e-lor (bach′e-lėr), *n.* **1,** a man who is not married; **2,** one who holds the first degree at a college or university; as, a *bachelor* of arts, etc.

back (bak), *n.* **1,** in humans and other animals having a backbone, the hinder or upper surface of the body from the neck to the end of the backbone; also, the corresponding part in other animals; **2,** the opposite of the front; the hinder part; as, the kitchen is at the *back* of the house; **3,** the side of anything away from, or out of sight of, the beholder; as, put the book at the *back* of the room; **4,** the part of a book where the leaves are sewed, glued, or stapled in; **5,** the part of a knife, sword, etc., opposite to the cutting edge; **6,** the vertical part of a chair, bench, or the like, against which one can lean when sitting; as, the *back* of a sofa:—*v.t.* **1,** to move backward or to the rear; as, to *back* a car; **2,** to second or support; as, we *back* Jorgenson for president; he *backed* up his proposal with a donation:—*v.i.* to go or move backward or to the rear:—*adj.* **1,** lying or being behind as to time, situation, or direction; as, *back* numbers of a magazine; a *back* porch; **2,** overdue; in arrears; as, *back* pay:—*adv.* **1,** to or toward the rear; **2,** to or toward a former place or state; as, to bring *back* a borrowed book; *back* to normal conditions; **3,** to or toward time past; **4,** in return; as, to pay *back*:—**back and forth,** move one way and then the other; as, to pace *back and forth*:—**back down,** give up a claim or attempt; as, to *back down* when caught in a lie:—**in back of,** behind; as, a garage *in back of* the house:—**back out,** decide not to do something; as, to *back out* of having a party at the last minute:—**back up, 1,** move backward; as, *back up* the car; **2,** to make an extra copy …work done on a computer; as, always ba… up your files when working on a comp…r.

back …on, bacon that is cut from the back… a pig, not the sides. Also called …n bacon.

…bench (bak′bench′), *n.* the seats in a …ment or legislative assembly for …bers who are not in the cabinet or a …er in the opposition parties:—**back…ncher,** a member of Parliament who …cupies a rear seat and seldom partici…ates in debates.

…ack-bone (bak′bōn′), *n.* **1,** the sp… …of a person or animal; **2,** firmn… moral courage; **3,** the most i… …rtant or strongest part of somet…g; as, a good goalie is the *backbone* … a hockey team.

back burner th… condition of receiving little atten…on or being given low priority; as, to place a minor task on the *back burner.*

back-door (bak′dōr′), *adj.* underhand; unworthily secret; as, his *backdoor* methods revolted us:—*n.* a door at the back of a building.

back-drop (bak′drop′), *n.* the rear curtain of a theatre's stage; also, a background.

back-field (bak′fēld′), *n.* in *football,* the players behind the front line.

back-fire (bak′fīr′), *n.* **1,** in a gasoline engine, an explosion of gas that occurs at the wrong time, or in the wrong part of the engine; **2,** a fire started to check a prairie fire by burning a space in its path:—*v.i.* to bring opposite results to those expected; as, our plot *backfired.*

back-gam-mon (bak′gam′on), *n.* a game with two players who move pieces around a board according to the roll of the dice.

BACKGAMMON BOARD

back-ground (bak′ground′), *n.* **1,** the distant parts of any scene or landscape, or the corresponding part of a picture; **2,** a surface upon which patterns or designs are drawn, printed, etc.; **3,** a place out of sight; a position that does not get attention; as, the timid student kept in the *background;* **4,** the events or experiences that lead up to something; as, to have a good *background* in math to do well in physics:—*adj.* pertaining to something that is in the background; as, *background* lighting; *background* reading.

back-hand (bak′hand′), *n.* **1,** backward-slanting handwriting; **2,** a backhanded stroke.

back-hand-ed (bak′han′did) or **back-hand** (bak′hand′), *adj.* **1,** made with the back of the hand, or with the hand turned backward; as, a *backhanded* stroke; **2,** not straightforward; insincere; as, a *backhanded* warning.

…al used to

back-ing (bak′ing), *n.* **1** … …upporters; **3,** strengthen (at the bac… aid, support.

back-lash (bak′l… …*n.* **1,** a strong negative reaction; … bill caused a backlash in the opp… camp; **2,** a violent reaction or … …ard movement (in machinery) … to worn or loose parts; **3,** a sna… …a reeled fishing line.

…log (bak′log′), *n.* a reserve or accumulation, as of unfilled orders.

back-pack (bak′pak′), *n.* a knapsack or bag worn on the back:—**backpacking,** hiking or camping with all the supplies in a backpack.

back-scratch-ing (bak′skrach′ing), *n.* **1,** the act of scratching a back; **2,** the giving and taking of favours for mutual benefit; granting reciprocal or equivalent favours; as, the politicians did a lot of *backscratching* just before the election.—*n.* **back′ scratch′er.**—*v.t.* and *v.i.* **1,** to scratch someone's back; **2,** to give and take for mutual benefit.

back-slap (bak′slap′), *v.i.* and *v.t.* [back-slapped, back-slap-ping], **1,** to slap (someone) on the back; **2,** to display excessive, outgoing sociability or outward friendliness:—*n.* such a display.—*n.* **back′slap′ping; back′slap′per.**

back-slash (bak′slash′), *n.* in *computing,* the backward diagonal on the keyboard [/], also known as the virgule or solidus, often used to separate elements in computer codes or Web addresses, as in http://www.

back-slide (bak′slīd′; bak′slīd′), *v.i.* [*p.t.* backslid (-slid′), *p.p.* backslid or backslid-den (-slid′n), *p.pr.* backslid-ing], to slip back, esp. to slip away from a religion, habit, etc.—*n.* **back′slid′er.**

back-space (bak′spās′), *v.i.* in *computing,* to move the cursor on a computer screen back one space:—*n.* the key at the top right corner of the keyboard that performs this function.

back-stab-ber (bak′stab′ėr), *n.* **1,** someone who stabs another in the back; **2,** someone who underhandedly or deceitfully attacks or betrays someone, esp. a friend.—*n.* and *adj.* **back′stab′bing.**

back-stop (bak′stop′), *n.* a screen or fence to stop balls from going too far; also, anything or anyone who serves as a stop.

back-track (bak′trak′), *v.i.* **1,** to reverse one's opinion or position; **2,** to retrace one's course or steps; **3,** to return to a previous point in a narrative or argument.

back-up (bak′up′), *n.* **1,** someone or something that serves as a substitute or an alternative; as, a *backup* goalie; **2,** in *computing,* a copy of computer data or files to be used if the originals are unavailable; **3,** an overflow or congestion of movement; as, the *backup* of traffic; **4,** musical accompaniment; as, she sang *backup.*—*n.* **back′up′ co′py; back′up′ sys′tem.**

back-ward (bak′wėrd), *adj.* **1,** directed to the rear; as, a *backward* look; **2,** behind in learning or progress; as, a *backward* part of a country:—*adv.* (also **back′wards**) **1,** toward the back; **2,** with the back forward; as, to have a hat on *backward*; **3,** opposite to the usual way; as, to spell *backward*.—*n.* **back′ward-ness.**

back-wa-ter (bak′wô′tėr), *n.* **1,** dammed-up, or stagnant, water; hence, **2,** an isolated place; as, we live in a cultural *backwater*.

back-woods (bak′woodz′), *n.pl.* forests or partly cleared land on the outskirts of a new settlement.

back-yard (bak′yärd′), *n.* a piece of land that is in back of a house or other building.

ba-con (bā′kun), *n.* the salted and dried or smoked meat of the hog, esp. that from the sides.

bac-te-ri-a (bak-tē′ri-a), *n.pl.* [*sing.* bacterium (bak-tē′ri-um)], a widely distributed group of tiny cells, invisible without a microscope, living on plant and animal tissues, dead or alive, and causing a great variety of processes and conditions affecting vegetable and animal life, as decay, fermentation, soil enrichment, and, in some cases, disease: differ from *virus*.—*adj.* **bac-te′ri-al.**

bac-te-ri-ol-o-gy (bak-tē′ri-ol′o-ji), *n.* the science that deals with bacteria.—*n.* **bac-te′ri-ol′o-gist.**

bad (bad), *adj.* [*comp.* worse, *superl.* worst], **1,** evil; morally wicked; vicious; as, *bad* company; **2,** of poor quality; defective; spoiled; as, *bad* eggs; *bad* housing conditions; legally worthless, as a coin; **3,** severe; as, a *bad* cold; **4,** ill; in poor health:—*n.* that which is wrong, defective, corrupting, or the like.—*adv.* **bad′ly.**—*n.* **bad′ness.**

bade (bād), *p.t.* of *bid.*

badge (baj), *n.* a distinctive mark, sign, or token to denote the occupation or achievements of the person by whom it is worn; as, a policeman's *badge*; the Roman toga was the *badge* of manhood; a *badge* of honour.

badg-er (baj′ėr), *n.* a hairy, flesh-eating, burrowing animal, about two feet long:—*v.t.* to tease; worry; pester; nag.

bad-lands (bad′landz′), *n.* barren lands where erosion has cut dry soil or soft rock into strange shapes; as, the Alberta *badlands*.

bad-min-ton (bad′min-ton), *n.* a tennis-like game in which feathered corks (shuttlecocks or birdies) are batted with light racquets to and fro across a net.

bad–mouth (bad′–mouth′), *v.t. Slang* **1,** to criticize or denounce severely, often unfairly; **2,** to spread malicious rumours or scandal; as, she *bad-mouthed* the opposition.

baf-fle (baf′l), *v.t.* [baf-fled, baf-fling], to check or interfere with (a person) by placing difficulties in his way; hence, to foil, or hamper (efforts or plans).

bag (bag), *n.* **1,** a soft container that is made of paper, plastic, or cloth and is usually open at the top; **2,** something that can be used like a bag, such as a woman's purse or suitcase; **3,** the amount contained in a sack; as, a *bag* of grain:—*v.t.* [bagged, bagging], **1,** to enclose in a bag; **2,** to secure or capture; as, to *bag* game:—*v.i.* to bulge; hang down like a full bag; as, jeans that *bag* at the knees.—*adj.* **bag′gy.**

ba-gel (bā′gl), *n.* a doughnut-shaped bread roll that is boiled briefly before it is baked.

bag-gage (bag′ij), *n.* **1,** the tents, clothing, utensils, etc., of an army; **2,** the suitcases, bags, packages, etc., that travellers take on a trip; luggage.

bag lady, *Colloq.* a homeless woman who carries her possessions in shopping bags.

bag-man (bag′man′), *Colloq. n.* **1,** a Canadian political party fundraiser; as, a Liberal Party *bagman*; **2,** one who collects money from illegal activities.

bag-pipe (bag′pīp′), *n.* a shrill Scottish musical instrument consisting of a leather bag from which air is forced by the player's arm into pipes.—*n.* **bag′pip′er.**

[1]**bail** (bāl), *v.t.* in *law*: **1,** to turn over (a defendant or prisoner) to persons who promise to be responsible for his or her appearance in court when summoned; as, the magistrate *bailed* the accused thief to Mr. Sanchez; **2,** to obtain the release of (a person) by promising to pay a certain sum if he or she does not appear in court or when wanted; as, Mr. Cohen *bailed* his friend out of jail; hence, to help someone out of a difficulty:—*n.* in law: **1,** temporary freedom given a defendant or prisoner, said to be out *on bail*, when security is given for his or her appearance when wanted; **2,** security so given.

[2]**bail** (bāl), *v.t.* **1,** to dip (water) out of a boat; **2,** to empty (a boat) by this process:—*n.* the dipper used in bailing.

bail-iff (bāl′if), *n.* **1,** a sheriff's officer.

bail out, *v.i.* **1,** leap, with a parachute, from an aircraft; **2,** escape from a situation.

bait (bāt), *n.* anything used to entice or lure fish or other animals with a view to catching them; hence, anything that attracts a person to do something; as, to use cookies to *bait* friends into helping with a project:—*v.t.* **1,** to prepare (a fishhook, trap, or snare) by placing bait so as to attract an animal; **2,** to torment or annoy; tease; as, to *bait* the opponent with accusations.

bake (bāk), *v.t.* and *v.i.* [baked, bak-ing], **1,** to cook or be cooked in an oven; as, she is *baking* cakes; the cake is *baking*; **2,** to dry or harden by dry heat; as, to *bake* pottery in a kiln.—*n.* **bak′er.**—*n.* **bak′er-y.**

bak-ing–pow-der (bāk′ing–pou′dėr), *n.* a

white powder used to bring about the quick rising of biscuits, cakes, etc.

bak-ing so-da, bicarbonate of soda.

bal-a-clav-a (bal′a-klav′a), *n.* a knitted woollen hat that covers the head and neck, except for the eyes.

bal-ance (bal′ans), *n.* **1,** an apparatus for weighing, consisting in its simplest form of a beam pivoted at its middle, with hooks, platforms, or pans suspended from the ends; **2,** the condition of a scale when the beam is about horizontal; hence, equality of any opposing forces; equilibrium or steadiness; **3,** general good sense; **4,** an equality between the two sides of an account; also, the excess shown on either side; **5,** the remainder of an amount due; as, the *balance* on a credit card; **6,** the amount of money in a bank account:—*v.t.* [balanced, balanc-ing], **1,** to weigh on a balance; **2,** to weigh in the mind; hence, to compare or estimate; as, we *balanced* the good against the bad; **3,** to find out the difference between the debits and credits of (an account); as, to *balance* a chequebook; **4,** to steady:—*v.i.* **1,** to be of the same weight, force, or amount as something else; as, the advantages of the two plans *balance*; **2,** to keep one's balance.—*adj.* **bal′anced.**

bal-co-ny (bal′ko-ni), *n.* [*pl.* balconies], a platform or gallery built to jut out from a wall, and enclosed by a balustrade or railing, positioned either on the outside or the inside of a building; as, an apartment *balcony*; a theatre *balcony*.

bald (bôld), *adj.* **1,** bare of hair; **2,** without the natural or usual covering of hair, feathers, fur, or foliage, upon the head, top, or summit; **3,** of birds, having a white head; as, a *bald* eagle; **4,** unadorned; bare; plain; as, a *bald* statement.—*adv.* **bald′ly.**—*n.* **bald′ness.**

bale (bāl), *n.* **1,** a large and closely pressed package of merchandise prepared for storage or transportation:—*v.t.* [baled, bal-ing], to make into bales; as, to *bale* cotton or hay.—*n.* **bal′er.**

bale-ful (bāl′fool), *adj.* full of deadly intent; destructive.—*adv.* **bale′ful-ly.**

balk (bôk), *v.i.* to stop short and refuse to go, as a stubborn horse:—*v.t.* to hinder or check; prevent (a person) from doing something:—*n.* **1,** a barrier; hindrance; **2,** in *baseball*, an incompleted pitch, entitling a runner to advance a base.—*adj.* **balk′y.**

[1]ball (bôl), *n.* **1,** a round or roundish body or mass; a sphere; esp., such a body, solid or inflated, used in playing a game; **2,** anything having a roundish shape like this; as, a *snowball*; **3,** a game played with a ball; **4,** in *baseball*, a pitched ball, not struck at, which does not pass over the plate between the levels of the batsman's shoulders and knees:—*v.t.* and *v.i.* to form into a ball.

[2]ball (bôl), *n.* a large, formal, social gathering for dancing.—*n.* **ball′room.**

bal-lad (bal′ad), *n.* **1,** a short narrative poem, suitable for reciting or singing; **2,** a simple song, often sentimental.

bal-last (bal′ast), *n.* **1,** heavy material carried to give steadiness or balance, as in a ship or a balloon; **2,** stones in the spaces between the ties of a railway track; **3,** that which helps to make a person or thing steady:—*v.t.* to steady with a weight; as, to *ballast* the bow of a canoe with a rock.

ball bearing (bôl′′ bār′ing), *n.* a bearing in which a shaft turns smoothly upon balls of metal that turn with it.—*adj.* **ball′-bear′ing.**

bal-let (bal′ā; ba-lā′), *n.* **1,** an elaborate, graceful, and artistic dance; **2,** the company of persons who perform the dance.—*n.* **bal-let′ dan′cer; bal-le-ri′na.**

bal-lis-tics (ba-lis′tiks), *n.pl.* the science of the motion of projectiles, as bullets, bombs, shells, etc.:—**ballistic missile,** a projectile that is launched and initially guided toward its target, arriving there due to the forces of gravity and inertia:—**go ballistic,** to become extremely angry, incensed, or irrational; as, he went *ballistic* after their team lost the game.

bal-loon (ba-lo͞on′), *n.* **1,** a small rubber bag filled with air or helium, used as children's toys or as decorations; **2,** a large airtight bag of prepared silk or other material, which when filled with a gas that is lighter than air, such as helium, rises and floats in the air: it can be attached to a basket or cabin to carry people up in the air:—*v.i.* **1,** to go up in a balloon; **2,** to expand or swell out.

bal-lot (bal′ut), *n.* **1,** a ticket paper, or other item used in voting; **2,** the system of secret voting by use of a printed or electronic form; **3,** the act of voting; as, the second *ballot*; also, the total number of votes cast:—**ballot box,** a sealed box in which voters deposit their completed ballots in an election:—*v.i.* to vote by ballot.

ball-park (bôl′pärk′), *n.* a park or stadium in which ball games, such as baseball, are played:—*adj. Colloq.* approximate or rough estimate; as, a *ballpark* figure or estimate.

bal-ly-hoo (bal′i-ho͞o′; bal′-i-ho͞o′), *n. Colloq.* **1,** sensational advertising; propaganda; **2,** noisy uproar:—*v.t.* loud promotion of a cause or product.

balm (bäm), *n.* **1,** an oily, gummy substance coming from certain trees or shrubs, used for healing or soothing; balsam; **2,** a lotion or ointment that soothes or heals; **3,** anything that heals or soothes; as, praise was *balm* to his wounded vanity.

balm-y (bäm′i), *adj.* [balm-i-er, balm-i-est], soft; mild; soothing; also, fragrant.—*n.* **balm′i-ness.**

ba-lo-ney (ba-lō′ni), *interj. Slang* nonsense.

bal-sa (bôl′sa; bäl′sa), *n.* a light wood used for airplane models, rafts, etc.

bal-sam (bôl′sam), *n.* **1,** an oily, fragrant substance obtained from certain trees and plants and used for medicine or in perfumery; balm; **2,** a kind of evergreen tree or shrub, yielding an oily, resinous substance; **3,** a flowering plant, with flowers like those of the Lady's slipper; **4,** Canada *balsam*, a fir.—*adj.* **bal-sam′ic.**

balsamic vinegar, an aromatic, aged Italian vinegar made from white grapes.

bal-us-ter (bal′us-tėr′), *n.* one of a set of small pillars that support the handrail of a parapet or balustrade.

bal-us-trade (bal′lus-trād′), *n.* a row of small pillars, or balusters, topped by a protective rail, as along the edge of a bridge, balcony, or staircase.

BALUSTRADE

bam-boo (bam-bōō′), *n.* a tropical, treelike plant of the grass family, with hard, thick, jointed stems, used for poles, canes, furniture, window blinds, etc.

bam-boo-zle (bam-bōō′zl), *v.t.* [-zled, -zling], *Colloq.* to trick; cheat; mislead; also, to puzzle.

ban (ban), *n.* **1,** the formal forbidding of an act, as by law; as, a *ban* on smoking on airplanes; **2,** condemnation, as by public opinion; **3,** excommunication by the church:—*v.t.* [banned, ban-ning], **1,** to curse; call evil down upon; **2,** to prohibit; forbid; as, noise is *banned* in the library.

ban-al (bān′al; ba-nal′; ba′nal), *adj.* trite; hackneyed; commonplace.

ba-nan-a (ba-nan′a), *n.* a tropical treelike plant that bears a long, hanging cluster of sweet fruit; also, the fruit.

[1]**band** (band), *n.* **1,** a thin, flat, flexible strip used for binding or supporting; a strip of trimming or lining, as on a hat or a sleeve; as, a rubber *band*; **2,** a stripe; as, a *band* of white around a pole:—*v.t.* to tie or mark with a band.

[2]**band** (band), *n.* **1,** a company united by a common purpose; as, a *band* of robbers or soldiers; **2,** a group of musicians; as, a school *band*:—*v.t.* and *v.i.* to unite; bring together into a company; to form a band.

band-age (ban′dij), *n.* a strip of cloth or tape used in dressing wounds, sprains, etc.:—*v.t.* [bandaged, bandag-ing], to dress, cover, or bind, as wounds, with a strip of any soft material.

ban-dan-a or **ban-dan-na** (ban-dan′a), *n.* a large handkerchief or scarf, with bright colours or patterns.

ban-dit (ban′dit), *n.* [*pl.* bandits or banditti (ban-dit′i)], an outlaw; robber.

band-stand (band′stand′), *n.* **1,** a platform or other stage, often with a roof, where concerts are held; **2,** any similar platform in an auditorium, ballroom, or nightclub for musicians or other performers.

band-wag-on (band′wag′un), *n.* a wagon carrying a band (in a parade): to climb or get *on the bandwagon*, to be on the popular or winning side, as in an election.

band-width (band′width′), *n.* **1,** in *telecommunications*, the capacity of a communications channel, measured in bits per second; the data transmission rate; **2,** the range of frequencies in a band, as a radio signal.

ban-dy (ban′di), *v.t.* [bandied, bandy-ing], **1,** to knock to and fro, as a ball; **2,** to give and take; exchange; as, to *bandy* words.

bane (bān), *n.* **1,** originally, poison: still used in names of plants; as, wolf's-*bane*; **2,** a cause of ruin or destruction; curse; as, drink is the *bane* of his existence.—*adj.* **bane′ful.**—*adv.* **bane′ful-ly.**

[1]**bang** (bang), *v.t.* **1,** to beat noisily; thump; as, to *bang* an anvil, drum, or piano; **2,** to shut or put down noisily; as, to *bang* a door:—*v.i.* **1,** to strike a noisy blow; as, to *bang* upon a piano or a door; **2,** to make a loud or sudden noise; as, the firecracker *banged*:—*n.* **1,** a heavy, noisy blow; whack; as, I gave the pan a *bang*; **2,** a loud, sudden noise; an explosive sound:—*adv.* suddenly; with a noisy sound; as, *bang* went another tire.

[2]**bang** (bang), *v.t.* to cut (the hair over the forehead) straight across:—**bangs,** *n.pl.* or, sometimes, **bang,** *sing.* hair cut to a short fringe over the forehead.

ban-gle (bang′gl), *n.* **1,** an ornamental ring worn upon the wrists and ankles; **2,** one of several slender bracelets worn together.

ban-ish (ban′ish), *v.t.* **1,** to drive out; condemn to exile; expel; as, to *banish* someone from a country; **2,** to send or drive away; as, to *banish* children from the living room; **3,** to drive out of the mind; as, to *banish* care or fear.—*n.* **ban′ish-ment.**

ban-is-ter or **ban-nis-ter** (ban′is-tėr), *n.* a baluster:—**banisters,** a balustrade of a staircase.

ban-jo (ban′jō), *n.* [*pl.* banjos], a stringed musical instrument somewhat like a guitar, having a long neck, and a body like a tambourine.—*n.* **ban′jo-ist.**

[1]**bank** (bangk), *n.* **1,** a ridge of earth; **2,** a heap, mound, or large mass; as, a *bank* of clouds or snow; **3,** the land at the edge or margin of a stream; **4,** a shallow place in the sea or at the mouth of a river; a shoal; **5,** a slope:—*v.t.* **1,** to cover (a fire) with ashes or packed coal, to prevent rapid burning; **2,** to pile up; as, he *banked* leaves against the wall:—*v.i.* in *aeronautics*, to tip an airplane when going round a curve or turning.

[2]**bank** (bangk), *n.* **1,** an institution that receives money from its depositors for safekeeping, lends money at interest, and assists in transactions requiring the transfer of money; **2,** a place where a large supply of something is kept; as, a food *bank*; a blood *bank*; a sperm *bank*:—*v.t.* to place (money) in a bank:—*v.i.* **1,** to have an account with a bank; **2,** *Colloq.* to rely; count; as, I *bank* on him to do his part.—*n.* **bank′ing; bank′book.**

[3]**bank** (bangk), *n.* a group of similar things together in a row; as, a *bank* of computers, a *bank* of switches.

bank-er (bangk′ėr), *n.* a person engaged in banking; **2,** a person or vessel employed in fishing off the Grand Banks.

bank machine. Same as **automated teller machine (ATM).**

bank note (bangk′ nōt), *n.* the paper currency of a country: issued in Canada by the Bank of Canada.

bank-rupt (bangk′rupt), *n.* a person who is legally declared to be unable to pay his or her debts, and whose property is divided among his or her creditors in proportion to their claims:—*adj.* unable to meet one's debts; also, destitute:—*v.t.* to make poor or insolvent.—*n.* **bank′rupt-cy.**

ban-ner (ban′ėr), *n.* a piece of cloth or other material with letters or pictures that represent something; an ensign; flag:—*adj.* unusually good; as, a *banner* year.

ban-nock (ban′uk), *n.* **1,** a flat, round cake made of flour, salt, and water; **2,** a flat cake made of oatmeal, wheat, or barley flour, usually without yeast or baking powder.

ban-quet (bang′kwit), *n.* an elaborate feast or large formal dinner:—*v.t.* and *v.i.* to feed elaborately; to feast.

ban-tam (ban′tam), *n.* **1,** a breed of small, but aggressive, fowl; **2,** a small pugnacious person; **3,** in *sports*, a class for players under 15 years old.—*adj.*; *bantam* hockey.

ban-tam-weight (ban′tam-wāt′), *n.* and *adj.* a boxer who weighs from 51 to 54 kilograms (113 to 118 pounds).

ban-ter (ban′tėr), *n.* good-natured teasing:—*v.t.* to make fun of; tease with good humour.—*adv.* **ban′ter-ing-ly.**

bap-tize (bap-tīz′), *v.t.* [baptized, baptizing], **1,** to sprinkle with water, or immerse in water, as a religious ceremony, esp. in admitting to a Christian church; **2,** to purify; test; **3,** to christen; name; as, the boy was *baptized* Jeremy.—*n.* **bap′tism.**—*adj.* **bap-tis′mal** (bap-tiz′mal).

bar (bär), *n.* **1,** a rigid piece of wood, metal, or other solid matter, long in proportion to its thickness; as, a *bar* of soap; a candy *bar*; **2,** a barrier; **3,** a bank of sand, gravel, etc., under water, obstructing the passage of ships; **4,** the professional body of lawyers; as, to be called to the *bar*; **5,** a counter over which liquor is sold as a beverage, or a room containing such a counter; **7,** a band or stripe; as, a *bar* of red in a border; **8,** in *music*, one of the series of upright lines drawn through a staff of written music, dividing it into equal measures of time; also, the space between two such bars or lines; **9,** a meteorological unit of atmospheric pressure:—*prep.* but; except; as, *bar* none:—*v.t.* [barred, bar-ring], **1,** to fasten with a bar; as, to *bar* a door or a window; **2,** to hinder; obstruct; block; as, the police *barred* the way.

barb (bärb), *n.* the sharp point extending backward in an arrow, fishhook, etc.:—*v.t.* to furnish with barbs.—*adj.* **barbed** (as, *barbed* wire).

bar-bar-i-an (bär-bâr′i-an), *n.* **1,** in ancient history, a foreigner; one not a Greek or a Roman, and therefore regarded as uncivilized; **2,** a person of uncultivated taste:—*adj.* rude; uncivilized; savage.—*adj.* **bar-bar′ic.**—*n.* **bar-bar′i-ty.**

bar-ba-rism (bär′ba-rizm), *n.* **1,** the state of being uncivilized; **2,** rudeness; ignorance of art and literature; **3,** a word or expression not used correctly.—*adj.* **bar′ba-rous.**

bar-be-cue (bär′be-kū′), *n.* **1,** any food broiled on a grill over hot coals or an open fire; the grill and its frame; **2,** an outdoor feast where food is so cooked and eaten:—*v.t.* to prepare and serve food in this manner.

bar-bell (bär′bel′), a metal bar to which weights are attached and used for lifting exercises.

bar-ber (bär′bėr), *n.* one whose business is shaving, haircutting, and hairdressing.

bar-bi-tu-rate (bär-bit′ū-rāt′; bär′bi-tū′rāt), *n.* one of a large group of drugs used to reduce tension, anxiety, etc.

bar code, a series of vertical lines or bars of varying widths, arranged to form a code readable by optical scanner and used for inventory control in organizations such as retail stores and the postal system.—*n.* **bar coding.**—*adj.* **bar coded.**

bard (bärd), *n.* in ancient times, a poet and singer who made and sang verses about heroes, etc.; hence, any poet; as, Shakespeare is called the *Bard* of Avon.

bare (bâr), *adj.* **1,** not covered; as, a *bare* hillside; esp., not covered with clothing; as, *bare* arms; **2,** unadorned; simple; plainly or scantily furnished; as, *bare* lodgings; **3,** empty; as, a *bare* cupboard; **4,** scanty; as, he earned a *bare* living:—*v.t.* [bared, bar-ing], to uncover; expose.—*n.* **bare′ness.**—*adj.* **bare′foot′; bare′head′ed.**

bare-back (bâr′bak′), *adj.* and *adv.* on a horse without a saddle.

bare-faced (bâr′fāst′), *adj.* unconcealed; bold; impudent; as, *barefaced* frauds.

bare-ly (bâr′li), *adv.* **1,** only just; hence,

time,

bar-gain

the terms of ..s, he had *barely* enough *gain* at $50 a lo..ly.

bought, or sold, at a ..an agreement on player was a *bargain*:— ... closed the *bar-* something offered as a conc... ...hing offered, tiations to influence the othe.. the DVD chip, agree to terms:—**bargaining table,** ...go- table where negotiations are carried on; the process of the negotiation itself; as, to bring an offer to the *bargaining table*:—*v.i.* to make a bargain or trade; also, to discuss the terms of an agreement; haggle.

barge (bärj), *n.* **1,** a large, roomy, flat-bottomed vessel, used for carrying freight or passengers; **2,** a large boat of a warship, used by a flag–officer:—*v.i.* to move clumsily, like a barge; as, to *barge* into the furniture; **2,** to push, shove, or thrust oneself rudely; as, to *barge* into line; to *barge* into the meeting.

bar-i-tone (bar′i-tōn′), *n.* **1,** a male voice between tenor and bass; also, a person with a voice that ranges between tenor and bass; **2,** a musical instrument that has this range; **3,** a musical part written for such a voice or instrument:—*adj.* having, or suited to, a baritone voice.

[1]**bark** (bärk), *n.* the outer covering of trees and other woody plants:—*v.t.* to strip bark or skin from; as, to *bark* a tree; *bark* one's shin.

[2]**bark** (bärk), *n.* the sound made by a dog or similar animal:—*v.i.* to utter a bark or sharp sound, as a dog; as, to *bark* out their names.

bar-ker (bär′kėr), *n.* a person, often with megaphone or amplifier, who attracts customers at a sideshow, circus, etc.

bar-ley (bär′li), *n.* **1,** a grain used as a food and in the manufacture of malt liquors; **2,** the plant yielding the grain.

bar mitz-vah (bär′ mits′vu), *n.* a religious ceremony for a Jewish boy when he reaches the age of 13, recognizing that he has become an adult and can take a full role in the Jewish religion:—*bas mitzvah* or *bat mitzvah,* a similar ceremony for a girl.

barn (bärn), *n.* a farm building for housing livestock, keeping tools, and storing hay, grain, and other produce.

bar-na-cle (bär′na-kl), *n.* **1,** a small sea animal living in a white shell and fastening itself to rocks or the bottoms of ships; **2,** a hanger-on.

barn-storm (bärn′stôrm′), *v.i.* and *v.t.* **1,** to perform plays, give lectures, or stage exhibitions in small towns; as, the Toronto Maple Leafs went on a *barnstorming* tour of Japan.

barn-yard (bärn′yärd′), *n.* a yard adjoining a barn:—*adj.* fit for a barnyard; as, *barnyard* manners.

ba-rom-e-ter (ba-rom′e... *n.* **1,** an instrument for measuring the ...ure of the air, used in showing height a... sea level and in forecasting weather; **2,** ... ...thing that gives notice of a change; a... of how ...interest rates as a *barometer* of how the market will behave.—*adj.* **bar′o-met′ric** (bar′o-met′rik) or **bar′-o-met′ri-cal.**

bar-on (bar′on), *n.* **1,** in Eng... ...′ō- one who held an estate direc... king; **2,** in European countries, lowest rank within the nob... wea...k itself; **3,** a person who... oil *baron*... power in a certain a... ess.—*adj.* **ba...attle** *baron*.—*n.fem.* ...i-al.

bar-racks (bar′... *n.pl.* **1,** a large structure or a row of buil...gs for lodging soldiers or workers; **2,** a building in which local detachments of the RCMP live, or an RCMP training centre.

bar-ra-cu-da (bar′a-kōō′da), *n.* a long, fierce, sharp-toothed, pikelike fish of tropical seas.

[1]**bar-rage** (ba-räzh′), *n.* **1,** a curtain of protective artillery or bombing fire under which an advance is made, or to prevent an enemy from advancing; **2,** an attack in words, blows, etc.; as, a *barrage* of questions.

[2]**bar-rage** (bär′ij), *n.* a dam on a stream or river.

bar-rel (bar′el), *n.* **1,** a round, bulging cask or vessel, greater in length than in width, usually of wood, with flat ends or heads; **2,** the quantity which a full barrel contains; **3,** a tubelike part; as, the *barrel* of a gun or of a fountain pen:—*v.t.* [barrelled, barrelling], to put or pack in a barrel:—*v.i.* to travel very fast; as, to *barrel* down the hill on a sled.

bar-ren (bar′en), *adj.* **1,** unable to bear, or not bearing, children or young; also, not producing fruit; as, a *barren* plant; **2,** not fertile; as, *barren* land; **3,** without profit; empty; lacking; as, *barren* labour:—*n.* (usually *barrens*), an area of empty land; wasteland:—**Barren Ground or Land**, the bare windswept Canadian tundra northwest of Hudson Bay.

bar-ri-cade (bar′i-kād′), *n.* a fortification made of such materials as are nearest to hand, and serving to obstruct an enemy or shield a besieged party:—*v.t.* [barricad-ed, barricad-ing], to obstruct or fortify with a barricade.

bar-ri-er (bar′i-ėr), *n.* **1,** anything that prevents progress or approach; as, a traffic *barrier*; a communication *barrier*; **2,** a fence or wall to keep people out.

barrier reef, a stretch of rock, coral, or sand close to a mainland shore and parallel to it, creating a lagoon.

bar-ring (bär′ing), *prep.* except for; as, *barring* delay, I shall arrive Tuesday.

bar-ris-ter (...is-tėr), *n.* a lawyer who argues ... superior courts; an attorney.

¹ba... (...r′ō), *n.* a flat, oblong frame ...ting handles (a *handbarrow*), or ...eel at one end and shafts at the ... (a *wheelbarrow*), for carrying ...g loads.

...ow (bar′ō), *n.* in early times, a ...nd of earth or stones raised over ...ve.

...r-ten-der (bär′ten′dėr), *n.* ... who serves liquor at a bar.

bar-ter (bär′ter), *v.t.* to ... exchange ... goods for something; as, to barter ... for a skateboard:—*n.* the trade ... exchange of one thing for another without the use of money.

bas-al (bās′al), *adj.* having to do with a base or foundation; used as a base; also, fundamental; basic.

basal metabolism, the minimum amount of energy needed to maintain an organism at rest, measured in oxygen consumption over time.

¹base (bās), *n.* **1,** the lowest part of something; the bottom; the part of a thing on which it rests; as, the *base* of a hill; the *base* of a statue; **2,** one of the principal or fundamental parts of which anything is made; as, the *base* of some soups is meat stock; a *base* of a word is a root word; **3,** the line or point from which an operation starts, as in surveying or in a race; **4,** in baseball and some other games, a station or goal; **5,** a secure or fortified location used as a starting point for operations, for storage of supplies, etc.; as, a military or naval *base*; **6,** in *chemistry,* a substance that combines with an acid to form a salt; an alkali:—*v.t.* [based, bas-ing], **1,** to found; establish; as, he *bases* his hopes on news reports; his business is *based* on honesty; **2,** to set on a base; as, to *base* a statue on concrete.—*adj.* **base′less.**

²base (bās), *adj.* **1,** inferior in quality; of little value; as, *base* materials; **2,** mixed with inferior metal; as, a *base* coin; **3,** morally bad; mean; vile; as, *base* motives; **4,** low or deep in sound; bass.—*adv.* **base′ly.**—*n.* **base′ness.**

base-ball (bās′bôl′), *n.* **1,** a game played with a bat and ball by nine players on a side, on a field with four stations, or bases, arranged in the shape of a diamond; **2,** the ball used in this game. Also, **base hit, baseline,** etc.

base-board (bās′bōrd′), *n.* a wide moulding running around the lower part of the wall, against the floor.

base-ment (bās′ment), *n.* the lowest story of a building, usually below the level of the ground.

¹bas-es (bās′iz), *n.pl.* of *base.*

²bas-es (bā′sēz), *n.pl.* of *basis.*

bash (bash), *v.t.* [bashed, bash-ing], **1,** *Colloq.* to strike ... blow; as, to *bash in* a door ...—*n.* a violent blow.

bash-ful (...), *adj.* shy; easily embarrassed; as, a *bashful* child.—*adv.* ...—*n.* **bash′ful-ness.**

ba-sic (bās′ik), *adj.* fundamental; essential; as, *basic* reasons; a *basic* wage, fact, ...—**basics,** the simplest but most important parts of something; as, reading, writing, and arithmetic are the *basics* of education.

BASIC (bās′ik), *n.* in *computing,* a simplified computer programming language that was designed for use by students and beginners: short for *B*eginner's *A*ll-purpose *S*ymbolic *I*nstruction *C*ode.

ba-si-cal-ly (bās′ik-li), *adv.* for the most part; chiefly; mainly; as, the response is *basically* correct, with a few minor errors.

ba-sil-i-ca (ba-sil′i-ka), *n.* [*pl.* basilicas], **1,** in ancient Rome, an oblong hall with columns along the two sides and a semicircular recess, or apse, at one end; **2,** a church built on such a plan.

ba-sin (bā′sn), *n.* **1,** a round, wide vessel for holding water or other liquid; a sink; **2,** the quantity such a vessel will hold; **3,** a hollow or enclosed place containing water, as a dock for ships; **4,** all the land drained by a river and its branches; **5,** a low place in land, usually containing water.

ba-sis (bā′sis), *n.* [*pl.* bases (bā′sēz)], **1,** a reason; cause; foundation; as, a *basis* for doubt; **2,** a fundamental part or ingredient.

bask (båsk), *v.i.* **1,** to lie in comfortable warmth, as in the sun or before a fire; **2,** to do well in the presence of a pleasant atmosphere or influence; as, to *bask* in the praise of the media.

bas-ket (bås′kit), *n.* **1,** a container used to hold and carry food, clothing, etc.; **2,** the amount that such a container will hold; **3,** a large metal ring with a net open at the bottom that is used as the goal in basketball; **4,** a score made in basketball; as, to score six *baskets.*

bas-ket-ball (bås′kit-bôl′), *n.* **1,** a game played on a basketball court by two teams of five players each, in which a large ball must be thrown into the opponent's basketlike goal placed high above the floor; **2,** the ball used in the game.

¹bass (bas), *n.* [*pl.* bass or basses], an edible fish of both fresh and salt water.

²bass (bās), *adj.* low-toned; deep; low in pitch; as, a *bass* note; a *bass* voice:—*n.* **1,** the lowest part in a musical composition; **2,** the lowest tones of a male voice or of an instrument; **3,** a musical instrument similar in shape to the violin: the largest in size and lowest in tone of all the stringed instruments: also called *bass viol;* **4,** a singer or an instrument with a bass part.

bas-si-net (bas′i-net′; bas′i-net), *n.* a basketlike baby's crib.

bas-soon (ba-so͞on′), *n.* a musical wind instrument of deep tone, having a long, curved mouthpiece and a wooden tube.

bass vi-ol (bās vī′al), *n.* Same as **bass** (def. 3).

bas-tard (bas′tėrd), *n.* **1,** a child born of unmarried parents; **2,** inferior; not genuine; **3,** *Slang* offensive; not pleasant.

[1]**baste** (bāst), *v.t.* [bast-ed, bast-ing], to sew temporarily with long, loose stitches; as, Monique *basted* her dress before she stitched it on the machine.—*n.* **bast′ings.**

[2]**baste** (bāst), *v.t.* [bast-ed, bast-ing], to moisten (roasting meat), esp. with its own juice, to make it tender and juicy.

bas-tille or **bas-tile** (bas-tēl′), *n.* a prison:—**the Bastille**, an old prison in Paris, destroyed by the people in 1789.

bas-tion (bas′chun; bas′ti-un), *n.* **1,** a part projecting out from the main body of a fortification; **2,** anything that is like a stronghold; as, a *bastion* of conservatism.

[1]**bat** (bat), *n.* **1,** a heavy stick, esp. one used to strike the ball in cricket, baseball, etc.; **2,** a turn to hit; **3,** *Colloq.* a hard blow; **4,** *Slang* a spree:—*v.t.* [bat-ted, bat-ting], to hit with a bat:—**at bat**, having a turn to hit in baseball or a similar game:—*v.i.* to use a bat in games; as, he *batted* once.—*n.* **bat′ter.**

[2]**bat** (bat), *n.* a small animal that flies by night and feeds on fruit and insects. It has a mouselike body and wings formed of skin stretched between the fore limbs, feet, and tail.

batch (bach), *n.* **1,** the quantity of bread, cookies, etc., baked at one time; **2,** a quantity of material to be used at one time; as, a *batch* of flour; **3,** a group or collection of similar things; as, a *batch* of letters; **4,** in *computing*, a group of records, jobs, programs, etc., treated as a single unit or performed in one run:—**batch file**, the file containing the commands of a computer operating system.

bate (bāt), *v.t.* to lower; diminish; moderate; as, with *bated* breath.

ba-teau (bå-tō′), *n.* [*pl.* bateaux (-tōz′)], a light, flat-bottomed river boat with tapering ends, used esp. on the St. Lawrence River by early French Canadians.

bath (båth), *n.* [*pl.* baths (bå*th*z)], **1,** a cleansing or washing of the entire body, esp. with water in a tub; **2,** the water, liquid, etc., used for bathing; **3,** a vessel holding water for bathing; as, a *bath*tub; a bird-*bath*; **4,** a building or room fitted up for bathing, having also a toilet, a sink, a bathtub or shower; as, a *bath*room. Also, **bath′robe′, bath′room′, bath′tub′.**

bathe (bā*th*), *v.t.* [bathed, bath-ing], **1,** to wash by putting into water, etc.; **2,** to wet; wash; as, the ocean *bathes* the shore; **3,** to surround; envelop; as, a landscape *bathed* in moonlight:—*v.i.* to take a bath.—*n.* **bath′er; bath′ing.**

bathing suit, a piece of clothing worn for swimming. Also called *swimsuit.*

ba-ton (bå′ton′; bat′un), *n.* **1,** a staff used as a badge of office or symbol of authority; **2,** the stick used by a band or orchestra leader to beat time; **3,** a long, thin stick used by a relay runner.

bat-tal-ion (ba-tal′yun), *n.* **1,** four companies of foot soldiers within one regiment; **2,** any large group organized to act together; as, a *battalion* of volunteers.

[1]**bat-ter** (bat′ėr), *v.t.* to strike with heavy, repeated blows; as, the sea *battered* the wall; the football team *battered* their opponents:—*v.i.* to strike repeatedly; as, he *battered* at the door.—*adj.* **bat′tered,** worn by hard use; as, a *battered* old car.

[2]**bat-ter** (bat′ėr), *n.* a stiff liquid mixture, as of flour, eggs, etc., beaten together before being cooked; as, pancake *batter.*

[3]**bat-ter** (bat′ėr), *n.* one who uses a bat, or is at bat in baseball.

bat-ter-ing ram (bat′ėr-ing ram′), *n.* a large iron-headed beam, used in ancient days to beat down the walls of besieged places; also, a heavy metal bar used esp. by firefighters and police officers to break down doors, walls, etc.

bat-ter-y (bat′ėr-i), *n.* [*pl.* batteries], **1,** an unlawful attack on another; as, he was arrested for assault and *battery*; **2,** two or more cannons placed together for combined action, usually under a single command; as, a field *battery*; also, the place where they are stationed; as, the forward *battery* on a battleship; **3,** an electric cell or group of cells supplying current and energy; as, a car *battery*, flashlight *batteries*; **4,** in *baseball*, the combination of pitcher and catcher; **5,** a number of like things used as a unit; as, a *battery* of lights.

bat-tle (bat′l), *n.* **1,** a fight between opposing forces, esp. one between armies or fleets; **2,** any hard struggle; as, the game was a *battle*:—*v.i.* [bat-tled, bat-tling], to fight; struggle. Also, **bat′tle-field′, bat′tle-ground′, bat′tle-ship′.**

bat-tle–axe or **bat-tle–ax** (bat′l-aks′), *n.* a broad-faced axe formerly used as a weapon in battle.

bat-tle-ment (bat′l-ment), *n.* a wall for defence, usually at the top of a building or tower, with openings through which, in ancient times, defenders shot at the enemy.

bau-ble (bô′bl), *n.* a trifling piece of finery; anything showy but without real value; a trinket; as, the prizes given at the fair were mere *baubles.*

baud (bäd), *n.* in *computing*, a measurement of data transmission speed in bits per second:—**baud rate**, the speed of data transmission measured in baud: the higher the baud rate, the better the response rate.

bawd-y (bôd′i), *adj.* lewd; obscene; as, *bawdy* talk, songs, or jokes.

bawl (bôl), *v.i.* to cry out loudly; howl; as, the child *bawled*; the cows *bawled*:—*v.t.* to call loudly; shout; as, to *bawl* instructions:—**bawl out**, *Colloq.* to scold or criticize loudly; as, to *bawl out* a misbehaving child.

[1]**bay** (bā), *n.* an arm of the sea in a sheltered recess or curve in the shore; as, Hudson *Bay*.

[2]**bay** (bā), *n.* **1,** the laurel tree; also, a shrub or tree resembling the laurel, the leaf (bay leaf) of which is used to give flavour to cooking; **2,** a garland or crown of laurel leaves, formerly given as a mark of honour to conquerors and successful poets.

[3]**bay** (bā), *n.* the deep-toned prolonged cry of a dog:—*v.i.* to bark with a deep sound; as, the hounds *bayed*.

[4]**bay** (bā), *n.* the position of a person or animal compelled to turn and face an enemy or a danger when no escape is possible; as, a soldier at *bay*; also, the position of the pursuers thus held off; as, the guard held five robbers at *bay*.

[5]**bay** (bā), *n.* **1,** a part of a building or other structure between columns, pillars, etc; **2,** a part of a wall that projects out and has a window or set of windows in it; as, a *bay* window; **3,** a compartment in a barn used to store hay or grain; **4,** a compartment or platform used for a special purpose; as, a loading *bay*.

[6]**bay** (bā), *adj.* reddish brown in colour:—*n.* a horse of a bay colour.

bay-o-net (bā′o-nit), *n.* a daggerlike weapon attached to the muzzle of a rifle:—*v.t.* [bayonet-ed, bayonet-ing], to stab with a bayonet.

bay-ou (bī′o͞o), *n.* [*pl.* bayous], a sluggish, marshy offshoot of a river or lake, as in the southern U.S.

ba-zaar (ba-zär′), *n.* **1,** a marketplace or street lined with shops; **2,** a hall or series of rooms with stalls for the sale of goods; **3,** a sale of articles, as in aid of a charity; as, a church *bazaar*.

ba-zoo-ka (ba-zo͞o′ka), *n.* a metal tube for launching electrically fired, armour-piercing rockets, esp. against tanks.

B.C. (bē′sē′), *abbrev.* for Before Christ, used in giving dates: Socrates died in 399 B.C., which means that he perished 399 years before the birth of Christ. Compare with *A.D.*

be (bē), *v.i.* [*present sing.* I am, you are, he is, *pl.* are; *p.t.* I was, you were, he was, *pl.* were; *p.p.* been; *p.pr.* be-ing], **1,** to exist; as, there *is* hope; **2,** to stay; remain; occupy a certain place; as, the lesson *is* on this page; **3,** to mean; signify; as, it *is* nothing to me; **4,** to coincide with; equal; as, it *is* I; the girl *is* my sister; **5,** to belong to the class or group of; as, the animal *is* a lion; **6,** to take place; happen; as, the meeting *is* tomorrow; **7,** as a helping verb used to form: **a,** the progressive form of other verbs; as, he *is* going; **b,** the passive voice; as, I *was* hit.

beach (bēch), *n.* the shore of a body of water which is washed by the waves, esp. the sandy or pebbly part:—*v.t.* and *v.i.* to haul up or land on a beach.

beach-comb-er (bēch′kōm′ėr), *n.* **1,** a long ocean wave rolling in; **2,** one who lives by gathering wreckage, etc., on a shore, esp. in the South Seas; **3,** in British Columbia, a person who retrieves loose logs for a fee.

beach-head (bēch′hed′), *n.* an area captured or secured by troops landing on a hostile shore.

bea-con (bē′kun), *n.* **1,** a fire, light, or radio signal used for warning or guidance, as for ships at sea or for airplanes on land; also, the structure bearing this signal, such as a lighthouse; **2,** anything that serves as a guide; as, faith was his *beacon*.

bead (bēd), *n.* **1,** a little ball of any material, such as wood, glass, metal, or plastic, pierced through and intended to be strung with others to form an ornament; **2,** any small round body; a drop or bubble; as, a *bead* of dew; *beads* of perspiration:—*v.t.* to ornament with beads.—*adj.* **bead′y.**

bea-gle (bē′gl), *n.* a small, short-legged hound, used esp. for hunting.

beak (bēk), *n.* **1,** the bill of a bird; also, the long, sharp mouth of some insects and other animals; **2,** anything pointed or shaped like the bill of a bird, as the prow of ancient war vessels or a *beak* of a pitcher.—*adj.* **beaked** (bēkt).

BEAK, DEF. 1

beak-er (bēk′ėr), *n.* **1,** a large drinking cup or vessel with a wide mouth; **2,** an open-mouthed glass or metal vessel with a projecting lip, used as a container in laboratories.

beam (bēm), *n.* **1,** a long heavy piece of wood or metal used in the framework of buildings and ships; **2,** the widest part of a ship; **3,** the bar of a balance on which the scale pans are hung; **4,** the chief timber of a plough; **5,** a ray of light given out by the sun or any other luminous body or a stream of radiation; as, the *beam* from a lamp; *beam* from a laser; **6,** in *gymnastics*, a balance beam; **7,** a smile:—*v.i.* to gleam; shine; as, his face *beamed* with joy.

bean (bēn), *n.* **1,** the seed or the long pod of a pod-bearing plant used as food; also, the plant itself; as, a lima, kidney, or string *bean*; **2,** any seed resembling a true bean; as, a coffee *bean*. Also, **bean′pole′**; **bean′stalk′.**

bean-bag (bēn′bag′), *n.* **1,** a small cloth

sack filled with dried beans used in games; **2,** a bag or cushion stuffed with pellets or beads that takes the shape around it; as, a *beanbag* chair.

bean-ie (bē′ni), *n.* a small brimless hat made of sections converging to the top.

[1]**bear** (bâr), *n.* **1,** a large four-footed animal with long shaggy fur, sharp claws, and a very short tail, as the brown *bear*, black *bear*, grizzly *bear*, polar *bear;* **2,** a person with rough, uncouth, or surly manners; **3,** on the stock exchange, one who tries to lower prices for his or her own advantage: opposite of *bull:*—**Bear,** in astronomy, either of two groups of stars in the Northern Hemisphere, called *Great Bear*, containing the *Big Dipper*, and the *Little Bear*, containing the *Little Dipper*.

[2]**bear** (bâr), *v.t.* [*p.t.* bore (bōr), *p.p.* borne (bōrn) or born (bôrn), *born* is properly used only in the passive voice of sense 6 when *by* does not follow; as, a son was *born* to him; he was *born* in 1800; a son *borne by* his first wife), *p.pr.* bear-ing], **1,** to support; hold up; as, the pillars *bore* all the weight; **2,** to carry; convey; as, this letter *bears* good news; **3,** to suffer or endure; stand; as, to *bear* pain or sorrow; **4,** to possess, wear, or use, as a weapon; **5,** to show; as, his past record *bears* proof of his guilt; **6,** to bring forth; as, she *bore* many children; **7,** to behave; as, he *bore* himself well:—*v.i.* **1,** to be capable of enduring trouble or pain; as, she *bears* up well under her grief; **2,** to be fruitful; as, this tree always *bears;* **3,** to press or weigh; as, he *bore* too hard on the tool and it broke; **4,** to refer; as, this *bears* on our talk:—**bear down, 1,** to press or push down; **2,** to try hard; as, to *bear down* and get the job done.—*adj.* **bear′a-ble.**

beard (bērd), *n.* **1,** the hair on the chin and cheeks of a man; **2,** anything resembling a beard, esp. the hairs on the heads of certain grains, as barley, and the hair on a goat's chin:—*v.t.* to take by the beard; hence, to oppose face to face; defy.—*adj.* **beard′less.**—*adj.* **beard′ed.**

bear-er (bâr′ėr), *n.* **1,** one who or that which carries; **2,** one who presents a cheque or other order for the payment of money.

bear-ing (bâr′ing), *n.* **1,** the act of one who endures or bears; **2,** behaviour; manner; as, the *bearing* of the princess; **3,** meaning; relation; as, this has no *bearing* on the subject; **4,** the act or power of producing; **5,** a part of a machine in which another part turns; as, ball *bearings;* **6,** (usually *bearings*), direction; way; as, he lost his *bearings* in the fog.

bear market, a stock market with falling prices: opposite of *bull market*.

beast (bēst), *n.* **1,** a four-footed animal, as distinguished from a bird, insect, fish, or human; **2,** *Colloq.* a brutal or rude person.—*adj.* **beastly, 1,** of or like a beast; **2,** *Colloq.* brutal; very unpleasant or nasty; as, a *beastly* remark.—*n.* **beast′li-ness.**

beat (bēt), *v.t.* [*p.t.* beat, *p.p.* beat-en (bēt′n), *p.pr.* beat-ing], **1,** to strike with many blows; **2,** to flap; as, the bird *beat* its wings; **3,** in *cooking,* to mix by stirring quickly; **4,** in *music,* to measure (time) by strokes; **5,** to defeat; conquer; as, the first team *beat* the second; **6,** *Colloq.* to confuse or bewilder; as, it *beats* me how he got here so soon:—*v.i.* **1,** to strike repeatedly; as, waves *beat* upon rocks; **2,** to throb; as, the heart *beats:*—*n.* **1,** a stroke that is made again and again; as, the *beat* of marching feet; **2,** a round frequently traversed; as, a police officer's *beat*; **3,** in *music,* the rise and fall of the stroke marking the divisions of time:—*adj. Colloq.* very tired; exhausted; as, to be *beat* after the long day.—*n.* **beat′er.**

beau-ti-cian (bū-tish′un), *n.* one who does hairdressing, manicuring, massaging, etc., in a beauty salon.—*v.t.* **beaut′i-fy.**

beau-ti-ful (bū′ti-fool), *adj.* possessing qualities that delight the mind and senses; lovely; as, a *beautiful* painting.—*adv.* **beau′ti-ful-ly.**

beau-ty (bū′ti), *n.* [*pl.* beauties], **1,** that combination of qualities that pleases the eye or ear, or satisfies in a moral sense; **2,** a particular grace or charm; as, the *beauty* of the country; **3,** a beautiful thing or person, esp. a lovely or beautiful woman.—*v.t.* **beau′ti-fy.**

bea-ver (bē′vėr), *n.* **1,** a small fur-bearing animal that lives both in water and on land, having a broad, flat, powerful tail, strong teeth formed for gnawing, and webbed hind feet: remarkable for the way in which it fells trees and dams streams; the national symbol of Canada; **2,** the fur of this animal; **3,** a man's high hat, formerly made of beaver fur.

be-bop (bē′bop′), *n.* a jazz style of music marked by off-hand composing, clashing harmonies, lack of restraint, and syncopation.

be-came (bi-kām′), *p.t.* of *become.*

be-cause (bi-kôz′), *conj.* for the reason that; since; as, we came in *because* it rained:—**because of,** on account of; as, I stayed late *because* of my work.

beck-on (bek′un), *v.i.* and *v.t.* to signal by a motion of the head or hand; also, to attract; call; as, pleasure *beckons.*

be-come (bi-kum′), *v.i.* [*p.t.* became (bi-kām′), *p.p.* become, *p.pr.* becom-ing], to come or grow to be; as, a teenager *becomes* an adult; to *become* excited:—*v.t.* to suit; be suitable for; as, that hat *becomes* you:—**become of,** to happen to; as, what has *become of* your old computer?

be-com-ing (bi-kum′ing), *adj.* proper; suitable; appropriate; as, a *becoming* hat; a *becoming* pride.—*adv.* **be-com′ing-ly.**

bed (bed), *n.* **1,** an article of furniture upon which one rests or sleeps; **2,** anything that serves as a bed or resting place; **3,** a portion of a garden; as, a *bed* of pansies; **4,** the base or bottom of anything; as, a *bed* of concrete; the *bed* of a river:—*v.t.* [bed-ded, bed-ding], **1,** to fix for the night; as, I *bedded* the horses; **2,** to plant; **3,** to set; fix; as, to *bed* a pole in concrete:—*v.i.* to go to bed; as, to *bed* down early. Also, **bed′ding′; bed′pan′; bed′post′; bed′ room′; bed′side′; bed′sore′; bed′spread′; bed′spring′; bed′time′.**

bed and breakfast, a small inn or hotel, often part of a private residence, that offers accommodations with breakfast for guests.

bed-bug (bed′bug′), *n.* a biting, blood-sucking, flat-bodied insect, of vile odour, infesting furniture, esp. beds.

bed-lam (bed′lam), *n.* any scene of uproar and confusion; as, the jail was a *bedlam* during the riot:—**Bedlam,** a former name for an English hospital for the mentally ill.

Bed-ou-in (bed′ō-in; bed′win), *n.* [*pl.* Bedouin or Bedouins], an Arab who is a nomadic herder in the deserts of the Middle East.

be-drag-gled (bi-drag′ld), *adj.* wet, soiled, and limp; as, a *bedraggled* dress.

bed-ridden (bed′rid′n), *adj.* confined to bed, as by age or illness.

bed-rock (bed′rok′), *n.* **1,** the solid rock underlying the looser upper crust of the earth; **2,** hence, the lowest state or bottom of a thing; as, my savings account has reached *bedrock.*

bed-side manner (bed′sīd′), *n.* the attitude and behaviour of a physician or other healthcare worker toward a patient; as, Dr. Jones had excellent *bedside manners.*

bee (bē), *n.* **1,** a winged insect with sucking and stinging organs; esp., the honeybee, which lives with many others in a hive, where it stores pollen and honey; **2,** a social meeting for work or amusement; as, a quilting *bee;* a spelling *bee.* Also, **bee′hive′; bees′wax′.**

beech (bēch), *n.* a wide-spreading tree with smooth, ash-grey bark and deep-green leaves, yielding hard timber and edible triangular nuts.—*n.* **beech′nut′.**

beef (bēf), *n.* **1,** the meat from cattle; **2,** [*pl.* beeves (bēvz) or beefs (bēfs)], a full-grown ox, bull, or cow, esp. when fattened for market; **3,** *Slang* an objection or complaint; as, what's your *beef* with this proposal?

beef-steak (bēf′stāk′), *n.* a thin broad piece, or slice, of beef that can be broiled or fried:—**beefsteak tomato,** a large tomato.

beef-y (bēf′i), *adj.* [beef-i-er, beef-i-est], fat; brawny; fleshy.—*n.* **beef′i-ness.**

bee-keep-er (bē′kē′pėr), *n.* someone who raises honeybees for their honey and wax; an apiarist.

bee-line (bē′līn′), *n.* **1,** the straight course of a bee returning to the hive with honey or pollen; **2,** the most direct way from one point to another; as, I made a *beeline* for home.

been (bin; bēn), *p.p.* of *be.*

beep (bēp), *n.* a high-pitched sound, esp. a carhorn:—*v.t.* and *v.i.* to make such a sound.

beeper (bē′pėr), *n.* a device that beeps, esp. an electric device; a pager.

beer (bēr), *n.* **1,** an alcoholic liquor generally brewed from malted barley and flavoured with hops; **2,** a non-alcoholic drink made from roots or plants, as root beer, ginger beer, etc.—*adj.* **beer′y.**

beet (bēt), *n.* a plant cultivated for its root, which serves as a vegetable and as a source of sugar; also, the red or white root.

bee-tle (bē′tl), *n.* a kind of insect having four wings, the outer pair being hard and shiny and serving as a protection to the inner pair, such as the ladybug, the sweet-potato weevil, and the cucumber beetle.

bee-tling (bē′tling), *adj.* jutting out; prominent; overhanging; as, bare and *beetling* cliffs; a *beetling* brow.

be-fall (bi-fôl′), *v.t.* [*p.t.* befell (bi-fel′), *p.p.* befall-en (bi-fôl′en), *p.pr.* befall-ing], to happen or occur to:—*v.i.* to come to pass; as, whatever *befalls.*

be-fit (bi-fit′), *v.t.* [befit-ted, befit-ting], to be worthy of; be suitable or appropriate for.—*adj.* **be-fit′ting.**

be-fore (bi-fōr′), *prep.* **1,** in front of; **2,** preceding in space, time, or rank; as, the lawn *before* the house; *before* 10 o'clock; a general comes *before* a colonel; **3,** in the presence or sight of; as, the prisoner was brought *before* the judge:—*adv.* in front; previously; formerly; as, you never looked like that *before:*—*conj.* **1,** previous to the time at which; as, I shall finish *before* I leave; **2,** rather than; as, he would die *before* he would betray his country.

be-fore-hand (bi-fōr′hand′), *adv.* in advance; as, do it *beforehand.*

be-friend (bi-frend′), *v.t.* to make friends; act as a friend; aid; as, to *befriend* a stray cat; to *befriend* a new student.

be-fud-dle (bi-fud′l), *v.t.* to confuse, as with liquor.

beg (beg), *v.t.* [begged, beg-ging], **1,** to entreat or ask for (food, money, etc.) as charity; **2,** to beseech; implore; as, I *beg* you to help me; **3,** to ask as a favour; as, I *beg* you to hand me that book:—*v.i.* to ask, or to live by asking for alms; as, he *begs* from door to door.—*n.* **beg′gar; beg′gar-y.**—*adj.* **beg′gar-ly.**

be-gan (bi-gan′), *p.t.* of *begin.*

be-gin (bi-gin′), *v.i.* [*p.t.* began (bi-gan′),

p.p. begun (bi-gun′), *p.pr.* begin-ning], **1,** to come into existence; arise; commence; as, life *began* many million years ago; the stream *begins* up in the hills; the story *begins* on page 30; **2,** to take the first step or do the first act; start; as, work *begins* tomorrow:—*v.t.* to commence.

be-gin-ner (bi-gin′ėr), *n.* one who is just starting in; one who has had no training or experience; a novice.

be-gin-ning (bi-gin′ing), *n.* **1,** origin; as, the *beginning* of the world; **2,** source; as, the *beginning* of all evil; **3,** the first part; as, the *beginning* of a book.

be-go-ni-a (bi-gō′ni-a; bi-gōn′ya), *n.* a plant with ornamental leaves and red, pink, or white flowers.

be-grudge (bi-gruj′), *v.t.* [begrudged, begrudg-ing], **1,** to envy (a person) the possession of (something); as, I *begrudge* him the honour; **2,** to give reluctantly or unwillingly; as, I *begrudge* the money.—*adv.* **be-grudg′ing-ly.**

be-guile (bi-gil′), *v.t.* [beguiled, beguil-ing], **1,** to deceive; **2,** to cause to pass pleasantly; as, to *beguile* many hours in reading; **3,** to amuse; as, to *beguile* children with stories.

be-half (bi-håf; bi-häf′), *n.* used only in phrases:—**in behalf of,** in the defence or interest of; as, he spoke *in behalf of* the plan; **on behalf of,** in the place of; for; as, the agent acts *on behalf of* his employer.

be-have (bi-hāv′), *v.t.* and *v.i.* [behaved, behav-ing], to conduct or carry (oneself); act in a certain way; as, he *behaves* himself well; also, to conduct (oneself) properly; as, make him *behave.*

be-hav-iour or **be-hav-ior** (bi-hāv′yėr), *n.* conduct; manners; the way of acting; as, the *behaviour* of lions.

be-hav-iour-ism or **be-hav-ior-ism** (bi-hāv′yėr-izm′), *n.* the psychological theory that only objectively observable behaviour is the basis for psychological theory and practice.

behaviour modification, psychotherapeutic techniques that aim to substitute appropriate behaviour for undesirable ones. Also called *behaviour therapy.*

be-head (bi-hed′), *v.t.* to cut off the head.

be-hest (bi-hest′), *n.* a command; order; as, on her *behest.*

be-hind (bi-hīnd′), *prep.* **1,** at the back of; as, to hide *behind* the door; **2,** inferior to; later than; after; as, he is *behind* in math; *behind* schedule; **3,** in support of; as, there is money *behind* the plan; **4,** remaining after; as, he left nothing but debts *behind* him:—*adv.* **1,** in the rear; as, to remain *behind*; **2,** backward; as, look *behind*; **3,** in arrears; as, he is *behind* in his dues; **4,** not on time; slow; late; as, to fall *behind* in chemistry.

be-hind-hand (bi-hīnd′hand′), *adj.* and *adv.* late; slow; behind, as in one's work.

be-hold (bi-hōld′), *v.t.* [*p.t.* beheld (bi-held′), *p.p.* beheld, *p.pr.* behold-ing], to look at; gaze upon; see.—*n.* **be-hold′er.**

be-hoove (bi-ho͞ov′), *v.t.* [*p.t.* behooved (-ho͞ovd′)], to be necessary; as, it *behooves* me to go.

beige (bāzh), *n.* a light-tan colour:—*adj.* of a light-tan colour.

be-ing (bē′ing), *n.* **1,** existence; life; as, to come into *being*; **2,** that which exists; esp., a person or animal:—*p.p.* of *be*; as, she is *being* very serious.

be-la-bour (bi-lā′bėr), *v.t.* **1,** to beat; pummel; **2,** berate; criticize; as, the media *belaboured* the politician; **3,** to overdo; go on excessively; as, to *belabour* the obvious point of the issue.

be-lat-ed (bi-lāt′id), *adj.* delayed; as, a *belated* report; a *belated* arrival.

belch (belch), *v.t.* and *v.i.* **1,** to discharge (gas) from the stomach through the mouth; **2,** to throw out with force; as, the volcano *belched* fire:—*n.* the act of belching.

be-lea-guer (bi-lē′gėr), *v.t.* to besiege; as, we *beleaguered* the fort; also, to torment; harass.

bel-fry (bel′fri), *n.* [*pl.* belfries], a bell tower, or that part of a tower in which a bell is hung.

be-lie (bi-lī′), *v.t.* [belied, bely-ing], **1,** to give a false notion of; as, his appearance *belies* his feelings; **2,** to fail to come up to or to accord with; as, his acts *belie* his words.

be-lief (bi-lēf′), *n.* **1,** the acceptance of something as true or desirable; confidence; as, a *belief* in physical activity; my *belief* in his innocence; **2,** creed; as, a religious *belief*; **3,** opinion; as, it is my *belief* that he is coming.

be-lieve (bi-lēv′), *v.t.* [believed, believ-ing], **1,** to accept as true; as, I *believe* the evidence; **2,** to trust the word of; place confidence in; as, I *believe* him; **3,** to think; as, I *believe* that honesty pays:—*v.i.* to have faith, trust, or confidence; as, to *believe* in God; *believe* in our cause:—**make believe,** to pretend; as, children like to *make believe.*—*adj.* **be-liev′ing; be-liev′a-ble.**—*n.* **be-liev′er.**

be-lit-tle (bi-lit′l), *v.t.* [belit-tled, belit-tling], **1,** to cause to appear small; as, he *belittled* the danger; **2,** to speak slightingly of; as, she *belittled* my work.

bell (bel), *n.* **1,** a hollow metal vessel, usually cup-shaped, that gives a ringing sound when struck with a clapper or hammer; **2,** anything that makes a ringing sound, as a doorbell, or is shaped like a bell, as the flare at the mouth of a horn; **3,** on shipboard, the time is indicated by strokes on a bell:—*v.t.* to put a bell on; as, to *bell* a cat or a sheep.

bell-bot-tom (bel′-bot′um), *adj.* flaring out below the knee to a bell shape; as, *bell-bottom* jeans:—**bell-bottoms**, pants that flare out below the knee to a bell shape.

bell-boy (bel′boi′), *n.* a hotel, club, or ship employee who attends to the wants of guests. Also, *Slang* **bell′hop′**.

belle (bel), *n.* a beautiful woman; a very popular girl or woman.

bel-li-cose (bel′i-kōs′), *adj.* quarrelsome; warlike.

bel-lig-er-ent (bi-lij′er-ent), *adj.* **1,** waging war; as, *belligerent* nations; **2,** quarrelsome; warlike; as, *belligerent* words; a *belligerent* person:—*n.* a nation or person at war; as, the *belligerents* took up arms.—*n.* **bel-lig′er-ence.**

bel-low (bel′ō), *v.i.* **1,** to roar like a bull; **2,** to make a similar noise; as, he *bellowed* with rage:—*v.t.* to utter with a loud, full voice; roar:—*n.* **1,** the roar of a bull or similar animal; **2,** a loud, deep cry or voice.

bel-lows (bel′ōz), *n.* [*pl.* bellows], **1,** an instrument for producing a current of air, used for various purposes, such as blowing fires, filling the pipes of an organ, or in accordions; **2,** the creased casing that connects the front and back of certain cameras.

bell-weth-er (bel′weth′ėr), *n.* **1,** a person, group, or event that sets the standard or that is an indicator of future trends; as, the *bellwether* for the global warming issue; **2,** any leader.

bel-ly (bel′i), *n.* [*pl.* bellies], **1,** the part of the body of a human or animal between the chest and the thighs, containing the stomach, bowels, etc.; the abdomen; **2,** the front or lower surface of the body of a human or an animal; **3,** the bulging part of any object; as, the *belly* of an airplane:—*v.i.* [bellied, belly-ing], to swell and extend; bulge out, as sails in the wind:—*v.t.* to cause to swell out.

be-long (bi-lông′), *v.i.* **1,** to be the duty, concern, or business; as, this work *belongs* to you; **2,** to be the property; as, the coat *belongs* to me; **3,** to be a part or member; as, the button *belongs* to my coat; she *belongs* to a book club; **4,** to have a characteristic place or niche; as, the book *belongs* on this shelf.

be-long-ings (bi-lông′ings), *n.pl.* the things a person owns; possessions; as, her *belongings* are in her backpack.

be-lov-ed (bi-luv′id; bi-luvd′), *adj.* dearly loved; as, a *beloved* pet:—*n.* one dearly loved.

be-low (bi-lō′), *prep.* **1,** farther down, or lower than, in place, rank, excellence, dignity, value, amount, price, etc.; as, the closet *below* the stairs; rank *below* captain; **2,** undeserving or unworthy of; beneath; as, *below* your dignity:—*adv.* **1,** into or to a lower place; as, go *below*; **2,** to a lower floor; downstairs; as, to go *below* during a storm.

belt (belt), *n.* **1,** a strip of leather, cloth, etc., worn around the body as a support for a garment, or as an ornament; **2,** any broad band, strip, or series of things; as, a *belt* of forts; **3,** a region, with a given character, or where a certain kind of vegetation grows; as, the timber *belt*; **4,** an endless band connecting two wheels or pulleys, and passing motion from one to the other; as, a fan *belt* in a car:—*v.t.* **1,** to encircle, as with a belt; **2,** to hit hard; as, to *belt* a ball out of the park.

be-lu-ga (be-lōō′ga), **1,** a white-toothed whale found from the Arctic to the Gulf of St. Lawrence; **2,** a large white sturgeon that is found in the Black and Caspian Seas, the largest inland fish in the world.

be-moan (bi-mōn′), *v.t.* to grieve for; bewail; as, to *bemoan* one's lot.

bench (bench), *n.* **1,** a long seat; **2,** a strong table on which mechanics do their work; as, a carpenter's *bench*; **3,** the seat where judges sit in court; hence, judges as a class; also, the court:—*v.t.* to keep or take a player out of a game.

bench-mark (bench′märk′), *n.* **1,** a standard or reference point against which other things are measured and compared; **2,** in *computing*, a test to determine the performance level of computer hardware or software.

bend (bend), *v.t.* [bent (bent), bend-ing], **1,** to strain or make taut, as the string of a bow; **2,** to curve or make crooked; as, he *bent* the iron rod; **3,** to turn; deflect; as, the glass *bent* the rays of the sun; **4,** to direct to a certain point; as, we *bent* our energies to the task; **5,** to force to submit or yield:—*v.i.* **1,** to become curved or crooked; as, the board *bent* under his weight; **2,** to turn toward or away from; as, the road *bends* to the left; **3,** to bow or stoop; hence, to submit; as, I *bend* to fate:—*n.* a turn or curve:—**the bends,** *Colloq.* cramps caused by a too-sudden change to normal air pressure from a high pressure, as in deep-sea diving—*n.* **bender,** *Slang* a spree, esp. drinking spree.

be-neath (bi-nēth′; bi-nē*th*′), *prep.* **1,** under; as, *beneath* the sky; **2,** under the pressure of; as, to sink *beneath* troubles; **3,** lower than; as, *beneath* the rank of captain; **4,** undeserving of; as, the letter was *beneath* his notice; unworthy of; as, the work was *beneath* him:—*adv.* in a lower place; below.

ben-e-dic-tion (ben′i-dik′shun), *n.* a blessing, esp. the short blessing pronounced at the end of a church service.

ben-e-fac-tor (ben′i-fak′tėr), *n.* one who has given help in the form of money or service.—*n.* **ben′e-fac′tion; be-nef′i-**

cence.—*adj.* **be-nef′i-cent.**

ben-e-fi-cial (ben′i-fish′al), *adj.* useful; helpful; profitable; as, *beneficial* climate, advice, or experiences.

ben-e-fi-ci-ar-y (ben′i-fish′ėr-i; ben′i-fish′i-er′i), *n.* [*pl.* beneficiaries], one who receives anything as a gift or benefit; esp., the person named in a will or an insurance policy to receive the inheritance.

ben-e-fit (ben′i-fit), *n.* **1,** a help; advantage; as, the *benefits* of an education, or of sunshine; **2,** a play, concert, etc., the proceeds of which go to a particular person or cause:—**benefits,** money paid to a person by the government or an insurance company; as, disability *benefits*; also, something of value that a worker receives from an employer in addition to regular pay, such as paid holidays, health insurance, or a pension:—*v.t.* [benefit-ed, benefit-ing], to do good to; help; as, the vacation *benefited* him:—*v.i.* to be helped; improve; as, he *benefited* from his rest.

be-nev-o-lent (bi-nev′o-lent), *adj.* kindly; charitable; generous; as, a *benevolent* nature.—*n.* **be-nev′o-lence.**

be-nign (bi-nīn′), *adj.* **1,** of a kind or gentle disposition; **2,** favourable; healthful; as, a *benign* sea breeze; **3,** in medical usage, harmless; as, a *benign* tumour: compare *malignant.*—*n.* **be-nig′ni-ty** (bi-nig′-ni-ti).—*adv.* **be-nign′ly.**

bent (bent), *adj.* **1,** curved; crooked; **2,** strongly inclined; set; as, he is *bent* on going:—*n.* a natural interest or ability; as, Tom has a *bent* for painting:—*p.t.* and *p.p.* of *bend.*

ben-zene (ben′zēn; ben-zēn′), *n.* a highly flammable, colourless liquid obtained from coal tar, used as a motor fuel, in the manufacture of chemical products, and in other processes.

ben-zine (ben′zēn; ben-zēn′), *n.* a flammable liquid obtained from petroleum used as a solvent in cleaning, dyeing, painting, etc., and as a motor fuel.

Be-o-thuk (bē-o*th*′uk; bē-ot′uk), *n.* **1,** the original inhabitants of Newfoundland, now extinct; **2,** a member of this group; **3,** the language of these people.

be-queath (bi-kwē*th*′), *v.t.* **1,** to give or leave by will; **2,** to hand down; as, the Greeks *bequeathed* to us a love of beauty.

be-quest (bi-kwest′), *n.* something given or left by will; a legacy; as, small *bequests* of money went to the charity.

be-rate (bi-rāt′), *v.t.* [berat-ed, berat-ing], to scold; rebuke severely.

be-reave (bi-rēv′), *v.t.* [bereaved (bi-rēvd′) or bereft (bi-reft′), bereav-ing], to deprive; leave desolate; as, *bereaved* of his children; fear *bereft* him of his wits.—*n.* **be-reave′ment.**

be-ret (be-rā′; be′rā), *n.* a flat, round, brimless cap of wool, felt, etc.

ber-i-ber-i (ber′i-ber′i), *n.* a disease caused by a lack of vitamin B1 (thiamine) in the diet.

ber-ry (ber′i), *n.* [*pl.* berries], **1,** any small pulpy fruit with many seeds, as the straw*berry*; **2,** the dry seed or kernel of certain plants; as, the coffee *berry*:—*v.i.* [berried, berry-ing], to gather berries.

ber-serk (bûr′sûrk), *adj.* destructively frenzied; as, he went *berserk* and punched his friend.

berth (bûrth), *n.* **1,** a bunk or bed for a passenger, as on a train, ship, or plane; **2,** a position or job; as, he has a good *berth* with the government; **3,** *nautical,* a place where a ship ties up or lies at anchor.

ber-yl (ber′il), *n.* a hard, lustrous gem in striking colours, two of the best known being emerald and aquamarine.

be-seech (bi-sēch′), *v.t.* [besought (be-sôt′), beseech-ing], **1,** to entreat; implore; as, I *beseech* you to hear me; **2,** to beg for; as, I *beseech* your favour.

be-set (bi-set′), *v.t.* [beset, beset-ting], **1,** to assail; harass; as, trouble *beset* him; his *besetting* sin; **2,** to hem in; surround; as, a spy is *beset* by danger.

be-side (bi-sīd′), *prep.* **1,** at, or by the side of; near by; as, sit *beside* me; **2,** in comparison with; as, my work is poor *beside* yours; **3,** away from; as, *beside* the point:—**beside oneself,** very upset or excited.

be-sides (bi-sīdz′), *adv.* in addition; also; as well:—*prep.* over and above; in addition to.

be-siege (bi-sēj′), *v.t.* [besieged, besieg-ing], **1,** to surround with armed forces; lay siege to; as, to *besiege* a city; **2,** to overwhelm, pester, or harass (a person, etc.) in any way, as with questions or requests; as, the company was *besieged* with requests for donations.

be-smirch (bi-smûrch′), *v.i.* **1,** to soil; **2,** to dishonour; sully; as, slander can *besmirch* a person's good name.

be-sought (bi-sôt′), *p.t.* and *p.p.* of **beseech.**

best (best), *adj.* [*superl.* of *good*], **1,** having the highest degree of goodness or excellence; as, he did the *best* work in class; **2,** most desirable; favourite; as, my *best* friend:—*n.* **1,** that which is finest; as, the *best* is none too good; **2,** the highest degree of excellence; as, she was at her *best* in the school play; **3,** good wishes; greeting; as, give her my *best* when you see her:—**at best,** under the most favourable conditions; as, to be third *at best*:—**get the best of,** to defeat; as, to not let nervousness *get the best of* you:—**make the best of,** to make do; do as well as possible with; as, to *make the best of* this bad situation:—*adv.* [*superl.* of ²*well*], **1,** in the most successful way; **2,** in the highest degree:—*v.t.* to get the better of; surpass. Also, **best′sell′er; best′sell′ing.**

bes-tial (best′yal; bes′chal), *adj.* like the beasts; brutish; savage.—*n.* **bes′ti-al′i-ty** (bes′ti-al′i-ti; bes′chi-al′i-ti).

be-stow (bi-stō′), *v.t.* to give or confer; as, to *bestow* a medal on a hero.

be-stride (bi-strīd′), *v.t.* [*p.t.* bestrode (bi-strōd′), *p.pr.* bestrid-ing], to mount, sit, or ride with one leg on each side; straddle; as, to *bestride* a horse, fence, log, etc.

bet (bet), *v.t.* [bet or bet-ted, bet-ting], to stake, risk, or wager (money or the like) that something will or will not happen, or that a contest or situation will end in a certain way; as, I *bet* a dollar that it will rain today; I *bet* him 10 dollars that our team would win:—*v.i.* **1,** to lay a wager; as, to *bet* on a horse; **2,** to believe strongly; as, I *bet* it will snow tomorrow:—*n.* **1,** a wager; as, to make a *bet*; **2,** the amount staked or wagered; **3,** that on which a wager is laid; as, this horse is a safe *bet.*

be-tray (bi-trā′), *v.t.* **1,** to give into the hands of an enemy by treachery; as, the double agent *betrayed* her country; **2,** to be faithless to; as, to *betray* a trust; **3,** to disclose; reveal, as a secret; **4,** to disclose unintentionally; as, his manner *betrays* uneasiness.—*n.* **be-tray′er; be-tray′al.**

be-troth (bi-trōth′; bi-trôth′), *v.t.* to promise to give (a daughter) in marriage:—**betrothed,** *n.* the person to whom one is engaged to be married.—*n.* **be-troth′al.**

bet-ter (bet′ėr), *adj.* [*comp.* of *good*], **1,** having good qualities in a higher degree; as, your work is *better* than it was; this computer is *better* than the old one; **2,** preferable; as, it is *better* to walk than to wait for a taxi; **3,** improved in health; **4,** larger; greater; as, I waited the *better* part of an hour:—*adv.* [*comp.* of [2]*well*], **1,** in a more excellent manner; as, you swim *better* than you did; **2,** more; as, you like swimming *better* now; *better* than 20 years:—*v.t.* **1,** to improve; as, he has *bettered* his condition; **2,** to surpass, as a record:—*n.* **1,** that which is *better* or more desirable; as, to rise from the good to the *better*; **2,** advantage; as, to get the *better* of an opponent; **3,** betters, superiors, as in social standing, rank, or position; as, to heed the advice of your *betters.*

bet-ter-ment (bet′ėr-ment), *n.* a bettering; an improvement, as of land, a railway, a road, or the like.

be-tween (bi-twēn′), *prep.* **1,** in the space or time that separates one thing from another; as, *between* dark and daylight; **2,** from one to another of; as, a look passed *between* them; **3,** by the joint action of; as, *between* us, we shall succeed; **4,** by comparison of; as, a choice *between* evils:—*adv.* in a place between other things.

bev-el (bev′el), *v.t.* [bevelled, bevel-ling], to give a sloping edge to; as, to *bevel* the edge of a table:—*v.i.* to slant or incline:—*n.* **1,** the slant or angle that one line or surface makes with another; **2,** an instrument used for drawing or measuring angles:—*adj.* slanting; as, a *bevelled* edge; *bevelled* glass.

bev-er-age (bev′ėr-ij), *n.* any kind of drink, as orange juice, milk, coffee, lemonade, wine, etc.

bev-y (bev′i), *n.* [*pl.* bevies], **1,** a company, collection, or group; **2,** a flock of birds; esp. of quail or larks.

be-ware (bi-wâr′), *v.i.* and *v.t.* be on one's guard (against); be wary (of).

be-wil-der (bi-wil′dėr), *v.t.* to perplex; confuse; puzzle; as, this exam *bewildered* us.—*n.* **be-wil′der-ment.**

be-witch (bi-wich′), *v.t.* **1,** to cast a spell over as by magic; as, the fairy *bewitched* the cow; **2,** hence, to fascinate; charm.—*adj.* **be-witch′ing.**—*adv.* **be-witch′ing-ly.**

be-yond (bi-yond′), *prep.* **1,** on the farther side of; as, *beyond* the hills; **2,** farther than; past; as, *beyond* the finish line; *beyond* five o'clock; **3,** out of the reach of; as, *beyond* medical aid; **4,** outside the experience or knowledge of; too much for; as, algebra was *beyond* him:—*adv.* at a distance; yonder:—*n.* that which lies on the farther side; the hereafter.

bi- (bī-), *prefix* meaning *two*; as, *bi*annual, *bi*cycle, *bi*lingual, etc.

bi-an-nu-al (bī-an′ū-al), *adj.* occurring twice a year.—*adv.* **bi-an′nu-al-ly.**

bi-as (bī′as), *adj.* slanting; diagonal; as, a *bias* seam:—*n.* **1,** the diagonal direction of a cut, seam, or stitching made to slant across the threads of material; as, to cut a skirt on the *bias*; **2,** a leaning of the mind toward a particular thing, desire, or opinion; prejudice:—*v.t.* [biased or biassed, bias-ing or bias-sing], to give a particular direction to; influence; as, newspapers *bias* our opinions.—*adj.* **bi′ased; bi′assed.**

bib (bib), *n.* an apronlike cloth tied under a child's chin to protect the clothes; also, the upper part of an apron.

Bi-ble (bī′bl), *n.* **1,** the sacred writings of the Christian religion, consisting of the Old and New Testaments, whether in the original tongue or translated; **2,** the Old Testament, which is sacred to the Jewish religion; **3,** a book of the sacred writings of any religion, as the Koran: **bible,** any book that is accepted as the highest authority in a particular field; as, the *Canadian Encyclopedia* is the *bible* of Canadiana.—*adj.* **Bib′li-cal; bib′li-cal** (bib′li-kal).

bib-li-og-ra-phy (bib′li-og′ra-fi), *n.* a list of writings about a given subject or of a given author, publisher, etc.

bi-car-bon-ate (bī-kär′bon-āt′; -it), *n.* a salt of carbonic acid:—**sodium bicarbonate,** a white substance, in the form of powder or crystals, used as a leaven in cooking, and as a medicine.

bi-cen-ten-ni-al (bī′sen-ten′i-al), *adj.* occurring every 200 years:—*n.* a 200th anniversary or its celebration.

bi-ceps (bī′seps), *n.* [*pl.* bicepses (bī′sep-sez)], the large muscle on the front of the upper arm.

BICEPS

bi-cker (bik′ėr), *v.i.* to squabble; wrangle; as, these boys and girls *bickered* over the name of their new team:—*n.* an angry or petty dispute; a wrangle.

bi-cul-tur-al (bī′kul′chėr-al), *adj.* involving, relating to, or having two cultures.—*n.* **bi′cul′tur-al-ism.**

bi-cus-pid (bī-kus′pid), *adj.* with two points or cusps:—*n.* in humans, one of eight teeth, placed in pairs, two on each side of each jaw, between the canines and the molars. (See *dentition*, illustration.)

bi-cy-cle (bī′sik-l), *n.* a light vehicle having a metal frame, two wheels, one behind the other, and a saddlelike seat for the rider, who propels the bicycle by means of pedals, and steers it by means of a handlebar:—*v.i.* [bicy-cled, bicy-cling], to ride on a bicycle—*n.* **bi′cy-clist.**

bid (bid), *v.t.* [*p.t.* bade (bad) or, in definition **3,** bid, *p.p.* bid-den (bid′n) or, in definition **3,** bid, *p.pr.* bid-ding], **1,** to command; order; as, he *bade* me tell everything; **2,** to offer by way of greeting; say; as, to *bid* someone welcome or goodbye; also, to invite; as, he *bade* me come again; **3,** to propose as a price for something, esp. at an auction; as, he *bid* 100 dollars for the antique vase; **4,** in *cards*, to state the number of tricks one expects to take:—*v.i.* to make an offer; offer a price:—*n.* **1,** an offer of a price, as at an auction; also, the amount offered; as, a *bid* of 50 dollars; **2,** the statement of a price, or the price itself, at which a person will do a piece of work; his *bid* on the new house was $150,000; **3,** in *cards* (a) the number of tricks stated, (b) a player's turn to bid; **4,** an attempt to obtain or become; as, the premier made a *bid* for re-election.—*n.* **bid′der.**—*n.* **bid′ding.**—*adj.* **bid′da-ble.**

bide (bīd), *v.t.* [*p.t.* bode (bōd) or bid-ed, *p.p.* bid-ed, *p.pr.* bid-ing], to wait for; as, you must *bide* your time.

bi-en-ni-al (bī-en′i-al), *adj.* **1,** occurring once in two years; as, a *biennial* convention; **2,** continuing or living for two years; as, *biennial* plants:—*n.* **1,** a plant that produces roots and leaves in the first year, and flowers, fruit, and seed in the second, and then dies; **2,** an event that occurs once in two years.

biff (bif), *v.t. Colloq.* to strike:—*n.* a sharp blow, as with a fist.

bi-fo-cal (bī-fō′kal), *adj.* having two focal points, as a lens:—*n.* a lens ground to form a combination of two lenses, one for near and the other for distant objects:—**bifocals,** eyeglasses with this type of lens.

big (big), *adj.* [big-ger, big-gest], **1,** large, bulky; as, a *big* house; a *big* load; **2,** boastful; pompous; as, *big* talk; **3,** grown up; as, *big* sister; **4,** important; serious; as, a *big* issue; a *big* mistake.

big-a-my (big′a-mi), *n.* the act of marrying a person while married to another. Compare *monogamy* and *polygamy.*—*n.* **big′a-mist.**

Big-foot (big′foot), *n.* a large, hairy creature that some people believe lives in the mountains of the Pacific Northwest. Also called *Sasquatch.*

big-horn (big′hôrn′), *n.* the wild sheep of the Rocky Mountains, known for their large curling horns and sure-footedness.

big-ot (big′ut), *n.* a person who is unreasonably and obstinately attached to his or her beliefs and opinions on such subjects as religion, morals, etc.; an intolerant and prejudiced person.—*adj.* **big′ot-ed.**—*n.* **big′ot-ry.**

bike (bīk), *n. Colloq.* bicycle or motorcycle.—*n.* **bik′er.**

bi-ki-ni (bi-kē′nē), *n.* **1,** a very brief, two-piece swimsuit for women; **2,** a brief one-piece swimsuit for men; **3,** low-cut briefs for men or women.

bi-lat-er-al (bī-lat′ėr-al), *adj.* having to do with two sides or two parties; as, a *bilateral* contract.

bile (bīl), *n.* **1,** the bitter, yellow or greenish fluid secreted by the liver to aid in the digestive processes; **2,** ill humour; irritation.

bilge (bilj), *n.* **1,** the bulging part of a cask; **2,** *Colloq.* worthless remarks; nonsense; **3,** the bottom of a ship up to the point where the sides become vertical:—**bilge water,** water that gathers in the bottom of a ship, always very disagreeable in odour:—*v.i.* [bilged, bilg-ing], **1,** to spring a leak by a break in the bilge; **2,** to bulge:—*v.t.* to stave in the bottom of (a ship).

bi-lin-gual (bī-ling′gwal), *adj.* of, or using, two languages; as, Canada is a *bilingual* nation.—*n.* **bi-lin′gual-ism.**—*adv.* **bi-lin′gual-ly.**

bil-ious (bil′yus), *adj.* **1,** caused by a disorder of the liver; due to too much bile; as, a *bilious* headache; **2,** bad-tempered; peevish.—*n.* **bil′ious-ness.**

bilk (bilk), *v.t.* to evade payment (of a debt); swindle; defraud.

[1]**bill** (bil), *n.* **1,** a draft of a proposed law presented to a legislature; **2,** an account of money owed for goods sold, services given, or work done; as, a plumbing *bill;* **3,** a piece of paper money; as, a 10-dollar *bill;* **4,** a promissory note; **5,** a printed advertisement; poster; **6,** a paper giving a list of items; as, the *bill* of the races; a *bill* of fare; **7,** in law, a written complaint or accusa-

tion:—*v.t.* **1,** to advertise by posters; enter on a program; announce; as, the actor was *billed* to appear in person; **2,** to make a bill of; enter on a bill; make a list of; as, these purchases will be *billed* next month; **3,** to charge (a person); send a statement of indebtedness to; as, please *bill* me without delay; **4,** to ship by freight; as, *billed* to Toronto.

[2]**bill** (bil), *n.* **1,** the beak of a bird; **2,** a similar beak in other animals, as the jaw of a turtle:—*v.i.* to join bills; show affection; as, doves *bill* and coo.

bill-board (bil′bōrd′), *n.* a board for outdoor poster displays.

bil-let (bil′et), *n.* **1,** a written order from a military officer directing the person to whom it is addressed to furnish a soldier with board and lodging; **2,** a place where a soldier is lodged; in the war, a rest camp; **3,** a situation; appointment; as, he had a comfortable *billet* in Montreal:—*v.t.* [billet-ed, billet-ing], to quarter or lodge; as, the government *billeted* the soldiers in private homes.

bill-fold (bil′fōld′), *n.* a folding wallet for money, cards, etc.

bil-liards (bil′yėrdz), *n.* a game played with solid balls and a cue on an oblong, cloth-covered table which is bounded by a raised, cushioned ledge.

bil-lion (bil′yun), *n.* in Canada, U.S., and France, one thousand millions, written 1,000,000,000; in Britain and Germany, a million millions, written 1,000,000,000,000. —*adj.* **bil′lionth** (bil′yunth).—*n.* **bil′lion-aire′.**

Bill of Rights, a statement of human rights and basic freedoms in a country: in Canada, first passed by Parliament in 1960.

bil-low (bil′ō), *n.* a great wave or rising of something, such as a large mass of water, smoke, or steam:—*v.i.* **1,** to rise or swell in a great mass; as, steam and smoke *billowed* from the chimneys; **2,** to swell out; bulge; as, the ship's sails *billowed* in the breeze.—*adj.* **bil′low-y.**

bil-ly (bil′i), *n.* a club, esp. a policeman's.

billy goat, *n. Colloq.* a male goat.

bi-month-ly (bī-munth′li), *adj.* and *adv.* occurring or appearing every two months; loosely (and less correctly) twice a month or semimonthly.

bin (bin), *n.* a box, crib, or enclosure, used for storage; as, a laundry *bin.*

bi-na-ry code (bīn′ėr-i), *n.* in *computing*, a computer coding system that uses the digits zero and one to represent all characters. Also, **bi′na-ry num′bers; bi′na-ry sys′tem.**

bi-na-tion-al (bī′nash′un-al), *adj.* relating to or involving two nations; as, a *binational* treaty.

bind (bīnd), *v.t.* [bound (bound), bind-ing], **1,** to tie up, as with a cord or band; **2,** to hold together; confine; restrain; as, cement *binds* bricks; ice *binds* the river in winter; this shoe *binds* my foot; **3,** to hold in bonds of affection, loyalty, duty, or law; as, *bound* by friendship or by a promise; *bound* as an apprentice; **4,** to finish or protect with a band or border; as, to *bind* an edge of a garment; **5,** to bandage; **6,** to fasten together and into a cover; as, to *bind* a book:—*v.i.* **1,** to tie up something; **2,** to have the force of a duty or necessity; as, ties that *bind*; **3,** to stick together in a mass; to become hard or stiff; as, clay *binds* when heated.—*n.* **bind′ing.**

bind-er (bīn′dėr), *n.* **1,** one who binds; as, a *bookbinder*; **2,** anything that binds, as tar on roads; **3,** a hard-covered folder, usually with rings or clips, that holds loose sheets of paper; **4,** a machine that cuts and binds grain.

bind-er-y (bīn′dėr-i), *n.* [*pl.* binderies], a place where books are bound.

binge (binj), *n. Slang* a spree, as eating or drinking.

bin-go (bing′gō), *n.* a game played by drawing numbered balls, discs, etc., and covering corresponding numbers on cards.

bin-oc-u-lar (bin-ok′ū-lėr; bī-nok′ū-lėr), *adj.* adapted to the use of both eyes at the same time; as, *binocular* glasses. Also, *n.pl.* **bin-oc′u-lars** (-lėrz), a device made of two small telescopes fastened together, used with both eyes, making distant objects appear closer and larger; field or opera glasses.

bi-nom-i-al (bī-nō′mi-al), *adj.* consisting of two terms, as *x* — *a*.

bi-o- (bī′ō-), *prefix* meaning *life*; as, *bio*chemistry, *bio*chemical, *bio*chemist, *bio*degradable, *bio*graphy, *bio*logical clock, *bio*logical weapon, *bio*logy, *bio*physics, *bio*psy, etc.

bi-o-de-grad-a-ble (bī′ō-de-grā′da-bl), *adj.* able to break down, rot, or decay by a natural process; as, *biodegradable* packaging.

bio-di-ver-si-ty (bī′ō-dī-vûr′si-ti; bī′ō-di-vûr′si-ti), *n.* the variety and number of species of plants and animals in a given area; as, biological *diversity*.

bio-en-gi-neer-ing (bī′ō-en′ji-nēr′ing), *n.* **1,** the application of engineering principles to the fields of biology and medicine to develop such things as artificial organs; **2,** genetic engineering.

bi-og-ra-phy (bī-og′ra-fi; bi-og′ra-fi), *n.* [*pl.* biographies], **1,** a history of a person's life; **2,** the branch of literature dealing with the written history of people's lives.—*n.* **bi-og′ra-pher.**—*adj.* **bi′-o-graph′ic** (bī′o-graf′ik); **bi′o-graph′i-cal.**

bi-ol-o-gy (bī-ol′o-ji), *n.* the science that includes both the study of plants (*botany*) and the study of animals ... ol′o-gist.—*adj.* bi′o-log′... bi′o-log′i-cal.

bi-on-ic (bī′ō-nik), *adj.* **1,** ... body parts; **2,** relating to ... mechanical systems that fu... ing organisms or parts of living ...

bio-sphere (bī′ō-sfēr′), *n.* those p... the earth in which living organisms exi...

bio-tech-nol-o-gy (bī′ō-tek-nol′o-ji), *n.* exploration of biological processes for industrial and other processes.

bi-ped (bī′ped), *n.* an animal with two feet. Humans and birds are bipeds.

bi-plane (bī′plān′), *n.* an airplane with two main supporting surfaces, usually one above the other. Compare *monoplane.*

birch (bûrch), *n.* **1,** a kind of tree, valued for its close-grained wood, with smooth outer bark, which in some varieties may be removed in thin, papery sheets; **2,** the wood of this tree:—*adj.* made of birch.

bird (bûrd), *n.* **1,** any member of a class of warm-blooded, feathered, egg-laying animals, having wings that enable most birds to fly; **2,** any small game bird, as distinguished from a waterfowl.

bird-ie (bûr′di), *n.* **1,** a little bird; **2,** in *golf,* a score of one less than par on a hole.

bird's–eye (bûrdz′–ī′), *adj.* **1,** seen from above, as if by a flying bird; as, a *bird's-eye* view of the city; hence, general; sweeping; not detailed; as, a *bird's-eye* view of the labour problem; **2,** marked with spots resembling a bird's eye; as, *bird's-eye* maple.

birth (bûrth), *n.* **1,** the act of coming into life; as, the *birth* of the baby; **2,** origin; beginning; as, the *birth* of a republic; **3,** descent; lineage.

birth control pill, an oral contraceptive for women.

birth-day (bûrth′dā′), *n.* the day of one's birth and the date on which this day falls in later years.

birth-mark (bûrth′märk′), *n.* a mark or blemish on the skin from birth.

birth-right (bûrth′rīt′), *n.* **1,** any right, privilege, or possession to which a person is entitled by birth; **2,** the rights or inheritance of the eldest in a family.

bis-cuit (bis′kit), *n.* **1,** a flat cake of unraised bread, baked hard and dry; a cracker; **2,** in Canada, a small piece of dough, usually unsweetened, raised with baking powder or baking soda, and baked.

bi-sect (bī-sekt′), *v.t.* to cut or divide into two equal parts.—*n.* **bi-sec′tion.**—*n.* **bi-sec′tor.**

bi-sex-u-al (bī′sek′shoo͞-al), *adj.* **1,** sexually attracted to both sexes; **2,** of or relating to both sexes; **3,** having sexual characteristics of both sexes; as, earthworms are *bisexual.*

bish-op (bish′up), *n.* **1,** in a Christian church, a clergyman of high rank, who is ...of a diocese or church district; **2,** ... in playing chess.—*n.* **bish′op-**...

bi-son (bī′zn), **1,** a wild, shaggy-... animal of North America, ... *buffalo,* extinct except in ... bison appears as an ... toba coat of arms; **2,** ... now extinct except ... huania.

bisque ... soup ... thick, rich, cream ... or tomatoes; **2,** a kind of ... ining finely chopped nuts ...

¹bit (bit), *n.* **1,** a tool ... for drilling holes; **2,** the cutting blade in a carpenter's plane; **3,** the ...ol, as a ... metal mouthpiece of a bridle; **4,** the ... key that enters and works a lock.

²bit (bit), *n.* **1,** a small piece of anything; a little; as, a *bit* of bread; **2,** a little while; as, wait a *bit*:—**not a bit,** not at all; none at all.

³bit (bit), *n.* in *computing,* the smallest unit of information that can be stored and used by a computer.

⁴bit (bit), *p.t.* and *p.p.* of *bite.*

bitch (bich), *n.* **1,** the female of the dog, wolf, fox, etc.; **2,** *Slang,* anything that is difficult; as, life's a *bitch;* **3,** a complaint; as, what's your *bitch?* **4,** an unpleasant woman:—*v.i.* to complain; as, to *bitch* about a job.

bite (bīt), *v.t.* [*p.t.* bit (bit), *p.p.* bitten (bit′n) or bit, *p.pr.* bit-ing], **1,** to seize, grip, or cut with the teeth; **2,** to sting; as, a spider *bit* him; **3,** to cut into; as, the saw *bites* the wood; **4,** to cause smarting pain to; sting; as, vinegar *bites* my tongue; the cold air *bit* her cheeks; **5,** to eat into; as, acid *bites* metal:—**bite the dust,** to fall dead or dying, as in combat; be defeated:—*v.i.* **1,** to seize an object with the teeth; as, the dog *bites;* **2,** to sting or pierce; as, insects *bite;* **3,** to cut or take hold; as, the saw *bites* well; **4,** to smart; as, mustard *bites;* **5,** to take a bait; as, the fish are *biting;* **6,** to eat away; as, acid *bites*:—*n.* **1,** the act of seizing with teeth; **2,** a wound made by the teeth or by a sting; as, a mosquito *bite;* **3,** a mouthful; a slight meal; a snack; as, to grab a *bite* on the way to work; **4,** a smarting sensation.—*n.* **bit′er.**—*adj.* **bit′ing.**

bit-map (bit′map′), *n.* in *computing,* a data file that corresponds to an electronic image bit by bit.

bit-ter (bit′ėr), *adj.* **1,** sharp and unpleasant to the taste; **2,** sharp; painful; as, *bitter* cold; grievous; as, *bitter* woe; **3,** severe; sarcastic; as, *bitter* words; **4,** relentless; as, a *bitter* enemy:—*n.* **1,** that which is hard or unpleasant; as, take the *bitter* with the sweet; **2, bitters,** liquor in which herbs or roots have been soaked.—*adv.* **bit′ter-ly.**—*n.* **bit′ter-ness.**

bit-ter–sweet (bit′ėr–swēt′), *adj.* mingling

… in … ring or … *pl.* bi-week- … two weeks:— … *adj.* and *adv.* occur- … *adj.* odd; grotesque; … *v.t.* [blabbed, blab-bing], to tell … ssly:—*v.i.* to tell tales; talk too … nd unwisely:—*n.* one who lets out … ts, or tells tales.—*n.* and *v.* **blab′ber.**

black (blak), *adj.* **1,** of the colour of coal or tar; opposite of *white*; **2,** almost without light; very dark; as, a *black* cellar; **3,** dismal; as, a *black* sky; threatening; sullen; as, *black* looks; **4,** without moral goodness; evil; as, *black* deeds; **5,** indicating disgrace; as, he got a *black* mark for conduct:—**Black,** of or having to do with people of African origin; as, *Black* history:—*n.* **1,** the colour of coal or tar; **2,** a black colour or dye:—**Black,** a person with dark skin who is of African origin:—*v.t.* to blacken, as boots.—*n.* **black′ness.**

black-ball (blak′bôl′), *v.t.* to vote against, or reject, by use of a blackball; to ostracize; as, to *blackball* someone from a club.

black-ber-ry (blak′bėr-i), *n.* [*pl.* blackberries], **1,** a bramble bearing a small, dark, juicy fruit, used in jams and pies; **2,** the fruit itself.

black-bird (blak′bûrd′), *n.* **1,** an English thrush; **2,** one of several North American birds related to the bobolink, including the redwing blackbird, the yellow-headed blackbird, and the purple grackle.

black-board (blak′bōrd′), *n.* a dark, smooth surface, often of slate, to be written or drawn upon with chalk, as in school classrooms: they are now often light green or another colour rather than black. Also called *chalkboard.*

black box, 1, a flight recorder that documents the performance of an aircraft and all events in flight; **2,** *Colloq.* any device that is mysterious to the user.

Black Death. Same as **bubonic plague.**

black-en (blak′en), *v.i.* to grow black or dark:—*v.t.* **1,** to make black; **2,** to speak evil of; as, to *blacken* a person's character.

black-fly (blak′flī′), *n.* a small black or grey fly that gives a painful bite and sucks blood.

Black-foot (blak′foot′), *n.* **1,** a confederacy of three groups of Algonquian peoples (the *Blackfoot*, the *Blood*, and the *Peigan*) from the western plains; **2,** the people or language of these groups.

black-head (blak′hed′), *n.* a small plug of dark fatty matter in a pore of the face.

black hole, 1, an object or region in outer space where the inward pull of gravity is so strong that no light or matter can escape; **2,** *Colloq.* something that consumes a great deal of money and effort without offering any real benefit.

black-jack, (blak′jak′), *n.* **1,** a small, flexible club with a weighted head; **2,** a card game, the strategy of which is to get 21 points:—*v.t.* to hit with a blackjack.

black list, a list of persons, companies, etc., judged worthy of punishment, exclusion, or the like:—**black-list** (blak′list′), *v.t.* to place the name of (a person or firm) on a black list.

black magic, witchcraft; magic practised for bad or evil purposes, esp. involving spells that employ evil spirits or occult powers.

black-mail (blak′māl′), *n.* **1,** the money or favour obtained from a person by a threat to tell something bad about him or her; **2,** an attempt to get money thus:—*v.t.* to get money or favour by threats.—*n.* **black′mail′er.**

black market, 1, the illegal buying or selling of goods that are regulated or restricted; **2,** the place where this activity takes place.

black-out (blak′out′), *n.* **1,** a temporary loss of consciousness; as, the pilot suffered a *blackout* in the steep dive; **2,** the shutting down of electrical power in a certain area, usually unintentionally; as, a *blackout* caused by broken wires; **3,** putting out of all lights, intentionally, as during an air raid; **4,** censorship, as of news, etc., during a war.

black sheep, a member of a group who is considered a disgrace; an outcast; as, my great-grandfather was considered the *black sheep* of the family because he was imprisoned for selling bootleg liquor during the Depression.

black-smith (blak′smith′), *n.* a person who works in iron, by heating it in fire, and then hammering it into shape.

blad-der (blad′ėr), *n.* **1,** in humans and other animals, a sac of elastic muscle in which fluid (urine) collects, esp. the fluid secreted by the kidneys; **2,** any sac or bag containing fluid or gas.

blade (blād), *n.* **1,** the cutting part of a knife or other instrument; **2,** a long, slender leaf, as of grass; **3,** the broad part of any leaf; **4,** a broad, flat object or part; as, the shoulder *blade*; **5,** a sword or swordsman; **6,** a dashing fellow.

blame (blām), *n.* **1,** an expression of disapproval; censure; **2,** responsibility for something that goes wrong or is done wrong; as, he bears the *blame*:—*v.t.* [blamed, blaming], **1,** to find fault with; reproach; **2,** to place responsibility for; as, she *blames* her errors on her sister:—**to blame,** at fault; as, she is *to blame*.—*adj.* **blam′a-ble.**—*adj.* **blame′less.**

blanch (blånch), *v.t.* **1,** to whiten; **2,** to scald quickly, so as to remove the skin; as, to *blanch* almonds:—*v.i.* to turn pale.

bland (bland), *adj.* **1,** soft-spoken; gentle; as, a *bland* manner; **2,** mild; soothing; plain; dull; as, a *bland* diet.—*adv.* **bland′ly.**

blan-dish (blan′dish), *v.t.* to flatter; coax; wheedle.—*n.* **blan′dish-ment.**

blank (blangk), *n.* **1,** any empty space; **2,** a space to be filled in on a form or document; as, to fill in the *blanks*; **3,** a printed form with empty spaces to be filled in; as, an order *blank*; **4,** a void; as, his mind was a *blank*; **5,** a cartridge having gunpowder, but no bullet:—*adj.* **1,** free from writing or print; as, a *blank* piece of paper; **2,** without variety or interest; as, a *blank* day; **3,** without expression; as, a *blank* look; **4,** unbroken; unmarked; as, *blank* silence; a *blank* wall.—*adv.* **blank′ly.**

blan-ket (blang′kit), *n.* **1,** a soft piece of cloth, used to cover a bed, a person, or an animal; **2,** any covering or thing that covers as a blanket does; as, a waterproof *blanket*; a *blanket* of flowers:—*v.t.* to cover with, or as with, a blanket.

blare (blâr), *n.* a loud sound like that of a trumpet:—*v.i.* [blared, blar-ing], to give forth a loud, brazen sound like that of a trumpet:—*v.t.* to sound loudly; as, the radio *blared*.

blar-ney (blär′ni), *n.* wheedling flattery:—*v.t.* to win over by smooth talk:—**Blarney Stone,** a stone in the wall of Blarney Castle, in Ireland, near Cork, said to confer the gift of blarney upon those who kiss it.

bla-sé (blä′zā′), *adj.* bored; glutted, as with pleasure, etc.

blas-pheme (blas-fēm′), *v.t.* [blasphemed, blasphem-ing], to speak profanely or impiously of (God or sacred things):—*v.i.* to talk irreverently.—*n.* **blas-phem′er.**—*n.* **blas′phe-my.**—*adj.* **blas′phe-mous.**

blast (blåst), *n.* **1,** a strong gust of wind; **2,** a forcible stream of air or gas from an opening; as, a *blast* of heat from a furnace; **3,** a sudden sound, as from a wind instrument; **4,** a sudden harmful influence upon plants or animals; a blight; **5,** an explosion, as of dynamite, used in blowing up rocks; also, the charge so used:—*v.t.* **1,** to cause to fade or wither; as, a late frost *blasted* the crops; **2,** to destroy; **3,** to break or shatter by an explosive.

blast–off (blast′–ôf′), *n.* the takeoff of a rocket or spacecraft at the moment when its fuel explodes and hurls it from its launching pad:—**blast off,** *v.i.* to launch a rocket or spacecraft.

bla-tant (blā′tant), *adj.* **1,** noisy; vociferous; **2,** vulgarly conspicuous; as, a *blatant* display of wealth.—*adv.* **bla′tant-ly.**

bla-ther (bla*th*′ėr; blå-), *n.* foolish talk.—*v.t.* and *v.i.* to speak foolishly.

[1]**blaze** (blāz), *n.* **1,** a fire; bright flame; **2,** intense direct light, as of the sun; **3,** brilliant display; splendour; **4,** a sudden outbreak; as, a *blaze* of fury:—*v.i.* [blazed, blazing], **1,** to burst into flame; burn; **2,** to glow or shine like a flame; as, his eyes *blazed*; **3,** to be lighted up, as a house.

[2]**blaze** (blāz), *n.* **1,** a white spot on the face of an animal; **2,** a mark made on a tree by removing a piece of the bark:—*v.t.* [blazed, blaz-ing], **1,** to mark (a tree), by chipping off bark; **2,** to indicate (a trail) by marking trees in this way.

blaz-er (blāz′ėr), *n.* a sports jacket for men; a similar jacket for women.

bla-zon (blā′zn), *n.* a showy display:—*v.t.* to proclaim; as, he *blazoned* the news abroad.

bleach (blēch), *v.t.* to whiten by a chemical process or by exposing to the sun's rays:—*v.i.* to become white:—*n.* the process of whitening or bleaching; also, a chemical used in the process.

bleach-ers (blēch′ėrz), *n.pl.* a roofless or temporary stand providing cheap seats at a game, such as baseball.

bleak (blēk), *adj.* **1,** exposed to wind and cold; desolate; unsheltered; as, a *bleak* house; **2,** piercing cold, as a wind; **3,** cheerless; as, a *bleak* day.—*n.* **bleak′ness.**

blear-y (blēr′i), *adj.* sore or dim from a watery discharge; as, *bleary* eyes:—**blear,** *v.t.* **1,** to make (the eyes) sore or watery; **2,** to dim or obscure (the sight).—*adj.* **blear′y–eyed′.**

bleat (blēt), *n.* the cry of a sheep, goat, or calf; also, any similar cry:—*v.i.* to utter any such cry.

bleed (blēd), *v.i.* [bled (bled), bleed-ing], **1,** to give forth or to lose blood; **2,** to lose sap or juice; as, the tree *bled* from trimming; **3,** to be filled with sympathy or pity; as, my heart *bleeds* for you:—*v.t.* **1,** to take blood or sap from; **2,** *Colloq.* to extort money from.

blem-ish (blem′ish), *n.* any defect or flaw; as, *blemishes* on a face:—*v.t.* to injure; mar; disfigure.

blend (blend), *v.t.* [blend-ed or blent (blent), blend-ing], to mix together, as colours, liquids, teas, ingredients, etc., so as to secure a certain quality or flavour:—*v.i.* to mingle; as, oil and water do not *blend*; merge; harmonize:—*n.* **1,** a thorough mixture; **2,** a shading or merging, as of one colour or flavour into another; **3,** a word that is made by joining parts of two or more words together, as "brunch."

blend-ed family (blend′ed), *n.* a family

consisting of children from more than one marriage; a step family.

bless (bles), *v.t.* [blessed or blest (blest), bless-ing], **1,** to make or declare holy; as, God *blessed* the seventh day; **2,** to call down the favour of God upon; as, the priest *blessed* the altar; **3,** to give happiness or favour to; as, to *bless* us with your sweet smile; **4,** to praise; extol; as, *bless* the Lord.—*adj.* **bless′ed.**—*n.* **bless′ed-ness.**

bless-ing (bles′ing), *n.* **1,** the favour of God; **2,** a prayer of thanks for such favour, as at a meal; a benediction; **3,** something that makes for happiness or well-being; as, good health is a *blessing.*

blew (blo͞o), *p.t.* of *blow.*

blight (blīt), *n.* **1,** any disease that causes plants to wither or decay; **2,** insects, fungi, or the like, which cause such a disease; **3,** anything that brings about ruin or decay; as, the *blight* of poverty:—*v.t.* to cause to wither; destroy.

blimp (blimp), *n. Colloq.* a small, motor-driven balloon; a dirigible.

blind (blīnd), *adj.* **1,** sightless; **2,** unable or unwilling to understand, judge, or realize; as, *blind* to one's own faults; **3,** heedless; unthinking; as, *blind* haste; **4,** without reason; as, *blind* instinct; **5,** hidden; as, a *blind* ditch; difficult to follow; as, a *blind* path; **6,** without an opening or outlet; as, a *blind* wall; a *blind* alley:—*n.* **1,** anything designed to obstruct vision, or light, as a window shade; **2,** something to mislead the eye or the understanding; a trick; **3,** a place or means of concealment, as in hunting:—*v.t.* **1,** to deprive of sight; also, to dazzle; as, the sunlight *blinded* him; **2,** to deprive of judgment; as, hate *blinded* him.—*adv.* **blind′ly.**—*n.* **blind′ness.**

blind-er (blīn′dėr), *n.* a blinker in a horse's bridle that prevents it from seeing objects beside or behind it.

blind-fold (blīnd′fōld′), *n.* a piece of cloth or other material tied to cover the eyes so the person can't see:—*v.t.* to cover the eyes of, as with a bandage:—*adv.* **1,** with the eyes covered and unable to see; as, to walk *blindfold*; **2,** without thinking clearly; hence, heedless; reckless; as, *blindfold* extravagance.

blind-side (blīnd′sīd′), *v.t.* [blind-sid-ed, blind-sid-ing], **1,** to surprise, startle, or take advantage of; as, she *blindsided* us with her plan to take over the project herself; **2,** to attack unexpectedly from the weak or unguarded side.—*adj.* **blind′sid′ed.**

blind spot, 1, an area of poor visibility; a spot where vision is poor; as, a *blind spot* in a car or on a hill; **2,** a subject about which a person is ignorant or prejudiced; **3,** the area of the retina that is insensitive to light.

blink (blingk), *v.i.* **1,** to wink quickly; **2,** to see through half-shut eyes; as, to *blink* at the sun; **3,** to twinkle; glimmer:—*v.t.* **1,** to wink (the eyes) rapidly; also, to turn (lights) off and on rapidly; **2,** to close the mind to:—*n.* **1,** a rapid winking; **2,** a glimmer, as of light.

blink-er (blingk′ėr), *n.* **1,** a leather flap placed one on each side of a horse's bridle to prevent it from seeing objects beside or behind it; a blinder; **2,** a blinking light used as a warning signal, as at a crossing.

blip (blip), *n.* **1,** a glowing spot on a radar screen to mark the position of an airplane, submarine, etc.; **2,** a temporary phenomenon; as, a *blip* in the economic recovery; **3,** a high-pitched electronic sound; a bleep.

bliss (blis), *n.* great happiness; perfect joy.—*adj.* **bliss′ful.**—*adv.* **bliss′ful-ly.**

blister (blis′tėr), *n.* **1,** a small bladderlike swelling of the skin, containing watery fluid, resulting from a burn, friction, etc.; **2,** any similar swelling, as of the surface of a leaf, or of paint, an air bubble in glass, etc.:—*v.t.* to cause blisters to rise on:—*v.i.* to become covered with blisters.

blithe (blī*th*), *adj.* gay; joyous; cheery; happy; as, a *blithe* spirit.—*adv.* **blithe′ly.**—*adj.* **blithe′some.**

blith-er-ing (bli*th*′ėr-ing), *adj.* talking nonsense; as, a *blithering* idiot.

blitz (blits), *n.* a lightning attack, as by use of tanks, bombs, aircraft, etc.; any such attack, campaign, or effort, esp. by propaganda; as, an advertising *blitz*:—*v.t.* to attack swiftly and violently.

bliz-zard (bliz′ėrd), *n.* a furious windstorm accompanied by fine driving snow and extreme cold.

bloat (blōt), *v.t.* **1,** to cause to swell, as with water or air; **2,** hence, to inflate; make vain; as, *bloated* with pride.

blob (blob), *n.* a drop of a thick liquid; as, a *blob* of paint; a daub or splash of colour:—*v.t.* to splotch, as with blobs.

bloc (blok), *n.* a coalition of (political, racial, or other) groups for a common purpose; as, the Communist *bloc.*

block (blok), *n.* **1,** a solid piece of wood, stone, metal, etc.; **2,** a form for moulding or shaping articles, as hats; **3,** the solid piece of wood on which an executioner chops off the heads; **4,** a stand on which articles are put up for sale by an auctioneer; **5,** a grooved pulley in a frame: often called *pulley block*; **6,** a connected row of houses or shops; a large building divided into separate houses or shops; **7,** a part of a city bounded by four streets: also called *square*; also, the length of one side of such a square; **8,** a number or section of things taken as a unit; as, a *block* of theatre seats; **9,** an obstacle; hindrance; hence, standstill; as, a road*block*:—*v.t.* **1,** to secure or hold up, as by square wooden supports; **2,** to obstruct; hinder; as, do not *block* my way; to *block* up the drain; **3,** to mould on a form; as, to *block* hats; **4,** to outline roughly; plan without details; **5,** in *football* or *basketball*, to check the progress of, or interfere with (an opponent or his play).—*n.* **block′age.**

block-ade (blok-ād′), *n.* the shutting up of a place, as a port, by ships or troops in order to prevent anything from coming in or going out, in the hope of forcing surrender:—**blockade runner,** a ship that evades the enemy's blockade:—*v.t.* [blockad-ed, blockad-ing], to surround (a place) with a blockade.

block-bust-er (blok′bus′tėr), *n.* **1,** something that is extremely successful; as, the play *The Producers* is a *blockbuster*; the *Star Wars* movies were *blockbusters*; **2,** a large, high-explosive bomb capable of destroying large areas:—*adj.* pertaining to a blockbuster; as, a *blockbuster* musical.

block heater, a small electrical heater mounted in the block of an engine to make starting easier in extremely cold weather.

block-house (blok′hous′), *n.* a fort, built of heavy timber, often made with a projecting upper storey, and with loopholes in the walls through which to shoot.

Bloc Québécois (blok′ kā′be′kwä′), *n.* a Canadian federal political party, made up of MPs from Québec, that advocates the separation of Québec from Canada.

blond or **blonde** (blond), *adj.* having light hair and fair skin; fair in colouring.—*n.masc.* **blond.**—*n.fem.* **blonde.**

blood (blud), *n.* **1,** in humans and other animals, the red fluid that circulates through the body, supplying it with nourishment and oxygen, and carrying away waste matter; **2,** kinship; relationship; as, near in *blood*; **3,** descent; esp., noble or royal lineage; as, a prince of the *blood*; **4,** bloodshed; violence; as, deeds of *blood*; **5,** a man of fire and spirit; as, a young *blood*; **6,** temper; anger; as, bad *blood* between them:—**in cold blood,** without feeling; in a cruel and deliberate way. Also, **blood′bank′; blood′bath′; blood count; blood donor; blood group** or **type; blood heat; blood′less′; blood money; blood plasma; blood poisoning; blood sugar; blood test; blood vessel.**

blood-cur-dling (blud′kûr′dling), *n.* frightening; terrifying.

blood-hound (blud′hound′), *n.* **1,** a powerful hound with long drooping ears, famous for its acute sense of smell, and used chiefly in tracking criminals; **2,** a person keen in pursuit; a detective.

BLOODHOUND

blood pressure, the amount of force that the blood has as it presses against the walls of the arteries while being pumped by the heart: blood pressure that is too high or too low can be dangerous to one's health.

blood-shed (blud′shed′), *n.* the shedding of blood, esp. of human beings; slaughter.

blood-shot (blud′shot′), *adj.* red and inflamed; as, *bloodshot* eyes.

blood-thirs-ty (blud′thûrs′ti), *adj.* cruel; murderous.

blood-y (blud′i), *adj.* [blood-i-er, blood-i-est], **1,** stained or running with blood; as, a *bloody* field; **2,** bleeding; as, a *bloody* nose; **3,** marked by much bloodshed; as, a *bloody* fight:—*v.t.* [bloodied, bloody-ing], to stain with blood.—*n.* **blood′i-ness.**

bloom (blo͞om), *n.* **1,** a blossom or flower; **2,** the state of being in flower or having flowers; as, the tulips are in *bloom*; **3,** a state or period of health and beauty; prime; as, the *bloom* of youth; **4,** a delicate, waxy, or powdery coating on certain fruits or leaves; **5,** a rosy flush on the cheeks:—*v.i.* **1,** to produce blossoms; flower; **2,** to glow with youth and freshness; flourish.

bloom-er (blo͞om′ėr), *n.* **1,** a fully developed or mature person; as, a late *bloomer*; **2,** *pl.* girls' or women's underpants, pyjama bottoms, etc.; **3,** *pl.* a short skirt and loose trousers gathered below the knee, formerly used by women for gymnastics.

bloop-er *n.* (blo͞o′pėr), *n.* **1,** an embarrassing mistake, esp. one made in public; a faux pas; **2,** in *baseball*, a fly ball that just barely reaches the outfield, or a soft, high-arching pitch.

blos-som (blos′um), *n.* **1,** the flower of a plant; **2,** the state of being in bloom; as, trees in *blossom*:—*v.i.* **1,** to put forth flowers; **2,** to flourish, grow, or develop; as, to *blossom* into an artist.

blot (blot), *n.* **1,** a spot or stain; **2,** a spot on the reputation; disgrace:—*v.t.* [blot-ted, blot-ting], **1,** to spot or stain, as with ink; **2,** to dishonour; stain with disgrace; **3,** to dry something with absorbent paper; as to *blot* the spill with a paper towel:—**blot out, 1,** to cancel; as, to *blot out* an obligation; **2,** to destroy utterly; as, Pompeii was *blotted out*; **3,** to darken or hide; as, a cloud *blots out* the moon:—*v.i.* to become blotted.

blotch (bloch), *n.* **1,** a large irregular spot, as of ink; **2,** a disfiguring spot or blemish on the skin:—*v.t.* to mark or disfigure with spots.—*adj.* **blotch′y.**

blouse (blouz; blous), *n.* an article of women's or girls' clothing, similar to a shirt, worn on the upper body.

¹blow (blō), *v.t.* [*p.t.* blew (blo͞o), *p.p.* blown (blōn), *p.pr.* blow-ing], **1,** to cause to move or send forward by a current of air; as, the wind *blows* the paper about; **2,** to force air upon, with the mouth or otherwise; as, *blow* out the light; **3,** to make or shape by causing to swell with air; as, to *blow* bubbles; **4,** to cause to sound by forcing air or steam through, as a wind instrument or a whistle; **5,** to clear by forcing air through, as a tube or a nostril; **6,** to shatter by explosives; also, to melt, by an electric overcharge, as a fuse; **7,** *Slang* to spend freely, as money:—*v.i.* **1,** to move flowingly, as the wind; **2,** to send forth air; send up a spout of water, as whales do in breathing out; **3,** to give forth sound when air or steam is forced through; as, the whistle *blew*; **4,** to pant; breathe with quick gasps; **5,** to be moved or carried by the wind; as, the curtains are *blowing*; **6,** *Colloq.* to brag:—*n.* a gale:—**blown,** *adj.*; as, *blown* glass. Also, **blow dryer.**

[2]**blow** (blō), *n.* **1,** a hard stroke with the hand or with a weapon; **2,** a calamity. Also, **blow′off′, blow′pipe′, blow′torch′, blow′up′.**

blow-er (blō′ėr), *n.* a device for producing an air current; as, a leaf *blower*.

blow-hole (blō′hōl′), *n.* **1,** a hole on the top of the head of a whale and some other animals used for breathing; **2,** a hole in the ice through which whales, seals, and other sea mammals are able to breath.

blow-out (blō′out′), *n.* the bursting of something, as a tire, caused by too much pressure from within.

blub-ber (blub′ėr), *v.i.* to weep noisily:—*v.t.* to utter sobbingly:—*n.* **1,** a noisy weeping; **2,** the fat of whales and some other animals.

bludg-eon (bluj′un), *n.* a short, heavy-headed stick used as a weapon:—*v.t.* to strike with, or as with, a club.—*n.* **bludg′eon-ing.**

blue (bloo͞; blū), *adj.* [blu-er, blu-est], **1,** of the colour of the clear sky; azure; **2,** gloomy; sad; dismal; as, the sad news made her *blue*; **3,** discoloured; as, my nose was *blue* with cold:—*n.* **1,** the colour between green and violet; **2,** a dye or powder that colours blue; **3, the blue,** the sky; the sea; **4, blues: a,** *Colloq.* usually with *the*, melancholy; low spirits; **b,** a melancholy kind of folk–song; a type of jazz, originated from Black spiritual songs:—*v.t.* [blued, blu-ing, or blue-ing], **1,** to make or dye the colour of the clear sky, or any hue like it; **2,** to treat with bluing.—*n.* **blue′ness.**

blue-ber-ry (bloo͞′-; blū′ber-i), *n.* [*pl.* blue-ber-ries], **1,** a shrub of the heath family, bearing round, blue, edible berries; **2,** the berry.

blue-bird (bloo͞′-; blū′bûrd′), *n.* a songbird of the thrush family: the male has a blue back.

blue box, a plastic container, often blue in colour, used to collect recyclable material.

blue–col-lar (bloo͞′–kol′ėr), *adj.* of or relating to industrial or manual workers who do not wear white shirts; working class; also, this type of attitude.

blue-grass (bloo͞′-; blū′gras′), *n.* **1,** a valuable pasture and lawn grass with slender, bluish-grey stems; **2,** a type of country music.

blue-jay (bloo͞′jā′), *n.* a bird of eastern North America, with bright blue plumage and a handsome crest, noted for its noisy, scolding cry.

blue line, one of two lines on a hockey rink midway between the centre-ice red line and the goal lines.

Blue-nose (bloo͞′-; blū′nōz′), *n.* **1,** a native of the Canadian maritime provinces, esp. Nova Scotia; **2,** the name of a famous Nova Scotian schooner, which was never defeated as the holder of the International Fisherman's Trophy, given to the fastest sailing vessel in the North Atlantic fishing fleets.

blue-print (bloo͞′print′), *n.* **1,** a copy of a building plan, map, or drawing, originally white lines on blue paper, but now often blue or black lines on white; **2,** any detailed plan or outline; as, a *blueprint* of the new school curriculum:—*v.t.* to make a blueprint or a detailed plan.

[1]**bluff** (bluf), *n.* **1,** a high, steep bank, cliff, or headland; **2,** a grove or clump of trees in the prairie provinces:—*adj.* **1,** rising steeply or boldly, as a cliff; **2,** abrupt but hearty in manner.—*n.* **bluff′ness.**

[2]**bluff** (bluf), *v.t.* and *v.i.* **1,** to mislead or fool (someone) by assuming a bold front or bold speech; **2,** to accomplish or attempt by pretence or bravado; as, to *bluff* a test:—*n.* **1,** a show of pretended confidence, knowledge, etc.; **2,** one who bluffs.—*n.* **bluff′er.**

blu-ing or **blue-ing** (bloo͞′ing), *n.* a bluish preparation used in laundering to make clothes white.

blun-der (blun′dėr), *n.* a stupid or careless mistake:—*v.i.* **1,** to make a mistake from stupidity, ignorance, etc.; **2,** to move clumsily, as in a dark room.—*n.* **blun′der-er.**

blunt (blunt), *adj.* **1,** having a thick or rounded edge or point; not sharp; as, *blunt* scissors; **2,** dull; not quick-witted; not sensitive; **3,** abrupt in speech or manner; plain-spoken:—*v.t.* **1,** to dull the edge or point of; as, to *blunt* a knife; **2,** to make less keen; as, fatigue *blunted* his wits.—*adv.* **blunt′ly.**—*n.* **blunt′ness.**

blur (blûr), *v.t.* [blurred, blur-ring], **1,** to make indistinct; as, fog *blurred* the road ahead; **2,** to dim (the senses or judgment); **3,** to stain; blemish; as, to *blur* a paper with blots:—*n.* **1,** a smudge; smear, as of ink; **2,** an indistinct or confused effect; as, the page was a *blur* to his tired eyes.

blurb (blûrb), *n.* *Colloq.* an announcement, esp. one of praise, as on a book jacket.

blurt (blûrt), *v.t.* to utter suddenly and impulsively; as, to *blurt* out a secret.

blush (blush), *v.i.* **1,** to become red in the face, as from shame, excitement, or confusion; 2, to feel shame; as, she *blushed* for his ignorance:—*n.* **1,** a reddening of the face from any emotion; **2,** a rosy tint; as, the *blush* of dawn.

blus-ter (blus′tėr), *v.i.* **1,** to blow gustily, as wind; to be rough and windy, as the weather; **2,** to talk in a noisy, threatening style:—*n.* **1,** the noise and violence of a storm, or of a high wind; **2,** noisy talk; empty threats.—*adj.* **blus′ter-y.**

B.N.A. Act, short for **British North America Act.**

bo-a (bō′a), *n.* **1,** a large, non-poisonous snake that crushes its prey by coiling around it, such as the boa constrictor, *anaconda*, and *python*; **2,** a long fur or feather scarf for women.

boar (bōr), *n.* a male pig; **2,** a wild hog found in Europe, Africa, and Asia.

board (bōrd), *n.* **1,** a thin, flat piece of sawn timber, longer than it is broad; **2,** a table for food, or spread with food; **3,** food; meals served, esp. at a fixed price; **4,** a group of persons with power to act or advise; as, a school *board*; **5,** pasteboard, as for a book cover; **6,** a flat piece of wood or other material prepared for a definite use; as, a diving *board*; an ironing *board*; a chess *board*:—**on board**, on a plane, train, bus, ship, or other conveyance:—*v.t.* **1,** to cover with boards; **2,** to furnish with food, or food and lodging, in return for money; as, to *board* students; **3,** to cause to be lodged and fed, as a horse at a stable; **4,** to get on (a plane, bus, ship, or train):—*v.i.* to get meals, or meals and lodging, regularly, at a fixed charge; as, I *board* at my aunt's.—*n.* **board′er.** Also, **board′ inghouse′; board′ing school′; board′room′; board′walk′.**

boast (bōst), *v.i.* to brag; praise oneself or one's belongings or deeds in loud terms; to exult:—*v.t.* to possess as a thing to be proud of; as, he *boasted* a fine ranch:—*n.* **1,** a proud, vainglorious speech; bragging; **2,** a cause of pride or vanity; as, his garden was his *boast*.—*n.* **boast′er.**—*adj.* **boast′ful.**—*adv.* **boast′ful-ly.**

boat (bōt), *n.* **1,** any kind of small open watercraft, named according to the power by which it moves; as, row*boat*; sail*boat*; motor*boat*; also, a ship; **2,** a long, narrow dish; as, a gravy *boat*:—*v.i.* to ride in a small open vessel; row; sail.—*n.* **boat′ing.** Also, **boat′house′; boat′load′.**

bob (bob), *n.* **1,** a jerking movement, as of the head; also, a curtsy; **2,** a weight, as on a pendulum or a plumb line; also, a cork or float on a fishing line; **3,** a style of haircut, shoulder length or shorter, for women or children; **4,** a bobsled:—*v.t.* [bobbed, bob-bing], **1,** to move (the head) with short jerky motions; **2,** to cut (a woman's or child's hair) to shoulder length or shorter:—*v.t.* **1,** to move jerkily; also, to curtsy; **2,** to fish with a float on the line.

bob-bin (bob′in), *n.* a spool or reel around which thread or yarn is wound.

bobby pin (bob′i pin′), *n.* a flat, wire hairpin with closed prongs.

bob-cat (bob′kat′), *n.* a lynx; wildcat.

bob-o-link (bob′o-lingk), *n.* a North and South American songbird.

bob-sled (bob′sled′), *n.* a long sled having two sets of runners, a steering wheel, and brakes, which moves on a steep, curving course made of icy snow:—*v.i.* [bob-sled-ded, bob-sled-ding], to ride or coast on a bobsled.

bob-tail (bob′tāl′), *n.* **1,** a short tail or a tail cut short; **2,** hence, an animal with such a tail.—*adj.* **bob′tailed′.**

bob-white (bob′hwīt′), *n.* **1,** a species of quail or partridge; **2,** its cry.

bode (bōd), *v.t.* [bod-ed, bod-ing], to be a sign or omen of; betoken; as, his lack of perseverance *bodes* ill for his future.

bod-ice (bod′is), *n.* **1,** the upper part of a woman's dress; **2,** a laced and often tight-fitting garment worn over a blouse or shirt.

bod-i-ly (bod′i-li), *adj.* having material form; belonging to the body; having to do with the body; as, *bodily* warmth:—*adv.* completely; in one body; as a whole; as, the class was sent out *bodily*.

body (bod′i), *n.* [*pl.* bodies], **1,** the physical form and substance of a person or an animal, living or dead; **2,** the trunk or main portion of a person, animal, or plant; also, the greater part of anything; as, the *body* of a letter; **3,** a person; as, she is a good *body*; **4,** a group of persons or things; as, a legislative *body*; a *body* of facts; the student *body*; **5,** a mass of matter; as, a heavenly *body*; **6,** consistency; substance; as, her hair has very little *body*.

bod-y-guard (bod′i-gärd′), *n.* a guard, of one or more, to protect a person; as, the president's *bodyguard*.

body language, communication by humans or animals through the movement or placement of the body or parts of the body, such as facial expressions or posture; as, to flirt using *body language*.

body shop, a garage that specializes in the repair of automobile bodies.

bog (bog), *n.* wet, spongy ground composed of partially decayed vegetation; a quagmire; marsh:—*v.i.* and *v.t.* [bogged, bog-ging], to sink, or cause to sink, in wet ground, or as if in a bog; to mire or hamper; as, to get *bogged* down with work.—*adj.* **bog′gy.**

bo-gan (bō′gan), *n.* a small bay, cove, or inlet (Canadian Atlantic provinces).

bo-gey (bō′gi), *n.* **1,** in *golf*, one stroke above par on a hole; **2,** a phantom, hobgoblin, or evil spirit.

bog-gle (bog′l), *v.i.* **1,** to shy away; as, the horse *boggled* at the jump; **2,** to hesitate or demur; **3,** to be overwhelmed; as, her mind *boggled* at the amount of homework she had to do:—*v.t.* **1,** to bungle; **2,** to overwhelm with wonder; as, the amount of information on the Internet *boggles* the mind.

bo-gus (bō′gus), *adj.* counterfeit; not genuine; sham; as, *bogus* money.

[1]**boil** (boil), *v.i.* **1,** to bubble from the action of heat; throw off bubbles of vapour; **2,** to be cooked in boiling water; **3,** to be violently agitated; seethe, as if boiling; **4,** to be excited, as by anger:—*v.t.* **1,** to heat (a liquid) to the boiling point, or temperature at which vapour rises in bubbles; **2,** to cook in a boiling liquid:—*n.* a bubbling from the effect of heat; as, the water came to a *boil.*—*adj.* **boiled**; as, *boiled* potatoes, *boiled* eggs.

[2]**boil** (boil), *n.* an inflamed, festering sore in the skin, caused by infection.

boil-er (boil′ėr), *n.* **1,** a strong metal vessel in which steam is produced, as for driving engines; **2,** a tank for storing hot water; **3,** a vessel in which things are boiled.

boil-er-plate (boil′ėr-plāt′), *n.* **1,** an unoriginal, standard, formulaic language; **2,** the steel plate used to make boilers.

bois-ter-ous (bois′tėr-us), *adj.* **1,** stormy; rough; as, a *boisterous* sea; **2,** noisily cheerful; as, *boisterous* laughter.—*adv.* **bois′ter-ous-ly.**—*n.* **bois′ter-ous-ness.**

bold (bōld), *adj.* **1,** courageous; fearless; as, a *bold* knight; **2,** steep; abrupt; as, a *bold* headland; **3,** clear; well-marked; as, *bold* strokes of a pen; **4,** showing courage or daring in thought or expression; as, *bold* ideas; **5,** audacious; rude; as, a *bold* child.—*adv.* **bold′ly.**—*n.* **bold′ness.**

bold-face, *n.* in *printing*, a type with thick, heavy lines; as, the entries in this dictionary are in *boldface.*—*adj.* **bold′faced′.**

bo-ler-o (bō-lâr′ō), *n.* **1,** a short, open, waist-length vest or jacket; **2,** a lively Spanish dance in 3/4 time.

bole (bōl), *n.* the trunk of a tree.

boll (bōl), *n.* the seed pod of a plant, as of cotton:—**boll weevil**, a greyish beetle that lays its eggs on cotton bolls, causing serious damage to the crop.

bo-lo-gna (bo-lo′nyå; bo-lō′nå), *n.* a sausage or sandwich meat of mixed beef, pork, chicken, or turkey, encased in a skin.

bo-lo-ney (bo-lō′ni), *n. Colloq.* **1,** bologna sausage; **2,** *interj. Slang* nonsense.

bolster (bōl′stėr), *n.* a long pillow; also, a cushioned pad or support:—*v.t.* to support; also, to boost or reinforce; as, to *bolster* her spirits.

bolt (bōlt), *n.* **1,** a short, heavy-headed arrow for a crossbow; a dart; **2,** hence, anything coming swiftly or suddenly; as, a *bolt* of lightning; **3,** a metal pin or rod for fastening together parts of machinery, furniture, etc., threaded to hold a nut; **4,** a sliding catch for a door or gate; that part of a lock that is shot or drawn back by the key; **5,** a roll of cloth, wallpaper, etc.; **6,** a sudden dashing or darting away, as of a horse; **7,** in politics, to withdraw support from one's own party:—*v.t.* **1,** to fasten with a sliding catch, as a door; **2,** to fasten together with bolts, as metal plates; **3,** to swallow (food) very rapidly, or without chewing; **4,** in politics, to break away from (one's party):—*v.i.* to dash away suddenly:—*adv.* stiffly.

bomb (bom; bum), *n.* a hollow iron ball or shell filled with an explosive, which may be exploded by a time fuse, or by the force with which it strikes:—*v.t.* to attack with bombs; drop bombs on; bombard. Also, **bomb′ shel′ter; bomb′ squad′.**

bom-bard (bom-bärd′; bum-bärd′), *v.t.* **1,** to attack with cannon, gunfire, or bombs; **2,** to assail persistently; as, they *bombarded* our neighbourhood with flyers.—*n.* **bom-bard′ment.**

bom-bas-tic (bom-bas′tik), *adj.* pompous; high-sounding.

bomb-er (bom′ėr), *n.* a heavy airplane, used in offensive warfare for dropping bombs; also, a person who bombs; as, a terrorist *bomber*.

bomb-shell (bom′shel′), *n.* **1,** an explosive missile; **2,** a devastating effect; as, his death came as a *bombshell*; **3,** something or someone that is amazing or stunning; as, Marilyn Monroe was considered to be a *bombshell*.

bo-na fi-de (bō′na fīd′; bō′na fī′dē), in good faith; genuine; without deceit.

bo-nan-za (bō-nan′za), *n. Colloq.* a lucky speculation.

bond (bond), *n.* **1,** that which fastens or confines; **2, bonds**, fetters; chains; imprisonment; **3,** a force or an influence that unites; as, the *bond* of kinship; **4,** an agreement binding a person to pay a certain sum of money, if certain conditions are not fulfilled; **5,** a certificate issued and sold by a corporation or government, and promising to pay the purchaser a specified sum by a certain date, with interest, usually in instalments; **6,** a guarantee that owners of goods, liable to a tax and held in a warehouse pending disposal, will pay the tax when the goods are removed:—*v.t.* **1,** to join something with a bond; **2,** to place under the conditions of a bond; as, the firm *bonded* its employees; **3,** to put (goods) into a bonded warehouse; **4,** to mortgage (property). Also, **bond′-hold′er′; bonds′man′; bonds′wo′man.**

bond-age (bon′dij), *n.* slavery; servitude.

bone (bōn), *n.* **1,** the hard, whitish material of which the skeleton of humans and other animals with backbones is composed; **2,** one of the separate pieces of this skeleton; **3,** a substance similar to bone; **4,** a piece of bone with meat on it; as, a soup *bone*:—*v.t.* [boned, bon-ing], to remove the bones from; as, to *bone* a chicken.

bon-fire (bon′fīr′), *n.* a large, outdoor fire.

bonk-ers (bông′kėrz), *n. Slang,* crazy.

bon-net (bon′it), *n.* **1,** a head covering worn by children; usually brimless, with ribbons or strings tied under the chin; also, a similar head covering formerly worn by women and girls; **2,** in Scotland, a soft woollen cap worn by men.

bon-spiel (bon′spēl′), *n.* a curling match (of clubs, towns, provinces, etc.).

bo-nus (bō′nus), *n.* a sum paid over and above what is strictly due.

bon-y (bōn′i), *adj.* [bon-i-er, bon-i-est], **1,** made of bone; like bone; as, *bony* tissue; **2,** full of bones, as a fish; **3,** having prominent bones; as, a *bony* arm; **4,** thin; gaunt; emaciated.

boo (bo͞o), *interj.* a sound to express scorn or disapproval, or to startle.—*v.t.* and *v.i.* [booed (bo͞od), boo-ing], to utter *boo*.

boo-by (bo͞o′bi), *n.* **1,** a stupid person; dunce; nitwit; **2,** in *games,* the player with the poorest score; as, he won the *booby* prize. Also, **boo′by hatch′; boo′by trap′.**

boo-gie–woo-gie (bo͞o′gi–wo͞o′gi), *n.* a jazz style of blues played (on the piano) with persistent bass rhythms.

book (book), *n.* a collection of sheets of paper or other writing material, fastened or bound together, and enclosed in a cover; **2,** a volume containing a composition of some length or a number of shorter ones; as, a text*book*; a *book* of verse; **3,** a main division, section, or part of a literary composition; as, a *book* of the Bible; **4,** in bridge, a minimum of six tricks, after which the counting of tricks won begins; **5,** in horse racing, a list of horses entered and the bets laid on them:—**the Book,** the Bible:—*v.t.* **1,** to record or register; as, to *book* an order; **2,** to engage beforehand; as, to *book* a caterer.—*adj.* **book′ish.**—*n.* **book′ish-ness.** Also, **book′ binder; book′case′; book′ends′; book′ jack′et; book′ lore′; book′ma′ker; book′man; book′mark′; book′sel′ler; book′store′.**

bookkeep-ing (book′kēp′ing), *n.* the work of recording business transactions in an orderly manner; the keeping of accounts.—*n.* **book′ keep′er.**

book-let (book′let), *n.* a small book with few pages, usually with a thin paper cover.

book-mark (book′märk′), *n.* **1,** something placed between the pages of a book to mark the reader's place; **2,** in *computing,* a shortcut to an Internet site stored in the Web browser software that allows you to return to a particular Web page:—*v.t.* to use a bookmark or as a bookmark.

book-worm (book′wûrm), *n.* **1,** an insect larva that feeds on the paste or leaves of books; **2,** a person very fond of books and reading.

Bool-e-an logic (bo͞o′lē-en), *n.* in *computing,* a system of symbolic logic devised by George Boole that allows computer users to limit their searches by using the words "and," "or," and "not."

¹boom (bo͞om), *n.* **1,** a long pole or spar attached to a ship's mast to extend the bottom of a sail; **2,** a similar pole attached to a derrick's mast to support or guide the load; **3,** a long pole that holds a microphone for making TV shows and movies; **4,** a chain or line of connected floating timbers used on a river to keep logs from drifting away; **5,** a large raft of logs being towed over water.

²boom (bo͞om), *n.* a deep, rumbling sound, as the roar of breakers or thunder:—*v.i.* and *v.t.* to make, or utter with, such a sound.

³boom (bo͞om), *n.* **1,** a sudden increase of business activity or in prices; also, rapid growth, as in population; as, there was a *boom* after World War II; **2,** a vigorous endorsement for office; as, a *boom* for president:—*v.i.* to grow or rise rapidly; become suddenly prosperous; as, the town *boomed* when gold was found:—*v.t.* to advertise (a town or a product) widely and actively; to advocate (a candidate) with vigour.

boom-er-ang (bo͞om′ėr-ang), *n.* **1,** a bent, flat piece of wood, originally used as a weapon by Australian natives, which, when thrown in a certain manner, returns to the thrower: now used mainly for sport; **2,** hence, anything that recoils to the disadvantage of its author.

BOOMERANG

¹boon (bo͞on), *n.* a favour; gift; blessing.

²boon (bo͞on), *adj.* jovial; merry; as, a *boon* companion.

boon-docks (bo͞on′doks′), *n.pl. Colloq.* the backwoods; rough, remote, or undeveloped area. Also called *boonies.*

boon-dog-gle (bo͞on′dog′l), *n. Colloq.* unnecessary and wasteful work that accomplishes very little, esp. government projects established for patronage purposes:—*v.i.* [boon-dog-gled, boon-dog-gling], to do unecessary and wasteful work; as, to procrastinate by *boondoggling.*

boon-ies (bo͞o′nēz), *n. Slang* backwoods, an underdeveloped area. Also called *boondocks.*

boor (bo͞or), *n.* **1,** a peasant or rustic; **2,** a clumsy, ill-mannered person; a lout.—*adj.* **boor′ish.**—*n.* **boor′ish-ness.**

boost (bo͞ost), *v.t.* **1,** to lift by pushing from behind; hoist; as, *boost* me over the fence; **2,** to raise; push up; increase; as, to *boost* wages; to *boost* the team spirit; **3,** to support; promote; as, *boost* someone for mayor:—*n.* a push or shove that helps someone to rise or advance; also, an increase or improvement; as, a *boost* to her chances of winning.—*n.* **boost′er.**

boot (bo͞ot), *n.* **1,** an outer covering for the foot, usually of leather or rubber, coming above the ankle; a high shoe; **2,** such a covering, either of leather or of rubber, and reaching either the knee or the hip:—**to boot,** besides, in addition; as, if we buy the computer, the company will throw in extra software *to boot*:—*v.t.* **1,** to put boots on (someone); **2,** to kick; **3,** to start or turn on the operating system of a computer.

boot camp, 1, a military basic training centre for recruits; **2,** a similar institution for civilian young offenders, to teach them socially acceptable behaviour.

booth (bo͞o*th*; bo͞oth), *n.* **1,** a temporary stall for the sale of goods; **2,** an enclosure to ensure privacy; as, a telephone *booth*; a voting *booth*; **3,** a partly enclosed space in a restaurant.

boot-leg-ger (bo͞ot′leg′ėr), *n. Slang* one who makes or sells something, esp. alcoholic liquors, computer software, etc., in violation of law.—*v.t., v.i.,* and *adj.* **boot′leg′.**—*n.* **boot′leg′ging.**

boo-ty (bo͞o′ti), *n.* [*pl.* booties], **1,** food, guns, etc., taken from the enemy in war; **2,** the plunder of thieves and robbers; **3,** any rich prize or gain.

booze (bo͞oz), *n. Colloq.* drink; liquor:—*v.i.* [boozed, booz-ing], to drink to excess.

bor-der (bôr′dėr), *n.* **1,** the edge of anything, as of a lake; **2,** a boundary or frontier, as of a country; **3,** a narrow strip along or around something; as, a dress with a lace *border*:—*v.t.* **1,** to surround or line with a border; as, to *border* a path with flowers; **2,** to come in contact with; lie next to; as, Canada *borders* the United States:—*v.i.* **1,** to touch; as, the park *borders* on the lake front; **2,** to come near to being; as, his ability *borders* on genius. Also, **bor′der-land′; bor′der-line′.**

[1]**bore** (bōr), *v.t.* [bored, bor-ing], **1,** to pierce or drill a hole in; as, to *bore* the ground; **2,** to form (a hole) by piercing or drilling; as, to *bore* a tunnel; **3,** to force (a passage) with effort; as, he *bored* his way through the crowd:—*v.i.* **1,** to make a hole; pierce; as, they *bored* all day; **2,** to be drilled by an instrument; as, this wood *bores* easily:—*n.* **1,** a hole made by piercing or drilling; **2,** hence, the hollow of a gun or tube; **3,** the inside diameter of a drilled hole; calibre; **4,** a high tidal wave or flow, esp. in a narrow channel or estuary.—*n.* **bor′er.**

[2]**bore** (bōr), *v.t.* [bored, bor-ing], to weary by tiresome repetition or by dullness; as, her complaining *bores* me:—*n.* a tiresome person or thing.—*adj.* **bor′ing.**—*n.* **bore′dom.**

[3]**bore** (bōr), *p.t.* of *bear*.

born (bôrn), *p.p.* of *bear* when used (in the passive) of *birth*:—*adj.* by birth or natural ability; as, to be a *born* musician.

born-a-gain (bôrn′-a-gen′; bôrn′-a-gān′), *adj.* **1,** of or relating to a renewed spiritual life, esp. evangelical Christians who have renewed their faith in Jesus Christ; **2,** renewed or new-found passion for a particular cause or idea; as, a *born-again* conservative.

borne (bôrn), *p.p.* of [2]*bear*.

bor-ough (bur′ō), *n.* **1,** an incorporated town or township that has its own government; **2,** in England, a town represented in Parliament.

bor-row (bor′ō), *v.t.* **1,** to obtain (something) with the understanding that it is to be returned; **2,** to copy; adopt; as, English has *borrowed* many words from Latin and German:—*v.i.* **1,** to obtain something on the promise to return it; as, he *borrowed* from his son; **2,** to copy or adopt another's thoughts or words; as, Shakespeare *borrowed* from old chronicles.—*n.* **bor′row-er.**

bos-om (bo͞o′zum; booz′um), *n.* **1,** the breast of a human being; **2,** the part of a garment that covers the breast; **3,** the breast as the seat of affections, passions, emotions, or desires; the heart; as, my *bosom* swells with pride; **4,** intimacy; privacy; as, in the *bosom* of the family; **5,** anything thought of as resembling the breast; as, the *bosom* of the sea:—*adj.* intimate; as, a *bosom* buddy.

boss (bôs), *n.* **1,** a projection, as of a rocky spur on a mountain or a stud on a shield; **2,** a superintendent, foreman, manager, or employer; someone who is in charge; **3,** a politician who controls a large number of votes:—*v.t.* to manage or tell someone what to do:—*v.i.* to be master.—*adj.* **boss′y.**

bot-a-ny (bot′a-ni), *n.* [*pl.* botanies], the scientific study of plants, their form, growth, classification, distribution, and importance to other forms of life.—*n.* **bot′a-nist.**—*adj.* **bo-tan′i-cal** (bo-tan′i-kal); **bo-tan′ic.**

botch (boch), *n.* bungled work:—*v.t.* to spoil; bungle; do clumsily.—*adj.* **botch′y.**

both (bōth), *adj.* the one and the other; not one only, but two; as, *both* boys were lost:—*pron.* the two; as, take *both*:—*conj.* alike; including; as, *both* men and women.

both-er (bo*th*′ėr), *v.t.* to annoy; worry; give trouble to; as, I am busy, don't *bother* me:—*v.i.* to take trouble; as, don't *bother* about dinner:—*n.* **1,** a source of worry; **2,** one who gives trouble.—*adj.* **both′er-some.**

bot-tle (bot′l), *n.* **1,** a hollow, narrow-necked vessel without handles, usually of glass or plastic; **2,** the contents of such a vessel; as, I drank a *bottle* of pop:—*v.t.* [bottled, bot-tling], **1,** to put into a bottle; **2,** to shut in or hold back; as, to *bottle* up one's feelings.—*n.* **bot′tler.**

bot-tle-neck (bot′l-nek′), *n.* figuratively, a

condition that checks progress; as, labour shortage is a *bottleneck* in industry; a traffic *bottleneck*.

bot-tom (bot′um), *n.* **1,** the lowest part of anything, as of a hill; **2,** the part underneath; the base, as of a barrel; **3,** the basis; essential point; as, he got to the *bottom* of the mystery; **4,** the ground under any body of water; **5,** low land bordering a river; **6,** the part of a vessel below the waterline; hence, a ship:—*adj.* lowest.—*adj.* **bot′tom-less.**

bottom line, **1,** the last line of a business report, showing how much money has been made or lost; **2,** the final result or most important part of something; as, the *bottom line* is that we lost the game.

bou-doir (bo͞o′dwär), *n.* a woman's private sitting room or dressing-room; a bedroom.

bough (bou), *n.* a large limb or branch of a tree.

bought (bôt), *p.t.* and *p.p.* of *buy*.

bouil-lon (bo͞o′yôn′; bool′yun), *n.* a clear soup made usually from beef, etc.

boul-der (bōl′dėr), *n.* a large stone, detached from its original bed, and rounded by water, weather, or moving ice.

bou-le-vard (bo͞o′le-värd′; bool′e-värd), *n.* a wide city street or avenue, often lined with trees.

bounce (bouns), *v.t.* [bounced, bounc-ing], **1,** to throw or toss (something) so that it will rebound; as, to *bounce* a ball; **2,** *Colloq.* to cause a cheque to be returned by a bank without being paid due to lack of funds in the account; as, to *bounce* a cheque:—*v.i.* **1,** to rebound; as, this ball won't *bounce*; **2,** to move suddenly and noisily; as, she *bounced* out of the room; **3,** *Colloq.* of a cheque, to be returned by a bank without being paid due to lack of funds in the account; as, my cheque *bounced*:—*n.* **1,** the rebound of an elastic body; a sudden bound or spring; as, she rose with a *bounce*; **2,** a person employed to keep order in a bar.—*n.* **bounc′er.**

[1]**bound** (bound), *v.i.* **1,** to leap or spring lightly; as, to *bound* from rock to rock; **2,** to rebound; bounce, as does a ball:—*n.* **1,** a light, springing step or leap; a rebound; **2,** the space covered by such a leap.

[2]**bound** (bound), *v.t.* **1,** to form the boundary of; as, the Pacific Ocean *bounds* Canada on the west; **2,** to name the countries or waters surrounding; as, to *bound* Canada:—*n.* **1,** a boundary; limit; **2, bounds,** extent of territory, as of a state; hence, range of action, thought, or the like; as, within the *bounds* of reason.

[3]**bound** (bound), *adj.* intending to go; going; as, to be *bound* for the sunny south.

bound-a-ry (boun′da-ri), *n.* [*pl.* boundaries], that which marks the extent or limit of anything, as a line that bounds a territory on a map, a fence around a property, etc.; also, the limit itself; as, this river forms a *boundary* between the two provinces.

bound-less (bound′lis), *adj.* unlimited; vast; as, *boundless* prairies.

boun-ti-ful (boun′ti-fool), *adj.* **1,** liberal; generous; as, a *bountiful* giver; **2,** plentiful; yielding abundantly; as, *bountiful* acres.

boun-ty (boun′ti), *n.* [*pl.* bounties], **1,** generosity in giving; also, generous gifts; as, this hospital is supported by the *bounty* of one woman; **2,** a premium or reward, esp. one offered or given by a government; as, to give a *bounty* for the capture of the terrorist.

bou-quet (bo͞o-kā′; bō′kā′), *n.* **1,** a bunch of flowers; **2,** aroma, as of herbs or wine; fragrance.

bour-geois (bo͞or′zhwä; boor-zhwä′), *n.* a member of the middle class of society; a business person:—*adj.* belonging to the middle class or having its characteristics.

bour-geoi-sie (bo͞or′zhwä-zē′), *n.* the middle classes of a nation or people; business people in general.

bout (bout), *n.* a test of skill, strength, or endurance; a contest; as, a boxing *bout*; **2,** a spell, period of time, or turn at something; as, a *bout* of spring cleaning; a *bout* of the flu.

bou-tique (bo͞o-tēk′), *n.* a small fashionable store or business with specialized goods or services.

bou-ton-nière (bo͞o′to-nyâr′), *n.* a man's buttonhole flower or bouquet.

[1]**bow** (bou), *v.t.* to bend (the head, body, or knee) to express greeting, thanks, or respect; as, to *bow* the head in prayer; **2,** to express (greeting, thanks, or respect) by bending the head, body, or knee; as, he *bowed* after his performance; **3,** to oppress; crush; as, sorrow has *bowed* her:—*v.i.* **1,** to bend, as in greeting, thanks, or respect; **2,** to yield; as, I *bow* to your wishes:—*n.* a bending of the head, body, or knee, in greeting, thanks, or respect.

[2]**bow** (bō), *n.* **1,** anything curved, as a rainbow; **2,** a weapon of elastic wood for shooting arrows; **3,** a rod strung with tightly stretched string, for playing instruments such as the violin; **4,** a knot with a loop or loops, as of ribbon for a gift, package, or the hair, or as on a shoelace:—**bow window,** a bay window:—*v.t.* to bend or curve like a bow:—*v.i.* to become bent or curved.—*n.* **bow′knot′; bow′shot′; bow′string′; bow′ tie′.**—*adj.* **bow′leg-ged** (-leg′id).

[3]**bow** (bou), *n.* the forward part of a boat, ship, airship, etc.:—*adj.* situated at or near the bow; as, the *bow* oar.

bow-els (bou′elz), *n.pl.* **1,** the intestines, esp. of humans; **2,** the innermost parts, as of the earth; as, to dig in the *bowels* of the earth.

bow·er (bou′ėr), *n.* **1,** a shelter made of boughs or twining plants; an arbour; **2,** one who bends or stoops or uses a bow; **3,** in certain card games such as euchre, a high card, often a jack.—*adj.* **bow′er-y.**

[1]**bowl** (bōl), *n.* **1,** a kitchen dish or vessel in shape more or less spherical; **2,** the contents of a bowl; as, the cat drank a *bowl* of milk; **3,** the hollow part of anything, as of a spoon; **4,** anything bowl-shaped, esp. a large, rounded stadium or amphitheatre for sporting events; as, the Varsity *Bowl*; **5,** a football game played after the regular season between two specially invited teams; as, the Super *Bowl.*

[2]**bowl** (bōl), *n.* **1,** a heavy ball used in lawn or pin bowling; **2,** the act of rolling a bowl:—*v.i.* **1,** to play at bowling; **2,** to roll a bowl or ball; **3,** to move rapidly and smoothly along; as, we *bowled* along the road:—*v.t.* **1,** to knock over; as, he *bowled* him off his feet; **2,** in the game of cricket, to throw (the ball) with a stiff arm.—*n.* **bowl′er.**

bowl·ing (bōl′ing), *n.* an indoor game played by rolling a heavy ball down a wooden lane (a bowling alley), the object of which is to knock down five or 10 pins at the end of the alley: fivepin bowling is popular in Ontario.

[1]**box** (boks), *n.* a slap on the face or a cuff on the ear:—*v.t.* to strike with the fist or hand:—*v.i.* to fight with fists, usually gloved in the sport of boxing.

[2]**box** (boks), *n.* an evergreen tree or shrub, much used for borders and hedges, which stays green all winter. Also called *boxwood.*

[3]**box** (boks), *n.* **1,** a square or rectangular case or container, of wood, cardboard, steel, etc., used to hold things, usually with a lid; **2,** the contents or the quantity that such a container can hold; as, to use up a *box* of paper; **3,** a compartment in a theatre, courtroom, etc.; as, the jury *box*; **4,** a shed or stall used as shelter for a sentry; **5,** in baseball, the place where the pitcher or the batter stands; as, the batter's *box*; **6,** the driver's seat on a coach or carriage; **7,** a trunk:—*v.t.* to enclose in a box; as, to *box* toys.

box·car (boks′kär′), *n.* a railway freight car with a roof and closed sides, usually with sliding doors.

box elder, a fast-growing shade tree with compound leaves, in Canada usually called the Manitoba maple.

box·er (boks′ėr), **1,** a person who takes part in the sport of boxing; **2,** a type of dog with a short, smooth tan or brownish coat, a sturdy build, and a short, square face:—**boxer shorts,** a type of loose underwear for men.

box·ing (bok′sing), *n.* the sport of fighting with the fists, esp. using boxing gloves.

Boxing Day, December 26, a legal holiday in most Canadian provinces: it was originally named for the British custom of giving boxed gifts to tradespeople and service workers after Christmas.

box office, 1, the place where tickets are sold in a theatre, stadium, or cinema; **2,** the income from ticket sales; as, a movie that made $150 million at the *box office*; **3,** total attendance at an event; **4,** the ability of a show or performer to attract an audience.

boy (boi), *n.* **1,** a male child, up to the age of about 14; a lad; **2,** a male servant; someone employed to do small jobs such as running errands; as, an errand *boy*, newspaper *boy*, etc.—*adj.* **boy′ish.**—*n.* **boy′hood.**

boy·cott (boi′kot), *v.t.* **1,** to refuse, in agreement with others, to buy from, sell to, or have dealings with (a person, firm, nation, etc.); **2,** to refuse as a group to use or purchase (a thing):—*n.* an organized refusal to have any dealings with a person, firm, or nation, or to buy a product, to protest something, or to change a policy.

boy·sen·ber·ry (boi′zn-ber′i; boi′sn-), *n.* a large, sweet fruit developed from crossing the raspberry, blackberry, and loganberry, relished as a dessert because of its fine flavour.

bra (brä), *n. Colloq.* Same as **brassiere.**

brace (brās), *n.* **1,** that which steadies a thing or supports it firmly, as a steel beam or timber in a building; also, a bandage or a steel support for a part of the body; **2,** a pair, esp. a pair of animals; as, a *brace* of pheasants; **3,** a curved line, as { or }, connecting two or more lines of print, staffs of music, etc.; **4,** a curved implement or handle used to hold a drill or bit; **5,** braces, suspenders; **6,** *pl.* a set off wires and bands used to straighten the teeth:—*v.t.* [braced, brac-ing], **1,** to steady; as, to *brace* a ladder; to *brace* one's courage; **2,** to prepare for something difficult or for a shock; as, we told her to *brace* herself for the bad news; **3,** to fill with energy; refresh; as, to *brace* yourself with a cold shower:—*v.i.* to rouse oneself to efforts; as, we told him to *brace* up.

brace·let (brās′lit), *n.* an ornamental band or chain for the wrist, arm, or ankle.

brack·et (brak′it), *n.* **1,** an L-shaped piece or framework of wood or metal projecting from a wall, as to support a shelf; **2,** one of a pair of marks, as [ ] or ( ), used to enclose a word, phrase, or numbers, or to mark off a part of the text from the rest; **3,** a group or category into which something can be placed; as, this marketing strategy concerns women in the 18-to-35-year-old *bracket*:—*v.t.* **1,** to enclose in brackets; as, to *bracket* a phrase; **2,** to place items together in a group or classify (things) together; as, to *bracket* her with the more mature athletes.

brag (brag), *v.i.* [bragged, brag-ging], to boast:—*n.* boasting.—*n.* **brag′ger; brag′gart.**

braid (brād), *n.* **1,** something plaited; as, a *braid* of hair; **2,** a flat band made of machine-plaited silk, cotton, or wool, used for binding or trimming:—*v.t.* **1,** to intertwine (three or more strands of hair, cloth, etc.); plait; **2,** to trim with braid.

braille or **Braille** (brāl), *n.* a system of printing for visually impaired people, using raised dots to be read by touch.

brain (brān), *n.* **1,** in humans and animals, the mass of nervous tissue filling the skull: the centre of the nervous system, which controls our thoughts and feelings; **2, brains,** *Colloq.* intelligence; as, she has *brains*; she is a *brain*:—*v.t.* to hit hard on the head (a person or animal).—*adj.* **brain′less; brain′y.**

brain drain, the loss of the most skilled or talented individuals in a country, region, or business sector, who leave for better opportunities elsewhere; as, the *brain drain* from Canada to the United States.

brain-storm (brān′stôrm′), *n.* a sudden thought as to how to solve a problem or create something new; as, to have a *brainstorm* about the name for our new mascot:—*v.t.* and *v.i.* to think hard to try to come up with new ideas; as, to *brainstorm* the concept; let's get together and *brainstorm.*

brain-wash (brān′wôsh′), *v.t.* to try to bring about a complete change in one's beliefs or convictions, esp. by suggestion, force, etc.; also, to persuade someone in an unfair way; as, some TV commercials *brainwash* people.

braise (brāz), *v.t.* [braised, brais-ing], to cook (meat) by browning first, and then simmering in very little liquid in a covered container.

brake (brāk), *n.* a device for slowing or stopping of a vehicle, such as a car, train, bus, bicycle, etc.:—*v.t.* [braked, brak-ing], to slow down or stop by applying a brake.

bram-ble (bram′bl), *n.* **1,** any prickly bush or shrub; **2,** the blackberry, raspberry, etc.

bran (bran), *n.* the outer coat or husk of wheat, rye, etc., used in cereal, flour, and bread when ground up.

branch (brånch), *n.* **1,** a shoot or limb from the main trunk of a tree, shrub, or plant; **2,** any member or part of a body or system; a department or subdivision; as, the executive *branch* of the government; a *branch* of a family; a *branch* of a library; a *branch* of the store; a *branch* of biology; **3,** a place in a computer program where there is a choice of one or more steps:—*adj.* **1,** turning off from the trunk or main body; as, the *branch* roads of a railway system; **2,** subordinate or subdivisional; as, a *branch* office; a *branch* store:—*v.i.* to send out a branch, or branches; to divide into branches; as, the firm has *branched* out into many cities; the road *branches* off from the main road:—**branch out,** to extend or add to something; as, Celia is *branching out* and listening to new types of music.

brand (brand), *n.* **1,** a charred or burning piece of wood; **2,** a mark burned with a hot iron upon animals, to indicate the owner, or upon things, often to indicate the producer; **3,** a type or kind of something; a trademark; hence, any particular kind or make of goods; as, they do not carry that *brand* of coffee:—**brand name,** the name of a particular product made by a certain company; as, "Crest" is the *brand name* of a well-known toothpaste:—*v.t.* **1,** to mark with disgrace; as, to *brand* him as a coward; **2,** to mark with, or as with, a brand; as, the cattle were *branded*; these words were *branded* upon my mind.

bran-dish (bran′dish), *v.t.* to wave or shake menacingly; flourish; as, they threatened us by *brandishing* their knives.

brand–new (brand′–nū′), *adj.* very new.

bran-dy (bran′di), *n.* [*pl.* brandies], an alcoholic liquor distilled from wine or other fermented fruit juice.

brash (brash), *adj.* **1,** brittle; **2,** *Colloq.* impudent; saucy; rash.

brass (brås), *n.* **1,** an alloy made of copper and zinc; **2,** the deep-yellow colour of brass; **3,** *Slang* impudence; as, he had the *brass* to say that; **4, brasses,** ornaments of brass; also, musical wind instruments of brass.—*n.* **bra′sier** (one who works in brass). Also, **brass band; brass ring; brass tacks.**

bras-siere (bra-zēr′), *n.* a woman's garment, worn under clothing, used to cover and support the breasts; a bra.

BRASSIERE

brat (brat), *n.* a child, esp. one who is unruly or impudent (used in contempt).

bra-va-do (bra-vä′dō; -vā′), *n.* [*pl.* bravadoes or bravados], pretence of courage or indifference; boastful defiance; as, timid people sometimes assume an air of *bravado.*

brave (brāv), *adj.* [brav-er, brav-est], **1,** fearless; courageous; as, a *brave* deed; **2,** showy; as, a *brave* display of flags:—*n.* a First Nations warrior:—**the brave,** all those who are brave:—*v.t.* [braved, brav-ing], to face or meet with courage; defy; as, he *braved* the storm.—*n.* **brav′er-y.**—*adv.* **brave′ly.**

bra-vo (brä′vō; brā′vō), *interj.* [*pl.* bravos], well done! good! excellent job!

brawl (brôl), *n.* a noisy quarrel or commotion; as, a hockey *brawl*:—*v.i.* to quarrel or wrangle noisily.—*n.* **brawl′er.**

brawn (brôn), *n.* **1,** firm, strong muscles; muscular strength; as, a fighter's *brawn.*—*adj.* **brawn′y.**

bray (brā), *n.* the loud, harsh cry of the ass; also, any similar sound, as the blast of a trumpet:—*v.i.* to utter a loud, harsh sound or cry.

bra-zen (brā′zn), *adj.* **1,** made of brass; like brass; **2,** loud and harsh; as, a *brazen* voice; **3,** impudent; shameless; as, a *brazen* manner:—*v.t.* to face with impudence; as, to *brazen* out a situation.—*adv.* **bra′zen-ly.**

breach (brēch), *n.* **1,** a gap or opening made by breaking through; as, a *breach* in a wall; **2,** the breaking of a law, contract, etc.; as, a *breach* of contract; **3,** a break in friendly relations; as, a *breach* between nations:—*v.t.* **1,** to make an opening; break through; **2,** to break or violate, as a contract.

bread (bred), *n.* **1,** a food made from flour or meal, moistened, raised, kneaded, and baked; **2,** livelihood; as, he works for his *bread:*—*v.t.* to cover with breadcrumbs before cooking.—*n.* **bread′board′; bread′stuff′.**

bread-fruit (bred′fro͞ot′), *n.* **1,** the large, round fruit of a tree native to the South Pacific islands, which, when roasted, somewhat resembles bread; **2,** the tree that bears this fruit.

breadth (bredth), *n.* **1,** the measure of a thing from side to side; width; hence, spaciousness; extent; **2,** a piece of fabric of a certain width; as, a *breadth* of carpet; **3,** freedom from narrowness; liberality; as, *breadth* of mind.

break (brāk), *v.t.* [*p.t.* broke (brōk), *p.p.* broken (brō′ken), *p.pr.* break-ing], **1,** to split or smash into pieces by a blow or strain; as, to *break* glasses; fracture, as a bone; **2,** to force (a path, hole, or the like) into or through something; **3,** to destroy the arrangement or completeness of; as, to *break* ranks; to *break* a 20-dollar bill; **4,** to weaken the force of; as, the haystack *broke* my fall; **5,** to set aside, violate, or fail to obey; as, to *break* a promise or a law; also, to escape from; as, he *broke* jail; **6,** to tell cautiously; disclose; as, to *break* news; **7,** to tame, as a horse; **8,** to plough or dig up, as ground; **9,** to make bankrupt; as, he *broke* the bank at Monte Carlo; **10,** to discontinue; as, to *break* off relations; **11,** to exceed; as, to *break* a swimming record; **12,** to interrupt, as silence or an electric circuit:—*v.i.* **1,** to separate into pieces suddenly; burst; as, the plate *broke;* **2,** to change abruptly in gait, tone, etc.; as, the horse *broke* into a gallop; three times his voice *broke* during the questioning; **3,** to fail in health; weaken; **4,** to burst forth violently, as a storm or cry; **5,** to force a way; as, he *broke* into the safe; **6,** to begin to be; as, day *breaks;* **7,** to discontinue relations; as, the firms *broke* with each other; **8,** *Slang* to occur or turn out in a given way; as, luck *broke* against him:—**break down, 1,** to fail to work; stop working; as, the car *broke down;* **2,** to become very upset; as, the witness *broke down* and cried:—**break in(to), 1,** to go in by force; as, the thief *broke into* the store; **2,** to get ready for use or work; as, to *break in* a new baseball glove; **3,** to interrupt; as, the special news report *broke into* the regular program:—**break out, 1,** to have a rash or other disorder of the skin; as, to *break out* in hives; **2,** to begin suddenly; as, the audience *broke out* in applause; **3,** to escape; as, to *break out* of jail:—**break up, 1,** to separate or scatter into parts; as, the crowd *broke up;* **2,** to bring or come to an end; as, the party *broke up* late; they *broke up* and stopped seeing each other; **3,** to laugh or cause to laugh; as, the comedian *breaks* me *up:*—*n.* **1,** the act of breaking; as, the *break* of day; **2,** something produced by breaking; as, a *break* in a wire; an interruption; as, a *break* in a conversation; to take a *break* from studying; **3,** a sudden fall in prices; as, a *break* in the stock market; **4,** *Colloq.* a blunder in speech or action; **5,** *Slang* a turn of fortune; as, it was a lucky *break* for me.—*adj.* **break′a-ble; break′neck.**—*n.* **break′age; break′down′; break′through′; break′up′.**

break-down (brāk′doun′), *n.* **1,** the failure to work or act properly; **2,** a failing in health, esp. a mental collapse. Also called *nervous breakdown.*

break-er (brāk′ėr), *n.* **1,** one who or that which smashes or breaks; as, a circuit *breaker;* **2,** a machine for crushing coal, rocks, etc.; **3,** a wave that dashes itself upon the shore in foam.

break-fast (brek′fast), *n.* the first meal of the day:—*v.i.* to eat breakfast.

break–in (brāk′–in′), *n.* the act of breaking in.

break point, in *computing,* the point in a computer program at which the operation may be interrupted.

break-through (brāk′thro͞o′), *n.* a sudden finding or advance; as, a *breakthrough* in finding a cure for a disease.

break–up (brāk′–up′), *n.* **1,** the fact of coming apart or separating; as, the *break-up* of a musical band; **2,** the breaking up of the ice layer on a lake or river in the spring; **3,** the time when this breaking of the ice layer takes place, esp. in northern Canada.

break-wa-ter (brāk′wô′tėr), *n.* a wall or dike built to break the force of the waves, as around a harbour.

breast (brest), *n.* **1,** the front part of the body between the neck and the abdomen; **2,** either one of the glands found on the chest of humans and some other mammals, serving, in females, for the secretion of milk; **3,** anything resembling the breast; as, the *breast* of a hill; **4,** the seat of the affections:—*v.t.* to face bravely; struggle; as, to *breast* the hurdles in life.

breast-bone (brest′bōn′), *n.* the thin, flat, vertical bone in the front of the chest to which the seven upper pairs of ribs are attached.

breath (breth), *n.* **1,** the air drawn into and forced out of the lungs; **2,** a single act of drawing air into or forcing air out from the lungs; hence, an instant; a pause; **3,** the power to breathe freely; as, to lose one's *breath*; hence, life; strength; **4,** a light breeze; as, a *breath* of fresh air; **5,** a whisper; as, a *breath* of scandal; **6,** a film produced by the breath, as on a mirror.—*adj.* **breath′less.**—*adv.* **breath′less-ly.**

breathe (brēth), *v.i.* [breathed, breath-ing], **1,** to use the lungs; be alive; as, the dying man still *breathes*; **2,** to rest from stress or action; pause; as, I can *breathe* again, now that the work is done; **3,** to blow softly, as wind:—*v.t.* **1,** to draw into and force out of the lungs; as, we *breathed* the fresh air; **2,** to exhale; give forth; as, he *breathed* a sigh of relief; the flower *breathes* perfume; **3,** to whisper softly; as, don't *breathe* a word of this.

breath-er (brēth′ėr), *n.* **1,** a person or animal that breathes, esp. in a certain way; as, a heavy *breather*; **2,** *Colloq.* a pause, break (for breath, rest, etc.); as, let's take a *breather* before going on with this work.

breath-tak-ing (breth′tā′king), *adj.* exciting; inspiring awe; as, a *breathtaking* view; a *breathtaking* performance.

bred (bred), *pt.* and *p.p.* of *breed.*

breech (brēch), *n.* **1,** the rear part of a firearm; **2,** the lower or back part; the buttocks; rump.

breech-es (brich′iz), *n.pl.* **1,** short trousers, fastened below the knee; **2,** *Colloq.* trousers.

breed (brēd), *v.t.* [bred (bred), breed-ing], **1,** to give birth to; **2,** to mate or raise, as animals or plants, for the purpose of maintaining or improving the stock; **3,** to train; rear; as, I was *bred* to be my father's successor; **4,** to nourish; cause; bring about; as, swamps *breed* mosquitoes; poverty *breeds* misery:—*v.i.* **1,** to bear young; **2,** to be born; come into being; as, crime *breeds* in slums:—*n.* race; stock; strain; as, a good *breed* of cattle.—*n.* **breed′er.**

breed-ing (brēd′ing), *n.* **1,** the producing of young; **2,** the training or bringing up of young; esp., the results of training; good manners; as, a person of good *breeding*.

breeze (brēz), *n.* **1,** a gentle wind; **2,** *Colloq.* something easy to do; as, this test was a *breeze*.—*adj.* **breez′y.**

brev-i-ty (brev′i-ti), *n.* [*pl.* brevities], briefness; shortness.

brew (brōō), *v.t.* **1,** to make, as beer, from malt and hops, by steeping, boiling, and fermenting; **2,** to make by steeping, as tea, or by mixing, as punch; **3,** to bring about; plot; as, to *brew* mischief:—*v.i.* **1,** to make a liquor by fermentation or steeping; **2,** to gather; grow in force; as, a storm *brews*:—*n.* a drink made by brewing.—*n.* **brew′er.**—*n.* **brew′er-y.**

brewis (brōō′′is), *n.* Same as **fish and brewis.**

bri-ar or **bri-er** (brī′ėr), *n.* **1,** any thorny plant or shrub; **2,** a thorn, as of a rose; **3,** a patch of thorny bushes; **4,** the European white-heath; **5,** a tobacco-pipe made from its root.

bribe (brīb), *n.* an offer of money or favour made or promised to a person to influence him or her to adopt a wrong course of action:—*v.t.* [bribed, brib-ing], to influence by a bribe.—*n.* **brib′er-y.**

bric-a-brac (brik′-a-brak′), *n.* small articles of artistic or sentimental value, displayed as ornaments; knick-knacks.

brick (brik), *n.* **1,** a material used in building or paving made from clay, moulded into blocks, usually oblong, and baked in the sun or in kilns; also, one of these blocks; **2,** anything shaped like such a block; as, a *brick* of ice-cream, cheese, or soap:—*v.t.* to lay bricks; wall in with bricks; as, to *brick* up a fireplace.—*n.* **brick′lay′er; brick′work′; brick′yard′.**

bride (brīd), *n.* a woman newly married, or about to be married.—*adj.* **brid′al.**

bride-groom (brīd′grōōm′), *n.* a man newly married, or about to be married. Also called *groom.*

brides-maid (brīdz′mād′), *n.* a girl or woman who attends a bride at her wedding.

bridge (brij), *n.* **1,** a structure built to carry a road or path across a river, valley, etc.; **2,** anything shaped like a bridge, as the upper part of the nose, the arch for the strings on a violin, or a mounting for artificial teeth; **3,** an observation platform above the deck of a ship for the officer in charge or the pilot; **4,** a movable passageway from a ship to the shore; **5,** a card game developed from the game of whist, played by two pairs of partners:—*v.t.* [bridged, bridg-ing], **1,** to build a bridge over; span; **2,** to pass; get over; as, he helped me *bridge* the difficulty.—*n.* **bridge′work′** (of teeth).

bri-dle (brī′dl), *n.* **1,** in a horse's harness, the headgear, with the bit and reins, by which the horse is governed; **2,** a check; restraint; as, to put a *bridle* on the tongue:—*v.t.* [bri-dled, bri-dling], **1,** to put a bit and reins on; **2,** to control, as, the temper.

brief (brēf), *adj.* **1,** short; not lengthy; as, a *brief* delay; **2,** said in a few words; condensed; as, a *brief* description:—*n.* a summary; esp., a lawyer's outline of the argument of a case:—*v.t.* to give short and concise information or instruction; as, the coach *briefed* the team before the game.—

adv. **brief′ly.**—*n.* **brief′ing.**

brief-case (brēf′kās′), *n.* a small, portable case for carrying documents, books, etc.

Bri-er (brī′ėr), *n.* in *sports,* the Canadian national championship curling competition, or bonspiel, for men.

brig (brig), *n.* **1,** a two-masted square-rigged vessel; **2,** a military or warship prison.

bri-gade (bri-gād′), *n.* **1,** a large unit of troops in an army; **2,** an organized body of people acting under authority; as, a fire *brigade.*

brig-a-dier (brig′a-dēr′), *n.* an officer in command of a brigade, ranking next below a major-general: more often called *brigadier-general.*

brig-an-tine (brig′an-tēn′, -tīn′), *n.* a two-masted square-rigged ship, unlike a brig in not having a square mainsail: it was often used as a pirate craft.

bright (brīt), *adj.* **1,** giving much light; shining, as the sun; **2,** vivid; as, *bright* green; **3,** lively; cheerful; **4,** clever; as, a *bright* idea; a *bright* child; **5,** favourable; hopeful; as, a *bright* future.—*adv.* **bright′ly.**—*n.* **bright′ness.**

bright-en (brīt′n), *v.i.* to grow clearer, lighter, or brighter; as, the day *brightens:*—*v.t.* to make light or bright; as, to *brighten* a room with flowers.

bril-liant (bril′yant), *adj.* **1,** sparkling; glittering; as, the *brilliant* light of a chandelier; **2,** very successful; distinguished; as, a *brilliant* reign; **3,** distinguished by splendid mental ability; as, a *brilliant* scientist:—*n.* a diamond or other precious stone, cut to show its sparkling quality.—*n.* **bril′liance; bril′lian-cy.**

brim (brim), *n.* **1,** the edge or brink, as of a lake; the rim, as of a cup; **2,** the projecting edge, as of a hat:—*v.i.* [brimmed, brimming], to be full to the very edge; as, her eyes *brimmed* with tears.—*adj.* **brim′less.**

brin-dled (brin′dld), *adj.* streaked with gray, brown, or tawny markings; as, a *brindled* cow.

brine (brīn), *n.* **1,** water that is extremely salty, such as pickle *brine;* **2,** the ocean.—*adj.* **brin′y.**

bring (bring), *v.t.* [brought (brôt), bringing], **1,** to cause (a person or thing) to come along; as, *bring* your cousin home; also, to fetch; as, *bring* me the new computer game; **2,** to carry; as, the boat *brought* me to land; **3,** to draw; attract; as, this speaker always *brings* a crowd; **4,** to cause, or to result in; as, winter *brings* snow; sleep *brings* relief; **5,** to sell for (a price); as, diamonds *bring* a large sum; **6,** to recall; as, that *brings* up a story; **7,** to persuade; as, I cannot *bring* myself to go; **8,** in *law,* to begin; as, to *bring* suit:—**bring about,** to make happen; cause; as, the Internet has *brought about* many changes in our lives:—**bring out,** to present to the public; as, the publisher is *bringing out* 10 new books this month:—**bring up, 1,** to care for or raise a child; as, to *bring up* a child to be honest; **2,** to mention; suggest; as, to *bring up* an issue during the meeting.

brink (bringk), *n.* the edge or top, esp. of a steep place; as, the *brink* of a pit; hence, verge; as, on the *brink* of ruin.

brinks-man-ship or **brink-man-ship** (bringks′man-ship′; bringk′man-ship′), *n.* the practice of manipulating dangerous situations and giving the impression of not compromising, esp. in international politics.

bri-quette or **bri-quet** (bri-ket′), *n.* a pressed brick of coal dust (for fuel or in barbecues).

brisk (brisk), *adj.* **1,** active; lively; swift; nimble; as, a *brisk* walker; **2,** burning freely, as a fire; **3,** keen; enlivening, as a wind.—*adv.* **brisk′ly.**

brist-le (bris′l), *n.* a short, stiff, coarse hair:—*v.i.* [bris-tled, bris-tling], **1,** to stand up in a stiff, prickly way, as an angry dog's hair; **2,** to be covered with bristly points; as, the battlefront *bristles* with bayonets; **3,** to show signs of anger or defiance; as, the class *bristled* with revolt.—*adj.* **bris′tly.**

Brit-ain (brit′un), *n.* Great Britain or the United Kingdom, made up of England, Scotland, and Wales.—*adj.* **Brit′ish.**

Brit-ish (bri′tish), *n.* **1,** a person who inhabits or originates from Great Britain; **2,** the language of these people:—*adj.* relating to the countries (England, Scotland, and Wales), the people, the language, or the culture of Great Britain.

British North America Act, an act passed by the British Parliament in March 1867, which established the Dominion of Canada. Also called the *B.N.A. Act.*

brit-tle (brit′l), *adj.* hard and easily broken; apt to break, as ice, glass, or bones.

broach (brōch), *n.* **1,** any pointed, spike-shaped tool, as a skewer for roasting meat; **2,** a tapered bit for boring holes, esp. in metal; a reamer:—*v.t.* **1,** to tap or pierce, as a keg of wine; **2,** to begin to talk about; as, to *broach* an unpleasant subject.

broad (brôd), *adj.* **1,** wide from side to side; **2,** spacious; vast; as, *broad* shoulders; **3,** liberal; as, *broad* views; **4,** open; clear; as, *broad* daylight; **5,** evident; plain; as, a *broad* hint; **6,** indelicate; as, a *broad* joke.—*adv.* **broad′ly.**

broad-axe or **broad-ax** (brôd′aks′), *n.* **1,** a broad-bladed axe for cutting timber; **2,** an ancient weapon with a wide blade.

broad-band (brôd′band′), *adj.* of or relating to a communications network with a wide variety of frequencies allowing the transmission of data, voice, video, etc.; as, a *broadband* network.

broad-cast (brôd′kåst′), *v.t.* [broadcast or broadcast-ed, broadcast-ing], **1,** to scatter or throw by hand, as seed; **2,** to spread abroad, as news; **3,** to send out (messages or information) by radio, television, or on the Internet:—*n.* **1,** a scattering of seed far and wide; **2,** anything broadcast by radio or television, as a program, speech, or game.—*n.* **broad′cast′er.**

broad-en (brôd′n), *v.i.* to grow wide or wider; as, the river *broadens* at this point:—*v.t.* to make wider or more liberal; as, education should *broaden* the mind.

broad-loom (brôd′lo͞om′), *n.* seamless carpet, a minimum of 1.8 metres wide.

broad–mind-ed (brôd′–mīn′did), *adj.* liberal in opinions; tolerant.

broad-side (brôd′sīd′), *n.* **1,** the entire side of a ship above the waterline; also, the broad unbroken expanse of anything; **2,** all the cannons or guns on one side of a warship; also, a discharge from all these at once; **3,** a sheet of paper printed on one side only, as a tract or advertisement; **4,** *Colloq.* a printed or verbal attack on some person:—*v.t.* to hit on the side; as, to *broadside* a car.

bro-cade (brō-kād′), *n.* a silken fabric woven with gold and silver threads, or ornamented with raised designs of flowers, etc.:—*v.t.* [brocad-ed, brocad-ing], to decorate or weave with a raised pattern.—*adj.* **bro-cad′ed.**

broc-co-li (brok′o-li), *n.* a green vegetable of the mustard family, related to the cabbage and cauliflower.

bro-chure (brō-shyo͝or′), *n.* a small, usually colourful pamphlet or booklet that advertises a product or service or provides information.

brogue (brōg), *n.* **1,** a pronunciation characteristic of a dialect; esp., the Irish pronunciation of English; **2,** a type of strong and comfortable shoe.

broil (broil), *v.t.* to cook directly over or under a hot fire or on a grill:—*v.i.* to be exposed to great heat; as, we *broiled* in the hot sun:—*n.* a broiled dish.

broil-er (broil′ėr), *n.* **1,** a utensil or device for cooking food directly over or under a fire; **2,** a young fowl suitable for broiling.

broke (brōk), *p.t.* of *break*:—*adj. Colloq.* having little or no money; as, to be *broke*.

[1]**bro-ken** (brō′ken), a *p.p.* of *break*.

[2]**bro-ken** (brō′ken), *adj.* **1,** not entire; in pieces; shattered; as, a *broken* dish; **2,** fractured; as, a *broken* bone; **3,** cut into; as, ground *broken* by ploughing; **4,** uneven; as, *broken* country; **5,** incomplete; disorganized; as, a *broken* set; *broken* ranks; **6,** interrupted; as, *broken* sleep; **7,** violated; as, a *broken* vow; **8,** trained to obedience; as, a *broken* horse; **9,** enfeebled; weak; as, *broken* health; **10,** subdued; crushed; as, a *broken* spirit; **11,** imperfectly spoken; as, *broken* French.—*adv.* **bro′ken-ly.**—*adj.* **broken-down; broken-hearted.**

bro-ker (brō′kėr), *n.* an agent for others in buying or selling anything, as real estate, stocks, bonds, etc.—*n.* **bro′ker-age.**

bron-chi-tis (bron-kī′tis; brong-kī′tis), *n.* an inflammation of the bronchi or bronchial tubes, which connect the windpipe or trachea and the lungs, causing coughs and chest pains.—*n.* **bron′chi.**—*adj.* **bron′chi-al.**

bron-co (brong′kō), *n.* [*pl.* broncos], in western North America, a small, half-tamed horse.

bron-to-saur-us (bron′to-sô′rus), *n.* a huge, plant-eating dinosaur (up to 25 metres long), with a small head and a long neck and tail.

bronze (bronz), *n.* **1,** an alloy or metallic mixture of eight or nine parts copper to one of tin; **2,** a work of art cast or wrought in this alloy; **3,** a yellowish or reddish brown, the colour of bronze:—*adj.* made of bronze; like bronze:—*v.t.* [bronzed, bronz-ing], to make the colour of bronze; tan; as, the sun *bronzed* his face.

brooch (brōch), *n.* an ornamental pin or clasp, worn on clothing, hats, etc.

brood (bro͞od), *n.* **1,** all the young of birds hatched at one time; **2,** all the young of one mother; also (*Colloq.*), all the children in one family; **3,** the eggs and larvae of bees when in the comb:—*v.t.* **1,** to sit on eggs, as a hen; **2,** to think about something long and moodily; as, to *brood* over losses:—*v.t.* to sit on and hatch (eggs).—*n.* **brood′er.**

brook (brook), *n.* a small, natural stream of water:—*v.t.* to bear; put up with; as, I will *brook* no delay.

broom (bro͞om), *n.* **1,** a long-handled brush used for sweeping; **2,** a shrub of the pea family, with stiff, slender branches.—*n.* **broom′stick′.**

broth (brôth), *n.* thin soup made by boiling meat, fish, or vegetables slowly in water.

broth-er (bru*th*′ėr), *n.* **1,** a male child of the same parents as oneself; **2,** a male member of a religious order who is not a priest; **3,** a male closely united to another or others by a common interest, such as a lodge, church, etc.

broth-er-hood (bru*th*′ėr-hood′), *n.* **1,** a group of men with similar interests and aims; a fraternity; as, the legal *brotherhood*; **2,** fellowship; kinship; as, the *brotherhood* of man.

broth-er–in–law (bru*th*′ėr–in–lô′), *n.* [*pl.* brothers-in-law], a brother of one's husband or wife, or husband of one's sister.

broth-er-ly (bru*th*′ėr-li), *adj.* like a brother; kind; friendly.—*n.* **broth′er-li-ness.**

brought (brôt), *p.t.* and *p.p.* of *bring.*

brow (brou), *n.* **1,** the forehead; **2,** the arch of hair over the eye; the eyebrow; **3,** the edge of a cliff; the top of a hill.

brow-beat (brou′bēt′), *v.t.* [*pl.* browbeat (-bēt′), *p.p.* browbeat-en (-bēt′n), *p.pr.* browbeat-ing], to frighten by stern looks or words; bully.

brown (broun), *adj.* of a dusky colour like chocolate or mud:—*n.* such a dark colour:—*v.i.* and *v.t.* to become or to make brown; as, to *brown* meat before stewing.

brown-ie (broun′i), *n.* **1,** a good-natured elf supposed to do certain useful household tasks by night; **2,** a thin flat chocolate cake with nuts in it; **3, Brownie,** a girl scout six to nine years of age.

browse (brouz), *n.* the tender shoots of shrubs and trees fit for the food of cattle, etc.:—*v.i.* [browsed, brows-ing], **1,** to nibble off twigs or grass; **2,** to read here and there in books; wander idly, as through an art gallery, etc.

brows-er (brou′zėr), *n.* in *computing,* a software program that allows the user to locate and view information on the Internet.

bruise (bro͞oz), *n.* an injury to the flesh that discolours the skin of people and plants:—*v.t.* [bruised, bruis-ing], to injure or hurt; as, to *bruise* one's leg; to *bruise* a tomato; to *bruise* a friend's feelings:—*v.i.* to show the effects of bruises; as, I *bruise* easily.

brunch (brunch), *n.* a late-morning meal that combines a late breakfast and an early lunch.—*v.i.* to eat brunch.

bru-nette or **bru-net** (bro͞o-net′), *adj.* having dark skin, hair, and eyes.—*n.masc.* **bru-net′.**—*n.fem.* **bru-nette′.**

brunt (brunt), *n.* the heaviest part of a shock or strain; as, to bear the *brunt.*

brush (brush), *n.* **1,** an implement made of bristles, feathers, or the like, fixed in a back or handle, used for cleaning, smoothing, applying paint, etc.; **2,** the tail of a fox; **3,** a slight battle; skirmish; **4,** the act of cleaning or smoothing with a brush; **5,** a thicket of small trees; **6,** branches cut from trees; brushwood; **7,** thin metallic plates or wires bound together, to conduct a current to or from an electric motor or dynamo:—*v.t.* **1,** to sweep, cleanse, or rub with a brush; as, to *brush* your hair or teeth; **2,** to remove, as with a brush; as, to *brush* crumbs away; **3,** to touch lightly in passing; graze:—*v.i.* to pass quickly with a casual touch; as, he *brushed* by me.—*adj.* **brush′y.**

brush-wood (brush′wood′), *n.* **1,** a dense growth of bushes; thicket; brush; **2,** cut branches, etc., suitable for a fire.

brusque (brusk; broosk), *adj.* abrupt; curt in manner or speech.—*adv.* **brusque′ly.**—*n.* **brusque′ness.**

Brus-sels sprouts, a food plant of the mustard family, with small, green, cabbagelike heads growing on a stalk.

bru-tal (bro͞o′tal), *adj.* savage; cruel; inhuman.—*adv.* **bru′tal-ly.**—*n.* **bru-tal′i-ty** (bro͞o-tal′i-ti).

brute (bro͞ot), *adj.* **1,** without intelligence; not human; **2,** like a wild beast; cruel:—*n.* **1,** a beast; esp., a wild beast; **2,** a savage person without human kindliness.—*v.t.* **bru′tal-ize.**—*adj.* **brut′ish.**

bub-ble (bub′l), *n.* **1,** a small, globelike film filled with air or gas; **2,** a small body of air or gas rising in a liquid, as in soda water, or held within a solid, as in ice or glass; **3,** anything unreal or fanciful; a delusion:—*v.i.* [bub-bled, bub-bling], **1,** to rise in bubbles; also, to form bubbles, as soda water; **2,** to make a gurgling sound, as a stream.—*adj.* **bub′bly.** Also, **bubble bath; bubble gum.**

bu-bon-ic plague (bū-bon′ik), a contagious disease (often fatal), marked by inflamed swelling of glands in the armpit or groin, chills and fever, and delirium: fleas from infected rats and squirrels carry it. Also called *Black Death.*

buc-ca-neer (buk′a-nēr′), *n.* a pirate; a sea robber.

buck (buk), *n.* **1,** the male of an animal, as the deer or rabbit, of which the female is called a *doe;* **2,** a sudden, vertical leap, as of an unruly horse; **3,** in football, a hard plunge into the opponents' line; **4,** *Slang* a dollar:—*v.i.* to leap suddenly into the air with arched back as a horse does to throw off a rider:—*v.t.* **1,** to throw off by a sudden leap; **2,** in football, to charge into (the opposing line); **3,** to resist or work against; as, to *buck* the system at work.

buck-board (buk′bōrd′), *n.* a light wagon with the seat set on a long, flexible board fastened without springs to the axles.

buck-et (buk′it), *n.* **1,** a pail for drawing water; **2,** any pail or holder in which something is collected or carried, as a dredge scoop; **3,** the amount a bucket holds; a bucketful.—*n.* **bucket seat.**

[1]**buck-le** (buk′l), *n.* **1,** a clasp for holding together the ends of a strap or the like; **2,** an ornament of similar shape for a dress, hat, etc.:—*v.t.* [buck-led, buck-ling], **1,** to fasten with a buckle; as, to *buckle* a seatbelt; **2,** to apply (oneself) with energy:—*v.i.* **1,** to be held together by means of a buckle; **2,** to set to work with energy; as, to *buckle* down to studying.

[2]**buck-le** (buk′l), *v.i.* [buck-led, buck-ling], to bend or warp, as metal, from pressure or heat; crumple up; as, his knees *buckled* from the weight:—*v.t.* to cause to buckle; crumple:—*n.* a bend, twist, or kink in a piece of metal.

buck-ler (buk′lėr), *n.* a small, round shield, or similar protection.

buck-saw (buk′sô′), *n.* a saw set in a deep, H-shaped frame and used with both hands for sawing firewood.

buck-shot (buk′shot′), *n.* coarse lead shot, used for large game.

buck-skin (buk′skin′), *n.* a soft, pliable leather made from the skin of a deer or sheep:—*adj.* made of buckskin.

buck-toothed (buk′tōōtht′), *adj.* having projecting teeth.

buck-wheat (buk′hwēt′), *n.* a plant grown for its triangular seeds, which are ground into flour or eaten whole, roasted and cooked; also, the flour.

bud (bud), *n.* **1,** a growth, as a lump or point on a plant, that may develop into a branch, stem, leaf, or flower:—*v.t.* [budded, bud-ding], to insert (a bud) into an opening cut in the bark of another plant; graft; as, to *bud* an apple on a quince stock:—*v.i.* to put forth new shoots; sprout.—*adj.* **bud′ding** (beginning to grow or develop; as, to be a *budding* actor).

Bud-dhism (bōōd′izm), *n.* the religion founded by Buddha and based on his teachings: an important religion in many countries of Asia.—*n.* and *adj.* **Bud′dhist.**

bud-dy (bud′-i), *n.* pal; very close friend; comrade.

budge (buj), *v.i.* [budged, budg-ing], to move from one's place; stir:—*v.t.* to cause to move.

budg-et (buj′it), *n.* **1,** a quantity or store; as, a *budget* of news; **2,** a statement by a person, corporation, or government, of estimated income and expenses for a definite period; also, a plan for the best division of such income among the expenses:—*v.t.* to plan the spending of (one's income or time) by making a budget; as, to *budget* time carefully in order to get everything done.

budg-ie (buj′i), *n. Colloq.* for **budg′er-i-gar′** (buj′ėr-i-gär′), an Australian parakeet with blue, green, yellow, and brown markings.

buff (buf), *n.* **1,** a thick, soft, dull-yellow leather made from the skin of a buffalo, ox, or similar animal; **2,** a soldier's coat made from this skin; **3,** a pale or faded yellowish-orange colour; **4,** a wheel covered with buff, used for polishing; **5,** a person who is very interested or good in some activity or subject; as, a computer *buff*:—*adj.* **1,** made of dull-yellow leather; **2,** of a faded yellowish-orange colour:—*v.t.* to polish with or as if with a buff.

buf-fa-lo (buf′a-lō′), *n.* [*pl.* buffalo or buffaloes], **1,** a kind of wild ox, as the Asiatic water buffalo, or the African Cape buffalo; **2,** in North America, the popular name for *bison*: the buffalo appears as an emblem on the Manitoba coat of arms.

BUFFALO

buf-fer (buf′ėr), *n.* **1,** a device to keep two objects or forces from colliding, as a fender or bumper, or as a *buffer* state; **2,** a machine that buffs or polishes; **3,** in *computing*, a storage area in a computer that holds information that is to be printed or transferred elsewhere, so that the main memory can continue to operate.

¹buf-fet (buf′it), *n.* **1,** a blow with the hand; **2,** any blow:—*v.t.* **1,** to strike with the hand or fist; knock about; **2,** to struggle against; as, to *buffet* the waves:—*v.i.* to fight; struggle.

²buf-fet (boo-fā′; bu′fā), *n.* **1,** a cupboard or sideboard for a dining room; **2,** (boo-fā′), a refreshment counter; also, a restaurant equipped with such counters; **3,** a light meal laid out on a buffet or table so that guests can serve themselves.

buf-foon (bu-fōōn′), *n.* one who amuses others by jokes, antics, etc.; a clown.—*n.* **buf-foon′er-y.**

bug (bug), *n.* **1,** one of a group of flattened insects, with or without wings, having a piercing or sucking mouth, as the squash bug; **2,** popularly, any crawling insect; **3,** *Colloq.* a disease germ; as, a flu *bug*; **4,** *Colloq.* a defect in the operation of a machine, esp. in a computer program, that keeps it from working properly; **5,** *Colloq.* a small microphone that is hidden in a place to pick up private conversations:—*v.t. Colloq.* **1,** to hide a microphone in; as, to *bug* an office; **2,** to bother or annoy someone; as, he was always *bugging* his sister.

bug-gy (bug′i), *n.* [*pl.* buggies], **1,** a light, one-seated carriage; **2,** a baby carriage.

bu-gle (bū′gl), *n.* **1,** a hunting horn; **2,** a trumpetlike brass wind instrument used for military calls:—*v.i.* and *v.t.* [bu-gled, bu-gling], to sound, or give forth (a sound) on, a bugle.—*n.* **bu′gler.**

build (bild), *v.t.* [built (bilt), build-ing], **1,** to construct by putting materials or parts together according to some plan or practice; **2,** to base or found; as, he *built* his hopes on his invention; **3,** to establish gradually, as a business:—*v.i.* to construct a building:—*n.* style of construction; as, the *build* of an automobile; also, figure; form; as, an athlete of sturdy *build.*—*n.* **build′er.**—*n.* **build′-up′.**—*adj.* **built′-in′.**

build-ing (bil′ding), *n.* **1,** the art or business of erecting buildings; **2,** the act of constructing, raising, or establishing; **3,** a structure covering a piece of land, and designed for a particular use, as a school, barn, hotel, office building, etc.

bulb (bulb), *n.* **1,** the rounded part, usually under ground, of some plant, as the onion, the lily, and the narcissus, where the plant food is stored; **2,** a rounded end of a glass tube, as of a thermometer; **3,** anything shaped like a bulb, such as a small glass globe containing an electric light filament.—*adj.* **bulb′ous.**

bulge (bulj), *n.* **1,** a swelling outward, as from pressure; **2,** the part of a wall, etc., designed to curve outward:—*v.i.* and *v.t.* [bulged, bulg-ing], to swell or bend outward.—*adj.* **bulg′y.**

bu-lim-ia (bo͞o-lē′mē-a), *n.* **1,** an eating disorder characterized by binging and purging, by self-induced vomiting; also called *bulimia nervosa*; **2,** excessive, insatiable appetite.—*n.* and *adj.* **bu-lim′ic.**

bulk (bulk), *n.* **1,** mass; volume; esp., great size; **2,** the main mass; the greater part; as, the *bulk* of his property.—*adj.* **bulk′y.**

bulk-head (bulk′hed′), *n.* **1,** an upright partition in a ship, separating watertight compartments; also, a similar partition in an aircraft; **2,** a structure built to resist the pressure of water, air, or earth; esp., a sea wall.

bull (bool), *n.* **1,** the male of any animal of the ox family or of various other large animals, as the whale, seal, moose, or elephant; **2,** a person who buys stocks, bonds, commodities, etc., because he or she thinks prices are going up and stocks, etc., can be sold at a profit: opposite of *bear.*—*adj.* **bull′ish.** Also, **bull′fight′; bull′frog′.**

bull-dog (bool′dôg′), *n.* a breed of short-haired, medium-sized dog with a heavy head and projecting lower jaw, remarkable for its courage and for its strong grip:—*adj.* having the qualities of a bulldog; courageous; tenacious.

bull-doze (bool′dōz′), *v.t.* [bulldozed, bull-doz-ing], **1,** to move earth, etc., with a bulldozer; **2,** to bully; compel by threats; as, to *bulldoze* someone into accepting the conditions.

bull-doz-er (bool′dōz′ėr), *n.* **1,** a machine for grading and roadbuilding: a powerful tractor, pushing a heavy, broad-nosed scraper; **2,** a person who forces another by bluster or violence; also, anything used to threaten; **3,** a heavy, powerful machine for bending and shaping metal into shorter and thicker form.

bul-let (bool′it), *n.* **1,** a small metal ball, made to be fired from a firearm; **2,** the heavy dot or other graphic at the beginning of items in some lists.—*adj.* **bul′let-ed** (as, a *bulleted* list).

bul-le-tin (bool′e-tin), *n.* **1,** a brief official report on some matter of public interest; as, a doctor's *bulletin* on a famous patient's condition; **2,** a magazine published regularly, containing reports of a club, society, or organization:—*v.i.* to publish or announce in a brief authorized statement.

bulletin board, *n.* **1,** a board on which notices and other items are posted, as at a school, store, or other public place; **2,** in *computing,* a message centre that operates by computer, so that someone can leave messages that other people can read on their own computer screens.

bull-head-ed (bool′hed′id), *adj.* blindly stubborn or headstrong; as, he was too *bullheaded* to be reasoned with.

bul-lion (bool′yun), *n.* uncoined gold or silver in lumps, bars, etc.

bull market, a stock market in which prices are rising: opposite of *bear market.*

bull pen, *n.* **1,** a pen for bulls; **2,** at a jail, an enclosure where rioting prisoners are confined; **3,** an area by a baseball field where relief pitchers warm up.

bull's–eye (boolz′–ī′), *n.* **1,** a bulging lens used to bring together the rays of light from a lantern upon a small spot; also, a lantern having such a lens; **2,** a round piece of thick glass in a floor or deck to admit light; **3,** the centre point of a target, or a shot that hits it; hence, anything esp. successful; **4,** a hard, round candy which looks like a marble.

bul-ly (bool′i), *n.* [*pl.* bullies], a coward who picks on or tries to rule weaker persons by cruelty or threats:—*v.t.* [bullied, bully-ing], to rule with bluster and threats:—*v.i.* to be noisy and overbearing.

bul-wark (bool′wėrk), *n.* **1,** a barrier or wall built for defence; an earthwork; rampart; breakwater; **2,** the boarding round the sides of a ship, above the level of the deck; **3,** any means of protection.

bum (bum), *n. Colloq.* **1,** a hobo; tramp; someone who does not work and tries to live by begging; **2,** a person who is thought of as bad or worthless; **2,** *Slang* the buttocks:—*v.i.* to loaf:—*v.t.* to take advantage of other people; beg; as, to *bum* money off one's friends. Also, **bummed; bum out; bum rap; bum steer.**

bum-ble–bee (bum′bl–bē′), *n.* a large bee with a yellow and black hairy body that makes a loud hum.

bum-bling (bum′bling), *adj.* blunderingly self-important.

bum-mer (bum′ėr), *n. Slang* **1,** a bad, unpleasant, or depressing experience; **2,** a loafer; a lazy or shiftless person.

bump (bump), *n.* **1,** a blow; collision; **2,** a swelling due to a knock or blow:—*v.t.* **1,** to bring violently together; as, to *bump* heads; **2,** to strike against; knock into:—*v.i.* to come together heavily.—*adj.* **bump′y.**

bumper (bump′ėr), *n.* **1,** a heavy rubber, metal, or plastic device on a car, truck, bus, etc., for absorbing shock from a collision and protecting the body of the car from damage; **2,** an overflowing cup; esp., one used for a toast; **3,** *Colloq.* anything unusually large:—*adj.* very large; as, a *bumper* crop. Also, **bumper car; bumper sticker.**

bump-kin (bump′kin), *n.* an awkward clumsy person; lout; rustic.

bun (bun), *n.* **1,** a sweetened, raised roll; **2,** a roll of hair worn on the top or back of the head.

bunch (bunch), *n.* **1,** a cluster, as of grapes; a bouquet, as of flowers; **2,** a collection of things of the same kind fastened together; as, a *bunch* of keys:—*v.i.* and *v.t.* **1,** to form into a cluster or bouquet; **2,** to gather into folds; **3,** to group together.

bun-dle (bun′dl), *n.* **1,** a number of things bound together; a parcel; as, a *bundle* of rags; a *bundle* of books; **2,** a quantity of something in one mass; as, a *bundle* of carpet:—*v.t.* [bun-dled, bun-dling], **1,** to tie in a mass or roll; **2,** to send off in a hurry; as, they *bundled* him out of town:—*v.t.* to pack up and start in haste; as, they *bundled* off before daylight; **3,** in *computing,* to sell a set of software together as a package in a computer.

bun-ga-low (bung′ga-lō′), *n.* a one-storey house or cottage.

bun-gee cord (bun′jē kôrd′), *n.* a stretchable cord of rubber or plastic that is often used to hold items in place.

bungee jumping, the sport of jumping from a high place using a long bungee cord attached to the ankles for safety.

bun-gle (bung′gl), *v.i.* and *v.t.* [bun-gled, bun-gling], to perform in a clumsy and unskillful manner:—*n.* a clumsy performance.—*n.* **bun′ gler.**

bun-ion (bun′yun), *n.* an inflamed swelling on the foot, usually on the big toe.

bunk (bungk), *n.* a shelf or recess used for a bed, as in a ship, camp, or the like:—*v.i.* to sleep in a bunk or bed.

bunk-er (bungk′ėr), *n.* **1,** a large bin, esp. for storing fuel on a ship; **2,** on a golf links, a sand trap or rough hazard; hence, an obstacle of any kind; **3,** a fortified chamber, usually below ground.

bun-ny (bun′i), *n.* a pet name for a rabbit; as, the Easter *bunny.*

bunt (bunt), *v.t.* and *v.i.* **1,** to butt or push, as with the head or horns; **2,** in baseball, to tap the ball a short distance within the infield by meeting it with a loosely held bat:—*n.* **1,** a push, as with horns; **2,** in baseball, a bunted ball.

buoy (boi; bo͞o′i), *n.* **1,** a floating object to show the position of rocks or shoals, or of a channel; **2,** a device to keep a person afloat: a *life buoy:*—*v.t.* to support; as, to *buoy* up one's hopes.

buoy-ant (boi′ant; bo͞o′yant), *adj.* **1,** able to float in a fluid, as cork; **2,** vivacious; light-hearted; cheerful.—*n.* **buoy′an-cy.**

bur-den (bûr′dn), *n.* **1,** something carried; a load; **2,** something endured, as a trouble or sorrow; **3,** the bearing of loads or packs; as, a beast of *burden;* **4,** the cargo-carrying capacity of a vessel; tonnage; **5,** a refrain or theme; as, the *burden* of a song:—*v.t.* **1,** to load; **2,** to put too much upon; oppress.—*adj.* **bur′den-some.**

bur-dock (bûr′dok′), *n.* a coarse weed with broad leaves and a prickly, clinging fruit.

bu-reau (bū′rō; bū-rō′), *n.* [*pl.* bureaus or bureaux (bū′rōz)], **1,** a low chest of drawers for clothing; **2,** an office or department; as, an employment *bureau;* information *bureau;* **3,** a government office or department.

bu-reauc-ra-cy (bū-rok′ra-si; bū-rō′kra-si), *n.* [*pl.* bureaucracies], **1,** government by an organized system of bureaus or departments; **2,** officials of such a government, spoken of as a whole.—*n.* **bu′reau-crat′** (bū′rō-krat′).

bur-ger (bûr′gėr), *n.* Same as **hamburger.**

bur-glar (bûr′glėr), *n.* one who breaks into a building to steal.—*n.* **bur′gla-ry.**

bur-i-al (ber′i-al), *n.* the act or ceremony of placing a body in the grave.

bur-ied (ber′ēd), *p.t.* of *bury:*—*adj.* that has been buried; as, *buried* treasure.

bur-ka (bûr′ka), *n.* the clothing traditionally worn by Muslim women, consisting of a veil and long, flowing robes that cover them from head to toe.

bur-lap (bûr′lap), *n.* a coarse fabric of jute or hemp, used for bags, curtains, etc.

bur-lesque (bûr-lesk′), *n.* **1,** a ridiculous imitation; a parody; **2,** a composition or play in which a trifling subject is treated with mock dignity, or a dignified subject with irreverence:—*v.t.* and *v.i.* [burlesqued, burles-quing], to ridicule by exaggeration:—*adj.* amusingly imitative.

bur-ly (bûr′li), *adj.* [bur-li-er, bur-li-est], strong and muscular.—*n.* **bur′li-ness.**

burn (bûrn), *v.t.* [burned (bûrnd) or burnt (bûrnt), burn-ing], **1,** to destroy or damage by fire or heat; **2,** to use or consume as fuel for heat or light; as, we *burn* oil; this lamp *burns* kerosene; **3,** to affect or injure by heat, acid, or the like; as, the sun *burned* her skin; **4,** to expose intentionally to the action of fire, as wood to make charcoal; **5,** in surgery, to apply heat or acid to; cauterize:—*v.i.* **1,** to be on fire; **2,** to suffer from, or be injured by, too much heat; **3,** to be inflamed with passion or desire; as, he *burns* to win fame; **4,** to feel a sensation of heat; as, his ears *burned;* **5,** to blaze; glow; be bright; as, the scene *burned* with colour:—*n.* an injury caused by fire; any damage caused by too much heat.—*n.* **burn′er.**

bur-nish (bûr′nish), *v.t.* to polish by rubbing, as metal:—*n.* polish; brightness.

burn-out (bûrn′out′), *n.* **1,** physical and mental exhaustion due to stress and overwork; as, after the exams were over, she experienced *burnout;* **2,** a person who is worn out from overwork, stress, or drug abuse; **3,** the shutting down of an engine on a jet or a rocket after the supply of fuel is exhausted or shut off.

burp (bûrp), *v.i. Slang* to belch.

burr (bûr), *n.* **1,** a thin ridge or roughness left by a tool in cutting or shaping metal; **2,** a small rotating drill used by dentists; **3,** a prickly, clinging seedcase; also, the plant that produces these; **4,** a person or thing that clings like a burr; **5,** a rough, guttural pronunciation of *r*:—*v.i.* and *v.t.* to pronounce with a rough or guttural sound; as, to *burr* one's *r's*.

bur-ro (bur′ō; boor′ō), *n.* [*pl.* burros], in the southwestern U.S., a small donkey.

bur-row (bur′ō), *n.* **1,** a hole in the ground, such as is dug by an animal as a refuge or nest; **2,** hence, a secluded dwelling place or place of retreat:—*v.i.* **1,** to dig a hole in the earth, as for shelter; **2,** to lodge in a burrow; **3,** to dig or search; as, he was *burrowing* in an old trunk:—*v.t.* to build by burrowing; as, to *burrow* a cave.

bur-sa-ry (bûr′sa-ri), *n.* a grant of money for support of a student at college or university.

burst (bûrst), *v.i.* [burst, burst-ing], **1,** to explode; break open; fly to pieces; as, our water heater *burst*; **2,** to break out into sudden action or expression of feeling; as, to *burst* into tears; **3,** to appear or disappear suddenly; as, a scene *burst* upon our view; **4,** to be full to overflowing; as, the bags are *bursting* with mail:—*n.* **1,** a violent or sudden breaking forth; as, a *burst* of applause; **2,** a broken place; as, a *burst* in a gas pipe; **3,** a rush; spurt; as, a *burst* of energy.

bur-y (ber′i), *v.t.* [buried, bury-ing], **1,** to place in a grave, tomb, etc.; **2,** to cover from sight; conceal, as treasure; **3,** to keep secret; as, to *bury* one's past; **4,** to engross; as, he *buried* himself in a book.

bus (bus) [*pl.* buses; busses], *n.* **1,** an omnibus; a large public vehicle with many rows of seats for carrying passengers; **2,** an electrical pathway that sends information from one part of a computer to another:—*v.t.* [bused, bus-ing or bussed, bus-sing] to send or go by bus; as, to *bus* students to school.

bush (boosh), *n.* **1,** a shrub or low-growing plant that develops some wood in its stem; **2,** an uncleared forest or bushy region, away from cities or towns.—*n.* **bush′man; bush′rang′er; bush′land.**

bushed (boosht), *adj. Colloq.* exhausted; fatigued.

bush-el (boosh′el), *n.* **1,** a unit of dry measure, containing four pecks, or 32 quarts; **2,** a container holding a bushel.

bush pilot, an airplane pilot who flies above Canada's vast bushlands to frontier outposts, esp. in northern Canada.

bush-whack-er (boosh′hwak′ėr), *n.* one used to travelling through dense bush afoot or by boat; also, someone who works or lives in the bush.

bush-y (boosh′i), *adj.* [bush-i-er, bush-i-est], **1,** growing thickly; as, *bushy* hair; **2,** overgrown with shrubs.

busi-ness (biz′nis), *n.* **1,** employment; regular occupation; **2,** duty; mission; as, I made it my *business* to see that the job was done; **3,** concern; as, it is no *business* of mine; **4,** affair; matter; as, the trial was an unpleasant *business*; **5,** a commercial enterprise; as, she started a hardware *business*; **6,** activity in trade; as, *business* was good last month:—*adj.* relating to commercial activities; as, a *business* deal.—*adj.* **busi′ness-like′.**—*n.* **busi′ness-per′son; busi′ness-man′; busi′ness-wo′man.** Also, **business administration; business class; business day; business cycle.**

busk (busk), *v.t.* to entertain, esp. perform music, in a public place, such as a subway or shopping mall, while seeking donations.—*n.* **busk′er; busk′ing.**

bust (bust), *n.* **1,** the upper front of the body; the breast or bosom, esp. of a woman; **2,** a piece of sculpture representing the head and shoulders.

[1]**bus-tle** (bus′l), *n.* noisy activity:—*v.i.* [bustled, bus-tling], to be noisily and fussily busy; to move in a busy and excited way.

[2]**bus-tle** (bus′l), *n.* a pad or a framework formerly worn under a woman's skirt just below the back of the waist.

bus-y (biz′i), *adj.* [bus-i-er, bus-i-est], **1,** at work; active; not idle; **2,** produced by industry or activity; as, the *busy* hum of the factory; **3,** full of activity; as, a *busy* crossing; **4,** in use, as a telephone line:—*v.t.* [busied, busy-ing], to keep constantly occupied; as, *busied* with housework.—*adv.* **bus′i-ly.**

bus-y-bod-y (biz′i-bod′i), *n.* [*pl.* busybodies], a person who meddles in the affairs of others.

but (but), *adv.* only; as, speak *but* a word:—*prep.* except; as, I can bear all *but* that:—*conj.* **1,** still; yet; as, poor *but* honest; **2,** on the contrary; as, you go, *but* I stay; **3,** that; as, I do not doubt *but* it is true; **4,** that not; as, who knows *but* he will succeed?

butch-er (booch′ėr), *n.* **1,** a person who kills and dresses animals for food; **2,** a meat dealer; **3,** a cruel, bloody murderer:—*v.t.* **1,** to kill and dress (animals) for food; **2,** to murder by violence; **3,** to botch or mangle; ruin.—*n.* **butch′er-y.**

but-ler (but′lėr), *n.* a manservant, usually the chief servant in a household.

[1]**butt** (but), *n.* **1,** the thicker, heavier, or lower part of anything, as of a whip or a gun; **2,** what is left after a part has been cut away or used up; **3,** any of several kinds of hinge or joint.

[2]**butt** (but), *v.t.* to strike with, or as with, lowered head:—*v.i.* to bump; collide; as, he *butted* into the table:—*n.* a push or sudden thrust with the head.

[3]**butt** (but), *n.* that at which anything is aimed; a target, esp. for ridicule; as, to be the *butt* of jokes.

butte (būt), *n.* an isolated tablelike hill.

but-ter (but′ėr), *n.* **1,** the fatty substance obtained from milk or cream by churning; **2,** any butterlike substance; as, peanut *butter;* peach *butter:*—*v.t.* to spread or season with butter.—*adj.* **but′ter-y.**

but-ter-fin-gers (but′ėr-fing′gėrz), *n. Colloq.* a clumsy, awkward, or careless person who tends to drop things; as, the goalie is a real *butterfingers.*—*adj.* **but′ter-fin′gered.**

but-ter-fly (but′ėr-flī′), *n.* [*pl.* butterflies], **1,** a day-flying insect with a long sucking beak, two long knobbed feelers, and four wings, often bright-coloured; as, the monarch *butterfly.*

but-ter-milk (but′ėr-milk′), *n.* the liquid left when the butterfat of milk has been removed after churning.

but-ter-scotch (but′ėr-skôch′), *n.* and *adj.* a taffy made of brown sugar and butter; as, a *butterscotch* sundae.

butter tart, a sweet, rich tart with a butter, brown sugar, syrup, raisin, and spice filling.

but-tock (but′uk), *n.* the part of the hip on which one sits; *pl.* the rump.

but-ton (but′n), *n.* **1,** a small disk or knob of bone, wood, glass, plastic, metal, etc., used for fastening or ornamenting a garment; **2,** anything like this, as the knob operating or turning on an electric switch, an elevator, a computer, etc.:—*v.t.* and *v.i.* to fasten with buttons.

but-ton-hole (but′n-hōl′), *n.* a stitched slit for a button to pass through:—*v.t.* [buttonholed, buttonhol-ing], **1,** to furnish with buttonholes; **2,** to edge (cloth) with the stitching used in making buttonholes; **3,** to engage (a person) in conversation, often against his or her will; as, to *buttonhole* someone in the hall.

but-tress (but′ris), *n.* **1,** brickwork or masonry built against a wall or building to support it; **2,** any prop or support:—*v.t.* to support with, or as with, a buttress; strengthen; brace.

buy (bī), *v.t.* [bought (bôt), buy-ing], **1,** to get by paying a price agreed on; as, to *buy* a snowboard; **2,** to gain at a sacrifice; as, to *buy* peace by yielding; **3,** to be the means of getting; as, money cannot *buy* happiness; **4,** to bribe:—*v.i.* to make a purchase; as, I cannot *buy* without money.—*n.* **buy′er.**

buzz (buz), *n.* **1,** a continuous humming sound, as of bees; **2,** a confused or blended murmur, as of voices:—*v.i.* **1,** to make, or speak with, a low hum; **2,** to be full of activity and talk; as, the school *buzzed* with rumours of a new principal; **3,** to fly an airplane low over something.

buz-zard (buz′ėrd), *n.* **1,** any of several hawklike birds of prey with a sharp beak and claws; **2,** the turkey buzzard, a blackish vulture that feeds only on dead flesh.

buzz-word (buz′wôrd′), *n. Colloq.* a new and important-sounding word that is used with a special meaning in a certain business or activity; as, Internet *buzzwords.*

by (bī), *prep.* **1,** beside or near to; as, a chair *by* the window; **2,** along; as, a road *by* the river; over; as, I came *by* the bridge; **3,** in, on, or at; as, *by* night; *by* land; **4,** past and beyond; as, to go *by* the spot; **5,** according to; from; as, known *by* his gait; to judge *by* appearances; **6,** not any later than; as, to finish *by* two o'clock; **7,** through the agency of; as, to send word *by* a messenger; **8,** through the action of; as, a novel *by* Margaret Atwood; **9,** because of; as, to succeed *by* industry; **10,** to or in the amount of; as, taller *by* several centimetres; the game was won *by* one goal; **11,** with regard to; as, he dealt well *by* me; **12,** with the witness of; in the name of; as, to swear *by* all that I value; **13,** in the measure of; as, sell tea *by* the kilogram; **14,** in the manner of; as, *by* accident; **15,** one point in the direction of; as, north *by* east:—*adv.* **1,** near; at hand; as, to stand *by;* **2,** aside; in reserve; as, put *by* some money; **3,** past; as, he drove *by.*

by-election (bī′e-lek′shun), *n.* an election between regular elections to fill one or more vacancies.

by-gone (bī′gôn′), *adj.* past; gone by:—*n.* a thing of the past.

by-law (bī′lô′), *n.* a rule or law made by a corporation, a city council, etc., for the regulation of its affairs; a local law.

by-line (bī′līn′), *n.* a line at the beginning or end of a newspaper article or magazine story that identifies the author.

by-pass (bī′pås′), *n.* **1,** a detour; shunt; **2,** a road to enable motorists to avoid cities, etc.; **3,** an operation to allow blood to pass around a damaged blood vessel; as, a heart *bypass:*—*v.t.* **1,** to detour; go around; **2,** to ignore or avoid; as, to *bypass* the instructions; **3,** to go over the head of (a superior, etc.).

by-prod-uct (bī′prod′ukt), *n.* something of value produced in a manufacturing process, other than the principal product; as, sawdust is a *byproduct* in a sawmill; buttermilk is a *byproduct* of butter; a secondary product.

by-stand-er (bī′stan′dėr), *n.* a person who looks on, but does not take part.

byte (bīt), *n.* in *computing,* a group of digits,

usually eight, that a computer stores as one unit in its memory.

by-way (bī′wā′), *n.* a side path; a road little known or used.

by-word (bī′wûrd′), *n.* **1,** a proverb or saying; **2,** an object of scorn or ridicule; as, her vanity made her a *byword.*

C

C, c (sē), *n.* [*pl.* C's, c's], **1,** the third letter of the alphabet; **2,** the Roman numeral for 100; **3,** in *music,* the first tone in the major scale of C; **4,** the third-highest mark, grade, or level.

cab (kab), *n.* **1,** an automobile for hire to passengers; a taxi; **2,** a public carriage drawn by one horse; **3,** on an engine, truck, steam shovel, crane, etc., the place for the operator.

cab-a-ret (kab′a-rā′; kab′a-rā′), *n.* a restaurant where music, dancing, etc., are provided for the patrons.

cab-bage (kab′ij), *n.* a vegetable with dense leaves forming a round, hard head.

cab-in (kab′in), *n.* **1,** a small hut or cottage; **2,** on a ship or airplane, an enclosed place for passengers.

cab-i-net (kab′i-nit), *n.* a piece of furniture or a closet having shelves or drawers, in which a number of articles are kept or displayed; as, a curio *cabinet;* a medicine *cabinet;* a filing *cabinet:*—**Cabinet,** a group of persons chosen by the head of a government as advisers in managing a country's affairs.

cabinet minister, the head of a department of the government; a member of the cabinet.

ca-ble (kā′bl), *n.* **1,** a chain or strong rope of hemp or wire strands, variously used, as for supporting suspension bridges, towing automobiles, mooring ships, etc.; **2,** an insulated bundle of wires used to carry electricity and messages: telephone, telegraph, television, and some Internet systems use cables:—*v.t.* and *v.i.* [ca-bled, ca-bling], to send a message by cable.

ca-ble-gram (kā′bl-gram′), *n.* a message sent by undersea cable.

cable television, an antennaless system in which television shows are sent through a cable instead of over the airwaves. Subscribers pay a fee for cable TV service in order to get better reception or to receive channels not available on open airwaves.

ca-boose (ka-bo͞os′), *n.* **1,** a kitchen on the deck of a ship; **2,** a small car in which train workers rest, sleep, or eat, generally attached to the end of a freight train.

ca-ca-o (ka-kā′ō; ka-kä′ō), *n.* **1,** a small evergreen tree of tropical America; **2,** the seeds of this tree, from which cocoa and chocolate are made.

cache (kåsh), *n.* **1,** a hidden store of food, supplies, etc.; **2,** a hiding place; as, the *cache* of the stolen merchandise; **3,** in *computing,* auxiliary computer memory that is designed to allow easy and quick access to temporarily stored data.

cack-le (kak′l), *n.* **1,** the cry, or clucking, of a hen or goose just after it has laid an egg; **2,** chatter; noisy, idle talk; as, the *cackle* of the diners drowned the music—*v.i.* [cackled, cack-ling], **1,** to cry like a goose or a hen; **2,** to giggle; prattle; as, they *cackled* too much to get anything done.

ca-coph-o-ny (ka-kof′o-ni), *n.* harsh, unpleasant, or discordant sound; as, a *cacophony* arose when the new orchestra began to practise: opposite of *euphony.*

cac-tus (kak′tus), *n.* [*pl.* cactuses or cacti (kak′tī)], a leafless desert plant with sharp spines along a fleshy stem and branches. Some kinds bear very showy flowers.

cad (kad), *n.* an ill-bred, ungentlemanly man.

CAD (kad), *abbrev.* in *computing,* short for *c*omputer-*a*ssisted *d*esign.

ca-dav-er-ous (ka-dav′ėr-us), *adj.* gaunt; ghastly, like a corpse.

cad-die or **caddy** (kad′i), *n.* [*pl.* caddies], a person who carries clubs for a golf player:—*v.i.* [caddied, caddy-ing], to be a caddie.

cad-dy (kad′i), *n.* [*pl.* caddies], **1,** a small box for holding tea; as, a tea *caddy;* **2,** any container; **3,** a caddie.

ca-dence (kā′dens), *n.* **1,** the rise and fall of the voice in reading or speaking; **2,** rhythm, as in music; **3,** in *music,* chords at the end of part of a composition.

ca-det (ka-det′), *n.* **1,** a student in a naval or military academy; **2,** a person receiving military training.—*n.* **ca-det′ship.**

ca-du-ce-us (ka-dū′sē-us), *n.* Hermes' staff with two intertwined serpents, used as a symbol by the medical profession.

CADUCEUS

café (ka-fā), *n.* a small, informal restaurant; also, the French word for coffee.

caf-e-te-ri-a (kaf′e-tē′ri-a), *n.* a restaurant where patrons order food at a counter and carry it on trays to provided tables.

caf-fe-ine (kaf′ēn′; kaf′ēn′) or **caf-fe-in,** *n.* the drug or stimulant in coffee and tea.

cage (kāj), *n.* **1,** a box or enclosure, usually

of bars or wire, used to confine birds or animals; **2,** anything like a cage in form or effect; as, a *cage* for baseball practice; a shark *cage*:—*v.t.* [caged, cag-ing], to confine; shut up in, or as if in, a cage.

caisse pop-u-laire (kes pop-ū-lâr′), *n.* (*pl.* caisses populaires) French-Canadian credit unions.

ca-jole (ka-jōl′), *v.t.* [cajoled, cajol-ing], to coax with flattery, etc.; wheedle; as, she *cajoled* the child into coming.—*n.* **ca-jol′er-y.**

Ca-jun (kā′jen), *n.* **1,** a descendant of French-speaking settlers of Louisiana from Acadia, esp. those expelled in the mid-eighteenth century from what became the Canadian Maritime provinces; **2,** the French dialect spoken by these people:—*adj.* of or having to do with the French-speaking people of Louisiana, their language, and their culture; as, *Cajun* cooking.

cake (kāk), *n.* **1,** a small mass of dough, sweetened and baked; as, layer *cake*; **2,** a small portion of thin batter or of ground-up meat, fish, potatoes, etc., cooked on a griddle, such as a pan*cake*; **3,** any small compressed or flattened mass; as, a *cake* of soap:—*v.i.* and *v.t.* [caked, cak-ing], to form or harden into a hard mass; as, the mud *caked.*

ca-lam-i-ty (ka-lam′i-ti), *n.* [*pl.* calamities], **1,** an event that causes widespread destruction, as a hurricane or an earthquake; **2,** a great personal misfortune, as the death of a loved one, loss of sight, etc.—*adj.* **ca-lam′i-tous.**

cal-ci-um (kal′si-um), *n.* a soft, white metal, found in combination with some other substance, as in lime, marble, chalk, or bone, and in food such as milk and cheese, required for strong teeth and bones.

cal-cu-late (kal′kū-lāt′), *v.t.* [calculat-ed, calculat-ing], **1,** to figure out by arithmetic; as, to *calculate* the cost of a house; **2,** to estimate in any way; as, to *calculate* the benefits of science; also, chiefly in *p.p.*, to intend; design; as, a program *calculated* to help business:—*v.i.* **1,** to make a computation or estimate; as, he *calculated* wrongly; **2,** *Colloq.* to plan; as, he *calculated* on arriving before dark.—*adj.* **cal′cu-lat′ed.**—*n.* **cal′cu-la′tion.**

cal-cu-la-tor (kal′kū-lā′tėr), *n.* a small electronic or mechanical machine that can solve number problems automatically.

cal-cu-lus (kal′kū-lus), *n.* any of several branches of higher mathematics using algebraic symbols.

cal-dron (kôl′drun), *n.* Same as **cauldron.**

ca-lèche (ka-lesh′), *n.* a light, two-wheeled, two-passenger carriage with a folding top, pulled by one horse.

cal-en-dar (kal′en-dėr), *n.* **1,** a method of reckoning time, esp. as to the length and divisions of a year; **2,** a chart, setting forth the days, weeks, and months of a year; **3,** a list of things to be done in order of time, or schedule of coming events; as, a court *calendar*; an events *calendar*:—*v.t.* to register; list.

¹calf (kåf), *n.* [*pl.* calves (kåvz)], **1,** the young of the cow; **2,** the young of certain other large mammals, as of the whale, elephant, seal, or moose; **3,** leather made of the skin of the calf: also called *calfskin.*

²calf (kåf), *n.* [*pl.* calves (kåvz)], the fleshy hinder part of the human leg, between the knee and the ankle.

calf-skin (kåf′skin′), *n.* leather made from the skin of a calf, used esp. for shoes and gloves.

cal-i-bre or **cal-i-ber** (kal′i-bėr), *n.* **1,** the inside diameter of the barrel of a pistol, gun, etc.; as, a .22 *calibre* revolver; **2,** mental capacity; degree of merit or importance; as, we play teams of our own *calibre.*

cal-i-co (kal′i-kō), *n.* [*pl.* calicoes or calicos], a cheap cotton cloth, usually printed with figured or flowered patterns:—*adj.* made of calico.

cal-i-per or **cal-li-per** (kal′i-pėr), *n.* a compasslike tool with two movable legs for measuring outside or inside diameters of pipes or distances between surfaces. Often used in plural.

cal-is-then-ics (kal′is-then′iks), *n.pl.* Same as **callisthenics.**

calk (kôk), *v.t.* Same as **caulk.**

call (kôl), *v.t.* **1,** to utter in a loud voice; as, to *call* the players; to announce, esp. with authority; as, the announcer *calls* the flight numbers; **2,** to summon or request to come; as, to be *called* home; **3,** to appeal to; as, she *called* for mercy; **4,** to bring up for action; as, to *call* a case in court; **5,** to arouse from sleep; **6,** to invite or summon to meet; as, to *call* delegates together; **7,** to issue a command for; as, to *call* a strike; **8,** to invite to a position; as, to *call* a minister; **9,** to direct; as, to *call* one's attention to something; **10,** to telephone to; as, he *called* me from St. John; **11,** to demand payment of (a loan); **12,** to give a name to; **13,** to regard as being; as, I *call* her my friend; **14,** to estimate; as, I should *call* it six kilometres; **15,** in *cards,* to require (a player) to show his or her hand; **16,** in *baseball,* to designate (a pitched ball) as a strike or a ball; **17,** in *sports,* to order (a game) to begin or end; as, the game was *called* at two o'clock:—*v.t.* **1,** to cry out loudly; **2,** to make a brief visit; **3,** to communicate by telephone; as, he *called* from St. John:—*n.* **1,** a loud shout, as for help; **2,** a summons; **3,** an invitation; as, a *call* to preach; **4,** need; occasion; as, she has no *call* to be offended; **5,** a short visit; **6,** the cry or note of an animal or bird:—*adj.* in business, payable on demand; as, a *call* loan.—*n.* **call′er.**

call-er (kôl′ėr), *n.* **1,** one who calls; esp., one who pays a brief visit; **2,** one who calls off or recites in a singsong the movements of a square dance.

call-ing (kôl′ing), *n.* **1,** a summons; **2,** a vocation or profession.

cal-li-o-pe (ka-lī′ō-pē′; popularly, kal′i-ōp′), *n.* a mechanical organ that produces tones by a set of whistles.

cal-lis-then-ics (kal′is-then′iks), *n.pl.* **1,** simple gymnastic exercises, without the use of special equipment; **2,** used as *sing.*, the science of such exercises.—*adj.* **cal′lis-then′ic.**

cal-lous (kal′us), *adj.* **1,** hardened, as the skin forming a callus; **2,** unfeeling; insensitive; as, he was *callous* to criticism.—*adv.* **cal′lous-ly.**—*n.* **cal′lous-ness.**

cal-low (kal′ō), *adj.* immature; raw; green; as, a *callow* youth.

cal-lus (kal′us), *n.* [*pl.* calluses], **1,** a thick, hard place on the skin, as on the palm of the hand; **2,** new growth at the ends of fractured bones serving to knit them.

calm (käm), *adj.* peaceful; undisturbed; not nervous or excited; as, a *calm* scene; a *calm* child:—*n.* stillness; peace and quiet; as, a *calm* after the storm:—*v.t.* to quiet; as, to *calm* an excited child:—*v.i.* to become calm; as, to *calm* down after a fight.—*adj.* **calm′ly.**—*n.* **calm′ness.**

cal-o-rie (kal′o-ri), *n.* a unit of heat or energy: used also to measure the heat or energy derived from foods.

cal-u-met (kal′ū-met′), *n.* a formerly used ceremonial, long-stemmed peace pipe of the First Nations people.

cal-um-ny (kal′um-ni), *n.* [*pl.* calumnies], a slanderous report; slander.—*v.t.* **ca-lum′ni-ate.**—*adj.* **ca-lum′ni-ous.**

calve (kåv), *v.i.* [calved, calv-ing], **1,** to bring forth young; as, cows, whales, elephants, and does are said to *calve*; **2,** to separate or break off in chunks, as of glaciers, which produce icebergs.

ca-lyp-so (ka-lip′sō), *n.* and *adj.* a lively Trinidadian jazz marked by syncopated rhythms and verse and loose rhyming; as, a *calypso* singer or dancer.

cal-yx (kā′liks; ka′liks), *n.* [*pl.* calyxes or calyces (kā′li-sēz′)], the outer sheath of a bud, composed of green sepals.

CALYX (C)

cam (kam), *n.* **1,** a device for changing circular to variable motion, often an oval or irregularly shaped wheel revolving with a shaft; **2,** short for *camera*:—CAM, in *computing*, computer-aided manufacturing. Also, **cam′shaft′.**

cam-ber (kam′bėr), *n.* **1,** the setting of the front wheels of a motor vehicle closer together at the bottom than at the top; **2,** any slightly convex surface.

cam-bi-um (kam′bi-um), *n.* the layer of soft tissue between the sapwood and the bark of trees, which develops into the new wood and the new bark.

came (kām), *p.t.* of *come.*

cam-el (kam′el), *n.* a large, four-footed, cud-chewing animal, of which there are two kinds: the Arabian camel or dromedary, with a single hump, and the Bactrian camel, with two humps, found only in Asia: used as beasts of burden in the desert, since they can go for several days without water.

cam-e-o (kam′i-ō), *n.* [*pl.* cameos], **1,** a gem, stone, or shell carved with a raised design; **2,** a brief appearance in a movie of a well-known actor.

cam-er-a (kam′ėr-a), *n.* an apparatus for taking photographs, movies, or videotapes; also, a similar device used in television to form a picture and send it out as an electronic signal for broadcasting.

cam-i-sole (kam′i-sōl), *n.* a woman's fancy undergarment, worn under a blouse or shirt.

cam-ou-flage (kam′oo-flåzh), *n.* **1,** disguise; concealment; pretence; as, her calm manner is mere *camouflage*; **2,** the art or practice of disguising guns, ships, soldiers, etc., to hide them from the enemy:—*v.t.* [camouflaged, camouflag-ing], to conceal by disguising; as, the soldiers' uniforms *camouflaged* them in the jungle.

camp (kamp), *n.* **1,** a collection of tents or other temporary dwellings; also, the ground on which these are set up; **2,** the people staying there; as, he belonged to a Gypsy *camp;* **3,** a summer residence in the country; **4,** one side in war, religion, politics, etc.; as, the republican *camp*:—*v.i.* to pitch a camp; live in a camp.—*n.* **camp′ing.**

cam-paign (kam-pān′), *n.* **1,** a series of military operations, conducted in a definite place, or with a single purpose; **2,** action organized to produce a certain result; as, a political *campaign*:—*v.i.* to take an active part in or go on a campaign.—*n.* **cam-paign′er.**

camp-er (kam′pėr), *n.* **1,** a person who camps; **2,** a car or trailer that is built for use on camping trips.

camp-fire (kamp′fīr′), *n.* **1,** a fire in a camp that is used for heat and cooking; **2,** a social gathering around a campfire.

cam-phor (kam′fėr), *n.* a whitish crystalline gum with pungent odour, obtained chiefly from the camphor tree of eastern Asia, and used in medicines, etc.

cam-pus (kam′pus), *n.* the grounds of a school, college, or university.

¹can (kan), *verb* [*p.t.* could (kood)], **1,** to be able to; have the power to; as, I *can* dance;

2, *Colloq.* to have the right or permission to; as, *can* I leave now?: distinguished from "may" in formal use; as, *may* I leave now?

[2]**can** (kan), *n.* **1,** a metal container for holding or preserving liquids, solids, or powders; as, a coffee *can*; **2,** the contents of or amount in a can; as, one *can* of peaches will be enough for lunch; **3,** any similar container; as, a garbage *can*:—*v.t.* [canned, can-ning], **1,** to preserve in sealed cans, as fruits or vegetables; **2,** *Slang* to stop; as, *can* that noise; also, to discharge; dismiss.

Can-a-da Day (ka′na-da), *n.* holiday on July 1 that celebrates the anniversary of *Confederation*, known formerly as *Dominion Day*.

Canada goose, a large wild goose of North America, with a black head and neck, white throat, and brownish-grey body.

Canada jay, a bird of the North American coniferous forest, having greyish feathers and a black-capped head.

Ca-na-di-an (ka-nā′dē-an), *n.* a person who lives in or comes from Canada:—*adj.* having to do with Canada.

Canadian English, the form of English spoken by English-speaking Canadians.

Canadian Forces or **Canadian Armed Forces**, the armed forces of Canada: the combined forces of the army (*Mobile Command*), navy (*Maritime Command*), and air force (*Air Command*).

Canadian French, the form of French spoken by French-speaking Canadians.

Ca-na-dien (ka-na-dyen′), *n.* the French word for a French Canadian.—*n.fem.* **Ca-na-dienne** (ka-na-dyen′).

ca-nal (ka-nal′), *n.* **1,** a human-made water channel, used for either navigation or irrigation; **2,** any tubelike part of the body; as, the alimentary *canal*.

ca-nar-y (ka-nâr′i), *n.* [*pl.* canaries], **1,** a small, yellow songbird, originally from the Canary Islands; **2,** a light-yellow colour:—*adj.* of a light-yellow colour.

ca-nas-ta (ka-nas′ta), *n.* a card game of the rummy family in which the aim is to meld sets of seven or more cards.

can-cel (kan′sel), *v.t.* [cancelled, cancelling or canceled, canceling], **1,** to cross out with a line or lines; mark so as to deprive of value; as, to *cancel* a stamp, a cheque; **2,** to take back; withdraw; as, to *cancel* an order; **3,** to balance; offset; as, this item *cancels* that; **4,** in *arithmetic*, to strike out (a common factor) from the numerator and the denominator of a fraction.—*n.* **can′cel-la′tion.**

Can-cer (kan′sėr), *n.* **1,** a northern constellation, the Crab; **2,** the fourth sign of the zodiac ♋, which the sun enters about June 22.

can-cer (kan′ser), *n.* **1,** a harmful, often deadly, tumour, or growth, that spreads and eats into the body; **2,** the diseased condition resulting from such a growth; **3,** something very bad that spreads in a harmful way; as, war is a *cancer* of humanity:—**Tropic of Cancer**, the northern boundary of the torrid zone; 23° 27′ north latitude.—*adj.* **can′cer-ous.**

Can-con (kan′kon′), *n.* *Colloq.* Canadian content, esp. the rules and regulations regarding radio and TV broadcasting quotas designed to promote Canadian artists; as, Bryan Adams is considered *Cancon*.

can-de-la-brum (kan′de-lā′brum; -lä′), *n.* [*pl.* candelabra or candelabrums], a large ornamental branched candlestick or an electric light similar to this.

can-did (kan′did), *adj.* **1,** outspoken; frank; as, a *candid* person; a *candid* opinion; **2,** unprejudiced; fair; **3,** not posed; as, a *candid* photograph.

can-di-date (kan′di-dāt′), *n.* one who offers himself or herself, or is proposed by others, as a contestant for an office, grade, honour, etc.—*n.* **can′di-da-cy.**—*n.* **can′di-da′ture.**

can-dle (kan′dl), *n.* **1,** a slender stick of tallow or wax enclosing a wick, burned to furnish light; **2,** anything resembling a candle in form or purpose:—*v.t.* [can-dled, can-dling], to test or examine (eggs) by holding between the eye and a small light.

can-dle-stick (kan′dl-stik′), *n.* a device for holding a candle.

can-dour or **can-dor** (kan′dėr), *n.* **1,** openness; frankness, as of speech; **2,** fairness; as, to judge with *candour*.

can-dy (kan′di), *n.* [*pl.* candies], something to eat made largely of sugar, usually cut or formed into small pieces:—*v.t.* [candied, candy-ing], to coat, cook, or preserve with sugar:—*v.i.* to turn into sugar; as, the syrup *candied*:—**candy bar**, a chocolate bar.

cane (kān), *n.* **1,** the woody, jointed stem of certain palms or grasses, as the bamboo or rattan; **2,** sugar cane; **3,** a walking stick:—*v.t.* [caned, can-ing], **1,** to beat, as with a walking stick; **2,** to furnish with parts made of cane; as, to *cane* chairs:—*adj.* made of cane, as a chair seat.

ca-nine (ka′nīn; kā′-; ka-nīn′), *adj.* **1,** pertaining to dogs; doglike; **2,** designating one of the four sharp-pointed teeth, found in most mammals, between the incisors and the bicuspids:—*n.* **1,** one of the canine teeth. (See *dentition*, illustration); **2,** a dog.

can-is-ter (kan′is-tėr), *n.* a box or small container, usually of metal, for holding tea, coffee, etc.

can-ker (kang′kėr), *n.* **1,** anything that destroys by gradual eating or wearing away, as an ulcer in animals, or rust in plants; **2,** a white sore that spreads, esp. in the mouth.—*adj.* **can′ker-ous.**

can-na-bis (kan′a-bis), *n.* the dried flower

of the hemp plant, which, when specially prepared, can be an intoxicant or hallucinogen. Compare *marijuana.*

can-ner-y (kan′ėr-i), *n.* [*pl.* canneries], a factory where fruit, meat, fish, or vegetables are canned.—*n.* **can′ner.**

can-ni-bal (kan′i-bal), *n.* **1,** a human being who eats human flesh; **2,** any animal that eats its own kind:—*adj.* like a cannibal.—*n.* **can′ni-bal-ism.**—*adj.* **can′ni-bal-is′tic.**

can-non (kan′un), *n.* [*pl.* cannon or cannons], a large mounted gun. Also, **can′non-ball′.**

can-not (kan′not), *verb* am, is, or are not able to; as, I *cannot* do this problem.

can-ny (kan′i), *adj.* [can-ni-er, can-ni-est], **1,** shrewd; cautious; as, a *canny* person; **2,** thrifty; frugal.—*adv.* **can′ni-ly.**

ca-noe (ka-nōō′), *n.* a light boat made of bark, canvas, thin wood, or other material and moved by paddles:—*v.i.* [canoed (ka-nōōd), canoe-ing], to paddle, or go in, a canoe.—*n.* **ca-noe′ing.**—*n.* **ca-noe′ist.**

can-on (kan′un), *n.* **1,** an established standard or principle; **2,** a law of a church; **3,** the accepted books of the Bible; **4,** a list of saints; **5,** a clergyman attached to a cathedral.

can-on-ize (kan′un-iz′), *v.t.* [canonized canoniz-ing], to declare (a deceased person) a saint; admit to the list of saints.—*n.* **can′on-i-za′tion.**

can-o-py (kan′o-pi), *n.* [*pl.* canopies], **1,** a covering fixed above a bed, hung over a throne, or held on poles over an important personage; **2,** any overhanging covering, as a *canopy* of trees:—*v.t.* [canopied, canopy-ing], to cover with, or as with, a canopy.

[1]**cant** (kant), *n.* **1,** the words and phrases peculiar to a certain trade, profession, or group, as the slang used by thieves; **2,** the insincere use of religious or moral speech; hypocrisy; **3,** a whining manner of speech, esp. that used by beggars.

[2]**cant** (kant), *n.* **1,** a sloping position; a slant or tilt; as, the *cant* of a roof; **2,** a sudden, forceful thrust resulting in a change of course or position:—*v.t.* **1,** to give a tilt or slant to; **2,** to push or pitch sideways; as, the wind *canted* the boat:—*v.i.* to lean; lean to one side.

can-ta-loupe (kan′ta-lōp′; -lōōp), *n.* a hollow, edible melon with a hard, rigid rind. Also, **can′ta-loup.**

can-tan-ker-ous (kan-tang′kėr-us), *adj. Colloq.* ill-tempered; quarrelsome; as, a *cantankerous* mood; a *cantankerous* person.—*n.* **can-tan′ker-ous-ness.**

can-ta-ta (kan-tä′ta), *n.* a choral composition, often sacred, with a story or play to be sung rather than acted.

can-teen (kan-tēn′), *n.* **1,** a place in a school, factory, camp, or military camp for the sale or distribution of food, drink, etc.; **2,** a small container used for carrying water or other drink when on the march; **3,** a box containing mess utensils for active-service use.

can-ter (kan′tėr), *n.* an easy gallop:—*v.i.* and *v.t.* to gallop, or cause (a horse) to gallop, without haste.

can-ti-lev-er (kan′ti-lē′vėr; -le′vėr), *n.* and *adj.* a bridge with two steelwork arms projecting from piers and joined directly together or by a suspended centre span.

can-to (kan′tō), *n.* [*pl.* cantos], a part or section of a long poem.

can-ton (kan′ton′), *n.* one of the political divisions of a country, province, etc.

Ca-nuck (ka-nuk′), *n. Colloq.* a Canadian.

can-vas (kan′vas), *n.* **1,** a coarse, heavy cloth of hemp, cotton, or flax, used for tents, sails, etc., and as material on which to paint in oil; **2,** an oil painting.

can-vass (kan′vas), *v.t.* **1,** to examine thoroughly; discuss in detail; as, we *canvassed* the subject from A to Z; **2,** to visit (a district, house, or person) in order to get votes or contributions, or make sales:—*v.i.* to seek orders, contributions, votes, etc.; as, to *canvass* for a charity:—*n.* **1,** a thorough examination or discussion; **2,** a solicitation of votes, orders, etc.—*n.* **can′vass-er.**

can-yon (kan′yun), *n.* a deep gorge or valley made by a river or stream.

caou-tchouc (kou′chōōk; kōō′chook; kou-chōōk′), *n.* rubber; India rubber.

cap (kap), *n.* **1,** a tight-fitting covering, esp. one with a peak and without a brim, for a person's head; as, a baseball *cap*; **2,** anything resembling a cap in form or use; as, a *cap* on a bottle; a mushroom *cap*; a nurse's *cap*; a *cap* and gown; **3,** a small quantity of explosive, enclosed in paper, for toy pistols, or in metal, for setting off cartridges, artillery shells, etc.; **4,** a capital or uppercase letter:—*v.t.* [capped, cap-ping], **1,** to cover, as with a cap; as, to *cap* a bottle; **2,** to match or surpass; as, his story *caps* mine.

ca-pa-ble (kā′pa-bl), *adj.* **1,** having skill or ability; as, a *capable* student, etc.; **2,** having the nature or spirit to do a given thing; as, he is quite *capable* of such a trick—*n.* **ca′pa-bil′i-ty.**

ca-pa-cious (ka-pā′shus), *adj.* roomy; able to hold much; as, a *capacious* trunk.

ca-pac-i-ty (ka-pas′i-ti), *n.* [*pl.* capacities], **1,** the power of receiving or holding; also, the amount that can be held; as, the *capacity* of a room, cup, etc.; **2,** mental ability; **3,** position; relationship; as, he served in the *capacity* of teacher.

[1]**cape** (kāp), *n.* a sleeveless outer garment worn loosely over the shoulders; also, a similar part of a garment, attached to a cloak or dress.

[2]**cape** (kāp), *n.* a point of land jutting out into the water; as, *Cape* Race.

[1]**ca-per** (kā′pėr), *n.* **1,** a playful leap or spring; **2,** a prank or scheme:—*v.i.* to skip or jump playfully; frolic.

[2]**ca-per** (kā′pėr), *n.* a kind of low, prickly shrub, grown in Europe:—**capers,** *pl.* buds of the caper, often pickled, used to flavour salads and sauces.

cap-il-lar-y (kap-i′lėr-i; kap′i-lėr′i), *n.* [*pl.* capillaries], a slender, hairlike tube; esp. very minute blood vessels, which connect the smallest arteries with the smallest veins:—*adj.* **1,** hairlike; slender; **2,** relating to the minute blood vessels of the body.—*n.* **cap′i-lar′i-ty.**

cap-i-tal (kap′i-tal), *adj.* **1,** punishable by death; involving the death penalty; as, *capital* crime; *capital* punishment; **2,** in writing and printing, designating one of the large letters, as A, B, C, etc., used at the beginning of a sentence, line of verse, proper noun, etc.; **3,** first in importance; chief; as, the *capital* points in a discussion; **4,** first-rate; as, a *capital* plan:—*n.* **1,** the city or town that is the seat of a government in a country or state; **2,** a capital letter; **3,** accumulated wealth available for use in business; as, he has plenty of *capital* to finance the invention; **4,** any resources.—*adv.* **cap′i-tal-ly.**

cap-i-tal-ism (kap′i-tal-izm), *n.* an economic system resting upon private ownership of wealth used in producing goods.—*n.* **cap′i-tal-ist.**—*adj.* **cap′i-tal-is′tic.**

cap-i-tal-ize (kap′i-tal-īz′), *v.t.* [capitalized, capitaliz-ing], **1,** to furnish (a business) with capital; as, the firm was *capitalized* at $100,000; **2,** to make profitable use of; as, a guide *capitalizes* on his knowledge of the woods; **3,** to print or write with capital letters; start (a word) with, or change (a small letter) to, a capital letter.—*n.* **cap′i-tal-i-za′tion.**

Cap-i-tol (kap′i-tl), *n.* **1,** in the U.S., the building in Washington, D.C., in which Congress meets:—**capitol,** the building in which a state legislature meets.

ca-pit-u-late (ka-pit′ū-lāt′), *v.i.* [capitulated, capitulat-ing], to surrender to an enemy on conditions agreed upon.

ca-pon (kā′pon), *n.* a castrated rooster fattened for eating.

ca-price (ka-prēs′), *n.* **1,** a sudden, unreasoning change of mind or conduct; whim; as, her refusal to go is mere *caprice*; **2,** the tendency to yield to whims.—*adj.* **ca-pri′cious** (ka-prish′us).

[1]**Cap-ri-corn** (kap′ri-kôrn′), *n.* **1,** a southern constellation, the Goat; **2,** the tenth sign of the zodiac [♑], which the sun enters about December 22.

[2]**Cap-ri-corn** (kap′ri-kôrn′), *n.* the Tropic of Capricorn, or southern boundary of the torrid zone, 23° 27′ south latitude.

cap-size (kap-sīz′), *v.i.* and *v.t.* [capsized, capsiz-ing], to upset; turn over (a boat).

cap-stan (kap′stan), *n.* **1,** an upright drum or cylinder, revolving upon a pivot, around which a rope or cable is wound, by means of which heavy weights are raised; **2,** a shaft that drives a tape consistently on a recording device.

cap-sule (kap′sūl), *n.* **1,** a small envelope of gelatin enclosing medicine, vitamins, etc., which can be swallowed whole; **2,** a seedcase, which bursts when ripe; **3,** a skinlike sac enclosing some part or organ of the body; **4,** a part of a space vehicle in flight:—*adj.* in a brief form; condensed; as, a *capsule* description.—*adj.* **cap′su-lar.**

cap-tain (kap′tin), *n.* **1,** one in authority over others acting in a group; a leader; as, the *captain* of a football team; **2,** in the army, an officer ranking below a major and above a lieutenant, and usually in command of a company; **3,** a person who is in command of a ship:—*v.t.* to act as leader or captain of; to lead.

cap-tion (kap′shun), *n.* the heading of an article, chapter, section, etc.; as, a *caption* on the front page of a newspaper, book, magazine, etc., often describing a picture, photo, etc.

cap-tious (kap′shus), *adj.* faultfinding; hard to please; as, his *captious* remarks irritated her.

cap-ti-vate (kap′ti-vāt), *v.t.* [captivat-ed, captivat-ing], to attract; charm; fascinate.—*n.* **cap′ti-va′tion.**

cap-tive (kap′tiv), *n.* a prisoner, esp. one taken in war:—*adj.* **1,** taken or held prisoner; as, a *captive* army; **2,** held within bounds, as if one were a prisoner; as, a *captive* audience.—*n.* **cap-tiv′i-ty; cap′tor.**

cap-ture (kap′tūr; chėr), *v.t.* [captured, captur-ing], to take or seize by force, skill, surprise, trickery, etc.; as, to *capture* a thief; to *capture* the attention; to *capture* a trophy:—*n.* **1,** the act of capturing; an arrest; **2,** the person or thing captured.

car (kär), *n.* **1,** a motor vehicle with four wheels and a motor; an automobile; **2,** any similar vehicle used to carry people or things, such as a railway car, trolley, etc.; **2,** the part of an airship or balloon in which freight, baggage, or passengers are carried; **3,** the cage of an elevator.

ca-rafe (ka-råf′; -räf′), *n.* a glass water bottle or decanter.

car-a-mel (kar′a-mel), *n.* **1,** a kind of candy, of various flavours, generally in the shape of a cube; **2,** burnt sugar used for colouring and flavouring foods.

car-at (kar′at), *n.* a unit of weight, one fifth of a gram, for precious stones; **2,** a **karat.**

car-a-van (kar′a-van′; kar′a-van′), *n.* **1,** a company of persons travelling together for safety, as across a desert or through dangerous country; **2,** any travelling group of people or vehicles; as, a *caravan* of military trucks; **3,** a large covered vehicle, usually with a living unit; a camper or van.

car-a-way (kar′a-wā), *n.* a plant of the parsley family, whose seed is used to flavour small cakes, rye bread, etc.

car-bine (kär′bīn), *n.* **1,** a short, light rifle; **2,** a light repeating rifle.

car-bo-hy-drate (kär′-bō-hi′drāt), *n.* an energy-producing compound of carbon, hydrogen, and oxygen, as sugar or starch.

car-bon (kär′bon), *n.* **1,** a nonmetallic element occurring pure in nature, as the diamond and as graphite, and found in combination in all animal and vegetable substances, esp. coal and charcoal; **2,** either of two rods of hard carbon used in an arc lamp, batteries, etc:—**carbon dioxide,** a gas made up of carbon and oxygen, an important part of the air we breathe:—**carbon monoxide,** a poisonous gas that cars and gas-burning engines produce.—*adj.* **car-bon′ic; car′bon-if′er-ous.**

car-bon-ate (kär′bon-āt′), *v.t.* to charge with carbonic-acid gas; hence, *carbonated* (or soda) water.

car-bun-cle (kär′bung-kl), *n.* a painful inflamed swelling, more severe than a boil.

car-bu-ret-or or **car-bu-ret-tor** (kä′bū-rāt′ėr), *n.* an apparatus used to mix air with gasoline in the form of a vapour or spray, as in the motor of an automobile.

car-cass (kär′kas), *n.* **1,** the dead body of an animal; **2,** contemptuously, the living or dead body of a human being.

[1]**card** (kärd), *n.* **1,** a stiff piece of paper or plastic, usually small and rectangular; as, a post*card*; baseball *card*; greeting *card*; report *card*; credit *card*; debit *card*, etc.; **2,** one of a set of 52 cards divided into four suits and marked with special symbols and numbers, used in playing various games: also called a *playing card*; **3,** a computer circuit board; as, an add-on *card*:—**cards,** any game or games played with playing cards; cardplaying:—**in the cards,** certain to happen:—**put (one's) cards on the table,** to be completely open about something.

[2]**card** (kärd), *n.* a toothed instrument for combing wool, flax, cotton, etc., to prepare it for spinning:—*v.t.* to comb with a card, as wool.

card-board (kärd′bôrd), *n.* stiff pasteboard used for cards, posters, boxes, etc.

car-di-ac (kär′di-ak′), *adj.* pertaining to the heart; as, *cardiac* nerves or muscles.

car-di-gan (kär′di-gan), *n.* a knitted woollen jacket or sweater.

car-di-nal (kär′di-nal), *adj.* **1,** chief; of first importance; as, justice is one of the *cardinal* virtues; **2,** of a rich red colour:—*n.* **1,** a high official in the Roman Catholic Church, appointed by the Pope, and of his council; **2,** a North American songbird, the male of which has bright-red plumage and a pointed crest:—**cardinal numbers,** the numbers *one, two, three,* etc., in distinction from the ordinal numbers, *first, second, third,* etc.:—**cardinal points,** the main directions of the compass: north, east, south, and west.

car-di-o-gram (kär′di-o-gram′), *n.* a graph or tracing showing the action of the heart. Also, **car′di-o-graph′.**

care (kâr), *n.* **1,** a burdened state of mind caused by doubt, fear, or anxiety; **2,** the cause of such doubt, fear, or anxiety; as, the *cares* of state weighed heavily upon the king; **3,** heed; caution; pains; as, take *care* in crossing the street; work done with *care*; **4,** charge or oversight; as, under a nurse's *care*:—*v.i.* [cared, car-ing], **1,** to be anxious, concerned, or interested; as, she *cared* only for dancing; also, to feel affection; as, she *cared* a great deal for her sister; **2,** to provide oversight or protection; as, the nurse *cared* for the children while the mother was away; **3,** to desire; wish; as, I do not *care* to go.

ca-reen (ka-rēn′), *v.t.* **1,** to rush headlong; lurch; **2,** to turn (a ship) over on one side, in order to clean or repair it:—*v.i.* to incline to one side; to lurch, as a ship in the wind; to career.

ca-reer (ka-rēr′), *n.* **1,** a swift or sweeping course; full speed; as, a horse in full *career*; **2,** a course of action in the life of an individual, a nation, etc.; **3,** an occupation or calling; as, a scientific *career*:—*v.i.* to move rapidly, as a speeding car.

care-free (kâr′frē′), *adj.* happy; unworried.

care-ful (kâr′fool), *adj.* **1,** done or made with care; as, a *careful* piece of work; **2,** attentive; concerned; as, the nurse is *careful* with his diet; **3,** watchful; cautious; as, *careful* with money.—*adv.* **care′-ful-ly.**—*n.* **care′ful-ness.**

care-less (kâr′lis), *adj.* **1,** not taking due care; inaccurate; as, a *careless* writer; *careless* work; **2,** unconcerned; heedless; as, *careless* of the outcome.—*adv.* **care′-less-ly.**—*n.* **care′less-ness.**

ca-ress (ka-res′), *n.* any act expressing affection, as a kiss or embrace:—*v.t.* to touch or stroke lovingly; fondle.

care-tak-er (kâr′tāk′ėr), *n.* one who takes care of places, persons, or things for someone else; a custodian or janitor.

Ca-rib-be-an (kâr′i-bē′en; kâ-ri′bē-en), *n.* a person who inhabits or originates from the West Indies:—*adj.* relating to the countries (Bahamas, Greater Antilles, Lesser Antilles), the people, the language, or the culture of the West Indies.

car-go (kär′gō), *n.* [*pl.* cargoes or cargos],

the goods or merchandise carried by a plane, train, or ship.

car-i-bou (kar′i-bo͞o), *n.* [*pl.* caribou or caribous], a large North American deer with antlers, which is related to the European reindeer.

car-i-ca-ture (kar′i-ka-tūr′; kar′i-ka-tūr′), *n.* a picture or description of a person or thing, in which the defects or peculiarities are so exaggerated as to appear ridiculous:—*v.t.* [caricatured, caricatur-ing], to make or give a caricature of.—*n.* **car′i-ca-tur′ist.**

ca-ri-es (kâr′i-ēz′; kâr′ēz), *n.* decay of the teeth, bones, or tissues.

car-il-lon (kar′i-lon′; ka-ril′yun), *n.* a set of fixed bells in a tower, usually operated from a keyboard.

car-mine (kär′min; -mīn), *n.* and *adj.* a deep purplish red or crimson.

car-nage (kär′nij), *n.* great slaughter, esp. in battle.

car-nal (kär′nal), *adj.* **1,** fleshly or sensual; **2,** worldly; **3,** sexual; as, *carnal* lusts or appetites.

car-ni-val (kär′ni-val), *n.* **1,** in some Roman Catholic countries, the season just before Lent, devoted to merrymaking; **2,** any revelry or feasting; a celebration; a fair or festival; **3,** a travelling amusement show, with sideshows, games, rides, etc.; **4,** a program of events having to do with a certain sport, institution, etc.; as, a winter *carnival.*

car-niv-o-rous (kär-niv′o-rus), *adj.* flesh- or meat-eating; as, dogs are *carnivorous.*—*n.* **car′ni-vore.**

car-ol (kar′ul), *n.* a song of joy or praise; as, a Christmas *carol*:—*v.t.* and *v.i.* [carolled, carol-ling], to sing joyfully.

ca-rouse (ka-rouz′), *n.* a drinking party:—*v.i.* [caroused, carous-ing], to take part in a drinking party.—*n.* **ca-rous′er; ca-rous′al.**

car-ou-sel or **car-rou-sel** (kâr′o-sel′; kar′o-sel′; -zel), *n.* a merry-go-round.

[1]**carp** (kärp), *v.i.* to find fault; nag; as, to *carp* at someone.—*adj.* **carp′ing.**

[2]**carp** (kärp), *n.* a freshwater fish that lives in ponds, sometimes to a great age, often used for food.

car-pel (kär′pel), *n.* the part of a plant that bears seeds; one of the parts of a compound ovary.

car-pen-ter (kär′pen-tėr), *n.* one who works in timber and builds or repairs the woodwork of houses, cabinets, etc.—*n.* **car′pen-try.**

car-pet (kär′pit), *n.* **1,** a thick woven or felted fabric used as a floor or stair covering; **2,** a soft covering upon which one may walk; as, a *carpet* of grass:—*v.t.* to cover with, or as with, a carpet.

car-riage (kar′ij), *n.* **1,** the act or business of carrying or transporting goods; also, the expense of carrying; **2,** a wheeled vehicle for carrying persons, esp. one drawn by horses; **3,** a wheeled support, as for a cannon; **4,** the moving part of a machine that carries another part, as in a typewriter; **5,** the manner of holding one's body; as, an erect *carriage*; **6,** a small vehicle that is pushed by hand and used to carry a baby or doll.

car-ri-er (kar′i-ėr), *n.* **1,** a bearer, as of letters; **2,** a person or firm whose business is to transport goods or persons; as, a mail *carrier*; an aircraft *carrier*; **3,** a person or thing that carries and transmits disease germs; **4,** a radio wave that transmits speech, music, images, or other signals.

car-ri-on (kar′i-un), *n.* decaying flesh.

car-ry (kar′i), *v.t.* [carried, carry-ing], **1,** to convey; transmit, as a cargo or a message; **2,** to support or sustain; as, the columns *carry* the weight of the building; **3,** to have upon one's person; as, to *carry* a scar; **4,** to hold (oneself); as, she *carries* herself well; also, to conduct (oneself); **5,** to win, as an election; **6,** to secure the passage of, as a bill in Parliament; **7,** to keep on hand for sale:—*v.i.* **1,** to bear or convey something; **2,** to have power to reach a distance, as a voice:—**carry on, 1,** to take part in; conduct; as, to *carry on* a conversation; **2,** to behave or talk in a foolish or overexcited way; as, quit *carrying on* so:—**carry out,** to put into action; accomplish; as, to *carry out* a plan:—*n.* [*pl.* carries], **1,** the distance over which something will travel; **2,** the act of carrying between two bodies of water; also, the distance crossed: also called *portage*; **3,** in *golf,* the distance from the spot where a ball is struck to the point where it first lands.

car-ry-all (kar′i-ôl′), *n.* **1,** a capacious vehicle for carrying passengers; **2,** a covered carriage; **3,** a large bag, basket, etc.

cart (kärt), *n.* **1,** a two-wheeled vehicle for carrying heavy goods; **2,** a light delivery wagon pulled by hand; **3,** a light, two-wheeled carriage:—*v.t.* to carry in or as if in a cart.—*n.* **cart′age; cart′er.**

carte blanche (kärt′blänsh′), *n.* absolute freedom of action; as, anything you say; I give you *carte blanche.*

car-tel (kär-tel′; kär′tel), *n.* an international association of rival firms to regulate prices and production so as to create a monopoly; as, OPEC is a petroleum *cartel.*

car-ti-lage (kär′ti-lij), *n.* an elastic tissue or gristle composing most of the skeleton of young animals and children, usually developing into bone: in adults, cartilage is found in the nose and outer ear.—*adj.* **car′ti-lag′i-nous** (kär′ti-laj′i-nus).

car-ton (kär′t′n), *n.* a pasteboard, cardboard, or plastic box; as, a milk *carton.*

car-toon (kär-to͞on′), *n.* **1,** a picture, esp. one in a newspaper or magazine, dealing with a public person or event in an exaggerated or satirical manner; as, the *cartoons* of the disaster aroused anger; **2,** a group of cartoons arranged in a short series in a newspaper; a comic strip; **3,** a movie or television program made up of a continuous series of drawings:—*v.t.* to draw a cartoon of:—*v.i.* to draw cartoons.—*n.* **car-toon′ist.**

car-tridge (kär′-trij), *n.* **1,** a case of metal, cardboard, or other material containing powder and a bullet, as for a firearm, or one charge of powder, as of dynamite; **2,** a case shaped like a cartridge, used as a container; as, a film *cartridge* for a camera; an ink or toner *cartridge* for a pen, printer, or copier; a cassette containing magnetic tape for playing or recording, such as a video- or audiotape; a case for storing information in a computer; a video game *cartridge;* etc.

cart-wheel (kärt′wēl), *n.* a handspring done sideways, with arms and legs extended.

carve (kärv), *v.t.* [carved, carv-ing], **1,** to produce by cutting; as, to *carve* a statue out of marble; **2,** to adorn by cutting; as, he *carved* a panel with floral designs; **3,** to cut, as meat; **4,** to make or get as if by cutting; as, he *carved* out a career for himself:—*v.i.* **1,** to work as a sculptor; **2,** to cut up meat.—*n.* **carv′er; carv′ing.**—*adj.* **carved.**

cas-cade (kas-kād′), *n.* **1,** a small waterfall or series of small falls; **2,** anything like this; as, a *cascade* of ruffles:—*v.t.* and *v.i.* to fall, or cause to fall, as a cascade; as, her hair *cascaded* over her shoulders.

[1]**case** (kās), *n.* **1,** any set of facts, conditions, or circumstances relating to a particular person or thing; as, the *case* of Mr. Jones; a *case* of robbery; **2,** an actual state of affairs; as, that was not the *case;* **3,** a certain form or instance of disease; also, the person having a given disease; a patient; as, there is a *case* of mumps in the house; **4,** a lawsuit; **5,** a person, family, or problem under the observation of a social-service organization; **6,** in *grammar,* the relation of a noun or pronoun to other words; as, the subject of a sentence is in the nominative *case;* **7,** *Colloq.* a peculiar person; as, he's an odd *case*:—**in case of,** in the event of; as, *in case of* fire, ring the alarm.

[2]**case** (kās), *n.* **1,** a covering or container; as, the *case* of a watch; a pillow*case;* a camera *case;* **2,** a container and its contents; as, a *case* of books; a suit*case;* also, the amount of this content; as, to buy canned peas by the *case;* **3,** a glass box used for exhibiting goods; as, a show*case;* **4,** a frame or casing, as of a window; **5,** in *printing, upper case* refers to the capital letters, and *lower case* refers to the small letters:—*v.t.* [cased, casing], to protect with a case; encase. Also, **case′ment; cas′ing.**

case-ment (kās′ment), *n.* a window made to open on hinges like a door.

cash (kash), *n.* **1,** money in the form of bills and coins; esp. ready money; as, I have no *cash* in my pocket; **2,** money or a cheque paid for an article at the time of purchase; as, a purchase made with *cash* instead of using a credit card:—*v.t.* to exchange for money in coin or bills; as, to *cash* a cheque.—*n.* **cash′book′.**

ca-shew (kash′o͞o; ka-sho͞o′), *n.* a tropical tree, or its kidney-shaped nut, which is used for food.

cash-ier (kash-ēr′), *n.* **1,** in a bank or business, a person who has charge of paying and receiving money; **2,** a person in a store who receives cash in return for merchandise.

cash-mere (kash′mēr; kash′mēr′), *n.* **1,** a soft woollen fabric made from the wool of the goats of Kashmir, Tibet, etc.; **2,** a shawl made of this; **3,** a soft woollen imitation of real cashmere.

cas-ing (kās′ing), *n.* **1,** a covering, as for a pillow; **2,** a framework, as of a window.

ca-si-no (ka-sē′nō), *n.* [*pl.* casinos], **1,** in Italy, a summer house; **2,** a room or building for entertainment and gambling.

cask (kåsk), *n.* **1,** a barrel-shaped, wooden vessel for holding liquids; a keg; **2,** the amount contained in a cask; as, a *cask* of molasses was consumed in a month; **3,** the cask and its contents; as, a *cask* of wine was shipped.

cas-ket (kås′kit), *n.* **1,** a small chest or box, as for jewels; **2,** a coffin.

cas-se-role (kas′e-rōl), *n.* **1,** a covered glass or earthen dish in which food is baked and served; **2,** food cooked and served in a casserole.

cas-sette (ka-set′), *n.* a small plastic box that holds magnetic tape that is played in a tape recorder.

cas-sock (kas′uk), *n.* a long, close-fitting gown worn by some clergymen.

cast (kåst), *v.t.* [*p.t.* and *p.p.* cast, *p.pr.* casting], **1,** to throw; hurl; as, to *cast* a fishing line; to *cast* stones; **2,** to send or turn in a certain direction; as, to *cast* a glance; to *cast* a shadow; **3,** to put off; shed; as, a snake *casts* its skin; **4,** to deposit, as a vote; **5,** to assign, as, the parts or actors in a play; **6,** to pour into a certain shape; as, to *cast* a bronze statue; **7,** to add; as, to *cast* up a column of figures:—*v.i.* **1,** to throw a fishing line; as, it was his turn to *cast;* **2,** to receive shape in a mould; **3,** in hunting, to search for game, or for a lost scent; hence, to search; as, he *casts* about for an idea:—*n.* **1,** the act or manner of throwing; the distance to which a thing can be thrown; **2,** a permanent turn, twist, or warp; as, a *cast* in the eye; **3,** calculation; the addition of columns of an account; **4,** the members of a company of actors to whom certain parts are assigned; **5,** something formed by moulding; as, a plaster *cast;* **6,** form; style;

bent; as, a gloomy *cast* of countenance; **7,** a tinge or hue; as, a greyish *cast*; **8,** in hunting, the scattering of hounds in search of a lost scent; **9,** a stiff bandage made of plaster and cloth, used for holding a broken bone or injured part of the body in place while it heals:—*adj.* shaped in a mould while fluid.

cas-ta-nets (kas′ta-nets′; kas′ta-nets′), *n.pl.* a pair of spoon-shaped shells of hard wood or ivory, clicked with the fingers to beat time, esp. in Spanish dances and music.

cast-a-way (kåst′a-wā), *n.* **1,** a person cast adrift at sea, or a shipwrecked person cast ashore; **2,** a social or moral outcast:—*adj.* **1,** shipwrecked; **2,** thrown aside; rejected.

caste (kåst), *n.* a distinct class of society, esp. as in India.

cas-ter (kås′-tėr), *n.* **1,** a small vessel for salt, vinegar, etc.; a cruet; also, a stand for a number of such vessels; **2,** a small roller on a swivel, or a set of rollers in a frame, used under furniture, etc., to permit easy moving. Also spelled **cast′or.**

cas-ti-gate (kas′ti-gāt′), *v.t.* **1,** to correct; chastise; **2,** criticize severely.

cast-ing (kåst′ing), *n.* an object formed by pouring (molten metal) into a mould; hence, cast iron; cast steel.

cast iron, iron that has been melted and shaped by being run into moulds.—*adj.* **cast–iron, 1,** made of cast iron; **2,** like iron; rigid; unyielding; as, a *cast-iron* will.

cas-tle (kås′l), *n.* **1,** a building or group of buildings fortified for defence; a fortress; **2,** any of these used now as a residence; **3,** anything resembling a castle; **4,** one of the pieces used in chess: also called *rook.*

cast-or (kås′tėr), *n.* Same as **caster.**

castor oil, a thick, yellowish oil from the castor bean, used as a laxative or lubricant.—*adj.* **cas′tor–oil′.**

cas-trate (kas′trāt), *v.t.* [castrat-ed, castrat-ing], to remove the male sex glands of (an animal); as, a steer is a *castrated* bull.

cas-u-al (kazh′ūal), *adj.* **1,** happening by chance; accidental; as, a *casual* meeting; **2,** uncertain; occasional; as, *casual* profits; **3,** having an air of indifference; relaxed; as, a *casual* manner.

cas-u-al-ty (kazh′ū-al-ti), *n.* [*pl.* casualties], **1,** a disaster; an accident; **2,** anyone hurt or killed accidentally:—**casualties,** in the army and navy, losses in general, caused by death, wounds, illness, desertion, or discharge.

cat (kat), *n.* a small flesh-eating animal, often kept as a household pet; also, any closely related animal, as the lion or tiger.—*adj.* **cat′like′; cat′ty.**

cat-a-clysm (kat′a-klizm), *n.* **1,** a deluge; flood; **2,** a violent upheaval, as an earthquake or a war.

cat-a-logue (kat′a-log′), *n.* **1,** a systematic list of names, places, books, etc., usually arranged alphabetically; **2,** a book or file containing such a list; as, a university *catalogue*; a store *catalogue*:—*v.t.* [catalogued, catalogu-ing], to make a list of; as, to *catalogue* a library. Also spelled **cat′a-log** [cataloged, catalog-ing].

cat-a-lyst (kat′a-list), *n.* **1,** a substance or agent that causes or speeds up chemical (or other) action between two other substances without itself undergoing change; **2,** someone or something that causes or speeds up a significant action or event without being directly involved.

cat-a-ma-ran (kat′a-ma-ran′), *n.* **1,** a raft or float of logs or pieces of wood lashed together, and propelled by sail, paddle, etc.; **2,** a craft with twin hulls.

cat-a-pult (kat′a-pult), *n.* **1,** in ancient times, a military engine for hurling stones, arrows, etc.; **2,** in modern times, a similar device for launching an aircraft from the deck of a ship; **3,** a slingshot:—*v.t.* to hurl (something) from a catapult:—*v.i.* to rush headlong; hurtle; as, the acrobat *catapulted* from a cannon into a net.

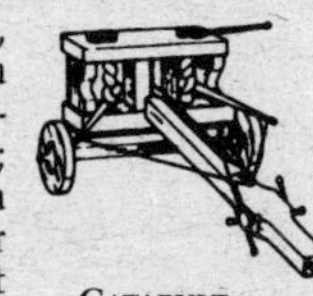

CATAPULT

cat-a-ract (kat′a-rakt′), *n.* **1,** a large waterfall; **2,** a furious rush of water; **3,** a disease that results in the clouding over of the eye lens, which can cause partial or total blindness.

ca-tas-tro-phe (ka-tas′trō-fi), *n.* a sudden calamity or widespread disaster; as, the terrorist attack on September 11, 2001, was a true *catastrophe.*

cat-call (kat′kōl′), *n.* a loud cry of disapproval, as from a theatre audience.

catch (kach), *v.t.* [caught (kôt), catch-ing], **1,** to lay hold of; seize; as, the brambles *caught* her dress; to *catch* a ball; **2,** to reach or be in time for; as, to *catch* a train; **3,** to overtake; as, I will *catch* you; **4,** to attract; as, to *catch* the eye or the attention; **5,** to learn by hearing, as a tune; **6,** to understand; as, to *catch* a meaning; **7,** to become infected with, as a disease or illness; as, to *catch* a cold; **8,** to come upon suddenly; surprise; as, to *catch* a thief in the act; the storm *caught* him; **9,** to take (fire); **10,** please; charm; as, the music *caught* the public's fancy:—*v.i.* **1,** to grasp; snatch; as, to *catch* at an opportunity; to *catch* at straws; **2,** to be seized and held; as, my dress *caught* in the door; **3,** to take hold, as fire; **4,** to take and keep hold, as a bolt; **5,** to be stuck, as a window:—*n.* **1,** a fastening, as a hook, door latch, etc.; **2,** a choking sensation in the throat; **3,** what is caught; as, a *catch* of fish; **4,** a trick or pitfall; as, a *catch* in a question; **5,** in ball games, the seizing of the ball before it touches the ground; **6,** a snatch of song; also, a round set to humorous words.—*n.* catch′er.—*adj.* catch′y.

catch-er (kach′ėr), *n.* a baseball player whose position is behind home plate.

catch-up (kach′up), *n.* Same as **ketchup.**

catch-word (kach′wûrd′), *n.* **1,** a word or phrase repeated as a slogan, esp. by a political party; **2,** any word placed prominently to catch the eye, as in a dictionary; **3,** an actor's cue.

cat-e-chism (kat′e-kizm), *n.* **1,** a small book of questions and answers for instruction in the Christian religion; **2,** a method of teaching by questions and answers; **3,** a set of questions to be answered.

cat-e-chize (kat′e-kīz′), *v.t.* [catechized, catechiz-ing], **1,** to instruct by questions and answers, esp. in the Christian religion; **2,** to question closely.—*n.* **cat′e-chist.**

cat-e-gor-y (kăt′e-go-ri), *n.* [*pl.* categories], a broad division or classification; as, there are three *categories* of matter: animal, vegetable, and mineral.—*adj.* **cat-e-gor′i-cal.**

ca-ter (kā-tėr), *v.i.* **1,** to provide or supply food; as, to *cater* for a banquet; **2,** to supply what is desired; as, some writers *cater* to popular taste.—*n.* **ca′ter-er.**

cat-er-pil-lar (kat′ėr-pil′ėr), *n.* a wormlike larva, usually of a butterfly or moth.

cat-fish (kat′fish′), *n.* [*pl.* catfish or catfishes], a scaleless fish with long, whiskerlike feelers around the mouth, as the bullhead.

cat-gut (kat′gut′), *n.* a dried and twisted cord made from the intestines of animals, usually sheep, used chiefly for the strings of musical instruments, tennis rackets, surgical stitches, etc.

ca-thar-tic (ka-thär′tik), *adj.* cleansing the bowels; purgative; as, *cathartic* herbs; also, anything that purifies or simplifies; as, a *cathartic* experience:—*n.* a purgative medicine; a physic; also, a purification or simplification.

ca-the-dral (ka-thē′dral), *n.* **1,** the principal church of a church district under the special charge of the bishop; **2,** any church of great size or importance.

cath-ode (kath′ōd), *n.* in *electrolysis*, the negative pole of a battery; a negatively charged electrode. Compare *anode*.

cath-o-lic (kath′o-lik), *adj.* **1,** universal; general; including all; as, he has a *catholic* taste in literature; **2,** liberal, as in thought or sympathies:—**Catholic, 1,** naming or having to do with the universal Christian church; **2,** naming or having to do with the Church of Rome:—*n.* a member of such a church.

cat-kin (kat′kin), *n.* a hanging, fingerlike flower cluster, as of the willow or birch.

cat-nap (kat′nap), *n.* a short, light sleep.

cat-nip (kat′nip), *n.* a common plant of the mint family, so called because cats like its pungent leaves.

cat-o'-nine-tails (kat′o-nīn′-tālz′), *n.* a whip with nine lashes of knotted cord, formerly used for flogging.

CAT scan (kat′ skan′), *abbrev.* short for *c*omputerized *a*xial *t*omography: computer-enhanced X-rays that produce a cross-sectional image and allow better medical diagnoses. Also called *CT scan*.

cat-tle (kat′l), *n.pl.* livestock; esp. cows, bulls, and steers, raised for profit.

Cau-ca-sian (kô-kā′zhan), *n.* loosely, a member of the white or light-skinned race, esp. peoples originally of Europe, North Africa, and the Middle East:—*adj.* **1,** pertaining to the white or light-skinned race; **2,** relating to the Caucasus area or mountains and the people of this area.

cau-cus (kô′kus), *n.* a meeting of political party leaders to discuss party policies or to choose party candidates.

cau-dal (kô′dal), *adj.* like, or near, the tail; as, the *caudal* fin of a fish.

caught (kôt), *p.t.* and *p.p.* of *catch*.

caul-dron or **cal-dron** (kôl′drun), *n.* a large kettle or boiler.

cau-li-flow-er (ko′li-flou′ėr), *n.* a vegetable related to the cabbage, with a white, compact flowering head.

caulk (kôk), *v.t.* to drive hemp rope fibre into the seams of (a ship) to stop leaks; also, to seal (a house) by putting a similar substance in cracks, as around doors and windows.—*n.* **caulk′ing; caulk′er.**

cause (kôz), *n.* **1,** a person who, or a thing which, makes something happen; as, the boy was the *cause* of the quarrel between them; **2,** a motive or reason; as, he had no *cause* for being angry; **3,** a subject, esp. one side of a question of wide interest, which is taken up by one or more persons and made into an issue, as in a political campaign; as, the temperance *cause*; **4,** in law, a ground for action; also, a lawsuit:—*v.t.* [caused, caus-ing], to bring about; effect.—*n.* **causa′-tion** (kô-zā′shun).—*adj.* **caus′-al.**

cause-way (kôz′wā), *n.* **1,** a raised path or road over wet ground, shallow water, or the like; **2,** a raised sidewalk.

caus-tic (kôs′tik), *adj.* **1,** having the power of gradually eating away or destroying by chemical action; as, *caustic* soda; **2,** sarcastic; biting; as, a *caustic* remark:—*n.* a substance which by chemical action burns or eats away animal tissues.—*adv.* **caus′ti-cal-ly.**

cau-ter-ize (kô′tėr-iz′), *v.t.* [cauterized, cauteriz-ing], to burn or sear with a hot iron, or with some caustic agent; as, to *cauterize* a wound with carbolic acid.—*n.* **cau′ter-i-za′tion.**

cau-tion (kô′shun), *n.* **1,** an act, word, or

the like that warns, as against danger; a warning; as, he heeded my *caution* against smoking; **2,** heedfulness; care in avoiding danger; as, handle chemicals with *caution*:—*v.t.* to warn of danger or to be careful.

cau-tious (kô′shus), *adj.* taking care to avoid danger or trouble; heedful.—*adv.* **cau′tious-ly.**

cav-al-cade (kav′al-kād′), *n.* **1,** a procession of persons; as, a *cavalcade* of stars; **2,** a series or sequence of scenes, etc.

cav-a-lier (kav′a-lēr′), *n.* **1,** formerly, a horseman; often, an armed horseman; a knight; **2,** an adventurer; **3,** a lady's escort; a gallant:—*adj.* **1,** happy; frank and carefree; **2,** haughty; offhand or unceremonious; as, a *cavalier* refusal.

cav-al-ry (kav′al-ri), *n.* [*pl.* cavalries], soldiers who fight on horseback; mounted troops; also, more recently, combat soldiers in armoured vehicles or helicopters, requiring great mobility.—*n.* **cav′al-ry-man.**

cave (kāv), *n.* a large hole in the earth, esp. a natural one:—**cave man,** a man of the Stone Age; hence, humorously, any man who is rough or overbearing, esp. toward women:—*v.i.* [caved, cav-ing], to fall in or down; as, the road *caved* in.

cav-ern (kav′ėrn), *n.* a large, underground cave.—*adj.* **cav′ern-ous.**

cav-i-ar or **cav-i-are** (kav′i-är′), *n.* the pickled eggs, or spawn, of the sturgeon, salmon, etc., eaten as a relish or delicacy.

cav-il (kav′il), *v.i.* [cavilled, cavil-ling], to find fault or object on trivial grounds; as, Benny *cavilled* at the suggestion that he tip the waiter.

cav-i-ty (kav′i-ti), *n.* [*pl.* cavities], a hollow place; a hole or hollow; as, a *cavity* in a tooth; a *cavity* in the ground.

ca-vort (ka-vôrt′), *v.i. Colloq.* to prance or caper about, as does a horse.

caw (kô), *n.* a cry like that of the crow:—*v.i.* to utter such a cry.

cay (kē; kā), *n.* Same as **key.**

cay-enne (kī-en′; kā-en′), *n.* a hot, biting pepper made from the seeds or fruit of certain plants: also called *red pepper, cayenne pepper.*

Ca-yu-ga (kā-ū′ga), *n.* **1,** Aboriginal people of the Cayuga nation, a member of the Six Nations Iroquois Confederacy; **2,** the Iroquoian language of the Cayuga people.

CB (sē′bē′), *abbrev.* a range of radio frequencies that can be used by private citizens, not the frequencies used by broadcasting stations, police departments, aircraft, etc.: short for *citizens' band.*

CD (sē′dē′), *abbrev.* short for *compact disc.*

CD bur-ner (sē′dē′ bûrn′ėr), *n.* a device that allows the user to record data on a recordable CD.

CD–ROM (sē′dē′–rom′), *abbrev.* short for compact *d*isc-*r*ead *o*nly *m*emory: in *computing,* a compact disc or storage device, shaped like a disk, that contains large amounts of information that can only be read (and not changed) on a computer with a CD-ROM drive.

cease (sēs), *v.i.* [ceased, ceas-ing], to come to an end; stop; as, at nightfall the singing of the birds *ceased*:—*v.t.* to discontinue; as, *cease* your quarrelling.—*adj.* **cease′less.**

ce-dar (sēd′ėr), *n.* **1,** an evergreen tree of the pine family, with a very durable and fragrant wood; **2,** any one of several related North American trees, as the white cedar, red cedar, etc.; **3,** the wood of any of these trees:—*adj.* relating to cedar; made of cedar; as, a roof of *cedar* shakes.

cede (sēd), *v.t.* [ced-ed, ced-ing], **1,** to give up or surrender, as a tract of land; **2,** to grant (a point), as in an argument.

CE-GEP (sē′jep′), *abbrev.* short for *C*ollège d'*E*nseignement *G*énéral *e*t *P*rofessionel (General and Vocational College): a community college in Québec that students attend between high school and university or to learn a skill or trade.

ceil-ing (sēl′ing), *n.* **1,** the inner overhead lining or covering of a room; **2,** an upper limit; as, a (price) *ceiling* on rents; **3,** the upper limit or height at which an airplane can fly.

cel-e-brate (sel′e-brāt′), *v.t.* [celebrat-ed, celebrat-ing], **1,** to perform publicly with suitable ceremonies; **2,** to make known with praise; honour; as, we *celebrate* the names of great Canadians; **3,** to observe suitably, as with a holiday and ceremonies; as, to *celebrate* Christmas, Hanukkha, Ramadan, or a birthday.—*n.* **cel′e-bra′-tion.**

cel-e-brat-ed (sel′e-brāt′id), *adj.* famous; illustrious.

ce-leb-ri-ty (se-leb′ri-ti), *n.* [*pl.* celebrities], **1,** fame; renown; **2,** a renowned or celebrated person; a public character.

ce-ler-i-ty (se-ler′i-ti), *n.* rapidity; speed.

cel-er-y (sel′ėr-i), *n.* a garden plant with long, light-green stalks, eaten as a vegetable; also, a stalk of this plant.

ce-les-tial (se-les′chal), *adj.* **1,** pertaining to the heavens; as, the stars are *celestial* bodies; **2,** heavenly; divine; as, *celestial* peace.

cel-i-bate (sel′i-bāt′; -bit), *n.* the state of celibacy:—*adj.* bound or resolved not to marry or have sexual intercourse.—*n.* **cel′i-ba-cy.**

cell (sel), *n.* **1,** a small, close room, as in a monastery or prison; **2,** a tiny mass of living matter, the unit of structure in both plants and animals; **3,** a small enclosed space, as in a honeycomb; **4,** in *electricity,* a vessel or small battery containing a fluid and two plates of different materials, or a similar apparatus, used to generate an electric current.—*adj.* **cel′lu-lar.**

cel-lar (sel′ėr), *n.* a room or group of rooms, generally underground or under a building, most often used for storage.

cel-lo or **′cel-lo** (chel′ō), *n.* [*pl.* cellos or celli (chel′ē)], the violoncello; a musical stringed instrument larger than the violin and deeper in tone.—*n.* **cel′list.**

cel-lo-phane (sel′o-fān′), *n.* a thin, transparent, waterproof material made from cellulose and used as a wrapper for many articles.

cellular phone, a portable, wireless telephone that operates using radiotelephone transmitting systems. Also called *cellphone.*

cel-lu-loid (sel′ū-loid′), *n.* a compound of camphor and cellulose nitrate: a flammable material used in making combs, brushes, films, etc., now often replaced by nonflammable plastics.

cel-lu-lose (sel′ū-lōs′), *n.* a substance related to starch, and forming the main part of plant tissue: used in making linen, paper, cellophane, rayon, plastics, etc.

Cel-si-us (sel′sē-us; sel′shus), *adj.* a scale that measures temperature, in which 0 degrees is the temperature at which water freezes, and 100 degrees, at which water boils. Also called *centigrade scale.*

Cel-tic (kel′tik; sel′tik), *adj.* having to do with a people including the Irish, Highland Scots, Welsh, Gaelic, and ancient Britons; also, the language of these people.

ce-ment (si-ment′), *n.* **1,** a substance usually made from clay and limestone and mixed with water to form a kind of mortar that soon hardens to the consistency of stone, used in building walls, laying floors, etc.; **2,** any similar substance that causes things to stick together, as glue or paste; **3,** the bony material that covers the root of a tooth; **4,** in *dentistry,* a material used for filling cavities:—*v.t.* **1,** to cause to stick together, as bricks; **2,** to cover or pave with cement.

cem-e-ter-y (sem′i-tėr-i), *n.* [*pl.* cemeteries], a burial ground; graveyard.

cen-o-taph (sen′ō-taf′), *n.* a monument or empty tomb erected in honour of a person buried elsewhere.

Ce-no-zo-ic (sen′e-zō′ik; se′ne-zō′ik), *adj.* relating to the geological era lasting from 65 million years ago to the present (following the Mesozoic period), and characterized by the rapid evolution of mammals and the appearance of humans. Compare *Mesozoic* and *Paleozoic.*

cen-ser (sen′sėr), *n.* a vessel with a perforated lid, in which incense is burned.

cen-sor (sen′sėr), *n.* **1,** in ancient Rome, one of the two magistrates who took the census and regulated morals; **2,** an official who examines books, plays, movies, etc., to prevent the publication or performance of anything considered immoral, harmful, or offensive; **3,** an official who, in time of war, examines all printed matter, mail, telegrams, etc., to suppress anything that might help the enemy; **4,** one who criticizes manners or morals:—*v.t.* to deal with as a censor.—*n.* **cen′sor-ship.**

cen-sure (sen′shyoor), *n.* blame; faultfinding:—*v.t.* [censured, censur-ing], to find fault with.—*adj.* **cen-sor′i-ous** (sen-sōr′i-us).

cen-sus (sen′sus), *n.* an official count of population: in ancient Rome, a registration of citizens and property for taxation purposes: in Canada, the national census is taken every five years, which includes statistics as to sex, race, age, employment, etc.

cent (sent), *n.* **1,** the hundredth part of a dollar; **2,** a coin of this value.

cen-te-na-ry (sen′ti-na-ri;), *n.* [*pl.* centenaries], a period of 100 years; also, a celebration of a 100th anniversary.—*n.* **cen′te-nar′i-an.**

cen-ten-ni-al (sen-ten′i-al), *adj.* relating to a period of 100 years:—*n.* the 100th anniversary of any event; also, the celebration of this anniversary; as, 1967 was Canada's *centennial.*

cen-ter (sen′tėr), *n.* Same as **centre.**

cen-ti-grade (sen′ti-grad′), *adj.* having 100 equal divisions called degrees; Celsius:—**centigrade thermometer,** a thermometer on which the distance between the freezing point of water, marked at 0°, and the boiling point, marked at 100°, is divided into 100 equal degrees.

cen-ti-me-tre (sen′ti-mē′tėr), *n.* a basic measure of length in the metric system, equal to one hundredth of a metre: abbreviated as *cm.*

cen-ti-pede (sen′ti-pēd′), *n.* a small, wormlike animal with a pair of legs for each body segment: it can have up to 170 legs.

cen-tral (sen′tral), *adj.* **1,** relating to the middle; situated in the middle; **2,** chief; leading; as, the *central* theme of a discussion.—*adv.* **cen′tral-ly.**

Cen-tral A-mer-i-can (sen′tral a-mer′i-kan), *n.* a person who inhabits or originates from the area between North and South America:—*adj.* relating to the countries (Guatemala, El Salvador, Honduras, Nicaragua, Costa Rica, Panama, and Belize), the people, the language, or the culture of this region.

cen-tral-ize (sen′tral-īz′), *v.t.* [centralized, centraliz-ing], to draw to one central point; to bring under one control; as, to *centralize* a government.—*n.* **cen′tral-i-za′tion.**

central processing unit (**CPU**), *n.* in

computing, the integrated circuits of the computer that control the computer system by processing instructions and managing the flow of information through the system.

cen-tre (sen′tėr), *n.* **1,** that point of a circle or sphere that is equally distant from every point of the circumference; **2,** a point about which something turns, or about which things are collected or people gather; as, the *centre* of a wheel; a shopping *centre*; **3,** the principal point or object; as, she is the *centre* of attention; **4,** a player whose position is in the middle of the playing area in basketball, football, hockey, etc.:—*v.t.* [centred, centring], **1,** to place (something) at the middle point; **2,** to gather to a point; concentrate, as the attention:—*v.i.* to gather at one point; converge toward a single point; as, his ambition *centred* on his son.

cen-trif-u-gal (sen-trif′ū-gal), *adj.* moving or tending to move away from a centre: opposite of *centripetal*:—**centrifugal force,** a force that tends to make a rotating body fly away from its centre, as mud is thrown from a moving wheel.

cen-trip-e-tal (sen-trip′e-tal), *adj.* tending to move toward the centre: opposite of *centrifugal.*

cen-tu-ri-on (sen-tū′ri-un), *n.* in Roman history, an officer commanding a company of about 100 soldiers.

cen-tu-ry (sen′choo-ri; sen′tū-ri;), *n.* [*pl.* centuries], **1,** a group of 100, esp. 100 years; **2,** each group of 100 years after some fixed date, as the birth of Christ; as, the years 1801 to 1900 inclusive belong to the nineteenth *century* A.D.; **3,** a score of 100 points; as, in cricket, to make a *century.*

ce-ram-ics (se-ram′iks), *n.pl.* used as *sing.*, the art of moulding and baking clays in the form of pottery, tiles, etc.; also, something made from clay in this way.—*adj.* **ce-ram′ic** (as, *ceramic* tiles).

ce-re-al (sē′ri-al), *n.* **1,** any grass that yields a grain or seed used for food, as rice, wheat, oats, etc.; **2,** any of these grains, in a natural state or as put on the market; **3,** a prepared or dry food, esp. a breakfast food, made from any of these grains:—*adj.* pertaining to edible grains or the grasses that produce them.

cer-e-bral (se-rē′bral; ser′e-bral), *adj.* **1,** of, or relating to, the brain; as, *cerebral* excitement; **2,** intellectual; as, *cerebral* music.

cer-e-mo-ni-al (ser′e-mō′ni-al), *adj.* relating to rites or formalities; as, *ceremonial* garb:—*n.* **1,** a system of rites, etc.; as, the *ceremonial* of coronation; **2,** behaviour required by custom on a given social occasion; as, court *ceremonial.*—*adv.* **cer′e-mo′ni-al-ly.**

cer-e-mo-ny (ser′e-mo-ni), *n.* [*pl.* ceremonies], **1,** a formal rite or observance; as, the marriage *ceremony*; the inaugural *ceremony*; **2,** behaviour regulated by the laws of strict etiquette; formality.—*adj.* **cer′e-mo′ni-ous.**

cer-tain (sûr′tin), *adj.* **1,** beyond question; sure; as, it is *certain* that day follows night; **2,** destined; inevitable; as, death is the *certain* end for all; **3,** fixed; settled; as, it is *certain* that we leave tomorrow; **4,** confident; as, I am *certain* of your loyalty; **5,** particular; one or some; as, to travel by a *certain* road; *certain* senators disagreed.—*adv.* **cer′tain-ly.**—*n.* **cer′tain-ty.**

cer-tif-i-cate (sėr-tif′i-kit), *n.* a formal, printed or written statement of a fact or privilege, signed by a public official or qualified person; as, a *certificate* of marriage; a medical *certificate*; a teacher's *certificate.*—*v.t.* (sėr-tif′i-kāt′), [-cat-ed, -cat-ing], **1,** to verify, or vouch for, in a written statement; as, to *certificate* a teacher; **2,** to issue a certificate.

cer-ti-fy (sûr′ti-fī′), *v.t.* [certified, certifying], **1,** to confirm or verify by a signed statement; as, the doctor *certified* that Byron had been vaccinated; **2,** to guarantee quality, value, or amount; as, to *certify* a cheque; to *certify* the safety of a car.—*n.* **cer′ti-fi-ca′tion.**

cer-ti-tude (sûr′ti-tūd′), *n.* assurance; certainty.

cer-vi-cal (sûr′vi-kal), *adj.* **1,** pertaining to the neck; as, a *cervical* vertebra; **2,** relating to the cervix; as, a *cervical* cap.

ces-sa-tion (se-sā′shun), *n.* a ceasing; a pause; stop; as, *cessation* of pain; *cessation* of hostilities.

ces-sion (sesh′un), *n.* a formal giving up to another; as, a *cession* of territory.

cess-pool (ses′pool′), *n.* **1,** a pit or well to receive drainage from sinks, toilets, etc.; **2,** a filthy place; as, Sodom was a *cesspool* of iniquity.

cha-dor (cha-dōr′), a large piece of cloth used as a cloak and veil by some Muslim women.

chafe (chāf), *v.t.* [chafed, chaf-ing], **1,** to rub with the hand, so as to restore warmth or sensation; as, to *chafe* numb hands; **2,** to wear away or make sore by rubbing; as, a frayed collar *chafes* the skin; **3,** to fret; irritate:—*v.i.* **1,** to rub; **2,** to be worn or made sore by rubbing; **3,** to be vexed; to fume; as, to *chafe* at the least delay.

chaff (chåf), *n.* **1,** the husks of grain, separated by threshing and winnowing; **2,** straw or hay cut fine for cattle; **3,** anything worthless.

cha-grin (sha-grin′; -grēn′), *n.* vexation due to disappointment, failure, or humiliation:—*v.t.* to vex; mortify; as, she was *chagrined* by the loss of her job.

chain (chān), *n.* **1,** a series of links or rings joined together to fasten or pull things or in jewellery; **2,** anything that binds or restrains;

3, a connected series or succession; as, a *chain* of events; **4,** a measure, used in surveying land, equal to 100 links or approximately 20 metres:—**chains,** imprisonment or bondage:—*v.t.* **1,** to fasten with a chain; **2,** to fetter; restrain.

chair (châr), *n.* **1,** a movable single seat with a back; **2,** a position of honour or authority; **3,** the seat from which a professor delivers his or her lectures; hence, the office or position of a professor; as, the *chair* of English at a university; **4,** the presiding officer of an assembly; chairperson; as, to address the *chair.*—*n.* **chair′-per-son; chair′man; chair′wo′man; chair′man-ship.**

chaise (shāz), *n.* a light carriage with a folding top and two wheels, drawn by one horse, and carrying two persons:—**chaise longue,** a long reclining chair in which one can stretch out.

cha-let (shal′ā; sha-lā), *n.* a Swiss-style, wide-eaved cottage or resort, usually in hilly country for skiing, etc.; also, any similar house.

chal-ice (chal′is), *n.* **1,** a goblet; **2,** the cup used in celebrating the Eucharist; **3,** the cup-shaped head of a flower, as of the tulip.

CHALICE, DEF. 1

chalk (chôk), *n.* **1,** a soft, whitish limestone, composed chiefly of tiny seashells; **2,** a chalklike material used to write with on a chalkboard:—**chalkboard,** a large green or black board used for writing on with chalk:—*v.t.* **1,** to rub or whiten with chalk; **2,** to mark or write with chalk:—**chalk up,** to score or earn, as to *chalk up* 10 points in a game.—*adj.* **chalk′y.**

chal-lenge (chal′inj), *n.* **1,** a summons or invitation to a fight or contest; a dare; **2,** a demand by a sentry that a passerby show who he or she is; also, a call or demand for proof that something is true or correct; **3,** an objection made to a person's serving on a jury; **4,** a job or task that calls for great effort:—*v.t.* [challenged, challeng-ing], **1,** to summon to a fight or contest; **2,** to invite; as, to *challenge* investigation; **3,** to take exception to; dispute, as a statement; the police *challenged* her story; **4,** to claim as due; as, he *challenges* respect by his honesty; **5,** to demand identification from; as, the sentry *challenged* him; **6,** in law, to object to (a juror).—*n.* **chal′leng-er.**

cham-ber (chām′bėr), *n.* **1,** a room, esp. a bedroom; **2,** a hall where a legislative or other government body meets; **3,** the government body itself; as, in Canada, the Senate is the upper *chamber* of Parliament; **4,** a group of persons organized for certain business purposes; as, the *Chamber* of Commerce; **5,** a hollow, enclosed space, as the part of a gun intended to hold the charge:—**chambers,** a set of rooms used as a dwelling or business office; as, a judge's *chambers.*

cham-ber-lain (chām′bėr-lin), *n.* the high court official who manages the household of a ruler or nobleman.

cha-me-le-on (ka-mē′li-un; ka-mēl′yun), *n.* **1,** a lizard that has the power to change its colour to match its surroundings; **2,** a person of changeable disposition.

cham-ois (sha′mwä; in def. 2, sham′i), *n.* **1,** a small antelope found on high peaks in Europe and Asia; **2,** a soft, thin leather, originally made from the hide of the chamois, but now prepared from other skins, and used for gloves, polishing cloths, etc.

champ (champ), *v.t.* and *v.i.* to bite or bite upon, noisily or impatiently; as, a horse *champs* the bit.

cham-pagne (sham-pān), *n.* **1,** a light, sparkling, almost colourless wine made originally in the northeastern part of France; **2,** in careless use, any sparkling wine.

cham-pi-on (cham′pi-un), *n.* **1,** a successful competitor against all rivals; as, the lightweight *champion* of Canada; **2,** a person who defends another or fights for a cause; as, a *champion* of free speech:—*adj.* above all rivals:—*v.t.* to defend or support.—*n.* **cham′pi-on-ship′.**

chance (chåns), *n.* **1,** the way things happen; fate; fortune; as, *chance* willed it; **2,** a possibility; probability; also, opportunity; as, a *chance* of a position; **3,** risk; as, to take a *chance:*—*adj.* accidental; unforeseen; as, a *chance* meeting:—**by chance, 1,** accidentally; as, to come upon this *by chance*; **2,** by some turn of events; as, to meet up with someone *by chance:*—*v.i.* [chanced, chanc-ing], to happen; as, it *chanced* to rain:—*v.t. Colloq.* to risk; as, I don't dare *chance* it:—**chance upon (on),** to happen to find or meet; as, to *chance upon* an old cabin in the woods.

chan-cel-lor (chån′se-lėr), *n.* **1,** in some European countries, the chief minister of state; **2,** in many universities, the honorary head:—**Chancellor,** in Great Britain: **1,** the highest judge of the realm, called *Lord Chancellor*; **2,** the minister of finance, called *Chancellor of the Exchequer.*—*n.* **chan′cel-lor-ship′; chan′cel-ler-y; chan′cer-y.**

chan-de-lier (shan′de-lēr′), *n.* a hanging light fixture, with branches for electric light bulbs, candles, etc.

change (chānj), *v.t.* [changed, chang-ing], **1,** to make different by substituting one thing for another; as, she *changed* her coat; he *changed* his job; **2,** to alter so as to make different in shape, size, colour, etc.; **3,** to exchange; as, to *change* books with someone; **4,** to give an equivalent for; as, to *change* a 20-dollar bill:—*v.i.* **1,** to vary; as, the weather *changes*; **2,** to be altered; as, her appearance has *changed* greatly; **3,** of the moon, to pass from one phase, or state, to another; as, the moon *changes* next week:—*n.* **1,** an alteration; a variation; as, a *change* of scenery; **2,** variety; as, she plays tennis almost every day, but likes golf as a *change;* **3,** small coins taken together, as opposed to paper money; **4,** the difference, returned to a purchaser, between the price of a purchase and the amount paid.—*adj.* **change′a-ble; change′less.**

chan-nel (chan′el), *n.* **1,** the bed of a stream; also, the deepest part of a bay, harbour, etc.; **2,** a strait separating two large bodies of land; as, the English *Channel;* **3,** a long groove or furrow; **4,** a course by which information, thought, etc., travels; as, news comes through the *channel* of the press; **5,** a means of carrying an electronic signal to a radio or television set through a certain range of frequencies:—*v.t.* [channelled, channel-ling], to cut or wear (a groove or way); as, the brook *channelled* its way through the rock.

chant (chånt), *v.t.* **1,** to sing; **2,** to praise in song; **3,** to intone, or sing on one prolonged note; recite musically:—*v.i.* **1,** to make melody with the voice; **2,** to intone; sing slowly and solemnly:—*n.* **1,** a song; esp. a solemn, measured song; **2,** a special musical composition, chanted or intoned, repeating the same words or tunes.—*n.* **chant′er.**

chant-ey (shån′ti; chån′ti), *n.* Same as **shanty.**

Cha-nu-ka (ha′nu-ka), *n.* Same as **Hanukkah.**

cha-os (kā′os), *n.* **1,** the utter confusion formerly supposed to have existed before the universe; **2,** hence, utter disorder.—*adj.* **cha-ot′ic** (kā-ot′ik).

chap (chap), *v.t.* [chapped, chap-ping], to cause to crack or become rough; as, cold *chaps* the skin:—*v.i.* to crack or become rough; as, my hands *chap* quickly:—*n.* **1,** a crack, as in the skin; **2,** a boy or man.

chap-el (chap′el), *n.* **1,** a place of public worship; a small church; **2,** a place of worship in a hospital, school, etc.; **3,** in Great Britain, a church belonging to neither the Church of England nor the Roman Catholic Church.

chap-er-one or **chap-er-on** (shap′ėr-ōn′), *n.* **1,** formerly, an older woman who accompanied a young, unmarried woman, or a group of young people, to the theatre, a dance, or other social function; **2,** an older person who attends and supervises parties, etc.; as, a *chaperone* at a school dance:—*v.t.* to act as chaperone to.

chap-lain (chap′lin), *n.* a clergyman who performs religious services in the army or navy, or in an institution, etc.

chaps (chaps; shaps; chops), *n.* seatless leather breeches or overalls open at the back, worn by those who ride horses as a protection against cacti, thorns, etc. Short for *cha-pa-ra-jos* (chä′pä-rä′hōs).

chap-ter (chap′tėr), *n.* **1,** a main division of a book; **2,** a local group that is part of a larger club or other organization; as, a Red Cross *chapter;* **3,** a specific period of life or time; as, a *chapter* in one's life.

char (chär), *v.t.* [charred, char-ring], **1,** to burn partially; **2,** to reduce to charcoal;—*n.* a small red-bellied brook trout.

char-ac-ter (kar′ak-tėr), *n.* **1,** a distinctive sign or mark; hence, the written or printed marks for letters and numbers; **2,** individuality; nature; the qualities that make a thing what it is, and different from other things; as, the *character* of mountain vegetation differs from that of a valley; **3,** a person possessing distinctive qualities; as, a great historical *character;* **4,** mental or moral nature; as, a person of high *character;* **5,** reputation; **6,** a testimonial; **7,** a person in literature, a movie, a television show, or a play; as, a Dickens *character;* a *character* in a movie.

char-ac-ter-is-tic (kar′ak-tėr-is′tik), *adj.* showing the distinctive qualities or traits of a person or thing; typical; as, her *characteristic* kindness:—*n.* a distinguishing or special quality, such as honesty, friendliness, shyness, tallness, etc.; as, the *characteristics* of a scholar, an athlete, a village, etc.

char-ac-ter-ize (kar′ak-tėr-īz′), *v.t.* [characterized, characteriz-ing], **1,** to describe as having specific qualities; as, the author *characterizes* his heroines as plain, but interesting; **2,** to mark or distinguish; be characteristic of; as, obstinacy *characterizes* the donkey.—*n.* **char′ac-ter-i-za′tion.**

cha-rade (sha-rād′; sha-räd′), *n.* a game in which a word is to be guessed from the acting out of each syllable, as *persuaded* from the acting of *purr, sway, dead.*

char-coal (chär′kōl′), *n.* a very dark or black porous substance produced by charring wood in the absence of air: used as fuel in outdoor cooking, in drawing pencils, and as a water or air filter.

chard (chärd), *n.* **1,** a beet, of which the thick stalk and large leaves are used as food, as the Swiss *chard;* **2,** the blanched leaves and stalk of the artichoke, used as food.

charge (chärj), *v.t.* [charged, charg-ing], **1,** to load, as a gun with ammunition, or a battery with electricity; **2,** to command; instruct; as, the judge then *charged* the jury; **3,** to accuse; blame; as, he was *charged* with murder; **4,** to demand, as a price; **5,** to pay later for something bought now; as, to *charge* this purchase on a credit card; **6,** to rush upon or attack:—*v.i.* **1,** to demand or set a price or sum due; as, he *charges* a reasonable fee for his services; **2,** to make an attack:—*n.* **1,** a quantity of material with which a firearm or other apparatus is loaded; as, a *charge* of gunpowder; **2,** an office or trust; responsibility; as, to be in *charge* of refreshments; **3,** a parish or congregation entrusted to the care of a minister; **4,** the price of an object; as, the *charge* is five dollars; **5,** an entry or account of what is owed; **6,** an accusation; as, a *charge* of theft; **7,** a violent onset or attack.—*adj.* **charge′a-ble.**

charg-er (chär′jėr), *n.* **1,** a spirited warhorse; **2,** an apparatus that provides an electrical charge to batteries, etc.

char-i-ot (char′i-ut), *n.* an ancient two-wheeled car used in war, state processions, and racing, drawn by two horses or, sometimes, by four.—*n.* **char′i-ot-eer′.**

char-i-ta-ble (char′i-ta-bl), *adj.* **1,** having to do with charity; as, UNICEF is a *charitable* organization; **2,** giving money or help to the poor or needy; generous; **3,** kind and understanding; as, a *charitable* comment, gesture.—*adv.* **char′i-ta-bly.**

char-i-ty (char′i-ti), *n.* [*pl.* charities], **1,** generosity to the poor; **2,** a gift to the poor; **3,** brotherly love and goodwill; **4,** leniency in judging others; **5,** an institution, founded by a gift, to help the needy, such as the Red Cross.

cha-ri-va-ri (sha-riv′a-rē′; shi′va-rē′), *n.* a mock serenade (to newlyweds), by beating on pans, blowing horns, etc. Also, *Colloq.* **shiv′a-ree′.**

char-la-tan (shär′la-tan), *n.* a quack, esp. a pretender to medical skill; an impostor.

char-ley horse (chär′li), *n. Colloq.* a cramp or stiffness, esp. in leg muscles.

charm (chärm), *n.* **1,** originally, a chanted verse supposed to have magic power; **2,** hence, anything that is thought to have magic power; **3,** something worn to bring good luck and avert ill luck; an amulet; **4,** a trinket worn on a watch chain, bracelet, etc.; **5,** a quality of appearance or personality that attracts others; attractiveness:—*v.t.* **1,** to bewitch; put a spell on; **2,** hence, to affect as if by magic; as, to *charm* away pain; **3,** to fascinate.—*adj.* **charm′ing.**—*adv.* **charm′ing-ly.**—*n.* **charm′er.**

chart (chärt), *n.* **1,** a map, esp. a map of any part of a body of water, marking dangerous ledges, ocean currents, islands, etc., for the use of mariners; **2,** the map of a ship's course; **3,** information in the form of tables, diagrams, graphs, etc.; as, a nurse's *chart*; sales *chart*:—*v.t.* **1,** to map out; **2,** to put (information) in the form of a chart.

char-ter (chär′ter), *n.* **1,** an official paper bestowing certain rights and privileges; **2,** a written permit from the authorities of a society to establish a chapter, lodge, or branch:—*v.t.* **1,** to grant a charter or permit to; **2,** to hire; as, to *charter* a bus.

Charter of Rights and Freedoms, a part of the Constitution of Canada that legally guarantees certain rights for all Canadians.

char-treuse (shär′tröz′), *n.* **1,** a pale yellowish-green colour; **2,** a syrupy alcoholic liqueur of this colour.

chase (chās), *v.t.* [chased, chas-ing], **1,** to pursue with intent to capture; as, to *chase* a fugitive; to hunt; **2,** to drive away; dispel; as, to *chase* crows; *chase* fears:—*n.* **1,** eager pursuit, esp. with the idea of capturing (a criminal) or driving away (an animal); **2,** hunters (collectively).

chasm (kazm), *n.* a deep cleft or gap (in the earth); a vast empty space.

chas-sis (shas′ē; shas′is), *n.* [*pl.* chassis (shas′iz)], **1,** the frame, machinery, and wheels of an automobile; **2,** the main frame of an airplane.

chaste (chāst), *adj.* **1,** virtuous; pure; **2,** simple and restrained in style or taste; unadorned.—*n.* **chas′ti-ty.**

chas-ten (chās′n), *v.t.* **1,** to punish for the purpose of making better; as, the teacher *chastened* her students; **2,** to subdue; bring low; as, criticism *chastens* a pompous writer.

chas-tise (chas-tīz′), *v.t.* [chastised, chastis-ing], to correct by punishment; as, to *chastise* a late student.—*n.* **chas′tise-ment.**

chat (chat), *v.i.* [chat-ted, chat-ting], to converse in an easy, familiar manner:—*n.* **1,** familiar, easy speech; an informal talk; **2,** a kind of songbird noted for its song.—*adj.* **chat′ty.**—*n.* **chat′ti-ness.**

cha-teau (shå′tō′), *n.* [*pl.* -teaux (-tōz′), **1,** a feudal castle; **2,** a stately (French) manor or country seat.

chat room, a place where group discussions are held in real time using an Internet service provider channel: participants converse via typed messages that all in the group can access.

chat-ter (chat′ėr), *v.i.* **1,** to utter sounds rapidly and indistinctly, as monkeys; **2,** to talk much and say little; **3,** to rattle, as parts of a machine in motion, or as teeth when one is shivering:—*n.* **1,** sounds like those of the magpie, monkey, etc.; **2,** idle, rapid talk; **3,** a rattling of the teeth, as from cold or fear.—*n.* **chat′ter-er.**

chat-ter-box (chat′ėr-boks′), *n. Colloq.* an incessant talker.

chauf-feur (shō′fėr; shō-fûr′), *n.* one whose business is to drive other people in an automobile.

cheap (chēp), *adj.* **1,** low in price; inexpensive; as, a *cheap* printer; **2,** low in quality; as, *cheap* goods are expensive in the long run; **3,** well worth the price; as, the used car was *cheap* at $8,000; **4,** easily secured; hence, of little value; as, *cheap* popularity; **5,** connected with things of low price or value; as, a *cheap* restaurant, movie, or store.—*adj.* **cheap′ly.**—*n.* **cheap′ness; cheap′skate′; cheap′ shot′.**

cheap-en (chēp′en), *v.t.* to lower in price or value:—*v.i.* to become cheap.

cheat (chēt), *n.* one who deceives or swindles another:—*v.i.* to act dishonestly; as, to *cheat* at cards:—*v.t.* **1,** to deceive; deprive of something by trickery; **2,** to escape; as, to *cheat* death.—*n.* **cheat′er.**

[1]**check** (chek), *n.* **1,** restraint; control; as, to keep one's thoughts in *check;* also, a person or thing imposing restraint; **2,** a stop or interruption; as, a journey without *check;* **3,** a ticket or metal disk that shows that a person has the right to claim something; as, a hat *check;* also, a ticket showing the amount of a bill; as, to pay the *check* in a restaurant; **4,** (preferably *cheque*), an order or draft on a bank for money; **5,** an examination into the accuracy of something; as, a *check* of a bank statement; **6,** a mark showing that something has been examined or verified:—**in check,** controlled; held back; as, to hold your temper *in check*:—*v.t.* **1,** to stop; as, to *check* the advance of the enemy; **2,** to examine for accuracy, or mark as having been examined or verified; **3,** to deposit for safekeeping; as, to *check* a coat; **4,** to get information for something; as, to *check* a dictionary for the proper spelling of a word:—**check in,** to register as a guest in a hotel, etc.:—**check off,** to mark as checked and found true or right; as, to *check off* items on the to-do list:—**check (up) on,** to find out about; seek more information about; as, to *check up on* a sick friend:—**check out,** to pay the bill for being a guest and leave; as, to *check out* of the hotel.

[2]**check** (chek), *n.* **1,** a pattern of squares of alternating colours, as on a checkerboard; **2,** any one of these squares; **3,** cloth showing this pattern:—*v.t.* to mark in checks.

check-er or **cheq-uer** (chek′ėr), *n.* **1,** one of the squares of a pattern marked in squares of alternate colours; also, the pattern itself; **2,** one of the pieces used in playing checkers:—**checkers,** a game played on a checkerboard by two persons, each with 12 pieces:—*v.t.* to mark with small squares of alternate colours; also, to mark similarly; as, sunlight through the leaves *checkered* the ground.—*n.* **check′er-board′.**

check-ered or **cheq-uered** (chek′ėrd), *adj.* **1,** varied; full of ups and downs; as, a *chequered* career; **2,** having a pattern of alternate squares or colours.

check-mate (chek′māt′), *n.* **1,** in *chess,* the putting of an opponent's king in such a position that he or she cannot escape; **2,** hence, a complete obstruction or defeat:—*v.t.* [checkmat-ed, checkmat-ing], to obstruct or defeat utterly; as, to *checkmate* a plan.

check-off (chek′ôf′), *n.* an arrangement whereby an employer deducts union dues from wages, and turns them over to the union.

check-room (chek′ro͞om′), *n.* a room where hats, coats, parcels, and baggage may be left temporarily.

check-up (chek′up′), *n.* an inspection; examination; as, a medical *checkup.*

ched-dar (ched′ėr), *n.* a hard yellow or white cheese of smooth, firm texture.

cheek (chēk), *n.* **1,** the side of the face below the eye; **2,** *Slang* saucy speech; effrontery; impudence.—*adj.* **cheek′y.**—*n.* **cheek′i-ness; cheek′bone′.**

cheep (chēp), *n.* a faint shrill note, as of a chick or bird; peep; chirp:—*v.t.* and *v.i.* to peep or chirp.

cheer (chēr), *n.* **1,** state of mind; esp. a state of gladness or joy; **2,** that which is furnished in the way of food or entertainment; as, Christmas *cheer;* **3,** a shout of joy, applause, or encouragement:—**cheerleader,** someone who leads people in cheering at a sports event:—*v.t.* **1,** to gladden; comfort; **2,** to greet, esp. with shouts of welcome; **3,** hence, to applaud; encourage:—*v.i.* **1,** to become hopeful or glad; as, he soon *cheered* up; **2,** to applaud.—*adj.* **cheer′y; cheer′less.**—*n.* **cheer′i-ness.**—*adv.* **cheer′i-ly.**

cheer-ful (chēr′fool), *adj.* **1,** in good spirits; happy; **2,** bringing cheer; as, a *cheerful* fire; **3,** willing; eager; as, a *cheerful* worker.—*adv.* **cheer′ful-ly.**—*n.* **cheer′ful-ness.**

cheese (chēz), *n.* a food made of the pressed curd of milk.—*adj.* **chees′y.**

cheese-cake (chēs′kāk′), *n.* **1,** a one-crust pie of cream or cottage cheese, sugar, eggs, milk, etc.; **2,** *Slang* a photograph of the figure (esp. the legs) of a beautiful woman.

cheese-cloth (chēz′clôth′), *n.* a thin, loosely woven cotton cloth.

chee-tah (chē′ta), *n.* a leopardlike, long-legged, swift, black-spotted member of the cat family, found in Africa and Asia.

chef (shef), *n.* a head cook, as of a hotel or restaurant; hence, any cook.

chem-i-cal (kem′i-kal), *adj.* **1,** pertaining to chemistry; as, a *chemical* experiment; **2,** produced by, or used in operations of, chemistry; as, a *chemical* compound:—*n.* a substance, such as alcohol, hydrogen, soda, etc., produced by, or used in, a chemical process.—*adv.* **chem′i-cal-ly.**

che-mise (she-mēz′), *n.* a woman's sleeveless, knee-length undergarment; also, a loose dress.

chem-is-try (kem′is-tri), *n.* **1,** the science that studies the nature of different kinds of substances, and of the laws that govern their combination and behaviour under various conditions; **2,** the way that people or things mix or go together; as, the right *chemistry* between two people.—*n.* **chem′ist.**

cheque or **check** (chek), *n.* an order or draft on a bank for money; also, a blank form on which such an order is written:—**chequebook,** a book of blank cheques.

cheq-uer (chek′ėr), *n.* Same as **checker.**

cher-ish (cher′ish), *v.t.* **1,** to protect; care for tenderly; **2,** to hold dear, as a memory; **3,** to cling to, as a hope.

cher-ry (cher′i), *n.* [*pl.* cherries], **1,** a tree related to the plum, bearing a small, smooth, fleshy fruit with a stone in the centre; also, the fruit or the wood of this tree; **2,** a bright red, like that of certain cherries:—*adj.* **1,** of the colour of ripe red cherries; **2,** made of cherry wood.

cher-ub (cher′ub), *n.* [*pl.* cherubs], **1,** a representation of a child, or the head of a child, with wings; **2,** a beautiful, innocent child; **3,** [*pl.* cherubim (cher′ū-bim; cher′oo-bim)], in the Bible, one of an order of angels.—*adj.* **che-ru′bic** (che-ro͞o′bik).

chess (ches), *n.* a game played by two persons, each with 16 variously shaped pieces, on a board of 64 squares.—*n.* **chess′board′.**

chest (chest), *n.* **1,** a strong case; a box with a lid; as, a sailor's *chest*; a tool *chest*; **2,** a large wooden piece of furniture having several drawers, used for holding or storing clothing, etc.; **3,** the quantity such a box contains; also, the box and the contents; as, a *chest* of tea; **4,** a place for keeping a fund of money; hence, the fund itself; as, a community *chest*; **5,** the breast or upper front part of the body enclosed by the ribs.

ches-ter-field (ches′tėr-fēld′), *n.* **1,** a large living-room sofa or divan with well-padded back and upright arms: also called *couch* and *sofa*.

chest-nut (ches′nut), *n.* **1,** a tree of the beech family, bearing nuts in a prickly burr; **2,** the nut or the timber of this tree; **3,** a reddish-brown colour; **4,** a horse of such colour; **5,** *Slang* an old or stale joke:—*adj.* **1,** made of the wood of the chestnut; **2,** reddish brown.

chev-ron (shev′run), *n.* **1,** a badge of two or more stripes meeting at an angle, on the coat sleeve of a noncommissioned officer, police officer, etc., to show his or her rank; **2,** any V-shaped figure, pattern, or design; as, the *chevrons* on a highway.

chew (cho͞o), *v.t.* to crush and grind with the teeth:—*v.i.* to bite repeatedly with the teeth:—*n.* **1,** the act of chewing:—**chewing gum,** a sweetened piece of gummy substance made from the gum of certain tropical trees.

chic (shik; shēk), *n. Colloq.* Parisian cleverness in dress; hence, smartness; style:—*adj.* stylish; as, a *chic* hat.

chi-can-er-y (shi-kān′ėr-i), *n.* **1,** trickery, esp. of a legal kind; **2,** sharp practice.

chick (chik), *n.* a young chicken or bird; **2,** a child; **3,** *Slang* a young girl.

chick-a-dee (chik′a-dē), *n.* a small, grey bird with a black cap.

chick-en (chik′en), *n.* **1,** the young of a fowl, esp. of the domestic fowl; **2,** a hen or rooster; **3,** the flesh of such fowl, prepared for the table; as, roast *chicken*.

chicken pox (chik′en poks′), *n.* a mild contagious disease of children, which is accompanied by a rash and fever.

chic-o-ry (chik′o-ri), *n.* **1,** a common Canadian weed with blue flowers, the leaves of which can be used as salad; **2,** the root of this plant, which, when roasted, is used as a coffee substitute.

chide (chīd), *v.i.* and *v.t.* [*p.t.* chid (chid) or chid-ed (chīd′ed), *p.p.* chid, chid-den (chid′n), or chid-ed, *p.pr.* chid-ing], to find fault (with); scold.

chief (chēf), *n.* a commander, leader, or principal person in an organization or group:—*adj.* principal; leading; most important; as, the *chief* news of the day.—*adv.* **chief′ly.**

chief-tain (chēf′tin), *n.* a leader or commander; esp. the military or civil head of a clan or tribe.

chif-fon (shi-fon′; shif′on), *n.* a soft, thin, transparent fabric:—*adj.* very light and sheer in weight; as, a *chiffon* veil; a *chiffon* cake.

chi-hua-hua (chi-wä′wä), *n.* one of the smallest of all dogs, from Mexico, with large pointed ears.

Chil-co-tin (chil′kō′tin), *n.* a group of Aboriginal peoples of southwestern British Columbia who speak an Athapascan language. Also called *Tsilhqot'in.*

child (chīld), *n.* [*pl.* children (chil′dren)], **1,** a boy or a girl; **2,** a son or a daughter; offspring; **3,** a baby; **4,** a descendant; as, a *child* of Abraham; **5,** a product, as of habit, environment, or temperament; as, a *child* of poverty.—*n.* **child′hood.**—*adj.* **child′less; child′ like.**

child-ish (chīl′dish), *adj.* **1,** like, or suitable to, a child; **2,** weak; foolish; as, a *childish* impulse in an adult.—*n.* **child′ishness.**

chi-li or **chil-li** (chil′i), *n.* **1,** a tropical plant, the pods of which, red when ripe, are dried and powdered to make cayenne pepper or hot seasoning for food; also, the pods; **2,** a dish flavoured with chili peppers, made with meat and usually beans.

chill (chil), *n.* **1,** coldness; **2,** a sudden coldness of body with shivering; as, *chills* and fever; **3,** a check upon enthusiasm; as, she put a *chill* on the party:—*adj.* **1,** cool; as, a *chill* breeze; **2,** unfriendly; not cordial; as, a *chill* welcome:—*v.t.* to make cold:—*v.i.* to become or feel cold.—*adj.* **chill′y.**—*n.* **chill′i-ness.**

chime (chīm), *n.* **1,** a set of bells musically attuned, as the bells in a clock tower; **2,** (often *chimes*), the music of such bells:—*v.i.* [chimed, chim-ing], **1,** to sound in harmony; as, to hear the bells *chiming*; **2,** to agree; as, your opinion *chimes* with mine:—*v.t.* to announce (the hour) by chimes.

chim-ney (chim′ni), *n.* [*pl.* chimneys], **1,** the upright tube or flue, made of brick, stone, etc., through which smoke and heated air may escape from a building; **2,** the part of a flue above a roof; **3,** a glass tube around the flame of a lamp:—**chimney sweep,** someone who cleans out chimneys.

chim-pan-zee (chim′pan-zē; chim′pan-zē′; chim′pan′zi), *n.* a blackish-brown anthropoid ape of Africa, smaller than the gorilla: they are among the most intelligent animals, making use of tools, as do humans.

chin (chin), *n.* the part of the face below the underlip; also, the rounded tip of the lower jaw:—*v.t.* [chinned, chin-ning], to pull (oneself) up while hanging by the hands from a horizontal bar, until one's chin is on a level with the bar.

chi-na (chī′na), *n.* **1,** porcelain or porcelain ware, brought originally from China; **2,** porcelain or earthenware dishes of any kind:—*adj.* made of porcelain.—*n.* **chi′na-ware′.**

Chi-nese (chī-nez′), *n.* **1,** a person who inhabits or originates from China; **2,** a group of related languages of these people:—*adj.* relating to the country, the people, the languages, or the culture of China.

¹chink (chingk), *n.* a narrow crack or opening; as, you can see through the *chink* in the wall:—*v.t.* **1,** to make fissures or cracks in; **2,** to fill the cracks of.

²chink (chingk), *n.* a sharp, ringing sound, as of glass or metal struck lightly:—*v.t.* to cause to jingle:—*v.i.* to jingle.

chi-nook (shi-nook′; chi-nōōk′; chi-nook′), *n.* and *adj.* **1,** a dry wind that blows at intervals down eastern Rocky Mountain slopes, esp. in Alberta and southward; **2,** a warm, moist, southwest ocean wind that blows along the British Columbia coast and southward; **3,** the largest kind of Pacific salmon.

chintz (chints), *n.* a cotton cloth, printed in coloured patterns, often with a smooth, glossy finish.

chip (chip), *v.t.* [chipped, chip-ping], **1,** to cut or break small bits or pieces from; **2,** to shape by cutting away small bits; as, to *chip* an arrow from flint:—*v.i.* to break off in small bits; as, these cups *chip* easily:—**chip in,** to give one's share of money or help; contribute; as, to *chip in* on a gift for a classmate:—*n.* **1,** a small piece, as of stone or wood, cut or broken off; also, the gap left; as, a *chip* in the saucer; a potato *chip*; **2,** a very small piece, as of a diamond; **3,** a counter or disk used in games; as, a poker *chip*; **4,** a tiny flake of material, usually silicon, that has been specially treated to carry the circuits needed to operate a computer; a microchip.

Chip-e-wy-an (chip′u-wī-en), *n.* the largest group of Athapaskan-speaking First Nation people in Manitoba, Saskatchewan, and the Northwest Territories.

chip-munk (chip′mungk), *n.* a small North American squirrel-like animal with brown fur and striped markings on its back.

chip-per (chip′ėr), *adj. Colloq.*, in good spirits; cheerful; as, I feel *chipper* today.

chi-rop-o-dist (kī-rop′o-dist; ki-rop′o-dist), *n.* one who treats ailments, esp. minor ailments, of the feet.—*n.* **chi-rop′o-dy.**

chi-ro-prac-tor (kī-rō-prak′tėr), *n.* one who treats bone, muscle, and nerve disorders by manipulating the joints, esp. the joints of the spine.—*n.* and *adj.* **chi′ro-prac′tic.**

chirp (chûrp), *n.* a short, cheerful note, as that of a bird:—*v.i.* **1,** to utter such a note; **2,** to talk merrily:—*v.t.* to utter (a sound) resembling a chirp.

chis-el (chiz′l), *n.* a steel-edged tool for cutting wood, stone, or metal:—*v.t.* and *v.i.* [chiselled, chisel-ling or chiseled, chisel-ing], **1,** to cut or engrave with such a tool; **2,** *Slang:* **a,** to cheat; **b,** to secure (something) by shrewd, often unfair, means.—*n.* **chis′el-ler, chis′e-ler.**

chit (chit), *n.* **1,** a letter, bill, note, etc.; **2,** a voucher for a small sum owed; **3,** a receipt.

chit-chat (chit′chat′), *n.* **1,** small talk; **2,** gossip.

chiv-al-ry (shiv′al-ri), *n.* **1,** the system of knighthood in the Middle Ages; **2,** the characteristics of an ideal knight, as courage, courtesy, respect for women, etc.; **3,** a body of knights; hence, a company of gallant gentlemen; **4,** well-mannered behaviour, esp. of a man.—*adj.* **chiv′al-rous.**

chlo-rine (klō′rēn; klō′rin), *n.* a heavy, poisonous, green-yellow gas of disagreeable odour used in bleaching, killing germs, and purifying water (as in swimming pools).—*v.t.* **chlo′rin-ate′.**—*n.* **chlo′rin-a′tion.**

chlor-o-phyll or **chlor-o-phyl** (klōr′ō-fil), *n.* the green colouring substance of plants: it uses sunlight to make plant food from air and water, known as *photosynthesis*.

choc-o-late (chok′o-lit), *n.* **1,** a food substance obtained by roasting and grinding cacao seeds; **2,** a small piece of candy made of, or coated with, this substance; **3,** a drink made from this food with milk and sugar:—*adj.* **1,** made of, or flavoured with, chocolate; **2,** of the dark-brown colour of chocolate.

choice (chois), *n.* **1,** selection; as, make your *choice*; also, power of selection; as, you have your *choice*; **2,** the thing or person chosen; as, the president is the *choice* of the society; **3,** the best or most desirable part or thing; as, this puppy is the *choice* of the litter; **4,** a number large enough to choose from; as, a *choice* of hats:—*adj.* [choic-er, choic-est], **1,** select; particularly fine; as, *choice* meats; **2,** selected with care; appropriate.

choir (kwīr), *n.* **1,** a group of trained singers, esp. in a church or school; **2,** the part of the church in which they sing.—*n.* **choir′boy′; choir′mas′ter.**

choke (chōk), *v.t.* [choked, chok-ing], **1,** to stop the breath of; stifle; as, this collar *chokes* me; **2,** to check the growth of by stifling, or as if by stifling; as, weeds *choked* the garden; to *choke* the fire; **3,** to cut down the air intake of the carburetor of (a motor) to enrich the mixture; as, to *choke* an engine; **4,** to block up; clog; as, rubbish *choked* the alley; **5,** to suppress (an emotion); as, to *choke* down anger:—*v.i.* **1,** to become suffocated; **2,** *Colloq.* to do badly in a tense situation because of nervousness; as, the Olympic skater *choked* and missed her jump:—*n.* **1,** the act or sound of strangling; **2,** the carburetor valve that regulates the air intake.

chok-er (chōk′ėr), *n.* **1,** *Colloq.* a necklace, high collar, wide scarf, etc., worn close about the neck or throat; **2,** anything that or anyone who chokes.

chol-er-a (kol′ėr-a), *n.* an infectious and often rapidly fatal disease.

chol-er-ic (kol′ėr-ik), *adj.* easily angered; quick-tempered; irascible.

cho-les-ter-ol (ka-les′te-rōl; ka-les′te-rol), *n.* a fatty white substance found in food from animals, which can build up in the blood vessels and cause health problems: the body produces most of its own cholesterol.

choose (chōōz), *v.t.* [*p.t.* chose (chōz), *p.p.* cho-sen (chō′zn), *p.pr.* choos-ing], **1,** to pick; select from a number; as, he *chose* the reddest apple; **2,** to prefer; see fit; as, he *chose* to run:—*v.i.* to make a choice.

[1]**chop** (chop), *v.t.* [chopped, chop-ping], **1,** to cut with repeated blows; as, to *chop* wood; **2,** to cut into very small pieces; as, to *chop* vegetables; **3,** to cut short, as words:—*v.i.* to make a quick stroke, as with an axe:—*n.* **1,** a small piece of meat containing a rib or section of bone; as, a lamb *chop;* **2,** a short, rough movement of the waves.

[2]**chop** (chop), *n.* a jaw:—**chops,** the mouth or the fleshy parts about it.

chop-per (chop′ėr), *n.* **1,** a person or thing that chops; **2,** a tool or device that chops; **3,** *Colloq.* a helicopter.

chop-py (chop′i), *adj.* [chop-pi-er, chop-pi-est], **1,** full of short, rough waves; as, a *choppy* sea; **2,** changeable; as, a *choppy* wind; **3,** short and quick; jerky; in spurts; as, *choppy* running.

chop-sticks (chop′stiks′), *n.pl.* two small sticks of wood, plastic, etc., used instead of a fork, esp. in Asian countries or to eat Asian food.

chor-al (kōr′al), *adj.* **1,** pertaining to a choir or chorus; as, *choral* singing; **2,** sung by a choir or chorus; as, a *choral* service.

[1]**chord** (kôrd), *n.* in *geometry,* a straight line joining two points on the circumference of a circle.

[2]**chord** (kôrd), *n.* in *music,* a combination of three or more tones sounded together and in harmony.

chore (chōr), *n.* **1,** a small job; **2,** any unpleasant or difficult task; as, studying for the chemistry exam is a real *chore*:—**chores,** small or odd jobs; the daily humdrum work of a farm or household.

chor-tle (chôr′tl), *v.i.* [chortled, chortling], to chuckle gleefully:—*n.* a low, deep, or inward laugh.

chor-us (kōr′us, kôr-), *n.* **1,** a group of persons singing together or their song; also, any utterance by a number of persons at one time; as, a *chorus* of shouts; **2,** a piece of music arranged to be sung by a number of voices all together; **3,** a refrain at the end of each verse of a song:—*v.t.* and *v.i.* to sing or utter all together.

chose (chōz), *p.t.* of *choose.*

cho-sen (chō′zen), *p.p.* of *choose.*

chow (chou), *n.* **1,** *Slang* food; **2,** a dog originating in China, having a muscular body, heavy coat, blue-black tongue, and short tail that curls over the back. Also called *chow chow.*

chow-der (chou′dėr), *n.* a soup made by stewing fish, clams, or a vegetable, usually with milk, potatoes, onions, etc.

Christ (krīst), *n.* **1,** the saviour, or the Messiah, whose coming was foretold by the ancient Hebrew prophets; **2,** Jesus of Nazareth, regarded by Christians as the Son of God and the true Messiah.

chris-ten (kris′n), *v.t.* **1,** to baptize; **2,** to name; as, to *christen* a ship; **3,** *Colloq.* to use for the first time; as, to *christen* the new car.—*n.* **chris′ten-ing.**

Chris-tian (kris′chan; krist′yan), *n.* a believer in the religion of Christ; a member of the Christian Church:—*adj.* **1,** believing in, or practising, the religion of Christ; **2,** pertaining to Christ, his followers, or his teachings; **3,** showing Christ-like qualities, as gentleness, forbearance, etc.:—**Christian name,** a person's first name.—*n.* **Chris′ti-an′i-ty.**

Christ-mas (kris′mas), *n.* the yearly festival (December 25) in honour of the birth of Jesus Christ.

chro-mat-ic (krō-mat′ik), *adj.* **1,** relating to colour; as, *chromatic* printing (in colours); **2,** in *music,* using or proceeding by half tones; as, a *chromatic* scale.

chrome (krōm), *n.* **1,** a bright colouring substance or pigment; as, *chrome* yellow, *chrome* green, *chrome* red; **2,** a shorter form of *chromium.*

chro-mi-um (krō′mi-um), *n.* a greyish-white, rust-resisting metallic element, much used in plating and trims, faucets, household wares, roller bearings, tools, dies, etc., and in alloys.

chro-mo-some (krō′mo-sōm′), *n.* a rod-shaped, threadlike structure that carries, in the nucleus of each plant and animal cell, the genes that convey hereditary characteristics: it is made up mainly of nucleoproteins containing DNA, coded hereditary information.

chron-ic (kron′ik), *adj.* **1,** continuing for a long time; as, he has a *chronic* back ache; **2,** habitual; as, a *chronic* complainer.—*adv.* **chron′i-cal-ly.**

chron-i-cle (kron′i-kl), *n.* a record of events in the order of their happening:—*v.t.* [chroni-cled, chroni-cling], to enter, as in a record.—*n.* **chron′i-cler.**

chro-nol-o-gy (kro-nol′o-ji), *n.* [*pl.* chronologies], **1,** the science that deals with events and arranges their dates in proper order; **2,** a table of events given in the order of their occurrence; as, a *chronology* of the war.—*adj.* **chron′o-log′i-cal** (kron′o-loj′i-kal).

chrys-a-lis (kris′a-lis), *n.* [*pl.* chrysalises or chrysalides (kri-sa′li-dēz′], **1,** the inactive or *pupa* stage through which an insect, esp. a moth or a butterfly, passes when it leaves the caterpillar or *larva* stage and before it reaches its winged or mature form; **2,** the case enclosing the insect during that stage; a cocoon.

CHRYSALIS OF A BUTTERFLY

chrys-an-the-mum (kris-an′the-mum), *n.* **1,** a plant with showy flowers that blooms late in the fall; **2,** a flower of this plant.

chub-by (chub′i), *adj.* [chub-bi-er, chub-bi-est], plump and round; as, a baby's *chubby* fists.—*n.* **chub′bi-ness.**

[1]**chuck** (chuk), *v.t.* **1,** to tap or pat under the chin affectionately or playfully; **2,** to fling away; throw; toss; as, *chuck* me the ball; to *chuck* an old proposal in the garbage:—*n.* a light tap; a pat under the chin.

[2]**chuck** (chuk), *n.* **1,** a clamp for holding a tool or piece of work in a lathe or drill press; **2,** a part of a side of beef or a carcass of lamb or mutton, including most of the neck, the shoulder, and about three ribs.

chuck-le (chuk′l), *n.* a quiet, suppressed laugh:—*vi.* [chuck-led, chuck-ling], to laugh quietly to oneself.

chuck-wag-on (chuk′wag′un), *n.* in Western Canada and U.S., a kitchen on wheels to provide meals for cowboys, lumbermen, etc.: the *chuckwagon* race at the Calgary Stampede is a popular event.

chum (chum), *n.* **1,** a roommate, as at school; **2,** a close friend:—*v.i.* [chummed, chum-ming], **1,** to occupy the same room; **2,** to be very friendly.—*adj.* **chum′my.**

chump (chump), *n.* **1,** a short, thick block of wood; **2,** *Slang* a fool, blockhead.

chunk (chungk), *n.* **1,** a short, thick piece; **2,** *Colloq.* a large amount; as, chores take up a large *chunk* of the weekend.—*adj.* **chunk′y.**

church (chûrch), *n.* **1,** a building for public Christian worship; **2,** the entire body of Christians; **3,** a regular service for Christian worship:—**Church,** a particular body or division of Christians; a denomination; as, the United *Church*:—*adj.* having to do with a church; as, *church* music; *church* architecture.—*n.* **church′go′ing.**

church-yard (chûrch′yärd′), *n.* ground about a church, often used for burial.

churl (chûrl), *n.* **1,** formerly, a person of low birth; **2,** a surly, ill-bred person.—*adj.* **churl′ ish.**—*adv.* **churl′ish-ly.**

churn (chûrn), *n.* a vessel in which milk or cream is made into butter:—*v.t.* **1,** to make (butter) by violently stirring cream; **2,** to stir by violent motion; as, the propeller *churned* the water:—*v.i.* **1,** to work a churn; **2,** foam; seethe; wash to and fro; as, the water *churns* around the rocks.

chute (shōōt), *n.* **1,** a slanting trough for sliding things down; as, a laundry *chute*; **2,** a rapid in a stream; a shoot; **3,** a toboggan slide; **4,** *Colloq.* a parachute:—*v.t.* [chut-ed, chut-ing], to send down a chute.

chutz-pah (hoot′spä), *n.* *Slang* boldness, effrontery; audacity; insolence.

ci-ca-da (si-kā′da; si-kä′da), *n.* [*pl.* cicadas], a large insect with four transparent wings, noted for the long, shrill, chirping sound made by the male.

ci-der (sī′dėr), *n.* apple juice: used as a drink or for making vinegar.

ci-gar (si-gär′), *n.* a roll of tobacco leaf, used for smoking.

cig-a-rette (sig′a-ret′), *n.* a small roll made of finely cut tobacco wrapped in thin paper for smoking.

cinch (sinch), *n.* **1,** a saddle girth firmly fastened in place by loops and knots; **2,** *Colloq.* a sure grip or hold; **3,** *Slang* a sure or easy thing:—*v.t.* **1,** to put a cinch upon; **2,** *Slang* to get a sure hold on.

cin-der (sin′dėr), *n.* **1,** a piece of partly burned coal or wood that has ceased to flame:—**cinders,** ashes.

cin-e-ma (sin′i-ma), *n.* a motion-picture theatre, a motion picture, or movies in general: short form of **cin′e-mat′o-graph.**

cin-na-mon (sin′a-mun), *n.* **1,** a tropical tree; also, its bark or the spice made from it; **2,** a red-brown colour.

cin-quain (sing′kān; sing′kwān), *n.* a poem or part of a poem that is five lines long and follows a set pattern.

ci-pher or **cy-pher** (sī′fėr), *n.* **1,** in *mathematics*, zero; naught [symbol 0]; **2,** hence, a person or thing without value or power; **3,** a secret manner of writing, or the key to it; a code:—*v.t.* and *v.i.* **1,** to work (arithmetical examples) with figures; calculate; **2,** to write in code.

cir-ca (sûr′ka), *prep.* about: used with dates and figures to show that they are not exact; as, Confucius was born *circa* 550 B.C.

cir-cle (sûr′kl), *n.* **1,** a plane surface bounded by a single curved line called its circumference, every part of which is equally distant from a point within it, called the centre; also, the curve bounding such a surface; **2,** any flat, round body; **3,** anything resembling a circle or part of a circle; as, the family *circle* in a theatre; **4,** a completed series; a system; cycle; round; as, the *circle* of the months; **5,** a number of persons grouped around a central interest or person; as, a *circle* of friends:—*v.i.* [cir-cled, cir-cling], to move in a circle; as, the airplane *circled* above:—*v.t.* **1,** to surround; as, a ring *circled* his finger; **2,** to revolve around; as, the earth *circles* the sun.—*n.* **cir′cler.**

cir-clet (sûr′klit), *n.* **1,** a small circle; **2,** a circular ornament for the head, arm, neck, or finger.

cir-cuit (sûr′kit), *n.* **1,** the boundary line around an area; also, the space enclosed; **2,** the distance around any space, whether circular or of other form; **3,** the act of going around anything; revolution; as, the *circuit* of the earth around the sun; **4,** the regular travelling from place to place of a judge or other person for the purpose of holding court or performing other specific duties; also, the territory or district over which he or she travels; **5,** the path of an electric current; **6,** a group of theatres under the same management:—**circuit breaker,** *n.* an automatic device for interrupting an electric current, esp. when the current load becomes too heavy:—**circuit board,** a printed circuit with electronic components.

cir-cu-i-tous (sėr-kū′i-tus), *adj.* round about; indirect; as, to go by a *circuitous* route.—*adv.* **cir-cu′i-tous-ly.**

cir-cu-lar (sûr′kū-lėr), *adj.* **1,** of, pertaining to, or like a circle; as, a *circular* saw; **2,** moving in a circle; as, *circular* motion; **3,** published for distribution to a group of persons; as, a *circular* letter:—*n.* a printed letter or advertisement for general distribution.—*adv.* **cir′cu-lar-ly.**

cir-cu-late (sûr′kū-lāt′), *v.i.* [circulat-ed, circulat-ing], **1,** to pass from place to place; as, he *circulated* among the guests; **2,** to move around in a course; move about; spread; as, in that heating system hot water *circulates* through the pipes; rumours *circulated* around the school; **3,** to be distributed, as a newspaper:—*v.t.* to send round; as, he *circulated* the report.

cir-cu-la-tion (sûr′kū-lā′shun), *n.* **1,** a going around; movement in a circuit; as, the *circulation* of air; **2,** the movement of blood through the blood vessels; **3,** the number of copies of a newspaper or magazine that are sold for each issue.—*n.* **cir′cu-la-to′ry sys′tem.**

cir-cum-cise (sûr′kum-sīz′), *v.t.* [circumcised, circumcis-ing], to cut off part or all of the foreskin.—*n.* **cir′cum-ci′sion.**

cir-cum-fer-ence (sėr-kum′fer-ens], *n.* **1,** the line that bounds a circle or any curved-plane figure; **2,** the distance around a circular body or area; circuit.

cir-cum-flex (sûr′kum-fleks′), *n.* an accent mark [^; ˆ; ˜] to denote a rising–falling tone, as in the French word *rôle* or Spanish *cañon* (canyon).

cir-cum-nav-i-gate (sûr′kum-nav′i-gāt′), *v.t.* [circumnavigat-ed, circumnavigat-ing], to sail completely around (the earth, an island, etc.).—*n.* **cir′cum-nav′i-ga′tion.**

cir-cum-scribe (sûr′kum-skrīb′), *v.t.* [circumscribed, circumscrib-ing], **1,** to draw a line around; **2,** hence, to restrict; as, to *circumscribe* the powers of a king.

cir-cum-spect (sûr′kum-spekt′), *adj.* cautious; considering all sides of a problem before acting.—*n.* **cir′cum-spec′tion.**

cir-cum-stance (sûr′kum-stans′), *n.* **1,** an incident, occurrence, or fact relating to another fact, and throwing light on its meaning, importance, etc.; **2,** a detail; as, one *circumstance* was overlooked; **3,** pomp; ceremony:—**circumstances, a,** the conditions under which an act occurs, such as time, place, or cause, etc.; as, the meeting occurred under peculiar *circumstances;* **b,** a condition or state of affairs; material welfare; as, he is living in poor *circumstances.*

cir-cum-stan-tial (sûr′kum-stan′shal), *adj.* **1,** consisting of, or based on, particular incidents or apparent facts; not direct; as, *circumstantial* evidence; **2,** detailed; as, a *circumstantial* report.

cir-cum-vent (sûr′kum-vent′), *v.t.* **1,** to get the better of by crafty means; get around; outwit; **2,** go around or avoid; as, to *circumvent* the big city.—*n.* **cir′cum-ven′tion.**

cir-cus (sûr′kus), *n.* **1,** a large level space surrounded by seats, usually within a tent, for displaying acrobatic feats, clowns, animals, etc.: circuses usually travel from town to town; **2,** the performance in such a space: also, the company of performers; **3,** in ancient Rome, an oval space surrounded on three sides by tiers of seats, used for chariot races, games, etc.

cir-rho-sis (si-rō′sis), *n.* a disease in which

the liver turns yellowish and becomes shrunken and deformed (often caused by drinking alcohol).

cir-rus (sir′us), *n.* and *adj.* a whitish, filmy, fleecy cloud formation at high altitude.

cis-tern (sis′tėrn), *n.* a tank or artificial reservoir, often underground, for storing water or other liquids.

cit-a-del (sit′a-del), *n.* **1,** a fortress, esp. one defending a city; **2,** any strongly fortified place; any refuge.

ci-ta-tion (sī-tā′shun), *n.* **1,** the quoting of a passage, as from a book; **2,** honourable mention, as for distinguished service; **3,** an official order to appear (in court); as, a traffic *citation.*

cite (sīt), *v.t.* [cit-ed, cit-ing], **1,** to summon to appear in court; **2,** to quote; as, a minister *cites* a passage from the Bible; **3,** to bring forward as proof; as, the lawyer *cited* the evidence; **4,** to give honourable mention to; **5,** to use as an example; refer to; as, to *cite* a magazine article when discussing how to write a good essay.

cit-i-zen (sit′i-zn), *n.* **1,** an inhabitant; a resident of a town or city; as, the *citizens* of Montréal; **2,** a member of a state or nation who enjoys political rights and privileges, such as voting, and in return pays taxes and gives his or her allegiance to the government; **3,** a civilian as distinguished from a soldier, police officer, etc.

citizens′ band, *n.* Same as CB.

cit-i-zen-ship (sit′i-zn-ship′), *n.* the status of a person who owes allegiance to the government in return for his or her political rights and privileges.

cit-ric (sit′rik), *adj.* pertaining to, or derived from, lemons, oranges, and other citrus fruits; as, *citric* acid.

cit-ron-el-la (sit′run-el′a), *n.* a sharp-smelling oil used to keep away insects, esp. mosquitoes; also used for perfume, liniment, and soap.

cit-rus (sit′rus), *adj.* of or relating to a group of trees and fruit including the orange, lemon, lime, citron, grapefruit, etc., which grow in warm climates.

cit-y (sit′i), *n.* [*pl.* cities], **1,** a large and important town; also, its inhabitants; **2,** in Canada and the U.S., a municipality or incorporated community having local self-government.

civ-ic (siv′ik), *adj.* of or relating to a city, a citizen, or citizenship; as, *civic* duty; *civic* rights:—**civics,** *n.pl.* used as *sing.* the study of city government or of good citizenship.

civ-il (siv′il), *adj.* **1,** of, relating to, or characteristic of a city, its government, or its citizens; as, *civil* duties; **2,** pertaining to civilians; not military or ecclesiastical; as, to be married in a *civil* ceremony; **3,** within a country or state; as, *civil* rights; **4,** formally polite; often, barely polite.—*adv.* **civ′il-ly.**—*n.* **ci-vil′i-ty.**

ci-vil-ian (si-vil′yan), *n.* and *adj.* one who is not, or pertaining to one who is not, a member of an armed service, such as army, navy, airforce, marines, or police force.

civ-i-li-za-tion (siv′i-li-zā′shun; -lī-zā′shun), *n.* **1,** the act of making or becoming less savage or barbarous; as, the *civilization* of humans has been a slow process; **2,** the state of being refined in manners; culture; refinement; a particular stage or type of this; as, Greek *civilization* is older than Roman; **3,** collectively, those countries that are in a high stage of development.

civ-i-lize (siv′i-liz′), *v.t.* [civilized, civilizing], to change from a primitive condition of life to a more developed one; instruct in the arts and refinements of life; enlighten.—*adj.* **civ′i-lized.**

civil liberty, the freedom of citizens to exercise their fundamental rights, such as freedom of speech, that are guaranteed by the Canadian Charter of Rights and Freedoms.

clack (klak), *n.* **1,** a confused hubbub of voices; as, a *clack* of tongues; **2,** a sharp, abrupt sound; as, the *clack* of belting in a mill.

clad (klad), a *p.t.* of *clothe*:—*p.adj.* dressed; clothed; as, he was *clad* in his best suit.

claim (klām), *v.t.* **1,** to demand or assert as one's own or one's due; as, to *claim* an inheritance; **2,** to call for; deserve; as, this matter *claims* our attention; **3,** maintain; as, I *claim* this to be true:—*n.* **1,** a demand for something as due; as, he put in a *claim* for damages; **2,** an assertion of a right to something; as, I have a *claim* to the property; **3,** the thing demanded, esp. a piece of land that a miner marks out; **4,** a statement that something is true; as, her *claim* that she saw a ghost.—*n.* **claim′ant.**

clam (klam), *n.* an edible shellfish with a hinged double shell, living partly or wholly buried in sand or mud:—*v.i.* [clammed, clam-ming], to dig for clams.—*n.* **clam′bake′.**

clam-ber (klam′bėr), *v.t.* and *v.i.* to ascend or climb with difficulty; as, to *clamber* up a rocky slope.

clam-my (klam′i), *adj.* [clam-mi-er, clam-mi-est], damp, soft, and cold.

clam-our or **clam-or** (klam′mėr), *n.* a loud and continued outcry; a loud and persistent demand:—*v.i.* to make noisy demands; as, to *clamour* for food.—*adj.* **clam′or-ous.**

clamp (klamp), *n.* a device, as a brace, clasp, or band, usually of wood or metal, used to hold or press things together:—*v.t.* to fasten or bind with a clamp:—**clamp down,** to be strict; as, the police *clamped down* on drinking-and-driving offenders.

clan (klan), *n.* **1,** a tribe or association of families, esp. in the Scottish Highlands, united under one chieftain, claiming common ancestry, and having the same surname; **2,** a group of people closely united by some common interest or pursuit; a set; clique.—*adj.* **clan′nish.**—*n.* **clans′man; clans′wo′man.**

clan-des-tine (klan-des′tin), *adj.* secret; private; underhanded; as, a *clandestine* meeting.—*adv.* **clan-des′tine-ly.**

clang (klang), *n.* a loud, ringing, metallic sound; as, the *clang* of an anvil:—*v.i.* to give out such a sound; as, the bells *clanged*:—*v.t.* to cause to give out such a sound; as, he *clanged* the cymbals.

clan-gour or **clan-gor** (klang′gėr; klang′ėr), *n.* a ringing, clanking, metallic sound, as of chains, bells, etc.

clank (klangk), *n.* a sharp, harsh, brief, metallic sound:—*v.t.* and *v.i.* to rattle.

clap (klap), *v.t.* [clapped, clap-ping], **1,** to strike together with a quick, sharp noise; **2,** to applaud by striking the hands together noisily; **3,** to put, place, etc., quickly and suddenly; as, they *clapped* him into jail; **4,** to strike or slap suddenly; as, he *clapped* me on the back:—*v.i.* **1,** to show approval by striking the hands together; **2,** to come together with a quick, sharp noise; as, the door *clapped* shut:—*n.* **1,** a loud noise made by, or as by, a sudden collision; as, a *clap* of thunder; **2,** applause; **3,** a slap; as, a *clap* on the back.

clap-board (klap′bōrd′; klab′ėrd), *n.* a long, narrow board, often thicker at one edge than at the other, used to cover the outside of wooden houses, esp. in the Maritimes:—*v.t.* to cover or line with such boards; as, to *clapboard* a house.

clap-per (klap′ėr), *n.* **1,** the tongue of a bell; **2,** one who claps hands; **3,** either of a pair of musical *bones*.

clap-trap (klap′trap′), *n.* empty, showy talk in order to gain applause.

clar-i-fy (klar′i-fī′), *v.t.* [clarified, clarifying], **1,** to make clear or pure; **2,** to make intelligible or plain; as, to *clarify* a statement:—*v.i.* to become clear, pure, or transparent; as, the syrup *clarified* as it heated.—*n.* **clar′i-fi-ca′tion.**

clar-i-net (klar′i-net; klar′i-net′), *n.* a tube-shaped, musical wind instrument, played by blowing into the mouthpiece and pressing the keys or covering the holes with the fingers.

clar-i-on (klar′i-un), *n.* a small, high-pitched, medieval trumpet; also, its sound:—*adj.* clear and loud; as, a *clarion* call.

clar-i-ty (klar′i-ti), *n.* clearness; as, the *clarity* of his speech; *clarity* of the air.

clash (klash), *v.i.* **1,** to make a loud, harsh noise by striking together; as, the cymbals *clashed*; **2,** to be in opposition; disagree; as, their interests *clashed*; **3,** not to match well; as, the shirt *clashes* with the suit:—*v.t.* to strike violently together; as, they *clashed* the cymbals:—*n.* **1,** the noise so produced; **2,** opposition; conflict; as, a *clash* of ideas.

clasp (klåsp), *n.* **1,** a hook to hold anything close; a fastening device; **2,** a grasp, as in shaking hands; a close embrace:—*v.t.* **1,** to fasten together with, or as with, a clasp; **2,** to enclose and hold with the arms; **3,** to grasp, as hands in a handshake.

class (klås), *n.* **1,** a number or body of persons with common characteristics, as social status, property, occupation, etc.; as, the middle *class*; **2,** a body of students taught by the same teacher, or engaged in similar studies; as, a *class* in physics; **3,** a meeting of such a group; as, to stay after *class;* **4,** a group of students who are to graduate in the same year; as, the *class* of 2002; **5,** a division or grading on the basis of quality; as, business *class* on an airplane; mail sent first *class*; **6,** *Colloq.* high quality or elegance; excellence; as, to have a lot of *class;* **7,** in *zoology,* a group of animals; in *botany,* a group of plants:—*v.t.* to arrange according to a system; classify. Also, **class′mate′; class′room′.**

clas-sic (klas′ik), *n.* **1,** any book or work of art that is, or may properly be regarded as, a standard; as, Shakespeare's plays, Mozart's music, etc.; **2,** esp., any Greek or Roman piece of literature or work of art; **3,** anything that is thought of as outstanding in its field; as, the 1937 Jaguar roadster is a *classic*; also, an author whose productions are of such excellence that they are regarded as standards:—**the Classics,** the literature of ancient Greece and Rome:—*adj.* **1,** pertaining to the highest class or rank in literature or art; as, *Anne of Green Gables* is a *classic* Canadian novel; **2,** pertaining to, or like, the Greek or Roman authors; **3,** being of very high quality; as, a *classic* movie; **4,** very typical and obvious; as, an accident as a *classic* example of careless driving.—*n.* **clas′si-cism; clas′si-cist.**

clas-si-cal or **Clas-si-cal** (clas′i-kl), *adj.* **1,** having to do with ancient Greece and Rome, or with their literature, art, and culture; as, the Parthenon is an example of *classical* Greek architecture; **2,** having to do with classical music: a form of music that follows certain formal rules and standards set down in Europe in the 1700s and early 1800s; as, Mozart's compositions are considered examples of *classical* music.

clas-si-fy (klas′i-fī′), *v.t.* [classified, classifying], to arrange in groups according to a system; as, to *classify* CDs by name.—*n.* **clas′si-fi′er; clas′si-fi-ca′tion.**—*adj.* **clas′si-fied.**

clat-ter (klat′ėr), *v.i.* **1,** to make a rattling sound; **2,** to talk idly and noisily:—*v.t.* to cause to make a rattling sound; as, to *clat-*

ter dishes:—*n.* **1,** a rattling noise; **2,** commotion; noisy talk.

clause (klôz), *n.* **1,** a separate part of a written agreement or document; a distinct condition; as, a *clause* in a treaty; a *clause* in an apartment lease that does not allow pets; **2,** a division of a sentence containing a subject and predicate of its own: in the sentence "I can go today, but I can't go tomorrow," there are two clauses connected by the conjunction "but."—*adj.* **claus′al.**

claus-tro-pho-bi-a (klos′trō-fō′bi-a), *n.* dread of enclosed or narrow places.

claw (klô), *n.* **1,** a sharp, hooked, horny nail on the foot of an animal or bird; **2,** the whole foot equipped with these nails; as, the owl held a mouse in its *claw*; **3,** the pincers of shellfish, such as crabs, lobsters, etc.; **4,** anything sharp and hooked like a claw, as the curved end of some hammerheads:—*v.t.* and *v.i.* to tear or scratch with, or as with, claws.

clay (klā), *n.* an earthy material, easily moulded when moist, but hard when baked, used in making pottery, bricks, etc.—*adj.* **clay′ey** [clay-i-er, clay-i-est].

clean (klēn), *adj.* **1,** free from dirt or filth; as, *clean* hands; **2,** unmixed with foreign matter; as, *clean* seed; **3,** pure; without moral or spiritual stain; as, he lives a *clean* life; a *clean* record; **4,** even; unobstructed; complete; as, a *clean* field; a *clean* sweep; **5,** skillful; well done; as, a *clean* hit; **6,** cleanly by habit; as, a *clean* housekeeper; **7,** shapely; as, a car with *clean* lines:—*adv.* **1,** so as to be clean; as, swept *clean*; **2,** wholly; entirely; as, she was wet *clean* through from the rain:—*v.t.* **1,** to remove dirt from; as, to *clean* house; **2,** to remove undesirable parts of; as, to *clean* a fish by removing its head, scales, etc.—*n.* **clean′ ness.**

clean-er (klēn′ėr), *n.* **1,** a person or business whose work is cleaning things; as, to take dirty clothes to the *cleaners*; **2,** a machine or substance that is used to clean; as, a carpet *cleaner*.

clean-ly (klen′li), *adj.* [clean-li-er, clean-li-est], careful to keep clean; neat:—*adv.* in a clean manner.—*n.* **clean′li-ness.**

cleanse (klenz), *v.t.* [cleansed, cleans-ing], to free from filth, guilt, sin, etc.—*n.* **cleans′er** (a cleaner such as soap, detergent, etc.).

clear (klēr), *adj.* **1,** bright; unclouded; as, a *clear* day; **2,** clean; pure; as, *clear* water; **3,** fresh; blooming; as, a *clear* skin; **4,** untroubled; as, a *clear* conscience; **5,** easily understood; plain; as, a *clear* explanation; **6,** audible; distinct; as, a *clear* voice; **7,** without further cost to be deducted; net; as, *clear* profit; **8,** unobstructed; as, a *clear* view; freed from obstruction; as, land *clear* of stumps:—*adv.* wholly, entirely; clean; as, I broke a piece *clear* off:—*v.t.* **1,** to make free from muddiness, cloudiness, smoke, stuffiness, etc.; **2,** to make plain; as, to *clear* up a puzzling situation; **3,** to free from obstruction; as, to *clear* the way; **4,** to remove; as, to *clear* away rubbish; **5,** to prove or declare to be innocent; as, to *clear* an accused person; **6,** to jump over or pass by without touching; as, the horse *cleared* the fence; **7,** to make beyond expenses; as, to *clear* 50 dollars:—*v.i.* to become clear.—*adv.* **clear′ly.**—*n.* **clear′ness.**—*adj.* **clear′–cut; clear′–head′ed; clear′sighted.**

clear-ance (klēr′ans), *n.* **1,** removal of obstructions; **2,** a certificate or permission for a vessel to leave or enter port or for an aircraft to take off or land; **3,** the clear space between two passing objects, or between a vehicle and the top of an arch, bridge, etc.:—**clearance sale**, the selling of merchandise at discounted prices in order to clear old inventory.

clear–cut (klēr′–kut′), *adj.* **1,** sharp and distinct; not ambiguous; as, *clear-cut* rules; **2,** relating to a method of lumbering in which all the trees in an area are cut down at the same time; as, a *clear-cut* forest:—*v.t.* [clear–cut, clear–cut-ting], to cut down all the trees in an area.—*n.* **clear-cutting; clear-cutter.**

clear-ing (klēr′ing), *n.* **1,** the act of removing obstructions; as, the *clearing* of land; **2,** a tract of land cleared of trees and bush.

cleat (klēt), *n.* **1,** a piece of wood or metal with branching arms, around which ropes are turned to prevent slipping; **2,** a strip of wood or metal fastened across a board, under a shelf, etc., to give support or strength, hold something in position, prevent slipping, or the like; as, the *cleats* on a gangplank, on football shoes, on a snowmobile, etc.

cleave (klēv), *v.t.* [*p.t.* cleft (kleft), cleaved (klēvd), clove (klōv), *p.p.* cleft, cleaved, cloven (klō′ven), *p.pr.* cleaving], to cut open; cut a way through; split; as, the axe *cleft* the log; the boat *cleaved* the water:—*v.i.* to split; divide; as, wood *cleaves* along the grain.—*n.* **cleav′age.**

cleav-er (klēv′ėr), *n.* a butcher's heavy hatchet or chopper for cutting meat or bone.

clef (klef), *n.* in *music*, a sign placed at the beginning of the staff to show the pitch of the notes on each line. The line on which the centre of the circle of the G clef falls is G; the line on which the dot of the F clef falls is F: the three clefs are *treble clef, bass clef,* and *tenor* or *alto clef*.

Clefs: Above, G clef; below, two forms of F clef.

cleft (kleft), *n.* a crack; crevice; as, the water trickled from a *cleft* in the rock:—*adj.* partly divided.

clem-ent (klem′ent), *adj.* **1,** forgiving; gentle; kind; as, a *clement* judge; **2,** mild; as, *clement* weather.—*n.* **clem′en-cy.**

clench (klench), *v.t.* **1,** to set closely together, as the teeth; close tightly, as the hands; **2,** to clinch or settle, as an argument; **3,** to grasp firmly; as, he *clenched* the ball:—*n.* a thing that grips or catches.—*n.* **clench′er.**

cler-gy (klûr′ji), *n.* [*pl.* clergies], the body of persons ordained for religious service, as ministers, priests, monks, pastors, and rabbis, etc.—*n.* **cler′gy-man.**

cler-ic (kler′ik), *n.* a member of the clergy.

cler-i-cal (kler′i-kal), *adj.* **1,** having to do with the clergy; as, *clerical* garb; **2,** pertaining to a clerk, writer, or copyist; as, *clerical* work.—*adv.* **cler′i-cal-ly.**

clerk (klärk; klûrk), *n.* **1,** a person, not of the clergy, with certain minor church duties; **2,** one who keeps records and does routine business; as, the town *clerk*; **3,** a general office assistant; typist; secretary; **4,** a salesperson in a store:—*v.i.* to act as a clerk; as, he *clerks* in a law office.—*n.* **clerk′ship.**

clev-er (klev′ėr), *adj.* **1,** skillful; as, a *clever* detective; **2,** mentally quick; talented; bright; as, a *clever* idea.—*adv.* **clev′er-ly.**—*n.* **clev′er-ness.**

clev-is (klev′is), *n.* a U-shaped piece of iron with a pin through the two holes at the end, for attaching to a wagon, tractor, draw bar, etc.

cli-ché (klē′shā′), *n.* an expression or idea worn, or made stale, by overuse; as, "bright and early"; "sadder but wiser"; a "fish out of water"; etc.

click (klik), *n.* a slight, sharp sound like the turning of a key in a lock:—*v.i.* **1,** to make such a sound; as, hail *clicked* against the window; **2,** *Colloq.* to fit or work together smoothly; as, everyone on the team *clicked* and got the job done quickly and without effort.

cli-ent (klī′ent), *n.* a person or company that uses the services or advice of another person or company; as, a lawyer's *client*; **2,** a customer or patron of a store or business:—**clientele,** a group of clients.

cliff (klif), *n.* a high, steep face of rock; a precipice.

cliff-hang-er (klif′hang′ėr), a story, movie, television show, etc., that is full of suspense, esp. an episode in a series in which the ending leaves the hero in a dangerous or unresolved situation.

cli-mate (klī′mit), *n.* **1,** the weather conditions of a place, esp. as regards temperature, moisture, wind, etc.; **2,** a region with certain conditions of weather, as of heat and cold, sunlight, etc.; as, a mild, sunny, or tropical *climate*; **3,** the main attitude or feeling that a certain group or place has; as, the *climate* of public opinion.—*adj.* **cli-mat′ic** (kli–mat′ik).

cli-max (klī′maks), *n.* **1,** a series of ideas or expressions increasing in force; also, the last of such a series; **2,** hence, the highest point of interest, excitement, or development; as, the *climax* of a play or movie.—*adj.* **cli-mac′tic.**

climb (klīm), *v.t.* **1,** to go up or down, esp. using both hands and feet; as, to *climb* a ladder; **2,** mount; ascend; rise; as, the sun *climbs* the heavens; **3,** to ascend by twining; as, a vine *climbs* a trellis:—*v.i.* **1,** to go up and down something, using both hands and feet; as, to *climb* out of (or into) a tree; **2,** to mount, ascend; rise; move upward; as, the plane *climbed* to 20000 metres; **3,** to rise by effort or achievement; as, to *climb* to the head of the class; *climb* to fame:—*n.* the act of climbing; as, a long, hard *climb*; also, a place to be ascended; as, there was a steep *climb* near the top.—*n.* **climb′er.**

clinch (klinch), *v.t.* **1,** to rivet; to fasten tightly; esp., to turn down the protruding point of (a nail); **2,** to confirm or settle, as a bargain or argument; **3,** to grasp tightly:—*v.i.* to grapple; seize one another, as in boxing:—*n.* **1,** the act of making a fastening on both sides of something; **2,** the fastening by which a tight hold is obtained; **3,** a struggle or scuffle at close grips, as in boxing; **4,** a kind of rope fastening.—*n.* **clinch′er.**

cling (kling), *v.i.* [clung (klung), cling-ing], **1,** to stick together or to something; as, snow *clings* to bushes; **2,** to adhere closely; stick; hold fast by embracing or entwining; hang on; as, a child *clings* to his or her mother's hand; ivy *clings* to a wall; **3,** hence, to be loyal; remain faithful.

clin-ic (klin′ik), *n.* **1,** a place where people can get medical help without having to stay in a hospital; **2,** any place where people can get help or learn certain skills; as, a reading *clinic*; **3,** the medical treatment of patients before a class of students for the instruction of the class; **4,** an institution, or department of a hospital, devoted to the study and treatment of disease or of problems of a particular type; as, an eye or blood donor *clinic*.—*adj.* **clin′i-cal.**

clink (klingk), *v.t.* to strike so as to make a slight, tinkling sound; as, they *clinked* glasses:—*v.i.* to make a tinkling noise; as, ice *clinks* in a glass:—*n.* a slight, tinkling noise; as, the *clink* of coins.

[1]clip (klip), *v.t.* [clipped, clip-ping], to clasp or hold tightly; fasten; as, he *clipped* the papers together:—*n.* a clasp, as for holding papers; any device for gripping; as, a paper *clip*; a tie *clip*; a money *clip*.

[2]clip (klip), *v.t.* [clipped, clip-ping], **1,** to cut or trim with shears or scissors, as hair, an article, a coupon, etc.; **2,** to cut short, as final letters, syllables, etc., from words:—*n.* **1,** the act of cutting off with shears; **2,** a quick rate of moving; as, to walk at a steady *clip*.

clip art, artwork, such as illustrations or other graphics, that can be copied into text without cost.

clip-board (klip′bōrd′), *n.* **1,** a small writing board with a clip at the top for holding papers; **2,** in *computing*, an area in some computer software that allows for the temporary storage of information, such as data, text, or graphics, to be inserted into another file.

clip-per (klip′ėr), *n.* **1,** one who or that which moves swiftly, as a horse or a ship; esp., a large sailing ship of the 1800s, built with fine lines and rigged to travel at a fast speed: also called *clipper ship*; **2,** a tool for clipping; as, fingernail *clippers*.

clip-ping (klip′ping), *n.* **1,** a story, picture, or advertisement cut out of a newspaper or magazine; **2,** anything that is cut off or clipped from something else; as, grass *clippings*; toenail *clippings*.

clique (klēk), *n.* a small, exclusive social group.—*adj.* **cli′quish** (klē′kish).

cloak (klōk), *n.* **1,** a loose outer garment, usually sleeveless; **2,** hence, that which covers or conceals; as, to escape under the *cloak* of the night:—*v.t.* to conceal; cover; disguise; as, to *cloak* grief with laughter; darkness *cloaked* the cabin.

cloak-room (klōk′ro͞om′), *n.* a place where coats, etc., may be left temporarily.

clob-ber (klob′ėr), *v.t. Slang* **1,** to batter; maul; wound; **2,** to defeat; win against; as, the Canadian women's and men's hockey teams *clobbered* their opponents in the 2002 Winter Olympics and won gold medals.

clock (klok), *n.* a mechanical or electronic stationary device for keeping time, larger than a watch:—**digital clock,** a clock that shows the time directly in numbers:—**analog clock,** a clock with a dial and hands that point to the time:—*v.t.* to measure time with a clock; as, the police *clocked* the speeding car at 130 km/h:—**clock in (out/off),** to register or punch in or out, esp. at the beginning or end of a workday; as, she *clocked* in at 8:30 a.m.—*adv.* and *adj.* **clock′wise.**—*n.* **clock′work′.**

clod (klod), *n.* **1,** a lump of earth, turf, or clay; **2,** a stupid or foolish person.—*adj.* **clod′dy.**

clod-hop-per (klod′hop′ėr), *n.* a clumsy person; boor; bumpkin; **2,** *pl.* heavy work shoes or boots.

clog (klog), *v.t.* [clogged, clog-ging], **1,** to hinder motion with a weight or burden; impede; **2,** hence, to hinder in any way; as, ignorance *clogs* progress; **3,** to obstruct; stop up; as, hair *clogs* a drain; traffic *clogged* the street:—*v.i.* **1,** to be hindered; **2,** to stick together:—*n.* **1,** a load or weight; hence, any hindrance or restraint; an obstruction or something that causes clogging; as, a *clog* in the drain; **2,** a shoe with a wooden sole; **3,** a dance by one wearing such shoes.

clois-ter (klois′tėr), *n.* **1,** a place of religious retirement; a monastery or convent; **2,** an arched way or covered walk along the outside walls of a monastery, university, college, etc., often surrounding an open court, or connecting buildings of a group:—*v.t.* to confine in, or as if in, a convent or monastery; seclude from the world.—*adj.* **clois′tered.**

clone (klōn), *n.* **1,** an organism or group of cells artificially produced from a common ancestor; **2,** the asexual reproduction of organisms; **3,** a person or thing that appears to be identical to another; a copy, duplicate, or facsimile; **4,** in *computing*, computer hardware or software, often designed by reverse engineering, to resemble more expensive, better-known brands; as, an IBM *clone*:—*v.i.* to produce an exact copy:—*v.t.* **1,** to create an organism from a clone cell; **2,** to make an exact copy; as, to *clone* a sheep.

[1]**close** (klōz), *v.t.* [closed, clos-ing], **1,** to shut, as a box, the mouth, a door, etc.; **2,** to fill; stop up; obstruct; as, to *close* an opening; **3,** to make an ending to; as, to *close* an argument; **4,** in *computing*, to terminate a file, window, application, etc.; as, save and *close* the Word file when you finish writing the report:—*v.i.* **1,** to come together; as, the waters *closed* over him; **2,** to grapple or fight at close quarters; **3,** to come to an ending:—*n.* conclusion; act of closing.

[2]**close** (klōs), *adj.* **1,** shut; closed; **2,** contracted; narrow; shut in; as, *close* quarters; **3,** stifling; without ventilation; as, this room is *close*; **4,** stingy; **5,** near in space, time, etc.; **6,** accurate; careful; as, *close* thinking; **7,** firmly knit; compact; tight; as, *close* weaving; **8,** dear; familiar; as, a *close* friend; **9,** almost equal; as, a *close* race or contest; **10,** fitting tightly or snugly, as a turban to the head; **11,** accurate; precise; as, a *close* translation; **12,** confined; kept within bounds; as, a *close* prisoner:—*adv.* **1,** near in space or time; as, follow *close* after me; **2,** tightly; closely together; as, *close* knit; **3,** secretly; in hiding; as, keep *close*.—*adv.* **close′ly.**—*n.* **close′ness.**

closed shop, an establishment that excludes nonunion labour.

close-fist-ed (klōs′fis′tid), *adj.* stingy.

close-lipped, close-mouthed (-lipt; -mou*th*d; -moutht), *adj.* talking little; secretive.

clos-et (kloz′it), *n.* **1,** a small room for privacy or retirement; **2,** a small room for storing things, as cloths, dishes, etc.; a cupboard:—*adj.* private; secret:—*v.t.* to shut up, as in a private room, esp. for secret conference.

close–up (klōs′–up′), *n.* a picture, or inspection, at close range.

clo-sure (klō′zhoor), *n.* **1,** a shutting up; ending; conclusion; as, the *closure* of a meeting; **2,** in parliamentary law, a way of ending a debate and taking an immediate vote.

clot (klot), *v.i.* [clot-ted, clot-ting], to thicken into a soft, sticky, semi-solid mass; as, blood *clots*:—*v.t.* to form into lumps of thickened fluid; as, souring *clots* milk:—*n.* a lumpish mass of some thickened fluid, esp. blood.—*adj.* **clot′ted.**

cloth (klôth), *n.* [*pl.* cloths (klô*thz*; klôths)], **1,** a woven fabric of wool, cotton, silk, linen, etc.; **2,** a piece of such fabric made for a certain use; as, a dish*cloth*; a table*cloth*; **3,** one's profession as shown by one's dress, esp. the profession of a clergyman:—**the cloth**, the clergy.

clothe (klō*th*), *.v.t.* [clothed or clad (klad), cloth-ing], **1,** to dress; **2,** to cover with, or as with, a garment; as, flowers *clothed* the field; old age *clothes* a person with dignity.

clothes (klōz), *n.pl.* **1,** garments; things worn to cover the body, such as shirts, pants, dresses, jackets, coats, etc. Also, **clothes′brush′; clothes′peg′; clothes′pin′.**

clothes-horse (klō*thz*′hôrs′; klō′-), *n.* **1,** a folding wooden frame with horizontal bars on which to dry or air clothes; **2,** *Colloq.* a person who has or buys a great deal of clothes, or who places a high value on being dressed stylishly.

clothes-line (klōz′līn), *n.* a rope or wire used to hang wet clothes on with clothespins so they can dry.

cloth-ing (klō*th*′ing), *n.* clothes; garments in general.

cloud (kloud), *n.* **1,** a visible mass of condensed water floating above the earth; **2,** a similar mass of smoke or dust; **3,** anything that threatens or darkens, as grief, disgrace, suspicion, etc.; **4,** anything that moves in or like a mass, as a large number of arrows, insects, birds, etc.:—*v.t.* **1,** to cover with a mist or cloud; **2,** hence, to make gloomy; as, grief *clouds* a face; **3,** to blacken; trouble; sully; as, a bad record *clouds* her reputation:—*v.i.* to grow cloudy; as, toward afternoon, the sky *clouded* over.—*adj.* **cloud′less.**

cloud-burst (kloud′burst′), *n.* a violent, unusually heavy downpour of rain.

cloud-y (kloud′i), *adj.* [cloudi-er, cloudi-est], **1,** pertaining to a cloud or clouds; **2,** overcast; threatening rain; **3,** vague; obscure; **4,** not transparent; as, a *cloudy* liquid; **5,** gloomy.—*n.* **cloud′i-ness.**

clout (klout), *n.* **1,** *Colloq.* a blow on the head with the hand; **2,** *Colloq.* influence or power; as, to have a lot of *clout* in a company:—*v.t. Colloq.* to strike; knock.

clove (klōv), *n.* **1,** the dried flower bud of a tropical evergreen tree of the myrtle family, used as spice; **2,** the tree.

clo-ven (klōvn), *p.p.* of *cleave*; as, a *cloven*, or cleft, hoof.

clo-ver (klō′vėr), *n.* a low-growing plant with three-parted leaves and sweet, round flower heads of red, white, yellow, or purple, used for fodder and to make soil richer.

clo-verleaf (klō′vėr-lēf′), *n.* a highway intersection allowing traffic to cross at different levels, and so called because its shape resembles the outline of a four-leaf clover.

clown (kloun), *n.* **1,** anyone who tells jokes or acts in a foolish way to make others laugh; as, a class *clown*; **2,** a jester; a person whose job is to make people laugh by doing tricks, acting silly, and wearing funny clothes, esp. at circuses, parades, parties, etc.; **3,** a person of coarse manners; a boor:—*v.i.* to act the clown; as, to *clown* around at the party.—*adj.* **clown′ish.**

cloy (kloi), *v.t.* **1,** to overdo or sate with food or something that is usually pleasurable, esp. with rich or sweet food; **2,** to weary by overdoing something; as, her constant attentiveness began to *cloy* him.—*adj.* **cloy′ing.**—*adv.* **cloy′ing-ly.**—*n.* **cloy′ing-ness.**

club (klub), *n.* **1,** a heavy stick; **2,** one of a suit, called *clubs*, of playing cards, marked with a black figure like a clover leaf; **3,** a number of persons united for a common purpose or mutual benefit; as, a swimming *club*; a hockey *club*; a yearbook *club*; **4,** a building or room occupied by such persons; **5,** a stick used to hit the ball in certain games, esp. golf:—*v.t.* [clubbed, clubbing], **1,** to beat with a club or stick; **2,** to give to a common cause; as, the town *clubbed* its resources to help the flood victims:—*v.i.* to combine for a common purpose; as, to *club* together to buy a new computer for the school.

cluck (kluk), *n.* a hen's call to her chicks:—*v.t.* to make a sound of suction in the side of the mouth; as, he *clucked* his disbelief.

clue (klōō; klū), *n.* anything that helps to solve a problem, plot, mystery, or difficulty; as, the result from the DNA test was the *clue* that solved the case.

clump (klump), *n.* **1,** a cluster or group, as of trees; **2,** a mass; lump, as of earth; **3,** a sound like that of heavy treading:—*v.i.* to tread heavily; as, the tired hikers *clumped* along the path.

clum-sy (klum′zi), *adj.* [clum-si-er, clum-si-est], **1,** awkward; heavy; lacking in ease or grace; as, a *clumsy* person or action; **2,** ill-made; unwieldy; not well made, said, or done; as, a *clumsy* tool; a *clumsy* excuse.—

adv. **clum′si-ly.**—*n.* **clum′si-ness.**

clung (klung), *p.t.* and *p.p.* of *cling.*

clus-ter (klus′tėr), *n.* **1,** a number of things, such as fruits, of the same kind growing or collected together; a bunch; **2,** a group; as, a *cluster* of islands:—*v.i.* and *v.t.* to grow, or gather, in bunches.

clutch (kluch), *v.t.* to grasp, seize, or grip strongly; as, to *clutch* a person's elbow:—*v.i.* to snatch or reach out eagerly; as, he *clutched* at the rope:—*n.* **1,** a tight grasp; **2,** a device for gripping or holding, as in a crane; also, a mechanical device that connects and disconnects the motor of a machine from certain other parts that do the work of the machine, as in an automobile; **3,** a nest of eggs; a brood of chicks:—**clutches,** grasping claws or hands; control or power; as, a bird in the *clutches* of a hawk; to be under someone's *clutches.*

clut-ter (klut′ėr), *n.* disorder; litter; mess:—*v.t.* to make untidy; disarrange; mess up.

co-or **co–** (cō-; cō–), *prefix* meaning *with another, together;* as, *co*exist, *co*host, *co*operate, etc.

coach (kōch), *n.* **1,** a large, closed, four-wheeled carriage; a stagecoach; **2,** a tutor, esp. one who prepares others for an examination; also, a director of athletics, dramatics, etc.; **3,** a closed, large automobile; **4,** a railway passenger car; **5,** a section of seats on a bus, train, or airplane that is less expensive than other sections:—*v.t.* to teach; direct; as, to *coach* a baseball team.

co-ag-u-late (kō-ag′ū-lāt), *v.t.* and *v.i.* [coagulat-ed, coagulat-ing], to clot or curdle; thicken; solidify; as, cooking *coagulates* the white of an egg.—*n.* **co-ag′u-la′tion.**

coal (kōl), *n.* **1,** a black, hard, burnable mineral, formed under the earth by the decay of the vegetation of prehistoric times, and used as a natural fuel; **2,** charcoal; **3,** a glowing or charred bit of wood, coal, etc.; an ember:—*v.t.* to furnish with coal, as a vessel:—*v.i.* to burn until becoming charcoal.—*n.* **coal′er; coal′ oil′; coal′ tar′.**

co-a-lesce (kō′a-les′), *v.i.* [coalesced, coales-cing], to grow together; blend; unite; as, the ends of the broken bone *coalesced;* the two groups *coalesced* to become one large one.

co-a-li-tion (kō′a-lish′un), *n.* and *adj.* a temporary alliance of persons or parties to work together for a special purpose; as, a *coalition* cabinet.

coarse (kōrs), *adj.* [coars-er, coars-est], **1,** of poor or inferior quality or appearance; rough; not smooth; as, *coarse* cloth; **2,** large in texture or size; as, *coarse* sand; *coarse* salt; **3,** not refined; gross; as, *coarse* manners.—*adv.* **coarse′ly.**—*n.* **coarse′ness.**—*adj.* **coarse′-grained′.**

coars-en (kōr′sn), *v.t.* and *v.i.* to turn, or become, large, rough, common, etc.

coast (kōst), *n.* **1,** the land forming the margin or boundary of the sea; the seashore; also, the region adjoining the sea; **2,** a slide downhill over snow or ice on a sled, skis, snowboard, etc.:—*v.i.* **1,** to sail along a shore, or from port to port; **2,** to ride along by the force of gravity, without power, as on a sled.—*adj.* **coast′al; coast′wise′.**—*n.* **coast′line′.**

coast guard (kōst′ gärd′), *n.* a coastal police force; also, a service for search and rescue at sea.

coat (kōt), *n.* **1,** a sleeved, outer garment covering the upper part of the body; **2,** any outside covering, as fur, skin, rind, etc.; also, any outer layer; as, a *coat* of paint:—*v.t.* to cover or spread over.—*n.* **coat-tail** (kōt′tāl′).

coat of arms, 1, a group of emblems signifying rank or achievement, originally granted to knights, noble families, or persons of distinction and adopted by their descendants; **2,** a shield or coat marked with such emblems.

coax (kōks), *v.t.* **1,** to wheedle; urge or influence with soft words or in a gentle way; as, to *coax* a child to go to bed; **2,** to handle with patience and skill; as, to *coax* a fire.—*adv.* **coax′ing-ly.**

co-ax-i-al cable (kō-ak′si-al), *n.* a cable with an outer insulated sheath composed of separately insulated wires overlying a similar inner core of insulated wires, used to conduct high-frequency signals, as of video and audio.

cob-ble (kob′l), *n.* a round stone, worn smooth by water, esp. one of a size used sometimes for street paving; a cobblestone:—*v.t.* [cob-bled, cob-bling], **1,** to pave with cobblestones; **2,** to repair; **3,** *Colloq.* to put something together hastily and clumsily; as, to *cobble* an essay.—*n.* **cob′ble-stone′.**

cob-bler (kob′lėr), *n.* **1,** one who mends boots and shoes; **2,** a clumsy worker; **3,** a cooling summer drink of iced wine and fruit juices; as, sherry *cobbler;* **4,** a deep-dish fruit pie with one crust.

co-bra (kō′bra; ko′bra), *n.* a large, poisonous snake of Asia and Africa, which, when irritated, swells its neck out like a hood.

cob-web (kob′web′), *n.* **1,** a spider's web or the material of which it is made; **2,** anything resembling the flimsy or entangling qualities of a cobweb. Also called *spiderweb.*

co-caine or **co-cain** (kō-kān′; kō′kān), *n.* a powerful drug extracted from the leaves of a South American shrub called *coca,* used to dull pain and as an illegal stimulant.

[1]**cock** (kok), *n.* **1,** the male of the common domestic fowl; a rooster; **2,** any male bird; **3,** a weather vane in the shape of a rooster;

4, a leader; as, *cock* of the school; **5,** a turn-valve, tap, faucet, etc.; **6,** the hammer of a firearm, or its position when raised; as, a gun at full *cock*.

[2]**cock** (kok), *n.* a tilting or turning upward, as of a hat or an eye:—*v.t.* **1,** to turn up or set jauntily on one side; tilt defiantly, as a hat; as, the dog *cocked* its ears when it heard the noise; **2,** to raise the hammer of (a gun) in readiness for firing.

cock-a-too (kok′a-to͞o), *n.* a white or brilliantly coloured parrot, often with a crest, found chiefly in Australia.

cock-er span-iel (kok′ėr span′yel), a spaniel, usually with long black, red, or cream-coloured hair and droopy ears.

cock-eyed (käk′īd′), *adj. Colloq.* **1,** tilted or askew; twisted to the side; as, a dog's *cock-eyed* ears; **2,** silly or impractical; off the mark; as, a *cockeyed* scheme; **3,** drunk.

cock-le (kok′l), *n.* **1,** an edible shellfish with two heart-shaped fluted shells; **2,** one of its shells; often called *cockleshell*; **3,** a frail or shallow boat; **4,** a species of weed found among grain; as, corn *cockle*, darnel, etc.

cock-ney (kok′ni), *n.* [*pl.* cockneys], a Londoner; esp., one born in the East End of London, and speaking a characteristic dialect:—*adj.* of or relating to cockneys.

cock-pit (kok′pit′), *n.* **1,** in airplanes, the place where the pilots sit; **2,** in small vessels, space aft lower than the deck; **3,** formerly, in a war vessel, the quarters of junior officers, used as a hospital during a battle; **4,** an enclosed space for cockfights.

cock-roach (kok′rōch′), *n.* a black or brown, beetlelike insect, sometimes pests in homes or restaurants.

cock-sure (kok′sho͝or′), *adj.* absolutely sure; positive.

cock-tail (kok′tāl), *n.* **1,** an iced, mixed drink made of alcoholic liquors, bitters, fruit juices, etc.; **2,** an appetizer of shellfish, mixed fruits, etc., served as a first course; as, a shrimp *cocktail*:—*adj.* pertaining to cocktail drinks; as, a *cocktail* party.

cock-y (kok′i), *adj. Colloq.* impudent; conceited; pert.

co-coa (kō′kō), *n.* **1,** a dark-brown powder made from the ground seeds of the cacao tree; **2,** a hot chocolate-tasting drink made from it and sugar and milk or water.

co-co-nut (kō′ko-nut′), *n.* **1,** the hard-shelled fruit of the coconut palm tree; **2,** loosely, the white meaty substance from it, prepared for use as food.

co-coon (ko-ko͞on′), *n.* the silky case spun by the larvae of many insects, such as caterpillars and silk worms, as a protection while they are in the inactive or *pupa* stage, and developing into butterflies, moths, etc.

cod (kod), *n.* [*pl.* cod or cods], a large, deep-sea food fish, found in the northern Atlantic.

cod-dle (kod′l), *v.t.* [cod-dled, cod-dling], **1,** to pet or pamper; treat tenderly; **2,** to stew gently; cook by allowing to stand in hot water.

code (kōd), *n.* **1,** a body of laws arranged in clear and regular order; as, the civil or penal *code*; **2,** a system of military or naval signals; **3,** any system of symbols used for messages to secure their brevity or secrecy; **4,** a body of principles or standards governing the conduct of a society, class, or profession, under certain conditions; as, the social *code*; a building *code*; the *code* of honour; **5,** in *computing*, a method of presenting information and instructions in a form that can be understood by the computer:—*v.t.* **1,** to put into code; as, to *code* a message; **2,** in *computing*, to write instructions for, or program, a computer.—*v.t.* **co′di-fy′**.—*n.* **co′di-fi-ca′tion; ge-ne′tic code.**

co-deine, co-dein (kō′di-ēn; ko′dēn), *n.* a drug derived from opium, used to calm or soothe nerves or excitement, and to allay pain.

cod-fish (kod′fish′), *n.* the cod or its flesh, esp. when cured and salted, served as food.

co-ed or **co–ed** (kō′ed′; kō′–ed′), *n. Colloq.* a student at a coeducational college or university.

co-ed-u-ca-tion (kō′ed-ū-kā-shun), *n.* the education of both male and female students in the same school.—*adj.* **co′ed-u-ca′tion-al.**

co-erce (kō-ûrs′), *v.t.* [coerced, coerc-ing], to compel by force; as, he *coerced* the prisoner into submission.—*n.* **co-er′cion.**

co-ex-ist (kō′eg-zist′), *v.i.* to exist together at the same time.—*n.* **co′ex-ist′ence.**

cof-fee (kôf′i), *n.* **1,** a drink made from the seeds, roasted and ground, of the tropical coffee plant; **2,** the seeds: often called *coffee beans;* **3,** the shrub or tree.—*n.* **cof′fee break′.**

cof-fer (kôf′ėr; kof′ėr), *n.* a casket, chest, or trunk in which to keep money or treasure:—**coffers,** a treasury; funds.

cof-fin (kôf′in), *n.* the case or chest in which a dead person is buried.

cog (kog), *n.* one of a series of teeth on the rim of a wheel that gives or transmits motion by interlocking with the teeth on another wheel.

co-gent (kō′jent), *adj.* forceful; convincing; as, a *cogent* reason.—*adv.* **co′gent-ly.**

cog-i-tate (koj′i-tāt′), *v.i.* [cogitat-ed, cogitat-ing], to reflect; ponder; think:—*v.t.* to think over; plan.—*n.* **cog′i-ta′tion.**

cog-nate (kog′nāt), *adj.* having the same nature or origin; related; thus, in "he dreamed a dream," "dream" is an object *cognate* with the verb "dreamed"; German and English are *cognate* languages:—*n.* a related word, language, person, or thing.

cog-ni-zant (kog′ni-zant; kon′i-zant), *adj.* having knowledge; aware.—*n.* **cog′ni-zance.**

co-hab-it (kō-hab′it), *v.i.* to live together as husband and wife, esp. when not married legally.

co-here (kō-hēr′), *v.i.* [cohered, coher-ing], to stick together in a mass, as mud; hold together, as cement and stone.

co-her-ent (kō-hēr′ent), *adj.* **1,** sticking together; **2,** logically connected and developed; consistent.—*adv.* **co-her′ent-ly.**—*n.* **co-her′ence; co-her′en-cy.**

co-he-sion (ko-hē′zhun), *n.* the action of sticking together; specifically, the force by which particles of the same material are held together; as, there is *cohesion* in clay, but not in gravel.—*adj.* **co-he′sive.**

co-hort (kō′hôrt), *n.* **1,** in ancient Rome, a body of soldiers of 300 to 600 men, or the tenth part of a legion; **2,** any body of soldiers or band of persons; **3,** *Colloq.* an associate.

coif-fure (kwä-fūr′), *n.* **1,** a headdress; **2,** the manner of arranging the hair.

coil (koil), *n.* **1,** anything wound in a circle or series of circles; a spiral; as, a *coil* of rope; **2,** a continuous spiral of pipe or wire for conducting hot water, electricity, or the like:—*v.t.* to wind into circles; as, to *coil* a rope:—*v.i.* to form coils.

coin (koin), *n.* **1,** a piece of metal legally stamped to be used as money; **2,** metal money:—*v.t.* **1,** to make (coins) by stamping pieces of metal; also, to change (metal) into coins; **2,** to invent (a word or phrase); as, to *coin* a phrase.

coin-age (koin′ij), *n.* **1,** the process of making pieces of money; **2,** the money made; **3,** the system of metal money used in a country; **4,** invention of new words and phrases.

co-in-cide (kō′in-sīd′), *v.i.* [coincid-ed, coincid-ing], **1,** to occur at the same time; as, their spare periods *coincide*; **2,** to occupy the same space exactly; **3,** to agree; be alike; as, my idea *coincides* with yours.—*adj.* **co-in′ci-dent.**

co-in-ci-dence (kō-in′si-dens), *n.* **1,** the condition of happening at the same time or of occupying the same space; **2,** agreement; **3,** a remarkable happening together of events, apparently accidental and unconnected; chance.

coke (kōk), *n.* **1,** coal from which some of the gases have been driven by intense heat: used for fuel; **2,** *Slang* cocaine.

col-an-der (kul′an-dėr; kol′an-dėr), *n.* a strainer; a kitchen utensil or container pierced with holes, used for draining off liquids from vegetables, pasta, etc.

cold (kōld), *adj.* **1,** producing or feeling chilliness; of low temperature: opposite of *hot*; esp., less hot than the human body; as, a *cold* wind; *cold* food; **2,** indifferent; not moved; as, the news left him *cold*; **3,** unresponsive; unfriendly; as, a *cold* greeting; **4,** chilling; depressing; as, *cold* comfort; **5,** spiritless; dull; **6,** not fresh, as a scent in hunting:—*n.* **1,** lack of heat; as, to feel the *cold*; **2,** the sensation produced by lack of heat; **3,** in *physics*, a temperature below the freezing point of water; as, five degrees of *cold*; **4,** cold weather; **5,** the shivering sensation caused by fear or despair; **6,** an inflammation of a mucous membrane, generally of the nose or throat.—*adv.* **cold′ly.**—*n.* **cold′ness; cold sore; cold war.**—*adj.* **cold–heart-ed.**

cold–blood-ed (kōld′–blud′id), *adj.* **1,** having blood that changes temperature as the nearby air or water becomes colder or warmer, such as fish, frogs, turtles, and snakes; **2,** having no feelings or emotions; cruel; as, a *cold-blooded* murderer.

cole-slaw (kōl′slô′), *n.* a salad made of finely cut raw cabbage, served with a sauce or dressing.

col-ic (kol′ik), *n.* sharp pain in the abdomen or bowels, esp. in infants.—*adj.* **col′ick-y.**

col-i-se-um (kol′i-sē′um), *n.* Same as **colosseum.**

col-lab-o-rate (ko-lab′o-rāt′), *v.i.* [-rat-ed, -rat-ing], **1,** to work jointly, esp. on a literary, artistic, or scientific project; **2,** to work treacherously with an invader or enemy of one's country; as, he *collaborated* with the terrorists.—*n.* **col-lab′o-ra′tion.**

col-lage (ko-läzh′), *n.* a picture that is made by gluing pieces of various textured material, such as paper, photographs, cloth, and yarn, to a surface.

col-lapse (ko-laps′), *n.* **1,** a falling in or together, as of a roof or a balloon; **2,** a sudden and complete failure, as of a government; **3,** general breakdown; as, a nervous *collapse*:—*v.i.* [collapsed, collaps-ing], **1,** to fall in or shrink together; **2,** to fail completely and suddenly; **3,** to break down physically.—*adj.* **col-laps′i-ble** (something that can be folded together; as, a *collapsible* chair).

col-lar (kol′ėr), *n.* **1,** the part of any garment that fits around the neck; also, an ornamental piece of lace, linen, silk, etc., worn around the neck; **2,** a leather or metal band for the neck of a dog or other animal; **3,** the part of a horse's harness that fits over the neck and shoulders and bears the strain of the load; **4,** in *mechanics*, a connecting ring or band:—*v.t.* **1,** to seize by the collar or as if by the collar; as, to *collar* a thief; **2,** to put a collar on.—*n.* **col′lar-bone′.**

col-lat-er-al (ko-lat′ėr-al), *adj.* **1,** side by side; parallel; **2,** connected with something but of minor importance; **3,** pertaining to something, as stocks or bonds, offered as security, in addition to one's note, or other promise to pay; **4,** descended from the same stock, but not in a direct line: opposed to *lineal*; as, my sister is my *collateral* relative; my father is my *lineal* relative:—*n.* something given, as stocks, bonds, or a house, as a pledge for the repayment of a loan.—*adv.* **col-lat′er-al-ly.**

col-league (kol′ēg), *n.* an associate in office, or in a profession; a coworker.

[1]**col-lect** (ko-lekt′), *v.t.* **1,** to gather together; **2,** to secure payment of (money due, bills, taxes, etc.); **3,** to make a hobby or study of collecting (something); as, to *collect* stamps, rare books, music CDs, DVDs, computer games, etc.:—*v.i.* **1,** to accumulate; as, scum *collects* on stagnant water; **2,** to meet or assemble; as, a crowd *collects*.

[2]**col-lect** (kol′ekt), *n.* a brief prayer, part of a church's ritual, suited to a particular occasion; as, a *collect* for peace.

col-lect-ed (ko-lek′tid), *adj.* calm; cool; undisturbed.—*adv.* **col-lect′ed-ly.**

col-lec-tion (ko-lek′shun), *n.* **1,** the process of gathering or assembling; as, garbage *collection*; the *collection* of a crowd at a fire; **2,** any assemblage of persons or things; esp. a group of books, stamps, paintings, or the like, gathered for display or study; **3,** the taking in of money due; also, the amount received; **4,** a contribution asked for; as, they took up two *collections* at the school.

col-lec-tive (ko-lek′tiv), *adj.* relating to, produced by, or affecting a number of individuals jointly, that is, a number of persons as if they were one body; as, the *collective* wisdom of the ages; *collective* action:—**collective noun,** a singular noun used to name a group or collection of individuals; as, "army" and "audience" are *collective nouns*:—**collective bargaining**, the negotiating of terms between union and employer respecting wages, hours, fringe benefits, etc.—*adv.* **col-lec′tive-ly.**

col-lec-tiv-ism (ko-lek′tiv-izm), *n.* the doctrine that the people should own and control the means of production and distribution; socialism.

col-lec-tor (ko-lek′tėr), *n.* a person who collects; as, an art *collector*; a tax *collector*.

col-lege (kol′ij), *n.* **1,** an institution of higher education that gives degrees or diplomas to its students upon completion of certain courses of study; as, a community *college*; **2,** the buildings and grounds of such an institution; **3,** a school within a university for special instruction; as, a teachers' *college*; **4,** an association of people having a common profession; as, the *College* of Physicians; **5,** *Colloq.* university.—*adj.* **col-le′gi-ate** (ko-lē′ji-it; -jit).

col-lide (ko-līd′), *v.i.* [collid-ed, collid-ing], to meet and strike together with force; crash; as, the two cars *collided*; also, to clash; conflict.

col-lie (kol′i), *n.* a large sheep dog with a shaggy coat, first used by Scottish farmers to guard sheep.

col-lier (kol′yėr), *n.* **1,** a coal miner; **2,** a ship for carrying coal.—*n.* **col′lier-y.**

col-li-sion (ko-lizh′un), *n.* the violent striking together of two bodies; a crash; also, a clash or conflict; as, a *collision* of opinions.

col-lo-qui-al (ko-lō′kwi-al), *adj.* used in ordinary conversation, but not usually in formal or literary language; as, "Canuck" is a *colloquial* word for Canadian.—*adv.* **col-lo′qui-al-ly.**—*n.* **col-lo′qui-al-ism.**

col-lo-quy (kol′o-kwi′), *n.* a somewhat formal conversation; conference; discussion; as, the students concerned held a *colloquy* at recess.

col-lu-sion (ko-lū′zhun), *n.* a secret agreement for an unlawful or evil purpose; as, *collusion* between witnesses in a lawsuit.

co-logne (ko-lōn′), *n.* a perfumed toilet water.

[1]**co-lon** (kō′lun′), *n.* a punctuation mark [:] used after the formal greeting with which a business letter begins, before a quotation of some length, and before a list, as of contents, illustrations, causes, etc.

[2]**colon** (kō′lun), *n.* the lower part of the large intestine.

colo-nel (kûr′nl), *n.* an officer's rank in the armed forces, ranking above lieutenant-colonel.—*n.* **colo′nel-cy.**

co-lo-ni-al (ko-lō′ni-al), *adj.* **1,** relating to a colony or colonies; **2,** of the time when a nation was a colony; as, *colonial* furniture:—*n.* a person who lives in a colony.—*n.* **co-lo′ni-al-ism.**

col-o-nize (kol′o-nīz′), *v.t.* [colonized, coloniz-ing], **1,** to migrate to and establish a colony in (a place); as, the French and English *colonized* Canada; **2,** to send colonists to; as, England *colonized* New Zealand.—*n.* **col′o-ni-za′tion.**

col-on-nade (kol′o-nād′), *n.* a row of columns, regularly spaced along the side or sides of a building.

col-o-ny (kol′o-ni), *n.* [*pl.* colonies], **1,** a body of people who leave their native country and settle in another land, but remain subject to the mother country; **2,** the country thus settled; **3,** a group of people allied by race, interests, etc., living together; as, an artist's *colony*; **4,** a group of plants or animals living together; as, a *colony* of honeybees.—*n.* **col′o-nist.**

col-or (kul′ėr), *n.* Same as **colour.**

co-los-sal (ko-los′al), *adj.* huge; vast.

col-os-se-um or **col-i-se-um** (kol′o-sē′um), *n.* a large building used as a theatre, stadium, or place of public entertainment; as, the *Colosseum* at Rome or Copps *Coliseum* in Hamilton, Ontario.

THE COLOSSEUM, ROME

co-los-sus (ko-los′us), *n.* [*pl.* colossuses (ko-los′us-iz) or colossi (ko-los′i)], **1,** a huge statue; **2,** any huge person or thing.

col-our or **col-or** (kul′ėr), *n.* **1,** that quality of an object by which one can see whether it is red, blue, yellow, etc.; **2,** any hue, tint, or shade; sometimes including black and white; **3,** a paint or pigment; **4,** complexion; **5,** a lively or interesting quality; as, to capture the *colour* of the quaint town:—**primary colours**, red, blue, and yellow:—**the colours**, the flag; as, a call to *the colours*:—*v.t.* **1,** to give a colour to; dye; **2,** to misrepresent; as, the witness *coloured* his story:—*v.i.* to blush.—*n.* **col′our-a′tion.**—*adj.* **colour–blind.**

col-our-cast (kul′ėr-kast′), *n.* a colour television broadcast.

col-oured (kul′ėrd), *adj.* **1,** having colour; not black or white; **2,** belonging to a race other than white, esp. black; pertaining to people of colour.

col-our-ful (kul′ėr-fo͝ol), *adj.* **1,** full of striking colour or colours; as, a *colourful* parade; **2,** exciting the fancy or imagination; as, *colourful* music.

col-our-less (kul′ėr-les), *adj.* **1,** having no colour; without colour; as, a gloomy, *colourless* landscape; **2,** not bright or vivid; not interesting; as, a *colourless* speaker.

colt (kōlt), *n.* a young horse, esp. a male under four or five years old; also, a young donkey, zebra, etc.

col-umn (kol′um), *n.* **1,** an upright pillar supporting or adorning any part of a building or standing alone as a monument; **2,** anything that by its form, position, or use suggests a pillar; as, the spinal *column*; a *column* of mercury; **3,** a vertical division on a printed page; as, the *columns* of a newspaper; **4,** a department in a newspaper or magazine, usually written by one person on one general subject; as, the society *column*; **5,** a body or file of soldiers or ships following one after the other.—*adj.* **co-lum′nar.**

col-um-nist (kol′um-nist), *n.* one who writes or edits a particular column in a newspaper or magazine.

co-ma (kō′ma), *n.* a state of prolonged unconsciousness and insensibility, produced by disease or injury.

comb (kōm), *n.* **1,** a toothed instrument of metal or plastic used to smooth, adjust, or hold in the hair; **2,** a toothed ornament for the hair; **3,** a toothed instrument used in grooming horses, separating and cleaning the fibres of flax or wool, etc.; **4,** the crest of a rooster; **5,** the crest of a hill or wave:—*v.t.* **1,** to dress (the hair) with a comb; **2,** to cleanse (flax or wool) with a comb; **3,** to search through; as, they *combed* the city for the fugitive.

com-bat (kom′bat; kum′bat), *n.* a struggle; fight, esp. between two military forces:—*v.i.* (kom′bat; kum′bat; kom-bat′), [combat-ed, combat-ing; if accented on the last syllable, combat-ted, combat-ting], to struggle; as, good *combating* with evil:—*v.t.* to oppose; resist.—*adj.* **com′ba-tive.**

com-bat-ant (kom′ba-tant; kum′ba-tant), *n.* a person who takes part in a fight or conflict:—*adj.* fighting.

com-bi-na-tion (kom-bi-nā′shun), *n.* **1,** something that is formed by combining things; as, a mule is a *combination* of a horse and a donkey; **2,** the act of combining; as, the *combination* of red and blue makes purple; **3,** a series of numbers or letters used to open a lock.

[1]**com-bine** (kom′bīn), *n.* a farm machine that harvests, threshes, and cleans grain in one continuous operation in the field.

[2]**com-bine** (kom-bīn′), *v.t.* [combined, combin-ing], to unite or join; as, to *combine* forces; to mix, as ingredients:—*v.i.* to unite; agree; as, two parties will *combine* to defeat a third:—*n.* (kom′bīn; kom-bin′), *Colloq.* a union; a joining of persons or parties in business or politics to effect a common purpose.—*adj.* **com-bined′.**

com-bus-ti-ble (kom-bus′ti-bl), *adj.* **1,** capable of taking fire and burning; as, gasoline, wood, and coal are *combustible*; **2,** excitable; fierce; as, a *combustible* temper:—*n.* an inflammable substance, as gasoline.—*n.* **com-bus′ti-bil′i-ty.**

com-bus-tion (kom-bus′chun), *n.* the act or process of burning.

come (kum), *v.i.* [*p.t.* came (kām), *p.p.* come, *p.pr.* com-ing], **1,** to move toward; draw near; as, *come* here; spring is *coming*; also, to arrive; **2,** to extend to a given point; as, the farm *comes* as far as the river; **3,** to amount to; as, the bill *comes* to $50; it all *comes* to the same thing; **4,** to become visible, audible, etc.; as, sounds *come* to the ear; **5,** to be descended or to be from a certain place; as, he *comes* from a humble family; she *comes* from Manitoba; **6,** to occur as a result; as, accidents *come* from carelessness; **7,** to happen; as, I don't know how we *came* to speak of it; **8,** to be available; exist; as, the T-shirt *comes* in different colours.

co-me-di-an (ko-mē′di-an), *n.* an actor who plays comic parts; also, a person whose work is entertaining others by telling jokes or doing funny things.—*n.fem.* **co-me′di-enne′** (ko-mē′di-en′). Also called *comic.*

com-e-dy (kom′e-di), *n.* [*pl.* comedies], an amusing play, movie, or television show with a happy ending:—**situation comedy,** a TV comedy show that uses the same characters in a series of programs.

come-ly (kum′li), *adj.* [come-li-er, come-li-est], **1,** fair to look upon; of pleasing appearance; as, a *comely* girl; **2,** suitable.—*n.* **come′li-ness.**

com-et (kom′it), *n.* a heavenly body, thought to be made of ice, frozen gases, and dust, that moves around the sun: it often has a bright head and a long, blazing train, or tail.

com-fort (kum′fėrt), *v.t.* to console or cheer (a person) in pain, grief, or trouble:—*n.* **1,** a person or thing that relieves distress or makes trouble easier to bear; as, a good friend is a *comfort*; **2,** enjoyment of freedom from mental or physical discomfort; **3,** contentment resulting from the satisfying of wants; also, the things that produce such a state; as, the *comforts* of home. Also, **com′fort food′; com′fort zone′.**

com-fort-a-ble (kum′fėrt-a-bl), *adj.* **1,** enjoying ease, contentment, or freedom from care; **2,** giving comfort; as, a *comfortable* chair.—*adv.* **com′fort-a-bly.**

com-fort-er (kum′fėrt-ėr), *n.* **1,** one who consoles or cheers; **2,** a quilted or padded bed covering of cotton, wool, feathers, or other material.

com-ic (kom′ik), *n.* **1,** a person who tells stories or jokes that make people laugh; a comedian; **2,** a comic strip or comic book:—*adj.* aiming to excite laughter; funny or amusing; as, a *comic* song. Also, **com′i-cal.**

com-ma (kom′a), *n.* a punctuation mark [,] used to indicate a slight separation of ideas or construction, as to set off a short quotation from the text, to separate words in a series, to separate parts of a name, a date, or an address, etc.

com-mand (ko-mand′), *v.t.* **1,** to give orders to, with authority; **2,** to have authority over; control; as, the captain *commands* her troops; **3,** to overlook or dominate, as from a height; **4,** to be able to obtain; as, to *command* good prices; to *command* respect:—*v.i.* to act as leader; rule:—*n.* **1,** authority; the right to command or control; as, a captain is in *command* of a company; **2,** an order; as, he gave the *command* to fire; **3,** a district or a body of troops under a naval or military officer; **4,** mastery; as, the *command* of a language; in *command* of one's temper; **5,** in *computing,* an instruction to a computer to perform a certain operation; keyboard commands; as, the *command* to alphabetize a list.

com-man-dant (kom′an-dant′; kom′an-dånt′), *n.* the officer in command of a troop, a military base, a navy yard, a training school, etc.

com-man-deer (kom′an-dēr), *v.t.* **1,** to compel (persons) to military service; **2,** to take forcibly (food, clothing, cars, etc.) for military purposes; **3,** *Colloq.* to seize for personal use.

com-mand-er (ko-man′dėr), *n.* **1,** a person in authority; **2,** a military leader or chief; **3,** a naval officer equal to the rank of lieutenant-colonel:—**commander-in-chief** [*pl.* commanders-in-chief], the person in supreme command of the armed forces.

com-mand-ment (ko-mand′ment), *n.* **1,** an order; injunction; law; **2,** any one of the Ten Commandments given by God to Moses.

com-mem-o-rate (ko-mem′o-rāt′), *v.t.* [commemorat-ed, commemorat-ing], to keep alive the memory of (a person, event, etc.), as by a celebration or a monument; as, the Peace Tower *commemorates* the Canadians killed in World War I.—*n.* **com-mem′o-ra′tion.**

com-mence (ko-mens′), *v.t.* and *v.i.* [commenced, commenc-ing], to begin.

com-mence-ment (ko-mens′ment), *n.* **1,** the beginning; origin; **2,** the occasion when degrees or diplomas are conferred at a school or a college; also, the graduation exercises.

com-mend (ko-mend′), *v.t.* **1,** to recommend as worthy of notice; as, to *commend* a movie; **2,** to praise; as, to *commend* a child for promptness.—*n.* **com′men-da′tion.**

com-mend-a-ble (ko-men′da-bl), *adj.* praiseworthy.—*adv.* **com-mend′a-bly.**

com-men-su-rate (ko-men′sū-rit; -shoor-), *adj.* corresponding in amount; proportionate; as, her skill is *commensurate* with her intelligence; pay *commensurate* with experience and the work performed.

com-ment (kom′ent), *n.* **1,** a spoken or written remark; esp., a note that explains, illustrates, or criticizes; **2,** talk; gossip; as, his unexpected departure caused *comment*:—*v.i.* (ko-ment′), to make observations or notes; as, to *comment* upon the news.

com-men-tar-y (kom′en-tėr-i; -ter′-), *n.* [*pl.* commentaries], **1,** an explanation; **2,** a series of notes explaining or interpreting parts of a book, etc.; also, a book of critical or explanatory notes; **3,** views, descriptions, or opinions, esp. by a radio or television commentator, on certain aspects of the news, such as sporting or entertainment events.

com-men-ta-tor (kom′en-tā′tėr), *n.* a person whose work is to comment on the news on television or radio; as, a news, sports, or fashion *commentator.*

com-merce (kom′ėrs), *n.* the buying and selling of goods, esp. on a large scale; trade.

com-mer-cial (ko-mûr′shal), *n.* an advertisement on television or radio:—*adj.* having to do with business or the advertising business; as, a *commercial* airliner, bank, commercial art, etc.—*adv.* **com-mer′cial-ly.**

com-mer-cial-ize (ko-mûr′shal-īz′), *v.t.* [commercialized, commercializ-ing], to make something into a money-making or business venture, sometimes implying that quality or standards have been reduced; exploit for profit; as, to *commercialize* football, Christmas.—*n.* **com-mer′cial-ism; com-mer′cial-i-za′tion.**

com-mis-er-ate (ko-miz′ėr-āt) [commiserat-ed, commiserat-ing], to feel or express pity for; sympathize with.—*n.* **com-mis′er-a′tion.**

com-mis-sar-y (kom′i-sėr-i), *n.* [*pl.* commissaries], **1,** one to whom some charge is committed by a superior; a deputy; **2,** in the army, an official in the department which has charge of provisions and supplies; **3,** a company store supplying food and equipment, as in a lumber or military camp; also, a lunchroom or cafeteria in a movie studio.

com-mis-sion (ko-mish′un), *n.* **1,** the doing or performing of some act, often implying wrongdoing; as, the *commission* of a crime; **2,** a matter entrusted to anyone to perform; as, he had a *commission* to buy land; **3,** the fee paid to an agent for doing business for another; as, the *commission* on the sale was $250; **4,** a group of persons appointed to perform certain duties; as, a *commission* to investigate housing; a Human Rights *Commission*; **5,** a document conferring military or naval rank or authority:—**out of commission,** out of active use or service; as, our copier is *out of commission*; the warship is *out of commission*:—*v.t.* **1,** to empower; delegate; as, I *commission* you to paint the picture; **2,** in the army and navy, to confer rank or authority upon; **3,** to put into service, as a warship.—*n.* **com-mis′sion-er.**

com-mit (ko-mit′), *v.t.* [commit-ted, commit-ting], **1,** to give (someone) into another's care for safekeeping, care, custody, etc.; as, to *commit* an invalid to a hospital; to *commit* a person for trial; **2,** to entrust (something) for safekeeping, as by writing down or memorizing; as, to *commit* thoughts to paper or a computer password to memory; **3,** to do (something foolish or wrong); as, to *commit* a folly or a crime; **4,** to involve (oneself) in difficulties; as, he refused to *commit* himself by talking; also, to pledge; as, I am *committed* to the cause.—*n.* **com-mit′ment.**—*n.* **com-mit′al.**

com-mit-tee (ko-mit′i), *n.* a group of persons elected or appointed to deal with a certain phase of a business, or to act on, consider, or report on one special matter; as, a *committee* for decorating the hall; a legislative *committee.*

com-mo-di-ous (ko-mō′di-us), *adj.* roomy; spacious.—*adv.* **com-mo′di-ous-ly.**

com-mod-i-ty (ko-mod′i-ti), *n.* [*pl.* commodities], something useful; an article of commerce that can be bought and sold, esp. raw materials produced by farming or mining, such as wheat, copper, corn, lumber, hogs, etc.:—**commodities,** goods; merchandise.

com-mo-dore (kom′o-dōr), *n.* **1,** a naval commanding officer ranking above a captain and below a rear admiral; **2,** a title of courtesy given to the president of a yacht club, the senior captain of a line of merchant ships, etc.

com-mon (kom′un), *adj.* **1,** belonging to, or shared by, more than one; general; as, cats are *common* pets; **2,** belonging, or relating, to a group or community; public; as, parks are *common* property; **3,** usual; frequent; as, a *common* saying; a *common* sight; **4,** of the ordinary kind; merely average in rank, ability, etc.; **5,** low; vulgar:—*n.* **1,** a tract of open public land; as, the village *common*; **2,** the average; as, a person above the *common*:—**in common,** equally with another or others; as, to have something in *common.*—*adv.* **com′mon-ly.**

com-mon-place (kom′un-plās′), *n.* **1,** an ordinary topic of conversation; also, an often-repeated remark; **2,** an everyday object or event; one that is not uncommon; as, using the Internet has become a *commonplace*:—*adj.* uninteresting; neither new nor striking; ordinary.

Commons (kom′unz), *n.* **1,** the House of Commons; **2,** members of the House of Commons.

common sense, *n.* good sense; sound, practical judgment; normal intelligence.—*adj.* **com′mon–sense′.**

com-mon-wealth (kom′un-welth′), *n.* **1,** the public; the whole body of people in a nation or state; **2,** a nation or state in which the people rule; **3,** a group of nations, persons, etc., united by some common bond or interest:—**Commonwealth (of Nations),** an association of countries that were once under British law and government.

com-mo-tion (ko-mō′shun), *n.* **1,** violent physical disturbance; as, the *commotion* of the raging sea; **2,** stir and confusion; tumult; as, a *commotion* in the crowd.

com-mu-nal (kom′ū-nal; ko-mū′nal) *adj.* relating to the community; belonging to the people; public; as, *communal* land.

com-mune (kō-mūn′), *v.i.* [communed, commun-ing], **1,** to feel an intimate understanding or hold intimate conversation or thoughts with; as, to *commune* with nature; **2,** to partake of Holy Communion.

com-mu-ni-cate (ko-mū-ni-kāt′), *v.t.* [communicat-ed, communicat-ing], **1,** to impart; convey; as, to *communicate* happiness; to *communicate* a disease; **2,** to make known; tell, as news; share or exchange information, feelings, or thoughts; as, to *communicate* our feelings for each other:—*v.i.* **1,** to receive Communion; **2,** to be connected; as, *communicating* rooms; **3,** to get into connection or touch, by letter, telephone, e-mail, etc.; speak or write to someone; as, to *communicate* by e-mail; she *communicates* with us regularly.—*adj.* **com-mu′ni-ca′tive; com-mu′ni-ca-ble.**

com-mu-ni-ca-tion (ko-mū′ni-kā′shun), *n.* **1,** the act of communicating; **2,** what is communicated; the information or ideas given:—**communications,** a system that is used to communicate, such as TV, radio, telephone, or e-mail.

com-mun-ion (ko-mūn′yun), *n.* **1,** fellowship; esp., religious fellowship; an intimate exchange of spiritual thoughts and feelings or rapport; **2,** a group of persons having the same religious beliefs:—**Communion,** the sacrament of Christ's Last Supper.

com-mu-ni-qué (ko-mū′ni-kā′), *n.* an official report, bulletin, or statement.

com-mu-nist (kom′ū-nist), *n.* one who believes in communism, or the theory that the people should own in common the means of production, such as mines, factories, etc., and should share in both the work and the returns:—**Communist,** a member of a political party holding these views, esp. formerly in the U.S.S.R.—*n.* **com′mu-nism; Com′mu-nism.**—*adj.* **com′mu-nis′tic.**

com-mu-ni-ty (ko-mū′ni-ti), *n.* [*pl.* communities], **1,** all the persons who live in one place, as the people of a town; hence, the public; also, the area or town itself; **2,** a group of persons, bound by ties of common interest; as, a *community* of artists; a religious *community*; **3,** likeness; similarity; as, *community* of interests.

community college, a post-secondary educational facility that offers training in technical skills and other generally practical matters.

com-mu-ta-tor (kom′ū-tā′tėr), *n.* a device used in a generator or motor for changing the direction of an electric current, esp. alternating to direct; usually it is a revolving cylinder that collects the current from, or distributes it to, the brushes.

com-mute (ko-mūt′), *v.t.* [commut-ed, commut-ing], to exchange for something different; esp., to reduce the severity of; as, to *commute* a sentence of imprisonment from 10 to five years:—*v.i.* to travel back and forth daily from and to work, esp. over a long distance.—*n.* **com-mut′er.**—*n.* **com′mu-ta′tion.**

com-pact (kom′pakt; kom-pakt′), *adj.* **1,** packed together tightly; as, a *compact* pile of newspapers; **2,** taking up a small amount of space or room; as, a *compact* stereo system; **3,** condensed; terse; as, a *compact* style:—*v.t.* (kom-pakt′), to pack together tightly; as, to *compact* leaves in a garbage bag:—*n.* (käm′pakt), **1,** a small case that is used to hold face powder; **2,** a car that is smaller than a regular-sized model; **3,** an agreement.—*n.* **com-pac′tor/com′pact-er** (a machine that compacts garbage into a tight bundle); **sub′com′pact.**—*adv.* **com-pact′ly.**—*n.* **compact′ness.**

compact disc or **compact disk** (**CD**), a small, round, flat plastic device that stores information such as music, pictures, or computer programs, and which is played using a laser beam, not a needle; also, a disc onto which data can be recorded: a *CD-ROM* (*c*ompact *d*isc—*r*ead *o*nly *m*emory) is a compact disc that cannot be recorded over.

com-pan-ion (kom-pan′yun), *n.* **1,** a comrade or associate; a person who spends time with another; a friend; **2,** a person paid to live or travel with another; **3,** one of a pair or set of objects designed to go together; as, a *companion* to a glove:—*v.t.* to accompany.—*n.* **com-pan′ion-ship.**—*adj.* **com-pan′ion-a-ble.**

com-pa-ny (kum′pa-ni), *n.* [*pl.* companies], **1,** companionship; society; as, I want *company* tonight; **2,** companions; associates; as, a person is known by the *company* he or she keeps; **3,** a guest or guests; **4,** a group of persons assembled; as, a ballet *company*; **5,** a business or commercial firm; **6,** a troupe of actors; **7,** a body of soldiers, esp. a section of infantry, normally commanded by a captain.

com-pa-ra-ble (kom′pa-ra-bl), *adj.* **1,** capable of being compared; as, the sound of cannon and the sound of thunder are *comparable*; **2,** worthy or fit to be compared; as, Westminster Abbey is *comparable* to Notre Dame.—*adv.* **com′pa-ra-bly.**

com-par-a-tive (kom-par′a-tiv), *adj.* **1,** involving the use of comparison; as, the *comparative* study of animals; **2,** measured by comparison with something else; as, we live in *comparative* comfort; **3,** in *grammar*, naming that form of an adjective or adverb, as "longer" or "sooner," that expresses a higher degree of the quality indicated by the simple form:—*n.* the comparative degree; also, a comparative form; as, "better" is the *comparative* of "good."—*adv.* **com-par′a-tive-ly.**

com-pare (kom-pâr′), *v.t.* [compared, compar-ing], **1,** to liken; describe as similar; as, the poets *compare* death to sleep; frozen corn does not really *compare* with fresh corn; **2,** to examine in order to discover likeness and unlikeness; as, to *compare* answers to the answer key; **3,** in *grammar*, to give the positive, comparative, and superlative degrees of (an adjective or adverb):—*v.i.* to be worthy of comparison with something else; as, rayon *compares* favourably with silk:—*n.* comparison; as, beauty beyond *compare.*

com-par-i-son (kom-pâr′i-sn), *n.* **1,** the act of comparing; as, to give a *comparison* between two Web sites; **2,** a likeness; similarity; as, there's no *comparison* between frozen and fresh corn; **3,** in *grammar,* the change in an adjective or adverb to show a difference in amount or quality.

com-part-ment (kom-pärt′ment), *n.* a separate part or division, as of an enclosed space; a separate section; as, the butter, cheese, meat, and vegetable *compartments* in a refrigerator:—**glove compartment,** an enclosed space in a car that holds small items such as gloves, maps, sunglasses, car registration, coins, etc.

com-pass (kum′pas), *n.* **1,** the boundary of an area; as, within the *compass* of a city; **2,** an instrument for determining direction by means of a needle pointing to the magnetic north; **3,** the range of tones possible to a given voice or instrument; **4,** an instrument for drawing and dividing circles, transferring measurements, etc., consisting of two small, upright rods joined together at the top by a hinge:—*v.t.* **1,** to go around or form a circle; as, a spacecraft *compassed* the earth; trees *compassed* the house; **2,** to bring about; achieve; as, he *compassed* his aims.

com-pas-sion (kom-pash′un), *n.* sorrow and pity for the sufferings of others.

com-pas-sion-ate (kom-pash′un-it), *adj.* merciful.—*adv.* **com-pas′sion-ate-ly.**

com-pat-i-ble (kom-pat′i-bl), *adj.* **1,** harmonious; consistent; mutually agreeable or suitable; as, this evidence is not *compatible* with your testimony; **2,** in *computing,* relating to computing devices that are able to operate with other components; as, this printer is *compatible* with the CPU.

com-pa-tri-ot (kom-pā′tri-ot; -pat′), *n.* a person from the same country.

com-pel (kom-pel′), *v.t.* [compelled, compel-ling], to oblige; force; as, a guilty conscience *compelled* him to confess.

com-pen-sate (kom′pen-sāt′), *v.t.* [compensat-ed, compensat-ing], to make a suitable return to; pay; as, to *compensate* you for your time:—*v.i.* to make up for something; supply an equivalent; as, nothing can *compensate* for loss of health.—*n.* **com′pen-sa′tion.**

com-pete (kom-pēt′), *v.i.* [compet-ed, compet-ing], to enter into a contest, game, or rivalry; contend; as, to *compete* in the Olympics.

com-pe-tence or **com-pe-ten-cy** (kom′pe-tens; kom′pe-tens-i), *n.* **1,** fitness; capability; ability; as, no one questions her *competence* to teach music; *competence* in French; **2,** a modest fortune; enough for comfort.

com-pe-tent (kom′pe-tent), *adj.* able; capable of doing what is needed.—*adv.* **com′pe-tent-ly.**

com-pe-ti-tion (kom′pe-tish′un), *n.* **1,** the act of competing; trying to win a contest or game; rivalry; **2,** a contest; a trial of ability, as in sport; as, the *competition* in skiing drew a crowd; **3,** the effort of rival concerns to secure as much business as possible by making concessions as regards price, terms of payment, etc.; a competitor or rival in business; as, a company tries to outperform its *competition.*—*adj.* **com-pet′i-tive** (kom-pet′i-tiv).—*n.* **com-pet′i-tor** (kom-pet′i-tėr).

com-pile (kom-pīl′), *v.t.* [compiled, compil-ing], to collect (data, facts, figures, literary extracts, etc.) from various sources and put into new form; as, to *compile* a table of contents, an index, or a list.—*n.* **com-pil′er.**—*n.* **com′pi-la′tion.**

com-pla-cent (kom-plā′sent), *adj.* pleased with oneself; self-satisfied.—*adv.* **com-pla′cent-ly.**—*n.* **com-pla′cence.**

com-plain (kom-plān), *v.i.* **1,** to give voice to grief, pain, resentment, or discontent; say that something is wrong or unfair; find fault with; be unhappy or annoyed; as, she *complained* of a headache; that her dinner was cold; that he was late; **2,** to make a formal report or statement that something is wrong; as, to *complain* to the police; **3,** to make an accusation; as, the prisoner *complained* of injustice.—*adv.* **com-plain′ing-ly.**

com-plaint (kom-plānt), *n.* **1,** the act of complaining; an expression of unhappiness; finding fault; as, *complaints* about the cold weather; **2,** the cause of complaining; as, her *complaint* was about his tardiness; **3,** a formal statement or report of complaining; a charge; as, to file a *complaint* with the ethics committee.

com-plai-sant (kom-plā′zant; kom′plā-zant′; kom-plā′sent), *n.* polite; courteous; agreeable; obliging; as, to be *complaisant* in your reception of visitors.

com-ple-ment (kom′ple-ment), *n.* **1,** the full number or quantity, a complete set; as, the orchestra has its *complement* of instruments; **2,** that which makes an incomplete thing complete; as, the sauce was a good *complement* for the chicken; **3,** one of two parts that together form a whole:—*v.t.* (kom′ple-ment′), to finish out; make whole; as, her accessories *complement* her suit.—*adj.* **com′ple-men′ta-ry.**

com-plete (kom-plēt′), *adj.* **1,** lacking nothing; entire; perfect; full; as, a *complete* pack of cards; **2,** absolute; as, a *complete* surprise; **3,** finished; as, her work is now *complete:*—*v.t.* [completed, complet-ing], to make whole or perfect; finish.—*n.* **complete′ness.**—*adv.* **com-plete′ly.**

com-ple-tion (kom-plē′shun), *n.* **1,** the act of completing something; as, a *completion* of the new highway; **2,** a completed condition; as, to see a project through to *completion*.

com-plex (kom′pleks; kom-pleks′), *adj.* **1,** made of various parts; not simple; as, a *complex* business organization; **2,** involved; intricate; complicated; as, a *complex* situation; a *complex* plan; a *complex* sentence:—*n.* (kom′pleks), **1,** something that is made up of many parts; as, a housing *complex*; **2,** a habitual emotional attitude toward a particular thing; as, a *complex* about performing in front of an audience.—*n.* **com-plex′i-ty.**

com-plex-ion (kom-plek′shun), *n.* **1,** the colour, texture, and appearance of the skin, esp. of the face; **2,** general aspect or character; as, his story gave a different *complexion* to the case.—*adj.* **com-plex′-ioned.**

com-pli-ant (kom-plī′ant), *adj.* inclined to consent; yielding; obliging.—*adv.* **com-pli′ant-ly.**—*n.* **com-pli′ance.**

com-pli-cate (kom′pli-kāt′), *v.t.* [complicat-ed, complicat-ing], **1,** to make confused or hard to understand; to make difficult; as, to *complicate* a project by using too many ambiguous statistics; **2,** to make worse or more severe; as, high blood pressure *complicated* her illness.—*adj.* **com′pli-cat′ed.**—*n.* **com′pli-ca′tion.**

com-plic-i-ty (kom-plis′i-ti), *n.* [*pl.* complicities], partnership in wrongdoing or crime.

com-pli-ment (kom′pli-ment), *n.* something pleasant said about a person or his or her work; praise; as, a *compliment* about his cooking:—**compliments,** formal greetings; best wishes; as, the new ambassador paid his *compliments* to the prime minister:—*v.t.* (kom′pli-ment′), to express approval of; praise.

com-pli-men-ta-ry (kom′pli-men′ta-ri), *adj.* **1,** conveying approval or admiration; **2,** given free; as, *complimentary* tickets.

com-ply (kom-plī′), *v.i.* [complied, com-ply-ing], to assent; yield; agree with rules, requests; as, we *complied* with the traffic laws.

com-po-nent (kom-pō′nent), *n.* part; ingredient; unit of a system, machine, or program; as, a stereo system has several different *components*, such as loudspeakers, a CD player, and a tuner:—*adj.* helping to make up or constitute; as, a monitor and a keyboard are *component* parts of a computer.

com-port (kom-pôrt′), *v.t.* to conduct or behave (oneself); as, he did not know how to *comport* himself at the formal dinner:—*v.i.* to agree; accord; harmonize; as, words that *comport* with actions.—*n.* **com-port′ment.**

com-pose (kom-pōz′), *v.t.* [composed, com-pos-ing], **1,** to form by putting things together; as, bronze is *composed* of copper and tin; **2,** to construct or put together; create; as, to *compose* a sentence, speech, piece of music, or drawing; **3,** to set (type); **4,** to settle or arrange (any matter) successfully; as, to *compose* a dispute; **5,** to calm; make tranquil; as, to *compose* one's mind; to *compose* oneself.—*n.* **com-pos′er.**

com-pos-ite (kom′poz-it), *adj.* **1,** made up of various distinct parts; as a *composite* picture; **2,** in *botany*, belonging to a group of plants with flowers that are made up of many small flowers, as the dandelion, daisy, etc.:—*n.* a compound.—*n.* **com-pos′i-tor.**

com-po-si-tion (kom′pō-zish′un), *n.* **1,** the act of creating an artistic work or composing; **2,** the work created, as a picture, a piece of music, an essay, etc.; **3,** a piece of writing done as a school assignment; **4,** the setting up of type; **5,** a substance formed by mingling various materials; **6,** the make-up of anything; as, what is the *composition* of this substance? the mineral *composition* of a rock.

com-post (kom′pōst), *n.* a rotted mixture of dead leaves, decaying vegetable matter, manure, etc., for fertilizing soils:—*v.t.* and *v.i.* to fertilize or convert into compost; produce compost; as, to *compost* garden clippings and leftover food.

com-po-sure (kom-pō′zhūr; -zhėr), *n.* calmness.

com-pound (kom-pound′), *v.t.* **1,** to mix or combine together, as two chemicals; **2,** to form by mixing, as a medicine; **3,** to make worse; as, complaining *compounded* the problem:—*adj.* (kom′pound; kom-pound′), composed of two or more elements:—*n.* (kom′pound), **1,** a combination of two or more elements or parts; **2,** in *chemistry*, a substance formed of two or more elements united in definite proportions.

compound sentence, a sentence having two (or more) independent clauses joined by a conjunction: each part can be a separate sentence on its own; as, "she went to work, and he stayed home" is a *compound* sentence.

compound word, a word made up of two or more parts that are words in themselves, such as "roadblock," "houseboat," "high-class," or "highway."

com-pre-hend (kom′pri-hend′), *v.t.* **1,** to understand; grasp the meaning of; **2,** to include; take in; as, Europe *comprehends* many nations.—*n.* **com′pre-hen′sion.**—*adj.* **com′pre-hen′si-ble.**

com-pre-hen-sive (kom′pri-hen′siv), *adj.* **1,** including much; full; complete; as, a *comprehensive* test of the course material covered; **2,** able to understand readily; comprehending.

com-press (kom-pres′), *v.t.* **1,** to press together; condense; **2,** in *computing,* to condense computer files to minimize storage space or transmission time required:—*n.* (kom′pres), a pad applied hot or cold to some part of the body to reduce inflammation.—*adj.* **com-press′i-ble; com-pressed′.**—*n.* **com-pres′sion.**

com-prise (kom-prīz′), *v.t.* [comprised, compris-ing], to consist of; include; as, the house *comprises* 12 rooms.

com-pro-mise (kom′prō-mīz′), *n.* **1,** a method of settling a dispute whereby each side yields something; as, after hours of dispute, they resorted to *compromise;* **2,** an agreement reached by mutual yielding; **3,** a line of action that follows a middle course; as, the plan adopted was a *compromise:*—*v.t.* [compromised, compromis-ing], **1,** to settle by mutual yielding; **2,** to expose to suspicion; endanger; as, such actions will *compromise* your reputation:—*v.i.* to make a compromise.

comp-trol-ler (kon-trōl′ėr), *n.* Same as **controller.**

com-pul-sion (kom-pul′shun), *n.* the act of compelling; force; also, the state of being compelled; constraint.

com-pul-so-ry (kom-pul′so-ri), *adj.* **1,** exercising force; required by law; as, *compulsory* driver's licence; **2,** obligatory; enforced; required; as, attending school for children is *compulsory.*—*adv.* **com-pul′so-ri-ly.**

com-punc-tion (kom-pungk′shun), *n.* a feeling (often slight or passing) of regret or uneasiness for wrongdoing; as, he felt *compunction* for the harsh words.

com-pute (kom-pūt′), *v.t.* [comput-ed, comput-ing], to figure; number; reckon; calculate; as, he *computed* his expenses.—*n.* **com′pu-ta′tion.**

com-put-er (kom-pūt′ėr), *n.* an electronic machine that is able to handle complicated mathematical and logical tasks at high speed by breaking them down into simple steps: it can store large amounts of information or data in a small space (memory) by changing them into a code:—**computer hardware,** the machine itself:—**computer software,** the programs that tell the machine what to do. Also, **computer game; computer graphics; computer literacy; computer science; computer virus.**

com-rade (kum′rid; kom′rad), *n.* a friend; a companion or buddy.—*n.* **com′rade-ship.**

[1]**con** (kon), *v.t.* [conned, con-ning], to study carefully; hence, to commit to memory.

[2]**con** (kon), *n.* and *adv.* the negative side; as, they argued the matter pro and *con;* the pros and *cons* of the debate.

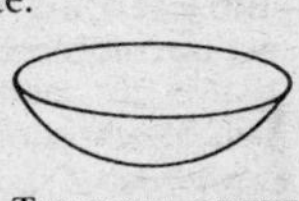

THE INSIDE OF THE BOWL IS CONCAVE.

con-cave (kon′kāv; kon-kāv′), *adj.* curved inward, as the inside of a spoon, circle, or ball: opposite of *convex.*—*n.* **con-cav′i-ty** (kon-kav′i-ti).

con-ceal (kon-sēl′), *v.t.* to hide; keep secret.—*n.* **con-ceal′ment.**—*adj.* **con-cealed′.**

con-cede (kon-sēd′), *v.t.* [conced-ed, conced-ing], **1,** to admit to be true; yield; as, he *conceded* the point in the debate; **2,** to grant (a right, privilege, etc.); as, to *concede* an advance in wages.

con-ceit (kon-sēt′), *n.* **1,** a too flattering belief in one's own powers; vanity; a too high opinion of oneself; **2,** a fanciful notion; a quaint thought.—*adj.* **con-ceit′ed.**

con-ceive (kon-sēv′), *v.t.* [conceived, conceiv-ing], **1,** to think of; imagine; **2,** to form (a purpose, design, etc.) in the mind; devise; as, to *conceive* a plot; **3,** to become pregnant with (young):—*v.i.* **1,** to think; imagine; as, I cannot *conceive* of her doing that; **2,** to become pregnant.—*adj.* **con-ceiv′a-ble.**—*adv.* **con-ceiv′a-bly.**

con-cen-trate (kon′sen-trāt′), *v.t.* [concentrat-ed, concentrat-ing], **1,** to bring to a common centre; as, the general *concentrated* his troops in the city; **2,** to fix (the attention or energies) on one course or object; **3,** to increase in strength by reducing bulk; as, to *concentrate* soup by boiling away excess liquid:—*v.i.* **1,** to come together in one place; as, population *concentrates* in the cities; **2,** to fix the attention; as, to *concentrate* on a problem.—*n.* **con′cen-trate** (as, orange *concentrate*).—*adj.* **con′cen-tra′ted** (as, *concentrated* orange juice).

con-cen-tra-tion (kon-sen-trā′shun), *n.* **1,** close attention; as, this math problem requires a great amount of *concentration;* **2,** a large gathering together; something concentrated; as, a large *concentration* of protesters gathered in front of the government building.

con-cen-tric (kon-sen′trik), *adj.* having a common centre; as, *concentric* circles.

CONCENTRIC CIRCLES

con-cept (kon′sept), *n.* a mental impression of an object; a general notion.

con-cep-tion (kon-sep′shun), *n.* **1,** the act of forming a mental image or impression; **2,** an idea or notion; **3,** the fertilization of the egg and the beginning of a new life in the body of the mother.

con-cern (kon-sûrn′), *v.t.* **1,** have to do with or be about; as, the article *concerns* pollution; **2,** to affect the welfare of; relate or belong to; interest or engage; as, that does not *concern* me; **3,** to make uneasy; as, don't let that *concern* you:—*n.* **1,** that which relates to one; one's business; as, that is my *concern*; **2,** interest; anxiety; **3,** a business firm or company.

con-cerned (kon-sûrnd′), *adj.* troubled or anxious; worried; as, to be *concerned* about her health:—**as far as one is concerned,** in one's opinion.

con-cern-ing (kon-sûr′ning), *prep.* relating to; regarding.

con-cert (kon-sûrt′), *v.t.* to plan together; settle by agreement:—*n.* (kon′sûrt), **1,** a musical entertainment; recital; **2,** musical harmony; as, the students like to sing in *concert*; **3,** agreement; cooperation; **4,** unison of voices; as, to recite in *concert*.

con-cer-ti-na (kon′sėr-tē′na), *n.* a small musical instrument somewhat like an accordion.

con-cer-to (kon-cher′tō; -châr), *n.* symphonic music for one or more solo instruments, as a piano or organ, with accompaniments for a full orchestra, playing a composition with three movements.

con-ces-sion (kon-sesh′un), *n.* **1,** the act of granting or yielding something; **2,** an acknowledgement or admission; **3,** a grant of a privilege, or of land, for some special purpose; **4,** a government grant of land forming a division of a township; **5,** a subdivision of land within a township; also, one of the roads (of a township) that run parallel.

conch (kongk; konch), *n.* a large spiral seashell; also, the animal in the shell.

con-cil-i-ate (kon-sil′i-āt′), *v.t.* [conciliated, conciliat-ing], to gain the goodwill of (a person); win over from hostility; as, her many kind deeds finally *conciliated* her enemy.—*n.* **con-cil′i-a′tion.**—*n.* **con-cil′i-a-tor.**—*adj.* **con-cil′i-a-tor′y.**

con-cise (kon-sīs′), *adj.* terse; brief; expressing much in few words; as, a *concise* description.—*adv.* **con-cise′ly.**—*n.* **concise′ness.**

con-clude (kon-klūd′; kon-klo͞od′), *v.t.* [conclud-ed, conclud-ing], **1,** to bring to an end; as, to *conclude* a speech; **2,** to arrive at an opinion by reasoning; infer; as, it grew so late, I *concluded* you were not coming; **3,** to settle; bring about as a result; as, after hours of bickering, he *concluded* the agreement:—*v.i.* to come to an end.

con-clu-sion (kon-klū′zhun; kon-klo͞o′zhun), *n.* **1,** the end or final part of something; as, the *conclusion* of a movie; **2,** something decided by thinking; a judgment or decision; as, to reach a *conclusion* that they are not coming:—**jump to conclusions,** to make a judgment too quickly, without enough information.—*adj.* **con-clu′sive.**

con-coct (kon-kokt′), *v.t.* **1,** to prepare, as food, by mixing various elements; **2,** to form; make up, as a plot.—*n.* **con-coc′tion.**

con-cord (kong′kôrd; kon′kôrd), *n.* agreement; peace; harmony.

con-course (kong′kōrs; kon′kōrs), *n.* **1,** a flowing together; as, a *concourse* of waters; **2,** an assembly or crowd; **3,** an open place where crowds gather or roads meet.

con-crete (kon′krēt; kon-krēt′), *adj.* **1,** actual; specific; capable of being seen, heard, tasted, etc.; not abstract; as, a table is a *concrete* object, but goodness is an abstract quality; **2,** consisting of the substance called *concrete*:—*n.* a mixture of cement, sand, gravel, and water that becomes very hard when dry, used for sidewalks, buildings, and roads:—**concrete poem,** a poem that uses words to make a visual image of the topic of the poem.—*adv.* **con′crete-ly.**

con-cur (kon-kûr′), *v.i.* [concurred, concur-ring], to agree or unite in action or opinion; as, all *concurred* in the decision.—*n.* **con-cur′rence.**—*adj.* **con-cur′rent.**

con-cus-sion (kon-kush′un), *n.* **1,** a shaking; shock; **2,** an injury, as to the brain or spine, from a blow or collision.

con-demn (kon-dem′), *v.t.* **1,** to blame; censure; declare to be wrong; as, to *condemn* television violence; **2,** to declare guilty; as, to *condemn* the guilty person to five years in prison; **3,** to declare to be forfeited or taken for public use; as, to *condemn* land; **4,** to pronounce unfit for use; as, to *condemn* a building because of fire damage.—*adj.* **con-dem′na-tor′y.**—*n.* **con′dem-na′tion.**

con-dense (kon-dens′), *v.t.* [condensed, condens-ing], **1,** to compress; make more close, compact, or dense; **2,** to reduce to fewer words; make shorter by taking out some parts; as, a condensed story; **3,** to change from a gas or vapour to a liquid, as steam to water; **4,** to increase in intensity, as an electric charge:—*v.i.* **1,** to become dense; **2,** to pass from gaseous or vaporous to liquid form.—*n.* **con′den-sa′tion; con-dens′er.**—*adj.* **con-densed′** (as, *condensed* milk).

con-de-scend (kon′de-send′), *v.i.* to stoop or come down voluntarily to the level of one's inferiors; show courtesies, often with a superior air; as, the great author *condescended* to join us.—*n.* **con′de-scen′sion.**

con-di-ment (kon′di-ment), *n.* a spicy seasoning for food, as pepper, mustard, relish, or ketchup.

con-di-tion (kon-dish′un), *n.* **1,** something that must exist if something else is to be or to take place; as, hard work is one of the *conditions* of success; **2,** state of being or of circumstances; as, the road is in bad *condition*; **3,** state of health; fitness for work, etc.; as, he is in good *condition*; **4,** rank; social position; as, a lady of high *con-*

dition:—**conditions,** a state of affairs; circumstances; as, poor working *conditions*:—*v.t.* **1,** to render fit; as, to *condition* a boxer; **2,** to be a condition for; as, health *conditions* success.—*adj.* **con-di′tioned.**

con-di-tion-al (kon-dish′un-al), *adj.* **1,** depending upon certain provisions or conditions; **2,** in *grammar,* containing a provisional clause; as, "if it rains, we will cancel the event."—*adv.* **con-di′tion-al-ly.**

con-do-lence (kon-dō′lens), *n.* expressed sympathy for another's sorrow; as, to send *condolences* over her loss.

con-do-min-i-um (kon′do-mi′nē-um), *n.* **1,** an apartment building in which each of the apartments is individually owned, rather than the whole building having one owner; **2,** an apartment in such a building. Also called *condo.*

con-done (kon-dōn′), *v.t.* [condoned, condon-ing], to forgive or overlook, as a fault or offence.—*n.* **con′do-na′tion.**

con-dor (kon′dor), *n.* a very large South American and Californian vulture found in the mountains.

con-duce (kon-dūs′), *v.i.* [conduced, conduc-ing], to lead or tend toward a result; contribute.—*adj.* **con-du′cive.**

con-duct (kon-dukt′), *v.t.* **1,** to guide; **2,** to manage; direct, as an orchestra; **3,** to behave (oneself); **4,** to carry; as, the canal *conducts* water; aluminum *conducts* heat; **5,** to carry on or carry out; as, to *conduct* a survey:—*v.i.* **1,** to direct; lead; **2,** to transmit electricity, heat, etc.:—*n.* (kon′dukt), **1,** personal behaviour or practice; **2,** management; guidance.—*n.* **con-duc′tion; con′duc-tiv′i-ty.**

con-duc-tor (kon-duk′tėr), *n.* **1,** a leader or guide; **2,** a manager; a director of a chorus or orchestra; **3,** an official who has charge of the passengers, collects fare, etc., on a bus, streetcar, or train; **4,** a substance that transmits energy; as, metals are good *conductors* of heat and electricity.

con-du-it (kon′doo-it; kon′dū-it), *n.* **1,** a canal or pipe for carrying water, etc.; **2,** an enclosed tube or passage for electric wires.

cone (kōn), *n.* **1,** a solid body that tapers uniformly to a point from a circular base; **2,** anything of similar shape; as, an ice-cream *cone*; **3,** the scaly, cone-shaped fruit of certain trees, as the pine, fir, etc.

con-fec-tion (kon-fek′shun), anything preserved in sugar; sweets; candy.

con-fec-tion-er-y (kon-fek′shun-er′i), *n.* [*pl.* confectioneries], **1,** candies, ice cream, cakes, etc.; **2,** the business of a confectioner.—*n.* **con-fec′tion-er.**

con-fed-er-a-cy (kon-fed′ėr-a-si), *n.* [*pl.* confederacies], a group or league made up of persons, states, or nations united for mutual support of any kind; an alliance; as, the Iroquois *confederacy*:—**the Confederacy,** the Confederate States of America: a league of 11 southern states that seceded from the United States in 1860 and 1861.

con-fed-er-ate (kon-fed′ėr-āt′), *v.t.* and *v.i.* [confederat-ed, confederat-ing], to unite in a league; as, Newfoundland *confederated* with Canada in 1949:—*adj.* (kon-fed′ėr-it), united by a league or agreement:—**Confederate,** pertaining to the U.S. Confederacy:—*n.* (kon-fed′ėr-it), **1,** a member of a league or union; **2,** an ally; accomplice:—**Confederate,** a person who sided with the U.S. Confederacy; a soldier of the U.S. Confederacy.

con-fed-er-a-tion (kon-fed′ėr-ā′shun), *n.* **1,** the act of forming an alliance or union, or the name of the alliance itself:—**Confederation,** the name given to the union of Ontario, Québec, Nova Scotia, and New Brunswick in 1867:—**the Confederation,** the 10 provinces and the territories of Canada.

con-fer (kon-fûr′), *v.t.* [conferred, conferring], to give or bestow; as, to *confer* a medal:—*v.i.* to consult with others; discuss; as, to *confer* with one's partner.

con-fer-ence (kon′fûr-ens; kon′frens), *n.* **1,** a meeting to discuss something; as, a teachers' *conference*; **2,** a group of teams or organizations; as, a football *conference*:—**press/media conference,** a meeting at which news reporters can ask questions.

con-fess (kon-fes′), *v.t.* **1,** to admit as true; esp., to acknowledge (a fault, crime, debt, etc.); **2,** to profess, as a religious belief; **3,** to hear a confession from: said of a priest:—*v.i.* **1,** to disclose the state of one's conscience to a priest; **2,** to make an acknowledgement or admission.

con-fes-sion (kon-fesh′un), *n.* **1,** the act of acknowledging or admitting; **2,** the act of making known one's sins to a priest; **3,** anything confessed.

con-fes-sor (kon-fes′ėr), *n.* **1,** one who admits or acknowledges a wrong; **2,** a priest who hears confessions.

con-fet-ti (kon-fet′i), *n.* small discs of coloured paper used in celebrating at weddings, festivals, etc.

con-fi-dant (kon′fi-dant′; kon′fi-dant′), *n.* an intimate friend to whom private matters are told.—*n.fem.* **con′fi-dante′.**

con-fide (kon-fīd′), *v.t.* [confid-ed, confid-ing], **1,** to put into another's trust or keeping; entrust; as, I will *confide* my daughter to your care; **2,** to tell in confidence; as, to *confide* your secret to me:—*v.i.* **1,** to have confidence or trust; as, to *confide* in military force; **2,** to entrust secrets; as, you can *confide* in me.—*adj.* **con-fid′ing.**

con-fi-dence (kon′fi-dens), *n.* **1,** belief; trust; as, I have *confidence* in his ability; **2,** boldness; self-assurance; as, he spoke with *confidence*; **3,** trusting intimacy; as, to speak in *confidence*; also, a secret.—*adj.*

con′fi-dent.—*adv.* **con′fi-dent-ly.**

con-fi-den-tial (kon′fi-den′shal), *adj.* **1,** private; secret; as, *confidential* information; also, intimate; as, he spoke in a *confidential* tone of voice; **2,** entrusted with secret matters; as, a *confidential* assistant.—*adv.* **con′fi-den′tial-ly.**

con-fig-u-ra-tion (kon-fig′ū-ra′shun), *n.* **1,** outline; contour; pattern; arrangement; as, the *configuration* of the constellation Orion; **2,** in *computing,* how hardware is arranged in a computer and selected options during set-up of the system.

con-fine (kon′fīn), *n.* a border, limit, or boundary; as, within the *confines* of a country:—*v.t.* (kon-fīn′), [confined, con-fin-ing], **1,** to restrict within limits; as, high dikes *confined* the sea; to *confine* an essay to a certain specific topic; **2,** to keep within doors; imprison; as, illness *confined* him to his room.—*n.* **con-fine′ment** (as, solitary *confinement*).

con-firm (kon-fûrm′), *v.t.* **1,** to establish more firmly; as, the book *confirms* my belief; **2,** to assure the truth of; verify; as, to *confirm* a report; **3,** to agree to or approve officially; as, the director *confirmed* the budget; **4,** to receive into church membership.—*n.* **con′fir-ma′tion.**

con-firmed (kon-fûrmd′), *adj.* settled, as in a habit; not likely to change; as, a *confirmed* bachelor.

con-fis-cate (kon′fis-kāt; kon-fis′kāt), *v.t.* [confiscat-ed, confiscat-ing], to take over (private property) by public authority, or by any authority; as, the police *confiscated* the smuggled goods; the teacher *confiscated* the student's comic books.—*n.* **con′fis-ca′tion.**

con-fla-gra-tion (kon′fla-grā′shun), *n.* a large and destructive fire.

con-flict (kon-flikt′), *v.i.* to clash; be in opposition; as, his story *conflicts* with mine:—*n.* (kon′flikt), **1,** a fight; struggle; battle; **2,** a clash between ideas, feelings, etc.; as, the *conflict* between duty and pleasure; **3,** a situation with opposing needs or conditions; as, to miss a meeting because of a *conflict* in your schedule:—**conflict of interest,** a situation in which a person has two opposing interests in the same matter.

con-flu-ence (kon′floo-ens), *n.* **1,** a flowing together, esp. of two rivers; **2,** the place where rivers flow together; **3,** a throng; crowd.—*adj.* **con′flu-ent.**

con-form (kon-fôrm′), *v.t.* to make like or similar; as, I will *conform* my tastes to yours:—*v.i.* to act in agreement with a standard, pattern, etc.; as, to *conform* to rules or to the ways of the world.—*n.* **con-form′ist; con-form-a′tion.**—*adj.* **con-form′a-ble.**

con-form-i-ty (kon-fôr′mi-ti), *n.* [*pl.* conformities], **1,** a correspondence in form, manner, or character; agreement; as, *conformity* of tastes; **2,** action in agreement with a standard, pattern, etc.; as, *conformity* to fashion.

con-found (kon-found′; kon′found′), *v.t.* **1,** to perplex; bewilder; confuse; **2,** to mistake for another; mix up; as, he *confounds* Kira with her twin; **3,** to damn: used as a mild curse.

con-front (kon-frunt′), *v.t.* **1,** to bring face to face; as, to *confront* a prisoner with evidence; **2,** to face defiantly or with hostility; as, to *confront* an enemy.—*n.* **con-fron-ta′tion.**—*adj.* **con-fron-ta′tion-al.**

con-fuse (kon-fūz′), *v.t.* [confused, confus-ing], **1,** to bewilder; perplex; embarrass; make uncertain; as, the difficult problem *confused* her; **2,** to mistake for another; as, to *confuse* the words "minor" and "miner."—*adv.* **con-fus′ed-ly.**

con-fu-sion (kon-fū′zhun), *n.* **1,** perplexity; loss of self-possession; as, in her *confusion,* she forgot to meet him; **2,** disorder; tumult; **3,** the mistaking of one person or thing for another.

con-geal (kon-jēl′), *v.t.* and *v.i.* to thicken by, or as if by, cold; as, fear *congealed* his blood.

con-gen-ial (kon-jēn′yal; kon-jē′ni-al), *adj.* **1,** sympathetic; having the same tastes; as, *congenial* friends; **2,** agreeable; naturally suited to one's nature; as, a *congenial* climate.—*adv.* **con-gen′ial-ly.**

con-gen-i-tal (kon-jen′i-tal), *adj.* existing at, or from, birth; as, a *congenital* disease, deformity, etc.; thus, a *congenital* liar.—*adv.* **con-gen′i-tal-ly.**

con-gest (kon-jest′), *v.t.* **1,** to cause (an organ or part of the body) to become too full of blood; **2,** to make too crowded; as, parades *congest* traffic.—*n.* **con-ges′tion.**

con-glom-er-ate (con-glom′er-ate), *n.* and *adj.* **1,** conglomeration or pertaining to conglomeration; as, a *conglomerate* rock; **2,** a large, diversified corporation:—*v.t.* and *v.i.* [conglomerat-ed, conglomerat-ing], to accumulate or gather in a mass; as, the members of the party *conglomerated* in the hall to listen to their leader's speech.

con-glom-er-a-tion (kon-glom′er-ā′shun), *n.* a compact mass or mixture of different things; as, a *conglomeration* of clay and pebbles, or of sense and nonsense.

con-grat-u-late (kon-grat′ū-lāt′) *v.t.* [congratulat-ed, congratulat-ing], to express sympathetic pleasure or praise to (a person) on account of some happy event or honour.—*adj.* **con-grat′u-la-tor′y.**—*n.* **con-grat′u-la′tion.**

con-gre-gate (kong′gre-gāt′), *v.i.* and *v.t.* [congregat-ed, congregat-ing], to assemble; gather together; as, people *congregated* in the town hall.

con-gre-ga-tion (kong′gre-gā′shun), *n.* **1,**

a gathering or collection of persons or things; **2,** a group of people meeting for religious worship or instruction.—*adj.* **con′gre-ga′tion-al.**

con-gress (kong′gres), *n.* **1,** a meeting, as of delegates for discussion; **2,** the chief lawmaking body of a republic:—**Canadian Labour Congress,** the Canadian confederation of trade unions:—**Congress,** the national lawmaking body of the U.S., composed of the Senate and the House of Representatives.—*adj.* **con-gres′sion-al.**—*n.* **con′gress–man; con′gress–wom′an.**

con-gru-ent (kong′groo-ent), *adj.* agreeing; corresponding; as, *congruent* triangles, which coincide when placed one over the other.—*n.* **con-gru′i-ty.**

con-ic (kon′ik), or **con-i-cal** (kon′i-kal), *adj.* shaped like a cone.

co-ni-fer (kō′ni-fėr; kon′i-fėr), *n.* a cone-bearing tree, as the spruce or pine, with evergreen needles.—*adj.* **co-nif′er-ous.**

con-jec-ture (kon-jek′tūr), *n.* the act of forming an opinion without definite proof; a guess:—*v.t.* and *v.i.* [conjectured, conjectur-ing], to guess.—*adj.* **con-jec′tur-al.**

con-join (kon-join′), *v.t.* and *v.i.* to join or connect together; unite; as, his memory and wit *conjoined* charmed his audience.—*adj.* **con-joined′.**—*adv.* **con-joint′ly.**

conjoined twins, identical twins, born with part of their bodies joined, and sometimes sharing organs. Also called *Siamese twins.*

con-ju-gal (kon′joo-gl), *adj.* of or relating to marriage; as, *conjugal* happiness.—*adv.* **con′ju-gal-ly.**—*n.* **con′ju-gal′i-ty.**

con-ju-gate (kon′joo-gāt′), *v.t.* [conjugated, conjugat-ing], in *grammar,* to give the various forms of (a verb) in order, as, "I am, you are, he is; we, you, they are."—*n.* **con-′ju-ga′tion.**

con-junc-tion (kon-jungk′shun), *n.* **1,** a joining together; union; as, to work in *conjunction* with someone; **2,** in *grammar,* a word, such as *and, if, but, as, or, though,* which is used to connect two words, phrases, clauses, or sentences.—*adj.* **con-junc′tive.**

con-jure (kon′joor; kun′jėr), *v.t.* [conjured, conjur-ing], **1,** to cause to appear or disappear as if by magic; **2,** (kon-jŏŏr′), to appeal to solemnly; implore; as, he *conjured* us to help:—*v.i.* to practise magical arts; also, to juggle.

con-jur-er or **con-jur-or** (kun′jėr-ėr), *n.* **1,** a magician; **2,** a juggler; **3,** a wizard.

conk (kongk), *v.t. Slang* to hit on the head:—**conk out,** to fail in operation, as the motor of a car or airplane; as, our car *conked out* before we reached our destination.

con-nect (ko-nekt′), *v.t.* **1,** to join or fasten together; as, a cable *connects* the keyboard to the computer; **2,** to join by personal relationship; as, to *connect* by marriage; **3,** to associate; as, I did not *connect* his name with his face:—*v.i.* to join; have a close relation.—*adj.* **con-nec′ting** (as, a *connecting* flight).

con-nec-tion (ko-nek′shun), *n.* **1,** the state of being joined; union; as, the *connection* of wires for the stereo system; **2,** the fact of being connected; as, a bad telephone *connection*; **3,** relationship by blood or marriage; hence, a relative, esp. a distant one; **4,** relationship by reason of a common interest or occupation; as, to make a good business *connection*; **5,** the linking of words or ideas in speech or thought; **6,** a connecting of two planes, trains, or other means of transportation; as, to have plenty of time to make our *connection* from Toronto to Edmonton.—*adj.* and *n.* **connec′tive.**

con-nive (ko-nīv′), *v.i.* [connived, conniving], to permit or help in secret what one should oppose or prevent; as, the jailer *connived* at his escape.—*n.* **con-niv′ance.**

con-nois-seur (kon′i-sûr′; -sûr′), *n.* one who is expert or competent in judging matters of art, taste, etc.

con-no-ta-tion (kon′ō-tā′shun), *n.* the suggested, implied, or associated significance, feeling, or atmosphere of a word, apart from its explicit meaning or denotation.—*v.t.* **con-note′**; thus, *house* connotes a refuge from the elements; *home,* a house plus warmth, love, toys, etc. Compare *denotation.*

con-quer (kong′kėr), *v.t.* **1,** to subdue by war; as, to *conquer* a country; **2,** to overcome by force of will, as a bad habit, fear, etc.; as, to *conquer* a fear of flying:—*v.i.* to be victorious.—*n.* **con′quer-or.**

con-quest (kong′kwest), *n.* a winning, subduing, or conquering, esp. by war; as, the Norman *Conquest* of England; also, that which is conquered, subdued, or won.

con-science (kon′shens), *n.* a sense of the rightness or wrongness of one's own acts; as, he has a guilty *conscience.*

con-sci-en-tious (kon′shi-en′shus), *adj.* **1,** careful to follow one's sense of right; as, a *conscientious* student; **2,** arising from one's feelings of right and wrong; as, *conscientious* objections.—*adv.* **con′sci-en′tious-ly.**—*n.* **con′sci-en′tious-ness.**

con-scious (kon′shus), *adj.* **1,** aware; as, *conscious* of a pain; to be *conscious* that she was not doing well in math; **2,** mentally awake; having possession of one's senses; as, the patient is *conscious*; **3,** known to oneself; done on purpose; intentional; as, a *conscious* sin.—*adv.* **con′scious-ly.**

con-scious-ness (kon′shus-nis), *n.* **1,** awareness of one's own existence, or of what is happening; being awake; as, when asleep, we lose *consciousness*; **2,** all that occurs in one's experience; one's sensations, thoughts, feelings, and actions; one's entire mental life.

con-script (kon-skript′), *v.t.* to force a (person) to serve in the army or navy; draft; also, to compel someone to do something; as, to *conscript* the children to clean up their rooms:—*adj.* (kon′skript), forced into military or naval service; as, a *conscript* army:—*n.* (kon′skript), a person so forced.—*n.* **con-scrip′tion.**

con-se-crate (kon′se-krāt′), *v.t.* [consecrat-ed, consecrat-ing], to set apart for a holy purpose; regard as sacred; as, to *consecrate* one's life to God; also, to devote oneself to something; as, to *consecrate* his life to art.—*n.* **con′se-cra′tion.**

con-sec-u-tive (kon-sek′ū-tiv), *adj.* following without a break; as, Monday and Tuesday are *consecutive* days.

con-sen-sus (kon-sen′sus), *n.* general agreement in opinion, testimony, or feeling; as, the *consensus* of the committee.

con-sent (kon-sent′), *n.* agreement; approval; compliance; as, by common *consent*:—*v.i.* to comply; yield; agree; give permission; as, the parents *consented* to let her go on the trip; he *consented* to buy the refreshments for the party.

con-se-quence (kon′se-kwens′), *n.* **1,** outcome; result; as, to suffer the *consequences* of an action; **2,** importance; as, a person of no *consequence*.

con-se-quent (kon′se-kwent′), *adj.* following as a result; as, the disorder *consequent* to the fire.—*adj.* **con′se-quen′tial.**

con-se-quent-ly (kon′se-kwent′li), *adv.* as a result; therefore; as, she slept in, and was *consequently* late for work.

con-ser-va-tion (kon′sėr-vā′shun), *n.* **1,** the act of conserving; **2,** the protection and careful use of natural resources, such as forests, lakes and rivers, minerals, and wild animals.—*n.* **con-ser-va′tion-ist** (someone who supports the conservation of the environment).

con-serv-a-tive (kon-sûr′va-tiv), *adj.* **1,** inclined to prefer existing institutions to new ones: in *politics,* conservatives generally believe that the government should hold to the values of the past and take a limited role in human affairs; **2,** not taking chances; cautious or careful; as, to be *conservative* about spending money; **3,** following a modest style; not showy; as, to dress in a *conservative* manner:—*n.* a conservative person.—*adv.* **con-serv′a-tive-ly.**

Conservative Party, in Canada, same as the **Progressive Conservative Party.**

con-serv-a-tor-y (kon-sûr′va-tėr-i), *n.* [*pl.* conservatories], **1,** a greenhouse, esp. a private one; **2,** a college for special study, as of music.

con-serve (kon-sûrv′), *v.t.* [conserved, con-serv-ing], **1,** to keep from waste or destruction; as, to *conserve* endangered species; **2,** to preserve with sugar:—*n.* (kon-sûrv′; kon′sûrv), preserved or candied fruit:—**conserves**, preserves; jam.—*n.* **con′ser-va′tor.**

con-sid-er (kon-sid′ėr), *v.t.* **1,** to think over with care; as, to *consider* the effects of one's actions; **2,** to take into account; allow for; as, to *consider* the price before buying; **3,** to respect; be thoughtful of; as, to *consider* the feelings of others; **4,** to regard as; believe; as, I *consider* him rude:—*v.i.* to reflect; as, to take time to *consider*.—*adj.* **con-sid′ered** (as, a doctor's *considered* opinion).

con-sid-er-a-ble (kon-sid′ėr-a-bl), *adj.* worthy of notice; important; not small; rather large; as, a *considerable* sum of money.—*adv.* **con-sid′er-a-bly.**

con-sid-er-ate (kon-sid′ėr-it), *adj.* thoughtful of others; kindly.—*adv.* **con-sid′er-ate-ly.**

con-sid-er-a-tion (kon-sid′ėr-ā′shun), *n.* **1,** careful thought; as, to take a thing into *consideration*; **2,** something taken, or worth taking, into account; a reason or motive; as, safety is the most important *consideration*; **3,** thoughtful regard for others; as, *consideration* for one's neighbours; **4,** payment or compensation for something; as, to get a small *consideration* for doing the job.

con-sid-er-ing (kon-sid′ėr-ing), *prep.* taking into account; allowing for; as, crops are good, *considering* the drought.

con-sign (kon-sīn′), *v.t.* **1,** to deliver formally; hand over; as, to *consign* a man to prison; **2,** to send, as merchandise; **3,** to assign.—*n.* **con-sign′ment.**—*n.* **con′sign-ee′.**

con-sist (kon-sist′), *v.i.* to be composed or made up; as, a day *consists* of 24 hours.

con-sist-en-cy (kon-sis′ten-si), *n.* [*pl.* consistencies], **1,** degree of firmness or thickness; as, this liquid has the *consistency* of syrup; **2,** harmony; agreement, as of one's deeds with one's statements.—*n.* **con-sist′ence.**

con-sist-ent (kon-sis′tent), *adj.* **1,** fitting in; in agreement; as, his story is *consistent* with facts; **2,** continuing without change, or with adherence to the same principles; as, a *consistent* Tory.—*adv.* **con-sist′ent-ly.**

[1]**con-sole** (kon-sōl′), *v.t.* [consoled, consol-ing], to comfort in sorrow.—*n.* **con′so-la′tion.**—*adj.* **con-sol′a-tor′y.**—*adj.* **con-sol′a-ble.**

[2]**con-sole** (kon′sōl), *n.* **1,** the part of a pipe organ at which the organist sits, containing the keyboard, stops, and pedals; **2,** a cabinet for a radio, television, etc., that sits directly on the floor; **3,** a display or control panel to monitor and interact with electrical devices such as a computer; **4,** a small

storage or control panel between bucket seats in a car; **5,** a cabinet or a table designed to stand against a wall.

con-sol-i-date (kon-sol′i-dāt′), *v.t.* and *v.i.* [consolidat-ed, consolidat-ing], to unite; combine; as, to *consolidate* two offices.—*n.* **con-sol′i-da′tion.**

con-som-mé (kon′so-mā′), *n.* a strong, clear soup made by boiling meat, vegetables, etc., in water.

con-so-nant (kon′so-nant), *n.* **1,** a sound made by closing or narrowing the mouth or throat, or by blocking the air by the lips, teeth, or tongue; **2,** a symbol of such a sound, that is not a vowel, as *b, c, d, f,* etc.:—*adj.* **1,** like a consonant; as, a *consonant* sound; **2,** harmonious; consistent; agreeing; as, an act *consonant* with one's beliefs.—*adv.* **con′so-nant′ly.**

con-sort (kon′sôrt), *n.* **1,** a husband or wife, esp. of a king or queen; **2,** an associate; **3,** a ship accompanying another:—*v.i.* (kon-sôrt′), to associate; keep company.

con-spic-u-ous (kon-spik′ū-us), *adj.* **1,** plainly visible; as, a *conspicuous* mistake; hence, striking; attracting attention; as, a *conspicuous* costume; **2,** distinguished; notable; as, the play was a *conspicuous* success.—*adv.* **con-spic′u-ous-ly.**

con-spire (kon-spīr′), *v.i.* [conspired, conspir-ing], **1,** to plan secretly together to do something unlawful; plot; **2,** to work with other factors toward a given result; as, events *conspired* to injure him.—*n.* **con-spir′a-cy** (kon-spir′a-si).—*n.* **con-spir′a-tor.**

con-sta-ble (kon′sta-bl; kun′sta-bl), *n.* a police officer, esp. one having minor duties.

con-stab-u-lar-y (kon-stab′ū-lẽr-i), *n.* [*pl.* constabularies], an armed force organized for police duty; provincial police.

con-stant (kon′stant), *adj.* **1,** standing firm in one's beliefs or affections; steadfast; faithful; as, a *constant* friend; **2,** regular in a habit; unchanging; as, *constant* speed; **3,** not stopping; going on all the time; as, *constant* rain; **4,** happening over and over; continuous; as, *constant* use of the school's computers.—*n.* **con′stan-cy.**—*adv.* **con′stant-ly.**

con-stel-la-tion (kon′ste-lā′shun), *n.* any group of fixed stars that form a pattern in the sky with a special name, as the Big Dipper, Sagittarius, etc.

THE CONSTELLATION SAGITTARIUS

con-ster-na-tion (kon′stẽr-nā′shun), *n.* terrified astonishment; dismay.

con-sti-pa-tion (kon′sti-pā′shun), *n.* a condition in which the bowels do not move freely enough.—*adj.* **con′sti-pat′ed.**—*v.* **con′sti-pate′.**

con-stit-u-en-cy (kon-stit′ū-en-si), *n.* [*pl.* constituencies], **1,** in Canada, an area that has its own representative in a provincial or federal government: also called *riding;* **2,** voters in such an area who elect a representative, as to Parliament.

con-stit-u-ent (kon-stit′ū-ent), *adj.* **1,** necessary in the make-up of something; as, a *constituent* part; **2,** being able to change a political constitution; as, a *constituent* assembly:—*n.* **1,** a necessary part; as, flour is a *constituent* of cake; **2,** a voter in a given district; as, the member addressed her *constituents.*

con-sti-tute (kon′sti-tūt′), *v.t.* [constitut-ed, constitut-ing], **1,** to make up or form; compose; as, 12 items *constitute* a dozen; **2,** to appoint; elect; as, he *constituted* himself judge of the contest.

con-sti-tu-tion (kon′sti-tū′shun), *n.* **1,** the way in which a thing is made up; as, the *constitution* of the earth; **2,** bodily strength; vitality; **3,** the fundamental law on which a nation, state, or group is organized; as, the national *constitution;* the organization's *constitution:*—**Constitution,** in Canada, the fundamental laws by which the country is governed: the Constitution Act of 1982 includes the *Charter of Rights and Freedoms.*

con-sti-tu-tion-al (kon′sti-tū′shun-al), *adj.* **1,** inherent in one's make-up; as, a *constitutional* liability to colds; **2,** relating to the fundamental law of a nation, state, or society; as, a *constitutional* amendment; *constitutional* monarchy; also, in harmony with such law:—*n. Colloq.* a walk taken for health's sake.

con-sti-tu-tion-al-i-ty (kon′sti-tū′shun-al′i-ti), *n.* agreement with the constitution, or fundamental law; as, the *constitutionality* of an act of Parliament.

con-strain (kon-strān′), *v.t.* **1,** to hold in check; restrain; as, the presence of the referee *constrained* the hockey players; **2,** to urge strongly; compel; as, to *constrain* a child to eat her vegetables.—*n.* **constraint′.**

con-strict (kon-strikt′), *v.t.* to bind; tighten; contract; draw together or make narrow at a single place; as, a tourniquet was applied around his cut to *constrict* the blood vessels so that the blood stopped flowing.—*n.* **con-stric′tion; con-stric′tor.**—*adj.* **con-stric′tive.**

con-struct (kon-strukt′), *v.t.* **1,** to fit together; arrange; build, as a house; **2,** to plan; compose; as, to *construct* a play.

con-struc-tion (kon-struk′shun), **1,** a putting together; the act or method of building; as, fireproof *construction;* also, the thing built; **2,** the business or work of building houses, apartments, offices, etc; as, a summer job in *construction;* **3,** understanding; as, to put a wrong *construction* on a letter; **4,** in *grammar,* the way in which words are related to one another in a sentence.

con-struc-tive (kon-struk′tiv), *adj.* tending to build up rather than to destroy; creative; helping to make better or useful; as, *constructive* ideas; *constructive* criticism.

con-strue (kon′strōō; kon-strōō′), *v.t.* [construed, constru-ing], **1,** to interpret; explain; as, his act was *construed* as a favour; **2,** in *grammar*, to apply the rules of syntax to (a sentence).

con-sul (kon′sul), *n.* **1,** an official commissioned by a government to promote his or her country's trade in a foreign city, and to protect its citizens; **2,** one of the two joint chief officials of the Roman Republic.—*adj.* **con′su-lar.**—*n.* **con′su-late.**

con-sult (kon-sult′), *v.t.* **1,** to ask advice of; **2,** to have regard to; as, he *consulted* my welfare:—*v.i.* to take counsel together; confer.—*n.* **con′sul-ta′tion.**

con-sult-ant (kon-sul′tant), *n.* a person who gives expert or professional advice.

con-sume (kon-sūm′), *v.t.* [consumed, consum-ing], **1,** to destroy, as by fire; as, the fire *consumed* most of the forest; **2,** to use up; waste; as, a car *consumes* fuel; leaving the lights on all the time *consumes* energy; **3,** to eat or drink, esp. a large amount; as, to *consume* several litres of water due to thirst; **4,** to take up all the attention or energy of; as, work *consumes* most of her time.—*n.* **con-sum′a-ble.**

con-sum-er (kon-sūm′ėr), *n.* a person or thing that consumes anything; esp., a person who buys goods to be used by himself or herself.

con-sum-mate (kon′su-māt′), *v.t.* [consummat-ed, consummat-ing], to complete; finish; fulfill; as, to *consummate* her life's ambition; to *consummate* a marriage (through sexual intercourse):—*adj.* (kon-sum′it; kän′sum-it), perfect; carried to the highest degree; as, a musician of *consummate* ability.—*n.* **con′sum-ma′tion.**

con-sump-tion (kon-sump′shun), *n.* **1,** a using up, as of food, energy, or other materials; also, the amount used up; **2,** tuberculosis of the lungs.—*adj.* **con-sump′tive.**

con-tact (kon′takt), *n.* **1,** a touch; touching; as, the *contact* of the plane wheels with the runway; **2,** a relation or connection; a meeting for conversation or consultation; **3,** an acquaintance that makes such a meeting possible or that can be of help or influence; as, he makes advantageous business *contacts*:—*v.i.* to touch together:—*v.t.* to get in touch with; as, to *contact* someone for more information.

contact lens, a thin plastic lens fitted over the pupil of the eyeball to correct faulty vision.

con-ta-gious (kon-tā′jus), *adj.* **1,** spreading easily from person to person; as, a *contagious* disease; **2,** exciting a similar action or feeling in others; as, *contagious* laughter.—*n.* **con-ta′gion; con-ta′gious-ness.**

con-tain (kon-tān′), *v.t.* **1,** to hold; as, the box *contained* video games; the bucket *contained* water; **2,** to include; as, ice cream *contains* sugar; **3,** to be equal to; as, a kilogram *contains* 1000 grams; **4,** to hold in check; as, to *contain* one's anger; **5,** to be a multiple of; as, 20 *contains* two, four, five, and 10.

con-tain-er (kon-tān′ėr), *n.* a receptacle used to hold or contain something, such as a box, can, bottle, jar, etc.

con-tam-i-nate (kon-tam′i-nāt′), *v.t.* [contaminat-ed, contaminat-ing], to pollute; make impure.—*n.* **con-tam′i-na′tion.**

con-tem-plate (kon′tem-plāt′), *v.t.* [contemplat-ed, contemplat-ing], **1,** to look at or to think about with attention; meditate on; as, to *contemplate* a painting; **2,** to intend; purpose; expect; as, not the results she had *contemplated*:—*v.i.* to meditate; reflect.—*n.* **con′tem-pla′tion.**—*adj.* **con′tem-pla-tive.**

con-tem-po-rar-y (kon-tem′po-rėr-i), *adj.* **1,** existing or occurring at the same time:—*n.* [*pl.* contemporaries], one who lives at the same time as another; as, Macdonald and Laurier were *contemporaries*; **2,** current; modern; as, Dennis Lee is a *contemporary* Canadian poet.

con-tempt (kon-tempt′), *n.* **1,** scorn, as of vile or mean acts; disdain; **2,** the state of being despised; disgrace; **3,** disregard of lawful orders; the crime of failing to obey or show respect for a judge or for proper courtroom procedure; as, *contempt* of court.—*adj.* **con-tempt′i-ble.**

con-temp-tu-ous (kon-temp′tū-us), *adj.* disdainful; scornful; as, a *contemptuous* smile.—*adv.* **con-temp′tu-ous-ly.**

con-tend (kon-tend′), *v.i.* **1,** to strive against opponents, as for a prize; **2,** to dispute; debate; claim; as, to *contend* that running is good for one's health; **3,** to fight or struggle; as, to *contend* with harsh conditions.—*n.* **con-tend′er.**

[1]**con-tent** (kon′tent; sometimes kon-tent′), *n.* **1,** the subject matter or thought, as of a magazine article, letter, etc.; **2,** (usually *contents*), all that is contained, as in a receptacle or book; also, the capacity, as of a measure:—**table of contents,** a list of chapter or section headings in a book, magazine, etc,

[2]**con-tent** (kon-tent′), *adj.* **1,** satisfied; happy; **2,** willing; as, I am *content* to go:—*v.t.* to satisfy; as, he is easily *contented*:—*n.* ease of mind.—*n.* **con-tent′ment.**—*adj.* **con-tent′ed.**

con-ten-tion (kon-ten′shun), *n.* **1,** a striving or struggling; dispute; quarrel; **2,** a point for which one argues; as, my *contention* is that the price is too high.

con-ten-tious (kon-ten′shus), *adj.* inclined to argue about trivial matters; quarrelsome.—*n.* **con-ten′tious-ness.**

con-test (kon-test′), *v.t.* to strive to win or hold, as a battlefield; to compete; **2,** to dispute; call in question; as, to *contest* an election:—*n.* (kon′test), a struggle for victory, as a game, race, fight, lawsuit, etc.; a competition or struggle; as, a dance *contest;* a science *contest.*—*n.* **con-test′ant.**

con-text (kon′tekst), *n.* the words just before and after a particular word, expression, or passage that determine its exact meaning; as, please do not quote me out of *context.*

con-tig-u-ous (kon-tig′ū-us), *adj.* touching; adjoining; also, near; as, a field *contiguous* to the village.—*adv.* **con-tig′u-ous-ly.**—*n.* **con-′ti-gu′i-ty.**

con-tin-ence (kon′tin-ens), *n.* self-restraint; moderation; esp., abstinence from sexual intercourse; also, the ability to control bowel discharge.

con-ti-nent (kon′ti-nent), *n.* one of the large divisions of land on the earth; as, the *continent* of North America:—**the Continent**, the mainland of Europe as distinguished from Great Britain:—*adj.* temperate; not indulging in passions; esp., sexually chaste; also, being able to control bowel or bladder discharge.

con-ti-nen-tal (kon′ti-nen′tal), *adj.* relating to a continent:—**Continental, 1,** relating to the mainland of Europe; as, *Continental* food; **2,** in U.S., having to do with the 13 colonies at the time of the Revolution; as, the *Continental* Congress:—*n.* **1,** an American soldier during the Revolution; **2,** an inhabitant of the mainland of Europe:—**continental shelf**, the relatively shallow slope of a continent beneath the sea before the steep descent to the ocean floor begins.

con-tin-gen-cy (kon-tin′-jen-si), *n.* [*pl.* contingencies], possibility; also, an event that may or may not happen; as, ready for any *contingency.*

con-tin-gent (kon-tin′jent), *adj.* **1,** possible, but uncertain; also, accidental; **2,** depending on something else, or on chance; as, her coming is *contingent* on the weather:—*n.* any unit or group in a gathering of representative units; as, the Alberta *contingent* at the convention.

con-tin-u-al (kon-tin′u-al), *adj.* **1,** occurring again and again; frequent; as, *continual* phone calls; **2,** going on without a break; ceaseless; as, *continual* snow.—*adv.* **con-tin′u-al-ly.**

con-tin-ue (kon-tin′ū), *v.t.* [continued, continu-ing], **1,** to keep on doing, without a break; as, he *continued* singing; also, to persevere in; **2,** to take up again after a break, as a story; **3,** to keep in office; **4,** to postpone, as a law case:—*v.i.* **1,** to remain in a place or condition; stay; as, to *continue* to work; **2,** to last; persist.—*n.* **con-tin′u-ance; con-tin′u-a′ tion.**

con-ti-nu-i-ty (kon′ti-nū′i-ti), *n.* [*pl.* continuities], **1,** unbroken succession; connectedness; **2,** a movie, television show, or play scenario; **3,** transitional remarks by a radio or television announcer, connecting the items on a program.

con-tin-u-ous (kon-tin′ū-us), *adj.* connected; unbroken.—*adv.* **con-tin′u-ous-ly.**

con-tort (kon-tôrt′), *v.t.* to bend or twist violently out of shape; distort.—*n.* **con-tor′tion; con-tor′tion-ist.**

con-tour (kon′toor; kon-to͝or′), *n.* an outline, as of a body, coast, mountain, etc.; also, an outline drawing:—*adj.* showing or fitting an outline or shape; as, a *contour* chair or seat; *contour* drawing:—**contour map**, a map with lines joining points of the same elevation above sea level:—*v.t.* to shape, fit, or show an outline or shape; to conform to a contour; as, a chair that *contoured* her body; sheets that *contoured* the bed; to *contour* a map.

con-tra-band (kon′tra-band′), *n.* **1,** anything forbidden to be brought into or out of a country, as firearms, endangered species, drugs, etc.; also, traffic in such goods; smuggling; **2,** smuggled goods:—*adj.* prohibited; forbidden.

con-tra-cep-tive (kon′tra-sep′tiv), *adj.* and *n.* a device or agent for the artificial prevention of conception.

con-tract (kon-trakt′), *v.t.* **1,** to draw closer together; condense; shorten and thicken, as a muscle; to make smaller; to wrinkle; as, to *contract* the brows; **2,** to get something bad; incur (a debt, disease, habit, etc.); **3,** (often kon′trakt), to enter upon by agreement, as an alliance or a marriage; **4,** in *grammar*, to shorten; as, to *contract* "do not" to "don't":—*v.i.* **1,** to shrink; **2,** (often kon′trakt), to make an agreement; as, to *contract* for the removal of snow:—*n.* (kon′trakt), **1,** a legal agreement between two or more people or groups; also, a written record of such an agreement; **2,** in cards, an undertaking to win a given number of tricks.

con-trac-tion (kon-trak′shun), *n.* **1,** a word formed by putting together two words with a certain letter or letters left out; as, "they're" is a *contraction* of "they are"; **2,** the act of contracting; as, the *contraction* of the heart.

con-trac-tor (kon-trak′tėr; kon′trak-tėr), *n.* **1,** one of the parties to a written agreement; **2,** one who undertakes to supply or construct something for a certain sum.

con-tra-dict (kon′tra-dikt′), *v.t.* **1,** to assert the opposite of (a statement); **2,** to deny the words of (a person).—*n.* **con′tra-dic′tion.**—*adj.* **con′tra-dic′to-ry.**

con-tral-to (kon-tral′tō), *n.* [*pl.* contraltos], **1,** the lowest female voice or part; **2,** a person with such a voice.

con-trap-tion (kon-trap′shun), *n. Colloq.* a gadget; makeshift device.

con-tra-ry (kon′trėr-i), *adj.* **1,** opposed; contradictory; conflicting; as, *contrary* opinions; **2,** opposite in direction; adverse; as, a *contrary* wind; **3,** (often kon-trâr′i), perverse; wayward; stubborn; liking to argue or oppose:—*n.* [*pl.* contraries], the opposite; as, if he says one thing, I believe the *contrary*; to the *contrary*, she does enjoy studying.—*adv.* **con′tra-ri-wise′** (conversely).

con-trast (kon-tråst′), *v.t.* to place or state in such a way as to show differences; compare so as to show unlikeness; as, to *contrast* these two species of animals:—*v.i.* to be very different, as shown by comparison; as, the white rose *contrasts* with her black dress:—*n.* (kon′trast), **1,** striking difference; opposition; **2,** the thing or quality showing such difference.

con-tra-vene (kon′tra-vēn′), *v.t.* to go contrary to; disobey; infringe; as, do not *contravene* the traffic laws.—*n.* **con′tra-ven′tion.**

con-trib-ute (kon-trib′ūt), *v.t.* [contribut-ed, contribut-ing], to give, as to some fund or purpose, alone or with others; furnish as a share; as, to *contribute* food and time to the food bank; to *contribute* toward the gift:—*v.i.* **1,** to help; assist; aid in the accomplishment of a purpose; as, every player *contributed* to the victory; **2,** to be of use; as, eating fruits and vegetables *contributes* to health.—*n.* **con′tri-bu′tion; con-trib′u-tor.**—*adj.* **con-trib′u-to′ry.**

con-trite (kon′trīt; kon-trīt′), *adj.* humble; repentant.—*n.* **con-tri′tion** (kon-trish′un).

con-trive (kon-trīv′), *v.t.* [contrived, con-triv-ing], **1,** to devise cleverly; invent; plan; **2,** to achieve by clever management; as, to *contrive* an escape.—*n.* **con-triv′ance.**

con-trol (kon-trōl′), *n.* **1,** a check; restraint; as, *control* of one's temper; **2,** effective authority; as, a teacher's *control* over a class:—**controls,** the instruments used to run a machine; as, the *controls* of an airplane:—*v.t.* [controlled, control-ling], **1,** to restrain; hold in check; as, to *control* one's anger; **2,** to govern; have power over, rule; **3,** to regulate; as, this dial *controls* the heat.

con-trol-ler (kon-trōl′ėr), *n.* **1,** a public official who examines accounts; **2,** someone or something that controls or regulates something; as, an air-traffic *controller;* **3,** a member of a board of control; **4,** in *computing,* an apparatus that controls and links several peripherals to a computer.

con-tro-ver-sy (kon′trō-vûr′si), *n.* [*pl.* controversies], a dispute; an argument.—*adj.* **con′tro-ver′sial.**

con-tro-vert (kon′trō-vûrt′; kon′trō-vûrt′), *v.t.* to dispute; contradict; oppose; as, he *controverts* your claim that he won the race.—*adj.* **con′tro-vert′i-ble.**

con-tu-sion (kon-tū′zhun), *n.* a bruise.

co-nun-drum (ko-nun′drum), *n.* a riddle.

con-va-les-cent (kon′va-les′ent), *adj.* **1,** getting well; as, a *convalescent* patient; **2,** having to do with recovery from an illness; as, a *convalescent* facility:—*n.* one who is getting well.—*n.* **con′va-les′cence.**—*v.i.* **con′va-lesce′.**

con-vec-tion (kon-vek′shun), *n.* the conveying of heat or electricity by the movement of heated or electrified gases or liquids:—**convection oven,** a small or full-size oven that quickly cooks food using forced heated air.

con-vene (kon-vēn′), *v.i.* and *v.t.* [convened, conven-ing], to come or call together; assemble.—*n.* **con-ven′er.**

con-ven-ience (kon-vēn′yens), *n.* **1,** suitability; fitness of place or time; **2,** ease in use or action; a saving of trouble or time; advantage; as, the *convenience* of a car; **3,** a handy device; **4, conveniences,** things that add to personal comfort, make work easier, etc.

con-ven-ient (kon-vēn′yent), *adj.* **1,** suited to one's needs or purposes; right for the situation; as, to meet at a *convenient* time; **2,** easy to reach or get to; handy; as, the house is *convenient* to the store.—*adv.* **con-ven′ient-ly.**

con-vent (kon′vent), *n.* a society, usually of women, living together and devoted to a religious life; also, the building occupied by such a society; a nunnery.

con-ven-tion (kon-ven′shun), *n.* **1,** a formal meeting; an assembly of delegates; as, a political *convention;* **2,** a diplomatic agreement; **3,** a fixed custom or usage; accepted way of acting; as, tipping is a North American *convention.*

con-ven-tion-al (kon-ven′shun-al), *adj.* **1,** in harmony with established customs; customary; as, *conventional* business clothes; **2,** regular; lacking in original thought; commonplace; as, to have *conventional* taste in food.—*n.* **con-ven′tion-al′i-ty.**

con-verge (kon-vûrj′), *v.i.* [converged, converg-ing], to tend to come together, as crowds at a place of interest; to approach each other, as spokes of a wheel, or lines drawn toward a common point.—*adj.* **con-ver′gent.**—*n.* **con-ver′gence.**

con-ver-sa-tion (kon′vėr-sā′shun), *n.* informal or familiar talk of persons with one another.—*adj.* **con′ver-sa′tion-al.**

[1]con-verse (kon-vûrs′), *v.i.* [conversed, convers-ing], to chat with a person:—*n.* (kon′vûrs), familiar talk; conversation.—*adj.* **con-ver′sant** (familiar).

[2]con-verse (kon′vûrs), *adj.* opposite:—*n.* the opposite of something else; as, "hot" is the *converse* of "cold."—*adv.* **con′verse-ly** (kon′vûrs-li; kon-vûrs′li).

con-vert (kon-vûrt′), *v.t.* **1,** to transform or change, as in form, substance, etc.; as, to *convert* the den into a home office; **2,** to bring (a person) to belief in a religion, course, opinion, etc.; **3,** to exchange for something else, as Canadian dollars to U.S. dollars:—*n.* (kon′vûrt), one who becomes a believer in something, as a religion or a political party; as, a *convert* to Islam; **2,** in *football*, the kicking of a field goal after a touchdown to score an extra point.—*n.* **con-ver′sion.**

con-ver-ti-ble (kon-vûr′ti-bl), *adj.* capable of being changed or transformed.—*n.* a car with a folding top.

con-vex (kon′veks; kon-veks′), *adj.* curved out like the outside of a circle, spoon, or ball; bulging; as, a *convex* mirror: opposite of *concave.*—*n.* **con-vex′i-ty.**

THE OUTSIDE OF THE BOWL IS CONVEX.

con-vey (kon-vā′), *v.t.* **1,** to carry; transport; as, the train *conveyed* the children to the mountains; **2,** to transmit; be a means of carrying; as, pipes *convey* gas; the cable *conveys* power to the computer; **3,** to transfer (property) from one person to another; **4,** to communicate some thought or feeling; make known; as, to *convey* agreement with a smile and a nod of the head.—*n.* **con-vey′er; con-vey′or; con-vey′or belt′.**

con-vey-ance (kon-vā′ans), *n.* **1,** the act of carrying from one place or person to another; **2,** anything used for carrying; esp., a vehicle; **3,** communication; **4,** a written title or deed to property.

con-vict (kon-vikt′), *v.t.* to prove or find guilty of a crime or offence:—*n.* (kon′vikt), **1,** a person found guilty of a crime; **2,** a person serving a term in prison.

con-vic-tion (kon-vik′shun), *n.* **1,** the finding that someone is guilty of a crime or offence; also, the state of being found guilty; **2,** a firm or settled belief.

con-vince (kon-vins′), *v.t.* [convinced, convinc-ing], to cause (a person) to see or feel a certain way about something; persuade.—*adj.* **con-vinc′ing.**—*adv.* **con-vinc′ing-ly.**

con-viv-i-al (kon-viv′i-al), *adj.* **1,** fond of feasting, drinking, merriment, etc.; **2,** happy; jovial.

con-voke (kon-vōk′), *v.t.* [convoked, convok-ing], to call together for a meeting; as, Parliament was *convoked* in June.—*n.* **con′vo-ca′tion.**

con-vo-lu-ted (kon′vō-lū′tid), *adj.* **1,** coiled, wound, folded together; **2,** complicated, involved; intricate; as, a *convoluted* plot in a story.—*n.* **con-vo-lu′tion.**

con-voy (kon-voi′), *v.t.* to accompany on the way, so as to guide or protect; to escort; as, the cruiser *convoyed* our ship into port:—*n.* (kon′voi), **1,** a protecting force accompanying ships, goods, persons, etc.; an escort; as, a *convoy* of trucks; **2,** the goods, ships, persons, etc., so escorted.

con-vulse (kon-vuls′), *v.t.* [convulsed, convuls-ing], **1,** to agitate or disturb violently; shake; **2,** to affect with spasms, as of laughter or anger.—*n.* **con-vul′sion.**—*adj.* **con-vul′sive.**

cook (kook), *v.t.* **1,** to prepare (food) by applying heat, as in boiling, baking, grilling, frying, microwaving, etc.; **2,** to invent falsely; as, to *cook* up an excuse:—*v.i.* to undergo cooking:—*n.* one who prepares food for the table.—*n.* **cook′er; cook′ing; cook′book′; cook′out′; cook′er-y.**

cook-ie (kook′i), *n.* [*pl.* cookies], **1,** a small, flat, sweet cake; **2,** in *computing*, a string of data recorded on a hard disk by a Web server to track the user's activities, likes, and dislikes at particular Web sites, accessed each time sites are visited.

cool (kōōl), *adj.* **1,** slightly or moderately cold; **2,** not admitting or retaining heat; as, *cool* clothes; **3,** calm; self-possessed; as, he was the only *cool* one in the mob; **4,** lacking in cordiality; as, a *cool* response; **5,** *Slang* excellent; hip; fashionable:—*v.t.* **1,** to make slightly cold; chill; **2,** to calm; quiet; as, his tears *cooled* my anger:—*v.i.* to become slightly cold:—*n.* a state or time of moderate cold; as, the *cool* of the evening.—*adj.* **cool′ish; cool′–head′ed.**—*adv.* **cool′ly.**—*n.* **cool′er; cool′ness.**

coop (kōōp), *n.* a cage or enclosure for fowl, rabbits, etc.; a pen:—*v.t.* to confine in a cage or pen; as, to be *cooped* up all day.

co-op-er-ate or **co–op-er-ate** (kō-op′ėr-āt′), *v.i.* [co-operat-ed, co-operat-ing], to act or work for a common end; work together; as, everyone *cooperated* in making the play a success.—*n.* **co-op′er-a′tion.**

co-op-er-a-tive or **co–op-er-a-tive** (kō-op′ėr-a-tiv; -ā′tiv), *adj.* **1,** working together for common ends; **2,** having to do with an organized group of people who work together for common ends and share their profits and losses; as, a *cooperative* shop for students.—*n.* **co–op,** *Colloq.* short form for *cooperative shop* or *store.*

co–opt (kō′–opt), *v.t.* to add or elect by combined action one or more persons to a committee, board, etc.

co-or-di-nate or **co–or-di-nate** (kō-ôr′di-nāt′), *v.t.* [co-ordinat-ed, co-ordinat-ing], **1,** to place in the same order or class; to make equal in rank or importance; **2,** to put in harmony; adjust; as, to *coordinate* movements in swimming; **3,** to orchestrate; organize; as, to *coordinate* an event, conference, etc.:—*v.i.* to harmonize:—*adj.* (kō–ôr′di-nit; nāt′), **1,** of the same rank or order, as the clauses of a compound sentence; **2,** pertaining to things of the same rank:—*n.* (kō-ôr′di-nit; nāt′), a person or thing of the same rank, order, or importance as another; an equal.—*n.* **co-or′di-na′tion.**—*adj.* **co-or′di-nat-ed.**

coo-tie (kōō′ti), *n. Slang* a louse.

cop (kop), *n. Colloq.* a police officer (*con*stable *o*n *p*atrol):—*v.t. Slang* to steal; seize; capture.

cope (kōp), *v.i.* [coped, cop-ing], to struggle or handle a difficult situation successfully; as, he is able to *cope* with difficulties.

co-pi-lot (kō′pī′lot), *n.* an assistant pilot in an aircraft.

cop-ing (kōp′ing), *n.* the top layer of a wall, often of brick or stone, usually sloping so as to shed water.

co-pi-ous (kō′pi-us), *adj.* plenteous; ample; abundant; as, a *copious* supply of pencils.—*adv.* **co′pi-ous-ly.**

cop-per (kop′ėr), *n.* **1,** a common reddish metal, easily worked, and an excellent conductor of heat and electricity: used to make pennies and other coins, electrical wire, and other products; **2,** something made of this metal; **3,** a coin, usually made of copper but sometimes of bronze; a cent:—*adj.* of or like copper.—*adj.* **cop′per-y.**

cop-u-late (kop′ū-lāt′), *v.i.* to unite in sexual intercourse.—*n.* **cop′u-la′tion.**

cop-y (kop′i), *n.* [*pl.* copies], **1,** an imitation; a reproduction; as, a *copy* of a portrait, dress, will, etc.; **2,** something to be set up in type, as a book, magazine, newspaper, etc.; **3,** a single one of a number of reproductions, as of a book, magazine, newspaper, tape, CD, etc.:—**copier (photocopier),** a machine that makes copies of letters, photographs, pictures, and other documents:—*v.t.* [copied, copy-ing], **1,** to make a likeness of; reproduce; duplicate; photocopy; as, to *copy* a report; **2,** to imitate; as, to *copy* the way the movie star walks and talks.—*n.* **cop′y-ist.**

cop-y-right (kop′i-rīt′), *n.* the exclusive legal right of an artist or author, or his or her agent, to reproduce, publish, etc., a literary or artistic work for a certain time:—*adj.* protected by copyright:—*v.t.* to secure a copyright for; as, to *copyright* a book, movie, piece of music, etc.

co-quette (kō-ket′), *n.* a flirtatious woman.—*adv.* **co-quet′tish-ly.**

cor-al (kor′al), *n.* **1,** a hard substance like limestone, varied and often brilliant in colour, built up of countless skeletons of certain animals that grow in shallow tropical seas, and often appearing at or above the surface as reefs or islands; **2,** one of the tiny animals that produce coral; **3,** the colour of orange red:—**coral reef,** a large formation of coral in shallow water:—*adj.* **1,** made of coral; **2,** red in colour, as coral.

cord (kôrd), *n.* **1,** a heavy string or small rope; **2,** a covered wire used to connect an electric device to a power outlet; **3,** a measure of firewood, usually the amount in a pile 2.4 m x 1.2 m x 1.2 m; **4,** any ropelike structure, as a tendon or nerve; as, the spinal *cord*:—**cords,** any binding force; as, the *cords* of friendship:—*v.t.* **1,** to bind with string or rope; **2,** to stack (wood) in cords.—*n.* **cord′age; cord′ing; cord′wood′.**

cor-dial (kôr′jal; kôrd′yal), *adj.* **1,** tending to revive or stimulate, as a medicine; **2,** hearty; sincere; as, a *cordial* manner:—*n.* a medicine, food, or drink that revives or stimulates.—*n.* **cor-dial′i-ty.**

cor-dil-le-ra (kôr′dēl-yâ′ra; kôr-dil′ėr-a), *n.* a mountain chain, esp. the chief mountain axis of a continent, as the Rocky Mountains, etc.

cord-less (kôrd′les), *adj.* pertaining to a device that operates without a cord, usually with a rechargeable battery; as, a *cordless* phone.

cor-don (kôr′don), *n.* a line or circle of soldiers, ships, etc., to guard a person or place; as, a *cordon* of police:—*v.i.* to put a restrictive barrier or cordon around something; as, to *cordon* off a stage.

cor-du-roy (kôr′dū-roi′; kôr′dū-roi′), *n.* **1,** a stout ribbed or corded cotton cloth with a velvety surface; **2, corduroys,** trousers or a suit made of corduroy:—*adj.* **1,** of or like corduroy; **2,** in Canada, made of logs laid crosswise, as a road or bridge.

core (kōr), *n.* **1,** the heart or innermost part of anything, esp. of certain fruits, such as apples, pears, etc.; **2,** the substance or essential point, as of an argument or a speech; **3,** a bar of soft iron forming the centre of an electromagnet:—*v.t.* [cored, cor-ing], to remove the core from, as an apple.—*n.* **cor′er.**

co-re-spond-ent (kō′ri-spon′dent), *n.* in a divorce suit, a defendant jointly charged with a husband or wife as guilty of adultery.

cork (kôrk), *n.* **1,** the light, elastic, outer layer of bark of a certain oak, used for floats for fishing, stoppers for bottles, bulletin boards, shoes, floor coverings, etc.; **2,** a stopper for a bottle or cask, esp. one made of cork:—*v.t.* **1,** to stop with a cork, as a bottle; **2,** to restrain; as, to *cork* up one's anger:—*adj.* made of cork.

cork-screw (kôrk′skrōō), *n.* a spiral wire or a screw, used for drawing corks from bottles:—*adj.* shaped like a corkscrew; as, a *corkscrew* path:—*v.i.* and *v.t. Colloq.* to follow, or cause to follow, a winding, zigzag course.

corm (kôrm), *n.* a short, fleshy or bulblike, underground stem, as of the *crocus* or *gladiolus*.

cor-mo-rant (kôr′mo-rant), *n.* **1,** a large, greedy sea bird that feeds on fish; **2,** a person who is greedy or covetous.

[1]**corn** (kôrn), *n.* **1,** a tall green plant that has large ears or cobs covered with rows of yellow or white kernels or seeds, eaten as a vegetable and used as feed for animals: used to make many other food products, such as corn oil, cornstarch, corn bread, cornflakes, cornmeal, etc.; maize; **2,** a grain or seed, esp. of a cereal plant; also, such a plant.—*adj.* **corn′fed′.**—*n.* **corn′field′; corn′stalk′; corn bread; corn chip; corn dog; corn roast.**

[2]**corn** (kôrn), *n.* a horny thickening of the skin, esp. on the toe or foot.

corn-cob (kôrn′kob′), *n.* **1,** the woody centre of an ear of corn, on which the grains are set; **2,** a tobacco pipe made of a corncob.

cor-ne-a (kôr′ni-a), *n.* the front, transparent part of the outer coat of the eyeball, which covers the iris and pupil and admits light to the interior.

corned (kôrnd), *adj.* preserved in brine or salt; as, *corned* beef.

cor-ner (kôr′nėr), *n.* **1,** an angle; the point where two lines, sides, or edges meet; as, the *corners* of a desk; also, the area near this angle; as, a *corner* of the attic; **2,** the intersection of two or more streets; **3,** a nook; a secluded place; **4,** a remote point; as, the *corners* of the earth; **5,** an awkward situation; as, your question put me in a *corner;* **6,** a monopolizing of the supply of something in order to raise the price; as, to have a *corner* on the market:—*v.t.* **1,** to drive into a corner; **2,** to force into a situation having no escape or into a difficult situation; as, to *corner* a burglar; to *corner* him to take on the job:—*adj.* **1,** located at a corner; as, a *corner* store; **2,** usable in a corner; as, a *corner* cupboard.

cor-ner-stone (kôr′nėr-stōn′), *n.* **1,** a stone at an angle of a building, esp. one laid at the formal ceremony preceding erection; **2,** anything of fundamental importance; as, faith is a *cornerstone* of most religions.

cor-net (kôr′nit; kôr-net′), *n.* a brass wind instrument somewhat similar to a trumpet.—*n.* **cor′net-ist; cor-net′tist.**

cor-nice (kôr′nis), *n.* **1,** an ornamental moulding on a wall near the ceiling; **2,** a horizontal projecting piece forming the top of a wall or column.

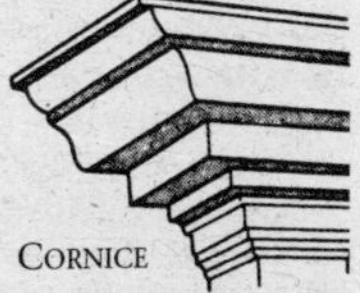

CORNICE

corn-starch (kôrn′stärch′), *n.* a white, floury starch made from corn, used in puddings and as a thickening for foods.

cor-nu-co-pi-a (kôr′nū-kō′pi-a), *n.* [*pl.* cornucopias], **1,** a horn full of fruit and flowers, symbolizing prosperity; **2,** hence, plenty; abundance; **3,** a cone-shaped holder for nuts, candy, etc.

corn-y (kôr′ni), *adj. Slang* stale; very old-fashioned; simple; sentimental; as, a *corny* joke; a *corny* story.

co-rol-la (ko-rol′a), *n.* the inner envelope of a flower, usually brightly coloured, and made up of the petals.

cor-ol-la-ry (ko-rol′a-ri; kôr′a-ler′i; kor′), *n.* **1,** an obvious inference or deduction; a result; **2,** in *geometry,* a proposition deduced from a proof already established.

co-ro-na (ko-rō′na), *n.* **1,** the dazzling halo of burning gases surrounding the sun, seen only during an eclipse; **2,** a crown; garland; something crownlike.

cor-o-na-ry (kor′o-nėr-i; -ner′i), *adj.* relating to a crown or to the *coronary* artery of the heart.—*n. Colloq.* a heart attack; as, he has had a *coronary* (thrombosis).

cor-o-na-tion (kor′o-nā′shun), *n.* the act or ceremony of crowning a king or queen.

cor-o-ner (kor′o-nėr), *n.* an officer, usually a medical doctor, whose chief duty is to find out the cause of any violent or mysterious death.

cor-o-net (kôr′o-net′; kor′o-nit), *n.* a small crown worn to show a high rank below that of a king, as of a duke or earl; **2,** an ornamental band or wreath worn around the head.

[1]**cor-po-ral** (kôr′po-ral), *n.* **1,** a noncommissioned officer in the army, next above a private; **2,** in the RCMP, a noncommissioned officer next below a staff sergeant.

[2]**cor-po-ral** (kôr′po-ral), *adj.* having to do with the body; as, *corporal* punishment.—*adj.* **cor-po′re-al.**

cor-po-ra-tion (kôr′po-rā′shun), *n.* a group of persons permitted by law to act as one person in carrying on a given kind of business, work, etc.—*adj.* **cor′po-rate** (kôr′po-rit).

corps (kōr), *n.* [*pl.* corps (kôrz)], **1,** a large unit of an army, containing two or more military divisions; **2,** a body of troops for special service; as, the signal *corps;* **3,** a body of persons associated in a common work; as, a *corps* of writers; the press *corps.*

corpse (kôrps), *n.* a dead body, usually a human body.

cor-pu-lent (kôr′pū-lent), *adj.* fat; having a large, fleshy body.—*n.* **cor′pu-lence.**

cor-pus-cle (kôr′pus-l), *n.* **1,** a minute particle of matter; **2,** one of the small cells of the blood.

cor-ral (ko-ral′; ko-räl′), *n.* **1,** a pen or enclosure for horses, cattle, etc.; **2,** an enclosure or circle of wagons formed to protect an encampment:—*v.t.* (ko-ral′), [corralled, corral-ling], **1,** to drive into, or secure in, a pen or enclosure; **2,** to hem in; surround.

cor-rect (ko-rekt′), *v.t.* **1,** to set straight; make right; remove errors from; mark errors in (something written or printed) for removal; as, to *correct* exams; **2,** to cure; as, to *correct* a bad habit; **3,** to reprove; as, the teacher *corrected* the student:—*adj.* **1,** exact; accurate; free from error; **2,** measuring up to a standard of morals, taste, manners, etc.; proper; as, *correct* behaviour.—*adv.* **cor-rect′ly.**—*n.* **cor-rec′tion; cor-rect′ness.**—*n.* and *adj.* **cor-rec′tive.**

cor-re-late (kôr′e-lāt′; kor-), *v.t.* to connect by mutual relation; as, to *correlate* biology and chemistry in the school program.

cor-rel-a-tive (ko-rel′a-tiv), *adj.* depending upon or naturally related to something else; as, the size and weight of a stone are *correlative* qualities; in *grammar*, so related that one implies the other; as, *either* and *or* are *correlative* conjunctions.—*n.* one of two related terms; as, *both, and; not only, but also; whether, or;* etc.—*n.* **cor′re-la′tion.**

cor-re-spond (kor′i-spond′), *v.i.* **1,** to be similar or equal in use, position, character, or amount; as, the number of places at the table *corresponds* to the number of invited guests; **2,** to agree; suit; match; harmonize; as, her actions do not *correspond* to our standards; **3,** to be similar to; be like; as, the French phrase "au revoir" *corresponds* to "goodbye"; **4,** to communicate by letter, e-mail, etc.—*n.* **cor′re-spond′ence.**

cor-re-spond-ent (kor′i-spond′ent), *n.* **1,** a person who corresponds with another by letter, e-mail, etc.; **2,** a person who sends in a news report to a newspaper, TV station, etc., esp. from a distant place; as, foreign *correspondents* during a war, crisis, etc.

cor-ri-dor (kor′i-dôr; kor′i-dėr), *n.* a long passage or hallway into which rooms open.

cor-rob-o-rate (ko-rob′ō-rāt′), *v.t.* [corroborat-ed, corroborat-ing], to confirm; make more certain; as, this evidence *corroborates* my opinion.—*n.* **cor-rob′o-ra′-tion.**—*adj.* **cor-rob′o-ra′tive; cor-rob′o-ra-tor′y.**

cor-rode (ko-rōd′), *v.t.* and *v.i.* [corroded, corrod-ing], to eat away or decay gradually, as by chemical action; disintegrate; rust; as, rust *corrodes* metal:—*n.* **cor′ro′sion.**—*adj.* **cor-ro′sive.**

cor-ru-gate (kôr′oo-gāt′; kor′ū-gāt′), *v.t.* [corrugat-ed, corrugat-ing], to shape in wrinkles or alternate ridges and grooves, as *corrugated* iron or paper:—*v.i.* to contract into wrinkles or folds.—*adj.* **cor′ru-gat′ed.**

cor-rupt (ko-rupt′), *v.t.* **1,** to injure; spoil; **2,** to make impure; debase; as, bad associations *corrupted* his morals; **3,** to bribe; as, to *corrupt* a witness:—*adj.* spoiled; depraved; dishonest; as, *corrupt* practices; full of errors; as, he spoke *corrupt* French.—*adv.* **cor-rupt′ly.**—*n.* **cor-rup′tion.**—*adj.* **cor-rup′tive; cor-rupt′i-ble.**

cor-sage (kôr′såzh′), *n.* **1,** a bouquet of flowers for a woman to wear; **2,** the bodice of a woman's dress.

cor-set (kôr′sit), *n.* **1,** a woman's tight-fitting undergarment with stays, worn formerly to support the figure or to modify its shape; **2,** a similar undergarment worn by men and women as a result of injury, etc.

cor-tege or **cor-tège** (kôr-tezh′; -tāzh′), *n.* a procession; retinue; as, a funeral *cortege.*

cor-tex (kôr′teks), *n.* [*pl.* cortices (kôr′ti-sēz)], **1,** a plant tissue lying below the epidermis, often storing starch; **2,** the outer layers of an organ, as of the brain.—*adj.* **cor′ti-cal.**

cor-ti-sone (côr′ti-zōn′; -sōn′), *n.* a hormone produced by the adrenal cortex and used esp. for treatment of arthritis, etc.

cor-vette (kôr-vet′), *n.* a small, fast, naval-escort warship.

co-sine (kō′sīn′), *n.* the ratio of the side adjacent to an acute angle of a right-angled triangle to the hypotenuse. Compare *sine.*

cos-met-ic (koz-met′ik), *n.* a preparation, as facial cream, powder, etc., used to beautify the skin, nails, or hair:—*adj.* designed to beautify the complexion, nails, or hair; also, superficial; as, *cosmetic* repairs.

cos-mic (koz′mik), *adj.* **1,** relating to the universe and its laws; as, *cosmic* dust, *cosmic* noise, or *cosmic* rays; **2,** vast (as to time or space).

cos-mo-pol-i-tan (koz′mo-pol′i-tan), *n.* a person of wide information and sympathies:—*adj.* **1,** at home anywhere; having broad interests and sympathies; sophisticated; **2,** belonging to the world; not restricted to one nation or race; as, *cosmopolitan* ideals. Also, **cos-mop′o-lite′** (koz-mop′o-līt′).

cos-mos (koz′mos), *n.* the universe conceived as a system of order and harmony (opposite of *chaos*).

cost (kôst), *v.t.* [*p.t.* and *p.p.* cost, *p.pr.* cost-ing], **1,** to be obtainable for (a certain price); as, the card *costs* $4.50; **2,** to cause to spend or lose; as, carelessness *cost* him his job:—*v.i.* to involve or cause expenditure, loss, etc.; as, the accident *cost* dearly:—*n.* **1,** a charge; expense; as, the *cost* of food; **2,** the price in terms of suffering, to work, etc.; as, at the *cost* of health:—**costs,** the expenses of a lawsuit.

co-star (kō′-stär′), *v.t.* and *v.i.* to share prominently in a movie, television show, play, performance, etc:—*n.* an actor who shares prominence with another.

cost-ly (kôst′li), *adj.* [cost-li-er, cost-li-est], **1,** involving great cost or expense, as of money or effort; **2,** causing a great loss; as, a *costly* victory because many lives were lost.—*n.* **cost′li-ness.**

cos-tume (kos′tūm; kos-tūm′), *n.* **1,** dress in general; style of dress; esp., the dress of a given time, period, class, purpose, etc.; as, a medieval *costume*; a riding *costume*; **2,** clothes worn to dress up as someone or something else; historical dress; fancy dress; as, to wear a pirate *costume* for Halloween:—**costume jewellery,** jewellery made from inexpensive material, not precious stones:—*v.t.* (kos-tūm′), [costumed, costum-ing], to provide with appropriate dress; as, to *costume* an actor for a part.—*n.* **cos-tum′er.**

co-sy or **co-zy** (kō′zi), *adj.* [co-si-er, co-si-est], warm and comfortable; snug:—*n.* [*pl.* cosies], **1,** a cover, padded, to keep a teapot warm; **2,** a corner seat.—*adv.* **co′si-ly.**

cot (kot), *n.* a small, light bed.

co-te-rie (kō′tė-ri; kō′tė-rē′), *n.* a set of intimate friends; a clique.

cot-tage (kot′ij), *n.* a small dwelling; also, a house at a summer resort.—*n.* **cot′tag-er.**

cot-ter pin (kot′ėr pin′), *n.* a split metal pin the ends of which are bent after insertion through a hole or slot.

cot-ton (kot′n), *n.* **1,** a white, fibrous down enclosing the seeds of the cotton plant; **2,** the plant producing this; **3,** thread or cloth made of processed cotton:—*adj.* pertaining to cotton; as, a *cotton* shirt.—*adj.* **cot′ton-y.**

cotton batting, thin layers of fluffy, absorbent cotton used for surgical dressings and padding in quilts.

cot-ton-tail (kot′n-tāl′), *n.* a wild brown or grey North American rabbit with a fluffy tail.

cot-y-le-don (kot′i-lē′dun), *n.* a part of a seed containing food for the young root, stem, and first true leaves: often appearing above ground at germination as the seed leaf, and later shrivelling up.—*adj.* **cot′y-le′don-ous.**

couch (kouch), *v.t.* **1,** to lay upon a bed or other resting place; **2,** to put into words; express; as, to *couch* a letter in strong terms; **3,** to lower, as a lance or spear for attack:—*v.i.* **1,** to lie down, as on a bed; **2,** to cower; hide:—*n.* a large piece of furniture for sleep or rest; lounge; any place for sleep or rest. Also called *chesterfield* and *sofa.*

cou-gar (ko͞o′gȧr), *n.* a large, tawny North American animal of the cat family. Also called *puma, panther,* or *mountain lion.* (See *puma,* illustration.)

cough (kôf), *v.i.* to force air from the lungs suddenly, with a sharp noise:—*v.t.* to expel from the lungs or air passages; as, he *coughed* up the bone:—*n.* **1,** the act or sound of coughing; **2,** an illness marked by a cough; as, to have a dry *cough.*

could (kood), **1,** *p.t.* of *can;* **2,** also, a modal auxiliary used to make a statement or question less strong or more polite; as, *could* you please hand me that?

cou-lee (ko͞o′li), *n.* in Western Canada, esp. in the Prairies, a deep, dry gulch with steeply sloping sides like those of a canyon.

coun-cil (koun′sil), *n.* **1,** a group of persons called together to discuss and settle problems, give advice, etc.; as, a student *council;* **2,** a lawmaking or governing body, as of a city or town; **3,** the deliberation of such a body.—*n.* **coun′cil-lor; coun′ci-lor.**

coun-sel (koun′sel), *n.* **1,** exchange of opinion; consultation; as, the general took *counsel* with his officers; **2,** instruction; advice; as, he was guided by his mother's *counsel;* **3,** prudence; foresight; **4,** an advocate or lawyer:—*v.t.* [counselled, counselling], **1,** to give advice to; **2,** to recommend; as, I *counsel* patience.

coun-sel-lor or **coun-se-lor** (koun′sel-ėr), *n.* **1,** a person who advises or guides; as, a guidance *counsellor;* **2,** a lawyer; as, the *counsellor* for the defence; **3,** a person who is in charge of activities at a children's camp.

[1]**count** (kount), *v.t.* **1,** to tell off (units) in order to find their number; sum up; as, *count* your dollars; **2,** to give the numerals in regular order to a certain point; as, *count* to 10 before you answer; **3,** to consider; as, she *counts* herself generous; **4,** to include in an enumeration; as, he *counted* only the best:—*v.i.* **1,** to tell off articles or numbers in order; **2,** to rely; as, we *count* on her consent; **3,** to be of worth or value; as, this doesn't *count* much; **4,** to have effect; as, his support *counted* heavily in the victory:—*n.* **1,** the act of numbering; as, a *count* of the students; **2,** the total ascertained; **3,** a charge against a person in a court of law; as, to be accused of five *counts* of burglary.

[2]**count** (kount), *n.* a title of nobility in France, Spain, Italy, etc.: about the same as British *earl.*

count-down (kount′doun′), *n.* a counting downwards before the launching of a rocket, missile, etc. (the counting ending ... 3, 2, 1, 0) to measure the precise period preceding blast- off.

coun-te-nance (koun′te-nans), *n.* **1,** the face; **2,** the expression of the face showing feeling or character; as, an angry *countenance;* a noble *countenance;* **3,** approval; support; as, to lend *countenance* to a plan; **4,** composure; as, he kept *countenance* despite the insult:—*v.t.* [countenanced, countenanc-ing], to support; favour; as, he *countenanced* the affair.

[1]**coun-ter** (koun′tėr), *n.* **1,** a person who keeps count; **2,** a small object used to keep score, as in a game; **3,** a long, flat surface where customers in restaurants, banks, or stores are served, or where things are displayed; also, counters in a kitchen or bathroom; **4,** a coinlike token.

[2]**coun-ter** (koun′tėr), *adj.* contrary; opposing; as, a *counter* opinion:—*n.* **1,** the opposite or contrary; as, *counter* to her instructions; **2,** in *boxing,* a blow to ward off a blow:—*v.i.* to make an opposite or contrary

attack:—*v.t.* **1,** to combat; oppose:—*adv.* in a contrary way; against.

coun-ter- (koun′tėr), *prefix* meaning *opposing, opposite, offsetting,* or *going against*; as, *counter*attack, *counter*clockwise, *counter*productive, *counter*terrorism, etc.

coun-ter-act (koun′tėr-akt′), *v.t.* to act in opposition to; neutralize; as, one medicine may *counteract* another.—*n.* **coun′ter-ac′tion.**

coun-ter-bal-ance (koun′tėr-bal′ans), *n.* a weight that balances another; hence, a power or influence that offsets another:—*v.t.* (koun′tėr-bal′ans), [counterbalanced, counterbalanc-ing], to balance, as with an equal weight; make up for; as, his unusual mental powers *counterbalanced* his physical weakness.

coun-ter-clock-wise (koun′tėr-klok′wiz′), *adj.* opposite to the direction in which the hands of a clock move.

coun-ter-feit (koun′tėr-fit), *v.t.* to copy or imitate exactly, as money, with intent to deceive or defraud:—*v.i.* to make imitations, esp. of money:—*adj.* made to resemble something genuine very closely, with intent to deceive; as, *counterfeit* money:—*n.* a copy made with intent to deceive; a forgery; as, this $100 bill is a *counterfeit.*—*n.* **coun′ter-feit′er.**

coun-ter-mand (koun′tėr-mand′; koun′-tėr-mand′), *v.t.* **1,** to cancel (a purchase); **2,** to issue instructions reversing (an order, plan, or the like); as, the general *countermanded* the march:—*n.* (koun′tėr-mand′), a contrary order.

coun-ter-march (koun′tėr-märch′), *n.* **1,** a reversal; a marching back; returning; **2,** in *drilling,* a sharp turn, as if around a post, and a march back parallel and close to the line of advance:—*v.i.* (koun′tėr-märch′; koun′tėr-märch′), to march back; make a countermarch.

coun-ter-part (koun′tėr-part′), *n.* a person or thing that corresponds closely to another; as, the right foot is a *counterpart* of the left; a duplicate; copy.

coun-ter-plot (koun′tėr-plot′), *n.* a plot in opposition.

coun-ter-sign (koun′tėr-sin′; koun′tėr-sin′), *v.t.* to sign (a document) already signed by another:—*n.* (koun′tėr-sin′), **1,** an additional signature to a document to make it of value; **2,** a word known to a special group, as a secret password.

count-ess (koun′tis), *n.* the wife or widow of a count or an earl; also, a lady who in her own right ranks with an earl or a count.

count-less (kount′lis), *adj.* innumerable; numberless.

coun-try (kun′tri), *n.* [*pl.* countries], **1,** a tract of land; region; as, level *country*; **2,** rural regions; as, we left the *country* for the city; **3,** one's native or adopted land; **4,** a territory with set borders that has a distinct existence as to name, language, government, etc.; a nation; as, Spain and other Mediterranean *countries*; **5,** the people of a nation as a whole; the public; as, the *country* voted for lower taxes:—*adj.* **1,** pertaining to the rural regions; as, *country* roads; **2,** unpolished; rustic; as, *country* ways.—*n.* **coun′try-side′; coun′-try-man; coun′try-wo′man.**

coun-ty (koun′ti), *n.* [*pl.* counties], **1,** a definite political district of a country, state, or province; **2,** the people belonging to this division; as, the *county* voted against the tax:—*adj.* pertaining to a county; as, *county* officials.

coup (ko͞o), *n.* a sudden, unexpected, and sometimes brilliantly successful move or stroke.

coup d'état (ko͞o′dā′tå′), *n.* an unexpected political change, usually the sudden overthrow of a government by force or an illegal measure.

cou-pé or **coupe** (ko͞o′pā′; ko͞op), *n.* **1,** a horse-drawn, four-wheeled, closed carriage for two, with an outside driver's seat; **2,** a closed, two-door automobile, often with only two seats.

cou-ple (kup′l), *n.* **1,** two persons or things of the same kind connected or thought of together; as, a *couple* of books; **2,** two persons, closely associated, who are thought of together because they are married, engaged, partners in a dance or game, etc.; as, a dancing *couple*:—*v.t.* [cou-pled, coupling], **1,** to join together, as railway cars; **2,** *Colloq.* to unite in pairs; unite in wedlock:—*v.i.* to pair off; mate.

cou-plet (cup′lit), *n.* two successive lines of rhymed verse.

cou-pon (ko͞o′pon), *n.* **1,** a printed piece of paper that can be traded for money or merchandise or used to get a cheaper price on a product or service; as, grocery *coupons*; dry-cleaning *coupons*; **2,** a dated, detachable certificate that may be clipped from a bond and presented for collection of interest.

cour-age (kûi′ij), *n.* boldness; fearlessness.—*adj.* **cou-ra′geous.**

cour-eur de bois (ko͞o′rûr′ de bwå′), *n.* formerly, a French or Métis fur trader or woodsman in Canada's North or Northwest.

cour-i-er (koor′i-ėr), *n.* **1,** a messenger, usually entrusted with important letters or documents to be delivered with great speed; **2,** a travelling attendant who arranges all the details of a trip, as tickets, hotel reservations, etc.; **3,** any person or company that carries messages, packages, etc., quickly; a messenger; as, the *courier* delivered the urgent package to our company:—*v.t.* and *v.i.* to send or ship by courier; as, to *courier* a package.

course (kōrs), *n.* **1,** the act of moving onward; progress in space; as, the *course* of the earth around the sun; progress in time; as, in the *course* of a week; **2,** ground to be passed over in a regular way; as, a golf *course;* **3,** a path; direction taken; as, a ship's *course;* **4,** a channel through which water flows; as, the *course* of a river; **5,** a succession; series of classes, etc.; as, a *course* of lectures; a physics *course;* **6,** method of procedure; as, a *course* of action; **7,** the part of a meal served at one time; as, the main *course;* **8,** in building, a layer of stone or bricks:—**of course,** naturally; certainly; as was to be expected:—*v.t.* [coursed, coursing], to pursue (game) with hounds:—*v.i.* to run; flow; as, tears *coursed* down her cheeks.

court (kōrt), *n.* **1,** an unroofed space wholly or partly surrounded by buildings or walls; **2,** a level space marked for playing games; **3,** a royal palace; also, the people in attendance at a palace; **4,** a prince or sovereign and his ministers considered as the ruling power; also, an official meeting of a sovereign and his or her councillors; **5,** a hall of justice; **6,** the judge or judges engaged in administering justice; also, the session at which they preside; as, traffic *court;* **7,** flattering attentions, respect, or honour paid to one in power; also, attention paid by a man to a woman in wooing her, esp. in former times:—*v.t.* **1,** to pay attention to as a lover, esp. in former times; woo; **2,** to seek favour of, by attention; as, *court* voters; **3,** to attempt to gain; seek, esp. something bad; as, to *court* disaster.

cour-te-ous (kûr′ti-us; kōrt′yus), *adj.* polite; considerate.—*adv.* **cour′te-ous-ly.**—*n.* **cour′te-ous-ness.**

cour-te-sy (kûr′te-si; kōr′te-si), *n.* [*pl.* courtesies], **1,** politeness; **2,** an act of kindliness or respect; **3,** kindness or generosity; as, a program presented through the *courtesy* of a large corporation.

court-house (kōrt′hous′), *n.* a public building in which courts of law are held.

court-ly (kōrt′li), *adj.* [court-li-er, court-li-est], polished; elegant; as, *courtly* manners.—*n.* **court′li-ness.**

court–mar-tial (kōrt′–mär′shal), *n.* [*pl.* courts-martial], a court made up of military or naval officers to try offences against military or naval law: also, a trial by such a court:—*v.t.* [court-mar-tialled, court-martial-ling or -tialed, -tial-ing], to try (a person) by such a court.

court-room (kōrt′rōōm′), *n.* a room where a court of law is held.

court-ship (kōrt′ship), *n.* attentions paid by a person to another, preparatory to marriage or mating; wooing.

court-yard (kōrt′yärd′), *n.* an enclosed space in or adjoining a large building, house, or castle.

cous-in (kuz′n), *n.* **1,** a son or daughter of one's uncle or aunt; **2,** any relative who has the same great-grandparent or other ancestor.

cove (kōv), *n.* **1,** a sheltered place or pass; esp., an inlet or creek on the coast; **2,** in *architecture,* a concave moulding.

cov-e-nant (kuv′e-nant), *n.* a compact or agreement:—*v.t.* and *v.i.* to promise by solemn agreement.

cov-er (kuv′ėr), *v.t.* **1,** to put or lay something over (a person or thing); as, to *cover* a box; **2,** to spread over the surface; lie over, so as to close or enclose; as, flowers *cover* the field; a lid *covers* the box; a shoe *covers* the foot; **3,** to hide; screen; as, clouds *cover* the mountain; to *cover* a mistake; **4,** to extend or pass over; as, the estate *covers* a wide area; we *covered* 90 kilometres today; **5,** to include; comprise; as, the course in biology *covers* genetics; **6,** to watch over or guard; as, roadblocks that *cover* all routes; **7,** in *journalism,* to report on a specific event; as, reporters *covered* the school's soccer match:—*n.* **1,** that which is laid on something else; as, a *cover* for a bed; **2,** the binding of a book, or the outside of a magazine, newspaper, CD, etc.; **3,** protection; as, to escape under *cover* of night; **4,** a thicket that may conceal game; **5,** the table equipment for the use of one person at a meal.

cov-er-age (kuv′ėr-ej), *n.* **1,** the amount of space or time given to a news event in the media; as, the television *coverage* of the terrorist bombings; **2,** the amount and extent of something covered by insurance; as, to have ample *coverage* on car insurance to meet liabilities; **3,** the number of people reached by a medium; **4,** the act of covering.

cov-er-alls (kuv′ėr-ôlz′), *n.* a one-piece, external work garment worn by mechanics, etc.

cov-er-ing (kuv′ėr-ing), *n.* **1,** that which covers, protects, or hides; as, a floor *covering;* **2,** the act of putting on a cover.

cov-er-let (kuv′ėr-lit), *n.* the outer cover of a bed; a bedspread.

cov-ert (kuv′ėrt), *adj.* concealed, secret; veiled; as, a *covert* scheme, threat, or glance.

cov-et (kuv′it), *v.t.* to long for (something that belongs to another).—*adj.* **cov′et-ous.**

[1]**cow** (kou), *n.* [*pl.* cows (kouz)], **1,** a full-grown female of the ox or bovine family, esp. of domestic cattle; **2,** a female of certain other large mammals, such as the moose, elephant, buffalo, whale, etc.

[2]**cow** (kou), *v.t.* to make afraid; as, the intruder *cowed* him.

cow-ard (kou′ėrd), *n.* a person lacking in courage; a shamefully timid person.—*adj.* and *adv.* **cow′ard-ly.**

cow-ard-ice (kou′ėr-dis), *n.* want of courage; shameful fear.

cow-boy (kou′boi′), *n.* in the western part of Canada and of the U.S., the former name for a person who tends cattle on a ranch and on a range, usually on horseback.—*n.fem.* **cow′girl′**. Now called *cowhand.*

cow-er (kou′ėr), *v.i.* to crouch down or move away, as from fear or shame; as, the dog *cowered* after being scolded for its bad behaviour.

cow-hand (kou′hand), *n.* Same as **cowboy.**

cow-hide (kou′hīd′), *n.* **1,** the skin or hide of a cow, esp. when tanned and dressed; the leather made from it; **2,** a whip of rawhide or of braided leather:—*adj.* made of cowhide:—*v.t.* [cow-hid-ed, cow-hid-ing], to flog or whip with a cowhide.

Cow-i-chan (kou′i-chen), *n.* **1,** the Salish people of Vancouver Island; **2,** a heavy sweater made of unbleached wool and having a knitted design on the front and back, esp. such a sweater knitted by the Cowichan people. Also called *Cowichan sweater.*

cow-lick (kou′lik′), *n.* a tuft of hair on the forehead that will not lie flat.

cow-ling (kou′ling), *n.* the metal covering of an aircraft engine.

coy (koi), *adj.* **1,** bashful; shy; **2,** pretending to be shy; coquettish.

coy-ote (koi′ōt; ki-ō′-ṭi), *n.* the prairie wolf, originally found only in western North America, but now also found elsewhere: most live and hunt alone.

co-zy (kō′zi), *adj.* Same as **cosy.**

CPU (sē′pē′ū′), *n.* Same as **central processing unit.**

crab (krab), *n.* **1,** any of various animals, most of which live in the sea, which have a broad, flattened body, 10 walking legs, and the abdomen, or so-called tail, curled under the body: many are used as food; **2,** *Colloq.* someone who is cross, surly, and bad-tempered; a grouch:—*v.i.* [crabbed, crab-bing], to fish for or catch crabs.—*adj.* **crab′bed** (kra′bid); **crab′by.**—*n.* **crab grass** (a coarse, creeping, weedy grass that infests lawns):—**catch a crab,** in *rowing,* to miss the water in making a stroke, or to fail to clear the water on a recovery stroke.—*n.* **crab′meat′.**

crab apple (krab), *n.* **1,** a tree bearing small, sour apples, often used in making jelly; also, the fruit.

crack (krak), *v.i.* **1,** to make a sharp, snapping noise, as a whip; **2,** to be broken without dividing completely; split; as, the glass *cracked* in hot water; **3,** to break or become rasping, as a voice:—*v.t.* **1,** to cause to pop or snap; as, to *crack* a whip; **2,** to break without separating completely; break open; as, to *crack* nuts; **3,** to tell (a joke); **4,** to hit with a sharp, hard blow; as, to *crack* your head on the cupboard door; **5,** to solve or break into; as, to *crack* the code; *crack* the safe:—*n.* **1,** a sudden, sharp noise; as, a *crack* of thunder; **2,** an incomplete break; as, a *crack* in the ice or in a glass; **3,** a broken note, as in a boy's voice when changing; **4,** a narrow space or opening; as, light through a *crack* in the door; **5,** *Colloq.* a sharp blow; as, he gave the boy a *crack* on the head:—*adj. Colloq.* first-rate; as, a *crack* shot.—*adj.* **crack′brained′** (*Colloq.* crazy).—*n.* **crack′down′** (*Slang* disciplinary action or of becoming more strict with rules or laws).

crack cocaine, *n. Colloq.* a powerful, extremely addictive form of cocaine.

crack-er (krak′ėr), *n.* **1,** a dry biscuit, often hard and crisp; **2,** a firecracker; **3,** a party favour that pops when pulled apart.

crack-le (krak′l), *v.i.* [crack-led, crack-ling], to make slight rustling or snapping noises, frequently repeated:—*n.* **1,** a slight, sharp, or snapping noise, esp. one that is often repeated; as, the *crackle* of a fire; **2,** the finely cracked glaze or surface of a kind of pottery, glass, or porcelain; also, ware having such a surface.—*adj.* **crack′ly.**

crack-pot (krak′pot′), *n. Colloq.* an eccentric or crazy person.

crack–up (krak′–up′), *n.* **1,** a crash, as of an airplane; **2,** *Colloq.* a mental or physical breakdown.—*v.i.* **crack up, 1,** to crash; **2,** *Colloq.* to break down; **3,** to laugh fitfully.

cra-dle (krā′dl), *n.* **1,** a baby's crib or bed, often on rockers or swinging; **2,** birthplace; origin; as, the *cradle* of liberty; **3,** anything resembling a baby's cradle, as a supporting frame placed under a ship or aircraft during construction, a trough on rockers used by miners in washing gold-bearing earth, the part of the telephone that holds the receiver, etc.; **4,** a frame of wood, fastened to a scythe, used in harvesting; also, the scythe:—*v.t.* [cra-dled, cra-dling], **1,** to place or rock in a cradle, or as if in a cradle; as, to cradle the tiny kitten in your arms; **2,** to shelter in infancy; as, the two brothers were *cradled* in luxury; **3,** to wash gold-bearing earth in a cradle; **4,** to reap with a cradle scythe.

craft (kråft), *n.* **1,** skill, esp. of the hand, such as sewing, pottery, etc.; **2,** deceit; cunning; **3,** a trade requiring artistic manual skill, such as woodworking; also, those engaged in such a trade; **4,** [*pl.* craft], a ship, boat, or aircraft.

crafts-man (kråfts′man), *n.* [*pl.* craftsmen (-men)], a skilled worker.—*n.* **crafts′manship′.**—*n.fem.* **crafts′wo′man.**

craft-y (kråf′ti), *adj.* [craft-i-er, craft-i-est], deceitful; wily; as, *crafty* schemes.—*adv.* **craft′i-ly.**—*n.* **craft′i-ness.**

crag (krag), *n.* a steep, rugged rock; also, a projecting point of a rock.—*adj.* **crag′gy.**

cram (kram), *v.t.* [crammed, cram-ming], **1,** to stuff; fill to overflowing; as, to *cram* the food into her mouth; **2,** to pack or crowd in; as, to *cram* the clothes in the messy closet; **3,** *Colloq.* to study intensively or prepare for, as for an examination; as, to *cram* the students for the upcoming exam:—*v.i.* **1,** to eat greedily; **2,** *Colloq.* to study hard for an examination; as, to *cram* for the English exam.

[1]**cramp** (kramp), *n.* **1,** an iron bar bent at the ends, used to hold together blocks of stone, timber, etc.; **2,** a piece of iron or steel, resembling a C, with a tightening screw, used for holding two things together: also called *clamp*:—*v.t.* **1,** to fasten or hold by a cramp; **2,** to hinder in action or growth; hamper; as, lack of knowledge *cramped* his progress; to *cramp* her style.

[2]**cramp** (kramp), *n.* a sudden, sharp, painful contracting of the muscles, due to sudden chill, strain, etc.:—**cramps,** a sharp pain in the stomach or abdomen:—*v.t.* and *v.i.* to suffer, or cause to suffer, from cramp; also, to crowd into a tight space.

cran-ber-ry (kran/bėr-i), *n.* [*pl.* cranberries], the small, tart, scarlet berry of a kind of bog plant, used to make sauce, jelly, and juice, and popular at Thanksgiving dinner with turkey; also, the plant.

crane (krān), *n.* **1,** a wading bird with very long legs, a long, straight bill, and a long neck that it stretches to full length in flight; **2,** a machine for raising and moving heavy weights; **3,** a mechanical arm or support, as an iron arm for utensils in a fireplace, or a boom for holding a movie or television camera:—*v.t.* and *v.i.* [craned, cran-ing], to stretch (the neck), in order to see better.

cra-ni-um (krā/ni-um), *n.* the skull, esp. the part enclosing the brain.—*adj.* **cra/ni-al.**

[1]**crank** (krangk), *n.* an arm fastened at right angles to a shaft, that is turned to make a machine work:—*v.t.* **1,** to work or start with a crank, as with a window; **2,** to start (a motor or a car):—**crank up,** to increase in speed, intensity, or momentum; as, the fundraising effort is *cranking up*.

[2]**crank** (krangk), *n. Colloq.* **1,** a person with a peculiar turn of mind; esp. one who pursues one idea exclusively; as, calls from *cranks;* **2,** an irritable person.

crank-shaft (krank/shåft/), *n.* the rotating shaft that turns or is turned by a crank.

crank-y (krangk/i), *adj.* [crank-i-er, crank-i-est], **1,** ill-tempered; irritable; **2,** eccentric; **3,** liable to upset, as a boat.—*adv.* **crank/i-ly.**—*n.* **crank/i-ness.**

cran-ny (kran/i), *n.* [*pl.* crannies], a crack or chink, as in a wall.

[1]**crash** (krash), *v.i.* **1,** to break to pieces with a loud noise, esp. on falling; as, the vase *crashed* to the floor; **2,** to break one's way noisily through something; as, to *crash* through a jungle; **3,** to make a noise as of breakage on a vast scale; as, the thunder *crashed;* **4,** to collide, as two automobiles; also, to come into violent contact with the ground, as an airplane; **5,** to fail, as a business enterprise, the stock market, etc.; **6,** in *computing,* to completely stop working, as from a loss of electrical power or because of hardware or software error:—*v.t.* **1,** to break (something) to bits with noise and violence; smash; **2,** to land (an airplane) so as to damage it:—*n.* **1,** a smashing or shattering; **2,** a sudden loud sound, as of violent breakage; as, the *crash* of the orchestra; **3,** an airplane landing in which the craft is damaged; **4,** an automobile collision; **5,** the failure of a business, stock market, etc.; also, a general business and financial collapse; as, the *crash* of 1929:—*adj.* showing a very great effort over a short time; as, a *crash* course in Spanish.

[2]**crash** (krash), *n.* a coarse linen or cotton used for towelling, upholstery, etc.

crass (kras), *adj.* thick; coarse; gross; as, *crass* stupidity, ignorance, or carelessness.

crate (krāt), *n.* a wickerwork basket, or a case made of wooden slats, used for shipping or storing goods:—*v.t.* [crat-ed, crat-ing], to pack in a crate, as apples.

cra-ter (krā/tėr), *n.* **1,** the cup-shaped cavity forming the mouth of a volcano; **2,** a hole in the earth, caused by an explosion, as of an artillery shell; also, on the moon, etc.

crave (krāv), *v.t.* [craved, crav-ing], **1,** to beg earnestly for; as, I *crave* your help; **2,** to long for (food); desire.—*n.* **crav/ing.**

cra-ven (krā/vn), *adj.* cowardly; base; as, a *craven* deserter:—*n.* an abject coward.

craw (krô), *n.* **1,** the crop of a bird or insect; **2,** an animal's stomach:—**stick in one's craw,** to irritate, be difficult to accept; as, his attitude *sticks in my craw.*

crawl (krôl), *v.i.* **1,** to move slowly by dragging the body along the ground; **2,** to go on hands and knees; **3,** to move very slowly; **4,** to be infested with creeping things; as, the ground *crawls* with ants; **5,** to feel as if live things were over one's body; as, to *crawl* with loathing; my skin *crawls:*—*n.* **1,** the act of creeping, or of making one's way with difficulty; slow motion; as, the traffic slowed to a *crawl;* **2,** a fast stroke in swimming.—*n.* **crawl/er.**

cray-fish (krā/fish/), *n.* [*pl.* crayfish or crayfishes], a shellfish related to, but much smaller than, the lobster, found in fresh water.

cray-on (krā/on), *n.* **1,** a stick of coloured wax, charcoal, chalk, etc., for drawing or writing; **2,** a drawing made with such material:—*v.t.* to draw with crayon.

craze (krāz), *n.* an intense but passing interest; infatuation; fad:—*v.t.* [crazed, craz-ing], to drive insane.—*adj.* **crazed.**

cra-zy (krā′zi), *adj.* [cra-zi-er, cra-zi-est], **1,** insane; mad; **2,** shaky; unsound, as a building; **3,** not sensible; foolish; silly; as, running barefoot in the snow is a *crazy* thing to do; **4,** *Colloq.* foolishly fond or eager; wildly enthusiastic; as, he is *crazy* about music.—*adv.* **cra′zi-ly.**—*n.* **cra′zi-ness.**

creak (krēk), *v.i.* to make a sharp, harsh, squeaking or grating sound:—*n.* a harsh, squeaking sound.—*adj.* **creak′y.**

cream (krēm), *n.* **1,** the rich, fat part of milk, that rises to the top, used for making butter, etc.; **2,** hence, the choicest part of anything; as, the *cream* of a story; *cream* of the crop; **3,** anything with the consistency of cream; as, shaving *cream*; **4,** a dessert or sweet made of cream, or like cream; as, ice *cream*; butter *creams*; **5,** a light-yellow colour; **6,** a soft cosmetic; as, cold *cream*:—*v.t.* **1,** to skim the cream from (milk): **2,** to put cream into (tea or coffee); **3,** to bring to the consistency of thick cream; as, to *cream* butter, or butter and sugar; **4,** to cook with a dressing of cream or with a sauce of creamlike consistency.—*adj.* **cream′y.**—*n.* **cream′er-y.**

crease (krēs), *n.* a mark or wrinkle left by a fold, as in paper:—*v.t.* [creased, creas-ing], to make a fold or wrinkle in; as, to *crease* a pair of pants:—*v.i.* to fall into folds or wrinkles; as, this dress *creases*.—*adj.* **creas′y.**

cre-ate (krē-āt′), *v.t.* [creat-ed, creat-ing], to cause to come into existence; make; originate; produce; also, to cause; occasion; as, to *create* a disturbance.

cre-a-tion (krē-ā′shun), *n.* **1,** the act of forming or originating; as, the *creation* of a new design; **2,** the thing made or originated:—**Creation,** the forming of the universe by God; also, the act by which it was created.—*adj.* **cre-a′tive.**

cre-a-tion-ism (krē-ā′shun-izm), *n.* the belief that the universe was created by God, as described in the Book of Genesis. Compare *evolutionism.*

cre-a-tor (krē-ā′tėr), *n.* one who makes or has the power to bring into existence:—**Creator,** the Supreme Being; God.

crea-ture (krē′tūr), *n.* **1,** any living being; an animal or a human being; **2,** a person who is the mere tool of another; **3,** a strange or frightening being; as, a *creature* from outer space.

crèche (krâsh), *n.* **1,** a public nursery for small children, esp. a day nursery; a day care; **2,** a model of the Christ child in a manger, displayed often at Christmas.

cre-dence (krē′dens), *n.* **1,** belief; as, he gave *credence* to the rumour; **2,** credential; as, he had a letter of *credence* with him.

cre-den-tials (kre-den′shalz), *n.pl.* documents given to a person to be presented by him or her in proof of identity, record, etc.; letters of introduction; references.

cred-i-ble (kred′i-bl), *adj.* **1,** trustworthy; as, a *credible* witness; **2,** believable; as, a *credible* story.—*adv.* **cred′i-bly.**

cred-it (kred′it), *n.* **1,** belief; trust; confidence in the truth of a statement or the truthfulness of a person; as, do not place much *credit* in gossip; **2,** good name; reputation; as, a citizen of *credit* and renown; **3,** acknowledgment of worth; honour; as, he is given *credit* for trying; also, a source of honour; as, he is a *credit* to his family; **4,** the sum remaining at a customer's disposal or in his favour, as on the books of a bank; **5,** a record of satisfactory standing or achievement; as, university entrance *credits*; also, a unit of work in school that counts toward graduation; **6,** an extension of time allowed a customer to pay; as, goods bought on *credit*; **7,** financial standing or reputation; as, his *credit* is good for a credit card; **8,** in bookkeeping, the right-hand side of an account: opposite of *debit*:—*v.t.* **1,** to believe; trust; have confidence in; as, I *credit* her story; **2,** to give (a person) credit or honour; as, I *credit* you with good intentions; **3,** to enter a sum in favour of (a customer on his account); as, *credit* me with 10 dollars.—*adj.* **cred′it-a-ble.**—*adv.* **cred′it-a-bly.**

cred-i-tor (kred′i-tėr), *n.* one to whom money is owed: opposite of *debtor*.

cre-do (krē′dō), *n.* any creed or formal statement of belief.

cred-u-lous (kred′ū-lus), *adj.* ready to believe almost anything; easily deceived or imposed upon.—*n.* **cre-du′li-ty** (kre-dū′li-ti).—*adv.* **cred′u-lous-ly.**

Cree (krē), *n.* [*pl.* Cree or Crees], **1**, a member of the Aboriginal people living in the central and western parts of Canada; **2**, the language of these people:—*adj.* relating to the Cree people, language, or culture.

creed (krēd), *n.* **1,** a brief, authoritative statement of religious belief; as, the Apostles' *Creed*; **2,** a set of opinions or principles on any subject, such as politics, science, etc.; as, a business *creed*.

creek (krēk), *n.* **1,** a small stream; **2,** a long, narrow bay or inlet; also, a stream emptying into a bay or inlet.

creep (krēp), *v.i.* [crept (krept), creep-ing], **1,** to move with the body near or touching the ground, as does a cat stalking a bird, or a human being on hands and knees; crawl; **2,** to feel as if touching crawly things; as, my skin *creeps* when I see a snake; **3,** to grow along the ground, or over a surface, as a vine; **4,** to move cautiously or stealthily:—*n.* **creeps,** *Colloq.* a prickly sensation in the skin or scalp; a feeling of being frightened or very uncomfortable; as, ghost stories give me the *creeps*.—*n.*

creep′er.—*adj.* **creep′y.**

cre-mate (krē-māt′; krē′māt), *v.t.* [cremat-ed, cremat-ing], to burn to ashes, as a corpse.—*n.* **cre′ma-tor; cre-ma′tion.**

crepe or **crêpe** (krāp), *n.* **1,** a soft fabric of silk, wool, cotton, or rayon, with a crinkled or wavy surface; **2,** a similar black silk fabric, used as a sign of mourning; **3,** (usually *crêpe),* a very thin pancake rolled up and stuffed with a filling. Also, **crepe paper; crepe rubber; crepe soles.**

crept (krept), *p.t.* and *p.p.* of *creep.*

cre-scen-do (kre-shen′dō; -sen′), *n.* in *music,* an increasing or swelling of sound to its highest loudness or intensity: opposite of *diminuendo.*

cres-cent (kres′ent), *adj.* **1,** thin and curved, as the new moon; **2,** shaped like the new moon when only a thin curved part of it is seen:—*n.* **1,** the figure of the moon in its first or last quarter; **2,** anything shaped like the new moon; as, a jewelled *crescent;* a *crescent* dinner roll.

cress (kres), *n.* a green water plant of the mustard family with crisp, peppery leaves, used in salads and for garnishing, as watercress.

crest (krest), *n.* **1,** a comb or tuft on the head of a bird; **2,** a tuft of feathers on a helmet, or the helmet itself; **3,** the top, as the ridge of a wave or the summit of a hill or ridge; the highest part of something; **4,** the device or figure at the top of a coat of arms; also, this device used by itself as a decoration or seal:—*v.t.* **1,** to serve as the crest of; as, woods *crest* the hills; **2,** to rise above; top.—*adj.* **crest′ed.**

CREST, DEF. 1

crest-fall-en (krest′fôl′en), *adj.* dejected; disheartened; dispirited.

cre-ta-ceous (kri-tā′shus), *adj.* containing or like chalk:—*adj.* and *n.* **Cretaceous,** in *geology,* a period succeeding the age of dinosaurs and reptiles during which the remains of early mammals and flowering plants were fossilized in chalk beds.

cre-tin (krē′tin), *n.* a person arrested in physical and mental development owing to a lack of thyroid secretion; someone affected by cretinism.

cre-vasse (kre-vas′), *n.* a deep fissure or cleft in a glacier.

crev-ice (krev′is), *n.* a narrow split or crack; as, a *crevice* in a wall or rock.

crew (kro͞o), *n.* **1,** the group of persons working on an aircraft, ship, or boat; **2,** a gang of persons working together; as, a road *crew;* **3,** a company or throng; as, a theatre *crew.*

crib (krib), *n.* **1,** a manger for feeding stock; **2,** a bin with slatted walls, for storing unshelled corn; **3,** a child's bed with high, railed sides; **4,** a heavy framework, for strengthening a building that is being moved; **5,** *Slang* an unfair aid, as a key or translation, used by students; **6,** in *cribbage,* discarded cards used by the dealer in scoring.—*v.t.* [cribbed, crib-bing], **1,** to put (grain) into a crib; **2,** *Colloq.* to steal and use as one's own; as, to *crib* a thought from Shakespeare:—*v.i. Colloq.* to use a crib, as in a recitation or test:—*adj.* pertaining to crib; as, *crib* notes.

crib-bage (krib′ij), *n.* a card game, usually for two, in which cards are discarded to form a *crib,* which adds to the dealer's score. The score is kept by moving pegs on a board with holes for them.

crib-bing (krib′ing), *n.* a framework of timber, as the lining of a mine, etc. Also, **crib′work′.**

crick (krik), *n.* a painful stiffness of the muscles of the neck or back.

[1]**crick-et** (krik′it), *n.* a popular British game somewhat like baseball, but with 11 players on each side and two wickets instead of bases.—*n.* **crick′et-er.**

[2]**crick-et** (krik′it), *n.* a black, hopping insect: the male makes a chirping sound by rubbing his forewings together.

crime (krīm), *n.* **1,** an act that breaks the law and makes the offender liable to punishment; also, a sinful or wicked deed; **2,** wrongdoing; law breaking.

crim-i-nal (krim′i-nal), *n.* one who is guilty of a grave offence against the law:—*adj.* having to do with crime or something like a crime; as, *criminal* acts; *criminal* law; *criminal* waste of food.—*adv.* **crim′i-nal-ly.**—*n.* **crim′i-nal′i-ty; crim′i-nol′o-gy.**

crimp (krimp), *v.t.* to fold or press into pleats; impart a wavy appearance to:—*n.* **1,** the act of waving, curling, or frilling; **2,** crimps, curled hair.—*adj.* **crimp′y.**

crim-son (krim′zn), *n.* a deep-red colour:—*adj.* deep red:—*v.t.* to colour deep red; as, the sunset *crimsons* the lake:—*v.i.* to blush; become red.

cringe (krinj), *v.i.* [cringed, cring-ing], **1,** to wince with pain; shrink or cower in fear; **2,** to fawn; be basely humble in manner, as a beggar:—*n.* a servile bow.

crin-kle (kring′kl), *v.i.* [crin-kled, crin-kling], **1,** to wrinkle; twist; become rippled; as, paper *crinkles;* **2,** to rustle, as stiff silk:—*v.t.* to cause to wrinkle or ripple:—*n.* a wrinkle; a fold.—*adj.* **crin′kly.**

crin-o-line (krin′o-lin), *n.* **1,** a stiff cloth used as a lining; **2,** a hoop skirt.

crip-ple (krip′l), *n.* a former term for a person or animal that is lame or physically disabled:—*v.t.* [crip-pled, crip-pling], **1,** to disable; **2,** to weaken; as, the depression *crippled* business.

cri-sis (krī′sis), *n.* [*pl.* crises (krī′sēz)], **1,** a turning point for better or worse in an illness; **2,** a turning point in the progress of anything, as in history.

crisp (krisp), *adj.* **1,** hard but brittle; as, *crisp* toast; *crisp* leaves; also, flaky; as, *crisp* pastry; **2,** brisk; decided; as, *crisp* speech; *crisp* sentences; **3,** fresh and firm; as, *crisp* lettuce and vegetables; **4,** fresh and bracing; as, *crisp* air; **5,** tightly curling; as, *crisp* hair:—*v.t.* and *v.i.* to make or become crisp.—*n.* **crisp′ness.**—*adj.* **cris′py.**—*adv.* **crisp′ly.**

criss-cross (kris′krôs′), *adj.* crosswise, crossed, as in the game of *tick-tack-toe* or a plaid pattern:—*v.t.* and *v.i.* to lie, cover, or go in a crisscross pattern; as, city streets *crisscross;* lines *crisscrossed* her skirt.

cri-te-ri-on (krī-tē′ri-un), *n.* [*pl.* criteria (krī-tē′ri-a)], a standard or rule by which to form a judgment; test; as, his words are no *criterion* of his thoughts.

crit-ic (krit′ik), *n.* **1,** a person skilled in judging art, literature, films, etc.; **2,** one who judges harshly.

crit-i-cal (krit′i-kal), *adj.* **1,** faultfinding; **2,** impartial and careful in forming judgments; **3,** decisive; important; as, a *critical* moment; **4,** involving risk or crisis; as, a *critical* operation; a patient in *critical* condition; **5,** having to do with a critic or critics; as, a book of *critical* success.—*adv.* **crit′i-cal-ly.**

crit-i-cism (krit′i-sizm), *n.* **1,** the act or art of judging and defining the merits of a scientific or artistic work; **2,** a harsh judgment; faultfinding; **3,** the principles or method of judging works of art.—*v.t.* and *v.i.* **crit′i-cize.**

croak (krōk), *v.i.* **1,** to utter a low, harsh sound like that of a raven or frog; **2,** to grumble; forebode evil; **3,** *Slang* to die:—*v.t.* to utter hoarsely or dismally:—*n.* a low, hoarse sound.—*n.* **croak′er.**

cro-chet (krō′shā), *v.t.* [crocheted (krō′shād), crochet-ing (krō′shā-ing)], to make (a fabric or article) by looping a thread into other loops with a single hooked needle; as, to *crochet* a sweater:—*v.i.* to make things in this manner; as, to *crochet* all day:—*n.* the kind of fabric thus made; as, a piece of *crochet.*

crock (krok), *n.* **1,** an earthenware pot or jar, esp. for kitchen use; **2,** *Slang* nonsense; untrue; as, the fact that she claims to be the best student in the class is a *crock.*

crock-er-y (krok′ėr-i), *n.* earthenware, esp. kitchen dishes, bowls, etc.

croc-o-dile (krok′o-dīl′), *n.* a tough-skinned, long-tailed, flesh-eating reptile, with a long, narrow head and pointed snout, found in the fresh waters of Africa, Asia, Australia, and the U.S.

cro-cus (krō′kus), *n.* one of the earliest spring-flowering bulbs, bearing purple, yellow, or white flowers: Manitoba's official floral emblem.

crone (krōn), *n.* a withered old woman; a hag.

cro-ny (krō′ni), *n.* [*pl.* cronies], a familiar friend; chum.—*n.* **cro′ny-ism.**

crook (krook), *n.* **1,** the bent or curved part of anything; **2,** a bent or hooked article or tool, as a shepherd's staff; **3,** a swindler; criminal:—*v.t.* to bend; as, to *crook* one's finger:—*v.i.* to curve; grow crooked.

crook-ed (krook′id), *adj.* **1,** bent; curved; not straight; as, a *crooked* path; **2,** not upright in conduct; dishonest.

croon (kro͞on), *v.i.* and *v.t.* to sing in a soft, plaintive, or sentimental manner:—*n.* the sound of such singing.—*n.* **croon′er.**

crop (krop), *n.* **1,** the amount, as of a grain or fruit, grown and gathered in one season; as, the corn *crop;* **2,** crops, plants grown for food, esp. grains and fruits; **3,** anything likened to a season's harvest; as, a *crop* of books; a *crop* of new players; **4,** a pouch in a bird's gullet where food is prepared for digestion; **5,** a stout horseback-riding whip; **6,** hair cut close or short:—*v.t.* [cropped, crop-ping], **1,** to mow; **2,** to bite off; as, the horse *cropped* the grass; **3,** to cut short, as hair, tail, ears, etc.:—*v.i.* **1,** to bite the tops off grass, etc.; **2,** to appear unexpectedly; as, an old friend *cropped* up yesterday.

crop-per (krop′ėr), *n.* **1,** one who raises farm crops on shares; also a crop plant; **2,** a disastrous failure; as, to come a *cropper.*

cro-quet (krō′kā), *n.* a lawn game in which wooden balls are driven by mallets from a starting stake, through a series of wire wickets to a turning-stake and back.

cro-quette (krō-ket′), *n.* a ball of minced meat, fish, or vegetables, seasoned and fried.

cross (krôs), *n.* **1,** an upright stake bearing a horizontal bar, or two stakes nailed together to form an X, an ancient Roman instrument of torture and death for slaves or foreign criminals; **2,** a sacred emblem, esp. of Christianity, as a symbol of the stake on which Jesus was crucified; **3,** any reproduction of this symbol, used as a shrine or monument; a crucifix; **4,** two intersecting straight lines, as the plus sign [+] or as the sign of multiplication [×]; **5,** such a mark used as a signature by one who cannot write; **6,** a badge of distinction; as, he received the Victoria *Cross;* **7,** suffering or affliction to be borne; **8,** an intermixture of breeds or varieties of plants

CROSSES: 1, LATIN; 2, GREEK; 3, ST. ANDREW'S; 4, MALTESE; 5, PAPAL.

or animals; as, a mule is a *cross* between a horse and an ass:—*v.t.* **1,** to put or lay across; as, to *cross* timbers in building; **2,** to draw a mark across; as, to *cross* a *t;* **3,** to go to the opposite side of; as, to *cross* a bridge; **4,** to meet and pass; as, my letter *crossed* his on the way; **5,** to intersect; **6,** to make the sign of the cross upon (oneself); **7,** to cancel; as, I *crossed* out a word; **8,** to thwart; hinder; as, he is not in a mood to be *crossed;* **9,** to cause to interbreed, as plants or animals of different kinds:—*v.i.* **1,** to go, move, or lie from one side to the other; **2,** to meet and pass, going in opposite directions; **3,** to interbreed:—*adj.* **1,** intersecting; **2,** opposed; contrary; as, to work at *cross* purposes; **3,** ill-tempered; peevish:—*n.* **crosscut saw**, any saw that cuts across the grain (opposite of *rip saw,* which cuts with the grain). Also, **cross′walk′;cross′ check′.**

cross-bow (krôs′bō), *n.* a weapon of the Middle Ages, having a bow across a wooden stock, which contained a groove for a stone or an arrow.

cross–ex-am-ine (krôs′–ig-zam′in), *v.t.* and *v.i.* to question closely; as, a lawyer *cross–examines* a witness who has already been questioned at a trial. Also, **cross′–ques′tion.**—*n.* **cross′–ex-am-in-a′tion.**

cross-ing (krôs′ing), *n.* a place where something crosses or is crossed; as, a school *crossing;* deer *crossing.*

cross–pol-li-nate (krôs′–pôl′i-nāt), *v.t.* to transfer pollen from one flower to the stigma of another (by wind, insects, or artificially), in order to fertilize it.—*n.* **cross′–pol-li-na′tion.**

cross-road (krôs′rōd′), *n.* **1,** a road that crosses a main road, or runs from one main road to another:—**crossroads, 1,** the place where two or more roads cross each other; **2,** a crucial point in something; as, to be at a *crossroads* in the program.

cross–sec-tion (krôs′sek′shun), *n.* a piece cut off at right angles to its length or axis; as, the *cross–section* of a fruit, a stalk, a girder, etc.

cross-wise (krôs′wīz′), *adv.* **1,** across; athwart; **2,** in the shape of a cross; as, the church was built *crosswise;* **3,** contrarily.

crotch (kroch), *n.* **1,** a hook or fork; esp., a forked prop or support; **2,** the point of separation into two parts or branches; as, a *crotch* of a tree; **3,** the place where the body or a pair of pants divides into two legs.

crotch-et-y (kroch′i-ti), *adj.* cantankerous; eccentric.

crouch (krouch) *v.i.* **1,** to stoop low, as if ready to spring; **2,** to cringe, as if in fear.

croup (kro͞op), *n.* a child's disease, not infectious, marked by difficult breathing, choking, loss of voice, and a harsh, gasping cough.—*adj.* **croup′y.**

¹crow (krō), *v.i.* [*p.t.* sometimes in sense **1,** crew (kro͞o); otherwise regular], **1,** to make a shrill sound, like that of a barnyard rooster; **2,** to boast in triumph; as, to *crow* over a victory; **3,** to utter a joyous cry:—*n.* the cry of a rooster.

²crow (krō), *n.* **1,** a large, black bird, harsh-voiced, highly intelligent, and often destructive, although they do eat thousands of harmful insects; **2,** any closely related bird, as a rook or raven; **3,** a crowbar.

crow-bar (krō′bär′), *n.* a long, straight iron bar, pointed or wedge-shaped at the working end, used as a lever.

crowd (kroud), *n.* **1,** a number of persons or things collected closely together; **2,** the masses, or common people; **3,** *Colloq.* a certain set of people; clique; as, a bad *crowd:*—*v.t.* **1,** to press (people or things) closely together; **2,** to fill too full; pack; stuff; **3,** to force (oneself or one's way) through; shove; push:—*v.i.* **1,** to assemble in large numbers; as, to *crowd* into a hall; **2,** to push; force oneself.—*adj.* **crowd′ed.**

crown (kroun), *n.* **1,** a wreath, as of flowers, for the head; **2,** a headdress of gold and jewels, worn by kings or queens on ceremonial occasions; a diadem; **3,** the monarch him- or herself, or the monarch's power; **4,** anything shaped like, or likened to, a crown; as, the *crown* of a hill, hat, or tooth; **5,** the top of the head; also, the head; **6,** completion; perfection; as, wisdom is the *crown* of age; **7,** an honour or championship; as, the boxing *crown;* **8,** the highest point of something; as, the *crown* of the hill; **9,** in Britain, a former silver coin worth five shillings; **10,** the heavy end of the shank of an anchor (see *anchor,* illustration):—**crown prince,** the immediate heir to a throne; **crown princess,** a woman or girl who is next in succession to a throne; also, the wife of a crown prince:—*v.t.* **1,** to put a crown upon the head of; hence, to invest with regal power; reward; honour; **2,** to occupy the topmost part of; complete; as, a dome *crowns* a building; success *crowns* a career; **3,** in dentistry, to place an artificial top upon (a tooth); **4,** *Colloq.* to hit on the head.—*n.* **crown′er.**

Crown corporation, a company or agency owned by the Canadian or a provincial government, such as Via Rail, Canada Post, and CBC.

Crown land, public land; land that is owned by the federal or a provincial government, which comprises nearly 90 per cent of all land in Canada.

crow's–feet (krōz′–fēt′), *n.* small wrinkles that form at the corners of the eyes, esp. of older persons.

crow's–nest (krōz′–nest′), *n.* a partly enclosed box or platform on the masthead of a ship, as shelter for the lookout person; also, any lookout or similar platform.

CRTC (sē′är′tē′sē′), *abbrev.* short for *C*anadian *R*adio-Television and *T*elecommunications *C*ommission: the federal regulator of all aspects of Canadian broadcasting.

cru-cial (kroo͞′shal), *adj.* important; decisive; as, a *crucial* test.—*adv.* **cru′cial-ly.**

cru-ci-ble (kroo͞′si-bl), *n.* **1,** an earthenware pot in which ores, metals, and the like are melted; **2,** an onerous test or trial.

cru-ci-fix (kroo͞′si-fiks), *n.* **1,** any image of Christ on the cross; **2,** a cross.

cru-ci-fix-ion (kroo͞′si-fik′shun), *n.* death upon a cross: **Crucifixion**, the death of Christ on the cross; also, a statue or picture representing this scene.—*v.t.* **cru′ci-fy′.**

crude (kroo͞d), *adj.* [crud-er, crud-est], **1,** in a raw state; unrefined; as, *crude* oil; **2,** uncultured; rude; as, *crude* manners; **3,** wanting in grace or taste; harsh in colour; as, a *crude* painting.—*adv.* **crude′ly.**

cru-el (kroo͞′el), *adj.* **1,** delighting in giving pain to others; merciless; hardhearted; **2,** painful; causing suffering, as a disease.—*adv.* **cru′el-ly.**—*n.* **cru′el-ty.**

cruise (kroo͞z), *v.t.* [cruised, cruis-ing], to sail about with no special destination; as, pirates *cruised* the China Sea:—*v.i.* **1,** to sail about in search of enemy ships or to protect merchant ships in time of war; **2,** to travel by boat from port to port; **3,** to make a like trip or move over land in an easy way; as, to *cruise* down the street in a car:—*n.* a voyage from place to place, esp. for enjoyment; as, a Caribbean *cruise*.

cruis-er (kroo͞z′ėr), *n.* **1,** a swift man-of-war with less armour than a battleship; **2,** a police car used for patrolling an area; **3,** a motorboat with a cabin for living on board; **4,** a person or thing that cruises.

cruising speed, the speed of a car, plane, or ship at which best use of fuel is obtained.

crul-ler (krul′ėr), *n.* a ring-shaped or twisted cake, fried brown in deep fat; a type of doughnut.

crumb (krum), *n.* **1,** the soft, inner part of bread; **2,** a fragment of bread, cake, etc.; **3,** a little bit; as, a *crumb* of evidence:—*v.t.* to break (bread) into little pieces.

crum-ble (krum′bl), *v.t.* [crum-bled, crum-bling], to break into crumbs or pieces:—*v.i.* **1,** to fall to pieces; **2,** to fall into decay or ruin.—*adj.* **crum′bly.**

crum-pet (krum′pit), *n.* a tea cake or thin muffin, usually toasted.

crum-ple (krum′pl), *v.t.* [crum-pled, crum-pling], to press into wrinkles; rumple:—*v.i.* to become wrinkled.

crunch (krunch), *v.t.* and *v.i.* **1,** to crush or grind noisily; as, feet *crunch* the ice; **2,** to chew noisily, as does a horse:—*n.* the act or sound of grinding or chewing noisily.

cru-sade (kroo͞-sād′), *n.* **1,** a vigorous movement for some cause, as against crime:—**Crusade**, any one of seven military expeditions of European Christians, in the eleventh, twelfth, and thirteenth centuries, to recover the Holy Land from the Muslims:—*v.i.* [crusad-ed, crusad-ing], to engage in a crusade.—*n.* **cru-sad′er.**

crush (krush), *v.t.* **1,** to press between two bodies; break to pieces by pressure; **2,** to squeeze; press into a mass; as, to *crush* berries; **3,** to bruise so as to change the normal condition; as, to *crush* a leg; **4,** to break down; ruin; conquer:—*n.* **1,** violent pressure; **2,** a crowd; **3,** *Colloq.* a strong and often foolish liking for a person; as, to have a *crush* on someone.—*n.* **crush′er.**

crust (krust), *n.* **1,** the hard outside covering on bread; also, a piece of this or of stale bread; **2,** any similar hard outside coating; as, a *crust* of ice over soft snow; the earth's *crust*; **3,** the pastry casing of a pie; **4,** *Slang* impudence:—*v.t.* and *v.i.* to cover, or become covered, with a crust.—*adj.* **crust′y.**—*adv.* **crust′i-ly.**—*n.* **crust′i-ness.**

crus-ta-cean (krus-tā′shan), *n.* any of a class of animals, most of which live in the water, having a crustlike shell, as crabs, lobsters, shrimps, etc., many of which are eaten as food.

crutch (kruch), *n.* **1,** a staff with a crosspiece to fit under the arm, used by lame or infirm persons; as, to use *crutches* because of a broken foot; **2,** any forked prop or support.

crux (kruks), *n.* [*pl.* cruxes (-ez); cruces (kroo͞′sēz)], **1,** a puzzle; anything hard to explain; **2,** a basic or essential point; as, this is the *crux* of the problem.

cry (krī), *v.i.* [cried, cry-ing], **1,** to call aloud; complain loudly; wail; exclaim; **2,** to shed tears; weep; **3,** of an animal or bird, to call loudly:—*v.t.* **1,** to announce publicly; as, to *cry* the hour of the night; **2,** to advertise or offer for sale; as, the pedlar *cries* his wares:—*n.* **1,** loud or passionate utterance; as, a *cry* of joy, fear, anger, pain, etc.; **2,** outcry; clamour; demand; **3,** the calling of goods for sale; as, the pedlar's *cry*; **4,** common report; rumour; **5,** the characteristic call of an animal; as, the *cry* of the wolf; **6,** a fit of weeping; **7,** a rallying call; as, a battle *cry*.

cry-ba-by (krī′bā′bi), *n.* one given to constant complaining.

cry-ing (krī′ing), *adj.* requiring action or redress; urgent; as, a *crying* evil.

crypt (kript), *n.* an underground vault, esp. one under a church.

cryp-tic (krip′tik), *adj.* not plain; secret, hidden, or ambiguous; difficult to understand; as, *cryptic* remarks.

cryp-to-gram or **cryp-to-graph** (krip′tō-gram′; -gråf′), *n.* a code or cypher; secret writing; also, a deciphering device.

crys-tal (kris′tal), *n.* **1,** transparent quartz; **2,** a body with regular flat surfaces formed by some substances when they solidify; as, *crystals* of ice; **3,** a glass of superior clearness; **4,** the glass over a watch dial:—*adj.* of or like crystal; consisting of transparent glass; clear.

crys-tal-line (kris′tal-īn′; kris′tal-in), *adj.* **1,** made of, or like, crystal; **2,** clear.

crys-tal-lize (kris′tal-īz′), *v.t.* [crystallized, crystalliz-ing], **1,** to cause to form grains or become crystalline; **2,** to give a fixed shape to; **3,** to coat with sugar crystals; as, to *crystallize* ginger:—*v.i.* **1,** to be converted into grains; become crystalline; **2,** to assume definite shape; as, his plans *crystallized* into deeds.—*n.* **crys′tal-li-za′tion.**

CSIS (sē′sis′), *abbrev.* short for *C*anadian *S*ecurity and *I*ntelligence *S*ervice: the federal counterespionage and security agency.

cub (kub), *n.* **1,** the young of the fox, bear, lion, wolf, etc.; **2,** an inexperienced youth.

cub-by-hole (kub′i-hōl′), *n.* a small, confined space.

cube (kūb), *n.* **1,** in *geometry*, a regular solid body with six equal square sides or faces; **2,** any body resembling this; as, sugar *cubes*; **3,** the product obtained when a number is multiplied two times by itself; as, 5 × 5 × 5 = 125, the *cube* of 5:—*v.t.* [cubed, cub-ing], **1,** to multiply (a number) twice by itself; raise to the third power; **2,** to form into cubelike shapes; as, to *cube* potatoes:—**cube root,** a number or quantity that multiplied by itself to the third power (or two times) gives the number; thus, 2 is the *cube root* of 8.—*adj.* **cu′bic.**—*adj.* **cu′bi-cal.**

cu-bi-cle (kū′bi-kl), *n.* a very small room, as a telephone booth, a private compartment in a public washroom, or a small bedroom in a dorm, etc.

cub-ism (kūb′izm), *n.* a modern school of painting and sculpture that uses geometric figures to suggest volume.

cuck-oo (kook′o͞o′), *n.* an ash-grey European bird noted for laying its eggs in the nests of other birds, and leaving them to the care of the nest owners; also, a North American bird that rears its own young: both so named from their characteristic two-noted love call; **2,** the call of the cuckoo:—*adj.* **1,** relating to the cuckoo; **2,** *Slang* silly; unbalanced.

cu-cum-ber (kū′kum-bėr), *n.* **1,** a creeping plant cultivated for its fruit, which is used in salads or to make pickles; **2,** the fruit itself.

cud (kud), *n.* food that certain animals, called *ruminants,* bring back into the mouth from the first stomach to be chewed; as, cows, sheep, goats, etc., chew the *cud.*

cud-dle (kud′l), *v.t.* [cud-dled, cud-dling], to embrace closely and lovingly; as, a mother *cuddles* a baby:—*v.i.* to lie close or snug; nestle; hug.

cudg-el (kuj′el), *n.* a thick stick used as a weapon:—*v.t.* [cudgelled, cudgel-ling], to beat with a stick.

[1]cue (kū), *n.* **1,** the tapering rod used to strike the ball in playing billiards, pool, and similar games; **2,** a pigtail; queue; **3,** a long line of people waiting. See **queue.**

[2]cue (kū), *n.* **1,** a hint; a suggestion as to what to do; as, that's my *cue* to leave; **2,** the last words of a speech or scene in a play or movie that indicate the time for another actor to enter or speak:—*v.t.* [cued, cue-ing or cu-ing], to give a person a cue; as, to *cue* him when it's time for him to walk on.

[1]cuff (kuf), *n.* a blow, as with the open hand:—*v.t.* to strike with the open hand.

[2]cuff (kuf), *n.* a band worn about the wrist, as on a sleeve; also, a fold about the bottom of a trouser leg:—**off the cuff,** without any preparation; as, to make a speech *off the cuff.*

cui-sine (kwi-zēn′), *n.* the kitchen or cooking department of a hotel, home, etc.; the style or quality of cooking; as, Italian *cuisine.*

cu-li-nar-y (kū′li-nėr-i), *adj.* pertaining to the kitchen or to cooking.

cull (kul), *v.t.* to pick out; select; gather:—*n.* something sorted out from the rest of a group, as inferior or worthless; as, the *culls* of an orchard.

cul-mi-nate (kul′mi-nāt), *v.i.* [culminat-ed, culminat-ing], to reach the highest point; come to a climax.—*n.* **cul′mi-na′tion.**

cul-pa-ble (kul′pa-bl), *adj.* guilty; criminal; blameworthy.—*adv.* **cul′pa-bly.**—*n.* **cul′pa-bil′i-ty.**

cul-prit (kul′prit), *n.* **1,** one formally accused of a crime; **2,** one guilty of a crime or doing something wrong; as, she was the *culprit* who lost the book.

cult (kult), *n.* **1,** a particular system of worship; **2,** devotion to a person, idea, theory, etc.; as, the nudist *cult*; **3,** the group of people so devoted; also, the object of their devotion:—*adj.* involved in or involving a cult; as, a *cult* film.

cul-ti-vate (kul′ti-vāt′), *v.t.* [cultivated, cultivat-ing], **1,** to till, as the soil; raise by tillage, as crops; **2,** to improve by care, labour, or study; **3,** to devote oneself to; as, to *cultivate* music; **4,** to seek the society of (a person or persons); as, to *cultivate* a friendship; **5,** to loosen the ground about (growing crops).—*n.* **cul′ti-va′tion.**

cul-ti-va-tor (kul′ti-vā′tėr), *n.* **1,** one who tills; **2,** a farm implement for loosening earth about crops.

cul-ture (kul′tūr; chėr), *n.* **1,** care given to the growth and development of animals and plants; **2,** the breeding of viruses or bacteria for scientific study; also, the product of such breeding; **3,** improvement of mind or body by practice or training; as, voice *culture*; physical *culture*; **4,** the training of the mental or moral powers; refinement; **5,** all the beliefs, habits, and customs that are common to a certain group of people at a certain time in history; the civilization of a race of people, including religion, arts, values, beliefs, social customs, etc.; as, Greek, Zulu, or Algonquian *culture*; **6,** the qualities found in a human society that is highly developed, such as art, science, and education.—*adj.* **cul′tur-al; cul′tured.**

cul-vert (kul′vėrt), *n.* a drain, sewer, conduit, etc., passing under a roadway.

cum-ber-some (kum′bėr-sum), *adj.* burdensome; clumsy.—*adv.* **cum′ber-some-ly.**

cu-mu-la-tive (kūm′ū-lā′tiv), *adj.* becoming larger by successive additions; as, *cumulative* interest (on money invested).

cu-mu-lus (kūm′ū-lus), *adj.* said of clouds that pile up in rounded masses above a horizontal base:—**cu′mu-lo-cir′rus,** or small, light, and filmy:—**cu′mu-lo-nim′bus,** thick, towering, and black (pouring rain):—**cu′mu-lo-strā′tus,** swelling up from a horizontal base.

cu-ne-i-form (kū-nē′i-fôrm), *n.* and *adj.* the wedge-shaped writing of ancient inscriptions found in Babylon, Persia, Assyria, etc.

CUNEIFORM WORD

cun-ning (kun′ing), *adj.* **1,** skillful; clever; done with skill or ingenuity; as, a *cunning* worker; a *cunning* escape; **2,** crafty; sly; designing; **3,** *Colloq.* pretty; cute; as, a *cunning* child:—*n.* skill; ability; also, deceit; craftiness.—*adv.* **cun′ning-ly.**

cup (kup), *n.* **1,** a small open vessel, usually with a handle, used mainly for drinking such things as coffee, tea, cocoa, and other hot drinks; **2,** something shaped like a cup; as, the *cup* of an acorn; **3,** the amount a cup holds; a cupful, equal to about 227 ml; as, two *cups* of milk; **4,** a cup-shaped prize of gold or silver; as, to win the Stanley *Cup*; **5,** one's portion of happiness or misery; as, to drain the *cup* of sorrow:—*v.t.* [cupped, cup-ping], to form a cup with; as, to *cup* one's hands.

cup-board (kub′ėrd), *n.* **1,** a closet or cabinet fitted with shelves for storing cups, plates, food, etc.; **2,** any small closet.

cu-pid-i-ty (kū-pid′i-ti), *n.* greed, esp. for money or wealth.

cu-po-la (kū′po-la), *n.* **1,** a domelike roof; a dome; **2,** any small, domelike structure above the roof of a building.

cur (kûr), *n.* **1,** a mongrel; a dog of mixed breed; **2,** a surly, ill-bred person.

cu-rate (kū′rit), *n.* **1,** a cleric in charge of a parish; **2,** an assistant to a priest or rector.

cu-ra-tor (kū-rā′tėr), *n.* one in charge of a museum, art gallery, etc.

curb (kûrb), *v.t.* **1,** to restrain; keep within bounds; as, to *curb* your appetite; **2,** to furnish with a protecting rim, as of stone; as, to *curb* a street:—*n.* **1,** that which checks, restrains, or subdues; as, he put a *curb* on his anger; **2,** a chain or strap attached to a horse's bit and used as a check; **3,** a protecting, raised concrete edge of a street.—*n.* **curb′stone.**

curd (kûrd), *n.* the thickened part of milk; as, cheese is formed of *curds*:—*v.t.* and *v.i.* to curdle.—*adj.* **curd′y.**

cur-dle (kûr′dl), *v.t.* [cur-dled, cur-dling], to thicken into curd:—*v.i.* to thicken; as, this milk has *curdled*.

cure (kūr), *n.* **1,** the act of healing; as, the *cure* for a disease; **2,** a method of treatment that cures; as, the rest *cure*; **3,** a remedy; as, quinine is a *cure* for malaria:—*v.t.* [cured, cur-ing], **1,** to heal; restore to health; **2,** to remedy or remove (an evil of any kind); as, he *cured* his dread of the dark; **3,** to preserve by salting, drying, etc.; as, to *cure* hams.—*adj.* **cur′a-ble; cur′a-tive.**

cur-few (kûr′fū), *n.* **1,** in medieval Europe, the ringing of a bell at a fixed hour in the evening as a warning that fires and lights were to be put out; the law that required this; also, the bell itself; **2,** any rule that something must end by a certain time of night; as, a *curfew* on the night before the big game; **3,** a time set by parents for their children to be at home.

cu-ri-o (kū′ri-ō′), *n.* [*pl.* curios], a rare object of art; a curiosity.

cu-ri-ous (kū′ri-us), *adj.* **1,** anxious to know; interested; prying; as, *curious* eyes; a *curious* mind; **2,** strange; full of mystery; as, a *curious* silence.—*adj.* **cu′ri-ous-ly.**—*n.* **cu′ri-os′i-ty.**

curl (kûrl), *n.* **1,** a small ring of hair; a ringlet; **2,** anything of similar shape; as, a *curl* of smoke; **3,** the act of forming, or state of being formed into, a curved or coiled shape; as, the *curl* of a wave; hair kept in *curl*:—*v.t.* to twist into ringlets or coils:—*v.i.* **1,** to grow or move in spirals; as, smoke *curled* lazily from the chimney; **2,** to play the game of curling.—*adj.* **curl′y.**

curl-er (kûr′lėr), *n.* **1,** a person or thing that curls; **2,** one who plays the game of *curling*.

curl-i-cue (kûr′li-kū′), *n.* a fancy flourish in handwriting.

curl-ing (kûr′ling), *n.* a game with two teams of four players each, in which heavy, polished stones are slid on ice toward a *tee*.

cur-rant (kur′ant), *n.* **1,** a small seedless raisin; **2,** a common garden shrub; also, its acid, red, black, or white berry, used for jellies and jams.

cur-ren-cy (kur′en-si), *n.* [*pl.* currencies], **1,** a passing from person to person; circulation, as of bank notes; **2,** general acceptance; as, the *currency* of a scientific theory; **3,** that which is generally used for money, as notes and coins; as, Canadian *currency* is based on the dollar.

cur-rent (kur′ent), *adj.* **1,** widely circulated; passing from person to person; **2,** now passing, as time; as, the *current* year; belonging to the present time; as, the *current* issue of a magazine; *current* events; **3,** generally accepted; common; as, *current* opinion:—*n.* **1,** a flow or passing; a body of air or water flowing in a certain direction; esp., the swift part of a stream; **2,** the flow, or rate of flow, of electricity; **3,** general course or tendency; as, the *current* of the present time.—*adv.* **cur′rent-ly.**

cur-ric-u-lum (ku-rik′ū-lum), *n.* [*pl.* curriculums (ku-rik′ū-lumz) or curricula (ku-rik′ū-la)], a regular course of study in a university, school, etc.; the required courses for a particular degree or certificate; the content of a particular course.—*adj.* **cur-ric′u-lar.**

¹cur-ry (kur′i), *n.* [*pl.* curries], **1,** a highly spiced sauce with cumin, cayenne, ginger, coriander, etc.; **2,** a dish of meat, rice, etc., cooked or seasoned with this sauce.

²curry (kur′i), *v.t.* **1,** to rub down and clean, as a horse:—**curry favour,** to try to gain favour, as by flattery, etc.

curse (kûrs), *n.* **1,** an oath; **2,** a prayer for injury to someone; **3,** that which brings or causes evil or trouble; also, the evil itself; as, crime is a *curse*; **4,** a word or words used in swearing; language that is considered rude:—*v.t.* [cursed, curs-ing], **1,** to wish, or bring, evil upon; blaspheme; **2,** swear; use bad language; **3,** to torment; to afflict; as, to be *cursed* with a bad temper:—*v.i.* to swear.—*adj.* **curs′ed.**

cur-sor (kûr′sėr), *n.* in *computing,* a marker on a computer screen that shows where the user is working; it usually blinks and may be a small line, a spot of light, an arrow, or another shape.

cur-so-ry (kûr′so-ri), *adj.* hasty; superficial; as, a *cursory* glance at a paper.

curt (kûrt), *adj.* **1,** short; **2,** abrupt; rude.

cur-tail (kûr-tāl′), *v.t.* to cut short; as, rain *curtailed* the exercises; reduce, as expenses.—*n.* **cur-tail′ment.**

cur-tain (kûr′tn; kûr′tin), *n.* **1,** a hanging covering or screen, usually of cloth, which can be drawn up or aside; as, a window *curtain*; **2,** a large hanging cloth or screen that separates the stage of a theatre from the audience; **3,** anything that serves to conceal; as, the fog was like a *curtain* over the city:—*v.t.* to furnish with draperies; enclose with a screen, etc.

curt-sy (kûrt′si), *n.* [*pl.* curtsies], a bow, made by bending the knees and lowering the body, made by girls and women:—*v.i.* [curtsied, curtsy-ing], to make a curtsy.

cur-va-ture (kûr′va-tūr; -chėr), *n.* a bending; curving; also, the amount of bending, as of a curved line or surface.

curve (kûrv), *n.* **1,** a bending without angles; also, that which is bent; **2,** in *baseball,* a ball so pitched as to turn from its expected course:—*v.t.* [curved, curv-ing], to cause to bend or turn from a straight line:—*v.i.* to bend; to turn.

cush-ion (koosh′un), *n.* **1,** a pillow or soft pad to sit, lie, or rest upon; **2,** anything resembling a cushion; as, a *cushion* of leaves:—*v.t.* **1,** to seat on, or as on, a soft pad; **2,** to furnish with a soft pad; **3,** to soften or reduce a shock, as a cushion would; as, soft snow *cushioned* her fall.

cusp (kusp), *n.* **1,** the point or elevation where two curves meet and stop, as on the crown of a tooth or apex of a leaf; **2,** one of the points of the crescent moon.

cus-pid (kus′pid), *n.* a tooth with only one point for tearing food; a canine tooth.

cus-tard (kus′tėrd), *n.* a sweet dessert made of eggs, milk, and sugar, baked or boiled.

cus-to-dy (kus′to-di), *n.* **1,** guardianship; care; as, the *custody* of the orphan; **2,** restraint of liberty; imprisonment; as, the accused was taken into *custody.*—*n.* **cus-to′di-an** (**1,** a guardian; **2,** a caretaker or janitor).

cus-tom (kus′tum), *n.* an established practice, habit, or usage; as, it is his *custom* to read in bed; the strange *customs* of these people:—**customs,** government taxes on imported goods, or the office that inspects these goods and collects the tax:—*adj.* **1,** made to order; as, *custom* clothes; **2,** doing only work that is ordered; as, *custom* tailors.—*adj.* **cus′tom-ar′y.**—*adv.* **cus′tom-ar-i-ly.**—*adj.* **cus′tom-built.**

cus-tom-er (kus′tum-ėr), *n.* one who buys; esp., one who buys regularly at a certain store; a patron.

cut (kut), *v.t.* [*p.t.* and *p.p.* cut, *p.pr.* cut-ting], **1,** to slash with a sharp-edged tool; as, to *cut* one's finger; to hew; as, to *cut* down a tree; to pierce; as, the sleet *cut* his skin; **2,** to shape, as a garment, with a sharp instrument; as, she *cut* the sleeves for the dress; **3,** to shorten or reduce in length or extent; trim; as, to *cut* the hair; *cut* expenses; **4,** figuratively, to grieve or hurt; as, the remark *cut* him to the quick; to penetrate, as if with a sharp-edged tool; as, the wind *cut* him to the bone; **5,** to pretend not to recognize; **6,** to cross; to intersect; as, the two railway lines *cut* one another; **7,** to dissolve or make less stiff; as, a dish detergent will *cut* the grease in washing dishes; **8,** *Colloq.* to absent oneself from (a lecture, class, or the like); as, to *cut* class:—**to cut teeth,** to have new teeth appear through the gums:—*v.i.* **1,** to make a gash; as, the knife *cuts* well; also, to admit of being cut or divided; as, this meat *cuts* easily; **2,** to pass through or across by a direct route; as, to *cut* across is shorter:—*n.* **1,** the act of slashing or separating by a sharp instrument; also, a slash or wound made by a sharp instrument; **2,** a sharp stroke, as with a whip; **3,** a passage or channel made by digging; as, a *cut* for a railway track; **4,** that which is severed or detached by a sharp instrument; a slice; as, a *cut* of cake; **5,** a straight, short passage; as, the path is a short*cut* to the house; **6,** the fashion of a garment; style; as, the *cut* of a coat; **7,** a reduction, as in price, expenses, etc.; as, a salary *cut*; **8,** absence, as from a lecture, class, etc.; **9,** the deliberate ignoring of an acquaintance; **10,** an engraved block of wood or metal from which a picture or the like is printed; also, the picture made from it:—*adj.* **1,** divided or separated; **2,** gashed, wounded; **3,** having the surface ornamented or fashioned, as a gem; **4,** reduced; as, dresses sold at *cut* prices:—**cut and dried, 1,** prearranged; **2,** boring; lifeless.

cute (kūt), *adj.* [cut-er, cut-est], *Colloq.* **1,** clever; shrewd; as, a *cute* trick; **2,** attractive because of daintiness, etc.; as, a *cute* child.

cu-ti-cle (kū′ti-kl), *n.* **1,** the outer layer of skin; the epidermis; **2,** dead skin, as that around the base of a fingernail.

cut-lass (kut′las), *n.* a short, heavy sword, with a wide, curved blade, used especially by sailors.

cut-ler (kut′lėr), *n.* one who makes, sells, or repairs knives or other cutting tools.

cut-ler-y (kut′lėr-i), *n.* **1,** edged or cutting tools collectively, as knives, scissors, etc.; esp., implements used in cutting or serving food; **2,** tools for preparing and eating food, such as a fork, spoon, knife, etc.; **3,** the business of a cutler.

cut-let (kut′lit), *n.* a slice of meat, generally of veal, pork, or mutton, cut from the ribs or leg of an animal, for frying or broiling; also, any preparation of fish, ground meat, or the like, shaped like a cutlet; a croquette.

cut-off (kut′ôf′), *n.* **1,** a device for shutting off a fluid, steam, etc., from an engine or mechanism, or the place where it is shut off; **2,** a road, passage, or channel that shortens the distance (across):—**cutoffs,** *Colloq.* jeans or pants that have been shortened by cutting, without hemming.

cut-out (kut′out′), *n.* **1,** a device to allow exhaust gases to bypass a car's muffler; **2,** a design or shape prepared for cutting, having been cut out of cardboard, paper, etc.; **3,** a switch or electric circuit breaker.

cut-ter (kut′ėr), *n.* **1,** one who cuts out and shapes anything, as garments; **2,** that which cuts; as, a cookie *cutter*; **3,** a light sleigh for two persons; **4,** a small, single-masted sailing vessel, or a boat used by ships of war; **5,** an armed boat used by the coastguard; as, a revenue *cutter*.

cut-throat (kut′thrōt′), *n.* a murderous villain; an assassin:—*adj.* murderous; ruthless.

cut-ting (kut′ing), *n.* **1,** a piece cut off something; clipping; as, a newspaper *cutting*; **2,** a stem or twig cut from a plant and able to grow roots and develop a new plant:—*adj.* **1,** sharp and able to cut; as, the *cutting* edge of a knife; **2,** hurting another's feelings; insulting; as, a *cutting* remark.

cy-an-ide (sī′an-īd′), *n.* any of the highly poisonous salts or esters of hydrocyanic acid.

cy-ber- (sī′bėr-), *prefix* pertaining to computers and/or networks, artificial intelligence, or virtual reality; as, *cyber*cash, *cyber*community, *cyber*netics, *cyber*punk, *cyber*sex, *cyber*space, *cyber*squatter, etc.

cy-ber-space (sī′bėr-spās), *n.* a special, intangible dimension of worldwide computer networks for online communications and data transmission and exchange; as, to lose an e-mail in *cyberspace*.

cy-cle (sī′kl), *n.* **1,** a period of time, or a round of events, that takes place regularly, as the four seasons; **2,** a complete series; esp., a group of stories surrounding a famous event or hero; as, the Arthurian *cycle*; a washing-machine *cycle*; **3,** an age or long period of time; **4,** a bicycle, tricycle, or motorcycle:—*v.i.* [cy-cled, cy-cling], to ride a cycle; as, he *cycled* to school.—*adj.* **cy′clic**—*n.* **cy′clist.**

cy-clone (sī′klōn), *n.* **1,** a violent storm in which the wind whirls inward toward a calm centre; **2,** loosely, any destructive storm.—*adj.* **cy-clon′ic** (sī-klon′ik).

cy-clo-tron (sī′klo-tron′; sik-), *n.* a device for increasing the speed of positive particles, esp. protons, etc., in order to bombard and split atoms.

cyl-in-der (sil′in-dėr), *n.* **1,** a solid or hollow body, long and round, with its two ends equal and parallel; **2,** any body having the form of a cylinder, as the piston chamber of a gasoline or steam engine, the barrel of a pump, a roller used in a printing press, etc.—*adj.* **cy-lin′dri-cal; cy-lin′dric.**

cym-bal (sim′bl), *n.* in *music*, either of two circular metal plates that, when clashed together or with a drumstick, produce a ringing sound.

cyn-ic (sin′ik), *n.* one who doubts the goodness of human nature and believes that each person has only a desire to further his or her own interests; hence, a sarcastic, sneering person; a faultfinder:—*adj.* sarcastic; doubting.—*adj.* **cyn′i-cal.**—*adv.* **cyn′i-cal-ly.**—*n.* **cyn′i-cism.**

cy-pher (sī′fėr), *n.* Same as **cipher.**

cy-press (sī′pres), *n.* **1,** a cone-bearing evergreen tree of the pine family; **2,** the wood of a cypress tree:—*adj.* pertaining to, or made of, cypress.

cyst (sist), *n.* in animals and humans, an abnormal sac or pouch filled with liquid or hard material.

czar (zär) or **tsar** (tsär), *n.* **1,** the title of the former emperors of Russia; **2,** a dictator; as, the *czar* of an industry.—*n.fem.* **cza-ri′na; tsa-ri′na.**

D

D, d (dē̄), *n.* [*pl.* D's, d's], **1,** the fourth letter of the alphabet, following C, or its sound; **2,** in *music,* the second tone in the major scale of C; **3,** the Roman numeral for 500; **4,** the fourth-highest mark, grade, or level.

dab (dab), *v.t.* [dabbed, dab-bing], to strike or touch lightly; smear in spots:—*n.* **1,** a soft blow; **2,** a quick, sharp stroke; **3,** a small, soft lump; **4,** a small portion.

dab-ble (dab′l), *v.t.* [dab-bled, dab-bling], to wet by dipping; spatter:—*v.i.* **1,** to paddle in water, as with the hands; **2,** to work at or do anything indifferently; as, to *dabble* in art.—*n.* **dab′bler.**

dachs-hund (däks′hoont′; daks′hoond′; dash′hund′; dash′und), *n.* a hound, usually black or brown, with a long body and very short, crooked legs.

dad or **dad-dy** (dad, da′di), *n. Colloq.* father.

dad-dy–long-legs (dad′i–lông′legz′), *n.* a small-bodied arachnid with long, slender legs.

daf-fo-dil (daf′ō-dil), *n.* a plant, grown from a bulb, with long, narrow leaves and large yellow or white spring-blooming flowers.

daft (dåft), *adj.* weak-minded; simple; foolish; crazy.

dag-ger (dag′ėr), *n.* **1,** a short, sharp, pointed knife; **2,** in printing, a mark † telling the reader to look elsewhere for more information.

dahl-ia (dāl′ya; däl′ya; dal′ya), *n.* **1,** a tall garden plant that grows from a bulb and bears in the early autumn large, showy flowers of red, yellow, white, etc.; **2,** the bulb or flower of this plant.

dai-ly (dā′li), *n.* [*pl.* dailies], a newspaper published every day:—*adj.* occurring, appearing, or done every day:—*adv.* on every day; day by day.

dain-ty (dān′ti), *n.* [*pl.* dainties], something choice or delicious; a choice bit of food:—*adj.* [dain-ti-er, dain-ti-est], **1,** delicious; **2,** pretty in a delicate way; as, a *dainty* ballerina; **3,** sensitive; having delicate tastes and feelings.—*adv.* **dain′ti-ly.**

dair-y (dâr′i), *n.* [*pl.* dairies], **1,** a place where milk is kept and made into butter and cheese; **2,** a farm, or part of a farm, where cows are kept and that produces and sells milk and milk products; **3,** a place where milk, butter, cheese, and other milk products are sold:—*adj.* pertaining to things made of milk; as, *dairy* products; *dairy* farm.—*n.* **dair′y-ing.**

da-is (dā′is; dās), *n.* [*pl.* daises (dā′is-ez; dās′ez)], a raised platform, as for a throne, seats of honour, or a lecture podium, in a large room or hall.

dai-sy (dā′zi), *n.* [*pl.* daisies], a flower of the aster family, with a brown or yellow centre surrounded by white, yellow, or pink petals; also, the plant itself.—*adj.* **dai′sied.**

Da-ko-ta (da-kō′ta), *n.* **1,** the Aboriginal people living in the southern plains of Western Canada and in the northwestern U.S.; **2,** the language of these people.

dale (dāl), *n.* a valley; glen; as, they went up hill and down *dale.*

dal-ly (dal′i), *v.i.* [dallied, dally-ing], **1,** to make sport; play; trifle, as with affections or an idea; **2,** to waste time; loiter; as, he *dallied* over his work.—*n.* **dal′li-ance.**

Dal-ma-tian (dal-mā′shun), *n.* a breed of dog like a pointer, with black and white spots; a coach dog.

[1]**dam** (dam), *n.* **1,** a bank or wall built so as to hold back a flow of water; **2,** water so held back:—*v.t.* [dammed, dam-ming], **1,** to provide with a dam; as, to *dam* a brook; **2,** to obstruct; restrain; confine; block; as, leaves *dammed* up the drain.

[2]**dam** (dam), *n.* a mother of certain animals, as sheep.

dam-age (dam′ij), *n.* **1,** injury or harm; as, the flood did *damage* to the town:—**damages,** money paid to one for injury or loss through the fault of another; as, the airline paid him *damages:*—*v.t.* [damaged, damaging], to injure.—*adj.* **dam′age-a-ble.**

dam-ask (dam′åsk), *n.* **1,** a figured fabric of silk, linen, wool, or other material, used esp. for tablecloths: so named for the city of Damascus, where it was originally made; **2,** hard, elastic steel decorated with wavy lines, and formerly used for sword blades; **3,** a deep-pink colour:—*adj.* **1,** pertaining to or coming from Damascus; **2,** made of damask; as, a *damask* tablecloth; **3,** of a deep-pink colour.

dame (dām), *n.* **1,** a female member of an order of knighthood: also used as a title of respect, corresponding to *sir;* **2,** a matron; an elderly woman.

damn (dam), *v.t.* [damned (damd), damning], **1,** to condemn; **2,** to doom to eternal punishment; **3,** to curse; call down a curse upon; **4,** to judge as bad, faulty, or a failure; as, the critics *damned* the movie:—*n.* **1,** saying the word "damn" as a curse; **2,** *Colloq.* the least little bit; as, to not be worth a *damn*:—*adj.* and *adv.* extremely, very; as, she's a *damn* good musician:—*interj. Slang* used to express anger, disappointment, etc.—*adj.* **dam′na-ble.**—*n.* **dam-na′tion.**

damp (damp), *n.* **1,** moisture; fog; **2,** a poisonous gas sometimes found in mines; **3,** depression of spirits:—*adj.* moist; a little wet; as, a *damp* cloth:—*v.t.* **1,** to moisten; **2,** to discourage; depress; **3,** to check; stifle; as, to *damp* a fire.—*adv.* **damp′ly.**—*n.* **damp′ness.**

damp-en (damp′en), *v.t.* **1,** to make moist or wet; **2,** to depress or discourage.

damp-er (damp′ėr), *n.* **1,** something that depresses, curbs, or discourages; as, to put a *damper* on fun; **2,** a movable plate to regulate a draft, as in a stove, fireplace, or furnace.

dance (dåns), *v.i.* [danced, danc-ing], **1,** to move the body and feet rhythmically in time to music; **2,** to skip about lightly; as, the child *danced* for joy; sunbeams *dance* in the room:—*v.t.* **1,** to give a dancing motion to; as, to *dance* the baby up and down; **2,** to perform; as, to *dance* a tango:—*n.* **1,** a rhythmical movement of the body and feet, usually to the accompaniment of music; **2,** a dancing party; as, a school *dance*; **3,** one round of dancing at such a party; as, may I have this *dance?* **4,** a piece of music for dancing; as, the band played a new *dance*.—*n.* **danc′er.**

dan-de-li-on (dan′di-lī′un), *n.* a common plant having yellow flowers and coarsely toothed leaves; also, its flower: the leaves and flowers are sometimes eaten in salads.

dan-druff (dan′druf), *n.* minute scales of dead skin that form on the scalp.

dan-dy (dan′di), *n.* [*pl.* dandies], **1,** a man who gives much attention to dress, esp. in former times; **2,** *Colloq.* something unusually fine or excellent:—*adj.* [dan-di-er, dan-di-est], *Colloq.* excellent; as, a *dandy* day.

dan-ger (dān′jėr), *n.* **1,** peril; exposure to loss, injury, or death; risk; as, the *danger* of an explosion was very grave; **2,** something that may cause loss, injury, etc.; the possibility that something bad or harmful will happen; as, the sign warned of *danger* ahead.

dan-ger-ous (dān′jėr-us), *adj.* **1,** unsafe; perilous; as, a *dangerous* road; **2,** likely to do harm; as, a *dangerous* criminal.

dan-gle (dang′gl), *v.i.* [dan-gled, dan-gling], **1,** to hang or swing loosely; **2,** to hang about anyone; follow; as, fans *dangle* about the rock star:—*v.t.* to cause to swing loosely; as, she *dangled* the toy in front of the kitten.

dank (dangk), *adj.* unpleasantly damp; moist; wet; as, a *dank* cellar.

dap-per (dap′ėr), *adj.* **1,** small and active; **2,** trim and neat in appearance.

dap-ple (dap′l), *adj.* spotted; as, a *dapple*-grey horse:—*n.* a spotted animal, esp. a horse:—*v.t.* [dap-pled, dap-pling], to decorate with spots.—*adj.* **dap′pled.**

dare (dâr), *v.i.* [*p.t.* dared (dârd), *p.p.* dared, *p.pr.* dar-ing], **1,** to have courage; be bold enough; venture; as, to *dare* to swim across Lake Ontario; **2,** to be bold or rude enough to do something; as, how *dare* you speak to me that way!—*v.t.* **1,** to have courage for; brave; as, to *dare* the perils of space travel; **2,** to challenge; as, he *dared* me to jump:—*n.* a challenge.

dare-dev-il (dâr′dev′l), *adj.* bold; reckless; as, a *daredevil* stunt:—*n.* a reckless, bold person.

dar-ing (dâr′ing), *n.* bravery; boldness:—*adj.* fearless; bold; courageous; willing to take chances.

dark (dark), *adj.* **1,** having little or no light; **2,** of colours, almost black; **3,** of a swarthy complexion; **4,** gloomy; as, a *dark* mood; **5,** secret; mysterious; as, a *dark* project; **6,** evil; as, a *dark* deed:—*n.* **1,** darkness; nightfall; **2,** secrecy; as, to work in the *dark*; **3,** ignorance; as, I am in the *dark* on the *subject*.—*adv.* **dark′ly.**—*n.* **dark′ness.**—*v.t.* and *v.i.* **dark′en** (to make dark; as, clouds *darkened* the sky; the sky *darkened*).

dark horse, an unexpected winner who or that is little known, as in a political contest or horse race.

dark-room (därk′rōōm,′), *n.* a room from which sunlight is excluded, for developing or printing films, etc.

dar-ling (där′ling), *n.* one dearly loved:—*adj.* **1,** tenderly loved; very dear; **2,** cute or charming; as, a *darling* dress.

darn (därn), *v.t.* to mend, as a hole in a fabric, by interweaving thread or yarn:—*n.* the place so mended:—*n., adj.,* or *adv.* a delicate form of *damn*.—*n.* **darn′ing.**

darn-ing nee-dle (därn′ing nē′dl), *n.* **1,** a long needle for darning; **2,** a dragonfly.

dart (därt), *n.* **1,** a thin, pointed arrowlike weapon, thrown by hand; **2,** an indoor game in which darts are thrown at a board or other target on a wall; **3,** a swift, sudden movement:—*v.t.* to throw out suddenly; as, to *dart* angry glances:—*v.i.* to move swiftly and suddenly; as, the child *darted* here and there.

dash (dash), *v.t.* **1,** to throw violently or hastily; as, he *dashed* the vase to pieces; **2,** to push aside; **3,** to spatter; to splash; as, they *dashed* him with water; **4,** to ruin; destroy; as, you *dash* my hopes; **5,** to do hastily; as, to *dash* off an e-mail:—*v.i.* **1,** to rush with violence; as, she *dashed* madly away; **2,** to strike on a surface violently; as, rain *dashed* against the window:—*n.* **1,** a violent blow; **2,** a little bit; as, a *dash* of pepper; **3,** spirit; energy; as, with vim and *dash*; **4,** a mark [–] used in writing, typing, or printing to mark a pause, break, or omission; **5,** the striking of a liquid against a surface; **6,** a sudden rush; as, a *dash* for freedom; **7,** a short race; as, a hundred-metre *dash*.

dash-board (dash′bōrd′), *n.* **1,** in cars, airplanes, etc., a panel with gauges and instruments; **2,** a splashboard or screen on a boat, carriage, etc.

dash-ing (dash′ing), *adj.* **1,** spirited; bold; as, a *dashing* soldier; **2,** showy; stylish.

da-ta (dā′tȧ; dä′tȧ), *n.pl.* [*sing.* datum (dā′tum; dä′tum)], **1,** a collection of facts to be used as a basis for study; facts or figures; information; as, he has collected the *data* for his essay; **2,** in *computing,* any information contained in a computer, including numbers, characters, and images.

data base or **database**, *n.* in *computing,* a large collection of information stored in a computer, organized for easy access and retrieval.

[1]**date** (dāt), *n.* **1,** the point of time at which something takes place or is done; as, the *date* on the letter; **2,** the period or era to which anything belongs; as, art of an early *date*; **3,** an engagement or appointment for a fixed time; as, a *date* to go to the movies; **4,** the person with whom one has a date; as, her prom *date*:—*v.t.* [dat-ed, dat-ing], **1,** to mark with a definite time; as, to *date* an invoice; **2,** to find the definite time of; **3,** to go out with someone on a regular basis; as, Yuri is *dating* Mira:—*v.i.* to belong to a certain time; as, this house *dates* back to the nineteenth century; **3,** to have a series of dates with someone; as, Yuri and Mira are *dating*.

[2]**date** (dāt), *n.* the edible fruit of the date palm tree, oblong in shape and enclosing a single seed.

da-tum (dā′tum), *n. Sing.* of *data.*

daub (dôb), *v.t.* **1,** to cover or smear with mud, plaster, etc.; **2,** to paint coarsely or unskillfully:—*v.i.* **1,** to put on plaster, mud, etc.; **2,** to paint poor pictures:—*n.* **1,** a smear; smudge; **2,** a picture poorly painted.—*n.* **daub′er.**

daugh-ter (dô′tėr), *n.* **1,** a female child; **2,** a female member of a race, country, ideology, etc.; as, a *daughter* of France, of freedom.

daughter board, in *computing,* a small circuit board that plugs into a larger board, such as the *mother board.*

daugh-ter–in–law (dô′tėr–in–lô′), *n.* [*pl.* daughters-in-law], a son's wife.

daunt (dônt; dänt), *v.t.* to frighten; dishearten; dismay.

daunt-less (dônt′lis; dänt′lis), *adj.* fearless; intrepid.

dav-en-port (dav′en-pôrt′), *n.* **1,** a long upholstered sofa with back and arms, esp. one that can be converted, or changed, into a bed; **2,** a small writing desk.

daw-dle (dô′dl), *v.i.* [daw-dled, daw-dling], to waste time; loiter; as, *dawdle* over work.—*n.* **daw′dler.**

dawn (dôn), *v.i.* **1,** to begin to grow light; as, when day *dawned*, the attack began; **2,** to become evident or plain; as, the solution to the problem finally *dawned* upon me; **3,** to begin to develop; as, with the moon landing, a new era *dawned* in space travel:—*n.* **1,** the first appearance of daylight; sunrise; **2,** a beginning or unfolding; as, the *dawn* of history.

day (dā), *n.* **1,** the period of light between sunrise and sunset; daylight; **2,** a period of 24 consecutive hours; **3,** an age or period; as, in Shakespeare's *day*; *days* of old; **4,** the number of hours per day allowed or permitted for work; as, an eight-hour *day*; **5,** a particular 24-hour period connected with some observance; as, a birth*day*; Boxing *Day*.

day-book (dā′book′), *n.* a bookkeeping journal or diary in which transactions are entered as they occur; a book recording daily all sales, purchases, receipts, etc.; a ledger or diary.

day-break (dā′brāk′), *n.* dawn.

daycare or **day care** (dā′kâr′), *n.* the care and supervision of children or elderly or disabled adults during the day outside the home:—**daycare centre,** the place where such activities take place.

day-dream (dā′drēm′), *n.* an idle fancy; a thought of pleasant things:—*v.i.* to indulge in fanciful waking dreams.

day-light (dā′līt′), *n.* **1,** the light of day; **2,** the time between dawn and dusk; **3,** daybreak; as, he arose at *daylight*:—**daylight-saving(s) time,** time that is reckoned one hour earlier than *standard time* and which thus gives an extra hour of daylight in the evening; as, when it is eight o'clock in the evening, standard time, it is nine o'clock *daylight-saving time.*

day-time (dā′tīm′), *n.* the period from dawn to sunset.

daze (dāz), *v.t.* [dazed, daz-ing], **1,** to confuse; stupefy; as, the blow *dazed* him; **2,** to dazzle; as, the display of Egyptian treasures *dazed* the spectators:—*n.* a state of confusion or bewilderment; as, to walk around in a *daze.*—*adj.* **dazed.**

daz-zle (daz′l), *v.t.* [daz-zled, daz-zling], **1,** to confuse with a glare of light; **2,** to bewilder or surprise with splendour; as, the beauty of her garden *dazzled* the guests:—*n.* glitter.—*adj.* **daz′zling.**—*adv.* **daz′zling-ly.**

de- (de-; dē-), *prefix* meaning **1,** *the opposite of*; as, *de*frost; **2,** *down*; as, *de*press; **3,** *away, off*; as, *de*port.

dea-con (dē′kun), *n.* **1,** a subordinate church official who assists in certain duties and ceremonies; a layman assisting the minister; **2,** an ordained member of the Christian clergy who ranks just below a priest.—*n.fem.* **dea′con-ess** (dē′kon-is).

dead (ded), *adj.* **1,** having ceased to live; as, a *dead* person; *dead*wood; *dead* plants; **2,** without life; inanimate, such as rocks; as, *dead* matter; **3,** inactive; broken; showing no force, motion, liveliness, etc.; as, a *dead* electric wire; a *dead* computer; a *dead* phone; **4,** disused; as, a *dead* language; **5,** complete; utter; as, a *dead* loss; *dead* silence:—*n.* **1,** one who has died; those who have died; as, the quick and the *dead*; **2,** the time of greatest inactivity or quietness; as, the *dead* of night:—*adv.* **1,** entirely; as, he is *dead* wrong; **2,** exactly; due; as, *dead* east.

dead-beat (ded′bēt′), *n.* **1,** in *physics*, a beat without a recoil; **2,** *Slang* one who doesn't pay one's bills; a sponger; **3,** a lazy person:—*adj.* **1,** relating to a beat without a recoil; **2,** pertaining to someone who doesn't pay his or her bills; as, a *deadbeat* parent; **3,** lazy; as, the *deadbeat* worker:—**dead beat,** *Colloq.* exhausted; as, to be *dead beat* after the race.

dead-en (ded′n), *v.t.* to deprive of force; lessen; make dull or weak; as, medicine to *deaden* pain.

dead end, **1,** a street or passageway that has no way out at the other end; **2,** a situation or course of action that does not lead to something further; as, this job was a *dead end*.—*adj.* **dead′–end′.**

dead-head (ded′hed′), *n.* **1,** *Colloq.* one who gets free tickets or passes for transportation, theatres, board, etc.; **2,** *Colloq.* a train, bus, etc., without passengers or a load; **3,** a submerged log or tree:—*v.i.* *Colloq.* to travel for free; also, to travel without passengers or a load; as, the subway train *deadheaded* to the end of the line.

dead heat, a tie in a race.

dead letter, **1,** a letter undelivered because of a faulty address, unreadability, etc.; **2,** anything that has lost its force; a law or regulation that is not enforced; as, this law is a *dead letter*.

dead-line (ded′līn′), *n.* the time limit for doing something, such as paying a debt, completing copy to go to press, or submitting an assignment.

dead-lock (ded′lok′), *n.* a standstill; the state of a contest when two opposing sides are so evenly balanced in strength or power that neither will give in and no progress can be made.—*adj.* **dead′locked.**

dead-ly (ded′li), *adj.* [dead-li-er, dead-li-est], **1,** causing death; fatal; as, AIDS is a *deadly* disease; **2,** relentless; as, a *deadly* enemy; **3,** resembling death; as, a *deadly* pallor:—*adv.* **1,** like death; as, *deadly* still; **2,** extremely; as, *deadly* dull; *deadly* serious.

dead-pan (ded′pan′), *adj.* expressionless; as, the clown's *deadpan* face was funny:—*n.* such an expression or manner or such a person:—*v.t.* [dead-panned, dead-panning], to act in this manner.

dead-wood (ded′wood′), *n.* **1,** wood that is no longer alive; **2,** anything useless, whether a person, object, or wording; as, she did little to help and was merely *deadwood*.

deaf (def), *adj.* **1,** unable to hear; unable to hear clearly; **2,** unwilling to listen or pay attention; as, *deaf* to persuasion.—*n.* **deaf′ness.**

deaf-en (def′en), *v.t.* to make deaf; stun with noise.—*adj.* **deaf′en-ing.**

deaf–mute (def′–mūt′), *n.* a person who cannot hear or speak.

[1]**deal** (dēl), *n.* **1,** a part; portion; an amount; as, a great *deal* of money; **2,** in card games, a distribution of cards to the players; also, a player's turn to distribute the cards; as, it's my *deal*; **3,** any distribution or redistribution; as, a new *deal*; **4,** a bargain or agreement; also, the result of such an agreement; as, to make a *deal*; to get a square *deal*:—*v.t.* [dealt (delt), dealing], **1,** to distribute (cards); **2,** to deliver; inflict; as, to *deal* a blow:—*v.i.* **1,** to buy and sell; trade; do business in; as, to *deal* in computer equipment; **2,** to behave; act; as, she *dealt* honourably with his associates; **3,** to be concerned with; be about; as, the chemistry lesson *dealt* with moles.—*n.* **deal′er.**

[2]**deal** (dēl), *n.* fir or pine wood cut into boards of a certain size; also, one of these boards:—*adj.* made of deal.

deal-er (dē′lėr), *n.* **1,** a person who buys and sells things; as, an automobile *dealer*; a drug *dealer*; **2,** a person who distributes cards in a card game; as, a blackjack *dealer*.

dean (dēn), *n.* **1,** the head of a group of clergy connected with a cathedral; **2,** the member of a university or college faculty who has charge of the students; **3,** the administrative officer of a college or university next below the president; **4,** a very illustrious or the oldest member, in years of service, among persons of similar calling; as, *dean* of Canadian scientists.

dear (dēr), *adj.* **1,** highly esteemed; beloved; **2,** often, as in correspondence, merely a polite form of address; as, *Dear* Sir; **3,** costly; also, charging high prices; as, that is a very *dear* restaurant; **4,** heartfelt; earnest; as, his *dearest* ambition:—*n.* a darling; loved one:—*adv.* at a high price:—*interj.* expressing surprise, pity, trouble, etc.; as, oh *dear*!—*adv.* **dear′ly.**

dearth (dûrth), *n.* want; sack; scarcity; as, a *dearth* of fresh fruit and vegetables during the winter months.

death (deth), *n.* **1,** the end of life of people, animals, or plants; also, the act of dying; **2,** total loss; end; as, the *death* of his hopes; the *death* of record albums; **3,** that which causes death; as, his disgrace was the *death* of his father:—**Death,** the destroyer of life: usually represented as a skeleton in black with a scythe. Also, **death′bed′; death′blow′; death′trap′.**

death-less (deth′lis), *adj.* never ending; never dying; as, *deathless* fame.

death-ly (deth′li), *adj.* [death-li-er, death-li-est], **1,** fatal; deadly; **2,** like death; as, a *deathly* stillness:—*adv.* to a degree like death; as, *deathly* pale.

debacle (dē-bä′kl; dē-ba′kl; de-bä′kl; de-ba′kl) *n.* **1,** a complete failure, disaster, or downfall, esp. a sudden collapse; as, the *debacle* of the stock market in 1929; **2,** the breakup of ice in the spring, and the ensuing flood.

de-bar (di-bär′), *v.t.* [debarred, debar-ring], to shut out; exclude; as, he was *debarred* from the game.

de-bark (di-bärk′; dē-bärk′), *v.i.* to go ashore from a vessel or aircraft:—*v.t.* **1,** to remove from a vessel or aircraft; as, to *debark* troops; **2,** to remove bark from a tree.—*n.* **de′bar-ka′tion.**

de-base (di-bās′; dē-bās′), *v.t.* [debased, debas-ing], to lower in value, quality, purity, etc.; as, to *debase* the country's currency.—*n.* **de-base′ment.**

de-bate (di-bāt′; dē-bāt′), *v.t.* [debat-ed, debat-ing], **1,** to discuss by presenting arguments for and against; as, he *debated* the issue; **2,** to think about; consider; as, she *debated* whether or not to go:—*v.i.* to argue or discuss a point:—*n.* **1,** an argument; discussion; **2,** a contest or formal presentation of arguments on both sides of a question by speakers before an audience.—*adj.* **de-bat′a-ble.**—*n.* **de-bat′er.**

de-bauch (di-bôch′; dē-bôch′), *v.t.* to corrupt, spoil, or seduce (a person):—*n.* an orgy; excessive indulgence in sensual pleasures.—*n.* **de-bauch′er-y.**

de-ben-ture (di-ben′tūr; chėr), *n.* an interest-bearing bond or other security, issued by the government or a corporation.

de-bil-i-tate (di-bil′i-tāt′; dē-bil′i-tāt′), *v.t.* [debilitat-ed, debilitat-ing], to weaken; as, a bad cold *debilitates* one's health.

de-bil-i-ty (di-bil′i-ti; dē-bil′i-ti), *n.* [*pl.* debilities], a weakness; lack of strength.

deb-it (deb′it), *n.* **1,** an entry in an account of something due; **2,** the left-hand, or debtor, side of an account; a liability: opposite of *credit*:—*v.t.* to charge (a sum due); enter a charge against (a person or an account); as, to *debit* a bank account.

debit card, a card, similar to a credit card, that allows the user to pay for purchases by electronically withdrawing money directly from the holder's bank account.

deb-o-nair (deb′o-nâr′), *adj.* cheerful; courteous; elegant; winsome; as, a *debonair* host.

de-brief (dē′brēf′), *v.t.* to question to obtain information after a mission or event; as, to *debrief* an intelligence agent upon his or her return from enemy territory.

de-bris or **dé-bris** (deb′rē; de-brē′ or dā′-brē; da-brē′), *n.* **1,** scattered fragments; rubbish; as, the yard was littered with paper and *debris*; **2,** piles of loose rock, as at the base of a mountain.

debt (det), *n.* **1,** that which one person or business owes to another; an amount owed; as, my *debts* total $1000; **2,** anything that is owed to one person from another; as, for your kindness to my mother, I owe you a *debt* of gratitude; **3,** the state of owing money, esp. more than one can pay; as, to be in *debt.*

debt-or (det′ėr), *n.* a person or company that owes money; also, one who is under obligation to another: opposite of *creditor.*

de-bug (di-bug′; dē-bug′), *v.t.* [de-bugged, de-bug-ging], **1,** in *computing,* to locate and remove problems or errors from a computer program; **2,** to remove hidden microphones from a room, building, etc.; **3,** to remove insects from a room, building, etc.

de-bunk (di-bungk′), *v.t.* to strip of false claims, etc.; deflate; expose; as, they *debunked* the popular hero.

de-but or **début** (dā-bū′; dā′bo͞o; de-bū′; dā′bū; deb′ū), *n.* **1,** the first formal appearance of a girl in society; **2,** a first appearance in public, on the stage, television, movies, in business, etc.; as, the *debut* of the new television show, magazine, band, etc.:—*v.t.* and *v.i.* to begin, introduce, or present to the public for the first time; as, to *debut* the new movie; the new television series *debuted* last week.

deb-u-tante or **déb-u-tante** (deb′ū-tänt′; dā′bo͞o′tänt′), *n.* a young woman who is making, or has recently made, her debut, or first appearance, in society.

dec-ade (dek′ād), *n.* **1,** a group of 10; **2,** a period of 10 consecutive years.

dec-a-dence (di-kā′dens; dek′a-dens), *n.* decay, as in morals, character, or quality.—*adj.* **dec′a-dent** (dek′a-dent; di-kā′dent).

de-caf (dē′kaf′), *n. Colloq.* short for decaffeinated coffee.

de-cal (dē′kal′; di-kal′), *n.* short for **de-cal-co-ma-ni-a** (di-kal′kō-mā′ni-a), the transfer of decorative designs or pictures from specially prepared paper to glass, wood, metal, or china.

de-camp (di-kamp′; dē-kamp′), *v.i.* to leave suddenly or secretly; run away; as, she *decamped* with my skateboard.

de-cant (di-kant′; dē-kant′), *v.t.* to pour

gently without disturbing the sediment, as wine from a bottle.

de-can-ter (di-kan′tėr; dē-kan′tėr), an ornamental glass bottle, with a stopper, used for wine or liquor; also, someone who decants.

de-cap-i-tate (di-kap′i-tāt′; dē-kap′i-tāt′), *v.t.* [decapitat-ed, decapitat-ing], to cut off the head of; behead.

de-cath-lon (di-kath′lon), *n.* an athletic contest of 10 separate events, such as runs, hurdles, vaults, jumps, and throws, in which all of the contestants take part.

de-cay (di-kā′), *v.i.* **1,** to decline from a condition of soundness or health; fail; as, business, beauty, or civilization may *decay*; **2,** to rot:—*n.* **1,** decline; gradual failure; as, the *decay* of the Roman Empire; **2,** rot; decomposition of animal or plant matter; as, tooth *decay*.

de-cease (di-sēs′), *v.i.* [deceased, deceas-ing], to die:—*n.* death.

de-ceased (di-sēst′), *adj.* dead, esp. recently dead:—**the deceased**, the dead person.

de-ceit (di-sēt′), *n.* **1,** the act or practice of misleading or cheating; as, he justified *deceit* as a means to an end; **2,** an instance of misleading; a trick.

de-ceit-ful (di-sēt′fool), *adj.* given to fraud and trickery; insincere; false.—*adv.* **de-ceit′ful-ly.**—*n.* **de-ceit′ful-ness.**

de-ceive (di-sēv′), *v.t.* [deceived, deceiv-ing], **1,** to cause (one) to believe what is untrue; as, do not *deceive* me, tell me the truth; **2,** to mislead; as, I was *deceived* by his looks.—*n.* **de-ceiv′er.**

De-cem-ber (di-sem′bėr), *n.* the twelfth and last month of the year, following November: it has 31 days.

de-cen-cy (dē′sen-si), *n.* [*pl.* decencies], **1,** propriety in speech, actions, or dress; decorum:—**decencies**, the requirements of a respectable or decent life, such as common courtesy, cleanliness, etc.

de-cent (dē′sent), *adj.* **1,** becoming; suitable; proper; as, *decent* behaviour; *decent* clothes; **2,** respectable; as, he comes from a *decent* home; **3,** passable; good enough; as, a *decent* living; a *decent* job.—*adv.* **de′cent-ly.**

de-cep-tion (di-sep′shun), *n.* **1,** the act of tricking or cheating; dishonesty; as, *deception* aided his escape; **2,** a piece of trickery; fraud.—*n.* **de-cep′tive-ness.**—*adj.* **de-cep′tive.**—*adv.* **de-cep′tive-ly.**

de-ci- (des′i-), *prefix* meaning a *tenth part; one-tenth*; as, *deci*mal, *deci*metre, etc.

dec-i-bel (des′i-bel′), *n.* the unit used to measure volume of sound; thus, soft radio music is about 35 decibels: most people talk at about 50 decibels.

de-cide (di-sīd′; dē-sīd′), *v.t.* [decid-ed, decid-ing], **1,** to settle; bring to a conclusion; as, he *decided* the matter without delay; **2,** to cause to make a decision; as, that evidence *decides* me in his favour:—*v.i.* **1,** to make up one's mind; as, I have *decided* to leave early; **2,** to give a judgment or decision; as, the jury *decided* in favour of the accused person.

de-cid-ed (di-sīd′id; dē-sīd′id), *adj.* **1,** definite; clear; as, a *decided* advantage; **2,** determined; resolute; as, a very *decided* person.

de-cid-ed-ly (di-sīd′id-li; dē-sīd′id-li), *adv.* definitely; certainly; as, she is *decidedly* intelligent.

de-cid-u-ous (di-sid′ū-us), *adj.* **1,** losing foliage every year; not evergreen; as, the oak is a *deciduous* tree; **2,** shed, or falling, at certain seasons; as, *deciduous* leaves.

dec-i-mal (des′i-mal), *adj.* based upon the number 10; as, the metric system is a *decimal* system of measurement:—**decimal fraction**, a fraction having as its denominator 10 or some power of 10, usually written as a number preceded by a dot, called the *decimal point*, as .7 = 7/10, .07 = 7/100:—*n.* a decimal fraction.

dec-i-mate (des′i-māt′), *v.t.* to kill a large part of; as, the fire *decimated* the forest; literally, to kill one in 10.

de-ci-pher (di-sī′fėr; dē-sī′fėr), *v.t.* to make out the meaning of; translate; figure out (esp. something written in secret characters); as, to *decipher* a code message.

de-ci-sion (di-sizh′un), *n.* **1,** the act of reaching an opinion; also, the opinion or judgment reached; as, he is quick in making *decisions*; a referee's *decision*; **2,** firmness; determination; as, she is a person of *decision*.

de-ci-sive (di-sī′siv), *adj.* **1,** final; conclusive; as, a *decisive* victory; **2,** prompt; positive; determined; as, *decisive* action.—*adv.* **de-ci′sive-ly.**

[1]**deck** (dek), *n.* **1,** a platform serving as a floor in a ship; also, the space between floors; **2,** a platform that is like the deck of a ship or boat; as, the *deck* at the back of a house; **3,** a pack of playing cards:—*v.t.* to furnish (a ship) with a deck.

[2]**deck** (dek), *v.t.* to put finery or ornaments on; adorn; decorate; as, she *decked* herself out in a new suit.

de-claim (di-klām′; dē-klām′), *v.i.* and *v.t,* **1,** to utter (words) in oratorical style; as, he does not speak naturally, he *declaims*; **2,** to recite in public.—*n.* **de-claim′er.**—*n.* **dec′la-ma′tion** (dek′la-mā′shun).

dec-la-ra-tion (dek′la-rā′shun), *n.* **1,** the act of announcing or proclaiming; as, the *declaration* of a holiday; **2,** that which is affirmed or proclaimed; also, the document embodying the proclamation; as, the *Declaration* of Independence.

de-clar-a-tive (di-klar′a-tiv), *adj.* making a statement or declaration; as, "The sun shone all day" is a *declarative* sentence.

de-clare (di-klâr′), *v.t.* [declared, declar-ing],

1, to make known; tell openly or publicly; proclaim formally; as, the government *declared* a holiday; she *declared* that nothing would persuade her to go; **2,** to affirm solemnly before witnesses; as, the accused man *declared* his innocence; **3,** to make a complete statement of (dutiable goods, etc.); as, a traveller, returning to Canada, must *declare* his or her purchases:—*v.i.* to make a statement; take sides for or against something; as, the students *declared* for self-government.—*n.* **de-clar′er.**

de-clen-sion (di-klen′shun), *n.* **1,** in *grammar*, the changes in form of nouns, pronouns, and sometimes adjectives in certain languages, such as Latin, Russian, and Ukrainian, to correspond to their use in the sentence; **2,** a sloping downward; descent; **3,** a falling away; deterioration; **4,** refusal.

de-cline (di-klīn′; dē-klīn′), *v.i.* [declined, declin-ing], **1,** to slope, bend, or lean downward; **2,** to sink toward the horizon, as the sun or a star; hence, to draw toward a close; as, day *declined*; **3,** to decay; fail; as, his vigour began to *decline*; **4,** to seek a lower level; as, interest rates have *declined*; **5,** to refuse in a polite way; as, I *decline* to go:—*v.t.* **1,** to refuse; as, to *decline* an invitation; **2,** to give the declension of; as, to *decline* a noun:—*n.* **1,** a settling; lessening; decay; as, the *decline* of day, of prices, of fame; **2,** a wasting away with disease; as, she went into a *decline*.

de-code (di-kōd′; dē-kōd′), *v.t.* [de-cod-ed, de-cod-ing], to convert secret writing into ordinary words; decipher; as, to *decode* a secret message.

de-com-pose (dē′kom-pōz′), *v.t.* [decom-posed, decompos-ing], **1,** to separate (something) into parts; as, a prism *decomposes* sunlight; **2,** to rot:—*v.i.* to decay.—*n.* **de′com-po-si′tion** (dē′kom-pō-zish′un).

de-com-press (dē′kom-pres′), *v.t.* **1,** to reduce or free from air pressure, as by means of an air lock, as in a submarine, airplane, etc.; as, the diver had to *decompress* before she could resurface; **2,** in *computing*, to restore to their normal size computer files that have been stored in compact form.—*n.* **de′com-pres′sion.**

de-con-tam-i-nate (dē′kon-tam′i-nāt′), *v.t.* to free from a harmful substance, as poison gas, radioactivity, etc.

dé-cor or **de-cor** (dā-kôr′), *n.* the decorative scheme of a room, stage setting, etc.; decoration.

dec-o-rate (dek′o-rāt′), *v.t.* [decorat-ed, decorat-ing], **1,** to adorn; as, to *decorate* a house for the holidays; **2,** to add paint, wallpaper, or new furnishings to a room; **3,** to confer a badge of honour, etc., upon; as, the general was *decorated* for bravery.—*n.* **dec′o-ra′tion; dec′o-ra′tor.**—*adj.* **dec′o-ra′tive.**

de-cor-ous (di-kōr′us; dek′ō-rus), *adj.* seemly; fit; proper; as, *decorous* behaviour.

de-cor-um (di-kōr′um), *n.* propriety of dress, language, and conduct; seemliness; dignity; as, to act with *decorum*.

de-coy (dē′koi; di-koi′), *n.* **1,** a deceptive trick or snare; a lure; **2,** a real or imitation bird used to attract live birds within shooting distance; **3,** a person used to lead another into a position of danger:—*v.t.* to draw into danger by a trick; entice.

de-crease (di-krēs′; dē′krēs), *v.i.* [decreased, decreas-ing], to grow less; diminish in number, strength, etc.; as, the government *decreased* its spending:—*v.t.* to cause to grow less:—*n.* (dē′krēs; dē-krēs′), a gradual lessening or falling off; also, the amount or degree of lessening.

de-cree (di-krē′), *n.* **1,** an ordinance; law; edict; **2,** in certain courts, the judgment or award of the court; as, a *decree* of divorce:—*v.t.* [decreed, decree-ing], to establish by law; as, to *decree* an amnesty:—*v.i.* to make a decision or law.

de-crep-it (di-krep′it), *adj.* broken down by age or use; as, a *decrepit* house.—*n.* **de-crep′i-tude** (dē-krep′i-tūd).

de-cry (di-krī′; dē-krī′), *v.t.* [decried, decry-ing], **1,** to condemn; censure; as, to *decry* pollution; **2,** to make little of; as, the ignorant may *decry* the value of education.

de-cryp-tion (dē′krip′shun), *n.* in *computing*, to decode or decipher transmitted information into a form that can be used by the user.

ded-i-cate (ded′i-kāt′), *v.t.* [dedicat-ed, dedicat-ing], **1,** to set apart by a solemn act or ceremony; as, to *dedicate* a church; **2,** to devote to some work, duty, or cause; as, to *dedicate* ourselves to peace; **3,** to address (a book or other work) formally to a patron or friend.—*n.* **ded′i-ca′tion.**

ded-i-cat-ed (ded′i-kāt′id), *adj.* **1,** devoted or committed to something; as, a *dedicated* musician; **2,** in *technology*, performing only one function; as, a *dedicated* fax line. Compare *dial-up*.

de-duce (di-dūs′; dē-dūs′), *v.t.* [deduced, deduc-ing], to arrive at (a conclusion) by reasoning; infer; as, from your accurate work, I *deduce* that you are an industrious student.—*adj.* **de-duc′i-ble.**

de-duct (di-dukt′; dē-dukt′), *v.t.* to take away; subtract; as, to *deduct* 10 per cent from the bill.—*adj.* **de-duct′i-ble.**

de-duc-tion (di-duk′shun; dē-duk′shun), *n.* **1,** subtraction; also, that which is taken away; as, she expected a *deduction* from her pay; **2,** the drawing of conclusions by reasoning from principles generally accepted as true; also, a conclusion thus reached:—**tax deduction**, an amount a taxpayer is allowed to subtract from the tax owed: that item is called a *deductible*.—*adj.* **de-duc′tive.**

deed (dēd), *n.* **1,** that which is done; an act; **2,** a brave action; exploit; as, *deeds* of prowess; **3,** a legal document for the transfer of ownership of real estate:—*v.t.* to convey by deed; as, he *deeded* the property.

dee-jay or **DJ** (dē′jā′), *n. Colloq.* disc jockey.

deem (dēm), *v.t.* to think; believe; judge; as, I *deem* it wise to call him back.

deep (dēp), *adj.* **1,** extending far down from the surface; not shallow; as, a *deep* hole; also, extending well back; as, a *deep* lot; **2,** penetrating; thorough; as, *deep* insight; **3,** difficult to understand; as, a *deep* subject; **4,** absorbed; involved; as, *deep* in study; **5,** low in pitch; as, a *deep* voice; **6,** profound; heavy; as, a *deep* sleep; **7,** dark; rich; as, a *deep* red; **8,** heartfelt; as, *deep* sorrow:—**the deep,** the sea:—*adv.* far down; far on; in the heart of; as, dig *deep*; *deep* in the jungle.—*adv.* **deep′ly.**—*v.t.* and *v.i.* **deep′en.** Also, **deep′–fry′; deep′ pocket′; deep′–root′ed; deep′–seat′ed.**

deep freeze or **deep–freeze** (dēp′–frēz′), *n.* **1,** a refrigerator for storing perishable foods at low temperatures; a freezer; **2,** the state of being frozen or like frozen; hidden or stored away; as, to keep her plans in *deep′-freeze′.*—*v.t.* **deep′freeze′.**

deer (dēr), *n.* [*pl.* deer], a swift, graceful, cud-chewing wild animal: the male deer and some female deer have branching horns, or antlers, which are shed and renewed every year.—*n.* **deer′skin′.**

MALE DEER

deer-fly (dēr′flī′), *n.* a blood-sucking small horsefly with mottled wings; in northern Canadian woods, it bites viciously, esp. in early summer.

de-face (di-fās′; dē-fās′), *v.t.* [defaced, defac-ing], to mar the appearance of; as, to *deface* a book with pencil marks.—*n.* **de-face′ment.**

de fac-to (di-fak′tō; dā-fak′tō; dē-fak′tō), *adj.* and *adv.* in fact; in reality; actually existing; as, *de facto* leader; she was, *de facto,* the leader.

de-fame (di-fām′; dē-fām′) *v.t.* [defamed, defam-ing], to injure or destroy the good name of; speak evil of; slander.—*n.* **de-fam′er.**—*n.* **def′a-ma′tion** (def′a-mā′shun).—*adj.* **de-fam′a-tor-y** (di-fam′a-tėr-i; dē-fam′a-tėr-i).

de-fault (di-fôlt′; dē-fôlt′; dē′fôlt′), *n.* **1,** failure to do something required by law; **2,** failure to pay one's debts; **3,** failure to start or to finish a game or contest; **4,** in *computing,* the automatic setting in a computer program unless the user cancels or overrides it; as, the *default* for the font:—*adj.* pertaining to default; as, a *default* penalty; the *default* setting on a computer:—*v.t.* and *v.i.* **1,** to fail to fulfill (a contract, esp. a financial contract); **2,** to fail to start or to finish; hence, to lose (a contest) through such a failure; **3,** in *computing,* to return to the original, automatic setting; as, the computer's font setting *defaults* to Times New Roman.—*n.* **de-fault′er.**

de-feat (di-fēt′; dē-fēt′), *v.t.* **1,** to overthrow or vanquish; as, to *defeat* an enemy; **2,** to bring to naught; frustrate; as, to *defeat* a purpose:—*n.* **1,** failure; as, the *defeat* of a plan or purpose; also, loss of a game or contest; **2,** overthrow, as of a government.—*n.* **defeat′ism; de-feat′ist.**

def-e-cate (def′e-kāt′), *v.i.* to void or excrete feces or waste matter from the bowels.

de-fect (di-fekt′; dē′fekt), *n.* **1,** a mental or physical abnormality; as, a birth *defect*; **2,** error; flaw; as, *defects* in writing:—*v.i.* to leave one's country or group permanently in order to join another; as, to *defect* from a company to work for the competition.

de-fec-tion (di-fek′shun), *n.* the act of abandoning a friend, company, country, duty, allegiance, etc.; desertion.

de-fec-tive (di-fek′tiv), *adj.* **1,** imperfect; incomplete; faulty; as, *defective* plumbing; a *defective* computer monitor; **2,** abnormal; deficient; as, *defective* eyesight:—*n.* a person or thing that is defective.

de-fence or **de-fense** (di-fens′; dē-fens′), *n.* **1,** resistance to attack; as, to fight in *defence* of one's country; **2,** one who or that which protects; a protector; protection; as, a coat is a *defence* against a cold wind; **3,** in *law,* the reply of the defendant to the charge against him or her; also, a lawyer or lawyers who defend an accused person; **4,** in *sports,* a player or players who try to stop the other team from scoring, as in hockey and basketball.—*adj.* **defence′less.**

de-fend (di-fend′), *v.t.* **1,** to protect from harm or violence; as, to *defend* a child from danger; **2,** to maintain or uphold, as one's legal rights, by argument or evidence; to contest, as a suit; **3,** to serve as a lawyer for a person who is accused of a crime.—*n.* **defend′er.**

de-fend-ant (di-fen′dant), *n.* **1,** a person sued in a court of law; **2,** a person in a court of law who has been charged with a crime; the accused.

de-fen-si-ble (di-fen′si-bl), *adj.* **1,** capable of being protected, as a military position; **2,** justifiable, as a point of view.

de-fen-sive (di-fen′siv; dē-fen′siv), *adj.* **1,** designed to guard or protect; as, *defensive* weapons; **2,** carried on in self-defence; as, *defensive* warfare; **3,** having to do with defence in sports; as, a *defensive* player in hockey:—*n.* the position of one warding off attack; as, she is always on the *defensive.*—*adv.* **de-fen′sive-ly.**

[1]**de-fer** (di-fûr′), *v.t.* [deferred, defer-ring], to put off until later; delay; postpone; as,

she *deferred* final action for a week.—*n.* **de-fer′ment.**

[2]**de-fer** (di-fûr′), *v.i.* [deferred, defer-ring], to yield; give in; bow (to); as, I *defer* to your judgment.

def-er-ence (def′ėr-ens), *n.* **1,** a yielding to the opinions or wishes of another; **2,** respect; as, *deference* to elders.—*adj.* **def′-er-en′tial** (def′ėr-en′shal).

de-fi-ance (di-fī′ans; dē-fī′ans), *n.* **1,** the act of challenging; a challenge; **2,** resistance; scornful opposition to authority.—*adj.* **de-fi′ant.**

de-fi-cien-cy (di-fish′en-si), *n.* **1**, a lack of something that is needed or important; as, vitamin *deficiency*; **2,** the amount by which something is lacking; shortage; as, a *deficiency* of $100 in the petty cash.—*adj.* **de-fi′cient.**

def-i-cit (def′i-sit), *n.* a shortage, as of money: opposite of *surplus.*

[1]**de-file** (di-fīl′; dē-fīl′), *v.t.* [defiled, defil-ing], **1,** to make foul or impure; as, to *defile* a stream with refuse; **2,** to bring dishonour upon; as, to *defile* a person's reputation.—*n.* **de-file′ment.**

[2]**de-file** (di-fīl′; dē-fīl′), *v.i.* [defiled, defil-ing], to march off in a line or in files:—*n.* (di-fīl′; dē′fīl), a long, narrow pass, as between mountains.

de-fine (di-fīn′), *v.t.* [defined, defin-ing], **1,** to state the exact meaning of; as, this dictionary *defines* words; **2,** to fix the limits of; as, to *define* the extent of a tract of land; **3,** to prescribe authoritatively; as, the duties of the treasurer were *defined* in the bylaws; **4,** to describe or tell in detail; make clear; as, to *define* our roles in a project.—*adj.* **de-fin′a-ble.**

def-i-nite (def′i-nit), *adj.* **1,** precise; exact; certain; clear; as, *definite* instructions; **2,** having fixed or distinct limits; as, a *definite* period of time:—**definite article,** the word *the*: so called because it limits the word it modifies.—*adv.* **def′i-nite-ly.**

def-i-ni-tion (def′i-nish′un), *n.* **1,** the act of explaining; **2,** an exact statement of the meaning of a word, term, or phrase.

de-fin-i-tive (di-fin′i-tiv), *adj.* final; conclusive; as, a *definitive* answer.

de-flate (di-flāt′; dē-flāt′), *v.t.* [deflat-ed, deflat-ing], **1,** to release air or gas from; as, to *deflate* a tire; **2,** to reduce (prices); also, to reduce the amount of (money in circulation); **3,** to expose a person's pretensions; as, her rebuff *deflated* his ego: opposite of *inflate.*—*n.* **de-fla′tion.**

de-flect (di-flekt′; dē-flekt′), *v.t.* to cause to turn from a straight line; as, the wall *deflected* the bullet.—*n.* **de-flec′tion; de-flec′tor.**

de-form (di-fôrm′; dē-fôrm′), *v.t.* **1,** to make unshapely; disfigure; **2,** to mar; deface.—*n.* **de-form′i-ty.**

de-fraud (di-frôd′; dē-frôd′), *v.t.* to cheat or deceive; deprive (one) of a possession, right, etc., by trickery or deceit.

de-fray (di-frā′; dē-frā′), *v.t.* to pay; settle; as, to *defray* the cost of a trip.—*n.* **de-fray′al.**

de-frost (di-frôst′; dē-frôst′), *v.t.* to remove frost or ice from or cause to thaw.—*n.* **de-frost′er.**

deft (deft), *adj.* neat and skillful in action; nimble; clever; as, piano playing requires *deft* fingers.—*adv.* **deft′ly.**—*n.* **deft′ness.**

de-funct (di-fungkt′; dē-fungkt′), *adj.* dead; extinct:—**the defunct,** the dead person(s).

de-fy (di-fī′; dē-fī′), *v.t.* [defied, defy-ing], **1,** to challenge or dare; resist; as, to *defy* an enemy; **2,** to act in contempt of; as, a criminal *defies* the law; **3,** to resist successfully; as, the problem *defied* solution.

de-gen-er-ate (di-jen′ėr-āt′; dē-jen′ėr-āt′), *v.i.* [degenerat-ed, degenerat-ing], to sink into a worse state; become inferior in goodness or quality:—*adj.* (di-jen′ėr-it; dē-jen′ėr-it), below the former or typical standard; degraded; as, *degenerate* times; inferior to the true or former type; as, *degenerate* offspring:—*n.* (di-jen′ėr-it; dē-jen′ėr-it), a degenerate person.—*n.* **de-gen′er-a-cy; de-gen′er-a′tion.**

de-grade (di-grād′; dē-grād′), *v.t.* [degrad-ed, degrad-ing], **1,** to reduce in grade or rank; deprive of honours, office, or dignity; as, to *degrade* a soldier; **2,** to lower morally; as, to tell lies *degrades* one.—*adj.* **de-grad′ed.**—*n.* **deg′ra-da′tion** (deg′ra-dā′shun).

de-gree (di-grē′), *n.* **1,** a step or grade in a series; **2,** rank in life; as, a person of low *degree*; **3,** a stage in progress; **4,** a title conferred by a college or university for completing a certain course of study or of special distinction; **5,** a relative amount, extent, quality; as, a good *degree* of skill; **6,** a unit for measuring temperature, as on the centigrade scale; **7,** a unit division on a mathematical or scientific instrument, as a compass; **8,** the 360th part of the circumference of a circle; **9,** in *grammar,* one of the three grades in the comparison of an adjective or adverb; as, "good," "better," "best" are the positive, comparative, and superlative *degrees* of "good"; **10,** in *music,* a line or a space on the staff for notes; also, a tone of a scale:—**by degrees,** gradually.

de-hy-drate (dē-hī′drāt), *v.t.* to remove water from; as, *dehydrated* (dē′hī-drā′tid) fruits or vegetables.

de-ice (dē′–is′; dē′–is′), *v.t.* to remove ice from; as, to *de–ice* the wings of an airplane.

de-i-fy (dē′i-fī′), *v.t.* [de-fied, deify-ing], to worship as a god; to make into a god; as, the druids *deified* the oak tree.—*n.* **de′i-fi-ca′tion.**

deign (dān), *v.i.* to condescend; think fit;

as, he did not *deign* to heed our request:—*v.t.* to grant; condescend.

de-i-ty (dē′-i-ti), *n.* [*pl.* deities], **1,** a god or goddess; a being worshipped as divine; **2,** the character, nature, or attributes of God:—**the Deity,** God.

dé-jà vu (dā′zhä′ vo͞o′; dā′zhä′ vü′), *n.* **1,** the feeling of having experienced something before, esp. when it is an illusion; as, to experience an event with the eerie sense of *déjà vu*; **2,** something tiresomely or unpleasantly familiar; as, the *déjà vu* of fashion trends.

de-ject-ed (di-jek′tid; dē-jek′tid), *adj.* downcast; sad; low-spirited.—*n.* **de-jec′tion.**

deke (dēk), *v.t. Slang* in *hockey*, to fool an opponent with a fake shot or movement; as, she *deked* the goalie.

de-lay (di-lā′; dē-lā′), *v.t.* **1,** to put off; postpone; hinder for a time; as, illness *delayed* my journey; **2,** to cause to be late; as, the snowstorm *delayed* the bus:—*v.i.* to act or proceed slowly:—*n.* a putting off; postponement; wait; as, a *delay* of two hours before takeoff.

de-lec-ta-ble (di-lek′ta-bl), *adj.* pleasing; delightful.—*adv.* **de-lec′ta-bly.**—*n.* **de′lec-ta′tion.**

del-e-gate (del′e-git), *n.* one sent to represent, and act for, others; as, the *delegates* to a convention:—*v.t.* (del′e-gāt′), [delegat-ed, delegat-ing], **1,** to send as an agent, with authority to act; as, I *delegate* you to deliver the message; **2,** to entrust, transfer, or commit duties; as, she *delegated* responsibility to her employees.

del-e-ga-tion (del′e-gā′shun), *n.* **1,** the act of authorizing a person or persons to act for others; **2,** a body of persons chosen so to act; a body of representatives.

de-lete (di-lēt′; dē-lēt′), *v.t.* to remove; cross out; destroy; take out (something written or printed); as, *delete* this comma:—**delete key,** in *computing*, the key on the computer keyboard that erases the last character input.—*n.* **de-le′tion.**

de-li (de′li), *n.* short for **delicatessen.**

de-lib-er-ate (di-lib′ėr-āt′), *v.t.* [deliberat-ed, deliberat-ing], to reflect on; think upon; consider carefully; as, to *deliberate* a question:—*v.i.* to think carefully; take counsel with oneself or others; as, to *deliberate* on a plan:—*adj.* (di-lib′ėr-it), **1,** careful; slow; cautious; as, a *deliberate* pace; **2,** slow in determining or acting; **3,** intended; as, a *deliberate* insult.—*adv.* **de-lib′er-ate-ly.**—*n.* **de-lib′er-a′tion.**

del-i-ca-cy (del′i-ka-si), *n.* [*pl.* delicacies], **1,** a dainty; a rare or delightful food; as, truffles are a *delicacy*; **2,** fineness of form or texture; as, the *delicacy* of a spider web; **3,** fineness of touch, as in writing or painting; **4,** sensitivity; as, *delicacy* of taste.

del-i-cate (del′i-kit), *adj.* **1,** pleasing to the taste; as, a *delicate* flavour; **2,** fine; dainty; exquisite in texture; as, *delicate* lace; **3,** of instruments, minutely accurate; as, a *delicate* scale; **4,** sensitive to injury or disease; as, a *delicate* child or plant; **5,** requiring skill or nicety; as, a *delicate* operation; **6,** soft or subdued, as a colour or scent; **7,** capable of making fine distinctions; as, a musician has a *delicate* ear; **8,** finely sensitive; as, a *delicate* touch; a *delicate* situation.—*adv.* **del′i-cate-ly.**

del-i-ca-tes-sen (del′i-ka-tes′en), *n.pl.* **1,** fine prepared foods, as cooked and smoked meats, cheese, salads, and preserves; table delicacies; as, German *delicatessen* are my favourite food; **2,** used as *singular*, a place where these are sold.

de-li-cious (di-lish′us), *adj.* highly pleasing, esp. to the taste.—*adv.* **de-li′cious-ly.**—*n.* **de-li′cious-ness.**

de-light (di-līt′; dē-līt′), *v.t.* to gratify or please greatly; charm; as, natural beauty *delights* the eye:—*v.i.* to take great pleasure or enjoyment; as, to *delight* in dancing:—*n.* **1,** an extreme degree of pleasure; high satisfaction; joy; **2,** that which causes pleasure.—*adj.* **de-light′ed; de-light′ful.**—*adv.* **de-light′ful-ly.**

de-lin-e-ate (di-lin′ē-āt′), *v.t.* [delineat-ed, delineat-ing], **1,** to mark out with lines; sketch; draw; **2,** to describe minutely and accurately in words; portray; as, an author *delineates* his or her characters.—*n.* **de-lin′e-a′tion.**

de-lin-quent (di-ling′kwent), *adj.* **1,** failing in duty; **2,** overdue; not paid, as taxes:—*n.* **1,** one who neglects a duty; **2,** a lawbreaker, esp. a youthful offender; as, a juvenile *delinquent.*—*n.* **de-lin′quen-cy.**

de-lir-i-um (di-lir′i-um; di-lir′ē-um), *n.* **1,** a temporary mental disorder, often caused by fever, and marked by wandering speech; **2,** excitement; wild enthusiasm.—*adj.* **de-lir′i-ous.**

de-liv-er (di-liv′ėr; dē-liv′ėr), *v.t.* **1,** to set free; save; as, *deliver* us from evil; **2,** to yield possession or control of, as a property; **3,** to give; hand over; transfer; as, to *deliver* a package; **4,** to send forth vigorously; as, to *deliver* a blow; **5,** to utter; as, to *deliver* a speech; **6,** to give birth to a baby, or help a woman to give birth.—*n.* **de-liv′er-ance.**

de-liv-er-y (di-liv′ėr-i; dē-liv′ėr-i), *n.* [*pl.* deliveries], **1,** the act of releasing; a setting free; **2,** a surrender; transfer; **3,** manner of speaking; as, a lecturer's *delivery*; **4,** a giving from one person to another; a handing over; as, a courier *delivery*; **5,** the act or manner of pitching a ball; **6,** childbirth.

dell (dėl), *n.* a secluded valley; glen.

del-ta (del′ta), *n.* **1,** the fourth letter of the Greek alphabet δ Δ; **2,** a fan-shaped alluvial deposit at the mouth of a river; as, the *delta* of the Fraser River; **3,** any triangular surface.

del-toid (del′toid), *n.* on the shoulder, a triangular muscle that raises the arm from the side.—*adj.* triangular.

de-lude (di-lūd′; dē-lūd′), *v.t.* [delud-ed, delud-ing], to mislead; deceive; as, to *delude* oneself with false hopes.—*n.* **de-lu′sion.**—*adj.* **de-lu′sive.**

del-uge (del′ūj; dāl′ūj), *n.* **1,** a heavy downpour; **2,** anything that overwhelms or floods; as, a *deluge* of protests greeted the new mayor:—**the Deluge**, the great flood of the time of Noah:—*v.t.* [deluged, delug-ing], **1,** to overflow; **2,** to overwhelm; as, they *deluged* her with questions.

deluxe (di-luks′; di looks′; dē-luks′; dē-looks′), of unusually fine quality; luxurious; expensive; as, a *deluxe* resort.

delve (delv), *v.i.* [delved, delv-ing], **1,** to work with a spade; **2,** to make earnest search for information; as, to *delve* into a subject.

dem-a-gogue or **dem-a-gog** (dem′a-gog), *n.* a political agitator or leader who gains and uses power by appealing to the ignorance or prejudice of the people.

de-mand (di-mand′; dē-mand′), *v.t.* **1,** to claim as due; exact; insist; as, to *demand* an apology; **2,** to question with authority; as, to *demand* another's name; **3,** to require; have urgent need for; as, the e-mail *demands* an answer; **4,** in *law*, to summon:—*n.* **1,** the act of claiming as due; as, a *demand* for payment; **2,** a desire to obtain; call; as, a great *demand* for computer games; **3,** the state of being sought after.—*adj.* **de-mand′ing.**

de-mean (di-mēn′), *v.t.* to lower in dignity; degrade; as, he *demeaned* himself by taking the bribe.

de-mean-our (di-mēn′ėr), *n.* behaviour; bearing; manner; as, a sophisticated *demeanour.*

de-ment-ed (di-men′tid), *adj.* insane; mad; crazy; out of one's mind.

de-men-tia (di-men′sha), *n.* **1,** mental or intellectual deterioration characterized by memory loss and often personality changes; **2,** madness; insanity.

de-mer-it (di-mer′it; dē-mer′it), *n.* and *adj.* **1,** something that deserves blame; a fault; **2,** a mark for failure or misconduct; as, to lose *demerit* points as a result of traffic violations.

dem-i- (dem′i), *prefix* meaning *half*; as, *demi*god, *demi*tasse, etc.

dem-i-god (dem′i-god′), *n.* an inferior god; a hero.

de-mise (di-mīz′), *n.* death; thus, on her *demise*, the house went to her daughter.

dem-i-tasse (dem′i-tȧs′), *n.* a small cup (of black coffee).

de-mo-bi-lize (dē-mō′bi-līz′; di-mō′bi-līz′), *v.t.* [demobilized, demobiliz-ing], to disband or dismiss, as troops; to change (an army or country) from a war to a peace footing; to discharge from military service.—*n.* **de-mo′bi-li-za′tion.**

de-moc-ra-cy (di-mok′ra-si), *n.* [*pl.* democracies], **1,** government by the people; government in which the people hold supreme power and delegate it to elected representatives; also, a nation or state so governed; as, Canada is a *democracy*; **2,** political or social equality as opposed to inherited rights and privileges.

dem-o-crat (dem′ō-krat), *n.* one who believes in and upholds democracy or the principles of popular government or social equality:—**Democrat,** in the U.S., a member of the Democratic Party.

dem-o-crat-ic (dem′ō-krat′ik), *adj.* **1,** pertaining to democracy, or government by the people; as, a *democratic* country; **2,** favouring equal rights or treatment for all people; friendly; appealing to many; as, a *democratic* supervisor:—**Democratic Party,** one of the two main political groups in the U.S.: so named in 1828.—*adv.* **dem′o-crat′i-cal-ly.**

dem-o-graph-ics (dem′ō-graf′iks; dem′o-graf′iks), *n.* the statistical study of populations in groups such as sex, age, income, etc.—*n.* **dem-o′graph-y; dem-o′grapher.**—*adj.* **dem′o-graph′ic.**—*adv.* **dem′o-graph′i-cal-ly.**

de-mol-ish (di-mol′ish), *v.t.* to pull down; destroy; wreck; as, they *demolished* the old house.

dem-o-li-tion (dem′ō-lish′un; dē′mō-lish′un), *n.* the act of tearing down; destruction.

de-mon (dē′mun), *n.* **1,** an evil spirit; a devil; **2,** a very cruel or wicked person; **3,** a person who has a lot of energy or determination; as, the energetic child was quite a little *demon.*—*adj.* **de-mon′ic** (di-mon′ik; dē-mon′ik); **de-mo′ni-ac′** (di-mō′ni-ak′); **de′mo-ni′a-cal** (dē′mo-nī′a-kl).

dem-on-strate (dem′un-strāt′), *v.t.* [demonstrat-ed, demonstrat-ing], **1,** to prove beyond a doubt; **2,** to teach by examples; illustrate; show clearly or explain; **3,** to show and explain publicly the good points of (an article or product); **4,** to take part in a public display to protest or to make demands for something; as, to *demonstrate* outside the factory for better working conditions.—*n.* **dem′onstra′tor.**—*adj.* **de-mon′stra-ble.**

dem-on-stra-tion (dem′un-strā′shun), *n.* **1,** the act of showing or proving; something that shows clearly or explains; **2,** a proof beyond any doubt; **3,** an outward expression of feeling; as, a kiss is a *demonstration* of affection; **4,** a public exhibition; as, a cooking *demonstration*; **5,** a show of military force; **6,** a show of public interest and sympathy, as by a street meeting or a parade; **7,** a public show or parade to protest or demand something; as, a *demon-*

stration against unfair taxes.

de-mon-stra-tive (di-mon′stra-tiv), *adj.* **1,** having the power of showing or proving; **2,** in *grammar*, serving to point out; as, *demonstrative* pronouns, such as *this* and *that*; **3,** showing the feelings, esp. affection, openly and strongly:—*n.* a pronoun that serves to point out the object to which it refers, as *this, that, these, those*.

de-mor-al-ize (di-mor′al-īz; dē-mor′al-īz), *v.t.* [demoralized, demoraliz-ing], **1,** to corrupt; lower the morals of; as, bad company will *demoralize* anybody; **2,** to weaken the courage, spirit, or energy of; throw into confusion; as, the loss of the team captain *demoralized* the hockey players.—*n.* **de-mor′al-i-za′tion.**

de-mote (di-mōt′; dē-mōt′), *v.t.* to reduce to a lower grade, position, or rank (at work, the army, etc.): opposite of *promote*.—*n.* **de-mo′tion.**

de-mur (di-mûr′), *v.i.* [demurred, demurring], to raise objections; as, he *demurred* at having to work late:—*n.* an objection or exception; protest.

de-mure (di-mūr′), *adj.* [demur-er, demurest], **1,** quiet; reserved; as, a *demure* child; **2,** affectedly modest, as in manner; coy.—*adv.* **de-mure′ly.**

den (den), *n.* **1,** the lair of a wild animal or beast; as, a lion's *den*; **2,** a cavern; cave; **3,** a cosy, private room in a house where a person can read, study, or watch television; **4,** something like a den, such as a haunt of criminals; **5,** a group of Cub Scouts.

Den-e (den′ā; den′ē), *n.pl.* the Athapaskan-speaking people of the Northwest Territories.

de-ni-al (di-nī′al; dē-nī′al), *n.* **1,** refusal to grant; as, *denial* of a request; **2,** contradiction; refusal to admit; as, the prisoner's *denial* of her guilt; **3,** refusal to acknowledge.

den-im (den′im), *n.* **1,** a coarse twilled cotton used for work and sports clothes, such as overalls and blue jeans, as well as hangings, upholstery, etc.; **2,** pants or overalls made from denim.

den-i-zen (den′i-zn), *n.* **1,** a naturalized (but not native) citizen, plant, or animal; **2,** an inhabitant; occupant; as, gnats are *denizens* of the air; **3,** someone or something that frequents a place.

de-nom-i-nate (di-nom′i-nāt′; dē-nom′i-nāt′), *v.t.* to name or call; designate; as, Maurice Richard was *denominated* the Rocket.

de-nom-i-na-tion (di-nom′i-nā′shun), *n.* **1,** a name; a descriptive title; **2,** a grouping of people or things under one name; designation; as, biology and chemistry come under the *denomination* of science; **3,** a class or division; esp., a religious sect; as, the Methodist *denomination*; **4,** a name for a certain class or unit in a series; as, in Canada, we have coins of many *denominations*.—*adj.* **de-nom′i-na′tion-al.**

de-nom-i-na-tor (di-nom′i-nā′tėr), *n.* in *arithmetic,* the part of a fraction below the line, showing into how many parts the number or units are to be divided; the divisor; as, in the fraction 1/4, 4 is the *denominator*. Compare *numerator*.

de-no-ta-tion (dē′nō-tā′shun), *n.* the literal or explicit meaning of a word as opposed to its *connotation*; thus, the *denotation* of "cattle" is *cows* or *livestock*, and the connotation is *unintelligent, driven beasts*. Compare *connotation*.

de-note (di-nōt′), *v.t.* [denot-ed, denoting], **1,** to show; indicate; mark out plainly; as, the hands of a clock *denote* the hour; **2,** to be a sign of; mean or signify; designate; as, the song of a robin *denotes* spring.

de-noue-ment or **dé-noue-ment** (dā′nōō′ män′), *n.* the solving of the mystery or plot of a play, story, novel, movie, etc.; the outcome or issue; as, the *denouement* of *Macbeth* is Macduff's killing of Macbeth.

de-nounce (di-nouns′; dē-nouns′), *v.t.* [denounced, denounc-ing], to accuse publicly; condemn; show strong disapproval; as, to *denounce* cruelty to animals.

dense (dens), *adj.* **1,** thick; heavy; as, a *dense* fog; closely packed together; as, a *dense* crowd; **2,** stupid; dull; as, *dense* ignorance; **3,** demanding concentration, profound; as, a *dense* book.—*n.* **dense′ness.**—*adj.* **dense′ly.**

den-si-ty (den′si-ti), *n.* [*pl.* densities], **1,** the state of being dense or close together; **2,** the amount of something within a unit or area; as, Japan has a higher population *density* than does Canada.

dent (dent), *n.* a small hollow or depression:—*v.t.* to make a small hollow in; as, to *dent* the fender of a car:—*v.i.* to receive dents; as, tin cans *dent* easily.

den-tal (den′tal), *adj.* **1,** pertaining to the teeth; as, *dental* health; **2,** having to do with a dentist or dentistry; as, a *dental* clinic; *dental* school; **3,** pronounced by the aid of the teeth; as, *t* and *d* are *dental* letters:—*n.* a dental sound, as *t, d*.

dental floss, disposable strong, thin, smooth thread, waxed or unwaxed, used to clean between the teeth.

den-tine (den′tēn; den′tin), or **den-tin** (den′tin), *n.* the hard, dense tissue that forms the main part of a tooth. (See *tooth*, illustration.)—*adj.* **den′ti-nal.**

den-tist (den′tist), *n.* one who is professionally trained to treat and take care of people's teeth and gums.—*n.* **den′tis-try.**

den-ti-tion (den-tish′un), *n.* **1,** the process or period of cutting teeth; **2,** the arrangement of the teeth.

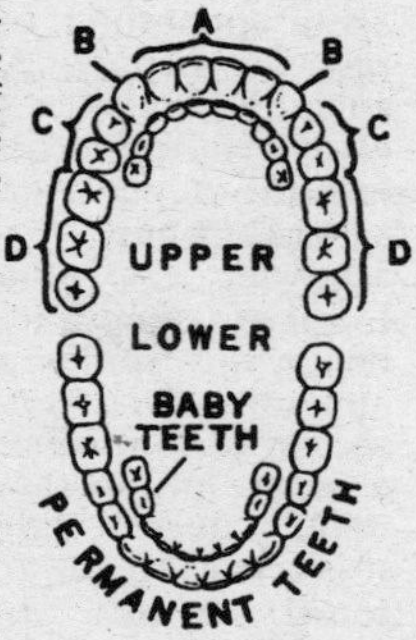

ARRANGEMENT OF THE TEETH OF A HUMAN BEING: A, INCISORS; B,B, CANINES; C,C, BICUSPIDS; D,D, MOLARS.

den-tures (den′tūrz; chėrz), *n.pl.* a set of artificial teeth.

de-nude (di-nūd′; dē-nūd′) *v.t.* [denud-ed, denud-ing], to make bare or naked; strip; remove the covering; as, to *denude* a hillside of trees.

de-nun-ci-a-tion (di-nun′si-ā′shun), *n.* a public accusation; also, condemnation of anything.

de-ny (di-nī′; dē-nī′), *v.t.* [denied, denying], **1,** to refuse to believe or admit; contradict; as, I *deny* his statement; **2,** to withhold; refuse to grant, give, or allow; as, to *deny* a favour.

de-o-dor-ant (dē-ō′dėr-ant), *n.* a preparation that destroys or disguises unpleasant odours, esp. a substance used under the arms or an air freshener:—*adj.* killing or disguising smells.—*v.t.* **de-o′dor-ize′.**

dé-pan-neur (dā-pa-nör′), *n. Colloq.* a convenience store in Québec, often shortened to *dep.*

de-part (di-pärt′; dē-pärt′), *v.i.* **1,** to go away; leave; **2,** to vary; change; as, to *depart* from a habit; **3,** to start on a journey.—*n.* **de-par′ture.**

de-part-ment (di-pärt′ment), *n.* **1,** a distinct division or branch of a whole; as, the English *department* at a university; **2,** a branch or field of business, study, or science; **3,** a division of government; as, the *Department* of Finance; **4,** in France and some Latin American countries, a division of local government, similar to a province:—**department store,** a store selling many kinds of goods, divided into departments, as for women's clothing, sporting goods, jewellery, electronics, etc.—*adj.* **de′part-men′tal.**

de-pend (di-pend′), *v.i.* **1,** to rely for support; as, the old man *depends* on his daughter; **2,** to be determined by; rest; as, his answer *depends* on his mood; **3,** to trust or rely; as, I *depend* on your word.

de-pend-a-ble (di-pen′da-bl), *adj.* reliable; trustworthy; as, *dependable* news; a *dependable* car or computer.—*adv.* **de-pend′a-bly.**—*n.* **de-pend′a-bil′i-ty.**

de-pend-ant (di-pen′dent), *n.* and *adj.* a person or of a person who relies on another for help or support; as, children are *dependants* of their parents; *dependant* children. Compare *dependent.*

de-pend-ence or **de-pend-ance** (di-pen′dens), *n.* **1,** the state of being influenced or determined by something; as, *dependence* of daylight on the sun; **2,** reliance; trust; **3,** that on which one relies; **4,** the state of needing aid; as, the *dependence* of children on their parents; **5,** drug addiction; as, *dependence* on alcohol.

de-pend-en-cy (di-pen′den-si), *n.* [*pl.* dependencies], **1,** the condition of relying on another; dependence; **2,** a country under the control of another country.

de-pend-ent (di-pen′dent), *adj.* **1,** hanging down; **2,** relying on someone or something else for support; **3,** conditioned by something; controlled or determined by; as, strength is *dependent* on health; **4,** in *grammar,* subordinate; as, a *dependent* clause. Compare *dependant.*

de-pict (di-pikt′; dē-pikt′), *v.t.* to portray; describe vividly in words.—*n.* **de-pic′tion.**

de-plete (di-plēt′), *v.t.* [deplet-ed, deplet-ing], to empty; reduce; exhaust; use up the quantity, value, or effectiveness of; as, to *deplete* Canada's natural resources.—*n.* **de-ple′tion.**

de-plor-a-ble (di-plōr′a-bl), *adj.* **1,** sad; lamentable; grievous; as, a *deplorable* accident; **2,** shameful; regrettable; as, *deplorable* behaviour.—*adv.* **de-plor′a-bly.**

de-plore (di-plōr′), *v.t.* [deplored, deploring], *v.t.* to lament; grieve for.

de-ploy (di-ploi′), *v.t.* to spread out on a wider front; as, to *deploy* troops.

de-pop-u-late (dē-pop′ū-lāt′), *v.t.* [depopulat-ed, depopulat-ing], to deprive of inhabitants; reduce the number of people in; as, war *depopulated* the country.—*n.* **de′pop-u-la′tion.**

de-port (di-pōrt′; dē-pōrt′), *v.t.* **1,** to banish; exile; remove; as, to *deport* criminal aliens; **2,** to behave (oneself); as, he *deported* himself with dignity.

de-por-ta-tion (dē′pōr-tā′shun), *n.* banishment; removal from the country.

de-port-ment (di-pōrt′ment; dē-pōrt′ment), *n.* conduct; behaviour; manners.

de-pose (di-pōz′; dē-pōz′), *v.t.* [deposed, depos-ing], **1,** to remove from a throne or other high station; deprive of office; **2,** to bear witness; testify under oath.—*n.* **de-pos′al; de-pos′er.**

de-pos-it (di-poz′it), *v.t.* **1,** to put or set down; place; as, to deposit a package inside the screen door; **2,** to put into a bank, as money or other valuable things; entrust to another for safekeeping; **3,** to pay money as a promise to do something or to pay more later; as, to *deposit* the first month's rent:—*n.* **1,** something committed to the care of another, such as money in a bank; **2,** a pledge; money given as a promise to pay more; as, a small *deposit* on a purchase;

3, something laid down; esp., solid matter through the action of nature that settles at the bottom of a liquid; sediment; as, gold *deposits*.—*n.* **de-pos′i-tor.**

dep-o-si-tion (dep′o-zish′un; dē′pō-zish′un), *n.* **1,** a putting out of office; dethronement; as, the *deposition* of a queen; **2,** a sediment; a laying down, as of sand or mud by a river; **3,** testimony under oath; **4,** the act of depositing or that which is deposited.

de-pot (dep′ō; dē′pō), *n.* **1,** a warehouse; **2,** a building for military supplies, food, etc.; **3,** in Canada, a bus or railway station.

de-prave (di-prāv′), *v.t.* [depraved, depraving], to make bad; to corrupt.—*adj.* **de-praved′.**—*n.* **de-prav′i-ty** (di-prav′i-ti).

dep-re-cate (dep′re-kāt′), *v.t.* [deprecat-ed, deprecat-ing], to express great disapproval of, or regret for; disparage; as, to *deprecate* drinking and driving.—*adj.* **dep′re-ca-to′ry.**

de-pre-ci-ate (di-prē′shi-āt′), *v.t.* [depreciat-ed, depreciat-ing], **1,** to lower the value of; as, to *depreciate* the currency; **2,** to speak slightingly of; belittle; as, to *depreciate* another's work:—*v.i.* to fall in value; become of less worth; as, used computer equipment *depreciates*.—*n.* **de-pre′ci-a′tion.**

dep-re-da-tion (dep′ri-dā′shun), *n.* a laying waste; a plundering; robbery; as, the *depredations* of the invaders.

de-press (di-pres′; dē-pres′), *v.t.* **1,** to press or thrust down; as, to *depress* the on button; **2,** to sadden; to cast down; as, bad news *depresses* us; **3,** to lower; make less active, as trade.—*adj.* **de-pressed′.**

de-pres-sion (di-presh′un; dē-presh′un), *n.* **1,** a sinking or falling in of a surface; as, a *depression* in the ground; **2,** low spirits; as, to sink into *depression* after a breakup; **3,** dullness of trade; also, the period of time in which business is dull and many people are out of work; as, the Great *Depression*.

de-prive (di-prīv′), *v.t.* [deprived, depriving], **1,** to take away from; as, to *deprive* her of her house; **2,** to keep from having, using, enjoying; as, to *deprive* a child from watching TV for misbehaving.—*n.* **dep′ri-va′tion** (dep′ri-vā′shun; dēp′rī-vā′shun).

depth (depth), *n.* **1,** deepness; distance below the surface, or from the observer in any direction; distance from top to bottom or from front to back; as, the *depth* of a swimming pool; the *depth* of the sky; the *depth* of a building lot; **2,** profoundness; wisdom; as, the *depths* of learning; a professor of *depth*; **3,** richness of tone or colour; **4,** the innermost part; as, the *depths* of a forest; the mid part; as, the *depth* of winter; **5,** that which is deep; as, the ocean *depths*:—**in depth**, in a thorough way; in detail; as, to study a problem *in depth*.

dep-u-ta-tion (dep′ū-tā′shun), *n.* **1,** the act of appointing, or giving power to, an agent or deputy; **2,** a group of people appointed to act or speak for others; as, a *deputation* of citizens called on the mayor.

de-pute (di-pūt′), *v.t.* **1,** to appoint as an agent or deputy; **2,** to send with power to act; delegate; as, to *depute* authority.

dep-u-ty (dep′ū-ti), *n.* and *adj.* [*pl.* deputies], someone or of someone appointed to act for another; an agent; a second in command; as, a police officer is a *deputy* of the law; a *deputy* mayor:—**deputy minister**, the senior civil servant in a Canadian government ministry.

de-rail (dē-rāl′), *v.t.* to cause (a train or trolley) to leave, or run off, the rails; also, to stop or block the progress of something; as, to *derail* the negotiations.—*n.* **de-rail′ment.**

de-range (di-rānj′), *v.t.* [deranged, deranging], **1,** to disorder; confuse; disturb; **2,** to make insane.—*adj.* **de-ranged′.**—*n.* **de-range′ment.**

der-by (dûr′bi; där′by), *n.* [*pl.* derbies], **1,** a stiff felt hat, with a dome-shaped crown and a narrow, curved brim; a bowler; **2,** a race or contest, as of horses, cars, bicycles, etc.; as, the Kentucky *Derby*; a bicycle *derby*.

der-e-lict (der′e-likt), *adj.* **1,** abandoned; deserted; **2,** unfaithful; neglectful; as, to be *derelict* in one's duty:—*n.* **1,** anything left, forsaken, or cast away; esp., a waterlogged ship; **2,** a human wreck; a hopeless outcast; a vagrant.—*n.* **der′e-lic′tion.**

de-ride (di-rīd′; dē-rīd′), *v.t.* [derid-ed, derid-ing], to mock; laugh at; jeer; ridicule.

de-ri-sion (di-rizh′un), *n.* the state or object of ridicule; scorn; contempt.—*adj.* **de-ri′sive** (dē-rī′siv).

de-riv-a-tive (di-riv′a-tiv), *adj.* obtained from a source; as, *derivative* words:—*n.* something formed from something else; esp., a word or substance formed from another; as, "hydroelectric" and "electricity" are *derivatives* of "electric."

derive (di-rīv′; dē-rīv′), *v.t.* [derived, deriving], **1,** to get from a source; as, to *derive* pleasure from a game; cocoa is *derived* from cacao seeds; **2,** to trace the origin of (a word); as, the word "garage" is *derived* from the French; **3,** to get or receive; as, to *derive* a great deal of satisfaction from volunteering at the Food Bank.—*n.* **der′i-va′tion.**

der-ma-tol-o-gy (dûr-ma-tä′lo-ji), *n.* the study and treatment of skin disorders.—*n.* **der-ma-tol′o-gist.**

de-rog-a-tor-y (di-rog′a-tėr-i), *adj.* tending to discredit; disparaging; as, "half-breed" is considered a *derogatory* term.

der-rick (der′ik), *n.* **1,** a machine equipped with ropes, gears, and pulleys for lifting and moving heavy weights, as on ships to load crates or to lift heavy nets filled with fish; **2,** a scaffolding built above an oil well, to which the drilling machinery is attached.

de-scend (di-send′; dē-send′), *v.i.* **1,** to go or come down from a higher to a lower level; as, the rain *descended*; **2,** to fall upon in force; as, the soldiers *descended* upon the city; **3,** to pass by inheritance or come down from; as, the house *descended* from father to daughter; also, to come down from earlier times; as, the custom *descended* from the ancient Greeks; **4,** to come down or be derived, as from a source; as, Prince William is *descended* from Queen Victoria:—*v.t.* to go down.

de-scend-ant (di-sen′dent), *n.* one who is descended from a given ancestor; offspring; as, modern racehorses are *descendants* of Arabian horses:—*adj.* (also, **descend-ent**), going or coming down; also, coming from an ancestor or source.

de-scent (di-sent′), *n.* **1,** change from a higher to a lower place; downward motion; as, the *descent* of an airplane; **2,** a sudden hostile invasion or attack; **3,** ancestry; as, she is of Ukrainian *descent*; **4,** a downward slope.

de-scribe (di-skrīb′), *v.t.* [described, describ-ing], **1,** to give a visual account of in words; as, he *described* the house; **2,** to tell or write about something; as, to *describe* the game in detail; **3,** to draw the outline of; as, *describe* a circle.—*adj.* **de-scrib′a-ble.**

de-scrip-tion (di-skrip′shun), *n.* **1,** the act of giving an oral or written account of something; **2,** a picture in words; **3,** a class; sort; kind; variety; as, his library contains books of every *description.*—*adj.* **de-scrip′tive.**

des-e-crate (des′i-krāt′), *v.t.* [desecrat-ed, desecrat-ing], **1,** to treat (something sacred) with contempt: opposite of *consecrate*; as, to *desecrate* the mosque by throwing stones through the windows; **2,** to treat something disrespectfully; as, to *desecrate* the rainforest.—*n.* **des′e-cra′tion.**

de-seg-re-ga-tion (dē′seg′ri-gā′shun), *n.* the process of abolishing racial segregation (separation) in schools, public resorts, buses, railways, etc., esp. in Southern U.S.—*v.t.* **de-seg′re-gate.**

[1]de-sert (di-zûrt′), *v.t.* **1,** to forsake; abandon; **2,** in military usage, to abandon without leave; as, to *desert* the army; **3,** to leave when needed or called for; as, words *deserted* me:—*v.i.* to run from duty; forsake a post.—*n.* **de-sert′er; de-ser′tion.**—*adj.* **de-sert′ed.**

[2]de-sert (di-zûrt′), *n.* often *deserts,* a deserved reward or punishment; as, he received his just *deserts.*

[3]des-ert (dez′ėrt), *n.* a wilderness; a remote, lonely place; esp., a vast expanse of dry, sandy waste with little plant life:—*adj.* pertaining to a wilderness or desert; as, cactus is a *desert* plant.—*adj.* **des-ert′ed** (desolate; having no people; as, a *deserted* island).

de-serve (di-zûrv′), *v.t.* [deserved, deserv-ing], to earn by service; be worthy of; merit; as, she *deserved* her promotion:—*v.i.* to be worthy.—*adj.* **de-serv′ing.**—*adv.* **de-serv′ed-ly.**

des-ic-cate (des′i-kāt′), *v.t.* to dry up; free from moisture; dehydrate; preserve by drying; as, to *desiccate* fruit, meat, etc.—*adj.* **des′ic-cat-ed** (as, *desiccated* farmland).

de-sign (di-zīn′), *v.t.* **1,** to draw or plan out; also, to plan and draw in detail; as, to *design* a house, bridge, airplane, or cover for a book; **2,** to mean; intend; as, a dictionary is *designed* to look up correct spellings and definitions of words:—*n.* **1,** an outline or sketch to serve as a pattern or to show how something will look, as for a dress, furniture, page of a book, building, car, etc.; **2,** purpose or intention; also, a plot; as, to perform the vicious act by *design,* not by accident; **3,** a certain pattern or arrangement of lines, colours, or shapes; as, the vase has fancy *designs*:—**designs,** sly or evil plans to get or take something; as, to have *designs* on her business or boyfriend.—*n.* **de-sign′er.**

des-ig-nate (dez′ig-nāt′), *v.t.* [designat-ed, designat-ing], **1,** to point out; indicate; show; as, to *designate* the boundaries of a country; **2,** to name; nominate; choose; as, the teacher *designated* Marcel to count the votes; **3,** to call by a special name or title; as, to *designate* her Project Leader.—*n.* **des′ig-na′tion.**

de-sign-ing (di-zīn′ing), *adj.* scheming; artful; cunning; as, a *designing* person:—*n.* the art of making or creating designs.

de-sir-a-ble (di-zīr′a-bl), *adj.* agreeable; attractive; pleasing; worth having; as, *desirable* qualities; a *desirable* job.—*n.* **de-sir′a-bil′i-ty.**

de-sire (di-zīr′; dē-zīr′), *v.t.* [desired, desir-ing], **1,** to wish earnestly for; crave; **2,** to express a wish for; ask; as, I *desire* your help:—*n.* **1,** a longing for the possession of some object; an earnest wish; **2,** a request; **3,** the object longed for.—*adj.* **de-sir′ous.**

de-sist (di-zist′; dē-zist′), *v.i.* to cease; stop; as, *desist* from talking.

desk (desk), *n.* a piece of furniture with a tablelike surface to support the paper, book, computer, etc., of a writer or reader, many having drawers.

desk-top (desk′top′), *n.* **1,** the surface of a desk; **2,** in *computing,* a computer that can fit on top of a desk:—*adj.* in *computing,* a microcomputer or other device that is designed to operate on top of a desk; as, *desktop* computer:—**desktop publishing,** in *computing,* the design and production of professional-quality typeset documents, using specially designed software programs, microcomputers, and laser printers.

des-o-late (des′ō-lāt′), *v.t.* [desolat-ed, desolat-ing], **1,** to lay waste; make unfit for inhabitants; as, an earthquake *desolated* the city; **2,** to overwhelm with sorrow:—*adj.* (des′o-lit; dez′ō-lit′), **1,** deprived of inhabitants; abandoned; deserted; **2,** in a condition of neglect or ruin; **3,** forlorn; miserable; as, to be *desolate* without one's friends.—*adv.* **des′o-late-ly.**—*n.* **des′o-la′tion.**

de-spair (di-spâr′), *v.i.* to lose all hope or expectation:—*n.* **1,** loss of hope or confidence; hopelessness; **2,** that which causes loss of hope; as, she is the *despair* of her mother.—*adj.* **de-spair′ing.**

des-patch (dis-pach′), *v.t.* and *n.* Same as **dispatch.**

des-per-a-do (des′pėr-ä′dō; des′pėr-ā′dō), *n.* [*pl.* desperadoes or desperados], a bold and reckless criminal.

des-per-ate (des′pėr-it), *adj.* **1,** without regard to danger; reckless; as, a *desperate* criminal; **2,** proceeding from despair; frantic; as, the swimmer made a *desperate* effort to reach shore.—*n.* **des′per-a′tion.**

des-pi-ca-ble (des′pi-ka-bl), *adj.* contemptible; mean; vile.—*adv.* **des′pi-ca-bly.**

de-spise (di-spīz′), *v.t.* [despised, despising], to look down upon; scorn; disdain.

de-spite (di-spīt′), *prep.* notwithstanding; in spite of; as, the player continued in the game *despite* her injuries.

de-spoil (di-spoil′), *v.t.* to rob; pillage; deprive of belongings; as, to *despoil* a house of all its treasures.—*n.* **de-spoil′er.**

de-spond (di-spond′), *v.i.* to lose hope or courage; become depressed.

de-spond-en-cy (di-spon′den-si), *n.* absence of hope; dejection; mental depression.—*n.* **de-spond′ence.**—*adj.* **de-spond′ent.**

des-pot (des′pot), *n.* an absolute ruler; tyrant; as, Nero was a *despot.*—*adj.* **des-pot′ic.**

des-pot-ism (des′pot-izm), *n.* **1,** absolute government; **2,** any absolute control; tyranny; as, the *despotism* of dictators.

des-sert (di-zûrt′), *n.* a course of fruit, ice cream, pie, cake, or pudding, served last at a meal.

des-ti-na-tion (des′ti-nā′shun), *n.* **1,** an end or objective; goal; **2,** the stated end of a journey; as, Moncton is my *destination.*

des-tine (des′tin), *v.t.* [destined, destining], **1,** to appoint to any purpose or end; as, she was *destined* for the stage; **2,** to settle in advance; foreordain; as, his hopes were *destined* (des′tind) to be realized.

des-ti-ny (des′ti-ni), *n.* [*pl.* destinies], **1,** lot or fortune; one's fate in life; as, it was his *destiny* to become prime minister; **2,** the succession of events in life considered as something beyond the power or control of a human; as, it is folly to whine against *destiny.*—*adj.* **des′tined** (as, to be *destined* for success).

des-ti-tute (des′ti-tūt′), *adj.* **1,** without means; penniless; impoverished; **2,** being wholly without something necessary or desirable; as, a person *destitute* of honour.—*n.* **des′ti-tu′tion.**

de-stroy (di-stroi′; dē-stroi′), *v.t.* **1,** to pull down; overturn; lay waste; undo; as, the fire *destroyed* the house; **2,** to kill; put an end to; as, to *destroy* a rabid animal; **3,** to render void; as, his acts *destroyed* his influence.

de-stroy-er (di-stroi′ėr; dē-stroi′ėr), *n.* **1,** a person or thing that destroys; **2,** a light, fast war vessel armed with guns, torpedoes, guided missiles, etc.

de-struct-i-ble (di-struk′ti-bl), *adj.* capable of being destroyed or ruined.

de-struc-tion (di-struk′shun), *n.* **1,** the act of destroying; ruin; as, fire completed the *destruction* of the city; **2,** a cause of ruin; as, gambling was his *destruction.*

de-struc-tive (di-struk′tiv), *adj.* **1,** causing desolation; ruinous; hurtful; as, a *destructive* insect; **2,** tearing down without building up; as, a *destructive* critic.—*adv.* **de-struc′tive-ly.**

des-ul-tor-y (des′ul-tėr-i), *adj.* passing from one thing to another without order or method; aimless; as, *desultory* browsing on the Internet.

de-tach (di-tach′; dē-tach′), *v.t.* **1,** to separate; disconnect; as, to *detach* a button from the coat; **2,** to separate or detail for a special duty; as, to *detach* troops to guard a pass.—*adj.* **de-tach′a-ble.**

de-tached (di-tacht′; dē-tacht′), *adj.* **1,** separate; unattached; as, a *detached* house; **2,** impartial; aloof; apart; as, a *detached* bystander.

de-tach-ment (di-tach′ment; dē-tach′ment), *n.* **1,** the act of separating; as, the *detachment* of a key from a keyring; **2,** a body of troops or ships separated from the main body and sent on special service; **3,** a standing apart or aloof; aloofness; isolation.

de-tail (di-tāl′), *v.t.* **1,** to relate minutely; enumerate; as, she *detailed* to us all her troubles; **2,** to appoint or choose for a special task; as, to *detail* her to collect the assignments; also, to select for a special duty; as, he *detailed* two men for guard duty:—*n.* (dē′tāl′; di-tāl′), **1,** a small part of a whole; a single item; as, the *details* of a scheme; such items considered together or taken one by one; as, a subject treated in great *detail;* to go into *detail;* **2,** a particular or minute account; **3,** a small group of people or body of troops assigned to special duty.

de-tain (di-tān′; dē-tān′), *v.t.* **1,** to hold back or delay; **2,** to keep in custody; as, to *detain* a suspect.

de-tect (di-tekt′; dē-tekt′), *v.t.* to discover; find out; as, to *detect* a criminal; to *detect* an odour.—*n.* **de-tec′tion.**

de-tec-tive (di-tek′tiv), *n.* **1,** a police officer whose work is to find out information that can be used to solve a crime; **2,** a private citizen who investigates crimes and mysteries or who finds out information about people; a sleuth: also called *private detective* or *private investigator:—adj.* fitted for, employed in, or connected with finding out; as, a *detective* agency.

de-tec-tor (di-tek′tėr), *n.* **1,** one who or that which detects; **2,** a device used to detect electromagnetic waves, radioactivity, heat, etc. Also, **lie detector; metal detector; smoke detector.**

de-ten-tion (di-ten′shun), *n.* **1,** the act of keeping back; a delay; **2,** confinement; restraint; as, to hold a suspect in *detention;* **3,** school punishment in which the student stays after class; as, the student was given a *detention* for misbehaving in class.

de-ter (di-tûr′; dē-tûr′), *v.t.* [deterred, deter-ring], to discourage or hinder, as by fear; restrain; dishearten; as, previous failures did not *deter* us from trying again.—*n.* **de-ter′ment.**

de-ter-gent (di-tėr′jent), *n.* a cleansing substance or agent, as soap.

de-te-ri-o-rate (di-tē′ri-ō-rāt′; dē-tē′ri-ō-rāt′), *v.t.* [deteriorat-ed, deteriorat-ing], to reduce the quality or value of; as, the rainy spell *deteriorated* the peach crop:—*v.i.* to grow worse; as, her health *deteriorated,* and she had to be hospitalized.—*n.* **de-te′ri-o-ra′tion.**

de-ter-mi-na-tion (di-tûr′mi-nā′shun), *n.* **1,** the act of deciding or settling of something; **2,** firmness; resolution; as, he spoke with *determination*; **3,** measurement or calculation; as, the *determination* of the amount of iron in the iron ore sample.

de-ter-mine (di-tûr′min; dē-tûr′min), *v.i.* [determined, determin-ing], to reach a decision; as, he *determined* on quick action:—*v.t.* **1,** to put an end to; **2,** to settle; as, to *determine* a case in court; **3,** to fix or decide upon beforehand; as, to *determine* the date for the game; **4,** to find out for oneself; as, to use a compass to *determine* one's location; **5,** to cause to come to a decision; as, this *determined* him to go at once; **6,** to establish as a result, or give a definite direction to; as, an accident *determined* his career.—*adj.* **de-ter′mi-nate** (-nit).

de-ter-mined (di-tûr′mind; dē-tûr′mind), *adj.* resolute; decided; strong-willed; as, he was a *determined* sort of person; a *determined* look.—*adv.* **de-ter′mined-ly** (di-tûr′mind-li; di-tûr′min-id-li or dē-tûr′mind-li; dē-tûr′min-id-li).

de-test (di-test′; dē-test′), *v.t.* to hate intensely; loathe; as, we *detest* people who cheat.—*adj.* **de-test′a-ble.**—*n.* **de′tes-ta′tion.**

de-throne (di-thrōn′; dē-thrōn′), *v.t.* [dethroned, dethron-ing], to remove from a throne; deprive of authority or power; as, to *dethrone* a king.—*n.* **de-throne′ment.**

det-o-nate (det′o-nāt′; det′), *v.t.* to explode; as, he *detonated* the charge of dynamite:—*v.i.* to explode; as, the bomb *detonated.*—*n.* **det′o-na′tion; det′o-na′tor.**

de-tour (di-tōōr′; dē′tōōr), *n.* a roundabout way; a path or road that is used temporarily because of an obstruction in a main road:—*v.t.* and *v.i.* to go or send by detour; bypass.

de-tract (di-trakt′; de-trakt′), *v.t.* and *v.i.* to take away; divert; as, the dark colour *detracts* a great deal from the beauty of the hall.—*n.* **de-trac′tion.**

de-train (dē-trān′), *v.i.* and *v.t.* to get off or remove from a railway train; as, the troops *detrained*; to *detrain* the freight.

det-ri-ment (det′ri-ment), *n.* that which injures or reduces in value; injury; damage; loss; harm; as, you cannot do evil without *detriment* to your reputation.—*adj.* **det′ri-men′tal.**

de-tri-tus (di-trī′tus), *n.* fragments of rock worn away or broken down by action of weather, glaciers, etc.; debris.

deuce (dūs), *n.* **1,** a card marked with a 2, or the side of a die marked with two spots; **2,** in *lawn tennis*, an even point score of 40 points each.

deutsche mark (doich mark), *n.* the basic monetary unit of Germany; also called *mark.*

de-val-ue (dē′val′ū) or **de-val-u-ate** (dē-val′ū-āt′), *v.t.* [de-val-ued, de-val-u-ing], **1,** to reduce the legal value (of currency); as, France *devaluated* the franc; **2,** to reduce something in value; depreciate; as, the accident *devalued* the price of the car.—*n.* **de′val′u-a′tion.**

dev-as-tate (dev′as-tāt′), *v.t.* [devastat-ed, devastat-ing], to lay waste; destroy; ruin; as, fire *devastated* the town.—*n.* **dev′as-ta′tion.**

de-vel-op (di-vel′up; dē-vel′up), *v.t.* **1,** to unfold gradually; make known in detail; as, he *developed* his strategies for winning the election; **2,** to make available for use; as, to *develop* a country's mineral wealth; **3,** to cause to grow; as, a balanced diet, fresh air, and exercise help to *develop* healthy bodies; **4,** in *photography*, to treat an exposed plate, print, or film with chemicals so as to bring out the picture:—*v.i.* to advance from one stage to another; to grow; as, caterpillars *develop* into butterflies; oak trees *develop* from acorns.

de-vel-op-er (di-vel′o-pėr; dē-vel′o-pėr), *n.* **1,** in *photography*, a chemical solution used to develop a film, plate, etc.; **2,** a person or company that builds real estate developments on a large scale.

de-vel-op-ment (di-vel′op-ment; dē-vel′op-ment), *n.* **1,** the act or process of developing; as, the *development* of the new day-care centre; **2,** an event or happening; as, the latest news *developments*; **3,** a group of houses or other buildings built by the same builder.

de-vi-ate (dē′vi-āt′), *v.i.* [deviat-ed, deviat-ing], to turn aside or stray, as from a course, plan, etc; as, to *deviate* from the main issue.—*n.* **de′vi-a′tion.**

de-vice (di-vīs′), *n.* **1,** a plan or scheme; trick; as, to use any *device* to win a game; **2,** an invention by people to be used for a certain purpose; apparatus; as, any tool or machine is a *device*; **3,** a design or pattern; a heraldic emblem; **4,** fancy or will; as, left to her own *devices*.

dev-il (dev′l), *n.* **1,** (often *Devil*), the supreme spirit of evil; Satan; **2,** a false god or demon; **3,** a wicked person; **4,** an unfortunate person; as, the poor *devil* deserves pity; **5,** a daring or reckless person; **6,** something very difficult or trying; as, a *devil* of a test:—*v.t.* [devilled, devil-ling or deviled, devil-ing], to tease; torment:—*v.i.* to season something with hot spices; as, *devilled* eggs.—*adj.* **dev′il-ish** (dev′l-ish).—*n.* **dev′il-ment; dev′il-ry; dev′il-try.**

de-vi-ous (dē′vi-us), *adj.* **1,** indirect; rambling; roundabout; as, *devious* paths; **2,** apart from the way of right and duty; cunning; as, *devious* methods.—*adv.* **de′vi-ous-ly.**

de-vise (di-vīz′), *v.t.* [devised, devis-ing], **1,** to think up or contrive; as, the prisoners *devised* a way to escape; **2,** to bequeath or give by will.

de-vis-er (di-vīz′ėr), *n.* one who contrives or invents.

de-vis-or (di-vīz′ėr), *n.* one who gives or bequeaths by will.

de-void (di-void′), *adj.* entirely without; lacking; as, *devoid* of sense.

de-volve (di-volv′), *v.i.* [devolved, devolv-ing], to be passed down or handed over; as, the duty *devolved* upon him.—*n.* **de′vo-lu′tion** (dē′vo-lū′shun).

de-vote (di-vōt′; dē-vōt′), *v.t.* [devot-ed, devot-ing], **1,** to dedicate or set apart; give attention, time, or help to; as, to *devote* the morning to studying; **2,** to give up wholly; as, to *devote* oneself to music.—*adj.* **de-vot′ed.**

dev-o-tee (dev′ō-tē′; dēv′ō-tē′; dev′ō-tā′), *n.* **1,** one entirely given up to a special interest; an enthusiast; as, a *devotee* of the theatre; **2,** one zealous in religion.

de-vo-tion (di-vō′shun; dē-vō′shun), *n.* **1,** the act of devoting or the state of being devoted; **2,** strong affection:—**devotions,** religious worship; prayer.—*adj.* and *n.* **de-vo′tion-al.**

de-vour (di-vour′; dē-vour′), *v.t.* **1,** of animals, to eat; as, the lions *devoured* their prey; **2,** to swallow greedily or ravenously; as, the hungry girl *devoured* the food; **3,** to destroy or lay waste; as, the fire *devoured* much timber; **4,** to take in eagerly with ears or eyes; as, to *devour* a new movie or CD.

de-vout (di-vout′), *adj.* **1,** devoted to religious thoughts and exercises; **2,** expressing piety; as, a *devout* prayer; **3,** sincere; as, accept our *devout* wishes for success.—*adv.* **de-vout′ly.**—*n.* **de-vout′ness.**

dew (dū), *n.* **1,** moisture from the night air condensed in small drops on the ground or other surface; **2,** anything refreshing like dew.—*adj.* **dew′y.**

dew–worm or **dew worm** (dū′–wûrm′; dū′ wûrm′), *n.* a variety of large earthworms found on lawns at night (often used for fishing).

dex-ter-ous (dek′stėr-us) or **dextrous** (deks′trus), *adj.* **1,** skillful with the hands; as, a *dexterous* worker; **2,** quick mentally; adroit; clever; **3,** done with skill; as, *dexterous* tricks.—*n.* **dex-ter′i-ty** (deks-ter′i-ti).

di-a-be-tes (dī′a-bē′tis; -tēz), *n.* a serious disease in which there is too much sugar in the blood when the body does not produce enough insulin, marked by excessive urination, .thirst, and hunger.—*n.* and *adj.* **di′a-bet′ic** (-bet′; -bēt′).

di-a-bol-ic (dī′a-bol′ik) or **di-a-bol-i-cal** (dī′a-bol′i-kal), *adj.* devilish; outrageously wicked; cruel; as, he has a *diabolic* temper.

di-ag-nose (dī′ag-nōz′; dī′ag-nōs′), *v.t.* [diagnosed, diagnos-ing], to determine the nature of something by examination, as a disease, from the symptoms; as, the doctor *diagnosed* her illness as bronchitis.

di-ag-no-sis (dī′ag-nō′sis), *n.* **1,** a finding based on a careful study of a person by a doctor to determine whether the person has a certain disease or unhealthy condition; **2,** any finding based on careful study aimed at learning why a certain problem exists; as, the techie's *diagnosis* concerning the malfunctioning computer.—*adj.* **di′ag-nos′tic.**

di-ag-o-nal (dī-ag′o-nal), *adj.* **1,** slanting; **2,** extending from one corner of a figure, as a square, to its opposite corner:—*n.* **1,** a straight line drawn or cut on a slant; **2,** a straight line drawn from one angle of a figure, as a square, to any other angle not adjacent; **3,** material with an oblique pattern.—*adv.* **di-ag′o-nal-ly.**

di-a-gram (dī′a-gram), *n.* a drawing or sketch of something, made for purposes of explanation, and giving in outline the most important parts; a plan or chart, as of a building, machine, etc.:—*v.t.* [diagrammed, diagram-ming], to illustrate by an outline or drawing.—*adj.* **di′a-gram-mat′ic.**

di-al (dī′al), *n.* **1,** a flat surface on which a pointer casts a shadow in such a way as to show the time of day; the face of a sundial; **2,** the face of a watch, clock, etc.; **3,** the front or face of an instrument that uses numbers, letters, or other marks to show how much there is of something, such as on some radios, TV sets, etc.; also, any plate on which a pointer marks revolutions, direction, pressure, etc.; as, the *dial* on a gas meter; **4,** in some older telephones, a movable device that is rotated to make connection with another telephone line:—*v.t.* [dialled, dial-ling], **1,** in telephoning, to connect to another line by operating a movable dial or to make a telephone call; as, *dial* 911 in an emergency; **2,** to use a dial, such as on a combination lock, radio, etc.

di-a-lect (dī′a-lekt), *n.* **1,** the special form of a language in a given region of a country or by a certain group of people; as, the Nova Scotia *dialect*; **2,** also, the customary speech of a certain group; as, Internet or computer *dialect*; **3,** the special language of a trade or profession, such as that of lawyers, business people, plumbers, etc.—*adj.* **di′a-lec′tal.**

di-a-logue or **di-a-log** (dī′a-log), *n.* **1,** a conversation between two or more persons; **2,** communication between two opposing sides; **3,** the words spoken by the characters in a novel, play, or movie:—**dialog box,** in *computing,* the window that appears on the computer screen asking the user for instructions and which disappears after it is completed.

dial tone, a low steady buzz or hum in a telephone when the receiver is lifted to show that the line is open and a number may be dialled, or when a connection is broken.

dial–up (dī′al–up′), *adj.* in *computing* and *technology,* a temporary (as opposed to a *dedicated*) connection made over the phone line between computers, using modems.

di-am-e-ter (dī-am′e-tėr), *n.* **1,** a straight line through the centre of a circle or another round object, dividing it in half; **2,** the length of a straight line through the centre of an object; hence, thickness or width of something that is round; as, the *diameter* of a tree.—*adj.* **di′a-met′ric** (dī′a-met′rik); **di′a-met′ri-cal.**—*adv.* **di′a-met′ri-cal-ly.**

di-a-mond (dī′a-mund), *n.* **1,** a brilliant, usually colourless, precious stone; crystallized carbon: the hardest known natural substance: used as precious jewels and as cutting or grinding tools; **2,** a plane figure with four equal straight sides and two acute and two obtuse angles; **3,** one of a suit, called *diamonds,* of playing cards, marked with a red figure like a diamond; **4,** in *baseball,* the space inside the lines connecting the bases; also, the entire playing field:—*adj.* resembling, or made of, a diamond.

di-a-per (dī′a-pėr), *n.* **1,** cotton or linen cloth woven in geometric patterns; **2,** a soft piece of folded cloth or a pad of other absorbent material worn as underpants by a baby.

di-a-phragm (dī′a-fram), *n.* **1,** the muscular partition that divides the chest from the abdomen; **2,** a vibrating disk, as in a telephone receiver or microphone; **3,** in a camera, optical instrument, etc., a perforated device for regulating the admission of light; **4,** a contraceptive device for women.

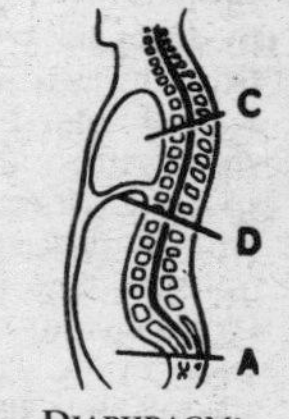

DIAPHRAGM: A, ABDOMINAL CAVITY; C, THORACIC CAVITY; D, DIAPHRAGM.

di-ar-rhe-a or **di-ar-rhoe-a** (dī′a-rē′a), *n.* extreme looseness of the bowels.—*adj.* **di′ar-rhe′al.**

di-a-ry (dī′a-ri), *n.* [*pl.* diaries], **1,** a personal record of daily events, thoughts, feelings, and experiences; **2,** a book for daily memorandums.—*n.* **di′a-rist.**

di-a-tribe (dī′a-trīb′), *n.* a bitter, abusive attack in words.

dice (dīs), *n.pl.* [*sing.* die (dī)], small cubes made out of plastic, wood, or other hard material, marked on the sides with one to six spots, used in games of chance:—*v.i.* [diced, dic-ing], to play with dice:—*v.t.* **1,** to decorate with patterns resembling cubes or squares; to checker; **2,** to cut into cubes or squares; as, to *dice* onions.—*n.* **dic′er.**

dick-er (dik′ėr), *v.i.* to bargain or trade on a small scale; as, to *dicker* with a store clerk:—*n.* a small bargain or deal.

di-cot-y-le-don (dī-kot′i-lē′don), *n.* a plant with two seed leaves; in this largest class of some 172 orders are the shrubs, deciduous trees, legumes, etc. Compare *monocotyledon.*—*adj.* **di-cot′y-le′don-ous.**

dic-tate (dik-tāt′), *v.t.* [dictat-ed, dictat-ing], **1,** to declare with authority; prescribe; **2,** to express orally for another to take down in writing; as, she *dictated* 10 letters to her administrative assistant:—*v.i.* to speak or show with final authority; as, the bad weather *dictated* that we hold the party indoors:—*n.* (dik′tāt), **1,** a command; as, the king's *dictates*; **2,** a controlling principle; as, the *dictates* of conscience.—*n.* **dic-ta′tion.**

dic-ta-tor (dik-tā′tėr; dik′tāt-ėr), *n.* **1,** one who says something for another to write; **2,** one who rules with absolute powers over a country and its people, esp. of modern political leaders such as Hitler, Stalin, Castro, and Milosevic, etc.; **3,** one exercising similar authority in any sphere; as, a *dictator* of styles.—*n.* **dic-ta′tor-ship.**

dic-ta-tor-i-al (dik′ta-tōr′i-al), *adj.* pertaining to one who gives commands or acts like a dictator; overbearing; imperious.

dic-tion (dik′shun), *n.* **1,** the manner of expressing ideas in words; choice of words in speaking or writing; **2,** clear and proper pronunciation in speaking and singing; as, to speak with perfect *diction.*

dic-tion-ar-y (dik′shun-ėr-i), *n.* [*pl.* dictionaries], **1,** a book that lists the words of a language, arranged alphabetically, and gives information about them such as the spelling, pronunciation, definition, usage, and etymology; a lexicon; vocabulary; **2,** a book of this kind that lists words of one language and gives their meaning in another; as, a French–English *dictionary*; **3,** a book that gives information about words related to a certain subject; as, a law, sports, business, computer, or Internet *dictionary.*

did (did), *p.t.* of *do.*

di-dac-tic (di-dak′tik; dī-), *adj.* pertaining to, or of the nature of, teaching; conveying instruction; as, a *didactic* poem.—*adv.* **di-dac′ti-cal-ly.**—*n.* **di-dac′ti-cism.**

did-dle (did′l), *v.i.* and *v.t. Colloq.* **1,** to jiggle; **2,** swindle; **3,** waste time; **4,** fiddle around with; as, to *diddle* with a button until it comes loose.

[1]**die** (dī), *v.i.* [died, dy-ing], **1,** to cease to live; expire; **2,** to decay; wither: said of plants or flowers; **3,** to long intensely; as, she is *dying* to hear your secret; **4,** figuratively, to fade; vanish; as, fame soon *dies*; **5,** to lose power or energy; as, the wind *died* down.

[2]**die** (dī), *n.* [*pl.* dies (dīz)], **1,** a metal form used in stamping coins, metals, etc.; **2,** tool used in cutting the threads of screws, bolts, etc.; **3,** a metal plate for threading a pipe or bar, with holes for receiving a punch; also, a form of cutter, used in a press, for shaping leather, paper, sheet metal, etc.

[3]**die** (dī), *n.* [*pl.* dice (dīs)], a small cube used in gaming; one of a pair of *dice.*

die-hard (dī′–härd′), *n.* a stubborn person who refuses to give in:—*adj.* **1,** staunchly loyal; as, *die-hard* fans; **2,** of a person who stubbornly resists change; as, a *die-hard* conservative.

die-sel (dē′zel), *n.* an internal-combustion engine in which crude oil is ignited by heat from air compression instead of by electric spark as in a gasoline engine.

[1]**di-et** (dī′et), *n.* a formal assembly or congress; esp., the parliamentary assembly of some countries.

[2]**di-et** (dī′et), *n.* **1,** one's customary food; **2,** manner of living, with special reference to food; as, a steady *diet* of song, dance, and wine; **3,** a prescribed course of food, intended as a health measure or to gain or lose weight:—*v.t.* to regulate the eating and drinking of (a person); as, he *dieted* himself back to health:—*v.i.* to eat or drink according to prescribed rules; as, to *diet* to lose weight.—*adj.* **di′e-tar-y.**

di-e-tet-ic (dī′e-tet′ik), *adj.* pertaining to diet; also, pertaining to a type of food that is low in calories, etc., or that belongs to restrictive diets:—**dietetics,** *n.pl.* used as *sing.,* that branch of science relating to diet or nutrition and its effects on the body.—*adj.* **di′e-tet′i-cal.**

di-e-ti-tian or **di-e-ti-cian** (dī′e-tish′an), *n.* one trained in dietetics or to plan meals with a proper proportion of various food elements.

dif-fer (dif′ėr), *v.i.* **1,** to be unlike or different; **2,** to disagree; dispute; quarrel.

dif-fer-ence (dif′ėr-ens), *n.* **1,** the state of being unlike or different; unlikeness; as, the *difference* between night and day; **2,** the way or amount of being different; as, the *difference* between the two beverages is the amount of sugar they have; **3,** controversy; quarrel; **4,** the amount by which numbers differ; remainder after subtraction; as, the *difference* between five and eight is three.

dif-fer-ent (dif′ėr-ent), *adj.* **1,** unlike; distinct; not the same; as, to have *different*-coloured shirts; **2,** not the same as each other; separate; as, cougar, mountain lion, and puma are three *different* names for the same animal; **3,** not like most others; as, to have *different* taste in music.—*adv.* **dif′fer-ent-ly.**

dif-fer-en-tial (dif′ėr-en′shal), *adj.* **1,** showing a difference; **2,** distinguishing; **3,** making use of differences; as, a *differential* gear.—*n.* **1,** a difference; **2,** a differential gear; **3,** a difference in rates.

dif-fer-en-ti-ate (dif′ėr-en′shi-āt′), *v.t.* [differentiat-ed, differentiat-ing], **1,** to observe or state an unlikeness between; as, to *differentiate* the various breeds of cattle; **2,** to mark (a person or thing) as unlike another; as, size *differentiates* the raven from the crow:—*v.i.* to acquire a distinctive character.—*n.* **dif′fer-en′ti-a′tion.**

dif-fi-cult (dif′i-kult), *adj.* **1,** not easy; hard to do, make, or understand, as a problem; **2,** not easily pleased or managed; hard to get along with; as, a *difficult* child or classmate.

dif-fi-cul-ty (dif′i-kul-ti), *n.* [*pl.* difficulties], **1,** the state of being hard to do; as, the *difficulty* of the task; also, great effort; as, he reached home with *difficulty*; **2,** something hard to do; an obstacle; trouble; hard work; as, he had *difficulty* in starting the car:—**difficulties,** a trying situation; embarrassment; esp., money trouble.

dif-fi-dent (dif′i-dent), *adj.* lacking self-reliance; shy; modest.—*n.* **dif′fi-dence.**

dif-frac-tion (di-frak′shun), *n.* **1,** the breaking of a ray of light into the colours of the spectrum or into dark and light bands; **2,** a similar breaking of wave motions, as of sound or electricity.—*v.t.* **dif-fract′.**

dif-fuse (di-fūz′), *v.t.* [diffused, diffus-ing], **1,** to send out; spread; scatter widely; as, the lamps *diffused* a pale light; **2,** in *physics*, to spread, as a gas or liquid, by mixing with another gas or liquid; as, to *diffuse* syrup in water:—*v.i.* to spread out in every direction:—*adj.* (di-fūs′), **1,** widely spread; scattered; **2,** wordy; as, a *diffuse* speaker.—*n.* **dif-fu′sion.**—*adv.* **dif-fuse′ly.**

dig (dig), *v.i.* [*p.t.* and *p.p.* dug (dug), *p.pr.* dig-ging], **1,** to work with a spade, hands, claws, etc., in breaking up or removing earth; **2,** to make a way (under, through, in); as, they *dug* through the thick forest:—*v.t.* **1,** to loosen or break up with a spade, hands, claws, etc.; as, to *dig* a garden; **2,** to make, as a hole, by breaking up or removing earth; to excavate; **3,** to bring up from underground; unearth; as, to *dig* potatoes; also, to bring to light; as, to *dig* up information; **4,** to thrust; poke; as, to *dig* spurs into a horse; **5,** *Slang* understand or appreciate; as, to *dig* this kind of music:—*n.* **1,** a poke or thrust; **2,** *Colloq.* a cutting or spiteful remark; **3,** an excavation site, esp. an archaeological one.—*n.* **dig′ger.**

di-gest (di-jest′; dī-jest′), *v.t.* **1,** to change (food) in the stomach and intestines into a form that the body can use; **2,** to think over carefully until one understands or until the material becomes a part of one's knowledge; as, to *digest* a book; **3,** to arrange in condensed form and systematic order; classify; as, the laws of the province were *digested*:—*v.i.* to undergo change, as food in the stomach and intestines, for use in the body; as, nuts and corn often do not *digest* easily:—*n.* (dī′jest), **1,** an orderly and classified arrangement of materials, usually in condensed form; as, a *digest* of the laws of the province; **2,** a brief summary; a condensed version of a written piece of material; as, he wrote a *digest* of the book.

di-gest-i-ble (di-jes′ti-bl; dī-jes′ti-bl), *adj.* capable of being changed in the stomach and intestines for use in the body.—*adv.* **di-gest′i-bly.**—*n.* **di-gest′i-bil′i-ty.**

di-ges-tion (di-jes′chun; dī-jes′chun), *n.* the act or process of changing food by action of juices in the stomach and intestines for use in the body; also, the power of digesting; as, a weak *digestion.*

di-ges-tive (di-jes′tiv), *adj.* pertaining to, or promoting, absorption of food by the body.

digestive system, the group of organs that digest food and eliminate waste from the body.

dig-it (dij′it), *n.* **1,** a finger or toe; **2,** any one of the numerals, esp. from 0 to 9.

dig-i-tal (di′ji-tl), *adj.* **1,** pertaining to fingers or toes; **2,** relating to numerals; **3,** relating to audio or video recording that uses numbers to store, send, receive, or display information; as, CDs hold music in *digital* form; **4,** in *computing*, relating to a computer that reads, writes, and stores information in the form of numbers expressed as binary digits, as opposed to an *analogue computer*; **5,** in *computing*, relating to computers and computing; as, the *digital* age:—**digital camera**, a camera that takes pictures without conventional film, using digital electronics.

digital photography, in *computing*, the method of taking pictures using digital electronics, whereby the image is digitally encoded and stored in a computer.

digital video disc. Same as DVD.

dig-ni-fy (dig′ni-fī), *v.t.* [dignified, dignifying], to exalt; confer honour upon; add distinction to; as, his presence *dignified* the meeting.

dig-ni-tar-y (dig′ni-tėr-i), *n.* [*pl.* dignitaries], one who holds a position of rank or honour; an influential person; as, a bishop is a *dignitary* of the church.

dig-ni-ty (dig′ni-ti), *n.* [*pl.* dignities], **1,** nobleness; true worth; a quality of being worthy and honourable that commands the respect of other people; as, a hard-working person of *dignity*; **2,** stateliness of manner or style; calm and serious manner; as, to walk away with *dignity* after tripping; **3,** high rank or office; as, the *dignity* of a king.—*adj.* **dig′ni-fied.**

di-gress (dī-gres′; di-gres′), *v.i.* to turn aside; get away from the main subject or line of argument.—*n.* **di-gres′sion.**

dike or **dyke** (dīk), *n.* **1,** a ditch; **2,** a mound or bank of earth along a ditch; a causeway; **3,** a wall, dam, or bank thrown up as a protection against the sea or floods; as, the *dikes* of Holland:—*v.t.* [diked, dik-ing], **1,** to enclose or protect with a dike; **2,** to drain by means of ditching or dikes.

di-lap-i-dat-ed (di-lap′i-dāt′ed), *adj.* in partial ruin from lack of care; rundown; neglected; as, a *dilapidated* old house.—*n.* **di-lap′i-da′tion.**

di-late (dī-lāt′; di-lāt′), *v.t.* [dilat-ed, dilat-ing], **1,** to enlarge or widen; as, to *dilate* the pupils of the eyes; **2,** to distend; as, to *dilate* the lungs with air:—*v.i.* **1,** to be extended or enlarged; **2,** to speak fully and copiously.—*n.* **di-lat′or; di-la′tion; dil′a-ta′tion.**

dil-a-tor-y (dil′a-tėr-i), *adj.* tending to cause delay; as, *dilatory* tactics; tardy; as, a *dilatory* reply.—*adv.* **dil′a-tor-i-ly.**

di-lem-ma (di-lem′a; dī-lem′a), *n.* a situation involving a choice between two or more alternatives; a difficult choice.

dil-et-tan-te (dil′e-tän′ti), *n.* one who dabbles in the fine arts, literature, or science as a pastime; also, a serious admirer of arts.

dil-i-gent (dil′i-jent), *adj.* industrious; careful.—*n.* **dil′i-gence.**

dill (dil), *n.* a tall plant with spicy leaves and seeds used in flavouring:—**dill pickle,** a large pickle seasoned with dill.

di-lute (di-lūt′; dī-), *v.t.* [dilut-ed, dilut-ing], **1,** to make weak or thin by mixing with something, esp. by adding water; **2,** to weaken the effect of something; as, to *dilute* a good story by boring details:—*adj.* weakened; thinned; as, a *dilute* mixture.—*n.* **di-lu′tion.**—*adj.* **di-lu′ted.**

dim (dim), *adj.* **1,** faint; obscure; not bright; as, the *dim* light of evening; **2,** shedding little light; as, *dim* headlights; **3,** hazy; ill-defined; vague; as, a *dim* figure in the shadows; **4,** not understanding or seeing clearly; as, eyes *dim* with tears:—*v.t.* [dimmed, dim-ming], to make less bright or distinct; dull:—*v.i.* to become indistinct; fade.—*adv.* **dim′ly.**—*n.* **dim′ness.**

dime (dīm), *n.* a coin of Canada and the U.S. worth 10 cents.

di-men-sion (di-men′shun), *n.* **1,** measurement in any one direction, as length, breadth, height, etc.:—**dimensions, 1,** size in terms of these measurements; **2,** size; importance; scope; as, an undertaking of large *dimensions.*—*adj.* **di-men′sion-al** (as, a three-*dimensional* figure).

di-min-ish (di-min′ish), *v.t.* **1,** to make less in amount, size, number, etc.; as, the recession *diminished* their savings; **2,** to weaken; impair; as, the power of wealth was *diminished*:—*v.i.* to grow less in amount or importance; decrease.

di-min-u-en-do (di-min′ū-en′dō), *adj.* and *adv.* in *music,* decreasing or softening in volume of sound: opposite of *crescendo.*

dim-i-nu-tion (dim′i-nū′shun), *n.* a decreasing; a making or growing less; as, a *diminution* in foreign trade.

di-min-u-tive (di-min′ū-tiv), *adj.* **1,** small or little; as, a *diminutive* dog; **2,** expressing smallness; as, "-let" is a *diminutive* ending:—*n.* a word formed from another to express a smaller thing of the same kind; as, *booklet,* a little *book.*

dim-ple (dim′pl), *n.* a small dent or hollow in the surface of anything, as in the cheek or chin:—*v.i.* [dim-pled, dim-pling], to form dimples:—*v.t.* to mark with dimples.

din (din), *n.* a continued and insistent noise; as, the *din* of traffic:—*v.t.* [dinned, din-ning], to repeat over and over persistently; as, she *dinned* into him the lesson of honesty:—*v.i.* to make a noise; as, cries *dinning* in his ears.

dine (dīn), *v.i.* [dined, din-ing], to eat dinner; as, to *dine* out twice a week:—*v.t.* to give a dinner for; feed; as, to wine and *dine* someone.

din-er (dīn′ėr), *n.* **1,** one who dines; **2,** a railway car in which meals are served: also called *dining car;* **3,** a small restaurant shaped like a dining car.

din-ette (dī′net′), *n.* an area used as a mini dining room; also, the furniture for this area.

ding (ding), *v.i.* **1,** to sound like a bell; **2,** to go on and on; reiterate:—*v.t.* **1,** to dent by hitting; as, to *ding* a car with another; **2,** to rei-terate endlessly; as, to *ding* it to someone:—*n.* a small dent.

ding-bat (ding′bat′), *n.* **1,** decorative typographical characters that are neither mathematical symbols nor letters and are largely ornamental; **2,** a silly or empty-headed person; a nitwit; **3,** a gadget or device the name of which is unknown or forgotten; a dingus; a thingamajig; **4,** an object, such as a stone or brick, that is thrown like a missile.

din-ghy (ding′gi), *n.* [*pl.* dinghies], any of various kinds of small rowboats, sailboats, lifeboats, liferafts, or a boat to go ashore from a larger boat.

din-gy (din′ji), *adj.* [din-gi-er, din-gi-est], dark and dirty; grimy; faded; dull; as, a *dingy* room; *dingy* curtains.—*adv.* **din′gi-ly.**—*n.* **din′giness.**

din-ner (din′ėr), *n.* **1,** the chief meal of the day, usually eaten in the evening; **2,** a formal party at which dinner is served in honour of some person or event.

din-ing room (dīn′ing ro͞om′), *n.* a room where meals are usually eaten.

dink-y (dingk′i), *adj. Colloq.* small.

di-no-saur (dī′no-sôr′), *n.* any of a great variety of huge reptiles that lived millions of years ago.—*adj.* **di′no-sau′ri-an.**

dint (dint), *n.* **1,** a mark left by a blow or pressure; a dent; **2,** force or power; as, the trunk was closed by *dint* of much effort:—*v.t.* to mark or dent.

di-o-cese (dī′ō-sēs; dī′ō-sis), *n.* the district in which a bishop has authority.—*adj.* **di-oc′e-san** (dī-os′e-san; dī-os′e-zan).

di-ode (dī′ōd), *n.* an electronic device with a cold pole (*anode*) and a heated negative pole (*cathode*), used as a rectifier (a means of changing alternating to direct current).

di-ox-ide (dī-ok′sīd), *n.* an oxide with two atoms of oxygen to the molecule, as carbon *dioxide* (CO_2).

dip (dip), *v.t.* [dipped, dip-ping], **1,** to put quickly into liquid and take out again; immerse; as, to *dip* one's finger into water; *dip* water from a brook; **3,** to lower and raise quickly, as a flag:—*v.i.* **1,** to immerse oneself; **2,** to enter slightly into anything; as, to *dip* into a book; **3,** to slope downward; as, the road *dips;* **4,** to sink; as, the sun *dipped* below the hills; **5,** to reach into to take something out; as, to *dip* into a bag for potato chips:—*n.* **1,** the act of putting into water temporarily; a short plunge; as, a *dip* in the ocean; **2,** a downward slope; as, a *dip* in the road; **3,** a liquid preparation used in cleaning or colouring; **4,** a sauce-like mixture for dipping food such as vegetables, potato chips, crackers, etc.

diph-thong (dif′thông), *n.* the union of two distinct vowel sounds which combine to form one continuous vowel sound, as in *oi*l, *ou*t, *ai*sle, b*oy*, etc.

di-plo-ma (di-plō′ma), *n.* an official document conferring some honour or degree; esp. a paper received upon graduation showing the completion of a course of study in school, university, or college.

di-plo-ma-cy (di-plō′ma-si), *n.* [*pl.* diplomacies], **1,** the art or practice of managing relations between countries or nations; **2,** skill in conducting affairs; tact.

dip-lo-mat (dip′lō-mat′), *n.* **1,** one who represents his or her country in conducting negotiations between nations; **2,** any person who is good at dealing with other people; a tactful person.—*adj.* **dip′lo-mat′ic.**—*adv.* **dip′lo-mat′ic-al-ly.**

dip-per (dip′ėr), *n.* **1,** a vessel with a long handle for scooping up a liquid; a ladle; **2,** a wrenlike bird skilled in diving:—**Dipper,** either of two groups of seven stars in the northern sky, arranged in the outline of a dipper: the *Big Dipper* and the *Little Dipper*.

dire (dīr), *adj.* [dir-er, dir-est], **1,** dreadful; as, the *dire* news of an explosion; **2,** extreme; as, in *dire* need.—*adv.* **dire′ly.**

di-rect (di-rekt′; dī-rekt′), *adj.* **1,** straight; as, a *direct* route; a *direct* flight to Charlottetown; **2,** straightforward; sincere; as, a *direct* answer; **3,** immediate; not coming through someone else; as, he had *direct* knowledge; hence, personal; as, under her *direct* supervision; **4,** in an unbroken line of descent; as, a *direct* heir:—*v.t.* **1,** to address (a letter); also, to address with a definite aim; as, he *directed* his remarks to the students; **2,** to aim or point; as, to *direct* one's attention to peace; **3,** to show or guide; as, to *direct* him to the station; **4,** to conduct or manage; as, to *direct* operations of a business; **5,** to order or instruct; as, to *direct* students to hand in their assignments:—*v.i.* to act as a guide.—*n.* **di-rect′ness; di-rec′tive.**

direct current (**DC**), an electric current that flows in only one direction at a constant rate, used in batteries, whereas ordinary household electricity uses *alternating current*.

di-rec-tion (di-rek′shun; dī-rek′shun), *n.* **1,** the act of controlling, managing, or guiding; management; **2,** instruction or command; as, he left *directions* for the employees; **3,** the address on a letter, etc.; **4,** a course or line of motion; as, he went in the opposite *direction*:—**directions,** information or instructions on how to get to a place or do a certain thing; as, to get *directions* to her office; *directions* on how to assemble the TV stand.

di-rect-ly (di-rekt′li; dī-rekt′li), *adv.* **1,** in a direct line or manner; as, to go *directly* to your room; **2,** at once; immediately; as, to go *directly* to the emergency room; **3,** exactly or absolutely; as, opinions *directly* opposite to hers.

di-rec-tor (di-rek′tėr; dī-rek′tėr), *n.* **1,** a person who manages; a manager; **2,** a member of the governing board of a company or society; **3,** a person who directs the performance of a play, movie, or television show.—*n.* **di-rec′to-rate.**

di-rec-to-ry (di-rek′to-ri; dī-rek′to-ri), *n.* [*pl.* directories], **1,** an alphabetical list of names, addresses, etc., usually a book or sign; as, a business *directory*; a telephone book *directory*; **2,** in *computing*, a list of computer files stored in memory on the hard drive or on a magnetic disk.

direct payment, electronic transfer of funds using a debit card or other similar device to move the funds from one's bank account to that of the seller.

dirge (dûrj), *n.* a funeral hymn; a song of mourning; a sad song or poem.

dir-i-gi-ble (dir′i-ji-bl), *adj.* capable of being guided; as, a *dirigible* balloon:—*n.* a cigar-shaped balloon, filled with gas and driven by motors; an airship.

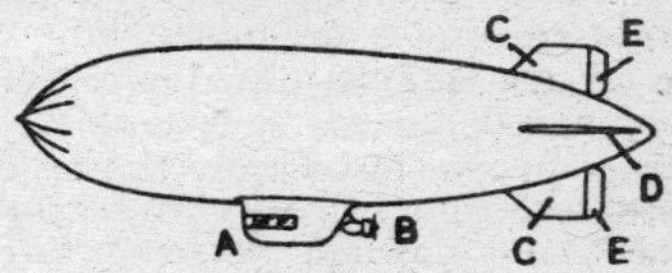

DIRIGIBLE:
A, CONTROL CAR; B, POWER CAR;
C, C, VERTICAL FIN; D, HORIZONTAL FIN;
E, E, RUDDER.

dirt (dûrt), *n.* **1,** mud; filth; as, streets full of *dirt*; **2,** foulness in action, speech, or thought; scandal; **3,** loose earth or soil, as in a garden.

dirt-y (dûr′ti), *adj.* [dirt-i-er, dirt-i-est], **1,** soiled; as, *dirty* hands; **2,** obscene; as, *dirty* language; **3,** base; low; mean; as, a *dirty* scoundrel; **4,** not clear, as water or colour; **5,** disagreeable, as weather:—*v.t.* [dirtied, dirty-ing], to soil.—*n.* **dirt′i-ness.**

dis- (dis), *prefix* meaning **1,** *not, opposite of*; as, *dis*honest, *dis*agree, etc.; **2,** *undo*; *reverse of*; as, *dis*assemble, *dis*mount, etc.

dis-a-bil-i-ty (dis′a-bil′i-ti), *n.* [*pl.* disabilities], **1,** the lack of power or ability to do something, esp. due to a physical or mental condition; **2,** that which deprives of power or ability, as old age or mental or physical impairment or illness; **3,** a disadvantage.

dis-a-ble (dis-ā′bl), *v.t.* [disabled, disabling], to deprive of power or ability; cripple; incapacitate; as, arthritis *disables* many people.—*adj.* **dis-a′bled.**

dis-a-buse (dis′a-būz′), *v.t.* [disabused, disabus-ing], to undeceive; set right; as, a program that *disabuses* people of racial hatred.

dis-ad-van-tage (dis′ad-vån′tij), *n.* **1,** unfavourable condition; obstacle; as, to work under *disadvantages;* to be at a *disadvantage* because she could not hear the lecturer; **2,** loss or harm; as, a rumour to his *disadvantage.—adj.* **dis-ad′van-ta′geous.**

dis-af-fec-tion (dis′a-fek′shun), *n.* **1,** discontent; **2,** ill will; disloyalty; as, *disaffection* among team players.—*adj.* **dis′affect′ed.**

dis-a-gree (dis′a-grē′), *v.i.* [disagreed, disagree-ing], **1,** to differ in opinion; also, to quarrel; as, to *disagree* over money; **2,** to be unlike; as, this answer *disagrees* with mine; **3,** to be unsuitable; have a bad or unpleasant effect on; be harmful; as, the climate *disagrees* with him; mushrooms *disagree* with her.—*n.* **dis′a-gree′ment.**

dis-a-gree-a-ble (dis′a-grē′a-bl), *adj.* unpleasant; distasteful; ill-tempered.—*adv.* **dis′a-gree′a-bly.**

dis-al-low (dis′a-lou′), *v.t.* to refuse to admit or allow (a claim, etc.).

dis-ap-pear (dis′a-pēr′), *v.i.* to pass from sight or existence; vanish.—*n.* **dis′appear′ance.**

dis-ap-point (dis′a-point′), *v.t.* **1,** to fail to fulfill the hope of; **2,** to balk.—*adj.* **dis′-appoint′ed.**—*n.* **dis′ap-point′ment.**

dis-ap-pro-ba-tion (dis′ap-rō-bā′shun), *n.* disapproval; unfavourable opinion.

dis-ap-prove (dis′a-pro͞ov′), *v.t.* [disapproved, disapprov-ing], **1,** to regard with disfavour; condemn; blame; **2,** to refuse assent to; reject:—*v.i.* to express an unfavourable judgment.—*n.* **dis′approv′al.**

dis-arm (dis-ärm′), *v.t.* **1,** to deprive of weapons; **2,** to make harmless; as, her honest admission *disarmed* her opponents:—*v.i.* to lay aside arms; reduce the size of armed forces; as, the country decided to *disarm.*

dis-ar-ma-ment (dis-är′ma-ment), *n.* **1,** the laying aside or depriving of weapons; **2,** the reduction of military, naval, and air forces.

dis-ar-range (dis′a-rānj′), *v.t.* [disarranged, disarrang-ing], to put out of order; disturb the order of.—*n.* **dis′arrange′ment.**

dis-ar-ray (dis′a-rā′), *v.t.* to throw into disorder:—*n.* **1,** disordered dress; **2,** confusion; disorder.

dis-as-ter (di-zås′tėr), *n.* a calamity; sudden misfortune; a serious accident, such as a flood, fire, train wreck, or plane crash.—*adj.* **dis-as′trous.**—*adv.* **dis-as′trous-ly.**

dis-a-vow (dis′a-vou′), *v.t.* to refuse to acknowledge; disclaim.

dis-band (dis-band′), *v.t.* to break up and dismiss (an organized body of people); as, to *disband* the protesters:—*v.i.* to disperse; as, the club *disbanded* after its meeting.—*n.* **dis-band′ment.**

dis-bar (dis-bär′), *v.t.* to expel a lawyer from the legal profession.

dis-be-lief (dis′bi-lēf′), *n.* lack of belief.

dis-be-lieve (dis′bi-lēv′), *v.t.* and *v.i.* [disbelieved, disbeliev-ing], to refuse to accept as true.—*n.* **dis′be-liev′er.**

dis-burse (dis-bûrs′), *v.t.* [disbursed, disburs-ing], to expend; pay out; as, a treasurer *disburses* money.—*n.* **dis-burs′er; disburse′ment.**

disc or **disk** (disk), *n.* **1,** a thin, round, flat object or plate, or anything like it, such as a coin, intervertebral disc, or phonograph record; **2,** a compact disc, DVD, or laser disc; **3,** (usually **disk**) in *computing,* a metal or plastic plate with a magnetic surface, used in a computer to store information; a diskette:—**disc jockey** or **disk jockey,** a person who provides and plays recorded music, punctuated with quips, commercials, etc., for a radio station, club, party, dance, etc.:—**disk drive,** in *computing,* an electronic computer device that reads and records information on a disk.

dis-card (dis-kärd′), *v.t.* **1,** to throw away as useless; as, to *discard* old notes; **2,** in card playing, to get rid of (a card or cards) as useless or extra:—*v.i.* to throw away a card or cards:—*n.* (also dis′kärd), **1,** the act of throwing away weak cards; also, the cards so thrown away; **2,** the act of discarding, or that which is cast aside as worthless.

dis-cern (di-zûrn′; di-sûrn′), *v.t.* **1,** to make out or perceive with the senses or mind; as, to *discern* a figure in the shadows; he *discerned* danger in the plan; **2,** to distinguish clearly; discriminate; as, to *discern* good from evil:—*v.i.* to see, make, or understand distinctions; as, to *discern* between right and wrong.—*n.* **dis-cern′er.**

dis-cern-i-ble (di-zûr′ni-bl; di-sûr′ni-bl), *adj.* visible; as, the hills are barely *discernible* in the mist.

dis-cern-ing (di-zûr′ning; di-sûr′ning), *adj.* of keen insight or discriminating judgment; acute.—*adv.* **dis-cern′ing-ly.**

dis-cern-ment (di-zûrn′ment; di-sûrn′ment), *n.* the act or power of distinguishing or discriminating; keenness of insight.

dis-charge (dis-chärj′), *v.t.* [discharged, discharg-ing], **1,** to relieve of a load or burden; unload; **2,** to remove, as a cargo from a ship or passengers from a train or plane; **3,** to let fly, as an arrow; to shoot, as a rifle; **4,** to set free; as, to *discharge* a prisoner; **5,** to release or dismiss, as employees; to end the services of; as, to *discharge* a jury, committee, etc; **6,** to give off; as, his wound *dis-*

charged blood; **7,** to pay off, as a debt; **8,** to perform, as a duty:—*v.i.* to get rid of a load or burden; to empty; as, the lake *discharged* into a river:—*n.* **1,** an unloading or emitting; as, the *discharge* of a ship; **2,** that which is unloaded; **3,** a firing or shooting off, as of rifles, arrows, dynamite; **4,** release from a burden, debt, accusation, confinement, responsibility; legal release, as of a prisoner; also, a certificate of release; as, a *discharge* from the army; **5,** dismissal; **6,** performance, as of a duty; **7,** a liquid or gas that is released.

dis-ci-ple (di-sī′pl), *n.* a pupil or follower who accepts the teachings of a leader or master and who helps to spread them; esp., one of the followers of Christ.

dis-ci-pli-nar-i-an (dis′i-pli-nâr′i-an), *n.* one who enforces strict rules and order.

dis-ci-pli-nar-y (dis′i-pli-nėr-i), *adj.* pertaining to strict training; corrective.

dis-ci-pline (dis′i-plin), *n.* **1,** strict training of mind or character; as, becoming an Olympic athlete takes years of *discipline;* **2,** obedience to rules and commands, as in a school, army, prison, etc.; as, a prison warden enforces *discipline*; **3,** punishment given by way of training or correction; **4,** branch or area of knowledge or study; as, mathematics and physics are related *disciplines*:—*v.t.* [disciplined, disciplin-ing], **1,** to train; drill; **2,** to punish.

dis-claim (dis-klām′), *v.t.* to disown; deny any connection with.—*n.* **dis-claim′er.**

dis-close (dis-klōz′), *v.t.* [disclosed, disclos-ing], **1,** to uncover; bring to light; as, the digging *disclosed* an old treasure; **2,** to make known; as, to *disclose* secrets.—*n.* **dis-clo′sure** (dis-klō′zhoor; dis-klō′zhėr).

dis-col-our (dis-kul′ėr), *v.t.* to spoil or change the colour of; stain:—*v.i.* to change colour or fade.—*n.* **dis-col′our-a′tion.**

dis-com-bob-u-late (dis′kom-bäb′û-lāt), *v.t. Colloq.* [discombobulat-ed, discombobulat-ing], to confuse; upset; disturb; as, she *discombobulated* all our plans for the party.—*adj.* **dis′com-bob′u-lat-ed.**—*n.* **dis′com-bob′u-la′tion.**

dis-com-fit (dis-kum′fit), *v.t.* to defeat; to upset or throw into confusion; hence, to disconcert; embarrass.—*n.* **dis-com′fi-ture.**

dis-com-fort (dis-kum′fėrt), *n.* **1,** the fact of not being comfortable; a lack of comfort; as, to feel *discomfort* on the lumpy bed; **2,** a feeling of embarrassment or confusion; as, to feel *discomfort* when people laugh at you; **3,** something that causes discomfort; as, living in the wilderness has many *discomforts*:—*v.t.* to make uneasy.

dis-com-pose (dis′kom-pōz′), *v.t.* [discomposed, discompos-ing], to disturb the peace or calm of; disarrange.—*n.* **dis′-com-po′sure.**

dis-con-cert (dis′kon-sûrt′), *v.t.* to disturb the calm or self-possession of: to disorder; as, sickness *disconcerted* his plans.

dis-con-nect (dis′ko-nekt′), *v.t.* to disunite; unfasten; break the connection; as, the phone line was *disconnected*; to *disconnect* a lamp by pulling the plug.—*n.* **dis′con-nec′tion.**

dis-con-so-late (dis-kon′sō-lit), *adj.* without hope; forlorn; sad or unhappy.

dis-con-tent (dis′kon-tent′), *n.* dissatisfaction; restlessness:—*adj.* not satisfied:—*v.t.* to dissatisfy.—*adv.* **dis′con-tent′ed.**

dis-con-tin-ue (dis′kon-tin′ū), *v.t.* [discontinued, discontinu-ing], to stop; cease doing; put an end to:—*v.i.* to cease; come to an end.—*n.* **dis′con-tin′u-ance.**

dis-cord (dis′kôrd), *n.* **1,** difference or lack of agreement; **2,** strife or conflict; **3,** a harsh noise; **4,** in *music,* lack of harmony.—*n.* **dis-cord′ance.**—*adj.* **dis-cord′ant.**

dis-count (dis-kount′; dis′kount), *v.t.* **1,** to deduct from an account, debt, or the like, for early payment; **2,** to get or advance money on, as a note not yet due, deducting interest for the period it still has to run; **3,** to make allowance for exaggeration in; ignore part of an account; disregard; as, they *discounted* his story of the accident; **4,** to reduce the importance of by considering beforehand; as, to *discount* the difficulties of the trip by careful planning; **5,** to sell at a discount; as, to *discount* clothing:—*n.* (dis′kount), **1,** a sum deducted from an account, bill, etc., for early payment; as, 10 percent *discount* for cash; **2,** a deduction made for interest from the face value of a bill, note, etc., when it is converted into cash or sold before it is due; **3,** the rate of interest so deducted; **4,** an amount subtracted from the regular price of something; as, to sell T-shirts at a 50 per cent *discount.*—*adj.* **dis′count-a-ble.**

dis-coun-te-nance (dis-koun′te-nans), *v.t.* to disapprove of; as, she *discountenances* smoking.

dis-cour-age (dis-kur′ij), *v.t.* [discouraged, discourag-ing], **1,** to lessen the courage of; dishearten; **2,** to try to prevent or deter; as, laws *discourage* crime.—*adj.* **dis-cour′aged.**—*n.* **dis-cour′age-ment.**

dis-course (dis′kōrs; dis-kōrs′), *n.* **1,** talk; conversation; **2,** a lecture, treatise, or sermon:—*v.i.* (dis-kōrs′), [discoursed, discours-ing], to talk; converse:—*v.t.* to send forth; utter; as, to *discourse* wisdom.

dis-cour-te-ous (dis-kûr′ti-us), *adj.* impolite; rude.—*n.* **dis-cour′te-sy.**

dis-cov-er (dis-kuv′ėr), *v.t.* **1,** to find, find out, or learn for the first time; as, to *discover* dinosaur bones; **2,** to find out; learn; as, to *discover* that your wallet is missing.—*n.* **dis-cov′er-er.**

dis-cov-er-y (dis-kuv′ėr-i), *n.* [*pl.* discoveries], **1,** a finding for the first time; as, the *discovery* of insulin by Banting and Best; **2,** the thing found out or discovered.

dis-cred-it (dis-kred′it), *v.t.* **1,** to refuse to believe; **2,** to destroy belief in or the reputation of; as, science *discredits* his theories:—*n.* **1,** loss of reputation; disgrace; **2,** doubt or disbelief; as, to bring old beliefs into *discredit*.

dis-cred-it-a-ble (dis-kred′it-a-bl), *adj.* disgraceful; unworthy.

dis-creet (dis-krēt′), *adj.* careful in speech and action; showing good judgment; as, *discreet* behaviour.—*adv.* **dis-creet′ly.**—*n.* **dis-creet′ness.**

dis-crep-an-cy (dis-krep′an-si), *n.* [*pl.* discrepancies], a difference; lack of agreement; as, the *discrepancy* between the two accounts.—*adj.* **dis-crep′ant.**

dis-crete (dis-krēt′; dis′krēt), *adj.* separate; detached; not continuous; as, photons of light and quanta of energy come in *discrete* units.

dis-cre-tion (dis-kresh′un), *n.* **1,** prudence; good judgment; **2,** freedom of choice or action; as, use your own *discretion.*

dis-crim-i-nate (dis-krim′i-nāt′), *v.t.* [discriminat-ed, discriminat-ing], to see or mark the difference between; distinguish; as, to *discriminate* good Web sites from bad ones:—*v.i.* **1,** to make a distinction; as, to *discriminate* between good and evil; **2,** to treat certain people unfairly or differently from others; as, do not *discriminate* against anyone because of race, religion, or gender.—*adv.* **dis-crim′i-nate-ly.**—*adj.* **dis-crim′i-na′tive.**

dis-crim-i-na-tion (dis-krim′i-nā′shun), *n.* **1,** the act of distinguishing; **2,** the ability to make fine distinctions; discernment; good judgment; **3,** the act or policy of treating people unfairly because of their race, religion, nationality, gender, or age.

dis-cur-sive (dis-kûr′siv), *adj.* rambling from one topic to another; digressing; as, his *discursive* remarks bored us.

dis-cus (dis′kus), *n.* [*pl.* discuses (dis′kus-ez) or disci (dis′kī)], a heavy disk of metal or stone to be thrown in athletic contests as a test of throwing strength.

dis-cuss (dis-kus′), *v.t.* to debate fully; talk over or write about a subject; consider.

dis-cus-sion (dis-kush′un), *n.* full and open consideration or argument; as, the assembly agreed after a two-hour *discussion*; also, talk or written item about a subject; as, her *discussion* in her report about endangered species was well informed.

dis-dain (dis-dān′), *v.t.* to scorn; look upon with contempt; as, he *disdained* our attempts to help:—*n.* contempt; scorn.—*adj.* **dis-dain′ful.**—*adv.* **dis-dain′ful-ly.**

dis-ease (di-zēz′), *n.* disorder of mind or body marked by definite symptoms, and often caused by an infection or growth; illness; sickness; any particular instance or kind of such disorder: people, animals, and plants can all suffer from diseases; as, heart *disease*; foot-and-mouth *disease*; Dutch elm *disease.*

dis-em-bark (dis′em-bärk′), *v.t.* and *v.i.* to remove from, or go ashore from, a vessel or aircraft; land; as, to *disembark* troops; to *disembark* at Québec City.—*n.* **dis-em′bar-ka′tion.**

dis-em-bod-ied (dis′im-bod′id), *adj.* free from a body, as a spirit, ghost, etc.

dis-en-chant (dis′en-chånt′), *v.t.* to set free from a charm, spell, or illusion; to disillusion.—*n.* **dis′en-chant′ment.**

dis-en-gage (dis′en-gāj′), *v.t.* [disengage, disengag-ing], **1,** to set free; release; as, to *disengage* one from a promise; **2,** to extricate; free (oneself); as, he *disengaged* himself from his commitments:—**disengaged,** *adj.* at liberty; not in use.—*n.* **dis′en-gage′ment.**

dis-en-tan-gle (dis′en-tang′gl), *v.t.* [disentan-gled, disentan-gling], **1,** to free from confusion; as, to *disentangle* truth from error; **2,** to unravel; as, to *disentangle* a ball of yarn.—*n.* **dis′en-tan′gle-ment.**

dis-fa-vour (dis-fā′vėr), *n.* **1,** disapproval; as, to look with *disfavour* on a scheme; **2,** the condition of being regarded with disapproval or dislike; as, he was in *disfavour.*

dis-fig-ure (dis-fig′ūr), *v.t.* [disfigured, disfigur-ing], to mar or injure in shape, form, or beauty.—*n.* **dis-fig′ure-ment.**—*n.* **dis-fig′u-ra′tion.**

dis-fran-chise or **dis-en-fran-chise** (dis-fran′chiz; dis-en-fran′chiz), *v.t.* to deprive of one's citizenship rights, voting, holding office, etc.

dis-gorge (dis-gôrj′), *v.t.* [disgorged, disgorg-ing], **1,** to discharge from, or as from, the throat with violence; to vomit; **2,** to give up unwillingly; as, to be forced to *disgorge* the stolen money:—*v.i.* **1,** to discharge contents; **2,** to surrender unlawful gains.

dis-grace (dis-grās′), *n.* **1,** shame; dishonour; **2,** the cause of shame; as, the roads are a *disgrace* to the town:—*v.t.* [disgraced, disgrac-ing], to bring shame, reproach, or dishonour upon.—*adj.* **dis-grace′ful.**

dis-grun-tle (dis-grun′tl), *v.t.* to make discontented or displeased; as, the voters' decision *disgruntled* him.

dis-guise (dis-gīz′), *v.t.* [disguised, disguising], **1,** to change in appearance so as to conceal the identity of (a person); as, they *disguised* him as a professor; **2,** to hide, conceal, or mask; as, to *disguise* one's intentions:—*n.* **1,** anything worn to conceal one's identity; **2,** anything, as a manner of speaking, assumed to deceive.

dis-gust (dis-gust′), *n.* strong distaste; loathing:—*v.t.* to offend by loathsome appearance, repulsive behaviour, etc.—*adj.* **dis-gust′ed.**

dish (dish), *n.* **1,** a plate or shallow bowl used for holding or serving food; also, anything so shaped; **2,** any special food; as, ice cream is a popular *dish*; **3,** a television antenna in the shape of a large dish, used to receive signals from a satellite:—*v.t.* to put into a dish for serving.—*n.* **dish′cloth′; dish′rag′; dish′wat′er.**

dis-heart-en (dis-här′tn), *v.t.* to discourage; as, failure *disheartened* her.

di-shev-el (di-shev′el), *v.t.* [dishevelled, dishevel-ling], to throw into disorder; to tousle; as, the children *dishevelled* his hair.—*adj.* **di-shev′elled.**

dis-hon-est (dis-on′est), *adj.* **1,** lacking in uprightness or fairness; not honest; as, lying is *dishonest*; **2,** inclined to cheat or deceive; as, a *dishonest* person; **3,** designed for unfair use; false; as, *dishonest* scales.—*n.* **dis-hon′es-ty.**

dis-hon-our (dis-on′ėr), *v.t.* **1,** to disgrace; bring shame upon; **2,** to refuse to pay (a bill or note):—*n.* disgrace; shame.

dis-hon-our-a-ble (dis′on′ėr-a-bl), *adj.* **1,** shameful; **2,** lacking in uprightness.

dis-il-lu-sion (dis′i-lū′zhun), *v.t.* to set free from a mistaken belief in the goodness or value of some person or thing; disappoint.

dis-in-clined (dis′in-klīnd′), *adj.* unwilling.—*n.* **dis-in′cli-na′tion.**

dis-in-fect (dis′in-fekt′), *v.t.* to cleanse from infection; purify of germs; as, to *disinfect* a bathroom.—*n.* **dis′in-fec′tion.**

dis-in-fect-ant (dis′in-fek′tant), *n.* a substance that destroys germs.

dis-in-gen-u-ous (dis′in-jen′ū-us), *adj.* not frank or candid; insincere; artfully simple; as, his excuse was *disingenuous.*

dis-in-her-it (dis′in-her′it), *v.t.* to cut off (an heir) from property or inheritance.

dis-in-te-grate (dis-in′ti-grāt), *v.t.* [disintegrat-ed, disintegrat-ing], **1,** to break into pieces; as, frost *disintegrates* rock; **2,** to destroy the unity of; as, to *disintegrate* society:—*v.i.* to crumble to pieces; as, limestone *disintegrates* rapidly.—*n.* **dis-in′te-gra′tion.**

dis-in-ter-est-ed (dis-in′ter-es-tid; dis-in′tris-tid), *adj.* **1,** not influenced by a personal or selfish motive; not prejudiced; fair; as, a *disinterested* judge; **2,** not concerned; not having any interests at all; not affected.—*adv.* **dis-in′ter-est-ed-ly.**

dis-joint (dis-joint′), *v.t.* **1,** to part at the joints; as, to *disjoint* a turkey; **2,** to put out of joint; as, to *disjoint* one's shoulder:—**disjointed,** unconnected; incoherent; as, a *disjointed* speech.

disk (disk), *n.* See **disc.**

dis-kette (dis′ket′), *n.* a small plastic magnetic disk used to store computer data; floppy disk.

disk operating system. Same as DOS.

dis-like (dis-līk′), *n.* a feeling of distaste; aversion:—*v.t.* [disliked, dislik-ing], to regard with distaste; not like; disapprove or object to; as, to *dislike* olives or gardening.

dis-lo-cate (dis′lō-kāt′), *v.t.* [dislocat-ed, dislocat-ing], to displace; put out of place; esp., to put out of joint; as, to *dislocate* a hip bone.—*n.* **dis′lo-ca′tion.**

dis-lodge (dis-loj′), *v.t.* [dislodged, dislodging], to remove from a resting place; drive from a hiding place.

dis-loy-al (dis-loi′al), *adj.* false to duty, government, or friends; faithless.—*n.* **disloy′al-ty.**—*adv.* **dis-loy′al-ly.**

dis-mal (diz′mal), *adj.* **1,** gloomy; depressing; as, *dismal* weather; **2,** depressed; melancholy, as a mood.—*adv.* **dis′mal-ly.**

dis-man-tle (dis-man′tl), *v.t.* [disman-tled, disman-tling], **1,** to strip or deprive of furniture, equipment, etc.; **2,** to take apart; as, to *dismantle* an engine.

dis-may (dis-mā′), *v.t.* **1,** to terrify; **2,** to dispirit; discourage:—*n.* **1,** terrified amazement, as at a great danger or disaster; **2,** discouragement, as at a hopeless task.—*adj.* **dis-mayed′.**

dis-mem-ber (dis-mem′bėr), *v.t.* to tear limb from limb; also, to tear or break into pieces; as, the animals *dismembered* their prey.

dis-miss (dis-mis′), *v.t.* **1,** to send away or permit to depart, as a class; **2,** to discharge from office or employment; fire; as, to *dismiss* the clerk for stealing; **3,** to refuse to consider further; as, to *dismiss* a matter from one's mind.—*n.* **dis-miss′al.**

dis-mount (dis-mount′), *v.i.* to get down, as from a horse, bicycle, etc.:—*v.t.* **1,** to remove (a rider) by force from a horse; **2,** to remove from a carriage, as a cannon; **3,** to remove from a setting, as a jewel.

dis-o-be-di-ence (dis′o-bē′di-ens), *n.* neglect or refusal to obey a rule or command.

dis-o-be-di-ent (dis′o-bē′di-ent), *adj.* refusing or neglecting to obey; as, a *disobedient* child.

dis-o-bey (dis′ō-bā′), *v.t.* and *v.i.* to refuse or fail to obey; as, to *disobey* parents.

dis-or-der (dis-ôr′dėr), *n.* **1,** lack of system or order; confusion; **2,** a commotion; esp., a riot; **3,** an unhealthy mental or physical condition; as, stomach *disorder*:—*v.t.* **1,** to throw into confusion; disarrange; **2,** to derange in health of mind or body.—*adj.* **dis-or′dered.**—*adj.* **dis-or′der-ly.**

dis-or-gan-ize (dis-ôr′gan-īz), *v.t.* [disorganized, disorganiz-ing], to throw into confusion; as, their arrival *disorganized* the meeting:—*adj.* **dis-or′gan-ized.**

dis-own (dis-ōn′), *v.t.* **1,** to reject; refuse to claim as one's own; as, to *disown* one's son; **2,** to renounce allegiance to; as, to *disown* one's flag.

dis-par-age (dis-par′ij), *v.t.* [disparaged, disparag-ing], to speak slightingly of; belittle; as, to *disparage* a rival.—*adv.* **dis-par′ag-ing-ly.**—*n.* **dis-par′age-ment.**

dis-par-i-ty (dis-par′i-ti), *n.* inequality; difference; as, the *disparity* in the ages of two girls.—*adj.* **dis′pa-rate** (-rit).

dis-pas-sion-ate (dis-pash′un-it), *adj.* free from passion; impartial; as, a *dispassionate* speech.—*adv.* **dis-pas′sion-ate-ly.**

dis-patch (dis-pach′), *v.t.* **1,** to send off promptly; as, to *dispatch* a messenger; **2,** to finish quickly; as, to *dispatch* a lunch; **3,** to put to death; kill:—*n.* **1,** promptness; as, she did her homework with *dispatch*; **2,** a message; esp., an official communication; **3,** an item of news; as, a *dispatch* from the U.S.; **4,** a putting to death.—*n.* **dis-patch′er.**

dis-pel (dis-pel′), *v.t.* [dispelled, dispel-ling], to drive apart; scatter; disperse; put an end to; as, the wind *dispelled* the fog, rumours.

dis-pen-sa-ry (dis-pen′sa-ri), *n.* [*pl.* dispen-saries], **1,** a place where medical advice and medicines are given free or very inexpensively; **2,** a place in a hospital where medication is kept.

dis-pen-sa-tion (dis′pen-sā′shun), *n.* **1,** distribution; **2,** divine management of the world; also, an instance of this; as, the flood was a *dispensation* of Providence; **3,** permission, esp. by a church official, to do something usually forbidden, or to omit something usually required.

dis-pense (dis-pens′), *v.t.* [dispensed, dis-pens-ing], **1,** to deal out in portions; **2,** to carry out; apply; as, to *dispense* justice:—**dispense with,** to do without; as, to *dispense with* formalities.

dis-perse (dis-pûrs′), *v.t.* [dispersed, dis-pers-ing], **1,** to scatter; as, to *disperse* a crowd; **2,** to spread; as, to *disperse* funds; also, to cause to vanish; as, the sun *dispersed* the mist:—*v.i.* to break up and depart; as, the meeting *dispersed.*—*n.* **dis-pers′al; dis-per′sion.**

dis-pir-it-ed (dis-pir′i-tid), *adj.* disheartened; discouraged; depressed.

dis-place (dis-plās′), *v.t.* [displaced, dis-plac-ing], **1,** to put out of place; **2,** to remove and replace with something else; as, to *displace* a car with a truck; **3,** to take the place of; as, the computer *displaced* the typewriter; **4,** to remove from office.—*n.* **dis-place′ment.**

dis-play (dis-plā′), *v.t.* **1,** to spread out; unfold; as, the peacock *displayed* its feathers; **2,** to exhibit; show off for others to see; put in view:—*n.* **1,** an exhibit; the act or fact of displaying; as, a *display* of trophies; **2,** a parade or show; as, a fashion *display*; **3,** in *computing,* the part of a computer that shows the information that is being worked on; the computer screen or monitor.

dis-please (dis-plēz′), *v.t.* [displeased, dis-pleas-ing], to offend; annoy; make angry; as, the results of the examination *displease* me.—*n.* **dis-pleas′ure** (dis-plezh′yoor; zhėr).

dis-pos-al (dis-pōz′al), *n.* **1,** arrangement; as, the *disposal* of merchandise on a store's shelves; **2,** the act of getting rid; removal; as, the *disposal* of garbage; **3,** control; command; as, to place money or other resources at one's *disposal.*

dis-pose (dis-pōz′), *v.t.* [disposed, dispos-ing], **1,** to arrange; distribute; **2,** to make willing; incline; as, weariness *disposed* him to give in:—**dispose of, 1,** to get rid of; throw away; give away; sell; as, to *dispose of* old clothes; *dispose* of one's property; **2,** to deal with or settle; as, to *dispose of* an issue before moving on; **3,** eat all; as, to *dispose of* the entire chicken.

dis-pos-a-ble (dis-pōz′a-bl), *adj.* **1,** meant to be thrown away after use instead of being used again; as, *disposable* diapers, razors, pens, etc.; **2,** available for use at the owner's discretion; as, *disposable* income.

dis-po-si-tion (dis′pō-zish′un), *n.* **1,** the act of placing or arranging; **2,** order; arrangement; as, the *disposition* of furniture in a room; **3,** the power of managing or distributing; as, to have the *disposition* of property; **4,** inclination; temper or habit of mind; as, a jealous *disposition.*

dis-pos-sess (dis′po-zes′), *v.t.* to oust; put out of possession; as, to *dispossess* a person of his or her home.—*n.* **dis′pos-ses′sion.**

dis-praise (dis-prāz′), *n.* and *v.* censure; blame.

dis-pro-por-tion (dis′prō-pōr′shun), *n.* lack of balance or symmetry; lack of proper relation in form, size, etc.—*adj.* **dis′pro-por′tion-ate.**

dis-prove (dis-pro͞ov′), *v.t.* [disproved, dis-prov-ing], to show to be untrue or unreasonable; as, to *disprove* a statement.

dis-pute (dis-pūt′), *v.i.* [disput-ed, disput-ing], to debate; argue; quarrel:—*v.t.* **1,** to contend for, by words or actions; as, the two countries *disputed* a strip of land on their border; **2,** to question the justice or fairness of; deny; as, to *dispute* election results:—*n.* an argument; also, a quarrel.—*n.* **dis′pu-ta′tion.**—*adj.* **dis-put′a-ble.**—*adj.* and *n.* **dis′pu-tant** (dis′pū-tant).

dis-qual-i-fy (dis-kwol′i-fī′; -kwôl′), *v.t.* [disqualified, disqualify-ing], **1,** to make unfit; disable; **2,** to deprive of a privilege; as, to *disqualify* a player.—*n.* **dis-qual′i-fi-ca′tion.**—*adj.* **dis-qual′i-fied.**

dis-qui-et (dis-kwī′et), *v.t.* to make uneasy; worry; as, his look *disquieted* her:—*n.* uneasiness; anxiety.—*n.* **dis-qui′e-tude.**—*adj.* **dis-qui′e-ted.**

dis-qui-si-tion (dis′kwi-zish′un), *n.* a formal discussion; dissertation.

dis-re-gard (dis′ri-gärd′), *v.t.* to fail to notice or give heed to; neglect; as, he *disregarded* instructions:—*n.* lack of attention; as, a *disregard* for her feelings.

dis-re-pair (dis′ri-pâr′), *n.* the state of needing repair, as of a building.

dis-rep-u-ta-ble (dis-rep′ū-ta-bl), *adj.* of bad reputation; not respectable.

dis-re-pute (dis′ri-pūt′), *n.* lack or loss of reputation; dishonour; ill repute.

dis-re-spect (dis′ri-spekt′), *n.* lack of courtesy or respect; rudeness; as, *disrespect* toward parents or elders.—*adj.* **dis′re-spect′ful.**

dis-robe (dis-rōb′), *v.i.* and *v.t.* [disrobed, disrob-ing], to undress; strip.

dis-rupt (dis-rupt′), *v.t.* to break apart; break up; put out of order or upset; as, to *disrupt* a lecture with her tardiness.—*n.* **dis-rup′tion.**

dis-sat-is-fac-tion (dis-sat′is-fak′shun), *n.* discontent; lack of satisfaction.

dis-sat-is-fy (dis-sat′is-fī′), *v.t.* [dissatisfied, dissatisfy-ing], to cause discontent to, as by lack of something; to fail to satisfy; as, the house *dissatisfied* her.—*adj.* **dis-sat′is-fied′.**

dis-sect (di-sekt′), *v.t.* **1,** to cut in pieces, in order to examine; as, to *dissect* a plant; **2,** to examine; analyze; as, to *dissect* a person's motives.—*n.* **dis-sec′tion.**

dis-sem-ble (di-sem′bl), *v.t.* [dissembled, dissem-bling], to hide under a false appearance; as, to *dissemble* one's feelings:—*v.i.* to conceal the truth by some pretence; ignore; as, to *dissemble* by making excuses.

dis-sem-i-nate (di-sem′i-nāt′), *v.t.* [disseminat-ed, disseminat-ing], to scatter, as seed; diffuse; spread abroad, as news.—*n.* **dis-sem′i-na′tion.**

dis-sen-sion (di-sen′shun), *n.* angry disagreement; strife.

dis-sent (di-sent′), *v.i.* to disagree in opinion; as, to *dissent* from a judgment:—*n.* a disagreement in opinion.

dis-sent-er (di-sen′tėr), *n.* a person who differs from the prevailing opinion:—**Dissenter**, in Great Britain, a member of a Protestant sect that has broken away from the established church.

dis-ser-ta-tion (dis′ėr-tā′shun), *n.* a lengthy and formal discourse, discussion, or treatise, esp. for a doctorate.

dis-sev-er (di-sev′ėr), *v.t.* to cut off; separate; disjoin.

dis-si-dent (dis′i-dent), *adj.* and *n.* disagreeing in opinion; as, the *dissident* members formed a new club.—*n.* **dis′si-dence.**

dis-sim-i-lar (di-sim′i-lėr; dis-sim′i-lėr), *adj.* unlike; as, *dissimilar* tastes.—*n.* **dis-sim′i-lar′i-ty.**

dis-sim-u-late (dis-sim′ū-lāt′), *v.i.* and *v.t.* [dissimulat-ed, dissimulat-ing], to dissemble; disguise; feign; pretend.—*n.* **dis-sim′u-la′tion.**

dis-si-pate (dis′i-pāt′), *v.t.* [dissipat-ed, dissipat-ing], **1,** to scatter in different directions; as, the wind *dissipated* the smoke; **2,** to waste foolishly; as, he *dissipated* his allowance:—*v.i.* **1,** to disperse; vanish; **2,** to engage in riotous amusement; esp., to drink to excess.—*n.* **dis′si-pa′tion.**—*adj.* **dis′si-pat-ed.**

dis-so-ci-ate (di-sō′shi-āt′), *v.t.* to sever relations; disunite; as, to *dissociate* oneself from a rude classmate.

dis-so-lu-ble (dis′o-lū-bl; di-sol′ū-bl), *adj.* able to be dissolved (as a substance or an assembly).

dis-so-lute (dis′ō-lūt′), *adj.* morally loose; given to vice or dissipation.

dis-so-lu-tion (dis′o-lū′shun), *n.* **1,** the act of separating or breaking up; as, the *dissolution* of a partnership; **2,** decay; ruin; death.

dis-solve (di-zolv′), *v.t.* [dissolved, dissolv-ing], **1,** to cause to be absorbed by a liquid; as, to *dissolve* salt in water; **2,** to break up; as, to *dissolve* a meeting; **3,** to put an end to; break up; as, to *dissolve* a partnership:—*v.i.* to be absorbed in a liquid.

dis-so-nant (dis′o-nant), *adj.* disagreeing (in sound); unharmonious; discordant; as, *dissonant* tunes or opinions.—*n.* **dis′so-nance.**

dis-suade (di-swād′), *v.t.* [dissuad-ed, dissuad-ing], to advise or counsel against; divert by persuasion from a purpose or action; as, they *dissuaded* him from going.—*n.* **dis-sua′sion.**

dis-tance (dis′tans), *n.* **1,** the extent of space between two objects or points; **2,** a far-off place; as, hills are blue in the *distance*; **3,** lack of familiarity; reserve; coldness; as, to keep one's *distance*:—*v.t.* [distanced, distanc-ing], **1,** to leave behind in a race; outstrip; as, to *distance* one's rivals; **2,** to be reserved; keep oneself from becoming familiar with someone or something; as, to *distance* oneself from office politics.

dis-tant (dis′tant), *adj.* **1,** far off in time, space, or relationship; as, a *distant* event; a *distant* cousin; **2,** separated by a certain amount; as, a store three kilometres *distant* from the school; **3,** reserved; not familiar; cold; as, she is *distant* with her employees.—*adv.* **dis′tant-ly.**

dis-taste (dis-tāst′), *n.* dislike; aversion; as, a *distaste* for seafood.—*adj.* **dis-taste′ful.**

dis-tem-per (dis-tem′pėr), *n.* **1,** a viral disease in dogs and other animals that is often fatal; **2,** disorder, uneasiness, or disturbance; as, political *distemper*; **3,** a type of paint and the process of using the water-based paint.

dis-tend (dis-tend′), *v.t.* to stretch out or

expand; as, to *distend* the stomach:—*v.i.* to swell; enlarge, as a balloon.—*n.* **dis-ten′sion; dis-ten′tion.**

dis-til or **dis-till** (dis-til′), *v.i.* [distilled, distil-ling], to fall in drops; trickle forth:—*v.t.* **1,** to let fall in drops; as, sap from a tree; **2,** to separate (a liquid) from a mixture by heating so as to form a vapour, which is carried off and condensed by cooling; **3,** to subject (a mixture) to this process; as, to *distil* water.—*n.* **dis′til-la′tion; dis-til′ler; dis′till-ate** (-lit; -lāt′).

dis-til-ler-y (dis-til′ėr-ī), *n.* [*pl.* distilleries], a place where liquids, esp. alcoholic liquors, are distilled.

dis-tinct (dis-tingkt′), *adj.* **1,** separate; different; **2,** clear to the senses; definite; as, a *distinct* sound or view; **3,** carefully thought out; lucid; as, a *distinct* statement.—*n.* **dis-tinct′ness.**—*adv.* **dis-tinct′ly.**

dis-tinc-tion (dis-tingk′shun), *n.* **1,** the act of noting clearly or marking off from others; **2,** a characteristic difference; as, the *distinction* between good and evil; **3,** special honour; eminence; excellence; as, an award of *distinction* in literature.

dis-tinc-tive (dis-tingk′tiv), *adj.* marking a difference; special; characteristic; as, a *distinctive* laugh or feature.—*adv.* **dis-tinc′tive-ly.**

dis-tin-guish (dis-ting′gwish), *v.t.* **1,** to mark off; tell apart; as, speech *distinguishes* humans from apes; **2,** to recognize by special features; as, to *distinguish* different makes of cars; **3,** to see clearly; **4,** to honour by a mark of preference:—*v.i.* to make a distinction; as, to *distinguish* between brown and tan.—*adj.* **dis-tin′guish-a-ble.**

dis-tin-guished (dis-ting′gwisht), *adj.* set apart, special in ability, achievement, etc.

dis-tort (dis-tôrt′), *v.t.* **1,** to change from the natural shape; as, to *distort* the features; **2,** to change the meaning of; as, he *distorted* what I said.—*n.* **dis-tor′tion.**

dis-tract (dis-trakt′), *v.t.* **1,** to divert; take someone's attention away from; as, the laughter of her friends *distracted* her from studying; **2,** to bewilder; perplex; as, the many changes *distracted* him; **3,** to make frantic; derange.—*adj.* **dis-tract′ed.**—*adv.* **dis-tract′ed-ly.**

dis-trac-tion (dis-trak′shun), *n.* **1,** a drawing away of the attention from an object; **2,** anything that diverts attention; **3,** bewilderment; mental confusion or distress; **4,** craze or frenzy.

dis-traught (dis-trôt′), *adj.* distracted; crazed (as with grief): the bereaved man was *distraught.*

dis-tress (dis-tres′), *v.t.* to inflict pain or grief upon; grieve:—*n.* **1,** physical or mental anguish; grief; **2,** misfortune; danger; trouble; as, a ship in *distress.*

dis-trib-ute (dis-trib′ūt), *v.t.* [distribut-ed, distribut-ing], **1,** to deal or give out; allot; as, to *distribute* books; **2,** spread; scatter; as, to *distribute* fertilizer; **3,** to sort; classify.—*n.* **dis′tri-bu′tion; dis-trib′u-tor.**—*adj.* **dis-trib′u-ted.**

dis-trib-u-tive (dis-trib′ū-tiv), *adj.* apportioning.—*n.* in *grammar,* a word that marks the distinction of members of a group: words such as *any, each, either, neither, every, everybody,* etc., are *distributives.*

distributed computing, in *computing,* computing that uses more than one computer, as a client-server network or the World Wide Web.

dis-trict (dis′trikt), *n.* **1,** an area of a country, province, state, or city marked off within definite limits for administration; as, a school *district;* **2,** a general region with a special use or character; as, a shopping *district.*

dis-trust (dis-trust′), *n.* lack of confidence or reliance; suspicion:—*v.t.* to have no faith in; to doubt; suspect.—*adj.* **dis-trust′ful.**

dis-turb (dis-turb′), *v.t.* **1,** to trouble; upset; make uneasy or nervous; as, the news of her illness *disturbed* him; **2,** to throw into confusion; agitate; **3,** to interfere with; break in on; interrupt; as, the noise *disturbed* her nap.—*n.* **dis-turb′ance.**

dis-u-nite (dis′ū-nīt′), *v.i.* and *v.t.* [disunit-ed, disunit-ing], to divide; separate.—*n.* **dis-un′ion.**

dis-use (dis-ūs′), *n.* the condition of not being in use; neglect.

ditch (dich), *n.* a trench cut in the earth:—*v.t.* **1,** to surround with a ditch; **2,** to send into a ditch; as, to *ditch* a car; **3,** *Colloq.* to get rid of; as, to *ditch* the old patio furniture.

dit-to (dit′ō), *n.* [*pl.* dittos], the same thing as has been said before:—*adv.* as before; likewise:—**ditto marks**, marks ["] written directly below something, as a list, used to avoid repetition.

di-ur-nal (dī-ûr′nal), *adj.* **1,** relating to the day or lasting a day; as, the *diurnal* revolution of the earth; occurring every day; daily; **3,** active during the daytime; as, *diurnal* insects.—*adv.* **di-ur′nal-ly.**

di-va (dē′va), *n.* **1,** a great female opera singer; a prima donna; **2,** any famous female singer; as, Céline Dion is a rock *diva.*

dive (dīv), *v.i.* [*p.t.* dived (dīvd) or dove (dōv), *p.p.* dived, *p.pr.* div-ing], **1,** to plunge head foremost, as into water; as, the shot plane *dived* toward the ground; **2,** to go quickly and completely into a place or activity; as, to *dive* into a tunnel; he *dived* into his work:—*n.* **1,** a plunge head foremost, as into water; **2,** a quick, steep movement downward; **3,** *Colloq.* poor or unkempt accommodation, restaurant, room, etc.

div-er (dīv′ėr), *n.* **1,** a person who plunges into water; **2,** a person who makes a business of going under the water, as an underwater explorer; **3,** any bird that dives for food, as a loon.

di-verge (di-vûrj′; dī-), *v.i.* [diverged, diverg-ing], **1,** to spread out from a point; **2,** to differ, as from a standard.—*n.* **di-ver′gence.**—*adj.* **di-ver′gent.**

di-verse (di-vûrs′; dī′vûrs; dī-vûrs′), *adj.* different; unlike; dissimilar; varied; as, to come from *diverse* backgrounds.

di-ver-si-fy (di-vûr′si-fī; dī-vûr′si-fī), *v.t.* [diversified, diversify-ing], to make various or balanced; give variety to; expand; as, hills *diversify* the view; to *diversify* a company; to *diversify* an investment portfolio.—*n.* **di-ver′si-fi-ca′tion.**

di-ver-sion (di-vûr′shun; di-vûr′zhun; dī-vûr′shun; dī-vûr′zhun), *n.* **1,** a turning aside from a set course; as, the *diversion* of a river; **2,** something that draws away attention; as, to create a *diversion* to get by the prison guard; **3,** a recreation; something that relaxes or amuses.

di-ver-si-ty (di-vûr′si-ti; dī-vûr′si-ti), *n.* [*pl.* diversities], difference; variety; as, *diversity* of plant life in an area.

di-vert (di-vûrt′; dī-vûrt′), *v.t.* **1,** to change the direction in which something moves; as, to divert a road; **2,** to turn from or to any direction or course; draw away; **3,** to entertain; amuse.

di-vest (di-vest′; dī-vest′), *v.t.* **1,** to strip; unclothe; **2,** to deprive, as of rights or office; despoil.

di-vide (di-vīd′), *v.t.* [divid-ed, divid-ing], **1,** to cut into two or more parts; split; **2,** to separate (a thing) from another or others; **3,** to separate into opposing sides; also, to cause to disagree; as, to *divide* the class, friends; **4,** to share, as money; **5,** in *arithmetic,* to perform the operation of division on or with; as, to *divide* 30 by 6; to *divide* 6 into 30:—*v.i.* **1,** to be separated into parts; **2,** to perform the operation of division with two numbers:—*n.* a watershed.

div-i-dend (div′i-dend), *n.* **1,** a share of the profits of a company or business; **2,** in *arithmetic,* a number or quantity to be divided by another number or quantity.

di-vid-er (di-vīd′er), *n.* **1,** someone or something that divides; **2,** a partition in a room; **3,** a separator in a binder, notebook, storage box, etc., usually made of cardboard:—**dividers,** an instrument used in mechanical drawing, for dividing lines, checking distances, etc.

div-i-na-tion (div′i-nā′shun), *n.* **1,** the act of foreseeing or foretelling; **2,** a forecast; guess.

[1]**di-vine** (di-vīn′), *adj.* [divin-er, divin-est], **1,** relating to God; from God; **2,** godlike; holy; **3,** superhumanly excellent; **4;** *Colloq.* excellent; superb; as, a *divine* meal:—*n.* a person who knows theology; a priest; clergyman.—*adv.* **di-vine′ly.**

[2]**di-vine** (di-vīn′), *v.t.* [divined, divin-ing], **1,** to foresee or foretell; **2,** to guess; perceive by reason or insight; as, she *divined* my purpose.—*n.* **di-vin′er.**

di-vin-i-ty (di-vin′i-ti), *n.* [*pl.* divinities], **1,** the state or quality of being godlike; **2,** a god or deity; **3,** the study of theology:—**the Divinity,** God.

di-vis-i-ble (di-viz′i-bl), *adj.* **1,** capable of being separated into parts; **2,** in *mathematics,* capable of division by a specified number without a remainder; as, 6 is *divisible* by 2.—*n.* **di-vis′i-bil′i-ty.**

di-vi-sion (di-vizh′un), *n.* **1,** a separation into parts; also, a portion or part; **2,** that which separates, as a partition; a dividing line; **3,** discord; difference in opinion; **4,** a department; as, the marketing *division* of a firm; **5,** in the army, a large unit complete in itself; **6,** in the navy, a section or unit of a fleet; **7,** the process of finding how many times one quantity contains, or is contained in, another.

di-vi-sor (di-vī′zėr), *n.* in *arithmetic,* the number or quantity by which the dividend is to be divided.

di-vorce (di-vōrs′), *n.* **1,** a legal dissolving of a marriage; **2,** disunion of things formerly united:—*v.t.* [divorced, divorc-ing], **1,** to release from the marriage contract legally; **2,** to separate; as, to *divorce* oneself from minor details in a company.

di-vor-cee or **di-vor-cée** (di-vōr′sē′; sā′), *n.* a divorced person, esp. a woman.

di-vulge (di-vulj′), *v.t.* [divulged, divulg-ing], to make known, as a secret; tell.

Di-va-li, Di-wa-li, or **De-wa-li** (di-vol′i; di-wol′i), *n.* an important Hindu festival that celebrates the beginning of the new year, also known as the *Festival of Light.*

diz-zy (diz′i), *adj.* [diz-zi-er, diz-zi-est], giddy; also, causing giddiness or lightheadedness; as, a *dizzy* height; to spin around until you get *dizzy.*—*n.* **diz′zi-ness.**

DNA (dē′en′ā′) *abbrev.* short for *deoxyribonucleic acid*: a self-replicating substance, found in the cells of all living things, that carries genetic information from the parents to their offspring.

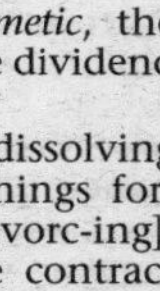

THE DOUBLE HELIX STRUCTURE OF DNA

do (do͞o), *v.t.* [*p.t.* did (did), *p.p.* done (dun), *p.pr.* do-ing], **1,** to perform; execute; as, to do one's work; **2,** to render; pay; give; as, to *do* a favour; **3,** to produce, esp. by art; as, to *do* a painting; **4,** to arrange; as, to *do* one's hair; put in order; as, to *do* a room; also, to prepare, as lessons; **5,** to achieve (a given speed); as, the car *did* 50 kilometres an hour in the school zone; **6,** *Colloq.* to cheat; as, he *did* me out of a job; **7,** *Colloq.* to visit as a tourist; as, to *do* Africa:—*v.i.* **1,** to try one's best to succeed; as, to *do* or die; **2,** to fare (well or ill); as, to *do* well in business; **3,** *Colloq.* to serve the purpose; as, this box will *do*:—*auxiliary verb* used: **1,** in sentences so phrased as to be emphatic; as, *do* tell me; never *did* I see so large an apple; **2,** in interrogative and negative sentences; as, when *do* you get back? the parade *did* not come this way:—*substitute v.* used to replace a verb or verb construction in order to avoid repetition; as, he walks as his father *does*.—*adj.* **do-a-ble** (do͞o′a-bl).—*n.* **do′er** (do͞o′ėr).

doc (dok), *n. Colloq.* **1,** doctor; **2,** documentary; **3,** in *computing,* a computer document.

doc-ile (dō′sīl; dos′il), *adj.* easy to teach; easily managed; as, a *docile* child.—*n.* **do-cil′i-ty** (dō-sil′i-ti).

[1]**dock** (dok), *n.* in a courtroom, the place reserved for the prisoner.

[2]**dock** (dok), *n.* **1,** an artificial basin or waterway for ships; **2,** a waterway between two piers; a wharf:—*v.t.* **1,** to bring to a pier and moor, as a ship; **2,** to join two spacecrafts together in space:—*v.i.* to arrive at a dock or become docked. Also, **dock′age, dock′yard′.**

[3]**dock** (dok), *n.* the fleshy part or stump of an animal's tail:—*v.t.* **1,** to cut off; **2,** to make a deduction from (wages); make less; as, to *dock* pay because of missed work days.

dock-et (dok′it), *n.* **1,** in *law,* a list of cases for trial; **2,** an agenda; **3,** a contents label.

docking station (dok′ing), *n.* in *computing,* a device that allows a laptop computer to be hooked up to additional accessories such as larger monitor, battery charger, and other peripherals.

doc-tor (dok′tėr), *n.* **1,** a licensed person who treats mental and physical disorders, diseases, or injuries, such as a physician, surgeon, dentist, psychiatrist, etc.; **2,** a person who holds the highest degree conferred by a university:—*v.t. Colloq.* **1,** to treat medically; as, to *doctor* a cold; **2,** to tamper with; alter; as, to *doctor* the financial records.—*n.* **doc′tor-ate.**

doc-trine (dok′trin), *n.* that which is taught; the principles or beliefs of a church, sect, or party.—*adj.* **doc′tri-nal** (dok′tri-nal; dok-trī′nal).

doc-u-ment (dok′ū-ment), *n.* **1,** a record; an official paper that gives information or evidence, such as a birth certificate, driver's licence, passport, etc.; **2,** in *computing,* a file of the work done within a computer program or application, esp. a text file:—*v.t.* **1,** to prove something by a document or documents; as, to *document* the accusations and order of events; **2,** to show or demonstrate; as, the video *documents* the stages of a butterfly.—*n.* and *adj.* **doc′u-men′ta-ry.**—*n.* **doc′u-men-ta′tion.**

doc-u-men-ta-ry (dok′ū-men′tėr-i; dok′ū-men′tri), *n.* a radio, movie, or television program that gives factual information about a real-life subject.

dod-der (dod′ėr), *v.i.* to shake; tremble; totter, as from weakness or age.—*adj.* **dod′der-ing.**

dodge (doj), *v.i.* [dodged, dodg-ing], **1,** to move aside quickly so as to escape something; **2,** to practise tricky devices:—*v.t.* to escape from, by dodging; as, to *dodge* a car:—*n.* **1,** an act of evasion; **2,** a clever trick.—*n.* **dodg′er.**

do-do (dō′dō), *n.* [*pl.* dodos or dodoes], **1,** a large extinct bird, with short legs and wings too small for flight, related to the pigeon; **2,** a stupid or old-fashioned person.

doe (dō), *n.* the female of the deer; also, the female of the antelope, rabbit, or hare.

does (duz), a *pr.t.* of *do.*

dog (dôg), *n.* **1,** a domesticated, four-legged animal, related to the wolf, of which there are many breeds, some ancient, found the world over; **2,** a device for bracing, holding, etc.; also, a catch or ratchet; **3,** *Colloq.* any sort of person; as, a lucky *dog*; a sly *dog*:—*v.t.* [dogged, dog-ging], to follow; track; trail.

dog–ear or **dog's–ear** (dôg′–ēr′; dôgz′–ēr′), *n.* the turned-down corner of a page in a book:—*v.t.* to disfigure (a book) in this way.—*adj.* **dog′–eared′** or **dog's′–eared′.**

dog-ged (dôg′ed), *adj.* stubborn; persistent.

dog-ger-el (dôg′ėr-el), *n.* **1,** trivial, comic, or inartistic verse; **2,** bad or inferior writing, esp. poetry or verse.—*adj.* crude, poorly constructed (rhymes).

do-gie or **do-gy** (dō′gi), *n.* in the western part of Canada and U.S., a stray or motherless calf.

dog-ma (dôg′ma), *n.* a principle, belief, or doctrine, accepted as authoritative, esp. one so accepted by the church.

dog-mat-ic (dôg-mat′ik) or **dog-mat-i-cal** (dôg-mat′i-kal), *adj.* **1,** pertaining to established doctrine or belief; **2,** making assertions in a positive manner, without proof; arrogant; as, a *dogmatic* old professor; **3,** asserted positively without proof; as, *dogmatic* opinions.—*adv.* **dog-mat′i-cal-ly.**

do–good-er (do͞o′–good′ėr), *n. Colloq.* a person who supports humanitarian or philanthropic causes, esp. one who is naive or unrealistic.

Dog-rib (dôg′rib′), *n.* **1,** a member of the Dene Aboriginal people of the Northwest Territories of Canada; **2,** the Athapaskan language of these people.

dog's–ear (dôgz′–ēr′) *n.* Same as **dog-ear.**

dog-sled (dôg′sled′), *n.* **1,** a sled pulled by teams of dogs, esp. in Northern Canada:—*v.i.* to travel by such a sled.

dog-wood (dôg′wood′), *n.* any of a group of trees or shrubs with hard close-grained wood, bearing in spring clusters of flowers, often surrounded by four pink or white petal-like parts.

do-gy (dō′gi), *n.* Same as **dogie.**

doi-ly (doi′li), *n.* [*pl.* doilies], a small mat of lace, linen, etc.

do-ings (do͞o′ings), *n.pl.* things that are done; actions; as, strange doings next door.

do-jo (dō′jō′), *n.* a school for the training of martial arts such as karate and judo.

dol-drums (dol′drumz), *n.pl.* **1,** the state of being calmed or at a standstill; as, a ship in the *doldrums;* **2,** a windless region near the equator where ships are often kept from moving; **3,** depression of mind; sadness, gloominess; as, to be in the *doldrums* after losing a pet.

do–it–your-self (do͞o′–it–ūr-self′), *n.* and *adj.* making, repairing, etc., done by oneself instead of hiring another.

dole (dōl), *n.* **1,** the dealing out of money, clothing, food, etc., for charity; **2,** the gifts themselves; **3,** a small portion; **4,** relief money given to unemployed people by their government:—*v.t.* [doled, dol-ing], **1,** to give as alms; **2,** to deal out sparingly or in small amounts.

dole-ful (dōl′fool), *adj.* sad; dismal; gloomy.—*adv.* **dole′ful-ly.**—*n.* **dole′fulness.**

doll (dol), *n.* **1,** a puppet or toy baby, child, or grown person; **2,** a pretty female.

dol-lar (dol′ėr), *n.* **1,** the basic unit of money used in Canada, the U.S., etc., equal to 100 cents: the Canadian dollar coin is called a *loonie;* **2,** a bank note, treasury note, coin, etc., worth 100 cents.

doll-y (dol′i), *n.* **1,** an appliance, as a low truck or frame, for moving heavy objects; **2,** a tool for holding rivets; **3,** a narrow-gauge yard engine; **4,** an apparatus for holding and moving a movie or television camera; **5,** an agitator for washing ores, etc.

dol-phin (dol′fin), *n.* **1,** an intelligent whalelike sea mammal with a long snout; **2,** an edible sea fish remarkable for its rapid changes of colour when out of water.

dolt (dōlt), *n.* a stupid person; a dunce; blockhead.—*adj.* **dolt′ish.**

do-main (dō-mān′), *n.* **1,** an estate owned in one's own right; **2,** a region under the rule of a monarch or government; dominion; realm; **3,** a field of thought or action; as, the *domain* of science; **4,** in *computing,* a group of networked computers that share a common address such as smith.com; the name of the Internet connection for a person, company, or organization; a domain name.

dome (dōm), *n.* **1,** a large rounded roof on a circular base; as, the *dome* of the Alberta legislature; **2,** any domelike object:—*v.t.* to top with, or shape like, a dome.

do-mes-tic (dō-mes′tik), *adj.* **1,** relating to one's home, household, or family; as, *domestic* chores; **2,** staying at home; fond of home; **3,** relating to, or made in, one's own country; not foreign; as, *domestic* trade; *domestic* products or produce; **4,** of animals, tame; living with people, as dogs; turned to the use of people, as cattle:—*n.* a household servant.

do-mes-ti-cate (dō-mes′ti-kāt′), *v.t.* [domesticat-ed, domesticat-ing], **1,** to accustom (a person) to a home or home life; **2,** to turn (an animal or plant) to the use of people; tame or cultivate.—*n.* **do-mes′ti-ca′tion.**

dom-i-cile (dom′i-sīl′), *n.* a place of abode; home:—*v.t.* [domiciled, domicil-ing], to establish in a fixed residence.

dom-i-nant (dom′i-nant), *adj.* controlling; ruling; also, most important; as, the *dominant* partner in a business.—*n.* **dom′i-nance.**

dom-i-nate (dom′i-nāt′), *v.t.* [dominat-ed, dominat-ing], **1,** to govern or control by power, size, or importance; rule; as, the Romans once *dominated* Europe; **2,** to occupy a commanding position; as, the mountain *dominates* the valley:—*v.i.* to exercise influence or control; as, the winning team *dominated* over their opponents.—*n.* **dom′i-na′tion.**

dom-i-neer (dom′i-nēr′), *v.i.* to exercise authority arrogantly or tyrannically; be overbearing.—*adj.* **dom′i-neer′ing.**

do-min-ion (dō-min′yun), *n.* **1,** supreme authority or control; rule; **2,** territory subject to a ruler or government; as, a king's *dominions:*—**Dominion, 1,** a self-governing country or territory in the *Commonwealth of Nations;* as, the *Dominion* of Canada was established in 1867; **2,** in Canada, under the control or authority of the federal government; also, relating to the country as a whole; national.

Dominion Day, formerly, the name of Canada's national holiday, July 1, which was officially changed to *Canada Day* in October 1982.

dom-i-no (dom′i-nō), *n.* [*pl.* dominoes or dominos], **1,** a loose cloak with a hood and mask, used as a masquerade costume; **2,** a flat, oblong, dotted piece of bone or wood used in playing a game:—**dominoes,** *n.pl.* used as *sing.* the game so played.

[1]don (don), *v.t.* [donned, don-ning], to put on; as, to *don* one's coat.

[2]don (don), *n.* **1,** a Spanish lord or gentleman; **2,** in British universities, a fellow, tutor, or head of a college; **3,** a person in charge of university or college student residences:—**Don** (dôn), Sir; Mr.: a title used in Spain.—*n. fem.* **Do′ña** (dō′nyä).

do-nate (dō-nāt′; dō′nāt), *v.t.* [donat-ed, donat-ing], to give to charity; contribute.—*n.* **do-na′tion; do′nor.**

done (dun), *p.p.* of *do.*

don-key (dong′ki), *n.* [*pl.* donkeys], **1,** an animal related to the horse, but smaller with longer ears, often used to pull or carry loads; an ass; **2,** a stupid or obstinate person.

do-nut (dō′nut′), *n.* Same as **doughnut.**

doo-dad (do͞o′dad′), *n. Colloq.* something the name of which is unknown or forgotten; a gadget.

doo-dle (do͞o′dl), *v.t.* and *v.i.* idly or aimlessly to scribble or trace designs, as when talking on a telephone or thinking of something else.

doo-hick-ey (do͞o′hi′ki), *n. Colloq.* a doodad or gadget.

doom (do͞om), *n.* **1,** destiny that cannot be escaped; **2,** destructive fate; **3,** the Last Judgment; as, the crack of *doom*; **4,** judgment; sentence:—*v.t.* **1,** to condemn; sentence; as, to *doom* a person to death; **2,** to destine; as, *doomed* to disappointment.

dooms-day (do͞omz′dā′), *n.* the end of the world; Judgment Day:—*adj.* something that has the potential of destroying the world; as, *doomsday* weapons.

door (dōr), *n.* **1,** a movable barrier, usually sliding or swinging on hinges, that opens and closes the entrance to a house, room, car, etc.; **2,** a means of entrance; doorway.

door-bell (dōr′bel′), *n.* a buzzer or bell outside a door that is used to signal someone is there.

door-knob (dōr′nob′), *n.* a round handle on a door that allows one to open the door.

door-step (dōr′step′), *n.* a step or flight of steps leading up to the outside door of a building.

door-way (dōr′wā′), *n.* **1,** an opening in a wall that leads in and out of a room or building and is closed by a door; **2,** a way of getting to some place or goal; as, a *doorway* to success.

dope (dōp), *n. Slang* **1,** harmful narcotic drugs; **2,** information; inside information, as on a horse race, stocks, etc.; **3,** a stupid person:—*v.t.* [doped, dop-ing], *Slang* to treat with drugs.

dork (dôrk), *n. Slang* a stupid or foolish person, esp. one who is socially inept; jerk; nerd.—*n.* **dork′i-ness.**—*adj.* **dork′y** [dork-i-er; dork-i-est].

dorm (dôrm), *n.* short for **dormitory.**

dor-mant (dôr′mant), *adj.* sleeping; temporarily inactive; as, plants lie *dormant* in the winter; a *dormant* talent.—*n.* **dor′mancy** (dôr′man-si).

dor-mer (dôr′mėr), *n.* a window built upright in a sloping roof; also, the structure that contains it. Also called *dormer window.*

dor-mi-tor-y (dôr′mi-tėr-i), *n.* [*pl.* dormitories], a building containing a number of bedrooms; as, a university *dormitory.*

dor-sal (dôr′sal), *adj.* pertaining to, or on or near, the back; as, a *dorsal* muscle; *dorsal* fin on a fish.

Dor-set (dor′set), *n.* an Aboriginal culture in northeastern Canada and northern Greenland, from around 500 B.C. to 1500 A.D.

dor-y (dôr′i), *n.* [*pl.* dories], **1,** a deep flat-bottomed rowboat with a sharp prow and flat, V-shaped stern, often used by saltwater fishers; **2,** an edible sea fish.

DOS (dos), *abbrev.* short for *d*isk *o*perating *s*ystem: in *computing,* a specialized computer program that provides an easy-to-use link between the user and a computer disk drive.

dose (dōs), *n.* **1,** a definite quantity of medicine to be taken at one time; **2,** a certain amount or portion of something; as, a *dose* of reality:—*v.t.* [dosed, dos-ing], to give medicine to.

dot (dot), *n.* **1,** a very small spot or point, as over an *i* or *j*; a speck; **2,** the character (period) used in electronic file names and Internet addresses, as in *.com*:—*v.t.* [dotted, dot-ting], **1,** to mark with dots; **2,** to be scattered here and there; as, flowers *dotted* the hillside.

dot-com (dot′kom′), *n.* an Internet address suffix denoting a commercial or business user:—*adj.* an Internet business; as, many *dotcom* companies went out of business in 2001.

dote (dōt), *v.i.* [dot-ed, dot-ing], **1,** to be feeble and foolish with age; **2,** to show excessive love; as, to *dote* on a grandchild.

dou-ble (dub′l), *adj.* **1,** being in pairs; as, *double* doors; a *double* bed; **2,** multiplied by two; twice as much or many; twice the size, strength, value, etc.; as, a *double* amount; **3,** combining two unlike qualities; as, his remark had a *double* meaning; **4,** folded over, as cloth or paper; **5,** in *botany,* having more than a single row of petals; as, a *double* nasturtium:—*n.* **1,** twice as much; twice the number or quantity; **2,** a substitute, understudy, or someone who does stunts, etc., for another; as, an action movie actor's *double*; **3,** a duplicate; that which looks very much like something else; **4,** a sharp turn made while running, as by a hunted animal, to throw pursuers off the track; hence, an evasive trick:—*v.t.* [dou-bled, dou-bling], **1,** to make twice as much; multiply by two; as, *double* five to get 10; **2,** to fold over; as, to *double* a piece of paper; **3,** to pass around; as, a ship *doubles* a cape:—

v.i. **1,** to increase to twice as much; as, his stock *doubled* in value; **2,** to turn and retrace the same course; as, the fox *doubled* back; **3,** to be a substitute or understudy; as, she *doubles* for the lead actor:—*adv.* by twos; in a pair; as, to ride *double*:—**double-dealing,** dishonest action; deceit.—*adv.* **dou′bly.**

dou-ble-click (dub′l-klik′), *v.t.* in *computing,* to depress a mouse button twice very quickly to launch or open a file.

dou-ble-cross (dub′l-krôs′), *v.t. Slang* to betray.

dou-ble-head-er (dub′l-hed′ėr), *n.* **1,** a train with two engines in front; **2,** in *baseball,* two games in succession on the one day (by the same two teams).

dou-blet (dub′let), *n.* **1,** one of a pair; **2,** a couple; **3,** a close-fitting garment for the upper part of the body, worn by men in western Europe from the fifteenth to the seventeenth century.

dou-bloon (dub-lo͞on′), *n.* an old Spanish gold coin; *Slang* the Canadian two-dollar coin; toonie.

doubt (dout), *v.i.* to waver in opinion or belief; be uncertain or undecided:—*v.t.* to distrust; question; as, to *doubt* one's eyes:—*n.* **1,** uncertainty of mind; unbelief; as, I have my *doubts*; **2,** an unsettled question; an objection; as, to answer a *doubt*; **3,** a state or condition of uncertainty; as, his life is in *doubt*.—*n.* **doubt′er.**—*adv.* **doubt′less.**

doubt-ful (dout′fool), *adj.* **1,** questionable as to result; as, a *doubtful* venture; **2,** questionable as to character; as, *doubtful* people; **3,** undecided; doubting; as, he was *doubtful* of her ability.—*adv.* **doubt′ful-ly.**

douche (do͞osh), *n.* and *v.* cleansing or flushing out of some cavity or organ of the body, etc.

dough (dō), *n.* a spongy paste of flour and other ingredients, esp. for bread, cookies, pies, etc.

dough-nut or **do-nut** (dō′nut′), *n.* a small cake of sweetened dough, fried in fat, often shaped like rings with holes in the middle.

Dou-kho-bors or **Du-kho-bors** (do͞o′ko-bōrz′), *n.pl.* a Christian sect driven by religious persecution from Russia to Western Canada in the 1890s: noted for its belief in pacifism and the rejection of church and government authority.

dour (do͝or), *adj.* stern, gloomy, or sour in manner; obstinate.

douse (dous), *v.t.* and *v.i.* **1,** to thrust into or pour a liquid over; as, he was *doused* in the pond; he was *doused* (or drenched) with water; **2,** *Slang* to put out (a light); as, *douse* the fire.

[1]**dove** (duv), *n.* a bird of the pigeon family, known by the cooing sounds it makes.

[2]**dove** (dōv), a *p.t.* of *dive.*

dove-tail (duv′tāl′), *n.* a tongue or a notch shaped like a dove's tail:—*v.t.* to fasten together by interlocking tongues and notches of this shape:—*v.i.* to fit closely and exactly; as, her strategies *dovertailed* with the company's overall objectives.

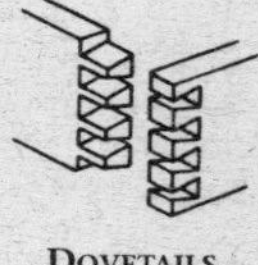
DOVETAILS

dow-a-ger (dou′a-jėr), *n.* **1,** a widow who holds property or title from her husband; **2,** *Colloq.* a dignified elderly woman.

dow-dy (dou′di), *n.* [*pl.* dowdies], a shabby, poorly dressed person:—*adj.* [dow-di-er, dow-di-est], lacking style.

dow-el (dou′el), *n.* a pin to fasten two pieces of wood or metal together: also called *dowel pin:*—*v.t.* [dowelled, dowelling], to fasten by such pins.

[1]**down** (doun), *n.* **1,** the first feathers of young birds; **2,** the soft underfeathers of birds; **3,** any velvety fuzz, as on a peach.

[2]**down** (doun), *adv.* **1,** from a higher to a lower position or degree: opposite of *up*; **2,** from an earlier to a later time; as, heirlooms are handed *down*; **3,** at once, as if on the counter; as, to pay 20 dollars *down*; **4,** to, or in, a lower state or condition, as of illness, defeat, etc.; as, to come *down* with a cold; to bring *down* one's price; **5,** from a greater to a lesser quantity; as, to boil *down*; **6,** seriously; as, to get *down* to work; **7,** upon paper; as, take *down* what she says:—*adj.* **1,** descending; as, a *down* elevator; **2,** in a lowered position; as, the curtain is *down*; **3,** in *golf,* behind one's opponent in holes or points; as, three *down*; **4,** ill; inactive; as, he is *down* with the flu; **5,** not working; out of order; as, the school computers are *down*:—*prep.* from a higher to a lower point on; as, to row *down* the stream:—*v.t.* to bring or put down; as, *down* the opponent; *down* the lemonade:—*n.* **1,** a descent; figuratively, a reverse of fortune; as, to have ups and *downs*; **2,** in *football,* any of the three chances that the team has to move forward at least 10 yards.

down-cast (doun′kast′), *adj.* **1,** directed downward; **2,** sad; discouraged.

down-fall (doun′fôl′), *n.* **1,** a falling downward; **2,** a sudden fall from rank, fortune, or reputation; disgrace; **3,** capture, as of a city.—*adj.* **down′fall′en.**

down-heart-ed (doun′här′tid), *adj.* downcast; sad.—*adv.* **down′heart′ed-ly.**

down-load (doun′lōd′), *v.t.* **1,** in *computing,* to transfer or copy data from one computer or source to another, esp. from a larger to a smaller; as, to *download* the program from the Internet; **2,** to shift the cost of a program from one level of government to another.

down-pour (doun′pōr′), *n.* a heavy rain.

down-right (doun′rīt′), *adj.* **1,** complete; as, *downright* stupidity; **2,** going straight to the point; blunt; as, an honest and *downright* person:—*adv.* (doun′rīt′; doun′rīt′), **1,** in plain terms; **2,** utterly; extremely; as, *downright* amazing.

down-stage (doun′stāj′), *adj.* and *adv.* toward the front of the stage.

down-stairs (doun′stârz′), *n.* the lower floor or floors of a building; as, she lives *downstairs*:—*adv.* on or to a lower floor; as, to go *downstairs*:—*adj.* (doun′stârz′), on a lower floor; as, a *downstairs* bedroom.

down-stream (doun′strēm′), *adj.* and *adv.* in the direction of the current.

Down syndrome or **Down's syndrome**, a congenital disorder caused by chromosome abnormality and resulting in mental retardation and physical deformities; also known as *trisomy 21.*

down-time (doun′tīm′), *n.* **1,** in *computing,* the period when a machine, esp. a computer, is not working due to some equipment failure or other problem; **2,** the time spent not working; leisure time.

down-town (doun′toun′), *n.* the main section, often the business section, of a town or city:—*adj.* and *adv.* in, to, or toward the centre of a town or city; as, to drive *downtown.*

down-trod-den (doun′trod′n), *adj.* oppressed.

down-ward (doun′wėrd), *adj.* moving from a higher to a lower level.

down-ward (doun′wėrd) or **downwards** (doun′wėrdz), *adj.* and *adv.* **1,** of or from a higher to a lower level or condition; as, a *downward* spiral; to move *downwards*; **2,** of or from an earlier time.

down-y (doun′i), *adj.* [down-i-er, down-i-est], **1,** made of, or covered with, soft feathers, hair, or wool; **2,** like down; soft.

dow-ry (dou′ri), *n.* [*pl.* dowries], **1,** the property a woman brings to her husband at marriage; **2,** an endowment or talent.

dowse or **douse** (dous), *v.i.* [dowsed, dowsing], to search for underground water, minerals, etc., by using a divining rod.

doze (dōz), *v.i.* [dozed, doz-ing], to sleep lightly; nap:—*n.* a light sleep; nap.

doz-en (duz′n), *n.* [*pl.* dozens or dozen], 12 things of a kind, taken together.

Dr. *abbrev.* **1,** a title used before a doctor's name; **2,** short for *Drive*; as, Maple *Drive.*

drab (drab), *adj.* [drab-ber, drab-best], **1,** of a dull greyish brown; **2,** uninteresting.

drae-ger-man (drā′gėr-man), *n.* a Maritime miner skilled in techniques of rescuing trapped miners, esp. in gas-filled mines.

draft or **draught** (dråft), *n.* **1,** a line drawing, sketch, or plan, as for an engine or building; **2,** a sketch or outline of something to be written or done; as, the first *draft* of a speech; **3,** a written order for the payment of money; also, a drawing of money from a bank or fund; **4,** a method of selecting people for compulsory military service, esp. in the U.S.; also, the people so selected; **5,** (also *draught*), the pulling of a load by beasts; as, horses used for *draft*; **6,** (also *draught*), a stream of air; as, a *draft* from an open door; **7,** (also *draught*), a device for controlling the air stream in a stove, furnace, fireplace, etc.; **8,** a taking away; drain; as, a *draft* on supplies; **9,** (also *draught*), the depth of water to which a ship sinks, esp. when loaded; **10,** (also *draught*), the hauling in of a net of fish; also, the quantity of fish caught in one haul; **11,** (also *draught*), a single drink; as, a *draught* of water; also, the act of drawing (liquid) from a cask, barrel, or the like; as, beer on *draught*:—*adj.* **1,** (also *draught*), used for pulling loads; as, *draft* animals; **2,** (also *draught*), served or drawn from a keg; as, *draft* beer; **3,** in *computing,* of a printer, poor print quality; as, *draft* mode:—*v.t.* **1,** to sketch, write, or draw in outline; **2,** to select (people) for compulsory military service.

draf-tee (dråf-tē′), *n.* one conscripted for military service, etc.

drafts-man (dråfts′man), *n.* [*pl.* draftsmen (-men)], one who makes plans, mechanical drawings, etc.

draft-y (dråf′ti), *adj.* [draft-i-er, draft-i-est], exposed to currents of air.

drag (drag), *v.t.* [dragged, drag-ging], **1,** to draw along by force; haul; **2,** to search the bottom of (a river or lake) with a drag or grapnel; **3,** in *computing,* to move material from one place to another on a computer screen, usually by using a mouse:—*v.i.* **1,** to trail along the ground; as, her skirt *dragged*; **2,** to move or go slowly; hence, to be slow and uninteresting; as, the speech *dragged*:—*n.* **1,** a device for searching the bottom of a river or lake; **2,** a sledge for hauling loads; **3,** a harrow for breaking up soil; **4,** anything that holds back progress; **5,** a kind of coach; **6,** *Slang* influence; pull; as, to have a lot of *drag* at the company; **7,** *Slang* a puff of a cigarette; **8,** a boring situation or person; as, she's a real *drag*; the movie was a *drag*; **9,** female clothes worn by a male.

drag and drop, in *computing,* a method of moving or otherwise manipulating computer files using the mouse and icons on the monitor screen.

drag-gle (drag′l), *v.t.* **1,** to wet or soil by dragging, as in mud; **2,** to lag behind.

drag-net (drag′net′), *n.* **1,** a net for drawing along the bottom of a river to catch fish, or along the ground to catch small game; **2,** a sweeping search for criminals, etc.

drag-on (drag′un), *n.* in mythology or folklore, a huge beast represented as a winged serpent, often with many heads, and breathing fire.

drag-on-fly (drag′on-flī′), *n.* [*pl.* dragonflies], an insect with a long, slender body, large eyes, and four narrow, finely veined wings: often called *darning needle.*

drain (drān), *v.t.* **1,** to draw off (a liquid) gradually; as, to *drain* water from a reservoir; **2,** to make empty; as, he *drained* the cup; **3,** to use up; exhaust; as, the race *drained* him of energy:—*v.i.* to discharge surface water; as, swamps *drain* into ditches:—*n.* **1,** a channel or pipe for useless water; **2,** a continuous demand; as, a *drain* on a country's resources.

drain-age (drān′ij), *n.* **1,** a flowing off of water; **2,** a system of pipes or streams for drawing off water; **3,** that which flows away.

drake (drāk), *n.* a male duck.

dram (dram), *n.* **1,** a unit of apothecaries' weight equal to about 3.89 grams; **2,** a unit of avoirdupois weight equal to about 1.77 grams; **3,** a small drink or small amount of something, esp. of alcoholic liquor.

dra-ma (drä′ma; dram′a), *n.* **1,** a play; a work, in prose or verse, intended for acting on a stage; **2,** that branch of literature concerned with plays; as, a student of *drama;* **3,** a movie or television story that is serious and not a comedy; **4,** any series of human events leading to a climax.—*adj.* **dra-mat′ic.**

dram-a-tize (dram′a-tīz′), *vi.* [dramatized, dramatiz-ing], **1,** to adapt or rewrite for the stage or film; as, to *dramatize* a novel; **2,** to portray anything vividly or in a dramatic manner.—*n.* **dram′a-tist.**—*n.* **dram′a-ti-za′tion.**

dra-me-dy (drä′me-di; dra′me-di), *Colloq.* a situation comedy with dramatic moments, esp. on television.

drank (drank), *p.t.* of *drink.*

drape (drāp), *v.t.* [draped, drap-ing], **1,** to cover with cloth; **2,** to arrange (cloth or hangings) in folds:—**drapes,** cloth that hangs in long, loose folds in front of a window; curtains.

dra-per-y (drā′pėr-ī), *n.* [*pl.* draperies], fabrics used for garments or hangings, esp. when hung loosely or in folds; also, the hangings or draped robes.

dras-tic (dras′tik), *adj.* acting rapidly and violently; severe; very strong or serious; as, a *drastic* remedy.—*adv.* **dras′ti-cal-ly.**

draught (dråft). See **draft.**

draw (drô), *v.t.* [*p.t.* drew (dro͞o), *p.p.* drawn (drôn), *p.pr.* draw-ing], **1,** to haul or drag; **2,** to pull out; haul up, as a fish net; **3,** to come to (a conclusion) by reasoning; **4,** to extend in length; as, to *draw* out a performance; **5,** to extract or bring out; remove; as, to *draw* a cork; to *draw* a winning ticket; **6,** to represent on paper with pen or pencil; **7,** to write in legal form; as, to *draw* up a will; **8,** to require in order to float; as, the boat *draws* two metres of water; **9,** to inhale; as, to *draw* a long breath; **10,** to receive; as, to *draw* one's pay; **11,** to obtain (money) from a bank; **12,** to attract; as, honey *draws* flies; **13,** to produce or gain; as, money *draws* interest; **14,** to select or obtain (a chance); as, to *draw* lots; **15,** to influence (someone) to reveal facts, talents, etc.; as, to *draw* someone out; **16,** to get (something) from a source; as, to *draw* inspiration from a book:—*v.i.* **1,** to move; as, to *draw* away; *draw* near; **2,** to attract; as, a good show always *draws;* **3,** to pull or haul something; to move something by pulling; **4,** to make a demand; as, to *draw* on a bank; **5,** to practise the art of making designs or pictures; **6,** to allow a current of air to pass; as, the chimney *draws* well:—*n.* **1,** the act or result of drawing; in particular, a lottery; **2,** a contest left undecided; a tie; **3,** the movable section of a drawbridge; **4,** the act of taking a pistol and aiming it.

draw-back (drô′bak′), *n.* a disadvantage; hindrance.

draw-bridge (drô′brij′), *n.* a bridge of which the whole or a part may be lifted up, let down, or drawn aside.

draw-er (drô′ėr; drôr), *n.* **1,** one who draws; a draftsman; **2,** (drôr), a sliding compartment in a piece of furniture such as a desk, cabinet, chest, etc., which is used for storing things:—**drawers** (drôrz), an undergarment for the lower part of the body.

draw-ing (drô′ing), *n.* **1,** the act of dragging, pulling, etc.; as, the *drawing* of a load, or of a sword; **2,** a picture made with a pen, pencil, chalk, etc.; a sketch; **3,** the art of making such a picture; **4,** the selection of a winning ticket in a raffle or lottery.

draw-ing room, a room for the reception of company, esp. in former times; parlour; also, a passenger railway train compartment.

drawl (drôl), *v.t.* and *v.i.* to speak in an affected, lazy manner:—*n.* **1,** a slow, lazy manner of speaking; **2,** a way of speaking in certain regions; as, a southern *drawl.*

[1]**drawn** (drôn), *p.p.* of *draw.*

[2]**drawn** (drôn), *adj.* **1,** left undecided; as, a *drawn* game; **2,** out of shape; twisted; as, a face *drawn* with grief; **3,** melted; as, *drawn* butter.

dread (dred), *v.t.* to look forward to with shrinking or fear:—*n.* fear, esp. of the future; **2,** fear mingled with awe:—*adj.* **1,** terrifying; **2,** inspiring fear mingled with awe; as, a *dread* employer.

dread-ful (dred′fl), *adj.* **1,** causing fear, terrible; as, *dreadful* noise; **2,** of poor quality; bad; awful; as, a *dreadful* essay.—*adv.* **dread′ful-ly.**

dream (drēm), *n.* **1,** thoughts, feelings, or pictures experienced or seen during sleep;

2, something imagined; daydream; as, a *dream* of greatness:—*v.t.* [*p.t.* and *p.p.* dreamt (dremt) or dreamed (drēmd), *p.pr.* dreaming], **1,** to see, think, or feel during sleep; **2,** to imagine or hope for; daydream:—*v.i.* **1,** to have thoughts, see pictures, etc., during sleep; **2,** to be lost in thought; daydream.—*n.* **dream′er.**

dream-y (drēm′i), *adj.* [dream-i-er, dream-i-est], **1,** like a dream; unreal; **2,** not awake to realities; **3,** soothing; as, *dreamy* music; **4,** *Colloq.* wonderful.—*adv.* **dream′i-ly.**—*n.* **dream′i-ness.**

drear-y (drēr′i), *adj.* [drear-i-er, drear-i-est], cheerless; gloomy; as, a *dreary* day.—*adv.* **drear′i-ly.**—*n.* **drear′i-ness.**

[1]**dredge** (drej), *n.* **1,** a device for scooping up mud, as from the bottom of a river; **2,** a device for gathering oysters:—*v.t.* [dredged, dredg-ing], **1,** to deepen, as a river channel; **2,** to scoop with a dredge; **3,** to gather, as information.—*n.* **dredg′er.**

[2]**dredge** (drej), *v.t.* [dredged, dredg-ing], to sprinkle with flour.

dregs (dregz), *n.pl.* **1,** the sediment of liquids; **2,** the worthless part of anything; as, *dregs* of society.

drench (drench), *v.t.* to wet thoroughly:—*n.* **1,** a drink or dose of medicine given to a horse, etc.; **2,** something that drenches, as a heavy rain.

dress (dres), *n.* **1,** a woman's or a girl's article of clothing that is a top and a skirt in one piece; **2,** a particular style of clothing; as, evening *dress;* **3,** any outer garb or appearance; as, trees in autumn *dress:*—*v.t.* **1,** to clothe; as, to *dress* a baby; **2,** to deck out; as, to *dress* a window; **3,** to make ready for use; as, to *dress* meat; **4,** to treat or bind up, as a wound; **5,** to straighten (a line of soldiers) in military drill; **6,** to arrange (hair):—*v.i.* **1,** to put on clothes; **2,** in *drilling,* to form into a straight line; as, "Right, *dress*!"

dress-er (dres′ėr), *n.* **1,** a chest of drawers with a mirror, for clothing; **2,** a cupboard for dishes, glasses, etc.; **3,** a bench used in dressing or preparing something for use; **4,** a surgeon's assistant who dresses wounds; **5,** a person who dresses, esp. in a certain way; as, a sloppy *dresser*; **6,** a person who dresses someone or something else; as, a *dresser* for a famous star; a window *dresser.*

dress-ing (dres′ing), *n.* **1,** the act of putting on clothes, treating a wound, etc.; **2,** material for stiffening fabrics; **3,** sauce for salads, etc.; **4,** stuffing, as for a turkey; **5,** a bandage, compress, etc., applied to a wound or sore.

dress-y (dres′i), *adj.* [dress-i-er, dress-i-est], **1,** given to showy dressing; **2,** *Colloq.* stylish; not casual; as, a *dressy* party.

drew (drōō), *p.t.* of *draw.*

drib-ble (drib′l), *v.i.* [drib-bled, drib-bling], **1,** to fall in drops; **2,** to drool:—*v.t.* **1,** to let fall in drops; give out in small portions; **2,** in *soccer* and *hockey,* to give slight kicks or shoves to (the ball or puck); **3,** in *basketball,* to bounce (the ball) rapidly along the floor; **4,** to drool:—*n.* a trickle of water.—*n.* **drib′bler.**

dried (drīd), *p.t.* of *dry.*

dri-er or **dry-er** (drī′ėr), *n.* **1,** a person or thing that dries something; **2,** an appliance or device that dries by blowing heated air; as, a clothes *drier;* hair *drier;* **3,** a substance added to paint or varnish to aid drying.

drift (drift), *n.* **1,** the direction in which anything is driven; tendency; meaning; as, the *drift* of a speech; **2,** that which is driven; as, a snow*drift;* **3,** in *geology,* loose rocks, earth, etc., carried by a glacier; **4,** the distance a ship is carried from its course by ocean or air currents or an airplane by air currents:—*v.t.* to drive along or heap up; as, the wind *drifts* dry leaves into piles:—*v.i.* **1,** to be carried along by a current or by circumstances; **2,** to gather or collect in heaps; **3,** to move without any purpose or goal.—*n.* **drift′er.**

drift-wood (drift′wood′), *n.* floating wood cast ashore by water.

drill (dril), *n.* **1,** a tool for boring holes; **2,** a machine for sowing seeds in rows; also, a row so planted; **3,** military exercises; **4,** thorough training by frequent repetition; as, a fire *drill:*—*v.t.* **1,** to pierce with a drill; bore (holes); **2,** to train (soldiers) in military exercises; **3,** to instruct thoroughly; as, to *drill* students; **4,** to sow in rows.—*n.* **drill′er.**

drink (dringk), *v.i.* [*p.t.* drank (drangk), *p.p.* drunk, *p.pr.* drink-ing], **1,** to swallow a liquid; **2,** to take alcoholic liquors habitually:—*v.t.* **1,** to swallow (a liquid); **2,** to absorb; suck in; as, plants *drink* water; **3,** to receive through the senses; as, to *drink* in a scene:—*n.* **1,** any liquid to be swallowed; as, a cool *drink;* **2,** the quantity of liquid to be swallowed; as, a *drink* of water; **3,** strong or intoxicating liquor; as, a rum *drink.*—*adj.* **drink′a-ble.**—*n.* **drink′er.**

drip (drip), *v.i.* [dripped, drip-ping], **1,** to fall in drops; as, the oil *drips* on the floor; **2,** to let fall drops; as, your umbrella *drips:*—*v.t.* to let fall in drops; as, the trees *drip* rain:—*n.* **1,** that which falls in drops; **2,** a projecting part so shaped as to throw off rain; **3,** the sound made by something dripping; as, the *drip* of the faucet.

drip-ping (drip′ing), *n.* the fatty juice from roasting meat.

drive (drīv), *v.t.* [*p.t.* drove (drōv), *p.p.* driven (driv′en), *p.pr.* driv-ing], **1,** to urge forward by force or threats; push forward forcibly; **2,** to control the motion of; steer, as an automobile; also, to carry in a driven vehicle; **3,** to carry on vigorously; to conclude; as, to *drive* a bargain; **4,** to put into a certain state; as, you *drive* me crazy; **5,** to overwork; as, he *drove* his employees to the limit:—*v.i.* **1,** to press, aim, or be moved forward steadily or with violence; **2,** to travel in a car, etc.; **3,** in *golf,* to strike the ball from a tee; also, a long hit in baseball and other games:—*n.* **1,** the act of sending forward; **2,** a road; as, Lakeshore *Drive;* also, a driveway; **3,** a trip in a car or other vehicle; **4,** a gathering together, or rounding up, as of cattle for branding, logs for floating, etc.; **5,** a campaign or strong organized effort; as, a fundraising *drive.*

driv-el (driv′el), *n.* **1,** idle silly talk; as, to descend to *drivel;* **2,** saliva drooling from the mouth:—*v.t.* and *v.i.* **1,** to talk nonsense; **2,** to drool (saliva).

drive–in (drīv′–in′), *adj.* built so that a patron can sit in his or her car while receiving service, as at a *drive-in* theatre, bank, restaurant, etc.:—*n.* a drive-in theatre.

driv-er (drīv′ėr), *n.* **1,** a person who drives a car or other vehicle; **2,** one who or that which forces something into motion or directs persons or things in motion; **3,** in *golf,* a wooden club for driving the ball from a tee: used for long shots; **4,** in *computing,* software that controls the operation of a peripheral device.

drive-way (drīv′wā′), *n.* a private passageway or road for vehicles, located between a house or building and the street.

driz-zle (driz′l), *v.i.* [driz-zled, driz-zling], to rain slightly or mistily:—*n.* fine, misty rain.—*adj.* **driz′zly.**

droll (drōl), *adj.* odd; amusing; as, a *droll* remark.—*n.* **droll′er-y.**

drom-e-dar-y (drom′i-dėr-i; drum′i-dėr-i), *n.* [*pl.* dromedaries], the Arabian, or one-humped, camel, noted for its speed.

drone (drōn), *v.i.* [droned, dron-ing], to utter a monotonous, humming sound; as, to *drone* through a lesson:—*v.t.* to read or speak in a monotonous or boring tone:—*n.* **1,** a dull monotonous tone; humming; as, the *drone* of bees; **2,** one of the pipes of a bagpipe; **3,** the male of a honeybee, which produces no honey; **4,** a lazy person.

drool (drōōl), *v.i.* **1,** to run at the mouth; drivel; **2,** to speak foolishly.

droop (drōōp), *v.i.* **1,** to sink or hang down, as from weariness; close, as eyelids; **2,** to fail or flag; as, his spirits *drooped:*—*v.t.* to let hang down; as, to *droop* the head:—*n.* the act of drooping.—*adj.* **droop′y.**

drop (drop), *v.i.* [dropped, drop-ping], **1,** to fall in small rounded masses of liquid; **2,** to fall; sink to a lower position; as, the hat *dropped;* **3,** to fall behind or below, as in rank; **4,** to grow lower in sound or pitch; as, her voice *dropped* to a whisper; **5,** to cease or end; as, the matter *dropped;* **6,** to come or go naturally or casually; as, to *drop* in for a visit:—**drop off, 1,** to fall asleep; **2,** to become less; weaken; as, sales have *dropped* off:—*v.t.* **1,** to let fall in tiny masses; as, to *drop* medicine from a spoon; **2,** to let fall suddenly; as, I *dropped* the book; **3,** to lower, as one's eyes or voice; **4,** to fell with a blow or weapon; **5,** to have done with; as, to *drop* an argument; *drop* a course; **6,** to deliver to a certain place or person; as, to *drop* a line or letter to someone; to *drop* off a package; **7,** to leave out or omit; as, to *drop* the "e" before adding "ing" to a word:—*n.* **1,** a small rounded mass of liquid; as, a *drop* of water; **2,** anything like a small rounded mass of liquid; as, cough *drops;* **3,** any very small quantity; **4,** a sudden descent or fall; as, a *drop* in prices; **5,** the depth or distance of a descent or fall; as, a sheer *drop* of 50 metres; **6,** something arranged to be lowered or hung from above; as, a curtain *drop;* **7,** a place where something may be left or dropped for someone else; as, a mail *drop.*—*n.* **drop′per; drop′let.**

drop down, in *computing,* a computer menu that drops down from the menu bar when selected by a mouse.

drop–kick (drop′–kik′), *n.* in *football,* a kick given to a ball as it rises or bounces after being dropped to the ground (not a *placement* or *punt*):—*v.t.* and *v.i.* kick a ball in this way; as, he *drop-kicked* a field goal.

drop-out (drop′out′), *n.* someone who leaves school, a course, an activity, a social group, etc.; as, a school *dropout;* a social *dropout;* a corporate *dropout.*—*v.i.* **drop′ out′.**

drought (drout), *n.* continued absence of rain or moisture.

[1]**drove** (drōv), *n.* **1,** a herd of animals driven in a body; **2,** a crowd of people, esp. when running along together.

[2]**drove** (drōv), *p.t.* of *drive.*

dro-ver (drō′vėr), *n.* **1,** one who drives cattle to market; **2,** a dealer in cattle.

drown (droun), *v.i.* to die from suffocation in water or other liquid:—*v.t.* **1,** to kill by plunging under water; **2,** to overpower or cover up one sound with a louder sound; as, the noise *drowned* out the music.

drowse (drouz), *v.i.* [drowsed, drows-ing], to be heavy with sleep; doze:—*v.t.* to spend (time) dozing; as, to *drowse* an afternoon away:—*n.* a light sleep, or doze.

drow-sy (drou′zi), *adj.* [drow-si-er, drow-si-est], **1,** not fully awake; sleepy; as, a *drowsy* feeling; **2,** making one sleepy; as, a *drowsy* sound.—*adv.* **drow′si-ly.**—*n.* **drow′si-ness.**

drudge (druj), *v.i.* [drudged, drudg-ing], to work hard at disagreeable tasks; slave:—*n.* one employed in disagreeable or hard work.—*n.* **drudg′er-y.**

drug (drug), *n.* **1,** a medicine, or a substance used in making medicine, used to treat or cure disease or pain in the body; **2,** a habit-forming substance, or narcotic, such as opium, nicotine, etc.; **3,** an article that sells slowly; as, a *drug* on the market:—*v.t.* [drugged, drug-ging], **1,** to give a drug to a person, esp. harmful or sleep-inducing drugs; **2,** to mix drugs with; as, to *drug* food; **3,** to render unconscious or put to sleep with a drug; as, she *drugged* herself with sleeping pills.

drug-gist (drug′ist), *n.* a licenced dealer in medicinal drugs. Also called *pharmacist.*

drug-store (drug′stōr′), *n.* a store where drugs and other miscellaneous goods, such as candy, perfumes, etc., are sold. Also called *pharmacy*.

dru-id or **Dru-id** (dro͞o′id), *n.* a priest of a religious cult of ancient Britain and Gaul.—*adj.* **dru-id′ic; dru-id′i-cal.**

drum (drum), *n.* **1,** a musical instrument consisting of a hollow cylinder with a cover stretched across the ends, and beaten with sticks or the hands; **2,** anything like a drum, as a cylinder for winding rope or wire, or a cylindrical container, as for oil:—*v.i.* [drummed, drum-ming], **1,** to beat or play a drum; **2,** to beat rapidly upon something with the fingers:—*v.t.* **1,** to cause to beat against something; as, to *drum* one's feet on the floor; **2,** to beat (up) or summon; as, to *drum* up trade; **3,** to repeat constantly; as, this idea has been *drummed* into me.

drum-mer (drum′ėr), *n.* **1,** one who plays a drum; **2,** *Colloq.* a salesperson.

drum-stick (drum′stik′), *n.* **1,** a stick for beating a drum; **2,** the lower joint of the leg of a chicken, turkey, etc.

drunk (drungk), a *p.p.* of *drink*:—*adj.* intoxicated:—*n. Slang* a drinking spree.

drunk-ard (drungk′ėrd), *n.* one who is habitually intoxicated or frequently drinks liquor.

drunk-en (drungk′en), *adj.* intoxicated; also, due to drink; as, a *drunken* stupor.—*adv.* **drunk′en-ly.**—*n.* **drunk′en-ness.**

dry (drī), *adj.* [dri-er, dri-est], **1,** without moisture or water; as, *dry* land; **2,** empty of water; as, a *dry* well; also, *Colloq.* thirsty; **3,** lacking in interest; as, a *dry* speech; **4,** harsh; as, a *dry*, hacking cough; **5,** shrewd and sharp; as, *dry* wit; **6,** *Colloq.* forbidding the sale of intoxicants; as, *dry* cities; *dry* laws:—*v.t.* and *v.i.* [dried, dry-ing], to make or become dry.—*n.* **dry′ness.**—*adv.* **dry′ly** or **dri′ly.**

dry cell, an electric cell, the current of which is produced by a chemical paste that cannot spill; a dry battery.

dry–clean (drī′–klēn′), *v.t.* to clean garments, etc., with an agent other than water, such as petroleum-based solvents.

dry dock (drī′dok′), *n.* a dock built so that the water can be pumped out after a ship has entered it, used for repairs, shipbuilding, etc.—*v.t.* and *v.i.* **dry′–dock′.**

dry-er (drī′ėr), *n.* Same as **drier.**

du-al (dū′al), *adj.* pertaining to two; composed of two; twofold; double; two matching or similar parts; as, *dual* ownership; a *dual*-engine plane.

du-al-ism (dū′al-izm), *n.* being of two parts, as in one human being (or universe) mind and matter, soul and body, good and evil, etc., the two parts or natures often being opposed or irreconcilable; duality.

dub (dub), *v.t.* [dubbed, dub-bing], **1,** to bestow knighthood upon by tapping the shoulder with a sword; **2,** to confer any title, name, or nickname upon; as, they *dubbed* her "Tommy"; **3,** to do awkwardly; as, to *dub* a golf stroke; **4,** to beat a drum; **5,** to replace the sound track of a movie, television show, or radio program with another version; as, to *dub* the Chinese movie with English dialogue; also, to add or rerecord the sound track:—*n. Slang* an awkward player.

du-bi-ous (dū′bi-us), *adj.* **1,** doubtful; as, a *dubious* venture; **2,** questionable; as, a person of *dubious* reputation.

duch-ess (duch′es), *n.* **1,** the wife or widow of a duke: a noble title or rank just below princess; **2,** a woman with the rank or authority of a duke.

duch-y (duch′i), *n.* [*pl.* duchies], the territory or dominion of a duke.

[1]**duck** (duk), *n.* **1,** a flat-billed waterfowl with short legs and neck and webbed feet; **2,** the female duck as distinguished from the male, or *drake*; **3,** *Colloq.* a pet or favourite.—*adj. Slang* **duck′y; duck′-tailed′.**—*n.* **duck′ling.**

[2]**duck** (duk), *v.t.* **1,** to plunge (the head) for an instant under water; also, to throw (a person) into the water; **2,** to bend down; as, to *duck* the head; **3,** *Colloq.* to avoid, as by quickly bowing the head; as, to *duck* a blow:—*v.i.* **1,** to take a quick dip into water; **2,** to move the head or body aside quickly; dodge:—*n.* **1,** a dip or quick plunge under water; **2,** a sudden lowering of the head.

duct (dukt), *n.* **1,** a canal, tube, or passage by which fluid is carried; **2,** a tube or vessel of the body, esp. one for carrying a secretion; as, tear *ducts;* **3,** a tube or pipe for cables, wires, etc.—*adj.* **duct′less.**

A

TEAR DUCT OPENING (A)

duc-tile (duk′tīl), *adj.* **1,** capable of being drawn out into strands; easily moulded; as, copper is highly *ductile;* **2,** easily influenced or led.

duct tape, a strong, silver-coloured tape used for sealing the joints in air ducts and for general repairs.

dud (dud), *n.* a shell that fails to explode; hence, a futile person or device.

dude (dūd), *n.* **1,** a man who is overrefined

in manner or dress; a dandy; **2,** a city person who spends time on a ranch, esp. for amusement; **3,** *Slang* any person.

duds (dudz), *n. Colloq.* clothes; rags; possessions.

due (dū), *adj.* **1,** owed or owing; payable; as, the rent is *due* today; **2,** suitable; proper; as, *due* courtesy; **3,** scheduled or expected; as, *due* at noon; **4,** caused by; as, an accident *due* to carelessness:—*adv.* exactly; directly; as, *due* west:—*n.* **1,** that which rightfully belongs to someone; as, give him his *due*:—**dues,** the money paid for membership in a club or organization.

du-el (dū′el), *n.* **1,** in former times, a combat between two persons to settle a quarrel or point of honour, usually planned beforehand and fought with deadly weapons before witnesses, called seconds; **2,** any conflict or contest between people, ideas, or things; as, a *duel* of wits:—*v.i.* [duelled, duel-ling or dueled, duel-ing], to fight a duel.—*n.* **du′el-ling; du′el-list.**

du-et (dū′et′), *n.* a musical composition for two performers.

duf-fel (duf′l), *n.* a camper's kit:—**duffel bag,** a large bag for carrying personal belongings, clothing, etc.

duf-fer (duf′ėr), *n. Colloq.* a stupid, dull, or incompetent person.

dug (dug), *p.t.* and *p.p.* of *dig.*

dug-out (dug′out′), *n.* **1,** a trench or cave used as a shelter against bombs, gunfire, etc.; **2,** in *baseball,* an enclosure next to the baseball field for the members of the two opposing teams to sit when not playing; **3,** a canoe hollowed out from a log.

duke (dūk), *n.* **1,** a member of the nobility next below a prince; **2,** the ruler of a duchy.—*n.* **duke′dom.**—*adj.* **du′cal.**

dul-cet (dul′sit), *adj.* sweet, esp. to the ear; as, *dulcet* tones or notes.

dull (dul), *adj.* **1,** not sharp-edged; blunt; as, a *dull* knife; **2,** lacking keenness or liveliness; as, a *dull* person; **3,** slow of understanding or action; not alert; as, a *dull* student; **4,** not clear or vivid; as, a *dull* colour; a *dull* sound; **5,** pointless; boring; as, a *dull* story:—*v.t.* and *v.i.* to make or become dull.—*adv.* **dul′ly.**—*n.* **dull′ness; dul′ness; dul′lard.**

du-ly (dū′li), *adv.* in a fit and becoming manner; regularly; as, *duly* elected officers.

dumb (dum), *adj.* **1,** unable to speak; as, to be struck *dumb* by the horrible tragedy; **2,** *Colloq.* stupid; foolish.—*n.* **dumb′ness.**

dumb-bell or **dumb–bell** (dum′bel′; dum′–bel′), *n.* **1,** one of a pair of weights, each consisting of two balls of wood or metal joined by a short bar that serves as a grip, used to build muscles; **2,** *Slang* an ignorant or stupid person.

dumb-found or **dum-found** (dum′found′; dum′found′), *v.t.* to amaze; make dumb with surprise or fear.—*adj.* **dumb′found′ed.**

dumb-wait-er (dum′wāt′ėr), *n.* a small elevator for moving dishes or supplies from one floor to another.

dum-my (dum′i), *n.* [*pl.* dummies], **1,** one who is silent; also, a stupid person; **2,** an imitation; hence, a copy of a human figure for showing clothing; **3,** in some card games, an exposed hand played by the partner; also, the player whose hand is exposed; **4,** a person who acts for another, when he or she seems to be acting for himself or herself; **5,** anything made to look like something else and be used in its place; a sample showing the general appearance of something; as, a *dummy* of a book:—*adj.* sham; counterfeit; as, a *dummy* drawer.

dump (dump), *v.t.* **1,** to unload; as, they *dumped* sand from the barrel; **2,** in *computing,* to transfer or delete stored data in a computer; as, to *dump* old and useless files; **3,** to print out such data:—*n.* **1,** a place for rubbish; as, the city *dump*; **2,** a heap of refuse.

dump-ling (dump′ling), *n.* **1,** a small mass of dough boiled in soup or stew; **2,** a shell of dough enclosing fruit or meat and either baked or boiled; as, an apple *dumpling.*

[1]**dun** (dun), *n.* **1,** an urgent request or demand for the payment of a debt; **2,** one who demands payment of a debt repeatedly:—*v.t.* [dunned, dun-ning], to plague by frequent demands for payment.

[2]**dun** (dun), *adj.* of a dull brownish or greyish colour.

dunce (duns), *n.* a dull, ignorant person; also, a student slow at learning.

dune (dūn), *n.* a low hill of drifted sand piled up by the wind, esp. along the seashore.

dung (dung), *n.* waste material from animals; manure.

dun-geon (dun′-jun), *n.* a dark underground cell for prisoners.

dunk (dungk), *v.t.* **1,** to dip something or somebody into liquid; **2,** in *basketball,* to jump and drop the ball through the hoop.

duo (dū′ō; do͞o′ō), *n.* [*pl.* duos (-ōz); dui (do͞o′i)], in *music,* a duet.

dupe (dūp), *n.* one who is easily tricked, or believes everything he or she is told:—*v.t.* [duped, dup-ing], to deceive by trickery.

du-pli-cate (dū′pli-kāt′), *v.t.* [duplicat-ed, duplicat-ing], **1,** to reproduce exactly; make a copy or copies of; as, to use a photocopier to *duplicate* documents; **2,** to do or make again; repeat; as, to *duplicate* a winning season:—*adj.* (dū′pli-kit), **1,** corresponding exactly with another; as, a *duplicate* key; **2,** double; twofold:—*n.* (dū′pli-kit), **1,** something exactly like another; a copy, as of a letter; **2,** exact likeness between two things; double; as, a *duplicate* dress.—*n.* **du′pli-ca′tion.**

du-plic-i-ty (dū-pli′si-ti), *n.* deceitfulness.

du-ra-ble (dū′ra-bl), *adj.* permanent and lasting; resisting wear; as, *durable* cloth.—*adv.* **du′ra-bly.**—*n.* **du′ra-bil′i-ty.**

du-ra-tion (dū-rā′shun), *n.* the time anything lasts; as, the *duration* of a game.

dur-ess (dū′res; dū-res′), *n.* **1,** compulsion, as by threat or violence: he signed under *duress*; **2,** imprisonment.

dur-ing (dūr′ing), *prep.* throughout the period of; in the time of; as, to talk *during* a film.

dusk (dusk), *adj.* dim; shadowy:—*n.* **1,** the dim light at the beginning and end of daylight; evening, just before dark; **2,** shadow; gloom.—*adj.* **dusk′y.**

dust (dust), *n.* **1,** fine, dry particles of earth or other matter; a cloud or film of such fine particles; **2,** the earth or its surface; the remains of a human body:—*v.i.* to remove dust from furniture, etc.:—*v.t.* **1,** to brush away dust from; as, to *dust* the table; **2,** to cover or sprinkle, as with powder.—*n.* **dust′er; dust′y; dust′i-ness.**—*adj.* **dust′less.**

Dutch (duch), *n.* **1**, a person who inhabits or originates from Holland; **2**, the language of these people:—*adj.* relating to the country, the people, the languages, or the culture of the Netherlands.

du-ti-ful (dū′ti-fool), *adj.* obedient and respectful; as, a *dutiful* child.—*adv.* **du′ti-ful-ly.**

du-ty (dū′ti), *n.* [*pl.* duties], **1,** the respectful, proper, or lawful behaviour; **2,** action required in a certain office or position; as, the *duties* of a chairperson; **3,** that which one is morally bound to do; **4,** a tax levied by the government for goods brought into a country.

DVD (dē′vē′dē′), *n. abbrev.* short for *d*igital *v*ideo *d*isc; also *d*igital *v*ersatile *d*isc, an optical storage device similar to a compact disc (CD), but larger.

dwarf (dwôrf), *n.* [*pl.* dwarfs (dwôrfs)], **1,** a person, animal, or plant much below usual size; **2,** in fairy tales, a very small person who often has magic powers:—*adj.* of smaller size or height than the average; as, a *dwarf* rose:—*v.t.* **1,** to hinder from growing to natural size; as, the drought *dwarfed* the corn; **2,** to cause to look small by comparison; as, the skyscraper *dwarfs* the store next to it.

dwell (dwel), *v.i.* [dwelt (dwelt) or dwelled (dweld), dwell-ing], **1,** to reside; live in a place; **2,** to think, write, or speak about at length; linger; as, to *dwell* on a subject.

dwell-ing (dwel′ing), *n.* a residence; a place where someone lives; one's home.

dwin-dle (dwin′dl), *v.i.* [dwin-dled, dwin-dling], to become gradually less; shrink.

dye (dī), *v.t.* [dyed, dye-ing], to stain or colour (fabric, shoes, hair, food, etc.):—*v.i.* to take colour in dyeing; as, this silk *dyes* well:—*n.* **1,** colouring matter used in dyeing; **2,** a colour produced by dyeing.

dyed–in–the–wool, *adj.* unchangeable; as, a *dyed-in-the-wool* Tory.

dy-ing (dī′ing), *p.p.* of [1]*die*:—*adj.* **1,** passing from life; as, a *dying* man; **2,** drawing to a close; as, the *dying* year; **3,** said or done at the time of death:—*n.* the act of passing from life.

dy-nam-ic (dī-nam′ik; di-nam′ik), *adj.* **1,** relating to power or physical energy; **2,** forceful.—*adv.* **dy-nam′i-cal-ly.**

dy-na-mite (dī′na-mīt′), *n.* a highly explosive mixture, usually made from nitroglycerine, used for blasting rocks, etc.:—*v.t.* [dynamit-ed, dynamit-ing], to destroy or blast by the explosion of dynamite.

dy-na-mo (dī′na-mō′), *n.* [*pl.* dynamos], **1,** a machine that converts mechanical energy into electric current; a generator; **2,** an energetic and forceful person.

dy-nas-ty (din′as-ti; dī′nas-ti), *n.* [*pl.* dynasties], a line or succession of sovereigns or leaders of the same family; as, the Tudor *dynasty*.—*adj.* **dy-nas′tic** (dī-nas′tik).—*n.* **dy′nast.**

dyne (dīn), *n.* in the *centimetre–gram–second* system, the force that, acting on a mass of one gram for one second, produces a velocity of one centimetre per second.

dys-en-ter-y (dis′en-tėr-i), *n.* a disease of the bowels, marked by severe inflammation and mucoid, bloody discharges.

dys-tro-phy (dis′trō-fi), *n.* a wasting disease that robs the muscles of power until the victim is helpless; as, muscular *dystrophy*.

E

E, e (ē), *n.* [*pl.* E's, e's], **1,** the fifth letter of the alphabet; **2,** *in music,* the third tone of the major scale of C.

e– (ē–), *prefix* meaning *electronic*; as, *e*-book, *e*-business, *e*-file, *e*-investing, *e*-mail, *e*-ticket, etc.

each (ēch), *pron.* every one of a number considered separately; as, *each* of the girls brings her lunch:—*adj.* every (one) of two or more taken separately; as, they study *each* lesson carefully.

ea-ger (ē′gėr), *adj.* full of keen desire; impatiently anxious to do or have something; as, he was *eager* to learn:—**eager beaver,** *Colloq.*

someone who is extremely diligent or eager.—*adv.* **ea′ger-ly.**

ea-gle (ē′gl), *n.* **1,** a bird of prey, akin to the hawks and kites, noted for its strength, size, and keen vision; **2,** in *golf,* a score of two strokes less than par on a hole:—**eagle eye,** exceptional sight.—*adj.* **ea′gle-eyed′** (having keen sight; keeping careful and alert watchfulness).

[1]ear (ēr), *n.* **1,** the entire organ of hearing; also, the outer, visible part of that organ; **2,** the sense of hearing; unusual ability to hear delicate sounds; as, she has an *ear* for music; **3,** attention; heed; as, give *ear* to what I say; **4,** the spike of a cereal plant, containing the grains; as, an *ear* of corn or wheat; **5,** anything like an external ear in shape.—*adj.* **ear′split′ting.**—*n.* **ear′ache′; ear′wax′.**

ear-drum (ēr′drum′), *n.* the middle ear; esp., the thin membrane between the outer and the middle ear.

ear-ful (ēr′fool′), *n. Colloq.* **1,** news; **2,** gossip; **3,** a scolding.

earl (ûrl), *n.* a British nobleman next below a marquis.—*n.* **earl′dom.**

ear-ly (ûr′li), *adj.* [ear-li-er, ear-li-est], **1,** near the beginning; as, *early* spring; **2,** before the usual time; in good time; as, an *early* riser:—*adv.* **1,** at or near the beginning; as, he arrived *early* in the week; **2,** before the usual time; in good time; as, he goes to bed *early*:—**early bird,** one who wakes up early or who arrives before others.—*n.* **ear′li-ness.**

ear-mark (ēr′mark′), *v.t.* to set aside for a particular purpose:—*n.* any distinguishing mark; as, the CD's *earmark* was its unique lyrics.

ear-muffs (ēr′mufs′), *n.* coverings for the ears in cold weather.

earn (ûrn), *v.t.* **1,** to receive pay for working; as, he *earns* $50 a day; **2,** to get something one deserves; as, he *earned* a rest or a bad reputation.—*n.pl.* **earn′ings.**

earned run (ûrnd′ run′) *n.* a run given up by a baseball pitcher that is not the result of an error:—**earned run average**, the calculated average of earned runs.

ear-nest (ûr′nist), *adj.* important; grave; as, life is *earnest.*

ear-phones (ēr′fōnz′), *n.* small speakers for listening to radios, telephones, etc., that fit in or over the ears; a headset.

ear-piece (ēr′pēs′), *n.* part of a device such as a hearing aid, stethoscope, or telephone that fits in or on the ear; an earphone; the parts of eyeglasses that fit on the ears.

ear-pierc-ing (ēr′pērs′ing), *adj.* extremely loud; deafening; earsplitting; as, the *earpiercing* sound of thunder.

ear-plug (ēr′plug′), *n.* **1,** an object of soft, pliable material such as rubber or wax that is inserted in the outer ear to protect against loud noise, water, etc.; **2,** an earphone that fits inside the ear.

ear-ring (ēr′ring′), *n.* an ear ornament.

ear-shot (ēr′shot′), *n.* the distance within which the voice can be heard; the range of hearing; as, to walk beyond *earshot.*

ear-split-ting (ēr′split′ing), *adj.* excessively loud or shrill; painfully noisy; deafening; earpiercing.

earth (ûrth), *n.* **1,** (also **Earth**) the planet on which we live, the third from the sun; **2,** the solid materials which compose its surface; dry land; **3,** ground; soil; as, rich *earth;* **4,** excessive amount; as, cost the *earth.*—*n.* **earth′ling.**

earth-en (ûr′then), *adj.* made of earth or baked clay; as, an *earthen* floor or jar.—*n.* **earth′en-ware′.**

earth-ly (ûrth′li), *adj.* **1,** pertaining to this world or to the present life; material; as, *earthly* possessions; **2,** possible; as, he has no *earthly* reason to go.—*n.* **earth′li-ness.**

earth-quake (ûrth′kwāk′), *n.* a sudden shaking, often violent, of the earth's surface, usually caused by a splitting and sliding of the rock foundation.

earth sci-ence (ûrth′ sī′ens), *n.* any of the sciences, such as geology or meteorology, that deals with the earth.

earth–shat-ter-ing (ûrth′–shat′ėr-ing), *adj.* **1,** very important; **2,** having a widespread, often traumatic effect; **3,** something revolutionary that challenges basic beliefs.

earth-ward (ûrth′wėrd), *adv.* toward the earth. Also, **earth′wards.**

earth-work (ûrth′wûrk′), *n.* an embankment made wholly or largely of earth.

earth-worm (ûrth′wûrm′), *n.* a burrowing worm that lives in the ground; an angle-worm.

earth-y (ûr′thi), *adj.* **1,** made of, or like, soil; as, *earthy* colours; **2,** open and direct, often coarse or crude; as, *earthy* language.—*n.* **earth′i-ness.**

ear-wig (ēr′wig′), *n.* a small insect with a pair of pincers, formerly supposed to creep into the ear.

ease (ēz), *n.* **1,** freedom from pain, labour, worry, trouble, difficulty, effort, etc.; as, a life of *ease;* run with *ease;* **2,** naturalness; as, *ease* of manner:—*v.t.* [eased, eas-ing], **1,** to free from pain, anxiety, stress, etc.; give relief to; as, medicine to *ease* pain; good news *eases* the mind; **2,** to loosen anything tight; as, to *ease* a band; also, to move gently; as, to *ease* a stretcher into an ambulance.

ea-sel (ē′zl), *n.* a frame for supporting an artist's canvas, a blackboard, or the like.

eas-i-ly (ēz′i-li), *adv.* **1,** without difficulty; readily; **2,** without doubt or question; as, *easily* the best video game; **3,** probably; as, we could *easily* have a snowstorm; **4,** comfortably; as, the patient rested *easily.*

east (ēst), *n.* **1,** that part of the heavens where the sun is seen to rise; **2,** one of the four points of the compass: opposite of *west*:—**East, 1,** the countries of Asia; **2,** in western Canada, the provinces east of Manitoba; in central Canada, the Atlantic provinces (N.B., N.S., P.E.I., and Newfoundland):—*adj.* coming from the direction of the east; as, an *east* wind; in the direction of the east; as, the *east* side of the street:—*adv.* in the direction of the east; as, facing *east*.

east-bound (ēst′bound′), *adj.* going eastward.

East-er (ēs′tėr), *n.* a festival of the Christian church to commemorate the resurrection of Jesus Christ, observed on a Sunday between March 21 and April 26.

east-er-ly (ēs′tėr-li), *adj.* **1,** eastward; as, an *easterly* direction; **2,** from the direction of the east; as, an *easterly* wind:—*adv.* in the direction of the east.

east-ern (ēs′tėrn), *adj.* **1,** grown or produced in the east; as, *eastern* potatoes; **2,** situated in the east; as, an *eastern* city:—**Eastern,** pertaining to Asia; Asian; as, *Eastern* religions.—*n.* **east′ern-er.**—*adj.* **east′ern-most.**

east-ward or **east-wards** (ēst′wėrd; ēst′wėrdz), *adj.* to or toward the east; as, steer an *eastward* course:—*adv.* to or toward the east; as, we journeyed *eastward*.

eas-y (ēz′i), *adj.* [eas-i-er, eas-i-est], **1,** free from troubles or worry; as, an *easy* life; **2,** comfortable; restful; **3,** not difficult; **4,** moderate; gentle; as, an *easy* pace; **5,** not exacting; as, an *easy* teacher; **6,** promiscuous.—*n.* **eas′i-ness.**

easy chair, a large, comfortable armchair for relaxation.

eas-y-go-ing (ēz′i-gō′ing), *adj.* relaxed and calm; unhurried; careless.

easy listening, music that is undemanding and conventional.

easy street, a state of wealth or financial independence; a worry-free existence.

eat (ēt), *v.t.* [*p.t.* ate (āt) or eat (et), *p.p.* eaten (ēt′n), *p.pr.* eat-ing], **1,** to chew and swallow, as food; **2,** to corrode; waste or wear away; as, the river *ate* away the banks:—*v.i.* **1,** to take food; as, we always *eat* here; **2,** to make a way (into), as by eating; as, acids *eat* into metal; expenses *eat* into one's money.—*n.* **eat′er.**

eat-a-ble (ēt′a-bl), *adj.* fit to eat.—*n.pl.* food.

eat-er-y (ē′tėr-i), *n. Colloq.* a restaurant or other enterprise that serves food.

eat-ing dis-or-der (ēt′ing dis-ôr′der), *n.* a psychological disorder, such as anorexia nervosa or bulimia, resulting from a neurotic fear of becoming overweight.

eaves (ēvz), *n.pl.* the lower edges of a roof which project a little from the building.

eaves-drop (ēvz′drop′), *v.i.* [eaves-dropped, eavesdrop-ping], to listen secretly to the private conversation of others.—*n.* **eaves′-drop′ping.**—*n.* **eaves′drop′per.**

eaves-trough (ēvz′trôf′), *n.* a trough or channel placed under the eves of a roof to carry away runoff water; a gutter.

ebb (eb), *n.* **1,** the going out of the tide; **2,** a decline; low state; as, his courage was at its lowest *ebb*:—*v.i.* **1,** to flow back or return; as, the tide *ebbs* to the sea; **2,** to decline; decay; as, his fortune *ebbs*.

eb-on-y (eb′un-i), *n.* [*pl.* ebonies], a hard, heavy, durable, black-coloured wood; also, the tree furnishing it:—*adj.* made of, or like, ebony; as, the *ebony* keys on a piano; black like *ebony*.

e-bul-lient (i-bul′yent), *adj.* enthusiastic; lively; exuberant; as, an *ebullient* youth.—*n.* **e-bul′lience.**

ec-cen-tric (ek-sen′trik), *adj.* **1,** odd; peculiar; not in the normal or usual way; as, an *eccentric* person has strange habits; **2,** out of centre; not revolving about its centre; elliptical, as the earth's course around the sun:—*n.* **1,** one who or that which is odd or peculiar; **2,** a circle or sphere not having the same centre as another circle or sphere with which it partly coincides.—*n.* **ec′cen-tric′i-ty** (ek′sen-tris′i-ti).

ec-cle-si-as-tic (i-klē′zi-as′tik), *adj.* pertaining to the church and its organization or government:—*n.* a person in holy orders; a clergyman; priest.—*adj.* **ec-cle′-si-as′ti-cal.**

ech-e-lon (esh′e-lon; āsh′), *n.* **1,** an arrangement of troops, ships, airplanes, etc., in a steplike formation; as, the troops marched in *echelon;* **2,** the grade or level in an organization or field; also, the people or group in that level; as, the top *echelon* in the company.

e-chin-a-cea (ek-i-nā′shu), *n.* **1,** a plant of the daisy family, esp. the purple cornflower; **2,** a herbal remedy made from this plant.

ech-o (ek′ō), *n.* [*pl.* echoes], **1,** the repetition of a sound caused by the throwing back of sound waves; **2,** any repetition or imitation:—*v.t.* [echoed, echo-ing], **1,** to give back or repeat a sound; as, the corridors *echoed* with footsteps; **2,** to repeat the sound of; imitate.

e-clair (ā-klâr′), *n.* a small, iced, oblong pastry containing whipped cream or custard.

e-clec-tic (e-klek′tic), *adj.* selected or made up of many styles, methods, systems, etc., or from many sources; heterogeneous; mixed; as, to have *eclectic* tastes in music:—*n.* a person who uses or has such an approach.

e-clipse (i-klips′), *n.* **1,** the obscuring of a celestial body, such as the sun, moon, or other planet, by another; **2,** an overshadowing; loss of importance, brilliance, or glory:—*v.t.* [eclipsed, eclips-ing], **1,** to darken or conceal, as one body overshadows another; **2,** to outshine; surpass, reduce in importance; as, his success *eclipsed* his father's.

E. co-li (ē.ʹkoʹlī), *n.* the bacterial *Escherichia coli,* which, in its toxic form, can cause gastrointestinal infections, resulting in dysentery and even death.

e-col-o-gy (i-kôlʹo-ji; ē-kôlʹo-ji), *n.* **1,** the scientific study of the relationships between living organisms and their environment; **2,** the set of relationships between these; as, human *ecology* studies the impact of people on the environment; **3,** the advocacy of the need to protect the natural environment.—*n.* **e-colʹo-gist.**

e-con-o-met-ric (ēʹko-no-metʹrik; eʹko-no-metʹrik), *n.* the application of mathematical and statistical methods to economic problems.

e-co-nom-ic (ēʹko-nomʹik; ekʹo-nomʹik), *adj.* relating to the production and use of wealth; as, the *economic* policy of a country:—**economics,** *n.pl.* used as *sing.* the science dealing with the production and use of wealth.—*n.* **e-conʹo-mist** (ē-konʹo-mist).

e-co-nom-i-cal (ēʹko-nomʹi-kal; ekʹo-nomʹi-kal), *adj.* thrifty; saving money or resources; using or operating with little waste.—*adv.* **eʹco-nomʹi-cal-ly.**

e-con-o-mize (ē-konʹo-mizʹ), *v.t.* [economized, economiz-ing], **1,** to use sparingly; **2,** to use to the best advantage:—*v.t.* to be careful in spending money; avoid extravagance; as, after two months of unemployment, she began to *economize.*

e-con-o-my (ē-konʹo-mi), *n.* [*pl.* economies], **1,** freedom from waste in the use of anything; thrift; **2,** the regulation and management of the resources of a group.—*n.* **e-conʹo-mist.**

e-co-sphere (ēʹkōʹsfēr; eʹkōʹsfēr), *n.* **1,** the parts of the universe that are able to sustain life; **2,** the biosphere of earth.

e-co-sys-tem (ēʹkōʹsisʹtem; eʹkōʹsisʹtem), *n.* a system formed by all the living plants and animals in one area or habitat, as well as their interactions with the environment.

e-co-ter-ror-ism (ēʹkōʹterʹėr-izm; eʹkōʹterʹėr-izm), *n.* **1,** violent, destructive, or disruptive activities carried out to further radical environmentalist goals; **2,** the deliberate destruction of the environment, as in wartime.—*n.* **eʹcoʹterʹror-istʹ.**

ec-ru (ekʹrōō; ā-krōōʹ; āʹkrōō), *adj.* pale brown; like unbleached linen in colour:—*n.* the colour of unbleached linen.

ec-sta-sy (ekʹsta-si), *n.* [*pl.* ecstasies], **1,** deep emotion, esp. rapturous joy; as, she felt *ecstasy* when he proposed; **2,** a hallucinogenic drug (MDMA).—*adj.* **ec-statʹic** (ek-statʹik).

ec-u-men-i-cal (ekʹū-menʹi-kal), *adj.* worldwide; universal; esp., of the Christian church as a whole: an ecumenical council would represent the entire Christian church.

ec-ze-ma (ekʹzi-m*a*; ekʹsi-m*a*), *n.* a skin disease usually attended by the formation of reddish scales and intense itching.

ed-dy (edʹi), *n.* [*pl.* eddies], a current of air, water, or the like, running opposite to the main current, thus taking on a circular motion; a small whirlpool:—*v.t.* and *v.i.* [eddied, eddy-ing], to move with a circular motion; whirl; as, smoke *eddies* from a chimney.

edge (ej), *n.* **1,** the thin, sharp, or cutting part of a knife or tool; **2,** extreme border; brink; margin; as, the *edge* of a chair; the *edge* of a brook; **3,** keenness; sharpness; as, her remarks had an *edge:*—*v.t.* [edged, edging], **1,** to furnish with a border; as, to *edge* a handkerchief with lace; **2,** to move carefully, little by little; as, to *edge* a car into traffic:—*v.i.* to move along little by little; as, to *edge* along a cliff.—*adj.* **edgʹy.**

edg-ing (ejʹing), *n.* a narrow border, as of lace, used as trimming.

edg-y (ejʹi), *adj.* **1,** nervous, irritable, tense, or anxious; **2,** unconventional and innovative; sharp-witted; as, to have an *edgy* sense of humour.

ed-i-ble (edʹi-bl), *adj.* fit to be used for food; as, the salmon is an *edible* fish.—*n.* **edʹi-bilʹi-ty.**

e-dict (ēʹdikt), *n.* a public order issued by an official authority and having the force of a law; a decree.

ed-i-fice (edʹi-fis), *n.* **1,** a building, esp. one that is large and imposing; **2,** a complex structure or organization.

ed-it (edʹit), *v.t.* **1,** to check, correct, and improve writing; as, to *edit* your term paper; **2,** to revise and prepare writing for publication; **3,** to prepare a film, video, or audio tape recording or the like by arranging and cutting the available materials; **4,** to direct the policies of (a newspaper, magazine, or the like).—*n.* **edʹi-tor.**

e-di-tion (i-dishʹun), *n.* **1,** the published form of a literary work; **2,** the number of copies, all exactly alike, of a book, magazine, or newspaper, published at or near the same time.

ed-i-tor-i-al (edʹi-tōrʹi-al), *n.* an article in a newspaper, magazine, etc., or a statement on television or radio, expressing the official opinions of the editors or publishers on some topic:—*adj.* connected with editors or their work.

ed-u-cate (edʹū-kāt), *v.t.* [educat-ed, educat-ing], to develop and improve, esp. mentally, by teaching or training; instruct; as, to *educate* children.—*adj.* **edʹu-ca-ble; edʹu-caʹtive.**

ed-u-ca-tion (edʹū-kāʹshun), *n.* **1,** the development of the mind and character through study, training, and experience, as by a system of study and discipline; also, the system itself; **2,** the knowledge and abilities gained by such training.—*adj.* **ed′u-ca′tion-al.**—*n.* **ed′u-ca′tion-al-ist; ed′u-ca′tion-ist.**

e-duce (i-dūs), *v.t.* to draw out; elicit; as, to *educe* a boy's faults (in order to correct them) or his virtues (to develop them).—*adj.* **e-duc′i-ble.**

eel (ēl), *n.* a long, snakelike fish with smooth, slimy skin.

ee-rie or **ee-ry** (ē′ri), *adj.* weird, strange, scary, and frightening; as, an *eerie* shriek.—*adv.* **ee′ri-ly.**—*n.* **ee′ri-ness.**

ef-fect (i-fekt′), *n.* **1,** result; consequence; **2,** impression; as, to do something for *effect;* **3, effects**, movable goods; personal property; as, household *effects:*—*v.t.* to accomplish; bring about; as, to *effect* a change in a plan.

ef-fec-tive (i-fek′tiv), *adj.* **1,** having the power to produce a desired result; as, an *effective* censorship; **2,** impressive; striking; as, an *effective* picture; **3,** operative; enforced; as, after a law is passed, time may elapse before it becomes *effective.*—*adv.* **ef-fec′tive-ly.**

ef-fec-tu-al (i-fek′tū-al), *adj.* producing, or having the ability to produce, a desired result.—*adv.* **ef-fec′tu-al-ly.**

ef-fem-i-nate (i-fem′i-nit), *adj.* having female qualities; overly refined.—*n.* **ef-fem′i-na-cy.**

ef-fer-ves-cent (ef′ėr-ves′ent), *adj.* **1,** bubbly or fizzy, as a gas escaping; **2,** enthusiastic, lively, and excited.—*n.* **ef′fer-ves′cence.**

ef-fete (e-fēt′), *adj.* decadent, ineffectual, weak; as, an *effete* government or civilization.

ef-fi-ca-cy (ef′i-ka-si), *n.* the power to produce desired results; as, the *efficacy* of a remedy.—*adj.* **ef′fi-ca′cious.**

ef-fi-cient (if-fish′ent), *adj.* capable; competent; able to get results; as, an *efficient* secretary.—*n.* **ef-fi′cien-cy.**

ef-fi-gy (ef′i-ji), *n.* [*pl.* effigies], a portrait, image, or other likeness of a person.

ef-flo-res-cence (ef′lo-res′ens), *n.* **1,** bloom or blossoming, as of flowers; **2,** coming to fullness, as of power, beauty, etc.—*adj.* **ef′flo-res′cent.**

ef-flu-ent (ef′loo-ent), *n.* that which flows out, as a stream from a lake, sewage from pipes, or lava from a volcano.

ef-fort (ef′ėrt; ef′ôrt), *n.* the putting forth of exertion, physical or mental; as, it takes *effort* to lift a rock or work out a problem; also, an attempt or endeavour; as, I shall make an *effort* to attend.—*adj.* **ef′fort-less;** **ef′fort-less-ly.**

ef-fron-ter-y (e-frun′tėr-i), *n.* [*pl.* effronteries], shamelessness, boldness, or audacity; rudeness.

ef-ful-gence (i-ful′jens), *n.* brilliance, radiance, or splendour, as of the sun.—*adj.* **ef-ful′gent.**

ef-fu-sion (i-fū′zhun), *n.* **1,** an act of pouring or gushing forth; as, an *effusion* of blood; **2,** an unrestrained outpouring of thought or feeling.—*adj.* **ef-fu′sive.**

e.g. *abbrev.* of "for example"; from the Latin *exempli gratia.*

[1]**egg** (eg), *n.* a reproductive body produced by females of animals, which may develop into a new individual; esp., the oval body produced by birds, insects, fish, and most reptiles, from which the young hatch out.—*n.* **egg′shell′; egg′ white′; egg′ yoke′.**

[2]**egg** (eg), *v.t.* to urge or incite; as, they *egged* him on to try his luck.

egg-head (eg′hed′), *n. Slang* an intellectual (term of contempt).

egg-nog (eg′nog′), *n.* a drink made of eggs beaten up with milk, sugar, spices, and often with alcohol.

egg-plant (eg′plant′), *n.* a cultivated plant or its large, purplish, egg-shaped fruit, used for food.

e-go (ē′gō; e′gō), *n.* **1,** the self; I; thus, his criticism bruised my *ego;* **2,** self-esteem; excessive self-esteem; conceit; egotism:—**ego trip,** *Colloq.* an act or series of acts undertaken to draw attention to oneself or to satisfy one's ego.

eg-o-ism (eg′ō-izm; ē′gō-izm), *n.* the belief that the aim of life is to perfect the self; hence, excessive interest in one's own concerns.—*n.* **e′go-ist.**—*adj.* **e′go-is′tic; e′go-is′ti-cal.**

eg-o-tism (eg′o-tizm; ē′go-tizm), *n.* the habit of talking or writing too much about oneself; conceit.—*n.* **eg′o-tist.**—*adj.* **eg′o-tis′tic; eg′o-tis′ti-cal.**

e-gress (ē′gres), *n.* **1,** a departure or going out; **2,** a means of leaving; an exit.

e-gret (ē′grit; eg′rit), *n.* a large wading bird of the heron family bearing, in the breeding season, long plumes drooping over the tail.

EGRET

eh (ā, e), *interj.* **1,** an expression of surprise or doubt; **2,** *Colloq.* an equivalent of "What did you say?"

ei-der-down (ī′dėr-down′), *n.* **1,** the soft breast feathers of the eider duck, used in pillows, coverlets, or the like; **2,** a down quilt.

eight (āt), *adj.* composed of one more than seven:—*n.* **1,** the number consisting of seven plus one; **2,** a sign representing eight units, as 8 or VIII.

eight-een (ā′tēn), *adj.* composed of ten more than eight:—*n.* **1,** the sum of seventeen and one; **2,** a sign representing eighteen units, as 18 or XVIII.

eight-eenth (ā′tēnth′), *adj.* next after the seventeenth: the ordinal of *eighteen*:—*n.* one of the 18 equal parts of anything.

eighth (āτth), *adj.* next after the seventh: the ordinal of *eight*:—*n.* one of the eight equal parts of anything.

eight-i-eth (ā′ti-eth), *adj.* next after the 79th: the ordinal of *eighty*:—*n.* one of the 80 equal parts of anything.

eight-y (ā′ti), *adj.* composed of one more than 79:—*n.* [*pl.* eighties], **1,** the sum of 79 and one; **2,** a sign representing 80 units, as 80 or LXXX.

ei-ther (ē′*th*ėr, ī′*th*ėr), *adj.* **1,** one or the other of two; as, come *either* today or tomorrow; **2,** each; as, along *either* bank:—*pron.* one of two; as, *either* of the two boys may go:—*conj.* in one of two cases: the correlative of *or;* as, *either* confess or die:—*adv.* also: used after a negative; as, he won't go, and she won't *either.*

e-jac-u-late (ē-jak′ū-lāt′), *v.t.* **1,** to eject suddenly; discharge; emit; to have an orgasm; **2,** to utter suddenly or vehemently; exclaim.—*n.* **e-jac′u-la′tion.**

e-ject (ē-jekt′), *v.t.* to throw or push out; as, to *eject* the tape from the VCR; expel; dismiss (from office); evict or turn out; as, to *eject* a tenant.—*n.* **e-jec′tor; e-jec′tion.**

eke (ēk), *v.t.* [eked, ek-ing], **1,** to manage to live on very little; as, to *eke* out a living by writing; **2,** to make something last longer by strict economy.

e-lab-o-rate (i-lab′o-rāt), *v.t.* [elaborat-ed, elaborat-ing], to work out with great care and detail:—*adj.* (i-lab′o-rit), worked out in detail; highly finished; as, an *elaborate* stage-setting; complicated; as, an *elaborate* plan.—*adv.* **e-lab′o-rate-ly.**—*n.* **e-lab′o-ra′tion.**

é-lan (ā′lôn), *n.* verve, energy, or enthusiasm; flair or style; as, to dance with *élan.*

e-lapse (i-laps′), *v.i.* [elapsed, elaps-ing], to pass or go by; as, hours *elapsed* as she read her new book.

e-las-tic (i-las′tik), *adj.* **1,** having the power of springing back to its original form after being stretched or pressed together, as rubber; **2,** able to rebound from a state of depression; as, an *elastic* disposition; **3,** flexible; easily changed; adaptable:—*n.* **1,** a narrow woven strip or band made in part of rubber; **2,** a rubber band.—*n.* **e-las′tic′i-ty** (i-las′tis′i-ti; ē′las-tis′i-ti).

e-late (i-lāt), *v.t.* [elat-ed, elat-ing], to fill with joy or pride; as, he was *elated* by the applause.—*adj.* **e-lat′ed.**—*n.* **e-la′tion.**

el-bow (el′bō), *n.* **1,** the joint between the upper and lower arm; also, the outer part or curve of this joint; **2,** a bend or angle like that of an elbow when the arm is bent; as, the *elbow* of a pipe:—*v.t.* and *v.i.* to jostle or push (a person), as with the elbows.

elbow grease, hard work; vigorous physical exertion; energy.

el-bow-ing (el′bō-ing), *n.* in *hockey*, illegal interference with an opponent using one's elbows.

elbow room, sufficient or adequate scope or space in which to move or work freely; unrestricted space.

[1]**eld-er** (el′dėr), *adj.* [a *comp.* of *old*], older; superior in rank or station; senior; as, an *elder* brother; the *elder* statesmen:—*n.* **1,** one who is older; **2,** a leader or ruler of a tribe or family.—*adj.* **eld′er-ly** (somewhat old).

eld-est (el′dest), *adj.* [a *superl.* of *old*], oldest of a number of people; as, the *eldest* son.

e-lect (i-lekt′), *v.t.* **1,** to choose or select by vote; as, to *elect* a new mayor; **2,** to choose or decide; as, we *elected* to play cards:—*adj.* chosen for office but not yet in charge; as, the president *elect.*—*n.* **e-lec′tion; e-lec′tor.**

e-lec-tion-eer (i-lek′shu-nēr′), *v.i.* [electioneered, electioneer-ing], to take an active part in an election; to work for the success of a particular candidate or party.

e-lec-tive (i-lek′tiv), *adj.* **1,** chosen by election, as an officer; filled by election, as an office; **2,** open to choice; not urgent; as, *elective* surgery:—*n.* a course of study that a student may choose, as distinguished from one that is compulsory.

e-lec-tric (i-lek′trik) or **e-lec-tri-cal** (i-lek′tri-kal), *adj.* **1,** pertaining to or connected with electricity, its production, transmission, or use; as, an *electric* guitar; *electric* eye; *electric* train; **2,** figuratively, as if charged with electricity; thrilling; exciting; as, an *electric* performance.—*n.* **e-lec-tri′cian.**

e-lec-tric-i-ty (ē′lek-tris′i-ti; el′ek-tris′i-ti), *n.* **1,** a form of energy produced by a current of charged particles, such as electrons, flowing quickly through a wire or other object: an important source of power to produce heat, light, and motion; **2,** electric current; **3,** excitement.

e-lec-tri-fy (i-lek′tri-fī), *v.t.* [electrified, electrify-ing], **1,** to charge with electricity; **2,** to equip for the use of electric power, as a railway; **3,** to thrill; startle; as, the acrobat's feat *electrified* the spectators.

e-lec-tro-cute (i-lek′tro-kūt), *v.t.* [electrocut-ed, electrocut-ing], to kill by an electric shock.—*n.* **e-lec′tro-cu′tion.**

e-lec-trode (i-lek′trōd), *n.* a conductor of electricity, such as the pole of a battery, vacuum tube, electrolytic cell, etc.

e-lec-trol-y-sis (i-lek′trol′i-sis), *n.* **1,** the breaking down of a chemical compound in solution by passing an electric current through it; **2,** the removal of unwanted hair with electrical current.

e-lec-tro-lyte (i-lek′trō-līt′), *n.* a compound capable of being broken down by an electric current.—*adj.* **e-lec′tro-lyt′ic.**

e-lec-tro-mag-net (i-lek′trō-mag′nit), *n.* a piece of soft iron made into a magnet by passing an electric current through a coil of wire wrapped around it.—*adj.* **e-lec′tro-mag-net′ic.**

e-lec-tron (i-lek′tron), *n.* an extremely small, subatomic, negatively charged particle, which is a component of every atom.

e-lec-tron-ic mail (i-lek′tron′ik māl′), *n.* Same as **e-mail.**

e-lec-tron-ics (i-lek′tron′iks), *n.* **1,** the scientific study of how electrons act and move; **2,** the devices that employ electrons, such as telephones, radios, televisions, and computers.

e-lec-tro-plate (i-lek′trō-plāt′), *v.t.* to cover with a thin coat of nickel, gold, chrome, etc., by means of electrolysis:—*n.* silver-plated articles.

e-lec-tro-scope (i-lek′trō-skōp′), *n.* an instrument for detecting small charges of electricity, and showing whether they are positive or negative.

el-e-gant (el′i-gant), *adj.* **1,** marked by refinement, grace, and good taste, as dress or manners; **2,** *Colloq.* excellent; very fine.—*adv.* **el′e-gant-ly.**—*n.* **el′e-gance.**

el-e-ment (el′i-ment), *n.* **1,** in *chemistry,* a substance which cannot be broken down into simpler substances, such as carbon, hydrogen, or oxygen; **2,** a simple part of a larger whole; an ingredient; **3,** a first or main principle of a subject which must be learned before the subject can be understood; **4,** a condition or place particularly suited to a person or thing; as, she is in her *element* on the stage:—**the elements,** the forces of nature.—*adj.* **el′e-men′tal.**

el-e-men-ta-ry (el′i-men′ta-ri), *adj.* dealing with the basic or simplest part; introductory; as, an *elementary* education.

el-e-phant (el′i-fant), *n.* the largest of living land animals, native to India and Africa, with thick, wrinkled hide, a long, flexible snout, or trunk, and two long, curved ivory tusks; the African elephant has large ears, and the Asian has small ones.

el-e-vate (el′i-vāt′), *v.t.* [elevat-ed, elevat-ing], to raise; lift; as, study *elevates* the mind; to *elevate* your feet.—*adj.* **el′e-vat′ed.**

el-e-va-tion (el′i-vā′shun), *n.* **1,** height above sea level of a certain place; **2,** a raised place; **3,** the act of raising or state of being raised.

el-e-va-tor (el′i-vā′tėr), *n.* **1,** a hoisting machine or lift; a cage that can be raised or lowered in a shaft, to carry people or goods from one level to another; **2,** a continuous belt or chain conveyer with buckets for raising sand, earth, etc.; **3,** a warehouse for the storage of grain.

e-lev-en (i-lev′en), *adj.* composed of one more than 10:—*n.* **1,** the number consisting of 10 plus one; **2,** a sign representing 11 units, as 11 or XI; **3,** a group of 11 things or people, such as a football or cricket team.

e-lev-enth (i-lev′enth), *adj.* next after the 10th: the ordinal of *eleven*:—*n.* one of the 11 equal parts of anything.

elf (elf), *n.* [*pl.* elves (elvz)], **1,** in fairy tales, a tiny goblin, dwarf, or fairy, sometimes mischievous, sometimes helpful to humans; **2,** a small creature.—*adj.* **elf′in.**—*adj.* **elf′ish.**

e-lic-it (i-lis′it), *v.t.* to draw out; extract; as, to *elicit* a reply.

el-i-gi-ble (el′i-ji-bl), *adj.* fit to be chosen or elected; meeting given requirements; as, the retired soldier is *eligible* for a pension.—*adv.* **el′i-gi-bly.**—*n.* **el′i-gi-bil′i-ty.**

e-lim-i-nate (i-lim′i-nāt′), *v.t.* [eliminat-ed, eliminat-ing], **1,** to get rid of; expel; **2,** to set aside; leave out of consideration.—*n.* **e-lim′i-na′tion.**

é-lite (ā-lēt′), *n.* **1,** the best or choicest members, the cream of a particular group; **2,** a small and privileged group.

e-lix-ir (i-lik′sėr), *n.* **1,** a substance formerly believed capable of changing baser metals into gold; also, a liquid formerly believed capable of prolonging life; **2,** hence, a remedy for all diseases or evils.

elk (elk), *n.* **1,** a large deer of North America, the male of which has very large antlers; **2,** a deer of Europe and Asia.

el-lipse (i-lips′), *n.* a closed curve that differs from an oval in that it has symmetrical ends.—*adj.* **el-lip′tic; el-lip′ti-cal.**

el-lip-sis (i-lip′sis), *n.* [*pl.* ellipses (-sēz)], **1,** the omitting of a word or words that are understood; as, "(*he*) who steals my purse steals trash"; **2,** in writing or printing, punctuation marks [...] that show something has been left out.

elm (elm), *n.* **1,** a tall, graceful shade tree; **2,** the hard, tough wood of this tree.

el-o-cu-tion (el′o-kū′shun), *n.* the art of effective public speaking.—*n.* **el′o-cu′tion-ist.**

e-lon-gate (ē′lông-gāt′; i-lông′gāt), *v.t.* and *v.i.* [elongat-ed, elongat-ing], to lengthen.—*n.* **e′lon-ga′tion.**

e-lope (i-lōp′), *v.i.* [eloped, elop-ing], to run away with a lover, usually to get married.—*n.* **e-lope′ment.**

el-o-quence (el′o-kwens), *n.* persuasive, forceful, and vivid use of language.—*adj.* **el′o-quent.**

else (els), *adv.* otherwise; besides; as, leave now or *else* you will be late:—*adj.* implying someone different or additional; as, somebody *else* has the book.

else-where (els′hwâr′), *adv.* in, at, or to another place; somewhere else.

e-lu-ci-date (i-lū′si-dāt′), *v.t.* explain; make clear; as, please *elucidate* this story of Atwood's.

e-lude (i-lūd′), *v.t.* [elud-ed, elud-ing], to escape or evade through cleverness; as, to *elude* an enemy.

e-lu-sive (i-lū′siv), *adj.* tending to slip away or escape; as, an *elusive* criminal; also, hard to get hold of or to understand; as, an *elusive* fact.—*adv.* **e-lu′sive-ly.**—*adj.* **e-lu′so-ry.**—*n.* **e-lu′sive-ness.**

e-ma-ci-ate (i-mā′shi-āt′), *v.t.* [emaciat-ed, emaciat-ing], to cause to waste away; to make thin; as, he was *emaciated* by hunger and fatigue.—*adj.* **e-ma′ci-at′ed.**

e-mail (ē′–māl′), *n.* electronic mail; messages sent electronically from one computer to another:—*v.i.* and *v.t.* to send electronic messages; as, *e-mail* me the information.

em-a-nate (em′a-nāt′), *v.i.* [emanat-ed, emanat-ing], to flow out, issue, emit, or proceed from a source, as light from the sun.—*n.* **em′a-na′tion.**

e-man-ci-pate (i-man′si-pāt′), *v.t.* [emancipat-ed, emancipat-ing], to set free from bondage or control; liberate.—*n.* **e-man′ci-pa′tion; e-man′ci-pa′tor.**

e-mas-cu-late (i-mas′kū-lāt′), *v.t.* **1,** to weaken or sap the strength of a person, idea, or thing; as, this film has been *emasculated* by the censor; **2,** to castrate or remove male identity from someone.

em-balm (em-bäm′), *v.t.* **1,** to treat (a dead body) to preserve it from decay; **2,** to hold in memory; preserve:—*n.* **em-balm′er.**

em-bank-ment (em-bangk′ment), *n.* a structure of earth, stones, etc., built to hold back water, to carry a roadway, or for some similar purpose.

em-bar-go (em-bär′gō), *n.* [*pl.* embargoes], **1,** an order of government forbidding ships of commerce to use its ports; also, a similar order forbidding transportation of certain freight; **2,** a prohibition:—*v.t.* to lay an embargo on.

em-bark (em-bärk′), *v.i.* **1,** to start out; **2,** to go on board a vessel; **3,** to engage in any affair; as, to *embark* in business.—*n.* **em′bar-ka′tion.**

em-bar-rass (em-bar′as), *v.t.* **1,** to disconcert; fluster; as, her manners *embarrassed* her mother; **2,** to worry; hinder; as, *embarrassed* by debt.—*n.* **em-bar′rass-ment.**

em-bas-sy (em′bas-si), *n.* [*pl.* embassies], **1,** the official residence of an ambassador and his or her staff in another country; **2,** an ambassador and staff in a diplomatic mission.

em-bat-tled (em-bat′ld), *adj.* **1,** assailed, troubled, or beset by difficulties, criticisms, etc.; as, even her enemies began to feel sorry for the *embattled* party leader; **2,** prepared for battle or war.

em-bed (em-bed′), *v.t.* [embed-ded, embed-ding], **1,** set firmly in surrounding matter; as, to *embed* the computer graphics; **2,** to plant something, such as an idea.

em-bel-lish (em-bel′ish), *v.t.* **1,** to beautify, decorate, or adorn; as, to *embellish* a cloak with fur; **2,** to add fanciful details to (a story) to make it more interesting.—*n.* **em-bel′lish-ment.**

em-ber (em′bėr), *n.* a live coal or small piece of wood, smouldering in ashes.

em-bez-zle (em-bez′l), *v.t.* [embez-zled embez-zling], to steal (funds entrusted to one's care); as, to *embezzle* a trust fund.—*n.* **em-bez′zler; em-bez′zle-ment.**

em-bit-ter (em-bit′ėr), *v.t.* to make hostile or resentful; as, his scolding *embittered* her because it was unjust.

em-bla-zon (em-blā′zn), *v.t.* **1,** to decorate brightly; as, a maple leaf was *emblazoned* on the flag; **2,** to spread widely; praise; extol.

em-blem (em′blum), *n.* a symbol or representation of an idea; as, the olive branch is an *emblem* of peace.—*adj.* **em′blem-at′ic; em′blem-at′i-cal.**

em-bod-y (em-bod′i), *v.t.* [embodied, embody-ing], **1,** to represent in bodily form; **2,** to express in a definite form; as, to *embody* thought in words; **3,** to collect into a united whole.—*n.* **em-bod′i-ment.**

em-boss (em-bôs′), *v.t.* to ornament with raised work; also, to raise above a surface; as, the name was *embossed* on the card.

em-brace (em-brās′), *v.t.* [embraced, embrac-ing], **1,** to hold in the arms with affection; **2,** to accept; adopt; turn to; to take up; enter on; as, to *embrace* a profession; **3,** to include; as, biology *embraces* botany and zoology:—*n.* the act of clasping in the arms; a hug.

em-broi-der (em-broi′dėr), *v.t.* **1,** to decorate or make beautiful with needlework; **2,** to exaggerate, as a story:—*v.i.* to do decorative needlework.—*n.* **em-broi′der-y.**

em-broil (em-broil′), *v.t.* to involve in strife; entangle; as, he became *embroiled* in the debate on the environment.

em-bry-o (em′bri-ō), *n.* [*pl.* embryos], **1,** the young of an animal in the earliest stages of its growth before birth or hatching; **2,** an undeveloped plant, contained in a seed; **3,** the first or undeveloped state of anything. Compare *fetus.*—*adj.* **em′bry-on′ic** (em′bri-on′ik).

e-mend (ē-mend′), *v.t.* to alter or correct; as, to *emend* a text.—*n.* **e′men-da′tion.**

em-er-ald (em′ėr-ald), *n.* **1,** a precious stone of a clear, deep-green colour; **2,** the colour of this stone.

e-merge (i-mûrj′), *v.i.* [emerged, emerg-ing], to rise up; come forth; appear; as, to *emerge* through the fog.

e-mer-gen-cy (i-mûr′jen-si), *n.* [*pl.* emergencies], a sudden or unexpected happening or situation, demanding prompt action; as, call 911 in an *emergency*.

em-er-y (em′ėr-i), *n.* a very hard, dark mineral substance used, when powdered, for grinding or polishing; as, *emery* board; *emery* cloth.

em-i-grant (em′i-grant), *n.* one who leaves his or her own country to settle in another:—*adj.* moving from one country to settle in another; as, *emigrant* labourers.

em-i-grate (em′i-grāt′), *v.i.* [emigrat-ed, emigrat-ing], to leave one's own country to settle in another; as, she *emigrated* to Canada from Chile.

é-mi-gré (ā′mē′grā′), *n.* an emigrant, esp. one who flees from political persecution; an exile.

em-i-nence (em′i-nens), *n.* a prominent position; high station or standing; as, to attain *eminence* as a lawyer.—*adj.* **em′i-nent.**—*adv.* **em′i-nent-ly.**

em-is-sar-y (em′i-sėr-i), *n.* [*pl.* emissaries], a person or agent sent on a mission, esp. of a secret nature; an envoy or representative.

e-mit (i-mit′), *v.t.* [emit-ted, emit-ting], to send forth; as, a stove *emits* heat.—*n.* **e-mis′sion.**

e-mo-tion (i-mō′shun), *n.* mental excitement; strong or intense feeling of love, hate, joy, awe, grief, etc.

e-mo-tion-al (i-mō′shun-al), *adj.* **1,** excitable; easily agitated; as, she has an *emotional* nature; **2,** tending to stir the feelings.—*adv.* **e-mo′tion-al-ly.**

em-pa-thy (em′pa-thi), *n.* the projecting of oneself imaginatively into another's personality in order to understand him or her better.

em-per-or (em′pėr-ėr), *n.* the supreme ruler of an empire.—*n.fem.* **em′press.**

em-pha-sis (em′fa-sis), *n.* [*pl.* emphases (em′fa-sēz)], **1,** importance; stress; as, to put too much *emphasis* on football; **2,** a particular stress of the voice on a word or words in reading or speaking.

em-pha-size (em′fa-sīz′), *v.t.* [emphasized, emphasiz-ing], **1,** to call attention to; as, he *emphasized* the fine points of the picture; **2,** to pronounce clearly and positively; stress; as, he *emphasized* each word.

em-phat-ic (em-fat′ik), *adj.* **1,** given emphasis to something; **2**, expressive; forceful; as, an *emphatic* gesture; **3**, definite; clear; positive; striking.—*adv.* **emphat′i-cal-ly.**

em-pire (em′pīr), *n.* **1,** a group of nations united under one ruler; as, the Roman *Empire*; **2,** any large area or activity controlled by a person or group; as, the Asper family controls a vast communications *empire*.

em-pir-i-cal (em-pēr′i-kal), *adj.* **1**, based on observation or experiment; **2**, verifiable by experiment or experience; **3**, based on practical experience.

em-ploy (em-ploi′), *v.t.* **1,** to make use of the services of; give occupation to; hire; as, he *employed* 10 people; **2,** to make use of; as, he *employed* his knowledge of Spanish in business:—*n.* the state of serving an employer for wages.—*n.* **em-ploy′ee; employ′er; em-ploy′ment.**

em-pow-er (em-pou′ėr), *v.t.* to give authority or opportunity to; enable.

emp-ty (emp′ti), *adj.* [emp-ti-er, emp-ti-est], **1,** containing nothing; vacant; as, an *empty* house; **2,** meaningless; having no force or sense; as, *empty* words:—*v.t.* [emptied, empty-ing], **1,** to remove the contents from; make vacant; **2,** to pour out; as, to *empty* the milk from a bottle:—*v.i.* **1,** to become empty; **2,** to discharge itself; as, the river *empties* into the ocean.—*n.* **emp′ti-ness.**

em-u-late (em′ū-lāt′), *v.t.* [emulat-ed, emulat-ing], to strive to equal or excel; imitate with the hope of equalling or excelling; as, to *emulate* great women.—*n.* **em′u-la′tion.**

e-mul-sion (i-mul′-shun), *n.* a liquid dispersed within another.—*v.t.* **e-mul′si-fy.**

en (en), *n.* **1,** the letter *n* as pronounced; **2,** a prefix (meaning *in, into, on,* etc.); as, *en*snare, *en*grave; a verbal intensive, as in *en*danger.

e-na-ble (i-nā′bl), *v.t.* [ena-bled, ena-bling], **1,** to make able or possible; as, the airplane *enables* us to travel faster than by train; **2,** make operational.

en-act (en-akt′), *v.t.* **1,** to make into law; as, to *enact* a bill; **2,** to act the part of; as, he *enacted* the hero.—*n.* **en-act′ment.**

e-nam-el (i-nam′el), *n.* **1,** a hard, glassy coating used to protect or decorate the surface of metals, glass, or porcelain, such as pots and pans; **2,** any hard, glossy covering like enamel, such as paint; **3,** the hard, white outer coating of the teeth:—*v.t.* [enamelled, enamel-ling], **1,** to cover or decorate with enamel; **2,** to apply a glossy surface to.

en-am-our (en-am′ėr), *v.t.* to inspire with love; charm.

en-camp (en-kamp′), *v.t.* to settle in camp:—*v.i.* to make camp; as, let's *encamp* here.—*n.* **en-camp′ment.**

en-case (en-kās′), *v.t.* [encased, encas-ing], to enclose in a case or box; surround with anything.

en-chant (en-chȯnt′), *v.t.* **1,** to charm by magic spells; bewitch; **2,** to fill with delight.—*n.* **en-chant′er.**—*n.* **en-chant′ment.**—*n.* **enchant′ ress.**

en-cir-cle (en-sûr′kl), *v.t.* [encir-cled, encircling], **1,** to surround; encompass; **2,** to make a circle around; go around.—*n.* **encir′cle-ment.**

en-close (en-klōz′), *v.t.* [enclosed, enclos-ing], **1,** to surround with a barrier; **2,** to insert; as, he *enclosed* the cheque in a letter.—*n.* **en-clo′sure.**

en-com-pass (en-kum′pas), *v.t.* to surround; encircle; as, enemies *encompassed* us.

en-core (äng-kōr′), *interj.* once more! again!—*n.* (äng′kōr), a repetition, as of a song, in response to a call by an audience:—*v.t.* (äng-kōr′; äng′kōr), [encored, encor-ing], to call for a repetition of (any part of a performance), by applause; also, to call upon (a person) for an encore.

en-coun-ter (en-koun′tėr), *v.t.* and *v.i.* to meet, particularly unexpectedly or in conflict:—*n.* a sudden or accidental meeting; a conflict.

en-cour-age (en-kûr′ij), *v.t.* [encour-aged, encourag-ing], **1,** to inspire with courage or hope; **2,** to help bring about or make happen; as, *encourage* recycling.—*n.* **en-cour′age-ment.**—*adv.* **en-cour′ag-ing-ly.**

en-croach (en-krōch′), *v.i.* **1,** to intrude upon another's rights or property; trespass; **2,** to go beyond normal limits.—*n.* **en-croach′ment.**

en-crust (en-krust′), *v.t.* to cover with, or as with, a crust; to coat; as, barnacles *encrusted* the hull.

en-crypt (en-kript′), *v.t.* **1**, to put into code; to encode; **2**, to scramble sensitive computer data to make it difficult or impossible to access.—*n.* **en-cryp′tion.**—*adj.* **en-cryp′ted.**

en-cum-ber (en-kum′bėr), *v.i.* to impede, restrict, or hinder; as, her long skirts *encumbered* her.—*n.* **en-cum′brance.**

en-cy-clo-pe-di-a or **en-cy-clo-pae-di-a** (en-sī′klo-pē′di-a), *n.* a work containing information on all branches of knowledge, with the articles arranged in alphabetical order.—*adj.* **en-cy′clo-pe′dic.**

end (end), *n.* **1,** the extreme limit or terminal point of anything; as, the *end* of a railway; **2,** death; **3,** that which is left over; as, odds and *ends*; **4,** purpose; goal; as, work to some good *end*; **5,** conclusion; as, bring the discussion to an *end*; **6,** in *football,* a player stationed at the end of the line:—*v.t.* **1,** to finish; **2,** to destroy; put to death:—*v.i.* **1,** to come to an end; as, the road *ends* here; **2,** to result; as, the argument *ended* in a fight; **3,** to die.

en-dan-ger (en-dān′jėr), *v.t.* to expose to danger; imperil; jeopardize; as, you *endanger* your health when you drink impure water:—*n.* **endangered species**, kinds of animals or plants that exist in such small numbers that they are likely to die out completely unless they are protected.—*n.* **en-dan′ger-ment.**

en-dear (en-dēr′), *v.t.* to make beloved; make (a person) dear or precious to another; as, his thoughtfulness *endeared* him to us.—*n.* **en-dear′ ment.**—*adj.* **en-dear′ing.**—*adv.* **en-dear′ ing-ly.**

en-deav-our (en-dev′ėr), *v.i.* to strive; attempt; as, the team *endeavoured* to win the game:—*n.* an effort or attempt.

en-dem-ic (en-dem′ik), *adj.* peculiar to a nation, group, or locality; as, *endemic* plants or diseases; thus, goitre is *endemic* in areas where iodine is lacking in the diet.

end-ing (en′ding), *n.* end; conclusion; completion.

en-dive (en′div; en′dīv), *n.* a plant with curling leaves, used as a salad.

end-less (end′lis), *adj.* **1,** lasting forever; without an end; **2,** having no ends; continuous; as, an *endless* chain.—*adv.* **end′-less-ly.**

en-do-crine (en′dō-krīn′; -krin), *adj.* relating to such glands as the thyroid, adrenal, and pituitary, or their secretions which regulate bodily functions.

en-dorse (en-dôrs′), *v.t.* [endorsed, endors-ing], **1,** to approve or support; as, Parliament *endorsed* the plan; **2,** to write one's name on the back of, as a cheque.—*n.* **en-dorse′ment.**

en-dow (en-dou′), *v.t.* **1,** to bestow a permanent fund or source of income upon; as, to *endow* a college; **2,** to equip or furnish; as, Nature *endowed* humans with reason.

en-dow-ment (en-dou′ment), *n.* **1,** property or a sum of money given to an institution, or devoted permanently to any cause; **2,** the act of making such a settlement; **3,** any talent that a person possesses by nature.

en-dure (en-dūr′), *v.t.* [endured, endur-ing], to bear up under; bear with patience:—*v.i.* **1,** to remain firm, as under suffering; **2,** to remain in existence; last.—*n.* **en-dur′ance.**—*adj.* **en-dur′a-ble.**

en-e-ma (en′i-ma; en-ē′ma), *n.* the injection of a fluid or gas into the rectum, esp. to produce bowel movement.

en-e-my (en′i-mi), *n.* [*pl.* enemies], **1,** one hostile to another; an adversary; **2,** a country at war with another; **3,** anything that is dangerous or harmful; as, laziness is an *enemy* of success.

en-er-get-ic (en′ėr-jet′ik), *adj.* full of life; active; vigorous; as, she is an *energetic* worker.—*adv.* **en′er-get′i-cal-ly.**

en-er-gy (en′ėr-ji), *n.* [*pl.* energies], **1,** capacities for work; power; force; vigour; as, he devoted all his *energy* to the task; **2,** the power needed to cause things to move or do other kinds of work; as, the sun, wind, gasoline, and electricity are all forms of *energy*.

en-er-vate (en′ėr-vāt′), *v.t.* [enervat-ed, enervat-ing], to deprive of nerve, force, or vigour; weaken.—*n.* **en′er-va′tion.**

en-fold (en-fōld′), *v.t.* to wrap up; infold; envelop; embrace.

en-force (en-fōrs′), *v.t.* [enforced, enforc-ing], **1,** to carry out; as, to *enforce* a law; **2,** to compel; impose; as, to *enforce* silence.—*adj.* **en-force′a-ble.**—*n.* **en-force′ment.**

en-fran-chise (en-fran′chīz), *v.t.* [enfran-chised, enfranchis-ing], **1,** to grant the right to vote; **2,** to free.—*n.* **en-fran′chise-ment** (en-fran′chiz-ment).

en-gage (en-gāj′), *v.t.* [engaged, engag-ing], **1,** to pledge or bind by oath or contract; **2,** a promise to marry; to betroth; **3,** to win and hold; as, to *engage* the attention; **4,** in *machinery,* to come into gear with; **5,** to secure for aid or employment; as, to *engage* a workman; **6,** to encounter, as in battle; **7,** to occupy the time or attention of; as, to *engage* someone in conversation:—*v.i.* **1,** to promise, or assume an obligation; as, he *engaged* to pay his father's debts; **2,** to occupy oneself; as, to *engage* in business; **3,** to enter a conflict; **4,** in *machinery,* to inter-lock.

en-gaged (en-gājd′), *adj.* **1,** busy or occu-pied; **2,** betrothed.

en-gage-ment (en-gāj′ment), *n.* **1,** betrothal; **2,** occupation; **3,** an appoint-ment; obligation; **4,** in *machinery,* the state of being in gear; **5,** a battle.

en-gag-ing (en-gāj′ing), *adj.* winning; pleasing; as, an *engaging* manner.

en-gen-der (en-jen′dėr), *v.t.* to beget; cause; as, poverty often *engenders* crime.

en-gine (en-jin), *n.* **1,** a machine by which power is used to do work; a motor; as, a steam *engine*; **2,** an apparatus for converting some form of energy, as heat, into mechanical power; esp., a railway locomotive; **3,** a tool; an instrument.

en-gi-neer (en′ji-nēr′), *n.* **1,** one who designs and constructs machines, bridges, etc.; as, an electrical *engineer*; **2,** one who has charge of and drives an engine or loco-motive; **3,** one of an army corps which constructs bridges, roads, etc.:—*v.t.* **1,** to plan or direct; as, he *engineered* the cam-paign; **2,** to plan and execute the construc-tion of (a road, canal, etc.).—*n.* **en′gi-neer′ing.**

En-glish (ing′lish), *n.* **1**, a person who inhabits or originates from England; **2**, the language of the people of England, Canada, most other Commonwealth countries, and the United States:—*adj.* relating to the coun-try, the people, the language, or the culture of England.

en-grave (en-grāv′), *v.t.* [*p.t.* engraved, *p.p.* engraved or engrav-en, *p.pr.* engrav-ing], **1,** to cut or carve, as in wood or metal; as, to *engrave* words on a monument; **2,** to cut (letters, figures, designs, etc.) on stone, wood, or a metal plate, as for printing; **3,** to impress deeply; as, the words were *engraved* upon his mind.—*n.* **en-grav′er; en-grav′ing.**

en-gross (en-grōs′), *v.t.* to absorb; occupy wholly; as, the book *engrossed* her.—*adj.* **en-gross′ing.**

en-gulf (en-gulf′), *v.t.* to swallow up, over-whelm, or overflow, as in a gulf; as, sorrow *engulfed* him.

en-hance (en-hŏns′), *v.t.* [enhanced, enhanc-ing], to increase in attractiveness or value; add to; as, a good education will *enhance* your earning power.

e-nig-ma (i-nig′ma), *n.* a mystery or riddle; a remark, act, or person not easily under-stood.—*adj.* **en′ig-mat′ic** (en′ig-mat′ik; ē′nig-mat′ik); **en′ig-mat′i-cal.**

en-join (en-join′), *v.t.* **1,** to direct with authority; command; as, the teacher *enjoined* the students to silence; **2,** to pro-hibit or restrain by judicial order.

en-joy (en-joi′), *v.t.* **1,** to take delight in; as, we *enjoyed* the book; **2,** to have the use or possession of; as, I *enjoy* keen eyesight.—*adj.* **en-joy′a-ble.**—*n.* **en-joy′ment.**

en-large (en-larj′), *v.t.* [enlarged, enlarg-ing], to make larger, bigger, or more com-prehensive; increase:—*v.i.* **1,** to become larger; **2,** to speak or write fully; as, he *enlarged* upon his theme.—*n.* **en-large′ment.**

en-light-en (en-līt′n), *v.t.* to furnish with increased knowledge; instruct.—*n.* **en-light′en-ment.**—*n.* **en-light′en-er.**

en-list (en-list′), *v.t.* **1,** to enroll (a person) for military service; **2,** to win over for a cause; as, to *enlist* support for the Red Cross:—*v.i.* to enroll for military service, or in any cause.—*n.* **en-list′ment.**

en-liv-en (en-līv′en), *v.t.* to make lively, active, or fun; to put life into.

en-mi-ty (en′mi-ti), *n.* [*pl.* enmities], ill will; hatred; hostility.

en-no-ble (e-nō′bl; en-nō′bl), *v.t.* [enno-bled, enno-bling], **1,** to dignify; exalt; **2,** to raise to the nobility.

en-nui (än′nwē), *n.* boredom from lack of something to do; tedium.

e-nor-mi-ty (i-nôr′mi-ti), *n.* [*pl.* enormi-ties], **1,** the state of being outrageous or monstrous; as, the *enormity* of his offence; **2,** a grave offence; **3,** huge size; vastness.

e-nor-mous (i-nôr′mus), *adj.* immense; extremely large; of great size or number.—*adv.* **e-nor′mous-ly.**—*n.* **e-nor′mous-ness.**

e-nough (i-nuf′), *adj.* sufficient:—*n.* a suf-ficient or adequate amount:—*adv.* in a suf-ficient degree; sufficiently; as, I've eaten *enough*:—*interj.* stop!

en-quire (en-kwīr′), *v.t.* Same as **inquire.**

en-rage (en-rāj′), *v.t.* [enraged, enrag-ing], to make intensely angry; provoke to fury.

en-rap-ture (en-rap′tûr), *v.t.* [enraptured, enraptur-ing], to delight; charm; enchant.

en-rich (en-rich′), *v.t.* **1,** to increase the wealth of; **2,** to make fertile, as soil; **3,** to improve, as the mind; **4,** to adorn.

en-roll or **en-rol** (en-rōl′), *v.t.* [enrolled, enrol-ling], to insert or write down in a register; enlist; as, to *enroll* men for the army:—*v.i.* to join or sign up for something; as, she *enrolled* in the art society.—*n.* **en-roll′ment; en-rol′ment.**

en route (än ro͞ot′), on the way; as, *en route* to Paris.

en-sconce (en-skons′), *v.t.* [ensconced, ensconc-ing], to settle comfortably, safely, or secretly.

en-sem-ble (än-som′bl; än′som′bl; än′-sänbl′′), *n.* **1,** all the parts of anything considered as a whole; **2,** a costume of two or more pieces, worn together; **3,** a group of performers, such as actors or musicians.

en-shrine (en-shrīn′), *v.t.* [enshrined, enshrin-ing], **1,** to enclose something as in a shrine; **2,** to preserve, cherish, or keep sacred.

en-shroud (en-shroud′), *v.t.* to cover completely; hide; as, fog *enshrouds* the city.

en-slave (en-slāv′), *v.t.* [enslaved, enslav-ing], to bring into bondage; deprive of freedom.—*n.* **en-slave′ment.**

en-snare (en-snâr′), *v.t.* [ensnared, ensnar-ing], to trap; snare.

en-sue (en-sū′), *v.i.* [ensued, ensu-ing], to follow; result; come afterward; as, the ship ran aground, and panic *ensued.*

en-suite (on-swēt′), *adj.* and *adv.* connected, adjoining; part of the whole; as, an *ensuite* bathroom.

en-sure (en-shoor′), *v.t.* [ensured, ensur-ing], to make sure or certain; to make safe; guarantee; as, it is difficult to *ensure* a happy outcome.

en-tail (en-tāl′), *v.t.* **1,** to necessitate; require; demand; as, success *entails* hard work; **2,** to leave (property), as money or land, to an heir or line of heirs, so that none of them can give or will it away.—*n.* **en-tail′ment.**

en-tan-gle (en-tang′gl), *v.t.* [entangled, entan-gling], **1,** to twist into a snarl; **2,** to get caught in or ensnare; as, he was *entangled* in a plot; **3,** to perplex; bewilder.—*n.* **en-tan′gle-ment.**

en-ter (en′tėr), *v.t.* **1,** to go or come into; as, he *entered* the house; **2,** to set down in writing; as, the clerk *entered* the account in the journal; **3,** to join; as, to *enter* a club; **4,** to go into or begin, as a business; **5,** to enroll as a competitor; as, he *entered* his horse in the race; **6,** to gain admission for; as, to *enter* a pupil in a school:—*v.i.* **1,** to go or come in; **2,** to take part; as, to *enter* into a discussion; **3,** to make a beginning, as into business; **4,** to come upon the stage, as an actor.—*n.* **en′trant.**

en-ter-prise (en′tėr-prīz), *n.* **1,** an undertaking of importance or danger; as, a daring *enterprise;* **2,** readiness to undertake such projects.—*adj.* **en′ter-pris-ing.**

en-ter-tain (en′tėr-tān′), *v.t.* **1,** to interest or amuse; as, she *entertained* the children with stories; **2,** to receive and treat hospitably; **3,** to harbour, as a grudge; **4,** to take into consideration; as, to *entertain* a proposal:—*v.i.* to receive guests.—*adj.* **en′ter-tain′ing.**—*n.* **en′ter-tain′ment.**

en-thrall (en-thrôl′), *v.t.* [enthralled, enthral-ling], **1,** to charm; **2,** to enslave.—*n.* **en-thrall′ment.**

en-thu-si-asm (en-thū′zi-azm), *n.* strong interest or feeling for something; as, the students took up soccer with *enthusiasm.*—*n.* **en-thu′si-ast.**—*adj.* **en-thu′si-as′tic.**—*adv.* **en-thu′si-as′ti-cal-ly.**

en-tice (en-tīs′), *v.t.* [enticed, entic-ing], to allure; tempt; lead on by arousing hope or desire.

en-tire (en-tīr′), *adj.* **1,** with no part omitted; whole; unbroken; complete; **2,** unqualified; as, my *entire* support.—*n.* **en-tire′ty.**

en-tire-ly (en-tīr′li), *adj.* **1,** wholly; **2,** solely; as, it is *entirely* his fault.

en-ti-tle (en-tī′tl), *v.t.* [enti-tled, enti-tling], **1,** to give a right to; as, this card *entitles* you to a seat; **2,** to give a name to.

en-ti-ty (en′ti-ti), *n.* being; essence; anything thought of as having real existence apart from its qualities and relations; thus, matter, space, time, and force are *entities.*

en-to-mol-o-gy (en′to-mol′o-ji), *n.* [*pl.* entomologies], that branch of zoology that studies insects.—*adj.* **en′to-mo-log′i-cal.**—*n.* **en′to-mol′o-gist.**

en-tou-rage (äñ′to͞o′rŏzh′), *n.* **1,** retinue; attendants; as, the queen's *entourage* accompanied her aboard the ship; **2,** surroundings.

en-trails (en′trālz), *n.pl.* **1,** the internal parts of animals; intestines; **2,** the inner workings of something.

[1]**en-trance** (en′trans), *n.* **1,** the act of entering; **2,** a door, passage, etc., through which one goes into a place; **3,** admission; permission to enter; as, he gained *entrance* at once.

[2]**en-trance** (en-trŏns′), *v.t.* [entranced, entranc-ing], to throw into a trance; delight; enrapture.—*adv.* **en-tranc′ing-ly.**

en-trap (en-trap′), *v.t.* [entrapped, entrap-ping], to catch in a trap; entangle; trick; beguile.—*n.* **en-trap′ment.**

en-treat (en-trēt′), *v.t.* to ask earnestly; beg or beseech.—*n.* **en-treat′y.**

en-trée (än′trā; äñ′trā′), *n.* **1,** the main dish of a meal; **2,** entrance; privilege of entering.

en-trench (en-trench′) , *v.t.* **1,** to establish solidly; safeguard; as, to *entrench* rights in the Charter; **2,** to surround or protect with trenches:—*v.i.* to trespass.—*n.* **en-trench′ment.**

en-tre-pre-neur (än′tri-pri-nûr′), *n.* one who

starts, organizes, and operates a business; one who acts as an entrepreneur.—*adj.* **en′tre-pre-neur′i-al.**—*n.* **en′tre-pre-neur′i-al-ism; en′tre-pre-neur′ism; en′tre-pre-neur′ship′.**

en-trust (en-trust′), *v.t.* **1,** to give (something) in trust to someone; as, to *entrust* funds to a bank; **2,** to confer a trust upon; as, to *entrust* a bank with funds.

en-try (en′tri), *n.* [*pl.* entries], **1,** the act of entering; entrance; **2,** a place through which one enters; **3,** the act of writing an item in a list, or record; also, the item.

en-twine (en-twin′), *v.t.* [entwined, entwin-ing], **1,** to wind around; twist together; **2,** very closely connected; as, our lives are *entwined.*

e-nu-mer-ate (i-nū′mėr-āt), *v.t.* [enumerat-ed, enumerat-ing], to count; list, to name one by one; as, Elections Canada just *enumerated* me.—*n.* **e-nu′mer-a′tion.**—*n.* **e-nu′mer-a′tor.**

e-nun-ci-ate (i-nun′si-āt; i-nun′shi-āt), *v.t.* [enunciat-ed, enunciat-ing], **1,** to declare; state; **2,** to utter:—*v.i.* to pronounce; as, a public speaker should *enunciate* clearly.—*n.* **e-nun′ci-a′tion.**

en-vel-op (en-vel′up), *v.t.* to cover; wrap up or in.—*n.* **en-vel′op-ment.**

en-ve-lope (en′ve-lōp′; on′ve-lōp′), *n.* **1,** a paper wrapper for enclosing letters sent by post, messenger, etc.; **2,** any similar covering; **3**, limit or edge; as, to push the *envelope.*

en-vi-a-ble (en′vi-a-bl), *adj.* exciting envy; arousing a wish for possession; desirable; as, an *enviable* record.—*adv.* **en′vi-a-bly.**

en-vi-ous (en′vi-us), *adj.* feeling, or characterized by, a desire to possess something belonging to another.—*adv.* **en′vi-ous-ly.**

en-vi-ron-ment (en-vī′run-ment), *n.* **1,** the natural conditions that make up the area in which a plant, animal, or person lives, such as air, water, and land; as, lizards are often found in a desert *environment;* **2**, all the conditions that surround or go with a certain person or thing; as, students with a supportive home *environment* excel in school.—*n.* **en-vi′ron-ment′al-ism.**—*adj.* **en-vi′ron-ment′al.**

en-vi-rons (en-vī′runz; en′), *n.* surroundings; suburbs; vicinity; as, the *environs* of Edmonton.

en-vis-age (en-viz′ij), *v.t.* **1,** to see in the mind's eye; visualize; as, he *envisaged* a new house; **2,** to contemplate possibilities.

en-voy (en′voi), *n.* a messenger or delegate, esp. a person sent on a special diplomatic mission.

en-vy (en′vi), *v.t.* [envied, envy-ing], **1,** to wish for (what is another's); as, I *envy* his health; **2,** to begrudge the excellence or prosperity of (another):—*n.* [*pl.* envies], **1,** ill will or jealousy felt because of the excellence or good fortune of another; **2,** a person or object exciting such feeling; as, she is the *envy* of her friends.

en-zyme (en′zīm), *n.* a protein produced by living organisms that promotes chemical, or catalytic, changes in other substances; thus, pepsin is a digestive *enzyme.*

e-on (ē′on; ē′un), *n.* **1,** an age; a period of time too long to measure, often exaggerated; as, it took me *eons* to write this essay; **2,** in *geology* and *astronomy*, one billion years.

ep-au-let or **ep-au-lette** (ep′o-let), *n.* a shoulder ornament on a military or naval uniform, usually signifying rank.

EPAULET

e-phem-er-al (i-fem′ėr-al), *adj.* existing only for a short time; short-lived; transitory.

ep-ic (ep′ik), *adj.* **1,** grand; noble; heroic; **2,** narrative: said of a poem:—*n.* a long narrative poem or story of heroic deeds; as, the film *Braveheart* is an *epic* about Scottish history.

e-pi-cen-tre (e′pi-sen′tėr), *n.* **1**, the point on the earth's surface directly above the focus of an earthquake; **2**, the focal point, centre, or heart of something; as, the *epicentre* of the crisis.

ep-i-cure (ep′i-kūr′), *n.* a person devoted to pleasure; also, one fond of the delicacies of the table.—*adj.* **ep′i-cu-re′an.**

ep-i-dem-ic (ep′i-dem′ik), *adj.* attacking many at the same time; as, illiteracy is a problem of *epidemic* proportions:—*n.* **1,** a general outbreak of a disease throughout a locality; **2,** a widespread occurrence of anything; as, an *epidemic* of cheap books.

ep-i-gram (ep′i-gram), *n.* **1,** a verse or short poem with a witty point; **2,** a wise thought given briefly, as "To err is human, to forgive, divine."—*adj.* **ep′i-gram-mat′ic.**

ep-i-lep-sy (ep′i-lep′si), *n.* a chronic disease of the nervous system, often attended by convulsions and loss of consciousness.—*adj.* and *n.* **ep′i-lep′tic.**

ep-i-logue or **ep-i-log** (ep′i-log′), *n.* **1,** an addition to a novel, play, etc., giving further comment, interpretation, or conclusion; **2,** a poem or speech at the end of a play.

E-piph-a-ny (i-pif′a-ni), *n.* a Christian festival (January 6) celebrating the appearance of Jesus to the Gentiles; **2,** in the Orthodox Church, the commemoration of the baptism of Jesus:—**epiphany**, a sudden, important, often illuminating discovery.

ep-i-sode (ep′i-sōd), *n.* an incident within a series of events; as, a comic *episode* in a tragic plot; an *episode* of the war.

ep-i-taph (ep′i-tôf), *n.* an inscription or writing on a tomb.

ep-i-thet (ep′i-thet), *n.* a word or phrase, often disparaging, expressing some characteristic quality, as "Toronto the Good."

e-pit-o-me (i-pit′o-mi), *n.* [*pl.* epitomes], **1,**

a typical or ideal example of something; **2,** a brief statement, summary, or synopsis of a literary work.—*v.t.* **e-pit′o-mize′.**

ep-och (ē′pok; ep′ok), *n.* **1,** an event or a point of time which marks the beginning of a new period in history; **2,** a period of unusual events.—*adj.* **ep′och-al** (ep′ok-al).

eq-ua-ble (ek′wa-bl; ē′kwa-bl), *adj.* **1,** steady; free from change; as, an *equable* climate; **2,** even and serene in temperament; tranquil.—*adv.* **eq′ua-bly.**

e-qual (ē′kwal), *adj.* **1,** the same in number, size, amount, or value; the same as; **2,** of the same rank or degree; evenly balanced; **3,** just; fair; as, an *equal* contest; **4,** strong or brave enough; as, *equal* to a task:—*n.* a person or thing of the same rank or value as another:—*v.t.* [equalled, equal-ling], to have the same size, rank, value, etc., with; match in some way; as, to *equal* another in height.—*adv.* **e′qual-ly.**

e-qual-i-ty (ē-kwol′i-ti; ē-kwôl′i-ti), *n.* [*pl.* equalities], sameness in size, rank, value, etc.

e-qual-ize (ē′kwal-īz), *v.t.* [equalized, equalizing], to make the same in size, rank, value, etc.; make equal.—*n.* **e′qual-i-za′tion; e′qual-iz′er.**

e-qua-nim-i-ty (ē′kwa-nim′i-ti; ek′wa-nim′i-ti), *n.* evenness of temper or mind; calmness; serenity.

e-quate (ē-kwāt′), *v.t.* [equat-ed, equat-ing], to make equal or treat as equal.

e-qua-tion (ē-kwā′zhun; ē-kwā′shun), *n.* in *mathematics,* a statement that two things are equal, as in "2 + 2 = 4."

e-qua-tor (i-kwā′tėr), *n.* **1,** an imaginary line around the earth, equally distant from the North and South Poles; **2,** a similar line dividing the sphere of the sky in two, called the *celestial equator.*—*adj.* **e′qua-tor′i-al** (ē′kwa-tōr′i-al).

e-ques-tri-an (i-kwes′tri-an), *adj.* pertaining to horses or horseback riding:—*n.* a person skilled in horseback riding.

e-qui-dis-tant (ē′kwi-dis′tant), *adj.* equally distant; as, the farm was *equidistant* from Regina and Saskatoon.

e-qui-lat-er-al (ē′kwi-lat′ėr-al), *adj.* having all sides equal.—*adv.* **e′qui-lat′er-al-ly.**

e-qui-lib-ri-um (ē′kwi-lib′ri-um), *n.* **1,** the state of balance between opposing forces, actions, or weights; **2,** even mental balance between opposing influences; hence, neutrality.

e-quine (ē′kwīn), *adj.* pertaining to a horse:—*n.* a horse.

e-qui-nox (ē′kwi-noks; ek′wi-noks), *n.* one of two times a year when the sun is directly over the equator, making the days and nights of equal length, the *vernal* (spring) *equinox* occurring about March 21, and the *autumnal* (fall) *equinox* about September 23.—*adj.* **e′qui-noc′tial** (ē′kwi-nok′shal).

e-quip (i-kwip′), *v.t.* [equipped, equipping], to fit out for any undertaking; as, to *equip* scouts with tents for camp.—*n.* **equip′ment.**

eq-ui-ta-ble (ek′wi-ta-bl), *adj.* impartial; just; fair; honest; as, an *equitable* decision.—*adv.* **eq′ui-ta-bly.**

eq-ui-ty (ek′wi-ti), *n.* [*pl.* equities], **1,** justice; fair dealing; **2,** the value of a property beyond the total amount owed on it; as, I have now an *equity* of $70,000 in my home.

e-quiv-a-lent (i-kwiv′a-lent), *adj.* equal in value; the same in meaning or effect; as, cheating is *equivalent* to lying:—*n.* a thing of the same value, weight, power, effect, etc.—*n.* **e-quiv′a-lence.**

e-quiv-o-cal (i-kwiv′o-kal), *adj.* of a doubtful or double meaning; vague; uncertain; as, an *equivocal* reply.

e-quiv-o-cate (i-kwiv′o-kāt′), *v.i.* [equivocat-ed, equivocat-ing], to speak with double meaning; evade the truth by a statement which can be understood in more than one way; lie.—*n.* **e-quiv′o-ca′tion.**

e-ra (ē′ra), *n.* **1,** a period of time starting from a given point; as, the Christian *era;* **2,** a period of time with notable characteristics; as, the machine *era;* **3,** one of the major divisions of geologic time.

e-rad-i-cate (i-rad′i-kāt′), *v.t.* [eradicat-ed, eradicat-ing], to destroy completely; get rid of; uproot; wipe out; as, to *eradicate* crime.—*n.* **e-rad′-i-ca′tion.**

e-rase (i-rās′), *v.t.* [erased, eras-ing], to rub or scrape out, esp. something written.—*n.* **e-ras′er; e-ra′sure** (i-rā′zhėr).

e-rect (i-rekt′), *v.t.* **1,** to construct; build, as a house; **2,** to raise upright, as a flagpole; **3,** to create, set up, or establish; as, to *erect* a new government:—*adj.* **1,** upright; not bent; as, an *erect* posture; **2,** raised; lifted up; as, to hold a banner *erect.*—*n.* **e-rec′tion** (i-rek′shun).

erg (ėrg), *n.* in the *metric system,* the unit of work or energy; namely, the work expended in overcoming a resistance of one dyne acting through a distance of one centimetre.

er-go-nom-ics (ėr′gi-no′miks), *n.* **1,** the study of the relationship between people and their working environments; **2,** the science of designing machines and equipment for maximum efficiency, productivity, safety, etc.—*adj.* **er′-go-nom′ic.**—*n.* **er′gon′o-mist.**

e-rode (i-rōd′), *v.t.* [erod-ed, erod-ing], **1,** to wear away; as, running water *erodes* rocks; **2,** to diminish in value; as, inflation *erodes* the value of our dollar:—*v.i.* to wear away gradually, as do rocks.

e-ro-sion (i-rō′zhun), *n.* the act of wearing away; gradual destruction or eating away: used esp. of the action of water on rock or soil; as, forests hinder soil *erosion.*

e-rot-ic (i-rot′ik), *adj.* amorous; relating to sexual love; as, an *erotic* poem.—*n.* **e-rot′i-cism.**

err (ûr), *v.i.* **1,** to go astray; **2,** to be mistaken.

er-rand (er′and), *n.* **1,** a short trip made to attend to some special business; **2,** the object for which the trip is made.

er-rat-ic (e-rat′ik), *adj.* having no fixed course; wandering; irregular; eccentric.—*adv.* **er-rat′i-cal-ly.**

er-ro-ne-ous (e-rō′ni-us), *adj.* incorrect; mistaken; wrong; as, an *erroneous* belief.—*adv.* **er-ro′ne-ous-ly.**

er-ror (er′ėr), *n.* a mistake; an inaccuracy; as, an *error* in a sum.

er-u-dite (er′oo-dīt; er′ū-dīt), *adj.* learned; scholarly.—*adv.* **er′u-dite′ly.**—*n.* **er′u-di′tion** (er′oo-dish′un; er′ū-dish′un).

e-rupt (i-rupt′), *v.i.* to burst forth violently, as a volcano, war, or disease:—*v.t.* to hurl out; as, a volcano *erupts* lava.—*n.* **e-rup′tion** (i-rup′shun).—*adj.* **e-rup′tive.**

es-ca-la-tor (es′ka-lā′tėr), *n.* a moving stairway that carries people from one floor to another in a store, airport, or other building.

es-ca-pade (es′ka-pād′; es′ka-pād′), *n.* a breaking loose from restraint; a foolish or reckless adventure.

e-scape (i-skāp′), *v.t.* [escaped, escap-ing], **1,** to flee from; avoid; as, to *escape* a task; **2,** to be unaffected by; as, he *escaped* the disease; **3,** to issue from unawares; as, a sigh *escaped* him; **4,** to elude the notice, memory, or understanding of; as, his name *escapes* me; **5,** to get away from; be saved from; as, to *escape* danger:—*v.i.* **1,** to get out of danger; avoid harm or capture; **2,** to break loose from confinement; as, to *escape* from prison; **3,** to flow out; as, gas *escapes* from a pipe; **4,** to slip away; as, to *escape* from memory:—*n.* **1,** a successful flight, as from prison; **2,** deliverance from harm or danger; as, a narrow *escape;* **3,** an outlet for water, steam, etc.; **4,** leakage; outflow; a temporary diversion from reality; as, adventure films provide an *escape* from routine.—*n.* **es-cap′ism** (es-kāp′izm).

es-carp-ment (es-kärp′ment), *n.* a long cliff; steep slope; sharp ridge; as, the Niagara *escarpment.*

es-chew (es-cho͞o′; es-chū′), *v.t.* to shun; abstain from; avoid; as, to *eschew* bad company; *eschew* drinking alcohol.

es-cort (es′kôrt), *n.* **1,** someone or something that goes along with another for protection or honour; **2,** a person accompanying another of the opposite sex in public:—*v.t.* (es-kôrt′), to act as escort.

es-crow (es′krō; es-krō′), *n.* an agreement, such as a bond or deed, placed in the care of a third party, not to be delivered (or in effect) until certain conditions are met.

Es-ki-mo (es′ki-mō′), *n.* Same as **Inuit.**

ESL, abbrev. for *E*nglish as a *s*econd *l*anguage; programs or courses to teach the language to students whose first language is not English.

e-soph-a-gus (i-sof′a-gus), *n.* the gullet; the tube that is part of the nutritional system from the throat to the stomach.

es-pe-cial (es-pesh′al), *adj.* particular; chief; special; exceptional of its kind; as, an *especial* friend.—*adv.* **es-pe′cial-ly.**

es-pi-o-nage (es′pi-o-nij; es′pi-ō-näzh′; es-pī′o-nij), *n.* the practice of spying, usually by governments, but also by industry.

es-pla-nade (es′pla-nād′), *n.* a public walk or roadway, often along a waterfront: a promenade.

es-pouse (es-pouz′), *v.t.* [espoused, espous-ing], **1**, to become a follower of; as, to *espouse* a cause; **2,** to wed.—*n.* **es-pous′al.**

e-spres-so (e-spre′sō′), *n.* strong, concentrated coffee made by forcing steam through finely ground, dark-roasted grounds.

es-say (es′ā), *n.* **1,** a literary composition on some special subject, usually of moderate length and expressing the personal views of the author; **2,** (often e-sā′), an attempt; experiment:—*v.t.* (e-sā′), to try.—*n.* **es′say-ist.**

es-sence (es′ens), *n.* **1,** the essential quality of something; that which is the real character of a thing; as, the *essence* of politeness is kindness; **2**, the extract of a substance; as, *essence* of peppermint; **3,** a perfume.

es-sen-tial (e-sen′shal), *adj.* **1,** pertaining to the real character of a thing; as, the *essential* element of a situation; **2,** necessary; indispensable; as, water is *essential* to life:—*n.* that which is a necessary element; as, the three Rs are the *essentials* of education.—*adv.* **es-sen′tial-ly.**

es-tab-lish (es-tab′lish), *v.t.* **1,** to fix firmly; settle; as, he has *established* a reputation for efficiency; **2,** to validate; to prove beyond doubt; as, to *establish* a claim; **3,** to create or found, as an institution.—*n.* **es-tab′lish-ment.**

es-tate (es-tāt′), *n.* **1,** property in land or buildings; esp., large possessions; **2,** in *law,* property in general; **3,** historically, an order or class of people, politically or socially distinct, as nobles or clergy.

es-teem (es-tēm′), *v.t.* **1,** to value highly; respect; prize; **2,** to think; consider; as, to *esteem* it a privilege:—*n.* a favourable opinion; respect; regard.—*adj.* **es′ti-ma-ble** (es′ti-ma-bl).—*adv.* **es′ti-ma-bly.**

es-thet-ic (es-thet′ik), *adj.* Same as **aesthetic.**

es-ti-mate (es′ti-māt′), *v.t.* [estimat-ed, estimat-ing], to reckon approximately; calculate (the amount, cost, or value); as, to *estimate* the cost of a job:—*n.* (es′ti-mit), **1,** a valuation of qualities; opinion; **2,** a judgment, esp. of the amount, cost, or value of anything.—*n.* **es′ti-ma′tion.**

es-trange (es′trānj′), *v.t.* [estranged, estrang-ing], to alienate; turn from affection to indifference or dislike; as, to *estrange* friends by neglect.—*n.* **estrange′ment.**

es-tu-ar-y (es′tū-ėr-i), *n.* [*pl.* estuaries], the wide mouth of a tidal river, where the stream meets the sea.

et cet-er-a (et set′ėr-a), and others of the same kind; abbreviated to *etc.*

etch (ech), *v.t.* **1,** to engrave a design on metal, glass, etc.; **2,** to impress clearly or deeply; as, the horror was *etched* in our minds:—*v.i.* to practise the art of etching.—*n.* **etch′er.**

etch-ing (ech′ing), *n.* **1,** a picture or design printed from an etched plate; also, the plate itself; **2,** the art or process of making etched plates.

e-ter-nal (i-tûr′nal), *adj.* **1,** without beginning or end; everlasting; unchanging; **2,** never ceasing; as, *eternal* chatter.—*adv.* **e-ter′nal-ly.**

e-ter-ni-ty (i-tûr′ni-ti), *n.* [*pl.* eternities], **1,** time without beginning or end; time everlasting; **2,** indefinite time; time that seems endless; as, to wait an *eternity*; **3,** life after death.

e-ther (ē′thėr), *n.* a liquid solvent or anesthetic, the vapour of which, when inhaled, produces unconsciousness and deadens pain.

e-the-re-al (i-thē′ri-al), *adj.* light; exquisite; airy; delicate; heavenly; not earthly; as, *ethereal* music.

eth-i-cal (eth′i-kal), *adj.* **1,** pertaining to questions of right and wrong; **2,** morally right or good; as, *ethical* behaviour.—*adv.* **eth′i-cal-ly.**

eth-ics (eth′iks), *n.pl.* **1,** used as *sing.*, the science of morals; **2,** used as *pl.*, moral principles or practice; as, every profession has its own *ethics.*

eth-nic (eth′nik), *adj.* of, or relating to, groups of people distinguished by speech, customs, characteristics, etc.; as, *ethnic* neighbourhoods.—*n.* **eth-nol′o-gy** (eth-nol′o-ji); **eth-nol′o-gist.**—*adj.* **eth′no-log′i-cal.**

ethnic cleansing, *n.* the systematic removal, expulsion, or extermination of an ethnic group from a region or country, usually involving violence.

eth-no-cen-tric (eth′nō-sen′trik), *adj.* **1**, the tendency to view and evaluate other cultures and people according to the assumptions of one's own group; **2**, a belief in the inherent superiority of one's own cultural or ethnic group; **3**, overly concerned or focussed on race or culture.—*n.* **eth′no-cen-tric′i-ty.**

eth-nog-ra-phy (eth-no′gra-fi), *n.* the scientific study of human cultures, their description, and classification.—*n.* **eth-nog′ra-pher.**

eth-nol-o-gy (eth-nol′o-ji), *n.* **1**, the scientific study of human cultural differences, their origins, relationships, characteristics, and distributions; **2**, cultural anthropology; **3**, the study of animal behaviour in general.—*n.* **eth-nol′o-gist.**—*adj.* **eth′no-log′i-cal.**

et-i-quette (et′i-ket′; et′i-ket′), *n.* **1**, rules of conventional social behaviour; **2**, the customary or official behaviour of a group or team; as, parliamentary *etiquette.*

et-y-mol-o-gy (et′i-mol′o-ji), *n.* [*pl.* etymologies], the study of the origin and meaning of words through history; also, the science treating of the origin and history of words.—*n.* **et′y-mol′o-gist.**—*adj.* **et′y-mo-log′i-cal.**

Eu-cha-rist (ū′ka-rist), *n.* **1,** in many Christian churches, the Holy Communion, or the sacrament of the Lord's Supper; **2,** the consecrated bread and wine used in that sacrament.

eu-chre (ū′kėr), *n.* a card game for two to four persons played with 24 cards, all cards below the nines (except the aces) being removed:—*v.t.* **1,** to defeat an opponent's bid by taking three of the five tricks; **2,** *Colloq.* to outwit; get the better of.

eu-gen-ics (ū-jen′iks), *n.pl.* used as *sing.*, the science of improving human and animal populations by careful selection of parents.

eu-lo-gy (ū′lo-ji), *n.* [*pl.* eulogies], high praise, either written or spoken, of the life or character of a person, esp. of a dead person.—*v.t.* **eu′lo-gize** (ū′lo-jīz).

eu-nuch (ū-′nuk), *n.* **1,** a man who has been castrated; **2,** someone who has been deprived of effective power.

eu-phe-mism (ū′fe-mizm), *n.* the use of a pleasing expression for a harsh or blunt one; as, *pass away* for *die* or *fib* for *lie.*—*adj.* **eu′phe-mis′tic.**

eu-pho-ny (ū′fo-ni), *n.* pleasantness of sound; as, the *euphony* of his accents charmed his audience.—*adj.* **eu-phon′ic.**

eu-ro or **Eu-ro** (ū′rō), *n.* the currency that was introduced in 2002 to replace the legal tender of 12 countries in the European union.

Eu-ro-pe-an (ū′ro-pē′en), *n.* a person wh[illegible] inhabits or originates from Europe:—*ad*[illegible] relating to the countries, the people, the lan[illegible]guages, the cultures, or the characteristics [illegible] Europe.

eu-tha-na-si-a (ū′tha-nā′zhi-a; -zi-a), [illegible] the killing, usually in a painless way, o[illegible] person or animal suffering from an inc[illegible]able disorder; mercy killing.

e-vac-u-ate (i-vak′ū-āt), *v.t.* [evacuat-ed, e[illegible] uat-ing], **1,** to empty; **2,** to abandon possession of; as, to *evacuate* a town; also, to withdraw (persons) from a place.—*n.* **e-vac′u-a′tion.**

e-vade (i-vād′), *v.t.* [evad-ed, evad-ing], **1,** to escape from by some trick; as, to *evade* pursuers or the law; **2,** to baffle or foil; as, a face which *evades* description; **3,** to fail to pay; as, he *evaded* paying taxes.

e-val-u-ate (i-val′yoo-āt′), *v.t.* to determine the worth of; appraise; as, this service cannot be *evaluated* in dollars.—*n.* **e-val′u-a′tion.**

e-van-gel-i-cal (ē′van-jel′i-kal; ev′an-jel′i-kal), *adj.* **1,** pertaining to the teachings of the Christian gospels; **2,** denoting certain fundamentalist Protestant Christian beliefs; **3,** holding beliefs of any kind with zealous, militant fervour. Also, **e-van-gel′ic.**

e-van-ge-list (i-van′je-list), *n.* **1,** one who spreads the Christian gospel, esp. a travelling preacher; **2,** any ardent, passionate devotee to a cause.—*adj.* **e-van′ge-lis′tic.**

e-vap-o-rate (i-vap′o-rāt), *v.i.* [evaporat-ed, evaporat-ing], **1,** to change from solid or liquid into vapour, as water into steam; **2,** to pass away without effect; as, his zeal soon *evaporated:*—*v.t.* **1,** to change into vapour; as, heat *evaporates* water; **2,** to dry or concentrate, by removing moisture; as, to *evaporate* fruit or milk.—*n.* **e-vap′o-ra′tor; e-vap′o-ra′tion.**

e-va-sion (i-vā′zhun), *n.* an artful escape, excuse, or avoidance; as, the *evasion* of a question.—*adj.* **e-va′sive.**—*adv.* **e-va′sive-ly.**

eve (ēv), *n.* **1,** the evening before a church festival or saint's day; as, Christmas *eve;* **2,** the period immediately before some important event; as, on the *eve* of departure.

e-ven (ē′ven), *adj.* **1,** level; smooth; as, an *even* surface; **2,** equal in quantity, size, ıumber; **3,** on the same line; parallel; as, ıe water is *even* with the top of a bucket; divisible by two without a remainder; six is an *even* number; **5,** impartial; fair; *even* justice; **6,** satisfied as to an account rudge; as, to get *even* with a person; **7,** ı; unruffled; as, an *even* temper; **8,** le; exact; as, an *even* mile:—*v.t.* **1,** to make smooth; as, to *even* a lawn; **2,** ke equal; as, to *even* up a score:—*adv.* ctly; just; as, *even* so; **2,** precisely; *even* as I spoke; **3,** quite; so much I never *even* spoke; **4,** used to ize or imply comparison; as, clear a child.—*adv.* **e′ven-ly.**—*n.* **e′ven-**

nd-ed (ē′ven–han′did), *adj.* fair; just; equitable.—*adv.* **e′ven–y.**—*n.* **e′ven–hand′ed-ness.**

ev′ning), *n.* the close of day and of night:—*adj.* pertaining to the the day; as, the *evening* meal.

evening dress, *n.* clothes, such as tuxedos and evening gowns, worn to formal social occasions; evening clothes.

EVENING GOWN

e-vent (i-vent′), *n.* **1,** an occurrence; incident; happening; **2,** the fact of something happening; as, in *event* of war; **3,** the result or outcome of an action; as, in any *event;* **4,** a single item in a programme of sports.—*adj.* **e-vent′ful** (i-vent′fool).—*adv.* **e-vent′ful-ly.**

e-ven-tu-al (i-ven′tū-al), *adj.* **1,** depending on a future or possible event; as, *eventual* succession to a throne; **2,** final; as, an *eventual* reward.—*adv.* **e-ven′tu-al-ly.**

ev-er (ev′ėr), *adv.* **1,** at any time; as, if I *ever* go; **2,** forever; always; as, the poor are *ever* with us; **3,** in any degree: used to strengthen an expression; as, study as hard as *ever* you can:—**ever so,** very; as, *ever so* much better.

ev-er-green (ev′ėr-grēn′), *n.* a tree or plant which remains green throughout the year, as the pine, cedar, holly, etc.:—*adj.* always green or fresh.

ev-er-last-ing (ev′ėr-lôs′ting), *adj.* **1,** endless; eternal; as, the *everlasting* hills; **2,** never ceasing; lasting too long; as, an *everlasting* noise:—*n.* **1,** any of various plants whose flowers keep their form and colour when dried; **2,** eternity.—*adv.* **ev′er-last′ing-ly.**

ev-er-y (ev′ri; ev′ėr-i), *adj.* **1,** all, taken one at a time; each; as, *every* dog has its day; **2,** all possible; as, *every* kindness.

ev-er-y-bod-y (ev′ri-bod′i; ev′ėr-i-bod′i), *pron.* every person; everyone.

ev-er-y-day (ev′ri-dā′; ev′ėr-i-dā′), *adj.* happening on each day; ordinary; usual; commonplace; as, *everyday* clothes.

ev-er-y-one (ev′ri-wun; ev′ėr-i-wun′), *pron.* every person; everybody.

ev-er-y-thing (ev′ri-thing′; ev′ėr-i-thing′), *pron.* all things; all that relates to a given matter; as, to tell *everything* about it.

ev-er-y-where (ev′ri-hwâr′; ev′ėr-i-hwâr′), *adv.* in all places or parts; as, they looked *everywhere*.

e-vict (ē-vikt′) *v.t.* to put out by force; expel, esp. by legal force; as, to *evict* a tenant.—*n.* **e-vic′tion.**

ev-i-dence (ev′i-dens), *n.* facts from which to judge; proof; testimony; as, *evidence* of guilt:—*v.t.* [evidenced, evidenc-ing], to prove; make evident or plain; indicate.

ev-i-dent (ev′i-dent), *adj.* clear to the eyes and mind; obvious; as, his dislike was *evident*.—*adv.* **ev′i-dent-ly.**

e-vil (ē′vl; ē′vil), *adj.* **1,** bad; wicked; sinful; as, *evil* acts; **2,** hurtful; disastrous; **3,** offensive; of ill repute; as, an *evil* name:—*n.* **1,** disaster; injury; anything that destroys happiness or well-being; **2,** sin; wrongdoing:

exercises; **4,** performance; as, in the *exercise* of duty.

ex-ert (eg-zûrt′), *v.t.* to put forth; bring to bear: to *exert* influence, willpower, etc.—*n.* **ex-er′tion.**

ex-hale (eks-hāl′; eg-zāl′), *v.t.* [exhaled, exhal-ing], to breathe out; give off; as, we *exhale* air in breathing; swamps *exhale* mist:—*v.i.* to rise in vapour.—*n.* **ex′ha-la′tion.**

ex-haust (eg-zôst′), *v.t.* **1,** to empty by letting out all the contents; use up; consume; drain; **2,** to weaken; wear out; use up, as strength or a supply of money; **3,** to discuss or treat thoroughly; as, to *exhaust* a topic:—*n.* **1,** the drawing off or escape of used fuel, as steam, gas, etc., from an engine; **2,** the steam, gas, etc., that escapes; **3,** an instrument or device for drawing off or letting escape, as bad air from a room, or used fuel from an engine.—*adj.* **ex-haust′ed; ex-haust′less; ex-haust′i-ble.**

ex-haus-tion (eg-zôs′chun), *n.* **1,** the act of draining or the state of being drained; **2,** utter fatigue.

ex-haus-tive (eg-zôs′tiv), *adj.* complete; thorough; as, *exhaustive* research, study, etc.—*adv.* **ex-haus′tive-ly.**

ex-hib-it (eg-zib′it), *v.t.* **1,** to show; as, he *exhibited* impatience; **2,** to show publicly; present formally or officially; as, to *exhibit* an artist's work:—*n.* **1,** an object or collection of objects offered for public view; as, an *exhibit* of paintings; **2,** in *law*, an article, paper, etc., marked to be used as evidence.—*n.* **ex-hib′-i-tor; ex′hi-bi′tion** (ek′si-bi′shun); **ex′hi-bi′tion-ist.**

ex-hil-a-rate (eg-zil′a-rāt′), *v.t.* [exhilarated, exhilarat-ing], to make joyous; gladden; enliven.—*n.* **ex-hil′a-ra′tion.**

ex-hort (eg-zôrt′), *v.t.* and *v.i.* to urge by appeal or argument, esp. to good deeds; advise; warn.—*n.* **ex′hor-ta′tion.**

ex-hume (eks-hūm′), *v.t.* **1,** to dig out of the earth; as, the judge ordered the corpse *exhumed*; **2**, revive.

ex-ile (ek′sīl), *v.t.* [exiled, exil-ing], to banish from home or country:—*n.* **1,** banishment, either forced or voluntary; as, to live in *exile;* **2,** a person banished from or living out of his or her own country.

ex-ist (eg-zist′), *v.t.* **1,** to have actual being; live; be; **2,** to be found; occur; as, salt *exists* in solution; to live in less-than-favourable circumstances; as, she was merely *existing* from hand to mouth.

ex-ist-ence (eg-zis′tens), *n.* **1,** the state of being; as, new truths come into *existence*; **2,** life; as, food is necessary for *existence;* **3,** manner of life; as, a happy *existence*; **4,** reality; as, he believes in the *existence* of devils.—*adj.* **ex-ist′ent; ex′is-ten′tial** (shal).

ex-it (eg′zit; ek′sit), *n.* **1,** the act of going out; **2,** a way out, as a door; **3,** the spot from which vehicles can depart a highway.

ex-o-dus (ek′so-dus), *n.* a going out; departure; as, a mass *exodus* from the city.

ex-on-er-ate (eg-zon′ėr-āt′), *v.t.* [exonerated, exonerat-ing], **1**, to free from blame; as, the jury *exonerated* the accused man; **2**, to relieve of responsibility or duty.—*n.* **ex-on′er-a′tion.**

ex-or-bi-tant (eg-zôr′bi-tant), *adj.* going beyond due limits; excessive; as, an *exorbitant* price.—*n.* **ex-or′bi-tance.**

ex-or-cize or **ex-or-cise** (ek′sôr-sīz′), *v.t.* [exorcized, exorciz-ing], **1**, to expel (an evil spirit), as by religious or magic ceremonies; to deliver or free from evil spirits; **2**, to remove an evil or malignant influence.—*n.* **ex′or-cism.**

ex-o-tic (eg-zot′ik; ek-sot′ik), *adj.* **1,** foreign, imported from another country; as, *exotic* plants, words, fashions, etc.; **2,** fascinating or beautiful, because strange or foreign.

ex-pand (eks-pand′), *v.t.* **1,** to spread or stretch out; **2,** to dilate; swell; as, to *expand* the chest; **3,** to give more details of; enlarge upon; as, *expand* your topic into an essay:—*v.i.* to increase in size.

ex-panse (eks-pans′), *n.* wide extent; unbroken stretch or area; as, an *expanse* of ocean or sky.—*n.* **ex-pan′sion.**

ex-pan-sive (eks-pan′siv), *adj.* **1,** capable of being spread or stretched out; **2,** widely extended; large; **3,** friendly, open; free and unrestrained in the expression of feeling; effusive; as, an *expansive* manner.—*adv.* **ex-pan′sive-ly.**

ex-pa-tri-ate (eks-pā′trē-it; eks-pā′trē-at), *n.* **1**, one who has lived abroad or away from his or her home for an extended period; **2**, an exile:—*adj.* **1,** living in a foreign country; **2,** exiled. Also called *expat.*

ex-pect (eks-pekt′), *v.t.* **1,** to look forward to as likely to happen; as, I *expect* the guests to arrive soon; **2,** *Colloq.* to suppose; as, I *expect* it is all for the best; **3,** to be pregnant; as, they are *expecting* twins.

ex-pect-ant (eks-pek′tant), *adj.* looking forward confidently; expecting.—*adv.* **expect-ant-ly.**—*n.* **ex-pect′an-cy.**

ex-pec-ta-tion (eks′pek-tā′shun), *n.* **1,** a looking forward to something; anticipation; as, in *expectation* of a good dinner; **2,** (usually *expectations*), the prospect of future benefit, esp. of advancement or wealth; as, his *expectations* are good.

ex-pe-di-en-cy (eks-pē′di-en-si), *n.* [*pl.* expediencies], **1,** suitableness; fitness for a purpose; **2,** the doing of something, regardless of fairness or justice, in order to gain a certain end; as, *expediency* made him refuse. Also, **ex-pe′di-ence.**

ex-pe-di-ent (eks-pē′di-ent), *adj.* **1,** fit for a special purpose; **2,** helpful toward self-interest; as, an *expedient* friendship:—*n.* **1,** that which acts as a means to an end; **2,** a device.—*adv.* **ex-pe′di-ent-ly.**

ex-pe-dite (eks′pi-dīt′), *v.t.* [expedit-ed, expedit-ing], to hasten; help forward; quicken; to carry out quickly; as, to *expedite* work.—*adj.* **ex′pe-di′tious.**

ex-pe-di-tion (eks′pi-dish′un), *n.* **1,** haste; dispatch; promptness; as, he did his work with *expedition*; **2,** a journey or voyage for some particular purpose; as, an exploring *expedition*; **3,** the body of persons engaged in such an enterprise.—*adj.* **ex′pe-di′tion-ar-y.**

ex-pel (eks-pel′), *v.t.* [expelled, expel-ling], **1,** to drive away; force out; as, to *expel* an enemy from a region; **2,** to turn out; send away; as, to *expel* someone from a club, school, or the like.

ex-pend (eks-pend′), *v.t.* to pay out; use up; spend; as, to *expend* strength, time, or money.—*adj.* **ex-pend′a-ble.**

ex-pend-i-ture (eks-pen′di-tūr), *n.* **1,** a spending, as of money, time, labour, etc.; **2,** that which is spent.

ex-pense (eks-pens′), *n.* **1,** money, labour, time, etc., laid out or spent; cost; as, the *expense* of a college education; **2,** a sacrifice or loss; as, he worked long hours at the *expense* of his health; **3,** a source or cause of spending; as, war is a great *expense.*

ex-pen-sive (eks-pen′siv), *adj.* costly; high-priced.—*adv.* **ex-pen′sive-ly.**

ex-pe-ri-ence (eks-pē′ri-ens), *n.* **1,** knowledge or skill gained by direct action, observation, enjoyment, or suffering; **2,** the actual observation or living through anything, as a series of events, or of feeling anything through sensation; **3,** anything lived through, enjoyed, or felt; as, war *experiences:*—*v.t.* [experienced, experiencing], to feel; live through; as, to *experience* hardship.—*adj.* **ex-pe′ri-enced** (eks-pē′ri-enst).

ex-per-i-ment (eks-per′i-ment), *n.* **1,** a trial or test to discover something previously unknown, or to confirm or disprove something; as, the *experiment* showed he was right; **2,** any procedure or policy tried for the first time:—*v.i.* (eks-per′i-ment), to find out something by testing; as, Bell *experimented* for years trying to perfect the telephone.—*n.* **ex-per′i-ment-er.**—*adj.* **ex-per′i-men′tal.**

ex-pert (eks-pûrt′; eks′pûrt), *adj.* skillful; clever; dextrous; having special knowledge; as, an *expert* photographer:—*n.* (eks′pûrt), one who is skilled or thoroughly informed in any particular subject; a specialist; as, a financial *expert.*—*adv.* **ex-pert′ly.**

ex-pi-ate (eks′pi-āt), *v.t.* [expiat-ed, expiat-ing], to atone or make amends for; as, he *expiated* his theft by restoring the plunder.—*n.* **ex′pi-a′tion.**

ex-pire (ek-spīr′), *v.i.* **1,** to die; **2,** to come to an end; as, his term *expired:*—*v.t.* [expired, expir-ing], to breathe out from the lungs.—*n.* **ex′pi-ra′tion** (eks′pi-rā′shun); **ex-pi′ry.**

ex-plain (eks-plān′), *v.t.* **1,** to make plain or clear; tell the meaning of; as, to *explain* a problem; **2,** to account for; as, to *explain* one's conduct.—*n.* **ex′pla-na′tion.**—*adj.* **ex-plan′a-tor-y** (eks-plan′a-tėr-i).

ex-ple-tive (eks′ple-tiv), *n.* **1,** an oath, curse, or swear word; as, his salty *expletives* startled her; **2,** in *grammar,* a word, such as *it* or *there,* used to fill in for the real subject; as, *it* is foolish to worry; *there* is nothing left.

ex-pli-ca-ble (eks′pli-ka-bl), *adj.* capable of being explained.

ex-plic-it (eks-plis′it) *adj.* **1,** plain; definite; expressed clearly and in detail; as, *explicit* instructions: compare *implicit;* **2,** blunt or outspoken.—*adv.* **ex-plic′it-ly.**

ex-plode (eks-plōd′), *v.i.* [explod-ed, explod-ing], **1,** to burst with sudden noise and violence; blow up; as, the bomb *exploded;* **2,** to break forth suddenly into laughter, anger, etc.; **3,** to increase very quickly in size, amount, etc.; as, the crowd *exploded:*—*v.t.* **1,** to cause to burst suddenly with a loud noise; as, to *explode* dynamite; **2,** to refute or disprove; as, Copernicus *exploded* the theory that the earth was the centre of the solar system.

ex-ploit (eks-ploit′), *v.t.* **1,** to make use of; work; develop; as, to *exploit* natural resources; **2,** to make use of for one's own profit; put to use selfishly; as, to *exploit* one's friends:—*n.* (eks′ploit; eks-ploit′), a remarkable deed or heroic act.—*n.* **ex-ploit′er; ex′ploi-ta′tion.**

ex-plore (eks-plōr′), *v.t.* [explored, exploring], **1,** to search or examine thoroughly; as, to *explore* a wound; **2,** to travel in or over (a region) to discover its geographical characteristics; as, to *explore* unknown islands; to investigate or explore anything new; as, she explored jazz and other forms of music.—*n.* **ex′plo-ra′tion; ex-plor′er.**—*adj.* **ex-plor′a-to-ry.**

ex-plo-sion (eks-plō′zhun), *n.* **1,** a sudden and violent bursting with a loud noise; as, the *explosion* of a bomb; **2,** a sudden and violent outburst, as of anger; **3,** any sudden increase; as, a population *explosion.*

ex-plo-sive (eks-plō′siv), *adj.* **1,** pertaining to explosion; likely or able to explode; as, dynamite is an *explosive* substance; **2,** controversial; as, *explosive* opinions; **3,** rapid or violent; as, *explosive* growth:—*n.* any substance, liquid, solid, or gaseous, which will explode or cause an explosion, as gunpowder, TNT, etc.—*adv.* **ex-plo′sive-ly.**

ex-po-nent (eks-pō′nent), *n.* **1,** one who supports, explains, or interprets; as, an *exponent* of democracy; **2,** a person or thing that represents a principle or theory;

as, Lévesque was the *exponent* of Québec sovereignty.

ex-po-nen-tial (eks′pō-nen′shal), *adj.* **1,** having to do with a mathematical exponent; **2,** extremely rapid increase; as, *exponential* growth.—*adv.* **ex-po-nen′tial-ly.**

ex-port (eks-pōrt′; eks′pōrt), *v.t.* **1,** to send or carry out (goods) to another country for sale; as, to *export* cattle; **2,** to send data from one computing system to another:—*n.* (eks′pōrt), **1,** (usually *exports*), goods sold and sent to a foreign country; also, their amount or value; **2,** the act or business of sending goods to a foreign country to be sold; as, the *export* of wheat is an important industry in Canada.—*n.* **ex′por-ta′tion; ex-port′er.**—*adj.* **export′a-ble.**

ex-pose (eks-pōz′), *v.t.* [exposed, exposing], **1,** to lay open to view; uncover; disclose; make known; as, to *expose* a secret, an opinion, or a villain; **2,** to leave without shelter or defence; as, to *expose* a child to the cold; **3,** to lay open or put in the way of; as, to *expose* a plant to the sun; *expose* a friend to blame; **4,** in *photography,* to subject (a film) to the action of light.

ex-po-sé (eks′pō′zā′), *n.* the public disclosure of the details of a scandal, crime, etc.

ex-po-si-tion (eks′pō-zish′un), *n.* an explanation or interpretation (as distinct from narration, description, or argument); a piece of writing that explains or interprets; **2,** an exhibition on a large scale; as, Canada has had two successful *expositions*: in 1967 and 1986.—*adj.* **ex-pos′i-to-ry.**

ex-po-sure (eks-pō′zhėr), *n.* **1,** a revealing or making known; as, the *exposure* of a crime; **2,** the state of being open or subject to attack, contamination, etc.; as, died of *exposure* to the elements; **3,** position; outlook; as, a house with a southern *exposure;* **4,** in *photography*, an exposing to light.

ex-pound (eks-pound′), *v.t.* to set forth, explain, or interpret.—*n.* **ex-pound′er.**

ex-press (eks-pres′), *adj.* **1,** plainly stated; special; definite; as, an *express* answer or wish; **2,** having to do with quick or direct transportation; as, an *express* train; **3,** pertaining to the business of transporting goods rapidly; as, an *express* company:—*adv.* **1**, by express; quickly; as, send the package *express*; **2,** clearly; definitely; mainly; for the purpose of; as, she came *expressly* to see the premier:—*n.* **1,** a fast railway train stopping only at principal stations; **2,** a system of transportation for mail, goods of small bulk, or the like; also, goods so forwarded:—*v.t.* **1,** to make known, esp. by language; utter; as, he *expressed* the idea clearly; **2,** to show; reveal; as, to *express* relief, joy, etc.; **3,** to represent; as, the symbol of the arrow *expresses* direction; **4,** to send by express.—*adj.* **ex-press′i-ble.**

ex-pres-sion (eks-presh′un), *n.* **1,** the act of expressing or revealing, esp. in words; manner of speech, change in tone of voice, etc., revealing thought and feeling; as, to speak with *expression;* **2,** a look on the face that betrays feeling; as, a joyous *expression*; **3,** a saying; as, "Never say die" is an old *expression.*

ex-pres-sive (eks-pres′iv), *adj.* full of meaning; serving to point out or express; as, a look *expressive* of sorrow.—*adv.* **ex-pres′sive-ly.**—*n.* **ex-pres′sive-ness.**

ex-press-ly (eks-pres′li), *adv.* **1,** particularly; specially; **2,** in direct terms; plainly; as, told *expressly* to go home.

ex-pro-pri-ate (eks-prō′pri-āt′), *v.t.* to take property from an owner, esp. for public use; as, the province *expropriated* the farmer's land for a new highway.—*n.* **ex-pro′pri-a′tion.**

ex-pul-sion (eks-pul′shun), *n.* **1,** a forcing out or away; **2,** banishment; as, the *expulsion* of the Acadians is a dark day in Canadian history.—*adj.* **ex-pul′sive.**

ex-qui-site (eks′kwi-zit), *adj.* **1,** delicately beautiful or charming; as, *exquisite* lace, *exquisite* workmanship; **2,** intensely or sensitively felt; as, *exquisite* joy.—*adv.* **ex′quisite-ly.**

ex-tem-po-ra-ne-ous (eks-tem′po-rā′ni-us), *adj.* made without preparation or study; extemporary.—*adv.* **ex-tem′po-ra′ne-ous-ly; ex-tem′po-rar-i-ly.**—*adj.* **ex-tem′po-rar -y** (eks-tem′po-rėr-i).

ex-tem-po-rize (ex-tem′po-rīz′), *v.i.* to sing, play an instrument, speak, etc., improvising music or words as one proceeds.—*n.* **ex-tem′po-ri-za′tion.**

ex-tend (eks-tend′), *v.t.* **1,** to lengthen, as a railway; prolong, as a visit; **2,** to enlarge; increase, as power, scope, influence, etc.; **3,** to straighten out, as the arm; **4,** to offer, as an invitation, friendship, etc.:—*v.i.* to reach, in time or distance; as, Canada *extends* from the Atlantic to the Pacific.—*adj.* to include; as, *extended* families include several generations.

ex-ten-sion (eks-ten′shun), *n.* **1,** the act of reaching or stretching out; **2,** the state of being lengthened; enlargement; **3,** an addition; as, an *extension* to a house; **4**, an electrical cable that allows appliances, etc., to be plugged into a distant electrical outlet; **5**, extra telephone.

ex-ten-sive (eks-ten′siv), *adj.* wide; comprehensive; far-reaching; as, *extensive* business interests; an *extensive* view.—*adv.* **exten′sive-ly.**

ex-tent (eks-tent′), *n.* the space or degree to which a thing is extended; size; length; limit; as, the *extent* of their land.

ex-ten-u-ate (eks-ten′ū-āt′), *v.t.* [extenuated, extenuat-ing], to offer excuses for; lessen the blame for.—*adj.* **ex-ten′u-at-ing** (mitigating; as, *extenuating* circumstances for being late).—*n.* **ex-ten′u-a′tion.**

ex-te-ri-or (eks-tē′ri-ėr), *adj.* **1,** outward; external; as, the *exterior* covering of a box; **2,** suitable for use outdoors; as, *exterior* paint:—*n.* **1,** the outer surface or the outside of anything; **2,** an outdoor scene; as, the film crew shot the *exteriors* in good weather.

ex-ter-mi-nate (eks-tûr′mi-nāt′), *v.t.* [exterminat-ed, exterminat-ing], to destroy utterly; root out; as, to *exterminate* moths.—*n.* **ex-ter′mi-na′tion; ex-ter′mi-na′tor.**

ex-ter-nal (eks-tûr′nal), *adj.* **1,** outside; exterior: opposite of *internal;* as, an *external* force; **2,** foreign; as, the *external* debt of a country; **3,** visible; as, *external* proof; **4,** superficial; not essential; as, *external* culture; **5,** auxiliary device in a computer system; as, an *external* modem:—*n.* **1,** an outward part; **2,** (often *externals*), outward form or ceremony; as, the *externals* of religion.—*adv.* **ex-ter′nal-ly.**

ex-tinct (eks-tingkt′), *adj.* **1,** no longer living or surviving; as, buffalo are almost *extinct;* **2,** no longer burning; gone out, as a fire; inactive, as a volcano; **3,** destroyed, as life or hope.—*n.* **ex-tinc′tion** (eks-tingk′shun).

ex-tin-guish (eks-ting′gwish), *v.t.* **1,** to put out, as a light; **2,** to destroy; as, to *extinguish* hope.—*n.* **ex-tin′guish-er.**

ex-tol (eks-tol′; eks-tōl′), *v.t.* [extolled, extol-ling], to praise highly; as, many people *extol* a low-fat diet.

ex-tor-tion (eks-tôr′shun), *n.* **1,** the act of obtaining by force or threat; **2,** unjust exaction, as of excessive interest on loans; **3,** that which has been exacted unlawfully.—*adj.* **ex-tor′tion-ate.**—*adv.* **ex-tor′tion-ate-ly.**—*n.* **ex-tor′tion-er.**—*v.t.* **ex-tort′.**

[1]**ex-tra** (eks′tra), *adj.* more than usual or needed; as, we made *extra* sandwiches for the party:—*n.* **1,** something additional; **2,** a newspaper special edition issued between regular editions; **3,** an actor appearing as part of a crowd in a film or play:—*adv.* exceptionally; as, *extra* fine silk.

[2]**extra-** (eks′tra-), *prefix* meaning *outside, besides,* or *beyond;* as, *extra*curricular, *extra*marital, *extra*mural, *extra*sensory, *extra*territorial, etc.

ex-tract (eks-trakt′), *v.t.* **1,** to pull out, as a tooth; **2,** to obtain from a substance by some process; as, to *extract* perfume from flowers; **3,** to get by effort; as, to *extract* money from a miser; **4,** to select, as a passage from a book; **5,** in *mathematics,* to calculate, as the root of a number:—*n.* (eks′trakt), **1,** that which has been extracted, or taken out; as, vanilla *extract;* **2,** a passage from a book, speech, etc.

ex-trac-tion (eks-trak′shun), *n.* **1,** the act of extracting; **2,** ethnic origin; descent; ancestry; as, a person of English *extraction.*

ex-tra-cur-ric-u-lar (eks′tra-ku-rik′ū-lėr), *adj.* **1,** outside the regular course of studies; as, athletics, debating, and dramatics are *extracurricular* activities; **2,** outside one's regular routine or duties.

ex-tra-dite (eks′tra-dīt′), *v.t.* **1,** to give up a prisoner or fugitive to the jurisdiction of another country; as, the murderer was *extradited* from the U.S.; **2,** obtain the extradition of someone from another country.—*n.* **ex′tra-di′tion.**

ex-tra-mur-al (eks′tra-mū′ral), *adj.* **1,** outside the limits or boundaries of a city, community, organization, school, institution, etc.; as, *extramural* activities or courses; **2,** between schools, universities, or colleges; as, *extramural* soccer. Compare *intramural.*

ex-tra-ne-ous (ek-strā′ni-us), *adj.* **1,** coming from without; external; foreign; as, no *extraneous* influences moulded the islanders' culture; **2,** not belonging or essential to a thing.

ex-tra-or-di-nar-y (eks-trôr′di-nėr-i; eks′tra-ôr′di-nėr-i), *adj.* **1,** unusual; **2,** remarkable; rare; **3,** a special function; as, an envoy *extraordinary.*—*adv.* **ex-tra-or′di-nar-i-ly.**

ex-trap-o-late (eks-tra′po-lāt′), *v.t.* and *v.i.* **1,** to infer or estimate by building upon known data; **2,** in *mathematics,* to predict values from those already known.

ex-trav-a-gant (eks-trav′a-gant), *adj.* **1,** exceeding reasonable limits; elaborate or showy; **2,** wasteful; needlessly lavish in spending; **3,** very high; exorbitant; as, *extravagant* prices.—*adv.* **ex-trav′a-gant-ly.**—*n.* **ex-trav′a-gance.**

ex-trav-a-gan-za (ek-strav′a-gan′za), *n.* **1,** a spectacular or lavish event; **2,** a drama or musical, as a comic opera, marked by fantastic plot, irregular form, farce, etc.

ex-treme (eks-trēm′), *adj.* **1,** of the highest degree; as, *extreme* old age; *extreme* danger; **2,** outermost; farthest away; as, the *extreme* ends of the world; **3,** most severe or strict; as, *extreme* measures; **4,** excessive; immoderate; as, *extreme* fashions; **5,** advanced; radical; as, *extreme* ideas; **6,** sports that are very dangerous and exciting; as, *extreme* skiing:—*n.* **1,** the extremity; the very end; **2,** the utmost degree of anything; **3,** excess; as, to go to *extremes.*—*adv.* **ex-treme′ly.**—*n.* **ex-trem′ist.**

ex-trem-i-ty (eks-trem′i-ti), *n.* [*pl.* extremities], **1,** the farthest point, or end; as, the western *extremity* of the bridge; **2,** a limb, such as an arm, hand, leg, or foot; **3,** the utmost degree; as, an *extremity* of pain; **4,** extreme need, distress, or desperation; as, people were driven to *extremities* by the drought.

ex-tri-cate (eks′tri-kāt′), *v.t.* [extricat-ed, extricat-ing], to free or set loose; as, to *extricate* an animal from a trap; also, to free from difficulties; disentangle; as, to *extricate* oneself from debt.

faint (fānt), *v.i.* to lose consciousness, as a result of great pain, loss of blood, shock, etc.:—*n.* the act or state of fainting:—*adj.* **1,** weak; about to faint; as, to feel *faint*; **2,** timid; as, a *faint* heart; **3,** dim; indistinct; weak; as, a *faint* sound or colour; **4,** feeble; inadequate; as, a *faint* attempt.—*n.* **faint′ness.**—*adv.* **faint′ly.**

[1]**fair** (fâr), *adj.* **1,** pleasing to the sight; as, a *fair* city; **2,** light in complexion; blond; as, *fair* skin; **3,** following the rules in a proper way; as, *fair* play; **4,** not cloudy; clear; as, today will be *fair*; **5,** honest; just; as, a *fair* judge; **6,** moderately good; as, a *fair* score; **7,** open to lawful pursuit; as, *fair* game; **8,** in *baseball*, not foul:—*adv.* in a fair manner; as, to play *fair*.—*adv.* **fair′ly.**—*n.* **fair′ness.**

[2]**fair** (fâr), *n.* **1,** a large public gathering for the sale or exhibition of farm products and animals, etc.; **2,** a large showing and selling of goods, products, or objects; as, a fall *fair*; **3,** any display or show of items of a certain kind; as, a school science *fair*.

fair-ly (fâr′li), *adv.* **1,** in an honest or fair way; as, to be treated *fairly*; **2,** for the most part; somewhat; rather; as, to leave *fairly* soon.

fair-way (fâr′wā′), *n.* in *golf*, the grassy lane between tee and putting green.

fair–weath-er (fâr′–weth′ėr), *adj.* loyal or reliable only in good times; as, a *fair-weather* friend.

fair-y (fâr′i), *n.* [*pl.* fairies], an imaginary being of graceful and tiny human form, with magical powers:—*adj.* having to do with, or like, fairies.

fair-y-land (fâr′i-land′), *n.* the home of the fairies; hence, an enchanting place.

fairy tale, 1, a children's imaginary story about fairies, witches, goblins, wizards, etc.; **2,** an untrue story often with an aim to mislead.

fait ac-com-pli (fâ′tå′kôn′plē′), *n.* an accomplished fact; a thing done, thereby making opposition useless.

faith (fāth), *n.* **1,** belief in God or other Supreme Being; **2,** belief in something without proof; as, he had *faith* that his son was safe; **3,** confidence or trust in another person; as, we had *faith* in our coach; **4,** a promise; as, he broke *faith* with us; **5,** a system of religious belief; as, the Buddhist *faith*.

faith-ful (fāth′fool), *adj.* **1,** loyal; devoted; as, a *faithful* friend; **2,** trustworthy; as, a *faithful* employee; **3,** accurate; true; as, a *faithful* testimony.—*adv.* **faith′ful-ly**—*n.* **faith′ful-ness.**

faith-less (fāth′les), *adj.* **1,** without faith; **2,** untrustworthy; disloyal.—*adv.* **faith′-less-ly.**—*n.* **faith′less-ness.**

fa-ji-ta (fa-hē′ta; fä-hē′ta), *n.* marinated strips of meat that are grilled or broiled and served on a tortilla with vegetables and spicy sauce.

fake (fāk), *v.t.* **1,** to pretend; as, she *faked* illness; in *football*, he *faked* a pass; **2,** to tamper with (in order to deceive); as, to *fake* a label; to counterfeit:—*n.* a deception; a person or thing that is not what it should be or seems to be: as, this so-called Rembrandt is a *fake*:—*adj.* sham; not genuine; as, a *fake* diamond.—*n.* **fa′ker.**

fa-la-fel or **fe-la-fel** (fe-lä′fel), *n.* a patty or ball consisting of a mixture of peas or beans and spices, fried, and served in a pita bread.

fal-con (fô′kun; fôl′kun), *n.* any one of several small, swift hawks, which can be trained for hunting.—*n.* **fal′con-ry** (fô′kn-r).

fall (fôl), *v.i.* [*p.t.* fell (fel), *p.p.* fall-en (fôl′en), *p.pr.* fall-ing], **1,** to drop from a higher to a lower place; as, the rain *fell*; to *fall* to your knees; **2,** to hang down; as, hair *falls* over the shoulders; **3,** to be overthrown; as, a city *falls*; **4,** to die; as, to *fall* in battle; **5,** to lose moral dignity or character; as, to *fall* from grace; **6,** to decrease; diminish in value or degree; as, prices *fall*; the thermometer *falls*; **7,** to slope, as land; **8,** to come by chance or by inheritance; as, this part *falls* to me; **9,** to pass gradually into some state of mind or body; as, to *fall* asleep; *fall* in love; **10,** to reach or strike; as, moonlight *fell* on the water; **11,** to occur; as, Thanksgiving always *falls* on Mondays:—*n.* **1,** the act of falling; **2,** something that has fallen; as, a heavy *fall* of rain; **3,** autumn; **4,** ruin or downfall; as, the *fall* of a city; **5,** decrease in price, value, etc.:—**falls,** a cascade; waterfall; as, Niagara *Falls*.

fal-la-cy (fal′a-si), *n.* [*pl.* fallacies], **1,** a mistaken idea; as, it is a *fallacy* that pigs are stupid and dirty animals; **2,** unsound reasoning.—*adj.* **fal-la′cious** (fa-lā′shus).

fall-en (fôl′en), *adj.* **1,** ruined; captured; overthrown; as, a *fallen* city or empire; **2,** dropped, as leaves, acorns, etc.; **3,** degraded; **4,** killed; as, *fallen* soldiers.

fal-li-ble (fal′i-bl), *adj.* liable to err; as, all humans are *fallible*.

fall-ing–out (fôl′ing–out′), *n.* [*pl.* fallings-out] *Colloq.* a quarrel.

fall–out (fôl′–out′), *n.* **1,** radioactive debris caused by a nuclear explosion; **2,** side effect or result; as, the *fall-out* of her lies.

fal-low (fal′ō), *n.* **1,** land that is ploughed, but left unseeded for a season; **2,** the ploughing of land without sowing it for a season, in order to increase its fertility:—*adj.* ploughed, but not seeded; as, a *fallow* field:—*v.t.* to make or keep fallow.

false (fôls), *adj.* [fals-er, fals-est], **1,** untrue; wrong; as, a *false* idea; *false* answer; **2,** disloyal; **3,** dishonest; lying; meant to deceive; as, a *false* witness or name; **4,** artificial; as, *false* nails; *false* teeth.—*adv.* **false′ly.**—*n.* **false′ness; false′hood.**

false alarm, 1, an emergency warning set

off unnecessarily; **2,** a situation that arouses unjustified alarm or excitement; as, her warning about bad weather was a *false alarm.*

fal-set-to (fôl-set′ō), *n.* [*pl.* falsettos], a voice, esp. a man's voice, pitched unnaturally high; also, one who sings with such a voice:—*adj.* pertaining to a *falsetto.*

fal-si-fy (fôl′si-fī), *v.t.* [falsified, falsifying], **1,** to make false; alter, so as to deceive; as, to *falsify* records; **2,** to prove to be false; disprove.—*n.* **fal′si-fi-ca′tion.**

fal-si-ty (fôl′si-ti), *n.* [*pl.* falsities], **1,** the quality of being untrue; **2,** that which is untrue; an error; falsehood.

fal-ter (fôl′tėr), *v.i.* **1,** to hesitate; waver; as, she started, then *faltered;* **2,** to move unsteadily; **3,** to speak hesitatingly; stammer:—*v.t.* to utter with hesitation; as, he *faltered* a few words.—*adj.* **fal′ter-ing.**

fame (fām), *n.* reputation; renown; popularity.—*adj.* **famed.**

fa-mil-iar (fa-mil′yėr), *adj.* **1,** well acquainted; intimate; as, *familiar* friends; **2,** well known; often seen or heard; common; as, a *familiar* sight; **3,** knowing something well; as, to be *familiar* with special effects technology; **4,** taking liberties; bold; **5,** informal; as, a *familiar* greeting.—*n.* **fa-mil′i-ar′i-ty.**

fa-mil-iar-ize (fa-mil′yėr-īz), *v.t.* [familiarized, familiariz-ing], **1,** to make (a person) feel well acquainted or at ease with something; as, to *familiarize* oneself with new surroundings; **2,** to make well known.

fam-i-ly (fam′i-li), *n.* [*pl.* families], **1,** a group of people related by blood, marriage, or adoption; **2,** the children alone of such a group; as, to start a *family;* **3,** a household; a group of persons under one roof; **4,** a body of persons descended from a common ancestor; tribe; clan; relatives; **5,** a group of things with some common characteristics; as, a mineral *family;* **6,** in *biology,* a classification of plants or animals, larger than a genus, but smaller than an order; as, the cat *family.* Also, **fam′i-ly law′; fam′i-ly plan′ning; fam′i-ly tree′.**

fam-ine (fam′in), *n.* **1,** extreme scarcity of food; starvation; **2,** shortage of some special thing; as, a wheat *famine.*

fam-ish (fam′ish), *v.t.* to destroy with hunger:—*v.i.* to suffer from extreme hunger.—*adj.* **fam′ished.**

fa-mous (fā′mus), *adj.* renowned; celebrated; as, a *famous* scientist or athlete.

fan (fan), *n.* **1,** any electric device with blades used to move currents of air; **2,** a small hand-held device, often one which unfolds into a semi-circular shape, moved to stir up the air; **3,** anything like a fan in shape; **4,** an enthusiast; as, a football *fan:*—*v.t.* [fanned, fan-ning], **1,** to winnow, or separate, as chaff from grain; **2,** to drive a current of air upon; cool the face of; kindle (a fire); **3,** hence, to rouse, as rage; **4,** *Slang* in *baseball,* to strike out (a batter).

fa-nat-ic (fa-nat′ik), *n.* **1,** one who holds extravagant and unreasonable views, esp. of religion; one who is carried away by his or her beliefs; **2,** a person who is much too serious or enthusiastic about something; as, a foreign film *fanatic:*—*adj.* **fa-nat′i-cal.**—*adv.* **fa-nat′i-cal-ly.**—*n.* **fa-nat′i-cism.**

fan-ci-er (fan′si-ėr), *n.* one who has a special interest in something; as, a cat *fancier;* a bird *fancier.*

fan-ci-ful (fan′si-fool), *adj.* **1,** led by imagination; **2,** unreal; as, a *fanciful* story; **3,** curiously designed.—*adv.* **fan′ci-ful-ly.**—*n.* **fan′ci-ful-ness.**

fan-cy (fan′si), *v.t.* [fancied, fancy-ing], **1,** to suppose; as, I *fancy* he will come; **2,** to imagine; as, she *fancies* herself to be prime minister; **3,** to take a liking to:—*adj.* [fan-ci-er, fan-ci-est], **1,** ornamental; not plain; decorated; elegant; as, *fancy* dress; *fancy* car; **2,** extravagant; as, *fancy* prices; **3,** superior to the average; high quality; as, *fancy* products; **4,** tricky; complicated; requiring skill; as, *fancy* footwork:—*n.* [*pl.* fancies], **1,** imagination; **2,** an idea; a notion or whim; **3,** a liking or fondness.

fancy–free (fan′si–frē′), *adj.* **1,** not in love; **2,** carefree.

fang (fang), *n.* a long, sharp tooth, as of a dog, wolf, or poisonous snake.

fan-ta-si-a (fan-tā′zi-a; -zhi-a; -zē′a), *n.* in *music,* **1,** a melody of well-known tunes; **2,** a composition of no fixed form that follows the composer's fancy.

fan-tas-tic (fan-tas′tik) or **fan-tas-ti-cal** (-tas′ti-kal), *adj.* **1,** imaginary; unreal; as, *fantastic* fears; **2,** odd; grotesque; as, shadows assume *fantastic* shapes; **3,** hard to accept as real; amazing; as, time travelling is a *fantastic* idea; **4,** very good; excellent; outstanding; as, the meal was *fantastic.*—*adv.* **fan-tas′ti-cal-ly.**

fan-ta-sy (fan′ta-si; fan′ta-zi), *n.* [*pl.* fantasies], **1,** imagination; **2,** a product of the imagination; **3,** a story, movie, etc., that deals with an imaginary world; as, *Lord of the Rings* is a fantasy novel and movie.

FAQ (ef′ā′kū′), *abbrev.* short for *frequently asked questions.*

far (fär), *adj.* [far-ther, far-thest or fur-ther, fur-thest], **1,** distant in time or space; as, the *far* past; a *far*-off land; **2,** more distant of two; as, the *far* side; **3,** reaching to great distances; as, a *far* journey:—*adv.* **1,** to or at a great, or definite, distance in time or space; as, to go *far;* to go only so *far;* **2,** by a great deal; very much; as, he is *far* wiser than I am.

far-a-way (fär′a-wā′), *adj.* **1,** distant; remote; **2,** dreamy; as, a *faraway* look.

farce (färs), *n.* **1,** a play or other work full

of exaggerated situations intended to be very funny; **2,** a ridiculous sham; as, the election was a mere *farce.*—*adj.* **far′ci-cal.**

fare (fâr), *v.i.* [fared, far-ing], **1,** to experience either good or bad fortune; as, to *fare* well or ill; **2,** to eat; be fed; as, I *fared* well at lunch:—*n.* **1,** the sum paid for a journey, as on a bus, train, airplane, or ship; **2,** a person paying this sum; passenger; **3,** food; meal; as, simple *fare* when camping.

Far East, the countries of eastern Asia, such as China and Japan.

fare-well (fâr′wel′), *interj.* goodbye!—*adj.* final; parting; as, a *farewell* tour:—*n.* (fâr′wel′), **1,** a wish of welfare at parting; a goodbye; **2,** a departure; as, a sad *farewell.*

far–fetched (fär′–fetcht′), *adj.* **1,** forced; strained; as, a *far-fetched* simile; **2,** unlikely; hard to believe; as, a *far-fetched* story.

farm (färm), *n.* an area of land where plants and animals are raised for food, esp. a place where this is done as a business:—*v.t.* and *v.i.* to cultivate (land); to own or work on a farm.—*n.* **farm′ing; farm′er; farm′house′; farm′ team′; farm′yard′.**

Far North, in Canada, the Arctic and subarctic regions.

far–reach-ing (fär′–rēch′ing), *adj.* having a wide influence or effect.

far-row (far′ō), *n.* **1,** a litter of pigs; **2,** *v.i.* and *v.t.* to give birth (to pigs).

far-see-ing (fär′sē′ing), *adj.* having foresight; farsighted.

far-sight-ed (fär′sīt′id), *adj.* **1,** able to see distant objects more clearly than near ones; **2,** having good judgment, with thought for the future; prudent. Compare *nearsighted.*—*n.* **far′sight′ed-ness.**

far-ther (fär′*th*ėr), *adj.* [*comp.* of *far*], more distant; as, the *farther* side:—*adv.* **1,** to or at a greater distance; as, to go *farther*; **2,** moreover.—*adj.* **far′ther-most′.**

far-thest (fär′*th*est), *adj.* [*superl.* of *far*], most distant:—*adv.* to or at the greatest distance.

far-thing (fär′*th*ing), *n.* formerly, a British coin worth one-fourth of a British penny.

fas-ci-nate (fas′i-nāt′), *v.t.* [fascinat-ed, fascinat-ing], **1,** to bewitch or hold motionless by some strange power; as, snakes are said to *fascinate* small birds; **2,** hence, to enchant; charm irresistibly; also, to attract and interest very much; as, this book *fascinates* me.—*adv.* **fas′ci-nat′ing-ly.**—*n.* **fas′ci-na′tion.**

fas-cism or **Fas-cism** (fash′izm), *n.* a centralized, one-party governmental system, suppressing unions and rival parties, and marked by aggressive nationalism, racism, and hostility to socialism: Italy and Germany were fascist states before World War II. Compare *Nazi.*—*n.* and *adj.* **fas′cist; Fas′cist.**

fash-ion (fash′un), *n.* **1,** the shape or form of anything; **2,** manner or way of doing something; as, he eats in an odd *fashion*; **3,** the prevailing style or custom at any time, esp. in dress; as, bustles and spats are no longer in *fashion*; a dress of the latest *fashion*:—*v.t.* to mould, shape, or form; as, to *fashion* a model out of clay.—*adj.* **fash′ion-a-ble.**—*adv.* **fash′ion-a-bly.**

¹fast (fåst), *adj.* **1,** securely fixed; attached; as, frozen *fast* in the snow; **2,** faithful; steadfast; as, *fast* friends; **3,** deep; sound; as, a *fast* sleeper; **4,** not fading; as, *fast* colours; **5,** rapid; swift; as, a *fast* runner; also, allowing quick motion; as, a *fast* track; **6,** ahead of the standard time; as, my watch is *fast*; **7,** wild; unrestrained; as, *fast* society:—*adv.* **1,** fixedly; firmly; **2,** rapidly; **3,** wildly; too free; **4,** deeply; as, *fast* asleep. Also, **fast′ lane′; fast′–talk′er; fast′ track′.**

²fast (fåst), *v.i.* to take little or no food because of health or religious or political beliefs:—*n.* the act or period of fasting.

fas-ten (fås′n), *v.t.* **1,** to fix securely, as a door; cause to hold together, as a dress; to attach to something else; as, to *fasten* a shelf to a wall; **2,** to keep fixed steadily, as one's attention; **3,** to attach, as blame:—*v.i.* to take hold; become attached.—*n.* **fas′ten-er; fas′ten-ing.**

fast food, food that can be prepared and served quickly, such as hamburgers and French fries. Also, **fast food restaurant.**

fast–for-ward or **fast for-ward** (fåst–fôr′wėrd), *n.* **1,** the control on an audiotape, videotape, or DVD player for advancing the tape rapidly; **2,** *Colloq.* any rapid change or advancement; as, her career is on *fast-forward.*—*v.t.* and *v.i.* **fastforward,** to advance an audiotape or videotape rapidly; as, to *fast-forward* past the commercial.

fas-tid-i-ous (fas-tid′-i-us), *adj.* hard to please; daintily particular.—*adv.* **fas-tid′i-ous-ly.**—*n.* **fas-tid′i-ous-ness.**

fast-ness (fåst′nes), *n.* **1,** swiftness; **2,** a stronghold; as, a mountain *fastness.*

fat (fat), *adj.* [fat-ter, fat-test], **1,** plump; fleshy; obese; **2,** greasy; rich; as, *fat* meat; **3,** well-filled or stocked; as, a *fat* wallet; **4,** profitable; as, a *fat* job; **5,** fertile; as, a *fat* soil:—*n.* **1,** an oily, yellow or white substance found in animal and vegetable tissues, which is an important source of energy for people, but harmful in excess; **2,** the best or richest part of anything:—*v.t.* [fatted, fat-ting], to make fat. Also, **fat′ cat′; fat′head′.**

fa-tal (fā′t'l), *adj.* **1,** causing death; as, a *fatal* accident; **2,** causing great harm; as, a *fatal* error.—*adv.* **fa′tal-ly.**—*n.* **fa′tal-ist; fa′tal-ism.**—*adj.* **fa′tal-is′tic.**

fa-tal-i-ty (fā-tal′i-ti), *n.* [*pl.* fatalities], **1,** a condition of being doomed by fate; as, a *fatality* attends everything she tries to do; **2,** a fatal influence; deadly quality; as, the *fatality* of cancer; **3,** a calamity; also, death in a disaster; as, there were two *fatalities* in the fire.

fate (fāt), *n.* **1,** a power beyond a person's control that is believed to determine events; **2,** that which is decided by fate; one's lot or destiny; **3,** the end or final result of something; outcome; as, to decide the *fate* of the moraine.—*adj.* **fat′ed.**

fate-ful (fāt′fool), *adj.* **1,** important; significant; as, tomorrow is the *fateful* day; **2,** prophetic; as, a *fateful* tolling of the bell; **3,** deadly; as, a *fateful* blow; **4,** controlled by fate.—*adv.* **fate′ful-ly.**

fa-ther (fä′*th*ėr), *n.* **1,** a male parent; **2,** an ancestor; **3,** one who stands in the relation of a father; **4,** an originator or founder; as, *Fathers* of Confederation:—**Father** a title for a clergyman, esp. a Roman Catholic priest:—**the Father,** God in the Christian religion:—*v.t.* **1,** to beget, adopt, or act as a father to (a child); **2,** to assume authorship of or accept responsibility for; as, to *father* a plan.—*n.* **fa′ther-hood.**—*adj.* **fa′ther-less; fa′ther-ly.**

fa-ther–in–law (fä′*th*ėr–in–lô′), *n.* [*pl.* fathers-in-law], the father of one's husband or of one's wife.

fa-ther-land (fä′*th*ėr-land′), *n.* one's native country.

Fa-ther's Day, the third Sunday in June, set aside to honour fathers.

Fathers of Confederation, the representatives from the original provinces of Canada who met to create the Dominion of Canada.

fath-om (fa*th*′um), *n.* a measure of length equal to 1.83 metres, used to measure the depth of water or length of ships:—*v.t.* **1,** to find the depth of (water); **2,** to reach an understanding of; as, I was able to *fathom* his meaning.

fath-om-less (fa*th*′um-lis), *adj.* **1,** so deep that the bottom cannot be reached; **2,** not possible to understand; as, a *fathomless* mystery.

fa-tigue (fa-tēg′), *n.* weariness resulting from labour; bodily or mental exhaustion:—*v.t.* and *v.i.* [fatigued, fatiguing], to weary; tire or become wearied.

fat-ten (fat′n), *v.t.* and *v.i.* to make or become fat.

fat-ty (fat′i), *adj.* [fat-ti-er, fat-ti-est], **1,** containing fat; **2,** greasy; oily.

fat-u-ous (fat′ū-us), *adj.* silly; as, a *fatuous* remark.—*n.* **fa-tu′i-ty.**

fau-cet (fô′set), *n.* a device for controlling the flow of liquid from a pipe or other container; a tap.

fault (fôlt), *n.* **1,** a weakness in character; **2,** a mistake or weak point in the way something works or is made; a flaw; as, a *fault* in an electrical wiring system; **3,** blame or responsibility for something; as, it was not his *fault*; **4,** a break in layers of rock that were previously continuous; as, earthquakes are likely to take place along a *fault*:—**find fault,** to complain; as, she was forever *finding fault*:—*v.t.* to find fault with someone or something; blame; as, to *fault* her for their tardiness.—*adj.* **fault′less.**—*n.* **fault′fin′der; fault′ line′** (a break in the earth).

fault-y (fôl′ti), *adj.* [fault-i-er, fault-i-est], imperfect; defective; as, *faulty* brakes.—*n.* **fault′i-ness.**

fau-na (fô′na), *n.* the animals belonging to a special region or period; as, the *fauna* of the African jungle.

faux pas (fō′pä′), *n.* a false step, as a breach of etiquette, manners, or morals; a tactless deed or word; blunder; as, to make a *faux pas* by addressing the prime minister by first name.

fa-vour or **fa-vor** (fā′vėr), *n.* **1,** an act of kindness; as, do me a *favour*; **2,** approval; as, she looked on with *favour*; **3,** partiality; special consideration; as, he asked no *favour*; **4,** a small gift or token; as, party *favours*:—*v.t.* **1,** to regard with goodwill; support or approve; **2,** to show partiality to; prefer; as, to *favour* soccer over baseball; **3,** to treat in a special or careful way; as, to favour an injured leg; **4,** to make possible or easy; as, fair weather *favours* our plan; **5,** to oblige; as, *favour* me with your attention; **6,** to look like (a person); as, she *favours* her mother.

fa-vour-a-ble (fā′vėr-a-bl), *adj.* **1,** expressing approval; as, a *favourable* article about a company; **2,** advantageous; as, *favourable* weather; **3,** giving assent; helpful.—*adv.* **fa′vour-a-bly.**

fa-vour-ite (fā′vėr-it), *n.* **1,** one who or that which is particularly liked or preferred; as, a *favourite* snack; **2,** a contestant thought to have the best chance of winning; as, this race horse was the *favourite*; **3,** in *computing,* bookmarks; the marking of frequently used Web sites on a Web browser that allows the user to go directly to the sites without retyping the address each time:—*adj.* preferred; best-liked; as, a *favourite* book.—*n.* **fa′vour-it-ism** (showing favour to a person or thing in an unfair way).

¹fawn (fôn), *n.* a deer less than one year old:—*adj.* of a light yellowish brown; as, she bought a *fawn* coat.

²fawn (fôn), *v.i.* **1,** to show pleasure or affection by wagging the tail, whining, etc., as a dog does; **2,** to seek favour by flattery and cringing behaviour.

fax (faks), *n.* [*pl.* faxes] **1,** a facsimile machine; **2,** the message sent by such a machine; a facsimile:—*v.t.* to transmit a message or document using such a machine; as, *fax* me a copy of your letter.

faze (fāz), *v.t. Colloq.* to disconcert; disturb; as, the errors didn't *faze* him.

fe-al-ty (fē′al-ti), *n.* in the feudal period,

the pledge of a vassal to be faithful to his lord; hence, loyalty; a pledge of allegiance.

fear (fēr), *n.* **1,** a feeling of alarm or dread of possible evil or danger; as, a *fear* of flying; **2,** reverence; as, the *fear* of God:—*v.t.* **1,** to regard with dread; be afraid of; as, to *fear* snakes; **2,** to revere:—*v.i.* to be afraid, worried, or anxious about what will happen; as, to *fear* that we were lost.

fear-ful (fēr′fool), *adj.* **1,** causing fear or awe; terrible; as, a *fearful* sight; **2,** full of alarm; timid; lacking courage.—*adv.* **fear′ful-ly.**

fear-less (fēr′lis), *adj.* without fear; not afraid; courageous; bold; daring.—*adv.* **fear′less-ly.**—*n.* **fear′less-ness.**

fea-si-ble (fē′zi-bl), *adj.* capable of being done; possible; as, a *feasible* scheme.—*n.* **fea′si-bil-i-ty.**

feast (fēst), *n.* **1,** a lavish meal; **2,** a festival in memory of an event, esp. a religious festival; **3,** anything pleasing to the taste or mind; as, the beautiful scenery was a *feast* for sore eyes:—*v.t.* **1,** to have or make a bountiful meal; **2,** to delight; as, to *feast* the eyes on beauty:—*v.i.* to partake of a feast.

feat (fēt), *n.* an act or deed displaying great courage, strength, skill, etc.; as, winning the gold medal by both the women's and men's hockey teams in the 2002 Winter Olympics was a remarkable *feat* for Canada.

feath-er (fe*th*′ėr), *n.* one of the light outgrowths that covers and protects the skin of a bird:—*v.t.* **1,** to cover or line with feathers; **2,** to turn the blade of (an oar) horizontally as it leaves the water:—*v.i.* **1,** to become covered with feathers; **2,** to feather one's oars while rowing.

feath-er-bed-ding (fe*th*′ėr-bed′ing), *n.* the forcing of an employer by a union to pay unnecessary employees.

feath-er-brain (fe*th*′ėr-brān′), *n.* a giddy, silly, or weak-minded person.

feath-er-weight (fe*th*′ėr-wāt′), *n.* in *sports,* the weight of a boxer between 54 and 57 kilograms.

feath-er-y (fe*th*′ėr-i), *adj.* like a feather in shape, lightness, or softness; as, a *feathery* fern.—*n.* **feath′er-i-ness.**

fea-ture (fē′tūr), *n.* **1,** something noticeable about a thing; as, the architectural *features* of a building; **2,** the chief attraction of a program, etc.; the main film of a motion-picture program; a full-length movie; **3,** a special story in a newspaper or magazine; **4,** any part of the face, as the eyes, chin, etc.; as, her best *feature* is her mouth:—**features,** the whole face:—*v.t.* [featured, featur-ing], **1,** to portray the features of; outline; **2,** to make prominent; as, the magazine will *feature* photos of the disaster:—*adj.* **1,** of a special story in a newspaper or magazine; as, a *feature* story for a newspaper; **2,** of a chief attraction of a program; as, *feature* film or presentation.

Feb-ru-a-ry (feb′roo-ėr-i), *n.* the second month of the year, with 28 days, except for every fourth year (*leap year*), when it has 29.

fe-ces or **fae-ces** (fē′sēz), *n.pl.* **1,** waste matter expelled from the bowels or intestines of people and animals; excrement; **2,** dregs; sediment.

fec-und (fē′kund; fek′und), *adj.* fruitful; prolific; as, a *fecund* mind (one rich in ideas).—*v.t.* **fe′cun-date′.**—*n.* **fe-cun′di-ty.**

fed-er-al (fed′ėr-al), *adj.* **1,** relating to a nation formed by the union of several smaller provinces, states, etc.; as, Canada has a *federal* government; **2,** (also **Federal**) having to do with the central government of Canada; as, the postal system is a *federal* responsibility:—**Federal,** in the U.S., favouring the North in the Civil War; as, a *Federal* soldier; also a person on the side of the Union in the Civil War.

fed-er-al-ism (fed′ėr-al-izm), *n.* **1,** a system of government in which power is distributed between the central and regional governments; **2,** in Canada, a support of Confederation and the central government as opposed to the provinces, esp. against Québec separatism.

fed-er-ate (fed′ėr-āt′), *v.t.* and *v.i.* [federat-ed, federat-ing], to combine (province, states, or societies) into a union.—*n.* **fed′er-a′tion.**

fe-do-ra (fi-dō′ra), *n.* a soft felt hat with the crown creased lengthwise and brim curved a little.

fee (fē), *n.* **1,** payment for a service, right, or privilege; as, a lawyer's *fee;* a licence *fee;* university *fees;* **2,** under the feudal system, land held from an overlord; also, the terms under which such land was held; a fief; as, to hold land in *fee.*

fee-ble (fē′bl), *adj.* [fee-bler, fee-blest], **1,** without strength; weak; frail; as, a *feeble* old woman; **2,** lacking in vigour; faint; as, a *feeble* effort.—*n.* **fee′ble-ness.**—*adj.* **fee′bly.**

fee-ble–mind-ed (fē′bl–mīn′did), *adj.* having little power to think or to learn.—*n.* **fee′ble–mind′ed-ness.**

feed (fēd), *v.t.* [fed (fed), feed-ing], **1,** to supply with food; as, to *feed* a homeless person; **2,** to put food into the mouth of; as, to *feed* a baby; **3,** to give as food; as, to *feed* meat to a dog; **4,** to nourish; as, soil *feeds* plants; **5,** to provide or supply with something; as, to *feed* information into a computer; to *feed* a fire with fuel:—*v.i.* to take food; as, the pup *fed* eagerly:—*n.* food for animals, esp. farm animals; fodder; as, chicken *feed.*—*adj.* and *n.* **feed′er.**

feed-back (fēd′bak′), *n.* **1,** a process by which a machine gets back information about how it is working and then adjusts itself according to this information; **2,**

information about how a process or plan is working; as, to get *feedback* from the public about a government program.

feel (fēl), *v.t.* [felt (felt), feel-ing], **1,** to examine by touch; as, to *feel* a person's pulse; **2,** to be aware of (something) by touch; as, I *felt* rain; **3,** to have a sense of; as, to *feel* pity; **4,** to be moved or disturbed by; as, to *feel* a slight; **5,** to be sure of, without proof; as, I *feel* it to be so:—*v.i.* **1,** to search by touch; grope; as, to *feel* for a pin; **2,** to be aware of being in some definite condition of mind or body; as, to *feel* faint; **3,** to have sympathy; as, to *feel* deeply for someone; **4,** to seem to the touch; as, the air *feels* damp:—*n.* a quality perceived by touch; as, the silky *feel* of velvet.

feel-er (fēl′ėr), *n.* **1,** an organ of touch, as one of a cat's whiskers; **2,** a remark made to draw out the opinions of others; as, to put out *feelers.*

feel-ing (fēl′ing), *n.* **1,** the sense, usually called *touch,* by which a person tells hot from cold, rough from smooth, etc.; **2,** any sensation of the skin, or of the body in general; as, a *feeling* of pain, cold, hunger, etc.; **3,** an emotion of hope, hate, love, etc.; **4,** emotional excitement; as, *feeling* over the game ran high; **5,** opinion; as, it is my *feeling* that you ought to go:—**feelings,** sensitive nature; one's pride; as, to hurt his *feelings.*

feet (fēt), *n.pl.* of *foot.*

feign (fān), *v.t.* and *v.i.* to pretend; as, to *feign* illness.—*n.* **feign′er.**

feint (fānt), *n.* a pretence; esp., a pretence of attack at one point while really attacking at another:—*v.i.* to make a sham thrust; as, to *feint* with the left hand and strike with the right.

feist-y (fī′sti), *adj. Colloq.* **1,** full of energy; spunky; exuberant; plucky; as, a *feisty* kitten; **2,** touchy; irritable.

fe-lic-i-tate (fe-lis′i-tāt′), *v.t.* [felicitat-ed, felicitat-ing], to congratulate; wish happiness to.—*n.* **fe-lic′i-ta′tion.**

fe-lic-i-ty (fe-lis′i-ti), *n.* [*pl.* felicities], **1,** great happiness; also, a source of happiness; **2,** a pleasing way of speaking or writing; also, a well-chosen expression.—*adj.* **fe-lic′i-tous.**

fe-line (fē′līn), *adj.* **1,** of, or relating to, a cat or the cat family; **2,** stealthy; sly; as, a *feline* movement in the darkness.

¹fell (fel), *p.t.* of *fall.*

²fell (fel), *n.* skin; pelt; hide; as, a *fell* of hair.

³fell (fel), *v.t.* **1,** to cause to fall; knock down, as by a blow; kill; as, to *fell* an enemy; **2,** cut down, as a tree; **3,** to fold over and sew down flat, as a seam:—*n.* **1,** cut-down trees; **2,** a seam made by felling.

⁴fell (fel), *adj.* cruel; savage; terrible; deadly; as, a *fell* disease.

fel-low (fel′ō), *n.* **1,** a companion; associate; equal; as, a *fellow* in misery; **2,** one of a pair; a mate; match; as, the *fellow* of this shoe; **3,** *Colloq.* a man or boy; anybody; as, a *fellow* has to eat; also, a girl's beau; **4,** an honoured member, as of certain learned societies; also, a graduate student supported by an endowment at a university or college:—*adj.* associated with others; as, *fellow* members.

fel-low-ship (fel′ō-ship′), *n.* **1,** membership in a group, society, etc.; also, the group itself; as, to admit to *fellowship*; **2,** friendly association; companionship; as, I enjoy his *fellowship*; **3,** a position endowed to enable the holder to continue study, free of expense for board, tuition, etc., as in a university.

¹fel-on (fel′un), *n.* a person who is guilty of a serious crime.

²fel-on (fel′un), *n.* a painful inflammation on a finger or toe, usually near the nail.

fel-o-ny (fel′o-ni), *n.* [*pl.* felonies], a serious crime, as murder or robbery.—*adj.* **fe-lo′ni-us** (fe-lō′ni-us).

¹felt (felt), *p.t.* and *p.p.* of *feel.*

²felt (felt), *n.* a fabric made of wool, hair, fur, or other material, matted or forced together by pressure:—*adj.* made of felt; as, a *felt* hat or slippers:—*v.t.* to mat into a mass; as, to *felt* wool together; also, to cover with felt.—*n.* **felt′ing.**

fe-male (fē′māl), *adj.* having to do with women or girls; belonging to the sex that can bear young:—*n.* a woman or girl; a person or an animal of the sex that can bear young.

fem-i-nine (fem′i-nin), *adj.* **1,** relating to women or girls; like women or girls; as, *feminine* characteristics; **2,** typical of or suitable for women or girls; as, *feminine* fashions; **3,** in *grammar,* of the gender to which names of females belong; as, "doe" and "sow" are *feminine* nouns: compare *masculine* and *neuter.*—*n.* **fem′i-nin′i-ty.**

fem-i-nism (fem′i-nizm), *n.* the belief that women should be given social, economic, and political status equal to that of men.—*n.* **fem′i-nist.**

fe-mur (fē′mėr), *n.* [*pl.* femurs (-mėrz), femora (fem′o-ra)], the thighbone, the longest and largest bone in the body (from hip to knee).

FEMUR

fen (fen), *n.* **1,** low, marshy land; **2,** a unit of money in the People's Republic of China.

fence (fens), *n.* **1,** a barrier or boundary of stone, wood, or other material, used mainly to keep people or animals in or out; **2,** a receiver of stolen goods:—*v.t.* [fenced, fencing], to enclose with a fence; as, to *fence* a field:—*v.i.* to practise the use of swords or foils.—*n.* **fenc′er.** Also, **fence′ sit′ter.**

fenc-ing (fen′sing), *n.* **1,** the art of using a foil or sword; **2,** materials used for making a fence; **3,** the fences on a plot of land.

fend (fend), *v.t.* to ward off, as a blow:—*v.i.* to provide; as, I must *fend* for myself.

fend-er (fen′dėr), *n.* **1,** a device on the front of a locomotive or streetcar to prevent or lessen injuries from collisions; **2,** a metal guard in front of a fireplace; **3,** a guard over an automobile, truck, or bicycle wheel. Also, **fend′er–bend′er.**

feng shui (fung′ shwā′), *n.* the Chinese practice of designing and arranging buildings, furniture, etc., to promote positive forces.

fen-nel (fen′el), *n.* a fragrant plant of the carrot family, the seeds of which are used in cooking and medicine.

fe-ral (fer′al), *adj.* **1,** wild; savage; as, a *feral* animal; **2,** deadly, as a disease; **3,** dismal.

fer-ment (fûr′ment), *n.* **1,** a substance, as yeast, that causes chemical change with effervescence; **2,** a state of excitement; unrest; as, the town is in a *ferment*:—*v.i.* (fėr-ment′), **1,** to be in a state of fermentation, as milk when it turns sour, or cider when it bubbles; **2,** to become stirred up or excited:—*v.t.* **1,** to cause fermentation in; **2,** to excite or stir up.

fer-men-ta-tion (fûr′men-t′shun), *n.* **1,** a change, such as is caused by yeast, producing gas bubbles, alcohol, or acid, as in the souring of milk, the working of cider, etc.; **2,** excitement; unrest.

fern (fûrn), *n.* any one of many flowerless plants with broad feathery, leaflike fronds, which grow throughout the world, usually in wet places.—*n.* **fern′er-y.**—*adj.* **fern′y.**

fe-ro-cious (fe-rō′shus), *adj.* savage; strong and fierce; as, a *ferocious* tiger.—*n.* **fe-roc′i-ty** (fe-ros′i-t).

fer-ret (fer′it), *n.* a small, weasel-like animal, often used to hunt rodents:—*v.t.* **1,** to hunt (rats, etc.) with ferrets; **2,** to search perseveringly for; as, to *ferret* out a secret:—*v.i.* to hunt with ferrets; search.—*n.* **fer′ret-er.**

fer-ry (fer′i), *n.* [*pl.* ferries], **1,** a boat used to carry passengers or vehicles across a river, lake, etc.; **2,** a place where such a boat lands:—*v.t.* [ferried, ferry-ing], **1,** to take across a body of water on a ferry; as, to *ferry* a car across a lake; **2,** to transport something, such as an automobile or airplane, from one place to another; **3,** to cross by ferry; as, to *ferry* the lake:—*v.i.* to go by ferry.

fer-tile (fûr′tl; fûr′tīl), *adj.* **1,** producing abundantly; fruitful; as, *fertile* land; **2,** capable of producing seed, eggs, pollen, or offspring; as, a *fertile* flower; **3,** capable of developing; as, a *fertile* seed or egg; **4,** able to produce many thoughts or ideas; as, a *fertile* imagination.—*n.* **fer-til′i-ty.**

fer-ti-lize (fûr′ti-līz′), *v.t.* [fertilized, fertil-iz-ing], **1,** to make productive; esp., to supply with plant food; as, to *fertilize* a lawn; **2,** to place pollen or sperm into a plant or female animal to develop a seed; pollinate or impregnate; as, bees *fertilize* flowers.—*n.* **fer′ti-li-za′tion; fer′ti-liz′er.**

fer-vent (fûr′vent), *adj.* warmly felt; intense; earnest; as, a *fervent* request.—*adv.* **fer′vent-ly.**—*n.* **fer′ven-cy.**

fer-vid (fûr′vid), *adj.* fiery in feeling; earnest; as, a *fervid* speech.—*adv.* **fer′vid-ly.**—*n.* **fer′vid-ness.**

fer-vour (fûr′vėr), *n.* glowing warmth of feeling; zeal; as, patriotic *fervour.*

fes-ter (fes′tėr), *v.i.* **1,** to become filled with pus; as, his wound *festered;* **2,** to linger painfully; cause a sore feeling; rankle; as, the insult *festered* in his mind:—*n.* a pus-forming sore.

fes-ti-val (fes′ti-val), *n.* **1,** a time of celebrating and feasting, usually in honour of some event; a special public celebration; as, a harvest *festival;* **2,** a series of entertainments or cultural events of the same kind over several days; as, a film or jazz *festival.*

fes-tive (fes′tiv), *adj.* **1,** suitable to a feast or holiday; **2,** joyous; bright; as, a *festive* room.—*n.* **fes-tiv′i-ty.**

fes-toon (fes-to͞on′), *n.* a decorative chain of flowers, etc., hung in curves; also, a carved likeness of such a chain:—*v.t.* to decorate with festoons, or decorative chains of flowers, etc.; as, the theatre was *festooned* with ivy.

fetch (fech), *v.t.* **1,** to go after and bring back; as, *fetch* me a pen; **2,** to sell for; as, the land *fetched* a high price.

fetching (fech′ing), *adj. Colloq.* charming; attractive; as, a *fetching* outfit.

fete or **fête** (fāt; fet), *n.* a festival; an entertainment; esp., an elaborate outdoor entertainment:—*v.t.* [fet-ed, fet-ing], to entertain as the guest of honour.

fet-id (fet′id; fē′tid), *adj.* stinking; as, *fetid* air; a *fetid* latrine.

fe-tish (fe′tish; fēt′-), *n.* an object of blind or unreasoning devotion; as, she makes a *fetish* of dress.

fet-ter (fet′ėr), *n.* **1,** a chain to bind the feet; **2,** a restraint; hindrance; as, the *fetters* of ignorance:—*v.t.* to put in chains; also, to hinder; restrain.

fe-tus or **foe-tus** (fē′tus), *n.* the child in the uterus from the third month of pregnancy until birth. Compare *embryo.*—*adj.* **fe′tal** or **foe′tal.**

feud (fūd), *n.* a quarrel or fight, generally of long standing, esp. between clans or families:—*v.i.* to take part in a feud or quarrel; as, to *feud* with a neighbour for years.

feu-dal (fū′d'l), *adj.* relating to the method of holding land in Western Europe in the Middle Ages:—**feudal system,** the form of political organization common in Western Europe in the Middle Ages, based on the relationship between lord and vassal, the vassal holding land from his lord in return for military and other service.—*n.* **feu′dal-ism.**

fe-ver (fē′vėr), *n.* **1,** a diseased condition or symptom marked by weakness, quick pulse, and high body temperature; **2,** a disease causing such symptoms, such as *yellow fever;* **2,** great excitement; as, a *fever* of anxiety.—*adj.* **fe′ver-ish; fe′vered.**

few (fū), *adj.* and *pron.* small in number; not many; as, a *few* steps; a *few* came late.—*n.* **few′ness.**

fez (fez), *n.* [*pl.* fezzes], a red felt, tasselled cap, formerly worn by Turkish men.

fi-an-cé (fē′än-sā′; fi-än′sā; *French*, fyän′sā′), *n.* a man engaged to be married.—*n.fem.* **fi′an-cée′** (fē′än-sā′; fi-än′sā; French, fyän′sā′).

fi-as-co (fi-ås′kō), *n.* [*pl.* fiascos or fiascoes], an ignominious failure; a breakdown.

fi-at (fī′at), *n.* a decree; command; as, a king's *fiat.*

fib (fib), *n.* a petty lie:—*v.i.* [fibbed, fibbing], to tell fibs.—*n.* **fib′ber.**

fi-bre or **fi-ber** (fī′bėr), *n.* **1,** one of many slender, threadlike parts forming certain plant and animal substances; as, flax *fibres;* nerve *fibres;* also, a substance made up of such parts; **2,** raw material that can be separated into threads and spun or woven; as, cotton, silk, or wool *fibre;* **3,** quality or character; as, a woman of tough *fibre.*—*adj.* **fi′broid.**

fi-bre-glass or **fi-ber-glass** (fī′bėr-glas′), *n.* finely spun glass filaments made into a woolly yarn, fabrics, building insulation, protecting boat hulls, etc.

fibre optics, 1, the transmission of light and information over thin fibres of glass or plastic; **2,** the fibres, usually bundled together, to carry data in such a way.—*adj.* **fi′bre–op′tic.**

fi-bro-my-al-gi-a (fī′brō-mī-al′jē-a), *n.* a condition characterized by chronic fatigue and the painful inflammation of muscles and soft tissues, esp. around the joints.

fi-brous (fī′brus), *adj.* **1,** threadlike; **2,** made of threadlike stuff; as, *fibrous* bark.

fib-u-la (fib′yoo-la), *n.* the outer, smaller bone of the leg below the knee. Compare *tibia.*

fick-le (fik′l), *adj.* uncertain; changeable; as, *fickle* weather.—*n.* **fick′le-ness.**

fic-tion (fik′shun), *n.* **1,** novels, short stories, etc., telling of imaginary events and characters; **2,** anything imagined or invented as contrasted with things that are real or true; as, that story of his wealth is a *fiction.* Compare *nonfiction.*—*adj.* **fic′tion-al.**

fic-ti-tious (fik-tish′us), *adj.* imagined; not real; as, a *fictitious* character.

fid-dle (fid′l), *n. Colloq.* a violin, esp. when used to play country or folk music:—*v.i.* [fid-dled, fid-dling], **1,** to play the violin; **2,** to trifle; play restlessly; as, to *fiddle* at writing:—*v.t. Colloq.* to play (a tune) on a violin; as, he can *fiddle* the latest folk-songs.—*n.* **fid′dler.**

fid-dle-head (fi′dl-hed′), *n.* the top curl of some ferns, eaten as a delicacy, esp. in New Brunswick and Nova Scotia.

fi-del-i-ty (fi-del′i-ti; fī-del′i-ti), *n.* [*pl.* fidelities], faithfulness to a person, cause, or trust; loyalty; trustworthiness.

fidg-et (fij′et), *v.i.* to be restless and uneasy; as, the boys *fidgeted* during the long play:—*v.t.* to make uneasy; worry; as, the heat *fidgets* me:—*n.* **1,** a restless person; as, the student is a *fidget* in class; **2,** the state of being restless:—**fidgets,** a fit of restlessness; as, to have the *fidgets.*—*adj.* **fidg′et-y.**

field (fēld), *n.* **1,** an open piece of farmland cleared for cultivation, pasture, etc., often enclosed by a fence or hedge; **2,** a plot of ground set aside for a special use; as, a football *field;* **3,** a region yielding some natural product; as, oil *fields;* corn *field;* **4,** the scene of military operations; a battlefield; also, a battle; **5,** in *sports,* all those who engage or compete in a contest or sport; as, in the marathon race, she led the *field;* **6,** in *baseball, cricket,* etc., the side not batting; **7,** the background against which a thing is seen; as, stars in a blue *field;* **8,** an open space; as, a *field* of snow; **9,** a range or sphere of activity; as, the *field* of art; **10,** part of a database containing a specific piece of information:—*v.t.* and *v.i.* in *cricket* or *baseball,* to catch or stop and return (a ball) from the field.—*n.* **field′er.** Also, **field′ goal′; field′ hock′ey; field′ test′; field′ trip′; field′work′.**

field mar-shal, in certain countries, a military officer above a general and next below the commander-in-chief. Also called *marshal.*

fiend (fēnd), *n.* **1,** an evil spirit; a devil; also, an unnaturally wicked or cruel person; **2,** *Colloq.* a person much given to a habit; as, a work *fiend;* a speed *fiend.*—*adj.* **fiend′ish.**—*adv.* **fiend′ishly.**

fierce (fērs), *adj.* [fierc-er, fierc-est], **1,** furiously violent and intense; as, a *fierce* fighter; *fierce* cold; **2,** cruel; savage; as, a *fierce* guard dog; **3,** very strong or eager; as, *fierce* determination.—*adv.* **fierce′ly.**—*n.* **fierce′-ness.**

fi-er-y (fī′ėr-i; fī′ri), *adj.* [fier-i-er, fier-i-est], **1,** hot and lively in feeling; as, a *fiery* speech; **2,** easily excited; as, a *fiery* temper; **3,** having a reddish glow like fire; as, a *fiery* sun; **4,** containing fire; burning; as, *fiery* wood.

fies-ta (fyās′tä; fi-es′ta), *n.* a religious festival; holiday; saint's day; also, a celebration.

fife (fīf), *n.* a shrill-toned musical instrument of the flute class:—*v.t.* and *v.i.* [fifed, fif-ing], to play (a tune) on a fife.—*n.* **fif′er.**

fif-teen (fif′tēn′), *adj.* composed of 10 more than five:—*n.* **1,** the sum of 14 and one; **2,** a sign representing fifteen units, as 15 or XV.—*adj.* **fif′teenth′.**

fifth (fifth), *adj.* next after the fourth: the ordinal of *five*:—*n.* one of the five equal parts of anything; also, the number-five item in a series.—*adv.* **fifth′ly.** Also, **fifth′ col′umn; fifth′ es-tate′; fifth′ wheel′.**

fif-ti-eth (fif′ti-eth), *adj.* next after the 49th: the ordinal of *fifty*:—*n.* one of the 50 equal parts of anything.

fif-ty (fif′ti), *adj.* composed of 10 more than 40:—*n.* [*pl.* fifties], **1,** the sum of 49 plus one; **2,** a sign representing fifty units, as 50 or L. Also, **fif′ty–fif′ty.**

fig (fig), *n.* **1,** a small, sweet, pear-shaped fruit, with many seeds, grown in warm countries, usually eaten as dried fruit; also, the tree that bears it; **2,** *Colloq.* the least amount; as, I don't care a *fig.*

fight (fīt) *v.i.* [fought (fôt), fight-ing], **1,** to strive in battle or in single combat; as, to die *fighting*; **2,** to strive against difficulties or opponents; as, to *fight* for a goal; **3,** to argue or quarrel; as, to *fight* over TV shows:—*v.t.* **1,** to strive against; make war upon; as, to *fight* an enemy, crime, disease, etc.; **2,** to engage in (a conflict); as, to *fight* a duel:—*n.* **1,** a battle; conflict with firearms, ships, armies, etc.; also, a physical conflict between persons; a brawl; **2,** a quarrel or argument; as, a *fight* between brother and sister about chores; **3,** any strife or struggle; as, the *fight* for lower taxes; **4,** a boxing match; **5,** willingness or eagerness to struggle; as, he is full of *fight.*

fight-er (fīt′ėr), *n.* **1,** any person who fights; **2,** a person who fights in the sport of boxing; a boxer; **3,** a fast warplane with a small crew.

fig-ment (fig′ment), *n.* something imagined; fiction; as, the ghost is a mere *figment* of your imagination.

fig-ur-a-tive (fig′ūr-a-tiv; fig′yėr-a-tiv), *adj.* expressing an idea or meaning in an unusual way, esp. by the use of language that tends to call up a picture; as, "armed to the teeth" is a *figurative* way of saying "completely armed."—*adv.* **fig′ur-a-tive-ly.**

fig-ure (fig′ūr; fig′yėr), *n.* **1,** a shape; outline; appearance; as, a *figure* in the fog; a slender *figure*; **2,** a person as he or she appears to others; as, the homeless person was a pitiful *figure*; also, a well-known or important person; as, a *figure* from history; **3,** a likeness of something; as, a *figure* on a coin; **4,** an illustrative drawing; **5,** a design or pattern, as in fabrics; also, a movement of a dance; **6,** a symbol of a number, as 1, 2, etc.; **7,** an amount shown in numbers; as, *sales* figures; **8,** price; as, sold at a high *figure*:—**figures,** calculations using numbers; arithmetic:—**figure of speech,** the saying of something in a fanciful manner in order to make it more striking or forceful:—*v.t.* [figured figur-ing], **1,** to calculate; as, to *figure* out the cost; also, to think; as, to *figure* out a way; **2,** to imagine; as, he *figures* himself a hero:—*v.i.* **1,** to be prominent; as, to *figure* in the news; **2,** to think or believe; as, I *figure* we'll be there by sunset; **3,** *Colloq.* to use arithmetic; as, she likes to *figure.*

fig-ure-head (fig′ūr-hed′; -yėr-), *n.* **1,** a carved image at the prow of a ship for decoration; **2,** a person who holds a high position but does not have real power; as, the queen was a mere *figurehead.*

figure skating, any ice-skating program that includes planned actions such as jumps, spins, and dance movements, usually set to music.—*n.* **fig′ure skat′er.**

fig-u-rine (fig′ūr-en′; yė), *n.* a small ornamental statuette, esp. of moulded and painted terra cotta or metalwork.

fil-a-ment (fil′a-ment), *n.* **1,** a fine wire or thread; **2,** in a flower, the stalk of a stamen. (See *flower*, illustration.)

fil-bert (fil′bėrt), *n.* the nut of the hazel.

filch (filch), *v.t.* to take by stealth; to steal.

[1]**file** (fīl), *n.* **1,** a folder or a case, for keeping papers, letters, cards, etc., in order; **2,** papers arranged in order; as, a *file* of patients' records; **3,** a row of persons or things, one behind another; **4,** in *computing*, a collection of data or programs stored in a computer under the same name:—*v.t.* [filed, fil-ing], **1,** to put (papers) away in order or store in a file; **2,** to send in to or put on an official record; as, to *file* a claim with an insurance company:—*v.i.* to march in line, one person or thing following behind another; as, to *file* out of a building during a fire drill.

[2]**file** (fīl), *n.* a steel tool with a rough face for smoothing, grinding, or wearing away surfaces, as wood, metal, etc.; as, a nail *file*:—*v.t.* [filed, fil-ing], to smooth or cut with a file; as, to *file* the rough edge of the door.—*n.* **fil′ing.**

fi-let mi-gnon (fē′le′mē′nyōn′), *n.* a round choice cut of tenderloin beef, sometimes garnished with pork or bacon.

file transfer protocol, in *computing*, the standard way of transferring a file between computers over the Internet.

fil-i-al (fil′i-al; fil′yal), *adj.* of a son or daughter or due from a child; as, *filial* respect.

fil-i-bus-ter (fil′i-bus′tėr), *n.* a long speech made merely to consume time in a legislature, esp. to prevent a bill from coming to a vote; use of dilatory tactics to thwart the will of a majority:—*v.i.* to use such tactics.—*n.* **fil′i-bus′ter-er.**

fil·i·gree (fil′i-grē′), *n.* ornamental lacelike work in gold or silver wire; also, any delicate pattern on anything, as of frost on a window:—*adj.* made of or like such work.

Fil·i·pi·no (fil′i-pē′nō), *n.* a person who inhabits or originates from the Philippines:—*adj.* relating to the country, the people, the language, or the culture of the Philippines.

fill (fil), *v.t.* **1,** to make full; as, to *fill* a glass; **2,** to close or stop up the pores or cavities of; as, to *fill* the cavity in the tooth; **3,** to satisfy, as with food; **4,** to take up all the space in; as, the crowd *filled* the room; **5,** to supply what is required by; as, to *fill* an order; *fill* a prescription; **6,** to perform the duties of; as, he *fills* the office well; **7,** to write information on a paper or form; as, to *fill* out an application form:—*v.i.* **1,** to become full; as, her eyes *filled* with tears; **2,** to become full of wind, as sails:—*n.* **1,** enough to satisfy; as, I ate my *fill*; **2,** anything put in to fill up a space; as, a *fill* of sand.—*n.* **fill′er; fill′ing** (as, pie *filling*).

fil·let (fil′et), *n.* **1,** a narrow band, esp. one worn around the forehead; **2,** a flat moulding separating other mouldings; **3,** (often fil′ā), in cooking, a boneless piece of meat or fish: also spelled *filet*:—*v.t.* **1,** to bind or ornament with a narrow band; **2,** to cut into fillets.

fil·ly (fil′i), *n.* [*pl.* fillies], a young mare; a female foal.

film (film), *n.* **1,** a thin layer, or coating, as of oil on water; **2,** a roll of plastic or other material, used in a camera for taking photographs; **3,** a movie:—*v.t.* **1,** to cover with a thin coating; **2,** to take a photograph or make a movie; as, to *film* the graduation ceremonies.

fil·ter (fil′tėr), *n.* any material, as sand, cloth, paper, or charcoal, used to strain out solid matter or impurities from liquids or gas; as, a coffee *filter*; also, an apparatus so used; as, a water *filter*:—*v.t.* and *v.i.* to pass (a liquid or gas) through a filter.—*n.* **fil·tra′tion** (fil-trā′shun).—*adj.* **fil′ter·a·ble** or **fil′tra·ble** (as, a *filterable* virus); **fil′tered** (as, *filtered* water).—*v.* and *n.* **fil′trate.**

filth (filth), *n.* **1,** loathsome dirt; as, *filth* covered her soccer uniform; **2,** dirty language or thought; obscenity.—*n.* **filth′iness.**—*adj.* **filth′y.**

fin (fin), *n.* **1,** one of the thin fanlike parts of a fish or water mammal, which helps to move and steer it through the water; **2,** a flat rubber shoe shaped like a fin, used by swimmers for greater speed in the water; a *flipper*; **3,** anything like a fin; as, an airplane *fin*.

fi·na·gle (fi-nā′gl), *v.t. Colloq.* **1,** to get by guile or underhanded means; as, he *finagled* passes to the game; **2,** to cheat.—*n.* **fi·na′gler.**

fi·nal (fī′nal), *adj.* **1,** coming at the end; last; as, the *final* page; **2,** putting an end to doubt; as, a *final* decision:—**finals,** *n.pl.* **1,** the last event or game in a series or match; **2,** the last examinations of the term in high school, college, or university.—*n.* **fi·nal′i·ty** (fī-nal′i-ti).—*n.* **fi′nal·ist.**—*v.t.* **fi′nal·ize′** (*U.S. Colloq.*).

fi·na·le (fi-nä′li; fi-nä′lā), *n.* **1,** the final part of an artistic performance; as, the last movement of a symphony or other musical composition, or the closing scene of an opera, play, etc.; **2,** the end of something; as, the *finale* of the campaign.

fi·nal·ly (fī′nal-i), *adv.* **1,** lastly; **2,** at last; as, they *finally* came; **3,** once and for all; as, to settle a matter *finally*.

fi·nance (fi-nans′; fī-nans′; fī′nans), *n.* the science of the management of money for a government, business, or person; also, matters dealing with money:—**finances,** income; funds; money matters; as, the family *finances* are low:—*v.t.* [financed, financing], to provide the money for; as, the bank *financed* the factory.—*adj.* **fi·nan′cial.**—*adv.* **fi·nan′cial·ly.**

fin·an·ci·er (fi-nan′si-ėr; fin′an-sēr′; fī′nan-sēr′), *n.* a person skilled in money matters or who deals with large sums of money.

finch (finch), *n.* any of various small songbirds, as the bunting, canary, sparrow, linnet, grosbeak, etc.

find (find), *v.t.* [found (found), find·ing], **1,** to discover by chance or accident; as, to *find* a toonie; **2,** to learn or discover something that was not known by observation or experiment; as, to *find* the answer to the problem; **3,** to reach; get to; as, the arrow *found* its mark; **4,** to determine and declare; as, the jury *found* him guilty; **5,** to look for and succeed in getting; as, to *find* a lost kitten; **6,** to get or obtain by effort; as, to *find* a job; **7,** to meet with a certain thing or condition; be located; as, to *find* kangaroos in Australia:—*n.* a valuable discovery; as, the rare antique piece on the Internet was a real *find*.

find·er (fīn′dėr), *n.* **1,** someone or something that finds; **2,** an extra lens on a camera, used to locate the object in the field of vision and to show on a very small scale the picture to be taken; as, a view*finder*.

¹fine (fīn), *n.* money paid as a penalty for breaking a law or rule; as, a library *fine*:—*v.t.* [fined, fin·ing], to punish by imposing a fine; as, to *fine* someone for speeding.

²fine (fīn), *adj.* [fin·er, fin·est], **1,** of superior quality; very good or excellent; as, *fine* silk; *fine* music; a *fine* meal; in *fine* health; **2,** slender; not coarse; as, a *fine* needle; *fine* sand; **3,** delicate; refined; as, *fine* manners; **4,** excellent in character; as, a *fine* student; **5,** pleasant; bright; as, a *fine* day; **6,** subtle; as, a *fine* distinction:—**fine art,** art concerned with the creation of beauty, as music and painting:—**fine print,** the small text or ambiguous language in a document, esp. a contract; also, something that is vague or obscure.—*adv.* **fine′ly.**—*n.* **fine′ness.**

fin-er-y (fīn′ėr-i), *n.* [*pl.* fineries], showy clothing or ornaments.

fi-nesse (fi-nes′), *n.* **1,** adroitness; delicate skill; artifice; as, he handled the diplomatic mission with *finesse;* **2,** at *cards,* esp. bridge, to try, as second or third player, to take a trick with a lower card, in the hope that a higher one is held by the right-hand opponent; as, he *finessed* the queen.

fine–tune (fīn′–tūn′), *v.t.* [fine–tuned, fine–tun-ing], to adjust precisely, refine, or improve something for optimal efficiency.

fin-ger (fing′gėr), *n.* **1,** one of the five separate divisions of the hand; esp., any one of four not including the thumb; **2,** any one of many mechanical devices used like a finger; **3,** a division of a glove into which a finger is put:—*v.t.* **1,** to touch; as, to *finger* objects on a counter; **2,** to play (an instrument) with the fingers.—*n.* **fin′ger-tip′.**

fin-ger-nail (fing′gėr-nāl′), *n.* the thin, hard covering on the end of the finger.

fin-ger-print (fing′gėr-print′), *n.* **1,** an impression made by the ridges at the tips of fingers on a surface, esp. that made with ink, taken for the purposes of identification; **2,** something that is characteristic or unique; that which identifies; as a DNA *fingerprint;* **3,** the pattern of ridges on the tips of someone's fingers, which are unique to each person:—*v.t.* to take fingerprints, usually as a means of identifying a person.

fin-ick-y (fin′i-ki), *adj.* affectedly fussy; precise or particular; fastidious; as, he was *finicky* about his food.

fin-ish (fin′ish), *v.t.* **1,** to bring to an end; complete; conclude; as, to *finish* a piece of work; **2,** to use until gone; use up; as, to *finish* the last of the cake; **3,** to put a final coat on or fix the surface of in some way; as, to *finish* wood cabinets with a dark stain; **4,** *Colloq.* to dispose of; render powerless; kill:—*v.i.* to come to an end; stop; as, the movie *finished* abruptly:—*n.* **1,** the completion; end; as, the *finish* of a race; **2,** the final coat or texture of a surface; as, wallpaper with a rough *finish;* wood with a smooth, dark *finish.*—*n.* **fin′ish-er.** Also, **fin′ish line′.**

fi-nite (fī′nīt), *adj.* having limits.

fiord or **fjord** (fyôrd), *n.* a long, narrow inlet, or arm of the sea, between high banks, as on the coast of Norway.

fir (fûr), *n.* a northern cone-bearing, evergreen tree, related to the pine tree, and valued for its resin and timber; also, the timber.

fire (fīr), *n.* **1,** the visible heat or light produced by burning; a spark or flame; **2,** wood, coal, or other burning fuel; as, a hot *fire* in the fireplace; **3,** a destructive burning; as, a forest *fire;* **4,** a discharge of firearms; as, the soldiers heard the *fire* of cannon; **5,** strong feeling; spirit; as, the speech lacked *fire;* **6,** brilliancy or light; as, the *fire* of a diamond:—*v.t.* [fired, fir-ing], **1,** to set on fire; as, to *fire* a haystack; **2,** to animate; excite; as, ambition *fires* his genius; **3,** to cause to explode; as, to *fire* a rifle; **4,** to apply intense heat to; as, to *fire* pottery; **5,** to dismiss from a job; discharge; as, the employer *fired* the lazy worker:—*v.i.* **1,** to become ignited; take fire; **2,** to discharge artillery; as, they *fired* at the enemy.—*adj.* **fire′less.** Also, **fire′ drill′.**

fire-arm (fīr′ärm′), *n.* a small weapon, as a rifle, revolver, pistol, etc., from which a shot is discharged by an explosive.

fire-brand (fīr′brand′), *n.* **1,** a piece of burning wood; **2,** one who kindles strife; esp., one who inflames the emotions of a crowd.

fire-crack-er (fīr′krak′ėr), *n.* a small roll of paper filled with gunpowder and set off by a fuse.

fire engine, a truck that carries firefighters and firefighting equipment to put out fires, esp. in buildings.

fire escape, a ladder or staircase that provides an escape from a burning building.

fire extinguisher, an apparatus, usually a portable tank containing chemicals, for immediate use in putting out a fire.

fire-fight-er (fīr′fī′tėr), *n.* a member of a fire department, whose job is to put out dangerous fires and rescue people from burning buildings; also, someone who puts out forest fires.

fire-fly (fīr′flī′), *n.* [*pl.* fireflies], a small beetle that gives off short flashes of light from the rear of its body when it flies in the dark.

fire hydrant, a street hydrant, to which a fire hose may be attached to a water main, esp. to put out fires.

fire-light (fīr′līt′), *n.* light from a fire; as, shadows dance in the *firelight.*

fire-man (fīr′man), *n.* Same as **firefighter.**

fire-place (fīr′plās′), *n.* a fireproof structure built to contain a fire for heating or cooking, attached to a chimney to carry away the smoke; a hearth.

fire-proof (fīr′pro͞of′), *adj.* made of material that resists fire; as, *fireproof* buildings:—*v.t.* to make fireproof.

fire-side (fīr′sīd′), *n.* **1,** the place near the fire; **2,** the hearth; home:—*adj.* happening near a fire or pertaining to the home; as, *fireside* comfort.

fire-wall (fīr′wôl′), *n.* **1,** a fireproof wall or plate manufactured to prevent the spread of fire in a building or vehicle; **2,** in *computing,* a security system that prevents the unauthorized use or access to a network and the data in it by hackers or others; **3,**

Slang maximum thrust; as, she slammed the gas pedal to the *firewall*.

fire-wood (fīr′wood′), *n.* wood for fuel.

fire-works (fīr′wûrks′), *n.pl.* devices, as firecrackers, rockets, etc., used in celebrations to make noise or a display of light in the sky.

[1]**firm** (fûrm), *adj.* **1,** compact; solid; as, *firm* muscles; a *firm* mattress; **2,** not easily moved; stable; as, a *firm* foundation; **3,** steady and vigorous; as, a *firm* step; **4,** steadfast; loyal; as, a *firm* belief; **5,** resolute; positive; as, he is *firm* of purpose; **6,** not likely to change; staying the same; as, a *firm* offer on the house:—*v.t.* to compact; fix firmly; as, to *firm* soil around a plant.—*adv.* **firm′ly.**—*n.* **firm′ness.**

[2]**firm** (fûrm), *n.* **1,** a partnership of two or more persons for doing business; **2,** the name under which a partnership operates; a business or company; as, a law *firm*.

fir-ma-ment (fûr′ma-ment), *n.* the sky.

first (fûrst), *adj.* **1,** earliest in time or order; as, the *first* page; **2,** foremost in importance, time, excellence, etc.; as, she was the *first* chess player in her class: also used as the ordinal of *one*:—*adv.* **1,** before everyone else, as in order, place, rank, etc.; **2,** sooner; rather; as, I would die *first*; **3,** for the first time; as, to *first* meet someone at the new job:—*n.* **1,** the beginning; **2,** any person or thing that is first; as, we were the *first* to go.

first aid, temporary treatment given to the sick or injured while awaiting regular medical treatment.—*adj.* **first′-aid′.**

first-born (fûrst′-bôrn′), *adj.* earliest produced or born; eldest:—*n.* the eldest.

first-class (fûrst′-klås′), *adj.* of the highest rank or quality.—*adv.* **first′class′** (with the best accommodations; as, to travel *first class*).

first-hand (fûrst′hand′), *adj.* obtained directly from the source; as, *firsthand* facts.—*adv.* **first′ hand′** (directly).

first-ly (fûrst′li), *adv.* first; in the first place: used with *secondly, thirdly,* etc.

first minister, the prime minister of Canada or the premier of a province.

First Nations, the Aboriginal people of Canada; as, he was elected head of the Assembly of *First Nations*.

first-rate (fûrst′-rāt′), *adj.* **1,** of the highest quality or class; very good; as, a *first-rate* writer; **2,** *Colloq.* very well; as, I feel *first-rate*:—*adv. Colloq.* excellently.

First World or **first world,** the industrialized capitalist countries of Western Europe, North America, and Asia-Pacific, as opposed to the *Second World*, or *Communist* bloc countries, and the *Third World*, the nonaligned countries of Asia and Africa.—*adj.* **first′-world′.**

fis-cal (fis′kal), *adj.* relating to financial matters; financial:—**fiscal year,** a 12-month financial period; financial year.

fish (fish), *n.* [*pl.* fish or fishes], **1,** an animal, usually with a scaly body and living in water, and breathing through gills instead of lungs; **2,** the flesh of fish used for food; **3,** in Newfoundland, cod:—*v.i.* **1,** to catch, or try to catch, fish; **2,** to search for anything hidden, buried, etc.; as, he *fished* in his pocket for a loonie; **3,** to seek to gain something by indirect means; as, he *fished* for information by sly questions:—*v.t.* **1,** to catch or try to catch (fish); **2,** to try to catch fish in; as, to *fish* a stream. Also, **fish′ and chips′; fish′ cake′; fish′eye′; fish′ farm′; fish′hook′; fish′mon′ger; fish′net′; fish′tail′.**

fish and brewis, in Newfoundland, a dish of salt cod and hardtack biscuit, soaked in water, and served with fried salt pork, onions, and other vegetables.

fish-er (fish′ėr), *n.* a person who fishes, either for a living or for sport. A sport fisher, also called *angler*.

fish-er-y (fish′ėr-i), *n.* [*pl.* fisheries], **1,** the business of catching fish; **2,** a fishing ground; **3,** a place for farming or processing fish.

fish-hook (fish′hook′), *n.* a hook that, when fastened to a line and baited, is used for catching fish.

fish-ing (fish′ing), *n.* the sport, activity, or occupation of catching fish. Also, **fish′ing lad′der; fish′ing line′; fish′ing pole′; fish′ing rod′; fish′ing stage′; fish′ing sta′tion.**

fish-y (fish′i), *adj.* [fish-i-er, fish-i-est], **1,** like fish in smell, taste, or appearance, or abounding in fish; **2,** *Colloq.* unlikely; questionable; as, the story sounds *fishy* to me.

fis-sion (fish′un), *n.* a splitting into parts; in *biology*, reproduction by cell division, as of bacteria; in *physics*, the splitting of an atomic nucleus, as by bombardment of uranium or plutonium with neutrons.

fis-sure (fish′yoor; -yėr), *n.* a narrow opening; a crack; a cleft; as, a *fissure* in the earth:—*v.t.* or *v.i.* [fissured, fissur-ing], to break or split.

fist (fist), *n.* the hand when closed or clenched: as, he struck with his *fist*.—*adj.* **fist′ic** (as, a *fistic* encounter).—*n.* **fist′icuffs; fist′ful.**

[1]**fit** (fit), *n.* **1,** a sudden, violent attack of disease, as of epilepsy or indigestion; as, a coughing *fit*; **2,** a sudden outburst, as of laughter or energy.

[2]**fit** (fit), *adj.* [fit-ter, fit-test], **1,** suitable; proper; as, a jewel *fit* for a queen; **2,** ready; prepared; as, the team is *fit* for work; **3,** in good condition; as, I feel *fit* again:—*v.t.* [fitted, fit-ting], **1,** to make suitable; adapt; as, I will *fit* my time to yours; **2,** to furnish with what is right, in size, shape, etc.; as,

can you *fit* me in shoes? **3,** to equip; prepare; as, to *fit* a girl for university; **4,** to be properly adjusted to; be suitable for; as, this dress *fits* me:—*v.i.* to be adapted to one; as, his gloves *fit* well:—*n.* the adaptation of one thing to another; as, this coat is an excellent *fit.*—*adv.* **fit′ly.**—*n.* **fit′ness; fit′ter.**

fit-ful (fit′fool), *adj.* changeable; capricious; also, irregular; erratic; restless; as, *fitful* sleep.—*adv.* **fit′ful-ly.**

fit-ting (fit′ing), *adj.* suitable; proper; as, you've come at a *fitting* moment:—**fittings,** *n.pl.* the equipment or necessary fixtures of a house, car, shop, etc.

five (fīv), *adj.* composed of one more than four:—*n.* **1,** the number consisting of four plus one; **2,** a sign representing five units, as 5 or V.

five-pin bowl-ing (fīv′-pin′ bōl′ing), *n.* in *sports,* a type of bowling using five pins instead of 10 and a smaller, lighter ball: invented in 1909 in Canada, originally for upper-crust businessmen who didn't want to overexert themselves during their lunch-hour games.

fix (fiks), *v.t.* **1,** to make fast or firm; as, they *fixed* a stake in the ground; **2,** to determine; as, they *fixed* the time for the meeting; **3,** to place definitely on a person, as blame, responsibility, etc.; **4,** to make fast or permanent, as a colour, a photographic negative, etc.; **5,** to direct or hold steadily, as the eyes; **6,** to repair; as, the plumber *fixed* the leak; **7,** to arrange; as, to *fix* one's hair:—*v.i.* to become fixed:—*n. Colloq.* an awkward or difficult situation; as, I'm in a *fix.*—*n.* **fix-a′tion.**—*adj.* **fixed.**—*adv.* **fix′ed-ly.**

fix-ture (fiks′tūr), *n.* **1,** something permanently attached to an office, house, etc.; as, an electric light *fixture;* plumbing *fixtures;* **2,** a person permanently placed; as, he's a *fixture* in our school.

fizz or **fiz** (fiz), *n.* **1,** a hissing sound; **2,** an effervescent or bubbling liquid, as soda water:—*v.i.* [fizzed, fizz-ing], to make a hissing noise.—*adj.* **fiz′zy.**

fiz-zle (fiz′l), *v.i.* [fiz-zled, fiz-zling], **1,** to make a hissing noise; **2,** *Colloq.* to fail miserably:—*n.* **1,** a hissing or spluttering; **2,** *Colloq.* a failure; as, he made a *fizzle* of his part in the game.

fjord (fyôrd), *n.* Same as **fiord.**

flab-ber-gast (flab′ėr-gast), *v.t. Colloq.* astound; amaze; esp. by startling news.

flab-by (flab′i), *adj.* [flab-bi-er, flab-bi-est], **1,** yielding to the touch; limp; not firm; as, *flabby* cheeks; **2,** feeble; weak; as, a *flabby* will.—*n.* **flab′bi-ness.**

flac-cid (flak′sid; flas′id), *adj.* flabby; soft; limp; as, *flaccid* muscles.

¹flag (flag), *n.* a piece of cloth bearing some design or symbol and often attached by one edge to a staff or stick, and intended to be spread or held aloft, as a national banner, signal, decoration, etc., used to represent a country, state, or other organization:—*v.t.* [flagged, flag-ging], **1,** to signal with, or as with, a flag; as, to *flag* a train; **2,** to place a flag upon; also, to deck with flags.—*n.* **flag′pole′; flag′-wav′ing; flag′-wav′er.**

²flag (flag), *v.i.* [flagged, flag-ging], to droop; lag; lose strength; as, his courage *flagged.*

³flag (flag), *n.* a large, flat slab of stone for pavements; a flagstone:—*v.t.* [flagged, flag-ging], to pave with flagstones.

flag-on (flag′un), *n.* a vessel for holding liquors, with a spout, a handle, and often a lid; flask; as, a wine *flagon.*

fla-grant (flā′grant), *adj.* openly wicked; outrageous; notorious; as, a *flagrant* crime.—*n.* **fla′gran-cy.**

flag-ship (flag′ship′), *n.* a ship that flies the flag of the commander of a fleet, or the largest or most important one in the fleet:—*n.* and *adj.* the most prominent or outstanding thing in a group; most prominent; as, a *flagship* store or company.

flag-staff (flag′ståf′), *n.* [*pl.* flagstaffs], a pole on which a flag is flown.

flag-stone (flag′stōn′), *n.* a large, flat stone used esp. for paving walks.

flail (flāl), *n.* an instrument consisting of a handle with a short stick hung loosely at one end, used for threshing grain by hand:—*v.t.* to thresh (with, or as if with, a flail):—*v.i.* to move about or fidget restlessly; as, the children *flailed* in the back seat of the car.

flair (flâr), *n.* aptitude; bent; instinct; knack; natural talent; as, a *flair* for public speaking.

flak (flak), *n.* **1,** anti-aircraft fire or guns; **2,** *Colloq.* intense criticism; as, to get *flak* from an employer for a glaring mistake.

flake (flāk), *n.* a small, thin chip or fragment of anything; as, a *flake* of soap, snow, dried paint, breakfast cereal, etc.:—*v.i.* [flaked, flak-ing], to break or come off in flakes; peel or scale off.—*adj.* **flak′y.**

flam-boy-ant (flam-boi′ant), *adj.* **1,** flaming; as, *flamboyant* colours; **2,** flowery; showy; as, *flamboyant* language or style; a *flamboyant* person; **3,** ornate; as, *flamboyant* architecture.

flame (flām), *n.* **1,** a burning gas or vapour, often orange or yellow and tonguelike in shape; **2,** a burning emotion or feeling; as, a *flame* of rage; **3,** *Colloq.* a sweetheart; as, she's an old *flame* of mine; **4,** *Slang* in *computing,* an angry or insulting remark or criticism made in an e-mail or posted to a newsgroup, esp. one made in haste, without thought:—**flames,** a state of blazing fire; as, the building was in *flames:*—*v.i.* [flamed, flam-ing], **1,** to burn with a flame;

burst into flame; as, the beacon *flamed* in the night; **2,** to show red or glow, as if burning; as, her face *flamed* with anger:—*v.t.* **1,** to subject to the action of flame; **2,** to send (a signal) by fire; **3,** in *computing,* to send someone an angry, ill-considered message by e-mail; to ramble on or rant about some boring subject.—*adj.* **flam′ing.**

fla-min-go (fla-ming′gō), *n.* [*pl.* flamingos or flamingoes], a long-legged, tropical wading bird, with pink or red plumage.

flamma-ble (flam′a-bl), *adj.* easily set on fire; inflammable: "flammable" is preferred to "inflammable," which can be ambiguous: the opposite is "nonflammable."

flange (flanj). *n.* a raised or projecting rim on a wheel to keep it in place upon a track, or on a pipe to give a place for attaching it to a wall, floor, etc.

flank (flangk), *n.* **1,** the fleshy part of an animal, between the ribs and hip; **2,** the side of anything, as of an army, building, etc.; as, the enemy attacked our right *flank*:—*v.t.* **1,** to stand at the side of; border; as, large trees *flanked* the road; **2,** to attack, go around, or guard the side of (an army).

flan-nel (flan′el), *n.* a soft, loosely woven cloth, usually made of wool, used for clothing, bedding, etc.:—**flannels,** garments made of this material, esp. men's trousers.

flan-nel-ette (flan′el-et′), *n.* a soft cotton cloth with a nap on one side.

flap (flap), *n.* **1,** anything broad and flat, hanging loose, and attached on one side only; as, the *flap* of an envelope; a tent *flap*; **2,** the motion of anything broad and flat swinging loosely and striking against something else; also, the sound thus made; **3,** a blow or slap; as, a *flap* of a beaver's tail; **4,** *Slang* a state of anger; as, to get into a *flap*:—*v.t.* [flapped, flap-ping], **1,** to strike with, or as with, a flap; **2,** to move to and fro; as, the bird *flaps* its wings:—*v.t.* to sway about loosely, often with a beating noise; as, the shades *flapped* against the windows.—*n.* **flap′per.**

flap-jack (flap′jak′), *n.* a cake of thin batter baked on a griddle; a pancake.

flare (flâr), *n.* **1,** a large, unsteady, glaring light; **2,** a fire or blaze serving as an emergency signal; **3,** a sudden bursting forth; as, a *flare* of trumpets; **4,** a spreading outward; as, the vase has a *flare* at the top:—*v.i.* [flared, flar-ing], **1,** to burn suddenly with a bright, unsteady flame; **2,** to spread outward; as, pants legs that *flare* at the bottom.

flash (flash), *n.* **1,** a sudden burst of light; as, a *flash* of lightning; **2,** a sudden outburst, feeling, or thought, as of merriment, wit, or genius; **3,** a momentary light displayed as a signal; **4,** cheap display or show; **5,** an instant; as, he saw it in a *flash*:—*v.t.* **1,** to send forth swiftly or suddenly; as, to *flash* a light; to *flash* a look; **2,** to send out in flashes; as, to *flash* a signal:—*v.i.* **1,** to shine for a moment with a sudden light; as, beacons *flash* at night; **2,** to appear suddenly; pass at great speed; as, the announcement *flashed* on the television screen.—*n.* **flash′er.** Also, **flash′ flood′.**

flash-back (flash′bak′), *n.* the interruption of a film, novel, etc., to present an earlier scene or episode; also, this scene.

flash-light (flash′līt′), *n.* **1,** a small, portable, battery-powered electric light; **2,** a sudden brilliant artificial light for taking photographs; also, the photograph so taken; **3,** a light that comes and goes in flashes, as a signal.

flash memory, in *computing,* a type of read-only memory that retains its data even after the power to the computer is turned off.

flash-y (flash′i), *adj.* [flash-i-er, flash-i-est], **1,** brilliant for a moment; **2,** gaudy; showy, but cheap-looking; as, *flashy* clothes.—*adv.* **flash′i-ly.**—*n.* **flash′i-ness.**

flask (flåsk), *n.* **1,** a narrow-necked bottle, made of glass, metal, or plastic, for holding liquids, powder, etc.; **2,** a bottle with flat sides; as, a pocket *flask*; **3,** a glass container used in laboratories to heat liquids.

[1]**flat** (flat), *adj.* [flat-ter, flat-test], **1,** having a level, horizontal surface; as, *flat* country; **2,** stretched out at full length; as, to lie *flat* on the ground; **3,** having a smooth and even surface, or nearly so, whether horizontal or not; as, the *flat* face of a cliff; **4,** broad and smooth, but not very thick; **5,** dull or uninteresting; as, a *flat* speech; tasteless or stale; as, *flat* food or wine; not clear or sharp; as, a *flat* sound; **6,** unqualified; downright; as, a *flat* refusal; **7,** based on a fixed unit; uniform; as, a *flat* rate for an oil change; **8,** deflated; as, a *flat* tire; **9,** *Colloq.* low-spirited; without energy; also, without funds; **10,** dull; not glossy; as, a *flat* paint or finish; **11,** in *music*: **a,** below the true pitch; as, a *flat* note; **b,** lowered by a half step; as, B *flat*:—*adv.* **1,** in a flat manner; as, he sprawled *flat* on the ground; **2,** positively; directly; as, he came out *flat* against the candidate; **3,** exactly, said of numbers; as, he ran 100 metres in 10 seconds *flat*; **4,** in *music,* below the true pitch; as, she sang slightly *flat*:—*n.* **1,** a level surface or plain; esp., low-lying country; as, the river *flats*; the *flat* of a hand; **2,** the smooth, wide part of a thing; as, the *flat* of a sword; **3,** a deflated tire; **4,** in *music,* a sign [♭] indicating a lowering of pitch by a half step; also, the note so lowered:—*v.t.* and *v.i.* [flat-ted, flat-ting], **1,** to make or become flat; **2,** to lower or become lower in pitch.—*adv.* **flat′ly.**—*n.* **flat′ness.** Also, **flat′bed′ scan′ner; flat′bread′; flat′car′; flat′fish′.**

[2]**flat** (flat), *n.* a set of rooms on one floor, forming complete living quarters; an apartment.

flat–foot-ed (flat′–foot′id), *adj.* **1,** having flat feet; **2,** firm; uncompromising; **3,** clumsy; **4,** forthright, blunt; as, a *flat-footed* way of speaking; **5,** unprepared; taken by surprise; as, I caught him *flat-footed.—n.* **flat′foot′** (*Slang* police officer).

flat-ten (flat′n), *v.t.* **1,** to make level or smooth; **2,** to beat down; as, the rain *flattened* the corn; **3,** to make dull or tasteless:—*v.i.* **1,** to become even or level; **2,** to become stale; as, pop *flattens* when it stands.

flat-ter (flat′ėr), *v.t.* **1,** to please, or seek to please, with praise which is usually insincere; as, to try to get a job by *flattering* the interviewer; **2,** to portray too favourably; as, the photograph *flatters* him; **3,** to please or make happy; as, to *flatter* someone by following in his or her footsteps:—*v.i.* to give false praise.—*n.* **flat′ter-y; flat′ter-er.**—*adj.* **flat′ter-ing.**

flat-top (flat′top′), *n.* **1,** *Colloq.* an aircraft carrier, esp. in the U.S.; **2,** a haircut similar to a crew cut.

flat-u-lent (flat′yoo-lent), *adj.* **1,** having or producing gas in the stomach or intestines; **2,** pompous or pretentious (in language); as, a *flatulent* style.

flat-ware (flat′wâr′), *n.* knives, forks, spoons, platters, plates, and saucers, used for eating and serving.

flat-worm (flat′wûrm′), *n.* any flat, unsegmented, parasitic worm, as the tapeworm.

flaunt (flônt; flänt), *v.t.* to show off; display impudently; as, the girl *flaunted* her new clothes:—*v.i.* **1,** to wave showily; as, flags *flaunting* in the wind; **2,** to make a showy appearance.—*adv.* **flaunt′ing-ly.**

flau-tist (flô′tist; flou′tist), *n.* a flute player; flutist.

fla-vour (flā′vėr), *n.* **1,** that quality that affects the sense of taste; as, a spicy *flavour* in a sauce; chocolate *flavour*; **2,** a substance that gives a particular taste to food or drink; **3,** a particular or characterizing quality; as, his stories have a *flavour* of the sea:—*v.t.* to give flavour to; as, to *flavour* the chicken with tarragon.

fla-vour-ing (flā′vėr-ing), *n.* an extract or substance added to food to give it a particular taste.

flaw (flô), *n.* **1,** a blemish; scratch; a weak spot; defect; crack; as, a *flaw* in the glass; **2,** a small fault or problem; as, a *flaw* in a plan.—*adj.* **flaw′less.**—*adv.* **flaw′less-ly.**

flax (flaks), *n.* a slender blue-flowered plant, the stem of which yields the fibres from which linen is spun, and the seeds from which linseed oil is made.—*adj.* **flax′en.**

flax-seed (flaks′sēd′; flak′sēd′), *n.* the seed of the flax, used in some organic foods such as bread, some medicine, and in the making of linseed oil.

flay (flā), *v.t.* **1,** to strip the skin from; skin; **2,** to scold; criticize or reprove severely or harshly.

flea (flē), *n.* a small, jumping, wingless, parasitic insect that sucks the blood of animals and people. Also, **flea′ col′lar; flea′ mar′ket.**

fleck (flek), *n.* a streak or spot; as, the bird had *flecks* of white on its breast:—*v.t.* to streak or spot; as, clouds *flecked* the sky.

fled (fled), *p.t.* and *p.p.* of *flee.*

fledge (flej), *v.i.* [fledged, fledg-ing], to acquire the feathers necessary for flight; as, some birds are quicker than others to *fledge* and fly:—*v.t.* to furnish with feathers for flying; as, the young birds are not yet *fledged*; to *fledge* an arrow.—*n.* **fledg′ling** or **fledge′ling.**

flee (flē), *v.t.* [fled (fled), flee-ing], to run away from; avoid; shun; as, to *flee* evil:—*v.i.* **1,** to run away, as from danger or evil; as, they *fled* from their burning homes; **2,** to vanish; disappear swiftly.

fleece (flēs), *n.* **1,** the woolly coat of a sheep; also, all the wool shorn from a sheep at one time; **2,** anything soft or woolly like the coat of a sheep, as clothing, towels, clouds, etc.:—*v.t.* [fleeced, fleec-ing], **1,** to shear (a sheep) of its wool; **2,** to rob; strip; as, the thieves *fleeced* him of all his money.—*adj.* **fleec′y.**

[1]**fleet** (flēt), *adj.* swift; nimble; as, a *fleet* deer:—*v.i.* to pass or fly quickly; as, the hours *fleeted* by.—*adv.* **fleet′ly.**—*n.* **fleet′ness.**

[2]**fleet** (flēt), *n.* **1,** a number of warships under one command; **2,** a number of vessels or vehicles moving together or under a single ownership; as, a *fleet* of taxis or trucks.

fleet-ing (flēt′ing), *adj.* passing quickly; as, a *fleeting* glance.—*adv.* **fleet′ing-ly.**

flesh (flesh), *n.* **1,** the soft muscular tissues beneath the skin that cover the bones of a human or animal body; muscles and other tissues; **2,** the meat of animals used as food; **3,** the soft, edible pulp of fruit and vegetables; **4,** the human body, as opposed to the soul; **5,** kindred, stock, or race; as, his own *flesh* and blood.—*adj.* **flesh′y.**—*n.* **flesh′i-ness.**

fleur–de–lis or **fleur–de–lys** (flûr′–dė–lē′; flûr′–dė–lēs′), *n.* [*pl.* fleurs-de-lis or fleurs-de-lys (flûr′–dė–lēz′)], **1,** the white iris; **2,** the emblem of the former royal family of France; **3,** the flower or symbol appearing on the flag and coat of arms of Québec.

FLEUR-DE-LIS

flew (flo͞o), *p.t.* of *fly.*

flex (fleks), *v.t.* to bend or move a muscle or a certain part of the body; as, he *flexed* his biceps.

flex-i-ble (flek′si-bl), *adj.* **1,** easily bent

without breaking; **2,** yielding to persuasion; hence, easily managed or led; tractable; **3,** adaptable; as, a *flexible* form of government; *flexible* working hours.—*adv.* **flex′i-bly.**—*n.* **flex′i-bil′i-ty.**

flex-or (flek′sėr), *n.* a muscle that bends an arm, leg, etc.

flex-time (fleks′tīm′), *n.* an arrangement whereby employees can select their own working hours within a certain framework.

flick (flik), *n.* **1,** a light, quick stroke, as of a whip or wrist; **2,** a streak or speck; fleck; as, a *flick* of dust; **3,** *Slang* a movie:—*v.t.* **1,** to whip or strike gently with a quick jerk, as with a whip; as, to *flick* the dust off one's coat; **2,** to turn on or off; as, to *flick* a switch.

[1]**flick-er** (flik′ėr), *v.i.* **1,** to waver, shine, or burn unsteadily, as a flame; **2,** to flutter; vibrate; quiver:—*n.* an unsteady light or movement.—*adj.* and *n.* **flick′er-ing.**—*adv.* **flick′er-ing-ly.**

[2]**flick-er** (flik′ėr), *n.* a woodpecker of North America; as, the yellow-shafted *flicker* is common in Canada.

fli-er or **fly-er** (flī′ėr), *n.* **1,** one who or that which flies, as a bird, insect, or pilot; **2,** anything that moves very rapidly, as an express train; **3,** *Colloq.,* a daring venture; as, he took a *flier* in stocks; **4,** (usually **flyer**), an advertising pamphlet or leaflet.

flight (flīt), *n.* **1,** the act, process, manner, or power of flying; **2,** a passage, or the distance travelled, through the air by an aircraft; as, the *flight* of a balloon, airplane, or rocket; hence, a swift passage; as, the *flight* of time; **3,** a scheduled trip by airplane; as, *Flight* 535 goes from Ottawa to Halifax; **4,** a hasty departure; as, the enemy took *flight*; also, the act of running or breaking away to be free; an escape; as, the convict took *flight*; **5,** a number of things or creatures, as birds, insects, arrows, etc., passing through the air together; as, the *flight* of the Canada geese; **6,** a soaring out beyond ordinary bounds; as, a *flight* of the imagination; **7,** a series of steps leading from one floor of a building to another. Also, **flight′ at-tend′ant; flight′ crew′; flight′ deck′; flight′ re-cord′er.**

flight-y (flīt′i), *adj.* [flight-i-er, flight-i-est], **1,** given to wild flights, as of fancy, humour, etc.; fickle; unsteady; **2,** mildly crazy.—*n.* **flight′i-ness.**

flim-flam (flim′flam′), *n. Colloq.* **1,** nonsense; **2,** a trick:—*v.t. Colloq.* [-flammed, -flamming] to trick; deceive.

flim-sy (flim′zi), *adj.* [flim-si-er, flim-si-est], **1,** light; thin; weak; without strength; as, a *flimsy* box; *flimsy* material; *flimsy* excuse; **2,** without reason; as, a *flimsy* argument.—*adv.* **flim′si-ly.**—*n.* **flim′si-ness.**

flinch (flinch), *v.i.* to draw back from pain, danger, fear, etc.

fling (fling), *v.t.* [flung (flung), fling-ing], **1,** to throw or cast from, or as if from, the hand; as, to *fling* stones into a lake; **2,** to put away violently; as, he was *flung* into prison; **3,** to jerk suddenly; as, he *flung* back his head; **4,** to send out; as, the lamp *flung* out a dim light; **5,** to throw aside or cast off; as, to *fling* caution to the winds:—*v.i.* to rush out or about impatiently; as, to *fling* out of the room:—*n.* **1,** a cast or throw; **2,** a sneer or gibe; as, a *fling* at politicians; **3,** a period, usually brief, of unrestrained pleasure; as, she has had her *fling* as a musician; **4,** a short affair; **5,** a lively dance; as, the Highland *fling.*

flint (flint), *n.* a hard kind of quartz or rock that strikes sparks from steel, used formerly before matches, to start fires.—*adj.* **flint′y.**

flint-lock (flint′lok′), *n.* an old form of gun, or the lock of such a gun, in which the charge was set off by a spark from a flint struck on steel.

flint-y (flint′i), *adj.* [flint-i-er, flint-i-est], **1,** composed of flint; **2,** hard like flint; **3,** hard; unyielding; as, a *flinty* heart.—*n.* **flint′i-ness.**

flip (flip), *v.t.* [flipped, flip-ping], **1,** to flick with the fingers; tap gently; as, to *flip* the ash from a cigar; **2,** to toss so as to turn over; as, to *flip* a coin or pancake:—*v.i.* to move jerkily; flap; as, the fish *flipped* in the boat:—*n.* **1,** a short, quick tap or flick; **2,** a somersault made from a standing position:—*adj. Colloq.* pert; flippant.

flip–flop (flip′–flop′), *n.* **1,** a sudden reversal or change of direction; as, the politician did a complete *flip-flop* on the contentious issue; **2,** a rubber sandal with a thong; **3,** a backward somersault; **4,** in *computing,* an electronic circuit, such as the one that is the basic component on most CPUs, that can be switched back and forth between two states:—*v.i.* to change abruptly or reverse direction.

flip-pant (flip′ant), *adj.* disrespectfully pert; saucy; as, a *flippant* child or a *flippant* answer.—*adv.* **flip′pant-ly.**—*n.* **flip′pancy; flip′pant-ness.**

flip-per (flip′ėr), *n.* **1,** a broad, flat limb or fin adapted for swimming, as those of seals; **2,** a flat rubber shoe shaped like a fin or flipper, used by swimmers for greater speed in the water; a fin.

flirt (flûrt), *v.t.* **1,** to toss to and fro jerkily; as, the bird *flirts* its tail; **2,** to throw with a jerk; as, they *flirted* water at each other:—*v.i.* **1,** to move jerkily; dart; also, to shift constantly from one thing to another; trifle; **2,** to try to gain someone's attention or affection through sexual or romantic behaviour; to be coquettish; **3,** to play, toy, or dally; as, to *flirt* with an idea:—*n.* **1,** a coquette; **2,** a sudden jerk or toss; as, the *flirt* of a fan.—*n.* **flir-ta′tion.**

flit (flit), *v.i.* [flit-ted, flit-ting], **1,** to move lightly from place to place; as, the butterfly *flitted* from flower to flower; **2,** to pass or dart along; as, the birds *flit* by.

flitch (flitch), *n.* **1,** the side of a hog salted and cured; as, a *flitch* of bacon; **2,** a section of a log.

float (flōt), *v.i.* to be buoyed or held up on the surface of a liquid or air; as, a boat *floats;* a balloon *floats:—v.t.* **1,** to cause to suspend, rest, or move gently on the surface of a liquid or air; as, the tide will *float* the boat again; to *float* logs down the river; to *float* balloons; **2,** to start or set going, as a company, scheme, or rumour:—*n.* **1,** anything that floats, as a raft, an anchored dock, a life preserver, a cork on a fishing line, a hollow metal ball in a tank or cistern, etc.; **2,** a low platform on wheels to carry an exhibit in a parade, or the exhibit so carried; also, a low underslung platform on wheels for carrying heavy loads.—*n.* **float′er; flo-ta′tion.**

flock (flok), *n.* **1,** a number of animals or birds of one kind keeping together; as, a *flock* of wild ducks; **2,** a large number of persons together; as, they came in great *flocks;* **3,** a group of people in the charge of some person; as, the minister preached to his *flock:—v.i.* to come together or move in crowds; as, people *flocked* to hear her sing.

floe (flō), *n.* a large mass of drifting ice.

flog (flog), *v.t.* [flogged, flog-ging], **1,** to whip; beat or strike with a rod; **2,** *Slang* to sell or try to sell something; as, to *flog* used computers.

flood (flud), *n.* **1,** a great flow of water; esp., a body of water overflowing its banks, often causing loss or damage; **2,** an abundant supply or outpouring of anything; as, a *flood* of light; a *flood* of music; a *flood* of criticism:—*v.t.* **1,** to cover or fill with water; as, to *flood* a valley; **2,** to supply; fill to excess; inundate; as, to *flood* a stage with light; *flood* the market with a new product; *flood* an engine.

flood-gate (flud′gāt′), *n.* a sluice or gate in a canal, etc., to regulate the flow of water; also, anything like a floodgate or that controls the movement of something; as, to open the *floodgates* for new applicants.

flood-light (flud′līt′), *n.* an artificial light of high intensity, used to illuminate playing fields, stages, exteriors of buildings, etc.

floor (flōr), *n.* **1,** the bottom surface of a room or hall; as, there is a pine *floor* in the kitchen; **2,** any bottom surface like a floor; as, the *floor* of the ocean; **3,** all the rooms on one level in a building; a storey; **4,** the main part of an assembly hall where members sit and speak; hence, the right to speak in an assembly; as, she has the *floor:—v.t.* **1,** to cover with a floor; **2,** to strike down; as, the boxer *floored* his opponent; **3,** to put to silence; confuse or surprise; as, that question on the exam *floored* the whole class. Also, **floor′board′; floor′ hock′ey; floor′ plan′.**

flop (flop), *v.t.* [flopped, flop-ping], to drop or let fall heavily; as, to *flop* a suitcase on the floor:—*v.i.* **1,** to move or jump about awkwardly; as, the fish *flops* in the boat; **2,** flap or swing, as a flag in the wind; **3,** to throw oneself heavily; as, to *flop* down on a couch; **4,** *Colloq.* to change over suddenly, as from one political party to another; **5,** *Slang* to fail:—*n.* **1,** *Colloq.* the act or sound of flopping; **2,** *Slang* a failure; as, the movie was a *flop* and lasted only two week in theatres.—*adj. Colloq.* **flop′py.**

flop-house (flop′hous′), *n. Slang* a cheap, run-down hotel.

floppy disk, in *computing,* a thin, flexible piece of plastic that stores computer data or information, and when inserted into a computer, allows the user to read, retrieve, and use the data. Also called *floppy* or *diskette.*

flor-a (flōr′a), *n.* the plants of a particular region or period of time.

flor-al (flōr′al), *adj.* of or resembling flowers; as, a *floral* arrangement.

flo-res-cent (flō-res′ent), *adj.* blossoming. Compare *fluorescent.*—*n.* **flo-res′cence.**

flor-id (flor′id), *adj.* **1,** bright in colour; flushed; as, a *florid* complexion; **2,** richly decorated; showy; as, a *florid* style.

flor-ist (flor′ist; flôr′ist), *n.* one whose business is growing or selling flowers.

floss (flôs), *n.* **1,** strands of silk used in embroidering, crocheting, etc.; **2,** the downy, silky substance in certain pods, as of milkweed; **3,** waxed or unwaxed dental floss used for cleaning between teeth:—*v.t.* and *v.i.* to use dental floss; as, to *floss* your teeth; you should *floss* every day.

flo-til-la (flō-til′a), *n.* **1,** a fleet of small vessels; **2,** a small fleet.

flot-sam (flot′sam), *n.* **1,** pieces of wreckage or lost cargo found floating, esp. after a shipwreck; **2,** miscellaneous or useless items. Compare *jetsam.*

flotsam and jetsam, 1, the objects left floating and washed ashore after a shipwreck; **2,** things considered useless and unimportant, esp. those discarded; **3,** people who are unemployed, homeless, or rejected by society.

[1]flounce (flouns), *n.* a gathered piece of cloth sewed by its upper border to the skirt of a dress; a deep ruffle:—*v.t.* [flounced, flounc-ing], to trim with deep ruffles.

[2]flounce (flouns), *n.* a jerk or sudden movement, often showing impatience; as, a *flounce* of the head:—*v.i.* [flounced, flounc-ing], to move suddenly and jerkily; as, to *flounce* out of a room.

[1]floun-der (floun′dėr), *v.i.* **1,** to plunge around; struggle awkwardly; stumble; as, to *flounder* through a swamp; **2,** to make mistakes; blunder; as, to *flounder* through a speech.

[2]**floun-der** (floun′dėr), *n.* a food fish with a flat body and both eyes on the same side.

flour (flour), *n.* **1,** the fine meal of ground wheat or other grain, used to make bread, cake, cookies, pasta, etc.; **2,** any fine, soft powder:—*v.t.* **1,** to grind into flour; **2,** to sprinkle flour upon.—*adj.* **flour′y.**

flour-ish (flûr′ish), *v.i.* **1,** to grow; prosper; thrive; be vigorous; as, palm trees *flourish* in the tropics; the civilization *flourished*; **2,** to make showy movements, as with a sword; **3,** to make ornamental strokes with a pen:—*v.t.* **1,** to swing or wave about or brandish; as, to *flourish* written proof in front of the guilty person; to *flourish* a sword; **2,** to ornament (letters) in writing:—*n.* **1,** a showy waving; as, a *flourish* of a flag, document, etc.; **2,** a decoration in handwriting; **3,** a showy musical passage played by trumpets, bugles, etc.

flout (flout), *v.t.* to insult; mock; disdain; scorn; as, to *flout* a kindness:—*n.* a scoffing remark or action.—*adv.* **flout′ing-ly.**

flow (flō), *v.i.* **1,** to move or run along as a fluid; as, water *flows*; blood *flows* in the body; **2,** to move in a steady, smooth way; as, the traffic *flowed*; **3,** to abound; be plentiful; as, wine *flows* at a feast; **4,** to pour out easily and plentifully; as, words *flow*; **5,** to come from; proceed; as, energy *flows* from health; **6,** to hang loose; as, her long hair *flows*; **7,** to rise, as the tide:—*n.* **1,** a flowing; as, the *flow* of a river; the *flow* of air from a fan; the *flow* of electricity through a wire; **2,** the amount of fluid passing through an opening or by a certain point in a given time; **3,** any easy, continuous movement or procedure; as, a *flow* of speech, music, or thought; **4,** the coming in of the tide.

flow chart, a schematic diagram or representation of the sequence of operations, and the relationships between them, in a system such as in manufacturing or data processing.

flow-er (flou′ėr), *n.* **1,** that part of a seed-bearing plant or tree from which the seed or fruit develops; a blossom; **2,** a plant grown for its blossoms, esp. for decoration; **3,** the best part; as, the *flower* of youth:—*v.i.* **1,** to blossom; as, fruit trees *flower* in the spring; **2,** to come to full growth.

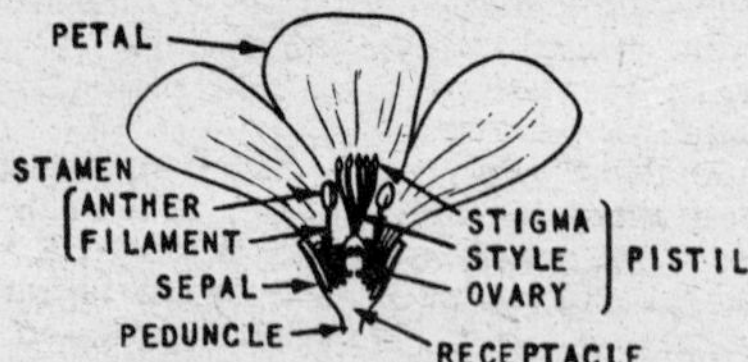

FLOWER, PARTLY CUT AWAY TO SHOW ITS PARTS

flow-er-y (flou′ėr-i), *adj.* **1,** abounding in, or like, flowers; **2,** full of showy words and phrases; as, *flowery* language.

flown (flōn), *p.p.* of *fly.*

FLQ (ef′el′kū′), *abbrev.* short for **Front de Libération du Québec.**

flu (flo͞o), *n.* short for *influenza.*

fluc-tu-ate (fluk′tū-āt′), *v.i.* [fluctuat-ed, fluctuat-ing], **1,** to rise and fall like waves; **2,** to keep changing or wavering, as prices or temperature; as, the price of gas *fluctuates* daily.—*n.* **fluc′tu-a′tion.**

flue (flo͞o), *n.* **1,** a pipe or passage for smoke, air, etc., as in a chimney or fireplace; **2,** the opening in an organ pipe or other wind instrument.

flu-ent (flo͞o′ent), *adj.* **1,** proceeding smoothly; flowing; **2,** ready or easy in the use of words, esp. in speaking; as, to be *fluent* in German.—*n.* **flu′en-cy.**

fluff (fluf), *n.* **1,** light down or fur nap, as a cotton ball or a kitten's fur; **2,** a mistake in speaking lines on stage, radio, television, etc.:—*v.t.* **1,** to puff up into a light mass; as, to *fluff* the hair; to *fluff* a pillow; **2,** on stage, radio, television, etc., to make an error in speaking one's lines; as, the mayor *fluffed* the difficult phrase.—*adj.* **fluff′y.**—*n.* **fluff′i-ness.**

flu-id (flo͞o′id), *adj.* **1,** capable of flowing; liquid or gaseous; **2,** having a relaxed, flowing appearance or style; as, the *fluid* movements of the dancer:—*n.* a substance that is capable of flowing, as a liquid or a gas.

[1]**fluke** (flo͝ok), *n.* **1,** the flattened, pointed end of an arm of an anchor; **2,** one of the broad lobes on the tail of a whale; **3,** the broad head of a harpoon, arrow, or lance.

[2]**fluke** (flo͝ok), *n.* a stroke of good or bad luck, esp. in a game.

flume (flo͞om), *n.* **1,** an artificial channel for carrying water; **2,** a gap or gorge through which a stream or river flows.

flung (flung), *p.t.* and *p.p.* of *fling.*

flunk (flungk), *v.t. Colloq.* to fail or cause to fail; as, she *flunked* the English test; his teacher *flunked* him in physics.

flunk-y or **flunk-ey** (flung′ki), *n.* **1,** a liveried servant, as a footman; **2,** a fawning and obedient person; toady; **3,** a drudge.

flu-o-res-cent (flo͞o′ėr-es′ent), *adj.* luminous when exposed to radiation:—**fluorescent lighting,** the light from a tubular electric lamp, the inside of which is coated with a phosphoric mixture that emits white light when electricity passes through the materials in the tube. Compare *florescent*; *phosphorescent.*—*n.* **flu′o-res′cence.**

flu-or-i-date (flo͞o′ėr-i-dāt′), *v.t.* to treat with fluoride; as, to *fluoridate* water.—*n.* **flu′o-ri-da′tion.**

flu-or-ide (flo͞o′ėr-īd′; -id), *n.* a fluorine compound, as sodium *fluoride*, NaF, which is added to drinking water and toothpaste to reduce tooth decay.

flu-or-ine (flōō′ėr-ēn′; -in), *n.* a poisonous, pungent, green-yellow, corrosive gaseous element (a member of the chlorine-bromine family).

flu-o-ro-scope (flōōr′e-skōp′), *n.* an instrument used by doctors for examining internal body structures by observing their shadows cast on a fluorescent screen when X-rays are passed through the structures.

flur-ry (flûr′i), *v.t.* [flurried, flurry-ing], to excite; confuse; bewilder; as, this question *flurried* her:—*n.* [*pl.* flurries], **1,** a sudden commotion or excitement; as, we were in a *flurry* at the news; **2,** a sudden gust of wind; **3,** light snow; as, snow *flurries.*

¹flush (flush), *v.t.* **1,** to redden; cause to blush; **2,** to excite; fill with elation; as, to be *flushed* with excitement; **3,** to wash or cleanse by a strong flow of water:—*v.i.* to blush; glow:—*n.* **1,** a blush; glow; **2,** a sudden rush, as of water; **3,** a thrill, as of excitement, elation, or pleasure; **4,** cards of one suit, as in poker:—*adj.* **1,** abundantly supplied, as with money; **2,** even; level; as, nail the board *flush* with the other; **3,** vigorous; spirited; full of life; **4,** in *printing,* not indented; aligned with one of the margins; as, *flush* right.

²flush (flush), *v.t.* to startle into flight, as birds.

flus-ter (flus′tėr), *v.t.* to confuse; excite; agitate:—*n.* agitation or confusion.

flute (flōōt), *n.* **1,** a musical wind instrument made of a long wooden or metal pipe with finger or metal stops (keys) and a hole across which the player blows; **2,** a long, rounded decorative groove, as in a column; **3,** a tall, slender wineglass, esp. one for champagne or other sparkling wine:—*v.i.* [flut-ed, flut-ing], to play on a flute:—*v.t.* to form grooves or folds in; as, to *flute* a ruffle.—*adj.* **flut′ed.**—*n.* **flut′ist; flut′ing.**

flut-ter (flut′ėr), *v.t.* to flap quickly without flying; as, the bird *flutters* its wings:—*v.i.* **1,** to flap the wings to move in a rapid and uneven way; as, the butterfly *fluttered* from flower to flower; **2,** to move quickly and irregularly; as, curtains *flutter* in the wind; **3,** to be confused; flit about aimlessly or restlessly; as, to *flutter* about at odd jobs:—*n.* **1,** a quick, irregular motion; vibration; as, the *flutter* of wings; **2,** a stir; excitement:—**flutter kick,** a short, rapid, up-and-down movement of the legs while using the crawl or the backstroke in swimming.

flux (fluks), *n.* **1,** any flow or discharge of matter; **2,** continuous flowing; constant change; as, in a state of *flux;* **3,** a substance used to promote fusing in metals, such as rosin:—*v.t.* to fuse or melt; make fluid.

fly (flī), *v.i.* [*p.t.* flew (flōō), *p.p.* flown (flōn), *p.pr.* fly-ing], **1,** to move through the air with wings, or as with wings by force of wind, or in an aircraft; as, birds *fly;* the ball *flew* over my head; we *flew* to Edmonton; **2,** to float in the air; as, the flag *flies;* **3,** to move or go swiftly; as, time *flies* when you're having fun; **4,** to run away; flee:—*v.t.* to cause to fly or float; as, to *fly* an airplane:—*n.* [*pl.* flies (flīz)], **1,** any of a large number of insects with a single pair of wings, such as the common housefly, *butterfly, firefly,* or *dragonfly;* **2,** a fishhook fitted with feathers to resemble an insect; **3,** in *baseball,* a ball batted so as to rise high in the air; **4,** a strip of material on a garment to cover or contain fastenings; a zipper, especially on a man's trousers; **5,** a piece of canvas stretched over something to form an extra roof. Also, **fly′a-way; fly′ ball′; fly′–by–night′; fly′–cast′ing; fly′–fish′ing; fly′–in′.**

fly-er (flī′ėr), *n.* Same as **flier.**

fly-ing (flī′ing), *adj.* **1,** moving through the air, as on wings; **2,** capable of gliding through the air; as, a *flying* squirrel; **3,** floating or moving freely, as a flag; **4,** moving rapidly; as, a *flying* horse; **5,** fleeting; brief; as, a *flying* visit:—**flying buttress,** an arched brace against the wall of a building to resist the outward thrust of the roof, as in the medieval cathedrals. Also, **fly′ing fish′; fly′ing sau′cer.**

fly-weight (flī′wāt′), *n.* a boxer of 49 kilograms or less.

fly-wheel (flī′wēl′), *n.* a heavy wheel used to stabilize the speed of a machine, esp. to carry a piston over dead centre.

FM or **fm** (ef′em′), *abbrev.* short for *frequency modulation,* one of the two main kinds of radio signals: the frequency of the radio wave is made higher or lower to match the sound being broadcast. Compare *AM.*

foal (fōl), *n.* the young of the horse or similar animal; a colt:—*v.i.* to give birth to a foal.

foam (fōm), *n.* the white substance or mass of tiny bubbles formed on a liquid by shaking or fermentation; froth:—*v.i.* to form or produce foam; as, the rabid dog *foamed* at the mouth; the sea *foamed* during the storm.—*adj.* **foam′y.**

fob (fob), *n.* **1,** a small pocket for a watch; **2,** a short watch-chain or ribbon; also, a small ornament at the end of it.

fo-cus (fō′kus), *n.* [*pl.* focuses (fō′kus-ez) or foci (fō′sī)], **1,** the point at which rays of heat, light, sound, etc., meet after being bent or turned from the straight lines in which they radiate; **2,** an adjustment of eyes, glasses, camera lenses, etc., to produce clear sight or images; **3,** a central point; centre of interest; as, the urgent matter was our immediate *focus:*—*v.t.* [focused, focus-ing or focussed, focus-sing], **1,**

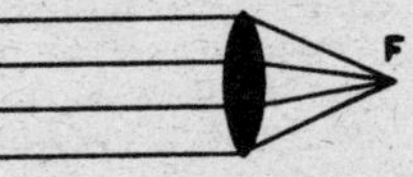

PARALLEL RAYS OF LIGHT BROUGHT TO A FOCUS (F) BY A CONVEX LENS

to adjust the focus of (eyes, a telescope, camera, etc.) to get a sharper picture; **2,** to bring into focus; **3,** to centre; concentrate; as, he *focused* his attention on history.—*adj.* **fo′cal.**

fod-der (fod′ėr), *n.* coarse food, such as dried cornstalks, for cattle.

foe (fō), *n.* **1,** an enemy or adversary; **2,** anything injurious; as, ill health is a *foe* to happiness.

foe-tus (fē′tus), *n.* Same as **fetus.**

fog (fog), *n.* **1,** a cloud of water vapour near the surface of the sea or land; **2,** any haziness, as on a mirror; **3,** bewilderment; confused state of mind; not alert; as, to be in a *fog* due to tiredness:—*v.i.* [fogged, fogging], to become clouded, as with a fog; as, the windshield *fogged* up:—*v.t.* to cover as with a fog; cloud.—*adj.* **fog′gy.**

fo-gey or **fo-gy** (fō′gi), *n.* [*pl.* fogies], a person of old-fashioned or dull habits and ideas.

fog-horn (fog′hôrn′), *n.* a siren or horn for warning ships in a fog.

foi-ble (foi′bl), *n.* a weak point; a failing or weakness of character; as, humorists write about the *foibles* of people.

[1]**foil** (foil), *n.* **1,** a thin, flexible, paperlike sheet of metal; as, aluminum *foil*; gold *foil*; **2,** a thin coat of metal placed on the back of a mirror to reflect light; also, such a coat placed under stones in jewellery to set off their brightness; **3,** anything that sets off another thing to advantage by contrast; as, his rudeness was a *foil* to her refinement.

[2]**foil** (foil), *n.* a long, thin sword with a blunt point, used in fencing.

[3]**foil** (foil), *v.t.* to prevent from carrying out a plan; to stop from succeeding; baffle; defeat; as, every attempt was *foiled* by the enemy.

foist (foist), *v.t.* to palm off; pass (something false or counterfeit) as genuine; as, to *foist* a fake gem on a buyer.

[1]**fold** (fōld), *v.t.* **1,** to double; bend over; as, to *fold* a letter; **2,** to clasp, as the hands; to bend close to the body; as, to *fold* one's arms; a bird *folds* its wings; **3,** to envelop; as, peaks *folded* in clouds:—*v.i.* **1,** to become closed by bending or doubling; as, the bird's wings *folded* up; **2,** to fail or close; as, the business *folded* due to a drop in sales:—*n.* a part doubled over another; also, a hollow or crease made by folding.—*adj.* **fold′ing** (as, a *folding* chair).

[2]**fold** (fōld), *n.* **1,** a pen for sheep; **2,** a flock of sheep; **3,** a body of religious believers:—*v.t.* to shut up (sheep) in a pen.

fold-er (fōl′dėr), *n.* **1,** a small folded circular, map, pamphlet, etc.; **2,** a cover for holding loose papers; **3,** in *computing,* a directory that contains a collection of files.

fo-li-age (fō′li-ij), *n.* leaves; all the leaves of a plant.

fo-li-ate (fō′li-it; -āt′), *adj.* **1,** covered with leaves; **2,** leaflike:—*v.t.* to beat into foil or divide into thin layers; also, to apply metal foil.

fo-li-o (fō′li-ō; fōl′yō), *n.* [*pl.* folios], **1,** a sheet of paper folded once; **2,** a book of the largest size, made of sheets of paper folded only once, with two leaves or four pages to each sheet; **3,** the size of a book so made; **4,** a folder for carrying loose papers, etc.; **5,** in *printing,* the number of a page:—*adj.* consisting of sheets of paper folded once; having the form or size of a folio; as, a *folio* edition:—*v.t.* to number the pages of (a book or manuscript).

folk (fōk), *n.* **1,** a race or nation; **2, folks** or **folk,** *pl.,* people of a certain type or group collectively; as, town *folk*; city *folk*; young *folk*; *folks* that like to travel; **3,** people in general; as, in this province, *folks* pay extra tax; **4, folks,** *Colloq.* one's own kindred; as, my *folks* are away:—*adj.* originating with the people of a certain area or way of life; as, a *folk* tale; *folk* art; *folk* music, etc. Also, **folk′ dance′; folk′ me′di-cine; folk′ mu′sic; folk′sing′er; folk′song′; folk′ways′.**

folk-lore (fōk′lōr′), *n.* the beliefs, legends, songs, customs, etc., handed down by a people over the years.

folk-tale or **folk–tale** or **folk tale** (fōk′tāl′), *n.* a story that has been told for many years and that has been passed down over time by word of mouth.

fol-li-cle (fol′i-kl), *n.* a small sac or gland for secretion or excretion; as, when the hair *follicles* dry up, baldness results.

fol-low (fol′ō), *v.t.* **1,** to go or come after; as, we *followed* the guide; **2,** to come after in time or rank; as, she *followed* her father in office; **3,** to go along; as, to *follow* a road; **4,** to strive after; aim at; as, to *follow* fame; **5,** to copy; imitate; as, your idea *follows* his; **6,** to accept as guide; obey; as, to *follow* advice or instructions; **7,** to practise as a profession; as, he *followed* medicine; **8,** to pay attention to; understand; as, to *follow* a lecture; **9,** to result from; as, illness *follows* neglect of health; **10,** to watch or observe closely; as, to *follow* her career:—*v.i.* **1,** to go or come after another; as, go ahead, and we will *follow*; **2,** to result from; as, it *follows* from your remark that you intend to leave.—*n.* **fol′low-er.**

fol-low-ing (fol′ō-ing), *adj.* coming after; next; as, the *following* year; read the *following* page:—*n.* **1,** a body of followers or supporters; as, a political leader with a very large *following*; **2,** those about to be mentioned; as, the *following* were there.

fol-ly (fol′i), *n.* [*pl.* follies], **1,** lack of sense, understanding, or good judgment; foolishness; **2,** a foolish act or idea.

fo-ment (fō-ment′), *v.t.* **1,** to bathe with warm liquids; **2,** to foster; excite; stir up; as, to *foment* a riot.—*n.* **fo′men-ta′tion.**

fond (fond), *adj.* **1,** affectionate; loving; **2,**

interested in; as, *fond* of music; **3,** cherished; as, my *fond* hope.—*adv.* **fond′ly.**—*n.* **fond′ness.**

fon-dle (fon′dl), *v.t.* [fon-dled, fon-dling], to caress; pet; as, to stroke and *fondle* a cat.

[1]**font** (font), *n.* **1,** a vessel to hold holy water or water for baptizing; **2,** a fountain or spring; **3,** source; as, the Internet is a *font* of information.

[2]**font** (font), *n.* in *printing* and *computing,* a complete assortment of one size and style of type; as, *fonts* on a computer.

food (fōōd), *n.* **1,** nourishment taken into the body to keep it alive, give it energy, and make it grow; also, any nourishing substance; **2,** solid nourishment in contrast to liquid.

food bank, a charitable organization that collects and distributes food, and sometimes other items, to the needy.

food-stuff (fōōd′stuf′), *n.* anything used as food or used to prepare food, esp. raw materials such as meats, cereals, and fruits; commodities.

fool (fōōl), *n.* **1,** a person of little sense, judgment, or intelligence; **2,** in former times, a jester or clown; **3,** a dupe; a victim of a joke; as, to make a *fool* of him:—*v.t.* to deceive or trick:—*v.i.* to trifle; act in a playful or silly way; as, to *fool* around in class.—*adj.* and *n.* **fool′ing.**—*n.* **fool′er-y; fool′har′di-ness.**—*adj.* **fool′har′dy; fool′proof′.**

fool-ish (fōōl′ish), *adj.* **1,** without reason or good judgment; **2,** silly; ridiculous like a fool.—*adv.* **fool′ish-ly.**—*n.* **fool′ish-ness.**

fools-cap (fōōlz′kap′), *n.* writing paper about 35 cm x 21 cm, originally watermarked with a jester's cap and bells; also, writing paper in general.

fool's gold (fōōlz′gōld′), *n.* iron pyrites, which looks like real gold.

foot (foot), *n.* [*pl.* feet (fēt)], **1,** that part of the leg on which humans and other animals walk or stand; **2,** the lowest part; base; as, the *foot* of a tree or a hill; **3,** the lowest part in rank; as, the *foot* of the class; **4,** the part of a boot or stocking that receives the foot; **5,** that part of anything where the feet lie; as, the *foot* of a bed; **6,** a measure of length, equal to 12 inches or about 30 cm; **7,** unmounted soldiers; infantry:—*v.t.* **1,** to add a foot to (a stocking or sock); **2,** to add up (a column of figures) and place the total at the bottom; **3,** *Colloq.* to pay; as, to *foot* the bill.—*adj.* **foot′sore′.**—*n.* **foot′path′; foot′stool′; foot′ wear′; foot′work′.**

foot-ball (foot′bôl′), *n.* **1,** a game played on a large field in which an inflated leather ball must be carried or kicked across the opposing team's goal line; **2,** the ball used in this game; **3,** in countries other than Canada and the U.S., the game of soccer.

foot-er (foot′ėr), *n.* a line of running text at the bottom of each page of a document.

foot-fall (foot′fôl′), *n.* a footstep; the sound of the tread of the foot.

foot-hill (foot′hil′), *n.* a low, outlying hill near the base of a mountain range.

foot-hold (foot′hōld′), *n.* a secure place to set foot; firm footing or position.

foot-ing (foot′ing), *n.* **1,** firm placing of the feet; foothold; as, to lose one's *footing;* **2,** a place to stand or walk; as, there was no *footing* along the cliff; **3,** relationship; basis; as, a friendly *footing;* **4,** the adding up, or the sum total, of a column of figures.

foot-lights (foot′līts′), *n.pl.* **1,** a row of lights along the front of the floor of the stage of a theatre; **2,** the stage or theatre as a profession.

foot-loose (foot′lōōs′), *adj. Colloq.* free to go anywhere or do anything; as, to be *footloose* and fancy free.

foot-man (foot′man), *n.* [*pl.* footmen (-men)], a male servant, usually in uniform, who attends a car or carriage, waits on tables, etc.

foot-note (foot′nōt′), *n.* a note of explanation at the bottom of a page in a book, magazine, etc.; also, an additional comment.

foot-print (foot′print′), *n.* **1,** the mark or impression made by a foot, as in mud, snow, etc.; **2,** the amount of space taken up by a structure, piece of equipment, or device; the space taken up on a desk surface by a computer.

foot-step (foot′step′), *n.* **1,** an act of stepping or placing one foot ahead of the other; a step; **2,** the sound of a step; **3,** the mark of a foot, as in the earth; footprint; track.

foo-zle (fōō′zl), *v.t. Colloq.* in *golf,* to bungle; as, he *foozled* the short putt.

fop (fop), *n.* a man who is fond of fine dress, esp. in former times; a dandy.—*n.* **fop′per-y.**—*adj.* **fop′pish.**

for (fôr), *prep.* **1,** in place of; as, Sarita ran base *for* Kimberly; **2,** as being; as, I took him *for* an honest person; **3,** in return for, in a trade; as, two pencils *for* 50 cents; **4,** because of; as, he could not walk *for* weakness; **5,** because of a hindrance or lack of; as, I'd go but *for* my lessons; pressed *for* time; **6,** on account of; in the interest of; as, do it *for* your mother; fear *for* his safety; **7,** in favour, support, or defence of; as, to vote *for* the liberal candidate; **8,** in spite of; as, *for* all his money, he has no influence; **9,** to the amount of; as, a bill *for* 50 dollars; **10,** as regards; as, so much *for* that point; a love *for* poetry; **11,** in comparison or contrast with; as, wise *for* her years; one success *for* every 10 failures; **12,** with the hope, intention, or expectation, of reaching, getting, doing, etc.; as, he left *for* Europe; to try *for* a prize; **13,** with a view to; for the purpose of; as, to go *for* a walk; **14,** suited to; as, a salve *for* burns; the person *for* the job; **15,** about; as, I don't care *for* cards; **16,** for the use of; as, textbooks *for* the class:—*conj.* because; since; seeing that; as, get up, *for* day is here.

for-age (for′ij), *n.* **1,** food for horses and cattle; **2,** a search for something, esp. food or provisions, as for an army:—*v.i.* [foraged, forag-ing], to go in search of something, esp. provisions:—*v.t.* to strip of provisions; plunder; ravage, as a land in wartime.—*n.* **for′ag-er.**

for-as-much as (fôr′az-much′az), *conj.* since; because.

for-ay (fôr′ā), *n.* **1,** in warfare, a raid; **2,** a brief, unusual attempt; as, an athlete's *foray* into music:—*v.i.* to plunder or ravage.

[1]**for-bear** (fôr′bâr), *n.* Same as **fore′bear.**

[2]**for-bear** (fôr-bâr′), *v.t.* [*p.t.* forbore (fôr-bōr′), *p.p.* forborne (fôr-bōrn′), *p.pr.* for-bear-ing], to refrain; keep from; as, he *forbore* to ask questions:—*v.i.* to restrain oneself; be patient.—*n.* **for-bear′ance.**

for-bid (fôr-bid′), *v.t.* [*p.t.* forbade or forbad (fôr-bad′), *p.p.* forbid-den (fôr-bid′n), *p.pr.* forbid-ding], **1,** to prohibit; not to allow; **2,** to command (a person) not to do.—*adj.* **for-bid′den; for-bid′ding.**

force (fōrs), *n.* **1,** energy; power; vigour; strength; violence; as, the *force* of the wind; **2,** power to convince or persuade; as, the *force* of an argument; **3,** real meaning, as of a word; **4,** (often *forces*), military or naval strength; armed men and women; warships or aircraft; as, armed *forces*; **5,** hence, any trained or organized body of persons; as, the police *force*; labour *force*; **6,** any powerful person or thing; as, a *force* for social reform; **7,** mental or moral strength; as, *force* of character; **8,** great numbers; as, the people ran out in full *force*; **9,** violence to persons or property; **10,** in *physics*, anything that causes or changes motion in a body; as, the *force* of gravity, electricity, heat, etc.:—*v.t.* [forced, forc-ing], **1,** to compel; as, to *force* her to talk; **2,** to push; get by strength; as, to *force* one's way; **3,** to produce by unnatural or special effort; as, to *force* a smile; **4,** to break open; as, to *force* a lock; **5,** to press or impose; as, to *force* a gift on someone; **6,** to hasten the growth of (a plant) artificially.

force-ful (fōrs′fool), *adj.* having vigour; strong; powerful; as, a *forceful* speech.—*adv.* **force′ful-ly.**—*n.* **force′ful-ness.**

for-ceps (fôr′seps), *n. sing.* and *pl.* pincers, pliers, or tongs, esp. those used by dentists, surgeons, watchmakers, etc.

for-ci-ble (fōr′si-bl), *adj.* **1,** vivid; convincing; powerful; as, *forcible* speech; **2,** accomplished by violence; as, a *forcible* entry.—*adv.* **for′ci-bly.**

ford (fōrd), *n.* a shallow part of a stream, which can be crossed on foot:—*v.t.* and *v.i.* to pass through (water, a stream, etc.) on foot.

fore (fōr), *n.* the front part, esp. on a ship or boat:—*adj.* and *adv.* at or near the front:—*interj.* used as a warning after hitting a ball on a golf course.

fore-and-aft (fōr′-and-åft′), *adj.* lengthwise of a ship; as, *fore-and-aft* sails.

fore-arm (fōr′ärm′), *n.* the arm between the wrist and the elbow.

fore-bear or **for-bear** (fōr′bâr), *n.* an ancestor.

fore-bode (fōr-bōd′), *v.t.* [forebod-ed, fore-bod-ing], **1,** to have a feeling or suspicion of (coming misfortune); foresee (evil); **2,** to be a sign or warning of; as, conditions *forebode* war.—*n.* and *adj.* **fore-bod′ing.**

fore-cast (fōr′kåst′), *n.* a prediction or foretelling, as of the weather:—*v.t.* (fōr-kåst′; fōr′kåst′), [forecast or forecast-ed, forecast-ing], to plan or calculate beforehand; to predict.

fore-check (fōr′-chek′), *v.t.* and *v.i.* in *hockey*, to block aggressively the progress of opposing team members to prevent them from organizing an offensive attack.

fore-close (fōr-klōz′), *v.t.* [foreclosed, fore-clos-ing], to terminate (a mortgage) by obtaining the legal right to the property mortgaged.—*n.* **fore-clo′sure.**

fore-fa-ther (fōr′fä′*th*ėr), *n.* an ancestor.

fore-fin-ger (fōr′fing′gėr), *n.* the first or index finger, next to the thumb.

fore-foot (fōr′foot′), *n.* [*pl.* forefeet (-fēt′)], a front foot of a four-legged animal.

fore-go (fōr-gō′), *v.t.* Same as **forgo.**

fore-go-ing (fōr-gō′ing), *adj.* coming ahead of something else; preceding.

fore-gone (fōr-gôn′; fōr′gôn), *adj.* settled in advance; as, a *foregone* conclusion.

fore-ground (fōr′ground′), *n.* that part of a picture or scene nearest the observer.

fore-hand (fōr′hand′), *adj.* in *tennis*, made, as a stroke, with the arm at the side, not extended across the body.

fore-head (fōr′id; fōr′hed′), *n.* the part of the face above the eyes; the brow.

for-eign (fôr′in), *adj.* **1,** belonging to another nation or country; as, a *foreign* language; **2,** not native; as, of *foreign* birth; **3,** not belonging or suitable; as, remarks *foreign* to the topic; a *foreign* object in the eye.—*n.* **for′eign-er.** Also, **for′eign aid′; for′eign ex-change′.**

fore-knowl-edge (fōr-nol′ij), *n.* the knowing of a thing before it happens or exists; as, she had *foreknowledge* of what we did.

fore-leg (fōr′leg′), *n.* either front leg, as of a horse, dog, etc.

fore-man (fōr′man), *n.* [*pl.* foremen (-men)], **1,** the person in charge of a group of workers; **2,** the chairperson and spokesperson of a jury.—*n. fem.* **fore′wom′an.**

fore-most (fōr′mōst), *adj.* first; most important; chief.

fo-ren-sic (fo-ren′sik), *adj.* **1,** relating to public debate or law courts; as, *forensic* eloquence; **2,** argumentative; **3,** relating to the application of science to law or police investigation; as, *forensic* medicine, pathology, etc.

fore-paw (fōr′pô′), *n.* a front foot of any animal that has claws.

fore-run-ner (fōr-run′ėr), *n.* **1,** a messenger sent in advance; harbinger; **2,** anything that precedes or foreshadows another; as, tulips and daffodils are *forerunners* of spring; **3,** a predecessor.

fore-see (fōr-sē′), *v.t.* [*p.t.* foresaw (fōr-sô′), *p.p.* foreseen (fōr-sēn′), *p.pr.* foresee-ing], to know or see beforehand.

fore-shad-ow (fōr-shad′ō), *v.t.* to point to as coming; warn; predict; as, dark clouds *foreshadow* a thunderstorm.

fore-sight (fōr′sīt′), *n.* **1,** knowing or seeing beforehand: opposite of *hindsight*; **2,** thought for the future; prudence.

fore-skin (fōr′skin′), *n.* the fold of skin covering the end of the penis, often removed by circumcision.

for-est (fôr′est), *n.* a growth of trees covering a large tract of land; wild woodland:—*adj.* of or relating to woodland; as, *forest* animals:—*v.t.* to cover with trees or woods.

fore-stall (fōr-stôl′), *v.t.* to hinder or prevent, by action taken in advance.

for-est-ry (fôr′est-ri), *n.* the science of developing, maintaining, and managing forests, as well as utilizing timber.—*n.* **for′est-er.**

fore-taste (fōr-tāst′), *v.t.* [foretast-ed, foretast-ing], to taste beforehand:—*n.* (fōr′tāst′), anticipation.

fore-tell (fōr-tel′), *v.t.* and *v.i.* [fore-told (fōr-tōld′), foretell-ing], to tell beforehand; predict; prophesy.

fore-thought (fōr′thôt′), *n.* **1,** the planning of something beforehand; **2,** heedfulness for the future.

for-ev-er (fôr-ev′ėr), *adv.* **1,** at all times; again and again; always; as, she was *forever* reading; **2,** through eternity; perpetually.

fore-warn (fōr-wôrn′), *v.t.* to caution in advance.—*n.* **fore-warn′ing.**

fore-wom-an (fōr′woom′an), *n.* **1,** a woman in charge of workers in a factory, workshop, etc.; **2,** a woman who presides over a jury.

fore-word (fōr′wûrd), *n.* a preface, esp. in a book; introductory note or remarks.

for-feit (fôr′fit), *n.* something lost because of a crime or fault; hence, a fine or penalty:—**forfeits,** a game in which one must perform a silly task to regain some article given:—*v.t.* to lose by neglect or fault; as, to *forfeit* a game by coming late; to *forfeit* a rental deposit:—*adj.* lost by neglect or crime.—*n.* **for′feit-er; for′fei-ture.**

[1]**forge** (fōrj), *v.i.* [forged, forg-ing], to go on steadily; as, to *forge* ahead.

[2]**forge** (fōrj), *v.t.* [forged, forg-ing], **1,** to shape (metal) by hammering while it is soft with heat; **2,** to shape; form; invent; **3,** to make a false imitation of; esp. to counterfeit (a signature):—*n.* **1,** an open fire for heating metal in preparation for hammering or shaping; **2,** a shop for heating and working metal; also, a blacksmith's shop.—*n.* **forg′er.**

for-ger-y (fōr′jėr-i), *n.* [*pl.* forgeries], **1,** the act of copying or imitating something, esp. a signature, with intent to deceive; **2,** a false signature; **3,** anything counterfeit.

for-get (fôr-get′), *v.t.* [*p.t.* forgot (fôr-got′), *p.p.* forgot-ten (fôr-got′n) or forgot, *p.pr.* forget-ting], **1,** to fail to remember or recall; **2,** to cease to think of; as, he has *forgotten* me; **3,** to fail to remember to take or do; as, I have *forgotten* to take my medicine; to *forget* to e-mail a reply; **4,** to neglect; disregard; as, to *forget* a debt:—*v.i.* to fail to remember.—*adj.* **for-get′ful.**—*n.* **for-get′ful-ness.**

for-give (fôr-giv′), *v.t.* [*p.t.* forgave (fôr-gāv′), *p.p.* forgiv-en (fôr-giv′en), *p.pr.* forgiv-ing], **1,** to cease to resent; to pardon; no longer blame; as, to *forgive* an unkindness; *forgive* him for doing it; **2,** to refrain from exacting, as a debt.—*adj.* **for-giv′ing; for-giv′a-ble.**—*adv.* **for-giv′ing-ly.**—*n.* **for-give′ness.**

for-go or **fore-go** (fôr-gō′), *v.t.* [*p.t.* forwent (fôr-went′), *p.p.* forgone (fôr-gôn′), *p.pr.* forgo-ing], to give up; deny oneself; abstain from; as, to *forgo* watching television.

fork (fôrk), *n.* **1,** a farm tool with two or more prongs and a handle, used for digging, picking up, carrying, etc.; as, a pitch*fork*; **2,** a small, pronged implement for the dining room or kitchen, used to pick up or hold food; **3,** anything branching like a fork; as, a *fork* in a road or a tree:—*v.t.* **1,** to make in the shape of a fork; **2,** to raise, throw, or dig with a fork; as, to *fork* hay:—*v.i.* to branch; as, the road *forks* here.

for-lorn (fôr-lôrn′), *adj.* forsaken; miserable; pitiful; as, a *forlorn* homeless person.

form (fôrm), *n.* **1,** the outward appearance or shape of anything; as, to have the *form* of a triangle; **2,** a body, esp. the human body; **3,** special arrangement or method of composition; as, poetic *form*; sonata *form*; **4,** established practice or ritual; as, *forms* of worship; **5,** a definite manner of doing something; etiquette; as, the *form* for an introduction; **6,** a standard of conduct; as, tattling is bad *form*; **7,** athletic fitness; as, he's in good *form* today; **8,** a mould or pattern; as, a *form* for jelly; **9,** a piece of printed paper with spaces left to be filled in; as, an application *form*; also, a printed letter, notice, etc., to be sent out in great numbers; as, the cable company sent out a *form* to all customers, advising of an increase in rates; **10,** a kind; variety; example; as, a tree is a *form* of plant life; **11,** a long bench without a back; **12,** in *grammar*, the composition of a word in reference to spelling, pronunciation, inflection, etc.; as, "narcissus" has two plural *forms*, "narcissuses" and "narcissi":—*v.t.* **1,** to give shape to; make; as, to *form* a figure out of clay; **2,** to mould by influence; train; as, education helps to *form* the mind; **3,** to go to make up; as, music *formed* the greater part of the program; **4,** to develop; bring into being; as, to *form* a habit; *form* a club; **5,** to construct (a word) by grammatical rules; as, to *form* the plural of a noun by adding *s*:—*v.i.* to take shape; as, lumps *formed* in the pudding.—*adj.* **form′less; form′a-tive.**

for-mal (fôr′mal), *adj.* **1,** according to established rules or conventions; as, a *formal* ceremony; **2,** suitable for wearing to an important ceremony or event, esp. in the evening; as, a *formal* dress; **3,** very proper and polite; not relaxed; as, a *formal* boss; having outward show but lacking reality; as, a *formal* friendship.—*adv.* **for′mal-ly.**

form-al-de-hyde (fôr-mal′de-hīd′), *n.* a pungent gas, used in solution as a preservative, antiseptic, and disinfectant.

for-mal-i-ty (fôr-mal′i-ti), *n.* [*pl.* formalities], **1,** rigid observance of forms or established rules; **2,** a regular order of procedure; as, legal *formalities*.

for-mat (fôr′mat), *n.* **1,** the whole style, shape, and size of a book, magazine, etc., including the paper, typeface, design, binding, etc.; **2,** a form or genre of writing; **3,** any system or arrangement for doing something; a plan; as, the *format* of a seminar; **4,** in *computing*, the way data is arranged, stored, and displayed in a computer; also, the method used for this:—*v.t.* **1,** to plan or arrange something in a certain way; **2,** in *computing*, to determine the way data is arranged, stored, and displayed in a computer; also, to divide a disk into specific sections and enter specific information to enable it to store data; as, to *format* a disk before copying a file onto it.

for-ma-tion (fôr-mā′shun), *n.* **1,** moulding or shaping; as, *formation* of character; **2,** that which is shaped; structure; as, rock *formations*; also, shape; form; as, the *formation* of the brain; **3,** arrangement of a body of troops or other people; as, marching *formation*; the *formation* of the football players.

for-mer (fôr′mėr), *adj.* **1,** preceding in time or order; as, *former* days; a *former* prime minister; **2,** the first of two things that were just named or mentioned; as, of the two speakers, I prefer the *former*: compare *latter*.

for-mer-ly (fôr′mėr-li), *adv.* in past time; before; as, he *formerly* lived in Spain.

for-mic (fôr′mik), *adj.* **1,** pertaining to a pungent, corrosive acid distilled from glycerine and oxalic acid (formerly from red ants); **2,** of ants.

for-mi-da-ble (fôr′mi-da-bl), *adj.* fear-inspiring; hard to deal with or overcome; as, a *formidable* army.—*adv.* **for′mi-da-bly.**

for-mu-la (fôr′mū-la), *n.* [*pl.* formulas or formulae (fôr′mū-lē′)], **1,** a set rule for doing something; as, the *formula* for happiness; **2,** in *mathematics*, a set of symbols and figures to express a rule; as, an algebraic *formula*; **3,** in *chemistry*, a list of the constituents of a compound, using symbols and figures; as, the *formula* for water is H_2O; **4,** the specified way of performing a ceremony or of expressing a faith or doctrine; **5,** a prescription, as for drugs; a recipe; as, baby's *formula*; a *formula* for making a soufflé.

for-mu-late (fôr′mū-lāt′), *v.t.* [formulated, formulat-ing], to put into a definite form; state in definite terms as, to *formulate* a law.—*n.* **for′mu-la′tion.**

for-ni-ca-tion (fôr′ni-kā′shun), *n.* sexual intercourse, esp. between unmarried people.—*v.i.* **for′ni-cate′.**

for-sake (fôr-sāk′), *v.t.* [*p.t.* forsook (fôr-sook′), *p.p.* forsak-en (fôr-sāk′en), *p.pr.* forsak-ing], to give up; abandon; as, his friends will not *forsake* him.

for-swear (fôr-swâr′), *v.i.* [forswore (fôr-swôr′), *p.p.* forsworn (fôr-swôrn′), *p.pr.* forswear-ing], to take an oath falsely:—*v.t.* **1,** to deny on oath; **2,** to renounce earnestly; **3,** to perjure (oneself).

fort (fōrt), *n.* **1,** a strongly fortified place; esp., a structure built for defence against enemy attack; **2,** an area where a large number of soldiers and weapons are regularly located; **3,** a trading post.

forte (fōrt; fôr′tā), *n.* one's strong point; special talent; as, her *forte* is music.—*adj.* (fôr′tā), in *music*, loudly.

forth (fōrth), *adv.* **1,** onward in time, place, or order; forward; as, from this day *forth*; **2,** out; outward; as, the sun sends *forth* light; **3,** away; as, to go *forth* and never return.

forth-com-ing (fōrth′kum′ing), *adj.* ready or about to appear; approaching; as, our *forthcoming* trip; a *forthcoming* answer.

forth-right (fōrth′rīt′), *adv.* straightforward; at once:—*adj.* direct; decisive; as, a *forthright* answer.

forth-with (fōrth′wi*th*′; fōrth′with′), *adv.* immediately; directly.

for-ti-eth (fôr′ti-eth), *adj.* next after the 39th: the ordinal of *forty*:—*n.* one of the 40 equal parts of anything.

for-ti-fi-ca-tion (fōr′ti-fi-kā′shun), *n.* **1,**

the act of building or strengthening military defences; **2,** a military work erected for defence; a fort; **3,** the addition of enrichment to food or drink.

for-ti-fy (fôr′ti-fī′), *v.t.* [fortified, fortifying], **1,** to strengthen by forts, walls, etc.; as, to *fortify* a town; **2,** to make strong; as, to *fortify* one's courage; **3,** to add enrichment to food or drink; as, to *fortify* bread or milk with extra vitamins and minerals.

for-tis-si-mo (fôr-tis′i-mō′), *adj.* in *music,* very loud:—*adv.* very loudly (stronger than *forte*).

for-ti-tude (fôr′ti-tūd′), *n.* strength of endurance or courage in pain or trouble.

fort-night (fôrt′nīt; fôrt′nit), *n.* a period of two weeks.—*adv.* **fort′night′ly.**

FOR-TRAN or **for-tran** (fôr′tran′), *n.* short for *formula translation*: in *computing,* high-level computer programming language used in science, mathematics, and engineering.

for-tress (fôr′tres), *n.* a fortified place; a stronghold.

for-tu-i-tous (fôr-tū′i-tus), *adj.* accidental; happening by chance; as, to many, the evolution of life is not *fortuitous.*

for-tu-nate (fôr′tū-nit), *adj.* **1,** bringing good fortune; as, a *fortunate* play; **2,** lucky; successful; as, a *fortunate* person.—*adv.* **for′tu-nate-ly.**

for-tune (fôr′tūn), *n.* **1,** the good or ill that happens to a person; chance; luck; as, the good *fortune* to find friends; **2,** wealth; riches; **3,** future fate; as, tell my *fortune.* Also, **for′tune cook′ie; for′tune tel′ler.**

for-ty (fôr′ti), *adj.* composed of one more than 39:—*n.* [*pl.* forties], **1,** the number consisting of 39 plus one; **2,** a sign representing forty units, as 40 or XL.

for-ty-ninth par-al-lel (fôr′ti–nīnth′ par′a-lel′), *n.* the 49th latitude north of the equator that forms the boundary between Canada and the United States from Lake of the Woods on the western Ontario border to the Pacific Ocean.

for-um (fōr′um), *n.* [*pl.* forums or fora (fōr′a)], **1,** the public meeting place in ancient Rome where the law courts, public offices, etc., were situated; **2,** a place of gathering for public discussion.

[1]**for-ward** (fôr′wėrd) or **for-wards** (fôr′wėrdz), *adv.* toward the front; on or onward; as, to march *forward*:—*interj.* on!

[2]**for-ward** (fôr′wėrd), *adj.* **1,** situated near the front; as, the *forward* ranks; **2,** early; ahead of time; as, *forward* crops; **3,** onward; as, a *forward* movement; **4,** ready; prompt; also, too confident; bold; rude; as, a *forward* manner:—*v.t.* **1,** to help on; advance; as, to *forward* a cause; **2,** to send on; as, to *forward* e-mails:—*n.* **1,** in *football,* a forward pass; **2,** in *basketball, soccer,* and *hockey,* a player whose position is at the front and who plays offence.—*n.* **for′ward-ness.**

fos-sil (fos′il), *n.* **1,** a petrified animal or plant; a trace or remnant of a prehistoric animal or plant, imbedded or preserved in the earth, in rocks, or in caves; **2,** *Slang* an old-fashioned person:—*adj.* **1,** petrified; like a fossil; **2,** out of date. Also, **fos′sil fu′el.**

FOSSIL, DEF. 1

fos-ter (fos′tėr), *v.t.* **1,** to nourish; rear up; as, to *foster* a child; **2,** to support; cherish; as, to *foster* ideas:—*adj.* giving, receiving, or sharing nurture or care, though not related by blood and not adopted; as, a *foster* parent.

fought (fôt), *p.t.* and *p.p.* of *fight.*

foul (foul), *adj.* **1,** offensive; disgusting; as, a *foul* taste or odour; **2,** dirty; soiled; as, *foul* linen; **3,** vulgar; obscene; as, *foul* language; **4,** morally offensive; odious; as, a *foul* crime; **5,** unfair; as, *foul* play; **6,** stormy; as, *foul* weather; **7,** clogged; as, a *foul* chimney; **8,** entangled; as, a *foul* rope; **9,** in collision; as, the ship ran *foul* of the rock:—*n.* **1,** in many games, as football, soccer, or hockey, a play or act that is against the rules; **2,** in *baseball,* a batted ball that first strikes the ground outside of the lines marking out the playing field:—*v.t.* **1,** to make impure; as, to *foul* the air; **2,** to dishonour; as, to *foul* one's name; **3,** to collide with or entangle; as, to *foul* a cable:—*v.i.* **1,** to become dirty; **2,** to come into collision, as two boats; to become entangled; **3,** in *baseball,* to hit a foul ball.—*adv.* **foul′ly.**—*n.* **foul′ness.** Also, **foul′ ball′; foul′ line′; foul′–mouthed′; foul′ play′; foul′–up′.**

[1]**found** (found), *p.t.* and *p.p.* of *find.*

[2]**found** (found), *v.t.* to lay the basis of; to originate; establish; as, to *found* a city or an institution.—*n.* **found′er.**

foun-da-tion (foun-dā′shun), *n.* **1,** the act of establishing; as, the *foundation* of a school; **2,** the groundwork of a structure; as, a stone *foundation*; **3,** basis; as, the rumour has no *foundation*; **4,** an endowment or gift of money to support an institution; **5,** an endowed institution or charity.

foun-der (foun′dėr), *v.i.* **1,** to fill and sink, as a ship; **2,** to go lame, as a horse; **3,** to fall down; collapse, as a building:—*v.t.* **1,** to cause (a ship) to fill with water and sink; **2,** to make (a horse) break down.

foun-dry (foun′dri), *n.* [*pl.* foundries], **1,** the place where metal casting is carried on; as, an iron *foundry*; **2,** the act or process of casting metals.

fount (fount), *n.* **1,** a spring of water; fountain; **2,** a source; font; as, a *fount* of information.

foun-tain (foun′tin), *n.* **1,** a natural spring of water; **2,** a spring or source; as, a *fountain* of truth; **3,** an artificial jet or spout of water; also, the apparatus for producing it; **4,** a reservoir, as for ink in a pen, or oil in a lamp; as, a *fountain* pen; **5,** a device that creates a small stream of water for drinking; as, a water *fountain* in a school.—*n.* **foun-tain-head** (foun′tin-hed′).

four (fōr), *adj.* consisting of one more than three:—*n.* **1,** the sum consisting of three plus one; **2,** a sign representing four units, as 4 or IV.

four-score (fōr′skōr′), *adj.* four times 20; 80; as, *fourscore* years.

four-some (fōr′sum), *n.* in certain games, such as golf or tennis, a match in which four players, two on a side, take part.

four-square (fōr′sqwâr′), *adj.* upright; honest:—*adv.* in a square form.

four-teen (fōr′tēn′), *adj.* consisting of one more than 13:—*n.* **1,** the number consisting of 13 plus one; **2,** a sign representing fourteen units, as 14 or XIV.

four-teenth (fōr′tēnth′), *adj.* next after the 13th: the ordinal of *fourteen*:—*n.* one of the 14 equal parts of anything.

fourth (fōrth), *adj.* next after the third: the ordinal of *four*:—*n.* one of four equal parts of anything; a quarter.—*adv.* **fourth′ly.**

fourth estate, the media, esp. the print media or press, as opposed to the other three estates of the nobility, the clergy, and the commons.

Fourth World, the poorest nations of the *Third World* (the nonaligned nations of Africa and Asia), esp. those with little or no natural resources, such as oil.

fowl (foul), *n.* [*pl.* fowl or fowls], **1,** a bird, esp. the common rooster or hen; **2,** any bird, esp. a wild bird hunted for food; **3,** the flesh of the domestic fowl used as food, as chickens, geese, turkeys, or ducks; poultry:—*v.i.* to hunt wild birds.

fox (foks), *n.* **1,** a wild animal related to the wolf, with pointed ears and a bushy tail, noted for its cunning; **2,** the fur of this animal; **3,** a sly person.—*adj.* **fox′y.**

fox-hole (foks′hōl′), *n.* a small hole dug by one or two soldiers for protection against gunfire.

fox-hound (foks′hound′), *n.* a hound trained to hunt foxes.

fox ter-ri-er, a small, active, alert wire-haired or smooth-haired dog of the terrier family.

fox-trot (foks′trot′), *n.* a dance in 2/4 or 4/4 time, performed by couples in a variety of short, quick steps; a two-step.—*v.i.* to dance a foxtrot.

fox-y (foks′i), *adj.* cunning; crafty; sly.

foy-er (fwå′yā′; foi′ėr), *n.* the lobby or entrance hall of a hotel, theatre, etc.

fra-cas (frå′kä′; frā′kas), *n.* a loud quarrel; brawl; uproar.

frac-tion (frak′shun), *n.* **1,** a fragment; a small part of a whole; **2,** in *mathematics*, a part or an indicated number of equal parts of a whole; as, in the *fraction* 7/8, the whole has been divided into eight equal parts, of which seven are indicated.—*adj.* **frac′tion-al.**—*adv.* **frac′tion-al-ly.**

frac-tious (frak′shus), *adj.* unruly; cross; as, a *fractious* child.—*adv.* **frac′tious-ly.**

frac-ture (frak′tūr), *n.* **1,** the act of breaking; **2,** a break, esp. of a bone; **3,** disruption:—*v.t.* and *v.i.* [fractured, fractur-ing], **1,** to break or crack; **2,** disrupt.

frag-ile (fraj′il; fraj′īl), *adj.* easily broken; delicate; frail; as, a *fragile* dish.—*n.* **fra-gil′i-ty.**

frag-ment (frag′ment), *n.* **1,** a part broken off from a whole; a portion, piece, or incomplete part; as, a *fragment* of a broken glass; **2,** a small or incomplete part; as, to remember only a *fragment* of the story.—*adj.* **frag′men-tar′y.**

frag-men-ta-tion (frag′men-tā′shun), *n.* **1,** the act of breaking into fragments; **2,** in *computing*, the scattering of computer files in chunks into many, often disconnected, areas of the hard disk, which dramatically slows the time needed to access and read these files:—*adj.* a bomb or other explosive device that scatters fragments upon detonation; as, a *fragmentation* grenade.

fra-grant (frā′grant), *adj.* sweet-smelling; having a pleasing odour; as, a *fragrant* spice, perfume, or flower.—*adv.* **fra′grant-ly.**—*n.* **fra′grance.**

frail (frāl), *adj.* **1,** fragile or easily broken; as, a *frail* stem; **2,** physically weak; as, a *frail* child; **3,** morally weak.—*adv.* **frail′ly.**

frail-ty (frāl′ti), *n.* [*pl.* frailties], **1,** weakness; as, *frailty* of character; **2,** a failing or sin due to moral weakness.

frame (frām), *v.t.* [framed, fram-ing], **1,** to put together; build; as, to *frame* a house; **2,** to invent; plan; as, to *frame* a conspiracy; express; as, to *frame* an answer; **3,** to surround or enclose with a stiff rim; as, to *frame* a picture; **4,** to set within a background or border; as, to *frame* a photographic shot with the doorway; **5,** *Slang* to falsify evidence to make a person look guilty:—*n.* **1,** anything built or made of parts fitted together; as, the *frame* of a ship; **2,** bodily structure; as, the slender *frame* of a girl; **3,** a structure of wood, metal, etc., for holding, enclosing, or supporting something; as, a *frame* of a door; a bicycle *frame*; a picture *frame*; **4,** one of a series of pictures that makes up a video or motion picture; **5,** in *computing*, the boxed areas on Web pages or in text documents that can be scrolled independently of one another; **6,** established order; system; as, the *frame* of society; **7,** in *bowling*, any of the 10 divisions of a game; in *pool*, the triangular form in which the balls are racked to begin a game:—**frame of mind**, the state of a person's thoughts or feelings; mood; as, to be in a positive *frame of mind.*—*n.* **fram′er.**

frame-work (frām′wûrk′), *n.* that which supports; a skeleton; as, the *framework* of a house or of the body.

franc (frangk), *n.* the French monetary unit; also a monetary unit of other countries, such as Switzerland, Belgium, Monaco, etc.

fran-chise (fran′chīz), *n.* **1,** citizenship; the right to vote; **2,** a special privilege granted by a government to a person or company; as, a *franchise* to run a bus line; **3,** an arrangement or licence to sell a company's products or services in a specific territory; also, the licensed business and territory; as, a fast-food *franchise.*

Fran-co-phone or **fran-co-phone** (frangk′kō-fōn′), *n.* a person whose first language is French.

fran-gi-ble (fran′ji-bl), *adj.* breakable; brittle; as glass.

[1]**frank** (frangk), *adj.* candid; outspoken; as, a *frank* opinion.—*adv.* **frank′ly.**—*n.* **frank′ness.**

[2]**frank** (frangk), *n.* a signature or mark that exempts mail matter from payment of postage:—*v.t.* to send postfree.

frank-furt-er (frangk′fėr-tėr), *n.* a highly seasoned beef and pork sausage.

frank-in-cense (frangk′in-sens′), *n.* a fragrant resin from balsam trees, burned as incense.

fran-tic (fran′tik), *adj.* wild; frenzied; as, *frantic* cries.—*adv.* **fran′ti-cal-ly.**

frat (frat), *n.* and *adj. Colloq.* a university fraternity; of or for a fraternity; as, to join the *frat*; a party at the *frat* house.

fra-ter-nal (fra-tûr′nal), *adj.* **1,** pertaining to, or like, a brother or brothers; as, *fraternal* love; **2,** naming or pertaining to a group or society of men who bind themselves together like brothers; as, a *fraternal* order.—*adv.* **fra-ter′nal-ly.**

fra-ter-ni-ty (fra-tûr′ni-ti), *n.* [*pl.* fraternities], **1,** brotherly relationship; **2,** a body of men joined by a common interest, esp. such an organization in universities and colleges.—*v.i.* **frat′er-nize′.**

frat-ri-cide (frat′ri-sīd′), *n.* **1,** the killing of a brother or sister; **2,** one who does so.

fraud (frôd), *n.* **1,** deceitfulness; trickery; **2,** a trick; **3,** one who cheats; a fake.

fraud-u-lent (frôd′ū-lent), *adj.* **1,** guilty of trickery; deceitful; dishonest; **2,** characterized by, or obtained by, unfair methods; as, *fraudulent* measures; *fraudulent* gains.—*adv.* **fraud′u-lent-ly.**—*n.* **fraud′u-lence; fraud′u-len-cy.**

fraught (frôt), *adj.* laden; filled; as, the voyage was *fraught* with danger.

[1]**fray** (frā), *n.* a riot; a fight; as, in the midst of the *fray.*

[2]**fray** (frā), *v.t.* and *v.i.* to rub; wear into shreds; as, a sleeve *frayed* at the edge; her nerves were *frayed* from the stress.

fraz-zle (fraz′l), *v.t.* and *v.i.* [fraz-zled, fraz-zling], **1,** to fray or ravel, as cloth; **2,** hence, to tire or wear out:—*n.* **1,** a ragged end; **2,** the state of being exhausted.

freak (frēk), *n.* **1,** a capricious change of mind; whim; **2,** an abnormal or deformed person, animal, or plant; **3,** something unusual; as, a *freak* of nature; **4,** *Slang* an enthusiast; fan; as a soccer *freak*:—*adj.* pertaining to freak; as, a *freak* snowfall in May.—*adj.* **freak′ish.**

freck-le (frek′l), *n.* a brownish spot on the skin, often caused by exposure to sunlight:—*v.t.* and *v.i.* [freck-led, freck-ling], to mark, or become marked, with freckles.

free (frē), *adj.* [fre-er, fre-est], **1,** having full personal and political liberty; as, a *free* people or country; **2,** loose; not attached; as, the *free* end of a rope; **3,** independent; as, a *free* church; **4,** at liberty; released; not caught or shut up; as, a *free* person or animal; **5,** not following rigid rules of form; as, *free* verse; **6,** not following the original exactly; as, a *free* translation; **7,** frank; also, informal; not troubled; as, a *free* and easy manner; **8,** lavish; generous; as, *free* with praise; abundant; as, a *free* flow of blood; **9,** clear of obstructions; open; as, a *free* field; a *free* course; a *free* afternoon; **10,** rid of or exempt from; as, *free* from disease or punishment; **11,** unhampered; not influenced by others; as, a *free* choice; **12,** given without cost; as, a *free* ticket; open to all; as, a *free* concert; **13,** impudent; as, a *free* tongue:—*v.t.* [freed, free-ing], **1,** to let go; set at liberty; as, to *free* an animal from a trap; **2,** to rid of; clear; as, to *free* someone of a charge of murder:—*adv.* without charge; as, to get in *free.*—*adv.* **free′ly.** Also, **free′ a′gent; free′ as-so-ci-a′tion; free′base′** (cocaine); **free′ en′ter-prise; free′ fall′; free′–for–all′; free′load′; free′ mar′ket; free′–range′; free′ ride′; free′ speech′; free′stand′ing; free′style′; free′ trade′; free′ wheel′ing.**

free-boot-er (frē′bo͞ot′ėr), *n.* one who roves in search of plunder, as the Elizabethan *freebooters* (Drake, Raleigh, etc.); a pirate; buccaneer.

free-dom (frē′dum), *n.* **1,** personal and political liberty; independence; as, slaves were given their *freedom*; the colonies won their *freedom*; *freedom* of speech; **2,** free use; as, to be given the *freedom* of a clubhouse; **3,** exemption from; lack of; as, *freedom* from disease; *freedom* from taxes; **4,** state of being clear or unmixed; as, *freedom* from impurities; **5,** ease; as, to move with *freedom*; **6,** frankness; as, *freedom* in expressing his feelings; **7,** undue familiarity; as, he assumes too much *freedom* with his elders.

free-hand (frē′hand′), *adj.* done or drawn by hand without the aid of ruler, compasses, etc.; as, a *freehand* sketch.

free-hold (frē′hōld′), *n.* **1,** the holding for life of land, etc., with the right to pass it on to one's heirs; **2,** land so held.

free-lance or **free lance** (frē′lans′), *n.* an independent writer, editor, actor, etc., who is not bound by contract to only one employer:—*v.i.* and *v.t.* [free-lanced, free-lanc-ing], to work or sell as a freelancer.—*adj.* **free′lance′**.—*n.* **free′lanc′er.**

Freemason (frē′mā′son), **1,** a member of a charitable fraternal organization (Free Accepted Masons), which exists worldwide, pledges to help each other, and has secret rites: also called *Mason;* **2,** formerly, a member of a secretive medieval guild of itinerant skilled stoneworkers.

free-think-er (frē′think′ėr), *n.* one who forms his opinions independently of authority, esp. in religious matters; an agnostic.

Free Trade Agreement, the bilateral free trade agreement between Canada and the United States that came into effect in 1989, superseded by the *North American Free Trade Agreement* (*NAFTA*) between Canada, the United States, and Mexico in 1994: abbreviated as *FTA*.

free verse, poetry marked by lack of rhyming and by irregular metre and line length.

free-ware (frē′wâr′), *n.* in *computing*, computer software available at no charge, usually over the Internet.

freeze (frēz), *v.t.* [*p.t.* froze (frōz), *p.p.* fro-zen (frō′zn), *p.pr.* freez-ing], **1,** to change from a liquid to a solid by cold; harden with cold; as, to *freeze* ice cream; **2,** to make very cold; as, the cold wind *froze* my hands; **3,** to chill, damage, or kill with cold; as, to *freeze* plants; **4,** to set or fix at a certain amount; as, to *freeze* rent rates:—*v.i.* **1,** to be changed into or covered with ice; as, the lake *freezes;* **2,** to be killed by cold or frost; as, the plants *froze* last night; **3,** to be or become very cold; **4,** to be chilled with fear or horror; as, deer often *freeze* at the glare of headlights; **5,** to stick or adhere because of cold; as, their hands *froze* to the oars:—*n.* **1,** a period of very cold weather; as a January *freeze;* **2,** the act of freezing; as, a *freeze* on pay raises.—*adj.* **freez′ing** (as, *freezing* rain).

free-zer (frēz′ėr), *n.* **1,** a separate part of a refrigerator that has a temperature below freezing, used to make ice, freeze food, and store frozen foods; **2,** a self-contained, stand-alone refrigerator used for this same purpose.

freight (frāt), *n.* **1,** the goods with which a vessel, car, truck, or aircraft is loaded; cargo; **2,** a method or business of transporting goods by land, air, or water; **3,** a train that carries goods; **4,** the sum paid for hauling goods:—*v.t.* **1,** to load with goods for hauling; **2,** to send (goods) by freight.

freight-er (frāt′ėr), *n.* **1,** one who loads a ship, train, truck, or aircraft with freight; **2,** one who sends goods by freight; **3,** a ship or aircraft for carrying freight.

French (french), *n.* **1,** a person who inhabits or originates from France or French Canada; **2,** the language spoken by these people:—*adj.* **1,** relating to the country or region, the people, the language, or the culture of France or French Canada.

French Canadian, 1, one of the French-speaking people of Canada; **2,** the language of these Canadians.—*adj.* **French–Canadian.**

French fry or **french fry,** potatoes cut in thin strips and fried in oil or deep fat until brown and crisp.

French horn, a musical wind instrument of the brass group, consisting of a long coiled tube ending in a flaring bell.

French immersion, a method of teaching the French language to predominantly English-speaking or non-French-speaking students by immersing them in the French language and culture; as, to spend the summer in *French immersion*.

fren-zied (fren′zid), *adj.* maddened; frantic; as, *frenzied* efforts to swim.

fren-zy (fren′zi), *n.* [*pl.* frenzies], **1,** violent mental derangement; delirium; **2,** wild excitement or enthusiasm.

fre-quen-cy (frē′kwen-si), *n.* [*pl.* frequencies], **1,** the repeated happening of anything at short intervals; as, the *frequency* of storms; **2,** the number of happenings in a given time; rate of occurrence; as, the *frequency* of a letter in a language; **3,** the cycles per second of an alternating current.

fre-quent (frē′kwent), *adj.* **1,** occurring often; as, *frequent* delays; **2,** habitual; as, a *frequent* visitor:—*v.t.* (frē-kwent′), to go to often or habitually; as, to *frequent* the theatre.—*adv.* **fre′quent-ly.**

fres-co (fres′kō), *n.* [*pl.* frescos or frescoes], **1,** the method or art of painting on plaster before it has dried; **2,** a painting made in this manner:—*v.t.* [frescoed, fresco-ing], to decorate or paint in fresco.

fresh (fresh), *adj.* **1,** new; not known or used before; as, a *fresh* sheet of paper; **2,** additional; different; as, to make a *fresh* start; **3,** recent; just made or arrived; as, a *fresh* report; **4,** newly gathered or produced; as, *fresh* grapes; not faded; as, *fresh* flowers; **5,** pure and cool; refreshing; as, *fresh* air; **6,** not preserved by salting or pickling; as, *fresh* ham; **7,** not salt; as, *fresh* water; **8,** not stale; not spoiled; as, *fresh* fish; **9,** not tired; vigorous; as, to feel *fresh* after a nap; **10,** not experienced; as, a *fresh* recruit; **11,** *Colloq.* bold; impudent; as, don't get *fresh.*—*adv.* **fresh′ly.**—*n.* **fresh′ness.**

fresh-en (fresh′en), *v.t.* refresh; revive; as, I *freshened* myself after a hard day's work:—*v.i.* to become brisk; as, the wind *freshens*.

fresh-et (fresh′et), *n.* a flood caused by melting snow or heavy rain.

fresh-man (fresh′man), *n.* [*pl.* freshmen (fresh′men)], a university student in his or her first year; also, esp. in the U.S., a first-year high school student:—*adj.* **1,** relating to a first-year student; as, a *freshman* course; **2,** a beginner; as, a *freshman* MP.

fresh-wa-ter (fresh′wô′tėr), *adj.* having to do with or living in water that is not salty; inland water; as, *freshwater* fish.

[1]**fret** (fret), *v.t.* [fret-ted, fret-ting], **1,** to chafe; wear or rub away; as, water *frets* a channel in a rock; **2,** to worry; irritate:—*v.i.* to be irritated; as, she *frets* over little things:—*n.* **1,** a worn spot; **2,** vexation; irritation.

[2]**fret** (fret), *n.* a small ridge or bar of wood, metal, ivory, etc., on the neck of certain stringed instruments, as the guitar, banjo, or mandolin, to regulate fingering.

fret-ful (fret′fool), *adj.* peevish; irritable; as, a *fretful* child.—*adv.* **fret′ful-ly.**—*n.* **fret′ful-ness.**

fret-work (fret′wûrk′), *n.* a kind of carved, raised, or open ornamental work.

fri-a-ble (frī′a-bl), *adj.* crumbling readily (to powder), as *friable* soil or rock.

fri-ar (frī′ėr), *n.* a brother, or member of any of certain religious orders; a monk.

fric-tion (frik′shun), *n.* **1,** the rubbing of one thing against another; **2,** the resistance or force one thing encounters when moving against another; as, ice has less *friction* than dirt; **3,** conflict; difference of opinion; as, *friction* between the opposing candidates.—*adj.* **fric′tion-al.**

Fri-day (Frī′dā), *n.* the sixth day of the week, before Saturday and after Thursday.

fried (frīd), *p.t.* and *p.p.* of *fry.*

friend (frend), *n.* **1,** a person bound to another by affection, esteem, and intimacy; a person that is liked; **2,** a sympathizer; helper; a supporter of a cause; as, a *friend* of the charity against abused animals; **3,** an ally.—*adj.* **friend′less.**

friend-ly (frend′li), *adj.* [friend-li-er, friend-li-est], **1,** like a friend; kind; **2,** not hostile; as, a *friendly* smile; **3,** played for mere sport; as, a *friendly* contest; **4,** favourable; as, a *friendly* breeze.—*n.* **friend′li-ness.**

friend-ship (frend′ship), *n.* the relationship or attachment between people arising from mutual affection and admiration; the relationship of being friends.

fri-er (frī′ėr), *n.* Same as *fryer.*

frieze (frēz), *n.* an ornamental or sculptured band around a wall.

frig-ate (frig′it), *n.* **1,** originally, a light, swift vessel propelled both by oars and sails; **2,** formerly, a fast, three-masted, square-rigged war vessel of the 18th and early 19th centuries; **3,** an escort war vessel that is smaller than a destroyer but larger than a corvette.

fright (frīt), *n.* **1,** violent fear; terror; alarm; **2,** *Colloq.* anything ugly or ridiculous in appearance; as, my hair is a *fright.*

fright-en (frīt′n), *v.t.* to terrify; alarm; startle; drive away; as, to *frighten* the cat away:—*v.i.* to make or become afraid.—*adj.* **fright′ened.**

fright-ful (frīt′fool), *adj.* **1,** terrible; dreadful; frightening; as, a *frightful* accident; **2,** *Colloq.* grotesque; ugly; as, a *frightful* dress.—*adv.* **fright′ful-ly.**

frig-id (frij′id), *adj.* **1,** very cold; freezing; as, *frigid* weather; **2,** unfriendly; stiff; formal; as, a *frigid* welcome.—*adv.* **frig′id-ly.**—*n.* **fri-gid′i-ty** (fri-jid′i-ti).

frill (fril), *n.* **1,** an ornamental edging made of a strip of material gathered on one edge; a ruffle; **2,** *Colloq.* an affectation of manner, speech, or dress; **3,** something that is not essential but desirable; as, the *frills* of the job contract included a company car.

fringe (frinj), *n.* **1,** a ravelled, frayed edge on a fabric; also, a separate ornamental border of hanging cords, tassels, etc.; **2,** any border or edging like a fringe; **3,** the part away from the middle; the edge; as, the *fringe* of society:—**fringe benefit,** employment benefits aside from regular salary, such as medical insurance, company car, etc.

frisk (frisk), *v.i.* to skip or dance in frolic or playfulness:—*v.t. Colloq.* to search someone for weapons, stolen items, drugs, etc., by running the hands quickly over the person's clothes; as, the police officer *frisked* the suspect.—*adj.* **frisk′y.**—*adv.* **frisk′i-ly.**

[1]**frit-ter** (frit′ėr), *n.* a fried cake made of batter, often containing meat, fruit, or other food; as, a corn *fritter.*

[2]**frit-ter** (frit′ėr), *n.* a fragment:—*v.t.* to cut or break into small pieces; hence, to waste; as, to *fritter* away one's time.

friv-o-lous (friv′o-lus), *adj.* **1,** of little importance; trivial; as, *frivolous* pastimes; **2,** not serious; giddy; as, *frivolous* people.—*n.* **fri-vol′i-ty** (fri-vol′i-t).

friz-zle or **frizz** (friz′l; friz), *v.t.* **1,** to curl (the hair); **2,** to fry with a sputter until crisp, as bacon; sizzle.—*adj.* **friz′zly; friz′zy.**

fro (frō), *adv.* away from; backward or back: used only in the phrase *to and fro.*

frock (frok), *n.* **1,** a loose upper garment worn by children and women; a dress; **2,** a monk's habit; **3,** a coarse outer garment worn by workers.

frog (frog), *n.* **1,** a small, tailless amphibian with smooth skin, webbed feet, and remarkable swimming and leaping ability; **2,** soreness in the throat.

frol-ic (frol′ik), *n.* **1,** a scene of merrymaking; **2,** a wild prank:—*v.i.* [frolicked, frol-ick-ing], to make merry; have fun; as, the children *frolicked* on the beach.—*adj.* **frol′ic-some.**

from (from), *prep.* **1,** indicating a starting

point in space, time, or a series; as, a letter *from* home; 10 metres *from* a post; *from* morning to night; *from* childhood on; *from* 10 to 20; **2,** indicating a place, person, or thing left behind; as, to go *from* school to the mall; **3,** indicating removal; as, take candy *from* a box; pick berries *from* a bush; steal candy *from* a baby; **4,** indicating separation or freedom; as, excused *from* school; free *from* disease; **5,** indicating some condition changed for another; as, to go *from* bad to worse; **6,** indicating origin or source; as, I translated *from* the French; weak *from* hunger; make bread *from* flour; **7,** indicating a model or copy; as, drawn *from* life.

frond (frond), *n.* the leaf of a fern, palm, or seaweed.—*adj.* **frond′ed.**

front (frunt), *n.* **1,** the foremost part of anything; as, the *front* of a book; **2,** the forehead; **3,** land that faces the sea, a river, stream, etc.; as, the beach *front;* the river *front;* **4,** in warfare, the scene of the actual fighting; **5,** an outward appearance that is different from what is real; as, to show a brave *front;* **6,** in weather, the division between two masses of air that have different temperatures; as, a cold *front*:—*adj.* situated at the foremost part; as, a *front* wall:—*v.t.* **1,** to stand, or be situated, opposite to; as, your house *fronts* mine; **2,** to confront; meet; as, to *front* danger; to *front* an enemy:—*v.i.* to have the front turned in a certain direction; as, his house *fronts* north.

front-age (frunt′ij), *n.* the boundary line (of a lot or building) fronting a street or road; the exposure.

fron-tal (frun′tal; fron′tal), *adj.* having to do with the front or forehead; as, a *frontal* artery:—*n.* the bone of the forehead.

Front de Libération du Québec, a Québec separatist organization active in the 1960s, whose use of terror and kidnapping triggered the October Crisis of 1970.

fron-tier (frun-tēr′; fron′tēr), *n.* **1,** the boundary of a country; **2,** the most remote settled part of a country, adjoining wild territory; **3,** any place or area of knowledge that has not yet been fully explored or developed; as, the *frontiers* of space:—*adj.* pertaining to, or situated near, the boundary of a country; as, a *frontier* custom; a *frontier* town.

fron-tis-piece (frun′tis-pēs′), *n.* **1,** a picture facing the front page or title page of a book; **2,** a façade or front of a building.

frost (frôst), *n.* **1,** minute frozen particles of dew or vapour; hoarfrost; **2,** a temperature low enough to cause freezing of water; freezing weather; **3,** *Slang* a failure:—*v.t.* **1,** to cover with frost, or with something like frost; **2,** to injure by frost; **3,** to cover (a cake) with icing.—*adj.* **frost′y; frost′ed; frost′bit-ten; frost′-free′.**—*n.* **frost′i-ness; frost′ line′.**

frost-ing (frôs′ting), *n.* **1,** a preparation of sugar mixed with a liquid, used in covering cakes or pastry: also called *icing;* **2,** a dull finish, as for metal or glass.

froth (frôth), *n.* a mass of small bubbles formed on the surface of a liquid, as by shaking or fermentation; foam:—*v.t.* to become covered with foam; as, the rabid dog *frothed* at the mouth.—*adj.* **froth′y.**—*n.* **froth′i-ness.**

fro-ward (frō′wėrd; frō′ėrd), *adj.* willful; disobedient; wayward; contrary.

frown (froun), *n.* a wrinkling of the brow showing displeasure; a scowl; a stern look:—*v.i.* **1,** to contract the brows in anger, deep thought, uncertainty, etc.; **2,** to show disapproval; as, to *frown* on gambling:—*v.t.* to rebuke or suppress by frowning; as, to *frown* a person down.

frow-zy or **frow-sy** (frou′zi), *adj.* slovenly; unkempt; dirty; as, a *frowzy* room or person.

fro-zen (frō′zn), *p.p.* of *freeze.*

frozen assets, property that for the present cannot be converted to cash for face value; as, a *frozen* loan.

fru-gal (froo͞′gl), *adj.* **1,** thrifty; economical; not wasteful; **2,** sparingly used or supplied; simple; as, a *frugal* meal.—*adv.* **fru′gal-ly.**—*n.* **fru-gal′i-ty.**

fruit (froo͞t). *n.* **1,** in general, a seed and all its enveloping parts; **2,** usually, a particular fruit, as the apple, peach, pear, etc., generally eaten raw, or cooked and used as a dessert; **3,** any product, result, or profit; as, the *fruit* of labour:—*v.i.* to produce fruit.—*adj.* **fruited,** laden with fruit.—*adj.* **fruit′y.**

fruit-ful (froo͞t′fool), *adj.* **1,** yielding fruit; fertile; as, a *fruitful* tree; *fruitful* soil; **2,** profitable; productive; as, *a fruitful* venture; a *fruitful* year.—*n.* **fruit′ful-ness.**

fru-i-tion (froo͞-ish′un), *n.* **1,** the bearing of fruit; **2,** realization or attainment; as, the *fruition* of his cherished hopes.

fruit-less (froo͞t′lis), *adj.* **1,** not bearing fruit; **2,** without result; useless; as, a *fruitless* effort.

frump (frump), *n.* a dowdy (or sometimes cross) woman or girl.—*adj.* **frump′y; frump′ish.**

frus-trate (frus′trāt), *v.t.* [frustrat-ed, frustrat-ing], **1,** to defeat or disappoint; thwart or oppose; bring to nothing; as, to *frustrate* a plan; **2,** to have a feeling of being discouraged, irritated, or helpless; as, the poorly written instructions *frustrated* her.—*adj.* **frus-tra′ted.**—*n.* **frus-tra′tion.**

frus-tum (frus′tum), *n.* in *geometry,* the part of a cone or pyramid left when the top is cut off parallel to the base.

fry (frī), *v.t.* [fried, fry-ing], to cook with fat or oil in a pan or on a griddle:—**small fry,** *Colloq.* **1,** children; **2,** unimportant people; **3,** young fish.—*n.* **fry′er** or **fri′er.**

FTA (ef′tē′ā′), *abbrev.* short for *Free Trade Agreement.*

FTP (ef′tē′pē′), *abbrev.* short for *file transfer protocol.*

fuch-si-a (fū′shi-a; fū′sha), *n.* **1,** a plant of the evening primrose family with drooping pink, red, or purple flowers; **2,** a bright red-purple or pink-purple colour.

fud-dled (fud′ld), *adj.* confused or muddled, as with alcoholic liquor; befuddled.—*v.t.* **fud′dle.**

fud-dy–dud-dy (fud′i–dud′i), *n. Slang* a fussy or old-fashioned person.

fudge (fuj), *n.* a candy made of a stiff, sugary mixture flavoured with maple, chocolate, nuts, etc.:—*interj.* nonsense:—*v.t.* [fudged, fudg-ing], **1,** to fake; falsely represent; as, he *fudged* the figures; **2,** to evade, gloss over, hedge or waffle; avoid confronting a problem; as, she *fudged* the issue:—*v.i.* **1,** to act indecisively or uncertainly; as, she always *fudged* on serious problems; **2,** to go beyond the proper limits; cheat; as, she *fudges* on the rules, on the exam.

fu-el (fū′el), *n.* **1,** material that can be burned to supply heat, as coal, wood, oil, etc.; **2,** anything that keeps an emotion active; as, the news adds *fuel* to his anger:—*v.t.* [fuelled, fuel-ling], to furnish with fuel; as, they *fuelled* the car for a long trip.

fuel cell, an electrochemical cell that produces electrical energy by burning a fuel, such as liquid hydrogen in oxygen, thereby generating power with little or no pollution.

fu-gi-tive (fū′ji-tiv), *adj.* **1,** fleeting; not lasting very long; as, a *fugitive* idea; **2,** fleeing from danger, pursuit, or duty; as, a *fugitive* convict:—*n.* one who flees; a runaway or deserter.

fugue (fūg), *n.* in *music,* a composition in which a number of parts, voices, or instruments successively repeat the theme to a climactic end.

ful-crum (ful′krum), *n.* [*pl.* fulcrums or fulcra (ful′kra)], the support, often wedge-shaped, on which a lever turns when it lifts something.

FULCRUM: A, LEVER; B, FULCRUM; C, WEIGHT.

ful-fill or **ful-fil** (fool-fil′), *v.t.* [fulfilled, fulfil-ling], **1,** to complete or accomplish; **2,** to do; carry (that which is promised, foretold, ordered, or expected); **3,** to satisfy, as a wish.—*n.* **ful-fill′ment.**

full (fool), *adj.* **1,** filled; having no empty space; as, a *full* pail; *full* stomach; **2,** well supplied; as, a *full* cupboard; **3,** rounded out; plump; as, a *full* figure; **4,** complete; filling the normal allowance, quota, etc.; as, a *full* hour; a *full* orchestra; *full* speed; **5,** having excess material arranged in folds; as, a *full* skirt; **6,** clear; distinct; as, a *full* tone:—*n.* the highest state, or extent; as, enjoy it to the *full*:—*v.t.* to give fullness to; as, to *full* a skirt:—*adv.* completely; quite: often with a hyphen; as, a *full-*blown rose; a bag *full* of apples.—*n.* **full′ness.**

full-back (fool′bak′), *n.* in *football,* one of the players farthest behind the line of scrimmage.

full–fledged (fool′–flejd′), *adj.* fully developed; as, a *full-fledged* lawyer.

full–time (fool′–tīm′), *adj.* involving the entire time needed for an activity; as, *full-time* teacher:—*adv.* for the customary number of hours; as, he works *full-time.*

full-y (fool′i), *adv.* completely; abundantly; as, *fully* equipped for school.

ful-mi-nate (ful′mi-nāt′), *v.t.* **1,** to explode; detonate; **2,** to denounce; as, he *fulminated* against the new law.—*n.* **ful′-mi-na′tion.**

ful-some (fool′sum; ful′sum), *adj.* offensive to good taste; excessive; immoderate; as, *fulsome* flattery.—*adv.* **ful′some-ly.**

fum-ble (fum′bl), *v.i.* [fum-bled, fum-bling], to grope or feel about in search; as, he *fumbled* in his pocket for a quarter:—*v.t.* **1,** to handle or manage awkwardly, or drop; as, to *fumble* the ball in a game; **2,** to handle something awkwardly; as, to *fumble* the pronunciation of a word.—*n.* **fum′bler.**

fume (fūm), *n.* smoke, vapour, or gas, esp. if offensive; as, the air was thick with toxic *fumes* after the explosion:—*v.i.* [fumed, fum-ing], **1,** to send forth smoke; **2,** to complain angrily; as, he *fumed* over his losses.

fu-mi-gate (fū′mi-gāt′), *v.t.* [fumigat-ed, fumigat-ing], **1,** to disinfect or purify with fumes; esp., to free of disease germs, insects, etc., with fumes; as, to *fumigate* a bug-infested apartment building; **2,** to perfume.—*n.* **fu′mi-ga′tion; fu′mi-ga′tor.**

fun (fun), *n.* **1,** a time of pleasure; mirth; sport; amusement; play; **2,** someone or something that causes enjoyment or amusement; as, he was a lot of *fun* at the party:—**make fun of,** to laugh at in a cruel or unkind way; tease.

func-tion (fungk′shun), *n.* **1,** the special work or use of anything; purpose or role; as, the *function* of the heart is to pump blood; the *function* of a judge is to interpret the law; **2,** a formal social or official ceremony; as, the award ceremony was the most important *function* of the year:—*v.i.* to perform the duty for which a person or thing is intended.—*adj.* **func′tion-al.**

function key, in *computing,* one of the 12 keys on a keyboard with a special function, which depends on the software the system is using: abbreviated as *F keys.*

fund (fund), *n.* **1,** a permanent supply of something; a stock; as, a *fund* of information; **2,** money set apart for carrying out some goal; as, she has a vacation *fund;* **3,** a stock in reserve:—**funds**, securities; money; as, to raise *funds* for a charity:—*v.t.* to provide funds for; as, to *fund* a sporting event.

fun-da-men-tal (fun′da-men′tal; -men′tl), *adj.* serving as a foundation or basis; essential; as, a *fundamental* reason:—*n.* a rule or principle that serves as the groundwork of a system; as, a *fundamental* of arithmetic.—*adv.* **fun′da-men′tal-ly.**

fun-da-men-tal-ist (fun′da-men′tal-ist), *n.* one who believes in a literal interpretation of the Bible (esp. its miracles, virgin birth, etc.) as essential to Christian faith—*n.* **fun′da-men′tal-ism.**

fund-rais-er or **fund–rais-er** (fund′rā′zėr), *n.* **1,** a person who procures monetary and other donations for an organization, esp. a nonprofit one; as, she was a volunteer *fundraiser* for the Cancer Society; **2,** an event designed to do this; as, an annual *fundraiser.*—*n.* and *adj.* **fund′ rais′ ing; fund′–rais-′ing.**—*v.i.* **fund′raise′; fund′– raise′** [fundraised, fundrais-ing; fund-raised, fund-rais-ing].

fu-ner-al (fū′nėr-al), *n.* the ceremony of burying a dead human body, or the services that take place at such a time:—*adj.* pertaining to, or fit for, a funeral.—*adj.* **fu-ne′r-al** (fū-nē′ri-al).

fun-gi-cide (fun′ji-sīd′), *n.* any substance that kills bacteria, moulds, mildews, etc.

fun-gus (fung′gus), *n.* [*pl.* fungi (fung′gī; fun′ji) or funguses (fung′gus-ez)], one of the plants without green colour, including yeasts, moulds, mushrooms, mildews, lichens, rusts, smuts, toadstools, etc., which feed upon other plants or decaying animal matter:—*adj.* pertaining to, or growing like, a fungus; as, *a fungus* growth.—*adj.* **fun′gal.**

funk (fungk), *n.* **1,** *Colloq.* panic; fright; as, to be in a blue *funk*; **2,** a type of music that combines blues, soul, and gospel:—*v.i.* to flinch or cower from fear; shrink from.

fun-nel (fun′el), *n.* **1,** a wide-mouthed vessel shaped like a cone with a tube or hole at the bottom, used for pouring liquids into a small opening; **2,** the smokestack of a steamship or steam engine.

fun-ny (fun′i), *adj.* [fun-ni-er, fun-ni-est], **1,** comical; droll; causing laughter; **2,** *Colloq.* strange; odd; peculiar; as, to feel *funny* after going on the scary ride.

fur (fûr), *n.* **1,** the thick, soft hair of certain animals; **2,** clothing made from fur; **3,** any light, fuzzy covering, as a coating on the tongue:—*adj.* lined or trimmed with fur, or made of fur:—*v.t.* [furred, fur-ring], to cover, line, or trim with fur.—*adj.* **furred.**

fur-be-low (fûr′bi-lō′), *n.* flounce, ruffle, etc. (on women's clothing).

fur-bish (fûr′bish), *v.t.* to polish; burnish; as, he *furbished* his medals; also, to restore.

fu-ri-ous (fū′ri-us), *adj.* **1,** very angry; mad; **2,** violent; extreme; strong and fierce; as, a *furious* storm.—*adv.* **fu′ri-ous-ly.**

furl (fûrl), *v.t.* to roll up and fasten to a mast, pole, etc., as a sail or flag.

fur-long (fûr′lông), *n.* a measurement equal to .2 kilometres.

fur-lough (fûr′lō), *n.* leave of absence; as, the soldier came home on *furlough*:—*v.t.* to give leave of absence to.

fur-nace (fûr′nis), *n.* an apparatus in which fuel is burned to make heat for various purposes, as to melt ores, heat a house, bake pottery, etc.; also, a hot place; as, the room was a *furnace.*

fur-nish (fûr′nish), *v.t.* **1,** to fit out or fit up with what is needed; as, to *furnish* a house; **2,** to provide; give; as, he *furnished* the money for the trip.

fur-nish-ings (fûr′nish-ingz), *n.pl.* **1,** the necessary fittings of a house; **2,** apparatus or fixtures of any kind.

fur-ni-ture (fûr′ni-tūr; -chėr), *n.* the necessary items of a house, a ship, or a business; outfit; esp., the movable articles of a house, as beds, chairs, tables, etc.

fu-ror (fū′rôr), *n.* **1,** rage; **2,** a great outburst of excitement or enthusiasm.

fur-row (fur′ō), *n.* **1,** a trench made in the ground by a plough; **2,** a groove; a wrinkle:—*v.t.* **1,** to plough; **2,** to make grooves or wrinkles in.

fur-ry (fûr′i), *adj.* **1,** covered with fur; as, a *furry* animal; **2,** like fur or made of fur.

fur-ther (fûr′*th*ėr), *adj.* **1,** more distant; as, the *further* field; **2,** additional; as, he needs *further* help:—*adv.* **1,** to a greater distance or degree; as, to go *further*; **2,** moreover; also; as, she remarked *further* that you were late:—*v.t.* to promote; help forward; as, he *furthered* my plans.

fur-ther-ance (fûr′*th*ėr-ans), *n.* advancement; aid.

fur-ther-more (fûr′*th*ėr-mōr′), *adv.* besides; in addition; also.

fur-ther-most (fûr′*th*ėr-mōst), *adj.* most distant or remote; as, the *furthermost* point inland.

fur-thest (fûr′*th*est), *adj.* and *adv.* most distant in time or space; as, the *furthest* island of the group.

fur-tive (fûr′tiv), *adj.* sly; secret; stealthy; as, *furtive* glances or actions.—*adv.* **fur′tive-ly.**—*n.* **fur′tive-ness.**

fu-ry (fū′ri), *n.* [*pl.* furies], **1,** violent anger; rage; **2,** great violence; fierceness; as, the *fury* of the storm; **3,** a violently angry person.

[1]**fuse** (fūz), *v.t.* [fused, fus-ing], **1,** to melt, esp. by heat, as metals; make liquid; **2,** to join or blend by melting:—*v.i.* **1,** to become melted, as by heat; **2,** to blend, as if melted.—*adj.* **fu′si-ble.**

[2]**fuse** (fūz), *n.* **1,** a small tube or casing filled with a material easily set on fire, or a cord saturated with such material, along which

fire will run: used for exploding gunpowder, dynamite, etc.; **2,** a piece of metal put in an electric circuit, that melts and breaks the circuit when the current gets too strong for safety: modern buildings use circuit breakers instead of fuses:—*v.t.* [fused, fusing], to melt together; to attach a fuse to.

fu-see (fū-zē′), *n.* **1,** a coloured railway flare; **2,** a friction match that will burn in the wind.

fu-se-lage (fū′ze-lij; fū′ze-läzh′), *n.* the body of an airplane, to which the wings and the tail are fastened, and which contains the controls, space for the pilot, passengers, cargo, etc.

fu-sil-lade (fū′zi-lād′), *n.* a rapid discharge of many firearms; an outpouring; as, a *fusillade* of questions.

fu-sion (fū′zhun), *n.* **1,** the act of melting, or state of being melted, together; as, the *fusion* of metals; **2,** a union or blending together; as, a *fusion* of ideas:—**fusion bomb,** a hydrogen bomb.

fuss (fus), *n.* **1,** unnecessary or disturbing activity, esp. in small matters; confusion; stir; **2,** a great show of interest or affection; as, to make a *fuss* over the new baby; **3,** a complaint:—*v.i.* **1,** to worry; **2,** to be busy over trifles; **3,** to show great interest or affection:—*v.t. Colloq.* to annoy or embarrass.—*adj.* **fuss′y.**

fu-tile (fū′tīl; fū′til), *adj.* **1,** without result; useless; as, *futile* shouting; **2,** of no importance; worthless.—*adv.* **fu′tile-ly.**—*n.* **fu-til′i-ty** (fū-til′i-t).

fu-ture (fū′tūr; -chėr), *adj.* yet to happen or come; as, a *future* event:—*n.* **1,** time yet to come; **2,** the future tense:—**future tense,** in *grammar,* a tense of a verb indicating action in time yet to come; as, I *shall go* tomorrow:—**future perfect,** in *grammar,* a tense of the verb indicating action taking place before a future time; as, when you arrive, I *shall have finished* the task.

fu-tu-ri-ty (fū-tū′ri-ti), *n.* [*pl.* futuri-ties], **1,** time to come; **2,** a future event.

fuzz (fuz), *n.* tiny particles of down, wool, etc., or something resembling this; as, peach *fuzz*:—*v.i.* to come off in small fluffy bits.—*n.* **fuzz′i-ness.**

fuzz′y (fuz′i), *adj.* [fuzz-i-er, fuzz-i-est], **1,** like, or covered with, loose fibres or hair; as, a *fuzzy* caterpillar; **2,** not clear; blurred; hazy; as, the picture is *fuzzy* on the old television set.

G

G, g (jē), *n.* [*pl.* G's, g's], **1,** the seventh letter of the alphabet, following F; **2,** in *music,* the fifth tone in the major scale of C.

gab (gab), *v.i. Colloq.* to talk much or idly:—*n.* idle talk; chatter; as, a gift of the *gab.*—*n.* **gab′ber.**

gab-ar-dine (gab′ėr-dēn′; gab′ėr-dēn′), *n.* **1,** a kind of woollen, cotton, or rayon cloth, with ribs, like serge; **2,** a garment made of gabardine; gaberdine.

gab-ble (gab′l), *v.i.* to make rapid, inarticulate sounds; as, the *gabbling* of geese.

ga-ble (gā′bl), *n.* **1,** the triangular part of a wall of a building between opposite slopes of a sloping roof; **2,** any similar construction, as over a window.

[1]**gad** (gad), *v.i.* [gad-ded, gad-ding], to go about without purpose; to ramble; as, to *gad* about all day.—*n.* **gad′der.**

[2]**gad** (gad), *n.* a goad, spike, or switch for loosening or breaking up ore, or rocks in a mine.

gad-a-bout (gad′a-bout′), *n. Colloq.* one who moves about aimlessly for gossip, excitement, or out of curiosity.

gadg-et (gaj′et), *n.* a device; contrivance; small tool or machine; as, kitchen *gadgets.*

Gael-ic (gāl′ik), *n.* the language or people of the Scottish Highlands, the Celts in Ireland, and the Isle of Man:—*adj.* having to do with these people or their language.

gaff (gaf), *n.* **1,** a large hook with a handle, used for getting large fish out of the water; **2,** a spar branching from the mast of a sailing vessel, to which is attached the top of a fore-and-aft sail; **3,** *Slang* a trial; ordeal; as, to stand the *gaff;* **4,** *Slang* a trick or hoax:—*v.t.* **1,** to seize (a fish) with a gaff; **2,** to trick or cheat.

gag (gag), *n.* **1,** something put in or across the mouth to hinder speech or sound; **2,** *Colloq.* a practical joke or trick; **3,** any remark, trick, or act done to get a laugh:—*v.t.* [gagged, gag-ging], **1,** to cover the mouth with a gag; **2,** to silence by force or law:—*v.i.* **1,** to strain, as in vomiting; not be able to swallow; choke; as, to *gag* on a piece of popcorn; **2,** to say something funny.

[1]**gage** (gāj), *n.* **1,** a promise; pledge; **2,** a pledge to appear and fight; **3,** a challenge to fight; a glove, cap, etc., thrown down as a challenge.

[2]**gage** (gāj), *n.* Same as **gauge.**

gai-e-ty or **gay-e-ty** (gā′e-ti), *n.* [*pl.* gaieties; gayeties], **1,** merriment; glee; jollity; **2,** elegance; brilliancy, as of dress.

gai-ly or **gay-ly** (gā′li), *adv.* **1,** merrily; happily; **2,** showily; as, to dress *gaily.*

gain (gān), *n.* **1,** advantage; profit; as, to be greedy for *gain*; **2,** increase; as, a *gain* in weight:—*v.i.* **1,** to obtain, as profit or advantage; earn; **2,** to win, esp. through effort; as, he *gained* his point; **3,** to obtain through an increase; as, to *gain* 10 kilograms in weight:—*v.i.* **1,** to improve; increase; as, to *gain* in knowledge; **2,** to advance; as, to *gain* on the runner ahead.—*n.* **gain′er.**—*adj.* **gain′ful.**

gain-say (gān′sā′), *v.t.* [gainsaid (gān′sād′; gān′sed′), gainsay-ing], to contradict; deny.

gait (gāt), *n.* a manner of walking or running; as, the old man's shuffling *gait.*

gai-ter (gā′tėr), *n.* **1,** a covering of cloth or leather for the lower leg or ankle, fitting over the top of the boot; **2,** a shoe with elastic strips at the sides; also, a kind of overshoe with a cloth top; **3,** a spat.

ga-la (gā′la; gä′la), *n.* a festival; a celebration:—*adj.* festive; as, *gala* attire.

gal-ax-y (gal′ak-si), *n.* [*pl.* galaxies (-siz)], **1,** a system of millions or billions of stars or suns many light years apart, making up the universe; **2,** an assemblage of famous persons:—**the Galaxy,** the Milky Way, to which our sun belongs: to the eye it appears as a luminous band across the sky.—*adj.* **ga-lac′tic.**

gale (gāl), *n.* **1,** a strong wind, less violent than a hurricane, which blows with a speed of 50–90 km/h; **2,** any strong wind; **3,** an outburst or sudden noise; as, *gales* of laughter.

¹gall (gôl), *n.* **1,** the bile, a bitter fluid separated out of the blood by the liver and stored in the gall bladder; **2,** anything bitter or distasteful; **3,** spite; hate; **4,** *Colloq.* insolence; as, she has a lot of *gall* to talk to her teacher that way.

²gall (gôl), *n.* a swelling or growth on the bark or leaves of numerous plants, esp. oaks, caused by, and growing around, the larva of certain insects or fungi.

³gall (gôl), *v.t.*, **1,** to chafe, or fret by friction, as a horse's collar; **2,** to vex; irritate; annoy:—*n.* a skin sore caused by chafing; a place rubbed bare; flaw.—*adj.* **gal′ling.**

gal-lant (gal′ant), *adj.* **1,** brave; high-spirited; chivalrous; as, a *gallant* knight; **2,** of noble or stately appearance; **3,** (ga-lant′; gal′ant), showing elaborate courtesy and respect to women:—*n.* (gal′ant; ga-lant′), **1,** a man of fashion; **2,** a beau; a man elaborately polite to women.—*n.* **gal′lant-ry.**

gall blad-der, a pear-shaped sac near the liver that receives and stores bile, which helps to digest food.

gal-le-on (gal′i-un), *n.* a large sailing vessel with a high stern and three or four decks, usually armed, used esp. by the Spaniards in the Armada from the 15th to the 17th century.

gal-ler-y (gal′-ėr-i), *n.* [*pl.* galleries], **1,** a long, narrow hall, often with windows on one side only; **2,** a platform projecting from the side and end walls of a theatre, church, assembly room, etc., containing seats; a balcony; **3,** the occupants of such seats; **4,** a building or room for exhibiting works of art, etc.; **5,** an underground passage for communication, as in a mine or an underground fort.—*adj.* **gal′ler-ied.**

gal-ley (gal′i), *n.* [*pl.* galleys], **1,** a low, flat, one-decked, sea-going vessel, propelled by sails and oars, used in ancient and medieval times; **2,** a large, open rowboat; **3,** the cooking quarters of a ship or aircraft; **4,** in *printing,* formerly, an oblong metal tray to hold composed or set type; also, a printer's proof, often called *galley* proof, made from such type on a long sheet of paper.

Gallic (gal′ik), *adj.* of or pertaining to France or its people; as, a *Gallic* shrug.

gal-li-vant (gal′i-vant′) or **gal-a-vant,** *v.i.* to play the beau or gallant; to gad about in search of passing pleasure or amusement.

gal-lon (gal′un), *n.* a unit of liquid measure: the imperial gallon equals 4.55 litres.

gal-lop (gal′up), *n.* **1,** the fastest gait of a horse or other four-footed animal, in which it takes all four feet off the ground in the same stride; **2,** a ride at this gait:—*v.i.* **1,** to run with leaps, like a horse; **2,** to ride a horse at a gallop; **3,** to hasten; move quickly; as, to *gallop* into the room:—*v.t.* to cause to move at a gallop; as, to *gallop* a horse.

gal-lows (gal′ōz; gal′us), *n.* [*pl.* gallowses], a structure consisting of two uprights with a crossbar on the top, used for hanging criminals.

gall-stone (gôl′stōn′), *n.* a crystalline fatty mass (sometimes a calcium salt) that forms in the gall bladder, liver, or bile duct, which can be painful and require surgery to remove.

ga-loot or **gal-loot** (ga-lo͞ot′), *n.* *Slang* a clumsy, awkward person.

ga-lore (ga-lōr′), *adj.* very many; abundant: used after the noun it modifies; as, pretty flowers *galore*:—*adv.* in great plenty.

ga-losh or **go-losh** (ga-losh′), *n.* any protective overshoe; esp., a high rubber overshoe.

gal-va-nize (gal′va-nīz′), *v.t.* [galvanized, galvaniz-ing], **1,** to coat or plate with metal, as iron with zinc, by means of electricity, used esp. formerly; **2,** to stimulate by applying an electric current to, as a muscle; **3,** to excite or shock, as if by electricity; as, to *galvanize* a person into action.—*adj.* **gal-van′ic.**

gal-va-nom-e-ter (gal′va-nom′e-tėr), *n.* an instrument that uses a magnetic needle or a coil in a magnetic field to detect and measure slight electric currents.

gambit (gam′bit), *n.* **1,** in *chess*, an opening move that sacrifices a pawn or piece in hope of an advantage; **2,** an opening move in a discussion, battle of wits, etc., in order to gain advantage.

gam-ble (gam′bl), *v.i.* [gam-bled, gambling], **1,** to play for money or a prize; **2,** to risk money on a possible happening; **3,** to run any great risk for the sake of uncertain gain; **4,** to bet:—*v.t.* **1,** to squander by playing for stakes; as, he *gambled* away his savings; **2,** to bet:—*n.* **1,** any game or act involving the risking of stakes; **2,** an act accompanied by uncertainty or by any special risk; as, investing in some stocks is quite a *gamble*; **3,** a bet or wager.—*n.* **gam′bler.**

gam-bol (gam′bul), *n.* a dancing or skipping about for joy or sport; frolic:—*v.i.* [gambolled, gambol-ling], to skip and dance about in play; as, the children *gambolled* in the park.

game (gām), *n.* **1,** sport or amusement; fun; frolic; also the device used; as, a board *game*; **2,** a contest carried on according to rules, success depending upon superiority in strength, skill, luck, etc.; as, the *game* of baseball, football, chess, cards, etc.; **3,** a single unit or division of play; as, four *games* in the first set at tennis; **4,** a scheme, or plan sometimes not praiseworthy; as, I've spoiled your little *game*; the *game* is up; **5,** wild animals, birds, or fish pursued by a hunter or fisher; also, their flesh used for food:—*v.i.* [gamed, gaming], to play for a stake or prize:—*adj.* **1,** pertaining to animals or birds hunted or taken for sport; **2,** *Colloq.* ready; spirited; plucky; as, he was a *game* athlete; **3,** ready; willing; as, are you *game* for a swim?—*adv.* **game′ly.** Also, **game′ bird′; game′ fish′; game′ plan′; game′ show′; game′ war′den.**

game-keep-er (gām′kēp′ėr), *n.* one in charge of wild animals or birds on a private preserve or estate.

game misconduct, in *hockey*, a penalty for a serious infraction, banishing a player from the ice for the remainder of the game.

game-ster (gām′stėr), *n.* one who habitually bets or plays for stakes; a gambler.

game winner, the goal or other score that wins the game.

gam-in (gam′in), *n.* a neglected street child; an outcast boy or girl; urchin.

gam-ma (gam′a), *n.* the third letter of the Greek alphabet γ, Γ:—**gamma rays,** penetrating short-wave radiations, similar to X-rays, emitted by radium, uranium, etc., and used in treating cancer.

gam-ut (gam′ut), *n.* **1,** the great scale or whole series of recognized musical notes; **2,** the major scale; **3,** the entire range of anything; as, to run the *gamut* from joy to despair.

gam-y (gām′i), *adj.* [gam-i-er, gam-i-est], **1,** abounding in game; **2,** plucky; ready; spirited; **3,** having the flavour of game.

gan-der (gan′dėr), *n.* **1,** a full-grown male goose; **2,** a simpleton.

gang (gang), *n.* **1,** a number of persons banded together for a particular purpose, esp. something illegal; a group of criminals; as, a *gang* of thieves; **2,** a group of young people from one area who form a group under a certain name, and who commit minor crimes and fight with other gangs; **3,** a group of workers under one foreman; as, a road *gang*, who repair roads; **4,** a social group; **5,** an outfit or set of tools or machines arranged for use together; as, a *gang* of snowplows:—*v.i.* (usually with *up*) to act against as a group; as, to *gang up* on the school bully. Also, **gang′bust′er; gang′land′.**

gan-gling (gang′gling), *adj.* spindly; awkwardly tall; lanky; as, a *gangling* youth.

gan-gli-on (gang′gli-un), *n.* [*pl.* ganglia or ganglions], **1,** a mass of nerve cells (as in the brain or spinal cord) serving as a nerve centre; **2,** a benign cyst formed on a joint or tendon; **3,** any centre of energy, force, or activity; as, the Internet is a vital *ganglion* of modern life.

gang-plank (gang′plangk′), *n.* a movable platform or bridge by which to enter or leave a ship; gangway.

gan-grene (gang′grēn′), *n.* dying or decomposing tissue, owing to interruption of blood circulation.—*adj.* **gan′gre-nous.**

gang-ster (gang′stėr), *n.* a member of a lawless gang; a criminal; mobster.

gang-way (gang′wā′), *n.* **1,** a movable platform or bridge between a wharf and a ship; gangplank; **2,** a passageway; aisle.

gan-ja (gän′ja), *n.* marijuana.

gant-let (gänt′let; gånt′let), *n.* Same as **gauntlet.**

gan-try (gan′tri), *n.* **1,** a large, bridgelike frame structure carrying a travelling crane; **2,** a bridge over several railway tracks carrying signals; **3,** a small overhead crane used in machine shops, mills, etc.; **4,** a frame for supporting barrels; **5,** a movable structure with platforms used to service and assemble a rocket; **6,** a structure for a road to carry a direction signal showing what lane to use.

gap (gap), *n.* **1,** an opening; passage; **2,** a pass in a mountain ridge; **3,** an unfilled interval; a blank or empty space; as, a *gap* in the conversation; **4,** a big difference in character, ideas, or opinions; as, a generation *gap*.

gape (gāp; gap; gåp), *v.i.* [gaped, gap-ing], **1,** to open the mouth wide, as from drowsiness, wonder, etc.; yawn; **2,** to stare with open mouth, as in amazement:—*n.* **1,** the act of opening the mouth and staring; **2,** a yawn; **3,** an opening; gap.

ga-rage (gar′äzh; ga-räzh′; gar′ij), *n.* **1,** a

building or part of a building used for parking a car; **2,** a building or place of business for repairing cars:—**garage sale**, a sale of personal belongings such as old furniture, toys, and clothes, often held in or in front of a garage.

garb (gärb), *n.* dress; clothing, esp. of a distinctive kind; as, the *garb* of surgeon, clown, artist, priest, etc.:—*v.t.* to clothe.

gar-bage (gär′bij), *n.* **1,** waste matter that is thrown away from a kitchen, market, store, etc.; **2,** any worthless material.

gar-ble (gär′bl), *v.t.* to corrupt; mutilate; distort (a story, text, etc.) so as to mislead; as, a *garbled* account of the accident.

gar-den (gär′dn), *n.* a piece of ground set aside for growing flowers, fruit, vegetables, etc.; also, a place set aside for the display of plant and animal life to the public; as, the botanical *gardens*:—*adj.* intended for or growing in a garden; as, *garden* tools, *garden* plants:—*v.i.* to labour in or cultivate a garden.

gar-den-er (gär-dn-ėr; gärd′nėr), *n.* one who gardens; also, one hired to care for a lawn or garden.

gar-de-ni-a (gär-dē′ni-a), *n.* **1,** any of a group of shrubs and trees cultivated for their fragrant yellow or white flowers; **2,** the flower of any of these, used often in corsages.

gar-gan-tu-an (gär-gan′tū-an), *adj.* unbelievably huge; enormous; as, a *gargantuan* appetite.

gar-gle (gär′gl), *n.* a medicinal, antiseptic, or other liquid for washing or rinsing the throat or mouth:—*v.t.* [gar-gled, gar-gling], to rinse or disinfect (the throat) with a liquid, kept moving by slowly expelling the breath:—*v.i.* to use a gargle.

gar-goyle (gär′goil), *n.* a grotesque waterspout or ornament in the form of an animal or human head, projecting from a gutter or corner of a building; as, the *gargoyles* of Westminster Abbey.

GARGOYLE

gar-ish (gâr′ish), *adj.* gaudy; showy (without taste); cheaply flashy; as, a *garish* dress, building, etc.

gar-land (gär′land), *n.* **1,** a wreath, as of flowers, branches, or leaves, worn on the head; **2,** an anthology:—*v.t.* to deck or adorn with a wreath.

gar-lic (gär′lik), *n.* a plant of the lily family, with a strong, biting taste: the bulb, which resembles a small onion, is used for flavour in cooking.

gar-ment (gär′ment), *n.* any article of clothing, as a dress, pants, etc.

gar-ner (gär′nėr), *n.* **1,** a storehouse for grain; a granary; **2,** an accumulation of anything:—*v.t.* **1,** to gather for safekeeping; store, as in a granary; gather up; as, to *garner* grain; **2,** to earn with effort; accumulate; as, to *garner* respect from her peers.

gar-net (gär′net), *n.* **1,** a semi-precious stone, used as a gem, usually deep red; **2,** a deep-red colour.

gar-nish (gär′nish), *n.* **1,** an ornament or decoration; **2,** something laid about food in a dish as a decoration, such as radishes, parsley, lemon slices, etc.:—*v.t.* **1,** to adorn; **2,** to decorate (food); as, to *garnish* potatoes with parsley.—*n.* **gar′ni-ture.**

gar-ni-shee (gär′ni-shē′), *v.t.* to seize by legal process a debtor's property; as, to *garnishee* wages.

gar-ret (gar′et), *n.* the uppermost part of a house, beneath the roof; an attic.

gar-ri-son (gar′i-sun), *n.* **1,** a body of troops stationed in a fort; **2,** the place where such soldiers are stationed:—*v.t.* **1,** to furnish (a place) with troops, usually to defend it; as, to *garrison* a town; **2,** to defend by means of a fort or forts manned by soldiers; as, they built a fort to *garrison* the pass.

gar-rote (ga-rot′; -rōt′), *n.* **1,** formerly, a Spanish method of execution by strangulation, using an iron collar; also, the device used; **2,** any method of strangulation, esp. during a robbery:—*v.t.* to disable or kill using a garrote; throttle.

gar-ru-lous (gar′ū-lus), *adj.* very talkative, esp. about unimportant things; wordy.—*adv.* **gar′ru-lous-ly.**—*n.* **gar-ru′li-ty.**

gar-ter (gär′tėr), *n.* a band or strap by which a stocking or sleeve is held up:—*v.t.* to bind or fasten with a garter.

garter snake, a small, harmless snake with yellow stripes along the back, common in North America.

gas (gas), *n.* **1,** one of the three basic forms of matter, along with *liquid* and *solid*, that is any airlike fluid, without shape or volume, tending to expand indefinitely; **2,** any combustible gaseous mixture used for cooking and heating; **3,** any similar fluid used as an anesthetic; esp., a mixture of nitrous oxide and oxygen: often called *laughing gas*; **4,** any fumes or vapour that make breathing difficult or impossible or are harmful in some other way; as, *gases* used in warfare; *tear* gas; **5,** *Colloq.* gasoline; petrol; **6,** accumulation of gas in the stomach or intestines:—*v.t.* [gassed, gas-sing], to poison by a gas.—*adj.* **gas′e-ous** (gā′si-us; ga′si-us).—*n.* **gas′ mask′.** Also, **gas′bag′; gas′ bar′; gas′ cham′ber; gas′–fired′; gas′light′; gas′ ped′al.**

gash (gash), *n.* a deep or gaping cut or wound:—*v.t.* to cut deeply; as, he *gashed* his hand with a sharp knife.

gas-ket (gas′kit), *n.* **1,** a band of metal, rubber, hemp, fibre paper, etc., to pack pistons and make joints leakproof; **2,** a cord used to tie a furled sail to a yard.

gas-o-line (gas′o-lēn′; gas′o-lēn′), *n.* an inflammable liquid commonly obtained by distilling petroleum and used esp. for fuel in cars, trucks, airplanes, boats, lawn mowers, and many other vehicles.

gasp (gåsp), *n.* a quick, painful effort to catch the breath; as, his breath came in *gasps*:—*v.i.* to catch the breath with the mouth open; as, she was *gasping* for air:—*v.t.* to emit with quick, painful breaths; as, he *gasped* his words in terror.

gas-tric (gas′trik), *adj.* pertaining to the stomach; as, *gastric* fluid; *gastric* ulcer:—**gastric juice**, a thin, digestive liquid, secreted by glands in the lining of the stomach.—*n.* **gas-tri′tis** (gas-trī′tis), inflammation of the lining of the stomach.—*n.* **gas′tro-en′ter-i′tis** (gas′trō-en′tėr-ī′tis), inflammation of the lining of the stomach and the intestines: also called *stomach flu* or *food poisoning*.

gas-tro-nom-ic (gas′tro-nom′ik), *adj.* pertaining to good eating: as, a *gastronomic* treat for dinner.

gate (gāt), *n.* **1,** an opening in a wall, fence, etc., to allow entrance or passage; **2,** a barrier, frame, or door that opens or closes such an entrance; **3,** a valve or door to stop or permit a flow, as of water, in a pipe, canal, etc.; **4,** the number of people paying to see an athletic contest; also, the amount of money taken in at the entrance gate.

gate-crash-er (gāt′krash′ėr), *n. Slang* someone who attends a party, concert, or other social function without an invitation or ticket.—*v.t.* **gate′crash′.**

gate-leg (gāt′leg′), *n.* and *adj.* a type of table with gatelike legs that can be folded to let the leaves drop.

gate-way (gāt′wā′), *n.* **1,** an opening in a wall or fence for entrance and exit; **2,** the frame or structure around a gate; **3,** an access means; as, the Internet is a *gateway* to information; **4,** in *computing*, hardware or software that allows communication between different computer networks. Also called *router*.

gath-er (ga*th*′ėr), *v.t.* **1,** to collect; bring together; as, to *gather* information; **2,** to pick and collect; as, to *gather* flowers; **3,** to summon; as, to *gather* one's strength; **4,** to amass gradually; as, to *gather* a fortune; **5,** to pucker; draw together; as, to *gather* a skirt; **6,** to conclude; infer; as, they *gathered* that she was leaving:—*v.i.* **1,** to collect; come together; as, people *gathered* on all sides; **2,** to generate pus, as an abscess; **3,** to increase; as, the storm *gathers*:—*n.* one of the folds in cloth, drawn together by a thread.

gath-er-ing (ga*th*′ėr-ing), *n.* the act or fact of bringing or coming together; as, a family *gathering*.

gauche (gōsh), *adj.* awkward; clumsy; boorish; tactless; as, a *gauche* comment.—*n.* **gau′che-rie** (gōsh′e-ri).

gaud-y (gôd′i), *adj.* [gaud-i-er, gaud-i-est], showy; vulgarly ornate; as, *gaudy* imitation jewellery.—*adv.* **gaud′i-ly.**—*n.* **gaud′i-ness.**

gauge or **gage** (gāj), *n.* **1,** any of various standards of measurement; **2,** a means of estimating or judging; a test; **3,** the distance between railway rails, standard gauge being 143.5 centimetres; **4,** any measuring or recording instrument, as one for measuring rainfall, wind velocity, steam pressure, diameter of a wire, etc.; **5,** the diameter of the barrel of a firearm:—*v.t.* [gauged, gaug-ing], **1,** to measure exactly; **2,** to ascertain the contents or capacity of; **3,** to make standard or uniform; **4,** to estimate; as, to *gauge* one's strength.

gaunt (gônt; gänt), *adj.* **1,** haggard and lean, as from hunger or suffering; **2,** barren and grim; desolate; as, a *gaunt* hillside.—*adv.* **gaunt′ly.**—*n.* **gaunt′ness.**

gaunt-let (gônt′let; gänt′let), *n.* **1,** in the Middle Ages, a mailed glove to protect the hand and wrist from wounds; **2,** a heavy glove with a long cuff; **3,** that part of such a glove that covers the wrist; **4,** a former punishment or torture in which a person ran between two files of men, who struck him as he passed:—**throw down/take up the gauntlet,** to give/accept a challenge:—**run the gauntlet, 1,** to undergo the punishment of a gauntlet; **2,** to do something regardless of the danger from all sides; as, the escaped convict *ran the gauntlet* of bullets as he ran across the field; **3,** to be exposed to an ordeal such as attack or criticism.

gauze (gôz), *n.* **1,** a thin, light, transparent fabric of silk, cotton, etc.; **2,** a thin, loosely woven cotton material, used for bandages.—*adj.* **gauz′y.**

gave (gāv), *p.t.* of *give*.

gav-el (gav′el), *n.* a small mallet used by a presiding officer, chairperson, or auctioneer to signal for order or attention.

ga-votte (ga-vot′), *n.* a lively French dance in 4/4 time, or the music for it.

gawk (gôk), *v.i. Colloq.* to stare stupidly:—*n.* a clumsy person; booby.

gawk-y (gôk′i), *adj.* [gawk-i-er, gawk-i-est], awkward; clumsy.—*adv.* **gawk′i-ly.**

gay (gā), *adj.* **1,** lively; merry; full of glee; cheerful; sportive; **2,** showy; bright-coloured; as, a *gay* red; **3,** addicted to pleasure; as, he leads a *gay* life; **4,** *Colloq.* homosexual:—*n. Colloq.* a homosexual.

gay-e-ty (gā′e-ti), *n.* Same as **gaiety.**

gay-ly (gā′li), *adv.* Same as **gaily.**

gaze (gāz), *v.i.* [gazed, gaz-ing], to look earnestly or steadily; stare; as, he *gazed* straight ahead:—*n.* a fixed, earnest look; stare.

ga-zelle (ga-zel′), *n.* a small, swift antelope of Africa and Asia, with large black eyes.

ga-zette (ga-zet′), *n.* **1,** a newspaper; **2,** an

official government journal that prints lists of promotions, appointments, etc.:—*v.i.* [gazet-ted, gazet-ting], publish in a gazette.

gaz-et-teer (gaz′e-tēr′), *n.* **1,** a dictionary of geographical names; **2,** someone who works for or publishes a gazette.

GDP (jē′dē′pē′), *abbrev.* short for *gross domestic product.*

gear (gēr), *n.* **1,** equipment for a certain activity; as, mountain-climbing or fishing *gear;* **2,** a harness for draft animals; **3,** a wheel having teeth that fit into the teeth of another wheel, which allows it to perform a certain function, such as transmitting power or changing timing; as, first, second, third, or reverse *gears* on a car or truck change the speed and power of the motor; **4,** a condition or arrangement in which the parts of a machine are adjusted to each other in order to act; as, to put a car in *gear;* **5,** a group of connected parts in a machine that have a certain purpose; as, the landing *gear* of an airplane:—**gear-wheel,** a wheel with teeth that fit into the cogs of another wheel:—*v.t.* **1,** to put into gear; **2,** to provide with a gear or gears:—*v.i.* **1,** to be in, or come into, gear; **2,** to fit to a certain purpose; make suitable; as, that computer game is *geared* to children.

gear-ing (gēr′ing), *n.* the parts of a machine by which motion is transmitted from one section to another.

gear-shift (gēr′shift′), *n.* a mechanism and lever for engaging and disengaging gears.

geck-o (gek′ō), *n.* [*pl.* geckos or geckoes], a species of small, insect-eating lizards with weak limbs, large heads, and suction pads on their feet.

geek (gēk), *n. Slang* **1,** someone who is single-minded or highly skilled in something, esp. technology, and often lacks social skills; as, a computer *geek;* **2,** someone lacking in social skills, who is uninteresting or inept; a nerd; **3,** formerly, a circus sideshow performer.—*adj.* **geeky.**

geese (gēs), *n.pl.* of *goose.*

Gei-ger count-er (gī′gėr), *n.* an instrument used to detect and measure radioactivity.

gei-sha (gā′sha), *n.* a Japanese hostess who is trained in dancing, singing, and making conversation, in order to entertain men.

gel-a-tin (jel′a-tin) or **gel-a-tine** (jel′a-tin; jel′a-tēn′), *n.* a transparent, tasteless substance extracted from the bones, hoofs, and other parts of animals by prolonged boiling, used in jelly desserts, photographic film, etc.; animal jelly.—*adj.* **ge-lat′i-nous.**

gel-ding (gel′ding), *n.* a castrated animal, esp. a horse.

gel-id (jel′id), *adj.* frozen; icy; as, *gelid* arctic blasts; the *gelid* tundra.

gem (jem), *n.* **1,** a precious stone; a jewel; **2,** any rare or special object or person; as, a *gem* of a picture; her assistant is a *gem;* **3,** a kind of muffin:—*v.t.* [gemmed, gem-ming], to adorn with, or as with, precious stones.

Gem-i-ni (jem′i-nī), *n.* **1,** a northern constellation, the Twins, containing two bright stars, Castor and Pollux, located in the Milky Way, opposite Orion and Taurus; **2,** the third sign of the zodiac; **3,** an annual Canadian television award; **4,** one of the spacecrafts, made for two people, launched by the U.S.

gen-darme (zhän′dårm′), *n.* in France, a member of an armed, uniformed police, trained as troopers or soldiers; also, any police officer.

gen-der (jen′dėr), *n.* in English *grammar,* any one of the three divisions (masculine, feminine, neuter) into which nouns and pronouns are put, according to whether the objects named are regarded as male, female, or neither. Also, **gen′der gap′; gen′der role′.**

gene (jēn), *n.* an element of an animal or plant reproductive cell by which hereditary characteristics (colour of hair, shape of leaf, etc.) are determined and transmitted, each individual resulting from a union of two such cells and receiving a set of genes from each of its parents.

gen-e-al-o-gy (jen′e-al′o-ji; -jē′), *n.* **1,** a recorded history of the descent of a person or his or her family from one or more ancestors; **2,** lineage; pedigree.

gen-er-a (jen′er-a), *n.pl.* of *genus.*

gen-er-al (jen′er-al), *n.* a military officer ranking higher than a colonel and usually placed in command of an army or one of the chief divisions of an army:—**in general,** as a rule; usually; generally; as, *in general,* January and February are the coldest months of the year:—*adj.* **1,** pertaining to or affecting one and all; universal; not limited; as, food is the *general* need of humans; a *general* epidemic; **2,** indefinite; not specific or detailed; as, a *general* outline; **3,** prevailing; usual; as, a *general* custom; **4,** whole; not local or divided; as, a *general* vote; the *general* public; **5,** not specializing in any one thing; as, a *general* store; **6,** indicating superiority of rank; as, the Governor *General.*

gen-er-al-i-ty (jen′ėr-al′i-ti), *n.* [*pl.* generalities], **1,** the greatest part; majority; as, the *generality* of humankind; **2,** a general statement, or one that is true as a rule but may have exceptions.

gen-er-al-ize (jen′ėr-al-īz′), *v.t.* [generalized, generaliz-ing], to derive general principles from; as, to *generalize* a law:—*v.i.* to draw general conclusions or notions from particular instances; as, to *generalize* that all politicians are self-serving.—*n.* **gen′er-al-i-za′tion.**

gen-er-al-ly (jen′ėr-al-i), *adv.* **1,** commonly; as a rule; in general; as, we *generally* go to the lake for summer vacation; **2,** in a broad sense; widely; in general; as, *generally* speaking, children go to school; **3,** extensively, but not universally; as, this condition exists *generally*.

gen-er-ate (jen′ėr-āt′), *v.t.* [generat-ed, generat-ing], **1,** to bring into existence, as plants, animals, etc.; **2,** to produce; as wind can *generate* electricity; an article that *generates* debate.

gen-er-a-tion (jen′ėr-ā′shun), *n.* **1,** the act or process of producing by natural or artificial means; as, the *generation* of electric power; **2,** a single step in a line of succession; as, a mother and son represent two *generations*; **3,** people born in the same period; as, the people of our *generation*; **4,** the average period of time between generations, considered about 30 years.

Generation X, the generation of esp. North Americans born between the early 1960s and the mid-1970s, after the baby boomers.

gen-er-a-tor (jen′ėr-ā′tėr), *n.* one who or that which causes or produces, esp. an apparatus that produces electricity from other forms of energy, such as by burning fuel.

ge-ner-ic (je-ner′ik), *adj.* **1,** general, not specific; **2,** having no quality or distinction from others in the group or class; **3,** a product that has no brand name; as, *generic* drugs; **4,** quality common to all members of a biological genus; **5,** in *grammar*, neither masculine nor feminine; as, "actor" is a *generic* noun.—*adv.* **ge-ner′i-cal-ly.**

gen-er-os-i-ty (jen′ėr-os′i-ti), *n.* [*pl.* generosities], the quality of being liberal; greatness of heart; as, she showed *generosity* in her dealings with her opponents.

gen-er-ous (jen′ėr-us), *adj.* **1,** characterized by liberality; **2,** unselfish; honourable; **3,** rich; abundant; as, a *generous* portion of beef; a *generous* harvest.—*adv.* **gen′er-ous-ly.**

gen-e-sis (jen′i-sis), *n.* **1,** a coming to birth; **2,** origin; creation, esp. of the world and human life.

ge-net-ic (ji-ne′tik), *adj.* relating to the science of heredity, esp. the accounting for variations traceable to the interaction of genes and environment.

genetic code, the way genetic information is stored in the DNA, which is the biochemical basis for heredity.

genetic engineering, the deliberate altering of genetic material in the cells of living organisms to produce different characteristics.

ge-net-ics (ji-net′iks), *n.pl.* used as *sing.*, the science of heredity, esp. the accounting for variations traceable to the interaction of genes and environment.—*adj.* **ge-net′ic.**—*n.* **ge-net′i-cist.**

gen-ial (jēn′yal; jē′ni-al), *adj.* **1,** favourable to comfort and growth; as, a *genial* climate; **2,** kindly; sympathetic; cordial; as, a *genial* disposition.—*adv.* **gen′ial-ly.**—*n.* **ge′ni-al′i-ty.**

ge-nie (jē′ni), *n.* Same as **jinni.**

Ge-nie (jē′ni), *n.* an annual Canadian award for feature films.

gen-i-tals (jen′i-talz), *n.pl.* the reproductive organs, esp. the external sex organs. Also called *genitalia.*

gen-ius (jēn′yus; jē′n-us), *n.* [*pl.* geniuses], **1,** [*pl.* genii (jē′n-ī′)], **a,** in *Roman religion*, a guardian spirit; hence, the controlling spirit of a place or person; **b,** in *Muslim lore*, a nature spirit; a jinni; **2,** remarkable ability or natural fitness for a special pursuit; as, a *genius* in computer technology; **3,** exceptional creative, intellectual, or artistic power; also, the one possessing it; **4,** a person who has a powerful influence over another.

gen-o-cide (jen′o-sīd′), *n.* the deliberate and systematic mass extermination of a group of people, esp. those belonging to a particular race, culture, or religion.—*adj.* **gen′o-cid′al.**

ge-nome or **ge-nom** (jē′nōm′; jē′nom′), *n.* the genetic material of an organism; as, the human *genome.*—*adj.* **ge-no′mic.**

gen-re (zhän′r), *n.* style, kind, or sort, esp. in works of literature, art, etc.; as, the novel is a literary *genre.*

gen-teel (jen-tēl′), *adj.* polite; well-bred, often used humorously or sarcastically.—*adv.* **gen-teel′ly.**

gen-tile or **Gen-tile** (jen′tīl), *n.* **1,** one who is not Jewish; **2,** a pagan; heathen; **3,** a Christian:—*adj.* **1,** non-Jewish; **2,** pagan; **3,** Christian.

gen-til-i-ty (jen-til′i-ti), *n.* [*pl.* gentilities], aristocracy or upper class; refinement; good manners; as, he has no claim to *gentility.*

gen-tle (jen′tl), *adj.* [gen-tler, gen-tlest], **1,** mild; not severe in manner; kind; as, a *gentle* nurse; **2,** light; not rough; as, a *gentle* touch; **3,** friendly; docile; not wild; as, a *gentle* dog; **4,** gradual; as, a *gentle* slope:—*v.t.* [gen-tled, gen-tling], to train; make docile; as, to *gentle* a pony.—*adv.* **gen′tly.**

gen-tle-man (jen′tl-man), *n.* [*pl.* gentlemen (-men)], **1,** a well-bred and honourable man; **2,** a polite form for "man"; as, show the *gentleman* in; **3,** formerly, a man born into a good family and having a high social position.—*adj.* **gen′tle-man-ly.**—*n.fem.* **gen′tle-wom′an.**

gen-try (jen′tri), *n.* **1,** people of education and breeding; **2,** formerly, in Britain, those ranking next below the nobility; **3,** people of a particular profession or group; as, the legal *gentry.*

gen-u-flec-tion (jen′ū-flek′shun), *n.* the bending of the knee (as in worship).

gen-u-ine (jen′ū-in), *adj.* **1,** real; not imitation; as, a *genuine* pearl; **2,** sincere; as, *genuine* affection.—*adv.* **gen′u-ine-ly.**

ge-nus (jē′nus), *n.* [*pl.* genera (jen′ėr-a)], a group of plants or animals that have certain fundamental likenesses, yet differ in minor characteristics; as, the lion, tiger, and lynx are different species of the same *genus.*—*adj.* **ge-ner′ic** (je-ner′ik).

Gen X (jen′ eks′), *n. abbrev. Slang* short for *Generation X.*—*n.* **Gen′–X′er.**

ge-o-des-ic or **ge-o-det-ic** (jē′o-des′ik; jē′o-det′ik), *adj.* relating to the science of measuring the size and shape of the earth by dividing its surface into triangles; as, a *geodesic* survey; *geodesic* dome.

ge-og-ra-phy (ji-og′ra-fi), *n.* [*pl.* geographies], **1,** the science that deals with the natural features of the earth, including its surface, its divisions into continents, its climates, plants, animals, inhabitants, and their distribution, industries, etc.; **2,** the natural features of a certain area; as, the *geography* of Venezuela—*n.* **ge-og′rapher.**—*adj.* **ge′o-graph′ic** (jē′o-graf′ik); **ge′o-graph′i-cal.**

ge-ol-o-gy (ji-ol′o-ji), *n.* [*pl.* geologies], the science of the structure of the earth's crust and the history of its successive physical changes, esp. as recorded in the rocks, soil, and other minerals.—*adj.* **ge′o-log′ic; ge′o-log′i-cal.**—*n.* **ge-ol′o-gist.**

ge-om-e-try (ji-om′e-tri), *n.* [*pl.* geometries], that branch of mathematics concerned with the properties and measurements of lines, angles, surfaces, and solids.—*adj.* **ge′o-met′ric; ge′o-met′ri-cal.**

ge-o-phys-i-cs (jē′o-fiz′iks), *n.* the scientific study that deals with the phenomena of the earth's physics such as oceanography, magnetism, meteorology, cosmic rays, seismology, etc.—*n.* **ge′o-phys′i-cist.**—*adj.* **ge′o-phys′i-cal.**

ger-bil (jûr′bl), *n.* a small furry animal like a mouse, with a long tail and long hind legs, often kept as a pet.

ger-i-at-rics (jer′i-at′riks), *n.* the branch of medicine dealing with old age and its diseases. Compare *gerontology.*

germ (jûrm), *n.* **1,** that from which anything springs; origin; as, the *germ* of an idea, etc.; **2,** the undeveloped beginning of an animal or plant; a sprout; seed; as, wheat *germ;* **3,** a miscroscopic microbe, esp. a bacterium that may cause disease.

Ger-man (jûr′men), *n.* **1,** a person who inhabits or originates from Germany; **2,** the language spoken by these people:—*adj.* relating to the country, the people, the language, or the culture of Germany.

ger-mane (jėr-mān′; jûr′mān), *adj.* closely pertinent; relevant; as, your remark is (not) *germane* to the argument.

ger-mi-cide (jûr′mi-sīd′), *n.* a substance used to destroy germs, esp. disease bacteria; a disinfectant.

ger-mi-nate (jûr′mi-nāt′), *v.t.* [germinated, germinat-ing], to sprout or bud; begin to develop:—*v.t.* to cause to develop; as, to *germinate* seeds.—*n.* **ger′mi-na′tion.**

ger-on-tol-o-gy (jer′on-tol′o-ji), *n.* the scientific study of the aging process and the problems associated with it. Compare *geriatrics.*—*adj.* **ge-ron′to-log′i-cal.**—*n.* **ger′ontol′o-gist.**

ger-ry-man-der (jer′i-man′dėr; ger′-), *v.t.* to divide, or change the boundaries of, a voting district so as to give a political party an unfair advantage; to manipulate; misrepresent:—*n.* the process or act of gerrymandering; also, the division itself.—*n.* and *adj.* **ger′ry-man′der-ing.**

ger-und (jer′und), *n.* a verbal noun; as, *seeing* is *believing.*—*adj.* **ge-run′di-al.**

ge-sta-po (ge-stä′pō), *n.* a high-handed secret police that uses terrorist tactics:—**Gestapo,** formerly, the secret police in Germany under the Nazi regime, which was known for its terrorist tactics.

ges-ta-tion (jes-tā′shun), *n.* **1,** the carrying of young in the womb; pregnancy; **2,** the formation and development of something, esp. in the mind.

ges-tic-u-late (jes-tik′ū-lāt′), *v.i.* [gesticulat-ed, gesticulat-ing], to make expressive motions, esp. while speaking; as, an orator *gesticulates* to emphasize a point.—*n.* **gestic′u-la′tion.**

ges-ture (jes′tūr), *n.* **1,** a movement of the face, body, or limbs, to express an idea or emotions; **2,** something said or done as a courtesy or for effect; as, her visit was a kindly *gesture:*—*v.i.* [gestured, gestur-ing], to make expressive motions.

get (get), *v.t.* [*p.t.* got (got), *p.p.* got or gotten (got′n), *p.pr.* get-ting], **1,** to acquire; win; realize; as, to *get* a new baseball glove; *get* first prize; *get* a job; **2,** to obtain by calculating; as, to *get* 40 by adding 20 and 20; **3,** to understand; as, to *get* an idea; **4,** to contract; catch; as, to *get* the measles; **5,** to receive as one's lot; as, to *get* the worst of it; to *get* 10 years' imprisonment; **6,** to learn; as, to *get* a lesson; **7,** to obtain by effort or some process; as, to *get* energy from food; *get* power from a waterfall; also, to prepare; as, to *get* dinner; **8,** to succeed in bringing about; bring into some state; as, to *get* the grass cut; *get* her talking; **9,** *Colloq.* to overcome; also, to catch or kill; as, he *got* his man:—*v.i.* **1,** to arrive; as, to *get* home by five; **2,** to bring oneself into a certain state; as, to *get* ready; *get* well; **3,** to become; as, to *get* hungry or tired.

get-a-way (get′a-wā′), *n.* **1,** *Colloq.* the start (of a race); **2,** *Colloq.* escape, as from pursuers, etc.; **3,** a vacation; also, the vacation place; as, a romantic *getaway*.

gew-gaw (gū′gô), *n.* a showy trifle.

gey-ser (gī′zėr), *n.* a hot spring that frequently spews jets of hot water, steam, and mud; also, anything like a geyser.

ghast-ly (gåst′li), *adj.* **1,** deathlike; pale; **2,** horrible; shocking; causing great fear; as, a *ghastly* crime.

ghet-to (get′ō), *n.* [*pl.* ghettos], **1,** a part of a city in which a minority group lives as a result of social and economic pressures; **2,** formerly, the only part of a city where Jews were permitted to live; **3,** something that is restricted or isolated like a city ghetto; as, a blue-collar job *ghetto*.

ghost (gōst), *n.* **1,** the spirit of a dead person, thought of as living in an unseen world, or as returning to earth in bodily form to haunt the living; **2,** a shadowy resemblance; as, the *ghost* of a smile; **3,** *Colloq.* a ghostwriter.—*adj.* **ghost′ly.**

ghostwriter (gōst′rī′tėr), *n.* one who writes books, speeches, articles, etc., for another who takes credit for them.

ghoul (gōōl), *n.* **1,** a grave robber; **2,** one who enjoys doing loathsome acts.—*adj.* **ghoul′ish.**

gi-ant (jī′ant), *n.* **1,** in *mythology* and *folklore*, a person of human form but of supernatural size and power; **2,** an unusually large person, animal, or plant; **3,** a person of unusual physical or mental strength, influence, or courage; as, to be a *giant* in her field:—*adj.* huge; unusually powerful; monstrous.

gib-ber (jib′ėr; gib′ėr), *v.i.* and *v.t.* **1,** to chatter rapidly and meaninglessly; as, monkeys *gibber*; **2,** to talk foolishly.

gib-ber-ish (gib′ėr-ish; jib′ėr-ish), *n.* **1,** rapid, disconnected talk; **2,** nonsense; as, his arguments were mere *gibberish*.

gib-bet (jib′et), *n.* a kind of gallows consisting of an upright post with an arm projecting from the top from which the bodies of executed criminals used to be hung and left as a warning:—*v.t.* **1,** to execute by hanging; **2,** to hang (the body of an executed person) on a gibbet as a warning; **3,** to expose to public ridicule or scorn.

gib-bous (gib′us), *adj.* bulging; swelling; humpbacked; as, the *gibbous* moon.

GIBBOUS MOON

gibe or **jibe** (jīb), *n.* a taunt or scoff; sneering or sarcastic expression:—*v.t.* [gibed, gib-ing], to sneer at; taunt; as, they *gibed* him for his mistakes:—*v.i.* to sneer; scoff; as, they *gibed* at her singing.

gib-lets (jib′litz), *n.* the internal organs of poultry, as heart, liver, gizzard, etc., used as food.

GIC (jē′ī′sē′), *abbrev.* short for *guaranteed investment certificate.*

gid-dy (gid′i), *adj.* [gid-di-er, gid-di-est], **1,** lightheaded; dizzy; **2,** causing dizziness or staggering; as, a *giddy* height; **3,** frivolous; fickle; as, a *giddy* young girl.—*adv.* **gid′di-ly.**—*n.* **gid′di-ness.**

gift (gift), *n.* **1,** something given; a present; **2,** the power to give or bestow; as, the position is in his *gift*; **3,** natural talent or ability; as, a *gift* for languages:—*adj.* of or for a gift; as, *gift* box; *gift* certificate.

gift-ed (gif′ted), *adj.* talented; endowed with unusual natural ability.

gig (gig), *n.* **1,** a light, two-wheeled, open carriage drawn by one horse; **2,** a ship's light boat, for the captain's use; **3,** *Slang* a performer's engagement, esp. for a specified time; as, to have a one-week *gig* at the new concert hall.

gig-a- (gig′a-) *prefix* meaning *one billion*; as in *giga*byte, *giga*hertz, etc.

gig-a-byte (gig′a-bīt′), in *computing*, a unit of data equal to one billion bytes or one thousand megabytes.

gi-gan-tic (ji-gan′tik), *adj.* huge; immense; of extraordinary size.

gig-gle (gig′l), *n.* a nervous, silly laugh:—*v.i.* [gig-gled, gig-gling], to laugh in a nervous, tittering manner, esp. in a high voice.—*adj.* **gig′gly.**

gi-go-lo (zhig′o-lō′), *n.* a professional male dancing partner or paid companion.

Gi-la mon-ster (hē′la), *n.* a poisonous, black-and-orange lizard of southwestern U.S. and northern Mexico deserts (about 50 centimetres long).

¹gild (gild), *v.t.* [gild-ed or gilt (gilt), gild-ing], **1,** to coat or cover with a thin layer of gold, or something resembling gold; **2,** to make (something) seem more attractive than it really is; gloss over; as, to *gild* a lie.—*n.* **gild′ing.**

²gild (gild), *n.* Same as **guild.**

¹gill (gil), *n.* an organ for breathing air under water, as in fish and amphibians.

²gill (jil), *n.* a unit of liquid measure equal to 142 millilitres.

gilt (gilt), *adj.* covered with, or of the colour of, gold; as, *gilt* chairs:—*n.* a thin layer of gold or something resembling it put on a surface: as, a picture frame covered with *gilt*.

gim-crack (jim′crak′), *adj.* and *n.* a showy but useless object, or relating to such; a gewgaw or of such.—*n.* **gim′crack′er-y.**

gim-mick (gim′ik), *n. Colloq.* **1,** a device by which a magician works a trick; **2,** any tricky or clever device or contrivance used to attract attention or obtain an end; as, an advertising *gimmick* to sell a company's new product.

¹gin (jin), *n.* an alcoholic liquor made from grain mash and flavoured with juniper berries, etc.

²gin (jin), *n.* **1,** a trap or snare; **2,** a machine for clearing cotton fibres of seeds; a cotton gin:—*v.t.* [ginned, gin-ning], to clear (cotton) of seeds with a cotton gin.

³gin (jin), *n.* a card game; as, *gin* rummy.

gin-ger (jin′jėr), *n.* **1,** a tropical plant cultivated for its spicy, sharp-tasting root; **2,** the dried, usually scraped, roots of such a plant used as a sweetmeat when candied; **3,** the powder obtained by grinding such dried roots, used as a spice or medicine; **4,** *Colloq.* courage; vim; spirit:—**ginger ale,** a nonalcoholic, carbonated drink flavoured with ginger.

gin-ger-bread (jin′jėr-bred′), *n.* **1,** a dark-coloured cake sweetened with molasses and flavoured with ginger, sometimes cut into various shapes and frosted; **2,** intricate wooden ornamentation or trimming, esp. on a house:—*adj.* gaudy; overornamented; as, *gingerbread* furniture.

gin-ger-ly (jin′jėr-li), *adv.* with extreme care; timidly:—*adj.* cautious; careful.

gin-ger-snap (jin′jėr-snap′), *n.* a thin, crisp molasses cookie flavoured with ginger.

ging-ham (ging′am), *n.* a cotton cloth, usually in two-coloured stripes, plaids, or checks.

gin-gi-vi-tis (jin′ji-vī′tis), *n.* inflammation of the gums.

gink-go or **ging-ko** (ging′kō; jing′kō), *n.* [*pl.* gingkoes; ginkgoes], a very old cone-bearing deciduous tree with fan-shaped leaves, native to and cultivated in Japan and China.

gip (jip), *v.* Same as *gyp.*

Gip-sy (jip′si), *n.* [*pl.* gipsies], Same as **Gypsy.**

gi-raffe (ji-raf′), *n.* a cud-chewing animal of Africa, remarkable for its long legs and neck, with spotted skin, and feeding on the leaves and twigs of trees: the tallest living animal, growing up to over 5.5 metres tall.

gird (gûrd), *v.t.* [gird-ed or girt (gûrt), gird-ing], **1,** to encircle or bind with a cord, belt, or the like; **2,** to encircle; **3,** to make ready; as, to *gird* oneself for combat.

gird-er (gûr′dėr), *v.* a main beam of wood, iron, or steel, used to support the weight of a structure; as, the steel *girders* of a bridge or skyscraper.

gir-dle (gûr′dl), *n.* something that surrounds, encircles, or confines, as a sash, belt, or a stretchy corsetlike woman's undergarment worn from the waist to the hips and used for slimming or support:—*v.t.* [gir-dled, gir-dling], **1,** to bind or surround with, or as with, a belt; **2,** to enclose; **3,** to cut the bark of (a tree or branch) clear around.

girl (gûrl), *n.* **1,** a female child; a young unmarried woman; **2,** a female employee; **3,** *Colloq.* a sweetheart; **4,** daughter.—*adj.* **girl′ish.**—*n.* **girl′hood.**

girth (gûrth), *n.* **1,** a band around an animal to hold a saddle, blanket, etc., in place; **2,** the measure around anything; as, the *girth* of a pillar; a man's *girth.*

gist (jist), *n.* the main point of a matter; substance; as, the *gist* of a story or speech.

give (giv), *v.t.* [*p.t.* gave (gāv), *p.p.* giv-en (giv′en), *p.pr.* giv-ing], **1,** to hand over as a present; as, I *gave* him a tie; **2,** to pay in exchange for something received or bought; as, to *give* her 20 dollars for that doll; he *gave* money for candy; **3,** to bestow freely; devote; as, he *gave* his life for art; **4,** to administer, as medicine or gas; **5,** to deliver, as a message; as, *give* her my love; **6,** to read, recite, or utter; as, to *give* a speech; **7,** to furnish; as, fire *gives* heat; **8,** to furnish as entertainment; as, to *give* a party; **9,** to put forth; as, *give* a jump or a shout; **10,** to impart; be the source of; as, to *give* someone a cold; the movie *gave* pleasure; **11,** to allot; assign; as, to *give* a child a name; **12,** to grant; as, to *give* permission; **13,** to entrust; as, I *give* it into your charge; **14,** to pledge; as, to *give* one's word; **15,** to present for action or consideration; as, to *give* a reason; **16,** to perform; present; as, to *give* a performance:—*v.i.* **1,** to present gifts; to contribute; bestow charity; as, he *gave* freely to the hospital; **2,** to yield, as to force, pressure, motion, etc.; as, the marshy ground *gave* under my feet; **3,** to afford a view or passage; as, the window *gives* on a court:—*n.* a yielding to pressure; elasticity; as, the *give* of new rubber.

giv-en (giv′en), *adj.* **1,** inclined; disposed; prone to; as, *given* to lying; **2,** stated; designated; as, to meet at a *given* time:—**given name,** the name given to a child by his or her parents or guardian.

giz-zard (giz′ėrd), *n.* the second stomach of birds, with thick, muscular walls for crushing and grinding food, often by means of pebbles previously swallowed.

gla-cier (gla′si-ėr; glā′shėr), *n.* a mass or river of ice, formed over a long period of time in high, cold regions, which moves very slowly down a mountain or through a valley until it melts.

glad (glad), *adj.* [glad-der, glad-dest], **1,** joyous; cheerful; **2,** pleased; as, I am *glad* that you came; **3,** causing joy; as, *glad* news; **4,** bright; beautiful; as, a *glad* sky.—*adv.* **glad′ly.**—*v.t.* and *v.i.* **glad′den.**

glade (glād), *n.* an open space in a forest.

glad-i-a-tor (glad′i-ā′tėr), *n.* in ancient Rome, a man trained or hired to fight for the amusement of the public.

glad-i-o-lus or **glad-i-o-la** (glad′i-ō′lus; gla-dī′ō-lus or glad′i-ō′la; gla-dī′ō-la), *n.* [*pl.* gladioluses or gladioli (glad′i-ō′lī; gla-dī′ō-lī)], a plant of the iris family, with sword-shaped leaves and spikes of coloured, showy flowers.

glam-our or **glam-or** (glam′ėr), *n.* **1,** magical charm; enchantment; as, the *glamour* of the moonlight; **2,** alluring charm of a person, place, or thing; as, the *glamour* of show business. The *-our* spelling is preferred for the noun, and the *-or* spelling for the words derived from it.—*adj.* **glam′or-ous.**

glance (glȧns), *n.* **1,** a swift, sideways look; **2,** a hasty look; as, a *glance* into a room; a *glance* at a paper:—*v.t.* [glanced, glanc-ing], **1,** to view with a quick movement of the eye; look quickly; as, to *glance* at the memo; **2,** to strike at a slant and fly off; as, the stone *glanced* off the tree.

gland (gland), *n.* an organ, such as the liver, kidneys, or pancreas, that secretes a special substance or substances to be used in, or discharged from, the body; as, the salivary, thyroid, adrenal, or pituitary *glands*.—*adj.* **glan′du-lar.**

glare (glâr), *n.* **1,** a brilliant light; dazzling brightness; as, the *glare* of the sun; **2,** a fierce, piercing look:—*v.i.* [glared, glar-ing], **1,** to shine with a dazzling light; as, the light *glared* through the windows; **2,** to look with fierce, piercing eyes; as, she *glared* at me when I spoke:—*v.t.* to express with a fierce look; as, he *glared* his disapproval.

glar-ing (glâr′ing), *adj.* **1,** dazzlingly bright; as, a *glaring* light; **2,** fierce; angry; as, *glaring* eyes; **3,** evident; extremely conspicuous; as, a *glaring* error.

glass (glȧs), *n.* **1,** a hard, brittle substance, usually transparent or translucent, made from sand mixed with soda, lime, and other chemicals, and shaped at high heat by pressing or blowing; **2,** an article made of this substance, or similar substance, as a mirror, drinking glass, window, telescope, etc.; **3,** the amount of anything contained in a drinking tumbler; as, a *glass* of milk:—**glasses,** spectacles; lenses; eyeglasses, made of glass or plastic:—*adj.* made of such a substance; as, *glass* beads:—*v.t.* to put into a jar, for preservation; as, to *glass* fruits.—*n.* **glass′ful; glass′mak′ing; glass′ware′.**

glass-y (glȧs′i), *adj.* [glass-i-er, glass-i-est], **1,** like glass in being smooth, transparent, etc.; **2,** staring without expression: said of the eye or look.—*adv.* **glass′i-ly.**

glau-co-ma (glô-kō′ma), *n.* an eye disease marked by pressure in the eyeball, which, if untreated, can lead to loss of sight.

glaze (glāz), *v.t.* [glazed, glaz-ing], **1,** to furnish or fit with glass; **2,** to cover or overlay with a thin coating of glass, or a substance resembling glass; hence, to make smooth and glossy; as, to *glaze* pottery or paper; **3,** in cooking, to coat with crystallized sugar or syrup; as, *glazed* fruit or doughnuts; **4,** to make (the eye) staring or glassy; as, fear *glazed* his eyes:—*v.i.* to become staring or glassy; as, his eyes *glazed*:—*n.* **1,** a substance used for glazing; **2,** a glossy or glazed surface; as, a *glaze* of ice.—*n.* **gla′zier** (glā′zhėr).

gleam (glēm), *n.* **1,** a brief, bright flash of light; a beam; **2,** something resembling a flash of light; as, a *gleam* of hope:—*v.i.* to send out rays of light; shine brightly; as, candles *gleamed* in the windows.—*adj.* **gleam′ing.**

glean (glēn), *v.t.* **1,** to gather (grain or other produce) that the reapers have left; **2,** to collect bit by bit; as, facts *gleaned* from many Web sites:—*v.i.* to gather grain left by reapers.—*n.* **glean′er.**

glee (glē), *n.* **1,** happiness; mirth; delight; **2,** a song, without musical accompaniment, for three or more voices, singing different parts in harmony:—**glee club,** a club organized to sing songs in harmony, esp. in former times.—*adj.* **glee′ful.**—*adv.* **glee′ful-ly.**

glen (glen), *n.* a narrow secluded valley.

glib (glib), *adj.* [glib-ber, glib-best], speaking or spoken with readiness and ease, but often with little sincerity or thought; as, a *glib* talker; a *glib* remark.—*adv.* **glib′ly.**

glide (glīd), *v.i.* [glid-ed, glid-ing], **1,** to flow, or move along smoothly or noiselessly; as, the boat *glided* through the water; **2,** of an aircraft, to travel through the air without using a motor or other form of power:—*n.* the act of moving along smoothly or noiselessly; also, a smooth, sliding step or motion, as in dancing.

glid-er (glīd′ėr), *n.* **1,** one who or that which moves along smoothly; **2,** a form of aircraft similar to an airplane, but without any engine or other form of power.

glim (glim), *n. Slang* light; candle.

glim-mer (glim′ėr), *n.* **1,** a faint, unsteady light; **2,** a glimpse or hint; as, a *glimmer* of hope:—*v.i.* to flicker; shine faintly and waveringly; as, lights *glimmer* in the distance.

glimpse (glimps), *n.* **1,** a hurried view; as, they caught a *glimpse* of her as she passed; **2,** a hint; a notion; as, a *glimpse* of what is to come:—*v.t.* [glimpsed, glimps-ing], to catch a hurried view of; as, they *glimpsed* the movie star as she hurried by.

glint (glint), *n.* a faint gleam; a flash:—*v.i.* to sparkle or flash; reflect light; as, the bracelet *glinted* in the sunlight.

glis-ten (glis′n), *v.i.* to sparkle; shine; gleam; as, her eyes *glistened* with tears:—*n.* glitter; sparkle.

glitch (glich), *n.* a malfunction, esp. a sudden, minor defect in a product or plan; a bug or a snag; as, a *glitch* in the computer software.

glit-ter (glit′ėr), *v.i.* **1,** to sparkle or flash, as diamonds; **2,** to be showy, as jewels:—*n.* **1,** brilliancy; sparkle; as, the *glitter* of gold; **2,** an attractive or showy quality; glamour; as, the *glitter* of Hollywood.—*adj.* **glit′ter-y.**

gloam-ing (glōm′ing), *n.* twilight; dusk.

gloat (glōt), *v.i.* to feast the eyes or mind in triumph, greed, or spite; as, a thief *gloats* over stolen jewels; to *gloat* over a rival's failure.

glob-al-i-za-tion (glō′bal-īz-ā′shun), *n.* the act of making something universal or worldwide in scope.—*v.t.* **glob′al-ize** [globalized, globaliz-ing].

global positioning system (glō′bl), *n.* a computerized system of satellites, transmitters, and receivers that uses radio signals to locate receivers on the surface of the earth with pinpoint accuracy: abbreviated as *GPS*.

globe (glōb), *n.* **1,** an object that is round like a ball; a ball; a sphere; **2,** a sphere showing a map of the earth (*terrestrial globe*); a similar sphere showing the arrangement of the heavenly bodies (*celestial globe*):—**the globe,** the earth.—*adj.* **glob′u-lar** (glob′ūlėr); **glob′al.**—*adv.* **glo′bal-ly.**

glob-ule (glob′ūl), *n.* a tiny globe-shaped particle; as, a *globule* of fat or spit.

gloom (gloom), *n.* **1,** partial darkness; **2,** unhappiness; low spirits; sadness; **3,** a sad look:—*v.i.* **1,** to be or become cloudy or partially dark; **2,** to frown or look sullen; be sad or unhappy.—*adj.* **gloom′y.**—*adv.* **gloom′i-ly.**—*n.* **gloom′i-ness.**

glor-i-fy (glōr′i-fī), *v.t.* [glorified, glorifying], **1,** to confer honour and splendour upon; as, to *glorify* a hero; **2,** to worship; adore; as, to *glorify* God; **3,** to give beauty, charm, or importance to, sometimes more than something actually is; as, to *glorify* a menial job.—*n.* **glor′i-fi-ca′tion.**

glor-i-ous (glōr′i-us), *adj.* **1,** praiseworthy; noble; as, a *glorious* victory; **2,** of splendid beauty; magnificent; as, a *glorious* scene; **3,** *Colloq.* delightful; as, *glorious* fun.—*adv.* **glor′i-ous-ly.**

glor-y (glōr′i), *n.* [*pl.* glories], **1,** distinction, fame, or honour, given to someone or something by others; **2,** splendour; radiant beauty; as, the *glory* of the sunset; **3,** a reason for pride; as, the Colosseum was the *glory* of ancient Rome; **4,** highest state of magnificence or accomplishment; as, the Olympic athlete in her *glory*; **5,** praise given in worship; as, *glory* be to God; **6,** in *art,* a halo:—*v.i.* [gloried, glory-ing], to rejoice or exult; as, to *glory* in one's power.

gloss (glôs), *n.* **1,** a smooth, glistening lustre; as, the *gloss* of satin; **2,** an insincere or false appearance; **3,** a glossary; **4,** an explanation:—*v.t.* **1,** to make smooth and lustrous; **2,** to give a fair appearance to; cover up or lessen by excuses; as, to *gloss* over a mistake; **3,** to explain.—*adj.* **gloss′y.**—*n.* **gloss′i-ness.**

glos-sa-ry (glos′a-ri), *n.* [*pl.* glossaries], a collection of notes, usually at the back of a book, explaining specialized, technical, or other unusual words specific to a book or text, or as used by some author.

glot-tis (glot′is), *n.* the small opening between the vocal cords in the larynx.

glove (gluv), *n.* **1,** a covering for the hand, of leather, wool, silk, etc., with a separate division for each finger; **2,** a padded covering to protect the hand in certain sports, as boxing, baseball, etc. Also, **glove′ box′; glove′ com-part′ment.**

glow (glō), *v.i.* **1,** to give off heat and light without flame; as, embers *glow* after a fire dies down; **2,** to be red; show brilliant colour; as, the sun *glows* in the west; **3,** to be warm or flushed, as from exercise; also, to have a shining, healthy colour; **4,** to burn with the fervour of emotion or excitement:—*n.* **1,** intense or shining light; **2,** redness, or brightness of colour; also, a healthy complexion; **3,** passion; ardour; **4,** warmth of body.

glow-er (glou′ėr), *v.i.* to stare threateningly or angrily; scowl; as, the angry man *glowered* at the boy.

glu-cose (gloo′kōs), *n.* **1,** a simple sugar in honey and most fruits; **2,** a syrup made from cornstarch, and used to sweeten food.

glue (gloo), *n.* **1,** a substance or adhesive used for sticking things together; **2,** any substance that is like glue:—*v.t.* [glued, gluing], to join with glue.—*adj.* **glue′y.**

glum (glum), *adj.* [glum-mer, glum-mest], gloomy; moody; sullen; as, a *glum* expression.—*adv.* **glum′ly.**

glut (glut), *n.* too large a supply; as, a *glut* of wheat on the market:—*v.t.* [glut-ted, glut-ting], **1,** to more than satisfy; as, he *glutted* his appetite with rich food; **2,** to oversupply; as, to *glut* the market with a product.

glu-ten (gloo′ten), *n.* a sticky substance, found in the flour of certain grains, esp. wheat, when the starch is removed.—*adj.* **glu′ti-nous.**

glut-ton (glut′n), *n.* **1,** one who eats too much; a greedy person; **2,** one who seems to have a great capacity for something; as, a *glutton* for punishment; **3,** a small flesh-eating and fur-bearing animal of the northern regions; the wolverine.—*adj.* **glut′ton-ous.**—*n.* **glut′ton-y.**

glyc-er-in (glis′ėr-in) or **glyc-er-ine** (glis′ėr-in; glis′ėr-ēn′), *n.* Same as **glycerol.**

gly-cer-ol (gli′se-rol; gli′se-rōl), *n.* a sweetish, colourless, sticky liquid obtained from oils, fat, etc., used as a sweetener and solvent, and in explosives, cosmetics, etc.

gly-col (glī′kol), *n.* an organic compound used as a solvent and as an antifreeze in cars.

gnarled (närld), *adj.* full of knots; distorted; twisted; as, an old, *gnarled* oak.

gnash (nash), *v.t.* and *v.i.* to strike or grind the teeth together, as in anger or in pain.

gnat (nat), *n.* a small, two-winged insect that stings or bites.

gnaw (nô), *v.t.* **1,** to bite off, or eat away, little by little; to corrode; **2,** to torment; cause pain or worry; as, remorse *gnawed* at her:—*v.i.* **1,** to bite repeatedly; as, to *gnaw* at a crust; **2,** to torment.

gnome (nōm), *n.* **1,** in *folklore,* a dwarf, supposed to live in the earth to guard the earth's treasures; **2,** a small, odd-looking person.

gno-mon (nō′mon), *n.* **1,** anything that points out the time of day by its shadow, as the arm of a sundial or a pillar; **2,** that part of a parallelogram left after a similar parallelogram has been cut from the corner.

GNP (jē′en′pē′), *abbrev.* short for *gross national product.*

gnu (nū; nōō), *n.* an African antelope with a mane, a flowing tail, humped shoulders, and curved horns. Also called *wildebeest.*

go (gō), *v.i.* [*p.t.* went (went), *p.p.* gone (gôn), *p.pr.* go-ing], **1,** to pass from place to place; travel; proceed; as, to *go* from Montréal to Toronto; *go* ahead; gossip *goes* through an office; a telegram *goes* by wire; **2,** to move away; depart; start; as, the train *goes* at five; the train has *gone*; **3,** to follow or be guided; as, to *go* by rule; she *goes* with the fashion; **4,** to be (in a certain condition); as, to *go* dirty; *go* unprepared; **5,** to be in working order; as, a clock or a computer *goes;* **6,** to make a particular motion; as, *go* like this; **7,** to make a particular sound; as, thunder *goes* "boom"; the cat *goes* "meow"; **8,** to have a certain wording or tune; as, the song *goes* like this; **9,** to result; as, the election *went* Conservative; **10,** to adopt certain views or a course of action; as, Cuba *went* Communist; to *go* to war; **11,** to lead; as, the road *goes* to the city; **12,** to pass by; elapse; as, an hour *goes* by quickly; **13,** to be known; as, she *goes* by the name of Kira; **14,** to be sold; as, a house *goes* at auction; the ring *went* for 200 dollars; **15,** to be missing; as, my ring is *gone*; **16,** to disappear; be abolished or lost; as, crime must *go*; his memory is *gone*; **17,** to be spent; as, my money *went* for rent; **18,** to die; as, all people finally *go*; **19,** to fail; give way; collapse; as, her mind *went*; the scaffolding *went*; **20,** to attend; as, she *goes* to Queen's; **21,** to become; as, to *go* crazy; *go* blind; **22,** to fit; belong; harmonize; as, this shoe *goes* on this foot; that book *goes* on that shelf; brown *goes* well with green; **23,** to be contained; as, three *goes* into nine:—**going to,** about to; intending to; as, I was just *going to* leave:—*v.t. Colloq.* to bet; wager; as, I'll *go* you one better:—*n. Colloq.* **1,** energy; enthusiasm; as, there is *go* in him yet; **2,** an agreement; as, it's a *go;* **3,** success; as, the business is a *go.*

goad (gōd), *n.* **1,** a sharp, pointed stick to urge on cattle; **2,** anything that urges one to action:—*v.t.* **1,** to drive with a goad; as, to *goad* cattle; **2,** to urge to action by irritating means; to drive; as, his taunts *goaded* me to try.

goal (gōl), *n.* **1,** a point marking the end of a race or journey; **2,** an aim; purpose; as, a *goal* in life; **3,** the place into, over, or through which the players in football, hockey, soccer, basketball, etc., must put the ball or puck in order to score; also, the score thus made.—*n.* **goal′keep′er; goal′ post′; goal′ten′der; goal′ie.**

goat (gōt), *n.* **1,** a small, very active, cud-chewing animal, with horns and a beard, much valued for its milk, flesh, and wool; **2,** *Colloq.* one who gets or takes the blame for another's deed; a scapegoat; one who is a butt for ridicule or jokes.—*n.* **goat′herd′.**

goat-ee (gō′tē′), *n.* a pointed beard (on chin or lower lip).

gob (gob), *n. Colloq.* a slimy lump or mass; as, a *gob* of paint.

[1]**gob-ble** (gob′l), *v.t.* [gob-bled, gob-bling], **1,** to swallow hastily or greedily; as, he *gobbled* his food; **2,** *Slang* to seize greedily; as, to *gobble* up all the tickets for the front seats of the show.

[2]**gob-ble** (gob′l), *n.* the cry of a male turkey:—*v.i.* [gob-bled, gob-bling], to utter this cry.

gob-bler (gob′lėr), *n.* a male turkey.

go–be-tween (gō′–bi-twēn′), *n.* one who goes from one person to another to make peace, do business, or settle difficulties; intermediary.

gob-let (gob′let), *n.* a drinking glass with a stem and a base.

gob-lin (gob′lin), *n.* an evil, mischievous, ugly spirit; gnome.

go–cart (gō′kärt′), *n.* **1,** a baby carriage with small front wheels, and a back that can be raised or lowered; **2,** a small wagon that children can ride in or pull; **3,** a baby walker; **4,** a small car used in racing.

god (god), *n.* **1,** a being thought of as having greater than human powers and traits; esp., one who is worshipped; **2,** anything believed to have divine powers, as an image, animal, phase of nature; **3,** a thing or person that is an object of supreme interest or devotion; as, money is her *god*; his mentor is his *god*:—**God,** in many religions, the Supreme Being: also called *the Creator, the Almighty; Jehovah.*—*n.* **god′hood.**—*adj.* **god′less; god′like.**

god-child (god′chīld′) *n.* a child for whose religious training a godparent or godparents, as sponsors, promise to assume responsibility at the baptism of the child; a goddaughter or godson.

god-dess (god′is), *n.* **1,** a female deity; as Venus is the *goddess* of love; **2,** a woman of unusual charm, beauty, or goodness; also, one who is respected.

god-fa-ther (god′fä′*th*ėr), *n.* a man who promises, as sponsor at the baptism of a child, to be responsible for the child's religious training.

god-head or **God-head** (god′hed′), *n.* **1,** divinity; **2,** God.

god-ly (god′li), *adj.* pious; obedient to the commands of God; as, the minister is a *godly* man.—*n.* **god′li-ness.**

god-mother (god′mu*th*′ėr), *n.* a woman who promises, as sponsor at the baptism of a child, to be responsible for the child's religious training.

god-par-ent (god′pâr′ent), *n.* a man or woman who promises, as sponsor at a child's baptism, to be responsible for the child's religious training.

god-send (god′send′), *n.* unexpected aid or good fortune that comes as if sent by God.

God-speed (god′spēd′), *n.* success; a wish for good luck, as to one going on a journey.

go–get-ter (gō′–get′ėr; gō′–get′ėr), *n. Colloq.* an enterprising person, esp. one who is aggressive in business.

gog-gle (gog′l), *v.i.* [gog-gled, gog-gling], to roll the eyes; stare with bulging eyes:—*adj.* staring; prominent; rolling; bulging; as, *goggle* eyes:—*n.* a strained or affected rolling or bulging of the eyes:—**goggles,** snug eyeglasses worn to protect the eyes from dust, particles, sun, etc.

go-ing (gō′ing), *n.* **1,** departure; as, her *going* was unexpected; **2,** the state of the ground or roads, as for travelling, racing, etc.; as, the *going* is good:—*adj.* working; successful; as, a *going* concern.

goi-tre or **goi-ter** (goi′tėr), *n.* a benign enlargement of the thyroid gland, often seen as a swelling on the front of the neck, usually caused by the lack of iodine in the diet.

gold (gōld), *n.* **1,** a precious metal, widely used for coins and jewellery, which is heavy and easily bent, and, when pure, of a bright yellow colour; **2,** money; wealth; **3,** the colour of gold; **4,** precious or pure quality; special; as, she has a heart of *gold*:—*adj.* of or like gold; as, a *gold* watch; *gold* medal; *gold* CD (big seller).

gold-en (gōl′den), *adj.* **1,** made of, or like, gold; **2,** shining; bright like gold; **3,** the colour of gold; deep, bright yellow; **4,** excellent; as, a *golden* opportunity; **5,** having to do with the 50th year in a series; as, a *golden* wedding anniversary. Also, **gold′en age′; gold′en hand′shake; gold′ en ju′bi-lee′; gold′en pa′ra-chute; gold′en re-triev′er.**

gold-en-rod (gōl′den-rod′), *n.* a summer- or fall-blooming common weed with wandlike stems and spike-shaped clusters of small, yellow flowers, the pollen of which sometimes causes allergic reaction.

golden rule, 1, the principle "do unto others as you would have them do unto you"; **2,** any basic guiding principle; as, the *golden rule* of computing is "always back up your data."

gold-eye (gōld′ī′), *n.* a silvery, herring-like game fish of cold-water lakes, as the Winnipeg *goldeye* (noted for its delectable flavour).

gold-fish (gōld′fish′), *n.* a small, gold- or orange-coloured freshwater fish native to East Asia, which is related to the minnow or carp and is often kept in ponds, bowls, or aquariums.

gold mine, 1, an excavation where gold ore is dug; **2,** a source of anything desired; as, the dictionary was a *gold mine* of information.—*n.* **gold′ min′ing; gold′ min′er.**

gold-smith (gōld′smith′), *n.* one who makes items out of gold, or who deals in gold plate.

golf (golf), *n.* a game played with a small, hard ball and long-handled clubs, on an outdoor course, or tract of land, called *links*, the object being to drive the ball into a series of holes with the fewest possible strokes:—*v.i.* to play the game of golf.—*n.* **gol′fer; golf club; golf course.**

go-losh (go-losh′), *n.* Same as *galosh*.

gon-do-la (gon′dō-la), *n.* **1,** a long, narrow, flat-bottomed boat, with high, pointed ends, moved, usually, by one oar, and used on the canals of Venice; also, a similar boat used on rivers; **2,** an open freight car with a flat bottom and low sides; **3,** a long car slung under a dirigible balloon for carrying passengers; **4,** a car suspended by a cable used to carry passengers to and from ski slopes, mountains, etc.; **5,** a booth above an enclosed hockey rink, used to broadcast games.—*n.* **gon′do-lier′.**

GONDOLA

gone (gôn), *p.p.* of *go*.

gong (gông), *n.* a saucer-shaped, metal bell that resounds when struck with a soft hammer; also, a similar device with a mechanical hammer, used as an alarm, etc.; as, a fire *gong*.

good (good), *adj.* [bet-ter, best], **1,** adapted to the end in view; suited to its purpose; as, fish are *good* to eat; a *good* saddle horse; **2,** efficient; as, a *good* doctor; a *good* driver; **3,** satisfactory in quality; as, *good* printer; **4,** giving pleasure; as, a *good* time; **5,** not less than; complete; as, a *good* kilometre; **6,** real; genuine; as, *good* money; **7,** considerable; as, a *good* distance; a *good* number; **8,** well-behaved; as, a *good* child; a *good* dog; **9,** morally excellent; virtuous; as, a *good* person; **10,** kind; benevolent; as, God is *good*; **11,** right; proper; as, a *good* rule to live by; **12,** favourable; advantageous; as, *good* news; **13,** of high or respectable birth;

as, to come of a *good* family; **14,** able to endure or perform; as, a coat *good* for two years; **15,** valid; sound; as, a *good* excuse; **16,** thorough; as, a *good* scolding; **17,** financially sound; trustworthy; as, a *good* debt:—*n.* **1,** whatever is excellent, right, desirable, or sound: opposite of *evil*; as, let *good* prevail; **2,** profit; advantage; welfare; as, I tell you for your own *good*; **3,** use; as, what *good* is it?—*interj.* an exclamation of approval.—*adj.* **good′–look′ing; good′–hu′moured.**

good-bye or **good–bye** or **good–by** (good′bī′; good′–bī′), *n.* a farewell; as, a fond *goodbye*:—*interj.* farewell!: a contraction of "God be with you."

good–for–noth-ing (good′fėr-nuth′ing), *n.* and *adj.* a useless or worthless person or thing.

good-ly (good′li), *adj.* [good-li-er, good-li-est], of considerable size; large; as, to eat a *goodly* amount of vegetables.

good-ness (good′nis), *n.* **1,** the state or quality of being good; excellence; **2,** virtue; kindness; as, from the *goodness* of her heart:—*interj.* an exclamation of surprise.

goods (goodz), *n.pl.* **1,** anything made to be bought and sold; merchandise; as, the *goods* at an auction; **2,** the things that belong to someone; belongings; as, to steal someone's *goods*.

goods and services tax, a tax collected on most goods and services, which was introduced into Canada in 1991: abbreviated as *GST*.

good-will or **good will** (good′wil′), *n.* **1,** kindly feeling; benevolence; **2,** good intention; well-wishing; as, you have my *goodwill*; **3,** the solid relationship and its value, as between a company and its customers.

goof (go͞of), *n. Slang* **1,** a silly, stupid, or gullible person; **2,** an error:—*v.i. Slang* to fail, blunder, etc.; as, to *goof* by forgetting about the meeting:—**goof off,** to waste time; evade responsibility:—**goof around,** to play around:—*v.t.* to bungle; as, to *goof* up the project.—*adj.* **goof′y.**

goon (go͞on), *n. Slang* **1,** a person hired by racketeers, unionists, etc., to terrorize by slugging, bombing, etc.; a thug hired as a strikebreaker; **2,** an awkward, stupid person.

goose (go͞os), *n.* [*pl.* geese (gēs)], **1,** a web-footed, flat-billed water bird, larger than a duck but smaller and more awkward than a swan; **2,** a female goose: in contrast to *gander*; **3,** the flesh of the goose, used as food; **4,** a silly person:—**Canada goose,** a common wild North American goose with black, brown, grey, and white colouring.

goose-ber-ry (go͞os′bėr-i; go͞oz′bėr-i), *n.* [*pl.* gooseberries], **1,** a sour, hairy berry, used in pies and jams; **2,** the bush that bears this berry.

goose bumps, a temporary roughness or bumpiness of the skin, resembling that of a plucked goose, caused by cold or fear. Also called *goose flesh*.

goose step, a stiff-legged parade step, esp. the type performed formerly by Nazi soldiers.

go-pher (gō′fėr), *n.* **1,** a ground squirrel of the prairies of North America; **2,** a ratlike, burrowing animal with large cheek pouches; **3,** a burrowing land tortoise of the southern U.S.; **4,** in *computing*, a computer program designed to search the Internet and read information and Web sites.

[1]**gore** (gōr), *n.* blood; esp., thick or clotted blood.—*adj.* **gor′y.**

[2]**gore** (gōr), *n.* **1,** a three-cornered or triangular piece of cloth sewed into a dress, sail, etc., to vary its width; **2,** one of the triangular or wedge-shaped pieces needed to make a dome-shaped object, as an umbrella, etc.; **3,** a piece of unassigned or remaining land after township lots are marked out:—*v.t.* [gored, goring], to piece with gores or a gore.

[3]**gore** (gōr), *v.t.* [gored, gor-ing], to pierce with, or as with, a horn; as, the bull *gored* him.

gorge (gôrj), *n.* **1,** the throat; **2,** that which is swallowed; **3,** a mass of anything that chokes up a channel; as, a *gorge* of ice in a river; **4,** a narrow passage, as between mountains, usually formed by a river that runs through it; a ravine:—*v.t.* [gorged, gorging], **1,** to eat a very large amount of food; swallow greedily; stuff oneself with food; **2,** to stop up:—*v.i.* to eat greedily.

gor-geous (gôr′jus), *adj.* beautiful; rich in colour; magnificent; showy.—*adv.* **gor′geous-ly.**

Gor-gon (gôr′gon), *n.* in *Greek mythology*, one of three snaky-haired sisters, so horrible that the beholder was turned to stone: one (Medusa) was slain by Perseus:—**gor′gon,** an ugly or repulsive woman.

go-ril-la (go-ril′a), *n.* a strong, central African ape, with a broad, heavy chest and shoulders, long arms, and short legs: the largest ape known.

gor-mand (gôr′mand), *n.* Same as **gourmand.**

gor-mand-ize (gôr′man-dīz′), *v.i.* [gormand-ized, gormand-iz-ing], to eat gluttonously; stuff with food.

gos-ling (goz′ling), *n.* a young goose.

gos-pel (gos′pel), *n.* **1,** good news or tidings; esp., the teachings of Jesus and the Apostles; **2,** anything believed as absolutely true; as, I take her word for *gospel*; **3,** any principle that guides actions and in which its supporters earnestly believe; **4,** a type of black church music of the southern U.S.:—**Gospel, 1,** the history of the life and teachings of Jesus Christ, contained in the first four books of the New Testament; **2,** any one of these books.

gos-sa-mer (gos′a-mėr), *n.* **1,** a light film or thread of a spider's web or cobweb; **2,** any very thin, filmy fabric:—*adj.* thin; delicate; gauzy; as, a *gossamer* scarf.

gos-sip (gos′ip), *n.* **1,** familiar or idle talk about the personal lives of others that is often not kind or true; talebearing; as, office *gossip*; *gossip* about movie stars; **2,** one who makes a habit of talking about other people and their affairs; tattletale:—*v.i.* to chat; tell idle tales about others; tattle; spread gossip.—*adj.* **gos′sip-y.**

got (got), *p.t.* and a *p.p.* of *get.*

Gothic (goth′ik), *adj.* **1,** characteristic of a style of architecture with pointed arches and steep roofs; **2,** pertaining to the Germanic Goths or their language; **3,** medieval:—*n.* **1,** a style of architecture; **2,** the language of the Goths:—**gothic,** *n.* in *printing,* a type of heavy font:—*adj.* **1,** barbarous; **2,** pertaining to a style of fiction that stresses the grotesque.

got-ten (got′en), a *p.p.* of *get.*

gouge (gouj), *n.* **1,** a curved, hollow chisel for scooping out grooves or holes; **2,** a groove or hole, made with, or as with, a gouge; **3,** *Colloq.* an extortion; swindle:—*v.t.* [gouged, goug-ing], **1,** to scoop out with, or as with, a gouge; **2,** *Colloq.* to extort; overcharge; as, that pricey restaurant *gouged* us.—*n.* **goug′er.**

gou-lash (go͞o′lash; go͞o′läsh), *n.* a highly seasoned stew of pieces of beef or veal, and vegetables.

gourd (go͞ord; gōrd), *n.* **1,** any of a number of fleshy, many-seeded fruits with hard shells, related to the melon, pumpkin, squash, etc.; also, the vine bearing this fruit; **2,** the dried shell of such fruits, used for cups, bowl, etc.; **3,** a bottle, cup, bowl, etc., made from a gourd shell.

gour-mand or **gor-mand** (go͞or′mand; gôr′mand), *n.* **1,** a glutton; **2,** a judge of fine foods; epicure; gourmet.

gour-met (go͞or′mā′), *n.* a judge of fine foods and drinks; an epicure:—*adj.* having to do with or suited for a gourmet; as, a *gourmet* cook; *gourmet* meals.

gout (gout), *n.* **1,** a form of arthritis that is marked by painful inflammation of the joints, esp. of the big toe; **2,** a splash or drop, as of rain or blood.—*adj.* **gout′y.**—*n.* **gout′i-ness.**

gov-ern (guv′ėrn), *v.t.* **1,** to control, manage, or direct; rule; as, to *govern* a nation, province, state, city, or other body; *govern* your temper; **2,** to decide; determine; influence; as, the financial report *governed* their decision; **3,** in *grammar,* to require to be in a particular grammatical mood, case, etc.; as, a transitive verb *governs* a noun in the objective case:—*v.i.* to rule.

gov-ern-ess (guv′ėr-nis), *n.* a woman employed to take care of, and often to teach, children in their own home.

gov-ern-ment (guv′ėrn-ment), *n.* **1,** control or management; as, the *government* of a nation, province, state, city, or other body; local *government*; **2,** the system of governing; method of ruling; as, a democratic *government*; **3,** a person or persons who govern; **4,** a territory or country governed.—*adj.* **gov′ern-men′tal.**

gov-er-nor (guv′ėr-nėr), *n.* **1,** an official who is in charge of an organization; as, the board of *governors* of a hospital; **2,** an elected official who is the head of a U.S. state; **3,** a person appointed to manage a colony or territory on behalf of a ruling country; **4,** a device attached to an engine, etc., to regulate its speed.

gov-er-nor gen-er-al [*pl.* governors general], a governor with deputy governors beneath him or her:—**Governor General,** in Canada and other Commonwealth countries, the representative of the king or queen appointed on the advice of the prime minister.

gown (goun), *n.* **1,** a woman's dress; esp., an elaborate, formal dress for special occasions; as, an evening *gown*; wedding *gown*; **2,** a long, loose robe worn by judges, priests, graduating students, etc.; **3,** any loose robe or similar garment; as, a night-*gown*; hospital *gown*:—*v.t.* to clothe with a gown.

GPS (jē′pē′es′), *abbrev.* short for *global positioning system.*

grab (grab), *v.t.* and *v.i.* [grabbed, grabbing], **1,** to seize suddenly by hand; snatch; as, the thief *grabbed* the purse; **2,** to take something in a sudden or hasty way; as, to *grab* a bite to eat:—*n.* a sudden snatch at something; as, to make a *grab* at a life preserver.

grace (grās), *n.* **1,** attractiveness; charm; esp., beauty and ease of motion or manner; as, the *grace* of a dancer; **2,** favour; goodwill; as, in the teacher's good *graces*; **3,** kindness; mercy; **4,** favour shown by granting a delay; as, three days' *grace* to hand in the history assignment; **5,** any charming quality, natural or affected; as, to be full of pleasant *graces*; **6,** a sense of right and wrong; as, he had the *grace* to apologize; **7,** a prayer of thanks before or after a meal; **8,** God's mercy or his divine favour:—*v.t.* **1,** [graced, gracing], to adorn; decorate; as, to *grace* the room with fresh flowers; **2,** to honour; favour; as, the prime minister's presence *graced* the banquet; **3,** to be blessed with; as, to be *graced* with a beautiful voice.—*adj.* **grace′ful; grace′less.**—*adv.* **grace′ful-ly; grace′less-ly.**

gra-cious (grā′shus), *adj.* **1,** kindly; courteous; also, merciful; as, the *gracious* king pardoned her; **2,** attractive and kind in manner and character.—*adv.* **gra′cious-ly.**

gra-da-tion (gra-dā′shun), *n.* **1,** a gradual change from one thing to another; as, *gradation* in colour from blue to purple; **2,** the act of arranging into a series in order of size, rank, colour, etc.; the series so formed; a step in such a series:—**gradations**, steps; stages; degrees.

grade (grād), *n.* **1,** a step or degree in rank, quality, order, etc.; **2,** position in a scale; as, a general holds the highest *grade* in the army; **3,** a class of persons or things of the same degree, rank, etc.; as, *grade* A meat; **4,** a division of the school course, consisting of a year of work; as, an elementary school has eight *grades*; also, the pupils in such a division; **5,** the mark or rating given to a student for school work; **6,** the rate at which a road, railway track, etc., slopes or inclines; also, the slope of a road, railway track, etc.; as, the train goes slowly on a downward *grade*:—*v.t.* [graded, grad-ing], **1,** to sort out according to size, quality, rank, or value; as, to *grade* meat; to arrange into classes; as, to *grade* children according to age; **2,** to level, or to ease the slope of, as a road; **3,** to assign a mark to; as, to *grade* test papers.—*n.* **grad′er.**

gra-di-ent (grā′di-ent), *n.* **1,** slope (or degree of slope), as of a road, ramp, etc.; **2,** in *physics*, the rate of change (as of pressure, temperature, electrical potential, etc.); **3,** a curve or graph showing such a rate of change:—*adj.* rising or descending by steps or degrees.

grad-u-al (grad′ū-al), *adj.* proceeding, or moving slowly, by degrees; not sudden; as, a *gradual* slope.—*adv.* **grad′u-al-ly.**

grad-u-ate (grad′ū-āt′), *v.t.* [graduat-ed, graduat-ing], **1,** to confer a degree or diploma upon; as, a university *graduates* students; **2,** to mark in grades or degrees; as, to *graduate* a measuring glass:—*v.i.* **1,** to receive a diploma or degree; as, she *graduated* from high school; **2,** to change gradually from one degree to another; as, the slope of the road *graduates*; **3,** to advance to some higher level or status; as, a baby *graduates* from a crib to a bed:—*adj.* (grad′ū-it), **1,** having received a degree; as, a *graduate* student; **2,** designed for one who has received a degree; as, a *graduate* course:—*n.* (grad′ū-it), one who has received a diploma or degree from a high school, college, or university.

grad-u-a-tion (grad′ū′ā′shun), *n.* **1,** a ceremony that honours people who have graduated; **2,** the act or fact of graduating.

graf-fi-ti (gra-fē′ti), *n.pl.* [*sing.* graffito (gra-fē′tō)], words or drawings scribbled or painted without permission and usually anonymously in a public place, as on a wall, sidewalk, rock, subway car, etc.

graft (gråft), *v.t.* **1,** to insert (a shoot) from one plant into another plant, on which it continues to grow; **2,** to transplant (living tissue) from one part of the body to another; as, to *graft* skin; **3,** *Colloq.* to get by unfair or dishonest means; extort; as, to *graft* money or votes:—*n.* **1,** the act of grafting; also, a shoot or piece of tissue used in grafting; **2,** the getting of money or positions by dishonest means; extortion.—*n.* **graft′er.**

gra-ham (grā′am), *adj.* made of whole-wheat flour; as, *graham* crackers.

Grail (grāl), *n.* the cup used by Jesus at the Last Supper, called the *Holy Grail*, famous in literature:—**grail**, something desirable that is the object of a pursuit, esp. a prolonged or difficult one.

grain (grān), *n.* **1,** the seedlike fruit of any cereal grass, such as oats, rice, wheat, etc.; also, the plant itself; **2,** any very small, hard particle; as, a *grain* of sand, salt, or sugar; **3,** any tiny bit; as, a *grain* of hope; **4,** a very small unit of weight, obtained from the weight of a grain of wheat; **5,** the arrangement of fibres or the texture of wood, stone, etc.; **6,** the nature or instincts of a person; as, dishonesty goes against my *grain*:—*v.t.* to paint in imitation of the grain of wood.

gram (gram), *n.* a unit or measure of weight or mass in the metric system, equal to one thousandth of a kilogram.

gram-mar (gram′ėr), *n.* **1,** the science that deals with the forms of words and their relation to each other in a particular language; **2,** the use of words according to this science; **3,** a book on this science.—*adj.* **gram-mat′i-cal** (gra-mat′i-kal).—*n.* **gram-mar′i-an** (gra-mâr′i-an).

gram-o-phone (gram′o-fōn′), *n.* one of the earliest machines producing speech or music from a record; phonograph.

gran-a-ry (gran′a-ri), *n.* [*pl.* granaries] a storehouse for grain.

grand (grand), *adj.* **1,** main; principal; as, the *Grand* Canal; **2,** magnificent; splendid; as, a *grand* ball; **3,** showing high social standing and wealth; as, a *grand* lady; **4,** dignified; noble; as, the *grand* manner; **5,** imposing; stately; impressive; as, a *grand* mountain; **6,** higher in rank than others of the same class; as, a *grand* duke; **7,** great in size, value, or consequence; as, a *grand* prize; *grand* climax; *grand* piano; **8,** including everything; as, a *grand* total; **9,** *Colloq.* very good; as, a *grand* time.

Grand Banks, a shoal, 93,000 square kilometres in area, southeast of Newfoundland, famous for fishing.

Grand Canyon, a gorge of the Colorado River, 217 miles long, 2,000 to 6,000 ft. deep.

grand-child (grand′child′), *n.* [*pl.* grandchildren (grand′chil′dren)], the child of one's son or daughter.

grand-daugh-ter (grand′dô′tėr), *n.* a daughter of one's son or daughter.

grand duke, 1, in certain countries of Europe, a sovereign duke, who is next below a king in rank; **2,** formerly, in Russia, a son of a czar.—*n.fem.* **grand duch′ess.**

gran-dee (gran-dē′), *n.* a person of high rank, esp. a Spanish or Portuguese nobleman.

gran-deur (gran′dūr), *n.* **1,** great power, rank, or fame; **2,** sublime beauty; as, the *grandeur* of the Rockies; **3,** social splendour.

grand-fa-ther (grand′fä′thėr), *n.* the father of one's father or mother; also, any forefather.—*adj.* **grand′fa′ther-ly.**

gran-dil-o-quence (gran-dil′o-kwens), *n.* the use of pompous, high-flown, or bombastic words or expressions.—*adj.* **gran-dil′o-quent.**

gran-di-ose (gran′di-ōs′), *adj.* **1,** imposing; impressive; **2,** pompous; showy; as, *grandiose* schemes.

grand jury, in the U.S., a group of jurors chosen to examine accusations against people, and decide whether or not to send them for trial to a regular court.

grand-ma (grand′mä′; gran′mä′; gram′mä′), *n. Colloq.* a grandmother.

grand-moth-er (grand′muth′ėr), *n.* the mother of one's father or mother.

grand-pa (grand′pä′; gran′pä′; gram′pä′), *n. Colloq.* a grandfather.

grand-par-ent (grand′pâr′ent), *n.* either parent of one's father or mother; a grandmother or grandfather.

grand slam, 1, in *bridge,* the (bidding and) taking of all 13 tricks; **2,** in *sports,* such as tennis, golf, etc., winning all the main tournaments in one season; **3,** in *baseball,* hitting a home run with the bases loaded.

grand-son (grand′sun′), *n.* a son of one's son or daughter.

grand-stand (grand′stand′), *n.* the principal covered seating place for the spectators at a racetrack, athletic field, etc.:—*n.* pertaining to something showy or pretentious; as, a *grandstand* strategy:—*v.i.* to act pretentiously to impress someone.

grange (grānj), *n.* a farm, esp. with all its buildings:—**Grange,** in the U.S., a national association of farmers; also, one of its lodges.

gran-ite (gran′it), *n.* a hard, durable rock, pink, whitish, or grey in colour, used for buildings, monuments, etc.

gra-no-la (gra-nō′la), *n.* a dry breakfast or snack food made of rolled oats, wheat germ, brown sugar or honey, and sometimes dried fruit and nuts.

grant (grant), *v.t.* **1,** to give or confer, esp. in response to a request; as, to *grant* permission; *grant* pardon; **2,** to agree to; admit as true; as, I'll *grant* you that you have a point in this argument:—**take for granted,** to be aware of without questioning or thinking about; as, to *take for granted* a friend's loyalty:—*n.* **1,** the act of granting or the thing granted; as, to receive a land *grant* from the government, to be used for farming; **2,** in *law,* a transfer of property; **3,** money that is provided for education, the arts, research, etc.; as, a *grant* to study AIDS.

gran-u-late (gran′ū-lāt′), *v.t.* [granalat-ed, granulat-ing], **1,** to form into small grains; as, to *granulate* metal; **2,** to roughen the surface of:—*v.i.* to form into small grains; as, maple syrup *granulates.*—*adj.* **gran′u-lar.**

gran-ule (gran′ūl), *n.* a small grain; also, a tiny particle of something.

grape (grāp), *n.* **1,** an edible, juicy, green or purple berry, growing in clusters on a vine and used for making wine, juice, jams, and raisins; **2,** the grapevine.

grape-fruit (grāp′frōōt′), *n.* a large, round, yellow fruit, with yellow or pink pulp, related to the orange, but larger and sourer.

grape-vine (grāp′vīn′), *n.* **1,** a vine on which grapes grow; **2,** a secret or informal way of passing news or rumours from person to person; as, to hear the news through the *grapevine.*

graph (gråf), *n.* a diagram showing by means of dots, lines, pictures, etc., the relationship between any two or more quantities or things; as, a *graph* of the temperature, hour by hour.

graph-ic (graf′ik) or **graph-i-cal** (graf′i-kal), *adj.* **1,** pertaining to the art of writing, drawing, engraving, etc.; as, *graphic* arts; **2,** illustrated by graphs, diagrams, etc.; **3,** vividly written or told; as, a *graphic* account of the accident.

graphical user interface, in *computing,* computer software that simplifies the use of programs, files, etc., by representing them as icons that can be manipulated with a mouse or other pointing device: abbreviated as *GUI* (gōō′i′).

graph-ics (graf′iks), *n.* **1,** the art and science of drawing; **2,** the product of this, esp. with relation to commercial design; **3,** the use of diagrams to calculate; **4,** in *computing,* computer-generated visual images.

graphics card, in *computing,* a circuit that allows computers to display and use graphics on a monitor.

graph-ite (graf′īt), *n.* a kind of soft black carbon used in lead pencils, lubricants, electrodes, coatings, etc.

grap-nel (grap′nel), *n.* **1,** a grappling iron, often with six hooks or claws; **2,** a small anchor with three or more flukes: used on boats, etc.

grap-ple (grap′l), *v.t.* [grap-pled, grap-pling], to grip and hold something fast:—*v.i.* to struggle in, or as in, a fight; as, to *grapple* in wrestling; to *grapple* with a problem:—*n.* **1,** a close fight; a close hold, as in wrestling; **2,** a mechanical device for seizing anything or for anchoring or joining boats, often called a *grappling iron.—n.* **grap′pler.**

grasp (gråsp), *v.t.* **1,** to seize; catch at; hold by clasping; as, to *grasp* the rope; **2,** to take hold of mentally; understand; as, to *grasp* the situation:—*v.i.* to try to seize; as, to *grasp* at power:—*n.* **1,** the grip of the hand; **2,** power of seizing; **3,** mental hold; comprehension; **4,** control; possession.

grasp-ing (gråsʹping), *adj.* greedy.

grass (grås), *n.* **1,** green herbage used to cover lawns, playgrounds, and sport fields and on which grazing animals feed; esp., plants having jointed stems and narrow leaves; **2,** land for grazing; any grass-covered ground; **3,** one of a family of green plants that have long, thin leaves and grow throughout the world, such as sugarcane, bamboo, reeds, and cereal grasses such as wheat, rice, and corn; **4,** *Slang* marijuana.—*adj.* **grass′y.**

grass-hop-per (grås′hop′ėr), *n.* any one of numerous slender, leaping, plant-eating insects, sometimes winged, which can do great damage to crops.

[1]**grate** (grāt), *v.t.* [grat-ed, grat-ing], **1,** to reduce to small particles by rubbing on a rough surface; shred; as, to *grate* cheese; **2,** to rub so as to produce a rasping sound; as, to *grate* fingernails on a chalkboard:—*v.i.* **1,** to produce a harsh noise by rubbing; **2,** to cause annoyance; as, her voice *grates* on me.

[2]**grate** (grāt), *n.* **1,** an iron frame of parallel or crossed bars; as, a *grate* on a prison window; **2,** a framework of iron bars to hold burning fuel; as, a fireplace *grate*:—*v.t.* [grat-ed, grat-ing], to furnish with iron bars; as, to *grate* a window.

grate-ful (grāt′fool), *adj.* **1,** thankful; appreciative; **2,** pleasant; soothing; as, a *grateful* massage.—*adv.* **grate′ful-ly.**—*n.* **grate′fulness.**

grat-er (grā′tėr), *n.* a device with a rough, perforated surface used to shred food, such as cheese, carrots, cabbage, potatoes, etc.

grat-i-fi-ca-tion (grat′i-fi-kā′shun), *n.* **1,** satisfaction; **2,** that which pleases; **3,** reward or recompense.

grat-i-fy (grat′i-fī), *v.t.* [gratified, gratifying], to please; indulge; humour; as, to *gratify* a taste for music.

[1]**grat-ing** (grāt′ing), *adj.* harsh; irritating.

[2]**grat-ing** (grāt′ing), *n.* a framework of crossed or parallel bars, used to cover an opening without shutting out light and air.

gra-tis (grā′tis), *adv.* without charge; free.

grat-i-tude (grat′i-tūd′), *n.* thankfulness.

gra-tu-i-tous (gra-tū′i-tus), *adj.* **1,** freely given; as, *gratuitous* information; **2,** without cause; unwarranted; as, a *gratuitous* insult.

gra-tu-i-ty (gra-tū′i-ti), *n.* **1,** a return for a service or favour, as a tip; **2,** a financial gift or bounty at retirement from the army; as a soldier's *gratuity.*

[1]**grave** (grāv), *v.t.* [*p.t.* graved, *p.p.* grav-en (grāv′en) or graved, *p.pr.* grav-ing], **1,** to shape by cutting with a chisel; sculpture; **2,** to cut, as letters, on a hard surface; engrave; **3,** to impress deeply, as on the mind:—*n.* **1,** a hole dug in the earth as a place of burial; any place of burial; **2,** death; destruction.—*n.* **grav′er; grav′ing; grave′yard′.**

[2]**grave** (grāv), *adj.* [grav-er, grav-est], **1,** needing serious thought; very dangerous or threatening; as, a *grave* problem; a patient in *grave* condition; **2,** of great importance; very serious; as, a *grave* responsibility; **3,** solemn in manner; serious; as, a *grave* face; **4,** not happy; dull; sombre; **5,** low in pitch, as in music.—*adv.* **grave′ly.**

grave accent (gråv), *n.* **1,** a mark [ˋ] over a vowel to show that it is pronounced, as in *belovèd*; **2,** in *French:* **a,** to distinguish words spelled alike, as *là* and *la*; **b,** to suggest an open *e,* as in *père.*

grav-el (grav′el), *n.* material consisting of pieces of rock and pebbles coarser than sand:—*v.t.* [gravelled, gravel-ling], to cover with gravel; as, to *gravel* a road.

grav-en (grāv′en), *adj.* **1,** sculptured; carved; engraved; **2,** deeply impressed:—**graven image,** an idol.

grave-stone (grāv′stōn′), *n.* a stone placed to mark a grave; a tombstone.

grav-i-ta-tion (grav′i-tā′shun), *n.* **1,** the force that draws all bodies in the universe toward one another; **2,** the force that draws all objects on the earth toward its centre; **3,** a natural movement toward a centre of attraction or influence; as, the *gravitation* of animals to a watering hole.—*v.i.* **grav′i-tate′.**—*adj.* **grav′i-ta′tion-al.**

grav-i-ty (grav′i-ti), *n.* [*pl.* gravities], **1,** seriousness; solemnity; as, the *gravity* of those attending a funeral; dignity, as of a judge; **2,** importance; serious significance; as, the *gravity* of war; **3,** the force that draws all objects on the earth toward its centre; also, gravitation of any kind.

gra-vy (grā′vi), *n.* [*pl.* gravies], **1,** the juice that comes out of meat in cooking; also, this juice made into a food dressing or sauce; **2,** *Slang* something that is easy or easily obtained. Also, **gra′vy train′.**

gray (grā), *n.* and *adj.* Same as **grey.**

[1]**graze** (grāz), *v.t.* [grazed, graz-ing], **1,** to feed growing grass to; to pasture; as, to *graze* cattle; **2,** to eat grass from:—*v.i.* to eat grass.—*n.* **graz′er.**

[2]**graze** (grāz), *v.t.* and *v.i.* [grazed, graz-ing], to touch, rub, or scrape lightly; to scratch, or become scratched, by rubbing:—*n.* a slight touch, scratch, or rub.

grease (grēs), *n.* **1,** melted animal fat; **2,** any thick, oily substance:—*v.t.* (grēs; grēz), [greased, greas-ing], **1,** to smear with grease; as, to *grease* a cake pan; **2,** to oil; lubricate; as, to *grease* a car.—*adj.* **greas′y** (grēz′i; grē′si).—*n.* **greas′i-ness.** Also, **greas′y spoon′.**

great (grāt), *adj.* **1,** large in size; big; vast; opposite of *small* or *little*; as, *great* plains stretch to the west; **2,** large in number; as, a *great* herd of cattle; **3,** prolonged; as, a *great* while; a *great* wait; **4,** extreme; as, *great* ignorance; *great* danger; **5,** plentiful; elaborate; as, a *great* feast; in *great* detail; **6,** of remarkable genius, skill, or character; noble; distinguished; excellent; as, a *great* artist; **7,** important; as, *great* things depend on her decision; **8,** considerable in size or intensity; as, a *great* storm; *great* pain; **9,** more than usual; as, take *great* precautions; **10,** more remote in relationship by one generation; as, a *great*-grandfather, a *great*-grandson; **11,** *Colloq.* having unusual skill or knowledge; as, he's *great* at swimming; **12,** *Colloq.* favourite; as, a *great* joke of his; **13,** *Colloq.* intimate; as, *great* friends; **14,** excellent; first-rate; as, a *great* vacation; that's *great*!—**Great War,** the war of 1914–18, which involved many nations of the world: also called *World War I.*—*adv.* **great′ly.**—*n.* **great′ness.**

great–aunt (grāt′–ånt′), *n.* a father's or mother's aunt; grandaunt.

Great Bear, the seven bright stars forming the Big Dipper, or Ursa Major.

great-coat (grāt′kōt′), *n.* in *military*, a heavy overcoat.

great–grand-child (grāt′–grand′child′), *n.* [*pl.* great-grandchildren (-chil′dren)], a child of one's grandson or granddaughter.

great–grand-fa-ther (grāt′–grand′fä′*th*ėr), *n.* the father of one's grandfather or grandmother.

great–grand-moth-er (grāt′–grand′mu*th*′ėr), *n.* the mother of one's grandfather or grandmother.

Great White North, *Slang* comic reference to Canada.

grebe (grēb), *n.* a diving bird with a short body, partly webbed feet, and almost no tail, related to the loon.

greed (grēd), *n.* intense and selfish hunger or desire; as, *greed* for wealth, power, etc.—*n.* **greed′i-ness.**

greed-y (grē′di), *adj.* [greed-i-er, greed-i-est], **1,** showing greed; desiring to have more than one needs or than one's share; **2,** wanting to eat or drink a very large amount.—*adv.* **greed′i-ly.**

Greek (grēk), *n.* **1,** a person who inhabits or originates from Greece; **2,** the language spoken by these people:—*adj.* relating to the country, the people, the language, or the culture of Greece.

green (grēn), *n.* **1,** the colour of growing grass or plants; a colour between blue and yellow; **2,** a grass plot or common; **3,** in *golf*, the closely cut turf around a hole:—**Green,** a supporter of protecting the environment; an environmentalist:—**greens, 1,** green leaves or branches cut for decorations; as, Christmas *greens*; **2,** spinach or similar vegetables, used for food:—*adj.* **1,** having the colour of green; **2,** covered with growing grass or plants; as, *green* hills and valley; **3,** fresh; full of life; **4,** having a sickly colour; **5,** unripe; as, *green* fruit; **6,** not dried; as, *green* wood; **7,** untrained; inexperienced; immature; as, a *green* employee; **8,** jealous; as, *green* with envy; *green*-eyed:—**Green,** environmentalist; as, the *Green* movement.

green-horn (grēn′hôrn), *n.* *Colloq.* an inexperienced person; a simpleton.

green-house (grēn′hous′), *n.* a house made of glass or clear plastic, with a controlled temperature, for growing flowers and plants year round.

greenhouse effect, the warming of the surface of the earth due to solar radiation being trapped in the planet's atmosphere by a layer of gases acting like a greenhouse.

greenhouse gas, any of several gases, such as carbon dioxide, that form the layer that acts as a greenhouse in the earth's atmosphere.

Greenwich mean time (grin′ij; -ich), the mean solar time of the first meridian at Greenwich, England, which is used as the basis of standard time everywhere in the world: abbreviated as *GMT*. Also called *universal time*.

green-wood (grēn′wood′), *n.* a forest in full leaf.

greet (grēt), *v.t.* **1,** to address courteously; welcome; **2,** to respond to; meet or receive; as, to *greet* the good news with cheers; **3,** to receive or meet, as with a demonstration; as, to *greet* the mayor with a parade; **4,** to appear before; as, a view of the sea *greets* us.

greet-ing (grēt′ing), *n.* an expression of goodwill, written or spoken; a welcome:—**greetings,** a friendly message that someone sends; as, holiday *greetings*.

gre-ga-ri-ous (gri-gâr′i-us), *adj.* **1,** of *animals*, living in flocks or herds; as, some wolves are *gregarious* hunters, for they prowl in packs; **2,** of *persons*, fond of company; sociable.

grem-lin (grem′lin), *n.* an imaginary, small, invisible mischievous being, humorously supposed to interfere with a process or mechanism, esp. an airplane; gnome.

gre-nade (gre-nād′), *n.* **1,** a bomb, usually thrown by hand or launched, containing explosives or chemicals; **2,** a flask containing chemicals that scatter when the container is thrown and broken: used for putting out fires.

gren-a-dier (gren′å-dēr′), *n.* originally, a foot soldier who threw grenades; now, any infantry soldier.

grew (gro͞o), *p.t.* of *grow.*

grey or **gray** (grā), *n.* any colour that is formed by mixing black with white:—*adj.* **1,** of the colour grey; hence, dull; as, a *grey* day; **2,** dismal; cheerless; **3,** old; mature; ancient; **4,** not distinct or specific in condition, character, etc.; vague; as, a *grey* area in the rules:—*v.t.* and *v.i.* to make or become grey:—*adj.* having the colour grey.—*adj.* **grey′ish.**

Grey Cup, 1, the annual trophy awarded to the champion Canadian football team; **2,** the game that decides this championship.

grey-hound (grā′hound′), *n.* a graceful, slender dog with long legs, keen sight, and great speed.

Greyhound

grid (grid), *n.* **1,** a grating of parallel or crisscrossed bars; **2,** something resembling a grid, as city streets; **3,** a gridiron for broiling meat, fish, etc.; **4,** numbered squares on a map, chart, etc., to facilitate in locating specific points; **5,** in *electricity,* a perforated lead plate in a storage battery; **6,** in *electricity,* an electrode in a vacuum tube of wire mesh for controlling the flow of electrons.

grid-dle (grid′l), *n.* a metal or soapstone plate used to cook food such as griddlecakes.

grid-dle-cake (grid′l-kāk′), *n.* a thin cake, usually made of wheat or buckwheat flour batter, and cooked on both sides on a griddle; a pancake or flapjack.

grid-i-ron (grid′ī′ėrn), *n.* **1,** an iron utensil with parallel bars, used for broiling meat, fish, or vegetables; grate; grill; **2,** a football field; **3,** anything resembling a gridiron, or marked with parallel lines.

grid-lock (grid′lok′), *n.* **1,** the complete paralysis of traffic, often caused by the blockage of grid streets; **2,** a deadlock, stalemate, or other similar situation; as, political *gridlock.*

grief (grēf), *n.* **1,** deep sorrow as a result of trouble, a death, etc.; also, the cause of sorrow; **2,** failure; disaster; as, his plans came to *grief.*—*adj.* **grief′-strick′en.**

griev-ance (grēv′ans), *n.* **1,** a real or fancied wrong or hardship; also, a cause of complaint; as, taxation without representation was the *grievance* of the Colonies; **2,** complaint by workers, esp. union workers, about unsatisfactory working conditions; as, the workers presented their *grievances* to their employers.

grieve (grēv), *v.t.* [grieved, griev-ing], to cause grief to; afflict mentally; as, his death *grieved* his friends:—*v.i.* to be in sorrow; be very sad; as, to *grieve* for a friend's tragedy.

griev-ous (grēv′us), *adj.* **1,** causing physical or mental suffering; severe; as, *grievous* wounds; *grievous* wrongs; **2,** showing grief; as, a *grievous* expression.

grif-fin (grif′in), *n.* a fabled monster with body and legs of a lion and wings and beak of an eagle.

grill (gril), *n.* **1,** a gridiron for broiling food; as, a barbecue *grill;* **2,** a dish of meat, fish, or vegetables cooked on a gridiron; **3,** a restaurant that serves grilled food:—*v.t.* **1,** to broil (meat, fish, etc.) on a gridiron; **2,** to torment, esp. with merciless questioning; as, police *grill* a criminal.

grim (grim), *adj.* [grim-mer, grim-mest], **1,** stern; forbidding; threatening; as, a *grim* expression; **2,** fierce; cruel; merciless; frightening; horrible; as, a *grim* story; a *grim* murder.

gri-mace (gri-mās′), *n.* a twisting of the face to show disgust or disapproval, or to provoke laughter; also, an unconscious twisting of the face in pain:—*v.i.* [grimaced, grimac-ing], to make faces.

grime (grīm), *n.* dirt rubbed or ground into the skin or other surface:—*v.t.* [grimed, grim-ing], to soil; make dirty.—*adj.* **grim′y.**—*n.* **grim′i-ness.**

grin (grin), *v.i.* [grinned, grin-ning], **1,** to show the teeth in smiling from pleasure; **2,** to show the teeth as the result of pain, anger, etc.; as, the cornered animal *grinned:*—*v.t.* to express by smiling; as, he *grinned* his delight:—*n.* a broad smile.

grind (grīnd), *v.t.* [ground (ground), grind-ing], **1,** to make into powder or small bits by crushing; as, to *grind* wheat, coffee, beef; also, to make by a crushing process; as, to *grind* flour; **2,** to sharpen by wearing down to a fine edge; as, to *grind* a knife; **3,** to rub together; grate; as, to *grind* the teeth; **4,** to oppress; harass; as, to *grind* a suspect down; **5,** to operate by turning a crank; as, to *grind* an organ:—*v.i.* to study hard:—*n. Colloq.* hard or tedious work; as, studying for the chemistry exam was a real *grind;* also, a student who studies hard.—*n.* **grind′er.**

grind-stone (grīnd′stōn′), *n.* a flat, round stone that turns on an axle, used to sharpen tools.

grip (grip), *n.* **1,** a tight grasp; a firm hold; as, take a *grip* on the rope; **2,** holding power; as, a dog with a strong *grip;* **3,** a handle; **4,** a particular way of clasping hands, as among members of a secret society; **5,** a mechanical device for holding something; **6,** mental or physical mastery; control; as, a good *grip* on the situation; get a *grip* (on yourself); **7,** *Colloq.* a valise or small suitcase; **8,** a person who adjusts props and scenery on a stage, television, or film set; **9,** grippe:—*v.t.* [gripped, gripping], **1,** to grasp firmly; seize; **2,** to get and retain the interest of; as, the vivid article *gripped* the reader:—*v.i.* to take a fast hold.

gripe (grīp), *v.t.* [griped, grip-ing], **1,** to cause pain in the bowels of; **2,** to distress; oppress; as, remorse *gripes* the mind:—*v.i.* **1,** to experience pain in the bowels; **2,** to complain; as, to *gripe* about the heavy workload:—*n.* **1,** a firm hold or grip; also, control; **2,** distress; oppression; as, the *gripe* of sorrow; **3,** complaint; as, what's your *gripe*?—**gripes,** pain in the intestines.

grippe (grip), *n.* a severe cold accompanied by fever and bodily aches; influenza.

grip-ping (grip′ing), *adj.* absorbing, intense; as, a *gripping* drama.

gris-ly (griz′li), *adj.* [gris-li-er, gris-li-est], horrible; ghastly; gruesome; grim.

grist (grist), *n.* grain to be ground; also, grain that has been ground:—**grist for the mill,** a source of profit or advantage.

gris-tle (gris′l), *n.* a transparent, tough, elastic substance found in animal tissue; cartilage.—*adj.* **gris′tly.**

grit (grit), *n.* **1,** tiny hard particles, as of sand; **2,** *Colloq.* strength of character; courage; endurance; as, to show true *grit*:—*v.i.* [grit-ted, grit-ting], to make a grating sound:—*v.t.* to grind; grate; as, to *grit* the teeth.—*adj.* **grit′ty.**

Grit (grit), *n. Colloq.* in Canadian politics, a dyed-in-the-wool Liberal; member of the Liberal party.

grits (grits), *n.* grain, such as wheat or oats, hulled and coarsely ground: used as a breakfast food.

griz-zled (griz′ld), *adj.* streaked with grey; grey-haired; as, a *grizzled* old man.

griz-zly (griz′li), *n.* [*pl.* grizzlies], a big, fierce bear of the western North America, with long claws and brown or black fur tipped with grey. Also called *grizzly bear*:—*adj.* [griz-zli-er, griz-zli-est], somewhat grey; grizzled.

groan (grōn), *n.* a low, deep sound of pain or sorrow; a moan:—*v.i.* **1,** to utter a deep sound of pain or sorrow; **2,** to creak, as a rusty hinge; **3,** to be overburdened or oppressed; as, the small chair *groaned* under the weight of the large man:—*v.t.* to express by groans; as, the audience *groaned* its disappointment.

groat (grōt), *n.* a trifling sum; as, not worth a *groat*:—**groats,** crushed grain such as oats.

gro-cer (grō′sėr), *n.* one who sells food and other household supplies; also, one who owns or runs a grocery.

gro-cer-y (grō′sėr-i), *n.* [*pl.* groceries], a grocer's shop; store that sells food and household supplies:—**grocery store,** a store that is smaller than a supermarket and is usually not part of a larger chain of stores:—**groceries,** food and household supplies.

grog (grog), *n.* **1,** an unsweetened mixture of rum or whisky with water; **2,** any intoxicating liquor.

grog-gy (grog′i), *adj.* [grog-gi-er, grog-gi-est], **1,** tipsy; drunk; **2,** dazed; staggering; as, *groggy* from lack of sleep.—*n.* **grog′gi-ness.**

groin (groin), *n.* **1,** the curved hollow where the thigh joins the body; **2,** the curved ridge made by the intersection of two arches:—*v.t.* to build or form with such ridges; as, to *groin* a roof.

groom (grōōm) *n.* **1,** a person who has charge of horses; **2,** a bridegroom; **3,** one of several officers of a royal household:—*v.t.* **1,** to feed, curry, and brush (a horse); **2,** to make neat and clean; as, a cat *grooms* itself daily; **3,** to prepare someone for a certain office, job, responsibility, or purpose; as, to *groom* her as a prime ministerial candidate.

groove (grōōv), *n.* **1,** a channel or furrow, esp. one cut by a tool or worn by flowing water; a rut; **2,** an unchanging way of living or working; routine; habit; **3,** *Slang* an excellent or pleasant experience; something that is fashionable; as, to be in the *groove*:—*v.t.* [grooved, groov-ing], to make a groove in; as, to *groove* a panel:—*v.i. Slang* to have an excellent or pleasant experience with something; enjoy oneself; as, to *groove* on the dance floor.—*adj.* **groovy.**

grope (grōp), *v.i.* [groped, grop-ing], **1,** to feel one's way with the hands, as in the dark; as, to *grope* in the dark for the light switch; **2,** to search in one's mind, as if feeling for something; as, to *grope* for the answer:—*v.t.* to search out, as in the dark; as, to *grope* one's way through a forest.

gros-beak (grōs′bēk′), *n.* any one of a number of songbirds, related to the finches; as, the rose-breasted *grosbeak* or the cardinal *grosbeak.*

gross (grōs), *adj.* **1,** thick; heavy; **2,** indelicate; not polite; coarse; vulgar; disgusting; as, *gross* remarks; *gross* habits; **3,** flagrant; glaring; obviously wrong or bad; as, *gross* errors; **4,** heavy; fat; **5,** very great; shameful; as, *gross* injustice; **6,** whole; total; as, *gross* income: distinguished from *net*:—*n.* **1,** 12 dozen; **2,** the entire amount.—*adv.* **gross′ly.**—*n.* **gross′ness.**

gross domestic product, the total value of all goods and services produced in a country in one year: abbreviated as *GDP.*

gro-tesque (grō-tesk′), *adj.* distorted; odd; fantastic; as, a *grotesque* mask; *grotesque* antics:—*n.* a painting or carving that combines human and animal forms in a fantastic way.

grotto (grot′ō), *n.* [*pl.* grottoes or grottos], **1,** a cavern in the earth; **2,** an artificial cavern, resembling a real cave.

grouch (grouch), *v.i. Colloq.* to grumble; sulk; be morose or ill-tempered:—*n.* one who acts in such a way.—*adj.* **grouch′y.**

[1]**ground** (ground), *p.t.* and *p.p.* of *grind*.

[2]**ground** (ground), *n.* **1,** the surface of the earth; the soil; land; **2,** a topic; subject; as, to be familiar with the *ground* covered in a seminar; **3,** land put to special use; as, a play*ground*; camp *ground*; **4,** distance or extent on a surface; as, to gain *ground* in football; **5,** cause; reason; as, a *ground* for argument; *grounds* for charging the suspect; **6,** in *painting*, a neutral background or undecorated part; **7,** the bottom of a body of water; as, the boat touched *ground*:—**grounds, 1,** lawns and gardens about a house, school, etc.; **2,** dregs; sediment; as, coffee or tea *grounds*:—*v.t.* **1,** to establish; as, to *ground* a government on proper principles; **2,** to bring to rest by touching the earth or bottom; as, to *ground* an airplane or a boat; **3,** to force to stay on the ground; as, the storm *grounded* the plane; also, to restrict someone from going somewhere or doing something as a form of punishment; as, to *ground* a teenager for breaking house rules; **4,** to teach the first principles or foundations to; as, to *ground* a class in science; **5,** in *electricity*, to connect an electric wire with the ground so that its circuit will be safely completed, as a wire conductor; **6,** in *baseball*, to hit a ball so that it bounces or rolls along the ground; hit a grounder; as, he *grounded* the ball:—*v.i.* **1,** to run upon land; as, the vessel *grounded*; **2,** in *baseball*, to hit a grounder:—*adj.* on or near the ground; as, the *ground* floor.

ground-break-ing (ground′brā′king), *adj.* **1,** original, innovative; unique; as, a *groundbreaking* achievement; **2,** relating to the ceremony of breaking ground to symbolize the start of a new project, such as building construction:—*n.* the ceremony symbolizing the start of such a project.—*n.* **ground′break′er.**

ground crew, 1, the personnel in charge of maintaining and repairing aircraft (chiefly technicians); **2,** people in charge of maintaining a baseball, soccer, or football field.

ground-er (groun′dėr), *n.* in *baseball*, etc., a ball that does not rise into the air when batted, but bounces or rolls on the ground.

ground-hog (ground′hog′) *n.* a plump, burrowing animal of the rat family. Also called *woodchuck*.

Groundhog Day, February 2, when the groundhog is supposed to come out, and, traditionally, if it sees its shadow and returns to the burrow, there will be six more weeks of winter.

ground-less (ground′lis), *adj.* without foundation or cause; as, *groundless* fear.

ground-work (ground′wûrk′), *n.* basis; foundation; fundamentals.

ground zero, 1, the centre of an explosion, esp. a nuclear one; as, the spot where the World Trade Center was located became known as *ground zero* after the 9/11 terrorist attacks; **2,** *Colloq.* a starting point; square one; as, to return to *ground zero*.

group (grōōp), *n.* **1,** a number of people or objects that belong together or are considered as a whole; as, the *group* of football players waited for the coach; **2,** a cluster; as, a *group* of houses; a *group* of people waited outside the bank:—*v.t.* to combine into a group; as, to *group* the items by weight and colour:—*v.i.* to gather in a group; as, the people *grouped* around the fire.

group-ware (grōōp′wâr′), *n.* in *computing*, software that can be used by several people at once on a network.

grouse (grous), *n.* [*pl.* grouse], **1,** any of several game birds having, usually, a mottled reddish-brown plumage, as the partridge, or ruffed grouse, spruce grouse, and the prairie chicken; **2,** *Colloq.* a complaint or complainer:—*v.i.* [groused, grous-ing], *Colloq.* to complain or grumble; as, she *groused* about her chores.

grove (grōv), *n.* a small wood or group of trees standing together; as, a maple *grove*; also, a group of cultivated fruit trees; as, an orange *grove*.

grov-el (grov′l; gruv′l), *v.i.* [grovelled, grovelling], **1,** to lie face downward in fear or in seeking favour; to crawl; as, to *grovel* before a king; **2,** to humble oneself basely.—*n.* **grov′el-ler.**

grow (grō), *v.t.* [*p.t.* grew (grōō), *p.p.* grown (grōn), *p.pr.* grow-ing], **1,** to produce by cultivation; as, to *grow* vegetables; **2,** to cause or allow to grow; as, to *grow* a beard:—*v.i.* **1,** to become bigger by natural development; as, puppies *grow* rapidly; **2,** to arise or spring up naturally; as, moss *grows* in damp places; **3,** to increase; as, to *grow* in understanding; the town's population *grew*; **4,** to become gradually; as, to *grow* stronger; **5,** to become attached, or become one; as, the broken bone *grew* together.—*n.* **grow′er.**

growl (groul), *n.* **1,** a deep, throaty, and threatening sound, as made by a dog; **2,** an angry, muttered complaint:—*v.i.* **1,** to snarl like a dog; **2,** to find fault in a surly tone; grumble:—*v.t.* to say in an angry, muttering tone; as, he *growled* his answer.

grown-up (grōn′up′), *n.* an adult.—*adj.* **grown′ -up′.**

growth (grōth), *n.* **1,** the progressive increase of animal or vegetable bodies; process of growing; as, the *growth* of a plant, child, etc.; **2,** increase; as, *growth* in skill; **3,** that which is produced; result; as, a season's *growth* of corn; **4,** an abnormal mass, such as a tumour, cancer, etc.

grub (grub), *v.t.* [grubbed, grub-bing], to dig up; root out of the ground, as stumps:—*v.i.* **1,** to dig in the earth; **2,** to drudge or toil; do menial labour; **3,** *Slang* to eat:—*n.* **1,** the wormlike larva of some insects; **2,** drudge; **3,** *Slang* food.—*adj.* **grub′by.**

grub-stake (grub′stāk′), *n.* **1,** money, supplies, etc., advanced to a prospector in return for a share in any profit from his or her discoveries; **2,** in Canada, the funds for food and other provisions; also, a store that sells such provisions.

grudge (gruj), *n.* lengthy, secret ill will against a person; as, to hold a *grudge*:—*v.t.* [grudged, grudg-ing], to envy; as, she *grudges* me my good luck; also, to begrudge; as, he *grudges* every dollar he spends.—*adv.* **grudg′ing-ly.**

gru-el (grōō′el), *n.* a thin porridge made by boiling oatmeal or flour in water or milk:—*v.t.* [gru-elled, gru-el-ling or gru-eled, gru-el-ing], *Colloq.* to question relentlessly; exhaust.

gru-el-ling (grōō′el-ing), *adj.* a severe, trying, or exhausting experience; as, the minivan was submitted to a *gruelling* road test.

grue-some (grōō′sum), *adj.* revolting and horrifying, repulsive; as, the decaying corpse was a *gruesome* sight.

gruff (gruf), *adj.* rough; surly; harsh; as, a *gruff* reply; hoarse; as, a *gruff* voice.—*adv.* **gruff′ly.**—*n.* **gruff′ness.**

grum-ble (grum′bl), *v.i.* [grum-bled, grum-bling], to murmur discontentedly; growl; find fault:—*v.t.* to mutter; as, he *grumbled* a reply:—*n.* a surly speech or reply; growl.—*n.* **grum′bler.**

grump-y (grump′i), *adj.* [grump-i-er, grump-i-est], surly; dissatisfied; as, a *grumpy* old man.—*adv.* **grump′i-ly.**—*n.* **grump′i-ness.**

grunt (grunt), *n.* **1,** the gruff sound made by a hog; also, any similar sound; as, the old woman bent down with a *grunt*; **2,** a fish that makes a grunting noise when caught:—*v.t.* to utter with a gruff sound; as, to *grunt* assent:—*v.i.* to make a grunting noise; as, the boy *grunted* as he lifted the heavy box.

GST (jē′es/tē′), *abbrev.* short for *goods and services tax.*

gua-no (gwä′nō), *n.* the manure of sea birds and bats, esp. from islands off the coast of Peru, used widely as fertilizer.

guar-an-tee or **guar-an-ty** (gar′an-tē′; gar′en-ti), *n.* **1,** anything that makes something else sure or certain; as, a *guarantee* of quality; **2,** a statement or certificate that something is as represented; as, a one-year *guarantee* goes with this scanner; **3,** in *law*: **a,** a promise made by one person that another will fulfill an agreement to a third; **b,** one who becomes surety for the performance of another's promises; **c,** property pledged as security for the performance of promises:—*v.t.* [guaranteed, guarantee-ing], **1,** to make sure; as, to *guarantee* success; **2,** to give a guarantee for; as, to guarantee a car for the first 50,000 kilometres; **3,** in *law*, to be legally responsible for.—*n.* **guar′an-tor** (gar′an-tôr; gar′an-tôr′).

guaranteed investment certificate (gar′an-tēd′), *n.* in Canada, a type of investment that guarantees a set rate of interest on deposit for a fixed term: abbreviated as *GIC*.

guard (gärd), *v.t.* **1,** to protect; preserve by caution; defend; keep safe; **2,** to watch over; as, to *guard* a prisoner; **3,** in *sports*, such as hockey, to stay close to a player from the other team to try to prevent him or her from scoring:—*v.i.* to watch; be cautious; as, to *guard* against disease:—*n.* **1,** defence against injury or attack; **2,** a state or duty of watchfulness or attention; as, be on *guard*; **3,** a position of defence, as in fencing; **4,** a device for protection; as, a mud*guard*; **5,** a person or body of people employed for control, as in a prison; **6,** in *sports*, a player whose job is to prevent scoring by the opposing team.

guard-ed (gär′did), *adj.* **1,** defended; protected; as, a heavily *guarded* fort; **2,** careful; cautious; as, a *guarded* answer.—*adv.* **guard′ed-ly.**—*n.* **guard′ ed-ness.**

guard-i-an (gär′di-an), *n.* **1,** one who legally has the care of a person who is young or who is not able to take care of himself or herself; a warden; as, a *guardian* of a child; **2,** one who or that which protects anything.

guards-man (gärdz′man), *n.* [*pl.* guards-men (-men)], **1,** a man employed for defence or watching; guard; **2,** an officer or soldier of any military body termed *Guards*.

guer-ril-la or **gue-ril-la** (ge-ril′a), *n.* and *adj.* one or pertaining to one who carries on irregular warfare; esp., one of a small, independent group engaged in harassing an enemy in wartime with raids, sabotage, etc.; as, the *guerrillas* ambushed the enemy troops; *guerrilla* warfare.

guess (ges), *n.* a hasty conclusion; an opinion formed without knowledge:—*v.t.* **1,** to form an opinion of without certain knowledge; **2,** to surmise; estimate; as, to *guess* the height of someone; **3,** to solve correctly by surmising; as, to *guess* a riddle; **4,** to think; suppose:—*v.i.* to form a chance judgment.

guest (gest), *n.* **1,** one who is entertained at the house or table of another; a visitor; **2,** a patron of a hotel, motel, or restaurant.

guff (guf), *n. Slang* foolish talk; nonsense.

guf-faw (gu-fô′), *n.* a coarse or loud burst of laughter:—*v.i.* to laugh noisily.

GUI (gōō′), *abbrev.* short for *graphical user interface.*

guid-ance (gīd′ans), *n.* **1,** direction; leadership; influence; **2,** the act of counselling students regarding their education and future prospects.

guide (gīd), *n.* **1,** one who or that which directs; **2,** a person hired to conduct travellers, explorers, campers, etc., in an unfamiliar place; also, a person who leads visitors through a museum, famous building, amusement park, etc.: also called *tour guide*; **3,** that by which one finds his or her way; a guidebook; guidepost; as, a restaurant *guide*:—*v.t.* [guid-ed, guid-ing], **1,** to lead; conduct; pilot; as, an usher at the movie theatre *guided* the people to their seats; **2,** to direct; instruct.

guide-book (gīd′book′), *n.* a book of information, esp. for travellers.

guide-post (gīd′pōst′), *n.* a post or sign to direct travellers at forks in a road or at crossroads.

guild or **gild** (gild), *n.* **1,** an association for mutual protection and aid of people in a common trade or profession; as, the Writers *Guild* of Canada; **2,** a society for a useful or charitable purpose.

guile (gīl), *n.* deceit; cunning; trickery; as, he's full of *guile*.—*adv.* **guile′ful-ly.**

guile-less (gīl′les), *adj.* innocent; frank; as, a *guileless* child.—*adv.* **guile′less-ly.**

guil-lo-tine (gil′ō-tēn′), *n.* **1,** a machine for cutting off a person's head by means of a knife that descends between two posts, esp. during the French Revolution; **2,** a device for cutting paper:—*v.t.* (gil′ō-tēn′), [guillotined, guillotin-ing], to behead or cut with a guillotine.

guilt (gilti), *n.* **1,** the fact of having done a wrong, esp. an act punishable by law; as, his *guilt* was proved by his own confession; **2,** wrongdoing; sin; as, she felt a lot of *guilt* for being disloyal to her friend.—*adj.* **guilt′less.**

guilt-y (gil′ti), *adj.* [guilt-i-er, guilt-i-est], **1,** responsible for a crime; having committed a wrong; as, he was judged *guilty* by the jury; **2,** having done something wrong; showing guilt; not innocent; as, to be *guilty* of eating the last chocolate bar; a *guilty* look.—*adv.* **guilt′i-ly.**

guin-ea pig (gi′ni′), *n.* **1,** a small, short-tailed rod- ent, usually white, black, or tan, originally from South America, often kept as a pet or used in biological research; **2,** a subject of a test or experiment; as, the students in her class are *guinea pigs* for the school's new conservation program.

GUINEA PIG

guise (gīz), *n.* **1,** manner or external appearance; likeness; disguise; as, the *guise* of a rock star; **2,** cloak or pretence; as, to cheat under the *guise* of friendship.

gui-tar (gi-tär′), *n.* a long-necked musical instrument with a hollow, wooden body and six or more strings, played with the fingers by plucking or strumming.

gulch (gulch), *n.* a narrow, deep valley or ravine; gorge.

gulf (gulf), *n.* **1,** an arm of the sea extending into the land, larger than a bay; **2,** a deep hollow in the earth; an abyss; **3,** wide separation or difference; as, the *gulf* between the two opposing sides.

gull (gul), a large, graceful, web-footed sea bird, usually white with grey or black markings, known all over the world, valuable as a harbour scavenger. Also called *seagull.*

gul-let (gul′it), *n.* the tube by which food travels from the mouth to the stomach; esophagus; also, the throat.

gul-li-ble (gul′i-bl), *adj.* easily fooled.—*n.* **gul′li-bil′i-ty.**

gul-ly (gul′i), *n.* [*pl.* gullies], a channel worn by water; a narrow ravine or ditch:—*v.t.* [gullied, gully-ing], to wear channels in.

gulp (gulp), *v.t.* **1,** to swallow hastily or greedily; **2,** to check; keep back; as, to *gulp* down angry words or tears:—*n.* a big swallow; a mouthful; a choke.

[1]**gum** (gum), *n.* the firm pink flesh around the teeth of human beings and animals.

[2]**gum** (gum), *n.* **1,** a sticky substance that comes out of certain trees and shrubs and hardens on the surface; as, *gum* arabic; spruce *gum*; **2,** any natural gum prepared for some industrial use, as to coat the back of stamps or envelopes, in drugs, or in chewing gum; **3,** a gum tree:—*v.t.* [gummed, gum-ming], to smear or fasten with gum:—*v.i.* to become stiff or sticky; to exude gum, as does a tree.—*adj.* **gum′my.**—*n.* **gum′ mi-ness.**

gum-bo (gum′bō), *n.* **1,** a silt or mud, as in the western prairies, that becomes sticky when wet; **2,** a soup thickened with okra pods; **3,** the okra plant and pod.

gum-drop (gum′drop′), *n.* a candy made of flavoured gelatin, cast in moulds, and sweetened with sugar.

gump-tion (gump′shun), *n. Colloq.* energy; initiative; spirit; as, he hasn't *gumption* enough to speak up for himself.

gum-shoe (gum′shōō′), *n.* **1,** a rubber shoe; **2,** *Colloq.* a detective:—**gumshoes,** sneakers; running shoes:—*v.i. Colloq.* to move about stealthily; sneak.

gum tree, a gum-yielding tree, as the sweet gum.

gum-wood (gum′wood′), *n.* wood from a gum tree.

gun (gun), *n.* **1,** a weapon for discharging bullets or shells through a metal tube by the force of an explosive, as a cannon, rifle, pistol, or revolver; **2,** any similar implement; as, a staple *gun*; **3,** a discharge of cannon given as an honour:—*v.i.* [gunned, gun-ning], to shoot or hunt with a gun:—*v.t.* to speed up a motor or engine suddenly; as, to *gun* the engine of a car.—*n.* **gun′fire′; gun′play′; gun′run′ner; gun′shot′.**

gun-boat (gun′bōt′), *n.* a small, armed patrol ship.

gun-man (gun′man), *n.* [*pl.* gunmen (-men)], **1,** an armed robber or murderer; **2,** a person skilled in the use of guns.

gun–met-al (gun′–met′l), *n.* and *adj.* **1,** a variety of bronze, formerly used in making cannons, etc., but now supplanted by steel; **2,** the colour of this bronze, dark grey with a blue or purple tinge.

gun-ner (gun′ėr), *n.* **1,** one who works a gun; **2,** one who hunts with a gun; **3,** in the navy, an officer in charge of the ship's ordnance or military supplies.—*n.* **gun′ner-y.**

gun-ny (gun′i), *n.* a strong, coarse fabric made from jute or hemp, used for bags, esp. *gunny* sacks.

gun-pow-der (gun′pou′dėr), *n.* an explosive powder made of sulphur, saltpetre, and charcoal, used in blasting, fireworks, and guns.

gup-py (gup′i), *n.* a tiny, tropical, live-bearing, freshwater fish, popular in home aquariums: the males have brilliant colouring.

gur-gle (gûr′gl), *n.* a broken, bubbling sound, as of a liquid when poured from a bottle:—*v.i.* [gur-gled, gur-gling], to make a low bubbling sound.

gush (gush), *n.* **1,** a sudden and free flow of liquid, as of blood from a wound, or of water from a spring; **2,** a violent outbreak, as of anger; **3,** *Colloq.* silly, sentimental talk or display of affection:—*v.i.* **1,** to flow out suddenly with force; flow abundantly; as, oil *gushed* from the well; **2,** *Colloq.* to display affection and enthusiasm in a silly, showy manner.—*adj.* **gush′y.**

gush-er (gush′ėr), *n.* **1,** *Colloq.* one who gushes; esp., one who makes a show of sentiment; **2,** an oil or gas well with a large natural flow.

gus-set (gus′it), *n.* **1,** a small triangular piece sewn into a garment, glove, etc., to make it stronger or roomier; **2,** a triangular metal plate used to strengthen angles and joints.

gust (gust), *n.* **1,** a sudden rush of wind; **2,** a violent outburst, as of laughter.—*adj.* **gust′y; gust′ing.**—*adv.* **gust′i-ly.**

gus-ta-to-ry (gus′ta-to-ri), *adj.* relating to the sense of taste; as the *gustatory* nerve, buds, etc.

gus-to (gus′tō), *n.* zest; relish; enjoyment; as, to eat or drink with great *gusto.*

gut (gut), *n.* **1,** the intestinal canal; **2,** catgut; **3,** a narrow channel; also, a gully:—*adj.* **1,** *Colloq.* from deep inside; as, *gut* instinct; **2,** *Slang* basic; fundamental; as, the *gut* problem in this plan:—*v.t.* [gut-ted, gut-ting], **1,** to extract the entrails from; **2,** to plunder, or empty; destroy the inside of; as, fire *gutted* the building.

gut-ter (gut′ėr), *n.* **1,** a trough under the eaves of a building to carry off rain water; **2,** a slope at the roadside to carry off surface water; **3,** any shallow trench:—*v.t.* to cut into, or make furrows in:—*v.i.* to become channelled, as the rim of a burning candle.

gut-ter-snipe (gut′ėr-snīp′), *n.* *Colloq.* a street urchin; gamin.

gut-tur-al (gut′ėr-al), *adj.* **1,** having to do with the throat; **2,** formed in the throat; harsh; as, a *guttural* sound:—*n.* a sound formed or modified in the throat, as *g* in *go* or *goose.*—*adv.* **gut′tur-al-ly.**

[1]guy (gī), *n.* a rope, chain, wire, etc., used to secure or keep something steady; as, the *guy* of a tent pole:—*v.t.* to fasten or steady with a guy.

[2]guy (gī), *n.* **1,** *Colloq.* any man or boy; **2,** *Colloq.* any person:—*v.t.* *Colloq.* to ridicule; as, his friends *guyed* him good-naturedly.

guz-zle (guz′l), *v.t.* and *v.i.* [guz-zled, guz-zling], to eat or drink greedily and to excess; as, to *guzzle* beer:—*n.* **guz′zler.**

gym (jim), *n.* **1,** *Colloq.* short for *gymnasium*; **2,** a course in physical education that is taught in a school or college.

gym-na-si-um (jim-nā′zi-um), *n.* [*pl.* gymnasiums (jim-nā′zi-umz) or gymnasia (jim-nā′zi-a)], a room or building with equipment for physical exercise or training and for indoor sports.

gym-nast (jim′nast), *n.* one who is expert in physical exercises or gymnastics, esp. one skilled in the use of gymnasium apparatus.

gym-nas-tics (jim-nas′tiks), *n.pl.* physical exercises for developing the body's muscles, agility, and balance.

gyn-e-col-o-gist (jin′i-kol′o-jist; jī′-; gī′-), *n.* a medical specialist who deals with the reproductive functions and diseases peculiar to women.—*n.* **gyn′e-col′o-gy.**

gyp (jip), *v.t.* *Slang* to swindle; cheat.

gyp-sum (jip′sum), *n.* a *common mineral,* calcium sulphate ($CaSO_4$ $2H_2O$), used for making plaster of Paris and for soil dressings or fertilizer.

Gyp-sy or **Gip-sy** (jip′si), *n.* [*pl.* Gypsies], **1,** a person belonging to a wandering group of people who are thought to have come from India hundreds of years ago; **2,** the language of the Gypsies: also called *Romany*; **3,** a person who looks or acts like a Gypsy.

gy-rate (jī′rāt; jī-rāt′), *v.i.* to whirl; revolve; spiral; as, a *gyrating* ballerina.—*n.* **gy-ra′tion.**

gy-ro-scope (jī′rō-skōp; gī′rō-skōp), *n.* an apparatus consisting of a wheel mounted in a ring so as to move freely in one or more directions: it is used to illustrate the laws of rotation, and to stabilize airplanes, ships, etc.—*adj.* **gy′ro-scop′ic** (jī′rō-skop′ik; gī′rō-skop′ik).

gy-ro-sta-tics (jī′rō-sta′tiks), *n.* in *physics,* the science that deals with rotating bodies.

H

H, h (āch), *n.* [*pl.* H's, h's], the eighth letter of the alphabet, following G.

ha-be-as cor-pus (hā′bi-us kôr′pus), in *law*, a writ requiring a prisoner to be brought before a judge or court to determine the justice of his or her detention.

hab-er-dash-er (hab′ėr-dash′ėr), *n.* a dealer in men's clothing and furnishings, as hats, ties, socks, etc.—*n.* **hab′er-dash′er-y.**

hab-it (hab′it), *n.* **1,** an action so often repeated as to become a fixed characteristic or addiction, and which is usually hard to stop or control; as, smoking is a bad *habit;* **2,** usual physical or mental condition or way of behaving or acting; custom; as, a cheerful *habit* of mind; it is his *habit* to get up at six; **3,** a special kind of clothing or outfit; as, a riding *habit;* **4,** the distinctive dress worn by members of a religious order; as, a nun's *habit*:—*v.t.* to dress; clothe.

hab-it-a-ble (hab′it-a-bl), *adj.* fit to be lived in; as, repairs have made the house *habitable.*

hab-it-ant (hab′i-tant), *n.* **1,** a dweller; permanent resident; **2,** (a′bē-tän′), in Canada (esp. Québec), a French-Canadian farmer.

hab-i-tat (hab′i-tat′), *n.* **1,** the natural abode of an animal or plant; as, a pond is a natural *habitat* for water lilies; **2,** a dwelling place; habitation.

hab-i-ta-tion (hab′i-tā′shun), *n.* **1,** an abode or dwelling place; **2,** the act of inhabiting or dwelling in; as, the house is ready for *habitation.*

ha-bit-u-al (ha-bit′ū-al), *adj.* **1,** formed or acquired by custom; usual; as, *habitual* promptness; **2,** given over to a regular practice, or habit; as, a *habitual* coffee drinker.—*adv.* **ha-bit′u-al-ly.**

ha-bit-u-ate (ha-bit′ū-āt′), *v.t.* and *v.i.* [-ated, -ating], to accustom; familiarize; as, to *habituate* her to hardship; to *habituate* to a large backyard.

ha-cien-da (ä-syān′dä; has′i-en′da), *n.* in Spanish America, a landed estate, as a ranch or plantation; an establishment for farming, mining, or stock raising.

[1]hack (hak), *v.t.* **1,** to cut unevenly or irregularly; **2,** *Slang* to tolerate; as, she couldn't *hack* the traffic and noise, so she moved to the country:—*v.t.* and *v.i.* **1,** in *computing,* to access a computer file or network without permission or through illegal means; **2,** *Colloq.* in *computing,* to change or refine a computer program:—*v.i.* **1,** to make rough cuts; **2,** to give short dry coughs:—*n.* **1,** a cutting or notching tool; **2,** a cut or gash; **3,** a short dry cough.

[2]hack (hak), *n.* **1,** a horse that may be hired for work; also, a saddle or carriage horse; a hackney; **2,** a carriage or hackney that may be hired; **3,** *Colloq.* a taxi; **4,** one who hires out his or her services for pay, esp. in literary work; a drudge:—*v.i.* **1,** to ride a horse; **2,** to drive a taxi; **3,** to work as a hack.

hack-er (hak′ėr), *n. Colloq.* **1,** a taxi driver; hackie; **2,** in *computing,* a person who accesses a computer file or network without permission or through illegal means; **3,** in *computing,* a person who enjoys experimenting with computers; also, someone who is interested in computers as a hobby; a computer buff; **4,** a person who enjoys a particular sport or game; as, an in-line skating *hack.*

hack-le (hak′l), *n.* **1,** any of the feathers on a bird's neck (esp. a rooster's), or the bristles on a dog's neck, that rise to indicate rage or anger; **2,** an artificial fishing fly made from a rooster's hackles.

hack-ney (hak′ni), *n.* [*pl.* hackneys], **1,** a horse used chiefly for riding or driving; **2,** a coach; or hack kept for hire:—*adj.* let out for hire; as, a *hackney* coach.

hack-neyed (hak′nid), *adj.* commonplace; trite; overused; as, a *hackneyed* phrase, such as "dry as a bone."

hack-saw (hak′sô′), *n.* a fine-toothed saw for cutting metal.

had (had), *p.t.* and *p.p.* of *have.*

had-dock (had′uk), *n.* a North Atlantic food fish of the cod family.

Ha-des or **ha-des** (hā′dēz), *n.* in the *Bible* and in *Greek mythology,* the place or abode below the earth of departed spirits; hell.

hae-mo-glo-bin (hē′mō-glō′bin; hem-), *n.* Same as **hemoglobin.**

hae-mo-phil-i-a (hēm′ō-fil′i-a; hem-), *n.* Same as **hemophilia.**

haem-or-rhage (hem′o-rij), *n.* Same as **hemorrhage.**

haem-or-rhoids (hem′o-roidz), *n.pl.* Same as **hemorrhoids.**

haft (håft), *n.* a handle, as of a cutting tool, dagger, or knife.

hag (hag), *n.* **1,** a witch; **2,** a wicked ugly old woman.

hag-gard (hag′ėrd), *adj.* worn and anxious in appearance; as, *haggard* from worry.

hag-gis (hag′is), *n.* a dish (esp. in Scotland) made of the heart, liver, etc., of a sheep or calf, highly seasoned, minced with onions and oatmeal, and boiled in a sheep's stomach.

hag-gle (hag′l), *v.i.* [hag-gled, hag-gling], to argue or wrangle, esp. about a price; as, to *haggle* over the price of a used car.

Hai-da (hī′da), *n.* **1,** a member of the Haida, Native peoples of western British Columbia and Alaska, who are known for their totem poles; **2,** the language of the Haida people:—*adj.* having to do with the Haida people or language.

hai-ku (hī′ko͞o), *n.* [*pl.* haiku or haikus], a form of poetry that originated in Japan, which is made up of three lines of different lengths that do not rhyme.

[1]**hail** (hāl), *n.* **1,** small, icy particles that fall from the sky under certain conditions such as thunderstorms; **2,** anything falling abundantly and with great force; as, a *hail* of shrapnel; *hail* of criticism:—*v.i.* to come down in the form of hail:—*v.t.* to shower; pour down; as, they *hailed* blows upon me.

[2]**hail** (hāl), *n.* a salutation; greeting:—*v.t.* **1,** to greet; salute; praise; as, he *hailed* me as I was entering the store; to *hail* the new leader; **2,** to get someone's attention by shouting or waving; accost; as, to *hail* a taxi:—**hail from,** to come from; as, she *hails from* the Northwest Territories.

hail-stone (hāl′stōn′), *n.* a single particle of hail or frozen rain.

hair (hâr), *n.* **1,** the mass of threadlike growths forming the coat or fur of an animal; the natural growth on a person's head and skin; any one of these threadlike growths; **2,** a hairlike fibre growing on the stems and leaves of plants; **3,** a very small distance, degree, or quantity; as, the bullet missed him by a *hair.*—*adj.* **hair′y; hair′less; hair′split′ting.**—*n.* **hair′i-ness.** Also, **hair′brush′; hair′cut′; hair′do′; hair′dres′ser; hair′ style′; hairs′breadth′.**

hair-pin (hâr′pin′), *n.* **1,** a two-pronged pin, as of wire or plastic, for holding the hair in place; **2,** a sharp U-shaped bend or turn, as in a road, river, etc.:—*adj.* something resembling a hairpin; as, a *hairpin* turn.

hair-spring (hâr′spring′), *n.* the delicate hairlike spring that regulates the balance wheel in a watch.

hal-berd (hal′bėrd) or **hal-bert** (hal′bėrt), *n.* a weapon of the Middle Ages that was a combination spear and battle-axe.

hale (hāl), *adj.* sound in body; robust; as, a *hale* old man.

half (håf), *n.* [*pl.* halves (håvz)], **1,** one of two equal parts; as, a *half* of an apple; **2,** in certain sports, one of the two equal time periods that make up a game:—*adj.* **1,** forming a half; amounting to half; as, a *half* kilogram; **2,** related through one parent only; as, a *half* brother or sister:—*adv.* **1,** to the extent or amount of a half; as, the gas tank is *half* full; **2,** partially; as, to be *half* asleep.

half-back (håf′bak′), *n.* in *football,* a player behind the forward line.

half-heart-ed (håf′här′ted), *adj.* uninterested; not enthusiastic; as, a *halfhearted* response to a suggestion.—*adv.* **half′-heart′ed-ly.**—*n.* **half′heart′ed-ness.**

half-life (håf′–līf′), *n.* **1,** in *nuclear physics,* the time required for half of the atoms of a radioactive element to disintegrate: thus, plutonium 238 has a *half-life* of some 50 years; **2,** in *biology,* the time required for half of the drug or substance in a living organism or ecosystem to be used up or eliminated.

half-mast (håf–måst′), *n.* a point near the middle of a mast or staff; as, a flag flies at *half-mast* in token of mourning or as a signal of distress.

half nelson, in *wrestling,* a hold consisting of thrusting an arm from behind under an opponent's arm and placing the hand on the nape of his or her neck.

half-track (håf′–trak′), *n.* a motor vehicle, the rear drive wheels of which operate on caterpillar treads, as in some army trucks.

half-way (håf′wā′), *adj.* **1,** situated midway between two points; as, a *halfway* house; **2,** midway between two states or conditions; as, twilight, the *halfway* state between night and day; **3,** partial; not extreme; as, *halfway* measures:—*adv.* **1,** midway; at half the distance; as, they met *halfway* between the two towns; **2,** partially; as, he *halfway* consented.

half-wit-ted (håf′–wit′ed), *adj.* mentally lacking; feeble-minded: considered offensive.—*n.* **half′–wit′.**—*adv.* **half′–wit′ted-ly.**

hal-i-but (hal′i-but; hol′i-but), *n.* [*pl.* halibut or halibuts], the largest of the flatfish, prized as food, found in the North Atlantic and Pacific oceans.

hal-i-to-sis (hal′i-tō′sis), *n.* offensive or bad breath.

hall (hôl), *n.* **1,** the main living room of a castle; **2,** a large building or room for entertainments; as, a dance *hall;* concert *hall;* dining *hall;* **3,** a public or government building; as, the City *Hall;* **4,** a university building used for residence, instruction, etc.; **5,** a passageway in a house or other building from which other rooms open; corridor; **6,** the passage or room just inside the entry to a house or building; **7,** a manor house.

hal-le-lu-jah (hal′e-lo͞o′ya), *n.* an exclamation or song of praise to God:—*interj.* praise be to God!

hall-mark (hôl′märk′), *n.* **1,** a mark or stamp of high quality, as on gold or silver articles; **2,** a distinguishing feature or attribute; as, attention to detail is a *hallmark* of an events coordinator; **3,** something that indicates good quality; as, loyalty is a *hallmark* of a true friend.

hal-lo or **hul-lo** (ha-lō′), *interj.* Same as **hello.**

hal-low (hal′ō), *v.t.* **1,** to make sacred; mark or set apart as holy; as, this ground has been *hallowed* by the brave men who died here; **2,** to honour as holy; revere.—*adj.* **hal′lowed.**

Hal-low-een or **Hal-low-e′en** (hal′ō-wēn′), *n.* the evening of October 31, which precedes All-Saints' Day or Allhallows, celebrated with fun, masquerading, and going door to door for treats.

hal-lu-ci-na-tion (ha-lū′si-nā′shun), *n.* **1,** the seeing or hearing of a thing or sound, seemingly (but not) real, as in some mental disorders; delusion; **2,** the object supposedly seen or heard.

hall-way (hôl′wā′), *n.* a corridor; entrance hall.

ha-lo (hā′lō), *n.* [*pl.* halos or haloes], **1,** a circle of light around a shining body, such as the sun or moon; **2,** in pictures, a bright ring drawn or painted around the head of a holy person or saint; **3,** the splendour or glory with which one endows a person or an object highly prized:—*v.t.* to surround with a halo.

hal-o-gen (hal′ō-jen), *n.* **1,** an element (chlorine, bromine, iodine, astatine, or fluorine) that forms a salt by uniting with a metal; **2,** a type of very bright and long-lasting lamp or bulb that uses halogen.

halt (hôlt), *n.* **1,** a stop or pause for a time; **2,** a hesitation or waiver; as, a *halt* in her testimony:—*v.i.* **1,** to come to a stop for a longer or shorter period; **2,** to hesitate or waiver; as, she *halted* before diving into the cold water:—*v.t.* to bring to a stop; as, to *halt* a horse.

hal-ter (hôl′tėr), *n.* **1,** a rope or strap for leading or fastening a horse or other animal; **2,** a rope for hanging criminals; **3,** a woman's or girl's top, tied behind the neck and back, leaving the arms and back bare:—*v.t.* to put a halter on an animal.

halt-ing (hôl′ting), *adj.* hesitating; faltering; as, *halting* speech.

halve (håv), *v.t.* [halved, halv-ing], **1,** to divide into two equal parts, as an apple; to share equally; **2,** to lessen by half; as, the teacher *halved* the assignment.

¹ham (ham), *n.* the thigh of an animal prepared for food; esp., the thigh of a hog, salted or smoked; also, the meat so prepared.

²ham (ham), *Colloq. n.* **1,** a licensed amateur radio operator; **2,** an ostentatious performer, esp. a stage or movie actor who overacts to get the audience's attention:—*adj.* **1,** pertaining to an amateur radio operator or the equipment; as, a *ham* radio; **2,** ostentatious; exaggerated:—*v.t.* and *v.i.* to overact; as, to *ham* her lines; he likes to *ham* it up.

ham-bur-ger, (ham′bûr-gėr) *n.* **1,** ground beef; **2,** a patty of cooked ground beef; **3,** a sandwich in the form of a round bun, made with such a patty. Also called *burger.*

ham–hand-ed (ham′–han′did), *adj. Colloq.* clumsy, awkward, or heavy-handed.

ham-let (ham′let), *n.* a small village.

ham-mer (ham′ėr), *n.* **1,** an instrument with a handle and an iron head, used for driving nails, beating metals, etc.; **2,** anything resembling this tool in its action or shape; as, the *hammer* of a piano that hits a string to make a sound:—*v.t.* **1,** to pound or beat with a hammer or a similar instrument; **2,** to drive into place by pounding; **3,** to produce by hard work; as, to *hammer* out a plan:—*v.i.* **1,** to strike heavy blows; **2,** to make a noise like that of a hammer blow; **3,** to work hard.

ham-mer-head (ham′ėr-hed′), *n.* a voracious species of shark with extensions from the head that give it a double-headed hammer appearance.

HAMMERHEAD SHARK

ham-mer-lock (ham′ėr–lok′), *n.* in *wrestling,* a hold in which one twists an opponent's arm and bends it behind his or her back.

ham-mock (ham′uk), *n.* a swinging bed or cot, usually of network or canvas, suspended between two supports by cords at the ends.

¹ham-per (ham′pėr), *n.* a large basket, often wickerwork with a cover, used to carry or hold clothes, food, etc.; as, a clothes *hamper*; picnic *hamper.*

²ham-per (ham′pėr), *v.t.* to obstruct; hinder; as, the snow *hampered* the traffic.

ham-ster (ham′stėr), *n.* a stout-bodied, ratlike, burrowing rodent of the Old World, with large cheek pouches for carrying grain, often raised as a pet.

ham-string (ham′string′), *n.* the large tendons at the back of the knee in humans or the back of the hock of quadruped animals:—*v.t.* **1,** to cripple by cutting these tendons; **2,** to disable or make ineffective; as, to *hamstring* a plan.

hand (hand), *n.* **1,** that portion of the human arm extending downward from the wrist, made up of the palm, four fingers, and a thumb, and fitted for grasping objects; also, a like part on an ape, an opossum, or certain other animals that grasp; **2,** an index or pointer on a dial; as, the *hands* of a clock; **3,** a measure of 10 centimetres: used chiefly in measuring the height of horses; **4,** deftness or skill; as, try your *hand* at this game; **5,** direction to the left or right; as, on the right *hand* of the passage; **6,** penmanship; handwriting; **7,** an employee who labours with his or her hands; **8,** a player in a game of cards; also, the cards held by a player; a single round in a game of cards; **9,** possession; control; as, the matter is in your *hands*; **10,** assistance; as, lend a *hand*; **11,** a pledge, esp. of betrothal; **12,** source; as, knowledge at first*hand*; **13,** one who is skilled at a particular thing; as, a hired *hand* to do yard work; **14,** a round of applause; clapping; as, to give the singer a big *hand*:—*v.t.* **1,** to pass or transfer by hand; as, *hand* me the book; **2,** to pass (down) from time past; as, these dishes were *handed* down to me from my grandmother; **3,** to lead or assist with the hand; as, he *handed* her into the car:—*adj.* pertaining to the hand; used or carried by the hand.—*adj.* **hand′like.**

hand-bag (hand′bag′), *n.* **1,** a satchel; **2,** a small bag to hold a wallet, powder, etc.; purse.

hand-ball (hand′bôl′), *n.* a game played in a walled court, or against a single wall, in which the players bat the ball against a wall with their gloved hands.

hand-bar-row (hand′bar′ō), *n.* a barrow, without a wheel, carried by four handles.

hand-bill (hand′bil′), *n.* a printed advertisement distributed by hand.

hand-book (hand′book′), *n.* a small guidebook; manual.

hand-breadth or **hand's–breadth** or **hand's breadth** (hand′bredth′; handz′–bredth′; handz′ bredth′), *n.* a measure of about 6.5 to 10 centimetres, the width of a hand.

hand-cuff (hand′kuf′), *n.* one of a pair of metal, braceletlike devices, locked around a prisoner's wrist to prevent his or her escape:—*v.t.* to restrain with handcuffs.

hand-ful (hand′fool), *n.* [*pl.* handfuls],**1,** the amount a hand can hold at one time; **2,** a small quantity or number; as, a *handful* of students remained after class.

hand-i-cap (han′di-kap), *n.* **1,** a disadvantage or advantage imposed on contestants in order to equalize chances of winning for all; also, a race, contest, or game in which such a condition exists; **2,** a hindrance; diadvantage; as, a sore leg is a *handicap* to a skater:—*v.t.* [handicapped, handicapping], **1,** to be a disadvantage to; **2,** to impose a handicap upon.—*n.* **hand′i-cap′per.**

hand-i-craft (han′di-kråft), *n.* a trade or craft requiring a skilled hand; manual skill; also, the items thus made.—*n.* **hand′i-crafts′man.**

hand-i-ly (han′di-li), *adv.* expertly; deftly; as, she won *handily*.

hand-i-work (han′di-wûrk′), *n.* **1,** work done by hand; **2,** anything done by personal effort or the result of such effort.

hand-ker-chief (hang′kėr-chif; -chēf), *n.* **1,** a square piece of cloth for wiping the face, nose, etc.; **2,** a piece of cloth worn around the neck; kerchief.

han-dle (han′dl), *n.* that part of a tool, vessel, etc., that is grasped, turned, or lifted by the hand:—*v.t.* [han-dled, handling], **1,** to hold, touch, or move with the hand; **2,** to manage; control; as, he *handled* the glider with skill; to *handle* the refreshments for the party; **3,** to deal with or treat in a given way; as, he *handles* complaints tactfully; **4,** to buy and sell; deal in; as, a broker *handles* stocks and bonds:—*v.i.* to act or move in a certain way; as, the car *handles* very well on icy roads.

hand-made (hand′mād′), *adj.* made by hand.

hand-maid or **hand-maid-en** (hand′mād′; hand′mā′den), *n.* a female servant or personal attendant.

hand-shake (hand′shāk′), *n.* the holding and shaking of another person's right hand as a greeting or to show friendship or agreement:—**golden handshake**, a generous sum of money given at early retirement.

hand-some (han′sum), *adj.* [handsom-er, handsom-est], **1,** pleasing to look upon; good-looking; as, the *handsome* young man; **2,** strong or dignified; as, a *handsome* black stallion; ample; generous; as, a very *handsome* gift or reward.—*adv.* **hand′some-ly.**—*n.* **hand′some-ness.**

hand-spring (hand′spring′), *n.* in *gymnastics,* a feat in which one places one or both hands on the ground and turns the body in the air so as to land on the feet.

hand-stand (hand′stand′), *n.* in *gymnastics,* the act of supporting the body with hands while the legs and body are stretched straight in the air.

hand-writ-ing (hand′rīt′ing), *n.* **1,** a person's style of penmanship; **2,** writing done by hand, rather than typed or printed by machine.

hand-y (han′di), *adj.* [hand-i-er, hand-i-est], **1,** skillful with the hands; as, to be *handy* with knitting needles; **2,** convenient; nearby; within easy reach; as, a *handy* stool to reach high shelves; **3,** helpful or easy to use; convenient; as, a *handy* kitchen gadget.—*n.* **hand′i-ness.**

hang (hang), *v.t.* [*p.t.* and *p.p.* hung (hung) or, in def. 3, hanged (hangd), *p.pr.* hanging], **1,** to attach to something above; suspend; as, to *hang* curtains; **2,** to fasten (something) so that it can swing to and fro; as, to *hang* a door; **3,** to suspend by the neck until dead; as, the murderer was *hanged*; **4,** to cause to droop; as, he *hung* his head; **5,** to decorate; as, she *hung* wallpaper:—*v.i.* **1,** to dangle; be suspended; **2,** to hover threateningly; as, ill fortune *hangs* over him; **3,** to rest; depend; as, my decision *hangs* on your answer; **4,** to die by hanging; **5,** to hold for support; as, *hang* on to me; **6,** to float above; be in the air over; hover; as, the smoke *hung* in the air; **7,** in *computing,* of a computer program or system, to stop operating suddenly or become stuck for some unexplained reason; as, my computer got *hung* up, so I needed to reboot:—**hang back,** to hold off; stay back:—*n.* **1,** the manner in which a thing hangs; as, the *hang* of a coat; **2,** *Colloq.*: **a,** the manner of doing or using; knack; as, to get the *hang* of the computer game; **b,** general idea; as, the *hang* of a story.

hang-ar (hang′ėr; hang′gär), *n.* a shed or building for housing airplanes and other aircraft.

hang-dog (hang′dôg′), *adj.* ashamed; cowering; as, a *hangdog* expression.

hang-er (hang′ėr), *n.* **1,** a wire, wood, or plastic frame on which clothes are hung; **2,** anything used to hang something, such as a hook for hanging a picture; **3,** someone who hangs something; as, a wallpaper *hanger;* **4,** a device used for hanging something.

hanger–on (hang′ėr–on′), *n.* [*pl.* hangers-on (-ėrz–on′)], **1,** one who, though not wanted, attaches himself or herself to another person, group, etc.; parasite; **2,** a dependent; follower; favour seeker.

hang-ing (hang′ing), *n.* **1,** the act of suspending; **2,** execution by suspending a person by the neck until dead:—**hangings,** covering, such as tapestry, for walls, windows, etc.

hang-man (hang′man), *n.* [*pl.* hangmen (-men)], formerly, a public officer whose duty it was to execute convicted criminals by hanging.

hang-nail (hang′nāl′), *n.* a small piece of loose skin around a fingernail.

hang-ov-er (hang′ō′vėr), *n.* **1,** *Colloq.* a survival from the past, as a custom; **2,** *Slang* nausea, headache, etc., resulting from too much drinking of alcohol the previous night.

hank (hangk), *n.* coil or skein, as of woollen or cotton yarn.

han-ker (hang′kėr), *v.i.* to yearn or crave; as, to *hanker* after pleasure.

Han-sard (han′sėrd), *n.* the official printed reports of the proceedings of British or Canadian Parliaments.

han-som (han′sum), *n.* a two-wheeled, horse-driven, covered cab, with an outside seat for the driver at the back. Also called *hansom cab.*

Ha-nuk-kah or **Ha-nuk-ah** or **Cha-nu-kah** (khä′nu-ka; hä′nu-ka), *n.* the Jewish celebration of the Festival of Lights, for eight days, usually in December.

hap-haz-ard (hap′haz′ėrd), *adj.* accidental; as, a *haphazard* remark:—*adv.* by chance:—*n.* a chance occurrence.

hap-less (hap′lis), *adj.* unlucky; unfortunate.—*adv.* **hap′less-ly.**

hap-pen (hap′en), *v.i.* **1,** to occur; as, how did it *happen?* **2,** to occur by chance; as, I *happened* to be there; **3,** to come upon by chance or accident; as, we *happened* on a house in the woods; **4,** to cause a change, esp. a bad change; as, what *happened* to the fax machine? It worked yesterday.

hap-pen-ing (hap′en-ing), *n.* an occurrence; an incident or event.

hap-py (hap′i), *adj.* [hap-pi-er, hap-pi-est], **1,** enjoying or expressing pleasure; glad; as, a *happy* girl with a *happy* smile; **2,** fortunate; lucky; as, a *happy* turn of events; **3,** pleased or willing; as, we would be *happy* to have you join us for dinner.—*adv.* **hap′pi-ly.**—*n.* **hap′pi-ness.**

hap-py–go–lucky (hap′i–gō–luk′i), *adj.* **1,** carefree; lighthearted; **2,** trusting to luck.

ha-ra-ki-ri or **ha-ri-ka-ri** (hå′ra–ki′ri; hå′ri–kå′ri), *n.* the Japanese ritual of suicide by disembowelling with a knife, formerly practised by the samurai or ruling class.

ha-rangue (ha-rang′), *n.* a public speech; usually, a loud, ranting address:—*v.i.* and *v.t.* [harangued, harangu-ing], to address in a loud, ranting speech.

har-ass (har′as; ha-ras′), *v.t.* **1,** to annoy or vex continuously; as, she was *harassed* by daily complaints; **2,** to plunder; lay waste; pillage; as, the troops *harassed* the village.—*n.* **har′ass-ment.**

har-bin-ger (här′bin-jėr), *n.* a herald; forerunner; as, the rooster is the *harbinger* of daybreak.

har-bour or **har-bor** (här′bėr), *n.* **1,** a partly sheltered portion of a sea, lake, etc., which serves as a port or haven for ships; **2,** any place of refuge or safety; shelter or sanctuary; as, a safe *harbour* among the trees:—*v.t.* **1,** to give lodging to; shelter; as, to *harbour* a criminal; **2,** to cherish; indulge; hold or keep within the mind; as, to *harbour* resentment:—*v.i.* to find or take shelter.

hard (härd), *adj.* **1,** solid; firm; not easily pierced or broken; as, *hard* bone; **2,** difficult; as, a *hard* task; **3,** difficult to bear; as, *hard* times; **4,** hardy; strong; as, *hard* as steel; **5,** done with exertion or energy; as, *hard* labour; **6,** industrious; as, a *hard* worker; **7,** harsh; unsympathetic; as, a *hard* boss; **8,** severe in action or effect; as, a *hard* winter; **9,** containing a high percentage of alcohol; as, *hard* liquor; **10,** violent; as, a *hard* rain; **11,** pronounced with the sound of *g* in "go" or *c* in "come," not soft like the *g* in "gin" or *c* in "cent"; **12,** *Colloq.* real; as, *hard* facts:—*adv.* **1,** vigorously; as, work *hard;* **2,** firmly; securely; as, bound *hard* and fast; **3,** with a struggle; as, friendship dies *hard;* **4,** close; near; as, *hard* by; **5,** severely; as, the loss bore *hard* on me.

hard–boiled (hard′–boild′), *adj.* **1,** boiled until hard; as, *hard-boiled* eggs; **2,** *Colloq.* callous; unyielding to appeal, argument, sentiment, etc.; tough; as, a *hard-boiled* person.

hard copy, documents printed on paper, esp. those produced by a computer.

hard drive, in *computing,* a hard plate or drive made from metal and coated with magnetic material, built into a computer to store and read a very large amount of information. Also called *hard disk drive.*

hard-en (här′dn), *v.t.* **1,** to make firm, solid, or unyielding; as, to *harden* steel; *harden* one's will; **2,** to toughen; make hardy; as, to *harden* the body:—*v.i.* to become firm, solid, harsh, unyielding, hardy, etc.—*n.* **hard′en-er.**—*adj.* **hard′ened.**

hard-head-ed (härd′hed′ed), *adj.* **1,** having shrewd judgment; practical; **2,** obstinate; stubborn.

hard-heart-ed (härd′här′ted), *adj.* unfeeling; cruel.—*n.* **hard′heart′ed-ness.**

har-di-hood (här′di-hood), *n.* robustness; boldness; audacity; impudence.

har-di-ly (här′di-li), *adv.* boldly.

hard-ly (härd′li), *adv.* **1,** with difficulty; **2,** scarcely; only just; almost not; as, he has *hardly* recovered; **3,** severely; as, to deal *hardly* with someone; **4,** not likely; probably not; as, you could *hardly* expect the plane to wait for you.

hard-ness (härd′nis), *n.* the quality or state of being solid, unyielding, etc.; as, the *hardness* of rock; *hardness* of heart.

hard-pan (härd′pan′), *n.* **1,** a hard, cementlike soil layer difficult to dig through; **2,** the fundamentals of something.

hard rock, a type of popular music with simple, fast songs, featuring amplified electric guitars and loud simple vocals and rhythms.

hard-ship (härd′ship), *n.* that which is hard to bear; sorrow, pain, or trouble; as, the *hardships* of early pioneers.

hard-top (härd′top′), *n.* a car designed to look like a convertible but with a rigid metal top; also, any car or motorboat with a permanent rigid top.

hard-ware (härd′wâr′), *n.* **1,** in *computing,* the physical components of a computer system, including such equipment as the CPU, monitor, keyboard, printer, etc. Compare *software;* **2,** articles manufactured from metal, as cutlery, kitchen utensils, tools, etc., which are used to make or fix other items.

hard-wood (härd′wood′), *n.* a heavy, close-grained wood, such as oak, maple, or cherry; deciduous trees, as opposed to coniferous:—*adj.* made or composed of hardwood; as, *hardwood* floors; *hardwood* forest.

har-dy (här′di), *adj.* [har-di-er, har-di-est], **1,** robust; capable of bearing hardship; **2,** bold; resolute; **3,** of plants, able to survive winter weather.—*n.* **har′di-ness.**

hare (hâr), *n.* a timid, swift-footed animal, like a rabbit, with a divided upper lip, long ears, and a short fluffy tail.

hare-brained (hâr′brānd′), *adj.* foolish; heedless; rash; as, a *harebrained* fool.

hare-lip (hâr′lip′), *n. usu. offensive,* a lip, usually the upper, that from birth is divided or cleft like that of a hare.

ha-rem (hâr′em; hā′rem), *n.* **1,** the part of a Muslim house where the women live; **2,** the wives and female relatives living in this part of the house.

hark (härk), *v.i.* to listen to:—**hark back,** to go back; as, her clothes *hark back* to the sixties.

har-le-quin (här′le-kwin; -kin), *n.* a buffoon or clown, usually masked, wearing spangled tights of many colours, and carrying a wooden sword or magic wand.

har-lot (här′lot), *n.* a prostitute.

harm (härm), *n.* **1,** injury; damage; **2,** moral evil or wrongdoing:—*v.t.* to hurt or damage.

harm-ful (härm′fool), *adj.* hurtful; injurious; damaging; as, *harmful* drugs.—*adv.* **harm′ful-ly.**

harm-less (härm′lis), *adj.* having no power to damage or hurt; as, a *harmless* snake; also, producing no ill effect; as, a *harmless* drug.—*adv.* **harm′less-ly.**

har-mon-ic (här-mon′ik), *adj.* **1,** relating to the science dealing with musical sounds or harmony; **2,** agreeing in sound; harmonious; concordant:—*n.* a tone, higher than the main tone, and heard along with it; an overtone:—**harmonics,** *n.pl.* used as *sing.* the science dealing with musical sounds.

har-mon-i-ca (här-mon′i-ka), *n.* a small musical wind instrument, provided with metal reeds, which is played by the mouth; a mouth organ.

har-mo-ni-ous (här-mō′ni-us), *adj.* **1,** combining so as to form a pleasing and agreeable whole; as, *harmonious* voices; **2,** agreeing in action and feeling; peaceable; friendly; as, *harmonious* neighbours.—*adv.* **har-mo′ni-ous-ly.**

har-mo-ni-um (här-mō′ni-um), *n.* a small organ that is played by forcing air through reeds; a reed organ.

har-mo-nize (här′mo-nīz′), *v.t.* [harmonized, harmoniz-ing], **1,** to arrange in musical harmony; **2,** to bring into agreement; as, to *harmonize* colours; **3,** to cause to agree; reconcile; as, to *harmonize* conflicting opinions:—*v.i.* **1,** to play or sing in harmony; **2,** to go suitably or pleasingly together; as, these colours *harmonize.*

harmonized sales tax, the tax that combines the goods and services tax

(GST) with the provincial sales tax in Nova Scotia, New Brunswick, and Newfoundland.

har-mo-ny (här′mo-ni), *n.* [*pl.* harmonies], **1,** the combination of parts so as to form an agreeable or connected whole; as, the *harmony* of motion in dancing; to work in *harmony*; **2,** agreement in feeling, opinions, etc.; as, *harmony* between Canada and the U.S.; **3,** the arrangement of similar passages, as in the Bible, so as to show their points of agreement or disagreement; as, a *harmony* of the four Gospels; **4,** in *music*, the combination of musical notes so as to form chords, or the science treating of this; also, the composition of a piece of music with reference to its chords; **5,** musical notes played or sung to go along with a melody.

har-ness (här′nes), *n.* **1,** the fittings used to attach a horse or other animal to a wagon, plough, or other vehicle to be pulled; **2,** any set of straps used to fasten or control something; as, a parachute *harness*:—*v.t.* **1,** to put a harness on; **2,** to make (something) produce power, by installing machinery; control and put to work; as, to *harness* the power of a waterfall to produce electricity.

harp (härp), *n.* a stringed musical instrument of triangular shape, played with the fingers:—*v.i.* **1,** to play on a harp; **2,** to dwell unduly on some particular subject; as, to *harp* on the dangers of riding a bicycle without a helmet.—*n.* **harp′er; harp′ist.**

har-poon (här-pōōn′), *n.* a long spear with a rope attached, used to strike and kill whales or large fish:—*v.t.* to strike or kill with a harpoon.—*n.* **har-poon′er.**

harp-si-chord (härp′si-kôrd), *n.* an instrument with wire strings and a keyboard, similar to the grand piano in form and arrangement, but sounding more like a harp, in general use before the piano.

Har-py (här′pi), *n.* in *Greek mythology*, a ravenous monster with a woman's head and a bird's body:—**harpy,** a greedy, grasping person.

har-ri-dan (har′i-dan), *n.* a disreputable, shrewish woman; a vicious old hag.

har-row (har′ō), *n.* a farming implement with sharp iron or wooden teeth, or sharp steel disks, for breaking up clods or covering sown seeds with earth:—*v.t.* **1,** to drive a harrow over; as, to *harrow* ploughed land; **2,** to distress deeply; as, his feelings were *harrowed* by his friend's misery.

har-ry (har′i), *v.t.* [harried, harry-ing], **1,** to plunder; lay waste; as, the invaders *harried* the country; **2,** to annoy or vex; worry; as, the upcoming exam *harried* her.

harsh (härsh), *adj.* **1,** wounding the feelings; cruel; severe; as, the *harsh* employer; a *harsh* punishment; **2,** rough or irritating to the hearing or touch; as, a *harsh* voice; a *harsh* piece of cloth; also, disagreeable; rigorous; as, a *harsh* climate.—*adv.* **harsh′ly.**—*n.* **harsh′ness.**

hart (härt), *n.* a male of the red deer over five years of age; a stag.

har-um–scar-um (hâr′um–skâr′um), *adj. Colloq.* reckless; irresponsible; wild; rash; as, a *harum-scarum* child:—*adv.* in such a way; as, to drive *harum-scarum*:—*n.* such a person.

har-vest (här′vist), *n.* **1,** a crop, as of grain or fruit, ready for gathering or already gathered; as, the corn *harvest*; **2,** the gathering in of such a crop; **3,** the season, usually late summer or early fall, for gathering in a crop; **4,** result; reward; as, his good marks are the *harvest* of hard work:—*v.t.* to gather in (a crop); as, to *harvest* wheat.—*n.* **har′vest-er.**

has (haz), *3rd pers. sing. pres.* of *have.*

has–been (haz′–bin′), *n. Colloq.* a person or thing once effective, useful, etc., but no longer so.

hash (hash), *v.t.* **1,** to chop into small pieces, as meat; **2,** to botch; bungle; **3,** to discuss in depth; as, to *hash* over the issues at hand:—*n.* **1,** a mixture of meat and vegetables, chopped into small pieces and cooked; also, the dish so prepared; **2,** a mixture or jumble; **3,** a botch; mess; **4,** *Slang* hashish.

hash-ish (hash′ēsh; hash′ish), *n.* a preparation of dried hemp, smoked, drunk, or chewed for its intoxicating or narcotic effect.

hasp (håsp), *n.* a hinged metal clasp for a door or a box, which folds over a staple and is fastened with a pin or padlock.

has-sle (ha′sl), *Colloq. v.t.* [hassled, hassling], to bother or annoy; as, to *hassle* her about the way she dresses:—*v.i.* to argue; as, to *hassle* with your parents:—*n.* **1,** something that bothers; a problem or difficulty; as, to take a taxi because parking is too much of a *hassle*; **2,** argument; fight.

has-sock (has′uk), *n.* **1,** a heavy, stuffed cushion, used to kneel or sit upon; a footstool; **2,** a tuft of coarse grass.

haste (hāst), *n.* **1,** quickness of movement; speed; **2,** undue, rash, or excessive speed; as, in her *haste*, she forgot her homework at home:—*v.t.* and *v.i.* [hast-ed, hast-ing], to hurry.

has-ten (hās′n), *v.t.* to cause (a person) to hurry; to urge (work) forward:—*v.i.* to move with speed; hurry; as, *hasten* home.

hast-y (hās′ti), *adj.* [hast-i-er, hast-i-est], **1,** speedy; hurried; as, a *hasty* departure; **2,** careless; superficial; done too quickly; as, *hasty* work; **3,** quick-tempered; impetuous.—*adv.* **hast′i-ly.**—*n.* **hast′i-ness.**

hat (hat), *n.* a covering for the head, usually with a crown and brim, worn outside for protection or decoration. Also, **hat′band′; hat′box′; hat′pin′.**

[1]**hatch** (hach), *n.* **1,** an opening in a deck, roof, floor, etc., often with a removable cover or trap door; a hatchway; **2,** any similar trap door or small opening; **3,** a cover for a hatch.

[2]**hatch** (hach), *v.t.* **1,** to produce young from; as, to *hatch* eggs; **2,** to produce (young) from eggs; as, to *hatch* chickens; **3,** to plot or plan; as, to *hatch* a scheme:—*v.i.* **1,** to yield young; as, the eggs *hatched* in three weeks; **2,** to come forth from the egg, as a young chick:—*n.* the brood of young produced at one time.—*n.* **hatch′er-y.**

hatch-et (hach′et), *n.* a small axe with a hammer head and short handle. Also, **hatch′et job′; hatch′et man′.**

hatch-way (hach′wā′), *n.* an opening, as in the deck of a vessel, for passage below; a hatch.

hate (hāt), *v.t.* [hat-ed, hat-ing], **1,** to dislike thoroughly; detest; **2,** to be averse to; dislike; as, I *hate* sewing:—*n.* extreme abhorrence or dislike; hatred.—*n.* **hat′er.**

hate-ful (hāt′fool), *adj.* deserving or causing hatred; abominable; as, murder is a *hateful* thing; also, displaying hatred; as, a *hateful* glance.—*adv.* **hate′ful-ly.**—*n.* **hate′ful-ness.**

ha-tred (hā′tred), *n.* intense dislike; enmity.

hat trick, 1, in *sports,* such as hockey, scoring of three goals in one game; **2,** any three similar successes; as, this election was a *hat trick* for the prime minister.

haugh-ty (hô′ti), *adj.* [haugh-ti-er, haugh-ti-est], proud; disdainful; conceited; as, a *haughty* classmate; a *haughty* gesture.—*adv.* **haugh′ti-ly.**—*n.* **haugh′ti-ness.**

haul (hôl), *v.t.* **1,** to pull or draw forcibly; to drag; **2,** to move or transport by pulling; as, to *haul* a load:—*v.i.* **1,** to change the course of a ship; as, the sailors *hauled* into the wind; **2,** to change direction; as, the wind *hauls* to the west:—*n.* **1,** a strong pull; **2,** a single pulling in of a net; also, the quantity of fish caught at one time; **3,** booty; loot; an amount collected; as, the thief made a good *haul*; a big *haul* of presents; **4,** the distance over which anything is drawn; as, a *haul* of 30 kilometres to the next town.—*n.* **haul′age; haul′er.**

haunch (hônch; hänch), *n.* **1,** the hip and buttocks of a human or other animal; the hind part; **2,** of meats, the leg and loin taken together; esp., a joint of venison or mutton.

haunt (hônt; hänt), *n.* a place of frequent meeting or resort; as, the *haunt* of outlaws; to return to our old *haunts* such as the diner:—*v.t.* **1,** to visit or return to a place as a ghost, spirit, or other strange form; as, the ghost *haunted* the old mansion; **2,** to visit frequently or habitually; **3,** to trouble persistently; as, dreams *haunt* me.

hau-teur (ō′tör′; hō-tûr′), *n.* haughtiness; arrogance; disdainful pride.

have (hav), *v.t.* [*pres. sing.* I have, you have, he has (haz), *pl.* have, *p.t.* and *p.p.* had (had), *p.pr.* hav-ing], **1,** to hold; possess; own; as, to *have* money; **2,** to be compelled; as, I *have* to sell it; **3,** to hold or harbour in one's mind; as, to *have* a grudge; **4,** in a general way, to engage in, experience, suffer, enjoy, etc.; as, to *have* a good time or an argument; to *have* a headache; **5,** to bear (a child); **6,** to cause to do or to be done; as, *have* her go; *have* this bill paid; **7,** to allow; permit; as, I will not *have* noise in the library; **8,** to obtain; get; as, he *has* his way; **9,** to state as a fact; as, the papers *have* it that the economy is in a recession; **10,** to beat; get the better of; as, he *had* me in that argument; **11,** to show; use; as, to *have* mercy; **12,** as a helping verb, used to form the present perfect, past perfect, and future perfect tenses of verbs, indicating action occurring before the present, past, or future; as, I *have* gone; I *had* gone; I *shall have* gone.

ha-ven (hā′ven), *n.* **1,** a sheltered anchorage for ships; **2,** any harbour or shelter.

have–not (hav′–not′), *adj.* a person or thing with little or no wealth or success; as, a *have-not* province.

hav-er-sack (hav′ėr-sak′), *n.* a strong canvas bag or pack for carrying provisions or rations, esp. on a march or hike.

hav-oc (hav′uk), *n.* devastation; ruin.

[1]**hawk** (hôk), *n.* any of several strong, swift-flying birds of prey, as falcons, buzzards, kites, etc.:—*v.i.* to hunt wild birds or game with the help of hawks.—*adj.* and *n.* **hawk′ing.**

[2]**hawk** (hôk), *v.t.* to peddle; offer goods for sale in a public place by calling out or shouting; as, to *hawk* hot dogs at the game.—*n.* **hawk′er.**

haw-thorn (hô′thôrn), *n.* any of several thorny trees or shrubs, with white or pink fragrant flowers and small red berries; also, the flower.

hay (hā), *n.* various grasses, clover, etc., cut and dried for fodder:—*v.i.* to make hay.

hay fe-ver, an allergy affecting the nose, eyes, and throat, caused by the pollen of certain plants, such as ragweed, goldenrod, etc.

hay-mak-er (hā′māk′ėr), *n.* **1,** one who handles hay, by spreading it, etc.; **2,** equipment for spreading and drying hay; **3,** *Slang* in *boxing,* a wild swinging blow.

hay-mow (hā′mou′), *n.* **1,** a mass of hay laid up in a barn; **2,** the part of a barn in which the hay is stored; hayloft.

hay-rick (hā′rik′), *n.* a large pile of hay stacked in the open air; a haystack.

hay·stack (hā′stak′), *n.* a stack or pile of hay in the open air; a hayrick.

hay·wire (hā′wīr′), *n.* wire for baling hay, esp. when tangled after removal from bales:—*adv.* and *adj. Slang* **1,** out of order; wrong; **2,** crazy; disturbed; as, he went *haywire.*

haz·ard (haz′ėrd), *n.* **1,** an old gambling game at dice, the precursor of craps; **2,** chance; risk; danger; **3,** in *golf,* an obstacle, such as rough ground, a stream, or a sand pit:—*v.t.* **1,** to subject to risk, or take the risk of; as, to *hazard* one's fortune; to *hazard* a loss; **2,** to offer; venture; as, to *hazard* a guess.—*adj.* **haz′ard·ous.**

hazardous waste, unwanted, toxic byproducts of industrial production or nuclear generation that could harm the environment.

[1]haze (hāz), *n.* **1,** a slight fog, mist, or smoke in the atmosphere; **2,** mental vagueness or confusion.—*n.* **ha′zi·ness.**

[2]haze (hāz), *v.t.* [hazed, haz·ing], to play practical jokes upon, as in college or university initiations; bully; as, to *haze* the new students.—*n.* **haz′er.**

ha·zel (hā′zl), *n.* **1,** any of various shrubs or small trees bearing a small, rounded, edible nut; **2,** the nut borne by this tree; a filbert; **3,** a light, reddish-brown colour:—*adj.* light reddish brown.—*n.* **ha′zel·nut′.**

ha·zy (hā′zi), *adj.* [ha·zi·er, ha·zi·est], **1,** covered by or blurred with haze; as, a *hazy* summer day; **2,** not clear; dim; blurred; as, a picture that is *hazy* around the edges; **3,** confused; as, *hazy* thinking.

H-bomb (āch′bom′), *n. abbrev.* for **hydrogen bomb.**

he (hē), *masc. pron.* of the third person [*nominative,* he; *possessive,* his (hiz); *objective,* him (him)]. **1,** one particular man or boy; as, where is Carlos? *He*'s absent; **2,** anyone; as, *he* who runs may read:—*n.* [*pl.* he's or hes (hēz)], a man or boy; male.

head (hed), *n.* **1,** the uppermost part of the body in humans, or, in most animals, the foremost part, containing the mouth, eyes, nose, ears, and brain; **2,** the top, front, or upper end of anything, as of a flagpole, paradecane, stairs, page, etc.; **3,** anything resembling a head; esp. the top part of a plant, or a round compact bloom; as, a *head* of lettuce; a *head* of clover; a *head* of a pin; **4,** imagination; intelligence; the power of the brain; mind; as, a story out of one's *head;* he talks over my *head;* a good *head* for figures; **5,** mental calm or control; as, to keep one's *head;* **6,** the front or foremost part of anything, as of a parade or an army; also, the bow of a ship; **7,** the position of command or leadership; as, to be at the *head* of a firm; also, a leader or chief; as, the prime minister is the *head* of the government; **8,** a separate topic; a class or subject; as, optics comes under the *head* of science; **9,** a head's length; as, the horse won by a *head;* **10,** a person; as, to charge so much per *head;* also, [*pl.* head], a single one; an individual; as, 50 *head* of sheep; **11,** an important or crucial point; crisis; as, the situation came to a *head;* **12,** source; beginning; as, the *head* of a river; **13,** force; pressure; as, a *head* of steam; **14,** a cape or promontory, as of land:—**heads,** the side of a coin showing a head:—*adj.* **1,** principal; chief; as, a *head* clerk; **2,** coming toward one; as, a *head* wind; **3,** placed at the front or top:—*v.t.* **1,** to lead; direct; as, to *head* an expedition; **2,** to take the first place in; as, she *heads* her class; **3,** to get in front of; as, to *head* off a horse; prevent; as, to *head* off a quarrel; **4,** in *soccer,* to strike the ball with the head:—*v.i.* **1,** to move in a given direction; as, to *head* south; **2,** to form a head, as a plant or flower. Also, **head′band′; head′phone′; head′room′; head′start′; head′wind′.**

head·ache (hed′āk′), *n.* a continuous pain in the head.

head·bang·er (hed′bang′ėr), *n. Slang* a fan of heavy metal music.

head·cheese (hed′chēz′), *n.* jellied meat made esp. from the head and feet of pigs, cut up, boiled, and pressed.

head·dress (hed′dres′), *n.* **1,** a covering, often ornamental, for the head; **2,** a manner of wearing the hair.

head·first, *adj.* and *adv.* **1,** headlong; as, a *headfirst* dive; to dive *headfirst;* **2,** in rash, thoughtless haste.—*adv.* **head′fore′most′.**

head·hunt·er (hed′hun′tėr), *n.* **1,** *Slang* an individual or company that recruits skilled personnel for corporations; **2,** someone who collects the heads of dead opponents as trophies.—*v.i.* **head′hunt′.**—*n.* and *adj.* **head′hunt′ing.**

head·ing (hed′ing), *n.* **1,** something at the top of a page, such as the title of a chapter, page, etc.; **2,** a title that sets apart or describes a section such as a chapter, paragraph, subject, or topic discussed; **3,** the direction of a vehicle as indicated by a compass; as, a *heading* of west.

head·land (hed′land), *n.* a cape or promontory.

head·light (hed′līt′), *n.* a bright light on the front of a car, bicycle, train, etc.

head·line (hed′līn′), *n.* a heading, often in large type, at the top of a newspaper or magazine column or at the beginning of an article; also, a similar title above an advertisement.—*n.* **head′lin′er** (the principal performer in a show).

head·lock (hed′lok′), *n.* in *wrestling,* a hold in which a wrestler locks his or her arm around an opponent's head.

head·long (hed′lông), *adv.* **1,** head foremost; **2,** rashly:—*adj.* **1,** rash; violent; thoughtless; as, a *headlong* decision; **2,** plunging headfirst.

head-man (hed′man′), *n.* [*pl.* headmen (-men′)], a leader; the chief.

head-mas-ter or **head mas-ter** (hed′mås′tėr; hed′ mås′tėr), the principal of a school, esp. a private school.

head–on (hed′–on′), *adj.* with fronts facing, esp. of collisions; as, the *head-on* collision stopped traffic all morning.

head-quar-ters (hed′kwôr′tėrz), *n.* [*pl.* headquarters], **1,** the residence, main location, or office of an army, police force, or another organization from which orders are issued; **2,** the main office of a business or an organization; **3,** any centre of activity or authority.

head-set (hed′set′), *n.* a pair of earphones, often with a microphone attached; as, he used the *headset* to answer the phone.

head-ship (hed′ship), *n.* the position of head, chief, or leader.

head-stone (hed′stōn′), *n.* **1,** a stone set at the head of a grave; **2,** a cornerstone.

head-strong (hed′strông), *adj.* ungovernable; self-willed; as, a *headstrong* child.

heads–up (hedz′–up′), *n. Colloq.* warning; notification; as, to give a *heads-up* about the possible problem:—*adj.* alert; resourceful; competent; as, a *heads-up* hockey player.—*interj.* **heads′ up′** (look out!).

head-wa-ters (hed′wô′tėrz), the source and upper waters of a stream.

head-way (hed′wā′), *n.* **1,** forward motion; progress; as, the ship made *headway* despite the storm; to make *headway* on the project; **2,** a clear space permitting passage under an arch, bridge, etc.; clearance.

head-y (hed′i), *adj.* [-ier, -iest], **1,** willful; rash; impetuous; as, a *heady* youth; a *heady* horse; **2,** intoxicating; as, *heady* wine.—*n.* **head′i-ness.**

heal (hēl), *v.t.* to restore to health; cure; make right; as, time *healed* the wound or bad feelings:—*v.i.* to become well or sound; the wound *healed.*—*n.* **heal′er.**

health (helth), *n.* **1,** freedom from pain or disease; vigour of body or mind; **2,** the condition of the body and mind, whether good or bad; as, these substances affect *health*; **3,** a toast to a person's health and happiness. Also, **health′ card′, health′ care′; health′ food′.**

health-ful (helth′fool), *adj.* promoting bodily welfare; giving health; as, *healthful* exercise; a *healthful* climate; *healthful* food.—*adv.* **health′ful-ly.**—*n.* **health′fulness.**

health-y (hel′thi), *adj.* [health-i-er, health-i-est-], **1,** having or being in a sound or wholesome condition; as, a *healthy* child; **2,** showing health; as, a *healthy* look; **3,** *Colloq.* healthful; **4,** large in amount; as, to have a *healthy* respect for the sea.—*adv.* **health′i-ly.**—*n.* **health′i-ness.**

heap (hēp), *n.* **1,** a number of things piled up together; **2,** *Colloq.* a large quantity; as, to be in a *heap* of trouble:—*v.t.* **1,** to make a pile of; **2,** to bestow generously or in large amounts; as, to *heap* gifts upon; **3,** to fill to overflowing; as, to *heap* a plate with food.

hear (hēr), *v.t.* [heard (hûrd), hearing], **1,** to perceive by the ear; take in sound; as, to *hear* a loud noise; **2,** to listen to; give heed to; pay attention to; as, to *hear* what he had to say; **3,** to become informed of; as, to *hear* news; **4,** to grant (a favour or a prayer):—*v.i.* **1,** to have the sense of hearing; **2,** to be told; as, I *heard* of his death; **3,** to listen.—*n.* **hear′er.**

hear-ing (hēr′ing), *n.* **1,** the sense by which sound is perceived; **2,** the distance over which a sound may be heard; as, to be within *hearing*; **3,** the act of getting information; **4,** a chance to be heard, esp. an official meeting or trial; attention; as, to get a *hearing* in court:—**hearing aid,** a device that makes sounds louder, worn on the ear by people who are hearing-impaired.

hear-say (hēr′sā′), *n.* rumour; gossip.

hearse (hûrs), *n.* a vehicle, such as a car or carriage, for carrying dead persons to the grave.

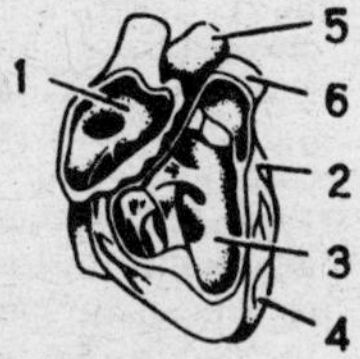

heart (härt), *n.* **1,** a hollow, muscular organ that pumps the blood through the body; **2,** hence, an essential part; as, the *heart* of a book; *heart* of the matter; also, the central or innermost part; as, the *heart* of a tree; **3,** tenderness; sympathy; as, one's *heart* goes out to a child; also, courage; as, I haven't the heart to tell her; **4,** a conventional figure representing a heart; as, a valentine *heart*; **5,** one of a suit, called *hearts,* of playing cards, marked with a red figure like a heart; **6,** memory; as, to learn by *heart*; **7,** liking; approval; as, after one's own *heart*:—**hearts,** a card game. Also, **heart′ache′; heart′beat′; heart′break′; heart′ bro′ken; heart′–rend′-ing; heart′sick′; heart′ string′.**

HEART PARTLY LAID OPEN TO SHOW: 1, RIGHT AURICLE; 2, LEFT AURICLE; 3, RIGHT VENTRICLE; 4, LEFT VENTRICLE; 5, AORTA; 6, PULMONARY ARTERY

heart attack, a sudden failure of the heart to work normally, often resulting in serious damage to the heart or body, or even death.

heart-break (härt′brāk′), *n.* intense sorrow; grief; distress; disappointment.—*n.* **heart′ break′er.**—*adj.* **heart′break′ing;**

heart′brok′ en.—*adv.* **heart′break′ing-ly.**

heart-burn (härt′bûrn′), *n.* a burning sensation in the lower chest region, caused by high acidity, indigestion, etc.

heart-en (här′tn), *v.t.* to give courage to; to cheer or inspire.

heart-felt (härt′felt′), *adj.* earnest; sincere; with true emotion.

hearth (härth), *n.* **1,** the floor or base of a fireplace, usually of brick or stone; **2,** the family circle; home.

hearth-stone (härth′stōn′), *n.* **1,** a flat stone forming a hearth; **2,** the fireside.

heart-land (härt′land′), *n.* an area that is central to a country, region, or culture; the most important part of an area; as, the industrial *heartland.*

heart-less (härt′lis), *adj.* **1,** without feeling or affection; **2,** cruel; merciless.—*adv.* **heart′less-ly.**—*n.* **heart′less-ness.**

heart-wood (härt′wood′), *n.* the hard inner wood of a tree trunk.

heart-y (här′ti), *adj.* [heart-i-er, heart-i-est], **1,** sincere; cordial; friendly; as, a *hearty* welcome; **2,** vigorous; strong; as, a *hearty* handclasp; **3,** abundant and nourishing; as, a *hearty* meal.—*adv.* **heart′i-ly.**—*n.* **heart′i-ness.**

heat (hēt), *n.* **1,** a form of energy due to the motion of invisible particles of matter and capable of passing from one body to another: produced by the sun, fire, friction, and certain chemical reactions; **2,** hotness; warmth; high temperature; as, the *heat* of summer; also, the sensation caused by heat; **3,** warm air supplied to a room or building; as, there was no *heat* in the building after the furnace broke down; **4,** intensity of feeling; rage; zeal; as, the *heat* of a quarrel; **5,** one race in an event that is made up of two or more races:—*v.t.* **1,** to make hot; **2,** to excite or arouse:—*v.i.* to become hot; as, an engine *heats* up.—*adj.* **heat′ed.**—*adv.* **heat′ed-ly** (hēt′id-li).

heat-er (hēt′ėr), *n.* a device, such as a stove, radiator, furnace, fireplace, etc., that provides heat, as to a building or car.

heath (hēth), *n.* **1,** a tract of waste or level land, covered with heather or other coarse vegetation, esp. in Great Britain; moor; **2,** an evergreen shrub; heather.

hea-then (hē′*th*en), *n.* [*pl.* heathens or, collectively, heathen], a person who is not religious; a pagan; idolater; barbarian:—*adj.* pertaining to the heathen; as, a *heathen* philosophy.

heath-er (he*th*′ėr), *n.* a small evergreen shrub with lavender flowers that blooms profusely in late summer.—*adj.* **heath′er-y.**

heave (hēv), *v.t.* [*p.t.* and *p.p.* heaved (hēvd) or hove (hōv), *p.pr.* heav-ing], **1,** to hoist or lift up with effort; **2,** to utter (a sob or sigh); **3,** to throw; hurl:—*v.i.* **1,** to be lifted up; swell up; **2,** to rise and fall alternately; as, the sea *heaves*; **3,** to struggle; strain; **4,** to haul; move; as, the ship *hove* in sight; **5,** to retch or try to vomit:—*n.* **1,** an effort to move or pull something; a lift; **2,** the act of throwing; **3,** a swell or rising; as, a *heave* of the breast.

heav-en or **Heav-en** (hev′en), *n.* **1,** the abode of God and the blessed; **2,** a state or condition of bliss; supreme happiness; as, she was in *heaven* when he asked her out on a date; **3,** the heavens, the firmament; sky.—*adj.* and *adv.* **heav′en-ward.**—*adv.* **heav′en-wards.**

heav-en-ly (hev′en-li), *adj.* **1,** pertaining to the sky; as, a *heavenly* body; **2,** pertaining to the abode of God; divine; as, *heavenly* joy; **3,** beyond compare; as, *heavenly* beauty.—*n.* **heav′en-li-ness.**

heav-y (hev′i), *adj.* [heav-i-er, heav-i-est], **1,** weighty; ponderous; as, a *heavy* load; **2,** large in extent, or effect; having more than the usual weight, size, or amount for its kind; as, a *heavy* rain; *heavy* sweater; **3,** oppressive; grievous; as, a *heavy* punishment; also, rough or hard to travel over; as, a *heavy* road; **4,** grave; serious; as, *heavy* reading; **5,** dejected; sad; as, a *heavy* heart; **6,** dull; stupid; as, a *heavy* mind; **7,** powerful; loud; as, a *heavy* voice; **8,** thick; coarse; as, *heavy* linen; **9,** loaded; as, a tree *heavy* with apples; **10,** dense, as storm clouds:—*n. Colloq.* a villain, as in a play, movie, etc.—*adv.* **heav′i-ly.**—*n.* **heav′i-ness.**

heavy hydrogen, a hydrogen isotope of twice the mass of ordinary hydrogen; deuterium.

heavy water, water in which the ordinary hydrogen atom is replaced by that of heavy hydrogen.

heav-y-weight (hev′i-wāt′), *n.* **1,** an amateur boxer of 81 kilograms or over; **2,** a person who is very important, powerful, or influential; as, a *heavyweight* in literature.

heck-le (hek′l), *v.t.* [heck-led, heck-ling], to question sharply or taunt, so as to annoy or confuse; as, to *heckle* a speaker or comedian.—*n.* **heck′ler.**

hect- or **hec-to-** (hekt-; hek′tō-), a *prefix* in the *metric system* meaning 100; as, *hect′*are (100 acres or 10,000 square metres), *hecto*gram (100 grams), *hecto*litre (100 litres), *hecto*metre (100 metres).

hec-tare (hek′târ′), *n.* a metric unit of land measure equal to 100 ares or 10,000 square metres (2.471 acres): abbreviated as *ha.*

hec-tic (hek′tik), *adj.* **1,** feverish; flushed and hot; **2,** exciting; wild; filled with activity; busy; as, a *hectic* lifestyle.

hec-tor (hek′tėr), *v.t.* and *v.i.* to bully; threaten; bluster:—*n.* a bully.

hedge (hej), *n.* **1,** a fence of bushes, shrubs, or low trees; **2,** a barrier:—*v.t.* [hedged, hedging], **1,** to enclose with a border of bushes or shrubs; **2,** to obstruct; hem in; surround; as, an army *hedges* in the enemy:—*v.i.* **1,** to bet on both sides in order to protect oneself against heavy loss; **2,** to speak evasively; avoid frank speech, esp. in answer to questions; as, the mayor *hedged* when asked about the homeless situation.

hedge-hog (hej′hog′), *n.* **1,** a spiny, insect-eating animal, with the power of rolling itself into a ball for defence; **2,** the North American porcupine, esp. in the U.S.

hedge-row (hej′rō′), *n.* a hedge or fence of small trees or shrubs.

heed (hēd), *v.t.* to notice; pay attention to; regard:—*n.* careful attention; notice; as, give *heed.*—*adj.* **heed′ful.**—*adv.* **heed′ful-ly.**—*n.* **heed′ful-ness.**

heed-less (hēd′lis), *adj.* careless; inattentive; neglectful.—*adv.* **heed′lessly.**—*n.* **heed′less-ness.**

hee-haw (hē′hô′), *n.* **1,** rude laughter; a guffaw; **2,** the braying of a donkey:—*v.i.* to laugh a loud or silly laugh.

[1]heel (hēl), *v.i.* to lean to one side; to list, as a ship:—*v.t.* to cause (a ship) to list.

[2]heel (hēl), *n.* **1,** the rounded back part of the foot, below the ankle; **2,** the corresponding part of a boot, shoe, or sock; **3,** anything resembling a heel in position or shape; as, the *heel* of a hand; a bread *heel*; **4,** a cad; a dishonourable or contemptible person:—*v.t.* **1,** to furnish with a heel; as, to *heel* boots; **2,** to urge forward; as, the collie *heels* sheep:—*v.i.* to follow closely; as, she taught her dog to *heel.*—*n.* **heel′ing.**

heft (heft), *n. Colloq.* **1,** weight; heaviness; **2,** importance:—*v.t. Colloq.* to try the weight of; as, he *hefted* the sack of sand:—*v.i.* to weigh.—*adj.* **heft′y.**

he-gi-ra or **he-ji-ra** (hej′i-ra; hi-jī′ra), *n.* **1,** Muhammad's flight from Mecca to Medina, A.D. 622, that marks the beginning of the Muslim era; **2,** any flight to safety; exodus. Also, **Hegira.**

heif-er (hef′ėr), *n.* a young cow that has not yet calved.

height (hīt), *n.* **1,** distance from the base to the top; of a person, stature; as, she is 165 centimetres in *height*; **2,** altitude; elevation; the distance anything rises above the earth or above sea level; as, the tower is 35 metres in *height*; **3,** the state of having great height; being high; as, his *height* was an asset; **4,** a mountain or hill; **5,** the highest point; top; summit; hence, the utmost degree; as, the *height* of success.

height-en (hīt′n), *v.t.* **1,** to raise; make higher; **2,** to intensify, as a colour; increase; aggravate; as, to *heighten* anger:—*v.t.* to rise in height; increase.

Heim-lich manoeuvre (hīm′lik′), *n.* an emergency procedure used on choking victims, in which sudden upward pressure is applied to the choker's upper abdomen to expel the obstruction.

hei-nous (hā′nus), *adj.* hateful; extremely wicked; as, a *heinous* crime.—*adv.* **hei′nous-ly.**—*n.* **hei′nous-ness.**

heir (âr), *n.* **1,** one who receives or has the right to receive an estate, title, etc., on the death of the owner; **2,** one who inherits anything, as property or characteristics; as, he fell *heir* to his father's temper.

heir-ess (âr′is), *n.* a woman or girl who inherits, or is heir to, title or property.

heir-loom (âr′lo͞om′), *n.* a piece of personal property handed down in a family for generations.

held (held), *p.t.* and *p.p.* of *hold.*

hel-i-cop-ter (hel′i-kop′tėr), *n.* a wingless aircraft lifted and propelled by large horizontal rotors or propellers, turned by motor power: it can move forward, backward, sideways, up, or down. Also called *chopper.*

he-li-o-graph (hē′li-ō-gråf′), *n.* an apparatus using a mirror for signalling (by Morse code) by reflecting flashes of sunlight:—*v.t.* and *v.i.* to signal by such a device.

he-li-um (hē′li-um), *n.* a very light gas that has no colour or smell and does not burn, used for inflating balloons and dirigibles because it is lighter than air.

hell or **Hell** (hel), *n.* **1,** in religion, the place below the earth where the wicked are punished after death; **2,** any place or condition of extreme misery or evil; **3,** the dwelling place of the dead.—*adj.* **hell′ish.**—*n.* **hell′ish-ness.**

Hel-len-ic (he-len′ik; -lē′nik), *n.* the Greek language:—*adj.* relating to early Greece, esp. its social and cultural aspects; as, *Hellenic* sculpture.

hel-lo or **hal-lo** or **hul-lo** (he-lō′; ha-lō′; hu-lō′), *interj.* an exclamation of informal greeting, surprise, or when answering the telephone:—*n.* a salutation; greeting.

helm (helm), *n.* **1,** the steering apparatus of a ship, esp. the tiller or the wheel; **2,** hence, any post of command or control; as, at the *helm* of the company.

hel-met (hel′met), *n.* a hard covering worn to protect the head in certain sports, warfare, dangerous work, etc.

helms-man (helmz′man), *n.* [*pl.* helmsmen (-men)], the person who steers a ship or boat; a pilot.

help (help), *v.t.* **1,** to give assistance to; support; **2,** to avoid; prevent; as, I cannot *help* his going; **3,** to distribute food to; serve; **4,** to remedy; as, nothing *helps* my headache:—*v.i.* to lend aid; be useful; as, she likes to *help*:—*n.* **1,** aid; support; act of helping; **2,** remedy; relief; **3,** that which forwards or promotes; **4,** a hired person, esp. someone paid to do housework; maid; as, she never has trouble with her *help.*—*n.* **help′er.**

help-ful (help′fool), *adj.* giving aid; beneficial; useful.—*adv.* **help′ful-ly.**—*n.* **help′ful-ness.**

help-ing (hel′ping), *n.* a portion of food served at the table.

help-less (help′lis), *adj.* unable to take care of oneself; feeble; dependent.—*adv.* **help′less-ly.**—*n.* **help′less-ness.**

hel-ter–skel-ter (hel′tėr–skel′tėr), *adj.* and *adv.* in hurried confusion; pell-mell:—*n.* disorder; hasty confusion.

hem (hem), *n.* the edge of material turned under and sewed down to prevent fraying:—*v.t.* [hemmed, hem-ming], **1,** to fold under and sew down the edge of (a cloth or garment); as, to *hem* a skirt; **2,** to shut in; surround; as, our opponents *hemmed* us in.

hem-a-tite or **haem-a-tite** (hem′a-tīt′; hēm′-), *n.* an important ore of iron, Fe_2O_3 (iron oxide).

he-ma-tol-o-gy or **hae-ma-tol-o-gy** (hē′ma-tol′o-ji), *n.* the branch of medical science that deals with the blood and its disorders.

hem-i-sphere (hem′i-sfēr), *n.* a half sphere; esp. a half of the earth. The equator divides the earth into the Northern and the Southern Hemispheres. A meridian divides the earth into the Eastern Hemisphere, including Europe, Asia, Africa, and Australia, and the Western Hemisphere, including North America and South America.

hem-lock (hem′lok), *n.* **1,** any of several evergreen trees of the pine family; also, the lumber from such a tree; **2,** any of several poisonous European plants of the parsley family.

he-mo-glo-bin or **hae-mo-glo-bin** (hē′mō-glō′bin; hem-), *n.* the red oxygen-carrying matter of the red corpuscles.

he-mo-phil-i-a or **hae-mo-phil-i-a** (hēm′ō-fil′i-a; hem-), *n.* a hereditary disease characterized by a tendency to excessive bleeding from the smallest cut, occurring esp. in males.

hem-or-rhage or **haem-or-rhage** (hem′o-rij), *n.* bleeding from the blood vessels, esp. a great or continuous flow of blood.

hem-or-rhoids or **haem-or-rhoids** (hem′o-roidz), *n.pl.* painful and itchy swelling and bleeding of the veins about the anus; piles.

hemp (hemp), *n.* a herb of Asia, the fibre of which is used for ropes and various kinds of coarse linen: the leaves and flowers are the source of the drug hashish or marijuana.—*adj.* **hemp′en.**

hem-stitch (hem′stich′), *n.* an ornamental stitch used in hemming, in which crosswise threads are pulled out and lengthwise threads fastened into small bundles; also, needlework so finished:—*v.t.* to finish with hemstitch.

hen (hen), *n.* the adult female of the domestic fowl or chicken; also, the female of other birds, such as turkey or pheasant.

hence (hens), *adv.* **1,** from this place, source, or time; as, a week *hence*; **2,** for this reason; as a result; as, she was sick; *hence*, she stayed home.

hence-forth (hens′fōrth′; hens′fōrth′) or **hence-for-ward** (hens′fôr′wėrd), *adv.* from this time on.

hench-man (hench′man), *n.* [*pl.* henchmen (-men)], a trusted follower; a political supporter.

hen-na (hen′a), *n.* a reddish-brown dye made from the leaves of the henna, a tropical Middle Eastern shrub with fragrant white or rose leaves.

hen-pecked (hen′pekt′), *adj. Colloq.* governed or domineered over by one's wife.

hen-ry (hen′ri), *n.* [*pl.* henrys], the unit for measuring induced currents; that is, the inducing of one volt by a current varying at the rate of one ampere per second.

hep-a-ti-tis (hep′a-tī′tis), *n.* a disease of the liver involving inflammation and often fever, jaundice, and other symptoms:—**hepatitis A,** also known as infectious hepatitis, a virus that causes jaundice and fever, and is transmitted in food:—**hepatitis B,** known as serum hepatitis, a severe viral infection, transmitted in blood and other bodily fluids:—**hepatitis C,** known also as non-A or non-B hepatitis, caused by different types of viruses and often resulting in chronic disease.

hep-ta- or **hept-** (hept′a-; hept-), *prefix* meaning seven; as, *hepta*gon, *hept*ane, etc.

hep-ta-gon (hep′ta-gon′), *n.* in *geometry*, a plane figure having seven sides and seven angles.

hep-tam-e-ter (hep-tam′e-tėr), *n.* and *adj.* a line or verse, or of a line or verse, with seven metrical feet.

her (hûr), *adj.* a possessive form of *she*, belonging to her; as, *her* book:—*pron.* the objective form of *she*; as, I see *her*; give *her* the book.

her-ald (her′ald), *n.* **1,** formerly, an official who made state proclamations, carried important messages, and assisted at public ceremonies; **2,** a messenger; forerunner; as, the bright morning sun was the *herald* of a beautiful day:—*v.t.* **1,** to introduce; proclaim; give a sign of; **2,** to greet with zeal; hail; as, the public *heralded* the new prime minister.

her-ald-ry (her′ald-ri), *n.* [*pl.* heraldries], **1,** the science that deals with coats of arms and of pedigrees; **2,** a coat of arms; **3,** pomp and splendour.—*adj.* **he-ral′dic.**

herb (hûrb; ûrb), *n.* a plant of which the stems, leaves, roots, or seeds are used for flavouring food or as a medicine, esp. parsley, basil, mint, sage, tarragon, etc.: it has a soft, juicy, not woody stem, which, after flowering, either dies completely, or withers to the ground.—*adj.* **herb′al; her′by.**—*n.* **herb′al-ist; herb′al tea′; her-bar′i-um; her′bi-cide; her′bi-vore.**

her-ba-ceous (hûr-bā′shus), *adj.* of the nature of an herb; also, planted with herbs.

herb-age (ûr′bij; hûr′bij), *n.* grass or herbs; pasturage.

her-biv-o-rous (hûr-biv′u-rus), *adj.* feeding on plants and grasses, as do horses and dairy cattle.

her-cu-le-an (hûr-kū′li-an; hûr′kū-lē′an), *adj.* **1,** of great strength or power (like Hercules); **2,** difficult; as, a *herculean* task.

herd (hûrd), *n.* **1,** a group of animals, esp. cattle, feeding or travelling together; **2,** a large crowd of people; **3,** the common people as a mass; mob; **4,** a person who herds animals; as, a goat*herd*:—*v.i.* **1,** to flock together, form, or gather into a large group; **2,** to associate:—*v.t.* to form (cattle) into a herd.

herds-man (hûrdz′man), *n.* [*pl.* herds-men (-men)], one who owns or tends cattle.

here (hēr), *adv.* **1,** in this place; as, I live *here*; in answer to a roll call, present; **2,** in this direction; hither; as, look *here*; **3,** at this point or moment; as, *here* she paused; **4,** in this world; as, *here* below:—*n.* this place; as, to know how to get there from *here*.

here-a-bout (hēr′a-bout′) or **here-a-bouts** (hēr′a-bouts′), *adv.* in this locality.

here-aft-er (hēr-åf′tėr), *adv.* **1,** after this; henceforth; in the future; as, *hereafter*, bring your own lunch; **2,** also, in the life to come:—*n.* **1,** the future; **2,** the life to come; as, to believe in the *hereafter*.

here-by (hēr-bī′), *adv.* by means of this.

he-red-i-tar-y (he-red′i-tėr-i), *adj.* **1,** descending from a person to his or her heir; as, a *hereditary* estate; **2,** holding rank or position by inheritance; as, a *hereditary* title; **3,** passed on from parent to child; as, *hereditary* diseases.

he-red-i-ty (he-red′i-ti), *n.* [*pl.* heredities], **1,** the passing on, through genes, from parent to child of physical or mental traits or characteristics, such as sex, colour of skin and hair, shape and size, likes and dislikes, etc.; **2,** hereditary traits; **3,** having to do with inheritance; **4,** coming from one's ancestors.

here-in (hēr-in′), *adv.* in this.

here-of (hēr-ov′), *adv.* of this; about this; as, we will speak further *hereof*.

here-on (hēr-on′), *adv.* on this; hereupon.

her-e-sy (her′e-s), *n.* [*pl.* heresies], an opinion or doctrine contrary to those commonly accepted on such subjects as religion, politics, or art.

her-e-tic (her′e-tik), *n.* and *adj.* one who holds an opinion contrary to accepted views.

here-to-fore (hēr′too-fōr′), *adv.* previously; formerly; until now.

here-up-on (hēr′u-pon′), *adv.* on this; hereon; at this point; immediately after this.

here-with (hēr-wi*th*′; hēr-with′), *adv.* with this; at this point.

her-it-age (her′i-tij), *n.* **1,** that which is handed down to an heir; inheritance; also, the lot or condition into which one is born; **2,** what has been handed down from the past to a people; the beliefs and customs that people take from earlier generations; as, Canadian *heritage*:—*adj.* pertaining to heritage; as, *heritage* art; *heritage* language.

Her (His) Majesty's Canadian Ship, the designation for Canadian naval vessels: abbreviated as *HMCS*; as, the *HMCS* Halifax is a frigate.

her-maph-ro-dite (hûr-maf′ro-dīt′), *n.* a plant or animal having both male and female sexual organs.

her-met-i-cal-ly (hûr-met′i-kal-i), *adv.* made airtight; as, a *hermetically* sealed container.—*adj.* **her-met′ic; her-met′i-cal.**

her-mit (hûr′mit), *n.* one who withdraws from society and lives alone; a recluse.

her-mit-age (hûr′mi-tij), *n.* **1,** the home of a recluse or hermit; **2,** a retreat away from people.

her-ni-a (hûr′ni-a), *n.* [*pl.* hernias (hûr′ni-az)], the pushing of part of the intestine through a break in the inner wall of the abdomen; a rupture.

he-ro (hē′rō), *n.* [*pl.* heroes], **1,** a person famed for courage or deeds of prowess; **2,** a person who is admired by others for great achievements or outstanding qualities; as, a literary *hero*; **3,** the chief character, usually male but also female, in a play, novel, film, etc.—*n.fem.* **her′o-ine** (her′ō-in), used esp. to distinguish female from male heroes in plays, literature, and films.

he-ro-ic (hē-rō′ik), or **he-ro-i-cal** (hē-rō′i-kal), *adj.* **1,** having the qualities of a hero; courageous; as, a *heroic* firefighter; **2,** worthy of a hero; bold; brave; as, a *heroic* rescue; **3,** having to do with heroes and their deeds; as, *heroic* stories; the *heroic* deeds described in Tolkien's *Lord of the Rings*.—*adv.* **he-ro′i-cal-ly.**

her-o-in (her′ō-in; hēr-), *n.* a white, crystalline, addictive narcotic powder derived from morphine.

her-o-ism (her′ō-izm), *n.* heroic conduct; high and noble courage.

her-on (her′un), *n.* a wading bird with long legs, neck, and bill, living in marshes, and feeding on fish, frogs, and insects.

her-pes (hûr′pēz), *n.* an acute viral disease, characterized by skin inflammation, in which clusters of blisters keep spreading on the mouth or genitals.

her-ring (her′ing), *n.* [*pl.* herring or herrings], a food fish found in North Atlantic and Pacific waters.

her-ring-bone (her′ing-bōn′), *adj.* **1,** composed of rows of short parallel lines slanting in opposite directions from a central rib, like the spine of a herring; **2,** in *skiing*, a way to climb a hill, with skis pointing outward.

herring choker, *Colloq.* a Canadian Maritimer, esp. one from New Brunswick.

hers (hûrz), *pron.* a possessive form of *she*, used alone: **1,** in the predicate, belonging to her; as, whose is that hat? it is *hers*; **2,** as a person or thing that belongs to her; as, which book do you have? I have *hers*.

her-self (hûr-self′), *pron.* **1,** a reflexive form of *her*; as, she cut *herself*; **2,** an emphatic form of *she*; as, she did it *herself*; **3,** her normal or usual self; as, she is now *herself* again.

hertz (hûrts), *n.* [*pl.* hertz], a frequency unit equal to one cycle per second: abbreviated as *Hz.*

hes-i-tant (hez′i-tant), *adj.* undecided; wavering; hesitating.—*n.* **hes′i-tan-cy; hes′i-tance.**

hes-i-tate (hez′i-tāt′), *v.i.* [hesitat-ed, hesitat-ing], **1,** to be uncertain or undecided; as, he *hesitates* about going; **2,** to be unwilling; as, I *hesitate* to take the risk; **3,** to pause for a moment; as, to *hesitate* before jumping; **4,** to stammer.

hes-i-ta-tion (hez′i-tā′shun), *n.* **1,** uncertainty; doubt; indecision; **2,** unwillingness; **3,** pause; **4,** a faltering in speech; stammering.

het-er-o- or **het-er-** (het′ėr-ō; het′ėr), *prefix* meaning different, other; as, *hetero*geneous, *hetero*sexual, etc.

het-er-o-ge-ne-ous (het′ėr-ō-jē′ni-us), *adj.* dissimilar; consisting of parts of different kinds: opposite of *homogeneous*; as, the *heterogeneous* population of Canada.

het-er-o-sex-u-al (he′tėr-ō-seks′shoo-al), *n.* and *adj.* one who is sexually attracted to a person of the opposite sex.—*n.* **het′er-o-sex′u-al′i-ty.**

hew (hū), *v.t.* [*p.t.* hewed, *p.p.* hewn (hūn) or hewed, *p.pr.* hew-ing], **1,** to cut or chop, as with an axe; as, to *hew* wood; **2,** to cut down (trees); **3,** to cut into shape; as, to *hew* out a beam:—*v.i.* **1,** to strike blows, as with an axe; **2,** to adhere; as, to *hew* to office policies.—*n.* **hew′er.**

hex (heks), *n. Colloq.* spell; enchantment; jinx; as, to put a *hex* on someone:—*v.t.* to jinx; bewitch.

hex-a-or **hex-** (heks′a-; heks-), *prefix* meaning six; as, *hexa*gon, *hexa*gram, *hex*ane, *hex*ose, etc.

hex-a-gon (hek′sa-gon′), *n.* a plane figure with six angles and six sides.—*adj.* **hex-ag′o-nal** (heks-ag′o-nal).

hex-am-e-ter (hek-sam′e-tėr), *n.* and *adj.* a line or verse, or of a line or verse, with six metrical feet.

hey (hā), *interj.* a word used to attract someone's attention or to show a certain feeling; as, *hey*, that was my candy bar that you ate!; *hey*, stop!

hey-day (hā′dā′), *n.* the time of greatest strength, vigour, bloom, etc.; as, the *heyday* of youth; the *heyday* of chivalry.

hi (hī), *interj.* an exclamation of greeting, similar to *hello.*

hi-a-tus (hī-ā′tus), *n.* **1,** a break or gap in space or time, as where something is missing; as, a *hiatus* in a manuscript; the professor was on *hiatus*; **2,** a slight pause between two vowels sounded separately, as *coo*perate; **3,** a separation or gap in a part of the body.

hi-ber-nate (hī′bėr-nāt′), *v.i.* [hibernat-ed, hibernat-ing], to pass the winter in a sleep-like state, as does the bear; to winter; also, to be inactive.—*n.* **hi′ber-na′tion.**

hi-bis-cus (hī-bis′kis; hi-), *n.* a shrub or small tree of the mallow family, found in tropical or temperate climates, having large, showy, bell-shaped white, pink, red, yellow, purple, or blue flowers.

hic-cup or **hic-cough** (hik′up), *n.* a sudden gasp of breath that one cannot control, producing a short, clicking sound: caused by a sudden tightening of the breathing muscles:—**hiccups,** the condition of having hiccups one after the other:—*v.i.* [hiccupped, hiccup-ping], to have hiccups.

hick (hik), *n. Slang* **1,** a farmer; rustic; **2,** an unsophisticated person:—*adj.* rustic; unsophisticated; as, a *hick* town.

hick-o-ry (hik′o-ri), *n.* [*pl.* hickories], a North American nut-bearing hardwood tree of the walnut family; also, the nut or the tough wood of this tree.

hid-den (hid′en), a *p.p.* of ²*hide:*—*adj.* **1,** put or kept out of sight; secret; as, a *hidden* doorway; **2,** obscure; as, a letter full of *hidden* meanings.

¹**hide** (hīd), *n.* **1,** the skin, raw or dressed, of an animal, used to make shoes, clothing, and other products; pelt; **2,** the human skin:—*v.t.* [hid-ed, hid-ing], *Colloq.* to whip.

²**hide** (hīd), *v.t.* [*p.t.* hid (hid), *p.p.* hidden (hid′n) or hid, *p.pr.* hid-ing], **1,** to conceal; keep secret or unknown; as, to *hide* a letter or a piece of news; **2,** to turn away; keep out of sight; shield; as, to *hide* one's face:—*v.i.* to conceal oneself or to be concealed.

hide–and–seek (hīd′–and–sēk′), *n.* a children's game in which some players hide and others seek or try to find them.

hide-bound (hīd′bound′), *adj.* **1,** having the skin or bark tight (said of cattle or trees); **2,** bigoted; narrow-minded.

hid-e-ous (hid′i-us), *adj.* frightful to look

upon; ugly; horrible to think of; as, a *hideous* monster.—*adv.* **hid′e-ous-ly.**—*n.* **hid′e-ous-ness.**

hide-out (hīd′out′), *n.* a safe place to hide; as, the cottage in the woods was a *hideout* for the fugitive.

hi-er-arch-y (hī′ėr-är′ki), *n.* **1,** a system of persons or things in graded ranks, order, etc.; as, the zoological *hierarchy* of *phylum, class, order, family,* and *species;* **2,** a government of clergy by graded ranks.

hi-er-o-glyph-ic (hī′ėr-ō-glif′ik), *n.* a picture or symbol that stands for a word, idea, or sound, used as one of the characters in the writing of the ancient Egyptians, etc.:—**hieroglyphics,** any form of writing in which pictures and symbols are used to present ideas; hence, any writing hard to read:—*adj.* **1,** pertaining to hieroglyphics; **2,** symbolic; **3,** illegible.

HIEROGLYPHICS

hi-fi (hī′fī′), *abbrev.* short for *high fidelity.*

hig-gle-dy–pig-gle-dy (hig′l-di–pig′l-di), *adv.* in disorder:—*adj.* jumbled together; topsy-turvy:—*n.* confusion; disarray.

high (hī), *adj.* **1,** far above the ground or sea level; as, a *high* plateau; also, tall; as, a *high* tree; a tower 30 metres *high;* **2,** noble; lofty; as, *high* aims; **3,** chief; important; as, *high* government officials; **4,** elated; lively; as, *high* spirits; **5,** intense or extreme; as, *high* speed; *high* favour; a *high* colour; **6,** strong, violent, or tempestuous; as, *high* winds; angry; as, *high* words; **7,** at the full; as, *high* tide; **8,** expensive; as, food is *high;* not low; as, prices are *high;* **9,** shrill or sharp; as, a *high* tone:—*adv.* **1,** to a great altitude or degree; as, hit a ball *high* in the air; **2,** extravagantly; as, to live *high;* **3,** proudly; as, to hold one's head *high;* **4,** in a shrill or loud pitch:—*n.* **1,** something that is high; a high place or point; as, a temperature that set a new *high* for this date; **2,** a weather condition in which there is a central area of air with higher pressure than the areas around it; **3,** *Slang* a state of elation or bliss, esp. produced by drugs.—*n.* **high′chair′; high′ def′i-ni′tion; high′ end′; high′ ex-plo′sive; high′ fash′ion; high′–five′; high′fli′er; high′ ground′; high′ jinks′; high′ jump′; high′ rise′; high′ rol′ler; high′ sign′; high′ tide′; high′ time′; high′ trea′son; high′ volt′age; high′ wire′.**—*adj.* **high′–grade′; high′–lev′el; high′–main′te-nance; high′–oc′tane; high′–pitched′; high′–pow′ered; high′–pres′ sure; high′–pro′ file; high′–risk′; high′–se-cu′ri-ty; high′–speed′; high′–spir′it-ed; high′–stakes′; high′–strung′; high′–top′.**

high-ball (hī′bôl′), *n.* **1,** a railway signal meaning to go ahead; **2,** an alcoholic drink diluted with soda water, ginger ale, etc., and served with ice in a tall glass:—*v.i.* *Slang* to go at full speed.

high-brow (hī′brou′), *n. Slang* a person highly educated or intellectual, or affecting to be so:—*adj. Slang* intellectual; cultured; as, *highbrow* music.

high-fa-lu-tin or **hi-fa-lu-tin** (hī′fa-lōō′tin), *adj. Colloq.* pretentious; pompous.

high fidelity, in *electronics,* reproduction of sound with very little distortion.

high-hand-ed (hī′han′did), *adj.* arbitrary; overbearing.—*adv.* **high′han′ded-ly.**—*n.* **high′ han′ded-ness.**

high-land (hī′land), *n.* high or mountainous land:—**Highlands**, a hilly region in northern and western Scotland.

high-ly (hī′li), *adv.* in a high degree; very much; as, *highly* coloured; favourably; as, to speak *highly* of someone; also, at a high price or rate; as, *highly* paid.

high–mind-ed (hī′–mīn′did), *adj.* honourable; having a lofty or noble character.

high-ness (hī′nes), *n.* the state or condition of being high; height:—**Highness**, a title of honour applied to persons of royal rank; as, Her Royal *Highness.*

high-road or **high road** (hī′rōd′), *n.* **1,** the best or easiest way; as, the *highroad* to obtaining consensus; **2,** a chief or much-travelled road or highway.

high school. Same as **secondary school.**

high-stick-ing (hī′stik′ing), *n.* in *hockey,* a penalty for interfering or striking another player with the stick above shoulder level; as, she got a two-minute penalty for *highsticking.*

high tech (tek), *n.* high technology; scientific technological developments, esp. in the field of electronics.

high–tech or **hi–tech** (hī′–tek′), *adj.* **1,** employing or involving technology that is high tech; **2,** a style of interior design that uses industrial material, etc.

high-way (hī′wā′), *n.* **1,** a main, public road between towns or cities; highroad; **2,** an expressway; **3,** any main or direct route; as, information *highway.* Also, **high′way rob′ber-y.**

high-way-man (hī′wā′man), *n.* formerly, a person on horseback who robbed on public roads by holding up his victims.

hi-jack or **high-jack** (hī′jak′), *v.t.* **1,** to commandeer or forcefully seize control of a vehicle, esp. an aircraft, and reroute it to another destination, usually for political or ideological reasons; as, the terrorists *hijacked* the planes and flew them into the World Trade Center and the Pentagon; **2,** to assume control of an organization, etc., often by deceit, and redirect it; as, the meeting was *hijacked* by extremists; **3,** to steal goods in transit, esp. by holding up vehicles in transit; as the bootleggers *hijacked* the truck convoy.

hi-jack-er or **high-jack-er** (hī′jak′ėr), *n.* *Colloq.* **1,** one who steals goods in transit, esp. by holding up trucks, boats, aircraft, etc.; **2,** one who forcefully causes a vehicle, esp. an aircraft, to be rerouted in order to reach another destination for financial gain or for political or ideological reasons; as, the terrorist *hijackers* flew the plane into the tower.

hike (hīk), *v.i.* [hiked, hik-ing], to tramp or walk, esp. for exercise or enjoyment:—*n.* a long walk or march.

hi-lar-i-ty (hi-lar′i-ti; hī-lâr′i-ti), *n.* [*pl.* hilarities], noisy merriment; jollity; fun; something that causes loud laughter.—*adj.* **hi-lar′i-ous** (hi-lâr′i-us; hī-lâr′i-us).

hill (hil), *n.* **1,** a natural elevation lower than a mountain; **2,** a small mound or heap; as, an ant hill:—*v.t.* to form into a mound; surround with a mound of earth; as, to *hill* potatoes.—*adj.* **hill′y.**—*n.* **hill′i-ness.**

hill-bil-ly (hil′bil′i), *n.* and *adj. Colloq.* a person from the mountains or backwoods, esp. of southern U.S.; as, *hillbilly* music.

hill-ock (hil′uk), *n.* a small hill.

hill-side (hil′sīd′), *n.* the sloping side of a hill.

hilt (hilt), *n.* a handle of a sword or dagger:—**to the hilt,** to the extreme; as, she was generous *to the hilt.*

him (him), *pron.* the objective case of *he*; as, they found *him.*

him-self (him-self′), *pron.* **1,** a reflexive form of *him*; as, he hurt *himself*; **2,** an emphatic form of *he*; as, he, *himself,* went; **3,** his normal or usual self; as, he is not *himself* today.

[1]**hind** (hīnd), *adj.* [hind-er, hind-most or hind-er-most], at the back or rear; as, the *hind* legs of a horse; the *hind*most legs of an ant.

[2]**hind** (hīnd), *n.* the female of the red deer, esp. in and after the third year: opposite of *stag* (def. 1).

[1]**hind-er** (hīn′dėr), *adj. comp.* of [1]*hind.*

[2]**hind-er** (hin′dėr), *v.t.* to keep back; slow up; delay; interfere; as, the snow *hindered* our progress.

hind-most (hīnd′mōst) or **hind-er-most** (hīnd′ėr-mōst), *adj. superl.* of [1]*hind.*

hindquar-ter (hīnd′kwôr′tėr), *n.* the back part of half a carcass, as of beef, lamb, or veal:—**hindquarters,** the posterior part of any four-legged animal.

hin-drance (hin′drans), *n.* the act of hindering; also, an obstruction.

hind-sight (hīnd′sīt′), *n.* seeing, after an event, what should or could have been done: opposite of *foresight* (def. 1).

Hin-du (hin′do͞o), *n.* and *adj.* **1,** a person, or of a person, believing in the religion of *Hinduism*; **2,** formerly, a person, or of a person, from India.

Hin-du-ism (hin′do͞o-izm), *n.* one of the predominant religions of India, characterized by a belief in polytheism, reincarnation, and a social order based on the caste system.

hinge (hinj), *n.* a jointed device or mechanism by means of which a movable part, as a door, gate, or lid, is made to turn or swing:—*v.t.* [hinged, hing-ing], to furnish or attach with a hinge:—*v.i.* to turn or depend, as on a hinge; as, my answer *hinges* on the decision you make.

hint (hint), *v.t.* to suggest slightly; refer to indirectly; as, to *hint* her suspicion:—*v.i.* to make an indirect suggestion; give a clue; as, to *hint* that she would not come:—*n.* **1,** an indirect or veiled suggestion; a clue; as, to give a *hint* for the solution to the problem; **2,** a very small amount of something that can barely be noticed; as, a *hint* of a smile.

hin-ter-land (hin′tėr-land′) *n.* **1,** an inland region; **2,** remote or undeveloped part of a country.

hip (hip), *n.* **1,** the widening fleshy part of the human body on either side below the waist, formed by the sides of the pelvis and the upper part of the thigh; the haunch; **2,** the hind portion of an animal, where the legs join the body; **3,** the seed pod of a rosebush; as, rose *hip* tea:—*adj. Slang* very interested or aware; stylish; as, *hip* musician, dresser. Also, **hip′ roof′; hip′ster, hip′ wa′ders.**

hip–hop (hip′–hop′), *n.* **1,** a style of U.S. black urban music that features rap-style lyrics and minimal instrumentation; **2,** the subculture associated with this music.—*n.* **hip′–hop′per.**

hip-po-drome (hip′ō-drōm′), *n.* **1,** a building or arena for circuses, games, theatricals, rodeos, equestrian events, etc.; **2,** in ancient Greece and Rome, an outdoor course used for chariot races, surrounded by seating for spectators.

hip-po-pot-a-mus (hip′o-pot′a-mus), *n.* [*pl.* hippopotamuses or hippopotami (hip′o-pot′a-mī)], a huge, herbivorous land and water animal, common near rivers, ponds, and lakes in Africa, with big head and mouth, thick hide, and short legs.

hire (hīr), *v.t.* [hired, hir-ing] **1,** to engage the service of, for a price; employ someone for wages; **2,** to secure the temporary use of, for a price; to rent; as, to *hire* a cab for a day; **3,** to grant the temporary use of, for a price; as, to *hire* out a limousine:—*n.* **1,** the act or fact of hiring; as, boats for *hire*; **2,** the wages paid for personal service; **3,** the price paid for the use of anything. Also, **hired′ gun′; hired′ hand′.**

hire-ling (hīr′ling), *n.* one who serves for wages, esp. one whose interest is centred in the wages rather than in the work:—*adj.* mercenary; working for pay.

hir-sute (hûr′sūt; hėr-so͞ot′), *adj.* rough with hair or bristles; hairy; as, a *hirsute* skin or face.

his (hiz), possessive form of *he*:—*adj.* belonging to him; as, this is *his* hat; this hat is *his*:—*pron.* a person or thing that belongs to him; as, I have my hat, and he has *his*.

His-pan-ic (hi-span′ik), *adj.* of or relating to Spanish-speaking people, esp. those in the U.S.:—*n.* a Spanish-speaking person, or someone of Spanish descent, esp. one living in the U.S.

hiss (his), *n.* **1,** the sharp sound made in the pronunciation of the letter *s*; also, this sound uttered as an exclamation of disapproval or contempt, like booing; **2,** a similar sound; as, the *hiss* of water in a kettle; the *hiss* of a snake:—*v.i.* to make a hiss, similar to booing; as, they *hissed* during her speech:—*v.t.* **1,** to express contempt for by hissing, similar to booing; as, the audience *hissed* the actors; **2,** to utter with a hiss; as, to *hiss* one's words.—*n.* **hiss′ing.**

his-tor-ic (his-tor′ik), *adj.* belonging to, connected with, or famous in history; as, a *historic* event or spot.

his-tor-i-cal (his-tor′i-kal), *adj.* **1,** of or pertaining to history; as, *historical* studies; **2,** based on history; as, a *historical* film; **3,** true to history; not legendary; as, a *historical* event.—*adv.* **his-tor′i-cal-ly.**

historical fiction, a story that is set in the past and includes accurate details of life during that period, and which can include real people, places, or events.

his-to-ry (his′to-ri), *n.* [*pl.* histories], **1,** a written narrative or record of past facts and events affecting one or more peoples, countries, institutions, sciences, etc., usually with comments and explanations; as, *histories* of the Canadian Confederation; **2,** the branch of learning that studies, records, and explains past facts and events, esp. as a subject in school; **3,** past facts or events referring to a particular person, nation, etc.; as, this house has a strange *history*; the *history* of Canada.—*n.* **his-tor′i-an.**

his-tri-on-ic (his′tri-on′ik), *adj.* **1,** pertaining to the stage or acting; dramatic; as, she has *histrionic* ability; **2,** overly dramatic, usually insincere; as, his *histrionic* outburst.—*n.* **his′tri-on′ics.**

hit (hit), *v.t.* hit, [hit-ting], **1,** to strike or give a blow to; as, to *hit* the table with a fist; **2,** to bring hard against something; as, to *hit* one's head on a post; **3,** to deliver; as, to *hit* a hard blow; **4,** to touch or reach; as, to *hit* the ceiling; **5,** to wound the feeling of; as, he was hard *hit* by failure:—*v.i.* **1,** to strike or deliver a blow; as, *hit* hard; **2,** to clash or collide; as, the two cars *hit* head-on; **3,** to come or light (upon); as, to *hit* upon the answer; **4,** *Colloq.* of internal-combustion engines, to fire or explode; as, the motor *hits* on all four cylinders:—*n.* **1,** a stroke or blow; the act or fact of hitting; **2,** a success; as, the song was a *hit*; **3,** in *baseball,* a ball so hit as to enable the batter to reach first base successfully; **4,** a subject or Web site found by searching the Internet; as, searching for that name on the Net produced thousands of *hits*:—*adj.* pertaining to a hit; as, a *hit* movie.—*n.* **hit′ter; hit′ list′; hit′ man′; hit′ pa-rade′.**—*adj.* **hit′-and-miss′; hit′-and-run′.**

hitch (hich), *v.t.* **1,** to fasten or tie; as, he *hitched* the pony to the post; **2,** to pull up with a jerk; raise; as, to *hitch* up the bottom of your pants; **3,** *Colloq.* to hitchhike; as, to *hitch* a ride home:—**get hitched,** *Slang* to get married:—*v.i.* **1,** to become fastened or entangled; **2,** to move jerkily; hobble:—*n.* **1,** a sudden pull or jerk; as, a *hitch* of the reins; **2,** a sudden stop or delay; obstacle or problem; as, the party went on without a *hitch*; **3,** something that hitches; a fastening; as, a trailer *hitch*; **4,** a kind of noose or knot, used, esp. on shipboard, for temporary fastening.

hitch-hike (hich′hīk′), *v.i.* [hitch-hiked, hitch-hik-ing], to travel by thumbing rides from motorists.—*n.* **hitch′hik′er.**

hi-tech (hī′-tek′), *abbrev.* short for *high-tech* or *high-technology.*

hith-er (hi*th*′ėr), *adv.* to or toward this place; here:—*adj.* nearer to the speaker.

hith-er-to (hi*th*′ėr-too͞′), *adv.* to this time; until now.

hith-er-ward (hi*th*′ėr-wėrd) or **hith-er-wards** (hi*th*′ėr-wėrdz), *adv.* to this place; in this direction.

HIV (āch′ī′vē′), *abbrev.* short for *human immunodeficiency virus.*

hive (hīv), *n.* **1,** a box, house, or nest for bees; **2,** a swarm of bees in a hive; **3,** a very busy place; also, a swarming multitude of people; as, the school gym is a *hive* of activity:—*v.i.* [hived, hiv-ing], to enter a hive, as bees; also, to live together in swarms; as, people *hive* in a city:—*v.t.* **1,** to put (bees) into a hive; **2,** to store, as honey.

hives (hīvz), *n.pl.* a skin condition marked by the appearance of a rash accompanied by intense itching, usually caused by allergies; urticaria.

HMCS (āch′em′sē′es′), *abbrev.* short for *Her (His) Majesty's Canadian Ship.*

ho (hō), *interj.* **1,** an expression of delight, surprise, mockery, etc.; **2,** an expression to gain attention; as, land *ho*!

hoard (hōrd), *n.* a secret store or treasure; a collection of things kept in reserve:—*v.i.* to lay up money or goods:—*v.t.* to lay up or store secretly; as, to *hoard* gold.—*n.* **hoard′er.**—*n.* **hoard′ing.**

hoar-frost (hōr′frost′), *n.* white frost; tiny ice particles from the moisture in the night air.

hoarse (hōrs), *adj.* [hoars-er, hoars-est], **1,** harsh or rough in sound; as, a *hoarse* voice; **2,** having a rough voice or making a rough, rasping sound; as, a *hoarse* foghorn.—*adv.* **hoarse′ly.**—*n.* **hoarse′ness.**

hoar-y (hōr′i), *adj.* [hoar-i-er, hoar-i-est], **1,** white or grey with age; as, *hoary* hair; **2,** old; venerable; ancient.

hoax (hōks), *n.* a mischievous trick or practical joke; also, a fraud:—*v.t.* to trick.

hob-ble (hob′l), *v.i.* [hob-bled, hob-bling], to walk with a limp or go unevenly; as, to *hobble* to the front door after spraining an ankle:—*v.t.* **1,** to make lame; **2,** to hamper, as a horse, by tying its legs loosely so that it cannot run away:—*n.* **1,** a limping walk; **2,** a rope or fetter for hobbling horses.

hob-by (hob′i), *n.* [*pl.* hobbies], a favourite interest or enjoyment in spare time.

hob-by-horse (hob′i-hôrs′), *n.* **1,** a stick with a replica of a horse's head, on which children pretend to ride; **2,** a wooden rocking horse; **3,** a favourite topic.

hob-gob-lin (hob′gob′lin), *n.* **1,** a mischievous elf; **2,** an evil sprite of frightful appearance; a bogey.

hob-nob (hob′nob′), *v.i.* [hob-nobbed, hob-nob-bing], to drink or talk together; be on intimate terms; as, the old friends *hobnobbed* during the entire semester.

ho-bo (hō′bō), *n.* [*pl.* hoboes or hobos], **1,** a poor, homeless person; vagrant; **2,** a person who goes from job to job; a migrant worker.

[1]**hock** (hok), *n.* the joint, as of a horse's hind leg, corresponding to the human ankle; also, a similar joint of a fowl's leg.

[2]**hock** (hok), *v.t. Slang* to pawn.

hock-ey (hok′i), *n.* a game originating in Canada played on ice skates in a rink by two teams of six persons to a side, with curved sticks with blades for controlling and shooting a rubber puck into the opposing team's goal. Also called *ice hockey*:—**ball hockey,** a similar game played outdoors, usually on pavement, using a tennis ball:—**field hockey,** a similar game played with a ball on an outdoor field:—**floor hockey,** a similar game played indoors on a floor, using a plastic puck or ring.

ho-cus-po-cus (hō′kus-pō′kus), *n.* **1,** meaningless words used as a formula by a magician or conjurer; **2,** sleight of hand; **3,** trickery; deception.

hod (hod), *n.* **1,** a wooden trough for carrying mortar or bricks; **2,** a coal scuttle.

hodge-podge (hoj′poj′), *n.* **1,** a stew of meat and vegetables; **2,** any motley mixture or jumble; as, a *hodgepodge* collection of CDs.

hoe (hō), *n.* a flat-bladed, long-handled garden tool for loosening soil, removing weeds, etc.:—*v.t.* [hoed (hōd), hoe-ing], **1,** to till or loosen with a hoe; **2,** to clear of weeds; as, she *hoed* her garden every week:—*v.i.* to work with a hoe.

hoe-down (hō′doun′), *n.* a lively, rollicking dance, as a square dance; also, an event featuring this type of dance.

hog (hog), *n.* **1,** a full-grown domestic swine raised for its meat; also, any of various similar animals, as the warthog; **2,** *Colloq.* a grasping or greedy person; as, a road *hog*; also, a coarse, dirty person; **3,** *Slang* a large motorcycle:—*v.t.* [hogged, hog-ging], *Slang* to take more than a fair share of; as, to *hog* all the cookies.

hogs-head (hogz′hed), *n.* **1,** a liquid measure equal to approximately 245 litres; **2,** a large cask holding up to 635 litres.

hog-wash (hog′wôsh′), *n. Colloq.* **1,** swill fed to hogs; **2,** empty phrases; worthless matter.

hoi pol-loi (hoi′ po-loi′), *n.* the common people; the masses: often used wrongly for "upper classes."

hoist (hoist), *v.t.* to raise aloft; as, to *hoist* a flag; to raise by means of a pulley or other tackle:—*n.* **1,** an apparatus for hoisting; a tackle; an elevator; **2,** *Colloq.* a push; a lift; **3,** the act of lifting.

ho-kum (hō′kum), *n. Slang* humbug; nonsense; bunk.

[1]**hold** (hōld), *n.* the interior of a ship or aircraft where cargo is stored.

[2]**hold** (hōld), *v.t.* [*p.t.* held (held), *p.p.* held, *p.pr.* holding], **1,** to have in one's hand or grasp; as, to *hold* a book; also, to keep in place; support; as, a shelf *holds* books; **2,** to control or have or keep possession of; as, to *hold* stocks in a company; *hold* a valid passport; also, defend; as, the defenders *held* the fortress; **3,** to contain; as, this bottle *holds* a litre; **4,** to restrain or check; as, *hold* your tongue; to detain; as, to *hold* a train; **5,** to believe or accept; as, to *hold* an opinion; to think; consider; as, the court *held* that the defendant was guilty; **6,** to keep in a particular state; as, to *hold* one's head erect; to *hold* someone in esteem; **7,** to maintain or carry on; as, to *hold* an argument; **8,** to conduct; as, the club *held* a meeting; also, to preside at; as, the judge *holds* court; **9,** to keep or observe (a festival); **10,** to occupy; have title to; as, to *hold* political office:—*v.i.* **1,** to keep a grasp on something; as, the anchor *holds*; **2,** to remain faithful; as, to *hold* to a purpose; **3,** to remain unbroken or unchanged; as, our ranks *held*; my offer still *holds* good; **4,** to keep going; as, to *hold* to one's course; **5,** to carry oneself; as, to *hold* still:—*n.* **1,** the act of holding; grasp; **2,** something that may be grasped for support; **3,** influence or control; as, the supernatural has a strong *hold* on him; get a *hold* of yourself; **4,** a way of interrupting a telephone call so that a person is not on the line but is not disconnected; as, to put the caller on *hold*; **5,** in *music*, a character placed over [↑] or under [↓] a note or rest to show that it is to be

prolonged; a pause:—*n.* **holding company**, a company organized to hold stocks or bonds of other companies, which it usually controls, in order to derive income from them. Also, **hold′out′; hold′o′ver.**

hold-er (hōld′ėr), *n.* a person or thing that holds; as, the *holder* of a world record: often used in compounds such as pot*holder*, knife*holder*, paper towel *holder*, etc.

hold-up (hōld′up′), *n.* **1,** a delay; as, the rain caused a *holdup* in the program; **2,** a robbery by someone who either has or pretends to have a weapon; as, a bank *holdup*.—*v.t.* **hold up.**

hole (hōl), *n.* **1,** an opening in or through something; as, a *hole* in the roof; **2,** a cavity in something solid; as, a *hole* in a tooth; **3,** an abrupt hollow in the ground, as a pit or cave; also, a deep place in a stream; as, a swimming *hole*; **4,** the burrow of an animal; a den, or hiding place; **5,** *Colloq.* a difficulty; predicament; as, to be in a financial *hole*; **6,** flaw, weakness; as, to have *holes* in her proposal; **7,** in *golf*: **a,** a cup, or hollow, in the putting green into which the ball is to be played; **b,** the part of a course from a tee to such a cup:—*v.t.* [holed, hol-ing], **1,** to drive or put into a hole; **2,** to make holes in; as, to *hole* a board for pegs:—*v.i.* **1,** to go into a hole; **2,** to make a hole; as, to *hole* through a wall; **3,** in *golf*, to put a ball in the hole.—*adj.* **hole′y.**

hol-i-day (ho′i-dā′), *n.* a day when most people do not work and business offices are closed, as in celebration of some event; as, Canada Day, Labour Day, Christmas, and New Year's Day are statutory *holidays*:—**holidays,** a period of rest from work or school; a vacation; as, the summer *holidays*:—*adj.* festive; as, in *holiday* dress.

ho-li-ness (hō′li-nis), *n.* the state or quality of being free from sin; saintliness:—**Holiness,** a title of the Pope.

hol-ler (hol′ėr), *v.i.* and *v.t. Colloq.* to shout; yell; as, he *hollered* for help.

hol-low (hol′ō), *n.* **1,** a cavity; empty space; as, the *hollow* of a tree; **2,** space between hills; a small valley:—*v.t.* to scoop out; as, he *hollowed* out the sand:—*adj.* **1,** having an empty space within; as, a *hollow* shell; **2,** sunken; haggard; as, a *hollow* face; **3,** unreal; insincere; as, *hollow* words of sympathy; **4,** deep or dull; muffled; as, a *hollow* roar:—*adv. Colloq.* completely; as, they beat us all *hollow*.—*adv.* **hol′low-ly.**—*n.* **hol′low-ness.**

hol-ly (hol′i), *n.* [*pl.* hollies], an evergreen shrub or tree, the glossy pointed leaves and red berries of which are much used as decorations at Christmas.

A SPRIG OF HOLLY

hol-ly-hock (hol′i-hok), *n.* a tall plant, much cultivated in gardens, that has large flowers of various colours.

hol-o-caust (hol′o-kôst′), *n.* a great destruction of lives or property, esp. by fire:—**Holocaust,** the mass killing of European Jews and others by Nazi Germany during World War II.

ho-lo-gram (hol′o-gram; hō′lo-gram), *n.* a three-dimensional image produced by patterns from lasers or other light sources.

hol-ster (hōl′stėr), *n.* a leather pistol case, carried at the belt or on a strap across the shoulder.

ho-lus–bo-lus (hō′lus–bō′lus), *adv. Colloq.* all at once; altogether; as, she swallowed the story *holus-bolus*.

ho-ly (hō′li), *adj.* [ho-li-er, ho-li-est], **1,** belonging to or dedicated to the service of God; as, the *Holy* Bible; **2,** perfect; divine; sinless; as, the *Holy* Spirit; *Holy* Grail; **3,** devoted to God; given over to piety; religious; as, the *holy* saints; *holy* person:—*n.* [*pl.* holies], a sacred thing; anything that is holy.

hom-age (hom′ij), *n.* **1,** reverence; respect; oath of loyalty; **2,** in feudal times, the ceremony in which a vassal promised loyalty and service to his lord in return for protection.

hom-bre (ôm′brā; om′bri), *n.* [*Spanish*, man], *Slang* fellow.

Hom-burg or **hom-burg** (hom′burg; hom′boorkh), *n.* a man's soft felt hat with partially rolled brim, worn with the crown dented lengthwise.

home (hōm), *n.* **1,** one's fixed residence or dwelling place; also, the unit of society formed by a family living together; **2,** an animal's or plant's dwelling or habitat; **3,** a person's native land; **4,** a place where something comes from or is typically found; as, Toronto is the *home* of the CN Tower; **5,** a place, such as an institution, for the care or relief of people with an illness or special needs; as, a nursing *home*; **6,** in various games, such as hide-and-seek, a goal or point to be reached; **7,** in *baseball*, the base at which the batter stands to hit and that a runner must reach to score a run:—**at home, 1,** at or in one's home; **2,** relaxed and comfortable; at ease; as, to feel *at home* with the new computer software program:—*adj.* **1,** having to do with or used in the home; as, *home* cooking; *home* computer; **2,** having to do with or being in a base or home area; as, a *home* hockey team:—*adv.* **1,** to or at home; **2,** to the heart or core; as, the blow struck *home*:—*v.i.* [homed, hom-ing], to return home as pigeons; also, to have a home; dwell. Also, **home′ base′; home′bod′y; home′ care′; home′com′ing; home′ comput′er; home′ fry′; home′grown′; home′ ice′; home′ in-va′sion; home′mak′er; home′ o′pen-er; home′own′er; home′ plate′; home′room′; home′shop′ping; home′ stretch′; home′ town′.**

home-land (hōm′land′), *n.* the country where a person was born.

home-less (hōm′les), *adj.* without a home; as, a *homeless* person needs shelter.

home-ly (hōm′li), *adj.* [home-li-er, home-li-est], **1,** homelike; plain; simple; as, *homely* meal; **2,** plain-featured; **3,** unpolished; unpretending; as, *homely* manners.

home-made (hōm′mād′; hōm′mād′), *adj.* made at home; not made in a factory or by a professional; as, a *homemade* cake; *homemade* gloves.

ho-me-o-path-ic or **ho′moe-o-path′ic** (hō′mi-ō-path′ik; hom′i-ō-path′ik), *adj.* naming or employing a method of treating disease in which small amounts of drugs are given that would, in healthy persons, produce effects like those of the disease.—*n.* **ho′me-o′pa-thy.**

home page, 1, in *computing,* the first computer screen that appears on the user's screen on opening the browser; **2,** the main page of an individual's or company's Web site.

ho-mer (hō′mėr), *n. Colloq.* in *baseball,* a *home run.*

home run, in *baseball,* a hit that allows the batter to run around all the bases and score a run.

home-sick (hōm′sik′), *adj.* sad and lonely because of being away from one's home and family.—*n.* **home′sick′ness.**

home-spun (hōm′spun′), *n.* **1,** cloth made of yarn spun at home; **2,** a loosely woven, woollen fabric:—*adj.* **1,** made at home; **2,** plain and homely.

home-stead (hōm′sted), *n.* **1,** a family home with the adjoining lands and buildings; **2,** formerly, in Western Canada, land granted by the federal government to settlers.—*n.* **home′stead′er.**

home-ward (hōm′wėrd), *adj.* and *adv.* toward home or one's native land; as, *homeward* bound.—*adv.* **home′wards.**

home-work (hōm′wûrk′), *n.* **1,** school lessons or studying done out of the regular class period; **2,** reading or research done to prepare for something; as, the mayor did her *homework* on the issue and had ready answers for the media; **3,** any task done at home.

hom-i-cide (hom′i-sīd′), *n.* **1,** the killing of a human being by another; **2,** one who kills another.—*adj.* **hom′i-cid′al.**

hom-i-ly (hom′i-li), *n.* **1,** a sermon; **2,** a tedious, moralizing lecture.

hom-i-ny (hom′i-ni), *n.* hulled, dried corn, or maize, coarsely ground or broken, used as a cereal and as a vegetable.

ho-mo-ge-ne-ous (hōmō-jē′nē-us; hom′ō-jē′nē-us), *adj.* uniform; of the same kind or nature; made up of similar parts: opposite of *heterogeneous*; as, a culturally *homogeneous* population.

ho-mo-gen-ize (ho-moj′en-īz′; hō′-), *v.t.* to make more uniform in texture by breaking down and blending the particles, esp. to break up the fat globules of milk to make it more uniform and prevent the cream from rising to the top.

hom-o-graph (hom′o-graf), *n.* a word that is spelled the same way as another word but has a different meaning, as a *bat* that is used in baseball, and a *bat* that lives in caves and flies.

hom-o-nym (hom′o-nim), *n.* any of two or more words, the same in sound but different in meaning and often in spelling, as *bat* (hitting stick) and *bat* (flying animal), and *pair, pare, pear*: both *homographs* and *homophones* are *homonyms.*

ho-mo-pho-bi-a (hō′mo-fō′bē-a), *n.* hatred or extreme fear of homosexuals, often involving discrimination or prejudice.

hom-o-phone (hom′o-fōn′), *n.* a word that has the same sound as another word but is spelled differently, as *to, too, two.*

ho-mo-sex-u-al (hō′mō-sek′shoo-al), *n.* and *adj.* one who is sexually attracted to a person of the same sex.—*n.* **ho′mo-sex′u-al′i-ty.**

hone (hōn), *n.* a fine-grained stone for sharpening razors and keen-edged tools:—*v.t.* [honed, hon-ing], **1,** to sharpen on such a stone; **2,** to make more effective; as, to *hone* one's skill in writing.

hon-est (on′est), *adj.* **1,** upright; just; as, an *honest* judge; truthful; sincere; as, an *honest* opinion; **2,** genuine; without fraud; as, *honest* weight; **3,** frank; expressing sincerity; as, an *honest* countenance.—*adv.* **hon′est-ly.**—*n.* **hon′es-ty.**

hon-ey (hun′i), *n.* **1,** a sweet, sticky substance, produced by honeybees from the nectar that they collect from flowers; **2,** sweetness; **3,** darling; sweetheart.

hon-ey-bee (hun′i-bē′), *n.* a bee that gathers nectar from flowers to make honey, often kept in hives for their wax and honey.

hon-ey-comb (hun′i-kōm′), *n.* **1,** a wax structure of six-sided cells made by bees to hold their honey and eggs; **2,** any similar structure:—*v.t.* and *v.i.* to fill, or become filled, with holes, passages, or cells; as, miners had *honeycombed* the ground beneath the town.

honey-dew (hun′i-dū′), *n.* **1,** a sweet liquid that exudes from some plants in hot weather; **2,** a pale-green muskmelon of sweet flavour and white flesh; the honeydew melon.

hon-eyed or **hon′ied** (hun′id), *adj.* **1,** covered or filled with honey; **2,** sweet; coaxing; flattering; as, *honeyed* words.

hon-ey-moon (hun′i-mo͞on′), *n.* **1,** a holiday spent together by a newly married couple; a wedding trip; **2,** a pleasant or peaceful period at the start of something; as, the *honeymoon* was over for the mayor two months after being elected when the media began criticizing his stand on several issues:—*v.i.* to spend a honeymoon.

hon-ey-suck-le (hun′i-suk′l), *n.* a climbing plant with fragrant white, red, or yellow tube-shaped flowers.

honk (hongk), *n.* **1,** the call of a wild goose; **2,** any sound resembling this; as, the *honk* of a car horn:—*v.i.* to make such a sound:—*v.t.* to sound or blow (a horn).

hon-o-ra-ri-um (on′o-râ′ri-um), *n.* [*pl.* honorariums or honoraria], **1,** a payment recognizing professional services for which propriety or law forbids a set price; as, an *honorarium* for speaking at the business luncheon; **2,** a fee for the services of a professional person.

hon-or-ar-y (on′ėr-a-ri), *adj.* **1,** given as a mark of honour, esteem, merit, etc.; as, an *honorary* title or degree; **2,** holding a position or office as an honour without its responsibilities, pay, etc.; as, *honorary* president.

hon-our or **hon-or** (on′ėr), *n.* **1,** respectful regard; high esteem; as, to show *honour* to a distinguished person; an outward mark of high esteem; as, military *honours*; **2,** glory; fame; as, Hector fought for the *honour* of Troy; **3,** distinction; as, the *honour* of being prime minister; also, a cause of glory; a credit; as, he is an *honour* to the town; **4,** uprightness; integrity; as, a man of *honour*; **5, honours,** distinguished standing in school or university; as, she graduated with *honours*:—**Honour,** a title of respect; as, his *Honour*, the mayor:—*v.t.* **1,** to treat with respect or deference; revere; **2,** to bestow marks of esteem upon; as, he was *honoured* with the title of captain; **3,** to accept and pay when due; as, the bank will *honour* my cheque. Also, **hon′our roll′; hon′our stu′dent; hon′our sys′tem.**

hon-our-a-ble or **hon-or-a-ble** (on′ėr-a-bl), *adj.* **1,** noble; illustrious; as, *honourable* deeds; **2,** upright; honest; as, an *honourable* person; an *honourable* purpose; **3,** in accord with honour; as, an *honourable* discharge; **4,** accompanied with honour or marks of respect; as, an *honourable* mention:—**Honourable,** a title of distinction of certain officials in government and law.—*adv.* **hon′our-a-bly.**

hood (hood), *n.* **1,** a soft wrapper or covering for the head, usually attached to a coat or jacket; **2,** something resembling such a head covering in shape or use; as, a *hood* over the stove; **3,** the hinged metal cover over the engine of an automobile; **4,** an ornamental fold hanging down the back of a gown worn by a graduate of a college or university, denoting, by its colour, the wearer's degree; **5,** *Slang* hoodlum:—*v.t.* to cover, or furnish with, or as with, a hood.—*adj.* **hood′ed.**

hood-lum (ho͞od′lum), *n. Colloq.* **1,** a young rowdy person; ruffian; **2,** a gangster.

hoo-doo (ho͞o′do͞o′), *n. Colloq.* **1,** a person or thing that causes bad luck; voodoo; **2,** a strangely shaped rock pillar caused by erosion, found in western North America, esp. Alberta:—*v.t.* [-dooed (do͞od), -dooing], to bring or cause bad luck; bewitch.

hood-wink (hood′wingk), *v.t.* to deceive; mislead.—*n.* **hood′wink′er.**

hoof (ho͞of), *n.* [*pl.* hoofs (ho͞ofs) or hooves (ho͞ovz)], **1,** the horny substance covering the toes of some animals, as horses; also, the whole foot; **2,** *Slang* a person's foot.—*adj.* **hoofed:**—*v.t. Colloq.* to walk or trample; as, to *hoof* it to school; *hoof* the ball:—*v.i. Slang* to dance.

hook (hook), *n.* **1,** a curved piece of metal, bone, etc., to hold or catch something; as, a crochet *hook*; a fish*hook*; coat *hook*; **2,** a curved instrument, as a sickle, for looping or cutting; **3,** a sharp bend or curve, as in a river or road; **4,** *Nautical* (*Colloq.*) an anchor; **5,** in *music*, a line or stroke at the end of the stem of a note to show that it is an eighth, sixteenth, etc.; **6,** in *baseball*, a curve; **7,** in *boxing*, a swinging blow; **8,** in *golf*, a stroke that is curved or pulled sharply to the left by a right-handed player, or to the right by a left-handed player; **9,** in *hockey*, an illegal check using a hockey stick:—**by hook or by crook,** by fair means or foul:—*v.t.* **1,** to catch with, or as with, a hook; as, to *hook* a fish; hence, to steal; also, to fasten with a hook or hooks; as, to *hook* the gate; **2,** in *hockey*, to use a hockey stick to check a player from the opposite team who has the puck; also, in other sports such as *golf* or *boxing*, to use a hook:—*v.i.* **1,** to bend or curve sharply; as, this road *hooks* to the left; **2,** to be fastened by a hook; as, this bikini top *hooks* in the front; **3,** to work as a prostitute.—*n.* **hook′er.**

hook-ah (hook′a), *n.* an Eastern smoking pipe with a long flexible tube for drawing the smoke through water contained in a vase.

hooked (hookt; hook′id), *adj.* **1,** curved like a hook; as, a *hooked* nose; **2,** made with a hook; as, a *hooked* rug; **3,** furnished with hooks; as, a *hooked* brassiere; **4,** *Slang* addicted; captivated; trapped; as, *hooked* on sleeping pills; **5,** *Slang* married or attached.

hook-up (hook′up′), *n.* **1,** a connecting system, with wires, etc., as of apparatus for computer, Internet, telephone, radio, or television reception or transmission; also, a system that links users with supply sources, such as gas, electricity, etc.; **2,** a chain of radio or television stations linked for a broadcast; as, a continent-wide *hookup*.

hook·y (hook′i), *n. Colloq.* be away from school without permission: used only in the expression *to play hooky*.

hoo·li·gan (hōō′li-gan), *n. Colloq.* a hoodlum; a young ruffian, esp. a member of a street gang.—*n.* **hoo′li·gan·ism.**

hoop (hōōp), *n.* **1,** a circular band or ring; also, anything shaped like a hoop; **2,** in *basketball*, the basket; **3,** a large circle of plastic, metal, or wood, used as a toy that is rolled along the ground or twirled around the body by children:—*v.t.* to bind with a hoop; encircle.

hoop skirt, formerly, a skirt expanded by means of a circular framework of wire, whalebone, etc.

hoo·ray (hoo-rā′), *interj.* Same as **hurrah.**

hoot (hōōt), *n.* **1,** the cry of an owl; as, a long *hoot* sounded through the woods; **2,** a sound like this cry; **3,** a shout of contempt:—*v.t.* to jeer with contemptuous shouts; as, to *hoot* their disapproval of the actor:—*v.i.* to utter a sharp cry, as an owl; **2,** to utter shouts of derision or contempt; as, the audience *hooted* and jeered at the speaker.

[1]**hop** (hop), *n.* a vine with small, greenish, cone-shaped flowers:—**hops**, the dried, ripened cones of this plant, used to give flavour to beer, ale, etc.:—*v.t.* [hopped, hop-ping], to flavour with hops:—*v.i.* to pick hops.

[2]**hop** (hop), *v.t.* [hopped, hop-ping], **1,** to jump over; as, to *hop* a fence; **2,** *Colloq.* to ride on a plane, bus, train, etc.; as, to *hop* a plane to Toronto:—*v.i.* **1,** to move by short jumps, using one leg only; **2,** to jump with both or all feet at once, as do frogs; **3,** *Colloq.* to travel by air, train, bus, etc., esp. a quick trip:—*n.* **1,** a short, brisk jump, esp. on one leg; **2,** *Colloq.* an informal dance; **3,** *Colloq.* a short trip on a plane, bus, train, etc.

hope (hōp), *n.* **1,** desire or wish accompanied by expectation; anticipation; confidence; as, an invalid's *hope* of speedy recovery; **2,** the thing desired; as, success in business was his constant *hope*; **3,** a cause or source of hope; as, she was the *hope* of her parents:—*v.t.* [hoped, hop-ing], to desire; expect; as, he *hopes* his efforts will be successful:—*v.i.* to cherish a desire; wish; as, we *hope* for better times.

hope·ful (hōp′fool), *adj.* **1,** full of confident expectations; as, he is *hopeful* that he will be able to go; **2,** promising success; as, *hopeful* news.—*adv.* **hope′ful·ly.**—*n.* **hope′ful·ness.**

hope·less (hōp′lis), *adj.* **1,** without expectation of good; despairing; as, *hopeless* grief; **2,** without promise of good; as, a *hopeless* situation.—*adv.* **hope′less·ly.**—*n.* **hope′less·ness.**

hop·per (hop′ėr), *n.* **1,** one who or that which hops; **2,** any of various leaping insects; as, the grass*hopper*; **3,** a wooden funnel through which grain passes into a mill, or any device like this.

hop·scotch (hop′skoch′), *n.* a child's game, in which the players hop or skip from one space to another of a design on the ground:—*v.i.* **1,** to play the game, or move as if so doing; **2,** *Colloq.* to travel about; as, she *hopscotched* around the globe.

horde (hōrd), *n.* **1,** a wandering tribe or clan; as, a *horde* of Mongols; **2,** a vast multitude, as of insects.

ho·ri·zon (ho-rī′zn), *n.* **1,** the line where the sky and earth, or the sky and sea, appear to meet; **2,** the range or limit of one's mental experience or interest; as, university can broaden your *horizons*.

hor·i·zon·tal (hor′i-zon′tal), *adj.* parallel to, or in the direction of, the line where earth meets sky; level; as, a ceiling is *horizontal*: opposite of *vertical*.—*adv.* **hor′i·zon′tal·ly.**

hor·mone (hôr′mōn), *n.* a chemical secretion made in organs or glands, such as the adrenal and pituitary, that excites or increases a vital process in remoter cells when carried to them by body fluids: hormones control body growth and development and regulate activities such as breathing, digestion, and perspiration.

horn (hôrn), *n.* **1,** a hard, usually pointed, outgrowth on the head of certain animals, esp. cattle, goats, deer, rhinoceroses, etc.; **2,** the material of which animals' horns are composed, or a similar material; **3,** anything made of or resembling the horns of an animal, as one of the ends of the moon when in crescent form; **4,** a musical wind instrument, usually made of brass, as a French horn, trumpet, tuba, trombone, etc.; **5,** a device in a car, truck, or other vehicle that can make a loud noise as a warning.—*adj.* **horned.**

hor·net (hôr′nit), *n.* a large type of wasp that inflicts a painful sting.

horn·y (hôr′ni), *adj.* [horn-i-er, horn-i-est], **1,** hard like horn; **2,** made of horn; **3,** having horns; **4,** *Slang* sexually excited.

hor·o·scope (hor′o-skōp′), *n.* **1,** the conjunction, or relative position, of the planets and stars at one's birth; **2,** the foretelling of the events of one's life from such position (not regarded as scientific); **3,** the diagram showing the 12 signs of the zodiac (used by astrologers).

hor·ren·dous (ho-ren′dus), *adj.* frightful; exciting terror.

hor·ri·ble (hor′i-bl), *adj.* **1,** terrible; dreadful; shocking; frightening; as, a *horrible* train wreck; **2,** *Colloq.* severe; extreme; unpleasant; awful; as, a *horrible* headache; a *horrible* smell.—*adv.* **hor′ri·bly.**

hor·rid (hor′id), *adj.* **1,** terrible; hideous; horrible; as, a *horrid* monster; **2,** *Colloq.* very bad or unpleasant; as, a *horrid* smell.

hor-ri-fy (hor′i-fī′), *v.t.* [horrified, horrifying], **1,** to fill or strike with great fear or dread; **2,** *Colloq.* to surprise in an annoying or unpleasant way; as, the mess in the kitchen *horrified* her parents.

hor-ror (hor′ėr), *n.* **1,** excessive fear; extreme dread; as, they were filled with *horror* at the thought of the terrorist attack; **2,** great disgust or aversion; as, she has a *horror* of dirt; **3,** that which causes dread; **4,** *Colloq.* very bad or unpleasant; as, her hair was a *horror.*

hors d'oeuvres (ôr′dûvr′), *n. French* an appetizer, as olives, radishes, and other finger foods, served at the beginning of a meal or alone as snacks.

horse (hôrs), *n.* **1,** a large, solid-hoofed, four-footed, grass-eating animal, used for pulling burdens or riding; **2,** mounted soldiers; cavalry; **3,** a framework for the support of anything; as, a clothes*horse*; saw*horse*; **4,** in *gymnastics,* a padded and raised wooden block used for vaulting:—**dark horse, 1,** in *horse racing,* a horse, the chances of success of which have been overlooked; esp. an unexpected winner; **2,** in *politics,* an unforeseen competitor:—*v.t.* [horsed, hors-ing], to mount on, or furnish with, a horse.

horse-back (hôrs′bak′), *n.* the back of a horse:—*adv.* on horseback.

horse-fly or **horse fly** (hôrs′flī′; hôrs′ flī′), *n.* [*pl.* horse-flies; horse flies], a large, two-winged fly that stings and sucks the blood of animals.

horse-hair (hôrs′hâr′), *n.* **1,** the hair of the mane or tail of a horse; **2,** cloth made from this hair.

horse-man (hôrs′man), *n.* [*pl.* horsemen (-men)], **1,** a rider on horseback; **2,** a person who is clever at managing horses; **3,** a horse rancher; **4,** *Slang* a member of the Royal Canadian Mounted Police.—*n.fem.* **horse′wom′an.**—*n.* **horse′man-ship.**

horse opera, *Slang* a play, movie, or television show about cowboys, rustlers, etc.; a western.

horse-play (hôrs′plā′), *n.* rough fun.

horse-power (hôrs′pou′ėr), *n.* a unit that measures the power of an engine; the amount of power required to raise about 250 kilograms 30.5 centimetres in one second; as, a boat with a 20-*horsepower* engine: abbreviated as *hp.*

horse-rad-ish (hôrs′rad′ish), *n.* **1,** a plant of the mustard family, the root of which is ground and used as a relish with meats, fish, etc.; **2,** the relish made from this root.

horse-shoe (hôrs′shōō′), *n.* **1,** a U-shaped metal shoe to protect the hoof of a horse; **2,** anything shaped like a horseshoe:—**horseshoes,** a game in which players throw a horseshoe or similar object so that it will land around a post in the ground.

horse-whip (hôrs′whip′), *n.* a leather whip for driving or managing horses:—*v.t.* [horse-whipped, horse-whip-ping], to flog with a horsewhip.

hor-sy or **hor-sey** (hôr′si), *adj.* **1,** fond of horses, racing, etc., or affecting the ways of those who are; as, *horsy* talk; **2,** *Slang* large and clumsy in appearance.

hor-ti-cul-ture (hôr′ti-kul′tūr), *n.* the art or science of growing vegetables, fruits, and flowers.—*adj.* **hor′ti-cul′tur-al.**—*n.* **hor′ti-cul′tur-ist.**

hose (hōz), *n.* [*pl.* hose], **1,** a covering for the leg; a sock or stocking; **2,** a tight-fitting covering for the legs and waist, formerly worn by men; **3,** flexible tubing for carrying liquids; as, a *hose* for sprinkling the lawn; a gas *hose*:—*v.t.* [hosed, hos-ing], **1,** to water or drench with a hose; **2,** *Slang* to cheat; as, the merchant at the exhibition *hosed* us.

ho-sier-y (hō′zhėr-i), *n.* stockings; hose.

hos-pi-ta-ble (hos′pi-ta-bl), *adj.* disposed to welcome guests with generosity and kindness; as, a *hospitable* host.—*adv.* **hos′pi-ta-bly.**

hos-pi-tal (hos′pi-tal), *n.* a place where doctors, nurses, and other medical workers provide treatment and care for the sick or injured.—*v.t.* **hos′pi-tal-ize′.**—*n.* **hos′pi-tal-i-za′tion.**

hos-pi-tal-i-ty (hos′pi-tal′i-ti), *n.* [*pl.* hospitalities], the entertaining of guests with kindness and liberality.

[1]host (hōst), *n.* a great number; a throng; as, a *host* of wildflowers.

[2]host (hōst), *n.* **1,** one who entertains others; also, one who provides food and lodging for pay; an innkeeper; **2,** a person who is the main performer on a television or radio variety show or talk show; **3,** an animal or plant organism that gives nourishment to a parasite; **4,** in *computing,* a computer that can be accessed by other users (known as clients) by modem through a network:—*v.t.* and *v.i.* to act as host.

Host (hōst), *n.* the consecrated bread or wafer used in Christian Holy Communion.

hos-tage (hos′tij), *n.* **1,** a person who remains in the hands of another as a guarantee that certain conditions will be fulfilled; as, prisoners of war are sometimes held as *hostages*; **2,** any pledge or guarantee.

hos-tel (hos′t'l), *n.* an inn or hotel.

host-ess (hōs′tes), *n.* **1,** a woman who receives and entertains guests; **2,** a woman who runs an inn; **3,** the main female performer on a television or radio variety show or talk show; **4,** an attendant in a restaurant who welcomes guests, conducts them to a table, etc.

hos-tile (hos′tīl; hos′til), *adj.* **1,** belonging to an enemy; as, *hostile* troops; **2,** unfriendly; as, *hostile* criticism.—*n.* **hos-til′i-ty.**

hos-tler or **os-tler** (hos′lėr; os′lėr), *n.* one who takes care of horses; a groom.

hot (hot), *adj.* [hot-ter, hot-test], **1,** of high temperature: opposite of *cold*; as, a *hot* stove; *hot* soup; **2,** fiery; passionate; as, a *hot* temper; **3,** having a sharp or biting taste, as spices; **4,** fresh; strong; as, a *hot* scent; **5,** *Colloq.* very active or successful; as, a *hot* young actor; **6,** *Slang* excellent; stylish; as, *hot* new clothes; **7,** *Slang* stolen; as, a *hot* car.—*adv.* **hot′ly.**—*n.* **hot′ness.**

hot-bed (hot′bed′), *n.* **1,** a bed of earth heated by decaying manure for forcing plants; **2,** any place or condition promoting rapid growth; as, a *hotbed* of intrigue, vice, treason, etc.

hot-blood-ed (hot′blud′id), *adj.* excitable; impetuous.

hotch-potch (hoch′poch′), *n.* a hodgepodge.

hot dog or **hot-dog** (hot′ dog′; hot′dog′), *n.* a heated wiener, usually in a split roll.—*v.i.* **hot′-dog′** [hot-dogged, hot-dog-ging], *Slang* to perform stunts.

ho-tel (hō-tel′), *n.* an establishment where lodging and usually food are provided for pay.

hot-head (hot′hed′), *n.* a rash, fiery-tempered person.—*adj.* **hot′head′ed.**

hot-house (hot′hous′), *n.* **1,** a building of glass or similar material, heated for growing or forcing flowers or vegetables; greenhouse; **2,** a hotbed; an environment conducive to growth; as, Silicon Valley North is a *hothouse* of Canadian high tech:—*adj.* **1,** grown in or for a hothouse; as, *hothouse* tomatoes; **2,** pertaining to a hotbed.

hot link, in *computing,* a hyperlink; an electronic connection that moves the user who clicks on it to another part of the document or to another document.

hound (hound), *n.* any of several breeds of dog, with large, drooping ears and very keen scent, originally trained for hunting:—*v.t.* **1,** to chase with hounds; **2,** to pursue; nag; pester; as, the reporters *hounded* the famous actor.

hour (our), *n.* **1,** the 24th part of a day; 60 minutes; **2,** the time of day; one of the points of time indicating such a period; as, clocks tell the *hours*; **3,** a particular or stated time; as, store *hours* are from 9 to 6; **4,** a unit of distance reckoned by the time taken to travel it; as, Regina is three *hours* from here.—*adj.* and *adv.* **hour′ly.**

hour-glass (our′glås′), *n.* a device consisting of two glass bulbs, one above the other, connected by a narrow neck, used for measuring time: it takes an hour for the sand, mercury, or water with which the uppermost bulb is filled to pass through the narrow neck to the lower bulb.

HOURGLASS

house (hous), *n.* **1,** a building for people to live in; also, the people living in a house; a household; **2,** a building for some particular purpose; as, a work*house*; court*house*; also, a shelter for animals; as, a dog*house*; **3,** family or race; as, the royal *house* of England; **4,** one of the divisions of a lawmaking body; as, the *House* of Commons; **5,** a theatre or its audience; **6,** a business firm or place of business:—*v.t.* (houz), [housed, hous-ing], **1,** to shelter or lodge; **2,** to store (goods); **3,** to secure; put into a safe place; as, to *house* a valuable collection in a case:—*v.i.* to take shelter.—*n.* **house′ ar-rest′; house′boat′; house′ brand′; house′break′er; house′ call′; house′ clean′ing; house′coat′; house′ful; house′ guest′; house′hus′band; House′ lead′er; house′plant′; house′ sit′ter; house′ style′; house′trail′er; house′ wares′.**

house-bro-ken (hous′brō′ken), *adj.* trained to live in a house (that is, to urinate, etc., in the proper place), as a cat, dog, etc.

house-fly (hous′flī′), *n.* [*pl.* houseflies], the common domestic fly that lives in or near houses.

house-hold (hous′hōld′), *n.* a group of persons living together; a family:—*adj.* **1,** pertaining to a family or home; domestic; as, *household* chores; **2,** very well-known; common; familiar; as, "Kleenex" has become a *household* word.

house-keep-ing (hous′kēp′ing), *n.* **1,** the management of domestic affairs; **2,** management of internal business affairs; routine tasks:—*adj.* pertaining to the management of a household, business, or routine tasks; domestic.—*n.* **house′keep-er.**

house-maid (hous′mād′), *n.* a girl or woman hired to do housework; a female servant.

House of Commons, **1,** in Canada, the elected representatives who meet in Ottawa to make laws and debate questions of government; **2,** the chamber in which these representatives meet.

house-warm-ing (hous′wôr′ming); *n.* a party celebrating a family's moving into a new home.

house-wife (hous′wīf′), *n.* **1,** [*pl.* housewives (-wīvz′)], the mistress of a home or who manages domestic affairs as the main occupation; **2,** (huz′if), [*pl.* housewives (huz′ivz)], a small case for sewing materials.

house-work (hous′wûrk′), *n.* the work done in a home, as cooking, cleaning, etc.; housekeeping.

hous-ing (houz′ing), *n.* **1,** the act of giving shelter; **2,** that which gives shelter; **3,** houses as a group; provision of homes for people; as, *housing* is a problem of a large city; **4,** in *mechanics,* a frame or support that protects the moving parts of a machine; as, the *housing* of gears in the rear axle of a motor vehicle.

hove (hōv), a *p.t.* and *p.p.* of *heave* (nautical).

hov-el (hov′el; huv′el), *n.* a wretched little cottage; a hut.

hov-er (hov′ėr; huv′ėr), *v.i.* **1,** to flutter over or about; as, the helicopter *hovered* over the bay; **2,** to wait near at hand; move to and fro near a place; as, to *hover* over a sick person; **3,** to waver; hesitate; fluctuate; as, the temperature *hovered* around 30 degrees Celsius.

how (hou), *adv.* **1,** in what manner or way; as, *how* did you do it? **2,** to what degree or extent; as, *how* far did you go? **3,** at what price; as, *how* much did you pay for it? **4,** in what condition; as, *how* are you? **5,** with what reason or meaning; as, *how* is it that you are late?

how-ev-er (hou′ev′ėr), *adv.* in whatever manner or degree; as, every donation, *however* small, is a help to the cause:—*conj.* nevertheless; in spite of that; as, I cannot, *however*, agree.

how-itz-er (hou′it-sėr), *n.* a short cannon that fires a shell at a high angle.

howl (houl), *n.* **1,** the long, wailing cry of a dog or a wolf; **2,** a cry of pain or distress; **3,** a loud shout of ridicule or amusement; as, *howls* and jeers from the audience:—*v.i.* **1,** to utter a loud, wailing cry, like a dog or wolf; **2,** to utter a prolonged cry of pain or distress; lament; **3,** to roar, yell, or shout; as, to *howl* with laughter:—*v.t.* to utter in a wailing tone:—**howl down,** to silence or deride by howling.

how-ler (hou′lėr), *n.* **1,** one who howls; **2,** a species of tropical monkey; **3,** *Colloq.* a glaring blunder.

how-so-ev-er (hou′sō-ev′ėr), *adv.* in whatever manner or degree; however.

how–to (hou′tōō′), *adj.* giving practical instruction or advice; as, *how-to* books:—*n.* [*pl.* how-tos], the instructions often contained in such books.

hp (āch′pē′), *abbrev.* short for *horsepower.*

HST (āch′es′tē′), *abbrev.* short for *harmonized sales tax.*

HTML (āch′tē′em′el′), *abbrev.* short for *hypertext markup language.*

http (āch′tē′tē′pē′), *abbrev.* short for *hypertext transfer protocol.*

hub (hub), *n.* **1,** the central part of a wheel; **2,** anything that resembles the centre of a wheel in position or importance; centre of activity; as, the *hub* of economic growth; **3,** in *computing,* a device that links computers together, esp. in a local area network. Also, **hub′cap′.**

hub-bub (hub′ub), *n.* uproar; tumult; as, the class was in a *hubbub* when the teacher returned.

hu-bris (hyōō′bris), *n.* excessive pride; arrogance; overconfidence.

huck-le-ber-ry (huk′l-ber′i), *n.* [*pl.* huckleberries], the blue-black, berrylike, edible fruit of a low-growing shrub; also, the shrub.

huck-ster (huk′stėr), *n.* **1,** a peddler or hawker; esp. one who deals in small items; **2,** a mean, tricky trader.

hud-dle (hud′l), *v.t.* and *v.i.* [hud-dled, hud-dling], to crowd or press together in disorder:—*n.* **1,** confusion; crowd; **2,** in *football,* the gathering together of the players of a team for the giving of signals, instructions, etc.

hue (hū), *n.* colour; tint; as, wildflowers of every *hue.*

huff (huf), *n.* a fit of ill humour; sudden offence taken:—*v.t.* and *v.i.* to bully or offend; to take offence.—*adj.* **huff′y.**

hug (hug), *n.* a close embrace:—*v.t.* [hugged, hug-ging], **1,** to embrace closely; as, to *hug* a child; **2,** to hold fast to; cling to; as, to *hug* a belief; **3,** to keep close to; as, to *hug* the shore.

huge (hūj), *adj.* [hug-er, hug-est], **1,** of great bulk; vast; very large; as, a *huge* mountain; **2,** great; as, the party was a *huge* success.—*adv.* **huge′ly.**

hula or **hu-la–hu-la** (hōō′la; hōō′la–hōō′la), *n.* a native Hawaiian women's dance, pantomimic and suggestive; also, the music.

hulk (hulk), *n.* **1,** the body of a wrecked or unseaworthy ship; **2,** an old, clumsy vessel; also, any clumsy object or person.

hulk-ing or **hulky** (hul′king; hul′ki), *adj.* clumsy; bulky; as, a *hulking* fellow.

¹hull (hul), *n.* the outer covering of certain fruits, vegetables, and grains:—*v.t.* to shell (peas), husk (corn), etc.

²hull (hul), *n.* the body or frame of a ship or airship.

hul-la-ba-loo (hul′a-ba-lōō′), *n.* uproar; confusion; hubbub; noisy disturbance.

hul-lo (hu-lō′), *n.* and *interj.* Same as **hello.**

hum (hum), *v.i.* [hummed, hum-ming], **1,** to make a sound without opening the lips, suggesting the sound of a prolonged *m*; **2,** to make a buzzing noise, as a bee in flight; to drone; **3,** to sing with lips closed; **4,** *Colloq.* to be in energetic motion or action; as, to make things *hum*:—*v.t.* to sing with the lips closed; as, to *hum* a song:—*n.* **1,** the noise made by bees and other insects in flying; a low sound like the letter *m*; **2,** a distant sound as of machinery in motion, airplanes in flight, etc.

hu-man (hū′man), *adj.* pertaining to, or characteristic of, a person or people; as, *human* progress; *human* kindness:—*n.* a human being. Also, **hu′man na′ture; hu′man race′; hu′man re-la′tions; hu′man re′sourc-es; hu′man rights′.**

hu-mane (hū-mān′), *adj.* having or exhibiting the feelings proper to humans and animals; benevolent; kind; as, *humane* laws.—*adv.* **hu-mane′ly.**—*n.* **hu-mane′-ness.**

human im-mu-no-de-fi-cien-cy virus, (im′ū-nō-di-fish′en-si), *n.* a retrovirus that causes AIDS: abbreviated as *HIV.*

hu-man-ism (hū′man-izm), *n.* **1,** a rationalistic philosophy that emphasizes the importance of human interests and values rather than supernatural ones; secular humanism; **2,** the study of the humanities and the liberal arts, esp. the Greek and Roman classics:—**Humanism,** the movement of the European Renaissance that emphasized the importance of rediscovering the Greek and Roman classics.—*n.* **hu′man-ist.**

hu-man-i-tar-i-an (hū-man′i-târ′i-an), *n.* a charitably inclined person; one who is devoted to the welfare of human beings:—*adj.* charitable; devoted to the welfare of people.—*n.* **hu-man′i-tar′i-an-ism.**

hu-man-i-ty (hū-man′i-ti), *n.* [*pl.* humanities], **1,** the human race; **2,** the nature that distinguishes humans from other creatures; **3,** charity toward others; kindness.

hu-man-ize (hū′man-īz′), *v.t.* and *v.i.* [-ized, -izing], to make kind, considerate, etc.; to civilize:—*v.i.* to become human.

hu-man-kind (hū′man-kīnd′), *n.* people collectively; human beings; humanity.

hu-man-ly (hū′man-li), *adv.* **1,** in a human or kind manner; as, to speak *humanly*; **2,** within human power or knowledge; as, we will do whatever is *humanly* possible.

hum-ble (hum′bl), *adj.* [hum-bler, hum-blest], **1,** not proud; as, a *humble* attitude; **2,** obscure; unassuming; not large or important; as, they lived in a *humble* cottage:—*v.t.* [hum-bled, hum-bling], to subdue; humiliate; as, the loss of her job *humbled* her.—*n.* **hum′ble-ness.**

hum-bug (hum′bug′), *n.* **1,** a fraud or sham; **2,** an impostor or deceiver; **3,** a kind of peppermint candy:—*v.t.* [humbugged, humbug-ging], to swindle.

hum-drum (hum′drum′), *adj.* dull; monotonous; as, a *humdrum* life:—*n.* **1,** monotony; **2,** a dull person; a bore.

hu-mer-us (hū′mėr-us), *n.* the bone of the upper arm from shoulder to elbow.

hu-mid (hū′mid), *adj.* damp; moist; as, a *humid* climate.—*n.* **hu-mid′i-ty.**

hu-mid-ex (hū′mi-deks), *n.* a combined measurement of temperature and humidity that shows what dry-air temperature would cause the same amount of discomfort as the temperature with the humidity: the scale was first devised in 1965 by Canadian scientists.

hu-mid-i-fy (hū-mid′i-fī′), *v.t.* [-fied, -fy-ing], to moisten or make humid.—*n.* **hu-mid′ i-fi′er.**

hu-mil-i-ate (hū-mil′i-āt′), *v.t.* [humiliat-ed, humiliat-ing], to humble; put to shame; make ashamed; as, his behaviour *humiliated* me.

hu-mil-i-a-tion (hū-mil′i-ā′shun), *n.* the act of putting to shame or the state of being put to shame; mortification.

hu-mil-i-ty (hū-mil′i-t), *n.* [*pl.* humilities], meekness; modesty; lack of pride.

hum-ming-bird (hum′ing-bûrd′), *n.* a small New World bird noted for its bright colours, ability to hover in one spot, and wings that during flight move so rapidly as to make a humming noise.

hum-mock (hum′uk), *n.* a knoll; a low rounded hill.

hu-mour or **hu-mor** (hū′mėr), *n.* **1,** a state of mind; mood; as, he is in a bad *humour*; **2,** the capacity to see or appreciate things that are funny; as, a sense of *humour*; **3,** the quality of being funny or amusing; as, the *humour* of a story:—*v.t.* to yield to the mood of; to indulge.—*n.* **hu′mor-ist.**—*adj.* **hu′mor-ous.**

hump (hump), *n.* a bulging lump, as that on the back of a camel or buffalo; also, a hill:—*v.t.* to make into such a shape; bend or curve, as the back.

hump-back (hump′bak′), *n.* **1,** one with a deformed or crooked back; a hunchback; **2,** a crooked back; **3,** a large whale with a rounded back. Also called *humpback whale.*—*adj.* **hump′backed′; humped; hump′y.**

humpf (humf), *interj.* a snort or grunt expressing doubt, disgust, disbelief, contempt, etc.

hu-mus (hū′mus), *n.* the black or dark substance in soils formed by the decay of vegetable matter, which nourishes the soil and helps plants grow.

hunch (hunch), *n.* **1,** a hump; a rounded lump; **2,** a strong feeling that something will happen, or happen in a certain way; as, to have a *hunch* that it would snow:—*v.t.* to round (the back); form a hump.

hunch-back (hunch′bak′), *n.* **1,** a person with a crooked back; **2,** a crooked back. —*adj.* **hunch′backed′.**

hundred (hun′dred), *adj.* composed of 10 times 10:—*n.* **1,** the number consisting of 10 times 10; **2,** a sign representing this number, as 100 or C.—*adj.* and *n.* **hun′dredth.**

hun-dred-fold (hun′dred-fōld′), *adj., adv.,* and *n.* a hundred times as much or as great.

hung (hung), a *p.t.* and *p.p.* of *hang.*

hun-ger (hung′gėr), *n.* **1,** a craving or need for food; **2,** any strong desire; as, a *hunger* for excitement:—*v.i.* **1,** to feel a desire or longing for food; **2,** to long eagerly for something; as, the boy *hungered* to be an artist.—*adj.* **hun′gry.**—*adv.* **hun′gri-ly.**

hunk (hungk), *n.* **1,** *Colloq.* a lump; large

piece; chunk, as of bread or meat; **2,** *Slang* a handsome man.

hun-ker (hungk′ėr), *v.i.* **1,** to crouch or squat, esp. close to the ground; as, she *hunkered* down; **2,** to take shelter; as, they *hunkered* down out of the wind; **3,** to stubbornly hold a position; as, the government *hunkered* down.

hunt (hunt), *v.t.* **1,** to pursue, or try to catch or kill (game or wild animals); **2,** to search through for something; as, to *hunt* the library for a book; **3,** to follow closely; hound; as, they *hunted* the fugitive over the countryside; **4,** to search after; as, to *hunt* gold:—*v.i.* **1,** to follow the chase; **2,** to seek; as, to *hunt* for gold:—*n.* **1,** the pursuit of game or wild animals; as, a deer *hunt*; **2,** an association of hunters; **3,** a search; as, a scavenger *hunt*.—*n.* **hunt′ing.**

hunt-er (hunt′ėr), *n.* **1,** one who pursues game; a huntsman; **2,** a horse or hound trained for use in hunting; **3,** one who searches or looks for something.

hunts-man (hunts′man), *n.* [*pl.* huntsmen (-men)], **1,** one who pursues game; **2,** one who manages a hunt or chase.

hur-dle (hûr′dl), *n.* **1,** a frame or framework of interwoven twigs, branches, etc., used in making fences; **2,** a fence or barrier to be leaped in steeple chasing or racing; **3,** any barrier or obstacle to be overcome; **4,** in Britain, a rude frame on which criminals were formerly dragged to execution:—**hurdles**, a race in which runners jump over a series of barriers or small frames:—*v.t.* [hur-dled, hur-dling], **1,** to leap over an obstacle while running; **2,** to surmount or overcome; as, to *hurdle* a difficulty.—*n.* **hur′dler.**

hur-dy–gur-dy (hûr′di–gûr′di), *n.* [*pl.* hurdy-gurdies], a musical instrument played by turning a crank, and pulled through the streets on wheels.

hurl (hûrl), *v.t.* **1,** to throw with violence; fling forcibly; as, he *hurled* the javelin; **2,** to cast down; overthrow; as, they *hurled* the despot from power; **3,** to utter with vehemence; as, to *hurl* threats:—*v.i.* in *baseball*, to pitch:—*n.* a cast; a violent throw.—*n.* **hurl′er.**

hurl-y–burl-y (hûr′li–bûr′li), *n.* tumult; confusion.

Hu-ron (hyoor′on; hyoor′än), *n.* [*pl.* Huron or Hurons], **1,** a member of the Native people who used to live in longhouses in the area between Lake Huron and Lake Ontario; **2,** the Iroquoian language of these people:—*adj.* having to do with these people or their language.

hur-rah (hoo-rä′; hu-rä′; hoo-rô′; hu-rô′), *interj.* expressing joy, triumph, applause, etc.:—*n.* a triumphant shout; a cheer:—*v.i.* to utter such a shout; to cheer.

hur-ray (hoo-rā′; hu-rā′), *interj.* Same as **hurrah.**

hur-ri-cane (hûr′i-kān; -kan), *n.* **1,** a violent tropical storm, originating in the Atlantic Ocean, with winds over 120 kilometres per hour, accompanied by rain, thunder, and lightning; **2,** any storm with similar wind velocity; **3,** a violent outburst.

hur-ried (hûr′id), *adj.* showing haste; hasty; rushed; as, a *hurried* meal.

hur-ry (hûr′i), *v.t.* [hurried, hurry-ing], to impel to greater speed; hasten; as, to *hurry* the children to school:—*v.i.* to act or move with haste; as, the woman *hurried* through the station:—*n.* haste; urgency.

hurt (hûrt), *v.t.* [hurt, hurt-ing], **1,** to injure or inflict physical pain upon; wound; as, the blow *hurt* his arm; **2,** to grieve; offend; upset; as, your indifference *hurts* me; **3,** to injure; impair or damage; harm; as, the frost *hurts* the crops:—*v.i.* to feel pain; as, my head *hurts*:—*n.* **1,** a wound or other injury causing physical pain; also, pain caused by such an injury; **2,** an injury or loss causing emotional pain; as, a *hurt* to one's pride; **3,** harm or damage of any kind.

hurt-ful (hûrt′fool), *adj.* injurious; harmful; damaging.

hur-tle (hûr′tl), *v.i.* [-tled, -tling], **1,** to move violently or noisily; move with great speed; rush with force; as, rocks *hurtled* through the air; **2,** to collide with a crash, clatter, or shock; as, the car *hurtled* into the tree:—*v.t.* to hurl; throw forcefully; as, to *hurtle* a stone across the lake.

hus-band (huz′band), *n.* a married man:—*v.t.* to manage, direct, or use with economy; as, to *husband* one's income.

hus-band-ry (huz′band-ri), *n.* **1,** agriculture; farming; as, animal *husbandry*; **2,** economical management.

hush (hush), *interj.* be still! silence!—*v.t.* **1,** to make silent; to calm; **2,** to conceal; suppress; as, to *hush* up scandal:—*v.i.* to become or keep quiet:—*n.* silence; as, in the *hush* of the night.

husk (husk), *n.* **1,** the dry outer covering of certain fruits or seeds, as that of an ear of corn; **2,** any rough, worthless outside covering:—*v.t.* to remove the husk from.—*n.* **husk′er.**

[1]**husk-y** (hus′ki), *adj.* [husk-i-er, husk-i-est], **1,** consisting of, or like, husks; **2,** dry and hoarse; as, a *husky* voice.—*adv.* **husk′i-ly.**—*n.* **husk′i-ness.**

[2]**hus-ky** (hus′ki), *adj.* [husk-i-er, husk-i-est], big and strong; well-developed; powerful; as, a *husky* wrestler:—*n.* [*pl.* huskies], a stalwart, well-developed person.

[3]**hus-ky** or **hus-kie; Hus-ky** or **Hus-kie** (hus′ki), *n.* [*pl.* huskies or Huskies], **1,** a large, strong dog with a thick, bushy coat, used in the Far North to pull dogsleds; a Siberian husky; **2,** any similar dog of the North that is used to pull sleds.

hus-sar (hoo-zär′), *n.* in European armies,

a soldier belonging to the light cavalry.

hus-sy (huz′i), *n.* **1,** a pert or saucy girl; wench; **2,** a woman, esp. of low morals (used in contempt); a promiscuous woman.

hus-tings (hus′tiṅgz), *n.pl.* **1,** a platform used for electioneering speeches; **2,** the campaign route; **3,** the political campaign as a whole.

hus-tle (hus′l), *v.t.* [hus-tled, hus-tling], **1,** to push or crowd roughly; jostle; as, to *hustle* him out the door; **2,** *Colloq.* to cause to be done quickly; as, to *hustle* work:—*v.t.* and *v.i.* **1,** *Colloq.* to promote aggressively; as, to *hustle* a new product; *hustle* to get new business; **2,** *Slang* to sell underhandedly; as, to *hustle* the naive customers; *hustle* as a living; **3,** *Slang* to lure someone into a gambling contest; as, to *hustle* pool; *hustle* in the pool hall:—*v.i.* **1,** to jostle; crowd; **2,** *Colloq.* to exhibit energy and alacrity; hurry:—*n.* **1,** a pushing or jostling; **2,** *Colloq.* activity; vigour; energy.—*n.* **hus′tler** (as, a pool *hustler*).

hut (hut), *n.* a small, roughly built shelter; a cabin or shanty.

hutch (huch), *n.* **1,** a bin, box, or chest in which things may be stored; as, a clothes *hutch*; **2,** a coop or pen for animals; as, a rabbit *hutch*; **3,** a cupboard or china cabinet.

hy-a-cinth (hī′a-sinth), *n.* a plant of the lily family with spikes of bell-shaped, and very fragrant, white, pink, yellow, blue, or purple flowers.

hy-brid (hī′brid), *n.* **1,** an animal or plant produced from the crossing of two distinct varieties or species; as, some roses are *hybrids*; **2,** anything formed of parts of unlike origin; esp. a compound word, as *cablegram*, the elements of which are derived from different languages; **3,** in *computing*, a computer with both analogue and digital systems:—*adj.* **1,** produced from two kinds or classes; as, the mule is a *hybrid* animal; **2,** composed of mixed elements; as, a *hybrid* word.—*v.t.* **hy′brid-ize.**

hy-dran-ge-a (hi-drān′ji-a), *n.* a shrub with large, round clusters of showy white, blue, or pink flowers.

hy-drant (hī′drant), *n.* a small structure located above ground near a street, with a pipe, valve, and spout, through which water may be drawn from an underground water main: used to provide water for fighting fires or washing streets.

hy-drate (hī′drāt), *n.* a compound formed by the chemical union of water with another substance; as plaster of Paris ($2CaSO_4 \cdot H_2O$) or copper sulphate ($CaSO_4 \cdot 5H_2O$).

hy-drau-lic (hī-drô′lik), *adj.* **1,** pertaining to water in motion; **2,** operated by water power; as, *hydraulic* brakes; **3,** accomplished by or having to do with water power; as, *hydraulic* engineering; **4,** hardening under water; as, *hydraulic* cement.

hy-dride (hī′drīd), *n.* a compound of hydrogen with another element.

hy-dro (hī′drō), *n.* **1,** power made from harnessing the force of water; short for *hydroelectric* power or *hydroelectricity*; **2,** electricity distributed by a power company:—**Hydro,** an electrical power company. Also, **hy′dro line′; hy′dro pole′; hy′dro pow′er; hy′dro sta′tion; hy′dro tow′er.**

hy-dro or **hydr-** (hī′drō-; hī′dr-), *prefix* meaning *water*; as, *hydro*carbon, *hydro*kinetic; *hydro*scope; *hydro*therapy, *hydr*oxide, etc.

hy-dro-e-lec-tric (hī′drō-e-lek′trik), *adj.* pertaining to electric energy generated by water power or steam.—*n.* **hy′dro-e-lec′tric′i-ty.**

hy-dro-gen (hī′drō-jen), *n.* a colourless, tasteless, odourless gaseous element that burns easily, and is the lightest of all known chemical elements: it combines with oxygen to form water.

hydrogen bomb, a nuclear-fusion bomb, in which atoms of a heavy hydrogen isotope are fused into helium under intense heat and pressure: it is much more powerful than an atom, or fission, bomb.

hy-drol-y-sis (hī-drol′i-sis), *n.* the breaking down of organic compounds by interaction with water.

hy-drom-e-ter (hī-drom′e-tėr), *n.* a float for measuring the specific gravity of liquids.

hy-dro-pho-bi-a (hī′drō-fō′bi-a), *n.* **1,** dread or fear of water; **2,** rabies.—*adj.* **hy′ dro-pho′bic.**

hy-dro-plane (hī′drō-plān′), *n.* **1,** a motorboat with a sloping bottom, the bow of which rises partly out of water when driven at high speed; hydrofoil; **2,** an aircraft so constructed that it can take off from, or alight on, a body of water; a seaplane.

hy-dro-pon-ics (hī′drō-pon′iks), *n.pl.* used as *sing.*, the science of growing plants in water, without soil, by using a solution with the proper plant foods; soilless gardening.

hy-drous (hī′drus), *adj.* **1,** containing water in combination; **2,** containing hydrogen.

hy-drox-ide (hī-drok′sīd), *n.* a compound containing the chemical unit [OH].

hy-e-na (hī-ē′na), *n.* a night-prowling, flesh-eating animal, somewhat resembling a wolf or large dog, with a laughlike cry, native to Africa and Asia.

hy-giene (hī′jēn; hī′ji-ēn), *n.* **1,** the science of treating and preserving health; **2,** the practice of cleanliness, as a part of preserving health; as, oral *hygiene.*—*n.* **hy′gi-en-ist** (hī′ji-en-ist).

hy-gi-en-ic (hī′ji-en′ik), *adj.* **1,** pertaining to health or to the science of treating and preserving health; **2,** not injurious to health; sanitary.

hy-grom-e-ter (hī-grom′e-tėr), *n.* an instrument for measuring atmospheric moisture.

hymn (him), *n.* **1,** a sacred song expressing praise or thanksgiving, usually part of a religious service; **2,** any song of praise, thanksgiving, etc.

hym-nal (him′nal; him′nl), *n.* a collection of sacred songs; a book of hymns.

hype (hīp), *n. Colloq.* exaggerated promotion or advertising; as, a lot of *hype* about the new action movie:—*v.t.* [hyped, hyping], **1,** to promote or advertise; the company *hyped* its new service; **2,** to excite or add interest; as, the famous athlete *hyped* the new athletic product.

hy-per (hī′pėr), *adj. Slang* overly excited or nervous.

hy-per- (hī′pėr), *prefix* meaning **1,** *over, beyond;* as in *hyper*charge; **2,** *excessive;* as, *hyper*acidity: opposite of *hypo-* (having a deficiency); **3,** of more than three dimensions; as in *hyper*space; **4,** not arranged in sequence; as in *hyper*text.

hy-per-bo-la (hī-pûr′bo-la), *n.* a curve formed by a conic section cut by a plane that makes a greater angle with the base than the side of the cone makes.

HYPERBOLA

hy-per-bo-le (hī-pûr′bol-lē′), *n.* extravagant exaggeration, used for emphasis or comic effect; as, "his arms dangled a *kilometre* out of his sleeves."

hy-per-link (hī′pûr-lingk′), *n.* in *computing,* a link in an electronic document, such as a Web page, that is designed to move the user, who clicks on it, to another part of the document or to another document: the hyperlink is usually displayed in a distinctive graphic or contrasting font or colour to distinguish it; also known as *hotlink* or *link*:—*v.t.* to use a hyperlink in this way.

hy-per-sen-si-tive (hī′pėr-sen′si-tiv), *adj.* oversensitive.

hypertext markup language (hī′pėr-tekst′), *n.* in *computing,* a set of codes used to lay out Web pages on the Internet: abbreviated as *HTML.*

hypertext transfer protocol, in *computing,* a standard way of transmitting data and for accessing and publishing information on the Internet in hypertext: abbreviated as *http.*

hy-phen (hī′fen), *n.* a punctuation mark [-] used to join compound words or word elements, as in *self-denial, two-day* trip, or *co-op;* also, to divide a word into syllables, esp. at the end of lines, as in *hy-phen-ate*:—*v.t.* to join (words) with, or separate (syllables) by, such a mark; hyphenate.

hy-phen-ate (hī′fen-āt′), *v.t.* [hyphenated, hyphenat-ing], to insert a hyphen between (two words) or between the syllables of (a word); to hyphen.

hyp-no-tism (hip′no-tizm), *n.* the act or method of producing a state of deep relaxation, resembling sleep, in which the mind readily responds to suggestions, esp. from the person who caused the state.—*n.* **hyp-no′sis;** **hyp′no-tist.**—*v.t.* **hyp′no-tize′** (hip′no-tīz).—*adj.* **hyp-not′ic** (hip-not′ik).

hy-po (hī′pō), *n.* short for *hyposulphite* (hī′pōsul′fīt), a photographic fixing agent.

hy-po- or **hyp-** (hī′pō-; hīp-), *prefix* meaning **1,** *below, underneath;* as in *hypo*dermic; **2,** less than normal; as in *hypo*tension; **3,** in a lower state of oxidation; as in *hypo*chlorous.

hy-po-chon-dri-a (hī′pō-kon′dri-a; hip′-), *n.* morbid anxiety about imagined illnesses; severe melancholy.—*n.* **hy′po-chon′dri-ac.**

hy-poc-ri-sy (hi-pok′ri-si), *n.* [*pl.* hypocrisies], a pretending to be what one is not; the putting on of an appearance of virtue that one does not possess.

hyp-o-crite (hip′ō-krit), *n.* one who puts on an appearance of virtue that one does not possess; as, she speaks of being honest and kind, but she is a *hypocrite* because she does not act that way.—*adj.* **hyp′o-crit′ical.**

hy-po-der-mic (hī-pō-dûr′mik; hip-), *adj.* **1,** pertaining to the tissues under the skin; as, a *hypodermic* injection; **2,** for use under the skin; as, a *hypodermic* needle:—*n.* **1,** the medicinal dose used in such an injection; **2,** the instrument used; syringe.

hy-pot-e-nuse (hī-pot′i-nūz′; hi-pot′i-nūz′), *n.* in *geometry,* the side of a right-angled triangle that is opposite the right angle.

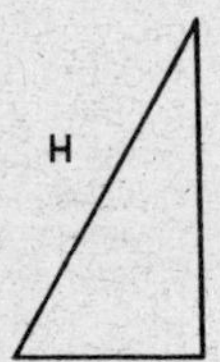

HYPOTENUSE

hy-poth-e-sis (hī-poth′e-sis; hi-poth′e-sis), *n.* [*pl.* hypotheses (hī-poth′e-sēz; hi-poth′e-sēz)], **1,** something that may or may not prove to be true for the sake of argument; **2,** an explanation of a set of facts that can be tested by further investigation.

hys-te-ri-a (his-tē′ri-a), *n.* **1,** a persistent nervous disorder, marked chiefly by uncontrolled emotional excitement and outbursts of senseless weeping and laughter; **2,** extreme excitement.

hys-ter-i-cal or **hys-ter-ic** (his-ter′i-kal; his-ter′ik), *adj.* **1,** pertaining to, or affected by, hysteria; **2,** violently emotional; uncontrolled; as, *hysterical* laughter; **3,** *Colloq.* very funny; as, a *hysterical* cartoon strip.—*adv.* **hys-ter′i-cal-ly.**

hys-ter-ics (his-ter′iks), *n.pl.* used as *sing.* a fit of nervous and uncontrollable laughing and crying; any hysterical outburst.—*n.* **hys-ter′ic** (a hysterical person).

Hz (āch′zed′), *abbrev.* short for *hertz.*

I

[1]I, i (ī), *n.* [*pl.* I's, i's], **1,** the ninth letter of the alphabet, following H; **2,** as a Roman numeral, 1.

[2]I (ī), *pron.* of the first person, [*nominative* I, *possessive* my, mine, *objective* me], the pronoun by which the speaker or writer denotes himself or herself.

i-amb (ī′amb) or **i-am-bus** (ī-am′bus), *n.* [*pl.* iambs, iambuses, or iambi (ī-am′bī′; ī-am′bē′)], in *verse metre*, a foot of two syllables, the first short or unaccented, the second long or accented: as, "In̆ sóoth/Ĭ kńow/not wh́y/Ĭ ám/sŏ sád" (*iambic* pentameter).—*adj.* and *n.* **i-am′bic.**

I-bar (ī′–bär′), *n.* in *computing*, the shape of the cursor of an I; also called *I-beam.*

i-bex (ī′beks), *n.* [*pl.* ibex or ibexes (ī′bek-siz)], a wild goat with large, backward-curving horns.

i-bis (ī′bis), *n.* [*pl.* ibises or ibis], a large, wading bird of the heron family, with a long, slender, curving beak, found in warm climates.

IC (ī′sē′), *abbrev.* short for *integrated circuit.*

ice (īs), *n.* **1,** frozen water; **2,** any substance resembling ice; as, menthol *ice*; **3,** a frozen dessert, made with fruit juices instead of cream; as, raspberry *ice*; **4,** cake frosting; icing; **5,** the frozen surface for skating, hockey, or curling:—*v.t.* [iced, icing], **1,** to freeze; **2,** to supply with ice; **3,** to cool by ice, as beverages or fruit; **4,** to cover, as cake, with frosting; **5,** in *hockey*, to shoot the puck from one's defensive zone past the goal line of the other team: called *icing*; **6,** *Slang* to kill:—*v.i.* to become icy cold or be covered with ice; freeze; as, an airplane's engine can *ice* up:—*adj.* **1,** of ice; as, *ice* cubes; **2,** having to do with ice; as, *ice* hockey; an *ice*boat. Also, **ice′bound′**; **ice′box′**; **ice′ bridge′**; **ice′cap′**; **ice′–cold′**; **ice′ cube′**; **ice′ dan′cer**; **ice′ field′**; **ice′ fish′ing**; **ice′ floe′**; **ice′–free′**; **ice′ jam′**; **ice′mak′er**; **ice′ pack′**; **ice′ pick′**; **ice′ sculp′ture**; **ice′ sheet′**; **ice′ shelf′**; **ice′ skate′**; **ice′ storm′**; **ice′ time′**; **ice′ wat′er**; **ice′wine′**.

ice age, a period of time when glaciers cover large parts of a region:—**Ice Age,** the most recent glacial epoch, or time when ice covered much of the earth, which began about 1.75 million years ago and ended about 10,000 years ago.

ice-berg (īs′bûrg′), *n.* a large mass of ice broken off from a glacier, and floating in the sea, often extending to a great height above and below the water, and which can be dangerous to ships. Also, **ice′berg′ let′tuce.**

ice-boat (īs′bōt′), *n.* **1,** a boat or frame mounted on runners and propelled by sails over ice; **2,** an icebreaker.

ice-break-er (īs′brāk′ėr), *n.* **1,** a heavily built steamboat with a very strong bow, used to break a channel in frozen rivers, lakes, or harbours; **2,** a dock used to protect against floating ice; **3,** *Colloq.* something that is said or done to reduce tension; as, her joke was the *icebreaker* at the formal luncheon.

ice cream, flavoured and sweetened frozen milk or cream, served as a dessert.

ice-house (īs′hous′), *n.* **1,** a dome-shaped house made from blocks of ice or snow, esp. one used by the Inuit, built as a temporary shelter while hunting or travelling: also called *igloo*; **2,** a building for storing ice; **3,** a pit or building for cold storage of meat and other food.

i-ci-cle (ī′sik-l), *n.* a hanging piece of ice, tapering downward to a point, formed by the freezing of dripping water.

ic-ing (īs′ing), *n.* a sweet, smooth coating or frosting for cakes, cookies, etc., made of sugar, butter, flavouring, etc. Also called *frosting.*

i-con or **i-kon** (ī′kon), *n.* **1,** an image; likeness; **2,** a sacred image or picture, as of the Virgin Mary, Christ, or a saint; **3,** in *computing*, a symbol or picture on the computer screen that represents an object, program, or command, such as file, print, etc.; as, the envelope *icon* represents e-mail.

i-con-o-clast (īkon′ō-klast), *n.* **1,** a breaker of images; **2,** one who opposes the use of icons in religion; also, one who destroys these images; **3,** one who attacks cherished beliefs or institutions.

ICU (ī′sē′ū′), *abbrev.* short for *intensive care unit.*

ic-y (īs′i), *adj.* [ic-i-er, ic-i-est], **1,** pertaining to, like, or covered with ice; as, *icy* pavements; cold; frosty; as, an *icy* road; *icy* gale; **2,** chilling in manner; indifferent; as, an *icy* welcome.—*adv.* **ic′i-ly.**—*n.* **i′ci-ness.**

ID (ī′dē′), *abbrev.* short for *identification.*

ID card, *abbrev.* short for *identification card.*

i-de-a (ī-dē′a), *n.* **1,** a mental picture of a thing; a thought, plan, or picture formed in the mind; as, his *idea* of an elephant; **2,** an ideal; also, a plan; as, he has the *idea* of becoming an actor; **3,** the purpose, point, or meaning of anything; as, the *idea* is to get votes; **4,** a supposition; fancy; as, I have an *idea* she will come; **5,** a certain belief or opinion; as, to have strong *ideas* about the environment.

i-de-al (ī-dē′al), *adj.* **1,** existing in imagination or fancy only; not real or practical; **2,** equal to one's highest wish; perfect; as, *ideal* weather:—*n.* any perfect person or thing, or one regarded as worthy of imitation:—**ideals,** standards for thinking or acting; as, a person of high *ideals.*—*adv.* **i-de′al-ly.**

i-de-al-ism (ī-dē′al-izm), *n.* **1,** the tendency to see things as they should be instead of as they are; **2,** the effort to live according to a standard of perfection; **3,** in *art* and *literature,* the effort to depict beauty and perfection rather than fact: opposite of *realism.*

i-de-al-ize (ī-dē′al-īz′), *v.t.* [idealized, idealiz-ing], to look upon as perfect, regardless of fact; as, she *idealizes* her son.—*n.* **i-de′al-i-za′tion.**

i-den-ti-cal (ī-den′ti-kal), *adj.* **1,** the very same; as, the *identical* spot; **2,** exactly alike; as, no two faces are *identical.*—*adv.* **i-den′ti-cal-ly.**

i-den-ti-fi-ca-tion (ī-den′ti-fi-kā′shun), **1,** the act of identifying; recognizing someone or something; as, to make an *identification* of the stolen coat; **2,** something that is used to prove who a person is; as, to show *identification* at a bank: abbreviated as *ID.*

identification card, a card that contains information to identify the holder, such as a photo, age, name, address, etc.: abbreviated as *ID card.* Also called *identity card.*

i-den-ti-fy (ī-den′ti-fi′), *v.t.* [identified, identify-ing], **1,** to make, consider, or treat as the same; consider the same; feel something in common with; as, he *identifies* money with happiness; be able to *identify* with someone; **2,** to prove to be the same or prove as one's own; recognize; as, I *identified* my umbrella; **3,** to recognize or classify, as a plant or a person.

i-den-ti-ty (ī-den′ti-ti), *n.* [*pl.* identities], **1,** sameness or likeness; as, the *identity* of this pen with the one I lost; **2,** the fact of being as represented; as, to establish one's *identity.*—*adj.* **i-dent′i-fi′a-ble.**

i-de-ol-o-gy (ī′di-ol′o-ji; id′-), *n.* **1,** the theory that ideas originate from sensation; **2,** the ideas, prejudices, beliefs, etc., that determine one's view of life; **3,** the set of beliefs or principles of an economic, political, or other system.

id-i-om (id′i-um), *n.* **1,** the language of a people; also, the dialect of a group or section; vernacular; as, the Newfoundland *idiom;* business *idiom;* **2,** the peculiar form or character of a language; **3,** an expression which, as a whole, has a meaning different from the meanings of the individual words joined together, as "to play it by ear" means "to do something spontaneously"; **4,** a method of expression characteristic of an individual; as, Shakespeare's *idiom.*

id-i-o-syn-cra-sy (id′i-ō-sing′kra-si), *n.* a peculiarity of one's disposition or behaviour; a mannerism.

id-i-ot (id′i-ut), *n.* **1,** a person lacking, from birth, the ability to learn; a person with a severe mental disability: now considered offensive; **2,** a fool; a dunce.

id-i-ot-ic (id′i-ot′ik), *adj.* **1,** pertaining to, or like, an idiot; **2,** senseless; foolish.—*n.* **id′i-o-cy.**

i-dle (ī′dl), *adj.* [i-dler, i-dlest], **1,** unused; doing nothing; as, the house stands *idle;* as, the team was *idle* until Saturday; **2,** useless; futile; of no importance; worthless; as, an *idle* rumour; **3,** not working; lazy; as, *idle* employees:—*v.i.* [i-dled, i-dling], **1,** to waste or lose time; do nothing; **2,** to run slowly in neutral gear, as an automobile engine:—*v.t.* to waste (time); as, to *idle* time; away gossiping.—*n.* **i′dle-ness.**—*n.* **i′dler.**—*adv.* **i′dly.**

i-dol (ī′d'l), *n.* **1,** an image of a god used as an object of worship, esp. a statue or similar figure; **2,** a person or thing greatly loved or adored; as, a movie *idol.*

i-dol-a-try (ī-dol′a-tri), *n.* [*pl.* idolatries], **1,** the worship of idols; **2,** extreme admiration for any person or thing.—*n.* **i-dol′a-ter.**—*adj.* **i-dol′a-trous.**

i-dol-ize (ī′d'l-īz′), *v.t.* [idolized, idolizing], **1,** to worship (an image regarded as a god, or as divine); to make an idol of; **2,** to love or admire to excess; as, to *idolize* a great basketball star.

i-dyll or **i-dyl** (ī′dil), *n.* **1,** a short poem describing a scene or event in country life; a similar prose description; **2,** an episode suitable for such a piece.

i-dyl-lic (ī-dil′ik), *adj.* **1,** pertaining to, or of the nature of, the idyll; **2,** charming and simple; as, an *idyllic* lifestyle.—*adv.* **i-dyl′li-cal-ly.**

i.e. (ī′ē′), *abbrev. Latin,* id est (that is).

if (if), *conj.* **1,** on the condition that; as, *if* I let you have the book, you must read it; **2,** supposing that; as, *if* I go to Québec, what is the best route to take? **3,** whether; as, he asked *if* he might go; **4,** although; as, even *if* the answer is correct, the work is not neatly done; **5,** whenever; as, *if* I have a question, I will come to you; **6,** that; as, is it all right *if* I borrow your pen?—*n.* a supposition or condition.

ig-loo (ig′lo͞o), *n.* **1,** an Inuit dome-shaped dwelling, made of blocks of snow or ice; **2,** any Inuit dwelling. Also called *icehouse.*

ig-ne-ous (ig′ni-us), *n.* and *adj.* produced by heat or fire, as an igneous rock (like granite); as, hardened lava is a type of *igneous* rock.

ig-nite (ig-nīt′), *v.t.* [ignit-ed, ignit-ing], to set on fire; cause to burn; as, to *ignite* wooden logs:—*v.i.* to catch fire; as, the paper *ignited* from sparks.

ig-ni-tion (ig-nish′un), *n.* **1,** the act of setting on fire; kindling; **2,** the state of being ignited; **3,** the means of producing fire; **4,** the electrical system, or the process of, starting the engine of a car, boat, or other vehicle.

ig-no-ble (ig-nō′bl), *adj.* **1,** not of noble birth; as, an *ignoble* family; **2,** of mean character or quality; degraded; vile; as, an *ignoble* act.—*adv.* **ig-no′bly.**

ig-no-min-i-ous (ig′nō-min′i-us), *adj.* disgraceful; humiliating; shameful; as, an *ignominious* punishment.—*n.* **ig′no-min-y.**

ig-no-ra-mus (ig′nō-rā′mus), *n.* an ignorant person.

ig-no-rance (ig′no-rans), *n.* lack of knowledge.

ig-no-rant (ig′no-rant), *adj.* **1,** lacking knowledge or education; uninformed; **2,** unaware; as, he was *ignorant* of the fact; **3,** showing, betraying, or caused by lack of knowledge; as, an *ignorant* reply.—*adv.* **ig′no-rant-ly.**

ig-nore (ig-nōr′), *v.t.* [ignored, ignor-ing], **1,** to disregard intentionally; as, to *ignore* a request; **2,** to overlook; as, to *ignore* her rudeness.

i-gua-na (i-gwä′na), *n.* a large herbivorous lizard with a row of spines along its back, found in very warm parts of the Americas.

i-kon (ī′kon), *n.* Same as **icon.**

il- (il-), *prefix* before *l* meaning **1,** *not, the opposite of*; as in *il*legal, *il*legible; *il*legitimate; *il*literate; **2,** *in, into, within*; as in *il*luminate.

ilk (ilk), *n.* family; breed; kind; type; as, thieves and others of that *ilk*.

ill (il), *adj.* [worse, worst], **1,** sick; not well; as, the child is *ill*; **2,** disagreeable; hostile; as, *ill* humour; *ill* will; **3,** bad or harmful; unfortunate; as, an *ill* turn; *ill* effects of bad weather:—*n.* **1,** a sickness or disease; **2,** evil: the opposite of *good*; **3,** something unfavourable or injurious; as, to work *ill* to one's neighbour; **4,** misfortune; as, social *ills*:—**ill at ease,** not comfortable; uneasy; as, to be *ill at ease* at her new job:—*adv.* **1,** badly; as, to fare *ill*; **2,** unkindly; as, to speak *ill* of someone. Also, **ill′–fa′ted; ill′–man′nered; ill′–o′mened; ill′–us′age.**

ill–bred (il′–bred′), *adj.* badly raised; impolite; rude.

il-le-gal (il-lē′gal), *adj.* against the law; unlawful; as, it is *illegal* to drive a car without a licence.—*n.* **il′le-gal′i-ty** (il′li-gal′i-ti).—*adv.* **il-le′gal-ly.**

il-leg-i-ble (il-lej′i-bl), *adj.* not readable; difficult to read; as, *illegible* handwriting; an *illegible* date on a coin.

il-le-git-i-mate (il′li-jit′i-mit), *adj.* **1,** born out of wedlock; **2,** unlawful; illegal; as, an *illegitimate* business.

ill–hu-moured or **ill–hu-mored** (ill–hū′mėrd), *adj.* cross; disagreeable; in a bad humour.

il-lic-it (il-lis′it; i-lis′it), *adj.* **1,** not allowed; illegal; as, *illicit* trade in drugs; **2,** not condoned according to custom; as, an *illicit* sexual act.

il-lim-it-a-ble (il-lim′it-a-bl), *adj.* immeasurable; vast; as, *illimitable* space.

il-lit-er-ate (il-lit′ėr-it), *adj.* **1,** uneducated; ignorant of letters or books; esp. unable to read or write at all; **2,** showing lack of learning; not able to read and write well enough to get by; as, an *illiterate* letter; *illiterate* student:—*n.* **1,** one unable to read or write; **2,** one who is illiterate in a certain field; as, a computer *illiterate*.—*n.* **il-lit′er-a-cy.**

ill-ness (il′nes), *n.* **1,** the state of being ill; **2,** a disease or malady; as, AIDS is a serious *illness*.

il-log-i-cal (i-loj′i-kal), *adj.* contrary to sound reason.

il-lu-mi-nate (i-lū′mi-nāt′), *v.t.* [illuminated, illuminat-ing], **1,** to give light to; as, halogen lights *illuminated* the room; **2,** to decorate with lights; as, the streets were *illuminated* for the holiday season; **3,** to make clear, as a difficult point; as, to *illuminate* the problem; **4,** formerly, to ornament (an initial letter on the borders of a page) with designs in colours, as in ancient manuscripts.—*n.* **il-lu′mi-na′tion.**

il-lu-mine (i-lū′min), *v.t.* [illumined, illumin-ing], to light up; brighten; as, the moon *illumines* the night; a smile *illumined* her face.

il-lu-sion (i-lū′zhun), *n.* **1,** an unreal or misleading appearance; as, that cloud gives the *illusion* of a castle; **2,** a false idea; a delusion; as, to have the *illusion* that she would be happier if she has more money.—*adj.* **il-lu′sive, il-lu′so-ry.**

il-lus-trate (il′us-trāt′; i-lus′trāt), *v.t.* [illustrat-ed, illustrat-ing], **1,** to make clear; as, to *illustrate* the definition of a word by a phrase in which the word is used; **2,** to make clear by means of pictures or diagrams; also, to ornament with pictures.—*adj.* **il′lus-trat′ed; il-lus′tra-tive** (il-lus′tra-tiv; il′us-trā′tiv).—*n.* **il′lus-trat′tor.**

il-lus-tra-tion (il′us-trā′shun), *n.* **1,** the process of making clear, or explaining, by the use of examples, comparisons, stories, etc.; as, falling leaves are a good *illustration* of the law of gravity; **2,** the art of ornamenting with pictures; **3,** that which makes clear, as a comparison or an example; **4,** that which decorates or clarifies a text, as a picture, diagram, map, etc.

il-lus-tri-ous (i-lus′tri-us), *adj.* famous; distinguished.—*adv.* **il-lus′tri-ous-ly.**

ill will, unfriendliness; hostility.

im- (im-), *prefix* before *b, m, p* meaning **1,** *not, the opposite of*; as in *im*perfect, *im*plausible, *im*politic; **2,** *in, into, within*; as in *im*plant; *im*plode.

im-age (im′ij), *n.* **1,** a statue, bust, or similar representation of a person or thing; as, an *image* of the saint; **2,** a close likeness; as, he is the *image* of his brother; **3,** a mental picture; an idea; representation; as, I have an *image* of the restaurant where we met; **4,** a reflection in a mirror or something seen through a camera lens, magnifying glass, etc.; as, to adjust the focus to make the *image* clear; **5,** in writing, a word or words used to suggest a certain picture in the mind; as, the words in the poem brought scenic *images* to my mind; **6,** public opinion about a person or thing; the way something is thought of by others; as, the advertising firm was hired to improve the politician's *image*:—*v.t.* [imaged, imaging], **1,** to form a likeness or picture of (something); portray; **2,** to represent to oneself; imagine; **3,** to picture vividly in words.

im-age-ry (im′ij-ri; im′ij-ėr-i), *n.* [*pl.* imageries], mental pictures, esp. as conveyed in words; also, language that causes the mind to form pictures.

im-ag-i-na-ble (i-maj′i-na-bl), *adj.* capable of being pictured by the mind; conceivable; as, the loveliest flowers *imaginable.*

im-ag-i-nar-y (i-maj′i-nėr-i), *adj.* existing only in the mind; unreal.

im-ag-i-na-tion (i-maj′i-nā′shun), *n.* **1,** the picture-forming power of the mind; the ability to form mental pictures of things not actually present; **2,** a product of this power; a mental picture or idea; a fancy; the ability of the mind to create something new or different, or to create a new or different use for something that already exists; as, to use your *imagination* to create a story.—*adj.* **im-ag′i-na′tive** (i-maj′i-na-tiv; i-maj′i-nā′tiv).

im-ag-ine (i-maj′in), *v.t.* and *v.i.* [imagined, imagin-ing], **1,** to form an idea or mental picture of (something); **2,** to suppose; guess; fancy; as, I can only *imagine* how she felt; **3,** to think or believe; as, I *imagine* that he's on his way here.

i-mam or **I-mam** (i-mäm′), *n.* **1,** a prayer leader in a mosque; **2,** a Shiite Muslim spiritual and civil leader.

im-be-cile (im′bi-sil; im′bi-sl), *adj.* **1,** feeble-minded; idiotic; silly; **2,** marked by stupidity; inane; as, an *imbecile* remark:—*n.* one of weak mind; a silly person.—*n.* **im′be-cil′i-ty.**

im-bed (im-bed′), *v.t.* Same as **embed.**

im-bibe (im-bīb′), *v.t.* [imbibed, imbibing], **1,** to drink; **2,** to receive or absorb into the mind; as, to *imbibe* knowledge.

im-bue (im-bū′), *v.t.* [imbued, imbuing], **1,** to cause to absorb; tinge deeply; dye; as, the setting sun *imbues* the lake with rose; **2,** to impress deeply; inspire; as, to *imbue* a citizen with patriotism.

im-i-tate (im′i-tāt′), *v.t.* [imitat-ed, imitating], **1,** to make a likeness of; copy; **2,** to follow as a model or pattern; mimic; as, to *imitate* the famous movie star; **3,** to look like; resemble; as, paper doilies are made to *imitate* lace ones.—*adj.* **im′i-ta′tive** (im′i-tā-tiv; im′i-tā′tiv).—*n.* **im′i-ta′tor.**

im-i-ta-tion (im′i-tā′shun), *n.* **1,** the act of copying or following a model; as, *imitation* is the sincerest form of flattery; **2,** a copy; as, an *imitation* of a famous painting:—*adj.* made to resemble something superior; as, *imitation* diamonds.

im-mac-u-late (i-mak′ū-lit), *adj.* **1,** absolutely clean; as, *immaculate* hands; **2,** without fault; stainless; pure.—*adv.* **im-mac′u-late-ly.**

im-ma-nent (im′a-nent), *adj.* indwelling; inherent; as, God is *immanent* in the universe.

im-ma-te-ri-al (im′ma-tē′ri-al), *adj.* **1,** not consisting of matter; without physical form; as, ghosts are *immaterial*; **2,** unimportant; as, *immaterial* details.

im-ma-ture (im′a-tūr′), *adj.* **1,** not ripe; not fully grown or developed; as *immature* fruit; **2,** not finished or perfected; crude; **3,** behaving in a childish way; not acting one's age; foolish.—*adv.* **im′ma-ture′ly.**—*n.* **im′ma-tu′ri-ty.**

im-meas-ur-a-ble (i-mezh′o͝or-a-bl), *adj.* incapable of being measured; limitless; as, the *immeasurable* heavens; *immeasurable* joy.

im-me-di-ate (i-mē′di-it), *adj.* **1,** closely related; as, one's *immediate* family; **2,** next; as, the *immediate* succession to the throne; **3,** direct; as, *immediate* cause; **4,** present; as, the *immediate* question; **5,** instant, urgent; as, *immediate* needs; **6,** near, at hand; as, the *immediate* neighbourhood; **7,** happening or coming at once, without delay; as, an *immediate* answer.

im-me-di-ate-ly (i-mē′di-it-li), *adv.* **1,** at once; **2,** closely; directly.

im-me-mor-i-al (im′me-mōr′i-al), *adj.* extending beyond the reach of memory or written record; as, life has existed on this earth from time *immemorial.*

im-mense (i-mens′), *adj.* vast; enormous; huge.—*adv.* **im-mense′ly.**—*n.* **im-men′si-ty.**

im-merse (i-mûrs′), *v.t.* [immersed, immersing], **1,** to plunge into some liquid; dip; as, to *immerse* clothes in water; **2,** to baptize by plunging (a person) entirely under water; **3,** to absorb the attention of; as, he was *immersed* in the new computer game.—*adj.* **im-mersed′.**—*n.* **im-mer′sion.**

im-mi-grant (im′i-grant), *n.* a person who leaves his or her native country and enters another country to settle there permanently; as, *immigrants* to Canada from Ukraine.

im-mi-grate (im′i-grāt′), *v.i.* [immigrat-ed, immigrat-ing], to leave a native country and enter another country, intending to settle there permanently.—*n.* **im′mi-gra′tion.**

im-mi-nent (im′i-nent), *adj.* threatening to happen; about to occur, said esp. of misfortune or danger; as, *imminent* danger.—*n.* **im′mi-nence.**

im-mo-bile (i-mō′bil; -bēl), *adj.* motionless; not movable.—*n.* **im′mo-bil′i-ty.**

im-mod-er-ate (im-mod′ẽr-it), *adj.* extreme; excessive; as, the *immoderate* use of jargon.—*adv.* **im-mod′er-ate-ly.**

im-mod-est (i-mod′est), *adj.* **1,** not decent or proper; as, *immodest* behaviour; **2,** forward; brazen; rude; as, *immodest* boasting.—*n.* **im-mod′es-ty.**

im-mor-al (i-môr′al), *adj.* **1,** contrary to what is considered right; lewd; as, *immoral* conduct; **2,** wicked; evil; unscrupulous; as, dishonesty is *immoral.*—*n.* **im′mo-ral′i-ty.**

im-mor-tal (i-môr′tal), *adj.* never dying; living or lasting forever; as, the ancient Greeks considered their gods *immortal*; an *immortal* poem; Mozart's *immortal* music:—*n.* **1,** one who never dies; **2,** one whose fame is undying; as, Shakespeare is considered an *immortal*:—**the immortals,** in Greek and Roman *mythology*, the gods.—*adv.* **im-mor′tal-ly.**—*n.* **im-mor-tal′i-ty.**—*v.t.* **im-mor′tal-ize.**

im-mov-a-ble (i-mo͞ov′a-bl), *adj.* **1,** incapable of being moved; firmly fixed; permanent; as, *immovable* rocks; **2,** firm; unchanging; not moving; **3,** umemotional, unfeeling.

im-mune (i-mūn′), *adj.* **1,** safe; free; as, *immune* from punishment; *immune* to criticism; **2,** protected from a particular disease; as, a vaccination makes one *immune* to smallpox.—*n.* **im-mu′ni-ty; im′mu-ni-za′tion.**—*v.t.* **im′mun-ize′.**

im-mure (i-mūr′), *v.t.* [immured, immuring], to confine within walls; shut up in, or as in, prison.

im-mu-ta-ble (i-mū′ta-bl), *adj.* unchangeable; unalterable.—*n.* **im-mu′ta-bil′i-ty.**

imp (imp), *n.* **1,** a little demon; offspring of the devil; **2,** an annoying or mischievous child.

im-pact (im′pakt), *n.* **1,** a collision; a forcible coming together of two objects; as, the *impact* of billiard balls or of a car crash; **2,** the force or effect of something; powerful influence or impression; as, she has a strong *impact* on the teenagers; technology has a strong *impact* on modern society:—*v.t.* **1,** to force something together by pressure; wedge or pack; **2,** *Colloq.* to affect someone or something; as, the bad weather *impacted* negatively the outdoor event:—*v.i.* **1,** to collide; as, the two cars *impacted*; **2,** *Colloq.* to have an effect; as, crime *impacts* heavily on society.—*adj.* **im-pact′ed** (as, an *impacted* tooth).

im-pair (im-pâr′), *v.t.* to make worse; lessen the quantity, excellence, value, or strength of; weaken; harm; as, reading in a dim light *impairs* the eyesight; drinking alcohol *impairs* the ability to drive.—*n.* **im-pair′ment.**

im-paired (im-pârd′), *adj.* **1,** drunk; of the operator of a vehicle under the influence of alcohol or drugs beyond the legally specified limit; as, driving while *impaired*; **2**, disabled or handicapped; as, hearing *impaired.*

im-pal-a (im-pal′a; im-päl′a), *n.* a small reddish or brown African antelope with curved horns, which can run very fast and make long, high leaps through the air.

IMPALA

im-pale or **em-pale** (im-pāl′; em-pāl′), *v.t.* [impaled, impal-ing], **1,** to pierce through with anything sharp; **2,** to kill by thrusting through and fixing with a sharp stake; **3,** to make powerless; as, the nation *impaled* the terrorists by cutting off their source of money.

im-pal-pa-ble (im-pal′pa-bl), *adj.* **1,** that cannot be felt or known by sense of touch; intangible; as, the *impalpable* air: said of gases, shadows, etc.; **2,** not perceptible or discernible mentally; as, *impalpable* difference between the two ideas.

im-pan-el or **em-pan-el** (im-pan′el; em-pan′el), *v.t.* [im-pan-elled, im-pan-el-ling or im-pan-eled, im-pan-el-ing], **1,** to enter on a list, or panel, for jury duty; **2,** to choose (a jury) from the list and swear in (as jurors for a trial).

im-part (im-pärt′), *v.t.* **1,** to bestow a share or portion of; give; as, flowers *impart* beauty to a room; **2,** to tell; disclose; as, to *impart* a secret.

im-par-tial (im-pär′shal), *adj.* not favouring one more than another; fair; just; as, a judge must be absolutely *impartial* in his or her decisions.—*n.* **im′par-ti-al′i-ty.**

im-pass-a-ble (im-pås′a-bl), *adj.* not capable of being traversed or travelled; as, an *impassable* swamp; an *impassable* road.

im-passe (im′pas′), **1,** a blind alley; **2,** a position from which there is no escape; a deadlock; as, to reach an *impasse* in negotiations.

im-pas-si-ble (im-pas′i-bl), *adj.* insensible to pain; apathetic; unfeeling.

im-pas-sioned (im-pash′und), *adj.* showing strong emotion; as, an *impassioned* speaker; an *impassioned* appeal for aid.

im-pas-sive (im-pas′iv), *adj.* feeling no emotion or pain; showing no feeling; unmoved; calm; insensitive; as, *impassive* faces; *impassive* murderer.

im-pa-tient (im-pā′shent), *n.* **1,** rebellious

against delay, restraint, etc.; restless, eager; as, she was *impatient* to leave; **2,** unable to tolerate or endure; intolerant; as, to be *impatient* of his lying; **3,** irritable; showing lack of control.—*adv.* **im-pa-tient-ly.**—*n.* **im-pa′tience.**

im-peach (im-pēch′), *v.t.* **1,** to charge (a person in public office), before a court, with misconduct in office; accuse; as, to *impeach* a judge or a president; **2,** to question or challenge (a person's honour, motives, etc.).—*adj.* **im-peach′a-ble.**—*n.* **im-peach′ment.**

im-pec-ca-ble (im-pek′a-bl), *adj.* faultless; flawless; as, his manners are *impeccable.*

im-pe-cu-ni-ous (im′pi-kū′ni-us), *adj.* lacking money; poor.

im-ped-ance (im-pēd′ans), *n.* the apparent resistance of a circuit to the flow of an alternating current.

im-pede (im-pēd′), *v.t.* [imped-ed, imped-ing], to obstruct or hinder; retard; as, snow and ice *impeded* our progress.

im-ped-i-ment (im-ped′i-ment), *n.* **1,** that which hinders or obstructs; an obstacle; **2,** a defect in speech, as a stammer.

im-pel (im-pel′), *v.t.* [impelled, impel-ling], to drive forward; force; compel; as, fear and remorse *impelled* him to confess; the breeze *impelled* the sailboat.

im-pend (im-pend′), *v.i.* **1,** to be at hand; threaten to happen; as, death *impends;* **2,** to be about to happen; be near; as, as a strike *impended,* negotiators tried to reach an agreement.—*adj.* **im-pend′ing.**

im-pen-e-tra-ble (im-pen′i-tra-bl), *adj.* **1,** not capable of being entered; allowing no entrance or passage; as, *impenetrable* forests; an *impenetrable* wall; **2,** not capable of being understood; as, an *impenetrable* plot; **3,** closed to reason, sympathy, etc.

im-pen-i-tent (im-pen′i-tent), *adj.* not sorry or repentant for one's sin:—*n.* a hardened sinner.—*n.* **im-pen′i-tence.**

im-per-a-tive (im-per′a-tiv), *adj.* **1,** in *grammar,* expressing command or exhortation; as, "Go!" and "Stop!" are verbs in the *imperative* mood: compare *indicative* and *subjunctive;* **2,** commanding; peremptory; authoritative; as, an *imperative* gesture of dismissal; **3,** necessary; urgent; as, it is *imperative* to leave at once:—*n.* **1,** in *grammar,* the mood expressing command; also, the form of a verb used in this mood; **2,** a command; **3,** something that is urgent or necessary.

im-per-cep-ti-ble (im′pėr-sep′ti-bl), *adj.* **1,** so small, slow, or gradual as hardly to be seen or felt; as, the *imperceptible* growth of a plant from day to day; **2,** too slight to be grasped by the mind; subtle; as, *imperceptible* shades of meaning.—*adv.* **im′per-cep′ti-bly.**

im-per-fect (im-pûr′fekt), *adj.* lacking perfection; faulty; incomplete:—**imperfect tense,** a tense of a verb that indicates action in the past going on but not completed; as, "she was walking:"—*n.* the imperfect tense, or a verb in that tense.—*adv.* **im-per′fect-ly.**—*n.* **im-per′fect-ness; im′per-fec′tion.**

im-pe-ri-al (im-pē′ri-al), *adj.* **1,** pertaining to an empire or an emperor; as, *imperial* policies; *imperial* majesty; **2,** splendid; magnificent; **3,** pertaining to the British Imperial System of measurement:—*n.* a small, pointed beard.—*adv.* **im-pe′ri-al-ly.**

im-pe-ri-al-ism (im-pē′ri-al-izm), *n.* **1,** the power or government of an emperor; **2,** the policy of any nation that aims at the acquisition of new territory and, usually, closer union of the territory already possessed.—*adj.* **im-pe′ri-al-is′tic.**—*n.* **im-pe′ri-al-ist.**

im-per-il (im-per′il), *v.t.* [imperilled, imperil-ling], to put in danger; endanger; as, to *imperil* one's life to save a child.

im-pe-ri-ous (im-pē′ri-us), *adj.* overbearing; urgent.—*adv.* **im-pe′ri-ous-ly.**

im-per-ish-a-ble (im-per′ish-a-bl), *adj.* enduring permanently; indestructible; immortal; as, he won *imperishable* fame.

im-per-me-a-ble (im-pûr′mi-a-bl), *adj.* not permitting passage, esp. of fluids; impervious; as, the skin is *impermeable* to water; *impermeable* rock.

im-per-son-al (im-pûr′sun-al), *adj.* **1,** not relating to any particular person or thing; as, an *impersonal* discussion; **2,** not existing as a person; as, fate and luck are *impersonal* forces; **3,** not affected by personal feelings; as, an *impersonal* corporation:—**impersonal pronoun,** an indefinite pronoun, such as *it, they, you,* or *one;* as, *it* is snowing; *they* say that *it* is becoming warmer; *you* shouldn't steal; *one* should always be honest:—**impersonal verb,** a verb that usually has *it* for a subject, used only in the third person singular; as, it *seems;* it *follows.*—*adv.* **im-per′son-al-ly.**

im-per-son-ate (im-pûr′sun-āt′), *v.t.* [impersonat-ed, impersonat-ing], to play the part of; mimic, esp. on the stage, television, or in film; as, to *impersonate* the legendary musician; to *impersonate* a security guard to get into the bank vault.—*n.* **im-per′son-a′tion; im-per′son-a′tor.**

im-per-ti-nent (im-pûr′ti-nent), *adj.* insolent; rude.—*n.* **im-per′ti-nence.**

im-per-turb-a-ble (im′pėr-tûr′ba-bl), *adj.* calm; serene; not easily excited; as, *imperturbable* composure.

im-per-vi-ous (im-pûr′vi-us), *adj.* not permitting entrance or passage; as, rubber boots are *impervious* to water and mud; *impervious* to insult.

im-pet-u-ous (im-pet′ū-us), *adj.* **1,** rushing with force and violence; as, an *impetuous* wind; **2,** acting with sudden energy; passionate; impulsive; as, an *impetuous* child.—*adv.* **im-pet′u-ous-ly.**—*n.* **im-pet′u-os′i-ty.**

im-pe-tus (im′pi-tus), *n.* **1,** the force or momentum by which a moving body tends to overcome resistance and go on moving; **2,** a moving force; stimulus; incentive; as, the desire for fame is an *impetus* to action.

im-pi-e-ty (im-pī′e-ti), *n.* [*pl.*impieties], **1,** lack of religious reverence; **2,** an act of irreverence or wickedness; lack of respect.—*adj.* **im′pi-ous.**—*adv.* **im′pi-ous-ly.**

im-pinge (im-pinj′), *v.i.* to strike (*on, upon, against*); as, sunshine *impinges* on the clear lake.

im-pish (imp′ish), *adj.* mischievous; as, an *impish* child; an *impish* smile.

im-pla-ca-ble (im-plā′ka-bl), *adj.* not able to be pacified or appeased; relentless; as, *implacable* hatred.—*adv.* **im-pla′ca-bly.**

im-ple-ment (im′pli-ment), *n.* an instrument, tool, or utensil; as, garden *implements*:—*v.t.* to make possible, or to put into effect; carry out; as, to *implement* a plan.

im-pli-cate (im′pli-kāt′), *v.t.* [implicat-ed, implicat-ing], to involve deeply; show connection; as, the accusation *implicated* a dozen people.

im-pli-ca-tion (im′pli-kā′shun), *n.* **1,** close connection; entanglement; **2,** something not expressed but suggested; a hint; as, *implications* of theft.

im-plic-it (im-plis′it), *adj.* **1,** understood, though not expressed; implied; as, an *implicit* threat: compare *explicit*; **2,** trusting in the word or authority of another without question; complete; absolute; as, *implicit* faith; *implicit* obedience.—*adv.* **im-plic′it-ly.**

im-plode (im-plōd′), *v.i.* [implod-ed, implod-ing], **1**, to burst inward; as, the vacuum tube *imploded*; **2,** to collapse or crumple inwardly; as, the political party *imploded*.—*n.* **im-plo′sion.**

im-plore (im-plōr′), *v.t.* [implored, imploring], to entreat earnestly and humbly; pray for; beg; as, to *implore* the king for mercy; *implore* aid; I *implore* you, please come.—*adv.* **im-plor′ing-ly.**

im-ply (im-plī′), *v.t.* [implied, imply-ing], **1,** to mean something not directly expressed; suggest; hint; as, silence *implies* consent; **2,** to involve as a result; as, wealth *implies* responsibility.

im-po-lite (im′pō-līt′), *adj.* discourteous; rude; having bad manners; disrespectful.—*adv.* **im′po-lite′ly.**—*n.* **im-po-lite′ness.**

im-pon-der-a-ble (im-pon′dėr-a-bl), *adj.* without weight; that which cannot be evaluated exactly:—*n.* problems, situations, etc., difficult to assess; as, the *imponderables* of war.

¹im-port (im-pōrt′; im′pōrt), *v.t.* **1,** to bring in from a foreign country, esp. for commercial purposes; **2,** in *computing*, to retrieve data from one program to another; as, she *imported* the graphics files into her text document:—*n.* (im′pōrt),**1,** an article brought from a foreign country; esp. merchandise intended for sale; **2,** in *sports*, an athlete who plays on a team other than his or her own country's, esp. an American professional football player who plays on a Canadian team for a short time.—*n.* **im-port′er.**

²im-port (im-pōrt′), *v.t.* to signify or express:—*v.i.* to have consequence; be of importance:—*n.* (im′pōrt), **1,** meaning; as, the *import* of a sentence; **2,** importance; as, a decision of great *import*.

im-por-tant (im-pôr′tant), *adj.* **1,** of much consequence, value, or meaning; significant; momentous; as, an *important* election; **2,** having an air of importance; pompous; as, she always behaves in an *important* manner; **3,** influential; as, an *important* book on nutrition.—*adv.* **im-por′tant-ly.**—*n.* **im-por′tance.**

im-por-ta-tion (im′pōr-tā′shun), *n.* the act or practice of bringing merchandise into a country from abroad; also, the merchandise so imported.

im-por-tune (im′pôr-tūn′; im-pôr′tūn), *v.t.* [importuned, importun-ing], to ask repeatedly; beg persistently.—*n.* **im′por-tu′ni-ty; im′por-tu′ner.**—*adj.* **im-por′tu-nate.**

im-pose (im-pōz′), *v.t.* [imposed, impos-ing], **1,** to lay (a burden, punishment, etc.) upon persons or property; apply by force; as, to *impose* taxes; **2,** to force (oneself); obtrude; take unfair advantage; as, to *impose* one's company on others:—*v.i.* to take advantage; presume; as, do not *impose* upon his kindness.

im-pos-ing (im-pōz′ing), *adj.* stately; impressive.

im-po-si-tion (im′pō-zish′un), *n.* **1,** the act of imposing a burden; **2,** the tax, punishment, etc., imposed; also, an excessive burden imposed; **3,** a trick; fraud.

im-pos-si-ble (im-pos′i-bl), *adj.* **1,** not capable of occurring or existing; not possible; as, time travel is still *impossible*; **2,** not convenient or easy; as, it is *impossible* to call a meeting for tomorrow; **3,** *Colloq.* utterly objectionable; intolerable; very unpleasant; hard to put up with or get along with; as, she's *impossible* to deal with.—*n.* **im-pos′si-bil′ity.**

im-post (im′pōst), *n.* a tax, esp. a duty levied by a government on imports into a country.

im-pos-tor (im-pos′tėr), *n.* one who attempts to deceive others by adopting a false name or character; a swindler.

im-po-tent (im′po-tent), *adj.* **1,** lacking

physical, mental, or moral power; weak; **2,** lacking sexual power (said of males).—*n.* **im′po-tence.**

im-pound (im-pound′), *v.t.* **1,** to shut in a pen; as, to *impound* stray animals; **2,** to seize and hold; as, the police *impounded* her car.

im-pov-er-ish (im-pov′ėr-ish), *v.t.* **1,** to make poor; as, his gambling *impoverished* him; **2,** to use up the strength or richness of; as, to *impoverish* land.—*n.* **im-pov′er-ish-ment.**

im-prac-ti-ca-ble (im-prak′ti-ka-bl) *adj.* that cannot be worked or used; as, an *impracticable* plan; an *impracticable* device.

im-prac-ti-cal (im-prak′ti-kal), *adj.* not inclined to pay attention to what is useful or profitable; not practical; unrealistic; as, a dress is an *impractical* outfit for outdoor activities.

im-pre-ca-tion (im′pri-kā′shun), *n.* the calling down of evil upon someone; a curse.

im-preg-na-ble (im-preg′na-bl), *adj.* **1,** unable to be captured by force; unconquerable; as, an *impregnable* fort; **2,** not to be overcome by temptation; as, a man of *impregnable* honesty.

im-preg-nate (im-preg′nāt), *v.t.* [impregnat-ed, impregnat-ing], **1,** to make pregnant; fertilize; **2,** to cause to be filled or saturated with; soak; as, to *impregnate* the charcoal with lighter fluid.—*n.* **im′preg-na′tion.**

im-pre-sa-ri-o (im′pre-sär′i-ō), *n.* the organizer, manager, or conductor of an opera, concert, ballet, or other musical company.

im-press (im-pres′), *v.t.* **1,** to mark by applying pressure; stamp; as, the king *impressed* the wax with the royal seal; **2,** to affect or influence deeply; as, the moving speech *impressed* me; **3,** to imprint or fix deeply on the mind; as, *impress* the fear of the law upon him; **4,** to enlist by force; as, to *impress* him into military service; to *impress* a vehicle for official police work:—*n.* (im′pres), **1,** a mark produced by pressure, as by a stamp; **2,** a distinguishing mark.

im-pres-sion (im-presh′un), *n.* **1,** the act of marking or stamping; also, the mark made; as, the *impression* of a seal on wax; **2,** the effect produced on the mind or emotions by something outside them; as, her first trip to Europe made a profound *impression* on her; **3,** a vague notion, remembrance, or belief; as, my *impression* is that I have seen you before; **4,** an imitation of the way someone speaks, acts, or looks; an impersonation; **5,** a mould, esp. of teeth and gums; **6,** the number of copies of a book in a single run; also, a single copy of such a book.—*adj.* **im-pres′sion-a-ble.**

im-pres-sive (im-pres′iv), *adj.* able to influence the mind or feelings; as, an *impressive* ceremony.—*adv.* **im-pres′sive-ly.**

im-print (im-print′), *v.t.* **1,** to mark by pressure; impress; **2,** to stamp or print, as letters, postmarks, etc., on paper; **3,** to impress (an idea) deeply on the mind:—*n.* (im′print), **1,** an impression or mark left by something; as, the *imprint* of a foot; poverty left an *imprint* on her character; **2,** the printer's or publisher's name, and the place and date of publication, printed on the title page or at the end of a book.

im-pris-on (im-priz′n), *v.t.* to put in jail or prison; restrain.—*n.* **im-pris′on-ment.**

im-prob-a-ble (im-prob′a-bl), *adj.* unlikely to happen, exist, or be true; as, an *improbable* result; an *improbable* story.—*adv.* **im-prob′a-bly.**—*n.* **im-prob′a-bil′i-ty.**

im-promp-tu (im-promp′tū), *adv.* and *adj.* without preparation; offhand; improvised; as, to speak *impromptu*; an *impromptu* party:—*n.* something that is made, done, or performed without preparation; improvisation.

im-prop-er (im-prop′ėr), *adj.* **1,** not suited to the purpose; as, *improper* gear for in-line skating; **2,** not according to good manners; indecent; as, *improper* conduct; **3,** incorrect; as, *improper* usage of words.—*adv.* **im-prop′er-ly.**

im-pro-pri-e-ty (im′prō-prī′e-ti), *n.* [*pl.* improprieties], **1,** the fact or quality of being improper; **2,** something, as in language or conduct, that is incorrect or indecent.

im-prov (im′prov′), *n. Colloq.* improvisation; an improvised role-playing in a public performance.

im-prove (im-pro͞ov′), *v.t.* [improved, improv-ing], **1,** to make better; as, to *improve* the mind; **2,** to use to advantage; as, to *improve* an opportunity:—*v.i.* to grow better, as in health; become better.

im-prove-ment (im-pro͞ov′ment), *n.* **1,** the act or fact of improving; making or becoming better; as, her work has shown a lot of *improvement*; **2,** a person or thing that is better; something that adds value; as, *improvements* to a house.

im-prov-i-dent (im-prov′i-dent), *adj.* lacking foresight; not providing for the future: opposite of *thrifty*.

im-pro-vise (im′prō-vīz′; im′prō-viz′) *v.t.* [improvised, improvis-ing], **1,** to compose without plan; make up on the spur of the moment, as role-playing, music, speech, or other performance; **2,** to contrive; as, we *improvised* a bed out of pine branches.—*n.* **im′pro-vi-sa′tion.**

im-pru-dent (im-pro͞o′dent), *adj.* lacking caution; heedless and rash; as, it is *imprudent* to stand under a tree during a thunderstorm.—*adv.* **im-pru′dent-ly.**—*n.* **im-pru′dence.**

im-pu-dent (im′pū-dent), *adj.* insolent; rude; disrespectful; as, an *impudent* reply.—*n.* **im′pu-dence.**

im-pugn (im-pūn′), *v.t.* to attack by argument; question; challenge; as, I do not *impugn* your veracity.

im-pulse (im′puls), *n.* **1,** a driving forward; the motion so produced, or the force producing it; as, *impulses* of the nervous system; **2,** a sudden, unthinking desire or inclination to act in a particular way; as, to give the homeless person money under an *impulse* of pity; **3,** tendency to act without thinking; as, many people are guided by *impulse* rather than by reason.—*adj.* **im-pul′sive.**—*adv.* **im-pul′sive-ly.**—*n.* **im-pul′sive-ness.**

im-pu-ni-ty (im-pū′ni-ti), *n.* freedom from punishment, injury, or loss; as, you cannot break the law with *impunity*.

im-pure (im-pūr′), *adj.* **1,** not clean; unwholesome; as, *impure* water; **2,** mixed with foreign or inferior substance; as, *impure* gold; **3,** bad; corrupt in thought, word, or deed; as, *impure* thoughts.—*adv.* **im-pure′ly.**—*n.* **im-pu′ri-ty.**

im-pute (im-pūt′), *v.t.* [imput-ed, imputing], to set to the account of; attribute or ascribe; blame; as, to *impute* a theft to poverty.—*n.* **im′pu-ta′tion** (im′pū-tā′shun); **im-pu-ta-bi′li-ty.**—*adj.* **im-pu′ta-ble; im-pu′ta-tive.**—*adv.* **im-pu′tab-ly.**

in (in), *prep.* **1,** within the bounds or limits of; as, lost *in* the woods; hurt *in* the hand; **2,** being surrounded by (circumstances, interests, etc.); as, *in* business; *in* trouble; **3,** within (a state, condition, occupation, etc.); as, *in* chains; *in* pain; **4,** within (a period of time); during; as, *in* winter; **5,** after; as, return *in* two days; **6,** at the time of; as, *in* the beginning; **7,** in the person or case of; as, you have a friend *in* me; **8,** in the range of; as, *in* mathematics; in the capacity of; as, it isn't *in* him to do that; **9,** made of; as, a statue *in* bronze; **10,** dressed in; as, a woman *in* black; **11,** expressed in; as, a letter *in* French; **12,** as a means of; as, *in* explanation:—*adv.* **1,** toward the inside; as, he went *in*; **2,** inside a place; at home; as, my mother is *in*; **3,** *Colloq.* stylish; as, chunky heels are *in*:—*adj.* **1,** incoming; as, the *in*-line of traffic; **2,** in power; as, the *in* party; **3,** *Colloq.* fashionable; as, the *in* style this year for hair; **4,** *Slang* in a certain relation; as, he's *in* bad with the officials:—*n. Colloq.* an influential position or approach; as, to have an *in* with the president of the company:—**ins,** *n.pl.* those in office or power:—**ins and outs,** all the details; as, to know the *ins and outs* of a business.

in- (in-), *prefix* before most letters except *b, l, m, p, r* meaning **1,** *not; the opposite of;* as in *in*accurate, *in*capable; **2,** *in, into, within;* as in *in*augurate, *in*bound, *in*breeding.

in-a-bil-i-ty (in′a-bil′i-ti), *n.* the condition of being unable; lack of power.

in-ac-ces-si-ble (in′ak-ses′i-bl), *adj.* not easy to get to or into; not obtainable or approachable; as, *inaccessible* heights.—*n.* **in′ac-ces′si-bil′i-ty.**

in-ac-cu-rate (in-ak′ū-rit), *adj.* incorrect; not exact; as, *inaccurate* figures made by *inaccurate* people.—*n.* **in-ac′cu-ra-cy.**

in-ac-tive (in-ak′tiv), *adj.* unable to move or act; not active; sluggish; idle; as, an *inactive* volcano.—*n.* **in-ac′tion.**—*n.* **in′ac-tiv′i-ty.**

in-ad-e-quate (in-ad′i-kwit), *adj.* not equal to some demand; not sufficient; as, *inadequate* resources.—*adv.* **in-ad′e-quate-ly.**—*n.* **in′ad′e-qua-cy** (in-ad′e-kwa-si).

in-ad-mis-si-ble (in′ad-mis′i-bl), *adj.* not to be granted, allowed, or conceded (as true); as, *inadmissible* evidence.

in-ad-vert-ent (in′ad-vûr′tent), *adj.* due to heedlessness; unintentional; thoughtless; as, an *inadvertent* insult.—*n.* **in′ad-vert′ence.**

in-ad-vis-a-ble (in′ad-vīz′a-bl), *adj.* not to be recommended; unwise.

in-al-ien-a-ble (in-āl′yen-a-bl), *adj.* that cannot be transferred or taken away; as, *inalienable* rights.

in-ane (in-ān′), *adj.* senseless; silly; as, an *inane* remark or smile.—*n.* **in-an′i-ty.**

in-an-i-mate (in-an′i-mit), *adj.* **1,** without life; as, *inanimate* rocks; **2,** deprived of life; as, an *inanimate* human body; **3,** dull; spiritless; as, *inanimate* conversation.—*adv.* **in-an′i-mate-ly.**

in-ap-pli-ca-ble (in-ap′li-ka-bl), *adj.* not fit, suitable, or relevant.

in-ap-pro-pri-ate (in′a-prō′pri-it), *adj.* not suitable, fit, or proper; as, an *inappropriate* dress or speech.—*adv.* **in′ap-pro′pri-ate-ly.**—*n.* **in′ap-pro′pri-ate-ness.**

in-ar-tic-u-late (in′är-tik′ū-lit), *adj.* **1,** not expressed in words; as, *inarticulate* rage; **2,** incapable of speech; as, *inarticulate* animals; surprise made him *inarticulate*; **3,** not jointed; as, a jellyfish has an *inarticulate* body.

in-ar-tis-tic (in′är-tis′tik), *adj.* **1,** not in accord with the principles of art; as, *inartistic* designs; **2,** lacking in appreciation of art; as, an *inartistic* nature; **3,** not graceful; not skillful; as, *inartistic* movements.—*adv.* **in′ar-tis′ti-cal-ly.**

in-as-much as (in′az-much′ az), *conj.* insofar as; because; as, *inasmuch as* you wish to, you may go.

in-at-ten-tion (in′a-ten′shun), *n.* failure to fix one's mind on a matter; heedlessness; as, he failed because of *inattention*.—*adj.* **in′at-ten′tive.**—*adv.* **in′at-ten′tive-ly.**

in-au-di-ble (in-ô′di-bl), *adj.* incapable of

being heard; as, an *inaudible* remark.—*adv.* **in-au′di-bly.**

in-au-gu-ral (in-ô-gū-ral), *adj.* pertaining to the dedication of a public building, the formal installation of a person in an office, etc.:—*n.* a speech made on such an occasion.

in-au-gu-rate (in-ô′gū-rāt′), *v.t.* [inaugurat-ed, inaugurat-ing], **1,** to admit or swear into office with special ceremony; as, to *inaugurate* a president; **2,** to make a formal beginning of; as, to *inaugurate* a custom; **3,** to celebrate the first public use of; as, to *inaugurate* a courthouse.—*n.* **in-au′gu-ra′tion.**

in-aus-pi-cious (in′ôs-pish′us), *adj.* unlucky; unfavourable; as, an *inauspicious* beginning.—*adv.* **in′aus-pi′cious-ly.**

in-born (in′bôrn′), *adj.* present at birth; innate; natural; inherited; as, an *inborn* sense of music.

in-breed-ing (in′brēd′ing), *n.* **1,** mating of individuals that are closely related; **2,** the self-fertilizing of plants.—*adj.* **in′bred′.**

in-cal-cu-la-ble (in-kal′kū-la-bl), *adj.* **1,** beyond estimate; hence, very great; as, he did *incalculable* harm; **2,** not dependable; as, a person *of incalculable* moods.

in-can-des-cent (in′kan-des′ent), *adj.* **1,** glowing with white heat; hence, brilliant; shining; **2,** giving off light by incandescence:—**incandescent lamp,** an electric lamp in which a filament gives off light as a result of intense heat; a light bulb.—*n.* **in′can-des′ cence.**

INCANDESCENT LAMP

in-can-ta-tion (in′kan-tā′shun), *n.* **1,** the use of charms or spells, sung or spoken, as a part of a magic ritual; **2,** the words used.

in-ca-pa-ble (in-kā′pa-bl), *adj.* **1,** not having power or ability; incompetent; as, *incapable* of walking; *incapable* workers; **2,** not open or susceptible to; as, *incapable* of improvement.—*n.* **in′ca-pa-bil′i-ty.**

in-ca-pac-i-tate (in′ka-pas′i-tāt′), *v.t.* [incapacitat-ed, incapacitat-ing], to make powerless or unfit; as, old age often *incapacitates* a person for hard labour.—*n.* **in′ca-pac′i-ty.**

in-car-cer-ate (in-kär′sėr-āt′), *v.t.* [incarcerat-ed, incarcerat-ing], to shut up in a prison; imprison; confine.

in-car-na-tion (in′kär-nā′shun), *n.* **1,** the taking on of material form; embodiment in human flesh; **2,** a person thought of as representing a principle, ideal, etc.; as, he is the *incarnation* of honesty:—**Incarnation,** in the Christian religion, the taking upon himself of human flesh by the Son of God in the person of Jesus.—*adj.* **in-car′nate.**

in-case (in-kās′), *v.t.* Same as **encase.**

in-cau-tious (in-kô′shus), *adj.* heedless; careless; unwary; indifferent.

in-cen-di-ar-y (in-sen′di-er′i), *adj.* **1,** pertaining to the malicious setting on fire of property; **2,** tending to stir up passion, strife, or violence; as, an *incendiary* article:—*n.* [*pl.* incendiaries], **1,** one who maliciously sets fire to property; **2,** one who excites quarrels; **3,** *Military,* a bomb that sets fire to its target: short for *incendiary bomb* (World War II).

[1]**in-cense** (in-sens′), *v.t.* [incensed, incensing], to make angry; enrage; as, the lie *incensed* her.

[2]**in-cense** (in′sens), *n.* **1,** any material that gives off perfume when burned; **2,** the smoke or odour of such material when burned, as in religious rites; **3,** any pleasant odour or perfume; as, the *incense* of flowers.

in-cen-tive (in-sen′tiv), *adj.* arousing to action; encouraging; motivating:—*n.* motive; as, a reward is an *incentive* to work.

in-cep-tion (in-sep′shun), *n.* beginning; initiation; first stage; as, *inception* of a new project.

in-ces-sant (in-ses′ant), *adj.* unceasing; constant; repeated; as, the *incessant* dripping of water.—*adv.* **in-ces′sant-ly.**

in-cest (in′sest), *n.* sexual intercourse between persons related within the degrees wherein marriage is forbidden by law.—*adj.* **in-ces′tu-ous.**

inch (inch), *n.* **1,** a unit of length equal to 2.54 centimetres or one twelfth of a foot; **2,** a small distance or degree; as, he came within an *inch* of being struck by the car:—*v.i.* to move slowly, a little bit at a time; as, the heavy traffic *inched* along.

in-ci-dence (in′si-dens), *n.* **1,** occurrence; as, the *incidence* of the car accident; **2,** the range or extent of occurrence or effect; as, the *incidence* of flu that year.

in-ci-dent (in′si-dent), *adj.* apt to happen; naturally belonging; as, the dangers *incident* to a career as a daredevil:—*n.* **1,** an episode; an event that adds to a larger event or experience; as, the pleasant *incident* that occurred on her trip; **2,** a minor conflict; something that causes trouble or problems; as, *incidents* along the border of the two countries.

in-ci-den-tal (in′si-den′tal), *adj.* occurring in connection with and addition to something else; as, a movie with *incidental* music; *incidental* worries:—**incidentals,** *n.pl.* relatively unimportant items, esp. minor expenses.

in-ci-den-tal-ly (in′si-den′tal-i), *adv.* by the way; along with something else; as, *incidentally,* I'm bringing a date to the party.

in-cin-er-a-tor (in-sin′ėr-ā′tėr), *n.* a furnace for burning waste matter.

in-cip-i-ent (in-sip′i-ent), *adj.* beginning to be or appear; as, an *incipient* disease.

in-ci-sion (in-sizh′un), *n.* **1,** the act of cutting into something; **2,** a cut made with a sharp instrument; as, a surgical *incision.*

in-ci-sor (in-sī′zėr), *n.* a cutting tooth; in humans, one of the four front teeth, between the canines, in either jaw. (See *dentition,* illustration.)

in-cite (in-sīt′), *v.t.* [incit-ed, incit-ing], to rouse; stir up; as, poor working conditions *incited* the workers to strike.—*n.* **in-cite′ment.**

in-ci-vil-i-ty (in′si-vil′i-ti), *n.* **1,** impoliteness; lack of courtesy; **2,** the state of being uncivil.

in-clem-ent (in-klem′ent), *adj.* harsh; severe; as, *inclement* weather, climate, leader.

in-cli-na-tion (in′kli-nā′shun), *n.* **1,** the act of bending or leaning toward something, esp. a bending of the head or body in reverence, recognition, etc.; a bow; **2,** a turning aside from a given direction or position; a slanting position; slope; as, the *inclination* of the Tower of Pisa; also, the amount of the slant; **3,** a liking; preference; as, an *inclination* for music; **4,** a tendency; as, older people have an *inclination* to become less active.

in-cline (in-klīn′), *v.t.* [inclined, inclining], **1,** to cause to lean; slant; as, to *incline* a board; **2,** to bow; as, to *incline* the head in acknowledgement; **3,** to give a tendency to; turn; dispose; as, this statement *inclines* me to believe:—*v.i.* **1,** to turn from a given direction; deviate; slant; lean; as, the road *inclines* to the west; **2,** to bow; **3,** be willing to; to have a preference; as, she's *inclined* to believe him; **4,** to be likely to; tend; as, moose are *inclined* to eat tender buds of trees and bushes:—*n.* (in-klīn′; in′klin), a slant; a sloping surface; as, we travelled up a steep *incline.*

in-close (in-klōs′), *v.t.* Same as **enclose.**

in-clude (in-klūd′; -klo͞od′), *v.t.* [includ-ed, includ-ing], **1,** to enclose within limits; contain as part of the whole; made up of; as, biology *includes* both botany and zoology; **2,** to make someone or something part of a group, etc.; as, to *include* her in the planning process; *include* the famous quote in the essay.—*n.* **in-clu′sion.**

in-clu-sive (in-klū′siv; -klo͞o′-), *adj.* **1,** containing a great deal; as, an *inclusive* survey; **2,** taking in the two extremes or limits mentioned and everything in between; as, read pages 300 to 350 *inclusive*:—**all-inclusive,** everything included; as, an *all-inclusive* resort, which includes meals, accommodations, use of facilities, etc.—*adv.* **inclu′sive-ly.**

in-cog-ni-to (in-kog′ni-tō′), *adj.* having one's true identity concealed or disguised; going under an assumed name; as, the famous movie star travelled *incognito* so that she would not be recognized.

in-co-her-ent (in′kō-hēr′ent), *adj.* **1,** consisting of parts that do not cling together; **2,** without logical connection; rambling; not making sense; as, an *incoherent* sentence.—*n.* **in′co-her′ence.**

in-com-bus-ti-ble (in′kom-bus′ti-bl) *adj.* unburnable; fireproof; as, asbestos is *incombustible.*

in-come (in′kum), *n.* the receipts, usually money, derived from labour, business, property, or capital; wages; salary:—**income tax,** a tax collected on the money earned by a person or business.

in-com-ing (in′kum′ing), *adj.* **1,** coming in; as, the *incoming* tide; **2,** beginning; coming into office; as, the *incoming* mayor:—*n.* the act of coming in; arrival.

in-com-pa-ra-ble (in-kom′pa-ra-bl), *adj.* not to be compared; unequalled; as, *incomparable* beauty.—*adv.* **incom′pa-ra-bly.**

in-com-pat-i-ble (in′kom-pat′i-bl), *adj.* **1,** incapable of existing together in harmony; **2,** inconsistent; as, desires *incompatible* with one's income.—*adv.* **in′com-pat′i-bly.**—*n.* **in′com-pat′i-bil′i-ty.**

in-com-pe-tent (in-kom′pi-tent), *adj.* **1,** unfit; without ability; as, an *incompetent* worker; **2,** not legally qualified.—*adv.* **in-com′pe-tent-ly.**—*n.* **in-com′pe-tence.**

in-com-plete (in′kom-plēt′), *adj.* not fully finished or developed; as, an *incomplete* design; not having all its parts; imperfect; as, an *incomplete* deck of cards.

in-com-pre-hen-si-ble (in′kom-pri-hen′si-bl), *adj.* not to be understood or grasped by the mind; as, *incomprehensible* points of view.—*adv.* **in′com-pre-hen′si-bly.**—*n.* **in′com-pre-hen′si-bi′li-ty.**

in-con-ceiv-a-ble (in′kon-sēv′a-bl), *adj.* incapable of being grasped by the mind or imagined; unbelievable; as, *inconceivable* cruelty.—*n.* **in′con-ceiv′a-bil′i-ty; in′-con-ceiv′a-ble-ness.**—*adv.* **in′con-ceiv′a-bly.**

in-con-gru-ous (in-kong′gro͞o-us), *adj.* unsuitable; inappropriate; inconsistent; as, his solemn manner was *incongruous* with the humorous situation.—*n.* **in′con-gru′i-ty.**—*adv.* **in-con′gru-ous-ly.**

in-con-se-quen-tial (in-kon′si-kwen′shal), *adj.* unimportant; trivial; irrelevant.—*adv.* **in-con′se-quen′tial-ly.**

in-con-sid-er-ate (in′kon-sid′ėr-it), *adj.* not heeding the wishes, thoughts, or feelings of others; thoughtless; as, an *inconsiderate* bully; an *inconsiderate* remark.—*adv.* **in′con-sid′er-ate-ly.**

in-con-sist-en-cy (in′kon-sis′ten-si), *n.* [*pl.* inconsistencies], **1,** lack of agreement; as, the *inconsistency* of two stories; **2,** a contradiction; as, testimony full of *inconsistencies.*

in-con-sist-ent (in′kon-sis′tent), *adj.* **1,**

not in keeping (with); as, stealing is *inconsistent* with honesty; **2,** self-contradictory; not logical; as, a person *inconsistent* in argument.—*adv.* **in′con-sist′ent-ly.**

in-con-so-la-ble (in′kon-sōl′a-bl), *adj.* not to be comforted; as, *inconsolable* grief.—*adv.* **in′con-so′la-bly.**

in-con-spic-u-ous (in′kon-spik′ū-us), *adj.* not noticeable; not prominent or striking; as, *inconspicuous* colours.—*adv.* **in′con-spic′u-ous-ly.**

in-con-stant (in-kon′stant), *adj.* subject to change; fickle; as, *inconstant* lovers.—*n.* **in-con′stan-cy.**—*adv.* **in-con′stant-ly.**

in-con-tro-ver-ti-ble (in-kon′tro-vûr′ti-bl), *adj.* indisputable; undeniable; as, this is the *incontrovertible* truth.—*adv.* **in-con′tro-ver′ti-bly.**

in-con-ven-ience (in′kon-vēn′yens), *n.* **1,** discomfort; trouble; as, an interruption in electrical service causes a great deal of *inconvenience*; **2,** that which causes trouble; a hindrance; annoyance; as, the late departure of the plane was an *inconvenience* to me:—*v.t.* [inconvenienced, inconvenienc-ing], to put to trouble; annoy; as, we might *inconvenience* our hosts if we stayed overnight.—*adj.* **in′con-ven′ient.** —*adv.* **in′con-ven′ient-ly.**

in-cor-po-rate (in-kôr′po-rāt′), *v.t.* [incorporat-ed, incorporat-ing], **1,** to combine into one body; unite; esp. to establish as a corporation, or group of people entitled by law to conduct a business as if they were one person; as, to *incorporate* a business, town, or club; **2,** to embody; include; put; as, to *incorporate* an idea into a story; **3,** to blend; mix, as one substance with another:—*v.i.* **1,** to unite with something else to form a single body; **2,** to become a corporation:—*adj.* (in-kôr′po-rit), **1,** closely united; united in one body; **2,** formed into, or united with others in, a body of persons authorized by law to conduct a business as one individual; incorporated.—*n.* **in-cor′po-ra′tion.**

in-cor-rect (in′ko-rekt′), *adj.* **1,** not according to model or rule; faulty; as, an *incorrect* copy; **2,** not according to fact; inaccurate; as, *incorrect* information; **3,** not in accordance with what is right or proper; improper; as, *incorrect* behaviour; *incorrect* dress.—*adv.* **in′cor-rect′ly.**

in-cor-ri-gi-ble (in-kor′i-ji-bl), *adj.* not capable of being corrected or set right; too accustomed to a bad habit to be reformed; as, an *incorrigible* drinker or liar.—*adv.* **in-cor′ri-gi-bly.**—*n.* **in-cor′ri-gi-bil′i-ty.**

in-cor-rupt-i-ble (in′ko-rup′ti-ble), *adj.* **1,** not liable to decay; as, gold is *incorruptible*; **2,** not open to bribery; honest; as, a person of *incorruptible* integrity.—*adv.* **in′cor-rupt′i-bly.**

in-crease (in-krēs′), *v.t.* and *v.i.* [increased, increas-ing], to make or become greater; enlarge; as, to *increase* the budget; the number of students *increases* year by year:—*n.* (in′krēs), **1,** grown in size, number, intensity, etc.; as, an *increase* in business; an *increase* in popularity; **2,** that which is added to the original number, stock, capital, etc.; as, an *increase* of 10 students.—*adv.* **in-creas′ing-ly.**

in-cred-i-ble (in-kred′i-bl), *adj.* hard to believe; unimaginable; amazing; as, *incredible* tales; *incredible* wealth.—*adv.* **in-cred′i-bly.**

in-cred-u-lous (in-kred′ū-lus), *adj.* **1,** indicating lack of belief; as, an *incredulous* smile; **2,** unbelieving; doubting; skeptical; as, even after the evidence was set before her, she was still *incredulous.*—*adv.* **in-cred′u-lous-ly.**—*n.* **in′cre-du′li-ty; in′cre′du-lous-ness.**

in-cre-ment (in′kre-ment; ing′kre-ment), *n.* an increase or addition, esp. one of several additions; as, an annual *increment* in salary, gain, growth, or profit.—*adj.* **in′cre-ment′al.**—*adv.* **in′cre-ment′al-ly.**

in-crim-i-nate (in-krim′i-nāt′) [incriminat-ed, incriminat-ing], to charge with, or involve in, a crime; implicate; as, his words *incriminated* him.—*n.* **in-crim′i-na′tion.**

in-crust (in-krust′), *v.t.* Same as **encrust.**

in-cu-bate (in′kū-bāt′; ing′kū-bāt′), *v.t.* [incubat-ed, incubat-ing], **1,** to sit upon (eggs) in order to hatch them; brood; **2,** to keep (eggs, embryos) under proper conditions, esp. of warmth, for them to hatch or develop; **3,** to cause something to develop; as, to *incubate* a plan:—*v.i.* **1,** to sit on eggs; brood; **2,** to develop or hatch.—*n.* **in′cu-ba′tion.**

in-cu-ba-tor (in′kū-bā′tėr; ing′kū-bā′tėr), *n.* **1,** an apparatus for hatching eggs by artificial warmth; **2,** an apparatus used in a hospital to help the growth of exceptionally small newborn babies, prematurely born babies, or babies with serious health problems; **3,** a device for growing and developing microorganisms, such as bacteria, under controlled conditions.

in-cul-cate (in′kul-kāt′; in-kul′kāt), *v.t.* [inculcat-ed, inculcat-ing], to impress upon the mind urgently; as, the mother tried to *inculcate* honesty on her children.—*n.* **in′cul-ca′tion.**

in-cum-bent (in-kum′bent), *adj.* **1,** lying or leaning with its weight on something else; **2,** pressing upon as a duty; as, it is *incumbent* upon every good citizen to vote:—*n.* the holder of an office:—*adj.* currently holding office; as, the *incumbent* premier.—*n.* **in-cum′ben-cy.**

in-cum-ber (in-kum′bėr), *v.t.* Same as **encumber.**

in-cur (in-kûr′), *v.t.* [incurred, incur-ring], to meet with, fall into, or bring down upon oneself; as, to *incur* hatred, punishment, debts, etc.

in-cur-a-ble (in-kūr′a-bl), *adj.* **1,** incapable of being healed; beyond the skill of medicine; as, an *incurable* disease; **2,** incapable of changing; as, an *incurable* pessimist:—*n.* a person diseased or handicapped beyond remedy.—*adv.* **incur′a-bly.**—*n.* **in-cur′a-bil′i-ty.**

in-cur-sion (in-kûr′shun), *n.* raid; inroad; invasion; interruption; as, an *incursion* into enemy territory; an *incursion* of the sea.

in-curve (in-kûrv′), *v.t.* and *v.i.* to curve inward:—*n.* (in′kûrv′), in *baseball*, a pitched ball that curves toward the batter.

in-debt-ed (in-det′id), *adj.* **1,** owing money; **2,** under obligation; owing gratitude; as, I am *indebted* to you for your kindness.—*n.* **in-debt′ed-ness.**

in-de-cent (in-dē′sent), *adj.* **1,** unfit to be heard or seen; as, *indecent* language or pictures; **2,** unbecoming; in bad taste; as, he spoke and left in *indecent* haste.—*adv.* **in-de′cent-ly.**—*n.* **in-de′cen-cy.**

in-de-ci-pher-a-ble (in′di-sī′fėr-abl), *adj.* that cannot be read; illegible; as, the note was *indecipherable.*

in-de-ci-sive (in′di-sī′siv), *adj.* **1,** not settling a matter; as, *indecisive* evidence; **2,** not positive; uncertain; hesitating; irresolute; as, an *indecisive* manner of speech.—*adv.* **in′de-ci′sive-ly.**—*n.* **in′de-ci′sion.**

in-de-co-rous (in′di-kō′rus; in-dek′or-us), *adj.* improper; violating the rules of good manners; as, *indecorous* conduct.

in-deed (in-dēd′), *adv.* in fact; in truth; really; as, I was *indeed* surprised.

in-de-fat-i-ga-ble (in′de-fat′i-ga-bl). *adj.* tireless; as, *indefatigable* exertion.—*adv.* **in′de-fat′i-ga-bly.**

in-de-fen-sib-le (in′di-fen′si-bl), *adj.* without defence; esp. not capable of being held, maintained, or justified; as, an *indefensible* argument.—*n.* **in′de-fen′si-bil′i-ty.**

in-de-fin-a-ble (in′di-fīn′a-bl), *adj.* that cannot be exactly described or explained.

in-def-i-nite (in-def′i-nit), *adj.* **1,** not exact; vague; uncertain; as, his answers were *indefinite*; **2,** having no fixed limit, amount, or number:—**indefinite article,** either of the words *a* or *an.*—*adv.* **in-def′i-nite-ly.**

in-del-i-ble (in-del′i-bl), *adj.* incapable of being erased; as, *indelible* ink; also, incapable of being forgotten; as, an *indelible* impression.—*adv.* **in-del′i-bly.**

in-del-i-cate (in-del′i-kit), *adj.* lacking refinement; offensive to modesty or propriety; coarse; as, *indelicate* remarks.—*adv.* **in-del′i-cate-ly.**

in-dem-ni-fy (in-dem′ni-fī′), *v.t.* [indemnified, indemnify-ing], to repay or compensate a person for loss, expense, or damage.—*n.* **in-dem′ni-fi-ca′tion.**

in-dem-ni-ty (in-dem′ni-ti), *n.* [*pl.* indemnities], **1,** insurance against loss, damage, or punishment; **2,** repayment for loss or injury; **3,** the salary paid to a Canadian Member of Parliament or Legislative Assembly.

in-dent (in-dent′), *v.t.* **1,** to give a zigzag outline to; notch; as, many small bays *indent* the coast; **2,** in writing or printing, to begin (a line) with a blank space; **3,** to make a depression in; dent; stamp; as, to *indent* the sand with footsteps.—*n.* **in′den-ta′tion; in-den′tion.**

in-den-ture (in-den′tūr), *n.* **1,** a dent; depression; indentation; **2,** a written agreement or contract, esp. one binding a person to a service:—*v.t.* [indentured, indentur-ing], to bind by a written agreement, as an apprentice.

in-de-pend-ence (in′di-pen′dens), *n.* freedom from support, control, or government by others.

in-de-pend-ent (in′di-pen′dent), *adj.* **1,** not relying on, supported by, or governed by others; free; as, Canada and the U.S. are *independent* nations; **2,** not easily influenced; not biased; as, an *independent* thinker; **3,** disinclined, through pride, to accept help; **4,** not connected with others; separate; as, an *independent* film company or store:—*n.* one who in politics, art, business, etc., acts or thinks for himself or herself or is not connected with others.

in-de-scrib-a-ble (in′di-skrīb′a-bl), *adj.* **1,** not sufficiently definite to be described; indefinite; vague; as, an *indescribable* pain; **2,** too great, beautiful, terrible, etc., to be described; beyond description; as, scenery of *indescribable* beauty.—*adv.* **in′de-scrib′a-bly.**

in-de-struct-i-ble (in′di-struk′ti-bl), *adj.* not capable of being broken up, ruined, or destroyed; durable; lasting.—*adv.* **in′de-struct′i-bly.**—*n.* **in′de-struct′i-bil′i-ty.**

in-de-ter-mi-nate (in′di-tûr′mi-nit), *adj.* not settled or fixed; indefinite; vague; as, an *indeterminate* sentence for a crime.

in-dex (in′deks), *n.* [*pl.* indexes (in′dek-sez) or indices (in′di-sēz′)], **1,** that which points out or indicates; a sign; as, busy factories are an *index* of prosperity; **2,** the finger next to the thumb; **3,** a pointer, as the hand on a dial; **4,** a list of subjects or names, usually at the end of a book, arranged alphabetically and telling on what page each subject or name is treated; also, in *computing*, a similar list in a computer program; **5,** in *printing*, a mark [☞] used to call attention to; **6,** a number showing the relative value or amount of something; as, the pollution or population *index*:—*v.t.* **1,** to provide (a book) with an alphabetical table of references; **2,** to indicate.

In-di-an (in′di-an; in′dē-an), *adj.* **1,** having to do with the country of India or the

East Indies or with the people, languages, and cultures found there; **2,** having to do with the original inhabitants of the Americas, their language or culture; Aboriginal.

Indian Ocean, a large ocean south of Asia between Africa and Australia: area, about 75.2 million square kilometres.

India rubber, *n.* Same as [1]*rubber* (def. 3).

in-di-cate (in′di-kāt′), *v.t.* [indicat-ed, indicat-ing], **1,** to point out; show; mark; as, signposts *indicate* the road; **2,** to suggest; also, to state briefly; as, her smile *indicated* that she was happy.—*n.* **in′di-ca′tion; in′di-ca′tor.**

in-dic-a-tive (in-dik′a-tiv), *adj.* **1,** pointing out; suggesting; as, cold hands are *indicative* of poor circulation; **2,** in *grammar,* designating, or having to do with, that mood of the verb used to state a fact or ask a direct question: compare *imperative* and *subjunctive*:—*n.* the indicative mood.—*adv.* **in-dic′a-tive-ly.**

in-dict (in-dīt′), *v.t.* to accuse; charge with a crime after finding evidence enough to warrant a trial; as, he was *indicted* for theft.—*n.* **in-dict′ment.**—*adj.* **in-dict′a-ble** (in-dīt′a-bl).

in-dif-fer-ent (in-dif′ėr-ent), *adj.* **1,** not caring or concerned about something; feeling no interest; as, a bad ruler is *indifferent* to the wishes of his or her people; **2,** neither good nor bad; mediocre; as, *indifferent* work; **3,** having no preference; taking neither side, as in an argument; as, he maintained an *indifferent* attitude.—*n.* **indif′ference.**

in-di-gence (in′di-jens), *n.* poverty; need.

in-dig-e-nous (in-dij′i-nus), *adj.* born or produced in a particular place or country; native; as, tobacco is *indigenous* to America.—*adv.* **in-dig′e-nous-ly.**

in-di-gent (in′di-jent), *adj.* very poor; needy; as, an *indigent* homeless person.

in-di-gest-i-ble (in′di-jes′ti-bl; in′dī-jes′ti-bl), *adj.* hard or impossible to digest.

in-di-ges-tion (in′di-jes′chun), *n.* difficulty in digesting food; the discomfort caused by such difficulty; dyspepsia.

in-dig-nant (in-dig′nant), *adj.* feeling anger and scorn because of unfair treatment.—*adv.* **in-dig′nant-ly.**—*n.* **in′dig-na′tion.**

in-dig-ni-ty (in-dig′ni-ti), *n.* [*pl.* indignities], an act or saying that injures the dignity of someone else; an insult; unfair treatment.

in-di-go (in′di-go′), *n.* [*pl.* indigos or indigoes], **1,** a manufactured blue dye, formerly obtained from the indigo plant; **2,** a deep violet blue: also called *indigo blue.*

in-di-rect (in′di-rekt′; in′dī-rekt′), *adj.* **1,** not straight; not in a direct line; as, an *indirect* road; **2,** roundabout; as, *indirect* taxation; **3,** not straightforward; as, an *indirect* reply.—*adv.* **in′di-rect′ly.**

in-dis-cern-i-ble (in′di-zûr′ni-bl), *adj.* that cannot be seen.

in-dis-creet (in′dis-krēt′), *adj.* not cautious or careful; unwise; imprudent; as, an *indiscreet* remark.—*adv.* **in′dis-creet′ly.**

in-dis-cre-tion (in′dis-kresh′un), *n.* **1,** rashness; lack of caution; **2,** an indiscreet or imprudent act.

in-dis-crim-i-nate (in′dis-krim′i-nit), *adj.* not distinguishing differences between one person or thing and another or others; not choosing or chosen carefully; as, an *indiscriminate* reader; *indiscriminate* reading.—*adv.* **in′dis-crim′i-nate-ly.**

in-dis-pen-sa-ble (in′dis-pen′sa-bl), *adj.* not to be done without; absolutely necessary; as, food is *indispensable* to life.

in-dis-posed (in′dis-pōzd′), *adj.* **1,** ill; unwell; **2,** unwilling; averse.

in-dis-po-si-tion (in′dis-po-zish′un), *n.* **1,** an illness, esp. one that is not serious; **2,** aversion; unwillingness.

in-dis-pu-ta-ble (in-dis′pū-ta-bl), *adj.* unquestionable; clearly evident.

in-dis-so-lu-ble (in-dis′o-lū-bl; in′di-sol′ū-bl), *adj.* **1,** that cannot be broken up or destroyed; **2,** forever binding, as a contract, agreement, etc.

in-dis-tinct (in′dis-tingkt′), *adj.* not distinct or clear; obscure; as, an *indistinct* sound.—*adv.* **in′dis-tinct′ly.**

in-dis-tin-guish-a-ble (in′dis-ting′gwish-a-bl), *adj.* not separable; blurred.

in-di-vid-u-al (in′di-vid′ū-al), *adj.* **1,** of or belonging to or meant for a single person or thing; as, *individual* lockers; *individual* servings; **2,** one's own; as, an *individual* style of speaking:—*n.* **1,** a single or separate person, animal, or thing; **2,** a distinct person; as, she's a real *individual* because she doesn't follow trends.—*adv.* **in′di-vid′u-al-ly.**

in-di-vid-u-al-i-ty (in′di-vid′ū-al′i-ti), *n.* [*pl.* individualities], **1,** the quality or state of existing separately, or apart from other persons or things; separate existence; **2,** the sum of all the characteristics that mark one person or thing as different and separate from another; personality.—*adj.* **in′di-vid′u-al-is′tic.**

in-di-vis-i-ble (in′di-viz′i-bl), *adj.* not capable of being divided into parts.—*n.* **in′di-vis′i-bil′i-ty.**

in-doc-tri-nate (in-dok′tri-nāt′), *v.t.* [-nated, -nating], to teach; impress deeply with a doctrine, principle, idea, etc.—*n.* **in-doc′tri-na′tion.**

in-do-lent (in′do-lent), *adj.* **1,** fond of ease; avoiding labour; lazy; lethargic; as, an *indolent* student; **2,** causing little or no pain; as, an *indolent* tumour.—*n.* **in′dolence.**

in-dom-i-ta-ble (in-dom′i-ta-bl), *adj.* unconquerable; stubborn; unyielding; as, an *indomitable* will.—*adv.* **in-dom′i-ta-bly.**

in-door (in′dōr′), *adj.* pertaining to the inside of a building; living, belonging, or done within doors; as, *indoor* sports; *indoor* lights.

in-doors (in′dōrz′; in′dōrz′), *adv.* in or into the house; as, to play *indoors.*

in-dorse (in-dôrs′), *v.t.* Same as **endorse.**

in-dorse-ment (in-dôrs′ment), *n.* Same as **endorsement.**

in-du-bi-ta-ble (in-dū′bi-ta-bl), *adj.* sure beyond doubt or question.—*adv.* **in-du′bi-ta-bly.**

in-duce (in-dūs′), *v.t.* [induced, induc-ing], **1,** to persuade; influence; prevail upon; as, money will *induce* him to go; **2,** to bring on; effect; cause; as, illness *induced* by stress; **3,** to arrive at (a conclusion or principle) from the observation or study of particular cases; infer; **4,** in *medicine,* to bring about artificially, esp. with drugs; as, to *induce* labour.—*n.* **in-duce′ment.**

in-duc-tance (in-duk′tans), *n.* in *electricity,* the capacity of a circuit for magnetic induction.

in-duc-tion (in-duk′shun), *n.* **1,** the introduction of a person into office; **2,** in *electricity,* the act or process by which a conductor becomes electrified when near, but not in contact with, a body that is charged; **3,** the process of reasoning by which a general conclusion is reached from a study of particular facts; **4,** the process of bringing about artificially; as the *induction* of labour.—*adj.* **in-duc′tive.**—*v.t.* **in-duct′.**

in-dulge (in-dulj′), *v.t.* [indulged, indulg-ing], **1,** to give way to; humour; as, the nurse *indulged* the sick child; **2,** to yield to; as, to *indulge* a love of chocolate:—*v.i.* to gratify one's desires, usually without restraint; as, to *indulge* in candy.

in-dul-gent (in-dul′jent), *adj.* yielding to the humour or wishes of another; as, an *indulgent* parent; also, too forbearing; too lenient.—*n.* **in-dul′gence.**

in-dus-tri-al (in-dus′tri-al), *adj.* **1,** having to do with, made by, or suitable for industry; as, *industrial* employees, *industrial* chemicals; **2,** having a highly developed industry; as, *industrial* countries.

in-dus-tri-ous (in-dus′tri-us), *adj.* diligent; hard-working; busy; as, an *industrious* worker.—*adv.* **in-dus′tri-ous-ly.**

in-dus-try (in′dus-tri), *n.* [*pl.* industries], **1,** steady application to a task; diligence; hard work; as, it takes a lot of *industry* to become successful; **2,** all forms of business and manufacture; **3,** in a more limited sense, the occupations that produce goods from raw materials, as distinguished from finance and commerce; the work of factories and manufacturing plants; **4,** a particular branch or type of manufacturing, trade, or business; as, the pulp and paper *industry*; the automobile *industry.*—*n.* **in-dus′tri-al-ist; in-dus′tri-al-i-za′tion.**—*v.t.* **in-dus′tri-al-ize′.**

in-dwell (in′dwel′), *v.t.* and *v.i.* to abide or exist in, as a spirit or principle.

in-e-bri-ate (in-ē′bri-āt′), *v.t.* [-ated, -ating], to make drunk; intoxicate (mentally or emotionally):—*n.* (-it), a habitual drunkard:—*adj.* drunken.—*adj.* **in-e′bri-a-ted.**—*n.* **in-e′bri-a′tion.**

in-ed-i-ble (in-ed′i-bl), *adj.* not fit to be eaten.—*n.* **in-ed′i-bil′i-ty.**

in-ef-fa-ble (in-ef′a-bl), *adj.* incapable of being expressed in words; beyond description; as, *ineffable* joy.—*adv.* **in-ef′fa-bly.**

in-ef-fec-tive (in′e-fek′tiv), *adj.* not producing, or unable to produce, the desired result; ineffectual; as, his urgent plea was *ineffective.*—*adv.* **in′ef-fec′tive-ly.**

in-ef-fec-tu-al (in′e-fek′tū-al), *adj.* without result; weak; unsuccessful; as, all his efforts were *ineffectual.*

in-ef-fi-cient (in′e-fish′ent), *adj.* **1,** not producing, or not capable of producing, the desired effect; as, *inefficient* labour; **2,** incapable; lacking in skill or in willingness to work well; as, an *inefficient* worker; **3,** wasteful; not working at peak performance; as, an *inefficient,* old furnace.—*n.* **in′ef-fi′cien-cy.**

in-el-e-gant (in-el′e-gant), *adj.* lacking in beauty, refinement, good taste, etc.

in-el-i-gi-ble (in-el′i-ji-bl), *adj.* **1,** unfit; unsuitable; not qualified; as, to be *ineligible* for employment insurance; **2,** not qualified legally for an office or position; as, his age makes him *ineligible* to be a bartender.—*adv.* **in-el′i-gi-bly.**—*n.* **in-el′i-gi-bil′i-ty.**

in-ept (in-ept′), *adj.* **1,** unsuitable; unfit; **2,** absurd; foolish; as, an *inept* remark; **3,** clumsy; inefficient.—*n.* **in-ep′ti-tude′.**

in-e-qual-i-ty (in′i-kwol′i-ti; in′i-kwôl′i-ti), *n.* [*pl.* inequalities], **1,** the quality of being unequal; difference of rank, station, size, number, etc.; **2,** unevenness, as in surface; changeableness in the condition of a person or thing; as, *inequalities* of temper, the weather, etc.

in-eq-ui-ta-ble (in-ek′wi-ta-bl), *adj.* unfair; unjust.

in-ert (in-ûrt′), *adj.* **1,** without power to move; lifeless; as, an *inert* mass of rock; **2,** slow; sluggish; **3,** having no active chemical powers; as, an *inert* drug.

in-er-tia (in-ûr′sha; in-ûr′shi-a), *n.* **1,** the tendency not to move, change, or exert oneself; **2,** in *physics,* that property of matter that causes a body at rest to stay motionless, or a body in motion to continue moving in the same direction, unless acted upon by some outside force.

in-es-cap-a-ble (in′es-kā′pa-bl), *adj.* that cannot be escaped; as, an *inescapable* conclusion.

in-es-ti-ma-ble (in-es′ti-ma-bl), *adj.* beyond measure or price; as, the work of our schools is of *inestimable* value.

in-ev-i-ta-ble (in-ev′i-ta-bl), *adj.* not to be escaped or shunned; unavoidable; certain to happen; happening very often; as, *inevitable* death; *inevitable* delays at the airport during March break.—*adj.* **in-ev′i-ta-bly.**

in-ex-act (in′eg-zakt′), *adj.* not exact or accurate; incorrect.—*adv.* **in′ex-act′ly.**

in-ex-cus-a-ble (in′eks-kūz′a-bl), *adj.* not to be excused or justified; as, *inexcusable* rudeness.—*adv.* **in′ex-cus′a-bly.**

in-ex-haust-i-ble (in′eg-zôs′ti-bl), *adj.* **1,** incapable of being used up; unfailing; as, *inexhaustible* resources; **2,** of tireless power, vigour, or strength; unwearied.

in-ex-o-ra-ble (in-ek′so-ra-bl), *adj.* not to be moved by persuasion; unyielding; unrelenting; as, an *inexorable* enemy.

in-ex-pe-di-ent (in′eks-pē′di-ent), *adj.* not advisable; not suitable or wise; as, it would be *inexpedient* to increase taxes now.—*n.* **in′ex-pe′di-en-cy.**

in-ex-pen-sive (in′eks-pen′siv), *adj.* cheap; costing little; low-priced.

in-ex-pe-ri-ence (in′eks-pē′ri-ens), *n.* lack of experience; lack of firsthand knowledge.—*adj.* **in′ex-pe′ri-enced.**

in-ex-pli-ca-ble (in-eks′pli-ka-bl), *adj.* not capable of being explained or understood; as, an *inexplicable* mystery.—*adv.* **in-ex′pli-ca-bly.**—*n.* **in-ex′pli-ca-bil′i-ty.**

in-ex-press-i-ble (in′eks-pres′i-bl), *adj.* not capable of being put into words; unutterable.—*adv.* **in′ex-press′i-bly.**

in-ex-tin-guish-a-ble (in′eks-ting′gwish-a-bl), *adj.* that cannot be put out, as a fire; unquenchable; that cannot be suppressed, as laughter.

in-ex-tri-ca-ble (in-eks′tri-ka-bl), *adj.* incapable of being untied or disentangled; hopelessly confused; incapable of being solved; as, an *inextricable* difficulty.—*adv.* **in-ex′tri-cab-ly.**

in-fal-li-ble (in-fal′i-bl), *adj.* **1,** incapable of failing; unerring; not capable of making a mistake; as, God is *infallible*; **2,** absolutely trustworthy; unfailing; as, an *infallible* remedy; an *infallible* friend.—*adv.* **in-fal′li-bly.**—*n.* **in-fal′li-bil′i-ty.**

in-fa-mous (in′fa-mus), *adj.* **1,** having a bad reputation; notorious; as, an *infamous* gangster; **2,** villainous; as, an *infamous* plot to kill someone.—*adv.* **in′fa-mous-ly.**

in-fa-my (in′fa-mi), *n.* [*pl.* infamies], **1,** public disgrace; dishonour; **2,** baseness; vileness; also, a disgraceful act.

in-fan-cy (in′fan-si), *n.* **1,** babyhood and early childhood; **2,** the first stage of anything; as, the *infancy* of a nation.

in-fant (in′fant), *n.* **1,** a baby; a young child; **2,** in *law*, a person who has not attained the age of 18:—*adj.* pertaining to, or intended for, babies or young children; as, *infant* diet; also, pertaining to the earliest stages of anything very young; undeveloped; as, an *infant* industry.

in-fan-ti-cide (in-fan′ti-sid′), *n.* the murder, or murderer, of an infant.

in-fan-tile (in′fan-til′), *adj.* **1,** childish; as, *infantile* behaviour; **2,** relating to infants; as, *infantile* diseases:—**infantile paralysis,** a spinal disease marked by inflammation of nerve cells, often resulting in permanent deformity; poliomyelitis.

in-fan-try (in′fan-tri), *n.* soldiers who are armed, equipped, and trained for service on foot; foot soldiers.—*n.* **in′fan-try-man.**

in-fat-u-at-ed (in-fat′ū-āt′ed), *adj.* showing foolish fondness; so inspired with an extravagant passion for something as to be wanting in sound judgment about it.—*n.* **in-fat′u-a′tion.**

in-fect (in-fekt′), *v.t.* **1,** to affect (a person or persons) with disease by spreading germs; as, to *infect* with a contagious disease; **2,** to taint or poison (a wound, instrument, drinking water, etc.) with germs; **3,** to affect or influence with a mood, feeling, or idea; as, her giggles *infected* her classmates; **4,** in *computing*, to contaminate a computer system with a virus.—*adj.* **infect′ed.**

in-fec-tion (in-fek′shun), *n.* **1,** the communication of disease germs; **2,** a disease communicated by germs in any manner; as, *infection* formed in the cut in my finger; **3,** in *computing*, the state of having a virus in a computer system.

in-fec-tious (in-fek′shus), *adj.* **1,** capable of spreading by means of germs; as, colds are *infectious*; **2,** readily communicated or spread; as, *infectious* laughter.—*adv.* **infec′tious-ly.**

in-fer (in-fûr′), *v.t.* [inferred, infer-ring], **1,** to arrive at (a conclusion) by reasoning rather than by being told; as, they *inferred* from her improved health that exercise was beneficial; **2,** (*loosely* and *incorrectly*) to indicate; imply; suggest; as, what are you *inferring* by that remark?—*n.* **in′fer-ence** (in′fėr-ens).

in-fe-ri-or (in-fē′ri-ėr), *adj.* **1,** lower in place, rank, or value; secondary; as, an *inferior* officer; **2,** second-rate; poor; as, *inferior* workmanship:—*n.* one who ranks below another.—*n.* **in-fe′ri-or′i-ty.**

inferiority complex, a strong and disturbing feeling that one is not as important or as good at activities as other people are; a feeling of inadequacy.

in-fer-nal (in-fûr′nal), *adj.* **1,** belonging to, or resembling, hell; hellish; **2,** fiendish;

outrageous; **3,** *Colloq.* tedious, disgusting; as, stop that *infernal* racket.—*adv.* **in-fer′nal-ly.**

in-fer-no (infûr′nō), *n.* [*pl.* -nos (nōz)], **1,** hell; **2,** a place or scene of flames, great heat, or distress; as, the blazing building became an *inferno.*

in-fest (in-fest′), *v.t.* to overrun; swarm in or over; trouble or annoy constantly or in numbers; as, moths *infested* the woollen material; sharks *infested* the water.—*n.* **in-fes-ta′tion.**

in-fi-del (in′fi-del), *n.* one who does not believe in a certain religion or religion in general:—*adj.* **1,** unbelieving; heathen; **2,** pertaining to, or like, infidels; as, *infidel* contempt for the faith.

in-fi-del-i-ty (in′fi-del′i-ti; in′fī-del′i-ti), *n.* [*pl.* infidelities], **1,** disbelief in religion or in a certain religion; **2,** the breaking of a trust; disloyalty, esp. of a spouse; unfaithfulness.

in-field (in′fēld′), *n.* in *baseball,* **1,** the space enclosed within the base lines; the diamond as distinguished from the *outfield;* **2,** the infield players, as a whole.—*n.* **in′field′er.**

in-fil-trate (in-fil′trāt), *v.t.* and *v.i.* **1,** to pass through (gaps, openings, etc.), or gain access; as, our scouts *infiltrated* the enemy lines; **2,** to permeate; as, sunlight *infiltrated* through the sheer curtains.—*n.* **in′fil-tra′tion.**

in-fi-nite (in′fi-nit), *adj.* **1,** without limit in greatness, power, knowledge, etc.; as, *infinite* wisdom; **2,** unlimited; endless; as, the universe is *infinite;* **3,** extreme; as *infinite* courage:—*n.* that which has no limit:—**the Infinite**, God; the Supreme Being.—*adv.* **in′fi-nite-ly.**—*n.* **in-fin′i-tude** (as, an *infinitude* of stars).

in-fin-i-tes-i-mal (in′fin-i-tes′i-mal), *adj.* too small to be measured; microscopic.—*adv.* **in′fin-i-tes′i-mal-ly.**

in-fin-i-tive (in-fin′i-tiv), *n.* in *grammar,* a part of the verb that expresses the general meaning of the verb without any inflection for person or number, usually having the same form as the stem of the present tense: often though not always used with *to*; as, he longs *to go*; this is a good road on which *to travel*; help me (to) *finish* the job: infinitives can be used as nouns, adjectives, adverbs, and in verb phrases:—*adj.* pertaining to, or formed with, the infinitive; as, an *infinitive* phrase.

in-fin-i-ty (in-fin′i-ti), *n.* [*pl.* infini-ties], **1,** the state of being infinite or beyond measure in time, space, number, etc.; boundlessness; **2,** space or time considered as boundless; **3,** an infinite quantity or number.

in-firm (in-fûrm′), *adj.* **1,** not well or sound physically; weak; **2,** weak of mind, will, or character; irresolute; wavering; as, a person *infirm* of purpose.—*n.* **in-fir′mi-ty.**

in-fir-ma-ry (in-fûr′ma-ri), *n.* [*pl.* infirmaries], a room or building in which the sick or injured are cared for, esp. in a school or other institution; also, a small hospital.

in-flame (in-flām′), *v.t.* [inflamed, inflaming], **1,** to set on fire; **2,** to excite; arouse; make angry; as, the speaker *inflamed* the crowd's anger; **3,** to put into a state of redness, swelling, and pain; as, the infection *inflamed* her throat.

in-flam-ma-ble (in-flam′a-bl), *adj.* **1,** easily set on fire; as, gasoline is *inflammable;* **2,** easily excited; as, an *inflammable* temper.

in-flam-ma-tion (in-fla-mā′shun), *n.* **1,** the act of inflaming; **2,** an unnatural condition of any part of the body, marked by redness, heat, swelling, and pain.

in-flam-ma-tor-y (in-flam′a-tėr-i), *adj.* **1,** tending to excite anger or rebellion; **2,** causing, or showing, inflammation.

in-flate (in-flāt′), *v.t.* [inflat-ed, inflat-ing], **1,** to swell out with air or gas, as a balloon or a tire; **2,** to puff up; to elate; as, the award *inflated* her ego; **3,** to raise beyond reason or the norm, as prices:—*v.i.* to become puffed up, elated, raised.—*adj.* **in-fla′ted.**

in-fla-tion (in-flā′shun), *n.* **1,** a situation in which the prices of goods and services rise, and the same amount of money will purchase less than it did before, as a result of too much paper money in circulation; **2,** the act of expanding something by filling it with air or another gas.

in-flect (in-flekt′), *v.t.* **1,** to change the pitch or tone of (the voice); **2,** to vary the form of (a word) so as to show grammatical changes in person, number, case, etc., as *he, his, him, they, their* or *theirs, them, sit, sat,* etc.; **3,** to bend:—*v.i.* to become inflected.—*n.* **in-flec′tion.**

in-flex-i-ble (in-flek′si-bl), *adj.* **1,** not able to be bent; rigid; as, an *inflexible* rod of iron; **2,** not to be moved by entreaty; unyielding; as, he has an *inflexible* will.—*adv.* **in-flex′i-bly.**—*n.* **in-flex′i-bil′i-ty.**

in-flict (in-flikt′), *v.t.* **1,** to cause by, or as if by, striking; as, to *inflict* a wound; **2,** to impose (a punishment or penalty) on someone.—*n.* **in-flic′tion.**

in-flo-res-cence (in′flo-res′ens), *n.* a flowering or blossoming.

in-flu-ence (in′flo͞o-ens), *n.* **1,** a power tending to produce results by indirect or invisible means; the power of personality; moral power; as, the *influence* of a good example; **2,** power arising from wealth or station; as, political *influence;* **3,** one who, or that which, exerts a power:—*v.t.* [influenced, influenc-ing], **1,** to have power over, physically or mentally; sway; **2,** to affect; as, weather *influences* crops.

in-flu-en-tial (in′flōō-en′shal), *adj.* having or exerting power; as, an *influential* citizen.—*adv.* **in′flu-en′tial-ly.**

in-flu-en-za (in′flōō-en′za), *n.* a severe infectious disease, frequently occurring in epidemic form, characterized by inflammation of the air passages, severe muscular pains, and headache: popularly called *flu.*

in-flux (in′fluks), *n.* an inflow; a pouring in; as, an *influx* of money into a bank.

in-fold (in-fōld′), *v.t.* Same as **enfold.**

in-form (in-fôrm′), *v.t.* to supply with knowledge; notify; tell; as, to *inform* him that the meeting was cancelled:—*v.i.* to give information, esp. in accusation; as, the neighbours *informed* against him.—*adj.* **in-form′a-tive.**—*n.* **in-form′ant; in-form′er.**

in-for-mal (in-fôr′mal), *adj.* **1,** not according to custom or rule; without ceremony; casual; relaxed; as, an *informal* dance; **2,** of language, used in everyday conversation and writing, but not appropriate for more serious or formal situations; colloquial; as, an *informal* talk.—*adv.* **in-for′mal-ly.**—*n.* **in′for-mal′i-ty.**

in-for-ma-tion (in′fôr-mā′shun), *n.* **1,** knowledge given or acquired; esp. knowledge of facts; also, news; as, *information* about words are found in a dictionary; **2,** a service provided to answer customer's questions and give other facts; as, to get someone's new telephone number by calling *information.*

information superhighway, in *computing,* the global high-speed communication network involving fibre-optical and coaxial cables linking ever-faster personal computers via the Internet, carrying data, voice, and video signals. Also called *information highway.*

information technology, in *computing,* the sum total of the systems involved in the storing, retrieving, and sending of information electronically using computers, the Internet, and other telecommunications hardware and software: abbreviated as *IT.*

in-frac-tion (in-frak′shun), *n.* the act of breaking; esp. the act of breaking a law or rule; as, speeding is an *infraction.*

in-fra-red (in′fra-red′), *adj.* relating to the penetrating, hot invisible rays that lie beyond the visible red end of the spectrum, such as sunlight, resistant wires, etc.: the rays are longer than those of the spectrum colours, but shorter than radio waves: these waves are used in wireless electronic communications, from TV remote controls to short-range computer networks.

in-fra-struc-ture (in′fra-struk′tūr), *n.* the basic foundations of a system such as public works, military operations, or computer networks.—*adj.* **in′fra-struc′tur-al.**

in-fre-quent (in-frē′kwent), *adj.* seldom occurring; as, *infrequent* visits; *infrequent* rains.—*adv.* **in-fre′quent-ly.**—*n.* **in-fre′quence; in-fre′quen-cy.**

in-fringe (in-frinj′), *v.t.* [infringed, infring-ing], to disregard or break, as a law; encroach:—*v.i.* to trespass; as, to *infringe* upon another person's privacy.—*n.* **in-fringe′ment.**

in-fu-ri-ate (in-fū′ri-āt′), *v.t.* [infuriat-ed, infuriat-ing], to enrage; madden; as, anything of a red colour is said to *infuriate* a bull.—*n.* **in-fu′ri-a′tion.**

in-fuse (in-fūz′), *v.t.* [infused, infusing], **1,** to introduce, as by pouring; **2,** to instill; inspire; as, to *infuse* a spirit of goodwill into a class; **3,** to steep in liquid; as, to *infuse* tea in boiling water.—*n.* **in-fu′sion.**

in-gen-ious (in-jēn′yus), *adj.* **1,** creative; gifted; clever; as, an *ingenious* mind; **2,** skillfully made or contrived; as, an *ingenious* device.—*n.* **in′ge-nu′i-ty.**

in-gen-u-ous (in-jen′ū-us), *adj.* frank; innocent; sincere; as, an *ingenuous* child.

in-gle (ing′gl), *n.* a fireplace or fire in a fireplace.

in-gle-nook (ing′gl-nook′), *n.* a corner by a fireplace or open fire; also, a seat near a fireplace.

in-glor-i-ous (in-glōr′i-us), *adj.* disgraceful; shameful; as, an *inglorious* defeat.

in-got (ing′got), *n.* a mass or bar of cast metal, such as gold, silver, or steel.

in-grained (in′grānd′; in′grānd′), *adj.* deeply rooted; fixed; as, an *ingrained* habit or vice.

in-grate (in′grāt), *n.* one who is ungrateful; a thankless person.

in-gra-ti-ate (in-grā′shi-āt′), *v.t.* [-ated, -ating], to work oneself into another's favour or good graces: as, he *ingratiated* himself with her by being attentive to her needs.

in-grat-i-tude (in-grat′i-tūd′), *n.* lack of thankfulness; ungratefulness.

in-gre-di-ent (in-grē′di-ent), *n.* a part of a compound or mixture; as, sugar is the principal *ingredient* of candy.

in-grown (in′grōn′), *adj.* **1,** grown into the flesh; as, an *ingrown* toenail; **2,** innate; inborn; ingrained; as, *ingrown* traits.—*adj.* **in′grow′ing.**

in-gulf (in-gulf′), *v.t.* Same as **engulf.**

in-hab-it (in-hab′it), *v.t.* to dwell in; live in; occupy; as, humans *inhabit* the earth; tigers *inhabit* the jungle.—*adj.* **in-hab′it-a-ble.**

in-hab-it-ant (in-hab′it-ant), *n.* a person or animal that inhabits a place for a length of time.

in-hale (in-hāl′), *v.t.* [inhaled, inhal-ing],

to draw into the lungs; to breathe in, as air, smoke, etc.—*n.* **in′ha-la′tion.**

in-har-mo-ni-ous (in′här-mō′ni-us), *adj.* **1,** unmusical; as, *inharmonious* sounds; **2,** conflicting; clashing; as *inharmonious* colours; **3,** disagreeable; unpleasant; as, *inharmonious* dinner guests.—*adv.* **in′har-mo′ni-ous-ly.**

in-her-ent (in-her′ent), *adj.* existing in something as a permanent or essential part; inborn; as, love of harmonious sounds is *inherent* in musicians; her *inherent* integrity.—*adv.* **in-her′ent-ly:**—*v.i.* **in-here′** (in) [inhered, inher-ing]; as, honesty *inheres* in him.

in-her-it (in-her′it), *v.t.* **1,** to come into possession of (property, as land or money) by right of succession or by will; as, she *inherited* her father's house; **2,** to derive (mental or physical qualities) from one's ancestors; receive by birth; as, to *inherit* intelligence, a strong love for writing, or blue eyes; **3,** to be heir to.—*n.* **in-her′i-tor.**

in-her-it-ance (in-her′i-tans), *n.* **1,** the act of inheriting, or coming into, property; **2,** property inherited; also, a trait or quality handed down from parent to offspring.

in-hib-it (in-hib′it), *v.t.* **1,** to restrain; hold in check; as, to *inhibit* a selfish impulse; **2,** to forbid.—*n.* **in′hi-bi′tion** (in′hi-bish′un).

in-hos-pi-ta-ble (in-hos′pi-ta-bl), *adj.* **1,** not disposed to welcome strangers or guests; as, an *inhospitable* host; **2,** barren; cheerless; as, an *inhospitable* shore.

in-hu-man (in-hū′man), *adj.* **1,** cruel; brutal; unfeeling; **2,** not human; having characteristics that are not natural, normal, or standard for humans; as, *inhuman* strength; *inhuman* working conditions.—*n.* **in′hu-man′i-ty.**

in-im-i-cal (in-im′i-kal), *adj.* **1,** unfavourable; adverse; as, lack of exercise is *inimical* to health; **2,** unfriendly; hostile; as, an *inimical* attitude.

in-im-i-ta-ble (in-im′i-ta-bl), *adj.*, matchless; impossible to imitate; as an *inimitable* style.—*adv.* **in-im′i-ta-bly.**

in-iq-ui-ty (i-nik′wi-ti), *n.* [*pl.* iniquities], **1,** wickedness; unrighteousness; **2,** a wicked act or crime; a sin.—*adj.* **in-iq′ui-tous.**

in-i-tial (i-nish′al), *adj.* **1,** placed at the beginning; first; as, the *initial* letter of a word; **2,** marking, or pertaining to, the beginning; earliest; as, the *initial* chapter in a book; the *initial* step in an undertaking:—*n.* a letter at the beginning of a word, name, paragraph, etc.:—**initials,** the first letter of each part of a person's name, sometimes used instead of a signature; as, *P.E.T.* are the *initials* of Pierre Elliott Trudeau:—*v.t.* [initialled, initial-ling or initialed, initial-ing], to mark with one's initial or initials.—*adv.* **in-i′tial-ly.**

in-i-tial-ize (i-nish′a-līz′), *v.t.* in *computing,* **1,** to format a computer disk or other similar device; **2,** to prepare a computer or other equipment for use; start or boot a computer.

in-i-ti-ate (i-nish′i-āt′), *v.t.* [initiat-ed, initiat-ing], **1,** to instruct in the first principles of anything; as, to *initiate* a student into the study of French; **2,** to begin; start; as, to *initiate* a new fashion; **3,** to introduce into a club, secret society, organization, etc., by special rites and ceremonies; as, to *initiate* new members into the student sorority by having them write an essay about themselves:—*n.* (i-nish′i-it), one who has been, or is about to be, initiated.—*n.* **in-i′ti-a′tion.**

in-i-ti-a-tive (i-nish′i-a-tiv), *n.* **1,** an introductory or first step; the lead; as, to take the *initiative* in a deal; **2,** a natural ability to take the lead; also, an ability to foresee what needs doing and to do it; as, people with *initiative* advance rapidly; **3,** the right, also the method, by which citizens may introduce new laws.

in-ject (in-jekt′), *v.t.* **1,** to drive or force into, as liquid through the skin with a needle; introduce, as a liquid; **2,** to throw in; interject; as, to *inject* humour into a story.—*n.* **in-jec′tion.**

in-ju-di-cious (in′jo͞o-dish′us), *adj.* **1,** unwise; lacking in judgment; as, an *injudicious* employee; **2,** not carefully thought out; as, *injudicious* advice; an *injudicious* remark.—*adv.* **in′ju-di′cious-ly.**

in-junc-tion (in-jungk′shun), *n.* **1,** a command; order; **2,** a writ to command or forbid certain proceedings; prohibition; as, to issue an *injunction* against a strike.

in-jure (in′joor), *v.t.* [injured, injur-ing], to harm; damage, physically or morally.—*adj.* **in-ju′ri-ous.**—*adv.* **in-ju′ri-ous-ly.**

in-ju-ry (in′joor-i), *n.* [*pl.* injuries], any hurt or harm; damage to one's person, property, rights, etc.

in-jus-tice (in-jus′tis), *n.* the quality of being unfair; lack of justice; also, an injury; a wrong.

ink (ingk), *n.* **1,** a coloured fluid used for writing or drawing with a pen, or for printing; **2,** a dark liquid that squid and octopuses release for protection; **3,** *Slang* publicity; as, the company got a lot of *ink* in the media on their new product:—*v.t.* **1,** to mark or smear with ink; **2,** to sign or put something in writing; as, to *ink* an agreement.

ink–jet printer (ingk′–jet′), *n.* a printer that forms characters and graphics by shooting tiny drops of ink from jets onto the surface of paper.

ink-ling (ingk′ling), *n.* a faint idea or suspicion; hint; as, an *inkling* of the truth.

ink-stand (ingk′stand′), *n.* **1,** a small container for ink, pens, etc.; **2,** a container for ink only; an inkwell.

inkwell (ingk′wel′), *n.* a container for ink, fitted into a desk or an inkstand.

ink-y (ingk′i), *adj.* [ink-i-er, ink-i-est], like or of ink; spotted with ink; black; dark; as, an *inky* blotter; *inky* darkness.

in-laid (in-lād′; in′lād′), *adj.* **1,** set into a surface for ornament; as, pearl *inlaid* in ebony; **2,** ornamented with inlay:—*p.t.* of *inlay.*

in-land (in′land), *adj.* **1,** pertaining to, or situated in, the interior of a country; away from the sea; as, an *inland* province or town; *inland* water; **2,** carried on within a country; as, *inland* commerce:—*adv.* (in′land′; in′land), toward the interior; as, to move *inland*:—*n.* (in′land; in′land′), the interior of a country.

in–law (in′–lô′), *n.* a relative by marriage instead of by birth, such as mother-in-law, father-in-law, brother-in-law, sister-in-law, daughter-in-law, and son-in-law.

in-lay (in-lā′), *v.t.* [inlaid (in-lād′), inlay-ing], to ornament (a surface) by setting in pieces of stones or beads, wood, metal, etc.; also, to set (pieces of metal, wood, etc.) into a surface:—*n.* (in′lā), materials for inlaying; also, a pattern or design formed by inlaying.

in-let (in′let), *n.* a small bay or creek along a coast, leading inland; an arm of the sea.

in–line skates (in′līn′ skāts), *n.* roller skates with the wheels in one row, one behind the other. Also, **in′–line′ skat′ing.**

IN-LINE SKATES

in-mate (in′māt), *n.* a member of a group of persons living under one roof, esp. a person confined in an institution; as, an *inmate* of a prison.

in-most (in′mōst), *adj.* most inward; deepest; as, my *inmost* wish is to be a great soccer player.

inn (in), *n.* **1,** formerly, a small hotel by the roadside for the lodging, feeding, and entertainment of travellers; **2,** a hotel or tavern.—*n.* **inn′keep′er.**

in-nate (in′nāt; i-nāt′), *adj.* inborn; natural; as, *innate* courtesy; *innate* talent for sports; *innate* dryness of the region.—*adv.* **in′nate-ly.**

in-ner (in′ėr), *adj.* **1,** internal; interior; inside; as, an *inner* lining; *inner* room; **2,** pertaining to the mind or soul; private; secret; as, the *inner* nature of humans; *inner* feelings.

in-ner-most (in′ėr-mōst), *adj.* farthest in from the outside; inmost.

in-ning (in′ing), *n.* in *baseball, cricket,* etc., one of the periods of the game during which one side is at bat or each side in turn is at bat once:—**innings,** the period when a person, group, or party is in power.

in-no-cent (in′ō-sent), *adj.* **1,** free from guilt or wrongdoing; blameless; **2,** pure in heart and life; simple and trusting; as, an *innocent* child; **3,** foolishly ignorant; naive; **4,** without evil effect; meaning no harm; as, an *innocent* joke; **5,** lacking; as, *innocent* of humour:—*n.* one who is free from, or unacquainted with sin; a naive person.—*adv.* **in′no-cent-ly.**—*n.* **in′no-cence.**

in-noc-u-ous (i-nok′ū-us), *adj.* harmless; as, an *innocuous* dose of medicine; *innocuous* comment.

in-no-va-tion (in′ō-vā′shun), *n.* **1,** the introduction of something new; **2,** a new custom, device, style, etc.; as, the Internet is a major *innovation* in sourcing information.

In-nu (in′o͞o), *n.* **1,** a member of the Algonquian people living in northern and eastern Québec and Labrador, who used to be known as Montagnais-Kapaski; **2,** the Algonquian language of the Innu people, similar to Cree.

in-nu-en-do (in′ū-en′dō), *n.* [*pl.* -does (dōz)], an indirect remark, reference, etc., that implies something derogatory; insinuation.

in-nu-mer-a-ble (i-nū′mėr-a-bl; in-nū′mėr-a-bl), *adj.* without number; countless; as, *innumerable* stars.

in-oc-u-late (in-ok′ū-lāt′), *v.t.* [inoculated, inoculat-ing], **1,** to produce a mild case of disease in (a person or animal) by the insertion of germs into body tissues in order to prevent future attacks; to vaccinate; as, to *inoculate* against small pox; **2,** to fill or infect the mind of (a person, community, etc.) with a feeling, opinion, or habit.—*n.* **in-oc′u-la′tion.**

in-of-fen-sive (in′o-fen′siv), *adj.* **1,** harmless; **2,** not disagreeable or disgusting.

in-op-er-a-tive (in-op′ėr-a-tiv), *adj.* not working; not in operation; ineffective.

in-op-por-tune (in-op′or-tūn′), *adj.* happening at the wrong time; unsuitable; inconvenient; as, an *inopportune* remark; the *inopportune* moment.—*adv.* **in-op′portune′ly.**

in-or-di-nate (in-ôr′di-nit), *adj.* too much; excessive; as, it took him an *inordinate* amount of time; *inordinate* vanity.

in-or-gan-ic (in′ôr-gan′ik), *adj.* without a living body; not belonging to the animal or vegetable kingdom; not part of, nor produced by, a plant or animal: rocks and metals are inorganic substances, while wood, bone, and blood are organic substances; also, artificial.

in-put (in′poot′), *n.* **1,** what is put in, as electricity supplied to a machine; **2,** in *computing,* data or information entered into a computer for processing or transmission; also, the place where the data enters a computer system; **3,** any comments or advice added; as, to get *input* from others on a plan:—*v.t.* [inputted or input, inputting], in *computing,* to enter information into a computer. Compare *keyboard.*—*n.* **in′put′ter.**

in-quest (in′kwest), *n.* **1,** an official inquiry, with the aid of a jury, esp. into the cause of a sudden death; also, the jury so appointed; **2,** any investigation.

in-quire or **en-quire** (in-kwir′; en-kwir′), *v.t.* [inquired, inquir-ing], to seek after by questions; investigate; as, to *inquire* the way to the station:—*v.i.* **1,** to ask; seek information; as, *inquire* at the office; **2,** to make examination or search; as, to *inquire* into a murder; to *inquire* about something; **3,** to ask concerning the whereabouts or welfare of someone; as, to *inquire* for or about a person.

in-quir-y or **en-quir-y** (in-kwīr′i; in′kwi-ri or en-kwīr′i; en′kwi-ri), *n.* [*pl.* inquiries], **1,** the act of seeking information, knowledge, etc.; research; **2,** an investigation; as, an *inquiry* into the cause of death; **3,** a question.

in-qui-si-tion (in′kwi-zish′un), *n.* **1,** inquiry; examination; esp. an official inquiry before a jury; also, the findings of the jury; **2,** any intense questioning or interrogation:—**Inquisition,** in the Roman Catholic Church, a court that was esp. active in the 15th and 16th centuries in seeking out and punishing heretics.—*n.* **in-quis′i-tor.**

in-quis-i-tive (in-kwiz′i-tiv), *adj.* given to asking questions; curious; as, a gossip is *inquisitive* about his or her neighbours.

in-road (in′rōd′), *n.* **1,** an invasion, esp. if sudden; entry by force; as, an *inroad* into enemy territory; **2,** an advance that destroys or decreases the thing attacked; as, the sea makes *inroads* upon the land; overwork makes *inroads* on endurance.

in-sane (in-sān′), *adj.* **1,** mentally disordered or ill; crazy; not mentally sound; **2,** very unreasonable or foolish; as, an *insane* desire to dance in the library; **3,** intended for the mentally disordered; as, an *insane* institution.—*adv.* **in-sane′ly.**—*n.* **in-san′i-ty.**

in-san-i-tary (in-san′i-ta-ri), *adj.* not clean; unhealthful; as, *insanitary* conditions.

in-sa-ti-a-ble (in-sā′shi-a-bl; in-sā′sha-bl), *adj.* immoderate; not to be satisfied; greedy; as, an *insatiable* appetite.

in-scribe (in-skrīb′), *v.t.* [inscribed, inscrib-ing], **1,** to mark, write, or engrave (letters or words) on parchment, brass, stone, etc.; as, to *inscribe* a date on a ring; **2,** to stamp deeply, as upon the memory; **3,** to address formally; dedicate; as, to *inscribe* a book to a friend; **4,** to enter or enroll on a list.—*n.* **in-scrib′er; in-scrip′tion.**

in-scru-ta-ble (in-skrōō′ta-bl), *adj.* unreadable; not to be understood; incomprehensible; as, his face was *inscrutable*; *inscrutable* destiny.—*adv.* **in-scru′ta-bly.**

in-sect (in′sekt), *n.* any of hundreds of thousands of kinds of small, boneless animals, including ants, bees, flies, mosquitoes, cockroaches, beetles, etc., with three pairs of jointed legs, body divided into three sections (head, thorax, and abdomen), and, usually, wings.

in-sec-ti-cide (in-sek′ti-sīd′), *n.* a poisonous substance, either a powder or liquid, for killing insects.

in-se-cure (in′si-kūr′), *adj.* **1,** not firm; unsafe; as, an *insecure* platform; **2,** not shielded from danger; not safe; as, an *insecure* position; **3,** unconfident; as, an *insecure,* timid person.—*adv.* **in′se-cure′ly.**—*n.* **in′se-cu′ri-ty.**

in-sen-sate (in-sen′sāt), *adj.* **1,** unfeeling; brutal; *insensate* fury; **2,** lifeless; as, *insensate* stones.

in-sen-si-ble (in-sen′si-bl), *adj.* **1,** lacking the power to feel; indifferent; as, *insensible* to beauty or to cold; **2,** too slow, gradual, or small to be perceived; as, the *insensible* motion of a clock's hands; **3,** unconscious; as, she fell *insensible* to the ground.—*adv.* **in-sen′si-bly.**—*n.* **in-sen′si-bil′i-ty.**

in-sep-a-ra-ble (in-sep′a-ra-bl), *adj.* incapable of being divided or parted; as, they were *inseparable* friends.—*adv.* **in-sep′a-ra-bly.**—*n.* **in-sep′a-ra-bil′i-ty.**

in-sert (in-sûrt′), *v.t.* to place in something or among things; introduce; as, to *insert* a coin into a slot:—*n.* (in′sûrt), that which is put in; inset; as, a coloured *insert* in a book or newspaper.—*n.* **in-ser′tion.**

in-set (in′set′), *n.* **1,** an extra page or pages inserted in a newspaper, magazine, etc.; **2,** a smaller drawing, map, etc., inserted within the border of a larger one; **3,** a piece of material inserted into a garment for decoration; **4,** a channel of water:—*v.t.* (in-set′), [inset, inset-ting], to put in; insert.

in-shore (in′shōr′), *adv.* near or toward the shore; as, to head *inshore*:—*adj.* (in′shōr′; in′shōr′), near, or moving toward, the shore; as, an *inshore* current; *inshore* fishers.

in-side (in′sīd′), *adj.* **1,** lying or being within; as, the *inside* pages of a newspaper; **2,** *Colloq.* private; from the inside of some group; as, *inside* information; *inside* job:—*adv.* within; as, to go *inside*:—*n.* **1,** that which is within; interior; as, the *inside* of a house; **2,** contents; as, to know the *inside* of a book:—**insides,** *Colloq.* the internal organs of the body:—*prep.* (in′sīd′), within; as, *inside* the box.

in-sid-er (in′sī′dėr), *n.* a person so situated that he or she is able to obtain reliable or special information not available to the general public:—*adj.* of or about an insider; as, an *insider* report.

insider trading, the illegal use of privileged (inside) information in buying and selling of stocks or other securities.

in-sid-i-ous (in-sid′i-us), *adj.* treacherous; working to harm secretly; as, *insidious* gossip.—*adv.* **in-sid′i-ous-ly.**

in-sight (in′sīt′), *n.* understanding; comprehension of the inner nature of things; as, *insight* into his character; *insight* into the industry.

in-sig-ni-a (in-sig′ni-a), *n.pl.* badges of honour or office; emblems of authority, rank, etc.; as, army *insignia.*

in-sig-nif-i-cant (in′sig-nif′i-kant), *adj.* **1,** without importance or force; as, his power is *insignificant;* **2,** trifling; mean; small; meaningless; as, an *insignificant* sum; *insignificant* remarks.—*adv.* **in′sig-nif′i-cant-ly.**—*n.* **in′sig-nif′i-cance.**

in-sin-cere (in′sin-sēr′), *adj.* false; not to be trusted; not honest; as, *insincere* praise.

in-sin-u-ate (in-sin′ū-āt′), *v.t.* [insinuat-ed, insinuat-ing], **1,** to penetrate; push (oneself) by slow or artful means, as an employee into a boss's favour; **2,** to hint or suggest indirectly; as, they *insinuated* that he lied.—*n.* **in-sin′u-a′tion.**

in-sip-id (in-sip′id), *adj.* **1,** without flavour; tasteless; as, *insipid* food; **2,** uninteresting; dull; as, an *insipid* novel.—*adv.* **in-sip′id-ly.**—*n.* **in-sip′id-ness; in′si-pid′i-ty** (in′si-pid′i-ti).

in-sist (in-sist′), *v.i.* **1,** to urge, wish, or command; as, the teacher *insists* on promptness; **2,** to maintain; make a stand; as, he *insists* that he is right.

in-sist-ent (in-sis′tent), *adj.* urgent; compelling attention; persistent; as, the *insistent* ringing of a bell.—*adv.* **in-sist′ent-ly.**—*n.* **in-sist′ence.**

in-so-bri-e-ty (in′sō-brī′e-ti), *n.* drunkenness.

in-so-far as (in′sō-far′ az), *conj.* to such an extent; as, *insofar as* I know, he is coming to the party.

in-sole (in′sōl), *n.* **1,** the inner sole of a shoe or boot; **2,** a removable, cushioned sole placed inside a shoe or boot.

in-so-lence (in′so-lens), *n.* insulting or haughty language or manner; impertinence; impudence; rudeness.—*adj.* **in′so-lent.**

in-sol-u-ble (in-sol′ū-bl), *adj.* **1,** not capable of being dissolved, or hard to dissolve in some liquid; as, fats are *insoluble* in water; **2,** not to be explained or solved; as, an *insoluble* mystery.—*n.* **in-sol′u-bil′i-ty; in-sol′u-ble-ness.**

in-sol-vent (in-sol′vent), *adj.* unable to pay all debts; bankrupt:—*n.* a person who cannot pay his debts.—*n.* **in-sol′ven-cy.**

in-som-ni-a (in-som′ni-a), *n.* sleeplessness, esp. chronic.

in-so-much as (in′sō-much′ az), *conj.* **1,** since; inasmuch as; as, *insomuch as* she's late, let's begin without her; **2,** to such a degree or extent as.

in-so-much that (in′sō-much′ that), *conj.* so; to such a degree or extent that; as, she worked so hard on the report *insomuch that* she got an excellent mark.

in-spect (in-spekt′), *v.t.* **1,** to examine closely and critically, in order to find possible faults or errors, to determine quality, etc.; **2,** to review and survey officially, as troops, meat, etc.—*n.* **in-spec′tor; in-spec′tion; in-spec′tor-ate.**—*adj.* **in-spec′tor-al.**

in-spi-ra-tion (in′spi-rā′shun), *n.* **1,** the act of drawing air into the lungs; **2,** the awakening of thought and the stirring of emotion that causes action or creation in art, literature, music, etc.; the effect upon the creative imagination of beauty, power, etc.; **3,** a person or thing that inspires; as, the Rockies have been an *inspiration* for many Canadian artists; **4,** the supernatural influence of a divine spirit, suggesting a message or a plan of action.—*adj.* **in′spi-ra′tion-al.**

in-spire (in-spīr′), *v.t.* [inspired, inspiring], **1,** to draw (air) into the lungs; **2,** to fill with thought or feeling; cause strong feelings or a wish to do something important; as, beauty *inspires* an artist; **3,** to cause an action, feeling, or thought; as, her determination *inspired* the whole team to do better; **4,** to control or guide by supernatural influence; as, God *inspired* the ancient prophets; **5,** to arouse or influence, as an idea, impulse, emotion, etc., in someone; as, his politics *inspired* his point of view.

in-sta-bil-i-ty (in′sta-bil′i-ti), *n.* [*pl.* instabilities], **1,** lack of steadiness; easily changed; as, the *instability* of the bridge or chemical; **2,** lack of emotional or mental balance.

in-stall (in-stôl′), *v.t.* **1,** to establish with the usual ceremonies in an office or position; **2,** to put into condition or position for use; as, to *install* a central vacuum system or kitchen cabinets; *install* the software from the floppy to the hard drive.—*n.* **in′stal-la′tion; in′stal′ler.**

in-stall-ment or **in-stal-ment** (in-stôl′ment), *n.* **1,** the act of establishing in a position or office; **2,** a portion of a sum of money that is to be paid in parts at stated times; as, to pay for the new computer in six *installments;* **3,** one of a number of parts of anything produced one part at a time; as, an *installment* of a serial story.

in-stance (in′stans), *v.t.* [instanced, instanc-ing], to refer to, or offer as an example:—*n.* **1,** something offered as an illustration or example; as, in this *instance,* the difference between the two plants is evident; **2,** occasion; as, she wanted, in this *instance,* to run away; **3,** a suggestion; request; as, at the *instance* of the teacher, they sang:—**for instance,** as an example; for example; such as; as, she wrote many things—*for instance,* songs, plays, movies, and novels.

in-stant (in′stant), *adj.* **1,** urgent; insistent; as, *instant* haste; *instant* hunger; **2,** immediate; as, *instant* death; *instant* hit; **3,** of food, requiring very little time or effort to prepare; as, *instant* cake, *instant* coffee:—*n.* **1,** a particular moment of time; as, do it this *instant;* **2,** a very small portion of time; as, it will take only an *instant.*

in-stan-ta-ne-ous (in′stan-tā′ni-us), *adj.* done at once; happening in one moment; as, an *instantaneous* reply.

in-stant-ly (in′stant-li), *adv.* at once; immediately.

in-stead (in-sted′), *adv.* **1,** in the place of; as, I will go *instead* of you; **2,** in its place; rather; as, she chose this *instead.*

in-step (in′step), *n.* the arched part of the upper side of the human foot between the toes and the ankle; also, the part of a shoe or boot that covers this part.

in-sti-gate (in′sti-gāt′), *v.t.* [instigated, instigat-ing], to prompt or urge on, usually in a bad sense; as, to *instigate* a strike.—*n.* **in′sti-ga′tion; in′sti-ga′tor.**

in-still or **in-stil** (in-stil′), *v.t.* [instilled, instil-ling], **1,** to pour in by drops; **2,** to introduce gradually; infuse; impart; as, to *instill* a sense of honesty into a child.

in-stinct (in-stingkt′), *adj.* charged or full of; as, creatures *instinct* with life:—*n.* (in′stingkt), **1,** a natural or inborn, rather than learned, impulse, esp. in animals, to do the necessary thing without taking conscious thought; as, it is the *instinct* of all animals to fear fire; **2,** a natural tendency or innate ability; as, her *instinct* told her not to go.—*adj.* **in-stinc′tive; in-stinc′tu-al.**—*adv.* **in-stinc′tive-ly.**

in-sti-tute (in′sti-tūt′), *v.t.* [instituted, institut-ing], **1,** to establish; found; originate; as, to *institute* a special fundraising program; **2,** to set in operation; start; as, to *institute* a new custom:—*n.* **1,** an established law or principle; **2,** a school, organization, or society set up for a special purpose; also, the building for this purpose; as, an *institute* of music; have lunch at the *institute.*

in-sti-tu-tion (in′sti-tū′shun), *n.* **1,** the act of establishing; as, the *institution* of new rules; **2,** any established law, practice, or social custom; as, marriage is an *institution* in many societies; **3,** an organization set up for some public purpose such as a hospital, school, library, prison, etc.; **4,** a place that cares for the mentally or physically disabled or the destitute; as, an *institution* for the blind.—*adj.* **in′sti-tu′tion-al.**

in-struct (in-strukt′), *v.t.* **1,** to teach; educate; as, to *instruct* a class in history; **2,** to furnish with orders or directions; as, to *instruct* a person to be early.—*n.* **in-struc′tor.**—*adj.* **in-struc′tive.**

in-struc-tion (in-struk′shun), *n.* **1,** the act or fact of teaching; **2,** the steps or rules involved in doing something; directions; as, read all the *instructions* before beginning the test; **3,** orders; as, our *instructions* are to meet at the library.

in-stru-ment (in′stroo-ment), *n.* **1,** a person or thing used to accomplish something; a means; **2,** a tool; as, surgical *instruments;* **3,** a device for producing musical sounds; as, a horn, piano, violin, and drum are all musical *instruments;* **4,** a device that controls or that records or measures information; as, the *instruments* on the dashboard of a car; **5,** in *law,* a formal writing; a document:—*v.t.* **1,** to equip with instruments; **2,** to orchestrate.

in-stru-men-tal (in′stroo-men′tal), *adj.* **1,** helping to bring about; as, he was *instrumental* in settling the quarrel; **2,** performed on, or composed for, a musical instrument or instruments; **3,** relating to instruments.—*n.* **in′stru-men-tal′i-ty.**

in-sub-or-di-nate (in′su-bôr′di-nit), *adj.* rebelling against authority; disobedient; mutinous:—*n.* someone who is insubordinate.—*n.* **in′sub-or′di-na′tion.**

in-sub-stan-tial (in′sub-stan′shal), *adj.* **1,** imaginary; unreal; as, this *insubstantial* story; **2,** not solid; flimsy; as, an old, *insubstantial* chair.

in-suf-fer-a-ble (in-suf′ėr-a-bl), *adj.* unbearable; as, *insufferable* pride.

in-suf-fi-cient (in′su-fish′ent), *adj.* not enough, as of quality, amount, power, etc.; as, *insufficient* light for reading.—*adv.* **in′suf-fi′cient-ly.**—*n.* **in′suf-fi′cien-cy.**

in-su-lar (in′sū-lėr), *adj.* **1,** relating to an island or to the inhabitants of an island, their customs, etc.; also, situated on an island; **2,** narrow-minded; prejudiced; as, *insular* ideas.—*n.* **in′su-lar′i-ty; in′su-lar-ism′.**

in-su-late (in′sū-lāt′; in′su-lāt′), *v.t.* [insulat-ed, insulat-ing], to separate; set apart; esp. to separate by, or enclose in, a material that will not conduct electricity, heat, sound, etc.; as, to *insulate* an attic to prevent cold from coming in during the winter.—*n.* **in′su-la′tion.**

in-su-la-tor (in′sū-lā′tėr; in′su-lā′tėr), *n.* a material or body that does not carry electricity, heat, or sound; a nonconductor, such as rubber.

in-su-lin (in′sū-lin), *n.* an extract from the pancreas of humans and animals, used in treating diabetes: it reduces the sugar content of the blood and urine.

in-sult (in′sult), *n.* **1,** an affront or indignity; **2,** a gross abuse in word or action:—

v.t. (in-sult′), to treat with intentional rudeness or abuse; say something bad about a person; offend.

in-su-per-a-ble (in-sū′pėr-a-bl), *adj.* not to be surmounted or overcome; as, *insuperable* difficulties.—*adj.* **in-su′per-a-bly.**

in-sup-port-a-ble (in′su-pōr′ta-bl), *adj.* unendurable; unjustifiable.

in-sur-ance (in-shoor′ans), *n.* **1,** a system of protection against financial loss resulting from fire, accident, death, etc.; **2,** a contract whereby one party, usually a company, guarantees to repay the other party for such loss, in return for the yearly payment of a smaller sum, called a *premium*; **3,** the premium; **4,** the amount of payment thus guaranteed; **5,** anything that is thought of as a protection against loss or damage; as, to get an extra goal in the hockey game for *insurance.*

in-sure (in-shoor′), *v.t.* [insured, insuring], **1,** to protect (a person), by a special contract, against financial loss resulting from fire, accident, theft, etc., in return for payments of a premium; as, to *insure* a car owner against theft or collision; **2,** to make such a contract about (property); as, the homeowner *insures* her house; **3,** to make such a contract about (one's life), providing for payment of a fixed sum to a specified person in case of one's death; as, he has *insured* his life for $150,000:—*v.i.* to protect oneself by insurance:—*v.t.* and *v.i.* to make certain; ensure; as, to *insure* a successful ending; *insure* that the door is locked.

in-sur-gent (in-sûr′jent), *adj.* rising against authority:—*n.* a rebel.—*n.* **in-sur′gence; in-sur′gen-cy.**

in-sur-mount-a-ble (in′sėr-moun′ta-bl), *adj.* unconquerable; as, *insurmountable* obstacles.

in-sur-rec-tion (in′su-rek′shun), *n.* active or open rebellion against authority, esp. against a government.

in-tact (in-takt′), *adj.* entire; uninjured; untouched; having all parts; whole; as, the house was *intact* after the earthquake.

in-take (in′tāk′), *n.* **1,** a thing or amount taken in, such as money; as, the store's *intake* was greater today because of the sale; **2,** a taking in, as of breath; the act of taking in; as, the *intake* of food; **3,** the opening where a fluid enters a pipe, channel, etc.

in-tan-gi-ble (in-tan′ji-bl), *adj.* **1,** not touchable; as, ghosts are *intangible*; **2,** vague; not easily expressed or defined; as, an *intangible* idea.—*adv.* **in-tan′gi-bly.**—*n.* **in-tan′gi-bil′i-ty.**

in-te-ger (in′ti-jėr), *n.* a whole positive or negative number or zero, as 1, 2, 3, –6, etc.

in-te-gral (in′ti-gral), *adj.* **1,** making a whole; complete; **2,** necessary as a part; as, sincerity is an *integral* part of friendship:—*n.* a whole made up of parts.

in-te-grate (in′ti-grāt′), *v.t.* **1,** to bring (the parts) together into a whole; unify; harmonize; as, to *integrate* the ideas of the group to form the official plan; **2,** to remove barriers (social, educational, legal, etc.) that separate groups; desegregate.—*n.* **in′te-gra′tion.**—*adj.* **in′te-gra′ted.**

integrated circuit, a semiconductor containing several miniature transistors and electronic circuits on a minute silicon chip: abbreviated as *IC.*

in-teg-ri-ty (in-teg′ri-ti), *n.* **1,** uprightness; virtue; honesty; as, the *integrity* of a person; **2,** soundness; as, the *integrity* of an argument; **3,** unbroken condition; completeness; wholeness; as, the *integrity* of the team or country.

in-tel-lect (in′te-lekt′), *n.* **1,** the powers of the mind that know and reason: distinguished from *feeling* and *will*; the mind; **2,** mental power; ability to reason; **3,** a person of high intelligence.

in-tel-lec-tu-al (in′te-lek′tū-al), *adj.* **1,** pertaining to the intellect or mind; as, *intellectual* interests; **2,** possessing a high degree of intellect or understanding; as, an *intellectual* person; **3,** demanding keen thinking; as, *intellectual* subjects:—*n.* an intelligent and well-educated person who has an interest in the arts and other activities of the mind.—*adv.* **in′tel-lec′tu-al-ly.**—*n.* **in′tel-lec′tu-al′i-ty.**

in-tel-li-gence (in-tel′i-jens), *n.* **1,** ability to learn, understand, and use what one has learned to the best advantage; understanding; mental ability; **2,** information or news, particularly secret information, as that secured for the government in wartime or by a business.

intelligence quotient, a number (derived from tests) that indicates one's relative level of intelligence; thus, a 10-year-old with a mental age of 12 would have an intelligence quotient of 120: abbreviated as *IQ.*

in-tel-li-gent (in-tel′i-jent), *adj.* **1,** able to learn, understand, and use what one has learned; possessing understanding; **2,** showing understanding; as, an *intelligent* answer; **3,** having intelligence or thinking capabilities; as, *intelligent* life in the universe; **4,** in *computing,* having certain capabilities.

in-tel-li-gent-si-a (in-tel′i-jent′si-a; -gent′-), *n.* the educated classes; intellectuals; elite.

in-tel-li-gi-ble (in-tel′i-ji-bl), *adj.* capable of being understood; clear; as, an *intelligible* explanation.—*n.* **in-tel′li-gi-bil′i-ty.**—*adv.* **in-tel′li-gi-bly.**

in-tem-per-ate (in-tem′pėr-it), *adj.* **1,** severe; not mild; as, an *intemperate* climate; **2,** lacking in moderation or self-control; violent; as, *intemperate* conduct; **3,** given to excess, esp. in the use of alcoholic liquors.—*n.* **in-tem′per-ance.**

in-tend (in-tend′), *v.t.* **1,** to plan; mean; as, we *intend* to stay; **2,** to design or destine (a person or thing) for some purpose; as, his daughter is *intended* for the legal profession; this speech was *intended* for the media.

in-ten-dant (in-ten′dant), *n.* **1,** a manager or superintendent; **2,** formerly, in New France, an official in charge of a district.

in-tense (in-tens′), *adj.* **1,** extreme; excessive; as, *intense* cold; **2,** violent; eager; earnest; very emotional; as, *intense* love.—*adv.* **in-tense′ly.**

in-ten-si-fy (in-ten′si-fī′), *v.t.* [intensi-fied, intensify-ing], to make greater in degree; as, to *intensify* pain.—*n.* **in-ten′si-fi-ca′tion.**

in-ten-si-ty (in-ten′si-ti), *n.* [*pl.* intensities], **1,** the state or quality of; being extreme; as, the *intensity* of anger or joy; **2,** strength or degree; as, *intensity* of light or colour.

in-ten-sive (in-ten′siv), *adj.* **1,** concentrated; thorough; as, an *intensive* study of literature; *intensive* thought; **2,** in *grammar*, giving emphasis or force; as, in the sentence "He did it himself," the word "himself" is *intensive*.—*adv.* **in-ten′sive-ly.**

intensive care unit, the section of the hospital that is devoted to the special medical treatment of dangerously ill patients: abbreviated as *ICU*.

in-tent (in-tent′), *adj.* **1,** concentrated; closely occupied; determined; as, he was *intent* on his work; **2,** having or showing deep feeling; as, an *intent* expression:—*n.* **1,** purpose; aim; as, study with *intent* to learn; **2,** meaning; significance; as, what was the *intent* of that comment?—*adv.* **in-tent′ly.**

in-ten-tion (in-ten′shun), *n.* that which is intended or planned; purpose; aim; as, to act with good *intention*; my *intention* was to become a dentist.

in-ten-tion-al (in-ten′shun-al), *adj.* done on purpose; deliberate; as, an *intentional* injury.

in-ter (in-tûr′), *v.t.* [interred, inter-ring], to bury.—*n.* **in-ter′ment.**

in-ter- (in′tėr–), *prefix* meaning **1,** *among, between, within*; as in *inter*continental, *inter*denominational, *inter*face, *inter*national, *inter*planetary, *inter*scholastic; **2,** *together, mutually, with one another*; as in *inter*action, *inter*fuse, *inter*lock, *inter*weave.

in-ter-cede (in′tėr-sēd′), *v.i.* [interced-ed, interced-ing], to act as peacemaker; mediate; also, to plead for another; as, I *interceded* for him with his father.

in-ter-cept (in′tėr-sept′), *v.t.* **1,** to seize or catch on the way; stop; as, the spy *intercepted* the message; **2,** to obstruct; cut off, as a view; **3,** to interfere with the course of; stop; as, to *intercept* a forward pass; *intercept* an aircraft or other vehicle.—*n.* **in′ter-cep′tion; in′ter-cept′or** or **in′ter-cept′er.**

in-ter-ces-sion (in′tėr-sesh′un), *n.* **1,** an attempt to restore friendship between persons who are unfriendly; the act of interceding; **2,** the act of pleading for someone else.—*n.* **in′ter-ces′sor.**

in-ter-change (in′tėr-chānj′), *v.t.* [interchanged, interchang-ing], **1,** to exchange the position of, by putting one thing or person in the place of another; **2,** to vary; alternate; as, to *interchange* study with play:—*n.* (in′tėr-chānj′), **1,** the exchange of two things, one for the other; as, an *interchange* of business cards; **2,** alternate succession; as, the *interchange* of seasons; the *interchange* of study with play; **3,** a cloverleaf connecting two or more highways.—*adj.* **in′ter-change′a-ble.**—*adv.* **in′ter-change′a-bly.**

in-ter-col-le-gi-ate (in′ter-ko-lē′-ji-it; -jit), *adj.* **1,** carried on, as games, between colleges, universities, or high schools; **2,** existing, as leagues among colleges, universities, or high schools.

in-ter-com (in′tėr-kom′), *n. Colloq.* short for *intercommunication system*: a two-way communication system between rooms or areas in a building, ship, aircraft, etc.

in-ter-course (in′tėr-kōrs), *n.* **1,** connection, correspondence, or communication between individuals, nations, etc.; as, the Internet makes *intercourse* between people of different countries much easier, faster, and cheaper; **2,** sexual intercourse.

in-ter-dict (in′tėr-dikt′), *v.t.* **1,** to prohibit or forbid officially; as, to *interdict* the purchase of alcohol; **2,** to cut off from the spiritual services of a church, esp. the Roman Catholic Church:—*n.* (in′tėr-dikt), **1,** a formal prohibition or censure of church privileges; **2,** an official prohibition.—*n.* **in′ter-dic′tion.**

in-ter-est (in′tėr-est), *n.* **1,** a feeling of concern or curiosity about something; also, that which arouses it or causes this feeling, such as a hobby; as, suspense gives *interest* to a story; collecting old coins is one of my *interests*; **2,** that which is of advantage; benefit; as, he acts for the public *interest*; **3,** a share or part ownership; as, he has an *interest* in the business; **4,** a sum paid by the borrower for the use of borrowed money; as, 10 per cent *interest* on a loan:—**interests,** the persons occupied in some field of business or industry, taken all together; as, the lumber *interests*:—*v.t.* **1,** to engage the attention of; arouse to curiosity, sympathy, etc.; as, the video game *interested* him; **2,** to cause to take an interest or a share in; as, can I *interest* you in a game of cards?

in-ter-est-ing (in′tėr-es-ting), *adj.* attracting, provoking, causing, creating, or holding attention, curiosity, or emotion; as, an *interesting* novel, movie, game, etc.—*adv.* **in′ter-est-ing-ly.**

in-ter-face (in′tėr-fās′), *n.* **1**, the point forming the common boundary between two bodies, regions, etc.; **2**, the point where two systems meet and interact; as, the *interface* between government and business; **3**, in *computing*, a software program that allows one computer to communicate and connect with others and other equipment; **4**, in *computing*, the way that a program is organized and displayed on the screen; as, the graphical user *interface*:—*v.t.* [interfaced, interfac-ing], in *computing*, to connect by means of such programs or to serve as such a connection; as, to *interface* the new printer with the computer:—*v.i.* to coordinate smoothly; act as an interface.

in-ter-fere (in′tėr-fēr′), *v.i.* [interfered, interfer-ing], **1**, to get in the way; interrupt or block; hinder; as, bad weather *interfered* with our travel plans; **2**, to meddle; get involved with the affairs of others without permission; as, to *interfere* with their argument; **3**, in *sports* such as *hockey* and *football*, to block an opposing player illegally.—*n.* **in′ter-fer′ence.**

in-ter-im (in′tėr-im), *n.* the time or period between happenings; the meantime; as, in the *interim*, you can research the subject:—*adj.* belonging to, or occurring or done in, an intervening period; temporary; as, an *interim* report.

in-te-ri-or (in-tē′ri-er), *adj.* **1**, inner; internal; as, *interior* walls of a house; **2**, far from the coast or frontier; inland; as, *interior* provinces; **3**, relating to a person's mental or spiritual being; private:—*n.* **1**, the inside or inner part, as of a building; **2**, the inland; as, Manitoba is in the *interior* of Canada; **3**, the domestic affairs of a nation; **4**, a person's mental or spiritual being:—**Interior**, the inland region of British Columbia.

interior decorator, someone who designs and decorates the interior of a room or building.

in-ter-ject (in′tėr-jekt′), *v.t.* to put or throw in; insert; as, to *interject* a question.

in-ter-jec-tion (in′tėr-jek′shun), *n.* **1**, the act of throwing in or interjecting; also, that which is thrown in; an exclamation; **2**, in *grammar*, a word or phrase that shows a sudden or strong feeling and is used as an exclamation, having no grammatical connection with what comes before or after; as, "Ouch!" and "Oh!" are *interjections*.

in-ter-lace (in′tėr-lās′), *v.t.* and *v.i.* [interlaced, interlac-ing], **1**, to join by weaving or lacing together; **2**, intermingle; intersperse; as, an article *interlaced* with vivid imagery.

in-ter-lard (in′tėr-lard′), *v.t.* to diversify; intermingle; interlace; as, to *interlard* a speech with jokes and anecdotes.

in-ter-line (in′tėr-līn′), *v.t.* [interlined, interlin-ing], **1**, to fit (a garment) with an extra lining beneath the usual one; **2**, to insert words or write between the lines of (a manuscript, essay, etc.).

in-ter-lock (in′tėr-lok′), *v.t.* and *v.i.* to lock or clasp together; connect.—*adj.* **in-ter-lock-ing** (as, *interlocking* bricks).

in-ter-loc-u-tor (in′tėr-lok′ū-tėr), *n.* **1**, someone who participates in a conversation; **2**, a questioner, esp. the person in the middle who questions the end persons.

in-ter-lop-er (in′tėr-lōp′ėr), *n.* an outsider who interferes; intruder; meddler.

in-ter-lude (in′tėr-lūd), *n.* **1**, a short entertainment given between the acts of a play; **2**, a short passage of music played between the stanzas of a hymn, parts of a church service, acts of an opera, parts of a song, etc.; **3**, any period of time coming between; interval; as, an *interlude* of outdoor activity in a school day.

in-ter-mar-riage (in′tėr-mar′ij; in′tėr-mar′ij), *n.* **1**, marriage between people of different religions, races, etc.; **2**, marriage between closely related people.—*v.i.* **in′ter-mar′ry** [intermar-ried, intermar-rying].

in-ter-me-di-ate (in′tėr-mē′di-it), *adj.* existing or lying in the middle; coming between; as, an *intermediate* swimming class; an *intermediate* car:—*n.* **1**, that which lies between; **2**, a go-between; **3**, a car next below the largest in size.—*adv.* **in′ter-me′di-ate-ly.**

in-ter-ment (in-tûr′ment), *n.* burial.

in-ter-mez-zo (in′ter-met′sō; -med′-), *n.* [*pl.* -mezzi (-tzē)], *n.* **1**, dramatic or musical entertainment between acts in parts of a larger musical composition, a play, opera, etc.; **2**, music connecting parts of a larger musical composition.

in-ter-mi-na-ble (in′tėr′mi-na-bl), *adj.* endless; exceptionally long and boring; as, an *interminable* speech.—*adv.* **in-ter′mi-na-bly.**

in-ter-min-gle (in′tėr-ming′gl), *v.t.* and *v.i.* [intermin-gled, intermin-gling], to mix together.

in-ter-mis-sion (in′tėr-mish′un), *n.* **1**, a short or temporary break; an interruption; a pause; **2**, an interval of time between two parts, as acts of a play, concert, etc.—*v.t.* **in′ter-mit′** [intermit-ted, intermit-ting].

in-ter-mit-tent (in′tėr-mit′ent), *adj.* ceasing for short periods and starting again; coming and going; as, *intermittent* rain.—*adv.* **in′ter-mit′tent-ly.**

in-tern or **in-terne** (in′tûrn; in-tûrn′), *n.* **1**, a resident doctor on a hospital staff, usually a recent medical graduate; **2**, any recent graduate training in other fields; **3**, an inmate; someone who is interned:—*v.i.* (in-tûrn′), to perform an intern's duties:—*v.t.* **1,** to hold or detain, as (enemy) aliens in time of war; **2,** to detain ships or persons in port.—*n.* **in-tern′ment.**

in-ter-nal (in-tûr′nal), *adj.* **1,** belonging to or for the use of the inside; inner: opposite of *external*; as, the *internal* parts of an engine; to suffer *internal* injuries; *internal* medicine; **2,** inherent; coming from within the thing itself; as, *internal* evidence; **3,** having to do with affairs within a company, organization, or country; domestic; as, *internal* mail or memos; *internal* products or affairs; **4,** subjective; as, *internal* feelings.—*adv.* **in-ter′nal-ly:—internal-combustion engine**, an engine used in motor vehicles, airplanes, boats, etc., in which the power is produced by the exploding of a fuel-and-air mixture inside the engine's cylinders.

in-ter-na-tion-al (in′tėr-nash′un-al), *adj.* relating to, carried on between, used by, or agreement between two or more nations or their people; as, *international* trade; *international* waters; *international* licence.—*adv.* **in′ter-na′tion-al-ly.**

international system of units. Same as SI.

In-ter-net (in′tėr-net′), *n.* a system of connected computer networks, used for e-mail, access to information, on-line discussions, and other features: short for *internetwork*. Abbreviated as *Net*.

Internet protocol, the numeric address, such as 10.255.255.255, that connects the user directly to a specific computer: abbreviated as *IP*.

Internet service provider, a company that provides access to the Internet via telephone line, cable, or satellite: abbreviated as *ISP*.

in-ter-pose (in′tėr-pōz′), *v.t.* [interposed, interpos-ing], **1,** to place or set between; **2,** to thrust in; put forth, in order to interfere; intrude; **3,** to introduce (a remark) into a conversation:—*v.i.* **1,** to come between parties in a quarrel; mediate; intervene; **2,** to interrupt; **3,** to be between.

in-ter-pret (in-tûr′pret), *v.t.* **1,** to explain the meaning of; as, to *interpret* a word or a difficult passage in another language; also, to take something that has just been said in one language and repeat it in another; **2,** to bring out the meaning of, as a poem, piece of music, a work of art, etc.; as, to *interpret* the role of Hamlet; **3,** to take one's own meaning from (words, actions, etc.); as, to *interpret* a friend's motives.—*n.* **in-ter′pre-ta′tion; in-ter′pret-er.**

in-ter-ro-gate (in-ter′o-gāt′), *v.t.* [interrogat-ed, interrogat-ing], to question; examine by asking questions; as, to *interrogate* a witness.—*adj.* **in′ter-rog′a-tor′y.**

in-ter-ro-ga-tion (in-ter′o-gā′shun), *n.* **1,** the act of asking questions; **2,** a question; inquiry:—**interrogation point** or **mark**, a mark [?] indicating a direct question or doubt. Also called *question mark*.

in-ter-rog-a-tive (in′te-rog′a-tiv), *adj.* indicating or containing a question; as, an *interrogative* glance; an *interrogative* sentence:—*n.* in *grammar*, a word that asks a question, as *why, where, who, what, when*.

in-ter-rupt (in′te-rupt′), *v.t.* **1,** to stop or hinder by breaking in upon; as, to *interrupt* a speech; to *interrupt* a speaker; **2,** to obstruct; as, a wall *interrupts* a view; **3,** to break the continuity of; as, only the clock's tick *interrupts* the silence.—*n.* **in′ter-rup′tion.**

in-ter-sect (in′tėr-sekt′), *v.t.* to cut across; divide; as, one line *intersects* another:—*v.i.* to cross each other.—*n.* **in′ter-sec′tion.**

in-ter-sperse (in′tėr-spûrs′), *v.t.* [interspersed, interspers-ing], **1,** to insert here and there; as, to *intersperse* comments in the reading of a play; **2,** to scatter about; place here and there among other things; as, to *intersperse* shrubs with flowers.

in-ter-state (in′tėr-stāt), *adj.* between states; as, *interstate* highways.

in-ter-stel-lar (in′tėr-stel′ėr), *adj.* between or among the stars; also, happening between or among the stars; as, *interstellar* space; *interstellar* travel.

in-ter-twine (in′tėr-twīn′), *v.t.* and *v.i.* [intertwined, interwin-ing], to twist; wind or coil together.

in-ter-val (in′tėr-val), *n.* **1,** the time or space between events, periods, etc.; break or pause; as, the *interval* between two illnesses; *interval* between snowstorms; **2,** a space between objects; as, an *interval* of five metres between tents; **3,** in *music*, the difference in pitch between two tones.

in-ter-vene (in′tėr-vēn′), *v.i.* [intervened, interven-ing], **1,** to come or be between (things or events); as, a minute *intervened* between his remarks; **2,** to step in; interfere, as a force to influence action; as, friends *intervened* when the two men quarrelled.—*n.* **in′ter-ven′tion.**

in-ter-view (in′tėr-vū′), *v.t.* to question in order to obtain information; conduct or have an interview:—*n.* **1,** a personal conference or meeting in which one person asks another person questions in order to obtain information; as, an *interview* by the police officer; **2,** a meeting at which a person is asked questions to determine whether he or she is qualified for a job or position; as, a job *interview*; **3,** in *journalism*, the act of talking with, or being questioned by, a reporter; **4,** the published or broadcasted account of such a conversation.—*n.* **in′ter-view′er.**

in-tes-tate (in-tes′tāt), *adj.* leaving no will; as, he died *intestate*.

INTESTINES: S.I., SMALL INTESTINE; L.I., LARGE INTESTINE; A, APPENDIX; R, RECTUM

in-tes-tine (in-tes′tin), *n.* a long, twisting tube extending from the stomach to the rectum, which helps to digest and absorb food and to eliminate waste matter: composed of the *large* and the *small intestine*; the bowels.—*adj.* **in-tes′ti-nal.**

in-ti-mate (in′ti-mit), *adj.* **1,** close in friendship; familiar; as, *intimate* friends; **2,** resulting from close study; as, an *intimate* knowledge of art; **3,** having to do with the inner nature of anything; innermost; personal; as, a person's *intimate* feelings; **4,** pertaining to sexual relations:—*n.* a close friend:—*v.t.* (in′ti-māt′), [intimat-ed, intimat-ing], to suggest; hint; make known indirectly; as, he *intimated* his disapproval of the plan.—*adv.* **in′ti-mate-ly.**—*n.* **in′ti-ma-cy.**

in-ti-ma-tion (in′ti-mā′shun), *n.* an indirect hint.

in-tim-i-date (in-tim′i-dāt′), *v.t.* [intimidat-ed, intimidat-ing], to frighten, esp. by threats; overawe; as, the thief *intimidated* her; the famous author *intimidates* me.—*n.* **in-tim′i-da′tion.**

in-to (in′to͞o; in′too), *prep.* **1,** to the inside of (a place, matter, occupation, state, etc.); as, come *into* the room; look *into* the affair; go *into* business; get *into* trouble; **2,** so as to hit against; as, to back the car *into* a tree; **3,** to the condition of; as, the rain later turned *into* snow; **4,** *Colloq.* very interested in or involved with; as, to be *into* hip-hop music.

in-tol-er-a-ble (in-tol′ėr-a-bl), *adj.* unbearable; not to be endured; as, *intolerable* heat; an *intolerable* insult.—*adv.* **in-tol′er-a-bly.**

in-tol-er-ant (in-tol′ėr-ant), *adj.* **1,** scorning difference of opinion, belief, or behaviour in others, esp. in religion and morals; **2,** not willing to accept as equals people of different races, religions, ideologies, etc.; **3,** unable to bear or endure; as, *intolerant* of pain.—*n.* **in-tol′er-ance.**

in-tone (in-tōn′), *v.t.* and *v.i.* to recite in a musical monotone; chant; as, the priest *intoned* the liturgy.—*n.* **in′to-na′tion.**

in-tox-i-cate (in-tok′si-kāt′), *v.t.* [intoxicat-ed, intoxicat-ing], **1,** to make drunk, as by alcoholic liquors; also, to introduce poisons or toxins into the body; **2,** to excite exceedingly; to elate; as, happiness *intoxicated* him.—*n.* **in-tox′i-ca′tion; in-tox′i-cant.**

in-trac-ta-ble (in-trak′ta-bl), *adj.* unmanageable; stubborn; not easily controlled; as, an *intractable* horse; an *intractable* temper.

in-tra-mu-ral (in′tra-mū′ral), *adj.* entirely within the limits of a city, community, organization, school, institution, etc.; as, *intramural* sports. Compare *extramural.*

in-tra-net (in′tra-net′), *n.* a computer network confined to one organization and its employees, although it may have several sites, as a multinational corporation.

in-tran-si-gent (in-tran′si-jent), *adj.* refusing to come to an understanding, agreement, etc.; uncompromising, as in politics, debates, etc.:—*n.* a person who refuses to come to an understanding, agreement, etc.

in-tran-si-tive (in-tran′si-tiv), *adj.* in *grammar*, not taking a direct object because none is needed to complete the action or the meaning: said of verbs; as, he *sits*; she *laughed*:—*n.* an intransitive verb. Compare *transitive*.—*adv.* **in-tran′si-tive-ly.**

in-treat (in-trēt′), *v.t.* Same as **entreat.**

in-trench (in-trench′), *v.t.* Same as **entrench.**

in-trep-id (in-trep′id), *adj.* bold; fearless; brave.—*adv.* **in-trep′id-ly.**—*n.* **in′tre-pid′i-ty; in-trep′id-ness.**

in-tri-cate (in′tri-kit), *adj.* entangled; complicated; involved; detailed; as, an *intricate* plot; an *intricate* carving; an *intricate* design or pattern.—*n.* **in′tri-ca-cy; in′tri-cate-ness.**

in-trigue (in-trēg′), *v.i.* [intrigued, intriguing], **1,** to carry on a secret plot; **2,** to engage in a secret love affair:—*v.t.* **1,** to arouse curiosity in; hence, to interest keenly; as, your plan *intrigues* me; **2,** to plot; perplex:—*n.* (in-trēg′; in′trēg), **1,** a plot; scheme; **2,** a plot in a movie, play, etc.; **3,** a secret love affair.—*adj.* **in-tri′guing.**

in-trin-sic (in-trin′sik), *adj.* relating to the inner nature; true; essential; as, a person's *intrinsic* worth.—*adv.* **in-trin′si-cal-ly.**

in-tro-duce (in′trō-dūs′), *v.t.* [introduced, introduc-ing], **1,** to bring in; usher in; as, he *introduced* me into the room; **2,** to bring into use or notice, esp. for the first time; as, to *introduce* a new fad; Newton *introduced* the theory of gravity; **3,** to make known or acquainted, as one person to another; as, please *introduce* me to your friend; **4,** to put into; insert; as, to *introduce* lime into the soil; **5,** to make known or bring to notice; as, to *introduce* the plays of Shakespeare to a class; **6,** to present in a formal manner; as, to *introduce* a bill into Parliament; **7,** to open; begin; start; as, a phrase may *introduce* a sentence.—*adj.* **in′tro-duc′to-ry.**

in-tro-duc-tion (in′trō-duk′shun), *n.* **1,** the act of introducing; as, the *introduction* of a new species to an area; **2,** the act of introducing people to each other; **3,** something that serves to introduce; as, an *introduction* to a computer science course; **4,** a part at the beginning of a book, play, etc., that tells something about it.

in-tro-spec-tion (in′trō-spek′shun), *n.* the act of observing or examining one's own mental processes.—*adj.* **in′tro-spec′tive.**

in-tro-vert (in′trō-vûrt′), *n.* one who is concerned with his or her own thoughts rather than other people, external events, or objects; opposite of *extrovert*:—*v.t.* to turn inward (one's attention, etc.).—*n.* **in′tro-ver′sion.**

in-trude (in-trōōd′), *v.i.* [intrud-ed, intrud-ing], to enter without invitation or welcome:—*v.t.* to thrust or force in; as, to *intrude* remarks into their conversation.—*n.* **in-trud′er; in-tru′sion.**—*adj.* **in-tru′sive.**

in-trust (in-trust′), *v.t.* Same as **entrust.**

in-tu-i-tion (in′tū-ish′un), *n.* knowledge that comes to one instinctively or without conscious thought, reasoning, or study; sudden insight; as, his *intuition* warned of danger.—*adj.* **in-tu′i-tive.**—*adv.* **in-tu′i-tive-ly.**

In-u-it (in′ū-it; in′ōō-it), *n.pl.* **1,** the Aboriginal peoples from Arctic areas of North America, Greenland, and eastern Siberia: formerly called *Eskimo*; **2,** any of the languages of these peoples:—*adj.* having to do with the Inuit people.

In-uk (in′ook), *n.* the singular form of *Inuit*: one Inuit.

In-uk-ti-tut (in-ook′ti-toot′), *n.* the language of the Inuit, which consists of many dialects.

in-un-date (in′un-dāt′), *v.t.* [inundated, inundat-ing], **1,** to fill to overflowing; flood; **2,** to spread over; overwhelm; as, the company hired students to *inundate* the area with advertising pamphlets.—*n.* **in′un-da′tion.**

in-ure or **en-ure** (in-ūr′; en-ūr′), *v.t.* [inured, inur-ing], to accustom; toughen; as, to *inure* oneself to cold weather:—*v.i.* (often *enure*, chiefly in legal sense), to come into use; take effect; as, the fund *inured* to his benefit.

in-vade (in-vād′), *v.t.* [invad-ed, invad-ing], **1,** to enter in a hostile manner; attack; as, the Romans *invaded* Gaul; worry *invades* the mind; **2,** to enter in great number; as, thousands of grasshoppers *invaded* the fields; **3,** to infringe upon; to violate; intrude; enter where one is not wanted; as, to *invade* the rights of a people; *invade* her privacy.—*n.* **in-vad′er.**

[1]in-val-id (in-val′id), *adj.* of no force, authority, or value; worthless; as, an *invalid* reason.

[2]in-val-id (in′va-lid; -lēd′), *n.* one who is weak or sick; also, a disabled person:—*adj.* **1,** sick; enfeebled by ill health; **2,** for a sick person; as, an *invalid* chair:—*v.t.* **1,** to make sick or weak; **2,** to relieve from active duty as a result of illness, disability, or injury; as, to *invalid* her out of the airforce.

in-val-u-a-ble (in-val′ū-a-bl), *adj.* priceless; exceedingly valuable.

in-var-i-a-ble (in-vâr′i-a-bl), *adj.* constant; unchanging.—*adv.* **in-var′i-a-bly.**

in-va-sion (in-vā′zhun), *n.* **1,** the act of entering in a hostile manner; an attack; **2,** the act of entering in great number; **3,** an attack of anything injurious, as a disease; **4,** an intrusion or infringement upon; as, an *invasion* of privacy.

in-vec-tive (in-vek′tiv), *n.* a violent, bitter attack in words; abusive language:—*adj.* abusive (of language or words).

in-veigh (in-vā′), *v.i.* to attack violently in words; rail; as, she *inveighed* against the new policy.

in-vei-gle (in-vē′gl), *v.t.* to trick or entice one into doing something; beguile; as, he *inveigled* me into cheating on the test.

in-vent (in-vent′), *v.t.* **1,** to create something new as a result of original study; originate; produce for the first time; as, to *invent* a machine; **2,** to make up; as, to *invent* a strange story or wild excuse.—*n.* **in-ven′tor.**—*adj.* **in-ven′tive.**

in-ven-tion (in-ven′shun), *n.* **1,** the act or fact of inventing; as, the *invention* of the telephone; **2,** something invented; as, the computer has become one of the most important *inventions* of modern times; **3,** the power to invent things; **4,** something made up, such as a story, excuse, etc.

in-ven-tor-y (in′ven-tôr-i), *n.* [*pl.* inventories], **1,** a catalogue or detailed list of goods or items on hand and their value; as, an *inventory* of books in the bookstore; **2,** the act of making such a list; **3,** all of the items listed; stock; as, a sale reduces a store's *inventory*:—*v.t.* [inventoried, inventory-ing], to make an inventory of; to include in a list; catalogue.

in-verse (in-vûrs′; in′vûrs), *adj.* directly opposite; reversed; as, in *inverse* order or ratio:—*n.* the direct opposite or something that is reversed or inverted; as, subtraction is the *inverse* of addition:—*v.t.* to invert; reverse.—*adv.* **in-verse′ly.**

in-vert (in-vûrt′), *v.t.* **1,** to turn upside down, inside out, or in an opposite direction; **2,** to reverse, as in meaning or order; as, to *invert* AB by making BA.—*adj.* **in-vert′ed.**—*n.* **in-ver′sion.**

in-ver-te-brate (in-vûr′ti-brāt′), *n.* an animal without backbone or spinal column, such as an arthropod:—*adj.* **1,** having no backbone; **2,** weak-willed.

in-vest (in-vest′), *v.t.* **1,** to lay out (money) for income or profit; as, he *invested* money in stocks; **2,** to spend time or energy in order to get some benefit; as, to *invest* many years studying to become a doctor; **3,** to clothe with an office, dignity, etc.; as, to *invest* a judge with the authority of her position; **4,** to give authority to; as, to *invest* her with power of attorney; **5,** to cover; as, smoke *invested* the sky:—*v.i.* to put money out for profit.—*n.* **in-vest′ment; in-ves′tor; in-ves′ti-ture** (sense 2).

in-ves-ti-gate (in-ves′ti-gāt′), *v.t.* and *v.i.* [investigat-ed, investigat-ing], to examine systematically; to make careful inquiry (about); as, to *investigate* the cause of a disaster.—*n.* **in-ves′ti-ga′tor; in-ves′ti-ga′tion.**

in-vet-er-ate (in-vet′ėr-it), *adj.* **1,** of long standing; deep-rooted; as, *inveterate* hatred; **2,** habitual; as, an *inveterate* liar.

in-vid-i-ous (in-vid′i-us), *adj.* likely to provoke ill will or envy; unfairly partial.

in-vig-o-rate (in-vig′o-rāt′), *v.t.* [invigorat-ed, invigorat-ing], to give vitality to; strengthen; as, the sea air *invigorated* her.

in-vin-ci-ble (in-vin′si-bl), *adj.* not to be overcome or subdued; unconquerable; unbeatable; as, an *invincible* will; *invincible* team.—*adv.* **in-vin′ci-bly.**—*n.* **in-vin′ci-bil′i-ty.**

in-vi-o-la-ble (in-vī′ō-la-bl), *adj.* **1,** sacred; not to be violated; as, *inviolable* territory; **2,** not to be broken; as, an *inviolable* promise; *inviolable* laws.

in-vi-o-late (in-vī′o-lit; -lāt′), *adj.* kept sacred or unbroken, as a promise, oath, etc.

in-vis-i-ble (in-viz′i-bl), *adj.* **1,** not capable of being seen; out of sight; hidden; as, clouds make the stars *invisible;* **2,** not capable of being seen because of small size; **3,** inconspicuous.—*adv.* **in-vis′i-bly.**—*n.* **in-vis′i-bil′i-ty.**

in-vi-ta-tion (in′vi-tā′shun), *n.* **1,** a request to a person to come to some place or to do something; also, the written or spoken form of such a request or the act of inviting; **2,** something that entices; as, her insolence was an *invitation* for punishment.

in-vite (in-vīt′), *v.t.* [invit-ed, inviting], **1,** to ask (a person) to come somewhere or to do something; as, *invite* him for a walk; **2,** to request; as, to *invite* an opinion; **3,** to tempt; be the cause of; as, the music *invites* us to dance; her poor attitude *invites* dislike from others.

in-vit-ing (in-vīt′ing), *adj.* tempting; alluring; as, an *inviting* meal.

in-vo-ca-tion (in′vō-kā′shun), *n.* **1,** a prayer; a supplication, esp. to a divine being; **2,** the act of conjuring up devils, or the magic words for doing so; incantation.

in-voice (in′vois), *n.* **1,** a written or printed list of goods or services sent to a purchaser, with their prices, quantity, and charges; also, the form used; **2,** the goods or services listed:—*v.t.* [invoiced, invoicing], to make an invoice of; to include in an invoice; to send an invoice to; as, when you finish the job, you can *invoice* us.

in-voke (in-vōk′), *v.t.* [invoked, invok-ing], **1,** to address in prayer or supplication; as, to *invoke* the Lord; **2,** to ask for earnestly; as, to *invoke* a blessing; **3,** to conjure up; as, to *invoke* evil spirits; **4,** to apply; as, Trudeau *invoked* the War Measures Act.

in-vol-un-tar-y (in-vol′un-tėr-i), *adj.* **1,** not under the control of the will; as, the beating of the heart is an *involuntary* activity; **2,** against one's will; compulsory; **3,** unintentional; as, an *involuntary* sigh; *involuntary* manslaughter.—*adv.* **in-vol′un-ta-ri-ly.**

in-volve (in-volv′), *v.t.* [involved, involving], **1,** to entangle; complicate; as, he *involved* his friends in the illegal scheme; **2,** to make difficult; complicate; as, these new facts certainly *involve* the mystery; **3,** to include as a necessity; require; as, a career *involves* hard work; **4,** to engage completely; as, study *involves* all my time.—*n.* **involve′ment.**

in-vul-ner-a-ble (in-vul′nėr-a-bl), *adj.* **1,** incapable of being injured; **2,** incapable of being answered or refuted; as, an *invulnerable* argument.—*n.* **in-vul′ner-a-bil′i-ty.**

[1]in-ward (in′wėrd), *adj.* **1,** situated within; internal; as, *inward* organs; **2,** of the inner self; as, *inward* happiness; **3,** toward the inside or centre; as, an *inward* curve; **4,** essential; as, the *inward* characteristics of this group.

[2]in-ward (in′wėrd) or **in-wards** (in′wėrdz), *adv.* **1,** toward the inside or centre; as, to bend *inward;* **2,** into or toward the mind; as, turn the thoughts *inward.*

in-ward-ly (in′wėrd-li), *adv.* internally; esp. in the mind or feelings; secretly; as, to grieve *inwardly.*

i-o-dine (ī′ō-dīn′; ī′ō-din; ī′ō-dēn′), *n.* **1,** a black-grey crystalline element found in mineral springs, seaweed, etc.; **2,** a solution of these crystals in alcohol used as an antiseptic.

i-o-dize (ī′ō-dīz′), *v.t.* to treat with iodine or an iodide (a wound, photographic plate, etc.); as, *iodized* salt.

i-on (ī′on), *n.* one of the particles bearing electrical charges that transmits an electric current through the air or other gases.

i-on-ize (ī′o-nīz′), *v.t.* and *v.i.* to change into ions.—*n.* **i′on-i-za′tion.**

i-o-ta (ī-ō′ta), *n.* **1,** a very small quantity; jot; as, there is not an *iota* of truth in the rumour; **2,** in the Greek alphabet, the ninth letter.

IP (ī′pē′), *abbrev.* short for *Internet protocol.*

IQ (ī′kū′), *abbrev.* short for *intelligence quotient.*

ir- (ir), *prefix* before *r* meaning *not;* as in *ir*reclai- mable, *ir*redeemable, *ir*reducible, *ir*refutable, *ir*remediable, *ir*reversible.

i-ras-ci-ble (i-ras′i-bl; ī-), *adj.* easily angered; showing anger; as, an *irascible* old man.

i-rate (ī-rāt′; ī′rāt), *adj.* angry, enraged.

ire (ir), *n.* anger; wrath.—*adj.* **ire′ful.**

ir-i-des-cent (ir′i-des′ent), *adj.* having changing, shimmering, rainbowlike colours, as an opal.—*n.* **ir′i-des′cence.**

i-ris (ī′ris), *n.* [*pl.* irises], **1,** the rainbow; also, a rainbowlike shimmer; **2,** the coloured portion of the eye around the pupil, which controls the amount of light that enters the eye; **3,** a plant with large, showy flowers and sword-shaped leaves.

I-rish (ī′rish), *n.* **1,** a person who inhabits or originates from Ireland; **2,** the language spoken in Ireland:—*adj.* relating to the country, the people, the language, or the culture of Ireland.

irk (ûrk), *v.t.* to weary; bore; annoy; as, it *irked* me to wait.

irk-some (ûrk′sum), *adj.* tedious; wearisome; dull; as, an *irksome* math lesson.

i-ron (ī′ėrn), *n.* **1,** a silver-white metal that can be melted and worked into tools and implements: the most common of all the metals, used over almost all the world in three commercial forms, *wrought iron, cast iron,* and *steel;* **2,** any tool or weapon made of iron, esp. a pistol, branding iron, or harpoon; **3,** firmness; rigidity; strength; as, a man of *iron;* **4,** in *golf,* any of several clubs with an iron head; **5,** a household appliance used to press wrinkles out of clothes; **6,** the chemical element that is needed in the body by all plants, animals, and people to live and grow:—**irons,** chains or fetters:—*adj.* **1,** pertaining to, or made of, iron; as, an *iron* bar; **2,** resembling iron in hardness, strength, etc.; as, an *iron* will:—*v.t.* **1,** to smooth with an iron; as, to *iron* clothes; **2,** to fetter.—*n.* **i′ron-er** (ī′ėr-nėr):—**iron lung,** a chamber enclosing all but the head, used to force normal lung action in patients. Also, **i′ron-clad′; i′ron-ware′; i′ron-wood′.**

Iron Age, the period of human culture when tools and weapons were made from iron, beginning, in Europe, about the eighth century B.C.

i-ron-ic (ī-ron′ik) or **i-ron-i-cal** (ī-ron′i-kal), *adj.* **1,** expressing the opposite of what is meant; disguisedly sarcastic; as, an *ironic* remark; **2,** describing a circumstance the reverse of what was, or might be, expected; as, an *ironic* turn of fate made him the rival of his best friend; **3,** showing or using irony.—*adv.* **i-ron′i-cal-ly.**

i-ro-ny (ī′ro-ni), *n.* [*pl.* ironies], **1,** hidden sarcasm; the expression of the opposite of what is really meant; as, ridicule disguised as praise is *irony;* **2,** any situation or event the opposite of what would normally be expected; as, the *irony* of it was that she was killed by her own invention.

Ir-o-quois (ir′u-kwä′), *n.* **1,** the Aboriginal people, originally living in Ontario, Québec, and New York State, who speak an Iroquoian language, including the Mohawk, Oneida, Onondaga, Cayuga, Seneca, Tuscaroran, Huron, and Cherokee peoples; **2,** the language of these peoples.—*adj.* **Ir-o-quoi′an.**

ir-ra-tion-al (ir-rash′un-al), *adj.* **1,** lacking reasoning powers, as beasts; **2,** without reason; as, an *irrational* fear.

ir-rec-on-cil-a-ble (ir-rek′on-sīl′a-bl; ir-rek′on-sīl′a-bl), *adj.* **1,** not adjustable, as a quarrel; unchangeably hostile, as two persons who have quarrelled; **2,** not in agreement; conflicting; as, his actions are *irreconcilable* with his promises.—*adv.* **ir-rec-′on-cil′a-bly.**

ir-reg-u-lar (ir-reg′ū-lėr), *adj.* **1,** not straight or symmetrical; not uniform in shape, order, etc.; rough; not smooth; as, *irregular* lines and figures; *irregular* surface; **2,** not according to rule or established method; as, an *irregular* proceeding; **3,** not usual or normal; as, an *irregular* heartbeat; **4,** in *grammar,* not following the regular rule for conjugation or inflection; as, "go" is an *irregular* verb.—*adv.* **ir-reg′u-lar-ly.**—*n.* **ir-reg′u-lar′i-ty.**

ir-rel-e-vant (ir-rel′i-vant), *adj.* not bearing upon the case; unrelated to the matter discussed; not pertinent; as, *irrelevant* evidence or arguments.—*adv.* **ir-rel′e-vant-ly.**—*n.* **ir-rel′e-vance; ir-rel′e-van-cy.**

ir-re-li-gious (ir′ri-lij′us), *adj.* lacking religion or respect for religion; profane; as, *irreligious* conduct.—*adv.* **ir′re-li′gious-ly.**

ir-rep-a-ra-ble (i-rep′a-ra-bl), *adj.* not capable of being repaired, restored, or remedied; as, his losses are *irreparable.*

ir-re-press-i-ble (ir′ri-pres′i-bl), *adj.* incapable of being checked or controlled; as, *irrepressible* laughter.

ir-re-proach-a-ble (ir′ri-prōch′a-bl), *adj.* blameless; faultless; as, *irreproachable* conduct.

ir-re-sist-i-ble (ir′ri-zis′ti-bl), *adj.* too strong or desirable to be resisted; overpowering; as, an *irresistible* temptation.—*adv.* **ir′re-sist′i-bly.**

ir-res-o-lute (i-rez′o-lūt′), *adj.* undecided; wavering; as, a woman *irresolute* in her decisions.—*n.* **ir-res′o-lu′tion.**

ir-re-spec-tive (ir′ri-spek′tiv), *adj.* regardless; as, all people must die, *irrespective* of wealth or power.—*adv.* **ir′re-spec′tive-ly.**

ir-re-spon-si-ble (ir′ri-spon′si-bl), *adj.* **1,** not to be held accountable; as, an *irresponsible* child; **2,** not trustworthy; as, *irresponsible* workers.—*adv.* **ir′re-spon′si-bly.**—*n.* **ir′re-spon′si-bil′i-ty.**

ir-re-triev-a-ble (ir′ri-trēv′a-bl), *adj.* not recoverable; not to be regained; as, an *irretrievable* loss; *irretrievable* computer file.—*adv.* **ir′re-triev′a-bly.**

ir-rev-er-ent (i-rev′ėr-ent), *adj.* disrespectful; showing a lack of respect or veneration, esp. for things held sacred.—*n.* **ir-rev′er-ence.**

ir-rev-o-ca-ble (i-rev′o-ka-bl), *adj.* incapable of being recalled or undone; as, an *irrevocable* act.

ir-ri-gate (ir′i-gāt′), *v.t.* [irrigat-ed, irrigat-ing], **1,** to supply with water, as land under cultivation, by means of ditches, channels, canals, pipes, sprinklers, etc.; **2,** to wash out, as a wound, with a flow of liquid, in order to clean or disinfect it.—*n.* **ir′ri-ga′tion.**

ir-ri-ta-ble (ir′i-ta-bl), *adj.* easily annoyed or angered; cranky; also, very sensitive.—*adv.* **ir′ri-ta-bly.**—*n.* **ir′ri-ta-bil′i-ty.**

ir-ri-tate (ir′i-tāt′), *v.t.* [irritat-ed, irritat-ing], **1,** to annoy or make angry; as, his pompous manner *irritates* me; **2,** to make sore; inflame; as, smoke *irritates* the eyes.—*n.* **ir′ri-ta′tion.**

ir-rup-tion (i-rup′shun), *n.* a bursting or rushing in; sudden invasion; as, an *irruption* of the enemy.

is (iz), *3rd pers. sing. pres.* of *be.*

i-sin-glass (ī-zing-glås′), *n.* **1,** a white semi-transparent substance or gelatin obtained from the air bladders of the sturgeon, cod, etc., used as an adhesive and as a clarifier; **2,** a mineral that readily separates into thin, semi-transparent sheets; mica.

Is-lam (is′lam; iz-), *n.* the Muslim religion, people, or territory; Mohammedan belief in one God, Allah.—*adj.* **Is-lam′ic.**

is-land (ī′land), *n.* **1,** a tract of land entirely surrounded by water; **2,** anything detached and isolated like an island; as, floating *islands* of ice; traffic *island.*—*n.* **is′land-er.**

isle (īl), *n.* a small island; usually *poetic,* except in proper names.

i-so-bar (ī′sō-bar′), *n.* a line on a map connecting places of equal barometric pressure.

i-so-late (ī′sō-lāt′; is′ō-lāt′), *v.t.* [isolat-ed, isolat-ing], to place alone and away from others; separate; as, the hospital *isolates* contagious cases.—*adj.* **i′so-lat-ed.**

i-so-la-tion (ī′sō-lā′shun; is′ō-lā′shun), *n.* a setting apart, or the state of being placed apart or in solitude; loneliness.

i-sos-ce-les (ī-sos′e-lēz′), *adj.* having two equal sides; as, an *isosceles* triangle.

ISOSCELES TRIANGLES

i-so-therm (ī′sō-thûrm′), *n.* a line on a map connecting points on the earth's surface having the same average temperature.—*adj.* **i′so-ther′mal.**

i-so-tope (ī′sō-tōp′), *n.* one of two or more forms of an element having the same place in the periodic table and having almost identical properties, but differing in atomic weight; as, uranium 235 and uranium 238 are *isotopes.*

ISP (ī′es′pē′), *abbrev.* short for *Internet service provider.*

is-sue (ish′ōō), *n.* **1,** the act of passing or flowing out; as, an *issue* of water, as from a tap; **2,** an outlet; also, the point of outlet, as the mouth of a river; **3,** that which is sent forth or produced; as, an *issue* of currency; a special *issue* of postage stamps; **4,** an edition of a book, newspaper, magazine, etc., esp. the entire number put out at one time; also, one copy of such a publication; **5,** offspring; progeny; as, to die without *issue*; **6,** the final result; outcome; as, the *issue* of an election; **7,** a point of contention between two parties; as, political *issues*; **8,** a subject that is being talked about or considered; a matter to be dealt with; as, unemployment is the main *issue* of the debate:—*v.t.* [issued, issu-ing], **1,** to send out; discharge; as, a crater *issues* smoke; **2,** to publish; send out officially; as, to *issue* a decree; *issue* a newspaper; **3,** to put into circulation; as, to *issue* currency:—*v.i.* **1,** to come or pass forth; as, blood *issues* from a cut; **2,** to arise, as from a source; as, a river *issues* from a lake; **3,** to end; as, the struggle *issued* in peace.—*n.* **is′su-ance.**

isth-mus (is′mus), *n.* [*pl.* isthmuses], a neck of land connecting two larger bodies of land; as, the *isthmus* of Panama.

it (it), *neut. pron.* of third person [*nominative* it, *possessive* its (its), *objective* it], the thing in question; as, Where is my book? *It* is on the table: also used impersonally; as, *it* is raining:—*n.* in children's games, the player whom the other players oppose.

IT (ī′tē′), *abbrev.* short for *information technology.*

I-tal-ian (i-tal′yen), *n.* **1,** a person who inhabits or originates from Italy; **2,** the language spoken by these people:—*adj.* relating to the country, the people, the language, or the culture of Italy.

i-tal-i-cize (i-tal′i-sīz′), *v.t.* [italicized, itali-ciz-ing], to print (words) in a slender, sloping style of type called *italics.*

itch (ich), *n.* **1,** a contagious skin disease causing great irritation; **2,** a sensation of irritation in the skin that makes one want to scratch; **3,** a constant and craving desire; restlessness; as, an *itch* to paint:—*v.i.* **1,** to have a feeling in the skin causing a desire to scratch; **2,** to have a longing; crave; as, he *itched* to go to Europe.—*adj.* **itch′y.**—*n.* **itch′i-ness.**

i-tem (ī′tem), *n.* **1,** a single thing; one of something; as, a list of *items* to take on vacation; **2,** a separate article, entry, etc.; a sum entered in an account; **3,** a piece of news; as, to read an *item* in the newspaper; watch a news *item* on television.

i-tem-ize (ī′tem-īz′), *v.t.* [itemized, itemiz-ing], to state by separate entries; give particulars of; make a list of items; as, to *itemize* a bill; *itemize* things to buy at the store.

it-er-ate (it′ėr-āt′), *v.t.* [iterat-ed, iterat-ing], to repeat; do or say again.—*n.* **it′er-a′tion.**

i-tin-er-ant (ī-tin′ėr-ant; i-), *adj.* passing from place to place; as, an *itinerant* worker:—*n.* one who travels from place to place.

i-tin-er-ar-y (ī-tin′ėr-ėr-i; i-tin′ėr-ėr-i), *n.* [*pl.* itineraries], **1,** a traveller's guide book; **2,** a plan for a trip or journey; **3,** a route actually taken; **4,** a record of a journey.

its (its), *adj.* the possessive form of the personal pronoun *it*: of or belonging to it; as, the tree has lost *its* leaves.

it-self (it-self′), *pron.* the intensive (emphatic) or reflexive form of *it*; as, he loved the work *itself*; the cat washes *itself*.

i-vo-ry (ī′vo-ri), *n.* [*pl.* ivories], **1,** the hard, white substance that forms the tusks of the elephant, walrus, etc.; **2,** the colour of ivory; creamy white; **3,** a substance resembling ivory; **4,** an article, as a carving, made of ivory: the sale of new ivory is now banned by many countries in an effort to protect the animals that are killed for their tusks:—**ivories,** *Slang* **1,** piano keys; **2,** dice; **3,** teeth:—*adj.* made of, or like, ivory.

i-vy (ī′vi), *n.* [*pl.* ivies], **1,** any of several clinging vines with shiny, green, ornamental leaves, as English ivy, Boston ivy; **2,** a similar plant, such as poison ivy.—*adj.* **i′vied.**

J

J, j (jā), *n.* [*pl.* J's, j's], the 10th letter of the alphabet, following I.

jab (jab), *v.t.* and *v.i.* [jabbed, jab-bing] to stab or poke with something pointed:—*n.* a sharp thrust; as, a *jab* of a needle, a finger, etc.

jab-ber (jab′ėr), *v.i.* and *v.t.* to talk rapidly and indistinctly; chatter:—*n.* chatter; unintelligible talk.

jack (jak), *n.* **1,** (often **Jack**), a young man; labourer; sailor; **2,** any one of several mechanical devices used for lifting a great weight, such as a car, a short distance off the ground; **3,** the male of any of several animals; as, a *jack*ass, etc.; **4,** in *cards*, any one of the four knaves or pages, ranking below the queen; **5,** a small flag used on a ship, as a signal or a sign of nationality; **6,** an electrical device, usually mounted on a wall, to receive a plug, such as a telephone or light plug:—**jacks,** a game using small pebbles or six-pointed metal pieces called jackstones, that players pick up quickly while bouncing a small ball:—*v.t.* **1,** to raise or hoist by means of a jack, lever, block, or other mechanical device; **2,** *Colloq.* to raise the level; as, to *jack* up the interest rates.

jack-al (jak′ôl), *n.* **1,** a doglike, flesh-eating pack animal of the plains of Africa and Asia that lives on small animals and carrion; **2,** one who does tedious work for another.

jack-a-napes (jak′a-nāps′), *n.* a conceited or impertinent person.

jack-ass (jak′ās′), *n.* **1,** the male donkey; **2,** a conceited fool; blockhead.

jack-et (jak′it), *n.* **1,** a short coat for the upper body, ending at the waist or hips; **2,** a covering similar to a jacket, for protection, insulation, etc., such as the skin of a potato, the covering for a record album, or the paper wrapping that protects the cover of a book; also, a water jacket for cooling an engine.

jack-ham-mer (jak′ham′ėr), *n.* a tool, often hand-held, such as a drill or hammer, that is driven by compressed air and is used to break up hard material such as rock, concrete, or pavement.

jack–in–the–box, a toy consisting of a box from which a figure springs out when the lid is released.

jack-knife (jak′nīf′), *n.* [*pl.* jack-knives (jak′–nīvz′)], **1,** a pocketknife, with blades that fold into the knife handle, larger and stronger than a penknife; **2,** a dive in which the diver bends forward while in the air to touch the toes and then straightens out:—*v.t.* [jackknifed, jackknif-ing], **1,** to use a jackknife; **2,** to cause to bend like a jackknife:—*v.i.* **1,** to bend like a jackknife; **2,** of jointed or connected vehicles, such as a tractor-trailer, to form a 90-degree angle at the connection when suddenly stopped or hit; as, the tractor-trailor *jackknifed* and turned over on the icy road when the driver suddenly hit the brakes.

jack–o'–lan-tern (jak′–o–lan′tėrn), *n.* **1,** a pumpkin hollowed out and cut to resemble a human face, used for decoration at Halloween, with a candle or light placed inside to show the carved face; **2,** a will-o'-the-wisp.

jack pine, an evergreen common to North America, the soft wood of which is often used to make wood pulp.

jack-pot (jak′pot′), *n.* **1,** in *poker*, a pot that keeps increasing until a player can open with a pair of jacks or better; **2,** any high or cumulative stakes, as in bingo, slot machines, or enterprise involving risk; a great gain; as, he hit the *jackpot* when he patented his invention.

jack-rab-bit (jak′rab′it), *n.* a hare of western North America, having very long ears and long hind legs.

jade (jād), *n.* **1,** a hard, semi-precious stone, usually green or white, often carved or used in jewellery; **2,** the green colour of jade; **3,** a worn-out or worthless horse; **4,** a disreputable woman; coquette:—*v.t.* [jad-ed, jad-ing], to wear out or tire:—*v.i.* to become worn out or tired.

jag (jag), *n.* a sharp, projecting point; a notch:—*v.t.* [jagged (jagd), jag-ging], to cut or tear unevenly.—*adj.* **jag′ged** (jag′ed).

jag-uar (jag′wär), *n.* a fierce, catlike, flesh-eating animal of tropical America, spotted like the leopard, but heavier and more powerful: now widely protected by law due to a large decrease in its population.

jail (jāl), *n.* a prison; esp. a lockup for persons guilty of minor offences, or for persons awaiting trial:—*v.t.* to imprison.—*n.* **jail′er.**

ja-lop-y (ja-lop′i), *n.* an old, ramshackle automobile.

[1]**jam** (jam), *v.t.* [jammed, jam-ming], **1,** to squeeze or press in tightly; crowd; push; as, to *jam* things into a box; block; as, to *jam* traffic; **2,** to crush or bruise; as, to *jam* one's finger in a heavy door; **3,** to push, place or shove hard; as, to *jam* the breaks of a car; **4,** to render (a machine or some movable part of it) unworkable by wedging; get stuck tight; as, to *jam* a window open with a stick; **5,** in *radio,* to send out signals that interfere with a broadcast:—*v.i.* **1,** to become tightly packed; as, the logs *jammed;* **2,** to become unworkable by the wedging of some part; stick; as, the engine *jammed;* **3,** to take part in a jam session:—*n.* **1,** a group of people or things that are crowded tightly together; as, a traffic *jam;* **2,** a difficult situation; as, we'll be in a *jam* if we miss our flight:—**jam session,** a meeting of musicians to enjoy the spontaneous and improvised performing of jazz or other type of music.

[2]**jam** (jam), *n.* a thick preserve, made by boiling fruit with sugar; as, raspberry *jam.*

jamb (jam), *n.* one of the side pieces of a door, window, fireplace, or other opening.

jam-bo-ree (jam′bo-rē′), *n.* **1,** a noisy revel or party; **2,** a Scout rally, esp. international or interregional.

jan-gle (jang′gl), *v.i.* and *v.t.* [jan-gled, jan-gling], **1,** to sound harshly or out of tune, as bells; **2,** to speak or utter in a loud, wrangling manner:—*n.* **1,** a discordant sound; **2,** a wrangling.

jan-i-tor (jan′i-tėr), *n.* a caretaker of a public building; someone who cleans and makes repairs to a building.

Jan-u-ar-y (jan′ū-a-ri), *n.* the first month of the year, with 31 days, before February.

ja-pan (ja-pan′), *n.* a hard, brilliant lacquer, varnish, coating, etc.:—*n.* objects ornamented with such lacquer:—*v.t.* **1,** to coat with a hard, black gloss; **2,** to lacquer with japan.

[1]**jar** (jär), *v.i.* [jarred, jar-ring], **1,** to give out a harsh sound; be discordant; **2,** to shake; vibrate, as doors and windows in an earthquake; **3,** to strike with harsh effect; as, his laugh *jars* on my nerves; **4,** to conflict; as, these colours *jar;* our ideas *jar:*—*v.t.* **1,** to make discordant; **2,** to cause to shake; rattle; as, the blast *jarred* the house:—*n.* **1,** a harsh sound; discord; **2,** a sudden shake or quivering; **3,** a conflict of opinion.—*adj.* **jar′ring.**

[2]**jar** (jär), *n.* **1,** a broad-mouthed vessel of earthenware or glass, with a removable lid; as, a Mason *jar;* **2,** a jar and its contents; as, I bought a *jar* of jelly; also, the amount a jar holds; as, we ate a *jar* of pickles.

jar-gon (jär′gun; jär′gon), *n.* **1,** confused talk that cannot be understood; **2,** a mixture of two or more languages, such as Pidgin English; **3,** the technical or special vocabulary of a profession, trade, etc.; as, business *jargon;* lawyers' *jargon;* computer *jargon;* **4,** language that is pompous and full of long, awkward, and often confusing words and sentences.

jas-mine or **jes-sa-mine** (jas′min; jaz′min; jes′a-min), *n.* a shrub of the olive family with shiny leaves and fragrant red, white, or yellow flowers; also, a perfume or tea made from the flowers.

jas-per (jas′pėr), *n.* an opaque, cloudy stone, usually red, brown, or yellow.

jaun-dice (jôn′dis; jän′dis), *n.* **1,** a disease of the liver characterized by yellowness of the eyeballs, skin, etc., also caused by too much bile in the system; **2,** an emotion such as jealousy, which distorts the judgment:—*v.t.* [jaundiced, jaundic-ing], **1,** to affect with jaundice; **2,** to affect with envy or prejudice.

jaunt (jônt; jänt), *n.* a short excursion or trip.

jaun-ty (jôn′ti; jän′ti), *adj.* [jaun-ti-er, jaun-ti-est], **1,** airy; carefree; as, to walk with a *jaunty* gait; **2,** smart in appearance; as, a *jaunty* outfit.—*adv.* **jaun′ti-ly.**—*n.* **jaun′ti-ness.**

ja-va (jav′a), *n. Colloq.* coffee.

Ja-va (jav′a), *n.* in *computing,* a programming language designed to create programs for computer networks and the Internet.

jave-lin (jav′lin; jav′e-lin), *n.* **1,** in *sports,* a long, thin, light spear used in a distance-throwing track-and-field event; also, this event; **2,** a similar spear used as a weapon.

jaw (jô), *n.* **1,** either of the two bony structures that frame the mouth and in which the teeth are set, the upper jaw being fixed, while the lower jaw is movable: also called *jawbone*; **2,** the lower part of the face; as, a square *jaw*; **3,** anything that resembles an animal's jaw in form or power of gripping; as, the *jaws* of a vise; **4,** mouth or entrance; as, the *jaws* of a chasm; **5,** *Slang* gossip; conversation:—*v.t.* and *v.i.* to talk (to) in a scolding way.

jay (jā), *n.* any of several noisy birds of the crow family, of Europe and North America, having bright-coloured plumage, and sometimes a crest; esp. in Canada and the U.S., the *bluejay*.

jay-walker (jā′wôk′ėr), *n.* one who crosses a street contrary to traffic regulations.—*v.i.* **jay′walk′.**—*n.* **jay′walk′ing.**

jazz (jaz), *n.* **1,** a kind of music developed by Black musicians in the southern United States, probably based on African rhythm and supposedly named for Jasbo Brown: it has a strong and lively rhythm, with musicians often improvising as they play; **2,** a dance to this music or similar music; **3,** *Slang* zeal; humbug; assorted things:—*v.t.* *Slang* **1,** to play (music) so as to make it resemble jazz; **2,** to make lively; as, to *jazz* up a party:—*v.i.* *Slang* **1,** to act in a lively manner; **2,** to lie.—*adj.* **jaz′zy.**

jeal-ous (jel′us), *adj.* **1,** characterized by suspicious fear or envy; envious; as, to be *jealous* of another's wealth; **2,** unwilling to have, or afraid of having, a rival in love; as, a *jealous* boyfriend; **3,** demanding exclusive loyalty; as, a *jealous* ruler; **4,** anxiously careful or watchful; as, to keep a *jealous* watch over a new bicycle.—*adv.* **jeal′ous-ly.**—*n.* **jeal′ous-y.**

jean (jēn), *n.* a twilled cotton cloth:—**jeans, 1,** overalls or work clothes made of this cloth; **2,** pants of this cloth: also called *blue jeans*.

jeep (jēp), *n.* a small trucklike vehicle, usually for four persons, used in the Allied armies during World War II:—**Jeep** (trademark), a similar civilian four-wheel-drive vehicle, capable of driving on rough terrain.

jeer (jēr), *v.t.* to sneer at; ridicule; as, the crowd *jeered* the losing team:—*v.i.* to speak in a sneering or sarcastic manner:—*n.* a sneer; coarse ridicule.

Je-ho-vah (ji-hō′va), *n.* [Hebrew, *Yahweh*], God; the Lord; the Almighty.

jell (jel), *v.i.* and *v.t.* **1,** to become jelly; **2,** *Colloq.* to crystallize or take definite form; as, our plans have not yet *jelled*.

jel-ly (jel′i), *n.* [*pl.* jellies], **1,** the juice of fruit, meat, etc., which becomes semi-solid and semi-transparent after boiling and cooling; **2,** any similar substance:—*v.i.* [jellied, jelly-ing], to become jelly; jell:—*v.t.* to cause to become jelly.

jel-ly-bean (jel′i-bēn′), *n.* a small, various-coloured, gelatinous candy in the shape of a bean.

jel-ly-fish (jel′i-fish′), *n.* [*pl.* jellyfish or jellyfishes], any of several swimming sea animals, with boneless, umbrella-shaped bodies, somewhat soft and transparent like jelly, some of which have long tentacles with stinging hairs.

jeop-ard-y (jep′ėr-di), *n.* risk; danger; as, the escape of the criminal put the safety of the community in *jeopardy*.—*v.t.* **jeop′ard-ize** [jeopardized, jeopardiz-ing].

jerk (jûrk), *v.t.* **1,** to give a quick pull, twist, or push to; as, he *jerked* off his coat; to *jerk* a fish out of water; **2,** to throw with a sudden, quick movement; **3,** to preserve meat slices by drying in the sun or over fire:—*v.i.* to move with or make a sudden convulsive movement:—*n.* **1,** a sudden, quick pull, twist, push, or throw; as, a *jerk* of the head; **2,** beef or other meat sliced into strips and dried in the sun or over a fire; **3,** *Slang* a disagreeable or stupid person.

jer-kin (jûr′kin), *n.* **1,** a short, close-fitting, sleeveless coat, often made of leather, formerly worn by men; **2,** a similar garment worn today.

jerk-wa-ter (jûrk′wô′tėr), *adj.* *Colloq.* small; unimportant; as, a *jerkwater* town.

jerk-y (jûr′ki), *adj.* [jerk-i-er, jerk-i-est], full of jerks; moving with sudden starts and stops; as, a *jerky* walk; not smooth; as, a *jerky* style of writing.—*adv.* **jerk′i-ly.**

jer-ry-built (jer′i-bilt′), *adj.* flimsy; built of cheap or inferior material; put together carelessly; as, a *jerrybuilt* house.

jer-sey (jûr′zi), *n.* **1,** a type of soft, stretchy cloth knitted from cotton, wool, or other material; **2,** a pullover shirt or sweater made from this material, often used as part of a sports uniform; as, a football *jersey*; **3,** a close-fitting garment for the upper body, often knitted:—**Jersey,** a type of light-brown dairy cow.

jess (jes), *n.* a strap fastened to a falcon's leg and attached to a leash.

jes-sa-mine (jes′a-min), *n.* Same as **jasmine.**

jest (jest), *n.* **1,** a joke; fun; mockery; as, many a true word is spoken in *jest*; **2,** the person or thing laughed at or jeered:—*v.i.* to joke; as, I was only *jesting*.

jest-er (jes′tėr), *n.* **1,** one who makes jokes; **2,** in medieval times, a court fool.

Jes-u-it (jez′ū-it), *n.* a member of the Society of Jesus, a Roman Catholic order founded by Ignatius Loyola in 1534:—**jesuit,** a crafty person; schemer.

Je-sus (jē′zuz), in the Bible, the Son of Mary, founder of Christianity. Also called *Jesus of Nazareth*, *Jesus Christ*, or *Christ*.

¹jet (jet), *v.t.* and *v.i.* [jet-ted, jet-ting], to shoot or spout out; spurt:—*n.* **1,** a stream of liquid or gas issuing from a small opening by great pressure; as, the whale spouts a *jet* of water; a *jet* of water from a geyser; **2,** a spout or nozzle for the issuing of a fluid or gas; as, a gas *jet*; **3,** a jet-propelled airplane; a jet plane:—**jet propulsion,** the propelling of airplanes, boats, etc., by use of heated gases emitted under pressure through a vent or orifice. Also, **jet′ boat′; jet′ en′gine; jet′ fight′er; jet′lin′er; jet′ set′; jet′ stream′.**

²jet (jet), *n.* **1,** a hard, black mineral, similar to coal, that is polished and used in making ornaments and buttons; **2,** the colour of jet; a deep, glossy black:—*adj.* **1,** made of, or like, jet; **2,** very black:—*adj.* **jet′-black′.**

jet lag, a feeling of fatigue after a long airplane flight through several time zones.

jet-sam (jet′sam), *n.* **1,** goods thrown overboard to ease a ship in danger of sinking; **2,** such goods when washed ashore; **3,** useless items that are thrown away. Compare *flotsam.*

jet-ti-son (jet′i-son), *v.t.* **1,** to throw cargo overboard, esp. to lighten a ship or airplane in distress; **2,** to throw away anything useless or a burden:—*n.* **1,** the act of jettisoning; **2,** the items jettisoned; jetsam.

jet-ty (jet′i), *n.* [*pl.* jetties], **1,** a structure extending into the water, used as a pier, breakwater, or wall to direct currents or break the force of waves; **2,** a landing pier; wharf.

jew-el (jo͞o′el; jū′el), *n.* **1,** a gem or precious stone, such as a diamond, ruby, or emerald; **2,** a valuable ornament or trinket set with gems; as, she willed her *jewels* to her granddaughter; **3,** a piece of precious stone used as a bearing in the works of a watch; **4,** a person or thing of great value or dearness:—*v.t.* [jewelled, jewel-ling], to adorn with, or supply with jewels, as a dress or watch.

jewel case, the plastic hinged case designed to hold CDs.

jew-el-ler or **jew-el-er** (jo͞o′el-ėr; jū′el-ėr), *n.* a person who makes, sells, or repairs jewellery and watches.

jew-el-ler-y or **jew-el-ry** (jo͞o′el-ri; jū′el-ri), *n.* personal ornaments, such as rings, necklaces, earrings, brooches, etc., often set with precious stones, and usually made of precious metal such as gold or silver.

jew's–harp or **jews′–harp** (jo͞oz′–härp′; jūz′–härp′), *n.* a small musical instrument, with a thin, flexible metal tongue which, when placed between the teeth and struck by the finger, produces a twanglike tone.

jib (jib), *n.* **1,** a three-cornered sail extending from the foremast of a vessel; **2,** the projecting arm or beam of a crane or other lifting machine:—*v.i.* [jibbed, jibbing] to refuse to move forward, going side to side.

¹jibe (jīb), *n.* Same as **gibe.**

²jibe (jīb), *v.i.* [jibed, jib-ing], *Colloq.* to agree; hang together.

³jibe or **gybe** (jīb), *v.i.* [jibed, jib-ing], to shift suddenly from one side to the other, as when a sail or boom snaps across in a following wind:—*v.t.* to cause to jibe.

jif-fy (jif′i), *n.* [jiffies], *Colloq.* an instant; a moment; as, to do it in a *jiffy.*

jig (jig), *n.* **1,** a quick, lively dance; also, music for such a dance; **2,** a particular kind of fishhook:—*v.i.* [jigged, jig-ging], **1,** to dance a jig; **2,** to fish with a jig.

¹jig-ger or **chig-ger** (jig′ėr), *n.* a small flea.

²jig-ger (jig′ėr), *n.* **1,** in *mechanics,* a device with a jerky up-and-down motion; **2,** a railway handcar, propelled by a gas motor or by pumping a lever up and down; **3,** in *nautical usage,* a small tackle, sail, or mast near the stern; **4,** *Colloq.* any gadget or device; **5,** a small measuring glass for liquor in prepared alcoholic drinks; a shot glass; also, the amount or contents in a jigger.

jig-gle (jig′l), *v.t.* and *v.i.* [-gled, -gling], to move with quick, short jerks; as, to *jiggle* the keys; his plump tummy *jiggled* when he danced:—*n.* a light, rapidly repeated jerky motion.

jig-saw (jig′sô), *n.* a narrow saw, moving vertically in a frame, used to cut curved or irregular patterns, as in scroll work:—**jigsaw puzzle,** a picture puzzle made up of various-shaped cardboard or wooden pieces that fit together, cut by a jigsaw.

ji-had or **je-had** (ji-häd′), *n.* **1,** a Muslim holy war; **2,** an exploit undertaken for a cause; as, the *jihad* against smoking.

jilt (jilt), *n.* a person who discards a previously accepted lover or suitor:—*v.t.* to discard or desert (a lover); as, she *jilted* her boyfriend.

jim-my (jim′i), *n.* [*pl.* jimmies], a short crowbar used esp. by burglars to gain entrance through doors or windows:—*v.t.* to pry open; as, to *jimmy* a safe, lock, window, etc.

jin-gle (jing′gl), *n.* **1,** a sharp, tinkling sound, as of bells or coins clinking; **2,** a pleasing or catchy verse or tune, easy to remember, often used in radio and television advertisements:—*v.i.* [jin-gled, jingling], **1,** to give a tinkling sound; as, the keys *jingled* in his pocket; **2,** to sound with a pleasing or catchy succession of rhymes:—*v.t.* to cause to jingle; as, to *jingle* coins, bells, etc.:—*v.i.* to make a jingling sound; as, the coins *jingled* in her pocket.

jin-go (jing′gō), *n.* [*pl.* jingoes], a supporter of an aggressive policy in foreign affairs; a blustering patriot.—*n.* **jin′go-ism; jin′go-ist.**—*adj.* **jin′go-is′tic; jin′go-ist.**—*adv.* **jin′go-is′ti-cal-ly.**

jinks (jingks), *n.pl. Colloq.* lively or boisterous pranks; frolic; as high *jinks.*

jin-ni or **jin-nee** (ji-nē′), *n.* [*pl.* jinn], in Islamic and Arabian folklore, a spirit made of fire, able to appear in both human and animal forms, and having a supernatural influence over humans for good and evil. Also called *genie* or *genius*.

jin-rik-sha or **jin-rick-sha** or **jin-rik-isha** (jin-rik′shä; jin-rik′shô), *n.* a small two-wheeled, person-drawn carriage; ricksha.

JINRIKSHA

jinx (jingks), *n. Slang* someone or something that brings bad luck; a hoodoo:—*v.t.* to bring bad luck (to).

jit-ney (jit′ni), *n. Slang* a car or bus that carries people for a small fare.

jit-ter-bug (jit′tėr-bug′), *n. Colloq.* one who, either alone or with a partner, dances rhythmically to swing music, using improvised acrobatic movements:—*v.i.* to dance in such a manner.

jit-ters (jit′ėrz), *n.pl. Slang* extreme nervousness; as, he has the *jitters.*—*adj.* **jit′ter-y.**

jiu-jit-su (jo͞o-jit′so͞o), *n.* Same as **ju-jit′su.**

jive (jīv), *n. Slang* **1,** swing or jazz music; also, this type of dance; **2,** the special vocabulary of swing or jazz enthusiasts; **3,** nonsense talk; slang:—*v.t.* and *v.i.* [jived, jiv-ing], **1,** to play or dance jive; **2,** *Slang* to kid; cajole.

JK (jā′kā′), *abbrev.* short for *junior kindergarten.*

job (job), *n.* **1,** a piece of work; task; as, a small painting *job*; **2,** anything one has to do; a responsibility; a duty; as, that's your *job*, not mine; **3,** any scheme for making money or securing private advantage, esp. dishonestly, at the expense of duty; **4,** work for pay; a position; employment; as, out of a *job*:—*adj.* **1,** done by the piece; as, *job* work; handled in the gross, or as a total; as, a *job* lot; **2,** related to employment or the place of work; as, a *job* injury:—*v.i.* [jobbed, job-bing], **1,** to do an occasional piece of work for wages; **2,** to work for one's own gain in a position of trust; **3,** to act as a wholesaler:—*v.t.* **1,** to buy up (goods) for resale in smaller quantities; **2,** to do, or cause to be done, by the lot or piece; subcontract; **3,** to speculate.

job-ber (job′ėr), *n.* **1,** one who buys in quantity, from a wholesaler or importer, and sells to a retailer; **2,** one who deals in odd or job lots; **3,** a pieceworker; **4,** an independent logger; **5,** a person who works dishonestly for one's own gain.

jock-ey (jok′i), *n.* [*pl.* jockeys], **1,** a professional horse rider hired to participate in a race; **2,** *Slang* one who drives or operates anything; as, a disc *jockey*; computer *jockey*:—*v.t.* and *v.i.* **1,** to ride (a horse) as a jockey; **2,** to bargain or direct (something or someone) for position or advantage; **3,** to trick.

jock-strap (jok′strap′), *n.* an athletic supporter for the genitals, worn by men participating in sports.

jo-cose (jo-kōs′), *adj.* full of jokes; humorous; playful.—*adv.* **jo-cose′ly.**—*n.* **jo-cose′ness; jo-cos′i-ty.**

joc-u-lar (jok′ū-lėr), *adj.* **1,** given to joking; as, a *jocular* person; **2,** humorous; comic; as, a *jocular* reply.

joc-und (jok′und; jō′kund), *adj.* jovial; merry; as, a *jocund* laugh.—*adv.* **joc′und-ly.**—*n.* **jo-cun′di-ty.**

jodh-purs (jod′pėrz), *n.pl.* a type of riding breeches, loose above the knee but tight below.

[1]**jog** (jog), *v.t.* [jogged, jog-ging], **1,** to push or shake slightly; nudge; **2,** to arouse; as, to *jog* the memory; **3,** to cause to travel at a slow trot; as, to *jog* a horse:—*v.i.* **1,** to run slowly, for exercise; **2,** to travel along at a slow trot, as an old horse:—*n.* **1,** a slight push or shake; **2,** an arousal; **3,** a slow trot; **4,** a slow, steady run.

[2]**jog** (jog), *n.* a notch; a sudden irregularity; as, a *jog* in the road:—*v.i.* [jogged, jogging], to make a jog; as, the road *jogs* to the right.

[1]**jog-gle** (jog′l), *v.t.* [jog-gled, jog-gling], to jerk slightly; nudge:—*v.i.* to totter; move in a jerking manner:—*n.* a sudden shake; jolt.

[2]**jog-gle** (jog′l), *n.* a joint in two adjacent pieces of building material, such as wood, consisting of a notch and tooth that fit together; also, such a notch or tooth:—*v.t.* [jog-gled, jog-gling], to fasten two things in this way.

john-ny-cake (jon′i-kāk′), *n.* a flat cake of cornmeal mixed with milk or water, eggs, etc., and baked.

Johnny Canuck, *Colloq.* **1,** a Canadian citizen or inhabitant, esp. a soldier during the world wars; **2,** the personification of Canada; as, *Johnny Canuck* is more than just a Mountie.

join (join), *v.t.* **1,** to unite; connect; put or bring together; as, to *join* a hose to a faucet; *join* hands; **2,** to unite in marriage; **3,** to become a member of; as, to *join* a club; **4,** to engage in, with others; participate; as, to *join* battle; **5,** to be next to; as, his yard *joins* ours; **6,** to meet; merge or come together; as, to *join* us at the game; *join* us at our table:—*v.i.* **1,** to be in contact; **2,** to become associated or united; also, to form an alliance; merge; as, two roads *join* at this point; the two small groups *joined* to make one large one:—**join forces,** to come together to support each other; as, our two teams *joined* forces to finish the job on time:—*n.* a joint; a joining.

join-er (join′ėr), *n.* **1,** one who or that which joins; **2,** a skilled worker who finishes the inside woodwork for houses; **3,** *Colloq.* someone who joins many organizations, clubs, etc.

joint (joint), *n.* **1,** the place where two or more things join; esp. the point where two bones of the body are joined, usually in such a way that they can move, such as the wrists, elbows, knees, and ankles; **2,** the part between two joinings; as, a *joint* in a grass stem; a *joint* between two plumbing pipes; **3,** a large piece of meat cut for roasting; **4,** *Slang* a low or disreputable establishment for eating and entertainment; also any place in general; **5,** *Slang* a marijuana cigarette:—*adj.* **1,** united; combined; as, *joint* efforts; **2,** used, held, or owned by two or more; as, *joint* property:—*v.t.* **1,** to connect by joints; **2,** to cut into pieces at the joints.—*adv.* **joint′ly.**

joint photographic experts group, in *computing* a file compression format for storing and transmitting high-quality photographic images electronically: abbreviated as *JPEG*.

joist (joist), *n.* a piece of timber to which the boards of a floor or ceiling are fastened for support.

joke (jōk), *n.* **1,** something said or done to cause mirth; a jest; something amusing; **2,** a laughingstock; as, he was the *joke* of the town; **3,** something trivial or not meant:—*v.i.* [joked, jok-ing], to jest; to tell or make jokes.

jok-er (jō′kėr), *n.* **1,** one who tells humorous stories or plays pranks; **2,** an extra card used in certain card games as the highest trump; **3,** *Colloq.* a clause in a legislative bill, a written agreement, etc., which is inconspicuous, but which actually changes the entire meaning of the document.

jol-ly (jol′i), *adj.* [jol-li-er, jol-li-est], **1,** full of fun; cheerful; as, a *jolly* time; **2,** causing or expressing happiness or joy; as, a *jolly* laugh:—*v.t.* [jollied, jolly-ing], *Colloq.* to flatter; make good-humoured fun of.—*n.* **jol′li-ness; jol′li-ty.**

Jolly Rog-er (roj′ėr), *n.* the emblem of piracy, which is a black flag with white skull and crossbones.

jolt (jōlt), *v.t.* to shake by sudden jerks; as, to *jolt* her out of her daydream:—*v.i.* to have a jerky motion; as, the old car *jolted* down the bumpy road:—*n.* **1,** a sudden jerk; as, the train stopped with a *jolt*; **2,** a sudden shock, dismay, or setback; as, the news of her accident was a *jolt*.

josh (josh), *v.t.* and *v.i. Colloq.* to tease; banter; ridicule good-naturedly:—*n.* a banter; as, he took the *joshing* in good part.

jos-tle (jos′l), *v.t.* and *v.i.* [jos-tled, jos-tling], **1,** to push against; elbow; as, we *jostled* one another in the subway; to *jostle* through the crowd; **2,** to collide; **3,** to be or live closely together; **4,** to contend.

jot (jot), *v.t.* [jot-ted, jot-ting], to make a brief note of; as, to *jot* down an address:—*n.* a very small particle or quantity; as, not a *jot* of hope.

jou-al or **joo-al** (zhwal; zhōō-al′), *n.* a dialect of Canadian French that was once considered uneducated and substandard: the word derives from the unique pronunciation for *cheval* (horse).

joule (joul; jōōl), *n.* **1,** in *electricity*, the unit of work or energy, namely, the unit of energy equal to the work done by a force of one newton acting through a distance of one metre; 10 million ergs; **2,** the International System of Units of measuring the amount of energy.

jounce (jouns), *v.t.* and *v.i.* [jounced, jounc-ing], to shake up and down; bounce or cause to bounce; jolt:—*n.* a jolt.

jour-nal (jûr′nal), *n.* **1,** a daily record of news or events; **2,** a newspaper, magazine, or other periodical; **3,** a diary; **4,** a book in which business transactions are entered daily; **5,** a ship's logbook; **6,** a record of the daily proceedings of a legislative body, organization, society, etc.; **7,** that portion of an axle or of a rotating shaft that rests on bearings.

jour-nal-ism (jûr′nal-izm), *n.* the occupation of researching, gathering, writing, editing, reporting, or presenting news for a newspaper, magazine, periodical, or for a radio or television station.—*adj.* **jour′nal-is′tic.**—*n.* **jour′nal-ist.**

jour-ney (jûr′ni), *n.* [*pl.* journeys], **1,** a trip from one place to another, esp. a long trip; as, a *journey* from Prince Edward Island to Nunavut; **2,** the amount of time consumed or space covered in travel:—*v.i.* to travel; take a long trip; as, to *journey* around the world.

jour-ney-man (jûr′ni-man), *n.* a craftsman or mechanic who has served his or her apprenticeship, or learned a trade and works for another, esp., formerly, by the day; also, a reliable or competent worker.

joust (jōōst; joust), *n.* **1,** a combat with lances between two mounted knights, usually as part of a tournament; **2,** a contest or competition:—*v.i.* **1,** to engage in combat with lances; **2,** to compete or engage in a competition.

jo-vi-al (jō′vi-al), *adj.* jolly; merry; happy; as, a *jovial* friend. *adv.* **jo′vi-al-ly.**—*n.* **jo′vi-al′i-ty; jo′vi-al-ness.**

jowl (joul; jōl), *n.* **1,** the jaw; esp. the under jaw; **2,** the cheek.

joy (joi), *n.* **1,** a feeling of happiness; gladness; delight; as, the holidays bring *joy*; to jump for *joy*; **2,** that which causes gladness or happiness; as, a thing of beauty is a *joy* forever; the *joy* of gardening:—*v.i.* to rejoice.—*adj.* **joy′less.**

joy-ful (joi′fool), *adj.* full of, showing, or causing gladness; as, *joyful* days; *joyful* news.—*adv.* **joy′ful-ly.**—*n.* **joy′ful-ness.**

joy-ous (joi′us), *adj.* having or causing happiness; glad; as, a *joyous* occasion.—*adv.* **joy′ous-ly.**—*n.* **joy′ous-ness.**

joy ride, 1, a pleasurable ride; **2,** a ride in a

recklessly driven vehicle, esp. in a stolen car; **3,** something done without regard to consequences.—*n.* **joy′ ri′der.**—*v.i.* **joy′–ride′.**

joy-stick (joi′stik′), *n. Slang* **1,** a lever in an aircraft that controls the vehicle's movement from side to side and up and down; **2,** in *computing,* a computer device for playing computer games, similar to the control column of an aircraft.

JPEG (jā′peg′), *abbrev.* short for *joint photographic experts group.*

ju-bi-lant (jo͞o′bi-lant), *adj.* showing great joy; exultant; as, *jubilant* over winning a game.—*adv.* **ju′bi-lant-ly.**

ju-bi-la-tion (jo͞o′bi-lā′shun), *n.* **1,** triumphant exultation; rejoicing; **2,** a celebration.

ju-bi-lee (jo͞o′bi-lē′), *n.* **1,** an important anniversary, such as the 25th or 50th, of any event; **2,** any occasion of rejoicing; also, a state of rejoicing; **3,** a year of special indulgence, which was formerly granted by the Pope every 25 years; **4,** a celebration every 50 years, in accordance with the Old Testament.

Ju-das (jo͞o′das), *n.* a traitor, esp. one who pretends friendship while betraying:—**judas,** a peephole; as, he peered out the *judas* hole.

judge (juj), *n.* **1,** the public official who presides in a court of law and hears and decides cases; **2,** a person appointed to decide the winner in a contest of skill, speed, etc., between two or more persons; as, an Olympic *judge;* **3,** one who has enough knowledge or experience to decide on the quality or value of anything; as, a *judge* of gems:—*v.t.* [judged, judg-ing], **1,** to hear and pass sentence on (a person or a matter), as in a court of law; **2,** to decide on the winner of a contest or settle an argument; as, to *judge* the figure-skating competition; **3,** to estimate; criticize; as, we *judged* him unfairly; **4,** to think or suppose; as, I *judged* this to be true:—*v.i.* **1,** to form an opinion after careful consideration; as, to *judge* in a debate; **2,** to hear and determine a case and pass sentence; **3,** to decide on the winner of a contest; as, to *judge* at the diving competition; **4,** to think; consider.

judg-ment or **judge-ment** (juj′ment), *n.* **1,** the act of passing sentence; also, the official decision of a judge or jury in a court of law; **2,** the mental process by which we are able to see differences and likenesses, and by which we are able to weigh values and make decisions; **3,** good sense; discernment; as, a person of good *judgment;* **4,** an estimate after careful consideration; opinion; as, in my *judgment* he is honest; **5,** any calamity attributed to the anger of God.

ju-di-ca-ture (jo͞o′di-ka-tūr; -chėr), *n.* **1,** a court of justice; judges collectively; **2,** the power to do justice by legal trial and judgment; **3,** the territory and matter over which the authority of a court extends.

ju-di-cial (jo͞o-dish′al), *adj.* **1,** pertaining to a judge, a court of law, or the administration of justice; as, *judicial* power; **2,** proceeding from, or inflicted by, a court of justice; as, a *judicial* decision; **3,** considering all aspects of a situation before deciding; impartial.

ju-di-ci-ar-y (jo͞o-dish′i-a-ri), *n.* [*pl.* judiciaries], the system of courts of justice in a country; also, the judges collectively:—*adj.* pertaining to judges, courts of justice, or the procedure of a court.

ju-di-cious (jo͞o-dish′us), *adj.* showing good judgment; wise; as, a *judicious* act.

ju-do (jo͞o′dō), *n.* a sport based on *jujitsu.*

jug (jug), *n.* **1,** a narrow-necked vessel, usually with a handle, for holding liquids; also, a pitcher; **2,** the vessel and its contents; as, a *jug* of water; also, the amount of liquid the vessel can hold; **3,** *Slang* jail.

jug-gle (jug′l), *v.t.* [jug-gled, jug-gling], **1,** to perform tricks with; to keep two or more objects in motion in the air at the same time by tossing and catching them as they fall; as, to *juggle* balls; **2,** to misrepresent; as, to *juggle* facts; **3,** to deal with several problems or tasks at the same time; as, to *juggle* school and a part-time job:—*v.i.* **1,** to perform entertaining tricks of a juggler; **2,** to play tricks so as to deceive; **3,** to manipulate several things at one time.—*n.* **jug′gler; jug′gler-y.**

jug-u-lar (jug′ū-lėr), *adj.* pertaining to neck, throat, or jugular vein.

jugular vein, one of two large veins on either side of the throat that return the blood from the head to the heart.

juice (jo͞os), *n.* **1,** the liquid part of fruits, meats, vegetables, etc.; **2,** a natural fluid in the body; as, digestive *juices.*—*adj.* **juic′y.**—*n.* **juic′i-ness.**

ju-jit-su or **jiu-jit-su** (jo͞o-jit′so͞o), *n.* the Japanese art of wrestling, which turns an opponent's own strength and weight against him or her.

juke-box (jo͞ok′ boks′), *n. Colloq.* an electric, automatic phonograph that usually operates when a coin is deposited in it.

ju-lep (jo͞o′lip), *n.* **1,** a drink made of brandy or whisky sweetened and flavoured; as, mint *julep;* **2,** a mixture of sugar, water, and flavouring.

ju-li-enne (jo͞o′li-en′; zhü′lyen′), *n.* a clear soup with chopped vegetables, esp. carrots, cut in thin strips:—*adj.* sliced in thin, long strips; as, carrots *julienne:*—*v.t.* [julienned, julien-ning] to cut into thin, long strips; as, to *julienne* carrots.—*adj.* **ju-li-enned′.**

Ju-ly (jo͞o-lī′), *n.* the seventh month of the year, with 31 days, between June and August.

jum-ble (jum′bl), *n.* **1,** a confused mass or mixture; disorder; hodgepodge; **2,** a thin round cake or cookie:—*v.t.* and *v.i.* [jum-bled, jum-bling], to mix in a confused mass; throw together messily.

jum-bo (jum′bō), *n. Colloq.* a large, clumsy animal, person, or thing:—*adj.* very large; as, *jumbo* olives; *jumbo* jet.

jump (jump), *n.* **1,** a leap, spring, or bound; a sudden rise; as, a *jump* in temperature; **2,** the space covered by a leap or bound; **3,** something to be leaped or hurdled; as, the third *jump* was easy; **4,** a sudden movement or start; **5,** an advantage; quick start; as, to get a *jump* on the opponents:—*v.i.* **1,** to leap or spring; **2,** to start suddenly; as, she *jumped* when she saw the mouse; **3,** to rise suddenly; as, prices *jumped* as the supply gave out:—*v.t.* **1,** to cause to leap; as, to *jump* a horse over a brook; **2,** to leap on or over; as, to *jump* the hedge; **3,** to jump upon or aboard; as, to *jump* a passing freight train; **4,** to seize in the owner's absence; as, to *jump* a mining claim. Also, **jump′ ball′; jump′ing jack′; jump′ing-off′ point′; jump′ rope′; jump′ seat′; jump′ shot′; jump′-start′; jump′ suit′.**

[1]**jump-er** (jump′ėr), *n.* a person or thing that jumps:—*n.* and *adj.* a short wire used as a temporary circuit connection or bypass; as, *jumper* cables.

[2]**jump-er** (jump′ėr), *n.* **1,** a loose outer jacket worn by workers; **2,** a girl's or woman's outer blouse reaching to the hips; **3,** a dress with no sleeves or collar, usually worn over sweaters or blouses.

jumpy (jum′pi), *adj.* **1,** moving in or like jumps; **2,** nervous; on edge.—*n.* **jump′i-ness.**

junc-tion (jungk′shun), *n.* **1,** the act of joining or state of being joined; **2,** a point of union, such as a station where two or more railway lines meet or cross.

junc-ture (jungk′tūr), *n.* **1,** the point at which two things join in time or space; joint; junction; **2,** a union of events, esp. a crisis.

June (jo͞on), *n.* the sixth month of the year, with 30 days, between May and July.

june-ber-ry (jo͞on′ber-i), *n.* Same as **saskatoon.**

June bug, a large brown beetle that emerges from the ground in late spring: its white larvae, or grubs, feed on the roots of plants, esp. grass.

jun-gle (jung′gl), *n.* **1,** any tract of land overrun with dense, tangled vegetation, usually tropical; **2,** something that is entangled; **3,** a fiercely competitive environment; as, the large city was an economic *jungle.*

jun-ior (jo͞on′yėr), *adj.* **1,** younger: used of a son named for his father; as, John Smith, *Junior;* **2,** of lower standing or rank; as, the *junior* partner in a firm; **3,** relating to young people; **4,** relating to students in grades 4 to 6:—*n.* **1,** a younger person; **2,** one of lower standing or rank; **3,** a grade 4 to 6 student.

junior kindergarten, a class, program, or school for children aged three or four that prepares them for kindergarten: abbreviated as *JK.*

ju-ni-per (jo͞o′ni-pėr), *n.* any of several evergreen trees or shrubs of the pine family, with blue, berrylike fruits, as the common juniper.

[1]**junk** (jungk), *n.* a jumble of worn-out articles that have no use or value; trash:—*v.t.* to cast off as worthless or unusable; also, to destroy or make unusable.

[2]**junk** (jungk), *n.* a kind of flat-bottomed Chinese or Japanese vessel with a high stern and square sails.

junk bond, risky but high-yielding bond of the type often used in leveraged buyouts and other corporate takeovers involving questionable credit.

jun-ket (jung′kit), *n.* **1,** milk that has been curdled, sweetened, and flavoured; **2,** a feast; a picnic; **3,** an often unnecessary excursion at public or company expense:—*v.i.* **1,** to feast or picnic; **2,** to go on a junket.

junk food, *Colloq.* popular foods that have little or no nutritional value and are often high in calories, such as candy, cookies, potato chips, and other snacks.

junk mail, unsolicited mail that generally consists of advertisements. Also, **junk′ e′-mail′; junk′ fax′.**

Ju-no (jo͞o′nō′), *n.* in *Roman mythology,* the wife of Jupiter and the goddess of birth, women, and marriage:—**Juno** Awards, Canadian music recording awards presented by the Canadian Academy of Recording Arts and Sciences.

jun-ta (jun′ta), *n.* **1,** in Spain and Latin America, an assembly for making or administering laws; **2,** a military group that seizes power and forms a government, esp. after a revolt; **3,** a junto.

jun-to (jun′tō), *n.* a secret group of people with a common cause.

Ju-pi-ter (jo͞o′pi-tėr), *n.* **1,** the ancient Roman supreme god (same as the Greek *Zeus*); **2,** the largest planet in the solar system, fifth from the sun, which takes 11.86 years to revolve around it.

ju-rid-i-cal (jo͞o-rid′i-kal), *adj.* pertaining to law, legal proceedings, or the office of a judge.

ju-ris-dic-tion (jo͞or′is-dik′shun), *n.* **1,** the right to apply legal authority; as, the *jurisdiction* of a court or nation; **2,** authority of a sovereign power; **3,** the district over which any authority extends.

ju-ris-pru-dence (jo͞o-ris-pro͞o′dens), *n.* **1,**

the science of law; **2,** a system of laws; a department or branch of law.

ju-rist (jŏŏr′ist), *n.* one skilled in the science of law; judge; lawyer.

ju-ror (jŏŏr′ėr), *n.* a member of a jury.

[1]**jury** (jŏŏr′i), *n.* [*pl.* juries], **1,** a body of persons selected and sworn to inquire into, or to try, matters of fact submitted to them in a court of law and to provide a verdict; **2,** a committee of experts selected to pass judgment on something, such as a contest, to award prizes, etc.

[2]**ju-ry** (jōō′i), *adj. Nautical,* for temporary use on a ship in an emergency; as, a *jury* mast.

ju-ry-man (jōō′ri-man), *n.* a juror.

just (just), *adj.* **1,** fair; impartial; as, the judge gave a *just* decision; **2,** based on reasonable grounds; as, a *just* accusation; **3,** exact; as, *just* weight; **4,** legally right; as, a *just* case; **5,** according to divine or human laws; upright; righteous; as, a *just* life; **6,** deserved; earned; as, *just* rewards:—*adv.* **1,** exactly; as, *just* how many? **2,** but now; a moment ago; as, he was *just* here; **3,** only; barely; as, *just* a little; **4,** very close; immediately; as, *just* around the corner; **5,** *Colloq.* simply; quite; as, *just* beautiful.

jus-tice (jus′tis), *n.* **1,** the principle or practice of dealing uprightly and fairly with others according to honour or law; **2,** absolute fairness; the condition of being proper or correct; as, the *justice* of a decision; **3,** legal administration; as, a court of *justice*; **4,** a judge:—**justice of the peace,** a public official with powers that are more limited than those of a judge:—**do justice to, 1,** to treat fairly; **2,** to see the good points of; **3,** show appreciation for; as, her compliments *did justice to* the wonderful party.

jus-ti-fy (jus′ti-fī′), *v.t.* [justified, justifying], **1,** to show or prove to be right or fair; warrant; as, the result *justified* the expense; **2,** to clear; free from blame; **3,** in *printing,* to line up lines so that they end evenly; as, to *justify* a margin:—*v.i.* **1,** to show lawful grounds for an act; **2,** in *printing,* to justify lines.—*adj.* **jus′ti-fied; jus′ti-fi′a-ble.**—*n.* **jus′ti-fi-ca′tion** (jus′ti-fi-kā′shun).

jut (jut), *v.i.* [jut-ted, jut-ting], to project; stick out; as, a peninsula *juts* into the sea:—*n.* a projection.

ju-ve-nile (jōō′vi-nī-l; jōō′vi-nīl), *adj.* **1,** childlike; youthful; immature; **2,** like, about, or for young people; as, *juvenile* literature:—*n.* **1,** a child or young person; **2,** a book for children; **3,** an actor in youthful roles.

juvenile delinquent, a person, under the age of legal responsibility, who commits illegal or criminal acts; in Canada, a young offender.

jux-ta-po-si-tion (juks′ta-pō-zish′un), *n.* a placing side by side or close together; also, this position:—*v.t.* **jux′ta-pose′** [juxtaposed, juxtapos-ing].

K

K, k (kā), *n.* [*pl.* K's, k's], the 11th letter of the alphabet, following J.

K (kā), *abbrev.* short for *kilobyte*.

kale (kāl), *n.* **1,** a plant belonging to the same family as the cabbage, with crisp, curly leaves, used as a vegetable; **2,** *Slang* money.

ka-lei-do-scope (ka-lī′dō-skōp′), *n.* **1,** an instrument containing small, loose bits of coloured glass and an arrangement of mirrors, in which the bits of glass are reflected in a variety of beautiful patterns when their position is changed by rotation of the instrument; **2,** anything that shows a succession of changing aspects.—*adj.* **ka-lei′do-scop′ic** (ka-lī′do-skop′ik).

kan-ga-roo (kang′ga-rōō′), *n.* [*pl.* kangaroos], an Australian marsupial, which has short forelegs, powerful hind legs with which it leaps, and a strong tail, used as a support in standing or leaping: the female has an external pouch in which she carries her young:—**kangaroo court,** an irregular or unauthorized court, as in a frontier area, among prison inmates, etc.; a mock court.

kar-a-oke (kâr′ē-ō′kē), *n.* **1,** a machine that plays prerecorded music, to which individuals sing popular songs; **2,** the performance of such songs.

kar-at (kar′at), *n.* a 24th part; a measure of the purity of gold, pure gold being 24 karats; as, 14 *karat* gold contains 14 parts gold and 10 parts alloy.

ka-ra-te (ka-rä′tē), *n.* a Japanese style of self-defence fighting in which the hands, elbows, feet, and knees are used as weapons.

ka-sha (kä′shä′), *n.* buckwheat, esp. the cooked food.

ka-ty-did (kā′ti-did′), *n.* a large, green insect similar to a grasshopper, so named because of the sound it makes.

kay-ak (kī′ak), *n.* **1,** originally, a lightweight Inuit canoe, made of animal skin stretched over a frame, and seating one person who propels it with one long paddle with a blade at both ends; **2,** any similar vessel.

ka-zoo (kå-zōō′), *n.* a toy musical instrument consisting of a tube containing a thin membrane of paper that vibrates to make a buzzing or humming sound when one blows into the tube.

Kb (kā′bē′), *abbrev.* short for *kilobit.*

KB (kā′bē′), *abbrev.* short for *kilobyte.*

k-byte (kā′bīt′), *abbrev.* short for *kilobyte.*

keel (kēl), *n.* **1,** the lowest timber or steel plate in the framework of a vessel, extending lengthwise along the bottom, and often projecting below the planking; **2,** a fin-shaped piece attached to the bottom of a sailboat that hangs down into the water to balance the boat; **3,** anything resembling a ship's keel:—*v.t.* and *v.i.* to turn up the keel (of); turn over; upset; fall; as, she nearly *keeled* over when she heard the bad news.

keen (kēn), *adj.* **1,** sharp; cutting; as, a *keen* blade; **2,** piercing; bitter; as, a *keen* wind; *keen* sarcasm; **3,** acute or sharp; as, *keen* eyesight; **4,** alert; quick; bright; as, a *keen* mind; **5,** eager; ardent; as, a *keen* fisher; **6,** *Slang* great; excellent.—*adv.* **keen′ly.**—*n.* **keen′ness.**

keen-er (kēn′ėr), *n. Colloq.* a student or other individual who is particularly eager, esp. one who is overzealous.

keep (kēp), *v.t.* [kept (kept), keep-ing], **1,** to watch; defend; as, to *keep* goal; **2,** to take care of; as, to *keep* dogs; to provide with lodging or food; as, to *keep* boarders; **3,** to manage; as, to *keep* a shop; *keep* house; **4,** to have and retain in use, ownership, or possession; as, whatever you find you may *keep*; **5,** to observe; fulfill; as, to *keep* a holiday or a promise; **6,** to guard; as, to *keep* a secret; **7,** to detain; hold back; as, to *keep* a student after school; the noise *kept* her from sleeping; **8,** to have on hand or in stock, as for sale; as, to *keep* shoes; **9,** to maintain; stay the same; as, to *keep* one's health; *keep* silence; *keep* a room clean; preserve; as, to *keep* food; **10,** to maintain (a record of events, transactions, diary, etc.); as, to *keep* books; to *keep* accounts; **11,** to put or hold in a safe place; as, to *keep* a car in a garage:—*v.i.* **1,** to remain or continue; as, to *keep* cheerful; *keep* quiet; *keep* on with one's work; **2,** stay; as, *keep* off the grass; **3,** to continue sweet, fresh, or unspoiled; as, perishable food will not *keep* for long if not refrigerated:—*n.* **1,** means of subsistence; maintenance; board and lodging; as, he worked for his *keep*; **2,** the stronghold of a castle.

keep-er (kēp′ėr), *n.* a person who takes care of or is in charge of something; as, a shop*keeper*, gate*keeper*, goal*keeper*, etc.

keep-ing (kēp′ing), *n.* **1,** maintenance; support; as, the *keeping* of bees or a dog; **2,** observance; as, the *keeping* of customs or a holiday; **3,** custody; charge; as, the book was given into his *keeping*; **4,** harmony; agreement; as, a formal speech in *keeping* with the solemn occasion.

keep-sake (kēp′sāk′), *n.* something kept in memory of the giver; a memento.

keg (keg), *n.* a small, strong barrel or cask; also, its contents; as, a *keg* of beer.

kelp (kelp), *n.* any of several large, brown seaweeds, a source of alkali, iodine, fertilizer, and other commercial products: also used as food.

Kelvin scale (kel′vin), *n.* temperature scale in which zero is equal to absolute zero (–273.15 degrees Celsius).

kennel (ken′el; ken′l), *n.* **1,** a doghouse; **2,** a place where dogs are bred and raised, or where owners may leave their dogs or cats to be cared for:—*v.t.* [kennelled, kennelling], to confine in a kennel; as, to *kennel* a dog:—*v.i.* to live or rest in a kennel.

kept (kept), *p.t.* and *p.p.* of *keep.*

ker-chief (kûr′chif), *n.* **1,** a piece of cloth worn on the head or around the neck; **2,** a handkerchief.

ker-nel (kûr′nl), *n.* **1,** a seed; a grain of wheat, corn, or other cereal; **2,** the softer, inner portion of a nut, fruit, stone, etc., sometimes used for food; **3,** the central or important part of anything; gist; as, the *kernel* of a plan, argument, or theory.

ker-o-sene (ker′o-sēn′; ker′o-sēn′), *n.* a thin, colourless oil, made from petroleum, and used as fuel in some lamps and stoves.

ketch (kech), *n.* a small sailing vessel with a large mainmast, and a smaller mizzenmast just forward of the rudder post.

ketch-up or **catch-up** (kech′up), *n.* a thick red sauce made from tomatoes, onions, spices, sugar, and salt, used to add flavour to foods.

ket-tle (ket′l), *n.* **1,** a metal vessel, usually with a lid, for heating liquids or cooking foods; **2,** a metal container with a small opening, used for heating water, esp. a teakettle, having a handle and a spout.

ket-tle-drum (ket′l-drum′), *n.* a drum consisting of a large hollow bowl of copper or brass, with parchment stretched over the opening.

KETTLE DRUM

[1]key (kē), *n.* **1,** a metal instrument for moving the bolt of a lock; a specially shaped device that fits into a lock to open or close it; **2,** anything resembling this instrument in use or form; as, a cardlike *key* for a hotel room; **3,** that which allows or hinders entrance or control; the most important element or part; as, Gibraltar is the *key* to the Mediterranean; hard work is the *key* to success; **4,** that by means of which a difficulty is removed or something difficult to understand or a problem is explained or solved; as, the *key* to a translation; a *key* to a code or cipher; an answer *key* at the back of a math book; **5,** in certain musical instruments, as the piano, and in computers, typewriters, and other similar devices, any of a series of levers by means of which the instrument is played or operated; **6,** the general pitch or tone of the voice; as, men usually speak in a lower *key* than women; also, tone of thought or expression; as, a poem in minor *key*; **7,** an arrangement or series of musical tones bearing a fixed relation to a given note, called the keynote; as, the *key* of G major:—*adj.* very important; major; as, *key* employees in a company:—*v.t.* **1,** to regulate the pitch of; as, to *key* a violin; **2,** to stimulate; make tense; as, the thought of the game *keyed* him up to a state of great excitement:—**key in,** in *computing,* to input information into a computer using a keyboard. Also, **key′chain′; key′less; key′ ring′.**

[2]**key** (kē), *n.* a low, small reef or island; cay; as, the Florida *keys.*

key-board (kē′bōrd′), *n.* **1,** the row of keys on a piano, organ, or other pianolike instrument, by means of which the instrument is played; as, an electronic *keyboard;* **2,** the bank of keys on a computer, typewriter, calculator, or any similar machine, by means of which the machine is operated; as, to replace the computer's *keyboard* with a newer one:—*v.i.* **1,** to type, input, or set data using a keyboard; **2,** to play an instrument using a keyboard. Compare *input.*

key-board-er (kē′bōrd′ėr), *n.* a person who types, inputs, or sets data using a keyboard on a computer, etc.

key-board-ist (kē′bōrd′ist), *n.* a person who plays a musical instrument that has a keyboard, such as a piano, organ, synthesizer, etc.

key-card (kē′kärd′), *n.* a plastic card with a magnetic tape used to perform a function, such as unlocking a door or accessing an automated teller machine.

key-hole (kē′hōl′), *n.* a small opening, as in a door or lock, for inserting a key.

key-note (kē′nōt′), *n.* **1,** in *music,* the first note of a scale; the note on which a scale or system of tones is based; **2,** the main idea or principle; as, the *keynote* of a plan:—*adj.* most important; principal; main; as, a *keynote* speaker at a conference:—*v.t.* [keynot-ed, keynot-ing], **1,** in *music,* to designate the keynote; **2,** *Colloq.* to present a keynote speech or address.

key-pad (kē′pad′), *n.* **1,** in *computing,* a separate numerical input device on the keyboard, usually on the right side, with function keys for efficient data input; **2,** any similar device that resembles a small keyboard used to operate electronic devices, such as telephones.

key-stone (kē′stōn′), *n.* **1,** the wedge-shaped stone at the topmost point of an arch, which holds the whole structure in place; **2,** something essential, on which other connected things depend; as, the fundraiser was the *keystone* of the program.

key-stroke (kē′strōk′), in *computing, n.* the stroke with a finger of a key on a keyboard:—*v.t.* [keystroked, keystrok-ing], to record data using a keyboard or similar device; type; as, she *keystroked* the essay on her computer.

key-word or **key word** (kē′wûrd′), *n.* **1,** a word that is the answer to a puzzle; **2,** in *computing,* a significant word that is used to refer to a computer document, database, or Web site.

kha-ki (kä′ki), *n.* **1,** a dull, yellowish-brown, tan, or olive-drab colour; **2,** a heavy cotton cloth of this colour, much used for uniforms; also, a uniform of this material:—*adj.* of a dull, yellowish-brown colour.

khan (kån), *n.* **1,** a Tatar, Turkish, or Mongol ruler in the Middle Ages; **2,** a title of respect in Iran, Afghanistan, India, etc.; **3,** an inn, esp. one in certain Asian countries, where caravans stop for the night.

kib-itz-er (kib′it-sėr), *n.* *Colloq.* **1,** one who looks on at a card game, and gives unrequested advice; **2,** a meddler; **3,** a joker; wisecracker:—*v.i.* **kib-itz** (kib′its).

ki-bosh (kī′bosh), *n.* *Slang* nonsense:—**put the kibosh on,** to veto or squelch.

kick (kik), *v.t.* **1,** to thrust at, or strike, with the foot; as, to *kick* a ball; *kick* a chair; **2,** *Slang* to quit or break free from something, as a habit:—*v.i.* **1,** to strike out with the foot or feet; as, to *kick* hard in a swimming contest; **2,** to spring back, as a gun after it has been fired; **3,** *Colloq.* to grumble; rebel; as, he *kicked* against staying indoors:—*n.* **1,** a blow with the foot; **2,** a burst of power or speed, as in a race; **3,** a backward spring, as of a gun; **4,** *Slang* an objection or protest; **5,** *Slang* thrill; excitement; as, to get a *kick* out of skiing; **6,** *Slang* a strong new interest or concern; as, to be on a money-saving *kick.* Also, **kick′box′ing; kick′er; kick′stand′; kick′-start′.**

kick-back (kik′bak′), *n.* **1,** a sudden and powerful recoil or reaction; **2,** *Slang* a giving back of part of a sum received as a commission, fee, etc., often as a result of a previous understanding, coercion, etc.

kick-off (kik′ôf′), *n.* **1,** in *football* and *soccer,* the opening of play by the kicking of the ball, at the beginning of the game or after a touchdown or goal; **2,** *Colloq.* the start of any activity; as, the *kickoff* of a campaign.

kid (kid), *n.* **1,** a young goat; also, its flesh; **2,** leather made from the skin of a kid, used esp. for shoes and gloves; **3,** *Colloq.* a child or young person:—*adj.* **1,** made of leather called kid; as, *kid* gloves; **2,** *Colloq.* younger; as, *kid* brother:—*v.i.* [kid-ded kid-ding], *Colloq.* to joke teasingly with someone:—*v.t. Colloq.* to tease.

kid-die or **kid-dy** (kid′i), *n.* [*pl.* -dies], *Slang* child.

kid-nap (kid′nap), *v.t.* [kidnapped, kid-nap-ping or kidnaped, kidnaping], to steal or carry off (a person) by force or fraud; as, to *kidnap* a child.—*n.* **kid′nap′per.**

kid-ney (kid′ni), *n.* [*pl.* kidneys], **1,** one of two bean-shaped glands situated in the back, near the spinal column, which separate waste matter from the blood, and pass it off in liquid form through the bladder; **2,** this organ in certain animals, used for food; **3,** sort or kind; disposition; as, to recruit these hard-working students and others of that *kidney*:—**kidney bean,** a reddish-brown, kidney-shaped bean.

kill (kil), *v.t.* **1,** to deprive of life or cause the death of; as, the frost *killed* the flowers; the farmer *killed* the chicken; the thief *killed* the guard; **2,** to destroy; as, to *kill* one's hopes; **3,** to use up; as, to *kill* time; *kill* the last bit of the lemonade; **4,** to reject; discard; as, to *kill* a legislative bill; **5,** *Colloq.* to cause great pain; hurt badly; as, my back is *killing* me:—*v.i.* to destroy life; as, it is a crime to *kill*:—*n.* **1,** in hunting, the act of killing; **2,** the animal or animals killed.

kill-er (kil′ėr), *n.* **1,** someone or something that kills; **2,** *Slang* something that is very taxing or arduous; as, that math test was a *killer.*

kiln (kil; kiln), *n.* a furnace or oven for burning, drying, or hardening something, as lime, bricks, pottery, tiles, etc.

ki-lo (kē′lō), *abbrev.* short for *kilogram* or *kilometre.*

ki-lo-bit (kē′lō-bit′), *n.* in *computing,* a measure of computer memory equal to 1024 bits of information; generally, one thousand bits: abbreviated as *Kb.*

ki-lo-byte (kē′lō-bīt′), *n.* in *computing,* a measure of computer memory equal to 1024 bytes of information: abbreviated as *K, KB,* or *kbyte.*

kil-o-gram (kil′ō-gram), *n.* a unit of weight or mass in the metric system equal to 1000 grams, or 2.2046 pounds avoirdupois: the symbol is *kg.*

kil-o-me-tre or **kil-o-me-ter** (kil′ō-mē′tėr; ki-lä′me-tėr), *n.* a measure of distance in the metric system equal to 1000 metres, or 3280.89 feet: the symbol is *km.*—*adj.* **kil′o-met′ric** (kil′ō-met′rik).

kil-o-watt (kil′ō-wät′; kil′ō-wôt′), *n.* an SI unit of electrical power equal to 1000 watts: the symbol is *kW*:—**kilowatt hour,** the energy expended, or work done, in one hour by one kilowatt.

kilt (kilt), *n.* a short pleated skirt, usually of tartan cloth, worn by men of the Scottish Highlands; also, any similar garment worn by women and girls:—*v.t.* **1,** to form into pleats; **2,** in Scotland, to tuck up (the skirts).

kil-ter (kil′tėr), *n. Colloq.* order; good condition; as, the schedule is out of *kilter.*

ki-mo-no (ki-mō′nō; ki-mō′na), *n.* [*pl.* kimonos], **1,** a loose outer robe, tied by a sash, worn by Japanese men and women; **2,** a similar garment sometimes worn as a dressing gown, robe, or housecoat.

kin (kin), *n.* **1,** a person's family or relatives; kinsfolk; kindred; as, my *kin* live in Hungary; **2,** family relationship:—*adj.* of the same ancestry; related; as, Josef is *kin* to me.

[1]**kind** (kīnd), *adj.* sympathetic; inclined to be considerate of others; friendly; caring; as, a *kind* employer; also, showing such sympathy or consideration; generous; as, a *kind* deed or remark.

[2]**kind** (kīnd), *n.* **1,** a natural group, class, or division; as, the cat *kind*; one of a *kind*; **2,** variety; sort; type; as, all *kinds* of food; **3,** nature; character; style; as, prose and poetry differ in *kind*:—**kind of,** *Colloq.* more or less; rather; somewhat; as, to be *kind of* hungry.

kin-der-gar-ten (kin′dėr-gär′tn), *n.* **1,** a class in school that comes before grade 1, in which teaching includes games, toys, songs, etc.; **2,** a school for younger children; a nursery school.

kin-dle (kin′dl), *v.t.* [kin-dled, kin-dling], **1,** to set fire to; as, the spark *kindled* the wood; **2,** to arouse or excite; stir; as, the speech *kindled* his anger; **3,** to make bright or shining; illuminate; as, enthusiasm *kindled* her face:—*v.i.* **1,** to catch fire; as, the wood *kindled* rapidly; **2,** to become excited or aroused; **3,** to become bright or glowing; as, his eyes *kindled* with joy.

kin-dling (kin′dling), *n.* material, easily lighted, for starting a fire, such as twigs, leaves, paper, or thin, dry wood.

kind-ly (kīnd′li), *adj.* [kind-li-er, kind-li-est], sympathetic; gracious; kind:—*adv.* **1,** in a kind or friendly manner; **2,** please; as, *kindly* remove your boots before entering; **3,** as a favour; as, she *kindly* helped me with my chores.—*n.* **kind′li-ness.**

kind-ness (kīnd′nis), *n.* **1,** the state or quality of being ready to do good to others; graciousness; **2,** a helpful or gracious act; as, she has done us many *kindnesses.*

kin-dred (kin′dred), *adj.* **1,** of like nature or character; as, football and soccer are *kindred* sports; also, congenial; as, *kindred* spirits; **2,** related by birth or marriage:—*n.* **1,**

relationship by birth or marriage; kinship; **2,** one's relatives.

ki-net-ic (ki-net′ik; kī-), *adj.* pertaining to, or resulting from, motion:—**kinetic energy,** the energy possessed by a moving body due to its motion, and equal to one half the product of its mass and the square of its velocity: opposite of *potential energy*:—**kinetics,** the branch of dynamics dealing with changes in motion as produced by unbalanced forces.

kin-folk or **kins-folk** (kin′fōk′; kinz′fōk′), *n.* relatives; kin.

king (king), *n.* **1,** a male sovereign or ruler, passed down from the previous ruler; **2,** something or someone who has power or importance that can be compared with that of a ruler or sovereign; as, a *king* of painters; the lion is sometimes called the *king* of beasts; **3,** the principal piece in the game of chess or checkers; **4,** in *cards,* a card that bears the picture of a king.—*adj.* **king′ly.**—*n.* **king′li-ness; king′ship.**

king-dom (king′dum), *n.* **1,** a country ruled by a king or queen, or the territory comprising such a country; **2,** a realm or sphere in which one has control; as, the *kingdom* of the mind; my home is my *kingdom;* **3,** one of the classes into which natural objects are divided; as, the animal, mineral, and plant *kingdoms.*

king-fish-er (king′fish′ėr), *n.* any of a family of bright-coloured, long-billed birds that feed on fish and insects.

king-pin (king′pin′), *n.* **1,** a main or large bolt, esp. one passing through an axle and acting as a pivot; kingbolt; **2,** *Colloq.* the chief person in an enterprise, company, etc.; also, the main or essential element; **3,** in *bowling,* the pin at the apex or centre.

king–size or **king–sized** (king′–sīz′; king′–sīzd′), *adj.* **1,** larger than usual or standard; as, a *king-size* chair; **2,** a bed that is larger than a queen-size, measuring 203 by 193 centimetres; **3,** for or of this type of bed; as, *king-size* sheets.

kink (kingk), *n.* **1,** a twist, curl, or loop in rope, wire, thread, hair, etc.; **2,** muscle stiffness or pain, as in the neck, etc.; cramp; **3,** a notion or odd whim; a twist in one's mind or disposition; quirk; **4,** problem; obtacle; as, your theory has many *kinks*:—*v.i.* to form twists or curls:—*v.t.* to cause to kink.—*adj.* **kink′y.**

kin-ship (kin′ship), *n.* **1,** relationship by birth or by marriage; **2,** any relationship; **3,** similarity in qualities or character; as, there is close *kinship* in their ideas.

kins-man (kinz′man), *n.* [*pl.* kinsmen (-men)], a male relative; a man related by birth or marriage.—*n.fem.* **kins′wom′an.**

kip-per (kip′ėr), *v.t.* to cure by cleaning, salting, and drying or smoking:—*n.* **1,** a salmon or herring so cured; **2,** a male salmon or sea trout during or after spawning season, when it is unfit to eat.

kis-met (kiz′met; kis-), *n.* fate; destiny.

kiss (kis), *n.* **1,** a touching with the lips in a caress or greeting; **2,** a slight touch; **3,** a kind of candy:—*v.t.* **1,** to touch with the lips as a sign of affection, greeting, etc.; **2,** to touch slightly; as, a soft breeze *kissed* the flowers:—*v.i.* **1,** to touch or salute a person with the lips; **2,** to touch gently.

[1]**kit** (kit), *n.* **1,** a special set of tools, equipment, information, articles of travel, etc.; as, a plumber's tool *kit;* first-aid *kit;* visitor's information *kit;* also, the box or bag holding such things; **2,** a set of parts to be put together to make something; as, a model-airplane *kit;* **3,** the uniform and equipment for an activity; as, a camping *kit.*

[2]**kit** (kit), *n.* **1,** a kitten; **2,** the young or the very small of certain fur-bearing animals, such as the beaver.

kitch-en (kich′en), *n.* a room in which cooking is done:—*adj.* of or for a kitchen; as, a *kitchen* sink. Also, **soup′ kitch′en.**

kitch-en-ette (kich′e-net′), *n.* a small, compactly arranged kitchen.

kite (kīt), *n.* **1,** a light frame of wood, covered with paper, plastic, cloth, or other thin material, to be flown in the air while held by a string; **2,** a bird of the hawk family, small or medium in size, with long, narrow wings.

kit-ten (kit′n), *n.* a young cat.

[1]**kit-ty** (kit′i), *n.* **1,** a pool, as in a poker game, contributed by players for a special purpose; also, the stakes; **2,** in some card games, an extra hand (or part of one) dealt to the table; **3,** money collected and used for any special purpose; as, a *kitty* for the school dance.

[2]**kit-ty** (kit′i), *n. Colloq.* a pet term for *kitten.*

klep-to-ma-ni-a (klep′to-mā′ni-a), *n.* an abnormal, often irresistible, impulse to steal.—*n.* **klep′to-ma′ni-ac.**

klutz (kluts), *n. Slang* a stupid or clumsy person, esp. one who is both physically and socially awkward.—*n.* **klutz′i-ness.**—*adj.* **klutz′y.**

knack (nak), *n.* cleverness in performance; ability to do something skillfully; special talent; as, she could never acquire the *knack* of playing the violin.

knap-sack (nap′sak′), *n.* a leather or canvas bag, worn strapped across the shoulders and carried on the back, used for clothes, camping equipment, books, etc.

knave (nāv), *n.* **1,** a dishonest or deceitful person; a rascal; **2,** a playing card with the figure of a soldier on it; a jack.—*n.* **knav′er-y; knav′ish-ness.**—*adj.* **knav′ish.**

knead (nēd), *v.t.* **1,** to mix and work into a mass, usually with the hands; as, to *knead* dough or clay; **2,** to work over or treat with the hands or fingers; massage; as, to *knead* the kinks out of the neck.

knee (nē), *n.* **1,** in humans, the joint between the thigh and the lower leg, or the area around it; **2,** the part of a garment covering this joint; as, the *knee* of your jeans is torn; **3,** anything resembling the human knee, esp. when bent, as a sharp angle in a pipe.

knee-cap (nē′kap′), *n.* a flattened, triangular, movable bone on the front part of the knee; patella:—*v.t.* [kneecapped, kneecapping], to shoot a person in the kneecap, esp. as punishment for betrayal in terrorist groups.

kneel (nēl), *v.i.* [knelt (nelt) or kneeled, kneel-ing], **1,** to bend the knee; as, he *knelt* to pick up his baseball cap; **2,** to rest on bent knees; as, to *kneel* in prayer.

knell (nel), *n.* **1,** the sound of a bell, esp. when tolled for a death or at a funeral; also, a sad sound; **2,** a sign of the ending or extinction of something; as, the fierce argument rang the *knell* of the possibility of reconcilation; to sound the death *knell* for her business:—*v.i.* to toll dolefully.

knew (nōō; nyōō), *p.t.* of *know.*

knick-er-bock-ers (nik′ėr-bok′ėrz), *n.pl.* short, wide breeches gathered at the knee; knickers:—**Knickerbockers**, descendants of the early New York Dutch; also New Yorkers in general.

knick-ers (nik′ėrz), *n.pl.* **1,** knickerbockers; **2,** *Colloq.* underwear.

knick-knack or **nick-nack** (nik′nak′), *n.* a trifle; toy; small ornament; trinket.

knife (nīf), *n.* [*pl.* knives (nīvz)], **1,** a cutting instrument with a sharp-edged blade or blades, set in a handle; **2,** a sharp-edged blade in a machine:—*v.t.* [knifed, knif-ing], **1,** to stab or cut with a knife; **2,** to move like a knife; as, the lightning *knifed* the ominous sky:—*v.i.* to move quickly through, as if by cutting; as, the speedboat *knifed* through the water.

knight (nīt), *n.* **1,** in the Middle Ages, a mounted warrior who served a king or lord; esp. one of noble birth who, after serving as page and squire, and pledging himself to chivalrous conduct, was admitted by solemn ceremonies to a high military rank; **2,** in modern times, esp. in Great Britain, a person raised to this honorary rank for great achievement or service to his or her country: a man so honoured has the title *Sir*, and a woman, *Dame*; **3,** a member of any of certain orders or societies; **4,** in *chess*, a piece bearing the figure of a horse's head:—*v.t.* to raise (a person) to the rank of knight.

knight-hood (nīt′hood), *n.* **1,** the character, rank, or dignity of a knight; **2,** knights as a class or body.

knight-ly (nīt′li), *adj.* [knight-li-er, knight-li-est], **1,** chivalrous; brave, gentle, and courteous; **2,** consisting of knights:—*adv.* bravely; courteously.

knit (nit), *v.t.* [knit or knit-ted, knit-ting], **1,** to form (a fabric, garment, etc.) by hand, using knitting needles, or by machine, by looping or weaving thread or yarn; as, to *knit* a sweater; **2,** to unite closely; lock together; as, he *knitted* his fingers; **3,** to draw together by a tie of some kind; as, common interests *knit* them to each other; **4,** to draw (the brow) into wrinkles:—*v.i.* **1,** to weave thread or yarn in loops by the use of needles; **2,** to become closely jointed or united; as, the broken bone *knitted* well.

knob (nob), *n.* **1,** the rounded handle of a door, drawer, umbrella, etc.; **2,** a round handle or button on a radio, television, computer, etc.; **3,** a round swelling, mass, or lump, as on the trunk of a tree; **4,** a rounded hill.—*adj.* **knob′by.**

knock (nok), *v.i.* **1,** to strike with a blow or bang, esp. to rap on a door; **2,** to collide; bump; to *knock* into someone; **3,** of machinery parts, to jar or pound noisily; **4,** *Slang* to make unfavourable comments; criticize:—*v.t.* **1,** to strike or beat; give a blow to; **2,** to strike (something) against something else; as, to *knock* one's head against a wall; **3,** *Slang* to criticize unfavourably; as, don't *knock* our idea unless you have a better one:—*n.* **1,** a sharp, quick blow; rap; **2,** a noise like that of a knock; as, a car engine *knock.*—*n.* **knock′er.** Also, **knock′down′; knock′-kneed′; knock′ out′.**

knoll (nōl), *n.* a small, rounded hill; mound.

knot (not), *n.* **1,** an interweaving or tying together of the parts of one or more threads, cords, ropes, etc., so that they will not slip or come apart; also, the tie so formed; **2,** a tight tangle of hair; **3,** something resembling a knot; a hard mass or lump; as, a *knot* in a muscle; **4,** a lump or knob in a piece of wood or in a tree; also, the hard, dark, roundish spot in a wooden board; **5,** a difficulty; hard problem; **6,** a group or cluster of people; **7,** a nautical mile (1,852 metres), the unit used in stating the speed of a moving ship, boat, or aircraft:—*v.t.* [knot-ted, knot-ting], **1,** to tie in a knot; **2,** to unite closely:—*v.i.* to form knots.—*adj.* **knot′ty.**

knot-hole (not′hōl′), *n.* a hole in a tree or in lumber caused by the rotting or falling out of a knot.

know (nō), *v.t.* [*p.t.* knew (nū), *p.p.* known (nōn), *p.pr.* know-ing], **1,** to perceive with the mind; understand clearly; as, he *knows* what he is doing; **2,** to recognize; identify; tell apart from others; as, she *knew* the new teacher; **3,** to be familiar with; be acquainted with; as, to *know* Spanish; she *knew* the famous singer, who went to her high school; **4,** to have information about; as, I *know* his reasons; **5,** to have in the memory; as, I *know* the names of all the bones; **6,** to be experienced or skilled in; as, he *knows* the art of jujitsu; **7,** to be certain; as, I *know* it is true:—*v.i.* to be informed; have certain knowledge.—*adj.* **know′a-ble.**

know–how (nō′–hou′), *n. Colloq.* the special ability, knowledge, or technical skill (usually from experience), enabling one to execute an operation efficiently.

know-ing (nō′ing), *adj.* **1,** having knowledge; intelligent; **2,** shrewd; showing special knowledge; as, a *knowing* look.

know-ing-ly (nō′ing-li), *adv.* **1,** in a knowing or shrewd way; **2,** intentionally.

know–it–all (nō′–it–ôl′), *n. Colloq.* someone who thinks that, and acts as if, he or she knows everything.

knowl-edge (nol′ij), *n.* **1,** that which has been acquired by study or observation; learning; information; **2,** understanding of a subject; as, a *knowledge* of history; **3,** skill; familiarity from experience; as, a *knowledge* of boating; **4,** extent of one's information; as, not to my *knowledge*; **5,** what is generally known; learning; as, scientific *knowledge*.—*adj.* **knowl′edge-a-ble.**

known (nōn), *p.p.* of *know*:—*adj.* generally recognized or accepted; as, a *known* fact.

knuck-le (nuk′l), *n.* **1,** the lump formed where the ends of two bones meet in a joint, esp. the joint of a finger; also, the area and the shape formed when the joints are bent; **2,** something similar to this in function or appearance; **3,** in *cooking*, the knee joint of a calf or pig:—*v.i.* [knuck-led, knuck-ling], **1,** in *marbles*, to place the knuckles on the ground in shooting; **2,** to yield or submit; as, make him *knuckle* under; **3,** *Colloq.* to apply oneself earnestly; as, she *knuckled* down to work:—**knuckle ball,** in *baseball*, a slow ball thrown with the thumb and little finger gripping the sides of the ball, the first joints of the other fingers tucked under and pressed against the top of the ball:—**knuckle–duster,** brass knuckles worn for rough fighting.

knurl (nûrl), *n.* **1,** a ridge, or series of ridges, as on a nut, coin, etc., to aid in gripping it; **2,** a knot or knob.—*adj.* **knurled.**

ko-a-la (kō-ä′la), *n.* a tailless, pouch-bearing animal of Australia with ash-grey, woolly fur, which resembles a small bear, but is, in fact, a distant relative of the kangaroo: it lives in eucalyptus trees and feeds on their leaves.

kohl-rab-i (kōl′rä′bi), *n.* [*pl.* kohlrabies], a cabbage with an enlarged, edible, turnip-like stem.

koo-doo (k o͞o′d o͞o), *n.* Same as **kudu.**

Koo-ten-ay or **Koo-te-nai** (koo′ten-ā′; k o͞o′ten-ē′), *n.* Same as **Kutenai.**

Ko-ran or **Qur-'an** (kō′ran; -rän; ko′ran; -rän), *n.* the sacred book of Islam, believed by the Muslims to be Allah's (God's) revelations to Muhammad by the archangel Gabriel.

ko-sher (kō′shėr), *adj.* **1,** of food, prepared according to the traditional rules and laws of the Jewish religion; as, *kosher* meat; **2,** pertaining to this type of food; as, a *kosher* deli; **3,** *Slang* legitimate; permissible; as, it's not *kosher* to chew gum in class.

kow-tow (kou-tou′), *n.* **1,** a former Chinese custom of kneeling and touching the ground with the forehead as a token of respect or worship; **2,** strict obedience:—*v.i.* to perform such an act; hence, to be obsequious.

kraal (kräl), *n.* **1,** a South African native village enclosed by a stockade; **2,** a sheepfold or cattle pen.

kraft (kråft), *n.* a strong wrapping paper, usually of brown colour, made from sulphate pulp.

krem-lin (krem′lin), *n.* a Russian citadel or fortress:—**the Kremlin, 1,** in Moscow, the place of government; **2,** the government of the former Soviet Union (USSR).

Krish-na (krish′na), *n.* the human form of the Hindu god Vishnu, usually pictured as a young man playing a flute.

kryp-ton (krip′ton), *n.* a rare inert gaseous element of the atmosphere (about one volume per million).

ku-dos (k o͞o′dōz; k o͞o′dōs; kū′dos), *n. Colloq.* **1**, compliments; expression of praise or credit; **2**, honour, award, or other recognition; as, *kudos* is due for her excellent marks.

ku-du or **koo-doo** (k o͞o′d o͞o), *n.* [*pl.* kudu or kudus; koodoo or koodoos], a large grey-brown African antelope with white markings, the male of which has long corkscrewlike horns.

kung fu (kung′ f o͞o′; koong′f o͞o), *n.* an ancient Chinese art of fighting, similar to *karate.*

Ku-te-nai or **Koo-te-nay** or **Koo-te-nai** (koo′ten-ā′; k o͞o′ten-ē′), *n.* [*pl.* Kutenai or Kutenais; Kootenay or Kootenays; Kootenai or Kootenais], **1,** a member of the Aboriginal peoples living in southeastern British Columbia and the northeastern United States; **2,** the language of the Kutenai people.

Kwan-za (kwon′za), *n.* an African-heritage cultural festival celebrated from December 26 to January 1.

L

L, l (el), *n.* [*pl.* L's, l's], **1,** the 12th letter of the alphabet, following K; **2,** the Roman numeral for 50; **3,** *abbrev.* short for *litre.*

lab (lab) *abbrev.* short for *laboratory.*

la-bel (lā′bl), *n.* **1,** a small slip of paper, cloth, metal, etc., attached to anything, indicating its maker, contents, size, owner, destination, etc.; a tag; as, a *label* on a garment; an address *label;* **2,** a short phrase or catchword applied to persons, things, or theories; **3,** a manufacturer's trademark, esp. of a recording company; **4,** in *computing,* a special symbol indicating the contents of an electronic file, etc.:—*v.t.* [labelled, label-ling], **1,** to mark with a label, as a medicine bottle; to put a label on; as, to *label* each box for storage; **2,** to classify; apply a descriptive word to; call or name; as, they *labelled* him a radical.

la-bi-al (lā′bi-al), *adj.* and *n.* relating to or formed by the lips, as *labial* consonants *b, p, m,* and rounded vowels *ō, o͞o.*

la-bor (lā′bėr), *n., adj., v.i.* Same as **labour.**

lab-o-ra-tor-y (lab′o-ra-tōr′i; la-bōr′a-tėr-i), *n.* [*pl.* laboratories], a place where scientific experiments and research are carried on, or where drugs, chemicals, etc., are made, or tested for purity or strength.

la-bor-i-ous (la-bōr′i-us), *adj.* **1,** difficult; requiring toil; as, the *laborious* task of planting new trees; **2,** hard-working; as, a *laborious* student.

la-bour or **la-bor** (lā′bėr), *n.* **1,** physical or mental toil; work; **2,** a difficult task; **3,** working people as a group or class, esp. workers who do physical work; as, laws benefiting *labour* as opposed to management:—*adj.* relating to labour:—**labour union,** an organization that protects and promotes the interests of workers:—*v.i.* **1,** to use muscular strength or mental capacity; toil; **2,** to be hard pressed; as, to *labour* under a difficulty; to move slowly and heavily; as, an old car *labours* up a hill; **3,** to strive; take pains; as, he *laboured* to understand the problem; **4,** to pitch and roll heavily, as a ship in a storm.—*n.* **la′bour-er.**

Labour Day, a holiday to honour working people, celebrated on the first Monday in September in North America.

la-boured (lā′bėrd), *adj.* produced with toil or care; not fluent; as, a *laboured* speech.

lab-y-rinth (lab′i-rinth), *n.* **1,** a maze or confusing network of passages winding into and about one another, so that it is difficult to find one's way through it; **2,** a confusing or puzzling state of affairs; **3,** in *Greek mythology,* the maze on the island of Crete in which the Minotaur was kept; **4,** the inner ear.—*adj.* **lab′y-rin′thine.**

lace (lās), *n.* **1,** an ornamental fabric of fine threads, as of linen, cotton, or silk, woven in a delicate open design; as, *lace* on a wedding gown; **2,** a cord or string, passed through eyelets or other holes to fasten together parts of a shoe, garment, etc.; as, a shoe*lace*:—*v.t.* [laced, lac-ing], **1,** to fasten with a lace; as, *lace* your shoes; **2,** to adorn or trim with lace; **3,** to weave or twine together; **4,** to lash; beat; as, the school basketball team *laced* its opponents in the second game; **5,** to add or intersperse; as, to *lace* the punch with alcohol; she *laced* her story with lofty adjectives; **6,** to mark with a loose, woven pattern like lace; as, many tiny cracks *laced* the old desk:—*v.i.* to be fastened with a lace or laces; as, the corset *laces* at the front.—*adj.* **lac′y.**

lac-er-ate (las′ėr-āt′), *v.t.* [lacerat-ed, lacer-at-ing], **1,** to tear, rip, or mangle; as, the claws of the grizzly bear *lacerated* his arm; **2,** to distress, as the feelings.—*n.* **lac′er-a′tion.**

lac-ing (lās′ing), *n.* **1,** the act of fastening with a lace; **2,** a cord, string, braid, etc., passed through eyelets to fasten something or serve as a trimming; **3,** *Colloq.* a beating or thrashing.

lack (lak), *v.t.* to be without; not to have; be in need of; as, his remarks *lack* common sense; I *lack* the money:—*v.i.* to have need; be short; as, he *lacks* in wisdom:—*n.* want; the state of being without something; need; as, *lack* of fresh air; *lack* of sleep.

lack-a-dai-si-cal (lak′a-dā′zi-kal), *adj.* lazily indifferent; listless.

lack-ey (lak′i), *n.* [*pl.* lackeys] **1,** a male attendant; a servant; a footman; **2,** someone who follows without question.

lack-lus-tre (lak′lus′tėr), *adj.* **1,** dull; lacking brightness; as, *lacklustre* eyes; **2,** uninteresting; not outstanding; mediocre; as, a *lacklustre* performance.

la-con-ic (la-kon′ik), *adj.* using few words; concise; pithy; terse; as, a *laconic* reply.

lacquer (lak′ėr), *n.* **1,** a varnish made of shellac dissolved in alcohol, and used to protect brass, silver, etc., from tarnish or to give a shiny appearance to wood, etc.; **2,** any of various varnishes made from resin, esp. one made from the sap of certain Oriental trees, and used for polishing wood and other surfaces; **3,** Chinese or Japanese woodwork finished with a hard, polished varnish and often inlaid with gold, etc.:—*v.t.* to paint with lacquer.

la-crosse (lå-krôs′), *n.* a field game played by two teams of 10 players each, in which the object is to send a small ball into the opponent's goal by means of a long stick with a net at one end, called a lacrosse stick.

LACROSSE STICKS

lac-te-al (lak′ti-al), *adj.* of, or relating to, milk; as, the *lacteal* fluid; *lacteal* ducts.

lac-tic (lak′tik), *adj.* of, relating to, or from milk; as, *lactic* acid.

lac-tose (lak′tōs), *n.* a white, sweetish powder made from evaporated whey and used in infant foods: also called *milk sugar* and *sugar of milk.*

lad (lad), *n.* a boy or youth; young man.

ladder (lad′ėr), *n.* **1,** a device for scaling or climbing, consisting usually of two long uprights connected by crosspieces, called *rungs*, forming steps; also, anything that resembles a ladder, as a run in a stocking; **2,** any means by which one mounts, ascends, or makes progress; as, the first step on the *ladder* to success.

lade (lād), *v.t.* [*p.t.* lad-ed, *p.p.* lad-en (lād′n) or lad-ed, *p.pr.* lad-ing], **1,** to load (goods); put a cargo aboard (a ship); **2,** to lift out or in with a scoop; bail; as, to lade water out of a vat; **3,** to burden; subjugate.

lad-en (lād′n), one form of the past participle of *lade:—adj.* **1,** loaded; burdened; as, *laden* with packages; **2,** oppressed or burdened in spirit; as, *laden* with sorrow.

lad-ing (lād′ing), *n.* **1,** the act of loading or of bailing; **2,** freight.

la-dle (lā′dl), *n.* a deep spoon or dipper, with a long handle, for scooping out liquids:—*v.t.* [la-dled, la-dling], to scoop out with a ladle.

la-dy (lā′di), *n.* [*pl.* ladies], **1,** in the United Kingdom and its colonies, a title for a noblewoman or one of authority over a house or an estate, of the same rank as a lord; **2,** a woman of good family or of high social position; a gentlewoman; **3,** a woman or girl with very polite manners and habits; **4,** any woman; as, the *lady* next door:—*n.* **la′dy-ship** (usually with *her, your,* etc.).

la-dy-bug (lā′di-bug′), *n.* a small, round-backed beetle, usually reddish or orange with black spots, which eats several kinds of insects that are harmful to plants: also called *ladybird.*

la-dy-like (lā′di-līk′), *adj.* befitting a lady; well-bred; as, *ladylike* behaviour.

la-dy's slip-per, any of a group of orchids with a slipper-shaped flower: the pink lady's slipper is the provincial floral emblem of Prince Edward Island.

[1]lag (lag), *v.i.* [lagged, lag-ging], to move slowly; fail to keep pace; fall behind; as, to *lag* behind other runners in a race; to *lag* in one's studies:—*n.* a falling behind in movement or progress; delay; as, a *lag* in the speed of a race or in the progress of work.

[2]lag (lag), *v.t.* to cover, as a steam boiler, to prevent loss of heat:—*n.* a piece of material used to insulate or cover a cylindrical object; a stave.

la-ger (lä′gėr), a light malt beer, aged from six weeks to six months after brewing.

lag-gard (lag′ėrd), *n.* one who acts or moves slowly; a backward person; as, she is a *laggard* in her studies:—*adj.* backward; slow.—*adv.* **lag′gard-ly.**

la-goon (la-gōōn′), *n.* **1,** a shallow lake or channel, usually near the sea, and connected with it; **2,** the shallow water inside an atoll, or ring-shaped coral island.

laid (lād), *v.t., p.t.* and *p.p.* of [3]*lay.*

lain (lān), *v.i., p.p.* of [2]*lie.*

lair (lâr), *n.* the den of a wild animal, such as a bear, wolf, etc.

la-i-ty (lā′i-ti), *n.* [*pl.* laities], **1,** lay people, as distinguished from the clergy; **2,** those outside any particular profession; as, legal jargon is sometimes difficult for *laity* to understand.

lake (lāk), *n.* a large body of fresh or salt water entirely surrounded by land.

la-ma (lä′ma), *n.* a Buddhist priest or monk of Tibet or Mongolia: the chief is called *Dalai Lama.—n.* **la′ma-ser′y.**

lamb (lam), *n.* **1,** the young of sheep; **2,** the flesh of young sheep, used as food; **3,** one who is gentle or innocent; **4,** a naive or inexperienced person; one who can be easily duped, fooled, or taken advantage of:—*v.i.* to bring forth or give birth to lambs.

lam-baste (lam-bāst′), *v.t. Colloq.* **1,** to beat severely; thrash; **2,** to criticize or scold harshly.

lame (lām), *adj.* [lam-er, lam-est], **1,** crippled or disabled, esp. in a leg or foot; not being able to walk well; limping; **2,** sore; painful; stiff; as, a *lame* shoulder; **3,** not sound or effective; weak; as, a *lame* excuse:—*v.t.* [lamed, lam-ing], to make lame.

la-ment (la-ment′), *v.i.* and *v.t.* **1,** to mourn; bewail; express deep sorrow or grief; **2,** to regret; as, she *lamented* her thoughtless actions:—*n.* **1,** an expression of sorrow or grief; **2,** a song or poem that expresses grief.

lam-en-ta-ble (lam′en-ta-bl), *adj.* **1,** regrettable; deplorable; unfortunate; as, a *lamentable* mistake; **2,** mournful; sorrowful; **3,** mediocre; inferior; as, a *lamentable* performance.—*adv.* **lam′en-ta-bly.**

lam-en-ta-tion (lam′en-tā′shun), *n.* an expression of grief; a lament.

lam-i-nat-ed (lam′in-ā′tid), *adj.* in the form of thin sheets or layers bonded together, as plywood:—*v.t.* **lam′i-nate′.**

lamp (lamp), *n.* **1,** in olden days, a vessel in which oil or other inflammable liquid was burned by means of a wick to produce light; **2,** today, any device for producing light by electricity, gas, etc. Also, **lamp′light′; lamp′post′.**

lam-poon (lam-po͞on′), *v.t.* to ridicule, satirize, or abuse (in prose or verse):—*n.* a bitter satire in writing; also, a light satire; spoof.

lam-prey (lam′pri), *n.* an eel-like, parasitic fish with large circular mouth, pouchlike gills, and horny teeth used to suck blood of its host.

LAN (lan), *abbrev.* short for *local area network.*

lance (låns), *n.* **1,** a weapon used in the Middle Ages consisting of a long shaft of wood with a sharp steel head; also, a soldier equipped with a lance; **2,** any sharp-pointed instrument resembling a lance, esp. one used by surgeons, etc.; a lancet:—*v.t.* [lanced, lanc-ing], **1,** to pierce with a lance; **2,** to cut open, as a boil, with a sharp knife or instrument.

lanc-er (lån′sėr), *n.* **1,** a person who uses a lance; **2,** formerly, a cavalry soldier armed with a lance.

lanc-ers (lån′sėrs), *n.* a square dance for four or more couples; also, the musical accompaniment.

lan-cet (lan′set), *n.* a small, pointed, two-edged surgical knife.

land (land), *n.* **1,** the solid part of the surface of the globe, which is not covered by water; **2,** a division of the earth's surface marked off by natural, political, or other boundaries; a country; district; also, the people of a country; a nation; **3,** soil; ground of a particular type; as, fertile *land;* **4,** property; real estate:—*v.t.* **1,** to set on land or shore; as, to *land* an airplane or passengers from a ship; **2,** to capture and bring to shore; as, to *land* a fish; **3,** *Colloq.* to win or gain; as, to *land* a prize or job; **4,** to bring to a destination; as, the train *landed* him in Toronto on time:—*v.i.* **1,** to bring or come down to the ground from the air; alight or come to earth; as, the plane *landed* on time; the missile *landed* in the ocean; **2,** to come or go ashore; disembark, as a passenger; **3,** to arrive at a destination; **4,** to come to the end of a course; get into a situation; as, she *landed* in jail. Also, **land′hold′er; land′own′er.**

lan-dau (lan′dô; lan′dou), *n.* **1,** a four-wheeled enclosed carriage with a top in two parts; **2,** a car with a similar roof.

land-ed (lan′did), *adj.* **1,** owning land; as, *landed* gentry; **2,** consisting of land; as, a *landed* estate:—**landed immigrant**, formerly, someone admitted into Canada legally but who is not a Canadian citizen. Also called *permanent resident.*

land-fall (land′fôl′), *n.* the first sighting of land after a voyage; also, the land so sighted.

land-fill (land′fil′), *n.* **1,** a way of disposing of garbage; **2,** the site where the trash is dumped; **3,** the material disposed of in this way:—*v.t.* **1,** to dispose of garbage in this way; **2,** to fill a garbage dump this way.

land-ing (lan′ding), *n.* **1,** the act of coming to land from the water or the air; as, an airplane *landing;* **2,** a place or platform, as a wharf, where passengers may embark or disembark, and where goods may be loaded or unloaded; **3,** a wide, flat platform, as at the end of a flight of steps.

land-la-dy (land′lā′di), *n.* [*pl.* landladies], **1,** a woman who rents her building, apartment, house, room, or land to others; **2,** the woman who manages a boarding house, rooming house, hotel, or inn; also, the wife of a landlord.

land-locked (land′lokt′), *adj.* **1,** surrounded or nearly surrounded by land; as, a *landlocked* bay; **2,** confined to waters shut off from the sea by some barrier; as, *landlocked* fish.

land-lord (land′lôrd′), *n.* **1,** one who owns a building, apartment, house, room, or land that is rented to others; **2,** a person who manages a boarding house, rooming house, hotel, or inn.

land-lub-ber (land′lub′ėr), *n.* one who is awkward or inexperienced on ships.

land-mark (land′märk′), *n.* **1,** an object that marks the boundary of a tract of land; **2,** a familiar or easily seen object that serves as a guide for a traveller or navigator; **3,** any event that marks or is associated with an important stage or turning point in history; as, the Internet is a *landmark* in communications.

land mine, an explosive, usually buried, that is designed to destroy personnel or vehicles, which set it off when their weight is placed on it.

land-scape (land′skāp′), *n.* **1,** a view of a large stretch of land or land and water; **2,** a picture, photograph, or painting of a view of such an area or a scene from nature; **3,** the landforms of a region; **4,** of a printed page, photo, etc., arranged so that its width is greater than its height; as, he printed the document in *landscape*: compare *portrait:*—*adj.* relating to landscape; as, *landscape* fabric; *landscape* design; *landscape* paintings:—*v.t.* and *v.i.* [landscaped, landscap-ing], to make an area more beautiful by planting trees, flowers, and other plants according to a plan; as, to *landscape* a backyard; to *landscape* using small shrubs.

land-slide (land′slīd′), *n.* **1,** the slipping of a mass of earth, stones, etc., down a steep slope; **2,** the material that slips down; **3,** a decisive, overwhelming victory in an election, etc.

lane (lān), *n.* **1,** a narrow, often winding

path or byway between hedges, fences, walls, etc.; an alley; **2,** an unpaved or little-used road, or a narrow street; any narrow way or track; **3,** a division of a road for a single line of traffic going in one direction; **4,** in *bowling*, the long strip of floor down which the ball is rolled; **5,** one of the courses fixed as routes for seagoing vessels or aircraft.

lang-syne or **lang syne** (lang′sīn′; -zīn′), *Scottish, adv.* long since; long ago:—*n.* times long ago.

lan-guage (lang′gwij), *n.* **1,** the power or ability to communicate ideas, thoughts, and feelings in words; human speech; **2,** the means of such expression, as letters, sounds, words, etc., current among members of a single people; as, the German *language;* **3,** the means of expression, as words, phrases, etc., peculiar to special fields of knowledge; as, technical, scientific, computer, or legal *language;* **4,** any style of verbal expression; as, plain *language;* **5,** any means of expressing ideas; as, the *language* of pictures; the *language* of flowers; body *language.*

language arts, subjects such as reading, writing, and spelling that teach students to develop their communications skills.

lan-guid (lang′gwid), *adj.* weak, as from exhaustion; dull; listless; disinterested.

lan-guish (lang′gwish), *v.i.* **1,** to lose strength or animation; become languid; as, the flowers *languished* in the hot sun; **2,** to pine away, as with longing; as, she *languished* for her friends back home; **3,** to suffer due to adversity; as, the captured animal *languished* in its small cage; **4,** to appeal for sympathy by pretending feebleness or fatigue.

lan-guor (lang′gėr), *n.* **1,** lack of energy; listlessness; **2,** dreaminess; a soft, tender mood; **3,** heaviness; oppressiveness; sluggishness; as, the *languor* of a humid day; **4,** apathy; disinterest.—*adj.* **lan′guor-ous.**

lank (langk), *adj.* **1,** lean; thin; as, a tall, *lank* figure; **2,** straight and limp, as hair that will not curl.—*adj.* **lank′y.**—*adv.* **lank′ly; lank′i-ly.**—*n.* **lank′ness; lank′i-ness.**

lan-o-lin (lan′ō-lin′), *n.* a fatty substance obtained from sheep's wool, which is purified and used in ointments, cosmetics, soaps, etc.

lan-tern (lan′tėrn), *n.* **1,** a transparent case enclosing a light and protecting it from wind, rain, etc.; **2,** the room at the top of a lighthouse where the light is kept.

[1]**lap** (lap), *n.* **1,** the loose part of a garment that may be doubled or folded over; the skirt of a coat or the overlapping part of a gown; a flap; **2,** that part of the clothing that rests upon the thighs and knees of a person in a sitting position; also, the front part of the body from the waist to the knees of a person who is sitting; as, the child sat in her *lap;* **3,** a place for supporting, sheltering, or rearing; as, the *lap* of luxury; **4,** that part of an object, as a shingle, that extends over another; also, the distance or amount of such extension; as, a *lap* of two centimetres; **5,** the length of a course or track that has to be passed over more than once in a race; as, to run three *laps* around the track; **6,** a stage of a journey or process; as, the final *lap* of the trip:—*v.t.* [lapped, lap-ping], **1,** to lay or fold over, as cloth; also, to wrap; as, she *lapped* herself in the warm blanket; **2,** to place over something else so as partly to cover it; as, to *lap* one shingle over another; **3,** to enfold; surround; as, *lapped* in luxury:—*v.i.* to lie partly over something; overlap; as, the boards *lap;* also, to be folded; as, the cuff *laps* back.

[2]**lap** (lap), *v.t.* [lapped, lap-ping], **1,** to lick up with the tongue, as liquid; as, the kitten *lapped* the milk; **2,** to splash gently against; as, the waves *lap* the shore:—*v.i.* **1,** to take up liquid with the tongue; **2,** to make a lapping or rippling sound:—*n.* the act or sound of lapping.

la-pel (la-pel′), *n.* the part of a garment that is folded back, esp. the fold at each side of a coat or jacket front, forming a continuation of the collar.

lapse (laps), *v.i.* [lapsed, laps-ing], **1,** to glide or slip slowly away; as, to *lapse* into unconsciousness; his attention *lapsed;* **2,** to slip or depart from a normal standard; fall into error; as, to *lapse* from good behaviour; **3,** to cease or to pass to another, as insurance, an estate, etc., because of the holder's failure to fulfill certain conditions; as, his licence *lapsed:*—*n.* **1,** a gliding or passing away slowly; as, the *lapse* of time; **2,** a slight mistake; a slip, as of memory, tongue, or pen; **3,** the loss of a claim, right, etc., through failure to use or renew it; as, a *lapse* of the permit; **4,** a passing into a lower rank or condition; as, a *lapse* into poverty; a *lapse* into drunkenness.—*adj.* **lapsed.**

lap-top (lap′top′), *n.* a small, lightweight, portable computer, usually having a flat screen and a rechargeable battery power source.

lar-ce-ny (lär′se-ni), *n.* [*pl.* larcenies], the unlawful taking away of another's property; theft.—*adj.* **lar′ce-nous.**—*adv.* **lar′ce-nous-ly.**

larch (lärch), *n.* any of a group of graceful trees of the pine family, with small cones and short needlelike leaves that drop in the fall; also, the wood of these trees, which is unusually durable.

lard (lärd), *n.* a white, greasy substance made from the fat of pigs, sometimes used in cooking:—*v.t.* **1,** to smear with lard; **2,** to insert strips of bacon or salt pork into (meat) before roasting; **3,** to embellish; enrich; as, to *lard* the speech with colourful anecdotes.

lard-er (lär′dėr), *n.* the place where household provisions are kept; a pantry; also, the stock or supply of food.

large (lärj), *adj.* [larg-er, larg-est], **1,** big; great in size; bulky; wide; extensive; more than the usual size, amount, or number; as, a *large* estate; a *large* collection of DVDs; **2,** wide in scope; broad in understanding and sympathy; as, a *large* mind:—**at large, 1,** free; unconfined; on the loose; escaped; as, the convict is *at large*; **2,** chosen to represent a whole section instead of one of its districts; as a whole; as, a delegate *at large*; the public *at large*.—*n.* **large′ness.**

large-ly (lärj′li), *adv.* to a great amount or extent; mostly; mainly; as, a region that is *largely* desert.

large–scale (lärj′–skāl′), *adj.* **1,** wide in extent or scope; widely occurring; as, *large-scale* attack; **2,** built or drawn large, as, *large-scale* map.

lar-gess or **lar-gesse** (lär′jes), *n.* **1,** liberal giving; generosity; **2,** a generous donation or gift.

lar-i-at (lar′i-at), *n.* **1,** a rope with a sliding noose, used for catching horses or cattle; a lasso; **2,** a rope for picketing horses.

COWBOY HOLDING A LARIAT, DEF. 1

[1]lark (lärk), *n.* **1,** any of various small European song-birds, as the skylark; **2,** any of many birds similar to larks but of different families, as the meadow lark.

[2]lark (lärk), *n.* a frolic; spree; an amusing adventure; something done for fun; as, to have a *lark* at the party:—*v.i. Colloq.* to frolic; have fun.

lar-va (lär′va), *n.* [*pl.* larvae (lär′vē)], **1,** the early, often wormlike, form of an insect's life cycle, in the stage between the egg and the pupa, such as a caterpillar, maggot, etc.; **2,** the early form of any animal that changes in form as it develops, such as a tadpole.—*adj.* **lar′val.**

lar-yn-gi-tis (lar′in-jī′tis), *n.* inflammation of the upper end of the windpipe, or larynx, often causing a faint, hoarse voice or a temporary loss of voice.

lar-ynx (lar′ingks), *n.* [*pl.* larynges (larin′jēz) or larynxes], an enlargement of the upper end of the windpipe, containing the vocal cords, which produce a person's voice.

las-civ-i-ous (la-siv′i-us), *adj.* lustful; lecherous; tending to excite sensual passion; as, a *lascivious* picture.

la-ser (lā′zėr), *n.* a device that produces a very narrow and very powerful beam of light that travels in a single direction; laser beams are used to melt or cut metal, send long-distance telephone, radio, and TV signals, perform surgical operatons, and print information from a computer. Short for *l*ight *a*mplification by *s*timulated *e*mission of *r*adiation:—*adj.* of or related to a laser; as, a *laser* beam; *laser* printer; *laser* surgery; *laser* disc.

[1]lash (lash), *v.t.* **1,** to strike or beat violently with a whip; flog; also, to beat upon; as, the waves *lashed* the shore; **2,** to rebuke or scold severely; **3,** to switch backward and forward like a lash; as, the puma *lashed* its tail; **4,** to stir up or arouse; as, the speaker *lashed* the crowd to fury; **5,** to criticize severely; as, the protesters *lashed* the government for its health policies:—*v.i.* **1,** to apply the whip; also, to rebuke severely; **2,** to rush, pour, or beat, as wind or rain:—*n.* **1,** the flexible part, or thong, of a whip; **2,** a stroke with a whip or anything used like a whip; as, a *lash* of sarcasm; **3,** one of the little hairs on the edge of the eyelid; an eyelash.

[2]lash (lash), *v.t.* to tie or bind with a rope or cord.

lass (las; lås), *n.* **1,** a girl or young woman; **2,** a sweetheart.

las-si-tude (las′i-tūd′), *n.* bodily or mental weariness; lack of energy; lethargy.

las-so (las′ō), *n.* [*pl.* lassos or lassoes], a rope with a slip-knot, used for catching horses and cattle; a lariat:—*v.t.* to catch with a noosed rope; as, she *lassoed* the steer.

[1]last (låst), *adj.* **1,** coming after all others in time, place, order, etc.; at the end; as, the *last* person to go; **2,** next before the present; most recent; as, *last* week; **3,** authoritative; conclusive; as, his writings are regarded as the *last* word in literary criticism; **4,** not likely; least likely; least fitted; as, he is the *last* person for the position:—*adv.* **1,** after all others; at the end; as, she came *last* in the race; **2,** on the time or occasion next preceding the present; most recently; as, when did you *last* see him? **3,** at the end; finally; as, pack your toothbrush *last*:—*n.* the person or thing that comes after all others; the end:—**at last,** finally; at the end of a long period of time; as, her dog came home *at last*:—**last straw,** the last of a series of events or things, which finally makes a person angry or causes an outburst; as, the student's late arrival was the *last straw* for the teacher.—*adv.* **last′ly.** Also, **last′–ditch′; last′ gasp′; last′ hur-rah′; last′ min′ute; last′ name′; last′ post′; last′ rites′; last′ word′.**

[2]last (låst), *v.i.* **1,** to continue; as, the play *lasted* three hours; **2,** to be enough for a given time; hold out; as, this coffee will *last* a week; **3,** to wear well; endure; as, the well-made running shoes *lasted* a long time.

latch (lach), *n.* a fastening device for a window, door, or gate, made of a small bar and catch:—*v.t.* and *v.i.* to fasten with a catch.

late (lāt), *adj.* **1,** coming after the usual or expected time; tardy; as, a *late* spring; a *late* lunch; **2,** far on toward the end of some period of time; as, a *late* hour of the day; the *late* 1900s; **3,** of recent date; not long past; as, a *late* occurrence or fashion; **4,** formerly in office; as, the *late* president of the company came to the event; **5,** deceased; dead; as, her *late* husband:—*adv.* **1,** after the usual, expected, or appointed time; as, to arrive *late*; **2,** toward the end of a certain time period; as, *late* in the fall; **3,** far into the day, night, etc.; as, to work early and *late*:—**of late**, recently; as, I have not seen you *of late*.—*n.* **late′ness.**

late-ly (lāt′li), *adv.* not long ago; recently; as, she has not been to class *lately*.

la-tent (lā′tent), *adj.* concealed; not visible; present, but not active; dormant; as, *latent* infection; *latent* discontent; *latent* ability.

lat-er-al (lat′ėr-al), *adj.* pertaining to, at, or coming from the side; as, a *lateral* pass in football; *lateral* thinking.—*adv.* **lat′er-al-ly.**

latex (lā′teks), *n.* **1,** a milky juice secreted by plants such as the rubber tree, milkweed, poppy, etc., which is the basis of rubber; **2,** a mixture of synthetic rubber and water used in paints, glues, etc.:—*adj.* of or relating to latex; as, *latex* paint; *latex* gloves.

lath (låth), *n.* [*pl.* laths (lå*thz*; låths)], one of the thin, narrow strips of wood nailed to the framework of a wall or building to support the plaster:—*v.t.* to cover with such strips.—*n.* **lath′ing.**

lathe (lā*th*), *n.* a machine that holds and turns articles of wood, metal, etc., while they are being cut, shaped, and polished with a fixed tool.

lath-er (la*th*′ėr), *n.* **1,** froth or foam made from soap and water; **2,** the foamy sweat of a horse:—*v.t.* to cover with froth or foam, as in shaving:—*v.i.* to form foam or suds.

Lat-in (lat′in), *n.* **1,** the language that was spoken in Ancient Rome and the Roman Empire; **2,** a person who speaks one of the languages that derives from Latin, such as Italian, French, Spanish, or Portuguese; **3,** a person born in or coming from Latin America: also called a *Latin American* or a *Latino*:—*adj.* **1,** having to do with the Latin language; as, a *Latin* phrase; **2,** having to do with languages that derive from Latin; also, these people; **3,** having to do with Latin America: also called *Latin American* or *Latino*.

Lat-in A-mer-i-can (la′tin a-mer′i-kan), *n.* a person who inhabits or originates from those parts of the Americas where Spanish and Portuguese are spoken:—*adj.* relating to the countries, the people, the languages, or the culture of this region.

lat-i-tude (lat′i-tūd′), *n.* **1,** the distance north or south of the equator measured in degrees, shown on a map by lines that run east and west, parallel to the equator: compare *longitude*; **2,** breadth; range; as, his remarks cover a wide *latitude* of subjects; **3,** degree of freedom of action or expresson; as, he was given great *latitude* in arranging the meeting; **4,** a region or locality; as, a warm *latitude*.

la-trine (la-trēn′), *n.* a toilet or privy, esp. in a camp, factory, etc.

lat-ter (lat′ėr), *adj.* **1,** the second of two things already mentioned: compare *former*; **2,** more recent; later; nearer to the end; as, the *latter* half of the century.

lat-tice (lat′is), *n.* **1,** crossed or interlaced open work of metal or wood; also, any pattern resembling lattice; **2,** a door, window, gate, trellis, etc., made of such work:—*v.t.* [latticed, lattic-ing], **1,** to cross or interlace (strips) as in a lattice; **2,** to furnish with a lattice.—*n.* **lat′tice-work′.**

laud (lôd), *v.t.* to praise; glorify; extol:—*n.* a hymn or song of praise.—*adj.* **laud′a-ble; laud′a-tor′y.**—*adv.* **laud′ab-ly.**—*n.* **laud′a-ble-ness.**

laugh (låf), *v.i.* to express mirth, enjoyment, or derision by a series of chuckling sounds; to make the sounds and movements of the face that show one is happy or finds something funny:—**laugh up (in) one's sleeve,** to laugh to oneself or secretively:—*v.t.* **1,** to express or utter with laughter; as, she *laughed* her pleasure; **2,** to move or affect by merriment or ridicule; as, we *laughed* her out of her bad mood:—*n.* the act of laughing or its sound.—*adj.* **laugh′a-ble.**—*n.* **laugh′er.**—*adv.* **laugh′ing-ly.**

laughing gas, a colourless gas, *nitrous oxide* (N_2O), which is used as an anesthetic in dentistry and often produces exhilaration and laughter.

laugh-ing-stock (låf′ing-stok′), *n.* a person who is the object of ridicule or who is poked fun of.

laugh-ter (låf′tėr), *n.* the act or sound of laughing.

laugh track, in a radio or television program, recorded laughter accompanying dialogue or action, which is added to the soundtrack.

¹launch (lônch; länch), *v.t.* **1,** to move or cause to slide into the water, as a boat or a ship; **2,** to send an aircraft, spacecraft, or another vehicle or device into the air; hurl; throw; catapult; send out: as, to *launch* a rocket, missile, or spear; **3,** to start off; commence; as, to *launch* a business; *launch* into a speech; **4,** in *computing*, to start a computer program:—*v.i.* **1,** to put to sea; **2,** to plunge or start swiftly and with vigour; as, he *launched* into a torrent of abuse; **3,** to enter on a new endeavour, such as a career; embark:—*n.* the act of launching; as, the *launch* of the space shuttle:—**launch(ing) pad, 1,** a platform from which to launch rockets or spacecraft; as, the *launch pad* at Cape Canaveral; **2,** any starting point for a mission, career, etc.

²launch (lônch; länch), *n.* **1,** the largest boat of a battleship; **2,** a large, open pleasure boat, usually driven by a motor.

laun-der (lôn′dėr; län′der), *v.t.* **1,** to wash or to wash and iron (clothes); **2,** to hide the origins or source of illegally obtained money by transferring to another party; as, the mob boss *laundered* his money to avoid being caught.—*n.* **laun′der-er.**

laun-dry (lôn′dri; län′dri), *n.* [*pl.* laundries], **1,** a commercial establishment, or a room in a home, where clothes and other fabrics are washed and ironed; **2,** articles sent to be washed or that have just been washed.

lau-re-ate (lô′rē-it; lô′rē-āt′), *adj.* decked or crowned with laurel as a sign of honour; hence, worthy of honour; distinguished:—*n.* someone honoured for great achievement, esp. in arts or sciences; poet laureate:—**poet laureate**, the official court poet of Great Britain; also, a distinguished poet or one honoured for his or her achievements in that field.—*n.* **lau′re-ate-ship′.**

lau-rel (lô′rel; lor′el), *n.* **1,** an evergreen shrub of southern Europe, used by the ancient Greeks and Romans as a symbol of fame and distinction: also called *bay* or *bay laurel*; **2,** any of several shrubs resembling the true laurel, esp. the flowering mountain laurel; **3,** a crown or wreath of bay given as a prize or honour:—**laurels**, fame; honour:—**rest on (one's) laurels**, to be satisfied with what one has already done.

la-va (lå′va), *n.* **1,** the red-hot melted rock that erupts from a volcano; **2,** the hardened rock that forms from the cooling of this melted rock.

lav-a-tor-y (lav′a-tôr′i), *n.* [*pl.* lavatories], **1,** a room for washing the hands and face; **2,** a basin fixed on a stand, usually with running water, for washing; **3,** a washroom or toilet.

lave (lāv), *v.t.* [laved, lav-ing], **1,** to wash; bathe; **2,** to flow or wash gently against; as, the calm sea *laves* the beach.

lav-en-der (lav′en-dėr), *n.* **1,** a plant related to the mint with aromatic lilac-coloured flowers and narrow woolly leaves, cultivated for its perfume and sometimes used, when dried, to sweeten and scent clothes, linens, air, etc.; **2,** the pale lilac colour of its flowers.

lav-ish (lav′ish), *adj.* **1,** very liberal; almost too generous; **2,** excessive; as, *lavish* praise:—*v.t.* to spend or bestow liberally or profusely; squander; waste.—*adv.* **lav′ish-ly.**—*n.* **lav′ish-ness.**

law (lô), *n.* **1,** a rule of action, established by authority or custom, for a nation or a group of people; **2,** a system or body of such rules or customs in a specific area or field; as, maritime *law*; social *law*; federal *law*; **3,** an act or enactment of a legislative, or lawmaking, body; **4,** the legal profession or the study of such a set of rules; **5,** in sports, games, etc., the generally accepted rules of procedure; as, the *laws* of football or hockey; **6,** trial in the courts; as, take it to *law*; **7,** in *science* or *mathematics*, a statement of what, under given conditions, invariably happens, or of relations between things in nature; as, the *law* of gravity; **8,** any similar statement about what is expected to happen in a certain situation; as, Murphy's *Law*; **9,** *Colloq.* a police officer or the police force; as, the *law* caught up with the thief. Also, **law′-a-bid′ing; law′break′er; law′giv′er; law′mak′er; law′mak′ing.**

law-ful (lô′fool), *adj.* **1,** according to law; right, not wrong; as, *lawful* acts; **2,** recognized by law; rightful; legal; as, *lawful* ownership.—*adv.* **law′ful-ly.**—*n.* **law′ful-ness.**

law-less (lô′lis), *adj.* **1,** without laws; **2,** not obedient to, or controlled by, authority; unruly.—*adv.* **law′less-ly.**—*n.* **law′less-ness.**

lawn (lôn), *n.* a plot of grass kept closely mowed, esp. around a house or other building.

lawn mow-er or **lawn-mow-er** (lôn′mou′ėr), *n.* a manual, gas, or electric machine with revolving blades used to cut grass.

law-suit (lô′so͞ot′), *n.* a case in a law court to settle a claim between two sides or enforce a right.

law-yer (lô′yėr), *n.* one who is trained and licensed to practise law by giving people advice about the law or representing them in court; an attorney.

lax (laks), *adj.* **1,** loose; not firm, tense, or rigid; **2,** careless; inexact; not strict; as, *lax* principles.—*adv.* **lax′ly.**—*n.* **lax′i-ty.**

lax-a-tive (lak′sa-tiv), *adj.* loosening; causing the bowels to move:—*n.* a medicine that causes the bowels to move.

¹lay (lā), *n.* **1,** a short lyric or poem intended to be sung; **2,** any poem or song.

²lay (lā), *adj.* **1,** having to do with persons outside the clergy; as, *lay* opinion; **2,** relating to those outside any particular profession; as, the *lay* mind usually cannot understand all the fine points of the law.

³lay (lā), *v.t.* [laid (lād), lay-ing], **1,** to cause to lie; place or put; set; as, to *lay* a card on the table; **2,** to bring or beat down; as, the blow *laid* him low; **3,** to produce and deposit (an egg); **4,** to bet; **5,** to impose, as a tax, burden, duty, etc.; **6,** to spread over a surface; as, to *lay* rugs; **7,** to keep down or quiet; suppress; make disappear; as, rain *lays* dust; to *lay* doubt; *lay* a ghost; **8,** to reduce to a certain condition; as, to *lay* waste a city; **9,** to set, in time or place; as, the scene was *laid* in ancient Rome; **10,** to place; impute; as, to *lay* blame for a crime on someone; **11,** to construct, as a floor, foundation, etc.; **12,** to present for consideration; as, to *lay* facts before a committee:—*v.i.* **1,** to produce eggs; **2,** to bet; **3,** on shipboard, to take up a position (as specified); as, to *lay* aft:—**lay off, 1,** to dismiss from a job; as, to *lay off* many workers; **2,** to stop, desist from teasing, etc.; as, we asked the bully to *lay off* the new student:—*n.* the manner or direction in which something lies; as, the *lay* of the land.

⁴lay (lā), *p.t.* of *²lie.*

lay-a-bout (lā′a-bout′), *n.* a lazy or shiftless person; an idler; a loafer.

lay-er (lā′ėr), *n.* **1,** one that lays; as, a brick*layer;* **2,** one thickness; a stratum, row, coating, etc.; as, a *layer* of earth; a *layer* of paint; a *layer* of chocolate icing:—*v.t.* to arrange or form in layers; as, to *layer* a cake.

lay-man (lā′man), *n.* [*pl.* laymen], **1,** a person not of the clergy; **2,** a person not belonging to a particular profession or not an expert in a particular field.

lay-off (lā′ôf′), *n.* **1,** the usually temporary discharge of an employee, esp. during a slowdown or shortage of work; **2,** the period of time the person is not working or is resting.

lay-out (lā′out′), *n.* **1,** plan; arrangement; design; makeup; as, the *layout* of a book, page, advertisement, house, etc.; **2,** an outfit or supply of tools, equipment, etc.; as, a carpenter's *layout;* **3,** the act of laying out.

lay-per-son (lā′pûr′sn), *n.* [*pl.* laypeople (lā′pē′pl) or laypersons] a man or woman not belonging to the clergy or to a particular profession; layman or laywoman.

laze (lāzi), *v.i. Colloq.* to lie, act, or enjoy (oneself) lazily; loaf; idle.

la-zy (lā′zi), *adj.* [la-zi-er, la-zi-est], **1,** disinclined to work; indolent; idle; as, the *lazy* boy slept all day; **2,** causing a lazy feeling; as, a *lazy* summer day; **3,** slow-moving; as, a *lazy* stream.—*adv.* **la′zi-ly.**—*n.* **la′zi-ness.**

LCD (el′sē′dē′), *abbrev.* short for *liquid crystal display.*

lea (lē), *n.* a grassy meadow; a stretch of pasture land.

leach (lēch), *v.t.* **1,** to filter or strain gradually (a liquid or powder); **2,** to permeate; **3,** to remove or drain; as, to *leach* happiness from life:—*v.i.* **1,** to filter through or be dissolved; **2,** to permeate (of an idea, etc.):—*n.* **1,** the process of leaching; **2,** a container used for leaching substances such as ashes, bark, etc.; **3,** a material or substance used for leaching; **4,** a chemical removed from soil by rain and other water.

¹lead (led), *n.* **1,** a soft, heavy, bluish-grey metallic element that is easily bent or shaped: one of the oldest known metals; **2,** a weight attached to a rope for sounding depths at sea; **3,** in *printing,* a thin strip of metal for separating lines of type; **4,** a stick of graphite in a pencil that makes marks, originally made of lead; **5,** bullets:—**leads,** strips of lead used for framing window panes, stained glass, etc.:—*adj.* consisting wholly or partly of lead:—*v.t.* **1,** to cover, fit, or join with lead; **2,** in *printing,* to spread (lines of type) by the insertion of thin metal strips.

²lead (lēd), *v.t.* [led (led), lead-ing], **1,** to conduct by the hand; as, to *lead* a child through a crowd; **2,** to conduct or guide by going on in advance; **3,** to guide or conduct by advice or counsel; **4,** to be first among; as, to *lead* one's class; **5,** to influence; as, hunger *led* him to steal; **6,** to direct; as, to *lead* the choir; **7,** to pass; spend; as, to *lead* a happy life; **8,** to play (a card) as the opening play of a trick:—*v.i.* **1,** to take the first place; **2,** to act as a guide, director, or manager; **3,** to take a course; extend in a direction:—**lead to,** to bring about; pave the way to; as, waste often *leads to* poverty:—*n.* **1,** guidance; example; **2,** first place or position; as, in the *lead;* also, the distance by which one competitor is in advance of another; **3,** in card games, the right to play first; also, the play thus made; **4,** something that may act as a guide; a tip or hint; clue; **5,** the principal actor in a play, movie, television show, etc.; also, his or her part; **6,** the top or introductory news story:—*adj.* first, most important, etc.; as, a *lead* singer, actor, etc.

lead-en (led′n), *adj.* **1,** made of lead; of the colour or weight of lead; heavy; **2,** dull; spiritless; as, a *leaden* step.

lead-er (lēd′ėr), *n.* **1,** one who guides, directs, or conducts; as, an orchestra *leader;* **2,** one who occupies, or is fitted to occupy, the first or chief place; as, a *leader* among the students; **3,** the piece of line or wire at the end of a fishing line to which the hooks are attached.—*n.* **lead′er-ship.**

leaf (lēf), *n.* [*pl.* leaves (lēvz)], **1,** one of the thin, flat parts of a plant, usually green, variously shaped, and borne on a stem or branch or growing from the roots; **2,** a petal; as, a rose *leaf;* **3,** foliage in general; as, a tree in *leaf;* **4,** a sheet of metal beaten thin; as, gold *leaf;* **5,** a sheet of paper, usually from a book or magazine; page; as, a loose-*leaf* notebook; **6,** any of various thin, flat, extra parts that are inserted into or folded out from a table, etc., to make it larger:—*v.i.* of a plant, to put forth foliage:—*v.t.* to glance quickly at and turn the pages of a book, magazine, etc.—*adj.* **leaf′y.**—*n.* **leaf′i-ness; leaf′age.**

leaf-let (lēf′let), *n.* **1,** a single division of a

compound leaf; **2,** a small or new leaf; **3,** a printed sheet or circular; pamphlet; small booklet; as, an advertising *leaflet.*

[1]league (lēg), *n.* **1,** an agreement entered into by two or more persons, organizations, or nations for their common good or purpose; also, the union so formed; **2,** an organization of groups of persons with a common interest, esp. sports teams that play against each other; as, a baseball, hockey, or bowling *league*; **3,** level or class; as, the contest was out of her *league*:—*v.t.* and *v.i.* [leagued, lea-guing], to combine or unite for mutual interests; as, they *leagued* together for protection.

[2]league (lēg), *n.* an old measure of distance equal to about five kilometres.

leak (lēk), *n.* **1,** a hole, crack, or other opening that accidentally lets anything, esp. a fluid, in or out; **2,** the escaping of gas or fluid; leakage; **3,** secret information that somehow becomes known; as, there was a *leak*, and details about the new federal budget got to the media prior to the official announcement:—*v.i.* **1,** to go in or out through a leak; as, water *leaks* in through a crack; **2,** to lose contents through a hole or a crack; as, a bucket *leaks*; **3,** to become gradually known; as, the news *leaked* out:—*v.t.* **1,** to allow something to enter or escape; as, the tire *leaks* air; **2,** to make known by accident or by a deliberate break in secrecy; as, she *leaked* the information to the media.—*n.* **leak′age.**—*adj.* **leak′y.**

[1]lean (lēn), *v.i.* [leaned, lean-ing], **1,** to slant from an upright position; go at an angle; not be straight up and down; as, the Tower of Pisa *leans*; **2,** to rest on something for support; as, to *lean* on a crutch; **3,** to rely or count on for support; as, she *leans* on her best friend in all things; **4,** to tend or be inclined to; have a tendency toward; favour; as, I *lean* toward his opinion; **5,** *Colloq.* to apply pressure; as, his parents *leaned* on him to study harder:—*v.t.* to place in a slanting position; as, he *leaned* the baseball bat against a tree:—*n.* the act or fact of leaning; as, the tree has a *lean* to the right.

[2]lean (lēn), *adj.* **1,** thin; lacking in fat; as, a *lean* athlete; *lean* meat; **2,** not productive; scarce; as, *lean* years; *lean* harvest:—*n.* meat with very little or no fat.—*n.* **lean′ness.**

lean–to (lēn′-tōō′), *n.* [*pl.* lean-tos], **1,** a building that rests against another structure and has a roof sloping one way only; **2,** a crude shelter or shed built against a tree, rock, etc.:—*adj.* having one slope or built against another structure; as, a *lean-to* roof.

leap (lēp), *v.t.* [leaped (lēpt) or leapt (lept), leap-ing], **1,** to pass over by a bound or jump, esp. a high, sudden jump; as, to *leap* a fence; **2,** to cause to jump or spring; as, to *leap* a horse over a hedge:—*v.i.* **1,** to jump or spring off the ground, water, etc., or from a high place; as, the fish *leaped* out of the water; **2,** to bound or move suddenly; as, my heart *leaps* up; to *leap* to help the crying child; **3,** *Colloq.* to embrace eagerly; as, to *leap* at the chance to go on the trip; **4,** to happen or appear suddenly; as, the new idea *leaped* to her mind:—*n.* **1,** the act of passing over with a bound; also, a jump; spring; **2,** the space covered in jumping; **3,** a sudden transition or choice; as, a *leap* of faith.

leap-frog (lēp′frog′), *n.* a game in which each player in turn places his or her hands on the bent back of another, and leaps over him or her:—*v.i.* [leap-frogged, leap-frog-ging], to jump in this fashion:—*v.t.* **1,** to jump over in this fashion; **2,** to evade or skip over; as, to *leapfrog* the obvious problem.

leap year, a year that contains 366 days, with February 29 being the extra day, occurring every four years.

learn (lûrn), *v.t.* [learned (lûrnd) or learnt (lûrnt), learn-ing], **1,** to acquire knowledge of, or skill in; as, to *learn* French; *learn* skateboarding; **2,** to gain information of; find out; as, I regret to *learn* the sad news; **3,** to memorize; as, to *learn* the periodic table:—*v.i.* to gain or receive knowledge or skill; as, she knows no calculus as yet, but she *learns* quickly; to *learn* to ski.—*n.* **learn′er.**

learn-ed (lûr′nid), *adj.* having much knowledge or education; scholarly; as, a *learned* professor.—*adv.* **learn′ed-ly.**

learn-ing (lûr′ning), *n.* **1,** the act or process of acquiring knowledge; as, a university is an institution of higher *learning*; **2,** knowledge or skill gained by study.

learning curve, 1, the rate of learning; **2,** a graph showing this.

learning disability, a term used to describe one of various kinds of problems that can cause a person to have difficulty in learning.

learnt (lûrnt), a *p.t.* and *p.p.* of *learn.*

lease (lēs), *n.* **1,** a written contract for the renting of land, buildings, equipment, vehicles, etc., for a specified time; **2,** property so rented; also, the time for which property is so rented; as, the car has a three-year *lease*:—*v.t.* [leased, leas-ing], **1,** to grant possession of, for a specified time, by a contract or lease; as, the owner *leases* the house to the tenant; **2,** to take possession of by lease; as, the tenant *leases* the house from the owner.

lease-hold (lēs′hōld′), *n.* the holding of property by lease or contract for a specified rate and fixed payments; also, the property so held.—*n.* **lease′hold′er.**

leash (lēsh), *n.* a strap or long cord or chain for holding or leading a dog or other animal:—*v.t.* to fasten or hold with a leash.

least (lēst), *adj.* [a *superl.* of *little*], smallest in degree, size, importance, etc.:—*adv.* in or to the lowest or smallest degree; as, to like this book *least* of all:—*n.* the smallest amount; as, to say the *least*:—**at least, 1,** not less than; as, *at least* eight hours of sleep; **2,** in any case; at any rate; as, he did poorly on the test, but *at least* he did not fail.

leath-er (le*th*′ėr), *n.* the skin of an animal, usually cattle, tanned and prepared for use; also, anything made of the skin so prepared, such as shoes, belts, gloves, purses, jackets, etc.—*adj.* **leath′er-y; leath′ern.**

[1]leave (lēv), *v.t.* [left (left), leav-ing], **1,** to fail to take; allow to remain behind; as, I *left* my book at home; **2,** to have remaining at death; as, they say she *left* three children; **3,** to allow to remain or continue in the same place or condition; as, the appeal *left* him indifferent; **4,** to depart or withdraw from; as, to *leave* a job; *leave* home; **5,** to deliver; as, the postman *leaves* letters; **6,** to give by will; bequeath; as, she *left* the money to charity; **7,** to refer (a matter) for decision; as, I *leave* the choice to you:—*v.i.* to go away; depart; as, the plane *leaves* in two hours.

[2]leave (lēv), *n.* **1,** official permission granted to be absent from work, school, or other duty; as, to be on a month's *leave* from work due to illness; also, the duration of such permission; **2,** permission to do something; as, to give them *leave* to go on the trip; **3,** departure; act of leaving; formal farewell.

[3]leave (lēv), *v.i.* [leaved, leav-ing], to put forth leaves; leaf.

leav-en (lev′en), *n.* **1,** a ferment mixed with a substance to render it light, as yeast in dough; **2,** an influence that cheers or lightens; as, humour is the *leaven* of life:—*v.t.* **1,** to make light or cause to rise by fermentation; to cause to ferment; as, yeast *leavens* dough; **2,** to mix with some modifying element; as, the teacher *leavens* constructive criticism with a little praise.

leaves (lēvz), *n.pl.* of *leaf.*

leav-ings (lēv′ingz), *n.pl.* what is left over; discarded remains; remnants.

lech-e-ry (lech′ėr-i), *n.* gross sensuality; lewdness; lasciviousness.—*adj.* **lech′er-ous;** as, a *lecherous* act; *lecherous* novels.

lec-tern (lek′tėrn), *n.* a stand used to hold a book or pages, used by a speaker; a reading desk, esp. that from which scripture lessons are read in a church.

lec-ture (lek′tūr), *n.* **1,** a prepared formal talk or address given to an audience on any subject, esp. for the purpose of instruction; as, a history *lecture* at a university; **2,** a lengthy reproof; scolding:—*v.i.* [lectured, lectur-ing], to deliver a formal talk; as, the professor *lectures* on economics:—*v.t.* **1,** to deliver a formal talk to; as, to *lecture* the class on economics; **2,** to rebuke; scold; as, to *lecture* the students on their poor test results.—*n.* **lec′tur-er.**

led (led), *p.t.* and *p.p.* of [2]*lead.*

LED (led), *abbrev.* short for *light-emitting diode.*

ledge (lej), *n.* **1,** a narrow, flat shelf or shelflike projection from an upright surface such as a wall, cliff, mountain, etc.; as, a window *ledge*; *ledge* of rock; **2,** a ridge of rock, esp. one underwater, not far from shore.

ledg-er (lej′ėr), *n.* the principal account book of a business, in which the final summaries of debits and credits are recorded.

lee (lē), *n.* **1,** the direction opposite to that from which the wind blows; **2,** the side of anything that is protected from the wind; as, the *lee* of the building; **3,** shelter; as, in the *lee* of the rock:—*adj.* **1,** pertaining to the part that is protected from the wind; as, the *lee* side of a ship; **2,** in the direction toward which the wind blows; as, a *lee* tide.

leech (lēch), *n.* **1,** any of various bloodsucking worms, usually water dwelling, formerly much used in medicine as a means of withdrawing blood from patients; **2,** one who gets all he or she can out of another; a hanger-on; **3,** the free or after edge of a sail: opposite of *luff*:—*v.t.* **1,** to bleed with leeches; **2,** to exhaust or drain resources; as, to *leech* fish from the sea:—*v.i.* to live like a leech; be a hanger-on.

leek (lēk), *n.* an onionlike vegetable, with long, thick green leaves and a narrow white bulb, used as food or flavouring.

LEEK

leer (lēr), *n.* a sly, sidelong look of malice or evil desire:—*v.i.* to look slyly or evilly.

leer-y or **lear-y** (lē′ri), *adj. Colloq.* **1,** suspicious; afraid; wary; **2,** wide-awake; knowing; cunning.

lees (lēz), *n.pl.* the sediment at the bottom of a container containing liquor, which occurs during fermentation; dregs.

lee-ward (lē′wėrd; lū′ėrd), *adj.* pertaining to the lee; away from the wind:—*adv.* toward the lee or sheltered side:—*n.* the lee side.

lee-way (lē′wā′), *n.* **1,** the sideward drift of a vessel caused by the wind; **2,** *Colloq.* extra room or time for action; margin; as, he has 10 minutes' *leeway* to catch the train.

[1]left (left), *adj.* **1,** naming or relating to that side of the human body that is toward the north when one faces east: opposite of *right*; **2,** placed or located on or for the left side; as, the *left* hand; *left* shoe:—*n.* **1,** the direction or region that lies on the left side; as, look to the *left*; **2,** in *politics*, a belief or party supporting social equality and liberal policies, often somewhat radical: so called because in some parliaments, this party is often seated on the left:—*adv.* to the left; as, to turn *left*.

[2]**left** (left), *p.t.* and *p.p.* of [1]*leave*.

left–hand (left′–hand′), *adj.* relating to, or situated on, the left side.

left–hand-ed (left′–han′did), *adj.* **1,** using the left hand with greater strength or skill than the right; **2,** done with, or adapted to, the left hand; **3,** going from right to left or counterclockwise; as, a *left-handed* screw; **4,** awkward; **5,** insincere; as, *left-handed* flattery.

left-ist (left′ist), *n.* and *adj.* one who is, or pertaining to someone who is, a member of, or sympathetic to, a party that supports social equality and liberal policies.

left-o-ver (left′ō′vėr), *n.* something that remains or is left, such as food after a meal; as, to have *leftovers* for dinner:—*adj.* relating to something that remains or is not used; as, *leftover* turkey; *leftover* paper.

leg (leg), *n.* **1,** one of the limbs that supports the body and by which humans and animals walk or stand; sometimes, in humans, the lower limb from knee to ankle; **2,** anything resembling a leg; as, a chair *leg*; **3,** the part of a piece of clothing covering the leg; as, pant *legs*; **4,** the course covered by a vessel on one tack; **5,** one part or stage of a trip or activity; as, the first *leg* of the race or journey; **6,** in *mathematics*, one of two sides of a triangle, the third being the base:—**not having a leg to stand on**, not having any reason, excuse, or defence:—**shake a leg, 1,** hurry up; **2,** dance.—*adj.* **leg′gy; leg′less; leg′like′.**

leg-a-cy (leg′a-si), *n.* [*pl.* legacies], **1,** a gift of money or other property left to someone in the will of a person who has died; **2,** anything that has been handed down from one's predecessors; as, his generosity was a *legacy* from his grandfather; **3,** in *computing*, hardware or software that has been replaced by newer versions.

le-gal (lē′g'l), *adj.* **1,** pertaining to law or lawyers; as, *legal* advice; **2,** permitted or authorized by law; lawful; as, a *legal* parking space; *legal* holiday; **3,** a size of paper, often used by lawyers and others, which is longer than standard letter size: it measures 22 by 35.5 cm (8 1/2 by 14 inches); as, to print a document on *legal*-size paper:—**legal tender**, money or currency lawfully valid for paying debts.—*n.* **le-gal′i-ty.**—*adv.* **le′gal-ly.** Also, **le′gal aid′; le′gal cli′nic; le′gal hol′i-day′.**

le-gal-ize (lē′gal-īz′), *v.t.* [-ized, i-zing], to make lawful; as, to *legalize* the sale of drugs.—*n.* **le′gal-i-za′tion.**

leg-ate (leg′it), *n.* **1,** an ambassador, delegate, or envoy; **2,** in the Roman Catholic Church, a representative of the Pope.

leg-a-tee (leg′a-tē′), *n.* in *law*, a person to whom money or other property is left by will.

le-ga-tion (li-gā′shun), *n.* **1,** an ambassador or envoy and his associates; **2,** the official residence of a diplomatic representative in a foreign country.

le-ga-to (li-gä′tō), *adj.* and *adv.* in *music*, in a smooth, flowing manner without breaks between notes: opposite of *staccato*.

leg-end (lej′end), *n.* **1,** a story or stories collectively handed down from the past by people, esp. a story that centres on a historic person or event but which cannot be proved to be true; as, Robin Hood is a figure from *legend*; **2,** the words of a title or inscription on a coin or medal; **3,** words that explain an illustration or map; caption.—*adj.* **leg′end-ar′y.**

leg-er-de-main (lej′ėr-de-mān′), *n.* **1,** sleight of hand; juggling; tricks; **2,** any deceit or trickery.

leg-ging (leg′ing), *n.* either of a pair of long coverings worn to protect the legs from cold or wet:—**leggings**, tight knit garment worn on the legs by children and women; also, warm trousers worn by children.

leg-i-ble (lej′i-bl), *adj.* capable of being read; easy to read; clear; distinct; as, *legible* handwriting.—*n.* **leg′i-bil′i-ty.**—*adv.* **leg′i-bly.**

le-gion (lē′jun), *n.* **1,** a large division of the ancient Roman army, made up of 3,000 to 6,000 foot soldiers; **2,** an army; any large military force; **3,** a vast number; as, *legions* of supporters:—**Legion**, the Royal Canadian Legion.

le-gion-ar-y (lē′jun-ėr-i), *adj.* belonging to, or consisting of, legions:—*n.* [*pl.* legionaries], a soldier of a legion; legionnaire.

le-gion-naire (lē′jun-âr′), *n.* and *adj.* a member of, or pertaining to, a legion; a legionary.

leg-is-late (lej′is-lāt′), *v.i.* [legislat-ed, legislat-ing], to make, pass, or enact a law or laws; as, to *legislate* against drug use:—*v.t.* to force using legislation; as, to *legislate* the strikers back to work.

leg-is-la-tion (lej′is-lā′shun), *n.* **1,** the act of making, passing, or enacting a law or laws; **2,** laws made, passed, or enacted.

leg-is-la-tive (lej′is-lā′tiv), *adj.* **1,** having the power to create and pass laws; as, Parliament is the *legislative* branch of the federal government; **2,** having to do with the making of laws; as, *legislative* policies:—**Legislative Assembly**, the group of representatives elected to the legislature in certain Canadian provinces and territories.

leg-is-la-tor (lej′is-lā′tėr), *n.* a person who makes or enacts laws; someone who belongs to a group that makes or enacts laws; member of a legislative body.

leg-is-la-ture (lej′is-lā′tūr), *n.* the lawmaking body of a country, province, or state: each Canadian province has a legislature.

le-git-i-mate (li-jit′i-mit), *adj.* **1,** lawful; rightful; legal; as, a *legitimate* claim to the property; **2,** born of wedded parents; **3,** according to accepted rules; as, a *legitimate* pass in football; **4,** reasonable; just; as, illness is a *legitimate* reason for absence; **5,** having hereditary rights; as, a *legitimate* heir to the throne:—*v.t.* (li-jit′i-māt′), [legitimat-ed, legitimat-ing], to permit or recognize by law; declare legal.—*n.* **le-git′i-ma-cy.**—*adv.* **le-git′i-mate-ly.**

leg-ume (leg′ūm; li-gūm′), *n.* **1,** a type of podlike fruit, as the pea and the bean; **2,** a plant bearing such fruit; **3,** the seed of such fruit used as food.—*adj.* **le-gu′mi-nous.**

lei-sure (lē′zhėr; lezh′ėr), *n.* spare time; a condition or time of not having to work and to do as one wishes; as, she enjoys gardening during her *leisure*:—*adj.* free; unoccupied by work; as, *leisure* hours.—*adj.* and *adv.* **lei′sure-ly.**

lem-ming (lem′ing), *n.* **1,** a short-tailed, mouselike rodent with furry feet, found in the Arctic: it was previously popularly believed, and now found to be untrue, that these animals periodically leaped to their death in herds; **2,** hence, a person who unthinkingly follows the crowd, esp. to his or her own destruction.

lem-on (lem′un), *n.* **1,** a small, juicy tropical fruit with pale-yellow skin and very acid juice with a sour taste, which is related to the grapefruit, orange, and lime; **2,** the tree, related to the orange, which bears this fruit; **3,** a pale or bright yellow colour; **4,** *Colloq.* a car or other machine that is badly made or has many things wrong with it:—*adj.* flavoured or coloured like a lemon; as, a *lemon* pie; *lemon* chiffon.

lem-on-ade (lem′un-ād′), *n.* a drink of sweetened water flavoured with lemon juice.

le-mur (lē′mėr; lem′ėr), *n.* any of various small, sharp-nosed, tree-dwelling woolly mammals, with large eyes and long furry tail, which are related to monkeys, found chiefly in Madagascar.

lend (lend), *v.t.* [lent (lent), lend-ing], **1,** to turn over to someone to use for a time; as, to *lend* him a book; **2,** to give someone money that must be paid back by a stated time, usually with interest; to make a loan; as, the bank *lent* us money to buy a car; **3,** to give (aid); provide; as, the light show *lends* excitement to the concert; **4,** to devote or accommodate; as, to *lend* oneself to a scheme:—**lend a hand,** help; as, to *lend a hand* to get the job done:—*v.i.* to make a loan or loans.—*n.* **lend′er.**

length (length), *n.* **1,** the measure of anything from end to end; as, the *length* of a boat; **2,** extent in space, degree, or time; as, the *length* of a movie or a vacation; **3,** a specified distance, as from head to tail of a horse; as, to win by a *length*; **4,** a single piece, as of a series of objects that may be connected; as, a *length* of pipe; **5,** a piece of something that is long; as, a *length* of rope; **6,** the fact or condition of being long; as, to sit through a movie in spite of its *length*; **7,** the quantity of a vowel measured by the time it takes to utter it; as, the *length* of *e* in "he" is greater than that of *e* in "bet":—**at length, 1,** in full detail; as, read the letter *at length*; **2,** at last; finally.

length-en (leng′then), *v.t.* to make long or longer; as, to *lengthen* a skirt:—*v.i.* to grow longer; as, the days *lengthen* in spring.

length-wise (length′wīz′), *adj.* and *adv.* in the direction from end to end or the length; longitudinally; as, a *lengthwise* measurement; we sleep *lengthwise* in bed. Also, *adv.* **length′ways.**

length-y (leng′thi), *adj.* [length-i-er, length-i-est], long; drawn out; tedious; too long; as, a *lengthy*, boring speech.—*adv.* **length′i-ly.**—*n.* **length′i-ness.**

le-ni-ent (lē′ni-ent; lēn′yent), *adj.* not severe; mild; merciful; as, a *lenient* judge.—*adv.* **le′ni-ent-ly.**—*n.* **le′ni-ency; le′ni-ence; len′i-ty.**

lens (lenz), *n.* **1,** a piece of glass or other transparent material, with one or both of its surfaces curved, used in cameras, eyeglasses, telescopes, etc., producing a change in the direction of rays of light, as a result of which, in some lenses, the rays that pass through make an image on a screen or a camera film and make objects look larger, clearer, or closer; **2,** a clear, colourless, lenslike part of the eye that focuses light onto the retina; **3,** something shaped like a lens.

lent (lent), *p.t.* and *p.p.* of *lend.*

Lent (lent), *n.* the 40 weekdays before Easter Sunday, observed in some Christian churches with fasting and penitence.—*adj.* **Lent′en.**

len-til (len′til), *n.* **1,** a pod-bearing plant (legume) of which the small, lens-shaped seeds are edible and the stalks are used for fodder; **2,** the seed of this plant.

len-to (len′tō), *adj.* in *music,* slow.—*adv.* slowly.—*n.* a slow musical passage.

Le-o (lē′ō), *n.* **1,** a northern constellation, the Lion; **2,** the fifth sign of the zodiac ♌, which the sun enters about July 22; also, a person born under this sign.

leop-ard (lep′ėrd), *n.* a large carnivorous cat of southern Asia and Africa, with a black-spotted tawny coat.

le-o-tard (lē′ō-tärd), *n.* **1,** a close-fitting, one-piece, shoulders-to-hips garment worn for dancing or exercising; **2,** tights.

lep-er (lep′ėr), *n.* a person who is afflicted with leprosy.

lep-re-chaun (lep′re-kôn′; -khôn′), *n.* in *Irish folklore*, a sprite or fairy, usually in the form of a little old man.

lep-ro-sy (lep′ro-si), *n.* [*pl.* leprosies], an infectious skin disease marked by external ulcers and a scaling off of dead tissue: also called *Hansen's disease.—adj.* **lep′rous.**

les-bi-an (lez′bē-en), *n.* **1,** a female homosexual; **2,** a resident of the Greek island of Lesbos.

le-sion (lē′zhun), *n.* a hurt; injury; in *medicine*, injury to the working or structure of an organ; as, a brain *lesion.*

less (les), *adj.* [a *comp.* of *little*], **1,** not so much; not so large; as, to eat *less* sugar; **2,** inferior; of lower rank or importance; as, no *less* a person than the director herself:—*prep.* minus; without; as, nine *less* seven equals two:—*adv.* in a lower degree; as, *less* famous:—*n.* a smaller quantity; as, to eat *less.*

les-see (les-ē′), *n.* one to whom a lease is granted; tenant.

less-en (les′n), *v.t.* to make smaller or fewer; reduce; decrease; as, to *lessen* the length of a rope; *lessen* working hours:—*v.i.* to become less; decrease in size, degree, or number; as, her headache *lessened.*

less-er (les′ėr), *adj.* [a *comp.* of *little*], smaller in size or amount; inferior; less; as, the *lesser* evil.

les-son (les′n), *n.* **1,** that which is assigned to a student to learn; **2,** the instruction given at one time; as, a math *lesson*; also, any activity that is taught for the purpose of learning something or gaining a skill; as, a swimming *lesson*; **3,** any person, experience, or event in life that gives knowledge or understanding or by which one learns; as, his accident taught him the *lesson* to drive more carefully; **4,** a reprimand; **5,** in a religious service, a reading from the Bible or other religious writings:—*v.t.* **1,** to instruct; **2,** to reprimand.

les-sor (les′ôr; les-ôr′), *n.* one who gives a lease or rents property to another.

lest (lest), *conj.* **1,** for fear that; as, in dread *lest* the thief returns; **2,** so that not; as, hurry *lest* you be too late.

[1]**let** (let), *n.* **1,** an obstacle; hindrance; **2,** in *tennis* and other racket games, a served ball that touches the net in going over and must be replayed.

[2]**let** (let), *v.t.* [let, let-ting], **1,** to permit; allow; as, *let* me try again; **2,** to cause to happen; **3,** to rent; lease; **4,** to allow (something) to escape, pass, go, or come; as, to *let* air out of a tire; *let* the cat out:—*v.i.* to be hired or leased; as, the house *lets* for $1,500 a month.

let-down (let′doun′), *n.* **1,** disappointment or dissatisfaction; as, losing the game was a huge *letdown*; **2,** decline or relaxation of effort; **3,** the descent of an airplane or spacecraft prior to landing.

le-thal (lē′thal), *adj.* **1,** deadly; fatal; causing or capable of causing death; as, a *lethal* dose; *lethal* chemicals; **2,** pertaining to death; **3,** destructive; as, a *lethal* invasion.

leth-ar-gy (leth′ėr-ji), *n.* [*pl.* lethargies], **1,** unnatural drowsiness; **2,** lack of interest; listlessness; apathy.—*adj.* **le-thar′gic** (li-thär′jik).

let-ter (let′ėr), *n.* **1,** a mark or character used to represent a sound and to spell words; an alphabetical symbol; **2,** a written or printed communication, usually in an envelope addressed to someone; as, a *letter* from my cousin; a *letter* of thanks; **3,** the exact or word-for-word meaning; as, the *letter* of the law; **4,** in *printing*, a special style of type or a single piece of type; **5,** an initial of an educational institution given as an achievement award, esp. in athletics:—**letters**, knowledge; learning; literature; as, a person of *letters*:—*v.t.* to mark with letters; print. Also, **let′ter-box′; let′ter car′ri-er; let′ter o′pen-er; let′ter–per′fect, let′ter–qual′i-ty.**

let-ter-head (let′ėr-hed′), *n.* **1,** the printed heading at the top of a sheet of stationery, usually containing the name and address of the sender; **2,** a sheet of paper so printed.

letter–size (let′ėr–sīz′), *adj.* relating to a regular size of paper, measuring 22 by 28 cm (8 1/2 by 11 inches), which is shorter than legal size; as, to copy the picture on regular *letter-size* paper.

let-tuce (let′us; let′is), *n.* a garden plant with large, green, crisp leaves, which are used in salads or as a garnish in sandwiches, etc.: iceberg, romain, leaf, bibb, etc., are types of lettuces.

let-up (let′up′), *n.* pause; cessation; as, it rained hard after a slight *letup.*

leu-ke-mi-a or **leu-kae-mi-a** (lū-kē′mi-a), *n.* a type of cancerous disease, often fatal, in which there is uncontrolled multiplying of the white blood cells.

leu-ko-cyte or **leu-co-cyte** (lū′kō-sīt′), *n.* the white blood corpuscle, useful in destroying harmful bacteria.

[1]**lev-ee** (lev′i; le-vē′), *n.* **1,** formerly, a morning reception, esp. by a person of high rank; **2,** any assemblage of guests; **3,** in Canada, a formal reception held usually during the day by a public official; as, a New Year's Day *levee.*

[2]**lev-ee** (le-vē′; lev′i), *n.* **1,** a wall or embankment built along a river to keep it from flooding adjoining land; **2,** a pier.

lev-el (lev′el; lev′l), *n.* **1,** an unbroken horizontal surface or line; **2,** equality of height; as, this house is on a *level* with that; **3,** a standard elevation; as, sea *level*; **4,** degree or position in a rank or scale; noise *level*; grade *level*; **5,** an instrument used to find or test a horizontal line; **6,** a flat, even surface; as the *level* at the top of the hill; **7,** a floor of a building; as, her office is on the third *level*; **8,** height; as, water at the highest *level*:—*adj.* **1,** having a flat, horizontal surface; as, *level* ground; **2,** equal to something else in height or importance; **3,** steady; judicious; well-balanced; as, a *level* head; *level* tone of voice:—*v.t.* [levelled, level-ling], **1,** to make smooth or flat in a horizontal plane; as, to *level* a road; **2,** to bring to the same plane, height, or condition as something else; equalize; specifically, to bring to the level of the ground; raze; **3,** to point; aim; direct; as, to *level* criticism at her:—*v.i.* **1,** *Colloq.* to be honest; as, to *level* with her and explain all the sordid details; **2,** to become flat or even; as, the ground *levels* off at this spot.—*n.* **lev′el-ler.**—*adj.* **lev′el–head′ed.**

level crossing, a crossing of a road and a railway on the same level: in the United States, known as a *grade crossing.*

le-ver (lē′vėr; lev′ėr), *n.* **1,** a bar used to move or lift a heavy object by prying; a crowbar; **2,** in *mechanics,* a rigid bar, fixed at one point, the fulcrum, around which it moves as on an axis, used to transmit or modify power; **3,** a projecting handle; as, a gearshift *lever* or a parking-brake *lever* in a car:—*v.t.* to pry, move, or operate like a lever.

le-ver-age (lē′vėr-ij; lev′ėr-ij), *n.* **1,** the action of a lever; **2,** the power gained by using a lever; **3,** advantage or power over someone or something; as, to use one's political *leverage*:—*v.t.* [leveraged, leveraging], to provide or enhance by using leverage; as, the corporation *leveraged* their technical knowledge.

le-vi-a-than (li-vī′a-than), *n.* **1,** in the Bible, a sea animal of enormous size; **2,** anything huge, as a whale or a large ship; **3,** a powerful person.

lev-i-ta-tion (lev′i-tā′shun), *n.* the supernatural or spiritualistic process or illusion of raising and suspending a body in the air without physical support.

lev-i-ty (lev′i-ti), *n.* [*pl.* levities], lack of seriousness; unseemly frivolity; unsteadiness.

lev-y (lev′i), *n.* [*pl.* levies], **1,** the act of enlisting persons or raising money under compulsion; **2,** the number or amount collected:—*v.t.* [levied, levy-ing], **1,** to raise or collect by force or order, as an army or a tax; **2,** to wage war:—*v.i.* to raise money by seizing property; as, to *levy* on an estate for a debt.

lewd (lo͞od), *adj.* **1,** lustful; lecherous; preoccupied with sex; **2,** obscene; vulgar; indecent.

lex-i-con (lek′si-kon), *n.* **1,** a dictionary, esp. of an ancient language, as Greek or Latin; **2,** the entire vocabulary of a certain subject, person, or language; **3,** inventory.

li-a-bil-i-ty (lī-′a-bil′i-ti), *n.* [*pl.* liabilities], **1,** the state of being held responsible for a loss, debt, wrong, crime, etc.; **2,** the state of being subject or susceptible to something or apt to do something; tendency; as, *liability* to disease or to error; **3,** something that hinders or holds back; a disadvantage; as, the car's lack of power is a real *liability*:—**liabilities,** debts; all the money that a person or business owes; the obligations that must be paid out of assets.

li-a-ble (lī′a-bl), *adj.* **1,** answerable; responsible by law; legally bound to pay; as, a person is *liable* for his or her debts; **2,** exposed to some damage, danger, misfortune, penalty, etc.; likely; as, a lazy student is *liable* to fail; to be *liable* to get sick after getting wet and cold; **3,** subject; as, to be *liable* to a fine.

li-aise (lē-āz′), *v.i.* [liaised, liais-ing), **1,** to act as a go-between or link between two or more groups; as, she *liaised* between the student council and the students; **2,** to establish a liaison.

li-ai-son (lē′ā-zon′; lē′ā-zōn′; lē-ā′zon), *n.* **1,** a connecting link; bond; union; coordination; as, a *liaison* between schools and school boards or between departments of the army, government, etc.; **2,** any close union; **3,** a sexual relationship; **4,** in *phonetics,* the carrying over of a final consonant to sound as the first letter of the next word, esp. one beginning with a vowel, as a *nold* crow (an old crow).

li-ar (lī′ėr), *n.* one who tells lies.

li-ba-tion (lī-bā′shun), *n.* **1,** the act of pouring out wine or other liquid as a ritual in honour of a god; **2,** the liquid so poured out; **3,** *Colloq.* the act of drinking, esp. alcohol; **4,** *Colloq.* a beverage, esp. alcohol.

li-bel (lī′bel; lī′bl), *n.* a malicious oral, written, or published statement or image tending to defame or to injure the reputation of another; also, the publishing of such a statement:—*v.t.* [libelled, libel-ling], to make or publish a malicious, injurious statement against; defame.—*n.* **li′bel-ler.**—*adj.* **li′bel-lous.**

lib-er-al (lib′ėr-al), *adj.* **1,** generous; as, a *liberal* supporter of the arts; **2,** abundant; plentiful; as, a *liberal* helping of dessert; **3,** free from narrowness in ideas; broad-minded; as, a *liberal* thinker; **4,** in *politics,* in favour of social and governmental change and progress; **5,** not exact or strict; as, a *liberal* translation of the French article:—*n.* any free-thinking or open-minded person; a progressive; an advocate of liberalism:—**Liberal, 1,** a member of a liberal political party; **2,** in Canada, a member of the Liberal Party.—*n.* **lib′er-al′i-ty.**—*adv.* **lib′er-al-ly.**

liberal arts, in college and university, the subjects such as languages, literature, history, and philosophy, known as the humanities, as distinguished from the technical and professional areas.

Liberal Party, one of the major political federal and provincial parties in Canada.

lib-er-ate (lib′ėr-āt′), *v.t.* [liberat-ed, liber-at-ing], to set free from restraint, bondage, injustice, etc.; release; as, to *liberate* slaves.—*n.* **lib′er-a′tor; lib′er-a′tion.**

lib-er-tine (lib′ėr-tēn′), *n.* one who gives free play to his or her evil impulses, appetites, and desires; a rake:—*adj.* loose in morals; dissolute.

lib-er-ty (lib′ėr-ti), *n.* [*pl.* liberties], **1,** freedom from control or bondage; freedom from the rules of others; independence; **2,** freedom to act, speak, and think as one pleases; **3,** an overstepping of the rules of propriety; undue freedom; as, to take *liberties* with a person; **4,** leisure; freedom from business; **5,** a privilege; permission.

Li-bra (lī′bra), *n.* **1,** a southern constellation, the Balance; **2,** the seventh sign of the zodiac [♎], which the sun enters about September 23; also, a person born under this sign.

li-brar-i-an (lī-brâr′i-an), *n.* someone who is in charge of a library, or someone trained in library science.

li-brar-y (lī′brâr-i), *n.* [*pl.* libraries], **1,** a collection of books, magazines, newspapers, periodicals, photos, CDs, DVDs, records, films, videotapes, computerized databases, etc., which are arranged according to a specific, logical system; **2,** a place where such materials are kept for use, sometimes for a fee, but not for sale; **3,** a room in a person's home with such a collection; **4,** a collection of materials having a common element; as, a *library* of jazz music; **5,** any collection of things similar to a library; **6,** in *computing,* a collection of computer files or programs that are stored and available for use.

li-bret-to (li-bret′ō), *n.* the words of an opera or other long musical composition.

lice (līs), *n.pl.* of *louse.*

li-cence or **li-cense** (lī′sens), *n.* **1,** legal authorization or permission to do or own something; also, the document that gives proof of such permission; as, a driver's *licence*; fishing *licence*; **2,** unrestrained liberty; abuse of freedom; **3,** freedom of thought, action, speech, etc.; **4,** deviation from established rules or form for effect; as, artistic *licence*. Also, **li′cence plate′.**

li-cense (lī′sens), *v.t.* [licensed, licensing], to authorize, or grant permission to, by law; to give a licence to someone; as, to *license* her to practise law.

li-cen-tious (lī-sen′shus), *adj.* lewd; unrestrained; dissolute.—*adv.* **li-cen′tious-ly.**—*n.* **li-cen′tious-ness.**

li-chen (lī′ken), *n.* a flowerless, leafless, mosslike plant, made up of an alga and a fungus, growing flat on solid surfaces such as rocks, tree trunks, etc.

lick (lik), *v.t.* **1,** to pass the tongue over; as, to *lick* a lollipop; **2,** to play or pass over lightly like a tongue, as do flames; **3,** *Colloq.* to beat; also, to conquer or defeat; as, our team *licked* our rivals:—*n.* **1,** the act of passing the tongue over something; **2,** a small amount; bit; as, she didn't do a *lick* of work; **3,** a deposit of natural salt, to which animals go for salt; as, salt *lick*; **4,** *Colloq.* a blow or hit; as, to get in your *licks* before being defeated.

lic-o-rice (lik′ō-rish), *n.* the dried root of a plant of the pea family, or an extract made from it, which is used in medicines and as flavouring in candy and liquors; also, the plant.

lid (lid), *n.* **1,** a movable cover for an opening, as of a container; a top; as, a *lid* of a jar or box; **2,** the covering of skin over the eye; eyelid.

¹lie (lī), *n.* **1,** an untrue statement; falsehood; **2,** anything that misleads or is intended to mislead:—**lie detector,** a device that detects changes in the body that are often associated with lying; polygraph:—*v.i.* [lied (līd), ly-ing], **1,** to speak a falsehood; **2,** to make false representations; as, figures never *lie.*

²lie (lī), *v.i.* [*p.t.* lay (lā), *p.p.* lain (lān), *p.pr.* ly-ing], **1,** to assume, or rest in, a reclining position; as, to *lie* in bed; **2,** to be in a flat or horizontal position; as, the tree *lay* in the road; **3,** to be situated; as, the town *lies* on the other side of the lake; also, to extend; as, there *lies* the path; **4,** to be; exist; as, the trouble *lies* in the engine; also, to remain; as, the factory *lay* idle all summer.

liege (lēj), *adj.* **1,** having the right to devotion and service; as, faithful to his *liege* lord; **2,** bound to give service and devotion, as to a feudal lord; **3,** loyal; faithful:—*n.* formerly, **1,** one bound to give service and devotion; a vassal; **2,** a sovereign; lord and master.

lien (lēn; lē′en), *n.* **1,** a legal claim upon property until a debt owing on it is paid; as, a *lien* on a house; **2,** security for payment.

lieu (lōō; lū), *n. French,* formerly, place; stead:—**in lieu of,** instead of; as, he used tape *in lieu of* string.

lieu-ten-ant (lef-ten′ant; lōō-ten′ant), *n.* **1,** one who acts for a higher authority; deputy: used also with names of ranks to indicate the next lower rank; as, *lieutenant* governor; *lieutenant* colonel; **2,** in the army or police force, a commissioned officer next below a captain; **3,** in the navy, a junior officer, equivalent to a captain; **4,** a similar rank in other military organizations.—*n.* **lieu-ten′an-cy.**

lieutenant governor or **Lieutenant**

Governor, the Queen's representative in each province, appointed by the federal government: a position that is held for five years.

life (līf), *n.* [*pl.* lives (līvz)], **1,** the particular quality that distinguishes an animal or a plant from rocks, earth, water, machines, etc.: something that has life can develop young like itself and can grow; **2,** the state of being alive; existence; as, *life* is precious; **3,** a living person; as, a *life* was saved by the operation; also, living beings collectively; as, human *life*; animal *life*; **4,** the period between birth and death; as, all the years of a person's *life*; **5,** a biography; as, the *life* of Pierre Elliott Trudeau; **6,** animation; vivacity; as, to be full of *life*; **7,** a manner of living; as, a *life* of hardship; city *life*; **8,** the time during which something is in use or in effect; as, the *life* of a car:—**as large (big) as life, 1,** as big as the living person or thing; **2,** in person:—**true to life,** as in real life; exactly:—*adj.* relating to life; as, *life* insurance; lifelong; as, *life* member. Also, **life′blood′; life′ cy′cle; life′ ex-pect′an-cy; life′ form′; life′–giv′ing; life′ his′to-ry; life′ in-sur′ance; life′ jack′et; life′less; life′long′; life′ mem′ ber; life′ part′ner; life′ pre-serv′er; lif′er; life′ raft′; life′sav′er; life′ sci′en-ces; life′ sen′tence; life′–size′; life′ skills′; life′style′; life′–sup-port′; life′–threat-′en-ing; life′work′.**

life-boat (līf′bōt′), *n.* a strong, open boat, carried on large boats or ships, for use in rescuing persons at sea.

life-guard (līf′gärd′), *n.* an expert swimmer who works at public beaches or pools, trained to look after the safety of swimmers.

life-like (līf′līk′), *adj.* **1,** looking as if alive; as, a *lifelike* picture; **2,** copying real life.

life-time (līf′tīm′), *n.* the period of time a person or animal lives or a thing lasts; the time of being alive:—*adj.* lasting or of this period of time; as, a *lifetime* achievement award.

lift (lift), *v.t.* **1,** to raise to a higher point; take up; pull up; pick up; as, to *lift* a heavy weight; **2,** to exalt; **3,** *Colloq.* to steal:—*v.i.* **1,** to rise or have the appearance of rising and going away; dissipate; as, the fog *lifts*; **2,** to go up; be raised to a higher level; as, their spirits *lifted* after hearing the good news:—*n.* **1,** the act of rising to a higher point; also, a rise; increase; as, a *lift* in prices; **2,** aid; assistance; hence, a free ride along one's way; **3,** an elevator; a hoist; a machine or device for lifting; as, a ski *lift*; **4,** a rope from the mast to the end of a yard below, supporting the yard; **5,** a happy feeling; a rise in spirits; as, my visit gave her a *lift*; **6,** the surgical tightening of skin; as, a face*lift*.—*n.* **lift′er.**

lift-off (lift′ôf′), *n.* the launching or take-off of a rocket, aircraft, spacecraft, or missile vertically into the air.

lig-a-ment (lig′a-ment), *n.* a band of tough, fibrous tissues that connect the ends of bones or hold an organ of the body in place.

lig-a-ture (lig′a-tūr′; -chōōr′), *n.* **1,** a tying or binding together; **2,** a narrow bandage; **3,** in *music*, a slur; **4,** in *printing*, two or more letters forming a single character, as *fl* or *œ*; **5,** in *surgery*, a thread or filament to tie blood vessels to stop bleeding.

[1]light (līt), *n.* **1,** the condition of illumination upon which sight depends; as, I need more *light*; **2,** anything that gives light, as the sun, a candle, an electric bulb, etc.; **3,** also, the brightness or radiance given off by these; **4,** something like light that leads to mental clearness and understanding; as, to throw *light* on a problem; **5,** the state of being visible, esp. in public; as, his crimes were brought to *light*; **6,** brightness; shining quality; as, the *light* in her eyes; **7,** a famous or model person; as, she is a shining *light*; **8,** something used to set fire to something else; as, we need a *light* to get the campfire going:—*adj.* **1,** clear; bright; not dark; **2,** pale in colour; as, her hair is *light*:—*v.t.* [light-ed or lit (lit), light-ing], **1,** to kindle, as a fire; also, to set on fire; burn; **2,** to cause to shine and give forth brightness; as, *light* the oil lamp; **3,** to give brightness to; as, the lamp *lights* up the room; **4,** to furnish with, or guide by, a light; as, to *light* someone on his way:—*v.i.* to become bright; as, her face *lit* up when we praised her.

[2]light (līt), *adj.* **1,** not heavy; of little weight; as, a *light* package; **2,** having less than the usual weight for its kind; as, a *light* truck; **3,** not burdensome; easy to endure, understand, or do; entertaining; as, *light* reading; *light* tasks; **4,** delicate; dainty; also, graceful; nimble; as, a *light* step; **5,** cheerful; as, a *light* heart; **6,** frivolous; fickle; **7,** small in amount; as, a *light* snowfall; **8,** of food, easily digested; as, a *light* snack; **9,** of wines and other alcoholic beverages, containing little alcohol; as, *light* beer; **10,** in food, low in fat or calories; as, *light* popcorn, mayonnaise, etc.; **11,** not heavily equipped; as, *light* infantry:—*adv.* in a light way; as, to travel *light*:—*v.i.* [light-ed or lit (lit), light-ing], to descend and rest; come down; settle; alight; land; come upon; as, the bird *lit* on the lawn; to *light* on the answer to the problem.—*adv.* **light′ly.**

light bulb, a glass bulb with a metal wire filament that glows brightly when electricity passes through it.

light–e-mit-ting di-ode (līt′–ē-mit′ing dī′ōd′), *n.* a semiconductor that glows when electric current is passed through it, such as the displays on digital clocks,

VCRs, and other devices: abbreviated as *LED*.

[1]**light-en** (līt′n), *v.t.* **1,** to make clear or bright; illuminate; brighten; as, to *lighten* the room with many windows; **2,** to make lighter in colour; as, to *lighten* her hair colour:—*v.i.* **1,** to become bright; **2,** to shine with flashes of lightning.

[2]**light-en** (līt′n), *v.t.* **1,** to reduce in weight, as a load; **2,** to make less burdensome; make less difficult to do or bear; as, he *lightened* my workload; **3,** to make or become more cheerful; as, she *lightened* my spirits.

light-er (lī′tėr), *n.* **1,** anything that ignites to produce a light or flame; as, a barbecue *lighter*; **2,** a large boat or barge used to load and unload ships not docked but lying at anchor.

light–foot-ed (līt′–foot′id), *adj.* nimble.

light-head-ed (līt′hed′id), *adj.* **1,** dizzy; also, delirious, as from fever; **2,** frivolous; silly.

light-heart-ed (līt′här′tid), *adj.* free from care; happy; cheerful; as, *lighthearted* laughter.—*adv.* **light′heart′ed-ly.**—*n.* **light′heart′ed-ness.**

light-house (līt′hous′), *n.* a tower or other structure with a brilliant light at the top, built near dangerous places along the coast, to warn and guide ships at night and during storms and fog.

light–mind-ed (līt′–mīn′did), *adj.* frivolous; silly.—*adv.* **light′–mind′ed-ly.**—*n.* **light′–mind′ed-ness.**

light-ning (līt′ning), *n.* a sudden flash of light in the sky, followed by thunder, caused by electricity as it travels between clouds or from clouds to the earth:—*adj.* very sudden or fast, like lightning; as, *lightning* speed.

lightning rod, a metal rod, fastened on a building and connected with the earth below, to protect the building from lightning by conducting the electric charge harmlessly into the ground.

light pen, in *computing*, a pen-shaped electronic device used to control or manipulate data on a computer terminal; as, to use a *light pen* to read a bar code.

light-ship (līt′ship′), *n.* a vessel carrying a warning light and moored at sea in a dangerous place to warn other ships or to mark a channel.

light-weight (lī′wāt′), *n.* **1,** someone who weighs less than average; **2,** something or someone of little importance or ability; as, he is an intellectual *lightweight*; **3,** a category or weight division in sports such as boxing, wrestling, weightlifting, etc.:—*adj.* **1,** having less than average weight; **2,** having little or no importance; **3,** relating to this weight division in certain sports; as, to win the *lightweight* wrestling title.

light–year or **light year** (līt′–yēr′), *n.* **1,** the distance that light travels in space in a year (about 9,460,500,000,000 kilometres), a unit of stellar distance; **2,** *Colloq.* a great distance.

lik-a-ble or **like-a-ble** (līk′a-bl), *adj.* easy to like; having a pleasing personality; popular.

[1]**like** (līk), *adj.* similar; exactly or nearly the same; as, *like* minds; in this and *like* situations:—*prep.* **1,** being the same as something else; similar; alike; as, this bike is just *like* mine; **2,** in a mood for; as, I feel *like* reading; **3,** characteristic of; as, it was *like* him to be kind; **4,** giving indications of; as, it looks *like* rain; **5,** in the manner of; the same way as; as, act *like* an adult; **6,** for example, such as; as, sports *like* hockey and baseball:—*n.* the equal of a person or thing; as, I have never seen its *like*:—**and the like**, and others of the same kind; and so on; etc.; as, peas, beans, corn, *and the like*.

[2]**like** (līk), *v.t.* [liked, lik-ing], **1,** to have a taste for; enjoy; find agreeable; as, to *like* skiing; to *like* him; **2,** to want; wish; as, would you *like* some vegetables?—*v.i.* to choose; prefer; as, we'll go, if you *like*:—**likes,** *n.pl.* the things one enjoys; as your *likes* and dislikes.

like-li-hood (līk′li-hood), *n.* probability; the fact of being likely.

like-ly (līk′li), *adj.* [like-li-er, like-li-est], **1,** probable; believable; as, a *likely* tale; **2,** suitable; promising; right for the time or purpose; fitting; as, a *likely* place for lunch; a *likely* candidate; **3,** expected; more or less certain to happen; as, it is *likely* to snow today:—*adv.* probably; as, we'll *likely* get homework.

like–mind-ed (līk′–mīn′did), *adj.* having the same ideas, opinions, or tastes; of the same mind; as, *like-minded* colleagues.

lik-en (līk′en), *v.t.* to compare; as, to *liken* life to a journey.

like-ness (līk′nis), *n.* **1,** resemblance; similarity; as, the *likeness* between the two brothers was amazing; **2,** a portrait; image; **3,** shape; external appearance; guise; as, an enemy in the *likeness* of a friend.

like-wise (līk′wīz′), *adv.* **1,** in a similar manner; as, watch him and do *likewise*; **2,** also; furthermore; as, she was a pianist, a singer, and *likewise* a dancer.

li-lac (lī′lak), *n.* **1,** a shrub with clusters of fragrant white, pink, or violet flowers; **2,** the flower of this shrub; **3,** the pale pinkish-violet colour of the flowers.

lilt (lilt), *n.* **1,** a light or lively tune; a merry song; **2,** light, rhythmic movement; as, the *lilt* of her step; **3,** a light, rhythmic, and pleasant way of speaking with a varied pitch:—*v.t.* to sing in a happy, rhythmic way:—*v.i.* to sing gaily; as, to *lilt* and play.

lil·y (lil′i), *n.* [*pl.* lilies], **1,** a plant with bell-shaped, brightly coloured flowers and a bulblike root: the *prairie lily* or *western red lily* is the provincial flower of Saskatchewan, and the white *garden lily* or *madonna lily* is the provincial flower of Québec; **2,** any other plant with flowers similar to a lily, such as the *water lily*:—*adj.* pure; pale; fragile.

lily of the valley, a low-growing plant with stalks of fragrant, bell-shaped flowers; also, the flowers.

LILY OF THE VALLEY

lily pad, one of the floating leaves of the water lily.

li·ma bean (lī′ma), *n.* a flat-podded bean; also, its seed, fresh or dried, eaten as a vegetable.

limb (lim), *n.* **1,** a leg or arm of a human or some other animal; also a bird's wing or a flipper; **2,** a main branch of a tree; **3,** an extension or projection; as, a *limb* of a building:—**out on a limb,** *Colloq.* in or into a dangerous, vulnerable, or exposed position; as, to go *out on a limb* by supporting the unpopular position.

lim·ber (lim′bėr), *adj.* **1,** flexible; **2,** supple; lithe:—*v.t.* and *v.i.* to make or become flexible or supple; as, to *limber* up before jogging.—*n.* **lim′ber·ness.**

lim·bo (lim′bō), *n.* **1,** a place or condition of confinement, oblivion, neglect, or uncertainty; as, to be kept in *limbo* about the job prospect: originally conceived to be a place between heaven and hell; **2,** a West Indian dance in which a person moves under a low pole while bent backwards.

¹lime (līm), *n.* a white powder obtained by the action of heating limestone, marble, bones, seashells, etc., and used in making cement, mortar, glass, fertilizer, etc.; calcium oxide or quicklime:—*v.t.* [limed, lim-ing], to treat (land) with lime.—*adj.* **lim′y.**

²lime (līm), *n.* **1,** a tropical tree bearing a small, juicy, green, lemonlike fruit; also, its small, sour fruit; **2,** a bright green colour; **3,** the linden.

lime·ade (līm′ād′), *n.* a drink made of lime juice, water, and sugar.

lime·light (līm′līt′), *n.* **1,** the brilliant, white light, formerly thrown upon the central figure or group on a stage, so called because it was produced by burning lime: also called *calcium light*; **2,** glare of publicity; centre of public attention; as, the famous singer enjoyed being in the *limelight.*

lim·er·ick (lim′ėr-ik), *n.* a nonsense or funny poem of five anapestic lines, with a rhyme scheme of *aabba*: the last line is usually the punch line.

lime·stone (līm′stōn′), *n.* a sedimentary rock used as building stone, for road construction, etc.

lim·it (lim′it), *n.* **1,** a border or boundary; that which confines, ends, or checks; as, the city *limits*; **2,** a point that cannot be passed; end; as, to reach the *limit* of one's endurance; **3,** the greatest amount or number that is officially allowed; as the speed *limit* near a school is 40 kilometres per hour:—*v.t.* to restrict; as, his share of the profits is *limited* to 25 per cent.—*n.* **lim′i·ta′tion.**—*adj.* **lim′it·less.**

lim·it·ed (lim′i-ted), *adj.* **1**, restricted; confined; circumscribed; as, a *limited* monarchy; **2**, including only a part of something; **3**, mediocre; lacking in scope, breadth, or originality; as, a *limited* actor; **4**, not excessive or unlimited; **5**, having a specific function; as, her *limited* role on the team; **6**, an incorporated business; **7**, a train or other vehicle with few stops; an express. Also, **lim′it·ed e·di′tion; lim′it·ed li′a·bil′i·ty.**

lim·o (lim′ō), *abbrev.* short for *limousine.*

lim·ou·sine (lim′oo-zēn′), *n.* a large automobile, often with a glass panel between the front, or driver's seat, and the back, or passengers' seats.

¹limp (limp), *n.* a limping, halting motion in walking or movement:—*v.i.* **1,** to walk in an uneven way, with less weight on one leg, usually because of pain or injury; **2,** to move haltingly; as, the old car *limped* uphill.

²limp (limp), *adj.* not stiff or firm; weak; drooping; as, *limp* hair; *limp* handshake; *limp* strategy.—*adv.* **limp′ly.**—*n.* **limp′ness.**

lim·pid (lim′pid), *adj.* transparent; sparklingly clear; intelligible; as, a *limpid* pool; *limpid* style of writing.

lin·age or **lin·e·age** (lī′nij), *n.* **1,** the number of printed or written lines in a piece of text; **2,** payment for written work based on the number of lines.

linch·pin (linch′pin′), *n.* **1,** an axle pin used to keep a wheel on; **2,** a crucial or key element; as, advertising was the *linchpin* of their marketing program; **3,** something vital or essential, esp. something that binds an organization or project together; as, she is the *linchpin* of the team.

lin·den (lin′den), *n.* a large tree with heart-shaped leaves and small clusters of cream-coloured flowers: also called *lime.*

¹line (līn), *n.* **1,** a mark having length, but very little width, made with pen, pencil, etc.; **2,** a wrinkle, as in the skin; a crease; as, laugh *lines*; **3,** a strong, slender string, cord, etc.; as, a clothes*line*; fishing *line*; **4,** a wire of a telephone or telegraph system; also, a telephone connection; **5,** a pipe system for transporting a liquid; as, a gas line; **6,** a boundary; as, they crossed the finish *line*; also, a limit; **7,** a plan or method; course of action or thought; as, a *line* of reasoning; **8,** a succession of persons or objects that form a line or row; as, a long waiting *line*; a *line* of tents; **9,** a profession; branch of business; as, her *line* of work is banking; **10,** a row of printed or written letters or words; as, a sonnet has 14 *lines*; **11,** family; descent; as, a *line* of kings; **12,** vehicles, cars, airplanes, trains, buses, ships, etc., making up a system of transportation; as, an air*line*, bus *line*; also, the company that owns the system; **13,** direction; route; as, a *line* of travel; **14,** outline; shape; contour; as, the *line* of the face; **15,** a brief letter, note, e-mail, etc.; as, drop me a *line* when you get a chance; **16,** *Colloq.* dishonest talk; as, don't hand me that *line*:—**lines**, the words of a part spoken by a performer in a movie, television show, play, etc.; as, the actors were not sure of their *lines*:—*v.t.* [lined, lin-ing], **1,** to draw lines upon; mark with lines; **2,** to form or make a line along; as, roses *line* the path; to *line* a street with trees; **3,** to arrange in a line, as soldiers:—*v.i.* to form a row. Also, **line′back′er; line′ dance′; line′ drive′; line′ graph′.**

²line (līn), *v.t.* [lined, lin-ing], to provide with an inside covering; as, to *line* curtains; to *line* a coat; to *line* gloves with fur.—*n.* **lin′er.**

lin-e-age (lin′i-ij), *n.* ancestry; also, all the descendants of one ancestor.

lin-e-al (lin′i-al), *adj.* **1,** pertaining to direct descent from an ancestor; hereditary; as, *lineal* heirs; **2,** linear.—*adv.* **lin′e-al-ly.**

lin-e-a-ment (lin′i-a-ment), *n.* **1,** [often *lineaments*] a feature; the features; **2,** profile; contour.

lin-e-ar (lin′i-ėr), *adj.* **1,** pertaining to, or composed of, lines; **2,** having or pertaining to length only; as, *linear* measure; **3,** straight; like a line; **4,** one-dimensional; **5,** logical; as, *linear* thinking.

line-man (līn′man), *n.* [*pl.* linemen (-men)], **1,** a person who repairs and maintains telephone, telegraph, or electrical power lines; **2,** in *surveying*, the one who carries tape, line, or chain; **3,** one who inspects rails on a railway track; **4,** in *football*, a player on a forward line.

lin-en (lin′en), *n.* **1,** thread spun from flax; **2,** the material made of this thread; **3,** articles made of this or similar material, as tablecloths, napkins, towels, sheets, etc.:—*adj.* made of linen or material similar to linen.

¹lin-er (lī′nėr), *n.* a large swift ship or airplane belonging to a regular system of transport.

²lin-er (līn′ėr), *n.* **1,** one who makes, fits or provides linings; **2,** a lining; material used in the inside of a garment; **3,** in *baseball*, a hard-hit ball that travels horizontally; **4,** someone who makes lines.

lines-man (līnz′man), *n.* [*pl.* linesmen (-men)], **1,** one who puts up or repairs telephone, telegraph, or electric power lines; lineman; **2,** in *hockey*, a person who is responsible for calling violations such as icing and offsides and conducting face-offs; **3,** in *football*, an official who records the distance gained or lost in each play; **4,** in *tennis*, an official who decides whether the ball lands inside or outside the boundary lines of the court.

line-up or **line–up** (līn′up′; līn′–up′), *n.* **1**, a list of players or performers on a team or in a group; **2**, the individuals on that list; as, he was included in the starting *line-up*; **3**, a queue of people waiting for some reason; as, a long *lineup* for tickets; **4**, a line of persons for the purposes of criminal identification; **5**, a group of people or things with a common purpose; as, the star-studded *lineup*; **6**, a schedule of events such as television programs; as, the network's fall *lineup*; **7**, merchandise or services available for sale.

lin-ger (ling′gėr), *v.i.* to delay; loiter; move or go away slowly; persist; as, the cool air *lingered*.—*adv.* **lin′ger-ing-ly.**

ling-e-rie (län′zhė-rā′; län′zhė-rē′; lân′zhė-rē′), *n.* women's undergarments, nightwear, etc.

lin-go (ling′gō), *n.* [*pl.* lingoes], dialect; often, humorously, any unusual or unfamiliar speech; jargon; language of a particular group or profession; as, baseball *lingo*; legal *lingo*.

lin-gual (ling′gwal), *adj.* **1,** pertaining to, or shaped like, the tongue; **2,** pertaining to languages; **3,** in *phonetics,* formed with the tongue (as a letter or sound):—*n.* in *phonetics*, a letter or sound formed by the tongue, as *l, r, th*, etc.

lin-guist (ling′gwist), *n.* one skilled in languages or linguistics.—*adj.* **lin-guis′tic.**

lin-guis-tics (ling-gwis′tiks), *n.* the scientific study of the structure and nature of language.

lin-i-ment (lin′i-ment), *n.* a healing or stimulating liquid rubbed on the skin.

lin-ing (līn′ing), *n.* an inside covering; also, the material of which such a covering is made; as, the *lining* of a coat.

link (lingk), *n.* **1,** a single loop or division of a chain; **2,** anything that serves to connect the parts of a series, as if by a chain; as, a photo album is a *link* to one's past; **3,** in *computing, hot link* or *hyperlink*:—*v.t.* and *v.i.* to connect, or be connected, by a link; join.—*n.* **link′age.—linking verb,** a verb requiring a predicate adjective, noun, or pronoun to complete it, as *to be, appear, seem, taste*, etc.; as, I *feel* ill.

links (lingks), *n.pl.* a golf course.

li-no-le-um (li-nō′lē-um), *n.* a hard, washable floor covering made of a hardened mixture of ground cork and linseed oil on a backing of burlap or canvas.

lin-seed (lin′sēd′), *n.* the seed of flax, esp. when used to make *linseed oil*; flaxseed.

linseed oil, a pale-yellow oil pressed from flaxseed, used in paint, varnishes, linoleum, etc.

lint (lint), *n.* **1,** the soft down obtained by scraping linen, used for dressing wounds; **2,** ravellings from textiles; fuzz; as, the *lint* in a clothes dryer.

li-on (lī′un), *n.* **1,** a powerful, flesh-eating mammal of the cat family, found in Africa and India: it has a smooth, light-brown coat, long tail, and the male has a darker, shaggy mane around the neck, head, and shoulders; **2,** a celebrated person who is much sought after by society; as, a business *lion*; **3,** a fierce or brave person.—*n.fem.* **li′on-ess.**

li-on-ize (lī′u-nīz′), *v.t.* [lionized, lionizing], to treat someone as important or as a celebrity; as, he was *lionized* in the media for scoring the winning goal.

lion's share, the largest or best part or portion; as, she grabbed the *lion's share* of the reward money.

lip (lip), *n.* **1,** one of the two fleshy borders of the mouth; **2,** an edge of anything hollow or surrounding an orifice; as, the *lip* of a cup; **3,** *Slang* insolence; back talk; as, don't give me any *lip*.—*n.* **lip′lin′er.**

lip reading, to surmise what a person is saying by reading or interpreting his or her lips and other gestures.

lip service, an insincere expression of support or loyalty; as, he paid *lip service* to the idea but did nothing to help.

lip-stick (lip′stik′), *n.* a stick of rouge or colouring for the lips.

lip–synch or **lip–sync** (lip′–singk′), *v.t* and *v.i.* to pretend to sing while moving one's lips in synchronization to a recording.

liq-ue-fy (lik′wi-fī′), *v.i.* and *v.t.* [liquefied, liquefy-ing], to become, or to change into, a liquid.

li-queur (li-kūr′; lē′kūr′), an alcoholic drink, sweetened and flavoured, as crème de menthe, chartreuse, etc.

liq-uid (lik′wid), *adj.* **1,** not solid; freely flowing; fluid; in the form of liquid; as, *liquid* soap; **2,** pure or clear in sound or appearance; as, *liquid* tones of voice; *liquid* eyes; **3,** smooth; flowing; as, *liquid* dance steps; **4,** smooth sounding, as the consonants *l* and *r*; **5,** in *finance*, easily and quickly salable for cash; as, *liquid* assets:—*n.* **1,** a form of matter that is not a gas or a solid and which flows freely, such as water; a liquid substance; **2,** any of the consonant sounds that can be drawn out like a vowel, such as *l*, *r*, and, sometimes, *m*, *n*, and *ng*.—*n.* **li-quid′i-ty.**

liq-ui-date (lik′wi-dāt′), *v.t.* [liquidat-ed, liquidat-ing], **1,** to pay off or settle, as a debt; **2,** to wind up or settle the affairs of (a business, estate, etc.) by turning the assets into cash, paying the debts in full or in whatever proportion may be possible, and dividing up what is left among the owners; **3,** to convert to cash; **4,** to get rid of, as by killing; abolish:—*v.i.* **1,** to wind up a business; **2,** to pay off or settle a debt.—*n.* **liq′ui-da′tion.**

liquid crystal display, the type of display used on many electronic devices, such as calculators or watches, in which the crystals are brighter or darker depending on the electrical current passed through them: abbreviated as *LCD*.

liq-uor (lik′ėr), *n.* **1,** a distilled alcoholic liquid substance, such as gin, vodka, or scotch; **2,** a liquid made of food and in which food is kept; **3,** a liquid for industrial use.

li-ra (lē′rä), *n.* [*pl.* lire (lē′rā), liri (lē′rē′), or liras] a unit of money in Italy, Malta, and Turkey.

lisp (lisp), *v.i.* to pronounce *s* and *z* incorrectly, giving them the sound of *th*:—*v.t.* to utter imperfectly:—*n.* the incorrect pronunciation of *s* and *z* as *th*.

[1]**list** (list), *n.* a series of names, items, etc.; a catalogue, roll, or register; as, a grocery *list*:—*v.t.* to catalogue, register, or enroll; make a list of; enter in a list.

[2]**list** (list), *n.* **1,** an edge or selvage of cloth; **2,** a narrow strip, band, or stripe:—*v.t.* **1,** to edge with a list; **2,** to cut a narrow strip, band, or stripe from the edge of something.

[3]**list** (list), *v.i.* to tilt toward one side, as a ship:—*n.* a leaning to one side, as of a ship.

lis-ten (lis′n), *v.i.* **1,** to try to hear; to pay attention in order to hear; as, to *listen* to the music; *listen* to what the teacher is saying; **2,** to heed; obey; as, to *listen* to your parents.—*n.* **lis′ten-er.**

list-ing (lis′ting), *n.* **1**, the act of making a series of names of people or things; **2**, the things included on such a roster or roll; as, the company's *listing* on the stock exchange; **3**, a property that a real estate agent is trying to sell; **4**, in *computing*, a printout of data or a program.

list-less (list′lis), *adj.* lacking energy or interest; spiritless; lethargic.—*adv.* **list′less-ly.**—*n.* **list′less-ness.**

lists (lists), *n.pl.* **1,** formerly, the barriers of a field where tournaments were held; **2,** any place or area of contest or controversy.

list–serv (list′–sûrv′), *n.* in *computing*, a computer program for the management of e-mail that allows subscribers to a specific mailing list to receive messages and information, and send messages to all subscribers, automatically.

lit (lit), *p.t.* and *p.p.* of *light*.

lit-a-ny (lit′a-ni), *n.* [*pl.* litanies], **1,** a certain form of prayer; esp. in a church service, a responsive prayer in which the clergyman repeats a series of petitions, to which the congregation makes responses; **2,** anything that is repeated or continuous; enumeration; as, a *litany* of complaints.

li-ter (lē′tėr), *n.* Same as **litre.**

lit-er-a-cy (lit′ėr-a-si), *n.* **1,** the ability to read and write; **2,** competence in some skill; as, computer *literacy.—adj.* **lit′er-ate.**

lit-er-al (lit′ėr-al), *adj.* **1,** following the given words or meaning; exact; as, a *literal* translation; **2,** precise; not exaggerated; as, the *literal* account of the accident; **3,** matter-of-fact; concerned with facts.—*n.* **lit′er-al-ness.**—*adj.* **lit′er-al–mind′ed.**

lit-er-al-ly (lit′ėr-a-li), *adv.* **1,** using words according to their exact or strict meaning; as, I didn't mean it *literally* when I said to jump in the lake; **2,** really, actually; as, *literally* millions of Web sites on the Internet.

lit-er-ar-y (lit′ėr-ėr-i), *adj.* **1,** relating to literature or the humanities; **2,** relating to books; as, a *literary* critic; **3,** scholarly; relating to professional writing; as, a *literary* periodical; **4,** enjoying or partaking of reading; knowledgeable about literature; as, a *literary* student.

lit-er-a-ture (lit′ėr-a-tūr′;-choŏr′), *n.* **1,** the written or printed productions of a country or period; esp. such poetry, prose, or other works that are notable for beauty of matter, style, etc., and which have lasting value; **2,** the occupation of authors; **3,** the body of writings on a given subject; as, the *literature* on music; **4,** literature as a course of study; **5,** a leaflet, booklet, or other printed material to advertise or promote something; as, advertising *literature* on a new computer.

lithe (līth), *adj.* [lith-er (līth′ėr), līth′est)], bending easily; supple.

li-thog-ra-phy (li-thog′ra-f), *n.* in *printing,* a process whereby the design or page is reproduced by photography on a thin metal plate curved to fit the printing-press cylinder, and transferred to paper by means of a rubber blanket that runs over another cylinder:—*v.t.* and *n.* **lith′o-graph′.**—*n.* **li-thog′ra-pher.**—*adj.* **lith′o-graph′ic.**

lit-i-gant (lit′i-gant), *n.* either party in a lawsuit:—*adj.* engaged in a lawsuit.

lit-i-gate (lit′i-gāt), *v.i.* [litigated, litigating], to carry on a lawsuit:—*v.t.* to contest in a lawsuit.

lit-i-ga-tion (lit′i-gā′shun), *n.* the act or process of carrying on a lawsuit; also, a lawsuit.

li-ti-gious (li-tij′us), *adj.* **1,** of or related to lawsuits; **2,** inclined to resort to lawsuits, esp. in an unreasonable manner; prone to sue for any reason; **3,** something that is debatable or disputable, esp. that which lends itself to argument in a court of law.

lit-mus (lit′mus), *n.* a violet-blue colouring matter obtained from lichens: it is turned red by an acid and restored to blue by an alkali:—**litmus paper,** a paper saturated with litmus and used for testing acid and alkali solutions:—**litmus test, 1,** a test using litmus paper to determine acidity or alkalinity; **2,** a test in which one factor is decisive.

li-tre or **li-ter** (lē′tėr), *n.* the basic metric unit of capacity or volume of liquids, etc.: one litre of water weighs one kilogram.

lit-ter (lit′ėr), *n.* **1,** a couch with a canopy, borne on persons' shoulders by means of long shafts; **2,** a cot or stretcher for carrying a sick or wounded person; **3,** straw, hay, etc., used as bedding for animals; also, the material, such as gravel, in a cat's litter box; **4,** odds and ends scattered about; also, bits of paper and other waste material lying around; rubbish; **5,** disarray, untidiness; **6,** young animals born at one time to the same mother; as, a *litter* of puppies:—*v.t.* **1,** to supply, as with straw, for bedding; **2,** to make (a place) untidy by scattering or leaving odds and ends about:—*v.i.* to bring forth young animals. Also, **lit′ter box′; lit′ter-bug′.**

lit-tle (lit′l), *adj.* [lit-tler, lit-tlest or less (les), least (lēst)], **1,** small in size or quantity; **2,** small in importance; **3,** brief in time or distance; as, a *little* while; **4,** petty; mean; as, a *little* mind:—*adv.* in small degree; not much; slightly; as, a *little* tired:—*n.* a small quantity, time, or distance; as, to have a *little* of this cake; as, to move a *little.*—*n.* **lit′tle-ness.**

lit-ur-gy (lit′ėr-ji), *n.* **1,** the prescribed ritual for public worship; **2,** a repertoire of ideas, etc.:—**Liturgy,** the eucharistic rite of the Eastern Orthodox Church.

liv-a-ble or **live-a-ble** (liv′a-bl), *adj.* **1,** fit or agreeable to live in or with; **2,** endurable; as, such a life is hardly *livable.*

[1]**live** (liv), *v.i.* [lived, liv-ing], **1,** to exist, or have life; **2,** to reside or dwell; as, to *live* in Ottawa; **3,** to continue to have life; endure; as, to *live* to be old; **4,** to pass life in a particular manner; as, to *live* happily; **5,** to win a livelihood; support oneself; as, to *live* by hard work; *live* on her pension; **6,** to be nourished; as, to *live* on vegetables and grains:—*v.t.* to pass or spend; as, to *live* a happy life.

[2]**live** (līv), *adj.* **1,** having life; alive; not dead; **2,** burning or glowing, as a hot coal; **3,** charged with electricity; as, a *live* wire; **4,** full of enthusiasm and energy; wide awake; as, a *live* club; **5,** of present interest; as, a *live* subject; **6,** of a television or radio program, aired while actually taking place, rather than being taped or filmed in advance; as, a *live* broadcast.

live-li-hood (līv′li-hood), *n.* a means of

existence; regular support; the way a person earns a living.

live-li-ness (līv′li-nis), *n.* cheerfulness; vigour.

live-long (liv′lông′), *adj.* whole; entire; as, the children played the *livelong* day.

live-ly (līv′li), *adj.* [live-li-er, live-li-est], **1,** animated; brisk; spirited; full of life and energy; as, a *lively* dance; **2,** alert; keen; as, a *lively* interest in politics; **3,** vivid; bright; as, a *lively* red; **4,** vigorous; cheerful; as, a *lively* manner; **5,** bounding back easily and quickly, as a ball.

liv-en (līv′en), *v.t.* and *v.i.* to make or become cheerful or lively; as, to *liven* up the party with dance music.

liv-er (liv′ėr), *n.* **1,** a large glandular organ in the upper part of the abdomen, which produces bile, absorbs fats, stores vitamins, and cleans the blood; **2,** the comparable organ in an animal used as food, such as a calf or chicken liver.

liv-er-y (liv′ėr-i), *n.* [*pl.* liveries], **1,** a particular costume worn by servants or by any other special group of persons; **2,** distinctive dress or appearance; **3,** the care of horses for pay; **4,** a stable where horses are boarded or hired out: also called *livery stable*; **5,** a business that hires out horses, carriages, cars, boats, etc.—*n.* **liv′er-y-man.**—*adj.* **liv′er-ied.**

live-stock (līv′stok′), *n.* domestic animals, such as horses, cattle, sheep, or hogs, raised on a farm or ranch for profit.

live wire, 1, *Colloq.* an energetic, active, alert, or aggressive person; as, the new coach is a real *live wire*; **2,** a wire carrying electrical current.

liv-id (liv′id), *adj.* **1,** black and blue; discoloured, as by a bruise; **2,** ashy pale, as with shock; **3,** red-coloured; flushed; as, *livid* with anger; **4,** *Colloq.* very angry; as, her rude remark made him *livid.*

liv-ing (liv′ing), *adj.* **1,** having life; alive; as, *living* beings; **2,** now existent; now in use; active; as, French is a *living* language; **3,** vigorous; active; as, a *living* hope; a *living* faith; **4,** exact; very; vivid; lifelike; as, he is the *living* image of his father; *living* colour; **5,** having to do with life or a certain way of life; as, poor *living* conditions; **6,** suitable for living; as, a *living* room:—*n.* **1,** state of existence; the fact or condition of being alive; **2,** mode of life; a certain way of life; as, plain *living*; country *living*; **3,** livelihood; as, to earn a *living* by tutoring in math:—**the living,** all who are alive. Also, **liv′ing col′our; liv′ing mu-se′um; liv′ing stand′ard; liv′ing wage′; liv′ing will′.**

liz-ard (liz′ėrd), *n.* a long, slender reptile, with a scaly body, four legs, and a long, tapering tail, usually found in warm climates.

lla-ma (lä′ma), *n.* a South American animal somewhat like the camel, but much smaller and without a hump: it is used as a beast of burden in the Andes and raised for its thick, soft wool, milk, and meat.

LLAMA

load (lōd), *v.t.* **1,** to put into or upon (a truck, ship, animal, etc.) as much as can be carried; **2,** to put (the cargo) into or upon a vehicle, ship, airplane, etc.; **3,** to burden; weigh down; as, to *load* a person with work; my heart is *loaded* with sorrow; **4,** to supply lavishly; as, to *load* a person with gifts; **5,** to put a cartridge into; as, to *load* a gun; **6,** to put materials into a machine; as, to *load* the dishwasher; **7,** in *computing,* to transfer information from one computer or storage device to another:—*v.i.* **1,** to put a cartridge into a gun; **2,** to put on, or take on, a cargo; as, the passengers *loaded* onto the bus:—*n.* **1,** the mass of weight usually lifted or carried at one time; cargo; as, this truck carries a huge *load* of lumber; **2,** a burden or worry; as, to take a *load* off my mind; **3,** the powder, bullet, etc., with which a gun is charged; **4,** the amount of electricity drawn from a given source; **5,** *Colloq.* any large amount of something; as, a *load* of homework.—*n.* **load′er.**

load-star (lōd′stär′), *n.* Same as **lodestar.**

load-stone (lōd′stōn′), *n.* Same as **lodestone.**

[1]**loaf** (lōf), *n.* [*pl.* loaves (lōvz)], **1,** a shaped mass of bread or cake, baked in one large piece; **2,** a dish of food made in the shape of a loaf of bread; as, meat *loaf.*

[2]**loaf** (lōf), *v.i.* to pass (time) in idleness; relax in a lazy way; do nothing; as, to *loaf* around all day.

loaf-er (lō′fėr), *n.* **1,** one who does not work; a lounger or idler; **2,** a moccasinlike sports shoe.

loam (lōm), *n.* **1,** a fertile soil of clay mixed with sand and decayed vegetable matter; **2,** a claylike mixture used for moulding and plastering.—*adj.* **loam′y.**

loan (lōn), *n.* **1,** something that is borrowed or lent; esp. a sum of money borrowed to be returned with interest; as, a bank *loan*; **2,** the act of lending; as, the *loan* of a book:—*v.t.* to give something as a loan; to lend (literally, in the physical sense; in figurative sense, use *lend*); as, she *loaned* me the money, the pen, etc.; but, he *lends* me a hand.

loan shark, *Colloq.* a person who charges excessive interest rates for loans: esp. associated with organized crime.

loathe (lō*th*), *v.t.* [loathed, loath-ing], to regard with extreme dislike or disgust; detest; as, I *loathed* the sight of food when I was seasick.—*n.* **loath′ing.**

loath-some (lōth′sum), *adj.* causing disgust; detestable; as, a *loathsome* disease.

lob (lob), *n.* a slow, soft shot, ball, or kick in a high arc:—*v.t.* and *v.i.* [lobbed, lob-bing], to propel or hit something in a high arc; as, to *lob* a volleyball.

lob-by (lob′i), *n.* [*pl.* lobbies], **1,** a hall or waiting room at the entrance to a hotel, theatre, apartment, or other building; **2,** persons or an organized group that try to influence the votes of members of a law-making body; as, the anti-smoking *lobby*:—*v.i.* [lobbied, lobby-ing], to act to change the way members of a legislature vote for a particular measure.—*n.* **lob′by-ist.**

lobe (lōb), *n.* any rounded projection or part; as, the *lobe* of the ear; the *lobe* of a leaf.

lob-ster (lob′stėr). *n.* a large shellfish with a hard outer shell, no backbone, and five pairs of legs, the first developed into powerful pinchers: often eaten as food. Also, **lob′ster-man; lob′ster pot′; lob′ster pound.**

lo-cal (lō′k'l), *adj.* **1,** relating to a particular place or places, esp. the town or neighbourhood one lives in; as, *local* school, library, park, customs, etc.; **2,** limited to a certain part of the body; as, a *local* sprain; *local* anesthetic; **3,** of a train, making all stops; **4,** serving a limited district; as, a *local* gas company:—*n.* **1,** a person from the area or from a specific locality; **2,** a train, bus, etc., that stops at all stations on a given route; **3,** a local branch of an organization, as a union.—*adv.* **lo′cal-ly.**—*v.t.* **lo′cal-ize′** (as, to *localize* an infectious disease).—*n.* **lo′cal-i-za′tion.**

local area network, in *computing,* a method of connecting together several computers that are close to each other, allowing them to share information and other resources: abbreviated as *LAN.*

lo-cale (lō′kal′; -käl′), *n.* a place or locality, esp. with reference to some event or circumstance connected with it.

lo-cal-i-ty (lō-kal′i-ti), *n.* [*pl.* localities], **1,** a general region, place, or district; neighbourhood; **2,** the state of belonging to a specific place.

lo-cal-ize (lō′ka-līz′), *v.t.* **1,** to identify the location of something; as, to *localize* the infection; **2,** restrict something to a particular area; **3,** to decentralize or make local; as, to *localize* responsibility to the community agency:—*v.i.* to be concentrated in a particular location or area; as, the infection *localized* in the lung.

lo-cate (lō-kāt′; lō′kāt), *v.t.* [locat-ed, locat-ing], **1,** to settle or establish in a particular spot; as, the firm *located* its office in Toronto; **2,** to mark out and determine the position of; as, to *locate* a gold mine; **3,** to find the position of; as, to *locate* the enemy:—*v.i.* to settle in a place.

lo-ca-tion (lō-kā′shun), *n.* **1,** a place where something is located; **2,** the act of locating:—**on location,** at a place outside the studio where a movie or television show is normally filmed.

loch (lokh), *n. Scottish* a lake; also, a bay or arm of the sea; as, *Loch* Ness.

¹lock (lok), *n.* **1,** a curl or piece of hair from the head; **2,** a tuft of wool, silk, etc.:—**locks,** the hair of the head; as, a girl with curly *locks.*

²lock (lok), *n.* **1,** a device for fastening a door, drawer, trunk, safe, etc., so that it can be opened only by a special key or a combination of turns of a knob; **2,** an enclosure between two gates in a canal or stream, used in raising or lowering boats or ships from one water level to another; **3,** the mechanism used to fire a gun; **4,** a hold; **5,** a sure thing:—*v.t.* **1,** to fasten or secure with, or as with, a lock; as, to *lock* a file cabinet; **2,** to make secure; to confine; to shut in, out, or up; as, to *lock* up a criminal; **3,** to make fast or rigid by the linking of parts; as, to *lock* the wheels of a truck; the ice *locked* the ship in place; **4,** in *computing,* to protect a file, disk, CD, etc., from changes, deletions, or access:—*v.i.* to become locked; as, the door *locks* automatically.—*n.* **lock′nut′.**

lock-er (lok′ėr), *n.* a small closet, cabinet, drawer, or compartment secured by a lock, used for storing personal belongings in a public place. Also, **lock′er room′.**

lock-et (lok′it), *n.* a small, ornamental, hinged case, often of gold or silver, made to hold a picture, lock of hair, or other small token or keepsake, and to be worn on a chain around the neck.

lock-jaw (lok′jô′), *n.* a form of the disease tetanus, in which the jaws become firmly locked together.

lock-out (lok′out′), *n.* the refusal of an employer to let his or her employees come to work unless they agree to his or her terms.

lock-smith (lok′smith′), *n.* a maker, installer, or repairer of locks and keys.

lock step or **lock-step, 1,** the method of marching in very close formation; **2,** standardized procedure that is unwittingly or slavishly followed, esp. in a rigid or inflexible manner.

lock-up (lok′up′), *n.* **1,** the act of locking up; **2,** *Colloq.* jail.

lo-co-mo-tion (lō′ko-mō′shun), *n.* the act of moving, or ability to move, from place to place.

lo-co-mo-tive (lō′ko-mō′t-iv), *adj.* **1,** moving from place to place; **2,** relating to a machine that moves about under its own power:—*n.* a railway car with an engine, used for pulling or pushing other railway cars.

loc·us (lō′kus), *n.* [*pl.* loci (-sī′, -kē, -kī′)], **1,** in *geometry,* a line or curve traced by a moving point; **2,** a place; site; locality; **3,** the position of a specific gene on a chromosome; **4,** the concentration or focus of activity; focal point.

lo·cust (lō′kust), *n.* **1,** a grasshopper; esp. one of a certain kind, destructive to vegetation, which migrates in great swarms; **2,** a cicada; **3,** a large North American tree, esp. the common locust, or false acacia, having rough bark, small, feathery leaves, and fragrant, yellow-white flowers; also, its wood; **4,** any of several other trees, as the honey locust.

lo·cu·tion (lō-kū′shun), *n.* a peculiar phrase; idiom; a particular style of speech; as, he used an odd *locution.*

lode (lōd), *n.* **1,** any deposit of metallic ore containing gold, silver, etc., found in a vein or crack in a rock; **2,** a vein filled with ore; **3,** an abundant source of something.

lode·star or **load·star** (lōd′stär′), *n.* **1,** the North Star, which is used as a point of reference in navigation to lead or guide; **2,** someone or something that serves as a guide or model; a guiding principle.

lode·stone or **load·stone** (lōd′stōn′), *n.* **1,** a kind of iron ore that is magnetic and attracts iron; **2,** anyone or anything that has great powers of attraction.

lodge (loj), *v.t.* [lodged, lodg-ing], **1,** to furnish with a temporary dwelling; **2,** to deposit for safety; **3,** to settle, or bring to rest, in some spot; as, to *lodge* the boat on the sand bar; **4,** to place formally before the proper authorities; as, to *lodge* a complaint:—*v.i.* **1,** to be deposited or come to rest; as, the kite *lodged* in the tree; **2,** to be a lodger; live in a place for a time:—*n.* **1,** a small house; cottage, esp. one used for a special purpose; as, a fishing *lodge;* **2,** the den of a wild animal or group of animals; as, a beaver *lodge;* **3,** a place where members of a local branch of a larger organization or society meet; also, the members themselves; **4,** an Aboriginal abode or household.

lodg·er (loj′ėr), *n.* one who lives in a room or apartment in another's house and pays rent.

lodg·ing (loj′ing), *n.* a place to sleep or live in for a while; as, *lodging* for the night:—**lodgings,** a room or rooms rented as living quarters in another person's home.

loft (lôft), *n.* a room or open space directly beneath a roof of a building; an attic; **2,** an open area, floor, or gallery above the main floor or under the roof; as, a hay *loft* in a barn; a choir *loft* in a church; **3,** an upper floor or open space of a building used as a work or storage area, as in a warehouse or business building:—*v.t.* and *v.i.* to propel high in the air; as, to *loft* a golf ball.

loft·y (lôf′ti), *adj.* [loft-i-er, loft-i-est], **1,** very high; as, a *lofty* redwoods; **2,** dignified; proud; as, a *lofty* manner; **3,** elevated in thought or language; as, *lofty* sentiments.—*adv.* **lof′ti·ly.**—*n.* **loft′i·ness.**

log (log), *n.* **1,** a bulky piece of felled timber, usually in its natural or unhewn state; **2,** a device consisting of a wooden float on a line and reel, used for measuring the rate of progress of a ship; **3,** a book in which the record of a ship's daily progress and other items of interest are entered: also called *log*book; **4,** any similar record of events; diary; as, a truck driver's *log;* an airplane's *log:*—*v.t.* [logged, log-ging], **1,** to fell and cut into logs, as a tree; **2,** to fell and remove the timber on (a tract of woodland); **3,** to enter in the logbook of a ship, airplane, etc.; also, to make a record of something in a log; as, to *log* the hours worked; **4,** to achieve in speed or distance; as, to *log* 700 kilometres in one day; to *log* 50 hours in one week:—*v.i.* to cut or transport logs:—**log in (on),** in *computing,* to enter into a computer the commands, such as a password or other identification, to open a program and begin a work session:—**log out (off),** in *computing,* to enter a command to terminate a program and a work session.—*n.* **log′ger.** Also, **log′ ca′bin; log′ chute′; log′ drive′; log′jam′; log′rol′ling.**

lo·gan·ber·ry (lō′gan-bėr-i), *n.* [*pl.* loganberries], **1,** a plant obtained by crossing the raspberry with the blackberry; **2,** the fruit of this plant.

log·a·rithm (log′a̩-rith′m; -ri*th*′m), *n.* the exponent, or index, of the power to which a given number must be raised in order to give a required number; as, the *logarithm* of 100 to the base 10 is 2, or of 1000, 3; the *logarithm* of 8 to the base 2 is 3: logarithmic tables are usually computed to the base of 10.

log·book (log′book′), *n.* **1,** a ship's or aircraft's diary or journal, recording its progress, position, daily occurrences, etc.: also called *log;* **2,** any record or diary.

log·ger·head (log′ėr-hed′), *n.* **1,** *Colloq.* a blockhead; stupid person; **2,** a carnivorous marine turtle with a large head; **3,** an iron tool with a long handle used to melt tar and other liquids:—**to be at loggerheads,** to dispute or quarrel.

log·ic (loj′ik), *n.* **1,** the science or art of reasoning that uses accurate information and thought to reach a conclusion; **2,** correct reasoning or thinking of any kind.—*n.* **lo·gi′cian** (lō-jish′an).

log·i·cal (loj′i-kal), *adj.* **1,** relating to reasoning; **2,** according to the rules of logic or correct reasoning; as, a *logical* conclusion; **3,** showing correct thinking; reasonable; sensible; as, a *logical* explanation; **4,** skilled in reasoning; as, a *logical* thinker.—*adv.* **log′i·cal·ly.**

lo·gis·tics (lō-jis′tiks), *n.* **1,** the branch of

military science dealing with the moving, quartering, and provisioning of armies; **2,** the planning and handling of the details of an elaborate operation.

lo-go (lō′gō′), *n.* a symbol or slogan used by companies and organizations to allow easy and explicit identification: an abbreviation of *logotype*.

loin (loin), *n.* **1,** that part of the body of an animal or human, on either side of the spine, between the lowest rib and the hip bone; **2,** a special cut of meat from this part of an animal; as, a pork *loin* chop:—**loins**, the lower abdomen, hips, and groin of a human; also, the reproductive organs or pubic region.

loin-cloth (loin′kloth′; loin′klôth′), *n.* a piece of material worn around the loins of a person, often as the only garment worn in tropical climates.

loi-ter (loi′tėr), *v.i.* to linger; saunter; dawdle; as, don't *loiter* on your way home from school.—*n.* **loi′ter-er.**

loll (lol), *v.i.* **1,** to lounge at ease; as, to *loll* in a chair; **2,** to hang out loosely; droop; as, the dog's tongue *lolls* out:—*v.t.* to permit (the tongue) to hang out; let droop.

lol-li-pop or **lol-ly-pop** (lol′i-pop), *n.* a lump of hard candy on a stick.

lone (lōn), *adj.* **1,** solitary; alone; only; as, a *lone* star in the sky; **2,** unfrequented; isolated; as, a *lone* road; **3,** preferring to be alone; as, a *lone* rider; **4,** lonely; as, a *lone* life.

lone-ly (lōn′li), *adj.* [lone-li-er, lone-li-est], **1,** solitary; without companions; as, a *lonely* traveller; **2,** not often visited; deserted; as, a *lonely* prairie road; **3,** depressed about being alone; missing other people; lonesome; as, a *lonely* person; **4,** causing a person to have this feeling; as, a train whistle is a very *lonely* sound.—*n.* **lone′li-ness.**

lone-some (lōn′sum), *adj.* [lonesom-er, lonesom-est], **1,** lonely; depressed about being alone; as, to feel *lonesome*; **2,** making one feel lonely; as, the *lonesome* hours he spent while away from home; **3,** desolate; not often visited; as, a *lonesome* place.

¹long (lông), *adj.* **1,** not short; covering great distance from end to end; as, a *long* road; **2,** extended in time; not brief; great duration; as, a *long* wait; **3,** far-reaching; as, a *long* memory; **4,** extended (to a specified measure) in space or time; having an exact length or time; as, 50 kilometres *long*; an hour *long*; **5,** of a vowel: **a,** sounded like its name; as, the *long a* in "hate," the *long e* in "eve," the *long u* in "use," etc.; **b,** taking more time to pronounce than the corresponding short sound, as the vowel in "palm" compared with the corresponding short vowel in "what":—*adv.* **1,** to a great length or extent of time; as, something *long* drawn out; **2,** at a distant point in time; as, *long* before the war; **3,** for a long time; as, to wait *long*; **4,** for or during a certain time; throughout; as, all night *long*. Also, **long′boat′; long′bow′; long′ dis′tance′; long′ face′; long′hair′; long′hand′; long′haul′; long′head′ed; long′horn′; long′ johns′; long′ jump′; long′-last′ing; long′-leg′ged; long′ -lived′; long′-lost′; long′-play′ing; long′-range′; long′run′; long′shot′; long′-stand′ ing; long′-suf′fer-ing; long′-term′; long week′end.**

²long (lông), *v.i.* to desire something eagerly; yearn; as, I *long* to go home.

lon-gev-i-ty (lon-jev′i-ti), *n.* great length of life.

long-house or **long house** (long′hous′; long′ hous′), *n.* the council house or communal dwelling of the Iroquois and of other First Nations peoples in North America.

long-ing (lông′ing), *n.* an earnest desire; wish; craving; as, a *longing* for wealth:—*adj.* showing a deep wish or a strong desire; as, a *longing* glance at the food.

lon-gi-tude (lon′ji-tūd′), *n.* the distance east or west on the earth's surface, measured in degrees, from the meridian of Greenwich, England, shown on a map by lines running north and south between the North and South poles. Compare *latitude.*

lon-gi-tu-di-nal (lon′ji-tū′di-nal), *adj.* **1,** relating to longitude or to length; **2,** running lengthwise; as, *longitudinal* veins on the wings of an insect; **3,** dealing with repeated observation of individuals or groups over a period of time; as, a *longitudinal* study or survey.

long-shore-man (lông′shôr′man), *n.* one who works about wharves, as in loading ships.

long–wind-ed (lông′–win′did), *adj.* **1,** tedious; long and drawn out; tiresome; as, a *long-winded* speaker; **2,** not easily becoming out of breath; as, a *long-winded* swimmer.

look (look), *v.i.* **1,** to direct the eyes upon something to see; as, to *look* at a picture; **2,** to front or face in a certain direction; as, my windows *look* out on a garden; **3,** to appear or seem; as, she *looks* happy; **4,** to pay attention; take care; as, *look* before you leap; **5,** to search; as, to *look* for the ball in the bushes:—*v.t.* **1,** to show by an expression of the face; as, he *looked* his contempt; **2,** to regard or survey with the eyes; as, he *looked* the boy up and down:—*n.* **1,** the act of looking; glance; as, I took a *look* at the picture; **2,** (often *looks*), appearance; **3,** expression of face; as, a pathetic *look*; **4,** a search or examination; as, to take a *look* for your lost pen.

look-out (look′out′), *n.* **1,** the act of watching for someone to come or something to happen; as, to be on the *lookout* for this suspect; **2,** a place for watching; also, a place from which to see a long way; as, from the *lookout*, they could see across the lake; **3,** a person engaged in watching.

[1]loom (lo͞om), *n.* a frame or machine for weaving cloth or thread.

[2]loom (lo͞om), *v.i.* **1,** to come into view in an indistinct and enlarged form; as, the buildings *loomed* dark above the deserted street; **2,** to appear or come into the mind as large, exaggerated, or threatening; as, fear *loomed* in her mind; the recession *loomed*.

[1]loon (lo͞oni), *n.* a fish-eating, diving water bird with short legs, webbed feet, and a back with small whitish spots: noted for its shrill cry.

[2]loon (lo͞on), *n.* a crazy, stupid, or ignorant person.

loon-ie (lo͞on′i), *n.* **1,** the Canadian dollar coin, which has a picture of a loon on the back side; **2,** the Canadian currency generally; as, the *loonie* is worth less than the U.S. dollar.

loon-y or **loon-ey** or **lun-y** (lo͞on′i), *Colloq. adj.* crazy; silly; foolish:—*n.* a crazy, silly, or foolish person.

loop (lo͞op), *n.* **1,** a folding or doubling of string, rope, etc., forming a ring or eye through which a cord may be run; a noose; **2,** a ring-shaped formation in a line, stream, road, etc.; **3,** a manoeuvre in which an airplane makes a circular turn in the air; **4,** anything that has or makes a loop; **5,** in *computing*, a program or sequence of instructions that are repeated; also, film or tape that is repeated continuously; **6,** a select group of influential people; inner circle:—*v.t.* to form into, furnish with, or fasten with loops:—*v.i.* to make a loop; move in a loop.

loop-hole (lo͞op′hōl′), *n.* **1,** a narrow opening in a wall for shooting through, as in a fort; **2,** a means of escape or evasion, esp. in law; as, a tax *loophole*.

loose (lo͞os), *adj.* [loos-er, loos-est], **1,** not held fast or attached tightly; as, a *loose* button; *loose* tooth; unbound; as, *loose* papers; **2,** free from bonds or fetters, as an escaped criminal; **3,** not tightly fitted; not snug; as, *loose* pants; **4,** wanting in accuracy or system; as, *loose* logic; **5,** vague; unfounded; as, *loose* ideas; **6,** not close or compact in substance or texture; as, *loose* soil; **7,** lax in principles; unstable morally; **8,** in *sports*, a ball, puck, etc., that is free and not in the possession of either team; as, a *loose* puck:—*adv.* in such a manner as not to bind; in a loose way; as, the keys hung *loose* at his belt:—*v.t.* [loosed, loos-ing], **1,** to set free; **2,** to relax (one's hold); **3,** to untie; unbind; **4,** to release or discharge, as an arrow.—*adv.* **loose′ly.**—*n.* **loose′ness.** Also, **loose′ can′non; loose′ end′; loose′-leaf′.**

loos-en (lo͞os′n), *v.t.* **1,** to make loose; as, to *loosen* a screw; **2,** to allow to become less rigid; as, to *loosen* discipline:—*v.i.* to become less tight, compact, or firm:—**loosen up,** to become more relaxed and less tense.

loot (lo͞ot), *n.* **1,** spoils, plunder, or booty taken in wartime; **2,** stolen goods, esp. something stolen by force; **3,** illicit gains; **4,** *Slang* any money; **5,** gifts received, esp. if plentiful; as, Halloween *loot*; **6,** the act of plundering:—*v.t.* **1,** to plunder; **2,** to rob, esp. on a large scale; **3,** to seize and carry off, esp. after riots or natural disasters; as, they went to *loot* their neighbourhood after the fire:—*v.i.* to engage in robbing or plunder, esp. in wartime.—*n.* **loot′er; loot′ing.**

lop (lop), *v.t.* [lopped, lop-ping], **1,** to cut off, as branches from a tree; **2,** to cut twigs, branches, etc., from; trim; **3,** to trim or eliminate anything that is irrelevant or unwanted:—*v.i.* to droop.

lope (lōp), *n.* an easy, swinging gait, as of a horse:—*v.i.* [loped, lop-ing], to move with an easy, swinging gait.

lop-sid-ed (lop′sīd′id), *adj.* larger or heavier on one side than on the other; leaning too far to one side; unevenly balanced; as, a *lopsided* load; *lopsided* building; *lopsided* competition.

lo-qua-cious (lō-kwā′shus), *adj.* talkative; wordy; garrulous.—*n.* **lo-quac′i-ty** (lō-kwas′i-ti).

lord (lôrd), *n.* **1,** a ruler or governor; master; one who has supreme power; **2,** in feudal times, a person from whom a vassal held land and to whom he owed service:—**Lord,** in the United Kingdom and some of its colonies, a title of a nobleman:—**the Lords,** the upper house of the British Parliament; the House of Lords:—**the Lord,** God; also, Jesus Christ:—*v.i.* to rule with absolute power; also, to act like a lord or act in a proud or bossy way toward others; as, to *lord* it over her peers.—*adj.* **lord′ly.**

lord-ship (lôrd′ship), *n.* **1,** the territory under the control of a lord; **2,** authority; control; ownership; **3,** in the United Kingdom and some of its colonies, the rank of a lord:—**Lordship,** a title or term of address to judges and noblemen.

lore (lōr), *n.* knowledge; esp. the body of traditions and facts about a particular subject; as, folk*lore*; bird *lore*.

lose (lo͞oz), *v.t.* [lost (lôst), los-ing], **1,** to cease to have, or to be deprived of, as by death, separation, accident, negligence, etc.; as, to *lose* a son; to *lose* a finger; to *lose* money; **2,** to fail to keep or sustain; as, to *lose* one's health; to *lose* interest in one's work; try not to *lose* this CD; **3,** to wander from; as, to *lose* one's way; **4,** to waste; let go by; as, to *lose* time; to *lose* an opportunity; **5,** to fail to keep in sight or follow mentally; forget or not know where something is; as, to *lose* track of something; *lose* a pen; **6,** to fail to win; as, to *lose* a game; **7,** to cause (a person) the loss of (a thing); as, sloppy work *lost* him his job; **8,** to obscure; submerge; as, the stream *lost* itself in the marsh; **9,** to ruin; destroy; as, the ship was *lost* at sea; **10,** to fail to see, understand, or hear; miss; as, to *lose* the point of the argument; **11,** to be completely taken up with; as, to *lose* yourself in the book:—*v.i.* **1,** to experience loss; **2,** to fall short of success; be defeated.—*n.* **los′er.**

loss (lôs), *n.* **1,** the state or fact of being lost or destroyed; as, the *loss* of an aircraft; also, that which is lost, or its value: compare *profit*; as, heavy business *losses*; **2,** failure to keep a thing; as, *loss* of wealth; *loss* of my favourite hat; **3,** failure to win or obtain; as, the *loss* of a contract; *loss* against our rival team; **4,** waste; as, *loss* of natural resources:—**losses,** the number of soldiers killed, wounded, or captured in battle.

[1]**lost** (lôst), *p.t.* and *p.p.* of *lose.*

[2]**lost** (lôst), *adj.* **1,** missing; as, a *lost* child; **2,** not won; as, a *lost* race; **3,** ruined; destroyed; as, a *lost* soul; **4,** preoccupied; as, *lost* in thought; **5,** wasted; as, *lost* efforts; **6,** no longer visible; as, *lost* in the distance; **7,** insensible; as, *lost* to honour; **8,** puzzled; uncertain; as, to feel *lost* in the new city. Also, **lost′ and found′; lost′ cause′.**

lot (lot), *n.* **1,** a method of deciding questions by drawing numbers, straws, etc., or by throwing blocks, dice, etc.; as, to choose by *lot*; also, the object or objects used; also, what falls to a person in such a decision; share; **2,** fortune; one's fate; as, it is not my *lot* to become famous; **3,** a portion or parcel; esp. a piece of land; as, a parking *lot*; an empty building *lot*; **4,** a number of objects in a group; as, the store has received a new *lot* of books; best of the *lot*; **5,** a great deal; as, to make a *lot* of noise:—*adv. Colloq.* very much; as, a *lot* bigger.

lo-tion (lō′shun), *n.* a liquid preparation or cosmetic for cleansing, protecting, healing, softening, or beautifying the skin; as, suntan *lotion*; hand *lotion.*

lot-ter-y (lot′ėr-i), *n.* [*pl.* lotteries], **1,** a scheme or contest for distributing prizes by lot to persons holding tickets corresponding to numbers drawn at random: many provinces hold lotteries to raise money for the government; also, charities hold lotteries to raise funds; **2,** an event or occurrence, the outcome of which is determined by fate or luck.

lot-to (lot′ō), *n.* **1,** a game resembling bingo, played with discs, and cards marked in squares; **2,** lottery.

lo-tus or **lo-tos** (lō′tus), *n.* **1,** a plant of the water lily family found in Egypt, or one that is held sacred in India; **2,** in Greek legend, a fruit supposed to cause forgetfulness of care; **3,** a plant of the pea family, with red, pink, or white flowers:—**lotus position,** a position in yoga in which the legs are crossed while seated.

loud (loud), *adj.* **1,** not low or quiet; having a great or strong sound; as, *loud* music; noisy; as, *loud* streets; **2,** striking; emphatic; as, *loud* protests; **3,** *Colloq.* showy or flashy in dress or manner; not in good taste; also, unpleasantly vivid; as, *loud* colours.—*adv.* **loud′ly.**—*n.* **loud′ness.**

loud-speak-er (loud′spēk′ėr), *n.* a device for making sounds louder, used to make announcements or to magnify the sound of music in public places: used in public address (PA) systems

lounge (lounj), *v.i.* [lounged, loung-ing], to move, act, or recline in a lazy, comfortable, or relaxed manner; as, to *lounge* on the porch during the heat wave:—*n.* **1,** a couch or sofa; **2,** a comfortable and informal parlour in a hotel, club, etc., in which a person can relax; **3,** a bar, often with live entertainment.—*n.* **loung′er.**

[1]**louse** (lous), *n.* [*pl.* lice (līs)], **1,** a small, flat, wingless insect living and feeding on the bodies of animals or humans; **2,** a similar insect that lives on plants:—*v.t.* [loused, lous-ing], to remove lice; delouse.—*adj.* **lous′y** (louz′i).

[2]**louse** (lous), *n.* [*pl.* louses], *Slang* a mean, detestable person; heel.—*adj.* **lous′y** (louz′i), *Slang* **1,** inferior; of poor quality; as, *lousy* grades; a *lousy* computer game; **2,** mean; as, a *lousy* trick; **3,** not skilled or good at; as, to be *lousy* in sports.

lout (lout), *n.* an awkward person; a clown or boor.—*adj.* **lout′ish.**

lou-vre or **lou-ver** (lōō′vėr), *n.* any one of a series of slits or openings for light and air, as in a gable, on a window, etc.:—**louvre boards,** sloping slats to keep rain out but let air and light in.

lov-a-ble or **love-a-ble** (luv′a-bl), *adj.* worthy of love or affection; endearing.—*n.* **lov′a-ble-ness.**

love (luv), *n.* **1,** warm and tender attachment or caring; as, mother *love*; also, passionate devotion; as, romantic *love*; **2,** strong liking; as, a *love* for music; **3,** a sweetheart; **4,** in *tennis,* no score:—*v.t.* [loved, lov-ing], **1,** to have a feeling of deep affection for; cherish; as, I *love* my sisters; **2,** to care for passionately; as, to *love* a boyfriend; **3,** to have sexual relations; **4,** to delight in; as, to *love* dancing.—*adj.* **love′less; love′sick′.**

love-bird (luv′bûrd′), *n.* a species of small African parrot that shows great affection for its mate:—**lovebirds,** two people who show great affection for each other and who are very much in love.

love-lorn (luv′lôrn′), *adj.* pining from love.

love-ly (luv′li), *adj.* [love-li-er, love-li-est], **1,** beautiful; charming; very pleasing to look at; admirable; as, a *lovely* child; a *lovely* man; **2,** very nice; delightful; as, *lovely* music.—*n.* **love′li-ness.**

lov-er (luv′ėr), *n.* **1,** one who has a deep affection for another; **2,** one who has a great liking for anything; as, a music *lover.*

lov-ing (luv′ing), *adj.* affectionate; devoted; as, a *loving* friend.—*adv.* **lov′ing-ly.**

¹low (lō), *adj.* **1,** not high or tall; close to the ground; as, a *low* mound; **2,** below the normal or usual level; as, *low* waters due to a lack of rain; *low* prices; **3,** deep in pitch; not loud or high; soft; as, a *low* voice; **4,** near the horizon; as, the sun is *low*; **5,** not advanced physically or mentally in development; as, a *low* organism; **6,** depressed; sad; as, *low* spirits; **7,** relatively small in amount, value, etc.; poor quality; bad; as, a *low* mark on the test; **8,** humble; as, a *low* station in life; **9,** unfavourable; as, a *low* opinion; **10,** vulgar; as, *low* thoughts; **11,** slow; as, at *low* speed; **12,** almost gone; used up; as, *low* in supplies or money; **13,** mean; as, a *low* trick; *low* blow:—*adv.* **1,** not high; as, to fly *low*; **2,** at a deep pitch; **3,** softly; **4,** at a small price; **5,** in humbleness, poverty, or disgrace:—*n.* something that is low; as, the temperature hit a new *low* last night.—*adj.* **low′ly; low′born′; low′brow′.** Also, **low′-ball′; low′ beam′; low′ blow′; low′ brow′; low′-budg′et; low′down′; low′-end′; low′fre′quen-cy; low′ gear′; low′-grade′; low′-in′come; low′-key′; low′-lev′el; low′ -life′; low′-ly′ing; low′-main′te-nance; low′ -pitched′; low′-pres′sure; low′-pro′file; low′ -rent′; low′-rise′; low′-risk′; low′ spir′its; low′-tech′; low′ tide′; low′-wa′ter mark′.**

²low (lō), *n.* the moo or soft call of cattle:—*v.i.* to moo.

¹low-er (lō′ėr), *v.t.* **1,** to let or bring down; let fall; as, to *lower* a curtain; **2,** to reduce in price or value; as, to *lower* the rent; *lower* taxes; **3,** to reduce the height of; as, to *lower* the level of the water; **4,** to weaken; as, illness *lowers* one's resistance; **5,** to humble; as, to *lower* the pride:—*v.i.* to sink; drop; diminish; decrease; become less, as in price or value.

²low-er (lō′ėr), *adj.* [*comp.* of ¹*low*], below in position, degree, rank, etc.; as, a *lower* drawer; *lower* step.

lower-case or **lower-case** (lō′ėr-kās′), in *printing,* the small letters, or letters not capitals. Compare *uppercase.*

low-er-most (lō′ėr-mōst′), *adj.* lowest. Compare *uppermost.*

lowest (lō′est), *superl.* of *low.*

lowest common denominator, 1, in mathematics, the least common denominator; **2,** the level of feelings, taste, and opinion of the majority: this is generally used in a derogatory manner to indicate unsophisticated and even undesirable attributes; **3,** the audience for such things.

low-land (lō′land), *adj.* pertaining to low, flat country:—*n.* low, level country.

low-ly (lō′li), *adj.* [low-li-er, low-li-est], humble; modest; also, low in position or rank:—*adv.* modestly; humbly.—*n.* **low′li-ness.**

loy-al (loi′al), *adj.* **1,** faithful, esp. to one's ruler, country, or government; **2,** true to friend, promise, or duty; **3,** showing faithfulness.—*n.* **loy′al-ty.**—*adv.* **loy′al-ly.**

loy-al-ist (loi′al-ist), *n.* one who supports the authority of one's ruler, country, or government, esp. in time of revolt:—**Loyalist, 1,** a United Empire Loyalist; **2,** any of the colonists who supported Britain during the American Revolution: many of them later left the United States and settled in Canada.

loz-enge (loz′inj), *n.* anything diamond-shaped, as a cough drop or candy, pane of glass, shield, design, etc.

lub-ber (lub′ėr), *n.* **1,** an awkward, clumsy person; **2,** a raw sailor.

lu-bri-cant (lo͞o′bri-kant), *n.* a substance, as oil or grease, for oiling machine parts to reduce friction.

lu-bri-cate (lo͞o′bri-kāt′), *v.t.* [lubricat-ed, lubricat-ing], **1,** to make smooth or slippery; **2,** to apply oil to in order to reduce friction, as in gears.—*n.* **lu′bri-ca′tion.**

lu-cent (lo͞o′sent), *adj.* transparent; clear.

lu-cid (lo͞o′sid), *adj.* **1,** clear; readily understood; as, a *lucid* explanation; **2,** characterized by mental soundness or clarity; as, she has *lucid* moments; **3,** clear; transparent; as, *lucid* water; **4,** shining.—*n.* **lu-cid′i-ty.**

lu-ci-fer (lo͞o′si-fėr), *n.* a friction match:—**Lucifer,** Satan.

luck (luk), *n.* **1,** the way some things happen by accident without being controlled or planned; chance; fortune, whether good or bad; as, the winner of the lottery is decided by *luck*; **2,** good fortune; success; as, I wish you good *luck.*

luck-i-ly (luk′i-li), *adv.* in a lucky way; by good luck; fortunately; as, *luckily,* it didn't rain on the day of the big game.

luck-less (luk′lis), *adj.* unfortunate; not having luck.

luck-y (luk′i), *adj.* [luck-i-er, luck-i-est], **1,** having or showing good fortune; as, a *lucky* winner; **2,** thought of as bringing good luck; as, a *lucky* penny; **3,** turning out well; favourable; as, a *lucky* venture; a *lucky* day.—*n.* **luck′i-ness.**

lu-cra-tive (lo͞o′kra-tiv), *adj.* profitable; money-making; as, a *lucrative* business.

Lud-dite (lud′īt), *n.* **1,** the 19th-century English movement of workers who destroyed machinery and factories in an effort to stop the spread of mechanization; **2,** someone who is opposed to technological change or progress.

lu-di-crous (lo͞o′di-krus), *adj.* ridiculous; absurd.

luff (luf), *v.i.* to sail close into the wind (usually with sails shaking); as, to *luff* past a buoy.—*n.* the forward edge of a fore-and-aft sail: opposite of *leech.*

lug (lug), *v.t.* [lugged, lug-ging], to pull, draw, or carry, with effort; as, to *lug* a suitcase onto the bus:—*v.i.* to move or tug heavily; as, the heavy wagon *lugged* up the hill:—*n.* a projecting piece to support or carry something; as, a tractor with *lugs.*

luge (lo͞ozh), *n.* **1**, a small, light racing sled for one or two people; **2**, the competition involving these sleds.

lug-gage (lug′ij), *n.* baggage; suitcases and bags that a traveller takes along on a trip.

lu-gu-bri-ous (lo͞o-go͞o′bri-us), *adj.* sad; mournful; as, a *lugubrious* air, tone(s), etc.

luke-warm (lo͝ok′wôrm′), *adj.* **1**, moderately warm; **2**, indifferent; not enthusiastic; as, a *lukewarm* greeting.

lull (lul), *v.t.* and *v.i.* to make or become quiet or calm; as, the storm *lulled;* also, to cause to sleep or rest; as, to *lull* the baby to sleep:—*n.* a lessening of noise, violence, or activity; temporary calm; as, a *lull* in a storm; a *lull* in sales.

lull-a-by (lul′a-bī′), *n.* [*pl.* lullabies], a soft song to lull small children to sleep.

lum-ba-go (lum-bā′gō), *n.* rheumatic pain in the muscles of the lower back.

lum-bar (lum′bär), *n.* and *adj.* the regions of the lower back, or loins; as, a *lumbar* nerve or vertebra.

[1]**lum-ber** (lum′bėr), *n.* **1**, timber that has been sawn into boards, planks, etc.; **2**, rubbish; articles of no value:—*v.i.* to cut and prepare timber for market:—*v.t.* to clutter; as, please don't *lumber* up this room.—*n.* **lum′ber-ing; lum′ber-jack′; lum′ber-man; lum′ber-yard′.**

[2]**lum-ber** (lum′bėr), *v.i.* to move or roll heavily and noisily along; as, the truck *lumbered* up the hill.

lu-mi-nar-y (lo͞o′mi-nėr-i), *n.* [*pl.* luminaries], **1**, a light-giving body, such as the sun or moon; **2**, a person who is a shining light, or leader, in his or her field.

lu-mi-nous (lo͞o′mi-nus), *adj.* **1**, giving light; bright; shining; as, *luminous* stars; **2**, easily understood; as, a *luminous* remark.—*n.* **lu′mi-nos′i-ty; lu′mi-nous-ness.**—*adv.* **lu′mi-nous-ly.**

lump (lump), *n.* **1**, a small, shapeless mass; as, a *lump* of clay; **2**, a swelling or bump; as, a *lump* on your head; **3**, something united in one body; as, to pay in one *lump:*—*adj.* related to a lump:—*v.t.* to unite in one body or amount; as, to *lump* expenses:—*v.i.* to form into a mass.

lump-ish (lump′ish), *adj.* heavy; dull; clumsy.

lump sum, a single payment that covers the total amount; as she paid off her car loan with a *lump sum.*

lump-y (lump′i), *adj.* [lump-i-er, lump-i-est], **1**, full of lumps; as, *lumpy* bread; **2**, like a lump; clumsy; lumpish.

lu-na-cy (lo͞o′na-si), *n.* [*pl.* lunacies], insanity; also, extreme foolishness.

lu-nar (lo͞o′nėr), *adj.* relating to the moon; as, a *lunar* eclipse; *lunar* landing; *lunar* month, *lunar* orbit; *lunar* year.

lu-na-tic (lo͞o′na-tik), *adj.* **1**, foolish; utterly absurd; as, *lunatic* notions; **2**, relating to the mentally ill; insane:—*n.* **1**, a mentally ill person; **2**, someone who acts in a wild and foolish way.

lunch (lunch), *n.* a light meal, usually eaten between breakfast and dinner; luncheon:—*v.i.* to eat a lunch.—*n.* **lunch′room′.** Also, **lunch′ box′; lunch′buck′et; lunch′coun′ter; lunch′ hour′; lunch′pail′; lunch′time′.**

lunch-eon (lun′chun), *n.* a light meal between breakfast and dinner; lunch, esp. a formal or special lunch to which guests are invited. Also, **lunch′eon-ette′; lunch′eon meat′.**

lung (lung), *n.* either of the two organs of breathing in humans and other air-breathing animals: located in the chest, lungs take in oxygen from the air and give out carbon dioxide into the air.

lunge (lunj), *n.* **1**, a sudden movement or rush forward; **2**, a sudden leap:—*v.i.* [lunged, lung-ing], **1**, to make a sudden thrust or movement forward; **2**, to plunge forward.

[1]**lu-pine** (lo͞o′pin), *n.* **1**, a garden plant of the pea family with blue, purple, yellow, or white flowers; **2**, the flower of this plant.

[2]**lu-pine** (lo͞o′pīn), *adj.* wolflike; savage.

[1]**lurch** (lûrch), *n.* a sudden roll to one side; as, the *lurch* of a ship; a swaying, staggering motion:—*v.i.* to stagger; as, the drunken man *lurched* down the street.

[2]**lurch** (lûrch), *n.* a difficult, embarrassing situation: used only in *to leave in the lurch.*

lure (lo͝or), *n.* **1**, anything that attracts by promising profit or pleasure; **2**, a decoy; artificial bait, esp. one used to catch fish; **3**, attraction; as, the *lure* of adventure:—*v.t.* [lured, lur-ing], to tempt with promise of profit or pleasure.

lu-rid (lo͞o′rid), *adj.* **1**, ghastly; pale; **2**, shining with a red glow; as, a *lurid* sky; **3**, shockingly vivid; as, a *lurid* tale; **4**, terrible; horrible; as, a *lurid* crime.

lurk (lûrk), *v.i.* **1**, to stay secretly in or about a place; as, the thief *lurked* in the bushes until the police had gone; **2**, to move about stealthily; **3**, to exist in secret; as, resentment *lurked* in his heart.

lus-cious (lush′us), *adj.* **1**, sweet and delicious; as, a *luscious* peach; **2**, pleasing to smell, hear, see, or feel.

lush (lush), *adj.* rich in growth or vegetation; healthy; as, *lush* meadows:—*n. Slang* a person who habitually drinks alcohol; a drunkard.

lust (lust), *n.* **1,** a strong, urgent desire to possess; as, a *lust* for gold; **2,** sinful, impure desire:—*v.i.* **1,** to have a very strong desire; crave; as, he *lusted* for power; **2,** to be filled with impure desire.—*adj.* **lust′ful.**

lust-i-ly (lus′ti-li), *adv.* heartily; with vigour or energy.

lus-tre or **lus-ter** (lus′tėr), *n.* **1,** the quality of shining by reflected light; gloss; **2,** brightness; **3,** splendour; renown; fame; **4,** a kind of pottery with a gleaming, metallic finish.

lus-trous (lus′trus), *adj.* gleaming; brilliant; as, *lustrous* eyes.

lust-y (lus′ti), *adj.* [lust-i-er, lust-i-est], vigorous; healthy.

lute (lūt), *n.* a stringed musical instrument with a body like that of a mandolin, used esp. in the 16th and 17th centuries.

Lutz or **lutz** (luts), *n.* in *figure skating,* a jump in which the skater takes off on one skate, does at least one complete rotation in the air, and lands on the other skate.

lux-u-ri-ant (lug-zhoor′i-ant; luks-ū′ri-ant), *adj.* **1,** abundant and vigorous in growth; **2,** profuse or elaborate.—*n.* **lux-u′ri-ance.**

lux-u-ri-ate (lug-zhoor′i-āt′; luks-ū′ri-āt′), *v.i.* [luxuriat-ed, luxuriat-ing], **1,** to grow abundantly; **2,** to revel or indulge without restraint.

lux-u-ri-ous (lug-zhoor′i-us; luks-ū′ri-us), *adj.* **1,** having a strong taste for costly pleasures or ease; **2,** lavishly furnished and comfortable; as, a *luxurious* hotel.

lux-u-ry (luk′shoo-ri; lug′zhoo-ri), *n.* [*pl.* luxuries], **1,** indulgence in costly pleasure or ease; **2,** something costly or difficult to get; **3,** anything beyond the merest necessity; **4,** a very rich, splendid, or costly way of living.

lye (lī), *n.* an alkali obtained from wood ashes, used in cleaning, making soap, etc.

[1]ly-ing (lī′ing), *p.p.* of *lie.*

[2]ly-ing (lī′ing), *n.* the act of telling lies; untruthfulness:—*adj.* untruthful.

lymph (limf), *n.* a transparent, colourless fluid in humans and animals, carried in vessels called *lymphatics.*

lym-phat-ic (lim-fat′ik), *adj.* relating to, or carrying, lymph:—*n.* a tiny vessel that carries lymph.

lynch (linch), *v.t.* to hang or put to death without a legal trial.—*n.* **lynch′ mob′.**

lynx (lingks), *n.* a large, fierce wildcat with short tail and tufted ears.

lyre (līr), *n.* a harplike musical instrument used by the ancients to accompany singing.

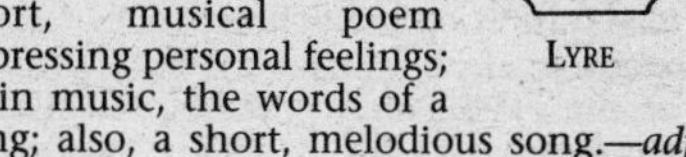

LYRE

lyr-ic (lir′ik), *adj.* suggesting song; like, or relating to, a songlike poem:—*n.* **1,** a short, musical poem expressing personal feelings; **2,** in music, the words of a song; also, a short, melodious song.—*adj.* **lyr′i-cal.**

M

M, m (em), *n.* [*pl.* M's, m's], **1,** the 13th letter of the alphabet, following L; **2,** the Roman numeral for 1000; **3,** *abbrev.* short for *metre;* **4,** *abbrev.* short for *mega-* (a million times or of); as, *mega*bit; *mega*ton; *mega*volt; *mega*watt.

ma (ma), *n. Colloq.* mama; mother.

ma'am (mam), *n.* the contraction for *madam.*

mac-a-ro-ni (mak′a-rō′ni), *n.* [*pl.* macaroni or macaronies], **1,** a food made of a flour paste dried in long, thin tubes or other shapes, which is cooked in boiling water; a type of noodle; **2,** a dandy; fop.

mac-a-roon (mak′a-ro͞on′), *n.* a small cake or cookie made of egg whites, crushed almonds or coconut, and sugar.

ma-caw (ma-kô′), *n.* a large, brightly coloured tropical parrot with a strong, hooked bill, a long tail, and a harsh voice, which is found in Central and South America.

[1]mace (mās), *n.* **1,** a large and heavy club, often spiked, formerly used as a war club; **2,** a staff carried by or before an official as a symbol of power; **3,** the bearer of such a staff.

[2]mace (mās), *n.* a fragrant spice ground from the dried outer covering of the nutmeg.

[3]mace (mās), *v.t.* [maced, mac-ing], to spray someone with a chemical aerosol irritant (Mace); as, the police officer *maced* the fleeing bank robber.

Mace (mās), *n.* a trademark for the chemical aerosol irritant used to temporarily disable someone: a type of tear gas.

Mach or **mach** (mok), *n.* the ratio of the speed of an object, such as an aircraft, to the speed of sound; as, *Mach* 2 is twice the speed of sound. Also called *Mach number* or *mach number.*

ma-che-te (ma-shet′ē; ma-chet′ē), *n.* a large, long, heavy, broad knife, used as a weapon and for cutting sugar cane and through heavy vegetation.

MACHETE

mach-i-na-tion (mak′i-nā′shun), *n.* **1,** a plotting or scheming to do evil; as, the *machinations* of an enemy; **2,** a clever or artful scheme or design; as, the *machinations* of the business rival.

ma-chine (ma-shēn′), *n.* **1,** any contrivance or apparatus designed to utilize motion and energy to produce power; a mechanism with moving and/or fixed parts that does a job or assists in performing a human job, such as a dishwasher, printer, computer, DVD player, robot, etc.; as, a sewing *machine*; fax *machine*; answering *machine*; **2,** a vehicle, esp. an automobile, aircraft, etc.; **3,** a basic device that makes it easier to do physical work or lightens human labour, such as a lever, pulley, wedge, screw, wheel, inclined plane, etc.; **4,** one who acts without thought or with unfailing regularity; **5,** an organization that controls the policies of a political party; as, the Conservative blue machine; **6,** a dispensing device; as, a pop *machine*; an automated teller *machine*:—*adj.* relating to a machine or machines; made by a machine.—*n.* **ma-chin′ist.** Also, **ma-chine′ code′; ma-chine′ gun′; ma-chine′ shed′; ma-chine′shop′; ma-chine′ tool′.**

ma-chin-er-y (ma-shēn′ėr-i), *n.* **1,** machines collectively; as, the *machinery* in a factory; **2,** the working parts of a machine; as, the *machinery* of a clock, elevator, etc.; **3,** any means by which something is kept in action or a desired result is gained; as, the *machinery* of law enforcement.

ma-cho (moch′ō), *adj.* **1,** exaggerated masculinity; aggressive virility; **2,** excessive pride in one's male attributes such as strength, virility, and aggressiveness:—*n.* a male who displays these attributes.—*n.* **ma-chis′mo** (mo-chēz′mō).

mack-er-el (mak′ėr-el), *n.* [*pl.* mackerel], **1,** a food fish, with a speckled and silver body, found in schools in the North Atlantic; **2,** any similar variety of fish:—**mackerel sky,** a sky covered with small white flecks of clouds.

mack-i-naw (mak′i-nô′), *n.* **1,** a short, double-breasted coat of thick, plaid, woollen material; **2,** a blanket of such material in bright colours, used by First Nations people, lumbermen, trappers, etc., of northern United States and Canada; **3,** a large, flat-bottomed boat used formerly on the upper Great Lakes.

mac-ro (mak′rō), *n.* in *computing,* abbreviated or shorthand instructions for frequently performed series of tasks; as, control plus P is the *macro* for print.

mac-ro- (mak′rō-), *prefix* meaning *large, great,* or *inclusive;* as in *macro*biotics, *macro*cosm, *macro*economics, *macro*physics, *macro*scopic: opposite of *micro-*.

ma-cron (mā′kron; ma-), *n.* a mark Æ over a vowel to show that it is pronounced long, as the *a* in *fate* (fāt).

mad (mad), *adj.* [mad-der, mad-dest], **1,** mentally disordered; insane; **2,** rashly foolish; as, he is *mad* to try to swim across the lake; **3,** carried away by strong feeling; excited; as, *mad* with delight; *mad* about mystery novels; **4,** rabid; as, a *mad* dog; **5,** wild; as, a *mad* rush; **6,** angry; showing or feeling anger; as, she was *mad* at him for being late.—*adv.* **mad′ly.**

mad-am (mad′am), *n.* a polite form of address for a woman; as, please follow me, *madam.*

Mad-am (mad′am), *n.* [*pl.* Mesdames (mā′ dåm′)], **1,** a complimentary or courtesy title before a woman's last name; as, *Madam* Sanchez; **2,** a title that denotes the rank or office of a woman; as, *Madam* Prime Minister.

mad-cap (mad′kap′), *n.* a wild, thoughtless, impulsive person:—*adj.* given to wild follies; reckless; foolish; as, a *madcap* adventure.

mad-den (mad′n), *v.t.* and *v.i.* to make, or become, crazed, excited, or furious.

made (mād), *p.t.* and *p.p.* of *make.*

mad-man (mad′man), *n.* [*pl.* madmen (-men)], **1,** a lunatic; insane man; **2,** a man who acts wildly, impulsively, or erratically; as, the *madman* tried to sky-dive off the bridge.—*n.fem.* **mad′wom′an.**

mad-ness (mad′nis), *n.* **1,** insanity; **2,** great foolishness; as, it was *madness* to drive so far in the snowstorm; **3,** great anger; rage.

Ma-don-na (ma-don′a), *n.* a picture or statue of the Virgin Mary.

mad-ri-gal (mad′ri-gl), *n.* **1,** a short love poem, which can be set to music; **2,** a musical setting for a medieval poem, written for several voices, without any instrumental accompaniment; **3,** a song in general.

mael-strom (māl′strom), *n.* **1,** a large, violent whirlpool; **2,** any widespread destructive influence or troublesome situation; as, the *maelstrom* of public unrest.

ma-es-tro (mīs′trō), *n.* [*pl.* maestros or maestri (mīs′trē)], a master of an art, esp. a great musical composer, conductor, or teacher.

Ma-fi-a (mof′ē-a), *n.* **1**, the criminal organization in the U.S. and elsewhere that engages in illegal activities such as racketeering, gambling, and drug dealing; **2**, the Sicilian secret society that began as a political movement and developed into the modern criminal organization:—**mafia, 1,** any similar criminal organization; as, the

Russian *mafia*; **2**, *Colloq.* any clique or tightly knit group, esp. one that dominates or controls some area; as, the literary *mafia*.

mag-a-zine (mag′a-zēn′; mag′a-zēn′), *n.* **1,** a publication, containing articles, stories, pictures, etc., and issued at regular times, usually weekly or monthly; as, a computer *magazine*; also, a similar newspaper publication or section in a newspaper; **2,** a television series, often news-related, which contains interviews, commentary, etc.; **3,** a place for storing military supplies, such as explosives or ammunition; **4,** a warehouse; **5,** a chamber in a gun containing a supply of cartridges; **6,** a chamber or space in a camera for storing film; also, a similar chamber or reservoir for other machines.

ma-gen-ta (ma-jen′ta), *n.* a purple-red dye; also, its peculiar shade of purplish red:—*adj.* of this colour.

mag-got (mag′ut), *n.* **1,** the wormlike larva of an insect, esp. the housefly, often found in decaying flesh, food, etc.; a grub; **2,** an impulse; notion; whim.—*adj.* **mag′got-y.**

mag-ic (maj′ik), *n.* **1,** the art, or pretended art, of compelling supernatural forces, as demons or spirits, to do one's bidding in the natural world: a part of all primitive religions; sorcery; witchcraft; **2,** any unexplainable, bewitching power; a powerful effect; enchantment; as, the *magic* of music; **3,** sleight of hand; the performing of certain tricks that seem impossible; the art of illusion; as, to have the tiger disappear by *magic*:—*adj.* pertaining to, produced by, or having magic; as, a *magic* touch.—*adj.* **mag′i-cal.**—*adv.* **mag′i-cal-ly.** Also, **mag′ic bul′let; mag′ic car′pet; mag′ic mush′room; mag′ic re′al-ism′; mag′ ic word′.**

ma-gi-cian (ma-jish′an), *n.* **1,** one skilled in performing magic tricks for entertainment; **2,** a person who supposedly has magical powers; wizard; sorcerer.

mag-is-trate (maj′is-trāt), *n.* **1,** a government official; **2,** a justice of the peace.—*n.* **mag′is-tra-cy** (maj′is-tra-si).—*adj.* **mag′is-te′ri-al.**

mag-ma (mag′ma), *n.* **1,** in *geology*, the molten, fluid matter deep in the earth from which igneous rock is formed: when ejected from volcanoes it is called *lava*; **2,** a mixture of fine solids and liquid forming a paste; **3,** insoluble solids suspended in water.

mag-nan-i-mous (mag-nan′i-mus), *adj.* great of mind; above pettiness; generous; forgiving; unselfish; noble.—*n.* **mag′na-nim′i-ty.**

mag-nate (mag′nāt; mag′nit), *n.* a person of rank or importance; esp. a person of power or influence in an industry; as, an oil *magnate*.

mag-ne-si-um (mag-nē′zhi-um; -shi-), *n.* a light, silver-white metallic element that burns with a hot, very bright white light, used in alloys, fireworks, flash bulbs, etc.

mag-net (mag′nit), *n.* **1,** lodestone; a variety of iron ore that has the natural property of attracting iron or steel; **2,** a bar or piece of iron or steel to which the power of attracting iron or steel has been artificially given; **3,** a person or thing that attracts; as, the new action movie was a *magnet* and drew a huge crowd.

mag-net-ic (mag-net′ik), *adj.* **1,** relating to a magnet, or its power of attraction; having the properties of a magnet; **2,** relating to the earth's magnetism; **3,** having the power to attract; winning; as, a *magnetic* smile:—**magnetic needle**, a light needle of magnetized steel, which, when suspended in a compass, points in the direction of the earth's magnetic poles, which is approximately north and south:—**magnetic field**, the space around a magnet or an electric current occupied by magnetic lines of force:—**magnetic pole**, **1,** either pole of a magnet where the lines of force converge; **2,** the north magnetic pole, which is currently located near Resolute Bay in the Canadian Arctic, extending over an elliptical zone about 160 kilometres: it is not fixed but is moving, and may leave Canada as early as 2004 before it moves north of Alaska and into Russia:—**magnetic north**, the point on the earth that compass needles point to, south of the North Pole, when free from other magnetic influences.

mag-net-ism (mag′ne-tizm), *n.* **1,** the property of a substance, naturally possessed by some substances, as lodestone, and artificially given to others, as iron or steel, of attracting certain substances according to fixed, physical laws; **2,** the science of magnetism; **3,** personal charm.—*v.t.* **mag′net-ize′** [magnetized, magnetiz-ing].

mag-ne-to (mag-nē′tō), [*n. pl.* magnetos], a small dynamo, with permanent magnets, for generating electric current.

mag-nif-i-cent (mag-nif′i-sent), *adj.* **1,** grand in appearance; splendid; as, a *magnificent* display of jewels; **2,** sublime; noble; impressive; as, a *magnificent* idea; **3,** beautiful; wonderful; as, a *magnificent* view of the ocean.—*adv.* **mag-nif′i-cent-ly.**—*n.* **magnif′i-cence.**

mag-ni-fy (mag′ni-fī), *v.t.* [magnified, magnify-ing], **1,** to cause to appear larger in size; as, a microscope *magnifies* objects seen through it; **2,** to make something seem greater or more important than it really is; exaggerate; as, he *magnifies* the danger.

mag-ni-fy-ing glass (mag′ni-fī′ing glas), *n.* a lens or combination of lenses that makes objects look larger than they are.

mag-ni-tude (mag′ni-tūd′), *n.* **1,** greatness of size; as, the *magnitude* of a mountain; **2,** importance, effect, or extent; as, the *magnitude* of a problem.

mag-no-li-a (mag-nōl′ya), *n.* an ornamental tree, with shiny, dark-green leaves, large white, purple, or pink flowers, and cone-shaped fruit, which grows in Asia and North America and blooms in the spring.

mag-pie (mag′pī′), *n.* **1,** a black-and-white bird of the crow family, noted for its incessant chatter; **2,** one who talks continuously; a chatterer.

ma-ha-ra-jah or **ma-ha-ra-ja** (mä′ha-rä′ja; mä′ha-rä′zha), *n.* in India, the title of a sovereign native king or prince, ranking above a *rajah.—n.fem.* **ma′ha-ra′ni; ma′ha-ra′nee** (mä′ha-rä′nē).

ma-hog-a-ny (ma-hog′a-ni), *n.* [*pl.* mahoganies], **1,** an evergreen tree that grows in tropical climates; **2,** the hard, usually reddish-brown wood of this tree, used for fine furniture and musical instruments; **3,** a dark, reddish-brown colour like this wood.

maid (mād), *n.* **1,** a girl or unmarried woman; maiden; virgin; **2,** a female servant, esp. a woman who does washing and cleaning:—**maid of honour**, an unmarried, principal bridal attendant at a wedding.

maid-en (mād′n), *n.* **1,** a girl or unmarried woman; maid; virgin; **2,** a horse that has not won a race:—*adj.* **1,** not married; **2,** pure; unsoiled; inexperienced; **3,** earliest or first; as, a *maiden* voyage; **4,** unused; untried; as, a *maiden* sword.—*adj.* and *adv.* **maid′en-ly.**

[1]**mail** (māl), *n.* **1,** the letters, newspapers, packages, etc., delivered by post; **2,** the government system for carrying letters, packages, etc.; the post office; **3,** something that carries the mail, as an airplane, boat, or other vehicle; **4,** the collection of items for mailing or arriving by mail; **5,** e-mail; **6,** voice mail:—*v.t.* and *v.i.* **1,** to post, or send by post; as, to *mail* a letter; **2,** to send mail electronically; as, to *mail* a response to an e-mail. Also, **mail′bag′; mail′ bomb′; mail′ box′; mail′er; mail′ing ad′dress; mail′ing list′; mail′man′; mail′ or′der; mail′ room′; mail′slot′.**

[2]**mail** (māl), *n.* **1,** in the Middle Ages, flexible body armour of metal rings, net, or scales linked together, used to protect the body during battle; hence, plate or other armour; **2,** the shell-like protective coat of some animals, as the turtle.

maim (mām), *v.t.* to deprive of the use of any necessary part of the body; cripple; disable.

main (mān), *adj.* **1,** chief; principal; first in size or importance; as, the *main* street; the *main* reason; **2,** sheer; as, by *main* strength:—*n.* **1,** any wide expanse, esp. the sea; as, to sail the *main*; **2,** a principal conduit or pipe carrying water, gas, electricity, etc., to or from a central location; as, a water *main*. Also, **main′ clause′; main′ course′; main′ drag′; main′line′; main′ stage′; main′stream′; main′ street′.**

main-frame (mān′frām′), *n.* in *computing*, a very powerful computer that is able to process huge amounts of information and supports simultaneously many users or terminals that are connected to it. Compare *personal computer* (*PC*).

main-land (mān′land′; mān′land), *n.* **1,** a continent; a broad stretch of land as contrasted with the islands off its coast or peninsulas; as, the small islands just off the *mainland*; **2,** in Newfoundland, the rest of Canada, not including Newfoundland and Labrador; **3,** in British Columbia, the region around Vancouver in southwestern B.C.

main-ly (mān′li), *adv.* principally; chiefly; for the most part.

main memory, *n.* in *computing*, the random-access memory or *RAM* of the *CPU*.

main-spring (mān′spring′), *n.* **1,** the principal spring, or driving spring, in a mechanism, such as a trigger or watch; **2,** a chief motive or reason; cause; as, her criticism was the *mainspring* of his defensive actions.

main-stay (mān′stā′), *n.* **1,** any of the large, strong ropes supporting the principal mast of a ship; **2,** the chief support; as, the *mainstay* of a cause.

main-tain (mān-tān′), *v.t.* **1,** to support or bear the expense of; as, the parents *maintain* their son at university; **2,** to sustain; keep unimpaired; continue or carry on in the same way; as, to *maintain* good grades by studying hard; *maintain* a good reputation; **3,** to continue; keep up; keep in good condition; take care of; as, to *maintain* a house fastidiously; *maintain* roads; **4,** to affirm and defend by argument, as a claim; as, to *maintain* her innocence; **5,** to retain possession of; hold to, as a belief; as, to *maintain* their religious convictions.—*n.* **main′te-nance.**

maize (māz), *n.* corn; field corn; also, its ears or kernels.

ma-jes-tic (ma-jes′tik) or **ma-jes-ti-cal** (ma-jes′ti-kal), *adj.* having or showing great dignity; stately; grand; as, the *majestic* ceremony; *majestic* Rockies.—*adv.* **ma-jes′ti-cal-ly.**

maj-es-ty (maj′es-ti), *n.* [*pl.* majesties], **1,** sovereign power or dignity; royal stateliness; nobility; **2,** a very grand and impressive quality; as, the *majesty* of the rising sun:—**Majesty**, the title of a sovereign ruler; as, Her *Majesty*, the Queen.

ma-jor (mā′jėr), *adj.* **1,** great or greater in number, extent, dignity, importance, or quality; as, the *major* meeting place was the town square; she worked the *major* part of the day; **2,** of full legal age:—**major scale,** in music, the most commonly used scale, consisting of eight tones arranged at intervals of a step or a half step:—*n.* **1,** a military officer next in rank above a captain; **2,** the course of study in post-secondary education in which a student specializes; as, computer sciences is my *major*; **3,** a person of full legal age:—*v.i.* to specialize in a certain subject; as, she *majored* in math.

ma-jor-i-ty (ma-jor′i-ti), *n.* [*pl.* majorities], **1,** the greater of two numbers looked upon as parts of a whole; **2,** the difference between this greater number and the smaller; as, in the class election she won by 24 to 18, a *majority* of six; **3,** the person, party, or group receiving the greatest number of votes, etc.; **4,** the greatest part; as, the *majority* of his music CDs are hip-hop; **5,** the full legal age; as, age of *majority*.

make (māk), *v.t.* [made (mād), mak-ing], **1,** to build; create; construct; fashion; as, to *make* a birdhouse or dress; **2,** to prepare for use; as, to *make* a garden or a bed; **3,** to get; win; as, to *make* friends; **4,** to profit or gain; clear; earn; as, to *make* 500 dollars; also, to score; as, we *made* 10 points in the game; **5,** to arrive at; draw near or into sight of; as, the ship *made* port at dusk; **6,** to cause to be or become; as, the club *made* him president; you *make* me happy; nuts *make* me sick; **7,** to cause; compel; as, to *make* her come to work on time; **8,** to perform; as, to *make* a gesture; **9,** to carry on, as war; **10,** to amount to; as, two and two *make* four; **11,** in electricity, to complete or close (a circuit); **12,** *Colloq.* to catch, as to *make* the 9:00 plane; **13,** to attend; as, I can't *make* your party tonight:—*v.i.* **1,** to move; as, he *made* toward the goal; **2,** to prepare; as, to *make* ready for a journey; **3,** to act in a certain manner; as, to *make* merry:—**make over**, to make different; change:—**make up**, **1,** to invent; as, to *make up* a story; **2,** to become friends again after a quarrel; **3,** to constitute; as, the team was *made up* of boys and girls; **4,** to apply makeup to a face:—*n.* **1,** character; style; build; as, students of her *make*; *make* of the dress; **2,** brand; model; act or method of manufacture; as, what *make* is this car?

make–be-lieve (māk′–bi-lēv′), *n.* pretence; imagination; pretending, as in the play of children:—*adj.* pretended; false.

mak-er (māk′ėr), *n.* a person or thing that makes something; a composer, producer, builder, manufacturer, or creator; as, a dress*maker*, watch*maker*, cabinet *maker*, coffee*maker*, decision *maker*:—**Maker**, God; as, to meet your *Maker*.

make-shift (māk′shift′), *n.* a thing that can be used for the time being until something better is obtained; substitute for a short period of time:—*adj.* temporary; as, a box may be used as a *makeshift* table; *makeshift* plans.

make-up or **make–up** (māk′-up′ or māk′–up′), *n.* **1,** the way the parts of anything are put together; composition; as, the *makeup* of a team; **2,** the dress, paint, powder, wigs, etc., used by an actor in a play, movie, or television show; **3,** cosmetics, such as powder, cream, lipstick, eye shadow, etc., used on the face to enhance one's appearance; **4,** the personality or character of a person; disposition; as, a quiet *makeup* of the child; **5,** a test, exam, or course taken by a student if the previous one was missed or failed.

mal- (mal-), *prefix* meaning **1,** *bad, ill, evil*; as in *mal*administration, *mal*evolent, *mal*odorous, *mal*practice, *mal*treatment; **2,** *poor, faulty, abnormal*; as in *mal*adjusted, *mal*formation, *mal*function, *mal*nutrition; **3,** *not*; as in *mal*content.

mal-a-dy (mal′a-di), *n.* [*pl.* maladies], **1,** a mental or physical disease, disorder, or ailment; **2,** a horrible or desperate condition or state; as, corruption is a societal *malady*.

ma-la-mute or **ma-le-mute** (ma′la-mūt′), *n.* a powerful breed of sled dog native to arctic regions in northern Canada and Alaska: it has a thick black-and-white or grey furry coat and a tail that curls over the back.

mal-a-prop-ism (mal′a-prop-izm′), *n.* **1,** the misuse of a word that is confused with one that sounds like another, often with humorous effects; **2,** the word so misused; as, being taken for "granite" (granted) is a perfect example of a *malapropism*.

ma-lar-i-a (ma-lâr′i-a), *n.* a disease caused by a parasite left in the blood by the bite of certain female mosquitoes, characterized by chills and fever.—*adj.* **ma-lar′i-al.**

mal-con-tent (mal′kon-tent′), *adj.* discontented, esp. with established authority; rebellious:—*n.* one who is discontented with the established order of things.

male (māl), *adj.* **1,** pertaining to the sex that can father young by fertilizing the female egg; **2,** consisting of men or boys; masculine; as, a *male* hockey team; **3,** having the characteristic of men or boys:—*n.* a human being, animal, or plant of this sex. Also, **male′ bond′ing; male′ chau′vin-ism′.**

mal-e-dic-tion (mal′e-dik′shun), *n.* **1,** a curse; **2,** slander.

mal-e-fac-tor (mal′i-fak′tėr), *n.* a wrongdoer; a criminal.—*n.* **mal′e-fac′tion.**

mal-e-mute (ma′le-mūt′), *n.* Same as **malamute.**

ma-lev-o-lent (ma-lev′o-lent), *adj.* wishing evil or injury to others; spiteful.—*adv.* **ma-lev′o-lent-ly.**—*n.* **ma-lev′o-lence.**

mal-ice (mal′is), *n.* evil desire to injure others; ill will; also, intent to commit an unlawful act that will harm someone.

ma-li-cious (ma-lish′us), *adj.* **1,** bearing ill will; filled with hatred or spite; as, a *malicious* person; **2,** arising from ill will; as, a *malicious* act.

ma-lign (ma-līn′), *v.t.* to speak of spitefully; slander; as, to *malign* an innocent person:—*adj.* **1,** possessed of an evil disposition; malicious; **2,** tending to injure; as, *malign* influences.—*n.* **ma-lign′er.**

ma-lig-nant (ma-lig′nant), *adj.* **1,** feeling or showing ill will; doing evil; malicious; **2,** in medical usage, infectious; as, *malignant* cholera; **3,** cancerous; as, a *malignant* tumour: compare *benign.*—*n.* **ma-lig′ni-ty; ma-lig′nan-cy.**

ma-lin-ger (ma-ling′gėr), *v.i.* to feign or pretend illness to escape a duty or work; shirk.—*n.* **ma-lin′ger-er.**

mall (môl), *n.* **1,** a public walk, often shaded by trees, which is closed to automobile traffic; a promenade; **2,** a shopping centre, esp. one that is enclosed and has a central walkway with shops, restaurants, etc., on either side.—*n.* **mall′ rat′.**

mal-lard (mal′ėrd), *n.* a large, common wild duck of the northern hemisphere: the male is marked by a greenish-black head, a white band around the neck, a reddish-brown chest, and grey back, while the female has a brownish body and blue bands on the wings.

mal-le-a-ble (mal′i-a-bl), *adj.* **1,** capable of being hammered or rolled out without being broken; as, gold, copper, and silver are *malleable* metals; **2,** of a person, flexible, adaptable, or yielding.

mal-let (mal′it), *n.* **1,** a short-handled hammer with a wooden or rubber head, used to drive a wedge or chisel; **2,** a wooden stick, hammerlike at one end, used for driving the balls in croquet or polo; **3,** a small, padded hammer used for playing some musical instruments such as xylophones, drums, and other percussion instruments.

malt (môlt), *n.* **1,** barley or other grain that has been sprouted in water and then dried for use in brewing and distilling; **2,** *Colloq.* beer or ale:—*v.t.* to make into, or with, malt:—*v.i.* to become malt:—*adj.* made with malt; as, beer and ale are *malt* liquors.

ma-ma or **mam-ma** or **mom-ma** (mä′mä), *n.* **1,** *Colloq.* mother; **2,** *Slang* a woman or wife.

mam-bo (mam′bō), *n.* a fast-tempo ballroom dance of Latin American origin:—*v.i.* to dance the mambo.

mam-mal (mam′al), *n.* a member of the large group of animals that are warm-blooded, have a backbone, usually have fur or hair on their bodies, and are usually born alive rather than hatched from eggs: female mammals feed their young by means of milk glands and include human beings, most of the common, four-footed, furry or hairy animals, such as cats, dogs, cattle, mice, etc., as well as elephants, bats, and whales.

mam-ma-ry (mam′a-ri), *adj.* pertaining to the breasts, or the gland in female mammals that secretes milk.

mam-mo-gram (mam′o-gram′), *n.* an X-ray for diagnosing tumours, etc., of the breasts.

mam-mon (mam′un), *n.* wealth; worldly gain, regarded as evil:—**Mammon,** greed; the god of greed.

mam-moth (mam′uth), *n.* an enormous, extinct, prehistoric elephant with long, curved tusks and a hairy body: the last ones died out about 10,000 years ago:—*adj.* gigantic; huge; colossal; as, the science-fiction movie was a *mammoth* production.

man (man), *n.* [*pl.* men (men)], **1,** a human being, male or female, used esp. formerly, now considered sexist language by some; the human race; humankind; as, all *men* were created equal; **2,** an adult male of the human race; an adult male person; **3,** a male employee or servant; valet; also, employees in general; **4,** a man possessed of male qualities in a high degree; as, he was quite the *man*; **5,** one of the pieces in chess, checkers, etc.; also, a male player in a game; **6,** a husband; as, *man* and wife; **7,** *Colloq.* boyfriend; lover; **8,** *interj. Colloq.* expletive to show strong emotion; as, *man*, am I tired!—*v.t.* [manned, man-ning], **1,** to furnish with workers, male or female; as, to *man* a ship, assembly line, etc.; **2,** to brace or nerve (oneself); as, she *manned* herself for the unpleasant task.

man-a-cle (man′a-kl), *n.* **1,** a handcuff; fetter; **2,** something that restrains or is used to restrain:—*v.t.* [mana-cled, mana-cling], to place handcuffs upon; put into chains; fetter.

man-age (man′ij), *v.t.* [managed, managing], **1,** to carry on; conduct; control; be in charge of something; as, to *manage* a store; **2,** to govern; make obedient; handle; gain control; as, to *manage* a wild pony; **3,** to bring about, esp. by clever means; contrive; as, he *managed* an escape; **4,** to direct or handle someone's professional career; **5,** to treat carefully; as, to *manage* money; **6,** to try to alter or do better; as, to *manage* stress:—*v.i.* **1,** to get along; get by or deal with, esp. in a difficult situation or with limited resources; as, to *manage* on a small income; **2,** to achieve one's goal; as, to *manage* to finish the project on time.—*adj.* **man′age-able.**

man-age-ment (man′ij-ment), *n.* **1,** the act of managing, directing, or controlling; as, skillful *management* saves money; **2,** skill in controlling or directing; **3,** those in charge of a business or enterprise; as, the *management* chooses the store's inventory.

man-ag-er (man′ij-ėr), *n.* **1,** one who manages, directs, or conducts anything; as, the *manager* of an office; *manager* of a baseball team; *manager* of a movie star; **2,** a person who conducts business or household affairs with skill and economy; as, a good *manager* of money.—*adj.* **man′age′ri-al.**

man-a-tee (man′a-tē′), *n.* a large, aquatic, herbivorous mammal found in tropical waters, popularly known as the *sea cow*.

man-da-rin (man′da-rin), *n.* **1,** in China, formerly a high public official; also, a high public official or bureaucrat in general; **2,** an influential or powerful person, esp. one who is also a member of an elite group; as, *mandarins* in the business community; **3,** a kind of small orange, with easily detachable rind and sweet pulp; tangerine; **4,** in Canada, a wildflower with small pink blooms:—**Mandarin**, the official language spoken in modern China.

man-date (man′dāt′), *n.* **1,** a command; an official order; **2,** political instructions from voters to their representatives in a legislature; **3,** in Canada, a term in office of a particular government; as, the Conservative Party's *mandate* lasted for nearly nine years:—*v.t.* (mandated, mandat-ing) to require by law or instruct someone to act in a certain way.—*adj.* **man′da-tor-y** (man′da-tôr′i).

man-di-ble (man′di-bl), *n.* **1,** a jawbone, usually the lower in fish and mammals; **2,** in birds, the upper or lower part of the beak; **3,** in insects or shellfish, one of the biting jaws.

man-do-lin (man′do-lin′; man′dl-in′; man′do-lin′), *n.* a guitar-like musical instrument with a pear-shaped sound box and metal strings arranged in pairs.

mane (mān), *n.* the long, thick hair on or about the neck and shoulders of certain animals, as the horse and the male lion; also, the long, thick hair on a person's head.

ma-neu-ver (ma-nōō′vėr; ma-nū′vėr), *n.* Same as **manoeuvre.**

man-ga-nese (mang′ga-nēz′), *n.* a hard, brittle, grey-white metallic element used in hardening steel, alloys, etc.

man-ger (mān′jėr), *n.* a long feeding trough in a barn, etc., for horses or cattle; also, formerly, a stall.

[1]**mangle** (mang′gl), *n.* a machine for ironing cloth between hot rollers:—*v.t.* [mangled, man-gling], to iron or press in a mangle.

[2]**man-gle** (mang′gl), *v.t.* [man-gled, mangling], **1,** to cut to pieces roughly; maim; mutilate by cutting, tearing, or hacking; **2,** to spoil in the making or doing; ruin; as, to *mangle* a composition; *mangle* a recipe.—*n.* **man′gler.**

man-go (mang′gō), *n.* [*pl.* mangoes or mangos], **1,** a tropical tree of the cashew family bearing a pear-shaped, sweet, juicy, yellow-red, edible fruit; **2,** the fruit.

man-grove (mang′grōv), *n.* a genus of tropical shore tree or shrub that spreads densely in swampy ground by sending down prop roots.

manhole (man′hōl′), *n.* an opening, usually with a cover, by which workers enter a tank, boiler, or sewer; utility access hole; sewer hole.

man-hood (man′hood), *n.* **1,** the state of being a man; **2,** men collectively; as, the *manhood* of a nation; **3,** courage; bravery; manliness.

ma-ni-a (mā′ni-a; mān′ya), *n.* **1,** mental illness marked by excitement and violence; **2,** excessive enthusiasm; a craze; as, a *mania* for collecting hockey cards.

ma-ni-ac (mā′ni-ak), *adj.* **1,** affected with mental illness that causes extreme excitement and violence; raving; as, a *maniac* fury; **2,** obsessively enthusiastic; maniacal:—*n.* **1,** an insane person; **2,** a person who behaves wildly or violently; as, she drives like a *maniac*; **3,** a person who is obsessively enthusiastic about something; as, a music *maniac*.—*adj.* **ma-ni′a-cal** (ma-nī′a-kal).

ma-nic (man′ik), *adj.* *Medical*, of (or having) mania or a disorder resembling mania; as, he is a *manic*-depressive (one who alternates between fits of mania and depression).

man-i-cure (man′i-kūr′), *n.* the cosmetic care of the hands and fingernails, esp. professional:—*v.t.* [manicured, manicur-ing], **1,** to care for (hands and fingernails), esp. trimming, cleaning, and polishing the fingernails; give a manicure to; **2,** to trim closely; as, to *manicure* a lawn.—*n.* **man′i-cur′ist.**—*adj.* **man′i-cured′.**

man-i-fest (man′i-fest′), *adj.* clear; apparent to the sight or understanding; as, the truth of that statement is *manifest*:—*v.t.* **1,** to make clear; show; as, to *manifest* anger; **2,** to show the list of (a ship's or plane's cargo); also, to record on such a list:—*v.i.* to appear:—*n.* the list or invoice of a cargo, freight, or passengers on a ship or plane; bill of lading.

man-i-fes-ta-tion (man′i-fes-tā′shun), *n.* a revelation, display, demonstration, or proof of the existence or nature of something; as, the *manifestation* of political feeling.

manifest destiny, **1,** the acceptance of something as inevitable; **2,** a policy that promotes imperialistic expansion as necessary:—**Manifest Destiny**, the 19th-century U.S. policy that held that expansion to the west and throughout North America was the country's right and duty.

man-i-fes-to (man′i-fes′tō), *n.* [*pl.* -toes (tōz)], a public proclamation or declaration of political measures, intentions, principles, etc.; as, a dictator's *manifesto*.

man-i-fold (man′i-fōld), *adj.* **1,** various in kind or quality; numerous; as, *manifold* favours; **2,** comprehensive; as, *manifold* wisdom; **3,** multifunctional:—*v.t.* **1,** to make many copies; **2,** to multiply:—*n.* **1,** one copy of many; **2,** a pipe with two or more outlets along its length, used for connecting one pipe with others; **3,** something composed of many diverse elements, parts, applications, etc.—*adv.* **man′i-fold′ly.**

man-i-kin or **man-ni-kin** (man′i-kin), *n.* **1,** a dwarf; little man; **2,** a model of the human body (often of detachable parts for study); **3,** an artist's or dressmaker's model (usually, *mannequin*) or dummy; also, a person who models clothes.

ma-nil-a, ma-nil-la, Ma-nil-a, or **Ma-nil-la** (ma-nil′a), *n.* and *adj.* **1,** a hemplike fibre, or relating to this fibre, which is used for ropes, textiles, paper, etc.; as, *manila* hemp; *manila* paper; *manila* rope; **2,** a light brown or yellow colour; as, *manila* envelope.

ma-nip-u-late (ma-nip′ū-lāt′), *v.t.* [manipulat-ed, manipulat-ing], **1,** to operate or work skillfully, as tools, by means of the hands; **2,** to treat or influence artfully; control the action of, by skillful management; **3,** to falsify, as books in bookkeeping; **4,** to examine or treat by using the hands therapeutically, as in physiotherapy; **5,** in *computing*, to change or move data, etc.—*n.* **ma-nip′u-la′tion.**—*adj.* **ma-nip′u-la′tive.**

man-i-tou (man′i-tōō′), **man-i-tu** (-tōō′), or **man-i-to** (-tō′), *n.* **1,** in Algonquian religion, a good or evil spirit regarded with awe and reverence; **2,** a being, fetish, or charm of supposed supernatural power.

man-kind (man′kīnd′), *n.* **1,** the human race as a group, considered by some as sexist; humankind; humanity; **2,** men, as distinguished from women.

man-ly (man′li), *adj.* [man-li-er, man-li-est], having the admirable qualities befitting a man; courageous; noble; dignified; resolute.—*n.* **man′ li-ness.**

man–made or **man-made** (man′–mād′), *adj.* **1,** made by humans; **2,** synthetic or artificial rather than natural; as, polyester is a *man-made* fibre.

man-na (man′a), *n.* **1,** in the Old Testament, the food miraculously supplied to the Israelites during their 40 years of wandering in the wilderness; **2,** anything greatly needed that is unexpectedly supplied; **3,** divine nourishment for the soul or spirit; **4,** sap from the ash tree and other plants, formerly used as a mild laxative.

manned (mand), *adj.* of a vehicle such as a spacecraft, transporting or operated by a human crew; as, a *manned* space station.

man-ne-quin (man′i-kin), *n.* **1,** a model of the human body (often of detachable parts for study); **2,** an artist's or dressmaker's model or dummy; manikin; **3,** a person who models clothes.

man-ner (man′ėr), *n.* **1,** method or way of acting or doing something; as, to speak in a rapid *manner*; walk in a gliding *manner*; **2,** sort; kind; species; as, what *manner* of person is he? all *manner* of fish in the bay; **3,** personal, habitual behaviour; as, her *manner* is kind; **4,** style in literature or art; as, a painting in the Renaissance *manner*; **5,** habit; custom, as of a race or nation; **6,** style or fashion; as, to dress in an eccentric *manner*:—**manners, 1,** social behaviour; etiquette; as, to have good or bad *manners*; **2,** rules of social conduct; as, the *manners* of today; **3,** politeness.—*adj.* **man′ner-ly; man′ner-less.**

man-ner-ism (man′ėr-izm), *n.* a distinctive, odd, or peculiar action, gesture, style of speech or dress, etc., esp. if affected or habitual.

ma-noeu-vre or **ma-neu-ver** (ma-nōō′vėr; ma-nū′vėr) *n.* **1,** a planned and supervised movement or change of position; an evolution; **2,** in war, a strategic change of position by troops or warships; **3,** a skillful or clever plan of action to obtain an objective, often meant to fool or trick someone; as, a clever *manoeuvre* with a basketball:—**manoeuvres,** strategic movements carried out as a training exercise; as, the fleet is on *manoeuvres* in the Mediterranean Sea:—*v.i.* [manoeu-vred (ma-nōō′vėrd), manoeu-vring], **1,** to perform certain movements, said of troops or war vessels; **2,** to manage with skill; as, the driver had to *manoeuvre* to put the car into the garage:—*v.t.* **1,** to cause to make certain movements, as troops; **2,** to handle skillfully.

man–of–war (man′–ov–wôr′), *n.* [*pl.* men-of-war (men′–ov–wôr′)], a large armed vessel belonging to a navy; warship.

man-or (man′ėr), *n.* **1,** in England, originally, a piece of land held by a nobleman, part of which he occupied, the rest being occupied and farmed by serfs; now, a landed estate held by a lord, part of which he rents to tenants; **2,** a large house or mansion on an estate with land.—*adj.* **ma-nor′i-al.**

man-pow-er (man′pou′ėr), *n.* **1,** the power supplied by human strength; **2,** the work force or number of workers available for a given task; as, construction *manpower*.

man-sion (man′shun), *n.* a large, expensive residence.

man-slaugh-ter (man′slô′tėr), *n.* the killing of a human being by another or others, unlawfully but without intention or premeditation; also, the killing of a person or persons in general. Compare *murder*.

man-ta or **manta ray** (man′ta; man′ta rā′), *n.* a large tropical ray (fish) with wide expanded fins at each side and slender whiplike tail.

man-tel or **man-tle** (man′tl), *n.* **1,** a structure of wood, marble, brick, etc., around and above a fireplace; **2,** the shelf, beam, or arch above a fireplace.

man-tel-piece (man′tl-pēs′), *n.* Same as **mantel.**

man-tis (man′tis), *n.* any of several insects with long, usually green bodies and rolling eyes, which prey on other insects and are noted for taking a position with the front legs folded as if praying. Also called *praying mantis.*

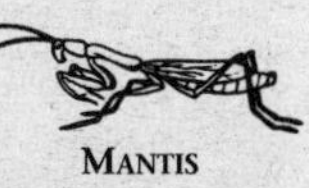
MANTIS

man-tle (man′tl), *n.* **1,** a loose cloak or cape; **2,** any enveloping covering; as, a tree in a *mantle* of bloom; **3,** part of the earth beneath the crust and above the outer core; **4,** the feathers on the back and wings of a bird; **5,** a conelike network of material that will not burn, which fits like a cap over a flame and gives light by glowing at high temperature:—*v.t.* [man-tled, man-tling], to cover with, or as with, a cloak; to disguise; envelope:—*v.i.* to become covered; as, her face *mantled* with blushes.

man-tra (man′tra; mun′tra; män′tra), *n.* **1,** a mystical hymn or other incantation repeated in prayer or meditation; **2,** a watchword, slogan, or motto; as, safety is our *mantra.*

man-u-al (man′ū-al), *adj.* **1,** pertaining to, or done by, the hands; as, *manual* skill; *manual* work; **2,** requiring physical rather than mental effort or ability; as, *manual* labour; **3,** not operating automatically; nonelectric or nonelectronic; as, a *manual* typewriter; a car's *manual* transmission:—*n.* **1,** a small instruction book for easy reference; a handbook or guidebook; as, a car owner's *manual*; **2,** a systematic exercise in the handling of a weapon; as, the *manual* of arms in the army; **3,** the keyboard of an organ, played with the hands.—*adv.* **man′u-al-ly.**

man-u-fac-ture (man′ū-fak′tūr), *v.t.* [manufactured, manufactur-ing], **1,** to make a product in large amounts by hand or machinery; **2,** to make over into a more useful form; as, to *manufacture* yarn from wool; **3,** to invent or make up; as, to *manufacture* an excuse for being late:—*n.* **1,** the making, usually on a large scale, of articles by hand, machinery, or a combination of processes, esp. in a factory; the act of manufacturing; **2,** anything made by these processes; also, such articles collectively; **3,** an industry; as, the car *manufacture*; **4,** production in general.—*n.* **man′u-fac′tur-er.**

ma-nure (ma-nŏŏr′; ma-nūr′), *n.* any fertilizing substance, esp. waste products of animals such as cattle or chickens, used for enriching the soil:—*v.t.* [manured, manur-ing], to enrich, as a field or garden, with fertilizing substances.

man-u-script (man′ū-skript′), *adj.* written by hand:—*n.* **1,** formerly, a book or paper written by hand; **2,** a book or paper written by hand, typewriter, or computer; **3,** an unpublished copy of a book, article, or another piece of writing, typed or written by hand; the author's copy; **4,** writing, as opposed to printing.

man-y (men′i), *adj.* [*comp.* more, *superl.* most], consisting of a great number; as, *many* students:—*n.* a great number; as, *many* of us like sports:—*pron.* a large number; as, *many* went to the demonstration.

map (map), *n.* **1,** a representation, on a flat surface, of the earth or some portion of it, showing the relative size and position of the parts or places represented, such as oceans, rivers, mountains, countries, cities, roads, etc.; **2,** a chart of the sky, showing the stars, planets, etc.; **3,** anything similar to a map in function; representation; as, a road *map*; gene *map*:—*v.t.* [mapped, map-ping], to picture or lay down in a chart; describe clearly; show on a map:—**map out,** to plan in detail; as, to *map out* a journey.

ma-ple (mā′pl), *n.* **1,** any of a large group of trees of the north temperate zone with deeply indented leaves and two-winged fruits, valued for their wood and for the sap of certain varieties, esp. the sugar maple, which is used in making a kind of sugar and syrup; **2,** the wood of any of these trees, which is strong and hard and used to make furniture:—*adj.* pertaining to this type of tree, wood, flavour, etc.; as, *maple* syrup; *maple* sugar; *maple* ice cream. Also, **ma′ple bush′; ma′ple but′ter.**

maple leaf, 1, the leaf of the maple tree; **2,** the emblem of Canada, which appears on the Canadian flag:—**Maple Leaf,** the Canadian flag.

maple syrup, the thick, sticky, sweet liquid made from the sap of the sugar maple.

mar (mär), *v.t.* [marred, mar-ring], **1,** to disfigure; damage; as, to *mar* a painting or a table; **2,** to injure; ruin; spoil the quality of; as, rain *marred* the outdoor event.

ma-ra-ca (ma-ra′ka), *n.* a percussion instrument consisting of a dried gourd or similar container with loose pebbles, beans, or seeds in it, which is shaken by a handle, usually in pairs.

mar-a-schi-no (mar′a-skē′nō; mar′a-shē′nō), *n.* a cordial or liqueur made by fermenting a small, black cherry, the marasca:—**maraschino cherries,** cherries flavoured in a syrup of this or similar cordial.

mar-a-thon (mar′a-thon′), *n.* **1,** a foot race of 42.195 kilometres (26 miles, 385 yards), run over roads and open ground rather than around a track: it is an event in the Olympics; **2,** any contest or task requiring prolonged endurance or that is difficult; as, a dance *marathon*; studying for and taking exams at the end of the term was a *marathon*.

ma-raud (ma-rôd′), *v.t.* to plunder:—*v.i.* to rove in search of plunder; as, wild beasts *maraud* at night.—*n.* **ma-raud′er.**

mar-ble (mär′bl), *n.* **1,** a hard limestone, white or streaked or mottled with various colours, capable of taking a fine polish, used in buildings, floors, fixtures, and sculptures; **2,** anything like such stone in hardness, smoothness, or coldness; **3,** a sculptured piece of such stone; **4,** a small glass, clay, or stone ball, formerly made of marble, used in the game of marbles:—**marbles, 1,** a children's game played with these balls; **2,** a collection of sculpture in marble; **3,** *Slang* common sense; sanity; as, did you lose your *marbles*?—*adj.* **1,** made of, or like, marble in appearance; as, a *marble* countertop; *marble* cake; **2,** cold; hard; unfeeling:—*v.t.* [mar-bled, mar-bling], to stain or vein like marble.—*adj.* **mar′bled.**—*n.* **mar′bling.**

march (märch), *n.* **1,** a regular, measured step or walk, esp. of soldiers; the act of marching; **2,** the distance passed over in marching from one place to another; as, a *march* of 15 kilometres; **3,** steady onward movement; as, the *march* of years; **4,** a musical composition to be played as troops march; also, any composition with a similar beat or characteristics; **5,** a walking demonstration:—*v.t.* **1,** to cause to move at a march; **2,** to cause to go by force; as, to *march* the criminal off to prison:—*v.i.* **1,** to move with regular steps, as done by members of a band, people in a parade, soldiers, etc.; **2,** to walk in a steady, determined way; **3,** to move or advance in a steady way; as, time *marches* on.—*n.* **march′er; march′ing or′ders.**

March (märch), *n.* the third month of the year, between February and April, with 31 days.

March break, in Canada, a school holiday in March, about a week long.

mare (mâr), *n.* the female of the horse, donkey, zebra, etc.

mar-ga-rine or **mar-ga-rin** (mär′ja-rin), *n.* a soft, smooth butter substitute made from vegetable oil and colouring or flavouring.

mar-gin (mär′jin), *n.* **1,** a border; edge; as, the *margin* of a pool; **2,** the unprinted, unwritten, or untyped edge of a page or a computer screen; **3,** an amount in reserve, as of money or time; extra part; as, he allowed a *margin* of 100 dollars for the trip; **4,** the difference between the cost of a product and the selling price.—*adj.* **mar′gin-al.**—*n.* **mar′gi-na′li-a; mar′gin-al-i-za′tion.**—*v.t.* **mar′gin-al-ize′** [marginalized, marginaliz-ing].

ma-ri-a-chi (mor′ē-och′ē), *n.* **1**, a Mexican street band; **2**, the music performed by such groups.

mar-i-gold (mar′i-gōld), *n.* **1,** any of a group of strong-scented garden plants of the aster family, with showy orange, yellow, red, or variegated flowers; **2,** any of numerous other yellow-flowered plants, as the marsh marigold; **3,** the flower of any of these.

ma-ri-jua-na or **ma-ri-hua-na** (ma′ri-wä′na; mä′ri-wä′na), *n.* a narcotic obtained from the dried leaves and flowers of the hemp plant and smoked in cigarettes; cannabis; also, the plant.

ma-rim-ba (ma-rim′ba), *n.* a musical percussion instrument, similar to a xylophone, consisting of graduated lengths of hardwood, each with a sounding box, which are played upon with wooden mallets.

ma-rine (ma-rēn′), *adj.* **1,** pertaining to, living in, or formed by the sea, ocean, or other large body of water; as, *marine* plants; *marine* deposits; **2,** naval; having to do with ships and boats; relating to commerce at sea; as, *marine* law; *marine* supply store; **3,** having to do with soldiers who serve on warships:—*n.* **1,** a soldier who once served only at sea, but now serving on land and in the air: Canada does not have marines; **2,** the navy of a nation; also, in some nations, the executive department dealing with naval affairs; **3,** the collective mercantile and naval shipping of a country; as, the merchant *marine*; **4,** a picture of a sea scene:—**Marine,** a member of the U.S. Marine Corps.

mar-i-ner (mar′i-nėr), *n.* a sailor or seaman; one of a ship's crew.

mar-i-o-nette (mar′i-o-net′), *n.* a doll moved from above by strings attached to the legs and arms, as in a puppet show; a puppet.

mar-i-tal (mar′i-t'l), *adj.* relating to marriage or the married state; as, *marital* vows.

mar-i-time (mar′i-tīm′), *adj.* **1,** pertaining to, or bordering upon, the sea; as, a *maritime* city; **2,** living near the sea; as, *maritime* people; **3,** relating to sea trade or navigation:—**Maritime,** of or having to do with the Maritime provinces.

Maritime provinces or **the Maritimes,** the three provinces on the Atlantic coast of Canada, consisting of New Brunswick, Nova Scotia, and Prince Edward Island: when Newfoundland is included, they are called the *Atlantic provinces*.

[1]**mark** (märk), *n.* **1,** the target at which one aims, as in shooting; an aim or goal; as, to hit the *mark* with an arrow; **2,** a visible imprint, as a line, scratch, chip, spot, stain, etc.; as, an ink *mark*; *mark* on the wooden floor; **3,** a sign by which anything is known; a brand, label, trademark, etc.; **4,** a trait; distinguishing feature; as, a *mark* of

integrity; **5,** high position; distinction; as, a person of *mark*; **6,** a figure or letter indicating a student's level or grade; **7,** a boundary or limit; a set standard; as, to fall below the *mark*; **8,** a line, object, etc., serving to indicate position; marker; as, a book*mark*; **9,** a line, sign, or symbol written or printed to indicate something; as, a check *mark*; exclamation *mark*; **10,** *Colloq.* an easy target for swindlers; **11,** in *computing*, a symbol or character used to find a specific point in a data file, etc.:—*v.t.* **1,** to make a mark by scratching, chipping, spotting, etc.; **2,** to furnish with an identifying sign, as on clothes; **3,** to characterize or indicate, as by a sign; as, faith and courage *mark* the leader; **4,** to single out or select, as by a sign; as, they *marked* him for promotion; **5,** to notice; observe; as, *mark* my words; **6,** to rank or grade, as examination papers; **7,** to set apart by or as if by a boundary; as, to *mark* out a tennis court:—*v.i.* **1,** being able to mark or be marked; as, this wooden table *marks* easily; a pen that *marks* on laminated surfaces; **2,** to grade or determine the level; as, the coach *marks* severely.—*n.* **mark′er.**

²mark (märk), *n.* **1,** the monetary unit of Germany, equal to 100 pfennigs: officially called *deutsche mark*; **2,** a former English and Scottish monetary unit; **3,** a former European unit of weight used for measuring gold and silver.

marked (märkt), *adj.* **1,** ranked or graded; as, *marked* papers; **2,** having a distinguishing mark or marks upon it; as, a *marked* bill; *marked* floor; **3,** noticeable; conspicuous; clearly defined; as, *marked* ability in music; **4,** object of suspicion, etc.; as, a *marked* man.—*adv.* **mark′ed-ly** (mär′kid-li).

mar-ket (mär′ket), *n.* **1,** a store or other place for the sale or purchase of goods, esp. of a certain type of product; as, a *meat* market; super*market*; **2,** a public place for buying and selling goods or services; as, a farmers' *market*; **3,** buyers of a certain type; as, the teenage *market*; **4,** buying and selling of a particular type of product; as, the lumber *market*; **5,** a region or country where something can be sold; as, Canada is a *market* for coffee; **6,** the state of trade as shown by rate or price; as, a dull *market*; **7,** demand for something that is for sale; as, there is a big *market* for DVDs; **8,** the stock market:—*v.i.* to deal in a public place where provisions are exposed for sale; buy or sell goods or provisions; go shopping; as, to *market* on weekends:—*v.t.* **1,** to offer for sale, or to sell; **2,** to promote a product for sale.—*adj.* **mar′ket-a-ble.** Also, **mar′ket–driv′en; mar′ket e-con′o-my; mar′ket-er; mar′ket gar′den; mar′ket-ing; mar′ket-ing board′; mar′ket-place′; mar′ket price′; mar′ket re′search; mar′ket share′; mar′ket val′ue.**

mar-ket-ing (mär′ket-ing), *n.* the process by which companies try to find buyers for their products or services through market research, advertising, public relations, promotions, packaging, etc.

mar-ket-place or **mar-ket place** (mär′ket-plās′; mär′ket plās′), *n.* **1,** a place in which a market is held, often an open space in a square; **2,** the world of business; **3,** an exchange of works, opinions, and ideas.

marks-man (märks′man), *n.* [*pl.* marks-men (-men)], one skilled in shooting.—*n.* **marks′man-ship′.**

mark-up (märk′up′), *n.* **1**, the amount added to the cost to get the selling price; profit; **2**, in *computing*, computerized document preparation; as, *markup* language.

mar-lin (mär′lin), *n.* a large marine game fish related to the swordfish.

mar-ma-lade (mär′ma-lād′), *n.* a thick preserve or jam made of oranges or other fruits boiled with sugar.

¹ma-roon (ma-rōōn′), *n.* one who is left alone or abandoned in a deserted or isolated place:—**Maroon**, originally, fugitive slaves, living in the wilder parts of the West Indies and Surinam; also, their descendants:—*v.t.* **1,** to abandon someone in a deserted or isolated place; as, to *maroon* sailors on a deserted island as punsihment; **2,** to leave someone alone or helpless; strand; as, to *maroon* someone in a cabin without a car for the weekend.

²ma-roon (ma-rōōn′), *n.* a dark brown-red colour:—*adj.* of the colour of maroon.

mar-quee (mär-kē′), *n.* **1,** a large tent, esp. one with open sides, often used for special events, parties, entertainment, etc.; **2,** a permanent canopy over the entrance to a building, theatre, or other structure; **3,** a bright sign over the entrance of a theatre, etc., listing the shows, such as plays or films, and their stars; **4**, the ability to attract an audience; as, this actor is a *marquee*:—*adj.* skilled (of an actor or athlete); as, a *marquee* player.

mar-quis (mär′kwis; mär-kē′) or **marquess** (mär′kwis), *n.* a nobleman ranking below a duke and above an earl or count; also, the title used for such a person.—*n.fem.* **mar-quise′** (mär-kēz′).

mar-riage (mar′ij), *n.* **1,** the act of legally uniting a man and woman in wedlock; the wedding ceremony; **2,** the state of being wedded or married; the relation existing between husband and wife; **3,** a close association or union; as, a *marriage* of colours and textures.—*adj.* **mar′riage-a-ble.**

mar-row (mar′ō), *n.* **1,** the soft tissue filling the cavities of bones; **2,** the real meaning or significance of anything; the most important part; as, liberty is the *marrow* of our civilization; **3,** an edible squash; vegetable marrow.

mar-ry (mar′i), *v.t.* [married, marry-ing], **1,**

to legally unite as husband and wife; as, the minister *married* the couple; **2,** to take in marriage; wed; as, Tomas *married* Maria; **3,** to give (a son or daughter) in wedlock; as, to *marry* a daughter; **4,** to associate closely; unite; as, to *marry* the colours of the fabrics with the colour of the walls:—*v.i.* to enter into the state of wedlock; take someone for one's husband or wife; become married.

Mars (märz), *n.* **1,** the Roman god of war; **2,** the planet next to the earth, the fourth from the sun: it is the seventh-largest planet in the solar system, has two moons, with a year of 687 days, diameter of about 6,787 kilometres, and an orbit of about 228 million kilometres from the sun.—*adj.* and *n.* **Mar′tian.**

marsh (märsh), *n.* an area of soft, low land that is partly or completely covered by water; a swampy tract of land.—*adj.* **marsh′y.**

mar-shal (mär′shal), *n.* **1,** an official of high rank who superintends and regulates ceremonies; **2,** in some foreign armies, an officer of highest rank: also called *field marshal*; **3,** in the U.S., a law officer of a municipal or federal jurisdiction; an officer who has certain police duties: sometimes, the head of a fire or police department:—*v.t.* [marshalled, marshal-ling], **1,** to arrange or dispose in order, as facts or military forces; as, to *marshal* the points in a debate; *marshal* the troops; **2,** to lead; guide; conduct.

[1]**marsh-mal-low** (märsh′mel′ō; märsh′mal′ō), *n.* **1,** a confection made from egg whites, sugar, corn syrup, starch, and gelatin, beaten to a creamy consistency and coated with powdered sugar; **2,** *Slang* someone who is very timid and unassertive.—*adj.* **mash′mal′low-y.**

[2]**marsh mal-low,** a coarse plant of the mallow family with large, five-petalled, white or rose-coloured flowers, growing in salt marshes, the roots of which were formerly used to make marshmallows.

mar-su-pial (mär-sū′pi-al), *n.* an order of mammal, like the kangaroo, opossum, etc., that carries its young in an abdominal pouch containing the teats:—*adj.* of or related to this order of mammals; also, pouchlike.

mart (märt), *n.* a market; store; as, a drug *mart.*

mar-ten (mär′t'n), *n.* **1,** a small animal of the weasel family with short legs and a long, thin body; **2,** the valuable fur of this animal.

mar-tial (mär′shal), *adj.* **1,** of, like, or suited to war; **2,** military; as, *martial* music; *martial* law; **3,** like or suited for a warrior; brave; as, *martial* arts.—*adv.* **mar′tial-ly.**

mar-tin (mär′tin), *n.* **1,** in Europe, a bird of the swallow family that builds a mud nest on the walls of buildings; **2,** in America, an insect-eating bird of the swallow family, nesting in colonies, and having blue-black plumage and a forked tail.

mar-ti-ni (mär-tē′ni), *n.* a cocktail originally made of gin and dry vermouth: nowadays, it can be made with a variety of liquors and flavourings.

mar-tyr (mär′tėr), *n.* **1,** one who dies rather than forsake or betray a faith, cause, or principle; **2,** one who suffers keenly or sacrifices much, esp. for a cause or principle; **3,** a person who pretends to suffer greatly in order to gain sympathy:—*v.t.* **1,** to put to death for loyalty to some belief, principle, or religion; **2,** to persecute; torture; torment.

mar-tyr-dom (mär′tėr-dum), *n.* **1,** death or suffering for the sake of a faith or cause; as, the *martyrdom* of Joan of Arc; **2,** the state of being a martyr; **3,** great suffering.

mar-vel (mär′v'l), *n.* someone or something that is extraordinary, outstanding, unusual, or astonishing; a wonder; as, she is a *marvel* at organizing parties:—*v.i.* [marvelled, marvel-ling or marveled, marvel-ing], to be struck with wonder, amazement, or astonishment; as, to *marvel* at a person's courage.

mar-vel-lous or **mar-vel-ous** (mär′vel-us), *adj.* **1,** causing wonder or great admiration; scarcely to be believed; amazing; as, a *marvellous* sight; **2,** not probable; **3,** very good, excellent; splendid; as, a *marvellous* day; *marvellous* effort.—*adv.* **mar′vel-lous-ly.**

Marx-ist (märk′sist), *n.* a believer in, or follower of, the Communist theory of Marx and Engels that a classless society will eventually replace a capitalistic one.—*n.* **Marx′ism.**

mas-car-a (mas-kar′a; mas-kär′a), *n.* a cosmetic for colouring the eyelashes to make them appear darker and thicker.

mas-cot (mas′kot′; mas′kut), *n.* **1,** a person or thing that is supposed to bring good luck; as, the team's *mascot* is a bulldog; **2,** a person in a costume representing a team and acting as a cheerleader.

mas-cu-line (mas′kū-lin), *adj.* **1,** pertaining to men or boys; **2,** manly; powerful; virile; **3,** having qualities of, or suitable for, men or boys; mannish; **4,** in *grammar,* designating the gender of words that name male persons, animals, or things; as, the French words stylo, homme, and chien are *masculine* nouns: compare *feminine* and *neuter.*—*n.* **mas′cu-lin′i-ty.**

mash (mash), *n.* **1,** a soft or pulpy mass or mixture; **2,** a warm mixture of bran and water for horses and other animals; **3,** bruised malt or meal soaked in hot water for making brews:—*v.t.* **1,** to mix, as malt, with hot water, in brewing; **2,** to change into a soft, pulpy state by crushing or beating; as, to *mash* potatoes or turnips.—*n.* **mash′er.**

mask (måsk), *n.* **1,** a full or partial cover for the face to disguise it, protect it, or aid in breathing; also, a caricatured false face; as, a Halloween *mask;* hockey *mask;* surgical *mask;* oxygen *mask;* ski *mask;* **2,** a disguise or pretence; as, to hide sorrow under a *mask* of laughter; **3,** a likeness of a human face made of clay, wax, or a similar material; **4,** a cosmetic treatment for the face; **5,** in classical drama, a huge figure of a head worn by actors to identify the character played; **6,** masque; masquerade; an old form of drama characterized by masks, music, and pantomime:—**gas mask,** a covering for the head and face, attached to a breathing device, to protect against poisonous gases that are found in mines or that are used in warfare:—*v.t.* **1,** to cover with, or as with, a mask; **2,** to hide or cover up; as, the picture *masked* the crack in the wall; her laughter *masked* her true feeling of sadness:—*v.i.* to put on a mask; be disguised.—*n.* **mask′er.**

A B C

MASKS: A, COSTUME; B, JESTER'S; C, SCUBA

mas-och-ism (mas′o-kizm′), *n.* **1,** the enjoyment of pain or mistreatment; **2,** the deriving of sexual gratification from pain or from physical or emotional abuse:—*n.* **mas′och-ist.**—*adj.* **mas′och-ist′ic.**—*adv.* **mas′och-is′ti-cal-ly.**

ma-son (mā′sn), *n.* a builder in stone, brick, etc.; bricklayer:—**Mason,** a *Freemason.*

ma-son-ry (mā′sn-ri), *n.* [*pl.* masonries], **1,** the art or occupation of a builder in stone or brick; **2,** a structure made of stone or brick; **3,** the trade of a mason.

masque or **mask** (måsk), *n.* **1,** a masquerade; **2,** an old form of drama, characterized by music, dancing, dialogue, and spectacular pageantry, performed by bands of amateur actors in court and castle, popular in the 16th and 17th centuries.

mas-quer-ade (mås′kėr-ād′), *n.* **1,** a ball or festive gathering where masks and costumes are worn; **2,** the mask and costume worn at this type of gathering; **3,** an acting or living under false pretences; as, his show of ethics is a *masquerade;* **4,** a disguise:—*v.i.* [masquerad-ed, masquerad-ing], **1,** to take part in a ball where the guests are disguised by masks and costumes; **2,** to take the part or character of another for amusement or deceit; disguise oneself; as, to *masquerade* as the heir to a fortune.—*n.* **mas′quer-ad′er.**

mass (mas), *n.* **1,** a quantity of matter or collection of things united into one body that has no particular shape; pile or lump; **2,** a large quantity or number; as, a *mass* of corrections; **3,** bulk; size; **4,** the main part; majority; **5,** the amount of matter in an object or body, which causes a thing to have a certain weight from the pull of gravity:—**the masses,** the common, ordinary, average people; general population; as, this ad campaign was aimed at *the masses:*—*adj.* **1,** of or including many people or things; as, a *mass* protest; **2,** on a large scale; as, *mass* market; *mass* media:—**mass production,** the use of machinery and often assembly lines to make large quantities of a product, such as a car, often using a standard design template:—*v.t.* to collect or gather into a lump or body; arrange in close relation; as, to *mass* shrubbery:—*v.i.* to make or gather into a lump or group. Also, **mass′ com-mu′ni-ca′tion; mass′ mar′ket; mass′ me′di-a; mass′mur′der; mass′num′ber; mass′tran′ sit.**

Mass or **mass** (mas), *n.* the main religious service in the Catholic Church and some other Christian churches; also, the music for this service.

mas-sa-cre (mas′a-kėr), *n.* **1,** the needless killing of many people or animals with violence and cruelty; wholesale slaughter or murder; **2,** *Colloq.* defeat:—*v.t.* [massa-cred (mas′a-kėrd), massa-cring (mas′a-kring; mas′a-kėr-ing;)], **1,** to slaughter in great numbers; **2,** *Colloq.* to defeat badly; as, our rival soccer team *massacred* us.

mas-sage (ma-säzh′; ma-säj′), *n.* a method of treating the body, for health purposes, by rubbing and kneading with the hands in order to enhance blood circulation and relax muscles and joints:—*v.t.* [massaged, massaging], to rub and knead with the hands; give a massage to.

mas-seur (må-sûr′), *n.* a man who massages professionally.—*n. fem.* **mas-seuse′** (må-söz′).

mas-sive (mas′iv), *adj.* **1,** weighty; huge; bulky; having great size or mass; as, a *massive* dinosour; **2,** extensive; substantial; widespread; as, a *massive* overdose; *massive* changes; **3,** imposing; impressive.

mast (måst), *n.* **1,** a long, round spar or pole of iron or timber set upright on the keel and through the decks of a vessel, to support the sails and rigging; **2,** any upright pole; as, a flag *mast.*

mas-tec-to-my (ma-stek′to-mi), *n.* the surgical removal of the breast, or part of the breast, usually to remove cancerous tissue.

mas-ter (mås′tėr), *n.* **1,** a person who rules or commands; a director; employer; owner; **2,** a man who is the head of a household, college, university, or school; also, a male teacher at a private school, esp. in Britain; **3,** an expert; skilled worker; **4,** a winner in a contest; **5,** a great artist; also, a painting by a great artist;

as, a gallery of old *masters*; **6,** the commander or captain of a merchant vessel; **7,** a graduate degree; as, to get a *master* in history; **8,** original copy of a recording, text, etc.; as, to make photocopies of the *master*.—**Master, 1,** a person holding an advanced university degree; as, a *Master* of Arts; **2,** a title used before the names of young boys, esp. formerly; **3,** a legal title:—*adj.* **1,** main; as, a *master* bedroom; **2,** controlling; as, *master* switch; **3,** chief; skilled; as, a *master* carpenter; **4,** original; as, *master* copy; *master* file:—*v.t.* **1,** to subdue or overcome; tame; as, to *master* a task; *master* a wild horse; **2,** to become an expert in; become skillful at; as, to *master* in-line skating; **3,** to make an original. Also, **mas′ter bed′room′; mas′ter key′; mas′ter-mind′; mas′ter of cer′e-mo′nies; mas′ter-stroke′; mas′ter switch′.**

mas-ter-ful (mås′tėr-fool), *adj.* **1,** commanding; powerful; expert; as, a *masterful* speaker; **2,** domineering.—*adv.* **mas′ter-ful-ly.**

mas-ter-ly (mås′tėr-li), *adj.* characteristic of a chief or expert; as, he played with a *masterly* touch:—*adv.* like, or with the skill of, an expert; skillfully.

mas-ter-piece (mås′tėr-pēs′), *n.* **1,** an outstanding work or accomplishment, esp. in the arts; **2,** a thing that surpasses in excellence everything else done by the artist or maker; as, Cervantes's *Don Quixote* is his *masterpiece*; **3,** anything made with extraordinary skill.

mas-ter-y (mås′tėr-i), *n.* [*pl.* masteries], **1,** dominion; power; rule, as of a country; **2,** superiority or triumph, as in a contest; **3,** skill in, or full knowledge of, a subject.

mast-head (måst′hed′), *n.* **1,** the top of a mast, esp. the top of a lower mast, used for a lookout; **2,** in newspapers, magazines, etc., the part that gives the title and that lists owners, publishers, editors, subscription rates, dates of publication, address, etc.

mas-tic (mas′tik), *n.* and *adj.* **1,** a brown resin used in varnish, chewing gum, etc.; **2,** a quick-drying cement or mortar used as a sealant in construction.

mas-ti-cate (mas′ti-kāt′), *v.t.* [masticated, masticat-ing], to grind (food) with the teeth; chew; also, to crush to a pulp.—*n.* **mas′ti-ca′tion.**

mas-tiff (mås′tif), *n.* one of a breed of dogs that were originally used as hunting dogs and now used as a watchdog or guard dog: it is extremely large, with a deep, powerful chest, short hair, and drooping ears.

mas-to-don (mas′to-don), *n.* a huge, extinct, forest-dwelling, elephantlike animal that was found in Asia, Europe, and North America.

mas-tur-ba-tion (mas′tėr-bā′shun), *n.* sexual stimulation without intercourse.

[1]**mat** (mat), *n.* **1,** a flat piece of coarse, woven fabric, made of straw, grass, rags, carpeting, etc.; **2,** such a fabric placed before a door for wiping the feet or as a floor covering; **3,** anything thickly grown or tangled, as hair, weeds, or wool; **4,** a piece of material placed under a dish, lamp, or other object to protect a surface or used as an ornament; **5,** a thick, resilient pad used on the floor of a gymnasium or other sports area to protect someone who falls or jumps:—*v.t.* [mat-ted, mat-ting], to mass, knot, or twist together; cover with mats:—*v.i.* to become closely tangled.

[2]**mat** or **matte** (mat), *adj.* dull; not shiny; lustreless but uniform: said of surfaces and colours:—*n.* **1,** a decorative border of paper, cardboard, silk, etc., used to set off or protect a picture; **2,** a dull finish on a gilded, painted, or paper surface; as, to order photos in *mat*:—*v.t.* [matted, matting], **1,** to mount something on a mat; **2,** to put a border on a picture; **3,** to produce a dull finish; **4,** to provide with a mat.

mat-a-dor (mat′a-dôr′), *n.* the bullfighter appointed to kill the bull with a sword at the end of a bullfight.

[1]**match** (mach), *n.* **1,** anything that agrees with, or is exactly like, another thing; as, these two socks are a *match*; **2,** two things or persons that go together well; as, this tie and that jacket are a good *match*; **3,** an equal; one able to cope with another; **4,** a game or contest; as, a hockey *match*; **5,** a marriage; also, a marriageable person; **6,** in *computing*, a record, file, data, etc., that is identical to another:—*v.t.* **1,** to be the same; **2,** to go together well; **3,** to compete with successfully; equal; as, their team *matched* ours; **4,** to find a suitable person or thing; as, to *match* her qualifications with a job position:—*v.i.* to agree with, or be like, someone or something; harmonize; as, this tie *matches* with these pants. Also, **match′mak′er; match′pen′al-ty; match′point′; match′up′.**

[2]**match** (mach), *n.* **1,** a slender piece of wood or cardboard tipped with material that is easily lit by friction, used for starting fires, lighting cigarettes, etc.; **2,** a wick that burns at a certain speed, used for firing cannon and guns. Also, **match′book′; match′box′; match′stick′.**

match-less (mach′lis), *adj.* not capable of being equalled; peerless.

mate (māt), *n.* **1,** a companion or associate; as, a play*mate*; class*mate*; room*mate*; **2,** a partner in marriage; a husband or wife; also, a lover; **3,** one of a pair of animals or birds for breeding; as, the lion's *mate*; **4,** one of a pair; as, the *mate* to a shoe; **5,** a merchant ship's officer ranking below the captain; **6,** an assistant:—*v.t.* and *v.i.* [mated, mat-ing], **1,** to match; **2,** to marry; **3,** of animals, to pair; as, Canada geese *mate* for life.

ma-te-ri-al (ma-tē′ri-al), *adj.* **1,** consisting of matter or substance; physical, not spiritual; **2,** pertaining to bodily wants; as, the *material* needs of the poor; **3,** important; noticeable; as, a *material* improvement; **4,** in *law*, influential; as, a *material* witness:—*n.* **1,** the substance of which anything is made; **2,** fabric for clothing; as, cotton *material*; **3,** information; ideas; as, research *material* for the essay; **4,** potential; as, she is manager *material*.

ma-te-ri-al-ism (ma-tē′ri-al-izm), *n.* **1,** the doctrine that all reality (including thought, will, feeling) can be explained only in terms of matter; **2,** the preference of and emphasis on material possessions and physical comfort over intellectual or spiritual values.—*n.* **ma-te′ri-al-ist.**—*adj.* **ma-te′ri-al-is′tic.**

ma-te-ri-al-ize (ma-tēr′ē-a-līz′), *v.t.* [materialized, materializ-ing], **1,** to give substance, reality, or form to; take on a physical form; **2,** to express (an idea) through outward objects; become real; as, to *materialize* an idea in a statue:—*v.i.* **1,** to become a fact; **2,** to appear or assume actual form.

ma-te-ri-al-ly (ma-tē′rē-a-li), *adv.* **1,** with respect to body or substance; physically; **2,** actually; considerably; as, his gift helps *materially*.

ma-ter-nal (ma-tûr′nal), *adj.* pertaining to motherhood or to one's mother; motherly; as, *maternal* love; *maternal* grandparents.—*adv.* **ma-ter′nal-ly.**

ma-ter-ni-ty (ma-tûr′ni-ti), *n.* [*pl.* maternities], the state of being a mother; motherhood; motherly qualities:—*adj.* related to motherhood; of or for pregnant women or women giving birth; as, *maternity* clothes; *maternity* ward; *maternity* leave.

math (math), *abbrev.* short for *mathematics*.

math-e-mat-i-cal (math′i-mat′i-kal) *adj.* **1,** pertaining to, performed by, or defined by mathematics; **2,** exact; precise; accurate; as, they measured the distance with *mathematical* precision.—*adv.* **math′e-mat′i-cal-ly.**

math-e-ma-ti-cian (math′i-ma-tish′an), *n.* one skilled or educated in mathematics; a mathematics expert.

math-e-mat-ics (math′i-mat′iks), *n.pl.* (used with a *sing. v.*) the science that deals with numbers, quantities, and shapes, and the way they are measured and the relations between them; as, *mathematics* comprises arithmetic, algebra, geometry, and calculus.

mat-i-nee or **mat-i-née** (mat′i-nā′), *n.* a play or other performance taking place in the afternoon.

mat-ri-cide (mat′ri-sīd′; mā-), *n.* **1,** the murder of a mother by her son or daughter; **2,** a person who murders one's mother.

ma-tric-u-late (ma-trik′ū-lāt′), *v.t.* to enroll, admit, or register a student (or candidate for a degree) in a college or university:—*v.i.* to gain admission, or right of admission, to such an institution.—*n.* **ma-tric′u-la′tion.**

mat-ri-mo-ny (mat′ri-mō′ni), *n.* marriage; the act or state of being married; also, the relationship between two married people.—*adj.* **mat′ri-mo′ni-al.**

ma-trix (mā′triks), *n.* [*pl.* matrices (mā′tri-sēz′) or matrixes], **1,** any die or mould for casting or shaping (an object); **2,** the rock in which a fossil, gem, etc., is embedded; **3,** a papier-mâché or plaster impression of type used in electrotypy or stereotypy (printing from page plates cast in type metal); **4,** something from which something else develops; **5,** in *mathematics*, a series of related things laid out in rows and columns; **6,** the intercellular material that surrounds tissue cells; **7,** a dot-matrix printer; **8,** *Slang* in *computing*, the sum total of all present-day computer networks.

ma-tron (mā′trun), *n.* **1,** a married woman or widow, esp. one who is dignified and middle-aged or older; **2,** a woman who supervises or manages the housekeeping in a hospital, school, dormitory, or other public institution, esp. in former times or in Britain; **3,** a woman whose duty it is to maintain order among inmates in a female prison:—**matron of honour,** a married, principal bridal attendant at a wedding; a married maid of honour.

ma-tron-ly (mā′trun-li), *adj.* like or pertaining to a matron; dignified; sedate; as, a *matronly* manner.

matte (mat), *n.*, *adj.*, and *v.t.* Same as ²**mat.**

mat-ted (mat′id), *adj.* **1,** covered with a mat or mats; made of mats; **2,** closely tangled together; as, *matted* hair.

mat-ter (mat′ėr), *n.* **1,** substance, as opposed to mind, spirit, etc.; **2,** the substance of which physical things are made, which has weight and takes up space: all things are made up of matter, and matter can be a solid, liquid, or gas; **3,** an instance of, or occasion for, something; as, a *matter* of habit; a laughing *matter*; **4,** the content of a book or speech; as, subject *matter*; **5,** anything sent by mail; as, second-class *matter*; **6,** importance; **7,** affair; business; anything to be dealt with or thought about; a subject that is given attention; as, this *matter* needs prompt action; financial *matters*; **8,** a problem; trouble; as, to deal with this urgent *matter* immediately; **9,** amount; space; as, a *matter* of 10 days or kilometres; **10,** pus; **11** body substance; as, grey *matter*; **12,** material set up in type; also, material printed from type:—**no matter, 1,** it is not important; **2,** regardless of; as, *no matter* how much he rests, he is always tired:—*v.i.* **1,** to be of importance;

as, health *matters*; **2,** to form or secrete pus; fester.

mat-ter-of-fact (mat′ėr-ov-fakt′), *adj.* literal; practical; not imaginative; unemotional; as, a *matter-of-fact* response to the delicate question.

mat-ting (mat′ing), *n.* **1,** a coarse fabric of straw, hemp, grass, etc., used for covering floors, for mats, etc.; **2,** mat making; **3,** a dull finish and this process.

mat-tress (mat′ris), *n.* **1,** a thick, soft pad, made of strong material, used for sleeping on, which usually fits within the frame of the bed; **2,** a similar pad filled with air or water; as, an air *mattress*.

ma-ture (ma-tūr′; ma-toor′; ma-choor′), *v.i.* [matured, matur-ing], **1,** to become ripe; develop fully; become an adult; **2,** to fall due for payment, as a bond, mortgage, loan, etc.:—*v.t.* to bring to full growth or completion; perfect:—*adj.* [matur-er, matur-est], **1,** ripe; full-grown; developed; as, *mature* fruit; *mature* individual; **2,** having to do with or suitable for an adult; as, a movie for *mature* audiences; **3,** perfected; ready for use, as a plan, wine, cheese, etc.; **4,** due, as a bond, mortgage, loan, etc.—*n.* **ma-tu′ri-ty.**

maud-lin (môd′lin), *adj.* **1,** easily moved to tears; weakly sentimental; as, *maudlin* sympathy; **2,** sentimental or tearful brought on by drinking too much alcohol; drunkenly silly.

maul or **mall** (mol; môl), *n.* a large, heavy hammer:—*v.t.* **1,** to beat or bruise; **2,** lacerate, mangle, or mutilate; as, the tiger *mauled* its prey; **3,** treat in a rough manner.

mau-so-le-um (mô′sō-lē′um), *n.* **1,** a stately, magnificent tomb; **2,** a large, dismal or bleak room or building.

mauve (mōv), *n.* a soft lilac, violet, or purple colour.

ma-ven or **ma-vin** (mā′ven), *n.* one who is particularly knowledgeable in some area; an expert; as, a literary *maven*.

mav-er-ick (mav′ėr-ik), *n.* **1,** an unbranded animal, esp. a lost calf running at large; **2,** *Colloq.* one who bolts his group or party and becomes an independent; **3,** *Colloq.* a person or group that is unconventional; rebel or nonconformist.

maw (mo; mô), *n.* **1,** the stomach of an animal; **2,** in birds, the craw or crop; **3,** something perceived as voracious or insatiable; as, the *maw* of the media.

mawk-ish (mok′ish; môk′ish), *adj.* foolishly or sickeningly sentimental; as, a *mawkish* lover.

max-im (mak′sim), *n.* a general truth or rule expressed briefly; proverb; as, "Waste not, want not" is a useful *maxim*.

max-i-mum (mak′si-mum), *n.* [*pl.* maximums or maxima (mak′si-ma)], the greatest possible number, quantity, or degree: opposite of *minimum*; as, the gas tank of our car holds a *maximum* of 40 litres:—*adj.* greatest in quantity or highest in degree; as, the *maximum* speed limit.

may (mā), *auxiliary v.* [*p.t.* might (mīt)], **1,** to be allowed or to be free to; as, you *may* go; **2,** to be likely, but not certain; as, it *may* rain; **3,** it is hoped that; would that, expressing the earnest desire, or wish, of the speaker; as, *may* the report prove untrue; *may* fortune be good to you; **4,** used to express purpose, contingency, concession, or choice; as, I keep busy that I *may* not become bored; she will attend the party come what *may*; he *may* be large, but he is agile; they *may* fly, or they *may* take a train.

May (mā), *n.* the fifth month of the year, with 31 days, between April and June:—**May Day,** a spring festival on May 1 to celebrate the coming of spring, and in some countries, esp. socialist ones, an international workers' day celebration.

may-be (mā′bē), *adv.* perhaps; possibly; as, *maybe* she'll come tomorrow:—*n. Colloq.* an uncertain reply; uncertainty; as, Will she come? *Maybe.*

may-day (mā′dā′), *n.* an international distress signal used in emergencies by aircraft and ships: from the French, "m'aidez" (help me).

may-hem (mā′hem; mā′em), *n.* **1,** the crime of willfully injuring a person by causing mutilation or loss, as of a limb or organ: a form of *maim*; **2,** violence; destruction; **3,** confusion; disorder; chaos.

may-on-naise (mā′o-nāz′; mā′o-nāz′), *n.* a thick, rich sauce or seasoned dressing for salads, sandwiches, and other foods, made of egg yolks, vegetable oil, and vinegar or lemon juice, beaten together until thick.

may-or (mā′ėr; mâr), *n.* the chief official or head of the government of a city, town, village, or borough.—*n.* **may′or-al-ty.**

maze (māz), *n.* **1,** a confusing network, as of passages, through which it is hard to find one's way; tangle; labyrinth; **2,** any complicated situation or complex pattern, design, system, process, or arrangement; **3,** confusion of mind; bewilderment.—*adj.* **ma′zy.**

MB (em′bē′), *abbrev.* **1,** short for *megabyte*; **2,** short for *Manitoba*.

Mc-In-tosh (mak′in-tosh′), *n.* popular red eating apple discovered and developed in Canada.

me (mē), *pron.* the objective case of *I*, the pronoun of the first person, used as a direct or indirect object or an object of a preposition; as, help *me*; give *me* the book; come with *me*.

me-a cul-pa (mā′a kul′pa; mē′a kul′pa), *n.* a formal acknowledgement of one's fault or error: Latin for "through my fault":—*interj.* expressing this admission.

mead·ow (med′ō), *n.* **1,** a field used for pasture; also, a field in which hay is grown; **2,** a piece of low, wet land by a river or stream; **3,** in mountain valleys in British Columbia, a piece of grassy land that is surrounded by trees.—*adj.* **mead′ow·y.**

mea·gre or **mea·ger** (mē′gėr), *adj.* **1,** lacking in flesh; lean; thin; **2,** poor; scanty; as, a *meagre* meal; **3,** lacking richness or quality; unfertile; as the *meagre* soil of a desert.—*adv.* **mea′gre·ly.**—*n.* **mea′gre·ness.**

[1]**meal** (mēl), *n.* **1,** coarsely ground grain, esp. ground corn or other grain; **2,** anything else that is ground to a powder.

[2]**meal** (mēl), *n.* the food served or eaten at one time, such as breakfast, lunch, or dinner.

meal·y (mēl′i), *adj.* [meal-i-er, meal-i-est], **1,** like meal; powdery, dry, and soft; as, *mealy* soil; **2,** covered with meal; floury; **3,** pale.

meal·y–mouthed (mē′li–mouthd′; moutht′), *adj.* afraid or unwilling to speak out plainly or bluntly; using soft words.

[1]**mean** (mēn), *v.t.* [meant (ment), meaning], **1,** to intend; as, he *means* to go; she *means* mischief; he did not *mean* to be rude; **2,** to express a certain thought; signify; as, charity *means* love; that nice gesture *meant* a lot to her; **3,** to refer to; designate; as, I *mean* you; **4,** to design or intend for a purpose; as, a pitcher is *meant* for holding and pouring a liquid; **5,** to have the sense of; be defined as; as, what does that word *mean*? **6,** to have a certain effect; as, having a long-haired dog or cat *means* extra work in grooming.

[2]**mean** (mēn), *adj.* **1,** not kind or good; nasty; cruel; as, a *mean* bully; **2,** hard to handle or deal with; tough; as, a *mean* storm; **3,** humble; common; as, of *mean* birth; **4,** inferior; ordinary; as, a *mean* grade of meat; **5,** poor; shabby; as, a *mean* house; **6,** lacking in generosity; stingy; as, a *mean* man; **7,** lacking in honour; base; as, a *mean* motive; **8,** *Slang* excellent; skillful; expert; as, a *mean* Caesar salad; *mean* tennis player; play a *mean* harmonica.—*n.* **mean′ness.**—*adv.* **mean′ly.**

[3]**mean** (mēn), *adj.* **1,** occupying the middle position between two extremes; average; middle point, condition, or action; as, a *mean* height; *mean* temperature; **2,** average in quality or degree; **3,** intermediary:—*n.* **1,** a condition, quality, course of action, etc., that is midway between two extremes; as, grey is the *mean* between black and white; **2,** moderation:—**means, 1,** that by which something is done or accomplished; as, a boat was the *means* of rescue; **2,** wealth; money or property; available resources; as, a woman of independent *means.*

me·an·der (mē-an′dėr), *v.i.* **1,** to follow a winding course, as a river; **2,** to wander aimlessly:—*n.* **1,** a winding course; **2,** the act of wandering aimlessly.

mean·ing (mēn′ing), *adj.* expressive; full of significance; important; as, a *meaning* glance:—*n.* **1,** goal; intention; what is intended; as, the *meaning* of her visit; **2,** that which is meant; as, the *meaning* of a word.—*adv.* **mean′ing·ly.**—*adj.* **mean′ing·ful.**

mean·ing·less (mēn′ing-lis), *adj.* without meaning or sense; not significant.

meant (ment), *p.t.* and *p.p.* of [1]*mean.*

mean·time (mēn′tīm′), *adv.* **1,** in the time between two occasions; meanwhile; as, the program was late starting; *meantime,* we read our books; **2,** at the same time; the teacher read the poem out loud; *meantime,* we followed along in our books:—*n.* the time between two occasions; as, dinner was delayed; in the *meantime,* she did her homework.

mean·while (mēn′wīl′; mēn′hwīl′), *adv.* **1,** in the time between two occasions; meantime; as, the program was late starting; *meanwhile,* we read our books; **2,** at the same time; the teacher read the poem out loud; *meanwhile,* we followed along in our books:—*n.* the time between two occasions; the intervening time; as, dinner was delayed; in the *meanwhile,* she did her homework.

mea·sles (mē′zlz), *n.pl.* used as *sing.* **1,** a contagious disease caused by a virus, common esp. among children, marked by fever, coughing, other coldlike symptoms, and itching small red spots on the skin; also, the red spots; **2,** any similar disease, such as German measles; **3,** a disease of cattle and pigs caused by tapeworm larvae.

meas·ure (mezh′ėr), *n.* **1,** the size, quantity, or capacity of a thing, as found by a rule or by comparison with a standard; also, the act or process for this purpose; **2,** a unit of measurement, as a litre, centimetre, etc.; also, an instrument for measuring, as a tape measure; **3,** a system of measurement; as, dry *measure;* **4,** an amount; degree; as, a small *measure* of pity; **5,** a reasonable limit; as, honesty knows no *measure;* **6,** a course of action; as, preventive *measure;* safety *measure;* **7,** an act of legislation; **8,** rhythm, as in poetry; **9,** in *music,* the time of a piece; also, the group of notes between two bars on a staff; a bar of music; **10,** a way of judging something; a standard; as, grades in school are not necessarily a true *measure* of intelligence:—*v.t.* [measured, measur-ing], **1,** to find out the extent, size, or volume of, by comparison with a fixed or known standard; **2,** to give out; allot; as, to *measure* out rations; **3,** mark off (size, rate, etc.); as, a speedometer *measures* the rate of speed:—*v.i.* **1,** to find dimensions, volume, etc.; **2,** to extend or be of a given length; as, the room *measures* 12 metres.—*adj.* **meas′ur·a·ble.**

meas·ured (mezh′ėrd), *adj.* **1,** regulated or determined by some standard; **2,** uniform; regular; also, rhythmical; as, *measured* steps; **3,** carefully considered; as, *measured* words.

meas·ure·ment (mezh′ėr-ment), *n.* **1,** the act of finding size, quantity, amount, etc., by a standard or by measuring; **2,** the size or quantity found by measuring; **3,** a system of units of measure.

meat (mēt), *n.* **1,** animal flesh used as food, esp. that of mammals: not poultry and fish; **2,** the food parts within a shell, rind, etc.; as, the *meat* of a nut; **3,** the main or essential part of something; the significant content or substance; core; as, the *meat* of the issue or argument; *meat* of the news story; **4,** *Slang* an activity, subject, etc., that is pleasurable or easy for someone; as, math is her *meat*; playing guitar is his *meat.—adj.* **meat′y; meat′less.** Also, **meat′ and po-ta′toes; meat′ball′; meat′head′; meat′ hook′; meat′ loaf′; meat′ mar′ket; meat′pack′ing.**

Mec·ca (mek′a), *n.* the city in Saudi Arabia that was the birthplace of Muhammad and thus, the holiest city in Islam:—**mecca, 1,** a place that attracts people for some reason; as, Niagara Falls is a tourist *mecca*; **2,** a centre of activity or interest; as, McGill University has long been a medical *mecca*.

me·chan·ic (mi-kan′ik), *n.* a skilled worker, esp. one who understands the construction and use of machinery and tools; one skilled at fixing or working with machines; artisan or machinist; as, an auto *mechanic:—adj.* relating to manual labour, esp. machinery and tools; mechanical.

me·chan·i·cal (mi-kan′i-kal), *adj.* **1,** relating to, or made by, machinery; using or having to do with machines or tools; **2,** done without thought, as a machine, as if from force of habit; without any feeling or expression; automatic; as, *mechanical* movements; **3,** run by machinery; as, a *mechanical* piano; **4,** relating to the science of mechanics.—*adv.* **me·chan′i·cal·ly.**

me·chan·ics (mi-kan′iks), *n.pl.* used as *sing.* **1,** the science of machinery; **2,** the branch of science or physics that deals with motion and with the effect of force on bodies in motion or at rest; also, the application of these principles to design, construction, etc.; **3,** the way in which some action is carried out; technique; workings; as, the *mechanics* of baseball pitching; the *mechanics* of a sewing machine; **4,** the details of a process, activity, etc.; as, the *mechanics* of planning a party or wedding.—*adj.* **mech′a·nis′ tic.**—*v.t.* **mech′a·nize′**[mechanized, mechaniz-ing].

mech·a·nism (mek′a-nizm), *n.* **1,** the structure or arrangement of the working parts of a machine of any kind; as, the *mechanism* of a watch; **2,** a mechanical device; **3,** any system of interworking parts; the arrangement of the parts of a large or complicated system; as, the *mechanism* of the federal government; **4,** the philosophical theory that all things are formed mechanically or materially; **5,** patterns that determine psychological behaviour under certain circumstances; as, defence *mechanism*.

med·al (med′l), *n.* a coinlike piece of metal marked with a design or with words to commemorate some event, achievement, deed, etc., or to serve as a reward or decoration for merit; as, Olympic gold *medals.—n.* **med′al·list** or **med′al·ist.**

me·dal·lion (mi-dal′yun), *n.* **1,** a large, round medal; **2,** a design or decorative panel, often oval or circular, used in lace, carpets, textiles, portraits, carvings, etc.; **3,** round or oval piece of boneless, cooked meat; as, beef *medallions*.

med·dle (med′l), *v.i.* [med-dled, med-dling], to interfere with what does not concern one in a rude or unwanted way; as, he loses his friends, because he *meddles* too much in their business.—*n.* **med′dler.**

med·dle·some (med′l-sum), *adj.* apt to interfere in the affairs of others.

me·de·vac or **me·di·vac** (me′de-vak′; me′di-vak′). *n.* **1**, evacuation by air of sick or wounded to medical care; **2**, the aircraft used in such evacuations; air ambulance:—*v.t.* to transport by air a sick or wounded person to medical care.

me·di·a (mē′dē-a), *n.pl.* **1,** a *pl.* of *medium*; **2,** the means of public or mass communication, such as newspapers, television, and radio, often regarded collectively, used with *pl.* or *sing.* verbs; as, the *media* often run/runs sensational stories; **3,** the group of individual reporters and others who make up the mass communications industry; as, several *media* were present at the news conference:—*adj.* relating to the media; as, *media* coverage; *media* event.

me·di·ae·val (mē′dē-ē′val; mē′dē′val; me′dē-ē′val; me′dē′val), *adj.* Same as **medieval.**

me·di·an (mē′di-an), *adj.* **1,** in the middle; related to the middle; **2,** relating to or near a plane that divides something, such as an animal, into the right and left halves; **3,** in *statistics*, relating to the midpoint, having an equal amount above and below a certain point in distribution; as, the *median* age of the town's population:—*n.* **1,** the middle point or part of something; **2,** a point or number in a series, having the same numbers of points or numbers before as after it; as, in the series 4, 5, 8, 16, 22, the *median* is 8; **3,** in *mathematics*, a straight line from the midpoint of the side opposite a triangle's vertex; **4,** on a major road or highway, the barrier or area between the opposite lanes of traffic.

me·di·ate (mē′dē-āt′), *v.i.* [mediat-ed,

mediat-ing], to act as a peacemaker between those who are openly disagreeing and assist in reaching agreement; as, to *mediate* between union and management:—*v.t.* to bring about by acting as an agent between opponents; as, to *mediate* a compromise:—*adj.* (mē′dē-it), **1,** not direct; acting by or through some intervening person or thing; **2,** intermediate.

me-di-a-tion (mē′dē-ā′shun), *n.* the act of intervening or interceding in a conflict, often as a neutral third party.

me-di-a-tor (mē′dē-ā′tėr), *n.* one who intervenes to effect agreement or compromise; peacemaker.

med-ic (med′ik), *n.* **1**, a health care professional, esp. a doctor or intern; **2**, a physician or surgeon who is a member of the military medical corps; **3**, a medical student.

med-i-cal (med′i-kal), *adj.* **1,** relating to the study and use of medicine, or the treatment of disease; as, a *medical* school; requiring *medical*, not surgical, attention; **2,** relating to one's health; as, to be absent for *medical* reasons:—*n. Colloq.* a thorough medical examination by a physician.—*adv.* **med′i-cal-ly.**—*n.* **med′i-ca′ tion.** Also, **med′i-cal doc′tor; med′i-cal ex-am′in-er; med′i-cal of′fic-er; med′i-cal prac-ti′tion-er.**

me-dic-i-nal (mi-dis′i-nal), *adj.* **1,** having the power to cure or relieve disease, pain, etc.; **2,** similar to medicine, as in smell, taste, etc.—*adv.* **me-dic′i-nal-ly.**

med-i-cine (med′i-sin), *n.* **1,** the science that deals with the understanding, prevention, non- surgical treatment, and cure of disease; **2,** any drug, remedy, or other substance used to prevent, treat, or cure disease or to relieve pain or injuries; **3,** a traditional First Nations ceremony or practice believed to have magical healing powers; **4,** something that is disagreeable but necessary. Also, **med′i-cine ball′; med′i-cine bun′dle; med′i-cine cab′i-net; med′i-cine man′; med′i-cine wheel′.**

medicine man or **medicine woman**, *n.* Same as **shaman.**

me-di-e-val or **me-di-ae-val** (mē′dē-ē′val; mē′dē′val; me′dē-ē′val; me′dē′val), *adj.* **1,** relating to, or characteristic of, the Middle Ages, a period extending approximately from A.D. 500 to A.D. 1500; **2,** *Colloq.* old-fashioned; extremely outmoded or conservative.

me-di-o-cre (mē′dē-ō′kėr), *adj.* of medium quality; commonplace; ordinary; so-so; as, a *mediocre* essay.—*n.* **me′di-oc′ri-ty** (mē′dē-ok′ri-ti).

med-i-tate (med′i-tāt′), *v.i.* [meditat-ed, meditat-ing], **1,** to think deeply; reflect; as, to *meditate* upon your goal in life; **2,** to reflect deeply, or pray, esp. as a religious ritual, often reaching a trancelike state:—*v.t.* to consider; plan; contemplate; as, to *meditate* a change.—*n.* **med′i-ta′tion.**—*adj.* **med′i-ta′tive.**

me-di-um (mē′dē-um), *n.* [*pl.* media (mē′dē-a) (def. 2 and 3) or mediums], **1,** that which comes between or in the middle between two extremes; also, a middle size; **2,** a means of communication or expression; that by which or through which something is done; as, the newspaper is an advertising *medium;* she expresses herself through the *medium* of art; books are sometimes produced in two *media*: print and electronic; **3,** the space, substance, or condition in which bodies exist or move; environment; as, water is the *medium* in which we swim; rich soil is the best *medium* for most plants; also, a substance through which something acts or is carried; as, the air is a *medium* for sound; **4,** a person who claims to receive messages from the spirit world:—*adj.* middle; moderate; as, cloth of *medium* weight; *medium* steak, not rare.

med-ley (med′li), *n.* [*pl.* medleys], **1,** a jumbled mixture or confused mass; hodgepodge; **2,** in *music*, a composition made up of passages selected from different songs or pieces.

me-dul-la (mi-dul′a), *n.* **1,** in *botany*, the spongy centre of a stem; pith; **2,** in *zoology*, the marrow of bones; also, the centre of an organ or other structure:—**medulla ob′lon-ga′ta**, a broadening of the spinal cord where it enters the skull to become a brain centre controlling breathing, blood circulation, and other necessary involuntary functions.

meek (mēk), *adj.* **1,** mild of temper; patient; gentle; humble; **2,** easily imposed upon; submissive; spiritless.—*adv.* **meek′ly.**—*n.* **meek′ness.**

meet (mēt), *v.t.* [met (met), meet-ing], **1,** to come upon by chance or by arrangement; come face to face with; as, he *met* her on his way to school; **2,** to keep an appointment with; as, she *met* her friend at 8:00 at the restaurant; **3,** to be at the place of arrival of; as, I *met* the bus at the station; **4,** to connect with; join; as, this path *meets* the main road; **5,** to oppose in a battle, contest, etc.; **6,** to be introduced to; as, I'd like you to *meet* my parents; **7,** to experience; as, he *met* strange adventures; **8,** to be perceived by; to catch the attention of; as, to *meet* the eye; **9,** to equal; satisfy; cope with; as, will you *meet* my demands?—*v.i.* **1,** to collect in one place; assemble; congregate; **2,** to come together; **3,** be joined; **4,** become introduced; **5,** contend:—**meet with, 1,** to experience; as, to *meet with* bad weather; **2,** to talk with; unite in company; as, to *meet with* a client:—*n.* a gathering or assembly for some definite purpose, esp. a contest or competition; as, a track *meet.*

meet-ing (mēt′ing), *n.* **1,** a coming together of persons; assembling; as, a *meeting* of members of Parliament; **2,** an assembly; a gathering for a special purpose, as social, business, or religious; congregation; convention; **3,** a place where two or more things come together; union; a junction, as of roads.

meg-a (meg′a-), *prefix* meaning **1,** *great, very large, a lot;* as in *mega*buck, *mega*city, *mega*deal, *mega*dose, *mega*flop, *mega*hit, *mega*project, *mega*star, *mega*store, *mega*structure, *mega*vitamin; **2,** a million times (or of) (abbreviated as *M*); as in *mega*bit, *mega*cycle, *mega*joule, *mega*ton (explosive force of a million tons of TNT), *mega*volt, *mega*watt.

meg-a-byte (meg′a-bīt′), *n.* in *computing,* **1,** a unit of computer data storage memory that is equal to 1,048,576 bytes; **2,** generally, one million bytes: abbreviated as *MB.*

meg-a-hertz (meg′a-hûrts′), *n.* one million *hertz* or cycles per second, which is a measure of radio frequency or the clock rate of a computer chip; as, the first Pentium chip ran at only 100 *megahertz*: abbreviated as *MHz.*

meg-a-lo- or **meg-al-** (meg′a-lō-; meg′al-), *prefix* meaning *great, very large;* as in *megalo*mania (mania for greatness), *megal*opolis, *megalo*saur.

meg-a-phone (meg′a-fōn′), *n.* a large, funnel-shaped horn or speaking trumpet used to increase the sound of the voice or to carry it a long distance.

mel-an-chol-y (mel′an-kol′i), *n.* [*pl.* melancholies], **1,** a gloomy state of mind or mood; depression of spirits; sadness; **2,** a thoughtful mood:—*adj.* **1,** dejected; downcast; sad; depressed; gloomy; as, she was *melancholy* because her friend could not come to the party; **2,** causing this feeling; as, a cold, rainy, *melancholy* day; **3,** showing or expressing sadness; as, a *melancholy* look or song.—*adj.* **mel′an-chol′ic.**

mel-a-no-ma (mel′a-nō′ma), *n.* [*pl.* melanomas or melanomata], **1,** a usually malignant, dark-coloured tumour on the skin; **2,** skin cancer.

me-lee (mā′lā′; mā′lā′) or **mêlée** (me-lā′), *n.* **1,** a confused conflict between opposing fighters; **2,** a brawl; **3,** a confused, disordered, or hectic state.

mel-lif-lu-ous or **mel-lif-lu-ent** (me-lif′loo-us; me-lif′loo-ent), *adj.* flowing sweetly and smoothly; musical; as, a *mellifluous* song, voice, etc.

mel-low (mel′ō), *adj.* **1,** soft, juicy, and sweet, because of ripeness; as, a *mellow* peach; **2,** of a delicate, rich flavour; well matured; as, *mellow* wine or; cheese; **3,** soft; rich; loamy, as soil; **4,** soft; full; pure; rich, as a colour or sound; **5,** softened by age or maturity; as, a *mellow* grandparent; **6,** relaxed; pleasant; laid-back:—*v.t.* and *v.i.* to make or become ripe, gentle, sweet, or relaxed (*Colloq.*); as, sorrow *mellowed* her nature; stop worrying so much; *mellow* out!

mel-o-dra-ma (mel′o-drä′ma; mel′o-drä′ma; mel′o-dram′a), *n.* **1,** a highly exciting drama with exaggerated emotions, usually with a happy ending; **2,** sensational or exaggerated language or behaviour.—*adj.* **mel′o-dra-mat′ic.**—*adv.* **mel′o-dra-mat′i-cal-ly.**

mel-o-dy (mel′o-di), *n.* [*pl.* melodies], **1,** an agreeable arrangement of sounds; **2,** musiclike quality; **3,** a song or tune; as, the *melody* was simple; **4,** the principal part in a song or piece of music; the air; as, the sopranos carry the *melody.*—*adj.* **me-lod′ic** (mi-lod′ik); **me-lo′di-ous** (mi-lō′dē-us).

mel-on (mel′un), *n.* **1,** a trailing plant of the gourd family, which grows on a vine; also, its edible, juicy fruit, such as a muskmelon, watermelon, honeydew melon, or cantaloupe; **2,** a pinky yellow colour; **3,** something that is rounded like a melon; **4,** *Slang* extra profits or dividends divided among shareholders; windfall.

MELON

melt (melt), *v.i.* **1,** to be changed from a solid to a liquid state, often by heat; as, ice *melts;* **2,** to dissolve; as, sugar or chocolate *melts* in the mouth; **3,** to waste away; grow gradually less; as, his anger *melts* under her charm; **4,** to disappear; vanish, as if by dissolving; as, the fog *melts* away; they *melted* into the crowd; **5,** to become gentle or tender; as, my heart *melts;* **6,** to blend as colours:—*v.t.* **1,** to change from a solid to a liquid state; as, heat *melts* butter; **2,** to make something disappear; dissolve; as, the sun *melts* the fog; coffee *melts* the sugar; **3,** to make gentle; soften; as, his kindness *melted* her heart. Also, **melt′down′; melt′ing point′; melt′ing pot′; melt′wa′ter.**

mem-ber (mem′bėr), *n.* **1,** one who belongs to a group or society; as, a team *member;* **2,** a part of the body or plant, esp. a leg, arm, wing, branch, etc.; **3,** the penis; **4,** one part of any whole:—**Member,** someone who is elected to a legislature; as, a *Member* of Parliament (*MP*); *Member* of the Provincial Parliament (*MPP*).

mem-ber-ship (mem′bėr-ship), *n.* **1,** the state of being a member; **2,** all the persons belonging to an organization; also, the total number of members.

mem-brane (mem′brān), *n.* **1,** a thin, soft sheet of tissue that serves as a cover, connection, or lining in an animal or vegetable body; as, the *membrane* in the ears or eyes; **2,** any similar material, such as plastic.—*adj.* **mem′bra-nous.**

me-men-to (me-men′tō), *n.* [*pl.* mementos or mementoes], that which serves as a reminder of a person, thing, event, or place in the past; souvenir; token; keepsake.

mem-o (mem′ō), *n. Colloq. abbrev.* short for *memorandum.*

mem-oir (mem′wär), *n.* **1,** a record or account of events written from the author's personal knowledge or experience; **2,** a biography; autobiography; biographical sketch or notice; **3,** a scholarly report; memorandum.

mem-o-ra-bil-i-a (mem′ėr-a-bil′ē-a; mem′ėr-a-bil′ya), *n.pl.* **1**, souvenirs and collectibles of memorable events; mementos; **2,** things, events, or experiences worth remembering.

mem-o-ra-ble (mem′o-ra-bl), *adj.* worthy of being remembered; notable; as, a *memorable* vacation.—*adv.* **mem′ora-bly.**

mem-o-ran-dum (mem′o-ran′dum), *n.* [*pl.* memorandums or memoranda (mem′o-ran′da)], **1,** a brief note to remind someone of something or to help one to remember; **2,** a brief, informal note, letter, or report; **3,** an informal diplomatic communication that summarizes the main points; **4,** a summary of the terms of a contract, etc. Often abbreviated as *memo.*

me-mor-i-al (mi-môr′ē-al), *adj.* **1,** in memory of a person or an event; commemorative; as, a *memorial* address; *memorial* service for the victims of the September 11 tragedy; **2,** pertaining to memory:—*n.* **1,** a thing, day, etc., serving to keep alive the memory of a place, person, etc.; as, a statue as a *memorial* to the fallen soldiers; **2,** a record or account of something; **3,** a written statement of facts addressed to a person or persons in authority, usually accompanied by a request or protest, esp. in the U.S.

mem-o-rize (mem′o-rīz′), *v.t.* [memorized, memoriz-ing], to commit to memory; to learn by heart; as, to *memorize* lines in a play.

mem-o-ry (mem′o-ri), *n.* [*pl.* memories], **1,** the ability or power to remember things; also, the act of remembering; **2,** a particular person, thing, period, or experience remembered; as, a trip to the circus is one of my earliest *memories*; **3,** all that can be remembered; **4,** the length of time within which past happenings are remembered; as, it happened within grandmother's *memory*; **5,** reputation after death; as, his *memory* is honoured; **6,** in *computing,* the part of a device, esp. a computer, in which information can be input and stored and from which it can be retrieved; also, the amount of information that can be stored. Also, **mem′o-ry bank′; mem′o-ry board′; mem′o-ry card′.**

memory chip, a device that stores information in the form of electrical charges.

men (men), *n.pl.* of *man.*

men-ace (men′is), *n.* **1,** a danger or evil that threatens and can cause harm; as, the *menace* of flood; **2,** *Colloq.* a nuisance:—*v.t.* [menaced, menac-ing], to threaten; put in danger; as, the forest fire *menaced* the nearby community.—*adj.* **men′ac-ing.**—*adv.* **men′ac-ing-ly.**

me-nag-er-ie (mi-naj′ėr-i; mi-nazh′ėr-i), *n.* **1,** a place where wild animals are kept; **2,** a collection of wild animals, kept in cages, for exhibition; **3,** a motley or incongruous collection of things, animals, or people.

mend (mend), *v.t.* **1,** to repair (that which is broken or worn); fix; as, to *mend* a torn sleeve; **2,** to make better; correct; reform; as, the prisoner *mended* her ways:—**mend fences,** to improve (a relationship) through negotiation:—*v.i.* to grow better or stronger; improve; heal; as, the child who had been ill *mended* rapidly:—*n.* **1,** the act of growing better; as, she is on the *mend* after her illness; **2,** a repaired part of something.

men-da-cious (men-dā′shus), *adj.* lying; false; dishonest; as, a *mendacious* suspect; a *mendacious* story.—*n.* **men-da′cious-ness; men-dac′i-ty** (men-das′i-ti).—*adv.* **men-da′cious-ly.**

me-ni-al (mē′nē-al; mēn′yal), *n.* **1,** a domestic servant, esp. one who does lowly or degrading work; **2,** a flunky:—*adj.* relating to, or suitable for, a servant; lowly; humble; as, a *menial* task.—*adv.* **me′ni-al-ly.**

men-in-gi-tis (men′in-jī′tis), *n.* a serious inflammation of the membranes of the brain and spinal cord.

men-stru-a-tion (men′stro͞o-ā′shun), the menses or monthly discharge of blood and tissue from the uterus (womb) through the vagina, occurring between puberty and menopause in nonpregnant women; period:—*v.i.* **men′stru-ate′** [menstruated, menstruat-ing].—*adj.* **men′stru-al.**

men-su-ra-tion (men′soo-rā′shun; men′shoo-rā′shun), *n.* **1,** the act or process of measuring; **2,** in *mathematics,* the branch of applied geometry dealing with the finding of lengths, areas, and volumes.

men-tal (men′tl), *adj.* **1,** relating to the mind; intellectual; as, *mental* exercise; *mental* health; **2,** done by the mind; as, to make a *mental* note of something; **3,** having to do with a disorder or disease of the mind; as, *mental* illness; **4,** relating to a place where mental illness is treated; as, a *mental* hospital; **5,** *Slang* crazy or insane: considered offensive.—*adv.* **men′tal-ly.**—*n.* **men-tal′i-ty.** Also, **men′tal block′; men′tal case′; men′tal hand′i-cap; men′tal note′; men′tal re′tar-da′tion.**

men-thol (men′thol; men′thôl), *n.* a solid, white, chrystalline substance with a mint-like odour, obtained from oil of peppermint and used in medicine, toiletries, cigarettes, and as a flavouring.—*adj.* **men′tho-lat′ed.**

men-tion (men′shun), *n.* **1,** a brief notice;

a light or chance remark; a statement or reference; as, a *mention* of the accident in the newspaper; **2,** an award of honour; as, to receive an honourable *mention* for one's effort or achievement:—*v.t.* to speak briefly of; name; refer to; disclose; as, he did not *mention* you; don't *mention* the surprise party to her.

men-tor (men′tôr; men′tėr), *n.* a wise, experienced, and faithful adviser, friend, or teacher:—*v.t.* to act as a mentor to someone; as, to *mentor* the new employee.—*n.* **men′tor-ship.**—*n.* and *adj.* **men′tor-ing.**

men-u (men′ū), *n.* **1,** a bill of fare; a list of food and drinks that are available in a restaurant or other eating establishment, along with their prices; the printed material on which the list appears; also, the dishes served; **2,** in *computing,* a list of program topics, commands, or options shown on a computer or television screen, often in a menu bar, which enables the user to make a selection; **3,** any list of topics or options; as, a *menu* of activities.

mer-can-tile (mûr′kan-tīl′; mûr′kan-til; mûr′kan-tēl), *adj.* having to do with, or engaged in, trade; relating to merchants; mercenary.

Mer-ca-tor pro-jec-tion or **Mer-ca-tor's pro-jec-tion** (mėr-kā′tėr prō-jek′shun; mėr-kā′tėrz prō-jek′shun), *n.* the use of lines on flat maps to show latitude and longitude: the distortion in the polar areas results from trying to show a global surface as a flat rectangle.

mer-ce-nar-y (mûr′si-nėr-i), *n.* [*pl.* mercenaries], **1,** a hired, professional soldier, usually by a foreign army; **2,** anyone who does something strictly for money:—*adj.* **1,** acting only for pay or reward; eager for money; **2,** prompted by greed; as, a *mercenary* crime.

mer-chan-dise (mûr′chan-dīz′; mûr′chan-dīs′), *n.* goods or articles that are bought and sold:—*v.t.* [merchandised, merchandising], **1,** to buy and sell goods or articles; **2,** to promote (goods, persons, ideas) through advertising, publicity, etc.—*n.* **mer′chan-dis-er.**—*n.* and *adj.* **mer′chan-dis-ing.**

mer-chant (mûr′chant), *n.* **1,** one who buys and sells goods wholesale for profit, esp. one who carries on trade on a large scale; **2,** a storekeeper or retailer; a person who owns or is in charge of a store; **3,** in Newfoundland, a business person involved in trade in the fishing industry:—*adj.* relating to, or employed in, business or trade; as, *merchant* ships. Also, **mer′ chant bank′; mer′chant ma-rine′; mer′chant na′vy.**

mer-ci-ful (mûr′si-fool), *adj.* full of mercy; tender-hearted; compassionate.—*adv.* **mer′ci-ful-ly.**

mer-ci-less (mûr′si-lis), *adj.* without mercy or pity; unfeeling; cruel.—*adv.* **mer′ci-less-ly.**

mer-cu-ri-al (mėr-kyoor′ē-al), *adj.* **1,** lively; quick; fickle; changeable, esp. with regard to mood; as, *mercurial* nature; **2,** containing mercury.

mer-cu-ry (mûr′kū-ri), *n.* a heavy, liquid, silver-white metal, which is a chemical element, used in thermometers, batteries, etc.; quicksilver:—**Mercury, 1,** the smallest planet in the solar system, closest to the sun; **2,** in ancient Roman mythology, the god who served as a messenger for other gods; also, the god of commerce, who was eloquent, quick-witted, and deceitful.

mer-cy (mûr′si), *n.* [*pl.* mercies], **1,** willingness to forgive an offender, or to treat him or her with kindness; pity; leniency; as, the judge showed *mercy* to the criminal; **2,** willingness to help suffering; **3,** an act of kindness; **4,** something one is thankful for; a blessing; as, it's a *mercy* that someone saw the smoke and called the fire department:—**at the mercy of,** in the power of; as, the thief was *at the mercy of* his captors:—**mercy killing,** euthanasia; painlessly killing a suffering person or animal.

mere (mēr), *adj.* [*superl.* mer-est], nothing but; no more than; only; simple; slight; insignificant; as, this error is a *mere* typo; her injury is a *mere* scratch.

mere-ly (mēr′li), *adv.* simply; purely; only; nothing more than; as, he was not unkind, *merely* thoughtless.

merge (mûrj), *v.t.* [merged, merg-ing], **1,** to cause (something) to be absorbed into, or be joined with, something else; **2,** in *computing,* to combine files, data, etc., from various sources into one:—*v.i.* **1,** to be absorbed; lose separate character or identity; as, the two small banks *merged* with a larger one; **2,** of traffic, to come together or blend with other traffic; of a lane, to come together with another; as, to *merge* with the other lane of traffic; this lane *merges* with the left one:—*n.* **1,** the act of merging; **2,** in *computing,* the combining of data from various sources; as, to use mail *merge* to produce letters.

merg-er (mûr′jėr), *n.* the act of merging; the legal combination of two or more business corporations, estates, etc., into one.

me-rid-i-an (me-rid′ē-an), *adj.* **1,** relating to the highest point reached by a heavenly body, as the sun, in its daily course; **2,** relating to, or characteristic of, the point of greatest success or splendour (of a person, state, etc.):—*n.* **1,** the highest point, as of success, wealth, fame, etc.; **2,** an imaginary circle around the earth, passing through the North and South poles and any given place; also, either section or a line on a map representing a meridian; **3,** a curved line on a surface of revolution that intersects with a plane containing the axis of revolution.

me-ringue (ma-rang′), *n.* a mixture of beaten egg whites and sugar, often baked until brown and used as a topping on pies, cakes, or puddings or made into small cakes or shells.

mer-it (mer′it), *n.* **1,** due reward; the fact of having value or worth; having a good quality; as, her essay had *merit;* **2,** the condition of deserving; as, we are treated according to our *merits;* **3,** excellence; worth; that which deserves praise; as, the *merit* of honesty; **4,** the right or wrong of anything; as, to judge a case on its *merits*:—*v.t.* to deserve; to be worthy of something; as, her performance *merits* praise.

mer-i-toc-ra-cy (mer′i-tôk′ra-si), *n.* [*pl.* meritocracies], **1**, a system that rewards talent and achievement; **2**, leaders selected according to their abilities and not because of their wealth or lineage; **3**, a government, society, or other group that is governed by these principles.

mer-i-tor-i-ous (mer′i-tōr′ē-us), *adj.* deserving of reward or praise; as, *meritorious* conduct.—*adv.* **mer′i-tor′i-ous-ly.**

mer-maid (mûr′mād′), *n.* **1,** a legendary sea nymph with the upper body of a woman and the tail of a fish; **2,** *Colloq.* a woman or girl who is a strong swimmer.—*n.masc.* **mer′man′.**

mer-ry (mer′i), *adj.* [mer-ri-er, mer-ri-est], full of mirth and fun; very happy; jolly; pleasant.—*adv.* **mer′ri-ly.**—*n.* **mer′ri-ment.**

mer-ry–go–round (mer′i–gō–round′), *n.* **1,** a large, revolving, circular platform fitted with figures in the form of horses and other animals or seats, on which persons ride; a carousel; **2,** a whirl of fast-paced activity; as, a *merry-go-round* of parties.

mesh (mesh), *n.* **1,** one of the openings between the threads of a net or of a wire screen; also, the material used; **2,** any network, or something that entangles; as, the *meshes* of a spider's web; **3,** in machinery, the uniting or engaging of the teeth of two gear wheels so that power can be passed along from one to the other:—*v.t.* **1,** to catch or entangle in or as in a net; **2,** to bring together; coordinate; as, to *mesh* your ideas with ours:—*v.i.* **1,** to become entangled; **2,** to fit together; be coordinated or harmonious; as, your ideas do not *mesh* with ours; **3,** in machinery, to unite with one another, as of gear teeth.

mes-mer-ism (mez′mėr-izm′; mes′mėr-izm′), *n.* the producing of a hypnotic sleep or trance in which the subject's behaviour and sensations are easily influenced by suggestion; hypnotism.

mes-mer-ize (mez′mė-rīz′; mes′mė-rīz′), *v.t.* **1,** to hypnotize; **2,** to fascinate or enthrall; as, the magnificent scenery *mesmerized* her.

me-so or **mes-**(me′zō-; me′sō-; or mez′-; mes′-), *prefix* meaning *middle, intermediate;* as in *meso*derm, *meso*morph, *meso*sphere.

Me-so-zo-ic (mez′e-zō′ik; mes′e-zō′ik), *adj.* relating to the geological era lasting from 245 to 66 million years ago (following the Paleozoic and preceding the Cenozoic periods), and characterized by the end of the dinosaurs and the appearance of early birds and animals. Compare *Cenozoic* and *Paleozoic.*

mess (mes), *n.* **1,** a number of persons who take their meals together, esp. soldiers or sailors; also, the place the meal is eaten or the meal itself; **2,** a social organization in the armed forces; also, the place where they meet; **3,** an area that is dirty and unpleasant, with useless or unwanted things lying around; **4,** a state of confusion; a situation that is unpleasant or hard to deal with; a muddle; a botch; **5,** a dirty or untidy person:—*v.t.* to provide food for:—**mess up, 1,** to muddle; as, he *messed up* the job; **2,** to soil; make dirty or untidy; as, don't *mess up* your room; **3,** interfere with; ruin; spoil; as, the broken cable line *messed up* the television signal; **4,** confuse; as, the traumatic incident *messed up* his mind:—*v.i.* **1,** to eat together, esp. soldiers or sailors; **2,** *Colloq.* to interfere with; trifle; as, to *mess* with the set plans:—**mess about/around, 1,** *Colloq.* to busy oneself without accomplishing anything; putter; waste time; **2,** *Slang* to have sexual relations.

mes-sage (mes′ij), *n.* **1,** a word, notice, etc., written, spoken, or otherwise delivered, usually brief, from one person to another; **2,** an official communication; an inspirational communication; sermon; as, the prime minister's *message;* the religious leader's *message;* **3,** a piece of communication to be delivered by a messenger; **4,** a lesson, moral, or other point contained in a literary or artistic work; **5,** a television or radio advertisement:—*v.t.* [messaged, messag-ing], to send or transmit a message; as, to *message* the document by e-mail, fax, etc.

message board, *n.* **1**, a bulletin board for displaying notices and messages; **2**, an electronic bulletin board; **3**, an electronic system that allows authorized users to access messages to and from others in the group over the Internet; **4**, an electronic board that displays information in an arena, train station, airport, etc.

mes-sag-ing (mes′ij-ing), *n. Colloq.* the sending and receiving of communications, esp. of electronic mail or other types of electronic communication between computers, PDAs, and other similar devices.

mes-sen-ger (mes′en-jėr), *n.* **1,** one who carries messages, packages, etc., from one place to another; courier; also, one who does errands; **2,** a herald or bringer of news; forerunner; as, cooler, shorter days is the *messenger* of the end of summer.

Mes-si-ah (mi-sī′a), *n.* **1,** in *Christianity,* Jesus Christ; **2,** in *Judaism,* the deliverer or long-awaited saviour of the Jews:—**messiah**, someone thought of as a saviour of a cause, group, people, or country.

mess-y (mes′i), *adj.* [mess-i-er, mess-i-est], disorderly; soiled; botched; complicated; as, a *messy* room; a *messy* job; a *messy* predicament.—*adv.* **mess′i-ly.**—*n.* **mess′i-ness.**

met (met), *p.t.* and *p.p.* of *meet.*

me-ta- or **met-** (me′ta-; met′-), *prefix* meaning **1,** *later, after, beyond, behind, of a higher form*; as in; *met*estrus, *meta*carpus, *meta*language; **2,** *change*; as in *meta*bolism, *meta*morphosis; **3,** *more comprehensive*; as in *meta*physics; **4,** *similar in chemical makeup*; as in *meta*phosphate, *meta*protein.

me-tab-o-lism (mi-tab′o-li′zm), *n.* the process of synthesizing and breaking down food matter into living cells, or protoplasm, which in turn is broken down into simpler substances, or waste matter, thereby releasing energy for vital processes.

met-al (met′l), *n.* **1,** any of a number of solid, heavy, lustrous substances, such as gold, tin, lead, aluminum, copper, etc., that conduct heat and electricity and that can be drawn into fine threads, hammered into thin plates, and melted by heat; **2,** an alloy, which is a mixture of some of these substances, such as brass (copper and zinc); **3,** the material, as broken stone, used for making a road or as ballast for a railway track; **4,** spirit; temper; substance; mettle; as, a hero of fine *metal*:—**heavy metal, 1,** a type of rock music that is electronic, highly amplified, and has a strong, hard beat; **2,** a metal that has a very high density and is often poisonous, such as mercury or lead:—*adj.* made of or for metal; as, a *metal* cup; *metal* detector:—*v.t.* to cover with metal.—*adj.* **me-tal′lic** (mi-tal′ik).

met-al-lur-gy (met′l-ûr′ji), *n.* the art and science of refining metals from ores, making alloys, and treating them to give them desired properties.—*n.* **met′al-lur′gist.**

met-a-mor-pho-sis (met′a-môr′fo-sis), *n.* [*pl.* metamorphoses (met′a-môr′fo-sēz′)], change of form, shape, structure, character, or condition; transformation; esp. a striking change in the form and habits of an animal as it grows and develops from the egg to the adult stage; as, the *metamorphosis* of a caterpillar into a moth; *metamorphosis* of a child into a young adult.—*v.t.* **met′a-mor′phose** [metamorphosed, metamorphos-ing].—*adj.* **met′a-mor′phic.**

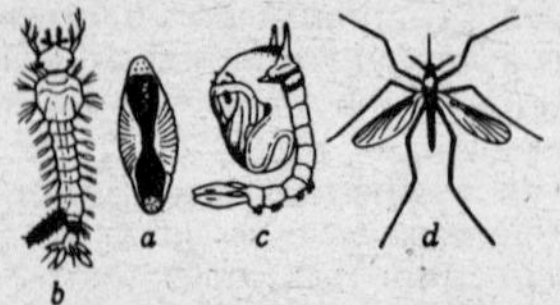

METAMORPHOSIS OF A MOSQUITO
A. EGG B. LARVA C. PUPA D. ADULT

met-a-phor (met′a-fôr′; met′a-fėr), *n.* a figure of speech to describe a person, place, or thing in which a name, action, or term ordinarily applied to a certain object is applied to another in order to suggest a likeness between them: distinguished from *simile* by not having *like* or *as* to introduce it; as, in "His voice cut through the silence," 'cut' is a *metaphor.*—*adj.* **met′a-phor′i-cal** (met′a-for′i-kal).—*adv.* **met′a-phor′i-cal-ly** (met′a-for′i-kal-i).

met-a-physics (met′a-fiz′iks), *n.* the branch of philosophy that deals with the nature, character, and causes of being and knowing; **2,** any abstract philosophical theory or reasoning, esp. one that is considered overly subtle or obscure.

[1]mete (mēt), *v.t.* [met-ed, met-ing], to give out by measure; apportion; distribute; as, to *mete* out rewards.

[2]mete (mēt), *n.* limit, extent, or boundary; as, *metes* and bounds.

me-te-or (mē′tē-ėr; mē′tē-ôr′), *n.* a mass of metallic or rocky matter coming from outer space that glows and burns as it enters and passes through the earth's atmosphere at high speed, often resembling a streak of light and burning up; shooting star.—*adj.* **me′te-or′ic** (mē′tē-ôr′ik; mē′tē-or′ik).

me-te-or-ite (mē′tē-ėr-īt′), *n.* a body of stone or metal that has fallen to the earth from outer space; a meteor that has fallen to earth without totally burning up.

me-te-or-ol-ogy (mē′tē-o-rol′o-ji), *n.* the science that deals with the atmosphere, esp. its changes in temperature, moisture, etc.: applied to weather forecasting.—*adj.* **me′te-or-o-log′i-cal.**—*n.* **me′te-or-ol′o-gist.**

[1]me-ter (mē′tėr), *n.* Same as **[1]metre, [2]metre.**

[2]me-ter (mē′tėr), *n.* **1,** an instrument for measuring and recording the passage of liquids, gases, or electric current; as, a water *meter*; **2,** any other instrument that measures time or amount; as, a parking *meter*; postage *meter*; taxi*meter*; speedo*meter*; thermo*meter*:—*v.t.* **1,** to measure with a meter; **2,** to provide something in regulated or measured amounts; as, to *meter* the cookies to each child; **3,** to use a meter; as, to *meter* the outgoing mail; **4,** to provide with a meter; as, to *meter* the new taxis or parking spaces.

me-tered (mē′tėrd), *adj.* **1,** measured amounts; as, *metered* doses; **2,** provided with a meter; as, a *metered* taxicab.

meth-am-phet-a-mine (meth′am-fet′a-mēn′; meth′am-fet′a-min′), *n.* a stimulant drug that is often used illegally: popularly known as *speed.*

meth-ane (meth′ān), *n.* a light, colourless, odourless, highly inflammable gas (CH_4, a compound of hydrogen and carbon): its chief forms are natural gas, marsh gas, and the fire damp of coal mines.

meth-od (meth′ud), *n.* **1,** an established order or regular way of doing something; as, a *method* of teaching; **2,** an orderly arrangement of ideas, subjects, etc.:—**Method,** an acting technique whereby the performer attempts to assimilate completely the behaviour, appearance, and other features of the character portrayed.

me-thod-i-cal (me-thod′i-kal), *adj.* **1,** arranged in an order; as, a *methodical* outline; **2,** devoted to a method or order; systematic; as, a *methodical* employee.—*adv.* **me-thod′i-cal-ly.**

me-tic-u-lous (me-tik′ū-lus), *adj.* unduly careful of details; precise; fastidious; as, his enunciation was *meticulous.*

Mé-tis (mā′tē; mā-tē′; mā-tēs′), *n.* [*pl.* Métis], a person who is the descendant of a French, Scottish, or English father and Cree or Ojibwa mother; a member of such a distinct cultural group.

me-ton-y-my (me-ton′i-mi), *n.* a figure of speech in which not the literal word but one associated with it is used; as, the *pen* is mightier than the *sword*; the *kettle* boils.

[1]**me-tre** or **me-ter** (mē′tėr), *n.* **1,** the arrangement of a line of poetry into measured groups of words or syllables, called feet, which gives a regular beat to the line; **2,** in *music,* rhythm or time.

[2]**me-tre** or **me-ter** (mē′tėr), *n.* the standard unit of length in the metric system, equal to 100 centimetres or 39.37 inches: abbreviated as *m.*

[1]**met-ric** (met′rik), *adj.* having to do with the metric system of measurement:—**metric system,** a decimal system of weights and measures using the *metre* as the unit of length, the *gram* as the unit of weight or mass, and the *litre* as the unit of capacity: many countries, including Canada, use an expanded version of the metric system, call the SI (Système international d'unités), but the U.S. still uses a system based on feet, miles, pounds, gallons, etc.

[2]**met-ric** (met′rik), *adj.* Same as **metrical.**

met-ri-cal (met′ri-kl), *adj.* **1,** relating to, like, or composed in metre or rhythm; as, a *metrical* translation; a *metrical* effect; **2,** relating to measurement; metric.—*adv.* **met′ri-cal-ly.**

met-ro (met′rō), *n.* **1**, a major metropolitan area; **2**, a subway; as, she rode the Montreal *metro*:—**Metro,** *Colloq.* an informal name for a large city such as Toronto, Vancouver, etc.; as, she lived in *Metro* for many years:—*adj.* pertaining to, of, or for a metro or Metro; as, *metro* council; *Metro* Toronto.

met-ro-nome (met′ro-nōm′), *n.* an instrument that beats time with adjustable, regular ticks or flashes, used esp. in practising music to enable the person to keep time.

me-trop-o-lis (mi-trop′o-lis), *n.* **1,** the chief city or capital of a country, province, state, or region; **2,** a principal centre of population and civilization; **3,** a metropolitan bishop's principal diocese or see.

met-ro-pol-i-tan (met′ro-pol′i-tan), *adj.* **1,** relating or belonging to a large city or metropolis; as, *metropolitan* police; *metropolitan* transit system; **2,** relating to an ecclesiastical metropolis:—*n.* **1,** a resident of a large city; **2,** a Roman Catholic or Anglican archbishop; **3,** an Eastern Orthodox bishop ranking above an archbishop and below a patriarch.

met-tle (met′l), *n.* spirit; courage; temperament; as, to try one's *mettle;* show your *mettle.*—*adj.* **met′tled; met′tle-some.**

mew (mū), *n.* the cry of a cat; meow:—*v.i.* to utter a sound or cry of a cat or resembling the cry of a cat; meow.

mez-za-nine (mez′a-nēn′; mez′a-nēn′), *n.* **1,** in a building, an extra floor between two others, usually the first and second, often in the form of a gallery; **2,** in a theatre, the lowest balcony or its first few rows.

mez-zo–so-pra-no (met′sō–so-prå′nō; met′sō–so-pra′nō; med′zō-; me′zo-), *n.* [*pl.* mezzosopranos], a voice or part between soprano and alto, or one with such a voice.

MHz (em′āch′zed′), *abbrev.* short for *megahertz.*

MIA (em′ī-ā′), *abbrev.* short for *missing in action.*

mi-as-ma (mī-az′ma), *n.* [*pl.* miasmas or miasmata (-ma-ta)], *n.* **1,** poisonous germs, etc., in the atmosphere; **2,** a corrupting or oppressive influence or atmosphere; as, a *miasma* of lies and deceit.

mice (mīs), *n.pl.* of *mouse.*

Mic-mac or **Mi'k-maq** (mik′mak′), *n.* [*pl.* Micmac or Micmacs; Mi'kmaq], **1,** a member of the Aboriginal peoples living in the Maritimes and in the Gaspé region of Québec; **2,** the Algonquian language of the Micmac people.

mi-cro (mī′krō), *n. abbrev.* short for *microcomputer, microprocessor,* or *microwave*:—*adj.* very small; miscroscopic; small-scale; as, *micro* particles; *micro* level.

mi-cro– or **micr-** (mī′krō-; mikr-), *prefix* meaning **1,** *very small, abnormally small;* as in *micro*biology, *micro*cassette, *micro*chip, *micro*cosm, *micro*dot, *micro*economics, *micro*fiche, *micro*graph, *micro*organism; **2,** *with or of a miscroscope;* as in *micro*dissection, *micro*surgery; **3,** *one millionth;* as in *micro*gram, *micro*metre.

mi-crobe (mī′krōb′), *n.* a living animal or plant so tiny as to be seen only under the microscope; a bacterium, esp. a bacterium carrying disease.

mi-cro-com-put-er (mī′krō-kum-pū′tėr), *n.* in *computing,* a small computer, often called a *personal computer* or *PC*, that has all its functions stored in the same unit and is designed to be used by one person at a time: abbreviated as *micro*: compare *mainframe.*

mi-cro-film (mī′kro-film′), *n.* film on which printed or graphic images have been reduced to a very small size, viewed with a projector that enlarges the images; as, one month of the *Globe and Mail* newspaper can be stored on two rolls of *microfilm*; also, such an image:—*v.t.* to photograph or reproduce something on microfilm.

mi-crom-e-ter (mī-krom′i-tėr), *n.* **1,** an instrument for measuring minute distances (often with a telescope or microscope); **2,** a caliperlike instrument with a spindle and a finely threaded screw used for precise measurements; **3,** in U.S., one millionth of a metre.

mi-cro-or-gan-ism (mī′krō-ôr′gan-izm), *n.* a very tiny, one-celled, living organism (such as bacteria, viruses, fungi, yeasts, algae, and protozoans) that can be seen only with a miscroscope.

mi-cro-phone (mī′kro-fōn′), *n.* an instrument that strengthens or passes along sound waves by means of electricity: it is used to make sound louder, to broadcast radio and television shows, and to record sound for movies, DVDs, CDs, and other recordings: abbreviated as *mike.*

mi-cro-proc-es-sor (mī′krō-pros′es-ėr), *n.* in *computing,* a single chip that contains everything a computer needs to process information: abbreviated as *micro.*

mi-cro-scope (mī′kro-skōp′), *n.* an optical instrument with a lens or lenses for making very tiny objects, which are too small to see with the eye alone, appear larger: often used in science to study bacteria, body cells, etc.; also, any similar instrument that magnifies.

mi-cro-scop-ic (mī′kro-skop′ik), *adj.* **1,** seen or discovered by means of, or relating to, a microscope; **2,** having the power of, or similar to, a microscope; as, a *microscopic* eye; **3,** very small; invisible without a microscope; as, a *microscopic* insect or plant.

mi-cro-wave (mī′kro-wāv′; mī′krō-wāv′) *n.* **1,** an electromagnetic wave that has a very short length, used in radar and to send long-distance television signals: abbreviated as *micro*; **2,** *Colloq.* a microwave oven:—*v.t.* [microwaved, microwav-ing] to cook using a microwave oven.

microwave oven, an oven that uses microwaves to cook foods much more quickly than an electric or gas oven.

mid (mid), *adj.* at or in the middle: often used in combination and hyphenated when attributive or followed by a capitalized word; as, my *mid* finger; to be in *mid* ocean; *mid*-ocean storm; *mid*-September.

mid- (mid-), *prefix* middle; as, *mid*air; *mid*day; *mid*point; *mid*-Atlantic; *mid*term; *mid*way; *mid*winter.

mid-day (mid′dā′), *n.* the middle of the day; noon:—*adj.* at noon; as, the *midday* meal.

mid-dle (mid′l), *n.* a point or part halfway between two given points, ends, or sides; centre; as, the *middle* of a river; *middle* of the movie:—*adj.* **1,** halfway between two given points; at or near the centre and away from the sides, front and back, or the beginning and end; as, the *middle* point of a line; *middle* seat; **2,** intermediate; in-between; medium; as, *middle* age.—*n.* and *adj.* **mid′dling.** Also, **mid′dle C′; mid′dle class′; mid′dle ear′; Mid′dle East′; mid′dle name′.**

mid-dle-aged (mid′l-ājd′), *adj.* neither young nor old: said of a person between the ages of about 40 and 60 years.

Middle Ages, the period in European history between ancient times and the Renaissance, from A.D. 476 (the year of the fall of the Western Roman Empire) to about A.D. 1450.

mid-dle-man (mid′l-man′), *n.* [*pl.* middlemen (-men′)], one who acts as a go-between or intermediary, esp. one who buys goods from the producer to sell to the retailer or consumer.

midg-et (mij′et), *n.* **1,** a very little person who is physically well-proportioned: sometimes considered offensive; **2,** anything that is smaller than usual; **3,** in *sports,* a category in Canadian amateur sports, such as hockey or softball, for ages 16 to 17 or 18; also, a player belonging to this group:—*adj.* **1,** diminutive; **2,** much smaller than usual for its type; as, a *midget* car; **3,** in *sports,* of or for players 16 to 17 or 18 years old; also, of or for very young or small players; bantam; as, a *midget* hockey league.

mid-land (mid′land), *adj.* inland; in the interior; in the central part of a country; as, a *midland* farming district:—*n.* the interior of a country.

mid-night (mid′nīt′), *n.* **1,** the middle of the night; 12:00 at night; **2,** anything like midnight; deep darkness or gloom:—*adj.* **1,** relating to the middle of the night; as, the *midnight* sun; burn the *midnight* oil; **2,** deep in intensity, dark, or gloomy; as, *midnight* blue.

mid-riff (mid′rif), *n.* **1,** the part of the body between chest and abdomen; diaphragm; the middle part of the body; **2,** a garment that exposes or covers this part or the part of a garment that covers this part.

midst (midst; mitst), *n.* the middle; the central place or time; during; among; as, in the *midst* of danger; in the *midst* of the crowd; in the *midst* of summer; a famous person in our *midst*:—*prep.* amid; among; as, *midst* the excitement.

mid-sum-mer (mid′sum′ėr), *n.* the middle of summer; also, the period about June 21, the longest day of summer:—*adj.* in or like the middle of the summer; as, *midsummer* heat.

mid-way (mid′wā′), *adj.* and *adv.* halfway; in the middle; as, *midway* between our two towns:—*n.* **1,** an amusement park at a fair, circus, or carnival, usually including rides, games, and sideshows; as, the *midway* at the Canadian National Exhibition in Toronto; **2,** the middle point of something.

mid-wife (mid′wīf′), *n.* **1,** a person who assists women in childbirth; **2,** someone who helps to produce something, as change.

mid-win-ter (mid′win′tėr), *n.* the middle of winter; also, the period about December 21, the shortest day of winter:—*adj.* in or like the middle of winter; as, *midwinter* blues.

miff (mif), *v.t.* and *v.i. Colloq.* to offend or be offended; put in a bad humour; vex:—*n.* **1,** a huff or bad mood; **2,** a petty or trivial argument.

¹might (mīt), *n.* great force or power of body or mind; as, to push with all your *might*; study with all your *might*.

²might (mīt), *p.t.* of *may*.

might-y (mīt′i), *adj.* [might-i-er, might-i-est], **1,** powerful; very strong physically, intellectually, etc.; as, a *mighty* warrior; *mighty* ruler; **2,** of unusual size, amount, etc.; great; extraordinary; as, a *mighty* wave:—*adv. Colloq.* very or exceedingly; extremely; as, *mighty* glad.—*adv.* **might′i-ly.**—*n.* **might′i-ness.**

mi-graine (mī′grān′), *n.* a severe, often recurring, headache, usually affecting one side of the head only, often accompanied by nausea and dizziness.

mi-grate (mī′grāt′), *v.i.* [migrat-ed, migrat-ing], **1,** to move from one country or locality to another for permanent residence; **2,** to travel periodically, esp. with the seasons, from one climate or feeding ground to another, as do many birds, whales, etc.—*n.* **mi-gra′tion** (mī-grā′shun).—*adj.* **mi′gra-tor-y.**—*n.* and *adj.* **mi′grant.**

mi-ka-do (mi-kä′dō), *n.* a former title for the emperor of Japan.

mike (mīk), *abbrev. Colloq.* short for *microphone*.

Mi'k-maq (mik′mak′), *n.* Same as Micmac.

mild (mīld), *adj.* **1,** gentle; kind; calm; as, a *mild* grandmother; **2,** moderate in quality or degree; not harsh, sharp, sour, or bitter; as, *mild* detergent; *mild* cheese; **3,** temperate; not severe; rather warm; as, *mild* weather.—*adv.* **mild′ly.**

mil-dew (mil′dōō′; mil′dū′), *n.* **1,** any of several kinds of tiny fungi, found on plants or decaying substances; **2,** a disease of plants produced by these fungi; **3,** spots of mould or fungus caused by their growth on food, cloth, leather, paper, etc., usually when exposed to dampness:—*v.t.* to affect with mildew:—*v.i.* to be affected with mildew; as, leather *mildews* when it remains damp.—*adj.* **mil′dewed′; mil′dew′y.**

mile (mīl), *n.* a nonmetric measure of length or distance equal to about 1.609 kilometres:—**nautical mile**, a way of measuring distance for sea or air travel, equal to about 1,852 metres.

mile-age or **mil-age** (mīl′ij), *n.* **1,** an allowance for travelling expenses, at so much per mile; **2,** total distance in miles, as of travel; as, the *mileage* from Ottawa to Montreal; **3,** the number of miles that a vehicle can travel on a certain amount of fuel; as, her new small car gets excellent *mileage*; **4,** *Colloq.* the use that one gets from something; as, to get good *mileage* from tires, an old joke, etc.

mile-stone (mīl′stōn′), *n.* **1,** formerly, a stone marker by a road used to show distances; **2,** any significant event in history, a person's life, etc., that marks a definite stage; as, graduating from university was a *milestone* in her life.

mi-lieu (mil-yoo′; mē-lū′; mē-lyö′), *n.* [*pl.* milieux or milieus], setting or environment, esp. the physical and social surroundings; as, social and cultural *milieu*.

mil-i-tant (mil′i-tant), *adj.* **1,** at war; also, warlike; fighting; as, a *militant* nation; **2,** combative or aggressive, esp. in promoting a cause; as, a *militant* anti-racist:—*n.* **1,** one who fights; **2,** one who is aggressive in promoting a cause.

mil-i-ta-rism (mil′i-ta-rizm′), *n.* **1,** a disposition to uphold a nation's power by means of a strong army and navy; **2,** a warlike policy; the policy of readiness to fight on slight grounds; **3,** rule or government by military interests.—*n.* **mil′i-ta-ris′tic** (mil′i-ta-ris′tik).

mil-i-tar-y (mil′i-tėr′i), *adj.* **1,** relating to soldiers, arms, or war; as, *military* force; **2,** performed or supported by soldiers; also, suitable for soldiers or war; as, *military* rule; *military* uniforms; *military* bravery:—*n.* the army; troops; soldiers.

mil-i-tate (mil′i-tāt′), *v.i.* [militated, mili-tat-ing], to have force or weight; tell: usually followed by "against"; as, her record *militated against* her.

mi-li-tia (mi-lish′a), *n.* **1,** a body of citizens enrolled and trained for the defence of a state or nation as a regular military force but not called into active service except in an emergency; reserve army; **2,** any small, unofficial military force.

milk (milk), *n.* **1,** a white fluid produced by

the mammary glands of female mammals and used by their young as food; **2,** this fluid taken by humans from certain animals, such as cows, goats, and sheep, and used as food; **3,** the white juice of certain plants; as, the *milk* of a coconut; **4,** any whitish fluid resembling milk:—*v.t.* **1,** to draw milk from; as, to *milk* a cow; **2,** to draw a liquid as if by milking, as venom, sap, etc.; **3,** to exploit or take advantage of; as, to *milk* the association's treasury; *milk* the situation for all its worth. Also, **milk′fat′; milk′run′; milk′ shake′; milk′weed′.**

milk-y (mil′ki), *adj.* [milk-i-er, milk-i-est], **1,** containing milk, or like milk; whitish; cloudy; as, *milky* water; **2,** yielding milklike juice, as do certain plants; **3,** weak; timid.

Milky Way, 1, the galaxy or island universe to which our sun and the planets that orbit it belong; **2,** a white, faintly luminous band that can be seen across the night sky, which is made up of billions of stars.

¹mill (mil), *n.* the thousandth part of a dollar or one tenth of a cent: used in accounting only.

²mill (mil), *n.* **1,** a building equipped with machinery to grind grain; as, a flour *mill*; **2,** any machine for grinding solid substances, as coffee, pepper, etc., for finishing or transforming raw materials, or for extracting juice or sap; as, a cider *mill*; **3,** a manufacturing plant; as, a steel *mill*; a paper *mill*; **4,** any unpleasant or exhausting experience; also, anything resembling an assembly line or mechanical process, esp. something concerned with large output only for profit; as, to go or be put through the *mill*; puppy *mill*:—*v.t.* **1,** to grind (grain), cut or saw (timber), roll or press (steel); crush (ore), etc., in a mill; **2,** to make a raised border around the edges of (a coin); **3,** to make frothy, as chocolate, by churning or whipping:—*v.i.* **1,** to move aimlessly in circles; as, the cattle *milled* about the pen; **2,** to move confusedly, as a crowd.

mil-len-ni-um (mi-len′ē-um), *n.* [*pl.* millenniums or millennia], **1,** a period of 1000 years; **2,** the thousand years that, according to the Bible, Christ is expected to reign on earth; **3,** any period of joy, peace, prosperity, and righteousness; **4,** a thousand-year anniversary; as, we celebrated the *millennium* in the year 2000.

mill-er (mil′ėr), *n.* **1,** one who owns or works a mill, esp. a flour mill; **2,** any moth with wings that appear as if they are powdered with flour.

mil-let (mil′it), *n.* **1,** a grain-bearing grass used as food; **2,** the seed of this grass, used in cereals and some breads.

mil-li- (mil′i-), *prefix* meaning *a thousandth part*; as in *milli*ampere, *milli*gram, *milli*joule, *milli*metre, *milli*litre.

mil-lion (mil′yun), *n.* **1,** one thousand times one thousand: written 1,000,000; **2,** an indefinitely large number; very many; as, I told you a *million* times not to do that.—*n.* and *adj.* **mil′lionth.**

mil-lion-aire (mil′yun-âr′), *n.* **1,** one who has a million or more dollars, pounds, etc., in currency and property; **2,** a very rich person.

mil-li-pede or **mil-le-pede** (mil′i-pēd′), *n.* any of the many-footed arthropods with 25 to 100 body segments, most having two pairs of legs.

mill-stone (mil′stōn′), *n.* **1,** one of two flat, circular stones used for grinding grain in a mill; **2,** something that crushes or grinds; **3,** a heavy burden; as, the old, unreliable car was a *millstone* around her neck.

milque-toast (milk′tōst′), *n.* one who is particularly timid, meek, or unassertive.

mime (mīm), *n.* **1,** a performance without words; a pantomime; **2,** one who performs pantomime; as, he is a *mime* artist; **3,** one who mimics or imitates:—*v.t.* and *v.i.* [mimed, mim-ing], **1,** to perform without using words; **2,** to mimic or imitate; as, to *mimic* a facial expression.

mim-e-o-graph (mim′ē-o-gråf′), *n.* a machine for duplicating letters, drawings, etc., by means of a stencil:—*v.t.* to make copies in this way.

mim-ic (mim′ik), *n.* one who imitates, esp. to make fun of the person or thing imitated; mime:—*v.t.* [mim-icked, mim-ick-ing], **1,** to imitate closely, esp. to ridicule (a person) by imitating his or her manners, characteristics, etc.; **2,** to copy strictly; as, to *mimic* her style of dress; **3,** to resemble; as, some fish *mimic* rocks:—*adj.* **1,** imitative; **2,** mock; pretending to be real; as, *mimic* warfare.—*n.* **mim′ic-ry.**

mince (mins), *v.t.* [minced, minc-ing], **1,** to cut or chop into very small pieces; grind; as, to *mince* onions or meat; **2,** to tell in part or by degrees, lessen the harshness of; as, to *mince* matters; **3,** to utter or move with assumed elegance or daintiness; as, she *minces* her words:—*v.i.* to talk or walk with assumed elegance or daintiness.

mince-meat (mins′mēt′), *n.* **1,** a sweet mixture of raisins, lemon peel, fruit, spices, and sometimes meat, chopped fine and used as a filling for pies; **2,** minced meat.

mind (mīnd), *n.* **1,** memory; recollection; as, to call to *mind*; **2,** one's thoughts, opinions, etc.; as, to speak one's *mind*; **3,** the part of a person that is aware, knows, thinks, feels, wills, etc.; consciousness, as opposed to matter; **4,** the understanding or intellect; as, he has a good *mind*; **5,** sanity; as, to lose one's *mind*; **6,** the use of the mind; one's thoughts or attention; as, to keep her *mind* on her driving:—*v.t.* **1,** to pay attention to; take care; as, *mind* your step; *mind* your manners; *mind* your own business; **2,** to be troubled by; object to; as, to *mind* the heat; **3,** to obey; as, *mind* your parents; **4,** to watch; take care of; as, to *mind* the baby:—*v.i.* **1,** to be troubled; feel annoyance; as, never *mind* if you can't do it; **2,** to be careful; as, *mind* you put on your jacket. Also, **mind′–al′ter-ing; mind′–bend′ing; mind′–blow′ing; mind′–bog′gling; mind′ game′; mind′ –numb′ing; mind′read′er; mind′set′; mind's′ eye′.**

mind-ed (mīn′did), *adj.* **1,** disposed or inclined; intending; as, *minded* to swim; **2,** having a mind of a certain kind or with a certain interest; as, a pure-*minded* person; she is mathematically *minded.*

mind-ful (mīnd′fool), *adj.* taking thought or heed; heedful; attentive; as, *mindful* of one's curfew.—*adv.* **mind′ful-ly.**

mind-less (mīnd′lis), *adj.* **1,** forgetful; disregarding; careless; as, *mindless* of danger; **2,** without good sense; foolish; **3,** not requiring intelligence; as, a *mindless* chore.

[1]**mine** (mīn), *n.* **1,** in mining, an excavation from which minerals, precious stones, etc., are dug; also, a deposit of ore or coal; **2,** an inexhaustible supply of anything or a source of great wealth; as, she is a *mine* of information about photography; **3,** an underground passage or cavity under an enemy's fortification in which a high explosive is set off; **4,** a case containing high explosives, moored where it will destroy enemy ships; **5,** a bomb or other explosive charge that is hidden shallowly under the ground, set to explode when something or someone touches it:—*v.t.* [mined, min-ing], **1,** to get by digging underground; as, to *mine* gold; **2,** to dig into, as for ore or metals; **3,** to destroy slowly or secretly; undermine; **4,** to place or lay bombs or other explosives under land or water:—*v.i.* to carry on the work of digging for metals, coal, etc.—*n.* **min′er; min′ing.**

[2]**mine** (mīn), a possessive form of the personal pronoun *I,* meaning *belonging to me;* as, Whose hat is that? It is *mine;* your hat is red, and *mine* is blue.

min-er-al (min′ėr-al), *n.* **1,** any solid, hard, usually crystalline substance that is not alive and that is neither animal nor vegetable in origin, such as lead, iron, gold, and quartz; **2,** a substance obtained by mining, esp. ore; **3,** any of certain chemical elements that are important to the nutrition of humans, animals, and plants, such as calcium, iron, magnesium, etc.:—*adj.* pertaining to, containing, or mixed with minerals, or a mineral; as, *mineral* ore; *mineral* water.

min-er-al-o-gy (min′ėr-al′o-ji; min′ėr-al′a-ji), *n.* the scientific study of minerals, including their structure, classification, etc.—*n.* **min′er-al′o-gist.**

min-gle (ming′gl), *v.t.* [min-gled, min-gling], **1,** to combine by mixing; blend; **2,** to associate:—*v.i.* **1,** to mix or blend; **2,** to enter into close relation; mix; socialize; as, to *mingle* with the crowd; to enjoy *mingling* at parties.

mi-ni- (mi′nē-) *prefix* meaning *small;* as in *mini*bike, *mini*bus, *mini*car, *mini*computer, *mini*skirt, *mini*van.

min-i-a-ture (min′ē-a-choor′; min′ē-a-chûr; min′i-), *n.* **1,** a very small painting, esp. a portrait, often worn inside a locket or other piece of of jewellery, esp. formerly; **2,** a small model or copy of any object:—*adj.* on a very small scale; tiny; as, *miniature* golf.—*v.t.* **min′i-a-tur-ize′** [miniaturized, miniaturiz-ing], to make small.

min-i-mize (min′i-mīz′), *v.t.* [minimized, minimiz-ing], to reduce to the smallest degree, part, or proportion; make little of; as, to *minimize* one's illness.

min-i-mum (min′i-mum), *n.* [*pl.* minimums or minima (min′i-ma)], **1,** the least quantity possible or allowable: opposite of *maximum;* **2,** the lowest point reached or recorded, as of temperature:—*adj.* lowest; least possible or allowable; as, the *minimum* mark for being accepted at a university; *minimum*-security prison; *minimum* wage.

min-ing (mīn′ing), *adj.* **1,** relating to the excavation of metals, ores, precious stones, etc.; **2,** relating to the laying of explosives:—*n.* **1,** the act or business of working mines for ores or minerals; **2,** the act or process of planting explosive mines:—*p.pr.* of *mine.*

min-ion (min′yun), *n.* **1,** a fawning servant or agent who obeys without question: sometimes considered derogatory; **2,** a favourite; a pet, esp. formerly; as, a monarch's *minion;* **3,** a petty official; **4,** in *printing,* a size of type (7-point).

min-is-ter (min′is-tėr), *n.* **1,** a cabinet member who is entrusted by the head of the government with the direction of a department; as, *minister* of finance; prime *minister;* **2,** a diplomatic agent, below an ambassador, sent to a foreign country to represent his or her own government; **3,** a clergyman or pastor of a church:—*v.i.* **1,** to serve or act as pastor; **2,** to give aid by doing helpful things; take care of; as, to *minister* to the poor or sick.—*adj.* **min′is-te′ri-al.**—*n.* **min′is-tra′tion.**

min-is-try (min′is-tri), *n.* [*pl.* ministries], **1,** service; **2,** the service of one who preaches a religion; **3,** a department of government under the direction of a cabinet minister; as, the *Ministry* of Finance; also, the building of such a department; **4,** the clergy; **5,** the body of government ministers as a group; **6,** the term of service of a minister; **7,** the governing period under a prime minister.

mink (mingk), *n.* **1,** an animal somewhat like the weasel, in the wild, living part of the time in or near water; **2,** its valuable fur; also, the garment made of this fur.

min-now (min′ō), *n.* [*pl.* minnow or minnows], **1,** a tiny freshwater fish of the carp family; **2,** loosely, any of several very small freshwater fish.

mi-nor (mī′nėr), *n.* **1,** a person of either sex under full legal age; **2,** a subject next in importance to a student's major subject:—*adj.* **1,** unimportant; not critical; smaller; lesser; as, a *minor* injury; **2,** in *music,* less by half a step than the major interval; designating a scale, chord, etc., in which such intervals occur; **3,** in *sports,* relating to a children's amateur team; as, *minor* soccer.

mi-nor-i-ty (mi-nôr′i-ti; mi-nor′i-ti; mī-nôr′i-ti), *n.* [*pl.* minorities], **1,** the smaller of two unequal numbers or parts of a group; less than half; **2,** the state of being under age; **3,** a group of people who are of a different race, nationality, or religion than a larger group living in the same area; as, the francophone *minority* in Canada:—*adj.* relating to a minority; as, a *minority* group.

Min-o-taur (min′o-tôr′; mī′ no-tôr), *n.* in *Greek mythology,* a monster with a bull's head and man's body, which inhabited the labyrinth of King Minos of Crete: it was slain by Theseus.

MINOTAUR

min-strel (min′strel), *n.* **1,** in the Middle Ages, a poet, singer, and musician; **2,** in the late 19th and early 20th centuries, one of a group of comic variety performers with blackened faces, who sang songs, told jokes, etc., based on black culture.—*n.* **min′strel-sy.**

[1]**mint** (mint), *n.* **1,** any of a large family of spicy-leaved plants, as the peppermint, used for flavouring such foods as jelly, ice cream, gum, tea, candy, etc.; **2,** the aroma or flavour of mint; **3,** candy flavoured with mint.

[2]**mint** (mint), *n.* **1,** a place where coins and paper money are produced under government authority and supervision; **2,** an abundant supply; a vast amount; as, this stereo system cost a *mint;* **3,** any source of invention or supply:—*v.t.* **1,** to produce money in a mint; **2,** to invent or coin; as, to *mint* an expression:—*adj.* perfect; flawless; as, a vintage car in *mint* condition.

min-u-et (min′ū-et′), *n.* **1,** a graceful and stately dance in triple measure, popular esp. in the 18th century; **2,** the music for such a dance; **3,** music having a similar style and rhythm.

mi-nus (mī′nus), *adj.* **1,** indicating subtraction; as, the *minus* sign; **2,** indicating a negative quantity; less than zero; as, the temperature last night was *minus* three:—*n.* the sign [–] indicating subtraction:—*prep.* **1,** less; as, five *minus* two; **2,** *Colloq.* deprived of; as, he was pulled out of the water *minus* his shoes and wallet.

[1]**min-ute** (min′it), *n.* **1,** the 60th part of an hour or of a degree of an arc; **2,** a short time; a moment; as, wait a *minute;* **3,** an official note; a memorandum:—**minutes,** the official record made of the proceedings of a meeting:—**up-to-the-minute,** up-to-date; latest; as, the information on this Web site is *up-to-the-minute.*

[2]**mi-nute** (mī-noot′; mī-nūt′; mi-), *adj.* **1,** tiny; as, a *minute* particle; **2,** precise; detailed; careful and exact; as, a *minute* description; **3,** petty.—*adv.* **mi-nute′ly.**

min-ute-man (min′it-man′), *n.* [*pl.* minutemen (-men′)], in the American Revolution, a citizen ready to arm at a minute's notice.

min-u-ti-a (mi-noo′shē-a; mi-nū′shē-a; -sha), *n.* [*pl.* -tiae (shē-ē′)], a small, precise, or trivial detail: usually *pl.*

mir-a-cle (mir′a-kl), *n.* **1,** an act or happening in the material or physical world that seems to depart from the laws of nature or to go beyond what is known of these laws; a wonder; a marvel; **2,** any event that is very amazing, lucky, or surprising; as, it's a *miracle* that she came at all.—*adj.* **mi-rac′u-lous.**

mi-rage (mi-räzh′), *n.* **1,** an illusionary image, usually upside down and often distorted, of some object actually beyond the range of sight, reflected in the sky over deserts, oceans, and plains: mirages are common in hot countries, esp. in sandy deserts, where travellers often imagine they see a body of water where no water exists; **2,** anything that is not what it seems or that cannot come true; an illusion.

mire (mīr), *n.* **1,** deep mud; wet earth; slush; dirt; **2,** an onerous situation or predicament that is difficult to overcome:—*v.t.* [mired, mir-ing], **1,** to soil; **2,** to cause to be stuck in the mud; as, to *mire* the wheels of a car; **3,** to cause to be in a difficult situation; as, this project was *mired* with debt:—*v.i.* to sink in mud.—*adj.* **mir′y.**

mir-ror (mir′ėr), *n.* **1,** a looking glass, which is made of glass with a thin coating of silver, aluminum, or other metal on the back; **2,** any smooth, shiny surface that reflects images, as water or polished metal; **3,** that which gives a true likeness; **4,** a model; a pattern:—*v.t.* to reflect; imitate; as, a lake *mirrors* a tree; her hair *mirrors* her friend's:—*adj.* like, of, or for a mirror; as, *mirror* image.

mirth (mûrth), *n.* noisy, social merriment; laughter; joy.—*adj.* **mirth′ful.**

mis- (mis-), *prefix* meaning *wrong, wrongly, bad,* or *badly;* as in *mis*belief, *mis*count, *mis*deal, *mis*direct, *mis*information, *mis-*

quote, *mis*read, *mis*rule.

mis-an-thrope (mis′an-thrōp′; miz′an-thrōp′), *n.* one who hates or distrusts humankind.—*adj.* **mis′an-throp′ic.**—*n.* **mis-an′thro-py.**

mis-ap-pre-hend (mis′ap-ri-hend′), *v.t.* to fail to understand.—*n.* **mis′ap-pre-hen′sion.**

mis-ap-pro-pri-ate (mis′a-prō′prē-āt′), *v.t.* (misappropriat-ed, misappropriat-ing], to apply to a wrong use or purpose, esp. to use (another's money) as one's own; embezzle; as, to *misappropriate* public funds.—*n.* **mis′ap-pro′pri-a′tion.**

mis-be-have (mis′bi-hāv′; mis′bē-hāv′), *v.i.* [misbehaved, misbehav-ing], to act in a wrong or improper fashion.—*n.* **mis′be-hav′iour.**

mis-cal-cu-late (mis-kal′kū-lāt′), *v.t.* and *v.i.* [miscalculat-ed, miscalculat-ing], to make a mistake in; misjudge; as, to *miscalculate* a distance.—*n.* **mis′cal-cu-la′tion.**

mis-car-riage (mis′kâr′ij; mis′kar′ij; mis-kâr′ij; mis-kar′ij), *n.* **1,** failure; mismanagement; as, *miscarriage* of justice; **2,** a premature and involuntary expulsion of a human fetus before it is viable.

mis-car-ry (mis′kâr′i; mis′kar′i; mis-kâr′i; mis-kar′i), *v.i.* [miscarried miscarry-ing], to go astray or go wrong; fail; as, my plans *miscarried*:—*v.t.* and *v.i.* to lose a fetus; have or suffer a miscarriage; abort.

mis-cel-la-ne-ous (mis′e-lā′nē-us), *adj.* **1,** consisting of several kinds mixed together; **2,** many-sided; consisting of various qualities.—*adv.* **mis′cel-la′ne-ous-ly.**

mis-cel-la-ny (mis′e-lā′n), *n.* [*pl.* miscellanies], a collection of various things of different kinds:—**miscellanies**, a book containing a variety of literary compositions.

mis-chief (mis′chif), *n.* **1,** harm; injury; damage; misfortune; as, to do someone *mischief*; **2,** discord; as, to make *mischief* between friends; **3,** vexatious behaviour; also, a tendency to cause annoyance or do pranks or tease; as, there was more *mischief* than evil in him; **4,** one who acts in an annoying manner; as, that child is a *mischief*.

mis-chie-vous (mis′chi-vus), *adj.* **1,** producing injury or damage; **2,** full of pranks; teasing; suggesting mischief; as, a *mischievous* wink; **3,** annoying; irritating.—*adv.* **mis′chie-vous-ly.**

mis-con-cep-tion (mis′kon-sep′shun), *n.* a false opinion; wrong understanding.

mis-con-duct (mis-kon′dukt), *n.* **1,** improper or wrong behaviour; **2,** in *hockey*, a major penalty lasting five minutes or more; as, he got a game *misconduct* for fighting:—*v.t.* (mis′kon-dukt′), to manage or handle badly; as, to *misconduct* a business.

mis-con-struc-tion (mis′kon-struk′shun), *n.* misunderstanding; the giving of a wrong meaning to something; as, the *misconstruction* of a word or an act.

mis-con-strue (mis′kon-stro͞o′), *v.t.* [misconstrued, misconstru-ing], to get the wrong meaning from; misinterpret; as, you *misconstrue* my words.

mis-cre-ant (mis′krē-ant), *n.* a villain; wrongdoer:—*adj.* villainous.

mis-cue (mis-kū′), *n.* **1,** a mistake or blunder; **2,** a faulty shot in billiards:—*v.t.* [miscued, miscu-ing], to make such an error; as, she badly *miscued* her entrance.

mis-deed (mis-dēd′), *n.* a wrong act; a crime; offence.

mis-de-mean-our or **mis-de-mean-or** (mis′di-mēn′ėr), *n.* **1,** a wrongdoing, esp. a minor one; **2,** in U.S. law, an offence less serious than a felony, similar to a summary conviction offence in Canada.

mis-di-rect (mis′di-rekt′; mis′dī-rekt′), *v.t.* **1,** to give false or incorrect instructions to; **2,** to direct incorrectly or aim badly; also, to place a wrong address on, as a letter, e-mail, etc.; **3,** to apply wrongly, as one's talents.

mi-ser (mī′zėr), *n.* one who accumulates or hoards money for its own sake, often living poorly in order to avoid spending money; a greedy, stingy person.—*adj.* **mi′ser-ly.**—*n.* **mi′ ser-li-ness.**

mis-er-a-ble (miz′ėr-a-bl; miz′ra-bl), *adj.* **1,** very unhappy; wretched; **2,** worthless; poor in quality; very bad; inferior; as, *miserable* food; **3,** causing discomfort, trouble, or unhappiness; as, a *miserable* cold; *miserable* weather; **4,** mean; as, a *miserable* old man.—*adv.* **mis′er-a-bly.**

mis-er-y (miz′ėr-i), *n.* [*pl.* miseries], extreme pain, distress, or misfortune; great unhappiness; wretchedness; also, something that causes this or such conditions; as, homeless people often live in *misery*.

mis-fire (mis-fīr′), *v.i.* [misfired, misfir-ing], **1,** to fail to work as expected; as, the engine *misfired*; **2,** to miss a target, goal, or intended effect; as, the scheme *misfired*:—*n.* failure of something to work as expected.

mis-fit (mis′fit′; mis-fit′), *n.* **1,** anything that does not fit; **2,** a person in a position or group for which she or he is unfitted or unsuited.

mis-for-tune (mis-fôr′chun), *n.* **1,** bad luck; as, the *misfortune* of losing the final game; **2,** an unlucky, unfortunate, or distressing event or accident; as, getting stranded in the snowstorm was a great *misfortune* for the group.

mis-giv-ing (mis-giv′ing), *n.* doubt or uncertainty; anxiety; apprehension.

mis-guide (mis-gīd′), *v.t.* [misguid-ed, misguid-ing], to mislead; lead in the wrong way; to influence to wrong actions, conduct, or thought:—*adj.* **mis-guid′ed.**

mis-han-dle (mis-han′dl), *v.t.* [mishandled, mishan-dling], **1,** to maltreat; to treat roughly or harshly; mistreat; as, to *mishandle* the horse; **2,** to manage something badly, clumsily, or incompetently; as, to *mishandle* the delicate situation.

mis-hap (mis′hap′; mis-hap′), *n.* ill fortune; an unlucky accident, esp. one that is not serious; as, to have a *mishap* and spill orange juice all over the table.

mish-mash (mish′mash′), *n.* a collection of unrelated things; a confused jumble; a hodgepodge.

mis-in-form (mis′in-fôrm′), *v.i.* and *v.t.* to give incorrect or false information (to); mislead.

mis-in-ter-pret (mis′in-tûr′pret), *v.t.* **1,** to misunderstand; **2,** to give a wrong explanation of.—*n.* **mis′in-ter′pre-ta′tion.**

mis-judge (mis-juj′), *v.t.* [misjudged, misjudg-ing], to form a wrong or unjust opinion of:—*v.i.* to be mistaken in opinion.—*n.* **mis-judg′ment.**

mis-lay (mis-lā′), *v.t.* [mislaid (mis-lād′), mislay-ing], **1,** to lose temporarily; put in the wrong place unintentionally, where it cannot be found easily; as, to *misplace* a book; **2,** lose.

mis-lead (mis-lēd′), *v.t.* [misled (mis-led′), mislead-ing], to deceive; give a wrong idea to.

mis-man-age (mis-man′ij), *v.t.* [mismanaged, mismanag-ing], to manage badly or not honestly; as, the financial officer *mismanaged* the company's accounts.—*n.* **mis-man′age-ment.**

mis-match (mis′mach′), *n.* a bad or unsuitable match or fit:—*v.t.* (mis′mach′) to match or fit together incorrectly or badly; as, to *mismatch* socks.

mis-no-mer (mis-nō′mėr), *n.* **1,** a wrong or unsuitable naming or terming of a person or thing; as, speedy is a *misnomer* for her old 486 computer; **2,** the wrong or erroneous name of a person in a legal document.

mi-sog-y-nist (mi-soj′i-nist), *n.* one who hates women:—*adj.* pertaining to a hatred of women.—*n.* **mi-sog′y-ny.**—*adj.* **mi-sog′y-nis′ tic; mi-sog′y-nous.**

mis-place (mis-plās′), *v.t.* [misplaced, misplac-ing], **1,** to put in a wrong place; mislay; **2,** to bestow on an undeserving object; as, he *misplaced* his trust.—*n.* **misplace′ment.**—*adj.* **mis-placed′**; as, *misplaced* loyalties.

mis-play (mis-plā′), *n.* in *sports* and *games*, a wrong or improper play, as in baseball:—*v.tr.* to play wrongly or improperly; as, she *misplayed* the card in the game of hearts.

mis-print (mis-print′), *v.t.* to print incorrectly:—*n.* (mis′print′; mis-print′), a mistake in printing.

mis-pro-nounce (mis′pro-nouns′), *v.t.* and *v.i.* [mispronounced, mispronouncing], to speak with a wrong sound or accent.—*n.* **mis′pro-nun′ci-a′tion** (mis′pro-nun′sē-ā′shun).

mis-rep-re-sent (mis′rep-ri-zent′), *v.t.* to report incorrectly, willfully or carelessly; represent wrongly.—*n.* **mis′rep-re-sen-ta′tion.**

[1]**miss** (mis), *v.t.* **1,** to fail to hit, reach, or connect in some way; as, to *miss* the mark; *miss* the ball; **2,** to feel the need or absence of; as, he *misses* his mother; **3,** to escape by good luck; avoid; as, he just *missed* the snowstorm; **4,** to fail to meet or catch; as, to *miss* a train; **5,** to let go by; fail to grasp, attend, etc.; as, to *miss* a chance; *miss* basketball practice; **6,** to fail to hear, notice, or understand; as, he *missed* that point; **7,** to not do what is expected or intended; fail to do; as, to *miss* a question on an exam; *miss* a day of school; **8,** to fail to keep an appointment or meet someone; as, I *missed* you at the conference because I was running late:—*v.i.* **1,** to fail to make a hit; **2,** to fail to secure, attain, do, etc.; as, to *miss* out on all the fun:—*n.* a failure to hit, reach, see, obtain, etc.

[2]**miss** (mis), *n.* [*pl.* misses], **1,** a young girl or woman; **2,** an unmarried woman; **3,** a way of addressing a woman or girl whose name or marital status is not known; as, excuse me, *miss*:—**Miss, 1,** a title sometimes used before the name of a girl, an unmarried woman, or a married woman who prefers to use her maiden name: compare *Mrs.* and *Ms.*; **2,** the title used for the female winner of certain contests; as, *Miss* Canada.

mis-sile (mis′il; mis′īl′), *n.* **1,** an object, as a spear, arrow, bullet, etc., that is thrown, hurled, or shot through the air; **2,** a guided or ballistic rocket.

miss-ing (mis′ing), *adj.* **1,** lost; as, to find a *missing* pet; **2,** lacking; as, something is *missing* in this soup; **3,** absent; as, to be *missing* from class.

missing link, **1,** a hypothetical primate that is believed to be the evolutionary link between humans and apes; **2,** something that is missing but is required to complete a series or solve a problem.

mis-sion (mish′un), *n.* **1,** the act of sending, or state of being sent, with specific powers, to do a special service or job; as, his *mission* was to rescue the stranded people; **2,** a business or duty on which one is sent; any errand; **3,** one's life work; a calling; a purpose or task in life that one feels chosen for or required to do; as, her *mission* in life was to help the poor; **4,** an organization or a centre for doing religious and charitable work; a place where missionaries do their work; **5,** a body of people sent on some special work; **6,** in military action, a task given to an individual or to a whole unit; **7,** in air warfare, a flight assignment for one aircraft or a whole group of aircraft; also, aircraft or spacecraft sent on a specific operation; **8,** a group of specialists or leaders sent to a foreign country for a specific purpose:—**missions,** missionary work.

mis-sion-ar-y (mish′un-ėr-i), *n.* [*pl.* missionaries], a person who is sent by a church to spread the knowledge of a religion and teach people about it, esp. in foreign lands:—*adj.* pertaining to missions or to missionaries; as, *missionary* service; also, characteristic of missions or missionaries; as, with *missionary* convictions.

mis-sive (mis′iv), *n.* **1,** an official letter or message; **2,** any letter or message, esp. a lengthy or serious one.

mis-spell (mis-spel′), *v.t.* [mis-spelled or mis-spelt, mis-spel-ling], to spell a word incorrectly.

mis-state (mis-stāt′), *v.t.* [mis-stat-ed, mis-stat-ing], to state falsely or incorrectly; misrepresent.—*n.* **mis-state′ment.**

mis-step (mis′step′), *n.* **1,** a wrong step; **2,** a wrong act; blunder; as, a *misstep* could lose her the election.

mist (mist), *n.* **1,** visible water vapour in the atmosphere, at or near the earth's surface; fog; haze; **2,** anything that dims or obscures the sight or the mind; as, a *mist* of tears; *mist* of confusing statistics:—*v.i.* to rain or become covered in very fine drops:—*v.t.* **1,** to cover in fine drops of moisture; **2,** to spray with water, as a plant.—*n.* **mist′i-ness.**

mis-take (mi-stāk′), *v.t.* [*p.t.* mistook (mi-stook′), *p.p.* mistak-en (mi-stāk′en), *p.pr.* mistak-ing], **1,** to misunderstand; as, to *mistake* a meaning or a motive; **2,** to put wrongly in place of another person or thing; identify wrongly; as, he *mistook* her for her sister:—*v.i.* to err in judgment or opinion; be wrong:—*n.* an error; fault; misunderstanding.—*adj.* **mis-tak′a-ble.**

mis-tak-en (mi-stāk′en), *adj.* **1,** wrong; as, a *mistaken* idea; **2,** wrong in judgment; as, he is *mistaken*; **3,** misunderstood; as, a *mistaken* meaning.—*adv.* **mis-tak′en-ly.**

¹mis-ter (mis′tėr), *n. Colloq.* **1,** a way of speaking to a man whose name is not known; as, hey, *mister*, you dropped your keys; **2,** husband:—**Mister,** a title of address to a man, used before a man's name or office title: when written, usually abbreviated as *Mr.*; as, *Mr.* MacMillan; *Mr.* Speaker.

²mis-ter (mis′tėr), *n.* a device used to spray plants, hair, etc., with fine water vapour.

mis-tle-toe (mis′l-tō), *n.* an evergreen parasitic plant with white waxen berries, which grows and feeds on trees: often used as a Christmas decoration.

mis-treat (mis-trēt′), *v.t.* to treat wrongly; abuse.

mis-tress (mis′tris), *n.* **1,** a woman at the head of a family, school, etc.; also, a woman with authority or power; as, she is *mistress* of her own business; **2,** a woman skilled in anything; as, a *mistress* of archery; **3,** a female owner of a pet; as, the dog ran up to its *mistress*; **4,** a female paramour; a woman who has a sexual relationship with another woman's husband.

mis-tri-al (mis-trī′al; mis-trīl′), *n.* **1,** an invalid trial due to procedural error; **2,** in the U.S., a trial in which jurors are not able to agree on a verdict.

mis-trust (mis-trust′), *n.* lack of confidence; suspicion:—*v.t.* to lack confidence; doubt; suspect.—*adj.* **mis-trust′ful.**—*adv.* **mis-trust′ful-ly.**

mist-y (mis′tē), *adj.* [mist-i-er, mist-i-est[, **1,** made up of water particles suspended in the air; **2,** clouded or obscured by mist; as, *misty* mountains; **3,** indistinct, vague; **4,** sentimental; as, to feel *misty*; **5,** tearful; as, *misty* eyes.

mis-un-der-stand (mis′un-dėr-stand′), *v.t.* and *v.i.* [misunderstood (mis′un-dėr-stood′), misunderstand-ing], to take (a person, remark, etc.) in a wrong sense; mistake the meaning of (words or actions).

mis-un-der-stand-ing (mis′un-dėr-stan′ding), *n.* **1,** disagreement; a quarrel; as, a *misunderstanding* between friends; **2,** a mistake as to meaning or motive.

mis-use (mis-ūs′), *n.* **1,** wrong use; improper use or application; **2,** abuse:—*v.t.* (mis′ūz′), [misused, misus-ing], **1,** to use wrongly; **2,** maltreat; abuse; as, to *misuse* a horse is cruel.

¹mite (mīt), *n.* any of various tiny, sometimes microscopic, arachnids that live as parasites on animals, insects, plants, and stored food, sometimes transmitting disease.

²mite (mīt), *n.* **1,** any small contribution; **2,** a very small object or quantity; a small child; **3,** in *sports*, the beginner's level for very young children, ages 5 to 8; **4,** a player at this level:—*adv. Colloq.* slightly; somewhat; as, to be a *mite* nervous.

mit-i-gate (mit′i-gāt′), *v.t.* [mitigat-ed; mitigat-ing], to make less severe or painful; soften; alleviate; as, time *mitigates* grief.—*adj.* **mit′i-gat′ing** (as, *mitigating* circumstances).

mi-tre or **mi-ter** (mī′tėr), *n.* **1,** a kind of crown or tall cap with two peaks, worn by archbishops, bishops, and abbots at special ceremonies, as a symbol of office; **2,** a slanting joint, as at corners in mouldings, edgings, fabric, etc.: also called *mitre joint*:—*v.t.* **1,** to place a mitre on a bishop or abbot; to raise to the office of a bishop or abbot; **2,** to join on a

BISHOP'S MITRE

WOODWORKER'S MITRE

slanting line at a corner or make such a joint; also, to cut such a shape or finish (a hem) in such a way.

mitt (mit), *n.* **1,** a kind of woman's glove without fingers or with half fingers; **2,** a glove with a thick protective pad over the palm, worn on one hand and used in baseball to catch the ball; **3,** a padded mitten for a specific use; as, an oven *mitt*; **4,** mitten.

mit-ten (mit′n), *n.* **1,** a glove for keeping the hands warm, esp. in winter, covering the four fingers together and the thumb separately; **2,** mitt (def. 1).

mix (miks), *v.t.* **1,** to unite or blend different items, ideas, etc., into one mass, unit, or compound; **2,** to make by putting ingredients together; as, to *mix* a cake; **3,** to confuse; jumble; as, to *mix* facts; *mix* up my papers with his; **4,** to blend or combine visual or audio recordings:—*v.i.* **1,** to become united in a compound; as, oil will not *mix* with water; **2,** to mingle; associate; socialize; take part; as, to *mix* with the crowd; to *mix* well; **3,** to participate or become involved; as, to *mix* in our personal business:—*v.t.* and *v.i.* to crossbreed:—*n.* **1,** a food that is sold partly prepared, with some ingredients already mixed in; as, a cake *mix*; cocktail *mix*; **2,** any group of different things; as, an unusual *mix* of guests at the dinner; **3,** several combined ingredients; as, trail *mix*; **4,** the blending or merging of visual or audio sounds; **5,** the act of mixing; **6,** a crossbred animal.—*n.* **mix′er.**

mixed (mikst), *adj.* **1,** composed of different kinds; as, *mixed* nuts; **2,** for persons of both sexes; as, a *mixed* softball team; **3,** not restricted to one class, background, race, etc.; as, a *mixed* crowd; **4,** unclear; vague; as, to send *mixed* signals; **5,** both negative and positive; as, *mixed* reviews of a movie. Also, **mixed′ dou′bles; mixed′drink′; mixed′farm′ing; mixed′feel′ings; mixed′ mar′riage; mixed′ me′di-a; mixed′ me′ta-phor.**

mixed num-ber, a whole number and a fraction, as $4^1/_2$ or 3.1416.

mix-ture (miks′chur), *n.* **1,** the state of being blended or mingled; **2,** a compound or mass formed of two or more different things.

mix–up or **mix-up** (miks′up′), *n.* **1,** a confusion or misunderstanding, esp. a mistake resulting from this; as, there was a *mix–up,* and our luggage was lost; **2,** a fight or brawl, esp. a confused one; as, the team captain was involved in a *mix-up*.

mne-mon-ic (ni-mon′ik), *adj.* **1,** of or related to attempting to aid the memory; **2,** of or related to memory in general:—*n.* a device, such as a formula, code, or rhyme, that makes remembering easier; as, "i before e except after c" is a *mnemonic* for correct spelling.

moan (mōn), *v.i.* **1,** to utter a low sound from, or as from, pain or sorrow; **2,** to emit a similar sound; as, the wind *moaned* through the trees; **3,** *Colloq.* to complain using such a sound; as, she *moaned* when asked to do the dishes; quit *moaning*:—*v.t.* to utter in a low wail:—*n.* **1,** a low, drawn-out sound of sorrow or pain; **2,** any similar sound; as, the *moan* of the wind; **3,** a complaint.

moat (mōt), *n.* a deep, wide ditch around a fortress, castle, or town, usually containing water; used formerly to protect against enemies.

mob (mob), *n.* **1,** the common people: considered as offensive by some; **2,** a rude, disorderly, or overly excited crowd; **3,** a crowd; **4,** *Colloq.* a criminal gang:—**Mob,** *Colloq.* the Mafia or organized crime:—*v.t.* [mobbed, mob-bing], to attack in a disorderly crowd; also, to assemble en masse or crowd:—*adj.* pertaining to or like a mob; as, *mob* violence; *mob* rule.

mo-bile (mō′bīl′; mō′bil), *adj.* **1,** easily moved or able to move easily; portable; as, a *mobile* home; *mobile* phone; *mobile* troops; **2,** flowing freely, as some liquids; **3,** easily changing in expression, position, etc.; as, a *mobile* face:—*n.* a type of decorative sculpture in which parts hang from wires or strings so that they can move freely in the air.—*n.* **mo-bil′i-ty.**

mo-bi-lize (mō′bi-līz′), *v.t.* [mobilized, mobiliz-ing], **1,** to call and prepare for active service; as, to *mobilize* an army or a navy; **2,** to assemble for a specific purpose; as, to *mobilize* support for a project.—*n.* **mo′bi-li-za′tion.**

mob-ster (mob′stėr), *Colloq.* a member of a criminal gang, the Mob, or other crime syndicate; gangster; criminal.

moc-ca-sin (mok′a-sin), *n.* **1,** a soft leather sandal with a soft sole and no heel, originally made and worn by North American Aboriginal peoples; **2,** any similar shoe.

mock (mok), *v.t.* **1,** to ridicule; mimic in fun or contempt; make fun of; deride; **2,** to defy or scorn; as, to *mock* the law; **3,** to deceive; tantalize; as, the mirage in the desert *mocked* the travellers:—*n.* **1,** ridicule; **2,** a jeer or gibe; **3,** an object of ridicule:—*adj.* false; not real; as, a *mock* battle.

mock-er-y (mok′ėr-i), *n.* [*pl.* mockeries], **1,** the act of making fun of a person or thing; **2,** ridicule; **3,** a poor or disrespectful imitation; as, to make a *mockery* of the judicial system; **4,** an empty sham.

mock-ing-bird (mok′ing-bûrd′), *n.* a North American songbird about the size of a robin, noted for imitating the calls of other birds: common esp. in the southern U.S.

mock-up or **mock–up** (mok′up′; mok′–up′), *n.* **1,** usually a full-sized model built accurately to scale, of a machine, weapon, airplane, etc., for instructional, test, or display purposes; **2,** a rough layout of printed matter, design, etc.

mod-al (mōd′al), *adj.* **1,** pertaining to a manner, form, or mode; **2,** in *grammar,* **a,** of a verb; as, *modal* auxiliaries (*may, might, must, can, would, should*); **b,** *modal* adverbs (*never, perhaps, certainly,* etc.), which indicate the speaker's point of view, or degrees of certainty; **c,** *mood* in verbs (assertion, doubt, command); **3,** a style of music in a particular mode.

mode (mōd), *n.* **1,** way, method, or manner of doing something; behaviour; as, a *mode* of speech; holiday *mode;* **2,** usual custom; fashion; style of dressing; **3,** in *grammar,* a certain form of a verb indicating whether or not the verb states a fact, a command, a condition, etc.; as, the indicative, imperative, or subjunctive *modes*: often called *mood;* **4,** in *music,* major or minor scale; scale system or patterned arrangement; **5,** in *computing,* the type of operation or a specific way in which a program, computer, printer, or other machine operates; as, safe *mode;* print *mode.*

mod-el (mod′el), *n.* **1,** a pattern of something to be made, copied, or imitated; a standard copy; **2,** a small-sized, exact, and detailed representation of something to be made; as, an engine or airplane *model;* **3,** a conceptual representation of something; as, a *model* of a lesson; **4,** a clay or wax figure for a statue; **5,** a certain style, design, or type of a manufactured product; as, a Toyota Camry is a popular car *model;* **6,** a person who poses for a photographer or artist; **7,** a person whose job is to display new clothes, jewellery, cosmetics, etc., as in an advertisement or a fashion show; **8,** a person or thing that is a good example, to be imitated; as, let the Olympic athlete be your *model:*—*v.t.* [modelled, model-ling or modeled, model-ing], **1,** to form or mould; as, to *model* a head in clay; **2,** to wear or display; as, to *model* the latest fashions in the Paris show; **3,** to represent something conceptually; as, to *model* a lesson:—*v.i.* **1,** to shape objects out of clay; make designs; **2,** to pose, as for a photographer or artist, or to display clothes, etc., in an advertisement or fashion show:—*adj.* **1,** serving as a pattern; **2,** worthy of being imitated.—*n.* and *adj.* **mod′el-ling** or **mod′el-ing.**

mo-dem (mō′dem′), *n.* in *computing,* a computing device that encodes data for transmission over telephone, cable, or fibre-optic lines, which allows one computer to send and receive information from another machine.

mod-er-ate (mod′ėr-āt′), *v.t.* [moderat-ed, moderat-ing], **1,** to keep within bounds; make less violent, intense, or extreme; as, to *moderate* rage, heat, etc.; **2,** to preside over, as a meeting:—*v.i.* to become less violent or intense; as, the storm gradually *moderated:*—*adj.* (mod′ėr-it), **1,** not extreme; calm; mild; **2,** limited; mediocre; medium:—*n.* a person who does not have extreme views, esp. in politics, religion, etc.—*n.* **mod′er-a′tion.**—*adv.* **mod′er-ate-ly.**

mod-er-a-tor (mod′ėr-ā′tėr), *n.* **1,** one who or that which regulates or restrains; mediator; **2,** a presiding elected official in the United Church of Canada; **3,** the presiding officer of a town council, assembly, meeting, etc.; **4,** a chairperson or officiator of a debating team, television or radio panel, etc.

mod-ern (mod′ėrn), *adj.* **1,** having to do with the present time or recent past; recent; as, DVDs, personal computers, and cell phones are *modern* inventions; *modern* language or art; **2,** up-to-date; not old-fashioned; as, *modern* furniture; *modern* hairstyle or clothes:—*n.* a person of recent and present times; also, one up-to-date in his or her views or manners.—*n.* **mod′ern-ism; mo-der′ni-ty.**—*adj.* **mod′ern-is′tic.**

mod-ern-ize (mod′ėr-nīz′), *v.t.* and *v.i.* [modernized, moderniz-ing], to make like, adapt to, or adopt present usage, taste, or speech; as, to *modernize* the old kitchen.

mod-est (mod′ist), *adj.* **1,** not boastful or vain of one's own worth; not conceited; **2,** retiring; not showy; plain and simple; as, the *modest* little house; **3,** not excessive or extreme; as, a *modest* ambition; **4,** pure; chaste; decent and proper in a quiet way, as in one's attire or actions.—*adv.* **mod′est-ly.**

mod-es-ty (mod′is-ti), *n.* **1,** regard for what is proper in behaviour or manner; **2,** reserve concerning one's own worth; lack of conceit; **3,** freedom from what is extreme; moderation; simplicity; as, *modesty* in dress.

mod-i-cum (mod′i-kum), *n.* a small or moderate amount; as, a *modicum* of common sense.

mod-i-fy (mod′i-fī′), *v.t.* [modified, modify-ing], **1,** to change slightly; as, to *modify* an idea or plan; **2,** to limit; reduce; make less extreme; **3,** in *grammar,* to qualify or limit the meaning; as, adjectives *modify* nouns.—*n.* **mod′i-fi-ca′tion.**—*n.* **mod′i-fi′er.**

mod-u-late (moj′u-lāt′; mod′ū-lāt′), *v.t.* [modulat-ed, modulat-ing], **1,** to vary the tone of; as, to *modulate* the voice; **2,** to tone down; as, to *modulate* the volume on the radio; **3,** to regulate, adjust, or moderate anything:—*v.t.* and *v.i.* in *music,* to pass from one key to a related key.—*n.* **mod′u-la′tion.**

mod-ule (moj′o͞ol; mod′ūl), *n.* **1,** a separate unit of a spacecraft, used for a specific operation; as, a landing *module;* **2,** in *computing,* any device that is a separate unit and that can be added to the computer system, such as a printer, disk drive, mouse, etc.; **3,** anything that is part of a larger system; as, an educational *module.—adj.* **mod′u-lar.**

mo-gul (mō′gl), *n.* **1,** a powerful, important person; a magnate; as, a movie *mogul;* industry *mogul;* **2,** the small mounds or bumps on some ski slopes; **3,** the style of skiing that uses these:—**Mogul,** a Mongolian, esp. one of the rulers of India between the 16th and 19th centuries.

mo-hair (mō′hâr′), *n.* **1,** the silky hair of the Angora goat; **2,** a woven material made from this; **3,** an imitation of such a material.

Mo-hawk (mō′hôk′), *n.* [*pl.* Mohawk or Mohawks], **1,** a member of the Aboriginal peoples who originally lived in northeastern New York State but now live mostly in southern Ontario and Québec: members of the Six Nation Iroquois Confederacy; **2,** the Iroquoian language of the Mohawk people; **3,** a type of hairstyle in which the head is shaved, leaving only a narrow, brushlike strip of hair along the middle of the head, from the forehead to the back of the neck.

moil (moil), *v.i.* **1,** to toil; drudge; **2,** to move about in confusion:—*n.* **1,** drudgery; **2,** confusion; turmoil.

moist (moist), *adj.* **1,** slightly wet; damp; humid; **2,** tearful; as, *moist* eyes.

mois-ten (mois′n), *v.t.* and *v.i.* to make or become damp or slightly wet.

mois-ture (mois′chûr), *n.* **1,** a small or moderate degree of dampness; **2,** water or other liquid in small quantity in the air as vapour or condensed on a surface.—*v.t.* **mois′tur-ize′** [moisturized, moisturiz-ing].

[1]**mo-lar** (mō′lėr), *n.* a broad-surfaced tooth, used for grinding. (See *dentition,* illustration.):—*adj.* **1,** used for, or capable of, grinding; **2,** pertaining to molar teeth.

[2]**mo-lar** (mō′lėr), *adj.* of or relating to a mole.

mo-las-ses (mō-las′iz), *n.* [*pl.* molasses], a dark-coloured syrup, obtained as a byproduct in the making of sugar; treacle; also, a lighter version used as a table syrup or in baking.

mold (mōld), *n.* Same as [1]**mould,** [2]**mould,** [3]**mould.**

[1]**mole** (mōl), *n.* a dark-coloured raised spot on the skin.

[2]**mole** (mōl), *n.* a tiny, burrowing, worm-eating animal with soft, blackish-brown or grey fur, imperfectly developed eyes, and broad, powerful forefeet with which it digs underground tunnels.

[3]**mole** (mōl), *n.* a spy or someone working undercover for an extended period within an organization in order to gain a position of trust.

[4]**mole** (mōl), *n.* the molecular weight of a substance in grams.

[5]**mole** (mōl), *n.* **1,** a sea wall, jetty, or breakwater; **2,** the harbour established by the construction of this.

[6]**mole** (mōl), *n.* a spicy Mexican sauce.

mol-e-cule (mol′i-kūl′), *n.* **1,** the smallest quantity of any substance that can exist separately and still retain the characteristics of the substance, made up of two or more atoms; a group of atoms bound together by chemical forces and acting as a physical unit; **2,** loosely, any tiny particle.—*adj.* **mo-lec′u-lar** (mo-lek′ū-lėr).

mole-hill (mōl′hil′), *n.* **1,** a little mound made by the burrowing of a mole; **2,** a small, trivial hindrance or difficulty; as, to make a mountain out of a *molehill.*

mo-lest (mo-lest′), *v.t.* **1,** to interfere with; disturb; pester; **2,** to abuse or attack, esp. sexually.—*n.* **mo′les-ta′tion.**

mol-li-fy (mol′i-fī′), *v.t.* [mollified, molli-fy-ing], to calm; soften; pacify; make less severe.

mol-lusk or **mol-lusc** (mol′usk), *n.* any of numerous soft-bodied, backboneless, usually hard-shelled animals, such as oysters, clams, snails, mussels, scallops, octopuses, etc.

mol-ly-cod-dle (mol′ē-kod′l), *v.t.* [molly-coddled, mollycod-dling], to pamper; as, she *mollycoddled* her child:—*n.* one so pampered or accustomed to being so spoiled.

molt (mōlt), *v.i.* Same as **moult.**

mol-ten (mōl′ten), *adj.* melted by heat; as, *molten* iron, lava, etc.

mom (mom), *n. Colloq.* mother.

mo-ment (mō′ment), *n.* **1,** a short period of time; an instant; **2,** a certain point in time; as, they left at the same *moment;* **3,** the present time; as, the woman of the *moment;* **4,** importance; as, news of great *moment.*

mo-men-tar-y (mō′men-tėr′i), *adj.* lasting only for, or done in, an instant; as, a *momentary* rage.—*adv.* **mo′men-tar-i-ly.**

mo-men-tous (mō-men′tus), *adj.* very important; of great consequence; as, a *momentous* decision; *momentous* occasion.

mo-men-tum (mō-men′tum), *n.* **1,** in *physics,* the force of motion in a moving body as measured by the product of its weight and speed; **2,** impetus gained by motion, as of an object, event, idea, etc.; as, the fundraising campaign gained *momentum* as more volunteers joined to help canvass.

mon-arch (mon′ėrk; mon′ork′), *n.* **1,** a supreme ruler or sovereign, who rules for life, as a king, queen, emperor, etc.; also, the hereditary ruler of a constitutional monarchy; **2,** the chief of its class or kind; as, the lion is *monarch* of all beasts; **3,** a North American migrating butterfly with orange and black wings.—*adj.* **mo-nar′chal** (mo-när′kal); **mo-nar′chi-cal** (-ki-kal).

mon-arch-ist (mon′ėr-kist), *n.* one who believes in, or supports, a government ruled by a king, queen, emperor, etc.—*n.* **mon′arch-ism.**

mon-arch-y (mon′ėr-ki; mon′or-ki), *n.* [*pl.* monarchies], **1,** a state ruled by a monarch whose power is supreme: called *absolute monarchy*; **2,** a state with a constitution that limits the monarch's powers, such as Great Britain: called a *limited* or *constitutional monarchy*; **3,** a kingdom; an empire.

mon-as-ter-y (mon′as-tėr-i), *n.* [*pl.* monasteries], a house of seclusion occupied by persons, esp. monks or nuns, bound by vows to a religious life; also, the monks or nuns in this community.—*adj.* **mon′as-te′ri-al.**

mo-nas-tic (mo-nas′tik), *adj.* **1,** pertaining to monasteries or to monks and nuns and their manner of life; as, *monastic* discipline; **2,** pertaining to anything similar; secluded; solitary; disciplined; austere; celibate; as, the hermit led a *monastic* life.—*n.* **mo-nas′ti-cism.**—*adv.* **mo-nas′ti-cal-ly.**

Mon-day (mun′dā; mun′di), *n.* the second day of the week, following Sunday and before Tuesday.

mon-e-tar-y (mon′i-tėr′i; mun′i-tėr′i), *adj.* **1,** of or relating to money; as, a *monetary* gift; **2,** pertaining to coinage or currency; as, the dollar is the *monetary* unit of Canada.

mon-ey (mun′i), *n.* [*pl.* moneys or monies], **1,** coins, paper bills, gold, etc., issued by a government and used as a means of exchange in buying or selling products or services; also, banknotes, cheques, drafts, etc., used as a means of exchange; **2,** any system of using objects in this way; **3,** a large amount of money; wealth; as, to be in the *money* after winning the lottery; **4,** moneys; sums of money. Also, **mon′ey-bag′; mon′ey-bags′; mon′ey belt′; mon′ey-chang′er; mon′ey-grub′ber; mon′ey laun′der-er; mon′ey laun′der-ing; mon′ey-lend′er; mon′ ey-mak′er; mon′ey or′der.**

mon-ger (mung′gėr; mong′gėr), *n.* **1,** a dealer, trader, or broker; as, a fish*monger*; **2,** someone who promotes or exploits something, esp. something undesirable; as, a war*monger*:—*v.t.* to sell, trade, or peddle something.

mon-goose (mong′gōōs′; mon′goos′), *n.* [*pl.* mongooses], a small, ferretlike carnivorous animal of Africa and Asia, noted for its ability to kill poisonous snakes.

mon-grel (mung′grel; mong′grel), *adj.* **1,** of a mixed breed or kind; **2,** of mixed origin:—*n.* **1,** a mutt; **2,** any animal of mixed breed or kind.

mon-i-tor (mon′i-tėr), *n.* **1,** someone who or something that warns or advises; as, the *monitors* in an airplane's cockpit; **2,** in a school, a student given a special duty such as assisting teachers with attendance taking, keeping order in the hall, etc.; **3,** a television set or speaker used in a broadcasting studio to check what is being broadcast; **4,** in *computing*, a computer screen that displays information visually; **5,** a television screen that displays information from a computer, VCR, DVD, etc.; **6,** a device that detects high levels of radiation or other toxic contamination; **7,** an ironclad warship, having low sides and one or more mounted with guns; **8,** a large lizard of Africa, Asia, and Australia, reputed to give warning of crocodiles:—*v.t.* to watch over, keep track of, or check regularly; as, to *monitor* the student's progress in math:—*v.i.* to act as monitor.

monk (mungk), *n.* a member of a religious order, who has taken vows and lives in a monastery apart from the world.—*adj.* **monk′ish.**

mon-key (mung′ki), *n.* [*pl.* monkeys], **1,** one of a family of animals of the primate order that have long arms and legs, hands with thumbs, and a long tail: they usually live in trees, are very good climbers, and are among the most intelligent animals; **2,** *Colloq.* a mischievous person:—*v.i.* **1,** to play around with something in a foolish way; tamper; as, to *monkey* with the switches of the new machine; **2,** to fool around; waste time; as, quit *monkeying* around and get to work.

monkey wrench, **1,** a hand tool with an adjustable jaw, useful for turning a nut, bolt, etc.; **2,** something that disturbs or upsets something; as, to throw a *monkey wrench* into her plans.

mo-no- or **mon-** (mon′ō-; mon-), *prefix* meaning *one, single, alone*; as in *mono*culture, *mono*hydroxy, *mono*layer, *mono*lingual, *mono*nucleosis.

mon-o-chrome (mon′ō-krōm′), *n.* a picture in one colour or in different shades of one colour or in black and white only (photography).

mon-o-cle (mon′o-kl), *n.* an eyeglass for one eye.

mon-o-cot-y-le-don (mon′ō-kot′i-lē′dun), *n.* a seed plant having a single seed leaf, or *cotyledon*, in the embryo. Compare *dicotyledon.*—*adj.* **mon′o-cot′y-lē′don-ous.**

mo-nog-a-my (mo-nog′a-mi), *n.* **1,** marriage to one person at a time: compare *bigamy* and *polygamy*; **2,** of animals, having only one mate.—*adj.* **mo-nog′a-mous.**

mon-o-gram (mon′ō-gram′), *n.* a decorative character formed of two or more letters, often a person's initials, combined or interwoven, used on towels, clothing, jewellery, stationery, table linens, etc.

mon-o-graph (mon′ō-gråf′), *n.* a short

treatise on one particular subject, esp. a vocation; as, a *monograph* on chemical engineering.

mon-o-lith (mon′ō-lith), *n.* **1,** a single large stone, used in architecture or sculpture, as a statue, pillar, etc.; **2,** a person or thing resembling such an object in appearance, size, rigidity, etc., esp. a large corporation or organization.

mon-o-lith-ic (mon′ō-lith′ik), *adj.* **1,** massively solid; **2,** solid, single, and uniform; as, a *monolithic* culture or party.

mon-o-logue or **mon-o-log** (mon′ō-log′), *n.* **1,** a long speech by one person in conversation; **2,** a long speech by one person in a movie, play, etc.; **3,** a dramatic scene in which only one person speaks; **4,** a comedy routine performed by a host of a television talk show at the beginning of the program.

mon-o-ma-ni-a (mon′ō-mā′ni-a), *n.* an obsession or craze in regard to a single subject, idea, or interest; as, to have a *monomania* about computer games.—*n.* **mon′o-ma′ni-ac.**—*adj.* **mon′o-ma-ni′a-cal** (mon′ō-ma-nī′a-kl).

mon-o-plane (mon′ō-plān′), *n.* an airplane with one main supporting surface, consisting of one wing on each side of the body: most planes today are monoplanes. Compare *biplane*.

mo-nop-o-ly (mo-nop′o-li), *n.* [*pl.* monopolies], **1,** the exclusive or near exclusive control and possession of anything, esp. of some commercial product or of some public service: compare *oligopoly*; **2,** the commodity or service so controlled; **3,** a company that has such control; as, VIA Rail is a Canadian *monopoly*; **4,** a grant, charter, or right of monopoly by a government; **5,** complete control over any situation, as if by a monopoly; as, she thinks that she has a *monopoly* on all good ideas.—*v.t.* **mo-nop′o-lize** [monopolize, monopolz-ing].

mon-o-rail (mon′ō-rāl′), *n.* a railway, often elevated, with a single rail on which cars run, sometimes suspended; also, this type of system.

MONORAIL

mon-o-syl-la-ble (mon′ō-sil′a-bl), *n.* a word of one syllable; as, "Go," "red," and "star" are *monosyllables*.—*adj.* **mon′o-syl-lab′ic.**

mon-o-the-ism (mon′ō-thē′izm), *n.* the belief in one God or deity only.—*adj.* **mon′o-the-is′tic.**

mon-o-tone (mon′ō-tōn′), *n.* **1,** utterance of one syllable after another without change of pitch or key; **2,** sameness of style or colour, as in writing or painting:—*adj.* **1,** without change of pitch or key; **2,** the same style or colour.

mo-not-o-nous (mo-not′n-us), *adj.* constantly the same; the same pitch or key; lacking variety; tiresome; dull; as, a *monotonous* voice; *monotonous* work; *monotonous* speech or lecture; *monotonous* bus ride.—*n.* **mo-not′o-ny.**

mon-soon (mon-so͞on′), *n.* **1,** a strong, steady wind of the Indian Ocean and southern Asia that blows from the northeast in winter and from the southwest in summer; **2,** the rainy season of the southwest monsoon; **3,** any similar wind.

mon-ster (mon′stėr), *n.* **1,** an abnormal or deformed animal or plant; as, a five-legged calf is a *monster*; **2,** a huge imaginary animal of grotesque form, such as a dragon or the Minotaur; **3,** something very huge, deformed, or hideous; **4,** a person who is wicked, cruel, or evil; **5,** any person or thing that is very large; as, a *monster* of a storm:—*adj.* huge; as, a *monster* truck; *monster* storm.

mon-strous (mon′strus), *adj.* **1,** not natural, esp. in an ugly or frightening way; abnormal; **2,** enormous; huge; as, a *monstrous* elephant; **3,** horrible; causing disgust; evil; as, a *monstrous* crime; **4,** absurd.—*adv.* **mon′strous-ly.**—*n.* **mon-stros′i-ty.**

mon-tage (mon′tåzh′; mōn′täzh′), *n.* **1,** in *motion pictures* or *television*, a technique of cutting and arranging film for a picture so that it tells a consecutive story or produces a desired effect; **2,** several pictures combined to make one composite picture; **3,** the process of combining various elements and the result obtained.

Mon-ta-gnais (mon′ten-yā′; mon′tanyē′), *n.* [*pl.* Montagnais], a member of the Aboriginal peoples living in eastern and northern Québec and Labrador. See *Innu*.

month (munth), *n.* **1,** one of the 12 parts into which the year is divided, each containing about four weeks: called *calendar month*; **2,** the period of 28 days from new moon to new moon: called *lunar month*.

month-ly (munth′li), *adj.* **1,** performed, payable, happening, or published once a month; as, a *monthly* bill; a *monthly* magazine; **2,** of or for a month; as, *monthly* sales:—*adv.* once a month; every month; as, she pays her bills *monthly*:—*n.* [*pl.* monthlies], **1,** a magazine, periodical, etc., published once a month; **2,** *Colloq.* menses.

mon-u-ment (mon′ū-ment), *n.* **1,** anything that keeps alive the memory of a person or event, as a pillar, statue, building, gravestone, etc.; **2,** a conspicuous and lasting example; an achievement worthy to be remembered; as, a *monument* of science.—*adj.* **mon′u-men′tal.**

mooch (mo͞och), *v.i.* **1,** to beg, sponge, or scrounge; as, she *mooched* off her friends; **2,** to steal; **3,** to loiter, sneak, or wander about aimlessly:—*v.t.* **1,** to beg or cadge; as, to *mooch* money from his parents; **2,** to steal:—*n.* someone who begs or scrounges trying to get things for free; a sponge; a parasite.—*n.* **mooch-er.**

[1]**mood** (mōōd), *n.* in *grammar*, one of the forms that the verb can take to show the manner in which the action or state, expressed by the verb, is to be understood, whether as a fact, wish, command, etc.

[2]**mood** (mōōd), *n.* **1,** a state of mind; humour; as, children in a joyous *mood;* **2,** a bad temper; as, to be in a *mood;* **3,** atmosphere, tone, etc.; as, the *mood* at the new spa was very serene.

mood-y (mōōd′i), *adj.* [mood-i-er, mood-i-est], **1,** subject to changes in the state of mind or temper; **2,** often ill-humoured or depressed; sullen.—*adv.* **mood′i-ly.**

moon (mōōn), *n.* **1,** the heavenly body that revolves around the earth once every 29.5 days; **2,** any heavenly body that revolves about a planet; **3,** a month; as, to be away for many *moons;* **4,** anything shaped like the moon, whether in its full or crescent phase; **5,** moonlight:—*v.i.* to wander or look about listlessly:—*v.t.* and *v.i.* to reveal the buttocks. Also, **moon′-faced′; moon′scape′; moon′shine′; moon′walk′.**

moon-beam (mōōn′bēm′), *n.* a ray of light from the moon.

moon-light (mōōn′līt′), *n.* the light reflected off the moon:—*adj.* **1,** lighted by the moon; **2,** occurring by moonlight; as, a *moonlight* cruise:—*v.i. Colloq.* to hold or do two jobs at once, esp. one by night as well as a regular full-time job.

moon-struck or **moon-strick-en** (mōōn′struk′; mōōn′strik′en), *adj.* **1,** romantically mesmerized or captivated; **2,** mentally ill; dazed or crazed.

[1]**moor** (moor), *n.* a tract of open, barren land, esp. in Great Britain.

[2]**moor** (moor), *v.t.* to secure (a vessel) in a particular place by a cable or anchor:—*v.i.* to become moored (a vessel).

moor-ing (mōōr′ing), *n.* **1,** a place where boats or aircraft can be secured; an anchorage; **2,** the act of making fast or securing a boat or aircraft with lines or anchors; **3,** the equipment or devices used to secure a craft; **4,** a source of stability or security; as, emotional *moorings.*

moose (mōōs), *n.* [*pl.* moose], the largest member of the deer family, related to the European elk, found in the forests of Canada and the northern U.S.: it has a heavy body with large humped shoulders, long legs, a large head, and the male has very large antlers. Also, **moose′hide′; moose′milk′.**

moose pasture, *Slang* in Canada, a worthless mining claim.

moose yard, in Canada, a wooded area where moose spend winter for protection and food, and where the snow has been trodden down by the moose.

moot (mōōt), *v.t.* to propose for discussion; also, to argue, debate, or discuss (a question):—*adj.* open for discussion; debatable; hypothetical; as, a *moot* question:—**moot point,** something that is no longer relevant or important.

mop (mop), *n.* **1,** a bundle of cloth or strings or a sponge fastened to the end of a long handle and used for washing floors, cleaning walls, etc.; **2,** a thick head of hair like a mop:—*v.t.* [mopped, mop-ping], **1,** to clean with a mop; as, to *mop* a floor; also, to remove with a mop; as, to *mop* up dust; **2,** to wipe; as, to *mop* the brow.

mope (mōp), *n.* one who is dull or out of spirits:—*v.i.* [moped, mop-ing], to be listless or low-spirited; move slowly in a dull or sad way; as, the children *moped* around the house because it was raining.

mo-raine (mo-rān′), *n.* a ridge or heap of rocks or gravel gathered by a glacier and deposited at its edge or base.

mor-al (môr′al; mor′al), *n.* **1,** the lesson about right and wrong taught by a fable, story, or event; **2, morals,** standards of conduct; belief or actions in matters of right and wrong; also, conduct; behaviour:—*adj.* **1,** referring to right and wrong; ethical; as, *moral* standards; a *moral* sense; **2,** virtuous; good; honest; as, a *moral* way of living; *moral* people; **3,** able to distinguish between right and wrong; as, humans are *moral* beings; **4,** having to do with the mind or spirit rather than with action; as, *moral* support.—*adv.* **mor′al-ly.**

mo-rale (mo-rål′), *n.* the mental state that enables people to sustain courage, enthusiasm, hope, confidence, etc., in the face of danger or discouragement; as, defeat did not rob the team of its *morale; morale* at the office was low after many people were let go.

mo-ral-i-ty (mo-ral′i-ti; mô-ral′i-ti), *n.* [*pl.* moralities], **1,** morals; standards of conduct; as, middle-class *morality;* **2,** virtuousness; upright behaviour; acting in the proper way; **3,** the right or wrong of something.

mor-al-ize (môr′al-īz′; mor′al-īz′), *v.t.* [moral-ized, moraliz-ing], **1,** to make moral, or improve the morals of; **2,** to explain or interpret in moral terms:—*v.i.* to talk at length about right and wrong, duty, goodness, truth, etc.—*n.* **mor′al-ist; mor′al-iz′er; mor′al-i-za′tion.**

mo-rass (mo-ras′; mô-ras′), *n.* **1,** a swamp; tract of soft, wet ground; bog; **2,** a disordered or difficult situation, esp. one that is a hindrance or impedes progess; as, a *morass* of detail.

mor-a-to-ri-um (môr′a-tôr′ē-um; mor′a-tôr′ē-um), *n.* **1,** in *law*, an enactment to allow a debtor or bank to delay payment of money due; **2,** the period that such an act is in force; **3,** a temporary cessation, pause, or prohibition of an activity.

mo-ray (môr′ā; mo-rā′), *n.* a voracious, bright-coloured, marine eel with sharp, knife-like teeth, found in warm seas, esp. coral reefs.

mor-bid (môr′bid), *adj.* **1,** relating to disease; as, a *morbid* condition; **2,** sickly; **3,** gloomy; unwholesome; as, a *morbid* imagination; **4,** gruesome; horrible; as, a *morbid* account of his death.—*adv.* **mor′bid-ly.**

mor-dant (môr′dnt), *adj.* **1,** caustic or biting; as, *mordant* wit; **2,** cleaning or corroding; **3,** burning, pungent, or smarting:—*n.* a corroding or cleansing substance:—*v.t.* to use or treat with mordant.

more (mōr), *adj.* [*comp.* of *many* and *much*], **1,** greater in number, amount, quantity, extent, etc.; as, we know *more* people than you; you have *more* energy and *more* time than I; **2,** additional; extra; as, one *more* word:—*adv.* **1,** to a greater degree or amount; as, to work *more* than her friend; **2,** again; in addition; as, we shall see her once *more*; **3,** used often to form the comparative of adjectives and adverbs; as, *more* hopeful; *more* hopefully:—*pron.* **1,** a greater quantity, number, etc.; **2,** something further or additional.

more-o-ver (môr-ō′vėr; môr′ō-vėr), *adv.* not only that; besides; in addition.

morgue (môrg), *n.* **1,** a building, place, or room where bodies of persons found dead are placed for identification; mortuary; **2,** the archives or reference material storage area at newspaper or periodical offices, at television or radio stations, etc.

mor-i-bund (môr′i-bund′; mor′i-bund′), *adj.* in a dying condition; near death; becoming obsolete; as, the *moribund* old tree.

morn-ing (môr′ning), *n.* the early part of the day, from midnight or sunrise to noon:—*adj.* pertaining to the morning; early; as, a *morning* walk.

mor-on (mōr′on′), *n.* **1,** a person whose mental ability or intelligence is below normal: considered offensive; **2,** *Colloq.* a stupid person.—*adj.* **mo-ron′ic.**

mo-rose (mo-rōs′; mô-rōs′), *adj.* sullen; gloomy; bad-tempered.

morph (môrf), *n.* a distinct form of an organism or species:—*v.t.* **1,** in *computing*, to use a computer to alter or change a digital image into another so that the first image transforms seamlessly into the second; as, the programmer *morphed* the photo; **2,** to change something, esp. to transform it radically:—*v.i.* **1,** of an image, to change seamlessly; **2,** to become changed, esp. radically.

mor-phine (môr′fēn), *n.* a drug made from opium and used in medicine to deaden pain or to produce sleep.

mor-phol-o-gy (môr-fol′o-ji), *n.* **1,** the science of the form and structure of plants and animals, as opposed to *physiology*, the science of functions and life processes; **2,** the study of the forms of words; also, such a system or process in language.

Morse code (môrs), *n.* a telegraphic system of dots and dashes, which represent the letters of the alphabet, transmitted by sounds, flashes, etc., formerly the most common way of sending long-distance messages.

mor-sel (môr′sel), *n.* a small piece, esp. of food; a little bit; a tidbit.

mor-tal (môr′tal), *n.* a being subject to death; a human being:—*adj.* **1,** subject to death; as, *mortal* humans; **2,** causing death; fatal; as, a *mortal* wound; causing spiritual death; deadly; as, *mortal* sin; **3,** involving death; as, *mortal* combat; **4,** filled with desire to kill; as, a *mortal* enemy; **5,** extreme; intense; as, *mortal* fear; **6,** accompanying death; as, *mortal* agony; **7,** belonging to human beings; as, *mortal* fame.—*adv.* **mor′tal-ly.**

mor-tal-i-ty (môr-tal′i-ti), *n.* [*pl.* mortalities], **1,** the condition of being subject to death; **2,** death; destruction, esp. on a large scale; as, the *mortality* from war or disease; **3,** the number of deaths in a given period in a given area; death rate.

mor-tar (môr′tėr), *n.* **1,** a hard, bowl-like vessel in which substances are pounded or ground with a pestle; **2,** a short cannon used for shells at a high angle; **3,** a building adhesive made of cement, lime, sand, and water and used between bricks or stone and in masonry or plastering.

mor-tar-board (môr′tėr-bôrd′), *n.* **1,** a square board with a handle on the underside, for holding mortar; **2,** an academic cap, with a flat, projecting top, worn esp. by graduating students.

mort-gage (môr′gij), *n.* a legal agreement by which a person borrows money from a bank, trust company, etc., to buy property or borrows against the value of real estate that is already owned, the property serving as the security in case the debt is not paid; also, the actual deed or paper:—*v.t.* [mortgaged, mortgag-ing], **1,** to make over (property) as security to one to whom a debt is owed; as, to *mortgage* our house; **2,** to pledge, esp. against something risky; as, to *mortgage* a medical career by promoting unconventional methods.

mor-ti-cian (môr-tish′an), *n.* an undertaker.

mor-ti-fy (môr′ti-fī′), *v.t.* [mortified, mortify-ing], **1,** to subdue or control by self-denial or discipline; as, to *mortify* the appetites; **2,** to embarrass; put to shame; as, his rudeness *mortified* me; **3,** to hurt, as someone's feelings:—*v.i.* to be affected with gangrene.—*n.* **mor′ti-fi-ca′tion.**—*adj.* **mor′ti-fy-ing.**

mor-tu-a-ry (môr′cho͞o-a-ri), *n.* **1,** a

morgue; **2,** a place, such as in a funeral home or cemetery, where dead bodies are kept before burial or cremation:—*adj.* relating to death, burial, or cremation.

mo-sa-ic (mō-zā′ik), *n.* **1,** a design or picture made of small pieces of coloured glass, stone, tile, etc., inlaid in some other material; **2,** a piece of work so made; **3,** such a process; **4,** something made up of different or diverse parts or elements; as, Canada is often called a cultural *mosaic*:—*adj.* made of or like mosaic; as, a *mosaic* mural.

mosh (mosh), *v.i. Slang* to slam dance; to dance in a violent way by intentionally knocking into others, usually at a rock concert:—*v.t.* to intentionally knock into others while dancing.—*n.* **mosh′pit′; mosh′er; mosh′ing.**

Mos-lem (moz′lem; mos′lem), *n.* and *adj.* Same as **Muslim.**

mosque (mosk), *n.* a Muslim temple or place of worship.

MOSQUE

mos-qui-to (mus-kē′tō), *n.* [*pl.* mosquitoes or mosquitos], a small, two-winged insect found in all parts of the world, esp. in hot, damp places, the female of which punctures the skin of humans and animals, feeding on the blood it sucks out: when they bite, some mosquitoes pass on dangerous diseases, such as malaria, yellow fever, and West Nile virus.

moss (mos; môs), *n.* **1,** a spore-bearing, small-leaved, flowerless plant that grows in the shade like a thick mat on damp ground, trees, rocks, etc.; **2,** any similar plant.—*adj.* **moss′y.**

most (mōst), *adj.* [*superl.* of *many* and *much*], **1,** greatest in number, quantity, degree, etc.; as, this house has the *most* rooms; **2,** to a great extent or amount; majority; nearly all; as, *most* students enjoy summer holidays:—*pron.* the greatest number, part, quantity, or value; as, *most* of the students went to the game:—*n.* **1,** the greatest number or amount; as, give him the *most*; it'll take me two hours at the *most* to finish my essay; **2,** *Slang* the best; greatest; fantastic; as, this band is the *most*!—*adv.* **1,** in the greatest degree; for the most part; as, I like plums *most*; **2,** used often to form the superlative of adjectives and adverbs; as, *most* hopeful; *most* hopefully.—*adv.* **most′ly.**

mote (mōt), *n.* a tiny particle of dust.

mo-tel (mō-tel′), *n.* a hotel primarily for motorists, usually with direct access to the outdoor parking lot.

moth (môth; moth), *n.* [*pl.* moths (mo*th*z; mô*th*z; moths, môths)], **1,** any of numerous, four-winged, night-flying insects, related to the butterfly, but less brightly coloured, having antennae that are not knobbed, smaller wings, and larger bodies; **2,** an insect of this kind, the larva of which feeds on wool, fur, etc. Also, **moth′ball′; moth′-eat′en.**

moth-er (mu*th*′ėr), *n.* **1,** a female parent of humans and animals; also, a female who acts or serves as a mother; as, a step *mother*; foster *mother*; etc.; **2,** origin or source; as, oppression is the *mother* of revolt; necessity is the *mother* of invention; *mother* lode; **3,** a title given to the head of a religious house for women; mother superior:—*adj.* **1,** native; as, one's *mother* tongue; *mother*land; *mother* country; **2,** pertaining to something considered to be nurturing like a mother; as, *mother* nature; *mother* earth; den *mother*; **3,** pertaining to the main ship, aircraft, or spacecraft; as, *mother* ship:—*v.t.* **1,** to give birth to; **2,** to act as a mother to; **3,** to be the origin of.—*adj.* **moth′er-ly; moth′er-less.** Also, **moth′er fig′ure; moth′er's al-low′ance.**

moth-er-board (mu*th*′ėr-bôrd′), *n.* in *computing*, the main printed circuit of an electronic device such as a computer, which usually contains the CPU and memory and often has ports or sockets for other devices such as printers, keyboards, mouses, etc.

moth-er-hood (mu*th*′ėr-hood), *n.* **1,** the state of being a mother; **2,** all the mothers of a country, region, etc., as a group; **3,** the characteristics of a mother.

moth-er–in–law (mu*th*′ėr–in–lo′; -lô′), *n.* [*pl.* mothers-in-law], the mother of one's husband or wife.

moth-er–of–pearl (mu*th*′ėr–ov–pûrl′), *n.* the hard, rainbow-tinted lining of certain mollusk shells, including that of the pearl oyster, used for buttons, ornaments, etc.

Moth-er's Day (mu*th*′ėrz), the second Sunday in May, in honour of mothers.

mo-tif (mō-tēf′), *n.* **1,** the subject or main idea of a work of art or literature; **2,** in *music*, a theme that may be repeated many times with variations; **3,** a unit of design; **4,** an ornamental pattern sewn on a piece of clothing.

mo-tion (mō′shun), *n.* **1,** the act or process of moving from one place or position to another; action, as opposed to rest; as, the ceaseless *motion* of the waves; **2,** one single or particular way of moving; as, slow *motion*; **3,** a gesture; as, a beckoning *motion*; **4,** a formal proposal made in a meeting requiring a vote or decision; as, a *motion* to adjourn:—*v.i.* to express one's meaning in a gesture instead of words:—*v.t.* to guide or invite by a gesture; as, he *motioned* me in.—*adj.* **mo′tion-less; mo′tion sick′ness.**

motion pic-ture (pik′chėr), a series of pictures of persons and things in action taken in rapid succession to form a continuous moving picture: also called *movie* and *cinema*:—**motion pictures**, the movie industry.

mo-ti-vate (mō′ti-vāt′), *v.t.* [motivated, moti-vat-ing], to give someone a motive or reason to do something; create interest; as, obtaining good grades *motivates* students to study harder; the enthusiastic speaker *motivated* them to start their own businesses.—*n.* **mo′ti-va′tion; mo′ti-va′tor.**—*adj.* **mo′ti-va′tion-al** (as, *motivational* speaker).—*adv.* **mo′ti-va′tion-al-ly.**

mo-tive (mō′tiv), *n.* **1,** that which causes a person to act as he or she does under certain circumstances; the inner reason for any act; as, hunger might be the *motive* for stealing; **2,** in *art, literature,* and *music,* the main idea or theme; motif:—*adj.* **1,** causing motion; as, *motive* power; **2,** relating to movement.

mot-ley (mot′li), *adj.* **1,** consisting of different colours; **2,** composed of various kinds or characteristics; as, a *motley* crowd:—*n.* **1,** a diverse mixture; **2,** a garment of various colours, formerly worn by jesters.

mo-tor (mō′tėr), *n.* **1,** an engine that produces action or mechanical power, often used to make other machines work, such as washing machines, vacuum cleaners, electric fans, printers, etc.; as, an electric *motor;* **2,** an automobile; motor vehicle; **3,** anything that produces motion:—*adj.* **1,** having to do with motors or with motor-driven vehicles; as, a *motor* vehicle; *motor* hotel; **2,** having to do with motion, esp. the motion of the body; imparting action; as, *motor* nerves:—*v.i.* and *v.t.* to travel or transport by a motor vehicle; as, to *motor* along the road. Also, **mo′tor-bike′; mo′tor-boat′; mo′tor-cade′; mo′tor-car′; mo′tor-coach′; mo′tor-cy′cle; mo′tor-cy′clist; mo′tor home′; mo′tor-ist′; mo′tor-mouth′; mo′tor pool′; mo′tor sco′oter; mo′tor-sport′; mo′tor-ve′hi-cle.**

mo-tor-man (mō′tėr-man), *n.* [*pl.* motor-men (-men)], one who operates a motor, esp. on a locomotive, streetcar, or subway train.

mot-tle (mot′l), *v.t.* [mot-tled, mot-tling], to mark with spots of various colours:—*n.* a spot, blotch, or pattern of these.

mot-to (mot′ō), *n.* [*pl.* mottoes or mottos], **1,** a short sentence, phrase, or single word, suggesting some guiding principle; slogan or maxim, as, don't drink and drive; **2,** a quotation used as a chapter heading, a slogan, or an inscription on an object.

[1]**mould** or **mold** (mōld), *n.* fine, soft soil rich in decayed matter.

[2]**mould** or **mold** (mōld), *n.* **1,** a hollow form into which anything is poured to be shaped, as melted metals and plastics, jelly, puddings, etc.; **2,** the shape in which a thing is cast; form; **3,** kind; character; type; as, a person of honest *mould;* **4,** bodily shape or form:—*v.t.* **1,** to fashion in, or as in, a form; as, to *mould* a candle; to *mould* butter; **2,** to shape into a mass of the desired consistency; knead, as dough; **3,** to influence the quality of something or someone; as, to *mould* public opinion.

[3]**mould** or **mold** (mōld), *n.* a fuzzy bluish or greenish surface growth, composed of fungi, that develops chiefly on decaying animal or vegetable matter under warm, moist conditions, spreading by means of tiny spores and forming dense, feltlike mats:—*v.i.* to become covered with mould.—*adj.* **mould′y** or **mold′y, 1,** covered with mould; **2,** having a stale, damp smell; **3,** decaying.

mould-er or **mold-er** (mōl′dėr), *v.i.* to crumble to dust by natural decay; deteriorate.

mould-ing or **mold-ing** (mōl′ding), *n.* **1,** anything made in or by a mould or form; **2,** an ornamental strip, usually of wood, used on a wall, cornice, picture frame, etc.

moult or **molt** (mōlt), *v.i.* to cast off and renew the hair, feathers, etc.:—*v.t.* to shed, as the skin, hair, horns, etc.:—*n.* the shedding of hair, feathers, etc., or the season when such shedding takes place.

mound (mound), *n.* **1,** a bank of earth or stone; also, a small hill; **2,** in *baseball,* the raised ground in the centre of the infield from which the pitcher throws the ball to the batter; **3,** any large pile or heap; as, a *mound* of laundry; a *mound* of papers.

[1]**mount** (mount), *n.* a high hill; mountain, used esp. before a name; as, *Mount* Everest.

[2]**mount** (mount), *v.t.* **1,** to climb, ascend, or get up on; as, to *mount* a platform, staircase, or horse; **2,** to set up for use; as, to *mount* a camera; also, to be equipped with; as, the television studio *mounts* four main cameras; **3,** to set up or arrange for exhibition or display; set firmly in place; as, to *mount* photographs on the display wall; **4,** to put on, or furnish with, a horse:—*v.i.* **1,** to rise or increase; as, his debts *mounted* steadily; **2,** to get up on a horse, platform, etc.:—*n.* **1,** a saddle horse or other animal for riding; **2,** that on which something, as a photograph or drawing, may be fixed or mounted.

moun-tain (moun′ten), *n.* **1,** a natural elevation of rock or earth rising high above the level of the surrounding country; a towering hill; **2,** anything huge; **3,** a heap or pile; mount; large quantity; as, a *mountain* of papers on the desk:—*adj.* having to do with a mountain or mountains; as, *mountain* air; *mountain* people.—*adj.* **moun′tain-ous, 1,** having many mountains; **2,** like a mountain; very high or large; as, *mountainous* waves. Also, **moun′tain bike′; moun′tain range′; moun′tain sheep′; moun′ tain-side′; moun′tain-top′.**

moun-tain-eer (moun′tin-ēr′), *n.* **1,** a mountain dweller; **2,** a mountain climber.

mountain goat, a pure-white goatlike

animal of the northwestern U.S. and Canada; also, any goat that lives in the mountains.

mountain lion, a large, wild North American animal of the cat family. Also called *cougar, puma,* or *panther.* (See *puma,* illustration.)

moun-te-bank (moun′ti-bangk′), *n.* **1,** formerly, a person who sold quack medicines, esp. from a public platform; **2,** a person who tricks or deceives people; swindler.

Moun-tie or **Moun-ty** (moun′ti), *n. Colloq.* a member of the *Royal Canadian Mounted Police (RCMP).*

mount-ing (moun′ting), *n.* **1,** the act of rising, climbing, etc.; **2,** a support, fixture, or setting; as, the *mounting* of a jewel or picture; the *mounting* of a camera.

mourn (môrn), *v.i.* and *v.t.* to grieve (for); sorrow (over); lament; as, to *mourn* the death of a close friend.—*n.* **mourn′er.**

mourn-ful (môrn′fool), *adj.* sad; doleful; also, gloomy.—*adv.* **mourn′ful-ly.**

mourn-ing (môr′ning), *n.* **1,** the act of grieving; **2,** an outward expression of sorrow, as the wearing of black clothes; **3,** the clothes themselves.

mouse (mous), *n.* [*pl.* mice (mīs)], **1,** a small rodent related to, but smaller than, the rat, with a pointed nose, large, sharp front teeth, soft fur, and a long tail; **2,** in *computing,* a small hand-operated pointing device that directs the cursor on a computer screen without the use of the keyboard, allowing the operator to manipulate data and graphics: shaped similar to a mouse; as, to move the *mouse* across the *mouse* pad; **3,** *Slang* a black eye; as, to get a *mouse* after being punched in the eye:—*v.i.* (mouz), [moused, mous-ing], **1,** to watch for or catch mice; **2,** to prowl and pry.—*n.* **mous′er** (mous′ėr; mouz′ėr).—*adj.* **mous′y.**

mousse (mo͞os), *n.* **1,** a frozen dessert made of whipped cream, sweetened and flavoured; **2,** a dish with fish, gelatin, and whipped cream, made in a mould; **3,** a foam for styling hair.

mous-tache (mus′tash′; mu-stash′), *n.* Same as **mustache.**

mouth (mouth), *n.* [*pl.* mouths (mou*th*z)], **1,** the opening in the face through which a person or animal takes food and drink into the body; the space behind the opening containing the teeth and tongue; **2,** this opening, as the channel of voice or speech; **3,** an opening or outlet; as, the *mouth* of a jug, tunnel, river, cave, etc.; **4,** *Colloq.* talkativeness; boastfulness; impudence; as, she has quite a *mouth* on her:—**mouth organ,** a small musical wind instrument, held horizontally against the lips and played by blowing or sucking air through it; a harmonica:—*v.t.* (mou*th*), **1,** to utter with a swelling or pompous voice; rant; **2,** to move the mouth in a certain way, either very distinctly or without sound; as, to *mouth* each word slowly so that all could understand:—*v.i.* **1,** to make faces; grimace; **2,** to declaim; **3,** to move the lips without sound.—*adj.* **mouth′y.**

mouth-ful (mouth′fool), *n.* [*pl.* mouthfuls], **1,** as much as can be put into the mouth at one time; **2,** a small amount; **3,** a very long word, phrase, or sentence; also, a meaningful comment.

mouth-piece (mouth′pēs′), *n.* **1,** that part of a wind instrument that is held in or against the player's mouth and through which he or she blows the air to produce the tone; **2,** any apparatus that goes or fits into the mouth, as on a tobacco pipe, snorkle, bridle, etc.; **3,** the part of a telephone receiver into which one speaks; **4,** a publication, organization, group, or person who speaks for others; as, he was the *mouthpiece* of the Alliance Party.

mouth–to–mouth, of or having to do with a method of artificial resuscitation in which the rescuer places his or her mouth tightly over the mouth of a person who has stopped breathing and forces air into the person's lungs.

mouth-wash (mouth′wosh′; -wôsh′), *n.* a liquid, usually flavoured, used for rinsing out the mouth and freshening the breath.

mouth-wa-ter-ing or **mouth–wa-ter-ing** (mouth′wot′ėr-ing), *adj.* **1,** very appealing to the taste, smell, or sight; **2,** tempting.

mov-a-ble or **move-a-ble** (mo͞ov′a-bl), *adj.* **1,** capable of being carried from one place to another; **2,** changing from one date to another; as, a *movable* holiday:—**movables,** goods or furniture that can be carried from place to place; personal property.

move (mo͞ov), *v.t.* [moved, mov-ing], **1,** to change from one place or position to another; as, to *move* a table; **2,** to set in motion; as, the breeze *moves* the grass; **3,** to cause to act; to impel; as, no argument could *move* him to consent; **4,** to arouse the feelings of; as, to *move* an audience to tears; **5,** to put (a formal motion) before a meeting; as, I *move* that we adjourn; **6,** to cause (the bowels) to act:—*v.i.* **1,** to change place or position; also, to advance; as, time *moves* on; **2,** to change one's residence; **3,** to take action; **4,** to live; pass one's life or time; as, to *move* in bad company; **5,** to apply (for); as, to *move* for a new trial; **6,** to act: said of the bowels:—*n.* **1,** a changing of place or position; as, a *move* in chess; **2,** a step in carrying out a plan; **3,** a change of residence.—*n.* **mov′er.**

move-ment (mo͞ov′ment), *n.* **1,** the act of changing place; any change of position; **2,** a joint effort directed toward a desired end; as, the peace *movement;* **3,** the delicate mechanism of a watch, clock, or other machine; **4,** a main division of a long musical composition; **5,** an emptying of the bowels and the matter emptied.

mov-ie (mōōv′i), *n.* a story or other work of entertainment or education, presented in the form of a motion picture. Also called *cinema, film,* or *motion picture*:—**movies, 1,** the showing of a movie, or a theatre where the movies are shown; as, to go to the *movies* every Tuesday; **2,** the movie industry.

mov-ing (mōōv′ing), *adj.* **1,** changing place or position; **2,** causing motion or action; **3,** that which moves or is able to move; as, the *moving* parts of a machine; **4,** pertaining to change of residence, job, etc.; as, a *moving* company; **5,** stirring the emotions; as, a *moving* graduation speech. Also, **mov′ing side′walk′; mov′ing tar′get′.**

[1]**mow** (mō), *v.t.* [*p.t.* mowed (mōd), *p.p.* mowed or mown (mōn), *p.pr.* mow-ing], **1,** to cut down with a scythe or a machine; as, to *mow* hay; **2,** to cut grass, grain, etc., from; as, to *mow* a lawn; **3,** to kill (living beings) as if mowing down grain; as, the guns *mowed* down the enemy:—*v.i.* to cut grass, grain, etc.—*n.* **mow′er.**

[2]**mow** (mou), *n.* **1,** a heap of hay, grain, etc., stored in a barn; **2,** the compartment in a barn for hay or grain:—*v.t.* to stow in a mow.

mox-ie (mok′sē), *n. Slang* **1,** courage, determination, nerve; **2,** aggressive energy, pep, initiative; **3,** skill, expertise, know-how.

MP or **M.P.** (em′pē′), *abbrev.* short for *Member of Parliament.*

MPP or **M.P.P.** (em′pē′pē′), *abbrev.* short for *Member of the Provincial Parliament.*

Mr. (mis′tėr), *abbrev.* [*pl.* Messrs. (mes′rz)], short for *Mister.*

Mrs. (mis′iz), *abbrev.* [*pl.* Mmes.], a title sometimes used before the name of a married woman. Compare *Miss* and *Ms.*

Ms. or **Ms** (miz), *abbrev.* [*pl.* Mses. or Mses; Mss. or Mss], a title used before a woman's name when it is not known or does not matter whether she is married or single. Compare *Miss* and *Mrs.*

much (much), *adj.* [*comp.* more, *superl.* most], great in quantity, extent, or degree; as, they left with *much* noise:—*adv.* **1,** to a great degree or extent; greatly; as, she is *much* quicker than her brother; how *much* does it cost? **2,** nearly; as, *much* of a size; **3,** frequently; as, he doesn't go *much* to the movies:—*n.* a great quantity; as, *much* has been said about this.

muck (muk), *n.* **1,** moist manure; **2,** a mixture of rich earth and decayed matter, esp. when used as a fertilizer; **3,** anything filthy or dirty:—*v.t.* **1,** to fertilize with manure; **2,** to make dirty; **3,** *Colloq.* to spoil or mess up.—*adj.* **muck′y.**

muck-rake (muk′rāk′), *v.i.* [muckraked, muckrak-ing], to look for and reveal scandal or corruption, esp. concerning public figures.

mu-cous (mū′kus), *adj.* pertaining to, like, or producing mucus:—**mucous membrane,** the moist lining of the nose, throat, and other passages of the body that open to the outside.

mu-cus (mū′kus), *n.* the slimy substance secreted by the mucous membrane.

mud (mud), *n.* soft, wet earth; mire:—*adj.* pertaining to or of mud; as, *mud* flat; *mud*hole; *mud* pie; *mud*room; *mud*slide; *mud*slinging.

mud-dle (mud′l), *n.* a state of confusion or disorder; a mess; also, mental confusion:—*v.t.* [mud-dled, mud-dling], **1,** to confuse or stupefy; mix up; **2,** to make a mess of; bungle; mismanage; as, to *muddle* accounts; **3,** to make disordered; as, to *muddle* up the papers:—*v.i.* to act ineffectively and haphazardly; as, to *muddle* along.

mud-dy (mud′i), *adj.* [mud-di-er, mud-di-est], **1,** thick with mud; **2,** cloudy; not clear; dull; as, *muddy* coffee; *muddy* water; **3,** confused; as, *muddy* ideas:—*v.t.* [mud-died, muddy-ing], to make dirty; as, to *muddy* the waters.

mud-guard (mud′gärd′), *n.* a casing over a cycle or vehicle wheel to catch or deflect mud, water, snow, etc.

[1]**muff** (muf), *n.* a warm, soft roll of fur or cloth with open ends into which the hands may be thrust for protection against cold, used by women and girls esp. formerly.

[2]**muff** (muf), *n.* in games such as baseball, a clumsy miss, or failure to keep hold of a ball:—*v.t.* and *v.i.* to handle clumsily; fail to hold (a ball); bungle.

muf-fin (muf′in), *n.* a small, cup-shaped, usually sweetened bread, often served hot with butter.

muf-fle (muf′l), *v.t.* [muf-fled, muf-fling], **1,** to cover up so as to deaden the sound of; stifle; as, to *muffle* a bell; **2,** to wrap up closely and warmly.

muf-fler (muf′lėr), *n.* **1,** a scarf worn around the neck; **2,** a device for deadening noise; as, the *muffler* of an automobile engine or musical instrument.

mug (mug), *n.* **1,** a heavy, earthen glass, or metal cup with a handle; also, its contents or a mugful; as, bring a *mug* of ale; **2,** *Slang* face or mouth; as, he got hit in the *mug*:—*v.t.* [mugged, mug-ging], to suddenly attack someone in order to rob the person, esp. on the street:—*v.i. Slang* to make humorous faces, esp. in front of a crowd or camera:—*adj.* pertaining to, of, or for a mug; as, *mug* shot.

mug-gy (mug′i), *adj.* [mug-gi-er, mug-gi-est], warm, damp, and very humid; oppressive; as, a *muggy* day.

Mu-ham-mad (moo-ham′id; moo-hom′id), *n.* the Arab prophet from Mecca and founder of Islam: his teachings and words are preserved in the Koran.

muk-luk (muk′luk), *n.* **1,** a traditional Inuit boot made of soft hide; **2,** a similar boot or slipper.

mu-lat-to (moo-lat′ō; moo-lot′ō; mū-lat′ō), *n.* [*pl.* mulattos or mulattoes], a person of one black parent and one white parent.

mul-ber-ry (mul′bėr-i), *n.* [*pl.* mulberries], a tree with broad leaves and a sweet, edible, berrylike dark red or white fruit: the white mulberry was originally grown for its leaves, on which silkworms fed; also, a dark-reddish colour.

mulch (mulch), *n.* a layer of plant matter, such as bark, leaves, straw, paper, etc., used to protect the roots of trees and plants, keep soil moist, control weeds, prevent erosion, nourish the soil:—*v.t.* to cover with mulch.

mule (mūl), *n.* **1,** an animal bred from a donkey and a mare, often used as a work animal; **2,** *Colloq.* a stubborn person; **3,** a kind of spinning machine; **4,** *Slang* a drug courier; one who smuggles illicit drugs; **5,** an open-heeled slipper or shoe.—*adj.* **mul′ish.**—*n.* **mul′ish-ness.**

[1]**mull** (mul), *v.t.* and *v.i. Colloq.* to reflect; ponder; as, all day, she *mulled* over the proposition.

[2]**mull** (mul), *v.t.* of wine, cider, or beer, to make hot with spices; as, *mulled* wine.

mul-ti (mul′tē-), *prefix* meaning *many, much, more than one*; as in *multi*form, *multi*millionaire, *multi*disciplinary; *multi*faceted; *multi*function; *multi*grain; *multi*lateral; *multi*layered; *multi*level; *multi*lingual; *multi*national; *multi*party; *multi*plex; *multi*polar; *multi*processing; *multi*purpose; *multi*racial; *multi*stage; *multi*user; *multi*vitamin.

mul-ti-cul-tur-al (mul′tē-kul′chėr-al; mul′tī-kul′chėr-al), *adj.* of or having many distinct cultures existing side by side in the same place or group; as, Canada is a *multicultural* country.

mul-ti-fa-ri-ous (mul′ti-fâ′rē-us), *adj.* many and diverse; as, *multifarious* talents.

mul-ti-me-di-a (mul′tē-mē′dē-a; mul′tī-mē′dē-a), *adj.* something that uses or involves more than one medium of communication; as, a *multimedia* presentation:—*n.* in *computing,* the use of text, sound, graphics, and video in one package.

mul-ti-ple (mul′ti-pl), *n.* a number or quantity that contains another number or quantity an exact number of times; as, 12 is a *multiple* of 6; also, the result of the multiplication of one number by another:—*adj.* **1,** being more than one; many; as, *multiple* personality; **2,** having many parts; as, *multiple*-choice questions; **3,** repeated many times.

multiple sclerosis, a degenerative disease of the spinal cord and brain that causes muscle weakness, speech and visual defects, and eventually, permanent paralysis.

mul-ti-pli-cand (mul′ti-pli-kand′), *n.* a number to be multiplied by another.

mul-ti-pli-ca-tion (mul′ti-pli-kā′shun), *n.* **1,** the act or process of increasing in number; as, a *multiplication* of details; **2,** in *mathematics*, the operation, shown by the sign ×, by which a number (the *multiplicand*) is taken a given number of times (the number of times being indicated by the *multiplier*), to form a result called the *product*; as, 5 (the *multiplicand*) × 2 (the *multiplier*) = 10 (the *product*); **3,** procreation (of people and animals) or propagation (plants).

mul-ti-pli-er (mul′ti-plī′ėr), *n.* **1,** the number that tells how many times another number is to be taken or multiplied; **2,** someone or something that multiplies.

mul-ti-ply (mul′ti-plī′), *v.t.* [multiplied, multiply-ing], **1,** to cause to increase in number or quantity; **2,** to repeat or take (a number or quantity) a given number of times; as, to *multiply* 4 by 3 means to take 4 three times, getting a result of 12; **3,** to cause to propagate or reproduce; breed:—*v.i.* **1,** to increase in number or extent; as, experiences *multiply* as one grows old; **2,** to procreate or propagate; as, weeds *multiply* rapidly if not controlled.—*n.* **mul′ti-plic′i-ty.**

mul-ti-task-ing (mul′tē-tas′king), *n.* **1,** the ability, process, or act of doing more than one task or job at the same time; as, cooking while watching television is *multitasking*; **2,** in *computing,* the ability of one unit to perform two or more operations, processes, or programs at the same time:—*adj.* having the capability of multitasking.—*v.t.* and *v.i.* **mul′ti-task′.**

mul-ti-tude (mul′ti-tood′; mul′ti-tūd′), *n.* **1,** a great number of people or things; crowd; **2,** people in general; as, the *multitude* came to hear her sing.—*adj.* **mul′ti-tu′di-nous.**

mum (mum), *n. Colloq.* **1,** chrysanthemum; **2,** mother:—*adj.* and *interj.* silent; be silent; as, *mum's* the word.

mum-ble (mum′bl), *v.t.* and *v.i.* [mumbled, mum-bling], **1,** to mutter, or speak indistinctly; **2,** to chew (food) lightly with partly closed lips or without closing the teeth:—*n.* a muttering.

mum-bo jum-bo or **mum-bo–jum-bo** (mum′ bō jum′bō; mum′bō-jum′bō), *n.* **1,** gibberish; meaningless ritual; nonsense; **2,** an idol; a superstition that is worshipped; fetish.

mum-my (mum′i), *n.* [*pl.* mummies], **1,** the body of a human being or animal embalmed in the ancient Egyptian manner; **2,** *Colloq.* mother.

mumps (mumps), *n.pl.* used as *sing.* a contagious viral disease, esp. of children, marked by inflammation and swelling of the glands that secrete saliva, in the lower cheeks and around the jaw, making it difficult to chew or swallow.

munch (munch), *v.t.* and *v.i.* to chew with a crunching noise, esp. with great pleasure; as, to *munch* on the tasty treats.

mun-dane (mun′dān), *adj.* **1,** relating to the world or worldly matters; worldly; as, *mundane* affairs; **2,** ordinary; routine; everyday; as, *mundane* daily chores.

mu-nic-i-pal (mū-nis′i-pal), *adj.* pertaining to a city or town, or to its local self-government; as, *municipal* buildings; *municipal* court; *municipal* district.

mu-nic-i-pal-i-ty (mū-nis′i-pal′i-ti), *n.* [*pl.* municipalities], a town, city, or district with local self-government; also, this government as a body.

mu-nif-i-cence (mū-nif′i-sens), *n.* generosity; liberality.—*adj.* **mu-nif′i-cent.**

mu-ni-tion (mū-nish′un), *n.* ammunition and war material: often used in *pl.*

mu-ral (myoo′ral), *adj.* pertaining to a wall; on a wall:—*n.* a large painting or design on a wall.

mur-der (mûr′dėr), *n.* **1,** the unlawful intentional killing of a human being by another: compare *manslaughter*:—**capital murder**, slaying with deliberate intent; **2,** *Colloq.* difficult, dangerous, very unpleasant, or damaging; as, the heat was *murder*; the job was *murder*; harsh detergents are *murder* on the skin:—*v.t.* **1,** to kill (a person) deliberately, esp. in a cruel fashion; **2,** *Colloq.* to spoil; ruin; as, to *murder* a song; **3,** *Slang* defeat; destroy; as, our team *murdered* them.—*adj.* **mur′der-ous.**—*n.* **mur′der-er; mur′der-ess.**

murk or **mirk** (mûrk), *n.* **1,** darkness; **2,** anything that is unclear or confusing.

murk-y or **mirk-y** (mûr′ki), *adj.* [murk-i-er, murk-i-est], **1,** dark; gloomy; cloudy; as, a *murky* night; *murky* water; **2,** unclear or confusing; obscure; as, *murky* reasoning.

mur-mur (mûr′mėr), *n.* **1,** a low, indistinct, often continous sound, as of voices, a running stream, etc.; **2,** a grumbling complaint in a low, muttering tone; a grumble:—*v.i.* **1,** to make a continuous sound like the hum of bees; speak in a low voice; **2,** to grumble:—*v.t.* to utter something complainingly or in a low voice.

Mur-phy's Law (mûr′fēz lô), *n.* a popular observation to the effect that what can go wrong, will go wrong, or anything that can go wrong, will.

mus-cle (mus′l), *n.* **1,** a fibrelike tissue that contracts and expands, thus producing movement in a human or animal body such as lifting, walking, running, breathing, digesting food, circulating the blood, etc.; **2,** a particular body part made up of this tissue; as, arm *muscles*; **3,** bodily strength; physical power; as, to require extra *muscle* to move these heavy boxes; **4,** influence or power; as, to use political *muscle*:—*adj.* powerful (as a motor or vehicle); as, *muscle* cars:—*v.i. Colloq.* [mus-cled, mus-cling], to use force to gain something; as, to *muscle* through the line of people:—*v.t. Colloq.* to move someone or something by force or intimidation; as, to *muscle* him out of the room; *muscle* him to accept the terms.—*adj.* **mus′cu-lar.** Also, **mus′cle-bound′; mus′cle fi′bre; mus′cle-man′.**

mus-cu-lar dys-tro-phy (mus′kū-lėr dis′trō-fi), *n.* an irreversible disease of the muscles that causes the eventual wasting of muscles.

muse (mūz). *v.i.* [mused, mus-ing], to meditate in silence; think deeply; dream:—*v.t.* to consider, think, or say something thoughtfully:—*n.* **1,** a state of meditation; **2,** someone or something that gives creative artists inspirations:—**Muse,** in Greek mythology, one of the nine goddesses who oversaw the fine arts and sciences.

mu-se-um (mū-zē′um), *n.* a building or room in which objects of value or interest, esp. of scientific, artistic, literary, historical, cultural, or technological interest, are kept, preserved, and displayed:—**museum piece**, **1,** something worthy of being displayed in a museum; **2,** someone or something that is very old-fashioned or outdated; as, that computer is a real *museum piece*.

¹mush (mush), *n.* **1,** a porridge of corn meal boiled in water, esp. in the U.S.; **2,** any soft, thick mixture like mush; **3,** *Colloq.* sentimentality.—*adj.* **mush′y.**

²mush (mush), *interj.* in northern Canada and Alaska, a shout ordering sled dogs to move along:—*v.i.* to travel, esp. with a dogsled, over snow.—*n.* such a journey.

mush-room (mush′rōōm′; mush′room′), *n.* **1,** a fast-growing fungus, usually shaped like an umbrella, some kinds of which are poisonous, such as *toadstools*, and some can be eaten, such as chanterelle, morel, oyster, portobello, shiitake, and truffle mushrooms; **2,** anything like this fungus in appearance or quickness of growth; **3,** pinkish beige, the colour of mushrooms:—*adj.* **1,** made from or with mushrooms; as, *mushroom* omelette; **2,** like mushrooms in appearance; as, *mushroom* clouds; **3,** like mushrooms in quickness of growth or development:—*v.i.* to appear suddenly or grow and spread rapidly; as, the small party *mushroomed* into a huge celebration.

mu-sic (mū′zik), *n.* **1,** the art of making pleasing or harmonious combinations of vocal or instrumental tones that express feelings or ideas; **2,** harmony; melody; **3,** a musical composition; also, the written or printed score of a musical composition; **4,**

any succession of melodious sounds; as, the *music* of the birds or the breeze:—*adj.* pertaining to, of, or for music; as, *music* box; *music* hall; *music* stand; *music* theatre; *music* video.

mu-si-cal (mū′zi-k'l), *adj.* **1,** relating to music; as, *musical* chairs; *musical* comedy; *musical* ride; **2,** full of music; melodious; as, a *musical* voice; *musical* sound of the stream; **3,** skilled in music:—*n.* a light, amusing play or movie that includes songs and dancing, as well as, usually, spoken dialogue; musical comedy; as, well-known *musicals* include *The Sound of Music, West Side Story,* and *My Fair Lady.*—*adv.* **mu′si-cal-ly.**

mu-si-cian (mū-zish′an), *n.* one who is skilled in some field of music; also, a person who performs music, esp. professionally.

musk (musk), *n.* **1,** a substance with a strong odour, obtained from the male musk deer, and used in perfumes; **2,** the odour of or resembling musk; **3,** a similar substance produced by other animals, such as the muskrat.—*adj.* **musk′y.**

mus-keg (mus′keg′), *n.* a bog or marsh formed in a depression or hollow of the land surface by accumulation of water, moss, and thick layers of decaying vegetation, found esp. in the Precambrian Shield of Canada.

mus-kel-lunge or **mus-ke-lunge** (mus′ke-lunj′) or **mas-ki-nonge** (mas′ki-nong′; mas′ki-nonj′), *n.* [*pl.* muskellunge or muskellunges; muskelunge or muskelunges; maskinonge or maskinonges], a large game fish of the pike family, found in freshwater lakes and rivers of North America, esp. the Great Lakes: a valuable food and game fish.

mus-ket (mus′kit), *n.* an early riflelike gun formerly carried by foot soldiers, prior to the invention of the rifle.

mus-ket-eer (mus′ke-tēr′), *n.* **1,** a foot soldier armed with a musket; **2,** a royal bodyguard in 17th- and 18th-century France.

mus-ket-ry (mus′ki-tri), *n.* **1,** the art of firing small arms; also, the fire of small arms; **2,** muskets collectively; **3,** musketeers collectively.

mus-kie or mus-ky (mus′kē), *n. Colloq.* a muskellunge.

musk-rat (musk′rat′), *n.* a ratlike water rodent of North America, with dark-brown fur, webbed hind feet, and a musky odour; also, the fur.

Mus-lim (muz′lim; mooz′lim; mus′lim; moos′ lim) or **Mos-lem** (moz′lem; mos′lem), *n.* a member of the religion of Islam:—*adj.* of or having to do with this religion; as, a *Muslim* temple.

mus-lin (muz′lin), *n.* a soft, plain-weave cotton cloth of various weights, used for dresses, sheets, drapes, etc.:—*adj.* made of muslin.

muss (mus), *n. Colloq.* confusion; disorder; mess:—*v.t. Colloq.* to disarrange, as clothing or hair; also, to soil.—*adj. Colloq.* **mus′sy.**

mus-sel (mus′l), *n.* any of several edible shellfish, which are related to clams and found in freshwater and saltwater.

MUSSEL

must (must), *auxiliary v.* [*p.t.* had to or must], **1,** to be required, obliged, or compelled; as, he *must* go; he *had to* go; **2,** to be logically necessary or likely; as, this *must* be what she means; **3,** to be absolutely certain or necessary; as, people *must* have food and water to live:—*n.* **1,** something that is obligatory; as, reading this book for this course is a *must*; **2,** *Colloq.* something that should not be missed; as, visiting the CN Tower is a *must* on your trip to Toronto.

mus-tache or **mous-tache** (mus′tash′; mu-stash′), *n.* **1,** the hair growing on a man's upper lip; **2,** hairs near the mouth on some animals.

mus-tang (mus′tang′), *n.* the small, hardy, half-wild horse of the western North American plains.

mus-tard (mus′tėrd), *n.* **1,** a plant with yellow flowers and long, slender seed pods; **2,** a yellow or brownish-yellow sharp-tasting paste or powder, made from the seeds of this plant, used to give flavour to meats and other foods; **3,** the yellow or brownish-yellow colour of mustard paste or powder.

mus-ter (mus′tėr), *n.* **1,** a gathering; esp. an assembly of troops; **2,** the number of troops thus assembled; **3,** any collection or assembly:—*v.t.* **1,** to assemble, esp. troops for inspection, for actual warfare, etc.; convene; **2,** to collect and show; **3,** to summon; rouse; as, to *muster* one's courage.

mus-ty (mus′ti), *adj.* [mus-ti-er, mus-ti-est], **1,** spoiled by dampness; mouldy; as, *musty* books; **2,** spoiled by age; stale.—*n.* **mus′ti-ness.**

mu-ta-ble (mū′ta-bl), *adj.* changeable; inconstant.—*n.* **mu′ta-bil′i-ty.**

mu-tant (mūt′ant), *n.* **1,** a new variety, esp. a distinct form of plant or animal resulting from genetic change; **2,** *Slang* something suggesting genetic mutation, such as a freakish appearance:—*adj.* produced by or related to genetic mutation.

mu-ta-tion (mū-tā′shun), *n.* **1,** change; variation; **2,** change in structure, esp. one that appears suddenly in a species and is inheritable; as, gene *mutations* or bud *mutations,* as in the producing of the nectarine from the peach or the navel (seedless) from the seeded orange; mutant.

mute (mūt), *n.* **1,** one who cannot speak or who remains silent: considered offensive by some; **2,** a contrivance to deaden, muffle, or soften the sound of a musical instrument; **3,** a mute button on a telephone, television, etc., which temporarily prevents sound from being transmitted:—*adj.* **1,** silent; speechless; as, the child stood *mute*; **2,** unable or lacking the ability to speak:—*v.t.* [mut-ed, mut-ing], **1,** to muffle or soften the tone of; **2,** to suppress the volume of or prevent sound from being transmitted from (a television, telephone, speaker, etc.).—*adj.* **mut′ed.**

mu-ti-late (mū′ti-lāt′), *v.t.* [mutilat-ed, mutilat-ing], **1,** to cut off or remove a necessary part of (as an arm or leg); **2,** to spoil or destroy; as, to *mutilate* a library book.—*n.* **mu′ti-la′tion.**

mu-ti-neer (mū′ti-nēr′), *n.* one who is guilty of rebellion against authority.

mu-ti-ny (mū′ti-ni), *n.* [*pl.* mutinies], rebellion against authority, esp. rebellion of soldiers or sailors against their officers:—*v.i.* [mutinied, mutiny-ing], to rise against authority.—*adj.* **mu′ti-nous.**

mutt (mut), *n. Colloq.* **1,** a mongrel dog; **2,** a person considered to be stupid.

mut-ter (mut′ėr), *n.* a murmur:—*v.i.* **1,** to speak indistinctly in a low voice; **2,** to make a low, rumbling noise, as does thunder; **3,** to grumble:—*v.t.* to utter indistinctly.

mut-ton (mut′n), *n.* the flesh of a sheep used as food.

mu-tu-al (mū′choo͞-al), *adj.* **1,** interchanged; given and received; reciprocal; as, *mutual* admiration; **2,** shared; as, a *mutual* friend; *mutual* love of science; *mutual* fund.

muz-zle (muz′l), *n.* **1,** the projecting jaws and nose of an animal; snout; **2,** a guard or cover for the mouth of an animal to prevent its biting; **3,** the mouth of a gun:—*v.t.* [muz-zled, muz-zling], **1,** to enclose the mouth of, to prevent biting; **2,** to restrain from free expression of opinion; as, to *muzzle* the newspapers.

muz-zy (muz′i), *adj.* **1,** muddled, confused, absent-minded; **2,** dull, gloomy, blurred, indistinct, vague.

MVP (em′vē′pē′), *abbrev.* in *sports*, short for *most valuable player*.

my (mī), *adj.* a possessive form of *I:* belonging or relating to me; as, this is *my* hat:—*interj.* expressing surprise; as, oh *my*!

my-o-pi-a (mī-ō′pē-a), *n.* **1,** nearsightedness; **2,** shortsightedness; lack of imagination.—*adj.* **my-op′ic** (-op-; -ōp-).

myr-i-ad (mir′ē-ad), *n.* a very large number; as, a *myriad* of stars:—*adj.* innumerable; diverse; as, *myriad* stars.

my-self (mī-self′), *pron.* [*pl.* ourselves (our-selvz′)], **1,** an emphatic form of *I* or *me*; **2,** a reflexive form of *me*; as, I hurt *myself*; **3,** my natural self; my usual self; as, I am not *myself* today.

mys-ter-y (mis′tėr-i), *n.* [*pl.* mysteries], **1,** something secret, hidden, or unexplained; as, the cause of the murder is a *mystery*; **2,** that which is beyond human understanding; as, the *mystery* of the creation of life; **3,** a book, movie, television show, or other fictional work in which a crime or other unexplained problem has to be solved.—*adj.* **mys-te′ri-ous** (mis-tē′rē-us).—*adv.* **mys-te′ri-ous-ly.**

mys-tic (mis′tik), *n.* one who believes that he or she can have direct spiritual communication with God or another deity:—*adj.* **1,** having a hidden meaning; mysterious; **2,** magical; occult.—*adj.* **mys′ti-cal.**—*n.* **mys′ti-cism.**

mys-ti-fy (mis′ti-fī′), *v.t.* [mystified, mystify-ing], to bewilder; puzzle; confuse; as, his actions *mystify* me.—*n.* **mys′ti-fi-ca′tion.**

myth (mith), *n.* **1,** a traditional story often founded on some fact of nature, or an event in the early history of a people, and embodying some religious belief of that people; **2,** any imaginary or fictitious person, thing, or event.—*adj.* **myth′i-cal.**—*n.* **myth′mak-ing.**

my-thol-o-gy (mi-thol′o-ji), *n.* [*pl.* mythologies], **1,** a body of myths in which are recorded a people's beliefs concerning their origin, gods, heroes, etc.; **2,** the study of these beliefs.—*n.* **my-thol′o-gist.**—*adj.* **myth′o-log′i-cal** (mith′o-loj′i-kal).

N

N, n (en), *n.* [*pl.* N's, n's], the 14th letter of the alphabet, following M:—**N,** *abbrev.* **1,** short for *newton*; **2,** short for *nitrogen*.

nab (nab), *v.t.* [nabbed, nab-bing], *Colloq.* to catch or seize unexpectedly; grab; arrest; as, the police *nabbed* the thief.

na-bob (nā′bob′), *n.* **1,** a native ruler in India; **2,** a very rich or important person; as, the nattering *nabobs* of negativity.

na-dir (nā′dėr; -dēr′), *n.* **1,** the point of the heavens or celestial sphere directly under the observer: opposite to *zenith*; **2,** the lowest point (of anything); as, he had reached the *nadir* of his fortunes.

NAF-TA (naf′ta), *abbrev.* short for *North American Free Trade Agreement.*

[1]nag (nag), *n.* **1,** a small horse; **2,** any horse, esp. one that is worn out; **3,** *Colloq.* a racehorse.

[2]nag (nag), *v.i.* [nagged, nag-ging], to scold or find fault continually, often about little things; as, she *nagged* at him to stop smoking:—*v.t.* to torment with tiresome insistence; as, the boys *nag* their mother for sweets:—*n.* a person who continually badgers or finds fault; as, he is such a *nag.*—*adj.* **nag′ging.**—*adv.* **nag′ging-ly.**

naif or **naïf** (nä-ēf′), *adj.* Same as **naive** or **naïve.**

nail (nāl), *n.* **1,** the thin, hard layer at the end of a finger or a toe; also, a claw; **2,** a slender, short bar or rod of metal, with a head at one end and a point at the other, used chiefly for driving into woodwork or other material to hold two pieces together:—**hit the nail on the head,** *Colloq.* to guess or understand correctly; do or say something just right:—*v.t.* **1,** to fasten with a nail; as, to *nail* a lid down; **2,** to clinch, accomplish, or make certain; as, I *nailed* my argument by showing the figures; to *nail* the difficult jump; **3,** to answer or disprove; as, he *nailed* her in the lie; **4,** to hold; as to *nail* one's eyes on something; **5,** to arrest or catch; as, to *nail* the thief; **6,** hit or punch; as, to *nail* the ball and get to second base.

na-ive or **na-ïve** (nä-ēv′), *adj.* artless; natural; unaffected; not sophisticated; credulous; not having experience or knowledge; believing or accepting things without question; as, a *naive* boy from the country.—*n.* **na-ive-té′** or **na-ïve-té′** (nä′ēv′tā′; nä-ē′vi-tā′).—*adv.* **na-ive′ly.**

na-ive-ty or **na-ïve-ty** (nä′ēv′ti′; nä-ē′vi-ti′), *n.* Same as **naiveté** or **naïveté.**

na-ked (nā′kid), *adj.* **1,** entirely undressed; nude; bare; as, *naked* babies; **2,** bare; without its usual covering; as, a *naked* hillside; a *naked* maple tree in winter; **3,** nothing to hide or disguise; plain; without addition; as, the *naked* truth:—**naked eye,** the eye alone; without the aid of a telescope, microscope, or similar glass; as, bacteria cannot be seen with the *naked eye.*

nam-by–pam-by (nam′bi–pam′bi), *adj.* weakly sentimental in writing or talking; affectedly nice; weak:—*n.* [*pl.* namby-pambies], such a person.

name (nām), *n.* **1,** the term or title by which a person or thing is called or known; also, family, clan, etc.; as, to keep our family *name* honourable; **2,** character; reputation; fame; as, she has made a *name* for herself in music; **3,** a word or phrase, esp. abusive, used to describe someone or something; as, don't call her *names:*—*v.t.* [named, nam-ing], **1,** to give a name to; as, to name a kitten; **2,** to appoint for a special purpose; specify; as, to *name* the day; *name* a new captain of the team; **3,** to mention, specify, or identify; as, I asked him to *name* the major cities in Ontario; **4,** to settle on; decide; as, to *name* your price:—*adj.* **1,** famous; popular; celebrated; well-known; as, a *name* brand; *name* actor; **2,** pertaining to, of, or for a name; as, *name* tags.—*adj.* **name′less.** Also, **name′–cal′ling; name′ –drop′ping.**

name-ly (nām′li), *adv.* that is to say; to state more particularly; as, three tools are needed, *namely,* a saw, a hammer, and a plane.

name-sake (nām′sāk′), *n.* one who is named for another, or has the same name as another; as, she is her grandmother's *namesake.*

nan-ny or **nan-nie** (nan′i), *n.* [*pl.* nannies], **1,** a person trained to care for children; a nursemaid; **2,** *Colloq.* a nanny goat; **3,** any protective person or thing, esp. one that is overprotective:—*adj.* relating to, of, or for a nanny; as, a *nanny* state.

nanny goat, a female goat.

nan-o- or **nan-no** (nan′o-), *prefix* meaning **1,** one billion; as in *nano*second; **2,** anything extremely small; as in *nano*technology, *nanno*plankton.

[1]nap (nap), *n.* a short sleep, esp. during the day; a doze:—*v.i.* [napped, nap-ping], **1,** to take a nap, or short sleep; doze; **2,** to be inattentive or off one's guard; as, don't let me catch you *napping* during class.

[2]nap (nap), *n.* short hairs or fuzz on the surface of some fabrics, such as velvet; the pile.

nape (nāp; nap), *n.* in humans or animals, the back of the neck.

nap-kin (nap′kin), *n.* **1,** a small square piece of cloth or paper used at meals and held across the lap for protecting the clothing or for wiping the fingers or lips; serviette; **2,** a sanitary napkin.

nar-cis-sus (när-sis′us), *n.* [*pl.* narcissuses or narcissi (när-sis′ī′ or när-sis′ē)] a spring-flowering plant that grows from a bulb, having white or yellow flowers with a cup-shaped part at the centre:—**Narcissus,** in *Greek mythology,* a handsome young man who fell in love with his own image in a pool and was changed into a narcissus flower.—*n.* **nar′cis-sist** (someone who is conceited or admires oneself excessively; egotist).—*adj.* **nar′cis-sis′tic.**

nar-co- (när′kō-; när′kō′-), *prefix* meaning **1,** *numbness, stupor;* as in *narco*lepsy, *narco*ma, *narco*sis; **2,** *narcotic drug;* as in *narco*analysis.

nar-cot-ic (när-kot′ik), *n.* **1,** a drug that produces drowsiness or sleep, and which lessens pain by making the nerves dull, often becoming addictive; **2,** an illegal, behaviour-altering, addictive drug, such as marijuana, LSD, heroin, cocaine, etc.; **3,** anything that produces a narcotic effect:—*adj.* **1,** having the power to produce drowsiness, sleep, or insensibility to pain;

2, pertaining to, of, or for illegal drugs; as, a *narcotics* police officer; **3,** having a narcotic effect; as, the *narcotic* tone of her voice.

nar-rate (nâr′āt′; nar′āt′; na-rāt′), *v.t.* [narrat-ed, narrat-ing], **1,** to tell (a story), esp. in a book; give an account of (events or happenings); relate; as, he *narrated* his adventures; **2,** to serve as a commentator or narrator of a movie, play, etc.—*n.* **nar-ra′tion.**

nar-ra-tive (nâr′a-tive; nar′a-tiv), *n.* **1,** a story or tale; an account of real or imaginary happenings; **2,** the part of a story that gives the description of events as opposed to the dialogue; **3,** the technique or practice of storytelling:—*adj.* having to do with storytelling; of the nature of a story; as, a *narrative* poem.

nar-ra-tor (nâr′āt′ėr; nar′āt′ėr; na-rāt′ėr) *n.* **1,** a person who speaks along with the action of a film, play, television show, etc., to tell the audience what is going on or to give background information; **2,** anyone who tells or writes a story.

nar-row (nâr′ō; nar′ō), *adj.* **1,** not broad or wide; of little breadth or width; as, a *narrow* lane; **2,** small in amount or extent; as, to move within a *narrow* range; miss by a *narrow* margin; **3,** lacking wide knowledge or breadth of view; having little imagination; limited; as, a *narrow* mind; **4,** exact; as, a *narrow* investigation:—*v.t.* to make smaller in width or extent; to limit or restrict:—*v.i.* to become less wide; lessen or contract.—*n.* **nar′row-ness.**—*adv.* **nar′row-ly** (barely).

nar-rows (nâr′ōz; nar′ōz), *n.* a thin or narrow part in a body of water.

na-sal (nā′zal), *adj.* **1,** having to do with the nose; as, *nasal* congestion; **2,** pronounced through the nose; as, *m, n,* and *ng* represent *nasal* sounds; **3,** relating to any similar sound; as, a *nasal* voice:—*n.* a nasal sound, or a letter used to represent it.—*adv.* **na′sal-ly.**—*v.t.* **na′sal-ize′** [nasalized, nasaliz-ing].

nas-cent (nas′ent; nā′sent), *adj.* **1,** beginning to develop or come into being; immature; as, a *nascent* culture, city, etc.; a *nascent* larva; **2,** in *chemistry*, uncombined: said of an element at the instant of its being set free from a compound, when it has unusual energy and combining power; as, a *nascent* condition.

nas-ty (nas′ti), *adj.* [nas-ti-er, nas-ti-est], **1,** dirty; filthy; **2,** disgusting to taste or smell; as, a *nasty* odour; **3,** obscene; indecent; **4,** troublesome; serious; harmful; as, a *nasty* cut; *nasty* car accident; *nasty* flu; **5,** ill-natured; mean; cruel; **6,** unpleasant; as, a *nasty* day; *nasty* habit.—*n.* **nas′ti-ness.**

na-tion (nā′shun), *n.* **1,** the people of one country, as Canada, living under one government; **2,** a race of people having the same religion and customs, but not always living in the same country or speaking the same language; as, the Jewish *nation*; **3,** a large and organized tribe; also, the region occupied by such a tribe; as, the Cree *Nation*; **4,** a place that has certain borders, its own form of government, and is not part of any larger area of government; a country; as, rain is predicted for all parts of the *nation* this weekend.

na-tion-al (nash′u-nal; nash′nul), *adj.* having to do with or belonging to a nation; as, the prime minister called a *national* election:—*n.* a citizen of a certain nation; as, Swiss *nationals*.—*adv.* **na′tion-al-ly.**

na-tion-al-ism (nash′u-na-lizm′; nash′na-lizm′), *n.* **1,** patriotic devotion; loyalty; a sense of national unity; **2,** a feeling of belonging to a certain nation and of wanting it to rule itself independently; as, *nationalism* led to a demand for independence; **3,** a desire for a people to retain and promote its culture, traditions, language, religion, etc.; as, *nationalism* among Ukrainian-Canadians.

na-tion-al-ist (nash′u-na-list′; nash′na-list′) *n.* a person who supports belonging to a certain nation and its independence; as, a Québec *nationalist*.—*adj.* **na′tion-al-is′tic.**

na-tion-al-i-ty (nash′u-nal′i-ti; nash′nal′i-ti), *n.* [*pl.* nationalities], **1,** one's connection with a particular nation by birth or citizenship, or one's political status because of this connection; as, her *nationality* is Hungarian; **2,** a group of people having the same homeland, language, and culture; ethnic group; as, Canada is a mosaic with many *nationalities*.

na-tion-al-ize (nash′u-na-līz′; nash′na-līz′), *v.t.* [nationalized, nationaliz-ing], **1,** to put under the control of the government, as the health system, land, railways, etc.; **2,** to make or change into a nation; as, Sir John A. Macdonald *nationalized* Canada.—*n.* **na′tion-al-i-za′tion; na′tion-al-iz′er.**

na-tive (nā′tiv), *adj.* **1,** pertaining to one's birth, the place of one's birth, or where one grew up; as, one's *native* land or language; a *native* Albertan; **2,** born or produced in, or belonging to, a country; indigenous; as, *native* plants; *native* people of New Zealand; **3,** produced by nature; not artificial; natural; as, *native* copper; **4,** inborn; not acquired; natural; as, *native* charm; **5,** in *computing*, installed into or designed for a specific computer system by the manufacturer; as, *native* software:—*n.* **1,** one who is born or grew up in a given country or place; as, she is a *native* of Newfoundland; **2,** an animal, plant, or group of people that has lived in a place from the earliest times.

Native people, the Aboriginal inhabitants of North America or their descendants; as, many *Native people* live in Canada.

na-tiv-i-ty (na-tiv′i-ti; nā-tiv′i-ti), *n.* [*pl.* nativities], **1,** birth; **2,** the time, place, and manner of birth:—**Nativity,** the birth of Christ; depiction of this; Christmas.

nat-u-ral (nach′ûr-al; nach′ral), *adj.* **1,** pertaining to one's nature; innate; inborn; not needing to be taught; as, *natural* gifts; **2,** occurring in the ordinary course of things; usual; ordinary; as, a *natural* result; **3,** true to life; as, a *natural* likeness; **4,** pertaining to the world and the things in it; as, *natural* science; **5,** made or found in nature; not caused or produced by people; not artificial; as, *natural* fruit juice; *natural* sweetener; **6,** having to do with nature, as opposed to people; as, gravity is a *natural* law; **7,** not pretended or artificial; as, a *natural* performance; **8,** related by birth; **9,** in *music,* written without sharps or flats; as, the *natural* scale of C:—**natural history, 1,** the study of plants, minerals, and natural objects in general, esp. the study of animals with relation to their life, habits, etc.; **2,** a book or other work about the plant and animal life of a certain place or region; as the *natural history* of Baffin Island; **3,** a compilation of facts about a natural development; as, a *natural history* of a butterfly:—**natural language,** a form of interaction between humans and computers using natural human language rather than artificial or invented language such as BASIC:—*n.* **1,** a person who has a natural talent or ability; as, she is a *natural* as a soccer player; **2,** an off-white or fawn colour; **3,** in *music,* a sign [♮] placed on a line or space of the staff to remove the effect of a preceding sharp or flat.

nat-u-ral-ism (nach′ûr-a-lizm′; nach′ra-lizm′), *n.* **1,** in *art* and *literature,* the presenting of nature and life realistically without idealizing them; realism; **2,** in *philosophy,* the doctrine that everything can be traced to natural causes; **3,** in *theology,* the doctrine that true religion may be learned from observing nature and does not depend on supernatural experiences; **4,** instinct-based action.

nat-u-ral-ist (nach′ûr-a-list′; nach′ra-list′), *n.* **1,** one who makes a special study of natural objects, as plants, minerals, and esp. animals; **2,** one who practises naturalism.

nat-u-ral-ize (nach′ûr-a-līz′; nach′ra-līz′), *v.t.* [naturalized, naturaliz-ing], **1,** to admit (someone of foreign birth) to citizenship; **2,** to accept or adopt, as a foreign word or custom; **3,** to introduce and make grow, as a foreign plant; **4,** to make or seem to make natural:—*v.i.* to become a citizen.—*n.* **nat′u-ral-i-za′tion.**

nat-u-ral-ly (nach′ûr-a-li; nach′ra-li), *adv.* **1,** in a normal, natural way or manner; as, to act *naturally*; **2,** by nature; without anything artificial; as, she was *naturally* clever at music; to be *naturally* blond; **3,** as might be expected; as, *naturally,* I was pleased when I won.

natural resource, something supplied by nature that is important for human life, such as water, minerals, and plants, and which can be exploited economically.

na-ture (nā′chûr), *n.* **1,** real character; qualities that naturally belong to a person or thing; personality; as, she has an affectionate *nature*; **2,** kind or sort; type; as, things of this *nature*; **3,** the outdoor world; wildlife; as, the beauties of *nature*; **4,** the physical universe as a whole, including what it is, what happens in it, such as weather, and what is in it, such as animals, plants, mountains, and oceans; anything that is not made by people; as, the laws of *nature.*

naught or **nought** (not; nôt), *n.* **1,** nothing; as, all her efforts were for *naught*; **2,** a cipher or zero; the character [0] used to represent an arithmetical value of nothing.

naugh-ty (not′i; nô′ti), *adj.* [naugh-ti-er, naugh-ti-est], **1,** bad; wayward; mischievous; disobedient; as, a *naughty* puppy; **2,** improper; lacking in taste.—*adv.* **naugh′ti-ly.**—*n.* **naugh′ti-ness.**

nau-se-a (noz′ē-a; nozh′a; nos′ē-a; nosh′a; nô′zē-a; nô′zha; nô′sē-a; nô′sha), *n.* **1,** sickness of the stomach, with a desire to vomit, as in seasickness; **2,** loathing; disgust.—*adj.* **nau′seous.**—*v.t.* **nau′se-ate** [nauseat-ed, nauseat-ing].

nau-ti-cal (not′i-kal; nô′ti-kal), *adj.* pertaining to ships, sailors, or navigation; maritime:—**nautical mile,** approximately 1,852 metres, used to measure distance on the water or in the air.—*adv.* **nau′ti-cal-ly.**

na-val (nā′val), *adj.* pertaining to war vessels or a navy; as, a *naval* officer; a *naval* power.

na-vel (nā′val), *n.* **1,** the depression or mark in the centre of the abdomen of people and other mammals that is made when the cord connecting a newborn baby to its mother is cut; **2,** a middle point:—**navel orange,** a type of seedless orange that has a similar formation on one end.

nav-i-ga-ble (nav′i-ga-bl), *adj.* **1,** capable of being travelled over by a boat or aircraft; as, a *navigable* stream; **2,** capable of being steered; as, a *navigable* balloon; an easily *navigable* boat.—*n.* **nav′i-ga-bil′i-ty; nav′i-ga-ble-ness.**

nav-i-gate (nav′i-gāt′), *v.i.* [navigat-ed, navigat-ing], **1,** to travel by water or air; **2,** to sail or direct a ship or an aircraft:—*v.t.* **1,** to travel on or over a certain body of water in any type of ship, or by air in any aircraft; as, to *navigate* the St. Lawrence River; **2,** to steer, control, or manage a ship or an aircraft; **3,** *Colloq.* to steer oneself; as, to *navigate* oneself through a throng of people.

nav-i-ga-tion (nav′i-gā′shun), *n.* **1,** the science of determining where a ship or aircraft is, how far it has travelled, and in what direction it is going; **2,** the act of navigating; as, the severe storm made *navigaton* of the airplane difficult.

nav-i-ga-tor (nav′i-gā′tėr), *n.* **1,** a person who plans and directs the course of a ship or aircraft; as, Jacques Cartier was a brilliant *navigator*; **2,** one who explores by sea; **3,** a mechanism responsible for the course of aircraft or missiles.

na-vy (nā′vi), *n.* [*pl.* navies], **1,** the warships of a nation; **2,** (often **Navy**) the sea war force and defence of a nation's armed forces, including ships, shipyards, shops, officers, personnel, etc.; as, in Canada, the *navy* is called the Maritime Command:—**navy blue,** a dark blue colour like that of some naval uniforms.

Na-zi (nät′sē; nat′sē), *n.* [*pl.* Nazis], a member of the National Socialist German Workers' Party, founded by Adolf Hitler: it was the controlling party of Germany between 1933 and 1945. Compare *fascism*:—*adj.* concerning, of, for, or like a Nazi.—*n.* **Na′zism; Na′zi-ism.**

n.b. or **N.B.** (en′bē′), *abbrev.* short for *nota bene* (note well).

NDP (en′dē′pē′), *abbrev.* short for *New Democratic Party*.

near (nēr), *adj.* **1,** not distant in time, place, or degree; close by; **2,** intimate; dear; close in feeling or relationship; as, a *near* friend; **3,** done or missed by a narrow margin; close; as, a *near* escape; *near* accident; **4,** closely related; as, a *near* relative; **5,** very similar; as, *near* leather; **6,** direct or quick; as, to go by the *nearest* way; **7,** mean or stingy; **8,** on the left-hand side of a vehicle, animal, or team:—*adv.* **1,** not distant in time, place, or degree; as, the winter holidays are *near*; **2,** almost; approximately; as, *near* dead with cold; **3,** closely; as, as *near* as I can tell:—*prep.* close to or by; as, she sat *near* the stream:—*v.i.* and *v.t.* to come close (to); approach.—*n.* **near′ness.**

near-by (nēr′bī′), *adj.* not far off; close; as, a *nearby* store:—*adv.* near; close; at hand; as, my friend lives *nearby*.

near-ly (nēr′li), *adv.* **1,** almost; almost but not quite; practically; as, *nearly* frozen; **2,** closely; as, *nearly* related.

near-sight-ed (nēr′sīt′id), *adj.* **1,** able to see objects with distinctness only when they are closer to the eyes; **2,** without thought for the future. Compare *farsighted*.—*n.* **near′sight′ed-ness.**—*adv.* **near′sight′ed-ly.**

neat (nēt), *adj.* **1,** tidy; trim; clean and in good order; fastidious; as, a *neat* room; *neat* employee; **2,** simple and elegant; well made; as, a *neat* costume; **3,** brief; cleverly phrased; as, a *neat* reply; **4,** skillful; deft; clever; as, a *neat* job of carpentry; *neat* trick; **5,** *Colloq.* very good; fine; excellent; as, a *neat* idea; *neat* party; **6,** of an alcoholic drink, without a mix; straight.—*adv.* **neat′ly.**—*n.* **neat′ness.**

neb-u-la (neb′ū-la), *n.* [*pl.* -lae (-lē′; -lī′) or -las], **1,** any luminous, cloudlike mass of gaseous matter or misty star clusters far out in space; as, the Great *Nebula* in Andromeda; **2,** an opaque spot on the cornea of the eye; **3,** cloudiness in the urine; **4,** an oily medicinal preparation for use in an atomizer.—*adj.* **neb′u-lar; neb′u-lous.**

nec-es-sar-i-ly (nes′i-sâr′i-li; nes′i-ser′i-li), *adv.* in a way that must be or that cannot be avoided; as, the old car is not *necessarily* scrap.

nec-es-sar-y (nes′i-ser′i), *adj.* **1,** existing or happening naturally; true according to natural laws; as, a *necessary* conclusion; **2,** not to be done without; essential; required; as, food is *necessary* to life; *necessary* information for an essay; **3,** unavoidable; inevitable; certain; as, tiredness is a *necessary* result of a lack of sleep:—**necessaries,** *n.pl.* things that cannot be done without, such as food and shelter.

ne-ces-si-tate (ne-ses′i-tāt′), *v.t.* [necessitat-ed, necessitat-ing], to make unavoidable; as, illness *necessitated* her absence from school.

ne-ces-si-ty (ne-ses′i-ti), *n.* [*pl.* necessities], **1,** great need of aid or help; the fact of being necessary; as, send for me in case of *necessity*; the *necessity* of sleeping; **2,** something greatly needed; as, vegetables are *necessities* for health; *necessity* is the mother of invention; **3,** extreme poverty; **4,** that which compels one to act in a certain way; as, he felt the *necessity* of leaving immediately:—**necessities,** the things needed for a decent living.

neck (nek), *n.* **1,** that part of the body connecting the head with the shoulders; **2,** the part of a garment that fits closely around the neck; the collar; **3,** a long, extended, usually narrow part of an object, esp. if near one end; as, the *neck* of a bottle; *neck* of a guitar:—**neck and neck,** being equal or even in a race or contest; as, the marathon runners were *neck and neck* as they crossed the finish line.

neck-lace (nek′lis), *n.* a decorative chain, as of gold or silver, or a string of beads, pearls, jewels, etc., worn around the neck.

neck-tie (nek′tī′), *n.* a narrow scarf or band worn around the neck and tied in a knot or bow in front; tie (def. 3).

nec-ro- or **necr-** (nek′rō-; nekr-), *prefix* meaning *dead, death,* or *corpse*; as in *necro*mancy (predicting the future by communicating with the dead), *necro*philia (obsession with death and corpses), *necro*phobia (fear of death or corpses), *necro*polis (cemetery), *necr*osis (decay of body or bone tissue).

nec-tar (nek′tėr), *n.* **1,** in *mythology*, the drink of the gods; **2,** any delicious beverage; **3,** a sweet fluid in plants, esp. in the flowers, used by bees in making honey; **4,** a concentrated, undiluted drink made from fruit; as, peach *nectar.*

nec-tar-ine (nek′ta-rēn′), *n.* a kind of peach with a smooth, thin skin and firm pulp.

need (nēd), *n.* **1,** lack of anything desired, important, or useful; as, he felt the *need* for sleep; **2,** something that must be done; obligation; as, there is no *need* to shout; **3,** necessity; time of trouble or difficulty; as, a friend in *need* is a friend indeed; **4,** urgent want; poverty; being poor or in difficulty:—**needs,** something that is useful, important, or wanted; as, the *needs* of a newborn baby:—*v.t.* to be in want of; require; have use for; as, I *need* a new notebook:—*v.i.* **1,** to be necessary; as, it *needs* to be done; **2,** to be under obligation; have to; as, she *need* not go.—*adj.* **need′y.**

need-ful (nēd′fool), *adj.* **1,** necessary; required; **2,** needy.—*adv.* **need′ful-ly.**

nee-dle (nē′dl), *n.* **1,** a small, sharp-pointed steel instrument furnished with an eye to hold thread, used for sewing; **2,** a thin, straight rod used in knitting or, when hooked at the end, for crocheting; **3,** anything sharply pointed like a needle, as the leaf of a pine, spruce, or fir tree; **4,** any of various other things that are long, thin, and pointed, often used on a measuring device to indicate something; as, the magnetic *needle* of a compass; the needle on a speedometer or barometer; **5,** a hollow tube with a sharp, thin point that is used to inject medicine or other liquid into the body; hypodermic syringe:—*v.t.* [nee-dled, nee-dling], to annoy, tease, torment, or provoke; as, she *needled* him about his error.

need-less (nēd′lis), *adj.* unnecessary; useless; not needed.—*adv.* **need′less-ly.**

nee-dle-work (nē′dl-wûrk′), *n.* hand sewing; embroidery done by hand.

ne'er-do-well (nâr′-do͞o-wel′), *n.* one who does nothing worthwhile; worthless person.

ne-fa-ri-ous (ne-fâr′ē-us), *adj.* extremely wicked; villainous; as, *nefarious* practices, schemes, etc.

ne-ga-tion (ni-gā′shun), *n.* **1,** denial; as, he shook his head in *negation*; **2,** the opposite or absence of something real or positive; as, death is the *negation* of life.

neg-a-tive (neg′a-tiv), *adj.* **1,** expressing or implying refusal or denial; meaning "no"; as, he gave me a *negative* answer; **2,** lacking positive qualities; not forceful or influential; not helpful or friendly; pessimistic; as, a *negative* sort of person; **3,** naming the kind of electricity made in silk by rubbing it on glass: the opposite of *positive*; **4,** in *mathematics*, naming a quantity to be subtracted; minus; pertaining to a number less than zero; **5,** showing that a disease or harmful condition is not present; as, her tests came back *negative*; **6,** harmful; as, *negative* side effects:—*n.* **1,** a refusal or denial; **2,** the side of a question that denies what the opposite side upholds; as, to support the *negative* in a debate; **3,** in *mathematics*, a quantity less than zero; also, its symbol; **4,** in *photography*, an image on a film that is developed into a print, sometimes called a *positive*; **5,** a word expressing denial, as the words *no, not, neither*:—*v.t.* [negatived, negativ-ing], **1,** to deny the truth of; contradict; **2,** to refuse assent to; veto; **3,** to counteract; neutralize; **4,** disprove.

ne-glect (ni-glekt′), *n.* **1,** failure to do that which should be done; negligence; as, her garden showed *neglect*; **2,** habitual lack of attention; disregard; as, his friends resented his *neglect*; **3,** carelessness:—*v.t.* **1,** to fail (to act or to do something), by carelessness or design; disregard, ignore, or avoid; as, to *neglect* one's chores; **2,** to slight; pay little attention to; as, to *neglect* a warning; **3,** to leave uncared for; as, the boy *neglects* his dog.—*adj.* **ne-glect′ed.**

ne-glect-ful (ni-glekt′fool), *adj.* careless; disregardful.—*adv.* **ne-glect′ful-ly.**

neg-li-gee or **neg-li-gée** or **neg-li-gé** (neg′li-zhā′; neg′li-zhā′), *n.* **1,** a loose, sheer lounging gown worn by women; **2,** easy, informal, or incomplete dress in general.

neg-li-gent (neg′li-jent), *adj.* **1,** careless; heedless; inattentive; **2,** neglectful.—*adv.* **neg′li-gent-ly.**—*n.* **neg′li-gence.**

neg-li-gi-ble (neg′li-ji-bl), *adj.* small, trifling, or unimportant; not worth consideration.

ne-go-tia-ble (ni-gō′sha-bl), *adj.* **1,** transferable to another, as a cheque or promissory note (usually by endorsement); **2,** being easily or able to be negotiated; **3,** being able to be traversed or accomplished; as, a difficult but *negotiable* road or obstacle.

ne-go-ti-ate (ni-gō′shē-āt′), *v.t.* [negotiat-ed, negotiat-ing], **1,** to talk over a problem or an issue in order to reach an agreement or to make arrangements; put through, obtain, or arrange for; as, to *negotiate* a sale, loan, or peace treaty; **2,** to sell, convert into cash, or transfer to another for a consideration; as, to *negotiate* business papers representing money value or credit, such as bonds, stocks, cheques, etc.; **3,** to go safely on or over or deal with successfully; as, I knew the horse could *negotiate* the jump:—*v.i.* to treat with others in political or business affairs in order to reach an agreement; as, the union leaders *negotiated* with the managers.—*n.* **ne-go′ti-a′tor; ne-go′ti-a′tion; ne-go′ti-at′ing.**—*adj.* **ne-go′ti-at′ed.**

Ne-gro (nē′grō), *n.* [*pl.* Negroes], a black person of African descent, now considered offensive by many: see *Black*:—*adj.* relating to this people.

neigh-bour or **neigh-bor** (nā′bėr), *n.* **1,** one who lives next to, near, or nearest another; as, a next-door *neighbour*; **2,** a person or thing that is near or next to another; as, Canada and the United States are *neighbours*; **3,** a fellow being; as, love thy *neighbour*:—*adj.* pertaining to someone or something that is next to or near another; as, a *neighbour* country:—*v.t.* and *v.i.* to adjoin.

neigh-bour-hood or **neigh-bor-hood** (nā′bėr-hood′), *n.* **1,** the region nearby; vicinity; as, it is in the *neighbourhood* of the river; **2,** all the people living near one another or within a certain range; as, the *neighbourhood* welcomed the new people; **3,** one particular area that is within a large city or town and that has certain characteristics of its own; as, the grocery store is in our *neighbourhood*; **4,** *Colloq.* an approximate degree, extent, or amount; range; as, a distance in the *neighbourhood* of 50 kilometres:—*adj.* for or of a neighbourhood; as, a *neighbourhood* park.

neigh-bour-ing or **neigh-bor-ing** (nā′bėr-ing), *adj.* living or being near; adjoining; close by; as, the *neighbouring* village.

neigh-bour-ly or **neigh-bor-ly** (nā′bėr-li), *adj.* friendly; kindly; like a good neighbour.—*n.* **neigh′bour-li-ness.**

nei-ther (nē′*th*ėr; nī′*th*ėr), *pron.* not the one nor the other; as, I want *neither* of the books:—*adj.* not either; as, *neither* book will do:—*conj.* **1,** not either; not (one or the other): often with *nor*; as, *neither* the book *nor* the CD; **2,** nor; nor yet; and ... not; as, I do not know; *neither* can I guess.

nem-e-sis (nem′i-sis), *n.* [*pl.* nemeses (nem′i-sēz′)], **1,** retributive justice whereby the punishment fits the crime; as, a fear of divine *nemesis*; **2,** someone who carries out justice and punishes another for crimes or evil deeds; **3,** a powerful, long-time rival or opponent; as, a business magnate's *nemesis* took over the company:—**Nemesis,** in *Greek mythology*, the goddess of retribution.

ne-o- (nē′ō-), *prefix* meaning *new, recent, modern, new and revised*; as in *neo*classical, *neo*conservative, *neo*fascist, *neo*liberal, *neo*plasm (new growth, as in a tumour), *neo*traditional.

Ne-o-lith-ic (nē′ō-lith′ik), *adj.* in *archaeology*, pertaining to the later stone age (New Stone Age), which began around 10,000 B.C., marked by use of polished stone implements and the beginnings of agriculture and domesticated animals (the *Neolithic* Age).

ne-on (nē′on), *n.* an inert, odourless and colourless gaseous element of which traces occur in the atmosphere (15 parts in a million), used in vacuum tubes to light up signs and lamps because it glows when an electric current is passed through it:—*adj.* **1,** pertaining to, of, or for neon; as, a *neon* sign over a store; **2,** relating to anything resembling neon; very bright; fluorescent; **3,** gaudy.

ne-o-phyte (nē′ō-fīt′), *n.* **1,** a beginner; novice; **2,** a newly ordained priest or one just entering a convent; **3,** a convert.

neph-ew (nef′ū), *n.* **1**, the son of one's brother or sister; **2**, the son of a brother-in-law or a sister-in-law.

Nep-tune (nep′tōōn′; nep′tūn′), *n.* **1,** in *Roman mythology*, the god of the sea, comparable to *Poseidon* in *Greek mythology*; **2,** the fourth-largest planet in the solar system, and the eighth-closest planet to the sun.

nerd or **nurd** (nûrd), *n. Slang* **1**, someone who is obsessively studious or single-minded, esp. one lacking in social skills; as, a computer *nerd*; **2**, a foolish, inept, or uninteresting person.

nerve (nûrv), *n.* **1,** one of the cordlike fibres that connect the brain and spinal cord with all parts of the body and carry messages to and from the brain; **2,** boldness; coolness in danger; courage; strength of the mind or will; as, skydiving takes *nerve*; **3**, the fact of being rude or impolite; audacity; as, she had a lot of *nerve* criticizing me like that; **4,** stress; nervousness; as, to drink herbal tea to calm your *nerves*:—*v.t.* [nerved, nerv-ing], to arouse courage or strength in; brace oneself; as, she *nerved* herself for the competition.

nerve-less (nûrv′lis), *adj.* **1,** without nerves; **2,** lacking vigour or strength; paralysed; weak; as, the pen fell from her *nerveless* grasp; **3,** lacking boldness or courage; cowardly; **4,** calm; cool; self-controlled; not nervous; as, a *nerveless* competitive skater.—*adv.* **nerve′less-ly.**—*n.* **nerve′less-ness.**

nerv-ous (nûr′vus), *adj.* **1,** pertaining to, or made of, nerves; as, epilepsy is a *nervous* disorder; **2,** having weak nerves; **3,** easily excited; not relaxed; tense; as, a *nervous* performer; she is *nervous* about giving the speech; **4,** forceful; vigorous; as, he is full of *nervous* energy; **5,** restless or uneasy; timid; afraid; as, to be *nervous* in the dark; a *nervous* smile.—*adv.* **nerv′ous-ly.**—*n.* **nerv′ous-ness.**

nervous system, the system in the body made up of the brain, spinal cord, and nerves.

nest (nest), *n.* **1,** the bed or place, of grass, mud, twigs, or other materials, made or chosen by a bird for the hatching of its eggs and rearing of its young; **2,** a hatching place for insects, turtles, fish, snakes, etc.;

lair or den; as, a hornet's *nest*; **3,** the inhabitants of a nest; **4,** a cozy retreat or residence; shelter; **5,** a place for something harmful or undesirable; hotbed; as, a *nest* of political corruption; **6,** a number of boxes, bowls, tables, etc., one fitting inside another; also, any collection of things that are made to fit inside each other; **7,** in *computing*, data contained within other data:—**nest egg**, money saved for the future:—*v.i.* **1,** to build and occupy a nest; **2,** to fit or place (an object) inside another:—*v.t.* to place in, or as if in, a nest.

nes-tle (nes′l), *v.i.* [nes-tled, nes-tling], **1,** to lie close, and snug; as, a child *nestles* in her mother's arms; **2,** to settle down or lie in a comfortable place; as, to *nestle* in a chair:—*v.t.* **1,** to cherish or cuddle; as, she *nestled* the kitten in her arms; **2,** to settle comfortably; as, to *nestle* the children in their beds.

nest-ling (nest′ling; nes′ling), *n.* **1,** a young bird recently hatched and not yet able to fly; **2,** a young child:—*adj.* recently hatched.

[1]net (net), *n.* **1,** a fabric made of thread, cord, or rope woven or knotted together, leaving evenly spaced openings, used for catching, stopping, or holding things; as, a fishing *net*; **2,** a net used as a goal or dividing line in such games as tennis, volleyball, hockey, or soccer; as, a goalie *net*; **3,** any fine openwork fabric used for bridal veils, laces, etc.; **4,** that which entraps; an entanglement; as, the criminal cannot escape the *net* of justice; a snare; **5,** a network; **6,** in *computing*, a system of computers linked together:—*adj.* of or like net or netting; as, *net* stockings:—*v.t.* [net-ted, net-ting], **1,** to make into a net or network; **2,** to catch in a net; as, to *net* a fish; **3,** to entrap by clever means; snare; **4,** to cover or protect with a net; **5,** to hit (a ball) into a net.

[2]net (net), *adj.* **1,** remaining after the deduction of all necessary expenses; as, *net* gain; **2,** excluding all waste, refuse, etc.; as, *net* weight; **3,** after everything has been taken into account; final; as, the *net* result:—*n.* **1,** the net amount, sum, result, etc.; **2,** the essential point:—*v.t.* [net-ted, net-ting], to earn as clear profit; as, the deal *netted* $20,000.

Net (net), *abbrev.* short for *Internet.*

net-i-quette, (ne′ti-ket′), *n. Colloq.* network etiquette; the unwritten set of rules for communication over the Internet.

net-ting (net′ing), *n.* **1,** the act or method of making nets; **2,** a fabric made of meshes or crossed wires; as, fish *netting*; wire *netting* for windows; **3,** fishing with a net; **4,** network.

net-tle (net′l), *n.* any of a group of coarse plants having prickles or stinging hairs:—*v.t.* [net-tled, net-tling], **1,** to sting, with or as with nettles; **2,** to provoke; irritate; vex; as, his remark *nettled* me.

net-work (net′wûrk′), *n.* **1,** an openwork fabric made by interlaced threads; **2,** any system of lines that cross like those in a net; as, a *network* of roads, routes, railways, telephone lines, vines, wires, etc.; **3,** a group of radio or television stations that are joined together so that they can use the same broadcasts; **4,** in *computing*, a set of computers linked together, allowing them to communicate and share information with one another; **5,** a group of people who share information:—*v.i.* to cooperate with a group of people, esp. to gain personal or business benefits:—*v.t.* and *v.i.* in *computing*, to link (computers or other machines) to allow for the exchange of information.

neu-ro- or **neur-** (noor′o-; noor-; nūr′ō-; nūr-), *prefix* meaning *nerve*; as in *neur*algia (acute intermittent face or head pain along the course of a nerve), *neur*itis (nerve inflammation), *neuro*logy (study of nerves), *neur*on (nerve cell), *neuro*path (a specialist on nerves, or a patient abnormally given to nerve disease), *neuro*science (science of nerves), *neuro*surgery (surgery on part of the nervous system).

neu-ro-sis (noo-rō′sis; nū-rō′sis), *n.* [*pl.* -ses (-sēz)], any mild mental or emotional disorder in which anxiety, fixed ideas, obsessive behaviour, and complaints, which are not traceable to a physical cause, dominate the mind, such as *hypochondria*: less serious than *psychosis*, in which there is a breakdown of personality and loss of touch with the real world.—*adj.* **neu-rot′ic.**

neu-ter (noo′tėr; nū′tėr), *adj.* **1,** in *grammar*, neither masculine nor feminine; as, "book" is a *neuter* noun: compare *feminine* and *masculine*; **2,** in *botany*, having no sex, as certain plants; **3,** in *zoology*, without fully developed sex organs; as, the worker bees are *neuter*; **4,** neutral:—*n.* a neuter word or organism:—*v.t.* **1,** to spay, castrate, or alter; **2,** to deprive of power or force.

neu-tral (noo′tral; nū′tral), *adj.* **1,** not affected by a special or personal interest; indifferent; as, my feelings on the matter were altogether *neutral*; **2,** not taking sides in a quarrel, debate, war, etc.; as, a *neutral* colleague; *neutral* nation; **3,** belonging to a neutral nation or area; as, *neutral* ships; **4,** neither good nor bad; neither one thing nor another; with no decided characteristics; **5,** neither acid nor alkaline; **6,** having little or no colour; as, grey is *neutral*:—*n.* **1,** one who does not take sides in a dispute or conflict; **2,** the position of gears (in a car) in which no power is sent from the engine to the wheels.—*adv.* **neu′tral-ly.**—*n.* **neu-tral′i-ty.**

neu-tral-ize (noo′tral-īz′; nū′tral-īz′), *v.t.* [neutralized, neutraliz-ing], **1,** to render inactive; make of no effect; counteract; as, to *neutralize* the effects of a poison; **2,** to make neutral chemically or electrically; **3,** to make (a country, region, etc.) neutral; as, to *neutralize* small nations; **4,** *Slang* to kill, eliminate, or make powerless; as, to *neutralize* the enemy.—*n.* **neu′tral-i-za′tion; neu′tral-iz′er.**

neu-tron (noo′tron; nū′tron), *n.* a minute constituent of an atomic nucleus, about the mass of a proton, but without either positive or negative charge: found in all atoms except hydrogen:—**neutron bomb,** a bomb designed to destroy life but not structures such as buildings and other inanimate objects by giving off a large amount of radiation with a minimal amount of blast.

nev-er (nev′ėr), *adv.* **1,** not ever; not at any time; as, I have *never* seen such a beautiful sight before; **2,** in no degree; under no condition: used for emphasis; as, *never* fear.

nev-er-the-less (nev′ėr-*th*ė-les′), *adv.* and *conj.* notwithstanding; in spite of that; yet; however; still; anyway; as, I won't be able to go, but, *nevertheless,* thanks for asking me.

new (nōō; nū), *adj.* **1,** made for the first time; not existing before; as, a *new* dress; a *new* house; **2,** lately made, produced, invented, or discovered; modern; as, a *new* type of computer monitor; **3,** beginning afresh; recurring anew; as, a *new* year; *new* start in life; *new* moon; **4,** freshly made or grown; as, *new* cheese; *new* peas; **5,** not yet used or worn; as, a *new* broom; *new* suit; *new* trail; **6,** changed in character, health, etc.; as, I feel like a *new* person; **7,** different from that previously existing, known, or used; as, a *new* language; a *new* race of settlers; **8,** being in a place or condition for only a short time; as, a *new* job; **9,** unfamiliar; as, a *new* experience:—*adv.* newly; recently; as, a field of *new*-mown hay.—*n.* **new′ness.**

new-bie (nōō′bē; nū′bē), *n. Slang* a novice or beginner, esp. one who is new at computer technology or the Internet; as, he is a *newbie* in our newsgroup.

new-born (nōō′bôrn′; nū′bôrn′), *adj.* **1,** very recently or just born; as, a *newborn* baby; **2,** born anew; regenerated; as, *newborn* determination:—*n.* a recently born baby; as, diapers for *newborns.*

new-com-er (nōō′kum′ėr; nū′kum′ėr), *n.* one who has lately arrived.

New Democratic Party, a Canadian democratic-socialist political party, which was founded in 1961: abbreviated as *NDP.*

new-fan-gled (nōō′fang′gld; nū′fang′gld), *adj.* novel; of a new kind; inclined to new theories, fashions, etc.: sometimes derogatory; as, *newfangled* ideas or notions.

new-ly (nōō′li; nū′li), *adv.* **1,** not long ago; recently; lately; as, *newly* cut flowers; **2,** anew; as, a *newly* upholstered sofa; **3,** in a different way; as, *newly* styled hair.

new-ly-wed (nōō′li-wed′; nū′li-wed′), *adj.* and *n.* recently married.

news (nūz), *n.* **1,** recent or fresh information; any report about something that has recently happened; as, we have no *news* of the accident; *news* about the family; **2,** recent events reported in the media. Also, **news′break′; news′mag′a-zine′; news′ mak′er; news′ per′son; news′ room′; news′stand′; news′worth′y.**

news-cast (nōōz′kåst′; nūz′kåst′), *n.* a radio or television broadcast of news reports:—*v.t.* to broadcast (news).—*n.* **news′cast′er.**

news-group (nōōz′grōōp′; nūz′grōōp′), *n.* in *computing,* an electronic forum for discussion of a particular topic on the Internet; as, she posted several messages to our *newsgroup.*

news-let-ter (nōōz′let′ėr; nūz′let′ėr), a written or printed letter or report presenting news in an informal way to a specific group.

news-pa-per (nōōz′pā′pėr; nūz′pā′pėr), *n.* **1,** a daily or weekly paper containing recent news, editorials, columns, advertisements, pictures, etc.; **2,** the company that publishes a newspaper; **3,** the paper that makes up a newpaper; newsprint; as, to wrap the breakable china in *newspaper.*

news-print (nōōz′print′; nūz′print′), *n.* a cheap, coarse paper made from wood pulp, used mostly for newspapers.

news-reel (nōōz′rēl′; nūz′rēl′), *n.* a short motion picture of current events.

newt (nūt), *n.* any of several small, harmless, brightly coloured animals resembling lizards, with smooth skin, short legs, and long tails, found in water or damp places.

new-ton (nōōt′n; nūt′n), *n.* in the SI system, the absolute unit of force required to accelerate one kilogram one metre per second squared: abbreviated as *N.*

new wave, *n.* **1,** in the 1950s and 1960s, a movement in French cinema that used experimental techniques in photography; **2,** a new trend in a specific field; as, a *new wave* in fashion; **3,** a type of rock music of the late 1970s and early 1980s that was influenced by punk and was often characterized by synthesizer music and lyrics expressing discontent:—*adj.* pertaining to, of, or for new wave; as, *new wave* music.

New World, North and South America; the Western hemisphere. Compare *Old World.*

New Year's Day, the first day of the year, celebrated in Canada and in many other countries as a legal holiday; January 1.

next (nekst), *adj.* **1,** immediately following in order; as, the *next* day; *next* person in line; **2,** nearest in time, place, degree, or rank; as, the *next* street; *next* store:—*adv.* immediately succeeding; in the nearest time, place, or order; as, you go *next*; *next* closest store:—*prep. Colloq.* nearest to; as, you sit *next* the end:—**next to, 1,** beside; as, sit *next to* me; **2,** nearly; as, *next to* nothing was left in the burglarized house; **3,** following in order; as, *next to* reading, her favourite pastime was playing soccer.

next door, *adv.* in or at the nearest house, building, or room; as, to move *next door*:—*adj.* of the nearest house, building, or room: often hyphenated; as, a *next-door* neighbour.

next of kin, *n.* [*pl.* next of kin], a person's nearest blood relative or relative by marriage.

nib (nib), *n.* **1,** the point of anything, esp. of a pen; **2,** a bird's bill or beak; **3,** any point or end.

nib-ble (nib′l), *v.t.* and *v.i.* [nib-bled, nib-bling], **1,** to bite a little at a time; eat quickly in little bites; as, to *nibble* lettuce; the mouse *nibbled* at the cheese; **2,** to bite or nip gently or playfully:—*v.i. Colloq.* to be somewhat interested in; as, to *nibble* at stamp collecting:—*n.* a small bite.

nice (nīs), *adj.* [nic-er, nic-est], **1,** dainty; attractive; as, the child looked *nice* in the new outfit; **2,** requiring care and accuracy; exact; as, a *nice* experiment; *nice* problems; **3,** able to find or feel small differences; subtle; as, a *nice* ear for music; *nice* distinctions; **4,** requiring the best; too particular; scrupulous; as, he is too *nice* about his food; **5,** pleasing; agreeable; good; kind; as, she is a *nice* person; **6,** well-behaved; as, they are *nice* children; **7,** pleasant; agreeable; as, to have a *nice* time; *nice* day for a picnic.—*adv.* **nice′ly.**—*n.* **nice′ness.**

ni-ce-ty (nī′si-ti), *n.* [*pl.* niceties], **1,** a dainty, elegant, or delicate thing; as, the *niceties* of life; **2,** a very small difference, point, or detail; as, to learn the *niceties* of drawing; **3,** accuracy; careful attention to details; as, to describe the scene with great *nicety*; **4,** the point at which a thing is just right; as, baked to a *nicety*; **5,** subtlety.

niche (nich; nēsh), *n.* **1,** a recess or hollow in a wall, as for a statue, vase, etc.; **2,** a condition, activity, or position esp. suitable to a person or thing; as, she found a *niche* in business; **3,** a place occupied by an organism in its environment; also, its role; **4,** a specialized market:—*adj.* pertaining to, for, or of a niche; as, *niche* marketing.

nick (nik), *n.* **1,** a notch; slit; to make a *nick* in the piece of wood; **2,** a broken place in any edge or surface; cut, scratch, or chip; as, a *nick* in the table; **3,** the exact or critical point (of time); as, he arrived in the *nick* of time:—*v.t.* **1,** to cut notches in; **2,** to hit upon exactly; strike at the right place or proper moment.

nick-el (nik′l), *n.* **1,** a hard, silver-white, metallic element, which is often combined with other metals; **2,** in Canada and the U.S., a coin of the value of five cents, made of nickel and copper.

nick-name (nik′nām′), *n.* a familiar form of a given name, as "Bill" for "William," or a wholly new name given in derision, sport, or familiarity, as "Red" for someone with red hair:—*v.t.* [nicknamed, nicknaming], to give a nickname to; call by a familiar name; as, they *nicknamed* him "Red."

nic-o-tine (nik′o-tēn′), *n.* a pungent, addictive, colourless poison contained in tobacco and used as an insecticide and in some medicines.

niece (nēs), *n.* **1,** the daughter of one's brother or sister; **2,** the daughter of a brother-in-law or sister-in-law.

nif-ty (nif′ti), *adj. Slang* [nif-ti-er, nif-ti-est], smart; clever; attractive; stylish; as, a *nifty* joke; *nifty* outfit.

nig-gard-ly (nig′ėrd-li), *adj.* **1,** stingy; miserly; as, a *niggardly* person; **2,** scanty, as a meal:—*adv.* stingily; miserly; scantily; meanly.—*n.* **nig′gard-li-ness.**—*n.* and *adj.* **nig′gard.**

nig-gle (nig′l), *v.i.* [nig-gled, nig-gling], **1,** to putter; work fussily; **2,** to trifle; **3,** to find fault; carp; irritate; as, quit *niggling* about my being late:—*v.t.* **1,** to work out with too elaborate care; **2,** to deceive; **3,** *Colloq.* to nag; as, quit *niggling* me:—*n.* a complaint.—*adj.* **nig′gling.**—*n.* **nig′gler.**

night (nīt), *n.* **1,** the time from sunset to sunrise; **2,** the close of the day; **3,** the darkness of night:—*adj.* of or relating to the night; as, *night* blindness; *night* owl; *night* school; *night* shift.

night-fall (nīt′fol′; nīt′fôl′), *n.* the coming of darkness at evening.

night-gown (nīt′goun′), *n.* a loose dresslike garment worn in bed by women and girls.

night-hawk (nīt′hôk′), *n.* **1,** any of a group of American birds, not properly hawks, which fly at night; **2,** a person who stays up late at night.

night-ie or night-y (nī′ti), *n. Colloq.* Same as **nightgown.**

night-in-gale (nīt′n-gāl′; nī′ting-gāl′), *n.* any of several small European reddish-brown thrushes noted for the melodious song of the male, heard most often at night.

night-ly (nīt′li), *adj.* **1,** happening, coming, or occurring at night; as, the army made *nightly* marches; **2,** occurring every night; as, he does *nightly* exercises:—*adv.* night by night; every night; at or by night; as, she sang *nightly* at the club.

night-mare (nīt′mâr′), *n.* **1,** a terrifying dream accompanied by a feeling of helplessness; **2,** any frightful or horrible experience or haunting fear like a bad dream; **3,** an extremely unpleasant situation; as, the traffic at the end of the long weekend was a *nightmare*.

nil (nil), *n.* nothing; zero; as, in that game, his score was absolutely *nil.*

nim-ble (nim′bl), *adj.* **1,** quick and active; alert; clever; as, a *nimble* mind; **2,** lively; brisk; swift; agile; as, *nimble* feet or fingers.—*adv.* **nim′bly.**—*n.* **nim′ble-ness.**

nim-bus (nim′bus), *n.* **1,** a rain cloud, heavy and grey; **2,** any kind of cloud enveloping a person or thing; **3,** a halo or circle about the heads of divinities, saints, sovereigns, etc., on medals and pictures.

nin-com-poop (nin′kom-po͞op′; ning′kom-po͞op′), *n. Colloq.* a silly or stupid person; fool.

nine (nīn), *adj.* composed of one more than eight:—*n.* **1,** the number consisting of eight plus one; **2,** a sign representing nine units, as 9 or ix.

nine-teen (nīn-tēn′), *adj.* composed of 10 more than nine:—*n.* **1,** the sum of 18 and one; **2,** a sign representing nineteen units, as 19 or XIX.—*adj.* **nine-teenth′.**

nine-ti-eth (nīn′ti-eth), *adj.* next after the 89th: the ordinal of *ninety*:—*n.* one of the 90 equal parts of anything.

nine-ty (nīn′ti), *adj.* composed of one more than 89:—*n.* [*pl.* nineties], **1,** the number consisting of 89 plus one; **2,** a sign representing ninety units, as 90 or XC.

nin-ny (nin′i), *n.* [*pl.* -nies (-iz)], *n.* a foolish person; simpleton; dunce.

ninth (nīnth), *adj.* next after the eighth: the ordinal of *nine*:—*n.* one of the nine equal parts of anything.

nip (nip), *v.t.* [nipped, nip-ping], **1,** to pinch; to cut off the end of; clip; bite; as, the dog *nipped* him in the ankle; **2,** to pinch in; as, to *nip* a dress at the waist; **3,** to blight; blast; destroy, as by frost; **4,** *Colloq.* to defeat; **5,** *Colloq.* to steal; as, the mugger *nipped* her purse.—*adj.* **nip′py** [nip-pi-er, nip-pi-est].

nip-per (nip′ėr), *n.* **1,** one who or that which pinches or cuts off; **2,** the large claw of a crab or lobster; **3,** a horse's front tooth; **4,** *Colloq.* a small child; **5,** in the Maritimes and Newfoundland, a glove to protect hands when handling lines; **6,** in Newfoundland, a mosquito:—**nippers,** any of various tools with jaws, such as forceps, pliers, tongs, etc.

nip-ple (nip′l), *n.* **1,** that part of a breast through which a baby or young animal draws milk; **2,** the mouthpiece of a baby's bottle; **3,** a similar projection on a male's chest; **4,** anything resembling a nipple in appearance or function.

nit-pick (nit′pik′), *v.t.* and *v.i.* to be overly critical in finding fault, esp. unjustified criticism of insignificant details; as, he was *nitpicking* all the new ideas; she *nitpicks* about every detail.—*n.* **nit′pick′ing; nit′pick′er.**—*adj.* **nit′pick′y.**

ni-trate (nī′trāt), *n.* **1,** a salt of nitric acid; **2,** potassium or sodium nitrate, extensively used as a fertilizer:—*v.t.* to use nitrate on.

ni-tre or **ni-ter** (nī′tėr), *n.* a white crystalline salt (potassium nitrate), used in making gunpowder, fertilizer, etc. Also called *saltpetre.*

ni-tric ac-id (nī′trik as′id), a very powerful acid that eats into and destroys flesh, wood, metal, etc., and is used in making explosives, dyes, fertilizers, etc.

ni-tro- or **nitr-** (nī′trō-; nitr′-), *prefix* meaning **1,** a compound of nitrogen or its acids, as *nitro*bacteria, *nitro*cellulose, *nitro*glycerin, *nitro*hydrochloric acid (aqua regia); **2,** the presence of the NO_2 radical, as in *nitro*benzene, *nitro*paraffin.

ni-tro-gen (nī′trō-jen), *n.* a chemical element that is a colourless, odourless, tasteless gas, and which forms about 80 per cent of Earth's atmosphere and is found in all living things: abbreviated as *N.*—*adj.* **ni-trog′e-nous** (nī-troj′i-nus).

ni-trous (nī′trus), *adj.* **1,** containing nitrogen; **2,** containing nitre or saltpetre; **3,** having less oxygen than compounds designated by nitric:—**nitrous oxide** (N_2O), a colourless gas of sweetish odour and taste, used as a mild anesthetic, esp. by dentists. Also called *laughing gas.*

nit-wit (nit′wit′), *n. Colloq.* a simpleton; stupid person.

nix (niks), *n.* and *interj. Slang* nothing; no; stop!; I disagree, refuse, etc.:—*adv.* no; not at all:—*v.t.* to veto, reject, or cancel; as, the committee *nixed* the building plans.

no (nō), *n.* [*pl.* noes (nōz)], **1,** a denial; a refusal or negative response by saying "no"; as, my *no* was received in silence; **2,** a negative vote; as, my *no* lost her the election:—**noes,** the voters in the negative; as, the *noes* have it:—*adv.* **1,** not so; as, *No,* I cannot go: opposite of *yes*; **2,** not any; not at all; as, he is *no* better; hand in your essays *no* later than Friday; **3,** not; as, whether or *no*:—*adj.* not any; as, there are *no* classes on the weekend:—**no-holds-barred, 1,** without rules or restrictions; as, a *no-holds-barred* game; **2,** complete; as, a *no-holds-barred* effort.

No-bel Prize (nō-bel′ prīz′), *n.* an international award established by Alfred B. Nobel and given each year since 1901 for important work in the fields of physics, chemistry, medicine, literature, economics, and advancing the cause of peace.

no-bil-i-ty (nō-bil′i-ti), *n.* [*pl.* nobilities], **1,** the quality of being lofty in character, mind, or rank; **2,** the rank or body of persons of noble birth; aristocracy.

no-ble (nō′bl), *adj.* [no-bler, no-blest], **1,** lofty or great in character or mind; outstanding; distinguished; as, a *noble* woman; *noble* deed; **2,** high in rank or title in society; of ancient lineage or descent; as, of *noble* birth; **3,** stately in appearance; grand; magnificent; splendid; as, *noble* architecture; the Rockies are a *noble* sight:—*n.* a peer or person of high rank or title.—*adv.* **no′bly.**—*n.* **no′ble-ness.**

no-ble-man (nō′bl-man), *n.* [*pl.* noblemen (-men)], a man of noble rank or title.—*n. fem.* **no′ble-wom′an.**

no-bod-y (nō′bod′i; nō′bud′i; nō′bud-i), *pron.* no one; no person; not anybody; as, *nobody* came to the party:—*n.* [*pl.* nobodies], a person of no importance or influence; as, she felt like a *nobody* because no one came to her party.

noc-tur-nal (nok-tûr′nal), *adj.* **1,** done or occurring at night; as, a *nocturnal* visit; **2,** active at night; as, the bat is a *nocturnal* animal.—*adv.* **noc-tur′nal-ly.**

noc-turne (nok′tûrn′), *n.* **1,** a quiet, dreamy song without words (usually for piano); **2,** a painting of a night scene.

nod (nod), *n.* **1,** a quick bending of the head, used as a sign of greeting, assent, approval, drowsiness, etc.; **2,** approval or recognition; as, the proposal received a *nod* from the committee:—*v.t.* [nod-ded, nod-ding], **1,** to say by means of a nod; as, he *nodded* his farewells; **2,** to incline or bend with a quick movement; as, to *nod* one's head:—*v.i.* **1,** to swing or sway quickly; as, flowers *nod* in the breeze; **2,** to bend the head in token of assent or as a salute; **3,** to be drowsy; bend the head forward sleepily.

node (nōd), *n.* **1,** a knot; knob; swelling; **2,** a hard swelling on a tendon or bone; **3,** the point on the stem of a plant from which a leaf springs; **4,** in *computing,* a junction or terminal in a computer network; **5,** a predicament or complication in a story, etc.—*adj.* **nod′al.**

N
N

PLANT NODES

nod-ule (noj′o͞ol), *n.* a little knot or swelling; irregular, rounded lump; as, a nodule on a plant, on the body, or on a rock—*adj.* **nod′u-lar; nod′u-lous.**

no-ël or **no-el** (nō-el′), *n.* a Christmas carol:—**Noël** or **Noel**, Christmas.

noise (noiz), *n.* **1,** sound, esp. when loud, confused, unwanted, or disagreeable; as, the *noise* of traffic; **2,** any sound; **3,** unwanted disturbance, such as static, in a radio or television signal; **4,** in *computing,* useless information on a computer:—**noises,** *Colloq.* words or actions that express a certain sentiment and usually attract attention; as, the group made unsympathetic *noises* about the federal budget:—*v.t.* [noised, nois-ing], to spread by rumour; as, the report was *noised* abroad:—*adv.* **nois′i-ly.**—*adj.* **nois′y.**—*n.* **nois′i-ness.**

noise-less (noiz′lis), *adj.* **1,** silent; still; **2,** making little sound; as, a *noiseless* engine.—*adj.* **noise′less-ly.**—*n.* **noise′less-ness.**

noi-some (noi′sum), *adj.* **1,** injurious to health; harmful; as, *noisome* gases; **2,** offensive; disgusting; bad-smelling; objectionable; as, *noisome* odours; a *noisome* sight.—*adv.* **noi′some-ly.**—*n.* **noi′some-ness.**

no-mad (nō′mad′), *n.* **1,** a member of a roving tribe or group of people, such as Bedouins, Inuit, etc., who have no fixed home but wander about in search of game, pasture, etc.; **2,** any person who wanders about aimlessly from place to place:—*adj.* **1,** pertaining to, of, or for a nomad; **2,** wandering; roving.—*adj.* **no′mad-ic.**—*n.* **no′mad′ism.**

nom de plume (nom′de plo͞om′), *n.* [*pl.* noms de plume (nom′de plo͞om′)], a pen name; pseudonym; as, she wrote her novel under a *nom de plume.*

no-men-cla-ture (nō′men-klā′chėr; nō′men-kla′chėr), *n.* **1,** the system of names or terms used for things, as in an art or science; as, the *nomenclature* of botany, chemistry, etc.; **2,** the process, act, or fact of naming.

nom-i-nal (nom′i-nal), *adj.* **1,** existing in name only; not real or actual; as, though the president was the *nominal* head of the company, her son actually ran it; **2,** so small as to be hardly worth mentioning; as, we paid only the *nominal* sum of one dollar for the old, used car; **3,** relating to or of names; as, a *nominal* list of students:—*n.* in *grammar,* a word that functions as a noun.—*adv.* **nom′i-nal-ly.**

nom-i-nate (nom′i-nāt′), *v.t.* [nominat-ed, nominat-ing], **1,** to propose or name for an office; as, to *nominate* a person for election; **2,** to propose for an honour; as, the song was *nominated* for a Juno award; **3,** to designate or name.—*n.* **nom′i-na′tor; nom′i-na′tion.**

nom-i-na-tive (nom′i-nā′-tiv), *adj.* **1,** nominated or appointed by nomination for office; **2,** (nom′i-na-tive) naming the case of the subject of a verb; as, in the sentence "I am ready," "I" is in the *nominative* case:—*n.* **1,** the case of the subject of a verb; the nominative case; **2,** a word in this case.

nom-i-nee (nom′i-nē′), *n.* **1,** one who is named or proposed for an office or duty; someone who is nominated; as, the *nominee* for premier; **2,** someone who is proposed for an honour; as, she is a *nominee* for a Gemini award.

non- (non-), *prefix* meaning *not, lack of,* or *opposite of;* as in *non*aligned, *non*cooperation, *non*essential, *non*issue, *non*productive, *non*resistant, *non*smoking, *non*verbal, *non*zero.

non-a-ge-na-ri-an (non′a-je-nâr′ē-an; nō′na-je-nâr′ē-an), *n.* and *adj.* one or relating to one who is 90 years old or between 90 and 100 years old.

non-cha-lance (non′sha-lons′), *n.* lack of interest; easy unconcern; indifference; as, he pretended *nonchalance* to cover his embarrassment.—*adj.* **non′cha-lant′.**

non-com-mis-sioned (non′ko-mish′und), *adj.* not having a certificate to engage in a service; not having a commission:—**non-commissioned member,** in Canada, any member, other than an officer, of the Canadian Forces:—**noncommissioned officer,** an enlisted person (in the RCMP, etc.) who has risen to the rank of sergeant or corporal and who has authority over other enlisted persons.

non-com-mit-tal (non′co-mit′al), *adj.* not revealing one's opinion or purpose; not meaning yes or no; as, his answer was wholly *noncommittal.*

non-con-duc-tor (non′kon-duk′tėr), *n.* any substance, such as rubber, through which heat, light, sound, electricity, etc., will not pass readily; an insulator.

non-con-form-ist (non′kon-fôr′mist) *n.* and *adj.* one or of one who does not conform to, or agree with, established beliefs or customs:—**Nonconformist,** a Protestant or pertaining to a Protestant who does not belong to the Church of England.—*n.* **non′con-form′i-ty.**

non-de-script (non′di-skript′), *adj.* **1,** not easily described or classified; of no particular character; as, a *nondescript* colour; **2,** odd, drab; uninteresting; as, she wore a *nondescript* dress:—*n.* a nondescript thing or person.

none (nun), *pron.* **1,** not any; as, I will have *none* of it; **2,** not one; no one or ones: used as *sing.* or *pl.*; as, we needed a ball, but *none* was to be had; *none* of them were there:—*adv.* not at all; not in the least; as, she felt *none* the better for his trip.

non-en-ti-ty (non-en′ti-ti), *n.* [*pl.* -ties (-tiz)], **1,** a person of no influence, importance, or individuality; as, he is a *nonentity*; **2,** an imaginary thing that does not exist; **3,** the state of not existing.

none-the-less (nun′*th*ė-les′), *adv.* nevertheless; however; as, although she did not feel well, she went to school *nonetheless.*

non-fic-tion (non-fik′shun), *n.* prose, such as biographies, histories, and reference books, that are not fiction or imaginary; also, the category in literature with these kinds of works. Compare *fiction.*

non-par-ti-san (non-pär′ti-zen; non-por′ti-sen), *adj.* not strongly in favour of, influenced by, or affiliated with a cause or a party; as, a *nonpartisan* candidate.

non-plus (non′plus), *v.t.* [nonplussed (non′plust), nonplus-sing], to throw into complete perplexity; bring to a standstill; as, I was *nonplussed* as to how to settle the quarrel:—*n.* inability to decide or proceed; state of perplexity; as, to be at a *nonplus.*—*adj.* **non-plussed′.**

non-re-stric-tive (non′ri-strik′tiv), *adj.* **1,** not restrictive; **2,** in *grammar,* not limited, such as a clause or phrase that gives description but is not necessary to the sense of a sentence; as, the boy, *who was tall and strong,* won the match: distinguished from *restrictive*; as, the boy *who was wearing the red shirt* won the match.

non-sense (non′sens′; non′suns), *n.* **1,** talk or action without sense; language without meaning; **2,** absurdity; foolishness; as, it's *nonsense* to say that you can jump that far; **3,** things of little worth; trifles; as, why spend money for such *nonsense*? **4,** impudence; unacceptable behaviour, talk, or action; as, the teacher does not stand for any *nonsense* from her students:—*interj.* absurd.—*adj.* **non-sen′si-cal.**

non-start-er (non-stär′tėr), *n.* **1,** a person or thing that does not start; **2,** *Colloq.* a useless person, thing, or idea; **3,** *Colloq.* a person or thing with a limited chance of success or effectiveness.

non-stop (non′stop′), *adj.* and *adv.* **1,** without a stop; as, a *nonstop* flight; to fly *nonstop* from New York to Montreal; **2,** without a break; as, a *nonstop* work schedule; to work *nonstop*:—*n.* a nonstop flight or trip.

noo-dle (nōō′dl), *n.* **1,** a narrow strip of dried dough, or pasta, made of flour, water, and egg, which comes in different sizes and shapes and is used in soups, stews, etc.; **2,** *Colloq.* a simpleton; stupid person; **3,** *Slang* the head; as, use your *noodle* to figure out the problem:—*v.i.* [noo-dled, noo-dling], **1,** to improvise casually on a musical instrument, esp. jazz music; **2,** to waste time; be unproductive.

nook (nook), *n.* **1,** a cozy, out-of-the-way place; a secluded spot; **2,** a corner in a room; **3,** a sheltered recess out of doors.

noon (nōōn), *n.* the middle of the day; 12:00 P.M.:—*adj.* pertaining to midday.

no one (nō′wun′), *pron.* nobody; no person; not one person; as, *no one* came to the meeting.

noose (nōōs), *n.* **1,** a loop in a rope, made with a slipknot, as in a lasso, which binds closer the more tightly it is drawn; **2,** any snare or nooselike thing:—*v.t.* [noosed, noos-ing], **1,** to catch or capture in or as if in a noose; **2,** to make a noose on or in something.

Noot-ka (nōōt′ka; noot′ka), *n.* [*pl.* Nootka or Nootkas], **1,** a member of the Aboriginal peoples living mainly on Vancouver Island; **2,** the Wakashan language of the Nootka.

nor (nôr), *conj.* and not: a negative connecting word used after the negatives *neither* and *not* to continue or complete their meaning; as, he has neither money *nor* friends; she is neither tall *nor* short; not a word *nor* a sign betrayed him.

norm (nôrm), *n.* a standard; model; pattern; average; the median or average of achievement in a large group; as, class marks above the *norm*; temperatures below the *norm*; social *norms*.

nor-mal (nôr′mal), *adj.* **1,** as it should be; healthy and natural; as, she has a *normal* temperature; **2,** according to rule; regular; typical; serving as a standard or model; as, a *normal* school day:—*n.* the usual or ordinary condition, quantity, etc.; as, the rain raised the river one metre above *normal.*—*adv.* **nor′mal-ly.**—*n.* **nor-mal′i-ty; nor′mal-cy.**

north (nôrth), *n.* **1,** one of the four points of the compass; the point opposite to the south, or to the left of a person facing the sunrise; **2,** a section of country lying north of another; as, the *north* of Canada:—**the North,** *n.* **1,** in Canada, the northern parts of the provinces from Québec westward and the territories lying north of these provinces; **2,** in the U.S., that district lying generally north of the Ohio River and the southern boundary of Pennsylvania; the states that fought for the Union in the Civil War; **3,** the northern part of the world:—*adj.* having to do with, situated in, toward, or coming from, the north; as, a *north* wind:—**North Pole**, the northernmost part of the earth, near the middle of the Arctic Ocean:—**North Star**, the bright star that is very nearly over the North Pole: also called *Polaris*:—*adv.* to the north; toward the north; as, walk *north* one block.—*n.* **north′land.**

North American Free Trade Agreement, the trilateral free trade agreement between Canada, the United States, and Mexico that superseded the *Free Trade Agreement* in 1994: abbreviated as *NAFTA*.

north-east (nôrth-ēst′; nôr-ēst′), *n.* **1,** the point of the compass halfway between north and east; **2,** a place or region lying in the direction of that point:—*adj.* having to do with the northeast, or in, at, of, toward, or from the northeast; as, a *northeast* wind:—*adv.* toward the northeast; as, to travel *northeast.*—*adj.* **north-east′ern.**—*adj.* and *adv.* **north-east′ward.**—*adv.* **north-east′ ward-ly; north-east′wards.**

north-east-er (nôrth-ē′stėr; nôr-ē′stėr), *n.* a violent wind or storm blowing from the northeast.

north-east-er-ly (nôrth-ē′stėr-li; nôr-ē′stėr-li), *adj.* and *adv.* from, coming from, or toward the northeast.

north-er-ly (nôr′*th*ėr-li), *adj.* pertaining to the north, or situated in, toward, or coming from the north; as, a *northerly* wind:—*adv.* toward the north:—*n.* [*pl.* northerlies], a wind or storm from the north.

north-ern (nôr′*th*ėrn), *adj.* in, from, or toward the north; as, a *northern* course; a *northern* wind:—**Northern**, relating to, of, or in the North.—*adj. superl.* **north′ern-most.**

north-ern-er or **North-ern-er** (nôr′*th*ėr-nėr), *n.* **1,** a person living in, or coming from, the north; **2,** a person living in or coming from the Canadian Far North; **3,** a person living in or coming from the part of the U.S. north of the southern boundary line of Pennsylvania.

northern lights, the streams of bright light and colour seen in the northern sky at night, best observed in the Arctic regions. Also called *aurora borealis*.

north–north-east (nôrth′–nôrth-ēst′; nôr′–nôr-ēst′) *n.* 22° 30′ east of due north; the point of the compass halfway between north and northeast:—*adj.* having to do with the north-northeast, or in, at, of, toward, or from the north-northeast:—*adv.* toward the north-northeast; as, to travel *north-northeast*.

north–north-west (nôrth′–nôrth-west′; nôr′–nôr-west′), *n.* 22° 30′ west of due north; the point of the compass halfway between north and northwest:—*adj.* having to do with the north-northwest, or in, at, of, toward, or from the north-northwest:—*adv.* toward the north-northwest; as, to travel *north-northwest*.

north-ward (nôrth′wėrd), *adj.* and *adv.* to or toward the north; leading to the north:—*n.* a northern region or direction.—*adv.* **north′wards.**—*adj.* and *adv.* **north′ward-ly.**

north-west (nôrth-west′; nôr-west′), *n.* **1,** the point of the compass halfway between north and west; **2,** a place or region lying in the direction of that point:—*adj.* having to do with the northwest, or in, at, of, toward, or from the northwest; as, a *northwest* wind:—*adv.* toward the northwest; as, to travel *northwest.*—*adj.* **north-west′ern.**—*adj.* and *adv.* **north′west′ ward.**—*adv.* **north-west′ward-ly; north-west′ wards.**

north-west-er or **nor′west-er** (nôrth-wes′tėr; nôr-wes′tėr), *n.* a strong wind or storm blowing from the northwest.

north-west-er-ly (nôrth-wes′tėr-li; nôr-wes′tėr-li), *adj.* and *adv.* from, coming from, or toward the northwest.

nose (nōz), *n.* **1,** in humans and other animals, that part of the face or head containing the nostrils for breathing and nerves of smell; **2,** the sense of smell; as, the deer has a keen *nose*; **3,** anything that protrudes like a nose, as a spout or a bow of a ship or aircraft; **4,** the ability to sense or search out things; as, a reporter with a *nose* for news; **5,** the aroma, perfume, or bouquet, as of wine:—**on the nose,** exactly; as, to guess the number *on the nose*:—**by a nose,** a very small difference; as, to win *by a nose*:—*v.t.* [nosed, nos-ing], **1,** to smell, scent, or detect; **2,** to rub or push with the nose or front; as, horses *nose* each other; the boat *nosed* its way through the ice:—*v.i.* **1,** to smell or scent; **2,** to pry into another person's affairs; snoop; **3,** to move forward cautiously. Also, **nose′bleed′; nose′dive′; nose′piece′.**

nos-tal-gi-a (no-stal′ja; ni-stal′ja), *n.* **1,** homesickness; **2,** a longing for something in the past; longing for the return of some former condition or circumstance; as, to think with *nostalgia* of one's childhood days; **3,** something that reminds one of former conditions or circumstances; as, the vinyl records are *nostalgia* to her.—*adj.* **nos-tal′gic.**

nos-tril (nos′tril), *n.* one of the two external openings in the nose: the nostrils are the passageways through which air is pulled into the body by the lungs and through which air is expelled.

nos-trum (nos′trum), *n.* **1,** a medicine recommended as a cure-all; as, an old woman's *nostrums*; **2,** a patent or quack medicine; **3,** a pet remedy for a social evil; as, political *nostrums*.

nos-y or **nos-ey** (nō′zi), *adj.* [nos-i-er, nos-i-est] *Colloq.* **1,** inquisitive; prying; **2,** curious about things that are not one's business; as, she is *nosy* because she listens to other people's phone calls.

not (not), *adv.* a word that expresses denial, prohibition, or refusal; in no way; as, he will *not* go.

no-ta be-ne (nō′ta ben′ē; nō′ta bē′nē), note well: abbreviated as *n.b.*

no-ta-ble (nō′ta-bl), *adj.* **1,** worthy of attention; memorable for any reason; outstanding; important; as, a *notable* event; a *notable* documentary; **2,** distinguished; eminent; as, a *notable* speaker was the guest of honour; **3,** perceptible; as, a *notable* difference between the two items:—*n.* a person or thing of distinction; as, many *notables* attended the ceremony.—*n.* **no′ta-ble-ness.**—*adv.* **no-ta-bly.**

no-ta-ry or **no-ta-ry pub-lic** (nō′ta-ri; nō′ta-ri pub′lik), *n.* [*pl.* notaries; notaries public], **1,** an official permitted by law to witness or certify contracts, etc., or to record the fact that a certain person swears something is true, etc.; **2,** in Québec, a person who can perform all the functions of a lawyer except pleading in court.

no-ta-tion (nō-tā′shun), *n.* **1,** the act or practice of recording by marks or symbols; **2,** a brief note, esp. as a reminder or explanation; as, he made a *notation* in the margin of his report; **3,** a system of signs or symbols used in place of language, for brevity or clearness, esp. the system of numbers, letters, and signs used in arithmetic and algebra and the signs used in writing or printing music.

notch (noch), *n.* **1,** a small nick or V-shaped cut in the edge or on a surface of something; also, such a nick as a means of recording something; **2,** a narrow pass through mountains, etc.; **3,** one of a series of holes in a belt, shoe, etc.; **4,** one of a series of indentations on the side opposite the spine of a book, such as a dictionary, that allows a reader to find a particular section quickly and easily; **5,** *Colloq.* a degree or step; as, to speed up a *notch*:—*v.t.* **1,** to nick or cut into small hollows; **2,** to keep count of by nicks; **3,** *Colloq.* to score.

note (nōt), *n.* **1,** a brief memorandum or record to assist the memory; as, speaker's *notes*; **2,** a brief explanation or comment; as, the margin *notes* make the book clearer; **3,** a short, informal letter or message; as, drop me a *note* about your plans; **4,** a formal letter from one government to another; **5,** characteristic quality; a hint or suggestion; as, a *note* of sadness in her voice; **6,** reputation; fame; distinction; as, an author of *note*; **7,** notice; attention; as, a matter worthy of *note*; **8,** in *music*, a written sign or character representing the pitch and relative length of a tone; also, a single tone itself, as made by a musical instrument or the voice; **9,** a legal paper acknowledging a debt, and promising payment; as, a promissory *note*; a bank *note*; **10,** an observation, written or unwritten:—**compare notes,** to exchange ideas or opinions; as, to *compare notes* about a movie:—**make a note of,** to write down as something to be remembered; as, to *make a note of* the changes to the plan:—*v.t.* [not-ed, not-ing], **1,** to make a memorandum of; record; as, he *noted* the date of the meeting on his PDA; **2,** to make mention of; **3,** to observe; notice; pay attention to; as, she *noted* the beauty of the scenery; **4,** to be well-known for; as, she was *noted* for her innovative architectural designs.

note-book (nōt′book′), *n.* **1,** a book with blank pages in which notes, drawings, etc., are made, esp. a student's book for notes, assignments, etc.; **2,** a portable computer that is smaller than a laptop but larger than a PDA.

not-ed (nō′tid), *adj.* well-known; celebrated; famous; as, a *noted* musician.—*adv.* **not′ed-ly.**—*n.* **not′ed-ness.**

note-wor-thy (nōt′wûr′*thi*), *adj.* worthy of notice; remarkable.—*adv.* **note′wor′thi-ly.**—*n.* **note′wor′thi-ness.**

noth-ing (nuth′ing), *pron.* not anything; as, she has *nothing* to do today:—*n.* **1,** a thing of no value, use, or importance; as, the scratch is *nothing*; **2,** a nobody; **3,** nothingness; something that does not exist; **4,** zero; as, 12 minus 12 equals *nothing*:—*adv.* in no degree; not at all; not in any way; as, the copy is *nothing* like the original.—*n.* **noth′ing-ness.**

no-tice (nō′tis), *n.* **1,** a taking heed; attention; observation; as, to take *notice* of events; **2,** advance information; warning; action that shows that something is about to happen; as, he received *notice* to vacate the building; at a moment's *notice*; **3,** a printed announcement or sign; as, a *notice* of a marriage; *notice* about the lost kitten on the bulletin board; **4,** a brief printed article or paragraph on a book, movie, play, etc.; a review; **5,** a formal announcement terminating an agreement; as, to give *notice* to an employer, landlord, etc.:—*v.t.* [noticed, notic-ing], **1,** to see or observe; regard; **2,** to make remarks upon; speak of; **3,** to pay polite attention to; as, she didn't even *notice* me.

no-tice-a-ble (nō′ti-sa-bl), *adj.* **1,** capable of being easily observed or noticed; as, a *noticeable* lack of interest; **2,** conspicuous; likely to attract attention; **3,** worthy of attention; significant; notable; as, her last book was a *noticeable* one.—*adv.* **no′tice-a-bly.**

no-ti-fy (nō′ti-fī′), *v.t.* [notified, notify-ing], **1,** to give warning or information to; as, to *notify* the employees of a new policy; **2,** to make known; declare; publish; announce.—*n.* **no′ti-fi′er.**—*n.* **no′ti-fi-ca′tion.**

not-ion (nō′shun), *n.* **1,** a vague or general idea; as, I have no *notion* what he means; **2,** a theory or belief; as, that is the common *notion*; **3,** inclination; a whim; a sudden or odd desire to do something; as, to have a *notion* to climb a mountain:—**notions,** small articles used in sewing, such as pins, thread, needles, ribbons, etc.; sundries.

no-to-ri-e-ty (nō′to-rī′i-ti), *n.* [*pl.* notorieties], the state of being well known, esp. in an undesirable or bad way; infamy.

no-tor-i-ous (nō-tôr′ē-us), *adj.* commonly known; noted; famous, usually in a bad sense; infamous; as, a *notorious* criminal; a *notorious* meddler.—*adv.* **no-to′ri-ous-ly.**—*n.* **no-to′ri-ous-ness.**

not-with-stand-ing (not′with-stan′ding; not′*with*-stan′ding), *prep.* in spite of; as, *notwithstanding* the rain, she walked to the store:—*adv.* nevertheless; still; however; all the same; as, his mother forbade his going, but he went, *notwithstanding*:—*conj.* although:—**notwithstanding clause,** section 33 of the Canadian Charter of Rights and Freedoms, which allows a provincial or the federal government to override provisions of the Charter.

nought (nôt), *n.* Same as **naught.**

noun (noun), *n.* in *grammar*, a word used to name a person, place, idea, or thing, acting as the subject of a verb (the *dog* jumped), object of a verb (close the *door*), or object of a preposition (she ran across the *street*).

nour-ish (nûr′ish), *v.t.* **1,** to feed (a plant or animal) with the material necessary to keep it alive and make it grow; **2,** to foster; encourage; as, the doctor *nourishes* hope in her patients; **3,** to enrich; as, to *nourish* soil; *nourish* the mind and spirit.—*n.* **nour′ish-ment.**

no-va (nō′va), *n.* [*pl.* -vae (vē; vī); -vas (vaz)], a star that explodes, sending huge masses of matter into space, and suddenly flashes out with unusual brilliancy and then gradually grows fainter.

[1]**nov-el** (nov′el), *adj.* **1,** modern; unknown formerly; of recent origin; as, not many years ago, DVDs were *novel* things; **2,** new or unusual; as, a *novel* idea for a book; a *novel* theory.

[2]**nov-el** (nov′el), *n.* **1,** a story, with a plot, long enough to fill one or more volumes, presenting fictional characters and actions as they might occur in real life; **2,** the literary branch relating to such works.

nov-el-ette (nov′e-let′), *n.* a short novel.

nov-el-ist (nov′e-list), *n.* a writer of novels.

nov-el-ty (nov′el-ti), *n.* [*pl.* novelties], **1,** unusualness; newness; the fact or condition of being new or different; as, the new game was fun at first, but the *novelty* soon wore off; **2,** something new; a change or innovation; as, not so long ago, the Internet was a *novelty*:—**novelties,** small, usually inexpensive, items for sale, such as toys, games, trinkets, etc.

No-vem-ber (nō-vem′bėr), *n.* the 11th month of the year, with 30 days, between October and December.

nov-ice (nov′is), *n.* **1,** a beginner; an inexperienced person, as to a job or activity; **2,** a monk or nun who has entered a religious order but has not yet taken final vows.

now (nou), *adv.* **1,** at the present time; as, she moved from Campbellton and *now* lives in Moncton; **2,** a short time ago; quite recently; as, he left just *now*; **3,** immediately; at once; as, I am going *now*; **4,** under the present circumstances; as, *now* what can we do? **5,** used without any idea of time; as, oh, come *now*, don't do that; *now* you know better than that; **6,** next; as, you have filled in your name and address, and *now* complete the questionnaire; **7,** nowadays; as, *now* it is possible to travel through space:—*conj.* since; now that; as, I need not stay, *now* that you are here:—*n.* the present moment.

now-a-days (nou′a-dāz′), *adv.* these days; now; as, *nowadays*, most people own a television set.

no-where (nō′wâr′; nō′hwâr′), *adv.* not in, at, or to any place; as, she was *nowhere* to be seen:—*n.* **1,** a place that does not exist; **2,** an obscure or distant place or state; as, suddenly, the storm came from *nowhere*:—*adj. Slang* not important; not satisfactory; as, a *nowhere* job.

nox-ious (nok′shus), *adj.* **1,** harmful; injurious; deadly; as, *noxious* gases; **2,** capable of corrupting; as, *noxious* ideologies.—*adv.* **nox′ious-ly.**—*n.* **nox′ious-ness.**

noz-zle (noz′l), *n.* **1,** a projecting mouthpiece or spout, as on a hose or pipe, through which liquid can be discharged; as, a *nozzle* of a garden hose; **2,** *Slang* nose.

nth (enth), *adj.* **1,** the last in a series of infinitely increasing or decreasing amounts, values, etc.; **2,** very great; utmost; extreme; as, the house was decorated to the *nth* degree for the holidays.

nu-ance (nōō′äns′; nū′äns; nōō-äns′; nū-äns′), *n.* **1,** a delicate shade, tone, colour, meaning, feeling, or expression; as, a *nuance* of green; a poem full of *nuance*; **2,** a subtle distinction; as, the *nuance* between the meaning of the two words.

nub (nub), *n.* **1,** knob; lump; knot; **2,** the gist, essence, or point (of a story).

nu-cle-ar (nōō′klē-ėr; nū′klē-ėr), *adj.* **1,** having to do with a nucleus; as, *nuclear* particles; **2,** having to do with the nucleus of an atom; as, *nuclear* physics; **3,** using power from the nucleus of an atom; as, a *nuclear*-powered submarine; **4,** having to do with nuclear weapons; as, a *nuclear* war; *nuclear* bomb:—**nuclear energy,** power or energy that can be released from the nucleus of an atom. Also, **nu′cle-ar med′i-cine; nu′cle-ar pow′er; nu′cle-ar re-ac′tor; nu′cle-ar weap′on.**

nu-cle-us (nōō′klē-us; nū′klē-us), *n.* [*pl.* nuclei (nōō′klē-ī or nū′klē-ī; nōō′klē-ī or nū′klē-ē) or nucleuses (nōō′kli-us-ez; nū′kli-us-ez)], **1,** a kernel; a central or most important part or thing about which other matter collects; anything that serves as the centre of growth or development; as, his few books became the *nucleus* of the club's library; **2,** in *biology*, the tiny central part of a seed or animal cell, necessary to growth and development; **3,** in *physics*, the central part of an atom, which contains protons and neutrons and has a positive charge of electricity.

AN ATOM, WITH NUCLEUS AT CENTRE

nude (nōōd; nūd), *adj.* bare; naked; unclothed:—*n.* **1,** a naked person or figure, esp. in a work of art, photo, etc.; **2,** the state of being naked.—*n.* **nud′ism.**

nudge (nuj), *v.t.* [nudged, nudg-ing], to touch or push gently, as with the elbow, in order to gain attention, provide encouragement, or to move along:—*v.i.* to move gradually; as, to *nudge* through the crowd:—*n.* a gentle touch or poke, as with the elbow.

nug-get (nug′it), *n.* **1,** a lump of gold or other precious metal found in the earth; **2,** a valuable piece of something; as, a *nugget* of information; **3,** any piece or lump of something.

nui-sance (nōō′sans; nū′sans), *n.* anything that offends, annoys, or causes trouble; a bother; as, the child was becoming a *nuisance* with her screaming.

null (nul), *adj.* **1,** of no force or value; not binding; invalid; as, the cheque was crossed out and marked *null* and void; **2,** insignificant; unimportant; **3,** relating to zero, nil, or nothing:—*n.* zero; nil; nothing:—*v.t.* to make null; nullify.—*n.* **nul′li-ty.**

nul-li-fy (nul′i-fī′), *v.t.* [nullified, nullifying], **1,** to deprive of effect or legal force; invalidate; as, to *nullify* a decision or a law; **2,** to make of no value; destroy; cancel.—*n.* **nul′li-fi-ca′tion.**

numb (num), *adj.* **1,** physically deprived of feeling or motion; as, *numb* fingers from cold; **2,** emotionally deprived of feeling; unresponsive; as, to be *numb* with grief:—*v.t.* to deprive of sensation; benumb, as by cold, anesthetic, etc.; paralyze.—*adv.* **numb′ly.**

num-ber (num′bėr), *n.* **1,** a total of units, persons, or things taken together; sum; as, to find out the *number* of students present; **2,** the figure, sign, or word that stands for this total; as, the *number* 20, six, etc.; **3,** a certain numeral by which one person or thing is identified from others; as, a phone *number*; locker *number*; **4,** a considerable but not exact amount; as, a *number* of people were present; **5,** one of a series; as, the October issue *number* of a magazine; **6,** one in a series of items on a program; as, a dance *number* in a performance; **7,** a song or music piece; as, 10 *numbers* on the music CD:—*v.t.* **1,** to count; enumerate; as, to *number* the persons in the crowd; **2,** to put a number on; assign a number; **3,** to amount to; total; as, the class *numbers* 25; **4,** to include; as, we *number* her among our friends; **5,** to limit the number of; as, her days are *numbered.*

number cruncher, *Slang* **1,** a powerful computer able to process vast amounts of data and calculations very rapidly; **2,** a person, such as a researcher or accountant, who is chiefly concerned with numbers and data.

num-ber-less (num′bėr-lis), *adj.* **1,** having no number; **2,** very many; countless; as, *numberless* stars in the sky.

number one, *Slang* **1,** oneself; as, to look after *number one*; **2,** someone or something that is the best or first in importance, rank, etc.; as, our team is *number one*:—*adj.* best or first in importance, rank, quality, etc.

nu-mer-al (nōō′mėr-al; nū′mėr-al), *n.* a word, sign, symbol, or figure representing a number or quantity; as, the Arabic *numerals* are 1, 20, 50, etc.; the Roman *numerals* are I, XX, L, etc.

nu-mer-a-tor (nōō′mė-rā′tėr; nū′mė-rā′tėr), *n.* **1,** in fractions, the number above the line; as, in the fraction 7/8, the *numerator* is 7: compare *denominator*; **2,** a person or thing that takes a count or numbers; as, a census *numerator.*

nu-mer-i-cal (nōō-mer′i-kal; nū-mer′i-kal),

adj. having to do with, or expressed in, numbers; as, *numerical* equations.—*adv*. **nu-mer′i-cal-ly.**

nu-mer-ous (nōō′mėr-us; nū′mėr-us), *adj*. consisting of a great number; very many; as, *numerous* mistakes on a test.—*adv*. **nu′mer-ous-ly.**—*n*. **nu′mer-ous-ness.**

nu-mis-mat-ics (nōō′miz-mat′iks; nōō′mis-mat′iks; nū′miz-mat′iks; nū′mis-mat′iks), *n.pl*. used as *sing*., the collecting, study, or science of coins, medals, etc.—*adj*. **nu′mis-mat′ic.**—*n*. **nu-mis′ma-tist.**

num-skull or **numb-skull** (num′skul′), *n*. a stupid person; blockhead; dunce.

nun (nun), *n*. a woman living under certain vows in a convent and devoted to a religious life: nuns do not marry, usually live together as part of a group, and do charitable work such as nursing, teaching, and helping the poor.

nun-ner-y (nun′ė-ri), *n*. [*pl*. nunneries], a convent or place where nuns live.

nup-tial (nup′shal; nup′chal), *adj*. **1,** pertaining to marriage or the ceremony; as, the *nuptial* day; **2,** of animals, pertaining to the mating season:—**nuptials,** a wedding; wedding ceremony; marriage.

nurse (nûrs), *n*. **1,** formerly, one who cared for another's young child or children; **2,** a person who is specially trained to take care of sick people and carry on other medical duties, such as assisting in surgery: nurses work in hospitals, private homes, or nursing homes, where elderly or ill people are cared for:—*v.t.* [nursed, nurs-ing], **1,** to breast-feed (an infant); **2,** to caress or treat fondly; as, the little girl was *nursing* her doll; *nurse* a cup of coffee; **3,** to care for or wait upon in sickness; **4,** to encourage; cherish; tend; harbour; make grow; promote; as, to *nurse* an industry, a grudge, a fire, a plant, etc.:—*v.i.* **1,** of a baby, to suck milk from a mother; suckle; **2,** to care for the sick or infirm; work as a nurse.

nurse-maid (nûrs′mād′), *n*. a person whose job it is to take care of another's child or children; nanny (def. 1).

nurs-er-y (nûr′sė-ri; nûrs′ri), *n*. [*pl*. nurseries], **1,** a room where young children or babies sleep or play; **2,** a daycare centre; **3,** a nursery school; **4,** a place or garden for raising and selling young trees and plants; **5,** any place or environment like a nursery.

nursery rhyme, a short rhyming song or poem for children.

nursery school, a school for young children who are not old enough to go to kindergarten.

nur-ture (nûr′chėr), *n*. **1,** food; nourishment; **2,** feeding; promotion of growth; education; training, esp. of children:—*v.t.* [nurtured, nurtur-ing], **1,** to bring up; educate; **2,** to nourish; feed; **3,** to cultivate.—*n*. **nur′tur-er.**

nut (nut), *n*. **1,** the dry fruit of certain trees, as the walnut, pecan, almond, etc., consisting of a kernel, or seed, enclosed in a hard, woody or leathery shell; **2,** the kernel itself; **3,** a small metal block with a threaded hole, used to screw on a bolt to make it fast; **4,** *Slang* the head; **5,** *Slang* an eccentric or crazy person; **6,** a person who has a great interest in something; enthusiast; as, a motorcycle *nut*.—*adj*. **nut′ty.**

nut-crack-er (nut′krak′ėr), *n*. **1,** an instrument for cracking nuts; **2,** a European bird of the crow family, feeding on nuts, seeds, and insects.

nut-meg (nut′meg′), *n*. **1,** the hard, nutlike, sweet-smelling kernel of the seed of an East Indies tree, which is grated and used as spice; **2,** the evergreen tree that bears this seed.

nu-tri-ent (nōō′trē-ent; nū′trē-ent), *n*. **1,** the special elements found in food that people, animals, and plants need to live and grow, such as proteins and vitamins; **2,** anything that nourishes and promotes growth:—*adj*. promoting growth; nourishing; as, milk is a *nutrient* fluid.

nu-tri-ment (nōō′tri-ment; nū′tri-ment), *n*. that which provides nourishment; food.

nu-tri-tion (nōō-trish′un; nū-trish′un), *n*. **1,** food; nourishment; **2,** the act of taking in food; **3,** the process by which an animal or plant uses food to promote growth.—*adj*. **nu-tri′tion-al.**—*adv*. **nu-tri′tion-al-ly.**—*n*. **nu-tri′tion-ist.**

nu-tri-tious (nōō-trish′us; nū-trish′us), *adj*. promoting growth; nourishing.—*adv*. **nu-tri′tious-ly.**—*n*. **nu-tri′tious-ness.**

nu-tri-tive (nōō′tri-tiv; nū′tri-tiv), *adj*. **1,** nourishing; nutritious; **2,** having to do with the process of food and growth in the body; as, the intestines play a major role in the *nutritive* process.

nuz-zle (nuz′l), *v.t.* [-zled, -zling], **1,** to rub or poke with the nose, muzzle, etc.; as, the pony *nuzzled* the boy's shoulder; **2,** to root up with the nose; as, the pig *nuzzled* the acorns:—*v.i.* **1,** to snuggle; nestle; as, the boat *nuzzled* the shore; **2,** to work with the nose or snout.

ny-lon (nī′lon′), *n*. a strong, elastic, synthetic fabric used for clothing, rope, machine parts, utensils, brush bristles, etc.:—**nylons,** women's stockings made of this material:—*adj*. of or pertaining to nylon; as, a *nylon* brush.

nymph (nimf), *n*. **1,** in *mythology*, a lesser goddess of nature, living in the mountains, woods, streams, etc.; **2,** in *zoology*, a pupa or chrysalis; also, an immature insect stage like an undeveloped adult form, seen in bugs, grasshoppers, etc.

O

O, o (ō), *n.* [*pl.* O's, o's], **1,** the 15th letter of the alphabet, following N; **2,** as a numeral, zero; **3,** anything shaped like the letter O; **4,** *abbrev.* short for *oxygen*:—*interj.* a word used in earnest address, as in prayer, pledge, etc.; as, *O* Canada! is our country's national anthem.

oaf (ōf), *n.* an awkward or foolish person; a lout.

oak (ōk), *n.* **1,** any of several large European and American trees bearing a one-celled fruit, the acorn, in a woody cup, and yielding a strong, tough wood used as timber or for making furniture; **2,** the wood of this tree:—*adj.* made of oak.—*adj.* **oak′en.**

oar (ôr), *n.* **1,** a light pole with a broad, flat or spoon-shaped blade at one end, used for rowing or steering a boat; **2,** one who rows a boat; an oarsman:—*v.t.* to row.

oars-man (ôrz′man), *n.* [*pl.* oarsmen (-men)], a man who rows; a rower.—*n.fem.* **oars′wom′an** (ôrz′woom′an).

o-a-sis (ō-ā′sis), *n.* [*pl.* oases (ō-ā′sēz)], **1,** a fertile place in a desert; **2,** any place or thing that is thought of as giving comfort or relief.

oat (ōt), *n.* (usually *oats*), a cereal plant or its seed, used as food for people and animals, esp. for horses.

oath (ōth), *n.* [*pl.* oaths (ō*th*z; ōths)], **1,** a solemn declaration that one speak the truth; as, the witness swore an *oath* to tell the truth; **2,** a profane use of the name of God or of any sacred thing; a swear word or curse.

oat-meal (ōt′mēl′), *n.* **1,** ground or rolled oats; meal made from oats; **2,** porridge or pudding made from this meal or from rolled oats.

ob- (ob-), *prefix* meaning **1,** *opposite* or *inverse*; as in *ob*verse; **2,** *to* or *toward*; as in *ob*ject; **3,** *in the way of*; as in *ob*vious; **4,** *completely*; as in *ob*solete (in this sense, often called an *intensive*). Note that in some compounds, the *b* may change; as in *oc*cur, *of*fer, *op*press, etc.

ob-du-rate (ob′doo-rit; ob′dū-rit), *adj.* **1,** not to be moved by appeals to the feelings; hard-hearted; **2,** unrepentant; **3,** stubborn; unyielding; firm.—*n.* **ob′du-ra-cy** (ob′door-a-si; ob′dū-ra-si).

o-be-di-ence (ō-bē′dē-ens), *n.* the act of yielding to control by others; submission to authority.—*adj.* **o-be′di-ent.**—*adv.* **o-be′di-ent-ly.**

o-bei-sance (ō-bā′sans; ōbē′), *n.* **1,** a movement or bending of the body that shows obedience or respect; a bow; **2,** deference or homage.

ob-e-lisk (ob′e-lisk), *n.* **1,** a four-sided, tapering stone pillar shaped at the top like a pyramid; **2,** in books, a mark of reference resembling a cross or dagger [†].

o-bese (ō-bēs′), *adj.* very fat.—*n.* **o-bese′ness; o-bes′i-ty** (ō-bē′si-ti).—*adv.* **o-bese′ly.**

o-bey (ō-bā′), *v.t.* **1,** to submit to the rule or authority of (a law or a person); to follow or mind; as, to *obey* the rules; to *obey* one's parents; **2,** to respond to the guidance or control of; as, a horse *obeys* the rein:—*v.i.* to yield; do as bidden.

o-bit (ō′bit; ō-bit′), *n. Colloq.* an obituary notice.

o-bit-u-ar-y (ō-bich′o͞o-ėr′i), *n.* [*pl.* obituaries], a printed notice of the death of a person, esp. one with a brief account of his or her life:—*adj.* pertaining to a person's death; as, an *obituary* notice.

[1]**ob-ject** (ob-jekt′), *v.i.* **1,** to offer opposition; as, he *objected* to my idea; **2,** to feel or express disapproval:—*v.t.* to urge as a reason against a plan, proposal, etc.; as, when asked to speak, she *objected* her lack of preparation.

[2]**ob-ject** (ob′jikt; ob′jekt′), *n.* **1,** that which can be seen or touched; **2,** a person or thing arousing some action or feeling; as, an *object* of charity; **3,** an aim; as, my *object* in school is to learn; **4,** in *grammar,* a word or clause governed by a verb: called *direct object* when immediately affected by the action of the verb, and *indirect object* when less directly affected; as, in the sentence "he gave (to) the boy money for a hat," "money" is the *direct object,* and "boy" the *indirect object,* of the verb "gave"; also, a word governed by a preposition; as, "hat" is the *object* of the preposition "for."

ob-jec-tion (ob-jek′shun), *n.* **1,** a feeling or expression of opposition or disapproval; **2,** a reason against anything.

ob-jec-tion-a-ble (ob-jek′shu-na-bl), *adj.* **1,** liable or open to opposition; **2,** arousing disapproval; undesirable; unpleasant.—*adv.* **ob-jec′tion-a-bly.**

ob-jec-tive (ob-jek′tiv), *n.* **1,** the end or goal toward which any action is directed; an aim or goal; **2,** that which exists outside the mind; an outward fact; reality; **3,** in *grammar,* the objective case; also, a word in the objective case; **4,** the lens of a microscope or telescope nearest to the object observed:—*adj.* **1,** serving as an end or goal of action or feeling; as, the *objective* point of military operations; **2,** having to do with an outward fact, or that which exists outside the mind, rather than with thoughts or feelings; not influenced by personal bias; impersonal: opposite of *subjective*; **3,** in *grammar*, naming the case of the object of a verb or a preposition.—*adv.* **ob-jec′tive-ly.**—*n.* **ob′jec-tiv′i-ty; ob-jec′tive-ness.**

ob-li-gate (ob′li-gāt′), *v.t.* [obligated, obligat-ing], to make someone do something because of a contract, promise, or feeling of duty, or because it is required by law; as, she was *obligated* to pay the parking ticket.

ob-li-ga-tion (ob′li-gā′shun), *n.* **1,** the binding power of a vow, promise, contract, or sense of duty; **2,** any duty imposed by law, by social relations, or by goodwill; as, the *obligations* of good citizenship; **3,** the state of being bound to perform some duty or to do something burdensome; as, under *obligation* to pay a debt; **4,** a written deed or bond by which one binds oneself to do a thing; a contract; a promise.—*adj.* **ob-li-ga-to-ry** (o-blig′a-tôr′i; ob′li-ga-tôr-i).

o-blige (o-blīj′), *v.t.* [obliged, oblig-ing], **1,** to compel by force, moral, legal, or physical; as, the police officer *obliged* his young prisoner to walk in front; **2,** to place under obligation; as, I was *obliged* to her for her help; **3,** to render a favour to; as, he *obliged* the audience with an encore.

o-blig-ing (o-blī′jing), *adj.* willing to do favours; courteous; kindly; as, an *obliging* neighbour.—*adv.* **o-blig′ing-ly.**

o-blique (ō-blēk′; o-blēk′), *adj.* neither horizontal nor vertical; slanting; also, neither perpendicular nor parallel.—*adv.* **o-blique′ly.**—*n.* **o-bliq′ui-ty** (ō-blik′wi-ti; o-blik′wi-ti).

o-blit-er-ate (o-blit′ė-rāt′; o-blit′ė-rāt′), *v.t.* [obliterat-ed, obliterat-ing], to erase or blot out; destroy all traces of; as, to *obliterate* a mark; time *obliterates* sorrow.—*n.* **o-blit′er-a′tion.**

o-bliv-i-on (o-bliv′ē-un), *n.* **1,** the state of being unaware or unconscious of one's surroundings; as, she was in *oblivion*; **2,** the state of being forgotten; **3,** forgetfulness of the past.—*adj.* **o-bliv′i-ous.**

ob-long (ob′long; ob′lông), *adj.* longer than broad: said usually of a figure that is rectangular or nearly so; as, an *oblong* box:—*n.* a rectangle or figure longer than it is broad.

ob-nox-ious (ob-nok′shus), *adj.* **1,** hateful; offensive; odious; **2,** very rude.—*adv.* **ob-nox′ious-ly.**—*n.* **ob-nox′ious-ness.**

o-boe (ō′bō), *n.* a high-pitched musical instrument of the woodwind group with a penetrating tone.—*n.* **o′bo-ist.**

OBOE

ob-scene (ob-sēn′), *adj.* **1,** offensive; repulsive; impure in language or action; indecent; lewd; **2,** excessive; as, an *obscene* flaunting of wealth.—*adv.* **ob-scene′ly.**—*n.* **ob-scen′i-ty** (ob-sen′i-ti).

ob-scure (ob-skūr′), *adj.* **1,** not clear or distinct; as, an *obscure* view; **2,** shadowy; dim; dark; as, an *obscure* room; **3,** not easily understood; as, an *obscure* meaning; **4,** illegible; as, faint and *obscure* writing; **5,** remote; unknown; as, he lived in an *obscure* little village; **6,** humble; inconspicuous; as, she occupied an *obscure* position:—*v.t.* [obscured, obscur-ing], **1,** to darken; hide from view; **2,** to disguise; render less intelligible.—*n.* **ob-scu′ri-ty; ob-scure′ness.**—*adv.* **ob-scure′ly.**

ob-se-qui-ous (ob-sē′kwē-us), *adj.* servile; fawning, usually in order to gain a selfish end.—*adv.* **ob-se′qui-ous-ly.**—*n.* **ob-se′ qui-ous-ness.**

ob-ser-vance (ob-zûr′vans), *n.* **1,** the act of keeping, or of paying attention to, laws or customs; as, the *observance* of the holiday; **2,** an act, as a ceremony, performed in token of worship or respect; **3,** the act of watching.

ob-ser-vant (ob-zûr′vant), *adj.* **1,** quick to notice; attentive; perceptive; **2,** watchful; mindful of duties or authority.—*adv.* **ob-ser′vant-ly.**

ob-ser-va-tion (ob′zėr-vā′shun), *n.* **1,** the act, power, or habit of seeing and noting; thorough, careful notice; **2,** that which is noticed or learned; **3,** a remark, judgment, or conclusion based on something noticed; **4,** the fact of being seen; as, he tried to avoid *observation*; **5,** the accurate examination of natural objects or events for the purpose of recording their cause, effect, etc.; as, *observation* of an eclipse.—*adj.* **ob′ser-va′tion-al.**

ob-ser-va-to-ry (ob-zûr′va-tôr′i), *n.* [*pl.* observatories], **1,** a building or place fitted up with a telescope and other instruments for studying astronomical and meteorological occurrences; **2,** a place equipped for observing nature; **3,** a tower or other high place built to give an extensive view.

ob-serve (ob-zûrv′), *v.t.* [observed, observ-ing], **1,** to take notice of; **2,** to watch closely; study; **3,** to keep or celebrate; commemorate; as, to *observe* Canada Day; **4,** to remark; as, she *observed* that the day was almost over; **5,** to comply with; as, to *observe* the social conventions:—*v.i.* **1,** to take notice; **2,** to comment.—*n.* **ob-serv′er.**—*adj.* **ob-serv′a-ble.**

ob-sess (ob-ses′), *v.t.* to rule the mind of; preoccupy; haunt; as, the idea *obsessed* him:—*v.i.* to engage in this type of thinking; as, she became *obsessed* with mystery novels.—*n.* **ob-ses′sion.**

ob-so-lete (ob′so-lēt′; ob′so-lēt′), *adj.* gone out of use; as, *obsolete* technology; no longer practised or accepted; as, an *obsolete* custom.—*adj.* **ob′so-les′cent.**—*n.* **ob′so-les′cence.**—*adv.* **ob′ so-lete′ly.**

ob-sta-cle (ob′sta-kl), *n.* that which hinders or stands in the way; an obstruction; impediment; hindrance; as, she overcame several *obstacles*, such as serious illness, and became an Olympic champion.

ob-stet-rics (ob-stet′riks), *n.pl.* used as *sing.* or *pl.* the science or branch of medicine dealing with the care and treatment of women before, during, and after childbirth.—*n.* **ob′ste-tri′cian.**—*adj.* **ob-stet′ric; ob-stet′ri-cal.**

ob-sti-nate (ob′sti-nit), *adj.* **1,** not yielding to argument, persuasion, or entreaty; headstrong; firm in opinion or purpose; stubborn, esp. perversely adherent to an opinion, etc.; **2,** not yielding to treatment; persistent, as a disease or illness; as, an *obstinate* cough.—*adv.* **ob′sti-nate-ly.**—*n.* **ob′sti-na-cy; ob′sti-nate-ness.**

ob-strep-er-ous (ob-strep′ėr-us), *adj.* noisy; unruly; turbulent; as, an *obstreperous* child.

ob-struct (ob-strukt′), *v.t.* **1,** to block up or close so as to prevent passage; **2,** to impede, prevent, or retard the progress of; as, to *obstruct* work; **3,** to be in the way of; cut off from sight; as, to *obstruct* the view.—*n.* **ob-struc′tion; ob-struc′tion-ist.**—*adj.* **ob-struc′tive** (as, *obstructive* tactics).

ob-tain (ob-tān′), *v.t.* to get possession of; gain; as, to *obtain* knowledge:—*v.i.* to be established in practice or use; prevail or be in fashion; as, that custom still *obtains* here.—*adj.* **ob-tain′a-ble.**

ob-trude (ob-trood′), *v.t.* [obtrud-ed, obtrud-ing], to thrust forward boldly:—*v.i.* to force oneself upon others; intrude.

ob-tru-sive (ob-troo′siv; ob-troo′ziv), *adj.* unduly inclined to push forward; intrusive; brash.

ob-tuse (ob-toos′; ob-tūs′), *adj.* **1,** not pointed or acute; blunt; **2,** of angles, greater than a right angle; **3,** dull or stupid; lacking understanding; as, an *obtuse* person.—*adv.* **ob-tuse′ly.**—*n.* **ob-tuse′ ness.**

ob-verse (ob-vûrs′; ob′vûrs′), *n.* **1,** the front surface, esp. of a coin or medal, with the main design on it: opposite of *reverse*; **2,** a corollary, different aspect, or counterpart of a fact or truth; as the science of medicine and its *obverse*, witchcraft:—*adj.* **1,** facing toward the observer; **2,** opposite; counterpart; **3,** having a base that is narrower than the top; as, an *obverse* leaf.

ob-vi-ate (ob′vē-āt′), *v.t.* [obviat-ed, obviat-ing], to remove, or clear away, beforehand, as difficulties or objections; to anticipate, foresee, and prevent.

ob-vi-ous (ob′vē-us), *adj.* easily understood or seen; clear; evident; plain; as, the effect is *obvious*.—*adv.* **ob′vi-ous-ly.**—*n.* **ob′vi-ous-ness.**

oc-ca-sion (o-kā′zhun), *n.* **1,** a particular or special event or celebration; as, to make her birthday an *occasion*; **2,** occurrence; as, on the *occasion* of her last visit; **3,** something that leads to unexpected results; an incidental cause; as, his carelessness was the *occasion* of the whole trouble; **4,** need; reason; as, having *occasion* to buy food; no *occasion* for anger; **5,** a favourable chance or opportunity; as, he seized the *occasion* to speak:—*v.t.* to cause; give rise to; as, the new company policy *occasioned* widespread dissatisfaction among employees.

oc-ca-sion-al (o-kā′zhu-nal), *adj.* **1,** happening now and then but not regularly; as, *occasional* visits; **2,** meant for, or suitable to, a special event; as, an *occasional* ceremony; **3,** acting as the cause of something; **4,** designed to be used only from time to time; as, *occasional* dishes.—*adv.* **oc-ca′sion-al-ly.**

oc-clu-sion (o-kloo′zhun), *n.* **1,** in *dentistry*, the shutting or fitting together of the cusps of the upper and lower teeth (in biting); **2,** in *chemistry*, absorption; as the *occlusion* of hydrogen by palladium; **3,** *medical*, closure or obstruction, as of the pores, arteries, etc.; **4,** in *meteorology*, the front that forms when a cold front overtakes a warm front and forces the warm air upward; an occluded front.—*v.t.* **oc-clude′** [occlud-ed, occlud-ing].

oc-cult (o-kult′; ok′ult′), *adj.* concealed; secret; mysterious: usually said of supernatural magic, alchemy, or astrology; as, the *occult* sciences.

oc-cu-pant (ok′ū-pant), *n.* one who dwells in, has possession of, or uses a house, property, or other place; as, that apartment has no *occupant*.—*n.* **oc′cu-pan-cy.**

oc-cu-pa-tion (ok′ū-pā′shun), *n.* **1,** the act of holding in possession or occupying; also, the time during which a property or position is held; **2,** regular business, employment, calling, or vocation; as, her *occupation* is dentistry; **3,** seizure or control; as, a military *occupation*.—*adj.* **oc′cu-pa′tion-al.**

oc-cu-py (ok′ū-pī′), *v.t.* [occupied, occupying], **1,** to take possession of; dwell in; as, to *occupy* an apartment; **2,** to fill or cover the time or space of; as, household duties *occupy* his day: **3,** to employ; busy; as, to *occupy* oneself with work; **4,** to hold; fill; as, to *occupy* the office of mayor.

oc-cur (o-kûr′), *v.i.* [occurred, occur-ring], **1,** to happen or take place; as, this mistake must not *occur* again; **2,** to be found; exist; as, such plants *occur* in abundance in the Northwest Territories; **3,** to come to mind; as, did it *occur* to you to go?—*n.* **oc-cur′rence.**

o-cean (ō′shan), *n.* **1,** the vast body of salt water covering three-quarters of the globe; also, any one of its chief divisions; as, the Atlantic, Pacific, Indian, and Arctic *oceans*;

Atlantic *Ocean;* **2,** a vast expanse or amount; as, an *ocean* of tears.—*adj.* **o′ce-an′ic.**

o-cean-og-ra-phy (o′sha-nog′ra-fi), *n.* geography or study dealing with the ocean.—*n.* **o′cean-og′ra-pher.**—*adj.* **o′cean-o-graph′ic; o′cean-o-graph′i-cal.**—*adv.* **o′cean-o-graph′i-cal-ly.**

o-ce-lot (os′e-lot′; ō′se-lot′), *n.* a nocturnal leopard-like cat, yellowish grey with elongated fawn-coloured spots edged in black, found in the southwestern U.S. and Central and South America.

o-chre or **o-cher** (ō′kėr), *n.* **1,** a fine clay (an ore of iron), pale yellow, orange, and red, used as paint pigments; **2,** a colour, esp. dark yellowy orange.

o′-clock (o-klok′), *adv.* according to the clock: short for *of the clock;* as, eight *o'clock.*

oc-ta-gon (ok′ta-gon′), *n.* a plane figure of eight sides and eight angles.—*adj.* **oc-tag′o-nal** (ok-tag′o-nal).

oc-tane (ok′tān′), *n.* a hydrocarbon, C_8H_{18}, obtained in the refining of petroleum: valuable for its high volatility:—**octane number,** a number used in grading the antiknock quality of a gasoline; as, a high-octane gasoline has a high *octane number.*

oc-tave (ok′tiv; ok′tāv′), *n.* **1,** in *music,* **a,** an interval of eight steps, as from C in the scale to the C next above or below; **b,** the series of tones comprised in such an interval; **c,** the harmonic combination of two tones at such an interval; **d,** the eighth note in the ordinary musical scale; **2,** any group of eight:—*adj.* consisting of eight.

Oc-to-ber (ok-tō′ber), *n.* the tenth month of the year, with 31 days, between September and November.

oc-to-ge-nar-i-an (ok′to-ji-nâr′ē-an), *n.* one who is between 80 and 90 years old:—*adj.* being between 80 and 90 years old.

oc-to-pus (ok′to-pus), *n.* [*pl.* octopuses or octopi (ok′to-pī′)], **1,** a sea mollusc with a large head and eight arms with suckers with which it holds on to its prey; **2,** any organization with several branches, esp. one with a harmful, far-reaching hold on the public.

oc-u-lar (ok′ū-lėr), *adj.* **1,** pertaining to the eye or to eyesight; **2,** resembling the eye; **3,** depending on, or seen by, the eye; as, *ocular* evidence.

oc-u-list (ok′ū-list), *n.* a physician who is skilled in the treatment of eye diseases; an *ophthalmologist.* Compare *optician* and *optometrist.*

odd (od), *adj.* **1,** not paired or matched with another; as, an *odd* glove; **2,** not exactly divisible by two; as, seven is an *odd* number; **3,** left over after equal division; extra; as, you may have the *odd* one; **4,** additional; as, 50 and some *odd* kilometres; also, plus a few more; as, 30 *odd;* **5,** unusual; as, an *odd* occurrence; **6,** eccentric; strange; peculiar; as, an *odd* person; **7,** occasional; as, *odd* jobs; **8,** not occupied; as, *odd* moments.—*adv.* **odd′ly.**—*n.* **odd′i-ty.**

odds (odz), *n.pl.* **1,** inequality; **2,** advantage; superiority of one as compared with another; as, the *odds* are in her favour; **3,** probability; as, the *odds* are that he will succeed; **4,** in betting, an advantage in the amount wagered to compensate for a smaller chance of winning; as, *odds* of five to one.

ode (ōd), *n.* **1,** a lyric poem expressing noble sentiments in a dignified style; **2,** anything, such as an artistic creation, that honours or glorifies something; as, her film is an *ode* to Canadian jazz legend Oscar Peterson.

o-di-ous (ō′dē-us), *adj.* **1,** deserving of or causing hatred; **2,** repulsive or offensive; as, his conduct was *odious.*—*adv.* **o′di-ous-ly.**—*n.* **o′di-ous-ness; o′di-um.**

o-dom-e-ter (ō-dom′i-tėr), *n.* an instrument or device that measures how far a vehicle has travelled: usually, a part of the *speedometer.*

o-dour or **o-dor** (ō′dėr), *n.* **1,** a scent; smell, whether pleasant or offensive; **2,** repute; as, in bad *odour;* **3,** characteristic or quality; as, the *odour* of hypocrisy.—*adj.* **o′dor-ous; o′dour-less; o′dor-if′er-ous.**

oe-soph-a-gus (i-sof′a-gus), *n.* Same as **esophagus.**

of (uv; ov), *prep.* **1,** from; as, to cure *of* an illness; north *of* the city; **2,** forced by; as, he did it *of* necessity; **3,** about; concerning; as, talk *of* success; news *of* her friend; **4,** in; as, quick *of* speech; 12 years *of* age; **5,** belonging to, related to, or connected with; as, the tip *of* the iceberg; **6,** containing; having; consisting of; as, a glass *of* milk; a person *of* great wisdom; a line *of* trees; **7,** made from; as, a house *of* cards; **8,** named; identity; as, the province *of* Québec; **9,** by; origin; as, the writings *of* Leacock; **10,** before, in telling time; as, 20 *of* six:—**of late,** lately.

off (of; ôf), *adv.* **1,** away from a place; as, to run *off;* to set *off* on a journey; **2,** from, so as not to be on; as, take *off* your coat, gloves, and hat; also, on one's way; as, he is *off* to town; **3,** into the condition of; as, to drop *off* to sleep; **4,** so as to stop the flow of; as, to turn *off* the gas; **5,** so as to end or be rid of; as, to break *off* a friendship; to shake *off* a feeling; **6,** in full; as, to pay *off* a mortgage; **7,** away from work; as, he has a day *off;* **8,** less: as, 10 per cent *off* for cash; **9,** into operation; as, the bomb went *off;* **10,** distant in time; as, holidays are two months *off:*—*adj.* **1,** on the far side of a vehicle; as, the *off*-side wheel; **2,** removed; not on; as, he stood with his hat *off;* **3,** not in use; disconnected; as, the heat is *off;* the computer was *off* all day; **4,**

given up; cancelled; as, the party is *off*; **5,** wrong; mistaken; as, he is *off* in his estimate; **6,** out of order; not functioning properly; unwell; as, he is feeling *off* today; **7,** unlucky; as, it is an *off* day for her; **8,** not up to the usual standard; as, his playing was *off* today; **9,** provided for; situated; as, she is well *off*; **10,** not very probable; as, an *off* chance; **11,** inferior; not fresh; as, the milk is *off*:—*prep.* **1,** away from; as, take your hands *off* the table; removed from; as, the captain of the hockey team was taken *off* the ice; **2,** distant from; as, a kilometre *off* shore; **3,** temporarily relieved of: as, he is *off* duty; **4,** less than; as, 10 per cent *off* the regular price:—*v.t. Slang* to kill or murder; as, the mobster *offed* the drug dealer.

off–col-our or **off–col-or** (ôf′–kul′ėr; ôf′–kul′ ėr), *adj.* **1,** varying from standard colour, as a gem; **2,** improper; as, an *off-colour* story.

of-fence or **of-fense** (o-fens′), *n.* **1,** a crime or illegal act; as, the *offence* landed him in jail; **2,** the act of offering an injury; as, rude behaviour is an *offence*; **3,** the state of being offended; **4,** an attack or assault; **5,** in *sports*, the part of a team that attacks, scores goals, etc.; **6,** the role of performing this.—*adj.* **of-fence′less.**

of-fend (o-fend′), *v.t.* **1,** to displease or make angry; vex or annoy; **2,** to hurt or cause pain:—*v.i.* **1,** to transgress; sin; to do wrong; as, to *offend* against the law; **2,** to do anything displeasing.—*n.* **of-fend′er.**

of-fen-sive (o-fen′siv), *adj.* **1,** insulting; as, *offensive* actions; **2,** disagreeable; repulsive; disgusting; as, an *offensive* odour; **3,** used in attack; as, *offensive* weapons; **4,** in *sports*, ready to or used to attack in an attempt to score; as, the *offensive* line:—*n.* an aggressive method or attitude; as, to take the *offensive*.—*adv.* **of-fen′sive-ly.**—*n.* **of-fen′sive-ness.**

of-fer (of′ėr; ôf′ėr), *n.* **1,** a proposal; **2,** a price bid; as, an *offer* on a house; **3,** an attempt or endeavour; as, to make an *offer* of resistance:—*v.t.* **1,** to present for acceptance or refusal; as, to *offer* money; **2,** to proffer; as, to *offer* help or advice; **3,** to propose; as, to *offer* a plan; **4,** to attempt to make, give, or put up; as, to *offer* resistance:—*v.i.* to present itself; appear; arise; as, a favourable opportunity soon *offered*.

of-fer-ing (of′ėr-ing; ôf′ėr-ing), *n.* **1,** the act of making a present or proposal; **2,** that which is offered or given; a gift, esp. a contribution to a church.

off-hand (of′hand′; ôf′hand′), *adj.* **1,** done without preparation; as, an *offhand* speech; **2,** informal; **3,** impolite or curt; as, *offhand* remarks:—*adv.* (of′hand′; ôf′hand′), without preparation; as, to say something *offhand*.—*adj.* **off′hand′ed.**—*adv.* **off′hand′ed-ly.**

of-fice (of′is; ôf′is), *n.* **1,** a place for the transaction of business; as, a doctor's *office*; an express *office*; **2,** the people who work in such a place; the staff; **3,** a position of trust, authority, or responsibility; as, the *office* of prime minister; **4,** a religious ceremony or rite; **5,** a service of kindness; as, through the good *offices*.

of-fi-cer (of′i-sėr; ôf′i-sėr), *n.* **1,** a person empowered to perform a public duty; as, a police *officer*; **2,** one elected or appointed to manage the affairs of an organization; as, the chief executive *officer*; **3,** in the army or navy, one appointed, esp. by commission, to a position of rank and authority; as, a commissioned *officer*.

of-fi-cial (o-fish′al), *n.* **1,** one who holds an office; an officer; as, the government *official*; **2,** in *sports*, the referee, umpire, or other individual who enforces the rules; as, hockey *officials*:—*adj.* **1,** pertaining to an office; as, *official* duties; **2,** derived from the proper authority; authorized; as, an *official* ruling; **3,** formal or ceremonial; as, *official* greetings.—*n.* **of-fi′cial-dom.**—*adv.* **of-fi′cial-ly.**

of-fi-ci-ate (o-fish′ē-āt′), *v.i.* [officiat-ed, officiat-ing], **1,** to perform the duties of an office, etc.; **2,** to carry out any type of function or ceremony; **3,** to act as a referee or umpire; as, she *officiated* at the hockey game.

of-fi-cious (o-fish′us), *adj.* **1,** too bold in offering services, esp. where they are not wanted or needed; meddling; **2,** domineering; **3,** unofficial or informal.—*adv.* **of-fi′cious-ly.**—*n.* **of-fi′cious-ness.**

off-ing (of′ing; ôf′ing), *n.* **1,** the open sea, visible from shore; **2,** distance; future; as, a job in the *offing*.

off–key (of′–kē′; ôf′–kē′), *adj.* and *adv.* **1,** in music, not in the correct musical key; **2,** improper; not well timed; as, *off-key* remarks.

off–line (of′–līn′; ôf′–līn′), *adj.* and *adv.* in *computing*, not connected to or under the control of a computer or computer network; as, an *off-line* printer; to work *off-line*.

off-load or **off–load** (of′lōd′; ôf′lōd′), *v.t.* **1,** to unload; as they *offloaded* the truck's cargo; **2,** to pass on or get rid of something, esp. something unpleasant; as, the government *offloaded* the expensive services to save money; **3,** in *computing*, to unload or transfer (information or data) to a peripheral device.

off–ramp (of′–ramp′; ôf′–ramp′), *n.* a sloping roadway that is an exit from a limited-access highway. Compare *on-ramp*.

off-set (of′set′; ôf′set′; of-set′; ôf-set′), *v.t.* [offset, offset-ting], **1,** to make up for; compensate; balance; as, her talent *offsets* her bad manners; **2,** to place out of line; **3,** to print using offset printing; as, to *offset* the brochure:—*n.* (of′set′; ôf′set′), **1,** that which proceeds or develops from something else; an offshoot; **2,** one thing that makes up for another; a compensation:—*adj.* pertaining to, of, or for offset:—**offset printing**, a process by which an inked impression is made on a rubber-covered roller and then transferred to paper.

off-shoot (of′sho͞ot′; ôf′sho͞ot′), *n.* **1,** a lateral branch from a main stem; **2,** anything that springs from a main stock; outgrowth; **3,** descendant; as, the *offshoot* of a noble house.

off-shore (of′shōr′; ôf′shōr′), *adj.* **1,** moving toward the sea; **2,** located out from the shore; **3,** outside the country; abroad; as, *offshore* banking:—*adv.* away from, or at some distance from, the shore; as, to drill for oil *offshore*.

off-side or **off-sides** (of′sīd′; ôf′sīd′; -sīdz′), *n.* in *football* and *hockey*, the act of being ahead of a certain line of play and hence ineligible to receive the ball or puck; as, the referee called many *offsides* in this game:—*adj.* **1,** of a player who is ahead of the puck or ball and therefore in an illegal position; **2,** of or relating to such a position; as, an *offside* pass:—*adv.* in the offside position; as, he was caught *offside*, and the play was whistled to a stop.

off-spring (of′spring′; ôf′spring′), *n.* [*pl.* offspring], **1,** a child or children; a descendant or descendants of a plant or animal; **2,** the result, product, or effect; offshoot; as, hockey helmets are the *offspring* of years of head injuries.

off–stage or **off-stage** (of′–stāj′; ôf′–stāj′), *adj.* **1,** in the area off the stage not normally seen by the audience; as, an *off-stage* whisper; **2,** nonperforming; as, her *off-stage* life was dull; **3,** away from the public eye; as, *off-stage* negotiations:—*adv.* behind the stage, in private, or away from the public eye; as, the negotiations took place *off-stage*.

off–the–rec·ord (of′–*th*ė–rek′ėrd; ôf′–*th*ė–rek′ėrd) *adj.* and *adv.* **1,** not intended for publication or release of news; as, the mayor's *off-the-record* remarks; the mayor made her remarks *off-the-record*; **2,** not to be written or recorded in the minutes of a meeting.

off–white (of′–wīt′; of′–hwīt′; ôf′–), *n.* a greyish-white colour:—*adj.* having a touch of grey in the white.

of-ten (of′en; of′ten; ôf′en; ôf′ten), *adv.* happening again and again; frequently.—*adv.* **of′ten-times′**.

o-gle (ō′gl; og′l), *v.t.* and *v.i.* [o-gled, o-gling], **1,** to eye or stare with familiar, lecherous, or amorous glances; as, to *ogle* someone; quit *ogling*; **2,** to regard greedily or with very interested attention:—*n.* an amorous or too familiar look or stare.—*n.* **o′gler.**

o-gre (ō′gėr), *n.* **1,** in fairy tales, a monster or giant who eats people; **2,** a cruel, ugly, brutal, or feared person.

oh (ō), *interj.* **1,** an exclamation of wonder, surprise, sorrow, shame, pain, etc.; **2,** an exclamation of understanding.

ohm (ōm), *n.* the unit of electrical resistance; the resistance of a circuit in which one volt produces a current of one ampere.

oil (oil), *n.* **1,** a greasy or fatty substance of animal, vegetable, or mineral origin, used variously as a lubricant, fuel, medicine, food, etc.; **2,** in *art*, **a,** a pigment mixed with oil; oil-colour; oil paint; **b,** a picture painted with this material:—*v.t.* **1,** to lubricate with oil; as, to *oil* the rusty hinges of the door; **2,** to smooth the way; as, she *oiled* the whole process; **3,** *Colloq.* to bribe.—*n.* **oil′er.**—*adj.* **oil′y.** Also, **oil′ field′; oil′ lamp′; oil′ paint′ing; oil′ patch′; oil′ rig′; oil′ slick′; oil′ tank′er; oil′ well′.**

oil-cloth (oil′kloth′; oil′klôth′), *n.* a coarse waterproof cloth coated with oil or oil paint, used for covering floors, shelves, tables, etc.

oil-skin (oil′skin′), *n.* **1,** a cloth treated with oil and made waterproof; **2,** waterproof clothing made of such cloth.

oint-ment (oint′ment), *n.* a medicinal semisolid preparation applied to the skin to heal or beautify; a salve.

OK, O.K., or **o-kay** (ō-kā′), *adj., adv., n.,* and *interj. Colloq.* all right; correct:—*v.t.* [OK'd, OK'ing], to endorse or acknowledge; as, the engineer and conductor *OK'd* the despatcher's orders.

o-kra (ō′kra), *n.* a plant cultivated for the seed pods, which are used as vegetables and in soups; gumbo.

old (ōld), *adj.* [old-er or eld-er, old-est or eld-est], **1,** having existed or lived many years; aged; as, an *old* oak; an *old* man; **2,** having an appearance of age; as, an *old* face; **3,** having reached a certain age; as, 21 years *old*; **4,** decayed by time; as, an *old* ruin; **5,** ancient; out of date; as, *old* customs; *old* coins; **6,** long used; not new; as, *old* shoes; **7,** long practised; as, *old* habits; **8,** belonging to the past; as, one's *old* home; **9,** long experienced; as, she is an *old* hand at that work; **10,** former; as, *old* students; **11,** tiresome; boring; as, her patter gets *old* fast:—*n.* **1,** former times; as, in days of *old*; **2,** a person of a specified age; as, a two-year-*old*; **3,** old people as a whole. Also, **old′ age′; old′–age′ home′; old′–age′ pen′sion; old′ age′ se-cur′i-ty; old′ coun′try; old′ growth′; old′ guard′; old′ hand′; old′ hat′; old′ mas′ter; old′ school′; old′–time′; old′–tim′er; old′ wives′′ tale′.**

old-en (ōl′den), *adj.* ancient; bygone; as, in *olden* times.

old–fash-ioned (ōld′–fash′und), *adj.* **1,** having or adhering to old ideas or customs; as, an *old-fashioned* person; **2,** out of style; out of date; outmoded; as, *old-fashioned* clothes.

old-world (ōld′-wûrld′), *adj.* **1,** of or relating to ancient times:—**Old World,** relating to the Eastern Hemisphere, esp. Europe; the world known before the discovery of the Americas: compare *New World.*

ol-fac-to-ry (ol-fak′to-ri; ol-fak′tri; ōl-), *adj.* pertaining to smelling; as, an *olfactory* nerve.

ol-i-gar-chy (ol′i-gär′ki; ŏ′li-), *n.* [*pl.* -chies (kiz)], *n.* **1,** a rule by a few, often vested in a clique, junta, or dominant class; **2,** the state or organization so governed; **3,** the members of such a group.—*n.* **ol′i-garch′.**—*adj.* **ol′i-gar′chic; ol′i-gar′chi-cal.**

ol-i-gop-o-ly (ol′i-gop′o-li; ŏ′li-), *n.* a state in which there exists a near-monopoly, with limited competition. Compare *monopoly.*

ol-ive (ol′iv), *n.* **1,** an Old World evergreen cultivated for its oily fruit; **2,** the fruit of this tree, which is brownish black when ripe; also, its wood; **3,** a dull yellowish-green colour, as of an unripe olive:—*adj.* of a dull yellowish-green or yellowish-brown colour:—**olive branch,** a gesture of goodwill or a sign of peace; as, to offer an *olive branch* to end the hostilities.

O-lym-pic games or **O-lym-pics** (ō-lim′pik), *n.pl.* **1,** in ancient Greece, a festival of athletic contests, music, poetry, drama, etc., celebrated every four years in honour of Zeus; in modern times, various international athletic contests held every four years in a chosen city (since 1896): they include track and field, swimming, pole-vaulting, skating, etc.: there are Summer Olympic games and Winter Olympic games.—*n.* **O-lym′pi-ad, 1,** the four-year interval between Olympic celebrations; **2,** the modern Olympic games celebration.

om-buds-man (om′budz′man; om′boodz′man) *n.* an official appointed by a government or other organization to investigate complaints by citizens, employees, the general public, etc.—*n.fem.* **om′buds-wom′an.**

o-me-ga (ō-meg′a; ō-mē′ga; ō′mā-ga), *n.* **1,** the last letter of the Greek alphabet; **2,** the last; the end; as, I am *alpha* and *omega*, the beginning and the end.

om-e-lette or **om-e-let** (om′e-let; om′let), *n.* a dish consisting of eggs and milk, often with other ingredients, beaten together, browned in a pan, and folded over.

o-men (ō′men), *n.* a prophetic sign of some future event; prediction.

om-i-nous (om′i-nus), *adj.* foreboding evil; threatening; a bad omen; as, the dark clouds overhead had an *ominous* look.—*adv.* **om′i-nous-ly.**

o-mis-sion (ō-mish′un), *n.* **1,** the act of omitting; state of being left out; **2,** something left out or neglected.

o-mit (ō-mit′), *v.t.* [omit-ted, omit-ting] **1,** to leave out; fail to include; as, tell me everything and do not *omit* a single detail; **2,** to neglect; leave undone.

om-ni-bus (om′ni-bus′; om′ni-bus), *n.* **1,** a book that includes several previously published works; as, an Atwood *omnibus;* **2,** a large four-wheeled public vehicle for passenger traffic over a fixed route; bus:—*adj.* including or providing for many different objects or cases; as, an *omnibus* bill was introduced into Parliament.

om-nip-o-tent (om-nip′o-tent), *adj.* all-powerful; almighty; as, an *omnipotent* ruler:—**the Omnipotent,** God.—*n.* **om-nip′o-tence; om-nip′o-ten-cy.**—*adv.* **om-nip′o-tent-ly.**

om-ni-pres-ent (om′ni-prez′ent), *adj.* present everywhere at the same time.—*n.* **om′ni-pres′ence.**

om-nis-cient (om-nish′ent), *adj.* knowing all; infinitely wise.—*n.* **om-nis′cience.**

om-niv-o-rous (om-niv′o-rus), *adj.* **1,** eating both animal and vegetable food, as bears, crows, etc.; **2,** figuratively, taking in everything with the mind; as, an *omnivorous* reader.—*n.* **om′ni-vore.**

on (on), *prep.* **1,** upon; supported by; as, to sit *on* a chair; **2,** in contact with the upper surface of; as, we live *on* the earth; **3,** covering; as, shoes *on* one's feet; **4,** along or by; situated by the edge of; as, Paris is *on* the Seine; **5,** in the state of; as, *on* fire; *on* sale; also, with a view to; as, to go *on* business; to go *on* a trip; **6,** toward; as, have pity *on* the needy; **7,** forming part of; as, *on* the committee; **8,** following; as, they are *on* his trail; **9,** in the direction of; as, the door opens *on* a lawn; from above in the direction of; as, the sun shone *on* the porch; **10,** about; concerning; as, an address *on* the environment; with reference to; as, to unite *on* a plan; **11,** at the time of; as, *on* June first; **12,** against or hanging from; as, a picture *on* the wall; **13,** upon the event of; as, she saw him *on* his arrival; **14,** by means of; as, to play *on* a violin; **15,** as witness; by the strength of; as, *on* my honour; **16,** after; in addition to; as, he made error *on* error:—*adv.* **1,** forward; as, to go *on*; without interruption; longer; as, to talk *on* and *on*; at or toward something; as, to look *on;* **2,** in such a way as to cover, support, etc.; as, put *on* your coat; **3,** into action or use; as, to turn *on* the gas; **4,** in progress; as, the fight is *on:*—*adj.* taking place; as, the television program is *on* tonight.

once (wuns), *adv.* **1,** at one time; formerly; as, *once* upon a time; this was *once* my home; **2,** one time only; as, to read it over *once*; **3,** at any time; ever; as, if *once* they lose heart, their cause will be lost:—*n.* one time; as, once is enough:—*conj.* as soon as; whenever; as, it will be a beautiful building *once* it is finished:—**at once, 1,** together; simultaneously; as, all talk *at once*; **2,** immediately; as, do it *at once*.

on-com-ing (on′kum′ing), *adj.* advancing; approaching; as, the *oncoming* snowstorm:—*n.* an approach; as, the *oncoming* of the snowstorm.

one (wun), *adj.* **1,** a; a single (person or thing); single; as, *one* person at a time; no *one* human can do that; **2,** a person named; as, I sold it to *one* Bill Chan; a certain; as, *one* day long ago; some; as, we'll go there *one* day very soon; **3,** united; as, they answered with *one* voice; to be forever *one*; **4,** the same; as, don't put all your eggs in *one* basket; they were all going in *one* direction; **5,** only; as, the *one* thing to do:—*n.* [*pl.* ones (wunz)], **1,** the first number in counting by units; also, its symbol, as 1, I, or i; also, any person or thing designated by the number; as, who has number *one*? **2,** a person or thing; as, never a *one*; pick me out some good *ones*; if this *one* is right, the other is wrong; what a *one* he is to get into trouble; *one* for all, and all for *one*:—*pron.* **1,** a single person or thing; as, *one* of them was lost; may I take *one* now?; they saw *one* another often; *one* by *one*; *one* is wise, another foolish; **2,** any person or thing, equivalent to the French "on"; as, *one* must eat to live; *one* can hardly sleep because of the noise.—*n.* **one′ness.**

on-er-ous (on′ėr-us; ōn′ėr-us), *adj.* **1,** burdensome; troublesome; weighty; as, an *onerous* duty; **2,** in *law*, having obligations that outweigh the benefits.

one-self (wun-self′), *pron.* **1,** a reflexive form of *one*; **2,** an emphatic form of *one*; **3,** one's true self.

on-ion (un′yun), *n.* **1,** a plant of the lily family, having a strong-smelling bulb used as food; **2,** the bulb of the plant.

on-ion-skin (un′yun-skin′), *n.* a thin, tough, translucent paper.

on–line (on′–līn′), *adj.* **1,** in *computing*, relating to, for, or of computers that are directly connected with a central computer or networked with several others and are ready to operate; **2,** being connected to the Internet:—*adv.* done while connected to another computer or network; as, to search *on-line* for databases on the topic.

on-look-er (on′look′ėr), *n.* a spectator, esp. a passive one; a casual observer.

on-ly (ōn′li), *adj.* **1,** without any other of the same kind or type; alone; sole; single; as, the *only* person there; an *only* daughter; **2,** best; finest; most suitable; as, it is the *only* perfume for me:—*adv.* **1,** without anyone or anything else; no more than; merely; solely; as, *only* six people showed up; **2,** at the very least; as, *only* too true; **3,** as recently as; as, *only* last week; **4,** in the final analysis; as, that will *only* make matters worse; **5,** except that; **6,** not until:—*conj.* except for the fact that; but; as, I'd go to the library, *only* I'm too tired.

on-o-mat-o-poe-ia (on′ō-mat′o-pē′ya), *n.* **1,** the forming of a word by imitating the sound associated with the thing or action named, such as *buzz, mumble, hiss, splash, trickle, cuckoo*; imitative harmony; **2,** the use of such words in poetry, etc.—*adj.* **on′o-mat-o-poe′ic** (-pē′ik).

on–ramp (on′–ramp), *n.* a sloping roadway that is an entrance to a limited access highway. Compare *off-ramp*.

on-rush (on′rush′), *n.* **1,** a violent onset; assault; headlong dash forward; as, an *onrush* of air, troops, etc.; **2,** a harsh attack, physical or verbal.

on-set (on′set′), *n.* **1,** an assault; attack; **2,** a first step or stage; beginning; commencement; as, the *onset* of the flu.

on-side (ōn′sīd′), *adj.* and *adv.* **1,** in *sports*, such as football, and hockey, according to the rules, being in the proper position for play: compare *off-side*; **2,** *Colloq.* in agreement with something or someone; as, the MPs are now *onside* with the new policy.

on-slaught (on′slôt′), *n.* **1,** a furious attack; **2,** a great deal; abundance; as, an *onslaught* of fan letters.

on-to (on′tōō), *prep.* **1,** to a position on or upon; as, she stepped *onto* the ice; **2,** *Colloq.* aware of; as, I'm *onto* your plan.

o-nus (ō′nus), *n.* a burden; duty; obligation; responsibility; as, the *onus* of proof is on you.

on-ward (on′wėrd), *adj.* advancing; as, the *onward* march of troops:—*adv.* (also *onwards*) forward; as, to move *onward*.

on-yx (on′iks), *n.* a kind of quartz in layers of various colours, such as brown, black, red, and white, often used as a gemstone.

oo-mi-ak (ōō′me-ak′), *n.* Same as **umiak**.

ooze (ōōz), *n.* **1,** a gentle flow, as of a stream through a marsh or sweat from pores; **2,** the process of seeping; **3,** mud or slime; **4,** any thick substance, esp. an unpleasant one; as, the primal *ooze*:—*v.i.* [oozed, ooz-ing], **1,** to flow gently; as, the water *oozed* through a crack in the wall; **2,** to leak or come out gradually; as, the news *oozed* out; **3,** to exude moisture; **4,** to emit (a quality); as, she *oozed* with charm:—*v.t.* **1,** to give off slowly; as, the sponge *oozed* moisture; **2,** to exude, emit, or radiate; as, he *oozes* confidence.—*adj.* **oo′zy.**

o-pal (ō′pal), *n.* a stone having constantly changing and delicate colours, often used as a gemstone.—*adj.* **o′pal-es′cent** (ō′pal-es′ent).—*n.* **o′pal-es′cence.**

o-paque (ō-pāk′), *adj.* **1,** not allowing light to pass through; as, *opaque* window shades; **2,** having no lustre; dull; not shining; as, an *opaque* surface; **3,** difficult to understand; obscure; as, *opaque* poetry; **4,** stupid, obtuse, or thickheaded.—*n.*

o-paci-ty (pas′); **o-paque′ness.**

o-pen (ō′pen), *adj.* **1,** not shut; unclosed; allowing things to pass through; as, an *open* door; **2,** unsealed or unstopped, as a letter or a bottle; **3,** uncovered or exposed; not enclosed; as, an *open* porch; **4,** not obstructed; as, a river *open* to navigation; **5,** having a clear space; clear of trees; as, *open* country; away from shore or land; as, the *open* sea; **6,** unfilled; unoccupied; vacant; as, the position is still *open*; **7,** undecided; as, an *open* question; **8,** mild; free from ice and snow; as, an *open* winter; **9,** unfolded or spread out; as, an *open* newspaper; **10,** not hidden; in plain view; as, *open* lawlessness; unreserved; frank; candid; as, an *open* criticism; **11,** public; free to all; unrestricted; as, an *open* meeting; **12,** unbiased; not prejudiced; ready to hear or to receive suggestion; as, an *open* mind; **13,** generous; as, to give with an *open* hand; **14,** frank; sincere; as, an *open* countenance; **15,** ready for business; doing business; as, the store is *open* 24 hours; **16,** in operation; as, an *open* mike; **17,** without protective covering; as, an *open* wound; **18,** available or accessible; as, the chemistry course is still *open*; **19,** without restriction; as, *open* season on politicians; **20,** in *sports,* of a player who is not closely covered by an opponent; as, to pass the puck to the *open* forward; **21,** generous; as, to be *open* with one's time; an *open* hand:—*v.t.* **1,** to unclose or unlock, as a window or door; **2,** to spread out or unfold, as a fan; **3,** to break the seal of or untie, as an envelope or package; **4,** to remove obstructions from; as, to *open* a road; **5,** to begin; as, to *open* the discussion; to *open* the bidding; **6,** to start or make available, as a business; as, to *open* a store; **7,** to unburden; as, to *open* one's mind to a friend; **8,** to offer for settlement, use, etc.; as, to *open* undeveloped land; **9,** in *computing,* to call up or access a computer file, document, or graphic in order to work with it:—*v.i.* **1,** to unclose itself; as, the door *opened;* **2,** to commence; as, the movie *opened* with an action scene; **3,** to lead to; as, the door *opens* into the hall; **4,** to unfold; as, the bud slowly *opened* in the sun; **5,** to become more clearly visible; as, the view *opened* before our eyes; **6,** to be shown or performed for the public; as, the play *opens* tonight:—*n.* **1,** any wide, clear space; outdoors; as, we lived in the *open* all summer; **2,** an opening; **3,** an undisguised or frank state or condition; as, to bring the problem into the *open*; **4,** a contest or tournament that allows both professionals and amateurs to compete; as, the Canadian *Open* is the leading golf tournament in Canada.

o-pen-ing (ō′pen-ing), *n.* **1,** the act of making, or the fact of becoming, open; **2,** a hole; gap; passage; aperture; as, an *opening* in a fence; **3,** a space in a woods with few trees and little undergrowth; a clearing; **4,** the first steps; a beginning; as, the *opening* of a trial; **5,** an opportunity or a chance; also, a vacant position; as, she applied for the *opening* in the bank; **6,** the beginning; the first performance of a play; as, tonight is the *opening* for the play; **7,** the initial series of moves in a game; as, the *opening* of her chess game was unique; **8,** the official ceremony to mark the start of a new business, building, etc.; as, tonight is the official *opening* for the new school library:—*adj.* first in order; as, the *opening* speech at the conference.

o-pen-ly (ō′pen-li), *adv.* without secrecy; as, he was *openly* envious of his friend.

o-pen-ness (ō′pen-nis), *n.* **1,** the state of being open; **2,** lack of secrecy; frankness; sincerity; as, *openness* of manner.

op-er-a (op′ėr-a), *n.* a drama set to music and produced with scenery and costumes.—*adj.* **o′per-at′ic** (op′ėr-at′ik).

op-er-ate (op′ėr-āt′), *v.i.* [operat-ed, operat-ing], **1,** to work; act; as, the engine *operates* smoothly; **2,** to produce or have a certain effect; as, many drugs *operate* harmfully on the body; **3,** to perform a surgical operation on the human body; as, she *operated* on the patient:—*v.t.* **1,** to cause to work; as, to *operate* a machine; **2,** to manage; work; as, to *operate* a business.

op-er-a-tion (op′ėr-ā′shun), *n.* **1,** the act, method, result, etc., of operating; **2,** regular action; as, the machine is in *operation*; **3,** action; a working; as, by *operation* of the law of gravitation, objects fall to earth; **4,** a surgical procedure upon the living body to remove diseased parts, treat an injury or ailment, correct a defect, etc.; **5,** a series of movements of an army or fleet; as, naval *operations*; **6,** a business, esp. one that is large; as, a large-scale farming *operation*; **7,** in *mathematics*, the manipulation of numbers by specific processes; as, addition and subtraction are two of the most common *operations* in mathematics; **8,** in *computing,* a single action performed by a computer program.

op-er-a-tive (op′ėr-a-tiv; op′ėr-ā′tiv), *adj.* **1,** having the power of acting; **2,** having effect; also, in operation; as, an *operative* law; **3,** concerned with work, either with the hands or with machinery; as, an *operative* art; **4,** having to do with surgical operations; as, *operative* surgery; **5,** effective or significant; as, education is the *operative* word:—*n.* (usually op′ėr-a-tiv), **1,** an artisan or skilled worker; as, *operatives* in a factory; **2,** a spy; **3,** a private investigator.

op-er-a-tor (op′ėr-ā′tėr), *n.* **1,** one who or that which works or acts; **2,** one who is employed by a telephone company to give information and assist customers; **3,** one who runs a machine; as, a computer *operator;* **4,** someone who owns or operates a business; **5,** an unscrupulous person who manipulates rules and people for gain; as, a smooth *operator.*

op-er-et-ta (op′ėr-et′a), *n.* a short, often humorous, musical play.

oph-thal-mol-o-gist (of′thal-mol′o-jist; op′thal-mol′o-jist), *n.* a physician skilled in eye functions and anatomy as well as treatment of eye diseases; an *oculist.* Compare *optician* and *optometrist.*

o-pi-ate (ō′pē-it; ō′pē-āt′), *n.* **1,** a medicine containing, or made from, opium, that causes sleep; **2,** anything that soothes; as, Karl Marx said, "Religion is the *opiate* of the people":—*adj.* soothing; quieting; as, an *opiate* drink.

o-pin-ion (ō-pin′yun), *n.* **1,** belief; appraisal; judgment; what one thinks about any subject; as, that is my *opinion* about the issue; **2,** estimation; as, I have a good *opinion* of him; **3,** the formal statement of an expert; as, a doctor's *opinion*; to get a second *opinion*; **4,** the prevailing view; the belief shared by most people; as, public *opinion*; **5,** in law, the formal decision of a judge or a court and the reasons for it; as, the judge's *opinion* was a long document.—*adj.* **o-pin′ion-at′ed.**

o-pi-um (ō′pē-um), *n.* **1,** a powerful narcotic drug used to cause sleep and dull pain, made from the juices of a certain kind of poppy; **2,** something having a stupefying or dulling effect.

o-pos-sum (o-pos′um), *n.* [*pl.* opossum or opossums], a small, four-legged American marsupial with dark-greyish fur, long nose, and a prehensile tail; if captured or in danger, it pretends to be dead. Also called *possum*; as, playing *possum.*

OPOSSUM

op-po-nent (o-pō′nent), *n.* one who works against, or takes the opposite side from, another in a debate, race, game, etc.; a rival, adversary, or antagonist:—*adj.* acting against each other; as, *opponent* forces in a volleyball game.

op-por-tune (op′ėr-tōōn′; op′ėr-tūn′), *adj.* well-timed; convenient; suitable; as, this is an *opportune* time to start the campaign.—*adv.* **op′por-tune-ly.**—*n.* **op′por-tun′ist.**

op-por-tu-ni-ty (op′ėr-tōō′ni-ti; op′ėr-tū′ni-ti), *n.* [*pl.* opportunities], convenient time or occasion; a good chance; as, I have not had the *opportunity* to e-mail him.

op-pose (o-pōz′), *v.t.* [opposed, oppos-ing], **1,** to stand in the way of; resist; to object to; as, to *oppose* a candidate's election; **2,** to set up in opposition or in contrast; **3,** to place opposite:—*v.i.* to be in opposition.

op-po-site (op′o-zit), *adj.* **1,** placed or standing in front of; across from; facing; as, the *opposite* side of the street; the houses were *opposite* to each other; **2,** completely different; contrary; as, in the *opposite* way; **3,** antagonistic; much different; as, *opposite* opinions:—*n.* something that is contrary or in marked contrast; as, "slow" is the *opposite* of "fast":—*prep.* **1,** facing or across from; as, to stand *opposite* the door; **2,** in the theatre, played in a complementary role; as, to play *opposite* her:—*adv.* on the opposite side or position; as, she sat *opposite* me at the table.—*adv.* **op′po-site-ly.**

op-po-si-tion (op′o-zish′un), *n.* **1,** the act of placing one thing opposite or against another; also, the state of being so placed; **2,** resistance; as, *opposition* to authority; **3,** something that is opposite or contrary to another, esp. a political party not in power; **4,** contrast; **5,** something that is an obstacle; **6,** diametrically opposed; as, the sun and Jupiter are in *opposition*:—**Opposition,** in a parliamentary system, the second-largest political party after the government.

op-press (o-pres′), *v.t.* **1,** to crush by hardships or severity; treat with cruelty; as, the cruel ruler *oppressed* his subjects; **2,** to weigh heavily upon; burden; as, sorrow *oppressed* him.—*n.* **op-pres′sor; op-press′ion.**

op-pres-sive (o-pres′iv), *adj.* **1,** unreasonably burdensome; as, *oppressive* laws; **2,** unjustly severe; tyrannical; as, an *oppressive* coach; **3,** overpowering, as, the *oppressive* heat and humidity.

opt (opt), *v.i.* to choose to do something; make a choice:—**opt out,** *Slang* to choose not to do something; as, she *opted out* of hockey.

op-tic (op′tik), *adj.* **1,** pertaining to the eye or to vision; as, an *optic* nerve; **2,** relating to, of, or for the science of optics.

op-ti-cal (op′ti-kal), *adj.* **1,** pertaining to the science of light and vision; **2,** pertaining to eyesight; **3,** constructed to aid vision; as, *optical* instruments; **4,** relating to, of, or for optics; **5,** in *computing,* the software that allows scanners to recognize printed or handwritten characters; as, *optical* character recognition.

op-ti-cian (op-tish′an), *n.* one who makes or sells eyeglasses, contact lenses, etc. Compare *oculist, ophthalmologist,* and *optometrist.*

op-tics (op′tiks), *n.pl.* used as *sing.* **1,** the science of light and its properties, vision, or other radiation such as ultraviolet and infrared radiation; as, fibre *optics;* **2,** the laws of vision and of making lenses, as for microscopes, telescopes, etc.

op-ti-mism (op′ti-mizm), *n.* **1,** the belief that everything in life happens for the best; **2,** the inclination to look on the best side of things: opposite of *pessimism.*—*n.* **op′ti-mist.**

op-ti-mis-tic (op′ti-mis′tik), *adj.* expecting things to turn out well; looking at the good side of a situation rather than at the bad side; as, she remained *optimistic* even after she lost her job.

op-ti-mum (op′ti-mum), *adj.* and *n.* best; most favourable; as, *optimum* conditions for growth.

op-tion (op′shun), *n.* **1,** the right or power of choosing; as, you have the *option* of taking it or leaving it; **2,** the act of choosing; choice; **3,** that which can be or is chosen; **4,** a right, usually purchased, to buy or sell something at a specified price within a specified time; **5,** in *football*, the play in which there is the choice of running with or passing the ball.—*adj.* **op′tion-al.**—*adv.* **op′tion-al-ly.**

op-tom-e-trist (op-tom′i-trist), *n.* one who examines and tests the eyes for the purpose of fitting glasses and contact lenses to correct any visual defect. Compare *oculist, ophthalmologist,* and *optician.*—*n.* **op-tom′e-try.**

opt–out (opt′–out′), *adj.* a provision allowing someone to decide not to do something; as, the contract had an *opt-out* clause.

op-u-lence (op′ū-lens), *n.* great riches, wealth, or affluence.

op-u-lent (op′ū-lent), *adj.* **1,** wealthy; rich, esp. ostentatiously so; **2,** luxurious; abundant; sumptuous; as, an *opulent* life of ease.

o-pus (ō′pus), *n.* [*pl.* opera (ō′pėr-a; op′ėr-a) or opuses], **1,** in *music*, a work or composition; as, *opus* 47 of Beethoven (the Kreutzer sonata); **2,** any artistic work, whether literary or musical, numbered or not.

or (ôr), *conj.* **1,** a connecting word introducing the second of two (or the last of several) possibilities; as, this book *or* that; go *or* stay, as you please; any city, town, *or* village: often used after *either* or *whether* to complete the sense; as, we'll go either tomorrow *or* Sunday; it is all the same whether you go *or* stay; **2,** that is; in other words; as, draw a triangle, *or* a figure with three sides and three angles; **3,** otherwise; or else; as, hurry, *or* you will be late; **4,** used to indicate an uncertain or approximate quantity; as, three *or* four choices.

or-a-cle (or′a-kl), *n.* **1,** among the ancients, the reply of a god, through an inspired priest, to a question or petition; **2,** the place where a god was consulted; a shrine; **3,** the person through whom the god spoke; **4,** a prophet or person of great wisdom; **5,** a prediction.—*adj.* **o-rac′u-lar** (o-rak′ū-lėr).

or-al (ōr′al), *adj.* **1,** spoken; not written; as, an *oral* quiz; **2,** of or pertaining to the mouth; as, the *oral* cavity; **3,** using speech and the lips, esp. in instructing the deaf; as, *oral* teaching; **4,** taken through the mouth; as, *oral* medicine; **5,** of or relating to the initial stage of development in psychoanalytical theory; as, the *oral* stage:—*n.* a verbal exam.—*adv.* **or′al-ly.**

or-ange (or′inj; ôr′enj), *n.* **1,** an evergreen tree with fragrant flowers and a deep golden-coloured or reddish-yellow juicy fruit; **2,** the fruit itself; **3,** the golden or reddish-yellow colour of such fruit:—*adj.* **1,** pertaining to such fruit; as, an *orange* grove; **2,** of a deep golden or reddish-yellow colour.

or-ange-ade (or′inj-ād′; ôr′enj-ād′), *n.* a drink of orange juice, sugar, and water.

o-rang–u-tan (ō-rang′–ōō-tan′; ôr′ang–ōō′tan) or **o-rang-ou-tang** (ō-rang′oo-tang′), *n.* a large, reddish-brown ape of Borneo and Sumatra.

o-ra-tion (o-rā′shun), *n.* **1,** a formal and dignified public speech, esp. one delivered on a particular occasion; as, a funeral *oration*; **2,** a speech given in a pompous or overblown manner.

or-a-tor (or′a-tėr), *n.* a public speaker, esp. one of skill and power.—*n.* **or′a-tor-y.**—*adj.* **or′a-tor′i-cal.**

orb (ôrb), *n.* a globe or sphere, esp. one of the celestial bodies, as the moon.

or-bit (ôr′bit), *n.* **1,** the bony cavity that contains the eye; **2,** the course followed by one celestial body around another, as the path of the earth around the sun; **3,** the area in which something or someone functions or has an influence; as, the *orbit* of the Liberal Party:—*v.t.* **1,** to revolve around; to circle; as, the space shuttle *orbited* the earth; **2,** to put into a circular path around; as, they *orbited* the new space station.—*adj.* **or′bit-al.**

or-chard (ôr′chėrd), *n.* a place where fruit or nut trees are grown; also, the trees themselves.

or-ches-tra (ôr′kes-tra), *n.* **1,** a large group of musical performers that usually includes strings, woodwinds, brass, and percussion instruments; **2,** the collection of instruments on which they play; **3,** in a theatre or opera house, the place occupied by the musicians; as, seats near the *orchestra*; **4,** the front part or all of the main floor of a theatre; as, seats in the *orchestra*:—*adj.* relating to, of, or for an orchestra; as, *orchestra* seats.—*adj.* **or-ches′tral.**

or-ches-trate (ôr′kes-trāt′), *v.t.* and *v.i.* [-trated, -trating], **1,** to compose or arrange (music) for an orchestra; **2,** to arrange matters to achieve some desired ends; as, she *orchestrated* the resignation of the president.—*n.* **or′ches-tra′tion.**

or-chid (ôr′kid), *n.* **1,** any one of a large family of plants bearing blossoms with two similar petals and a third (the lip), which is usually enlarged and often oddly shaped; **2,** the blossom of any of these plants; **3,** a light purple colour.

or-dain (ôr-dān′), *v.t.* **1,** to invest into the clergy by a special ceremony or rite;

2, to give orders for; decree; regulate by law; **3,** to predestine; foreordain.—*n.* **or′di-na′tion.**

or-deal (ôr′dēl), *n.* **1,** an ancient method of trial by fire, combat, etc., to determine the guilt or innocence of an accused person, the person being judged guilty if harmed; **2,** a severe or difficult trial or experience; as, the *ordeal* of studying for final exams.

order (ôr′dėr), *n.* **1,** sequence; succession; as, alphabetical *order*; also, regular arrangement; as, the house is in *order*; **2,** a fixed method of acting; established custom; as, the *order* of church worship; **3,** public observance of law; as, *order* in the streets; **4,** working condition; as, the automated teller machine was out of *order*; **5,** rule; command; as, by *order* of the prime minister; **6,** a direction to buy, sell, or supply goods; as, an *order* for books; also, the goods bought or sold; **7,** a written direction to pay money; as, a money *order*; **8,** a rank, degree, or class in the social scale; as the *order* of nobility; **9,** a group of persons united in a society, esp. as an honour; as, *Order* of Canada; **10,** a monastic society; as, the Franciscan *order*; also, the rank or degree of a priest or clergyman; as, the *order* of deacon, priest, bishop, etc.; **11,** a badge indicative of an honour or membership in a society; as, he wore all his *orders*; **12,** in *botany* and *zoology*, a group larger than the family and smaller than the class; as, butterflies and moths belong to the same *order*; **13,** in *architecture*, the form of a column and the capital just above it; as, the Doric, Ionic, and Corinthian *orders* of Greek architecture; **14,** a serving of food in a restaurant; as, an *order* of fries:—*v.t.* **1,** to command; as, to *order* someone to appear before court; **2,** to regulate or manage; direct; **3,** to give an order for; as, to *order* pizza.

order–in–council (ôr′dėr–in–koun′sel), *n.* [*pl.* orders-in-council], in Canada, an official order or decree issued by the authority of the governor general (federal) or lieutenant governor (provincial).

or-der-ly (ôr′dėr-li), *adj.* **1,** neat or tidy; as, an *orderly* room; also, having regard for order and system; as, an *orderly* person; **2,** well conducted or managed; as, an *orderly* meeting; **3,** methodical; as, done in an *orderly* manner; **4,** well behaved; peaceable; as, an *orderly* crowd:—*n.* [*pl.* orderlies], **1,** a soldier who attends an officer to carry out his or her orders; **2,** a person who acts as an attendant in a hospital.—*n.* **or′der-li-ness.**

or-di-nal (ôr′di-nal), *n.* **1,** a book of instructions for Christian ceremonies; **2,** an ordinal number:—**ordinal number,** one of the numbers (*first, second, third,* etc.) showing order or position in a series: distinguished from *cardinal numbers* (*one, two, three,* etc.):—*adj.* **1,** being of or showing position or order; **2,** relating to, of, or for a plant or animal order.

or-di-nance (ôr′di-nans), *n.* **1,** an authoritative rule, law, or decree; as, a city *ordinance* against unlicensed cats; **2,** an established religious ceremony or rite.

or-di-nar-i-ly (ôr′di-na-ri-li), *adv.* usually; commonly; in most cases; normally; as, *ordinarily*, he orders fries with his burger.

or-di-nar-y (ôr′di-nâr-i), *adj.* **1,** usual; customary; regular; normal; as, he followed his *ordinary* routine; **2,** commonplace; not distinguished; as, an *ordinary* dress; an *ordinary* student; **3,** second-rate; below average; boring; inferior; as, a dull, *ordinary* speech.

or-di-nate (ôr′di-nit; ôr′di-nāt′), *n.* in *plane geometry*, one of two lines used in fixing a point on a graph.

ORDINATE

ord-nance (ôrd′nans), *n.* **1,** the heavy guns used in warfare; artillery; **2,** military supplies, such as ammunition, weapons, army vehicles, etc.; **3,** the branch of the military that deals with such supplies.

ore (ōr), *n.* a metal-bearing mineral or rock, esp. one containing sufficient metal to be commercially valuable.

or-gan (ôr′gan), *n.* **1,** a part of a plant or animal fitted for a special use; as, the ear is the *organ* of hearing; **2,** a medium of public communication, as a newspaper, political or company newsletter, etc.; **3,** an agency by which something is done; as, the court is an *organ* of justice; **4,** a large, musical wind instrument with one or many sets of pipes, sounded by air blown from bellows and played by one or more keyboards; as, a pipe *organ*; **5,** a similar instrument that produces sound electronically; **6,** a small, simple wind instrument; as, she plays the mouth *organ*.—*n.* **or′gan-ist.**

or-gan-ic (ôr-gan′ik), *adj.* **1,** of, relating to, or affecting some organ of the body; as, an *organic* disease; **2,** relating to, or derived from, something that lives or has lived; as, fossils are remains of *organic* bodies; **3,** belonging to, or inherent in, the organization or constitution of something; fundamental; as, an *organic* fault; **4,** having a systematic arrangement of parts; as, an *organic* whole; **5,** of food, grown without artificial fertilizers, pest controls, etc.; as, *organic* vegetables; **6,** made up of plant or animal matter; as, *organic* fertilizer; **7,** something containing carbon; **8,** harmonious fitting together; as, *organic* unity; **9,** systematic or natural development; as, *organic* growth; **10,** fundamental; essential; as, the heroine is an *organic* part of the book.—*adv.* **or-gan′i-cal-ly.**

or-gan-ism (ôr′gan-izm), *n.* **1,** any living plant or animal, esp. one composed of parts performing special duties but dependent upon each other; **2,** anything like such a body in having many parts, special functions, etc.; as, the social *organism.*

or-gan-i-za-tion (ôr′gan-i-zā′shun; -ī-zā′shun), *n.* **1,** the act of grouping and arranging related parts into one whole, or the condition of being so organized; as, the *organization* of a campaign; the *organization* of a club; **2,** a body made up of parts dependent upon one another but each functioning separately; also, the way in which the separate parts of a living being are united in a whole; as, the *organization* of the human body; **3,** a body of persons united for some end or work; an association; **4,** a company or business.

or-gan-ize (ôr′gan-īz′), *v.t.* [organized, organiz-ing], **1,** to cause to unite and work together in orderly fashion; as, to *organize* volunteers for a campaign; **2,** to unionize; as, they *organized* the factory; **3,** to arrange in good order by systematic planning; as, to *organize* one's facts:—*v.i.* **1,** to arrange parts into a systematic, coherent whole; **2,** to become organized, esp. with regard to a labour union.—*n.* **or′gan-iz′er.**

or-gasm (ôr′gazm), *n.* the highest point of excitement, esp. the climax of the sexual act.—*adj.* **or-gas′mic.**

or-gy (ôr′ji), *n.* [*pl.* orgies], **1,** among the ancient Greeks and Romans, a secret celebration in honour of the gods, esp. the god of wine, accompanied by wild singing, dancing, sexual activity, etc.; **2,** a drunken revel, esp. one that is excessive and lacking in any control; **3,** something resembling such activity; as, an *orgy* of destruction.—*adj.* **or′gi-as′tic** (ji-); as, *orgiastic* rites.

or-i-ent (ôr′i-ent), *n.* the east: opposite of *west:*—**Orient,** the, countries of Asia or the Far East, esp. east Asia:—*adj.* bright; clear; lustrous, as pearls:—*v.t.* (ôr′i-ent′), **1,** to place so as to face the east; **2,** to place (a person or oneself) in right relation to unfamiliar conditions; **3,** to make or become familiar with something new; **4,** to focus or aim a story or other communication at a particular group; as, to *orient* the program toward New Canadians:—*v.i.* **1,** to face the east; **2,** become aligned or adjusted.—*adj.* **or′i-en′tal; Or′i-en′tal.**—*n.* **Or′i-en′tal** (an Asian person: sometimes considered offensive); **o′ri-en-ta′tion.**

or-i-fice (ôr′i-fis), *n.* a mouth or other opening, such as a hole or vent.

or-i-gin (ôr′i-jin), *n.* **1,** a source; beginning; as, a word of French *origin;* **2,** parentage; ancestry; as, she comes from good *origins;* **3,** in *mathematics,* the point of intersection of coordinate axes; **4,** the point of attachment of a muscle.

o-rig-i-nal (o-rij′i-nal), *adj.* **1,** of or relating to the beginning; first in existence or order; initial; preceding all others; primary; as, the *original* edition of a book; *original* cast of a play; **2,** not copied; as, an *original* painting; not translated; as, he read the story in the *original* French; **3,** new; not imitative or derivative; as, an *original* idea; **4,** able to create or invent something new; as, an *original* writer:—*n.* **1,** that from which anything is copied; as, the *original* of that picture is in the museum; **2,** the literary text, or the language of such a text, from which a translation is made; **3,** an unusual person; a character; an eccentric; as, he is an *original.*—*adv.* **o-rig′i-nal-ly.**

o-rig-i-nal-i-ty (o-rij′i-nal′i-ti), *n.* [*pl.* originalities], **1,** the ability to create or make something new; as, the *originality* of an inventor; **2,** the quality of being new or novel; as, the *originality* of a story.

o-rig-i-nal-ly (o-rij′i-na-li), *adv.* from the start; at first.

o-rig-i-nate (o-rig′i-nāt′), *v.t.* [originat-ed, originat-ing], to bring into existence; invent; create; as, to *originate* a style of dancing:—*v.i.* to begin to exist; start; as, the fire *originated* in the garage; the flight *originated* in Calgary.—*n.* **o-rig′i-na′tion; o-rig′i-na′tor.**

or-i-ole (ôr′ē-ōl′), *n.* **1,** any of various black-and-yellow songbirds of the Old World, similar to the crow, that build hanging nests; **2,** any of various American songbirds that build hanging nests, as the orange-and-black Baltimore oriole and the black-and-chestnut orchard oriole; esp. the Baltimore oriole.

O-ri-on (ō-rī′un), *n.* **1,** a constellation of seven stars near the celestial equator: noted for its belt of three bright stars; **2,** in *Greek mythology,* a great hunter who was loved by the goddess Diana.

or-na-ment (ôr′na-ment), *n.* **1,** anything that adorns; decoration; as, Christmas tree *ornaments;* **2,** a thing or person that adds beauty, honour, or grace to the surroundings:—*v.t.* (ôr′na-ment), to adorn; bedeck; as, to *ornament* a hall with holly.—*adj.* **or′na-men′tal.**—*n.* **or′na-men-ta′tion.**

or-nate (ôr-nāt′), *adj.* **1,** elaborately decorated or adorned; **2,** marked by an elaborate, flashy, showy, or florid style, esp. in rhetoric or writing; as, an *ornate* speech.

or-ner-y (ôr′nėr-i), *adj.* grumpy; cantankerous; ugly or mean in disposition; hard to manage.—*n.* **or′ner-i-ness′.**

or-ni-thol-o-gy (ôr′ni-thol′o-ji), *n.* **1,** the branch of zoology that deals with birds; **2,** a book or other study on this subject.—*n.* **or′ni-thol′o-gist.**—*adj.* **or′ni-tho-log′i-cal.**

or-phan (ôr′fan), *n.* **1,** a child whose parents are dead; **2,** a young animal that has lost its mother; **3,** something that is deprived of protection or support; as, *orphan* technology:—*adj.* being without parents:—*v.t.* to deprive a child or young animal of a parent or parents.

or-phan-age (ôr′fan-ij), *n.* an institution or home for the care of orphans.

or-tho-(ôr′thō-), *prefix* meaning *straight, (up)right, correct;* as in *ortho*graphy (correct spelling), *ortho*logy (the art of using words correctly).

or-tho-don-tist (ôr′tho-don′tist), *n.* a dentist who specializes in straightening teeth and other teeth irregularities.

or-tho-dox (ôr′tho-doks), *adj.* **1,** holding what is regarded as the correct or sound opinion, esp. in regard to religion; as, an *orthodox* Muslim; **2,** approved; accepted; typical; customary; also, conventional; as, *orthodox* behaviour:—**Orthodox,** of, or relating to Orthodox Judaism or the Eastern Orthodox Church.—*n.* **or′tho-dox′y.**

or-tho-pe-dic (ôr′tho-pē′dik), *adj.* of or related to the branch of medicine that deals with the treatment of bones, muscles, and the skeletal system; as, *orthopedic* shoes.

or-tho-pe-dics or **or-tho-pae-dics** (ôr′tho-pē′diks), *n.* the branch of medicine that deals with the treatment of bones, muscles, and the skeletal system.

os-cil-late (os′i-lāt′), *v.i.* [oscil-lat-ed, oscil-lat-ing], **1,** to swing to and fro, as a clock's pendulum; vibrate; **2,** to waver, as in purpose or opinion; fluctuate; vacillate; **3,** to alternate or vary, as an electric current; as, a vacuum tube *oscillates.*—*n.* **os′cil-la′tion; os′cil-la′tor.**

os-mo-sis (os-mō′sis; oz-), *n.* **1,** the tendency of liquids to pass through a porous membrane or partition that separates them: living cells depend on osmosis for most of their activity; **2,** the gradual assimilation of knowledge, esp. if effortlessly or unconsciously absorbed; as, she learned French by *osmosis* while living in Montreal.—*adj.* **os-mot′ic** (os-mot′ik).

os-prey (os′pri; os′prā), *n.* a large fish-eating hawk.

os-si-fy (os′i-fī′), *v.t.* and *v.i.* [-fied, -fying], **1,** to change, or become changed, into bone, or hard like bone; **2,** to make or become hard, inflexible, or unprogressive.—*n.* **os′si-fi-ca′tion.**

os-ten-si-ble (os-ten′si-bl), *adj.* professed; apparent; as, an *ostensible* reason.—*adv.* **os-ten′si-bly.**

os-ten-ta-tion (os′ten-ta′shun), *n.* unnecessary show; ambitious, pretentious, or vain display.—*adj.* **os′ten-ta′tious.**

os-te-o- (os′ti-ō′-), *n. prefix* meaning *bone;* as in *osteo*myelitis (inflammation of bone marrow), *osteo*porosis (a disease causing porous and brittle bones).

os-te-op-a-thy (os′ti-op′a-thi), *n.* a system of medicine which, while recognizing the value of ordinary medical and surgical treatment, holds that disease is chiefly due to displacements of parts of the body, esp. of the vertebrae of the spinal column, and in healing lays stress on working the displaced parts into place with the hands, along with conventional therapies.—*n.* **os′te-o-path′.**—*adj.* **os′te-o-path′ic.**

ost-ler (os′lėr), *n.* Same as **hostler.**

os-tra-cize (os′tra-sīz′), *v.t.* [-cized, -cizing], **1,** in *ancient Greece,* to banish temporarily by popular vote; **2,** to exclude from social fellowship, privileges, etc.; as, his club *ostracized* him for his radical opinions.

os-trich (os′trich), *n.* a swift-running African bird with long legs and a long neck, which cannot fly but can run very fast: the largest known bird.

oth-er (u*th*′ėr), *adj.* **1,** not the same; different; as, I have *other* matters to attend to; **2,** additional; extra; further; added; more; as, I have *other* sisters; **3,** opposite; as, the *other* side of the street; **4,** alternating; second; as, every *other* line; **5,** those not already mentioned; remaining; **6,** recently; as, the *other* day:—*adv.* otherwise; as, she could not do *other* than help him:—*pron.* and *n.* **1,** the second person or thing of two; as, one or the *other* of you must do it; some students stayed, *others* left; they played against each *other;* **2,** a different person or thing; as, do good to *others;* have you any *other?;* there will be many *others* here; the few *others* I have.

oth-er-wise (u*th*′ėr-wīz′), *adv.* **1,** in a different way; differently; as, you evidently think *otherwise;* **2,** in different conditions or respects; as, I know him professionally, but not *otherwise:*—*conj.* else; as, it was told to me in confidence, *otherwise* I would tell you:—*adj.* different; as, the facts were *otherwise.*

ot-ter (ot′ėr), *n.* [*pl.* otter or otters], **1,** a fish-eating animal with webbed feet that lives in and near the water; **2,** the fur of this animal.

ot-to-man (ot′ō-man), *n.* **1,** a cushioned footstool; **2,** a small, padded, backless seat:—**Ottoman,** pertaining to the Turks or Turkey, as the *Ottoman* Empire (a dynasty about 1300 A.D.).

ouch (ouch), *interj.* an exclamation expressing sudden pain or annoyance.

ought (ôt), *v.i.* [no other form], **1,** to be or feel bound, obliged, or under obligation; as, we *ought* to finish our work; we *ought* to have paid the workers; **2,** to be expected; as, this top *ought* to fit the jar; you *ought* to have been able to go; **3,** to be forced by necessity; as, we *ought* to go at once if he is to catch his plane; **4,** to need; as, this shirt *ought* to have long sleeves.

ounce (ouns), *n.* **1,** a unit of measuring weight in the imperial system equal to about 28 grams or 1/16 of a pound avoirdupois; **2,** a unit of measuring weight in the apothecary system equal to about 31 grams or 1/12 of a pound in either troy or apothecaries' weight; **3,** fluid ounce; a unit for measuring liquids in the imperial system equal to about 28 cm^3 or 1/20 of a pint; **4,** a small amount; as, "an *ounce* of prevention is worth a pound of cure."

our (our), *adj.* a possessive form of the personal pronoun *we*: **1,** belonging to us; as, *our* house; **2,** of or relating to us; as, *our* children; *our* friends; in *our* midst.

ours (ourz), a possessive form of the personal pronoun *we*, used alone: **1,** as *adj.* in the predicate, belonging to us; as, whose car is that? it is *ours*; **2,** as *pron.*, a person or thing that belongs to us; as, their car is black, but *ours* is blue.

our-selves (our-selvz′), *pron.* **1,** a reflexive form of *us*; our own selves; as, we fooled *ourselves* instead; we praised *ourselves* for a job well done; **2,** an emphatic form of *we*; as, we painted the room *ourselves*; **3,** usual or normal selves; as, to feel *ourselves* again after our illness.

oust (oust), *v.t.* to drive, push, or turn out; as, to *oust* a person from a position.—*n.* **oust′er.**

out (out), *adv.* **1,** outdoors; not within doors; as, stay *out* in the fresh air; not in; not at home; absent; as, she is *out* today; the doctor is *out*; not within the limits; as, he is *out* of town; at liberty; as, *out* on bail; **2,** abroad; away from home; forth; as, to go *out* to India; to send a chair *out* to be fixed; **3,** not in a state or condition; as, *out* of practice; my elbow is *out* of joint; not in power or office; as, the Conservatives are *out*; **4,** forth from concealment; into view; as, the sun came *out*; he brought *out* an old bag; in or into full bloom; as, the flowers are *out*; into the open; as, the story came *out*; **5,** to or at a conclusion or end; resolved; determined; as, the fire burned *out*; to figure *out* a problem; March went *out* like a lion; **6,** from one's possession or use to another's; as, the bank lends *out* money; **7,** in error; as, your estimate is *out* by a large margin; **8,** minus; as, she is *out* five dollars; **9,** so as to clear of obstruction; as, to sweep *out* a room; **10,** on strike; as, the workers are *out*; **11,** loudly; without restraint; as, to speak *out*; **12,** in *baseball*, not at bat, as a team; fielding; also, deprived of the right to continue at bat or to continue a run around the bases for a score; **13,** away from the inside; as, the water rushed *out* of the hole; **14,** away from the usual place; as, the doctor has stepped *out* for a minute; **15,** so as to be available for use; as, to give *out* free tickets; **16,** not a choice; not possible; as, the beach this weekend is *out* unless I get my homework done; **17,** not in style; no longer popular; as, wide collars are *out* this year; **18,** exhausted; as, we're *out* of coffee; **19,** not possible, not to be considered; as, *out* of the question:—*adj.* **1,** external; as, *out* surface; **2,** distant; outlying; as, the *out* lands; **3,** directed outward or away from the centre; as, the *out* basket; **4,** *Colloq.* openly homosexual; as, an *out* gay person:—*prep.* out of; through; as, to step *out* the door; look *out* the window:—*n.* **1,** one who is not in office or power; **2,** in *baseball*, the side not having its inning; a player who is retired; a play in which a player is retired; **3,** *Colloq.* an escape route or excuse; as, to have an *out* for not attending the meeting:—*v.i.* to become known; as, the truth will *out*:—*v.t.* **1,** in *sports*, to hit or throw (a ball) outside the playing area; **2,** *Colloq.* to force out.

out– (out), *prefix* meaning **1,** *surpassing, exceeding, better than, more than, beyond*; as in *out*flank, *out*fox, *out*guess, *out*live, *out*manoeuvre, *out*number, *out*play, *out*rank, *out*reach, *out*score, *out*shoot, *out*smart, *out*work; **2,** *away from, extending*; as in *out*flow, *out*pour, *out*stretch; **3,** *separate, outside*; as in *out*back, *out*building, *out*take.

out–and–out (out′–n–out′), *adj.* complete; thorough; utter; great; as, an *out-and-out* injustice; an *out-and-out* liar.

out-bid (out-bid′), *v.t.* [outbid, outbidding], to offer to pay more for something than (another person); as, she *outbid* all other bidders at the auction.

out-board (out′bôrd′), *n.* **1,** an outboard motor; a portable gasoline engine with a propeller and tiller, clamped on to the stern of a boat; **2,** a boat with such a motor:—*adj.* situated away from the centre of a ship or airplane.

out-bound (out′bound′), *adj.* outward bound; leaving a port, railway terminal, etc.; as, an airplane *outbound* for Rome.

out-break (out′brāk′), *n.* **1,** a sudden bursting forth; an epidemic; as, an *outbreak* of the flu; **2,** a revolt; riot.

out-burst (out′bûrst′), *n.* **1,** a breaking forth; an eruption or outbreak; as, an *outburst* of anger; *outburst* of tears; **2,** an explosion or surge of activity.

out-cast (out′kast′), *n.* one who is driven from home, friends, or country; an exile; a pariah:—*adj.* **1,** friendless; homeless; **2,** forlorn; wretched.

out-class (out-klås′), *v.t.* to surpass or excel in quality, skill, etc.

out-come (out′kum′), *n.* the result or consequence of an act; as, the *outcome* of the vote.

out-crop (out′krop′), *n.* and *v.i.* in *geology*, a vein or stratum of rock or mineral that emerges on the surface.

out-cry (out′krī′), *n.* [*pl.* outcries], **1,** a loud cry; clamour; uproar; confused noise;

2, a protest, esp. a vehement one; as, a public *outcry* against the new tax.

out-dat-ed (out-dā′ted), *adj.* old-fashioned; obsolete; as, an *outdated* typewriter.

out-dis-tance (out-dis′tans), *v.t.* [outdistanced, outdistanc-ing], **1,** to outstrip; surpass, outrun, esp. in a race; **2,** to surpass by a wide margin; put to shame; as, she *outdistanced* all other candidates.

out-do (out-dōō′), *v.t.* [*p.t.* outdid (-did′), *p.p.* outdone (-dun′), *p.pr.* outdo-ing], to surpass; excel.

out-door (out′dōr′), *adj.* not inside the walls of a building; done, used, or played in the open air; as, *outdoor* sports.

out-doors (out′dōrz′), *n.* the world outside of the walls of buildings; as, to spend the summer months in the great *outdoors*:—*adv.* outside of a building; in the open air; as, playing *outdoors*.

out-er (out′ėr), *adj.* on the outside; exterior; farther out; as, *outer* garments; *outer* regions.

outer space, **1,** space immediately beyond the air around the earth; **2,** interplanetary or interstellar space.

out-er-most (out′ėr-mōst′), *adj.* farthest outside; farthest from the centre or inside; as, the *outermost* layer of birch bark.

out-field (out′fēld′), *n.* **1,** in *baseball*, the part of the field outside or beyond the diamond; **2,** the players who play in the outfield; also, the position.—*n.* **out′field′er.**

out-fit (out′fit), *n.* **1,** all the articles required for a special purpose; equipment; as, a camping *outfit*; a hockey *outfit*; **2,** a group of people who work together, esp. in the military; as, to be in the same *outfit* of the armed forces:—*v.t.* (out′fit′), [outfitted, outfit-ting], to furnish with an outfit; to provide the necessary clothing or equipment for some work or activity.—*n.* **out′fit′ter.**

out-go-ing (out′gō′ing), *adj.* **1,** leaving; departing; as, *outgoing* mail; **2,** going out of office; retiring; as, the *outgoing* president; **3,** friendly and talkative; extroverted; sociable; as, she is very *outgoing*.

out-grow (out-grō′), *v.t.* [*p.t.* outgrew (-grōō′), *p.p.* outgrown (-grōn′), *p.pr.* outgrow-ing], **1,** to excel in growing; as, weeds *outgrow* crops; **2,** to grow away from; as, to *outgrow* a habit; **3,** to become too big for; as, to *outgrow* clothes.

out-growth (out′grōth′), *n.* anything that grows out of anything else; a result.

out-house (out′hous′), *n.* **1,** a building belonging to, but apart from, a main house, as a barn, stable, etc.; **2,** an outdoor toilet; a privy.

out-ing (out′ing), *n.* **1,** a short excursion or pleasure trip; esp., a party or a walk in the open air; **2,** an appearance in a game or athletic competition; as, his first *outing* in goal; **3,** any public appearance; as, her first *outing* as an author.

out-land-ish (out-lan′dish), *adj.* strange; unfamiliar; odd; as, *outlandish* habits.

out-last (out-last′), *v.t.* to last longer than; outlive; as, these shoes will *outlast* the others.

out-law (out′lô′), *n.* **1,** one who is deprived of the benefits and protection of the law; **2,** one who flees from the law; a lawless wanderer; criminal; **3,** one who is unconventional and does not conform to established practices; as, an *outlaw* poet:—*v.t.* **1,** to deprive of legal benefits and protection; as, to *outlaw* a criminal; **2,** to remove from legal control; to put beyond the power of the law to enforce or collect; as, to *outlaw* a debt; **3,** to make illegal; as, to *outlaw* gambling.

out-lay (out′lā′), *n.* **1,** that which is spent, either money or effort, in an undertaking; cost; expenditure; as, an *outlay* of several thousand dollars; *outlay* of energy; **2,** the act of spending:—*v.t.* to spend; as, to *outlay* money for home renovations.

out-let (out′let), *n.* **1,** a means of escape; as, games are an *outlet* for a child's energy; **2,** a passage or way out; as, the *outlet* of a lake; **3,** a place in a wall where an electric device can be plugged in; **4,** a store that sells merchandise, esp. that of a particular manufacturer; as, a retail *outlet*.

out-line (out′līn′), *n.* **1,** a line showing the outer limits of an object; **2,** a drawing, or manner of drawing, showing shapes or contours, without light and shade; **3,** a draft or sketch of a story, speech, etc.; **4,** a summary or general description of the main points of something; as, an *outline* of Canadian history:—*v.t.* [outlined, outlin-ing], **1,** to draw the outline of; **2,** to state the plan of; **3,** to summarize; give the main features of; as, she *outlined* the content of the geography course.

out-look (out′look′), *n.* **1,** a view seen from a point of vantage, as from a window; **2,** the place from which such a view is obtained; lookout; **3,** the present state or future prospect of things; as, a favourable *outlook*; **4,** point of view; attitude; as, a happy *outlook* on life.

out-ly-ing (out′lī′ing), *adj.* far from the centre or main body; remote; as, the *outlying* regions of the city.

out-mod-ed (out-mōd′id), *adj.* **1,** out of fashion; **2,** obsolete; no longer accepted; as, *outmoded* theories, doctrines, etc.

out–of–date (out′–ov–dāt′), *adj.* no longer in fashion or use; as, *out-of-date* styles in dress; *out-of-date* computer.

out–of–the–way (out′–ov–*th*ė–wā′), *adj.* **1,** hard to reach or find; remote; hidden; as, an *out-of-the-way* village; **2,** strange; unusual; as, *out-of-the-way* events.

out-pa-tient (out′pā′shent), *n.* a patient who receives treatment at a hospital, but who does not stay overnight.

out-place-ment (out′plās′ment), *n.* the process of helping downsized and other terminated employees, esp. executives, find new employment.

out-port (out′pôrt′), *n.* a small fishing village, esp. an isolated one in Newfoundland.

out-post (out′pōst′), *n.* **1,** a soldier, or troops, stationed at a distance from the main army to guard from surprise attack; **2,** the place so occupied; **3,** an outlying frontier settlement; **4,** anything that is apart or isolated from the main body or organization.

out-put (out′poot′), *n.* **1,** the amount put out or produced, as from a mine, mill, etc.; the yield; **2,** the act of putting forth something; as, the *output* of energy from a generator; **3,** in *computing,* any information, as a printout, that comes out of a computer and can be understood by the user.

out-rage (out′rāj), *n.* **1,** gross insult or wrong; a cruel or violent act; **2,** angry feelings caused by an injury or insult; as, they expressed *outrage* over the new taxes:—*v.t.* [out-raged, out-rag-ing], **1,** to inflict shame or wrong upon; to injure violently or grievously; **2,** to be contrary to; as, his profanity *outraged* all decency; **3,** make furious; produce anger or resentment.

out-ra-geous (out-rā′jus), *adj.* **1,** very cruel or wrong; as, an *outrageous* crime; **2,** very bad or insulting; shocking; offensive; as, *outrageous* language; **3,** highly unusual or unconventional; as, *outrageous* clothes.

out-ride (out-rīd′), *v.t.* [*p.t.* outrode (-rōd′), *p.p.* outrid-den (-rid′n), *p.pr.* outrid-ing], **1,** to ride better or faster than; outstrip in riding; as, the scout *outrode* his pursuers; **2,** to withstand; as, to *outride* the storm.

out-rig-ger (out′rig′ėr), *n.* **1,** the brace holding an oarlock out from the side of a racing shell (to give better leverage); **2,** a native canoe with a timber rigged out from the side to prevent tipping; **3,** a similar supporting extension in a vehicle or building.

out-right (out′rīt′; out′rīt′), *adv.* **1,** not by instalments; all at once; as, to buy a house *outright*; **2,** at once; immediately; instanteously; as, killed *outright*; **3,** straightforwardly; without reserve; directly; honestly; as, stated the problem *outright*:—*adj.* (out′rīt′), **1,** downright; straightforward; out-and-out as, an *outright* denial; **2,** undisputed; as, an *outright* winner.

out-run (out-run′), *v.t.* [*p.t.* out-ran (-ran′). *p.p.* outrun, *p.pr.* outrun-ning], **1,** to run faster than; get ahead of by running; escape from; **2,** to pass beyond; exceed; as, her ambition *outran* her ability.

out-set (out′set′), *n.* a start; the beginning, as of a business or journey.

out-shine (out-shīn′), *v.t.* [*p.t.* and *p.p.* outshone (-shon′), *p.pr.* outshining], **1,** to shine more brightly than; surpass in brightness; **2,** to excel; outdo; surpass; as, she *outshines* the rest of the class in biology:—*v.i.* to shine out.

out-side (out′sīd′), *n.* **1,** the part of anything that is on the surface or that is seen; the external part; **2,** the farthest limit; as, I shall return in a week at the *outside*:—*adj.* **1,** of or on the surface; exterior; external; as, the *outside* door; **2,** of or from one who does not belong to a group; as, *outside* help; **3,** apart from one's regular duties; as, *outside* interests; **4,** very unlikely; as, an *outside* chance:—*adv.* **1,** on or to the outer side; as, painted green *outside*; **2,** outdoors; as, to go *outside*:—*prep.* (out′sīd′; out′sīd′), **1,** beyond the limits of; on the outer side of; as, a cabin outside of town; **2,** except; as, *outside* her promptness, she was not a good employee.

out-sid-er (out′sīd′ėr), *n.* **1,** one not belonging to a given group, set, etc.; **2,** a long shot; a competitor not expected to win; as, the *outsider* was the surprise winner; **3,** in Northern Canada, a person who lives in heavily populated, usually southern, parts of Canada; as, residents of Toronto are considered to be *outsiders* by the people of the Northwest Territories.

out-skirts (out′skûrts′), *n.pl.* edge or edges; outlying part or parts; as, she lives on the *outskirts* of the city.

out-source (out′sôrs′) *v.t.* [outsourced, outsourc-ing], the subcontracting of manufacturing or other work to outside sources; farming out.—*n.* **outsourcing.**

out-spo-ken (out-spō′ken), *adj.* free or bold of speech; frank; as, he was *outspoken* in his criticism.—*adv.* **out′spo′ken-ly.**

out-stand-ing (out-stan′ding), *adj.* **1,** prominent; conspicuous; excellent; superior; as, an *outstanding* author or student; **2,** unpaid; as, *outstanding* debts.

out-strip (out-strip′), *v.t.* [outstripped, out-strip-ping], **1,** to outrun, as in a race; **2,** to excel; surpass.

out-ward (out′wėrd), *adj.* **1,** of or on the outside; external; superficial; as, *outward* appearance; **2,** away from the shore; as, the *outward* course of a ship; **3,** visible; apparent; as, *outward* show:—*adv.* (also **out-wards**) **1,** from the inside; toward the outside; as, to move *outward*; to face *outward*; **2,** away from a place; as, the ship was *outward* bound.

out-ward-ly (out′wėrd-li), *adv.* on the surface; in appearance; as, she remained *outwardly* calm.

out-weigh (out′wā′), *v.t.* **1,** to weigh more than; **2,** to exceed in value, importance, etc.; as, the plan's merits *outweighed* its defects.

out-wit (out-wit′), *v.t.* [outwit-ted, outwit-ting], to get the better of by superior skill or cunning; as, to *outwit* an opponent.

out-worn (out′wôrn′), *adj.* **1,** worn out; as, *outworn* shoes; **2,** out-of-date; obsolete; as, an *outworn* point of view; *outworn* machinery.

o-val (ō′vl), *adj.* shaped like an egg; elliptical:—*n.* anything eggshaped; an ellipselike curve with one end broader than the other.

o-va-ry (ō′va-ri), *n.* [*pl.* ovaries], **1,** in a female animal, the reproductive organ in which the ova, or egg cells, are formed; **2,** the part of a plant in which the seeds are formed. (See *flower,* illustration.)

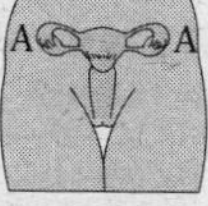

OVARIES (A)

o-va-tion (ō-vā′shun), *n.* **1,** enthusiastic applause; **2,** a hearty public tribute; as, the Canadian Olympic team received a tremendous *ovation.*

ov-en (uv′en), *n.* an enclosed chamber for baking, heating, or drying, esp. one inside a stove or range.

o-ver (ō′vėr), *prep.* **1,** above in position, authority, dignity, excellence, etc.; as, the sky is *over* our heads; a captain is *over* a lieutenant; a governor rules *over* the state; **2,** across; from one side to another; as, to jump *over* a ditch; **3,** on the surface of; upon; covering; as, to wear a cape *over* the shoulders; to wander *over* the plains; **4,** more than; as, he spent *over* 100 dollars; **5,** during; throughout; as, to stay *over* the weekend; **6,** along; as, to drive *over* a new road; **7,** on account of; concerning; as, to weep *over* defeat; argue *over* money; **8,** all through; as, the smile spread *over* her face:—*adv.* **1,** from beginning to end; as, to talk the matter *over;* **2,** from one to another; as, to make *over* property; from one side to the other; as, to cross *over* to Canada; to go *over* to the enemy; **3,** in addition; remaining; in excess; as, all that is left *over;* **4,** so as to bring the under side up; as, to turn a coin *over;* so as to be upright no longer; as, to topple *over;* **5,** from end to end; throughout; as, a landscape dotted *over* with trees; **6,** again; once again; as, to do a thing *over;* **7,** down from the edge, top, or brim; as, the water is running *over;* **8,** at an end; finished; as, all is *over;* **9,** *Colloq.* successfully; with the effect planned; as, the show went *over* the first night; **10,** cover; as, paint it *over;* **11,** pass across; as, to climb *over:*—*adj.* **1,** external; **2,** extreme; **3,** extra; left over.

o-ver- (ō′vėr-), *prefix* meaning **1,** *excessively;* as in *over*abundance, *over*achieve, *over*act, *over*age, *over*bite, *over*blown, *over*book, *over*burden, *over*capacity, *over*cautious, *over*confident, *over*cook, *over*crowd, *over*develop, *over*dose, *over*dress, *over*act, *over*emphasize, *over*exert, *over*extend, *over*heat, *over*indulge, *over*kill, *over*much, *over*nice, *over*optimistic, *over*pay, *over*populated, *over*priced, *over*protective, *over*qualified, *over*react, *over*ripe, *over*sell, *over*simplify, *over*sleep, *over*spend, *over*stay, *over*step, *over*stock, *over*stress, *over*strung, *over*stuffed, *over*tax, *over*tired, *over*train, *over*use, *over*value, *over*weight, *over*zealous; **2,** *extra;* as in *over*sized, *over*time; **3,** *outer, external;* as in *over*alls, *over*coat, *over*shoe; **4,** *completely;* as in *over*all, *over*joyed; **5,** other senses; as in *over*drive, *over*dub, *over*land, *over*lay, *over*lie, *over*lord, *over*pass, *over*ride, *over*seas, *over*shadow, *over*shoot, *over*skate, *over*trump.

o-ver-all (ō′vėr-ôl′), *adj.* **1,** including everything; total; as, *overall* costs; **2,** general; viewed as a whole; as, *overall* improvement; **3,** end to end; as, *overall* length:—*adv.* **1,** in the circumstances; as, *overall,* it was a good game; **2,** when all is included; as, she finished second *overall;* **3,** all over; as, the paint used *overall;* **4,** from one end to the other; as, 100 metres *overall.*

o-ver-alls (ō′vėr-ôlz′), *n.pl.* loose-fitting trousers supported by shoulder straps, worn over, or in place of, other garments.

o-ver-awe (ō′vėr-ô′), *v.t.* [overawed, overaw-ing], to hold in check through fear, respect; hold spellbound; as, the guest's manner *overawed* us.

o-ver-bal-ance (ō′vėr-bal′ans), *v.t.* [overbalanced, overbalanc-ing], **1,** to be greater than, in weight or influence; outweigh; **2,** to upset the balance of; throw off balance:—*v.i.* to capsize; to lose one's balance:—*n.* an excess of something.

o-ver-bear (ō′vėr-bâr′), *v.t.* [*p.t.* overbore (-bōr′), *p.p.* overborne (-bōrn′), *p.pr.* overbear-ing], **1,** to bear down, as by greater physical weight or force; overthrow; **2,** to overcome; triumph over.

o-ver-bear-ing (ō′vėr-bâr′ing), *adj.* **1,** haughty; domineering; as, his attitude is so *overbearing* that even his friends don't like it; **2,** overpowering; predominant.

o-ver-board (ō′vėr-bōrd′), *adv.* **1,** over the side of a ship or boat, into the water; as, to fall *overboard;* **2,** extremely enthusiastic, esp. excessively so; as, to go *overboard* with her praise.

o-ver-cast (ō′vėr-kåst′), *v.t.* [overcast, overcast-ing], **1,** to cover over; cloud; overshadow; darken; as, the sky is *overcast;* **2,** (ō′vėr-kåst′), to take long, loose stitches over the edges of (a seam) to prevent unravelling:—*v.i.* to become cloudy or gloomy:—*adj.* **1,** clouded over; as, an *overcast* day; **2,** gloomy; **3,** sewn with an overcast stitch:—*n.* **1,** a covering, esp. with clouds; **2,** an overcast stitch.

o-ver-charge (ō′vėr-chärj′), *v.t.* [overcharged, overcharg-ing], **1,** to load too heavily; as, to *overcharge* a battery; **2,** to ask too high a price from; as, to *overcharge* customers; **3,** exaggerate; overstate:—*v.i.* to charge too much:—*n.* (ō′vėr-chärj′), **1,** too heavy a load, as of electricity; **2,** too high a price.

o-ver-coat (ō′vėr-kōt′), *n.* **1,** a heavy, outdoor coat worn in cold weather; **2,** a protective layer of paint, etc.

o-ver-come (ō′vėr-kum′), *v.t.* [*p.t.* overcame (-kām′), *p.p.* overcome, *p.pr.* over-com-ing], **1,** to defeat; prevail over; become master of; as, to *overcome* fear; **2,** to overpower; as, terror *overcame* him:—*v.i.* to be victorious.

o-ver-do (ō′vėr-do͞o′), *v.t.* [*p.t.* overdid (-did′), *p.p.* overdone (-dun′), *p.pr.* overdo-ing], **1,** to carry too far; exaggerate; **2,** to weary by overwork; **3,** to cook too long:—*v.i.* to work too hard; do too much.

o-ver-draft or **o-ver-draught** (ō′vėr-draft′), *n.* **1,** a cheque or draft drawn in excess of one's bank account or credit balance; **2,** the act of doing this; **3,** a stream of air in a furnace.

o-ver-draw (ō′vėr-drô′), *v.t.* [*p.t.* overdrew (-dro͞o′), *p.p.* overdrawn (-drôn′), *p.pr.* over-draw-ing], **1,** to exaggerate; overstate; as, her story of the robbery was greatly *overdrawn*; **2,** to draw against (a bank account) by writing a cheque for a sum greater than the amount on deposit.

o-ver-due (ō′vėr-dū′), *adj.* **1,** unpaid at the time for payment; as, an *overdue* account; **2,** not on hand at the scheduled time; as, the plane is *overdue*.

o-ver-es-ti-mate (ō′vėr-es′ti-māt′), *v.t.* [overestimat-ed, overestimat-ing], to set too high a value on; as, he *overestimates* his own ability:—*n.* (ō′vėr-es′ti-mit), too high a valuation or estimate.

o-ver-flow (ō′vėr-flō′), *n.* **1,** the spreading of water or other liquid beyond its proper limits; an act of overflowing; **2,** the excess water or liquid; also, an outlet for excess liquid; **3,** excess; superabundance; as, an *overflow* of enthusiasm:—*v.t.* and *v.i.* (ō′vėr-flō′), to flood; overrun; spread all over.

o-ver-grow (ō′vėr-grō′), *v.t.* [*p.t.* overgrew (-gro͞o′), *p.p.* overgrown (-grōn′), *p.pr.* over-grow-ing], **1,** to cover; grow over; as, the path is *overgrown* with weeds; **2,** to outgrow:—*v.i.* **1,** to grow too large or too fast; **2,** to become overrun or grown over.

o-ver-hand (ō′vėr-hand′), *adj.* **1,** down from above; as, an *overhand* blow; **2,** grasping with the hand over the object, and with the palm downward; as, an *overhand* grip; **3,** in *baseball* and other sports, thrown with the arm swung above the shoulder; as, an *overhand* pitch:—*n.* the simplest kind of knot:—*adv.* (ō′vėr-hand′), with the palm of the hand down; as, to haul in a fishline *overhand*. Compare *underhand*.

o-ver-hang (ō′vėr-hang′), *v.t.* [overhung (-hung′), overhang-ing], **1,** to jut over; project above; as, trees *overhang* the road; **2,** to threaten, menace, or loom; as, the threat of war *overhangs* the country:—*v.i.* to project over and beyond something; as, the ledge *overhangs* several centimetres:—*n.* (ō′vėr-hang′), **1,** a part of something, such as a building or mountain, that projects; **2,** the extent of the projection; as, an *overhang* of 50 centimetres; **3,** excess supply; as, an inventory *overhang*.

o-ver-haul (ō′vėr-hôl′), *v.t.* **1,** to examine thoroughly in order to make repairs; **2,** to overtake; catch up with; **3,** make extensive changes; as, to *overhaul* the school curriculum:—*n.* a thorough examination for maintenance and repair; as, an *overhaul* of the old car.

o-ver-head (ō′vėr-hed′), *adv.* above one's head; as, stars shine *overhead*:—*adj.* (ō′vėr-hed′), **1,** situated or operating above one's head; as, *overhead* ventilation; **2,** referring to the cost or expenses of a business that are directly chargeable not to any particular department, but to the running of the business as a whole:—*n.* (ō′vėr-hed′), **1,** overhead expenses; as, rent and utilities are items in our *overhead*; **2,** a device that projects objects from transparencies onto a screen or wall; as, an *overhead* projector; **3,** large transparencies used in these projectors.

o-ver-hear (ō′vėr-hēr′), *v.t.* and *v.i.* [overheard (-hûrd′), overhear-ing], to hear a remark or conversation that one is not intended to hear.

o-ver-joyed (ō′vėr-joid′), *adj.* made very glad; completely filled with joy; delighted; as, she was *overjoyed* at the news.

o-ver-lap (ō′vėr-lap′), *v.t.* [overlapped, over-lap-ping], **1,** to lie so as to partly cover; as, each shingle *overlaps* the one below; also, to lay so as to cover the edge of something; **2,** to coincide partly with; as, the treasurer's duties *overlap* those of the secretary:—*v.i.* **1,** to lie so that part of one thing covers part of another; **2,** to coincide in part:—*n.* (ō′vėr-lap′), **1,** the extension, or amount of extension, of one thing over the edge of another; **2,** that which partly covers, or laps over, something.

o-ver-lay (ō′vėr-lā′), *v.t.* [overlaid (-lād′), overlay-ing], to spread or cover (a surface) with something; superimpose:—*n.* (ō′vėr-lā′), that which is laid on, as a covering.

o-ver-load (ō′vėr-lōd′), *v.t.* to load, or burden, too heavily; as, to *overload* the truck with furniture:—*n.* (ō′vėr-lōd′), too large a load, esp. an electrical one; as, the power *overload* blew the circuit.

o-ver-look (ō′vėr-look′), *v.t.* **1,** to look down on from above; as, the room *overlooks* Niagara Falls; **2,** to keep an eye on; watch over; manage; superintend; **3,** to fail to see; miss; as, I *overlooked* part of the problem; **4,** to disregard deliberately; pass over without noticing; ignore; as, she *overlooked* her friend's rude remark.

o-ver-night (ō′vėr-nīt′), *adv.* **1,** in or during the night; as, it happened *overnight*; **2,** very quickly; suddenly; as, to learn guitar *overnight*:—*adj.* (ō′vėr-nīt′), **1,** lasting through a night; as, an *overnight* trip by train; **2,** for a night or short visit; as, an *overnight* bag; *overnight* guests; **3,** rapid;

sudden; as, an *overnight* sensation.

o-ver-power (ō′vėr-pou′ėr), *v.t.* **1,** to crush by superior force; subdue; overcome; **2,** to affect greatly; as, she was *overpowered* by grief and sorrow.—*adj.* **o′ver-pow′er-ing.**

o-ver-rate (ō′vėr-rāt′), *v.t.* [overrat-ed, overrat-ing], to set too high a value upon; as, to *overrate* one's ability.

over-reach (ō′vėr-rēch′), *v.t.* **1,** to defeat (oneself) by reaching too far or attempting too much; **2,** to get the better of (another) by trickery; **3,** to reach above or beyond:—*v.i.* **1,** to exaggerate; go to excess; **2,** of horses, to strike the heel of the forefoot with the hind foot.

o-ver-rule (ō′vėr-rōōl′), *v.t.* [overruled, overrul-ing], **1,** to set aside; nullify; as, the judge *overruled* a previous decision; **2,** to decide against; disallow; as, the chairman *overruled* my objections.

o-ver-run (ō′vėr-run′), *v.t.* [*p.t.* overran (-ran′), *p.p.* overrun, *p.pr.* overrun-ning], **1,** to grow or spread over in great quantity or numbers; as, weeds had *overrun* the garden; the enemy *overran* the country; **2,** to run beyond; overshoot; as, to *overrun* first base; **3,** overflow; as, the river *overruns* its banks:—*v.i.* to overflow:—*adj.* infested; plagued; as, the *overrun* garden:—*n.* **1,** the act of overrunning, esp. with regard to costs; **2,** the amount of the cost overrun; **3,** printed material in excess of the amount ordered.

o-ver-seas (ō′vėr-sēz′; ō′vėr-sēz′), *adv.* and *adj.* abroad; across the sea; as, serve CUSO *overseas*; *overseas* flights.

o-ver-sea (ō′vėr-sē′; ō′vėr-sē′), *adj.* of, to, or from countries across the sea; as, an *oversea* flight.

o-ver-see (ō′vėr-sē′), *v.t.* [*p.t.* oversaw (-sô′), *p.p.* overseen (-sēn′), *p.pr.* oversee-ing], to keep watch over; superintend; supervise; manage; inspect.—*n.* **o′ver-se′er.**

o-ver-shad-ow (ō′vėr-shad′ō), *v.t.* **1,** to darken or obscure with or as with a shadow; **2,** to cause (something) to lose importance or significance; as, his early success was *overshadowed* by his later failures; **3,** outweigh; appear more important than; exceed in importance; as, Wayne Gretzky *overshadowed* his teammates.

o-ver-shoe (ō′vėr-shōō′), *n.* a waterproof shoe or boot, generally of rubber, worn over another shoe, for protection against wetness, snow, or cold.

o-ver-sight (ō′vėr-sīt′), *n.* **1,** failure to see or think of something; **2,** a slip or mistake resulting from such failure; **3,** supervision; as, he has general *oversight* of the students at lunch time.

o-ver-spread (ō′vėr-spred′), *v.t.* [overspread, overspread-ing], to cover the surface of; spread over; as, a mossy carpet *overspread* the ground.

o-ver-state (ō′vėr-stāt′), *v.t.* [overstated, overstat-ing], to state or express too strongly; exaggerate.—*n.* **o′ver-state′ ment.**

o-ver-step (ōvėr-step′), *v.t.* [overstepped, overstep-ping], to go beyond; exceed; as, he *overstepped* his authority.

o-vert (ō′vėrt), *adj.* publicly or openly performed; not secret or hidden; as, the bombing of the city was an *overt* act of war.—*adv.* **o′vert-ly.**

o-ver-take (ō′vėr-tāk′), *v.t.* [*p.t.* overtook (-took′), *p.p.* overtak-en (-tāk′en), *p.pr.* overtak-ing], **1,** to catch or come up with; **2,** to come upon suddenly; take by surprise; as, the storm *overtook* us.

o-ver-tax (ō′vėr-taks′), *v.t.* **1,** to tax too heavily; **2,** to lay too great a burden upon; as, to *overtax* one's strength.

o-ver-throw (ō′vėr-thrō′), *v.t.* [*p.t.* overthrew (-thrōō′), *p.p.* overthrown (-thrōn′), *p.pr.* overthrow-ing], **1,** to cause to fall or to fail; as, to *overthrow* a government; **2,** to overturn; upset; as, to *overthrow* a chair; **3,** in *sports*, to throw past the intended target; as, he *overthrew* second base:—*n.* (ō′vėr-thrō′), ruin; defeat, as of an army.

o-ver-time (ō′vėr-tīm′), *n.* **1,** extra time worked beyond regular working hours; as, to work three hours of *overtime*; **2,** the pay for this time; as, to receive *overtime* for her work; **3,** in *sports*, an extra amount of playing time to decide the winner of a game that is tied:—*adv.* beyond regular hours; as, to work *overtime*:—*adj.* of or for extra work; as, *overtime* work.

o-ver-tone (ō′vėr-tōn′), *n.* in *music*, **1,** a harmonic or partial tone; **2,** a higher or secondary tone attending the production of a basic one; **3,** an implication or suggestion; as, the article had accusatory *overtones*:—*v.t.* (ō′vėr-tōn′), in *photography*, to give too much tone (to).

o-ver-ture (ō′vėr-tūr), *n.* **1,** a preliminary offer or proposal; as, an *overture* of peace; **2,** music composed and played as the prelude to a larger piece of work, such as an opera.

o-ver-turn (ō′vėr-tûrn′), *v.t.* **1,** to cause to upset or turn over; as, to *overturn* a chair; **2,** to overthrow; bring to ruin; **3,** in *law*, to reverse a decision; as, the court *overturned* the previous verdict:—*v.i.* to upset:—*n.* (ō′vėr-tûrn′), an upsetting; as, the *overturn* of a political party.

o-ver-ween-ing (ō′vėr-wēn′ing), *adj.* conceited; arrogant; also, excessive; exaggerated; as, *overweening* pride.

o-ver-whelm (ō′vėr-hwelm′), *v.t.* **1,** to submerge; flood; as, he was *overwhelmed* with applause; **2,** to crush utterly; as, to *overwhelm* a person by harsh criticism.—*adj.* **o′ver-whelm′ing.**

o-ver-work (ō′vėr-wûrk′), *v.t.* **1,** to place too much work upon; **2,** to exhaust with excess work; **3,** to overuse; as, to *overwork* buzz words:—*v.i.* to work beyond one's strength:—*n.* (ō′vėr-wûrk′) work beyond one's capacity; too much work.

o-ver-wrought (ō′vėr-rôt′), *adj.* **1,** excited; unstrung; agitated; **2,** too elaborately adorned; overdone.

o-vi- (ō′vi-), *prefix* meaning *egg* or *ovum*; as in *ovi*duct (a tube by which eggs pass from the ovary to the uterus or egg sac), *ovi*parous (producing eggs that are expelled from the body, as of birds, some reptiles, and fishes), *ovi*ferous (bearing eggs), *ovi*form (egg-shaped), *ovi*positor (a special egg-laying organ, as in crickets and grasshoppers).

o-vule (ō′vūl), *n.* **1,** in *plants*, an undeveloped seed; **2,** in *female animals*, a little or undeveloped ovum, or germ cell.

o-vum (ō′vum), *n.* [*pl.* ova (ō′va)], the female germ cell or seed; egg.

owe (ō), *v.t.* [owed, ow-ing], **1,** to be under obligation to pay; as, to *owe* 50 dollars; **2,** to be indebted for; as, I *owe* my success to you:—*v.i.* to be in debt.

ow-ing (ō′ing), *adj.* due as a debt:—**owing to,** because of.

owl (oul), *n.* any one of a group of night-flying birds of prey, which have large heads and eyes, short hooked bills and sharp claws, and a distinctive call or hoot.—*adj.* **owl′ish.**

own (ōn), *adj.* **1,** belonging to the individual person or thing; as, your *own* house; the sun's *own* light; **2,** of the same parents; as, my *own* sister:—*v.t.* **1,** to be the possessor of; as, I *own* this book; **2,** to acknowledge, admit; confess; as, to *own* a fault; **3,** to grant; as, I *own* the truth of your argument:—*v.i.* confess to; as, to *own* up to the lie:—*n.* something belonging to oneself; as, a room of my *own*.

own-er (ōn′ėr), *n.* one who owns or possesses; a proprietor.—*n.* **own′er-ship.**

ox (oks), *n.* [*pl.* oxen (ok′sen)], **1,** a steer, or castrated male of the family of domestic cattle, esp. one that has been trained to do hauling and farm work; **2,** any of several animals related to domestic cattle, as the wild ox and the musk ox.

ox-bow (oks′bō′), *n.* **1,** a U-shaped or S-shaped bend in a river; **2,** the land enclosed by it; **3,** the wooden frame in the shape of a U that fits around an ox's neck and into the horizontal yoke.

ox-ford (oks′fėrd), *n.* **1,** a low shoe, laced or tied over the instep; **2,** a type of cloth often used in making shirts; as, *oxford* cloth.

ox-ide (ok′sīd′), *n.* a compound of oxygen with another element.

ox-i-dize (ok′si-dīz′), *v.t.* and *v.i.* [oxidized, oxidiz-ing], to combine with oxygen; make into or coat with oxide.—*n.* **ox′i-diz′er.**—*n.* **ox′i-da′tion.**

ox-y- (ok′si-), *prefix* meaning **1,** *containing oxygen*; as in *oxy*acetylene, *oxy*calcium; **2,** *sharp, acute, pointed, acid*; as in *oxy*gen, *oxy*moron.

ox-y-gen (ok′si-jen), *n.* a gaseous element without odour, colour, or taste, forming about 1/5 of the total volume of the atmosphere: essential to life and part of many substances, such as water, acids, etc.: abbreviated as *O*.

ox-y-gen-ate or **ox-y-gen-ize** (ok′si-jen-āt′; ok′si-jen-īz′), *v.t.* [oxygenated, oxygenat-ing; oxygenized, oxygeniz-ing], to mix or enrich with oxygen.—*n.* **ox′y-gen-a′tion.**

ox-y-mo-ron (ok′si-mō′ron), *n.* a figure of speech combining opposite or contradictory ideas, as *cruel kindness, bitter sweet, make haste slowly, falsely true, jumbo shrimp*: often used to give point to an epigram, etc.

oys-ter (ois′tėr), *n.* a shellfish, valued as food, having a rough, hinged shell, and living in shallow water of sea coasts.

o-zone (ō′zōn′), *n.* a bluish gas, O_3, with the odour of weak chlorine, formed by the discharge of electricity through air or by exposure to ultraviolet radiation: a powerful oxidizing agent, used in bleaching, sterilizing water, etc.:—**ozone layer,** a layer of ozone in the upper atmosphere that absorbs ultraviolet radiation from the sun.

P

P, p (pē), *n.* [*pl.* P's, p's], the 16th letter of the alphabet, following O.

pace (pās), *n.* **1,** a step; the space covered by a step in walking; **2,** gait, or manner of moving; **3,** a certain gait of a horse; **4,** rate of speed; as, to keep the *pace*:—*v.t.* [paced, pac-ing], **1,** to measure by steps; as, to *pace* off 50 metres; **2,** to walk over with even steps; as, the guard *paces* his round; **3,** in racing, to set the *pace* for:—*v.i.* **1,** to walk with long, even steps; **2,** to go at a *pace*, as a horse; **3,** to walk back and forth repeatedly.—*n.* **pac′er.**

pach-y-derm (pak′i-dûrm′), *n.* **1,** any thick-skinned, hoofed quadruped, as the elephant or rhinoceros; **2,** *Colloq.* a person lacking sensitivity.

pa-cif-ic (pa-sif′ik), *adj.* **1,** peacemaking; as, *pacific* words; **2,** peaceful; tranquil; as, *pacific* waters:—**Pacific Ocean,** the largest ocean (about 180 million square kilometres), lying between Australia and Asia and North and South America.—*adv.* **pa-cif′i-cal-ly.**

pac-i-fi-er (pas′i-fi′ėr), *n.* **1,** someone or

something that soothes and pacifies; **2,** a rubber nipple, teething ring, etc., for babies to bite or suck.

pac-i-fist (pas′i-fist), *n.* one who opposes violence, esp. war, and who believes in, and works for, peace among nations.—*n.* **pac′i-fism.**

pac-i-fy (pas′i-fī′), *v.t.* [pacified, pacifying], to calm; soothe; appease; as, to *pacify* an angry mob.—*n.* **pac′if-i-ca′tion.**

pack (pak), *n.* **1,** a bundle tied up for carrying, esp. on the back of a person or animal; a backpack; **2,** a full set of things; as, a *pack* of cards; **3,** a number of animals or people of the same kind living or hunting together; as, a *pack* of hounds; a *pack* of thieves; **4,** a large area of floating cakes of ice driven close together; **5,** a division of Scouting; as, a *pack* of Brownies:—*v.t.* **1,** to stow away, arrange compactly, or press into a bundle; as, to *pack* clothes for a trip; **2,** to fill (a receptacle or space) entirely; as, to *pack* a suitcase with clothes; **3,** to crowd together; as, to *pack* people into a room; **4,** to press into a hard mass; as, to *pack* earth; **5,** to fill in (a joint or crack) to prevent leaking; **6,** to send away; as, to *pack* him off in a hurry; **7,** to arrange unfairly to suit one's own ends; as, to *pack* a jury; **8,** to give in; as, he *packed* it in; **9,** *Colloq.* to wear or carry; as, to *pack* a gun; **10,** have an impact; as, to *pack* a punch; **11,** to carry in a pack; as, they *packed* the supplies into camp:—*v.i.* **1,** to press or crowd together into a hard mass; as, ice *packs* together; **2,** to stow things for safety or for carrying; **3,** to admit of being stowed; as, these articles *pack* well; **4,** to depart or move in haste; as, she sent him *packing*; **5,** to quit; as, she *packed* up and left.—*n.* **pack′er.** Also, **pack′horse′; pack′sack′; pack′ sad′dle.**

pack-age (pak′ij), *n.* **1,** a bundle or bale of goods; a parcel; packet; **2,** things grouped together and thought of as one; as, the vacation *package* included all meals:—*v.t.* [packaged, packag-ing], **1,** to wrap or make into a package; as, the film was *packaged* with the camera when we bought it; **2,** to present or put something together for mass appeal or for a certain purpose; as, to *package* a product, a book, a vacation, software, etc:—*adj.* several things grouped together; as, a *package* deal.—*n.* **pack′ag-er.**

pack-et (pak′it), *n.* **1,** a small bundle or parcel; package; **2,** a group of characters transmitted from one computer to another over a network; **3,** *Slang* a lot of money.

pack-ing (pak′ing), *n.* **1,** the act of packing; **2,** material, as paper, plastic foam, bubble wrap, etc., used to protect goods packed for carrying; **3,** material used to make something airtight or watertight; as, to seal the pipe joint with *packing*; **4,** the gauze or other material used to fill a wound; **5,** the processing of meat for sale; as, meat *packing*:—*adj.* relating to, of, or for packing; as, a meat *packing* company.

pact (pakt), *n.* an agreement or contract; as, the girls made a *pact* not to tease each other.

[1]**pad** (pad), *v.i.* [pad-ded, pad-ding], to walk noiselessly, as a cat does.

[2]**pad** (pad), *n.* **1,** a soft cushion used to fill a hollow space, lessen pressure or friction, protect from blows, etc.; padding; as, hockey *pads*; **2,** the cushionlike part of the foot of some animals, as a dog and cat; **3,** a number of sheets of paper stuck together at one end, used for writing or drawing; a tablet; **4,** the floating leaf of certain water plants, as the water lily; **5,** a cushioned, inked block used for inking a rubber stamp; as, a stamp *pad*; **6,** the area for the takeoff and landing of helicopters or rockets, etc.; as, the space shuttle lifted off the *pad* at noon; **7,** *Colloq.* a place where someone sleeps or lives; as, her new *pad* is right downtown:—*v.t.* [pad-ded, pad-ding], **1,** to stuff with cushions or pads; line, as a coat; **2,** to expand with unnecessary material; as, to *pad* a newspaper story; **3,** to inflate or expand in a fraudulent way; as, they *padded* their expense accounts.

pad-ding (pad′ing), *n.* **1,** material used to pad; stuffing; **2,** material of no value used to fill up space; **3,** extra, unnecessary material; as, *padding* in a news story; **4,** an inflated amount, esp. in a fraudulent way; as, their expense accounts had a lot of *padding*.

pad-dle (pad′l), *n.* **1,** a short oar with a broad blade at one or both ends, used to propel a canoe or other small boat; **2,** a short, broad-bladed instrument used for stirring, mixing, etc.; **3,** one of the wide boards of a water wheel or a paddle wheel; **4,** a small, flat racket with a handle, used to hit the ball in table tennis and other games:—*v.i.* and *v.t.* [pad-dled, pad-dling], to propel (a canoe or boat) with a *paddle*:—*v.i.* to wade; to dabble in water with the hands or feet.

pad-dock (pad′uk), *n.* an enclosure near a stable or racetrack where horses are exercised.

pad-dy (pad′i), *n.* rice in the husk; a rice field.

pad-lock (pad′lok′), *n.* a removable lock that hangs by a curved bar, hinged at one end and snapped shut at the other:—*v.t.* to fasten with such a lock.

pad-re (pȧd′ri), *n.* **1,** *Colloq. Military* a chaplain; **2,** a Christian priest or monk, esp. in Europe and Latin America.

pa-gan (pā′gan), *n.* **1,** someone with religious beliefs that are different from those of the major religions; **2,** formerly, a heathen; one who was not Christian, Jewish, or Muslim; **3,** a person having no religious beliefs:—*adj.* heathen; irreligious; related to, of, or for pagans.—*n.* **pa′gan-ism.**

[1]**page** (pāj), *n.* **1,** in the days of chivalry, a boy, usually of high birth, attending on a

person of distinction as the first stage in the process of his training toward knighthood; **2,** a messenger in a lawmaking body, such as the House of Commons, or in a hotel:—*v.t.* [paged, pag-ing], **1,** to serve as a page; **2,** to call for or summon a person by calling out his or her name or by tracking down that person by phone, etc.; as, the receptionist *paged* the person I was calling; **3,** to call someone electronically by means of a device known as a pager or a beeper.

[2]**page** (pāj), *n.* **1,** one side of a leaf, as of a book; also, what is written or printed on it:—*v.t.* [paged, pag-ing], to arrange or number in pages; **2,** in *computing,* the information available at one location on the Internet or on a computer screen; as, a Web *page*:—*v.i.* [paged, pag-ing], **1,** to flip or rapidly scan through the pages of a book; as, she *paged* through the book quickly; **2,** in *computing,* to display a page of text on the screen; as, she *paged* down trying to find the material.

pag-eant (paj′ant), *n.* **1,** a brilliant, stately display or procession in celebration of an event or in honour of a person; **2,** any public show or entertainment; as, she starred in the school *pageant.*—*n.* **pag′eant-ry.**

pag-er (pā′jėr), *n.* a small, wireless electronic device worn or carried by individuals that allows them to receive messages from another person via radio signals; a beeper.

pa-go-da (pa-gō′da), *n.* in the Far East, a sacred tower or temple of many storeys, usually built in the form of a pyramid and richly painted and ornamented.

PAGODA

paid (pād), *p.t.* and *p.p.* of *pay.*

pail (pāl), *n.* **1,** an open vessel of wood or metal with a handle, for carrying liquids; a bucket; **2,** the amount a pail will hold; as, a *pail* of milk.—*n.* **pail′ful.**

pain (pān), *n.* **1,** suffering of body; an ache; as, a *pain* in the stomach; **2,** distress of mind; sorrow; **3,** *Colloq.* someone or something that is annoying; a nuisance; as, she is a real *pain*; a *pain* in the neck:—**pains,** diligent effort; as, he took great *pains* with his work:—*v.t.* **1,** to cause bodily suffering to; **2,** to make uneasy; grieve; as, her impoliteness *pained* her teacher.

pain-ful (pān′fool), *adj.* **1,** full of pain; causing pain; as, a *painful* injury; **2,** causing worry or concern; **3,** difficult, as a task.—*adv.* **pain-ful-ly.**

pains-tak-ing (pānz′tāk′ing), *adj.* taking great pains; careful; as, a *painstaking* worker:—*n.* the act of taking great care.—*adv.* **pains′tak′ing-ly.**

paint (pānt), *v.t.* **1,** to depict in paints; as, to *paint* a portrait; **2,** to describe vividly; as, to *paint* a scene in words; **3,** to coat or cover with colour; as, to *paint* a house; **4,** to coat, as with paint; swab; as, the surgeon *painted* the patient's stomach before performing the operation:—*v.i.* **1,** to practise the art of making pictures with colour; **2,** to cover something with paint:—*n.* **1,** a colouring substance composed of pigment mixed with oil or water; **2,** cosmetic rouge.

paint-er (pān′tėr), *n.* **1,** a person whose work is painting things, such as walls, buildings, etc.; **2,** a person who paints pictures; an artist; as, Picasso was a great *painter*; **3,** a rope attached to the front of a boat, used for tying it to a dock or other object.

paint-ing (pān′ting), *n.* **1,** the act, art, or work of a painter; **2,** a picture in colours.

pair (pâr), *n.* **1,** two things of a kind, similar in form, intended to be used together, or corresponding to each other in some way; as, a *pair* of eyes; a *pair* of shoes; **2,** a single thing composed of two like parts; as, a *pair* of scissors; **3,** two people or animals that go or work together; as, a *pair* of oxen; **4,** two cards of the same value or denomination; as, a *pair* of kings; **5,** in *sports,* two contestants who act as a team; as, a skating *pair*; **6,** in Parliament, members of different parties in a legislative body who agree that neither will vote on a given motion:—*v.i.* to join in couples; mate; as, we *paired* for the science project:—*v.t.* **1,** to come together in couples; as, the coach *paired* them in the dance competition; **2,** to match; form a pair.

pa-ja-ma (pa-jåm′a; pa-jam′a), *n.* Same as **pyjama.**

pal (pal), *n. Colloq.* an intimate friend; chum; comrade; as, she has pen *pals* all over the world; *pals* at school.

pal-ace (pal′as; pal′is), *n.* **1,** the official residence of a king, queen, or other ruler; **2,** a magnificent house that is large or impressive and resembles a royal residence; as, she lives in a real *palace*; **3,** a public building, esp. one with a particular function; as, a movie *palace.*

pal-a-din (pal′a-din), *n.* **1,** a knightly or heroic champion; **2,** a dedicated supporter, esp. of a cause.

pal-ate (pal′at; pal′it), *n.* **1,** the roof of the mouth; **2,** the sense of taste; as, a delicate *palate.*—*adj.* **pal′a-tal.**

pa-la-tial (pa-lā′shal), *adj.* pertaining to, or resembling, a palace; magnificent; spacious.

[1]**pale** (pāl), *adj.* [pal-er, pal-est], **1,** wanting in colour; as, a face *pale* from illness; **2,** dim; not bright; as, *pale* blue:—*v.i.* [paled, pal-ing], **1,** to turn white or lose colour; **2,** to decline or decrease in importance; grow weaker; my troubles *pale* compared to hers:—*v.t.* to make dim or pale.—*n.* **pale′ness.**

[2]**pale** (pāl), *n.* **1,** a pointed stake or fence

picket; **2,** a place enclosed by such a fence; **3,** a district with clearly marked bounds; **4,** limits or bounds:—*v.t.* [paled, pal-ing], to enclose or fence with pales.

pa-le-o- or **pa-lae-o-** (pā′li-ō; pal), *prefix* meaning *very old* or *ancient*; as in *paleo*ecology (the study of prehistoric organisms and their environment), *paleo*ntology (the branch of geology dealing with the treating of fossil remains of plants and animals).

Pa-le-o-lith-ic or **Pa-lae-o-lith-ic** (pā′li-ō-lith′ik; pal′), *adj.* relating to the Old Stone Age or earliest period of human development, when crude stone tools were used.

Pa-le-o-zo-ic or **Pa-lae-o-zo-ic** (pā′li-ō-zō′ik; pal′), *adj.* relating to the geological era lasting from 590 to 245 million years ago (preceding the Mesozoic period), and characterized by the development of fish and sea plants, the first amphibians, and land plants and reptiles: coal and oil were produced then. Compare *Cenozoic* and *Mesozoic.*

pal-ette or **pal-let** (pal′it), *n.* **1,** a thin wood, porcelain, metal, or plastic plate with a hole for the thumb, used by artists for mixing and holding colours; **2,** the colours or other elements used in creating a piece of art; **3,** in *computing,* the range of colours and shapes available to the user.

pal-in-drome (pal′in-drōm′), *n.* a word, phrase, sentence, or number that reads the same forward and backward; as, dad, Hannah, or February 20, 2002 (digitally, 2002 2002) are all *palindromes.*

¹pall (pôl), *n.* **1,** a heavy, velvet covering for a coffin, hearse, or tomb; also, the coffin itself; **2,** any heavy, dark covering; as, a *pall* of smoke.

²pall (pôl), *v.i.* to become distasteful or wearisome; lose power to interest; to become tired of; as, too much joking *palls* on him:—*v.t.* to satiate or fill; as, to *pall* the appetite.

pall-bear-er (pôl′bâr′ėr), *n.* one of the persons who carry or attend the coffin at a funeral.

pal-li-ate (pal′i-āt′), *v.t.* [palliat-ed, palliat-ing], **1,** to excuse or cause to appear less wrong; as, to *palliate* a fault; **2,** to ease without curing; as, to *palliate* a disease.—*n.* **pal′li-a′tion.**

pal′li-a-tive (pal′ē-ā′tiv; pal′ē-a′tiv), *n.* something that eases without curing, as a drug:—*adj.* serving to alleviate without curing; as, *palliative* care for the terminally ill.

pal-lid (pal′id), *adj.* **1,** pale; lacking in colour; as, a *pallid* face; **2,** lacking vitality or sparkle; as, a *pallid* performance.—*n.* **pal′lid-ness.**

pal-lor (pal′ėr), *n.* lack of colour, as in the face; paleness.

¹palm (päm), *n.* **1,** the inner surface of the human hand, between the fingers and the wrist; **2,** the part of a glove that covers this area of the hand; **3,** a unit of length of about 10 centimetres used to measure the height of horses; a hand:—*v.t.* **1,** to conceal in or about the hand, as in a sleight-of-hand trick; as, the magician *palmed* the card; **2,** to pass by fraud; as, to *palm* off worthless stock on investors; **3,** touch with the palm of the hand; to handle.

²palm (päm), *n.* **1,** a tropical tree with a crown of large fan-shaped leaves generally radiating from the summit of a slender trunk from which no large branches grow; **2,** a leaf of the tree, formerly used as an emblem of victory; **3,** victory; honour.

palm-is-try (päm′is-tri; pal′), *n.* the practice of reading character or foretelling the future from the lines and marks on the palm of the hand.—*n.* **palm′ist.**

palm-y (päm′i), *adj.* [palm-i-er, palm-i-est]; **1,** abounding in palm trees; **2,** flourishing; prosperous; as, *palmy* days.

pal-o-mi-no (pal-o-mē′nō), *n.* a creamy or golden-coloured saddle horse with white tail and mane.

pal-pa-ble (pal′pa-bl), *adj.* **1,** capable of being touched or felt; tangible; **2,** easily seen; manifest; plain; as, a *palpable* error.—*adv.* **pal′pa-bly.**

pal-pi-tate (pal′pi-tāt′), *v.i.* to beat or throb rapidly, as the heart; to flutter.—*n.* **pal′pi-ta′tion.**

pal-sy (pôl′zi), *n.* [*pl.* palsies], paralysis; loss of sensation, or of power to move or to control motion, in any part of the body:—*v.t.* [palsied, palsy-ing], to paralyze.—*adj.* **pal′sied.**

pal-ter (pôl′tėr), *v.i.* to use deceit or trickery; to trifle or equivocate, esp. in speech.

pal-try (pôl′tri), *adj.* [pal-tri-er, pal-tri-est], **1,** worthless; contemptible; **2,** small; measly or meagre; as, a *paltry* gift.—*n.* **pal′tri-ness.**

pam-per (pam′pėr), *v.t.* to humour; gratify; indulge (a person) in every wish:—*adj.* overindulged or spoiled; as, a *pampered* child.

pam-phlet (pam′flet), *n.* a small unbound book, usually with a paper cover or no cover; a booklet; brochure; as, the candidate distributed *pamphlets* before the election.

pan- (pan-), *prefix* meaning *all, whole, general*; as in *pan*-Canadian (relating to all of Canada or all Canadians), *pan*chromatic (sensitive to any colour; as a *panchromatic* film), *pan*theism (the doctrine that God exists, not as a person, but as manifest in all forms of matter, including humans and every natural object).

pan (pan), *n.* **1,** a broad, shallow metal or earthenware dish for cooking and other household uses; **2,** any similar vessel, as either of the dishes for holding things weighed on scales, or the shallow receptacle for washing out gold from dirt or gravel; **3,** in old-fashioned guns, the hollow part of the lock that held gunpowder for firing the gun; **4,** *Slang* the human face; **5,** a critical, negative review; as, the book review was a *pan*:—*v.t.* [panned, pan-ning], **1,** in mining, to wash (gravel or dirt) in a pan to separate out the gold; **2,** to cook in a pan; as, to *pan* oysters; **3,** *Colloq.* to ridicule , esp. with regard to an artistic endeavour; as, she *panned* the new play.

pan-a-ce-a (pan′a-sē′a), *n.* a remedy or medicine for all ills; a cure-all.

pan-cake (pan′kāk′), *n.* a thin cake made of batter fried in a pan or on a griddle:—**pancake landing,** an emergency manoeuvre in which an airplane is stalled and drops straight down, much like a pancake onto a grill.

pan-cre-as (pan′kri-as; pang′kri-as), *n.* a large, fleshy gland near the stomach that helps digestion: the pancreas of animals, when cooked for food, is called sweetbread.—*adj.* **pan′cre-at′ic.**

pan-da (pan′da), *n.* **1,** the lesser panda of the Himalayas is a raccoonlike, rusty-coloured animal; **2,** the giant panda of Asia is bearlike, with white-and-black markings.

pan-de-mo-ni-um (pan′di-mō′ni-um) *n.* **1,** a place of lawless disorder; **2,** wild uproar; utter confusion.

pan-der (pan′dėr), *n.* **1,** someone who exploits the weaknesses of others; **2,** a pimp or panderer.—*v.i.* to cater to the baser passions; as, to *pander* to people's appetite for gossip.

pan-der-er (pan′dėr-er), *n.* a pimp; an exploiter of lust and desire, esp. sexual.

pane (pān), *n.* **1,** a square or oblong piece of glass in a window or door; **2,** a panel or section of panels in a wall or door.

pan-e-gyr-ic (pan′i-jir′ik), *n.* praise formally written or spoken in honour of a person or event; any high praise.

pan-el (pan′el), *n.* **1,** a division or section of a wall, ceiling, or door, raised above, or sunk below, the surrounding parts; as, a wooden door with glass *panels*; **2,** a thin board on which a picture is painted; also, the picture itself; **3,** a list of persons summoned to serve as jurors; also, an entire jury; **4,** an ornamental strip placed lengthwise on a dress or skirt; **5,** a group of speakers organized specially for discussing, judging, etc.; as, a *panel* of experts; **6,** a board with dials and controls for operating something; as, an instrument *panel* of an airplane:—*v.t.* [paneled, panel-ing], to form, fit, or decorate with panels; as, she *panelled* the walls with pine.—*n.* **pan′el-ist** or **pan′el-list; pan′el-ling** or **pan′el-ing.**

pang (pang), *n.* **1,** a violent, sudden pain; as, *pangs* of hunger; **2,** a sudden, bitter emotion; as, *pangs* of remorse:—*v.t.* to torment; cause great pain.

pan-han-dle (pan′han′dl), *v.t.* and *v.i.* to beg for money or food, esp. on the streets:—*n.* **1,** a handle of a pan; **2,** a narrow strip of land that juts out from a larger area, esp. another country or state.—*n.* **pan′han′dler.**

pan-ic (pan′ik), *n.* **1,** sudden, extreme fright; as, the fire in the theatre caused *panic*; **2,** sudden, general fear, alarm, and distrust, esp. in financial circles; as, the closing of several banks caused a *panic*; **3,** *Colloq.* someone who is very funny; as, she is a real *panic*:—*adj.* caused by fear or alarm; as, a *panic* flight; *panic* selling:—*v.i.* to feel sudden fear; as, don't *panic*:—*v.t* to fill (someone) with panic.—*adj.* **pan′ick-y.**

pan-o-ply (pan′o-pli), *n.* [*pl.* panoplies] **1,** a complete suit of armor; **2,** ceremonial attire; **3,** any complete covering, esp. one that protects; **4,** a splendid array; as, a *panoply* of movie stars.—*adj.* **pan′o-plied.**

pan-o-ra-ma (pan′o-rä′ma; pan′o-ram′a), *n.* **1,** a picture giving a view in every direction, seen from a central standpoint; **2,** a picture seen a part at a time as it is unrolled or unfolded and made to pass before the spectator; **3,** a complete view of a region; **4,** a scene that moves constantly before one, as from the window of a moving train; **5,** a general view of a subject, esp. a comprehensive one; as, a *panorama* of Canadian history.—*adj.* **pan′o-ram′ic.**

pan-sy (pan′zi), *n.* [*pl.* pansies], **1,** a common garden plant of the violet family, with blossoms of rich colour and velvety texture; also, its flower; **2,** *Slang* an effeminate man, esp. a homosexual: often considered offensive.

pant (pant), *v.i.* **1,** to breathe rapidly; gasp; as, the walk uphill made him *pant*; **2,** to desire earnestly; yearn:—*v.t.* to utter with a gasp:—*n.* **1,** a short, rapid breath; **2,** a puffing sound; as, the *pant* of an engine:—**pants,** an outer garment covering the legs individually from waist to ankles; trousers.

pan-ther (pan′thėr), *n.* **1,** a large American wildcat: also called *cougar, mountain lion,* and *puma* (see *puma,* illustration); **2,** the leopard; **3,** less frequently, the jaguar.

pan-tie or **pan-ty**(pan′ti), *n.* short underpants, with closed crotch, worn by children and women: often used in plural.

pan-to-mime (pan′to-mīm′), *n.* **1,** a series of actions, chiefly gestures and facial expressions, that express meaning without words; mime; **2,** a play presenting meaning through gestures, without any talking:—*v.i.* [pantomimed, pantomim-ing], to express oneself without using words:—*v.t.* to express without words.—*adj.* **pan′to-mim′ic.**

pan-try (pan′tri), *n.* [*pl.* pantries], a room or closet, usually near the kitchen, for storing food, dishes, etc.

pap (pap), *n.* **1,** soft food for infants; **2,** pulp of fruits; **3,** something that lacks substance; as, his ideas are pure *pap*; **4,** *Colloq.* political patronage:—**Pap smear,** a cancer test of the cervix.

pa-pa or **pop-pa** (på-pä′), *n. Colloq.* a child's name for *father*.

pa-pa-cy (pā′på-si), *n.* [*pl.* papacies], the office, dignity, or term of authority of the Pope:—**Papacy,** the government of the Roman Catholic Church.

pa-pal (pā′pal), *adj.* of or pertaining to the Pope, or to the Roman Catholic Church.

pa-per (pā′pėr), *n.* **1,** a material made of finely divided fibres from rags, wood pulp, etc., commonly in the form of a thin, smooth, flexible sheet, used for writing, drawing, printing, photocopying, etc.; **2,** a piece or sheet of this material; **3,** a packet wrapped in this material; **4,** a newspaper or journal; **5,** an essay or special article; as, a *paper* read before a club; **6,** a legal document; **7,** banknotes or bills of exchange: called *commercial paper*; **8,** a written examination; **9,** *Colloq.* free theatre tickets; **10,** wallpaper:—**papers,** collection of documents; as, the Macdonald *papers* are in the National Archives:—*adj.* **1,** having to do with paper; as, a *paper* cutter; **2,** made of paper; as, *paper* dolls; **3,** having no reality; existing only on paper; as, *paper* profits; **4,** resembling paper; thin:—**paper money,** notes issued by a government, a bank, etc., and used as currency:—*v.t.* **1,** to cover or line with paper; as, to *paper* the walls; **2,** to give out free passes to fill a theatre; as, she *papered* the house.—*adj.* **pa′per-y.**

pa-pier–mâché (pā′pėr–ma-shā′; på′pyā′–mä′ shā′), *n.* paper pulp, mixed with glue or paste, moulded into various shapes, and then dried to harden.

pa-poose (pa-pōōs′), *n.* in North America, an Aboriginal baby.

pap-ri-ka (pa-prē′ka; pap′ri-ka), *n.* mildly pungent, red spice made from the dried ripe fruit of certain peppers.

pa-py-rus (pa-pī′rus), *n.* [*pl.* papyruses or papyri (pa-pī′ri)], **1,** a kind of Egyptian reed from which the ancients made paper; **2,** the paper made from the pith of this plant; **3,** a manuscript or writing on papyrus.

par (pär), *n.* **1,** full or normal value; as, the stock is below *par*; **2,** equality; equal footing; as, the worker is not on a *par* with the others; **3,** normal conditions; as, to feel below *par*; **4,** in *golf*, the standard number of strokes for a given course or hole; as, the hole was a *par* three; **5,** the value of the currency of a country compared to another's; as, Canada's dollar was once at *par* with that of the U.S.:—*adj.* relating, to, or of a par; as, a *par*-three hole:—*v.t.* [parred, par-ring], in *golf*, to equal the standard number of strokes set for a hole or a course.

[1]par-a- (par′a-), *prefix* meaning **1,** *beside*; *beyond*; *aside from*; as in *para*llel; *para*normal; **2,** in *medicine*, *secondary*, *abnormal*, *like*; as in *para*typhoid; **3,** *protecting*; as in *para*chute, *para*sol; **4,** *like a parachute*; as in *para*sailing, *para*gliding.

par-a-ble (par′a-bl), *n.* a made-up story, usually about something that might naturally occur, from which a moral may be drawn.

pa-rab-o-la (pa-rab′o-la), *n.* in *geometry*, the curve formed when a cone is cut by a plane parallel to one of its sides; the curve described by a projectile.—*adj.* **par′a-bol′ic.**

par-a-chute (par′a-shōōt′), *n.* a folding apparatus, umbrella-shaped when open, used in descending from a balloon or airplane high in the air:—*adj.* relating to something dropped in this way; as, *parachute* troops:—*v.t.* **1,** to drop in this manner; **2,** to introduce a well-known personality from outside the riding into an election race to win the seat:—*v.i.* to descend using a parachute.

pa-rade (pa-rād′), *n.* **1,** a show; pompous display; as, a *parade* of wealth; **2,** a military display, or review of troops; **3,** a place of assembly for exercising and inspecting troops; **4,** any march or procession; as, a Santa Claus *parade*; **5,** a promenade or public place for walking; **6,** a series of people or things, esp. in quick succession; as, a *parade* of criminals before the court:—*v.t.* [parad-ed, parad-ing], **1,** to assemble and form (troops, etc.) in military order, as for review; **2,** to march over or through; as, to *parade* the city; **3,** to make a display of; as, she *paraded* her wealth:—*v.i.* **1,** to walk about so as to exhibit or show oneself; **2,** to take part in a formal march.

par-a-dise (par′a-dis′), *n.* **1,** the place in which the souls of the righteous abide after death; heaven; **2,** a state of bliss; **3,** a place or condition of perfect beauty or happiness; as, a tropical *paradise*.

par-a-dox (par′a-doks), *n.* **1,** something that seems absurd or unbelievable, yet may be true; **2,** a statement that appears contradictory; as, "the child is father of the man" is a *paradox*; **3,** a self-contradiction; as, "I always lie" is a *paradox*.—*adj.* **par′a-dox′i-cal.**

par-af-fin (par′a-fin), *n.* **1,** a tasteless, waxy substance obtained from wood, coal, etc., and used to make candles, seal jars, etc.; paraffin wax; **2,** in Britain, kerosene; paraffin oil.

par-a-gon (par′a-gon′, par′a-gun), *n.* a model of excellence or perfection.

par-a-graph (par′a-gråf′), *n.* **1,** a small section of a piece of writing, dealing with one topic; a short passage; **2,** a reference mark [¶] indicating the beginning of a paragraph; **3,** an item in a newspaper, magazine, etc.:—*v.t.* **1,** to arrange in paragraphs; **2,** to write a brief passage about.

par-a-keet (par′a-kēt′), *n.* any of several small, slender parrots with long, tapering tails, which are noted for their chattering and their brightly coloured plumage.

par-al-lel (par′a-lel′), *adj.* **1,** equally distant from each other at all points; as, *parallel* lines; **2,** having the same course; as, *parallel* roads; **3,** similar; corresponding; as, *parallel* circumstances; **4,** having similar parts; **5,** in *computing,* relating to the simultaneous performing of more than one instruction at the same time; as, *parallel* processing:—*n.* **1,** a line or plane equally distant at all points from another line or plane; **2,** one of the imaginary lines drawn on the surface of the earth, or one of the lines drawn on a map or globe, parallel to the equator, that mark degrees of latitude; **3,** a person or thing closely resembling another; **4,** a presentation of resemblance; as, to draw a *parallel* between two careers:—*v.t.* [paralleled, parallel-ing], **1,** to compare; **2,** to be parallel with; **3,** to correspond to:—*adv.* in a parallel relationship; as, the road and river run *parallel.*—*n.* **par′al-lel-ism.**

par-al-lel-o-gram (par′a-lel′o-gram), *n.* a four-sided plane figure, the opposite sides of which are equal and parallel.

PARALLELOGRAMS

parallel port, in *computing,* a device that allows a computer to communicate with another machine by sending several bits simultaneously over separate routes; as, the *parallel port* is connected to the laser printer.

pa-ral-y-sis (pa-ral′i-sis), *n.* [*pl.* paralyses (pa-ral′i-sēz′)], **1,** the loss of feeling or of power to move in one or more parts of the body; palsy; **2,** a state of complete inactivity from lack of power to move; **3,** helplessness; inability to act; as, the snowstorm caused a *paralysis* of transportation.—*adj.* **par′a-lyt′ic.**

par-a-lyze or **par-a-lyse** (par′a-līz′), *v.t.* [paralyzed, paralyz-ing], **1,** to affect with paralysis; **2,** to unnerve; render useless, helpless, or ineffective; as, the snowstorm *paralyzed* the city; fear *paralyzed* him.

par-a-mount (par′a-mount′), *adj.* above all others; supreme; as, of *paramount* importance.

par-a-noi-a (par′a-noi′a), *n.* **1,** a mental disorder marked by delusions, esp. of persecution or grandeur; **2,** in general, the excessive mistrust of others.—*n.* **par′a-noi′ac.**

par-a-pher-na-li-a (par′a-fėr-nā′li-a), *n. pl.* **1,** personal belongings; as, trappings, finery, regalia, etc.; **2,** equipment; apparatus, esp. that used for a specific purpose; as, photographic *paraphernalia.*

par-a-phrase (par′a-frāz′), *n.* the rewording of the sense or meaning of a passage, text, etc., in clearer, simpler, or more precise terms:—*v.t.* and *v.i.* [paraphrased, paraphrasing], to reword in such a way; as, to *paraphrase* an awkward sentence; I don't understand, so please *paraphrase.*

par-a-pleg-ic (par′a-plej′ik; -plēj′ik), *n.* and *adj.* one whose entire lower half of the body is paralyzed.—*n.* **par′a-ple′gi-a** (-plē′).

par-a-site (par′a-sīt′), *n.* **1,** one who lives at another's expense, usually by flattery; a toady or sycophant; **2,** an animal or plant that lives on or within another, called the host, at the latter's expense.—*adj.* **par′a-sit′ic** (par′a-sit′ik); **par′a-sit′i-cal.**

par-a-sol (par′a-sôl′), *n.* a small, light umbrella used as a sunshade.

par-a-troops (par′a-trōōps′), *n.* troops trained and equipped to drop by parachute for battle action behind enemy lines.—*n.* **par′a-troop′er.**

par-boil (pär′boil′), *v.t.* to cook partially by boiling.

par-cel (pär′sl), *n.* **1,** a bundle or package; **2,** a separate part; as, a *parcel* of land:—*v.t.* [parcelled, parcel-ling], **1,** to divide into parts; distribute; as, to *parcel* out fruit; **2,** to do up in a package.

parcel post, 1, a postal rate for large or heavy packages; **2,** the packages so handled.

parch (pärch), *v.t.* **1,** to roast slightly; dry by heating; as, to *parch* corn; **2,** to dry up by heat exposure; **3,** to make thirsty:—*v.i.* to become very dry, hot, or thirsty.

parch-ment (pärch′ment), *n.* **1,** the skin of a sheep, goat, etc., dressed and prepared for writing purposes; **2,** a deed or document on such a skin; as, he referred to his high school diploma as his *parchment*; **3,** paper resembling this material.

par-don (pär′dn), *v.t.* **1,** to free from punishment; forgive; as, to *pardon* a criminal: **2,** to overlook; excuse:—*n.* **1,** forgiveness; **2,** polite indulgence, esp. to indicate that the speaker did not understand; as, I beg your *pardon*; **3,** an official act setting one free from penalty.—*adj.* **par′don-a-ble.**

pare (pâr), *v.t.* [pared, par-ing], **1,** to cut or shave off the outside or ends of; peel; as, to *pare* an apple; **2,** to lessen; reduce; as, to *pare* expenses; **3,** to remove or cut away excess; whittle; trim; as, to *pare* wood or a picture; *pare* expenses.

par-ent (pâr′ent), *n.* **1,** a father or mother; the source of any living thing, as a plant; **2,** cause; origin; as, the *parent* of the revolution:—*adj.* relating to, of, or for a parent; as, a *parent* company:—*v.t.* **1,** to produce or originate; **2,** to act as a parent:—*v.i.* to be a parent.—*adj.* **pa-ren′tal.**

par-ent-age (pâr′en-tij), *n.* **1,** fatherhood or motherhood; **2,** birth or descent; ancestry; lineage; as, of noble *parentage.*—*n.* **par′ent-hood′.**

pa-ren-the-sis (pa-ren′thi-sis), *n.* [*pl.* parentheses (pa-ren′thi-sēz′)], **1,** an explanatory word, phrase, or clause put into a sentence that is grammatically complete without it: indicated by round brackets like these ( ); **2,** either or both of the round brackets ( ); **3,** a digression, interlude, or interval.—*adj.* **par′en-thet′ic; par′en-thet′i-cal.**

pa-ri-ah (pâr′i-a; pa-rī′a), *n.* **1,** a social outcast; **2,** originally, a low Hindu caste in India); **3,** any person or thing that is despised or disdained; as, the state was a *pariah.*

pa-ri-mu-tu-el (par′i-mū′tū-el; cho͞o), *n.* **1,** a form of betting (on horse races) in which those who bet on the winners divide the stakes less a percentage for management and taxes; **2,** the race or bet itself; **3,** the machine used to record the bet and compute the payoff.

par-ing (pâr′ing), *n.* **1,** the act of cutting from a surface; **2,** the part cut off.

par-ish (par′ish), *n.* **1,** a church district under the charge of a clergyman; **2,** those who live in that district or area; **3,** in England, a county subdivision; **4,** a congregation; also, the locality covered by its activities; **5,** in New Brunswick, a county subdivision like a township; **6,** in Québec, a political and ecclesiastical unit:—*adj.* pertaining to, or maintained by, a church, congregation, or district; as, a *parish* school.—*n.* **parish-ion-er** (pa-rish′un-ėr).

par-i-ty (par′i-ti), *n.* **1,** equality, as in character status, amount, etc., **2,** in *finance,* equality in the value of the currency or products of two countries; **3,** in *mathematics,* the relationship between two integers: they are said to have the same *parity* if both are either odd or even; **4,** in *computing,* a method of detecting errors in binary code transmission, known as *parity* bit.

park (pärk), *n.* **1,** a tract of ground set apart as a public place for recreation or wildlife refuge; **2,** a large extent of woods and fields attached to a country house; **3,** a train of artillery; an artillery encampment; as, a *park* of artillery; **4,** an enclosed area of a sports stadium; as, a ball*park*; **5,** an area designated for a specific purpose; as, an industrial *park* or an amusement *park*; **6,** a gear position in an automobile transmission that acts as a brake; as, to put the car in *park*; **7,** in *computing,* the disengagement of the head of the hard disk to protect it from damage when the computer is moved; as, modern computers have automatic *park*:—*v.t.* **1,** to enclose, as in a park; **2,** to collect and station in order; as, to *park* artillery; **3,** to place and leave for a time; as, she *parked* the car; **4,** to place a spacecraft in a temporary orbit; as, they *parked* the space shuttle; **5,** *Colloq.* to place temporarily; as, he *parked* the children with their grandparents:—*v.i.* to place and leave a vehicle temporarily.—*n.* **park′ing.**

par-ka (pär′ka), *n.* a fur jacket, fleece-lined coat, or heavy woollen shirt, with hood attached for protecting the head from the cold: worn in the Yukon, Alaska, etc.

park-way (pärk′wā′), a broad road or highway, often divided by, or bordered with, trees, shrubs, grass, etc.

par-lance (pär′lans), *n.* way of speaking; idiom; language; as legal, military, or newspaper *parlance.*

par-lay (pär′lā; li), *v.t.* and *v.i.* **1,** to bet one's original wager plus its winnings on another race, contest, etc.; **2,** to exploit any asset successfully; as, to *parlay* to fame one's voice, beauty, skill, etc.:—*n.* a series of bets in which the original wager plus all its winnings are gambled.

par-ley (pär′li), *n.* [*pl.* parleys], a conference or discussion, esp. one with an enemy:—*v.i.* to hold a conference, esp. with an enemy, with a view to peace.

par-lia-ment (pär′li-ment), *n.* a general council; a meeting of the people or their representatives to consider matters of common interest:—**Parliament, 1,** the supreme lawmaking body of Canada, consisting of the Senate and the House of Commons; **2,** the similar body in Great Britain, consisting of the House of Lords and the House of Commons; **3,** a similar assembly in certain other countries; **4,** the legislative bodies in the Canadian provinces; **5,** the group of individuals who make up such legislatures: they are known as *Members of Parliament*; **6,** the place where they meet:—**Parliament Hill, 1,** the hill overlooking the Ottawa River, etc., on which Canada's parliament buildings stand at Ottawa, Ontario; **2,** the government of Canada in general; as, the announcement from *Parliament Hill* about the new tax bill.—*adj.* **par′lia-men′ta-ry.**

par-lour or **par-lor** (pär′lėr), *n.* **1,** a room for conversation and the reception of visitors, in a private dwelling, inn, or club, esp. formerly; **2,** a room or building used for a certain type of business; as, a beauty *parlour*; funeral *parlour*; **3,** in Canada, a tavern or hotel where beer is served:—**beer parlour,** a tavern or beverage room where beer is served.

pa-ro-chi-al (pa-rō′ki-al), *adj.* **1,** of or pertaining to a parish or church district; as, a *parochial* school; **2,** narrow; local; limited in scope; as, *parochial* mentality.

par-o-dy (par′o-di), *n.* [*pl.* parodies], **1,** a humorous imitation of a serious writing or musical composition; **2,** a work of this sort; **3,** a satirical imitation of anything; **4,** something done so badly that it is an inferior imitation; a travesty:—*v.t.* [parodied, parody-ing], **1,** to write a humorous imitation of; as, to *parody* a song; **2,** to mimic something in a satirical way; **3,** to imitate poorly.

pa-role (pa-rōl′), *n.* **1,** word of honour; esp., a promise given by a prisoner of war that in return for partial freedom or privileges, he or she will not try to escape, not take up arms within a given time, etc.; **2,** the freeing of a prisoner before his or her time is up, on certain conditions; **3,** the duration of the conditions; **4,** a password or watchword:—*v.t.* [paroled, paroling], to release a prisoner with the stipulation that certain conditions are met.

par-ox-ysm (par′ok-sizm), *n.* **1,** a spasm, convulsion, or fit of acute pain, recurring at intervals; **2,** a sudden and violent outburst of emotion; a fit of any kind; as, a *paroxysm* of rage.—*adj.* **par′ox-ys′mal.**

par-ri-cide (par′i-sīd′). *n.* the murder, or murderer, of a close relative, esp. a parent.

par-rot (par′ut), *n.* **1,** a tropical bird with a hooked bill and brilliant feathers that can be taught to repeat words; **2,** someone who mindlessly repeats the words or actions of others without understanding them:—*v.t.* to repeat by rote without understanding; as, the class *parroted* the teacher's words:—*v.i.* to jabber incessantly like a parrot.

par-ry (par′i), *v.t.* [parried, parrying], **1,** to ward off or deflect; as a blow; **2,** to evade or avoid; as, to *parry* a question:—*v.i.* **1,** to ward off or turn something aside; as, to *parry* with the arms; **2,** to evade or dodge; as, to *parry* the question:—*n.* [*pl.* parries], a warding off or evasion, as of a blow.

parse (pärs; pärz), *v.t.* [parsed, pars-ing], in *grammar* **1,** to analyze or describe (a sentence) by stating the parts of speech and their relation to one another; **2,** to state the part of speech of a word and its value in a sentence; **3,** in *computing*, to break down (input) into simple components.

par-si-mo-ni-ous (pär′si-mō′ni-us), *adj.* excessively frugal; close; stingy; miserly.—*n.* **par′si-mo-ny.**

pars-ley (pärs′li), *n.* a garden plant, the leaves of which are used as a garnish and for flavouring.

pars-nip (pärs′nip), *n.* a plant with an edible carrotlike root.

par-son (pär′sn), *n.* **1,** a clergyman in charge of a parish, esp. a Protestant one; a rector; **2,** *Colloq.* any minister or preacher.

par-son-age (pär′sn-ij), *n.* the residence of a minister in charge of a parish, esp. a house owned by a church or parish and set aside for the use of the minister; a rectory.

part (pärt), *n.* **1,** something less than the whole; as, *part* of a pear; a piece, section, or division; an individual portion; **2,** a share in action, duty, or responsibility; as, to do one's *part*; **3,** an essential member or organ; as, *part* of the body; automobile *parts*; **4,** a side in a quarrel; as, they took his *part*; **5,** a character assigned to an actor in a play, movie, television show, etc.; also, the words spoken by that character; as, he took the *part* of Hamlet; **6,** a division of the hair of the head by a straight line; as, he calls it a wide *part*, but he is really going bald; **7,** in *music*, one of the melodies in a harmony; as, a bass *part*; **8,** one of a given number of equal quantities into which a number, quantity, or object may be divided; as, three is the third *part* of nine:—**parts, 1,** a region or section; as, to live in these *parts*; visit foreign *parts*; **2,** ability or talent; as, a person of *parts*:—*v.t.* **1,** to divide into two or more pieces or sections; **2,** to disunite; force to go apart; **3,** to separate; as, to *part* the fighters:—*v.i.* **1,** to divide into two or more parts; break; as, the rope *parted*; **2,** to separate; as, to *part* from a friend:—*adv.* not full or complete; partial; partly; as, a mule is *part* horse and *part* donkey.—*adj.* **part′ed.**

par-take (pär-tāk′), *v.i.* [*p.t.* partook (pär-took′), *p.p.* partak-en (pär-tāk′en), *p.pr.* partak-ing], **1,** to have or receive a share in common with others; as, humans *partake* of the ability to talk; **2,** to take a portion; as, to *partake* of food; **3,** to participate in; as, to *partake* in the festivities.—*n.* **par-tak′er.**

par-tial (pär′shal), *adj.* **1,** inclined to favour one side or party; biased; prejudiced; as, a judge should not be *partial*; **2,** having a liking for; as, she is *partial* to chocolate; **3,** not entire; incomplete; as, a *partial* view of the building.—*adv.* **par′tial-ly.**—*n.* **par′ti-al′i-ty** (pär′shi-al′i-ti; pär-shal′i-ti).

par-tic-i-pate (pär-tis′i-pāt′), *v.i.* [participat-ed, participat-ing], to share with others; to take part; as, everyone *participated* in the fun.—*n.* **par-tic′i-pa′tor; par-tic′i-pa′tion.**—*n.* and *adj.* **par-tic′i-pant.**

par-ti-ci-ple (pär′ti-si-pl), *n.* a part of a verb used as both verb and adjective; as, in "running, the woman caught the train," the *participle* "running" shows action as a verb, and describes the noun "woman" as an adjective.—*adj.* **par′ti-cip′i-al.**

par-ti-cle (pär′ti-kl), *n.* **1,** a very small piece; a bit; as, sand *particles*; **2,** the smallest possible amount of anything; as, not a *particle* of courage; **3,** in *grammar*, a short, subordinate part of speech, as a conjunction, article, preposition, or interjection.

par-tic-u-lar (pär-tik′ū-lėr), *adj.* **1,** distinct from others; as, a *particular* kind of paint; **2,** special; unusual; as, of *particular* importance; **3,** exact; nice; as, *particular* in dress; **4,** detailed; precise; as, a *particular* report:—*n.* a detail; as, the *particulars* of the story.—*n.*

par-tic′u-lar′i-ty.—*v.t.* and *v.i.* **par-tic′u-lar-ize′** [particularized, particulariz-ing].

par-tic-u-lar-ly (pär-tik′ū-lėr-li), *adv.* **1,** in detail; in a particular manner; as, *particularly* accurate; **2,** especially; as, he *particularly* wanted to go.

par-ti-san (pär′ti-zn), *n.* **1,** a devoted, sometimes prejudiced, follower, esp. of a political cause or faction; **2,** a guerrilla:—*adj.* pertaining to, or strongly in favour of, a person, cause, or faction, esp. a political party or faction.

par-ti-san-ship (pär′ti-zan-ship′), *n.* loyalty; esp., unreasonable loyalty to a person or cause.

par-ti-tion (pär-tish′un), *n.* **1,** the act of dividing or the state of being divided; **2,** a separation; a dividing wall, as in a building; **3,** a section or division:—*v.t.* **1,** to divide into shares or parts; **2,** to divide by walls.

part-ly (pärt′li), *adv.* in part; not wholly or completely; as, the clothes are *partly* dry.

part-ner (pärt′nėr), *n.* **1,** one who is associated with another or others for mutual benefit or united action; as, a business *partner;* **2,** one who shares something with another; as, *partners* in misery; **3,** in *games,* one who plays with another on a side against opponents; as, each player has a *partner;* **4,** one who dances with another; **5,** a husband, wife, or significant other.

part-ner-ship (pärt′nėr-ship), *n.* **1,** joint interest or ownership; **2,** the union of two or more persons in the same business; **3,** the people so associated.

par-tridge (pär′trij), *n.* **1,** any of various Old World game birds allied to the quails and pheasants; **2,** in America, any of a number of similar game birds, as the bob-white, quail, and ruffed grouse.

par-ty (pär′ti), *n.* [*pl.* parties], **1,** a number of persons united for a particular purpose; group; faction; as, a political *party;* **2,** one who has an interest in an affair, as one of the two sides in a lawsuit; **3,** a social gathering, esp. one to mark a special occasion; as, a dinner *party;* **4,** any group of people who act together; as, the search *party* found the lost child.

pass (pås) *v.i.* [*p.t.* passed (påst), *p.p.* passed or past, *p.pr.* pass-ing], **1,** to go from one place or condition to another; move along; as, the parade *passes* down the street; **2,** to move from one to another; circulate freely, as money; **3,** to elapse or go by; as, the night *passed* slowly; **4,** to make or force one's way; as, to *pass* through a crowd; **5,** to go unnoticed; as, his action *passed* without rebuke; **6,** to be approved, as a bill or law; **7,** to go through a test with success; as, to *pass* her driver's test; **8,** to decide on the quality of something; as, to *pass* on someone's work; **9,** in *cards,* to let one's turn go by without playing or bidding; **10,** to be known or accepted; as, to *pass* for a lawyer; **11,** to end; as, old customs *pass* and new ones take their place; **12,** to happen; occur; as, to see what *passed:*—*v.t.* **1,** to go by, through, beyond, etc.; as, to *pass* the house; **2,** to cause or allow to go; hand; as, to *pass* the butter; also, to give to someone; cause to circulate; as, to *pass* bad money; **3,** to spend time; as, to *pass* the day; **4,** to exceed; as, it *passes* belief; **5,** to give as a judgment; as, to *pass* sentence; **6,** to utter or pronounce; as, to *pass* an opinion; **7,** to give legal status to (a bill or law); **8,** to go through (a test) successfully; **9,** to examine and approve: as, to *pass* a candidate:—*n.* **1,** a narrow passage, as in the mountains; **2,** a permit or ticket allowing free admission or passage; as, a backstage *pass;* **3,** critical condition; as, matters have come to a sad *pass;* **4,** in *sports,* the act of throwing the ball, puck, etc., from one player to another; **5,** in an examination, a standard that satisfies examiners without securing honours.—*n.* **pass′er.**—*adj.* **pass′a-ble.**—*adv.* **pass′a-bly** (moderately).

pas-sage (pas′ij), *n.* **1,** course or progress; as, the *passage* of time; **2,** a journey; esp., a voyage; as, a *passage* to India; **3,** a way by which one passes; a hall or corridor; as, an underground *passage;* **4,** the right to go; as, a free passage; **5,** legal enactment; as, the *passage* of a law; **6,** a single portion of a book, speech, etc.; **7,** a conflict; as, a *passage* at arms.—*n.* **pas′sage-way′.**

pass-book (pås′book′), *n.* a book in which the deposits and withdrawals of a bank's customer are recorded; a bankbook.

pas-sé (på′sā′), *adj.* out-of-date; old-fashioned; superseded; as, that style is *passé.*

pas-sen-ger (pas′en-jėr), *n.* one who travels usually at a stated fare by a public conveyance, as a plane, boat, train, bus, taxi, etc.

pass-er-by or **pass-er–by** (pås′ėr-bī′), *n.* [*pl.* passersby or passers-by], one who goes past.

pass-ing (pas′ing), *n.* the act of going by or past:—*adj.* **1,** moving by; going by; as, the *passing* train; **2,** lasting only a short time; brief; as, a *passing* interest in swimming.

pas-sion (pash′un), *n.* **1,** any intense feeling or emotion, as joy, fear, love, etc.; **2,** an outburst of rage; **3,** love; intense desire; enthusiasm; as, a *passion* for music; **4,** the object of love, interest, etc.; as, video games are my *passion.*—*adj.* **pas′ sion-ate.**

pas-sive (pas′iv), *adj.* **1,** suffering without resisting; submitting; **2,** not acting but acted upon; **3,** in *grammar,* indicating that form of the transitive verb that carries the idea that the subject is acted upon: opposite of *active;* as, in the sentence, "the boy was thrown from the horse," the subject "boy" receives the action expressed in the *passive* form "was thrown."—*adv.* **pas′sive-ly.**—*n.* **pas-siv′i-ty** (pa-siv′i-ti); **pas′siv-ism.**

pass-key (pås′kē′), *n.* **1,** a private key; **2,** a master key that opens a group of locks.

pass-port (pås′pōrt), *n.* **1,** an official paper

from one's own government giving one permission to travel in a foreign country; **2,** anything that opens the way to success; as, education is a *passport* to success.

pass-word (pås′wûrd′), *n.* **1,** a secret word or phrase known only to those on guard and to those allowed to pass the guard; a watchword; **2,** in *computing*, a series of characters that must be typed in to allow authorized users to log on to a computer system.

past (påst), *adj.* **1,** having formerly been; gone by; as, the *past* generation; **2,** just gone by; last; as, the *past* hour; **3,** thoroughly experienced; as, a *past* master:—*n.* **1,** time gone by; as, memories of the *past*; **2,** previous life or history; as, we know nothing of his *past*; **3,** in *grammar*, the past tense:—*adv.* by; beyond; as, he just walked *past*:—*prep.* beyond in time, age, or condition; as, he is *past* 18; she is *past* cure:—**past tense,** in *grammar*, a tense of the verb indicating time gone by; as, she *went*:—**past perfect,** a tense of the verb indicating action that took place before a time in the past; as, when we arrived, she *had gone*.

pas-ta (pås′ta; pas′ta), *n.* a food made by mixing flour, water, and sometimes eggs into a paste or dough, which is formed into different shapes and boiled in water; noodles; macaroni.

paste (pāst), *n.* **1,** a sticky mixture, often of flour and water, used for making things stick together; **2,** dough prepared for pie crust, pasta, etc.; **3,** a pureed preparation, as of fish, nuts, or other foods, finely ground to a creamy consistency; as, anchovy or almond *paste*; also, a jellylike confection; as, Turkish *paste*; **4,** a hard, glassy mixture used for making artificial gems:—*v.t.* [past-ed; past-ing], **1,** to cover or fasten with a sticky mixture; as, to *paste* the photos in the album; **2,** in *computing*, to transfer material from one location to another; as, to *paste* data from one file to another; **3,** to cover as by pasting; as, to *paste* the bulletin board with messages; **4,** *Slang* to hit hard or beat; as, she *pasted* him a good one; **5,** *Slang* to defeat.—*n.* **past′ing.**—*adj.* **past′y.**

paste-board (pāst′bōrd′), *n.* stiff material made by pressing paper pulp or pasting together sheets of paper:—*adj.* anything flimsy or substandard, as if made of pasteboard.

pas-tel (pas-tel′), *n.* **1,** a soft, pale shade of any colour; **2,** a crayon of ground colouring matter mixed with gum, or the ground pigment paste itself; **3,** a drawing made with such crayons, or the art of drawing with them; **4,** a light, short prose study:—*adj.* done in subdued tints; as, the interior was in *pastel* shades.

pas-teur-ize (pas′tūr-iz′, pas′tėr-iz′), *v.t.* [pasteurized, pasteuriz-ing], to heat a liquid, as milk, to a temperature high enough to destroy harmful germs without destroying the nourishing value of the liquid.—*n.* **pas′teur-i-za′tion.**

pas-time (pas′tīm′), *n.* diversion; sport; amusement; any activity that fills time agreeably.

pas-tor (pås′tėr), *n.* a Christian minister in charge of a church and congregation.

pas-to-ral (pås′to-ral), *adj.* **1,** pertaining to the duties of a minister; as, *pastoral* calls; **2,** pertaining to shepherds or the shepherd's life; as, *pastoral* poetry; **3,** of or relating to country life in general, esp. an idealized version of it:—*n.* a poem, play, music, painting, etc., depicting country life.

pas-try (pās′tri), *n.* [*pl.* pastries], **1,** desserts, as pies, tarts, etc., made with a rich crust, usually enclosing fruit or meat; **2,** the dough used to make these foods.

pas-tur-age (pås′tūr-ij), *n.* land used for grazing cattle or other animals.

pas-ture (pås′tūr), *n.* land or grass on which cattle feed:—*v.t.* [pastured, pastur-ing], to supply with grass or pasture:—*v.i.* to graze.

past-y (pās′ti, pas′ti), *adj.* **1,** something that is similar to paste; **2,** pale and unhealthy; as, a *pasty* complexion:—*n.* [*pl.* pasties], a British pie, usually of highly seasoned meat, covered with a crust.

[1]**pat** (pat), *n.* **1,** a light, quick blow with the hand or fingers; as, a *pat* on the back; **2,** a small shaped lump, as of butter; **3,** a light sound or tap:—*v.t.* [pat-ted, pat-ting], to strike gently with a flat surface, esp. with the hand or fingers; stroke gently.

[2]**pat** (pat), *adj.* [pat-ter, pat-test], **1,** suitable; as, a *pat* answer; **2,** resolute; as, to stand *pat*:—*adv.* aptly; readily.

patch (pach), *n.* **1,** a piece of material, as cloth or metal, put on to cover a hole or to strengthen a worn place; **2,** a small piece; **3,** a spot or blotch of colour; as, the cat had a *patch* of white on its side; **4,** a piece of cloth or bandage put over a wound or injury for protection; a dressing; as, an eye *patch*; a small area; as, a *patch* of ice:—*v.t.* **1,** to cover or strengthen by putting on a patch; **2,** to mend, esp. clumsily; **3,** to piece together with pieces of material; as, to *patch* a quilt; **4,** to settle; mend; as, to *patch* a quarrel.—*n.* **patch′work′.**—*adj.* **patch′y.**

pâ-té (på′tā′), *n.* a meat paste, used in sandwiches, pies, or with crackers, etc.

pa-tel-la (pa-tel′a), *n.* [*pl.* patellae (pa-tel′ē; pa-tel′ī)], the knee cap.

Patella, labelled "A"

pa-tent (pā′tent; pat′ent), *adj.* **1,** open for anyone to view or to read: said esp. of an official paper that confers a privilege; as, letters *patent*; **2,** medicines; **3,** (usually pā′tent), evident; plain; as, his honesty was *patent*:—*n.* **1,** a privilege granted by the government that gives to an inventor the sole right of making, using, or selling his or her invention for a definite number of years; **2,** the thing so protected; as, she owned several *patents*; **3,** the documents granting this protection:—*v.t.* to grant or secure the sole right to; as, she *patented* her invention.—*adj.* **pat′ent-a-ble.**—*adv.* **pat′ent-ly** (pā′tent-li).—*n.* **pat′ent-ee′** (a person granted a patent).

pa-ter-nal (pa-tûr′nal), *adj.* **1,** pertaining to a father; as, *paternal* advice; **2,** inherited from a father; **3,** related through the father; as, a *paternal* uncle.—*n.* **pa-ter′ni-ty** (fatherhood); **pa-ter′nal-ism.**

path (påth), *n.* [*pl.* paths (på*thz*)], **1,** a road; footpath; **2,** a track; **3,** a course of conduct or action.—*adj.* **path′less.**

pa-thet-ic (pa-thet′ik), *adj.* arousing sympathy and pity; pitiful; as, a *pathetic* story:—**pathetic fallacy,** in *literature*, the portraying of nature as having human feeling; as, the *angry* sea; the sky *weeps*.—*adv.* **pa-thet′ical-ly.**

path-o- (path′ō-), *prefix* meaning *suffering* or *feeling*; as in *patho*logy (the science of the cause, nature, and course of diseases).

pa-thos (pā′thos), *n.* that quality that excites sympathy and pity.

path-way (påth′wā′), *n.* **1,** a narrow footpath; **2,** any course or road.

pa-tience (pā′shens) *n.* the condition or quality of being patient; as, she had great *patience* with her baby sister.

pa-tient (pā′shent), *adj.* **1,** enduring pain, hardship, etc., without complaint; **2,** tolerant; tender; forgiving; **3,** untiring in labour; persevering; as, a *patient* worker; **4,** waiting with calmness; as, the *patient* customer:—*n.* one under the care of a doctor or who receives medical attention; as, the *patient* waited for two hours to see her doctor.

pa-ti-o (på′ti-ō′; pä′tyō), *n.* [*pl.* patios], **1,** an open courtyard within a house or other building; **2,** an outdoor space near a house that is usually used for cooking, eating, or relaxing.

pa-tois (pat′wa; på′twä′), *n.* [*pl.* patois], a local or provincial dialect that differs from the accepted standard; jargon; as, the Dutch *patois* of South Africa.

pa-tri-arch (pā′tri-ärk), *n.* **1,** a founder or head of a family or tribe; esp. one of the early ancestors of the Jews; **2,** an aged and venerable man; **3,** in the Eastern Orthodox Churches, a bishop of the highest rank.—*adj.* **pa′tri-ar′chal** (pā′tri-är′kal).

pa-tri-cian (pa-trish′an), *n.* **1,** a member of the ancient Roman aristocracy: opposite of *plebeian*; **2,** a person of noble birth; aristocrat; **3,** someone with refined manners and tastes:—*adj.* **1,** pertaining to the ancient Roman aristocracy; **2,** noble; aristocratic; **3,** relating to refined manners and tastes.

pat-ri-cide (pat′ri-sīd′), *n.* **1,** one who murders his or her own father; **2,** such a murder.

pat-ri-mo-ny (pat′ri-mo-ni), *n.* [*pl.* patrimonies], **1,** property inherited from a father or other ancestor; **2,** property settled upon a religious institution for its support.—*adj.* **pat-′ri-mo′ni-al.**

pa-tri-ot (pā′tri-it; pāt′ri-ot), *n.* one who loves his or her government or country.—*adj.* **pa′tri-ot′ic** (pā′tri-ot′ik).

pa-tri-ot-ism (pā′tri-ot-izm), *n.* love of one's country.

pa-trol (pa-trōl′), *n.* **1,** a guard; police officer; **2,** the act of going on the rounds of a district in order to protect it; **3,** a body of soldiers on guard or reconnoitring duty; **4,** a division of eight Scouts or Guides in a troop:—*v.t.* [patrolled, patrol-ling], **1,** to go or walk round in order to protect; as, a police officer *patrols* her beat; **2,** to act as a guard to (a camp, sea coast, etc.).

pa-trol-man (pa-trōl′man), *n.* [*pl.* patrolmen (-men)], a policeman or watchman whose duty it is to patrol a certain beat or district.—*n.fem.* **pa-trol′wom′an.**

pa-tron (pā′trun), **1,** a guardian or protector; **2,** an upholder or supporter; as, a *patron* of music or painting; **3,** in business, a regular customer; **4,** a person who lends his or her support to a social or charitable event:—*adj.* aiding, or acting as guardian; as, *patron* saints.

pa-tron-age (pā′trun-ij; pat′), *n.* **1,** special favour or encouragement; guardianship or protection; **2,** the act of buying goods or services regularly from one supplier; **3,** politically, the power to control nominations or to give jobs, favours, etc.:—*adj.* relating to, of, or for patronage; as, a *patronage* appointment by the premier.

pa-tron-ize (pā′trun-īz′, pat′) *v.t.* [patronized, patroniz-ing], **1,** to act as guardian or benefactor toward; support or protect; favour; **2,** to treat with condescension; **3,** to deal with regularly as a customer; as, to *patronize* a store.—*n.* **pa′tron-iz′er.**—*adj.* **pa′tron-iz′ing.**

[1]**pat-ter** (pat′ėr), *v.i.* **1,** to mumble or mutter something over and over rapidly; **2,** to talk glibly:—*v.t.* to mumble indistinctly:—*n.* **1,** rapid, cheap, fluent talk; **2,** jargon of a specific group; as, marketing *patter*.

[2]**pat-ter** (pat′ėr), *n.* a quick succession of light sounds:—*v.i.* **1,** to run with quick, short steps; **2,** to strike with a quick succession of light taps.

pat-tern (pat′ėrn), *n.* **1,** a model, sample, or specimen; **2,** anything cut out or formed into a shape to be copied; as, a *pattern* for a dress; **3,** an example to follow, esp. a good example; **4,** a design or figure; as, the *pattern* in a carpet:—*v.t.* **1,**

to make in imitation of; copy; as to *pattern* a dress after a model; **2,** to decorate, as with a design:—*v.i.* to follow a pattern or example.

pat-ty (pat′i), *n.* [*pl.* patties], **1,** a small, cup-shaped shell of pastry, holding meat or other ground ingredients; **2,** a round, flat cake of chopped food such as meat or fish; as, a hamburger *patty*; **3,** a round, flat candy; as, a peppermint *patty*; **4,** a small pie; **5,** a half-moon pastry filled with spicy meat; as, a Jamaican *patty*.

pau-ci-ty (pô′si-ti), *n.* small number (of); fewness; scarcity; as, a *paucity* of workers, supplies, evidence, etc.

paunch (pônch; pänch), *n.* the abdomen; the belly and its contents, esp. one that bulges out like a potbelly.

pau-per (pô′pėr), *n.* a very poor person, esp. one who is supported by the public or by charity—*n.* **pau′per-ism.**—*v.t.* **pau′per-ize** [pauperized, pauperiz-ing].

pause (pôz), *n.* **1,** a temporary stop or rest; interruption; as, a *pause* in the day's work; **2,** an intermission or break in speaking or reading; **3,** a break in writing indicated by a punctuation mark; **4,** a mark in music over or under a note or rest to show that it is to be prolonged: also called *hold*; **5,** a hesitation; **6,** the control on the VCR, CD player, etc., that allows the user to interrupt the operation; as, to put the movie on *pause*:—*v.i.* [paused, paus-ing], to make a short stop; wait; as, to *pause* for breath.

pave (pāv), *v.t.* [paved, pav-ing], **1,** to cover with stones, bricks, etc.; as, to *pave* a street; **2,** to make smooth or easy; as, the explorers *paved* the way for those who followed.—*n.* **pav′er.**

pave-ment (pāv′ment), *n.* **1,** a roadway or floor covered or laid with stone, brick, tile, etc.; **2,** any material, as of stones, concrete, etc., used in covering a road, pathway, or floor.

pa-vil-ion (pa-vil′yun), *n.* **1,** a light, ornamental building, as in a garden; **2,** a large tent with a peaked roof; **3,** a temporary open building for shelter, entertainment, etc.

pav-ing (pāv′ing), *n.* **1,** the surfacing of a road or sidewalk; **2,** material for covering roads, walks, etc.; also, the surface itself; as, stone or brick *paving*.

paw (pô), *n.* **1,** the foot of an animal that has claws, as a cat, dog, tiger, etc.; **2,** *Colloq.* a hand:—*v.t.* **1,** to scrape or beat with the feet; as, the horse *pawed* the ground; **2,** to handle (something) roughly; **3,** to strike wildly with the hands; as, to *paw* the air:—*v.i.* **1,** to scrape or touch something with the forefoot; **2,** to handle a thing awkwardly; grope clumsily.

[1]pawn (pôn), *n.* **1,** something given or deposited as a pledge for the payment of a debt or return of a loan; **2,** the state of being so pledged; as, my watch is in *pawn*; **3,** a hostage:—*v.t.* to give as security for a loan; as, to *pawn* a ring:—*v.t.* to pledge or deposit something in this manner.

[2]pawn (pôn), *n.* **1,** in *chess*, a piece of lowest value; **2,** a person deliberately used or sacrificed by another.

pawn-bro-ker (pôn′brō′kėr), *n.* someone whose business it is to lend money on goods left with him or her.

pawn-shop (pôn′shop′), *n.* a shop run by a pawnbroker.

pay (pā), *v.t.* [paid (pād), pay-ing], **1,** to give money to, in return for work done or goods received; as, to *pay* workers; **2,** to discharge, as a debt, by giving over the money required; **3,** to be profitable or worth doing; as, it will *pay* you to do what I say; **4,** to give without any sense of obligation; as, to *pay* a compliment; **5,** to allow to run out; to pass out through the hands; as, we *paid* out all the slack in the rope; **6,** to give, do, say, or make; as, to *pay* attention in class:—*v.i.* **1,** to make recompense; discharge a debt; as, he always *pays* promptly; **2,** to make suitable return for effort; be worthwhile; as, the business *pays* well; it *pays* to be honest:—*n.* money given for work done; wages; salary.—*n.* **pay′er.**

pay-a-ble (pā′a-bl), *adj.* due, as a bill.

pay-ee (pā-ē′), *n.* the one to whom money is paid or payable.

pay-ment (pā′ment), *n.* **1,** the act of giving money for wages, a debt, etc.; **2,** that which is given to discharge a debt, etc.; as, her car *payments* were $200 per month.

PC (pē′sē′), *abbrev.* short for **1,** in *computing, personal computer*; **2,** *Progressive Conservative*; **3,** *politically correct;* **4,** *postal code.*

PDA (pē′dē′ā′), *abbrev.* short for *personal digital assistant.*

pea (pē), *n.* **1,** a pod-bearing plant of the same family as the bean, widely grown as a vegetable; **2,** its round, green seed, which is used for food; **3,** a related plant; as, the sweet *pea*.

peace (pēs), *n.* **1,** a state of rest or calm; quiet, esp. freedom from war or disorder; **2,** friendly relations between persons; **3,** a treaty or agreement to end a war.—*n.* **peace′mak′er; peace′keep′er; peace′keep′ing.**

peace-a-ble (pēs′a-bl), *adj.* **1,** not quarrelsome; **2,** calm; quiet.

peace-ful (pēs′fool), *adj.* **1,** free from war or commotion; **2,** mild; calm; undisturbed; quiet; as, a *peaceful* evening.—*adv.* **peace′ful-ly.**

peach (pēch), *n.* **1,** a sweet, juicy fruit, with yellow flesh, a downy, red-tinted yellow skin, and a large, rough stone containing one large seed; **2,** the tree bearing this fruit; **3,** a soft yellowish-pink colour; **4,** *Colloq.* a pleasing or admired person.

pea-cock (pē′kok′), *n.* **1,** the male bird of the peafowl, noted for its long, handsome tail feathers, marked with iridescent, eyelike spots; **2,** *Colloq.* a vain person.—*n. fem.* **pea′hen′.**

pea jacket, a short, heavy, woollen overcoat, worn esp. by sailors.

peak (pēk), *n.* **1,** the sharp-pointed top of a mountain or hill; **2,** a mountain standing alone; **3,** a pointed end of anything; as, the *peak* of a roof; **4,** the most intense or highest point; as, the *peak* of happiness; **5,** the visor of a cap; **6,** the narrow part of a vessel's bow or stern:—*v.i.* to reach maximum; as, unemployment *peaked* in February:—*v.t.* to cause to reach maximum:—*adj.* approaching a maximum; as, to work at *peak* efficiency.

[1]**peaked** (pēkt), *adj.* pointed; as, a *peaked* roof; also, projecting; as, a *peaked* cap.

[2]**peak-ed** (pēk′id), *adj. Colloq.* sharp-featured; thin; wan; sickly; as, a *peaked* face.

peal (pēl), *n.* **1,** a loud sound or succession of sounds, as of thunder, bells, etc.; as, a *peal* of laughter; **2,** a set of bells, or a musical phrase rung on them:—*v.i.* to give forth loud sounds, as a bell or organ:—*v.t.* to cause to sound loudly; as, to *peal* a bell.

pea-nut (pē′nut′), *n.* **1,** a yellow-flowered plant of the pea family, the pods of which ripen under the ground; **2,** the nutlike seed or fruit of these plants; **3,** *Colloq.* a person who is short or otherwise insignificant:—**peanuts**, *Slang* an insignificant or small amount; as, to work for *peanuts.*

pear (pâr), *n.* **1,** a sweet, juicy fruit related to the apple, with a spherical base tapering toward the stalk; **2,** the tree that bears this fruit.

pearl (pûrl), *n.* **1,** a small, smooth, lustrous gem formed as a growth inside the shells of oysters or other shellfish; **2,** something resembling a pearl in shape, size, colour, or value; **3,** a pale, greyish-white colour:—**mother of pearl**, the tinted lining of the shell of various shellfish.—*adj.* **pearl′y.**

peas-ant (pez′ant), *n.* **1,** one who tills the soil; a farmer or farm labourer; **2,** a country person; **3,** an ill-mannered person; a boor:—*adj.* relating to, of, or for peasants; rustic; boorish; as, a *peasant* dress; *peasant* manners.

peas-ant-ry (pez′ant-ri), *n.* the class consisting of those who till the soil; peasants; farmers.

peat (pēt), *n.* a substance formed of partly decayed vegetable matter in swamps and marshy places and used for fuel and fertilizer.—*adj.* **peat′y.**

peb-ble (peb′l), *n.* **1,** a small stone; a stone worn smooth by water; **2,** a rough, grainy, or dimpled texture.—*adj.* **peb′bly.**

pe-can (pi-kan′; pi-kän′; pē′kan), *n.* **1,** a kind of hickory tree of the southern U.S.; **2,** its oblong, smooth, thin-shelled nut; **3,** the wood of this tree.

pec-ca-dil-lo (pek′a-dil′ō), *n.* [*pl.* -dilloes or -dillos], a trifling fault; as, the boy's *peccadillos.*

[1]**peck** (pek), *n.* **1,** in the system of U.S. dry measure, a capacity of one quarter of a bushel; or eight quarts; 8.8 litres; **2,** a vessel for measuring out a peck; **3,** a lot; a great deal; as, a *peck* of trouble.

[2]**peck** (pek), *v.t.* **1,** to strike with the beak; as, the bird *pecked* my hand; **2,** to strike with a pointed instrument, as a pick; **3,** to pick up with the beak; as, the hen *pecks* corn; **4,** *Colloq.* to eat sparingly; as, she *pecks* at her food:—*v.i.* **1,** to make strokes with the beak or a sharp instrument; **2,** to pick up food with the beak:—*n.* **1,** a quick, sharp stroke, as with the beak; **2,** a mark made by a blow with a pointed instrument; **3,** a light, quick kiss; as, a *peck* on the cheek.

pec-tin (pek′tin), *n.* a white, water-soluble substance found in ripe fruit, etc., used as a jellying agent in various foods, pharmaceuticals, and cosmetics.

pec-to-ral (pek′to-ral), *adj.* of or placed on the chest; as, a *pectoral* muscle.

pe-cul-iar (pi-kūl′yėr), *adj.* **1,** one's own; individual; belonging to a particular person or place; as, a tree *peculiar* to British Columbia; **2,** strange; odd; as, her actions are *peculiar.*—*n.* **pe-cu′li-ar′i-ty.**

pe-cu-ni-ar-y (pi-kū′ni-er-i), *adj.* of or concerned with money; financial; as, *pecuniary* losses.

ped- (ped-), or **pe-do-** (pē′dō-), or **pedi-** (ped′i-), *prefix* meaning **1,** *foot;* as in *ped*al, *ped*estrian, *pedi*cure (foot care), *pedo*meter (an instrument that measures the distance walked); **2,** *child;* as in *ped*agogy (teaching), *pedi*atrician; **3,** *soil;* as in *pedo*logy (the branch of science that studies soil).

ped-a-gogue (ped′a-gog), *n.* a school teacher, esp. a dogmatic one.—*adj.* **ped′a-gog′i-cal** (ped′a-goj′i-kal).

ped-al (ped′l), *adj.* concerning or operated by a foot:—*n.* the treadle, or foot-operated lever, of a machine, vehicle, organ, piano, or harp; as, the brake *pedal* of the car:—*v.t.* and *v.i.* [pedalled, pedal-ling], to move or operate by working a pedal or pedals; as, to *pedal* a bicycle.

ped-ant (ped′ant), *n.* one who makes a show of his or her learning, esp. with regard to formal rules.—*adj.* **pe-dan′tic.**

ped-dle (ped′l), *v.i.* [ped-dled, ped-dling], **1,** to travel about selling small wares; **2,** to be concerned with trifles; to piddle:—*v.t.* **1,** to sell from house to house; hawk; **2,** to deal out little by little; **3,** *Colloq.* to sell (drugs) illegally.

ped-dler or **ped-lar** (ped′lėr), *n.* **1,** one who travels around selling small articles; a hawker; **2,** someone who sells illegal drugs; as, a drug *peddler*.

ped-es-tal (ped′es-t'l), *n.* **1,** the base of a column; also, the support of a statue, lamp, etc; **2,** any base or foundation; **3,** a position of high regard, admiration, or idolization; as, he put her on a *pedestal*.

pe-des-tri-an (pi-des′tri-an), *n.* one who travels on foot; a walker:—*adj.* **1,** walking; on foot; as, a *pedestrian* crossing; **2,** slow-moving; dull; uninspired; ordinary; as, *pedestrian* argument or writing.

pe-di-a-tri-cian (pe′di-a-trish′an), *n.* a specialist in the care of infants and the treatment of children's diseases.

ped-i-cel (ped′i-s'l), *n.* a slender flower stem branching from a peduncle. (See illus. under *peduncle*.)

ped-i-gree (ped′i-grē′), *n.* **1,** a record or list of ancestors of a person or animal; **2,** lineage; ancestry; as, a person of noble *pedigree*:—*adj.* relating to, of, or for a purebred; as, a *pedigree* dog.

ped-lar (ped′lėr), *n.* Same as **peddler**.

pe-dun-cle (pi-dung′kl), *n.* the main stem of a flower or cluster of flowers.

peek (pēk), *v.i.* to look slyly, as through half-closed eyes; look through a crevice or crack; peep:—*n.* a peep; a sly glance.

peel (pēl), *v.t.* **1,** to strip off an outer covering from; as, to *peel* an orange; **2,** to strip off; as, to *peel* bark from a tree:—*v.i.* to come off; as, bark *peels*:—*n.* skin or rind; as, lemon *peel*.

¹peep (pēp), *v.i.* **1,** to chirp; cry, as young birds; **2,** to speak in a weak, high voice:—*n.* **1,** chirp; squeak; **2,** a baby chick.

²peep (pēp). *v.i.* **1,** to look through a crack or from a hiding place; look slyly; peek; **2,** to begin to appear; as, the moon *peeped* from behind a cloud:—*n.* **1,** a quick, sly look; **2,** a glimpse; peek; as, I took a *peep* at the first chapter; **3,** first appearance, as of the sun.—*n.* **peep′er.**

¹peer (pēr), *n.* **1,** a person of the same rank; an equal or associate; as, a jury of his *peers*; **2,** a member of nobility; a nobleman.—*n. fem.* **peer′ess.**

²peer (pēr), *v.i.* **1,** to look closely or out of curiosity; as, they all *peered* at me; **2,** to peep out; come into sight; as, the sun *peered* from behind the cloud.

peer-age (pēr′ij), *n.* **1,** the rank or dignity of a noble; **2,** the whole body of nobles; **3,** a record or list of peers.

peer group, people of about the same age, social status, etc., within a community.

peer-less (pēr′lis), *adj.* without equal; matchless; as, a *peerless* voice.

peeve (pēv), *v.t.* and *v.i.* [peeved, peev-ing], to become or make bad-tempered:—*n.* the person or thing disliked, or that annoys; as, his pet *peeve* is people talking in a movie theatre.—*adj.* **peeved** (pēvd).

pee-vish (pē′vish), *adj.* childishly fretful; hard to please; discontented; as, a *peevish* disposition.

peg (peg), *n.* **1,** a pointed wooden or metal pin used as a fastening; as, a clothes*peg*; a tent *peg*; **2,** a piece of wood serving as a nail; as, to hang one's coat on a *peg*; **3,** a step or degree; as, he took her down a *peg*:—*v.t.* [pegged, peg-ging], **1,** to fasten with pegs; **2,** to mark by driving in small stakes of wood; as, to *peg* out a mining claim; **3,** *Colloq.* to categorize; as, to *peg* her as the class clown:—*v.i.* **1,** to work steadily; as, to *peg* away at one's lessons; **2,** *Colloq.* to keep (prices, etc.) at the same level.

Pe-king-ese (pē′king-ēz′; pē′king-ēs′) or **Pe-kin-ese** (pē′kin-ēz′; pē′kin-ēs′), *n.* [*pl.* Pekingese or Pekinese], **1,** a small, pug-nosed, long-haired dog, originally from China; **2,** a person from Beijing (Peking); also, the language from this area.

pe-koe (pē′kō), *n.* a choice black tea that is superior since the leaf is picked young with the down still on it.

pel-i-can (pel′i-kan), *n.* a large, web-footed waterbird that has a large pouch attached to the lower jaw of its huge bill.

pel-let (pel′it), *n.* **1,** a little ball, as of food or medicine; **2,** a missile; bullet.

pell–mell or **pell-mell** (pel′–mel′; pell′mell), *adv.* **1,** in a disorderly manner; **2,** headlong; in a great hurry; frantically; as, to rush out *pell-mell*.

¹pelt (pelt), *n.* a raw hide; the untanned skin of an animal.

²pelt (pelt), *v.t.* to strike with a number of missiles; as, to *pelt* pebbles at the windows:—*v.i.* **1,** to strike repeated blows with something thrown; **2,** to beat down heavily, as, rain or hail; **3,** to run quickly; as, she *pelted* past us:—*n.* **1,** a blow from something thrown; **2,** a rapid speed:—**full pelt,** (at) full speed; as, to ride *full pelt*.

pel-vis (pel′vis), *n.* [*pl.* pelvises or pelves (pel′vēz)], in human anatomy, the basin-shaped structure of bones that supports the spinal column and to which the lower limbs are attached; in animals, a similar structure where the backbone and hipbones meet.—*adj.* **pel′vic.**

pem-mi-can or **pem-i-can** (pem′i-kan), *n.* **1,** in North America, an Aboriginal food made of dried lean meat pounded into a paste with fat and pressed into cakes; **2,** a concentrate of dried beef, raisins, suet, and sugar, which keeps for a long time: used by explorers and as emergency rations during expeditions.

¹pen (pen), *n.* **1,** a small enclosure, esp. one

for confining animals; a coop; **2,** any small enclosed area; as, a baby's play*pen*:—*v.t.* [penned (pend) or pent (pent), pen-ning], to shut up in, or as if in, a pen or enclosure.

[2]**pen** (pen), *n.* **1,** an instrument for writing or drawing with ink; as, a ballpoint *pen*; **2,** a style of writing; **3,** an author:—*v.t.* [penned, pen-ning], to write or compose, with or as with a pen, as a letter, article, etc.

pe-nal (pē′nal), **1,** *adj.* having to do with punishment or with punished persons; as, *penal* laws; *penal* labour; a *penal* colony; **2,** meriting punishment; as, a *penal* offence.

pe-nal-ize (pē′nal-īz′), *v.t.* [penalized, penaliz-ing], **1,** to inflict a penalty upon; as, the referee *penalized* our football team; **2,** to put at a disadvantage; as, poverty *penalizes* certain students.

pen-al-ty (pen′al-ti), *n.* [*pl.* penalties] **1,** legal punishment for breaking the law; as, the *penalty* for murder is death; **2,** a fine; forfeit; **3,** a punishment or handicap imposed for the breaking of a rule; as, a two-minute hockey *penalty* for slashing.

penalty box, a special bench in hockey and some other sports where players serve penalties.

pen-ance (pen′ans), *n.* **1,** an act of devotion, often prescribed, to show sorrow or repentance for a sin; **2,** hardship or suffering as a result of a mistake or wrongdoing.

pen-cil (pen′sil), *n.* **1,** a stick formerly of black lead but now of graphite, generally encased in wood, metal, or plastic, and used for writing, drawing, etc.; **2,** any similar device, as, an eyeliner *pencil*:—*v.t.* [pencilled, pencil-ling], to write or sketch with a pencil; as, she *pencilled* in the time of her class.—*adj.* **pen′cilled.**

pen-dant or **pen-dent** (pen′dent), *n.* something hanging, esp. a hanging ornament.

pen-dent or **pen-dant** (pen′dent), *adj.* **1,** hanging; swinging; as, a *pendent* bough; **2,** overhanging; jutting over, as, a *pendent* rock; **3,** undetermined; in suspense; pending.

pend-ing (pen′ding), *adj.* not yet finished or decided; pendent; as, a *pending* trial:—*prep.* **1,** during; as, *pending* the negotiations for peace, an armistice was declared; **2,** until; as, *pending* his arrival, we did nothing.

pen-du-lous (pen′dū-lus), *adj.* hanging down; swaying; as, *pendulous* branches, fruits, etc.

pen-du-lum (pen′dū-lum), *n.* an object suspended from a fixed point so that it is free to swing to and fro; as, the *pendulum* of a grandfather clock.

pen-e-trate (pen′i-trāt′), *v.t.* [penetrated, penetrat-ing], **1,** to enter into; pierce; **2,** to soak through; spread itself through; permeate; as, the dampness *penetrated* his clothes; **3,** to understand; grasp in the mind; as, to *penetrate* a secret:—*v.i.* **1,** to pierce something; **2,** to affect the feelings or mind deeply.—*adj.* **pen′e-trat′ing.**

pen-e-tra-tion (pen′i-trā′shun), *n.* **1,** the act of entering or piercing; **2,** mental acuteness or keenness; sagacity.

pen-guin (peng′gwin; pen′gwin), *n.* a large black and white Antarctic seabird that cannot fly but uses its winglike appendages as paddles in swimming.

pen-i-cil-lin (pen′i-sil′in), *n.* any of various antibiotics produced naturally by moulds or synthetically, able to prevent the growth of disease-causing bacteria: it is useful in the treatment of such infections as pneumonia.

pen-in-su-la (pen-in′sū-la), *n.* a piece of land almost surrounded by water but still connected to a larger body of land; as, Nova Scotia is a large *peninsula*.—*adj.* **pen-in′su-lar.**

pe-nis (pē′nis), *n.* the male organ of sexual intercourse.

pen-i-tence (pen′i-tens), *n.* sorrow for sin or wrongdoing; repentance.—*adj.* and *n.* **pen′i-tent.**—*adj.* **pen′i-ten′tial.**

pen-i-ten-tia-ry (pen′i-ten′sha-ri), *adj.* **1,** pertaining to penance; **2,** pertaining to prisons or reformatories; **3,** making a person liable to imprisonment; as, a *penitentiary* offence:—*n.* [*pl.* penitentiaries], a prison in which convicts are confined.

pen-knife (pen′nīf′), *n.* [*pl.* penknives (pen′ nīvz′)], a small pocketknife.

pen-man-ship (pen′man-ship), *n.* the art or style of handwriting; as, good *penmanship*.

pen name or **pen-name** (pen′nām′), *n.* a pseudonym; nom de plume.

pen-nant (pen′ant), *n.* **1,** a long, narrow naval flag or streamer; **2,** a small, triangular flag; **3,** in *sports*, a flag given to a champion team; **4,** championship.

pen-ni-less (pen′i-lis), *adj.* without a penny; very poor; destitute.

pen-ny (pen′i), *n.* [*pl.* pennies], **1,** in Canada and the U.S., one cent; **2,** [*pl.* pence (pens)], in England and some other Commonwealth countries, a coin equal to one one-hundredth of a pound; **3,** a sum of money; as, to cost a pretty *penny*; **4,** a trivial amount; as, it cost just *pennies*.

pe-nol-o-gy (pi-nol′o-ji), *n.* **1,** the science of reforming and rehabilitating criminals; **2,** the practice and study of managing prisons.

[1]**pen-sion** (pen′shun), *n.* **1,** a certain sum paid regularly by a government, employer, or corporation to a person retired after a long period of service; **2,** an allowance paid by governments to provide for certain needy people; as, old-age *pensions*:—*v.t.* to

grant a regular allowance of money to.

[2]pen-sion (pän′syôn•′; pän-syōn•′), **1,** in Europe, a hotel, boarding house, or boarding school; **2,** room and board.

pen-sion-er (pen′shun-ėr), *n.* a person who receives a pension.

pen-sive (pen′siv), *adj.* **1,** engaged in, or given to, serious thought; musing; as, a *pensive* mood; a *pensive* nature; **2,** expressing serious thought; as, a *pensive* magazine article.

pent (pent), *adj.* shut or penned up.—*adj.* **pent′-up′** (as, *pent-up* emotions).

pen-ta-or **pent-** (pen′ta-; pent-), *prefix* meaning *five;* as in *penta*cle, *penta*gram, *penta*meter, *penta*thlon.

pen-ta-gon (pen′ta-gon), *n.* in *geometry*, a figure with five sides and five angles.—*adj.* **pen-tag′o-nal** (pen-tag′o-nal).

pen-tam-e-ter (pen-tam′e-tėr), *n.* a verse or line of five metrical feet; as, an iambic *pentameter.*

pen-tath-lon (pen-tath′lon), *n.* **1,** an athletic track-and-field contest of five events, esp. the long jump, 200-metre dash, 1500-metre run, javelin throw, and discus throw of the traditional Olympic Games; **2,** in the modern pentathlon, a contest consisting of five different events in swimming, running, fencing, shooting, and riding.

Pen-te-cost (pen′ti-käst′), *n.* **1,** a Christian celebration on the seventh Sunday after Easter to commemorate the descent of the Holy Spirit on the apostles: also called *Whitsunday;* **2,** a Jewish religious festival, about seven weeks after Passover, celebrating the harvest and the giving of the Ten Commandments to Moses: also called *Shavuot.*

Pen-te-cos-tal (pen′ti-käs′tl), *n.* a member of one of several Protestant fundamentalist churches that believes in the importance of the human spirit as demonstrated through faith healing, speaking in tongues, and other such charismatic displays:—*adj.* relating to this church.

pent-house (pent′hous′), *n.* **1,** a house or apartment built on a roof or top floor(s) of a building, esp. a luxurious residence; **2,** a shed or roof sloping from a wall or building; **3,** a sloping covering like an awning, canopy, etc.

pe-nult (pē′nult; pi-nult′), *n.* the second-last thing in a series, as a syllable of a word.—*adj.* **pe-nul′ti-mate.**

pen-um-bra (pi-num′bra), *n.* the partial, as distinct from the total, shadow, esp. that which surrounds the total shadow of the moon, or of the earth, during an eclipse.

pen-u-ry (pen′ū-ri), *n.* want of the necessities of life; extreme poverty.—*adj.* **pe-nu′ri-ous.**

pe-on (pē′on), *n.* **1,** in Latin America and in the southern U.S., a labourer, often unskilled, esp. one forced to work to pay a debt; **2,** any menial worker.

pe-o-ny (pē′o-ni), *n.* [*pl.* peonies], a garden plant that springs up in a cluster of red shoots; also, one of its large, usually double, red, pink, or white flowers.

peo-ple (pē′pl), *n.* **1,** a body of persons united into a community, race, tribe, nation, etc.; inhabitants; as, the Canadian *people;* **2,** men, women, and children; as, only 10 *people* were present; **3,** the persons of a particular place or group; as, country *people;* **4,** the populace; the masses; as, the *people* rebelled against the new law; **5,** relatives; as, my own *people*:—*v.t.* [peo-pled, peo-pling], to fill with inhabitants; as, to *people* a country.

pep (pep), *n. Colloq.* liveliness; energy; vim; as, the puppy was full of *pep*:—*v.t.* [pepped, pepping], to stimulate; invigorate (often used with *up*); as, to *pep up* a boring speech.—*adj.* **pep′py.**

pep-per (pep′ėr), *n.* **1,** a hot seasoning made of the ground berries of a tropical plant; also, the plant which bears these berries; **2,** a plant, the red berries of which make a similar hot seasoning; **3,** a garden plant, the hollow red or green fruit of which is used as a vegetable:—*v.t.* **1,** to season with pepper; **2,** to sprinkle or strew thickly; as, the story was *peppered* with negative innuendoes; **3,** to shower or pelt with small missiles.

pep-per-mint (pep′ėr-mint), *n.* **1,** a strong-smelling plant of the mint family; **2,** an oil prepared from it; **3,** a candy flavoured with this oil.

pep-per-y (pep′ėr-i), *adj.* **1,** containing pepper; pungent; **2,** hot-tempered; fiery; spirited.

pep-sin or **pep-sine** (pep′sin), *n.* **1,** an enzyme formed in the gastric juice of animals as a natural aid to digestion; **2,** a preparation from this substance used in medicine.

pep-tic (pep′tik), *adj.* **1,** digestible or aiding digestion; caused by pepsin, as *peptic* ulcers.

per (pėr), *prep.* **1,** *Colloq.* through; by means of; by; as, *per* bearer; *per* the teacher's instructions; **2,** for or in each; as, two dollars *per* person; one computer *per* classroom; 1000 revolutions *per* second.

per- (pûr-), *prefix* meaning *thoroughly* or *completely;* as in *per*fervid (ardent), *per*vert (corrupt).

per-am-bu-late (pėr-am′bū-lāt′), *v.t.* [perambulated, perambulat-ing], to walk through:—*v.i.* to stroll about.—*n.* **per-am′bu-la′tion.**

per an-num (an′um), by the year; yearly; as, five per cent *per annum.*

per-ceive (pėr-sēv′), *v.t.* [perceived, perceiv-ing], **1,** to become aware of through the senses; see, hear, feel, taste, or smell; **2,** to understand; comprehend; realize; as, she *perceived* that he was upset and changed the subject.

per cent or **per-cent** (pėr-sent′), *n.* in or to every hundred; as, six *per cent* of a dollar is six cents; five *per cent* of 200 is 10: symbol [%].

per-cent-age (pėr-sen′tij), *n.* **1,** a certain part or number in each hundred; **2,** any part or proportion of a whole; ratio; as, a large *percentage* of students graduate; **3,** *Colloq.* profit, gain, or advantage; as, what's the *percentage* in finishing school?

per-cep-ti-ble (pėr-sep′ti-bl), *adj.* capable of being known through the senses.—*adv.* **per-cep′ti-bly.**—*n.* **per-cep′ti-bil′i-ty.**

per-cep-tion (pėr-sep′shun), *n.* **1,** power or ability to become aware of something through the senses; **2,** a mental impression; also, understanding.—*adj.* **per-cep′tive.**

[1]**perch** (pûrch), *n.* **1,** a spiny-finned freshwater fish of which the yellow perch is the commonest variety; **2,** any of various spiny-finned, saltwater fishes, as the ocean perch and the white perch.

[2]**perch** (pûrch), *n.* **1,** a rod or pole on which birds sit or roost; **2,** any high seat; **3,** an advantageous position:—*v.i.* to sit on a high seat; roost; as, the guest speaker was *perched* on the stool.

per-cip-i-ent (pėr-sip′i-ent), *adj.* seeing or perceiving keenly or readily.—*n.* **per-cip′i-ence.**

per-co-late (pûr′kō-lāt′), *v.i.* [percolated, percolat-ing], to pass, as a liquid, through very small spaces; to filter; as, water *percolates* through sand:—*v.t.* **1,** to cause to pass through very small spaces; to filter; **2,** to pass boiling water through in order to extract a flavour; as, to *percolate* coffee.

per-co-la-tor (pûr′ko-lā′tėr), *n.* anything that filters, esp. a coffeepot in which boiling water filters through ground coffee.

per-cus-sion (pėr-kush′un), *n.* **1,** a violent crashing together of two bodies; **2,** the striking of sound waves against the eardrum; **3,** musical instruments played by striking them; also, such instruments or their players considered as a group:—*adj.* relating to, of, or for percussions; as, *percussion* instruments.

per-di-tion (pėr-dish′un), *n.* **1,** loss of all happiness after death; damnation; **2,** hell.

per-emp-to-ry (per-emp′tėr-i, pėr-emp′to-ri), *adj.* **1,** positive; final; allowing no discussion; as, a *peremptory* command; **2,** dogmatic or dictatorial.—*adv.* **per-emp′to-ri-ly.**

per-en-ni-al (pėr-en′i-al), *adj.* **1,** lasting throughout the year, as, *perennial* summer; **2,** living more than one year; living on from year to year; as, *perennial* plants; **3,** enduring; as, *perennial* youth; **4,** constantly recurring; repeating again and again; as, *perennial* problems:—*n.* a plant that lives more than one year.

per-fect (pûr′fekt), *adj.* **1,** complete; finished; whole; **2,** without defect or blemish; as, a *perfect* apple; a *perfect* diamond; **3,** lacking nothing; exact; as, a *perfect* likeness; **4,** of the highest type of excellence; as, a *perfect* answer; **5,** very skilled or accomplished; as, a *perfect* defence; **6,** utter; entire; as, a *perfect* stranger:—*v.t.* (pėr-fekt′; pûr′fekt), **1,** to complete or finish; as, to *perfect* an invention; **2,** to bring to final excellence; as, to *perfect* one's writing ability.

perfect tense, in *grammar*, any of three tenses of the verb, called more specifically *present perfect, past perfect*, and *future perfect*, which indicate action that has taken place before the time of the present, the past, or the future; as, I *have seen*, I *had seen*, I *shall have seen*, esp. the present perfect:—*n.* in *grammar*, the present perfect tense.

per-fec-tion (pėr-fek′shun), *n.* **1,** completion; as, the *perfection* of the plan was left to the captain of the team; **2,** completeness; as, to bring a plan to *perfection*; **3,** that which is faultless; also, highest excellence or skill; as, the *perfection* of the child's playing amazed the musician.—*n.* **per-fec′tion-ist.**

per-fect-ly (pûr′fekt-li), *adv.* **1,** in a perfect manner; **2,** exactly; completely; as, *perfectly* still.

per-fid-i-ous (pėr-fid′i-us), *adj.* treacherous; faithless; disloyal; as, a *perfidious* friend.—*adv.* **per-fid′i-ous-ly.**—*n.* **per′fi-dy.**

per-fo-rate (pûr′fo-rāt′), *v.t.* [perforated, perforat-ing], **1,** to pierce; **2,** to make a hole or a series of holes in, esp. for ease of separation; as, to *perforate* sheets of postage stamps.—*n.* **per′fo-ra′tion.**

per-form (pėr-fôrm′), *v.t.* **1,** to do; carry out; execute; as, to *perform* a task; *perform* an illegal operation on the computer; **2,** to discharge; fulfill; as, to *perform* a duty; **3,** to represent; render; portray; as, to *perform* a part in a school play:—*v.i.* **1,** to act a part; as, to *perform* on the stage; **2,** to exhibit skill in public; as, to *perform* on the piano.—*n.* **per-form′er.**

per-form-ance (pėr-fôr′mans), *n.* **1,** the carrying out of something; execution; completion; as, the *performance* of a duty; **2,** a thing done; deed; feat; **3,** a public exhibition, esp. on the stage.

per-fume (pėr-fūm′), *v.t.* [perfumed, perfum-ing], to fill with a pleasant odour; scent; as, flowers *perfumed* the night air:—*n.* [pûr′fūm; pėr-fūm′] **1,** a pleasing scent; a fragrance; **2,** a fluid mixture esp. prepared to give out a pleasing odour.—*n.* **per-**

fum′er; per-fum-er-y.

per-func-to-ry (pėr-fungk′to-ri), *adj.* done halfheartedly, carelessly, or as if to get rid of a duty; as, a *perfunctory* inspection.—*adv.* **per-func′to-ri-ly.**

per-haps (pėr-haps′), *adv.* possibly; maybe; it may be.

per-i- (per′i-), *prefix* meaning **1,** *around, about;* as in *peri*patetic (walking around or about), *peri*phery (perimeter or outside); **2,** *near;* as in *peri*gee (the point in the moon's orbit where it is nearest the earth); *peri*helion (the point in a planet's or comet's orbit where it is nearest the sun).

per-il (per′il), *n.* exposure to injury; danger; risk:—*v.t.* [perilled, peril-ling], to expose to danger or risk.—*adj.* **per′il-ous.**

per-im-e-ter (pe-rim′e-tėr), *n.* the outer boundary or circumference of an area; as, the *perimeter* of a field.

pe-ri-od (pē′ri-ud), *n.* **1,** a definite portion of time, the beginning and end of which are fixed; **2,** any space of time as, a *period* of rainy weather; also, a number of years looked on as an era; as, the World War II *period;* **3,** a full pause at the end of a complete sentence; **4,** a dot [.] used as a mark of punctuation at the end of a complete declarative sentence or after an abbreviation; **5,** a complete sentence, esp. a complex one; **6,** a part of the school day; as, a lunch *period;* **7,** in *sports,* the divisions of the playing time; as, her goal in the third *period* won the game; **8,** *Colloq.* a menstrual cycle.

pe-ri-od-ic (pē′ri-od′ik), *adj.* **1,** pertaining to a definite period of time; **2,** occurring at intervals, esp. at regular times; as, *periodic* fever; **3,** designating a kind of sentence so framed that the thought is not complete until the end.

pe-ri-od-i-cal (pē′ri-od′i-kal), *adj.* **1,** pertaining to a definite period of time; **2,** occurring at intervals; **3,** published at regular intervals:—*n.* a periodical magazine.—*adv.* **pe′ri-od′i-cal-ly.**

pe-riph-er-al (pėr-if′ėr-al), *n.* in *computing,* a supplemental device that is connected to a computer, such as a keyboard, mouse, printer, etc.

per-i-scope (per′i-skōp′), *n.* an upright tube with lenses and mirrors so arranged that a person below a certain level, as below ground or sea level, can view objects on or above that level; as, the submarine's *periscope.*

per-ish (per′ish), *v.i.* **1,** to lose life; decay, spoil, or die; as, fruit *perishes* quickly in the heat; **2,** to be destroyed or come to nothing; as, empires *perish.*

per-ish-a-ble (per′ish-a-bl), *adj.* liable to decay; easily spoiled; as, *perishable* food.—*n.pl.* **per-ish-a-bles,** something, esp. food, that is easily spoiled.

per-i-win-kle (per′i-wing′kl), *n.* a creeping evergreen plant, esp. the common myrtle, which has shiny leaves and blue or white flowers.

per-jure (pûr′jėr), *v.t.* [perjured, perjur-ing], to make (oneself) guilty of swearing falsely, or breaking a vow; as, to *perjure* oneself.—*n.* **per′jur-er.**

per-ju-ry (pûr′jėr-i), *n.* [*pl.* perjuries], **1,** the willful breaking of an oath or solemn promise; **2,** willful giving under oath of false testimony, usually in a court of law.

[1]**perk** (pûrk), *v.t.* **1,** to lift quickly; as, the little bird *perked* up its head; **2,** to make (oneself) trim or neat; as, to *perk* oneself out in new clothes:—*v.i.* **1,** to hold up the head saucily; **2,** to become brisk or jaunty.

[2]**perk** (pûrk), *n. Colloq.* a perquisite or fringe benefit.

[3]**perk** (pûrk), *v.t.* **1,** to brew coffee; percolate; **2,** to stir into activity; as, to *perk* up the economy.

perk-y (pûr′ki), *adj.* [perk-i-er, perk-i-est], pert; lively; jaunty; cheerful; energetic; as, a *perky* personality.

per-ma-nent (pûr′ma-nent), *adj.* lasting; durable; continuing in the same state; as, a *permanent* job:—*n. Colloq.* a chemical hair treatment that produces a long-lasting curl; a permanent wave.—*adv.* **per′ma-nent-ly.**—*n.* **per′ma-nence.**

permanent resident, Same as **landed immigrant.**

per-me-ate (pûr′mē-āt′), *v.t.* [permeat-ed, permeat-ing], **1,** to pass through the pores or crevices of; penetrate; as, water *permeates* sand; **2,** spread itself through; pervade; as, gas *permeates* a room.—*n.* **per′me-a′tion.**—*adj.* **per′me-a-ble.**

per-mis-si-ble (pėr-mis′i-bl), *adj.* tolerable; allowable; as, *permissible* conduct.

per-mis-sion (pėr-mish′un), *n.* **1,** the act of allowing; **2,** consent; authorization; as, he asked for *permission* to leave early.

per-mit (pėr-mit′), *v.t.* [permit-ted, permit-ting], **1,** to allow by not trying to prevent; tolerate; as, swimming is *permitted* in the creek; **2,** to give consent to; authorize; as, to *permit* food in the study lounge:—*v.i.* to give consent; allow; as, if the weather *permits,* I shall go:—*n.* (pûr′mit), a written licence to do something, as to drive an automobile.

per-mu-ta-tion (pûr′mū-tā′shun), *n.* **1,** alteration, esp. a radical one; **2,** the process of rearranging; **3,** any of the ways of arranging a number of objects, letters, etc.; thus, the possible *permutations* of *a, b, c,* are *abc, acb, bac, bca, cab, cba.*

per-ni-cious (pėr-nish′us), *adj.* highly injurious; destructive; deadly; as, smoking is a *pernicious* habit.

per-nick-et-y (pėr-nik′et-i), *adj.* Same as **persnickety.**

per-ox-ide (pėr-ok′sīd′), *n.* a compound that contains a large proportion of oxygen; as, hydrogen *peroxide.*

per-pen-dic-u-lar (pûr′pen-dik′ū-lėr), *adj.* **1,** at right angles to a given line or surface; **2,** perfectly upright; also, steep; as, a *perpendicular* hill:—*n.* **1,** a line or plane at right angles with another; **2,** a vertical line or direction.—*adv.* **per′pen-dic′-u-lar-ly.**

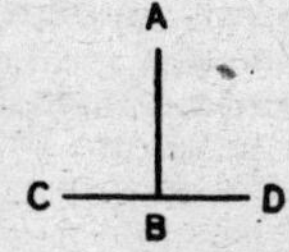

LINE AB IS PERPENDICULAR TO CD

per-pe-trate (pûr′pi-trāt′), *v.t.* [perpetrated, perpetrat-ing], to do; perform; commit: usually in a bad sense; as, to *perpetrate* a crime.—*n.* **per′pe-tra′tion; per′pe-tra′tor.**

per-pe-tu-al (pėr-pet′ū-al), *adj.* **1,** never ceasing; continuous; endless; everlasting; as, *perpetual* motion; **2,** happening over and over without stopping; as, *perpetual* complaining.—*adv.* **per-pet′u-al-ly.**

per-pet-u-ate (pėr-pet′ū-āt′), *v.t.* [perpetu-at-ed, perpetuat-ing], to make everlasting; to continue indefinitely.—*n.* **per-pet′-u-a′tion; per-pet′u-a′tor; per′pe-tu′i-ty** (pûr′pi-tū′i-ti).

per-plex (pėr-pleks′), *v.t.* **1,** to fill with uncertainty or doubt; to puzzle; distract; **2,** to complicate something.—*adj.* **per-plexed′.**—*n.* **per-plex′i-ty.**

per-qui-site (pûr′kwi-zit), *n.* a gain or profit attaching to an office, above the usual wage or salary, as a tip or gratuity, a company car, etc.; a perk.

per-se-cute (pûr′si-kūt′), *v.t.* [persecut-ed, persecut-ing], **1,** to keep on inflicting injury upon; to oppress, esp. for political or religious reasons; **2,** to harass or treat cruelly; annoy; vex.—*n.* **per′se-cu′tor.**

per-se-cu-tion (pûr′si-kū′shun), *n.* **1,** the continued infliction of unjust pain or punishment; as, political *persecution*; **2,** the state of being unjustly treated; repeated injury of any kind.

per-se-ver-ance (pûr′si-vēr′ans), *n.* refusal to give up; continued effort, esp. under a handicap; persistence.

per-se-vere (pûr′si-vēr′), *v.i.* [persevered, persever-ing], to persist steadfastly in a purpose or undertaking.—*adj.* **per′se-ver′ing.**—*adv.* **per′se-ver′ing-ly.**

per-sist (pėr-sist′; pėr-zist′), *v.i.* **1,** to continue steadily or obstinately in saying or doing something; as, she persisted until she solved the mystery; **2,** to continue to last or endure; as, his cold *persists.*

per-sist-ence (pėr-sis′tens; pėr-zis′tens), *n.* **1,** continuous effort, esp. in spite of obstacles or opposition; **2,** lasting quality; as, the *persistence* of an illness.—*n.* **per-sist′en-cy.**

per-sist-ent (pėr′sis′tent; pėr-zis′tent), *adj.* **1,** persisting; persevering; as a *persistent* worker; **2,** continuing for a long time; enduring; lasting; as, a *persistent* rain.—*adv.* **per-sist′ent-ly.**

per-snick-et-y or **per-nick-et-y** (pėr-snik′et-i or pėr-nik′et-i), *adj. Colloq.* fussy; overprecise; finicky; as, the actor was *persnickety* about her wardrobe and makeup.

per-son (pûr′sn), *n.* **1,** a human being as distinguished from a thing or an animal; an individual; **2,** the body of a human being; bodily appearance; **3,** in *grammar*, one of the three classes of personal pronouns, the *first person* referring to the person speaking, the *second person* to the person spoken to, and the *third person* to the person or thing spoken of; also, any of the corresponding distinctions in verbs.—**per′son-a-ble.**

per-son-al (pûr′sun-al), *adj.* **1,** relating to, or peculiar to, a person and his or her private affairs; private; intimate; as, *personal* letters; **2,** pertaining to the outward appearance, looks, nature, or character of a person; as, *personal* beauty; *personal* hygiene; *personal* integrity; **3,** given, performed, etc., in person, or by oneself; as, a *personal* greeting; **4,** relating to a certain person; as *personal* remarks; **5,** movable; as, *personal* property; **6,** in *grammar*, expressing person; as, *personal* endings in verbs; "I," "you," "he," "she," "it," etc., are *personal* pronouns.

personal computer, in *computing,* a small computer meant to be used on its own by one person: abbreviated as *PC.* Compare *mainframe.*

personal digital assistant, a hand-held, wireless personal computer that functions as a personal organizer, sending and receiving electronic messages, scheduling, maintaining telephone directories, etc.: abbreviated as *PDA.*

personal identification number, a password or secret code that allows the user access to such things as bank accounts through automated teller machines (ATMs) and computers: abbreviated as *PIN.*

per-son-al-i-ty (pûr′su-nal′i-ti), *n.* [*pl.* personalities], **1,** the quality or fact of being a person and not a thing; **2,** that which makes one human being different from another; individuality; **3,** outstanding qualities of character; as, she has a lot of *personality*; **4,** a person who has such qualities; **5,** someone who is well-known; a celebrity; as, he is a radio *personality.*

per-son-al-ly (pûr′sun-al-i), *adv.* **1,** in person; by oneself; directly; as, to attend to business *personally*; **2,** as a person; as, *personally*, he is charming; **3,** as far as I am concerned; as, *personally*, I would prefer to stay home.

per-son-i-fi-ca-tion (pėr-son′i-fi-kā′shun), *n.* **1,** a figure of speech by which things, qualities, or abstract ideas have a personal nature given to them; as, "the cruel waves" is a *personification* of "waves"; **2,** a striking example of some quality; as, she is the *personification* of neatness.

per-son-i-fy (pėr-son′i-fī′), *v.t.* [personified, personify-ing], **1,** to regard, treat, or represent (a thing, quality, or idea) as a person; **2,** to be a striking example of; represent; embody; as, this business executive *personifies* power.

per-son-nel (pûr′so-nel′), *n.* **1,** all the people employed in any business, public service, factory, office, etc.; **2,** the division of the organization having to do with those employed there; human resources; as, to enquire at *personnel* about a job:—*adj.* relating to, of, or for personnel; as, the *personnel* department.

per-spec-tive (pėr-spek′tiv), *n.* **1,** the art of drawing an object on a flat surface in such a way as to give one the impression that the viewer is looking at the object itself; **2,** a view that includes things in the distance as well as things nearby; **3,** the ability to see things in their right relation to each other; as, a true *perspective* of historical events; **4,** the right relationship of things to each other; as, to look at the causes of our team's defeat in *perspective.*

per-spi-ca-cious (pûr′spi-kā′shus), *adj.* mentally keen; penetrating; discerning.—*n.* **per′spi-cac′i-ty; per′spi-cu′i-ty.**—*adj.* **per-spic′u-ous.**

per-spi-ra-tion (pûr′spi-rā′shun), *n.* the act of secreting sweat; also, the sweat secreted.

per-spire (pûr-spīr′), *v.t.* and *v.i.* [perspired, perspir-ing], to secrete moisture through the skin; to sweat.

per-suade (pėr-swād′), *v.t.* [persuad-ed, persuad-ing], to win over to a point of view; to convince by argument, advice, entreaty, etc.; as, he *persuaded* his mother to let him go on the trip.

per-sua-sion (pėr-swā′zhun), *n.* **1,** the act of persuading, the power to persuade, or the state of being persuaded by argument or entreaty; **2,** a conviction; belief, generally religious; as, of Jewish *persuasion*; **3,** kind or sort; as, writers and others of that *persuasion.*

per-sua-sive (pėr-swā′siv), *adj.* having power to convince or influence; as, a *persuasive* argument.—*adv.* **per-sua′sive-ly.**

pert (pûrt), *adj.* **1,** saucy; bold; impertinent; as, a *pert* answer; **2,** lively or animated.—*adv.* **pert′ly.**

per-tain (pėr-tān′), *v.i.* to belong; also, to relate or refer to something; as, the e-mail *pertains* to business.

per-ti-nent (pûr′ti-nent), *adj.* fitting or appropriate; to the point; as, a *pertinent* remark.—*adv.* **per′ti-nent-ly.**—*n.* **per′ti-nence; per′ti-nen-cy.**

per-turb (pėr-tûrb′), *v.t.* **1,** to agitate; disturb greatly, esp. in mind; **2,** to confuse or disorder.—*n.* **per′tur-ba′tion** (pûr′tėr-bā′shun).

pe-ruse (pi-rōōz′), *v.t.* [perused, perus-ing], **1,** to read, esp. to read with care and attention; **2,** *Slang* to read over casually; skim.—*n.* **pe-rus′al.**

per-vade (pėr-vād′), *v.t.* [pervad-ed, pervad-ing], to pass or spread through every part of; as, an appetizing aroma *pervades* the kitchen.—*adj.* **per-va′sive.**

per-verse (pėr-vûrs′), *adj.* **1,** willfully wrong; set against doing right; **2,** obstinate or stubborn, usually in a wrong action; **3,** petulant; ill-tempered; as, a *perverse* child; **4,** wicked or perverted.—*adv.* **per-verse′ly.**—*n.* **per-verse′ness.**

per-ver-sion (pėr-vûr′zhun; pėr-vûr′shun), *n.* **1,** a turning from the true or proper use, purpose, or meaning; as a *perversion* of justice; **2,** an abnormal or deviant act, esp. with regard to sexuality.

per-ver-si-ty (pėr-vûr′si-ti), *n.* [*pl.* perversities], **1,** willful refusal to do right; **2,** stubbornness; contrariness.

per-vert (pėr-vûrt′), *v.t.* **1,** to turn from the true end or proper purpose; misuse; **2,** to give a wrong meaning to purposely; as, to *pervert* what someone has said:—*n.* (pûr′vûrt), one who has turned from right to wrong or practises sexual deviance.—*adj.* **per-vert′ed.**

pes-ky (pes′ki), *adj. Colloq.* troublesome; annoying; as, *pesky* weather; *pesky* flies.

pe-so (pā′sō), *n.* [*pl.* -sos (-sōz; sōs)], *n.* the monetary unit of several Latin American countries, as of Mexico.

pes-si-mism (pes′i-mizm), *n.* **1,** the belief that there is more evil in the world than good; **2,** a habit of looking on the dark side of life or things: opposite of *optimism.*—*n.* **pes′si-mist.**—*adj.* **pes′si-mis′tic.**

pest (pest), *n.* **1,** an animal, insect, or plant that destroys crops or causes other damage; as, mice are common household *pests*; **2,** a widespread, fatal, contagious disease; as smallpox; a plague or pestilence; **3,** anything or anyone very mischievous or annoying; as, he is such a *pest.*—*adj.* **pes-tif′er-ous.**

pes-ter (pes′tėr), *v.t.* to annoy or harass; vex; bother, esp. with petty irritations; as, he *pestered* his sister with questions.

pes-ti-lence (pes′ti-lens), *n.* **1,** a widespread, infectious, fatal disease; **2,** anything that is destructive.—*adj.* **pes′ti-len′tial.**

pes-ti-lent (pes′ti-lent), *adj.* **1,** poisonous; deadly; **2,** bad for health, morals, or society; **3,** making mischief; vexatious.

pes-tle (pes′l; pes′tl), *n.* a tool for pounding substances to a powder in a mortar:—*v.t.* and *v.i.* [pes-tled, pestling], to pound with a pestle.

pet (pet), *n.* **1,** a tame animal, as a dog, cat, bird, or fish, kept by people as a companion; **2,** a person treated with special affection; a favourite; as, a teacher's *pet*:—*adj.* **1,** kept or treated as a pet; as, my *pet* goldfish; **2,**

favourite; as, a *pet* project; **3,** showing affection; as, a *pet* name:—*v.t.* [pet-ted, pet-ting], to fondle and indulge; as, she *petted* the puppy on the head.

pet-al (pet′al), *n.* one of the parts, usually bright-coloured, of the flower of a plant. (See *flower,* illustration.).—*adj.* **pet′alled** or **pet′aled.**

pet-it or **pet-ty** (pet′i), *adj.* in *law,* minor; as, a *petit* crime.

pe-tite (pe-tēt′), *adj.* small and trim in figure, generally when referring to females; as, she is *petite.*

pe-ti-tion (pe-tish′un), *n.* **1,** an earnest request or entreaty; **2,** a formal request directed to someone in authority, asking for some action to take place; as, to *petition* for a new traffic light; **3,** a document containing a request supported by many signatures; as, a *petition* to city council:—*v.t.* **1,** to present a formal request to; **2,** to solicit or ask for earnestly.—*n.* **pe-ti′tion-er.**

pet-ri-fy (pet′ri-fī′), *v.t.* [petrified, petrifying], **1,** to change into stone; **2,** to make motionless with amazement or fear; as, the approach of danger *petrified* him:—*v.i.* to become stone or of a stony hardness.—*n.* **pet′ri-fac′tion** (-fak′shun).

pet-ro- or **pet-ri-** or **petr-** (pet′rō-; pet′rē-; petr-), *prefix* meaning **1,** *rock;* as in *petrography* (the study of rocks); **2,** *petroleum;* as in *petro*latum (a basis for ointments).

pe-tro-le-um (pe-trō′li-um), *n.* a thick, oily liquid that can burn easily and is usually found underground: it is obtained from the earth by means of wells, and is the source of gasoline, kerosene, etc.

pet-ti-coat (pet′i-kōt′), *n.* a loose underskirt or slip worn by women and girls, esp. formerly.

pet-ti-fog-ging (pet′i-fog′ing), *adj.* mean; dishonest in petty matters; as, a *pettifogging* lawyer, transaction, etc.

pet-ty (pet′i), *adj.* [pet-ti-er, pet-ti-est], **1,** trifling; unimportant; as, a *petty* quarrel; **2,** small-minded; occupied with trivial things; as, *petty* people.—*n.* **pet′ti-ness.**

pet-u-lant (pet′ū-lant), *adj.* fretful; cross; impatient; pettish; as, a *petulant* answer.—*adv.* **pet′u-lant-ly.**—*n.* **pet′u-lance.**

Pe-tun (pe-to͞on′) *n.* [*pl.* Petun or Petuns], an Aboriginal people who were part of the Huron Nation, originally living in Central and Southern Ontario, but now living in Oklahoma, where they are known as the Wyandot.

pe-tu-ni-a (pi-tū′ni-a), *n.* a common garden plant with funnel-shaped flowers, usually white, pink, or purple.

pew (pū), *n.* one of the long, fixed benches in a church.

pew-ter (pū′tėr), *n.* **1,** a lustrous metal, silvery grey in colour, made of tin and lead, or of tin and some other metal, as copper; **2,** dishes or utensils made of this metal:—*adj.* made of pewter; as, a *pewter* tray.

phal-anx (fal′angks; fa′langks), *n.* **1,** among the ancient Greeks, a company of heavy-armed soldiers drawn up in a close rank; **2,** any compact body of persons united for some purpose; **3,** [*pl.* phalanges (fa-lan′jēz)], a bone of the fingers or toes.

phan-tom (fan′tum), *n.* an apparition; spirit; ghost:—*adj.* having no substance but said to have been seen; as, a *phantom* ship.

Phar-aoh or **phar-aoh** (fâr′ō; fā′rō), *n.* the title of the rulers of ancient Egypt; tyrant.

phar-ma-cy (fär′ma-si), *n.* [*pl.* pharmacies], **1,** the art of preparing and selling medicines; **2,** a place where medicines are prepared and sold; an apothecary's shop; a drugstore.—*adj.* **phar′ma-ceu′ti-cal** (as, a *pharmaceutical* chemist).—*n.* **pha′ma-col′o-gy** (study of drugs); **phar′ma-co-poe′ia** (a list, or stock, of drugs); **phar′ma-cist.**

phase (fāz), *n.* **1,** in *astronomy,* a particular appearance presented by the moon or a planet at a given time; as, the full moon is a *phase* of the moon; **2,** one stage or period in the development of a person or thing; as, she's just going through a *phase; phase* one of the plan; **3,** one side of a subject; as, a *phase* of history:—*v.t.* [phased, phas-ing], **1,** to plan and execute in stages; as, the school *phased* in the new textbooks; **2,** to make the parts or stages syncronized.

pheas-ant (fez′ant), *n.* **1,** a large, Old World game bird with brilliant feathers; **2,** any of various birds that look like the pheasant, as the ruffed grouse.

phe-nom-e-non (fi-nom′i-non; fi-nom′i-nun), *n.* [*pl.* phenomena (fi-nom′i-na)], **1,** any natural fact or event that can be seen; as, a tornado is a natural *phenomenon;* **2,** something uncommon, as snow in summer.—*adj.* **phe-nom′e-nal.**

phew (fū), *interj.* an exclamation of disgust, discomfort, surprise, relief, etc.

phil-an-throp-ic (fil′an-throp′ik) or **phil-an-throp-i-cal** (-throp′i-kal), *adj.* **1,** loving humans, esp. as shown through charitable and humanitarian activities; **2,** a benevolent act or organization; as, a *philanthropic* society.

phi-lan-thro-pist (fi-lan′thro-pist), *n.* one who loves and seeks to benefit humans, esp. one who uses his or her wealth for this.—*n.* **phi-lan′thro-py.**

phi-lat-e-ly (fi-lat′e-li); *n.* the collecting and study of postage stamps.—*n.* **phi-lat′e-list.**

phil-har-mon-ic (fil′här-mon′ik), *adj.* fond of music, as, a *philharmonic* concert, orchestra, society, etc.:—*n.* a symphony orchestra or other musical group; as, the Winnipeg *Philharmonic* Choir.

phil-o- or **phil-** (fil′ō-; fil-), *prefix* meaning *loving* or *liking*; as in *phil*anderer (a person who carries on many affairs), *philo*logy (the love or study of literature).

phi-los-o-pher (fi-los′o-fėr), *n.* **1,** a student of philosophy; **2,** any person who thinks deeply or makes judgments about the nature of life; **3,** one who keeps calm and courageous in misfortune; as, she was a *philosopher* despite the tragedy.

phi-los-o-phy (fi-los′o-fi), *n.* [*pl.* philosophies], **1,** the study of the principles that cause, control, or explain facts and events; **2,** the calmness of temper characteristic of a philosopher; resignation; **3,** a particular system of beliefs or views that determines how a person acts; a guide to living.—*adj.* **phil′o-soph′i-cal** (fil′o-sof′i-kal); **phil′o-soph′ic.**

phlegm (flem), *n.* **1,** a thick mucus, or sputum, from throat or lungs, as during a cold; **2,** apathy, sluggishness; **3,** self-possession; coolness.

phleg-matic (fleg-mat′ik) or **phleg-mat-i-cal** (fleg-mat′-i-kal), *adj.* **1,** relating to phlegm; **2,** sluggish; not easily excited; cool; unemotional; as, a *phlegmatic* person.—*adv.* **phleg-mat′ical-ly.**

phlox (floks), *n.* a plant that bears showy clusters of white, reddish, or purplish flowers.

pho-bi-a (fō′bi-a), *n.* a morbid fear or dread of a particular situation or thing; as, flying is a common *phobia*.

phoe-nix (fē′niks), *n.* **1,** a mythical bird, symbol of immortality, said to have lived 500 or 600 years in the Arabian desert, burned itself to ashes on a funeral pyre, and risen to a new life of youth and beauty; **2,** any person or thing that is renewed like the mythical bird.

¹phone (fōn), *n.* any simple speech sound, as a vowel or consonant.

²phone (fōn), *n. Colloq.* a telephone:—*v.t.* and *v.i.* [phoned, phon-ing], *Colloq.* to call someone on the telephone.

pho-net-ics (fo-net′tik), *n.* the study of the sounds people make when they speak and of how these sounds are produced.—*adj.* **pho-net′ic** (having to do with the sounds of speech).

pho-nics (fon′iks), *n.* a way of teaching people to read by showing how the letters used in writing stand for certain speech sounds.—*adj.* **phon′ic.**

pho-no- or **phon-** (fō′nō-; fōn-), *prefix* meaning *sound*; as in *phono*gram (a sound recorder), *phono*logy (the science of sounds).

pho-no-graph (fō′nō-graf′), *n.* a record player.—*adj.* **pho′no-graph′ic.**

pho-ny or **pho-ney** (fō′ni), *adj.* **1,** sham; fake; bogus; as, *phony* money; **2,** hypocritical or insincere:—*n.* **1,** a fake; **2,** a hypocrite.

phos-pho-res-cent (fos′fo-res′ent), *adj.* **1,** giving light without heat by certain bodies, such as phosphorus and decaying wood, and by some insects and sea animals; **2,** giving off light following exposure and absorption of radiation by a substance: compare *fluorescent.*—*n.* **phos′pho-res′cence.**

phos-pho-rus (fos′fo-rus), *n.* a yellowish-white, waxy, poisonous substance that has an unpleasant odour and easily bursts into flame: used in making safety matches, pyrotechnics, fertilizer, etc.—*adj.* **phos′pho-rous** (fos′fo-rus; fos-for′us).—*adj.* **phos-phor′ic.**

pho-to (fō′tō), *n. Colloq.* a photograph.

pho-to- or **phot-** (fō′tō-; fōt-), *prefix* meaning **1,** *light*; as in *photo*chemistry, *photo*sensitive; **2,** *photography*; as in *photo*composition, *photo*essay, *photo*play.

pho-to-cop-y (fō′tō-kop′i) *n.* [*pl.* photocopies], an exact copy of something written or printed on a page, made by a special photographic process:—*v.i.* and *v.t.* [photocop-ied, photocop-y-ing], to make a copy using this process:—*n.* **pho′to-cop′i-er** (a machine that makes photographic copies).

pho-to-en-gra-ving (fō′tō-en-grā′ving), *n.* **1,** a process by which photographs are reproduced in relief on metal plates for printing; **2,** a picture so printed.

pho-to-fin-ish-ing (fō′tō-fin′i-shing), *n.* the process of developing film and printing pictures.—*v.t.* and *v.i.* **pho′to-fin′ish.**—*n.* **pho′to-fin′ish-er.**

pho-to-gen-ic (fō′tō-jen′ik), *adj.* **1,** photographing well, used esp. of a person who is artistically a good subject; **2,** phosphorescent.

pho-to-graph (fō′tō-gråf), *n.* a picture produced by exposing to the light a plate or film made sensitive to light by being coated with certain chemicals, or in digital photography, on a disk:—*v.t.* to take a picture of, by exposing a sensitized plate, film, or disk to the action of light.—*n.* **pho-tog′ra-pher** (fō-tog′ra-fėr).—*adj.* **pho′to-graph′ic.**

pho-tog-ra-phy (fō-tog′ra-fi), *n.* **1,** traditionally, the art or process of making pictures by the action of light on a material, as paper, glass, or celluloid, that has been coated with a film of chemicals to make it sensitive to light; **2,** in digital photography, the image is digitally encoded and stored in a computer.

pho-ton (fō′ton), *n.* in *physics*, the smallest unit of light energy, called a quantum; a corpuscle of light.

pho-to-syn-the-sis (fō′tō-sin′the-sis), *n.* in living plants, the forming of carbon-hydrogen compounds from water and carbon dioxide by the action of sunlight on the green colouring matter (chlorophyll).

phrase (frāz), *n.* **1,** in *grammar*, a group of

related words not containing a subject and a predicate; as, "to the city" is a *phrase*; **2,** any brief, pithy expression containing a single idea; **3,** a characteristic style or manner of talking; as, speaking in the simple *phrase* of the day:—*v.t.* [phrased, phrasing], to put into words, esp. into suitable words; as, he *phrased* his apology carefully.—*adj.* **phras′al.**

phra-se-ol-o-gy (frā′zi-ol′o-ji), *n.* [*pl.* phraseologies], selection and arrangement of words; manner of expression; as, legal *phraseology* contains many repetitions.

phylum (fī′lum), *n.* in *biology*, a basic or primary division, larger than a class, of the animal or vegetable kingdom, as the vertebrates, molluscs, crustaceans, etc.

phys-i-cal (fiz′i-k'l), *adj.* **1,** relating to natural science, or to the natural features and changes in the universe; as, *physical* geography; **2,** pertaining to the world around us, or to the material rather than to the mental or spiritual; as, the *physical* world; **3,** pertaining to the science of physics; as, *physical* changes in matter; **4,** pertaining to the body; as *physical* weakness.

phy-si-cian (fi-zish′an), *n.* one skilled in the art of healing and legally qualified to treat disease; a doctor of medicine.

phys-ics (fiz′iks), *n.pl.* used as *sing.* the science that deals with matter and its ability to perform work or energy, including the study of mechanics, heat, light, sound, electricity, nuclear physics, cryogenics, etc.—*n.* **phys′i-cist.**

phys-i-og-no-my (fiz′i-og′no-mi), (fiz′i-on′o-mi); *n.* [*pl.* physiognomies], **1,** the face; esp. the peculiar form or expression of the face; **2,** the art of judging the personality or character of an individual by studying the face; **3,** outward appearance, as of a landscape.

phys-i-og-ra-phy (fiz′i-og′ra-fi), *n.* physical geography; the study of the earth's natural features, as climate, surface, etc.

phys-i-ol-o-gy (fiz′i-ol′o-ji), *n.* [*pl.* physiologies], that branch of biology that deals with the functions of the organs, tissues, cells, etc., in living plants, animals, and human beings. Compare *morphology.*—*adj.* **phys′i-o-log′i-cal.**

phys-i-o-ther-a-py (fiz′i-ō-ther′a-pi) *n.* healing by the use of massage, exercise, light, heat, etc.

phy-sique (fi-zēk′), *n.* the structure and appearance of the body; as, the football player has a powerful *physique.*

phy-to- or **phyt-** (fī′tō-; fīt-), *prefix* meaning *plant*; as in *phyto*chemistry, *phyto*geography, *phyto*logy (the study of plants), *phyto*toxic.

[1]**pi** (pī) *n.* in *mathematics*, the Greek letter π, designating the ratio of the circumference of a circle to its diameter, about 3.1416.

[2]**pi** (pī), *n.* **1,** a jumble of printing type; **2,** any mixture.

pi-an-ist (pē′a-nist), *n.* a person who plays the piano.

pi-an-o (pē-an′ō; pyan′ō), *n.* [*pl.* pianos], a large musical instrument, enclosed in a case and played from a keyboard, which, when struck, operates hammers that strike wires, giving forth musical tones.

pi-ca (pi′ka), *n.* a printer's unit of measurement equivalent to approximately 4 mm; 12-point type.

pic-a-yune (pik′i-yūn′), *adj.* and *n.* anything small or trifling; as, his quibbling was *picayune.*

pic-co-lo (pik′o-lō′), *n.* [*pl.* piccolos], a small, flute-shaped instrument with very shrill tones, an octave higher than the tones of the ordinary flute.

pick (pik), *n.* **1,** a heavy tool for breaking earth or rock; a pickaxe; **2,** a pointed instrument used for piercing or pecking; as, an ice *pick*; **3,** the amount of a crop gathered at one time; a picking; **4,** choice; as, take your *pick*; **5,** the best of anything; as, the *pick* of the lot; **6,** a small piece of plastic or other hard material used to play a guitar, banjo, or other such instrument:—*v.t.* **1,** to strike or break open with a sharp instrument or with the beak; pierce or peck; as, to *pick* a hole; **2,** to open by a sharp instrument; as, to *pick* a lock or safe; **3,** to lift or raise; as, to *pick* up something fallen; **4,** to pluck or gather; as, to *pick* berries; **5,** to choose or select; as, to *pick* the best one; **6,** to bring about by choice or intention; provoke; as, to *pick* a quarrel; **7,** to rob; as, to *pick* a pocket; **8,** to separate with the fingers; as, to *pick* rags; **9,** to clean or clear of something; as, to *pick* a chicken; **10,** to pluck the strings of (a musical instrument); as, to *pick* a banjo:—*v.i.* **1,** to eat slowly and daintily; **2,** to pilfer; as, to *pick* and steal; **3,** *Colloq.* to find fault; nag.—*n.* **pick′er.**

pick-axe or **pick-ax** (pik′aks′), *n.* a hand tool for digging with a wooden handle and a curved or straight iron head pointed at one end or at both ends.

pick-er-el (pik′ėr-el), *n.* a kind of freshwater fish of the pike family, used for food; sometimes, the pike, walleye, etc.

pick-et (pik′it), *n.* **1,** an upright pointed stake, used in making fences, for tethering a horse, etc.; **2,** in warfare, a military guard stationed at a given place to prevent surprise by an enemy; a sentry; **3,** one or more persons appointed by a labour union to watch at a factory, shop, etc., during a strike, to persuade or otherwise influence nonunion workers not to work there; **4,** any person or persons appointed by an organization to watch at a given place for any purpose:—*v.t.* **1,** to fence with pointed stakes; as, to *picket* a farm; **2,** to fasten to a stake; to tether; as, to *picket* a horse; **3,** to watch or guard; as, to *picket* a certain position; **4,** to place on guard; as, to *picket* soldiers for duty:—*v.i.* to serve as a picket.

pick-le (pik′l), *n.* **1,** brine or a mixture of salt and water used for preserving meat, fish, etc.; also, vinegar, with or without spices, for preserving vegetables, fruit, meat, etc.; **2,** something preserved in pickle; esp. a small pickled cucumber; **3,** *Colloq.* an embarrassment; difficulty:—*v.t.* [pickled, pick-ling], to preserve in brine or vinegar.

pick-pock-et (pik′pok′it), *n.* a thief who steals purses or the contents of pockets.

pick-up (pik′up′), *n.* **1,** a small delivery truck; **2,** reception of sound or light, as by radio or television; **3,** the act of picking up something; as, there is no garbage *pickup* today; **4,** a quick increase in speed; as, her sports car has amazing *pickup*; **5,** *Colloq.* the act of improving; **6,** the pivot arm with the needle of a record player:—*adj.* **1,** related to, of, or for pickups; as, a *pickup* truck; **2,** not organized beforehand; impromptu; as, a *pickup* hockey game.

pic-nic (pik′nik), *n.* **1,** a short trip by a pleasure party carrying its own food for an outdoor meal; **2,** *Colloq.* an easy or pleasant experience; as, the chemistry course is no *picnic*:—*v.i.* [picnicked, picnick-ing], to go on, or hold, an outdoor pleasure party.—*n.* **pic′nick-er.**

pic-to-graph (pik′tō-gråf′), *n.* a picture expressing an idea, as in the picture-writing of prehistoric peoples; hieroglyph; symbol; as, computer icons are a type of *pictographs*.

pic-tor-i-al (pik-tōr′i-al), *adj.* **1,** pertaining to, shown by, or containing, pictures; as, a *pictorial* magazine; **2,** suggesting a picture or clear mental image; as, *pictorial* description.—*adv.* **pic-tor′i-al-ly.**

pic-ture (pik′tūr; chėr), *n.* **1,** a painting, drawing, or photograph of a person, object, scene, etc.; **2,** a likeness or image; as, she is the *picture* of her mother; representation; as, he was the *picture* of health; **3,** a vivid portrayal in words; as, the speaker drew a *picture* of future prosperity; **4,** a mental image; as, my mind carried a *picture* of the beautiful scene; **5,** what is seen on the television or movie screen; as, the *picture* is fuzzy on this set; **6,** a motion picture or movie:—*v.t.* [pictured, pictur-ing], **1,** to present in a painting, drawing, etc.; as, the artist *pictured* a country scene; **2,** to describe vividly in words; **3,** to form a mental image of; imagine; as, I *pictured* myself in his place.

pic-tur-esque (pik′tūr-esk′), *adj.* **1,** giving a vivid impression, as a picture does; as, a *picturesque* description of one's travels; **2,** suitable to be drawn or painted as an interesting or striking picture; as, *picturesque* mountain scenery.—*adv.* **pic′tur-esque′ly.**—*n.* **pic′tur-esque′ness.**

pie (pī), *n.* **1,** a prepared dish consisting of meat, fruit, etc., baked in a pastry crust; **2,** something that can be shared; as, the movie made a lot of money, and the actors wanted a piece of the *pie*.

piece (pēs), *n.* **1,** a part of anything; a fragment; as, a *piece* of bread; a plot or division; unit; as, a *piece* of land; *piece* of furniture; **2,** a fixed quantity or size in which goods or various articles are made up for sale; as, this fabric comes at 12 metres to the *piece*; **3,** a separate instance, example, or performance; as, a bad *piece* of business; a fine *piece* of writing; **4,** a single object of a group; as, each *piece* in the set; **5,** a single, distinct, literary or artistic composition; as, a *piece* of music; **6,** the amount of work done as a distinct job; as, the work is paid for by the *piece*; **7,** a coin; as, a five-cent *piece*; **8,** *Slang* a gun; **9,** one of the counters used in board games; as, she moved the chess *piece*:—*v.t.* [pieced, piec-ing], **1,** to enlarge or mend by adding material; as, to *piece* a skirt; **2,** to make by joining sections together; as, to *piece* together the broken statue.

piece-meal (pēs′mēl′), *adv.* in portions or parts; by degrees; gradually; as, the work was done *piecemeal*:—*adj.* done in stages or parts; as, a *piecemeal* project.

pier (pēr), *n.* **1,** a support for an arch, bridge, etc., **2,** a projecting part of a wall, such as a buttress; **3,** a wharf or dock built out over the water in order to provide a landing–place for boats.

pierce (pērs), *v.t.* [pierced, pierc-ing], **1,** to puncture or run through; stab; as, the knife *pierced* her hand; **2,** to make a hole in; as, she *pierced* her ears and nose for earrings; **3,** to affect deeply; as, to *pierce* the heart with sorrow; **4,** to force a way through; as, they *pierced* the enemy lines; **5,** to see through or solve, as a mystery:—*v.i.* to enter; penetrate; as, the sun *pierced* through the clouds.—*adj.* **pierc′ing** (penetrating; as, the *piercing* shout broke the quiet).

pi-e-ty (pī′e-ti), *n.* [*pl.* pieties], **1,** devotion to religion; **2,** reverence for God; **3,** honour and devotion to parents.

pig (pig), *n.* **1,** a hoofed, two-toed animal; a hog, esp. a young one; also, the meat used for food; **2,** *Colloq.* a greedy or selfish person; **3,** an oblong mass of metal, esp. of iron or lead, formed by being run into moulds when melted; **4,** *Slang* an offensive term for a police officer; **5,** *Slang* a sexist or racist:—*v.i.* [pigged, pig-ging], **1,** to give birth to pigs; **2,** to eat greedily or otherwise behave like pigs.—*n.* **pig′ger-y; pig′pen′; pig′sty′.**

pi-geon (pij′un), *n.* a bird, often domesticated, with stocky body, short legs, long wings, and handsome plumage.

pi-geon-hole (pij′un-hōl′), *n.* **1,** a hole in

which pigeons nest; **2,** a small, open, boxlike space in a desk, case, etc., for documents or letters:—*v.t.* [pigeonholed, pigeonhol-ing], **1,** to place (letters, documents, etc.) in such a boxlike space; to file; **2,** to lay aside and forget; shelve; as, the committee *pigeonholed* the proposal.

pi-geon-toed (pij′un-tōd′), *adj.* with the toes turned in.

pig-gish (pig′ish), *adj.* like a pig; stubborn, greedy, or dirty.—*adv.* **pig′gish-ly.**—*n.* **pig′gish-ness.**

pig-gy-back (pig′i-bak′), *adj.* and *adv.* **1,** on the shoulders or back; as, he carried the boy *piggyback;* **2,** being part of something larger or more important:—*v.t.* to connect or align something with something larger or more important; as, to *piggyback* the promotion with the advertising campaign.

pig-head-ed (pig′hed′id), *adj.* obstinate or stubborn.

pig iron, crude iron, as it comes from the blast-furnace cast into moulds, or pigs.

pig-ment (pig′ment), *n.* **1,** any substance used to give colouring, esp. dry colouring matter which, when mixed with the proper fluid, forms paint; **2,** the colouring matter in persons, animals, or plants.—*n.* **pig′men-ta′tion.**

Pig-my (pig′mi), *n.* Same as **Pygmy.**

pig-skin (pig′skin′), *n.* **1,** the hide of a pig or the leather made from it; **2,** in *sports,* a football; **3,** *Colloq.* a saddle.

pig-tail (pig′tāl′), *n.* **1,** hair twisted into a braid, usually hanging down from the back of the head; **2,** a long twist of tobacco.

[1]**pike** (pīk), *n.* **1,** a weapon formerly carried by foot soldiers, consisting of a long wooden shaft with a spearhead at one end; **2,** a sharp point or spike.

[2]**pike** (pīk), *n.* a large, freshwater fish with a pointed head, found esp. in the Great Lakes in North America.

[3]**pike** (pīk), *n.* **1,** a road on which a charge is made for driving; a road with a tollgate; a turnpike; **2,** any main road:—*v.i.* [piked, pik-ing], to move rapidly.

pik-er (pīk′ėr), *n. Slang* **1,** an overcautious gambler, esp. one who bets only small amounts; **2,** one who does things in a cheap or small way; a petty person; quitter; shirker.

[1]**pile** (pīl), *n.* **1,** a mass or heap; as, a *pile* of sand; **2,** a heap of wood for burning a body; a pyre; **3,** *Colloq.* a great quantity; a lot; **4,** *Slang* a fortune:—*v.t.* [piled, pil-ing], **1,** to place or throw in a heap; arrange; as, to *pile* old magazines; **2,** to accumulate; amass; as, he *piled* up a big fortune; **3,** to fill; load; as, to *pile* a car full of people:—*v.i.* **1,** to form a mass or heap; accumulate; as, the snow *piled* up around the door; **2,** to press forward in a mass; crowd.

[2]**pile** (pīl), *n.* **1,** a timber driven into the ground, as for a wharf, foundation for a building, etc.; also, metal or concrete columns similarly used; **2,** a pointed stake or post:—**pile driver,** a machine for driving piles into the ground:—*v.t.* [piled, pil-ing], to drive piles into.

[3]**pile** (pīl), *n.* **1,** nap of cloth; esp., the furry or velvety surface of velvet, plush, carpet, etc.; **2,** short, soft hair; down.

piles (pīlz), *n.* hemorrhoids, or painful swelling or bleeding of veins under the skin of the anus.

pil-fer (pil′fėr), *v.t.* and *v.i.* to steal in small amounts.—*n.* **pil′fer-er.**

pil-grim (pil′grim), *n.* **1,** one who travels from a distance to visit some sacred place; **2,** a traveller:—**Pilgrim,** a Puritan settler of the first colony in Massachusetts in 1620.

pil-grim-age (pil′gri-mij), *n.* a long journey, esp. to some sacred place.

Pi-li-pi-no (pi′li-pē′nō), *n.* the official language of the Philippines, which is based on *Tagalog.*

pill (pil), *n.* **1,** medicine prepared in the form of a small ball, tablet, or capsule; **2,** something disagreeable that must be accepted; as, defeat was a bitter *pill;* **3,** *Slang* a disagreeable person.

pil-lage (pil′ij), *n.* **1,** the act of plundering, or robbing openly, esp. in war; **2,** booty; spoil:—*v.t.* and *v.i.* [pillaged, pillag-ing], to plunder, or rob openly; despoil; sack.—*n.* **pil′lag-er.**

pil-lar (pil′ėr), *n.* **1,** a column to support a structure or to serve as a monument; **2,** any support or mainstay; as, a *pillar* of society.—*adj.* **pil′lared.**

pil-lo-ry (pil′o-ri), *n.* [*pl.* pillories], an old instrument used to punish offenders publicly, consisting of a wooden frame supported by an upright post, and having holes through which the head and hands of a person were passed and secured:—*v.t.* [pilloried, pillory-ing], **1,** to punish (an offender) by putting into a pillory; **2,** to expose to public disgrace or ridicule.

PILLORY

pil-low (pil′ō), *n.* a case filled with feathers or other soft material to support the head of a person lying down:—*v.t.* to place on a pillow.

pi-lot (pī′lut), *n.* **1,** one who steers a ship; one licensed to conduct a ship in or out of a port or in waters where sailing is difficult or dangerous; **2,** one who is licensed to fly any kind of aircraft; **3,** a guide of any sort; as, the Prime Minister is the *pilot* of our national affairs; **4,** a device on a machine that guides or starts other parts; **5,** a premier of a television show:—*v.t.* **1,** to direct the course of (a vessel, airship, etc.); **2,** to guide or escort through difficulties; as, she *piloted* the bill through Parliament.—*adj.* **1,**

serving as a guide, or as a test unit; as, a *pilot* plant, dye, parachute, television program, etc.; **2,** serving to start a larger device; as, a *pilot* lamp, light, etc.

pi-men-to (pi-men′tō), *n.* [*pl.* pimentos], **1,** allspice; an unripe fruit, dried and used as a flavouring; also, the tree bearing it; **2,** Same as **pimiento.**

pi-mien-to or **pimento** (pi-myen′tō; pi-men′tō), *n.* [*pl.* pimientos; pimentos], a variety of sweet pepper, used as a vegetable, stuffing for olives, etc.

pim-ple (pim′pl), *n.* a small, inflamed swelling of the skin, often containing pus.—*adj.* **pim′pled; pim′ply.**

pin (pin), *n.* **1,** a short piece of wire with a sharp point at one end and a round head at the other, used for fastening things together; **2,** a piece of wood, metal, etc., having a similar use or appearance; as, a clothes*pin*, a hair*pin*, a hat*pin*, etc.; **3,** an ornament, badge, or jewel fitted with a pin and a clasp; as, a fraternity *pin*; **4,** a bolt or peg; **5,** a wooden roller; as, a rolling *pin*; **6,** a wooden peg, shaped like a bottle, that is a target in bowling:—*v.t.* [pinned, pinning], **1,** to fasten with, or as with, a pin; as, to *pin* a pattern on cloth; **2,** to hold fast in one position; as, the steering wheel *pinned* him in the wrecked car; **3,** to hold or keep (a person) to an obligation, course of action, etc.; as, to *pin* him down to his promise; **4,** to finalize or establish firmly; as, to *pin* down the date of the party. Also, **pin′cush′ion; pin′point′; pin′wheel′.**

PIN (pin), *abbrev.* short for *personal identification number*.

pin-ball (pin′bôl′), *n.* and *adj.* a mechanical game played on a sloping board, the aim being to cause a ball, driven by a spring, to fall into the highest-numbered hole(s).

pin-cers or **pinch-ers** (pin′sėrz; pin′chėrz), *n. pl.* sometimes used as *sing.* **1,** an instrument with two handles and jaws working on a pivot, used for gripping things; nippers; **2,** the claws of lobsters, crabs, etc.

pinch (pinch), *v.t.* **1,** to squeeze or nip between the thumb and a finger, or between two hard edges; as, to *pinch* a finger in a door; **2,** to press on so as to hurt; as, the shoe *pinches* my toe; **3,** to oppress or distress; as, to be *pinched* by poverty; **4,** to make thin or worn; as, to be *pinched* with hunger; **5,** *Slang* to arrest; **6,** *Slang* to steal:—*v.i.* **1,** to press hard; as, my shoe *pinches*; **2,** to be mean or miserly:—*n.* **1,** a squeeze or nip, as with the fingers and thumb; **2,** painful pressure; as, the *pinch* of poverty; **3,** a sudden difficulty or necessity; emergency; as, anything will do in a *pinch*; **4,** as much as can be held between the thumb and a finger; as, a *pinch* of salt; **5,** *Slang* an arrest; **6,** *Slang* a theft.

¹pine (pīn), *n.* **1,** a kind of cone-bearing tree having clusters of evergreen needlelike leaves; **2,** the timber of the tree.—*adj.* **pin′y** or **pin′ey.**

²pine (pīn), *v.i.* [pined, pin-ing], **1,** to grow thin and weak from distress, anxiety, etc.; **2,** to long intensely; as, to *pine* for absent friends.

pine-ap-ple (pīn′ap′l), *n.* **1,** a tropical plant with spiny leaves, bearing a large fruit somewhat resembling a pine cone; **2,** the edible, juicy fruit of this plant.

ping (ping), *n.* a slight ringing sound, as from a bullet's flight through the air, or from the bullet's striking something.

¹pin-ion (pin′yun), *n.* **1,** the last group of bones of a bird's wings; **2,** a wing; **3,** a feather:—*v.t.* **1,** to bind the wings of, or to clip off the pinion of; as, to *pinion* a bird; **2,** to bind or confine; shackle; as, to *pinion* a person's arms.

²pin-ion (pin′yun), *n.* a wheel, the cogs of which come into gear with those of a larger toothed wheel or rack, so that motion is imparted from one to the other; also, in a pair of gears, the smaller gear.

¹pink (pingk), *v.t.* **1,** to cut the edges of (cloth, leather, paper, etc.) in points or scallops, esp. with *pinking* shears; **2,** to prick or pierce, as with a sword.—*adj.* **pink′ing.**

²pink (pingk), *n.* **1,** a very pale red; **2,** a garden plant with sharp-pointed leaves and red, pink, or white flowers, which are either fringed or ruffled and have a sweet, spicy fragrance; also, the flower; **3,** the highest degree; the peak; as, in the *pink* of perfection:—*adj.* of a very pale-red colour.—*adj.* **pink′ish.**

pink-ie or **pink-y** (ping′ki), *n. Colloq.* the smallest finger on the hand.

pin-na-cle (pin′a-kl), *n.* **1,** a small tower or turret above the rest of a building; **2,** a high point like a spire; as, a *pinnacle* of rock; **3,** the highest point; as, few people reach the *pinnacle* of fame.

pi-noch-le or **pi-noc-le** (pē′nuk′l), a game of cards, the object of which is the making of certain card combinations of differing point values.

pint (pīnt), *n.* a measure of capacity in the imperial system equal to 0.57 litres; half a quart.

pin-to (pin′tō), *n.* [*pl.* pintos or pintoes], in the Western U.S. and Canada, a mottled or spotted horse or pony:—*adj.* spotted; mottled.

pi-o-neer (pī′o-nēr′), *n.* one who goes before to prepare the way for others, esp. an original settler in a frontier country:—*v.i.* to prepare a way:—*v.t.* to open up (new country) or take the lead in (new causes); to act as a pioneer; as, the company *pioneered* the sale of small, inexpensive computers.

pi-ous (pī′us), *adj.* **1,** showing reverence

for God; religious; devout; as, *pious* nuns; **2,** done under pretence of religion; as, *pious* deception; **3,** high-minded.—*adv.* **pi′ous-ly.**

pip (pip), *n.* **1,** a small seed, as of an apple, orange, etc.; **2,** *Colloq.* something exceptional or extraordinary; **3,** *Slang* a minor ailment; as, it gives me the *pip*; **4,** a disease of poultry or birds, marked by a thick mucus in mouth and throat; **5,** any of the spots on dice, dominoes, playing cards, etc.

pipe (pīp), *n.* **1,** any long, hollow tube; as, a water *pipe*; **2,** a tube of clay, wood, etc., with a bowl for smoking tobacco, blowing bubbles, etc.; **3,** a high-pitched voice; as, the *pipe* of a child; **4,** the note or call of a bird or insect; **5,** a musical wind instrument consisting of a hollow tube, as a flute; **6,** one of the graduated tubes in which the notes of some organs, called *pipe* organs, are produced:—**pipes, 1,** the bagpipe; **2,** *Colloq.* vocal cords; voice; as, this singer has great *pipes*:—*v.t.* [piped, pip-ing], **1,** to play on a musical pipe; as, to *pipe* a tune; **2,** to utter in a high key; as, to *pipe* a song; **3,** to furnish with pipes; as, to *pipe* a house for water; **4,** to carry through a pipe or tube; as, to *pipe* water into a city:—*v.i.* **1,** to play on a pipe; **2,** to speak shrilly.—*adj.* **pipe′ful.**—*n.* **pipe′line′.** Also, **pipe′ clean′er; pipe′ dream′** (unrealistic ambition or goal)**; pipe′ fit′ter.**

pip-er (pīp′ėr), *n.* one who plays on a pipe, esp. one who plays on a bagpipe.

pip-ing (pīp′ing), *n.* **1,** the music of a pipe; also, a shrill sound; as, the *piping* of birds; **2,** a system of tubes for drainage, gas, etc.; **3,** a narrow fold of material used in trimming clothing:—*adv.* hissing; sizzling; as, *piping* hot:—*adj.* tranquil; as, *piping* times of peace.

pi-quant (pē′kant), *adj.* **1,** agreeably sharp to the taste; as, a *piquant* sauce; **2,** arousing interest or curiosity; having a lively charm; as, *piquant* remarks; a *piquant* face.—*n.* **pi′quan-cy.**

pique (pēk), *n.* slight anger or resentment, esp. as a result of wounded pride; as, she left the party in a fit of *pique*:—*v.t.* [piqued (pēkt), piqu-ing (pē′king)], **1,** to wound the pride of; irritate; displease; **2,** to pride or value (oneself); as, she *piqued* herself on her ability; **3,** to stir or arouse; as, to *pique* the curiosity.

pi-ra-cy (pī′ra-si), *n.* [*pl.* piracies], **1,** robbery upon the high seas or the hijacking of an aircraft; **2,** the using, without permission, of another's literary work, invention, copyrighted or patented material, etc., esp. for profit; as, software *piracy* is a huge problem.

pi-ra-nha or **pi-ra-ña** (pi-rän′ya; pi-rän′a), *n.* a small voracious, carnivorous South American fish.

pi-rate (pī′rit), *n.* **1,** a robber on the high seas or hijacker of an aircraft; **2,** anyone using lawless methods in gaining something, esp. one who uses another's literary work or copyrighted or patented material for profit without permission, or claims it as his or her own product; **3,** a ship engaged in robbery on the high seas:—*v.t.* and *v.i.* [pirat-ed, pirat-ing], **1,** to rob at sea or hijack an aircraft; **2,** to take and publish without permission or payment, esp. of copyrighted works, such as CDs or computer software programs.—*adj.* **pi-rat′ic** (pī-rat′ik); **pi-rat′i-cal; pi′rat-ed** (as, *pirated* software).

pir-ou-ette (pir′o͞o-et′), *n.* a whirl or turn made on the toes (by a person or a horse):—*v.i.* [-etted, -et-ting], to turn or spin in one spot.

Pis-ces (pis′ēz), *n.* **1,** an equatorial constellation, the Fishes (south of Andromeda); **2,** the 12th sign of the zodiac (♓), which the sun enters about February 21; also, a person born under this sign.

pis-ta-chi-o (pis-tä′shē-ō; pis-tā′shē-ō), *n.* [*pl.* pistachios], **1,** a small tree of Asia and southern Europe, or its nut, the kernel of which is used for flavouring; **2,** the flavouring; **3,** the greenish colour of the kernel.

pis-til (pis′til; pis′tl), *n.* in *botany*, the seed-bearing organ in the centre of a flower.

pis-tol (pis′tl), *n.* a small, short gun intended for use with one hand, such as the revolver and the automatic: usually called a handgun.

pis-ton (pis′tun), *n.* a closely fitting disk or cylinder designed to slide to and fro within a larger hollow tube or cylinder.

¹pit (pit), *n.* **1,** a hole or cavity in the earth; **2,** the shaft of a mine, or the mine itself; **3,** a deep gulf; abyss; **4,** a hole used for trapping; a pitfall; **5,** a small scar, such as that left by smallpox, acne, or other skin disorders; **6,** a depression in some part of the body; as, the arm*pits*; **7,** in the theatre, the area where the orchestra is located; **8,** the area in a casino where gambling takes place; **9,** an enclosed place set aside for dog-fighting, cock-fighting, etc.; **10,** that part of the floor of an exchange where a special business is carried on; as, a grain *pit*; **11,** in *sports*, the auto racing area where the cars are refuelled or serviced; **12,** at a rock concert, the area where the violent dancing, or moshing, takes place; a mosh pit:—**the pits,** *Colloq.* the worst possible thing or situation; as, the math exam was *the pits*:—*v.t.* [pit-ted, pit-ting], **1,** to mark with small pits; as, acne had *pitted* his face; **2,** to match or set to fight against another; as, to *pit* one's strength against a foe; **3,** to place in a pit.

²pit (pit), *n.* the kernel or stone of certain fruits, as the peach, cherry, date, etc.:—*v.t.*

[pit-ted, pit-ting], to remove the pits of.

pi-ta (pē′ta), a flat bread that can be stuffed with filling, such as falafel.

[1]**pitch** (pich), *n.* **1,** a thick, sticky, black substance, soft when heated, left over after distillation of coal tar, wood tar, petroleum, or turpentine, much used in roofing, waterproofing, paving, and filling seams in ships: commonly called *tar*; **2,** the sticky resin of certain trees:—*v.t.* to cover or smear with pitch or tar.

[2]**pitch** (pich), *v.t.* **1,** to fix in or on the ground; set up; as, to *pitch* a tent; **2,** throw or fling; as, to *pitch* hay; to *pitch* horseshoes; **3,** in *music,* to determine the key of; start, as a tune, by sounding the keynote; **4,** in *baseball,* to throw (the ball) to the batter; **5,** *Colloq.* to try to influence others (with an idea or to do something); as, she *pitched* her promotional idea to her client:—*v.i.* **1,** to fall headlong; as, to *pitch* forward; **2,** to fix the choice; decide; as, they finally *pitched* on the right candidate; **3,** to rise alternately forward and aft as a ship in heavy seas; to toss; **4,** in *baseball,* to throw the ball to the batter; act as pitcher:—*n.* **1,** a plunging forward or down; as, a headlong *pitch* from a ladder; **2,** the act or manner of throwing or tossing; as, a good *pitch* in baseball; **3,** a tossing motion, as of a ship in a storm; **4,** degree or rate; as, the highest *pitch* of excitement; **5,** the tone of a voice; **6,** slope; as, the *pitch* of a roof; **7,** the distance between two successive threads of a screw; **8,** in *music,* the highness or lowness of a sound or a tone; **9,** the density of printed characters; **10,** *Colloq.* actions or behaviour designed to influence others, esp. to buy something; as, her sales *pitch* fell flat.

[1]**pitch-er** (pich′ėr), *n.* **1,** one who throws or hurls; **2,** in *baseball,* the player who throws the ball to the batter.

[2]**pitch-er** (pich′ėr), *n.* a container, usually with an open spout and a handle, used to hold or pour liquids; a jug.

pitch-fork (pich′fôrk′), *n.* a fork with a long handle for tossing hay, straw, etc.:—*v.t.* to toss, as hay or straw, with, or as with, a pitchfork.

pit-e-ous (pit′i-us), *adj.* exciting sorrow or sympathy; mournful.—*adv.* **pit′e-ous-ly.**

pit-fall (pit′fôl′), *n.* **1,** a hole lightly covered, used for trapping; a trap; **2,** any hidden source of trouble, danger, or temptation; as, the *pitfalls* of the proposed plan.

pith (pith), *n.* **1,** the soft, spongy substance in the centre of the stem of some plants; **2,** any similar soft tissue, as the marrow in a bone; **3,** energy or force; vigour; **4,** gist; substance; importance; as, the *pith* of her speech.—*adj.* **pith′less.**—*n.* **pith′ hel′met.**

pith-y (pith′i), *adj.* [pith-i-er, pith-i-est], **1,** like or full of the soft, spongy substance called pith; **2,** forcible; full of meaning; as, Mordecai Richler was noted for his *pithy* sayings.—*adv.* **pith′i-ly.**

pit-i-a-ble (pit′i-a-bl), *adj.* **1,** deserving sympathy; as, he was in a *pitiable* condition; **2,** poor; mean; as, *pitiable* makeshifts.—*adv.* **pit′i-a-bly.**

pit-i-ful (pit′i-fool), *adj.* **1,** miserable; sad; as, a *pitiful* sight; **2,** small; meagre; as, a *pitiful* amount; **3,** contemptible; as, a *pitiful* crime.—*adv.* **pit′i-ful-ly.**

pit-i-less (pit′i-lis), *adj.* without sympathy or mercy.—*adv.* **pit′i-less-ly.**

pit-tance (pit′ans), *n.* **1,** a small allowance, esp. of money; small wage or salary; as, my income is a mere *pittance*; **2,** an extremely small amount.

pit-ter–pat-ter (pit′ėr–pat′ėr), *n.* and *adv.* a rapid succession of light beats or taps; as, the *pitter-patter* of raindrops.

pi-tu-i-tar-y (pi-tū′i-ta-ri), *adj.* and *n.* a small two-lobed gland at the base of the brain; hormones secreted by the lobes control the growth or size of the body, metabolism, and other body functions.

pit-y (pit′i), *n.* [*pl.* pities], **1,** a feeling of sorrow for the suffering of others; mercy; as, they took *pity* on the pathetic creatures; **2,** a reason for regret or grief; as, it is a *pity* he was not promoted with the other employees:—*v.t.* [pitied, pity-ing], to sympathize with; to feel sorry for; as, she *pitied* the abandoned dog.

piv-ot (piv′ut), *n.* **1,** a fixed pin or short shaft on which some object, as a ball or wheel, turns; **2,** that on which something important depends; a critical factor:—*v.t.* to place on, or supply with, a pivot:—*v.t.* to turn on a pivot.—*adj.* **piv′ot-al.**

pix-el (pik′sl; pik′sel′), *n.* in *computing,* one of the individual, tiny dots that is the smallest element of a graphic image on a computer screen, television, etc.

pix-y or **pix-ie** (pik′si), *n.* [*pl.* pixies], **1,** in old folktales, a fairy; elf; **2,** any small, mischievous person.

piz-za (pēt′sa), *n.* an Italian highly flavoured pie made of a crust and toppings such as tomato sauce, cheese, meat, anchovies, vegetable, pineapples, etc., and baked in a hot oven.

plac-ard (plak′ärd′), *n.* a printed bill or notice posted in a public place, as an advertisement; a poster:—*v.t.* (plak′ärd′; pla-kärd′), **1,** to advertise by a bill posted publicly; **2,** to post a bill or notice on.

place (plās), *n.* **1,** originally, an open space, as a public square, in a town or city; sometimes, a part of a street; also, a city or town; **2,** a particular location; a point in space; as, that is a good *place* to fish; **3,** rank; social position; esp. high rank; **4,** a position; job; **5,** in a race, a position among the winning competitors; **6,** in *arithmetic,* the position occupied by a figure in relation to the other figures of a series; **7,** a building devoted to a special purpose; as, a *place* of business; **8,** the location of a given body; as, it is out of *place*; **9,** duty; as, it is your *place* to do it; **10,** position in order; as, in the first *place*; **11,** a particular spot in a surface; as, a sore *place* on my arm:—*v.t.* [placed, plac-ing], **1,** to put in a particular spot or position; **2,** to put in office or authority; **3,** to identify by connecting with some place, circumstance, etc.; as, we *placed* him as a former neighbour; **4,** to put; as, I *place* trust in him; **5,** to finish in a certain position or rank in a race; as, she *placed* third in the science fair.

pla-ce-bo (pla-sē′bō), *n.* [*pl.* -bos or -boes (-bōz)], **1,** a nonmedicinal pill or other substance given to please a patient or to reinforce his or her desire to get well: used chiefly for its psychological effect; **2,** a nonmedicinal substance used as a control to test the effectiveness of a medicine; **3,** something of no real value used to pacify or mollify someone.

place kick (plās′ kik), *n.* a placing of the ball on the ground in order to kick a field goal: it is neither a convert after a touchdown nor a dropkick.—*v.t.* and *v.i.* **place′kick′.**

plac-id (plas′id), *adj.* calm; peaceful.—*adv.* **plac′id-ly.**—*n.* **pla-cid′i-ty.**

pla-gi-a-rism (plā′ji-a-rizm; plā′ja-rizm), *n.* stealing the ideas, words, or writings of another, and passing them off as one's own.—*n.* **pla′gi-ary; pla′gi-a-rist.**—*v.t.* and *v.i.* **pla′gi-a-rize** [plagiarized, plagiarizing].

plague (plāg), *n.* **1,** a deadly, epidemic disease; **2,** anything very troublesome or causing misery; **3,** *Colloq.* a nuisance:—*v.t.* [plagued, plagu-ing], **1,** to afflict with disease, evil, or disaster; **2,** to trouble or annoy greatly.—*adj.* **pla′guy** (plā′gi).

plaid (plad), *n.* **1,** a squared or checkered woollen cloth; tartan; **2,** a garment made of a large rectangle of such material, worn by the Highlanders of Scotland; **3,** any material with such a pattern; also, the pattern:—*adj.* having a squared or checkered pattern; as, a *plaid* skirt.

plain (plān), *adj.* **1,** level; flat; even; **2,** clear; evident; easy to see or hear; as, in *plain* sight; **3,** easily understood; as, your meaning is *plain*; **4,** unlearned; unpolished; simple in manners; as, a *plain*, blunt person; **5,** frank; direct; sincere; as, a *plain* speech; **6,** not luxurious; as, *plain* living; **7,** without ornament; as, *plain* furniture; **8,** all of one colour; as, a coat of *plain* material; **9,** without beauty; homely; as, a *plain* face; **10,** by itself; without anything added; as, a *plain* hamburger without condiments:—*adv.* clearly:—*n.* **1,** a wide stretch of level land; a flat expanse:—**plains,** great tracts of level country without trees.—*adv.* **plain′ly.**

plain-spo-ken (plān′spō′ken), *adj.* candid; frank in speech; blunt.

plain-tiff (plān′tif), *n.* one who brings suit in a court of law.

plain-tive (plān′tiv), *adj.* expressing sorrow; mournful; sad; as, a *plaintive* song.

plait (plāt; plat), *n.* **1,** a flattened fold made by doubling cloth over upon itself; a pleat, as in a skirt; **2,** a braid, as of hair:—*v.t.* **1,** to double over in folds; pleat; **2,** to braid or interweave.

plan (plan), *n.* **1,** a drawing, diagram, or map showing the outline or design of anything; as, an architect's *plan* of a building; **2,** the arrangement of parts according to a fixed design; **3,** a way of doing something; **4,** a scheme or project worked out in advance; as, she had a *plan* for her class project:—*v.t.* [planned, plan-ning], **1,** to make a sketch or design of; outline; **2,** to arrange beforehand; as, she has already *planned* her vacation for next year:—*v.i.* make a plan; as, he *planned* for his early retirement.

[1]**plane** (plān), *n.* a carpenter's tool for smoothing wood:—*v.t.* [planed, plan-ing], to make something, as a board, smooth with such a tool; as, to *plane* a tabletop:—*v.i.* to work with a plane.

[2]**plane** (plān), *adj.* flat; level; even; as, a *plane* surface:—*n.* **1,** a flat or even surface; **2,** a grade, degree, or level of knowledge or attainment; as, a high *plane* of living; high intellectual *plane*; **3,** an airplane.

plan-et (plan′it), *n.* **1,** in *astronomy*, any celestial body revolving around the sun or other star, and shining by reflected light; **2,** one of the nine bodies revolving around the sun.—*adj.* **plan′e-tar′y.**

plan-e-tar-i-um (plan′i-târ′i-um), *n.* [*pl.* planetariums or planetaria (plan′i-târ′i-a)], **1,** a model of the planetary system, showing the planets, their motions round the sun, their relative sizes, etc.; **2,** a device that projects images of planets and other celestial bodies onto a domed surface; **3,** a domed building or room containing such a device.

plank (plangk), *n.* **1,** a long, broad piece of sawn timber thicker than a board; **2,** an item in the platform of a political party:—*v.t.* **1,** to cover with thick boards; **2,** *Colloq.* to lay down, as on a plank; **3,** *Colloq.* to pay; as, to *plank* down money; **4,** to cook on a board; as, to *plank* salmon.—*n.* **plank′ing.**

plank-ton (plangk′tun), *n.* the floating or drifting microscopic plant and animal life of seas and lakes, such as algae, used by fish as food.

plant (plant), *n.* **1,** a member of the vegetable kingdom, usually with roots in the soil, from which it draws part of its food in the form of minerals and water, and with stems, branches, leaves, and flowers above the ground, as a bush, herb, or tree; **2,** a sprout or young shoot ready for transplanting; **3,** the tools, machinery, fixtures, and sometimes buildings, of any trade or business; as, a manufacturing *plant*; **4,** the equipment of an institution, as a university, college, or hospital:—*v.t.* **1,** to put into the ground for growth; as, to *plant* seed; **2,** to provide or prepare with seeds, roots, etc.; as, to *plant* a garden; **3,** to fix firmly; place; as, he *planted* his feet firmly; **4,** to establish, as a colony; **5,** to implant or introduce, as an idea; as, she *planted* the idea of a party in his head.

plan-ta-tion (plan-tā′shun), *n.* **1,** a place where anything is sown, set out, or cultivated; as, a *plantation* of trees; **2,** a large estate, esp. in America, where crops are cultivated; **3,** a colony.

plant-er (plan′tėr), *n.* **1,** the owner or cultivator of a plantation; **2,** a person who sows or plants; **3,** a planting machine; **4,** a container in which plants are grown inside a house, on a patio, etc.

plaque (plåk), *n.* **1,** a thin, flat plate of wood or metal used as a wall ornament, to mark historic sites, or given as an award; **2,** the thin film left by food on the surface of the teeth, which often contains bacteria and can cause cavities and gum disease; **3,** a fatty deposit in arteries.

plas-ma (plaz′ma), *n.* **1,** the colourless watery part of the blood in which the red and white corpuscles float; **2,** the liquid part of milk in which the fat globules are suspended.

plas-ter (plås′tėr), *n.* **1,** a mixture of lime, sand, and water, which hardens on drying, used for coating walls and partitions of buildings; **2,** a substance with medicinal qualities, which is spread upon cloth and applied to some part of the body as a remedy or for cosmetic purposes; as, a mustard *plaster*:—*v.t.* **1,** to cover with plaster; as, to *plaster* the walls; **2,** to treat with a plaster; **3,** to cover closely or smooth, as if with plaster; as, she *plastered* her wet hair down; **4,** to cover something densely, esp. to excess; as, she plastered the town with election posters:—**plaster of Paris,** a white powder of calcium sulphate or gypsum, used, when mixed with water, for finishing walls, making moulds, casts, statues, etc.

plas-tic (plas′tik), *adj.* **1,** capable of being formed or moulded; as, clay or wax are *plastic* materials; **2,** quick to receive impressions; as, *a plastic* mind; **3,** giving form to matter; creative; as, *plastic* art; **4,** of, pertaining to, or characteristic of, moulding or modelling; **5,** made of plastic; as, a *plastic* cup; **6,** artificial; lacking in originality; insincere:—*n.* **1,** any of various nonmetallic synthetic compounds used instead of glass, wood, metal, etc.; **2,** something made of plastic; **3,** *Colloq.* a credit card or credit cards; as, she used *plastic* to buy the DVD player.

plate (plāt), *n.* **1,** a thin, flat piece of metal or glass, rigid, and of uniform thickness; as, armour *plate*; **2,** a shallow, usually circular, dish from which food is eaten; **3,** the food on such a plate; a plateful; also, food served to one person at a meal; **4,** a piece of metal on which something is engraved; as, a door *plate*; name *plate*; **5,** a print made from an engraved metal surface; also, the surface; **6,** in *photography,* a thin sheet of glass treated with chemicals to make it sensitive to light, on which a picture is taken; **7,** household articles, esp. utensils, made of gold or silver; **8,** a thin piece of rubber, metal, etc., fitted to the mouth, and holding artificial teeth; also, a device for straightening irregular teeth; **9,** in *baseball,* the home base; **10,** a cut of beef from the lower part of the side; **11,** in *architecture,* a horizontal timber upon which the lower ends of the rafters are set; **12,** the mould of a page or section of type; **13,** an automobile's licence plate:—*v.t.* [plat-ed, plat-ing], **1,** to coat with metal; **2,** to cover with sheets of metal.

pla-teau (pla-tō′), *n.* [*pl.* plateaux (-tō′) or plateaus (-tōz′)], **1,** an elevated tract of flat land that is higher than the area surrounding it; tableland; **2,** the period of time during which progress stops, slows, or stabilizes; as, the winning hockey team hit a *plateau*; **3,** a level of accomplishment; as, she reached the 1000-metre *plateau*:—*v.i.* to stabilize or level off; as, the land *plateaued* beyond the sharp rise.

plat-en (plat′n), *n.* **1,** in a printing press, the flat part or cylinder that brings the paper against the type; **2,** in a typewriter, the roller; **3,** in *computing,* the roller in a computer printer against which the type strikes; **4,** the glass surface of a photocopier or flatbed scanner.

plat-form (plat′fôrm′), *n.* **1,** a structure raised above the level of the ground or of the main floor, as a stage for public speakers, or along the tracks at a railway station; **2,** a statement of principles and policies, as of a political party; **3,** in *computing,* the combination of hardware and software that provides the basis for the computer's operation; **4,** the thick layer in the sole of a shoe to provide additional height to a person.

plat-i-num (plat′i-num), *n.* a heavy, silver-white, precious metal much used as a catalyst, and for jewelry.

plat-i-tude (plat′i-tūd′), *n.* a commonplace or dull remark, esp. when used as though fresh or profound.

pla-toon (pla-to͞on′), *n.* **1,** a small unit of soldiers; **2,** any similar group, esp. one with a common interest; as, a *platoon* of police; **3,** in *sports,* a group of players specifically trained to function as a unit; as, the defensive *platoon*:—*v.t.* to alternate two or more players in the same position.

plat-ter (plat′ėr), *n.* a large, flat dish for serving meat, poultry, vegetables, etc.

plat·y·pus (plat′i-pus), *n.* [*pl.* -puses], a small, aquatic, egg-laying Australian mammal with a ducklike bill.

plau·dit (plô′dit), *n.* **1,** applause, esp. by clapping; **2,** enthusiastic praise or approval; as, he won the *plaudits* of his audience.

plau·si·ble (plô′zi-bl), *adj.* **1,** seeming to be true; having the appearance of truth; as, a *plausible* excuse; **2,** persuasive; as, a *plausible* speaker.—*n.* **plau′si-bil′i-ty.**—*adv.* **plau′si-bly.**

play (plā), *v.i.* **1,** to move lightly or capriciously; flutter, as leaves in the wind; **2,** to sport or frolic; **3,** to take part in a game; also, to gamble; **4,** to perform on a musical instrument; **5,** to act on the stage, in a movie, or a television program; **6,** to dally; trifle; **7,** to be accepted; as, the idea *played* well in the west:—*v.t.* **1,** to take part in; as, to *play* checkers; also, to compete with, in a game; as, our team *played* the champion team; **2,** to put into action in a game or contest, as by laying a card on the table; **3,** to imitate in fun; as, to *play* house; **4,** to perform; as, to *play* a comedy; also, to perform music on; as, to *play* the violin; **5,** to act in the character of; as, to *play* Othello; *play* the fool; **6,** to set in action; as, to *play* a trick; **7,** to operate continuously; as, to *play* a hose on the grass:—*n.* **1,** brisk, sometimes irregular, motion; as, the *play* of light and shade; **2,** freedom or room to act; as, to give one's arm full *play* in throwing a ball; **3,** action or use; as, all their resources were brought into *play*; **4,** exercise, esp. in a contest of strength or skill; as, the *play* of a duellist's sword; **5,** a game or sport; **6,** recreation; **7,** gambling; as, to lose money at *play*; **8,** any single action in a game; also, one's turn to move a piece, lay down a card, etc.; as, it is your *play*; **9,** fun; jest; as, she did it in *play*; **10,** conduct; as, fair *play*; **11,** a drama intended for the stage; also, its performance. Also, **play′bill′; play′book′; play′boy′; play′go′er; play′-off′; play′pen′, play′room′.**—*adj.* **play′a-ble.**

play·er (plā′ėr), *n.* **1,** a person who plays a game or a musical instrument; as, a hockey *player*, piano *player*; **2,** a machine that reproduces something that was recorded before; as, a CD or DVD *player*; **3,** an actor; as, she was the leading *player* in the theatre; **4,** a major participant; as, he is a *player* in financial industry.

play·ful (plā′fool), *adj.* full of play; lively; as, a *playful* kitten.

play·ground (plā′ground′), *n.* **1,** a plot of ground, esp. outdoors, set aside for children's play, usually with swings, slides, and other such equipment; **2,** any area set aside for recreation or other pleasurable activity.

play·house (plā′hous′), *n.* **1,** a theatre; **2,** a house for children's play.

play·mate (plā′māt′), *n.* someone who plays or takes part in games with another; a friend or companion.

play·thing (plā′thing′), *n.* a toy.

play·wright (plā′rīt′), *n.* a writer of plays; a dramatist.

pla·za (plå′za), *n.* **1,** a shopping centre; **2,** an open square or marketplace surrounded by buildings.

plea (plē), *n.* **1,** an excuse or apology; **2,** an appeal or entreaty; **3,** the defendant's answer to the charges in a lawsuit; as, a *plea* of not guilty.

plead (plēd), *v.i.* [*p.t.* and *p.p.* plead-ed or pled (pled), *p.pr.* plead-ing], **1,** to argue or reason in support of a cause against another; **2,** to argue before a court of law; as, to *plead* for an acquittal; **3,** to beg earnestly; pray; to ask for something with deep feeling; as, to *plead* for mercy:—*v.t.* **1,** to defend by arguments; as, to *plead* a case; **2,** to answer, as to a charge; as, to *plead* not guilty; **3,** to offer as an excuse; as, to *plead* poverty.—*n.* **plead′er.**

pleas·ant (plez′ant), *adj.* **1,** pleasing; delightful; enjoyable; agreeable; as, a *pleasant* smell; a *pleasant* day; **2,** characterized by charming manners or behaviour; cheerful; as, a *pleasant* person.

pleas·ant·ry (plez′ant-ri), *n.* [*pl.* pleasantries], **1,** merriment; lively talk; banter; **2,** a laughable speech; a joke.

please (plēz), *v.t.* [pleased, pleas-ing], **1,** to gratify; give enjoyment to; as, to *please* a parent; **2,** to be the will of; suit; as, may it *please* the court to call our next witness:—*v.i.* **1,** to give satisfaction or enjoyment; as, we strive to *please*; **2,** to like or choose; as, to do as you *please*:—*adv.* **1,** used to ask a person politely to do something; as, *Please* stand up; **2,** yes; as, More coffee? *Please.*—*adj.* **pleas′ing** (giving pleasure; pleasant; enjoyable; as, a *pleasing* smile).

pleas·ur·a·ble (plezh′ėr-a-bl), *adj.* delightful; gratifying; as, a *pleasurable* occasion.—*adv.* **pleas′ur-a-bly.**

pleas·ure (plezh′ėr), *n.* **1,** a feeling of delight or satisfaction; enjoyment; as, it was a *pleasure* meeting you; **2,** a source of delight; a joy; as, she played just for the *pleasure* of it; **3,** choice; wish; as, I await your *pleasure*:—*adj.* related to, of, or for something that gives pleasure or enjoyment; as, a *pleasure* ride; *pleasure* craft.

pleat (plēt), *n.* a fold, as of cloth doubled over upon itself; a plait:—*v.t.* to fold in pleats.—*adj.* **pleat′ed.**

pleb (pleb), *abbrev.* short for *plebeian.*

ple·be·ian (pli-bē′an; pli-bē′yan), *adj.* **1,** originally, pertaining to the common people of ancient Rome; **2,** vulgar or common; as, *plebeian* tastes:—*n.* **1,** one of the common people of ancient Rome: opposite of *patrician*; **2,** any person of common or lower classes; a commoner; **3,** a vulgar person.

pleb-i-scite (pleb′i-sīt′; -sit), *n.* a direct vote of all the people; as, the Charlottetown Accord was defeated in the 1992 *plebiscite*.

pledge (plej), *n.* **1,** anything given or considered as a security or guarantee; a pawn; **2,** the state of being given as security; as, goods held in *pledge*; **3,** a drinking of a health as an expression of goodwill; also, a person so pledged; **4,** an agreement or promise to do or not to do something; **5,** a token or sign of goodwill; as, a *pledge* of friendship; **6,** the promise of a donation; as, her *pledge* to the charity was for $100; **7,** the donation itself:—*v.t.* [pledged, pledg-ing], **1,** to give as security or guarantee; as, to *pledge* one's honour; to put in pawn; as he *pledged* his watch; **2,** to bind by a promise; as, to *pledge* oneself to secrecy; **3,** to drink to the health of; **4,** to promise to donate, as to a charity; as, he *pledged* $100.

ple-na-ry (plē′na-ri; plen′), *adj.* full; complete; absolute; as, *plenary* powers or authority.

plen-ti-ful (plen′ti-fool), *adj.* **1,** yielding abundance; as, a *plentiful* harvest; **2,** existing in great quantity.—*adv.* **plen′ti-ful-ly.**—*n.* **plen′ti-ful-ness.**

plen-ty (plen′ti), *n.* [*pl.* plenties], a condition of abundance; as, horn of *plenty*:—*pron.* a full supply; more than enough; large number or scope; as, there is *plenty* of food; *plenty* of trouble:—*adj.* abundant; more than enough; ample; as, two pieces of bread will be *plenty*:—*adv. Colloq.* very; as, it's *plenty* hot.

pleth-o-ra (pleth′ėr-a), *n.* excess; too much; abundance; as, a *plethora* of mistakes on the test.

pli-a-ble (plī′a-bl), *adj.* **1,** easily bent; flexible; **2,** easily influenced; docile.—*adj.* **pli′a-bly.**—*n.* **pli′a-bil′i-ty.**

pli-ant (plī′ant), *adj.* **1,** easily bent; pliable; as, a *pliant* twig; **2,** easily influenced.—*adj.* **pli′ant-ly.**—*n.* **pli′an-cy.**

pli-ers or **ply-ers** (plī′ėrz), *n.pl.* used as *sing.* small pincers for bending wire, holding small objects, or cutting things.

[1]**plight** (plīt), *n.* a state or condition, usually unfavourable or dangerous; a predicament; as, they found us in a sorry *plight*; the *plight* of underdeveloped countries.

[2]**plight** (plīt), *n.* a pledge or solemn promise, esp. in marriage:—*v.t.* **1,** to pledge, as one's faith; **2,** to promise, esp. in marriage; as, to *plight* one's troth; **3,** to betroth or marry.

plod (plod), *v.i.* [plod-ded, plod-ding], **1,** to walk slowly and heavily; trudge; **2,** to drudge or toil steadily and with perseverance:—*v.t.* to walk over heavily and slowly.—*n.* **plod′der.**

plop (plop), *n.* the sound made by a smooth object's dropping into water without splashing:—*v.i.* [plopped, plop-ping], to fall with a plop:—*v.t.* to drop (something) with a plop.

plot (plot), *n.* **1,** a small area of ground; as, a *plot* of land; **2,** a plan of a piece of land, an estate, etc.; a diagram; chart; map; **3,** a scheme or plan; esp., a secret conspiracy; as, a *plot* to steal the treasure; **4,** the plan of a play, novel, movie, television show, etc.:—*v.t.* [plotted, plot-ting], **1,** to lay plans for; scheme; as, to *plot* a crime; **2,** to make a plan or map of; as, to *plot* a course of action; **3,** to locate or show on a map or chart:—*v.i.* to scheme; as, to *plot* against an enemy.—*n.* **plot′ter.**

plough (plou), *n.*, *v.t.*, and *v.i.* Same as **plow.**

plow or **plough** (plou), *n.* **1,** a farming implement for cutting and turning up the soil in preparation for planting; **2,** any implement that works in a similar way by cutting, shoving, furrowing, etc.; as, a snow*plow*:—*v.t.* to turn up with such an implement; till; as, to *plow* a field:—*v.i.* **1,** to break or turn up soil with, or as with, a plow; **2,** to move onward by cutting or pushing a way; as, the ship *plowed* on; we *plowed* through the mud.

ploy (ploi), *n.* a calculated move to gain an end; a trick.

pluck (pluk), *v.t.* **1,** to pull off, out, or up; as, to *pluck* weeds; **2,** to pick or gather; harvest; as, to *pluck* grapes; **3,** to pull or twitch; as, to *pluck* the strings of a guitar; **4,** to strip completely of feathers; as, to *pluck* a goose:—**pluck up,** to summon; as, *pluck up* your courage:—*v.i.* to give a sudden pull; tug:—*n.* **1,** spirit; courage; as, a person of *pluck*; **2,** a pull; snatch; tug.

pluck-y (pluk′i), *adj.* [pluck-i-er, pluck-i-est], brave; courageous; full of spirit.—*adv.* **pluck′i-ly.**

plug (plug), *n.* **1,** a piece of wood, rubber metal, etc., used to fill or stop a hole; **2,** a device to make an electrical connection; **3,** a cake of pressed tobacco; **4,** a point in a water system where a hose may be attached; a fire hydrant:—*v.t.* [plugged, plug-ging], **1,** to stop or make tight with a piece of wood, cork, etc.; as, to *plug* a leak; **2,** to advertise, as a song, book, or other product or event, by reference to it on radio, television, etc.—*v.i. Colloq.* to work hard; plod:—**plug in,** to make an electrical connection by inserting a plug into a socket.

plug–in (plug′–in), *n.* **1,** in *computing*, an accessory software program that can be used to alter or enhance a central application; **2,** any device that plugs into something else; **3,** an electrical outlet or plug.

plum (plum), *n.* **1,** a tree somewhat like the peach and cherry; also, its red, green, purple, or yellow, smooth-skinned fruit; **2,** something like this fruit in sweetness or shape; as, a sugar*plum*; **3,** a raisin when used in cooking; **4,** a dark-purple colour; **5,** a choice or best part; a desirable job or appointment:—*adj.* relating to, of, or for a plum; as, *plum* pudding; a *plum* job.

plum-age (plo͞om′ij), *n.* **1,** a bird's feathers; **2,** bright and ornamental costume.

plumb (plum), *n.* **1,** a small weight fastened to a cord, used by builders to test the accuracy of vertical work; **2,** a similar weight used to find the depth of water; a plummet; **3,** the perpendicular or vertical:—*adj.* vertical; upright:—*adv.* **1,** vertically; **2,** *Colloq.* completely; entirely; as, *plumb* crazy:—*v.t.* **1,** to test with a plumb line; **2,** to straighten; make vertical; as, to *plumb* up a wall; **3,** to sound (the depth of water) by a plummet; **4,** to get to the bottom of; solve; probe.

plumb-er (plum′ėr), *n.* a person who supplies, repairs, or installs bathroom fixtures, water pipes, gas pipes, etc.

plumb-ing (plum′ing), *n.* **1,** the occupation of putting in or repairing the piping and other fittings for the water or gas supply or sewage disposal of a building; **2,** the pipes and fittings so installed.

plumb line, **1,** a cord attached to a plumb; **2,** a vertical line.

plume (plo͞om), *n.* **1,** a long and beautiful feather or tuft of feathers; **2,** a feather worn as an ornament:—*v.t.* [plumed, plum-ing], **1,** to clean and adjust; preen; as, a bird *plumes* its feathers; **2,** to adorn with feathers or with fine clothes; **3,** to feel proud of (oneself); as, to *plume* oneself on one's skill.

plum-met (plum′it), *n.* a weight attached to a plumb line:—*v.i.* to plunge; drop or fall straight down; as, the rocket *plummeted* to earth.

plump (plump), *adj.* well-filled or rounded out; fleshy; as, a *plump* figure:—*v.i.* **1,** to grow round or full; **2,** to support, esp. an electoral candidate; as, to *plump* for a person; **3,** to drop sharply or abruptly; as, the stock market *plumped*:—*v.t.* to cause to fill out or become round.

plun-der (plun′dėr), *n.* the act of robbing or taking by force; also, that which is taken; booty:—*v.t.* to rob by open force, esp. in war.—*n.* **plun′der-er.**

plunge (plunj), *v.t.* [plunged, plung-ing] **1,** to thrust suddenly into a liquid or into any substance that can be penetrated; **2,** to place suddenly in an unexpected condition; as, to *plunge* a friend into difficulty:—*v.i.* **1,** to dive, fall, or rush, as into water; **2,** to enter suddenly; as, to *plunge* into danger:—*n.* a sudden dive or leap; a headlong rush.—*n.* **plung′er** (**1,** a person or thing that dives; **2,** a rubber suction device with a handle that is used to unclog drains).

plunk (plungk), *v.t.* and *v.i.* **1,** to pluck or twang (the strings of a banjo, etc.); **2,** to throw down; as, he *plunked* down a loonie; **3,** to hit abruptly, as a baseball:—*n.* a plunking or twanging sound.

plu-per-fect (plo͞o′pûr′fekt), *adj.* in *grammar,* the tense that shows an action as complete before a given past time; past perfect; as, he *had gone* when I *arrived; had gone* is the *pluperfect* (completed action) in relation to *arrived.*

plu-ral (ploor′al), *adj.* **1,** consisting of more than one; **2,** in *grammar,* relating to the form of a word that names more than one; as, "girls" is a *plural* noun:—*n.* in *grammar,* that form of a word that names more than one; as, *computers* is the plural of *computer, women* of *woman, oxen* of *ox, sons-in-law* of *son-in-law.*

plu-ral-i-ty (ploo-ral′i-ti), *n.* [*pl.* pluralities], **1,** the state of consisting of more than one; **2,** the larger number; the majority; **3,** in *politics,* the number of votes one candidate receives more than any other candidate, esp. if it is not an absolute majority.

plus (plus), *adj.* **1,** extra; as, *plus* value; **2,** and more; as, 100 *plus*; **3,** indicating addition; as, the *plus* sign; **4,** indicating a positive quantity; as, a *plus* three:—*n.* **1,** an extra quantity; an addition; **2,** the plus sign [+]:—*prep.* with the addition of; and; as, 14 *plus* 12 makes 26.

plush (plush), *n.* thick, soft cloth with a pile or nap longer than that of velvet:—*adj.* **1,** made of such a fabric; **2,** luxurious.

plu-to-crat (plo͞o′tō-krat′), *n.* a member of a group that governs or influences a government by virtue of its wealth; a rich person.—*n.* **plu-toc′ra-cy.**

plu-to-ni-um (plo͞o-tō′ni-um), *n.* a radioactive element that is fissionable and is used in some nuclear reactors and weapons.

¹ply (plī), *v.t.* [plied, ply-ing], **1,** to work at steadily; as, to *ply* a trade; **2,** to use diligently or earnestly; as, to *ply* an oar; **3,** to urge; offer something persistently to; as, to *ply* one with food:—*v.i.* **1,** to run regularly on a fixed course between two parts or places, as does a boat; **2,** to work diligently.

²ply (plī), *n.* [*pl.* plies], a thickness or layer, as in a carpet or facial tissue; a turn or twist.

ply-wood (plī′wood′), *n.* a building material made of two or more layers, or plies, of wood glued together.

PM or **P.M.** (pē′em′), *abbrev.* short for *prime minister.*

P.M. or **p.m.** (pē′em′), *abbrev.* in the afternoon and evening, between noon and midnight: short for *post meridiem.* Compare *A.M.*

pneu-mat-ic (nū-mat′ik; noo-), *adj.* **1,** pertaining to air; **2,** inflated with air; as, a *pneumatic* tire; **3,** made to work by air pressure or vacuum; as, a *pneumatic* drill.

pneu-mo-ni-a (nū-mō′ni-a; noo-), *n.* inflammation of the tissues of the lungs.

[1]**poach** (pōch), *v.t.* to cook food such as eggs or fish in boiling water or other liquid.

[2]**poach** (pōch), *v.t.* and *v.i.* to hunt or fish, without permission, on another's property or out of season.—*n.* **poach′er.**

pock (pok), *n.* **1,** a small swelling (like a blister or pimple), as in smallpox; **2,** the scar left by such a swelling; as, *pock*marked by chickenpox:—*v.t.* to mark or scar with pocks or pits.

pocket (pok′it), *n.* **1,** a small pouch or bag attached to a garment, for carrying small articles; **2,** a small netted bag in a billiard table for catching the balls; **3,** in a mine, a cavity or place where a deposit of ore is found; as a gold *pocket*; **4,** the region marked by a sudden variation in the density of the air, which causes an airplane to drop suddenly; an air pocket; **5,** an isolated area or group; as, a *pocket* of poverty:—*v.t.* **1,** to put into a pocket; **2,** to take unlawfully, as profits; **3,** to receive (an insult) without showing any feeling:—*adj.* small-sized; as, a *pocket* calculator.—*n.* **pock′et-ful′.**

pock-et-book (pok′it-book′), *n.* a small case or folder for carrying money, papers, etc., in the pocket; a billfold.

pock-et-knife (pok′it-nīf′), *n.* [*pl.* pocket-knives (-nīvz′)], a small knife with blades that close into the handle.

POCKETKNIFE

pock-mark (pok′märk′), *n.* **1,** a scar or small hole in the skin, as one left by smallpox; **2,** a similar mark on any surface.

pod (pod), *n.* **1,** a seed vessel, esp. of the pea, bean, etc.; **2,** any protective covering; **3,** a school of marine mammals, such as whales.

po-di-um (pō′di-um), *n.* **1,** a small raised platform for an orchestra leader, public speaker, etc.; lectern; **2,** in *botany,* a support, as a stalk.

po-em (pō′im), *n.* a composition in verse; a piece of poetry.

po-et (pō′it), *n.* one who writes verses, esp. one who writes such verse or poetry as is characterized by beauty of thought and language.—*n.fem.* **po′et-ess.**

po-et-ic (pō-et′ik) or **po-et-i-cal** (pō-et′i-kal), *adj.* **1,** connected with, or characteristic of, poetry or poets; as, *poetic* language; **2,** written in verse; as, Milton's *poetic* works.—*adv.* **po-et′i-cal-ly.**

po-et-ry (pō′it-ri), *n.* **1,** the art of expressing beautiful or elevated thought or feeling in verse; **2,** a poem or poems as a whole.

poign-ant (poin′ant; poin′yant), *adj.* **1,** acute; excessive; as, *poignant* thirst; **2,** piercing; keenly felt; as, *poignant* regrets; **3,** keen; as, *poignant* wit.—*n.* **poign′an-cy.**

poin-set-ti-a (poin-set′-i-a), *n.* a plant on which tiny greenish flowers are surrounded by large, showy, bright-red, petal-like leaves.

point (point), *n.* **1,** the sharp or tapering end of a thing; as, the *point* of a pin; a pencil *point*; a *point* of land; **2,** a particular or separate part; detail; as, the *points* of an argument; a trait; as, *points* of character; also, the most important feature of a speech, story, action, etc.; as, you missed the *point*; **3,** purpose; as, she gained her *point*; **4,** a particular spot or position; as, a certain *point* on a road; also, a definite degree or stage; as, the boiling *point*; a turning *point*; **5,** the unit of scoring in certain games; **6,** a dot printed or written; period; decimal point; **7,** one of the 32 equal divisions of the compass or one of the points marking them; **8,** a physical feature in an animal, esp. one by which excellence is judged; **9,** in *hockey,* the location inside the opponent's blue line that is most advantageous to set up scoring attempts; as, he shot from the *point*:—*adj.* made with the needle; as, *point* lace:—*v.t.* **1,** to sharpen; as, to *point* a pencil; **2,** to give liveliness or force to; show the purpose of; as, to *point* a moral; **3,** to show the direction of; as, to *point* the way; **4,** to direct or aim; as, to *point* a gun; **5,** to separate with a decimal point; as, to *point* off figures; **6,** to fill the joints of (masonry) with mortar and smooth with a trowel; **7,** to show the presence of (game) by standing in a certain position, as some hunting dogs do; **8,** to indicate; direct attention to; as, to *point* out errors:—*v.i.* **1,** to call attention by extending the finger; as, it is rude to *point*; **2,** to face; tend (to or toward); be directed; **3,** to indicate the presence of game by standing in a certain position, as do some dogs; **4,** in *computing,* to move the cursor on the screen with a mouse or other such device; **5,** to indicate; as, all evidence *points* to suicide.

point–blank (point′–blangk′), *adj.* aimed straight at the mark; direct; blunt; as, a *point-blank* question:—*adv.* (point′–blangk′), directly.

point-ed (poin′tid), *adj.* **1,** sharpened; having a sharp end, as a needle; **2,** direct; telling; as, *pointed* repartee; also, having a personal application; as, a *pointed* allusion.

point-er (poin′tėr), *n.* **1,** a thing that points or shows position; **2,** a breed of large hunting dog with short hair and long ears, trained to point, that is, to stop and show the place where game is hidden; **3,** a timely hint; suggestion; tip; **4,** a rod or other device used to indicate things on a chalk board, etc.; **5,** in *computing,* the arrow-shaped symbol that indicates the position of the cursor on the screen.

point-less (point′lis), *adj.* without purpose

or meaning; having no point; as, a *pointless* argument.

point of view, the way a person looks at or judges something; viewpoint; perspective.

poise (poiz), *n.* **1,** equilibrium; balance; **2,** the manner of carrying the head and body; **3,** mental balance; self-possession; as, she kept her *poise* under trying conditions:—*v.t.* and *v.i.* [poised, pois-ing], to balance:—*v.i.* [poised, pois-ing], to hover:—*v.t.* to balance.

poised (poizd), *adj.* confident; composed; as, she remained *poised* during the oral examination.

poi-son (poi′zn), *n.* **1,** a substance that causes injury or death to a living body by chemical action when taken in or absorbed: common poisons include arsenic and lead, the substance contained in the bite of many snakes and insects, and the sap in some plants; **2,** an influence that damages the character:—*v.t.* **1,** to injure or kill by some deadly substance; **2,** to put a deadly substance into or upon; as, to *poison* food; **3,** to corrupt; as, to *poison* his mind.—*adj.* **poi′son-ous.**

poison ivy, a common vine with leaves formed of three leaflets, the mere touch of which brings out, on many persons, a painful, itching rash: another form of the plant is poison oak.

poke (pōk), *v.t.* [poked, pok-ing], **1,** to thrust or push against, esp. with a pointed object; prod; as, to *poke* the fire; **2,** to thrust (in or out); as, to *poke* one's head out of the door:—*v.i.* **1,** to thrust or push; as, to *poke* at the fire; **2,** to move lazily; dawdle.—*n.* **1,** a thrust or push; **2,** *Colloq.* a punch; as, he took a *poke* at me.

poke check, in *hockey*, the defensive manoeuvre of poking the puck away from the puck carrier with the hockey stick.

[1]**pok-er** (pōk′ėr), *n.* a rod of metal used for stirring fires.

[2]**pok-er** (pōk′ėr), *n.* a card game in which two or more players bet on the value of their hands.

pok-y or **poke-y** (pōk′i), *adj.* [pok-i-er, pok-i-est], *Colloq.* **1,** slow; dull; **2,** small; cramped; as, a *poky* closet; **3,** shabby.

po-lar (pō′lėr), *adj.* **1,** pertaining to, or situated near, either pole of the earth; **2,** pertaining to either pole of a magnet.

polar bear, a large bear with heavy white fur that lives in the far north.

Po-la-ris (pō-lâr′is; -la′), *n.* the polestar, or North Star.

po-lar-ize (pō′lar-īz′), *v.t.* **1,** in *magnetism* and *electricity*, to give opposite magnetic properties to the poles of a bar, coil, battery, etc.; **2,** in *optics*, the process of affecting light or radiant heat so that the paths of the vibrations become straight lines, circles, or ellipses.—*n.* **po-lar′i-ty; po′lar-i-za′tion.**

[1]**pole** (pōl), *n.* **1,** either of the two ends of the axis of a sphere, esp. either of the two ends of earth's axis, called the *North Pole* and the *South Pole*; **2,** either of the two terminals or ends of a magnet, electric battery, etc.

[2]**pole** (pōl), *n.* **1,** a long piece of wood or metal; as, a fishing *pole*; also, an upright timber, such as a mast; as, a telegraph *pole*; **2,** the position in a race in the front row on the inside; as, he won the *pole* position in qualification:—*v.t.* [poled, poling], to push with a pole; as, to *pole* a boat:—*v.i.* to propel a boat with a pole.

pole-star (pōl′stär′), *n.* **1,** the North Star, or Polaris, a guide to navigators and explorers; **2,** a guiding light or principle; guide.

po-lice (pō-lēs′), *n.* **1,** that part of a government that enforces the laws, investigates crimes, makes arrests, and keeps order; **2,** the individuals in this department; **3,** any group that fulfills similar functions; as, military *police* or language *police*:—*v.t.* [policed, polic-ing], **1,** to watch, protect, and keep in order by means of police officers; **2,** to perform the functions of a police force:—*adj.* connected with the police; as, *police* protection.

police dog, the German shepherd dog, or any of a variety of wolflike dogs, trained to aid police.

police officer, a member of a police force.—*n.* **po-lice-man; po-lice′wom′an.**

[1]**pol-i-cy** (pol′i-si), *n.* [*pl.* policies], **1,** wise management of public affairs; **2,** a course of conduct; as, it is good *policy* not to meddle; esp. a line of conduct of a government, business corporation, etc.; as, an immigration *policy*.

[2]**pol-i-cy** (pol′i-si), *n.* [*pl.* policies], a document containing a contract of insurance between an insurance company and the person or persons insured. Also, **pol′i-cy-hol′der; pol′i-cy-mak′ing.**

po-li-o (pōl′i-ō), *n.* an infectious disease that esp. attacks children, causing a paralysis, sometimes permanent, of muscles of the arms and legs, for which a vaccine has been developed that has all but eradicated the disease: also called *infantile paralysis* or *poliomyelitis*.

Pol-ish (pō′lish), *n.* **1,** a person who inhabits or originates from Poland; **2,** the language spoken by these people:—*adj.* relating to the country, the people, the language, or the culture of Poland.

pol-ish (pol′ish), *v.t.* **1,** to make smooth or glossy by rubbing; as, to *polish* brass; **2,** to make polite or cultured; **3,** to perfect or improve; as, she *polished* her essay:—*v.i.* to become smooth or glossy:—*n.* **1,** the act of polishing; **2,** a smooth glossy surface; **3,** a mixture for making a surface smooth and glossy; as, shoe *polish*; **4,** elegance of manners.—*n.* **pol′ish-er.**

po-lite (po-līt′), *adj.* [polit-er, polit-est], **1,** well-bred; refined; as, *polite* society; **2,** courteous; as, a *polite* child.

pol-i-tic (pol′i-tik), *adj.* **1,** prudent; shrewd; as, a *politic* adviser; **2,** useful; advisable; as, a *politic* decision; **3,** political; as, the body *politic.*

po-lit-i-cal (po-lit′i-kal), *adj.* associated with the science of government or the management of public affairs.

pol-i-ti-cian (pol′i-tish′an), *n.* **1,** a person who is elected to or running for public office, such as a mayor, member of Parliament, premier, or prime minister; **2,** any person who works for a political party or is involved in politics; **3,** someone who is mainly interested in his or her own advancement and selfish ends, esp. a schemer who uses underhanded methods; as, a sly *politician.*

pol-i-tics (pol′i-tiks), *n.pl.* used as *sing.* **1,** the science or art of government; political science; **2,** one's political opinions; the party to which one belongs; someone's attitudes and beliefs about government; as, her *politics* are very conservative.

pol-ka (pōl′ka), *n.* **1,** a lively dance of Bohemian origin, performed by two persons; **2,** music suitable for such a dance.

polka dot, one of the small round dots used to form regular patterns on textile fabrics and other objects; as, a *polka dot* tie.

poll (pōl), *n.* **1,** a survey of a group of people to find out what they think about a subject; as, they took a *poll* on that question; **2,** a count of persons, or the resulting number; a list of persons, as of those entitled to vote at an election; **3,** an election; **4,** the number of votes recorded at an election; **5,** (usually *polls*), the place where votes are cast; **6,** a tax on each person: also called *poll tax*; **7,** the head, esp. the part of it on which hair grows:—*v.t.* **1,** to lop, clip, or shear; as, to *poll* trees or sheep; also, to cut the horns of (cattle); **2,** to enroll, as for voting; **3,** to examine or record the votes of; as, to *poll* a jury; **4,** to receive votes from; as, he *polled* a large majority; **5,** to cast or drop into a ballot box; as, to *poll* one's vote; **6,** in *computing,* to test or check to see when data will be sent or received.

pol-len (pol′en), *n.* the fine powder produced by the anthers of a flower, which, when carried to the pistil, usually of another flower, fertilizes the seeds.

pol-li-nate (pol′i-nāt′), *v.t.* [pollinat-ed, pollinat-ing], to carry and drop pollen upon the pistil of (a flower) for fertilization, as bees do.—*n.* **pol′li-na′tion.**

pol-li-wog or **pol-ly-wog** (pol′i-wog′), *n.* a tadpole, or immature frog.

pol-lut-ant (po-lo͞ot′ent), *n.* something that is harmful to living things, esp. toxic substances or gas; as, car exhaust is a *pollutant.*

pol-lute (po-lūt′), *v.t.* [pollut-ed, pollut-ing], **1,** to make unclean; as, to *pollute* water with filth or chemicals; **2,** to destroy the purity of; corrupt.

pol-lu-tion (po-lo͞o′shun), *n.* **1,** the condition of being polluted; as, air *pollution* is a serious problem; **2,** things that pollute; as, the *pollution* in the lake is killing the fish.

po-lo (pō′lō), *n.* a game similar to field hockey, in which the players are mounted on horses and equipped with long-handled mallets:—**water polo,** a ball game played in the water by swimmers.—*n.* **po′lo-ist.**

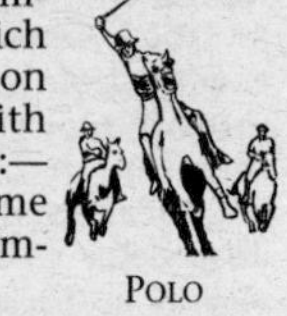
Polo

pol-troon (pol-tro͞on′), *n.* a mean-spirited, lazy coward.

pol-y- (pol′i-), *prefix* meaning *many*; as in *poly*morphic (having various forms), *poly*nuclear (having many nuclei), *poly*theism (belief in many gods).

pol-y-es-ter (pol′ē-es′tėr; pol′ē-es′tėr), *n.* an artificial fibre made from chemicals, often used for making clothes.

po-lyg-a-my (po-lig′-a-mi), *n.* the practice or state of having more than one wife or more than one husband at the same time. Compare *bigamy* and *monogamy.*—*adj.* **po-lyg′a-mous** (po-lig′a-mus).

pol-y-glot (pol′i-glot′), *adj.* containing, or made up of, several languages; as, a *polyglot* dictionary.

pol-y-gon (pol′i-gon; pol′i-gun), *n.* in *geometry,* a closed plane figure of three or more straight sides.

pol-y-syl-la-ble (pol′i-sil′a-bl), *n.* a word of many syllables.

pome-gran-ate (pom′gran′it; pom′i-gran′it; pum′gran′it; pum′i-gran′it), *n.* **1,** a tropical Asiatic tree yielding a fruit with a thick rind and a very seedy, crimson pulp, of pleasant, acid taste; **2,** the fruit of this tree.

Pom-er-a-ni-an (pom′er-ā′ni-an), *n.* a small dog with long, thick, black or white, silky hair, bushy, curled-up tail, and pointed muzzle.

pom-mel or **pum-mel** (pum′el), *n.* **1,** the knob on a sword hilt; **2,** the ridge on the front of a saddle:—*v.t.* [pommelled, pommel-ling or pummelled, pummel-ling], to beat, esp. with the fists.

pomp (pomp), *n.* display; magnificence.

pom-pon or **pom–pon** or **pom–pom** or **pom-pom** (pom′pon; pom′pom′), *n.* **1,** an ornamental tuft or ball of silk, feathers, etc., for hats or other articles of clothing; **2,** a chrysanthemum with small, round flowers.

pom-pous (pom′pus), *adj.* self-important; pretentious; as, a *pompous* speaker.—*n.* **pom-pos′i-ty.**

pon-cho (pon′chō), *n.* [*pl.* ponchos], a loose type of clothing made of a large piece of material with a hole in the middle for the head to go through, worn over other clothes to keep a person warm or dry.

pond (pond), *n.* **1,** a small, shallow body of fresh, usually still water that is completely surrounded by land: it can be formed by nature or dug by people; **2,** a lake.

pon-der (pon′dėr), *v.t.* to consider carefully; think about:—*v.i.* to reflect.

pon-der-ous (pon′dėr-us), *adj.* **1,** very heavy; **2,** laboured; dull; as, a *ponderous* style of writing.

pon-tiff (pon′tif), *n.* a bishop, esp. the Pope.—*adj.* **pon-tif′i-cal.**

pon-toon (pon-to͞on′), *n.* **1,** a small, low, flat-bottomed boat; **2,** a flat-bottomed boat, a raft, a hollow metal cylinder, etc., used to support a temporary floating bridge; a pontoon bridge; **3,** a boatlike attachment on the bottom of an airplane to enable it to land on water.

po-ny (pō′ni), *n.* [*pl.* ponies], **1,** a horse of any one of certain small breeds; as, a Shetland *pony*; **2,** *Colloq.* a racehorse; **3,** a small liqueur glass; **4,** in the U.S., a literal translation into English of some foreign text, used by students in preparing lessons; a crib or trot. Also, **po′ny-tail.**

pooch (po͞och), *n. Slang* a dog.

poo-dle (po͞o′dl), *n.* one of a breed of intelligent, curly-haired dogs, of the standard, miniature, and toy varieties.

[1]**pool** (po͞ol), *n.* **1,** a large tank of water for swimming and diving, set either into the ground or above it; **2,** a small body of still water; a pond; **3,** a small body of any standing liquid; as, a *pool* of water near the open window.

[2]**pool** (po͞ol), *n.* **1,** a game played on a special table, with balls that are shot with a cue into the pockets at the edge of the table; **2,** in betting games, the total amount of the player's bets; the money at stake; **3,** a combination of persons, rival business corporations, etc., united for some special purpose, intended to result in profit to all involved; also, the resources combined in furtherance of this end; as, to ride to school in a car *pool*:—*v.t.* to put into a common fund for a joint undertaking or in order to share the profits; as, they *pooled* their money to buy lunch.

poop (po͞op), *n.* **1,** the raised deck in the stern of a vessel; also, the stern itself; **2,** *Slang* excrement; **3,** *Slang* inside information, esp. up-to-date or secret news; as, the *poop* sheet; to get all the *poop* about the scandal:—*v.t. Slang* to exhaust; as, the hard job *pooped* her.—*adj.* **pooped.**

poor (po͝or), *adj.* **1,** having little or no means; lacking riches; **2,** lacking in good qualities such as strength, beauty, or dignity; **3,** inferior in skill or execution; as, a *poor* piece of work; **4,** wretched; feeble; also, spiritless; **5,** of no great value; as, in my *poor* opinion; **6,** not fertile; as, *poor* soil; scanty; as, a *poor* harvest; **7,** worth feeling sorry for; deserving pity or care; as, the *poor* rabbit shivered from the cold.—*adj.* **poor′ly.**

pop (pop), *n.* **1,** a short, sharp, quick sound; **2,** *Colloq.* father; **3,** a bubbling non-intoxicating drink; as, soda *pop*; **4,** *Colloq.* short for popular; as, she enjoyed listening to *pop* (music):—*v.t.* [popped, pop-ping], **1,** to cause to burst open by heat; as, to *pop* corn; **2,** to strike or knock sharply; as, he *popped* the ball; **3,** to push or thrust suddenly; as, she *popped* her head through the door:—*v.i.* **1,** to make a short, sharp, quick sound as, the balloon *popped*; **2,** to move quickly; dart; as, to *pop* in or out; **3,** come suddenly into view; to burst open with a sound:—*adv.* suddenly.

pop-corn (pop′kôrn′), *n.* **1,** a kind of corn with small, hard grains which, when exposed to heat, burst open with a sharp noise, or pop, and become white and puffy; **2,** the white, puffed kernels.

Pope (pōp), *n.* **1,** the Bishop of Rome and head of the Roman Catholic Church; **2,** the head of the Coptic Church; **3,** the patriarch of the Eastern Orthodox Church:—**pope,** a dignitary with great power.

pop-lar (pop′lėr), *n.* a fast-growing, slender tree with shiny, heart-shaped leaves, rough bark, and soft wood; also, the wood.

pop-o-ver (pop′ō′vėr), *n.* a hot bread or muffin made of a batter of eggs, milk, and flour, thoroughly beaten: when baked, it becomes a hollow shell.

pop-py (pop′i), *n.* [*pl.* poppies], any of a number of plants with showy red, yellow, orange, or white flowers; also, the flower of a poppy plant: the seeds are used to make medicine and drugs.

pop-py-cock (pop′i-kok′), *n.* and *interj. Colloq.* nonsense.

pop-u-lace (pop′ū-lis), *n.* the common people; the masses; the general public.

pop-u-lar (pop′ū-lėr), *adj.* **1,** having to do with the general public; as, *popular* taste; a *popular* form of government; **2,** suitable for the majority; as, *popular* music; **3,** held in favour by many people; as, a *popular* writer; **4,** within the means of the average purchaser; as, *popular* prices.—*adv.* **pop′u-lar-ly.**—*v.t.* **pop′u-lar-ize** [popularized, populariz-ing].

pop-u-lar-i-ty (pop′ū-lar′i-ti), *n.* the state of being liked and admired by many people.

pop-u-late (pop′ū-lāt′), *v.t.* [populated,

populat-ing], **1,** to furnish with inhabitants; settle; move to an area; as, to *populate* a country; **2,** to inhabit; as, squirrels *populate* the parks of most cities.

pop-u-la-tion (pop′ū-lā′shun), *n.* **1,** the total number of people of a country, state, town, etc.; **2,** the people themselves; also, any one group of the people or animals; as, the adult *population* or the deer *population*; **3,** the process of furnishing with inhabitants or populating.

pop-u-lous (pop′ū-lus), *adj.* containing many inhabitants.—*n.* **pop′u-lous-ness.**

por-ce-lain (pôr′se-lin; pôrs′lin), *n.* and *adj.* **1,** a fine, white, glazed earthenware, unusually hard, and so thin that light can be seen through it; **2,** dishes or ornaments of such material:—*adj.* looking like porcelain; as, she has *porcelain* skin.

porch (pôrch), *n.* **1,** a partly enclosed approach to a doorway, extending from the main wall of a building and having a separate roof but usually open at the sides; **2,** a veranda; piazza.

por-cu-pine (pôr′kū-pīn′), *n.* an animal similar to the rat and beaver, with spines or sharp quills in its hairy coat, which protect it from its enemies.

[1]**pore** (pôr), *n.* a tiny hole or opening, esp. one of many in the skin through which perspiration is discharged; also, a similar opening in a plant.

[2]**pore** (pôr), *v.i.* [pored, poring], to study with close attention; ponder; as, to *pore* over lessons.

pork (pôrk), *n.* the meat of pigs or hogs, used for food.

pork-er (pôr′kėr), *n.* a pig or hog fattened for food.

porn or **por-no** (pôrn; pôr′no), *abbrev. Slang* short for *pornography* or *pornographic*.

por-nog-ra-phy (pôr-nog′ra-fi), *n.* writings, pictures, movies, etc. intended to arouse sexual desire.—*adj.* **porn′no-graph′ic.**

por-ous (pôr′us), *adj.* full of tiny holes through which a fluid may pass or be absorbed.—*n.* **po-ros′i-ty** (po-ros′i-ti).

por-poise (pôr′pus), *n.* **1,** a warm-blooded sea mammal, belonging to the whale family, with a round head and a blunt snout; **2,** a dolphin.

por-ridge (pôr′ij), *n.* a food made by boiling oatmeal or other cereal slowly in water or milk until it thickens; as, oatmeal *porridge*.

[1]**port** (pôrt), *n.* **1,** a place where vessels arrive and depart; a harbour; as, the *port* of Halifax; **2,** a harbour town.

[2]**port** (pôrt), *n.* **1,** a round opening or window in the side of a ship, through which air and light may enter, or out of which cannons may be discharged; a loophole in a wall, fort, etc.: also called *porthole*; **2,** in *computing*, a connection that allows a computer to be connected to other devices; as, she connected the modem to the serial *port*; **3,** an outlet, as for steam or water.

[3]**port** (pôrt), *n.* the left side of a boat, ship, or aircraft as one faces the front or bow: opposite of *starboard*:—*adj.* on the left side of a ship; as, a *port* cabin:—*v.t.* to turn to the port, or left, side of a ship; as, to *port* the helm.

[4]**port** (pôrt), *n.* a strong, sweet wine, usually dark red in colour.

port-a-ble (pôr′ta-bl), *adj.* **1,** capable of being easily carried; as, a *portable* computer; **2,** in *computing*, of or related to programs that can be used on different types of computers; **3,** something that can be transferred; as, *portable* pensions:—*n.* a temporary building on the grounds of a school, used as an extra classroom; as, I have math in the *portable*.

por-tage (pôr′tij; pôr-täzh′), *n.* **1,** the carrying of boats, goods, etc., overland from one navigable lake or river to another; **2,** the overland route taken; **3,** any cargo to be carried, or the cost of such carriage:—*v.i.* and *v.t.* to carry boats, goods, etc., or to travel in this way.

por-tal (pôr′t'l), *n.* **1,** a gateway; entrance; **2,** in *computing*, a Web site that functions as an entry to the Internet by providing links to other sites.

por-tend (pôr-tend′), *v.t.* to give warning in advance of something that is to happen; as, clouds *portend* a storm.

por-tent (pôr′tent; pôr′tent), *n.* an omen or sign, esp. of calamity to come.

por-ten-tous (pôr-ten′tus), *adj.* **1,** foreshadowing evil; threatening; as, a *portentous* dream; **2,** remarkable; extraordinary.

por-ter (pôr′tėr), *n.* **1,** one who carries luggage, as at airports, railway stations, and hotels; **2,** an attendant in a sleeping car or parlour car of a train; **3,** a person who maintains a building; **4,** a dark-brown, bitter beer.

port-fo-li-o (pôrt-fō′li-ō; pôrt-fōl′yō), *n.* [*pl.* portfolios], **1,** a case for carrying loose papers, drawings, etc.; a briefcase; **2,** the office of a minister of the government; as, the *portfolio* of defence; **3,** samples of one's work; as, her art *portfolio*; **4,** a range of securities and investments.

port-hole (pôrt′hōl′), *n.* **1,** a round opening, or window, in the side of a ship; **2,** an opening in the wall of a fort, blockhouse, etc., through which to shoot.

por-ti-co (pôr′ti-kō′), *n.* [*pl.* porticoes or porticos], a colonnade or walk covered by a roof supported on columns, esp. a porch with columns at the front of a building.

por-tion (pôr′shun), *n.* **1,** a piece or part of anything; as, a *portion* of pie; **2,** a share, or a part given; as, she gave a *portion* of her allowance to charity:—*v.t.* **1,** to divide into shares; **2,** to give a share to.

port-ly (pôrt′li), *adj.* [port-li-er, port-li-est], corpulent; stout; as, a *portly* chef.—*n.* **port′li-ness.**

por-trait (pôr′trit; pôr′trāt), *n.* **1,** a picture of a person; a likeness; as, the Mona Lisa is a famous *portrait;* **2,** a realistic description of something in words; **3,** in *computing,* printing or displaying a page that is higher than it is wide: compare *landscape.*—*n.* **por′trai-ture.**

por-tray (pôr-trā′) *v.t.* **1,** to make a likeness of; depict; **2,** to describe in words; **3,** to play the part of; as, to *portray* Hamlet.

por-tray-al (pôr-trā′al), *n.* the act or fact of portraying something.

Por-tu-guese (pôr′che-gēz′; pôr′che-gēs′), *n.* **1,** a person who inhabits or originates from Portugal; **2,** the language spoken by the people of Portugal and Brazil:—*adj.* relating to the country, the people, the language, or the culture of Portugal and Brazil.

[1]**pose** (pōz), *v.i.* [posed, pos-ing], **1,** to assume and keep an attitude; as, the model *posed* for an hour; **2,** to pretend to be what one is not; as, he *posed* as an expert:—*v.t.* **1,** to place in a suitable attitude; as, to *pose* a person for a portrait; **2,** to put or set forth; as, she *posed* a question:—*n.* **1,** attitude or position; **2,** a mental attitude assumed for the sake of effect.

[2]**pose** (pōz), *v.t.* [posed, pos-ing], to perplex.

Po-sei-don (pō-sīd′n), *n.* in *Greek mythology,* the god of the sea, comparable to *Neptune* in *Roman mythology.*

pos-er (pō′zėr), *n.* **1,** one who poses; an affected person; **2,** a perplexing or baffling problem.

po-si-tion (po-zish′un), *n.* **1,** the place where a thing is set or placed; situation; as, the *position* of a house; **2,** the manner in which anything is placed or arranged; as, an awkward sleeping *position;* **3,** social standing or rank; **4,** employment; job; **5,** mental attitude toward any subject; as, a conservative *position;* **6,** a correct or proper place; as, take your *positions;* **7,** in *sports,* the function or place of an individual player; as, her *position* was goalie:—*v.t.* to put in position or locate; as, the conductor *positioned* the altos behind the sopranos.

pos-i-tive (poz′i-tiv), *adj.* **1,** clearly stated; as, a *positive* assertion; uttered with authority; as, *positive* instructions; **2,** leaving no doubt; as, proof *positive;* **3,** of real, practical value; as, self-reliance is a *positive* virtue; **4,** confident; sure; as, people were once *positive* that the sun moved around the earth; **5,** in *grammar,* naming the simplest form of an adjective or adverb; as, "easy" is a *positive* form, and "easier" is comparative; **6,** in *arithmetic,* a quantity larger than zero; a plus quantity; **7,** naming the kind of electricity formed on a glass rod when it is rubbed with silk: as opposed to the electricity on the silk, which is called *negative;* **8,** in *photography,* matching the original in the distribution of light and shade: opposite of *negative;* **9,** of a medical test, showing that a disease or condition is present; as, to test *positive* for AIDS; **10,** *Colloq.* utter; absolute; as, a *positive* beauty:—*n.* **1,** in *grammar,* the simplest degree of comparison; also, an adjective or adverb in that degree; **2,** a photographic plate, film, or slide, reproducing the light and shade of the original: opposite of *negative,* in which the light and shade of the original are reversed; **3,** a number greater than zero.—*adv.* **pos′i-tive-ly.**

pos-i-tron (poz′i-tron), *n.* in an atom, a particle of positive electricity having a mass and charge equal to that of the electron.

pos-se (pos′i), *n.* **1,** a number of persons summoned by a sheriff to assist in carrying out the law; **2,** *Colloq.* a criminal gang; **3,** *Slang* a group of friends or hangers-on; as, here comes the star with her *posse.*

pos-sess (po-zes′), *v.t.* **1,** to own; have; as, to *possess* great wealth; **2,** to feel a very strong influence that takes over one's mind or will; as, he was *possessed* by a dream of going to the Olympics; **3,** to occupy; seize; as, to *possess* a city during war.—*adj.* **possessed′ 1,** as if in the power of evil spirits; crazy; **2,** being self-possessed or calm.

pos-ses-sion (po-zesh′un), *n.* **1,** control; occupancy; as, *possession* of a town by an enemy; **2,** the thing owned; as, a small *possession;* **3,** in *sports,* control of the puck or ball; as, the Rangers took *possession;* **4,** *Colloq.* owning or holding illegal drugs; as, he was arrested for *possession:*—**possessions,** property.

pos-ses-sive (po-zes′iv), *adj.* **1,** showing ownership, or a desire to own; as, a *possessive* manner; **2,** in *grammar,* naming the case used to express ownership, origin, etc., as "Ashley's" in the expression "Ashley's book":—*n.* the possessive case; also, a word in that case.

pos-ses-sor (po-zes′ėr), *n.* one who owns or holds something.

pos-si-bil-i-ty (pos′i-bil′i-ti), *n.* [*pl.* possibilities], **1,** anything that may happen; as, snow is a *possibility* today; **2,** the chance that a thing may happen; as, the *possibility* of failure.

pos-si-ble (pos′i-bl), *adj.* **1,** capable of existing or coming into being; capable of happening; as, the *possible* result of an act; **2,** available; worth considering; as, a *possible* candidate.

pos-si-bly (pos′i-bli), *adv.* **1,** according to what is possible; as, I can't *possibly* be in two places at once; **2,** it is possible that; perhaps; as, she is 80, *possibly* 90, years old.

[1]**post** (pōst), *n.* an upright piece of timber, metal, etc., used esp. as a support for something:—*v.t.* **1,** to fasten, as a notice, to a wall; **2,** to make known by means of notices fastened to a wall; **3,** to place (a person's name) on such a notice; **4,** to put notices upon (a place) forbidding entrance or warning against use; as, to *post* an unsafe bridge; to *post* a trout stream.

[2]**post** (pōst), *n.* **1,** a system of carrying and delivering letters; the mail; **2,** a single delivery of mail; as, was there anything in today's *post*? **3,** an electronic message:—*v.i.* to travel with speed:—*v.t.* **1,** to send by mail, esp., to drop, as a letter, into a letterbox; **2,** to place an electronic message on a newsgroup or other discussion group on the Internet; as, he *posted* his views; **3,** in bookkeeping, to transfer (an entry or item) from journal to ledger; **4,** *Colloq.* to inform fully; as, keep me *posted*:—*adv.* speedily.—*adj.* **post′al** (having to do with mail or post offices; as, put the *postal* code on the envelope.—*n.* **post′box′; post′free′.**

[3]**post** (pōst), *n.* **1,** a place where a person or thing is stationed; **2,** a position of trust; **3,** a trading settlement; **4,** a military station; also, the soldiers occupying it:—*v.t.* to station.

post- (pōst-), *prefix* meaning *after*; as in *post*glacial, *post*graduate, *post* meridiem (P.M. or afternoon), *post*natal (after birth), *post*nuptial (after marriage), *post*prandial (after dinner).

post-age (pōs′tij), *n.* the cost of sending letters by mail; also, the stamps and labels:—**postage stamp,** a government stamp to be pasted on mail as a sign that postage has been paid.

post-al (pōs′tal), *adj.* of or pertaining to the post office or mail service; as, *postal* rates.

postal code, a code designed to speed up the processing of mail sorted by machines: in Canada, this code is a mixture of letters and numbers, as M8Z 4X6.

post card or **post-card** (pōst′kärd′), *n.* a private, often scenic card for sending messages and mailing, to which a stamp must be attached.

post-date (pōst′dāt′), *v.t.* [-dated, -dat-ing], to date something with a date later than the current one; as, a *postdated* cheque or invoice.

post-er (pōs′tėr), *n.* **1,** a placard or bill put up in a public place, as on a wall, to advertise or announce something; **2,** a work of art, often reproduced on a large piece of paper.

pos-te-ri-or (pos-tē′ri-ėr) *adj.* **1,** later; **2,** rear; hinder:—*n.* the rump; buttocks.

pos-ter-i-ty (pos-ter′i-ti), *n.* **1,** a person's descendants, considered as a group; **2,** future generations.

post-haste (pōst′hāst′), *adv.* quickly.

post-hu-mous (pos′tū-mus), *adj.* **1,** born after the death of the father; as, a *posthumous* child; **2,** published after the death of an author; as, a *posthumous* book; **3,** arising or occurring after one's death; as, *posthumous* fame.—*adv.* **post′hu-mous-ly.**

post-mark (pōst′märk′), *n.* an official mark stamped upon mail to show the place and date of mailing and to cancel the stamp:—*v.t.* to stamp thus.

post-mor-tem (pōst′môr′tem), *adj.* happening after the death of the person involved; as, the *postmortem* examination of a body:—*n.* an examination made of a body after death, esp. to find the cause of death; autopsy.

post office, 1, the Crown corporation that handles the mail; **2,** any local office of this department.

post-paid (pōst′pād′), *adj.* having the postage paid in advance.

post-pone (pōst-pōn′), *v.t.* [postponed, postpon-ing], to put off to another time; as, to *postpone* the game because of rain.—*n.* **post-pone′ment.**

post-script (pōst′skript), *n.* a written addition to a book, article, etc., esp. a paragraph added to a letter after the writer's signature: abbreviated as *PS.*

post-sec-ond-ar-y (pōst-sek′un-dâr′i), *adj.* relating to education beyond secondary school.

pos-ture (pos′tūr), *n.* the way a person holds or carries the body when standing, sitting, or walking; personal bearing or carriage:—*v.t.* [postured, postur-ing], to place in a particular attitude:—*v.i.* to take a certain position, esp. an artificial or affected pose.

post-war (pōst′wôr′), *adj.* after any war, as contrasted with *prewar.*

pot (pot), *n.* **1,** a metal or earthenware vessel used for cooking; **2,** the quantity such a vessel will hold; **3,** such a vessel with its contents; as, a *pot* of soup; **4,** a vessel of earthenware for holding growing plants; as, a flower *pot*; **5,** *Slang* marijuana; **6,** *Colloq.* a sum of money made up as a bet by contributions from a group, to go to one of them; **7,** *Colloq.* a large sum of money:—*v.t.* [pot-ted, pot-ting], **1,** to transplant into a pot; **2,** to shoot (a bird or animal) for food, as with a potshot.—*adj.* **pot′bel′lied.**—*n.* **pot′hold′er.**

pot-ash (pot′ash′), *n.* a salt of potassium, esp. impure potassium carbonate, a white salt obtained from wood ashes, and used in fertilizers.

po-tas-si-um (po-tas′i-um), *n.* a soft, very light, bluish-white metal, found only in union with other substances, and used in making fertilizers, soaps, etc.

po-ta-to (po-tā′tō), *n.* [*pl.* potatoes], **1,** a

plant related to the tomato, grown for its starchy, edible tubers; **2,** one of these tubers used as food; **3,** the sweet potato or yam.

po-tent (pō′tent), *adj.* **1,** powerful; mighty; having great strength or force; as, a *potent* drug; **2,** having great authority or influence; as, a *potent* leader.—*n.* **po′ten-cy.**

po-ten-tate (pō′ten-tāt′), *n.* a ruler who has great power or authority; a monarch; sovereign.

po-ten-tial (pō-ten′shal), *adj.* **1,** capable of existing, but not yet in existence; possible, but not actual; as, a country with great *potential* wealth; **2,** in *grammar*, expressing power or possibility, as the word "can" in the sentence "I can come":—*n.* **1,** something that is possible; **2,** a quality that can be developed; promise; as, her athletic *potential;* **3,** the amount of electrical force in an electrical conductor, usually measured in volts:—**potential energy**, the energy possessed by a body due to its condition or structure rather than to motion, such as a tightly coiled spring: opposite of *kinetic energy*.—*n.* **po-ten′ti-al′i-ty.**

pot-hole (pot′hōl′), *n.* **1,** a cylindrical hole left in a river's rocky bed from the action of whirling gravel or boulders, as at Rockwood, Ontario; **2,** a hole left in a road by action of frost, erosion, etc.

po-tion (pō′shun), *n.* a drink, esp. of liquid medicine or poison.

pot-latch (pot′lach′), *n.* **1,** a winter festival, esp. among the Aboriginal people of the North American Pacific Coast, at which extravagant gifts were exchanged chiefly for fame or prestige: modern potlatches are less elaborate and more ceremonial; **2,** *Colloq.* any social event or ceremony.

pot-luck (pot′luk′), *n.* and *adj.* **1,** whatever food is available for a meal; as, a *potluck* dinner; **2,** a meal to which guests bring food to be shared.

pot-pie (pot′pī′), *n.* **1,** a meat and vegetable pie; **2,** a meat stew with dumplings.

pot-pour-ri (pō′poo-rē′), *n.* any mixture or medley, as of spices, songs, writings, edibles, perfumes; esp. a fragrant mixture of dried flowers and spices.

pot-tage (pot′ij), *n.* a stew or thick soup of meat and vegetables.

pot-ter (pot′ẽr), *n.* a maker of vessels of earthenware, stoneware, etc.

potter's field, a plot of ground set aside for the burial of unidentified persons and of persons who have neither friends nor money.

pot-ter-y (pot′ẽr-i), *n.* [*pl.* potteries], **1,** pots, dishes, vases, etc., moulded from moistened clay and hardened in ovens or kilns; **2,** a place where such ware is manufactured; **3,** the art of making it.

pouch (pouch), *n.* **1,** a bag or sack of any sort; as, a letter carrier's *pouch;* **2,** in certain animals, such as marsupials, any baglike part, as that in which the female kangaroo carries its young.

poul-tice (pōl′tis), *n.* a moist mixture of herbs and other medicines, usually heated, spread on a cloth, and applied to a sore or inflamed spot:—*v.t.* [poulticed, poulticing], to apply such a mixture to (a sore place).

poul-try (pōl′tri), *n.* domestic fowl, as chickens, turkeys, etc., raised for their meat and eggs.

pounce (pouns), *n.* a sudden swooping attack; as, the *pounce* of a cat on a toy mouse:—*v.i.* [pounced, pounc-ing], to spring suddenly or unexpectedly; as, the terrier *pounced* on the ball.

[1]**pound** (pound), *n.* **1,** a measure of avoirdupois weight, equal to 16 ounces or about 454 grams; also, a measure of troy weight, equal to 12 ounces (about 373 grams); **2,** the unit of money in various countries, including Great Britain, where it is officially called the *pound sterling;* it is written with the symbol [£]: 20 pounds is £20.

[2]**pound** (pound), *n.* **1,** a place for confining or keeping stray animals; as, a dog *pound;* **2,** a shelter for livestock; **3,** an enclosure for trapping wild animals; as, a buffalo *pound;* **4,** an area or space where fish are caught or kept; **5,** any place of confinement, esp. for lawbreakers; **6,** a place for holding impounded items; as, a car *pound*:—*v.t.* to confine, as in a pound.

[3]**pound** (pound), *v.t.* **1,** to beat; strike forcibly; **2,** to reduce to powder; **3,** to make solid by blows; tamp, as loose earth; **4,** to walk with heavy steps; as, she *pounded* the pavement:—*v.i.* **1,** to deal blows; **2,** to beat heavily or steadily, as waves against the seashore; **3,** to beat heavily or throb; as, my heart *pounded*:—*n.* **1,** a blow; **2,** the sound of a blow.

pound key, the button on the telephone marked with the symbol "[#]".

pour (pōr), *v.t.* **1,** to cause to flow in a steady stream; as, to *pour* a glass of milk; **2,** to send forth freely; **3,** utter freely; talk openly; as, she *poured* out her story:—*v.i.* **1,** to flow down freely; **2,** to rain heavily; **3,** to proceed freely in large amounts; as, the ants *poured* into the picnic basket:—*n.* a heavy rain.

pout (pout), *v.i.* **1,** to push out the lips, as in sullenness, contempt, or displeasure; **2,** to sulk:—*v.t.* to push (the lips) out; pucker:—*n.* **1,** a sullen puckering of the lips; **2,** a fit of sullenness or sulkiness; as, the child was in a *pout.*

pov-er-ty (pov′ẽr-ti), *n.* **1,** the state of being poor; being without money for things that are necessary to life; want; **2,** any lack of excellence in quality; scarcity; as, a *poverty* of ideas.

pow-der (pou′dėr), *n.* **1,** any dry substance in fine particles; a fine dust; **2,** an explosive in powder form; as, blasting *powder*; **3,** a fine, dustlike cosmetic for use on the skin; as, face *powder*; **4,** a fine, light snow; as, this *powder* is great for skiing; **5,** *Slang* to leave quickly or abruptly, esp. to run off; as, he took a *powder* after he heard the police were looking for him:—*v.t.* **1,** to reduce to powder; pulverize; **2,** to dust with powder; to decorate, as with powder; as, an ornament *powdered* with gilt stars; **3,** to sprinkle for flavouring; as, to *powder* cake with icing sugar:—*v.i.* **1,** to use powder; as, she *powders* lightly; **2,** to be reduced to powder; as, sugar *powders* easily.—*adj.* **pow′der-y.**

pow-er (pou′ėr), *n.* **1,** ability to act or to do something; as, the *power* to fly; the *power* to think; **2,** strength; vigour; as, the *power* of a blow; **3,** rule; influence; as, to have *power* over a group; also, official right to rule; authority; as, the *power* to levy taxes; **4,** a person or thing of great influence; as, he is a *power* in the city; **5,** an influential nation; as, the U.S. is a great *power*; **6,** any form of force or energy to do work; as, mechanical or electrical *power*; **7,** the magnifying capacity of a lens; **8,** the result of multiplying a number by itself a given number of times; as, 27 is the third *power* of three, that is, 3 × 3 × 3 = 27:—*v.t.* to provide with power; as, electricity *powers* the lawn mower:—*adj.* **1,** powered by a motor; as, a *power*boat; *power* mower; *power* drill; **2,** relating to, of, or for power; as, a *power* plant; *power*house; *power* play; *power* steering; *power* trip.

pow-er-ful (pou′ėr-fool), *adj.* having great power, influence, or strength; as, the actor had a *powerful* voice.

pow-er-less (pou′ėr-les), *adj.* without power; not able to do something; helpless.

pow-wow (pou′wou′), *n.* **1,** a public feast or dance, esp. one intended to secure religious or magical aid in a hunt, war, etc., as among the North American Aboriginal people; **2,** the working of magic, as in the cure of disease; **3,** a worker of magic; an Aboriginal shaman; **4,** a meeting with or of Aboriginal peoples; **5,** *Colloq.* any meeting or conference, often a political one:—*v.i. Colloq.* to hold such a meeting.

prac-ti-ca-ble (prak′ti-ka-bl), *adj.* capable of being done, practised, or used; as, fire prevention is *practicable*; a *practicable* idea.—*adv.* **prac′ti-ca-bly.**—*n.* **prac′ti-ca-bil′i-ty.**

prac-ti-cal (prak′ti-kal), *adj.* **1,** relating to, or obtained through, experience or use; as, *practical* wisdom; **2,** capable of being put to use; useful; as, a *practical* suggestion; **3,** inclined to useful action rather than thought; as, a *practical* disposition.—*n.* **prac′ti-cal′i-ty.**

prac-ti-cal-ly (prak′ti-kal-i), *adv.* **1,** nearly; almost; as, his painting is *practically* worthless; **2,** through actual experience or practice; as, he is *practically* familiar with all types of computers; **3,** virtually; in fact, though not in name; as, she is *practically* the president; **4,** in a useful or practical way.

prac-tice (prak′tis), *n.* **1,** custom; habit; as, the *practice* of getting up early and exercising before going to school; **2,** the putting of knowledge to actual use; as, the *practice* of good manners; **3,** the exercise of any profession; as, the *practice* of medicine; **4,** regular exercise as a means to learning; as, *practice* makes perfect; **5,** time set aside for exercise or drill in some activity; as, hockey *practice.*

prac-tise or **prac′tice** (prak′tis), *v.t.* [practised, practis-ing], **1,** to do in reality; as, to *practise* what you preach; **2,** to do frequently or as a rule; as, to *practise* self-control; **3,** to work at, as a profession; as, to *practise* law; **4,** to perform in order to learn; as, to *practise* baseball; *practise* piano:—*v.i.* **1,** to do something as a habit; **2,** to follow a profession; **3,** to do something often in order to learn.

prac-ti-tion-er (prak-tish′un-ėr), *n.* a person who is engaged in any profession, esp. medicine or law.

prag-mat-ic (prag-mat′ik), *adj.* concerned with practical values or consequences, or with the testing of an idea by experience; as, a *pragmatic* method.—*n.* **prag′ma-tism; prag′ma-tist.**

prai-rie (prâr′i), *n.* **1,** a large, treeless tract of level or rolling grassland:—**the Prairies,** the plain in Western Canada that covers parts of Manitoba, Saskatchewan, and Alberta.

prairie dog, a small burrowing animal resembling a woodchuck, so called because it barks: it lives in large, underground colonies in parts of Western Canada and the U.S.

PRAIRIE DOG

prairie lily, a North American lily, which is an orange flower with purplish-black spots: Saskatchewan's official floral emblem.

Prairie Provinces, Alberta, Manitoba, and Saskatchewan; also known as *the Prairies.*

praise (prāz), *n.* approval; applause:—*v.t.* [praised, prais-ing], **1,** to speak well of; approve; **2,** to glorify or extol a god.—*adj.* **praise′ wor′thy.**

prance (pråns), *v.i.* [pranced, pranc-ing], **1,** to move by springing or bounding from the hind legs, as a high-spirited horse; **2,** to ride a prancing horse; **3,** to swagger; strut; **4,** to dance; caper:—*v.t.* to cause (an animal) to prance:—*n.* a prancing or swaggering.—*n.* **pranc′er.**

prank (prangk), *n.* a mischievous trick.—*n.* **prank′ster.**

prate (prāt), *v.i.* [prat-ed, prat-ing], to talk idly:—*v.t.* to prattle; utter idly.

prattle (prat′l), *v.t.* and *v.i.* [prat-tled, prat-tling], to babble; chatter meaninglessly:—*n.* chatter; babble.—*n.* **prat′tler.**

prawn (prôn), *n.* an edible, shrimplike shellfish with reddish-brown spots.

pray (prā), *v.i.* **1,** to address words or thoughts to a god; **2,** to make a petition to a human being or authority:—*v.t.* **1,** to make request of; beseech; as, to *pray* the court for relief; **2,** to bring about by praying.

prayer (prâr), *n.* **1,** earnest entreaty, esp. that offered to a god with thanks and praise; **2,** *Colloq.* a hope or chance; as, the team hasn't a *prayer* of winning.

pray-ing man-tis (prā′ing man′tis), *n.* Same as **mantis.**

pre-(prē-), *prefix* meaning *before* (in time, place, rank, etc.) or *beforehand;* as in *pre*arrange, *pre*conceived, *pre*decease (die before), *pre*concerted (arranged beforehand), *pre*cursor (forerunner), *pre*disposed, *pre*exist, *pre*fabricate, *pre*figure (foreshadow), *pre*heat, *pre*judge, *pre*medical, *pre*natal (before birth), *pre*ordain, *pre*school, *pre*shrunk, *pre*view, *pre*vocational.

preach (prēch), *v.i.* and *v.t.* **1,** to talk or teach publicly on a religious subject; as, to *preach* a sermon; **2,** to advise on moral, religious, or social subjects; as, his teacher *preached* to him.—*n.* **preach′er.**

pre-am-ble (prē′am′bl, prē-am′bl), *n.* **1,** an introduction to a speech or writing; **2,** an introduction to a statute or law, giving the reason for passing the law; as, the *preamble* to the Constitution.

pre-car-i-ous (pri-kâr′i-us), *adj.* **1,** depending on circumstances; uncertain; **2,** dangerous; risky; not safe or secure.—*adv.* **pre-car′i-ous-ly.**

pre-cau-tion (pri-kô′shun), *n.* care taken beforehand to prevent harm, loss, etc.—*adj.* **pre-cau′tion-ar′y.**

pre-cede (prē-sēd′), *v.t.* and *v.i.* [preced-ed, preced-ing], to go before in time, place, rank, or importance; as, the calm *preceded* the storm.—*adj.* **pre-ced′ing** (coming before in time, place, importance; as, the *preceding* sentence).—*n.* **pre′ced-ence.**

prec-e-dent (pres′i-dent), *n.* something said or done in the past, that serves as a model or authority for the future:—*adj.* (pri-sēd′ent), going before.

pre-cept (prē′sept), *n.* a rule of conduct or action to be used as a guide.—*n.* **pre-cep′tor** (pri-sep′tėr).

pre-ces-sion (pri-sesh′un), *n.* a going before or forward:—**precession of the equinoxes,** the earlier occurrence of the equinoxes each year owing to the westward motion of the equinoxes on the ecliptic (the sun's apparent path), caused by the slow and regular shifting of the earth's axis in space (forming a completed cone of motion once every 26,000 years): precession is the result of the sun's and moon's action on the mass of matter about the earth's equator.

pre-cinct (prē′singkt), *n.* esp. in the U.S. **1,** a boundary; also, the region within it; **2,** a small district marked off, as for voting or police purposes:—**precincts,** the surrounding regions.

pre-cious (presh′us), *adj.* **1,** of great price or value; as, *precious* metals; **2,** very dear; greatly loved; as, my *precious* child; highly esteemed; as, a *precious* privilege; **3,** *Colloq.* thorough; extreme; as, a *precious* nuisance.—*n.* **pre-cious-ness.**

prec-i-pice (pres′i-pis), *n.* **1,** the steep, nearly vertical face of a cliff or rock; **2,** a dangerous situation.

pre-cip-i-tate (pri-sip′i-tāt′), *v.t.* [precipitated, precipitat-ing], **1,** to throw headlong; **2,** to hurry on rashly; bring to a crisis; as, his act *precipitated* the disaster; **3,** to cause to change from vapour to liquid or solid, and fall, as rain or snow; **4,** in *chemistry,* to cause to separate in solid form from a solution, as salt crystals from brine:—*n.* (pri-sip′i-tāt′, pri-sip′i-tit), any solid substance that separates from a solution:—*adj.* (pri-sip′i-tit), **1,** rash; hasty; as, a *precipitate* departure; **2,** falling or rushing headlong, as a waterfall.

pre-cip-i-ta-tion (pri-sip′-i-tā′shun), *n.* any form of water that falls from the sky, including rain, snow, hail, and sleet.

pre-cip-i-tous (pri-sip′i-tus), *adj.* very steep, as a cliff.

pré-cis (prā′sē), *n.* [*pl.* précis (prā′sēz; prā-sēz′)], a concise or shortened statement; a summary or abstract of the main points in a piece of writing:—*v.t.* to condense or summarize; make a précis.

pre-cise (pri-sīs′), *adj.* **1,** exact; careful; as, a *precise* speaker; *precise* measurements; **2,** keeping closely to rule; prim.—*adv.* **pre-cise′ly** (in a precise or accurate way; exactly; as, the class starts *precisely* at 9:30).

pre-ci-sion (pri-sizh′un), *n.* the quality of being precise or exact; as, it takes *precision* to be good at math.

pre-clude (pri-klōōd′; klūd′), *v.t.* [preclud-ed, preclud-ing], to shut out; prevent; make impossible.

pre-co-cious (pri-kō′shus), *adj.* showing unusual mental development for one's age; as, a *precocious* child.—*adv.* **pre-co′cious-ly.**—*n.* **pre-coc′i-ty** (-kos′).

pred-a-tor (pred′a-tėr), *n.* **1,** an animal that lives by hunting other animals; as, lions are *predators;* **2,** anyone or anything that preys on others:—*adj.* relating to, of, or for a predator; as, a *predator* state.

pred-a-tor-y (pred′a-tėr-i), *adj.* living by plunder, or by preying on others; as, a *predatory* tribe or beast.—*adj.* **pre-da′cious.**

pred-e-ces-sor (prē′di-ses′ėr; pred′i-ses′ėr; pred′i-ses′ėr), *n.* a person who has gone before another, as in the same office, position, etc.: opposite of *successor.*

pre-des-ti-na-tion (pri-des′ti-na′shun), *n.* **1,** the doctrine that from eternity God has determined whatever is to be, esp. with regard to the salvation or damnation of souls; **2,** the condition of being predestined:—*v.t.* **pre-des′ti-nate′** [predestinated, predestinat-ing].—*adj.* **pre-des′tined** (tind).

pre-dic-a-ment (pri-dik′a-ment), *n.* an unpleasant, difficult, or dangerous situation.

pred-i-cate (pred′i-kāt′), *v.t.* [predicat-ed, predicat-ing]; to declare (something) to be true or characteristic of something else; as, to *predicate* the wetness of water:—*n.* (pred′i-kit), in *grammar,* the part of a sentence that makes a statement about the subject; as, in the sentence, "Tomas caught the ball," the expression "caught the ball" is the *predicate*:—*adj.* (pred′i-kit), belonging in the predicate; as, in the sentence, "This is my hat," the word "hat" is a *predicate* noun.—*n.* **pred′i-ca′tion.**

pre-dict (pri-dikt′), *v.t.* and *v.i.* to tell or make known beforehand; foretell; as, it is hard to *predict* the weather.

pre-dic-tion (pri-dik′shun), *n,* **1,** an act of foretelling or predicting something; **2,** the thing predicted.

pre-di-lec-tion (prē′di-lek′shun), *n.* a preconceived liking; a preference.

pre-dis-pose (prē′dis-pōz′), *v.t.* [predisposed, predispos-ing], **1,** to incline beforehand; as, good humour in strangers *predisposes* us to like them; **2,** to make liable or subject, as to a disease; as, to be *predisposed* to colds.—*n.* **pre′dis-po-si′tion.**

pre-dom-i-nant (pri-dom′i-nant), *adj.* superior in numbers, strength, influence, etc.—*n.* **pre-dom′i-nance.**

pre-dom-i-nate (pri-dom′i-nāt′), *v.i.* [predominat-ed, predominat-ing], to be superior in power or influence; prevail.

pre-em-i-nent or **pre–eminent** (pri-em′i-nent; pri–em′i-nent), *adj.* highly superior to others; distinguished from others who are eminent; outstanding.—*n.* **pre–em′i-nence.**

preen (prēn), *v.t.* and *v.i.* **1,** to cleanse and smooth (the feathers) with the beak; **2,** to dress or groom (oneself) with care.

pref-ace (pref′is), *n.* an introduction, as to a book, preceding the body of the work:—*v.t.* [prefaced, prefac-ing], **1,** to introduce (a book, speech, etc.) by some act or statement; **2,** to serve as an introduction to; as, the program was *prefaced* by a talk.—*adj.* **pref′a-tor-y** (pref′a-tėr-i).

pre-fer (pri-fûr′), *v.t.* [preferred, preferring], **1,** to like (something) more than something else; as, to *prefer* candy to vegetables; **2,** to offer for consideration; as, to *prefer* a claim.

pref-er-a-ble (pref′ėr-a-bl; pref′ra-bl), *adj.* more desirable; as, death is *preferable* to slavery.

pref-er-a-bly (pref′ėr-a-bli), *adv.* rather than something else; by choice; as, come soon, *preferably* in the morning.

pref-er-ence (pref′ėr-ens), *n.* **1,** choice of one thing rather than another; **2,** that which is favoured or chosen.—*adj.* **pref′er-en′tial.**

pre-fix (prē′fiks), *n.* a syllable, or syllables, placed at the beginning of a word to modify its meaning, as *sub-* in the word "subway," and *super-* in the word "supermarket":—*v.t.* (prē-fiks′), to place before, or at the beginning of, anything; as, he *prefixed* "Doctor" to her name.

preg-nant (preg′nant), *adj.* **1,** about to have young; carrying unborn young; **2,** fruitful; fertile; **3,** full of meaning; important; as, a *pregnant* thought; *pregnant* pause.—*n.* **preg′nan-cy.**

pre-hen-sile (prē-hen′sīl), *adj.* adapted for seizing or grasping, as a monkey's tail; as, *prehensile* fingers or toes.

pre-his-toric (prē′his-tôr′ik) or **pre-his-tor-i-cal** (prē′his-tôr′i-kal), *adj.* relating to the time before there were written records.

prej-u-dice (prej′ū-dis), *n.* **1,** an opinion, often unfavourable, formed without a fair examination of the facts; bias; **2,** injury or harm resulting from hasty or unfair judgment; **3,** a strong feeling against another person or the group to which he or she belongs because of race, religion, status, etc.:—*v.t.* [prejudiced, prejudic-ing], to cause to form an opinion, usually unfavourable, before examination of the facts; as, your story *prejudiced* me against him.

pre-j-u-di-cial (prej′ū-dish′al), *adj.* injurious; damaging; as, his bad record was *prejudicial* to him.—*adv.* **prej′u-di′cial-ly.**

pre-lim-i-nar-y (pri-lim′i-nėr-i), *adj.* introductory; preparatory:—*n.* [*pl.* preliminaries], an introductory act or step.

prel-ude (prel′ūd; prē′lūd), *n.* **1,** a preface; something preceding and preparing for something of greater importance; as, a lie may be the *prelude* to a quarrel; **2,** a piece of music played as an introduction to a musical composition:—*v.t.* and *v.i.* [preluded, prelud-ing], to precede; preface; introduce.

pre-ma-ture (prē′ma-tūr′; prē′ma-choor′), *adj.* coming before the usual or proper time; too early; untimely; as, a *premature* baby is one that is born a month or more early.

pre-med-i-tate (prē-med′i-tāt′), *v.t.* and

v.i. [premeditat-ed, premeditat-ing], to think over carefully or plan beforehand.—*n.* **pre-med-i-ta′tion.**

pre-mi-er (prē′mi-ėr; prem′yėr), *adj.* **1,** foremost; chief; highest or most important; first in rank or quality; as, Shakespeare was the *premier* playwright of his day; **2,** earliest in time:—*n.* (prē′mi-ėr; prė-mēr′; prem′yir), **1,** the chief officer of a state; a prime minister; **2,** in Canada, the head of a provincial or territorial government.

pre-miere or **première** (prė-myâr′), *n.* the first public performance of a play, movie, or other such work:—*v.t.* [premiered, premier-ing], to present (a play, movie, etc.) for the first time; as, to *premiere* a movie to a small group:—*v.i.* to give a first public performance or showing; as, the film she directed *premiered* last night.

prem-ise (prem′is), *n.* **1,** a statement accepted as true, from which a conclusion is to be drawn; **2,** in *logic,* one of the first two statements of a form of argument called a syllogism; as, major *premise,* humans must eat to live; minor *premise,* Carlos is a human; conclusion, Carlos must eat to live:—**premises, 1,** facts previously stated, as in a legal document; **2,** the property, such as lands, houses, etc., that is the subject of a legal document; **3,** a house or building with its grounds.

pre-mi-um (prē′mi-um), *n.* **1,** a reward or prize for excelling, as in a competition; **2,** a sum agreed upon as the price to be paid for a contract of insurance; **3,** an amount exceeding the par value of something; as, the stock sold at a *premium*; **4,** that which is given in return for a loan of money, over and above the interest; as, she paid a *premium* of $500 for a loan of $10,000:—**put (place) a premium on,** to value something highly; as, parents put a *premium* on good grades:—*adj.* of higher value or quality; as, *premium* ice cream is more expensive.

pre-mo-ni-tion (prē′mo-nish′un), *n.* **1,** a warning in advance; as, a *premonition* of a flood; **2,** a foreboding; a feeling that something is about to happen.—*adj.* **pre-mon′i-tor-y** (pri-mon′i-tėr-i).

pre-oc-cu-pied (prē-ok′ū-pīd′), *adj.* **1,** lost in thought; absorbed; **2,** already occupied or in use.—*n.* **pre-oc′cu-pa′tion.**

pre-oc-cu-py (prē-ok′ū-pī′), *v.t.* [preoccupied, preoccupy-ing], to fill the mind of; hold the attention of.

prep-a-ra-tion (prep′a-rā′shun), *n.* **1,** the act of making fit or ready for use; as, the *preparation* of dinner took an hour; **2,** a state of readiness; **3,** that which makes fit or ready; as, *preparations* for war; **4,** a substance, as a medicine or a salve, made up or compounded for a special use.—*adj.* **pre-par′a-tor′y** (pri-par′a-tėr-i).

pre-pare (pri-pâr′), *v.t.* [prepared, prepar-ing], **1,** to fit for some purpose or make ready for use; as, to *prepare* a house for occupancy; to *prepare* food; **2,** to make (a person) mentally ready or fit for something; as, to *prepare* students for university; **3,** to provide or fit out; as, to *prepare* an expedition:—*v.i.* to make things or oneself ready; as, to *prepare* for cold weather; to *prepare* for bad news.—*n.* **pre-par′ed-ness.**

pre-pay (prē′pā′), *v.t.* [prepaid, prepay-ing], to pay, or pay for, in advance.—*n.* **pre-pay′ment.**

pre-pon-der-ance (pri-pon′dėr-ans), *n.* superiority in power, influence, number, or amount; as, there was a *preponderance* of women in the audience.

prep-o-si-tion (prep′o-zish′un), *n.* in *grammar,* a part of speech, as *to, from, by,* etc., used with a noun or pronoun in the objective case, to show the relation between the noun or pronoun and some other word or words in the sentence; as, in "a bag for the mail," the word "for" is a *preposition* showing a relation between "bag" and "mail."—*adj.* **prep′o-si′tion-al.**

pre-pos-sess-ing (prē′po-zes′ing), *adj.* tending to win favour, love, affection, confidence, etc.; attractive.

pre-pos-ter-ous (pri-pos′tėr-us), *adj.* contrary to common sense; absurd; silly; foolish.—*adv.* **pre-pos-ter-ous-ly.**

pre-req-ui-site (prē-rek′wi-zit), *n.* that which is required before something else can follow; as, reading is a *prerequisite* of all other studies:—*adj.* required before something else can follow.

pre-rog-a-tive (pri-rog′a-tiv), *n.* a right or privilege belonging to a person, class, or body of persons, by virtue of rank or position; as, the *prerogatives* of a sovereign, of a citizen, etc.

[1]**pres-age** (pres′ij), *n.* **1,** a sign or omen foretelling what is going to happen; **2,** a feeling of what is going to happen; a foreboding.

[2]**pre-sage** (pri-sāj′), *v.t.* [presaged, presag-ing], **1,** to give a warning or sign of; **2,** to foretell.

Pres-by-te-ri-a-nism (prez′bi-tir′ē-a-nizm), *n.* the established Church of Scotland, founded by John Knox during the Protestant Reformation of the mid-16th century: an important church in Canada, the United States, and many former British colonies.—*n.* and *adj.* **Pres′-by-te′ri-an.**

pre-scribe (pri-skrīb′), *v.t.* [prescribed, prescrib-ing], **1,** to advise the use of (a medicine or treatment); as, the doctor *prescribed* antibiotics for her infection; **2,** to set down as a rule of action; as, to *prescribe* laws:—*v.i.* **1,** to write or give medical directions; **2,** to give laws, rules, or directions.

pre-scrip-tion (pri-skrip′shun), *n.* **1,** a

written order from a doctor for a certain medicine or treatment; **2,** the act of setting down rules, laws, etc.; **3,** anything that is prescribed; **4,** a formula.

presence (prez′ens), *n.* **1,** the state of being in a certain place; **2,** nearness; immediate neighbourhood; as, in the *presence* of danger; **3,** one's appearance or bearing; as, a girl of pleasing *presence:*—**presence of mind**, quickness of thought or action in an emergency.

[1]**pres-ent** (prez′ent), *adj.* **1,** being at hand or in sight at a given place; as, all the students were *present* in class; **2,** existing now; as, my *present* situation:—*n.* the time now here; as, I do not know at *present*:—**present tense**, in *grammar,* a tense of the verb that indicates an action now going on; as, he *runs*:—**present perfect**, in *grammar*, a tense of the verb indicating: **1,** action begun in the past and continuing to the present; as, I *have waited* an hour; **2,** an action the results of which are still going on; as, he *has stolen* my dog; **3,** an action just completed; as, I *have done* the deed.

[2]**pre-sent** (pri-zent′), *v.t.* **1,** to introduce (one person) to another; as, let me *present* her to you; **2,** to bring (oneself) into the presence of someone; as, he *presented* himself before the judge; **3,** to bring to the view or attention of the public; as, to *present* a play; **4,** to submit; hand in; as, to *present* a bill; **5,** to give as a gift; as, we *presented* a CD to him; also, to give a gift to; as, we *presented* him with a CD; **6,** to display; offer to view; as, he *presented* a sad appearance.

[3]**pres-ent** (prez′ent), *n.* a gift; anything given or presented; as, a birthday *present.*

pre-sent-a-ble (pri-zen′ta-bl), *adj.* **1,** suitable to be offered, given, or introduced; **2,** suitable in appearance; fit to be seen.

pres-en-ta-tion (prez′en-tā′shun; prē′zen-tā′shun), *n.* **1,** the act of presenting; **2,** something that is presented.

pres-ent-ly (prez′ent-li), *adv.* **1,** at the present time; now; as, she is *presently* studying to be a doctor; **2,** in a little while; soon; before long; as, I shall be there *presently.*

pre-serv-a-tive (pri-zûr′va-tiv), *n.* a substance that tends to prevent decay or injury; as, sugar, vinegar, or salt can be used as a *preservative* in jams and pickles:—*adj.* acting as a preservative.

pre-serve (pri-zûrv′), *v.t.* [preserved, preserv-ing], **1,** to keep from injury; save; protect; **2,** to keep (fruit or vegetables) from spoiling by canning, pickling, cooking with sugar, etc.; **3,** to keep up; maintain; as, to *preserve* peace:—*n.* **1,** (usually *preserves*), fruit or vegetables preserved with sugar; **2,** a place set apart for keeping wildlife, fish, or vegetation protected; **3,** a special place or activity considered to be exclusive to a person or group.—*n.* **pre-serv′er; pres′er-va′tion** (prez′ėr-vā′shun).

pre-side (pri-zīd′), *v.i.* [presid-ed, presid-ing], **1,** to direct or control; as, to *preside* over a corporation; **2,** to act as chairman of a meeting; as, at the meeting, Sylvie *presided.*

pres-iden-cy (prez′i-den-si), *n.* [*pl.* presidencies], the office, or term of office, of a president.

pres-i-dent (prez′i-dent), *n.* **1,** the chief officer of a company, university, college, club, etc.; **2,** (often *President*), the highest executive officer of a modern republic; **3,** someone who presides, as over a meeting.

pres-i-den-tial (prez′i-den′shal), *adj.* of or relating to a president; as, a *presidential* election.

press (pres), *v.t.* **1,** to bear down upon; **2,** to compress; squeeze; as, to *press* fruit to extract juice; also, to squeeze out; as, to *press* juice from a fruit; **3,** to thrust or push; as, to *press* a crowd back; **4,** to embrace; hug; as, she *pressed* the baby to her; **5,** to urge; entreat; as, we *pressed* him to stay; **6,** to hasten or urge; as, heavy anxiety *pressed* him on; **7,** to thrust upon others; impose; as, she *pressed* opinions upon them; **8,** to smooth or shape by pressure; as, to *press* clothes; **9,** to place in an urgent situation; as, to be *pressed* for time; **10,** to apply steady force; to push; as, to *press* the buzzer:—*v.i.* **1,** to bear down heavily; **2,** to hasten; strive eagerly; as, we *pressed* to the gate; **3,** to urge or impel to action; as, time *presses*; **4,** to harass or apply pressure; as, the team was *pressing* but failed to score:—*n.* **1,** the act of pushing forward; **2,** a dense crowd; **3,** a machine that presses or stamps anything; as, a printing *press;* **4,** newspaper and magazine literature, or those who write and publish it; print media; mass media; as, the power of the *press;* a statement issued by the *press;* also, a notice, article, etc., in the media; as, the new film got good *press;* **5,** urgent demand; as, the *press* of business; **6,** an upright cupboard, as for clothes.—*n.* **press′er.** Also, **press′board′; press′ box′; press′ con-′fer-ence; press′ gal′ler-y; press′ kit′; press′re-lease′; press′room′; press′sec′re-ta-ry; press′ work′.**

pres-sure (presh′ėr), *n.* **1,** a bearing down upon; as, the *pressure* of a roller on a lawn; **2,** weight on the mind; distress; as, the *pressure* of worry; **3,** burden; oppression; as, the *pressure* of high expenses; financial *pressures;* **4,** weight of influence or authority; as, parental *pressure* changed his mind; **5,** urgent demand on one's time or energies; as, the *pressure* of work; **6,** in *physics,* force exerted on a body so as to tend to change its shape or lessen its volume.—*v.t.* [pressured, pres-sur-ing], to put pressure on; to force or influence strongly; as, she *pressured* them into attending the art exhibit.

pres-sur-ize (presh′ėr-īz′), to maintain

normal air pressure, esp. in an airplane at high altitudes or when descending.

pres-tige (pres-tēzh′; pres′tij), *n.* reputation or influence resulting from past achievement or associations:—*adj.* something that has or gives prestige; as, a *prestige* position:—*adj.* **pres-ti′gious.**

pre-sum-a-ble (pri-zūm′a-bl), *adj.* probable; to be expected; as, the *presumable* results of an act.—*adv.* **pre-sum′a-bly.**

pre-sume (pri-zūm′), *v.t.* [presumed, presum-ing], **1,** to take for granted; suppose; **2,** to venture; dare (to do something); as, to *presume* to offer advice:—*v.i.* to take liberties; act with unwarranted boldness.

pre-sump-tion (pri-zump′shun), *n.* **1,** boldness; arrogance; **2,** acceptance and belief of something not fully proved; as, the argument is based on *presumption*; **3,** that which is taken for granted.

pre-sump-tu-ous (pri-zump′tū-us), *adj.* presuming something without having the right or permission; too bold or overconfident.

pre-sup-pose (prē′su-pōz′), *v.t.* [presupposed, presuppos-ing], to take for granted in advance.

pre-tence or **pre-tense** (pri-tens′; prē′tens), *n.* **1,** make-believe; a putting on of a false appearance in order to hide what is real; deception; as, she made a *pretence* of friendship; **2,** ostentation; a false show; display; as, a humble person without *pretence*; **3,** a claim, esp. a false one; as, she had no *pretence* to knowing how to ski.

pre-tend (pri-tend′), *v.t.* **1,** to make believe; as, he *pretends* to be rich; **2,** to make a false show of; as, to *pretend* friendship:—*v.i.* **1,** to put forward a claim, true or false; as, to *pretend* to a title; **2,** to play at make-believe.—*n.* **pre-tend′er.**

pre-ten-sion (pri-ten′shun), *n.* **1,** a claim made, whether true or false; **2,** outward show; display, esp. an ostentatious one.

pre-ten-tious (pri-ten′shus), *adj.* **1,** making claims to importance, worth, etc., esp. if undeserved; as, a *pretentious* book; **2,** made or done for show or display; as, a *pretentious* house.

pre-text (prē′tekst), *n.* a pretence or excuse; a false motive put forward to conceal the real one.

pret-ty (prit′i), *adj.* [pret-ti-er, pret-ti-est], **1,** pleasing to look at; attractive; **2,** nice; fine; as, a *pretty* wit; **3,** often used slightingly; bad, terrible; as, a *pretty* mess:—*adv.* fairly; moderately; as *pretty* well.—*adv.* **pret′ti-ly.**—*n.* **pret′-ti-ness.**

pret-zel (pret′s'l), *n.* a hard biscuit, made in a twisted form and glazed, and salted on the outside.

pre-vail (pri-vāl′), *v.i.* **1,** to be victorious; triumph; as, right will *prevail*; **2,** to be or become widespread; be in general use; as, the English language *prevails* in North America; **3,** to persuade; as, she finally *prevailed* on him to go.—*n.* **prev′a-lence.**—*adj.* **prev′a-lent; pre-vail′ing.**—*adv.* **prev′a-lent-ly.**

pre-var-i-cate (pri-var′i-kāt′), *v.i.* [prevaricat-ed, prevaricat-ing], to stray from the truth; lie.—*n.* **pre-var′i-ca′tor; pre-var′i-ca′tion.**

pre-vent (pri-vent′), *v.t.* **1,** to stop or keep from happening, doing, etc.; as, regular brushing *prevents* tooth decay; **2,** to keep someone from doing something; hold back or stop; hinder; as, the flu *prevented* her from going to the school dance.—*n.* **pre-ven′tion.**—*adj.* **pre-vent′a-ble** or **pre-vent′i-ble.**

pre-ven-tion (pri-ven′shun), *n.* the act or fact of preventing something; as, fire *prevention.*

pre-ven-tive or **pre-ven-ta-tive** (pri-ven′tiv; pri-ven′ta-tive), *adj.* something that serves or intends to prevent or hinder; as, *preventive* medicine:—*n.* that which hinders; esp. something that wards off disease.

pre-view (prē′vū′), *n.* **1,** an advance showing of a movie, play, or show before its regular opening; as, a sneak *preview*; **2,** any advance showing or example; as, they got a *preview* of the new exhibit; **3,** in *computing,* to view the document on screen before actually printing it:—*v.t.* to view before or in advance.

pre-vious (prē′vi-us), *adj.* coming or made before something else; earlier; preceding; as, he spoke of you in a *previous* letter.—*adv.* **pre′vi-ous-ly.**

pre-war (prē-wôr′), *adj.* before any war, as contrasted with *postwar.*

prey (prā), *n.* **1,** any animal hunted or killed by another animal for food; **2,** a person who is a victim of another person or of anything that is hostile or evil; a victim:—**bird of prey** or **beast of prey,** a bird or beast that kills and devours other animals:—*v.i.* **1,** to plunder for the sake of booty; **2,** to seize and devour an animal as food; **3,** to bother or irritate; to exert a destructive influence; as, his guilt *preyed* upon his mind.

price (prīs), *n.* **1,** worth; value; as, stereo equipment of great *price*; **2,** something, usually money, given or asked in exchange for a thing; cost; **3,** reward; as, to set a *price* on a terrorist's head; **4,** the cost at which something is obtained; as, the *price* of victory was the loss of a thousand lives:—*v.t.* [priced, pric-ing], **1,** to set a price on; **2,** *Colloq.* to inquire the price of; as, to *price* goods in various stores.

price-less (prīs′lis), *adj.* **1,** too valuable to be bought at any price; invaluable; **2,** very funny or odd; as, a *priceless* anecdote.

prick (prik), *n.* **1,** a dot or mark made by a pointed instrument; also, the instrument;

2, a sharp, stinging pain; **3,** remorse:—*v.t.* **1,** to pierce with something pointed; **2,** to mark out by puncturing; **3,** to pain or sting, as with remorse; **4,** to erect or raise; as, a dog *pricks* up its ears; **5,** to spur; urge; as, to *prick* a horse on:—*v.i.* to feel or produce a sharp, stinging pain; as, pine needles *prick*.

prick-le (prik′l), *n.* **1,** a sharp point, esp. a small, slender projection growing from the surface of a plant; **2,** a slight stinging sensation:—*v.t.* [prick-led, prick-ling], **1,** to give a stinging sensation to (the skin); **2,** to cover with small dots:—*v.i.* to tingle.—*n.* **prick′li-ness.**

prick-ly (prik′li), *adj.* **1,** having small sharp points or thorns; thorny; as, a *prickly* rose bush; **2,** something difficult or thorny; as, a *prickly* situation; **3,** touchy or easily irritated; as, he has a very *prickly* personality.

pride (prīd), *n.* **1,** a high opinion of one's own qualities; conceit; **2,** haughtiness; disdain; **3,** dignity; self-respect; as, she has great *pride* in her abilities; **4,** a person or thing that is highly regarded; as, the new baby is their *pride* and joy:—*v.t.* [prid-ed, prid-ing], to be proud of; to think highly of; as, she *prides* herself on her speech.

priest (prēst), *n.* one with authority, ranking below a bishop, to perform religious rites and services.—*n.fem.* **priest′ess.**—*n.* **priest′hood.**—*adj.* **priest′ly.**

prig (prig), *n.* a conceited person who is overly particular about speech, conduct, etc.—*adj.* **prig′gish.**

prim (prim), *adj.* [prim-mer, prim-mest], **1,** extremely neat or precise; **2,** overly proper, decorous.—*adv.* **prim′ly.**

pri-ma don-na (prē′ma don′a), [*pl.* prima donnas], **1,** the principal female singer in an opera or concert; **2,** any temperamental, haughty person.

pri-mal (prī′mal), *adj.* **1,** first; original; **2,** primary; chief.

pri-ma-ri-ly (prī′ma-ri-li), *adv.* **1,** at first; originally; **2,** principally.

pri-ma-ry (prī′mar-i), *adj.* **1,** first in time; original; as, the *primary* meaning of a word; **2,** relating to the education level of young children, esp. under the age of 12; **3,** basic; fundamental; as, the *primary* colours; **4,** chief; principal; as, a *primary* purpose; **5,** pertaining to the large flight feathers of a bird's wing:—*n.* [*pl.* primaries], **1,** that which is first in rank, place, or importance; **2,** in the U.S., a district meeting of the voters of a party to name candidates for a coming election; **3,** (also *primary election*), a preliminary election in which parties nominate their respective candidates; **4,** one of the large flight feathers in a bird's wing; **5,** one of the primary colours.

primary colour, one of the three basic colours—red, yellow, and blue—that can combine with the others to make all the other colours.

pri-mate (prī-māt′), *n.* a member of the highest order of mammals [the *Primates*], which includes humans, monkeys, apes, lemurs, etc.

[1]**prime** (prīm), *adj.* **1,** first in time; original; **2,** chief; principal; as, a matter of *prime* importance; **3,** first in excellence or value; as, a *prime* grade of beef:—*n.* **1,** the early stage or beginning, as of a day, year, etc.; **2,** the spring of life; youth; also, the period of the greatest health, beauty, etc.; as, a person in the *prime* of life; **3,** the best one of a group or the best part of anything; **4,** in mathematics, a prime number; **5,** the prime rate, which is the lowest interest rate that banks give to their best customers.—*n.* **prim′a-cy** (prī′).

[2]**prime** (prīm), *v.t.* [primed, prim-ing], **1,** to prepare (a gun) for firing; also, to prepare (a pump) to lift water, by pouring water into it; **2,** to cover with the first coat of paint or plaster; **3,** to instruct (a person) beforehand as to what must be said; as, the lawyer *primed* the witness before she put him on the stand.—*n.* **prim′er** (prīm′ėr); **prim′ing.**

prime minister or **Prime Minister**, the head of the government in Canada, Great Britain, and other parliamentary democracies: abbreviated as *PM*.

prime number, a whole number, such as 2, 3, 5, 7, and 11, that cannot be divided evenly except by itself and by 1.

pri-mer (prim′ėr), *n.* **1,** a small book from which children receive their first lessons in reading; **2,** a textbook containing the first principles of any subject; **3,** paint or other such material used to prepare a surface for painting; **4,** someone who applies such material.

pri-me-val (prī-mē′val), *adj.* pertaining to the earliest age or time; primitive; original.—*adv.* **pri-me′val-ly.**

prim-i-tive (prim′i-tiv), *adj.* **1,** belonging to the earliest ages; first; as, *primitive* humans lived by hunting and fishing; **2,** characterized by the style of early times; **3,** simple or crude; as, he built a *primitive* hut out of leaves and branches.

pri-mor-di-al (prī-môr′di-al), *adj.* **1,** existing from the beginning; original; as, *primordial* matter; **2,** in *biology*, earliest formed in the course of growth, as leaves, fruit, etc.; also, in a rudimentary or developing stage, as tissues, germ cells, etc.

primp (primp), *v.t.* and *v.i. Colloq.* to dress for show, esp. with exaggerated care; to preen.

prince (prins), *n.* **1,** a ruler or sovereign, esp. of a small state; **2,** the son of a king, queen, or other ruler; **3,** a male member of a royal family or of a high order of nobility; **4,** the husband of a queen; **5,** a distinguished member of a class of men; as, a merchant *prince.—adj.* **prince′ly.**

prin-cess (prin′ses′), *n.* **1,** the daughter or granddaughter of a sovereign; **2,** the wife of a prince; **3,** a female member of a royal family; **4,** *Colloq.* a female who acts, or is treated, like a princess.

prin-ci-pal (prin′si-pal), *adj.* highest in rank, value, or importance; main; foremost; chief; as, the *principal* reason for his failure was his lack of confidence:—*n.* **1,** a leader; the chief person in authority; **2,** the head of a school; **3,** a sum of money drawing interest; **4,** a person or group of persons for whom an agent acts.—*adv.* **prin′ci-pal-ly.**

prin-ci-pal-i-ty (prin′si-pal′i-ti), *n.* [*pl.* -ities], the territory of a prince or princess or the country from which he or she obtains his or her title.

prin-ci-ple (prin′si-pl), *n.* **1,** a truth or law on which other truths, laws, etc., are based; as, *principles* of government; **2,** a settled rule of action; as, *principles* of conduct; **3,** honesty; uprightness; as, a person of *principle*; moral *principles*; **4,** a natural law, esp. one that is utilized in the construction and operation of a machine; as, an automobile engine works on the *principle* of the expanding power of gases; the *principle* of uncertainty.

print (print), *n.* **1,** a mark or character made by pressure; as, a foot*print* or finger*print*; **2,** a stamp or die for making an impression; also, that which has received the impression; **3,** letters produced from type; as, the child's book was in large *print*; **4,** the state of being in published form; as, the story has just gone into *print*; **5,** anything produced by type, from a photographic image, or from an engraved plate, as a newspaper, engraving, etc.; **6,** cloth decorated with a printed design; **7,** a copy of a photograph; as, the *print* will be ready in an hour; **8,** a painting or other picture reproduced by printing:—*v.t.* **1,** to make an impression on; as, their feet *print* the sand; **2,** to fix or stamp in or on something; as, to *print* footsteps in the sand; **3,** to reproduce from type, engraved plates, etc., as books, pictures, newspapers, etc.; **4,** to make in letters, like those of type; as, a child *prints* a letter; **5,** in *photography*, to produce (a picture) from a negative; **6,** in *computing*, to produce with a computer printer a printout of the text or image on the computer screen:—*v.i.* to make letters like those used in type; as, the child *prints* well.

printed circuit, in *computing*, electronic circuits, used in computers and other electronic appliances, that are composed of printed or etched electrical paths of conductive material on insulated sheets.

print-er (prin′tėr), *n.* **1,** a person or business that prints books, magazines, or other such material; **2,** in *computing*, a machine used to print information from a computer; as, a laser *printer*; **3,** any similar device that prints.

printing press, a machine that prints letters, words, or pictures on paper.

print-out (print′out), *n.* in *computing*, the printed material that comes out of a computer printer.

pri-or (prī′ėr), *adj.* going before in time, order, or importance; previous:—*n.* the head of a monastery; also, in an abbey, the religious officer next below an abbot.—*n. fem.* **pri′or-ess.**

pri-or-i-ty (pri-or′i-ti), *n.* the state of being first in rank, time, or place.

prism (prizm), *n.* **1,** a solid object with ends that are parallel and exactly the same in size and shape, and sides that are parallelograms; **2,** such a solid, usually three-sided, made of glass, crystal, or a similar substance, that breaks up a ray of light into the colours of the rainbow.—*adj.* **pris-mat′ic** (priz-mat′ik).

PRISMS

pris-on (priz′n), *n.* **1,** a place of confinement or detention for criminals; a jail; **2,** time spent in such an institution; confinement; custody; as, he spent much of his early years in *prison*; **3,** any place that confines or restricts; as, the small town was a *prison* to the boy, who wanted to see the world.

pris-on-er (priz′n-ėr; priz′nėr), *n.* **1,** anyone held against his or her will, as a person under arrest, in jail, or captured in war; **2,** anyone who is not free to act for some reason; as, she was a *prisoner* of her own personality.

pris-sy (pris′i), *adj. Colloq.* affectedly prim or precise.

pris-tine (pris′tēn; -tin; tīn), *adj.* **1,** original; former; as, *pristine* condition; **2,** unsullied or unspoiled; pure; as, its *pristine* purity.

pri-va-cy (prī′va-si), *n.* [*pl.* privacies], **1,** the state of being away from public view; seclusion; retirement; **2,** secrecy; as, to plot a scheme in *privacy*.

pri-vate (prī′vit), *adj.* **1,** concerning or belonging to oneself alone; personal; not public; as, one's *private* affairs; **2,** away from public view or knowledge; secret; as, he obtained *private* information; **3,** not holding a public position; as, a *private* citizen; **4,** not for people in general; not public; as, a *private* school:—*n.* a common soldier; the lowest rank in the Canadian army and airforce.—*adv.* **pri′vate-ly.**

pri-va-teer (prī′va-tēr′), *n.* **1,** an armed ship,

privately owned, but permitted by the government to attack the enemy's ships during wartime; **2,** the commander or one of the crew of such a ship:—*v.i.* to sail in, or as, a privateer.

pri-va-tion (prī-vā′shun), *n.* need; hardship; want of the usual comforts of life.

priv-i-lege (priv′i-lij), *n.* a special favour or right granted to a person or body of persons:—*v.t.* [privileged, privileg-ing], to give some particular right to; allow; as, employees are *privileged* to buy at a discount.

priv-y (priv′i), *adj.* **1,** for private, not public, use; personal; as, the *privy* purse; **2,** secretly informed; as, to be *privy* to a plot:—**Privy Council, 1,** in Canada, a body of honorary advisers to the prime minister, appointed by the Governor General, which includes former and current Cabinet ministers, etc.; **2,** a similar council in Britain:—*n.* [*pl.* privies], an outdoor toilet.—*adv.* **priv′i-ly.**

prize (prīz), *n.* **1,** a reward offered or won in a contest; **2,** anything of value; **3,** that which is taken from an enemy in war; esp. a captured vessel:—*adj.* **1,** given a prize; as a *prize* painting; **2,** worthy to be given a prize; as, a *prize* student; **3,** given as a prize; as, he won the *prize* trophy:—*v.t.* [prized, priz-ing], to value or esteem highly; as, to *prize* a gift.

pro (prō), *adv.* on the affirmative side; as, they argued *pro* and con:—*n. Colloq.* a professional; expert; as, a golf *pro*; a math *pro*.

pro- or **pro–** (prō- prō–), *prefix* meaning **1,** *substituting*; as in *pro*noun; **2,** *supporting*; as in *pro*-choice, *pro*-union, **3,** *prior, before*; as in *pro*cambium, *pro*phet, **4,** *in front of, forth*; as in *pro*duce, *pro*ject.

prob-a-bil-i-ty (prob′a-bil′i-ti), *n.* [*pl.* probabilities]; **1,** the quality or state of being likely; **2,** something likely to happen; **3,** chance; as, the *probabilities* at present are against snow.

prob-a-ble (prob′a-bl), *adj.* **1,** likely; expected; **2,** giving grounds for belief; having the appearance of truth; as, a *probable* explanation.

prob-a-bly (prob′a-bli), *adv.* almost certain or definite; likely; as, it will *probably* rain.

pro-bate (prō′bāt), *v.t.* [probated, probat-ing], to prove the validity of a will:—*adj.* having jurisdiction over wills; as, a *probate* court:—*n.* legal proof of a will, or a copy of a will with the certificate of its legal proof.

pro-ba-tion (prō-bā′shun), *n.* **1,** a trial or test of a person's character, ability, etc.; also, the period of trial; **2,** a system of releasing offenders under supervision before they have served their full sentence.—*adj.* **pro-ba′tion-al; pro-ba′tion-ar-y.**—*n.* **pro-ba′tion-er.**

probe (prōb), *n.* **1,** a device or tool used to explore or test something; as, the space *probe* headed toward Venus; **2,** slender, flexible surgical instrument for examining a wound, cavity, etc.; **3,** a searching inquiry; as, to conduct a *probe* into poverty:—*v.t.* [probed, prob-ing], **1,** to examine with a probe; **2,** to inquire into closely.

prob-i-ty (prō′bi-ti), *n.* integrity, uprightness; honesty; as, a woman of *probity*.

prob-lem (prob′lem), *n.* **1,** a question hard to understand; a matter hard to solve or settle; as, to have a *problem* choosing the right gift; **2,** something that is to be worked out or solved; as, a math *problem*.—*adj.* **prob′lem-at′i-cal.**

pro-bos-cis (prō-bos′is), *n.* [*pl.* proboscises or proboscides (-i-dēz′)], **1,** the trunk of an elephant; **2,** the long snout of certain other animals, as the tapir; **3,** the elongated mouth parts of certain insects; **4,** *Colloq.* a person's nose, esp. a large one.

pro-ce-dure (prō-sē′dūr), *n.* **1,** a course of action; a proceeding; as, his *procedure* in the matter was very fair; **2,** a system of proceeding; manner of conducting a business transaction, a lawsuit, etc.; **3,** the established manner of conducting a meeting.

pro-ceed (prō-sēd′), *v.i.* **1,** to go on or forward; advance; continue acting, speaking, etc.; as, to *proceed* on a journey; *proceed* with your speech; **2,** to issue; result; as, the tides *proceed* from the attraction of the sun and moon; **3,** to carry on a series of actions in a systematic manner.

pro-ceed-ing (prō-sēd′ing), *n.* **1,** a transaction, as in business; **2,** a course of conduct; **3,** an action in a law suit:—**proceedings,** the record of the business accomplished at a meeting of a society, board of directors, etc.

pro-ceeds (prō′sēdz), *n.pl.* results from a transaction, esp. the amount of money realized from a sale or other business activity; as, the *proceeds* of the fundraiser.

pro-cess (prō′ses; pros′es), *n.* **1,** progress; course; as, the house is in *process* of construction; **2,** a continuous action or series of actions that lead to the accomplishment of a result; as, getting an education is a long *process*; **3,** in industry, esp. manufacturing, a method of operation or treatment that brings about a certain result; as, the *process* of making glass; **4,** an official written summons to appear in court; **5,** an outgrowth or projecting part, esp. on a bone:—*v.t.* **1,** to subject to a special treatment or process; as, to *process* leather; *process* cheese; **2,** in *computing*, to perform tasks that manipulate data using software; as to *process* data.

pro-ces-sion (prō-sesh′un), *n.* **1,** the act of going on or forward, esp. in an orderly way; **2,** a formal parade; as, a religious *procession*; **3,** a group of people moving forward in an orderly fashion; as, a wedding *procession*.

pro-ces-sor (prō′ses′ėr), *n.* a person or thing that processes something; as, a word *processor* or a food *processor*.

pro-claim (prō-klām′), *v.t.* to make known publicly; declare; publish abroad; announce; as, to *proclaim* Friday a holiday.

proc-la-ma-tion (prok′la-mā′shun), *n.* **1,** the official act of announcing publicly; **2,** that which is announced; a formal announcement.

pro-cliv-i-ty (prō-kliv′i-ti), *n.* a natural inclination; tendency: used esp. in a bad sense; as, she has a *proclivity* for exaggeration.

pro-cras-ti-nate (prō-kras′ti-nāt′), *v.i.* [procrastinat-ed, procrastinat-ing], to delay, esp. without good reason; put off action from day to day; postpone; as, even though the assignment was due the next day, she *procrastinated* and went to the mall instead.—*n.* **pro-cras′ti-na′tion.**

pro-cre-ate (prō′kri-āt′), *v.t.* and *v.i.* to produce offspring; as, couples marry and *procreate.*—*n.* **pro-cre-a′tion.**

pro-cure (prō-kūr′), *v.t.* [procured, procur-ing], **1,** to get; obtain; **2,** to cause or bring about; as, she *procured* his arrest.—*n.* **pro-cure′ment; pro-cur′er.**

prod (prod), *n.* **1,** a pointed implement for pricking, as a goad or pointed stick; **2,** a prick; **3,** a poke or dig:—*v.t.* [prod-ded, prod-ding], **1,** to punch or poke with a pointed instrument; **2,** to urge.

prod-i-gal (prod′i-g'l), *adj.* reckless with money; lavish; wasteful:—*n.* a spendthrift.—*n.* **prod′i-gal′i-ty.**

pro-di-gious (prō-dij′us), *adj.* **1,** unusually great in size, quantity, etc.; enormous; **2,** marvellous; amazing.

prod-i-gy (prod′i-ji), *n.* [*pl.* prodigies], **1,** anything both unusual and unnatural; as, comets were once thought of as *prodigies*; **2,** anything causing wonder; a marvel; as, a *prodigy* of learning; **3,** a person, esp. a child, unusually gifted or precocious.

[1]**pro-duce** (prō-dūs′), *v.t.* [produced, pro-duc-ing], **1,** to exhibit or bring to view; as, he *produced* the papers from the safe; **2,** to yield or bring forth; as, trees *produce* fruit; **3,** to manufacture; **4,** to lead to; as, wealth *produces* comfort; **5,** to bring a play, movie, television show, etc., before the public.

[2]**prod-uce** (prod′ūs), *n.* that which is brought forth or yielded, esp. the products of farm and garden, such as fresh fruit and vegetables.

pro-duc-er (prō-dūs′ėr; prō-dōōs′ėr), *n.* **1,** a person or thing that produces something; as, Québec is a leading *producer* of maple syrup; **2,** a person in charge of producing a play, movie, television show, etc.

prod-uct (prod′ukt), *n.* **1,** that which is yielded by nature, or made by labour, thought, manufacture, etc.; as, farm or factory *products*; fiction novels are *products* of the imagination; **2,** in *mathematics,* the result obtained by multiplying two or more numbers together; as, the *product* of 1, 3, and 5 is 15.

pro-duc-tion (prō-duk′shun), *n.* **1,** that which is yielded by nature or made by labour, thought, etc.; **2,** a performance on the stage, on television, on the radio, in a movie, etc.; also, the staging and presenting of such a performance; **3,** the act of producing.

pro-duc-tive (prō-duk′tiv), *adj.* **1,** having the power to create something; creative; **2,** creating in abundance; fertile; as, *productive* soil; **3,** causing to exist; as, *productive* labour.

pro-duc-tiv-i-ty (prō′duk-tiv′i-ti; pro′-), *n.* the ability to produce things; also the quality and rate of production.

pro-fane (prō-fān′), *adj.* **1,** not sacred or holy; **2,** having to do with this world only; as, *profane* history; **3,** showing disrespect or irreverence; vulgar; coarse; as, *profane* language:—*v.t.* [profaned, profan-ing], **1,** to treat (something sacred) with irreverence, contempt, or abuse; **2,** to put to an improper use.—*n.* **prof′a-na′tion** (prof′a-nā′shun).

pro-fan-i-ty (prō-fan′i-ti), *n.* [*pl.* profanities], irreverent or vulgar conduct or speech.

pro-fess (prō-fes′), *v.t.* **1,** to make a public statement of (one's belief, intentions, etc.); as, to *profess* allegiance to one's country; **2,** to pretend; claim; as, to *profess* friendship; he *professed* to have expert knowledge.—*adv.* **pro-fess′ed-ly.**

pro-fes-sion (prō-fesh′un), *n.* **1,** the act of declaring; declaration; as, a *profession* of friendship; **2,** a calling or vocation, esp. one that requires special education; as, the *professions* of medicine and law; **3,** all the persons engaged in any one calling of this kind.

pro-fes-sion-al (prō-fesh′un-al), *adj.* **1,** pertaining to, or associated with, a profession; as, *professional* duties; **2,** pertaining to sport or other activity engaged in for profit or pay, or to the act or practice of engaging in a sport for pay; as, a *professional* boxer; *professional* golf; *professional* soccer player; **3,** done in a skillful way, as if by a professional; as, a *professional* job of building the deck:—*n.* **1,** one who engages in a sport or other pleasurable pursuit for gain; **2,** a person who works in a profession, such as a lawyer, doctor, dentist, etc.: opposite of *amateur*.

pro-fes-sor (prō-fes′ėr), *n.* **1,** a teacher of the highest rank in a college or university; **2,** loosely, a teacher; **3,** one who makes an open declaration of his or her opinions, esp. concerning religion.—*adj.* **prof′es-**

sor′i-al (prof′e-sōr′i-al; prō′fe-sōr′i-al).

prof-fer (prof′ėr), *v.t.* to offer for acceptance; as, to *proffer* help:—*n.* an offer.

pro-fi-cient (prō-fish′ent), *adj.* thoroughly skilled; expert; as, *proficient* in drawing.—*n.* **pro-fi′cien-cy.**

pro-file (prō′fīl), *n.* **1,** outline or contour; as, the *profile* of a mountain; **2,** a side view of a human face, or a drawing, photograph, etc., made from it; **3,** a short description of a person or thing; as, a *profile* of the new teacher:—*v.t.* [profiled, profil-ing], to outline or describe something or someone in this way.

prof-it (prof′it), *n.* **1,** gain in money; the amount by which income exceeds expenses in a given time: compare to *loss*; **2,** benefit or advantage:—**profits,** the gain, as from the operation of a business, after all expenses, charges, etc., have been met:—*v.i.* and *v.t.* to benefit; as, to *profit* from a transaction; the transaction *profited* him.—*adv.* **prof′it-a-bly.**

prof-it-a-ble (prof′i-ta-bl), *adj.* **1,** making or giving a profit; **2,** giving a gain or benefit; as, a *profitable* study session.

prof-li-gate (prof′li-gāt′), *adj.* **1,** given up to vice; dissolute; **2,** recklessly extravagant:—*n.* a vicious or immoral person.—*n.* **prof′li-ga-cy.**

pro-found (prō-found′), *adj.* **1,** deep, as to space; as, the *profound* depths of the ocean; **2,** deep, as to mental state; thorough; as, *profound* thought; *profound* learning; **3,** deep, as to feeling; intense; as, *profound* sorrow; **4,** bowing low; **5,** humble; lowly; **6,** coming from the depths; as, a *profound* sigh.—*adv.* **pro-found′ly.**

pro-fun-di-ty (prō-fun′di-ti), *n.* [*pl.* profundities], **1,** deepness; depth; **2,** depth of thought, knowledge, feeling, etc.; **3,** that which is deep in any sense.

pro-fuse (prō-fūs′), *adj.* **1,** pouring forth freely; giving or given with great generosity; as, *profuse* kindness; **2,** produced or shown in great abundance; as, *profuse* foliage.—*adv.* **pro-fuse′ly.**—*n.* **pro-fu′sion** (-fū′zhun).

pro-gen-i-tor (prō-jen′i-tėr), *n.* an ancestor; forefather.

prog-e-ny (proj′e-ni), *n.* offspring; children; descendants or a descendant.

prog-no-sis (prog-nō′sis), *n.* a forecast, esp. by a doctor about the probable course of a disease.

prog-nos-ti-cate (prog-nos′ti-kāt′), *v.t.* to predict or foretell (from present signs); prophesize; foreshadow.—*n.* **prog-nos′ti-ca′tion.**

pro-gram or **pro-gramme** (prō′gram), *n.* **1,** a brief outline giving in order the features that make up a public entertainment, ceremony, etc.; as, a concert *program*; **2,** the features that make up such an entertainment; **3,** a clearly defined plan of action in any undertaking; as, a town improvement *program*; **4,** in *computing,* a set of instructions telling a computer how to carry out a job:—*v.t.* [programmed; program-ming or programed; program-ing], **1,** in *computing,* to enter instructions into a computer or other machine so that it can perform a function; as, she *programmed* the new computer; **2,** to include in a program; as, he *programmed* an evening of entertainment.

pro-gram-mer or **pro-gram-er** (prō′gram′ėr), *n.* in *computing,* someone skilled at developing computer programs.

[1]**pro-gress** (prō′gres; prog′res), *n.* **1,** a moving forward; as, the *progress* of a boat; **2,** advancement or improvement; as, the patient made slow *progress* to recovery; **3,** growth or development; as, the *progress* of a campaign:—**in progress,** happening at the time; going on; as, it is a work *in progress.*

[2]**pro-gress** (prō-gres′), *v.i.* **1,** to move forward; as, time *progresses*; **2,** to grow; improve; develop; as, science *progresses.*

pro-gres-sion (prō-gresh′un), *n.* the act or method of advancing.

pro-gres-sive (prō-gres′iv), *adj.* **1,** moving forward step by step; as, *progressive* improvement; **2,** ready to accept new ideas or to introduce changes for the sake of improvement; as, a *progressive* schoolteacher; **3,** in *grammar,* designating a form (of a verb) that expresses an action as going on; as, I *am thinking* (present progressive); in December he *was working* (past progressive or imperfect):—*n.* one who believes in, and works for, changes and reforms, esp. in political matters:—**Progressive,** a supporter of the Progressive Conservative Party in Canada.—*adv.* **progres′sive-ly.**

Progressive Conservative Party, one of the major political parties in Canada. Also called the *Conservative Party,* the *Conservatives,* and the *Tories.*

pro-hib-it (prō-hib′it), *v.t.* **1,** to forbid by law; as, the law *prohibits* fishing in the spring; **2,** to hinder; prevent.—*adj.* **pro-hib′i-to-ry.**

pro-hi-bi-tion (prō′i-bish′un; prō′hi-bish′un), *n.* **1,** the act of forbidding, esp. the forbidding by law of the manufacture and sale of intoxicating drinks; **2,** a law or injunction forbidding something:—**Prohibition,** the period around the 1920s when countries such as Canada outlawed the manufacture and sale of alcoholic beverages.—*n.* **pro′hi-bi′tion-ist.**

pro-hib-i-tive (prō-hib′i-tiv), *adj.* tending to forbid, prevent, or hinder; as, *prohibitive* prices keep us from buying.

[1]**pro-ject** (prō-jekt′), *v.t.* **1,** to throw or

shoot forward; **2,** to cause (a beam of light, a shadow, etc.) to fall on a surface; as, to *project* a picture on a screen; **3,** to plan (something to be done, a course of action, etc.):—*v.i.* to jut out; extend forward; as, a bay window *projects*.—*n.* **pro-jec′tion; pro-jec′tion-ist; pro-jec′tor.**

[2]**project** (prō′jekt; proj′ekt), *n.* **1,** a design; scheme; plan; **2,** in school, a problem or lesson intended to make students rely on their own effort and natural ability; **3,** a group of houses or apartment buildings built and operated as a unit; as, a housing *project*.

pro-jec-tile (prō-jek′tīl; prō-jek′til), *n.* something thrown or shot forward, esp. a ball, shell, torpedo, etc., intended to be shot from a cannon.

pro-jec-tion (prō-jek′shun), *n.* **1,** a part that projects; as, the roof *projection*; **2,** the act or fact of projecting; as, televisions use rear *projection*.

pro-jec-tor (prō-jek′tėr), *n.* **1,** a machine that shows a picture on a screen by means of a beam of light and special lenses; as, a motion picture *projector*; **2,** someone who plans or projects.

OVERHEAD PROJECTOR

pro-le-tar-i-at (prō′le-târ′i-it), *n.* **1,** in the Marxist sense, the industrial working class; **2,** the labouring class; earners of day wages.—*adj.* **pro′le-ta′ri-an.**

pro-lif-ic (prō-lif′ik), *adj.* **1,** producing young or fruit abundantly; fertile; as, a *prolific* vine; **2,** producing ideas or results abundantly; as, a *prolific* writer.

pro-lix-i-ty (prō-lik′si-ti), *n.* wordiness; long-windedness.—*adj.* **pro′lix** or **pro-lix′.**

pro-logue or **pro-log** (prō′log), *n.* **1,** an introduction or preface to a poem, drama, etc., esp. verses spoken or sung by an actor before the performance of a play or an opera; **2,** the actor who delivers these verses; **3,** an introduction to a book or novel; **4,** any introductory action or event.

pro-long (prō-lông′), *v.t.* to lengthen in time or space; draw out; extend; as, to *prolong* a conversation; to *prolong* a line.—*n.* **pro′lon-ga′tion.**

prom-e-nade (prom′i-näd′; i-näd′), *n.* **1,** a walk for pleasure or exercise; **2,** a place for walking; **3,** *Colloq.* prom; a ball or dance:—*v.i.* [promenad-ed, promenad-ing], to walk for pleasure.

prom-i-nent (prom′i-nent), *adj.* **1,** standing or jutting out; projecting; **2,** conspicuous; noticeable; as, a *prominent* store window; **3,** distinguished; as, a *prominent* scientist.—*n.* **prom′i-nence.**

pro-mis-cu-ous (prō-mis′kū-us), *adj.* **1,** made up of a random mixture of unrelated parts or individuals; as, a *promiscuous* assembly; **2,** not confined to one person (used esp. of sexual intercourse); not discriminating; as, *promiscuous* hospitality; **3,** casual; accidental; un-planned.—*n.* **prom′is-cu′i-ty** (prom′-).

prom-ise (prom′is), *n.* **1,** a pledge that one will or will not do something; **2,** a cause or ground for hope or expectation; as, a *promise* of fair weather:—*v.i.* [promised, promising], **1,** to pledge or engage to do or not to do something; **2,** to give reason for hope or expectation; as, the garden *promises* well:—*v.t.* **1,** to pledge or engage (to do or not to do); as, he *promised* to go; **2,** to agree to give to, or get for, someone; as, he *promised* her a position; **3,** to give reason to expect (something); as, the day *promised* rain.—*n.* **prom′is-er.**—*adj.* **prom′is-sor-y** (prom′i-sėr-i).

promissory note, a written agreement to pay a certain sum of money on demand or at a fixed date.

prom-on-tor-y (prom′un-tėr-i), *n.* [*pl.* promontories], a high point of land extending into a body of water.

pro-mote (prō-mōt′), *v.t.* [promot-ed, promot-ing], **1,** to raise to a higher rank or class; as, the teacher *promoted* her to the sixth grade; **2,** to set up or organize, as a business venture; **3,** to help the growth or development of; as, to *promote* interest in outdoor sports; **4,** to advertise or publicize; as, to *promote* cancer research.—*n.* **pro-mot′er.**

pro-mo-tion (prō-mō′shun), *n.* **1,** the act or fact of promoting; as, she got a *promotion* to vice-president; **2,** an activity designed to help the selling of something; as, the *promotion* of the new breakfast cereal.

prompt (prompt), *adj.* **1,** ready and quick to act; as, *prompt* to forgive; **2,** done or given without delay; as, *prompt* service; **3,** on time; not tardy; as, you must learn to be *prompt*:—*v.t.* **1,** to rouse to action; incite; **2,** to suggest; inspire; as, generosity *prompted* the gift; **3,** to remind or help (a speaker at a loss for words):—*n.* in *computing*, the symbol that appears on the computer screen to indicate that the computer is ready to receive input.—*n.* **prompt′er; prompt′ness.**—*adv.* **prompt′ly.**

prom-ul-gate (prom′ul-gāt′; prōmul′gāt), *v.t.* [promulgat-ed, promulgat-ing], to make known formally and officially; proclaim; as, to *promulgate* a law.

prone (prōn), *adj.* **1,** naturally disposed or inclined; as, she is *prone* to forget; **2,** lying face downward.

prong (prông), *n.* one of the pointed ends of a fork; also, any sharp point or sharp-pointed instrument.

pro-noun (prō′noun), *n.* a word that refers to, or is used in the place of, a noun or name, as, "this," "which," "he," "she," "who," etc.—*adj.* **pro-nom′i-nal.**

pro-nounce (prō-nouns′), *v.t.* [pronounced, pronounc-ing], **1,** to utter the sounds of; as, to *pronounce* a name; **2,** to declare; as, they *pronounced* him a failure; **3,** to speak or utter with formal solemnity; as, to *pronounce* a benediction:—*v.i.* **1,** to utter words, esp. with care and precision; enunciate; **2,** to speak with confidence or authority.—*adj.* **pro-nounce′a-ble.**—*n.* **pro-nounce′ment.**

pro-nounced (prō-nounst′), *adj.* strongly marked; easy to notice; obvious; decided; as, a *pronounced* change in the weather.

pron-to (pron′tō), *adj.* and *adv. Slang* quick(ly); prompt(ly).

pro-nun-ci-a-tion (prō-nun′sē-ā′shun), *n.* the act or manner of uttering the sounds that form words.

proof (prōōf), *n.* **1,** the means by which something is shown to be true or correct; **2,** convincing evidence; as, *proof* of guilt; **3,** a test or trial; as, "the *proof* of the pudding is in the eating"; **4,** in *photography*, a trial print from a negative; **5,** in *printing*, an impression taken from type for correction; **6,** in *science* or *mathematics*, the process of checking to make sure that a certain statement is true:—*adj.* **1,** used in proving or testing; **2,** of a standard strength or purity; as, *proof* whisky; **3,** capable of resisting; as, *proof* against infection.

proof-read (prōōf′rēd′), *v.t.* and *v.i.* to read over a piece of writing in order to correct errors, etc.; as, the boy had failed to *proofread* his essay.—*n.* **proof′read′ing; proof′read′er.**

prop (prop), *v.t.* [propped, prop-ping], **1,** to support by placing something under or against; as, to *prop* up a book; **2,** to sustain; support; as, to *prop* up a friend's courage:—*n.* **1,** a support or stay used to keep something from falling; **2,** an object used as part of a scene in a play, television show, or movie, not including the costumes and scenery; property.

prop-a-gan-da (prop′a-gan′da), *n.* **1,** any organization or scheme for spreading special opinions or beliefs, esp. by distortion or dishonesty; as, Communist *propaganda*; **2,** the opinions or beliefs thus spread.—*n.* **prop′a-gan′dist.**

prop-a-gate (prop′a-gāt′), *v.t.* [propagated, propagat-ing], **1,** to cause to increase or multiply by natural reproduction; as, to *propagate* plants; **2,** to spread from person to person; as, to *propagate* news.—*n.* **prop′a-ga′tor; prop′a-ga′tion.**

pro-pane (prō′pān), *n.* a methane gas, C_3H_8, obtained from petroleum, used as a fuel.

pro-pel (prō-pel′), *v.t.* [propelled, propelling], to push or urge forward; drive onward; as, to *propel* the canoe with a paddle.

pro-pel-lant (prō-pel′ant), *n.* an explosive charge that propels, esp. fuel plus an oxidizing agent used in rocket engines; a propelling agent.—*adj.* **pro-pel′lent.**

pro-pel-ler (prō-pel′ėr), *n.* **1,** a device, usually a revolving shaft with blades, for causing an airplane or a ship to move forward; **2,** one who or that which drives forward.

pro-pen-si-ty (prō-pen′si-ti), *n.* [*pl.* propensities], natural inclination or tendency; as, a *propensity* to exaggerate.

prop-er (prop′ėr), *adj.* **1,** suitable; fitting; appropriate; as, *proper* clothes for wet weather; **2,** belonging naturally to some person or thing; characteristic; as, trees *proper* to a region; **3,** according to accepted usage; correct; conventional; respectable; as, *proper* table manners; **4,** in a narrow or restricted sense; as, the spider is not an insect *proper.*—*adv.* **prop′er-ly.**

proper noun or **proper name**, a noun that names one particular person, place, or thing and begins with a capital letter, such as Clayton Brown; St. John's; Pacific Ocean; Rocky Mountains.

prop-er-ty (prop′ėr-ti), *n.* [*pl.* properties], **1,** any quality or attribute that belongs to a thing, or one that esp. marks it; as, sourness is a *property* of vinegar; **2,** ownership; as, the duties and rights of *property*; **3,** the thing owned; possessions, namely, real estate, movable goods, etc.:—**properties** or **props**, all the stage furnishings and articles required by actors in performing a play, television show, or movie, except scenery and the costumes of the actors.

proph-e-cy or **proph-e-sy** (prof′i-si), *n.* [*pl.* -cies], **1,** a foretelling or prediction of future events; **2,** something that is said in this way; as, Orwell had many accurate *prophecies* in *1984.*—*v.t.* **proph-e-sy** (prof′i-sī′) [prophesied, prohe-sy-ing].—*n.* **proph-et; proph′et-ess.**

pro-phet-ic (prō-fet′ik), *adj.* **1,** pertaining to the foretelling of future events or to one who foretells; as, the *prophetic* gift; **2,** containing a prophecy; as, a *prophetic* vision.

pro-pi-tious (prō-pish′us), *adj.* **1,** favourably inclined; gracious; **2,** favourable; suitable, as *propitious* weather.

pro-po-nent (prō-pō′nent), *n.* an advocate or supporter; as, he is a *proponent* of state ownership and state medicine.

pro-por-tion (prō-pōr′shun), *n.* **1,** the relation between the size, amount, or degree of one thing and the size, amount, or degree of another; ratio; as, the *proportion* of weekdays to weekends is five to one; **2,** proper or just share; as, what is my *proportion* of the profits? **3,** a proper or balanced relationship between the parts of a thing; as, the dog's short legs are not in *proportion* to its body; **4,** a part or share; as, a large *proportion* of the earth is covered by water; **5,** in *mathematics*, a statement of equality between two ratios; as, 4:8 = 6:12 is a *proportion*:—**proportions**, dimensions; size; as, the house has large *proportions*:—*v.t.* **1,** to cause (one thing) to be in suitable relation to another; as, to *proportion* one's expenses to one's income; **2,** to give suitable dimensions to.—*adj.* and *n.* **pro-por′tion-al.**—*adj.* **pro-por′tion-ate.**

pro-pos-al (prō-pō′zal), *n.* **1,** the act or fact of proposing; suggesting; **2,** a plan or suggestion; as, our *proposal* to have art classes; **3,** an offer of marriage.

pro-pose (prō-pōz′), *v.t.* [proposed, proposing], **1,** to put forward for consideration; suggest; as, he *proposed* that I should go; I *proposed* a later date; **2,** to suggest someone for an office; nominate:—*v.i.* **1,** to make an offer of marriage; **2,** to form a plan; make known a plan; **3,** to intend; purpose; as, I *propose* to stay at home.

prop-o-si-tion (prop′o-zish′un), *n.* **1,** that which is offered for consideration; a proposal; **2,** the formal statement of a topic to be discussed; **3,** in *mathematics*, the statement of a theorem or problem for solution.

pro-pound (prō-pound′), *v.t.* to offer for discussion or debate; to set forth, as a question, problem, etc.

pro-pri-e-tar-y (prō-prī′e-ta-ri), *adj.* **1,** pertaining to an owner; **2,** holding property; **3,** held under patent, trademark, etc.; as, a *proprietary* drug.

pro-pri-e-tor (prō-prī′e-tėr), *n.* one who has a legal title to property; an owner; as, the *proprietor* of a farm.—*n.* **pro-pri′e-tor-ship′.**

pro-pri-e-ty (prō-prī′e-ti), *n.* [*pl.* proprieties], **1,** fitness or suitability; also, correctness of manners or conduct; **2, proprieties**, the manners expected in polite society.

pro-pul-sion (prō-pul′shun), *n.* the act of propelling, or the state of being propelled.

pro-rogue (prō-rōg′), *v.t.* and *v.i.* to end the meetings of a legislative assembly; as the Parliament at Ottawa *prorogued* on July 15.—*n.* **pro′ro-ga′tion.**

pro-sa-ic (prō-zā′ik), *adj.* **1,** of or pertaining to prose; **2,** commonplace; unimaginative; dull.

pro-scribe (prō-skrīb′), *v.t.* [proscrib-ed, proscrib-ing], **1,** to put (a person) outside the protection of the law; outlaw; banish; **2,** to condemn; prohibit; as, free speech is still *proscribed* there.—*n.* **pro-scrip′tion.**

prose (prōz), *n.* ordinary spoken or written language without the metre, rhyme, rhythm, etc., of poetry: distinguished from verse:—*adj.* pertaining to composition that is not verse.—*adj.* **pros′y.**

pros-e-cute (pros′i-kūt′), *v.t.* [prosecut-ed, prosecut-ing], **1,** to follow up or pursue (an undertaking) in order to complete it; as, to *prosecute* an investigation; **2,** to bring legal proceedings against (someone):—*v.i.* **1,** to conduct the case against a person accused of crime; **2,** to carry on a lawsuit.—*n.* **pros′e-cu′tion; pros′e-cu′tor.**

pros-pect (pros′pekt), *n.* **1,** a scene spread out before the sight; view; outlook; as, a *prospect* of green, rolling prairie; **2,** a looking forward to, esp. that which one looks forward to, or expects; expectation; as, a *prospect* of fair weather; **3,** a possible customer or client:—*v.t.* and *v.i.* (pros-pekt′; pros′pekt), to search or explore, esp. for gold, oil, etc.; as, thousands *prospected* for gold in the Yukon.

pro-spec-tive (pro-spek′tiv), *adj.* **1,** concerned with the future; **2,** expected; hoped for; as, *prospective* profits; *prospective* clients.

pro-spec-tor (pro-spek′tėr; pros′pek-tėr), *n.* one who explores a region, searching for oil, gold, etc., in the earth.

pro-spec-tus (pro-spek′tus), *n.* a printed outline of a forthcoming book or a new enterprise (to win financial support for it).

pros-per (pros′pėr), *v.i.* to thrive; make progress; flourish.

pros-per-i-ty (pros-per′i-ti), *n.* the condition of doing very well or being successful; as, they brought *prosperity* to the town.

pros-per-ous (pros′pėr-us), *adj.* having wealth or good fortune; being successful; as, she is a *prosperous* business person.

pros-tate (pros′tāt), *n.* the male reproductive gland.

pros-ti-tute (pros′ti-tūt′), *v.t.* to devote to a low or unworthy purpose; as, to *prostitute* one's talents:—*n.* anyone who enters into sex relations for pay, or who devotes oneself to unworthy matters.—*n.* **pros′ti-tu′tion.**

pros-trate (pros′trāt), *adj.* **1,** lying face down on the ground; bending to the ground; in token of defeat, humility, or worship; as, the vanquished foe, *prostrate* before the victor; **2,** flung down to the ground; as, the *prostrate* pillars of a ruined temple; **3,** overcome, as with emotion; also, drained of vitality; lifeless; as, a *prostrate* industry:—*v.t.* (pros-strāt′), [prostrat-ed, prostrat-ing] **1,** to humble (oneself) by lying face down on the ground; as, to *prostrate* oneself before the conqueror; **2,** to exhaust; as, she is *prostrated* with fatigue.—*n.* **pros-tra′tion.**

pro-tag-o-nist (prō-tag′o-nist), *n.* **1,** the leading character in a play, television show, movie, story, or novel; **2,** the person who acts that part.

pro-tect (prō-tekt′), *v.t.* **1,** to shield from harm; guard; shelter; as, quills *protect* a porcupine from danger; **2,** in *computing*, to restrict access to files, data, etc.—*adj.* **pro-tec′tive.**—*n.* **pro-tec′tor.**

pro-tec-tion (prō-tek′shun), *n.* **1,** the act of keeping in safety; **2,** the state of being kept in safety; **3,** that which keeps safe; defence; security; as, an overcoat is a *protection* against a cold wind; **4,** the placing of duties on imported goods for the encouragement of home industry, a policy opposed to that of free trade:—**protection money**, money extorted by gangsters under the threat of violence.—*n.* **pro-tec′tion-ist** (one opposed to free trade).

pro-tec-tive (prō-tek′tiv), *adj.* helping to protect; as, a *protective* covering.

pro-tec-tor-ate (prō-tek′tėr-it), *n.* **1,** government by a person appointed to rule in place of a king; **2,** the relation of a great nation to a weak one that it defends and partly controls; also, the period during which this control is maintained; **3,** the nation so defended and controlled.

pro-té-gé (prō′te-zhā; prô′tā′zhā′), *n.* one who is mentored or under the guardianship or care of another.—*n.fem.* **pro′té-gée.**

pro-te-in (prō′tē-in; prō′tēn), *n.* a substance containing nitrogen, found as a vital element in all living organisms, animal and vegetable: protein is an essential part of any diet, and is contained in meat, fish, dairy products, eggs, nuts, peas, beans, etc.

pro-test (prō-test′), *v.i.* to make a formal declaration of disapproval or dissent:—*v.t.* **1,** to affirm or assert; as, the defendant *protested* that he was telling the absolute truth; **2,** to object to; dissent from; as, to appeal to a higher court is to *protest* the judgment of the lower; **3,** to make a formal statement of refusal to honour or pay; as, to *protest* a cheque:—*n.* (prō′test), **1,** a formal declaration of opinion against something; **2,** a formal notification that a note, cheque, etc., will not be honoured or paid.

Prot-es-tant (prot′es-tant), *adj.* of or relating to any of the branches of the Christian church that do not belong to the Roman Catholic or the Orthodox Church: Protestant churches include Anglican, Baptist, Lutheran, Presbyterian, United, and many others:—*n.* a member of a Protestant church.—*n.* **Prot′es-tant-ism.**

prot-es-ta-tion (prot′es-tā′shun), *n.* **1,** a solemn declaration; as, *protestations* of friendship; **2,** a formal objection or protest; as, a *protestation* against war or against unjust taxes.

pro-to-col (prō′tō-kol′), *n.* **1,** the proper courtesies in ceremonies of state, esp. the etiquette governing official visits between heads of states and their ministers; **2,** in *computing*, the rules that govern the mode of data transmission between computers over a network.

pro-ton (prō′ton), *n.* one of the basic constituents, or particles, of an atom's nucleus: it carries, or consists of, a charge of positive electricity.

pro-to-plasm (prō′tō-plazm), *n.* the essential living substance of both animal and plant cells: it is usually a colourless, jelly-like substance, in which tiny grains of solid matter are suspended.—*adj.* **pro′to-plas′mic** (plaz′).

pro-to-type (prō′tō-tīp′), *n.* an original; model; pattern; as, the *prototype* of the Avro Arrow was way ahead of its time.

Pro-to-zo-a (prō′tō-zō′a), *n.* a phylum, or division, of animals, such as the *amoeba*, chiefly microscopic and aquatic, consisting of a single cell and reproducing by fission (splitting and dividing).—*n.* and *adj.* **pro′to-zo′an.**

pro-tract (prō-trakt′), *v.t.* **1,** to draw out; prolong, as a meeting; **2,** to draw to scale.—*n.* **pro-trac′tion.**—*adj.* **pro-tract′ed.**

pro-trac-tor (prō-trak′tėr), *n.* an instrument for measuring angles.

PROTRACTOR

pro-trude (prō-trōōd′), *v.t.* and *v.i.* [protrud-ed, pro-trud-ing], to stick out; project; as, to *protrude* the tongue; pencils *protrude* from his pocket.—*n.* **pro-tru′sion.**

pro-tu-ber-ant (prō-tū′bėr-ant), *adj.* swelling out beyond the surrounding surface; bulging; as, a *protuberant* nose.—*n.* **pro-tu′ber-ance.**

proud (proud), *adj.* **1,** having or exhibiting too great self-esteem; overbearing; haughty; as, a *proud* dignitary with her *proud* airs; **2,** having worthy self-respect; as, too *proud* to beg; **3,** having a feeling of glad satisfaction; gratified; as, *proud* of his daughter's success; **4,** noble; magnificent; as, a *proud* old castle.—*adv.* **proud′ly.**

prove (prōōv), *v.t.* [*p.t.* proved (prōōvd), *p.p.* proved or prov-en (prōōv′en), *p.pr.* prov-ing], **1,** to test by an experiment; as, to *prove* the purity of copper; **2,** to demonstrate by reasoning or evidence; as, to *prove* a theorem in geometry; **3,** to cause to be accepted as genuine; as, to *prove* a will:—*v.i.* to turn out to be; be found to be; as, the new coat *proved* warm.

prov-erb (prov′ûrb), *n.* **1,** a short, homely saying, expressing a truth in few words; an adage, as "a stitch in time saves nine"; **2,** a byword.

pro-ver-bi-al (pro-vûr′bi-al), *adj.* **1,** contained in, or resembling, proverbs; as, *proverbial* wisdom; **2,** widely spoken of or known; as, her kindness is *proverbial*.—*adv.* **pro-ver′bi-al-ly.**

pro-vide (prō-vīd′), *v.t.* [provid-ed, provid-ing], **1,** to supply or furnish (a thing) for use; as, to *provide* food and lodging; also, to outfit or equip (a person); as, to *provide* a child with books; **2,** to set forth as a condition; stipulate; as, her will *provided* that a new hospital be built:—*v.i.* to make preparations in advance; as, to *provide* against cold weather.

pro-vid-ed (prō-vīd′id), *conj.* on condition that; if; as, I'll go, *provided* you go.

prov-i-dence (prov′i-dens), *n.* **1,** prudence; foresight; also, prudent management; thrift; **2,** an instance of divine care; as, her recovery was God's special *providence*:—**Providence**, God; as, to trust in *Providence*.

prov-i-dent (prov′i-dent), *adj.* **1,** mindful of the future; prudent; **2,** economical; thrifty.—*adv.* **prov′i-dent-ly.**

prov-i-den-tial (prov′i-den′shal), *adj.* **1,** of or by divine foresight; as, a *providential* recovery from illness; **2,** fortunate.—*adv.* **prov′i-den′tial-ly.**

prov-ince (prov′ins), *n.* **1,** a division of an empire or country; as, Alberta is a *province* of Canada; **2,** a country governed by a distant authority; **3,** limits or range; a proper sphere of action; as, this task is outside your *province*:—**provinces**, regions remote from a capital or a very large city; as, a company left London for the *provinces*.

pro-vin-cial (prō-vin′shal), *adj.* **1,** of or belonging to a division of an empire or country; as, *provincial* government; **2,** countrified; crude; **3,** restricted to the ideas and customs of one special region; **4,** narrow; limited:—*n.* **1,** an inhabitant of a province; **2,** an uncultivated person.—*n.* **pro-vin′cial-ism.**

pro-vi-sion (prō-vizh′un), *n.* **1,** preparation; care beforehand; as, *provision* must be made for a long journey; **2,** (often *provisions*), a supply or stock of food; as, *provisions* for the winter; **3,** a condition; proviso; stipulation; as, a *provision* in a contract:—*v.t.* to supply with something, esp. food.—*adj.* **pro-vi′sion-al** (temporary).—*n.* **pro-vi′sion-er.**

pro-vi-so (prō-vī′zō), *n.* [*pl.* provisos or provisoes], a conditional clause or stipulation, as in a deed or will.

prov-o-ca-tion (prov′o-kā′shun), *n.* **1,** that which excites to anger or resentment; as, he gets upset on the slightest *provocation*; **2,** the act of provoking; as, the *provocation* of a quarrel.—*adj.* **pro-voc′a-tive** (pro-vok′a-tiv).

pro-voke (prō-vōk′), *v.t.* [provoked, provok-ing], **1,** to excite; stir up; as, to *provoke* a laugh; **2,** to irritate; rouse; incite; as, to *provoke* another to anger.—*adj.* **pro-vok′ing.**

prow (prou), *n.* the forward end or part, as the nose of an airplane or ship; the bow.

prow-ess (prou′es), *n.* **1,** daring; bravery; valour; **2,** very great skill or ability; as, he was noted for his *prowess* as a cellist.

prowl (proul), *v.i.* to move about stealthily; as, wolves *prowl* for food:—*v.t.* to roam over, as woods or fields, in search of prey:—*n.* a roving for prey or plunder; as, beasts on the *prowl*.—*n.* **prowl′er.**

prox-im-i-ty (proks-im′i-ti), *n.* nearness; closeness; as, *proximity* to danger.

prox-y (prok′si), *n.* [*pl.* proxies], **1,** authority to act for another; **2,** the document giving the authority; as, to vote by *proxy*; **3,** a person who is given authority to act for another.

prude (prood), *n.* a person who is extremely or affectedly proper in dress, speech, or behaviour.—*adj.* **prud′ish.**—*n.* **prud′er-y.**

pru-dent (proo′dent), *adj.* **1,** mindful of the future; using judgment and foresight; cautious; as, a *prudent* shopper; **2,** showing forethought; as, a *prudent* act.—*n.* **pru′dence.**—*adj.* **pru-den′tial.**

[1]**prune** (proon), *v.t.* [pruned, prun-ing], **1,** to cut unnecessary twigs or branches from (a vine, bush, or tree); trim; **2,** to cut out or clear away the useless parts of; as, the author *pruned* his novel:—*v.i.* to remove useless branches or parts.—*n.* **prun′er.**

[2]**prune** (proon), *n.* a kind of plum, esp. one that has been dried or is capable of being dried without fermentation.

pru-ri-ent (proo′ri-ent), *adj.* lustful; lewd; as, *prurient* longings.—*n.* **pru′ri-ence.**

[1]**pry** (prī), *v.i.* [pried, pry-ing], to look or peer closely and inquisitively; inquire into anything and everything; as, some people *pry* into other people's affairs.—*adj.* **pry′ing.**

[2]**pry** (prī), *v.t.* [pried, pry-ing], **1,** to raise or open with a lever; **2,** to budge or move with difficulty; as, you can't *pry* the child away from the piano:—*n.* a lever.

PS (pē′es′), *abbrev.* short for *postscript*.

psalm (säm), *n.* a sacred song or poem.—*n.* **psalm′ist.**

pseu-do or **pseu-do-** (sū′dō), *adj.* and *prefix* meaning *false, sham, pretended*; as in *pseudo*aquatic (found in moist regions) and *pseudo*volcano (one that emits smoke or flame, but no lava).

pseu-do-nym (sū′do-nim), *n.* a fictitious or false name taken by a writer; a pen name; nom de plume; as, Great Owl was the *pseudonym* of Archibald Belaney.

psy-che (sī′ki), *n.* the human soul, mind, or spirit; as, the failure left him with a bruised *psyche*.

psy-chi-a-trist (si-kī′a-trist), *n.* a medical doctor who is specially trained to treat people who have serious mental disorders.—*n.* **psy-chi-a-try** (sī-kī′a-tri), the study and treatment of mental disorders.

psy-chic (sī′kik), *n.* a person sensitive to forces that cannot be explained by any known laws; a medium:—*adj.* **1,** concerning the soul or mind; spiritual; **2,** lying outside the realm of known physical processes; as, *psychic* forces; **3,** sensitive to forces of this kind; as, a *psychic* person.—*adj.* **psy′chi-cal.**

psy-cho- (sī′kō-), *prefix* meaning *mental* or *mind* (processes); as in *psycho*analysis (the treating of neuroses, etc., on the theory that many desires, repressed by the conscious mind and persisting in the unconscious to the harm of one's mental life and conduct, can be directed into better channels through an analysis of the patient's emotional history); *psycho*analyze.

psy-chol-o-gi-cal (sī-ko-loj′i-kl), *adj.* **1,** having to do with psychology; **2,** having to do with the mind; as, she suffers from a *psychological* problem.

psy-chol-o-gy (sī-kol′o-ji), *n.* [*pl.* psychologies], the science that studies the mind, particularly the human mind, and its activities.—*adj.* **psy′cho-log′i-cal** (sī′ko-log′i-kal).—*n.* **psy-chol′o-gist.**

psy-cho-path (sī′kō-path′), *n.* a person with an antisocial personality disorder characterized by a tendency toward violence or irresponsible acts and a lack of empathy.

psy-cho-sis (sī′kō′sis), *n.* [*pl.* psychoses (-sēz)], severe mental disorder that lacks any apparent physical cause, or is accompanied by some organic damage, as in alcoholism, brain tumours, etc.: a *psychosis* is primarily a mental disorder, while a *neurosis* is primarily a nervous disorder.—*adj.* **psy-chot′ic.**

psy-cho-ther-a-py (sī′kō-ther′a-pi), *n.* the use of such aids as suggestion, hypnosis, and psychoanalysis to cure mental and nervous disorders.

pter-o-dac-tyl (ter′ō-dak′til), *n.* a flying reptile of the dinosaur era: it had large wings (about 5.5 metres across) between the hind leg and the very long fourth digit of the forelimb.

pto-maine (tō-mān′), *n.* **1,** a substance, usually poisonous, found in decaying organic matter:—**ptomaine poisoning,** the illness caused by eating contaminated food; food poisoning.

pu-ber-ty (pū′bėr-ti), *n.* the earliest age at which one can beget or bear children.

pub-lic (pub′lik), *adj.* **1,** pertaining to the people as a whole; as, the *public* welfare; **2,** common to all; open to general use; as, a *public* park; a *public* library or school; **3,** generally known; not secret; as, the facts were made *public*; **4,** serving the people; as, a *public* utility:—*n.* **1,** the people in general or as a whole; as, the media informed the *public*; **2,** a special section or group of the people; as, the voting *public*.—*adv.* **pub′lic-ly.**

pub-li-ca-tion (pub′li-kā′shun), *n.* **1,** the act or business of printing and placing on sale; as, the *publication* of books; **2,** something that is published, as a book, magazine, etc.; **3,** making known to the public; as, this information is not for *publication*.

pub-lic-i-ty (pub-lis′i-ti), *n.* **1,** the state of being open to common knowledge; notoriety; public notice; as, unfavourable *publicity*; a *publicity* seeker; **2,** news that advertises through the media; as, theatrical *publicity*.—*v.t.* **pub′li-cize′** [publicized, publiciz-ing].—*n.* **pub′li-cist.**

pub-lish (pub′lish), *v.t.* **1,** to make generally known; as, to *publish* one's intentions; also, to proclaim, as an edict; **2,** to print and offer for sale, as a book, magazine, etc.—*n.* **pub′lish-er; pub-lish-ing.**

puck (puk), *n.* in *hockey*, a hard rubber disk pushed or driven along the ice with a hockey stick.

puck-er (puk′ėr), *v.t.* to draw up into small folds; wrinkle; as, in perplexity, he *puckered* up his brow:—*v.i.* to become drawn up into folds; as, the cloth *puckered* badly after being wet:—*n.* a small fold or wrinkle.

pud-ding (pood′ing), *n.* a kind of soft food, often a dessert, made of flour, milk, eggs, flavouring, etc.; as, butterscotch *pudding* or rice *pudding*.

pud-dle (pud′l), *n.* **1,** a small pool of dirty water; **2,** a mixture of clay and water used as a watertight covering or filling:—*v.t.* [pud-dled, pud-dling], **1,** to make muddy; **2,** to work water into (clay) so as to make a mixture through which water cannot pass; **3,** to stir or process, as impure metal.—*n.* **pud′dler.**

pudg-y (puj′i), *adj.* [pudg-i-er, pudg-i-est], short and fat; as, a *pudgy* hand.—*n.* **pudg′i-ness.**

pu-er-ile (pū′ėr-īl′; -il), *adj.* **1,** pertaining to childhood; **2,** immature; foolish; as a *puerile* remark; a *puerile* display of temper.

puff (puf), *n.* **1,** a short, quick blast, as of wind, steam, gas, breath, etc.; also, the accompanying sound or vapour; as, one may both hear and see the *puffs* of a locomotive; **2,** a soft pad; as, a powder *puff*; **3,** a light pastry shell filled with whipped cream, custard, etc.; as, a cream *puff*; **4,** in dressmaking, a piece of material gathered on two sides so as to stand out in the centre; **5,** exaggerated praise; as, the critic gave the new play quite a *puff*; **6,** a loose mass or roll of hair:—*v.i.* **1,** to send out air, smoke, breath, etc., in puffs; **2,** to breathe quickly and hard, as a runner; **3,** to swell with air; **4,** to swell with importance:—*v.t.* **1,** to emit or blow out, with whiffs or little blasts; **2,** to cause to swell, as with wind, or, figuratively, with importance; as, to *puff* out the cheeks; **3,** to praise in too high terms; as, to *puff* a book; **4,** to arrange in puffs, as the hair, dress material, etc.—*adj.* **puf′fy.**

puf-fin (puf′in), *n.* a North Atlantic sea bird, about 30 centimetres long, black above and white below, with short neck and bright-coloured, grooved beak.

puff-y (puf′i), *adj.* [puff-i-er, puff-i-est], **1,**

swollen; bloated; as, infection made his hand *puffy*; **2,** breathing hard; puffing; as, a *puffy* old man; **3,** blowing in little gusts; as, a *puffy* wind.

pug (pug), *n.* **1,** a small stocky dog with short, broad nose, wrinkled face, and tightly curled tail; **2,** a turned-up nose, reminiscent of the dog's; a *pug* nose; **3,** *Colloq.* a boxer.

pu-gi-list (pū′ji-list), *n.* a prize fighter; a boxer.—*adj.* **pu′gil-is′tic.**—*n.* **pu′gil-ism.**

pug-na-cious (pug-nā′shus), *adj.* desiring to fight; quarrelsome.

puke (pūk), *v.i.* and *v.t. Colloq.* to vomit:—*n.* **1,** the act of throwing up; **2,** *Slang* someone who is contemptible.

pul-chri-tude (pul′kri-tūd′), *n.* great physical beauty.

pull (pool), *v.t.* **1,** to draw out or toward one by exerting force; as, to *pull* a nail; *pull* a tooth; **2,** to draw in any direction; drag; haul; as, she *pulled* her wagon behind her; **3,** to pluck up by the roots; as, to *pull* weeds; **4,** to rend or tear; as, to *pull* down the Berlin Wall; **5,** to work by stretching; as, to *pull* candy; **6,** to go or move to a certain place; as, to *pull* into the lot; **7,** to hurt or strain, esp. by stretching too hard; as, to *pull* a muscle; **8,** *Colloq.* to do something characteristic of; as, he *pulled* a Chrétien; **9,** in *sports*, to remove or take out, as, to *pull* the goalie or pitcher:—*v.i.* **1,** to draw forcibly; tug; **2,** *Colloq.* express sympathy; to root for; as, we are *pulling* for you:—**pull off,** *Colloq.* to succeed; as, she managed to *pull* it *off*:—*n.* **1,** the act of pulling; a tug; as, he gave my sleeve a *pull*; **2,** a hard climb; as, a long *pull* up the mountain; **3,** a handle or cord by which something is pulled; **4,** injury, esp. by stretching too hard; as, a groin *pull*; **5,** a contest; as, a tractor *pull*; **6,** *Slang* influence.

pull-down menu, in *computing*, the list that scrolls down and is displayed on the computer screen when an item on the menu toolbar is selected.

pul-ley (pool′i), *n.* [*pl.* pulleys], a tackle that consists of a wood or metal frame for a wheel with a grooved rim, into which fits a rope or chain, used for hauling, lifting, and pulling, or for changing the direction of a pull.

pul-mo-nar-y (pul′mo-nėr-i), *adj.* pertaining to the lungs; as, pneumonia is a *pulmonary* disease.

pulp (pulp), *n.* **1,** the soft fleshy part of fruit, plant stems, etc.; **2,** the inner fleshy part of a tooth; **3,** any soft, wet mass; as, wood *pulp*; **4,** cheaply published books or magazines containing sensational material, often poorly written; as, *pulp* fiction.—*adj.* **pulp′y.**

pul-pit (pool′pit), *n.* **1,** a raised platform or desk in a church, from which the sermon is delivered; **2,** the preaching profession.

pulp-wood (pulp′wood′), *n.* soft wood, as spruce, etc., used in making paper.

pul-sate (pul′sāt; pul-sāt′), *v.i.* [pulsat-ed, pulsat-ing], **1,** to throb; beat, as the heart; **2,** to quiver; vibrate with life or feeling; as, a voice *pulsates*.—*n.* **pul-sa′tion.**

pulse (puls), *n.* **1,** the throbbing or beating in an artery as the blood is pumped through, esp. as felt on the inside of the wrist, at the temple, or elsewhere on the human body; **2,** a stroke or beat occurring at regular intervals similar to this; as, the *pulse* of flashing lights; **3,** a general feeling or sentiment; as, the *pulse* of the nation:—*v.t.* [pulsed, puls-ing], to beat or throb, as an artery.

pul-ver-ize (pul′vėr-īz′), *v.t.* [pulverized, pulveriz-ing], to crush, grind, or beat into powder or dust; as, to *pulverize* sugar:—*v.i.* to become dust; as, even rocks *pulverize* in time.

pu-ma (pū′ma), *n.* a large tawny, North American wildcat. Also called *cougar*, *mountain lion*, and *panther*.

PUMA

pum-ice (pum′is), *n.* a hard, light porous volcanic rock, used for cleaning or polishing; also in powdered form.

pum-mel or **pom-mel** (pum′el), *v.t.* [pummelled, pummel-ling or pommelled, pommel-ling], to beat, esp. with the fists:—*n.* the act of beating with the fists.

¹pump (pump), *n.* a machine for raising or moving liquids or for compressing gases by means of pressure or suction; as, a gas *pump*:—*v.t.* **1,** to raise or draw, as water, by means of a pump; **2,** to remove water or gases from; as, to *pump* a boat dry; **3,** to draw out by artful questions; as, to *pump* a secret, or a friend; **4,** to force, as does a pump; as, the heart *pumps* blood to all parts of the body; **5,** to increase; as, to *pump* up the volume; **6,** to remove the contents; as, they *pumped* his stomach:—*v.i.* **1,** to work a pump; as, to *pump* faster; **2,** to work like a pump; as, your heart *pumps* too fast.—*n.* **pump′er.**

²pump (pump) *n.* a woman's shoe with no fastenings.

pump-kin (pump′kin; pum-kin; pung′kin), *n.* a vine or plant that bears large yellow or orange fruit, like squashes; also, the fruit, used esp. for pies, as feed for animals, and during Hallowe'en as an ornament.

pun (pun), *n.* a play on words; a form of jesting expression in which one word is used with two meanings, or two different words pronounced nearly alike are used close together, as in "*stand* by what you say or you will *stand* the penalty" and "rain falls, but it goes up again in dew time":—*v.i.* [punned, pun-ning], to make or utter a pun; as, he is always *punning*.

[1]**punch** (punch), *n.* **1,** a tool for making dents or holes; **2,** a machine tool for stamping and forming sheet metal articles; **3,** a blow or thrust, esp. with the closed fist:—*v.t.* **1,** to strike with the fist; **2,** to drive along; as, to *punch* cattle; **3,** to press down on the key or keys of (a machine); as, to *punch* a computer keyboard; **4,** to make (a hole) in; **5,** to cut or mark with a tool; **6,** to give emphasis to; as, to *punch* up a story:—*v.i.* **1,** to hit with the fist; as, to *punch* hard; **2,** to make a hole; as, this tool *punches* cleanly.

[2]**punch** (punch), *n.* a drink made of rum, whisky, or other liquor, with water, lemon juice, sugar, etc.; also, a drink made from fruit juices, sweetened and flavoured.

punch line, the final line or sentence of a joke that is essential to understand it.

punc-til-i-ous (pungk-til′i-us), *adj.* nice or precise in conduct; as, *punctilious* etiquette.—*n.* **punc-til′i-ous-ness.**

punc-tu-al (pungk′tū-al), crompt; arriving or appearing at the proper time.—*adv.* **punc′tu-al-ly.**—*n.* **punc′tu-al′i-ty.**

punc-tu-ate (pungk′tū-āt′), *v.t.* [punctuat-ed, punctuat-ing], **1,** to mark or set off the parts of, with a period, comma, semicolon, etc.; as, to *punctuate* a paragraph; **2,** to emphasize; as, he *punctuated* his remarks with gestures; **3,** to interrupt at intervals, or now and then; as, cheers *punctuated* the speaker's words.

punc-tu-a-tion (pungk′tū-ā′shun), *n.* in writing or printing, the marking, or setting off, of words, phrases, sentences, etc., by the use of certain special marks:—**punctuation marks** include the comma [,], semicolon [;], period [.], question mark [?], exclamation mark [!], dash [—], parentheses [( )], brackets [ ], and quotation marks ["..."].

punc-ture (pungk′tūr), *n.* a hole or wound made by something pointed; as, a *puncture* in a tube; also, deflation, as of a balloon:—*v.t.* [punctur-ed, punctur-ing], **1,** to make a hole in, or pierce, as with a pointed instrument; prick; as, the nail *punctured* our tire; **2,** to deflate; destroy; as, a sharp reproof may *puncture* pride.

pun-dit (pun′dit), *n.* **1,** a learned man; scholar (originally a Hindu); **2,** an authority, expert, or teacher, sometimes used ironically; as, political *pundits.*

pun-gent (pun′jent), *adj.* **1,** stinging; pricking; biting; as, a *pungent* acid; **2,** piercing; keen; as, *pungent* wit; **3,** sarcastic; caustic; as, *pungent* satire.—*adv.* **pun′gent-ly.**—*n.* **pun′gen-cy.**

pun-ish (pun′ish), *v.t.* **1,** to cause (a person) to pay the penalty for a crime or fault; as, to *punish* a criminal; **2,** to inflict the penalty for (something); as, to *punish* disobedience; **3,** to treat harshly or roughly.—*adj.* **pu′ni-tive; pun′ish-a-ble; pun′ish-ing.**

pun-ish-ment (pun′ish-ment), *n.* **1,** the act or fact of punishing; **2,** the way in which someone is punished; as, her *punishment* was a $100 fine; **3,** *Colloq.* rough treatment; as, toys built to take a lot of *punishment.*

Pun-ja-bi or **Pan-ja-bi** (pun-job′ē; pun-jab′ē), *n.* **1,** a person who inhabits or originates from the Punjab, the northwestern region of India and Pakistan; **2,** the language spoken by these people:—*adj.* relating to the region, the people, the language, or the culture of Punjab.

punk (pungk), *n.* **1,** partly decayed wood; tinder; **2,** a substance (made of decayed vegetable matter) used to light fireworks; **3,** a young person, esp. a criminal or hoodlum; **4,** a style of music; as, *punk* rock.

[1]**punt** (punt), *n.* a flatbottom boat.

[2]**punt** (punt) *v.t.* and *v.i.* to drop a football from the hands and kick it *before* it strikes the ground: in a dropkick, the ball is kicked *after* it rebounds from the ground:—*n.* such a kick.

pu-ny (pū′ni), *adj.* [pu-ni-er, pu-ni-est], **1,** undersized; weak; as, a *puny* baby; **2,** feeble; halfhearted; as, a *puny* effort.

pup (pup), *n.* **1,** a young dog; a puppy; **2,** the young of several other mammals, as of the seal; **3,** *Colloq.* an inexperienced young person; as, a mere *pup.*

pu-pa (pū′pa), *n.* [*pl.* pupae (pū′pē) or pupas], the stage in the life of an insect when it is in a cocoon or case: the pupa is the stage between the caterpillar and the butterfly.—*adj.* **pu′pal.**—*v.i.* **pu′pate** (to become a pupa, chrysalis, or cocoon).

[1]**pu-pil** (pū′pl; pū′pil), *n.* a young person under the care and instruction of a teacher.

[2]**pu-pil** (pū′pl; pū′pil), *n.* the dark centre in the iris of the eye, through which rays of light pass to the retina.

pup-pet (pup′it), *n.* **1,** a small doll or figure, esp. one moved by wires from behind a screen in a mock drama, called a *puppet show*; a marionette; **2,** a person or group that is completely under the control of another; as, the king was the *puppet* of his ministers:—*adj.* controlled (by another) as, a *puppet* state.

pup-py (pup′i), *n.* [*pl.* puppies], **1,** a young dog; **2,** an inexperienced or naive young person.

pur-chase (pûr′chis), *v.t.* [purchased, purchas-ing], to get by paying money; buy; as, to *purchase* a new computer:—*n.* **1,** the act or process of buying; as, the *purchase* of a new laptop; **2,** the thing bought; as, he examined his *purchase*; **3,** a firm hold or grasp to help one to move something or to keep oneself from slipping; as, to take a *purchase* on a rock with a crowbar.—*n.* **pur′chas-er.**

pure (pûr), *adj.* [pur-er, pur-est], **1,** free from

any foreign matter that might lower its quality; clear; clean; as, *pure* spring water; **2,** free from evil or fault; innocent; as, she has a *pure* conscience; **3,** sheer; mere; nothing but; as, *pure* foolishness.—*n.* **pure′ness; pur′ist.**—*adv.* **pure′ly.**

pu-rée (pū-rā′), *n.* a thick paste, made of meat, beans, etc., boiled and strained through a sieve; also, food processed in a blender:—*v.t.* [pu-reéd, pu-rée-ing], to make such a paste.

pure-ly (pūr′li), *adv.* entirely; merely; as, I have a *purely* unselfish interest in it.

pur-ga-tive (pûr′ga-tiv), *adj.* having the power of cleansing:—*n.* a medicine for the purpose of cleansing the system of waste and impurities; a cathartic or physic.—*n.* **pur-ga′tion.**

pur-ga-to-ry (pûr′ga-to-ri), *n.* **1,** in Roman Catholic theology, a place or state in which those who die in the grace of God are cleansed by suffering; **2,** any place of temporary torment or misery.

purge (pûrj), *v.t.* [purged, purg-ing], **1,** to cleanse or free from impurities; **2,** to clear of guilt; free from sin; as, to *purge* one's mind of evil thoughts; **3,** to cause the evacuation of the bowels or stomach; **4,** to remove or rid an organization of someone or something seen as undesirable; as, to *purge* the party:—*n.* **1,** the act or process of cleansing or freeing from impurities; **2,** a purgative; **3,** the elimination of undesirables; as, a political *purge*.

pu-ri-fy (pū′ri-fī′), *v.t.* [purified, purifying], **1,** to make clean; to free from impurities; as, use a filter to *purify* the water; **2,** to make ceremonially clean, as by baptism.—*n.* **pu′ri-fi-ca′tion.**

pu-ri-tan (pū′ri-tan), *n.* **1,** one who is very strict in his or her religious life or attitude toward worldly pleasures; **2,** sometimes, one who is bigoted and narrow-minded:—**Puritan,** a member of a group in the 1500s and 1600s who wanted to "purify" the Church of England by making its services simpler and by living strictly according to the teachings of the Bible.—*adj.* **pu′ri-tan′i-cal.**

pu-ri-ty (pū′ri-ti), *n.* **1,** freedom from impurities; as, *purity* of spring water; **2,** virtue; innocence; freedom from evil; as, *purity* of thought; **3,** accuracy; refined elegance; as, *purity* of style.

[1]**purl** (pûrl), *v.t.* and *v.i.* **1,** to edge with a chain of loops, as in knitting; **2,** to invert stitches for a ribbed effect.

[2]**purl** (pûrl), *v.i.* to flow with a gentle murmur, as a stream; to swirl, as an eddy.

pur-loin (pûr-loin′), *v.t.* and *v.i.* to steal; pilfer; filch; as, he *purloined* the key to the car.

pur-ple (pûr′pl), *n.* **1,** a colour resulting from a mixture of red and blue; formerly, a deep crimson; **2,** a robe of this colour formerly worn by royalty; **3,** royal power or dignity; **4,** great wealth or high rank; as, born to the *purple*:—*adj.* of the colour of blended blue and red.—*adj.* **pur′plish.**

pur-port (pûr′pōrt), *n.* meaning; sense; substance; as, the *purport* of his reply was that he would do what we wished:—*v.t.* (pûr-pōrt′; pûr′pōrt), to profess; as, the book *purported* to be a real account of the author's experiences in the jungle.

pur-pose (pûr′pus), *n.* **1,** settled intention; design; aim; as, her *purpose* in consenting was merely to help her friends; **2,** end; result; as, he saved his money, but to little *purpose*, because his children spent it foolishly:—*v.t.* [purposed, purpos-ing], to intend; resolve; as, I *purpose* to go on with my studies.— *adj.* **pur′pose-ful.**

pur-pose-ly (pûr′pus-li), *adv.* intentionally; deliberately; on purpose; as, he hit me *purposely*.

purr (pûr), *n.* a low murmuring sound, as made by a cat when it is comfortable or contented:—*v.i.* [purred, purr-ing], to make such a sound; as, the car *purred* on my lap.

purse (pûrs), *n.* **1,** a small bag or pouch for money and other items; a handbag or pocketbook; **2,** a sum of money given as a prize or gift; as, the winner of the race claimed a *purse* of $10,000; **3,** money; treasury; as, the public *purse*:—*v.t.* [pursed, purs-ing], to pucker or wrinkle as, to *purse* the lips.

purs-er (pûr′sėr), *n.* on an airplane or ship, the officer who has charge of the accounts.

pur-sue (pėr-sū′), *v.t.* [pursued, pursu-ing], **1,** to follow with the aim of overtaking; chase; as, to *pursue* a thief; **2,** to seek; engage in; as, to *pursue* pleasure; **3,** to go on with; continue; as, to *pursue* an inquiry; **4,** to follow; engage in (studies, a profession, etc.).—*n.* **pur-su′er; pur-su′ance** (in *pursuance* of).—*adj.* **pur-su′ant** (to).

pur-suit (pėr-sūt′), *n.* **1,** the act of following or seeking; chase; as, the *pursuit* of game; **2,** occupation; employment; as, scientific or mercantile *pursuits*.

pus (pus), *n.* the yellowish-white substance produced by infection in sores, abscesses, etc.—*adj.* **pus′sy.**

push (poosh), *v.t.* **1,** to press against with force, for the purpose of moving; as, to *push* the door; **2,** to urge forward or extend by effort; as, to *push* one's interests; **3,** to demand urgently; press; urge; as, to *push* a debtor; **4,** *Colloq.* to sell, esp. illegal drugs; as, they *push* drugs; **5,** *Colloq.* to near or approach; as, she's *pushing* 40:—*v.i.* **1,** to make a steady forward effort; as, the army *pushed* on; **2,** to press hard in order to move:—*n.* **1,** a thrust; force applied; a shove; **2,** *Colloq.* enterprise; energy; as, I admire his *push*.—*n.* **push′er.**

push-up (poosh′up), *n.* an exercise done

by lying face down, then raising and lowering the body by straightening and bending the arms.

puss-y (poos′i), *n. Colloq.* [*pl.* pussies], a cat.

pussy willow, a dwarf willow that bears furry buds along its branches.

pus-tule (pus′tūl), *n.* a small, inflamed swelling on the skin, as a pimple or blister full of pus.

put (poot), *v.t.* [put, put-ting], **1,** to move so as to place (something) in some position; to place; set; as, *put* on your hat; **2,** to cause to be in a certain condition; as, to *put* things in order; *put* one's parents to shame; **3,** to state; propose; as, to *put* a question; **4,** to assign; set a value on (a thing); as, *put* a price on the desk; **5,** to express; as, to *put* a thought into words; **6,** to apply; set; as, he *put* himself to the task; **7,** to throw or hurl with an upward and forward motion of the arm; as, to *put* a shot; **8,** to force or urge; as, to *put* a horse through its paces:—*v.i.* to go; proceed; as, to *put* out to sea.—*adv.* remain in place; as, stay *put.*

pu-tre-fy (pū′tri-fī′), *v.t.* [putrefied, putrefy-ing], to rot; corrupt:—*v.i.* to decay or become rotten.—*n.* **pu′tre-fac′tion; pu-tres′cence.**—*adj.* **pu-tres′cent.**

pu-trid (pū′trid), *adj.* **1,** corrupt; rotten; **2,** foul.—*n.* **pu′trid-ness; pu-trid′i-ty.**

putt (put), *n.* in *golf,* a short, careful stroke to play the ball into a hole:—*v.t.* and *v.i.* to drive (a golf ball) into a hole.

put-tee (put′i), *n.* **1,** a strip of cloth wrapped spirally from ankle to knee, esp. by soldiers, sportsmen, etc.; **2,** a stiff, heavy leather legging.

[1]**put-ter** (put′ėr), *n.* in *golf,* a short club used for playing the ball into a hole.

[2]**put-ter** (put′ėr), *v.i.* to tinker or work aimlessly, lazily, or with little purpose; as, to *putter* around the house; *putter* around at gardening.

put-ty (put′i), *n.* a cement of whiting and linseed oil used for filling cracks, holding panes in window sashes, etc.:—*v.t.* [puttied, putty-ing], to fill, as a crack or a hole, with such cement.

puz-zle (puz′l), *n.* **1,** something that perplexes, confuses, or bewilders; **2,** a toy or problem made to tax one's skill or ingenuity; **3,** a problem; riddle:—*v.i.* [puz-zled, puz-zling], to be perplexed; as, to *puzzle* over a mystery:—*v.t.* **1,** to perplex; entangle; **2,** to solve by clever thinking; as, to *puzzle* out a riddle.—*n.* **puz′zler.**

Pyg-my or **Pig-my** (pig′mi), *n.* [*pl.* Pygmies or Pigmies], one of several short peoples (under 150 centimetres) of southwest Africa:—**pygmy,** any very small person or thing; a dwarf; also, anything that is smaller than average:—*adj.* dwarflike; very small; as, a *pygmy* chimpanzee.

py-ja-ma or **pa-ja-ma** (pi-jä′ma), *n.* a sleeping garment consisting of jacket and trousers.

py-lon (pī′lon), *n.* a slender tower or shaft flanking a gateway or marking a course for air flights: the Canadian war memorial on Vimy Ridge has two beautiful *pylons* rising from its base.

pyr-a-mid (pir′a-mid), *n.* **1,** in *geometry,* a solid body standing on a triangular, square, or polygonal base, with triangular sides that meet in a point at the apex or top; **2,** anything having the shape of a pyramid:—**The Pyramids,** a group of Egyptian monuments built by the early kings to serve as their tombs:—*v.t.* and *v.i.* to build in the form of a pyramid; to pile up.—*adj.* **py-ram′i-dal** (pi-ram′i-dal).

PYRAMIDS

pyre (pīr), *n.* a pile of wood for burning a corpse; a funeral pile.

py-rite (pī′rīt), *n.* iron disulfide (FeS_2), a bright, brass-yellow mineral used in making sulphuric acid.

py-ro- (pī′rō-), *prefix* meaning *fire* or *heat;* as in *pyro*maniac (one with a mania for setting fires), *pyro*technics (display of fireworks).

py-thon (pī′thun; pī′thon), *n.* a large, nonpoisonous Old World serpent that crushes its prey.

Q

Q, q (kū), *n.* [*pl.* Q's, q's], the 17th letter of the alphabet, following P.

[1]**quack** (kwak), *n.* the cry of a duck, or a harsh sound like it:—*v.i.* to utter a quack.

[2]**quack** (kwak), *n.* **1,** an unskilled person who claims to have skill in medicine; **2,** one who pretends to have knowledge that he or she does not really possess:—*adj.* making false claims; not genuine.—*n.* **quack′er-y.**

quad (kwod; kwôd), *n. Colloq.* **1,** quadrangle; **2,** quadruped; **3,** quadruplet; **4,** quadruple; **5,** quadrilateral; **6,** quadrant; **7,** quadriplegic; **8,** *Slang* quadriceps.

quad-ran-gle (kwod′ran′gl; kwôd′-; kwod-rang′gl; kwôd-), *n.* **1,** in *geometry,* a plane figure with four angles and four sides; **2,** a four-sided court or space, surrounded by buildings, as on a college or university campus; **3,** the buildings surrounding such a space.—*adj.* **quad-ran′gu-lar.**

quad-rant (kwod′rant; kwôd′-), *n.* **1,** one quarter of the circumference of a circle, an arc of 90 degrees; **2,** the area bounded by such an arc and the lines from its ends to the centre of the circle; **3,** an instrument used in surveying, astronomy, etc., to measure altitude.

quad-ri- or **quad-ru-** or **quadr-** (kwod′ri; kwôd′ri or kwod′roo; kwôd′roo or kwodr; kwôdr), *prefix* meaning *four* or *square*; as in *quadr*angle, *quadr*ant, *quadri*lateral, *quadru*ped.

quad-ri-ceps (kwod′ri-seps′; kwôd′ri-seps′), *n.* the large extensor muscle on the front of the thigh.

quad-ri-lat-er-al (kwod′ri-lat′ėr-al; kwôd′-), *n.* a plane figure bounded by four straight lines and having four angles, as a parallelogram, square, rectangle, and trapezoid:—*adj.* having four sides.

quad-ri-ple-gic (kwod′ri-plē′jik; kwôd′ri-plē′jik), *n.* and *adj.* one, or pertaining to one, who is paralyzed from the neck down, in all four limbs.

quad-ru-ped (kwod′-roo-ped; kwôd′-) *n.* a four-footed animal, such as a cat, dog, or bear:—*adj.* having four feet; as, a horse is a *quadruped* animal.

quad-ru-ple (kwod′roo-pl; kwôd′-; kwod-ro͞o′pl; kwôd-), *adj.* fourfold; composed of, or including, four parts:—*n.* (kwod′roo-pl; kwôd′-), **1,** a sum or quantity four times as great as another; **2,** in *skating*, a four-revolution jump:—*v.t.* (kwod-ro͞o′pl; kwôd-; kwod′roo-pl; kwôd′-), [quadru-pled, quadru-pling], to multiply by four:—*v.i.* to increase fourfold.—*n.*, *v.*, and *adj.* **quad-ru′pli-cate′.**

quad-ru-plet (kwod-ru′plet; kwôd-ru′plet; kwod-ro͞o′plet; kwôd-ro͞o′plet; kwod′ru-plet; kwôd′-) *n.* **1,** a combination of four of one kind; one of a group of four; **2,** one of four children born at one birth.

quaff (kwåf), *v.t.* to drink in deep drafts:—*v.i.* to drink deeply.

quag (kwag), *n.* soft, miry ground; quagmire.—*adj.* **quag′gy.**

quag-mire (kwag′mīr′), *n.* **1,** wet, boggy ground that yields under the feet; **2,** a perplexing situation, as of sinking into a morass of troubles.

[1]**quail** (kwāl), *n.* [*pl.* quail or quails], any of several small birds with a plump body, short tail, and brownish feathers, often hunted as game: often called *partridge*, *pheasant*, and *ruffed grouse*.

[2]**quail** (kwāl), *v.i.* to shrink from pain or danger; lose heart; cower.

quaint (kwānt), *adj.* pleasingly odd or interesting in appearance or manner, esp. attractive because of an old-fashioned daintiness or prettiness; as, a *quaint* little dollhouse.—*n.* **quaint′ness.**

quake (kwāk), *v.i.* [quaked, quak-ing], **1,** to shake from internal shock or convulsion; as, the earth *quakes*; **2,** to tremble or shake with fear, cold, etc.; quiver:—*n.* a shaking or trembling, esp. an earthquake.

qual-i-fi-ca-tion (kwol′i-fi-kā′shun; kwôl′-), *n.* **1,** the act of making, or the state of being, fit or qualified; **2,** that which makes a person or thing fit for a special task, position, etc.; fitness; **3,** that which limits; a restriction; as, he told the story with the *qualification* that it be kept secret for a week.

qual-i-fied (kwol′i-fīd′; kwôl′-), *adj.* **1,** fitted; adapted; as, she is well *qualified* for the task; **2,** limited; as, *qualified* praise.

qual-i-fy (kwol′i-fī′; kwôl′-), *v.t.* [qualified, qualify-ing], **1,** to make fit for any office, occupation, sport, etc.; as, his work *qualified* him to compete for the prize; **2,** to alter slightly; change; limit; as, to *qualify* a statement; **3,** to moderate; lessen; soften; as, to *qualify* a rebuke; **4,** to give legal authorization to; as, the province has *qualified* her to practise medicine; **5,** in *grammar*, to limit the meaning of (a word); as, adverbs *qualify* verbs, adjectives, or other adverbs:—*v.i.* to be or become competent or fit for any office or employment; as, she *qualified* for the information technology position.—*n.* **qual′i-fi′er.**

qual-i-ty (kwol′i-ti; kwôl′-), *n.* [*pl.* qualities], **1,** that which distinguishes one person or thing from another; **2,** the essential nature of a person or thing; a characteristic; as, elasticity is a *quality* of rubber; she has many wonderful *qualities*, such as friendliness, confidence, and intelligence; **3,** degree of excellence; as, a fine *quality* of wool; **4,** the amount of worth or value of something; as, the *quality* of a good education.—*adj.* **qual′i-ta′tive** (as, a *qualitative* analysis).

qualm (kwäm; kwôm), *n.* **1,** a feeling of illness or faintness that lasts only a moment; **2,** a sudden fear; **3,** uneasiness of conscience.—*adj.* **qualm′ish.**

quan-da-ry (kwon′de-ri; kwon′dri), *n.* [*pl.* quandaries], a state of hesitation or doubt; uncertainty.

quan-ti-ty (kwon′ti-ti; kwôn′-), *n.* [*pl.* quantities], **1,** amount; bulk; as, this bag contains one bushel in *quantity*; **2,** any uncertain, usually considerable, amount; as, to buy cat food in *quantity*; **3,** the relative time occupied in uttering a sound or syllable; **4,** in *mathematics*, anything that can be increased, divided, or measured.—*adj.* **quan′ti-ta′tive** (as, a *quantitative* analysis).

quan-tum (kwän′tum), *n.* [*pl.* quanta], **1,**

in *physics*, the quantum theory holds that the energy of the electrons is discharged in specific, or discrete, amounts (or quanta); **2,** an amount; **3,** anything that can be measured or counted. Also, **quan′tum jump′; quan′tum leap′.**

quar-an-tine (kwor′an-tēn′; kwôr′-), *n.* **1,** the time during which an incoming vehicle, person, or object is detained and inspected for contagious diseases; **2,** the means taken to enforce this inspection; **3,** the place of detention; **4,** any enforced restriction placed on a person, thing, or place because of contagious disease; isolation:—*v.t.* (kwor′an-tēn′; kwôr′-; kwor′an-tēn′; kwôr′-), [quarantined, quarantining], to keep (a person or thing) away from others; isolate.

quark (kwork; kwôrk), *n.* **1,** in *physics*, any of the six elemental particles that carry a small electric charge: the basis for all matter; **2,** a soft, low-fat, European cheese.

quar-rel (kwor′el; kwôr′-), *n.* **1,** an angry dispute; a petty fight; argument; **2,** a cause for dispute; as, he has no *quarrel* with us; **3,** a disagreement or falling out; a breach of friendship:—*v.t.* [quarrelled, quarrel-ling], **1,** to dispute violently; fight; **2,** to disagree; fall out; argue; **3,** to find fault; as, to *quarrel* with a decision.—*adj.* **quar′rel-some.**

[1]**quar-ry** (kwor′i; kwôr′i), *n.* [*pl.* quarries], **1,** an open excavation or hole from which stone is obtained by cutting or blasting; **2,** a plentiful source:—*v.t.* [quarried, quarrying], to dig or take from, or as from, an excavation or hole; extract.

[2]**quar-ry** (kwor′i; kwôr′i), *n.* [*pl.* quarries], **1,** an animal that is hunted; prey; game; as, a lion's *quarry*; **2,** anyone or anything that is chased or pursued.

quart (kwôrt), *n.* **1,** a unit of measure for liquids in the imperial system, equal to about 1.14 litres; **2,** a vessel containing a quart, or its contents.

quar-ter (kwôr′tėr), *n.* **1,** one of the four equal parts into which a thing may be, or is, divided; **2,** three months or a fourth of one year; **3,** one half of a semester at school, university, or college; **4,** a fourth of a dollar, or 25 cents; also, a coin of this value; **5,** one of the four cardinal points of the compass; any part or division of the earth; as, humans came from all *quarters*; **6,** a particular place or district; as, the Latin *Quarter* in Paris; **7,** one of the four limbs of an animal with the parts near it; as, a *quarter* of beef; **8,** the aspect or phase of the moon when halfway between new and full; **9,** in *sports*, one of four equal divisions or periods in a game such as football, basketball, etc.; **10,** a time of 15 minutes, equal to one fourth of an hour; as, a *quarter* to nine:—**quarters,** lodgings; a place to live or stay:—*adj.* consisting of, or equal to, a fourth part of something; as, a *quarter* hour:—*v.t.* **1,** to divide into fourths, or quarters; **2,** to furnish with food and lodging; as, to *quarter* soldiers in a town.

quar-ter-back (kwôr′tėr-bak′), *n.* in *football*, a player just behind the line of scrimmage, who calls the signals and conducts the field strategy in the huddles.

quar-ter-ly (kwôt′tėr-li), *n.* [*pl.* quarterlies], a publication issued once every three months:—*adj.* **1,** consisting of, or containing, a fourth part; **2,** coming, or falling due, once every three months:—*adv.* once in each quarter.

quartet or **quar-tette** (kwôr-tet′), *n.* **1,** a musical composition for four voices or instruments; **2,** the four performers of such a composition; as, a barbershop *quartet*; **3,** anything made up of four.

quartz (kwôrts), *n.* a very common, colourless or coloured, hard mineral, found in masses or in brilliant crystals, and used in watches, clocks, and radio and television transmitters: many semi-precious stones, such as agates, amethysts, onyx, and jasper, are forms of quartz.

qua-sar (kwā′zär′′ kwā′zėr′), *n.* an immense, starlike object that sends out powerful radio waves and very bright light: quasars are located at very great distances from the earth, and therefore their properties are uncertain.

quash (kwosh), *v.t.* **1,** to crush, as a rebellion; **2,** to stop, as a lawsuit; to set aside (by a judge), as an indictment (owing to an irregularity).

qua-si (kwa′zi; kwa′si; kwā′zī; kwā′sī), *adj.* similar, resembling; as, a *quasi* win; a *quasi* office.

qua-si- (kwa′zi-; kwa′si-; kwā′zī-; kwā′sī-), *prefix* meaning *as it were, as if, virtually, seemingly, pseudo, to some degree*; as, *quasi*-historical, *quasi*-technical.

qua-ver (kwā′vr), *n.* **1,** a shaking or trembling, as of the voice; **2,** a trill in singing or playing; **3,** in *music*, an eighth note:—*v.i.* to quiver; vibrate:—*v.t.* to utter or sing with trills.

quay (kē; kā), *n.* a permanent wharf, often of stone, where ships may load or unload.

quea-sy or **quea-zy** (kwē′zi), *adj.* [quea-si-er, quea-si-est; quea-zi-er, quea-zi-est], **1,** nauseated; easily upset; as, a *queasy* stomach; **2,** causing nausea; **3,** squeamish; overscrupulous; as, a *queasy* conscience; **4,** causing squeamishness.—*n.* **quea′si-ness.**

queen (kwēn), *n.* **1,** a woman who rules a country as the head of a royal family; **2,** the wife or widow of a king; **3,** a woman who is a leader in a certain sphere or situation; as, a *queen* of the battlefield; **4,** a female bee, ant, etc., usually the only one in the group able to lay eggs; **5,** a playing card bearing a conventional drawing of a queen; **6,** in *chess*, the piece ranking next to the king; **7,** the best or chief of her kind; as, a *queen* of industry.—*adj.* **queen′ly.**—*n.* **queen′li-ness.**

queen-size or **queen-sized** (kwēn′-sīz′; kwēn′-sīzd′), *adj.* **1,** larger than usual or standard; as, *queen-size* pantyhose; **2,** a bed that is smaller than a king-size but larger than a double, measuring about 153 by 208 centimetres; **3,** for or of this type of bed; as, *queen-size* sheets.

queer (kwēr), *adj.* **1,** differing from the ordinary or normal; droll; strange; **2,** giddy; faint; sick; as, a *queer* feeling; **3,** *Colloq.* questionable or shady, as of character; **4,** *Slang* pertaining to a homosexual:—*n. Slang* a homosexual, often considered offensive:—*v.t. Slang* **1,** to spoil; upset; to interfere with; as, to *queer* one's chances for a job; **2,** to place in an embarrassing situation; as, he *queered* himself at the party.—*n.* **queer′ness.**

quell (kwel), *v.t.* **1,** to suppress or subdue; put an end to; as, to *quell* a riot; **2,** to pacify.

quench (kwench), *v.t.* **1,** to put out; extinguish; as, to *quench* a fire; **2,** to suppress; stifle; as, to *quench* a desire for revenge; **3,** to relieve; slake; as, to *quench* thirst.—*adj.* **quench′a-ble; quench′less.**

quer-u-lous (kwer′ū-lus; kwer′oo-lus) *adj.* **1,** complaining; fretful; as, a *querulous* old man; **2,** whining; grumbling; as, a *querulous* voice.

que-ry (kwē′ri), *n.* [*pl.* queries], **1,** a question; an inquiry; **2,** a question mark [?]:—*v.t.* [queried, query-ing], **1,** to inquire into; ask; **2,** to express a doubt in regard to; as, to *query* his loyalty:—*v.i.* to ask questions.

quest (kwest), *n.* **1,** a search; as, an animal in *quest* of food; **2,** in medieval romance, an expedition, usually by a knight, for a particular object; as, the *quest* for the Holy Grail:—*v.i.* to search; seek.

ques-tion (kwes′chun), *n.* **1,** the act of asking or inquiring; **2,** that which is asked; **3,** the subject under discussion or to be decided upon; issue; as, the *question* before the meeting; **4,** dispute, doubt, or objection; as, beyond *question*, these are the facts:—**question mark,** an interrogation point; a mark [?] of punctuation in writing or printing put at the end of a question:—*v.t.* **1,** to ask; examine by queries; **2,** to consider doubtful; **3,** to challenge; take exception to; as, I *question* that statement:—*v.i.* to make inquiries.—*n.* **ques′tion-er.**—*adv.* **ques′tion-ing-ly.**

ques-tion-a-ble (kwes′chun-a-bl), *adj.* **1,** open to question or doubt; **2,** arousing suspicion; as, a *questionable* character; a *questionable* answer.

ques-tion-naire (kwes′chun-âr′), *n.* a list of questions submitted to a number of persons, whose replies serve as the basis of a report on a subject.

queue (kū), *n.* **1,** a braid of hair hanging down the back; a pigtail; **2,** a line of people, automobiles, etc., awaiting their turn to proceed; **3,** in *computing*, a number of stored items of data, programs, commands, or jobs to be performed or processed in a certain order; as, a printing *queue*:—*v.i.* [queued, queu-ing], **1,** to line up; as, we *queued* up for the new movie; **2,** in *computing*, to arrange data, jobs, etc., in a queue.

quib-ble (kwib′l), *n.* a skillful evasion of the point in question by advancing a trifling argument or by using words with a double meaning; avoidance of dealing with the main point or problem:—*v.i.* [quib-bled, quib-bling], to avoid the truth or main point by a skillful but trifling objection.—*n.* **quib′bler.**

quiche (kēsh), *n.* a pastry shell filled with ingredients such as eggs, milk, cheese, vegetables, meat, etc., and baked in an oven.

quick (kwik), *adj.* **1,** rapid; swift; as, *quick* in action; **2,** nimble; as, *quick* on one's feet; **3,** prompt to respond to impressions; alert; as, a *quick* mind; **4,** accurate; unhesitating; ready; as, a *quick* eye; *quick* wit; **5,** easily excited; hasty; as, a *quick* temper; **6,** sensitive; as, a *quick* ear; **7,** done or happening in a short time; brief; as, a *quick* glance at her notes:—*adv.* with haste; rapidly; fast:—*n.* **1,** living beings; as, the *quick* and the dead; **2,** the tender, sensitive skin under the fingernails; as, to cut the nails down to the *quick*; **3,** the seat of the feelings and emotions; as, she was hurt to the *quick*; **4,** the essence; as, the *quick* of the argument.—*adv.* **quick′ly.**—*n.* **quick′ness.**

quick-en (kwik′en), *v.i.* **1,** to come to life; become alive; **2,** to act or move more rapidly:—*v.t.* **1,** to increase the speed of; hasten; as, to *quicken* one's steps; **2,** to bring to life; **3,** to make keen; arouse; kindle.—*n.* **quick′en-er.**

quick-sand (kwik′sand′), *n.* **1,** a bed of wet, loose sand that allows any heavy object that comes upon it to sink; **2,** a precarious situation that is like quicksand.

qui-es-cent (kwī-es′ent), *adj.* calm; still; tranquil.—*n.* **qui-es′cence.**

qui-et (kwī′et), *adj.* **1,** without sound; silent; as, a *quiet* night; also, not loud; soft; as, a *quiet* moan; **2,** not moving; still; as, *quiet* hands; **3,** tranquil; peaceful; secluded; as, a *quiet* countryside; **4,** peaceable; gentle; as, a *quiet* disposition; **5,** informal; as, a *quiet* wedding; **6,** not showy; modest; as, *quiet* colours:—*v.t.* to make peaceful; as, to *quiet* a child:—*v.i.* to become still or calm; as, the wind has *quieted*:—*n.* **1,** freedom from motion, noise, or disturbance; **2,** gentleness or composure of manner; **3,** peace; rest.—*n.* **qui′e-tude; qui′et-ness.**—*adv.* **qui′et-ly.**—*v.t.* and *v.i.* **qui′et-en.**

quill (kwil), *n.* **1,** a large, strong bird's feather; also, the hollow shaft of a feather; **2,** a pen made from a feather, esp. in former times; **3,** a long, sharp spine, as of a porcupine.

QUILL

quilt (kwilt), *n.* a bed cover made by stitching together two layers of fabric, usually in an ornamental pattern, with a layer of soft material between; also, any warm bed cover:—*v.t.* to stitch and interline (layers of cloth) in the manner of a quilt:—*v.i.* to do quilting; make a quilt.—*n.* **quilt′ing.**

qui-nine (kwī-nēn′; kwī′nīn), *n.* a bitter, colourless drug obtained from the bark of the cinchona tree and used esp. in treating malaria.

quin-que- (kwin-kwe′-), *prefix* meaning *five*; as in *quinque*nnial.

quin-quen-ni-al (kwin-kwen′i-al), *adj.* and *n.* occurring every five years, or lasting five years.

quint (kwint), *n. Colloq.* quintuplet.

quin-tes-sence (kwin-tes′ens), *n.* the concentrated essence, or most perfect embodiment, of anything; as, the *quintessence* of vanity.—*adj.* **quin′tes-sen′tial.**—*adv.* **quin′tes-sen′tial-ly.**

quin-tet or **quin-tette** (kwin-tet′), *n.* **1,** a group of five persons or things; **2,** a musical composition for five voices or instruments.

quin-tu-plet (kwin′tū-plet), *n.* **1,** a combination of five of one kind; **2,** one of five children born at one birth.

quip (kwip), *n.* **1,** a clever, funny, or sarcastic remark; **2,** an evasion of a point by clever use of words; a quibble; **3,** something odd:—*v.i.* [quipped, quip-ping], to make such a remark.—*adj.* **quip′py.**

quire (kwīr), *n.* **1,** a pack of 24 or 25 uniform sheets of paper; **2,** a set of folded leaves of paper in a book or manuscript.

quirk (kwûrk), *n.* **1,** a sudden twist or turn, as of a pen in writing; **2,** a quick turn of fancy; a quip; **3,** a clever evasion of the truth in speaking; **4,** a strange or peculiar way of acting; idiosyncrasy; as, this printer has many *quirks*; sometimes it works, and sometimes it doesn't.

quit (kwit), *v.t.* [quit-ted or quit, quit-ting], **1,** to pay off (a debt); **2,** to stop; give up; as, to *quit* work; *quit* smoking; **3,** to go away from; as, to *quit* a neighbourhood; **4,** in *computing,* to end or clear (a job, program, etc.) from the memory of the computer:—*v.i.* **1,** to stop doing something; as, to *quit* at noon; **2,** to leave a job or position; resign; **3,** in *computing,* to exit:—*adj.* free; as, we're *quit* of that person.

quite (kwīt), *adv.* **1,** totally; completely; as, *quite* mistaken; **2,** to a considerable extent; rather; as, *quite* cold.

quit-ter (kwit′ėr), *n.* one who gives up too easily in the face of problems or difficulty.

[1]quiv-er (kwiv′ėr), *n.* a light case for carrying or holding arrows.

[2]quiv-er (kwiv′ėr), *n.* a trembling or shivering:—*v.i.* to shake or tremble, as from excitement.

quix-ot-ic (kwiks-ot′ik), *adj.* **1,** absurdly chivalrous, romantic, or idealistic: after Don Quixote; **2,** impulsive.

quiz (kwiz), *n.* [*pl.* quizzes], **1,** an absurd or puzzling question; **2,** an informal oral or written examination of a student or class; a short test:—*v.t.* [quizzed, quiz-zing], **1,** to examine informally; **2,** to question or interrogate; as, the police officer *quizzed* the suspect.

quiz-zi-cal (kwiz′i-kal), *adj.* **1,** comical; humorously serious; as, a *quizzical* look; **2,** questioning; puzzling; **3,** odd.

quor-um (kwôr′um), *n.* the number of members of a committee, etc., that the rules require to be present in order that business may legally be transacted; also, a special group.

quo-ta (kwō′ta), *n.* **1,** the part of a total that any individual or group is to contribute or receive; a share; as, each class paid its *quota* toward the school picnic; **2,** the amount or percentage of a certain type of thing or people that is allowed; maximum set amount; as, fishing *quotas* to prevent overfishing.

quot-a-ble (kwōt′a-bl), *adj.* suitable for quoting from, as an author, famous person, etc.

quo-ta-tion (kwō-tā′shun), *n.* **1,** the repeating of another's exact words; **2,** the words repeated; **3,** a passage from a book, etc.; **4,** the current market price of something, or a statement of this; as, a *quotation* on wheat:—**quotation mark,** a mark of punctuation placed at the beginning ["] and end ["] of a word or passage to show that it is quoted, or to set off the title of a newspaper, magazine article, story, poem, etc.: a quotation within a quotation is usually enclosed in single quotation marks [' ']; as, "the boy said, 'I am going home.'"

quote (kwōt), *v.t.* [quot-ed, quot-ing], **1,** to repeat (another's words, either written or spoken); as, I *quoted* your magazine article; **2,** to repeat a passage from; refer to as an authority; as, to *quote* Pierre Berton; **3,** to give the present price of:—*v.i.* to repeat the words of another; as, she *quoted* accurately:—*n.* **1,** in *printing,* a quotation mark; **2,** *Colloq.* a quotation.

quo-tient (kwō′shent), *n.* the result obtained when one number is divided by another; as, if 10 is divided by 5, the *quotient* is 2.

Qur-'an (ko-ran′; -rän′; kō-ran′; -rän′), *n.* Same as **Koran.**

R

R, r (är), *n.* [*pl.* R's, r's], the 18th letter of the alphabet, following Q:—**the three R's**, reading, 'riting, and 'rithmetic.

rab-bet (rab′it), *n.* **1,** a groove or slot cut out of the edge or face of a board, etc., so that another piece may be fitted into it to form a joint; **2,** a joint so made:—*v.t.* and *v.i.* to cut such a groove in.

rab-bi (rab′ī), *n.* [*pl.* rabbis (rab′īz)], in the Jewish religion, a teacher and interpreter of the law and ritual.—*adj.* **rab-bin′i-cal.**

rab-bit (rab′it), *n.* a small, short-tailed animal of the hare family that has soft fur, large front teeth, long ears, and a short tail.

rab-ble (rab′l), *n.* a noisy crowd or mob:—**the rabble**, the common people, esp. those of the lowest class:—**rabble-rouser**, a person who incites people, esp. to violence; a demagogue.

rab-id (rab′id), *adj.* **1,** furious; raging; **2,** extremely unreasonable; excessively zealous; as, a *rabid* reformer; **3,** infected with rabies; as, a *rabid* dog.

ra-bi-es (ra′bi-ēz; rā′bēz), *n.* an infectious and often fatal disease of the dog and other animals, esp. flesh-eating animals; hydrophobia: often transmitted to a person by the bite of an infected animal.

rac-coon or **ra-coon** (ra-kōōn′), *n.* a greyish-brown, tree-dwelling animal of North America, with a bushy, ringed tail.

[1]**race** (rās), *n.* **1,** a competitive contest of speed, as in running or swimming; as, a relay *race* or a bicycle *race*; **2,** any contest or rivalry; as, a political *race*; **3,** a swift current of water, or the channel for such a current; as, a mill *race*:—*v.i.* [raced, rac-ing], **1,** to run swiftly; as, to *race* a motor; **2,** to try to beat in a speed contest; as, I'll *race* you to the corner.—*n.* **rac-er** (rās′ėr).

[2]**race** (rās), *n.* **1,** the descendants of a common ancestor; a family; **2,** a people or group of peoples united by a common language, religion, or culture; as, the English *race*; **3,** a division of humans, made up of tribes descended from a common stock; as, the Negroid *race*; **4,** a class of persons with common interests and traits; as, the *race* of artists.—*adj.* **ra′cial** (rā′shal).

rac-ism (rās′izm), *n.* fear or dislike of a race other than one's own, or the doctrine that some races are inferior to others.—*n.* **rac′ist.**

[1]**rack** (rak), *n.* **1,** a framework on or in which articles are arranged, held, or displayed; as, a coat *rack*; a towel *rack*; **2,** a frame of bars above a manger for holding fodder; **3,** a set of antlers; **4,** a bar with teeth on one side that engage the teeth of a gear.

[2]**rack** (rak), *n.* **1,** in former times, an instrument for torturing the body by stretching and straining the limbs; **2,** intense physical or mental anguish:—*v.t.* **1,** to stretch, as on the rack; **2,** to subject to great pain or anguish: as, remorse *racked* him; **3,** to strain; exert to the utmost; as, to *rack* one's brain for a word.

[3]**rack** (rak), *n.* Same as **wrack.**

[1]**rack-et** (rak′it), *n.* **1,** a clattering noise; din; noisy talk or play; **2,** *Colloq.* a dishonest trick or scheme; esp., an organized activity of the criminal underworld, such as the extortion of money from merchants by threats of violence; *Slang* any business:—*v.i.* to make a loud and confused noise.

[2]**rack-et** or **rac-quet** (rak′it), *n.* a round or oval frame with tightly laced strings in a crisscross pattern and a handle at the end, used in tennis, badminton, etc.

rack-et-eer (rak′e-tēr′). *n.* a criminal who carries on illegal business, esp. by extorting money by threats.

ra-con-teur (ra′kōn•′tûr′), *n.* one skilled or clever at telling stories.

ra-coon (ra-kōōn′), *n.* Same as **raccoon.**

rac-y (rās′i), *adj.* **1,** full-flavoured; piquant; as, *racy* fruit; **2,** lively; spirited; as, a *racy* style; **3,** suggestive or risqué; something close to being improper; daring; as, a *racy* story.

ra-dar (rā′där), *n.* a device that sends out radio waves of ultra high frequency and locates a distant object, such as an airplane or ship, by the radio waves reflected from the object: acronym for *ra*dio *d*etecting *a*nd *r*anging.

ra-di-al (rā′di-al), *adj.* arranged like the spokes of a wheel.—*adv.* **ra′di-al-ly.**

ra-di-an (rā′di-an), *n.* an arc of a circle equal in length to the radius; also the angle at the centre measured by such an arc (about 57.3°).

ra-di-ant (rā′di-ant), *adj.* **1,** sending out rays of light or heat; as, the *radiant* sun; shining; brilliant; as, *radiant* beauty; **2,** beaming with joy, delight, etc.; as, a *radiant* face; **3,** coming out in rays from some source; as, the *radiant* energy of the sun:—**radiant energy**, energy issuing from any source, as electromagnetic waves, sound, heat, light, X-rays, gamma rays, etc.:—**radiant heating**, heating as by electric coils, steam, or hot-water pipes, etc., installed in floors or walls:—*adv.* **ra′di-ant-ly.**—*n.* **ra′di-ance.**

ra-di-ate (rā′di-āt′) *v.t.* [radiat-ed, radiat-ing], **1,** to send out in rays; as, a lamp *radiates* light; **2,** to spread abroad; as, to *radiate* happiness:—

v.i. **1,** to send forth beams; shine; glow; **2,** to come out in rays, as heat from a fire; **3,** to come out from a centre; as, the spokes of a wheel *radiate* from the hub.

ra-di-a-tion (rā′dē-ā′shun), *n.* **1,** light or other energy that radiates through the air; as, the sun's rays are a form of *radiation*; **2,** certain rays given off by radioactive material; as, *radiation* from a nuclear explosion is dangerous.

ra-di-a-tor (rā′di-ā′tėr), *n.* **1,** a set of pipes heated by hot water or steam, used sometimes for heating a room; **2,** an appliance used to cool a motor.

rad-i-cal (rad′i-k'l), *adj.* **1,** having to do with a root or origin; deep-seated; fundamental; as, a *radical* cure; **2,** advocating extreme change, esp. in politics; as, a *radical* speech:—*n.* **1,** (often **Radical**), a person who wishes to root out old customs and institutions, rather than to reform them; esp. in politics; an extremist; **2,** a root; a fundamental part or principle; **3,** a word or root from which other words are formed; **4,** in *chemistry*, a group of atoms (part of a molecule in a compound) that act as a single atom; as, the radical [OH]: also, *radicle*; **5,** in *mathematics*, a quantity considered as the root of another quantity: shown by use of the radical sign [√]; the sign itself.—*adv.* **rad′i-cal-ly.**

ra-di-o (rā′di-ō), *n.* [*pl.* radios], **1,** any message, music, etc., transmitted or received by means of electromagnetic waves without the use of wires between sender and receiver; also, this system of sending and receiving messages; **2,** equipment for transmitting messages in this way, esp. an instrument for receiving such messages:—*adj.* having to do with radio; as, *radio* supplies; a *radio* program:—**radio frequency**, vibrations too high to be heard by the human ear: over 10,000 cycles per second.—*v.t.* [radioed, radio-ing[, to send or receive messages in this way; as, the pilot *radioed* the control tower.

ra-di-o-ac-tive (rā′di-ō-ak′tiv), *adj.* giving off radiant energy in the form of particles or rays (alpha, gamma, etc.) by the breakdown of atomic nuclei of radium, thorium, uranium, etc.

ra-di-ol-o-gy (rā′di-ol′o-ji), *n.* the science of radiant energy and its uses, esp. in diagnosing and treating disease by X-rays.

rad-ish (rad′ish), *n.* **1,** a garden plant of the mustard family, with a pungent root; **2,** the root, which is eaten raw.

ra-di-um (rā′di-um), *n.* a rare white metal found in various minerals: its atoms break down into lead and other metals, giving off rays that are used in treating cancer, etc.

ra-di-us (rā′di-us), *n.* [*pl.* radii (rā′di-ī) or radiuses], **1,** a straight line from the centre of a circle to its circumference, or from the centre of a sphere to its surface; **2,** a circular area measured by a given radius; as, two schools within a *radius* of a kilometre; **3,** a bone in the forearm.

raf-fle (raf′l), *n.* a lottery in which people buy tickets for the chance of winning something:—*v.t.* [raffled, raf-fling], to dispose of by selling chances on; as, to *raffle* off a car.

raft (råft), *n.* a floating framework of logs or boards:—*v.t.* to convey on such a float.

Raft

raft-er (råf′tėr), *n.* a sloping beam that helps support the roof of a house.

rag (rag), *n.* **1,** a worn or torn piece of cloth; a shred; **2,** *Colloq.* a newspaper, magazine, or other publication, esp. one of inferior quality:—**rags,** tattered or worn-out clothes; as, the homeless children were dressed only in *rags*:—*v.t.* [ragged (ragd), rag-ging], **1,** *Colloq.* to play (music) with a catchy shifting of the beat; play in ragtime; **2,** *Slang* to tease; also, to scold; **3,** in *hockey*, to control the puck, esp. to kill time during a penalty; as, he *ragged* the puck for a long time.

rag-a-muf-fin (rag′a-muf′in), *n.* a ragged, dirty person, esp. a child.

rage (rāj), *n.* **1,** uncontrolled anger; as, he flew into a terrible *rage*; **2,** violence; fury; **3,** anything for the moment popular or fashionable; a fad; as, pointed shoes are the *rage* this spring:—*v.i.* [raged, rag-ing], **1,** to be furiously angry; **2,** to act or speak violently; **3,** to have furious force; as, the tornado *raged* through the countryside.

rag-ged (rag′id), *adj.* **1,** having holes or tears resulting from wear; torn; as, a *ragged* coat; **2,** clothed in tatters; as, a *ragged* child; **3,** rough; jagged; as, a *ragged* stone.

ra-gout (ra-goo͞′), *n.* a stew of meat and vegetables, which is highly seasoned.

rag-time (rag′tīm′), a dance music in fast, syncopated rhythm: of Black origin, it was a forerunner of jazz.

rag-weed (rag′wēd′), *n.* a coarse weed with small, yellowish-green flowers with pollen that often causes hayfever.

raid (rād), *n.* **1,** a hostile invasion; a sudden attack; as, an air *raid*; **2,** a forced entrance by police, to make arrests or seize stolen goods:—*v.t.* to conduct or make a raid on.

[1]**rail** (rāl), *n.* **1,** a bar of wood or metal placed level between two posts, as in a fence; **2,** a wooden or iron barrier to keep persons from falling; as, a hand*rail*; **3,** one of the two metal bars forming a track for trolley cars or trains; **4,** a railway; as, to travel by *rail*:—*v.t.* to enclose with bars; as, to *rail* in an exhibit.

[2]**rail** (rāl), *v.i.* to use bitter, scornful, or reproachful language; to rant or complain bitterly; as, to *rail* against the new rules.—*n.* and *adj.* **rail′ing.**

rail-ing (rāl′ing), *n.* **1,** material for rails; **2,**

a fence or barrier made of rails and held up by posts; as, a *railing* on a stairway.

rail-road (rāl′rōd′), *n.* in the U.S., a railway:—*v.t. Colloq.* to put through rapidly; as, to *railroad* a bill through a legislature.

rail-way (rāl′wā′), *n.* **1,** a path or track made of two metal rails on which a train runs; **2,** a system of transportation in which people and goods are moved along such tracks, including the trains, tracks, and stations, and the workers who operate the system.

rain (rān), *n.* **1,** water falling in drops condensed from moisture in the air; **2,** the fall of such drops; as, a heavy *rain*; **3,** a shower of anything, esp. a heavy, fast fall; as, a *rain* of angry words:—*v.i.* to fall in drops, or like rain; as, it *rained* all day:—*v.t.* to pour down like rain; as, to *rain* blows on someone.—*adj.* **rain′less; rain′y.** Also, **rain′drop′; rain′proof′; rain′storm′.**

rain-bow (rān′bō′), *n.* **1,** an arc or bow, containing the colours of the spectrum, formed in the sky opposite the sun by the reflection of the sun's rays from drops of falling rain, spray, or mist; **2,** something that resembles a rainbow with many colours; as, a *rainbow* trout.

rain-coat (rān′kōt), *n.* a coat made from waterproof material, used to keep a person dry when it rains.

rain-fall (rān′fôl′), *n.* **1,** the falling of rain; a shower; as, a heavy *rainfall* overnight; **2,** the amount of rain that falls during a definite period on any given area.

rain forest, a dense forest in an area that has high rainfall throughout the year.

rain-y (rā′ni), *adj.* [rain-i-er, rain-i-est], having a lot of rain; as, a *rainy* day.

raise (rāz), *v.t.* [raised, rais-ing], **1,** to set upright; lift up; **2,** to stir up; to rouse from sleep; **3,** to erect; construct; as, to *raise* a building; **4,** to cause to come into existence; as, to *raise* a smile; to *raise* trouble; **5,** to grow, breed, or take care of; as, he *raised* cattle; **6,** to procure; collect; muster; as, to *raise* money, armies, etc.; **7,** to bring up for consideration (a question, claim, etc.); **8,** to cause to increase in degree, amount, intensity, etc.; as, to *raise* prices, the voice, one's courage; **9,** to terminate; put an end to (a blockade); **10,** to cause (bread) to rise; **11,** to make higher in rank or power; as, to *raise* a prince to the throne; **12,** to rear; bring up (children); **13,** in *cards*, to increase a bet; as, I *raise* you five dollars:—*n.* **1,** an increase in salary or wages; **2,** in cards, an increased bet; as, a *raise* of five dollars; **3,** any increase in amount or value.

rai-sin (rā′zn), *n.* a sweet, dried grape that is eaten as a snack or used in cooking.

ra-jah or **ra-ja** (rä′ja), *n.* a Hindu king or prince; a *maharajah.*

[1]rake (rāk), *n.* a farm or garden tool with teeth at one end of a long handle, used for loosening or smoothing soil, or for gathering loose matter, such as dead leaves, hay, etc.:—*v.t.* [raked, rak-ing], **1,** to gather, smooth, or loosen with a rake; as, to *rake* the lawn; **2,** to gather by diligent effort; as, to *rake* up evidence; to *rake* a few dollars together; **3,** to search carefully; as, to *rake* the library for a special book; **4,** in military language, to direct gunfire along the length of; as, to *rake* the deck of a ship:—*v.i.* **1,** to work with a rake; **2,** to make a close search.

[2]rake (rāk), *n.* a slant or tilt; as, the *rake* of a hat; also, a slant from the perpendicular, as of a ship's mast or funnel:—*v.i.* and *v.t.* [raked, rak-ing], to slant, or cause to slant, as a mast.—*adj.* **rak′ish.**

[3]rake (rāk), *n.* a person of loose morals; a libertine.

ral-ly (ral′i), *v.t.* [rallied, rally-ing], **1,** to bring together and restore to order; as, she *rallied* the spectators to cheer louder; **2,** to call together for any purpose:—*v.i.* **1,** to return to order; **2,** to come together for action; be aroused to vigorous action; as, to *rally* round the flag; **3,** to recover strength; as, to *rally* from fever; **4,** in *tennis*, to send the ball rapidly back and forth over the net:—*n.* [*pl.* rallies], **1,** a restoring or recovery of order and discipline, as among defeated troops; **2,** a quick sharp rise after a dip; as, a *rally* in prices; **3,** a mass meeting, esp. one to show support for some person or cause; as, a protest *rally*; **4,** in *tennis*, the repeated return of the ball in play until one player misses.

ram (ram), *n.* **1,** a male sheep; **2,** in *war*, esp. in former times, a heavy pole for battering a wall; as, a battering *ram*:—*v.t.* [rammed, ramming], **1,** to strike or butt against; as, he *rammed* the table; **2,** to pack with sharp blows; as, to *ram* earth into a hole; **3,** to pack hastily; cram; as, she *rammed* her clothes into the bag.

RAM (ram), *abbrev.* short for *random-access memory.*

Ra-ma (rä′ma), *n.* a human form of the Hindu god Vishnu, who is known for his goodness and justice toward people.

Ram-a-dan (ram′a-don′; ram′a-don′), *n.* the ninth month of the Muslim year, during which the faithful practice daily fasting.

ramble (ram′bl), *v.i.* [ram-bled, ram-bling], **1,** to wander or rove aimlessly about; to stroll for pleasure; **2,** to talk or write at length and aimlessly; as, he *rambled* on and on; **3,** to grow or spread at random, as vines; as, the climbing roses *rambled* over the wall:—*n.* a leisurely, aimless stroll.—*n.* **ram′bler.**

ram-bling (ram′bling), *adj.* **1,** wandering at will; **2,** built on no single plan; growing or spreading at random; as, a *rambling* garden; **3,** loose and unorganized; as, a *rambling* tale.

ram-bunc-tious (ram-bungk′shus), *adj.* wild, boisterous, or unruly behaviour.

ram-i-fi-ca-tion (ram′i-fi-kā′shun), *n.* **1,** the act, manner, or arrangement of branching; **2,** a small branch or offshoot; as, a *ramification* of a tree or a nerve; **3,** a dividing or separating into branches; **4,** a division of anything complex; **5,** a consequence or result; as, the *ramification* of his act was severe:—*v.t.* and *v.i.* **ram′i-fy′** [ramified, ramify-ing], (to divide into parts or branches; to grow by such division).

ramp (ramp), *n.* a sloping roadway or inclined surface by which persons or vehicles may go from one level to another; as, a wheelchair *ramp.*

ram-page (ram-pāj′; ram′pāj), *n.* a fit of excitement or rage:—*v.i.* (rampāj′; ram′pāj), [rampaged, rampag-ing], to dash about in a wild rage:—*adj.* **ram-pa′geous.**

ramp-ant (ram′pant), *adj.* **1,** showing a fierce, high spirit; violent; as, the *rampant* foe; **2,** bold and unchecked; as, *rampant* crime; also, growing rankly, as weeds; **3,** reared on the hind legs, with one foreleg raised above the other, as a lion on a coat of arms.

ram-part (ram′pärt; ram′pėrt), *n.* **1,** an embankment or earthen wall, built around a fort for better defence; **2,** any protection against danger; **3,** the high, very steep banks along a river gorge.

ram-rod (ram′rod′), *n.* **1,** a rod used for ramming down the charge of a gun that loads through the muzzle; **2,** a harsh, demanding disciplinarian.

ram-shack-le (ram′shak-l), *adj.* **1,** loose; tumble-down; rickety; as, a *ramshackle* cottage; **2,** poorly constructed or designed; as, a *ramshackle* committee.

ran (ran), *p.t.* of *run.*

ranch (ranch), *n.* **1,** in western Canada and the U.S., a farm for the raising of cattle, horses, or sheep in large herds; **2,** a large farm for a special crop; as, a fruit *ranch*; **3,** the owners or workers on such a farm; as, the entire *ranch* went into town:—*v.i.* to manage, or work on, a ranch.—*n.* **ranch′er; ranch′man.**

ran-cid (ran′sid), *adj.* not fresh; having the rank, tainted smell or taste of spoiled fat.—*n.* **ran′cid-ness.**

ran-cour or **ran′cor** (rang′kėr), *n.* deep spite or malice; a bitter, cherished grudge.—*adj.* **ran′cor-ous.**

ran-dom (ran′dum), *adj.* done without aim or purpose; guided by chance; as, a *random* guess:—**at random,** without definite direction or aim; as, books picked *at random.*

random-access memory, in *computing,* the device or process that allows stored information to be quickly and easily accessed: abbreviated as *RAM.*

rang (rang), *p.t.* of *ring.*

range (rānj), *v.t.* [ranged, rang-ing], **1,** to set in a row or in regular order; as, to *range* cups on a shelf; also, to classify; as, to *range* books by subjects; **2,** to put (oneself) in a certain position with reference to others; as, he *ranged* himself with the conservatives; **3,** to wander over; as, cattle *range* the plains:—*v.i.* **1,** to wander; roam; as, he lets his fancy *range*; **2,** to vary within certain limits; as, the library's collection *ranges* from books to videos and CDs; **3,** to be found, or to occur, over a certain area; as, this plant *ranges* northward to the Yukon:—*n.* **1,** a line or row; series; chain, as of hills or mountains; as, the Rockies are a *range* of mountains; **2,** direct line; as, in *range* with my window; **3,** the limits of space or time included or covered; scope; extent; as, the whole *range* of history; **4,** the limits within which something varies; as, her voice has a *range* of two octaves; **5,** a tract of land over which cattle graze; **6,** the distance to which a gun, cannon, etc., can shoot; as, a *range* of one kilometre; also, the distance of the target from the gun; **7,** a place for target practice; as, a rifle *range*; **8,** the area over which a plant or animal may be found; as, the *range* of the violet; **9,** a large cooking stove; **10,** in Ontario and Québec, a row of lots in a township concession.

ran-ger (rān′jėr), *n.* a person whose job is to guard and look after a forest or natural area; as, a park *ranger* or forest *ranger*:—**Ranger,** a senior Girl Guide, aged 15 or older.

ran-gy (rān′ji), *adj.* [rang-i-er, rang-i-est], **1,** long in limb, lean and muscular, as animals or persons; **2,** adapted to ranging or wandering far and wide.

[1]rank (rangk), *n.* **1,** a row or line of persons or objects; also, an orderly arrangement, esp. a line of soldiers side by side; **2,** high station or position; as, a woman of *rank*; **3,** a grade of social or official position; as, the *rank* of duke; *rank* of admiral; **4,** degree of worth or eminence; as, an athlete of the first *rank*:—**ranks, 1,** the army as a whole; **2,** the body of privates, as distinguished from the officers; as, the captain was reduced to the *ranks* for disobedience:—**rank and file, 1,** the whole body of common soldiers; **2,** the common people:—*v.t.* **1,** to place in rows; draw up (soldiers) in line; **2,** to include in a certain class, order, or division; as, to *rank* students by their marks; **3,** to be of higher rank than (another); outrank; as, a major *ranks* a captain:—*v.i.* **1,** to hold a certain grade or position; as, she *ranks* high in her classes; **2,** to form into divisions or classifications; **3,** *Slang* to complain or criticize; carp; as, she is always *ranking* on me.

[2]rank (rangk), *adj.* **1,** plentiful and coarse

in growth; as, *rank* vegetation; **2,** producing too freely; as, *rank* soil; **3,** coarse; strong in taste or smell; as, *rank* fat; **4,** gross; inexcusable; extreme; as, *rank* carelessness; **5,** absolute or complete; as, he is a *rank* amateur.

ran-kle (rang′kl), *v.i.* [ran-kled, ran-kling], **1,** to fester or cause irritation or anger; **2,** to cause mental pain or irritation; as, the insult *rankled*.

ran-sack (ran′sak), *v.t.* **1,** to make a thorough search of; as, I *ransacked* my desk in vain; **2,** to pillage; to plunder; as, the enemy *ransacked* the town.

ran-som (ran′sum), *n.* **1,** the returning of a captive or seized property upon payment of a price; as, they negotiated the *ransom* of the prisoners from the enemy; **2,** the sum so paid or demanded; as, the million-dollar *ransom*:—*v.t.* **1,** to free from prison, slavery, or punishment, by a payment; **2,** to set free on receipt of a payment.

rant (rant), *n.* noisy, empty speech:—*v.i.* to speak loudly and at length; to rave on.—*n.* **rant′er.**—*adj.* **rant′ing.**

[1]**rap** (rap), *v.i.* [rapped, rap-ping], **1,** to strike a quick, sharp blow; to knock; **2,** *Slang* to talk or discuss; as, we *rapped* all night:—*v.t.* **1,** to strike sharply; **2,** to utter sharply as, to *rap* out a command; **3,** *Colloq.* to criticize or rebuke:—*n.* **1,** a quick, sharp blow or knock; a tap; as, she heard the *rap* at the window; **2,** *Colloq.* punishment or rebuke, esp. a prison sentence; **3,** *Slang* a conversation, talk, or discussion; as, the subject came up in the *rap*:—*adj.* pertaining to, of, or for raps; as, a *rap* session; *rap* sheet.

[2]**rap** (rap), *n.* a form of music in which lyrics are spoken or chanted to a rhythm without instruments:—*v.i.* [rapped, rapping], to perform such music.

ra-pa-cious (ra-pā′shus), *adj.* **1,** seizing by violence; as, *rapacious* pirates; **2,** greedy; grasping; as, a *rapacious* money lender.—*n.* **ra-pac′i-ty** (ra-pas′i-ti).

rape (rāp), *v.t.* [raped, rap-ing], **1,** to take by force or destroy; as, the *rape* of the country's forests; **2,** to sexually assault or ravish someone against their will, esp. a woman;—*n.* **1,** a taking or carrying off by force; **2,** the act of sexual assault.—*n.* **rap′ist.**

rap-id (rap′id), *adj.* very quick, fast, or swift; as, to run at a *rapid* rate; a *rapid* runner:—**rapids,** *n.pl.* a place in a river where the water rushes swiftly because of a steep slope in the riverbed.—*n.* **ra-pid′i-ty.**—*adv.* **rap′id-ly.**

rap-ine (rap′īn; rap′in), *n.* the act of plundering or of carrying off property ruthlessly or by force; destruction.

rap-port (rå′pôr′; ra-pōr′), *n.* a sympathetic relationship; harmony; as, he had a *rapport* with his audience: used of speakers, singers, actors, etc.

rapt (rapt), *adj.* **1,** carried away with delight; enraptured; **2,** absorbed; engrossed; as, he gave *rapt* attention to his book.

rap-ture (rap′tūr), *n.* the state of being transported or carried away with great joy; extreme delight or pleasure.—*adj.* **rap′turous.**—*adv.* **rap′tur-ous-ly.**

[1]**rare** (râr), *adj.* [rar-er, rar-est], **1,** thin; not dense; as, a *rare* atmosphere; **2,** scarce; not frequent; as, on one of his *rare* visits to the country; **3,** unusual; precious; as, *rare* old baseball cards.—*n.* **rar′i-ty** (rar′i-ti; râr′i-ti):—*v.t.* **rar′e-fy′** [rarefied, rarefy-ing].—*adv.* **rare′ly.**

[2]**rare** (râr), *adj.* [rar-er, rar-est], not cooked through; underdone; as, *rare* beef.

ras-cal (ras′k′l), *n.* someone who does things that are naughty or mischievous but not really harmful; scoundrel; rogue.—*adj.* and *adv.* **ras′cal-ly.**—*n.* **ras-cal′i-ty.**

[1]**rash** (rash), *n.* an eruption of the skin, showing red spots; as, she developed a *rash* after touching that poison ivy.

[2]**rash** (rash), *adj.* **1,** hasty in thought or act; reckless; as, he was *rash* to drive that car; **2,** done, made, or given through lack of caution; as, a *rash* promise.

rasp (råsp), *v.t.* **1,** to rub or scrape with, or as with, a file or other rough instrument; **2,** to irritate or grate (on); as, her voice *rasps* on my nerves:—*v.i.* **1,** to scrape or grate roughly; **2,** to make a harsh, grating noise:—*n.* **1,** a rough file with a toothed rather than a ridged surface; **2,** the act of rasping or scraping; **3,** a harsh, grating noise; as, the *rasp* of rusty hinges.

rasp-ber-ry (raz′bėr-i), *n.* [*pl.* raspberries], **1,** the seedy, edible fruit, usually red or black in colour, of a prickly shrub or vine; **2,** the shrub or vine; **3,** *Slang* a sound made by vibrating the lips and tongue, expressing disapproval; as, to give him a *raspberry*.

rat (rat), *n.* **1,** a gnawing animal that looks like a mouse but is larger; **2,** *Colloq.* someone who is frequently found in the same place; as, a *mall* rat; **3,** *Colloq.* a person who is considered mean, sneaky, or destructive:—*v.i.* [rat-ted, rat-ting], **1,** to hunt or catch rats; **2,** *Colloq.* to betray or inform on; as, she *ratted* on us to the teacher.—*n.* **rat′ter.**

rat-chet (rach′it), *n.* **1,** a hinged tongue that drops into the notches of a toothed wheel and prevents it from turning backward; **2,** the toothed wheel; **3,** a mechanism or device consisting of the toothed wheel and the tongue.

rate (rāt), *n.* **1,** the amount or number of one thing measured in units of another; as, a *rate* of 8 kilometres per second; **2,** a fixed charge for a certain amount of material, piece of work, length of time, etc.; as, the mechanic's *rate* is $25 per hour; **3,** a relative standard in respect to manner, style, etc.; as, to drive at a fast *rate*; to spend at an extravagant *rate*; **4,** class; quality; as, first-*rate* food:—**at any rate**, in any case:—*v.t.* [rat-ed, rat-ing], **1,** to settle or fix the value, rank, or degree of; **2,** to consider; regard; as, we *rate* her among the best authors:—*v.i.* to be estimated or ranked; as, he *rated* very high in his class.

rath-er (rå*th*′ėr), *adv.* **1,** more willing; gladly; sooner; as, I would *rather* read than write; **2,** on the contrary; instead; as, she took the side road *rather* than the main highway; **3,** more accurately; as, a pale purple, or *rather*, a deep lavender; **4,** somewhat; to a certain extent; as, it is *rather* warm.

rat-i-fy (rat′i-fī′), *v.t.* [ratified, ratify-ing], to accept, approve, or endorse in an official way; make valid by signing; as, Parliament *ratified* the bill.—*n.* **rat′i-fi-er; rat′i-fi-ca′tion.**

rat-ing (rāt′ing), *n.* **1,** the act of classifying according to relative value; **2,** position, rank, or class; as, our school has a high academic *rating*; **3,** a measurement of the popularity of a television show, radio program, etc.; as, the news program has the highest *rating*.

ra-tio (rā′shi-ō; rā′shō), *n.* [*pl.* ratios], the relation in number, degree, or quantity existing between two things; proportion; as, the *ratio* of average to brilliant students is 10 to 1.

ra-tion (rā′shun; rash′un), *n.* **1,** a definite quantity of food or supplies allowed to a person or an animal; **2,** any fixed or stated share; as, a daily *ration* of sugar:—*v.t.* **1,** to furnish with a fixed allowance of food, supplies, etc.; **2,** to distribute food, supplies, etc., on a limited basis.

ra-tion-al (rash′un-al), *adj.* **1,** having the power to reason or think connectedly; as, she is a *rational* being; **2,** based on, or in accordance with, reason; intelligent; not foolish; as, *rational* thought or conduct.—*n.* **ra′tion-al′i-ty; ra′tion-al-ist.**—*v.t.* **ra′tion-al-ize′** [rationalized, rationaliz-ing].

rat-tle (rat′l), *v.i.* [rat-tled, rat-tling], **1,** to produce short, sharp noises in quick succession; clatter; as, a door *rattles* in the wind; **2,** to talk in a noisy rapid manner; prattle; as, she *rattled* on for an hour; **3,** to move with a clatter; as, the wagon *rattled* along the road:—*v.t.* **1,** to cause to make a succession of rapid, sharp noises; as, the wind *rattles* the shutters; **2,** to utter in a rapid, noisy way; as, he *rattled* off his speech; **3,** to confuse or daze; as, this unexpected news *rattled* him:—*n.* **1,** a series of short, sharp, clattering sounds following one another quickly; as, the *rattle* of hail against the windows; **2,** anything for making a rattling sound, as a child's toy.

rat-tler (rat′lėr), *n.* **1,** anything that makes a rattling noise; **2,** a rattlesnake.

rattle-snake (rat′l-snāk′), *n.* a poisonous snake with hard bony rings or scales on the tail that make a rattling sound.

rau-cous (rô′kus), *adj.* **1,** hoarse; rough; as, a *raucous* voice; **2,** boisterous and disorderly; as, the *raucous* party.

rav-age (rav′ij), *v.t.* [ravaged, ravag-ing], to lay waste; pillage; plunder:—*v.i.* to work havoc; as, the enemy *ravaged* the country:—*n.* destruction by violence; ruin; waste; as, the *ravages* of the storm.

rave (rāv), *v.i.* [raved, rav-ing], **1,** to act or talk madly; **2,** to speak enthusiastically; as, he *raved* about her singing; **3,** to rage, as a high wind; **4,** *Colloq.* to attend a rave party:—*n.* **1,** enthusiastic praise in reviews etc.; as, the play got *raves*; **2,** a party, often illicit and lasting all night, in a warehouse or other nontraditional venue, featuring loud, alternative music and dancing; as, it was morning when she got back from the *rave*.—*adj.* **rav′ing.**

ra-ven (rā′ven), *n.* a large bird of the crow family, noted for its glossy-black colour:—*adj.* like a raven; jet black and shining.

rav-en-ous (rav′-en-us), *adj.* **1,** very hungry; rapacious; starving; as, *ravenous* beasts of prey; **2,** extremely sharp; greedy; as, a *ravenous* appetite.—*adv.* **rav′en-ous-ly.**—*n.* **rav′en-ous-ness.**

ra-vine (ra-vēn′), *n.* a long, deep hollow, formed by the action of a stream or torrent; a mountain gorge; gully.

rav-ish (rav′ish), *v.t.* **1,** to seize and remove by force; rape; **2,** to affect overpoweringly, as with delight, rapture, grief, etc.; as, they were *ravished* by the divine music.—*n.* **rav′ish-er; rav′ish-ment.**

rav-ish-ing (rav′ish-ing), *adj.* very charming or attractive; as, a *ravishing* voice.

raw (rô), *adj.* **1,** uncooked; as, a *raw* potato; **2,** without the covering of the skin; as, a *raw* spot on the hand; **3,** in its natural form or state; unprepared; as, *raw* silk; **4,** crude; inexperienced; unpractised; as, *raw* recruits; **5,** cold and damp; as, *raw* weather.—*n.* **raw′ness.**

raw-boned (rô′bōnd′), *adj.* having little flesh; gaunt; lean.

raw-hide (rô′hīd′), *n.* **1,** untanned skin or hide, as of cattle; **2,** a whip made of a roll or braid of tanned leather.

raw material, any substance, such as coal, wood, or cotton, that is still in its natural state and has not been refined, manufactured, or processed.

[1]**ray** (rā), *n.* **1,** a single line of light appearing to stream from a bright centre or source; as, a *ray* of sunlight; also, light or illumination; as, they studied by the *ray* of the lamp; **2,** a glimmer; trace; as, a *ray* of hope; **3,** one of a number of thin lines

spreading from a common centre like the spokes of a wheel; **4,** a beam of energy, electricity, etc.; as, an X-*ray*; **5,** something that resembles a ray, as one of the yellow, petal-like flowers around the dark disk of a black-eyed Susan, one of the radiating arms of a starfish, etc.:—*v.t.* to send forth (light):—*v.i.* to shine forth; radiate.—*adj.* **ray′less.**

[2]**ray** (rā), *n.* a saltwater fish with a broad, flat body and a thin tail such as the skate and the torpedo.

ray-on (rā′on), *n.* an artificial, shiny, silklike fabric made from wood or cotton fibre spun into thread.

raze (rāz), *v.t.* [razed, raz-ing], to level to the ground; tear down, as a building.

ra-zor (rā′zėr), *n.* a sharp-edged instrument used in shaving.

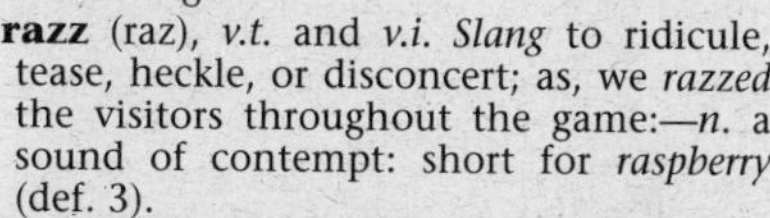

Ray

razz (raz), *v.t.* and *v.i. Slang* to ridicule, tease, heckle, or disconcert; as, we *razzed* the visitors throughout the game:—*n.* a sound of contempt: short for *raspberry* (def. 3).

RCMP (är′sē′em′pē′), *abbrev.* short for *Royal Canadian Mounted Police.*

Insignia of the RCMP

re- (rē-), *prefix* meaning **1,** *in return, mutual;* as in repay; **2,** *against;* as in resist; **3,** *back, backward;* as in recall; **4,** *off, away, down;* as in refuge, relax; **5,** *repeated action;* as in reduplicate; **6,** *an intensive;* as in redolent; **7,** *a negative;* as in resign; **8,** *again, renew;* as in reread; **9,** *back to a previous or better state;* as in reform, recondition.

reach (rēch), *v.t.* **1,** to stretch out; as, the children *reached* out their hands; **2,** to touch or grasp; as, they could not *reach* the railing; **3,** to get in touch with someone; communicate; as, I tried to *reach* you all day; **4,** to arrive at or come to; attain; as, to *reach* a goal; **5,** to extend as far as; penetrate to; as, this road *reaches* the lake:—*v.i.* **1,** to extend the hand so as to touch or seize something; **2,** to endeavour to obtain something; as, to *reach* for fame:—*n.* **1,** the act or power of stretching out the arm in order to touch or grasp something; also, the distance one can stretch; as, he has a long *reach;* **2,** the distance within which one can touch, observe, etc.; as, she lives within *reach* of town; **3,** an unbroken stretch, as of water.

re-act (ri-akt′), *v.i.* **1,** to rebound; act back or as a boomerang; as, his cruelty to his friend *reacted* back on him and made him suffer; **2,** to respond to an influence or stimulus; as, the patient *reacted* favourably to the doctor's treatment; **3,** in *chemistry,* to undergo change; as, inert substances are those that are slow to *react.*

re-ac-tion (rē-ak′shun), *n.* **1,** the fact of reacting or responding; as, her *reaction* to the question; **2,** a condition in nature that occurs as a direct result of something else; as, for every action, there is an equal and opposite *reaction;* **3,** in *chemistry,* a process by which substances are changed into new substances; as, the *reaction* between iron and water creates rust.

re-ac-tion-ar-y (rē-ak′shun-ėr-i), *n.* [*pl.* reactionaries], a person who favours a return to former conditions, esp. with regard to social or political change:—*adj.* pertaining to, or favouring, a return to a former state of affairs; as, a *reactionary* political party.

re-ac-tor (ri-ak′tėr), *n.* **1,** anything that reacts; **2,** a condenser used to modify the current of an alternating current circuit; **3,** an apparatus in which a controlled chain reaction of atomic fission may be maintained for the production of fissionable material, radioactive isotopes, or power; an atomic pile: also called *nuclear reactor.*

read (rēd), *v.t.* [read (red), read-ing], **1,** to look at and understand the meaning of something written or printed; to peruse; as, to *read* a book; **2,** to utter aloud something written or printed; as, she *reads* the story to the class; **3,** to discover, by observation, the meaning of certain lines or marks on; as, to *read* palms; to *read* a thermometer; **4,** to make a study of; as, to *read* about cats in the encyclopedia; **5,** to interpret (dreams or riddles); also, to foretell (the future); **6,** to show; indicate; as, the thermometer *reads* 15 degrees; **7,** in *computing,* to locate and retrieve data from a storage device or other source electronically; as, the scanner *reads* the bar code, and the price appear on the cash register:—*v.i.* **1,** to peruse written or printed matter; **2,** to learn from written or printed matter; as, to *read* about politics; **3,** to utter aloud written or printed words; as, he often *reads* to us; **4,** to have a special form; as, the passage *reads* thus.

read-er (rē′dėr), *n.* **1,** someone who reads; as, she is a very fast *reader;* **2,** a book used by students for learning and practising the skill of reading; **3,** in *computing,* a device that reads and interprets electronic information from CD-ROMs, bar codes, etc.; **4,** someone employed to read or proofread manuscripts for publishers; **5,** someone who reads aloud or recites written passages to an audience, as in church.

read-i-ly (red′i-li), *adv.* in a willing way; without difficulty; easily; as, she *readily* agreed to complete her homework.

read-ing (rēd′ing), *n.* **1,** the act of one

who reads; perusal of written or printed matter; **2,** utterance aloud of the words of books, letters; **3,** a public recital; as, to give a *reading* from Kipling; **4,** a form of a particular passage in a book; as, various *readings* of a passage may be found in different editions of Shakespeare; **5,** written or printed matter to be perused; as, *Lord of the Rings* is good *reading;* **6,** the manner of interpreting something written; as, an actor's *reading* of her lines; **7,** that which is shown by an instrument; as, the *reading* of our gas meter is taken monthly.

re-ad-just (rē′a-just′), *v.t.* to set in order again; set right once more.

read-only memory, in *computing,* the device or process that allows stored information to be accessed quickly and easily but not manipulated: abbreviated as *ROM.*

read-out or **read–out** (rēd′out′), *n.* in *computing,* information from a computer in a printed form that can be read by the user.

read-y (red′i), *adj.* [read-i-er, read-i-est], **1,** in condition for immediate action; as, I am *ready* to go; prepared for instant use; as, your dinner is *ready;* **2,** quick; prompt; as, *ready* payment; **3,** mentally fit or prepared; willing; as, *ready* to obey; **4,** on the point of; about to; as, that tree is *ready* to fall; **5,** awaiting use; available; as, *ready* cash.—*adv.* **read′i-ly.**—*n.* **read′i-ness.**

read-y–made or **read-y-made** (red′i–mād′), *adj.* **1,** not made to individual order; made in standard forms; as, *ready-made* clothing; **2,** prepared beforehand; as, a *ready-made* speech.

re-al (rē′al), *adj.* **1,** not imaginary; actually existing as a thing, or occurring as a fact; as, *real* events; a *real* illness; **2,** genuine; not imitation; as, *real* silk; **3,** in *law,* pertaining to land or buildings; as, *real* property.

real estate, land and the buildings, plants, water, etc., that are on the land.

re-al-ism (rē′al-izm), *n.* **1,** concern with the practical and real; **2,** the theory that art and literature should present life and nature as they really are, even when sordid or disgusting: opposite of *idealism.*—*n.* **re′al-ist.**

re-al-is-tic (rē′al-is′tik), *adj.* **1,** looking or presenting people and scenes as they actually are; true to life; as, a *realistic* novel; **2,** dealing with real life; seeing things as they really are; as, to be *realistic* enough to know that we may lose the game.

re-al-i-ty (rē-al′i-ti), *n.* [*pl.* realities], **1,** the state or quality of being real or actual; as, we believe in the *reality* of what we see; **2,** that which exists or is actual; a fact; as, the *reality* proved less horrible than his fear.

re-al-ize (rē′al-īz′), *v.t.* [realized, realizing], **1,** to bring into actual existence; **2,** to accomplish; as, he *realized* his plan to go abroad; **3,** to see clearly; understand; as, she *realized* her error; **4,** to obtain as profit; as, she *realized* $50 from the sale:—*v.i.* to turn property into money; as, to *realize* on a building.—*n.* **re′al-i-za′tion.**

re-al-ly (rē′al-i), *adv.* **1,** actually; as a matter of fact; she didn't *really* want to go; **2,** very much; truly; as, a *really* difficult test.

realm (relm), *n.* **1,** a kingdom; an empire; **2,** any region or state; **3,** a field or area of interest, knowledge, influence, or activity; as, the *realm* of science.

real time, 1, in *computing,* the time needed for a computer to complete a task; **2,** something that happens almost immediately; as, the news broadcast was in *real time.*

re-al-tor (rē′al-tėr; -tôr′), *n.* a dealer in real estate.

re-al-ty (rē′al-ti), *n.* real estate; landed property.

[1]**ream** (rēm), *n.* **1,** 20 quires, or about 500 sheets of paper:—**reams**, a large amount; as, she wrote *reams* of notes.

[2]**ream** (rēm), *v.t.* **1,** to enlarge or taper (a hole), esp. in metal; **2,** *Colloq.* to reprimand severely; as, she *reamed* out the new recruit for his mistakes.

ream-er (rēm′ėr), *n.* **1,** one who or that which reams, esp. a tool with sharp edges for enlarging or tapering holes; **2,** a device for squeezing fruit, consisting of a dish with a ridged, cone-shaped centre.

reap (rēp), *v.t.* **1,** to cut down and gather in crops; as, to *reap* grain; **2,** to cut a crop from; as, to *reap* a field; **3,** to receive as reward; as, to *reap* the benefit of hard study:—*v.i.* to cut and gather grain.—*n.* **reap′er.**

re-ap-pear (rē′a-pēr′), *v.i.* to come into view again.

[1]**rear** (rēr), *n.* **1,** the back or the part that is away from the front; as, the door at the *rear* of the room; **2,** *Colloq.* the buttocks; **3,** that part of the military that is farthest from the front line:—*adj.* pertaining to, or situated at, the back part; as, *rear* stairs.

[2]**rear** (rēr), *v.t.* **1,** to raise or lift up; as a snake *rears* its head; **2,** to construct; erect; as, to *rear* a palace; **3,** to bring up and educate; as, to *rear* children; **4,** to breed; grow; as, to *rear* horses:—*v.i.* to rise up on the hind legs, as a horse.

re-ar-range (rē′a-rānj′), *v.t.* [rearranged, rearrang-ing], to put back in order or place; to change the position of.

rea-son (rē′zn), *n.* **1,** an explanation given for a belief, act, etc.; as, she gave no *reason* for leaving; **2,** the grounds for an opinion or the motive of an act; as, there were *reasons* for his belief; **3,** the power to understand or think; as, the sick man lost his *reason;* **4,** sanity; common sense; as, to bring a naughty child to *reason:*—*v.i.* **1,** to exercise the power of thinking; to draw logical conclusions; **2,** to argue; as, you cannot *reason* with a stubborn person:—*v.t.* **1,** to persuade by argument; as, to *reason* a child out of his fears; **2,** to prove or explain by means of the intellect; as, to *reason* out a solution.—*n.* **rea′son-er.**

rea-son-a-ble (rē′zn-a-bl), *adj.* **1,** having the power to think clearly and to reach sound conclusions; as, a *reasonable* being; **2,** governed by reason; just; as, a *reasonable* employer; **3,** moderate or fair; as, a *reasonable* charge; **4,** sound or sensible; as, a *reasonable* decision.—*adv.* **rea′son-a-bly.**

rea-son-ing (rē′zn-ing), *n.* **1,** the process of reaching conclusions by careful and connected thinking; **2,** a line of argument; a presentation of reasons; as, the students understood the teacher's *reasoning.*

re-as-sure (rē′a-shoor′), *v.t.* [reassured, reassur-ing], to give back courage to; give new confidence to; as, the mother *reassured* her child.—*n.* **re′as-sur′ance.**

re-bate (re′bāt; ri-bāt′), *n.* money paid back; discount; as, she got a *rebate* of 10 dollars on the books she bought:—*v.t.* [rebated, rebat-ing], **1,** to discount or pay back money; **2,** to diminish.

[1]**re-bel** (ri-bel′), *v.i.* [rebelled, rebel-ling], **1,** to take up arms against the law or government; **2,** to resist any authority.

[2]**reb-el** (reb′′l), *n.* **1,** one who takes up arms against his or her government or resists its laws; **2,** one who resists any authority:—*adj.* opposing or resisting authority.

re-bel-lion (ri-bel′yun), *n.* **1,** the act of taking up arms, or the state of being in revolt, against the government; as, the *Rebellion* of 1837 did not amount to much in Ontario; **2,** defiance of any authority.—*adj.* **re-bel′lious.**

re-boot (rē-bo͞ot), *v.t.* and *v.i.* in *computing,* to restart a computer by turning it off and then powering it up and loading its operating system again:—*n.* an act of rebooting.

re-bound (ri-bound′), *v.i.* **1,** to spring or fly back from that which has been struck; as, the puck *rebounded* off the boards; **2,** to recover; as, she *rebounded* after a long illness:—*n.* (rē′bound′), the act of springing back or recovering.

re-buff (ri-buf′), *n.* a sudden check; repulse; defeat:—*v.t.* to refuse or repel sharply; snub (someone).

re-build (rē′bild′), *v.t.* [rebuilt (rē′bilt′), rebuild-ing], to construct again.

re-buke (ri-būk′), *n.* a sharp reproof; scolding:—*v.t.* [rebuked, rebuk-ing], to censure sharply; as, to *rebuke* a child.

re-but-tal (ri-but′al), *n.* the answering, refuting, or contradicting of the arguments of one's opponent in a debate:—*v.t.* **rebut′.**

re-cal-ci-trant (ri-kal′si-trant), *adj.* and *n.* refusing to comply, submit, obey, etc.; stubbornly defiant; as, this student is *recalcitrant.*

re-call (ri-kôl′), *v.t.* **1,** to order or summon back; as, the automaker *recalled* the model because of faulty brakes; **2,** to remember; recollect; as, to *recall* a name; **3,** to withdraw; annul; as, to *recall* a decision:—*n.* **1,** the act of summoning or calling back; **2,** the ability to remember; **3,** the request for the return of faulty products; as, the auto *recall* was huge; **4,** power by which an unsatisfactory public official may be put out of office by vote of the people.

re-cant (ri-kant′), *v.t.* to withdraw publicly (something previously believed or said):—*v.i.* to renounce formally an opinion previously held.

re-ca-pit-u-late (rē′ka-pit′ū-lāt′), *v.t.* [recapitulat-ed, recapitulat-ing], to sum up the chief points of; as, after listening to the speakers, she *recapitulated* their main arguments:—*v.i.* to repeat briefly what has been said at length.—*n.* **re′ca-pit′u-la′tion.**

re-cap-ture (rē′kap′tūr), *n.* the act of seizing or taking again; as, the *recapture* of a town:—*v.t.* [recaptured, recaptur-ing], to seize or take again; also, to recollect.

re-cast (rē′kåst′), *v.t.* [recast, recast-ing], **1,** to plan or lay out anew; as, I must *recast* the first chapter; **2,** to mould or cast again; as, to *recast* a medal.

re-cede (ri-sēd′), *v.i.* [reced-ed, reced-ing], **1,** to fall back; retire; as, the tide *recedes;* **2,** to withdraw, as from a claim or proposal; **3,** to slope or incline backward; as, his forehead *recedes.*—*adj.* **re-ced′ing** (as, a *receding* hairline).

re-ceipt (ri-sēt′), *n.* **1,** the act of getting, or state of having received, something given, sent, etc.; as, the *receipt* of the e-mail; in *receipt* of news; **2,** a written acknowledgment of anything, usually money or goods; as, he signed a *receipt* for the couriered package:—**receipts,** that which is taken in, as distinguished from what is paid out; as, yesterday, our store had over $5,000 in *receipts.*

re-ceiv-a-ble (ri-sēv′a-bl), *adj.* due; payable; as, accounts *receivable.*

re-ceive (ri-sēv′), *v.t.* [received, receiv-ing], **1,** to get (a gift, message, payment, etc.) from another; as, I *received* your letter; **2,** to be informed of; as, to *receive* news; **3,** to admit to one's company; greet; entertain; as, to *receive* guests; **4,** to serve as a holder for; as, a box to *receive* books; **5,** to get; experience: as, to *receive* a shock; **6,** to buy stolen goods:—*v.i.* **1,** in *sports,* to catch or possess a kicked ball; as, they elected to *receive;* **2,** to change or convert electromagnetic waves into sound or picture signals that one can hear or see, as does a radio or television.

re-ceiv-er (ri-sēv′ẽr), *n.* **1,** one who or that which takes or holds; **2,** a device that can receive radio or television signals and convert them into sound; **3,** the part of a telephone that receives the electric waves and turns them into sound; **4,** a person appointed by a court to hold and manage the property of a bankrupt person or firm; **5,** in *football,* the team or player to whom the ball is kicked.—*n.* **re-ceiv′er-ship′.**

re-cent (rē′sent), *adj.* **1,** pertaining to time not long past; as, a *recent* occurrence; **2,** new; modern; fresh; as, a *recent* book.—*adv.* **re-cent-ly.**

re-cep-ta-cle (ri-sep′ta-kl), *n.* **1,** anything, such as a cup, barrel, or vault, used to hold other things; **2,** in a plant, the part of the stalk to which the parts of the flower are attached.

re-cep-tion (re-sep′shun), *n.* **1,** the act of receiving, or the state of being received; as, the *reception* of news; **2,** the act or manner of welcoming; as, a cool *reception;* **3,** a formal entertainment; as, a *reception* was held in honour of the mayor and her husband; **4,** the quality of signals received by a radio or television set.—*n.* **re-cep′tor** (a sensory nerve ending for reception of stimuli).

re-cep-tion-ist (ri-sep′she-nist), *n.* someone whose job is answering telephones, giving information, and greeting visitors.

re-cep-tive (ri-sep′tiv), *adj.* ready to receive; open to ideas or suggestions; as, she had a *receptive* mind and was eager to learn.

re-cess (rē′ses; ri-ses′), *n.* **1,** a brief time during which work ceases; an intermission; as, the school *recess;* **2,** a receding part or space that breaks the line of a wall; an alcove or niche:—*v.t.* (ri-ses′), to put back; set into a recess:—*v.i.* to adjourn or take a recess or intermission.

re-ces-sion (ri-sesh′un), *n.* in *economics,* a temporary decline in business, characterized by falling levels of production and of employment.

re-ces-sive (ri-ses′iv), *adj.* **1,** receding; tending to recede, or go back; **2,** in *biology,* relating to a character, or characteristic, that does not appear in the immediate but may be transmitted to later, offspring: opposite of *dominant* character.

rec-i-pe (res′i-pē′), *n.* **1,** a set of directions for mixing or preparing anything, as in cooking; as, a good *recipe* for cake; **2,** general directions for accomplishing a result; as, there is no *recipe* for success.

re-cip-i-ent (ri-sip′i-ent), *n.* one who receives; as, a *recipient* of high honours:—*adj.* receiving or ready to receive.

re-cip-ro-cal (ri-sip′ro-kl), *adj.* **1,** mutual; done, given, or offered by each to the other; as, *reciprocal* benefits; **2,** corresponding; equivalent; as, to ask for *reciprocal* privileges; **3,** in *grammar,* showing mutual action or relation: used of certain pronouns; as, in the sentence "the student and teacher spoke to each other," "each" and "other" are *reciprocal* pronouns, showing that the student spoke to the teacher and the teacher spoke to the student:—*n.* **1,** that which is given or done by each to the other; an equivalent; **2,** in *mathematics,* the quotient obtained by dividing the number 1 by another number; as, the *reciprocal* of 3 is 1/3.—*adv.* **re-cip′ro-cal-ly.**

re-cip-ro-cate (ri-sip′ro-kāt′), *v.t.* [reciprocat-ed, reciprocat-ing], **1,** to give and take in exchange; as, they *reciprocate* each other's affection; **2,** to give something in return for; as, to *reciprocate* a favour; **3,** in *mechanics,* to cause to move to and fro:—*v.i.* **1,** in *mechanics,* to move to and fro; **2,** to interchange; make an exchange with one another; **3,** to pay back; make a return; as, she *reciprocated* with a gift.—*n.* **rec′i-proc′i-ty** (res′i-pros′i-ti).

re-cit-al (ri-sīt′al), *n.* **1,** a telling of the details of an event; narration; as, a *recital* of one's adventures; also, the thing told; a story; **2,** an entertainment, usually consisting of music, instrumental or vocal.

re-cite (ri-sīt′), *v.t.* [recit-ed, recit-ing], **1,** to repeat aloud from memory; declaim; as, to *recite* a poem; **2,** to tell in detail; relate; as, to *recite* the story of a trip; **3,** to enumerate; list; as, she *recited* her grievances to the teacher:—*v.i.* to repeat something from memory.

reck-less (rek′lis), *adj.* not thinking of consequences or danger; rash; careless; as, a *reckless* driver; *reckless* spending.

reck-on (rek′un), *v.t.* **1,** to count or number; compute; as, to *reckon* the cost; **2,** to look upon as being; consider; as, we *reckon* him a friend; **3,** *Colloq.* to think; suppose; as, I *reckon* it will rain:—*v.i.* **1,** to depend or rely; as, he *reckoned* on our votes; **2,** to make calculations.

reck-on-ing (rek′un-ing), *n.* **1,** calculation, computation, or the result of it; **2,** a settling of accounts, as between debtor and creditor; **3,** a calculated guess; **4,** in *navigation,* the determining of a ship's or aircraft's position:—**dead reckoning,** the use of the log and compass, owing to cloudiness, fog, etc.

re-claim (ri-klām′), *v.t.* **1,** to demand or obtain the return of; as, to *reclaim* a book; **2,** to reform; as, to *reclaim* a criminal; **3,** to bring under cultivation; as, to *reclaim* swampy land.—*n.* **rec′la-ma′tion.**

re-cline (ri-klīn′), *v.i.* [reclined, reclin-ing], to lie down for rest or repose:—*v.t.* to cause to lean or lie back; as, he *reclined* his tired body on the cot.

re-cluse (ri-kloos′; rek′loos), *n.* one who lives alone; a hermit.—*adj.* **re-clu′sive.**

rec-og-ni-tion (rek′og-nish′un), *n.* the fact of recognizing or being recognized; being known; as, a look of *recognition* came over her.

rec-og-nize (rek′og-nīz′), *v.t.* [recognized, recogniz-ing], **1,** to know the identity of; recall as having known before; as, to *recog-*

nize a voice; **2,** to admit acquaintance with; salute; as, she *recognized* her old friend with a smile; **3,** to take formal notice of; acknowledge; as, for many years, America did not *recognize* China; **4,** to appreciate; as, to *recognize* true worth; to accept or acknowledge that someone or something has a certain value; as, Gretzky is *recognized* as one of the greatest hockey players; **5,** to concede as true; admit; as, I *recognize* that you are right; **6,** in a meeting, to acknowledge (someone) as the person entitled to be heard at the time.—*n.* **rec′og-ni′tion.**

re-coil (ri-koil′), *v.i.* **1,** to start back or shrink, as in horror, fear, etc.; as, they *recoiled* at the sight of the mangled body; **2,** to spring back; kick, as a gun; **3,** to retreat or fall back; as, the enemy *recoiled;* **4,** to come back to the starting point; as, evil *recoils* on the doer:—*n.* **1,** a shrinking back; **2,** a rebound; **3,** the springing back or kick of a gun or spring; **4,** the distance it moves.

rec-ol-lect (rek′o-lekt′), *v.t.* to call back to the mind; remember.

rec-ol-lec-tion (rek′o-lek′shun), *n.* **1,** the act of remembering; also, the power of remembering; as, age often impairs the *recollection*; **2,** a person's memory or the time over which it extends; as, the coldest winter in my *recollection*; **3,** something remembered; as, childhood *recollections*.

rec-om-mend (rek′o-mend′), *v.t.* **1,** to give in charge or trust; **2,** to offer to the favour, attention, or use of another; speak in favour of; as, to *recommend* a student for the program; **3,** to advise; suggest; as, I *recommend* a change of diet.

rec-om-men-da-tion (rek′o-men-dā′shun), *n.* **1,** the act of offering to favourable notice; **2,** something that procures or deserves favourable attention; as, a neat appearance is a good *recommendation*; **3,** something recommended or advised; as, the committee's *recommendation* is to wait.

rec-om-pense (rek′om-pens′), *v.t.* [recompensed, recompens-ing], **1,** to give an equivalent to (a person); reward; repay; as, she *recompensed* him for his loyalty; **2,** to make amends for; atone for; as, to *recompense* a loss:—*n.* something given by way of reward or amends.

rec-on-cile (rek′on-sīl′), *v.t.* [reconciled, reconcil-ing], **1,** to restore peace between; as, to *reconcile* brothers who have quarrelled; **2,** to adjust; settle; as, to *reconcile* differences; **3,** to make content or submissive; as, to *reconcile* a person to his fate; **4,** to make consistent; as, it is hard to *reconcile* her words with her actions.—*n.* **rec-on-cil′i-a′tion** (rek′on-sil′ē-ā′shun).

re-con-nais-sance (ri-kon′i-sans), *n.* **1,** the making of a preliminary survey, as for military or scientific purposes; **2,** a party of people sent on such a survey.

rec-on-noi-tre or **rec-on-noi-ter** (rek′o-noi′tėr; rē′ko-noi′tėr), *v.t.* and *v.i.* [reconnoitred (-tėrd), reconnoi-tring], to explore and investigate, esp. for military or scientific purposes.

re-con-sid-er (rē′kon-sid′ėr), *v.t.* **1,** to think over or ponder again; as, to *reconsider* a proposal; **2,** in a legislative body, to bring up (a bill or motion) for renewed deliberation.—*n.* **re′con-sid′er-a′tion.**

re-con-struct (rē′kon-strukt′), *v.t.* to rebuild; remodel.—*n.* **re′con-struc′tion.**

¹re-cord (ri-kôrd′), *v.t.* **1,** to write out or set down in some permanent form; as, to *record* events; ; **2,** to put sounds or images on a tape, disk, or other device; as, they planned to *record* the concert live; **3,** to mark, display, or indicate; as, the clock *records* time.

²rec-ord (rek′ôrd; rek′ėrd), *n.* **1,** the act of writing down or recording facts or events for the purpose of history or evidence; also, what is written or recorded; as, she keeps a *record* of her day in a dairy; **2,** an official report, written or printed, of public acts; as, a legislative *record;* a court *record;* **3,** the body of facts, known and preserved, giving the history of a person or thing; as, the prisoner's *record;* **4,** a vinyl disk on which music or other sounds can be stored to be played back on a phonograph, or record player; **5,** in *sports*, the best performance so far officially recognized; as, the track team broke two *records:—adj.* best, greatest, or most remarkable of its kind up to a given time; as, *record* heat.

re-cord-er (ri-kôr′dėr), *n.* **1,** a person whose business it is to keep an official record; as, a *recorder* of wills; **2,** any of various devices that register mechanically or electronically; as, a tape *recorder;* **3,** a soft-toned flute, played in vertical position.

RECORDER

re-count (ri-kount′), *v.t.* to tell or repeat in full the particulars of; recite:—*n.* (rē′kount), a second counting, as of votes.

re-coup (ri-ko͞op′), *v.t.* **1,** to make up for; indemnify; compensate; as to *recoup* one's losses; **2,** pay back; reimburse (for damage, loss, etc.).

re-course (ri-kōrs′; rē′kōrs), *n.* **1,** an appeal for aid or protection; **2,** the person to whom one appeals, or the thing to which one turns.

re-cov-er (ri-kuv′ėr), *v.t.* **1,** to get back or regain; as, to *recover* one's health; to *recover* lost property; **2,** to make up for; make good the loss or waste of; as, to *recover* lost time; **3,** to find again; as, to *recover* a scent:—*v.i.* **1,** to regain health, strength, or any former state; **2,** to win a lawsuit.—*adj.* **re-cov′er-able.**—*n.* **re-cov′er-y.**

rec-re-ate (rek′ri-āt′), *v.t.* and *v.i.* [recreated, recreat-ing], to revive or refresh, as after toil or exertion; amuse; divert.

re-cre-ate (rē′kri-āt′), *v.t.* [re-created, re-creat-ing], to create again.—*n.* **re-cre-a′tion.**

rec-re-a-tion (rek′ri-ā′shun), *n.* refreshment of mind or body after toil; play; amusement; as, she listened to music for *recreation.*

re-crim-i-na-tion (ri-krim′i-nā′shun), *n.* an accusing in return, or counter accusation; as *recrimination* is a defence of weak minds:—*v.i.* **re-crim′i-nate′.**

re-cruit (ri-kro͞ot′), *n.* **1,** someone newly enlisted in the armed forces; **2,** one who has just joined any organization; as, in some companies, new *recruits* are called new hires:—*v.t.* **1,** to gather together; to add to, or supply with, fresh members, esp. athletes to a college or university; **2,** to enlist soldiers, sailors, etc.:—*v.i.* to obtain fresh supplies of members.—*n.* **re-cruit′er.**

rec-tan-gle (rek′tang′gl), *n.* a four-sided figure with four right angles.—*adj.* **rec-tan′gu-lar.**

rec-ti-fy (rek′ti-fī′), *v.t.* [rectified, rectify-ing], **1,** to correct; as, to *rectify* an error; to remedy; as, to *rectify* abuses; **2,** to refine or purify (liquids) by distillation; **3,** in *electricity*, to change (an electric current) from alternating to direct:—*adj.* **rec′ti-fi′a-ble.**—*n.* **rec′ti-fi-ca′tion; rec′ti-fi-er.**

rec-ti-lin-e-ar (rek′ti-lin′i-ėr), *adj.* **1,** moving in straight lines; **2,** bounded or formed by straight lines; **3,** in *optics*, corrected (as a lens) so as not to distort straight lines.

rec-ti-tude (rek′ti-tūd′), *n.* rightness of intention and action; honesty; uprightness.

rec-tor (rek-tėr), *n.* **1,** in some Christian churches, a clergyman or priest in charge of a parish; **2,** the head of a university, college, or school.—*n.* **rec′to-ry.**

rec-tum (rek′tum), *n.* the lower end of the large intestine.

re-cum-bent (ri-kum′bent), *adj.* lying down; reclining; as, a *recumbent* figure.

re-cu-per-ate (ri-kū′pėr-āt′), *v.t.* [recuperat-ed, recuperat-ing], to regain (one's health):—*v.i.* to recover from illness, losses, etc.; as, it took her weeks to *recuperate* from the flu.—*n.* **re-cu′per-a′tion.**

re-cur (ri-kûr′), *v.i.* [recurred, recur-ring], **1,** to go back, as in memory or in speech; as, he *recurred* to his former opinion; **2,** to come back or return; as, a thought *recurs* to the mind; **3,** to come again, or at intervals, as malaria.—*n.* **re-cur′rence.**—*adj.* **re-cur′rent.**

re-cy-cle (rē-sī′kl), *v.t.* **1,** to recover waste products to be used again; as, to *recycle* the metal from old cars; **2,** use over again with little or no change; **3,** adapt something to a new use; as, to *recycle* the old tires into flowerbeds:—*v.i.* to practise recycling.

red (red), *n.* **1,** the colour of blood, that part of the visible spectrum having the longest wavelength; **2,** any colouring matter that produces this colour:—**Red, 1,** a communist or revolutionary socialist; **2,** loosely, any radical:—*adj.* [red-der, reddest], **1,** of the colour of blood; **2,** pertaining to or favouring revolution; as, a *red* agitator; **3,** inflamed or sore; as, *red* eyes.—*n.* **red-ness.**

red-den (red′n), *v.t.* to make red:—*v.i.* to become red; blush; flush.

red-dish (red′ish), *adj.* somewhat red; tinged with red.

re-deem (ri-dēm′), *v.t.* **1,** to buy back, recover, or rescue; **2,** to exchange or turn in for a prize; as, she *redeemed* the discount coupon on the pizza; **3,** to make good; perform; as, to *redeem* a promise; **4,** to make up for; as, to *redeem* a fault; **5,** to pay off (a promissory note or a mortgage).—*n.* **re-deem′er** (ri-dēm′ėr); **re-demp′tion.**—*adj.* **re-deem′a-ble; re-deem′ing.**

red-hand-ed (red′-han′did), *adj.* **1,** with bloodstained hands; **2,** in the very act of doing something bad or wrong; as, to be caught *red-handed* (in a crime); violent.

red-let-ter (red′-let′ėr), *adj.* memorable; lucky; as, a *red-letter* day.

red-o-lent (red′ō-lent), *adj.* **1,** sweet-smelling; as, *redolent* of newly mown hay; **2,** suggestive (of).—*n.* **red′o-lence.**

re-doubt-a-ble (ri-dout′a-bl), *adj.* formidable; commanding respect; as, a *redoubtable* opponent: often used ironically.

re-dress (ri-dres′), *v.t.* **1,** to right (a wrong); **2,** to correct or do away with (abuses):—*n.* (ri-dres′; rē′dres), **1,** the act of setting right; as, *redress* of grievances; **2,** compensation for a wrong or loss; as, to seek *redress* in the courts.

re-duce (ri-dūs′), *v.t.* [reduced, reduc-ing], **1,** to make less in value, size, etc.; lessen; lower; as, to *reduce* a debt; **2,** to bring from a higher to a lower rank or position; degrade; as, to *reduce* an officer to the ranks; **3,** to consume less; as, environmentalists recommend that we *reduce*, reuse, and recycle; **4,** to bring into order; as, to *reduce* spelling to rules; **5,** to bring to a specified condition; as, she *reduced* her family to despair; **6,** to change into some other physical state; as, to *reduce* sugar to syrup; **7,** in *arithmetic*, to change from one form to another without changing the value, as kilograms to grams; **8,** in *chemistry*, to remove nonmetallic elements from; as, to *reduce* iron ore; **9,** in *surgery*, to restore (a displaced part) to its right position; also, to set; as, to *reduce* a fracture.—*adj.* **re-duc′i-ble.**—*n.* **re-duc′tion** (ri-duk′shun).

re-dun-dant (ri-dun′dant), *adj.* exceeding what is needed; superfluous in writing or speaking; too full or too wordy.—*n.* **re-dun′dance.**

red-wood (red′wood′), *n.* the very large evergreen tree that grows on the Pacific coast of North America; the giant sequoia.

reed (rēd), *n.* **1,** any of certain tall, coarse grasses that grow in wet places; also, one of their jointed hollow stems; **2,** a musical instrument that uses a reed, such as a clarinet, saxophone, or oboe; **3,** a thin, elastic tongue attached to the mouthpiece of certain musical instruments, as the clarinet.—*adj.* **reed′y.**

reef (rēf), *n.* a sandbar or a shelf of rock at or just below the surface of the water.

reek (rēk), *n.* vapour, steam, or smoke; also, a disagreeable odour:—*v.i.* to send out vapour or unpleasant fumes; as, this room *reeks* of smoke.—*adj.* **reek′y.**

[1]**reel** (rēl), *n.* **1,** any of various devices with a revolving frame for winding yarn, wire, rope, etc.; **2,** a device for winding and unwinding line in fishing; **3,** in motion pictures, a strip of film held by one spool:—*v.t.* **1,** to wind on a frame or bobbin; **2,** to draw in by winding a line on a reel; as, to *reel* in a trout; **3,** to tell rapidly and easily; as, to *reel* off a long story.

[2]**reel** (rēl), *v.i.* **1,** to stagger or sway from side to side in walking; **2,** to turn round and round; whirl; feel dizzy; as, his head *reeled;* **3,** to give way; waver; as, the whole line *reeled:*—*n.* the act of staggering or swaying.

[3]**reel** (rēl), *n.* **1,** a lively country or folk dance; **2,** the music for such a dance.

re-fer (ri-fûr′), *v.t.* [referred, refer-ring], **1,** to send or direct a person to an authority for information or decision; as, they *referred* the question to experts; **2,** to direct or send somewhere for information or help; as, to *refer* students to the Internet; **3,** to attribute or explain something as due to a certain cause; as, I *refer* his actions to ignorance:—*v.i.* **1,** to make mention of something; allude; as, she *referred* frequently to progress; **2,** to turn to something; apply; as, he *referred* frequently to his notes; **3,** to point or call attention; as, that sign *refers* to a footnote; **4,** to direct one person to another for information or recommendation; as, she had permission to *refer* to the president of the company.—*adj.* **ref′er-a-ble.**

ref-er-ee (ref′ėr-ē′), *n.* one to whom a matter in dispute is handed over for decision and settlement; an umpire:—*v.t.* and *v.i.* [refereed, referee-ing], to umpire; as, to *referee* a hockey game.

ref-er-ence (ref′ėr-ens), *n.* **1,** the act of submitting a matter for settlement or of applying for information; **2,** a standard source of information that may be consulted; as, a dictionary is a book of *reference*; the Internet is a source of *reference;* **3,** a passing allusion; as, she made no *reference* to politics; **4,** a passage or note in a book, article, etc., directing attention to some other book or passage; a citation; also, the book or passage to which attention is directed; **5,** a person to whom inquiries may be addressed regarding another person; **6,** a written statement about a person's character or ability; **7,** regard; respect; as, with *reference* to your request:—*adj.* used for information or research; as, a *reference* book.

ref-er-en-dum (ref′ėr-en′dum), *n.* [*pl.* referendums (ref′ėr-en′dumz) or referenda (ref′ėr-en′da)], **1,** the submitting of a legislative act to the vote of the people for approval or rejection; as, in 1992, the country rejected the Charlottetown Accord in a *referendum;* **2,** the right of the people to vote upon a legislative act; **3,** a direct popular vote on a proposed measure.

re-fine (ri-fīn′), *v.t.* [refined, refin-ing], **1,** to make pure; clear from impurities, dross, or worthless matter; as, to *refine* sugar; **2,** to polish; free from coarseness, rudeness, etc.; improve; as, to *refine* one's table manners.—*adj.* **re-fined′.**—*n.* **re-fine′ment.**

re-fin-er-y (ri-fīn′ėr-i), *n.* [*pl.* refineries] a place where anything is refined or made pure; as, an oil *refinery.*

re-flect (ri-flekt′), *v.t.* **1,** to throw or give back (rays of light, heat, or sound); **2,** to give back or show an image of, as does a mirror; **3,** to give back as a result; as, his act *reflects* honour upon him:—*v.i.* **1,** to consider carefully; think; **2,** to cast reproach, blame, etc.; as, her faulty grammar *reflects* upon her lack of education.—*n.* **re-flec′tor.**

re-flec-tion (ri-flek′shun), *n.* **1,** the act of throwing back; as, the *reflection* of light; **2,** that which is reflected, as an image; also, an effect or influence; as, the *reflection* of early associations on the character; **3,** careful consideration or thinking; as, this question requires prolonged *reflection;* **4,** criticism; reproach; as, a *reflection* on one's honesty; **5,** a remark, thought, or opinion; as, that was a profound *reflection.*—*adj.* **re-flec′tive.**

re-flex (rē′fleks), *adj.* **1,** thrown back; recoiling; as, *reflex* consequences; **2,** in *physiology*, showing automatic response to some outside stimulus; as, *reflex* action:—*n.* **1,** an image or reflection; as, public opinion is often a *reflex* of the newspapers; **2,** in *physiology*, an involuntary movement of some part of the body in response to a stimulus.

re-flex-ive (ri-flek′siv), *adj.* in *grammar*, indicating an action which the subject performs upon himself or herself; as, "cut" in the sentence "he cut himself" is a *reflexive* verb:—**reflexive pronoun**, a pronoun that, though used as the object of a verb, is invariably identical with the subject, as "herself" in the sentence "she hurt herself accidentally."—*adv.* **re-flex′ive-ly.**

re-for-est-a-tion (rē′fôr-is-tā′shun; for-), *n.* the replanting (of deforested land) with trees.—*v.t.* **re-for′est** (-for).

re-form (ri-fôrm′), *v.t.* to improve or make better by changing the form, removing the faults, or correcting or ending abuses; as, to *reform* the calendar, a thief, the courts:—*v.i.* to abandon evil ways:—*n.* a change for the better; a removal of some evil or abuse; as, *reforms* in the education system; also, improvement in character:—*adj.* pertaining to reform; as, a *reform* movement.—*n.* **re-form′a-tor-y; re-form′er.**

ref-or-ma-tion (ref′ôr-mā′shun), *n.* the act of changing for the better; improvement, esp. in social, political, or religious affairs:—**Reformation,** the great religious movement begun by Martin Luther in the 16th century, which resulted in the establishment of Protestantism.

re-fract (ri-frakt′), *v.t.* to bend from a straight line; as, to *refract* rays or waves of light, heat, or sound (in passing through media or layers of different density).—*n.* **re-frac′tion.**

re-frac-to-ry (ri-frak′tėr-i), *adj.* **1,** disobedient; hard to manage; as, a *refractory* puppy; **2,** resisting heat; hard to work or fuse, as ore or metals; **3,** not yielding to treatment, as a disease or wound.

[1]**re-frain** (ri-frān′), *n.* a phrase or verse repeated at intervals in a poem or song; a chorus.

[2]**re-frain** (ri-frān′), *v.i.* to hold oneself back; restrain oneself; as, to *refrain* from comment.

re-fresh (ri-fresh′), *v.t.* **1,** to make fresh again; revive; as, to *refresh* flowers; **2,** to restore after fatigue; as, rest *refreshes* the body; **3,** to quicken; as, to *refresh* the mind; **4,** in *computing,* to renew data stored in memory; **5,** in *computing,* to reload a Web page from its source.

re-fresh-ment (ri-fresh′ment), *n.* **1,** the act of reviving, or state of being revived; restoration of strength, liveliness, etc.; **2,** that which restores or revives, esp. food, drink, or rest:—**refreshments**, food and drink served to guests.

re-frig-er-ate (ri-frij′ėr-āt′), *v.t.* and *v.i.* [refrigerat-ed, refrigerat-ing], to cool or become cool; as, to *refrigerate* meat to keep it from spoiling.—*n.* **re-frig′er-a′tion.**

re-frig-er-a-tor (ri-frij′ėr-ā′tėr), *n.* a storage device used to keep things cold, esp. the kitchen appliance where food and other perishable things are kept cool.

ref-uge (ref′ūj), *n.* **1,** a place of safety from trouble or danger; a shelter or secure retreat; as, to seek *refuge* from the storm; **2,** one who or that which protects or defends from danger or misfortune; as, she is my *refuge.*

ref-u-gee (ref′ū-jē′), *n.* one who flees for safety, esp. from political or religious persecution, to a foreign land.

re-fund (ri-fund′; rē′fund′), *v.t.* and *v.i.* to give back or pay back (money); as, the game was cancelled and the money for the tickets was *refunded:*—*n.* (rē′fund′), the money paid back.

re-fus-al (ri-fūz′al), *n.* **1,** the act of rejecting or denying; **2,** the right to refuse or take something before others are given an opportunity to take it; as, the right of first *refusal.*

[1]**re-fuse** (ri-fūz′), *v.t.* [refused, refus-ing], **1,** to decline to take; be unwilling to accept; **2,** to decline to do or grant; deny; as, to *refuse* help:—*v.i.* to decline to take an offer; decline to do something.

[2]**ref-use** (ref′ūs), *n.* waste material; trash; rubbish:—*adj.* worthless.

re-fute (ri-fūt′), *v.t.* [refut-ed, refut-ing], to prove to be false or wrong; to overthrow by argument or proof.—*adj.* **ref′u-ta-ble** (ref′ū-ta-bl; ri-fūt′a-bl).—*n.* **ref′u-ta′tion** (ref′ū-tā′shun).

re-gain (ri-gān′), *v.t.* **1,** to get back; recover; as, to *regain* a fortune; **2,** to reach again; as, to *regain* shelter.

re-gal (rē′gal), *adj.* **1,** royal; fit for a king or queen; **2,** resplendent; magnificent.

re-gale (ri-gāl′), *v.t.* [regaled, regaling], to entertain in regal manner; feast; delight; as, he *regaled* us with anecdotes.

re-gard (ri-gärd′), *v.t.* **1,** to observe closely; look upon attentively; as, she *regarded* him with a frown; **2,** to consider; as, I *regard* her as an enemy; **3,** to heed; respect; as, *regard* my words; she does not *regard* her mother's wishes; **4,** to relate to; concern; as, the matter *regards* your happiness; **5,** to esteem; admire; as, I *regard* him highly:—*n.* **1,** a look or gaze; **2,** close attention or notice; **3,** care; consideration; as, *regard* for others; **4,** respect; affection; as, I hold him in high *regard:*—**regards**, good wishes; as, my best *regards* to your mother.

re-gard-ing (ri-gär′ding), *prep.* about; in respect to; as, a meeting *regarding* the new gym.

re-gard-less (ri-gärd′lis), *adj.* careless; negligent; heedless; with no thought or regard for; in spite of; as, *regardless* of danger:—*adv.* anyway; as, it was snowing, but she left *regardless.*

re-gat-ta (ri-gat′a), *n.* a boat race or series of boat races.

re-gen-cy (rē′jen-si), *n.* [*pl.* regencies], **1,** the office of a temporary ruler; **2,** a person or body of persons governing for another; **3,** the office, powers, or government of such a person or body; **4,** the period during which someone rules for another.

re-gen-er-ate (ri-jen′ėr-āt′), *v.t.* [regenerat-ed, regenerat-ing], **1,** to renew spiritually; **2,** to make a change for the better in;

reform; as, the economic system needs to be *regenerated*; **3,** to produce anew; as, the body *regenerates* tissue; **4,** to fill with new life or power:—*adj.* (ri-jen′ėr-it), **1,** having new life; **2,** spiritually reborn; as, a *regenerate* soul.—*n.* **re-gen′er-a′tion.**

re-gent (rē′jent), *n.* **1,** a person appointed to govern while the rightful ruler is unable to do so, or until he or she is able to take the throne; **2,** in certain universities, a member of the governing board:—*adj.* ruling in place of another; as, a *regent* prince.

re-gime (rā-zhēm′), *n.* **1,** a system of government; as, the communist *regime*; **2,** a time when a certain ruler or government is in power; as, the *regime* of Queen Victoria; **3,** a systematized method of living; as, a daily *regime*.

reg-i-men (rej′i-men), *n.* **1,** a regulated course of diet, exercise, sleep, etc., prescribed for some special purpose; **2,** orderly government; control.

reg-i-ment (rej′i-ment), *n.* an organized body of soldiers under the command of a colonel:—*v.t.* to systematize; subject to discipline, as if part of a military unit.—*n.* **reg′i-men-ta′tion.** —*adj.* **reg′i-ment′al.**

re-gion (rē′jun), *n.* **1,** an indefinitely large section of land; a district; as, the Rocky Mountain *region*; **2,** one of the divisions or portions into which the earth, the sea, or the air may be thought of as divided; as, the inner *regions* of the earth; the upper *regions* of the atmosphere; **3,** a division or part of the body; as, the *abdominal* region.—*adj.* **re′gion-al** (having to do with or happening in a certain large area; as, we won the *regional* soccer tournament).

reg-is-ter (rej′is-tėr), *n.* **1,** an official written record; as, a *register* of births and deaths; also, a book for keeping such a record; **2,** a person who keeps a record; as, a *register* of deeds; **3,** a device that records; as, a cash *register*; **4,** a device for regulating the entrance of heated air to a room; **5,** the compass or range of a voice or an instrument:—*v.t.* **1,** to enter in a list or formal record; enrol; as, to *register* students at the university; **2,** to mark or read; as, the thermostat *registers* 20 degrees; **3,** to indicate by facial expression; as, to *register* surprise:—*v.i.* to write one's name in a list or record; as, to *register* at a hotel.—*n.* **reg′is-trar′; reg′is-try.**

reg-is-tra-tion (rej′i-strā′shun), *n.* the act of enrolling or entering on an official list; as, high school *registration* starts today.

re-gret (ri-gret′), *v.t.* [regret-ted, regret-ting], **1,** to look back upon, or recall, with remorse or distress; as, to *regret* one's mistakes; **2,** to feel sorry about or grieve over; as, he *regretted* leaving:—*n.* **1,** sorrow for the loss or want of something; as, *regret* for vanished friendships; **2,** distress of mind over some past event with the wish that it had been otherwise; as, *regret* for harsh words; **3,** sadness; disappointment; as, I hear with *regret* that you will not come:—**regrets,** a polite expression of refusal in answer to an invitation.—*adj.* **re-gret′ful; re-gret′ta-ble.**—*adv.* **re-gret′ful-ly; re-gret′ta-bly.**—*n.* **re-gret′ful-ness.**

reg-u-lar (reg′ū-lėr), *adj.* **1,** according to some established rule, order, or custom; occurring on a fixed date; as, a *regular* holiday; without a break; as, in *regular* succession; fully qualified; as a *regular* student; orthodox; as, a *regular* Liberal; orderly or methodical; as, *regular* habits; unvarying, steady, or uniform; as, a *regular* pulse; **2,** following a certain design; symmetrical; as, *regular* features; **3,** permanent; as, the *regular* army; **4,** in *grammar*, following the usual rules of declension, comparison, or conjugation; **5,** *Colloq.* thorough or absolute; as, she is a *regular* bookworm:—*n.* **1,** a soldier belonging to a standing army; **2,** *Colloq.* a repeat customer or visitor; as, she's a *regular* at the restaurant.—*adv.* **reg′u-lar-ly.**—*n.* **reg′u-lar′i-ty.**

reg-u-late (reg′ū-lāt′), *v.t.* [regulat-ed, regulat-ing], **1,** to govern according to rule, method, or established custom; as, to *regulate* one's conduct; **2,** to put or keep in proper order; as, to *regulate* a household; **3,** to adjust a machine or device to some desired or standard condition; as, to *regulate* a thermostat.—*n.* **reg′u-la′tor.**

reg-u-la-tion (reg′ū-lā′shun), *n.* **1,** the act of adjusting; as, the *regulation* of temperatures; also, the state of being adjusted; **2,** a rule or law; as, hospital *regulations*:—*adj.* conforming to a regular style, method, or rule; as, a *regulation* uniform.

re-gur-gi-tate (rē-gûr′ji-tāt′), *v.t.* **1,** to pour or throw back; surge or rush back, esp. from the stomach; as cows *regurgitate* the food, which forms their cuds; **2,** to repeat anything; as, the student *regurgitates* memorized facts.

re-ha-bil-i-tate (rē′ha-bil′i-tāt′), *v.t.* **1,** to restore (a former state, rank, privilege, etc.); reinstate; **2,** to reestablish (in social position); clear the character or reputation; **3,** to put on a firm basis, as the currency of a country.—*n.* **re′ha-bil′i-ta′tion.**

re-hearse (ri-hûrs′), *v.t.* [rehearsed, rehears-ing], **1,** to narrate; tell the story of; as, she *rehearsed* the most interesting events of her career; **2,** to practise in preparation for a public performance; as, to *rehearse* a play, a scene in a movie, or a piano solo.—*n.* **rehears′al** (a practice session before an actual performance).

reign (rān), *n.* **1,** supreme rule; royal power; **2,** the time during which a ruler holds sway; as, the *reign* of King George; **3,** the period when someone has great power or influence over others; as, Elvis had a long *reign* as king of rock 'n' roll:—*v.i.* **1,** to exercise authority or power; rule; **2,** to hold sway; prevail; to have great influence; as, terror *reigned* in the village.

re-im-burse (rē′im-bûrs′), *v.t.* [reimbursed, reimburs-ing], to repay (a person); as, to *reimburse* the delivery people for the loss of their time.—*n.* **re′im-burse′ment.**

rein (rān), *n.* **1,** either of two leather straps fastened to rings in the ends of the bit of a horse or other animal as a means of guiding and controlling it; **2,** (often *reins*), any means of restraint or control; as, the *reins* of government:—**give rein to,** allow to be unchecked or uncontrolled; as, to *give rein* to grief:—*v.t.* **1,** to hold in, direct, or stop, by means of reins; as, to *rein* a horse; **2,** to restrain; control; as, to *rein* in one's anger.

re-in-car-na-tion (rē′in-kär-nā′shun,) *n.* **1,** the rebirth of the soul in a new body; **2,** the rebirth of something, as an idea, in a new form; a new embodiment:—*v.t.* **re′in-car′nate** [reincarnated, reincarnat-ing].

rein-deer (rān′dēr′), *n.* [*pl.* reindeer or reindeers], a large deer with branched antlers, found in northern countries and sometimes used as a draft animal or for food and clothing: wild reindeer of North America are caribou.

re-in-force (rē′in-fōrs′), *v.t.* [reinforced, reinforc-ing], to give new strength to; support; strengthen; as, to *reinforce* the foundations of a building.—*n.* **re′in-force′ment.**

re-in-state (rē′in-stāt′), *v.t.* [reinstated, reinstat-ing], to restore to a former position; as, to *reinstate* a suspended student.

re-it-er-ate (re-it′ėr-āt′), *v.t.* [reiterat-ed, reiterat-ing], to do or say again and again; as, to *reiterate* a denial.—*n.* **re-it′er-a′tion.**

re-ject (ri-jekt′), *v.t.* **1,** to throw away as worthless; discard; as, to *reject* all imperfect specimens; **2,** to refuse to take; decline; as, to *reject* an offer of assistance; **3,** to refuse to grant, believe, or agree to; as, to *reject* a suggestion.—*n.* **re-jec′tion** (the act of rejecting or the thing that is rejected).

re-joice (ri-jois′), *v.i.* [rejoiced, rejoic-ing], to feel or express joy or gladness; as, I *rejoice* in your happiness:—*v.t.* to make joyful; gladden; as, the sight of her gifts *rejoiced* him greatly.—*n.* **re-joic′ing.**

re-join (rē′join′), *v.t.* to join again; return to after separation:—*v.i.* (ri-join′), to make answer to a reply; retort.

re-join-der (ri-join′dėr), *n.* a reply; retort.

re-ju-ve-nate (ri-jo͞o′ve-nāt′), *v.t.* to make young again; restore youth, vigour, etc.; to renew; refresh.—*n.* **re-ju′ve-na′tion.**

re-lapse (ri-laps′), *v.i.* [relapsed, relaps-ing], **1,** to fall back into a former bad state or habit; as, he *relapsed* into carelessness; **2,** to fall back into illness after a state of partial recovery:—*n.* a slipping back; a setback.

re-late (ri-lāt′), *v.t.* [relat-ed, relat-ing], **1,** to tell (a story); recite; narrate; **2,** to show a connection between; as, to *relate* poverty and crime:—*v.i.* **1,** to refer or allude (to); have to do (with); as, the letter *relates* to his success; **2,** to understand and get along with others; to be connected with other people; as, she *relates* well to others.

re-lat-ed (ri-lā′tid), *adj.* **1,** belonging to the same family; as, the two cousins were *related*; **2,** having something in common; as, crabs, lobsters, and *related* sea animals.

re-la-tion (ri-lā′shun), *n.* **1,** the act of narrating or telling; also, the thing narrated or told; **2,** a connection between two or more things; as, the *relation* of lack of nourishment to disease; **3,** reference; regard; as, in *relation* to the matter of which you spoke; **4,** connection by birth or marriage; also, a relative:—**relations,** dealings; affairs; as, foreign *relations*; business *relations*; public *relations*.

re-la-tion-ship (ri-lā′shun-ship′), *n.* **1,** the fact of being related or connected to another person; **2,** a connection between ideas or things; as, a strong *relationship* between good marks and studying.

rel-a-tive (rel′a-tiv), *n.* **1,** that which refers to, or is thought of in its connection with, something else; **2,** a person connected with another by blood or marriage; **3,** in *grammar,* a word, such as the pronouns *who, which, that,* which refers to an antecedent:—*adj.* **1,** having or expressing connection with, or reference to, something; as, their conversation was *relative* to business; **2,** comparative; as, the *relative* speed of field hockey and ice hockey; **3,** having meaning only in connection with something else; as, "more" and "less" are *relative* terms; **4,** in *grammar,* referring to an antecedent; as, a *relative* pronoun.—*adv.* **rel′a-tive-ly.**—*n.* **rel′a-tiv′i-ty.**

re-lax (ri-laks′), *v.t.* **1,** to slacken; make less tight or firm; as, to *relax* one's hold; **2,** to make less strict, harsh, or severe; as, to *relax* rules of conduct; **3,** to relieve from strain; ease; as, watching a good sitcom *relaxes* one's mind:—*v.i.* **1,** to become less tight, firm, or severe; **2,** to cease from effort; lessen tension; rest; as, to *relax* after a day in school.—*n.* **re′lax-a′tion.**

re-lay (rē′lā), *n.* a new or additional supply of something to relieve another:—**relay race,** a race in which a number of contestants replace one another, each covering a definite part of the course:—*v.t.* (ri-lā′), to send as if by successive messengers; as, to *relay* a message to the teacher.

re-lease (ri-lēs′), *v.t.* [released, releas-ing], **1,** to set free; as, the man was *released* from prison; **2,** to free from obligation or penalty; as, to *release* a person from a promise; **3,** to deliver from pain, care, etc.; **4,** to permit the showing or sale of; to provide to the public; as, to *release* a book:—*n.* **1,** the act of setting free; the state of being set free; **2,**

deliverance from pain, anxiety, distress, etc.; **3,** a freeing from an obligation or a penalty; as, *release* from debt; **4,** a device for holding or freeing part of a machine; as, a *release* on an automobile hood; **5,** a placing on the market or before the public; as, the *release* of a film; **6,** a letter or document granting freedom from something; as, the parent signed a *release* allowing them to go on the class trip; **7,** in *computing,* the edition or version number of the software.

rel-e-gate (rel′e-gāt′), *v.t.* [-gated, -gating], **1,** to send or put away; exile; **2,** to remove, often to a less desirable place; as, to *relegate* furniture to the attic.

re-lent (ri-lent′), *v.i.* to become less harsh, severe, or cruel; to become more merciful; as, the tyrant *relented.*

re-lent-less (ri-lent′les), *adj.* going on and on in a strict or harsh way; not stopping or letting up; as, the *relentless* rain.—*adv.* **re-lent′less-ly.**

rel-e-vant (rel′e-vant), *adj.* bearing on the matter in hand; pertinent; as, a *relevant* story to this discussion.—*n.* **rel′e-van-cy.**

re-li-a-ble (ri-lī′a-bl), *adj.* trustworthy; fit to be depended upon; as, a *reliable* baby sitter; *reliable* news.—*n.* **re-li′a-bil′i-ty.**—*adv.* **re-li′a-bly.**

re-li-ant (ri-lī′ant), *adj.* having confidence; depending, as upon a person or thing.—*n.* **re-li′ance.**

rel-ic (rel′ik), *n.* **1,** that which remains; a survival; a trace or memorial, as of a custom, period, people, etc.; as, arrowheads are *relics* of primitive peoples; **2,** anything held in religious reverence as having belonged to a martyr or saint; **3,** a souvenir or memento.

[1]**re-lief** (ri-lēf′), *n.* **1,** the release in whole or in part from pain, grief, want, etc.; comfort; ease; **2,** that which aids or relieves; as, exercise is a *relief* from studying; **3,** release from a task or duty; as, the nurse's *relief* arrived at midnight; **4,** charitable help given to those in need; also, help given in time of danger or difficulty; **5,** fresh supplies of people, animals, food, etc., esp. fresh troops, coming to take the place of those tired out in action.

[2]**re-lief** (ri-lēf′), *n.* **1,** the raising of a sculptured design from a flat surface; as, the figures carved in *relief* on the wall; **2,** sharpness of outline, due to contrast; as, a tower in bold *relief* against the sky:—**relief map,** a map that shows the height or depth of land and water areas by using different colours and shadings.

THE SPIRES OF A CATHEDRAL IN RELIEF

re-lieve (ri-lēv′), *v.t.* [relieved, reliev-ing], **1,** to remove; reduce in severity; lessen; as, to *relieve* pain; **2,** to free from suffering, distress, etc.; to help; as, to *relieve* a famine-stricken people; **3,** to release from a post; take the place of; as, she *relieved* the guard at midnight; **4,** to set off; bring out by contrast; as, a white collar *relieves* a black dress.

re-li-gion (ri-lij′un), *n.* **1,** belief in a divine or superhuman power, esp. in a personal god; **2,** the outward acts and practices of life that grow out of the worship of such a god; **3,** any system of faith and worship; as, the Christian *religion*; **4,** anything that is very strongly believed in or seriously practised; as, hockey is a *religion* in many parts of Canada.

re-li-gious (ri-lij′us), *adj.* **1,** having to do with religion; as, Christmas is a *religious* holiday; **2,** following the practices of a religion very closely; as, the rabbi is very *religious.*

re-lin-quish (ri-ling′kwish), *v.t.* to give up; leave; surrender; as, to *relinquish* a claim.—*n.* **re-lin′quish-ment.**

rel-ish (rel′ish), *n.* **1,** a taste or preference; as, a *relish* for adventure; also, enjoyment; as, he ate his meal with *relish*; **2,** the quality that makes a thing pleasurable; as, novelty gave *relish* to the journey; **3,** a condiment that is a mixture of chopped vegetables and spices, which adds flavour to food and stimulates the appetite:—*v.t.* **1,** to enjoy; take pleasure in; as, to *relish* gossip; **2,** to eat with pleasure or zest; as, he *relishes* his dinner.

re-load (rē′lōd), *v.t.* and *v.i.* **1,** to load a camera, gun, etc., again; **2,** in *computing,* to get a new version of information, such as a Web page, that is already stored in the computer's memory.

re-luc-tant (ri-luk′tant), *adj.* **1,** unwilling; disinclined; as, *reluctant* to admit defeat; **2,** marked by unwillingness; as, a *reluctant* acceptance.—*n.* **re-luc′tance.**

re-ly (ri-lī′), *v.i.* [relied, rely-ing], to trust; have confidence; depend; as, you can *rely* on her.

re-main (ri-mān′), *v.i.* **1,** to stay behind when others go; as, only she *remained* in the room; **2,** to be left after a part has been used, taken away, lost, or destroyed; as, only the walls of the house *remain*; **3,** to be left for further consideration or action; as, that *remains* to be seen; **4,** to continue in the same state; as, he *remained* happy at school.

re-main-der (ri-mān′dėr), *n.* **1,** the portion left after anything is taken away; the rest; as, the *remainder* of one's life; **2,** in *arithmetic,* the quantity left after subtraction; as, 9 – 3 leaves a *remainder* of 6; **3,** the part, less than the divisor, left over after division; as, 17 ÷ 4 leaves a *remainder* of 1.

re-mains (ri-mānz′), *n. pl.* **1,** the part or parts left; as, the *remains* of a meal; **2,** ruins; relics, esp. of antiquity; as, the extensive *remains* of ancient Rome; **3,** a dead body; corpse.

re-mark (ri-märk′), *v.t.* **1,** to take note of; observe; as, we *remarked* his worried look; **2,** to utter briefly and casually; mention; as, he *remarked* that he would be in Toronto today:—*v.i.* to comment upon something:—*n.* **1,** observation; notice; comment; as, his unusual outfit made him an object of *remark*; **2,** a brief or casual comment or statement; as, we laughed at her *remarks*.

re-mark-a-ble (ri-mär′ka-bl), *adj.* worthy of observation or comment; extraordinary; as, *remarkable* wit.—*adv.* **re-mark′a-bly.**

re-me-di-al (ri-mē′dē-ul), *adj.* meant to improve or cure a problem; as, *remedial* reading classes help people to read better.

rem-e-dy (rem′i-di), *n.* [*pl.* remedies], **1,** anything designed to cure or relieve illness; a helpful medicine; **2,** that which removes or corrects a problem; a relief; as, the best *remedy* for fear of exams is to be prepared:—*v.t.* [remedied, remedy-ing], **1,** to cure, or cause to improve, with medicine; as, to *remedy* a cough; **2,** to repair; make right; correct (a problem).—*adj.* **reme′di-a-ble.**

re-mem-ber (ri-mem′bėr), *v.t.* **1,** to retain in the mind; recall; as, I don't *remember* how to play chess; **2,** to keep in mind carefully; know by heart; as, to *remember* an important historic date; **3,** to carry greetings from; as, *remember* me to her; **4,** to give a present to; tip; as, *remember* the waiter:—*v.i.* to possess or use the faculty of memory; as, he doesn't *remember* from one day to the next.

re-mem-brance (ri-mem′brans), *n.* **1,** the act or power of recalling to, or keeping in, the mind; recollecting; **2,** the state of being held in, or recalled to, mind; memory; as, in *remembrance* of someone; **3,** the length of time over which one's memories extend; as, a remarkable event in my *remembrance*; **4,** that which is remembered; also, a memento or keepsake:—**remembrances**, greetings showing regard.

Remembrance Day, observed in Canada each November 11, the day is set aside to honour those who served in the Canadian armed forces since World War I.

re-mind (ri-mīnd′), *v.t.* to bring to the mind of; cause to recollect.—*n.* **remind′er.**—*adj.* **re-mind′ful.**

rem-i-nis-cence (rem′i-nis′ens), *n.* **1,** the act of recalling or remembering; **2,** something remembered, esp. a particular event or experience that is remembered and told:—**reminiscences**, the collection of past experiences; as, *reminiscences* of school days:—*v.t.* and *v.i. Colloq.* **rem′i-nisce′** [-nisced, -niscing] (to recall past experiences; as, she *reminisced* about her summer at camp).

rem-i-nis-cent (rem′i-nis′ent), *adj.* **1,** bringing memories of the past; as, a *reminiscent* scene; **2,** given to recalling the past; dwelling on the past; as, a *reminiscent* letter; **3,** suggestive; as, a poem *reminiscent* of Burns.

re-miss (ri-mis′), *adj.* careless; neglectful; lax; as, she is *remiss* in keeping her engagements.—*n.* **re-miss′ness.**

re-mis-sion (ri-mish′un), *n.* **1,** the act of cancelling, as a fine or debt; also, forgiveness, as of sins or other offences; **2,** temporary lessening; as, a *remission* of pain; **3,** abatement of symptoms of a disease; as, her cancer is now in *remission*.

re-mit (ri-mit′), *v.t.* [remit-ted, remit-ting], **1,** to forgive or pardon; as, to *remit* sins; **2,** to send (money) in payment of debts or bills due; **3,** to refrain from demanding or insisting upon; as, to *remit* a fine; **4,** to make less severe; relax; as, to *remit* one's watchfulness:—*v.i.* **1,** to moderate, abate, or lessen in force; slacken; **2,** to send money, as in payment of goods.—*n.* **remit′tance; re-mit′ter.**

rem-nant (rem′nant), *n.* **1,** that which is left over or survives; as, the *remnant* of the defeated army; **2,** remainder, esp. a short length of fabric, the last of a piece, offered at a low price.

re-mon-strate (ri-mon′strāt), *v.i.* [remonstrat-ed, remonstrat-ing], to urge or put forward strong reasons against some act or course; as, to *remonstrate* against low wages.—*n.* **re-mon′ strance.**

re-morse (ri-môrs′), *n.* anguish of mind caused by sense of guilt; bitter reproach of oneself; repentance; as, she was filled with *remorse* after hitting her sister.—*adj.* **remorse′ful.**—*n.* **re-morse′ful-ness.**

re-morse-less (ri-môrs′lis), *adj.* cruel; merciless; pitiless.—*n.* **re-morse′less-ness.**

re-mote (ri-mōt′), *adj.* [remot-er, remot-est], **1,** far off in time; as, *remote* centuries; **2,** distant in place; as, *remote* lands; **3,** far removed; not closely related; as, his remarks were *remote* from the subject; a *remote* cousin; **4,** slight; not plainly seen; as, a *remote* likeness; a *remote* possibility:—*n. abbrev.* short for *remote control.*

remote control, 1, the control of a machine or device from a distance by using radio waves, electricity, or similar method; **2,** the device used to so control something such as a television set: often abbreviated as *remote.*

re-mov-al (ri-mo͞o′val), *n.* the act of taking away; as, we need help with the garbage *removal*.

re-move (ri-mo͞ov′), *v.t.* [removed, removing], **1,** to take from its place; transfer from one place to another; as, to *remove* toys from a counter; **2,** to put an end to; push out of the way; as, to *remove* a hindrance; **3,** to dismiss; displace; as, to *remove* a person from office:—*v.i.* to go from one place to another; change residence:—*n.* a step or interval; removal; as, unemployment is but one *remove* from poverty.—*n.* **re-mov′er.**—*adj.* **re-mov′a-ble.**

re-mu-ner-ate (ri-mū′nėr-āt′), *v.t.* [remunerat-ed, remunerat-ing], to pay (someone) in return for service, time spent, products, etc.—*n.* **re-mu′ner-a′tion.**—*adj.* **re-mu′ner-a-tive.**

ren-ais-sance (ren′e-säns′; ri-nā′sans;), *n.* a revival of interest and effort in any line of endeavour, esp. in art or literature:—**Renaissance**, the period of a great revival of learning and classical art in Europe during the 15th and 16th centuries, marking the transition from medieval to modern civilization.

rend (rend), *v.t.* [rent (rent), rend-ing], **1,** to tear apart with violence; split; as, the wind *rends* the sail; **2,** to take away by force or violence.

ren-der (ren′dėr), *v.t.* **1,** to give in return; pay back; as, to *render* blow for blow; **2,** to pay, as something owed; as, to *render* homage; **3,** to present for payment; as, to *render* an account; **4,** to utter as final; as, to *render* a decision; **5,** to perform or represent; as, to *render* a portrait; **6,** to furnish; give; as, to *render* aid; **7,** to cause to be; make; as, to *render* a house fit for habitation; **8,** to translate; as, to *render* French into English; **9,** to express or interpret, as music; **10,** to extract and purify (lard) by melting.—*n.* **ren-di′tion** (-dish′).

ren-dez-vous (rän′dā-vōō′; rän′dā-vōō′), *n.* [*pl.* rendezvous (rän′dā-vōōz′; rän′dā-vōōz′)], **1,** an appointed place of meeting; **2,** a meeting by appointment; as, he had a *rendezvous* with his friends:—*v.i.* and *v.t.* to meet or bring together at a certain place; as, we plan to *rendezvous* in the park.

ren-e-gade (ren′i-gād′), *n.* one who denies or gives up his faith; a deserter or outlaw.

re-nege (ri-nig′; ri-neg′; -nēg′), *v.i.* **1,** at *cards,* to fail to follow suit when required to do so; revoke; **2,** to go back on a promise or an agreement.

re-new (ri-nū′), *v.t.* **1,** to cause to become new once more; bring back the youth and strength of; revive; as, spring *renews* the earth; **2,** to take up again; resume; as, she *renewed* her piano lessons; **3,** to grant or obtain an extension of; as, to *renew* a magazine subscription; **4,** to replace; as, to *renew* furniture.—*n.* **re-new′al.**

re-nounce (ri-nouns′), *v.t.* [renounced, renounc-ing], **1,** to disown; cast off; as, to *renounce* an heir; **2,** to abandon; surrender; as, to *renounce* a claim; **3,** in *cards,* to renege or revoke.

ren-o-vate (ren′ō-vāt′), *v.t.* [renovat-ed, renovat-ing], to make as good as new; restore to a former or better condition of freshness; as, to *renovate* a house.—*n.* **ren′o-va′tion.**

re-nown (ri-noun′), *n.* fame; celebrity; as, a woman of great *renown.*—*adj.* **re-nowned′.**

[1]rent (rent), *p.t.* and *p.p.* of *rend:*—*n.* a tear; a hole or slit made by tearing, as in cloth.

[2]rent (rent), *n.* a fixed amount payable at a stated time or times for the use of property:—*v.t.* **1,** to lease; hire; hold or use without ownership, in consideration of stated, regular payments; as, to *rent* a house from the owner; **2,** to give possession of, in return for rent; lease; as, to *rent* a house to a tenant:—*v.t.* to be leased or to let; as, the house *rents* for $2,000 a month.—*n.* **rent′er.**

rent-al (ren′tal), *n.* **1,** something that is rented; as, the cottage is a summer *rental;* **2,** the amount of money paid or received as rent.

re-nun-ci-a-tion (ri-nun′si-ā′shun), *n.* the act of disowning, casting off, or giving up.

re-or-gan-ize (rē′ôr′gan-īz′), *v.t.* and *v.i.* [reorganized, reorganiz-ing], to arrange or organize anew; change to a more satisfactory form or system; as, to *reorganize* a club or files.—*n.* **re′or-gan-i-za′tion.**

re-pair (ri-pâr′), *v.t.* **1,** to put in good condition again after decay, injury, etc.; mend; renovate; as, to *repair* a roof; **2,** to remedy; set right; as, to *repair* a mistake:—*n.* **1,** the act of restoring to a sound condition, or the state of being thus restored; **2,** (usually *repairs*), the results of such restoration; as, he made the needed *repairs* on the barn; **3,** general condition in regard to soundness, need of repair, etc.; as, the house is in good *repair.*—*adj.* **rep′a-ra-ble.**

rep-a-ra-tion (rep′a-rā′shun) *n.* **1,** the act of remedying a mistake, a wrong, an injury, etc.; as, he made *reparation* for his neglect; **2,** that which is done by way of amends; **3,** reparations, money paid in compensation, as for war damages.

rep-ar-tee (rep′är-tē′), *n.* a quick-witted, clever reply; also a conversation full of such replies; as, she is expert at *repartee.*

re-pa-tri-ate (rē-pā′tri-āt′), *v.t.* **1,** to restore people, such as prisoners-of-war or refugees, to their own country; **2,** to return something, such as a constitution, to the country to which it applies; as, Trudeau *repatriated* the constitution to Canada.

re-pay (ri-pā′), *v.t.* [repaid (ri-pād′), repaying], **1,** to pay back, as money; **2,** to pay back money to; as, to *repay* a creditor; **3,** to make a return to; as, to *repay* one for past kindnesses.—*n.* **re-pay′ment.**

re-peal (ri-pēl′), *v.t.* to cancel; take back; revoke; as, to *repeal* an amendment:—*n.* a cancelling; an abolition; as, the *repeal* of a law.—*adj.* **re-peal′a-ble.**

re-peat (ri-pēt′), *v.t.* **1,** to do or speak a second time; as, to *repeat* a command; **2,** to say over from memory; recite; as, to *repeat* the alphabet; **3,** to say after another; tell; as, to *repeat* gossip:—*v.i.* to say or do anything over again:—*n.* the act of doing or saying over again; also, something done or said again; repetition.—*n.* **re-peat′er.**—*adv.* **re-peat′ed-ly.**

re-pel (ri-pel′), *v.t.* [repelled, repel-ling], **1,** to force back; check the advance of; as, to *repel* invaders; **2,** to reject; refuse to consider; as, to *repel* an offer; **3,** to cause disgust in; as, the idea *repels* me.—*adj.* **re-pel′lent.**

re-pent (ri-pent′), *v.i.* **1,** to feel regret or sorrow on account of something done or left undone; **2,** to change one's way because of regret for sin:—*v.t.* to feel regret or sorrow for; as, to *repent* hasty words.—*n.* **re-pent′ance.**—*adj.* **re-pent′ant.**

re-per-cus-sion (rē′pėr-kush′un), *n.* **1,** reaction or consequence; as, the *repercussions* of staying up late before the big exam; **2,** a forcing or throwing back of one thing by another, as waves from a sea wall; **3,** reflection; echo; reverberation (as of sound).

rep-er-toire (rep′ėr-twär′), *n.* a list of pieces (plays, operas, songs, etc.), that a performer or company is ready to perform: often called *repertory,* which may also be a collection, or a place where the collection is stored.

rep-e-ti-tion (rep′i-tish′un), *n.* the act of doing or saying something more than once; a repeating; also, that which is repeated; as, this work is a *repetition* of what you did yesterday.—*adj.* **rep′e-ti′tious; re-pet′i-tive.**

re-place (ri-plās′), *v.t.* [replaced, replac-ing], **1,** to put back in place; as, to *replace* the books on the shelf; **2,** to fill the place of; as, a new house *replaces* the old one; **3,** to supply an equivalent in place of or to take the place of; as, the coach *replaced* the goalie after the other team scored several times.

re-place-ment (ri-plās-ment), *n.* **1,** the act as, of replacing or being replaced; as, you need a *replacement* for the broken window; **2,** a person or thing that takes the place of another; as, the *replacement* for the goalie.

re-plen-ish (ri-plen′ish), *v.t.* to fill up again; stock in abundance; as, to *replenish* food supplies.

re-plete (ri-plēt′), *adj.* completely filled, esp. with food.—*n.* **re-ple′tion.**

rep-li-ca (rep′li-ka), *n.* **1,** a copy of a work of art, esp. one made by the original artist; **2,** any exact copy or duplicate; as, a *replica* of a tall ship.

re-ply (ri-plī′), *n.* [*pl.* replies], **1,** something spoken, written, or done by way of an answer; a response; as, he sent in his *reply* to the advertisement; **2,** the act of answering:—*v.i.* [replied, reply-ing], to say or write something in answer; as, to *reply* to a request.

re-port (ri-pôrt′), *v.t.* **1,** to give an oral or written account of, esp. an official statement; as, to *report* the results of an investigation; **2,** to make a charge or accusation against; as, to *report* an offender:—*v.i.* **1,** to make, prepare, or present a written or oral statement; **2,** to present oneself at a given place; as, to *report* for work:—*n.* **1,** an official or authorized presentation of facts; as, a government *report*; the *report* of a case at law; **2,** a school assignment that requires giving information about something; as, a book *report*; **3,** something widely talked of; rumour; hearsay; **4,** fame; reputation; as, a person of good *report*; **5,** a loud and sudden noise; the sound of an explosion; as, the *report* of a pistol.

report card, a written account sent from school to parents or guardians, giving information on a student's work, behaviour, etc.

re-port-er (ri-pōr′tėr), *n.* one who reports, esp. a person who collects news for a newspaper, magazine, television station, radio station, etc.—*adj.* **rep′or-to′ri-al.**

[1]**re-pose** (ri-pōz′), *v.t.* [reposed, repos-ing], to lay or place one's trust; as, to *repose* one's faith in her honesty.

[2]**re-pose** (ri-pōz′), *v.t.* [reposed, repos-ing], to place in a position of rest; lay down to rest; as, to *repose* oneself on a bed:—*v.i.* **1,** to lie at rest; **2,** to sleep; **3,** to be supported:—*n.* **1,** rest; **2,** sleep; **3,** quietness of manner.

re-pos-i-tor-y (ri-poz′i-to-ri), *n.* **1,** a place for storing and safekeeping, as a bank, warehouse, etc.; **2,** a place of sale or exhibition; museum; **3,** any storehouse; as, the Canadian tundra is a *repository* of untapped mineral wealth; **4,** a burial vault or tomb; **5,** a person in whom one confides.

rep-re-hen-si-ble (rep′ri-hen′si-bl), *adj.* blamable; deserving reproof or rebuke.—*v.t.* **rep-re-hend** (rep′ri-hend′).

rep-re-sent (rep′ri-zent′), *v.t.* **1,** to show a likeness of; portray; as, this statue *represents* Prime Minister Mackenzie King; **2,** to make (oneself) out to be; describe (oneself); as, she *represents* herself as belonging to the nobility: **3,** to act for or speak in place of; as, she *represents* her father in the business; **4,** to take or act the part of; as, he *represented* a clown in the movie; **5,** to stand for or be a symbol of; as, letters *represent* sounds.

rep-re-sen-ta-tion (rep′ri-zen-tā′shun), *n.* **1,** the act of standing for or representing; also, the state of being represented, esp. in a legislative body; as, each of the 10 provinces is given *representation* in the Senate; **2,** a picture, statue, etc., that portrays something; an image; as, a scale-model *representation* of a real airplane; **3,** a statement of fact or an argument in behalf of someone or something; as, she made false *representations*; **4,** a sign or symbol.

rep-re-sent-a-tive (rep′ri-zen′ta-tiv), *n.* **1,** someone or something that is typical or shows the main features of a group; as, he was a splendid *representative* of the Canadian businessperson; **2,** one who has power or authority to act for another or others; **3,** a member of a legislative body, elected by the people; as, she is one of the *representatives* from Manitoba; **4,** a salesperson; as, one of our sales *representatives* will call:—**Representative,** in the U.S., a member of the lower house in Congress, or in a state legislature:—*adj.* **1,** serving as an example; representing, or portraying a group or type; a *representative* selection of your writing; **2,** acting, or having power to act for another or others, esp. in government; **3,** founded on representation by elected delegates; as, *representative* government.

re-press (ri-pres′), *v.t.* **1,** to keep under control; check; as, to *repress* a wish; *repress* anger; **2,** to crush; subdue; as, to *repress* a rebellion.—*n.* **re-pres′sion.**—*adj.* **re-pres′sive.**

re-prieve (ri-prēv′), *n.* **1,** a temporary delay in carrying out the sentence of a judge; **2,** a temporary relief from pain or escape from danger:—*v.t.* [reprieved, repriev-ing], **1,** to grant a delay in the execution of; as, to *reprieve* a condemned prisoner; **2,** to free for a time from pain or danger.

rep-ri-mand (rep′ri-mand′), *n.* a severe reproof or rebuke:—*v.t.* (rep′ri-mand′, rep′ri-mand′), to rebuke severely for a fault, esp. to reprove officially.

re-pris-al (ri-prīz′al), *n.* **1,** a retaliation inflicted upon an enemy in return for an injury or loss suffered; **2,** any repayment of injury with injury.

re-proach (ri-prōch′), *n.* **1,** the act of scolding or rebuking; censure; as, a *reproach* for their lateness; **2,** the cause or object of blame, scorn, or shame; as, the tenement district is a *reproach* to the town:—*v.t.* **1,** to charge with something wrong or disgraceful; rebuke or blame; as, he *reproached* the bad driver for carelessness; **2,** to bring shame or dishonour upon; disgrace.—*adj.* **re-proach-ful.**

rep-ro-bate (rep′rō-bāt′), *n.* a sinful or wicked person; a scoundrel:—*v.t.* [reprobat-ed, reprobat-ing], to disapprove of strongly; condemn:—*adj.* given up to sin; wicked.

re-pro-duce (rē′prō-dūs′), *v.t.* [reproduced, reproduc-ing], **1,** to bring about or show again; repeat; as, to *reproduce* a play, a movie, a sound, or a gesture; **2,** to bear, yield, or bring forth (offspring); **3,** to copy; make an image of; as, to *reproduce* a person's features in marble; *reproduce* the document by using a photocopier.—*n.* **re′pro-duc′tion.**—*adj.* **re-pro-duc-tive.**

re-prove (ri-prōōv′), *v.t.* [reproved, reproving], to blame; rebuke; as, to *reprove* a naughty child.—*n.* **re-proof′.**

rep-tile (rep′tīl), *n.* **1,** any of a class of cold-blooded, air-breathing, scaly animals, usually egg-laying, as snakes, lizards, alligators, and turtles; **2,** a mean, debased person.—*adj.* **rep-til′i-an.**

re-pub-lic (ri-pub′lik), *n.* **1,** a state or country in which the supreme power is held by the voting public, which elects its own representatives and executive officers, who are responsible directly to the people; **2,** the form of government of such a state or country.—*adj.* and *n.* **re-pub′li-can.**

re-pu-di-ate (ri-pū′di-āt′), *v.t.* [repudiated, repudiat-ing], **1,** to refuse to recognize; disown; as, to *repudiate* an old friend; **2,** to decline to acknowledge or pay; as, to *repudiate* a debt; **3,** to reject; refuse to honour; as, to *repudiate* authority; to *repudiate* a statement.—*n.* **re-pu′di-a′tion.**

re-pug-nant (ri-pug′nant), *adj.* **1,** highly distasteful or disagreeable; as, a *repugnant task*; **2,** contrary; opposed; as a course *repugnant* to one's principles.—*n.* **re-pugnance.**

re-pulse (ri-puls′), *v.t.* [repulsed, repulsing], **1,** to drive back; beat off; as, to *repulse* an attack; **2,** to drive away by coldness, lack of sympathy, etc.:—*n.* **1,** the act of forcefully driving back; also, a defeat or setback; as, the army met with a *repulse*; **2,** a decided refusal; rejection; as, his request met with another *repulse*.—*n.* **re-pul′sion.**

re-pul-sive (ri-pul′siv), *adj.* disgusting; loathsome; as, a *repulsive* sight.

rep-u-ta-ble (rep′ū-ta-bl), *adj.* having a good reputation; decent; respectable.—*adv.* **rep′u-ta-bly.**

rep-u-ta-tion (rep′ū-tā′shun), *n.* **1,** good name or standing; honour; as, the artist has achieved world *reputation*; **2,** the general opinion held of a person, whether good or bad; as, he has a *reputation* for meanness.

re-pute (ri-pūt′), *v.t.* [reput-ed, reput-ing], to regard or consider; as, she is *reputed* to be rich:—*n.* the estimation, good or bad, in which a person, place, or thing is held; also, fame; as, a person of *repute*.—*adv.* **re-put′ed-ly.**

re-quest (ri-kwest′), *n.* **1,** the act of asking for something; as, a *request* for information; **2,** that which is asked for; as, to grant a *request*; **3,** the condition of being in demand; as, he is in great *request* as a public speaker:—*v.t.* **1,** to ask for; express a wish for; as, to *request* a favour; **2,** to ask (someone) to do something; as, she *requested* him to make haste.

re-qui-em (rek′wē-em; rē′kwē-em), *n.* a solemn musical service, hymn, Mass, etc., for the dead.

re-quire (ri-kwīr′), *v.t.* [required, requiring], **1,** to demand or insist upon; as, to *require* promptness at school; **2,** to have need of; call for; as, this will *require* haste.

re-quire-ment (ri-kwīr′ment), *n.* something that is needed or demanded; as, computer skills are a *requirement* of the job.

req-ui-site (rek′wi-zit), *n.* anything that cannot be done without; a necessity; as, honesty is a *requisite* of fine character:—*adj.* so needful that it cannot be done without; necessary; as, a *requisite* amount of food.

req-ui-si-tion (rek′wi-zish′un), *n.* **1,** a formal, written demand or claim; as, a *requisition* for office supplies; **2,** the form used for such a request; as, fill out the *requisition*; **3,** condition of being demanded or put to use; as, his new car was in constant *requisition* for family errands:—*v.t.* **1,** to demand; claim by authority; as, to *requisition* supplies; **2,** to make a demand upon, esp. for military supplies.

re-scind (ri-sind′), *v.t.* to annul; repeal; cancel; as, to *rescind* a law.

res-cue (res′kū), *n.* the fact of saving or freeing someone or something from danger, imprisonment, violence, etc.; as, the police aided in the *rescue* of the kidnapped boy:—*v.t.* [rescued, rescu-ing], to save or free from danger, violence, or imprisonment; as, the firefighters *rescued* the entire family.—*n.* **res′cu-er.**

re-search (ri-sûrch′; rē′sûrch), *n.* careful study or investigation of something in an effort to find new information by experiment or by a thorough examination of sources; as, much time, money, and effort are being devoted to cancer *research*:—*v.t.* to do research on; as, she *researched* Egypt for her report.—*n.* **re-search′er.**

re-sem-ble (ri-zem′bl), *v.t.* [resembled, resem-bling], to be similar to in appearance or character; as, the brothers *resemble* each other.—*n.* **re-sem′blance.**

re-sent (ri-zent′), *v.t.* to be angry because of; be indignant at; as, to *resent* criticism.—*adj.* **re-sent′ful.**

re-sent-ment (ri-zent′ment), *n.* strong anger or displeasure, often accompanied by a feeling of ill will, because of a real or fancied wrong, insult, etc.

res-er-va-tion (rez′ėr-vā′shun), *n.* **1,** the act of holding back or hiding; **2,** uncertain feeling; doubt; a limiting condition; as, they gave their consent with *reservations*; **3,** accommodations arranged for in advance, as in a hotel, on an airplane, etc.; **4,** a tract of public land set aside for some special use, such as an Aboriginal reserve.

re-serve (ri-zûrv′), *v.t.* [reserved, reserv-ing], **1,** to set aside or arrange for in advance; as, to *reserve* a room; **2,** to keep as one's own; keep control of; as, she *reserves* all rights in this book:—*n.* **1,** the act of setting aside, keeping back, or excepting; restriction; qualification; as, to accept a report without *reserve*; **2,** that which is kept in store for future use or for a particular purpose; extra supply; as, a large *reserve* of ammunition; **3,** a tract of land set apart for a special purpose, esp. for Aboriginal people; as, an Aboriginal *reserve*; **4,** restraint in speech and manner; **5,** funds kept on hand by a bank as a basis for credits:—**reserves,** a body of troops withheld from action and kept in readiness as reinforcements.

re-served (ri-zûrvd′), *adj.* **1,** reticent; keeping one's thoughts and feelings to oneself; also, undemonstrative; as, a *reserved* manner; **2,** set aside; arranged for, or capable of being arranged for, in advance; as, *reserved* seats.

res-er-voir (rez′ėr-vwär′; rez′ėr-vwôr′), *n.* **1,** a place where anything, esp. water, is collected and stored for current and future use; **2,** a part of an apparatus or instrument in which a liquid is held; **3,** a reserve supply; a storehouse; as, the library is a *reservoir* of information.

re-side (ri-zīd′), *v.i.* [resid-ed, resid-ing], **1,** to dwell for a length of time; live; as they *reside* in the country; **2,** to exist as a fixed or essential quality, characteristic, right, etc.; as, the power to issue currency *resides* in the national government.—*n.* and *adj.* **res′i-dent.**

res-i-dence (rez′i-dens), *n.* **1,** the place where one lives; a settled or permanent home; **2,** the act or fact of living in a place for a period of time; also, the period during which one lives in a place; as, during his *residence* abroad; **3,** a building where students live; dormitory.

res-i-dent (rez′i-dent), *n.* someone who lives in a certain place; as, a *resident* of Saskatchewan.

res′i-den′tial (rez′i-den′shul), *adj.* used or suitable for living; as, a *residential* area has many parks.

res-i-due (rez′i-dū′), *n.* that which remains after something has been removed; as, ash is the *residue* of the campfire.—*adj.* **re-sid′u-al** (-zid′).

re-sign (ri-zīn′), *v.t.* **1,** to give up; quit; surrender; as, to *resign* an office or job; to *resign* hope; **2,** to submit calmly; reconcile; as, she *resigned* herself to staying at home:—*v.i.* to withdraw from a position or office.—*adj.* **re-signed′.**

res-ig-na-tion (rez′ig-nā′shun), *n.* **1,** the act of giving up or yielding; a withdrawal; also, the official or written notice of such withdrawal; as, she handed in her *resignation*; **2,** patient submission; accepting problems or difficulties patiently; as, she accepted the loss with *resignation*.

re-sil-i-ent (ri-zil′i-ent), *adj.* **1,** springing back to a former position or shape; elastic; **2,** able to recover quickly, such as after illness or misfortune; buoyant; as, a *resilient* temperament.—*n.* **re-sil′i-ence.**

res-in (rez′in), *n.* **1,** a hardened or dried

brownish or yellowish substance obtained from certain trees, such as the pine and the fir, and used in making varnish, medicine, etc.; **2,** a similar synthetic material.—*adj.* **res′in-ous.**

re-sist (ri-zist′), *v.t.* **1,** to stop or repel; to succeed in standing against, warding off, etc.; as, the armour *resisted* all weapons; **2,** to strive against; oppose; as, they *resisted* the invaders; **3,** to not accept; keep from giving in; as, to *resist* temptation:—*v.i.* to offer opposition; refuse to obey or agree.

re-sist-ance (ri-zis′tans), *n.* **1,** the act of opposing; as, *resistance* to arrest; an underground *resistance*; **2,** power to ward off disease; as, his body lacked *resistance*; **3,** retarding force; as, air *resistance* to an airplane; **4,** the opposition of a substance to an electric current.—*adj.* **re-sist′ant; re-sist′less.**

re-sis-tor (ri-zis′tėr), *n.* in an electric circuit, a device providing resistance for protection or control.

re-size (ri-sīz′), *v.t.* **1,** to alter the size of something; **2,** in *computing,* to scale, esp. a graphic, to fit the screen without altering its basic shape.

res-o-lute (rez′o-lūt′), *adj.* having a fixed purpose; determined; firm; as, a *resolute* will.—*adv.* **res′o-lute-ly.**

res-o-lu-tion (rez′o-lū′shun), *n.* **1,** fixed determination; purpose, or firmness of purpose; as, a person of *resolution*; **2,** that which is determined; as, we seldom keep our New Year's *resolutions*; **3,** a formal proposal or statement voted on in a legislative assembly or public meeting; as, they passed a *resolution* banning cats from roaming freely; **4,** the fact of settling or solving something, such as a problem or a quarrel; as, to finally reach a *resolution* in the dispute; **5,** the sharpness or clarity of an image, such as a picture on a video or computer screen; **6,** the act of reducing a chemical compound to a simpler form or to component parts.

re-solve (ri-zolv′), *v.t.* [resolved, resolving], **1,** to determine by vote; decide; as, they *resolved* that no additional funds should now be paid out; **2,** to explain; clear up; as, he *resolved* all doubts by confessing everything; **3,** to reduce by breaking up; transform; as, the argument *resolves* itself into three heads:—*v.i.* **1,** to make up one's mind; come to a determination; decide firmly; as, he *resolved* to do better; **2,** to change to some simpler form or state; **3,** to pass or adopt a resolution:—*n.* **1,** fixed purpose; determination; **2,** that which has been determined on; a resolution.—*adj.* **re-solv′a-ble.**

res-o-nant (rez′o-nant), *adj.* **1,** echoing back; resounding; able to return, reinforce, or prolong sound; as, *resonant* walls; **2,** round, full, and vibrant in sound.—*n.* **res′o-nance; res′o-na′tor.**

re-sort (ri-zôrt′), *v.i.* **1,** to go often, habitually, or in numbers; **2,** to go or turn to for help, relief, or the gaining of an end; as, to *resort* to violence:—*n.* **1,** the act of turning to; as, a *resort* to arms; **2,** the person or thing applied to for aid; recourse; refuge; as, a last *resort*; **3,** a place much visited; as, a summer *resort*.

re-sound (ri-zound′), *v.i.* **1,** to sound loudly; as, his voice *resounded* far; **2,** to be full of sound; echo; as, the woods *resound* with song.

re-sound-ing (ri-zound′ing), *adj.* **1,** a long, loud sound; as, a *resounding* bang; **2,** clear or certain; as, a *resounding* success.

re-source (ri-sōrs′; rē′sōrs), *n.* **1,** knowledge of what to do in an emergency or difficulty; as, a person of *resource*; **2,** that to which one turns in a difficulty or emergency; as, flight was his only *resource*:—**resources,** a stock or reserve upon which one can draw when necessary; wealth in money, property, raw materials, etc.; as, a country's natural *resources*.

re-source-ful (ri-sōrs′fool), *adj.* **1,** abounding in resources or riches; as, a *resourceful* country; **2,** capable of meeting unusual demands or sudden needs; as, a *resourceful* manager can make ends meet when resources are scarce.

re-spect (ri-spekt′), *n.* **1,** regard for worth; honour and esteem; consideration; as, we have a lot of respect for your opinion; **2,** a polite attitude toward or consideration for someone who is older, of higher rank, etc.; as, to show *respect* for old age; **3,** a special point or particular detail to be considered; as, in certain *respects*, the book is good; **4,** relation, reference, or regard; as, with *respect* to your question:—**respects,** expression of good will or regard; as, to pay one's *respects*:—*v.t.* **1,** to honour or esteem; as, the world *respects* a good person; also, to obey; as, to *respect* the law; **2,** to feel esteem for; defer to; heed; as, to *respect* a parent's advice; **3,** to relate to; concern; **4,** to avoid intruding upon; as, to *respect* her privacy.—*n.* **re-spect′er.**

re-spect-a-ble (ri-spek′ta-bl), *adj.* **1,** worthy of regard or esteem; as, an honest and *respectable* merchant; **2,** of moderate excellence or size; passably good; as, a *respectable* income; **3,** presentable; as, a *respectable* suit of clothes.—*adv.* **re-spect′a-bly.**—*n.* **re-spect′a-bil′i-ty.**

re-spect-ful (ri-spekt′fool), *adj.* showing, or marked by, proper regard, esteem, or courtesy; polite; as, it is not *respectful* to call a senior citizen by his or her first name.—*adv.* **res-pect′ful-ly** (as, he bowed *respectfully* to the queen).

re-spec-tive (ri-spek′tiv), *adj.* belonging to each of several persons or things; separate;

particular; as, the boys took their *respective* positions in line.

re-spec-tive-ly (ri-spek′tiv-li), *adv.* as relating to each; in the order named; as, the red, blue, and green T-shirts are for Ari, Gina, and Katlin, *respectively*.

res-pi-ra-tion (res′pi-rā′shun), *n.* the act or process of breathing; as, artificial *respiration* performed on persons rescued from the sea.—*n.* **res′pi-ra′tor.**

re-spir-a-tor-y (ri-spīr′a-tėr-i; res′pi-ra-tėr-i), *adj.* having to do with breathing or the organs involved in breathing; as, lung cancer is a *respiratory* disease.

re-spire (ri-spīr), *v.t.* and *v.i.* [respired, respir-ing], to breathe; inhale and exhale.

res-pite (res′pit), *n.* **1,** a putting off; postponement, esp. in the carrying out of a sentence; as, the murderer was granted a *respite*; **2,** a brief period of rest; as, a *respite* from doing homework:—*v.t.* [respit-ed, respit-ing], to grant a respite to.

re-splend-ent (ri-splen′dent), *adj.* shining brilliantly; intensely bright; as, the heavens were *resplendent* with stars.—*n.* **re-splen′dence.**

re-spond (ri-spond′), *v.i.* **1,** to return an answer; make a reply; as, to *respond* to a question; **2,** to act or show some feeling in answer or sympathy; as, to *respond* to a friend's need; **3,** to react; as, to *respond* quickly to medicine.—*n.* and *adj.* **re-spond′ent.**

re-sponse (ri-spons′), *n.* something said or done as an answer; as, the computer's *response* slowed as more people logged onto the Internet.

re-spon-si-bil-i-ty (ri-spon′si-bil′i-ti), *n.* [*pl.* responsibilities], **1,** the state or fact of being answerable or accountable; as, I will assume no *responsibility* for debts contracted by you; **2,** that for which one is answerable or accountable; a duty or charge; as, this work is your *responsibility*; **3,** ability to meet obligations; as, a bank checks people's *responsibility* before granting them a loan.

re-spon-si-ble (ri-spon′si-bl), *adj.* **1,** involving trust, duty, or obligation; as, she is capable of holding a *responsible* position; **2,** answerable; accountable; as, a guardian is *responsible* to the law; I will not be *responsible* for his debts; **3,** able to answer for one's conduct; trustworthy; as, only a *responsible* person can hold this position; **4,** being the cause of; you are *responsible* for the budgie's escape.—*adv.* **re-spon′si-bly.**

re-spon-sive (ri-spon′siv), *adj.* **1,** containing answers or responses; as, *responsive* glances; **2,** easily moved; sympathetic; as, a *responsive* audience.

[1]rest (rest), *n.* **1,** freedom from motion; as, a machine at *rest*; freedom from work or activity; as, a day of *rest*; freedom from disturbance of mind or spirit; peace of mind; **2,** sleep; as, a good night's *rest*; **3,** a place of quiet or repose; a shelter or lodging; as, a sailor's *rest*; **4,** that on which anything leans for support; as, a back *rest*; **5,** in *music* and in *reading aloud,* a pause or a sign indicating such a pause:—*v.i.* **1,** to stop moving or acting; pause; relax; as, to *rest* from work; **2,** to take repose; sleep; as, I *rested* well all night; **3,** to lie dead; as, the unknown soldier *rests* in his tomb; **4,** to be supported; as, the house *rests* upon its foundation; to lean; as, her hand *rested* upon the arm of the chair; to be fixed; as, his eyes *rested* on the book; **5,** to rely; depend; as, the success of this campaign *rests* on you; to be based or founded; as, the case *rested* on the evidence of one person; **6,** to remain for action or accomplishment; as, the matter *rests* with you:—*v.t.* **1,** to place at rest or in repose; as, *rest* yourself after a hard day's work; **2,** to lean; as, he *rested* his arm on the table; **3,** to base or ground; as, we *rest* our hopes in her.

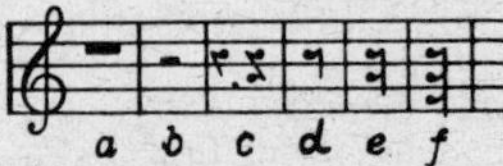

MUSICAL RESTS: A, WHOLE NOTE; B, HALF NOTE; C, QUARTER NOTE (TWO FORMS); D, EIGHTH NOTE; E, SIXTEENTH NOTE; F, THIRTY-SECOND NOTE

[2]rest (rest), *n.* **1,** what remains or is left over; the remainder; as, the *rest* of the book; **2,** the others; those who remain; as, the *rest* of the party:—*v.i.* to be and to continue to be; stay; as, we *rest* satisfied.

res-tau-rant (res′to-ränt′), *n.* a public place that prepares and serves meals or refreshments.

rest-ful (rest′fool), *adj.* **1,** giving repose; as, *restful* sleep; **2,** tranquil; peaceful; as, a *restful* hour.

res-ti-tu-tion (res′ti-tū′shun), *n.* **1,** the act of giving back to the rightful owner that which has been taken away or lost; **2,** the act of making good any loss, injury, or damage.

rest-less (rest′lis), *adj.* **1,** always active or in motion; as, a *restless* child; *restless* waves; **2,** eager for change; as, a *restless* spirit; **3,** affording no repose; uneasy; as, a *restless* night.—*adv.* **rest′less-ly.**—*n.* **rest′less-ness.**

re-stor-a-tive (ri-stōr′a-tiv), *adj.* having the power to bring back to a former condition or place; as, a *restorative* medicine:—*n.* something which has power to restore, esp. a medicine used to bring back health or to restore strength or consciousness.

re-store (ri-stōr′), *v.t.* [restored, restor-ing], **1,** to bring back to a former or original condition; as, to *restore* health; to *restore* a painting; *restore* a person to office; **2,** to bring back to the owner; as, to *restore* a lost pet.—*n.* **res′to-ra′tion.**

re-strain (ri-strān′), *v.t.* to check; hold back; as, I could not *restrain* my desire to laugh.

re-straint (ri-strānt′), *n.* **1,** the act of holding back or hindering from action of any kind; **2,** the state of being held back or hindered; **3,** that which limits or hinders; **4,** reserve; as, to speak with *restraint.*

re-strict (ri-strikt′), *v.t.* to keep within bounds; to confine or limit; as, to *restrict* a patient to a certain diet.

re-stric-tion (ri-strik′shun) *n.* **1,** the act or fact of restraining; as, to be open without *restriction*; **2,** anything that restricts, esp. a law or rule; as, a *restriction* against skateboards in the mall.

re-stric-tive (ri-strik′tiv), *adj.* **1,** limiting; restraining; as, *restrictive* trade laws; **2,** in *grammar,* limiting and necessary to identify the antecedent; as, people *who work hard* succeed: opposite of *nonrestrictive* (nonidentifying); as, idlers, *who seldom work hard,* rarely succeed.

re-sult (ri-zult′), *n.* **1,** consequence; outcome; as, the *result* of hard work; **2,** in *arithmetic,* the answer to a problem or example:—*v.i.* **1,** to follow as a consequence or effect; as, benefits will *result* from this law; **2,** to end; lead to something as an outcome; as, the quarrel *resulted* in a fight.—*adj.* and *n.* **re-sult′ant.**

re-sume (ri-zūm′), *v.t.* [resumed, resuming], **1,** to take up again after interruption; begin again; as, to *resume* work; **2,** to take or occupy again after leaving; as, he *resumed* his seat.—*n.* **re-sump′tion.**

ré-su-mé or **re-su-me** or **re-su-mé** (rez′zoo-mā′; rez′zoo-mā′), *n.* curriculum vitae; a summary or outline of one's education, skills, and experience prepared when applying for a new job, etc.

re-sur-gence (ri-sûr′jens), *n.* a rising again (into life); as, *resurgence* of hope.—*adj.* **re-sur′gent.**

res-ur-rect (rez′u-rekt′), *v.t.* **1,** to raise from the dead; **2,** to revive or bring again to notice or use; as, to *resurrect* an old style.—*n.* **res′ur-rec′tion.**

re-sus-ci-tate (ri-sus′i-tāt′), *v.t.* [resuscitat-ed, resuscitat-ing], **1,** to bring back to life from apparent death; as, artificial respiration to *resuscitate* a drowning person; **2,** to restore or revive anything; as, to *resuscitate* the flagging economy.—*n.* **re-sus′ci-ta′tion; re-sus′ci-ta′tor.**

re-tail (rē′tāl), *n.* the sale of goods in small quantities to the general public rather than to a dealer or distributor: opposite of *wholesale*:—*adj.* pertaining to, or engaged in, the sale of goods in small quantities; as, *retail* price; *retail* store; *retail* merchant:—*v.t.* (ri-tāl′; rē′tāl), **1,** to sell in small quantities; **2,** to tell in detail; pass on to others; as, to *retail* gossip:—*v.i.* to sell at retail price; as, this cloth *retails* for $20 a yard.

re-tain (ri-tān′), *v.t.* **1,** to hold or keep in possession, practice, control, use, etc.; as, she *retained* her lead in the race; **2,** to engage by payment of a fee beforehand; as, to *retain* a lawyer; **3,** to keep in mind; remember; as, he *retains* faces well; **4,** to keep in a certain or same position or condition; as, the pan *retained* the heat.—*n.* **re-tain′ment.**

re-tain-er (ri-tān-ėr), *n.* **1,** one kept in the service of a person of high rank or position; as, a lord's *retainers*; **2,** a person or thing that keeps possession; **3,** an advance fee paid to a barrister, adviser, consultant, etc.; **4,** a dental device that keeps teeth straightened or in place.

re-tal-i-ate (ri-tal′i-āt′), *v.i.* [retaliat-ed, retaliat-ing], to give like for like, esp. evil for evil; as, to *retaliate* upon a person for an insult:—*v.t.* to repay (an injury or wrong) with something of the same kind.—*n.* **re-tal′i-a′tion.**—*adj.* **re-tal′i-a-tor-y.**

re-tard (ri-tärd′), *v.t.* to cause to move less quickly; to hinder; delay; as, the heavy snow *retarded* traffic.—*n. Slang* an offensive term for a mentally retarded person or someone who is stupid or foolish:—*n.* **re-tar-da′tion.**

retch (rech), *v.i.* to try to vomit; strain, as in vomiting.

re-ten-tion (ri-ten′shun), *n.* **1,** the act of keeping in one's power or possession; **2,** the state of being kept in possession; **3,** the act or power of keeping things in mind; memory.—*adj.* **re-ten′tive.**—*n.* **re-ten-tiv′i-ty.**

ret-i-cent (ret′i-sent), *adj.* **1,** disposed to be silent; reserved in speech; **2,** restrained or reserved in general.—*n.* **ret′i-cence.**

ret-i-na (ret′i-na), *n.* the inner sensitive coating of the eyeball containing the ends of the nerves of sight: upon the retina are focused the images of objects.

re-tire (ri-tīr′), *v.i.* [retired, retir-ing], **1,** to go to one's room or other place of privacy; as, to *retire* after a long journey; **2,** to withdraw; retreat; as, to *retire* from a field of battle; **3,** to withdraw from business, or active life, esp. at a certain age; as, people no longer automatically *retire* at age 65; **4,** to go to bed:—*v.t.* **1,** to withdraw; as, to *retire* forces; **2,** to withdraw (currency) from circulation, or (securities) from the market; **3,** to cause to give up active service; as, to *retire* an employee with a pension; **4,** in *baseball,* to put out a batter or to end the turn of the opposing side.

re-tired (ri-tīrd′), *adj.* **1,** apart or withdrawn from society; secluded; as, a *retired* life; **2,** having given up business or active life; as, a *retired* physician.

re-tire-ment (ri-tīr′ment), *n.* **1,** the act or

state of retiring, or the fact of being retired from work; **2,** the time when this takes place.

re-tir-ing (ri-tīr′ing), *adj.* modest; shy; reserved; avoiding attention or notice; as, her *retiring* nature.

[1]**re-tort** (ri-tôrt′), *n.* a quick, witty, or angry reply; as, her insulting remark brought a quick *retort*:—*v.t.* and *v.i.* to answer sharply, wittily, or angrily.

[2]**re-tort** (ri-tôrt′), *n.* a (glass) vessel with a long tube, in which substances are distilled or decomposed by heat.

re-touch (rē′tuch′), *v.t.* **1,** to touch up; improve by going over; as, to *retouch* a photo; **2,** to repair or improve makeup or colour hair:—*n.* **1,** the act of touching up; as, this photo needs a *retouch*; **2,** the thing retouched.

re-trace (ri-trās′), *v.t.* [retraced, retrac-ing], to go over again; as, to *retrace* one's steps.

re-tract (ri-trakt′), *v.t.* and *v.i.* **1,** to draw back or in; as, the cat can *retract* its claws; muscles *retract*; **2,** to take back (something said or written).—*n.* **re-tract′a-bil′i-ty; re-trac′tion.**—*adj.* **re-tract′a-ble; re-trac′tive.**

re-tread (rē′tred′), *v.t.* **1,** to put a new tread on a worn tire; regroove; **2,** to alter someone or something superficially:—*n.* (rē′tred′), **1,** a recapped tire; **2,** a person or thing that is presented as new but in reality is the same; as, the politician was really a *retread*.

re-treat (ri-trēt′), *n.* **1,** the act of withdrawing or retiring, esp. the retiring of troops before an enemy; also, the signal for retiring; **2,** a place of safety or shelter; as, the cabin in the forest is my *retreat*:—*v.i.* to withdraw; retire; as, the water *retreats* from shore.

re-trench (ri-trench′), *v.t.* **1,** to reduce; as, to *retrench* unnecessary expenses; **2,** to take away; as, to *retrench* privileges:—*v.i.* to cut down expenses.—*n.* **re-trench′ment.**

ret-ri-bu-tion (ret′ri-bū′shun), *n.* reward or punishment suitable to a good or bad action, esp. loss or suffering considered as just punishment for wrongdoings.—*adj.* **re-trib′u-tive.**

re-trieve (ri-trēv′), *v.t.* [retrieved, retriev-ing], **1,** to recover; get back; regain; as, to *retrieve* a lost book; **2,** in *computing,* to locate and restore data stored on the hard drive; **3,** to repair the harm done by; as, to *retrieve* a misfortune; **4,** to fetch; as, he taught his dog to *retrieve* the ball; **5,** revive; as, to *retrieve* one's good name:—*v.i.* to find and bring back; as, he trained his dog to *retrieve*.

re-triev-er (ri-trēv′ėr), *n.* a dog trained to find and bring in game: a Labrador retriever and golden retriever are two popular breeds.

ret-ro-(ret′rō-), *prefix* meaning **1,** *backward, in reverse*; as in *retro*grade (moving in reverse direction or backwards); **2,** *situated behind*; as in *retro*sternal (behind the breastbone).

ret-ro-ac-tive (ret′rō-ak′tiv), *adj.* extending in scope or effect to matters that have occurred in the past; as, a *retroactive* law.

ret-ro-spect (ret′rō-spekt′; rē′trō-), *n.* a looking back on things past; a review of the past; as, life is pleasant in *retrospect*.—*n.* **ret′ro-spec′tion.**—*adj.* **ret′ro-spec′tive.**

re-turn (ri-tûrn′), *v.i.* **1,** to come or go back to a place, person, or condition; as, to *return* to one's home; **2,** to begin or appear again; as, spring *returns*; **3,** to come or go back in thought or consideration; as, to *return* to the subject; **4,** to reply; make answer:—*v.t.* **1,** to bring, send, carry, or put back; restore; as, to *return* a borrowed CD; **2,** to say in reply; as, to *return* an answer; also, to repay; as, to *return* a visit; **3,** to yield; as, the fields *returned* a good crop; **4,** to give back (an official report); as, to *return* the results of an election; **5,** in various games, to strike or play (the ball) back:—*n.* **1,** a coming or going back; as, a *return* from a vacation; **2,** a restoring or giving back; as, a *return* of lost keys; **3,** that which is restored or given back; **4,** profit or yield; as, a good *return* on an investment; **5,** an official record or statement; as, a tax *return*:—**returns, 1,** results; as, election *returns*; **2,** proceeds; as, the *returns* from the sale; **3,** exchange or giving back; as, no *returns* after Christmas:—*adj.* pertaining to a return or repeat; as, a *return* journey; a *return* engagement.—*adj.* **re-turn′a-ble.**

re-un-ion (rē-ūn′yun), *n.* **1,** the act of coming or bringing together again; **2,** a gathering of persons who were once closely associated but who have been separated; as, a class *reunion*; family *reunion*.

re-u-nite (rē′ū-nīt′), *v.t.* [reunit-ed, reunit-ing], **1,** to bring together again; **2,** to reconcile:—*v.i.* to become joined again.

re-vamp (rē-vamp′), *v.t.* **1,** to renew the vamp, or upper (of a shoe); **2,** to patch, reconstruct, or renovate.

re-veal (ri-vēl′), *v.t.* **1,** to make known; disclose; as, a chance word *revealed* his secret ambition; **2,** to display; unveil; expose to view; as, the curtain rose to *reveal* a forest scene.

re-veil-le (rev′i-li), *n.* a morning signal, as of bugle, drum, etc., to awaken and call people to the day's duties, as in a camp or military garrison.

rev-el (rev′el), *v.i.* [revelled, revel-ling], **1,** to make merry; **2,** to take great delight; as, to *revel* in music:—*n.* a riotous or noisy festivity; merrymaking.—*n.* **rev′el-ler.**—*n.* **rev′el-ry.**

rev-e-la-tion (rev′e-lā′shun), *n.* **1,** the telling or making known of something secret or private; **2,** that which is made known.

re-venge (ri-venj′), *v.t.* [revenged, reveng-ing], **1,** to inflict pain or injury in return for; as, to *revenge* an insult; **2,** to avenge a wrong done to; as, to *revenge* oneself:—*n.* **1,** the returning of injury for injury; **2,** the desire to return evil for evil; as, her heart was still filled with *revenge*; **3,** a chance to obtain satisfaction; as, to give a loser at cards his *revenge*.—*adj.* **re-venge′ful.**

rev-e-nue (rev′e-nū′), *n.* **1,** the sum that is yielded by an investment of any kind; income; **2,** the general income of a government from taxes, customs, and other sources.

re-ver-ber-ate (ri-vûr′bėr-āt′), *v.i.* [reverberat-ed, reverberat-ing], to resound; to echo; as, thunder *reverberates* in the mountains:—*v.t.* to cause (sound) to echo; also, to reflect (heat or light).—*n.* **re-ver′ber-a′tion.**

re-vere (ri-vēr′); *v.t.* [revered, rever-ing], to regard with respectful and affectionate awe; to honour; venerate.

rev-er-ence (rev′ėr-ens), *n.* a feeling of great respect and honour, mixed with love; as, she felt great *reverence* in the cathedral.

rev-er-end (rev′ėr-end), *adj.* worthy of reverence or deep respect:—**Reverend,** a title of respect given to clergymen; as, the *Reverend* Smith presided.—*n. Colloq.* a clergyman.

rev-er-ent (rev′ėr-ent), *adj.* feeling or expressing respect and affection mingled with awe; deeply respectful.—*adj.* **rev′er-en′tial.**—*n.* and *v.t.* **rev′er-ence** [reverenced, reverenc-ing].—*adv.* **rev′er-ent-ly.**

rev-er-ie (rev′ėr-i), *n.* **1,** a daydream; **2,** deep musing; dreaminess; the state of being lost in thought or dreams.

re-verse (ri-vûrs′), *adj.* **1,** turned backward; opposite; back to front; as, in *reverse* alphabetical order; **2,** causing an opposite motion; as, the *reverse* gear in a car:—*n.* **1,** the direct contrary or opposite, generally a backward, motion; as, to put the car in *reverse*; **2,** the back or less important side, as of a coin: opposite of *obverse*; **3,** a change for the worse; as, business *reverses*; **4,** a check or defeat; as, the enemy met with a *reverse*:—*v.t.* [reversed, revers-ing], **1,** to turn back; **2,** to cause to move in an opposite direction; **3,** to exchange; transpose; as, to *reverse* positions; **4,** to set aside or annul; as, to *reverse* a judgment:—*v.i.* to move in an opposite direction.—*adj.* **re-vers′i-ble.**—*n.* **re-ver′sal.**—*adv.* **re-verse′ly; re-vers′i-bly.**

re-vert (ri-vûrt′), *v.i.* **1,** to go back to an idea, purpose, condition, etc.; **2,** to return to the original owner or his or her heirs; **3,** in *biology*, to return to an earlier type.—*n.* **re-ver′sion** (ri-vûr′shun; ri-vûr′zhun).—*adj.* **re-vert′i-ble.**

re-view (ri-vū′), *n.* **1,** a going over anything again to consider or examine something; **2,** an examination by a higher court of a decision of a lower court; **3,** a lesson studied or recited again; **4,** a general survey; as, a *review* of the news; **5,** a criticism or critique, esp. of a new publication, movie, television show, play, work of art, etc.; **6,** a magazine or newspaper featuring criticisms of new books, movies, television shows, plays, etc.; **7,** an official military inspection:—*v.t.* **1,** to study or examine again; as, to *review* notes before an exam; **2,** to go over in order to make corrections; revise; examine critically; **3,** to write an opinion about a book, play, movie, television show, etc.; as, to *review* a concert; **4,** to look back on; as, to *review* one's life; **5,** to inspect (troops):—*v.i.* to write criticisms of books, movies, television shows, plays, works of art, etc.—*n.* **re-view′er.**

re-vile (ri-vīl′), *v.t.* [reviled, revil-ing], to address with abusive language; heap abuse upon; as, to *revile* a rival.

re-vise (ri-vīz′) *v.t.* [revised, revis-ing], **1,** to go over and examine in order to correct or update; **2,** to change and correct; as, to *revise* a manuscript; *revise* an old dictionary; **3,** to reconsider; amend; as, to *revise* one's opinion.—*n.* **re-vi′sion** (ri-vizh′un).

re-viv-al (ri-vīv′al), *n.* **1,** a bringing back, or the state of being brought back, to life, consciousness, or energy; as, the *revival* of flagging spirits; a *revival* of trade; **2,** a bringing or coming back to public attention and use; as, the *revival* of an old fashion or style; **3,** a new performance of an old play, opera, or movie; as, the festival of *revivals* of old movies; **4,** a reawakening of religious fervour; also, the series of meetings held with this purpose in view.—*n.* **re-viv′al-ist.**

re-vive (ri-vīv′), *v.i.* [revived, reviv-ing], **1,** to come back to life; **2,** to return to consciousness, as after a fainting spell; **3,** to return to vigour or activity; as, learning *revived* in the 15th century:—*v.t.* **1,** to restore to life; **2,** to give new vigour to; as, efforts to *revive* interest in handicrafts; **3,** to bring back from a state of neglect; as, to *revive* old songs; **4,** to recall (memories).

re-voke (ri-vōk′), *v.t.* [revoked, revok-ing], to cancel; repeal; annul; as, to *revoke* a law or a licence:—*v.t.* in *cards*, to fail to follow suit when one could and should:—*n.* in *cards*, a failure to follow suit when one could and should.—*adj.* **rev′o-ca-ble.**—*n.* **rev′o-ca′tion.**

re-volt (ri-vōlt′; ri-volt′), *n.* an uprising against authority; rebellion; as, only a handful joined in the failed *revolt*:—*v.i.* **1,** to cause a revolt; to rebel; **2,** to turn from something in disgust or loathing; as, the civilized mind *revolts* against cannibalism:—*v.t.* to disgust.—*adj.* **re-volt′ing** (very offensive; as, the *revolting* smell of the garbage).

rev-o-lu-tion (rev′o-lū′shun; -lo͞o′), *n.* **1,**

the turning of a body, esp. a heavenly body, around a central point or axis; rotation; **2,** the course or motion of such a body around another body in a fixed orbit; as, the *revolution* of the earth around the sun; also, the time it takes to complete such a revolution; **3,** any far-reaching change in habits of thought, methods of labour, manner of life, etc.; as, the 20th century saw a *revolution* in transporation, from the horse and buggy to the space shuttle; the Industrial *Revolution*; **4,** a sudden change in the government of a country; the overthrow of one form of government and the setting up of another; as, the Russian *Revolution*; American *Revolution*.—*n.* **rev′o-lu′tion-ist.**

rev-o-lu-tion-ar-y (rev′o-lū′shun-ėr-i), *adj.* **1,** associated with a sudden and complete change in thought, method, government, etc.; as, the *Revolutionary* War; **2,** leading to or causing great change; as, the Internet is a *revolutionary* way of researching:—*n.* [*pl.* revolutionaries], a believer in sudden and complete change.

rev-o-lu-tion-ize (rev′o-lū′shun-īz′), *v.t.* [revolutionized, revolutioniz-ing], to cause an entire change in the government, affairs, or character of; as, computers have *revolutionized* every facet of life.

re-volve (ri-volv′), *v.i.* [revolved, revolv-ing], **1,** to turn around on an axis; rotate; as, the earth *revolves* once in 24 hours; wheels *revolve*; **2,** to move in a curved path around a centre, as the moon around the earth; **3,** to occur regularly; come round again and again; as, the seasons *revolve*:—*v.t.* **1,** to turn over and over in the mind, as an idea or plan; **2,** to cause to turn.—*adj.* **re-volv′ing.**

re-volv-er (ri-vol′vėr), *n.* **1,** something that turns around or revolves; **2,** a pistol with several bullet chambers in a cylinder that revolves, bringing a fresh cartridge into position, so that several shots may be fired without reloading.

re-vue (ri-vū′), *n.* a musical show reviewing, satirizing, or parodying current fashions, events, etc.

re-vul-sion (ri-vul′shun), *n.* a sudden and violent change, esp. of feeling; a sharp recoil; as, a *revulsion* of feeling from a popular favourite.

re-ward (ri-wôrd′), *n.* **1,** something given in return; as, this prize is a *reward* for diligence; **2,** money offered for service or for the return of something lost; as, to offer a $100 *reward* for our lost kitten:—*v.t.* **1,** to give a reward to someone; **2,** make a return to (somebody) or for (something); as, to *reward* her courage.—*adj.* **re-ward′ing.**

re-write (rē′rīt′), *v.t.* and *v.i.* [*p.t.* rewrote (rē′rōt′), *p.p.* rewrit-ten (rē′rit′n), *p.pr.* rewrit-ing], to revise or write in different words; write (something) again.

rhap-so-dy (rap′so-di), *n.* [*pl.* rhapsodies], **1,** a piece of literature, highly emotional in tone; **2,** an utterance of extravagant feeling; as, he went into *rhapsodies* over the hockey game; **3,** in *music*, an instrumental composition, emotional in tone and irregular in form.

rhet-o-ric (ret′o-rik), *n.* **1,** the art of correct and forceful language, written or spoken; **2,** the use of words to impress or convince an audience; **3,** a false or exaggerated use of language; as, the report is all *rhetoric*.—*adj.* **rhe-tor′i-cal.**

rheu-ma-tism (rōō′ma-tizm), *n.* a disease causing stiffness and pain in the muscles and joints.—*adj.* and *n.* **rheu-mat′ic.**

rhine-stone (rīn′stōn′), *n.* a colourless paste gem made in imitation of a diamond.

rhi-no- or **rhin** (rī′nō′-; rīn-), *prefix* meaning *nose*; as in *rhino*plasty (nose plastic surgery).

rhi-noc-er-os (ri-nos′ėr-us), *n.* a massive thick-skinned, three-toed, herb-eating animal of tropical Asia and Africa, having either one or two hornlike projections on the snout.

rhi-zome (rī′zōm), *n.* any rootlike stem that sends out roots from its lower surface and leafy shoots from its upper surface.

rho-do-den-dron (rō′dō-den′dron), *n.* a shrub with shiny, usually evergreen leaves and large clusters of variously coloured bell-shaped flowers.

rhom-boid (rom′boid), *n.* a four-sided plane figure with equal opposite sides and two acute and two obtuse angles.

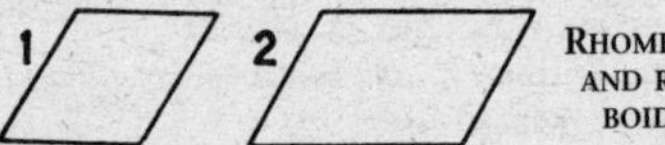

RHOMBUS (1) AND RHOMBOID (2)

rhom-bus (rom′bus), *n.* [*pl.* rhombuses or rhombi (-bī, -bē)], an equilateral, four-sided figure having oblique angles: if one pair of sides is greater than the other, the figure is called a *rhomboid.*

rhu-barb (rōō′bärb), *n.* **1,** a plant with large green leaves and long, fleshy, reddish stems or stalks; **2,** the stalks of this plant used as food; **3,** a medicine made from the roots of a certain kind of rhubarb; **4,** *Slang* a heated dispute or argument.

rhyme or **rime** (rīm), *n.* **1,** the identity in sound of the final sounds or syllables of two or more words; as, the words "side," "cried," and "guide" are *rhymes*; **2,** verse or poetry that consists of lines ending in a rhyme or a series of rhymes:—*v.i.* [rhymed, rhyming], **1,** to end in identical sounds; as, "bone" and "stone" *rhyme*; **2,** to compose verses:—*v.t.* to make (lines of poetry or songs) rhyme.—*n.* **rhym′er.**

rhythm (ri*th*′m), *n.* **1,** in *prose* and *poetry*,

the harmonious rise and fall of the sounds of language, produced by patterns, more or less regularly repeated, of stressed and unstressed syllables; **2,** in *music*, the ebb and flow of sound in measured intervals of time set off by beats; **3,** in any action, the regular repetition of movement or sound; as, the *rhythm* of the pulse; the *rhythm* of the workers.—*adj.* **rhyth′mic; rhyth′mi-cal.**

rib (rib), *n.* **1,** in humans and other animals, one of the set of long, flat, curved bones joined in pairs to the spine, which encircle and protect the cavity of the chest; **2,** anything like a rib, as a ridge in fabrics or knitted work, a rod in an umbrella frame, one of the curved pieces of timber that shape and strengthen the side of a ship, etc.; **3,** the main vein of a leaf; **4,** a sparerib or other cut of meat containing this bone:—*v.t.* [ribbed, rib-bing], **1,** to enclose or strengthen with, or as with, ribs; as, to *rib* an umbrella; **2,** *Colloq.* to tease.

ri-bald (rib′ald), *adj.* **1,** coarse, crude, or indecent; low; as a *ribald* song; **2,** noisy and profane; as, *ribald* mirth.

rib-bon (rib′un), *n.* **1,** a woven strip of fabric used for trimming, tying back the hair, etc.; **2,** a fabric strip; as, a printer *ribbon*; **3,** a shred; as, torn to *ribbons*; **4,** something that resembles a ribbon; as, a *ribbon* of light; **5,** a prize or award in a contest; as, he won several *ribbons* for his baking.

ri-bo-fla-vin (rī′bō-flā′vin), *n.* a factor of the vitamin B complex, found in milk, fresh meat, eggs, leafy vegetables, etc.: it is necessary for growth.

rice (rīs), *n.* **1,** a grass, valuable for its seed, grown in wet soil in a warm climate; **2,** the seed or grain itself, the chief article of food in many parts of Asia.

rich (rich), *adj.* **1,** having much money or many possessions; wealthy; **2,** expensive; valuable; as, *rich* clothing; **3,** great in amount; abundant; as, *rich* forests full of animal life; **4,** fertile; as, *rich* soil; productive; as, a *rich* mine; **5,** heavily spiced or seasoned; made with large quantities of butter, eggs, sugar, etc.; as, a *rich* pudding or cake; **6,** having depth and vividness; as, a *rich* colour; **7,** mellow and full in sound; as, a *rich* voice; **6,** highly humorous or entertaining; as, a *rich* situation:—**the rich,** those who have wealth.—*n.* **rich′ness.**

rich-es (rich′iz), *n.pl.* things that make a person rich, such as money or property; wealth.

Rich-ter scale (rik′tėr skāl′), a scale ranging from 1 to 10 that is used to measure the strength of earthquakes, with the lower numbers being the less severe: named for Charles Richter, the scientist who developed it.

rich text, in *computing*, that which includes the codes for special effects such as boldface, italics, etc.

rick-et-y (rik′it-i), *adj.* **1,** shaky; likely to collapse; as, a *rickety* chair; **2,** infirm; tottering; feeble.

rick-sha or **rick-shaw** (rik′shä′), *n.* Same as **jinriksha.**

ric-o-chet (rik′o-shā′; -shet′), *n.* a skipping or rebounding of anything, as of a missile over the ground or of a stone over the surface of the water:—*v.i.* to so skip or rebound and glance off; as, the ball *ricocheted* off the wall.

rid (rid), *v.t.* [rid-ded or rid, rid-ding], to free, as of a burden; clear; as, to *rid* oneself of an unpleasant task; *rid* a room of flies.—*n.* **rid′dance.**

[1]**rid-dle** (rid′l), *n.* **1,** a puzzling question or problem so worded that it is hard to understand; **2,** a person or thing that is difficult to understand; a mystery:—*v.t.* [riddled, rid-dling], to explain; solve; as, to *riddle* this question for me:—*v.i.* **1,** to solve riddles; **2,** to speak with doubtful meaning.—*n.* **rid-dler.**

[2]**rid-dle** (rid′l), *v.t.* **1,** to fill with holes, as with gunshots; as, the bored hunters *riddled* the sign with bullets; **2,** permeate or spread throughout; as, the manuscript was *riddled* with errors.—*n.* a coarse screen or sieve.

ride (rīd), *v.i.* [*p.t.* rode (rōd), *p.p.* rid-den (rid′n), *p.pr.* rid-ing], **1,** to be carried on the back of a horse or other animal; **2,** to be borne on or in a vehicle of any kind; as, to *ride* on a bicycle; *ride* in a car; **3,** of a vessel, to float or move over a surface; lie at anchor; **4,** to serve as a means of travel; as, this horse *rides* well:—*v.t.* **1,** to sit upon and manage; as, to *ride* a horse; *ride* a bicycle; **2,** to be carried on; as, to *ride* the waves; **3,** to take part in, as a race; **4,** to cause to ride; as, he *rode* the baby on his back; **5,** to oppress; as, the foreman *rode* his workers:—*n.* **1,** the act of riding; as, it was a great *ride*; **2,** a journey in a vehicle, on a bicycle, horse, etc.; as, a horseback *ride*; **3,** something ridden on or in, esp. for fun at an amusement park; as, the roller coaster *ride*.

ridge (rij), *n.* **1,** a range of hills or mountains; **2,** the projecting backbone of an animal; **3,** the angle formed by the meeting of two sloping sides; as, the *ridge* of a roof; **4,** any raised strip or line; as, the *ridges* in plowed ground:—*v.t.* and *v.i.* [ridged, ridging], to mark, or become marked, with raised lines, or ridges.

rid-i-cule (rid′i-kūl′), *n.* words, looks, or acts intended to make fun of someone, or to make something seem absurd:—*v.t.* [ridiculed, ridicul-ing], to make fun of, esp. in an unkind way; as, the teammates *ridiculed* the new player.

ri-dic-u-lous (ri-dik′ū-lus), *adj.* deserving or exciting ridicule or laughter; very foolish or silly.

rid-ing (rid′ing), *n.* an electoral district or constituency arbitrarily divided off for administrative and voting purposes: Metropolitan Toronto is comprised of several such ridings.

rife (rīf), *adj.* **1,** common; widespread; as, gossip is *rife* in the school; **2,** abounding; as, the office is *rife* with gossip.

rif-fle (rif′l), *v.t.* and *v.i.* **1,** to shuffle cards by dividing the deck in two, raising the corners or edges slightly, and allowing them to fall alternately together; **2,** to turn the pages of a book rapidly:—*n.* **1,** a method of shuffling cards, or of leafing rapidly through a book; **2,** a ripple, as on water; **3,** in a mining sluice, the lining of wooden slats, etc., arranged with grooves or openings between them for catching and holding particles of gold; **4,** any such slat, groove, or opening.

riff-raff (rif′raf′), *n.* **1,** the scum of society; **2,** trash; scraps.

[1]**ri-fle** (rī′fl), *v.t.* [ri-fled, ri-fling], **1,** to ransack and rob; as, the safe was *rifled*; **2,** to make off with; steal.

[2]**ri-fle** (rī′fl), *n.* a firearm with a long barrel that is spirally grooved inside to secure greater accuracy in firing:—*v.t.* [ri-fled, ri-fling], to groove (a gun barrel) spirally.—*n.* **ri′fle-man.**

rift (rift), *n.* **1,** an opening made by splitting; a cleft, as a crevice in a rock; **2,** any opening or separation; as, a *rift* in friendship; a *rift* in a fog:—*v.t.* and *v.i.* to split; burst open.

rig (rig), *v.t.* [rigged, rig-ging], **1,** to furnish (a ship) with spars, ropes, sails, etc.; **2,** to make; equip; as, to *rig* up a fishing pole; **3,** to dress; as, she *rigged* herself out in an old costume; **4,** to manipulate fraudulently; as, to *rig* the election, a boxing match, quiz show, etc.:—*n.* **1,** a special arrangement of sails, masts, etc., on a ship; as, a square *rig*; **2,** the structure and equipment for a special purpose, such as drilling for oil; as, working on an oil *rig*; **3,** *Colloq.* a tractor trailer or large transport truck; as, to drive the big *rigs*; **4,** *Colloq.* an odd style of dress; outfit; as, a cowboy's *rig.*

rig-ging (rig′ing), *n.* **1,** the ropes, chains, etc., by which the masts and spars of a vessel are supported, and the sails trimmed or set; **2,** any gear or tackle, esp. that used in logging.—*n.* **rig′ger.**

right (rīt), *adj.* **1,** straight; as, a *right* line; **2,** just; honourable; as, it is *right* to fulfill one's obligations; **3,** fit; suitable; as, the *right* person for the job; **4,** correct; not mistaken; as, her opinion is usually *right*; **5,** in good condition; well; healthy; as, to be all *right*; **6,** meant to be placed or worn so as to be seen; as, the *right* side of a rug; the *right* side of a jacket; **7,** naming the side of the body on which are the arm and hand, which many people naturally use for writing, carrying, etc.: opposite of *left*:—*adv.* **1,** in a direct line; as, he went *right* to the place; **2,** justly; honourably; truthfully; as, to act *right*; **3,** suitably; properly; as, nothing has been done *right*; **4,** exactly; as, *right* now; **5,** in the direction of the right side; as, then you should turn *right*; **6,** very; as, *right* honourable:—*n.* **1,** that which is proper, just, honourable: opposite of *wrong*; as, to fight for the *right*; **2,** the right-hand side; **3,** something to which one has a moral or legal claim; as, to defend one's *rights*; **4,** in *politics*, the conservative party: opposite of *left*:—*v.t.* **1,** to restore to proper condition; correct; as, to *right* an injustice; **2,** to make straight or upright; as, to *right* a chair:—*v.i.* to go back to a natural, generally an upright, position.

right an-gle, an angle of 90 degrees formed by two straight lines perpendicular to each other.

right-eous (rī′chus), *adj.* **1,** just; upright; honourable; as, a *righteous* sovereign; **2,** justifiable; as, *righteous* indignation.—*adv.* **right′eous-ly.**—*n.* **right′eous-ness.**

right-ful (rīt′fool), *adj.* **1,** having a just claim according to law; as, the *rightful* heir; **2,** just; fair; as, a *rightful* claim; **3,** held by just claim; as, a *rightful* inheritance.—*n.* **right′ful-ness.**

right-hand (rīt′-hand′), *adj.* **1,** pertaining to, or situated on, the right; **2,** chiefly relied upon; as, my *right-hand* person; **3,** intended for the right hand, as a glove.—*adj.* **right′-hand′ed.**

right-ly (rīt′li), *adv.* **1,** honestly; uprightly; as, duty *rightly* performed; **2,** properly; suitably; as, she is *rightly* called our benefactor; **3,** correctly; in accordance with fact; as, you are *rightly* informed.

right triangle, a triangle with one right angle.

rig-id (rij′id), *adj.* **1,** stiff; immovable; as, the *rigid* bone of the upper jaw; **2,** strict; severe; unbending; unchanging; as, someone with *rigid* ideas.—*n.* **ri-gid′i-ty** (ri-jid′i-ti).

rig-ma-role or **rig-a-ma-role** (rig′ma-rōl′; rig′a-ma-rōl′), *n.* **1,** complicated, finicky, difficult-to-understand procedure, esp. one that is very long; **2,** foolish, disconnected talk; nonsense:—*adj.* incoherent; frivolous.

ri-gor mor-tis (rī′gėr; ri′gėr môr′tis), *n.* the stiffening of the body soon after death.

rig-our (rig′ėr), *n.* **1,** strictness; severity; as, to enforce a law with *rigour*; **2,** severity of climate; hardship; as, the *rigours* of Arctic life.—*adj.* **rig′or-ous.**

rim (rim), *n.* **1,** a border, edge, or margin, esp. when round or raised; as, a glass *rim*; **2,** the outer part of the wheel of a car or bicycle to which the tire is attached:—*v.t.* [rimmed, rim-ming], **1,** to furnish with a border or edge; **2,** to serve as a border around; as, silver *rims* the cup.

rind (rīnd), *n.* the outer skin or coat of a thing; as, the *rind* of a lemon; the *rind* of cheese; also, the bark of a tree.

[1]**ring** (ring), *n.* **1,** any circular band or hoop, esp. a small ornamental hoop, as of gold or platinum, often set with gems, worn as an ornament or distinctive mark; as, an engagement *ring;* a school *ring;* **2,** an ornament for the ear; as, an ear*ring;* **3,** anything circular in shape; as, a key *ring;* a *ring* of smoke; **4,** any circular arrangement; as, a *ring* of dancers; **5,** an arena or space used for contests or displays; as, a boxing *ring;* a circus with three *rings;* **6,** a group of persons working together secretly, often toward some unlawful end; as, a drug trafficking *ring:*—*v.t.* [ringed, ring-ing], **1,** to put a ring around; encircle; hem in; **2,** to fit or decorate with a ring or rings; **3,** to put a ring through; as, to *ring* the nose of a bull; **4,** in certain games, such as horseshoes, to throw a loop over (a peg).

[2]**ring** (ring), *v.i.* [*p.t.* rang (rang), *p.p.* rung (rung), *p.pr.* ring-ing], **1,** to sound musically or resound, as a bell when struck; **2,** to cause a bell to sound; as, to *ring* for service; **3,** to sound loudly and clearly; as, his voice *rang* out; **4,** to give the impression of a quality; as, her excuse *rings* false; **5,** to be filled with a buzzing sound; as, my ears *ring;* **6,** to resound; echo; as, the woods *ring* with song; **7,** to be known far and wide; be famous; as, his deeds *ring* through the country:—*v.t.* **1,** to cause (particularly a bell or other metal object) to give forth a resonant sound; **2,** to announce or proclaim by a bell; as, to *ring* the hours; **3,** to summon, control, or otherwise affect by a bell signal; as, to *ring* up a friend on the telephone; *ring* up the curtain:—*n.* **1,** the sound made by a blow on metal; as, the *ring* of a hammer on iron; also, any similar sound; as, the musical *ring* of glass; **2,** a summons by, or as by, a bell; as, the *ring* of an alarm; **3,** a characteristic quality of spoken or written words; as, her words have the *ring* of sincerity; **4,** any echoing or repeated sound; as, the *ring* of applause.—*n.* **ring′er.**

ring-lead-er (ring′lēd′ėr), *n.* the leader of a number of persons banded together, usually for some unlawful act.

ring-let (ring′lit), *n.* **1,** a small ring; **2,** a curl or lock of hair.

rink (ringk), *n.* **1,** an outdoor expanse of ice marked off for skating or hockey playing; as, a hockey rink; **2,** an artificial sheet of ice in a building, for skating, or a floor for roller skating; **3,** the building that contains this.

rinse (rins), *v.t.* [rinsed, rins-ing], **1,** to put through clear water to remove all traces of soap; as, to *rinse* clothes; **2,** to wash lightly; as, to *rinse* the mouth:—*n.* **1,** a light wash, esp. to remove soap; **2,** a liquid that temporarily changes the colour of a person's hair.

ri-ot (rī′ut), *n.* **1,** disorderly or uproarious behaviour; revelry; **2,** a disturbance of the public peace by a number of persons who are often ready for violence; as, a labour *riot;* **3,** unrestrained display on growth; as, a *riot* of colour; a *riot* of weeds; **4,** *Colloq.* someone or something that is very funny or enjoyable; as, Ralph always referred to Alice as a *riot;* that joke was a *riot:*—*v.i.* **1,** to raise an uproar; engage in a public disturbance; **2,** to eat and drink without restraint; revel.—*n.* **ri′ot-er.**—*adj.* **ri′ot-ous.**—*adv.* **ri′ot-ous-ly.**

rip (rip) *v.t.* [ripped, rip-ping], **1,** to tear or cut with violence; as, she *ripped* open the package; he *ripped* off the bandage from his arm; **2,** to undo the seam of by cutting or pulling out the stitches; as, please *rip* both sleeves; **3,** to saw (wood) along, or with, the grain; **4,** *Colloq.* to swindle; as, she *ripped* us off:—*v.i.* **1,** to become torn apart; as, my skirt *ripped;* **2,** *Colloq.* to criticize severely; as, the coach *ripped* into the team:—*n.* **1,** a rent made by the breaking of stitches; also, a tear; **2,** *Colloq.* a swindle; as, it was a real *rip*-off .

ripe (rīp), *adj.* [rip-er, rip-est], **1,** grown to maturity; ready for harvest as, *ripe* fruit is sweetest; **2,** just right for use; mellow; as, *ripe* ale; **3,** advanced to a high degree; mature; as, *ripe* wisdom; **4,** ready; prepared; as, *ripe* for action.

rip-en (rī′pen), *v.t.* and *v.i.* to become ripe; as, cherries *ripen* faster than apples.

rip-ple (rip′l), *n.* **1,** a tiny wave on the surface of water; as, the stone made rings of *ripples;* **2,** any slight, curling wave; as, *ripples* of hair; **3,** the sound made by gentle waves of water, or a sound like it; as, a *ripple* of mirth:—*v.t.* [rip-pled, rip-pling], to make small curling waves upon or in; as the wind *ripples* the water:—*v.i.* **1,** to become ruffled or waved on the surface; **2,** to sound like running water; as, the laughter of children *rippled* below us.

rise (rīz), *v.i.* [*p.t.* rose (rōz), *p.p.* ris-en (riz′n), *p.pr.* ris-ing], **1,** to go from a lower position to a higher; mount; ascend; as, a bird or lift *rises;* **2,** to extend upward; reach or attain; as, the building *rises* to a height of over 20 metres; also, to slope upward; as, *rising* ground; **3,** to get up from kneeling sitting, or lying down; stand up; as, to *rise* from bed; **4,** to appear above the horizon, as the sun; **5,** to come into view or existence; as, hills *rose* on my right; also, to have an origin; as, this river *rises* in the north; **6,** to swell up, as bread dough in fermentation; **7,** to increase in value, force, intensity, etc.; as, gas is expected to *rise* in price; his fears *rose;* **8,** to thrive; prosper; also, to be promoted in rank; as, to *rise* in the world; **9,** to revolt; rebel; as, to *rise* against authority; **10,** to prove equal to something; as, to *rise* to one's opportunities; **11,** to live again; as, to *rise* from the dead:—*n.* **1,** the act of going up; ascent; **2,** the distance anything rises or ascends; as, the *rise* of a step; **3,** a small hill; **4,** appearance above the horizon; **5,** origin; source; as, the *rise* of a river; **6,** increase in value, amount, etc.; as, a steady *rise* of prices; **7,** an advance in power or rank.

ris-er (rīz′ėr), *n.* **1,** one who rises, esp. with reference to the hour of rising; as, we are all late *risers*; **2,** the upright part of a step or stair.

ris-i-ble (riz′i-bl), *adj.* **1,** having the power to laugh; as, humans are the only *risible* animals; **2,** laughable; ridiculous; as *risible* jokes; **3,** used in laughing; as, *risible* muscles.—*n.* **ris′i-bil′i-ty** (*pl.* sensitiveness to the ridiculous).

risk (risk), *n.* possibility of loss or injury; peril:—*v.t.* **1,** to expose to danger; as, to *risk* life and limb; **2,** to hazard; as, to *risk* a battle.

risk-y (ris′ki), *adj.* dangerous; involving the possibility of loss or injury; as, skydiving is a *risky* sport.

ris-qué (rēs′kā′), *adj.* daringly close to being improper or indelicate; as, a *risqué* story.

rite (rīt), *n.* **1,** the prescribed form for conducting a solemn ceremony; also, the ceremony; as, funeral *rites*; **2,** anything considered important or required; as, a *rite* of passage.

rit-u-al (rit′ū-al), *adj.* pertaining to formal, solemn ceremonies; as, *ritual* observances:—*n.* **1,** a set form for conducting a solemn, esp. a religious, ceremony; **2,** a book of such forms; **3,** any action that is often repeated in the same way; as, pancakes are a Sunday morning *ritual*.—*n.* **rit′u-al-ism**; **rit′u-a-list**.—*adj.* **rit′u-a-lis′tic**.

ri-val (rī′val), *n.* one who strives to equal or surpass another in some way; a competitor; as, *rivals* in soccer:—*v.t.* [rivalled, rival-ling], to try to equal or surpass; compete with; also, to be the equal of or match for; as, Toronto *rivals* Montreal in banking:—*adj.* competing; as, *rival* hockey teams.—*n.* **ri′val-ry**.

riv-er (riv′ėr), *n.* **1,** a large stream of water flowing in a definite channel into another stream, or into a lake or sea; **2,** an abundant flow of something that resembles a river; as, a *river* of blood.

river horse, *n.* Same as **hippopotamus**.

riv-et (riv′it), *n.* a metal bolt with a head on one end, used to fasten together two or more pieces of wood, metal, etc., by passing it through holes and hammering down the plain end to form another head:—*v.t.* **1,** to secure with, or as with, such a bolt; as, to *rivet* parts of a car; **2,** to make firm or secure; as, to *rivet* a friendship; **3,** to fix (the eyes, mind, etc.) attentively.—*n.* **riv′et-er**.—*adj.* **riv′et-ing** (completely absorbing).

riv-u-let (riv′ū-lit), *n.* **1,** a little stream; **2,** a stream of liquid; as, a *rivulet* of sweat.

roach (rōch), *n.* **1,** a household insect pest; a cockroach; **2,** *Slang* the butt of a marijuana cigarette.

road (rōd), *n.* **1,** a public way for travel; highway; **2,** a way or means by which anything is reached; as, the *road* to happiness; **3,** a course.—*n.* **road′bed′**; **road′block′**; **road′house′**; **road′side′**; **road′way′**.

roam (rōm), *v.i.* to wander about aimlessly; ramble:—*v.t.* to wander over; as, to *roam* the countryside.

roan (rōn), *adj.* reddish brown, black, on chestnut, thickly sprinkled with grey or white; as, a *roan* horse:—*n.* **1,** a roan colour; **2,** a horse of that colour.

roar (rōr), *n.* **1,** the deep, full cry of a large animal; as, the *roar* of a tiger; **2,** any loud, confused noise; as, the *roar* of traffic; **3,** loudly expressed mirth; as, a *roar* of laughter:—*v.i.* **1,** to cry with a loud, full, deep sound; as, a lion *roars*; **2,** to cry loudly, as in pain, distress, or anger; **3,** to laugh loudly; **4,** to make a loud, confused noise, as wind, waves, passing vehicles, etc.:—*v.t.* to utter boisterously; cry aloud; as, he *roared* his defiance.

roast (rōst), *v.t.* **1,** to cook before a fire or in a closed oven; **2,** to dry and brown by heating; as, to *roast* peanuts; **3,** to criticize severely; as, the critics *roasted* the new film; **4,** to honour with a roast ceremony:—*v.i.* to be cooked by heat, as before a fire or in an oven:—*n.* **1,** a piece of meat cooked, or suitable to be cooked, before a fire or in an oven; as, a *roast* of veal, beef, or pork; **2,** a ceremony that honours someone through good-natured mock insults:—*adj.* **roasted**.—*n.* **roast′er**.

rob (rob), *v.t.* [robbed, rob-bing], **1,** to take something forcibly away from; as, to *rob* a person; to steal from; as, to *rob* a bank; **2,** to deprive (a person) of something unjustly; as, to *rob* people of their rights:—*v.i.* to commit a theft.—*n.* **rob′ber**.

rob-ber-y (rob′ėr-i), *n.* the unlawful act of taking money or property that belongs to someone else.

robe (rōb), *n.* **1,** a long, loose outer garment, esp. one indicating rank or honour; as, a graduation *robe*; **2,** a wrap or covering; as, a bath*robe*:—**robes**, state or ceremonial costume; as, *robes* of office:—*v.t.* and *v.i.* [robed, rob-ing], to dress in, or put on, a robe.

GRADUATION ROBES

rob-in (rob′in), *n.* **1,** a small European bird of the thrush family; the robin redbreast; **2,** a North American thrush somewhat like the English robin, but larger.

ro-bot (rō′bot), *n.* **1,** a humanlike machine that does manual and routine work for human beings; an automaton; **2,** one who acts or works mechanically; a brutal, insensitive (but efficient) person.—*n.* **ro′bot-ry; ro-bot′ics.**—*adj.* **ro-bot′ic.**

ro-bust (rō-bust′), *adj.* **1,** strong; vigorous; sturdy; as, *robust* health; **2,** in *computing,* reliable (not brittle) under even the worst conditions, quickly recovering from a fault or other problem.

[1]**rock** (rok), *n.* **1,** a large mass of stone or of stony matter; also, stony fragments; **2,** mineral matter; a bed or mass of one mineral; **3,** that which resembles such a mass in firmness; a firm support; **4,** a stone, esp. a large gem; as, a diamond is often called a *rock;* **5,** a curling stone:—**the Rock,** a popular name for Newfoundland.—*adj.* **rock′y.**

[2]**rock** (rok), *v.t.* **1,** to move to and fro, or backward and forward; as, to *rock* a cradle, etc.; also, to move or swing (a baby) in a cradle; **2,** to lull to sleep; **3,** to cause to vibrate or shake; as, the explosion *rocked* the building; **4,** to distress, disturb, or shock; as, the news *rocked* him:—*v.i.* **1,** to move backward and forward; as, to *rock* in a rocking chair; **2,** to sway or reel; **3,** to play rock 'n' roll music:—*n.* **1,** a rocking movement; **2,** the period of rocking; **3,** rock 'n' roll music.

rock-er (rok′ėr), *n.* **1,** a chair mounted on two curved pieces of wood or springs that allow it to rock back and forth; **2,** the curved pieces of wood or metal on which the chair or other object, such as a cradle, rocks; **3,** a rock 'n' roll performer.

rock-et (rok′it), *n.* **1,** a device that is propelled at great speed by the force of burning gases being released from the rear: often used to launch spacecraft and power guided missiles; **2,** a space vehicle or missile that is powered by such an engine; **3,** a type of firework that is shot through the air by gunpowder or other explosive:—*v.i.* to dart swiftly ahead or travel very quickly; as, the flames *rocketed* into the air.—*n.* **rock′et-ry.**

rock 'n' roll or **rock–and–roll,** a popular form of music that originated in the 1950s, which is characterized by amplified instruments, a heavy rhythmic beat, and simple lyrics.

rod (rod), *n.* **1,** a straight, slender stick of wood or metal; as, a fishing *rod;* **2,** a unit of length once used for measuring land, equal to about five metres; **3,** *Slang* a revolver.

rode (rōd), *p.t.* of *ride.*

ro-dent (rō′dent), *n.* any one of various gnawing animals, such as rats, mice, squirrels, and beavers.

ro-de-o (rō′dē-ō′), *n.* **1,** a roundup or driving together of cattle to be branded; also, the enclosure; **2,** an exhibition of cowboys' skill in cattle roping, horsemanship, etc.

roe (rō), *n.* the eggs of a fish.

rogue (rōg), *n.* **1,** a dishonest person; cheat; **2,** a mischievous person; as, a playful little *rogue:*—*adj.* **1,** an animal that lives apart from the herd and is often vicious; as, a *rogue* elephant; **2,** a human who displays similar tendencies; as, a *rogue* trader.—*adj.* **ro′guish.**

roil (roil), *v.t.,* **1,** to make (water, etc.) muddy by stirring (sediment or dregs); **2,** to vex; disturb.—*adj.* **roiled** (in a vexed or agitated state).

role or **rôle** (rōl), *n.* **1,** a part or character taken by an actor in a play, movie, television program, etc.; **2,** any assumed part; as, to take on the *role* of team leader:—**role model,** someone whom another person imitates or follows.

roll (rōl), *v.t.* **1,** to cause to move onward by turning over and over; as, to *roll* a ball; **2,** to move or push along on casters or wheels; as, to *roll* a wheelchair; **3,** to wrap upon itself or on some other object; as, to *roll* a rug; **4,** to wrap up; as, to *roll* oneself in a blanket; **5,** to cause to sway sidewise, as a ship; **6,** to utter or express with a deep, vibrating sound; as, the organ *rolls* forth its music; **7,** to level with a heavy revolving cylinder; as, to *roll* a lawn; **8,** to pronounce with a prolonged trilling sound; as, to *roll* one's r's:—*v.i.* **1,** to move onward by turning over and over; as, a ball *rolls* down a hill; **2,** to run on wheels; as, the wagon *rolls* along; **3,** to rock, as does a ship; **4,** to sweep along, as do waves; **5,** to give forth a long, deep, rumbling sound; as, the thunder *rolls;* **6,** to form, when being wound, the shape of a ball or cylinder; as, the cloth *rolls* easily; **7,** to rise and fall in gentle slopes, as land; **8,** to flatten under some kind of roller; as, dough *rolls* easily; **9,** *Colloq.* to pile up; as, debts *roll* up quickly:—*n.* **1,** the act of turning over and over, or of tossing from side to side; **2,** the state of being rolled; **3,** that which revolves; a roller; as, a towel *roll;* **4,** anything wrapped upon itself in the form, or nearly the form, of a cylinder; as, a *roll* of pennies; **5,** a list of persons, generally official in character; as, a class *roll;* **6,** a kind of biscuit or bread, rolled or rounded; as, a dinner *roll;* **7,** a continued, deep sound, as of a beaten drum, thunder, etc.; **8,** a swell or unevenness on a surface, as of a rough sea.

roll-er (rōl′ėr), *n.* **1,** anything that turns round and round, or over and over; as, a paint *roller* or hair *rollers;* **2,** a small wheel (or set) attached to something so it can be moved; as, a chair on *rollers;* **3,** a long, huge wave; **4,** a kind of pigeon that turns somersaults in the air; **5,** a canary with a trilling song:—**rolling stock,** railway vehicles.

roller coaster, an amusement park ride in which a set of open cars travels very fast on tracks that form steep hills and sharp turns.

roller skate, a shoe or boot that fastens to a plate with wheels attached to the bottom, worn for skating on paved surfaces.—*v.i.* **roll′er–skate′** [roller–skated, roller–skating] (to move along on roller skates).

roll-ing (rōl′ing), *adj.* **1,** moving along by turning over and over; as, a *rolling* ball; **2,** moving on, or as on, wheels; as, a *rolling* chair; **3,** rising and falling in gentle slopes; as, *rolling* countryside; **4,** rumbling; as, *rolling* thunder:—*n.* **1,** the act of a person or thing that rolls; also, a person who works with a rolling tool; **2,** a deep sound.

ro-ly–po-ly (rō′li–pō′li), *adj.* short and fat; dumpy; as, a *roly-poly* baby:—*n.* such a person or thing.

ROM (rom), *abbrev.* short for *read-only memory.*

Roman Catholic Church (rō′man), a Christian church that is headed by the Pope.

ro-mance (rō-mans′; rō′mans′), *n.* **1,** a love affair, esp. an idealized one; **2,** a long tale of adventure, love, or great deeds, esp. one set in past times; as, *Ivanhoe* is a well-known *romance*; **3,** a series of acts or happenings that are strange and fanciful; **4,** a disposition to delight in what is fanciful; **5,** a falsehood:—*v.i.* [romanced, romancing], **1,** to invent fanciful stories; **2,** to indulge in dreamy imaginings:—**Romance**, any of the languages descended from Latin, such as Italian or French.—*n.* **ro-manc′er.**

Roman numeral, a number in the system used by the ancient Romans, in which letters are used instead of numbers: I = 1, V = 5, X = 10, L = 50, C = 100, D = 500, and M = 1000.

ro-man-tic (rō-man′tik), *adj.* **1,** pertaining to, or like, what is imaginary, sentimental, idealistic, or having to do with a love affair; fanciful; impractical; as, a *romantic* dinner, movie, or getaway; *romantic* ideas; **2,** pertaining to, or suggesting, what is strange or heroic; as, *romantic* literature; **3,** of a disposition to ignore what is real and delight in what is fanciful; as, a *romantic* novel; **4,** pertaining to a style of literature, art, or music, which places more value on imagination than on things as they are.

ro-man-ti-cism (rō-man′ti-sizm), *n.* **1,** the quality of being imaginative, sentimental, or extravagantly ideal; **2,** a movement in Europe at the end of the 18th century to restore imagination and feeling to literature, art, and music.—*n.* **ro-man′ti-cist.**

romp (romp), *n.* **1,** carefree, boisterous play; as, a *romp* in the snow; **2,** an easy victory; as, the hockey game was a *romp* for the home team:—*v.i.* **1,** to play in a rough manner; **2,** to win easily.

roof (ro͞of), *n.* **1,** the top covering of a building; **2,** any similar top covering; as, a car *roof*; the *roof* of the mouth:—*v.t.* to cover with a roof.—*n.* **roof′er.**

¹rook (rook), *n.* **1,** a European bird with glossy black plumage, similar to the crow; **2,** a cheat, esp. at dice or cards:—*v.t.* and *v.i.* to cheat; defraud.—*n.* **rook′er-y.**

²rook (rook), *n.* a piece used in chess: also called *castle.*

rook-ie (rook′i), *n.* **1,** a first-year player in a league of professional sport (hockey, football, baseball, etc.); **2,** any new recruit or beginner without experience:—*adj.* inexperienced; as, a *rookie* politician.

room (ro͞om; room), *n.* **1,** a space separated by partitions from the rest of the structure in which it is located; as, a living room; **2,** space; as, there is *room* in this closet for their coats; **3,** opportunity; as, *room* for development or improvement:—*v.i.* to occupy or rent a room or rooms:—*v.t.* to accommodate with a room or lodgings.—*n.* **room′er; room′ful.**

room-y (ro͞om′i), *adj.* [room-i-er, room-i-est], having plenty of room; large; spacious; as, a *roomy* garage.—*n.* **room′i-ness.**

roost (ro͞ost), *n.* **1,** the pole, perch, etc., upon which a bird rests at night; **2,** a number of fowls resting together; **3,** a temporary nesting place:—*v.i.* to sit or sleep upon a perch or pole.

roost-er (ro͞os′tėr), *n.* the domestic cock; a male chicken.

¹root (ro͞ot), *n.* **1,** that part of a plant, usually growing downward into the soil, that holds the plant in place and absorbs and stores food; **2,** any underground part of a plant, esp. a large part suitable for food, as a beet, turnip, carrot, etc.; **3,** anything like a root in position, use, etc.; as, the *root* of a tooth; **4,** a cause or source; as, the *root* of the problem; **5,** in *arithmetic*, a number that, when used as a factor a given number of times, produces a given number; as, since 2 × 2 × 2 = 8, 2 is the third *root* of 8; **6,** the basic part of a word, apart from prefixes, suffixes, etc.; as, "roll" is the *root* of "roller" and "rolling":—**roots**, the feeling of belonging to a certain place; as, my *roots* are in the country:—*v.t.* **1,** to plant and fix in the earth; **2,** to implant deeply; as, his dislike was *rooted* in fear; **3,** to tear or dig up by the roots; to destroy; as, to *root* out vice:—*v.i.* **1,** to take root; as, the bulbs began to *root* in March; **2,** to become firmly or permanently established.—*n.* **root′let** (a little root).

²root (ro͞ot), *v.t.* **1,** to dig with the snout, as swine; **2,** to get by searching or hunting; as, to *root* out a secret:—*v.i.* **1,** to turn up the earth with the snout; **2,** to rummage.

³root (ro͞ot), *v.i. Colloq.* to support a team or a contestant by cheering, applauding, etc.; as, to *root* for the home team.—*n.* **roo′ter.**

root beer, a soft drink that was originally flavoured with the roots of plants such as sassafras and sarsaparilla.

rope (rōp), *n.* **1,** a thick, stout cord made of several strands of hemp, cotton, or other fibre, twined together; **2,** a collection of things braided or twined together in a line or string; as, a *rope* of pearls; **3,** a stringy thread formed in a liquid:—*v.t.* [roped, roping], **1,** to fasten or tie with a rope; **2,** to mark or enclose by means of a rope; as, to *rope* off a field; **3,** to lasso; as, to *rope* a steer:—*v.i.* to form stringy threads, as syrup does.—*adj.* **rop′y.**

ro-sa-ry (rō′za-ri), *n.* [*pl.* rosaries], **1,** a string of beads for counting a series of prayers to be said one after the other in a certain order; **2,** the series of prayers thus recited; **3,** a rose bed or rose garden; a place where roses grow.

[1]**rose** (rōz), *n.* **1,** a thorny shrub, erect or climbing, bearing showy, fragrant flowers; also, the flower; **2,** the most typical colour of a rose; deep pink; **3,** a certain shape in which diamonds are cut.—*adv.* **ros′i-ly.**—*n.* **ros′i-ness.**—*adj.* **ros′e-ate′.**

[2]**rose** (rōz), *p.t.* of *rise.*

rose-mary (rōz′mėr-i), *n.* [*pl.* rosemaries], a fragrant evergreen shrub: the leaves are used as a seasoning and in making perfume.

ro-sette (ro-zet′), *n.* an ornament, as a knot or bunch of ribbon, made into the shape of a rose.

rose-wood (rōz′wood′), *n.* a valuable hard, dark-red wood, usually fragrant, yielded by various tropical trees and used for fine furniture; also, any of the trees from which such wood is obtained.

Rosh Ha-sha-nah or **Rosh Ha-sha-na** or **Rosh Ha-sho-na** or **Rosh Ha-sho-nah** (rosh′ ha-shon′a; ho-shô′na), the Jewish New Year, celebrated in late September or early October.

ro-sin (roz′in), *n.* the resin, or solid substance, that remains after distilling crude turpentine:—*v.t.* to rub with rosin; as, to *rosin* the bow of a violin.

ros-ter (ros′tėr), *n.* **1,** an enrolment or list of names; **2,** a schedule or program; as, the *roster* of the day's events.

ros-trum (ros′trum), *n.* [*pl.* rostrums or rostra (ros′tra)], a pulpit, platform, or stage for public speaking; dais.

ros-y (rōz′i), *adj.* [ros-i-er, ros-i-est], **1,** like a rose; red; blooming; blushing; **2,** favourable; hopeful; as, *rosy* prospects.

rot (rot), *v.i.* [rot-ted, rot-ting], **1,** to decay; as, the fruit was *rotting* in the orchard; **2,** deteriorate, weaken, or disintegrate; **3,** to languish; as, she was left to *rot* in prison:—*n.* **1,** process of decay; **2,** the state of being decayed; **3,** decayed matter; **4,** a disease of certain animals, esp. sheep; as, foot *rot*; also, a disease or decay of plant tissues; as, dry *rot.*

ro-ta-ry (rō′ta-ri), *adj.* **1,** turning or rotating; **2,** having parts that turn around; as, a *rotary* blade on a lawn mower.

ro-tate (rō-tāt′; rō′tāt), *v.t.* [rotat-ed, rotating], **1,** to cause to turn on, or as on, an axis; as, to *rotate* a wheel; **2,** to alternate or change about; as, to *rotate* crops:—*v.i.* **1,** to turn around on its own centre of axis; revolve; **2,** to take turns at anything; as, the members of the club *rotated* in office.—*adj.* **ro′ta-tor-y.**—*n.* **ro-ta′tor.**

ro-ta-tion (rō-tā′shun), *n.* **1,** the fact of rotating around a centre point; as the *rotation* of a wheel; also, one complete cycle; **2,** regularly organized sequencial changes; as, crop *rotation.*

rote (rōt), *n.* **1,** the repeating of words over and over to learn them, without paying much attention to their meaning; as, to learn rules by *rote*; **2,** routine.

ro-tor (rō′tėr), *n.* a part that revolves in a stationary part, esp. in an electrical machine.

rot-ten (rot′n), *adj.* **1,** decayed; spoiled; as, *rotten* eggs; **2,** likely to break; not firm; weak; as, a *rotten* plank; **3,** corrupt; dishonest; as, a *rotten* criminal; **4,** *Colloq.* very bad or poor; as, to feel *rotten*; *rotten* grades.—*adv.* **rot′ten-ly.**—*n.* **rot′ten-ness.**

ro-tund (rō-tund′), *adj.* **1,** plump; rounded out; as, a *rotund* baby; **2,** full-toned; rich; as, a *rotund* voice.

ro-tun-da (rō-tun′da), *n.* **1,** a round hall or room, esp. one with a dome; **2,** the lobby or foyer of a hotel, theatre, etc.

rouge (ro͞ozh), *n.* a red powder or paste used for colouring the cheeks and lips: often called *blush*:—*v.t.* and *v.i.* [rouged, roug-ing], to colour with rouge; redden.

rough (ruf), *adj.* **1,** having an uneven surface; not smooth; bumpy or jagged; as, a *rough* road; *rough* cloth; **2,** not polished; unfinished; as, *rough* diamonds; *rough* sketches; *rough* draft of an essay; **3,** harsh; violent; forceful; as, *rough* treatment; *rough* sports; **4,** stormy; as, *rough* weather; **5,** not refined; rude in character; as, *rough* manners; **6,** approximate; not exact or detailed; as, a *rough* estimate; **7,** unpleasant or difficult; hard to deal with or get through; as, a *rough* day at the office:—*n.* **1,** a low, coarse person; a rowdy; **2,** a crude or unfinished condition; as, diamonds in the *rough*; **3,** in *golf,* the long grass bordering a fairway:—*v.t.* **1,** to make rough; ruffle; as, the bird *roughed* its feathers; **2,** to shape or sketch roughly; as, to *rough* in an outline; **3,** to treat in a mean or violent way; as, to they *roughed* him up:—**rough it,** to do without conveniences, as on a camping trip.—*adv.* **rough′ly.**—*n.* **rough′-ness.**—*adj.* and *adv.* **rough′shod′**; as, to ride *roughshod* (domineer) over.

rough-age (ruf′ij), *n.* coarse food, as bran, vegetable fibre, etc., used in the diet to stimulate bowel movement.

rough-en (ruf′n), *v.t.* to destroy the

smoothness of; as, the wind *roughens* one's skin:—*v.i.* to become uneven or coarse on the surface.

rou-lette (rōō-let′), *n.* **1,** a game of chance played with a revolving disc marked off in red and black sections; **2,** small, consecutive punctures, as between some postage stamps, to facilitate their separation.

round (round), *adj.* **1,** like, or nearly like, a circle or sphere in shape; as, a *round* plate; an apple is *round*; **2,** having a curved surface; as, a *round* cheek; **3,** semicircular; as, opposed to pointed; as, a *round* arch; also, moving in a circle; as, a *round* dance; **4,** full or whole; as, a *round* dozen; **5,** going from, and returning to, the same place; as, a *round* trip; **6,** full in sound; not jarring; as, the *round* tones of a voice; **7,** outspoken; frank; as, a *round* scolding; **8,** brisk; as, a good *round* pace:—**in round numbers,** expressed approximately, as in even tens, dozens, etc.:—*n.* **1,** a circle or sphere; also, a curved part; **2,** a fixed course or route; a beat; routine; as, the day's *round* of duties; **3,** a series of events or acts; as, a *round* of cheers; **4,** one of a series of regular periods, esp. in a game or contest; as, the *rounds* in a fight; a *round* of golf; **5,** a rung of a ladder; **6,** a cut of beef between the rump and the leg; **7,** a simultaneous volley of shots, each soldier firing once; also, the ammunition needed for such a volley, or enough for a single shot; **8,** a song sung by several persons or groups starting one after the other at intervals:—*v.t.* **1,** to give a curved or rounded form to; **2,** to travel on pass around; as, they *rounded* the corner; **3,** to bring to complete perfection or finish; as, to *round* out a plan; **4,** to drive in, or gather together; as, to *round* up cattle; **5,** of a number, to make it more simple or less exact by changing it; as, *round* off the total to the nearest one hundred:—*v.i.* **1,** to become curved, spherical, or circular in form; **2,** to grow full, complete, or perfect; develop:—*adj.* **1,** in the neighbourhood; near by; as, they waited *round* for orders; **2,** in a circle or group; as, to gather *round*; **3,** in a circular motion; as, the earth goes *round*; **4,** from one side or party to another; as, she came *round* to our belief; **5,** in a complete circuit from person to person, or point to point; as, enough food to go *round*; **6,** by outside measure; as, a hole two centimetres *round*; **7,** so as to face in the opposite direction; as, to turn *round*:—*prep.* **1,** about; on every side of; as, a wall *round* a town; **2,** taking a curved or bent course to the other side of; as, walk *round* the corner.—*n.* **round′ness.**—*adv.* **round′ly.**

round-a-bout (round′a-bout′), *adj.* indirect; not straightforward; as, *roundabout* methods:—*n.* **1,** a detour; **2,** a short jacket, as for boys or sailors.

round-trip or **round–trip** or **round trip** (round′trip), *n.* a trip that includes going to a place and then returning to the starting point:—*adj.* pertaining to, of, or for a roundtrip; as, the *roundtrip* airfare.

round-up (round′up′), *n.* **1,** the herding together and corralling of cattle; **2,** the people and horses that herd them; **3,** any similar drive or roundup; as, a *roundup* of criminals.

rouse (rouz), *v.t.* [roused, rous-ing], **1,** to awaken; also, to stir to thought or action; she was *roused* by an urgent phone call; **2,** to bring into existence; as, to *rouse* indignation; **3,** to cause to move or become active; stir up; as, the dogs *roused* the ducks:—*v.i.* **1,** to awake from sleep; **2,** to show signs of activity; as, the crowd *roused* at the sound of a shot:—*adj.* stirring; as, a *rousing* cheer.

[1]**rout** (rout), *n.* **1,** a total defeat as of an army or team; as, the game turned into a complete *rout*; **2,** disorder resulting from such a defeat; **3,** a noisy crowd; mob:—*v.t.* to defeat and put to flight.

[2]**rout** (rout), *v.t.* **1,** to root up, as with the snout; **2,** to dig out, as with a gouging tool; **3,** *Colloq.* to drag by force; as, to *rout* someone out of bed.

route (rōōt; rout), *n.* **1,** a way or road travelled; course; journey; **2,** a regular series of stops for a vehicle, delivery person, etc.; as, a bus *route*:—*v.t.* [routed, rout-ing], to send or ship forward; as, to *route* the parcel.

rout-er (rou′tėr), *n.* **1,** a tool used in routing; **2,** in *computing*, a device that allows many computer networks to communicate and exchange information: also called *gateway*.

rou-tine (rōō-tēn′), *n.* **1,** a customary course of action in business, pleasure, or duty; as, my after-school *routine*; **2,** an act or part of an act performed for a show; as, her standup *routine* is very funny:—*adj.* according to routine; regular or repeated; as, a *routine* job.—*adv.* **routinely.**

rove (rōv), *v.t.* and *v.i.* [roved, rov-ing], to wander aimlessly (over); to ramble; as, buffaloes *roved* over the land.—*n.* **rov′er.**

[1]**row** (rō), *n.* **1,** a series of persons or things in a line; as, a *row* of seats in the theatre; **2,** a series of things, one right after the other, with no breaks in between; as, she was sick five days in a *row*; **3,** a line of houses side by side on a street; also, the street.

[2]**row** (rō), *v.i.* **1,** to move a boat by means of oars; as, she has learned to *row*; **2,** to be moved by means of oars; as, the boat *rows* easily:—*v.t.* **1,** to propel by means of oars; **2,** to carry in a boat; as, she *rowed* her across:—*n.* the act of moving a boat by oars; also, a trip taken in a rowboat.

[3]**row** (rou), *n.* a noisy quarrel; brawl; fight; they got into a *row* over sharing:—*v.i.* to quarrel.

row-boat (rō′bōt′), *n.* a boat propelled by means of oars.

row-dy (rou′di), *n.* [*pl.* rowdies], a rough person; ruffian:—*adj.* [row-di-er, row-di-est], disorderly; rough; noisy or rude; a few *rowdy* students disturbed the rest.—*n.* **row′di-ness; row′dy-ism.**

roy-al (roi′al), *adj.* **1,** pertaining to or belonging to a king or queen; as, the *royal* household; **2,** pertaining to, or connected with, a kingdom; as, the *royal* navy; **3,** suited to or like a king or queen; regal; as, the *royal* treatment; **4,** *Colloq.* extreme; as, a *royal* pain:—*n.* a small sail:—**the royals,** members of the royal family.—*n.* **roy′a-list.**—*adv.* **roy′al-ly.**

Royal Canadian Mounted Police, the federal police force of Canada that also functions as a provincial and territorial force in all areas except Ontario and Québec: abbreviated as *RCMP* or *Mountie*.

roy-al-ty (roi′al-ti), *n.* [*pl.* royalties], **1,** the station, dignity, etc., of a monarch; **2,** the king or queen; also, any person of sovereign rank; as, *royalty* was present at the theatre; **3,** regal nature or quality; **4,** a tax paid to the crown; **5,** a share of the profits paid to the owner for the use of a property; **6,** a percentage paid to an inventor or author for the use of a patent or copyright; as, *royalties* from the sale of a book.

rub (rub), *v.t.* [rubbed, rub-bing], **1,** to cause (a surface) to undergo friction and pressure; as, to *rub* one's face with a towel; **2,** to touch with a scraping or brushing movement; as, the wheel *rubbed* my dress; **3,** to cause to move over something with pressure; as, to *rub* the eraser over the paper; **4,** to cleanse or scour by rubbing; as, she *rubbed* the silver with a cloth; **5,** to erase; as, to *rub* out a mark; **6,** to cause to penetrate; spread; as, to *rub* wax on a floor:—*v.i.* **1,** to move along a surface with pressure; scrape; as, two things *rub* together; **2,** to get along with difficulty; as, to *rub* along somehow:—*n.* **1,** the use of friction and pressure upon a surface; a rubbing; as, give the table a good *rub*; **2,** that which makes progress difficult; a hindrance; as, there's the *rub*.—*n.* **rub′down′.**

rub-ber (rub′ėr), *n.* **1,** one who polishes, erases, massages, or rubs in any way; **2,** anything used for erasing, polishing; as, a *rubber* on a pencil; **3,** the prepared, solidified sap from various tropical trees, used for waterproofing, insulating, etc.; caoutchouc: also called *India rubber*; **4,** an article made of this, as an overshoe or an elastic band; as, my *rubbers* got soaked:—*adj.* made of, like, or pertaining to rubber.—*adj.* **rub′ber-y.**

rub-bish (rub′ish), *n.* anything valueless; trash.

rub-ble (rub′l), *n.* rough, broken stone, brick, etc., or masonry built from it.

ru-by (ro͞o′bi), *n.* [*pl.* rubies], **1,** a precious stone, varying in colour from carmine to crimson; **2,** the deep-red colour of the stone.

ruck-sack (ruk′sak′), *n.* a knapsack for hikers, etc.

ruck-us (ruk′us), *n.* row; noisy disturbance; uproar.

rud-der (rud′ėr), *n.* **1,** a broad, flat piece of wood or metal, hinged vertically to the stern of a vessel and used for steering; **2,** a similar part in an airplane.—*adj.* **rud′der-less.**

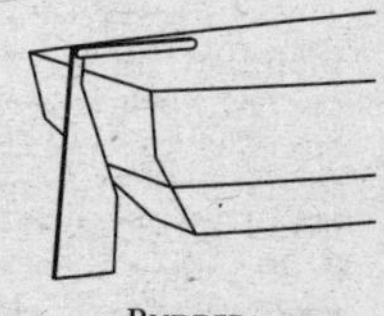
RUDDER

rud-dy (rud′i), *adj.* [rud-di-er, rud-di-est], **1,** red or reddish; as, a warm, *ruddy* glow; **2,** having the colour of good health; as, a *ruddy* complexion.—*n.* **rud′di-ness.**

rude (ro͞od), *adj.* [rud-er, rud-est], **1,** impolite; disrespectful; as, *rude* behaviour; **2,** crude; unskillful; as, a *rude* carving; **3,** rough; severe; as, a *rude* awakening.—*adv.* **rude′ly.**—*n.* **rude′ness.**

ru-di-ment (ro͞o′di-ment), *n.* **1,** one of the first principles of an art, science, etc.; as, the *rudiments* of algebra; **2,** in *biology*, a part or organ partially developed; as, the *rudiments* of antlers.—*adj.* **ru′di-men′ta-ry.**

rue (ro͞o), *v.t.* [rued, ru-ing], to be sorry for; wish undone; as, he shall *rue* his wicked deeds:—*n.* remorse; regret.—*adj.* **rue′ful.**

ruff (ruf), *n.* **1,** a large pleated or fluted collar, worn in the 16th and 17th centuries; **2,** anything like such a collar, as a prominent growth of feathers round the neck of a bird.—*adj.* **ruffed.**

ruffed grouse, a North American game bird, which is conspicuous with a black band near the tip of the tail, and a crest on the head: often called *partridge, pheasant,* and *quail*.

ruf-fi-an (ruf′i-an; ruf′yan), *n.* a brutal, lawless person; one given to cruel deeds:—*adj.* brutal; cruel; violent; as, *ruffian* rage.

ruf-fle (ruf′l), *n.* a pleated or gathered strip of material used as a trimming:—*v.t.* [ruffled, ruf-fling], **1,** to draw into folds or plaits; **2,** to furnish or adorn with plaited or gathered strips; **3,** to cause to stand up or out; as, a bird *ruffles* its feathers; **4,** to disturb slightly or make ripples upon; as, the wind *ruffled* the pond; **5,** to disarrange; disorder; as, he *ruffled* her hair; **6,** to annoy or upset; as, the player *ruffled* the goalie:—*v.i.* **1,** to form small folds; **2,** to become vexed or annoyed.

rug (rug), *n.* **1,** a heavy floor covering, usually made in one piece and often of a size to cover only part of the floor; **2,** *Slang* a toupee or wig.

rug·by (rug′bi), *n.* in *sports,* a kind of football first played at Rugby, Warwickshire, England, the forerunner of modern Canadian and U.S. football.

rug·ged (rug′id), *adj.* **1,** having an uneven surface; rough; as, *rugged* country; **2,** steep and rocky; as, a *rugged* cliff; **3,** crude; plain; as, a *rugged* grandeur; **4,** hard; austere; harsh; as, a *rugged* character; **5,** healthy; strong; sturdy.—*n.* **rug′ged·ness.**

ru·in (ro͞o′in), *n.* **1,** overthrow; destruction; downfall; as, political *ruin;* **2,** a cause of destruction; **3,** the state of decay or desolation:—**ruins,** the remains of a building destroyed or fallen into decay; as, the *ruins* of an old castle:—*v.t.* to pull down, overthrow, or destroy; as, the scandal *ruined* her career.—*n.* **ru′in·a′tion.**

ru·in·ous (ro͞o′i-nus), *adj.* **1,** bringing or causing ruin; destructive; as, a *ruinous* war; **2,** dilapidated; as, a barn in a *ruinous* state.—*adv.* **ru′in·ous·ly.**

rule (ro͞ol), *n.* **1,** a standard or principle of conduct; as, the golden *rule;* school *rules;* an established usage or law, as in arithmetic or grammar; **2,** government; authority; as, a country under foreign *rule;* **3,** usual course of action; as, she works late as a *rule;* **4,** that which may be generally expected; as, scholarship is the *rule* in a university; **5,** a straight-edged strip of wood or metal, marked off in units such as centimetres, used in drawing lines or measuring:—*v.t.* [ruled, rul·ing], **1,** to govern; as, to *rule* a country; **2,** to guide, influence, or control; as, he was *ruled* by hatred; **3,** to establish by a decision, as does a court; **4,** to mark with lines by the use of a ruler:—*v.i.* **1,** in *law,* to decide a point; **2,** to exercise superior authority; as, he *ruled* over the country for 10 years.

rul·er (ro͞ol′ėr), *n.* **1,** one who governs; as, a wise *ruler;* **2,** a strip of wood, metal, etc., used in drawing lines or in measuring.

rul·ing (ro͞ol′ing), *adj.* chief; predominant:—*n.* **1,** a decision laid down by a judge or court; **2,** the act of making lines; also, ruled lines.

rum (rum), *n.* a strong, alcoholic liquor made from molasses or the juice of the sugar cane.

rum·ble (rum′bl), *n.* **1,** a low, heavy, rolling sound; as, the *rumble* of city traffic or thunder; **2,** *Slang* a street fight, esp. between gangs:—*v.i.* and *v.t.* [rum·bled, rum·bling], to make or cause to make rumbling sounds.

ru·mi·nant (ro͞o′mi-nant), *n.* and *adj.* any hoofed, four-footed animal that chews a cud, esp. the cow, bison, goat, deer, camel, giraffe, and llama.

ru·mi·nate (ro͞o′mi-nāt′), *v.i.* [ruminat·ed, ruminat·ing], **1,** to chew the cud; **2,** to meditate or muse; reflect; as, to *ruminate* on the future.—*n.* **ru′mi·na′tion.**

rum·mage (rum′ij), *n.* a thorough search made by turning things over in a disorderly way:—*v.t.* [rummaged, rummag·ing], to search thoroughly by turning over the contents of; ransack:—*v.i.* to make a thorough but disorderly search; as, to *rummage* in a closet.

rummage sale, a sale of used clothes, furniture, and other household items, esp. in order to raise funds for charity.

rum·my (rum′i), *n.* a card game in which the aim is to match cards into sets of the same denomination or sequences of the same suit.

ru·mour or **ru·mor** (ro͞o′mėr), *n.* **1,** talk; hearsay; **2,** a current story that has not been verified; as, a *rumour* of strikes:—*v.t.* to spread by report.

rump (rump), *n.* the hind part of an animal; the buttocks; also, a cut of beef from this part.

rum·ple (rum′pl), *n.* a wrinkle or crease:—*v.t.* and *v.i.* [rum·pled, rum·pling], to wrinkle; muss; as, to *rumple* cloth.

rum·pus (rum′pus), *n.* and *adj.* a disturbance; brawl; clamour:—**rumpus room,** a (basement or attic) recreation room.

run (run), *v.i.* [*p.t.* ran (ran), *p.p.* run, *p.pr.* run·ning], **1,** to go on the feet at a speed faster than a walk; depart suddenly; **2,** to hurry; rush; as, he *ran* through his work too fast; **3,** to travel; proceed; as the express *runs* 120 kilometres an hour; **4,** to make regular trips; as, a bus *runs* between Oakville and Hamilton; **5,** to move in a stream; flow, as a river; **6,** to act; be in action; operate; as, the car will not *run;* **7,** to extend; be placed; as, a path *runs* round the house; **8,** to become unfastened; ravel; as, a thread *runs* in a stocking; **9,** to engage in a contest; be a competitor; as, to *run* for office; **10,** to climb; creep; trail; as, the vine *runs* along the wall; **11,** to be written or related; as, so the story *runs;* **12,** to spread or dissolve; as, dye *runs;* **13,** to discharge a fluid; ooze; as, the nose *runs;* a sore *runs;* **14,** in *computing,* to make a computer execute programs or commands:—*v.t.* **1,** *Colloq.* to cause to move or operate; as, to *run* a computer; to *run* a theatre; **2,** to thrust; stick; as, to *run* a pin into one's finger; **3,** to drive or dash forcibly; as, to *run* one's head against a wall; **4,** to do by running; as, to *run* errands; **5,** to go through (some danger) successfully; as, to *run* a blockade; **6,** to expose oneself to; as, to *run* a temperature or *run* a risk; **7,** to permit to mount up, as debts; **8,** to sew with small, even stitches; as, to *run* a seam; **9,** in *computing,* to execute a computer's commands; **10,** *Colloq.* to fail to stop; as, to *run* a stop sign:—*n.* **1,** the act or power of going at a pace swifter than a walk; **2,** a trip or journey; progress; as, the train made its usual *run*; **3,** the act of flowing or that which flows; as, a *run* of maple sap; **4,** a course or succession; repetition; as, a *run* of bad luck; **5,** the average kind; as, the *run* of workers; **6,** a place passed over frequently by animals; also, an enclosed place for animals; **7,** a herd of animals or school of fish moving together; **8,** a period of operation; as, the play had a year's *run*; **9,** sudden and pressing demand; as, a *run* on a bank; **10,** in *baseball*, the unit of scoring made by running to home plate after touching all three bases; **11,** a brook; **12,** free use or enjoyment; as, the *run* of a friend's house.—*adj.* and *n.* **run′–in′**; **run′off′**.

run-a-way (run′a-wā′), *n.* **1,** one who escapes or leaves; a person who runs away; as, a teenage *runaway*; **2,** the act of running away; **3,** a fugitive:—*adj.* **1,** escaping from control; as, a *runaway* train; **2,** happening very quickly or easily; as, a *runaway* victory.

run-down (run′doun′), *adj.* **1,** having bad health; sick or tired; as, to get sick when you are *rundown*; **2,** needing to be fixed; falling apart; as, a *rundown* apartment.

[1]**rung** (rung), *n.* a crosspiece or round bar or rod, esp. of a ladder or a chair.

[2]**rung** (rung), *p.p.* of *ring*.

run-ner (run′ėr,), *n.* **1,** one who runs, as a racer, a messenger, etc.; **2,** one of the long, narrow pieces on which a sleigh, skate, or sled moves; **3,** a long strip of carpet in a hallway or stairway; **4,** a slender, trailing branch that takes root at the end or at the joints; also, a plant that spreads in this way; **5,** in *baseball*, a player who is on base or trying to reach a base; as, the *runner* rounded second; **6,** a smuggler; as, a rum *runner*; **7,** a running shoe.

run-ner–up (run′ėr–up′), *n.* [*pl.* runners-up], a person or team that finishes in second place in a race or contest.

runt (runt), *n.* **1,** any undersized animal, esp. the smallest and weakest of a litter; **2,** a person of stunted growth.

run-way (run′wā′), *n.* **1,** a long, narrow roadway used by airplanes for taking off and landing; **2,** a beaten way or path along which animals pass; **3,** a fenced place; as, a *runway* for dogs; **4,** a raised platform in a theatre or fashion show.

rup-ture (rup′tūr), *n.* **1,** a bursting or breaking apart; **2,** the state of being broken or violently burst apart; **3,** a breach or an interruption of friendly relations; **4,** a hernia:—*v.t.* [ruptured, ruptur-ing], **1,** to burst violently apart; **2,** to cause a hernia to; **3,** to bring about a breach of (friendship):—*v.i.* to suffer a breach or break.

ru-ral (ro͞o′ral), *adj.* pertaining to or like the country or country life.

ruse (ro͞oz), *n.* a trick; fraud or deceit.

[1]**rush** (rush), *n.* any of certain plants growing in wet ground, having long hollow stems, which are used for making chairs, baskets, etc.

[2]**rush** (rush), *v.i.* **1,** to move with great speed; press forward with violent haste; **2,** to act with extraordinary haste or eagerness; as, to *rush* through one's work; **3,** in *sports*, to advance the puck or ball toward the opponent's goal:—*v.t.* **1,** to cause to move or act with great speed; hurry; as, to *rush* an order; **2,** to make an attack upon and occupy; to charge; as, to *rush* a fortification; **3,** in *sports*, to carry (the ball or puck) forward:—*n.* **1,** a driving forward with eagerness and haste; **2,** a sudden migration; as, a gold *rush*; **3,** *Colloq.* extraordinary activity; as, the holiday *rush*:—*adj.* requiring haste; as, a *rush* job.

rush hour, a time of day when many people are travelling either to or from work.

rus-set (rus′it), *n.* **1,** a reddish-brown colour; **2,** cloth, esp. homespun, of such colour; **3,** a kind of winter apple:—*adj.* reddish brown in colour.

rust (rust), *n.* **1,** the reddish-brown or orange matter formed on iron and steel and some other metals through exposure to air; red oxide of iron; **2,** anything like rust, as mildew on wheat, corn, etc.; **3,** a reddish-brown colour:—*v.i.* **1,** to form rust; **2,** to grow worthless because of idleness:—*v.t.* to cause to rust.—*n.* **rust′i-ness.**—*adj.* **rust′less; rust′proof′**.

rus-tic (rus′tik), *n.* a person reared in the country, esp. one who is unpolished:—*adj.* **1,** relating to the country; **2,** simple; artless; **3,** awkward; crude.—*n.* **rus-tic′i-ty.**

rus-tle (rus′l), *n.* a soft, crackling sound, such as that made by leaves:—*v.i.* [rus-tled, rus-tling], to make a soft, crackling sound, as taffeta or tissue paper when moved or crumpled:—*v.t.* **1,** to cause to make such a sound; **2,** to steal (cattle).—*n.* **rus′tler.**

rust-y (rus′ti), *adj.* [rust-i-er, rust-i-est], **1,** covered with rust; as, a *rusty* nail; **2,** having the look or colour of rust; **3,** not as good as it should be because of not being used or practised; as, my tennis game is *rusty*.

rut (rut), *n.* **1,** a hollow track or groove made by a wheel; **2,** a fixed habit, esp. a boring routine:—*v.t.* [rut-ted, rut-ting], to cut into hollows; make wheel tracks in.—*adj.* **rut′ty.**

ru-ta-ba-ga (ro͞o′ta-bā′ga), *n.* **1,** the yellow turnip; **2,** any table turnip washed, waxed, and ready for market.

ruth-less (ro͞oth′lis), *adj.* cruel; without mercy; savage; as, a *ruthless* fighter; a *ruthless* business person.—*adv.* **ruth′less-ly.**—*n.* **ruth′less-ness.**

rye (rī), *n.* **1,** a hardy cereal plant closely related to wheat; **2,** its seed, used in making bread and alcoholic beverages; **3,** the whisky distilled from this.

S

S, s (es), *n.* [*pl.* S's, s's], **1,** the 19th letter of the alphabet; **2,** anything having the shape of an S.

Sab-bath (sab′ath), *n.* **1,** the Christian Sunday, or the first day of the week, observed as a day of rest and worship; **2,** the seventh day of the week, observed by the Jews and certain others as a day of rest, commencing at sunset on Friday and ending at sunset on Saturday.

sab-bat-i-cal (sa-bat′i-kl), *adj.* a period of absence for study, travel, rest, etc.; as, a *sabbatical* leave or year (originally every seventh for teachers in colleges, etc.).

sa-ble (sā′bl), *n.* **1,** a small, flesh-eating animal of Europe and Asia that is similar to the mink ; **2,** the fur of this animal:—*adj.* very dark; black; as, *sable* night.

sa-bo-tage (sab′o-tåzh′; -tij), *n.* malicious or wanton destruction, esp. of an employer's property during a strike, or of a country's resources or equipment in wartime.—*n.* **sab′o-teur′** (-tûr).—*v.t.* [sab-o-taged, sab-o-taging], to damage or destroy by sabotage; as, *sabotage* the phone lines of a building.

sa-bre or **sa-ber** (sā′bėr), *n.* a cavalry sword with a curved blade, today used mainly in the sport of fencing:—*v.t.* to cut down with a sabre.

sabre–toothed tiger, a fierce tigerlike mammal with long, curved, upper canine teeth: it lived about 12,000 years ago.

sac (sak), *n.* a baglike part of a plant or an animal, often containing a fluid.

sac-cha-rin (sak′a-rin), *n.* a crystalline substance about 400 times sweeter than sugar, used as a sugar substitute and in the manufacture of candy, jam, etc.—*adj.* **sac′char-rine** (-rin; -rīn′).

sa-chet (sa′shā; sa-shā′), *n.* a small bag or cushion filled with a perfume in the form of powder; also, the powder.

[1]**sack** (sak), *n.* **1,** a bag; esp. a large coarse bag open at one end, for holding grain, potatoes, etc.; **2,** a sackful; as a *sack* of sugar; **3,** *Slang* dismissal; as, to get the *sack:*—*v.t.* to put into a bag.—*n.* **sack′ful.**

[2]**sack** (sak), *n.* the plundering by soldiers of a town taken in war; as, the *sack* of Rome by the Vandals:—*v.t.* **1,** to plunder or pillage; ravage; **2,** to rob; ransack.

sac-ra-ment (sak′ra-ment), *n.* **1,** a religious act or ceremony regarded as an outward, visible sign of inward, spiritual grace, as baptism and the Eucharist, or Lord's Supper; **2,** (also *Sacrament*), the consecrated elements of the Eucharist.—*adj.* **sac′ra-ment′al.**

sa-cred (sā′krid), *adj.* **1,** set apart for religious uses; consecrated; holy; as, a *sacred* edifice; **2,** pertaining to religion; as, *sacred* literature; **3,** to be treated with reverence; not to be violated; as, a *sacred* trust.

sac-ri-fice (sak′ri-fīs′), *n.* **1,** the act of presenting an offering to a god; **2,** that which is offered; anything offered or consecrated to a god; **3,** the giving up of something in order to gain something else; as, the *sacrifice* of leisure time for money; also, self-sacrifice; **4,** a price below cost; as, the house sold at a *sacrifice:*—*v.t.* (sak′ri-fīs′), [sacrificed, sacrific-ing], **1,** to offer to a god; **2,** to give up for the sake of some other person or object; as, to *sacrifice* health for riches; **3,** to sell at a loss:—*v.i.* to offer up a sacrifice.—*adj.* **sac′ri-fi′cial** (sak′ri-fish′al):—**sacrifice bunt,** in *baseball*, the bunting of the ball by the batter in such a way that, though he or she is put out, a base-runner advances:—**sacrifice fly,** when there are fewer than two outs, a long fly that enables a runner to score from third base.

sac-ri-le-gious (sak′ri-lē′jus; sak′ri-lij′us), *adj.* treating sacred things irreverently; profane.—*n.* **sac′ri-lege.**

sac-ro-sanct (sak′rō-sangkt′), *adj.* very holy, sacred, or inviolable: said of persons, obligations, laws, things, etc. (often ironically).

sad (sad), *adj.* [sad-der, sad-dest], **1,** full of grief; mournful; doleful; **2,** causing mournfulness; as, a *sad* event.—*v.t.* and *v.i.* **sad′den.**

sad-dle (sad′l), *n.* **1,** a padded leather seat for a rider on horseback; also, the seat of a bicycle; **2,** anything shaped like a saddle, as a cut of meat consisting of the two loins; **3,** a ridge between two hills or summits:—*v.t.* [sad-dled, sad-dling], **1,** to equip with a seat for a rider; **2,** to burden or embarrass; as, to be *saddled* with debt.—*n.* **sad′dler.**

sa-dism (sād′izm; sad′), *n.* a form of sex perversion marked by love of cruelty; any abnormal tendency to inflict pain.—*n.* **sa′dist.**—*adj.* **sa-dis′tic.**

saf-a-ri (sa-fär′i; suf′a-rē′), *n.* an expedition or journey, esp. for hunting or photographing animals (as in eastern Africa).

[1]**safe** (sāf), *adj.* [saf-er, saf-est], **1,** free from danger or harm; as, *safe* and sound; **2,** out of danger; secure; as, the soldier was *safe* from pursuit; **3,** incapable of doing injury or harm; securely kept, as a prisoner; **4,** reliable; trustworthy; involving no risk of loss; as, a *safe* investment; **5,** in *baseball*, reaching base without being put out.—*adv.* **safe′ly.**

[2]**safe** (sāf), *n.* a steel chest, usually fireproof

or burglar-proof, specially designed for safeguarding money and other valuables.

safe-guard (sāf′gärd′), *n.* a person or thing that guards or protects; a means of security; defence; as, traffic lights are a *safeguard* for both pedestrians and motorists:—*v.t.* to protect or defend.

safe-keep-ing (sāf′kēp′ing), *n.* care; protection.

safe-ty (sāf′ti), *n.* freedom from danger, injury, or damage; security:—*adj.* protecting against accident or injury; as, *safety* devices.—*n.* **safe′ty–pin′; safety belt; safety glass; safety net; safety valve.**

saf-flow-er (saf′flou′ėr), *n.* a flowering thistlelike plant, the seeds of which are used to make a cooking oil.

saf-fron (saf′run), *n.* **1,** a purple-flowered, fall-blooming species of crocus; **2,** the yellow colour obtained from the dried stigmas of this plant, used as a dye and in medicine; **3,** a deep-yellow colour:—*adj.* deep yellow.

sag (sag), *v.i.* [sagged, sag-ging], **1,** to sink or droop in the middle, from weight or pressure; as, the wire *sags;* **2,** to lean to one side; become lopsided; as, the door *sags;* **3,** to lose firmness; weaken; as, his spirits sagged:—*n.* the fact or the extent of sinking or drooping under weight or pressure; as, the *sag* of a door.

sa-ga (sä′ga), *n.* **1,** a story of heroic achievement or marvellous adventure, as in heroic Scandinavian legends; **2,** any long story of adventure with many episodes.

sa-ga-cious (sa-gā′shus), *adj.* having good judgment; shrewd; as, a *sagacious* ruler.—*n.* **sa-gac′i-ty** (sa-gas′-i-ti).

[1]**sage** (sāj), *adj.* [sag-er, sag-est], wise; shrewd:—*n.* an extremely wise person.

[2]**sage** (sāj), *n.* **1,** a plant of the mint family, whose spicy, dull-green leaves are used for flavouring meats, soups, etc.

Sag-it-ta-ri-us (saj′i-târ′i-us), *n.* **1,** the 9th sign of the zodiac (♐); **2,** a constellation, the Archer (a centaur drawing his bow).

said (sed), *p.t.* and *p.p.* of *say.*

sail (sāl), *n.* **1,** a sheet of canvas or cloth that is rigged to the masts and spars of a vessel and extended to catch the wind; **2,** all the sails of a ship; as, under full *sail;* **3,** (*pl.* sail), any ship; as, a squadron of 50 *sail;* **4,** an excursion in a sailboat; as, we went for a *sail;* **5,** anything resembling a sail, as the arms of a windmill:—*v.i.* **1,** to be driven or propelled by the force of the wind upon spread canvas; **2,** hence, to go by water; as, we *sailed* to Liverpool; **3,** to begin a voyage; as, the ship *sailed* at noon: **4,** to glide smoothly; as, the eagle *sailed* through the air:—*v.t.* **1,** to pass over in a ship; as, to *sail* the seas; **2,** to navigate or steer (a ship). *n.* **sail′boat′; sailboard.**

sail-or (sāl′ėr), *n.* **1,** a member of the crew of a vessel; a seaman; **2,** someone who sails for pleasure.

saint (sānt), *n.* **1,** a person of exceptionally upright or holy life; **2,** one of the blessed in heaven; **3,** in the Roman Catholic Church, an exceptionally godly person, who, after death, is declared holy by the church:—*v.t.* to canonize; declare officially to be a saint.—*adj.* **saint′ly.**—*n.* **saint′hood; saint′li-ness.**

Saint Ber-nard (sānt bûr′nard′), *n.* a very large, powerful dog with thick brown-and-white hair, first bred by monks at the monastery of St. Bernard in the Swiss Alps and used to find people lost in the snow.

[1]**sake** (sāk), *n.* **1,** purpose; cause; as, for the *sake* of argument; **2,** one's own welfare or the welfare of others; as, for my own *sake;* for my country's *sake.*

[2]**sa-ke** (sä′kē or sa′kē), *n.* a Japanese winelike alcoholic beverage made from fermented rice and usually served heated.

sa-la-cious (sa-lā′shus), *n.* lewd; tending to provoke lust; as, *salacious* magazines, pictures, etc.

sal-ad (sal′ad), *n.* a cold dish, as of lettuce with vegetables, fruit, meat, fish, etc., mixed with, or covered by, dressing.

sal-a-man-der (sal′a-man′dėr), *n.* **1,** a small, lizardlike but scaleless animal living in water or damp places: formerly fabled to live unharmed in fire; **2,** hence, one who can bear intense heat.

sa-la-mi (sa-lä′mi), *n.* a salted, garlic-flavoured sausage, dried or smoked so as to keep indefinitely in a dry atmosphere.

sal-a-ry (sal′a-ri), *n.* [*pl.* salaries], a regular, periodic payment for services; as, teachers receive a monthly *salary.*—*adj.* **sal′a-ried.**

sale (sāl), *n.* **1,** the act of selling; the exchange of a commodity or goods for an agreed price; as, to arrange for the *sale* of a house; **2,** a disposal of goods at a reduced price, by auction or in some other special way; as, the store is holding its annual *sale;* **3,** a chance to dispose of goods; a demand for goods; as, there is a great *sale* on toys at Christmas.—*adj.* **sal′a-ble.**—*n.* **sal′a-bil′i-ty.**

sales-per-son (sālz′ pûr′sn), *n.* [*pl.* salespeople or salespersons], a person whose business it is to sell goods. Also called a *salesclerk, sales representative, salesman,* or *saleswoman.*—*n.* **′sales′man-ship′.**

sales tax (sālz′ taks), money that is collected as tax on the price of the goods sold.

sa-li-ent (sā′li-ent), *adj.* **1,** outstanding; conspicuous; noticeable; as, a *salient* angle (of a defended position):—*n.* projecting line of battle, trenches, etc.

sa-line (sā′līn), *adj.* **1,** consisting of or containing salt or a salt; as, a *saline* solution; **2,** pertaining to salt; salty; as, a *saline* taste.—*n.* **sa-lin′i-ty.**

Sa-lish (sā′lish), *n.* **1,** an Aboriginal people in British Columbia and the northwestern United States, consisting of several groups: Coastal Salish, the Interior Salish, and the Straits Salish; **2,** the languages of the Salish people.

sa-li-va (sa-lī′va), *n.* the watery fluid secreted by the salivary glands and discharged into the mouth; spit.—*adj.* **sal′i-var-y** (sal′i-vėr-i).

sal-low (sal′ō), *adj.* of a pale, sickly yellow colour; as, the *sallow* complexion of a confined invalid.—*n.* **sal′low-ness.**

salm-on (sam′un), *n.* [*pl.* salmon], **1,** a silver-scaled, salt-water or fresh-water fish, prized as a game and food fish; **2,** the orange-pink colour of cooked salmon flesh:—*adj.* of an orange-pink colour:—**salmon trout, 1,** any of various large salmonlike fishes of North American lakes and rivers; **2,** the smaller European sea trout.

salm-on-ber-ry (sam′un-ber-i), *n.* [*pl.* salm- onberries], **1,** a large bush of the Pacific coast with red flowers and pink, edible fruit; **2,** the fruit of this bush, which resembles a raspberry.

sal-mo-nel-la (sal-mun-el′la), *n.* [*pl.* salmonellae or salmonellas], **1,** bacterium that can cause diseases such as food poisoning; **2,** an illness caused by this bacterium.

sa-lon (sa-lon′; så′lōn′), *n.* [*pl.* salons (så′lon′; så′lônz′)], **1,** a large reception-room; **2,** a boutique or shop of fashionable products or services; as, a beauty *salon*; **3,** an art gallery; also, the paintings or sculpture exhibited there.

salt (sôlt), *n.* **1,** a white, crystalline substance found in sea water, mineral springs, etc., and used universally for seasoning foods and preserving meats; **2,** anything that, like salt, gives flavour or character; savour; **3,** in *chemistry*, a compound, generally crystalline, formed by the union of an acid with a base; **4, salts,** in *medicine*, a substance resembling salt, used as a cathartic:—*adj.* **1,** flavoured or seasoned with salt; **2,** preserved with salt; **3,** growing in salt water; as, *salt* weed:—*v.t.* **1,** to preserve with salt; as, to *salt* meat; **2,** to sprinkle or season with salt; **3,** to furnish with salt; as, to *salt* cattle.—*adj.* **salt′y.**—*n.* **salt′i-ness.**

salt-pe-tre or **salt-pe-ter** (solt′pē′′tėr; sôlt′ pē′tėr), *n.* a white, crystalline compound used in making gunpowder and matches, and in preserving foods. Also called *nitre.*

salt-water (sôlt′wô′tėr), *adj.* having to do with or living in the ocean, rather than in the fresh water of lakes, rivers, etc.; as, *salt-water* fish.

sa-lu-bri-ous (sa-lū′bri-us), *adj.* healthful; wholesome; as, a *salubrious* climate.

sal-u-tar-y (sal′ūtėr-i), *adj.* **1,** producing health; as, *salutary* exercises; **2,** promoting good; as, *salutary* reforms.

sal-u-ta-tion (sal′ū-tā′shun), *n.* the act or manner of addressing or greeting another; also, the words or the gestures used.

sa-lute (sa-lūt′), *n.* **1,** a greeting; **2,** a gesture, bow, etc., expressing welcome, respect, etc.; **3,** in the army and navy, a gesture or position prescribed for respectful recognition of a superior officer, consisting of raising the fingers to the cap; also, the discharge of cannon, the lowering and raising again of a flag, etc., as a mark of honour:—*v.t.* [salut-ed, salut-ing], **1,** to address with words or gestures of greeting; **2,** in the army and navy, to honour or receive with an official salute or with a formal demonstration, as a discharge of guns, the lowering of a flag, etc.; as, the private *saluted* the captain; the fleet *saluted* the king with a discharge of 21 guns:—*v.i.* to make a gesture of respect.

sal-vage (sal′vij), *n.* **1,** the act of saving a ship or goods from the sea, from a wreck, from a fire, etc.; **2,** the ship or the goods so saved; **3,** payment given to those who help to save property under such circumstances:—*v.t.* [salvaged, salvaging], to save (a ship or goods) from destruction.

sal-va-tion (sal-vā′shun), *n.* **1,** the act of saving; rescue; **2,** the setting free of the soul from sin and from eternal punishment; **3,** that which saves or rescues; as, a raft was their *salvation* from the sea.

salve (såv), *n.* **1,** an ointment or greasy mixture, used for the relief and healing of wounds and sores on the skin; **2,** anything that calms, soothes, or pacifies:—*v.t.* to calm, soothe, or pacify; as, the compliment *salved* his wounded pride.

sal-vo (sal′vō), *n.* **1,** a simultaneous discharge of artillery, etc., often as a salute; **2,** a burst of cheers; as, a *salvo* of applause.

sam-ba (sam′ba), *n.* a Brazilian dance of African origin, distinguished by a dip with knee-bending and springing up in time to the music.

same (sām), *adj.* **1,** being one; identical; as, he goes to the *same* school as his sister; **2,** similar in kind or quality; as, suits of the *same* cloth; **3,** equal; as, the *same* distance; **4,** just mentioned; as, these *same* words:—*pron.* the identical person or thing; as, give me more of the *same.*—*n.* **same′ness.**

sam-o-sa (sa-mō′sa or sô-mō′sa), *n.* an Indian appetizer or snack food consisting of fried triangular pastries filled with meat or vegatables.

sam-ple (sam′pl), *n.* a specimen; model; pattern; also, a part of something, by which the whole is judged; as, she showed us a *sample* of the silk:—*v.t.* [sam-pled, sam-pling], to test by trying a small piece; as, to *sample* candy.

san-a-tor-i-um (san′a-tōr′i-um), *n.* [*pl.* sanatoria (san′a-tōr′i-a) or sanatoriums], an institution for the care of invalids; a sanitarium.

sanc·ti·fy (sangk′ti-fī′), *v.t.* [sanctified, sanctify-ing], **1,** to make holy; set apart for some sacred use; as, "God blessed the seventh day and *sanctified* it"; **2,** to purify (human beings) from sin.—*n.* **sanc′ti-fi-ca′tion.**

sanc·ti·mo·ni·ous (sangk′ti-mō′ni-us), *adj.* making a hypocritical show of piety or holiness; as, a *sanctimonious* TV evangelist.

sanc·tion (sangk′shun), *n.* formal approval or consent by those in authority:—**sanctions,** a legal term given to coercive measures imposed for securing obedience to law, as by a group of nations withholding loans, freezing assets abroad, imposing a blockade, etc.:—*v.t.* to approve; authorize; as, their parents *sanctioned* the marriage.

sanc·ti·ty (sangk′ti-ti), *n.* [*pl.* sanctities], **1,** holiness; purity; **2,** sacredness; solemnity; as, the *sanctity* of a cathedral; **3, sanctities,** sacred objects, duties, etc.

sanc·tu·ar·y (sangk′tū-ėr-i), *n.* [*pl.* sanctuaries], **1,** a place of shelter and protection; as, a *sanctuary* for wildfowl; **2,** hence, security; shelter; as, to seek *sanctuary* from the world; **3,** a consecrated place; a church or temple.

sand (sand), *n.* **1,** dry soil composed of fine particles of crushed or worn rock, found chiefly along the shores of large bodies of water or in deserts; **2, sands,** a mainly sandy area; **3, sands,** moments; time: from the custom of measuring time by sand in an hourglass; as, the *sands* of time run fast:—*v.t.* **1,** to smooth or polish with sandpaper; as, *sand* the shelves before painting them; **2,** to sprinkle, mix, or rub with sand; as, to *sand* floors. Also, **sand′bank′; sand′bar′; sand′box′; sand′cas′tle; sand′ dune′.**

san·dal (san′dl), *n.* an open shoe made up of a sole that is attached to the foot by straps or ties, originally worn by the ancient Greeks and Romans.

san·dal·wood (san′dl-wood′), *n.* **1,** a tree that grows in the Malay Archipelago and India; **2,** the close-grained fragrant wood of this tree, used for fine carving, and valued for the perfume that it yields: three varieties grow in Canada.

sand·bag (sand′bag′), *n.* a bag filled with sand, used as a weapon, to protect fortifications against enemy fire or buildings, etc., against flooding, strong winds, etc.:—*v.t.* **1,** to bank or place sandbags to protect, as protective dikes, etc.; **2,** to hit or knock down as with a sandbag weapon; **3,** to coerce; intimidate; bully; thwart; **4,** to entrap; to create overconfidence in an opponent by downplaying one's skill or potential; as, she *sandbagged* the player across the poker table.

sand·bar (sand′bär), *n.* a shallow place in a body of water, where sand has built up to form a ridge.

sand·er (san′dėr), *n.* **1,** a power tool for sanding or sandpapering; **2,** a vehicle used to spread sand on icy roads.

sand·pa·per (sand′pā′pėr), *n.* a heavy paper with a coating of sand on one side, used for smoothing and polishing:—*v.t.* to smooth or polish with sandpaper.

sand·stone (sand′stōn′), *n.* a rock composed chiefly of quartz sand hardened into a solid mass by a natural cement.

sand·wich (sand′wich; san′wij), *n.* two or more slices of fresh or toasted bread with meat, cheese, or other filling between them:—*v.t.* to place (a person or thing) between two others.

sand·y (san′di), *adj.* [sand-i-er, sand-i-est], **1,** entirely or chiefly composed of or covered with sand; as, *sandy* soil, *sandy* beach; **2,** of a yellowish-red colour; as, *sandy* hair.—*n.* **sand′i-ness.**

sane (sān), *adj.* [san-er, san-est], **1,** mentally sound or healthy; **2,** coming from a sound mind; sensible; showing good sense; as, a *sane* suggestion.

sang (sang), *p.t.* of *sing.*

san·guine (sang′gwin), *adj.* **1,** of the colour of blood; ruddy; as, a *sanguine* complexion; **2,** hopeful; confident; as, *sanguine* of victory.—*adj.* **san′gui-na-ry.**

san·i·tar·i·um (san′i-târ′i-um), *n.* [*pl.* sanitariums or sanitaria (san′-i-târ′i-a)], a place for the care of invalids or the treatment of certain diseases; also, a sanatorium.

san·i·tar·y (san′i-tėr-i), *adj.* **1,** clean and free of germs, hygienic, preserving health; as, *sanitary* conditions; **2,** relating to health; as, *sanitary* laws

san·i·ta·tion (san′i-tā-shun), *n.* the science and practice of bringing about conditions that protect health, such as collecting garbage, providing safe drinking water, and building sewer systems; hygiene.

san·i·ty (san′i-ti), *n.* soundness of mind.

sank (sank), *p.t.* of *sink.*

San·ta Claus (san′ta klôz), in *nursery lore,* a chubby, white-bearded old man who represents the spirit of Christmas and who brings children gifts on Christmas Eve in a sleigh drawn by eight reindeer.

[1]**sap** (sap), *n.* the watery juice of a tree or plant that carries food and other materials. The sap of certain trees is used to make products such as rubber, sugar, maple syrup, etc.—*adj.* **sap′less.**

[2]**sap** (sap), *v.t.* [sapped, sap-ping], **1,** to wear away by digging beneath; undermine; as, the flood waters *sapped* the foundations of the house; **2,** to weaken; wear away; as, continual defeats *sapped* his courage.

sa·pi·ent (sā′pi-ent), *adj.* wise, intelligent: often ironical.—*n.* **sa′pi-ence.**

sap·ling (sap′ling), *n.* **1,** a flexible young tree; **2,** hence, a youth.

sap-phire (saf′īr), *n.* **1,** a precious stone, hard and transparent, and of a deep-blue colour; **2,** the deep-blue colour of this gem.

sar-casm (sär′kazm), *n.* a bitter, cutting remark; also, ironical language expressing scorn or contempt.—*adj.* **sar-cas′tic.**—*adv.* sar-cas′ti-cal-ly.

sar-coph-a-gus (sär-kof′a-gus), *n.* [*pl.* -gi (-jī); -guses], a stone coffin, esp. for a distinguished person, as that of King Tutankhamen of Egypt, which was unearthed in 1922.

sar-dine (sär-dēn′; sär′dēn), *n.* a small fish of the herring family, often packed tightly and preserved in oil for use as food.

sar-don-ic (sär-don′ik), *adj.* sneering; mocking; bitterly ironic or derisive; as, the *sardonic* grin of the murderer.

sa-ri (sä′rē), *n.* [*pl.* saris], a length of cotton or silk material wrapped around the body, as in the traditional outer clothing of Hindu women.

sa-rong (sa-rông′), *n.* the chief garment of both sexes in Malaysia and the East Indies: it is a long strip of cloth, worn tucked around the waist like a skirt.

sar-to-ri-al (sär-tō′ri-al), *adj.* relating to clothing or tailoring; as, *sartorial* splendour or elegance of her prom dress.

¹sash (sash), *n.* [*pl.* sashes], an ornamental band, ribbon, etc., worn around the waist or over the shoulder.

²sash (sash), *n.* [*pl.* sashes or sash], a frame into which the glass of a window or door is fitted.

sa-shi-mi (sa-shē′mē), *n.* a Japanese dish of thinly sliced raw fish.

sas-ka-toon (sas′ka-tōōn′), *n.* a small shrub, *Amelanchier canadensis,* of which 13 species grow in Canada: the fruit is a purple berry, sweet and juicy, of which large quantities are harvested and preserved in Western Canada. Also called *serviceberry, juneberry,* and *shadbush.*

Sas-quatch (sas′kwoch), *n.* a large, hairy, humanlike creature thought to live in the mountains of the Pacific Northwest. Also known as *Bigfoot.*

sas-sy (sa′si), *adj.* **1,** rude; disrespectful; impudent; saucy; **2,** energetic; lively; vigorous; **3,** chic; smart; stylish; as, a *sassy* outfit.—*adv.* **sas′si-ly.**—*n.* **sas′si-ness.**

sat (sat), *p.t.* and *p.p.* of *sit.*

Sa-tan (sā′tn), *n.* the Devil.

sa-tan-ic (sa-tan′ik), *adj.* pertaining to, or like, Satan; devilish; wicked; as, *satanic* wickedness.

sat-ay (sa′tā or sa-tā′) *n.* a dish of southeast Asia consisting of skewered meat or fish that is barbecued and usually served with a peanut sauce.

satch-el (sach′el), *n.* a small bag, usually of fabric or leather, often with a shoulder strap, used to carry books and personal belongings, papers, etc., esp. to and from school.

sate (sāt), *v.t.* [sat-ed, sat-ing], **1,** to satisfy fully (an appetite or desire); **2,** to supply with an excess of something; as, he was *sated* with flattery.

sat-el-lite (sat′e-līt′), *n.* **1,** a heavenly body revolving around a larger one; as, the moon is a *satellite* of the earth; **2,** an artificial body put into orbit from earth to collect information, transmit radio and TV signals, etc.; **3,** a state economically or politically dependent on a more powerful one:—**satellite dish,** a dish-shaped device used to receive or transmit signals transmitted from orbiting satellites.

SATELLITE

sa-ti-ate (sā′shi-āt′), *v.t.* [satiat-ed, satiat-ing], to gratify to excess; as, to *satiate* one's appetite.—*n.* **sa-ti′e-ty** (sa-tī′e-ti).

sat-in (sat′in), *n.* a closely woven, glossy silk fabric:—*adj.* made of or like this silk.

sat-ire (sat′īr), *n.* **1,** a poem, essay, story, etc. that uses humour to expose and ridicule evil or folly; **2,** biting sarcasm or ridicule.—*adj.* **sa-tir′ic** (sa-tir′ik); **sa-tir′i-cal.**

sat-is-fac-tion (sat′is-fak′shun), *n.* **1,** the act of supplying a need or desire; also, the act of paying off, compensating, contenting, etc.; **2,** the condition of having one's wishes filled or of being gratified, paid off, contented, etc.; contentment; **3,** that which satisfies or gratifies; as, your visit will be a great *satisfaction.*

sat-is-fac-to-ry (sat′is-fak′to-ri), *adj.* sufficient; adequate; producing satisfaction; as, his mark in math was only *satisfactory.*—*adv.* **sat′is-fac′to-ri-ly.**

sat-is-fy (sat′is-fī′), *v.t.* [satisfied, satisfy-ing], **1,** to content; fill the wishes of; as, they were *satisfied* with the new house; also, to gratify to the full; as, to *satisfy* one's hunger; **2,** to free from doubt; convince; as, the explanation *satisfied* the child:—*v.i.* to give gratification; as, riches do not always *satisfy.*

sat-u-rate (sat′ū-rāt′), *v.t.* [saturat-ed, satu-rat-ing], to cause to become soaked; to fill to the limit of capacity for absorbing; as, to *saturate* the ground with water.—*n.* **sat′u-ra′tion.**

Sat-ur-day (sat′ėr-di; -dā′), *n.* the seventh-day of the week, the day after Friday and before Sunday.

Sat-urn (sat′ėrn), *n.* **1,** the second-largest planet in the solar system, and the sixth-closest to the sun. It is surrounded by large rings made up of particles of ice and water; **2,** the ancient Roman god of agriculture.

sat-ur-nine (sat′ėr-nīn′), *adj.* gloomy; sluggish; taciturn; as, a *saturnine* countenance, temper, person, etc.

sat-yr (sat′ėr; sā′tėr), *n.* in *mythology*, a forest god, represented with long, pointed ears, short horns, and the tail of a horse or goat, who indulged in drunken merriment and lustfulness.

sauce (sôs), *n.* **1,** a liquid or semi-liquid dressing or seasoning for food, usually poured or spooned on top of food; also, any highly seasoned mixture of ingredients, used as a relish; as, chili *sauce;* **2,** stewed fruit; as, apple*sauce*; **3,** *Colloq.* insolence; impudence **4,** *Colloq.* alcohol:—*v.t.* [sauced, sauc-ing], **1,** to prepare or serve with a sauce; **2,** *Colloq.* to be insolent or impudent to someone.

sauce-pan (sôs′pan′), *n.* a small metal pan or pot, with a handle, used in cooking.

sau-cer (sô′sėr), *n.* a shallow dish, esp. one to hold a cup.

sau-cy (sô′si), *adj.* [sau-ci-er, sau-ci-est], rude; impudent; also, bold, lively, or sexually suggestive; as, a *saucy* smile.—*adv.* **sau′ci-ly.**—*n.* **sau′ ci-ness.**

sauer-kraut (sour′krout′), *n.* finely sliced cabbage, fermented in a brine made of its own juice.

sault (sōō), *n.* a rapid or waterfall, as at *Sault* Ste. Marie.

sau-na (sô′na), *n.* **1,** a small room or enclosure filled with steam from pouring water on hot rocks: originated in Finland; **2,** the time spent in such a heat bath for invigorating or therapeutic purposes.

saun-ter (sôn′tėr; sän′tėr), *v.i.* to wander idly; stroll; as, to *saunter* along the beach:—*n.* **1,** a leisurely manner of walking; **2,** an idle walk or ramble.

sau-sage (so′sij), *n.* ground, highly seasoned meat, often stuffed into a thin, tubelike casing.

sau-té (sô′tā, sô-tā′, or sō-tā′), *v.t.* to fry food lightly and quickly in a small amount of oil or fat in a open pan over high heat.—*adj.* **sau′téed.**

sav-age (sav′ij), *adj.* **1,** relating to the forest or wilderness; wild; as, *savage* country; **2,** cruel; fierce; as, *savage* beasts; **3,** uncivilized; barbaric; as, *savage* tribes:—*n.* **1,** an uncivilized person; a barbarian; **2,** a fierce, brutal person.—*adv.* **sav′age-ly.**

sav-age-ry (sav′ij-ri), *n.* [*pl.* savage-ries], **1,** the condition of being wild or uncivilized; **2,** brutal roughness or cruelty.

sa-van-na or **sa-van-nah** (sa-van′a), *n.* a grassy, open plain in the tropics or subtropics; a prairie.

sa-vant (sa-vänt′), *n.* a person of learning, esp. one famed for scientific research.

[1]**save** (sāv), *v.t.* [saved, sav-ing], **1,** to bring out of danger; rescue; as, the soldier *saved* his comrade's life; also, to preserve from damage, decay, etc.; as, rubber overshoes *save* shoes; **2,** to spare; avoid; as, to *save* trouble; prevent the waste of; as, to *save* time; **3,** to refrain from spending; hoard; as, to *save* money; **4,** to free from the power and result of sin; as, to *save* souls:—*v.i.* **1,** to refrain from spending or wasting money or supplies; **2,** to put away money a little at a time:—*n.* a play in hockey or soccer in which the goalie prevents a goal from being scored.—*n.* **sav′er.**

[2]**save** (sāv), *prep.* except; not including; as, he attended every game *save* one.

sav-ing (sāv′ing), *adj.* **1,** preserving from sin or destruction; as *saving* faith; **2,** redeeming; compensating; as, a *saving* sense of humour; **3,** economical; not wasteful; as, a very *saving* individual; labour-*saving* device:—*n.* **1,** economy; as, the habit of *saving;* **2,** rescue; **3, savings,** money saved; as, *savings* account:—**savings bond,** debenture; an instrument issued by governments or public companies promising to repay a certain amount of money at a fixed rate, often on a fixed date; as, *savings bonds* issued by the government of Canada are one of the most risk-free investments available:—*prep.* except.

sav-iour or **sav-ior** (sāv′yėr), *n.* one who rescues or saves:—**Saviour,** in Christianity, Jesus Christ.

sa-voir faire (sav′wär′ fâr′), *n.* the knowledge of the ways of the world and the appropriate things to do in any given situation; tact; polished certainty; graceful confidence; as, many people envy James Bond his *savoir faire.*

sa-vor-y (sā′vėr-i), *n.* a fragrant herb of the mint family, used in cooking.

sa-vour or **sa-vor** (sā′vėr), *n.* flavour; taste; characteristic; as, a spicy *savour:*—*v.t.* to appreciate or enjoy the taste or smell of food or an experience; as, *savour* the fancy meal; *savour* every moment of the trip.—*adj.* **sa′vour-y.**

sav-vy (sa′vi) *n. Colloq.* practical know-how; insight; shrewdness:—*adj.* having practical knowledge or intuitive insight; well informed; as, the media-*savvy* politician:—*v.t* and *v.i.* [sav-vied, sav-vy-ing], to understand or know.

[1]**saw** (sô), *p.t.* of *see.*

[2]**saw** (sô), *n.* a cutting tool with a thin toothed blade, worked mechanically or by hand; also, a cutting machine having one or more such blades:—*v.t.* [*p.t.* sawed (sôd), *p.p.* sawn (sôn) or sawed, *p.pr.* saw-ing], **1,** to cut with a saw; as, to *saw* wood; **2,** to form or fashion with such a tool; as, he *sawed* the board so that it fitted into place:—*v.i.* **1,** to be cut with a saw; as, the wood *saws* easily; **2,** to use a saw; **3,** to cut.

[3]**saw** (sô), *n.* a proverb; an adage.

saw-dust (sô′dust′), *n.* the fine particles or chips that result when wood is sawn.

saw-horse (sô′hôrs′), *n.* a rack or frame to hold sticks of wood while they are being sawn by hand.

saw-mill (sô′mil′), *n.* a mill where logs are sawn into lumber by machines; also, a sawing machine.

sax-o-phone (sak′so-fōn′), *n.* a musical instrument consisting of a metal tube with keys and a reed mouthpiece. Also called *sax.*

say (sā), *v.t.* [said (sed), say-ing], **1,** to utter in words; tell; **2,** to declare; state as a decision; assert; as, I *say* he shall go; **3,** to estimate; assume; as, *say* he has ten houses, how long will he keep them? **4,** to recite; repeat; as, to *say* a poem:—*n.* **1,** something that one has said or intends to say; as, to have one's *say;* **2,** one's turn or right to express an opinion; as, it's your *say* next; also, the right to decide; as, the teacher has the whole *say.*

say-ing (sā′ing), *n.* that which is often said; a proverb or maxim.

scab (skab), *n.* **1,** a crust formed over a wound or sore to protect it as it heals; **2,** a disease of animals, esp. sheep, characterized by spots that resemble scabs; also, a similar disease of plants; **3,** *Slang* a non-union worker, esp. one who takes a striker's job.—*adj.* **scab′by.**

sca-bi-es (skā′bi-ēz′), *n.* a contagious skin disease of humans and animals, due to a parasite, the itch mite.

scaf-fold (skaf′uld), *n.* **1,** a temporary structure serving as a support for workers while building, painting, etc., in high places; **2,** an elevated platform on which the execution of criminals takes place by hanging, beheading, etc.

scaf-fold-ing (skaf′ul-ding), *n.* **1,** a scaffold or series of scaffolds; **2,** the materials used in erecting scaffolds.

scal-a-wag, scal-la-wag (skal′a-wag′), or **scal-ly-wag** (skal′i-wag′), *n. Colloq.* a disreputable person; good-for-nothing; one who will not work; a scamp; rascal.

scald (skôld), *v.t.* **1,** to burn or injure, as does hot liquid; also, to burn with steam; **2,** hence, to cause pain as if by burning; as, hot tears *scalded* her face; **3,** to bring near to the boiling point; as, to *scald* milk; **4,** to rinse or dip in boiling water; as, to *scald* dishes; to *scald* tomatoes:—*n.* a burn or injury from hot liquid or steam.

¹scale (skāl), *n.* **1,** one of the pans or dishes of a balance; **2,** (usually *scales*), the balance itself; **3,** any instrument or machine for weighing:—*v.t.* [scaled, scal-ing], to weigh by means of scales.

²scale (skāl), *n.* **1,** one of the thin, bony or horny plates forming the outer covering of many fish, lizards, snakes, etc.; **2,** any thin plate resembling a scale; **3,** one of the small flaky pieces of dead skin which fall off in certain diseases:—*v.t.* [scaled, scal-ing], to strip (a fish) of scales:—*v.i.* **1,** to form or drop scales; separate and come off in thin layers; **2,** to become rough and hard; become crusted.—*adj.* **scal′y.**—*n.* **scal′i-ness.**

³scale (skāl), *n.* **1,** a measure consisting of a series of marks, laid down at definite, regular distances along a line; as, the *scale* on a tape measure; **2,** a basis for a system of numbering; as, the decimal *scale;* **3,** a series of numbers, similar objects, etc., that progress from a low to a high point or degree; as, the *scale* of marks in the math test ranged from 47 to 98; **4,** the relation between the actual size of an object and the size of the object as it appears in a drawing, painting, etc.; as, a drawing of a house on the *scale* of one metre to one centimetre; **5,** any standard for judging or estimating; **6,** in *music,* a series of tones in a regular order, whether ascending or descending; also, a succession of tones beginning on a certain keynote; as, the *scale* of F:—*v.t.* [scaled, scal-ing], **1,** to climb up; as, to *scale* a wall; **2,** to reduce in accordance with a settled ratio or scale; as, to *scale* down expenses; **3,** to make (a drawing, etc.) in accordance with a definite scale.

sca-lene (skā-lēn′), *adj.* in *geometry,* having three unequal sides; as, a *scalene* triangle.

scal-lion (skal′yun), *n.* an onionlike plant; a leek; green onion.

scal-lop (skol′up; skal′up)′, *n.* **1,** a saltwater shellfish with two fan-shaped, usually ribbed, shells, that are hinged together; **2,** the muscle by which the shell is closed, valued for food; **3,** one of a series of curves that form an ornamental edge, as on lace, linens, etc.:—*v.t.* **1,** to cut the edge or border of, in a series of curves; **2,** to mix with crumbs, butter, etc., and bake; as, to *scallop* tomatoes:—*adj.* **scal′loped.**

scalp (skalp), *n.* the skin on the top of head, normally covered with hair:—*v.t.* to cut off the skin and hair of the head of an enemy.

scal-pel (skal′p'l). *n.* a surgeon's small, light, straight knife with very sharp blade for operations and dissections.

scal-per (skal′pėr), *n.* one who buys stocks, tickets for games, etc., and resells them (sometimes illegally) at a profit:—*v.t.* and *v.i.* **scalp** (*Colloq.*)

scam (skam), *n.* a fraud, cheat, trick, or swindle; as, the insurance *scam* was uncovered by the police:—*v.t.* [scammed, scamming], to cheat, defraud or swindle; to obtain something by underhanded or improper methods.—*n.* **scam′mer.**

scamp (skamp), *n.* a rascal; a worthless person; a playful person.

scam-per (skam′pėr), *v.i.* to run or skip quickly; as, the frightened rabbit *scampered* away:—*n.* a hasty flight.

scan (skan), *v.t.* [scanned, scan-ning], **1,** to look at the details of; scrutinize or examine carefully; as, Columbus *scanned* the horizon for land; **2,** to read over quickly; as, *scan* the newspaper; **3,** to use a special machine to check for certain information; as a metal detector *scans* airline passengers; **4,** to convert data to electronic format; as, *scan* a picture onto a computer; **5,** to test or mark (a line of poetry) to show the kind of metrical structure used:—*n.* the act or fact of scanning; as, a brain *scan.*

scan-dal (skan′dal), *n.* **1,** a cause of reproach; also, shame; disgrace; as, cuts to hospital funding are a *scandal;* **2,** careless or malicious gossip injurious to another's reputation; backstabbing.

scan-dal-ize (skan′dal-īz′), *v.t.* [scandalized, scandaliz-ing], to offend or shock by an opinion, action, etc.

scan-dal-ous (skan′dal-us), *adj.* **1,** tending to harm the good name or reputation of someone; as, *scandalous* rumours; **2,** shocking; disgraceful; as, *scandalous* neglect of the homeless.

scan-ner (skan′ėr), *n.* a device or machine that scans; as, a metal detector *scanner,* brain *scanner,* image *scanner.*

scant (skant), *adj.* **1,** barely enough; as, a *scant* supply of food; **2,** a little less than; as, it weighs a *scant* gram:—*v.t.* to stint; limit the supply of.

scant-y (skan′ti), *adj.* [scant-i-er, scant-i-est], barely sufficient; scarcely enough; as, *scanty* supplies.

scape-goat (skāp′gōt′), *n.* **1,** one who bears the blame for others; **2,** in an ancient Jewish custom, a goat selected by lot, on whose head the high priest laid the sins of the people, after which it was driven into the wilderness.

scar (skär), *n.* **1,** the mark left after a wound or burn heals; **2,** any mark like a scar; as, knife *scars* on the table; **3,** a lasting effect caused by grief, trouble, etc.:—*v.t.* [scarred, scarring], to mark with, or as with, a scar:—*v.i.* to form a scar.

scarce (skârs), *adj.* [scarc-er, scarc-est], **1,** not common; rare; as, real diamonds are *scarce;* **2,** not plentiful; not equal to the demand; as peaches are *scarce* this year.—*n.* **scarce′ness.**—*n.* **scar′ci-ty.**

scarce-ly (skârs′li), *adv.* **1,** almost not; barely; as, I *scarcely* saw him before he left; **2,** surely not; hardly; as, you can *scarcely* run as fast as that.

scare (skâr), *v.t.* [scared, scar-ing], to strike with sudden terror; frighten:—*n.* a sudden fright or panic.—*adj.* **scar′y.**

scare-crow (skâr′krō′), *n.* **1,** a figure, usually a crude representation of a person, dressed in ragged clothes, set up to frighten birds and animals away from crops; **2,** a person dressed in rags.

scare-mon-ger (skâr′mon′gėr; skâr′mun′gėr), *n.* an alarmist; one who spreads alarming or frightening rumours, esp. needlessly; one who encourages panic.—*n.* **scare′mon′ger-ing.**

scarf (skärf), *n.* [*pl.* scarfs or scarves (skärvz)], **1,** a piece of cloth worn on the head or around the neck or shoulders for ornament or warmth; **2,** a cover, often long and narrow, used on a bureau, piano, etc.:—*v. Colloq.* to eat or drink quickly

scar-let (skär′lit), *n.* a bright-red colour tinged with orange:—*adj.* **1,** of a scarlet colour; **2,** promiscuous; as, a *scarlet* woman.

scar-let fe-ver (fē′vėr), a highly contagious disease, characterized by a severe sore throat, high fever, and scarlet rash.

scat (skat), *interj. Colloq.* Go!—*n.* **1,** the excrement of a wild animal; **2,** improvised jazz singing with nonword vocals that usually imitate the sound of musical instruments:—*v.t.* [scat-ted, scat-ting], to sing in this fashion:—*v.i.* to leave quickly.

scath-ing (skāth′ing), *adj.* severe; bitter; as, *scathing* remarks.—*adv.* **scath′ing-ly.**

scat-ter (skat′ėr), *v.t.* **1,** to throw here and there; strew; as, to *scatter* clothes about a room; *scatter* seed; **2,** to drive apart; disperse; as, the soldiers *scattered* the mob:—*v.i.* to separate and go in different directions; as, the covey of quail *scattered.*

scat-ter-brain (skat′ėr-brān′), *n.* someone who is disorganized, thoughtless, or flighty; one who lacks concentration.—*adj.* **scat′ter-brained′.**

scav-en-ger (skav′en-jėr), *n.* **1,** any animal, bird, etc., that eats refuse or the remains of dead animals or a person who looks through garbage for useful objects that have been thrown away; **2,** a person or thing that feeds or lives off something or someone:—**scavenger hunt,** a game played by individuals or teams, the object of which is to collect a list of specified items, usually with a time limit, and often outdoors over a wide area.—*v.t.* **sca′venge** [sca′venged, sca′veng-ing].

sce-na-ri-o (si-nâr′i-ō; si-nä′ri-ō), *n.* [*pl.* scenarios], **1,** the complete, detailed story of the plot of a play, novel, or film, including the cast of characters and acting directions; **2,** projected sequence of events or course of action; as, taking into account this *scenario,* the project will take two years to complete.

scene (sēn), *n.* **1,** one of the parts into which an act of a play is divided; **2,** the painted background, hangings, etc., used on the stage to picture the place where the action is going on; **3,** the time, place, or circumstances in which the action of a play, story, occurrence, etc., takes place; as, the *scene* of the play is a farm; **4,** a particular episode or happening of a story, play, etc.; as, the storm *scene* in *David Copperfield;* **5,** a display of strong feeling or emotion; as, to make a *scene;* **6,** a landscape; view.

scen-er-y (sēn′ėr-i), *n.* **1,** painted hangings, screens, etc., used on a stage; the background; **2,** a landscape, or general way a place looks.

sce-nic (sē′nik; sen′ik), *adj.* **1,** pertaining to the stage; **2,** pertaining to a landscape; also, offering beautiful views of nature.

scent (sent), *n.* **1,** odour; fragrance; **2,** the sense of smell; as, hounds have a keen *scent;* **3,** an odour left lingering about a place by a person or animal; as, the dogs caught the wolf by following his *scent;* **4,** hence, the trail or track, as of a criminal; **5,** a perfume:—*v.t.* **1,** to smell; **2,** hence, to get a hint of; as, to *scent* trouble; **3,** to perfume; as, handkerchiefs *scented* with lavender.—*adj.* **scent′less.**

scep-tic (skep′tik), *n.* Same as **skeptic.**

scep-tre or **scep-ter** (sep′tėr), *n.* a ruler's staff; an emblem of authority or power.

sched-ule (sked′ūl; shed′ūl′), *n.* **1,** a list of things to be done in a certain order of time; as, according to the *schedule*, the job will take a month; also, a timetable; **2,** the normal or expected time for something to happen; as, open on *schedule*; **3,** a slip of paper containing a list or inventory; as, a *schedule* of household goods:—*v.t.* [scheduled, schedul-ing], **1,** to include in a list or schedule; as, I'll *schedule* your speech for tomorrow; **2,** to make a list or schedule of; as, to *schedule* one's possessions.

sche-ma (skē′ma), *n.* **1,** a diagram, outline, or proposal; a conceptual framework; **2,** the underlying pattern or structure, esp. in psychology or philosophy.

scheme (skēm), *n.* **1,** a carefully arranged and systematic plan; a system; as, a *scheme* for old-age pensions; **2,** an underhanded plan; plot; as, a *scheme* to rob a house; **3,** an arrangement or system in which everything is related or in harmony; as, the colour *scheme* of a costume:—*v.t.* [schemed, schem-ing], to design or plan; plot:—*v.i.* to form a plot or plan.—*adj.* **sche-mat′ic.**

schism (skizm; sizm), *n.* **1,** a split or division of a group into opposing factions; **2,** a division of a Church or religious body into two separate entities.

schiz-oid (skiz′oid′), *adj.* **1,** schizophrenic; **2,** of a person or personality, divorced from reality; **3,** something with inconsistent, contrary elements; as, the *schizoid* political platform:—*n.* a person who manifests such symptoms.

schiz-o-phre-ni-a (skiz′ō-frē-ni-a), *n.* a psychosis or form of mental disease marked by delusions, hallucinations, and withdrawal.

schnit-zel (shnit′sil), *n.* a thin slice of meat, esp. veal, but also pork, coated in breadcrumbs and spices and fried.

schol-ar (skol′ėr), *n.* **1,** one who has acquired thorough and expert knowledge in one or more fields of learning; **2,** formerly, one who attends a school or learns from a teacher:—*adj.* **schol′ar-ly.**

schol-ar-ship (skol′ėr-ship′), *n.* **1,** money given to a student to enable him or her to follow or continue a course of study; **2,** the practice of gaining knowledge or learning.

scho-las-tic (sko-las′tik), *adj.* relating to learned people, students, schools, education, academic life, etc.

[1]**school** (sko͞ol), *n.* **1,** a place that holds regular classes for learning and teaching; as, the new *school* was opened yesterday; **2,** a regular meeting or session at which instruction is given and received; as, there will be no *school* tomorrow afternoon; **3,** the whole body of students, teachers, and staff in any educational institution; as, the *school* is happy over the victory; **4,** the followers or imitators of a teacher or leader; as, the Platonic *school* of philosophy; **5,** a division of a university devoted to one branch of learning; as, a *school* of dentistry. Also, **school′book′; school′ boy′; school′child′; school′chil′dren; school′girl′; school′house′; school′ing; school′mate′; school′room′; school′tea′ cher; school′work′; school′yard′:**—*v.t.* to train or instruct in, or as in, a school.

[2]**school** (sko͞ol), *n.* a great number of fish or other water animals of the same kind feeding or swimming together; a shoal:—*v.i.* to swim together in great numbers.

school board, **1,** a group of people, usually elected, that oversees the administration of schools in a given area; **2,** the body responsible for the administration of schools in a given geographic area; **3,** the area that the group oversees.

schoon-er (sko͞o ′nėr), *n.* **1,** a vessel with two or more masts, rigged so that the sails stretch along the length of the ship rather than across from side to side; **2,** a covered wagon, formerly used by pioneers on the western prairies; a prairie schooner; **3,** a tall beer or sherry glass.

schwa (shwä), *n.* an inverted *e* [ə], used in some dictionaries as a diacritical (or pronunciation) mark to indicate a slurred vowel sound in an unaccented syllable; as, *a* in *a*go or *e* in ag*e*nt.

sci-ence (sī′ens), *n.* **1,** a body of knowledge that results from the study of things in nature and in the universe, along with the forces that affect these things; **2,** a specific area of science, such as biology, chemistry, or physics; **3,** knowledge, or the pursuit of knowledge, of things as they are, and of why they act as they do; also, the classification and systematic arrangement of such knowledge, and the formulation, where possible, of general laws, or truths, deduced from it; as, the *science* of snowboarding.

science fiction, stories about possible future scientific developments, often of travel through space or time. Also called *sci-fi*.

sci-en-tif-ic (sī′en-tif′ik), *adj.* **1,** relating to, or used in, a science; as, *scientific* instruments; **2,** in accordance with the methods of science; applying the laws of science; as, *scientific* approach.—*adv.* **sci′en-tif′i-cal-ly.**

scientific method, the systematic application of the principles and procedures of natural science that generally involves the observation of phenomena and the formulation and testing of hypotheses.

sci-en-tist (sī′en-tist), *n.* a person who is learned in science; also, a person whose profession is in the area of science.

sci–fi (sī′–fī′), *n.* and *adj.* Same as **science fiction.**

scim-i-tar or **scim-i-ter** (sim′i-tėr), *n.* a Middle Eastern sword with a curved blade.

scin-til-la (sin-til′a), *n.* a particle; iota: used figuratively (with a negative); as, there is not a *scintilla* of truth in the rumour.

scin-til-late (sin′ti-lāt′), *v.i.* **1,** to give off sparks, fire, or firelike particles; **2,** to twinkle, as stars; **3,** figuratively, to be witty or clever.—*n.* **scin′til-la′tion.**

sci-on (sī′un), *n.* **1,** the sprout or shoot of a plant, cut off and used for planting or grafting; **2,** a descendant; heir, esp. of a distinguished family.

scis-sors (siz′ėrz), *n.pl.* an instrument, smaller than shears, with two sharp blades that open and close on a pivot, and cut when they meet.

scle-ro-sis (skli-rō′sis), *n.* [*pl.* -oses (-sēz)], **1,** the hardening of a part of the body, esp. of the nervous system, due to overgrowth of fibrous connective tissue, esp. multiple *sclerosis*; **2,** the hardening of a plant's cell wall, as by the formation of wood.

¹scoff (skôf), *v.i.* to show scorn or contempt by mocking language; to jeer; as, do not *scoff* at the mistakes of others:—*v.t.* to mock or jeer at:—*n.* an expression of scorn or contempt:—*n.* **scoff′er.**

²scoff (skôf), *v.t.* to eat food quickly and greedily; to wolf down; as, she *scoffed* down the food because she was very hungry:—*n.* a large meal, esp. of seafood.

scold (skôld), *v.i.* to reprimand sharply or rudely:—*v.t.* to find fault with; rebuke severely; as, the teacher *scolded* the student for being late:—*n.* **scold′ing.**

sconce (skons), *n.* an ornamental bracket, fastened to a wall, originally holding one or more candlesticks, but now for electric wall lights.

scone (skōn), *n.* **1,** a rich tea biscuit, with currants or raisins.

scoop (sko͞op), *n.* **1,** a large long-handled ladle for skimming or dipping out liquids; **2,** a shovel for snow, coal, etc.; also, a small utensil, shaped like a shovel, for dipping out flour, sugar, etc., from a bin or bag; **3,** the act of dipping out or making a hollow; **4,** any gesture or motion like that made with a scoop; as, with a *scoop* of his hand, he splashed water into my face; **5,** the hollow left from scooping; **6,** the quantity dipped out in one scoop; as, two *scoops* will be enough; **7,** the scoop-like bucket of a dredging machine, water wheel, etc.; **8,** *Colloq.* the securing and publishing of a piece of news before a rival (or rivals); also, the article printed:—*v.t.* **1,** to take out or up with a scoop; **2,** to make hollow.

scoot (sko͞ot), *v.i. Colloq.* **1,** to walk or run hastily; dart; scurry off; **2,** to skim along, as a bird.

SCOOTER

scoot-er (sko͞ot′ėr), *n.* **1,** a child's toy vehicle, hung low on two wheels, and propelled by pushing one foot against the ground; **2,** a light motorcycle; as, motor *scooter*; **3,** a small motorized vehicle used by elderly or disabled people.

scope (skōp), *n.* **1,** extent of understanding; range of mental activity; as, a book beyond the *scope* of secondary school students; **2,** the field covered; range of subjects embraced; as, a book limited in *scope*; **3,** room or outlet for action; as, he craved ample *scope* for his abilities.

scorch (skôrch), *v.t.* **1,** to burn lightly the surface of; as, to *scorch* linen; **2,** to parch; wither; as, a hot sun *scorches* grass.—*n.* **scorch′er.**—*adj.* **scorch′ing.**

score (skōr), *n.* **1,** the number of points, runs, etc., made in a game, contest, or test; as, the *score* was five to one; a *score* of 85 per cent on the test; **2,** a debt; bill; also, a grudge; as, to pay off old *scores;* **3,** a line, groove, or mark that has been drawn, cut, or scratched on a surface; **4,** [*pl.* score], twenty; as, three *score* and ten; **5,** in *music*, a copy of a composition showing all the parts for all the instruments or voices; **6, scores**, a great many; as, *scores* of people were there:—*v.t.* [scored, scor-ing], **1,** to make or record a certain score; **2,** to win (a run, a point, etc.); hence, to achieve (a hit, success, etc.); **3,** to grade (test papers); **4,** to notch or mark with lines, scratches, etc., as wood or paper:—*v.i.* **1,** to keep the tally in a game; **2,** to win points in a game; **3,** *Slang* to obtain illegal drugs; **4,** *Slang* to have sex with someone. Also, **score′board′; score′card′; score′sheet′.**

scorn (skôrn), *n.* extreme contempt; haughty disdain and indignation:—*v.t.* **1,** to hold in extreme disdain; reject with contempt; as, to *scorn* underhanded methods.—*adj.* **scorn′ful.**—*adv.* **scorn′ful-ly.**

Scor-pi-o (skôr′pi-ō′), *n.* **1,** a southern constellation, the Scorpion; its brightest star is Antares; **2,** the eighth sign of the zodiac [♏], which the sun enters about October 24.

scor-pi-on (skôr′pi-un), *n.* an animal of the same class as the spider, five to twenty centimetres in length. Each of the front legs is equipped with a pair of pincers, and the tip of the tail has a poisonous sting.

scotch (skoch), *v.t.* to put an end to; as, to *scotch* a riot.

scot–free (skot′–frē′), *adj.* safe; unpunished; as, the prisoner went *scot-free.*

Scot–tish (skot′–ish), *n.* **1,** a person who inhabits or originates from Scotland; **2,** the Gaelic language spoken by these people:—*adj.* relating to the country, the people, the language, or the culture of Scotland.

scoun-drel (skoun′drel), *n.* a low, worthless rascal.—*adj.* **scoun′drel-ly.**

[1]**scour** (skour), *v.t.* **1,** to scrub hard with some rough material, in order to make clean and shiny; as, we *scoured* the pots and pans; **2,** to wash or clear of dirt, grease, etc., by rubbing with soap and water, flushing, etc.; as, to *scour* a rug; to *scour* a pipe:—*n.* the act of scouring; as, she gave the floor a good *scour.*—*n.* **scour′er.**

[2]**scour** (skour), *v.t.* to go through thoroughly, as on a search; as, the police *scoured* the city for the criminal.

scourge (skûrj), *n.* **1,** one who or that which afflicts or destroys; as, the *scourge* of pestilence; **2,** a means of inflicting punishment; hence, harsh punishment; **3,** a whip used to inflict pain or punishment:—*v.t.* [scourged, scourg-ing], **1,** to grieve or torment greatly; harass; as, the plague *scourged* the land; **2,** to whip severely.

scout (skout), *n.* **1,** a person sent out to obtain and bring back information; esp., a soldier sent out to obtain information about the enemy; **2,** a person who seeks out new information in sports or entertainment, such as finding talented new people or players or the strategy of opposing teams; as a *scout* from the hockey team; **3,** the act of gathering such information; **4,** a member of the Boy Scouts or the Girl Guides:—**scout's honour,** a saying affirming honesty, based on the scout's oath:—*v.i.* **1,** to act as a scout; to go about for purposes of securing information; esp., to ascertain the movements, position, strength, etc., of an enemy; **2,** to act as a scout in sports or entertainment; **3,** to perform the duties of a boy scout or a girl scout.—*n.* **scout′mas′ter.**

Scout-ing (skout′ing), *n.* the activities of scouts, the international youth organization founded in 1908 by Robert Baden-Powell.

scow (skou), *n.* a large flat-bottomed boat with square ends, used to carry garbage and other refuse to be dumped.

scowl (skoul), *v.i.* to wrinkle the brows in displeasure, anger, etc.:—*n.* an angry wrinkling of the brow.

scrab-ble (skrab′l) *v.i.* **1,** to scramble (on hands and knees); **2,** scrape, scratch, or paw; as, the cat *scrabbled* at the litter.—**Scrabble,** *n.* a game played by forming words with letters of the alphabet on small blocks: the rarer consonants, like *j* or *z*, carry higher scoring values.

scrag-gly (skrag′li), *adj.* **1,** messy, as a beard; **2,** jagged, irregular, or splintered, as rocks.

scrag-gy (skrag′i), *adj.* **1,** lean, thin, or bony; **2,** scraggly.

scram (skram), *interj. Slang* Go!

scram-ble (skram′bl), *v.i.* [scram-bled, scram-bling], **1,** to clamber, climb, or move along on the hands and feet; as, to *scramble* over sand dunes; **2,** to struggle eagerly or roughly for something; as, the children *scrambled* for the candy:—*v.t.* **1,** to toss together or mix at random; **2,** to prepare (eggs) by cooking the mixed yolks and whites:—*n.* **1,** a disorderly struggle; **2,** a climb.

scram-bler (skram′blėr), *n.* **1,** a device that scrambles electronic signals such as those for television or telephone; **2,** a person or device that does this.

[1]**scrap** (skrap), *n.* **1,** a small piece, cut or broken off; **2,** worn out, discarded, or broken machinery, or used and discarded metal of any kind; junk metal; **3, scraps,** odds and ends; esp., small pieces of food left over from a meal:—*adj.* in the form of fragments or pieces; as, *scrap*-metal:—*v.t.* [scrapped, scrap-ping], **1,** to break up; discard, as broken machinery; **2,** to give up something as useless or unwanted; as *scrap* the idea.

[2]**scrap** (skrap), *v.i. Slang* to fight; quarrel; also, to box:—*n. Slang* a scuffle; a fight with blows or words.—*n.* **scrap′per.**—*adj.* **scrap′py.**

scrap-book (skrap′book′), *n.* a blank book for pasting in clippings, pictures, etc.

scrape (skrāp), *v.t.* [scraped, scrap-ing], **1,** to drag harshly or gratingly; as, to scrape a chair along the floor; **2,** to remove by rubbing with something sharp or rough; as, to *scrape* paint from a door; also, to remove paint, paper, etc., from; as, to *scrape* furniture; *scrape* walls; **3,** to gather or accumulate in small amounts, with effort; as, to *scrape* together a small sum:—*v.i.* to manage by being extremely economical; as, to pinch and *scrape*:—*n.* **1,** the act, noise, or effect of harsh rubbing or grating; **2,** a difficult or awkward situation; as, if he had obeyed his mother, he would not be in this *scrape.*—*n.* **scrap′er.**

scratch (skrach), *v.t.* **1,** to mark or tear the surface of, with something rough or pointed; as, to *scratch* a table with a pin; **2,** to cancel or erase; as, *scratch* this item out; **3,**

to scrape or rub lightly with the fingernails, etc.; as, he *scratched* his cheek; **4,** to strike on an uneven surface; as, to *scratch* matches:—*v.i.* **1,** to make a grating noise; as, the chalk *scratches;* **2,** to cause irritation or pain by rubbing; as, the collar *scratches:*—*n.* **1,** a mark or tear made by something pointed or rough; **2,** a slight wound or cut, as that made by a pin; **3,** a grating sound, as of chalk on a slate; **4,** the starting line in a race; also, the beginning; as, we will start this work from *scratch.*—*n.* **scratch′er.**—*adj.* **scratch′proof.**

scratch pad, 1, a notepad; **2,** in *computing,* a high-speed memory for the temporary storage of data.

scrawl (skrôl), *v.t.* and *v.i.* to write or draw hastily, or in badly formed characters:—*n.* careless handwriting; a scribble.

scraw-ny (skrô′ni), *adj.* [scraw-ni-er, scraw-ni-est], lean; thin; bony; skinny.

scream (skrēm), *n.* a sharp, shrill cry, as of fear or pain:—*v.i.* to utter such a cry:—*v.t.* to utter in a loud, piercing voice; as, to *scream* a warning.

scree (skrē), *n.* loose rock, debris, or pebbles at the base of a cliff or on a mountain slope, glacier, etc.

screech (skrēch), *n.* **1,** a harsh, shrill cry, as of fright or pain, or noise; as, the *screech* of car brakes; **2,** a strong rum drink of Newfoundland:—*v.i.* to utter a harsh, shrill cry:—*v.t.* to cry out in a shrill voice.

screen (skrēn), *n.* **1,** a light, covered framework, partition, or curtain, that protects or conceals; as, the nurse put a *screen* around his bed; **2,** anything in the nature of a protective curtain; as, a smoke*screen;* the villain was concealed behind a *screen* of shrubbery; **3,** a frame covered with wire or cotton fabric to exclude insects; as, a window *screen;* **4,** a coarse sieve for separating coal, gravel, etc., into different sizes; **5,** a flat surface that reflects light, used to show movies or slides; **6,** the surface on which images from a movie, television, or computer appear:—*v.t.* **1,** to shut off from danger, observation, etc.; shelter or conceal; protect; **2,** to sift through a coarse sieve; **3,** to project (a picture) upon a screen; **4,** to go through carefully to separate; as, *screen* phone calls. Also, **screen′ door′; screen′ing; screen′ play′; screen′ test′; screen′writ′er.**

screen saver, a program that replaces the image on a computer monitor after a given amount of time with either a blank screen or moving images to prevent damage to the screen.

screw (skrōō), *n.* **1,** a slender, naillike, round bar of metal, with a spiral groove, or thread, for holding together pieces of wood, metal, etc.; **2,** anything resembling such a device; **3,** a contrivance to propel steamships, motorboats, etc.: also called *screw propeller;* **4,** a turn of a screw; as, give it another *screw:*—*v.t.* **1,** to tighten or fasten with, or as with, a screw; **2,** to twist or distort; as, to *screw* up one's face; **3,** *Slang* to cheat or take advantage of someone; as, *screw* him out of his money:—*v.i.* to turn with a motion like a screw.

screw-ball (skrōō′bôl′), *n.* **1,** a baseball pitch that breaks in a direction opposite to a curve ball; **2,** a silly, zany, crazy, or eccentric person or thing:—*adj.* zany or whimsical; as a *screwball* comedy film.

screw-dri-ver (skrōō′drī′vėr), a tool with a blunt blade, the tip of which fits into a slot in the head of a screw, and is used for turning the screw.

screw–top (skrōō′–top′), *n.* and *adj.* the cover or lid of a container that is secured and held in place by a screw thread; the container itself; as, a *screw-top* jar. Also called *screw cap.*

screw–up (skrōō′–up′), *n. Slang* a mess; a blunder; something botched; a person who ruins something; a bungler.—*v.t.* **screw up** (to tighten, as a screw; also, to bungle, flub, or mess up something).

screw-y (skrōō′i), *adj. Slang* **1,** unpractical; as, a *screwy* proposal; **2,** misleading; **3,** unbalanced; eccentric; irrational (of a person).

scrib-ble (skrib′l), *v.t.* [scrib-bled, scrib-bling], **1,** to write hastily and carelessly; **2,** to cover (paper, books, etc.) with careless or meaningless scrawls:—*v.i.* to scrawl:—*n.* hasty, sloppy writing.

scrib-bler (skrib′lėr), *n.* **1,** one who scribbles; **2,** a book for writing in; a student notebook.

scribe (skrīb), *n.* **1,** in former times, a skilled person who copied manuscripts, or acted as an official or public secretary; **2,** among the Jews, in ancient times, a teacher and lawgiver; **3,** *Colloq.* a writer, author.

scrim-mage (skrim′ij), *n.* **1,** a general quarrel or fight; a tussle; **2,** in *football,* play following the snapping back of the ball when both teams are lined up; **3,** in *sports,* practice play.

scrimp (skrimp), *v.i.* **1,** to be sparing or frugal; as, *scrimp* and save; **2,** to skimp; allow too little of; as, to *scrimp* on repairs.

scrip (skrip), *n.* **1,** paper currency, esp. that issued for temporary reasons; **2,** a document or certificate declaring the holder to have the right to receive something such as a plot of land, stocks, or bonds; as, Métis land *scrip;* **3,** any receipt, list, or scrap of paper.

script (skript), *n.* **1,** ordinary handwriting; written characters; also, style of writing; not printing; **2,** typeface that is an imitation of writing; **3,** in motion pictures, plays, television shows, or other such spoken performances, a written summary of the action, the cast of characters, etc. Also, **script′writ′er; script′writ′ing.**

Scrip-ture (skrip′tûr), *n.* the Bible: chiefly in *pl.* with *the*:—**scripture,** any sacred writing; as, the Buddhist *scriptures*.

scroll (skrōl), *n.* **1,** a manuscript of paper or parchment in the form of a roll; **2,** a spiral, ornamental design in carving or printing:—*v.i.* in a computer, using the control keys to view different areas of a document or graphics.

scroll bar, the long, narrow section at the bottom or side of a computer screen where the operator is able to move up and down or from side to side in a document.

scro-tum (skrō′tum), *n.* in male mammals, the pouch of skin enclosing the testicles.

scrounge (skrounj), *v.t.* and *v.i. Slang* to hunt about for and take without permission or at no cost; pilfer.

[1]**scrub** (skrub), *v.t.* [scrubbed, scrub-bing], **1,** to wash by hard rubbing; as, to *scrub* clothes; **2,** to rub hard with a wet cloth or brush; as, to *scrub* floors, woodwork, hands, etc.; **3,** *Colloq.* to cancel; as, *scrub* the event; *scrub* the space shuttle launch:—*n.* the act or process of cleaning by hard rubbing.

[2]**scrub** (skrub), *n.* **1,** a shrub, tree, bush, etc., stunted or inferior in growth; also, a growth of thicket of such stunted trees; as, pine *scrub;* **2,** a plant or animal that is inferior in size, quality, or breed; **3,** in sports, a member of a non-first-class team; as, the varsity played the *scrubs:—adj.* **1,** mean or small; also, below normal size; stunted; **2,** consisting of, or pertaining to, players who are not members of a regular team; as, a *scrub* game.—*adj.* **scrub′by.**

scruff (skruf), *n.* the back of the neck; the loose skin at the back of the neck.

scrum (skrum), *n.* **1,** a disorderly crowd, esp. of reporters around a celebrity or politician; **2,** the ensuing interrogation; as, the media *scrum;* **3,** a rugby scrummage:—*v.i.* [scrummed; scrum-ming], to act or engage in a scrum; as, the reporters *scrummed* after the political incident was announced.

scrump-tious (skrump′shus), *adj. Slang* delightful; enjoyable; first-rate; delicious; as, we had a *scrumptious* time; *scrumptious* dinner.

scrunch (skrunch), *v.t.* to crunch, crumple, squeeze, or crush; as *scrunch* your hair, paper:—*v.i.* **1,** to crouch; hunch; as, children *scrunched* into a ball; **2,** make a crunching sound:—*n.* the act or sound of crunching.

scru-ple (skrōō′pl), *n.* **1,** regard to what is right or moral and what should be done; honesty; as, the criminal had no *scruples;* **2,** a feeling of doubt, uneasiness, or uncertainty arising from one's conscience; as, he had *scruples* about disregarding his mother's advice:—*v.i.* [scru-pled, scru-pling], to hesitate on grounds of conscience; as, he *scrupled* to leave his work so long.

scru-pu-lous (skrōō′pū-lus), *adj.* **1,** conscientious; attentive to details: as, a *scrupulous* student; **2,** unswerving; strict; as, *scrupulous* honesty.

scru-ti-neer (skrōō.′ti-nēr′), *n.* **1,** one who oversees or scrutinizes voting procedures and counting of ballots in an election; **2,** a person or who examines or observes something:—*v.t.* and *v.i:* to act as a scrutineer.

scru-ti-nize (skrōō′ti-nīz′), *v.t.* and *v.i.* [scrutinized, scrutiniz-ing], to inspect closely; examine carefully.—*n.* **scru′ti-ny.**

scu-ba (skū′bu), *n.* the special air tanks worn by swimmers for breathing under water: acronym for *s*elf-*c*ontained *u*nderwater *b*reathing *a*pparatus.—*n.* **scu′ba di′ving, scu′ba diver:**—*v.* **scu′ba dive.**

scud (skud), *v.i.* [scud-ded, scud-ding], to run or move swiftly; of a ship, to run before a gale with little or no sail spread:—*n.* **1,** the act of scudding; **2,** foam or spray driven by the wind; **3,** a long-range missile.

scuff (skuf), *v.t.* **1,** to wear a rough place on the surface of; as, to *scuff* new shoes; **2,** to shuffle or drag (the feet):—*v.i.* **1,** to become rough on the surface; as, soft leather *scuffs* easily; **2,** to drag the feet in a slovenly manner:—*n.* a rough or worn spot.

scuf-fle (skuf′l), *v.i.* [scuf-fled, scuf-fling], **1,** to fight or struggle in a confused, disorderly manner; **2,** to drag or shuffle the feet in a slovenly fashion; scuff:—*n.* a close grappling; a confused or disorderly struggle or fight.

scull (skul), *n.* **1,** an oar used at the stern of a boat and worked from side to side to propel the boat forward; **2,** one of a pair of short, light oars; **3,** a boat, usually for racing, propelled by short oars:—*v.i.* and *v.t.* to propel or move (a boat) with an oar used at the stern.—*n.* **scull′er.**

scul-ler-y (skul′ėr-i), *n.* formerly, a back kitchen for washing and storing pots, pans, etc.

sculp-tor (skulp′tėr), *n.* one who practises the art of carving, cutting, or modelling figures or designs in wood, stone, etc.

sculp-ture (skulp′tūr), *n.* **1,** the art of fashioning figures or other objects in stone, metal, wood, or clay; **2,** a piece of such work:—*v.t.* [sculptured, sculptur-ing], to carve, chisel, model, cast, in stone, wood, clay, or metal. Also, **sculpt** (skulpt).

scum (skum), *n.* **1,** a layer of impurities that forms on the surface of a liquid; **2,** anything worthless or vile; hence, low, worthless people.—*adj.* **scum′my.**—*n.* **scum′bag′** (a despicable, contemptable, or very unpleasant person).

scup-per (skup′ėr), *n.* a hole, tube, or gutter in the side of a ship to carry off water from the deck:—*v.t. Slang* **1,** sink; as, to *scupper* a ship; **2,** prevent, ruin; as, to *scupper* a plan.

scur-ri-lous (skûr′i-lus), *adj.* grossly or obscenely vulgar, damaging, or abusive; as, a *scurrilous* attack, speaker, journal, etc.—*n.* **scur-ril′i-ty.**

scur-ry (skur′i), *v.i.* [scurried, scurry-ing], to hasten or move rapidly along:—*n.* [*pl.* scurries], a scampering.

scur-vy (skûr′vi), *n.* a disease caused by lack of Vitamin C, as in fresh fruit and vegetables, and marked by great weakness, thinness of the body, bleeding gums, etc.

[1]**scut-tle** (skut′l), *v.i.* [scut-tled, scut-tling], to hasten or hurry away:—*n.* a hurried flight.

[2]**scut-tle** (skut′l), *n.* a small opening with a lid, as in the roof of a house, or in the deck, bottom, or side of a ship; also, the lid covering such an opening:—*v.t.* [scut-tled, scut-tling], **1,** to sink (a ship) by cutting holes in the bottom or sides; **2,** to destroy or dismiss; as, *scuttle* a plan.

[3]**scut-tle** (skut′l), *n.* a deep metal vessel or bucket for holding a small quantity of coal.

scut-tle-butt (skut′l-but′), *n.* **1,** a rumour, gossip; as, what's the *scuttlebutt* about the new boss? **2,** originally, the cask containing fresh drinking water on a ship's deck.

scuz-zy (sku′zi), *adj.* [scuzz-i-er, scuzz-i-est], *Colloq.* disgusting; sleazy; squalid; shabby; disreputable; squalid; as the *scuzzy* shack.—*n.* **scuzz; scuzzball.**

scythe (sīth), *n.* a cutting instrument for mowing grain, grass, etc., by hand.

sea (sē), *n.* **1,** a body of salt water, smaller than an ocean; as, the Aegean *Sea;* **2,** an inland body of water; as, the *Sea* of Galilee; **3,** the ocean as a whole; **4,** a billow or large wave; the swell of the ocean or other body of water in a storm; as, the high *sea* kept on after the storm; **5,** a large quantity; anything like the sea in vastness; as a *sea* of troubles; a *sea* of faces.

sea-board (sē′bōrd′), *n.* the land bordering the sea or ocean; the seacoast or seashore:—*adj.* near or on the seacoast.

sea-coast (sē′kōst′), *n.* the coast, or land bordering upon the sea or ocean; seashore.

sea-cow (sē′kou′), *n.* same as **manatee.**

sea-far-er (sē′fâr′ėr), *n.* a person who travels by sea or follows the life of a sailor.—*adj.* **sea′far′ing.**

sea-food (sē′fo͞od′), *n.* **1,** any edible animal from the sea, esp. fish and shellfish; **2,** any edible fish, including freshwater varieties.

sea-go-ing (sē′gō′ing), *adj.* **1,** seafaring; **2,** suitable or fitted for use on the open sea; as, a *seagoing* yacht.

seagull (sē′gul′), *n.* one of several web-footed aquatic birds, esp. the herring gull.

sea horse (sē′–hôrs′), *n.* **1,** in *mythology*, a fabulous creature, half horse and half fish; **2,** a small fish with a head resembling that of a horse.

[1]**seal** (sēl), *n.* **1,** a large fish-eating animal with flippers and sleek, shiny fur, found in cold ocean waters. Seals are mammals that live mainly in the water and rest on land; **2,** sealskin.

[2]**seal** (sēl), *n.* **1,** a stamp or die engraved with a device, image, etc., used for making an impression in wax or some similar substance; **2,** wax or a similar substance fixed upon a letter or document and stamped with an emblem or design as proof of genuineness; **3,** anything that closes another thing securely in order to prevent its being opened or tampered with; hence, anything that secures; a pledge; as, a *seal* of silence on his lips; **4,** a decorative stamp used in sealing a letter or package; as, a Christmas *seal*:—*v.t.* **1,** to fasten with a device so that it cannot be tampered with; as, to *seal* a letter; **2,** to set or affix a seal to; as, to *seal* a deed; **3,** to ratify or confirm; as, the bargain was *sealed;* **4,** to keep secure or secret; as, to *seal* documents for later examination; **5,** to settle (a person's fate) once and for all; **6,** to enclose; confine; as, a fly *sealed* in amber; **7,** to close tightly, as a pipe, a jar of fruit, etc.; also, to fill up the cracks of.—*n.* **seal′er.**

sea legs, the ability to adjust to a ship's movement, to walk steadily, and avoid seasickness; the recovery from a bout of seasickness; as, to get your *sea legs* back.

sea level, the level of the sea halfway between high and low tide: used as the standard in measuring the height of land; as, 100 metres above *sea level.*

sea lion, any of several large seals of the Pacific Ocean.

SEA LION

seam (sēm), *n.* **1,** the line formed by sewing together two edges of material; **2,** a visible line of junction or union, as between two boards; **3,** a layer or bed of mineral or rock; as, a *seam* of copper ore:—*v.t.* **1,** to join or sew together, as the parts of a garment; **2,** to scar; line; as, the wind had *seamed* his face with wrinkles.—*adj.* **seam′less.**

sea-man (sē′man), *n.* [*pl.* seamen (-men)], a sailor; mariner.—*n.* **sea′man-ship.**—*adj.* **sea′man-ly.**

seam-stress (sēm′stres), *n.* a woman who does sewing for a living.

seam-y (sēm′i), *adj.* [seam-i-er, seam-i-est], **1,** showing or having seams, esp. roughly finished seams; **2,** hence, rough; harsh and unpleasant; as, the *seamy* side of life.

sé-ance (sā′äns; sā′äns′), *n.* a session or meeting, as of a society; esp. a meeting of spiritualists to receive messages from the dead.

sea-plane (sē′plān′), *n.* a plane so constructed that it can take off from or land on the surface of the water.

sea port (sē′pōrt′), *n.* a town, harbour, or port that can be reached by seagoing vessels.

sear (sēr), *v.t.* **1,** to cause to dry up or wither; scorch; as, the summer sun *sears* the fields; **2,** to burn or scorch the surface; cauterize; as, to *sear* a wound, *sear* meat; **3,** to render callous or unfeeling, as the conscience:—*adj.* (also *sere*), withered; dried, as leaves.

search (sûrch), *v.t.* **1,** to seek; as, to *search* out the truth; **2,** to look for something by examining carefully the contents of (a place or object), the clothing of (a person), etc.; as, to *search* a room; to *search* a prisoner for weapons; **3,** to probe; try or test; as, to *search* one's heart:—*n.* **1,** the act of seeking or looking for something; **2,** a careful investigation; examination.

search engine, a software program that allows the searching and retrieval of data and files, esp. from the Internet.

search-ing (sûr′ching), *adj.* penetrating; thorough; keen; as, a *searching* glance.—*adv.* **search′ing-ly.**

search-light (sûrch′līt′), *n.* a powerful electric light that can throw a beam of light in any direction, used for searching or signalling; also, the beam.

search party, a crew of individuals organized to look for lost persons or things; as, the *search party* went into the bush, following the clues.

search war-rant (sûrch′–wor′ant), *n.* a written order giving a police officer authority to search a house or building and seize evidence.

sea-scape (sē′skāp′), *n.* a view, or picture, of the sea.

sea-shore (sē′shōr′), *n.* the land bordering the sea; seacoast.

sea-sick (sē′sik′), *adj.* suffering from nausea caused by the pitching and rolling of a boat.—*n.* **sea′sick′ness.**

sea-side (sē′sīd′), *n.* the shore along the sea; the seashore.

sea-son (sē′zn), *n.* **1,** one of the four periods into which the year is divided, as spring, summer, autumn, and winter; **2,** any particular time; as, the holiday *season;* **3,** a suitable, convenient, or legal time; as, the fishing *season:*—*v.t.* **1,** to bring to the best state for use; as, to *season* timber; **2,** to make palatable, as with salt or spices; also, to make more delightful; as, he *seasoned* his lecture with humour:—*v.i.* to become fit for use; as, timber *seasons* well in the open air.

sea-son-a-ble (sē′zn-a-bl), *adj.* **1,** occurring or coming in good or proper time; as, *seasonable* advice; **2,** in keeping with the time of year; as, *seasonable* weather.

sea-son-al (sē′zn-al), *adj.* relating to or influenced by certain periods of the year; as, *seasonal* rates; *seasonal* diseases; *seasonal* trades; *seasonal* labour.—*adv.* **sea′son-al-ly.**

sea-son-ing (sē′zn-ing), *n.* that which is added to give more flavour to food, as salt, pepper, garlic, and other spices.

season ticket or **season's ticket**, a ticket or pass allowing the holder to attend all games or performances for a specified period; as, *season tickets* to the Raptors games.

seat (sēt), *n.* **1,** an object on which one sits; a bench, chair, or stool; **2,** that part of a chair, stool, or bench, on which one sits; **3,** that part of the body on which one sits; also, the part of a garment covering it; as, the *seat* of her jeans; **4,** the place where anything flourishes; location; site; centre; as, the brain is the *seat* of the intellect; a university is a *seat* of learning; **5,** a capital town or city; as, a county *seat;* **6,** the right to sit; specifically, membership; as, a *seat* on the stock exchange; **7,** room or space for a spectator; as, *seats* for a football game:—*v.t.* **1,** to place on a chair or bench; cause to sit down; **2,** to furnish with places to sit; as, this hall *seats* 800 persons.

seat-belt (sēt′belt′) *n.* a strap or set of straps holding a person in place in the seat of a car, airplane, or other moving vehicle, to help prevent injury in the case of an accident or sudden stop. Also called a **safety belt.**

sea-ward (sē′wėrd), *adj.* going toward, or situated in the direction of, the sea:—*adv.* toward the sea.—*adv.* **sea′wards.**

sea water, the salt water in the sea or coming from it.

sea-way (sē′wā′), *n.* **1,** a route by sea; **2,** an inland passage for ocean-going ships, as the Saint Lawrence Seaway.

sea-weed (sē′wēd′), *n.* any plant growing in the sea, as kelp.

sea-wor-thy (sē′wûr′*th*i), *adj.* fit for a voyage on the open sea; as, a *seaworthy* boat.—*n.* **sea′wor′thi-ness.**

se-cant (sē′kant), *n.* **1,** a straight line that cuts a curve in two points; **2,** a ratio in trigonometry.

se-cede (su-sēd′), *v.i.* [seced-ed, seced-ing], to withdraw formally from fellowship, union, or association; esp., to withdraw from a political or religious body.—*n.* **se-ces′sion** (si-sesh′un).

se-clude (si-klo͞od′), *v.t.* [seclud-ed, seclud-ing], **1,** to withdraw or keep apart from others; to place in solitude; isolate; **2,** to hide from view; screen:—*n.* **se-clu′sion.**—*adj.* **se-clu′ded.**

sec-ond (sek′und), *adj.* **1,** immediately following the first; next to the first in order of place or time; **2,** next to the first in value, excellence, merit, dignity, or importance; as, a *second* lieutenant; **3,** being of the same kind as another that has gone before; another; as, a *second* Trudeau; additional; as, a *second* helping; **4,** in *music*, rendering a part next to the highest in pitch and importance; as, a *second* violin:—*adv.* **sec′ond-ly:**—*n.* **1,** one who or that which is next to the first in place, rank, excellence, or power; **2,** one who helps or supports another, as in a duel or boxing match; **3,** a unit of time; the 60th part of a minute; **4,** hence, *Colloq.* a short space of time; as, wait just a *second;* **5,** an article of merchandise of a grade inferior to the best; as, these *seconds* are very cheap:—*v.t.* **1,** to act as an assistant or supporter of; assist; **2,** in parliamentary practice, to support a motion, resolution, or nomination proposed by another.—*adj.* and *n.* **sec′ond-ar-y.**

sec-ond-ar-y school (sek′un-dâ′ri sko͞ol′), *n.* the school that students attend after elementary school and junior high school, and before college or university. Also called *high school.*

second banana, *Colloq.* someone who is in a secondary, supporting, or inferior role; as, to play *second banana* to someone: originally, the supporting comedian in a vaudeville or burlesque show.

sec-ond–class (sek′und–klås′), *adj.* **1,** next below the highest; as, to travel *second-class;* **2,** mediocre or inferior; as, the *second-class* essay; **3,** politically, economically, or otherwise disadvantaged; as *second-class* citizens.

sec-ond–de-gree (sek′und–di-grē′), *adj.* **1,** crimes that are next below the most serious; as, *second-degree* murder; **2,** burns that cause blistering but no permanent damage.

sec-ond–guess (sek′und–ges′), *v.t.* **1,** to criticize, question, or correct in hindsight; **2,** to predict or anticipate; to outguess; as, to *second-guess* the outcome:—*v.i.* to criticize after the fact.

sec-ond-hand (sek′und-hand′), *adj.* **1,** not new; as, *secondhand* furniture; **2,** dealing in goods that are not new; as, a *secondhand* shop; **3,** heard or learned indirectly; as, *secondhand* news:—**secondhand smoke**, smoke from a cigarette or other tobacco product involuntarily inhaled, esp. by a non-smoker.

second nature, a behaviour or skill so often performed and repeated that it becomes automatic; as, swimming is *second nature* to her.

sec-ond–rate (sek′und–rāt′), *adj.* mediocre or inferior quality or value; as, a *second-rate* book.

second–string (sek′und–string′), *adj.* **1,** relating to backup players; **2,** the quality of not being first-class; as, *second-string* singers.—*n.* **second string** (backup players who replace starters who are injured or cannot play for other reasons; relievers; replacements).

second thoughts, 1, reservations and reconsiderations about a previous decision; new opinions after consideration; change of mind; **2,** doubt or apprehension about a prior decision.

second wind, 1, the recovering of energy after initial exhaustion; as, after five kilometres, she got her *second wind;* **2,** any restored energy, strength, or vigour; as, the steel industry got a *second wind.*

Second World or **second world,** during the Cold War, the industrialized Communist bloc countries, as opposed to *First World* and *Third World.*

se-cre-cy (sē′kre-si), *n.* [*pl.* secrecies], **1,** the state or quality of being secret or hidden; concealment; as, done in *secrecy;* **2,** the habit of keeping information to oneself.

se-cret (sē′krit), *adj.* **1,** concealed; private; as, *secret* information; **2,** withdrawn from public view or knowledge; as, a *secret* treaty; also, operating in secrecy; as, a *secret* society; **3,** permitting concealment; secluded; as, a *secret* chamber; **4,** mysterious; unknown; as, the *secret* operations of nature:—**secret service**, government detective service:—*n.* **1,** that which is purposely concealed or left untold; **2,** something not widely known; as, the *secrets* of science; **3,** a hidden reason or cause; as, unselfishness is the *secret* of his happiness; **4,** secrecy; as, prepared in *secret.*—*adv.* **se′cret-ly.**

sec-re-tar-y (sek′re-tėr-i; sek′ri-ter′i), *n.* [*pl.* secretaries], **1,** a person in business whose job is to assist another person by doing such work as typing letters, answering the telephone, and keeping records. Also known as an *administrative assistant;* **2,** an official of a company or society in charge of records and correspondence; **3,** a state executive who superintends the business of a government department; as, the *secretary* of Sstate; **4,** a writing-desk.—*adj.* **sec′re-tar′i-al** (sek′ri-târ′i-al).

se-crete (sē-krēt′), *v.t.* [secret-ed, secret-ing], **1,** of an animal or plant, to give off a liquid from some part of the body; produce; as, the liver *secretes* bile; **2,** to hide or conceal; as, *secrete* assets in a overseas bank account.—*n.* **se-cre′tion.**

se-cre-tive (si-krē′tiv), *adj.* inclined to keep things to oneself; not frank or open; reticent—*adv.* **se-cre′tive-ly.**

sect (sekt), *n.* a number of persons who, following a teacher or leader, hold certain opinions in common, esp. certain religious opinions.—*n.* and *adj.* **sec-tar′i-an.**

sec-tion (sek′shun), *n.* **1,** one part of a whole thing; as, a *section* of a pie; **2,** a division or subdivision of a book, chapter, or other document; as, the last *section* of the book; **3,** a division of a store, library, etc.; as, the history *section* of the school library; **4,** a distinct part of a country, people, community, etc.; as, the business *section* of the city; **5,** the act of cutting; separation by cutting; **6,** a part or portion cut off; **7,** a representation of an object cut in two crosswise or lengthwise; as, the cross-*section* of a tomato:—*v.t.* to divide or cut into sections or parts; as, *section* an orange.

sec-tion-al (sek′shun-al), *adj.* **1,** relating to a section or district; local; as, *sectional* strife; **2,** consisting of parts; as, a *sectional* bookcase.

sec-tor (sek′tėr), *n.* **1,** a distinct section or area of an economy; as, the business or tourism *sector*; **2,** the area enclosed by two radii and the arc of a circle, ellipse, or other curve cut by them.

sec-u-lar (sek′ū-lėr), *adj.* **1,** relating to things of the world or to things not sacred; worldly; as, *secular* art; relating to matters of the earth and humankind, rather than with a god or gods and religion; as, *secular* courts; **2,** not bound by monastic communities; as, a parish priest belongs to the *secular* clergy.—*v.t.* **sec′u-lar-ize′.**—*n.* **sec′u-lar-i-za′tion.**

secular humanism, 1, the philosophy or belief that human values should prevail over religious ones; **2,** secularism in general.

se-cure (si-kūr′), *adj.* **1,** free from fear, care, or worry; **2,** safe; free from danger; as, *secure* against attack; in safekeeping; as, the prisoners are *secure;* affording safety; as, a *secure* retreat; firm or steady; as, a *secure* foundation; **3,** confident; as, *secure* of welcome; certain; assured; as, the victory is *secure:*—*v.t.* [secured, secur-ing], **1,** to make safe; protect; **2,** to guarantee repayment of; as, he gave a mortgage to *secure* the loan; also, to protect oneself against the loss of; as, he took a mortgage to *secure* the loan; **3,** to make fast; latch or lock; as, to *secure* a door; also, to place in custody; as, to *secure* a prisoner; **4,** to gain possession of; as, to *secure* wealth.—*adv.* **se-cure′ly.**—*adj.* **se-cur′a-ble.**

se-cu-ri-ty (si-kū′ri-ti), *n.* [*pl.* securities], **1,** the state or quality of being safe or protected; certainty; **2,** a means of safety or protection; as, insurance offers *security;* **3,** something given as a guarantee of performance or payment; as, he offered stock as *security* for the loan; **4,** one who becomes responsible for another; a surety; **5, securities,** bonds or stock that may be bought and sold.

security blanket, 1, a blanket or toy carried by a child to reduce anxiety; **2,** any object that is a source of comfort and security; something that dispels anxiety; as, my lucky charm is my *security blanket.*

security guard, someone hired to provide protection and maintain order; as, the *security guard* stationed at the front desk.

se-dan (si-dăn′), *n.* **1,** a car with two or four doors, a front and back seat, a permanent roof, and a trunk; **2,** formerly, a portable covered chair or vehicle accommodating one passenger, usually slung between two poles and carried by two men: also called *sedan chair.*

se-date (si-dāt′), *adj.* calm; composed; serious; as, a *sedate* student:—*v.t.* make sleepy or calm by administering a sedative.

sed-a-tive (sed′a-tiv), *n.* and *adj.* a remedy or drug that calms or soothes by lessening excitement, irritation, etc.—*n.* **se-da′tion.**

sed-en-ta-ry (sed′en-ta-ri), *adj.* **1,** requiring much sitting and little physical activity; as, typing is a *sedentary* occupation; **2,** caused by sitting; as, a *sedentary* ailment.

sed-i-ment (sed′i-ment), *n.* **1,** the solid substance that settles at the bottom of a liquid; dregs; **2,** sand, gravel, mud, etc., deposited, as by water—*adj.* **sed′i-men′ta-ry.**—*n.* **sed′i-men-ta′tion.**

se-di-tion (si-dish′un), *n.* agitation against a government, just short of insurrection or treason; the stirring up of discontent, rebellion, or resistance against lawful authority.—*adj.* **se-di′tious.**

se-duce (si-dūs′), *v.t.* [seduced, seduc-ing], to entice into sexual activity; to lead away from the paths of right, duty, or virtue, by flattery, promises, etc.; lead astray; tempt to do wrong.—*n.* **se-duc′er; se-duc′tion.**—*adj.* **se-duc′tive.**

sed-u-lous (sed′ū-lus), *adj.* steadily industrious; diligent in application and attention; as, a *sedulous* worker, *sedulous* flattery.—*adv.* **sed′u-lous-ly.**

¹see (sē), *v.t.* [*p.t.* saw (sô), *p.p.* seen (sēn), *p.pr.* see-ing], **1,** to perceive with the eyes; behold; **2,** to discern mentally; understand; as, to *see* a meaning; **3,** to accompany or escort; as, he *saw* the visitor to the door; **4,** to find out or learn by observation or experience; as, he wished to *see* what the result would be; **5,** to have personal experience of; as, he *saw* service in the war; **6,** to make sure; as, *see* that you address him properly; **7,** to visit, call on, or talk with; as, we went to *see* her; **8,** to admit to one's presence; receive; as, she refused to *see* us; **9,** to date or have a romance; as, they are *seeing* each other:—*v.i.* **1,** to possess or use the power of sight; **2,** to understand or discern; **3,** to consider; reflect; as, will you do it? I will *see;* **4,** to take care; attend; as, *see* to the dinner; **5,** to look: used only in the imperative; as, *See!* here he comes!

²see (sē), *n.* the official local seat of a bishop; the diocese of a bishop; the office or authority of a bishop:—**Holy See**, the seat of the papacy; the papal court or authority.

seed (sēd), *n.* [*pl.* seed or seeds], **1,** that part of a flowering plant that holds the germ of life, capable of developing into another plant; **2,** any small, seedlike fruit; as, dandelion or grass *seed;* **3,** a source or origin; as, *seeds* of discord; **4,** offspring; descendants; as, the *seed* of Jacob:—**to go to seed, 1,** to develop seed; **2,** *Colloq.* to become shabby; to lose vitality or vigour:—*v.i.* **1,** to sow seed; **2,** to mature or produce seed; also, to shed seed:—*v.t.* **1,** to sow with seed, as a lawn; **2,** to remove the seeds from.—*n.* **seed′er.**—*adj.* **seed′less.**

seed-ling (sēd′ling), *n.* **1,** a plant grown from a seed; **2,** a young plant or tree.

seed money, money invested to get a business or other project started.

seed-y (sēd′i), *adj.* [seed-i-er, seed-i-est], **1,** full of seed; having run to seed; **2,** *Colloq.* shabby; threadbare.

seek (sēk), *v.t.* [sought (sôt), seeking], **1,** to go in search of; **2,** to aim at; as, to *seek* wealth; **3,** to ask or appeal for; as, to *seek* aid; **4,** to resort to; as, he *sought* the theatre for recreation; **5,** to attempt or try; as, he *sought* to undo the harm he had done:—*v.i.* to search for; inquire; make efforts to find someone or something.

seem (sēm), *v.i.* **1,** to appear; look; have the semblance of; as, the sky *seems* clear; **2,** to appear to exist; as, there *seems* little difference of opinion; **3,** to appear to one's own mind or imagination; as, I *seemed* to be floating in space.—*adj.* **seem′ing.**—*adv.* **seem′ing-ly.**

seem-ly (sēm′li), *adj.* [seem-li-er, seem-li-est], fit or becoming; decent; proper; as, *seemly* behaviour.—*n.* **seem′li-ness.**

seen (sēn), *p.t.* of *see.*

seep (sēp), *v.i.* to leak out or flow slowly; ooze.

seep-age (sēp′ij), *n.* **1,** a slow leaking through; **2,** the liquid that leaks through.

se-er (sē′ėr), *n.* **1,** one who sees; **2,** (sēr), one who claims to foresee the future; a prophet.

seer-suck-er (sēr′suk′ėr), *n.* a thin linen or cotton fabric, usually striped and of a crinkly or puckered weave.

see-saw (sē′sô′), *n.* **1,** a game or piece of play equipment in which children, sitting or standing on opposite ends of a balanced board, move alternately up and down; also, the board; **2,** any movement to and fro or up and down:—*v.i.* to move up and down or to and fro.

seethe (sē*th*), *v.i.* [*p.t.* seethed, *p.p.* seethed or, rarely, sod-den (sod′n), *p.pr.* seething], **1,** to boil; as, a *seething* pot; to move in violent agitation; as, a *seething* whirlpool; **2,** to be violently agitated or angry; as, the crowd *seethed* with excitement.

seg-ment (seg′ment), *n.* **1,** any of the parts into which an object naturally separates or divides; a section; as, a *segment* of a grapefruit; **2,** in *geometry,* a part cut off from a figure by one or more lines; esp., the part of a circle included between an arc and its chord.—*n.* **seg′men-ta′tion.**

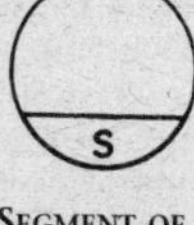

SEGMENT OF A CIRCLE

seg-re-gate (seg′ri-gāt′), *v.t.* **1,** to separate from others; cut off; set apart; isolate; **2,** in *science,* to put into a new or separate class.—*adj.* **seg′re-ga′ted.**—*n.* **seg′re-ga′tion.**

seigneur (sân′yûr′) or **seign-ior** (sēn′yėr), *n.* in French Canada, the holder of a **seign′eur-y** (sân′yû-ri) or **seign′ior-y** (sēn′yėr-i), a landed estate, held (until 1854) by feudal tenure (esp. along the St. Lawrence River).

seine (sān; sēn), *n.* a large fishing net equipped with sinkers and floats:—*v.t.* [seined, sein-ing], to catch (fish) with such a net:—*v.i.* to fish with a seine.

seis-mo-graph (sīs′mō-gråf′; sīz′), *n.* an instrument that automatically records the time, intensity, and direction of earthquakes.

seis-mol-o-gy (sīs-mol′o-ji), *n.* the science of earthquakes, their causes, etc.

seize (sēz), *v.t.* [seized, seiz-ing], **1,** to take possession of forcibly or suddenly; as, soldiers *seized* the fort; **2,** to grasp; snatch; take hold of; as, *seize* him by the arm; **3,** to take into legal custody on a warrant or capture; as, the officers *seized* the kidnappers; **4,** to grasp mentally; understand:—**seize** (*up*), to become stuck owing to excessive heat, etc.; as, his motor *seized up* from lack of oil.

sei-zure (sē′zhūr; -zhėr), *n.* **1,** the act of taking forcible possession; **2,** a sudden attack, or loss of control of the body, as of a disease; as, epilepsy causes *seizures.*

sel-dom (sel′dum), *adv.* rarely; not often.

se-lect (si-lekt′), *v.t.* to pick out from among a number; choose; as, to *select* a movie to see:—*adj.* **1,** carefully chosen or picked out; **2,** hence, of great excellence; choicest or best; as, a volume of *select* poems; **3,** exclusive; made up of chosen persons; as, a *select* club.—*n.* **se′lec-tiv′i-ty; se-lec′tor.**—*adj.* **se-lec′tive.**—*adv.* **se-lec′tive-ly.**—*n.*

se-lec-tion (si-lek′shun), *n.* **1,** the act of choosing; choice; as, the *selection* of one from so many is difficult; **2,** the thing or things chosen; as, the Scott novel is my *selection;* **3,** a part of a book, a piece of music, etc.; as, he read a *selection* from Shakespeare.

[1]self (self), *n.* [*pl.* selves (selvz)], **1,** the entire person or character of an individual; that which makes one person quite different from others; personality; **2,** a phase or side of a person's character that may show itself under certain conditions or at specific times; as, her nobler *self;* **3,** personal or private interest; as, *self* was always present in his thoughts.

[2]self– (self–), *prefix* meaning *of, by, in,* or *to oneself* or *itself;* as, *self*-addressed, *self*-appointed, *self*-awareness, *self*-centred, *self*-cleaning, *self*-confidence, *self*-confident, *self*-consciousness, *self*-conscious, *self*-control, *self*-controlled, *self*-defence, *self*-denial, *self*-denying, *self*-destruct, *self*-employed, *self*-esteem, *self*-examination, *self*-explanatory, *self*-fulfilling, *self*-government, *self*-governing, *self*-help, *self*-importance, *self*-important, *self*-improvement, *self*-interest, *self*-made, *self*-pity, *self*-possession, *self*-possessed, *self*-preservation, *self*-reliance, *self*-reliant, *self*-respect, *self*-respecting, *self*-restraint, *self*-sacrifice, *self*-sacrificing, *self*-service, *self*-serving, *self*-sufficiency, *self*-sufficient, *self*-supporting.

self–de-ter-mi-na-tion (self′–di-tûr′mi-nā′shun), *n.* **1,** the freedom of a people or cultural group to decide their political status; independence; the right to choose one's own form of government; **2,** the freedom of the individual to act independently without consulting others; free will.—*adj.* **self′–de-ter′mined; self′–de-ter′ min-ing.**

self–ev-i-dent (self′–ev′i-dent), *n.* obvious or clear; axiomatic; something that does not need explanation or proof.—*adv.* **self′–ev′i-dent-ly.**—*n.* **self′–ev′i-dence.**

self-ish (sel′fish), *adj.* **1,** putting one's own wishes and advantages before the wishes and advantages of others; **2,** prompted or marked by undue regard for oneself; as, a *selfish* act.—*adv.* **self′ish-ly.**—*n.* **self′ish-ness.**

self–right-eous (self′–rī′chus), *adj.* **1,** absolutely certain of one's own virtue and the correctness of one's beliefs; **2,** smugly moralistic, piously certain; **3,** narrow-minded; hypocritical; sanctimonious; as, self-righteous disregard for the opinions of others.—*adv.* **self′–right′eous-ly.**—*n.* **self′–right′eous-ness.**

self-same (self′sām′), *adj.* identical, the very same; as, they got the *selfsame* video game.

self–start-er (self′–stär′tėr), *n.* **1,** someone who is motivated and needs no external supervision; as, she is a *self-starter* who can take over immediately; **2,** an engine that has its own starter.

sell (sel), *v.t.* [sold (sōld), sell-ing], **1,** to give in return for a price, esp. money; as, this store *sells* shoes; also, to act as a salesperson of; as, he *sells* insurance; **2,** to promote or advertise the merits of an idea, concept, product, etc.; as, *sell* a concept to a client; **3,** to betray for a reward; as, to *sell* secrets to the enemy:—*v.i.* **1,** to dispose of for a price; **2,** to find a market; as, raspberries *sell* at a lower price in summer than in winter.

seller (sel′ėr), *n.* **1,** a person who sells something; **2,** a product that sells in a certain way; as, that book is a best-*seller*.

sell–off (sel′–ôf′), *n.* **1,** the sale of a quantity of securities; as, the stock *sell-off* led to a decline in share price; **2,** divestiture; the sudden selling of assets; **3,** privatization of government holdings; as, the government *sell-off* included Crown corporations.

sell-out (sel′out′), *n.* **1,** an event that succeeds in selling all of its tickets; as, the rock concert was a *sellout* within hours; **2,** a betrayal or double cross; **3,** one who betrays.

selt-zer (selt′sėr), *n.* **1,** naturally carbonated mineral water; **2,** any bubbly, effervescent water; soda water.

selves (selvz), *n.pl.* of *self*.

se-man-tics (si-man′tiks), *n.pl.* used as *sing.* the science of the meaning and sense development of words, together with the effect of language symbols upon the intellectual, emotional, and psychological life of the individual: the Canadian Institute of General Semantics was founded in Montreal in 1956.—*adj.* **se-man′tic.**

sem-a-phore (sem′a-fōr′), *n.* **1,** a system or apparatus for signalling using lanterns, flags, or mechanical arms, esp. on railways.

sem-blance (sem′blans), *n.* outward appearance; hence, pretence; as, a *semblance* of truth.

se-men (sē′men), *n.* [*pl.* semina], the whitish fertilizing fluid of the male reproductive organs.—*adj.* **sem′i-nal.**

se-mes-ter (si-mes′tėr), *n.* **1,** an academic session or term lasting half the year, esp. one of the two terms of a college or university year; **2,** a six-month period.

sem-i (sem′i-), *prefix* meaning *half, partly,* or *imperfectly*, or twice (in a specified period), as in *semi*circle, *semi*conscious, and *semi*weekly, respectively. Also, *semi*dark, *semi*detached, *semi*gloss, *semi*sweet, etc.

sem-i-an-nu-al (sem′i–an′ū-al), *adj.* occurring, published, due, etc., each half year, or twice a year; as, *semi-annual* interest payments.—*adv.* **sem′i–an′nu-al-ly.**

sem-i-cir-cle (sem′i-sûr′kl), *n.* half of a circle.—*adj.* **sem′i-cir′cu-lar.**

sem-i-co-lon (sem′i-kō′lun), *n.* a mark of punctuation [;], indicating a separation in the parts of a sentence greater than that marked by a comma but less than that of a period.

sem-i-con-duc-tor (sem′i-kon-duk′tėr), *n.* a material, such as silicon, that conducts electricity better when it is heated: widely used in television sets, radios, and computers.

sem-i-fi-nal (sem′i-f ī′nal) *n.* a game or round that comes just before the final one, and must be won to participate in the final.—*n.* **sem′i-fi′-nal-ist.**

sem-i-month-ly (sem′i-munth′ly), *adj.* occurring or done every half month, or twice a month:—*n.* [*pl.* semi-monthlies], anything published or produced twice a month:—*adv.* at intervals of half a month.

sem-i-nal (sem′i-nal), *adj.* **1,** original; essential; creative; having great influence over future delevopments; as, Leacock's *seminal* work in Canadian literature; **2,** containing or having to do with seed or semen; **3,** something that has the power to create or originate.—*adv.* **sem′i-nal-ly.**

sem-i-nar (sem′i-när′), *n.* **1,** any meeting for exchanging and discussing special information; as, a *seminar* on new technology; **2,** a small group meeting, esp. of students at a university, discussing, researching, or studying a particular topic under an instructor.

sem-i-nar-y (sem′i-nėr′i), *n.* [*pl.* seminaries], **1,** a school or college that trains students to be priests, ministers, or rabbis; **2,** a private school or academy, usually one which prepares students for college.

sem-i-pre-cious (sem′i-presh′us), *adj.* not among the most valuable; used of gems, such as the opal and amethyst, to distinguish them from *precious* gems, such as the diamond and ruby.

Sem-it-ic (se-mit′ik), *adj.* pertaining to the Semites, esp. Jews; a speech family comprising esp. Hebrew, Arabic, Assyrian, and Aramaean.—*n.* **Se′′mite′** (se′′mīt′).

sem-i-tone (sem′i-tōn′), *n.* in *music,* a tone at an interval of half a tone from a given tone: also called *half step* and *the interval.*

sem-i-trail-er (sem′i-trāl′ėr), *n.* a large trailer (with four or more wheels) attached to a tractor cab for hauling heavy loads.

sem-i-week-ly (sem′i-wēk′li), *adj.* occurring, published, or produced twice a week:—*n.* [*pl.* semiweeklies], anything published or produced twice a week:—*adv.* at intervals of half a week.

sem-o-li-na (sem′-o-lē′na), *n.* the hard, coarse byproducts of milled wheat, used to make pasta and other foods.

sen-ate (sen′it), *n.* **1,** in ancient Rome, the supreme legislative and administrative body; **2,** in modern times, an assembly or council of citizens with governmental powers; a legislative body:—**Senate,** the upper and smaller branch of the legislature, in such countries as Canada, the U.S., France, and Australia.

sen-a-tor (sen′a-tėr), *n.* a member of the senate, or upper house of a legislature.

sen-a-tor-i-al (sen′*a*-tōr′i-al), *adj.* **1,** referring to, or befitting, a senator or a senate; as, *senatorial* dignity; **2,** entitled to elect a senator; as, a *senatorial* district.

send (send), *v.t.* [sent (sent), send-ing], **1,** to cause to go, often to some special destination; as, to *send* a messenger; to *send* a child to school; **2,** to cause to be carried; as, to *send* a letter, greetings, or news; **3,** to cause to come or happen; bestow; as, fate *sent* much happiness to him; **4,** to throw or drive, as a ball; **5,** to cause a certain feeling or condition; as, the joke *sent* the audience into gales of laughter:—*v.i.* to send word of some kind; as, he *sent* for me; I *sent* to warn him.—*n.* **send′er.**

send-off (send′-ôf′), *n.* an act of farewell, expressing goodwill and demonstrating affection and best wishes for someone undertaking a new venture, such as a trip, new job, etc.; as, to give a retiring person a great *send-off.*

Sen-e-ca (sen′u-ku) *n.* **1,** a member of the Aboriginal group originally living in western New York State and now in Ontario. The Seneca are part of the Six Nations Iroquois Confederacy; **2,** Iroquoian language of these people.

se-nile (sē′nīl; -nil), *adj.* showing the mental or physical weaknesses usually associated with old age; now, generally known as dementia.—*n.* **se-nil′i-ty** (dotage).

sen-ior (sēn′yėr), *adj.* **1,** higher in rank or office; older in standing or longer in service; as, the *senior* member of the firm; **2,** older in years: generally used after a person's name, often in abbreviated form, *Sr.*, to distinguish the older of two persons having the same name; as, John Moore, *Sr.*; **3,** connected with the last year of a secondary school or college/university course:—*n.* **1,** one who is older than others, or higher in rank or office; **2,** a student in the final year of secondary school or college/university; **3,** short for *senior citizen.*—*n.* **sen-ior′i-ty** (sēn-yor′i-ti).

senior citizen, an older person, esp. one who is retired from work.

sen-sa-tion (sen-sā′shun), *n.* **1,** the use of the senses: the ability to see, hear, touch, taste, or smell; **2,** a bodily feeling, usually produced by an external object or condition; as, a *sensation* of warmth; also, a mental feeling or emotion; as, a *sensation* of fear; **3,** a state of general excitement or interest; as, the new pianist produced a great *sensation*; also, the cause of the excitement.

sen-sa-tion-al (sen-sā′shun-al), *adj.* **1,** pertaining to bodily sensation; **2,** extraordinary; as, a *sensational* escape; **3,** exciting; thrilling; as, a *sensational* novel.

sense (sens), *n.* **1,** any one of the special faculties of the body by which impressions are received from the outside world; as, the *senses* of sight, smell, hearing, taste, or touch; **2,** bodily feeling; sensation; as, a *sense* of pleasure or pain, heat or cold; **3,** understanding; judgment; as, he is a man of *sense*; a *sense* of the fitness of things; good *sense* of direction; **4,** lively appreciation; as, a *sense* of humour:—*v.t.* [sensed, sensing], **1,** to perceive; be aware of; as, to *sense* hostility; **2,** *Colloq.* to understand; as, I *sense* your meaning.

sense-less (sens′lis), *adj.* **1,** without feeling; unconscious, as a person in a faint; **2,** foolish; meaningless; as, a *senseless* argument.—*adv.* **sense′less-ly.**—*n.* **sense′less-ness.**

sen-si-bil-i-ty (sen′si-bil′i-ti), *n.* [*pl.* sensibilities], **1,** the capacity to feel; as, the *sensibility* of the skin; **2,** sensitiveness; capacity for emotion, in contrast to intellect; esp., acute feelings of delight, sorrow, appreciation, etc., in response to impressions; as, the *sensibility* of an artist.

sen-si-ble (sen′si-bl), *adj.* **1,** having good common sense; reasonable; as to be *sensible* enough to not drink and drive; **2,** capable of affecting the senses; noticeable; as, a *sensible* rise in temperature; **3,** capable of being grasped by the mind; as, a *sensible* difference; **4,** conscious; aware; as, I am *sensible* of your kindness to me.—*adv.* **sen′si-bly.**

sen-si-tive (sen′si-tiv), *adj.* **1,** quick to receive impressions from external objects or conditions; as, a *sensitive* skin; **2,** responding to or recording slight shades or changes of sound, light, etc.; as, a *sensitive* photographic film; **3,** easily moved; impressionable; also, easily offended; touchy.—*n.* **sen′si-tiv′i-ty.**—*adv.* **sen′si-tive-ly.**—*v.t.* **sen′ si-tize′.**

sen-sor (sen′sôr), *n.* a device that is able to detect and measure light, temperature, or other physical properties; as, carbon monoxide *sensors*.

sen-so-ry (sen′so-ri), *adj.* **1,** pertaining to the senses or to sensation; as, *sensory* impressions; **2,** conveying messages from the organs of sense, as the eyes, ears, etc., to the brain; as, *sensory* nerves.

sen-su-al (sen′shoo-al; sen′sū-al), *adj.* **1,** associated with the pleasures of the body or senses; not mental or spiritual; as, a *sensual* life; **2,** indulging in the sexual pleasures.—*n.* **sen′su-al′i-ty; sen′su-al-ism; sen′su-al-ist.**

sen-su-ous (sen′shoo-us; sen′sū-us), *adj.* **1,** appealing to the senses; as, *sensuous* music; **2,** sensitive to the beauty of colour, tone, texture, etc.; **3,** attractive sexually.—*adv.* **sen′suous-ly.**

sent (sent) *p.t.* of *send*.

sen-tence (sen′tens), *n.* **1,** in *grammar*, a series of words usually containing a subject and a predicate and expressing a complete thought; **2,** in *law*, judgment pronounced by a court; also, a penalty imposed:—*v.t.* [sentenced, sentenc-ing], to pronounce judgment or impose a penalty upon; as, the judge *sentenced* the thief to two months' imprisonment.

sen-ti-ent (sen′shi-ent; sen′shent), *adj.* **1,** able to feel or perceive; conscious: opposite of *inanimate;* **2,** experiencing sensation.—*n.* **sen′ti-ence.**

sen-ti-ment (sen′ti-ment), *n.* **1,** an opinion or attitude of mind based on, or strongly influenced by, feeling or emotion; as, a person of strong patriotic *sentiment;* **2,** a feeling or emotion, as of pity or affection; **3,** a thought or opinion as distinct from the words in which it is expressed; as, I like the *sentiment* but not the language.

sen-ti-men-tal (sen′ti-men′tal), *adj.* **1,** easily moved to pity, sympathy, etc.; also, given to indulging one's emotions freely, or too freely; as, a *sentimental* friend; **2,** appealing to the emotions; as, *sentimental* poetry.—*adv.* **sen′ti-men′tal-ly**—*n.* **sen′ti-men-tal′i-ty.**—*n.* **sen′ ti-men′tal-ism; sen′ti-men′tal-ist.**

sen-ti-nel (sen′ti-nl), *n.* a person who watches or guards; esp., a soldier on guard at a camp or fort; a sentry; a lookout.

sen-try (sen′tri), *n.* [*pl.* sentries], a person stationed as a sentinel or guard to keep watch.

se-pal (sē′pal; sep′al), *n.* one of the leaflike sections of the calyx, outside the coloured petals of a flower, usually green in colour.

SEPALS (S)

sep-a-rate (sep′a-rāt′), *v.t.* [separat-ed, separat-ing], **1,** to part or divide; disunite; set apart; as, please *separate* the pens from the pencils; **2,** to come in between; keep apart; as, a hedge *separates* the two gardens:—*v.i.* **1,** to part; withdraw from each other or from one another; scatter; as, rain began to fall, and the crowd *separated* in a hurry; **2,** of a married couple, to make an agreement to live apart while still remaining legally married:—*adj.* (sep′a-rit; sep′rit), **1,** divided; no longer united; as, they have turned the second floor into two *separate* apartments; **2,** distinct; different; single; as, each *separate* item on a bill.—*n.* **sep′a-ra′tion; sep′a-ra′tor.**—*adj.* **sep′a-ra-ble.**—*adv.* **sep′a-rate-ly.**

separate school, a publicly funded school for students of the religious minority (usually Roman Catholics); denominational schools.—*n.* **separate school board.**

sep-a-rat-ist (sep′a-ra-tist; sep′ra-tist), *n.* someone who advocates political or ecclesiastical independence for his or her group or region; as, Québec *separatists* often call themselves sovereigntists:—*adj.* characteristic of the policies or beliefs of separatists.—*n.* **sep′a-rat-ism.**

se-pi-a (sē′pi-a), *n.* **1,** a dark reddish-brown colour; **2,** a brownish tint used in early photography; **3,** a dark-brown pigment made from an inky fluid ejected by the European cuttlefish.

Sep-tem-ber (sep-tem′bėr), *n.* the ninth month of the year, between August and October, with 30 days.

sep-tic (sep′tik); *adj.* and *n.* infected by germs; as, *septic* poisoning; putrefying:—**septic tank,** a sewage tank in which solid waste is decomposed by bacterial action.

sep-tu-a-ge-na-ri-an (sep′tū-a-ji-nâ′ri-an), *n.* a person who is 70, or between 70 and 80, years old.

se-pul-chral (se-pul′kral), *adj.* **1,** pertaining

to a tomb or to the burial of the dead; **2,** gloomy or funereal; as, a *sepulchral* mansion; **3,** deep and solemn; as, a *sepulchral* voice.—*n.* **sep′ul-chre.** Also spelled **sep′ul-cher.**

se-quel (sē′kwel), *n.* **1,** a succeeding part; continuation; result; as, the *sequel* of his fiery speech was a riot in the streets; **2,** a complete story that continues from where an earlier story ended; as, a *sequel* to a movie.

se-quence (sē′kwens), *n.* **1,** the act of following; the coming of one thing after another; as, the *sequence* of cause and effect; **2,** the order in which things occur or are arranged; as, the *sequence* of words in a sentence; **3,** a series; as, a *sequence* of plays; **4,** an event that follows another.

se-quen-tial (sē-kwen′shal), *adj.* **1,** following in a connected series or sequence; serial; **2,** in the order of time; **3,** following.—*n.* **se-quen′ti-al′i-ty.**—*adv.* **se-quen′tial-ly.**

se-ques-ter (si-kwes′tėr), *v.t.* **1,** to seize by court order as security for a debt, claim, etc.; **2,** to confiscate (esp. by a government).

se-ques-tered (si-kwes′tėrd), *adj.* secluded; retired; quiet.

se-quin (sē′kwin), *n.* a small spangle or shiny metal ornament used to decorate dresses, etc.

se-quoi-a (si-kwoi′a), *n.* either of two evergreen trees of California, called *big tree* and *redwood* respectively, which grow to immense size and have a reddish-brown bark and pointed leaves.

ser-e-nade (ser′e-nād′), *n.* **1,** music sung or played at night, often by a lover under his or her beloved's window; **2,** a piece of music suitable to such an occasion:—*v.t.* and *v.i.* [serenad-ed, serenad-ing], to sing or play a serenade in honour of (a person).

ser-en-dip-i-ty (ser-en-di′pi-ti), *n.* the ability to make discoveries by accident; good luck or fortune; as, his success was due to serendipity, not planning.—*adj.* **ser-en-dip′i-tous.**—*adv.* **ser-en-dip′i-tous-ly.**

se-rene (se-rēn′), *adj.* **1,** clear and calm; as, a *serene* summer day; **2,** placid; composed.—*adv.* **se-rene′ly.**—*n.* **se-ren′i-ty** (si-ren′i-ti).

serf (sûrf), *n.* **1,** originally, a slave; **2,** in the Middle Ages, a poor farm worker who belonged to the land that person tilled, and stayed with the land whenever it was sold.—*n.* **serf′dom.**

serge (sûrj), *n.* a woollen material, woven with fine diagonal ridges, used for dresses, suits, and coats; the RCMP uniform is made of red serge.

ser-geant (sär′jent), *n.* **1,** in Canada, an officer in the military ranking above master corporal but below warrant officer; **2,** a police officer ranking above detective or constable but below inspector or staff sergeant.

sergeant-at-arms (sär′jent-at-ärmz′), *n.* [*pl.* sergeants-at-arms], an officer of a judicial, legislative, or deliberative body, who is responsible for keeping order at meetings.

sergeant major, 1, an officer ranking above staff sergeant major in the RCMP; **2,** an officer ranking below inspector in the Ontario Provincial Police; **3,** in the U.S., the highest rank of noncommissioned officer; **4,** in the U.K., a warrant officer.

se-ri-al (sē′ri-al), *adj.* consisting of parts or units that follow one another; esp., published in successive parts or numbers; as, a *serial* story:—*n.* a long story that is broken up into smaller parts that are published or broadcast in successive instalments.—*adv.* **se′ri-al-ly.**

serial killer, a person who kills repeatedly over a period of time, often following the same pattern of behaviour:—*n.* **serial killing.**

serial number, *n.* a number given to a member of a large group to identify one from the others, as with soldiers, cars, or appliances.

se-ries (sē′riz), *n.* [*pl.* series], **1,** a number of similar things or events following one another in regular order or succession; as, a short *series* of lectures; **2,** a set of books, movies, programs, games, etc. that deal with the same subject, or are otherwise related to each other; as, a TV *series*; baseball *series*:—**series circuit**, an electric circuit in which the cells, conductors, or units are connected positive pole to negative pole so that the current passes through each in succession: opposite of *parallel circuit.*

ser-if (ser′if), *n.* in *printing,* a fine projecting and decorative cross stroke at the top or bottom of a letter.

se-ri-ous (sē′ri-us), *adj.* **1,** responsible; earnest; as, a *serious* student; **2,** not trifling; not comic; as, a *serious* play; **3,** demanding thought and attention; as, *serious* reading; **4,** disastrous or dangerous; as, *serious* consequences.—*adv.* **se′ri-ous-ly.**—*n.* **se′ri-ous-ness.**

ser-mon (sûr′mun), *n.* **1,** a formal talk or lecture based on a moral or religious subject, as part of a church service; **2,** any serious talk or address.

ser-pent (sûr′pent), *n.* **1,** a snake, esp. a large one; **2,** a sly, deceitful person.

ser-pen-tine (sûr′pen-tīn′; sûr′pen-tēn′), *adj.* **1,** snakelike or like a serpent; **2,** winding in coils or curves; as, the *serpentine* course of a stream; **3,** sly and crafty; as, *serpentine* wisdom:—*n.* (sûr′pen-tēn′), a kind of dull green, sometimes mottled, rock that takes a high polish.

ser-rat-ed (ser′ā-tid), *adj.* having sawlike

notches, as of leaves, knives, etc.; also, **ser′rate**; as, a *serrate* leaf of hydrangea.

se-rum (sē′rum), *n.* [*pl.* serums or sera (sē′ra)], **1,** fluid taken from the blood of an animal that has been inoculated with a given disease, and used to fight the disease in human beings; **2,** the yellowish, clear, watery fluid that remains after blood has coagulated.

ser-vant (sûr′vant), *n.* a person who works for another person, doing jobs such as cooking, cleaning, or gardening. People who work for the government are often called **civil servants** or **public servants.**

serve (sûrv), *v.t.* [served, serv-ing], **1,** to attend or wait upon; work for; **2,** to obey and honour; as, to *serve* God; **3,** to put on the table and distribute, as food; as, to *serve* breakfast; also, to wait upon (persons) in a restaurant or store; as, to *serve* a customer; **4,** to be of use to; as, the car *served* him very well all summer; the coat *served* her for a pillow; **5,** to defend; take the part of; as, to *serve* one's country; also, to promote; make a contribution to; as, to *serve* science; **6,** to treat; deal with; act toward; as, he *served* me shamefully; **7,** to deliver, as a legal writ or summons; **8,** to undergo; as, to *serve* a prison sentence; **9,** in games, such as tennis, to put (the ball) into play:—*v.i.* **1,** to be employed by another; be a servant, slave, or employee; **2,** to discharge the duties of an office or employment; as, to *serve* in the army or navy; to *serve* on a committee; **3,** to be sufficient; act as substitute; answer the purpose; as, rain will not *serve* as an excuse for absence; **4,** in games, such as tennis, to put (the ball) into play by sending it to an opponent as the first stroke:—*n.* in games, as tennis, the act of serving (the ball); also, the ball as served or the turn for serving; as, whose *serve* is it?—*n.* **serv′er.**

serv-ice (sûr′vis), *n.* **1,** duty or function performed or required; as, have you need of our *services*? also, the manner of performing work; as, poor hotel *service;* **2,** a set of implements for special use; as, a silver tea *service*; dinnerware *service* for eight; **3,** any formal religious ceremony; as, the funeral or wedding *service;* **4,** professional or official functions or duties; as, a lawyer's *services;* military *service*; **5,** employment; as, civil *service;* **6,** benefit; advantage; as, an education is often of great *service*; **7,** in games, such as tennis, that stroke of the ball that puts it into play; **8,** the state or position of a servant; as, he was in his master's *service* for 10 years:—*v.t.* [serviced, servic-ing], to put into, or maintain in, condition; put back into good shape; as, to *service* a car:—*adj.* having to do with or giving service; as, a *service* award.

serv-ice-a-ble (sûr′vis-a-bl), *adj.* **1,** useful; helpful; as, colonies may in many ways be *serviceable* to the parent country; **2,** having good wearing qualities; durable; practical; as, a *serviceable* pair of rubber boots.

ser-vice-ber-ry (sûr′vis-ber′i), *n.* Same as **saskatoon.**

service centre, a facility beside a major highway or other road that provides services such as restaurants, gas stations, garages, and toilets for travellers.

service charge, a fee or additional charge beyond the basic one, for services from a bank, ticket agent, etc.

service club, a volunteer association, often of business and professional people, whose aim is to support charitable activities and community well-being; as, members of the *service club* volunteer their time.

service industry, a group of enterprises that provides goods and materials to others but does not manufacture things itself.

service provider, a company that provides Internet access to computer users; as, my *service provider* uses high-speed cable modems.

service road, a local road that provides access to areas adjoining an expressway; an access road.

service station, a garage or establishment that services automobiles, supplying gas and oil and often repairs and maintenance. Also called a *gas station.*

ser-vi-ette (sûr′vi-et′), *n.* a cloth or paper table napkin.

ser-vile (sûr′vīl; sûr′vil), *adj.* **1,** pertaining to a slave; as, of *servile* origin; **2,** characteristic of a slave; as, *servile* fear; **3,** having an extreme desire to please others; cringing; slavishly humble; as, a *servile* flatterer.—*n.* **ser-vil′i-ty** (sûr-vil′i-ti).

serv-ing, *n.* a portion of food for one person; as, a *serving* of vegetables.

ser-vi-tude (sûr′vi-tūd′), *n.* **1,** slavery; bondage; **2,** service or labour enforced as a punishment; as, penal *servitude.*

ses-a-me (ses′a-mi), *n.* an East Indian herb that contains seeds that yield an oil and are used as food:—**open sesame**, any magical charm, password, etc., that removes barriers or brings about a desired end: from *Ali Baba and the Forty Thieves.*

ses-sion (sesh′un), *n.* **1,** a formal meeting of a council, club, court, legislative body, etc.; as, court is now in *session;* **2,** a series of such meetings; as, a *session* of Parliament; **3,** the time occupied by a single meeting or by a series of meetings, at a fixed time; as, a two-hour *session*; a two-month *session*; a band's recording *session.*—*adj.* **ses′sion-al.**

set (set), *v.t.* [set, set-ting], **1,** to place or fix in a certain position; as, they *set* the basket on the floor; **2,** to put (a hen) upon a nest of eggs, or (eggs) under a hen; **3,** to put in order; make ready for use; as, to *set* a table;

set a trap; **4,** to regulate (a clock); **5,** to cause to become stiff, as jelly; to make permanent or fast, as colours; **6,** to prepare (a broken bone) to heal; **7,** to fix (a price); **8,** to adapt, as words to music; **9,** to put into a special condition; as, to *set* a house on fire; **10,** to arrange (type) in words; **11,** to fix or determine; as, to *set* one's mind on, to, or against something:—*v.i.* **1,** to sink below the horizon, as the sun; **2,** to become firm, as jelly, or rigid, as cement; **3,** to apply oneself; as, to *set* to work; **4,** to flow or tend; as, the current *sets* to the north; **5,** to start; as, to *set* out on a journey; **6,** to fit; as, this coat *sets* well; **7,** to sit; hatch eggs; as, a *setting* hen:—*adj.* **1,** fixed or established; as, a *set* wage; **2,** immovable; obstinate; as, *set* in his ways; **3,** regular; formal; as, a *set* speech:—*n.* **1,** a number of things of the same kind, to be used in conjunction; as, a *set* of golf clubs; a *set* of encyclopedias; also, apparatus; as, a television *set;* **2,** a congenial group of persons; clique; as, the younger *set;* **3,** a series of games that counts as a unit, as in tennis; **4,** a setting, or scenery either for a play, movie, or television show; **5,** posture; as, the *set* of the head; **6,** fit; as, the *set* of a coat or a skirt.

set-back (set′bak′), *n.* a check to progress or advancement; a reverse.

set-screw (set′skrōō′), *n.* a screw to regulate tension on a spring, etc., or to prevent movement, as of a ring around a shaft.

set-tee (se-tē′), *n.* a long seat or short sofa with arms and a back.

set-ter (set′ėr), *n.* **1,** one who or that which sets; as, a type*setter;* **2,** a longhaired hunting dog trained to stand rigid and point on scenting prey.

set-ting (set′ing), *n.* **1,** the act of a person or thing that sets; **2,** that in which something is fastened, as the mounting of a jewel; **3,** the scene or scenery and stage properties for a play, book, movie, or television show; the background of a story; **4,** music composed for a written text.

set-tle (set′l), *v.t.* [set-tled, set-tling], **1,** to place in a fixed state or position; as, *settle* yourself in this hammock; also, to establish in business or in a home; as, they were finally *settled* in the new house; **2,** to make calm; free from unrest; as, you must *settle* your nerves; **3,** to agree on; as, to *settle* a price; adjust, as a quarrel; pay, as a bill; **4,** to free of dregs by causing them to sink; as, to *settle* coffee; **5,** to make firm or solid; as, to *settle* a roadway; **6,** to colonize; as, the French and English *settled* Canȧda; **7,** to dispose of; as, to *settle* an estate; bestow legally; as, to *settle* an annuity on someone; put into shape, as one's affairs:—*v.i.* **1,** to become fixed; assume a lasting form; **2,** to come to rest, as a bird; establish a residence, as a colonist; **3,** to become established in business or in a way of life; as, to *settle* down; **4,** to sink to the bottom of a liquid, as dregs; be cleared of dregs, as coffee; **5,** to become firm or solid, as a roadbed; find a permanent level, as the foundations of a building; **6,** to determine; as, to *settle* on a course of conduct; **7,** to pay a bill.—*n.* **set′tler.**

set-tle-ment (set′l-ment), *n.* **1,** the act of settling or establishing; also, the state of being fixed or established, as in a business or profession; **2,** the payment of an account; adjustment of a dispute; **3,** a legal gift; as, a marriage *settlement;* **4,** the process of colonizing; also, a colony, esp. one in a state of development; **5,** a small town or village; **6,** in a poor and crowded section of a large city, an institution providing instruction, entertainment, etc., for the people of the neighbourhood.

set-tler (set′lėr), *n.* a person who goes to live in a new area or country.

set–up (set′–up′), *n.* **1,** the arrangement of an organization; **2,** the layout of apparatus or equipment for a specific task; **3,** *Colloq.* a conspiracy or hoax; **4,** a plan of action; **5,** physical makeup; posture; physique; **6,** in *sports,* a play intended to allow a player to score; **7,** the position of the camera; **8,** a table setting, esp. in a restaurant; **9,** the ingredients and material needed to mix an alcoholic drink:—*v.t.* **set up, 1,** to build, raise, or assemble something; as, the police *set up* a road block; **2,** to create, found, or bring into existence; as, to *set up* the scholarship fund; **3,** to plan; make preparations; as, to *set up* the bank robbery; **4,** to place someone in power; as, to *set up* the dictator; **5,** to claim to be something; as, to *set* herself *up* as an authority; **6,** *Colloq.* to frame or incriminate; to cause to appear guilty; as, to *set up* to take the fall:—*v.i.* to begin operating a business.

sev-en (sev′en), *adj.* composed of one more than six:—*n.* **1,** the sum of one and six; **2,** a sign representing seven units, as 7 or VII.—*adj.* and *adv.* **sev′en-fold′** (seven times as much or as many).

sev-en-teen (sev′en-tēn′), *adj.* composed of ten more than seven:—*n.* **1,** the sum of sixteen and one; **2,** a sign representing seventeen units, as 17 or XVII.

sev-en-teenth (sev′en-tēnth′), *adj.* next after the sixteenth: the ordinal of *seventeen:*—*n.* one of the 17 equal parts of anything.

sev-enth (sev′enth), *adj.* next after the sixth: the ordinal of *seven:*—*n.* one of the seven equal parts of anything.

sev-en-ti-eth (sev′en-ti-eth), *adj.* next after the sixty-ninth: the ordinal of *seventy:*—*n.* one of the 70 equal parts of anything.

sev-en-ty (sev′en-ti), *adj.* composed of one more than 69:—*n.* [*pl.* seventies], **1,** the number consisting of 69 plus one; **2,** a sign representing seventy units, as 70 or LXX.

sev-er (sev′ėr), *v.t.* **1,** to divide or separate with violence; cut; as, they *severed* the cords that bound him; **2,** to put apart (two or more persons or things); divide: as, they *severed* all ties with each other:—*v.i.* to part; be torn apart—*n.* **sev′er-ance.**

sev-er-al (sev′ėr-al), *adj.* **1,** more than two but not many; some; as, *several* members of the club arrived late; **2,** distinct; separate; as, they went their *several* ways.—*adv.* **sev′er-al-ly.**

severance pay, the payment made, in addition to regular wages and benefits owing, to an employee upon termination of employment, often based on length of service.

se-vere (si-vēr′), *adj.* [sever-er, sever-est], **1,** strict; stern; as, *severe* methods of discipline; **2,** austere; serious, grave in manner; **3,** extreme; sharp; violent; as, *severe* anguish; **4,** hard to bear or undergo; trying; as, a *severe* test; **5,** extremely plain; as, a *severe* dress.—*adv.* **se-vere′ly.**—*n.* **se-ver′i-ty** (si-ver′i-ti).

sew (sō), *v.i.* [*p.t.* sewed (sōd), *p.p.* sewn (sōn) or sewed (sōd), *p.pr.* sew-ing] **1,** to work with needle and thread; **2,** to do dressmaking for a living:—*v.t.* **1,** to put together, as a dress, etc., by means of stitches; **2,** to join or fasten to something with stitches, as a ruffle on a skirt; **3,** to close or mend by sewing; as, to *sew* up a tear.

sew-age (sū′ij), *n.* foul liquids or waste matter carried off by sewers from homes and other buildings.

sewed (sōd), *p.t.* of *sew.*

¹sew-er (sū′ėr), *n.* an underground pipe to carry off water, waste, etc.; a public drain.

²sew-er (sō′ėr), *n.* a person who sews.

sew-er-age (sū′ėr-ij; sōō), *n.* **1,** a drainage system (of pipes or sewers) to carry off the refuse matter of a town or city; **2,** sewage.

sewing machine, *n.* a mechanical device that sews, usually having an electric motor to run it.

sewn (sōn), *p.p.* of *sew.*

sex (seks), *n.* **1,** the physical characteristics that make a human being, animal, or plant distinctively male or female; **2,** one of the two divisions of animals or plants, called male and female; gender; **3,** the manner in which humans and animals reproduce young.—*adj.* **sexed; sex′y** (*Slang*); **sex′u-al.**—*adv.* **sex′u-al-ly.**

sex-a-ge-nar-i-an (sek′se-je-nâr′i-an), *n.* one who is 60 years old, or between 60 and 70.

sex-ism (**sek′sizm′**) *n.* prejudice against a person or persons because of his, her, or their sex.—*adj.* **sex-ist.**

sex offender, a person who is convicted of having committed a sexual crime.

sex symbol, a celebrity renowned for his or her sex appeal; as, Mae West was a *sex symbol* of the 1930s.

sex-tant (seks′tant), *n.* an instrument used by mariners esp. for observing the altitude of the sun in order to determine latitude and longitude at sea.

sex-tet or **sex-tette** (seks-tet′), *n.* **1,** a musical composition for six performers or voices, or the six performers; **2,** any group of six.

sexual abuse, unwanted sexual advances.

sexual assault, the criminal behaviour that includes forcing another into unwanted sexual contact, esp. sexual intercourse.

sexual harassment, repeated unwanted, offensive sexual advances or remarks, esp. of a woman in the workplace, which may extend to blackmail and coercion.

sexual intercourse, **1,** coitus; sexual union; the genital contact between individuals, esp. the insertion of the penis in the vagina; **2,** any sexual encounter between individuals involving genital contact.

sexual orientation, one's general sexual tendency, outlook, or direction of interest; as, her *sexual orientation* was heterosexuality.

sexually transmitted disease, any of a number of diseases that are transmitted by sexual contact, such as AIDS, gonorrhea, syphilis, etc.

shab-by (shab′i), *adj.* [shab-bi-er, shab-bi-est], **1,** threadbare or worn; as, *shabby* clothes; **2,** poorly dressed; seedy; **3,** petty or unworthy; mean; as, that was a *shabby* trick.—*adv.* **shab′bi-ly.**—*n.* **shab′bi-ness.**

shack (shak), *n.* **1,** a roughly built cabin or shanty, as of logs, etc.; **2,** a shabby old house; hut or shed.

shack-le (shak′l), *n.* **1,** (usually *shackles*), anything that confines the arms or legs so as to prevent free action, as a strap or chain; a fetter; handcuff; **2,** hence, anything that restrains or prevents free action; **3,** any of various fastenings, as a link for coupling cars:—*v.t.* [shack-led, shack-ling], **1,** to embarrass or hinder; **2,** to join or fasten with a shackle.

shad-bush (shad′boosh′), *n.* Same as **saskatoon.**

shade (shād), *n.* **1,** partial darkness caused by cutting off rays of light; **2,** a spot not exposed to the sun; a shady place; hence, a secluded retreat; **3,** something that cuts off or softens the rays of light; esp., a screen or curtain fitting close to a windowpane and adjustable so as to regulate the amount of light admitted; or, a lampshade; **4,** a special degree or variety of a colour; as, this *shade* of blue is difficult to match; tints and *shades;* **5,** a slight degree or amount; a trace; as, there was a *shade* of doubt in his voice; **6,** a shadow; a ghost or phantom; an unreal thing; **7, shades,** the shadows that gather as light fails; darkness; dimness; as, the *shades* of night; *Slang* sunglasses:—*v.t.* [shad-ed, shad-ing], **1,** to screen from light or heat; **2,** to darken or make dim; **3,** to mark or paint with varying degrees of light or colour:—*v.i.* to merge or change by slight degrees; as, the sunset *shaded* from a flame colour to pale yellow.

shad-ow (shad′ō), *n.* **1,** comparative darkness, or shade, caused by cutting off the direct rays coming from the sun or other source of light; **2,** a dark figure or image projected by a body or person cutting off the direct light from a given source; as, his figure cast a *shadow* on the wall; **3,** that which follows inseparably or closely; as a *shadow* in soccer; a constant companion; as, Jane is Mary's *shadow;* **4,** a reflection, as in water; hence, an imaginary likeness; **5,** the darker portion of a picture; **6,** protection; as, under the *shadow* of the Almighty; **7,** a weakened counterpart; a mere semblance; as, after her illness, she was a mere *shadow* of her former self; **8,** a ghost; phantom; wraith; **9,** an unsubstantial or unreal thing: **10,** slightest trace; as, without a *shadow* of excuse:—*v.t.* **1,** to darken; cloud; **2,** to indicate indirectly or in outline; **3,** to keep under observation or follow closely; as, the detective *shadowed* the suspect.—*adj.* **shad′ow-y.**

shad-ow–box-ing (shad′ō-bok′sing), *n.* as training or exercise, to spar with an imaginary opponent:—*v.i.* **shad-ow–box** [shad-ow–boxed, shad-ow–box-ing].

shad-y (shād′i), *adj.* [shad-i-er, shad-i-est], **1,** giving shade or shelter; as, a *shady* tree; **2,** sheltered from the glare of light or heat; as, a *shady* path; **3,** *Colloq.* questionable; of doubtful honesty or legality; as, *shady* business deals.—*n.* **shad′i-ness.**

shaft (shåft), *n.* **1,** the long stem or handle of an arrow or similar missile; also, an arrow; spear; dart; **2,** any long, slender part resembling the stem of an arrow, as the stalk of a plant or the handle of a golf club, hockey stick, axe, hammer, etc.; **3,** the long, narrow, vertical or slanted opening; as, mine *shaft;* elevator *shaft;* **4,** the pole of a wagon or carriage; **5,** in an engine or a machine, a bar to hold or to help move wheels or other rotating parts; **6,** a ray or beam of light; as a shaft of sunlight; **7,** the body of a column between the base and the top.

shag (shag), *n.* **1,** mass of messy and tangled hair, or a type of hairstyle made up of layers; **2,** a coarse nap on cloth or carpet; as, *shag* carpet; **3,** a coarse-cut tobacco:—*v.t.* *Slang* in *baseball*, to chase and catch (balls) in batting practice; as, to *shag* flies; *Slang* in Britain, to have sex with someone.

shag-gy (shag′i), *adj.* [shag-gi-er, shag-gi-est], **1,** rough-haired; as, a *shaggy* dog; **2,** unkempt; tangled.—*n.* **shag′gi-ness.**

shah (shä), *n.* *Persian* the title of Iran's former ruler.

¹shake (shāk), *v.t.* [*p.t.* shook (shook), *p.p.* shak-en (shāk′en), *p.pr.* shak-ing], **1,** to move with a quick back and forth motion; as, a baby *shakes* a rattle; **2,** to cause to tremble; as, chills *shook* his body; **3,** to cause (a person) to waver or doubt; also, to weaken; impair; as, to *shake* a person's faith; **4,** to throw off or dispel; as, to *shake* off sleepiness; **5,** to loosen; unfasten; as, to *shake* out a sail:—*v.i.* to tremble; quake:—*n.* **1,** the act of moving or causing to move with a quick short motion; **2,** a drink made by mixing several ingredients together using a shaking or blending motion; as, a milk*shake*.

²shake (shāk), *n.* a thick red cedar shingle used for both roofing and siding.

shake-down (shāk′doun′), *n.* **1,** a makeshift bed; **2,** *Slang* extortion of money, as by blackmail; **3,** a careful search; **4,** a trial period or process of adjustment; **5,** a testing of something new such as a ship or aircraft and crew to detect any flaws.

shak-er (shāk′ėr), *n.* **1,** one who shakes; **2,** that from which something is shaken; as, a salt*shaker*.

shake-up (shāk′up′), *n.* a drastic reorganization, as of personnel or policy.

shak-y (shāk′i), *adj.* [shak-i-er, shak-i-est], **1,** ready to fall to pieces; unsteady, unsound; as, a *shaky* table; **2,** feeble; tottering; as, a shaky beginning.

shale (shāl), *n.* a rock formed of hardened clay, easily split into sheets, and somewhat resembling slate.

shall (shal), *auxiliary v.* [*p.t.* should (shood)], used in the first person to express simple futurity, and in the second and third persons to express command, determination, promise, etc.; as, I *shall* be in town tomorrow; "Thou *shall* not kill."

shal-lot (sha-lot′; sha′lit), *n.* **1,** an onionlike plant with small, pear-shaped edible bulbs; **2,** the bulb of this plant, used in cooking, having a flavour between that of onion and garlic.

shal-low (shal′ō), *adj.* **1,** not deep; as, a *shallow* stream; **2,** having no mental depth; superficial; as, a *shallow* mind:—*n.* a place where the water is not deep; a shoal.—*n.* **shal′low-ness.**

sham (sham), *n.* **1,** one who or that which deceives; a trick, fraud, pretence, or imitation; **2,** an ornamental cover for a pillow or bolster:—*adj.* **1,** feigned; false; as, a *sham* attack by the fleet; **2,** unreal; pretentious; as, *sham* finery:—*v.t.* [shammed, shamming], to make a pretence of, in order to deceive; feign; as, to *sham* death:—*v.i.* to pretend.

sha-man (shä′man or shā′man), *n.* in some religions, a priest or priestess who is believed to be able to influence the spirits. Also know as a *medicine man* or *medicine woman*, especially among the Native peoples of North America.

sham-ble (sham′bl), *v.i.* [sham-bled, sham-bling], to walk awkwardly and uncertainly, as if with weak knees; shuffle:—*n.* a shuffling gait.—*adj.* **sham′bling.**

sham-bles (sham′blz), *n.pl.* used as *sing.*, any scene of confusion, destruction, or disorder; a mess; as, the boys left the house a *shambles*.

shame (shām), *n.* **1,** a painful feeling caused by the knowledge that one has been guilty of something wrong, immodest, or dishonourable; also, that which causes a feeling of shame; **2,** disgrace; dishonour; **3,** a restraining sense of modesty or decency; **4,** something that should not be; something unfortunate or unwanted; as, it's a *shame* that we lost the game:—*v.t.* [shamed, sham-ing], **1,** to cause to blush with shame or guilt; **2,** to disgrace; as, to *shame* one's family; **3,** to make (a person) do a thing through a sense of decency; as, his friends *shamed* John into apologizing.—*adj.* **shame′faced′; shame′ful; shame′less.**—*adv.* **shame′less-ly.**

sham-poo (sham-pōō′), *v.t.* to wash (the head and hair) with soap and water, or other cleansing preparation:—*n.* **1,** the act of washing the hair; **2,** a special soap used in washing the hair.

sham-rock (sham′rok), *n.* a kind of three-leaved plant of the clover family: it is the national emblem of Ireland.

Shan-gri–La (shang-ri–lä′), *n.* **1,** a remote, imaginary paradise; utopia; **2,** a peaceful, idyllic hideaway.

shank (shangk), *n.* **1,** the leg; esp., in humans, the leg from the knee to the ankle; the shin; also, a corresponding part in animals; **2,** in dressed beef, a cut from the upper part of the foreleg; **3,** the portion of a tool, implement, etc., between the cutting or working part and the handle, as the stem of a key, bit, or drill, or the central part of an anchor; **4,** in a shoe, the part of the sole under the instep.

[1]**shan-ty** (shan′ti), *n.* [*pl.* shanties], a rude or roughly built shack or cabin, esp. in a logging camp.—*n.* **shan′ty-man** (a Canadian lumberjack).

[2]**shan-ty** (shan′ti), *n.* [*pl.* shanties], a sailor's song sung in rhythm with the work performed; as, "Blow the man down..." Also called *chantey*.

shape (shāp), *n.* **1,** the form or figure of a person or thing; outline; as, the *shape* of a boat; **2,** that which has form or figure, whether real or imaginary; a person or thing indistinctly seen; hence, a ghost; **3,** a pattern for guiding a cutter; a mould; **4,** concrete or definite form; as, to whip an idea into *shape;* **5,** *Colloq.* condition or state of being; as, his affairs were in bad *shape:*—*v.t.* [shaped, shap-ing], **1,** to make into a certain form; fashion; as, eyebrows *shaped* in a long curve; **2,** to adapt to a particular end; regulate; adjust; as, to *shape* plans:—*v.i.* to take form; develop; give signs of future form or fate.—*adj.* **shape′less.**—*n.* **shap′er.**

shape-ly (shāp′li), *adj.* [shape-li-er, shape-li-est], well–formed or pleasing in appearance.—*n.* **shape′li-ness.**

shard (shard), *n.* a piece or fragment of something broken, esp. of pottery or glass.

share (shâr), *n.* **1,** a certain portion or part that falls to an individual; as, he has had more than his *share* of trouble; **2,** an equitable part given or belonging to one of a number of persons claiming or owning something jointly; as, he received his *share* of the estate; **3,** one's proportional contribution of any kind to a joint undertaking; as, he gave his *share* of time and money to the club; **4,** one of the equal portions unto which a company's capital stock is divided, each represented by a certificate entitling the holder to a proportionate part of the earnings:—*v.t.* [shared, shar-ing], **1,** to give away a part of; divide and distribute; as, to *share* one's wealth; **2,** to possess in common; partake of, experience, enjoy, or suffer, with others; as, to *share* the common lot; *share* a bedroom:—*v.i.* to take part; as, to *share* in the fun.

sharecrop-per (shâr′krop′ẽr), *n.* one who works a landlord's farm and gives a share of the crops to the landlord as rent.

share-hold-er (shâr′hōl′dẽr), *n.* a stockholder; one who owns one or more of the transferable shares of the capital stock of a company or corporation.

share-ware (shâr′wâr′), *n.* computer software that is available to the user free of charge, often for a trial period.

shark (shärk), *n.* **1,** a large, saltwater, carnivorous, sharp-toothed fish, found mostly in warm seas and sometimes dangerous to people; **2,** *Slang* a swindler or cheat; as, loan *shark;* **3,** *Slang* a person unusually talented in some special line; as, a *shark* at mathematics.

SHARK

shark-skin (shärk′skin′), *n.* **1,** the smooth, shiny fabric of rayon and other fibres often used in suits; as, the band all wore *sharkskin* suits; **2,** the skin of a shark; **3,** any fabric in a similar pattern.

sharp (shärp), *adj.* **1,** having a very thin, fine edge that will cut easily; as, a *sharp* knife; **2,** ending in a fine point; as, a *sharp* needle; **3,** well defined; distinct; as, *sharp* features; *sharp* image on the computer screen; **4,** angular; abrupt; as, a *sharp* bend in the road; **5,** quick; keen; alert; as, a *sharp* eye; also, clever; shrewd; intelligent; **6,** close in dealing; hence, dishonest; unscrupulous; as, a *sharp* dealer;

card*sharp;* **7,** severe; intense; as, a *sharp* pain; **8,** piercing; shrill; penetrating; as, a *sharp* voice; **9,** acid; sour; tart; as, a *sharp* taste; **10,** frosty; cutting; as, *sharp* cold; **11,** quick; hasty; as, a *sharp* temper; **12,** sarcastic; bitter; as, a *sharp* tongue; **13,** fierce; violent; as, a *sharp* contest; **14,** in *music:* **a,** above the true pitch; as, a *sharp* note; **b,** raised by a half step; as, C *sharp*; the symbol [#] that indicates this:—*adv.* **1,** in *music,* above the true pitch; **2,** *Colloq.* promptly; precisely; as, six o'clock *sharp;* **3,** in a sharp manner; alertly; as, look *sharp:—n.* in *music,* a tone or note raised a half step in pitch; also, the sign [#] showing that a note is to be so raised:—*v.t.* and *v.i.* in *music,* to make (a note) higher in pitch by a half step; also, to sing or play above the correct pitch.—*adv.* **sharp′ly.** —*n.* **sharp′ness.**

sharp-en (shär′p'n), *v.t.* to make sharp or sharper; give point or keenness to; as, to *sharpen* a tool:—*v.i.* to become sharp.

sharp-shoot-er (shärp′shoō_t′ėr), *n.* an expert marksman or shooter.

shat-ter (shat′ėr), *v.t.* **1,** to break violently into many pieces; smash; as, to *shatter* a vase; **2,** to distress, derange, or disorder; as, the accident *shattered* his nerves; **3,** to defeat; ruin; as, *shattered* hopes:—*v.i.* to fly into pieces; break.—*adj.* **shat′ter-proof′.**

shave (shāv), *v.t.* [*p.t.* shaved (shāvd), *p.p.* shaved or shav-en (shāv′en), *p.pr.* shav-ing], **1,** to cut off or remove with a razor or similar sharp-edged instrument; to free (the face, chin, etc.) of hair; **2,** to cut in very thin slices; as, to *shave* ham; **3,** to come very close to; graze:—*v.i.* to use the razor to remove hair:—*n.* **1,** the act or operation of removing hair with a razor; **2,** any of various woodworking instruments for paring or smoothing the surface of wood; **3,** *Colloq.* a very small time or distance; also, a narrow escape; as, a close *shave.*

shav-er (shāv′ėr), *n.* **1,** one who, or that which, shaves; **2,** *Colloq.* a young boy; lad; as, he is a little *shaver.*

shav-ing (shāv′ing), *n.* a thin slice pared off with a knife or plane, as from a plank or board.

Sha-vu-ot or **Sha-bu-oth** (sha-vo͞o′ōt′; shov′o͞o-ot′), *n.* Same as **Pentecost** (def. 2).

shawl (shôl), *n.* a scarf made of a square or oblong piece of cloth, used chiefly by women as a loose outer covering for the shoulders or head.

she (shē), *fem.pron.* of the third person personal pronoun [*nominative* she, *possessive* her (hûr) or hers (hûrz), *objective* her], **1,** one particular female, woman, or girl, previously mentioned; as, where is Ann? *she* is here; **2,** any female animal, or thing personified as female:—*n.* a woman; any female.

sheaf (shēf), *n.* [*pl.* sheaves (shēvz)], **1,** a quantity of cut grain, laid lengthwise and bound together; **2,** any bundle of things tied together, as arrows, papers, etc.

shear (shēr), *v.t.* [*p.t.* sheared (shērd), *p.p.* sheared or shorn (shôrn), *p.pr.* shear-ing], **1,** to cut off or clip (hair, wool, etc.), esp. with large scissors or shears; **2,** to cut or clip wool or hair from; as, to *shear* sheep:—*n.* **shears: a,** any of various large cutting instruments, working much like scissors, by the crossing of cutting blades or edges; **b,** large scissors.—*n.* **shear′er.**

sheath (shēth), *n.* [*pl.* sheaths (shē*th*z)], **1,** a close-fitting cover or case for a sword or knife; **2,** any covering enclosing a part or organ of a plant or animal; **3,** a condom.

sheathe (shē*th*), *v.t.* [sheathed, sheath-ing], **1,** to put into, furnish, or cover with, a case; as, to *sheathe* a sword; **2,** to encase or protect with a covering; as, to *sheathe* a roof with tin.

sheath-ing (shē*th*′ing), *n.* that which covers or protects; esp., the protective boarding on the outside of a frame house.

sheaves (shēvs), *n.pl.* of the noun *sheaf.*

she-bang (shi-bang′), *n. Slang* **1,** a situation, concern, or organization; as, the whole *shebang*; **2,** an event or affair; **3,** a hut or shed.

¹shed (shed), *v.t.* [shed, shed-ding], **1,** to pour out; drop; spill; as, to *shed* tears; **2,** to cause to flow; as, to *shed* blood; **3,** to pour forth; spread about; as, the sun *sheds* light; **4,** to cause to flow off; as, oilskins *shed* water; **5,** to cast away loose, or let fall an outer covering; as, birds *shed* their feathers:—*v.i.* to cast off or let fall hair, feathers, etc.

²shed (shed), *n.* a small building or hut, used for sheltering animals, or for storing tools, supplies, farm implements, etc.; as, a tool shed.

sheen (shēn), *n.* lustre; radiance.

sheep (shēp), *n.* [*pl.* sheep], **1,** a timid, cud-chewing farm animal, related to the goat, valued for its wool, meat, and milk; other kinds of sheep live wild in mountain areas of Asia, southern Europe, and western North America; **2,** a timid, defenceless person, easily led.

sheep-ish (shēp′ish), *adj.* awkwardly bashful; somewhat silly; as, a *sheepish* look.

sheep-skin (shēp′skin′), *n.* **1,** the dressed skin of a sheep, preserved with the wool on, and used for garments; **2,** leather or parchment made from the skin of sheep; **3,** formerly, a document written on parchment; hence, *Colloq.* a graduation diploma.

¹sheer (shēr), *adj.* **1,** pure; utter; absolute; as, *sheer* exhaustion; **2,** very thin, fine, or transparent: said of fabrics; as, *sheer* pantyhose; **3,** straight up and down; perpendicular; steep; as, a *sheer* cliff:—*adv.* **1,** steeply; straight up and down; **2,** quite; completely.

²sheer (shēr), *v.i.* to turn from the course; swerve; as, the ship *sheered* to the north;

sheer away from the sensitive topic.

sheet (shēt), *n.* **1,** a large, broad, thin piece of any substance, as of cloth, glass or metal; as, a *sheet* of plywood; cookie *sheet;* **2,** a broad piece of linen or cotton, used as bedding; as, a bed*sheet;* **3,** a single piece of paper; **4,** a newspaper, esp. one of ill repute; **5,** a broad expanse or surface; as, a *sheet* of ice; **6,** a rope attached to the lower corner of a sail to hold and regulate it.—*n.* **sheet′ing.**

sheik (shēk; shāk), *n.* the head of an Arab family, tribe, or clan; a Muslim leader. Also, **sheikh.**

shek-el (shek′el), *n.* **1,** the monetary unit of modern Israel; **2,** an ancient Hebrew unit of weight and money; a coin; **3,** (*pl.*) *Slang* money.

shelf (shelf), *n.* [*pl.* shelves (shelvz)], **1,** a flat board, usually long and narrow, fastened to a wall or set into a bookcase or cupboard; **2,** something resembling a shelf in appearance or position, as a sandbank or a reef; as, the Continental *Shelf;* **3,** a flat projecting ledge of rock.

shelf ice, an expanse of ice extending from a riverbank or seashore like a shelf or sheet, anchored only on the shoreline and not on the bed of the sea, river, or lake.

shell (shel), *n.* **1,** a hard outside case or covering, as on a fruit, egg, nut, or seed, or on certain animals, as a crab, oyster, snail, or turtle; also, a husk, as on corn; **2,** a framework or skeleton, as of a building; **3,** a very light, long, narrow racing boat; **4,** a metal or paper case holding ammunition for a rifle, pistol, etc., or the bullet itself; **5,** [*pl.* shell], a metal projectile filled with explosive, for use in a cannon or mortar:—*v.t.* **1,** to take from the shell, pod, etc., as peas from the pod; **2,** to separate from the cob, as corn; **3,** to bombard; as, to *shell* an enemy fort.

shel-lac (she-lak′; shel′ak), *n.* a sticky, resinous substance used in making sealing wax, varnish, etc.; also, a solution of dry shellac, esp. in alcohol, used as a varnish to form a shiny protective covering for furniture, floors, etc.:—*v.t.* [shellacked, shellacking], **1,** to coat or treat with this substance; **2,** *Slang* to beat; defeat: as, our team was *shellacked.*

shell-fish (shel′fish′), *n.* a water animal having a shell to protect its body, as a clam, lobster, crab, and shrimp.

shell game, 1, a game or trick using three nut shells and a small object that the dealer manipulates and then asks spectators to bet on the position of; **2,** any confidence game; fraud, or swindle; as, that mining company was little more than a *shell game.*

shell shock, 1, post-traumatic stress disorder; combat fatigue; **2,** psychological trauma due to wartime combat exposure.

shel-ter (shel′tėr), *n.* **1,** anything that protects, covers, or shields; a refuge, esp. from the weather; a house or cabin; **2,** a place for homeless people to stay for a while; as, a community homeless *shelter;* **3,** the state of being protected, covered, or shielded; safety:—*v.t.* to protect; defend:—*v.i.* to take refuge; as, during the storm we *sheltered* in the cave.

[1]**shelve** (shelv), *v.t.* [shelved, shelv-ing], **1,** to place on a shelf; as, to *shelve* a book; **2,** to dismiss from service; as, to *shelve* an officer; **3,** to postpone indefinitely; as, to *shelve* a petition; **4,** to furnish with shelves, as a closet.—*n.* **shelv′ing.**

[2]**shelve** (shelv), *v.i.* [shelved, shelv-ing], to slope; as, the bottom *shelves* from the shore.

shelves (shelvz), *n.pl.* of the noun *shelf.*

she-nan-i-gans (shi-nan′i-ganz), *n.pl. Colloq.* **1,** mischief, horseplay; as, the teacher did not stand for the students' *shenanigans;* **2,** trickery, deliberate deception; as, the company's financial *shenanigans.*

shep-herd (shep′ėrd), *n.* **1,** a person who tends sheep; **2,** someone who guides, protects, or watches over a group of people; a member of the clergy:—*v.t.* to tend or guard, as sheep; also, to protect; lead.

sher-bet (shûr′bet), *n.* **1,** a frozen dessert like ice cream, made mostly of fruit juice, water, and sugar; **2,** a sweet powder or a sparkling drink made from this powder. Also called *sorbet.*

sher-iff (sher′if), *n.* **1,** in Canada, a law officer who carries out court orders; **2,** the chief law-enforcing officer of a county.

sher-ry (sher′i), *n.* [*pl.* sherries], a fortified wine originally made in Jerez, Spain.

shied (shīd), *p.t.* and *p.p.* of *shy.*

shield (shēld), *n.* **1,** a broad piece of metal or wood, or a frame covered with leather or a similar material, carried on the arm to protect the body in fighting; **2,** hence, any person or thing that serves to protect or ward off attack or injury; **3,** something shaped like a shield, such as a police badge:—*v.t.* to protect with, or as with, a shield; defend.

shift (shift), *v.t.* **1,** to transfer; as, to *shift* the blame; **2,** to exchange; substitute; as, to *shift* places in a boat; **3,** to change the gears (in a car); as, *shift* gears:—*v.i.* **1,** to change position; as, sand dunes *shift;* also, to veer; as, the wind *shifted* to the north; **2,** to make one's way; as, to *shift* for oneself:—*n.* **1,** a turning away from one thing to another; change; substitution; as, a *shift* of public enthusiasm toward a new leader; **2,** an expedient; as, to make one's way by *shifts;* hence, a trick; **3,** the system of working groups in relays; any one of these groups; as, an early *shift;* also, the working time of each group; as, an eight-hour *shift;* **4,** in *football,* a change in position of the line just before the ball is snapped:—**shift work,** a job done at set intervals, esp. at night; not standard working hours.

shift-less (shift′lis), *adj.* lazy; thriftless; taking no thought for the future.

shift-y (shif′ti), *adj.* [shift-i-er, shift-i-est], **1,** able to turn circumstances to advantage; **2,** hence, not to be trusted, deceitful.

shill (shil), *n.* a decoy, confederate, or accomplice of a gambler or huckster, who encourages spectators to buy or bet:—*v.i.* **1,** to promote a cause or product; as, she's *shilling* for the new corporation; **2,** to act as an accomplice, esp. in a scam.

shil-ling (shil′ing), *n.* a silver coin once used in Britain: value of twelve pence, or one-twentieth of a *pound sterling.*

shil-ly-shal-ly (shil′i-shal′i), *v.i.* to hesitate; trifle; be irresolute; as, don't *shilly-shally.*

shim (shim), *n.* a thin piece of wood, metal, etc., often tapered, for support or levelling:—*v.t.* to level or support something.

shim-mer (shim′ėr), *v.i.* to shine waveringly; gleam and glitter, as moonlight on the water:—*n.* **1,** a tremulous gleam; flicker; **2,** gloss; sheen, as, of satin.

shim-my (shim′i), *n.* **1,** vibration; a shaking; as, a *shimmy* in a steering wheel; **2,** *Colloq.* formerly, a type of a foxtrot dance done with a shaking motion:—*v.i.* **1,** to shake; quiver; vibrate; **2,** *Colloq.* to dance the shimmy.

shin (shin), *n.* the front part of the leg between the ankle and knee; shank:—*v.i.* [shinned, shin-ning], to climb a tree, pole, etc., by gripping it alternately with the arms and legs.

shin-dig (shin′dig), *n. Slang* **1,** a dance; **2,** a party or social affair.

shine (shīn), *v.i.* [shone (shon; shōn), shin-ing], **1,** to emit or give forth rays of light, as the sun or moon; also, to reflect light; gleam; sparkle; as, the lake *shone* in the sunlight; **2,** to be brilliant; excel in some particular line; as, he *shines* in English:—*v.t.* [*p.t.* and *p.p.* shined (shīnd)], *Colloq.* to cause to glisten; polish; as, to *shine* an automobile:—*n.* **1,** lustre; sheen; **2,** bright weather; sunshine; as, rain and *shine;* **3,** *Colloq.* a polish; as, my shoes need a *shine.*—*adj.* **shin′y.**

shin-er (shīn′ėr), *n.* **1,** one of many varieties of small silvery fishes; **2,** *Slang* a black eye (as from a bruise, etc.).

[1]**shin-gle** (shin′gl), *n.* **1,** one of the thin, oblong pieces of wood, slate, etc., used in overlapping rows for roofing and siding; **2,** a signboard, as on a doctor's office:—*v.t.* [shin-gled, shin-gling], **1,** to cover, as a roof, with shingles; **2,** to cut (the hair) progressively shorter toward the nape of the neck, so as to reveal the outline of the back of the head.

[2]**shingles** (shing′glz), *n.pl.* a painful skin eruption in the form of blisters that cluster along the course of a nerve, or spread about the body like a belt.

[1]**shin-ny** (shin′i), *v.i. Colloq.* to climb, using the shins: chiefly used with *up;* as, to *shinny up* a tree.

[2]**shin-ny** (shin′i), *n.* a kind of informal hockey without a net or referee; also, the stick used in playing it.

Shin-to (shin′tō′), *n.* the native religion of Japan, characterized by the veneration of nature and of ancestors and the divinity of the emperor:—*adj.* pertaining to the Shinto religion.—*n.* **Shin′to′i′sm; Shin′to′ist.**

ship (ship), *n.* **1,** any large seagoing vessel; **2,** a large sailing vessel with three, four, or five square-rigged masts; **3,** an airplane or a spacecraft:—*v.t.* [shipped, ship-ping], **1,** to load on a vessel; as, to *ship* cargo; **2,** to carry or transport by water; **3,** to send through any regular channel of transportation, as by rail; **4,** to fix in its proper place or position on a ship, as a mast or a rudder; **5,** to hire for service on a ship; as, to *ship* sailors:—*v.i.* **1,** to engage oneself for service on a vessel, as a sailor; **2,** to embark on a ship; as, to *ship* for Spain.—*n.* **ship′buil′der; ship′per; ship′yard′.**

ship-ment (ship′ment), *n.* **1,** the act of having goods transported; **2,** the goods transported; as, a *shipment* of toys.

ship-ping (ship′ing), *n.* **1,** the act or business of sending goods by water, land, or air; **2,** all the ships in a port or harbour; all the ships belonging to a country; tonnage.

ship-shape (ship′shāp′), *adj.* in good order; neatly arranged:—*adv.* neatly; orderly.

ship-wreck (ship′rek), *n.* the sinking or destruction of a ship at sea, or such a ship itself:—*v.t.* to cause to suffer a shipwreck.

shire (shīr; as an ending, -shėr; -shir), *n.* in England, a district or county.

shirk (shûrk), *v.t.* purposely to neglect, shun, or evade a duty or obligation; as, to *shirk* your responsibilites:—*v.i.* to avoid work; neglect a duty or obligation.—*n.* **shirk′er.**

shirr (shûr), *v.t.* to pucker a cloth or fabric by means of parallel gathers; in *sewing,* to draw up (cloth) by gathering on parallel running stitches; in *cookery,* to cook (eggs) in a buttered dish or casserole.—*adj.* **shirred.**—*n.* **shir′ring.**

shirt (shûrt), *n.* a piece of clothing worn on the upper body, usually having sleeves and a collar.—*n.* **shirt′ing.**

shish kebab (or **kabab; kebob**) (shish′ ki-bob′), *n.* cubed meat, such as beef or lamb, often marinated, cooked on a skewer, sometimes with vegetables.

shiv-a-ree (shiv′a-rē′), *n.* a mock serenade to newlyweds, with kettles, pans, horns, etc. Also called *charivari.*

[1]**shiv-er** (shiv′ėr), *v.i.* to tremble, as from cold or fright; to quiver; shake:—*n.* a trem-

bling from cold, fear, etc.—*adj.* **shiv′er-y.**

[2]**shiv-er** (shiv′ėr), *v.i.* and *v.t.* to break, or cause to break, into small pieces; shatter:—*n.* a small fragment splintered off by a fall or blow; a sliver.

[1]**shoal** (shōl), *n.* **1,** a large number; **2,** a school of fish, etc.; as, a *shoal* of dolphins.

[2]**shoal** (shōl), *adj.* of little depth; shallow; as, *shoal* water:—*n.* **1,** a shallow place in any body of water; a shallow; **2,** a sandbank or bar that shows only at low tide; **3,** hence, a hidden or unexpected danger:—*v.t.* to grow shallow.

[1]**shock** (shok), *n.* **1,** a forcible blow; impact; violent jar; as, the *shock* of a collision; **2,** an unexpected and violent jarring of the feelings; as, a *shock* of grief; **3,** the effect of the passage of an electric current through the body; as, he got a *shock* when he touched the live wire; **4,** a condition of the body caused by the blood's sudden failure to circulate properly, which can be brought on by an injury, heavy bleeding, a great fright, or emotional distress:—*v.t.* to strike with electricity, surprise, horror, disgust, etc.; as, the crime *shocked* the country.—*adj.* **shock′ing.**—*adv.* **shock′ing-ly.**

[2]**shock** (shok), *n.* a stack of sheaves of grain set upright together in a field to dry:—*v.t.* to collect and stack (sheaves of grain).

[3]**shock** (shok), *n.* a bushy mass, as of hair.

shock absorber, a device, such as a hydraullic piston, that absorbs shocks on automobiles, airplanes, and other vehicles.

shock treatment or **shock therapy, 1,** psychological technique for treating depressed patients with a combination of electric shocks and drugs; electroconvulsive therapy; **2,** any act intended to surprise or shake up a situation; sudden, harsh measure; as, *shock treatment* economics.

shock troops, 1, soldiers trained for assault, esp. those who lead an attack; **2,** an aggressive group of militants who lead advances, as in politics; as, the *shock troops* of the party.

shock wave, 1, a compressional wave caused by an explosion, such as an earthquake or supersonic boom; **2,** a violent disruption, reaction, or repercussion to a surprising event.

shod (shod), *p.t.* and *p.p.* of *shoe.*

shod-dy (shod′i), *adj.* inferior; of poor quality; not genuine; sham; pretentious; as, *shoddy* work; *shoddy* cloth; a *shoddy* aristocracy:—*n.* refuse fibre from carding or weaving wool; inferior material (esp. from reclaimed wool).

shoe (shōō), *n.* **1,** an outer covering for the human foot, made of leather, suede, cloth, satin, etc.; **2,** a U-shaped metal bar nailed on the hoof of a horse, donkey, etc.; **3,** something resembling a shoe in form or use, as the strip of steel fastened on the runners of a sleigh, or the lining inside the brake drum of a wheel:—*v.t.* [shod (shod), shoe-ing], **1,** to furnish with a shoe or shoes; as, the blacksmith *shod* the horse; **2,** to protect, strengthen, or ornament, by adding a tip, rim, etc., of harder material; as, to *shoe* a wooden pole with an iron point. Also, **shoe′box′; shoe′horn′.**

shoe-mak-er (shōō′māk′ėr), *n.* a person whose business it is to make or mend shoes.—*n.* **shoe′ mak′ing.**

shoe-string (shōō′string′), *n.* **1,** shoelace; **2,** *Colloq.* a very small, barely adequate amount of money; as, to run the business on a *shoestring*:—*adj.* **1,** long and thin; as, *shoestring* potatoes; **2,** a limited or inadequate amount of money; as, a *shoestring* budget.

shone (shon; shōn), *p.t.* and *p.p.* of *shine.*

shoo (shōō), *interj.* and *v.t.* go away! be off! used esp. in scaring away fowls.

shoo–in (shōō′–in′) *n. Slang* a certainty; something that is sure to happen or succeed; as, he was a *shoo-in* to win the election.

shook (shook), *p.t.* of *shake.*

shoot (shōōt), *v.t.* [shot (shot), shoot-ing], **1,** to let fly, send out, or discharge with sudden force; as, to *shoot* an arrow; **2,** to strike, kill, or wound with a missile discharged from a gun; **3,** to fire or discharge (a missile, weapon); **4,** to streak with different colours; as, the setting sun *shot* the sky with crimson; **5,** to move (a bolt) into or out of a fastening; **6,** to push forward; stick out; as, the snake *shot* out its tongue; **7,** to throw; as, to *shoot* dice; **8,** to flip or propel by a sharp, quick movement of the thumb or fingers; as, to *shoot* marbles; **9,** to pass or rush rapidly through or over; as, to *shoot* the rapids in a canoe; **10,** to photograph or film something:—*v.i.* **1,** to protrude or project; jut; as, the peninsula *shoots* out into the sea; **2,** to rush or flash along swiftly; as, the meteor *shot* through the sky; **3,** to bud; sprout; **4,** to dart with a stabbing sensation; as, a sharp pain *shot* up her arm; **5,** to discharge a missile from a gun; cause a gun, bow, etc., to let fly a missile; **6,** to grow rapidly; grow taller; **7,** to stream forth; spurt:—*n.* **1,** a young branch or growth; **2,** a shooting match; a hunt.

shooting star, a meteor that appears to be propelled across the sky, and that burns up as it enters earth's atmosphere.

shop (shop), *n.* **1,** a room or building where goods are sold at retail; a small store; as, a candy shop; **2,** a place where mechanics carry on their trade; as, an automobile repair *shop;* **3,** (usually *shops*), a factory; **4,** one's own business as a subject of conversation; as, to talk *shop:*—*v.i.* [shopped, shop-ping], to visit stores to look over or purchase goods.—*n.* and *adj.* **shop′ping.**—*n.* **shop′keep′er; shop′per.**

shop-lift-er (shop′lif′tėr), *n.* a person who steals goods from a shop or store while pretending to buy or inspect.—*n.* **shop′lift′ing.**

shopping centre, a separate group of stores, restaurants, and other businesses in one area with a common parking area. Also called a *shopping mall* or *shopping plaza,* and often shortened to *mall, plaza,* or *centre.*

shop talk, 1, discussion or gossip about one's business, esp. outside regular office hours; **2,** jargon or specialized vocabulary pertaining to one's business.

shop-worn (shop′wōrn′), *adj.* dirty, worn out, stale, or not fresh.

[1]**shore** (shōr), *n.* **1,** the land bordering on a body of water, as on the sea, a lake, etc.; **2,** dry land, as opposed to water; as, to go on *shore.*—*adj.* and *adv.* **shore′ward.**

[2]**shore** (shōr), *n.* a prop or support, esp. a timber used to prop up a ship in dock, a wall, etc.:—*v.i.* [shored, shor-ing], to prop, support, reinforce, etc.; used usually with *up;* as, *shore* up the wall with a beam.—*n.* **shor′ing.**

shorn (shōrn), *p.p.* of *shear.* Also, **sheared.**

short (shôrt), *adj.* **1,** brief in time; as, a *short* vacation; **2,** not long; of little length; as, a *short* piece of string; a *short* walk; **3,** below the average height; not tall; as, a *short* man; **4,** scant; deficient; as, a *short* supply of food; also, insufficiently provided with; as, to be *short* of cash; **5,** curt; abrupt; uncivil; as, a *short* answer; **6,** rich; flaky, as pastry; as, *short*bread cookies; **7,** of vowels: **a,** taking less time than the corresponding long sound, as the vowels in "fed" and "foot" compared with those in "fare" and "food"; **b,** sounded like *a* in "hat," *e* in "met," *i* in "sit," *o* in "hot," *u* in "but":—**short ton,** a weight of 2,000 pounds (907.19 kilograms): called *ton* in the U.S.:—**shorts,** *n.pl.* **1,** short, loose trousers; **2,** something that is short, such as a movie lasting a few minutes; **3,** men's underpants:—*adv.* **1,** abruptly; suddenly; **2,** less than what is desired or regular; as, to fall *short* of the mark.

short-age (shôr′tij), *n.* the amount by which anything is short; a deficit; as, his accounts last year showed a *shortage.*

short-bread (shôrt′bred′), *n.* a cookie made of flour, sugar, and butter or shortening.

short-cake (shôrt′kāk′), *n.* a cake resembling biscuit in texture, or a sweetened sponge cake, split and served with fruit between the layers; as, strawberry *shortcake.*

short circuit (shôrt sûr′kit), *n.* an electric circuit that allows too much current to flow through it, which may blow a fuse or start a fire:—*v.t.* **short–cir′cuit, 1,** apply a short circuit to; to stop working because of a short circuit; as, the stove *short-circuited;* **2,** bypass or avoid; **3,** impede or hinder.

short-com-ing (shôrt′kum′ing; shôrt′kum′ing), *n.* a failing; fault or weakness; as, the *shortcomings* of the cheap DVD player.

shortcut (shôrt′kut′), *n.* a quicker or shorter way to go somewhere or do something.

short-en (shôr′tn), *v.t.* **1,** to make short or shorter in time, extent, or measure; lessen; as, the new road will *shorten* our trip to town; **2,** to make crisp or short, as pastry, by using butter, lard, etc.:—*v.i.* to grow or become shorter or briefer.

short-en-ing (shôr′tn-ing), *n.* any kind of fat that makes pastry crisp, such as lard, butter, hydrogenated vegetable oils, etc.

short-fall (shôrt′fôl′), *n.* a failure to reach a goal, esp. a financial one; as, a *shortfall* of several million dollars.

short fuse, *Colloq.* a quick temper; the state of being easily angered; as, the tired student had a *short fuse.*

short-hand (shôrt′hand′), *n.* a system of rapid writing in which characters, symbols, or abbreviations are used for letters, words, phrases, etc., used by reporters and secretaries; stenography.

short–hand-ed (shôrt′–han′ded), *adj.* without a full complement of employees or players; as, to score a *short-handed* goal.—*n.* **short′–hand′ed-ness.**

short-horn (shôrt′hôrn′), *n.* a large heavy (red, white, and roan) breed of cattle with short, curved horns: used for beef and milk.

short list, a list of people or things chosen for final consideration; as, you have made the *short list* for the position.—*v.t.* **short′–list′** (to make such a list, to add to it, or place on it).

short-ly (shôrt′li), *adv.* **1,** soon; in a short time; **2,** in a few words; concisely; **3,** curtly; abruptly.

short–or-der (shôrt′–ôr′dėr) *adj.* pertaining to restaurant food that is cooked and served quickly; as, a *short-order* cook.

short–sight-ed (shôrt′–sīt′id), *adj.* **1,** seeing clearly at short distances only; unable to see far; **2,** due to, or marked by, lack of foresight; imprudent; as, a *short-sighted* business venture.

short-stop (shôrt′stop′), *n.* in *baseball,* the infielder who plays between second and third base.

short story, a work of fiction that is shorter than a novel, usually with very few characters and themes.

short–tem-per-ed (shôrt′–tem′pėrd), *adj.* easily angered; quick tempered; irascible; touchy, cantankerous.

short–term (shôrt′–tûrm′), *adj.* **1,** lasting for a brief period of time; **2,** with regard to financial operations, something that falls due or matures in a short period; as, *short-term* deposits.

[1]**shot** (shot), *n.* **1,** the discharge of a firearm; **2,** a bullet, shell, cannonball, etc.; also, anything let fly or discharged with force; **3,** the launching of a rocket or missile toward a target; as, a moon *shot*; **4,** [*pl.* shot], a small ball or pellet of lead, or a number of such pellets combined in one charge, and used in a shotgun; **5,** the distance that is or can be covered by a missile; hence, range; as, the soldiers were within gun*shot*; **6,** in *sports*, in certain games, such as hockey, basketball, or soccer, a stroke, throw, or effort to score a goal or point; **7,** hence, an attempt; a try; as, a *shot* at the title of champion; **8,** in *sports*, a heavy ball-shaped weight used by a shot putter, which is thrown in competition for distance; **9,** a marksman; as, he is a good *shot*; **10,** in *motion pictures*, the film record of a scene; also, the process of photographing a single scene; **11,** *Colloq.* a small amount of alcohol.

[2]**shot** (shot), *p.t.* of *shoot.*

shot-gun (shot′gun′), *n.* a gun with a smooth bore, for firing at short range: it is fired from the shoulder like a rifle.

shot-put (shot′poot′), *n.* a sports event in track and field that consists in heaving a heavy metal ball with an overhand thrust.—*n.* **shot′put′ter.**

should (shood), *auxiliary v.* past tense of *shall*, used: **1,** in quoting a thought or expression in which *shall* was originally used; as, "I *shall* stay until six" becomes "I said that I *should* stay until six"; "he *shall* not leave" becomes "I said that he *should* not leave"; **2,** to express doubt, uncertainty, condition, etc.; as, if it *should* rain, don't try to go; I *should* like to see the play, if it is a good one; **3,** to express duty or obligation that ought to be or ought to have been fulfilled; as, he *should* telephone this afternoon; he *should* have telephoned yesterday; you *should* not drink and drive.

shoul-der (shōl′dėr), *n.* **1,** either of the two projecting parts of the human body between the neck and the place where the arm joins the trunk; **2,** in animals, the forequarter; also, a cut of meat consisting of the upper joint of the foreleg and adjacent parts of the animal; **3,** the part of a garment that covers the shoulder; **4,** anything resembling a shoulder; as, the *shoulder* of a vase; **5,** the graded edge of a road:—*v.t.* **1,** to take upon the shoulder; as, to *shoulder* a pack; **2,** hence, to assume the responsibility of; as, to *shoulder* an obligation; **3,** to push with the shoulders; hence, to make (one's way) by pushing with the shoulders; as, he *shouldered* his way through the crowd.

shout (shout), *n.* a loud and sudden cry, as of joy, command, encouragement, etc.:—*v.i.* to make an outcry; as, he *shouted* with joy:—*v.t.* to utter with a loud voice; as, he *shouted* out his orders.

shove (shuv), *n.* a forcible push:—*v.t.* [shoved, shov-ing], **1,** to push (something) along; as, to *shove* a book across the table; **2,** to push or press roughly; crowd; as, she *shoved* me rudely:—*v.i.* to crowd against others.

shov-el (shuv′l), *n.* **1,** a tool consisting of a broad, flat scoop with a handle, for lifting and throwing dirt, snow, etc., or for digging; **2,** anything that resembles a shovel in shape or use; **3,** the amount that a shovel holds; as, a *shovel* of ashes:—*v.t.* [shovelled, shovel-ling], **1,** to take up and throw with such a tool; **2,** to gather up with, or as with, a shovel; as, to *shovel* one's food; **3,** to dig, clear, or clean out with this tool; as, to *shovel* a path through snow.—*n.* **shov′el-ler; shov′el-ful.**

show (shō), *v.t.* [*p.t.* showed (shōd), *p.p.* shown (shōn) or showed, *p.pr.* showing], **1,** to present to view; exhibit; as, *show* your stamps to me; to *show* anger; **2,** to make known; disclose; as, a fortune-teller claims to *show* the future; **3,** to make clear or explain (something); as, let me *show* just what I mean; hence, to teach; as, *show* me how to skate; **4,** to prove; demonstrate; as, I shall *show* that he is wrong; **5,** to indicate; point out; as, this *shows* who did it; **6,** to direct; as, to *show* a person to his seat; **7,** bestow or manifest; as, to *show* mercy:—*v.i.* to be visible or noticeable; as, pity *showed* in his face; the stain still *shows*:—*n.* **1,** the act of exhibiting or displaying; **2,** an exhibition or display; as, a dog *show;* **3,** an imposing or proud display; as, a *show* of wealth; **4,** a deceitful appearance or pretence; as, a *show* of enthusiasm; **5,** a play, movie, television or radio program, or other such entertainment. Also, **show′room′.**

show and tell, 1, an activity chiefly of primary school, in which young students bring items from home and explain them to classmates; **2,** any similar, informative public presentation

show-boat (shō′bōt′), *n. Colloq.* **1,** a showoff; someone who behaves flamboyantly or pretentiously; **2,** formerly, a riverboat used to present shows:—*v.i.* to show off or behave in a showy or ostentatious way; as, the star athlete loved to *showboat.*

show busi-ness, the entertainment industry, including such branches as theatre, film, and television.—*n. Colloq.* **show biz.**

show-case (shō′kās′), *n.* **1,** a case or cabinet for exhibiting items in a store or museum; **2,** a place or occasion to display something in such as way as to attract attention; as, the booklet *showcases* the Maritimes:—*v.t.* [show-cased, show-cas-ing], to exhibit advantageously; as, to *showcase* new singers.

show-down (shō′doun′), *n.* **1,** in the game of poker, a laying of cards, face up, on the table; **2,** hence, a full disclosure or confrontation of facts or plans; as, to force a *showdown*.

show-er (shou′ėr), *n.* **1,** a brief fall of rain, sleet, or hail; **2,** something resembling a shower; a brief outburst; as, a *shower* of stones; a *shower* of abuse; **3,** a party at which gifts are given to a future bride or future mother; **4,** a bath in which water sprays down on a person from an overhead fixture with small holes in it; this fixture itself, or an enclosed space containing it:—*v.t.* **1,** to cause a liquid to fall upon; as, he *showered* me with water; **2,** to bestow liberally upon a person; as, honours were *showered* on the hero:—*v.i.* **1,** to rain for a short time; **2,** to bathe in a shower.—*adj.* **show′er-y.**

show-ing (shō′ing), *n.* a display or exhibition; as, a *showing* of fall clothes; also, the impression made by a person's appearance or actions, or by a presentation of facts; as, a poor financial *showing*.

show jumping, a competition involving the riding of horses over obstacles in a set time limit, with penalties deducted for errors.

SHOW JUMPING

show-man (shō′man), *n.* **1,** a flamboyant and stylistic performer; **2,** one skilled in self-promotion; as, the mayor is a real *showman*; **3,** a show manager; impressario.—*n.* **show′man-ship′.**

shown (shōn) *p.t.* of *show*.

show–off (shō′–ôf′), *n.* **1,** someone who shows off; an exhibitionist; **2,** the act of showing off or flaunting:—*adj.* showy:—*v.t.* and *v.i.* **show off,** to display with pride; to seek attention through dramatic or flamboyant behaviour; as, to *show off* an excellent report; to like to *show off*.

show-piece (shō′pēs′), *n.* **1,** an outstanding example of its kind; as, the Lawren Harris painting is a real *showpiece*; **2,** something exhibited or displayed.

show-stop-per (shō′stop′ėr), *n.* **1,** a performance or performer that receives so much applause that the show is temporarily interrupted; **2,** a person or thing that draws great attention.

show-time (shō′tīm′), *n.* **1,** the time at which an event, such as a concert or film, is scheduled to begin; **2,** *Slang* the kickoff of an activity, esp. one involving showmanship or dramatic elements; as, it's *showtime* for our sale pitch.

show-y (shō′i), *adj.* [show-i-er, show-i-est], attracting attention; gaudy; as, a *showy* dress; a *showy* garden.—*adv.* **show′i-ly.**—*n.* **show′i-ness.**

shrank (shrangk), *p.t.* of *shrink*.

shrap-nel (shrap′nel), *n.* **1,** bullets of iron in a shell timed to explode and scatter its contents over a desired area or point; also the shells so charged; **2,** fragments of a bomb, mine, or shell that are scattered when exploded.

shred (shred), *n.* **1,** a long, narrow strip torn or cut off; a scrap or fragment; as, to tear a newspaper to *shreds*; **2,** a small amount; a bit; as, not a *shred* of evidence:—*v.t.* [*p.t.* and *p.p.* shred-ded or shred, *p.pr.* shred-ding], to tear or cut into strips; as, to *shred* cabbage.

shred-der (shred′ėr), *n.* **1,** a machine that shreds paper into small strips; **2,** anything that or anyone who shreds; **3,** *Slang* a person using a snowboard.

shrew (shrōō), *n.* **1,** a mouselike animal with a long snout, that feeds chiefly on insects and worms; **2,** a scolding, quarrelsome woman; as, *Taming of the Shrew*.—*adj.* **shrew′ish.**

shrewd (shrōōd), *adj.* sharp-witted; clever in practical affairs; keen; as, a *shrewd* politician:—*adv.* **shrewd′ly.**—*n.* **shrewd′ness.**

shriek (shrēk), *v.t.* and *v.i.* to cry out sharply; scream; as, he *shrieked* out the answer; he *shrieked* for help:—*n.* a piercing scream; a shrill outcry.

shrill (shril), *adj.* sharp and piercing in tone; as, a *shrill* cry:—*v.i.* and *v.t.* to speak in a piercing, sharp tone.—*adv.* **shril′ly.**—*n.* **shrill′ness.**

shrimp (shrimp), *n.* **1,** a small shellfish with a long tail that is related to the lobster, used for food; **2,** *Colloq.* a very small or puny person.

shrine (shrīn), *n.* **1,** a case or box in which sacred relics are kept; **2,** the tomb of a saint; **3,** any consecrated place or object, as a chapel or the statue of a saint; also, a place considered sacred because of its history; as, the old Montreal Forum was often called "the *shrine* of hockey":—*v.t.* [shrined, shrin-ing], to cherish as sacred; put in a sacred place; enshrine.

shrink (shringk), *v.i.* [*p.t.* shrank (shrangk) or shrunk (shrungk), *p.p.* shrunk or esp. as *adj.*, shrunk-en (shrungk′en), *p.pr.* shrink-ing], **1,** to contract; become smaller or shorter; as, the blanket *shrank* when it was washed; **2,** to draw back; recoil; as, to *shrink* from punishment or an unpleasant sight or thing:—*v.t.* to cause to contract or grow smaller; as, to *shrink* flannel by washing—*n.* **shrink′age.**—*adj.* **shrink′a-ble.**

shrink wrap, a clear plastic film that shrinks itself to the contours of the packaged good when heated.—*v.t.* **shrink′–wrap′** [–wrapped; –wrap-ping], to wrap an article in this manner:—*adj.* **shrink′–wrapped′,** software that is packaged for the mass market.

shriv-el (shriv′l), *v.t.* and *v.i.* [shrivelled, shrivel-ling], to wrinkle, wither, or dry up; as, the heat *shrivelled* the leaves of the plant; some plants *shrivel* quickly.

shroud (shroud), *n.* **1,** a dress or covering for the dead; **2,** anything that envelops and conceals; as, a *shroud* of mystery; **3, shrouds,** a set of ropes, usually two to five, connected by rope rungs, or ratlins, which support and steady the masts of a vessel:—*v.t.* **1,** to clothe (a corpse) in a shroud; **2,** to hide or conceal with a covering; veil; as, the grey mist *shrouded* the hills.

Shrove Tuesday, the day before Ash Wednes -day, a day of penitence and confession immediately preceding Lent. Also known as Pancake Day. Also, **Shrove Sunday**, the 50th day before Easter.

shrub (shrub), *n.* a woody plant not as tall as a tree; a bush. It usually has many separate stems starting near the ground rather than a single trunk.—*adj.* **shrub′by.**

shrug (shrug), *v.t.* and *v.i.* [shrugged, shrug-ging], to draw up or hunch (the shoulders) in doubt, surprise, contempt, lack of interest, etc.:—*n.* a drawing up or hunching of the shoulders; as, his answer was a *shrug.*

shrunk or **shrunk-en** (shrunk′en), *p.p.* of *shrink.*

shtick (shtik), *n.* **1,** a show business routine; a gimmick; **2,** a characteristic or special talent; as, his juggling *shtick*; **3,** something done to get attention.

shuck (shuk), *n.* a husk or pod; the outer covering of a nut; a shell:—*v.t.* to shell, as peanuts or oysters; husk, as corn.

shud-der (shud′ėr), *v.i.* to tremble or shake, as with fear or cold; to quake; shiver:—*n.* a sudden trembling, as from fear, aversion, cold, or excitement.

shuf-fle (shuf′l), *v.t.* [shuf-fled, shuf-fling], **1,** to shift from place to place or from person to person; as, we *shuffled* the money from hand to hand; **2,** to rearrange or mix up the order of (cards in a pack); **3,** to move or jumble together in a disorderly heap; as, to *shuffle* papers on a desk; **4,** to drag or trail (the feet) in walking or dancing; **5,** to slip off carelessly; as, to *shuffle* off a burden:—*v.i.* **1,** to shift things from one position to another; **2,** to rearrange the cards in a pack; **3,** to drag the feet in a slow, lagging manner; scuffle; as, he *shuffled* along in his big slippers; also, to dance with a sliding or scraping motion of the feet; **4,** to do something in a careless, clumsy manner; as, to *shuffle* through one's work:—*n.* **1,** the act of shifting, rearranging, etc.; esp., the rearranging of cards in a pack; **2,** a lazy, dragging gait or movement; also, a dance characterized by a scraping or sliding motion of the feet.—*n.* **shuf′fler.**

shuf-fle-board (shuf′l-bōrd′), *n.* a game in which disks are pushed with a cue along a flat surface toward numbered squares.

shun (shun), *v.t.* [shunned, shun-ning], to avoid; stay away from; as, to *shun* evil.

shunt (shunt), *v.t.* and *v.i.* **1,** to turn to one side; switch, as a car or train; **2,** to put off on someone else, as a task or duty; **3,** to change; shift; as an opinion or course; **4,** to divert blood or an electrical current using a surgical or electrical shunt..

shush (shush), *interj.* and *v.t.* to tell (someone) to be quiet.

shut (shut), *v.t.* [shut, shut-ting], **1,** to close, so as to prevent entrance or exit; as, to *shut* a gate; **2,** to bar or deny entrance to; as, the country *shut* its ports to trade; **3,** to prevent the entrance of; as, to *shut* out certain imports; **4,** to confine; imprison; as, to *shut* a child in his room; **5,** to keep from functioning by turning off the power; as, to *shut* off the radio; **6,** to bring together the parts of; as, to *shut* an umbrella or a book:—**shut out,** in *sports,* to prevent another team from scoring:—*v.i.* **1,** to become closed; as, the door *shut* with a bang; **2,** to cease working; as, the factory *shut* down for six weeks.—*n.* **shut′down′.**

shut-eye (shut′-ī′), *n. Slang* sleep; as, get some *shut-eye.*

shut-in (shut′-in′), *n.* someone confined indoors because of illness, disability, or other incapacity.

shut-out (shut′out′), *n.* in *sports,* a game in which one team does not score; the preventing of an opposing team from scoring; as, to pitch a *shutout.*

shut-ter (shut′ėr), *n.* **1,** a movable metal or wood cover or screen for a window; **2,** in *photography,* a device for regulating the exposure of a sensitive plate to light.

shut-ter-bug (shut′ėr-bug′), *n.* an enthusiastic amateur photographer.

shut-tle (shut′l), *n.* **1,** a train, bus, airplane, or other mode of transportation that makes short trips back and forth between two points; as, a space *shuttle* to the moon; **2,** in *weaving,* an instrument used to carry the thread of the weft, or woof, back and forth through the warp; **3,** in a sewing machine, the sliding holder that encloses the bobbin and carries the lower thread to meet the upper thread in order to form a single stitch; **4,** any similar device, as one used in tatting:—*v.t.* and *v.i.* [shut-tled, shut-tling], to move backwards and forwards like a shuttle.

shy (shī), *adj.* [shy-er or shi-er, shy-est or shi-est], **1,** easily scared away; timid, as a fawn; **2,** reserved; bashful; as, a *shy* girl; **3,** *Slang* short of; lacking; as, this pack is one card *shy*:—*v.i.* [shied, shy-ing], **1,** to start suddenly aside, as from fear; as, a horse that *shies*; **2,** to stay away from, out of doubt or dislike; as, to *shy* away from the large horse.—*adv.* **shy′ly.**—*n.* **shy′ness.**

shy-ster (shī′stėr), *n. Colloq.* one who carries on a business in a mean or tricky manner, esp. an unscrupulous lawyer.

SI (es′ī′), *abbrev.* the modern, standardized

metric measurement system, adopted by Canada, which is based on units of 10, such as metre, centimetre, litre, millilitre, gram, kilogram, etc: short for *Système international d'unités* (French for international system of units).

Si-a-mese twins (sī′a-mēz′ twinz′), *n.* Same as **conjoined twins.**

sib-i-lant (sib′i-lant), *n.* and *adj.* a hissing sound, esp. of a letter of the alphabet: the sibilants are *s, sh, z,* and *zh* (or any symbol representing one of these sounds).

sib-ling (si′bling), *n.* a brother or sister; individuals having at least one parent in common; as, *sibling* rivalry.

sick (sik), *adj.* **1,** in ill health; having a disease; **2,** affected with nausea; inclined to vomit; **3,** tired (of); as, *sick* of flattery; **4,** longing (for); as, *sick* for recognition; **5,** used by, or set apart for the use of, a person who is ill; as, a *sick*-bed; a *sick* benefit:—**the sick,** those who are ill.—*n.* **sick′ness.**

sick bay, a ship's hospital and drug dispensary.

sick-en (sik′en), *v.i.* **1,** to become ill; as, to *sicken* and die; **2,** to become tired of; as, to *sicken* of vain effort:—*v.t.* **1,** to make ill; as, the tainted meat *sickened* me; **2,** to disgust; as, vulgarity *sickened* her.—*adj.* **sick′ening.**—*adv.* **sick′en-ing-ly.**

sick-le (sik′l), *n.* a hand tool consisting of a curved steel blade fitted into a short handle, used to cut grass, etc.

sickle cell anemia, a severe hereditary disease, affecting primarily Blacks, caused by defective hemoglobin.

sick-ly (sik′li), *adj.* [sick-li-er, sick-li-est], **1,** habitually ailing; weak; as, a *sickly* baby; **2,** caused by, or characteristic of, illness; as, a *sickly* look; **3,** unfavourable to health; as, the *sickly* tropics; **4,** weak; faint; as, a *sickly* grin.—*n.* **sick′li-ness.**

side (sīd), *n.* **1,** one of the edges or lines that bound a surface; esp., in a rectangle, one of the longer lines as distinguished from the ends; **2,** one of the surfaces of a solid object; as, one of the six *sides* of a box; also, either of the surfaces of an object that has no appreciable thickness; as, the shiny *side* of a piece of silk; **3,** the particular surfaces of a structure that are not the top, bottom, front, or back; as, the *sides* of a house; **4,** a position to the right or to the left of the centre; as, he kicked the ball to the right *side* of the field; **5,** either lengthwise half of a person or an animal; as, a *side* of beef; **6,** a party or group upholding one view or aspect of a cause; **7,** line of descent through the father or mother; as, a cousin on my mother's *side*; **8,** a certain quality that a person or thing has; as, he has a funny *side*:—*adj.* **1,** pertaining to a side or sides; **2,** directed from or toward one side; as, a *side*step; **3,** placed or situated on one side; as, a *side* door; **4,** minor; incidental; secondary; as, a *side* issue:—*v.i.* [sid-ed, siding], to take the part of one against another; as, he invariably *sided* with them in the argument.

side-bar (sīd′bär′), *n.* **1,** a short news story, often boxed, that supports and adds to the main article; also, a similar feature in a book, etc.; **2,** anything that is complementary, subordinate, or secondary to the main function; as, the *sidebar* factors.

side-board (sīd′bōrd′), *n.* a piece of dining room furniture with drawers and compartments for holding silverware, dishes, linens, etc.; buffet.

side-burns (sīd′bûrnz′), *n.* the hair that grows along the side of a man's face, next to the ears.

side-car (sīd′kär′), *n.* **1,** a small single-wheeled, passenger vehicle that attaches to the side of a motorcycle; **2,** a cocktail consisting of brandy, orange liqueur, and lemon juice.

side dish, a food that accompanies the main course, often served on a separate plate.

side-kick (sīd′kik′), *n.* **1,** a companion, assistant, or confederate; **2,** the second, subordinate member of a duo or partnership; as, Watson is Holmes's *sidekick*.

side-line *n.* **1,** in *sports*, the line along the sides of the field; **2,** the sidelines; the area outside the playing surface that is out of bounds; as, to watch the game from the *sidelines*; **3,** an activity, such as a job, that is a secondary interest; **4,** a line on goods or merchandise that is produced in addition to the main function:—*v.t.* [side-lined; side-lin-ing] to remove from action or participation; the politician was *sidelined* by her opponent.

side ef-fect (sīd′ i-fekt′), *n.* a secondary effect of a drug, chemical, or other medicine, besides the intended effect; as, the *side effect* of producing drowsiness.

side-long (sīd′lông′), *adv.* sideways:—*adj.* directed to one side; as, a *sidelong* glance.

side-man (sīd′man′), *n.* a musician who accompanies the leader or soloist in a jazz or dance band.

side road, **1,** a minor or secondary road; a back road; **2,** in Ontario, a rural road laid out perpendicular to a concession road.

side-show (sīd′shō′), *n.* **1,** a minor show in addition to the main one; as, a circus *sideshow*; **2,** any minor activity, event, or issue; as, his problems are just a *sideshow*.

side-slip (sīd′slip′), *v.i.* and *v.t.* and *n.* in *flying, skiing, etc.,* to slip or travel sideways and downward by banking steeply on turn: opposite of *skid*.

side-split (sīd′split′), *n.* a split-level dwelling in which the floors are raised half a level on one side.—*adj.* **side′split′ting** (extremely funny).—*adv.* **side′split′ting-ly.**

side-step *v.t.* [side-stepped, side-step-ping], to evade or avoid something; as, to *sidestep* the real issue:—*v.i.* step sideways; move laterally:—*n.* a lateral step.—*n.* **side′-step′per.**

side street, a secondary or minor street, esp. one leading to or from a main road.

side-swipe (sīd′swīp′), *n.* **1,** a glancing blow along the side; **2,** a passing jibe or incidental verbal taunt:—*v.t.* [side-swiped, side-swip-ing], **1,** to hit along the side, esp. indirectly; as, to *sideswipe* the parked car; **2,** to attack offhandedly or indirectly.

side-track (sīd′trak′), *v.t.* **1,** to deflect or divert someone from something such as an objective, issue, etc.; as, on their hike over the mountain, the beautiful flowers *sidetracked* them, and they stopped to pick some; **2,** to put off for consideration at some future time; set aside; as, to *sidetrack* a legislative bill; **3,** to transfer (a car or train) from the main track to a siding:—*v.i.* to run a train upon a siding:—*n.* **1,** a secondary position or line of thinking; **2,** a railway siding.

side-walk (sīd′wôk′), *n.* a path or pavement beside a road or street for pedestrians.

side-ways (sīd′wāz′), *adv.* **1,** toward the side; as, to glance *sideways;* **2,** from the side; as, to see a thing *sideways;* **3,** with the side foremost; as, to turn *sideways:*—*adj.* directed or turned to one side; as, a *sideways* look.

sid-ing (sīd′ing), *n.* **1,** boarding, plywood, metal, or composition used for covering the sides of a building; **2,** a short railway track by the side of the main track, to which cars may be switched; a sidetrack.

si-dle (sī′dl), [si-dled, si-dling], to move sideways; sneak up; edge along, as if from shyness or fear; as, the boy *sidled* up to us.

siege (sēj), *n.* **1,** the surrounding of a fortified place by an army or fleet and the cutting off of supplies to compel its surrender; **2,** a persistent attempt to gain possession of something; as, he laid *siege* to her heart.

si-en-na (si-en′a), *n.* **1,** a yellowish-brown pigment containing iron and manganese; **2,** a reddish-brown pigment, *burnt sienna,* made from burning the former; **3,** the colour of either of these.

si-es-ta (si-es′ta), *n.* a sleep or rest taken during the hottest part of the day, as in Spain and Mexico; any midday or after-dinner rest or nap.

sieve (siv), *n.* **1,** a utensil with small holes or meshes, usually of wire, for separating solids from liquids or the finer from the coarser parts of a substance; as, a flour sieve; **2,** in *hockey,* a goalie who allows many goals.

sift (sift), *v.t.* **1,** to separate, as the finer part from the coarser, with a sieve, net, etc.; **2,** to put through a sieve; also, to sprinkle with a sieve; as, the cook *sifted* flour over the meat; **3,** to fall in a light, loose way, as if through a sieve; as, snow was sifting down; **4,** to examine critically; as, the jury *sifted* the facts in the case.—*n.* **sift′er.**

sigh (sī), *n.* **1,** a deep, audible breath expressing fatigue, sorrow, etc.; as, to heave a *sigh;* **2,** a similar sound; as, the *sigh* of the wind:—*v.i.* **1,** to breathe a sigh; as, to *sigh* with regret; **2,** to long; grieve; as, the old lady *sighs* for the past; **3,** to make a sound like sighing; as, trees murmur and *sigh:*—*v.t.* to express by sighs; as, she *sighed* her relief.

sight (sīt), *n.* **1,** the power of seeing; vision; as, eyeglasses help to correct defects in *sight;* **2,** the act of seeing; as, she was thrilled by her first *sight* of mountains; **3,** that which is seen; a view or spectacle; as, the sunset was a *sight* to remember; also, something ludicrous or grotesque; a fright; as, my hair is a *sight* on a windy day; **4,** the limit or range within which a person can see, or an object can be seen; as, in *sight;* out of *sight;* **5,** manner of looking at or considering something; opinion; as, in his *sight,* she did well; **6,** inspection; as, this report is intended for the *sight* of the committee only; **7,** any of several devices, as on a gun, optical instrument, etc., to help in guiding the eye or aim; **8,** careful aim or observation taken by means of such a device; as, take *sight* before firing:—**at sight, on sight,** as soon as seen; upon presentation to sight:—*v.t.* **1,** to see with the eye; as, to *sight* an object through the telescope; **2,** to direct by means of an aiming device; as, to *sight* a gun:—*v.i.* **1,** to aim a gun by means of a sight; **2,** to look carefully in a certain direction.—*adj.* **sight′less.**—*n.* **sight′se′er.**

sign (sīn), *n.* **1,** a board, plate, or other such object with words or numbers displaying the name of a business, giving information, etc.; as, an accountant's *sign;* a *sign* to keep off the grass; a stop *sign;* **2,** a symbol, emblem, or character typifying or representing an idea; as, the *sign* of the cross; **3,** that by which anything is made known; a mark; token; proof; as, his gift was a *sign* of his love; also, indication; evidence; as, there was no *sign* of anyone stirring in the house at that hour; **4,** an omen; as, the breaking of a mirror is said to be a *sign* of bad luck; **5,** a gesture or motion used instead of words to express some thought, command, or wish; as, the teacher gave the *sign* to rise; **6,** one of the 12 equal divisions of the zodiac or its symbol; **7,** in *arithmetic,* a symbol for adding, subtracting, multiplying, or dividing, as +, −, ×, or ÷:—*v.t.* **1,** to write one's name on or at the end of; as, to *sign* a letter; *sign* a cheque; **2,** to transfer (a right to property) by putting one's signature to a document; as, the old man *signed* away all his property; **3,** to hire by getting the signature of; as, to *sign* a person for a particular job:—*v.i.* **1,** to write one's signature; as, I am ready to *sign;* **2,** to signal; motion; as, he *signed* for them to approach; **3,** to use sign language.—*n.* **sign′er.**—*n.* **sign′board′; sign′ post′.**

sig-nal (sig′nal), *n.* **1,** a sign agreed upon for sending information, giving notice of danger, etc.; as, a train *signal;* **2,** that which brings about action; as, the fire alarm was the *signal* for leaving the building calmly in a single file:—*adj.* memorable; extraordinary; remarkable; as, a *signal* success:—*v.t.* [signalled, signal-ling], to communicate with by means of flags, lights, gestures, etc.; make signs to; as, the scoutmaster *signalled* the boys to return to camp:—*v.i.* to make signs.—*n.* **sig′nal-ler** or **sig′nal-er.**

sig-na-to-ry (sig′na-tōr′i), *n.* and *adj.* one bound jointly with others, esp. a state, country, or power, by a signed agreement or treaty.

sig-na-ture (sig′na-tūr), *n.* **1,** the name of a person in his or her own handwriting; autograph; **2,** in *music,* the signs at the beginning of a staff indicating key and time.

sig-net (sig′nit), *n.* **1,** a seal; esp., in England, one of the private seals of the monarch used instead of a signature; **2,** an imprint made by, or as by, a seal.

sig-nif-i-cance (sig-nif′i-kans), *n.* **1,** meaning; as, the full *significance* of his remark escaped me; **2,** importance; as, he must realize this is a matter of great *significance;* **3,** expressiveness; as, he gave the boy a look of deep *significance.*

sig-nif-i-cant (sig-nif′i-kant), *adj.* **1,** full of meaning; expressive; as, Caesar has come to be a *significant* name; also, suggestive; having some concealed or special meaning; as, a *significant* silence; **2,** important; conspicuous; as, *significant* progress.—*adv.* **sig-nif′i-cant-ly.**

sig-ni-fy (sig′ni-fī′), *v.t.* [signified, signify-ing], **1,** to show by a sign, mark or token; make known; declare; as, to *signify* one's consent; **2,** to denote; mean; as, that gesture *signifies* refusal:—*v.i.* to be of importance; to matter or count.—*n.* **sig′ni-fi-ca′tion.**

sign language (sīn lang′gwij), *n.* a way of communicating by using hand and body movements to represent words and ideas; used between people speaking different languages, and esp. by the hearing impaired.

sign–off (sīn′–ôf′), *n.* the action of ending a letter or radio or TV broadcast; as, it was Peter Gzowski's final *sign-off.*—*v.t.* **sign off, 1,** the make a final announcement of the end of a radio or TV broadcast; **2,** to log off a computer; **3,** to approve something; as, to sign off on the plans.

Sikh-ism (sē′kizm′), *n.* a religion founded in the Punjab in the early 16th century by Guru Nanak, which combines elements of Hinduism and Muslimism.—*n.* and *adj.* **Sikh.**

si-lence (sī′lens), *n.* **1,** the state of being still or mute; as, he listened in *silence;* **2,** entire absence of sound or noise; general stillness; as, there was *silence* in the courtroom; **3,** absence of mention; as, to pass over a subject in *silence:*—*v.t.* [silenced, silenc-ing], **1,** to cause to be still; as, to *silence* the dogs; **2,** to quiet; put to rest; as, to *silence* opposition; **3,** to force (guns) to cease firing—*n.* **si′lenc-er.**

si-lent (sī-lent), *adj.* **1,** saying nothing; mute; also, not given to frequent or many words; as, a *silent* man; **2,** quiet; still; free from noise; as, a *silent* place; **3,** not expressed; not spoken; as, a *silent* command; **4,** having a share, not publicly acknowledged, in a business; as, a *silent* partner; **5,** written, but not pronounced: said of a letter; as, the "b" in "doubt" is *silent.*—*adv.* **si′lent-ly.**

silent partner, a financial investor who takes no active role in the management of a business.

sil-hou-ette (sil′oo-et′), *n.* **1,** an outline drawing, esp. a profile portrait, filled in with solid colour, usually black; **2,** a dark outline of something against a lighter background; as the *silhouette* of the trees against the evening sky; **3,** the figure cast by a shadow, as on a wall or screen:—*v.t.* [silhouet-ted, silhouet-ting], to cause to appear in outline or silhouette; as, his form was *silhouetted* against the wall.

silicon (sil′i-kon′), *n.* a brown or grey non-metallic element, ranking next to oxygen in abundance, found in a combined state in minerals and rocks making up one quarter of the earth's crust: because of its semiconductor characteristics, widely used in making computers and other electronic devices, as well as glass, steel, etc.

sil-i-con chip, an integrated circuit constructed on a semiconductor, used in electronics applications such as computing.

silicone (sil′i-kōn), *n.* any compound made by replacing carbon with silicon in an organic substance: the chief silicones are oils, greases, resins, plastics, polishes, and synthetic rubber.

silk (silk), *n.* **1,** a fine, soft, lustrous fabric made from threads spun by silkworm larvae to form their cocoons; known for its strength and deep, rich colours when dyed; **2,** the thread as produced by the larvae; **3,** any similar thread, as that spun by certain spiders; **4,** anything like silk, as the down of the milkweed pod:—*adj.* made of silk.—*adj.* **silk′en; silk′y.**—*n.* **silk′i-ness.**

silk-screen (silk′skrēn′), *n.* **1,** a method of printmaking using a stencil on a screen of fine mesh such as silk; **2,** a print made using this process:—*adj.* made using this method; as, a *silkscreen* T-shirt.—*v.t.* **silk–screen,** to print or duplicate using silkscreen.

silk-worm (silk′wûrm′), *n.* the larva or caterpillar of a certain kind of moth. The silkworm makes a strong silk fibre in spinning its cocoon.

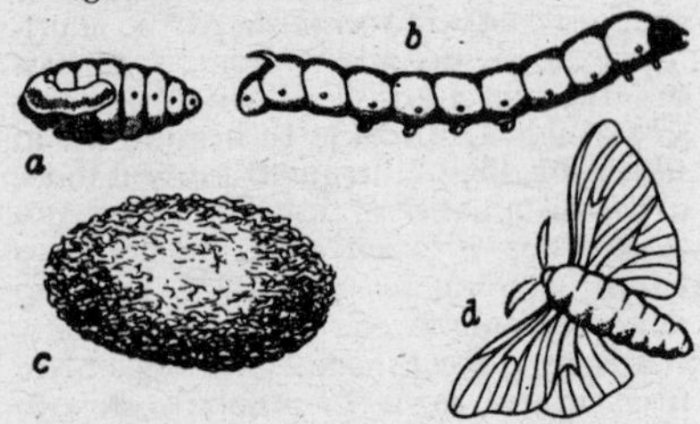

SILKWORM: *A*, PUPA; *B*, LARVA (CATERPILLAR); *C*, SILK COCOON ENCLOSING PUPA; *D*, ADULT FEMALE MOTH

sill (sil), *n.* **1,** a horizontal piece forming the foundation, or part of the foundation, of a structure; **2,** a threshold; as, a door *sill;* **3,** the bottom piece in a window frame.

sil-ly (sil′i), *adj.* [sil-li-er, sil-li-est], **1,** not intelligent or serious; not showing good sense; **2,** foolish; absurd; ridiculous; as, a *silly* answer.—*n.* **sil′li-ness.**

si-lo (sī′lō), *n.* [*pl.* silos], **1,** a pit or tower for storing and preserving green fodder or grain for farm animals; **2,** a deep hole in the ground used to store and launch guided missiles.

silt (silt), *n.* mud or fine earth suspended in, or deposited by, water:—*v.t.* and *v.i.* **1,** to choke, fill, or block with such deposit: usually with *up*; as, the channel is *silted up*; **2,** to ooze through crevices, as water carrying a fine sediment.

sil-van (sil′van), *adj.* Same as **sylvan.**

sil-ver (sil′vėr), *n.* **1,** a soft, shining, white metal, which is a chemical element, used for table implements, dishes, jewellery, etc.; **2,** anything made of this metal, as silverware or money; **3,** anything that has the lustre or colour of silver; as, cloth of *silver*:—*adj.* **1,** made of silver; as, a *silver* cup; **2,** having a soft, silvery lustre; as, *silver* dew; **3,** soft and clear, as the tones of a *silver* bell; hence, eloquent; as, a *silver* tongue; **4,** relating to silver; as, *silver* legislation; a *silver* mill:—*v.t.* **1,** to cover or coat with silver, or with something resembling it; **2,** to give a silverlike polish to; make the colour of silver:—*v.i.* to turn silvery white or grey; as, her hair *silvered* at a very early age.—*adj.* **sil′ver-y.**

silver bullet, *Colloq.* a magic cure-all or instanteous solution to a problem, esp. a long-standing one.—*adj.* **sil′ver–bul′let** (as, a *silver-bullet* solution).

sil-ver-fish (sil′vėrfish′), *n.* a wingless insect with silvery scales, long feelers, and bristly tail: it likes dampness, such as bathrooms, and lives on the starches and sugars of wallpaper, books, etc.

silver lining, a consolation; something hopeful in the midst of a gloomy sitiuation; as, every cloud has a *silver lining.*

sil-ver screen, the motion picture industry; movies in general.

sil-ver-smith (sil′vėr-smith′), *n.* a person who makes or repairs silver.

sil-ver–tongued (sil′vėr–tungd′) *adj.* an eloquent, persuasive, or particularly effective public speaker; as, the *silver-tongued* politician.

sil-ver-ware (sil′vėr-wâr), *n.* knives, forks, spoons, etc., sometimes made of silver or containing silver.

sil-vi-cul-ture (sil′vi-kul′tūr; chėr), *n.* forestry.

sim-i-an (sim′i-an), *adj.* pertaining to, or like, an ape or monkey:—*n.* an ape or monkey, as the gorilla and chimpanzee.

sim-i-lar (sim′i-lėr), *adj.* **1,** having a general likeness; like, but not exactly the same; as, pink and rose are *similar* colours; **2,** in *geometry*, shaped alike, but not of the same size, position, etc.; as, *similar* triangles.—*n.* **sim′i-lar′i-ty.**—*adv.* **sim′i-lar-ly.**

sim-i-le (sim′i-lē′), *n.* a figure of speech in which two different things having some likeness are compared by the use of *like* or *as*: as, the ice is *like* glass; the night is black *as* ink.

sim-mer (sim′er), *v.t.* **1,** to boil gently; **2,** to cook in liquid at or just below the boiling point:—*v.i.* **1,** to cook at or just below the boiling point; as, let the stew *simmer;* **2,** to make a gentle, low, murmuring sound, as a liquid about to boil: **3,** to be in a state of suppressed emotion; to be on the verge of breaking out; as, her temper was *simmering*:—*n.* **1,** a heated state at or near the boiling point; as, to cook meat at a *simmer*; **2,** a state of suppressed emotion or excitement.

sim-per (sim′pėr), *v.i.* to smile in an affected, silly, or self-conscious manner; smirk:—*n.* an affected smile; a smirk.

sim-ple (sim′pl), *adj.* [sim-pler, simp-lest], **1,** not mixed or compounded; as, a *simple* fraction; not divided into parts; as, a *simple* leaf; **2,** not involved or elaborate; easy to solve or understand; as, *simple* words; a *simple* problem; **3,** plain; as, *simple* food; unadorned; as, *simple* clothes; **4,** mere; unqualified; as, a *simple* fact; **5,** sincere; straightforward; as, a *simple,* unaffected manner; **6,** humble; of low rank or degree; as, *simple* folk; **7,** weak in intellect; foolish; as, a *simple* remark.—*n.* **sim′ple-ness.**

sim-ple-ton (sim′pl-tun), *n.* one who is foolish or gullible.

sim-plic-i-ty (sim-plis′i-ti), *n.* [*pl.* simplicities], **1,** the state or quality of being easy, clear, plain, or unaffected; as, *simplicity* of language; *simplicity* of dress; **2,** lack of cunning; sincerity; **3,** lack of common sense, or of average ability to judge.

sim-pli-fy (sim′pli-fī′), *v.t.* [simplified, simplify-ing], to make easier; make plainer to the understanding—*n.* **sim′pli-fi-ca′tion.**

sim-ply (sim′pli), *adv.* **1,** plainly; clearly; as, to write *simply;* **2,** without elaborate show; as, to dress *simply*; **3,** only; merely; as, it is *simply* a question of money; **4,** absolutely; as, you *simply* must go.

sim-u-late (sim′ū-lāt), *v.t.* to give a show or appearance of; imitate; as, to *simulate* insanity.—*n.* **sim′u-la′tion.**

si-mul-cast (sī′mil-kast′), *n.* a broadcast of the same program done simultaneously on radio and TV, on two or more channels or networks, or in two or more languages:—*v.t.* to broadcast in this way; as, to *simulcast* a concert.

sim-ul-ta-ne-ous (sim′ul-tā′ni-us; sī′), *adj.* happening, done, or existing at the same time; as, *simultaneous* explosions.—*adv.* **sim′ul-ta′ne-ous-ly.**

sin (sin), *n.* **1,** the breaking or violation of a moral or religious law; also, any instance of such violation, as dishonesty; **2,** any serious offence or bad action; as, a *sin* to chain up dogs for too long:—*v.i.* [sinned, sin-ning], **1,** to transgress, offend, or neglect a moral or religious law in any way; **2,** to commit evil deeds.—*adj.* **sin′ful.**—*n.* **sin′ful-ness; sin′ner.**

since (sins), *adv.* **1,** from a certain past time until now; as, he left six years ago and has not been seen *since*; **2,** at some time after a certain past event and before now; as, he was then treasurer, but has *since* been elected president; **3,** before this; ago; as, not long *since*:—*prep.* from the time of; during the time after; ever after; as, *since* his departure, I have not seen him:—*conj.* **1,** from and after a time when; as, I have not seen him *since* that happened; **2,** seeing that; because; as, *since* that is the case, I shall go.

sin-cere (sin-sēr′), *adj.* [sincer-er, sincer-est], honest; frank; as, a *sincere* man; genuine, real; as, a *sincere* friend; also, honestly felt or intended; as, *sincere* wishes for your success.—*adv.* **sin-cere′ly.**—*n.* **sin-cer′i-ty** (sin-ser′i-ti).

sine (sīn), *n.* in *mathematics*, the ratio of the side opposite an acute angle of a right-angled triangle to the hypotenuse. Compare *cosine*.

si-ne-cure (sī′ni-kūr′; sin′), *n.* a position requiring little or no work, yet that is well paying.

sin-ew (sin′ū), *n.* **1,** a tendon or tough piece of tissue joining muscle to bone; **2,** strength; power; energy; muscles; **3,** anything supplying strength; the mainstay of anything; as, money, the *sinews* of war.—*adj.* **sin′ew-less; sin′ew-y.**

sing (sing), *v.i.* [*p.t.* sang (sang), *p.p.* sung (sung), *p.pr.* sing-ing], **1,** to make musical sounds with the voice; **2,** to make a shrill or humming noise; as, a flying arrow *sings*; **3,** to make pleasant, melodious sounds like songs; as, the brook *sings* merrily; **4,** to celebrate or praise some event in verse; as, Virgil *sang* of the deeds of Aeneas; **5,** *Slang* to provide evidence, to turn informer, to snitch:—*v.t.* **1,** to utter with musical tones of the voice; as, to *sing* a song; to chant; as, to *sing* Mass; **2,** to celebrate in poetry; **3,** to lull by singing; as, to *sing* a child to sleep.—*n.* **sing′er.**

singe (sinj), *v.t.* [singed, singe-ing], **1,** to burn slightly or on the surface; scorch; **2,** to pass over a flame to remove the feathers or down; as, to *singe* a plucked chicken before cooking it:—*n.* a slight burn.

sin-gle (sing′gl), *adj.* **1,** consisting of one only; as, a *single* page; stand in a *single* file; **2,** not married; as, the resort is for *singles* only; **3,** performed by one person; having only one on each side; as, *single* combat; **4,** for the use of one person only; as, a *single* room; **5,** straightforward; sincere; as, a man of *single* purpose; **6,** in *botany*, having only one row of petals; as, a *single* tulip:—*v.t.* [sin-gled, sin-gling], to select (one person or thing) from others; as, they *singled* him out for honourable mention:—*v.i.* to make a base hit:—*n.* **1,** in *baseball*, a base hit; **2,** in *golf*, a game between two players; in *tennis*, (usually *singles*), a game with only one person on each side.

sin-gle–hand-ed (sing′gl–han′did), *adj.* done without aid or assistance.

sin-gle–mind-ed (sing′gl–mīn′did), *adj.* **1,** focussed on one goal or purpose; determined; devoted; **2,** inflexible; adamant; uncompromising; as, her *single-minded* pursuit of success.—*adv.* **sin′gle–mind′ed-ly.**—*n.* **sin′gle–mind′ed-ness.**

sin-gle-ness (sing′gl-nis), *n.* **1,** the state of being separate or alone; the state of being unmarried; **2,** freedom from selfish ends; sincerity; as, *singleness* of purpose.

single parent, a person, often a woman, who is raising a family without a partner.—*adj.* **sin-gle–par-ent** (relating to having one parent only; as, a *single-parent* family).—*n.* **sin′gle par′ent-hood′.**

sin-gle-ton (sing′gl-tun), *n.* a single thing, as distinguished from several, esp. the only card of a suit in a hand (of playing cards).

sin-gly (sing′gli), *adv.* **1,** individually; one by one; as, we took up each matter *singly;* **2,** without others; alone; single-handedly.

sing-song (sing′song′), *n.* and *adj.* a monotonous or unvaried tone or rhythm.

sin-gu-lar (sing′gū-lėr), *adj.* **1,** in *grammar*, relating to the form of a word naming one person or thing; as, the word "girl" is a *sin-*

gular noun; **2,** extraordinary; exceptional; as, *singular* strength; **3,** peculiar; strange; as, *singular* habits:—*n.* in *grammar*, that form of a word naming one person or thing; as, "man" is the *singular* of "men."—*n.* **sin′gu-lar′i-ty.**

sin-is-ter (sin′is-tẽr), *adj.* **1,** ill-omened; threatening; evil; as, a *sinister* look; **2,** base; dishonest; as, *sinister* intentions; **3,** left: applied in heraldry to the side of a shield on the left of the person bearing it.

sink (singk), *v.i.* [*pl.* sank (sangk) or sunk (sungk), *p.p.* sunk, *p.pr.* sink-ing], **1,** to become wholly or partly submerged, as in water; **2,** to descend gradually; as, the sun *sinks*; to slope downward; as, land *sinks* to the sea; **3,** to decline gradually, as in strength; also, to degenerate, as in morals; **4,** to become hollow: often said of the cheeks; **5,** to enter deeply; as, a thought *sinks* into the mind:—*v.t.* **1,** to cause to go to the bottom; as, to *sink* a boat in a river; **2,** to make by digging downward; as, to *sink* a well; also, to place in an excavation thus made; as, to *sink* a pipe; **3,** to invest or spend unprofitably; as, to *sink* money in worthless stocks; **4,** in *sports*, to make a ball go in a hole, basket, etc., as in golf, billiards, basketball:—*n.* **1,** a kind of metal or porcelain basin, as in a kitchen, with faucets and a drain to carry off dirty or excessive water; **2,** any slight hollow of land, esp. one that has little or no water outlet; **3,** a place of vice and corruption.—*n.* **sink′er.**

sin-u-ous (sin′ū-us), *adj.* **1,** winding or curving in and out; twisting; as, the *sinuous* path; **2,** moving smoothly, supplely; as a *sinuous* dancer.

si-nus (sī′nus), *n.* a natural cavity or hollow in bone, esp. the air cavity in the bones of the skull that connect to the nostrils.

si-nus-i-tis (sī′nu-sī′tis), *n.* a condition when sinuses become swollen and cause painful pressure.

Sioux (sōō), *n.* [*pl.* Sioux], **1,** an Aboriginal people living on the American Plains; also known as *Dakota*; **2,** the language of these people.—*adj.* **Siou′an.**

sip (sip), *v.t.* [sipped, sip-ping], to drink by taking a small portion at a time; as, she *sips* her hot chocolate:—*v.i.* to drink a liquid in sips:—*n.* a small taste or mouthful; as, a *sip* of tea.

si-phon (sī′fun), *n.* **1,** a pipe or tube bent like an inverted U, with one leg longer than the other, used for drawing off liquids from a higher to a lower level by means of air pressure; **2,** a bottle for carbonated water, fitted with a siphon, through which the water is forced by pressure of gas in the bottle:—*v.t.* **1,** to draw off by such a tube; **2,** to divert, redirect, or draw off gradually, esp. money; as to *siphon* funds illegally from the organization.

sir (sûr), *n.* **1,** a title or term of respect in addressing a man, used in place of the man's name, esp. an elder or a superior; **2,** (*Sir*), a title used for a man who has been knighted; as, *Sir* Paul McCartney.

sire (sīr), *n.* among animals, the male parent:—*v.t.* [sired, siring], to be or become the father of: used esp. of animals; as the lion *sired* four litters.

si-ren (sī′ren), *n.* **1,** a device that produces a shrill sound as a signal or warning; as, a *siren* on an ambulance, police car, fire truck; also, the sound produced; **2,** (often *Siren*), in *Greek mythology*, one of the sea nymphs who captivated sailors by her sweet singing; **3,** an alluring or captivating woman; a temptress; **4,** someone who sings beautifully:—*adj.* **1,** pertaining to, or like, a siren; **2,** bewitching; alluring; tempting.

sir-loin (sûr′loin′), *n.* a choice cut of beef, taken from the upper part of the loin.

sis-sy (sis′i), *n. Colloq.* an effeminate, timid, or cowardly person.

sis-ter (sis′tẽr), *n.* **1,** a woman or girl who has the same father and mother as another person; **2,** a female member of a group or club; **3,** a woman of the same religious society, order, or community as others; a nun.—*adj.* **sis′ter-ly.**

sis-ter-hood (sis′tẽr-hood′), *n.* **1,** the relationship between sisters; **2,** a number of women united by a common interest, as a religious society, club, or organization.

sis-ter–in–law (sis′tẽr–in–lô′), *n.* [*pl.* sisters-in-law], **1,** a husband's or wife's sister; **2,** a brother's wife.

sit (sit), *v.i.* [sat (sat), sit-ting], **1,** to rest with the weight of the body on the lower back and bottom; occupy a seat; as, to *sit* on a bench; to *sit* on the porch; **2,** to perch; as, the birds *sit* in the tree; **3,** to have place or position; be situated; as, the box *sits* on the floor; **4,** to fit; suit; as, the dress *sits* well; **5,** to press or weigh, as sorrow on the mind; **6,** to occupy a seat officially; be a member of a council or assembly; as, to *sit* in Parliament; **7,** to meet or hold a session, as a court; **8,** to cover eggs to be hatched, as does a fowl; **9,** to pose; as, to *sit* for a portrait:—*v.t.* **1,** to place or keep someone or something on a seat; as, to *sit* a child on a chair; **2,** to seat (oneself).—*n.* **sit′ter.**

sit–down (sit′–doun′), *adj.* **1,** relating to or of a labour dispute or other protest in which demonstrators occupy or obstruct entrance to something by sitting down; as, a *sit-down* protest; **2,** of a meal, served at a table; as, a *sit-down* dinner:—*n.* **1,** a protest or labour dispute involving this activity; **2,** a period of sitting; **3,** something done while seated; as, the opponents agreed to a *sit-down* to negotiate terms.

site (sīt), *n.* **1,** position or place; as, the *site* of a battle; **2,** a plot of land suitable for a building.

sit-ting (sit′ting), *adj.* **1,** resting on the haunches; seated; as, a *sitting* figure; **2,** pertaining to, or used for sitting; as, a *sitting* room:—*n.* **1,** the position or act of being seated; **2,** a session or meeting; **3,** the time during which one sits; as, a long *sitting;* **4,** a set of eggs for hatching.

sitting duck, a person or thing that is an easy target; a defenceless victim; as, she left herself a *sitting duck* in the contest.

sit-u-at-ed (sit′ū-āt′id), *adj.* having a position; located; placed.

sit-u-a-tion (sit′ū-ā′shun), *n.* **1,** position; location; as, the *situation* of a hospital; **2,** a combination of circumstances; as, a ludicrous *situation;* **3,** a position of employment; as, a *situation* as nurse.

sit–up (sit′–up′), *n.* a calisthenic exercise to condition the abdomen by raising the torso from the ground while lying flat.

six (siks), *adj.* composed of one more than five:—*n.* **1,** the number consisting of five plus one; **2,** a sign representing six units, as 6 or VI.

six-er (siks′ėr), *n.* the leader of one of the sixes, or groups of six, of Cub Scouts or Brownies.

Six Na-tions, the Iroquois Confederacy, formed in 1722, consisting of the Cayuga, Mohawk, Oneida, Onondaga, Seneca, and Tuscarora.

six-pence (siks′pens), *n.* formerly, a small British silver coin, of the value of six English pence, or about seven cents.

six-teen (siks′tēn′), *adj.* composed of ten more than six:—*n.* **1,** the sum of fifteen plus one; **2,** a sign representing sixteen units, as 16 or XVI.

six-teenth (siks′tēnth′), *adj.* next after the fifteenth: the ordinal of *sixteen:*—*n.* one of the 16 equal parts of anything.

sixth (siksth), *adj.* next after the fifth: the ordinal of *six:*—*n.* one of the six equal parts of anything.

sixth sense, intuition; keen perception or insight; as, she had a *sixth sense* about people.

six-ti-eth (siks′ti-eth), *adj.* next after the fifty-ninth: the ordinal of sixty:—*n.* one of the 60 equal parts of anything.

six-ty (siks′ti), *adj.* composed of one more than 59:—*n.* [*pl.* sixties], **1,** the number consisting of 59 plus one; **2,** a sign representing 60 units, as 60 or LX.

siz-a-ble or **size-a-ble** (sīz′ȧ-bl), *adj.* of considerable bulk; quite large; as, a *sizable* income.—*adv.* **siz′a-bly.**

[1]**size** (sīz), *n.* **1,** dimensions; bigness; as, to measure the *size* of a room; a building of great *size;* **2,** a measure showing how large something is; as, a medium *size;* a *size* four shoe:—*v.t.* [sized, siz-ing], **1,** to arrange in order of bulk, height, volume, or extent; **2,** *Colloq.* to form a conclusion, judgment, or opinion about; as, to *size* up a situation.

[2]**size** (sīz), *n.* any of various thin, sticky washes, used by painters, papermakers, etc., for glazing and stiffening the surface of various materials:—*v.t.* [sized, siz-ing], to prepare, stiffen, or cover with thin glue.—*n.* **siz′ing.**

siz-zle (siz′l), *v.i.* [siz-zled, siz-zling], to make a hissing or crackling sound, as in frying:—*n.* a hissing or crackling sound; as, the *sizzle* of the campfire.

ska (skä), *n.* a popular form of music that originated in Jamaica in the 1950s, which is generally considered a forerunner of reggae.

[1]**skate** (skāt), *n.* a broad, flat-bodied fish with a long, very narrow tail.

[2]**skate** (skāt), *n.* **1,** a shoe or boot with a metal runner attached to the bottom, used for gliding rapidly over ice; also called an *ice skate;* **2,** a shoe or boot with small wheels mounted on the bottom, used for moving over hard surfaces, such as streets and sidewalks; also called *roller skate* or *inline skate:*—*v.i.* [skat-ed, skat-ing], to move or glide along on skates.—*n.* **skat′er.**

skate-board (skāt′bōrd), *n.* a low, flat board that has wheels mounted on the bottom, used for riding. The rider usually balances in a standing position, while pushing off the ground with one foot from time to time:—*v.i.* to ride on a skateboard.—*n.* **skate′boar′der; skate′board′ ing.**

skating rink, **1,** an ice surface reserved for skating; **2,** the building housing that area; **3,** a surface or area, such as a smooth floor, used for roller or inline skating.

ske-dad-dle (ski-dad′l), *v.i. Colloq.* to run away in haste; scamper.

skeet (skēt), *n.* a kind of shooting sport popular since 1925: the shooter, from eight different angles, shoots in succession 25 clay targets.

skein (skān), *n.* **1,** a quantity of thread, yarn, etc., coiled together; **2,** something that is twisted and coiled as a skein; **3,** flying wild geese, etc.

skel-e-ton (skel′i-tun), *n.* **1,** the bony framework that supports the body of a person or animal; **2,** the supporting framework of anything, as of a building; as, the *skeleton* of the house.—*adj.* **skel′e-tal.**

skep-tic (skep′tik), *n.* **1,** a person of doubting mind; **2,** one who doubts the truth of any fact or theory, and questions the possibility of human knowledge of anything; **3,** one who doubts the truth of a religious belief, as Christianity. Also spelled **scep′tic.**—*adj.* **skep′ti-cal.**—*adv.* **skep′ti-cal-ly.**—*n.* **skep′ti-cism.**

sketch (skech), *n.* **1,** a simple, quickly made drawing; as, a crayon *sketch;* **2,** an outline; a rough draft or preliminary study; as, a *sketch* for a story; **3,** a short comedic segment in a show or program; **4,** a short and simple piece of literature:—*v.t.* to make an outline or sketch of; as, to *sketch* plans; to *sketch* a flower:—*v.i.* to make a sketch.—*n.* **sketch′er.**

sketch-y (skech′i), *adj.* [sketch-i-er, sketch-i-est], of the nature of a sketch; given in outline only; incomplete; as a *sketchy* description.—*adv.* **sketch′i-ly.**

skew (skū), *v.t.* **1,** to distort; to make biased, inaccurate, or unfair; as, to *skew* something in favour of the elites; **2,** to make crooked or place at an angle:—*v.i.* **1,** to twist or move obliquely; **2,** to look sideways:—*n.* **1,** a slant or slope; **2,** nonsymmetrical statistical distribution.—*adj.* **skewed** (as, *skewed* information).—*n.* **skew′ness.**

skew-er (skū′ėr), *n.* a pin of wood or metal for holding meat or vegetables in shape while cooking:—*v.t.* to fasten with, or as with, a skewer.

ski (skē; shē), *n.* [*pl.* ski or skis (skēz; shēz)], one of a pair of long, narrow pieces of wood, metal, or other material, to be fastened one on each foot for sliding or travelling over snow or water:—*v.i.* [skied (skēd; shēd), skiing], to slide on skis.—*n.* **ski′er; ski′ing; ski′ jump′; ski′ lift′.**

skid (skid), *n.* **1,** a device used on the wheel of a vehicle to check its motion; **2,** one of a pair or set of logs, rails, etc., used to form a track down which heavy objects roll or slide; **3,** a piece of timber on which a boat rests during the process of building or repair; **4,** a runner attached under an airplane to aid in landing; **5,** the act of sliding or slipping sideways; as, a *skid* on the ice:—*v.t.* [skid-ded, skid-ding], **1,** to cause to move on skids; **2,** to protect or check with a drag or skid:—*v.i.* to slip sideways on the road: said of an automobile.

skid row, *Colloq.* **1,** a run-down area of town inhabited by vagrants, the homeless, etc.; **2,** formerly, a logging road.

skiff (skif), *n.* a small, light boat that can be rowed.

skill (skil), *n.* knowledge of any art or science, with ability to use it; dexterity; as, *skill* in surgery.

skilled (skild), *adj.* **1,** expert; as, *skilled* in painting; **2,** having or requiring special training; as, *skilled* labour.

skil-let (skil′it), *n.* **1,** a shallow, metal vessel with a handle, used for frying; a frying pan; **2,** a long-handled saucepan.

skill-ful or **skil-ful** (skil′fool), *adj.* **1,** having expert training; clever; as, a *skillful* worker; **2,** showing expertise; as, *skillful* work.—*adv.* **skill′ful-ly.**

skim (skim), *v.t.* [skimmed, skim-ming], **1,** to remove floating substances from the top of; as, to *skim* milk; **2,** to take from the surface of a liquid, with a ladle or spoon; as, to *skim* cream from milk; **3,** to touch the surface of, lightly; as, the boat *skims* the water; **4,** to read hurriedly:—*v.i.* **1,** to pass lightly over a surface; also, to glide, as through the air; **2,** to read without thoroughness; as, to *skim* through a book:—**skim milk**, milk left after removal of cream.—*n.* **skim′mer.**

skimp (skimp), *v.t.* to be sparing with; as, to *skimp* material in making a dress:—*v.i.* to save; economize; be miserly; as, to *skimp* on ingredients in a recipe.—*adj.* **skimp′y.**

skin (skin), *n.* **1,** in humans and other animals, the outer covering of the body; **2,** the pelt or hide of an animal after it is removed from the body; **3,** rind; as, an orange or potato *skin*; **4,** a vessel made of an animal's skin, used to hold liquids; **5,** anything like a skin, as the outside covering of an airship:—*v.t.* [skinned, skin-ning], **1,** to strip the skin from; as, to *skin* a chicken before baking; **2,** to injure by scraping or removing the skin from; as, to *skin* an elbow while skateboarding; **3,** *Slang* to get the better of; cheat:—*v.i.* to become covered over with skin, as a wound.—*n.* **skin′ner.**

skin–deep (skin′–dēp′), *adj.* **1,** superficial or shallow; as, *skin-deep* beauty; *skin-deep* kindness; **2,** only as deep as the skin; as, a *skin-deep* cut.

skin diving, 1, a sport in which the diver swims underwater for long periods of time using a mask, flippers, and a snorkel, but without scuba equipment and diving suit; **2,** any underwater swimming activity, with or without scuba and other equipment.—*v.i.* **skin′–dive′** [skin–dived or skin–dove, skin–div-ing].—*adj.* **skin′–div′ ing.**—*n.* **skin′ div′er.**

skin-flint (skin′flint′), *n.* a miser; a stingy or avaricious person.

skinhead (skin′hed′), *n. Slang* **1,** a member of a group of youths, usually white, with close-cropped hair and often supporting white-supremacist or neo-Nazi causes; **2,** someone with a shaved head; a bald person.

skin-ny (skin′i), *adj.* [skin-ni-er, skinn-i-est], lean; without much flesh; very thin, especially in an unhealthy or unattractive way.—*n. Slang* inside information; the facts; gossip; as, to get the *skinny* on the new teacher.

skip (skip), *v.t.* [skipped, skip-ping], **1,** to jump lightly over; as, to *skip* rope; **2,** to pass over or omit; as, he *skipped* three pages in reading; to *skip* a meal; **3,** to bounce something across a surface; as, to *skip* stones across the lake:—*v.i.* **1,** to leap or bound lightly; move with light trips and hops; **2,** to pass along rapidly; hurry along, omitting portions, as in reading; **3,** bounce or glide across a surface; as, the schooner *skipped* along the ocean:—*n.* **1,** a light leap; **2,** an omission; a passing over.

skip-per (skip′ėr), *n.* the master of a small trading or fishing vessel; the master or captain of any ship or boat.

skirl (skirl), *n.* a shrill, piercing sound, esp. that of the bagpipe:—*v.i.* to play the bagpipes.

skir-mish (skûr′mish), *n.* **1,** a brisk fight or contest between two small groups or parties of soldiers during a war; as, a *skirmish* between two soccer teams; **2,** any slight struggle or encounter:—*v.i.* to engage in a skirmish.

skirt (skûrt), *n.* **1,** the lower and loose part of a coat, dress, or other garment; **2,** an outer garment for women and girls, covering the body below the waist; **3,** an edge or border:—*v.t.* **1,** to border; run or pass along the edge of; as, we *skirted* the town; **2,** to avoid something; as the politician *skirted* the serious issues.

skit (skit), *n.* **1,** a short comic sketch or play, as a revue; **2,** a short satire or humorous piece of writing.

skit-tish (skit′ish), *adj.* **1,** shy, excitable; nervous; easily frightened; as, a *skittish* horse; **2,** lively; high-spirited; as, a *skittish* fancy; **3,** uncertain; fickle.

skul-dug-ger-y (skul-dug′ėr-i), *n. Colloq.* mean trickery; dishonesty; craftiness: often humorous.

skulk (skulk), *v.i.* to hide or get out of the way in a sneaking or underhanded manner.—*n.* **skulk′er.**

skull (skul), *n.* in humans and other animals with a backbone, the skeleton or framework of the head.

skunk (skungk), *n.* **1,** a small North American mammal, usually black with white stripes, which gives forth a liquid of very offensive odour when frightened or attacked; **2,** *Colloq.* a contemptible person.—*adj.* **skun′ky.**

sky (skī), *n.* [*pl.* skies], **1,** the heavens or upper atmosphere above the earth; the region of the clouds and winds; **2,** heaven.—*adj.* and *adv.* **sky′ward.**

sky-div-ing (skī′dīv′ing), *n.* a type of parachute jumping in which the jumper falls through the air for a long distance before opening the parachute.—*v.i.* **sky′dive′** [sky-dived, sky-div-ing].—*n.* **sky′di′ver.**

sky-light (skī′līt′), *n.* a window in a roof or in the ceiling of a room that lets in outside light.

sky-line (skī′līn′), *n.* **1,** the line where land and sky, or water and sky, seem to meet; the horizon; **2,** the outline of mountains, trees, buildings, etc., against the sky; as, a city *skyline.*

sky-rock-et (skī′rok′it), *v.i.* **1,** to rise rapidly, as prices, etc.; **2,** succeed or become famous quickly; as, the Beatles *skyrocketed* to fame during the 1960s:—*n.* a firework that goes off high in the sky and showers coloured sparks and lights.

sky-scrap-er (skī′skrāp′ėr), *n.* a very tall building.

sky-way (skī′wā′), *n.* **1,** an airlane or air-travel route; **2,** an elevated highway, as over a railroad, harbour, or waterway; as, the Burlington *Skyway* bridge; **3,** an overhead walkway between two building, which is enclosed.

slab (slab), *n.* a thick piece of anything, as of marble, wood, or stone; also, a thick slice, as of bread or cheese.

slack (slak), *adj.* **1,** slow; lacking in vigour or energy; as, a *slack pace*; **2,** sluggish, as a backwater; **3,** relaxed; not tight; as, a *slack* wire; **4,** lazy; careless; as, a *slack* housekeeper; **5,** inactive; slow; as, business is *slack*:—*n.* **1,** that part of a wire, rope, etc., which is not stretched taut; **2,** a dull period, as in business; **3, slacks,** pants or trousers, especially when worn as casual wear:—*v.t.* **1,** to loosen or slacken (a rope); **2,** to slake (lime):—*v.i.* to be or become sluggish or slack; slacken.

slack-en (slak′en), *v.i.* **1,** to become less firm, tense, or rigid; **2,** to let up; become slower; as, the firewood business *slackens* in warm weather:—*v.t.* **1,** to make slower; relax; as, to *slacken* speed or efforts; **2,** to loosen; as, do not *slacken* the rope.

slack-er (slak′ėr), *n.* **1,** a person who shirks his work or his duty; **2,** an apathetic person.

slag (slag), *n.* **1,** the dross or dregs of melted metal; **2,** lava from a volcano:—*v.t.* to criticize or insult; as, the strikers were *slagging* the management.

slain (slān), *p.p.* of *slay.*

slake (slāk), *v.t.* [slaked, slak-ing], **1,** to quench; relieve; appease; as, to *slake* one's thirst; **2,** to combine chemically with water; as, to *slake* lime:—*v.t.* to be chemically mixed with water.

sla-lom (slä′lōm), *n.* **1,** a downhill snow skiing race over a zigzag course marked out by flags, posts, etc.; **2,** a similar race in water skiing, skateboarding, etc.; **3,** in water skiing, using one ski.

SLALOM

slam (slam), *v.t.* [slammed, slam-ming], **1,** to shut violently and noisily; **2,** to put, or throw, with force and loud noise; as, to *slam* down a book; **3,** to criticize or put down:—*v.i.* to bang; as, the door *slams*:—*n.* **1,** a blow; a bang; **2,** the act of shutting noisily; **3,** a criticism or insult.

slan-der (slan′dėr), *n.* the utterance of false reports about a person in order to defame or injure his or her reputation; also, the reports themselves:—*v.t.* to injure the reputation of (a person) by spreading false reports.—*n.* **slan′der-er.**—*adj.* **slan′der-ous.**

slang (slang), *n.* **1,** informal language or popular speech using new or made-up words and expressions that are humorous, exaggerated, impolite, etc., and that are generally not used in formal or written language; **2,** the language or jargon of a particular geographic area, group, or profession; as, business *slang.—adj.* **slang′y.**

slant (slant), *n.* **1,** an inclined plane; a slope; as, the *slant* of a roof; **2,** a point of view; attitude; as, he has a modern *slant* on the problem:—*v.t.* **1,** to give a sloping direction to; as, *slant* your ruler a little more; **2,** to present facts or ideas so that they favour one side or point of view; as, to *slant* the facts to make the movie more interesting:—*v.i.* to slope; as, tilt the easel so that it *slants* a bit:—*adj.* sloping.—*adj.* **slant′ing.**—*adv.* **slant′ing-ly.**

slap (slap), *n.* **1,** a blow with the open hand or something flat; **2,** an insult; a repulse:—*v.t.* [slapped, slap-ping], **1,** to strike with the open hand; **2,** to lay down with, or as with, a bang; as, to *slap* the report on the table.

slap-dash (slap′dash′), *adv. Colloq.* in a boldly careless manner; recklessly:—*adj.* dashing; impetuous; hasty: as, a *slapdash* style.

slap–hap-py (slap′–hap′i), *adj. Slang* **1,** as though dazed or bewildered; **2,** carefree; lighthearted; reckless; foolish.

slap-shot (slap′shot), *n.* in *hockey*, a fast, hard shot made with a quick stroke.

slap-stick (slap′stik′), *n.* physical comedy that depends upon farce and horseplay, etc.:—*adj.* crudely and noisily humorous; as, *slapstick* comedy.

slash (slash), *v.t.* **1,** to cut by striking violently and aimlessly with a knife or other sharp object; **2,** reduce sharply; as, to *slash* prices; **3,** in *hockey*, to swing at a player with a hockey stick:—*v.i.* to strike out violently and at random:—*n.* **1,** a long cut or gash; **2,** the act or fact of slashing; **3,** an oblique punctuation mark [/] that shows choice; **4,** a low, swampy area covered with brush.—*n.* **slash′er; slash′ing; slash′er mov′ie.**

slat (slat), *n.* a thin, narrow strip of wood, metal, or other such material.

slate (slāt), *n.* **1,** a kind of fine-grained rock that splits into thin layers; **2,** the dark bluish-grey colour of this rock; **3,** a thin plate of this rock prepared for use, as for roof covering, blackboards, garden tiles, etc.; **4,** a list of proposed candidates for nomination or election; **5,** *Colloq.* a schedule, list, or agenda:—*v.t.* [slat-ed, slat-ing], **1,** to cover with slate; **2,** to register or suggest (a person) for an office or an appointment.—*adj.* **slat′y.**

slather (sla*th*′ėr), *v.t. Colloq.* to spread thickly or lavishly; as, to *slather* butter on toast.

slaugh-ter (slô′tėr), *n.* **1,** the act of killing; great and wanton destruction of life; **2,** the killing of animals for food:—*v.t.* **1,** to kill with violence; **2,** to kill (animals) for food; **3,** *Colloq.* to defeat very badly; as, to *slaughter* a rival baseball team.—*n.* **slaugh′ter-er.**—*n.* **slaugh′ter-house′** (a place where animals are killed for food).

slave (slāv), *n.* **1,** a person owned by another and who can be sold like a piece of property; a bondsman; **2,** one who works like a slave; a drudge; **3,** a person who is controlled by a harmful habit or vice; as, a *slave* to junk food:—*adj.* pertaining to slaves; as, *slave* labour:—*v.i.* [slaved, slav-ing], to work like a slave; toil.—*adj.* **slav′ish.**—*n.* **slav′ish-ness; slav′er; slav′er-y.**

slave driver, 1, a hard taskmaster; an employer or supervisor who is overly demanding and inflexible; **2,** an overseer of slaves.

slave labour, 1, extremely difficult, esp. forced labour for little or no compensation; **2,** work done by slaves.

Sla-vey (slā′vi), *n.* [*pl.* Slavey or Slaveys], **1,** an Aboriginal people of northwestern Canada. Their name, *Awokanak*, means "slaves" from the Cree, who often enslaved them; **2,** the Athapaskan language of these people.

slaw (slô), *n.* sliced cabbage mixed with a dressing, served as a relish or salad.

slay (slā), *v.t.* [*p.t.* slew (slo͞o), *p.p.* slain (slān), *p.pr.* slay-ing], to kill or put to death by violence—*n.* **slay′er.**

slea-zy (slē′zi), *adj.* **1,** slippery; unprincipled; two-faced; revolting; as, *sleazy* conduct; a *sleazy* person; **2,** of *fabrics*, thin; flimsy; shoddy; inferior quality; as *sleazy* silk, rayon, muslin, etc.—*n.* **slea′zi-ness; sleaze.**

sled (sled), *n.* a vehicle on runners, used for coasting, or for carrying loads, on snow or ice:—*v.i.* and *v.t.* [sled-ded, sled-ding], to travel or carry by sled.—*n.* **sled′ding; sled′der.**

sledge (slej), *n.* a vehicle on runners for carrying heavy loads over snow or ice; a strong and heavy sled:—*v.i.* and *v.t.* [sledged, sledg-ing], to travel or carry on a sledge.

sledge-ham-mer (slej′ham′ėr), *n.* a large, heavy hammer with a long handle, used to drive large posts into the ground or break up heavy surfaces such as concrete and rocks; also used by blacksmiths;—*adj.* something clumsy or severe; as, *sledgehammer* methods:—*v.t.* and *v.i.* to strike as or with a sledgehammer.

sleek (slēk), *adj.* **1,** smooth; glossy; as, a *sleek* satin jacket; **2,** smooth or flattering in speech or manner; suave; as, a *sleek* salesperson; **3,** neat, trim, smooth, stylish, or elegant; as, a *sleek* car or restaurant.—*n.* **sleek′ness.**—*adv.* **sleek′ly.**

sleep (slēp), *n.* **1,** the natural condition for humans and animals of rest and not being awake, during which the body and mind regain strength and energy; slumber; **2,** any condition like sleep; as, death is called eternal *sleep*:—*v.i.* [slept (slept), sleep-ing], **1,** to be asleep; slumber; **2,** to be motionless; remain inactive:—*v.t.* **1,** to rest in (sleep); as, he *slept* a sound sleep; **2,** to spend, waste, or rid oneself of, by sleeping; as, he *slept* away half the morning; he *slept* off his headache; **3,** to provide with a place to sleep; as, the cottage *sleeps* eight.

sleep-er (slēp′ėr), *n.* **1,** one who sleeps; hence, one who likes to sleep; **2,** a horizontal beam, on or near the ground level, that serves as support for some structure above, as railway ties for rails; **3,** a sleeping car or berth in a train, truck, etc.; **4,** one-piece pyjamas for small children, usually with feet; **5,** something that initially is considered unpromising or unremarkable and is introduced quietly, but which becomes very popular or successful; as a *sleeper* movie breaking box office records.

sleep-ing bag (slēp′ing bag), *n.* a thickly padded, warm bag with a zipper in which a person may sleep outdoors or in a tent.

sleeping sickness, an infectious, tropical African disease transmitted by the tsetse fly, resulting in fever, lethargy, and often death.

sleep-less (slēp′lis), *adj.* going without sleep; not sleeping; as, to be *sleepless* the night before the exam.—*n.* **sleep′less-ness.**

sleep-walk-er (slēp′wô′kėr), *n.* someone who walks while asleep; a somnambulist.—*v.i.* **sleep′walk′.**—*n.* **sleep′walk′ing.**

sleep-y (slēp′i), *adj.* [sleep-i-er, sleep-i-est], **1,** inclined to, or ready for, slumber; drowsy; **2,** producing drowsiness; as, *sleepy* weather; **3,** drowsy; inactive; as, a *sleepy* town.—*adv.* **sleep′i-ly.**—*n.* **sleep′i-ness; sleep′y-head.**

sleet (slēt), *n.* driving rain that is partly frozen or that freezes as it falls:—*v.i.* to shower frozen rain.—*adj.* **sleet′y.**

sleeve (slēv), *n.* **1,** the part of a garment that covers the arm; **2,** something, as a part of a machine, that covers or protects another part; a flat or tubular cardboard cover used to protect something, such as a record.—*adj.* **sleeve′less.**

sleigh (slā), *n.* a vehicle, equipped with runners, for use on snow or ice, usually pulled by a horse:—*v.i.* to travel by sleigh.—*n.* **sleigh′ing.**

sleight of hand (slīt), *n.* skill or dexterity in using the hands to deceive or confuse onlookers, as in magic; legerdemain. Also, **sleight-of-hand.**

slen-der (slen′dėr), *adj.* **1,** narrow in proportion to length or height, esp. in a graceful and attractive way; slim; **2,** scanty; slight; scarcely sufficient; as, *slender* opportunities; to win by a *slender* margin.

slept (slept), *p.t.* of *sleep.*

sleuth (slo͞oth), *n.* a detective; investigator:—*v.t.* and *v.i.* to act as a detective; to investigate.

[1]**slew** (slo͞o), *p.t.* of *slay.*

[2]**slew** (slo͞o), *n.* a twist; turn:—*v.t.* and *v.i.* to swing around, yaw, or pivot on a fixed point; as, the sled *slewed* (*slued*) about on the ice.

[3]**slew** (slo͞o), *n.* a large amount of something; as, a *slew* of people at the rock concert.

slice (slīs), *n.* a thin, broad piece cut from something; as, a *slice* of bread:—*v.t.* [sliced, slic-ing], **1,** to cut into thin pieces or layers; as, to *slice* the entire cake; also, to cut into; as, *slice* open the melon; **2,** to cut (a layer) from something; as, to *slice* off a piece of meat:—*v.i.* to cut or move like a knife; as, the arrow *sliced* through the air.—*n.* **slic′er.**

slick (slik), *adj.* **1,** smooth; sleek; as, *slick* hair; slippery, as *slick* roads; **2,** smooth, clever, or skillful in speech and manners; as a *slick* presentation; **3,** *Slang*: **a,** tricky; sly; insincere; **b,** first-rate; as, a *slick* time:—*v.t.* to make smooth or glossy, as hair:—*n. Slang* **1,** a magazine printed on paper of glossy finish: opposite of *pulp*; **2,** a smooth area or patch on the surface of water; as, an oil *slick.*

slick-er (slik′ėr), *n.* a loose waterproof coat; raincoat.

slide (slīd), *v.i.* [*p.t.* slid (slid), *p.p.* slid or slid-den (slid′n), *p.pr.* slid-ing], **1,** to move smoothly over a surface, as over ice; glide; **2,** to move quietly or secretly; slip; as, he *slid* into a seat; **3,** to move or pass gradually or without being noticed; as, time *slides* by:—**to let slide,** to let (something) take care of itself; as, I'll *let* my lessons *slide* until tomorrow:—*v.t.* **1,** to push along; cause to slip into place; as, they *slid* the canoe into the water; **2,** to put quietly; slip; as, he *slid* his left hand into his pocket:—*n.* **1,** the act of sliding; **2,** a surface of snow or ice for sliding; **3,** any smooth slope or incline; **4,** a mass of earth, rock, or snow that slides down a mountain; **5,** a thin glass plate upon which is a picture to be projected on a screen; also, a plate of glass upon which is mounted a specimen for examination under a microscope; **6,** that part of a device upon which anything slides; also, the part that slides; **7,** a piece of playground equipment with a smooth, slanting surface to slide down.—*n.* **sli′der; slide′ gui-tar′; slide′ pro-jec′tor.**

slight (slīt), *adj.* **1,** slender; thin; frail; not strong; as, a *slight* figure; **2,** small in amount or degree; as, a *slight* trace of gas; **3,** not important; trivial; as, a *slight* difference in colour:—*v.t.* **1,** to treat with indifference; to snub; as, she *slighted* her guests; **2,** to neglect or perform carelessly; as, she was so engrossed in her music that she *slighted* her studies:—*n.* an act of discourtesy; a snub.—*n.* **slight′ness.**—*adv.* **slight′ly.**

slim (slim), *adj.* [slim-mer, slim-mest], **1,** slender; as, a *slim* figure; **2,** scant; slight; insufficient; as, a *slim* excuse; *slim* chance:—*v.t.* and *v.i.* [slimmed, slim-ming], to decrease in size; to become slender.

slime (slīm), *n.* **1,** soft, sticky mud; any sticky, dirty substance; **2,** a sticky external secretion of certain animals, such as fishes and snails, and of certain plants.—*adj.* **slim′y.**

sling (sling), *n.* **1,** a hand-held implement for hurling a missile, as a stone; **2,** the act of hurling or flinging; a throw; **3,** any of various devices for hoisting or lowering heavy articles, or for suspending a pack, etc., from the shoulder; **4,** a supporting bandage, as for a wounded arm:—*v.t.* [slung (slung), sling-ing], **1,** to hurl with, or as with, a sling; **2,** to hang (a hammock) so that it will swing or throw loosely; as, to *sling* a jacket over his shoulder; **3,** to place or suspend in a device for hoisting or lowering.

sling-shot (sling′shot′), *n.* a forked wooden or metal stick with a rubber band attached, for shooting small stones.

slink (slingk), *v.i.* [slunk (slungk) or slinked, slink-ing], to go furtively; sneak or steal along quietly.

slip (slip), *v.i.* [slipped, slip-ping], **1,** to glide or slide smoothly; as, the drawers *slip* in and out easily; **2,** to miss one's foothold; lose one's balance; **3,** to move or pass without being seen; as, she *slipped* into the room; **4,** to move suddenly out of place; as, the knife *slipped;* **5,** to escape; as, the address has *slipped* from my mind:—*v.t.* **1,** to put on or off with ease; as, to *slip* on a ring; *slip* off a coat; **2,** to cause to slide; as, to *slip* a rod into place; **3,** to lose or allow to escape; as, to *slip* a stitch; to cause to slide off; as, the horse *slips* his bridle; **4,** to escape from; as, his name has *slipped* my mind; **5,** to cut a small shoot from, in order to grow a new plant; as, to *slip* a rosebush:—*n.* **1,** the act of sliding or missing one's foothold; also, an escaping or eluding; as, to give someone the *slip;* **2,** a fault; an error; as, a *slip* in grammar; **3,** a cutting from a plant; **4,** a space between wharves for vessels; a dock; **5,** something that may be put on or off with ease, as a kind of undergarment, a pillowcase, etc.; **6,** a long narrow piece of something; a strip of paper; as, fill out the *slip* with your information; **7,** a slim person; as, a *slip* of a girl.

slip-cover (slip′kuv′ėr), *n.* **1,** a removable, fitted cover for a cushion or piece of furniture; **2,** a book jacket or dust cover.

slip-knot (slip′not′), *n.* a knot that slips along the cord around which it is formed.

slip–on (slip′–on′) *n.* and *adj.* clothes that can be put on or taken off easily; as, *slip-on* shoes.

slip-per (slip′ėr), *n.* a low, comfortable, lightweight shoe or sandal, usually intended for indoor wear; as, house *slippers*; ballet *slippers*.

slip-per-y (slip′ėr-i) *adj.* [slipper-i-er, slipper-i-est], **1,** having a surface so smooth or slimy as to yield no firm hold or footing; as, a *slippery* pavement; **2,** of persons, shifty; not trustworthy.—*n.* **slip′per-i-ness.**

slip-shod (ship′shod′), *adj.* **1,** wearing shoes down at the heel; **2,** hence, slovenly; careless; shabby.

slip-stream (slip′strēm′), *n.* **1,** the current of air or water behind a moving object such as a ship, airplane, or automobile; **2,** the pocket of reduced air pressure behind a moving vehicle that creates forward suction; **3,** something that propels one forward:—*v.i.* to drive in the slipstream of the vehicle ahead, as in a race.

slip–up (slip′–up′), *n. Colloq.* a mistake; error; as, minor *slip-ups* in grammar.

slit (slit), *v.t.* [slit, slit-ting], **1,** to cut or tear lengthwise or into long strips; as, to *slit* cloth for bandages; **2,** to cut or make a lengthwise opening in; as, to *slit* a skirt:—*n.* **1,** a long cut or tear; **2,** a narrow opening.

slith-er (shi*th*′ėr), *v.i.* **1,** to slip or slide, esp. on a loose or gravelly slope, with some noise or friction; **2,** to move in a twisting motion, esp. close to the ground; as, the snake *slithered* through the grass; **3,** to sneak; as, to *slither* through a crowd unnoticed.

sliv-er (sliv′ėr), *n.* **1,** a long, thin, sharp-pointed piece, as of wood, etc.; a splinter; as, *slivers* of glass; **2,** a scant amount; as, a *sliver* of hope:—*v.t.* and *v.i.* to break off or split into long, thin pieces.

slob (slob), *n.* **1,** soft or mushy ice or snow, esp. in Newfoundland and the sealing fields of the Arctic; **2,** *Slang* a clumsy, untidy, or slovenly person.—*adj.* **slob′bish.**

slob-ber (slob′ėr), *v.i.* **1,** to let saliva dribble from the mouth; drool; **2,** to show or express feeling gushingly; as, to *slobber* over the movie celebrity:—*v.t.* to wet by letting liquid run from the mouth; as, to *slobber* a dress; to spill so as to soil something; as, to *slobber* milk over a dress.—*adj.* **slob′ber-y.**

slog (slog), *v.i. Colloq.* **1,** to plod one's way heavily and with effort; toil; **2,** to hit hard; slug (a ball, opponent, etc.):—*n.* **1,** hard and persistent work; as, cataloguing the books in the library was a real *slog*; **2,** a hard blow or hit.

slo-gan (slō′gan), *n.* **1,** a war cry or rallying cry; **2,** a word or phrase used as a motto by a party or group, or as a catchword to advertise a product.

sloop (slo͞op), *n.* a one-masted sailboat with

a fore-and-aft rig, a mainsail, and a single jib.

slop (slop), *n.* **1,** water or other liquid carelessly spilled; **2,** poor, tasteless, or weak liquid food: used contemptuously; **3,** (often *slops*): **a,** refuse or waste water from kitchen or bedrooms; **b,** refuse or garbage used as food for swine:—*v.t.* [slopped, slopping], **1,** to soil by letting liquid fall upon; as, to *slop* the floor; **2,** to give leftover food or wet garbage to farm animals, esp. to pigs; as, to *slop* the pigs:—*v.i.* to be spilled; also, to overflow.

slope (slōp), *n.* **1,** a slanting line; also, a tilted surface; as, a ski *slope*; **2,** the degree of such a slant or tilt; as, a steep *slope*; **3,** any stretch of descending ground; esp. the land that descends toward the ocean; as, the Pacific *slope*:—*v.i.* and *v.t.* [sloped, slop-ing], to incline; slant; as, the ground *slopes*; to *slope* a roof.

slop-py (slop′i), *adj.* **1,** very wet; wet and dirty; as, clothes *sloppy* with mud; **2,** not neatly done or made; careless; messy; as, *sloppy* handwriting.—*adv.* **slop′pi-ly.**—*n.* **slop′piness.**

slosh (slosh), *v.i.* to splash about or flounder in slush, mire, etc.; as, to *slosh* through a puddle:—*v.t.* to stir in a fluid; as, to *slosh* a mop through a pail; to splash liquid; as, to *slosh* soup all over the counter.

slot (slot), *n.* **1,** a narrow groove or depression into which something fits or moves snugly; **2,** a narrow opening through which something can be slipped or inserted; as, a mail *slot* in a door; a *slot* for a coin in the vending machine; a *slot* in a computer; **3,** a place or position; as, third *slot* in the race:—**slot machine,** a coin-operated gambling machine; a one-armed bandit:—*v.t.* [slot-ted, slot-ting], to cut a slot or slots in.—*adj.* **slot′ted.**

sloth (slōth; slôth), *n.* **1,** laziness; indolence; a person who is lazy or not willing to work; **2,** a tree-dwelling animal of South and Central America that clings upside down to the branches: so called for its slow movements.—*adj.* **sloth′ful.**

slouch (slouch), *n.* **1,** a stooping or droop, as of the head or shoulders; **2,** an incompetent, lazy person:—*v.i.* to stand or move in a loose, ungainly manner.—*adj.* **slouch′y.**

[1]**slough** (slou; in def. 2, slo͞o), *n.* **1,** a miry place; a mud hole; **2,** (slo͞o), a swamp: also, an inlet from a river; **3,** a state of depression or gloom into which one sinks and from which it is difficult to free oneself; as, the *slough* of despair.

[2]**slough** (sluf), *n.* **1,** the cast-off skin of a snake or other animal; **2,** anything that has been or can be cast off, as dead tissue, a bad habit, etc.:—*v.i.* **1,** to come off or be shed, as the skin of a snake; **2,** to shed or cast the skin:—*v.t.* to cast off, as the skin; hence, to discard.

slov-en (sluv′n), *n.* an untidy, slipshod, or lazy person.

slov-en-ly (sluv′en-li), *adj.* [sloven-li-er, sloven-li-est], untidy in appearance; careless; not neat.—*n.* **slov′en-li-ness.**

slow (slō), *adj.* **1,** not rapid in motion; as, a *slow* march; **2,** not prompt; as, *slow* in arriving; **3,** taking a long time; as, a *slow* journey; **4,** not rash or hasty; as, *slow* to anger; **5,** behind the correct time; as, the clock is *slow*; **6,** not quick to learn or understand; **7,** tending to hinder rapid motion; as, a *slow* track; **8,** *Colloq.* dull; not lively; as, a *slow* party:—*adv.* in a manner not rapid:—*v.i.* to move with less and less speed; as, the train *slowed* down:—*v.t.* **1,** to cause to move with less speed; as, to *slow* down a car; **2,** to delay; as, heavy snow *slowed* up the traffic.—*adv.* **slow′ly.**—*n.* **slow′ness.**

slow-down (slō′doun′), *n.* a planned slowing down of production by either workers or management; the act of slowing down.

slow motion *n.* a film and video technique that shows action moving at a pace that is less than normal speed.—*adj.* **slow′-mo′tion** (as, a *slow-motion* action clip).

slow-poke (slō′pōk′), *n.* *Colloq.* a very slow-moving or lazy person.

sludge (sluj), *n.* **1,** the sediment that forms in water tanks, septic tanks, etc.; **2,** mud, ooze, slush, or mire; as, *sludge* on a riverbed; **3,** refuse from soap making, bleaching, oil refining, etc.—*adj.* **sludg′y.**

[1]**slug** (slug), *n.* **1,** an animal like a snail, except that it has no shell or only a very thin one; **2,** a piece of lead or other metal that is fired from a gun; **3,** a coin-shaped piece of metal used illegally in place of a coin in a vending machine or other coin machine.

[2]**slug** (slug), *v.t.* [slugged, slug-ging], to strike hard, esp. with the fist, as in boxing:—*n.* a hard blow, as with the fist or a club.—*n.* **slug′ger.**

slug-gish (slug′ish), *adj.* **1,** habitually lazy and idle; dull; slothful; **2,** inactive; slow; as, a *sluggish* river.—*adv.* **slug′gish-ly.**—*n.* **slug′gish-ness.**

sluice (slo͞os), *n.* **1,** an artificial channel for conducting water, having a gate, called *sluice gate,* to regulate the flow; **2,** a floodgate for controlling the flow of water; **3,** a channel through which anything flows; **4,** an inclined trough for washing gold ore, carrying down logs, etc.:—*v.t.* [sluiced, sluic-ing], **1,** to wash with water from, or as from, a sluice; as, to *sluice* gold; **2,** to draw off (water) by a channel or floodgate; **3,** to transport (logs) by such means.

slum (slum), *n.* **1,** a poor, densely populated street or district of a town or city; **2,**

slums, a neighbourhood composed of such streets:—*v.i.* [slummed, slum-ming], **1,** to visit such neighbourhoods for the purpose of study or charity, or out of curiosity; **2,** to go somewhere, do something, or associate with someone considered to be of lower social status.

slum-ber (slum′bėr), *v.i.* **1,** to sleep peacefully; **2,** to be in a state of rest or inactivity; as, his suspicions *slumbered*:—*n.* sleep.

slum-lord (slum′lôrd′), *n.* a landlord who rents substandard housing to tenants, esp. one who overcharges.

slump (slump), *v.i.* **1,** to fall or sink suddenly, as, to *slump* to the ground; **2,** to sink down heavily; slouch; as, he *slumped* in his chair; **3,** to fall or decline suddenly, as prices, stocks, business, etc.:—*n.* **1,** the act of sinking down; **2,** a sudden drop or decline; as, a *slump* in business.

slung (slung), *p.t.* and *p.p.* of *sling*.

slunk (slungk), *p.t.* and *p.p.* of *slink*.

slur (slûr), *v.t.* [slurred, slur-ring], **1,** to pass over hurriedly or briefly; as, to *slur* over an incident; **2,** to pronounce hastily or indistinctly (a sound or syllable), running together certain sounds; as, she *slurred* her words after her visit to the dentist; **3,** in *music,* to sing or sound (two or more successive tones of different pitch) without a break; also, to mark (notes that are to be so sounded) with the sign ⌢ or ⌣ :—*n.* **1,** a stain, smudge, or blot; **2,** a slight reproach or criticism, or a remark conveying such reproach; **3,** in *music,* a mark [⌢ or ⌣] connecting notes that are to be sung or played without a break; also, the notes to be so treated.

slurp (slûrp), *v.t.* to eat or drink noisily; as, to *slurp* the milkshake:—*v.i.* to make a sucking noise when eating or drinking:—*n.* **1,** a slurping sound; **2,** a mouthful.

slush (slush), *n.* **1,** partly melted snow; **2,** soft mud; **3,** silly, sentimental talk or writing; **4,** sweet, flavoured crushed ice.—*adj.* **slush′y.**

slush fund, a sum of money set aside, esp. for illegal purposes such as political bribery.

slut (slut), *n.* a woman of loose, promiscuous character; hussy; prostitute.

sly (slī), *adj.* [sly-er or sli-er, sly-est or sli-est], **1,** cunning, shrewd; working or acting secretly; underhanded; deceitful; as, a *sly* schemer; a *sly* scheme; **2,** playfully mischievous; roguish; as, a *sly* grin:—**on the sly,** in secret.—*adv.* **sly′ly** or **sli′ly.**

[1]**smack** (smak), *n.* a slight taste or flavour; tinge:—*v.i.* to convey a suggestion; as, this *smacks* of treason.

[2]**smack** (smak), *n.* **1,** a quick, sharp noise made by opening and closing the lips quickly; **2,** a loud, hearty kiss; **3,** a quick, resounding blow or slap:—*v.t.* **1,** to make a loud noise with (the lips); **2,** to strike or slap:—*v.i.* to strike or bump sharply making a loud noise; as, the door *smacked* shut.—*adj.* **smack′ing.**

[3]**smack** (smak), *adv.* straight into, directly; suddenly; exactly; as, to walk *smack* into the post; the basketball landed *smack* in the middle of the hoop.

[4]**smack** (smak), *n.* a small sailing vessel used in fishing; a fishing sloop.

smack-er (smak′ėr), *n. Slang* **1,** a loud kiss; **2,** a dollar.

small (smôl), *adj.* **1,** little in size, amount, number, degree, etc.; as, a *small* boy; a *small* school; a *small* dose; **2,** not important; insignificant; as, his opinion is of *small* value; **3,** doing business in a limited way; as, a *small* farmer; **4,** petty; not generous; narrow; as, a *small* remark:—**small fry, 1,** small or young fish; **2,** youngsters; **3,** people or things considered unimportant or petty (also called *small potatoes*).

small change, 1, coins of small denomination; **2,** something trivial or insignificant; as, the issue was *small change*.

small hours, the hours right after midnight; as, to study into the *small hours*.

small letter, a letter that is not a capital or upper-case letter; a lower-case letter; as, "R" is a capital letter, and "r" is a small letter.

small-pox (smôl′poks′), *n.* a contagious disease marked by fever and a characteristic skin eruption.

small screen, *Colloq.* television.

small talk, chitchat; gossip; casual conversation; as, to make *small talk* by the lockers.

small-time (smôl′-tīm′), *adj. Colloq.* insignificant, petty, or unimportant; as, *small-time* crooks.

smart (smärt), *v.i.* **1,** to feel a sharp stinging pain; as, my hand *smarts;* **2,** to cause a stinging sensation; as, iodine *smarts;* **3,** to suffer; have one's feelings wounded:—*n.* **1,** a quick lively pain; **2,** a pang of grief:—*adj.* **1,** causing a sharp, stinging sensation; also, severe; as, a *smart* thrashing; **2,** clever; shrewd; as, a *smart* business man; **3,** quick to learn; intelligent; bright; as, a *smart* child; of an inanimate object, guided or automated; as, a *smart* bomb or missile; **4,** amusingly witty as, a *smart* saying; **5,** up-to-date; fashionable; as, a *smart* gown; the *smart* set.—*adv.* **smart′ly.**—*n.* **smart′ness.**—*v.t.* **smart′en** (*up*).

smart card, a plastic card with a built-in microchip for credit or other banking transactions as well as security or identification functions.

smash (smash), *v.t.* to break (something) into pieces by dropping it, hitting it, or striking it against something else; as, to *smash* a vase, window, car:—*v.i.* **1,** to break into many pieces; as, fine glass *smashes* easily; **2,** to rush or be thrown violently against something; as, the car *smashed* into the fence; **3,** to go to pieces, as a business that fails:—*n.* **1,** an act or the sound of breaking to pieces; a crash; **2,** a violent collision; **3,** complete destruction or ruin; **4,** a resounding success; as a *smash* hit.—*adj.* **smash′ing.**

smash-up (smash′-up′), *n.* **1,** a serious accident; as a violent *smash-up*; **2,** a complete collapse or defeat.

smat-ter-ing (smat′ėr-ing), *n.* slight, superficial knowledge; small amount: used with *of*; as, I know a *smattering* of French; a *smattering* of Parmesan cheese on the pasta.

smear (smēr), *v.t.* **1,** to spread with anything greasy, oily, or sticky; daub; **2,** to spread (oil, paint, etc.) over something; **3,** to be or cause to be blurred or messy; as, water smeared the writing on the notepad; **4,** to harm or spoil someone's reputation; to slander:—*n.* **1,** a blot or stain; a streak; **2,** a false charge or criticism; as, a politician's *smear* tactics; the candidate's *smear* campaign of his opponent.

smell (smel), *v.t.* [*p.t.* and *p.p.* smelled (smeld) or smelt (smelt), *p.pr.* smell-ing], **1,** to perceive by means of the nose; obtain the scent of; as, to *smell* smoke; **2,** to inhale the odour of; as, to *smell* a flower; **3,** to suspect; detect; as, to *smell* trouble:—*v.i.* to have an odour or aroma; as, this room *smells* of lilacs; to *smell* of rotten eggs:—*n.* **1,** that quality of things that is perceived by the nose; an odour or aroma; as, the *smell* of freshly baked bread; **2,** the sense by which odours are perceived; **3,** the act of smelling; **4,** characteristic or aura of something; as the sweet *smell* of success.

smel-ly (smel′i), *adj.* [smel-li-er, smel-li-est] having a strong, bad odour; as, *smelly* old socks.

[1]**smelt** (smelt), *p.t* of *smell.*

[2]**smelt** (smelt), *n.* a small, silvery food fish found in northern waters.

[3]**smelt** (smelt), *v.t.* to fuse or melt (ore) in order to refine the metal; also, to obtain (metal) by this process.—*n.* **smelt′er; smelt′ing.**

smile (smīl), *n.* an expression on the face, particularly around the mouth, indicating amusement, pleasure, or affection; also, a facial expression conveying irony or contempt:—*v.i.* [smiled, smil-ing], **1,** to show a smile; look pleasant; as, the photographer told her to *smile*; **2,** to show pleasure or amusement, contempt or disdain, by smiling; **3,** to look with favour; as, fortune *smiled* upon his efforts:—*v.t.* to express by smiling; as, to *smile* assent.—*adj.* **smil′ing.**—*adv.* **smil′ing-ly.**

smirk (smûrk), *v.i.* to smile affectedly, smugly, or conceitedly:—*n.* an affected smile.

smite (smīt), *v.t.* [*p.t.* smote (smōt), *p.p.* smit-ten (smit′n), *p.pr.* smit-ing], **1,** to hit; strike with the hand, or with a weapon or implement; **2,** to strike with disaster; afflict; as, Egypt was *smitten* with plagues; **3,** to cause to strike; as he *smote* his staff upon the ground; **4,** to affect with the suddenness of a blow; as, a cry *smote* the silence; **5,** to affect with any strong feeling, as love, grief, fear, etc.; **6,** to cause to feel regret or sorrow; as, his conscience *smote* him; **7,** to captivate; as, he was *smitten* with her grace and beauty.

smith (smith), *n.* one who works or shapes metal with hammer and anvil.

SMITH'S TOOLS

smith-er-eens (smi*th*′ėr-ēnz′), *n.pl.* tiny fragments; as, to smash into *smithereens.*

smith-y (smith′i; smi*th*′i), *n.* [*pl.* smithies], a forge; a blacksmith's shop.

smock (smok), *n.* a long, loose blouse or garment worn to protect the clothing:—*v.t.* to trim (a blouse or dress) with gathers fastened into a pattern by fancy stitches.—*n.* **smock′ing.**

smog (smog), *n.* a mixture of smoke and fog; polluted air caused by the exhaust from cars and factories in larger cities.—*adj.* **smog′gy.**

smoke (smōk), *n.* **1,** the visible gas that escapes from a burning substance; **2,** a column, cloud, or mass of smoke; **3,** anything that resembles smoke, as fumes or vapour:—*v.t.* [smoked, smok-ing], **1,** to preserve (fish or meat) by exposure to smoke; **2,** to inhale and puff out the fumes of a cigarette, cigar, or pipe; as, to *smoke* a cigarette; **3,** to force out by smoke; as, to *smoke* out snakes:—*v.i.* **1,** to give out fumes, as a chimney; **2,** to inhale and puff out the fumes of a cigarette, cigar, or pipe; **3,** to give off anything like smoke—*n.* **smok′er; smok′ing.**—*adj.* **smoke′less.**

smoke detector, a device that detects and warns of the presence of smoke by sounding an alarm.

smoked meat, 1, a cured meat similar to corned beef or pastrami; **2,** meat cured by smoking.

smoke-free (smōk′-frē′), *adj.* **1,** pertaining to a place where smoking is not allowed; as, a *smoke-free* restaurant; **2,** free from smoke; **3,** giving off little or no smoke; as, a *smoke-free* campfire.

smoke-house (smōk′hous′), *n.* a building or room in which fish or meat is cured by smoke.

smoke screen, 1, smoke produced to conceal military or other operations from the enemy; **2,** something used to disguise or mislead; as, a *smoke screen* of disinformation.

smoke-stack (smōk′stak′), *n.* a tall chimney, as in a factory or on an ocean liner.

smok-y (smōk′i), *adj.*, [smok-i-er, smok-i-est], **1,** giving off a lot of smoke or filled with smoke; as, a *smoky* room; **2,** having the colour or taste of smoke; as, *smoky* glass; *smoky* deli meat.

smooth (smōōth), *adj.* **1,** not rough; even in surface or texture, as a new road; **2,** perfectly blended; free from lumps; as, *smooth* gravy; **3,** gently flowing, as a river; hence, serene; calm; pleasant; **4,** easy and polished; as, a *smooth* style in speaking or writing; **5,** flattering; fluent; as, *smooth* words; a *smooth* talker; **6,** without beard; as, a *smooth* face; **7,** steady in motion; not jerky or jarring; as, the *smooth* running of a car; **8,** of food and drinks, free from sharpness; not harsh or bitter to taste; pleasant; as, a *smooth* cheese or wine; **9,** free from trouble or problems; as, a *smooth* and carefree vacation:—*adv.* in a smooth manner; smoothly:—*v.t.* **1,** to remove roughness from; to make level or even; flatten; as, to *smooth* wrinkles out of a T-shirt; **2,** to make even, steady, or calm; **3,** to soothe; as, to *smooth* a person's feelings; **4,** to make easy; as, to *smooth* a person's way; also, to remove; to make easy or easier; take away troubles or problems; as, to *smooth* away difficulties.—*adv.* **smooth′ly.**—*n.* **smooth′ness.**

smooth-ie or **smooth-y** (smōō′thē), *n.* [*pl.* smoothies], **1,** a person who is a smooth talker; one who is polished, suave, and often insincere; **2,** a smooth, thick drink made with fruit and milk, ice cream, or yogurt.

smor-gas-bord (smôr′gas-bōrd′), *n.* **1,** a Swedish type of meal, buffet style, in which a variety of hot or cold meats, fish, sausage, cheese, salads, desserts, etc., are served; **2,** a mixture, mélange, or medley of something; as, a *smorgasbord* of fashion styles at the event.

smote (smōt), *p.t.* and *p.p.* of *smite.*

smoth-er (smuth′ėr), *v.t.* **1,** to kill by depriving of air; stifle; also, to deaden by suffocating, as a fire; **2,** to suppress or conceal; cover up; as, to *smother* one's anger; **3,** in *cookery,* to cover, as with onions, and cook in a covered dish; also, to cover thickly or overwhelm with something; as, the mudslide *smothered* the buildings; to *smother* someone with too much attention:—*v.i.* **1,** to be deprived of air; **2,** to be restrained:—*n.* a dense smoke or dust.

smoul-der or **smol-der** (smōl′dėr), *v.i.* **1,** to burn slowly, giving forth smoke with little or no flame; **2,** to burn or have strong feelings just beneath the surface; as, hate *smouldered* in his heart and eyes.

smudge (smuj), *n.* **1,** a smear or stain; **2,** a smouldering fire that produces a dense smoke for protecting fruit trees from frost or for keeping off insects:—*v.t.* and *v.i.* [smudged, smudg-ing], **1,** to smear or stain; mark; **2,** to keep away by a smudge.—*adj.* **smudg′y.**

smug (smug), *adj.* [smug-ger, smug-gest], self-satisfied; pleased with oneself to the point of annoying others; as, to say in a *smug* voice that you are the best student in the class.—*adv.* **smug′ly.**—*n.* **smug′ness.**

smug-gle (smug′l), *v.t.* and *v.i.* [smug-gled, smug-gling], **1,** to bring or send (goods) into or out of a country secretly and illegally; **2,** to carry or take secretly; as, to *smuggle* candy into the movie theatre.—*n.* **smug′gler** (smug′lėr); **smug′gling** (smug′gling).

smut (smut), *n.* **1,** a spot or stain made by soot or dirt; also, that which causes the spot; **2,** a disease affecting corn, wheat, etc.; **3,** obscene, offensive, or indecent language, pictures, etc., usually sexual in nature:—*v.t.* [smut-ted, smut-ting], **1,** to soil or blacken with, or as with, soot; **2,** to affect a plant with smut:—*v.i.* **1,** to become blackened by soot; **2,** to be affected by mildew or smut, as grain.—*adj.* **smut′ty.**

snack (snak), *n.* a small meal taken between regular meals:—*v.i.* to eat something as a snack; as, to *snack* on the potato chips:—**snack bar**, a small store, restaurant, or lunch counter where snacks and light meals are served or can be purchased.

sna-fu (sna-fōō′; sna′fōō′), *n.* (*pl.* snafus), *Slang* a confused, muddled, or chaotic situation: from *s*ituation *n*ormal *a*ll *f*ouled *u*p:—*adj.* utterly confused or chaotic:—*v.t.* [sna-fued, sna-fuing], to make disordered or chaotic.

snag (snag), *n.* **1,** the stump of a branch projecting from the trunk of a tree; **2,** some sharp or rough part of a tree sticking up from the bottom of a river or lake and dangerous to boats; **3,** a broken or decayed tooth; **4,** any unexpected obstacle or difficulty; as, a *snag* in a plan; **5,** a jagged pull or tear in cloth, nylon, etc.; as, a *snag* in her stocking:—*v.t.* [snagged, snag-ging], **1,** to catch or damage on a snag; **2,** to clear of obstructions or snags; **3,** to catch or obtain quickly or through good luck; as, to *snag* a couple of last-minute tickets for the sold-out concert.

snail (snāl), *n.* **1,** a small slow-moving land or water animal in the mollusk family, with a spiral shell into which it withdraws for protection; **2,** a person who is slow moving as a snail.

snail mail, *Slang* traditional surface mail handled by the postal system, as opposed to electronic mail.

snake (snāk), *n.* **1,** a long, legless, slim-bodied reptile that preys on insects and small animals: it has lidless eyes and is capable of swallowing prey larger than itself because of its extendable jaws: some varieties, such as cobras, are poisonous; **2,** a treacherous person:—*v.t.* [snaked, snak-ing], *Colloq.* to drag, esp. at full length; jerk; as, to *snake* a log out of a swamp:—*v.i.* to crawl along like a snake.—*adj.* **snak′y.**

snake oil, 1, formerly, phony cure-all or quack medicine, as that sold in fraudulent medicine shows; **2,** any fraudulent product; **3,** anything designed to deceive; **4,** nonsense, poppycock, or humbug.

snap (snap), *v.i.* [snapped, snap-ping], **1,** to break suddenly; as, the glass *snapped* in my hand; **2,** to snatch at something suddenly, esp. with the teeth; as, a dog *snaps* at a bone; **3,** to produce a sharp, sudden sound; as, twigs *snap* underfoot; **4,** to speak crossly or angrily; **5,** to sparkle; as, her eyes *snapped*:—*v.t.* **1,** to break off short; crack; **2,** to seize suddenly; as, the fish *snapped* up the bait; **3,** to cause to make a sudden, sharp sound; **4,** to close with a sharp sound; as, to *snap* down a lid; **5,** in *football*, to put (the ball) in play by passing it back from the line of scrimmage; **6,** to take a quick photograph of; as, to *snap* a picture:—*n.* **1,** the act of seizing suddenly; **2,** the sudden breaking of something stiff or tightly stretched; as, the *snap* of a wire; **3,** a sudden, sharp sound; **4,** a spring lock or catch; **5,** a kind of thin, crisp biscuit; a gingersnap; **6,** a sudden, short period of severe weather; as, a *cold* snap; **7,** *Colloq.* energy or vim; **8,** *Colloq.* something that is easy; a cinch; as, the math problems are a *snap*; **9,** a card game:—*adj.* **1,** done in haste or without much thought; as, a *snap* decision; **2,** closing with a click, or with a special closing device; as, a *snap* bracelet; **3,** *Colloq.* easy; requiring little effort; as, a *snap* university course.

snap-drag-on (snap′drag′un), *n.* a plant with showy white, yellow, reddish, or pink flowers that grow in clusters on a long stalk.

snap-pish (snap′ish), *adj.* **1,** likely to snap or bite; as, a *snappish* dog; **2,** sharp in speech; easily irritated.—*n.* **snap′pish-ness.**

snap-py (snap′i), *adj.* [snap-pi-er, snap-pi-est], **1,** sharp and irritable in speech; snappish; **2,** *Colloq.*: **a,** lively; brisk, as conversation; as, a *snappy* debate; **b,** stylish; fashionable; smart, as clothes.—*adv.* **snap′pi-ly.**—*n.* **snap′pi-ness.**

snap-shot (snap′shot′), *n.* **1,** a photograph taken quickly or informally; **2,** a brief, focussed view or impression of something; as, the written article gave a quick *snapshot* of the situation.

snare (snâr), *n.* **1,** a running noose or a loop of cord or wire for catching an animal or a bird; **2,** hence, anything that entangles, lures, or entraps; as, the soldiers set a *snare*, which led the enemy right into the ambush:—*v.t.* [snared, snar-ing], to catch with, or as with, a snare.—*n.* **snar′er.**

snare drum, a small drum with catgut strings, or snares, stretched across the lower head to produce a rattling sound when the upper head is beaten.

snark-y (snär′ki), *n.* sarcastic; irritable; snappish; short-tempered; crotchety; as, *snarky* comments.

[1]**snarl** (snärl), *v.i.* **1,** to make a growling noise, as an angry dog; **2,** to speak in harsh, surly tones:—*v.t.* to utter in a growl or in a harsh, surly tone:—*n.* **1,** the act of growling; **2,** a surly tone.—*adj.* **snarl′y.**

[2]**snarl** (snärl), *n.* **1,** a tangle or knot, as of yarn or hair; **2,** hence, a state of confusion; a complicated situation:—*v.t.* and *v.i.* to make or become tangled, confused, or complicated; as, the accident snarled traffic; his negative actions *snarled* her straightforward plans.

snatch (snach), *v.t.* to seize or grab suddenly, rudely, or illegally; as, the dog *snatched* the food from the table; the thief *snatched* the money from the till; the kidnappers *snatched* the child from the playground:—*v.i.* to try to seize something suddenly; as, the child *snatched* at a flower:—*n.* **1,** a hasty catch; kidnapping; **2,** a small fragment or amount; as, *snatches* of verse; **3,** a brief period; as, to work in *snatches*.—*n.* **snatch′er.**

snaz-zy (sna′zi), *adj. Slang* fancy, stylish, or fashionable; as, a *snazzy* new outfit.

sneak (snēk), *v.i.* to creep or move about secretly or slyly; slink; as, he tried to *sneak* into his sister's room:—*v.t.* to bring, put, or take something secretely or furtively; as to sneak a pen from her desk:—*n.* **1,** a person who is dishonest or who does things in a cunning, secret way; **2,** a petty thief; **3, sneakers,** canvas shoes with rubber soles; running shoes.—*adj.* **sneak′y.**—*adv.* **sneak′i-ly.**—*n.* **sneak′i-ness.**

sneak preview, a special showing of a movie or other show before it is released to the general public, often to test audience reaction.

sneer (snēr), *v.i.* **1,** to show contempt by an expression of the face, as by curling the lips; **2,** to speak contemptuously or with ridicule:—*n.* **1,** contempt or scorn shown in speech; **2,** a contemptuous smile.—*adj.* **sneer′ing.**—*adv.* **sneer′ ing-ly.**

sneeze (snēz), *n.* a sudden brief spasm of the breathing organs, causing a violent and audible rush of air out through the mouth and nostrils:—*v.i.* [sneezed, sneez-ing], to force air out through the nose and mouth in a sudden, violent way that cannot be stopped or controlled.

snick-er (snik′ėr), *n.* a half-suppressed laugh, often showing scorn, dislike, or disrespect; a giggle:—*v.i.* to laugh in this manner; giggle.

snide (snīd), *adj. Slang* sly; malicious; disparaging; as, *snide* remarks.

sniff (snif), *v.i.* **1,** to draw in the breath audibly through the nose; to clear the nose; **2,** to express contempt; as, he *sniffed* at the suggestion:—*v.t.* **1,** to smell quickly and audibly; as, the dog *sniffed* the baggage at the airport; **2,** to smell out; as, to *sniff* danger:—*n.* **1,** the act of smelling; **2,** an audible, often scornful, inhaling through the nose.

sniff-er (snif′ėr), *n.* **1,** one who sniffs, esp. someone who inhales drugs or other substances; as, a glue *sniffer;* **2,** a dog trained to detect drugs, explosives, etc., by smell; as, *sniffers* that check bags at an airport; **3,** *Slang* the nose.

snif-fle (snif′l), *v.i.* [snif-fled, snif-fling], to draw air through the nose audibly and repeatedly, as when crying or when sick with a cold:—*n.* **snif′fles, 1,** the act or sound of sniffling; **2,** a slight cold in the nose and head.

snif-ter (snif′tėr), *n.* **1,** a pear-shaped, short-stemmed goblet used primarily for drinking brandy; **2,** *Slang* a small drink of liquor.

snip (snip), *v.t.* [snipped, snip-ping], to cut or clip, with scissors or shears, in short, quick strokes:—*n.* **1,** a single cut with scissors; a clip; **2,** a small piece; bit.—*adj.* **snip′py,** *Colloq.* sharp; curt; esp. in an insolent or supercilious way.

snipe (snīp), *n.* [*pl.* snipe], **1,** wading birds of the sandpiper family; **2,** insulting or critical remarks; as, to make a *snipe* about an essay; **3,** shots fired from a hidden spot; **4,** the act of shooting from concealment:—*v.i.* [sniped, snip-ing], **1,** to hunt such birds; **2,** to criticize; to make a sly, underhanded or malicious attack; **3,** esp. in *war,* to shoot enemies, one by one, at a distance from ambush:—*v.t.* to shoot at someone, as an enemy, from hiding at long range.

snip-er (snīp′ėr), *n.* a person who shoots a gun at people from a hidden vantage place.

snit (snit), *n. Colloq.* a state of agitation, irritation, or annoyance; as, to be in a *snit.*

snitch (snich), *v.i. Slang* to inform on; tell; blab:—*v.t. Slang* to pilfer, steal:—*n.* an informer.

sniv-el (sniv′l), *v.i.* [snivelled, snivel-ling], **1,** to run at the nose; to sniffle; **2,** to cry in a complaining way.—*n.* **sniv′el-ler.**—*n.* and *adj.* **sniv′el-ling.**

snob (snob), *n.* **1,** someone who thinks he or she is better than others because of wealth or position; **2,** a person who claims great knowledge or taste in some area, and who looks down on the taste of others; as, an art *snob.*—*adj.* **snob′bish; snob′by.**—*n.* **snob′bish-ness; snob′ber-y; snob′bism.**—*adv.* **snob′bish-ly.**

snook-er (snŏŏk′ėr), *n.* a game like pool (or billiards) played with balls numbered 1 to 15, which must be sunk in order, with the difference that a red ball must be sunk each time before a coloured numbered one.—*v.t. Slang* to dupe, deceive, or defeat; as, he *snookered* his friend into doing his chores for him.

snoop (snōōp), *v.i.* to peer or pry in a sneaking way:—*n.* one who pries into other people's private affairs; as, a *snoop* who reads someone else's diary.

snoot-y (snōō′ti), *adj. Colloq.* snobbish; conceited; looking down one's nose (snoot); as, *snooty* people at the lavish event.—*adv.* **snoot′-i-ly.**—*n.* **snoot′i-ness.**

snooze (snōōz), *v.i. Colloq.* [snoozed, snoozing], to take a nap; doze:—*n.* **1,** a nap; **2,** *Slang* something that is boring and makes you sleepy; as, the professor's lecture on quantum physics was a real *snooze!*

snore (snōr), *v.i.* [snored, snor-ing], to breathe with a hoarse sound through the nose, or nose and mouth, in sleep:—*n.* a noisy breathing in sleep.—*n.* **snor′er.**

snor-kel (snôr′kl), *n.* a device for underwater breathing consisting of two vertical tubes (or one tube with two passages) for taking in and blowing out air: it permits swimming just under the surface of the water for long periods:—*v.i.* to swim using a snorkel.

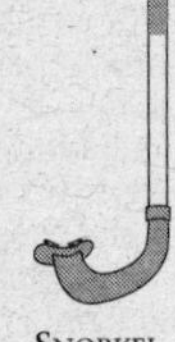

SNORKEL

snort (snôrt), *v.i.* **1,** to force the air out through the nose with a loud sound; **2,** to express feeling by such a sound; as, to *snort* with anger:—*v.i.* and *v.t.* to inhale a drug; as, to *snort* cocaine:—*n.* a loud, abrupt sound so made; as, a *snort* of rage:—*n. Colloq.* a small drink of liquor.

snot (snot), *n. Slang* **1,** mucus from the nose; **2,** an annoying, conceited, or unpleasant person.—*adj.* **snot′ty.**

snout (snout), *n.* **1,** the projecting nose, and often jaws, of a beast, esp. of a dog or hog; the muzzle; **2,** anything like a snout.

snow (snō), *n.* frozen water vapour in the form of white, feathery flakes, or crystals, falling from the sky; also, masses of such flakes lying on the ground:—*v.i.* to fall in frozen crystals:—*v.t.* **1,** to pour out thickly like falling snow, as confetti; **2,** to obstruct or shut in with masses of snow; as, the blizzard *snowed* us in.

snow-ball (snō′ball′), *n.* a small mass of snow that is packed together to resemble a ball:—*v.i.* to grow bigger very quickly; as, the company's debts *snowballed,* so it had to declare bankruptcy.

snow-bank (snō′bangk′), *n,* a large mass of snow piled up against something. Also called *snowdrift.*

snow-belt (snō′belt′), *n.* a region that receives heavy snowfall; as, Québec City is in a *snowbelt.*

snow-bird (snō′bûrd′), *n.* **1,** the junco, a blue-grey-and-white finch; the snow bunting; **2,** a person who winters in a warm climate; esp. someone from Canada who lives in the southern American states in the winter.

snow blower, a machine that clears snow by picking it up in its rotating spiral blades and expelling it through a chute to one side; a snow thrower.

snow-board (snō′bōrd′), *n.* a flat board that can be attached to boots, used to go down a snow-covered hill:—*v.* to go down a hill on a snowboard.—*n.* **snow′board-er; snow′board-ing.**

snow-bound (snō′bound′), *adj.* shut in by a heavy snowstorm.

snow-drift (snō′drift′), *n.* Same as **snow-bank.**

snow-fall (snō′fôl′), *n.* the amount of snow that falls in a certain amount of time or at a particular place.

snow-flake (snō′flāk′), *n.* a white feathery crystal or single crystal or flake of snow.

snow job, *Slang* an intensive effort to persuade someone through flattery and deception; as, the used car salesperson did a great *snow job* on us.

snow-man (snō′man′), *n.* snow packed and shaped into a figure similar to a person.

snow-mo-bile (snō′mō-bēl′), *n.* a small, usually open, motor vehicle that travels over snow on ski-like runners: Bombardier's Ski-Doo is one of the best-known snowmobiles in the world.—*n.* **snow′mo-bil′er; snow′mo-bil′ing.**

snow-plough (snō′plou′) or **snow-plow** (plou), *n.* **1,** a machine, usually a truck with a wide blade on the front, used to clear roads, tracks, etc., of heavy snow; **2,** in *skiing*, the act of using both skis turned inward to slow down or come to a stop:—*v.t.* and *v.i.* to remove snow with a snowplough:—*v.i.* to execute a slowplow.

snow-shoe (snō′shōō′), *n.* a network of rawhide or other material stretched upon a racket-shaped wooden frame, fastened by thongs to the foot and worn for travelling over deep snow.

snow-storm (snō′stôrm′), *n.* a storm with heavy snow and high wind.

snow tire, a tire specifically designed with deep treads or studs for added traction in snow or ice.

snow-y (snō′i), *adj.* [snow-i-er, snow-i-est], **1,** covered with, or full of, snow; **2,** white and fluffy like fresh snow; as, *snowy* linen; a *snowy* beard.

snub (snub), *v.t.* [snubbed, snub-bing], **1,** to check, answer, or interrupt with rude or scornful words; **2,** to treat with scorn; slight intentionally; **3,** to check the motion of; as, to *snub* a boat by means of a rope wound round a post:—*n.* **1,** an intentional slight; **2,** a check:—*adj.* short and slightly turned up; as, a *snub* nose.

snuck (snuk), *p.t.* of *sneak*.

[1]**snuff** (snuf), *n.* powdered tobacco, which is inhaled through the nose.

[2]**snuff** (snuf), *n.* the burned part of a wick:—*v.t.* **1,** to cut or pinch the charred part from; as, to *snuff* a candle; **2,** to put out (a candle); **3,** hence, to put a sudden end to; to kill; as, the accident *snuffed* out his life; the convict *snuffed* out his enemy.

snuf-fer (snuf′ėr), *n.* **1,** an implement with a long handle and small funnel used to snuff out a candle; **2, snuffers,** a scissors-like device used to trim or hold the wick of a candle or extinguish it.

snug (snug), *adj.* [snug-ger, snug-gest], **1,** sheltered and warm; cosy; as, a *snug* house; *snug* in bed; **2,** fitting closely; as, a *snug* jacket; **3,** modest but sufficient; as, a *snug* fortune.—*adv.* **snug′ly.**

snug-gle (snug′l), *v.i.* [snug-gled, snug-gling], to cuddle or nestle close for warmth and comfort:—*v.t.* to hold close, comfort, and make comfortable; as, to *snuggle* the crying baby.—*adj.* **snug′gly.**

so (sō), *adv.* **1,** in like manner or degree; as, I can run fast; *so* can she; today is not *so* hot as yesterday; **2,** to such a degree; as, this fabric is *so* old that it tears; **3,** as stated, indicated, or implied; as, I told you she would come, and *so* she did; hold your needle *so*:—*interj.* well: expressing surprise; as, *so* here you are:—*pron.* **1,** a person or thing already indicated; as, he is a poor student and will always remain *so*; **2,** approximately that which has been indicated; a little more or less; as, it costs a dollar or *so*:—*conj.* therefore; consequently: it is raining; *so* we must stay at home; she stayed home, *so* that she could study for her exam.

soak (sōk), *v.t.* **1,** to wet thoroughly; as, the rain *soaked* him; **2,** to wet so as to soften or clean; as, to *soak* dried apricots before cooking; to *soak* a shirt in bleach to remove the stain; **3,** to absorb; as, paper towels *soak* up spills; to *soak* up the warmth of the sun:—*v.i.* **1,** to become thoroughly wet; **2,** to enter by pores or small openings; as, water *soaks* into a sponge; also, to penetrate the mind, as words or ideas:—*n.* the act or process of wetting thoroughly.—*n.* **soak′er.**

soap (sōp), *n.* a substance for cleansing, made by combining fats or oils with an alkali, and which comes in the forms of bars, liquids, powders, or flakes:—*v.t.* to cover or wash with soap.—*adj.* **soap′y.**

soap-box (sōp′boks′), *n.* **1,** the temporary platform for public speakers; **2,** an outlet for someone's opinions; **3,** a child's cart, originally built out of soapboxes; as, to enter in the *soapbox* derby.

soap opera, *Colloq.* a regular television serial drama, usually melodramatic, emotional, etc., originally sponsored by a soap company.

soap-suds (sōp′sudz′), *n.* soapy water whipped into a froth or foam.

soar (sōr), *v.i.* **1,** to fly high, as a bird, seemingly without effort; mount upward with wings; **2,** to rise far above what is usual; as, prices *soared.*

sob (sob), *v.i.* [sobbed, sob-bing], to catch the breath convulsively; also, to weep with a convulsive heaving of the breast:—*v.t.* to utter while catching the breath; as, to *sob* out a confession:—*n.* **1,** a convulsive sigh; **2,** any similar sound.

so-ber (sō′bėr), *adj.* **1,** temperate by habit, esp. in the use of intoxicating liquors; **2,** not intoxicated or drunk; **3,** calm; steady; as, *sober* judgment; **4,** solemn; grave; serious; as, a *sober* face; **5,** plain; subdued; as, *sober* colours:—*v.t.* and *v.i.* to make or become sober.—*adv.* **so′ber-ly.**

so-bri-e-ty (sō-brī′e-ti), *n.* **1,** moderation; temperance, esp. in the use of liquor; **2,** calmness; seriousness; gravity.

so-bri-quet (sō′bri-kā′ or sō′bri-ket′), *n.* a nickname; epithet.

sob story, *Colloq.* an excessively sentimental story intended to arouse pity or sadness, esp. one that fails to do so; as, a *sob story* about being late.

so–called (sō′–kôld′), *adj.* called such, but usually not actually so; as, the *so-called* hero actually started the fire.

soc-cer (sok′ėr), *n.* a form of football in which the ball is controlled by the feet, legs, body, or head, and the use of the hands and arms is prohibited: many countries call this game *football.*

so-cia-ble (sō′sha-bl), *adj.* **1,** friendly; companionable; liking to be with other people; **2,** giving opportunity for friendly companionship; as, a *sociable* neighbourhood; **3,** marked by friendliness; not formal.—*adv.* **so′cia-bly.**—*n.* **so′cia-bil′i-ty.**

so-cial (sō′shal), *adj.* **1,** pertaining to human beings living in association with one another; as, her *social* life, as opposed to her business life; **2,** relating to human life in general; as, *social* welfare; **3,** sociable; **4,** pertaining to the life of people of wealth and fashion; as, the *social* event of the year; **5,** of insects, living in organized communities, as ants or bees do; as, bees and ants are *social* insects:—*n.* an informal, friendly gathering; as, a church *social*:—**social climber**, a person who tries to gain higher social status.—*n. Colloq.* **so′cial-ite′** (a member of fashionable society).—*adv.* **so′cial-ly.**—*v.i.* and *v.t.* **so′cial-ize.**

social contract, the philosophical belief that society was founded on a contract, or agreement, between individual citizens. Also called *social compact.*

Social Credit Party, a political party founded in the 1930s in Alberta on the principles of social credit.

so-cial-ism or **So-cial-ism** (sō′shal-izm), *n.* the economic, social, and political doctrine that holds that, for the greatest good of the people, the resources of a country and its industries should be placed permanently under public or government ownership and operation rather than owned by private individuals or corporations.—*n.* and *adj.* **so′cial-ist** or **So′cial-ist.**—*adj.* **so′cial-is′tic.**

social science, 1, the scientific study of human relationships and the way society works: history, government, economics, geography, sociology, and anthropology are social sciences; **2,** (usually *social studies*) the study of history, geography, and other social sciences as a subject in school.

social security, 1, benefits paid by the government to needy individuals through social insurance programs such as welfare, unemployment, and pensions:—**Social Security,** in the U.S., government programs covering unemployment, disability, and pensions.

social work, a profession that brings assistance to people with special needs, in areas such as health care, mental health, and family and child welfare:—**social worker,** a person trained to do this work.

so-ci-e-ty (sō-si′e-ti), *n.* [*pl.* societies], **1,** people in general, considered as living and working in relationship with one another; **2,** a certain group of people; as, the Canadian *society*; **3,** an organized body of persons united by a common interest or purpose; as, a debating *society*; the Cancer *Society*; **4,** fashionable or wealthy members of a culture or community; as, high *society*; **5,** a plant or insect community; **6,** association; companionship; as, to enjoy the *society* of those people.

socio-, *prefix* meaning *society, social,* or *sociological*; as, *socio*cultural, *socio*political, etc.

so-ci-ol-o-gy (sō′si-ol′o-ji; sō′shi-), *n.* the science of the origin, development, organization, functions, laws, etc., of human society.—*n.* **so′ci-ol′o-gist.**—*adj.* **so′ci-o-log′i-cal.**

[1]**sock** (sok), *n.* a knitted or woven covering for the foot and lower leg.

[2]**sock** (sok), *v.t. Slang* **1,** to strike or hit hard, esp. with the fist; **2,** to stow away; as, he *socks* his money in the bank.—*n. Slang* a blow.

sock-et (sok′it), *n.* a hollow into which something is fitted; as, the *socket* of the eye; the *socket* for a light bulb.

sod (sod), *n.* **1,** the top layer of the soil, containing the roots of grass; turf, usually cut square; **2,** the surface of the ground:—*v.t.* [sod-ded, sod-ding], to cover with turf or pieces of turf.

so-da (sō′da), *n.* **1,** the name given to either of two compounds of sodium: **a,** a white powdery substance, sodium bicarbonate, or baking soda; **b,** a white crystalline substance, sodium carbonate, or washing soda; **2,** carbonated water; also, a drink made with carbonated water and sweet flavouring, and sometimes ice cream. Also called *soda water, soda pop,* or *soft drink.*

sod-den (sod′n), *adj.* **1,** soaked; heavy with moisture; as, *sodden* shoes; **2,** badly cooked or baked; as, *sodden* piecrust; **3,** spiritless; dull; intoxicated; as, a *sodden* crowd; a *sodden* boor.

so-di-um (sō′di-um), *n.* a silvery-white, alkaline metallic element always occurring in nature in combination, as in common salt, rock salt, borax, etc.:—**sodium bicarbonate,** $NaHCO_3$ or *baking soda:*—**sodium carbonate,** Na_2CO_3 or *washing soda:*—**sodium chloride,** NaCl, or *common salt:*—**sodium hydroxide,** NaOH, a white *caustic* solid:—**sodium nitrate,** $NaNO_3$ a clear, odourless *salt* used mainly in fertilizers: also called *Chili saltpetre:*—**sodium peroxide,** Na_2O_2 a yellowish-white *powder,* used as an antiseptic:—**sodium sulphate,** Na_2SO_4 a white, crystalline *salt* (of Saskatchewan) used as a detergent.

so-fa (sō′fa), *n.* a long, upholstered seat with a back and arms. Also called *chesterfield* and *couch.*

soft (sôft), *adj.* **1,** easily yielding to pressure; lacking in hardness; as, *soft* eggs; **2,** easily moulded or shaped; as, *soft* wax; **3,** smooth, light, and yielding to the touch; as, *soft* fur; **4,** not glaring; as, a *soft* light; **5,** not loud; as, *soft* music; **6,** kind; courteous; mild or gentle; as, a *soft* answer; **7,** easily touched or moved; as, a *soft* heart; **8,** mild; as, *soft* winds; **9,** lenient; not strict; requiring little effort; as, a *soft* teacher; a *soft* job; **10,** in *pronunciation,* pronounced with the sound of "c" in "cell" or "g" in "gem"; not hard, like the "c" in "case" or "g" in "gate"; **11,** *Colloq.*: **a,** not in good physical condition; flabby; weak; lacking strength; as, *soft* muscles; to become *soft* from lack of exercise; **b,** containing no alcohol; as, *soft* drinks:—*adv.* quietly.—*adv.* **soft′ly.**—*n.* **soft′ie; soft′ness.**

soft-ball (sôft′bôl′), *n.* **1,** a game like baseball that uses a bigger, softer ball that is pitched underhand and a smaller diamond than in ordinary baseball; **2,** the ball used in this game.

soft drink, a sweet, carbonated drink made without alcohol.

sof-ten (sôf′n; sôf′en), *v.t.* and *v.i.* to make or become less hard, rough, loud, glaring, severe, strict, or rude.

soft–heart-ed (sôft′–här′ted), *adj.* kind; compassionate; sympathetic; tender.—*n.* **soft′– heart′ed-ness.**—*adv.* **soft′–heart′ed-ly.**

soft–ped-al (sôft′–ped′l), *v.t.* [–ped-alled, –ped-al-ling], **1,** to play down or refrain from emphasizing; as, she *soft-pedalled* her harsh stand on crime; **2,** to play piano with the soft pedal down.—*n.* **soft ped-al** (the pedal on the piano that softens or mutes the tone).

soft return, in *computing,* in word processing software, the automatic return at the end of a line of text that starts a new line, compared to hard return, that starts a new paragraph.

soft sell *n.* restrained, low-pressure selling.

soft soap *n.* **1,** semi-liquid soap; **2,** *Colloq.* flattery.

soft-ware (sôft′wâr), *n.* the programs that make a computer operate, the information and instructions for a computer, and storage media such as disks: opposite of *hardware,* which includes machinery such as a keyboard, a monitor, and a printer.

soft-wood (sôft′wood′), *n.* any light, easily worked wood, esp. that of cone-bearing trees, such as spruce or pine: opposite of *hardwood:*—*adj.* made of or containing softwood.

sog-gy (sog′i), *adj.* [sog-gi-er, sog-gi-est], soaked; sodden; as, *soggy* clothes; also, wet and heavy; as, *soggy* cake.—*n.* **sog′gi-ness.**

[1]soil (soil), *n.* **1,** the loose top layer of the earth's surface, as distinguished from solid rock; ground; earth; **2,** land; the country; as, to go back to the *soil.*

[2]soil (soil), *v.t.* **1,** to make dirty; stain, as, to *soil* the hands; **2,** to mar or sully; as a reputation:—*v.i.* to become stained or dirty:—*n.* **1,** dirt; stain; **2,** refuse; manure.

so-journ (sō′jûrn; so-jûrn′), *v.i.* to dwell for a time:—*n.* a short stay; as, a *sojourn* in the mountains.—*n.* **so-journ′er.**

sol-ace (sol′is), *n.* comfort in sorrow; consolation; as, to find *solace* in music:—*v.t.* [solaced, solac-ing], to comfort in sorrow; console, soothe, amuse.

so-lar (sō′lėr), *adj.* pertaining to, measured by, or proceeding from, the sun; as, *solar* rays; *solar* time:—**solar system,** the sun together with the planets, comets, and the other bodies that orbit the sun. Also, **solar cell; solar eclipse; solar energy; solar panel; solar power; solar radiation; solar year.**

so-lar-i-um (sō-lâr′i-um), *n.* **1,** a room, porch, balcony, etc., that is enclosed with glass to allow the maximum amount of sunlight in; **2,** a sun room in a hospital, etc., for medicinal sunbathing or therapeutic exposure to sunlight.

solar plexus, a massive network of nerves lying behind the stomach: it runs to the intestines, stomach, and glands of the upper abdomen; also, the region in front of this.

sold (sōld), *p.t.* and *p.p.* of *sell.*

sol-der (sol′dėr; sod′ėr), *n.* a metal or metallic alloy used, when melted, to join metal surfaces or to mend breaks in metal: a mixture of lead and tin is a common solder:—*v.t.* to join or patch with such an alloy:—**soldering iron,** a pointed, electric device used for soldering.

sol-dier (sōl′jėr), *n.* **1,** a person engaged in military service; **2,** someone who serves in the army who is not a commissioned officer; **3,** a person of military experience:—**soldier of fortune,** an adventurer; esp., a military person who serves any country or person for profit, adventure, or pleasure:—*v.i.* to serve in the army.—*adj.* **sol′dier-ly.**

[1]**sole** (sōl), *n.* a kind of flatfish, similar to a flounder, used for food.

[2]**sole** (sōl), *n.* **1,** the under side of the foot; **2,** the bottom of a shoe or slipper:—*v.t.* [soled, sol-ing], to furnish with a sole; to repair a sole.

[3]**sole** (sōl), *adj.* **1,** alone; only; single; as, the *sole* survivor; **2,** limited to one person or group; exclusive; as, to have *sole* use of something.—*adv.* **sole′ly.**

sol-e-cism (sol′e-sizm), *n.* **1,** an error or blunder, esp. in grammar or syntax; as, *I seen it; they was;* **2,** a breach of etiquette; bad manners.

sol-emn (sol′em), *adj.* **1,** attended with sacred rites or ceremonies; as, a *solemn* religious service; **2,** inspiring awe or fear; as, a *solemn* occasion; **3,** sober; serious; as, a *solemn* expression; **4,** grave; deliberate; as, a *solemn* oath.—*adv.* **sol′emn-ly.**—*v.t.* **sol′em-nize′.**

so-lem-ni-ty (so-lem′ni-ti) *n.* [*pl.* solemnities], **1,** a sacred rite or ceremony; **2,** a formal and grave celebration; **3,** impressiveness; seriousness; gravity.

so-lic-it (sō-lis′it), *v.t.* **1,** to ask for urgently; implore; entreat; seek; as, to *solicit* a favour; to *solicit* trade; **2,** to entice or proposition someone; esp., of a prostitute, to offer to have sexual relations with someone for money:—*v.i.* **1,** to seek orders, support, votes, etc.; **2,** to offer to have sex for money.—*n.* **so-lic′i-ta′tion.**

so-lic-i-tor (so-lis′i-tėr), *n.* **1,** one who seeks trade, votes, contributions, etc.; as, telephone *solicitors;* **2,** an attorney or lawyer; **3,** the civil law officer of a city, town, department, or government.

so-lic-it-ous (so-lis′i-tus), *adj.* anxious; concerned; careful; apprehensive; also, eager; as, *solicitous* to repay a debt.—*n.* **so-lic′i-tude.**

sol-id (sol′id), *adj.* **1,** having and keeping a shape despite pressure; not in the form of a fluid or gas; **2,** not hollow; as, a *solid* foundation; also, substantial; as, a man of *solid* means; **3,** all of a piece; the same throughout; as, *solid* silver or gold; **4,** unbroken; united; as, a *solid* line of defence; **5,** whole; uninterrupted; as, a *solid* hour:—*n.* **1,** one of the three basic forms of matter, along with liquid and gas; a body whose shape cannot be changed by pressure; a substance not fluid or gaseous, such as wood, rocks, and metals; **2,** in *geometry,* a body having length, breadth, and thickness; as, a prism is a *solid.*—*adv.* **sol′id-ly.**—*n.* **sol′id-ness; so-lid′i-ty** (so-lid′i-ti).

sol-i-dar-i-ty (so-li-dâr′i-ti), support and unity for an individual, group, or ideology.

so-lid-i-fy (so-lid′i-fī′), *v.t.* and *v.i.* [solidified, solidify-ing], to make or become hard or firm.—*n.* **so-lid′i-fi-ca′tion.**

so-lil-o-quy (so-lil′o-kwi), *n.* the act of talking to oneself; a dramatic monologue:—*v.t.* and *v.i.* **so-lil′o-quize′.**

sol-i-taire (sol′i-târ′), *n.* **1,** a game of cards played by one person; **2,** a gem, esp. a diamond, mounted alone in a ring, etc.

sol-i-tar-y (sol′i-tėr-i), *adj.* **1,** being by oneself; without companions; as, a *solitary* hermit; **2,** done, passed, or suffered alone; as, *solitary* confinement; **3,** rarely visited; remote; secluded; as, a *solitary* house; a *solitary* inn; **4,** only; single; as, a *solitary* example.

sol-i-tude (sol′i-tūd′), *n.* **1,** the state of being by oneself; loneliness; seclusion; **2,** a remote and lonely place.

so-lo (sō′lō), *n.* [*pl.* solos (sō′lōz) or soli (sō′lē)], **1,** a musical composition, or a part of one, played or sung by a single person; as, a violin *solo;* **2,** any performance, as an airplane flight, by one person:—*adj.* done by one person; as, a *solo* flight; also, performing alone; as, a *solo* violinist.—*n.* **so′lo-ist.**

sol-stice (sol′stis), *n.* either of the two times of the year when the sun is farthest from the earth's equator, either north of it or south of it: in the Northern Hemisphere, June 21 and 22 is the *summer solstice* (the longest day of the year), and December 21 and 22 is the *winter solstice* (the shortest day).

sol-u-ble (sol′ū-bl) *adj.* **1,** capable of being dissolved in a fluid, as sugar in water; **2,** capable of being solved or explained; as, a *soluble* physics problem.—*n.* **sol′u-bil′i-ty.**

so-lu-tion (so-lū′shun; lo͞o), *n.* **1,** the process of solving, or arriving at the answer to, a problem; an answer or explanation; **2,** the process by which a gas, liquid, or solid is dissolved in and mixed with a liquid; also, the resulting liquid; as, an ammonia *solution.*

solve (solv), *v.t.* [solved, solv-ing], **1,** to explain; find out; esp., to find the answer to or solution for (a problem); **2,** to make clear; unravel; as, to *solve* a mystery.

sol-vent (sol′vent), *adj.* **1,** capable of dissolving another substance; as, turpentine has a *solvent* action; **2,** able to pay one's debts:—*n.* any liquid, as water, alcohol, etc., capable of dissolving other substances; as, a *solvent* to remove paint.—*n.* **sol′vency.**

som-bre or **som-ber** (som′bėr), *adj.* **1,** dull; dark; dismal; gloomy; as, a *sombre* forest; **2,** serious; grave; melancholy; as, a *sombre* mood.

som·bre·ro (som-brâ′rō), *n.* [*pl.* sombreros], a kind of broad-brimmed hat made of straw or felt worn esp. in Latin America and the southwestern U.S.

SOMBRERO

some (sum), *adj.* **1,** a certain; particular, but not named; as, *some* boy did it; *some* other time; there were *some* people here today; **2,** of an indefinite number, amount, extent, quantity, etc.; as, have *some* potatoes; I have *some* money:—*pron.* **1,** particular persons not named; as, *some* came early; **2,** an indefinite number or amount; as, I'll have *some* of these pencils; *some* of the cake:—*adv.* about; nearly; as, *some* ten people came.

some·body (sum′bud′i; sum′bod-i), *pron.* a person unknown or not named:—*n.* [*pl.* somebodies], a person of importance.

some·day (sum′dā), *adv.* at some time in the future; as, *someday*, she will learn how to play hockey.

some·how (sum′hou), *adv.* in one way or another; by some means; in a way that is not known or stated; as, *somehow*, the raccoon got into the house.

some·one (sum′wun′), *pron.* a person unknown or not named; somebody.

som·er·sault (sum′ėr-sôlt), *n.* the act of rolling, springing, or leaping in which one turns heels over head:—*v.i.* to do a somersault.

some·thing (sum′thing), *pron.* **1,** a thing not definitely known, named, decided, or stated; **2,** a thing of unnamed amount or degree; as, one should give *something* to charity; **3,** a person or thing of importance; as, that seminar was quite *something*:—*adv.* to some degree, somewhat; as, a zebra looks *something* like a horse.

some·time (sum′tīm′), *adv.* **1,** at a time not exactly known or not definitely stated: as, *sometime* in June; **2,** at a time in the future, not yet decided upon; as, I will see you *sometime*.

some·times (sum′tīmz′), *adv.* once in a while; now and then; as, *sometimes*, it's very hot in Calgary.

some·what (sum′hwot′; sum′hwôt′), *pron.* **1,** an indefinite amount; **2,** a person or thing to some extent like another; as, he was *somewhat* of a philosopher:—*adv.* to an indefinite degree or extent; rather; as, *somewhat* tired.

some·where (sum′hwâr′), *adv.* **1,** in one place or another; as, we'll go *somewhere* quiet; **2,** in, at, or to a place not named or not known; as, the old photo album is *somewhere* in the attic; **3,** at an unknown or unnamed point; about; as, he was born *somewhere* around 1960:—**get somewhere,** to make progress; have some success; as, now, we're getting *somewhere* with this problem!

som·nam·bu·list (som-nam′bū-list), *n.* a sleepwalker.—*n.* **som·nam′bu·lism.**

som·no·lent (som′nō-lent), *n.* sleepy, or inducing sleep; as, a *somnolent* day, air, etc.—*n.* **som′no·lence.**

son (sun), *n.* **1,** a male child; a boy or man in relation to his parent or parents; **2,** any male descendant; **3,** a native of a particular country; **4,** a person thought of as the product of an age, civilization, etc.; as, a true *son* of the Middle Ages:—**the Son,** in *Christianity*, Jesus Christ.

so·nar (sō′när), *n.* a device used to locate submarines, schools of fish, icebergs, ocean depths, etc., by means of sound vibrations reflected from them.

so·na·ta (sō-nä′ta), *n.* a musical composition in three or four movements, usually for the piano.

song (sông), *n.* **1,** a series of rhythmic and tuneful musical sounds uttered vocally, as by a bird; **2,** music produced by the human voice; **3,** poetry; esp., a lyric or ballad that can be set to music; **4,** a musical composition to be sung; **5,** *Colloq.* a mere trifle; as, he sold it for a *song*. Also, **song′book; song′writ′er.**

song·bird (sông′bûrd′), *n.* **1,** a singing bird; **2,** an exceptional female singer.

son·ic (son′ik), *adj.* having to do with, or caused by, sound waves:—**sonic boom,** an explosive sound that occurs when aircraft travel at speeds faster than sound (1,225 kilometres per hour).—*adv.* **son′i·cal·ly.**

son–in–law (sun′–in–lô′), *n.* [*pl.* sons-in-law], the husband of one's daughter.

son·net (son′it), *n.* a poem, usually of 14 lines and 10 syllables in each line, arranged in any one of several rhyme schemes.

so·nor·ous (so-nōr′us), *adj.* **1,** resonant; giving a full or loud sound; as, *sonorous* bells; **2,** having a full, rich sound; as, *sonorous* poetry.—*adv.* **so·nor′ous·ly.**—*n.* **so·nor′i·ty; so·nor′ous·ness.**

soon (sōō), *adv.* **1,** in a short time; in the near future; as, it will *soon* be dark; **2,** shortly; quickly; as, he came *soon* afterwards; **3,** ahead of time; early; as, to take the cake out of the oven too *soon*; **4,** gladly; willingly; as, I'd just as *soon* read a book than play computer games; I'd *sooner* read a book than play computer games.

soot (soot; sōōt), *n.* the very fine black powder that gives smoke a greyish or black colour: it is formed when anything is burned, and is deposited in chimneys, fireplaces, etc.—*adj.* **soot′y.**

soothe (sōōth), *v.t.* [soothed, sooth-ing], **1,** to make quiet or calm; comfort or console; **2,** to make less severe, as pain; as, to *soothe* sore muscles.—*adj.* **sooth′ing.**—*adv.* **sooth′ing·ly.**

sooth·say·er (sōōth′sā′ėr), *n.* one who

claims to have the power of foretelling the future; a fortune-teller.—*n.* **sooth′say′ing.**

sop (sop), *n.* **1,** anything soaked, dipped, or softened in a liquid, as bread in broth; **2,** something given to pacify; as, a *sop* to injured feelings:—*v.t.* [sopped, sop-ping], **1,** to dip or soak, as biscuits in coffee; **2,** to mop up, as gravy with bread.—*adj.* **sop′py; sop′ping.**

so-phis-ti-cat-ed (so-fis′ti-kāt′id), *adj.* **1,** wise in the ways of the world; very cultured; **2,** drawing on high levels of knowledge; complex; complicated; as, a *sophisticated* software program.—*n.* **so-phis′ti-ca′tion.**

soph-ist-ry (sof′is-tri), *n.* reasoning that appears to be sound but is not so; a false argument; as, his ingenious *sophistry* deceived us.—*n.* **soph′ist.**

soph-o-more (sof′o-mōr′), *n.* in American universities, colleges, and high schools, a student in his or her second year.—*adj.* **soph′-o-mor′ic.**

so-po-rif-ic (sō′po-rif′ik; sop′), *adj.* and *n.* inducing sleep: used esp. of a medicine, drug, etc.

so-pra-no (so-prä′nō; so-pran′ō), *n.* [*pl.* sopranos], **1,** the highest singing voice for women and boys; **2,** a singer or musical instrument with such a voice or range.—*adj.* **so-pra′no.**

sor-cer-er (sôr′sėr-ėr), *n.* a magician; conjurer—*n.fem.* **sor′cer-ess.**

sor-cer-y (sôr′sėr-i), *n.* [*pl.* sorceries], witchcraft; magic; enchantment.

sor-did (sôr′did), *adj.* **1,** filthy; squalid; as, *sordid* slums; **2,** vile; immoral; base; degraded; as, *sordid* intentions.—*adv.* **sor′did-ly.**—*n.* **sor′did-ness.**

sore (sōr), *adj.* [sor-er, sor-est], **1,** tender or painful to the touch; inflamed; **2,** afflicted; grieved; as, her heart was *sore*; a *sore* subject; **3,** *Colloq.* angry; annoyed; resentful:—*n.* **1,** a painful or diseased spot on the body; an ulcer; **2,** a cause of trouble or distress.—*adv.* **sore′ly.**—*n.* **sore′ness.**

so-ror-i-ty (so-rôr′i-ti), *n.* a female club, esp. in a university or college.

sor-rel (sôr′el), *n.* **1,** any of several flowering herbs with sour-tasting leaves that are used in salads, soups, and sauces; **2,** a reddish-brown colour; **3,** a reddish-brown horse:—*adj.* reddish brown.

sor-row (sor′ō), *n.* **1,** mental pain caused by loss, regret, disappointment, etc.; grief; **2,** that which causes grief; trouble:—*v.i.* to feel sorrow; be sorrowful; grieve.—*n.* **sor′row-ful-ness′.**—*adj.* **sor′row-ful.**—*adv.* **sor′row-ful-ly.**

sor-ry (sor′i), *adj.* [sor-ri-er, sor-ri-est], **1,** feeling regret for one's own loss, disappointment, wrongdoing, etc.; as, to be *sorry* for being late; **2,** feeling pity, sadness, or regret for another; as, to be *sorry* to hear of his death; **3,** wretched; shabby; as, a *sorry* person; also, dismal; miserable; as, a *sorry* plight; **4,** not very good; poor; as, a *sorry* excuse.

sort (sôrt), *n.* **1,** a kind, type, or species; as, there are many *sorts* of roses; **2,** quality; character; as, material of this *sort* wears longest:—**out of sorts,** ill; out of humour; grouchy:—*v.t.* to place or arrange in different classes, according to kind or group; as, to *sort* beads by colour:—*adv.* **sort of,** *Colloq.* a little, somewhat; as, to be *sort of* tired.

sor-tie (sôr′tē), *n.* **1,** a sudden sally or attack, esp. of troops from a defensive position; **2,** an attack or mission by one military airplane; **3,** excursion, journey.

SOS (es′ō′es′), *n.* the international wireless distress signal [. . . – – – . . .] used by ships, aircraft, etc., to call for help; as, the Titanic sent an *SOS* before it sank.

souf-flé (so͞o-′flā′), *n.* a dish of eggs, milk, cheese, salmon, vegetables, etc., made light and fluffy by the adding of beaten egg whites before baking:—*adj.* puffed up.

sough (sou) *v.i.* to sigh, rustle, or murmur, as, the wind *soughing* in the trees.—*n.* such a sound.

sought (sôt), *p.t.* and *p.p.* of *seek.*

soul (sōl), *n.* **1,** that part of a person that is supposed to be the centre of mental and spiritual life, believed by many to survive death; **2,** the part that gives vigour and character; as, the *soul* of art; **3,** a person who leads and inspires; as, the *soul* of the team; **4,** a person; as, not a *soul* was there; **5,** personification; as, the *soul* of honour:—*adj.* pertaining to Black Americans or their culture; as, *soul* music; *soul* food.—*adj.* **soul′ful.**

[1]**sound** (sound), *adj.* **1,** whole; not hurt or damaged; in good condition; as, safe and *sound;* **2,** deep; as, *sound* slumber; **3,** healthy; not decayed; as, a *sound* tooth; **4,** founded on what is believed to be true and right; free from error; as, *sound* doctrine; carefully thought out; as, a *sound* plan; **5,** conservative; dependable; as, a *sound* business person; solvent; as, a *sound* business; **6,** legal; valid; as, a *sound* title; **7,** firm; safe; as, a *sound* floor; **8,** thorough; as, a *sound* thrashing:—*adv.* deeply; thoroughly; as, *sound* asleep.—*adv.* **sound′ly.**—*n.* **sound′ness.**

[2]**sound** (sound), *n.* **1,** that which is heard; the sensation perceived through the ear; as, the *sound* of a drum; a loud *sound;* **2,** meaning attached to what is heard; as, I don't like the *sound* of what you say; **3,** the distance to which a sound is audible; earshot; as, within *sound* of the bell; **4,** one of the distinct noises making up human speech; as, the "s" *sound:*—*v.t.* **1,** to cause to make a sound; as, to *sound* a bell; **2,** to cause (a sound) to be heard; to utter, play, etc.; as, to *sound* a high note; **3,** to examine or test by causing to give forth sound; as,

to *sound* the walls of a building; **4,** to order or announce by sound; as, to *sound* an alarm:—*v.i.* **1,** to make a noise or sound; **2,** to be played upon, as an instrument; make music; **3,** to give a certain impression when heard; as, her voice *sounds* sad; **4,** to pronounce or be pronounced; as, "sole" and "soul" *sound* alike.—*adj.* **sound′less′.**

³sound (sound), *v.t.* **1,** to measure the depth of (water, etc.), as by lowering a weighted line from the surface; to fathom; **2,** to examine indirectly; try to find out the opinions or attitude of; as, to *sound* a person out on a delicate subject:—*v.i.* **1,** to measure the depth of water; **2,** to dive deeply, as do whales.

⁴sound (sound), *n.* **1,** a long stretch of water, wider than a strait, connecting two large bodies of water, or lying between the mainland and an island; as, Long Island *Sound*; **2,** the air bladder of a fish.

sound bite, a brief, attention-grabbing statement included in televised news programs, esp. repeatedly.

sound-board (sound′bôrd′), *n.* **1,** in *computing*, a computer sound card; **2,** the thin resonate wood as in a violin or piano which enhances the fullness of the tone.

sound card, in computing, a circuit board added to a computer to allow the use of an audio system, including external speakers, microphones, etc., for multimedia.

sound effects, sounds, other than speech or music, that artificially imitate noises such as traffic, thunder, etc., for effect in a film, play, or radio program.

sound-ing board, 1, someone whose reactions to ideas or opinions serves as a test of their validity; **2,** a structure placed on stage or by a podium to direct sound at the audience; **3,** a means of making one's opinions more widely known; as, to use a newspaper column as a *sounding board*; **4,** sound board.

sound-proof (sound′prōōf′), *adj.* not allowing sound to pass in or out; as, a *soundproof* door:—*v.t.* to make a room or building soundproof.—*n.* **sound′proof′ing.**

soundtrack or **sound track, 1,** the music of a movie; the commercial recording of this music; **2,** the part of a motion picture film on which sound is recorded.

soup (sōōp), *n.* **1,** liquid food, or broth, made by simmering meat, fish, or vegetables in a large quantity of liquid; it often contains solid pieces of food and is served as a first course; **2,** anything with the consistency of or like soup, as heavy fog, muddy water, etc.—*adj.* **soup′y′.**

soup kitchen, a place where meals, esp. soup, are dispensed to the needy.

sour (sour), *adj.* **1,** having a tart, sharp, biting taste, as vinegar, lemons, or green fruit; **2,** acid, esp. as a result of fermentation; as, *sour* cream; **3,** spoiled, decayed, or rancid; as, *sour* milk; **4,** disagreeable; cross; as, a *sour* disposition:—*v.t.* **1,** to cause to become acid, fermented, or spoiled; **2,** to cause to become cross and disagreeable:—*v.i.* to become acid, fermented, or spoiled.—*n.* **sour′ness.**—*adv.* **sour′ly.**

source (sōrs), *n.* **1,** the beginning of a stream; **2,** that from which anything rises or originates; the origin; as, the Internet is a *source* of information; **3,** a primary reference, document, or person who supplies information:—*adj.* **1,** pertaining to a primary reference or document; as, a *source* book; **2,** in *computing*, a computer program or software written in its original programming language; as, *source* code:—*v.t.* **1,** to specify or identify the source of a quotation, etc.; **2,** to obtain a product or service from a specific supplier.

sour cream, a smooth, thick cream made sour with acids and used as an ingredient in soups, salads, and other dishes, or as a topping.

sour-dough (sour′dō′), *n.* **1,** a type of bread mix that has active yeast, of which a small amount is saved and used to make the next batch; **2,** a Canadian or Alaskan prospector, who usually carried dough from camp to camp for use as a leaven in making bread: see Robert Service's *Songs of a Sourdough* (1907).

sour grapes, an attitude of belittling something that is unattainable; as, pretending that she didn't want the job she didn't get is just *sour grapes*.

sour-puss (sour′poos′), *n. Colloq.* an irritable, grumpy, or sullen person; grouch; killjoy.

soused (sousd), *adj. Slang* intoxicated; drunk.

south (south), *n.* **1,** one of the four points of the compass; the point opposite to the north, or to the right of a person facing the sunrise; **2,** the section of a country lying to the south; as, the *south* of France:—*adj.* having to do with, or coming from, the south; as, a *south* wind:—*adv.* to the south; as, turn *south*:—**the South**, in the U.S., that district lying generally south of the Ohio River and the southern boundary of Pennsylvania; the southeastern U.S.:—**South Pole**, the southern end of the earth's axis.—*n.* **south′ern-er.**—*adj.* **south′ern; south′ern-most.**—*adj.* and *adv.* **south′er-ly; south′ward.**

South A-mer-i-can (south a-mer′i-kan), *n.* a person who inhabits or originates from the South American continent:—*adj.* relating to the countries, the people, the languages, or the culture of this continent.

south-east (south′ēst′), *n.* **1,** the point on the compass halfway between south and east; **2,** a region lying in the direction of that point:—*adj.* having to do with the southeast, or in or from the southeast; as, a *southeast* wind:—*adv.* toward the southeast.—*adj.* **south′east′ern**—*adj.* and *adv.* **south′east′er-ly; south′east′ward.**

south-east-er (south′ēs′tėr), *n.* a storm or gale coming from the southeast.

south-paw (south′pô′), *adj. Slang* left-handed, esp. in pitching a baseball:—*n.* a left-handed person.

south–south-east (south′–south′ēst′), *n.* halfway between southeast and south.

south–south-west (south′–south′west′), *n.* halfway between southwest and south.

south-west (south′west′), *n.* **1,** the point of the compass halfway between south and west; **2,** a region lying in the direction of that point:—*adj.* having to do with the southwest, or in or from the southwest:—*adv.* toward the southwest.—*adj.* **south′west′ern.**—*adj.* and *adv.* **south′west′er-ly;′ south′west′ward.**

south-west-er (south′wes′tėr), *n.* a strong wind or storm from the southwest.

sou-ve-nir (so͞o′vė-nēr′; so͞o′vė-nēr), *n.* a thing by which to remember a person or an event; a memento or keepsake; as, a jar of sand as a *souvenir* of Prince Edward Island.

sou′-west-er (sou′wes′tėr), *n.* **1,** a southwester; **2,** a painted canvas or oilskin hat with a brim that is wide at the back, worn in stormy weather by sailors and fishermen; **3,** an oilskin coat worn in stormy weather.

Sou′wester

sov-er-eign (sov′rin; sov′ėr-in), *adj.* **1,** chief; supreme; as, *sovereign* power; **2,** possessing absolute and independent power; as, a *sovereign* state; **3,** principal; greatest; also, best and most effective; as, a *sovereign* remedy:—*n.* a ruler, as a king, emperor, or queen.

sov-er-eign-ist or **sov-er-eign-tist** (sov′rin-ist′ or sov′ėr-in-ist′; sov′rin-tist′ or sov′ėr-in-tist′) *n.* a separatist; someone who supports sovereignty for Québec; an advocate of the separation of Québec from the rest of Canada:—*adj.* relating to, advocating, or promoting the independence of Québec from Canada.

sov-er-eign-ty (sov′rin-ti; sov′ėr-in-ti′), *n.* [*pl.* sovereignties], supreme power or dominion, whether vested in a monarch or, as in a limited monarchy or a republic, in the people.

sovereignty association, a proposal for the political independence of Québec from Canada while retaining other significant ties, such as economic links, in an association between sovereign states.

so-vi-et (sō′vi-et; sō′vi-et′), *n.* and *adj.* **1,** an elected council of workers in a Communist country; **2,** (usually *Soviet*), one of the local councils or governing bodies of the former Union of Soviet Socialist Republics, which were elected by the people, and which sent delegates to the higher congresses; **3,** the people or citizens of the former U.S.S.R.

[1]**sow** (sou), *n.* a female hog.

[2]**sow** (sō), *v.t.* [*p.t.* sowed (sōd), *p.p.* sown (sōn) or sowed, *p.pr.* sow-ing], **1,** to strew or scatter, as seed, upon the earth; **2,** to strew seed in, on, or over; as, to *sow* a lawn; **3,** to cause to grow or spread; as, to *sow* discord:—*v.i.* to strew or scatter seed for growing.

soy or **soya** (soi; soi′o), *n.* and *adj.* Same as **soybean.**

soy-bean or **soya bean** (soi′bēn′; soi′o), *n.* a protein-rich bean or legume, originally from Southeast Asia, used in making flour and oil and eaten as an additive in many foods or as a substitute for animal protein: soybeans grow in pods on leafy green bushes:—**soy milk** or **soybean milk,** a low-fat milk substitute made from soybean flour:—**soy sauce** or **soya sauce,** salty brown sauce made from fermented soybeans:—**soyburger** or **soya burger,** a hamburger made from soybean curd instead of ground beef.

spa (spä). *n.* **1,** a mineral-spring resort; **2,** a fashionable, commercial resort, hotel, or other establishment that offers beauty, health, and fitness services.

space (spās), *n.* **1,** the boundless expanse in which our universe moves, and all known things exist; as, outer *space;* **2,** the empty area of air that surrounds objects on the earth; as, to stare off into *space;* **3,** a definite, or limited, distance or area; room; an area to be filled in some way; as, the *space* between the desk and the wall; that advertisement takes up too much *space;* parking *space;* **4,** length of time; as, in the *space* of a few months; **5,** in *music,* one of the open places between the lines of the staff; **6,** in typewritten or printed matter, one of the open spaces separating letters or words:—*v.t.* [spaced, spac-ing], to arrange, as letters, words, or objects by separating them with spaces; as, *space* the words evenly; *space* the chairs out around the room.—*n.* **spac′ing; space′ age′; space′ bar′; space′ ca-det′; space′ pro′gram; space′ heat′er; space′ man′; space′ship′; space′ sta′tion; space′ walk′.**—*adj.* **spa′tial; space′–sav′ing.**

space-craft (spās′kråft), *n.* any vehicle used for travelling outside the earth's atmosphere. Also called *spaceship.*

space shuttle, a vehicle that is launched into space by a rocket and used repeatedly to carry people and supplies between earth and space.

space suit, a special airtight astronauts' suit that protects against radiation, heat, and cold and provides oxygen.

spa-cious (spā′shus), *adj.* **1,** having a lot of space; large and open; roomy; as, a *spacious* house; **2,** extensive; expansive; taking up a lot of space; as, a *spacious* forest.—*adv.* **spa′cious-ly.**—*n.* **spa′cious-ness.**

spade (spād), *n.* **1,** a digging tool, consisting of a broad, flat blade of iron with a long handle; **2,** one of a suit, called *spades,* of playing cards, marked with a black figure like a pointed spade:—*v.t.* [spaded, spad-ing], to dig or work [ground] with a spade; as, to *spade* a garden—*n.* **spade′ful′.**

spa-ghet-ti (spa-get′i), *n.* a noodle or pasta made of flour and water that is very thin, long, stringlike, and cooked by boiling.

spam (spam), *n.* **1,** an unsolicited advertisement or other message sent to a random number of groups or individuals over the Internet; **2,** these messages collectively:—*v.i.* [spammed, spam-ming], to send such messages:—*v.t.* to send such a message to a particular group or individual.—*n.* **spam′mer; spam′ming.**

span (span), *n.* **1,** the distance from the end of the thumb to the tip of the little finger when the thumb and fingers are extended wide open; also, regarded as a measure of length, 23 centimetres (9 inches); **2,** a limited space of time; as, the life *span* of a person; short attention *span*; **3,** any extent having two definite bounds; as, the *span* of a river; **4,** the distance between the supports of an arch, a beam; etc.; also, the sections of an arch; a beam, etc., between two supports, **5,** a pair of horses, harnessed as a team:—*v.t.* [spanned, span-ning], **1,** to measure by the extended thumb and fingers; **2,** to extend or stretch across; as, a plank *spanned* the gully.

span-gle (spang′gl), *n.* **1,** one of the tiny, shining, metallic disks used to ornament dresses; **2,** any small, glittering ornament:—*v.t.* [span-gled, span-gling], to adorn with bits of shining material.—*adj.* **span′gly.**

span-iel (span′yel), *n.* any of various small or medium-sized dogs with drooping ears and long, silky hair.

Span-ish (spa′nish), *n.* **1,** a person who inhabits or originates from Spain; **2,** the language spoken by these people:—*adj.* relating to the country, the people, the language, or the culture of Spain.

spank (spangk), *v.t.* to hit; to punish by striking the buttocks with the open hand or other flat object in order to punish; as, to *spank* the puppy for biting:—*n.* a slap.

spank-ing (spank′ing), *adv.* very; extremely; as, a *spanking* new suit:—*n.* the act of punishing by slapping on the buttocks.

[1]**spar** (spär), *n.* a mast, yard, boom, etc., on a vessel:—*v.t.* [sparred, spar-ring], to fit with spars.

[2]**spar** (spär), *v.i.* [sparred, spar-ring], **1,** to fight with the fists; to box; esp., to box skilfully or scientifically; **2,** to engage in a contest of words; wrangle.

spare (spār), *v.t.* [spared, spar-ing], **1,** to use in a frugal or saving manner; use rarely; as, *spare* the rod; **2,** to do without conveniently; as, can you *spare* this book? **3,** to refrain from; omit; as, I shall *spare* no expense; **4,** to save (a person) from something; to keep from being hurt or punished; not harm or destroy; as, this will *spare* me trouble; to chase away the cat in order to *spare* the life of the bird; **5,** to avoid injuring; treat carefully; as, to *spare* a person's feelings:—*adj.* [spar-er, spar-est], **1,** thin; lean; **2,** held in reserve; as, a *spare* tire; also, extra; as, *spare* cash:—*n.* **1,** a spare part; esp., a spare tire; **2,** in *bowling,* the knocking over of all the pins in two attempts; also, the score for this; **3,** a free period in school with no class.

spar-ing (spâr′ing), *adj.* **1,** frugal; **2,** scanty; limited; as, a *sparing* use of salt.—*adv.* **spar′ing-ly.**

spark (spärk), *n.* **1,** a tiny, burning particle thrown off by something that is on fire; **2,** any bright, small flash; **3,** hence, any sudden flash; as, a *spark* of genius; **4,** a small sign or particle; as, not a *spark* of life remained; **5,** the flash of light produced by a discharge of electricity between two conductors; **6,** the discharge of electricity in a spark plug; also, the mechanism controlling this discharge:—*v.i.* **1,** to send out sparks; **2,** to produce an electric spark:—*v.t.* to activate; to set off or cause to begin; as the negative comment *sparked* a heated debate.

spar-kle (spär′kl), *v.i.* [spar-kled, spar-kling], **1,** to give off light in small flashes; glisten; gleam; as, the calm lake *sparkled* in the sunlight; **2,** to flash; scintillate, as wit; **3,** to bubble, as wine; as, champagne is a wine that *sparkles*:—*n.* a gleam or glitter, as of gems; also, a flash, as of wit.—*adj.* **spar′kling.**

spar-kler (spär′klėr), *n.* **1,** someone or something that sparkles; **2,** a type of handheld firework that emits bright sparks when lit.

spark plug (spärk′plug′), *n.* a device used in many engines, such as the engine of an automobile, for igniting a mixture of air and gasoline vapour by means of an electric spark.

spar-row (spar′ō), *n.* a common songbird of the finch family that is small, brown or grey, commonly found in North America and most parts of the world.

sparse (spärs), *adj.* [spars-er, spars-est], thinly scattered; scant and thinly distributed; as, *sparse* vegetation.—*adv.* **sparse′ly.**

spasm (spazm), *n.* **1,** a sudden, violent, involuntary contraction, or shortening of the muscles; as, a coughing *spasm*; **2,** a sudden, violent, but brief movement, emotion, etc.; as, a *spasm* of laughter.—*adv.* **spas-mod′ic** (spaz-mod′ik); **spas-mod′i-cal-ly.**

spas-tic (spas′tik), *adj.* denoting a form of paralysis in which there is a sudden involuntary contraction of muscles.

[1]**spat** (spat), *n. Colloq.* a small, unimportant, or petty quarrel or fight:—*v.i.* [spatted, spat-ting], to engage in a petty quarrel.

[2]**spat** (spat), *n.* a kind of short cloth gaiter fastened under the instep.

[3]**spat** (spat), *p.t.* and *p.p.* of *spit.*

spate (spāt), *n.* a great outpouring; outburst; a flood; as, a *spate* of words, rumours, books, etc.

spat-ter (spat′ėr), *v.t.* **1,** to splash a liquid upon; soil by splashing; as, to *spatter* the tablecloth with grease; **2,** to scatter in drops or by splashing; as, to *spatter* milk over the floor; **3,** to cover, as with splashes; as, a field *spattered* with flowers:—*v.i.* to splash in drops:—*n.* **1,** a splashing or sprinkling; **2,** a spot so made; **3,** a pattering, as of rain.

spat-u-la (spat′ū-la), *n.* an implement with a broad, flat, fairly flexible blade, used to slide under foods in order to turn them over, or for mixing, stirring, scraping, scooping, or spreading mixtures such as icing, plaster, etc.: used by painters, cooks, etc.

spawn (spôn), *n.* **1,** the eggs of fish, oysters, and other water animals that lay great numbers of small eggs; **2,** offspring:—*v.t.* and *v.i.* **1,** to lay or produce (eggs or spawn); **2,** to produce (offspring) in great numbers:—*v.t.* to create a new idea or product; produce; as, the book *spawned* a TV series.

spay (spā), *v.t.* to sterilize (a female animal) by removing the ovaries.

speak (spēk), *v.i.* [*p.t.* spoke (spōk), *p.p.* spoken (spō′ken), *p.pr.* speak-ing], **1,** to utter words; talk; **2,** to tell; mention; as, do not *speak* of this; **3,** to make an address or speech; **4,** to convey ideas, though not in words; as, our actions *speak* for us:—*v.t.* **1,** to utter, as a word; pronounce; **2,** to express in words; as, to *speak* the truth; **3,** to use, or be able to use, in conversation; as, he *speaks* four languages.—*n.* **speak′ing.**

speak-er (spē′kėr), *n.* **1,** a person who talks, esp. articulately, and often in public; **2,** one who is able to converse in a particular language; as, a French *speaker*; **3,** someone who speaks as an advocate or on behalf of others; a spokesperson; **4,** a loudspeaker:—**Speaker,** the presiding officer of a legislative body; as, the *Speaker* of the House of Commons.—*n.* **speak′er-ship.**

speak-er-phone (spē′kėr-fōn′), *n.* a telephone or other communication device that includes a microphone and loudspeaker, allowing hands-free operation.

spear (spēr), *n.* **1,** a weapon with a long shaft and sharp, pointed head, to be thrust or thrown; a lance; **2,** an instrument with barbed prongs for catching fish; **3,** a slender blade or shoot; as, a *spear* of grass; asparagus *spear*:—*v.t.* to pierce or catch with a spear; as, to *spear* a vegetable with a fork.

spear-head (spēr′hed′), *n.* **1,** the end or point of a spear; **2,** a leading group, element, or force in a campaign or undertaking:—*v.t.* to lead or act as a spearhead; as, to *spearhead* the school's environmental campaign.

spear-mint (spēr′mint′), *n.* a pleasant-smelling, spicy herb, used to give flavour to foods, chewing gum, toothpaste, etc.: the leaves are shaped like the head of a spear; the common garden mint.

spe-cial (spesh′al), *adj.* **1,** characterizing a single person or thing, or a single class; as, the *special* qualities of a leader; **2,** designed for a particular purpose; as, a *special* course of study; **3,** particular; unusual, esp. in a good way; as, a *special* favour; a *special* point of interest; **4,** esteemed beyond others, intimate; as, a *special* companion:—*n.* **1,** something that is special or offered at a reduced price; as, a restaurant's *special*; the store's *special*; **2,** a television program that is not part of a regular series.—*adv.* **spe′cial-ly.**

special education, educational classes or programs adapted for students with special needs, such as those with physical or mental advantages or disadvantages.

special interest group, 1, a group or organization with common goals or purposes, esp. one that attempts to influence legislators; a lobby; **2,** people with a common interest in a particular topic, esp. those who engage in discussions over the Internet.

spe-cial-ist (spesh′al-ist), *n.* a person who limits himself to one particular field of work or study, esp. a doctor; as, an eye *specialist.*

spe-ci-al-i-ty (spesh′i-al′i-ti), *n.* **1,** the distinctive mark of a person or thing; as the *speciality* of an author's style; sauces are the chef's *speciality*; in *pl.* [specialities] details; particulars; **2,** a specialty (definitions 1, 2).

spe-cial-ize (spesh′al-īz′), *v.i.* [specialized, specializ-ing], to pursue a particular line of action or course of study; as, to *specialize* in science:—*v.t.* to modify or adapt for a particular purpose or use.—*n.* **spe′cial-i-za′tion.**—*adj.* **spe′cial-ized.**

spe-cial-ty (spesh′al-ti), *n.* **1,** a line of work or study to which one is particularly devoted; as, my *specialty* is music; **2,** an article dealt in exclusively or chiefly; as, their *specialty* is laptop computers; **3,** a speciality (definition 1).

spe-cies (spē′sēz; spē′shēz), *n.* [*pl.* species], **1,** a kind; variety; **2,** a group of animals or plants differing from each other in minor respects, and having certain common characteristics that clearly distinguish the group from other groups; as, coyotes and wolves are different *species* of the dog family.

spe-cif-ic (spi-sif′ik), *adj.* **1,** pertaining to a species; as, a *specific* name for an insect; **2,** definite or particular; precise; clearly stated; as, *specific* information; **3,** having some restricted, particular quality; as, a *specific* medicine; a disease *specific* to birds:—*n.* anything that is suited to a particular use or purpose:—**specific gravity,** the ratio of the weight of a given mass or volume of substance to that of an equal volume of water (for solids and liquids) or of hydrogen (for gases).

spe-cif-i-cal-ly (spi-sif′i-kal-i), *adv.* **1,** with respect to one particular point; **2,** definitely; in particular.

spec-i-fi-ca-tion (spes′i-fi-kā′shun), *n.* **1,** the act of stating or specifying in detail; **2,** specifications, the items of a detailed statement of requirements for carrying out some work or project; also, the statement; as, the *specifications* for a building.

spec-i-fy (spes′i-fī′), *v.t.* [specified, specifying], to mention or name particularly; state fully and clearly; as, to *specify* a time for the meeting.

spec-i-men (spes′i-men), *n.* **1,** a part that represents or shows the quality of the whole; sample; as, a *specimen* of ore; **2,** one of a group from which the characteristics of the entire group may be studied; as, an insect *specimen*: [*pl.* add *s*]; **3,** a sample of material for testing or examination; as, a urine or blood *specimen.*

spe-cious (spē′shus), *adj.* seeming to be right or logical, but not really so; apparently fair or just, but not genuine; as, *specious* arguments, reasoning, etc.—*adv.* **spe′cious-ly.**

speck (spek), *n.* **1,** a spot or flaw; blemish; as, a *speck* of decay in fruit; **2,** a very small thing; particle; as, a *speck* of dust:—*v.t.* to spot or stain with small spots; speckle.

speck-le (spek′l), *n.* a small spot in or on something; as, the *speckles* on a speckled trout:—*v.t.* [speck-led, speck-ling], to mark with speckles.

spec-ta-cle (spek′ta-kl), *n.* **1,** something displayed to view, esp. something unusual, impressive, or worthy of notice; a public exhibition; pageant; as, the fireworks display was quite a *spectacle*; **2,** a silly or embarrassing sight; as, to make a *spectacle* of oneself; **3,** **spectacles,** a pair of eyeglasses for assisting or correcting vision.

spec-tac-u-lar (spek-tak′ū-lėr), *adj.* sure to be noticed and remembered, very unusual or impressive; as, a *spectacular* view of the ocean:—*n.* a lavishly elaborate event or show, such as a television program, movie, or theatrical production.

spec-ta-tor (spek-tā′tėr; spek′tā-tėr), *n.* one who looks on or watches, as at a game, theatre, or parade; an observer.

spec-tral (spek′tral), *adj.* **1,** pertaining to, or like, a ghost; ghostly; as, a *spectral* light; **2,** pertaining to a spectrum; as, *spectral* analysis.—*adv.* **spec′ tral-ly.**

spec-tre or **spec-ter** (spek′tėr), *n.* **1,** a ghost or apparition; **2,** something that is feared or haunts the mind and emotions; as, the *spectre* of poverty.

spec-trum (spek′trum), *n.* [*pl.* spectra (spek′tra) or spectrums], **1,** the image formed when light is broken up into its constituent parts, and these are arranged according to their different wavelengths, as in the rainbow, or when light passes through a prism; **2,** a wide range; a variety; as, a broad *spectrum* of opinions.

spec-u-late (spek′ū-lāt′), *v.i.* [speculated, speculat-ing], **1,** to meditate; consider a subject from every side, without having all the facts or evidence, before forming an opinion; to guess; as, to *speculate* how the dinosaurs died; **2,** to buy or sell, with the idea of profiting by a rise or fall in prices; to take a risk in business that may pay off in profit; as, to *speculate* on a new invention.—*n.* **spec′u-la′tion; spec′u-la′tor.**—*adj.* **spec′u-la′tive.**

sped (sped), *p.t.* and *p.p.* of *speed.*

speech (spēch), *n.* **1,** the power of uttering sounds or words that are understandable; **2,** the expression of thought in words; the act of speaking; **3,** manner of speaking; as, his *speech* is indistinct; **4,** that which is spoken; words; remarks; **5,** a language or dialect; as, Italian is a musical *speech*; **6,** a formal talk, delivered in public.—*adj.* **speech′less.**—*n.* **speech′less-ness.**

speech recognition, 1, in *computing,* the devices and techniques that allow a user to operate a computer with just voice commands; **2,** the ability of a computer, using specialized software, to recognize and respond to the sounds of the human voice. Also called *voice recognition.*

speed (spēd), *n.* **1,** swiftness of motion; **2,** rate of motion; as, to reduce the *speed* of the car; **3,** in *photography,* the sensitivity of the film; the power of a lens or the time the shutter remains open; **4,** something or someone to one's liking or ability; as, singing is not her *speed*; **5,** methamphetamine:—*v.t.* [sped (sped) or speed-ed, speed-ing], to cause to move faster; accelerate; as, to *speed* up an engine; he *sped* the job to completion:—*v.i.* **1,** to move quickly; as, the car *sped* toward him; **2,** to move at too great a speed, faster than the law allows; as, he *sped* faster than the speed limit.—*n.* **speed′er; speed′ing; speed′ boat′; speed′ bump′; speed′-dial′; speed′-dial′ling; speed′ lim′it; speed′-read′; speed′ skat′er; speed′ trap′; speed′way′.**—*adj.* **speed′ y.**—*adv.* **speed′i-ly.**

speed-om-e-ter (spē-dom′e-tėr), *n.* a device on a vehicle, esp. an automobile, to show the speed in kilometres per hour.

[1]spell (spel), *n.* **1,** magic power to control a person's actions; **2,** a spoken word, or words, supposed to act as a charm; **3,** hence, fascination or power of great charm or attraction; as, the *spell* of her beauty.

[2]spell (spel), *v.i.* [spelled (speld) or spelt (spelt), spell-ing], to form words with letters:—*v.t.* **1,** to give, in order, the, proper letters of (a word); **2,** to make out or decipher with difficulty; as, to *spell* out an inscription; **3,** to make up or form; as, the letters d, o, g, *spell* "dog"; **4,** to indicate or mean; as, war *spells* hardship.

[3]spell (spel), *n.* **1,** a turn at work to relieve another; as, a *spell* at the oars; **2,** any short period of time; as, a hot *spell*; **3,** *Colloq.* a short attack of illness; as, a dizzy *spell*:—*v.t.* [spelled, spell-ing] to take the place of, or do a turn for; as, let me *spell* you at the oars.

spell-bind (spel′bīnd′), *v.t.* [spell-bound, spell-bind-ing], to capture and hold someone's attention as if by a spell; to fascinate; enchant.

spell-bound (spel′bound′), *adj.* fascinated; enchanted.

spell check, in *computing*, the verification of the correctness of the spelling of words in a document, esp. by use of a special software program:—*v.t.* the act of doing this task:—**spell check′er**, computer software that examines the spelling of words in a text, verifies their correctness, and amends them as needed.

spell-er (spel′ėr), *n.* **1,** one who spells, esp. one who spells in a particular way; as, a good *speller*; a poor *speller*; **2,** a book that teaches spelling.

spell-ing (spel′ing), *n.* **1,** the act of putting letters together to form words, or a school subject that teaches this; **2,** the correct written form of a word:—**spelling bee**, a contest to see who can spell the most words correctly.

spelt (spelt), a *p.t.* and *p.p.* of *spell*.

spend (spend), *v.t.* [spent (spent), spend-ing], **1,** to pay out, as money; **2,** to expend or use up, as strength or energy; to squander; to exhaust; as, to *spend* all your energy playing ball; **3,** to pass (time); as, I *spent* an hour shopping.—*n.* **spend′er.**

spend-thrift (spend′thrift′), *adj.* wasteful; extravagant:—*n.* one who spends money foolishly or wastefully.

spent (spent), *v.i.* and *v.t.*, *p.t.* and *p.p.* of *spend*:—*adj.* used up; consumed; exhausted; as, to be utterly *spent* after the race; a *spent* laser cartridge.

sperm (spûrm), *n.* the fertilizing fluid of male animals that can fertilize the egg of a female animal in order to produce new life; also, one of the many living germ cells that it contains.

sperm whale or **cach′a-lot′,** a large, toothed whale with a huge, flat head, that is found in all oceans: *Moby Dick* was of this species.

spew (spū), *v.t.* and *v.i.* to pour out; move in a strong, quick flow; to vomit; as, fire *spewed* from the building; the sick child *spewed* out the food.

sphere (sfēr), *n.* **1,** a round, solid body with a continuous surface, every point of which is equally distant from the point within called its centre; **2,** a globe or globelike body; a ball; also, a planet; **3,** extent or range of knowledge, influence, action, etc.; as, to seek a wider *sphere* for one's abilities; to be under a country's *sphere* of influence.—*adj.* **spher′i-cal** (sfer′i-kal).

sphe-roid (sfē′roid), *n.* a body nearly spherical, as the earth (an oblate *spheroid*, being flattened at the poles).

spiff-y (spi′fi), *adj. Colloq.* neat; smart; elegant; stylish; as, a *spiffy* dresser.

sphinx (sfingks), *n.* [*pl.* sphinxes (sfingk′sez)], **1,** in *Greek mythology*, a monster with the body of a winged lion and a woman's head and breasts who killed anyone who could not answer its riddle; **2,** any ancient Egyptian statues or images thus shaped; **3,** a mystifying or enigmatic person.

spice (spīs), *n.* **1,** aromatic seeds, leaves or other parts of a plant, ground or powdered, used for seasoning, as cinnamon, nutmeg, garlic, or pepper; **2,** that which gives flavour or zest; relish; as, a *spice* of humour:—*v.t.* [spiced, spic-ing], to season or flavour with spice or spices.—*adj.* **spic′y.**—*n.* **spic′i-ness.**

spider (spī′dėr), *n.* **1,** a small, wingless, eight-legged animal that belongs to the arachnid class of arthropods: it is capable of spinning silken threads, of which it makes cocoons for eggs, and in some instances, webs for catching prey; **2,** anything thought to resemble or recall a spider.—*adj.* **spi′der-y.**

spied (spīd), *p.t.* of *spy*.

spiel (spēl), *n. Slang* a talk or speech, such as a sales presentation or pitch:—*v.i. Slang* to talk or speak this way.

spig-ot (spig′ut), *n.* **1,** a plug or peg used to stop a cask; **2,** a tap.

[1]spike (spīk), *n.* **1,** a sharp point; **2,** any slender pointed object, as a kind of large nail; **3,** one of the metal pieces fastened to the soles of certain shoes used in sports, such as football and golf, to prevent slipping; **4,** a sudden increase, as in prices; **5,** a sudden but brief increase and decrease in voltage:—*v.t.* [spiked, spik-ing], **1,** to fasten or equip with large nails or sharp points; **2,** to run through or stab with a sharp point; **3,** to make (a gun, cannon, etc.) useless by driving a spike into an opening; **4,** hence, to make ineffective or suppress; as, to *spike* gossip; **5,** to add alcohol to a drink; **6,** to add zest, vitality, or spice to something; as, to *spike* the story with amusing anecdotes; **7,** to hit or drive something downward sharply; as, to *spike* a volleyball.—*adj.* **spik′y.**

[2]**spike** (spīk), *n.* **1,** an ear of grain; **2,** a long, often tapering, flower cluster, in which the flowers grow along the sides of the stalk, as in a hyacinth.—*n.* **spike′let** (a secondary spike).

spile (spīl), *n.* a spout or spigot driven into a hole bored in a tree, as the sugar maple, to drain off the sap.

spill (spil), *v.t.* [spilled (spild) or spilt (spilt), spill-ing], **1,** to permit to run over, or fall out of, a vessel or other container by accident; as, don't *spill* the water; **2,** to cause to be scattered, wasted, lost, etc.; as, to *spill* blood; **3,** to divulge; as, to *spill* their secret plans:—*v.i.* to flow over, fall out, be scattered, etc.; as, her hair *spilled* over her shoulders; the students *spilled* into the auditorium:—*n.* **1,** an overflowing or downpour, as of liquid or rain: **2,** a fall or tumble; as, a *spill* from a horse; **3,** the overflow of a dam, etc.

spill-o-ver (spil′ō′vėr), *n.* **1,** the act or process of overflowing; **2,** the amount that spills over; **3,** a byproduct or unintended consequence:—*adj.* effects beyond those intended; repercussions; as, a *spillover* effect.

spill-way (spil′wā′), *n.* a channel for carrying away the overflow of a dam, etc.

spin (spin), *v.t.* [*p.t.* spun (spun), *p.p.* spun, *p.pr.* spin-ning], **1,** to draw out and twist (fibre) into threads; as, to *spin* cotton; **2,** to form (a web or cocoon) by drawing out threads of fluid from a gland; said of spiders, silkworms, etc.; **3,** to draw out to some length; as, to *spin* a long story; **4,** to cause to whirl rapidly, as a top:—*v.i.* **1,** to engage in drawing out and twisting fibre into threads, or in making a thread as a spider does; **2,** to whirl or turn quickly around in circles; **3,** to feel dizzy from turning quickly; as, my head is *spinning*; *Colloq.* to move swiftly; as, to *spin* along on a bicycle:—*n.* **1,** the act of spinning; esp., a rapid whirling; **2,** *Colloq.* a short drive, as in an automobile; **3,** a special, biased interpretation to produce a favourable image; as, the bureaucrat put her own *spin* on the commission's findings.—*n.* **spin′ner; spin′ doc′tor.**

spin-ach (spin′ich; spin′ij), *n.* a common garden vegetable with dark green leaves, which are eaten raw in salads or cooked.

spi-nal (spī′nal), *adj.* pertaining to the backbone, or spinal column; as, the *spinal* fluid; a *spinal* puncture.

spinal cord, the thick band of nerve tissue running through the centre of the spine, which carries messages between the brain and the rest of the body.

spin-dle (spin′dl), *n.* **1,** in spinning, a long, thin rod, or a tapering stick, used for twisting and winding the thread; **2,** a slender rod or pin on which something turns.—*adj.* **spin′dling** (long and thin); **spin′dly.**

spin-drift (spin′drift), *n.* spray or foam blown up from the surface of a stormy sea.

spine (spīn), *n.* **1,** the bones down the centre of the back that support the body and protect the nerves of the spinal cord; the backbone, or spinal column; **2,** something like the backbone in position or function; **3,** the strip on the narrow edge of a book that joins the front cover to the back; **4,** hence, that which supports or strengthens; endurance or courage; as, the coward had no *spine* at all; **5,** a stiff, thorn-shaped or pointed growth on a plant, as the hawthorn or barberry, or on an animal, as the hedgehog or porcupine.—*adj.* **spined; spine′less; spin′y.**

SPINAL COLUMN

spin-na-ker (spin′a-kėr), *n.* a large triangular sail used with a light boom (spinnaker boom) on the side opposite the mainsail when a yacht is running before the wind.

spinning wheel, a hand- or foot-operated machine on which fibres, as cotton or wool, were twisted into thread or yarn: used before sewing machines were invented.

spin-off (spin′ôf′), *n.* something developed or established from an earlier product, such as a company, a television program, etc.; a byproduct.

spin-ster (spin′stėr), *n.* an unmarried woman, or one who is unlikely to marry.—*n.* **spin′ster-hood′.**

spi-ra-cle (spi′rē-kl), *n.* a small opening for taking in and expelling air or water, as in the whale or some crustaceans, insects, etc.; a blowhole or vent.

spi-ral (spī′ral), *adj.* **1,** winding around a fixed point or centre in increasingly larger circles, like a watch spring; **2,** winding about a cylindrical surface, like the thread of a screw, or the stripes on a candy cane:—*n.* a spiral curve; a curve like that of a watch spring or the thread of a screw; a coil:—*v.i.* and *v.t.* [spiralled, spiral-ling], to follow, or cause to follow, a spiral course; as, the smoke slowly *spiralled* upward; the airplane *spiralled* downward.—*adv.* **spi′ral-ly.**

spire (spīr), *n.* **1,** a slender leaf or blade, as of grass; **2,** a form that tapers to a point; esp., the slender, tapering top of a tower or steeple; also, a steeple.

spir-it (spir′it), *n.* **1,** the soul; the mental, nonphysical part of humans; of a dead person, the immortal part thought of as continuing to exist apart from the body; **2,** a supernatural being, as a sprite or fairy; a ghost; also, a being without a body; as, departed *spirits*; **3,** a person considered with reference to qualities of mind or character; as, the poet is a noble *spirit*; **4,** (often **spirits),** state of mind; mood; as, to be in low *spirits*; Christmas *spirit*; **5,** courage; energy and vim; as, the troops advanced with *spirit*; **6,** enthusiasm for an object, place, or concept; as, school *spirit*; **7,** real meaning; true intent; as, the *spirit* of the law, not just the letter of the law; also, the chief characteristic or influence; as, the scientific *spirit* of the 21st century; **8,** (usually *spirits*): **a,** any strong distilled alcoholic liquor, as brandy, whisky, etc.; **b,** an alcoholic solution of certain drugs that evaporate easily; as, *spirits* of ammonia:—**Spirit,** the third person of the Trinity: also called *Holy Spirit, Holy Ghost*:—*v.t.* to carry off (a person) suddenly and secretly; as, to *spirit* away the school mascot.—*adj.* **spir′it-less.**

spir-it-ed (spir′i-tid), *adj.* **1,** full of vigour or life; animated; lively; as, a *spirited* horse; **2,** having a certain feeling or spirit; as, a poor-*spirited* student; a mean-*spirited* bully.

spir-it-u-al (spir′it-ū-al), *adj.* **1,** pertaining to the mind or spirit, as distinguished from matter, the body, or the physical world; **2,** pertaining to the soul or higher nature of humans; pure; holy; **3,** pertaining to sacred or religious things; as, *spiritual* guidance:—*n.* a hymn or sacred song, esp. one originating among the black people of the southern U.S. in the 1800s.—*n.* **spir′it-u-al′i-ty.**—*adv.* **spir′it-u-al-ly.**

spir-it-u-al-ism or **spir-it-ism** (spir′it-ū-al-izm; spir′i-tizm), *n.* the belief that departed spirits communicate with the living, esp. through a medium, as by rapping, writing, etc.—*n.* **spir′it-u-al-ist.**

[1]**spit** (spit), *n.* **1,** a long pointed rod or bar, used to hold meat for roasting over an open fire or in a barbecue; **2,** a narrow point of land extending into the sea:—*v.t.* [spit-ted, spit-ting], to pierce with a spit; impale.

[2]**spit** (spit), *v.t.* [spat (spat) or spit, spit-ting], **1,** to eject (saliva, blood, etc.) from the mouth; **2,** to eject, emit, or expel; as, the cannon *spat* fire; to *spit* out words; to *spit* rain:—*v.i.* **1,** to eject saliva from the mouth; **2,** to make a hissing noise: said esp. of cats:—*n.* **1,** saliva; **2,** the act of ejecting saliva.—**spitting image,** exact likeness; as, she is the *spitting image* of her mother.—*n.* **spit′ter.**

spit-ball (spit′bôl′), *n.* **1,** a pellet of chewed paper, thrown or shot at someone as a prank; **2,** in *baseball*, an illegal pitch made to curve by moistening one side of the ball with saliva. Also called a *spitter*.

spite (spīt), *n.* ill will or hatred toward another; malice; as, to tear up the picture out of *spite*:—**in spite of,** despite; in defiance of; notwithstanding; even though there are opposing facts or conditions; as, to be angry *in spite of* her apology:—*v.t.* [spit-ed, spiting], to show malice toward; try to injure or baffle; annoy.—*adj.* **spite′ful.**—*adv.* **spite′ful-ly.**—*n.* **spite′ful-ness.**

spit-tle (spit′l), *n.* **1,** spit; saliva; **2,** the froth or spit that surrounds the larvae of certain insects.

spit-toon (spi-tōōn′), *n.* a vessel into which one may spit; a cuspidor.

splash (splash), *v.t.* **1,** to spatter or toss about; as, to *splash* water; **2,** to spatter or soil with water, mud, etc.:—*v.i.* **1,** to dash or spatter a liquid about in drops; as, don't *splash;* **2,** to move or proceed with a splashing noise; as, to *splash* into, or through, a puddle; **3,** to fall or fly about in drops; as, the paint *splashed* over the floor:—*n.* **1,** a spot or daub; as, I have a *splash* of mud on my dress; **2,** an irregular spot of colour; a blotch; as, the dog has a *splash* of black on his head; **3,** a noise as from sudden, violent contact with water; as, he plunged into the pool with a *splash*; **4,** someone or something that creates excitement; as, the new band caused a big *splash* in the city.—*adj.* **splash′y.**—*n.* **splash′er.**

splash-down (splash′doun′), *n.* the landing of a spacecraft in water; as, a *splash-down* in the Pacific Ocean.

splat-ter (splat′or), *v.t.* and *v.i.* to spatter; splash; as, the soup *splattered* over my new shirt.

splay (splā), *v.t., v.i.,* and *adj.* **1,** to spread out; turned outward; as *splay*-toed, *splay*-footed; to *splay* your fingers out; **2,** to bevel, as the outward edge of a doorway, window, etc.

spleen (splēn), *n.* one of the ductless glands near the stomach that filters and stores blood: part of the immune system.

splen-did (splen′did), *adj.* **1,** magnificent; gorgeous; inspiring; as, a *splendid* spectacle; **2,** very good, excellent; as, a *splendid* opportunity; **3,** grand; distinguished; illustrious; as, the *splendid* coronation.—*adv.* **splen′did-ly.**

splen-dour or **splen-dor** (splen′dėr), *n.* **1,** dazzling brightness; brilliance; as, the *splendour* of diamonds; **2,** magnificence; pomp; as, the *splendour* of a king's court.

splice (splīs), *v.t.* [spliced, splic-ing], **1,** to unite without knots, as two ropes, by interweaving the ends of the strands; **2,** to connect (pieces of wood, metal, film, or magnetic tape) by overlapping and sticking the ends together; **3,** to join, link, or unite something as if by splicing; **4,** to combine or unite genetic material; as, to *splice* genes:—*n.* the union, or place of union (of rope, wood, metal, film, magnetic tape, slopes, timbers, etc.) by splicing.—*adj.* **spliced.**—*n.* **splic′er.**

splint (splint), *n.* **1,** one of a number of thin strips of wood interwoven to form baskets, etc.; **2,** a straight, rigid device or appliance for holding in place a broken or fractured bone until it mends.

splin-ter (splin′tėr), *n.* a thin, sharp fragment of wood, metal, glass, etc., split or torn off lengthwise; a fragment:—**splinter group**, a faction, such as a political party or religious sect, that has broken away from a larger one:—*v.t.* and *v.i.* to split into long, thin pieces.—*adj.* **splin′ter-y.**

split (split), *v.t.* [split, split-ting], **1,** to divide, break, or cut lengthwise; as, to *split* wood; **2,** to break or tear apart; to shatter; as, the frost *splits* rocks; the loud noise *split* the air; **3,** to divide or break up into parts; as, to *split* a large class into several sections; **4,** to share or divide into equal parts; as, to *split* the cost of lunch:—**split hairs,** to make too fine distinctions:—*v.i.* **1,** to burst; break apart; as, my sleeve *split;* **2,** to divide lengthwise, or with the grain; as, wood *splits* easily; **3,** to separate into groups; as, a political party *splits:*—*n.* **1,** a break or crack; **2,** a division or separation, as in a group; **3,** an exercise in which the legs are opened straight out over the floor, in the air, or over an apparatus such as a balancing beam:—**split infinitive**, one with a word (esp. an adverb) between the *to* and the verb; as, *to boldly go* (justifiable when used to avoid ambiguity or awkwardness or for emphasis).

split–lev-el (split′–lev′el; split′–lev′l), *adj.* a dwelling or other building with floor levels divided so that each is about half a storey higher or lower than the one adjacent; as, *split-level* house.

split personality, a psychological disorder in which patients exhibit more than one distinct but dissociated personality; multiple personality; dissociative identity disorder.

splotch (sploch), *n.* a stain; daub; blotch:—*v.t.* to mark with stains or blotches.—*adv.* **splotch′y.**

splurge (splûrj), *n. Colloq.* a showy display by spending money extravagantly; as, after we wrote our final exams, we made a *splurge* and went to the expensive resort for a holiday:—*v.i.* to spend money excessively; as, to *splurge* on a new sports car.

splut-ter (splut′ėr), *v.i.* **1,** to speak hastily and confusedly; as, to *splutter* with excitement; **2,** to make a hissing noise; sputter; as, the candles *spluttered* in their holders:—*v.t. Colloq.* to utter in a quick, incoherent manner; to stammer:—*n.* a confused, spluttering noise or sound; stir.

spoil (spoil), *v.t.* [spoiled (spoild) or spoilt (spoilt), spoil-ing], **1,** to damage or impair the good qualities of; mar; as, the rain *spoiled* the party; **2,** to indulge (a child) with harmful effects on its character; pamper; as, to *spoil* a kitten by feeding it whenever it meowed:—*v.i.* to decay; as, food sometimes *spoils* in warm weather:—*n.* **spoils, 1,** pillage; plunder; booty; as, they shared the *spoils;* **2,** public offices and the gain derived from them, appropriated as plunder by the successful party in an election:—**spoilsport**, someone who spoils others' pleasure.—*adj.* **spoiled.**

[1]**spoke** (spōk), *p.t.* of *speak.*

[2]**spoke** (spōk), *n.* **1,** one of the bars of a wheel connecting the hub with the rim, as on a bicycle tire; **2,** a round or rung of a ladder:—*v.t.* to furnish with spokes.—*adj.* **spoked.**

[1]**spo-ken** (spō′ken), *p.p.* of *speak.*

[2]**spo-ken** (spō′ken), *adj.* **1,** expressed in speech; oral as opposed to written; as, *spoken* language; **2,** speaking in a certain way; as, a soft-*spoken* person.

spokes-per-son (spōks′pûr′sn), *n.* [*pl.* spokespersons or spokespeople (-pē′pl)], a person who speaks formally for another person, group, or organization; an agent or representative. Also, **spokes′man′, spokes′wom′an, spokes′mo′ del,** etc.

spon-dee (spon′dē), *n.* a poetic foot of two long or accented syllables [– –]; as, "Rōse frŏm theĭr/*sēa-wēed*/chāmbĕrs thĕ/mȳstĭcăl/chōir ŏf thĕ/*sēa-māids*" (Kingsley's *Andromeda*).

sponge (spunj), *n.* **1,** the porous elastic mass of horny fibres forming the skeleton of certain saltwater animals and capable of absorbing a large quantity of water; also, any of these animals; **2,** household sponges that were originally made from these animals but are now made of a synthetic material; **3,** any light, porous, or absorbent substance like a sponge, as raised dough; as, *sponge* cake:—*v.t.* [sponged, spong-ing], **1,** to cleanse, wipe out, or dampen with a sponge; as, to *sponge* the floor; **2,** to take up or absorb, as with a sponge; as to *sponge* the water off the counter; **3,** *Colloq.* to obtain by imposing upon someone; as, to *sponge* a dinner:—*v.i.* **1,** *Colloq.* to live as a parasite upon others, or to get something without paying for it, by imposing upon someone; **2,** to gather sponges.—*adj.* **spon′gy.**—*n.* **spong′er; spon′gi-ness**

spon-sor (spon′sėr), *n.* **1,** a company, business, or other group that pays for all or part of a television or radio show in order to advertise on the program; **2,** any person or group that endorses, pays, or lends support to a person, event, movement, etc.; as, the *sponsor* of the jazz festival; **3,** a godfather or godmother:—*v.t.* to endorse or support; be a sponsor for; as, to *sponsor* a bill in Parliament.—*n.* **spon′sor-ship.**

spon-ta-ne-ous (spon-tā′ni-us), *adj.* **1,** acting or springing from natural impulse; as, *spontaneous* applause; **2,** produced by internal forces rather than by an external cause; as, *spontaneous* combustion.—*adv.* **spon-ta′ne-ous-**

ly.—*n.* **spon′ta-ne′i-ty** (spon′ta-nē′i-ti).

spoof (spo͞of), *v.t.* and *v.i.* *Slang* **1,** to deceive as by a yarn or story; to hoax; **2,** to make light, exaggerated fun of someone or something; to parody; as, to *spoof* the candidate's gaffe.

spook (spo͝ok), *n.* a ghost or spirit; apparition: used humorously:—*v.t.* to scare or startle; as, to *spook* the horses:—*v.i.* to become scared or startled; as, to be *spooked* by the eerie sound.—*adj.* **spook′y.**

spool (spo͞ol), *n.* a hollow cylinder or reel of wood or metal, with a rim at each end, for winding thread, wire, tape, film, etc.:—*v.t.* **1,** to wind on a spool; as, to *spool* thread; **2,** in *computing*, to use a spooler.

spool-er (spo͞ol′ėr), *n.* in *computing*, a computing device that can temporarily store data to be printed at a later time, thereby allowing the main operating and processing systems to continue to function.

spoon (spo͞on), *n.* **1,** a utensil with a shallow bowl at the end of a handle, used in preparing, serving, or eating food; **2,** something resembling a spoon, as an oar with a curved blade, a fishing lure, etc.:—*v.t.* to use or take up with, or as with, a spoon.—*n.* **spoon′ful.**

spoon-er-ism (spo͞on′ėr-izm), *n.* the accidental interchange of two sounds; as, it is *k*ist-omary to *c*uss the bride; *d*ickens and *ch*ucks.

spoor (spo͞or), *n.* the track, trail, or scent of a (wild) animal; footprint.

spo-rad-ic (spō-rad′ik), *adj.* occasional; scattered; as, *sporadic* strikes; *sporadic* outbreaks of disease.—*adv.* **spo-rad′i-cal-ly.**

spore (spōr), *n.* a very small cell, occurring in flowerless plants, such as ferns and fungi, and in certain plantlike animals, capable of developing into a new plant or animal.

sport (spōrt), *n.* **1,** an athletic game or other activity in which people actively use the body, play according to certain fixed rules, and compete to win, as baseball or hockey; **2,** outdoor or indoor activity done for recreation or enjoyment, as hiking, swimming, or biking; **3,** a person judged as to how fairly she or he plays a game and reacts to winning or losing; as, a good *sport*; a poor *sport*:—*v.t.* to show off, or wear in public; as, to *sport* a diamond ring:—*adj.* (also *sports*), relating to, or suitable for, outdoor games, recreation, or enjoyment; as, a *sports* car; also, adapted to informal outdoor wear; as, *sports* clothes.—*n.* **sports′ bar′; sports′cast; sports′ coat′; sports′ jack′et; sports′ plex′; sports′ shirt′; sports′wear′; sports′writ′er.**—*adj.* **sport′ing; sport′y** (*Colloq.*)

sports car, a small, low car seating one or two people, designed for high speed and quick turns.

sports-man (spōrts′man), *n.* [*pl.* sportsmen (-men)], **1,** one who engages in sports, esp. racing or fishing: **2,** one who is fair and honourable in sports.—*adj.* **sports′man-like′.**—*n.* **sports′man-ship′.**—*n.fem.* **sports′woman.** Also, **sports′ per-son.**

spot (spot), *n.* **1,** a blot or mark; a discoloured place or stain; as, a *spot* of ink; **2,** a blemish; as, a *spot* on his reputation; **3,** locality; place; as, the exact *spot* where he fell; a popular *spot*; **4,** a small part of a surface, differing from the background in colour; as, *spots* on a playing card; **5,** a difficult or embarrassing situation; as, a tight *spot*:—*v.t.* [spot-ted, spot-ting], **1,** to mark with spots; discolour; stain; **2,** to disgrace or blemish; **3,** *Colloq.* to mark or note; recognize; as, we *spotted* the guilty man:—*v.i.* to become marked or stained; as, velvet always *spots* with water.—*adj.* **spot′ty; spot′ted.**—*n.* **spot′ter.**

spot check, a random, unannounced test or inspection; as, a traffic *spot check* for alcohol consumption.—*v.t.* **spot′-check′.**

spot-less (spot′les), *adj.* not having any marks, stains, flaws; completely clean; as, a *spotless* kitchen.

spot-light (spot′līt), *n.* **1,** a brilliant beam of light directed at a particular object or person, as an actor on a stage; also, the lamp or apparatus that throws this light; **2,** hence, prominence; public notice; as, his fight against pollution kept him in the *spotlight*:—*v.t.* [spotlight-ed or spot-lit, spotlight-ing], to light up or make prominent, as with a spotlight.

spouse (spouz), *n.* either one of a married couple; husband or wife.—*adj.* **spou′sal.**

spout (spout), *v.t.* **1,** to throw out (liquid) forcibly in a jet or stream, as does a pipe; **2,** to utter pompously or tiresomely; as, to *spout* poetry:—*v.i.* **1,** to come forth with violence in a jet or stream, as blood from a wound; **2,** to force out fluid in a jet or stream, as does a whale; **3,** to speak in a pompous manner:—*n.* **1,** the projecting tube, nozzle, etc., through which a liquid pours; as, the *spout* of a teapot; also, a trough or pipe for carrying rain off a roof; **2,** a stream or jet of liquid.

sprain (sprān), *n.* a severe twisting or straining of the muscles or ligaments around a joint:—*v.t.* to injure by wrenching or twisting severely; as, to *sprain* a wrist.

sprang (sprang), *p.t.* of *spring.*

sprawl (sprôl), *v.i.* **1,** to lie or sit in a careless, ungraceful position; as, to *sprawl* on the couch; **2,** to spread in an irregular, straggling manner, as a plant, a place, or a person's handwriting; as, the city *sprawls* for 50 kilometres:—*v.t.* to spread or cause to spread awkwardly or ungracefully:—*n.* an awkward spreading position or movement.—*adj.* **sprawl′ing.**

[1]**spray** (sprā), *n.* a small branch of a tree or plant, bearing leaves or flowers; sprig; a

bouquet; as, a *spray* (of flowers).

[2]**spray** (sprā), *n.* **1,** water driven in small drops or particles by the wind, the dashing of waves, etc.; **2,** medicine or other liquid applied or dispensed, in the form of fine drops of liquid or vapour, by an atomizer or spray can; as, hair *spray*; nose *spray*; air-freshener *spray*:—*v.t.* **1,** to apply fine drops of liquid or vapour to; as, to *spray* trees; **2,** to scatter (a liquid) in fine drops.—*n.* **spray′er.**

spread (spred), *v.t.* [spread (spred), spreading], **1,** to cause to cover a surface; as, to *spread* butter on bread; to *spread* fertilizer; also, to cover (a surface) with something; as, to *spread* bread with jam; **2,** to unfold; stretch forth; expand; as, the peacock *spreads* its tail; **3,** to publish or make widely known; as, to *spread* the good news; **4,** to place food upon; as, to *spread* the table; **5,** to communicate or carry from person to person; as, flies *spread* disease:—*v.i.* **1,** to be extended over a surface; as, smoke *spread* over the city; **2,** to be dispersed or scattered; as, rumours *spread*; **3,** to be forced apart, as rails:—*n.* **1,** extension; growth; as, the *spread* of civilization; **2,** the limit or area of expansion; as, the *spread* of an eagle's wings; **3,** a covering for a bed, table, etc.; **4,** *Colloq.* a table set with a fancy meal; a feast; **5,** any substance, as butter or jam, used to spread on bread or crackers; as, cheese *spread*.—*n.* **spread′er; spread-a-bil′i-ty.**—*adj.* **spread′a-ble.**

spread-sheet (spred′shēt′), *n.* in *computing*, computer software that allows the display of a large amount of data in rows and columns, similar to an accounting ledger, which allows for rapid, automatic calculations, adjustments, and other manipulations.

spree (sprē), *n.* a short burst of activity; as, a shopping *spree*.

sprig (sprig), *n.* **1,** a small branch; a twig or shoot; **2,** an ornamental figure or design in the form of a spray.

spright-ly (sprīt′li), *adj.* [spright-li-er, spright-li-est], vivacious; lively; spirited.—*n.* **spright′li-ness.**

spring (spring), *v.i.* [*p.t.* sprang (sprang) or sprung (sprung), *p.p.* sprung, *p.pr.* spring-ing], **1,** to leap; bound; as, to *spring* into action; **2,** to rise suddenly; dart out, as an animal from a covert; **3,** to start up or forth; appear; as, a breeze *sprang* up; weeds are *springing* up on the lawn; **4,** to result; have a beginning; as, superstitions *spring* from fear; **5,** to recoil; rebound; as, an elastic *springs* back; **6,** to become warped or bent, as a board; **7,** *Colloq.* to pay for; as, to *spring* for lunch:—*v.t.* **1,** to reveal or produce with unexpected suddenness; as, to *spring* a surprise; **2,** to release the catch of (a trap); also, to explode or discharge (a mine); **3,** to weaken by a crack or strain; as, I *sprang* my ankle playing tennis; also, to develop (an opening) at the seams; as, the roof *sprang* a leak; **4,** to set free from custody; as, to *spring* a prisoner from jail:—*n.* **1,** the act of springing; a leap; also, the length of the leap; **2,** a contrivance, usually of metal that yields to pressure and returns to its original form when the force is removed; as, bed *springs*; **3,** the quality of being elastic; as, the *spring* of a rubber band; also, the shooting back from a tense position; recoil; **4,** a natural fountain or supply of water rising to the surface of the earth; **5,** the season of the year between winter and summer:—*adj.* pertaining to the spring.—*adj.* **spring′y.**—*adv.* **spring′i-ly**—*n.* **spring′i-ness; spring′ break′; spring′ chick′en; spring′ e′qui-nox′; spring′ fe′ver; spring′ roll′; spring′ tide′; spring′time′; spring′ train′ing.**

spring-board (spring′bōrd′), *n.* **1,** a flexible board attached at one end used to spring high into the air in diving and in gymnastics; **2,** something that gets things moving quickly; a starting point; as, studying diligently is a *springboard* to success.

sprin-kle (spring′kl), *v.t.* [spring-kled, spring-kling], **1,** to scatter in small drops or particles; as, to *sprinkle* salt on food; **2,** to spray with small drops or particles; as, to *sprinkle* the lawn:—*v.i.* to rain lightly:—*n.* **1,** a light shower of rain; **2,** a small quantity; as, a *sprinkle* of salt:—**sprin′kler,** a device used to spray or sprinkle water over lawns, gardens, or roads, or to put out fires, as, a *sprinkler* system:—**sprinkles,** small bits of coloured candy used on top of ice cream, cake, cookies, etc.:—**sprinkling,** a small number or scattering of something, as, a *sprinkling* of wildflowers along the hillside.

sprint (sprint), *n.* **1,** a short race at full speed; **2,** a race over a short distance, such as the 100-metre dash:—*v.i.* to race or go a short distance at full speed by running, cycling, or driving; dash.—*n.* **sprin′ter.**

sprite (sprīt), *n.* **1,** an elf, goblin, or fairy; **2,** a person who possesses the qualities of a sprite; animated; peppy.

sprock-et (sprok′it), *n.* **1,** a toothlike projection as on the outer rim of a wheel, shaped so as to engage with the links of a driving chain; **2,** a wheel having such teeth on its rim.

sprout (sprout) *v.i.* **1,** to begin to grow; **2,** to put forth shoots, as the seed of a plant; **3,** to arise or develop; as, new houses *sprouted* along the road:—*v.t.* to cause to put forth shoots; as, to *sprout* plants indoors; to *sprout* whiskers:—*n.* **1,** a new shoot; bud; as, alfalfa or bean *sprouts*; **2,** a young person.

[1]**spruce** (spro͞os), *adj.* [spruc-er, spruc-est], smart; trim; neat:—*v.i.* and *v.t.* [spruced, spruc-ing], *Colloq.* to dress smartly; arrange in a neat and tidy manner; as, to *spruce* up a messy bedroom; to *spruce* up a bit.

[2]**spruce** (spro͞os), *n.* a coniferous, evergreen tree bearing cones and needle-shaped

leaves, and which grows in colder temperatures; also, its wood.

sprung (sprung), *p.p.* of *spring.*

spry (sprī), *adj.* [spry-er or spr-ier, spryest or spri-est], nimble; active; agile.—*adv.* **spry′ly.**—*n.* **spry′ness.**

spud (spud), *n. Colloq.* a potato.

spume (spūm), *n.* froth, foam; scum.

spun (spun), *p.t.* and *p.p.* of *spin.*

spunk (spungk), *n. Colloq.* courage; spirit; pluck.—*adj.* **spunk′y.**—*adv.* **spunk′i-ly.**—*n.* **spunk′i-ness.**

spur (spûr), *n.* **1,** a pointed instrument worn on the heel of a rider's boot, used to urge on a horse; **2,** anything that urges to action; an incentive; as, to offer a prize as a *spur* to good work; **3,** anything resembling a spur, as the hollow, projecting part of the flower in the larkspur and the columbine; **4,** a mountain ridge running out to the side from a range of mountains; **5,** the stiff, sharp spine on a rooster's leg; **6,** a bony growth on the heel of a foot or elbow; **7,** a short railway line connected with a main line at only one end; a short railway branch line over which regular service is not maintained:—*v.t.* [spurred, spur-ring], **1,** to prick with a spur; as, to *spur* a horse; **2,** to excite or drive on to action; as, to *spur* him to finish the assignment:—*v.i.* to travel with haste; press onward.

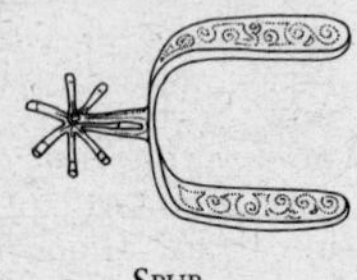

SPUR

spu-ri-ous (spū′ri-us), *adj.* not genuine; false; not authentic; as, *spurious* coins; *spurious* intentions.

spurn (spûrn), *v.t.* **1,** to push away, as with the foot; **2,** to reject with contempt; turn away from; as, to *spurn* sexual advances.

spurt (spûrt), *v.i.* to gush forth suddenly in a stream or jet; as, water *spurted* from the leak in the pipe:—*v.t.* to throw or force out in a stream or jet; squirt:—*n.* **1,** a sudden gushing forth of liquid; **2,** any brief and sudden outbreak, as of passion or anger; **3,** a sudden and extraordinary burst of strength or energy for a brief period, as in a race; as, to clean the room in *spurts*; also, a sharp and sudden increase in business, prices, etc.

sput-ter (sput′ėr), *v.i.* **1,** to throw out small particles, as sparks from burning wood; **2,** to spit small, scattered drops of saliva, as in rapid or excited speech; **3,** to speak rapidly and indistinctly; **4,** to make explosive sounds; as, the car's engine *sputtered* and then died:—*v.t.* to utter in an excited or confused way:—*n.* **1,** the act of sputtering; also, the sound; **2,** excited and indistinct talk.

spu-tum (spū′tum), *n.* spit or saliva, often mixed with mucus from nose, throat, or lungs.

spy (spī), *n.* [*pl.* spies], **1,** a person who enters an enemy's territory secretly in time of war, to gain information; **2,** one who keeps watch on others and gains information on them; as, a business *spy*; a secret agent; **3,** a type of apple:—*v.t.* [spied, spy-ing], **1,** to catch sight of, esp. at a distance; as, she *spied* a friend in the crowd; **2,** to watch closely or explore secretly; as, to *spy* out the land:—*v.i.* **1,** to make a careful examination; **2,** to watch others secretly; to act as a spy; as, to *spy* on the competitor.

squab-ble (skwôb′l; skwob′l), *n.* a noisy, minor quarrel; dispute:—*v.i.* [squabbled, squab-bling], to wrangle; to dispute noisily; as, to *squabble* over a toy.

squad (skwod; skwôd), *n.* **1,** a small party of about 12 soldiers assembled for drill, etc.; **2,** any small group of persons engaged in a common effort; as, a police *squad*; drug *squad*; football *squad.*

squad-ron (skwod′run; skwôd′run), *n.* **1,** any group of people in regular formation; **2,** a unit in the army, navy, or airforce that operates together; **3,** *Colloq.* a great number of people or things.

squal-id (skwol′id; skwôl′id), *adj.* **1,** extremely dirty and neglected; wretched; as, a *squalid* tenement; **2,** sordid, immoral; as, a *squalid* motive.—*n.* **squal′or.**

¹squall (skwôl), *n.* **1,** a sudden and violent gust of wind, often accompanied by rain, sleet, or snow; **2,** *Colloq.* commotion, trouble or danger of any sort.—*adj.* **squall′y.**

²squall (skwôl), *v.i.* and *v.t.* to weep, scream, or utter violently, as a child in pain:—*n.* a loud, harsh scream.

Squam-ish (skwäm′ish), *n.* **1,** an Aboriginal group living on the southwest coast of British Columbia, related to the Interior Salish tribes; **2,** the Salish language of these people.

squan-der (skwon′dėr; skwôn′dėr), *v.t.* to spend lavishly or wastefully or lose due to negligence or lack of prudence; as to *squander* money on frivolous things; to *squander* natural resources.

square (skwâr), *n.* **1,** a plane figure with four right angles and four equal sides; **2,** anything shaped like a square; as, a checkerboard with red and black *squares*; **3,** a city block consisting of a four-sided space on each side of which is a street and buildings; **4,** an open space or area, often used as a small park; **5,** an instrument, consisting usually of two straight edges at right angles to each other, used for measuring or laying out right angles; **6,** in *mathematics*, the product obtained by multiplying a number by itself; as, 4 is the *square* of 2; **7,** *Slang* a conservative or old-fashioned person:—*v.t.* [squared, squar-ing], **1,** to give (an object) the shape of a square; **2,** to cause (a line or side) to make a right angle with another; also, to bring into a position producing such an angle; **3,**

to balance (accounts); **4,** in *mathematics*, to multiply (a number) by itself:—*v.i.* to accord or agree; coincide; fit; as, his story does not *square* with mine:—*adj.* **1,** having the same shape as a square; **2,** forming a right angle; rectangular; as, a *square* outline; **3,** a unit of area having the same width and length; as, a room 100 *square* metres; **4,** straight and angular, rather than curved, in outline; as, a *square* jaw; **5,** true; honest; just; as, a *square* deal; **6,** balanced; settled, as accounts; **7,** *Colloq.* satisfying; substantial; as, a *square* meal; **8,** *Slang* conservative or old-fashioned:—*adv.* exactly; as, he hit the nail *square* on the head.—*adv.* **square′ly.**—*n.* **square′ness.**

square dance, a type of folk dance that is done by four or more couples who form a square at the beginning of the dance.—*v.i.* **square′- dance.**—*n.* **square′ dan′cing; square′ dan′cer.**

square–rigged (skwâr′–rigd′), *adj.* having rectangular sails stretched along yards which are slung horizontally to the mast: a brig is a *square*-rigged craft.

square root, the quantity that, when multiplied by itself (squared), produces a given quantity; as, 3 is the *square root* of 9.

[1]**squash** (skwosh; skwôsh), *n.* a green, yellow, orange, or white gourd that grows on a vine along the ground and is used as a vegetable; also, the vine bearing it.

[2]**squash** (skwosh; skwôsh), *v.t.* **1,** to beat or mash into pulp; to crush or pack closely together; **2,** to put down or suppress; as, to *squash* a rumour:—*v.i.* **1,** to fall in a soft, flattened mass; be crushed to a pulp, as from a fall; **2,** to be packed closely together; as, the people squashed into the small elevator:—*n.* **1,** a crushed object or mass; **2,** the sudden fall of something soft and heavy; also, the noise made when such a thing falls; **3,** a game similar to tennis, played in a walled court with rackets and a ball.

squat (skwot; skwôt), *v.i.* [squat-ted, squat-ting], **1,** to sit on the heels, or with knees drawn up; **2,** to crouch on the ground, as an animal; **3,** to settle on public land with a view to gaining title to it; also, to live on unoccupied land without permission or right:—*adj.* [squatter, squat-test], **1,** crouching; **2,** short and thick; as, a *squat* vase:—*n.* a squatting position.—*n.* **squat′ter.**—*adj.* **squat′ty.**

squawk (skwôk), *n.* a loud, harsh cry, as of a duck or hen:—*v.i.* **1,** to make a loud, harsh cry; as, the radio *squawked* when she turned it on; **2,** *Slang* to complain vehemently; protest; as, the students *squawked* when the teacher assigned extra homework.

squeak (skwēk), *n.* **1,** a short, shrill, sharp sound; as, the *squeak* of a mouse; **2,** a win or escape by a narrow margin:—*v.i.* **1,** to utter a short, shrill, sharp cry; **2,** to make a grating, disagreeable noise, as a rusty hinge; **3,** to win, attain, pass, or escape by a narrow margin; as, the student barely *squeaked* by on the exam.—*adj.* **squeak′y.**—*n.* **squeak′er.**

squeal (skwēl), *n.* a shrill, prolonged cry of pain or delight, as of a pig or child:—*v.i.* **1,** to make a shrill, prolonged cry; as, the tires *squealed* on the wet driveway; **2,** *Colloq.* to betray a plot or a companion in a crime or fault.

squeam-ish (skwēm′ish), *ads.* **1,** having a stomach easily upset or nauseated; **2,** easily shocked or disgusted; **3,** dainty; fastidious.—*adv.* **squeam′ish-ly.**—*n.* **squeam′ish-ness.**

squee-gee (skwē′jē), *n.* a T-shaped, rubber-edged tool for removing water from windows, etc.:—**squeegee kid,** a person who cleans, with a squeegee, the windshields of stopped cars, for money:—*v.t.* to use a squeegee.

squeeze (skwēz), *v.t.* [squeezed, squeez-ing], **1,** to exert pressure on; compress; as, to *squeeze* a tube of toothpaste; **2,** to draw forth by pressure; extract; as to *squeeze* water from a wet garment; also, to cause to yield juice; as, to *squeeze* a lemon; also, to get by extortion; as to *squeeze* money from someone; **3,** to thrust forcibly; crowd into too small a space; as, to *squeeze* people into a hall:—*v.i.* to press; force one's way; push; as, to *squeeze* through a crowd:—*n.* **1,** pressure; a crowding together; **2,** the act of squeezing; **3,** middleman profit; **4,** financial pressure or crisis; **5,** a bird; **6,** *Slang* a girlfriend or boyfriend.—*n.* **squeez′er.**

squelch (skwelch), *v.t.* to crush; silence by a rebuke; as, to *squelch* a quarrelsome child; to *squelch* a revolt:—*v.i.* to make a squashing sound, such as is made by walking through slush:—*n.* **1,** a suction sound; as the *squelch* of the mud; **2,** the act of crushing, silencing, or rebuking.—*adj.* **squelch′y.**

squib (skwib), *n.* **1,** a short, sarcastic, or satirical article (or speech), often malicious or abusive in tone; a lampoon; also, a short news filler; **2,** a broken firecracker, whose powder burns with a fizz; **3,** in *sports*, esp. football and baseball, a ball that is hit or kicked lightly:—*v.t.* and *v.i.* to write, speak, fire, hit, or kick a squib or as a squib.

squid (skwid), *n.* a tube-shaped, eight-armed, shellless mollusc, with two long tentacles, similar to an octopus, and sometimes used as food: they can be small or very large, as the giant squid, which can be over 15 metres long.

squig-gle (skwig′l), *n.* a short, wavy line; a curlicue; illegible writing:—*v.t.* [squig-gled, squig-gling], to scrawl or write undecipherably:—*v.i.* to wriggle or squirm.—*adj.* **squig′gly.**

squint (skwint), *n.* **1,** the condition of being cross-eyed; **2,** a sidelong, stealthy glance:—*v.i.* **1,** to look sideways; **2,** to have the eyes half closed, as in bright sunlight;

3, to be cross-eyed:—*v.t.* to half close (the eyes):—*adj.* **1,** looking sideways; **2,** cross-eyed.—*adj.* **squint′y.**

squire (skwīr), *n.* **1,** formerly, a young man who acted as a servant to a knight while training to become a knight himself; **2,** in the U.S., a justice of the peace, lawyer, or judge; **3,** in England, the chief landholder of a district; **4,** a lady's escort:—*v.t.* [squired, squir-ing], to accompany (a lady) as a squire or escort.

squirm (skwûrm), *v.i.* **1,** to twist about like an eel or a snake; wriggle; writhe; **2,** to act or feel nervous, embarrassed, or uneasy; as, to *squirm* when telling a lie.

squir-rel (skwir′el; skwur′el), *n.* a small, bushy-tailed, grey, black, or reddish-brown animal that lives mostly in trees and feeds largely on grains and nuts:—*v.t.* to store up or save; as, to *squirrel* away money for the car.

squirt (skwûrt), *v.i.* to gush forth in a stream or jet from a small opening; to spurt:—*v.t.* **1,** to force out in a quick jet; as, a squid *squirts* an inky liquid; **2,** to make wet by squirting; as, to squirt the flowers with a hose:—*n.* **1,** a small stream or jet squirted forth; **2,** an instrument for squirting water or other liquid; **3,** the act of squirting; **4,** *Slang* a small, impudent child; a kid.

squish (skwish), *v.t.* and *v.i. Colloq.* to squash; squeeze; as, to *squish* mud between the toes.—*adj.* **squish′y.**

stab (stab), *v.t.* [stabbed, stab-bing], **1,** to pierce with a pointed weapon, or as if with a pointed weapon; as, pain *stabbed* her leg; **2,** to wound the feelings of; as, conscience *stabbed* him with remorse:—*v.i.* **1,** to pierce something with a pointed weapon; **2,** to wound a person's feelings:—*n.* **1,** a thrust with a sharp-pointed weapon, or a sharp feeling of pain; **2,** a wound so made; **3,** an attempt; a try; as, to take a *stab* at the question.—*n.* **stab′ber; stab′bing.**

stab-i-lize (stā′bi-līz′; stab′i-līz′), *v.t.* [stabilized, stabiliz-ing], **1,** to make firm, steady, regular, or dependable; as, to *stabilize* one's life, or one's income; **2,** to secure or maintain the balance of (a boat or aircraft) by a special device.—*n.* **stab′i-li-za′tion; stab′i-liz′er; sta-bil′i-ty.**

¹sta-ble (stā′bl), *adj.* **1,** firm; securely established; hence, having permanence; continuing without change; as, *stable* institutions; a patient in *stable* condition; **2,** steadfast; unwavering; as, a man of *stable* purpose.—*adv.* **stab′ly.**

²sta-ble (stā′bl), *n.* **1,** a building, usually divided into stalls, in which horses, cattle, or other animals are housed; **2,** a group of race-horses belonging to a particular owner; also, a group of people or products under one management or affiliation; as, a profitable *stable* of nonfiction books; a *stable* of speed skaters:—*v.t.* [sta-bled, sta-bling], to put into, or keep in, such a building:—*v.t.* to be so lodged.

stac-ca-to (sta-kä′tō), *adj.* and *adv.* **1,** in *music*, played, or to be played, in an abrupt, disconnected fashion, with breaks between the notes: opposite of *legato*; **2,** expressed in this way; as, a *staccato* remark.

stack (stak), *n.* **1,** a large quantity of hay, wood, etc., piled up like a cone or mound; **2,** a somewhat orderly mass or heap; as, a *stack* of letters; **3,** a chimney; often, a vent for smoke, as on a factory; as, a smoke*stack*:—**stacks,** the area in a library where books are kept on shelves:—*v.t.* **1,** to heap or pile up; **2,** to cheat by arranging something secretely; as, to *stack* a deck of cards.—*adj.* **stacked.**

sta-di-um (stā′di-um), *n.* [*pl.* stadiums or stadia (stā′-di-a)], a large structure consisting of seats in tiers around a field or playing area that is used for sports events, concerts, rallies, etc.

staff (ståf), *n.* [*pl.* staffs or staves (ståfs; stāvz)], **1,** a pole, rod, or stick used as a support in walking or climbing, as a means of defence, or as an emblem or evidence of authority; **2,** a long, slender pole serving as a support; a flagpole; as, a flag*staff*; **3,** [*pl.* staffs], a body of persons engaged in a single task; as, a teaching *staff*; an office *staff*; also, in the army, a body of assistant advisory officers; **4,** [*pl.* staves], in *music*, the set of five horizontal lines and four intervening spaces on which the notes are written: also called *stave*:—*v.t.* to provide with employees; as, to *staff* an information desk.—*n.* **staf′fing; staf′fer.**

stag (stag), *n.* **1,** the full-grown male deer; a buck: opposite of ²hind; **2,** a gathering of men only to celebrate an event such as the upcoming marriage of the honoured guest:—*adj.* **1,** intended for, or restricted to, men only; as, a *stag* party; **2,** pornographic; as, a *stag* movie.

stage (stāj), *n.* **1,** a raised platform, as in a theatre or concert hall; **2,** the theatre; the theatrical profession; as, she is reluctant to leave the *stage*; **3,** a place or field of action; arena; as, the political *stage*; the scene of any celebrated event or career; as, London was the *stage* of her debut; **4,** a part, or lap, as of a journey; **5,** degree of progress in any business, process, etc.; a point or period of development; as, an advanced *stage* of civilization; **6,** a stage coach; **7,** a section of a rocket with its own engine and fuel:—*v.t.* [staged, stag-ing], **1,** to put (a play) on the stage; **2,** to put or make happen before the public; carry out; as, to *stage* a hunger strike.—*n.* **stag′ing; stage′craft′; stage′hand′; stage′ fright′.**—*adj.* **stag′y** (theatrical).

stage-coach (stāj′kōch), *n.* a large coach drawn by horses, used to carry passengers and mail between designated stops.

stag-ger (stag′ėr), *v.i.* to totter or reel; walk unsteadily; as, a drunkard *staggers*:—*v.t.* **1,** to cause to totter or reel; **2,** to shock; as, the truth *staggered* him; **3,** to make less sure or certain; as, the setback *staggered* his self-confidence; **4,** to alternate in time or position; as, to *stagger* working hours so that all employees can have some time off during the holiday season; to *stagger* chairs in a room so that everyone can see:—*n.* **1,** a reeling or tottering; unsteadiness; **2, staggers,** *n.pl.* used as *sing.* a nerve disease of horses, sheep, and cattle, marked by staggering and falling; often called *blind staggers*.

stag-nant (stag′nant), *adj.* **1,** not flowing; stale or foul from standing; as, *stagnant* water; **2,** not brisk; sluggish.

stag-nate (stag′nāt), *v.i.* **1,** to cease to flow or run; be or become motionless; **2,** to be or become inert or dull; **3,** to be or become foul or unwholesome.—*n.* **stag-na′tion.**

staid (stād), *adj.* quiet; sedate; steady; unadventurous; prim; as, a gathering of *staid* senators.

stain (stān), *n.* **1,** a discoloured spot or blot; **2,** a dye; as, walnut *stain*; **3,** the taint of guilt or crime; a stigma; as, a reputation without *stain*:—*v.t.* **1,** to blot or spot; soil; as, to *stain* a tie; **2,** to tinge with colouring matter; as, to *stain* wood; **3,** to tarnish or dim; to disgrace; as, a speeding ticket will *stain* your driving record:—*v.i.* to take or give a dye or stain.—*adj.* **stain′less.**—*n.* **stained′ glass′.**

stainless steel, a form of steel that does not rust or stain easily, often used for household products such as utensils, knives, pots, etc.

stair (stâr), *n.* **1,** any one of a set of steps or treads connecting different levels; **2,** one of these steps; as, a cat was sleeping on the top *stair*; **3,** (usually *stairs*), a flight of steps.

stair-case or **stair-way** (stâr′kās′; stâr′wā′), *n.* a flight of steps or stairs.

stake (stāk), *n.* **1,** a strong stick sharpened at one end and fixed into the ground as a marker or support; **2,** the post to which a person condemned to be burned is bound; hence, death by burning; **3,** (often *stakes*), something, esp. money, wagered or risked on an event, game, race, or contest; as, to play for high *stakes*; **4,** an interest or share in a business, investment, or other such activity:—**at stake,** risked or hazarded; as, the gold medal was at *stake*:—*v.t.* [staked, stak-ing], **1,** to fasten, support, or provide with stakes; as, to *stake* tomatoes; **2,** to mark the limits of; as, to *stake* a claim; **3,** to gamble or risk; bet; as, he *staked* all he had on the success of his invention.

sta-lac-tite (sta-lak′tīt), *n.* an iciclelike formation of calcium carbonate hanging from the roof of a cave: caused by the dripping of water with a high lime content.

sta-lag-mite (sta-lag′mīt), *n.* a cone of carbonate of lime, often formed under a stalactite and gradually uniting with it to form a column.

stale (stāl), *adj.* [stal-er, stal-est], **1,** not fresh or new; tasteless; dried out: used esp. of food; **2,** worn out by constant repetition or use; tedious; as, a *stale* joke; **3,** out of condition, as an athlete who is not in training or who has trained too hard or too long:—*v.t.* [staled, stal-ing], to make stale; destroy the novelty of:—*v.i.* to lose newness or freshness; wear out.

stale-mate (stāl′māt), *n.* **1,** in *chess*, a situation in which the king, not being in check, cannot move without being placed in check, and when no move can be made by any other piece; hence, a draw; **2,** a deadlock:—*v.t.* to bring to a deadlock or standstill.

[1]**stalk** (stôk), *n.* **1,** the main stem of a plant, or the stem of a leaf, flower, or fruit; as, bean *stalk*; corn *stalk*; **2,** any stemlike support, as of a wineglass.—*adj.* **stalk′y.**

[2]**stalk** (stôk), *v.t.* **1,** to approach (an animal or person) cautiously and under cover; **2,** to pursue or harrass a person unrelentingly:—*v.i.* to walk in a haughty manner:—*n.* **1,** the act of creeping up on an animal or person; **2,** a proud, haughty step.—*n.* **stalk′er; stalk′ing.**

stall (stôl), *n.* **1,** a stable; cattle shed; also, an enclosed space in a stable for one animal; **2,** a table on which goods are displayed for sale; as, a flower *stall*; **3,** a seat in the choir of a church; also, a church pew; **4,** a small compartment or cubicle; as, a shower *stall*; a toilet *stall*; **5,** a parking space; **6,** a delay using dishonest means; as, a *stall* tactic:—*v.t.* **1,** to place or keep in a stall; **2,** to cause to stick fast or stop; as, the snowdrifts *stalled* the train; unskilled driving *stalled* the engine:—*v.t.* **1,** to stick fast or stop, as in mud; **2,** to come to a forced standstill; cease running; **3,** to put off action; slow down; delay; as, to *stall* him until you return.

stal-lion (stal′yun), *n.* a male horse, esp. one kept for breeding purposes.

stal-wart (stôl′wėrt; stol′wėrt), *adj.* **1,** sturdy; strong and muscular; as, a man of *stalwart* build; **2,** brave; daring; as, a *stalwart* fighter:—*n.* a firm, loyal partisan.

sta-men (stā′men), *n.* the pollen-bearing and pollen-producing male part of a flower, consisting of an anther and a filament. (See *flower*, illustration.)

stam-i-na (sta′i-na), *n.pl.* used as *sing.*, vigour; strength or staying power; power of endurance; as, *stamina* to complete a long race.

stam-mer (stam′ėr), *v.i.* to hesitate or falter in speaking; stutter:—*v.t.* to utter with difficulty or hesitation; as, he *stammered* out an excuse:—*n.* **1,** hesitating or faltering speech; **2,** any difficulty in pronouncing; a stutter.—*n.* **stam′mer-er.**

stamp (stamp), *v.t.* **1,** to mark with a design by means of a die, pattern, etc.: as, to *stamp* a coin; **2,** to put a postage or other official stamp upon; as, to *stamp* a letter; **3,** to label; brand; as, our acts *stamp* our characters; **4,** to set (the foot) down heavily; **5,** to crush or grind (ore) into powder:—**stamp out**, to destroy; end; as, to *stamp out* crime:—*v.i.* to bring down the foot forcibly or with pressure:—*n.* **1,** a mark or design impressed upon a surface; as, the *stamp* on a coin; **2,** a die or instrument for stamping; **3,** a small piece of paper, sold by the government and stuck to a letter, document, etc., to show payment of a fee or tax; **4,** a characteristic mark or imprint; as, his actions bear the *stamp* of refinement; **5,** a heavy downward blow with the foot:—**stamp-ing ground**, *Colloq.* the place to which an animal or person habitually resorts.

stam-pede (stam-pēd′), *n.* **1,** a sudden, wild rush, as of a herd of frightened animals; **2,** any sudden, impulsive movement on the part of a crowd; a general rush; as, a *stampede* for the exits; **3,** a rodeo and fair; as, the Calgary *Stampede*:—*v.t.* [stamped-ed, stamped-ing], **1,** to put to sudden flight; as, to *stampede* cattle; **2,** to force to act in a careless or thoughtless way; as, to *stampede* us into buying something:—*v.i.* **1,** to be part of or cause a stampede; as, the cattle *stampeded* at the loud noise; **2,** to start off in a general panic; **3,** to act together from a sudden impulse; as, to *stampede* for the bargain counter.

stance (stans), *n.* **1,** posture; **2,** a position; attitude; as, to take an anti-smoking *stance*; **3,** in *golf*, the position of a player's feet when making a stroke.

stanch (stônch), *v.t.* and *adj.* Same as **staunch.**

stan-chion (stan′shun), *n.* an upright, supporting bar, post, or pillar, esp. one of two upright bars, or props, that hold an animal by the head in a stall.

stand (stand), *v.i.* [stood (stood), standing], **1,** to be stationary on the feet in an erect position; **2,** to be in a certain condition, attitude, or position; as, I *stand* ready to pay; he *stands* acquitted; **3,** to be a substitute; as, a pronoun *stands* for a noun; **4,** to remain firm or in force; as, the agreement *stands*; **5,** to maintain a certain attitude toward a question or a principle; as, he *stands* for free trade:—*v.t.* **1,** to set on the feet, or on end, in an upright position; put in place; as, *stand* the broom in the corner; **2,** to put up with; endure; as, to *stand* pain:—*n.* **1,** a stop or halt to maintain a position or to offer resistance; as, they made a *stand* at the river; **2,** position; place of standing; as, he took his *stand* behind the counter; **3,** a raised platform for spectators, usually with seats in tiers; **4,** a booth or station used for business; as, a hamburger *stand*; **5,** a piece of furniture on which things may be placed or kept; a small table; as, a magazine *stand*; **6,** a place where a person performs an official duty; as, a witness *stand*; **7,** a place where a vehicle stops or parks; as, a taxi *stand*.

stand–a-lone (stand′–a-lōn′), *n.* **1,** in *computing*, a computing device that is able to operate independently from a network or other system; **2,** any self-contained device that can function on its own; as, a *stand-alone* computer.

stand-ard (stan′dėrd), *n.* **1,** a figure, flag, etc., used as an emblem; as, to rally around the *standard*; **2,** an established measure of weight, length, quality, etc.; as, safety *standards* for cars; **3,** any state or degree that is accepted as the desirable one; as, high academic *standards*; **4,** an upright support; as, a lamp on a tall *standard*:—*adj.* **1,** serving as an accepted basis for comparison, reference, etc.; as, *standard* practice to tip servers in restaurants; **2,** of a certain or recognized level of excellence; as, *standard* English.—*v.t.* **stand′ard-ize′.**

standard of living, the level at which a country, group, or person lives, based on how well basic needs and wants are satisfied.

standard time, official measure of uniform time in a certain region.

standby (stand′bī), *n., adj.,* and *adv.* [*pl.* –bys], *Colloq.* **1,** one who, or that which, may be depended upon, esp. in emergencies; **2,** something or someone held in reserve; as, *standby* tickets; to fly *standby*.

stand-ing (stand′ing), *n.* **1,** a certain rank or position; as, the *standings* for the teams in a league; **2,** duration; **3,** location; **4,** length of experience, service, etc.; **5,** reputation; as, of high *standing*:—*adj.* **1,** that stands; in an upright or fixed position; as, to begin a race from a *standing* start; **2,** not moving or changing; permanent; as, a *standing* invitation; **3,** set by custom or by law. Also, **stand′ing com-mit′tee; stand′ing joke′; stand′ing or′der; stand′ing o-va′tion; stand′ing room′**

stand-off (stand′ôf′), *n.* a tie, deadlock, or draw; as, the contest was a *standoff*.—*adj.* **stand′off′ ish.**

stand-point (stand′point′), *n.* a position, principle, or standard from which things are considered or judged; a point of view; as, from the *standpoint* of justice, the man should be given a fair trial.

stand-still (stand′stil′), *n.* a complete stop; as, the snowstorm brought the town to a complete *standstill*.

stank (stangk), *p.t.* of *stink*.

stan-za (stan′zȧ), *n.* a group of lines or verses, varying in number, forming a unit or section of a poem or song.

¹sta-ple (stā′pl), *n.* **1,** the chief thing produced in a district; as, wheat is the *staple* of the Prairies; **2,** the principal part, or an important element, of something; chief item; as, bread is a *staple* of most meals; **3,** raw material for manufacture; **4,** the fibre of cotton, flax, or wool, as establishing its quality; as, wool of long *staple*:—*adj.* **1,** important because produced regularly and in large amounts; as, *staple* goods; **2,** in commerce, fixed; as, a *staple* demand:—*v.t.* [sta-pled, sta-pling], to sort according to the quality of its fibre; as, to *staple* wool.

[2]sta-ple (stā′pl), *n.* **1,** a small, U-shaped piece of metal, which may be driven into wood or other hard surface, to hold a hook, pin, or bolt in place; **2,** a similar piece of light wire bent to hold papers and other thin materials together:—*v.t.* [sta-pled, sta-pling], to hold together or fasten with a staple.—*n.* **sta′pler.**

star (stär), *n.* **1,** a celestial, gaseous body seen as a point of light in the night sky: our sun is the closest star to earth; **2,** a figure, the points of which make it look like a star, as an asterisk; **3,** in *astrology*, a planet supposed to influence a person's life; **4,** a brilliant, outstanding person in some field, esp. in music, film, television, stage, or athletics; as, rock *star*, movie *star*, baseball *star*; **5,** an actor who plays a leading part in a movie, play, or television show:—*v.t.* [starred, star-ring]. **1,** to deck or adorn with a star or something resembling a star, as an asterisk; **2,** to display or feature (a person) as the principal actor in a movie, television show, or play; as, this film *stars* a famous athlete:—*v.i.* **1,** to be illustrious or prominent; **2,** to appear as the principal actor in a movie, television show, or play; as, she *starred* in the television show:—*adj.* outstanding; excellent; as, the *star* athlete.—*adj.* **star′less; star′like; star′lit; star′-span′gled; star′-struck′; star′-studded.**—*n.* **star′burst′; star′dom** (as, he attained *stardom* on TV); **star′dust′; star′gaz′er; star′light′; star′ship′.**

star-board (stär′bėrd; stär′bōrd), *n.* the right side of a boat, ship, or aircraft as one faces forward: opposite of *port*:—*adj.* on the right side of a a boat, ship, or aircraft; as, a *starboard* cabin; the *starboard* engine:—*v.t.* to turn to the starboard side of a ship; as, to *starboard* the helm.

starch (stärch), *n.* **1,** a white, odourless, tasteless complex carbohydrate found in nearly all green plants and in potatoes and grains: it is a granular or powdery substance that is an important element in the diet; **2,** a commercial form of this substance used in laundering to stiffen fabrics or clothes; **3,** hence, stiffness of conduct or manner or vigour, strength:—*v.t.* to stiffen with starch:—*adj.* **starch′y,** of food, containing a high amount of starch; as, pasta is a *starchy* food:—*adj.* **starched,** of cloth, having been stiffened with starch; as, a *starched* shirt.

stare (stâr), *v.i.* [stared, star-ing], **1,** to look with eyes wide open; gaze fixedly in one direction; **2,** to glare, as lights, bright colours, etc.; as, the ink blob *stared* from the page:—*v.t.* to be visible to; confront; as, disaster *stared* them in the face; also, to embarrass or dismay by staring; as, she *stared* him down:—*n.* a fixed steady look with wide-open eyes.

star-fish (stär′fish′), *n.* a sea animal with a body shaped like a star: it usually has five arms, or rays.

stark (stärk), *adj.* **1,** stiff; rigid; bare; plain; harsh; bleak; as, a *stark* view of the frozen fields; **2,** in every way; utter; complete, esp. with a negative word; as, *stark* nonsense:—*adv.* wholly; absolutely; as, *stark* naked; *stark* raving mad.—*adv.* **stark′ly.**

star-ling (stär′ling), *n.* a bird, varying in plumage from brown with light speckles in winter to greenish black in summer, and found in great numbers in North America: it is a sociable bird, flying in large flocks and building near human habitations.

Star of David, a six-pointed star that is the symbol of the Jewish religion and of the country of Israel.

ISRAELI FLAG, SHOWING THE STAR OF DAVID

star-ry (stär′i), *adj.* [star-ri-er, star-ri-est], **1,** spangled or lighted with stars; as, a *starry* night; **2,** shining like stars; as, *starry* eyes.

start (stärt), *v.i.* **1,** to spring suddenly; leap; bound; **2,** to make a sudden involuntary movement, as of surprise, pain, or shock; **3,** to begin; set out; as, to *start* on a journey; to *start* in business; **4,** to come into operation or being; as, her vacation *starts* tomorrow:—*v.t.* **1,** to originate action in; set going; as, to *start* a clock; to *start* a fire; **2,** to rouse suddenly, as game; **3,** to originate; begin; as, to *start* a quarrel; **4,** to cause or help (a person) to begin; as, to *start* a man in business:—*n.* **1,** a sudden leap or bound; an involuntary movement, caused by surprise, fear, or joy; as, the prisoner gave a *start* when he heard the sentence; **2,** beginning; as, a *start* in business; **3,** a head or advantage; as, he had a good *start*.—*n.* **start′er.**

star-tle (stär′tl), *v.t.* [star-tled, star-tling], to cause to start or move suddenly; scare; shock; as, the noise *startled* her.—*adj.* **star′tled; star′tling.**

starve (stärv), *v.i.* [starved, starv-ing], **1,** to suffer or die from extreme hunger; **2,** to be very hungry; as, I am *starving*; **3,** to suffer from the lack of something; to need or want greatly; as, to be *starved* for attention:—*v.t.* **1,** to cause to suffer or die from hunger; **2,** to cause to suffer from the lack of something; deprive; as, to *starve* her of attention.—*n.* **star-va′tion.**

stash (stash), *v.t.* and *v.i.* *Slang* to hide or store away in a safe place (money or valuables) for future use:—*n.* a secure hiding place or something that is hidden; as, a *stash* of stolen diamonds.

state (stāt), *n.* **1,** the condition in which a person or thing is; as, a *state* of health; a confused *state* of affairs; *state* of emergency; **2,** one of the three conditions (solid, liquid, or gas) in which all matter exists; also, any condition or stage; as, the pupal *state* of an insect; **3,** a body of people united under one government; a nation; **4,** the territory or the civil powers of such a nation; as, the *state* provides medical care; **5,** one of several political units forming a federation; as, the *state* of Texas:—**the States,** the United States of America:—*adj.* **1,** pertaining to a state; as, a *state* tax; **2,** formal; ceremonious; as, *state* occasions:—*v.t.* [stat-ed, stat-ing], to utter clearly and formally; tell; declare; as, to *state* the facts.

state-craft (stāt′kråft′), *n.* the art of managing the political affairs of a nation or state; statesmanship.

stat-ed (stāt′id), *adj.* fixed; regular; as, a *stated* meeting; at *stated* times.

state-ly (stāt′li), *adj.* [state-li-er, stateli-est], having a grand or imposing appearance or manner; noble; majestic; as, a *stately* tree; a *stately* manor.—*n.* **state′li-ness.**

state-ment (stāt′ment), *n.* **1,** something that is stated; an idea expressed in speech or writing; as, this *statement* is wrong; **2,** the act of presenting or expressing formally in words; also, that which is so expressed; as, the prime minister issued a *statement* condemning the terrorists; **3,** a report or summary of financial condition; as, a bank or credit card *statement.*

state-of-the-art (stāt′-ov-thē-ärt′), *adj.* of the best or most advanced quality that is currently available; as, a CD-ROM with *state-of-the-art* graphics.—*n.* **state′ of the art′.**

state-room (stāt′ ro͞om′), *n.* a private room or compartment on a passenger vessel, in a railway car, etc.

states-person (stāts′pûr′sn), *n.* [*pl.* statespersons or statespeople (-pē′pl)], one skilled in public affairs and the art of government. Also, **states′ man′, states′wom′an.**—*adj.* **states′man-like′.** —*n.* **states′man-ship′.**

stat-ic (stat′ik), *n.* **1,** in *television* and *radio*, electrical charges in the air that interfere with broadcast signals; as, during the storm, there was only *static* on the television; also, the noise produced by this; **2,** *Slang* criticism; as, don't give me any *static*:—*adj.* **1,** pertaining to bodies at rest, or to forces in balance; **2,** standing still; inactive; not moving; **3,** in *television* and *radio*, caused by static:—**static electricity,** electricity that is motionless and does not flow in a current: the charges are produced by friction, creating sparks and causing clothes, hair, etc., to adhere.

static electricity, an electrical charge that is stationary as opposed to a current, and which is usually produced by friction.

sta-tion (stā′shun), *n.* **1,** a regular stopping place along the route of a train, bus, etc.; also, the buildings there; as, the subway *station*; **2,** a company or location for sending out broadcast signals; as, a rock *station*; a television *station*; **3,** a building or place that is used for a particular purpose; as, a gas *station*; a police *station*; **4,** a place where a person or thing usually remains; position; as, the guard took his *station* before the door; **5,** rank; standing; as, a woman of high *station*:—*v.t.* to set or place in a certain position; assign; as, to *station* troops on the border.

sta-tion-ar-y (stā′shun-ėr-i), *adj.* **1,** not to be or unable to be moved; fixed; as, a *stationary* bicycle; **2,** not moving or changing; remaining still; as, *stationary* arms; **3,** without change in condition, numbers, etc.; stable; as, a *stationary* population.

sta-tion-er-y (stā′shun-ėr-i), *n.* paper and other writing materials, such as pens, pencils, etc.

station wagon, a car with a rear door that can be used for loading and unloading, and a rear seat or seats that can be folded down.

sta-tis-tics (sta-tis′tiks), *n.pl.* **1,** numerical facts or data relating to a community, a special industry, etc., collected and arranged for study; **2,** *pl.* used as *sing.* the science of collecting and interpreting such data:—**statistic,** a single number in a set of statistics; as, the *statistic* for the number of smokers in the country.—*adj.* **sta-tis′ti-cal.**—*n.* **stat′is-ti′cian.**

stat-ue (stat′ū), *n.* the figure of a person or an animal, sculpted: carved, as in marble, moulded, as in clay, or cast, as in bronze.—*adj.* **stat′u-esque′.**—*n.* **stat′u-ette′.**

stat-ure (stat′ūr), *n.* **1,** the height of a person or an animal; as, a person of average *stature*; **2,** a level of achievement or development; as, a writer of great *stature.*

sta-tus (stā′tus), *n.* [*pl.* statuses], **1,** the position, state, or condition of a person, esp. as pertaining to the law; standing; as, the *status* of an alien; marital *status*; **2,** the position or condition of affairs; as, what is the present *status* of the negotiations? **3,** a person's rank or standing in society; as, to be *status*-minded; a *status* symbol.

status quo (stā′tus kwō′; stat′), *n.* the existing or present state of things.

stat-ute (stat′ūt), *n.* an ordinance or law passed by a law-making body.—*adj.* **stat′u-to-ry.**

statutory holiday, a public holiday established by law: in Canada, these include Christmas Day, Boxing Day, New Year's Day, Good Friday, Victoria Day, Canada Day, Labour Day, and Thanksgiving Day.

staunch or **stanch** (stånch; stônch), *adj.* **1,** loyal; as, a *staunch* friend; **2,** firm; strong; as a *staunch* believer in conservation; **3,** seaworthy, as a ship:—*v.t.* **1,** to stop the flow of; as, to *staunch* blood; **2,** to stop a flowing from; as, to *staunch* a wound.—*adv.* **staunch′ly.**

stave (stāv), *n.* **1,** one of the curved, narrow strips of wood forming the sides of a cask or barrel; **2,** a verse or stanza; **3,** in *music*, the set of five horizontal lines and four intervening spaces on which the notes are written; a staff:—*v.t.* [*p.t.* and *p.p.* staved (stāvd) or stove (stōv), *p.pr.* stav-ing], **1,** to knock a hole through the side of; as, to *stave* in a barrel or a boat; **2,** to keep back or drive away; as, to *stave* off disease.

stay (stā), *v.t.* **1,** to put off; postpone; as, to *stay* an execution; **2,** to satisfy for a time; as, to *stay* the stomach with a small snack:—*v.i.* **1,** to remain; wait; as, you must *stay* until I return; **2,** to dwell temporarily; as, to *stay* at a hotel; *stay* south for the winter:—*n.* **1,** a postponement; as, a *stay* of execution; **2,** a prop or support; esp., a rope or wire used to steady or support a mast or spar on a vessel; **3,** a stop or halt; sojourn; short visit; as, a *stay* of three days:—**stays,** a corset.

stead-fast (sted′fåst), *adj.* **1,** fixed firmly; immovable; as, the troops stood *steadfast*; **2,** steady; constant; as, *steadfast* faith.—*adv.* **stead′fast-ly.**

stead-y (sted′i), *adj.* [stead-i-er, stead-i-est], **1,** firmly fixed or supported; as, a *steady* foundation; **2,** constant in feeling or purpose; resolute; unwavering; as, a *steady* faith; **3,** regular; uniform; even; nonfluctuating; as, a *steady* tread; *steady* rain; *steady* prices; **4,** not easily upset or excited; calm; as, to have *steady* nerves; **5,** dependable; industrious; as, a *steady* employee:—*v.t.* and *v.i.* [steadied, steady-ing], to make or become steady.—*adv.* **stead′i-ly.**—*n.* **stead′i-ness.**

steak (stāk), *n.* a slice of fish, beef, or other meat, cut for broiling or frying.

steal (stēl), *v.t.* [*p.t.* stole (stōl), *p.p.* sto-len (stō′len), steal-ing], **1,** to take property by theft; take without permission, dishonestly, or illegally; as, to *steal* a car; to *steal* an idea; **2,** to take or get by surprise; as, to *steal* a kiss; **3,** to get or win by charm; as, to *steal* someone's heart by your kindness; **4,** in *baseball*, to run suddenly to the next base, without being advanced by a hit; as, to *steal* third base:—*v.i.* **1,** to take what belongs to another; as, she *steals* for a living; **2,** to move or act stealthily or secretly; as, to *steal* about on tiptoes; **3,** to gain gradually; as, the child *stole* its way into the man's heart:—*n.* **1,** the act of stealing; a theft; also, that which is stolen; **2,** a bargain.—*adj.* **sto′len.**

stealth (stelth), *n.* secret and quiet means used to accomplish something; secret action; as, to move with stealth in order not to be heard or seen:—*adj.* being undetectable or almost undetectable by radar or sonar, esp. of aircraft; as, a *stealth* bomber.—*adj.* **stealth′y.**

steam (stēm), *n.* **1,** the vapour or gas that rises from boiling water: steam is used for heating and cooking and as a source of energy; **2,** this vapour used as a source of power; as, the engine was driven by *steam*; **3,** a driving force, power, or momentum; as, to finish a race under her own *steam*:—*v.i.* **1,** to throw off visible vapour; as, a tea kettle *steams*; **2,** to rise or pass off in visible vapour; as, moisture *steams* from the earth; **3,** to move under the power of steam or as if by steam; as, the vessel *steamed* away; **4,** *Slang* to be very angry; as, the teacher *steamed* about the trick:—*v.t.* **1,** to expose to, or treat by, steam; **2,** to cook or soften with steam; as, to *steam* vegetables.—*adj.* **steamed; steam′y.**

steam-boat (stēm′bōt′), *n.* a boat driven by steam power.

steam engine, an engine that is powered by the force of steam.

steam-er (stēm′ėr), *n.* **1,** a steamship or steamboat; **2,** a special container in which food is steamed; as, a rice or vegetable *steamer*; **3,** a clam with a soft shell, usually cooked by steaming.

steam-rol-ler (stēm′rōl′ėr), *n.* a vehicle on heavy rollers that is used for crushing and smoothing road surfaces:—*v.i.* and *v.t.* **1,** to use a steamroller; **2,** to overwhelm using great force and pressure; as, the politician *steamrollered* the bill.

steam-ship (stēm′ship), *n.* a ship driven by steam power.

steed (stēd), *n.* a horse, esp. a spirited war or parade horse, used mostly in older stories; as, a knight and his *steed*.

steel (stēl), *n.* **1,** an alloy of iron and carbon, treated to make a hard, tough metal, which is used to make machines, cars, tools, frameworks for large buildings, etc.; **2,** strong or durable as steel; as, nerves of *steel*; **3,** any instrument or weapon of steel; **4,** a piece of steel for striking fire from flint:—*adj.* made of steel; as, a *steel* blade:—*v.t.* to make hard or strong; as, to *steel* one's courage.—*adj.* **steel′y.**

steel band, a band of West Indian origin made up of steel drums, which plays calypso-type music.

steel wool, a pad made of the fine threads of steel, used for cleaning and polishing.

¹steep (stēp), *adj.* **1,** having a sharp pitch or slope; nearly vertical; as, a *steep* cliff; **2,** *Colloq.* very high; as, *steep* prices:—*n.* a cliff or precipice.—*adv.* **steep′ly.**

²steep (stēp), *v.t.* **1,** to soak, usually in a liquid just below the boiling point; as, to *steep* tea; **2,** to soak or dye; hence, to saturate; fill thoroughly; as, the sun *steeped* the valley in sunshine:—*v.i.* to be soaked or steeped in a liquid.

stee-ple (stēpl), *n.* a high tapering tower above the roof of a church or other building.

stee-ple-chase (stēpl-chās′), *n.* **1,** a cross-country race on horseback; **2,** any race over a course made difficult with artificial obstacles.—*n.* **stee′ple-chas′ing; stee′ple-chas′er.**

[1]**steer** (stēr), *n.* a bull, or male of the family of domestic cattle, that has been castrated, esp. one that is raised for beef.

[2]**steer** (stēr), *v.t.* to direct or guide (a ship, automobile, etc.) by means of a rudder, wheel, or other gear:—*v.i.* **1,** to direct a ship, vehicle, etc., in its course; **2,** to direct one's course in a given direction; as, to *steer* toward shore; to *steer* clear of something; **3,** to obey the helm; be steered.—*n.* **steer′ing.**—*adj.* **steer′able.**

steer-age (stēr′ij), *n.* that part of a ship set aside for passengers paying the lowest rates.

steg-o-sau-rus or **steg-o-saur** (steg′o-sô′rus; steg′o-sôr′), *n.* a herbivorous dinosaur with a small head, heavy, bony plates, and sharp spines along the back.

stel-lar (stel′ėr), *adj.* **1,** relating to the stars; as, *stellar* photography; **2,** excellent; as, a *stellar* performance; **3,** relating to stars in film, theatre, music, etc.; as, a *stellar* cast.

[1]**stem** (stem), *n.* **1,** the main stalk of a plant; also, any slender stalk that bears a leaf, flower, or fruit; **2,** any shaft, support, or handle resembling the stalk of a plant; as, the *stem* of a wine glass; **3,** the curved wooden or metal piece to which the two sides of a ship are joined in the front; as, from *stem* to stern; **4,** the part of a word to which various endings may be attached; the root of a word; as, "word" is the *stem* of "wording":—*v.t.* [stemmed, stem-ming], to pluck the stem or stems from; as, to *stem* cherries:—*v.i.* to come from; originate; as, many Canadian place names *stem* from Aboriginal words.

[2]**stem** (stem), *v.t.* [stemmed, stem-ming], **1,** to stop or check; dam up; as, to *stem* a flow of water; **2,** to make headway against; as, to *stem* the tide.

stem cell, an unspecialized cell that can develop into any type of cell, from nerve cell to blood cell, reproducing indefinitely, creating massive potential for supplying transplant tissue: this issue is controversial because of the moral status of the embryo or fetus from which stem cells are taken.

stench (stench), *n.* a strong, disagreeable odour; very bad smell; stink.

sten-cil (sten′sil), *n.* **1,** a thin sheet of metal, paper, etc., cut with an open pattern, so that when it is placed on a surface and colour is spread over it, the design appears on the surface beneath; **2,** a design or decoration so made:—*v.t.* [stencilled, stencil-ling], to mark or decorate in this manner.

ste-nog-ra-phy (ste-nog′ra-fi), *n.* a rapid, abbreviated method of writing; shorthand; also, the process of taking dictation in shorthand notes and transcribing them.—*n.* **ste-nog′ra-pher.**—*adj.* **sten′o-graph′ic.**

step (step), *v.i.* [stepped, step-ping], **1,** to move the feet alternately, as in walking forward, backward, or sidewise; **2,** to walk, esp. a short distance; as, to *step* across the street; **3,** to take possession without effort; as, to *step* into a fortune; **4,** to place the foot (on); as, to *step* on a tack:—*v.t.* **1,** to set or place (the foot); as, *step* foot on land; **2,** to measure by steps; as, to *step* off 30 metres; **3,** to place the heel, or foot, of (a mast) in the socket:—*n.* **1,** the complete movement made in raising and setting down the foot, as in walking or dancing; a pace; also, the sound or mark made, as footstep or footprint; **2,** the distance gained in one such movement; hence, any short distance; as, just a few *steps* to the store; **3,** a degree of progress; as, a *step* nearer fame; **4,** a tread in a stairway; **5,** one of a series of actions or measures; as, the first *step* in an undertaking; **6,** in *music,* the interval between two successive degrees on a scale or staff.—*n.* **step′per; step′ping-stone′.**

step-broth-er (step′bru*th*′ėr), *n.* the son, by a former marriage, of one's stepfather or stepmother.

step-child (step′child′), *n.* [*pl.* stepchildren], the child, by a former marriage, of one's husband or wife.

step-daugh-ter (step′dô′tėr), *n.* the daughter, by a former marriage, of one's husband or wife.

step-fa-ther (step′fä*th*ėr), *n.* the husband of one's mother by a later marriage.

step-lad-der (step′lad′ėr), *n.* a short, portable set of steps, supported at the back by a hinged prop.

step-moth-er (step′mu*th*′ėr), *n.* the wife of one's father by a later marriage.

steppe (step), *n.* a vast, dry, level plain with low grass and few trees, found in southeastern Europe and parts of Asia; as, the *steppes* of Ukraine.

step-sis-ter (step′sis′tėr), *n.* the daughter, by a former marriage, of one's stepfather or stepmother.

step-son (step′sun′), *n.* the son, by a former marriage, of one's husband or wife.

ster-e-o (ster′i-ō), *n.* a radio, CD, or tape player that produces realistic sound by using two or more speakers; a stereophonic sound system:—*adj.* **1,** pertaining to stereophony; **2,** pertaining to stereoscopy.

ster-e-o- (ster′i-ō-), *prefix* meaning *three-dimensional, firm,* or *solid,* as in *ster′e-o-scop′ic,* *ster′e-os′co-py, or ster′e-o-scope′* (an optical instrument that gives three-dimensional effect to a photograph).

ster-e-o-phon-ic (ster′i-ōfon′ik), *adj.* pertaining to the use of several loud speakers so placed or combined as to impart greater realism or fidelity to sound recordings.—*n.* **ster′ē-o′phony.**

ster-e-o-type (ster′e-o-type′), *n.* **1,** an oversimplified image of a group that makes all of its members seem the same; as, the *stereotype* of women being more emotional than men; **2,** a person or thing conforming to such an image:—*v.t.* [stereo-typed, stereotyp-ing] to make or view as a stereotype.—*adj.* **ster′e-o-typ′i-cal; ster′e-o-typ′ic.**—*adv.* **ster′e-o-typ′i-cal-ly.**

ster-ile (ster′īl; ster′il), *adj.* **1,** not fertile or fruitful; unable to produce fruit, seed, crops, or young; **2,** free from living germs or microbes; as, a *sterile* bandage; **3,** without life or energy; empty; barren; as, a *sterile* and deserted street.—*n.* **ste-ril′i-ty.**

ster-i-lize (ster′i-lize′), *v.t.* **1,** to make free from germs or dirt; as, to *sterilize* pond water by boiling; **2,** to make unable to produce young.—*n.* **ster′i-li-za′tion; ster′i-li′zer.**

ster-ling (stûr′ling), *n.* the British system of money; as, pound *sterling*:—*adj.* **1,** of standard weight or purity; as, *sterling* silver; **2,** pure; genuine; of acknowledged worth; as, a *sterling* character.

¹stern (stûrn), *adj.* **1,** severe; rigorous; strict; as, *stern* discipline; **2,** forbidding; repelling; as, a *stern* look.—*adv.* **stern′ly.**

²stern (stûrn), *n.* the aft or rear part of a vessel.

ste-roid (stûr′oid′; stâr′oid′), any of a group of organic compounds, such as sterols and certain hormones, which are present in living animal and plant cells, used to treat various diseases. Compare *anabolic steroid.*

steth-o-scope (steth′o-skōp′), *n.* an instrument used by doctors for listening to the sounds made by the heart, lungs, etc.

ste-ve-dore (stē′vi-dōr′), *n.* one who loads and unloads ship cargoes.

stew (stū), *v.t.* and *v.i.* to boil slowly; simmer:—*v.i. Colloq.* to be agitated, worried, or nervous; as, to *stew* over debts:—*n.* **1,** a dish of food, usually of meat or fish and vegetables, prepared by simmering; as, chicken *stew*; **2,** *Colloq.* nervous anxiety; worry; as, to be in a *stew* over exams.

stew-ard (stū′ėrd), *n.* **1,** one who manages the household affairs of a family or institution; also, the manager of a large estate or farm; **2,** a person employed at a hotel, club, or on a ship, train, or airplane as a server or an attendant in staterooms; a flight attendant; **3,** one who controls financial affairs: as, the *steward* of a church.—*n.fem.* **stew′ard-ess.**—*n.* **stew′ard-ship′.**

¹stick (stik), *n.* **1,** a piece of wood, generally long and slender; a small branch from a tree or shrub; **2,** something long and slender like a stick, as a long piece of candy, gum, a cane, the baton of a musical director, etc.; **3,** a sports implement; as, a hockey or lacrosse *stick*:—**the sticks,** *Slang* a rural area; boondocks.

²stick (stik), *v.t.* [stuck (stuk), stick-ing], **1,** to puncture with a pointed instrument; prick; pierce; as, he *stuck* his hand with a pin; to cause (a pin or a needle) to go through fabric; **2,** to attach or hold in place by means of a point; to fasten in place by causing to adhere; as, to *stick* a stamp on an envelope; **3,** to push or thrust (something); as, he *stuck* the letter under the door:—*v.i.* **1,** to penetrate by means of a pointed end; as, the pin *stuck* in his arm; **2,** to adhere closely; as, dough *sticks* to the hands; **3,** to stay in one place; as, to *stick* close to home; **4,** to hold fast; as, he *sticks* to his ideals; **5,** to persist; persevere; as, to *stick* to a job; **6,** to protrude; as, his handkerchief *stuck* out of his pocket; **7,** to be checked; lose the power of motion; as, to *stick* in a rut; hence, to become blocked or jammed; as, an engine *sticks*; the door *sticks*; **8,** to be checked by fear; hesitate; as, to *stick* at nothing.

stick-er (stik′ėr), *n.* **1,** a label or other printed piece of paper with glue or gum on the back for fastening to a surface; **2,** a person or thing that adheres or pierces.

stick-han-dle (stik′han′dl), *v.i.* [han-dled, han-dling], **1,** to control and manoeuvre a puck in hockey; **2,** to skillfully manoeuvre; as to *stickhandle* around an issue.—*n.* **stick′han′dler.**

stick-y (stik′i), *adj.* [stick-i-er, stick-iest], **1,** tending to stick or adhere, like glue; **2,** hot and humid; as, *sticky* weather; **3,** *Colloq.* difficult; unpleasant; as, a *sticky* situation.—*n.* **stick′i-ness.**

stiff (stif), *adj.* **1,** not easily bent; rigid; firm; as, *stiff* cardboard; also, moved or bent with difficulty or with pain; as, a *stiff* knee; **2,** not easily operated; not working smoothly; as, a *stiff* engine; **3,** strong; severe; fresh; as, a *stiff* breeze; **4,** unnatural; formal; as, a *stiff* manner; **5,** firm; thick; not fluid; as, *stiff* gelatin; **6,** difficult; as, a *stiff* test; **7,** *Colloq.* high; dear; as, a *stiff* charge or prices:—*v.t. Slang* to cheat, snub, stick, or refuse to pay or tip; as, to *stiff* your friends with the lunch bill; to *stiff* someone in a business transaction:—*n. Slang* **1,** a corpse; **2,** a regular person; as, a lucky *stiff*; **3,** someone or something foolish.—*adv.* **stiff′ly.**—*n.* **stiff′ness.**

stiff-en (stif′en), *v.t.* and *v.i.* to make or become rigid, stiff, or less flexible; as, to *stiffen* from old age.

sti-fle (stī′fl), *v.t.* [sti-fled, sti-fling], **1,** to suffocate; smother; **2,** to put out (a fire);

also, to stop or muffle (sounds); **3,** to suppress; choke back; as, to *stifle* a yawn; to *stifle* rage; **4,** to discourage; hold back; as, to *stifle* her creativity.—*adj.* **sti′fling.**

stig-ma (stig′ma), *n.* **1,** [*pl.* stigmas], a mark of disgrace or dishonour; as, the *stigma* attached to a prison term; **2,** [*pl.* stigmata (stig′ma-ta)], a distinguishing mark; esp., the sign of some particular disorder; as, the *stigmata* of dementia; **3, stigmata,** marks resembling the wounds on the body of Christ, said to have appeared on the bodies of certain saints; **4,** [*pl.* stigmas], the upper part of a flower pistil on which the pollen falls (see illustration under *flower*).—*v.t.* **stig′ma-tize′.**—*adj.* **stig-ma′tic.**

sti-let-to (sti-let′ō), *n.* [*pl.* stilettos or stilettoes], **1,** a small, slender dagger; **2,** a tool for making holes in needlework; **3,** a high, thin heel on a woman's shoe.

[1]**still** (stĭl), *adj.* **1,** motionless; also, peaceful and calm; tranquil; as, a *still* pond; **2,** quiet; silent; as, a *still* evening; **3,** in *photography,* pertaining to static, nonmoving images; as, *still* picture; *still* photography:—*n. Poetic* stillness; profound silence:—*adv.* **1,** up to this time; up to any particular time; as, he is *still* sleeping; he was *still* sleeping when I saw him; **2,** nevertheless; in spite of something; as, though he failed, his friends loved him *still*; **3,** even; as, louder *still*:—*conj.* however; yet; as, he was in pain; *still* he uttered no sound:—*v.t.* to check motion, disturbance, or sound in; calm; put at rest; as, to *still* a baby; *still* one's fears.—*n.* **still′ness.**

[2]**still** (stil), *n.* an apparatus for distilling alcoholic liquors.

still-born (stil′bôrn′), *adj.* dead at birth.—*n.* **still′birth′.**

stilt (stilt), *n.* one of a pair of wooden poles, each with an elevated footrest that makes it possible to walk with the feet high above the ground; also, a similar support for a building.

stilt-ed (stilt′id), *adj.* pompous; stiffly formal; as, *stilted* speech.

stim-u-lant (stim′ū-lant), *n.* **1,** that which excites or spurs on; **2,** that which quickens some bodily function for a short time; as, caffeine in coffee or tea is a heart *stimulant.*

stim-u-late (stim′ū-lāt′), *v.t.* [stimulat-ed, stimulat-ing], **1,** to rouse to activity; animate; as, danger *stimulated* us to action; **2,** to produce greater activity in; as, the drug *stimulates* hormone production.—*n.* **stim′u-la′tion.**

stim-u-lus (stim′ū-lus), *n.* [*pl.* stimuli (stim′ūlī′)], **1,** something that rouses to action; as, the newspaper article about the successful entrepreneur was the *stimulus* I needed to work harder; **2,** something that excites an organ or tissue to a specific activity.

sting (sting), *n.* **1,** the sharp, often poisonous, organ with which certain animals, as the scorpion and bee, are armed; **2,** the thrust of such an organ; also, the wound made by it; **3,** keen, smarting, mental or physical pain; **4,** a complex undercover plan or strategy to entrap criminals; also, a swindle:—*v.t.* [stung (stung), sting-ing], **1,** to prick or wound with a sharp point; **2,** to cause a sharp, smarting physical or emotional pain to; as, cold *stings* the face; the cruel remark *stung* me:—*v.i.* **1,** to be sharply painful; as, my eyes *sting* from working on the computer too long; **2,** to be able to prick and wound; as, bees and wasps *sting.*—*n.* **sting′er.**—*adj.* **sting′ing.**

sting-ray (sting′rā′), *n.* a large, flat ocean fish that has a long whiplike tail with poisonous, stinging spines that can inflict a painful wound.

STINGRAY

stin-gy (stin′ji), *adj.* [stin-gi-er, stin-gi-est], **1,** meanly saving of something, esp. money; miserly; not generous; **2,** scanty; meagre; as, a *stingy* portion.—*n.* **stin′gi-ness.**

stink (stingk), *n.* **1,** an offensive odour; disgusting smell; **2,** *Colloq.* an outcry, ado; fuss; as, don't make such a *stink* about it; there was a big *stink* about the misappropriation of public funds:—*v.i.* [*p.t.* stank (stangk) or stunk (stungk), *p.p.* stunk, *p.pr.* stinking], **1,** to throw off a strong, offensive odour; **2,** *Colloq.* to be very bad in quality or unpleasant; as, this essay *stinks*; her job *stinks.*—*n.* **stink′er.**—*adj.* **stink′ing; stink′y.**—*adv.* **stink′ing-ly.**

stint (stint), *v.t.* to keep within narrow limits; skimp; as, to *stint* food; to limit to a scant allowance; as, to *stint* a child:—*v.i.* to be sparing or frugal:—*n.* **1,** a limit or bound; as, generosity without *stint*; **2,** a task assigned or the period of time doing it; as, his weekly *stint* was to cut the grass; a brief *stint* as a courier.—*adj.* **stint′ed.**

sti-pend (stī′pend), *n.* **1,** fixed pay for services; salary; **2,** a periodic payment, as a pension.

stip-ple (stip′l), *v.t.* to paint, speckle, or draw by means of light touches or dots:—*n.* the effect so produced.—*n.* **stip′pler; stip′pling.**

stip-u-late (stip′ū-lāt′), *v.t.* [stipulat-ed, stipulat-ing], to arrange or settle definitely; specify, as part of an agreement; as, he *stipulated* that he be paid in advance.—*n.* **stip′u-la′tion.**—*adj.* **stip′u-lat′ed.**

stir (stûr), *v.t.* [stirred, stir-ring], **1,** to change the position of; move; as, he *stirred* neither hand nor foot; **2,** to set in motion; as, the wind *stirred* the leaves; **3,** to shake or mix up the parts of, by moving, beating, poking, etc., with some utensil; as, *stir* the cake with a spoon; *stir* the fire with a poker; **4,** to move, agitate, or rouse; as, to *stir* men to pity:—*v.i.* **1,** to move or be moved; budge; as, he would not *stir* from his chair; **2,** to be in motion; as, the leaves *stirred* in the trees; **3,** to be roused or agitated; as, pity *stirred* in his heart:—*n.* **1,** the act of stirring or mixing; as, give the soup a *stir;* **2,** hustle; excitement; as, his announcement created quite a *stir.*

stir–fry (stûr′–frī′), *v.t.* [–fried, –frying], to cook finely chopped meat and vegetables over high heat in a lightly oiled pan or wok, stirring constantly:—*n.* a dish prepared in this manner.

stir-rup (stir′up; stûr′up), *n.* one of a pair of loop-shaped metal or leather supports for the feet of a horseback rider, attached to the saddle by a strap.

stitch (stich), *n.* **1,** in *sewing,* a single passing of a threaded needle in and out of the material; also, the section of thread left in the fabric; **2,** in *knitting, crocheting, embroidering,* and such work, a single complete movement of the needle or hook; also, the link or loop so formed; **3,** a particular type of stitch or arrangement of stitches, as the buttonhole stitch in needlework; **4,** the act of closing up a cut with a threadlike material to help it heal properly; **5,** a sudden, sharp pain; as, a *stitch* in the side:—**in stitches,** laughing very hard; as, the comedian had us in *stitches*:—*v.t.* to join by stitches; hence, to sew; also, to ornament by stitches:—*v.i.* to sew.—*n.* **stitch′er; stitch′ing.**

stock (stok), *n.* **1,** the capital of a corporation in the form of shares; **2,** the supply of goods that a merchant keeps on hand; as, to replenish the *stock* of CDs; **3,** hence, a supply of anything; as, a *stock* of information; **4,** domestic animals kept on a farm; livestock; **5,** raw material ready for manufacture; as, paper *stock;* **6,** the juices of meats, fish, or vegetables from which soups, gravies, etc., are made; **7,** the main stem or trunk of a plant or tree; also, a growing plant in which a graft is placed, as a quince *stock;* **8,** the race or line of a family; ancestry; as, he comes of old *stock;* **9,** the part of an implement or machine that serves as the body or main support for other parts, as the part of a gun to which the barrel, lock, etc., are attached, the cross-piece of an anchor, etc. (see illustration under *anchor*); **10,** a close-fitting wide band or cloth for the neck; **11,** a company of actors presenting one play after another:—**stocks,** an old instrument of punishment for minor offences, consisting of a wooden frame with holes in which to confine the hands, feet, and, sometimes, the head of offenders; as, to be put in the *stocks* for her crime:—**stock exchange,** the place where stocks, bonds, and other securities are traded in an organized manner; stock market; as, the Toronto *Stock Exchange;* also, the association of dealers and brokers who trade in securities:—*v.t.* to keep on hand; keep in supply of:—*adj.* **1,** on hand; in supply; as, a *stock* item; **2,** in common use, standard; as, a *stock* question regarding this issue.—*n.* **stock′room′.**—*adj.* **stocked.**

stock-ade (sto-kād′), *n.* **1,** a fence of upright posts or logs set close together in the earth, used as a defensive barrier or to form an enclosure for cattle or prisoners; **2,** the space so enclosed:—*v.t.* [stockad-ed, stockad-ing], to surround with, or defend by, such a fence.

stock-brok-er (stok′brōk′ėr), *n.* one who buys and sells shares of stock for others for a fee.—*n.* **stock′brok′ing; stock′bro′kerage; stock′ hold′er** (one who owns shares of capital stock in a corporation or joint stock company).

stock-ing (stok′ing), *n.* a close-fitting covering for the leg.

stock market, a place where stocks and bonds are bought and sold. Also called *stock exchange.*

stock-pile (stok′pīl′), *n.* a storage pile; a reserve supply for future use, esp. in case of emergency; as, a *stockpile* of food supplies:—*v.t.* [stock-piled, stock-pil-ling], to accumulate such a supply; as, to *stockpile* weapons.—*n.* **stock-pil-er.**

stock–still (stok′stil′), *adj.* completely still; motionless; as, she stood *stock-still.*

stock-y (stok′i), *adj.* [stock-i-er, stock-iest] short and stoutly built; as, a *stocky* wrestler.

stock-yard (stok′yärd′), *n.* a large pen where cattle, swine, and sheep are kept, usually before being shipped to market or to be slaughtered.

stodg-y (stoj′i), *adj.* **1,** boring; dull; as, a *stodgy* book; **2,** lacking in vivacity, old-fashioned; as a *stodgy* old man; **3,** bulky; stuffed; filling; as, *stodgy* cake.

sto-ic (stō′ik) or **sto-i-cal** (stō′i-kal), *adj.* self-controlled; able to suffer without complaining: from the ancient Greek philosophy *Stoicism* that promoted indifference to pain or pleasure; as, a seemingly *stoic* indifference to excessive heat.—*n.* **sto′ic.**—*adv.* **sto′i-cal-ly.**

stoke (stōk), *v.t.* and *v.i.* [stoked, stok-ing], **1,** to tend (a fire or furnace); **2,** to fuel; provoke; stimulate; as, her tardiness *stoked* the teacher's wrath.—*n.* **stok′er.**—*adj.* **stoked** (*Slang* excited; stimulated; inspired; as, to be *stoked* after winning the essay contest).

[1]**stole** (stōl), *p.t.* of *steal.*

[2]**stole** (stōl), *n.* **1,** a woman's long scarf, usually of fur or cloth, worn with the ends hanging in front; **2,** a long scarflike vestment worn by a bishop or priest.

sto-len (stō′len), *p.p.* of *steal.*

stol-id (stol′id), *adj.* not easily aroused or

excited.—*adv.* **stol′id-ly.**—*n.* **sto-lid′i-ty; stol′id-ness.**

stom-ach (stum′ak), *n.* **1,** a part of the digestive tract; in humans, the sac at the end of the gullet to which food goes when it is swallowed; **2,** the area of the body between the middle of the chest and the hips; **3,** desire; inclination; as, he had no *stomach* for revenge:—*v.t.* to put up with; tolerate; as, to be unable to *stomach* his diatribe.

stomp (stômp), *v.i.* to walk or step heavily and with force; to trample; as, the troops *stomped* through the village, flattening everything in their path.—*n.* a dance characterized by stomping.

stomping grounds, familiar territory; one's favourite, much-frequented, or habitual place of action; as, to return to old *stomping grounds*. Also called *stamping grounds*.

stone (stōn), *n.* **1,** a small piece of rock; **2,** the hard, nonmetallic mineral matter of which rock consists; **3,** a piece of rock cut and shaped for a special use; as, a hearth*stone*; **4,** a gem; as, a perfect ruby is a precious *stone*; **5,** something resembling a small stone in hardness and shape; as, a hail*stone*; **6,** the hard pit or seed of certain fruits, such as cherries and peaches:—*v.t.* [stoned, ston-ing], **1,** to pelt with pieces of rock; kill by hurling pieces of rock; **2,** to remove the stones, or pits, from; as, to *stone* dates:—*adj.* made of stoneware or earthenware.—*adj.* **stoned** (to be intoxicated or under the influence of drugs); **ston′y.**

Stone Age, an early period of human history when tools and weapons were made of stone rather than metal.—*adj.* **stone-age** (primordial; old-fashioned).

stone-wall (stōn′wôl′), *v.t.* to delay or stall; hinder or block; as, to *stonewall* the legislation:—*v.i.* to act unco-operatively, obstructively, or evasively.—*n.* **stone′wal′ler; stone′wal′ling.**

stood (stood), *p.t.* and *p.p.* of *stand.*

stooge (sto͞oj), *n. Slang* one who acts as an underling or a foil to another, esp. in a secretive or obsequious fashion; also, a straight man in a comedy team.

stook (sto͝ok), *n.* a pile or bundle of sheaves, esp. when stacked in a field:—*v.t.* to pile sheaves. Also called *shock*, esp. in U.S.—*n.* **stook′ing.**

stool (sto͞ol), *n.* **1,** a seat without a back, having three or four legs; **2,** a rest for the feet; also, a rest for the knees in kneeling.—**stools,** fecal matter; excrement.—**stool pi-geon, 1,** a decoy; **2,** *Colloq.* an informer; spy.

stoop (sto͞op), *v.i.* **1,** to bend the body down and, usually, forward; also, to carry the head and shoulders habitually bowed forward; **2,** to lower oneself to do something one should not do; as, she *stooped* to cheating on the exam; **3,** to submit; yield:—*n.* **1,** a bending down and forward, esp. of the head and shoulders; as, to walk with a *stoop*; **2,** a small porch or platform with steps (at the door of a house).—*adj.* **stooped.**

stop (stop), *v.t.* [stopped, stop-ping], **1,** to fill up (a hole or an opening); also, to close (a container); as, to *stop* a keg; **2,** to obstruct or make impassable; as, to *stop* a road; **3,** to check the progress or motion of; cause to come to a state of rest; as, to *stop* a car; cause to cease; as, to *stop* an annoyance; **4,** to desist from; as, *stop* all that noise; **5,** withhold something, esp. payment; as, to *stop* payment on the cheque:—*v.i.* **1,** to cease; desist; halt; **2,** *Colloq.* to break a journey; lodge; as, to *stop* at an inn:—*n.* **1,** a pause or delay; **2,** a halt; also, a halting place; **3,** a punctuation mark; **4,** any of several devices, as a block, peg, plug, or pin, to regulate or check motion, or to keep a movable part in place; as, a window *stop*; **5,** in *music*, any means or device for regulating pitch; also, in an organ, a set of pipes producing tones of the same quality.

stop-gap (stop′gap′), *n.* and *adj.* a temporary substitute; a makeshift or expedient; as, *stopgap* measures.

stop-page (stop′ij), *n.* the arresting of motion or action; also, the state of arrested motion; obstruction.

stop-per (stop′ėr), *n.* **1,** a plug that closes the opening of a bottle, jar, etc.; **2,** a person or thing that stops, obstructs, or attracts attention; as, a show *stopper*; **3,** in *baseball*, a relief pitcher.

stop-watch (stop′woch′), *n.* a watch that can be stopped to give the exact length of time that something takes.

stor-age (stōr′ij), *n.* **1,** the placing of goods in a warehouse, for safekeeping; also, the space thus occupied or the price charged for the service; **2,** in *computing*, the fact or process of, or device for, saving information in a computer; the space or memory on a computer for storing information; as, a computer with 30 gigabytes of memory or *storage* capacity. Also called *storage device.*

store (stōr), *n.* **1,** a great quantity or number; **2,** (often *stores*), an accumulation or supply kept in reserve or ready for use; **3,** a shop where goods are kept for sale; as, a convenience *store*; department *store*, grocery *store*; variety *store*:—**in store,** in reserve:—*v.t.* [stored, stor-ing], **1,** to furnish or stock; equip; as, a mind *stored* with knowledge; **2,** to collect; hoard; **3,** to put in a warehouse for safekeeping; **4,** to put information into a computer memory or onto a memory storage device such as a tape, CD-ROM, zip disk, or floppy disk; to back up data; as, to *store* the entire files of the project on a zip disk:—

adj. relating to a store; manufactured; as, *store* products; *store* counter; *store*-bought.—*n.* **store′front′; store′keep′er; store′room′.**

store-house (stōr′hous′), *n.* **1,** a building or other place where things are stored for future use; **2,** a large supply or source; as, the Internet is a *storehouse* of useful information.

stor-ey or **stor-y** (stōr′i), *n.* [*pl.* storeys; stories], a floor of a building, usually divided into rooms; as, a 50-*storey* tower.

stork (stôrk), *n.* a kind of wading bird with long legs and a long bill, symbolic of bringing new babies.

Stork

storm (stôrm), *n.* **1,** a violent disturbance of the atmosphere, often with a heavy fall of rain, snow, or hail; also, a thunderstorm; **2,** an outburst of passion or excitement; as, a *storm* of rage; **3,** a sudden violent attack on a fortified place:—**by storm,** with a sudden and powerful attack, or to become successful very quickly; as, to take a stronghold *by storm*; to take the theatre world *by storm*:—*v.t.* to attack suddenly with violence; as, to *storm* a fort:—*v.t.* **1,** to blow violently, or to rain, hail, snow, etc.; **2,** to rage.—*adv.* **storm′i-ly.**—*n.* **storm′i-ness.** Also, **storm cloud; storm sewer; storm trooper; storm window.**

storm-y (stôr′mē), *adj.* [storm-i-er, storm-i-est], **1,** having to do with a storm or storms; as, stormy weather; **2,** like a storm; noisy, violent, angry, etc.; as, to have a *stormy* relationship with many arguments.

stor-y (stōr′i), *n.* [*pl.* stories], **1,** real or imagined events narrated in prose or verse; a tale, either written or spoken; **2,** a report or statement; rumour; **3,** news article or segment; **4,** anecdote; as, to tell funny *stories* about his encounters with the legendary writer; *Colloq.* a lie; as, to tell absurd heroic *stories*; **5,** a storey. Also, **sto′ry-book′; sto′ry-line′; sto′ry-tel′ler.**

stout (stout), *adj.* **1,** brave; resolute; as, a *stout* soldier; **2,** tough; strong; as, the *stout* oak; **3,** bulky; thickset; heavy; as, a *stout* figure:—*n.* strong, dark porter, ale, or beer.—*adv.* **stout′ly.**—*n.* **stout′ness.**

stove (stōv), *n.* **1,** an electrical or gas kitchen appliance that is used for cooking food; **2,** an apparatus that burns fuel for producing heat with which to warm a room, etc.; as, a Franklin *stove*; **3,** a kiln.

stove-pipe (stove′pipe′), *n.* a large metal pipe used to carry smoke away from a stove.

stow (stō), *v.t.* **1,** to fill by close packing; as, to *stow* a trunk with articles; **2,** to store (a cargo) compactly; **3,** to hide away; conceal:—**stow away,** to be a stowaway.

stow-a-way (stō′a-wā′), *n.* one who hides on a ship, train, or airplane to travel for free.

strad-dle (strad′l), *v.t.* [strad-dled, strad-dling], **1,** to stand or sit astride of; as, to *straddle* a fence; **2,** *Colloq.* to support, or seem to support, both sides of; as, to *straddle* an issue:—*v.i.* **1,** to sit, stand, or walk with the legs wide apart; **2,** *Colloq.* to support, or seem to support, both sides of a question:—*n.* the act of straddling; also, the space between the legs of one who straddles.

strafe (strāf; sträf), *v.t.* to punish; subject to rapid fire, esp. machine-gun fire from low-flying aircraft.

strag-gle (strag′l), *v.i.* [strag-gled, strag-gling], **1,** to wander away from the main group; stray; ramble; as, on the hike, certain boys *straggled* behind the rest; **2,** to spread about; occur here and there; move or grow unevenly or in a crooked way; as, weeds *straggle* along a roadside; to *straggle* up a hillside.—*n.* **strag′gler.**—*adj.* **strag′gly.**

straight (strāt), *adj.* **1,** not crooked or curved; extending directly without change in direction; as, a *straight* line; **2,** honest; upright; as, *straight* living; **3,** logical; clear; as, *straight* thinking; **4,** accurate; in order, as accounts; as, to get information *straight*; **5,** orderly; tidy; **6,** serious; as, to keep a *straight* face; **7,** uninterrupted; as, five *straight* hits; **8,** not deviating from what is generally considered to be the norm; conventional; heterosexual; not under the influence of alcohol or drugs:—*adv.* **1,** directly; without swerving; as, the arrow flew *straight*; **2,** without delay; as, to come *straight* home.—*n.* **straight′ face′; straight′ness.**—*adj.* **straight′-faced′.**

straight-a-way (strāt′a-wā′), *n.* and *adj.* a track or course that extends in a straight line.

straight-en (strāt′n), *v.t.* **1,** to make free of turns or curves; as, to *straighten* a road; **2,** to arrange in a desired position or condition; as, to *straighten* a necktie; to *straighten* a room; **3,** to make clear; as, to *straighten* out a mystery:—*v.i.* to become straight.

straight-for-ward (strāt′fôr′wėrd), *adj.* proceeding in a direct course or manner; hence, honest; not complex.—*n.* **straight′for′ward-ness.**

straightjacket (strāt′jak′it), *n.* Same as **straitjacket.**

[1]**strain** (strān), *n.* **1,** stock; breed, or type of animal or plant; as, an ancient *strain* of cat; **2,** family line, ancestry; **3,** disposition; tendency; as, a strain of *violence*; **4,** manner; tone; sort; as, to speak in lofty *strain*; **5,** a vein or streak; as, a *strain* of humour; **6,** a tune or melody.

[2]**strain** (strān), *v.t.* **1,** to put to its utmost strength; exert as much as possible; as, to *strain* every muscle; stretch even beyond proper limits; as, to *strain* a muscle; **2,** to weaken or injure by excessive use; as, to *strain* one's voice; **3,** to put through a sieve; as, to *strain* soup; also, to remove by filter-

ing:—*v.i.* **1,** to make tremendous efforts; strive; **2,** to pass through a sieve or filter; be strained; **3,** to become injured by excessive use or exertion:—*n.* **1,** extreme stretching; tension; **2,** a violent effort; **3,** injury due to violent effort or to overwork.—*adj.* **strained.**

strain-er (strān′ėr), *n*, a device with small holes for separating liquids from solids.

strait (strāt), *n.* **1,** a narrow passage of water connecting two larger bodies of water; as, the *Strait* of Magellan; **2, straits,** perplexity; difficulties; as, financial *straits*:—*adj.* narrow; confining; strict; as, the *strait* and narrow path; a *strait*jacket.

strait-jack-et (strāt′jak-it′), *n.* **1,** a long-sleeved garment resembling a jacket, used to restrain violent individuals; **2,** anything that restricts or confines; as, a legal *straitjacket*:—*v.t.* to confine, restrict, or restrain like a straitjacket. Also called *straightjacket.*

strait-laced (strāt′lāst′), *adj.* very strict in conduct or morality; puritanical; prudish.

[1]**strand** (strand), *n.* the shore, as of an ocean:—*v.t.* **1,** to drive ashore; run aground; as, the storm *stranded* the ship on a reef; **2,** to leave in a state of embarrassment or difficulty; as, he was *stranded* in a strange city without money:—*v.i.* to run aground; become stranded.—*adj.* **strand′ed.**

[2]**strand** (strand), *n.* **1,** one of a number of flexible strings, as of wire or hemp, twisted together into a rope; **2,** anything similar to a strand, as of pearls, beads, or hair.

strange (strānj), *adj.* [strang-er, strang-est], **1,** belonging to some other person or place; as, to sleep in a *strange* bed; **2,** not familiar; as, a *strange* voice; **3,** odd; remarkable; unusual; as, *strange* ideas; **4,** reserved; shy; timid; as, to feel *strange* in her company; **5,** inexperienced; as, he is *strange* to the new work.—*adv.* **strange′ly.**

stran-ger (strān′jėr), *n.* **1,** a person from another place; as, "a *stranger* in a strange land"; **2,** a newcomer; visitor; as, *strangers* are welcome in this community shelter; **3,** a person not known to one; as, he was a *stranger* to me.

stran-gle (strang′gl), *v.t.* [stran-gled, stran-gling], **1,** to choke; kill by squeezing the throat; **2,** to suppress; as, to *strangle* an impulse; to *strangle* her musical ability:—*v.i.* to be choked or suffocated.—*n.* **stran′gu-la′tion; stran′gler.**

strap (strap), *n.* **1,** a narrow strip of leather, cloth, etc., used to fasten objects together or hold them in place; as, a shoe *strap*; **2,** a piece of leather used as a punishment tool:—*v.t.* [strapped, strap-ping], **1,** to fasten or bind with a strap; **2,** to punish with a strap.—*adj.* **strapped** (punished with a strap; also, suffering from a shortage, esp. of money; as, *strapped* for cash).

strap-ping (strap′ing), *adj.* tall and well built; robust; strong; as, a *strapping* youth:—*n.* **1,** material for a strap; **2,** punishment with a strap.

strat-a-gem (strat′a-jem), *n.* **1,** a trick for deceiving an enemy, esp. in war; **2,** any trick for gaining some advantage.

strat-e-gy (strat′i-ji), *n.* **1,** the art or science of war; the art of planning and manoeuvring troops or ships on a large scale; the plan itself; **2,** a careful plan, esp. long-range, for reaching a certain goal or in managing any affair; as, the government health-care *strategy*; a long-term *strategy* for building a client base and growing a company.—*adj.* **stra-te′gic; stra-te′gic-cal-ly.**—*n.* **strat′e-gist.**

strat-i-fy (strat′i-fī′), *v.t.* and *v.i.* to form, arrange, or harden in layers or strata; as, *stratified* rock:—*v.t.* to arrange or divide into distinct categories or classes; as, to *stratify* the population by income.—*n.* **strat′i-fi-ca′tion.**

stra-to–cu-mu-lus (strā′tō–kū′mū-lus), *n.* a low cloud or cloud layer made up of large dark masses that appear like mounds piled on top of one another, seen esp. in winter.

stra-to-sphere (strā′to-sfēr′; strat′o-sfēr′), *n.* **1,** the portion of the atmosphere that is 11 to 50 kilometres above the earth's surface; **2,** at the highest level of something; as, as the new estimate has reached the *stratosphere.*—*adj.* **stra′to-spher′ic.**

stra-tum (strā′tum; strat′um), *n.* [*pl.* strata (strā′ta; strat′a)], **1,** one of a series of layers of rock or earth; as, a *stratum* of rock between *strata* of clay; **2,** a specific area or layer of the sea or atmosphere; **3,** a class or statistical group in society; as, he belongs to the upper *stratum*; the lower-income *stratum.*

straw (strô), *n.* **1,** the stalk of grain; **2,** such stalks when cut and threshed, used for fodder, packing, etc.; **3,** anything practically worthless; as, clutching at *straws*; **4,** a narrow tube made of paper or plastic, used for sucking up liquids, or something resembling one; as, she drank her smoothie through a thick *straw*:—*adj.* **1,** made of straw; as, a *straw* hat; stuffed with straw; as, a *straw* mattress; **2,** of the colour of straw.

straw-ber-ry (strô′ber′i), *n.* [*pl.* strawberries], **1,** a sweet, fleshy, edible berry, red when fully ripe; also, the low-growing plant of which it is the fruit; **2,** the colour of this fruit.

stray (strā), *v.i.* to wander from a designated path; as, to *stray* from the main issue; err:—*adj.* **1,** wandering; lost; as, a *stray* dog; **2,** occasional; incidental; as, a *stray* remark:—*n.* a lost person or domestic animal; as, the puppy is a *stray.*

streak (strēk) *n.* **1,** a line differing in color from its background; stripe; **2,** a trait of character; as, a *streak* of meanness; **3,** layer; as, *streaks* of lean in bacon; **4,** a continuing pattern or series of events; as, a nine-game winning *streak*:—*v.t.* to mark with streaks:—*v.i.* to move very quickly; as, a shooting star *streaked* across the sky.—*adj.* **streak′y.**—*n.* **streak′er.**

stream (strēm), *n.* **1,** flowing water; a creek, small river, etc.; **2,** anything flowing forth like a stream; as, a *stream* of people; a *stream* of light; **3,** hence, a continued flow; drift; course; as, the *stream* of civilization; *stream* of consciousness; to go against the *stream* of current trends; **4,** in *computing*, a constant flow of information or data:—*v.i.* **1,** to flow or move continuously; run in a current; **2,** to pour or drip; as, rain *streams* off the umbrella; **3,** to wave or float in the air; as, banners *stream* in the air.—*n.* **stream′let.**

stream-er (strē′ėr), *n.* **1,** a long, narrow pennant or ribbon; **2,** a shaft of light, as in the northern lights.

stream-line (strēm′līn′), *v.t.* **1,** to shape in long smooth curves so as to offer the least resistance to air or water; as, to *streamline* the design of the boat; **2,** to reorganize or simplify a procedure, etc., for efficiency; as, to *streamline* the registration process at the university.—*adj.* **stream′lined′.**

street (strēt), *n.* a public road in a city or town, usually lined with buildings:—*adj.* pertaining to or happening in the streets; as, *street* door; *street* fighting; *street* hockey; *street* map.

street-car (strēt′kär′), *n.* an electric passenger car that runs on tracks laid on the surface of a street.

street people, 1, people who live mainly on the streets; homeless people; **2,** those who frequent the streets and other outdoor areas of their neighbourhoods; **3,** those who earn their living on the streets, as vendors, performers, and artists.

street-wise (strēt′wīz′), *adj. Colloq.* having the shrewdness, skills, experience, and resourcefulness to survive in the often-dangerous urban environment.

strength (strength; strengkth), *n.* **1,** the quality of being strong; muscular force; also, the ability to do or endure; **2,** firmness; toughness; as, the *strength* of a rope; **3,** power; vigour; intensity; as, *strength* of will; **4,** force in numbers; as, the *strength* of an army; **5,** attribute; positive quality; as, the main *strength* of the novel.—*v.t.* and *v.i.* **strength′en.**

stren-u-ous (stren′ū-us), *adj.* **1,** urgent; zealous; active; as, a *strenuous* reformer; **2,** full of or with great effort or exertion; as, a *strenuous* life; a *strenuous* climb.—*adv.* **stren′u-ous-ly.**

stress (stres), *n.* **1,** impelling physical force; pressure; as, to test the heavy metal to see how much *stress* it could take; **2,** mental or emotional pressure or strain; as, the *stress* of exams; **3,** importance; emphasis; accent; as, to place *stress* on a particular fact; to put the *stress* on the first syllable of the word:—*v.t.* **1,** to emphasize; as, to *stress* the importance of being on time; **2,** accent; as, *stress* the first word.—*adj.* **stressed; stress′ful.**—*adv.* **stress′ful-ly.**

stretch (strech), *v.t.* **1,** to draw out in length or width; hence, to draw taut; as, to *stretch* a rubber band; **2,** to extend; as, to *stretch* out an arm; to extend between two points; as, to *stretch* a tennis net; **3,** to strain; exert to the utmost; as, *stretch* every effort to get there; **4,** to exaggerate; as, to *stretch* the truth; **5,** to make the most of; as, *stretch* the loonies:—*v.i.* **1,** to spread; reach; as, the rope *stretched* across the street; **2,** to be able to be extended; as, elastic *stretches*; **3,** to extend or spread the body or limbs:—*n.* **1,** the act of straining or extending; **2,** reach; scope; extent; **3,** a continuous line, space, or time; as, a *stretch* of good road; **4,** *Colloq.* overstatement; exaggeration; as, it's a real *stretch* that you'll be able to finish your essay in two days.—*adj.* **stretch′a-ble; stretch′y.**

stretch-er (strech′ėr), *n.* a frame, usually covered with canvas, for carrying sick or injured people.

strew (stro͞o), *v.t.* [*p.t.* strewed (stro͞od), *p.p.* strewed or strewn (stro͞on), *p.pr.* strew-ing], **1,** to scatter; let fall loosely; as, to *strew* flowers on a path; **2,** to cover by scattering small objects; as, to *strew* a walk with pebbles; to *strew* clothes around the room.

stri-at-ed (strī′āt-id), *adj.* streaked; striped; furrowed; grooved; as *striated* rocks, shells, etc.—*n.* **stri-a′tion.**

strick-en (strik′en), *adj.* afflicted; affected by illness, age, misfortune, etc.; as, *stricken* with fear; *stricken* with rubella.

strict (strikt), *adj.* **1,** exacting; severe; exact; as, *strict* laws; **2,** rigid; unswerving; as, *strict* honesty; a *strict* secret; **3,** accurate; precise; as, the *strict* sense of a word.—*adv.* **strict′ly.**—*n.* **strict′ness.**

stride (strīd), *n.* **1,** a long step; also, the space covered by a long step; **2,** the fact of advancing; progress or improvement; as, to take great *strides* in improving working conditions:—*v.i.* [*p.t.* strode (strōd), *p.p.* strid-den (strid′n), *p.pr.* strid-ing], to walk with long steps:—*v.t.* to straddle; hence, to ride (a horse).

stri-dent (strī′dent), *adj.* **1,** shrill; harsh; grating; as, *strident* tones; **2,** emphatic, urgent; as, *strident* pleas for leniency.

strife (strīf), *n.* conflict; hostilities; rivalry.

strike (strīk), *v.t.* [*p.t.* struck (struk), *p.p.* struck or strick-en (strik′en), *p.pr.* strik-ing], **1,** to hit; dash against; **2,** to deal (a blow); also, to deal a blow to; as, John *struck* him in the face; **3,** to collide, or cause to collide, with; as, my foot *struck* the table; I *struck* my foot on the table; **4,** to come to the mind of; occur to; as, an idea *struck* her; **5,** to afflict or affect; as, horror *struck* him; illness *struck* her; **6,** to come upon; as, to *strike* gold; **7,** to conclude, as a bargain; as, to *strike* a deal; **8,** to cancel; as, the remarks were then *struck* (or *stricken*) from the record; **9,** to cause (a match) to ignite; **10,** to produce by printing; as, to *strike* off a new issue of stamps; **11,** to cause to sound; as, to *strike* a bell; also, to announce by sound; as, the clock *strikes* 12:—*v.i.* **1,** to deal a quick blow or thrust; make an attack; fight; **2,** to hit; collide; become stranded, as a ship; **3,** to proceed quickly, dart; as, they *struck* through the woods; **4,** to sound, as a bell or a clock; **5,** to cease from work in order to secure or prevent a change in working conditions or pay:—*n.* **1,** the act of striking; **2,** a stopping of work by a number of employees in order to secure or prevent a change in working conditions, rate of pay, etc.; **3,** a fortunate discovery of ore or oil; hence, any sudden success; **4,** in *baseball*, an unsuccessful attempt by the batter to hit the ball, or a ball so pitched that the batter should have struck at it; **5,** in *bowling*, the upsetting, by a player, of all the pins with the first ball bowled; also, the score so made:—**strike out, 1,** in *baseball*, to make an out by getting three strikes; **2,** to fail completely; as, to *strike out* when asking for a raise; **3,** to begin to move or go, set out; as, to *strike out* for the next destination.—*n.* **strike′out′; strike′break′er** (someone who substitutes for a striking worker; a scab).

strik-er (strīk′ėr), *n.* **1,** a person or thing that strikes; **2,** an employee who, with others, quits work in protest against existing or proposed working conditions, rates of pay, etc.

strik-ing (strīk′ing), *adj.* **1,** making a strong impression by being attractive or unusual; as, a *striking* view; **2,** being on strike; as, *striking* employees:—*n.* the act of striking.—*adv.* **strik′ing-ly.**

string (string), *n.* **1,** a thin cord; thick thread; twine; also, something used for tying; as, apron-*strings*; **2,** a set of things, as beads, arranged on a cord; as, a *string* of pearls; also, a series of things in, or as in, a line; as a *string* of jokes; a *string* of cars; **3,** a vegetable fibre, as of string beans; **4,** a tightly stretched cord for musical instruments that produces a tone; **5,** in *computing*, a sequential string of information:—**strings,** stringed musical instruments, such as a violin or cello:—*v.t.* [strung (strung), string-ing], **1,** to furnish (a bow, violin, etc.) with a string or strings; **2,** to thread on a cord, as beads; **3,** to form into a line or series; **4,** to fasten or hang with a cord; as, to *string* pictures on a wall; **5,** to take the strings from (beans); **6,** to fool or deceive; as, to *string* him along about her intentions:—*v.i.* **1,** to form strings; become stringy, as glue; **2,** to move along in a single file:—*adj.* relating to strings or string instruments; as, *string* ensemble; *string* bikini; *string* bean.

string bean (string′bēn′), *n.* a kind of green bean, grown and eaten in its edible pods; one of the pods.

stringed (stringd), *adj.* fitted with strings, as the violin, cello, mandolin, etc.

strin-gent (strin′jent), *adj.* strict; severe; as, *stringent* rules.—*n.* **strin′gen-cy.**

string-y (string′i), *adj.* [string-i-er, string-i-est], **1,** long and thin; wiry; as, a *stringy* athlete; **2,** full of fibres or strings; as, *stringy* meat; **3,** capable of being drawn out into strings, as glue.

strip (strip), *v.t.* [stripped, strip-ping], **1,** to make naked; deprive of a covering; hence, to rob; bare or deprive; as, to *strip* a man of his riches; to *strip* a tree of apples; **2,** to pull off (a covering); as, to *strip* bark from a tree:—*v.i.* to undress:—*n.* a long, narrow piece or area of anything; as, a *strip* of paper or cloth; a comic *strip*; an air*strip*.—*n.* **strip′per.**

stripe (strīp), *n.* **1,** a line, band, or streak; **2,** a strip of different colour or material attached to anything; as, a *stripe* on a uniform; **3,** distinctive sort or kind; as, they are persons of the same *stripe*:—*v.t.* [striped, strip-ing], to mark with lines or bands.—*adj.* **striped.**

strip mall, a small shopping centre, usually in a suburban area, with stores arranged in a row and not enclosed in a single building.

strive (strīv), *v.i.* [*p.t.* strove (strōv) or strived (strīvd), *p.p.* striv-en (striv′en) or strived, *p.pr.* striving,] **1,** to make an effort; try hard; as, to *strive* for success; **2,** to struggle; battle; as, the swimmer *strove* against the current.

strode (strōd), *p.t.* of *stride.*

stroke (strōk), *n.* **1,** the act of dealing a blow or the blow dealt; as, the *stroke* of a hammer; **2,** the act of hitting a ball in a game; as, a golf *stroke*; **3,** a sudden loss of consciousness and sensation as a result of stopping or blocking the blood flow to the brain: also called *apoplexy;* **4,** a sudden and vigorous effort, producing an impact or result; as, a *stroke* of genius; a *stroke* of luck; **5,** a gentle touch; as, a *stroke* of the hand; **6,** a single movement with an instrument; as, a pencil *stroke*; the result or mark made by such a movement; **7,** the sound of a bell or clock; also, the time marked; as, at the *stroke* of three; **8,** one of a series of repeated movements in air or water; as, the *stroke* of a swimmer; **9,** in *rowing*, the oarsman nearest the stern who sets the time; **10,** *Colloq.* to flatter or finesse for a purpose; as, to *stroke* your employer's ego in order to get a raise:—*v.t.* [stroked, strok-ing], **1,** to rub gently with the hand; **2,** to set the pace for (rowers); as, he *stroked* the crew for two years.

stroll (strōl), *n.* **1,** a quiet walk or ramble; as, a *stroll* in the park; **2,** *Colloq.* something achieved without great effort; as, winning the election was a *stroll*:—*v.i.* **1,** to wander on foot from place to place; to ramble; **2,** to get something without much effort; as, to *stroll* to success.—*adj.* **strol′ling.**

stroll-er (strol′ler), *n.* **1,** a baby carriage in which a child can sit upright; **2,** someone who strolls.

STROLLER

strong (strông), *adj.* **1,** physically powerful; muscular; robust; as, a *strong* horse; a *strong* physique; **2,** upright; firm; as, a *strong* character; **3,** powerful in wealth, numbers, or other resources; as, a *strong* party; also, of a specified numerical force; as, 9,000 *strong*; **4,** violent, as a high wind; **5,** ardent or warm, as the affections; **6,** vigorous or forceful, as an argument; **7,** stable or settled, as a government; **8,** intense, as a bright light; concentrated; as, *strong* tea or coffee; also, containing alcohol; as, *strong* drink; **9,** firm in opinion; ardent; as, a *strong* partisan; **10,** deeply rooted; positive; as, *strong* beliefs; **11,** solid; not easily broken; as, a *strong* plank.—*adv.* **strong′ly.**

strong-arm (strông′ärm′), *adj. Colloq.* relating to physical violence, coersion, or threats; as, *strong-arm* tactics:—*v.t.* to bully, threaten, or intimidate; as, to *strong-arm* someone into line.

strong-hold (strông′hōld′), *n.* a fort or fortress; a place of refuge; a central place for a particular group or having a specific characteristic; as, the Liberal *stronghold.*

strove (strōv), *p.t.* of *strive.*

struck (struk), *p.t.* and *p.p.* of *strike.*

struc-ture (struk′tūr), *n.* **1,** that which is built, as a bridge or a house; **2,** the manner in which something is built; as, the *structure* of automobiles has been improved; **3,** the form or arrangement of parts or elements; as, the *structure* of a flower.—*adj.* **struc′tur-al.**—*adv.* **struc′tur-al-ly.**

strug-gle (strug′l), *v.i.* [strug-gled, struggling], **1,** to put forth violent effort, as in trying to escape from a grasp; to fight; to do battle; **2,** to labour; strive; as, he *struggled* to keep from falling asleep in class:—*n.* **1,** a violent effort; **2,** a contest; strife.

strum (strum), *v.t.* and *v.i.* to pluck the strings (as of a guitar, banjo, etc.) in an easy or relaxed way; as, to *strum* a guitar.

strung (strung), *p.t.* and *p.p.* of *string.*

strut (strut), *v.i.* [strut-ted, strut-ting], to walk with a proud step or false dignity:—*n.* **1,** a proud and haughty walk; **2,** a brace or bar to support or receive weight or pressure in the direction of its length.

stub (stub), *n.* **1,** the stump of a tree, tooth, etc.; **2,** the short, blunt, remaining part of anything, as a ticket *stub*; a pencil *stub*; **3,** the part left in a chequebook after a cheque is torn out, used as a receipt:—*v.t.* [stubbed, stub-bing], to strike (one's toe) against some fixed object.—*adj.* **stub′by** (as, *stubby* bristles).

stub-ble (stub′l), *n.* **1,** the stumps of grain left in the ground after cutting; **2,** a short, rough, growth of unshaven hair; esp. on a man's face.—*adj.* **stub′bly.**

stub-born (stub′ėrn), *adj.* **1,** fixed in opinion or purpose; determined; obstinate; as, a *stubborn* child; **2,** obstinately followed or held to; as, a *stubborn* attempt; **3,** hard to change or treat; as, a *stubborn* cold; a *stubborn* stain.—*adv.* **stub′born-ly.**—*n.* **stub′born-ness.**

stuc-co (stuk′ō), *n.* [*pl.* stuccoes or stuccos], a kind of plaster used on inside walls or on the outside of houses:—*v.t.* [stuccoed (stuk′ōd), stucco-ing (stuk′ō-ing)], to cover with stucco.

stuck (stuk), *p.t.* and *p.p.* of *stick.*

[1]stud (stud), *n.* **1,** an upright timber or post in walls to which boards and other material are nailed; **2,** an ornamental or functional knob or nail projecting from a surface; as, a belt with brass *studs*; *studs* for pierced ears; metal *studs* on tires that improve traction; **3,** a device like a button used as a fastener; as, shirt *studs*:—*v.t.* [studded, stud-ding], **1,** to furnish with upright props; **2,** to adorn or set with studs; as, a sky *studded* with stars.—*adj.* **stud′ded.**

[2]stud (stud), *n.* **1,** a male horse, or stallion, kept for breeding; a stable of such horses; **2,** *Slang* a promiscuous man:—*adj.* pertaining to a stud; as, a *stud* farm.

stu-dent (stū′dent), *n.* **1,** a person who attends school; **2,** a person devoted to studying or learning; **3,** a close observer; as, a *student* of life.

stu-di-o (stū′di-ō), *n.* [*pl.* studios], **1,** the workroom of a painter, photographer, dancer, etc.; as, a dance *studio*; an artist's *studio*; a graphic designer's *studio*; **2,** a place where movies are filmed or where radio and television programs are produced; **3,** a company that produces movies or radio and television shows; **4,** a small, one-room apartment; as, to rent a *studio* apartment.

stu-di-ous (stū′di-us), *adj.* **1,** given to study; fond of books; as, a *studious* youth; **2,** thoughtful; earnest; as, *studious* attention.—*adv.* **stu′di-ous-ly.**—*n.* **stu′di-ousness.**

stud-y (stud′i), *n.* [*pl.* studies], **1,** the application of the mind to books, science, etc., for the gaining of knowledge; the act of studying; **2,** a special branch of learning; as, the *study* of genetics; **3,** careful examination of a particular question; as, a *study* of foreign trade; also, the result of such examination; as, this book is a *study* of the tariff; **4,** a room set apart for reading or writing:—*v.i.* [studied, study-ing], to devote oneself to the gaining of knowledge; as, he is *studying* at college:—*v.t.* **1,** to learn the details of; as, to *study* physics; **2,** to investigate or examine closely; think over carefully; as, to *study* labour disputes.

stuff (stuf), *n.* **1,** things in a group; a mass or collection of things; as, all the *stuff* on the table fell on the floor; **2,** the material of which anything is composed or may be made; **3,** the essential part of anything; as, he is of the *stuff* of heroes; **4,** something that is known but not named; as the *stuff* to make the grass grow; **5,** portable property; personal belongings; as, her *stuff* was on the desk; **6,** refuse; useless or unwanted matter; nonsense; as, get rid of all that *stuff*; **7,** knowledge or skill; as, the physicist knew his *stuff*:—*v.t.* **1,** to crowd, cram, or pack; as, to *stuff* clothes into a bag; also, to fill by cramming; as, to *stuff* a bag with clothes; **2,** to fill with specially prepared material; as, to *stuff* a chicken; **3,** to fill the skin of (a dead animal) so as to make it look lifelike; **4,** to put dishonest votes into (a ballot-box).

stuffed shirt, *Colloq.* a pompous, conceited, or prim person, esp. one who is very conservative.

stuf-fing (stuf′ing), *n.* **1,** material that is used to fill or pack something; as, the *stuffing* in a pillow; **2,** a seasoned mixture of food put inside some other kind of food; as, turkey *stuffing*.

stuff-y (stuf′i), *adj.* [stuff-i-er, stuff-i-est], **1,** closed or badly ventilated; as, a *stuffy* room; **2,** choked or stopped up, as with a cold in the head; **3,** too serious and formal; dull; boring; as, the principal is rather *stuffy*.—*n.* **stuff′i-ness.**

stul-ti-fy (stul′ti-fi′), *v.t.* to make ineffective; negate; as, this decision *stultifies* the other; **2,** to make foolish or absurd; as, don't *stultify* yourself.

stum-ble (stum′bl), *v.i.* [stum-bled, stum-bling], **1,** to trip or fall in walking; lose one's balance; **2,** to walk, act, or speak in an unsteady or clumsy manner; as, to *stumble* over the names; **3,** to blunder; to make an error:—**stumble on** or **upon,** to come upon by chance; as, to *stumble* on a valuable secret:—*n.* **1,** a tripping, as in walking; **2,** an error or blunder.

stumbling block, an obstacle or other impediment to progress.

stump (stump), *n.* **1,** that part of a tree that remains in the ground after the trunk is cut down; **2,** the part, as of an arm, tail, etc., remaining after the main part has been removed or worn down; a stub; **3,** a platform for political speaking: from the early custom of speaking from tree stumps:—*v.i.* to walk heavily:—*v.t.* **1,** to reduce or trim to a stump; remove stumps; *Colloq.*: **2,** to canvass (a district) making political speeches; **3,** to confuse, hinder, or baffle; as, he was *stumped* and could go no further; the question *stumped* her.—*adj.* **stumped; stump′y.**

stun (stun), *v.t.* [stunned, stun-ning], **1,** to make senseless by a blow; daze or overpower; **2,** to confuse, shock, or surprise greatly; as, her unpredictable action *stunned* him.—*adj.* **stun′ning** (very attractive or stylish; shocking).—*n.* **stun′ner.**

stung (stung), *p.t.* and *p.p.* of *sting.*

stunk (stungk), *p.t.* and *p.p.* of *stink.*

[1]**stunt** (stunt), *v.t.* to check or stop the growth or development of; dwarf.

[2]**stunt** (stunt), *n.* **1,** an attention-grabbing event, etc.; as, the outrageous contest was nothing more than a publicity *stunt*; **2,** a striking or daring feat or performance, as of strength or skill; as, daring acrobatic *stunts* on top of the CN Tower:—**stunt person,** a person who does the dangerous actions of an actor during the filming of a movie or television program.

stu-pe-fy (stū′pe-fi′), *v.t.* [stupefied, stupefying], to dull the senses of; make stupid; astonish.—*adj.* **stu′pe-fy-ing.**—*adv.* **stu′pe-fy-ing-ly.**—*n.* **stu′pe-fac′tion.**

stu-pen-dous (stū-pen′dus), *adj.* overpowering the senses by great size, speed, etc.; amazing; remarkable.—*adv.* **stu-pen′dous-ly.**

stu-pid (stū′pid), *adj.* **1,** not having intelligence or common sense, not smart; as, a *stupid* person; **2,** foolish; as, a *stupid* error; **3,** boring; **4,** exasperating; as, the stupid printer won't work.—*adv.* **stu′pid-ly.**—*n.* **stu-pid′i-ty.**

stu-por (stū′pėr), *n.* a condition of more or less complete unconsciousness; lethargy.

stur-dy (stûr′di), *adj.* [stur-di-er, stur-di-est], **1,** hardy; robust; stout; as, a *sturdy* oak; a *sturdy* brick house; **2,** firm and unyielding; as, a person of *sturdy* principles.—*adv.* **stur′di-ly.**—*n.* **stur′di-ness.**

stur-geon (stûr′jun), *n.* a large sharklike food fish, having rows of bony plates along the body: its eggs are the source of caviar.

stut-ter (stut′ėr), *v.i.* in speaking, to hesitate over or repeat the initial sounds of words; to stammer:—*v.t.* to utter with difficulty:—*n.* a stammer.

sty (stī), *n.* [*pl.* sties], **1,** a pen for pigs; **2,** a filthy or vile place; **3,** an inflamed swelling of the eyelid.

[1]**style** (stīl), *n.* **1,** a pointed instrument used by the ancients for writing upon wax tablets; hence, any of various similar instruments, as an engraver's tool; **2,** a characteristic manner of writing or speaking; as, a polished *style*; also, literary excellence; as, the speech lacked *style*; **3,** mode of expression or execution in any art; as, the Colonial *style* in architecture; **4,** manner of conduct or action; as, a graceful *style* of dancing; also, sophisticated or elegant appearance; as, she has *style*; hair*style*;

life*style*; **5,** fashion; as, a coat of the latest *style*:—*v.t.* [styled, styl-ing], **1,** to design or arrange something in a certain style or fashion; as, to *style* her hair; **2,** to term, name, or call; as, Wayne Gretzky is *styled* the Great One.

²style (stīl), *n.* the stemlike part of the pistil. (See illustration under *flower.*)

styl-ish (stīl′ish), *adj.* very fashionable; showing the latest style.—*adv.* **styl′ish-ly.**

styl-ist (stīl′ist), *n.* **1,** a writer or speaker who is a master of style or noted for a distinctive style; **2,** someone who creates, designs, or consults on styles; as, a hair*stylist*; a clothes designer or *stylist*.—*adj.* **sty-lis′tic; styl′ized.**—*adv.* **sty-lis′ti-cal-ly.**—*n.* **styl′i-za′tion.**

sty-lus (stī′lus), *n.* **1,** a style (definition 1); **2,** in *computing,* a pen-shaped device used to enter or change information on a computer screen, esp. graphic images; **3,** a sharp, needlelike device for cutting grooves in records or for reproducing their sound.

sty-mie (stī′mi), *n.* in *golf,* an opponent's ball lying directly between the player's ball and the hole of a putting green; the occurrence of this:—*v.t.* **1,** to hinder; block; obstruct; as, I was *stymied* by this move; **2,** to baffle or puzzle; as, to be *stymied* by the difficult chemistry problem; **3,** in *golf,* to block with a stymie.

suave (swāv; swäv), *adj.* polite, sophisticated, and smooth, often superficially; as, the *suave* host.—*n.* **suav′i-ty** (swävi-ti; swav′i-ti).

sub- (sub-), *prefix* meaning **1,** *under, below, beneath*; as in *sub*marine, *sub*zero, *sub*freezing, *sub*cutaneous; **2,** *inferior, smaller, lesser*; as in *sub*standard, *sub*division, *sub*heading, *sub*class, *sub*category, *sub*group, *sub*set, *sub*section, *sub*compact; **3,** *secondary*, as in *sub*committee, *sub*lease, *sub*tenant, *sub*lieutenant, *sub*continent, *sub*plot; **4,** *bordering,* as in *sub*tropical, *sub*arctic.

sub-con-scious (sub-kon′shus), *adj.* pertaining to mental activity of which one is not aware or existing in the subconscious:—*n.* unconscious mental functioning or processes.—*n.* **sub-con′scious-ness.**—*adv.* **sub-con′scious-ly.**

sub-cul-ture (sub′kul′chėr), *n.* **1,** a social group that is distinguished from the larger culture by its shared beliefs, behaviour, or customs; as, the criminal *subculture*; **2,** the culture of micro-organisms, such as bacteria, that are derived from another.

sub-di-rec-to-ry (sub′di-rek′to-ri), *n.* in *computing,* an index of files in storage that is part of the larger computer directory.

sub-di-vide (sub′di-vīd′), *v.t.* [sub-divided, sub-divid-ing], to separate the parts of into other parts:—*v.i.* to divide or separate again.

sub-di-vi-sion (sub′di-vizh′un), *n.* **1,** something divided into smaller parts, esp. a housing development partitioned into several building lots; as, to survey the new *subdivision*; **2,** each of the parts into which something is divided; **3,** the action of so dividing in this manner.

sub-due (sub-dū′), *v.t.* [subdued, subdu-ing], **1,** to conquer; defeat; as, to *subdue* an enemy; **2,** to bring under control; master; as, to *subdue* the ferocious animal; to *subdue* an impulse; **3,** to tone down; soften; as, to *subdue* your voice in the library.—*adj.* **sub-dued′.**

sub-ject (sub′jekt), *adj.* under the power or control of another; as, a *subject* nation:—**subject to, 1,** exposed; liable; as, he is *subject to* malaria; **2,** dependent on; bound by law; as, a plan *subject to* your approval:—*n.* **1,** a person under the control of another; esp., one who owes allegiance to a government or a sovereign; **2,** a person, animal, or thing made to undergo an operation or treatment; as, the *subject* of an experiment; **3,** the matter, theme, or topic about which something is said or written; **4,** in a sentence, the word or group of words of which something is said or asked, and which tell what the sentence is about; as, in "our vacation begins tomorrow," the *subject* is "our vacation": the verb "begins" shows what the subject is or does; **5,** an area of learning taught in school, university, etc.; as, biology is her best *subject*:—*v.t.* (sub-jekt′), **1,** to bring under control; **2,** to make liable; expose; as, to *subject* him to insult; **3,** to cause to undergo; as, to *subject* iron to heat; to *subject* the patient to many unpleasant tests.—*n.* **sub-jec′tion.**

sub-jec-tive (sub-jek′tiv), *n.* in *grammar,* the case of the subject:—*adj.* existing in the mind; not produced by outside objects: opposite of *objective*.—*adv.* **sub-jec′tive-ly.**—*n.* **sub′jec-tiv′i-ty.**

sub-ju-gate (sub′joo-gāt′), *v.t.* [sub-jugat-ed, subjugat-ing], to conquer; subdue, bring under control; as, to subjugate the unruly masses.—*n.* **sub′ju-ga′tion.**

sub-junc-tive (sub-jungk′tiv), *adj.* in *grammar,* pertaining to that mood of a verb that expresses state or action, not as a fact, but as something possible, desired, feared, conditional, or doubtful; as, "if I were athletic, I would join the soccer team":—*n.* the subjunctive mood. Compare *imperative* and *indicative.*

sub-li-mate (sub′li-māt′), *v.t.* **1,** in *chemistry,* to purify a solid by heating it to a gaseous state and condensing the vapour back to solid form; **2,** to change a primitive impulse, such as a sexual one, to one that is more acceptable by society.—*n.* **sub′li-ma′tion.**—*adj.* **sub-lim′i-nal** (below the threshold of consciousness; as, *subliminal* advertising messages).

sub-lime (sub-līm′), *adj.* [sublim-er, sublim-est], **1,** inspiring a feeling of awe, reverence, greatness, power, or grandeur; **2,** exalted; noble:—*n.* that which is lofty, awe-inspiring, or grand:—*v.t.* [sublimed, sublim-ing], to exalt or dignify:—*v.i.* **1,** in *chemistry*, to pass from solid to vapour form by heat, and, on cooling, back to solid form without becoming liquid: the Chinook winds sometimes do this to southern Alberta snows; **2,** sublimate (definition 1):—*v.t.* to dignify; exalt; ennoble; purify; as, his selfishness was *sublimed* to public devotion.—*adv.* **sub-lime′ly.**—*n.* **sub-lim′i-ty** (sub-lim′i-ti).

sub-ma-rine (sub′ma-rēn′), *adj.* living, situated, or used beneath the surface of the sea; under water; as, *submarine* plant life:—*n.* (sub′ma-rēn′), a vessel, usually a war vessel, that can be operated under water.—*n.* **sub′ma-rin′er.**

sub-merge (sub-mûrj′), *v.t.* [submerged, submerg-ing], **1,** to put or sink under water; as, to *submerge* a boat; **2,** to cover with water; flood; overwhelm; as, the employer *submerged* the new employee with work; **3,** to suppress; hide; keep below the surface; as, to *submerge* angry feelings:—*v.i.* to go or sink under water or out of sight.—*n.* **sub-mer′gence; sub-mer′sion** (sub-mûr′shun; sub-mûr′zhun).—*adj.* **sub-merged′.** —*n.* and *adj.* **sub-mers′i-ble.**

sub-mis-sion (sub-mish′un), *n.* **1,** the act of submitting a legal, official, or other document, proposal, etc., for consideration; also, the item submitted; as, the *submission* of university registration forms; **2,** the act of referring to the judgment, or yielding to the power or authority, of another; as, the *submission* of the city to the attacking army; **3,** humility or meekness.—*adj.* **sub-mis′sive.**—*adv.* **sub-mis′sive-ly.**—*n.* **sub-mis′sive-ness.**

sub-mit (sub-mit′), *v.t.* [submit-ted, sub-mit-ting], **1,** to present a legal, official, or other document, proposal, etc., for the judgment of another; as, to *submit* an offer or proposal; **2,** to yield (oneself) to the will of another:—*v.i.* to yield or surrender.

sub-or-di-nate (su-bôr′di-nit), *adj.* **1,** lower in rank, value, power, or importance; as, a *subordinate* rank; **2,** subject to another; as, a *subordinate* official:—**subordinate clause,** in *grammar*, designating the clause that modifies the prinicipal clause in a complex sentence; as, "When the phone rang (*subordinate*), we were eating dinner (principal)":—**subordinating conjunction,** in *grammar,* any conjunction that introduces a subordinate clause, such as when, because, since, after, before, etc.:—*n.* one who is below another in rank, power, etc.:—*v.t.* (su-bôr′di-nāt′), [subordinat-ed, subordinat-ing], **1,** to place in a lower order or rank; to treat as less important; **2,** to make subject or obedient.—*n.* **sub-or′di-na′tion.**—*adj.* **sub-or′di-nat-ed.**

sub-poe-na (sub-pē′na), *n.* a legal written order that a person appear in court (as a witness):—*v.t.* [-naed (-nid), -naing], to serve or summon a person or evidence with such writ.

sub-scribe (sub-skrīb′), *v.t.* [subscribed, subscrib-ing], **1,** to give or promise (a sum of money) to a cause; as, he *subscribed* $100 to the Cancer Society; **2,** to write or put (one's name) to a paper or document:—*v.i.* **1,** to order and pay for a magazine, newspaper, or other item or service delivered or offered at regular intervals; as, to *subscribe* to a CD music club; **2,** to agree; give assent; as, to *subscribe* to her views; **3,** to promise to give a certain sum; as, to *subscribe* to a charity; **4,** to sign one's name to a letter or other document.—*n.* **sub-scrib′er.**

sub-script (sub′skript′) *n.* and *adj.* a character or relating to a character situated below the line and usually to the right of a regular character: opposite of *superscript.*

sub-scrip-tion (sub-skrip′shun), *n.* **1,** an agreement to pay for and receive a certain number of newspapers, magazines, theatre tickets, CDs, etc.; as, our *subscription* to the book club has expired; **2,** a formal agreement to give or contribute a sum of money; also, the sum of money promised; **3,** the act of signing one's name by way of agreement.

sub-se-quent (sub′si-kwent), *adj.* following; coming after; happening as a result; as, *subsequent* events.—*adv.* **sub′se-quent-ly.**

sub-ser-vi-ent (sub-sûr′vi-ent), *adj.* servile; submissive; as, a *subservient* employee; subordinate; secondary; as, *subservient* demands.—*n.* **sub-ser′vi-ence.**

sub-side (sub-sīd′), *v.i.* [subsid-ed, subsid-ing], **1,** to sink or fall to the bottom; settle, as sediment; **2,** to sink to a lower level; as, the swollen river will *subside*; **3,** to become quiet or less violent or intense, as anger, fever, a storm, etc.

sub-sid-i-a-ry (sub-sid′i-a-ri), *adj.* and *n.* [*pl.* -aries], **1,** serving to aid or supplement; auxiliary; tributary; as, a *subsidiary* stream, valley, etc.; **2,** subordinate; secondary but related; as, a *subsidiary* company (one in which the controlling interest is owned by another company):—*n.* **1,** one who assists or supplies; **2,** a *subsidiary* person or organization.

sub-si-dize (sub′si-dīz′), *v.t.* to help or provide financial aid, esp. by a government; to make a grant or contribution; as, to *subsidize* a railway, hospital, the agricultural industry, etc.:—*n.* **sub′si-dy; sub′si-di-za′tion.**—*adj.* **sub′si-dized′.**

sub-sist (sub-sist′), *v.i.* **1,** to continue to be; exist; as, the regulations continue to *subsist* despite protest; **2,** to be supported, esp. barely; live; as, to *subsist* on minimum wage.

sub-sist-ence (sub-sis′tens), *n.* **1,** the act of existing or living; **2,** the means of staying alive; a livelihood; **3,** the minimum necessary to maintain life; the basic level of existence; as, *subsistence* farming.

sub-soil (sub′soil′), *n.* the layer of soil below the topsoil.

sub-stance (sub′stans), *n.* **1,** the real or essential part of anything; as, the *substance* of the candidate's platform is reducing national debt; **2,** the stuff, matter, or material of which something is made; **3,** the gist or real point of a speech or an article; **4,** a drug, esp. alcohol or illegal drugs; as, *substance* abuse; **5,** wealth; property.

sub-stan-tial (sub-stan′shal), *adj.* **1,** having real existence; actual; not imaginary; **2,** made of good substance; solid; strong; as, a *substantial* car that can stand ordinary wear and tear; **3,** of real worth; considerable; large; as, a *substantial* donation; also, nourishing; ample; as, *substantial* food; **4,** prosperous; responsible; as, *substantial* business men; **5,** real or true for the most part; virtual; as, *substantial* stories.—*adv.* **sub-stan′tial-ly.**

sub-stan-ti-ate (sub-stan′shi-āt′), *v.t.* to prove by evidence; verify; as to *substantiate* a charge, claim, etc.

sub-stan-tive (sub′stan-tiv), *adj.* **1,** real; permanent; having substance; **2,** substantial; considerable in amount; as, the poor essay required *substantive* editing; **3,** in *grammar*: **a,** expressing existence; as, "to be" is a *substantive* verb; **b,** of the nature of a noun or used as a noun; as, a *substantive* clause.—*adv.* **sub′stan-tive-ly.**

sub-sti-tute (sub′sti-tūt′), *n.* a person or thing that takes the place of another; as, we had a *substitute* today because our teacher was ill:—**substitute teacher**, someone who temporarily replaces a teacher who cannot perform his or her function because of illness or some other reason:—*v.t.* [substitut-ed, substitut-ing], to put in the place of another person or thing:—*v.i.* to take the place of another; as, to *substitute* for a teacher.—*n.* **sub′sti-tu′tion.**

sub-stra-tum or **sub-strate** (sub-strā′tum; sub′strāt), *n.* [*pl.* substrata; substrates], **1,** an underlayer, or stratum, as of rock or soil; **2,** a basis or foundation; as, a *substratum* of truth; a strong substrate of a building.

sub-tend (sub-tend′), *v.t.* **1,** in *geometry*, to lie opposite to; as, the chord that *subtends* an arc; **2,** in *botany*, to fold or enclose in an axil; as, a leaf *subtends* a bud.

sub-ter-fuge (sub′tėr-fūj′), *n.* a scheme, excuse, or trick by which one seeks to escape from a difficulty, or the action of using subterfuge; as, the spy tried to use *subterfuge* to evade prosecution.

sub-ter-ra-ne-an (sub′te-rā′ni-an), *adj.* **1,** below the surface of the earth; underground; as, a *subterranean* cave; **2,** hidden; secret; as, *subterranean* manoeuvres.

sub-tle (sut′l), *adj.* [sub-tler, sub-tlest], **1,** delicate; elusive; not obvious; obscure; as, a *subtle* odour; **2,** clever; discerning; keen; as, a *subtle* mind; **3,** artful; crafty; cunning; as, a *subtle* scheme: **4,** intricate; hard to follow; as, *subtle* reasoning.—*n.* **sub′tle-ty.**—*adv.* **sub′tly** (sut′li).

sub-tract (sub-trakt′), *v.t.* to take away (a part) from the whole.—*n.* **sub-trac′tion.**

sub-urb (sub′ûrb), *n.* a residential district on the outskirts of a city.—*adj.* **sub-ur′ban.**—*n.* **sub-ur′ban-ite′** (one who lives in a suburb); **sub-ur′ban-i-za′tion.**

sub-vert (sub-vûrt′), *v.t.* **1,** to turn upside down; overthrow (a government); **2,** to ruin or corrupt, as a person's principles.—*n.* **sub-ver′sion.**—*adj.* **sub-ver′sive.**

sub-way (sub′wā′), *n.* **1,** an underground railway powered by electricity and found in major cities such as Toronto, Montreal, London, and New York; **2,** an underground passage under a street for water or gas pipes, wires, etc.; an underpass.

suc-ceed (suk-sēd′), *v.t.* **1,** to take the place of; be the successor of (a ruler); **2,** to follow or come next; as, Friday *succeeds* Thursday:—*v.i.* **1,** to become heir (to); as, he *succeeded* to the family estate; **2,** to do something very well, or to have something turn out well; to be successful; meet with success; as, all his plans *succeeded*; he *succeeded* in finding what he wanted to know.

suc-cess (suk-ses′), *n.* **1,** the favourable end or result of an undertaking; the gaining of wealth, fame, etc.; **2,** a person or thing that turns out well; as, his book was a great *success*.—*adj.* **suc-cess′ful.**—*adv.* **suc-cess′ful-ly.**

suc-ces-sion (suk-sesh′un), *n.* **1,** a following of one person or thing after another; as, things happened in quick *succession*; also, a series: as, a *succession* of misfortunes; **2,** the act or right of succeeding to the place, office, property, title, or throne of another; **3,** natural change in ecosystems as plants and animals adapt to and modify environments until balance is reached.—*adj.* **suc-ces′sive.**—*adv.* **suc-ces′sive-ly.**

suc-ces-sor (suk-ses′ėr), *n.* one who follows, or takes the place of, another: opposite of *predecessor.*

suc-cinct (suk-singkt′), *adj.* concise; terse; expressed in few words; as, a *succinct* narrative.—*adv.* **suc-cinct′ly.**

suc-cour (suk′ėr), *v.t.* to help or relieve (someone) in difficulty or distress; as, to *succour* the homeless:—*n.* **1,** relief; aid; help; **2,** one who or that which brings help.

suc-cu-lent (suk′ū-lent), *adj.* **1,** full of juice; tasty and moist; as, *succulent* fruit or steak; **2,** in *botany*, a plant that has thick leaves or stems adapted for conserving large quantities of water; as, most cactuses are *succulent* plants:—*n.* such a plant.—*n.* **suc′cu-lence.**—*adv.* **suc′cu-lent-ly.**

suc-cumb (su-kum′), *v.i.* **1,** to yield or submit; **2,** hence, to die.

such (such), *adj.* **1,** of that kind; of the like kind; as, pens, pencils, and *such* things; **2,** the same; as, this flour is *such* as I have always used; **3,** a certain or particular; as, on *such* a date; **4,** so great, so good, so bad, etc.; as, he is *such* a fool; he did *such* great work that he received honours:—**such as,** for example; as, ingredients *such as* onions, garlic, carrots, and celery:—*pron.* **1,** a certain person or thing of that kind; also, these or those; as, pencils, pens, markers, and *such*; **2,** a person or thing implied or already stated; as, *such* was our goal:—*adv.* **1,** so much; to a specific degree; especially; as, *such* strong athletes; **2,** in such a way; as, the room was arranged *such* as to allow easy access to the windows.

suck (suk), *v.t.* **1,** to draw (a liquid) into the mouth by action of the lips and tongue; as, to *suck* on a milk shake with a straw; **2,** to draw a liquid from (something) with the mouth; as, to *suck* an orange; **3,** to hold or keep in the mouth and lick; as, to *suck* on a candy; **4,** to drink in or absorb; as, a paper towel *sucks* up moisture; **5,** to draw in or engulf, as does quicksand; **6,** to consume, as if by suction; as, this hard work *sucked* all the energy from us:—*v.i.* **1,** to draw milk from the breast or udder; **2,** *Slang* to be bad, inadequate, substandard; as, the movie *sucks*; this work *sucks*; the substitute teacher *sucks*:—**to suck up,** acting with exaggerated attentiveness, esp. in return for something; to brown-nose; as, *to suck up* to the new coach:—*n.* **1,** the act of drawing in a liquid; **2,** *Slang* someone who is a spoil sport, sore loser, or poor team player; **3,** a brown-noser.—*adj.* **suck′y.**

suck-er (suk′ėr), *n.* **1,** a person or thing that sucks; a young animal; a suckling; **2,** a shoot of a plant from the roots or the lower part of the stem; **3,** in some animals, a disk-shaped organ by which they adhere to other animals; **4,** *Colloq.* a lollipop; **5,** *Slang* a person easily taken in; a gullible person.

suck-le (suk′l), *v.t.* [suck-led, suck-ling], to nurse at the breast or udder; as, the animal *suckled* its newborn:—*v.i.* to draw milk from the breast.

PIGLETS SUCKLING

suck-ling (suk′ling), *n.* a baby or young animal that nurses at the breast.

suc-tion (suk′shun), *n.* **1,** the force of drawing or pulling a solid, liquid, or gas that is caused by lowering the air pressure on its surface; **2,** the act or condition of sucking; **3,** the drawing of liquid, dust, etc., into a container as air is withdrawn from it; as, liquid is drawn into a straw by *suction*; **4,** the sticking together of two bodies when the air between them is removed. Also, **suc′tion cup′; suc′tion pump′.**

sud-den (sud′n), *adj.* **1,** happening unexpectedly; as, a *sudden* turn for the worse; **2,** quickly done; hasty; as, a *sudden* job:—**all of a sudden,** in a sudden way; as, *all of a sudden,* the phone went dead.—*adv.* **sud′den-ly.**—*n.* **sud′den-ness.**

sudden death, an extra play to break a tie game in which the first to score wins.—*adj.* **sud′den–death′** (as, *sudden-death* overtime).

suds (sudz), *n.pl.* soapy water; also, the froth or bubbles floating on it.—*adj.* **sud′sy** (sud′zi).

sue (sū), *v.t.* [sued (sūd), su-ing (sū′ing)], to start an action in law against (a person); prosecute; as, to *sue* a person for libel:—*v.i.* **1,** to entreat, beg, or petition; as, to *sue* for pardon; **2,** to begin a lawsuit; as, to *sue* for damages.

suede (swād), *n.* soft, unglazed, fuzzy leather, used for gloves, shoes, purses, clothes, etc.; as, blue *suede* shoes.

su-et (sū′it), *n.* the hard fat around the kidneys and loins of mutton and beef: it is sometimes used in cooking and other products.

suf-fer (suf′ėr), *v.t.* **1,** to feel or endure; as, to *suffer* pain; bear up under; as, to *suffer* a wrong; **2,** to experience, esp. something bad; as, the car *suffered* a great deal of damage:—*v.i.* **1,** to feel pain, distress, or loss; **2,** to sustain loss or damage; as, illness made his work *suffer.*—*adj.* **suf′ fer-a-ble.**—*n.* **suf′fer-er.**

suf-fer-ance (suf′ėr-ans), *n.* **1,** implied consent or permission; as, he remained in the house on *sufferance* only; **2,** the ability to endure; endurance; as, cruelty beyond *sufferance.*

suf-fer-ing (suf′ėr-ing), *n.* **1,** the bearing of physical or mental pain; **2,** the pain borne; the loss or injury endured; as, the *suffering* of war.

suf-fice (su-fīs′; su-fīz′), *v.i.* [sufficed, suff-ic-ing], to be enough or sufficient; as, *suffice* it to say that they will get the job done:—*v.t.* to be sufficient for; satisfy; as, the small amount *sufficed* him.

suf-fi-cient (su-fish′ent), *adj.* equal to the need; enough; as, *sufficient* wood for the fireplace for the winter.—*n.* **suf-fi′cien-cy.**—*adv.* **suf-fi′cient-ly.**

suf-fix (suf′iks), *n.* a syllable or syllables, added at the end of a word or word stem, to form a new word related in meaning, as *-ant* in "assistant" or *-ion* in "erection":—*v.t.* (su-fiks′), to add (a syllable) to the end of a word in order to form a new word.

suf-fo-cate (suf′o-kāt′), *v.t.* [suffocated,

suffocat-ing], **1,** to choke or to kill by smothering and stopping the breath of; **2,** to smother; to stifle; to make uncomfortable due to lack of fresh air; as, this heat is *suffocating* me; the cramped room *suffocated* her; **3,** to impede or restrict; as, high taxes were *suffocating* consumer spending:—*v.i.* **1,** to be choked or stifled; to die from the lack of oxygen; **2,** to be smothered or cramped; as, she was *suffocating* in the small town; **3,** to be impeded or restricted.—*n.* **suf′fo-ca′tion.**—*adj.* **suf′fo-cat-ing.**

suf-frage (suf′rij), *n.* **1,** a vote upon a measure or candidate; **2,** the right to vote; also, the act of voting.

suf-fuse (su-fūz′), *v.t.* [suffused, suffus-ing], to spread over; as, a blush *suffused* her cheeks.—*n.* **suf-fu′sion.**

sug-ar (shoog′ėr), *n.* **1,** a sweet substance obtained usually from sugarcane or the sugar beet, but also from many other plants, such as the maple tree: it comes in crystal, powder, or liquid form and is used to sweeten foods; **2,** any sweet substance like sugar obtained from or found in corn, milk, blood, etc.:—*v.t.* **1,** to mix or sprinkle with sugar; as, to *sugar* berries; **2,** to make less disagreeable, esp. on the surface; as, to *sugar*coat the situation:—*v.i.* **1,** to turn into sugar; as, syrup *sugars* if boiled too long; **2,** to make maple sugar.—*adj.* **sug′ar-y.**

sug-ar-cane (shoog′ėrkān), *n.* a tall, jointed, maizelike tropical grass that is pressed for its sap, which is dried into sugar.

sug-gest (su-jest′), *v.t.* **1,** to propose, as a plan or method; as, to *suggest* ways to conserve energy; **2,** to cause (an idea) to come to a person's mind through some natural connection or relationship; to imply; as, crocuses *suggest* spring; yawning *suggests* that a person is tired.

sug-ges-tion (su-jes′chun), *n.* **1,** the act of proposing something; also, the thing proposed; as, we accepted his *suggestion* for a ride; **2,** the process by which an idea causes another idea to come to mind through some natural connection; a hint or trace; also, the idea thus brought to mind; as, a *suggestion* of fear in his eyes.

sug-ges-tive (su-jes′tiv), *adj.* **1,** tending to bring thoughts, ideas, etc., to the mind; **2,** tending to bring to the mind something improper or indecent, or something of a sexual nature; evocative; risqué.

su-i-cide (sū′i-sīd′), *n.* **1,** the act of intentionally taking one's own life; as, to commit *suicide*; **2,** a person who kills himself or herself intentionally; **3,** a dangerous or destructive action; as, a professional *suicide*; a *suicide* mission.—*adj.* **su′i-cid′al** (ready to commit suicide).

suit (sūt), *n.* **1,** a legal action or process brought before a judge or jury: also, *lawsuit*; as, the *suit* was about defamation of character; **2,** a set of clothes made to be worn together, such as trousers or a skirt with a matching jacket; also, clothing for a special purpose or condition; as, a gym *suit*; birthday *suit*; **3,** any of the four sets in a deck of cards; **4,** *Slang* a business executive, esp. one who always wears a suit; as, the boardroom was filled with *suits*:—*v.t.* **1,** to fit; adapt; as, *suit* your words to the occasion; **2,** to be proper or suitable to; become; befit; as, your behaviour does not *suit* your position; **3,** to please; satisfy; as, I hope this will *suit* you; **4,** to be becoming to; flatter; as, this colour *suits* you..

suit-a-ble (sūt′a-bl), *adj.* right or correct for the purpose; fitting; becoming; appropriate.—*adv.* **suit′a-bly.**—*n.* **suit′a-bil′i-ty; suit′a-ble-ness.**

suit-case (sūt′kās′), *n.* a flat travelling bag with a handle, for carrying clothes and other items.

suite (swēt), *n.* **1,** a group of connected rooms in a hotel, motel, apartment, etc.; **2,** a matching set of furniture; a set; as, a bedroom or dining room *suite*; **3,** instrumental composition with several movements; **4,** a group of attendants; retinue; as, a king and his *suite*.—*adj.* **suit′ed.**

suit-or (sūt′ėr), *n.* **1,** one who sues; **2,** one who petitions; **3,** a potential buyer of a business; **4,** a man who courts a woman, esp. with the purpose of marrying her.

sulk (sulk), *v.i.* to be in a bad mood or ill-humoured; to refuse to talk; as, she *sulked* when they ignored her suggestion:—*n.* the state or act of sulking; as, to be in a sulk.—*adj.* **sulk′y** (**1,** bad-humoured; **2,** a two-wheeled vehicle for harness racing).—*adv.* **sulk′i-ly.**

sul-len (sul′en), *adj.* **1,** gloomy; unsociable; as, a *sullen* disposition; **2,** dismal; lowering; as, *sullen* weather.—*adv.* **sul′len-ly.**

sul-ly (sul′i), *v.t.* [sullied, sully-ing], to tarnish or soil; dirty or stain; as, to *sully* her reputation; to *sully* the clean floor.

sul-phur (sul′fėr), *n.* a yellow, nonmetallic element, found in many places and in various forms, which burns with a blue flame and a suffocating odour, and is used in manufacturing gunpowder and matches, as a disinfectant, in medicine, etc.:—*adj.* **sul′phu-rous** (sul′fūrus; sul-fū′rus); **sul-phu′ric** (sul-fū′rik):—**sulphur dioxide,** SO_2, a colourless, suffocating gas, easy to liquefy: used for industrial and agricultural purposes such as in making sulphuric acid and as a preservative, etc.: it is a pollutant:—**sulphuric acid,** H_2SO_4, a corrosive, colourless, oily liquid made from SO_2, used in the chemical industry.

sul-tan (sul′tan; sool-tän′), *n.* a Muslim ruler, esp. in former times:—**Sultan,** formerly, the emperor of Turkey.

sul-try (sul′tri), *adj.* [sul-tri-er, sul-tri-est], **1,** very hot, close, moist, and oppressive;

as, a *sultry* day; **2,** marked by heat, as of passion or lust; sensual.

sum (sum), *n.* **1,** the total of two or more numbers, quantities, etc.; the whole; **2,** the amount resulting from addition; as, 5 is the *sum* of 3 + 2; **3,** a problem in arithmetic; **4,** a quantity, as of money; as, to pay a huge *sum* for the house; **5,** summary; summation; substance; as, the *sum* of the evidence:—*v.t.* [summed, sum-ming], **1,** to add into one amount; **2,** to condense into few words; summarize; as, to *sum* up the main points of the meeting:—*v.i.* to make a summary; to review; as, and now, let me *sum* up.

su-mac or **su-mach** (sho͞o′mak; sū′mak), *n.* **1,** a shrub or small tree with divided green leaves turning to a vivid red in the fall, and clusters of flowers followed by red or white berries: some sumac leaves can cause a rash when touched; **2,** the dried leaves and roots of the sumac, used in tanning and dyeing.

sum-ma-rize (sum′-a-rīz′), *v.t.* [summarized, summariz-ing], to sum up; to review the main points; as, to *summarize* the evidence.

sum-ma-ry (sum′a-ri), *n.* [*pl.* summaries], a brief account containing the sum or main points of a fuller account; a synopsis:—*adj.* **1,** giving the general idea; brief; concise; **2,** performed instantly and without formalities; as, *summary* punishment.—*adv.* **sum′ma-ri-ly** (instantly; immediately).

sum-ma-tion (sum-ā′shun), *n.* a final adding, totalling, or summing up (of conditions, influences, qualities, etc.); as, Maugham's *summation* of Tolstoy.

sum-mer (sum′ėr), *n.* the hottest season of the year, between spring and fall; the season of the year when the sun shines most directly; in the Northern Hemisphere, the period from the summer solstice, about June 21, to the autumnal equinox, about September 22:—*adj.* characteristic of, suitable for, or occurring during the summer; as, a *summer* suit; a *summer* thunderstorm; *summer* school:—*v.i.* to pass the summer; as, to *summer* at the shore.—*n.* **sum′mer-time′**.—*adj.* **sum′mer-y.**

sum-mer-sault (sum′ėr-sôlt′), *n.* and *v.* Same as **somersault.**

sum-mit (sum′it), *n.* **1,** the top or highest point of a mountain or hill; **2,** the highest point, degree, or level; the top; as, the *summit* of his sports career was winning an Olympic medal; **3,** meetings or talks held by highest government officials; as, a *summit* meeting with the G8 leaders.

sum-mon (sum′un), *v.t.* **1,** to require the presence of; order to appear in court; **2,** to send for; call; as, to *summon* a doctor; **3,** to arouse; gather up; as, to *summon* one's strength.

sum-mons (sum′unz), *n.* [*pl.* summonses (sum′un-zez)], **1,** an official order to appear somewhere or do something, esp. in court on a certain day; **2,** a document containing such a notice; **3,** a call to duty.

sump (sump), *n.* **1,** the bottom of a mine shaft or crankcase where water or oil collects; **2,** a cesspool: a *sump* pit is drained by a *sump* pump.

sump-tu-ous (sump′tūus), *adj.* costly; lavish; as, a *sumptuous* feast.—*adv.* **sump′tuous-ly.**

sun (sun), *n.* **1,** the star around which the earth and other planets of our solar system revolve, and which gives us light and heat; **2,** a heavenly body which, like our sun, is the centre of a system of planets; **3,** sunshine:—*v.t.*and *v.i.* [sunned, sun-ning], to expose to the sun's rays for warming, drying, etc; to bask in the sun; as, she *sunned* in the backyard.—*adj.* **sun′-baked′; sun′-drenched′; sun′less.**—*n.* **sun′beam′; sun′dress′; sun′room′; sun′shade′** (as a hat, parasol, or awning).

sun-bathe (sun′bā′), *v.* [sunbathed, sunbath-ing], to lie in the sun; spend time in the sun; to tan.—*n.* **sun′ bath′-er; sun′bath′ing.**

sun-burn (sun′burn′), *n.* an inflammation and redness of the skin caused by prolonged exposure to the sun, which can cause serious damage to the skin:—*v.t.* and *v.i.* to burn by excessive exposure to the sun.—*adj.* **sun′burned′** or **sun′ burnt′.**

sun-dae (sun′di), *n.* a serving of ice cream topped with a syrup, fruit, whipped cream, or nuts.

sun dance, a religious ceremony held annually in midsummer by some Aboriginal Plains tribes.

Sun-day (sun′di; dā), *n.* the first day of the week, after Saturday and before Monday.

sun-di-al (sun′dī′al), *n.* an instrument for showing the time by the casting of a shadow from an indicator (the gnomon) on a dial. (See illustration under *gnomon.*)

sun-down (sun′doun′), *n.* sunset.

sun-dried, (sun′drīd′), *adj.* dried naturally by the sun; as, *sun-dried* tomatoes.

sun-dry (sun′dri), *adj.* various; several; as, *sundry* school supplies:—**sundries,** *n.pl.* various articles too small or too numerous to be specified.

sun-flow-er (sun′flou′ėr), *n.* a tall plant with large leaves and round, flattened, bright-yellow flowers, that resemble the sun: the seeds are eaten raw, baked, or pressed into an oil.

sung (sung), *p.p.* of *sing.*

sun-glass-es (sun′glås′iz), *n.* eyeglasses with specially coloured or shaded lenses to protect the eyes from sunlight or the sun's glare.

sunk (sungk), *p.t.* and *p.p.* of *sink.*

sunk·en (sungk′en), *adj.* **1,** below the surface, depressed; as, a *sunken* ship; *sunken* gardens; **2,** hollow; depressed; lower; as, *sunken* eyes or cheeks; *sunken* bathtub.

sun·light (sun′līt′), *n.* the light of the sun.—*adj.* **sun′lit′.**

sun·ny (sun′i), *adj.* [sun-ni-er, sun-ni-est], **1,** bright; cheerful; as, a *sunny* disposition; **2,** exposed to the warmth and light of the sun; as, a *sunny* room.

sun·rise (sun′rīz′), *n.* **1,** the daily appearance of the sun above the horizon; **2,** the time at which the sun appears; early morning; **3,** the brightening of or the colour of the sky at that time; **4,** the east.

sun·screen (sun′skrēn′), *n.* **1,** something, as a lotion or cream, that protects the skin from sunburn by blocking harmful ultraviolet rays; as, sunblock is a strong form of *sunscreen*; **2,** a sunshade.

sun·set (sun′set′), *n.* **1,** the daily disappearance of the sun below the horizon; **2,** the time at which the sun disappears; following dusk; evening; **3,** the colours of the sunset sky; **4,** the west; **5,** a declining period, esp. old age; as, *sunset* years.

sun·shine (sun′shīn′), *n.* **1,** the light, warmth, or rays of the sun; also, the place where they fall; **2,** brightness; cheerfulness.

sun·spot (sun′spot′), *n.* a dark patch or spot on the sun's disk, thought to be a cyclonic sunstorm that affects the earth's magnetism, etc.

sun·stroke (sun′strōk′), *n.* an illness caused by being exposed to too much heat from the sun, which results in high body temperature, dizziness, and weakness, and which can lead to the loss of consciousness or even death.

sun·tan (sun′tan′), *n.* a darkening of the skin caused by exposure to the sun.—*adj.* **sun′tanned′.**

su·per- (sū′pėr-), *prefix* meaning *above, over, higher, extra, extremely, superior,* as in *super*abundant, *super*conductivity, *super*critical, *super*hero, *super*model, *super*mom, *super*structure.

su·per (sū′pėr), *n.* **1,** *Colloq.* superintendent; **2,** the removable upper story of a beehive where the honey is stored:—*adj. Colloq.* esp. good or fine; ouststanding; excellent; as, to do a *super* job on the project.

su·per·an·nu·ate (sū′pėr-an′ūāt′), *v.t.* to retire on pension, as from age or infirmity.—*adj.* **su′per-an′nu-at′ed, 1,** retired (on pension); **2,** antiquated; obsolete.—*n.* **su′per-an′nu-a′tion** (the pension paid to a retired person).

su·perb (sū-pûrb′), *adj.* **1,** grand; proud; stately; as, a *superb* residence; **2,** rich; elegant; as, *superb* attire; **3,** exceedingly good; of finest quality; excellent; as, *superb* acting.—*adv.* **su-perb′ly.**

su·per·charge (sū′pėr-chärj′), *v.t.* [-charged, charg-ing], **1,** to charge greatly or excessively, esp. with emotion; as, to *supercharge* the atmosphere with tension; **2,** to increase the power of an engine using a supercharger.—*adj.* **su′per-charged′.**

su·per·cil·i·ous (sū′pėr-sil′i-us), *adj.* contemptuously haughty; proud.—*adv.* **su′per-cil′i-ous-ly.**—*n.* **su′per-cil′i-ous-ness.**

su·per·ego (sū′pėr-ē′gō′), *n.* in psychoanalytical theory, the part of the psyche that acts as the conscience and imposes moral standards.

su·per·fi·cial (sū′pėr-fish′al), *adj.* **1,** lying on the surface only; not deep; as, *superficial* wounds; **2,** not thorough; hasty; as, a *superficial* examination; **3,** shallow; without substance or importance; as, a *superficial* character.—*adv.* **su′per-fi′cial-ly.**

su·per·flu·ous (sū′pûr′floo-us), *adj.* beyond what is necessary or desirable; excessive; as, *superfluous* remarks.—*adv.* **su′per′flu-ous-ly.**

su·per·high·way (sū′pėr-hī′wā′), *n.* a divided public highway, esp. designed and constructed for speedy, but safe, travel.

su·per·hu·man (sū′pėr-hū′man), *adj.* **1,** beyond what is human; seeming to exceed human powers; as, *superhuman* strength; **2,** supernatural; divine; as, *superhuman* beings.

su·per·in·tend·ent (sūpėr-in-tend′ent), *n.* **1,** a person who directs, administers, or manages something; as, a *superintendent* of schools; a police or military *superintendent*; **2,** someone who is responsible for the repair or cleaning of an apartment or office building; a caretaker:—*v.t.* to have, or exercise, the charge or oversight of; supervise and direct.—*n.* **su′per-in-tend′ence.**

su·pe·ri·or (soo-pir′i-ėr; sū-), *adj.* **1,** higher in place, position, rank, dignity, or office; as, a *superior* officer; **2,** of higher or better quality; preferable; as, this cloth is far *superior*; **3,** not stooping (to); not yielding (to); as, *superior* to petty jealousies; **4,** pretending to be better than others; too proud; arrogant; as, a *superior* attitude:—*n.* **1,** one who is better, greater, or higher in rank; **2,** the head of a religious community; as, a Mother *Superior.*—*n.* **su-pe′ri-or′i-ty.**

superiority complex, the belief that one is better than everyone else; an exaggeratedly high opinion of oneself.

su·per·la·tive (sōō-pûr′la-tiv; sū), *adj.* **1,** best, highest, or greatest in degree; as, a man of *superlative* wisdom; **2,** in *grammar,* the form of an adjective or adverb that describes the highest, the best, or the most of something; as, "best" is the *superlative* adjective of "good":—*n.* the superlative degree; also, a superlative form; as, "best" is the *superlative* of "good."

su-per-man (sōō′pėr-man′; sū′), *n.* [*pl.* super-men (-men)], a man of unusual strength and ability, or with more than human powers; the comic book, television, and movie hero.—*n.fem.* **su′per-wo′man.**

su-per-mar-ket (sōō′pėr-mär′kit; sū′), *n.* a large store that sells food and other non-food items, such as cleaning and health-care products, and in which customers can serve themselves and pay as they leave.

su-per-nat-u-ral (sū′pėr-nat′ūral), *adj.* outside, or exceeding, the laws of nature; not part of normal human powers or understanding; as, *supernatural* beings such as aliens, ghosts, and monsters:—*n.* that which is outside the usual course of nature.

su-per-no-va (sū′pėr-nō′va), *n.* the explosion of a very large star, which burns extremely brightly, millions of times brighter than the sun, for a short period before fading away.

su-per-nu-mer-ar-y (sū′pėr-nu′mėr-a-ri), *n.* a person or thing above the usual number or complement, esp. one not on a regular staff, as an army officer, or an actor who does bit parts:—*adj.* more than needed; superfluous.

su-per-sat-u-rat-ed (sū′pėr-sat′ū-rāt′id), *adj.* concentrated or saturated beyond normal; as, a *supersaturated* solution.—*n.* **su′per-sat′u-ra′tion.**

su-per-script (sū′pėr-skript′), *n.* and *adj.* a character or relating to a character situated above the line and usually to the right of a regular character: opposite of *subscript.*

su-per-sede (sū′pėr-sēd′), *v.t.* [super-seded, supersed-ing], to take the place of; supplant; as, automobiles *superseded* carriages.

su-per-son-ic (sōō′pėr-son′ik; sū′), *adj.* of sound, having a frequency higher than can be heard by the human ear; of speed, faster than the speed of sound in air (about 1,180 kilometres per hour).—*n.pl.* **su′per-son′ics.**

su-per-sti-tion (sōō′pėr-stish′un; sū′), *n.* **1,** belief in, fear of, or reverence for the unknown or mysterious; **2,** beliefs or practices, often of a religious character, based on fear of the unknown; also, any popular belief in the power of omens, charms, etc.—*adj.* **su′per-sti′tious.**

su-per-vise (sōō′pėr-vīz′; sū′pėr-vīz′) *v.t.* [supervised, supervis-ing], to oversee; watch over; superintend; direct; manage; as, a senior employee *supervised* the trainee.—*adj.* **su′per-vi′so-ry.**—*n.* **su′per-vi′sion; su′per-vi′sor.**

su-pine (sū′pīn), *adj.* lying on the back: opposite of *prone.*

sup-per (sup′ėr), *n.* the evening meal; the last meal of the day: also called *dinner.*—*adj.* **sup′per-less.**—*n.* **sup′per-time.**

sup-plant (su-plant′), *v.t.* **1,** to take the place of; as, computers have *supplanted* typewriters; **2,** to take the place of (another), sometimes by underhanded means.

sup-ple (sup′l), *adj.* [sup-pler, supplest], easily bent; flexible; graceful; as, a *supple* gymnast.

sup-ple-ment (sup′li-ment), *n.* **1,** that which completes an unfinished thing or adds something to a completed thing; esp., a part at the end of a book or an article adding information or making corrections; **2,** something added to a thing to make it better; as, a vitamin *supplement*:—*v.t.* (sup′li-ment′), to make additions to; complete.—*adj.* **sup′ple-men′tal; sup′ple-men′ta-ry.**—*adv.* **sup′ply** (sup′lē).

sup-pli-cate (sup′li-kāt′), *v.t.* [supplicat-ed, supplicat-ing], **1,** to ask for humbly and earnestly; as, to *supplicate* divine blessing; **2,** to address or appeal to in prayer:—*v.i.* to pray or beseech humbly and earnestly.—*n.* **sup′pli-ant′; sup′pli-ca′tion.**

sup-ply (su-plī), *v.t.* [supplied, supplying], **1,** to furnish; provide; as, to *supply* people with food; to *supply* food for people; **2,** to make up for; fill; as, to *supply* a lack:—*n.* [*pl.* supplies], **1,** the act of furnishing what is needed; **2,** that which is needed; an amount required; as, a winter's *supply* of salt; **3,** the total amount available:—**supplies,** food and other such necessary items; as, to have enough *supplies* for a three-day hike:—**supply teacher,** a substitute teacher.—*n.* **sup-pli′er.**

sup-port (su-pōrt′), *v.t.* **1,** to bear the weight of; as, the pedestal *supports* the statue; **2,** to endure; bear; as, he *supported* his agony bravely; **3,** to encourage; sustain; assist; **4,** to verify; prove; corroborate; as, the figures *support* my claim; **5,** to aid, favour, or defend, as a political party; **6,** to provide for; as, to *support* a family; **7,** in *computing,* be compatible with; as, my operating system *supports* this software program:—*n.* **1,** the act of maintaining or upholding; **2,** one who or that which maintains or upholds; a prop; pillar; as, he is the chief *support* of the cause; the column is a strong *support* for the roof; **3,** maintenance; livelihood; **4,** one who furnishes means of living; as, she is the *support* of the family; **5,** the money paid to a divorced spouse to maintain his or her lifestyle; **6,** in *computing,* technical advice or help; as, technical *support* for this complicated new software program was provided by the manufacturer:—*adj.* of or relating to a person, group, or thing that supports; as, *support* group; *support* hose; *support* staff.—*n.* **sup-port′er; sup-port′ group.**—*adj.* **sup-port′a-ble; sup-port′ing; sup-port′ive.**

sup-pose (su-pōz), *v.t.* [supposed, suppos-ing], **1,** to accept as true; imagine; think; believe; as, to *suppose* there could be life on Mars; **2,** to assume as a basis of argument;

as, but *suppose* you lose; **3,** to imply; require as a condition; as, creation *supposes* a creator:—*v.i.* to think; imagine.—*n.* **sup′po-si′tion.**—*adv.* **sup-pos′ed-ly.**—*adj.* **sup-posed′.**

sup-pos-i-to-ry (su-poz′i-tėr-i), *n.* a medical preparation, in the form of a cone or cylinder, that melts at body temperature, inserted into a body cavity, as the vagina or rectum (to stimulate bowel action).

sup-press (su-pres′), *v.t.* **1,** to subdue; crush; as, to *suppress* a revolt; **2,** to keep in; restrain; as, to *suppress* a cough; to *suppress* anger; **3,** to conceal; also, to stop the publication of; as, to *suppress* news.—*n.* **sup-pres′sion; sup-pres′sor.**—*adj.* **sup-pres′sive; sup-pres′sant** (as, cough *suppressant*).

su-prem-a-cy (sū-prem′a-si; sōōprem′a-si), *n.* the highest authority or power; the state of being supreme.

su-preme (sū-prēm′; sōōprēm), *adj.* **1,** highest in power or authority; as, a *supreme* court; **2,** highest in degree; greatest possible; as, *supreme* indifference; *supreme* sacrifice; **3,** crucial; most important; as, the climax is the *supreme* moment in the movie.—*adv.* **su-preme′ly.**

Supreme Court, 1, the highest court in Canada, consisting of nine judges, which acts as the final authority for any disputed court case; **2,** a similar court in other countries or provinces.

sur-charge (sûr′chärj), *n.* **1,** an additional or extra charge or tax; **2,** an exorbitant burden:—*v.t.* (su′r-chärj′), to levy an extra charge; overcharge; overload.

sure (shoor), *adj.* [sur-er, sur-est], **1,** knowing and believing; confident; as, I am *sure* you will succeed; **2,** destined; certain; as, you are the *sure* winner of any race; **3,** dependable; reliable; as, the only *sure* way; **4,** firmly fixed; as, a *sure* foundation; a *sure* grip:—*adv. Colloq.* surely; as, *sure* as fate:—*interj.* of course; as, *sure*, you can go.—*n.* **sure′ness.**—*adv.* **sure′ly.**

sure-ty (shoor′ti; shoor′i-ti), *n.* [*pl.* sureties], **1,** certainty; assurance; **2,** that which makes for security; esp., a money guarantee against loss or damage; **3,** one who makes himself liable, or responsible for certain acts of another, as for the payment of a debt.

surf (sûrf), *n.* the waves of the sea as they break in foam upon the shore:—*v.t.* and *v.i.* **1,** to ride on a wave on a surf board, etc.; **2,** to browse, skim, or scan; as, to *surf* the Net; to *surf* TV.—*n.* **surf′er; surf′ing.**

sur-face (sûr′fis), *n.* **1,** the outside part of a solid body, or the upper face of a body of liquid; as, a rough *surface*; the *surface* of a lake; **2,** external or outward appearance:—*adj.* **1,** pertaining to the top or surface; **2,** insincere; as, *surface* politeness:—*v.t.* [surfaced, surfac-ing], to give an outside covering or polish to; to cover with something; as, to *surface* a road:—*v.i.* to come to or emerge on the surface; as, whales *surfaced* near our boat; evidence *surfaced* about the killer.

surf-board (sûrf′bōrd′), *n.* a long, flat board, usually made of a strong, light plastic covered with fibreglass, which helps it float: it is used to ride a breaking wave to shore.

sur-feit (sûr′fit), *n.* **1,** indulgence to excess, esp. in eating or drinking; **2,** fullness or sickness caused by such excess:—*v.t.* to feed to excess; satiate.

surge (sûrj), *n.* **1,** a large wave, swell, or billow; **2,** a great rolling motion; rush; as, the *surge* of a mob; **3,** a sudden high increase; as, the *surge* of house sales:—*v.i.* [surged, surging], to rise high and roll; swell; rise suddenly; as, prices *surged.*

surge protector or **surge suppressor,** a device that protects electronic equipment from power-surge damage.—*n.* **surge′ protec′tion.**

sur-geon (sûr′jun), *n.* a medical doctor trained to perform surgery.

sur-ger-y (sûr′jėr-i), *n.* [*pl.* surgeries], **1,** the branch of medicine that deals with treating injuries, deformities, or diseases by cutting into the body to remove, repair, or replace affected parts; **2,** a place where a medical operation is performed.—*adj.* **sur′gi-cal** (sûr′ji-kl).

sur-ly (sûr′li), *adj.* [sur-li-er, sur-li-est], ill-humoured; uncivil; rudely abrupt; hostile.—*n.* **sur′li-ness.**

sur-mise (sûr-mīz′; sûr′mīz), *n.* a thought or conjecture based upon little evidence; a guess:—*v.t.* and *v.i.* (sûr-mīz′), [surmised, surmis-ing], to guess, or make a guess, on insufficient evidence.

sur-mount (sûr-mount′), *v.t.* **1,** to overcome; conquer; as, to *surmount* difficulties; **2,** to be placed at the top of; as, a castle *surmounts* the hill.

sur-name (sûr′nām′), *n.* originally, a name, often descriptive, added to the first name, as in "Charles the Bold"; now, the last or family name, often shared by all the members of one family:—*v.t.* (sûr′nām′; sûr-nām′), [surnamed, surnam-ing], to give a surname, or additional name, to; as, Alexander was *surnamed* the Great.

sur-pass (sėr-pås′), *v.t.* **1,** to exceed; go beyond the limits of; as, wonders that *surpass* belief; **2,** to excel; be better than; as, he *surpasses* all others in wisdom.—*adj.* **sur-pas′sing.** —*adv.* **sur-pas′sing-ly.**

sur-plus (sûr′plus), *n.* that which remains over and above what is used or required; excess; leftover: opposite of *deficit*:—*adj.* exceeding what is used or needed.

sur-prise (sėr-prīz′), *n.* **1,** the act of coming upon or attacking unexpectedly; as, the enemy was taken by *surprise*; **2,** the feeling aroused by what is sudden and strange; wonder; astonishment; **3,** a sudden or unexpected event or fact; as, his dismissal came as a *surprise*; her birthday party was a *surprise*:—*adj.* unexpected; as, a *surprise* gift; *surprise* party; *surprise* attack:—*v.t.* [surprised, surprising], **1,** to take unawares; come upon or attack without warning; as, they *surprised* the conspirators; **2,** to strike with wonder, as does something unexpected; as, her kindness *surprised* me.—*adj.* **sur-prised′; sur-pris′ing.**—*adv.* **sur-pris′ing-ly.**

sur-re-al (sūr-rēl′), *adj.* having dreamlike qualities; bizzare; fantastic; unreal; associated with the surrealism artistic movement.—*adv.* **sur-re′al-ly.**

sur-re-al-ism or **Sur-re-al-ism** (su-rē′al-izm), *n.* a 20th-century movement in art and literature that tried to show activities of the subconscious mind by images without order, as in a dream.—*adj.* **sur-re′al-is′tic.**—*n.* and *adj.* **sur-re′al-ist.**

sur-ren-der (su-ren′dėr), *v.t.* **1,** to yield (oneself) under pressure to the power of another; **2,** to resign possession of; give up; as, to *surrender* arms; *surrender* one's claim to property; **3,** to yield (oneself) to an influence or emotion:—*v.i.* to yield; give up the struggle; give up; accept defeat:—*n.* the act of yielding to an outside influence; also, the giving up of a claim or privilege.

sur-rep-ti-tious (sûr′ep-tish′us), *adj.* done by stealth, by secret, or by improper means; as, a *surreptitious* entry, will, plan, etc.—*adv.* **sur′rep-ti′tious-ly.**

sur-ro-gate (sûr′ōgāt′; -git), *n.* and *adj.* **1,** a court that probates wills, administers estates, etc.; **2,** a substitute; something or somewho who takes the place of another; deputy; esp. for a judge, bishop, etc.

surrogate mother, 1, a woman who bears a child for another who is unable to do so; **2,** someone who acts as a substitute mother.

sur-round (su-round′), *v.t.* **1,** to enclose on all sides; as, the suburbs *surround* the city; **2,** to encircle or cause to be encircled; as, to *surround* oneself with luxuries.

sur-round-ings (su-roun′dingz), *n.pl.* **1,** neighbourhood; **2,** the things or conditions that are around a person, animal, or thing; environment; as, many animals adapt to their *surroundings*.—*adj.* **sur-round′ing.**

sur-tax (sûr′taks′), *n.* a tax added to a normal tax, often graduated, as that on incomes above a specific level.—*v.t.* to levy a surtax on.

sur-veil-lance (sûr-vāl′ans; sûr-vāl′yans), *n.* **1,** a close watch; supervision, as by detectives; **2,** a security system installed in a building to detect illegal entry.

sur-vey (sėr-vā), *v.t.* **1,** to gather and record detailed information, opinions, or views of a person or group about certain topics or issues; as, to *survey* shoppers about customer service; **2,** to examine closely, with respect to condition, value, etc.; appraise; as, to *survey* a factory; **3,** to measure and determine the boundaries or other features of (a portion of land):—*n.* (sûr′vā; sėr-vā), **1,** the act of looking over or examining carefully; **2,** a formal or informal poll about some topic or issue; as, a *survey* of what students eat at lunch; also, an investigation, often of official nature; as, a *survey* of unemployment; **3,** a summary or outline of a broad subject; **4,** the process of determining the exact measurements, outline, position, etc., of any part of the earth's surface; also, an accurate plan and description, based on these measurements.—*n.* **sur-vey′ing; sur-vey′or.**

survival (sėr-vī′val), *n.* the fact of surviving; continuing to live, esp. after or due to an adverse situation or condition; as, the *survival* of many endangered species depends on many factors:—**survival of the fittest** or **natural selection**, the process in nature by which animals that are better able to live under or adapt to certain conditions survive, and the weaker ones die out.

sur-vive (sėr-vīv′), *v.t.* [survived, surviv-ing], **1,** to live or continue to live longer than (others); as, to *survive* a parent; **2,** to outlive; also, to live beyond or through (an event, state, etc.); as, to *survive* a tornado; *survive* the Ice Age:—*v.i.* to remain alive or in existence; endure.—*n.* **sur-viv′al; sur-vi′vor.**

sus-cep-ti-ble (su-sep′ti-bl), *adj.* **1,** capable of; admitting to process, etc.; as, a statement *susceptible* of proof; **2,** capable of being changed, influenced, or easily affected by a stimulus, etc.; vulnerable; as, a person *susceptible* to flattery; *susceptible* to pain; **3,** sensitive; impressionable; easily influenced; as, a *susceptible* child.—*n.* **sus-cep′ti-bil′i-ty.**

su-shi (sū′shē′), *n.* a Japanese dish of raw fish, rice, vegetables, and other ingredients, served in delicate, intricate shapes.

sus-pect (sus-pekt′), *v.t.* **1,** to conjecture; believe; suppose; as, I *suspect* that illness kept her home; **2,** to believe in the possible guilt of, without having definite proof; as, the police *suspected* her of the crime; **3,** to consider as questionable; doubt; as, to *suspect* the accuracy of a report; **4,** to be aware of; realize or sense; as, I didn't *suspect* a thing:—*n.* (also sus′pekt), a person believed, but not proved, to be guilty of crime:—*adj.* that can be doubted or misstrusted; uncertain; as, a *suspect* remedy for her illness.—*adj.* **sus-pect′ed.**

sus-pend (sus-pend′), *v.t.* **1,** to cause to hang down; as, to *suspend* a rope from a roof; **2,** to hold, as if hanging; as, particles of dust are *suspended* in the air; **3,** to delay; hold undecided; as, to *suspend* judgment; **4,** to set aside or waive temporarily; disregard for a time; as, to *suspend* a rule; **5,** to debar, or keep out, for a time, from some privilege, office, etc.; as, to *suspend* a student.—*n.* **sus-pen′sion.**

sus-pend-ers (sus-pen′dorz), *n.pl.* two straps or bands worn over the shoulders to hold up a pair of pants or a skirt.

sus-pense (sus-pens′), *n.* a state of uncertainty, doubt, or anxiety; as, the *suspense* in the movie was almost unbearable:—*adj.* relating to something that contains suspense; as, a *suspense* novel.—*adj.* **suspense′ful.**

suspension bridge, a bridge suspended from cables that are stretched between two towers.

sus-pi-cion (sus-pish′un), *n.* **1,** the feeling or imagining that something is wrong; mistrust; doubt; **2,** a notion or inkling; as, a *suspicion* of trouble; **3,** a very small amount; hint; trace; as, a *suspicion* of humour; **4,** the condition of being suspected of a crime or wrongdoing.

sus-pi-cious (sus-pish′us), *adj.* **1,** inclined to imagine without proof; distrustful; as, a *suspicious* parent; **2,** open to unbelief; questionable; as, a *suspicious* alibi; **3,** showing, or suggesting, doubt or suspicion; as, a *suspicious* glance.—*adv.* **sus-pi′cious-ly.**

sus-tain (sus-tān′), *v.t.* **1,** to support, as weight or pressure; **2,** to maintain or keep up, as an argument; continue; as, to *sustain* a friendship; **3,** to keep going; as, food *sustains* life; **4,** to suffer; undergo, as a loss; **5,** to bear up under; receive, suffer; undergo; as, to *sustain* injuries or a blow; **6,** to keep up the spirit of; as, his faith *sustained* him; **7,** to confirm; bear out; as, to *sustain* an accusation with proof; **8,** to uphold, as a decision.—*n.* **sus′te-nance** (sus′ti-nans) (something that provides life or strength).—*adj.* **sus-tained′.**

su-ture (sū′tūr; so͞o′chėr), *n.* **1,** the act of sewing; **2,** in *surgery*, the drawing together of the edges of a wound by stitches; also, the thread used for this purpose; **3,** a joining together or junction, as of the bones of the skull, valves of a mollusc, etc.:—*v.t.* [sutured, sutur-ing], to join or stitch up with a suture.

svelte (svelt), *n.* lithe; supple; slender.

swab (swob), *n.* **1,** a mop for cleaning decks, floors, etc.; **2,** an absorbent piece of cotton, pad, sponge, etc., used in surgery, or for cleaning wounds and applying medicine: sometimes attached to a small stick:—*v.t.* to clean, wipe, or treat with a swab.—*n.* **swab′ber.**

swag (swag), *n.* *Slang* plundered goods; loot; booty.

swag-ger (swag′ėr), *v.i.* to strut about; also, to boast noisily; brag:—*n.* an affected, insolent walk or strut; also, noisy boastfulness.—*adj.* **swag′ger-ing.**—*adv.* **swag′ger-ing-ly.**

swale (swāl), *n.* a meadow, often marshy and rank with vegetation.

[1]**swal-low** (swol′ō; swôl′ō), *n.* any one of several small insect-eating migratory birds, with long, forked tail and pointed wings, noted for graceful, swift flight.

[2]**swal-low** (swol′ō; swôl′ō), *v.t.* **1,** to transfer, as food, from the mouth to the stomach through the esophagus; **2,** to absorb; as, expenses *swallow* up income; engulf; as, night *swallowed* the earth; **3,** to endure quietly; repress; as, to *swallow* anger at the insult; **4,** to accept as true without asking for proof; as, to *swallow* an improbable story:—*v.i.* to perform the act of taking down food or liquid; as, to *swallow* quickly:—*n.* the act of swallowing; also, the amount swallowed at one time.

swam (swam), *p.t.* of *swim.*

swamp (swomp), *n.* wet, marshy land; bog:—*v.t.* **1,** to cause to sink in a swamp or bog; **2,** to fill with water; as, to *swamp* a boat; **3,** to overwhelm; submerge; as, the business was *swamped* by old debts; **4,** to remove or clear of bush, shrubs, and trees.—*adj.* **swamp′ish; swamp′y; swamped** (overwhelmed).—*n.* **swamp′land′.**

swan (swon), *n.* a large, graceful aquatic bird, related to ducks and geese, with a long neck and usually white feathers. Also, **swan′ dive′; swan′ song′.**

swank (swangk), *n.* *Slang* elegance, style, pretentiousness:—*adj.* *Slang* pretentiously stylish, smart, fashionable, elegant:—*v.i.* *Slang* to swagger; show off.—*adj.* **swank′y.**

swap (swop), *v.t.* *Colloq.* to exchange; barter; trade; as to *swap* knives.—*n.* *Colloq.* an exchange.—*n.* **swap′per.**

swarm (swôrm), *n.* **1,** a large number of moving birds, animals, insects, etc.; as, a *swarm* of locusts; **2,** a large number of bees, accompanied by a queen, leaving one hive to establish a new home in another; also, a colony of bees settled in a hive permanently; **3,** a great number; a crowd; as, a *swarm* of people:—*v.i.* **1,** to move about in great numbers; as, people *swarmed* into the theatre: **2,** to be crowded; as, the town *swarmed* with soldiers; **3,** of bees, to leave a hive in a swarm to form a new colony:—*v.t.* to throng; as, people *swarmed* the streets.—*n.* **swarm′ing.**

swarth-y (swôr′*th*i; swôr′thi), *adj.* [swarth-i-er, swarth-i-est], of a dusky colour; dark-skinned.—*n.* **swarth′-i-ness.**

swash-buck-ler (swosh′buk′lėr; swôsh′buk′lėr), *n.* a blustering swaggerer or adventurer, esp. associated with daring, romantic feats; also, a novel or movie dealing with such a person.

swas-ti-ka (swos′ti-ka; swôs′ti-ka; swas′ti-ka), *n.* a crosslike symbol, dating from ancient times, shaped like four capital Ls joined together: adopted by Nazi Germany as the national emblem and later by other racial hate

SWASTIKA

groups, esp. anti-Semitic groups.

swat (swot), *v.t.* to strike quickly or sharply; as, to *swat* a fly:—*n.* a sharp slap or smack:—*n.* **swat′ter** (as, fly *swatter*).

swath (swôth), *n.* **1,** the amount of grass cut, or the space left clear, by a single sweep of a mower, etc.; **2,** a large, broad strip or belt of something; as, a *swath* of fine sand in front of the cabin.

swathe (swāth), *v.t.* [swathed, swath-ing], **1,** to bind with a band or bandage; **2,** to wrap; enclose; as, to *swathe* oneself in blankets; moonlight *swathed* the lake:—*n.* a bandage.

sway (swā), *v.i.* **1,** to move or swing from side to side, or backward and forward, as treetops in a breeze; **2,** to lean to one side; waver; as, the tightrope dancer *swayed* and fell into the net:—*v.t.* **1,** to cause to bend or to move backward and forward, or from side to side; **2,** to cause to lean to one side; bias; as, to *sway* opinion; to *sway* the jury; **3,** to influence by power; direct; rule; as, to *sway* the lives of a people:—*n.* **1,** the act of swaying; **2,** a controlling force or influence; as, under the *sway* of anger; **3,** rule or control; as, the *sway* of the press over public opinion.

swear (swâr), *v.i.* [*p.t.* swore (swōr), *p.p.* sworn (swōrn), *p.pr.* swear-ing], **1,** to make a solemn declaration to the truth of what is affirmed; **2,** to make a solemn vow or promise; **3,** to give evidence on oath; **4,** to use profane language:—*v.t.* **1,** to declare solemnly; **2,** to vow or promise solemnly; **3,** to cause (a person) to take an oath.—*n.* **swear′ing.**

sweat (swet), *n.* **1,** the salty moisture that is given off through the pores of the skin; perspiration; **2,** moisture given off by any substance; **3,** the act of perspiring; also, the condition of one who is perspiring; **4,** *Colloq.* hard work; drudgery:—*v.i.* [*p.t.* and *p.p.* sweat or sweat-ed, *p.pr.* sweat-ing], **1,** to perspire; **2,** to form moisture in drops on the outside; as, a glass of cold water *sweats*; **3,** *Colloq.* to labour hard; drudge:—*v.t.* **1,** to cause to perspire freely; as, to *sweat* a horse; **2,** to wet with perspiration; **3,** to employ at long hours of work for very low wages; **4,** *Colloq.* to worry about; as, don't *sweat* it.—*adj.* **sweat′y.**—*n.* **sweat′band′; sweat′bath′; sweat′pants′; sweat′shirt′; sweat′shop′; sweat′suit′.**

sweat-er (swet′ėr), *n.* a piece of clothing that is knitted or crocheted from wool or other fibres and worn, usually for warmth, on the upper part of the body.

sweat lodge, a structure heated by pouring water over hot stones, used by certain Aboriginal tribes for ritualistic religious or medicinal purposes.

sweep (swēp), *v.t.* [swept (swept), sweep-ing], **1,** to brush or clean with a broom, brush, etc.; as, to *sweep* a floor; **2,** to remove or clean away; as, to *sweep* up bits of paper; **3,** to drive, flow over, or carry along or off, with force; as, waves *swept* the deck; **4,** to pass lightly over or across; as, to *sweep* the strings of a guitar; **5,** to scan or gaze at; move or traverse swiftly; as, to *sweep* the horizon; **6,** to win overwhelmingly or in a series of contests, etc.; as, to *sweep* the election:—*v.i.* **1,** to clean or clear away dirt with a brush, broom, etc.; **2,** to pass with speed or force; as, the cavalry *swept* down the field; **3,** to move with stateliness or dignity; **4,** to extend in a continuous line or curve; as, the lawn *sweeps* down to the river:—*n.* **1,** the act of sweeping, clearing out, or getting rid of; **2,** a sweeping motion; as, a *sweep* of the arm; **3,** the range of such a motion; **4,** a bend or curve, as of a drive; **5,** one who makes a business of cleaning chimneys; as, a chimney *sweep*; **6,** a long pole, attached to a post, for drawing a bucket from a well; **7,** a long oar for moving or steering a boat; **8,** successive victories in a contest; as, she won every race, so it was a clean *sweep*; **9,** a thorough examination of an area, by police for drugs, etc.; also for electronic monitoring devices.—*n.* **sweep′er.**—*adj.* **sweep′ing.**

sweep-stake (swēp′stāk′), *n.* a winning of all the stakes or prizes by one contestant or bettor: *pl.* used as *sing.* or *pl.*, a lottery in which each buys a stake or ticket to form a common fund, which goes as a prize to the winner or in shares to several winners; as, the Irish *sweepstakes*: a form of gambling.

sweet (swēt), *adj.* **1,** tasting like sugar or honey; **2,** not bitter, sour, or salty; as, *sweet* milk; *sweet* butter; **3,** fragrant; as, *sweet*-smelling roses; **4,** pleasing in sound; soft; as, the *sweet* tones of a violin; **5,** charming or attractive in manner or appearance; **6,** gentle; mild; as, a *sweet* disposition; **7,** profitable; beneficial; as, a *sweet* deal:—*n.* **1,** one dearly loved; a darling; **2,** a tart, pudding, etc.; dessert; **3,** **sweets,** confectionery or candy.—*n.* **sweet′ness.**—*adj.* **sweet′ened; sweet′ ish.**—*adv.* **sweet′ly.**

sweet-bread (swēt′bred′), *n.* the pancreas of a young animal, cooked for food.

sweet-en (swēt′n), *v.t.* to make sweet; as, to *sweeten* tea:—*v.i.* to become sweet.

sweet-heart (swēt′härt′), *n.* one who is beloved; a lover; also, an endearing person.

sweet pea, a plant with slender, climbing stems and fragrant flowers of various colours; also, the flower.

sweet potato, the sweet, starchy root of a tropical plant, cooked and eaten as a vegetable; also, the vine.

swell (swel), *v.i.* [*p.t.* swelled (sweld), *p.p.* swol-len (swōl′en) or swelled, *p.pr.* swell-ing], **1,** to increase in size, volume, force, importance, value, etc.; as, her sprained ankle began to *swell*; I hope that profits will *swell* this year; the music *swelled* to a climax; **2,** to be inflated or bulge, as sails; **3,** to be puffed up; as, to *swell* with pride; **4,** to rise above the surrounding surface; as, the ground *swells*:—*v.t.* **1,** to cause to rise or increase; fill; puff up; **2,** to inflate with pride; **3,** in *music*, to play or sing (notes) with gradual increase and decrease of volume:—*n.* **1,** the act of swelling; an increase in volume, force, value, etc.; **2,** in *music*, gradual increase and decrease of sound; **3,** a long, continuous wave; **4,** *Colloq.* a very fashionable person:—*adj. Colloq.* excellent or good; fine; as, a *swell* party.—*n.* **swel′ling.**—*adj.* **swol′len.**

swel-ter (swel′tėr), *v.i.* to suffer from the heat; perspire freely.—*adj.* **swel′ter-ing.**

swept (swept), *p.t.* and *p.p.* of *sweep.*

swerve (swûrv), *v.i.* and *v.t.* [swerved, swerv-ing], to turn aside quickly, or cause to turn aside, from a direct course; as, the driver *swerved* to avoid hitting the cat crossing the road:—*n.* a sudden turning aside.

swift (swift), *adj.* **1,** rapid; quick; fast; alert; as, the *swift* movement of the boat; **2,** happening quickly; as, a *swift* reply; **3,** clever:—*n.* a bird, related to the hummingbird, but resembling the swallow.—*adv.* **swift′ly.**

swig (swig), *n. Colloq.* a deep swallow of a liquid, often liquor:—*v.t.* and *v.i. Colloq.* to drink deeply; gulp; as, to *swig* a cool drink.

swill (swil), *n.* **1,** liquid food for animals, esp. kitchen refuse given to pigs; **2,** garbage; refuse:—*v.t.* to drink or gulp greedily; guzzle.

swim (swim), *v.i.* [*p.t.* swam (swam), *p.p.* swum (swum), *p.pr.* swim-ming], **1,** to propel or push oneself forward in the water, with the arms and legs, as do humans, or with fins and tail, as do fish, etc.; **2,** to float on a liquid; **3,** to be carried along smoothly by a current; **4,** to overflow; as, eyes *swimming* with tears; **5,** to be dizzy; as, my head *swims*; also, to reel or seem to reel; as, the room *swam* before her eyes; **6,** to be in or covered by a liquid; as, the sundae was *swimming* in chocolate syrup:—*v.t.* **1,** to cause to swim or float; as, to *swim* cattle across a stream; **2,** to traverse by swimming; as, to *swim* a lake:—*n.* swimming, esp. as a sport.—*n.* **swim′mer; swim′ ming; swim′suit′; swim′ trunks′; swim′ wear′.**—*adj.* **swim′ming.**—*adv.* **swim′ming-ly.**

swin-dle (swin′dl), *v.t.* and *v.i.* [swin-dled, swin-dling], to get money or property from (someone) on false pretences; cheat:—*n.* the act of cheating; also, a fraudulent scheme.—*n.* **swin′dler.**

swine (swīn), *n.* [*pl.* swine], **1,** any animal of the hog family; **2,** a person with greedy or coarse habits.—*adj.* **swin′ish.**

swing (swing), *v.i.* [swung (swung), swing-ing], **1,** to move to and fro regularly, as the pendulum of a clock. **2,** to turn on, or as on, a hinge, or axis; as, the gate *swings* open; **3,** to move with a loose, free, swaying gait; **4,** to turn or wheel round; veer, as the wind; as, she *swung* around when I called:—*v.t.* **1,** to cause to move to and fro; as, to *swing* a child in a hammock; **2,** to move or wave to and fro; brandish, as a cane; **3,** to cause to turn or wheel about; **4,** to put up so as to hang freely; as, to *swing* a hammock; hang on hinges; as, to *swing* a gate; **5,** to manage successfully; as, to *swing* a business deal:—*n.* **1,** the act of swinging; also, the distance through which an object swings; **2,** a loose, free gait; **3,** an apparatus, usually a rope holding a seat, for swinging; **4,** strongly marked rhythm, as of poetry or music; **5,** a type of jazz music suitable for dancing; **6,** activity, movement; as, to get into the *swing* of things:—**in full swing,** at the highest point of activity; as, the party was *in full swing* when I arrived:—*adj.* **1,** relating to the music of swing; as, a *swing* band; **2,** being capable of changing an opinion on an issue or of swinging either way; as, a *swing* vote.

swipe (swīp), *n.* **1,** a vigorous blow, as with a club; **2,** a strong criticism; as, to take a *swipe* at the politicians:—*v.i.* and *v.t.* [swiped, swip-ing], **1,** to hit with force; **2,** *Slang* to steal; **3,** to run a magnetic card through an electronic device in order to pay for something, obtain data, etc.

swirl (swûrl), *v.i.* to move with a circular or whirling motion:—*v.t.* to cause to eddy or whirl:—*n.* **1,** a whirl or eddy; **2,** a curve or twist; as, a *swirl* of hair.

swish (swish), *n.* a rustling sound, or the movement that makes it:—*v.t.* to brandish, as a cane; cause to make a rustling sound:—*v.i.* to move with a rustling sound.—*adj.* **swish′y.**

switch (swich), *n.* **1,** a thin, flexible twig or rod; **2,** a blow with such a switch or whip; **3,** a movable section of rail for shifting cars from one track to another; **4,** a device for making, breaking, or shifting electric circuits; **5,** a change or shift from one thing to another, esp. a change that is not expected; as, to make a *switch* in the seating arrangement:—*v.t.* **1,** to whip or lash with a switch; **2,** to swing or jerk; as, the horse *switched* its tail; **3,** to shift (cars) to another track; **4,** to shift to another circuit, or on or off a circuit; as, to *switch* off the light; **5,** to change or shift something; as, we *switched* seats:—*v.i.* **1,** to shift to another track; **2,** hence, to change course suddenly; **3,** to change or shift.

switch-board (swich′bōrd′), *n.* a central board or panel with switches or plugs controlling and combining electric circuits.

swiv-el (swiv′l), *n.* **1,** anything that turns on a headed bolt or pin or that can turn freely; as, office chairs turn on a *swivel*; **2,** a link in two parts connected by a bolt or pin, so that each part can turn independently:—*v.t.* and *v.i.* [swivelled, swivel-ling], to turn on a swivel.—*n.* **swiv′el chair.**

swoll-en (swōl′en), *p.p.* of swell.

swoon (swo͞on), *v.i.* to faint:—*n.* a faint.

swoop (swo͞op), *v.i.* to sweep (down) swiftly and suddenly; pounce; as, the eagle *swoops* down upon its prey:—*n.* a sudden downward plunge, as of a bird of prey.

sword (sōrd), *n.* **1,** a weapon, esp. in former times, consisting of a long pointed blade, with one or two sharp edges, set in a handle or hilt, and kept, when not in use, in a sheath or scabbard; **2,** the symbol of military power, of justice, or of vengeance; **3,** conflict or war; as, to resort to the *sword.*—*n.* **swords′man.**

sword-fish (sōrd′fish′), *n.* a large, edible sea fish with an upper jaw that lengthens out into a swordlike projection.

swore (swōr), *p.t.* of *swear.*

sworn (swōrn), *p.p.* of *swear.*—*adj.* bound by oath; as, a *sworn* enemy.

swum (swum), *p.p.* and one of the past tenses of *swim.*

swung (swung), *p.t.* and *p.p.* of *swing.*

syc-a-more (sik′a-mōr′), *n.* **1,** a North American tree with broad leaves and smooth bark that peels off in thin layers; **2,** a fig tree of Syria and Egypt; **3,** in Europe and Asia, a kind of maple.

syc-o-phant (sik′ō-fant), *n.* a servile flatterer; brown-noser; parasite; someone who sucks up.—*adj.* **sy′co-phan′tic.**—*adv.* **sy′cophan′tically.**

syl-la-ble (sil′a-bl), *n.* **1,** a unit of pronunciation consisting of a vowel sound, or a vowel sound grouped with one or more consonant sounds, pronounced by a single impulse of the voice, and forming either a complete word or one of the units that, together, make a word; as, "dog" is the first *syllable* of "dog-mat-ic"; **2,** the written or printed letters corresponding, though not always exactly, to a syllable as pronounced.—*adj.* **syl-lab′ic** (si-lab′ik).—*n.* **syl-lab-i-ca′tion.**—*v.t.* **syl-lab′if-y** (to divide into syllables).

syl-la-bus (sil′a-bus), *n.* [*pl.* syllabi (sil′a-bī) or syllabuses], **1,** a manual or directory of courses, programs, etc.; **2,** a brief statement of the main points of a lecture, book, etc.

syl-lo-gism (sil′ō-jizm), *n.* a form of logic or reasoning consisting of a major premise, a minor premise, and a conclusion; as, all humans are mortal; AB is a human; therefore AB is mortal.

syl-van (sil′van), *adj.* **1,** pertaining to woods, forests, or trees; rustic; as, a *sylvan* deity; **2,** wooded; as, a *sylvan* scene. Also, **sil′van.**

sym-bol (sim′bl), *n.* **1,** something that stands for or represents something else; an emblem; as, the maple leaf is the *symbol* of Canada; **2,** a mark, character, combination of letters, etc.; as, the letters of the alphabet are *symbols*; the sign ÷ is the *symbol* of division; H_2O is the chemical *symbol* for water.—*adj.* **symbol′ic** (sim-bol′ik); **sym-bol′i-cal.**—*adv.* **sym-bol′i-cal-ly.**

sym-bol-ize (sim′bul-īz′), *v.t.* [symbolized, symboliz-ing], to stand for, or represent; as, the lily *symbolizes* purity; also, to represent by means of a symbol.—*n.* **sym′bol-ism.**

sym-me-try (sim′i-tri), *n.* [*pl.* symmetries], **1,** the balanced structure of an object, the halves of which are alike; as, the *symmetry* of a sphere or of a butterfly; **2,** beauty of proportion; balance.—*adj.* **sym-met′ri-cal** (si-met′ri-kal).

sym-pa-thy (sim′pa-thi), *n.* [*pl.* sympathies], **1,** the sharing of another's emotions; agreement; as, I feel *sympathy* with your indignation; **2,** compassion for another's trouble; as, to feel *sympathy* for the homeless; **3,** harmony or agreement of affections or tastes; congeniality; **4,** friendly understanding and interest.—*adj.* **sym′pa-thet′ic.**—*v.i.* **sym′pa-thize.**

sym-pho-ny (sim′fo-ni), *n.* [*pl.* symphonies], **1,** harmony of sound; **2,** an agreeable blending of any kind; as, a *symphony* in blue and grey; **3,** an elaborate musical composition, consisting of three or four movements, for a full orchestra; also, a large orchestra that plays symphonies or other such musical pieces.—*adj.* **sym-phon′ic.**

sym-po-si-um (sim-pōzi-um), *n.* **1,** a conference organized to discuss a particular subject; **2,** a meeting or social gathering for the free exchange of ideas; **3,** a collection of brief essays in which writers express their views on a given topic.

symp-tom (simp′tum), *n.* **1,** any change or special condition in the body or its functions, as an evidence of disease; **2,** a sign of the existence of something; as, a *symptom* of unrest.—*adj.* **symp′to-mat′ic.**

syn-a-gogue (sin′a-gog′), *n.* a place or building used for worship and instruction in the Jewish religion.

syn-chro-nize (sing′kro-nīz′), *v.t.* **1,** to cause to agree in time, speed, or rate of vibration; **2,** to assign to the same date or period of time:—*v.i.* to coincide as to date, period of vibration, rate, etc.; to happen at the same time or rate.—*n.* **syn′chro-nism; syn′chro-ni-za′tion.**—*adj.* **syn′chro-nized; syn′chro-nous.**

syn-co-pate (sing′kōpāt′), *v.t.* in *music,* to begin a tone on an unaccented beat and sustain it through the next accented beat, or on the last half of a beat and sustain it through the first half of the next; in *grammar,* to contract (a word) by omitting a letter, as in *e'er* for *ever.*—*n.* **syn′co-pa′tion.**—*adj.* **syn′co-pa-ted.**

syn-di-cate (sin′di-kāt′; kit), *n.* a group or company of persons formed to carry out a particular enterprise, esp. one requiring much capital; as, a newspaper *syndicate;* also, a cartel:—*v.t.* (sin′di-kāt′), [syndicat-ed, syndicat-ing], **1,** to form into a syndicate; **2,** to manage, control, or sell to or through a syndicate; as, to *syndicate* a newspaper column; **3,** to sell a television show or series to local stations.—*adj.* **syn′di-cat-ed.**

syn-drome (sin′drōm′), *n.* **1,** a group of symptoms that together indicate a certain disease or abnormality; as, irritable bowel *syndrome;* **2,** a set of ideas, opinions, or behaviour that form an identifiable, characteristic pattern; as, the empty nest *syndrome.*

syn-od (sin′ud), *n.* **1,** a church council, or meeting, to consult on religious matters; **2,** any deliberative assembly or council.

syn-o-nym (sin′o-nim), *n.* a word having the same or nearly the same meaning as another; as, "small" is a *synonym* of "little": opposite of *antonym.*—*adj.* **syn-on′y-mous** (**1,** having the same or similar meaning; **2,** very closely connected; as, mosquitoes are *synonymous* with cottage country in early summer).

syn-op-sis (si-nop′sis), *n.* [*pl.* synopses (si-nop′sēz)], a condensed statement or summary, as of a book or play.—*adj.* **syn-op′tic.**

syn-tax (sin′taks), *n.* that part of *grammar* that deals with the relationship of the words in a sentence, esp. the structure and word order.—*adj.* **syn-tac′ti-cal.**

syn-the-sis (sin′thi-sis), *n.* [*pl.* syntheses (sin′thi-sēz′)], the combining of separate elements, substances, or parts to make a new form or whole.—*adj.* **syn-thet′ic** (made artifically with chemicals; not found in nature; as, *synthetic* fabrics).—*v.t.* **syn′the-size′.**

syr-inge (sir′inj), *n.* an appliance for ejecting liquid in a jet under pressure, used in gardening, surgery, and esp. for injecting a liquid into the body:—*v.t.* [syringed, syring-ing], to wash or cleanse by the use of a syringe.

syr-up (sir′up), *n.* **1,** a thick, sticky liquid made from the juice of fruits, herbs, etc., boiled with sugar; **2,** any similar liquid; as, maple *syrup.*—*adj.* **syr′up-y.**

sys-tem (sis′tem), *n.* **1,** a group or combination of parts or units functioning together as a whole according to some common law or purpose; as, the solar *system;* **2,** an orderly collection of rules and principles; as, the metric *system;* **3,** an orderly grouping of facts and objects; as, a filing *system;* **4,** regular routine; hence, efficiency; **5,** the human body considered as a unit; **6,** in *computing,* a computer system is the total of hardware and software units functioning together.—*adj.* **sys-′tem-at′ic; sys-tem′ic; sys′tem-at′i-cal.**—*v.* **sys′tem-a-tize.**

T

T, t (tē), *n.* [*pl.* T's, t's], **1,** the 20th letter of the alphabet, following S; **2,** anything with the shape of a T:—*adj.* shaped like a T; as, a *T*-bone.

tab (tab), *n.* **1,** a small flap or tag or projecting piece attached to the edge of something, such as a garment; as, a zipper *tab;* **2,** a projecting piece on a file folder or card, which can be labelled to assist in filing; **3,** *Colloq.* account; check; as, to keep close *tab* on his work; **4,** *Colloq.* a bill or cheque; as, put it on my *tab;* **5,** in *computing,* a tab key on a keyboard; tabulator; also, this function.

tab-by (tab′i), *n.* [*pl.* tabbies], a domestic cat, esp. a female, yellowish grey and marked with black.

tab-er-nac-le (tab′ėr-nak′l), *n.* **1,** a place of worship, esp. one erected temporarily; **2,** a Jewish temple; **3,** in some churches, an ornamental box resting on the altar and containing the sacred host:—**Tabernacle,** the movable structure used by the Israelites as a place of worship in the wilderness.

ta-ble (tā′bl), *n.* **1,** a piece of furniture consisting of a flat smooth top supported by legs; **2,** the persons sitting around a table; as, a *table* of bridge; **3,** food; fare in general; as, to set a fine *table;* **4,** an arrangement of words, facts, figures, etc., in systematic order for reference; as, statistical *tables;* **5,** a thin slab of wood, stone, metal, etc., with a flat surface, esp. one on which an inscription may be written or carved; tablet; **6,** a flat surface of land; plateau:—**table of contents,** a list of information or contents in a book, magazine, etc.; synopsis:—*adj.* pertaining to, of, or for a table; as, *table* mat, *table* salt:—*v.t.* [tabled, tabling], **1,** to lay aside so as to postpone consideration of; as, to *table* a report; shelve; **2,** to put forth for consideration, as a proposal; **3,** to lay (something) upon a table; **4,** to put in list form; tabulate.—*n.* **ta′ble-cloth′.**

tab-leau (tab′lō′; tå′blō′), *n.* [*pl.* tableaux (tab′lōz; tå′blō′) or tableaus (tab′-lōz)], **1,** a representation, as of a scene from history, in which silent and motionless living models pose; **2,** a vivid description; a remarkable scene.

ta-ble-land (tā′bl-land′), *n.* a plateau; elevated level stretch of land.

ta-ble-spoon (tā′bl-spoo͞n′), *n.* **1,** a large spoon used in preparing, serving, and eating meals; **2,** a unit of measure in cooking, equal to about 15 millilitres, or three times as much as a teaspoon.—*n.* **ta′ble-spoon′ful.**

tab-let (tab′lit), *n.* **1,** a small flat piece of some hard material, as wood or stone, for writing or drawing upon; **2,** blank sheets of paper fastened together at one end and used for writing; a writing pad; **3,** a flat panel, often of stone, brass, or bronze, fastened in a wall and bearing an inscription; **4,** medicine in the form of a small, flat disk or pellet; **5,** a small, flat cake of soap, candy, etc.

table tennis, *n.* a game that is similar to tennis, played on a table with paddles and a small, hollow plastic ball.

tab-loid (tab′loid), *n.* a newspaper, small in size, and usually containing many photographs and sensational material:—*adj.* condensed; concentrated.

ta-boo or **ta-bu** (ta-boo͞′), *n.* a system or practice in which certain things are held sacred, and contact with them is forbidden; **2,** a ban or prohibition:—*v.t.* to place under a ban; forbid; prohibit:—*adj.* **1,** set apart; made untouchable or sacred; **2,** prohibited by social custom; as, bad manners are *taboo.*

tab-u-lar (tab′ū-lėr), *adj.* **1,** flat; having a tablelike surface; as, a *tabular* rock; **2,** organized or arranged in list form; **3,** calculated using a table or list.

tab-u-late (tab′ū-lāt′), *v.t.* [tabulat-ed, tabulat-ing], to set up, or arrange in, a systematic outline or list, usually in columns; as, to *tabulate* data.—*n.* **tab′u-la′tion.**

tac-it (tas′it), *adj.* implied, but not stated outright; as, a *tacit* agreement.—*adv.* **tac′it-ly.**

tac-i-turn (tas′i-tûrn), *adj.* silent or reserved; disinclined to talk.—*adv.* **tac′i-turn-ly.**—*n.* **tac′i-tur′ni-ty.**

tack (tak), *n.* **1,** a small, sharp-pointed nail with a wide, flat head; as, upholstery *tacks;* **2,** a rope for lashing down the lower forward corner of certain sails; also, the corner of the sail so held down; **3,** the direction of a ship as determined by the position of her sails; **4,** a change in a ship's direction to take advantage of side winds; **5,** any course or policy of action:—*v.t.* **1,** to fasten with tacks; as, to *tack* a poster up on a bulletin board; **2,** to stitch lightly together; **3,** to attach with a tack or as with a tack; as, to *tack* a bow on a dress; **4,** to change the course of (a vessel):—*v.i.* **1,** to change the course of a vessel; **2,** to change a course of policy or action:—**tack on,** to add something extra at the end; as, to *tack on* delivery charges to a bill.

tack-le (tak′l), *n.* **1,** an instrument consisting of pulleys and ropes, used for raising or lowering weights, such as the sails of a ship, cargo, etc.; **2,** equipment used for a certain activity or sport; gear; as, fishing *tackle;* **3,** in *football,* the act of seizing and stopping an opponent who is running with the ball; also, a player in the line next to either end player, or the position next to either end position:—*v.t.* [tack-led, tack-ling], **1,** to grapple with (a person); try to solve (a problem); as, to *tackle* an extra assignment; **2,** to fasten with ropes and pulleys; **3,** to seize and stop by a tackle, as in football.

tack-y (tak′i), *adj.* [-ier, -iest], **1,** sticky, as varnish, glue, etc., before dry or tape; **2,** *Colloq.* of poor quality or cheap; shabby; **3,** *Colloq.* not stylish; **4,** *Colloq.* in bad taste; offensive.

ta-co (täk′ō), *n.* a tortilla with a filling such as meat, cheese, lettuce, etc.

tact (takt), *n.* natural ability to deal wisely, carefully, and sensitively with others; skill in saying and doing the appropriate thing.—*adj.* **tact′ful.**

tac-tic (tak′tik), *n.* any plan or method of action to reach a goal.

tac-tics (tak′tiks), *n.pl.* **1,** the science or practice of handling military or naval forces in the presence of an enemy; **2,** any skillful manoeuvring to gain an end; such a procedure.—*adj.* **tac′ti-cal.**—*n.* **tac-ti′cian.**

tac-tile (tak′tīl; til), *adj.* **1,** pertaining to the sense of touch; as, *tactile* organs; **2,** perceptible by touch; as, *tactile* qualities; tangible.

tact-less (takt′lis), *adj.* lacking, or not showing, readiness to say and do the most suitable thing; lacking tact or diplomacy; inconsiderate.—*n.* **tact′less-ness.**

tac-tu-al (tak′tū-al; tak′choo͞-al), *adj.* **1,** caused by touch; as, *tactual* impressions; **2,** tactile.

tad-pole (tad′pōl′), *n.* a frog or toad in an immature, or larva, stage, with, gills, a tail, and no legs.

tae kwon do (tī′ kwon′ dō′), *n.* a modern Korean style of self-defence, similar to karate.

taf-fe-ta (taf′i-ta), *n.* a shiny, fine, rustling silk or rayon, slightly stiffened, used esp. as dress material; also, a similar fabric.

taf-fy (taf′i), *n.* **1,** chewy candy made with butter and brown sugar, maple syrup, or molasses; **2,** a candy made of hot maple syrup poured on snow until it hardens.

tag (tag), *n.* **1,** an attached identifying or information card or label made of paper, plastic, metal, or other material; as, a price *tag;* dog *tag;* **2,** a children's game in which a player who is "it" chases the others in order to touch, or "tag," them; **3,** a reinforcement at the end of a shoestring, to stiffen it; **4,** a loose end; **5,** in *baseball,* the act of putting out a runner by touching him or her with the ball or with the hand holding the ball; **6,**

in *computing*, a code inserted before or after data to identify them or show how they are to be interpreted or used; **7,** a nickname; **8,** a motto, cliché, or saying:—*v.t.* [tagged, tagging], **1,** to fix a tag to; **2,** in the game of tag, to catch by touching; **3,** in *baseball*, to put out (a runner) by touching him or her with the ball; **4,** to follow closely and persistently; **5,** to place a traffic-violations ticket on a vehicle; **6,** in *computing*, to code (data):—*v.i.* to follow another closely.—*n.* **tag′ger.**

Ta-ga-log (tag′a-log′; ta-gol′og), *n.* [*pl.* Tagalog or Tagalogs], **1,** a person who inhabits or originates from certain areas of the Philippines, esp. Luzon; **2,** the language spoken by these people:—*adj.* relating to the region, the people, the language, or the culture of Tagalog.

Tahl-tan (tol′tan′), *n.* [*pl.* Tahltan or Tahltans], **1,** the Aboriginal people living in northwest British Columbia; **2,** the Athapaskan lanugage of these people.

tai chi or **Tai Chi** or **tai chi chuan** or **Tai Chi Chuan** (tī′ chē′; -jē′; -chwon′), *n.* a Chinese form of slow movements used for meditation and self-defence.

tai-ga (tī′ga), *n.* the dense, damp pine forests of northern Canada and Siberia, just south of the tundra.

tail (tāl), *n.* **1,** the hindmost part of an animal, extending beyond the rest of the body, usually having a long, thin shape; **2,** something resembling a tail in position, shape, etc.; as, a comet's *tail*; *tail* of a shirt; **3,** the end part of anything; as, the *tail* of a show or parade; **4,** the side of a coin opposite the side bearing the impression of a head; **5,** a plane or planes at the rear of an airplane to give it balance:—**tails**, a man's formal evening wear:—*v.t.* to furnish with a tail:—*v.i.* to follow close behind and watch; tag.

tai-lor (tā′lėr), *n.* one whose business it is to make and repair outer garments for men and women:—*v.i.* to follow the trade of a tailor:—*v.t.* **1,** to work on and fit (clothes); as, to *tailor* a suit to fit; **2,** to make, adjust, or adapt in a special way or for a specific purpose; as, to *tailor* products and services for individual customers.—*n.* **tai′loring.**—*adj.* **tai′lored** (custom-made); **tailor-made** (perfectly made, fitted, or suited).

tail-pipe (tāl′pīp′), *n.* a pipe at the back of a vehicle, etc., that emits exhaust gas from an engine.

tail-spin (tāl′spin′), *n.* **1,** the descent of an airplane, nose down and tail spinning in circles overhead; **2,** *Colloq.* a state of emotional confusion or distress.

taint (tānt), *n.* a spot, trace, or tinge of decay, corruption, or pollution:—*v.t.* **1,** to spoil by mixing with something unpleasant or poisonous; infect; **2,** to defile; corrupt:—*v.i.* to become spoiled, as meat.

take (tāk), *v.t.* [*p.t.* took (took), *p.p.* tak-en (tāk′en), *p.pr.* tak-ing], **1,** to lay hold of, as with the hands; grasp; as, to *take* a puppy in one's arms; also, to seize or capture; as, the troops *took* the city; **2,** to assume possession of; as, she *took* the store on a year's lease; also, to buy regularly; subscribe to; as, I *take* this magazine every month; **3,** to eat, drink, or inhale; as, to *take* breakfast; to *take* gas; **4,** to carry; as, *take* your purse; also, to conduct or escort; as, to *take* a guest home; **5,** to remove; subtract; as, to *take* three from five; also, to steal; as, to *take* another's idea; **6,** to experience; feel; as, to *take* pride in one's work; **7,** to perform, do, make, etc.; as, to *take* piano lessons; *take* a picture; *take* notes in class; **8,** to require; as, this report *took* a lot of time; **9,** to pick out; choose; as, *take* the largest apple; **10,** to be infected with; catch; as, to *take* cold; **11,** to attract the attention of; please; as, the hat *took* her fancy; **12,** to accept as true; assume; as, do not *take* me as a fool:—*v.i.* **1,** to have the intended effect; act; be successful; as, the vaccination *took*: **2,** to proceed; go; as, they *took* to the boats; **3,** to prove attractive; as, the song *took*:—*n.* **1,** the amount of money made, received, or stolen; as, the thief's *take* in the robbery; **2,** the amount or quantity received or taken, said esp. of fish; **3,** a portion or scene of a movie, television program, or recording that is photographed or recorded without interruption; as, *take* three; **4,** *Colloq.* assessment or response; as, to do a double *take*; what's your *take* on this matter?—*n.* **tak′er.**

take-off (tāk′ôf′), *n.* **1,** a parody, copy, or imitation; as, a *takeoff* of an actor; **2,** a place from which one makes a start in running or jumping; **3,** the act of an aircraft rising up in flight from the ground.

take-out or **take–out** (tāk′out′), *n.* food that is ordered and taken away to be eaten:—*adj.* relating to, of, or for food intended to be eaten elsewhere; as, *takeout* Chinese food.

take-o-ver or **take–o-ver** (tāk′ō-vėr), *n.* in business, the act of taking control or ownership of a company by buying up a certain amount of the company's stock.

tak-ing (tāk′ing), *adj.* **1,** attractive; pleasing; as, a *taking* personality; **2,** contagious, as a disease:—*n.* the act of gaining possession:—**takings**, the amount taken or received; receipts.

talc (talk), *n.* a soft, fine-grained mineral, greasy to the touch, used in paper and plastics manufacture, talcum powders, etc.

tal-cum (tal′kum), *n.* talc:—**talcum powder**, a skin powder of finely pulverized talc.

tale (tāl), *n.* **1,** that which is told; an imaginary story; fable; folk tale; **2,** an account of real events; as, the sad *tale* of how the house burned down; **3,** false report or piece of gossip.

tal-ent (tal′ent), *n.* **1,** an ancient weight and coin; **2,** mental ability; skill; cleverness; **3,** a special, natural or inborn ability for a particular business, art, or profession; as, artistic *talent*; **4,** a skilled person or a group of skilled persons; as, the baseball scout was looking for new *talent.—adj.* **tal′ent-ed.**

tal-is-man (tal′is-man; tal′iz-man), *n.* [*pl.* talismans], **1,** a figure engraved on a stone or ring, supposed to possess magical powers; a charm; an amulet; **2,** any similar thing, esp. something that acts like a charm or seems magical.

talk (tôk), *v.i.* **1,** to utter words; express and try to communicate thoughts through speech; **2,** to speak familiarly; converse; **3,** to confer; discuss; as, to *talk* with one's doctor; **4,** to chatter; gossip; **5,** to communicate ideas without speech; as, to *talk* by gestures:—*v.t.* **1,** to speak of; discuss; as, to *talk* business; **2,** to speak a language fluently; as, to *talk* French; **3,** to influence or affect by speech; as, they *talked* him into going to the game:—*n.* **1,** speech; conversation; as, an evening of friendly *talk*; **2,** a subject of discussion; as, the *talk* of the town; **3,** rumour; as, there is *talk* of a strike; **4,** meaningless speech; as, idle *talk*; **5,** a conference; as, peace *talks*; **6,** an informal address; as, a short *talk* on e-business.—*adj.* **talk′a-tive.**

talk-er (tôk′ėr), *n.* a person who talks, usually one who talks fast, well, or a lot; as, she's a real *talker* because she tells such interesting stories of her experiences.

tall (tôl), *adj.* **1,** of more than average height; as, a *tall* girl; **2,** of a certain specified height; as, the man is 176 centimetres *tall*; **3,** *Colloq.* exaggerated; difficult; as, a *tall* tale; *tall* order.

tal-low (tal′ō), *n.* the hard fat of animals, as beef or mutton suet, melted and used for making candles, soap, lubricants, etc.:—*adj.* made of tallow.—*adj.* **tal′low-y.**

tal-ly (tal′i), *n.* [*pl.* tallies], **1,** originally, a stick on which scores were recorded by notches; **2,** anything on which a score or account is kept; **3,** a count or record of votes, points, etc.; a score; **4,** a duplicate; counterpart:—*v.t.* [tallied, tally-ing], to keep score of; count; reckon and record:—*v.i.* **1,** to keep score; **2,** to match; balance; as, the two accounts *tally*.

tal-on (tal′un), *n.* the claw of a bird of prey; as, the *talon* of a hawk, owl, or eagle.

ta-ma-le (ta-mä′li), *n.* a Mexican dish of chopped meat and cornmeal, seasoned with red pepper, wrapped in cornhusks, dipped in oil, boiled or steamed, and served hot.

tam-bou-rine (tam′boo-rēn′), *n.* a small hand drum, with pairs of little metallic disks attached to the rim, played by shaking or striking it with the knuckles.

tame (tām), *adj.* [tam-er, tam-est], **1,** changed from a wild state; made useful to live or work with humans; domesticated; **2,** harmless; gentle; also, without fear; as, these squirrels are very *tame*; **3,** tedious; dull; as, the debate was *tame*:—*v.t.* [tamed, tam-ing], **1,** to make (an animal) useful to humans; domesticate; as, to *tame* an elephant; also, to make less wild or timid; as, to *tame* a bird; **2,** to crush the spirit or courage of; subdue.—*adv.* **tame′ly.**—*n.* **tam′er.**—*adj.* **tam′ a-ble** or **tame′a-ble.**

tamp (tamp), *v.t.* **1,** in blasting, to fill in (a hole containing the charge) with clay, earth, etc.; **2,** to drive in or down by repeated light strokes; as, the gardener has *tamped* down the sod.—*n.* **tamp′er.**

tam-per (tam′pėr), *v.i.* to meddle so as to injure or alter something; as, to *tamper* with a lock or mail.

tan (tan), *n.* **1,** oak bark, or other bark containing tannic acid, used in treating hides; **2,** a yellowish-brown colour, like that of such bark; **3,** a darker colour given to the skin by exposure to the sun:—*v.t.* [tanned, tan-ning], **1,** to convert (raw hide) into leather by treating with tannic acid or with mineral salts; **2,** to make darker by exposure to the sun; **3,** *Colloq.* to thrash; beat:—*v.i.* **1,** to be made into leather; **2,** to become darker in the sun:—*adj.* yellowish brown.—*n.* **tan′ner.**

tan-dem (tan′dem), *adv.* one behind another:—*adj.* arranged one behind the other, as horses, or seats on a bicycle:—*n.* **1,** a pair of horses harnessed one before the other; **2,** a carriage with horses one behind the other; also, the horses grouped in tandem; **3,** a bicycle with seats tandem; **4,** a vehicle with two attached parts, as a tractor-trailer.

TANDEM BICYCLE

tang (tang), *n.* **1,** a strong, sharp taste, flavour, or odour; also, a distinctive characteristic; **2,** a trace or hint; **3,** the part of a knife or similar tool that fits into the handle.—*adj.* **tang′y.**

tan-gent (tan′jent), *adj.* **1,** touching; **2,** in *geometry*, touching a line or surface at one point only but not passing through it:—*n.* a tangent line or surface.

tan-ger-ine (tan′je-rēn′; tan′je-rēn′), *n.* **1,** a small, juicy fruit that is related to the orange, with a skin that peels away easily; **2,** a reddish-orange colour like the colour of this fruit.

tan-gi-ble (tan′ji-bl) *adj.* **1,** touchable; capable of being felt by the touch; **2,** definite; real; not imaginary; as, *tangible* proof.—*adv.* **tan′gi-bly.**

tan-gle (tang′gl), *v.t.* [tan-gled, tan-gling], to knot so as to make difficult to unravel; entangle:—*v.i.* to be or become entangled:—*n.* **1,** a snarl; a confused mass; as, a *tangle* of string; **2,** a confused state; **3,** *Colloq.* an argument.

tan-go (tang′gō), *n.* [*pl.* tangos], a ballroom dance, originally from South America, in two-four time and with a great variety of steps.

tank (tangk), *n.* **1,** a large cistern, basin, or circular container for holding water or other fluid; as, an oil *tank*; gas *tank*; **2,** a kind of armoured vehicle, built like a caterpillar tractor and equipped with guns: used in warfare for advancing over rough ground:—*v.t.* to put or store in a tank.

tank-er (tangk′ėr), *n.* a ship, truck, or airplane built with tanks for carrying oil or other liquids in bulk.

tan-nic (tan′ik), *adj.* pertaining to, or obtained from, any bark, as oak or hemlock, which produces tan or tannin:—**tannic acid,** a strong acid obtained from tea, sumac, etc., and used in tanning, dyeing, and medicine: also called *tannin.*

tan-ta-lize (tan′ta-līz′), *v.t.* [tantalized, tantaliz-ing], to tease by exciting hopes or fears that will not be realized.

tan-ta-mount (tan′ta-mount′), *adj.* equivalent, or equal to, in effect, value, or importance; as, silence may be *tantamount* to consent.

tan-trum (tan′trum), *n.* a sudden outburst of temper or passion.

Tao-ism (tou′izm; dou′izm), *n.* the Chinese religion and philosophy, developed from the teachings of Lao-Tzu around 500 B.C., which emphasizes harmony and balance: the popular form of this religion adopted polytheism and a belief in magic.—*n.* and *adj.* **Tao′ist.**—*adj.* **Tao-is′tic.**

¹tap (tap), *n.* **1,** a pipe through which liquor is drawn from a cask; **2,** a faucet, spout, or spigot for drawing or turning off water; **3,** a plug or cork that closes a hole in a barrel; **4,** liquor drawn from a cask; **5,** a tool for cutting screw threads on an inner surface, as of a nut; **6,** in *electricity*, a device for making connection with a wire:—*v.t.* [tapped, tap-ping], **1,** to furnish with a spigot; **2,** to pierce the side of a cask or the bark of a tree in order to draw out liquid; **3,** to draw or let out (liquid); **4,** to make connections so as to draw from or extract from; employ; use; as, to *tap* secret sources of information; **5,** to make connection with (a wire) so as to draw off current; **6,** to cut in on a telephone line and secretly listen to another person's conversation; to wiretap; as, to *tap* a telephone.

²tap (tap), *v.t.* [tapped, tap-ping], **1,** to strike or touch lightly; as, she *tapped* me on the shoulder; **2,** to cause to strike or touch lightly; as, he *tapped* his foot impatiently:—*v.i.* to strike light blows:—*n.* a light blow or touch; pat; rap.

tape (tāp), *n.* **1,** a long, narrow band of paper, plastic, or other material, having a sticky substance on one side and used for wrapping, fastening, or sealing things; **2,** any long, narrow band of cloth, steel, paper, etc.; **3,** the rope or line stretched across the track to mark the finish of a race; **4,** a narrow strip of cloth, paper, or steel, marked for measuring length; **5,** a long narrow piece of magnetic plastic for recording sound, or sounds and pictures; as, video*tape*, audio*tape*, or magnetic *tape*:—*v.t.* [taped, tap-ing], **1,** to bind or cover with tape; as, he *taped* the handle of his tennis racket; **2,** to measure off with a tape; **3,** to record sounds or images on magnetic tape.—*n.* **tape′ deck′.**

ta-per (tā′pėr), *n.* **1,** a long, slender candle; **2,** a gradual lessening of thickness toward a point; as, the *taper* of a cone:—*v.i.* and *v.t.* **1,** to narrow to a point; **2,** to decrease gradually; as, the rain *tapered* off by morning.

tape recorder, a device that records sound on magnetic tape so that it can be played back later.

tap-es-try (tap′es-tri), *n.* [*pl.* tapestries], an ornamental fabric in which a picture or design is woven, used as a wall hanging or furniture covering.

tap-i-o-ca (tap′i-ō′ka), *n.* a starchy, granular substance prepared from the roots of the cassava plant, used for puddings and as a thickening.

taps (taps), *n.pl.* in the army and navy, the last signal of the day, on drum or bugle, ordering lights out: taps are also sounded over the grave of a soldier or sailor.

tar (tär), *n.* a thick, black, sticky, oily substance obtained from wood, coal, peat, etc., used to pave roads, waterproof roofs, and in making many industrial products:—*v.t.* [tarred, tar-ring], to cover with, or as with, tar; as, to *tar* a road.

ta-ran-tu-la (ta-ran′choo-la), *n.* a large, hairy spider with a bite that is painful but generally not dangerous, found in many warm countries.

tar-dy (tär′di), *adj.* [tar-di-er, tar-di-est], **1,** moving or progressing slowly; sluggish; as, *tardy* growth; **2,** not prompt; late.—*adv.* **tar′di-ly.**—*n.* **tar′di-ness.**

tar-get (tär′git). *n.* **1,** formerly, a small shield or buckler; **2,** a mark set up for archery, rifle, or artillery practice; **3,** one who or that which is made the object of attack, criticism, ridicule, etc.; as, he is the *target* of abuse; **4,** a goal:—*v.t.* **1,** to aim for; **2,** set as a goal or target.

tar-iff (târ′if; tar′if), *n.* **1,** a schedule of duties or taxes placed by a government on goods entering, or leaving, the country; **2,** a tax or duty levied according to such a schedule; **3,** any schedule of rates, charges, etc.; as, he asked for a copy of the new *tariff.*

tar-mac (tär′mak′), *n.* a paved runway, flight strip, or apron at an airport or in front of a hangar.

tar-nish (tär′nish), *v.t.* **1,** to dull the brightness of; discolour or stain; **2,** to lose purity or quality; as, to *tarnish* a reputation:—*v.i.* to lose brightness; as, silver *tarnishes* easily:—*n.* dullness; loss of polish; stain; corrosion.

tarp (tärp), *abbrev.* short for *tarpaulin.*

tar-pau-lin (tär-pô′lin; tär′po-lin), *n.* a piece of heavy, waterproof canvas or other material used as a protective covering from moisture: abbreviated as *tarp.*

[1]**tart** (tärt), *adj.* **1,** sharp to the taste; sour; not sweet; as, a *tart* jelly; **2,** severe; cutting; harsh; as, a *tart* reply.—*adv.* **tart′ly.**—*n.* **tart′ness.**

[2]**tart** (tärt), *n.* a small pastry shell without a top crust, filled with fruit, jam, or custard.

tar-tan (tär′tan), *n.* a woollen cloth, woven with a plaid pattern, worn particularly in the Scottish Highlands: Scottish clans or families have their own tartan:—*adj.* of, or in the pattern of, tartan.

tar-tar (tär′tėr), *n.* **1,** a whitish-yellow substance often found on teeth; **2,** an acid substance, present in grape juice, that is deposited on the inside of wine casks during fermentation:—**tartar sauce**, a sauce made of mayonnaise, relish, etc., served with fish.

task (åsk), *n.* **1,** a piece of work given out to be done; job or duty; as, daily *tasks*; **2,** in *computing,* a job assigned to, or performed by, a computer:—**take to task**, to censure:—*v.t.* to burden with work.—*n.* **task′mas′ter.**

task-bar (tåsk′bar′), *n.* in *computing,* a bar, usually at the bottom of the computer screen, containing icons and text indicating programs and functions.

task force, a temporary military group assigned a specific job or operation; also, any other similar group; as a *task force* to study the traffic congestion problem in the town.

tas-sel (tas′l), *n.* **1,** a hanging ornament made of a tuft of threads or cords of silk, wool, etc.; as, a *tassel* on a mortarboard; **2,** the hanging flower or head of certain plants; as, corn *tassels*:—*v.i.* [tasselled, tasselling], to put forth hanging flowery heads:—*v.t.* to trim with, or make into, tassels.

taste (tāst), *v.t.* [tast-ed, tast-ing], **1,** to perceive or know by the tongue and palate; as, I *taste* vanilla in the cocoa; **2,** to test the flavour of, by eating or drinking a little; as, to *taste* the sauce; **3,** to experience; as, to *taste* the joys of living:—*v.i.* **1,** to try food by the tongue or palate; **2,** to have a certain flavour; as, candy *tastes* sweet:—*n.* **1,** the flavour of a substance as perceived by the tongue and palate; as, a spicy *taste*; **2,** a little bit or piece, esp., a small portion tasted; as, take a *taste*; **3,** the sense by which the flavour of substances is perceived; **4,** liking or inclination; as, a *taste* for reading; **5,** ability to see what is beautiful; as, she has good *taste* in art.—*n.* **tast′er.**

taste-ful (tāst′fool), *adj.* marked by good taste.—*adv.* **taste′ful-ly.**—*n.* **taste′ful-ness.**

taste-less (tāst′les), *adj.* **1,** having little or no flavour; **2,** marked by bad taste; as, a *tasteless* comment.

tast-y (tā′sti), *adj.* [tast-i-er, tast-i-est], pleasing to the sense of taste; having a good flavour; as a *tasty* treat.

tat-ter (tat′ėr), *n.* **1,** a loose-hanging rag:—**tatters**, ragged clothing; rags.—*adj.* **tat′tered** (torn or hanging in shreds, ragged; as a *tattered* old coat).

tat-tle (tat′l), *v.i.* [tat-tled, tat-tling], **1,** to chatter; **2,** to tell tales; tell someone what another person has done wrong; gossip; tattletale; as, to *tattle* on a classmate:—*v.t.* to tell (tales or secrets):—*n.* trifling or idle talk; gossip; tattletale.—*n.* **tat′tler; tat′tling.**

tat-tle-tale (tat′l-tāl′), *n.* someone who gossips or tells of someone else's wrongdoing; informer; tattle.

[1]**tat-too** (ta-tōō′), *n.* **1,** a drum or bugle signal to call soldiers to their quarters; **2,** a presentation of military exercises for entertainment; **3,** a continuous beating or strumming; as, he beat a *tattoo* on the desk:—*v.i.* and *v.t.* [tattooed (ta-tōōd′), tat-too-ing], to beat continuously.

[2]**tat-too** (ta-tōō′), *n.* [*pl.* tattoos], a design made by puncturing the skin and rubbing indelible stain or dye into the punctures:—*v.t.* [tattooed (ta-tōōd′), tattoo-ing], to mark with tattoos.—*n.* **tat-too′er; tat-too′ing; tat-too′ist.**

taught (tôt), *p.t.* and *p.p.* of *teach.*

taunt (tônt; tänt), *n.* a bitter or mocking gibe:—*v.t.* to ridicule with bitter, sarcastic, or insulting language; make fun of; as, they *taunted* him on his failure to make the team.

taupe (tōp), *n.* a greyish-brown colour.

Tau-rus (tô′rus), *n.* **1,** the Bull, a northern constellation, near Gemini and Aries; **2,** the second sign of the zodiac (♉), which the sun enters about April 20; also, a person born under this sign.

taut (tôt), *adj.* **1,** stretched or drawn tight, as a stretched rope; **2,** tense; strained; as, *taut* nerves; **3,** in good condition.

tau-tol-o-gy (tô-tol′o-ji), *n.* needless repetition of an idea in different words; as, to *descend down*, or *necessary essentials*; redundance.

tav-ern (tav′ėrn), *n.* **1,** an inn, esp. in former times; a hotel, esp. one in a rural section; **2,** a place where liquors are sold to be drunk on the premises; a bar.

taw-dry (tô′dri), *adj.* [taw-dri-er, taw-dri-est], showy but cheap; gaudy; as, *tawdry* jewellery.—*n.* **taw′dri-ness.**

taw-ny (tô′ni), *adj.* [taw-ni-er, taw-ni-est],

tan-coloured; of a yellowish-brown colour.

tax (taks), *n.* **1,** a charge or duty on income or property, imposed by a government; as, public services such as schools, hospitals, roads, etc., are supported by the *taxes* paid by the people; **2,** a heavy or oppressive burden; as, a *tax* on one's patience:—*v.t.* **1,** to impose a rate or duty upon, esp. for the support of a government; as, to *tax* all incomes above a certain amount; to *tax* imported goods; **2,** to burden; oppress; as, to *tax* the mind with too much detail; **3,** to accuse; as, to *tax* a person with bribery.—*adj.* **tax′a-ble; tax′-free′** (exempt from tax).—*n.* **tax′pay′er.**

tax-a-tion (taks-ā′shun), *n.* **1,** the act or system of raising money for public use by imposing a charge or duty upon persons or property; **2,** the sum, or tax, imposed.

tax-i (tak′si), *n.* [*pl.* taxis or taxies], a car that can be hired to take a person somewhere; a taxicab:—*v.i.* [taxied, taxi-ing or taxy-ing, taxies or taxis], **1,** of an aircraft, to run along on water or land, as when preparing to rise or after landing; **2,** to ride in a taxicab:—*v.t.* **1,** to cause to taxi, as of an aircraft; **2,** to carry something in or as if in a taxi.

tax-i-cab (tak′si-kab′), *n.* a vehicle provided with a meter that measures and records the fare according to the distance travelled; taxi.

tax-i-der-my (tak′si-dûr′mi), *n.* the art of preparing, stuffing, and mounting the skins of dead animals to give them a lifelike appearance.—*n.* **tax′i-der′mist.**

ta-xo-, or **ta-xi-**, or **tax-** (tak′so; tak′sē; taks), *prefix* meaning *arrangement*; as in *taxonomy* (classification of organisms).

tea (tē), *n.* **1,** a shrub of eastern Asia, cultivated for its leaves; **2,** the dried leaves of the tea plant; **3,** the drink obtained by pouring boiling water on these leaves; **4,** any of various mild beverages resembling tea; as, beef *tea*; herbal *tea*; **5,** in Britain, a light afternoon meal at which tea is served; **6,** an afternoon social affair where tea is served.—*n.* **tea′ bag′; tea′ bis′cuit; tea′room′.**

teach (tēch), *v.t.* [taught (tôt), teaching], **1,** to instruct; educate; as, to *teach* a student; **2,** to give instruction in; as, to *teach* history; **3,** to show or explain how to perform some physical action or skill; as, to *teach* him to ride a bike; **4,** to inform; help to learn; show by example; as, experience has *taught* me to work carefully:—*v.i.* to give instruction; engage in teaching; work as a teacher in a school.

teach-er (tēch′ėr), *n.* a person whose profession is teaching or instructing.

teach-ing (tēch′ing), *n.* **1,** the profession of instructing or educating; as, he went into *teaching*; **2,** that which is taught; as, the *teachings* of Jesus or the prophet Muhammad.

tea-cup (tē′kup′), *n.* **1,** a cup, usually smaller than a coffee cup, in which tea is served; also, any cup of this size; **2,** the amount that such a cup holds; a teacupful.

teak (tēk), *n.* **1,** a tall southeast Asian tree; **2,** its hard, durable timber much used in the making of ships and furniture.

tea-ket-tle (tē′ket′l), *n.* a covered kettle with a spout and handle, in which water is heated.

teal (tēl), *n.* **1,** a swift, small, freshwater wild duck: in Canada, teals are blue-winged and green-winged; **2,** a blue-green colour.

team (tēm), *n.* two or more work horses, oxen, etc., harnessed together to one plow, cart, or carriage; **2,** a number of persons working or playing together; as, a basketball *team*; a *team* of firefighters:—*v.t.* **1,** to join together in a team; as, to *team* horses; **2,** to transport with a team; as, to *team* lumber:—*v.i.* **1,** to make one's living by driving a team; **2,** to work with a group or team; as, he *teamed* up with the other students to work on the project.

team-mate (tēm′māt′), *n.* a person on the same team as another; a fellow worker or player.

team-ster (tēm′stėr), *n.* **1,** the driver of a team of horses or other animals; **2,** one whose business is driving a truck, esp. on long hauls.

team-work (tēm′wûrk′), *n.* smooth work done by several persons acting as a unit to reach the same goal, as distinguished from work done by one person alone; as, superior *teamwork* won us the science prize.

tea-pot (tē′pot′), *n.* a vessel with a spout, handle, and cover, for making and serving tea.

¹tear (târ), *v.t.* [*p.t.* tore (tōr), *p.p.* torn (tōrn), *p.pr.* tear-ing], **1,** to pull apart; as, I *tore* my jeans when I fell; **2,** to cut deeply; gash; as, to *tear* the flesh; **3,** to produce or cause by the action of pulling apart; as, to *tear* a hole in paper; **4,** to remove by force; as, he *tore* the plant up by the roots; **5,** to cause great pain to; as, it *tore* his heart to leave his friend:—*v.i.* **1,** to part on being pulled or roughly handled; as, the cloth *tears* easily; **2,** to move or act with force or excited haste; as, to *tear* across the street:—*n.* **1,** the act of tearing; also, damage caused by tearing; **2,** a hole made by pulling apart; as, there is a large *tear* in my coat.

²tear (tēr), *n.* a small drop of salty, watery liquid secreted by a gland of the eye, or tear duct:—**tears,** the fact of crying from pain or sadness; as to burst into *tears.*—*n.* **tear′drop′.**—*adj.* **tear′ less.**

tear-ful (tēr′fool), *adj.* shedding tears; weeping.—*adv.* **tear′ful-ly.**

tease (tēz), *v.t.* [teased, teas-ing], **1,** to comb or unravel (wool or flax); separate the fibres of; **2,** to roughen the surface of, or raise the nap; as, to *tease* cloth; **3,** to make hair fuller by combing it backward, from the ends to the scalp; **4,** to annoy by petty requests or by good-natured ridicule; make fun of:—*n.* **1,** one who teases; flirt; **2,** the act of teasing.—*n.* **teas′er.**

tea-spoon (tē′spo͞on′), *n.* **1,** a small spoon; **2,** a unit of measure used in cooking, equal to 5 millilitres, or one-third of a tablespoon.—*n.* **tea′spoon-ful.**

teat (tēt), *n.* the nipple on the breast or udder through which milk passes.

tech-ie (tek′i), *n. Colloq.* in *computing,* a person who is skilled in technology, esp. in computers; also, someone who has an avid interest in technology.

tech-ni-cal (tek′ni-kal), *adj.* **1,** having to do with the industrial or mechanical arts and sciences, which uses science to deal with practical problems; as, engineering is a *technical* field of study; **2,** having to do with a certain occupation, profession, or field; as, medicine uses many *technical* words; **3,** having to do with technique; as, she has mastered the *technical* side of piano playing, but her style is very rigid and not very appealing; **4,** according to strict and exact rules or judgment; as, to be *technical,* that animal is a bison, not a buffalo:—**technical support**, in *computing,* assistance, often free of charge, available by a manufacturer to a user of hardware or software products, esp. by phone or e-mail.—*adv.* **tech′ni-cal-ly.**

tech-ni-cal-i-ty (tek′ni-kal′i-ti), *n.* [*pl.* technicalities], **1,** the quality of belonging to, or being characteristic of, a particular occupation or science; as, the *technicality* of scientific language; **2,** a small point, formally exact, but often of a quibbling nature and relevant only to someone who specializes in a certain field; as, he was acquitted on a legal *technicality.*

tech-ni-cian (tek-nish′an), *n.* a person who has skill in some technical field; an expert in the use of certain instruments or machinery; as, a computer *technician.*

tech-nique (tek-nēk′), *n.* the method of handling details or fundamentals in the practice of any fine art or science, or in doing anything that requires special skill; a method or plan of action.

tech-nol-o-gy (tek-nol′o-ji), *n.* **1,** the science of industrial arts and manufacture; the use of tools, machines, inventions, and scientific principles to do work and solve problems; **2,** the terms used in science, art, etc.—*adj.* **tech′no-log′i-cal.**

ted-dy (ted′i), *n.* **1,** a teddy bear; **2,** a woman's undergarment consisting of a top and panties.

teddy bear or **Teddy bear**, a child's toy somewhat like a small stuffed bear (in plush): named after Theodore Roosevelt, U.S. president (1907).

te-di-ous (tē′dē-us), *adj.* wearisome; tiresome; very boring; as, *tedious* work.—*n.* **te′di-um** (boredom).

[1]**tee** (tē), *n.* in *golf,* **1,** a small pointed plastic or wooden pin with cupped top on which a ball is placed for the first stroke on a hole; **2,** the place or area set apart for making the first stroke on a hole:—*v.t.* and *v.i.* [teed (tēd), tee-ing], to place (a ball) on a tee and hit it off the tee to start playing a hole; as, he *teed* off early in the morning.

[2]**tee** (tē), *n.* the letter T; also, something shaped like a T, as a metal beam.

teem (tēm), *v.i.* to be very productive; be full; be stocked or crowded to overflowing; as, the city *teemed* with tourists.

teen-ag-er or **teen–ag-er** (tēn′āj′ėr), *n.* a person in his or her teens (between the ages of 13 and 19).—*adj.* **teen′age′** or **teen′–age′; teen′aged′** or **teen′–aged′.**

teens (tēnz), *n.pl.* the years of one's age marked by numbers ending in *-teen,* from 13 to 19; as, a girl in her *teens.*

tee-ny or **teen-sy** (tē′ni; tēn′si), *adj. Colloq.* tiny.

tee-pee (tē′pē), *n.* Same as **tepee.**

tee-ter (tē′tėr), *v.t.* and *v.i.* **1,** to seesaw or cause to seesaw; sway from side to side; stand or move in an unsteady way; **2,** to vacillate:—*n.* a seesaw; a swaying motion.

tee-ter-tot-ter (tētėr–tot′ėr), *n.* a seesaw.

teeth (tēth), *n.pl.* of *tooth.*

teethe (tē*th*), *v.i.* [teethed, teeth-ing], to cut teeth; also, to grow or develop teeth.—*n.* **teeth′er; teeth′ing.**

tee-to-tal-ler or **tee-to-tal-er** (tē′tō′tal-ėr), *n.* a total abstainer from intoxicating liquors.—*adj.* **tee-to′tal.**—*n.* **tee′to′tal-ist; tee-to′tal-ism.**

tel-e- (tel′e-), *prefix* meaning **1,** *at a distance;* as in *tele*communication (communication at a distance), *tele*photo (relating to a photographic lens used for distant objects), *tele*scope; **2,** *telephone, telegraph, television;* as in *tele*banking, *tele*conference, *tele*marketing, *tele*gram, *tele*cast, *tele*play, *tele*thon.

tel-e-cast (tel′e-kast′), *n.* a program broadcast by television program.

tel-e-com (tel′e-käm′), *n. abbrev.* short for *telecommunication.*

tel-e-com-mu-ni-ca-tion (tel′i-ko-mū-ni-kā′shun), *n.* the process of sending messages or broadcasts at a distance by telephone, radio, television, computer, etc.; also, the system used to send such a message, or the message itself.

tel-e-gram (tel′e-gram′), *n.* a message sent by telegraph.

tel-e-graph (tel′e-gråf′), *n.* a piece of equipment or system for sending and receiving messages at a distance by means of electronic signals carried by wires or cables, used esp. in former times:—*v.t.* to send by means of such an instrument; as, to *telegraph* news; also, to send a message to by such means; as, to *tele-*

graph a friend:—*v.i.* to send a message by telegraph.—*adj.* **tel′e-graph′ic.**—*n.* **te-leg′ra-pher** (te-leg′ra-fėr); **te-leg-ra-phy** (te-leg′ra-fi).

te-lep-a-thy (te-lep′a-thi), *n.* the apparent transferring of thought from one mind to another other than through the recognized sense organs.

tel-e-phone (tel′e-fōn′), *n.* an instrument for transmitting speech over wires or through the air over a distance by means of electricity:—*v.t.* [telephoned, telephon-ing], to send (a message) by telephone; also, to, communicate with by telephone; as, to *telephone* a friend:—*v.i.* to send a message by telephone; call or talk by telephone.—*adj.* **tel′e-phon′ic.**—*n.* **tel′e-phon′er; te-leph′o-ny.**

tel-e-pho-to (tel′i-fō′tō), *adj.* relating to the process of photographing distant objects; as, to photograph an object using a *telephoto* lens.

tel-e-scope (tel′e-skōp′), *n.* an optical instrument used for viewing objects at a distance, esp. the moon, stars, planets, etc.: it makes distant objects seem much closer and larger:—*v.t.* [telescoped, telescop-ing], **1,** to drive or force together, as colliding railway cars, so that one part slides into another, like sections of a collapsible telescope; **2,** to condense:—*v.i.* to be forced together in this manner.—*adj.* **tel′e-scop′ic** (tel′e-skop′ik).

tel-e-vise (tel′e-vīz′), *v.t.* and *v.i.* [televised, televis-ing], to broadcast or be broadcast by television.

tel-e-vi-sion (tel′e-vizh′un), *n.* **1,** the process of sending and receiving, by means of electronic signals, images and sounds; **2,** a device used to receive such signals and display images on a screen; television set; **3,** programs broadcast in this way; as, to watch *television* after finishing homework; **4,** the business or industry that produces and broadcasts programs on television.

tell (tel), *v.t.* [told (tōld), tell-ing], **1,** to relate in words; narrate or write; as, to *tell* a story; **2,** to say; utter; as, to *tell* a lie; **3,** to disclose; confess; as, to *tell* a secret; **4,** to decide; as, I cannot *tell* what is best to do; also, to recognize; as, to *tell* the difference; **5,** to order; command; as, he *told* his dog to sit; **6,** to make known by some sign or indication; as, a thermometer *tells* how hot or cold it is:—*v.i.* **1,** to give an account; as, he *told* of days gone by; **2,** to play the informer; as, Jeanne *told* on Aaron; **3,** to have a marked effect; as, each blow *told.*

tell-er (tel′ėr), *n.* **1,** one who tells, discloses, narrates, etc.; as, a story writer is sometimes called a *teller* of tales; **2,** a bank clerk who counts, receives, and pays out money over the counter; **3,** a bank machine; ATM; **4,** one who counts the votes in a legislative body, meeting, etc.

tell-ing (tel′ing), *adj.* striking; impressive; as, his words had a *telling* effect.

tell-tale (tel′tāl′), *adj.* revealing or betraying (something intended to be secret); as, a *telltale* blush:—*n.* **1,** a tattler; informer; **2,** something that reveals, indicates, or monitors information.

te-mer-i-ty (te-mer′i-ti), *n.* boldness; rashness; as, the employee had the *temerity* to criticize her employer.

tem-per (tem′pėr), *v.t.* **1,** to mix to the proper degree of softness; as, to *temper* clay; also, to soften or ease; as, to *temper* a rebuke with a smile; **2,** to bring to the proper degree of hardness or toughness; as, to *temper* steel; **3,** to reduce; moderate; as, sympathy *tempers* grief:—*n.* **1,** the degree of hardness, softness, toughness, etc., of a substance, as of steel, clay, or mortar; consistency; **2,** disposition or mood or feeling; as, he is in a bad *temper* today; **3,** anger; as, to show *temper*; **4,** control of one's anger or emotions; as, to lose one's *temper.*—*adj.* **tem′pered.**

tem-per-a-ment (tem′pėr-a-ment), *n.* disposition; a person's nature; the characteristic mental and emotional makeup of a person; as, an artistic *temperament*; an outgoing *temperament.*

tem-per-a-men-tal (tem′pėr-a-men′tl), *adj.* **1,** easily upset or made angry; as, a *temperamental* ruler; **2,** unpredictable; as, a *temperamental* laser printer; **3,** having to do with temperament; caused by one's nature.—*adv.* **tem′per-a-men′tal-ly.**

tem-per-ance (tem′pėr-ans), *n.* **1,** moderation; avoidance of extremes, esp. in eating and drinking; **2,** moderation in, or abstinence from, the use of alcoholic liquors.

tem-per-ate (tem′pėr-it), *adj.* **1,** inclined not to eat or drink to excess; moderate; also, seldom using alcoholic liquors; **2,** calm; restrained; showing self-control; as, a *temperate* disposition; **3,** free from extremes of heat or cold; as, a *temperate* climate.—*adv.* **tem′per-ate-ly.**—*n.* **tem′per-ate-ness.**

tem-per-a-ture (tem′pėr-a-tūr), *n.* **1,** the degree or amount of heat or cold as measured by a thermometer; **2,** the degree of heat of the human body; as, normal body *temperature* is 37 degrees Celsius; **3,** an excess of body temperature; fever; as, a child, when ill, often has a high *temperature.*

tem-pest (tem′pest), *n.* **1,** a violent windstorm, usually accompanied by rain, hail, etc.; **2,** any violent tumult or agitation; uproar; as, a *tempest* of fury.

tem-pes-tu-ous (tem-pes′tū-us), *adj.* stormy; agitated; as, *tempestuous* seas; a *tempestuous* relationship.

tem-plate (tem′plāt) or **tem-plet** (tem′plit), *n.* **1,** a thin pattern of wood or metal serving as a gauge or guide, esp. a flat plate or strip with holes for use in riveting, drilling, etc.; **2,** in a wall, a horizontal stone, timber, etc., to take and distribute the weight of a girder, beam, etc.; **3,** in *computing,* a particular, frequently used pattern, which is stored for use in various programs or parts of programs; as, a spreadsheet *template.*

[1]**tem-ple** (tem′pl), *n.* **1,** a building dedicated to the worship of a deity; as, a Mayan *temple;* **2,** one of the three successive buildings for Jewish worship in ancient Jerusalem; **3,** a Jewish synagogue; **4,** a building for Christian public worship, esp. a Mormon church.

[2]**tem-ple** (tem′pl), *n.* the flat part of the head at each side, between the eye and the upper part of the ear.

tem-po (tem′pō), *n.* **1,** characteristic speed and rhythm; as, the *tempo* of city life; **2,** in *music,* the relative pace or time.

tem-po-ral (tem′po-ral), *adj.* **1,** limited in time; not eternal or everlasting; **2,** worldly or earthly; **3,** pertaining to civil matters or to affairs of political life; secular; not of the church; as, *temporal* powers; **4,** relating to the temples of the head.

tem-po-rar-y (tem′po-rėr-i), *adj.* continuing for a limited time only; not permanent; as, *temporary* relief.—*adv.* **tem′po-rar-i-ly.**

tem-po-rize (tem′po-rīz′), *v.i.* [tempo-rized, temporiz-ing], **1,** to put off an action or decision in order to gain time; **2,** to take part in discussions or negotiations for the purpose of delay.

tempt (tempt), *v.t.* **1,** to persuade or try to persuade a person to do something wrong or forbidden; to entice; as, to *tempt* someone to cheat; **2,** to attract; invite; as, some foods *tempt* me more than others.—*adj.* **tempt′ing.**—*n.* **tempt′ er; tempt′ress.**

temp-ta-tion (temp-tā′shun), *n.* **1,** the act of being tempted; **2,** an enticement; as, the open wallet was a *temptation* to steal.

ten (ten), *adj.* composed of one more than nine, or twice five:—*n.* **1,** the sum of five and five; **2,** a sign representing 10 units, as 10 or X.

ten-a-ble (ten′a-bl), *adj.* capable of being held, maintained, or defended, as, a *tenable* theory.

te-na-cious (te-nā′shus), *adj.* **1,** holding on to something firmly; as, the political party has a *tenacious* hold on power; not letting go; as, the *tenacious* grip of a bulldog; **2,** especially capable of retaining or remembering; as, a *tenacious* mind; **3,** clinging; as, *tenacious* burrs stuck to my clothing.—*n.* **te-nac′i-ty** (te-nas′i-ti).

ten-ant (ten′ant), *n.* **1,** a person or business that has use or possession of property for a certain length of time in return for the payment of rent; **2,** an occupant of a place:—*v.t.* to hold as a tenant; occupy.—*adj.* **ten′ant-less.**—*n.* **ten′an-cy.**

[1]**tend** (tend), *v.i.* **1,** to move or go in a certain direction; as, the point to which an argument *tends;* also, to exhibit a natural tendency toward something; as, her talents *tend* toward music; **2,** to be likely to have a certain result; as, ill health *tends* to produce irritation.

[2]**tend** (tend), *v.t.* to attend to; take care of; protect; as, the shepherd *tends* his sheep; to have charge of; as, *tending* goal.

tend-en-cy (ten′den-si), *n.* [*pl.* tendencies], **1,** direction; trend or movement in some direction; as, there was a *tendency* toward anarchy in the state; **2,** natural bent or inclination; as, he had a *tendency* to get angry easily.

[1]**tend-er** (ten′dėr), *n.* **1,** a person who attends or takes care of; as, a bar*tender;* **2,** a small car containing coal and water, attached behind a locomotive; **3,** a small vessel attending and supplying a larger one, with fuel, provisions, etc.; **4,** a small boat used to land passengers from a ship.

[2]**ten-der** (ten′dėr), *v.t.* **1,** to offer something formally; as, to *tender* one's resignation; **2,** to offer money in payment of a debt; **3,** to make an offer to buy or supply products or services; as, to *tender* for a contract.—*n.* an offer, bid, or proposal; also, the thing offered:—**legal tender,** currency that a lender must, by law, accept when it is offered in repayment of money owed.

[3]**ten-der** (ten′dėr), *adj.* **1,** easily chewed or cut; **2,** not hardy or tough; as, the *tender* shoots of a plant; also, easily hurt or injured; as, *tender* skin; **3,** easily touched by pain, grief, love, or kindness; as, a *tender* heart; also, gentle; kind; loving; as, *tender* words; **4,** young; as, at the *tender* age of two.—*adv.* **ten′der-ly.**—*n.* **ten′der-ness.**

ten-der-foot (ten′dėr-foot′), *n.* [*pl.* tender-feet (-fēt′)], **1,** a person who has had no exposure to rough living or hardships; esp. a greenhorn or newcomer to pioneer life in the West; **2,** a novice or inexperienced person.

ten-der-ize (ten′dėr-īz′), *v.t.* to make tender; esp. meat, by pounding or marinating.

ten-der-loin (ten′dėr-loin′), *n.* the tenderest part of a loin of beef or pork.

ten-di-ni-tis (ten′di-nī′tis), *n.* inflammation of a tendon, often from overuse.

ten-don (ten′dun), *n.* a tough cord or band of fibrous tissue attaching a muscle to a bone, to another muscle, or to an organ of the body.

ten-dril (ten′dril), *n.* **1,** a slender shoot of a climbing plant, often in spiral form, used by the plant to attach itself to a structure; **2,** anything that resembles this part of a plant, as a curl, a ringlet, or a *tendril* of smoke.

ten-e-ment (ten′e-ment), *n.* a building with rental apartments or rooms, esp. one with cheap rents, run-down, and in a poor area of a city.

ten-et (ten′it), *n.* a principle or belief.

ten-fold (ten′fōld′), *adj.* and *adv.* 10 times as much or as great.

ten-nis (ten′is), *n.* a game played by two or four people; players use tennis rackets to hit a ball back and forth over a net stretched across a court.

ten-or (ten′ėr), *n.* **1,** general character or state; as, the angry *tenor* of the debate; **2,** general tendency, direction, or course; as, the *tenor* of a person's life; **3,** the second highest adult male singing voice; also, a part written for this voice; **4,** one who sings such a part; also, a musical instrument like a viola with a range just above the bass:—*adj.* relating to; as, *tenor* saxophone.

[1]**tense** (tens), *adj.* [tens-er, tens-est], stretched tight; rigid; as, *tense* muscles; showing or feeling mental strain; high-strung:—*v.t.* [tensed, tens-ing] to stretch tight; as, she *tenses* her muscles:—*v.i.* to become tense; as, he *tensed* up before the competition.—*adv.* **tense′ly.**

[2]**tense** (tens), *n.* in *grammar*, the form a verb takes to indicate the time of an action or state of being, past, present, or future.

ten-sile (ten′sil), *adj.* **1,** relating to tension or the act of stretching; **2,** capable of being stretched or strained; as, *tensile* wire.

ten-sion (ten′shun), *n.* **1,** the act of stretching; **2,** the state of being stretched or strained; as, too much muscle *tension* can cause pain; **3,** mental strain; intensity of feeling; stress; **4,** strained relations; as, *tension* between relatives.

tent (tent), *n.* a portable shelter, usually of nylon, canvas, or another flexible material, supported by poles and ropes, often fastened down by pegs driven into the ground:—*v.i.* to camp out in a tent.

ten-ta-cle (ten′ta-kl), *n.* **1,** a long, thin, flexible appendage of an animal (esp. invertebrates) used for feeling, grasping, or moving; **2,** a sensitive hair or filament on parts of a plant.

A SQUID'S TENTACLES

ten-ta-tive (ten′ta-tiv), *adj.* **1,** done as a trial or experiment; as, a *tentative* solution (to a problem); not final, provisional; as, a *tentative* agreement; **2,** timid, uncertain; as, a *tentative* statement.

ten-ter-hooks (ten′tėr-hooks′), *n.* hooks that hold cloth (stretched on a framework or tenter):—**to be on tenter-hooks,** to be in a state of painful suspense.

tenth (tenth), *adj.* next after the ninth: the ordinal of 10:—*n.* one of the 10 equal parts into which anything is or may be divided.

ten-u-ous (ten′ū-us), *adj.* **1,** thin; slender; slight; as, a *tenuous* hold (on life); **2,** flimsy; unsubstantial; meagre; as, a *tenuous* plot (to a story).

ten-ure (ten′ūr), *n.* **1,** the right, or manner, of holding real estate; as, land *tenure*; **2,** the period during which a position or office is held; as, do so during my *tenure* of office; **3,** the right of permanent employment after certain conditions have been met; as, the professor was given *tenure* after 10 years of teaching.

te-pee or **tee-pee** or **ti-pi** (tē′pē), *n.* a cone-shaped tent, originally made of animal skins or tree bark, used by some native North Americans as a dwelling, esp. among the Plains tribes. Compare *wigwam.*

tep-id (tep′id), *adj.* **1,** moderately warm; lukewarm; as, a *tepid* bath; **2,** not enthusiastic; as, a *tepid* response (to a proposal).

ter-cen-te-na-ry (tûr-sen′ti-na-ri), *adj.* comprising 300 years; as, a *tercentenary* celebration:—*n.* the 300th anniversary of an event.

ter-i-ya-ki (târ′ē-ya′kē), *n.* **1,** in Japanese cooking, fish, meat, or vegetables marinated in soy sauce, etc., and then broiled or grilled; **2,** the sauce.

term (tûrm), *n.* **1,** a fixed period of time; the time during which a thing lasts; as, a *term* of office; the school's fall *term*; a prison *term*; **2,** a word or expression, esp. one belonging to a particular art, business, etc.; as, "investment" is a financial *term*; **3,** in *mathematics*, one of the parts of a proportion or ratio:—**terms, 1,** conditions or arrangements; as, *terms* of a sale; **2,** relationship; as, to be on good *terms* with a person:—*v.t.* to name or call; as, the police *termed* his mysterious death murder.

ter-mi-nal (tûr′mi-nal), *adj.* **1,** relating to a fatal illness; **2,** having to do with the end of a railroad, bus, or airline service; as, a *terminal* station; **3,** at the end; coming last; growing at the end of a shoot or branch; as, a *terminal* bud:—*n.* **1,** a limit or boundary; **2,** the departure and arrival building for train, bus, or air passengers; **3,** in *computing,* a device for entering and receiving data from a computer, most often by using a keyboard and monitor; **4,** a facility for storing products like oil or grain at the end of a pipeline or railroad; **5,** one end of an electrical circuit.

ter-mi-nate (tûr′mi-nāt′), *v.t.* [terminated, terminat-ing], **1,** to bring to an end; to finish; as, the two countries *terminated* friendly relations; **2,** to dismiss or fire (an employee):—*v.i.* to end; as, the contract *terminates* in June.—*n.* **ter′mi-na′tion.**

ter-mi-nol-o-gy (tûr′mi-nol′o-ji), *n.* the special terms or expressions belonging to a science, art, or business; as, the *terminology* of nuclear physics; nomenclature.

ter-mi-nus (tûr′mi-nus), *n.* [*pl.* terminuses or termini (tûr′mi-nī′)], **1,** a limit or goal; **2,** an end of a railway, bus, or airline; the town and station there.

ter-mite (tûr′mīt), *n.* any of an order of small ant-like insects that live in large colonies: some species eat cellulose and can cause much damage to anything made of wood.

tern (tûrn), *n.* any of a subfamily of aquatic birds with long, narrow wings, a forked tail, a pointed bill and, typically, black and white markings.

ter-race (ter′is), *n.* **1,** a paved area next to, or on the roof of, a house or building, often used for social gatherings; patio; **2,** a flat area made on the side of a hill or slope to provide a level surface for growing crops:—*v.t.* [terraced, terrac-ing], to furnish with a terrace or terraces; as, to *terrace* a lawn.

ter-ra–cot-ta (ter′a–kot′a), *n.* reddish-brown unglazed pottery of baked clay or earth; also, its reddish-brown colour.

ter-rain (te-rān′; ter′ān), *n.* a piece of ground considered for the physical features that make it suitable for a special purpose; as, landing aircraft, camping, military manoeuvres, etc.

ter-rar-i-um (tûr-âr′ē-um′), *n.* an enclosed glass or plastic container for keeping live plants or small animals such as turtles and snakes.

ter-res-tri-al (te-res′tri-al), *adj.* **1,** consisting of earth or land; as, the *terrestrial* globe; consisting of land as distinguished from water; as, *terrestrial* portions of the earth; **2,** belonging to the earth, not to the heavens; as, a *terrestrial* being; **3,** existing on land, not in the water, trees, or air; as, *terrestrial* animals.

ter-ri-ble (ter′i-bl), *adj.* **1,** causing fear or suffering; dreadful; as, a *terrible* disaster; **2,** extreme; very damaging; as, a *terrible* storm; **3,** extreme; excessive; as, a *terrible* hurry.—*adv.* **ter′ri-bly.**

ter-ri-er (ter′i-ėr), *n.* an active, intelligent dog, usually of small size, and noted for its alertness and gameness, esp. in killing rats and mice: used to hunt burrowing animals.

ter-rif-ic (te-rif′ik), *adj.* **1,** causing fear or terror; alarming; dreadful; as, a *terrific* explosion; **2,** excessive; extreme; as, a *terrific* amount of work; **3,** excellent; extraordinary; as, a *terrific* speech.

ter-ri-fy (ter′i-fī′), *v.t.* [terrified, terrify-ing], to fill with great alarm or terror; frighten greatly; as, the storm *terrified* him.—*adj.* **ter′ri-fy′ing.**

ter-ri-to-ri-al (ter′i-tôr′ē-al), *adj.* having to do with a territory or territories.

ter-ri-tor-y (ter′i-tôr-i), *n.* [*pl.* territories], **1,** a large tract of land; region; as, Canada covers a large *territory*; also, an assigned district; as, the salesperson's *territory* covers the entire province; **2,** the entire extent of land and water under the control of one ruler or government; as, Canadian *territory*:—**Territory,** a region of a country that is not a province or state; as, the Yukon *Territory*.

ter-ror (ter′ėr), *n.* **1,** very great fear; alarm; **2,** a person or thing causing great fear; as, the tyrant was a *terror* to his subjects.—*adj.* **ter′ror–strick′en.**

ter-ror-ism (ter′ėr-ism) *n.* the use or threat of violence to gain a political or ideological goal.—*n.* **ter′ror-ist.**

ter-ror-ize (ter′ėr-īz′), *v.t.* [terrorized, terroriz-ing], **1,** to fill with great alarm or fear; reduce to a state of terror; **2,** to govern by methods which arouse fear.

terse (tûrs), *adj.* [ters-er, ters-est], concise or brief; exactly to the point; as, a *terse* literary style.—*adv.* **terse′ly.**—*n.* **terse′ness.**

ter-ti-a-ry (tûr′shi-a-ri; -sha-ri), *adj.* and *n.* **1,** third, in rank, degree, class, etc.; as, a *tertiary* defence (in football); **2,** in *geology*, the Third Period of rock formations, from 60 to 12 million years ago: the great reptiles had disappeared, the mammals were beginning, and the great mountains (Alps, Andes, Himalayas, etc.) were forming.

test (test), *n.* **1,** trial; proof; as, his character was put to a *test*; examination; as, a *test* in keyboarding; **2,** a criterion or standard by which a person or thing may be gauged; as, self–control is the *test* of a person's power; **3,** in *chemistry*, an experiment for discovering the presence of any particular substance in a compound:—*v.t.* **1,** to give a *test* to; examine; question; as, to *test* a person's ability; **2,** in *chemistry*, to try to find a particular substance in; as, to *test* alcohol for poison.—*n.* **test′er.**

tes-ta-ment (tes′ta-ment), *n.* a written document in which a person provides for the disposal of property after death; as, the phrase *last will and testament*:—**Testament,** **1,** either of the two main parts of the Bible; **2,** a book containing only the New Testament.—*adj.* **tes′ta-men′ta-ry** (bequeathed by will).

tes-ti-cle (tes′ti-kl) or **tes′tis** (tes′tis), *n.* [*pl.* testicles; testes (-tēz)], either of the two male sex glands that produce sperm and the hormone testosterone.

tes-ti-fy (tes′ti-fī′), *v.i.* [testified, testify-ing], **1,** to give evidence in a court of law; as, the witness *testified* in the prisoner's behalf; to declare something as true under oath; **2,** to make a statement of truth, based on knowledge or first-hand experience; **3,** to serve as evidence; as, her paintings *testify* to her ability as an artist:—*v.t.* to declare solemnly on oath; bear witness to.—*n.* **tes′ti-fi′er.**

tes-ti-mo-ni-al (tes′ti-mō′ni-al), *n.* **1,** a writing or certificate regarding the character, ability, etc., of a person, or the value of a thing; **2,** a token of respect, acknowledgement of services, etc., presented to a person.

tes-ti-mo-ny (tes′ti-mo-ni), *n.* [*pl.* testimonies], **1,** evidence; proof; as, fossil-bearing rocks give *testimony* to life in former ages; **2,** a formal statement made under oath in a court of law; as, the witness's *testimony* was very clear.

test tube, a small glass tube with a closed, rounded bottom, used in laboratory tests and experiments.

testy (tes′ti), *adj.* [tes-ti-er, tes-ti-est], touchy; irritable.—*adv.* **tes′ti-ly.**—*n.* **tes′ti-ness.**

tet-a-nus (tet′a-nus), *n.* an acute, infectious, often fatal, disease marked by muscular spasms or rigidity caused by a bacillus that enters through wounds.

tête-à-tête (tāt′-a-tāt′; tâ′-tå-tât′), *n.* confidential, friendly talk between two persons:—*adj.* face to face; confidential.

teth-er (te*th*′ėr), *n.* **1,** a rope or chain to fasten an animal; **2,** the limit of a person's strength or resources; as, she was at the end of her *tether*:—*v.t.* to tie with a rope or chain.

Tex–Mex (teks–meks), *n. Colloq.* a Texan style of cooking that has adapted elements from Mexican cuisine: generally a more moderate use of hot flavours like chilies:—*adj.* relating to the blend of Texan and Mexican cooking, and other cultural elements, characteristic of the southwestern U.S.

text (tekst), *n.* **1,** the main body of any written or printed matter, separate from the illustrations, notes, etc.; **2,** the subject of a discussion, speech, etc.; theme; **3,** a book used for instruction; a *text*book.

text-book (tekst′book′), *n.* a standard book of instruction in a branch of study; as, a chemistry *textbook*.

text box, in *computing*, an area inside a window (rectangular viewing area) on a screen where a person can type or edit text.

tex-tile (teks′tīl; teks′til), *n.* [*pl.* textiles], fabric or cloth:—*adj.* relating to the production of; as, *textile* mill.

tex-ture (teks′tūr), *n.* **1,** the structure or arrangement of threads making up a fabric; as, satin has a smooth *texture*; **2,** composition; structure; as, the compact *texture* of clay; **3,** the way a surface feels to the touch; as, rough, smooth, soft, bumpy, etc.

than (*th*an), *conj.* **1,** in comparison with; as, you are taller *than* Maria; **2,** used to show a preference; as, I'd rather stay home *than* go to the concert; **3,** besides; but; as, no one other *than* my parents can help me.

thank (thangk), *v.t.* to express gratitude to:—**thanks,** *n.pl.* expression of gratitude.—*adj.* **thank′ful.**

thank-less (thangk′lis), *adj.* **1,** ungrateful; not feeling or expressing gratitude; as, a *thankless* child; **2,** not gaining gratitude; unprofitable; as, a *thankless* task.—*adv.* **thank′less-ly.**

thanks-giv-ing (thangks′giv′ing; thangks-giv′ing), *n.* the act of expressing gratitude:—**Thanksgiving Day,** in Canada, an annual holiday for feasting, and giving thanks for the success of the harvest: originally a religious festival: celebrated on the second Monday in October.

that (*th*at), *adj.* [*pl.* those (*th*ōz)], **1,** indicating someone or something at a distance in time or space; the farther; as, please take *that* chair upstairs; who are *those* people; **2,** pointing out a single, particular, or known thing or person; as, ask *those* people best able to pay; **3,** the other; the second; the latter; as, on this side and *that* side:—*demonstrative pron.* **1,** a person or thing at a distance; not this; as, *that* is not fair; these must stay, *those* may go; **2,** a person or thing already indicated or to be indicated; as, so *that* is what he said; *that* is the man you mean; **3,** the other, second, or farther person or thing; as, this wood is softer than *that*:—*relative pron.* **1,** who or whom; which; as, the man *that* you saw; **2,** in, on, or at which; when; as, all those years *that* he was gone; also, for which; as, the reason *that* he came:—*conj.* **1,** used to introduce a clause which is the object or the subject of a verb; as, he said *that* he would come; *that* he lied is bad; **2,** with a purpose; as, work *that* you may succeed; **3,** with the result; as, I am so sleepy *that* I can hardly see; **4,** to express a wish; as, oh, *that* you were here!—*adv.* to a certain amount or degree; as, I'm tired but not *that* tired.

thatch (thach), *n.* a roof or covering made of straw, reeds, palm leaves, etc.; also, the material used:—*v.t.* to cover or roof with straw, reeds, etc.; as, they *thatched* the cottage last week.

thaw (thô), *v.i.* **1,** to melt or become liquid, as ice or snow; **2,** to change from a solid to a liquid because of a rise in temperature; as, take the meat out of the freezer so it can *thaw* out; **3,** to become warmer or friendlier; to unbend; as, his manner *thawed* perceptibly:—*v.t.* to cause to melt:—*n.* the melting of ice or snow as a result of warm weather; also, a state of weather when ice and snow melt.

the (*th*ė when unaccented before a consonant, as in *the cat*; *th*ē or *th*i when unaccented before a vowel, as in *the ear*; *th*ē when emphatic or alone), *adj.* or *definite article* **1,** pointing out a specific or known person or thing; as, *the* boy in the back row; *the* book I gave you; **2,** a; any; every; as, *the* cow is a useful animal; **3,** that which is, or those who are; as, *the* beautiful; *the* great; **4,** being best, greatest, or most important; as, *the* event of the year:—*prep.* a; to each; as, 20 lines to *the* page:—*adv.* to that degree; by that amount; as, *the* sooner you clean your room, *the* sooner you can go out.

the-a-tre or **the-a-ter** (thē′a-tėr), *n.* **1,** a building or place where plays, movies, etc., are presented; **2,** dramatic art; the drama; **3,** a place where important action takes place; as, Waterloo was once the *theatre* of battle.

the-at-ri-cal (thi-at′ri-kal), *adj.* **1,** having to do with the theatre, a dramatic performance, or actors; as, *theatrical* costumes; **2,**

suitable for, or characteristic of, the stage; conspicuous; as, a *theatrical* entrance.

theft (theft), *n.* **1,** the act of stealing; robbery; **2,** the property stolen; as, the *theft* amounted to ten dollars.

their (*th*âr), *adj.* a possessive form of the personal pronoun *they*: **1,** belonging to them; of them; as, *their* house; **2,** coming from them; as, *their* kindness.

theirs (*th*ârz), a possessive form of *they*, used alone: **1,** as *adj.* in the predicate, belonging to them; as, whose is that car? it is *theirs*; **2,** as *pron.*, a person or thing that belongs to them; as, our car is blue, *theirs* is black.

them (*th*em), *pron.* objective case of *they*.

theme (thēm), *n.* **1,** the subject or topic of a speech, essay, etc.; **2,** a short essay or composition on a given subject; **3,** in *music*, an often recurring series of notes forming the subject of a composition or the main melody of a song, movie, television show, or particular entertainer.

them-selves (*th*em-selvz′), *pron.* the plural form of *himself, herself,* and *itself*; the emphatic form of *they* or reflexive form of *them*; as, they *themselves* are going; they caused *themselves* much trouble.

then (*th*en), *adv.* **1,** in that case; therefore; in consequence; as, go *then* and buy what we need; if you must, *then* do it; **2,** next; immediately after; as, wash it; *then* dry it; **3,** at that time; as, *then* Rome fell; **4,** later; at another time; as, come *then* instead:—*adj.* existing at the time mentioned; as, the *then* poet laureate:—*n.* a time mentioned; as, by *then* he was ready.

the-ol-o-gy (thē-ol′o-ji), *n.* [*pl.* theologies], **1,** the study of religion; **2,** a system of religious beliefs.—*adj.* **the′o-log′i-cal** (thē-o-loj′i-kal).—*n.* **the′o-lo′gian.**

the-o-ret-i-cal (thē′o-ret′i-kal) or **the-o-ret-ic** (thē′o-ret′ik), *adj.* **1,** relating to, or depending on, abstract principles or theories; **2,** based on ideas rather than on fact or experience; not practical; as, *theoretical* knowledge.—*adv.* **the′o-ret′i-cal-ly.**

the-o-rize (thē′o-rīz′), *v.i.* [theorized, theoriz-ing], to form or express a theory.

the-o-ry (thē′o-ri), *n.* [*pl.* theories], **1,** a statement of the fundamental principles of an art or science rather than the actual practice of it; as, the *theory* of music; **2,** a set of facts or ideas generally accepted as an explanation of some event or condition in nature; as, the *theory* of relativity; **3,** a view or opinion, not necessarily based on facts; a guess; conjecture; as, her *theory* of the crime.—*n.* **the′o-rist.**

ther-a-py (ther′a-pi), *n.* in *medicine*, the treatment of any disease, physical or mental, without surgery; as, chemo*therapy*, psycho*therapy*, etc.—*n.pl.* **ther′a-peu′tics** (the science and art of healing).—*adj.* **ther′a-peu′tic** (healing; curative).—*n.* **ther′a-pist′** (a person trained to give a certain kind of therapy).

there (*th*âr), *adv.* **1,** in or at that place; not here; as, put the book *there*; **2,** to or toward that place; as, I will go *there* today; **3,** in that matter, respect, etc.; as, you're wrong *there*, I think; **4,** used preceding a verb or in questions to introduce a sentence; as, is *there* time? *there* is time:—*interj.* **1,** expressing defiance, triumph, etc.; as, I won't go. So *there*! **2,** expressing sympathy; as, *there, there*, don't worry.

there-a-bouts (*th*âr′a-bouts) or **there-a-bout** (*th*âr′a-bout′), *adv.* near that place, time, number, etc.; nearly.

there-aft-er (*th*âr-åf′tėr), *adv.* after that; thereupon.

there-by (*th*âr-bī′), *adv.* **1,** by that means; **2,** near by; **3,** in that connection; as, *there-by* hangs a tale.

there-fore (*th*âr′fôr), *adv.* for that reason; on that account.

there-in (*th*âr-in′), *adv.* **1,** in or into this or that place, time, etc.; **2,** in this or that respect; as, *therein* you err.

ther-mal (thûr′mal), *adj.* **1,** having to do with heat; as, a *thermal* unit; helping to retain heat; as, *thermal* underwear; **2,** warm; hot; as, *thermal* baths or springs.

ther-mom-e-ter (thėr-mom′e-tėr), *n.* an instrument for measuring temperature and temperature changes, esp. one consisting of a sealed glass tube partly filled with mercury or another liquid: the expansion or contraction of the liquid due to heat changes is indicated on a scale marked off in degrees on the side of the tube.

ther-mo-nu-cle-ar (thûr′mō-nū′kli-ėr), *adj.* using heat energy released in nuclear fission.

ther-mos (thûr′mos), *adj.* an insulated container used to keep liquids either hot or cold:—**Thermos,** a trademark name for a brand of such containers.

ther-mo-stat (thûr′mō-stat′), *n.* a device that automatically controls the temperature of something; as, you can reduce the amount of fuel you use by lowering your *thermostat*.

the-sau-rus (thi-sō′rus), *n.* [*pl.* thesauruses or thesauri], a reference book that contains groups of words that share a similar meaning; as, I often use a *thesaurus* to make my writing more interesting.

these (thēz), *adj.* and *pron. pl.* of *this*: opposite of *those*; as, *those* are yours, but *these* are mine.

the-sis (thē′sis), *n.* [*pl.* theses (thē′sēz)], **1,** something laid down or stated; esp., a statement by a person who undertakes to support it by argument; **2,** a long essay, based on original research, offered by a candidate for an advanced degree at a college or university.

they (*thā*), *personal pron.* **1,** nominative plural of *he, she,* or *it;* **2,** people in general; as, so *they* say.

thick (thik), *adj.* **1,** large in diameter; coarse; as, a *thick* stem; **2,** with a large distance between its opposite sides or surfaces; not thin; as, a board two inches *thick;* a *thick* book; **3,** of dense texture, consistency, etc.; not flowing easily; as, *thick* glue; **4,** close together; abundant; as, *thick* foliage; also, densely set or overgrown; as, a garden *thick* with weeds; **5,** stupid; dense; **6,** not clear; muddy; foggy; as, the air was *thick* with smoke:—*adv.* (also **thickly**) close together; following closely or quickly; as, the blows came *thick* and fast:—*n.* the most intense moment; the place where action is liveliest; as, the *thick* of combat.—*n.* **thick′ness.**—*adj.* (figuratively) **thick′-skinned′; thick′-wit′ted.**

thick-en (thik′en), *v.t.* to make (a liquid) less thin; as, to *thicken* gravy:—*v.i.* **1,** to become denser; as, the clouds *thicken;* **2,** to become complicated; as, the plot *thickens.*

thick-et (thik′it), *n.* a dense growth of tangled shrubs, trees, etc.

thick-set (thik′set′), *adj.* **1,** closely planted; **2,** having a short, stout body; as, a *thickset* fighter.

thief (thēf), *n.* [*pl.* thieves (thēvz)], a person who steals or robs.

thieve (thēv), *v.t.* and *v.i.* [thieved, thiev-ing], to steal; rob.—*n.* **thiev′er-y.**

thigh (thī), *n.* **1,** in a person, the muscular part of the leg between the knee and the hip; **2,** the corresponding part in other animals.

thim-ble (thim′bl), *n.* a small cover that is worn when sewing to protect the tip of the finger that pushes the needle.

thim-ble-ber-ry (thim′bl-ber′i), *n.* any species of raspberry or blackberry having thimble-shaped fruit.

thin (thin), *adj.* [thin-ner, thin-nest], **1,** small in diameter; fine; slim; slender; **2,** with a small distance between its opposite sides or surfaces; not thick; as, a *thin* book; **3,** transparent; sheer; as, *thin* material; **4,** of a liquid, flowing easily; watery; **5,** lacking density; rarefied; as, *thin* air; **6,** high-pitched; shrill; faint; as, a *thin* voice; **7,** lacking roundness or plumpness of figure; gaunt; **8,** scanty; lacking substance or vigour; as, *thin* blood; **9,** few and far apart; scanty; as, *thin* vegetation:—*v.t.* [thinned, thin-ning], **1,** to make *thin* or less dense; **2,** to reduce in numbers:—*v.i.* to become less dense or numerous; as, the crowd *thinned* when it started to rain.—*n.* **thin′ness.**—*adj.* (figuratively) **thin′-skinned′** (sensitive; easily hurt).

thing (thing), *n.* **1,** any item which may be perceived through the senses; as, a stone, a tree, etc.; any physical object; **2,** a particular act, event, or affair; as, this *thing* must not occur again; **3,** a person or animal thought of in a certain way; as, that dog is a friendly *thing;* **4,** an object that is not known or named; as, what is that green *thing* crawling on your arm:—**things, 1,** personal possessions; baggage; as, get your *things;* **2,** circumstances; as, *things* are improving; **3,** an activity or interest that appeals to or suits a person; as, music is just her *thing.*

think (thingk), *v.i.* [thought (thôt), think-ing], **1,** to develop ideas; to form a conception, opinion, or judgment; **2,** to consider; to meditate; muse; **3,** to have in mind, or call to mind, a thought, idea, or image of something; as, to *think* of a picture; **4,** to have an opinion or judgment; as, he *thinks* well of you; **5,** to purpose, plan, or intend; as I had not *thought* of going until tomorrow:—*v.t.* **1,** to occupy the mind with; imagine; as, *think* no evil; **2,** to review or examine mentally; as, to *think* out a problem; **3,** to hold as an opinion; as, you may *think* what you please.—*n.* **think′er.**

third (thûrd), *adj.* next after the second: the ordinal of three:—*n.* one of the three equal parts of anything.

Third World, *n.* the economically developing countries of Africa, Asia, South and Central America. Compare *First World.*

thirst (thûrst), *n.* **1,** a desire for drink; also, the sensation relieved only by drinking: usually a feeling of dryness and heat in the mouth, throat, and stomach; **2,** a great craving; a yearning; as, a *thirst* for fame:—*v.i.* **1,** to desire drink; **2,** to be eager; as, to *thirst* for revenge.—*adj.* **thirst′y.**

thir-teen (thûr′tēn′), *adj.* composed of one more than 12:—*n.* **1,** the sum of 12 plus one; **2,** a sign representing thirteen units, as 13 or XIII.

thirteenth (thûr′tēnth′), *adj.* next after the twelth: the ordinal of thirteen:—*n.* one of 13 equal parts of anything.

thir-ti-eth (thûr′ti-eth), *adj.* next after the twenty-ninth: the ordinal of thirty:—*n.* one of the 30 equal parts of anything.

thir-ty (thûr′ti), *adj.* composed of one more than 29:—*n.* [*pl.* thirties], **1,** the number consisting of 29 plus one; **2,** a sign representing thirty units, as 30 or XXX.

this (*this*), *adj.* [*pl.* these (*thēz*)], **1,** indicating something or someone near in time or space; as, will you mail *this* letter for me? *these* guests came; **2,** pointing out a single, particular, or known thing or person; as, *this* whole matter is a joke; *these* students are best able to do the work; **3,** the first; the nearer; the former; as, *this* side and that:—*demonstrative pron.* **1,** a person or thing near at hand; not that; as, *this* is my house; **2,** a person or thing just indicated or to be indicated; as, I have heard *this* before; *this* is the violinist who is outstanding; **3,** the first or nearer person or thing; as, *this* is a better cake than that:—*adv.* to the amount or extent mentioned; so; as, I expected the test to be hard, but not *this* hard.

this-tle (this′l), *n.* a plant of the aster family with rough, thorny stems, finely divided, prickly leaves, and mainly purple flowers: most often found growing wild.—*adj.* **this′tly.**—*n.* **this′tle-down′** (silky fibres attached to thistle seeds, enabling them to be wind-borne).

thong (thông), *n.* **1,** a thin leather strap or string for fastening something; **2,** the lash of a whip.

Thor (thôr), *n.* the Scandinavian god of thunder, war, and strength, for whom Thursday is named.

thor-ax (thō̆r′aks), *n.* **1,** in the human body, the chest, containing the heart, lungs, etc.; **2,** in insects, the middle of the three main sections of the body.—*adj.* **tho-rac′ic** (thō-ras′ik).

thorn (thôrn), *n.* **1,** in plants, a sharp point on a branch or stem; **2,** any tree or shrub that has thorns; as, a haw*thorn*; **3,** anything that annoys; causes trouble:—**a thorn in one's side,** a continuing irritation. *adj.* **thorn′less.**—*n.* **thorn′i-ness.**

thorn-y (thôrn′i) *adj.* [thorn-i-er, thorn-i-est] **1,** full of thorns, prickly; as, a *thorny* bush; **2,** causing trouble; difficult; as, a *thorny* problem.

thor-ough (thûr′ō), *adj.* **1,** finished; complete; not superficial; as, a *thorough* cleaning; **2,** accurate; careful; as, a *thorough* worker.—*n.* **thor′ ough-ness.**

thor-ough-bred (thûr′ō-bred′), *adj.* **1,** of pure and unmixed breed; as, a *thoroughbred* dog; **2,** outstanding or very special; as, a *thoroughbred* car:—*n.* an animal of pure breed:—**Thoroughbred,** a special type of racing or jumping horse originally bred in England.

thor-ough-fare (thûr′ō-fâr′), *n.* a street, road, or passage open at both ends; **2,** in the *Maritimes,* a water passage between lakes or ponds of the same level.

those (thōz), *adj.* and *pron.*; *pl.* of *that*: opposite of *these*.

though (thō), *conj.* **1,** notwithstanding the fact that; as, I shall go, *though* it is late; **2,** even if; although; as, *though* he is going, I will stay; **3,** as if; as *though*; as, they huddled in the corner as *though* they were afraid:—*adv.* nevertheless; however.

thought (thôt), *n.* **1,** mental activity; meditation; reflection; **2,** that which the mind conceives, considers, remembers, or imagines; an idea; opinion; notion; **3,** the power of imagining and reasoning; intellect; **4,** concern; care; worry; as, please show some *thought* for the children; **5,** a way of thinking, or a group of ideas or beliefs, characteristic of a period, nation, class, society, etc.; as, modern *thought*, etc.

thought-ful (thôt′fool), *adj.* **1,** thinking; full of thought; **2,** considerate of others; kind.—*adv.* **thought′ful-ly.**—*n.* **thought′ful-ness.**

thought-less (thôt′lis), *adj.* **1,** not thinking; careless; **2,** without consideration for others.—*adv.* **thought′less-ly.**—*n.* **thought′less-ness.**

thou-sand (thou′zand), *adj.* **1,** composed of 10 times 100; **2,** indefinitely great in number:—*n.* **1,** the number consisting of 10 hundreds; **2,** a sign representing this number, as 1000 or M; **3,** a large number.

thou-sandth (thou′zandth), *adj.* next after the 999th: the ordinal of thousand:—*n.* one of the 1000 equal parts of anything.

thrash (thrash), *v.t.* **1,** to discuss thoroughly, or over and over; as, to *thrash* out the solution to a problem; **2,** to beat or flog:—*v.i.* to toss or move wildly; as, the patient with a high fever *thrashed* about in bed.

thread (thred), *n.* **1,** a thin, twisted strand of flax, cotton, silk, or other fibrous substance; **2,** a filament; anything threadlike; as, a *thread* of glass or metal; a fibre; **3,** something running through and connecting the parts of anything; as, the *thread* of a story; **4,** the spiral ridge of a screw or nut:—*v.t.* **1,** to put a *thread* through the eye of (a needle); **2,** to string (beads); **3,** to move in a winding, twisting way; as, to *thread* a narrow street; also, to make (one's way) with difficulty.

thread-bare (thred′bâr′), *adj.* **1,** worn down to the threads; shabby; as, *threadbare* upholstery; **2,** overused or worn-out; as, a *threadbare* plot to a play or story.

threat (thret), *n.* **1,** the statement of an intention to hurt or punish; as, he never carried out his *threats*; **2,** a warning of coming evil or danger; **3,** a person or thing that can be dangerous or harmful; as, the tornado was a *threat* to the houseboats.

threat-en (thret′n), *v.i.* to give notice of coming evil or danger:—*v.t.* **1,** to warn of punishment or injury; as, the law *threatens* criminals with punishment; **2,** to be a sign or give evidence of (a coming event or coming calamity); as, the clouds *threaten* a storm; **3,** to be the cause of danger or harm; as, second-hand smoke *threatens* our health.—*adj.* **threat′en-ing.**—*adv.* **threat′en-ing-ly.**

three (thrē), *adj.* composed of one more than two:—*n.* **1,** the number consisting of two plus one; **2,** a sign representing three units, as 3 or III.

three-fold (thrē′fōld′), *adj.* triple; in three layers, forms, etc.; consisting of three:—*adv.* (thrē′fōld′), in a threefold manner; triply.

thresh (thresh), *v.t.* or *v.i.* to separate seeds or grain from plants by beating or striking.—*n.* **thresh′er** (a person or a machine that threshes).

thresh-old (thresh′ōld; thresh′hōld), *n.* **1,** the stone, plank, or piece of timber at the base of a doorway; **2,** a point of beginning or entering; the place or time of entrance; as, she was at the *threshold* of making a new discovery.

threw (thrōō), *p.t.* of *throw*.

thrift-y (thrif′ti), *adj.* [thrift-i-er, thrift-i-est], careful in the use of money; not extravagant: opposite of *improvident.*—*n.* **thrift, thrift′i-ness.**

thrill (thril), *v.t.* to fill with intense emotion; stir deeply; as, the great actor *thrilled* her audience:—*v.i.* **1,** to experience a sharp tingling sensation or a wave of emotion; as, they *thrilled* with delight; **2,** to quiver; as, his voice *thrilled* with anger:—*n.* **1,** a tingling, vibrating sensation; **2,** a sudden, strong feeling of emotion.—*n.* **thrill′er** (a sensational story, play, etc.)

thrive (thrīv), *v.i.* [*p.t.* throve (thrōv) or thrived, *p.p.* thriv-en (thriv′en) or, rarely, thrived, *p.pr.* thriv-ing], **1,** to prosper by industry, economy, and good management; **2,** to increase or prosper in any way; succeed; **3,** to grow sturdily; increase; flourish.—*adj.* **thriv′ing.**

throat (thrōt), *n.* **1,** the front part of the neck between the collar-bone and the chin; also, the passage from the mouth to the stomach or lungs; **2,** a narrow entrance or passage; as, the *throat* of a cannon.

throb (throb), *v.i.* [throbbed, throb-bing], **1,** to beat, as the pulse; sometimes, to beat with more than usual force; palpitate; **2,** to thrill, as with joy:—*n.* **1,** a strong pulsation or beat; **2,** a thrill; as, a *throb* of joy.

throm-bo-sis (throm-bō′sis), *n.* the forming of a blood clot, or thrombus, in a blood vessel, causing local stoppage of circulation (often fatal if in brain or heart).

throne (thrōn), *n.* **1,** the chair of state of a king, queen, etc.; **2,** the power or authority of a queen or king; as, she has a claim to the *throne*:—*v.t.* [throned, thron-ing], to place in a position of power; raise to the *throne*.

throng (thrông), *n.* a multitude or great number; a crowd:—*v.t.* to crowd into; fill; as, soldiers *thronged* the streets:—*v.i.* to assemble in great numbers.

throt-tle (throt′l), *v.t.* [throt-tled, throt-tling], **1,** to strangle or choke by pressure on the windpipe; **2,** to shut off fuel from; as, to *throttle* an engine:—*n.* a valve to control the supply of fuel to an engine.

through (thrōō), *prep.* **1,** from beginning to end; as, *through* life; *through* a tunnel; *through* thick and thin; **2,** in, at one place and out, at another; as, to bore *through* a plank; **3,** in the midst of; as, to walk *through* the woods; **4,** by means of; as, *through* the influence of a friend; **5,** on account of; by reason of; as, he departed *through* fear of being discovered:—*adv.* **1,** from end to end, or from side to side; as, to drive a nail *through*; **2,** from the beginning to the end; as, he played the music *through*; **3,** completely; as, to be wet right *through*:—*adj.* **1,** extending from one place or point to another: as, a *through* passage; a *through* bolt; **2,** transporting passengers or freight from one place to another without stop or change of cars; as, a *through* train:—**to be through,** to be finished; as, are you *through* with the computer?

through-out (thrōō-out′), *adv.* everywhere; in every part; as, the jewellery is gold *throughout*:—*prep.* during; in every part of; as, *throughout* the year.

throw (thrō), *v.t.* [*p.t.* threw (thrōō), *p.p.* thrown (thrōn), *p.pr.* throw-ing], **1,** to fling or hurl with the arm; pitch; toss; as, to *throw* a stone; **2,** to give forth or cast; as, the lamp *threw* a faint light; she *threw* him a quick glance; **3,** to upset; to make (someone) fall; as, his horse *threw* him; the wrestler *threw* his opponent; **4,** to suddenly put or place in a particular position, state, etc.; as, the fire *threw* the people into confusion:—*n.* the act of *throwing*, casting, or flinging.—*n.* **throw′back′** (a person or a thing that reflects aspects of an earlier era):—**to throw away, throw out,** to get rid of something no longer wanted, esp. garbage.—*adj.* **throw′a-way′** (wasteful; as, the *throwaway* society).

thrush (thrush), *n.* any of a large family of songbirds, most often of plain colour, but sometimes with spotted throat and breast: the wood thrush and hermit thrush are common in North America.

thrust (thrust), *v.t.* [thrust, thrust-ing], **1,** to push or shove forcibly; as, he *thrust* the package into the car; **2,** to pierce; as, their swords *thrust* him through:—*v.i.* to attack, with a pointed weapon; as, to *thrust* with a dagger:—*n.* **1,** a violent or sudden push; **2,** a stab; as, the *thrust* of a sword.

thud (thud), *n.* a dull sound:—*v.i.* [thud-ded, thud-ding], to make, or strike so as to make, a dull sound; as, the apples *thudded* on the ground.

thug (thug), *n.* a violent criminal; a ruffian.

thumb (thum), *n.* **1,** the short, thick finger on the hand, closest to the wrist; **2,** the part of a glove which covers the thumb:—*v.t.* **1,** to look quickly through pages; as, to *thumb* through a magazine; **2,** to make something dirty by or as if by repeated handling with the thumb; as, don't *thumb* up your new book.—*n.* **thumb′-tack′.**

thump (thump), *n.* **1,** a hard, heavy blow; as, he hit him a *thump* on the back; **2,** a heavy fall, or the sound of it; as, the tree fell with a *thump*:—*v.t.* to pound; strike, or beat with dull, heavy blows; as, she *thumped* on the door:—*v.i.* to pound or throb; as, her heart *thumped* with fear.—*n.* **thump′er.**

thun-der (thun′dėr), *n.* **1,** the loud, rumbling or crashing noise that follows a flash of lightning; **2,** any similar loud noise; as, the *thunder* of the guns:—*v.i.* **1,** to make thunder; **2,** to send out a sound like thunder; as, the sea *thundered* against the rocks.—*adj.* **thun′der-ous.**—*n.* **thun′der-clap′; thun′der-cloud′; thun′der-er.**—*adj.* **thun′der-struck′.**

thun-der-bolt (thun′dėr-bōlt′), *n.* **1,** a flash of lightning accompanied by a clap of thunder; **2,** something swift, sudden, and terrible, like lightning and thunder; as, the news of the bank's failure was like a *thunderbolt.*

thun-der-head (thun′dėr-hed′), *n.* a large rounded mass of dark cloud, often seen before a thunderstorm.

thun-der-storm (thun′dėr-stôrm′), *n.* a storm with thunder and lightning.

Thurs-day (thûrz′di; dā), *n.* the day after Wednesday and before Friday.

thus (*th*us), *adv.* **1,** in this way or in this manner; as, write it *thus;* **2,** to this degree or extent; as, *thus* far; **3,** as a consequence; so; therefore; as, *thus* plants need light.

thwart (thwôrt), *adj.* situated or placed across something:—*n.* a rower's seat in a boat, extending from side to side:—*v.t.* to successfully oppose; baffle; outwit; as, to *thwart* an enemy.

thyme (tīm), *n.* an herb with small aromatic leaves, used for seasoning.

thy-roid (thī′roid), *n.* and *adj.* a large gland in the neck which secretes hormones controlling the body's rate of growth and the rate at which it burns up food for energy.

ti-ar-a (ti-ä′ra; tī-âr′a; ti-âr′a), *n.* a small, jeweled crown, usually worn by a woman; as, a diamond *tiara.*

tib-i-a (tib′i-a), *n.* the inner and larger of the two bones between knee and ankle; the shinbone. Compare *fibula.*

tic (tik), *n.* the habitual, convulsive twitching of a muscle, esp. of the face.

[1]**tick** (tik), *v.i.* to make a slight, quick, regularly repeated sound; as, a watch *ticks:*—*v.t.* **1,** to mark or check off with dots or other small marks; as, he *ticked* each item as he came to it; **2,** to mark off or record by repeated ticking sounds:—*n.* **1,** a light, repeated ticking sound; **2,** time shown by the sound made by a clock; an instant; **3,** a tiny mark, as a dot, check, etc., used in checking off, or in marking something for attention.

[2]**tick** (tik), *n.* **1,** a tiny, blood-sucking, spider-like animal that attaches itself to the skin of dogs, cows, and other mammals: can spread disease to humans; **2,** various lice-like parasites that infest birds, sheep, bats, etc.

tick-et (tik′it), *n.* **1,** a certificate or card which entitles the holder to certain stated privileges, such as admission to an entertainment, transportation by air, rail, or ship, etc.; **2,** a small card stating price, size, etc., of goods; a label or tag; **3,** a notice for someone to pay a fine or go to court for breaking a traffic law; as, a speeding *ticket:*—*v.t.* to mark by a label; to give notice to a person to pay a fine or go to court.

tick-le (tik′l), *v.t.* [tick-led, tick-ling], **1,** to touch lightly so as to produce a peculiar nervous tingle; **2,** to please or amuse; as, your speech *tickled* me:—*v.i.* to feel a tingling sensation; as, my ear *tickles:*—*n.* a peculiar thrill or tingle, or the touch causing this sensation.

tick-lish (tik′lish), *adj.* **1,** sensitive to tickling; **2,** delicate to handle or cope with; as, a *ticklish* problem; **3,** risky; unstable; unsteady; as, *ticklish* footing.—*n.* **tick′lish-ness.**

tick-tack-toe (tik′–tak–tō′), *n.* **1,** a game in which the object is for two players to place alternately three crosses or circles in a row, diagonally, or straight up and down, in a nine-square grid: the first person to do so is the winner.

tid-al (tīd′al), *adj.* relating to, or affected by, the tide; as, a *tidal* river; *tidal* flats:—**tidal wave,** a huge powerful ocean wave caused by an underwater earthquake or by a heavy storm at sea: often called by the Japanese name, *tsunami.*

tid-bit (tid′bit′), *n.* **1,** a small but good piece of food; **2,** an interesting bit of information or news.

tide (tīd), *n.* **1,** the regular rise and fall twice every day of the oceans and the bodies of water connected with them: tides are caused by the pull of gravity from the moon and sun, and they change from high to low and low to high about every 12 hours; **2,** anything which increases and decreases, like the tide; as, the *tide* of events:—*v.t.* [tid-ed, tid-ing], to help (a person) along; assist in time of need; as, this money will *tide* him over until he gets a job.

ti-dings (tī′dingz), *n.pl.* news; information; a message; as, glad *tidings.*

ti-dy (tī′di), *adj.* [ti-di-er, ti-di-est], **1,** trim; neat; orderly; **2,** considerable; as, a *tidy* sum of money:—*v.t.* and *v.i.* [tidied, tidy-ing], to make neat; put things in proper order:—*n.* **ti′di-ness.**

tie (tī), *v.t.* [tied, ty-ing], **1,** to attach by a cord or rope drawn together and knotted; as, to *tie* a tag to a box; to *tie* flowers in a bunch; **2,** to bind together the parts of, by a cord that is drawn up and knotted; as, to *tie* a shoe; **3,** to make a knot or bow in; as, to *tie* a scarf; also, to form (a knot, bow, etc.) by looping and securing the ends of a cord or rope; **4,** to restrict or limit; as, his business *ties* him down; **5,** to equal in score; make the same score as; as, we *tied* the other team in football; **6,** to join together; connect; as, scientists *tie* the poor weather to the volcanic eruption:—*v.i.* **1,** to form a bow or knot; as, the sash *ties* in the back; **2,** to make the same score:—*n.* **1,** something, as a band, rope, or ribbon, used to bind, draw, or fasten together; **2,** a plank or rod to which the rails of a railroad track are attached; **3,** something tied, as a ribbon, and used as a fastening or ornament, esp. a necktie; **4,** a relationship or connection; as, business *ties*; **5,** a common interest which unites; as, a strong family *tie*; **6,** equality of numbers, as of votes; equal scores in a contest, race, etc.

tier (tēr), *n.* a number of rows or layers arranged one above the other; as, a wedding cake often has several *tiers*; there were *tiers* of seats in the theatre.

tiff (tif), *n.* **1,** a slight quarrel; spat; **2,** a fit of anger or resentment; huff; ill humour.

ti-ger (tī′gėr), *n.* a large, fierce wild cat, with yellow-orange fur and black cross-stripes: lives in parts of Asia and is one of the largest members of the cat family.—*n.fem.* **ti′gress.**

tight (tīt), *adj.* **1,** not loose; fastened firmly; as, a *tight* knot; compact; as, a *tight* weave; **2,** closely built, so that water or other liquid cannot pass through; as, a *tight* barrel; also air*tight*; water*tight*; **3,** fitting close to a part of the body, usually too close for comfort; as, a *tight* glove; **4,** having little room or space; close or confined; as, it was a *tight* squeeze; **5,** not easily obtained; not plentiful; as, during a depression, money is *tight*; **6,** *Colloq.* stingy:—*adv.* **tightly**; as, she held on *tightly*:—**tights,** *n.pl.* close-fitting clothing for the lower part of the body, worn by actors, acrobats, etc. Also called *leotards*:—*adv.* so as to be tight; as, hold on *tight*.—*adj.* **tight′-fist′ed; tight′-lipped′.**

tight-en (tīt′n), *v.t.* and *v.i.* to make or become tight; as, to *tighten* a screw.

tight-rope (tīt′rōp′), *n.* a taut or stretched rope or cable on which acrobats balance themselves while performing.

til-de (til′dė), *n.* **1,** in *computing*, the character [~], often found on upper left key on a keyboard: can be used to indicate the home directory of a particular user; as, ~smith is the home directory of a user named smith; **2,** a pronunciation mark [~] used to denote the Spanish ñ, as in cañon, señor: also used in pronunciation keys of dictionaries.

tile (tīl), *n.* a thin slab of baked clay, stone, etc., used for roofing, floors, wall decoration, etc.; **2,** a pipe made of baked clay and used as a drain:—*v.t.* [tiled, til-ing], to cover with tiles.

[1]**till** (til), *n.* a money drawer such as one found in a store.

[2]**till** (til), *prep.* to the time of; as far as; as, wait *till* one o'clock:—*conj.* **1,** until; to the time when; as, wait *till* I return; **2,** before; unless; as, he won't come *till* you call him.

[3]**till** (til), *v.t.* to prepare for seed, as by ploughing; cultivate; as, to *till* the soil.

till-er (til′ėr), *n.* a handle or bar used to turn a rudder to steer a boat.

tilt (tilt), *v.i.* to lean or tip; as, the tall building began to *tilt*:—*v.t.* to raise one end or side higher than the other; slant or tip; as, to *tilt* a wheelbarrow:—*n.* **1,** the act of tipping; the state of being tipped; as, the *tilt* of her head; **2,** a slanting position; as, the bench was on a *tilt*:—**full tilt,** full speed or force; as, she ran down the hill at full *tilt*.

tim-ber (tim′bėr), *n.* **1,** wood suitable for carpentry, shipbuilding, etc.; **2,** a large, thick piece of wood prepared for use; **3,** wooded land from which timber may be obtained.—*adj.* **tim′bered.**—*n.* **tim′ber-line′** (the line on a mountain above which trees do not grow; in Canada, a line across the northern part of the country: no trees grow north of this line).

tim-bre (tim′bėr; taṅ′br), *n.* the quality or tone identity of a sound (determined by the number and character of its overtones) that makes it distinct from other sounds; as, the *timbre* of a voice, violin, etc.

time (tīm), *n.* **1,** the moment when something happens or occurs; as, his father was away at the *time* of the fire; **2,** the period during which something is going on; as, the play continued for two hours' *time*; **3,** the regular or appointed hour when something is supposed to begin, take place, or end; as, it is *time* for lunch; **4,** the proper moment for something to happen; opportunity; as, this is the *time* to buy; **5,** a definite or precise moment as shown by a clock; as, the *time* for his departure is five o'clock; **6,** a period with more or less definite limits; an age; as, in the *time* of Julius Caesar; ancient *times*; **7,** a period marked by definite physical characteristics; as, summer*time*; day*time*; **8,** a period characterized by special qualities, experiences, or conditions; as, good *times*; hard *times*; **9,** the period required or consumed in performing an action; as, the winner's *time* was 11.5 seconds; **10,** one of a series of repeated actions; as, do this exercise five *times*; **11,** the lapse or passing of all the days, months, and years, taken as a whole; as, *time* will make him forget; **12,** a system of reckoning or measuring the passage of hours, days, etc.; as, solar *time*; standard *time*; **13,** the rate at which something is done; as, to run in double-quick *time*; **14,** in *music*, the arrangement of the rhythmic beats of a composition into equal measures included between successive bars; as, two-four *time*; also, the tempo at which a passage or composition should be, or is, played; **15,** a period long enough for something to be done; as, I have no *time* to finish this work:—

times, an indication that one number is to be multiplied by another; often used in place of the multiplication sign (×); as, five *times* two is ten:—*v.t.* [timed, tim-ing], **1,** to adapt to the occasion; arrange the time of; as, I will *time* my visit to suit your convenience; **2,** to regulate; as, to *time* the speed of a machine; **3,** to find out or record the speed of; as, to *time* a runner.—*adj.* **time′less; time′worn′.**—*n.* **time′keep′er.**

time-ly (tīm′li), *adj.* [time-li-er, time-li-est], suitable to the time or occasion; well-timed; as, *timely* help.—*n.* **time′li-ness.**

tim-er (tīm′ėr), *n.* a person or instrument that shows or records the passage of time; as, a stop-watch or a kitchen *timer.*

time-ta-ble (tīm′tā′bl), *n.* **1,** a list of the times when airplanes, buses, trains, boats, etc., arrive and depart from various stations or terminals; **2,** a schedule or plan for events or personal activities.

tim-id (tim′id), *adj.* shy; not brave or bold; easily frightened.—*adv.* **tim′id-ly.**—*n.* **timid′i-ty.**

tim-or-ous (tim′ėr-us), *adj.* **1,** fearful of danger; nervous; as, he spoke in a *timorous* voice; **2,** expressing fear or alarm; as, a *timorous* expression.

tim-pa-ni (tim′pa-nē′), *n.pl.* kettledrums.—*n.* **tim′pa-nist** (one who plays a set of timpani).

tin (tin), *n.* **1,** a silvery-white, soft metal that is a chemical element; used to make many useful articles such as boxes, cans, and pans: it protects things from rust and is often used to coat other metals; **2,** something made out of tin; as, a *tin* of cookies:—*adj.* made of tin or coated with tin; as, a *tin* can:—*v.t.* [tinned, tin-ning], **1,** to cover with tin, or with tinned iron; **2,** to put into tins, as food.

tin-der (tin′dėr), *n.* any dry material that catches fire easily, esp. when used to start a fire: wood shavings, dry pine cones, and paper can all be tinder.

tine (tīn), *n.* a tooth or spike; a prong, esp. of a fork.

tin-foil (tin′foil′), *n.* a very thin sheet of tin, aluminum, or other metal used for wrapping.

ting (ting), *n.* a tinkling sound, as of a single stroke on a small bell. Also, **ting′–a–ling′.**

tinge (tinj), *v.t.* [tinged, ting-ing or tinge-ing], **1,** to stain slightly with colour; dye faintly; **2,** to give a certain characteristic flavour or quality to; as, envy *tinged* all his remarks:—*n.* **1,** a slight degree of some colour; tint; **2,** a touch; trace; as, there was a *tinge* of sarcasm in her remarks.

tin-gle (ting′gl), *v.i.* [tin-gled, tin-gling], to feel or have a stinging sensation or pricking pain; as, his fingers *tingled* with the cold:—*n.* a stinging sensation or pain, as from cold or a slap.

tink-er (tingk′ėr), *n.* in former times, a person who travelled around mending pots, pans, and other such household items:—*v.i.* to fix or work with something in an unskilled or casual way; as, Anna likes to *tinker* with old computers.

tin-kle (ting′kl), *n.* a small, quick, sharp, ringing sound; as, the *tinkle* of a bell:—*v.i.* and *v.t.* [tin-kled, tin-kling], to make or cause to make such a sound.

tin-sel (tin′sel), *n.* **1,** a fabric originally of silk, or silk and wool, covered or woven with gold and silver threads; **2,** strips of glittering, metallic material, used as an inexpensive trimming, as for Christmas trees; **3,** something showy but of little value; false show; pretence:—*v.t.* [tinselled, tinsel-ling], to decorate with, or as with, tinsel.

tint (tint), *n.* **1,** a slight colouring; a pale tinge; as, just a *tint* of gold in the hair; **2,** a delicate or pale colour or a pale tinge of a colour; as, her dress and shoes were different *tints* of blue:—*v.t.* to give a slight colouring to.

ti-ny (tī′ni), *adj.* [ti-ni-er, ti-ni-est], extremely small; minute.

¹tip (tip), *n.* **1,** the point or end of anything; as, the *tip* of a finger; **2,** a small piece or part attached to the end of a thing; as, the *tip* of a pen.

²tip (tip), *v.t.* [tipped, tip-ping], **1,** to slant or tilt; raise at one end or side; as, to *tip* a chair; **2,** to overturn; cause to lose balance; as, to *tip* a vase over:—*v.i.* to lean, slant, or fall over; as, the boat *tipped* dangerously.

³tip (tip), *v.t.* [tipped, tip-ping], **1,** to strike or hit lightly; to give a slight blow to; as, his bat just *tipped* the ball; **2,** to give a small amount of money for a service; as, she *tipped* the waiter very generously:—**to tip off,** to give someone private or secret information:—*n.* **1,** a light blow or tap; **2,** a small amount of money for a service, beyond the normal amount due; **3,** a friendly hint; useful information; as, a safety *tip.*—*n.* **tip′–off′** (a warning; advance secret information; in *basketball,* a jump ball at the start of a game).

tip-sy (tip′si), *adj.* [tip-si-er, tip-si-est], almost drunk; unsteady or foolish from the effect of liquor.

tip-toe (tip′tō′), *v.i.* [tiptoed, tiptoe-ing], to walk or stand on the toes; walk softly; as, the nurse *tiptoed* down the hall.

ti-rade (tī-rād′ tī′), *n.* a long, vehement speech, esp. of blame or abuse.

¹tire (tīr), *n.* covering for a wheel of a car, truck, bicycle, or other such vehicle: it can be made of rubber or other materials and is usually filled with air, although some are solid rubber.

²tire (tīr), *v.t.* [tired, tir-ing], to exhaust or wear out the strength, interest, or patience of; as, hard work *tired* him:—*v.i.* to become physically weary; as, her grandmother *tires* easily.—*adj.* **tir′ing** (as, a *tiring* flight).

tired (tīrd), *adj.* **1,** weary; exhausted; fatigued; as, a *tired* mother; **2,** no longer interested; bored or annoyed; as, they got *tired* of waiting for the speaker.—*n.* **tired′ness.**

tire-less (tīr′lis), *adj.* unwearying; not to be wearied; as, *tireless* hands.—*adv.* **tire′less-ly.**

tire-some (tīr′sum), *adj.* wearisome; tedious; as, a *tiresome* journey; also, annoying; boring; as, *tiresome* talk.

tis-sue (tish′ōō′; tish′ū), *n.* **1,** a soft, thin paper used as a handkerchief; **2,** the cells and connecting parts that form the structure and substance of any part of an animal or plant; as, bone *tissue*; **3,** a web or network; as, a *tissue* of lies:—**tissue paper,** very thin, soft paper used to pack or wrap up delicate articles, gifts, etc.

ti-tan (tī′tan), *n.* a person or group of enormous strength (like the fabled giants of Greek mythology).—**Titan,** the largest satellite of Saturn.—*adj.* **ti-tan′ic.**

tit-il-late (tit′i-lāt′), *v.t.* [-lated, -lating], to tickle or excite pleasurably; as, to *titillate* the fancy, palate, etc.

ti-tle (tī′tl), *n.* **1,** the name of a book, song, movie, poem, play, etc.; **2,** a designation of dignity, rank, or distinction, generally used in front of a person's name; as, *Professor* Martini; **3,** a championship; as, our school won the hockey *title* last year; **4,** the legal right to property, esp. real estate; as, a *title* to land; also, the paper giving such right:—*v.t.* [ti-tled, ti-tling], to entitle; give a name to; as, the writer titled her book *The Big Cheese*.

tiz-zy (tiz′i), *n.* [*pl.* -zies], *Colloq.* a state of nervousness or agitation.

to (tōō; when not emphatic, too), *prep.* expressing: **1,** in the direction of; towards; as, on my way *to* work; they drove across the country from west *to* east; **2,** as far as; so as to arrive at or be in; as, he came *to* my office today; **3,** against; opposite; as, face *to* face; compared with; as, the score was 6 *to* 4; **4,** into the possession of; as, give the book *to* John; **5,** in agreement or harmony with; as, words set *to* music; true *to* life; **6,** fitting; for; as, a key *to* the car; five kilos *to* a bag; a room *to* himself; **7,** within the scope of; as, *to* my knowledge he has not come; **8,** till or until; as, I shall stay *to* midnight; before; as, ten minutes *to* five:—used to introduce an infinitive: **1,** in a noun construction; as, she began *to* sing; *to* err is human; **2,** expressing purpose; as, we work *to* succeed; **3,** completing the meaning of a preceding adjective or noun; as, fit *to* wear:—also used **1,** to introduce an indirect object; as, take the briefcase *to* her mother; **2,** to show a relation to a noun or adjective; as, you were always so kind *to* him:—*adv.* **1,** in or into a position or contact; as, the wind blew the door *to;* **2,** to the normal position or condition; as, she came *to* slowly.

toad (tōd), *n.* any tailless, froglike amphibian which breeds in water but lives on land: related to frogs but with a broader body and rougher, drier skin.

toad-stool (tōd′stōōl), *n.* any umbrella-shaped fungus that grows on decaying matter, esp. a poisonous mushroom.

toad-y (tōd′i), *n.* [*pl.* toadies], one who caters to the rich or powerful for the sake of gain or favour:—*v.t.* and *v.i.* [toadied, toady-ing], to flatter in order to gain reward.

[1]toast (tōst), *n.* sliced bread browned by heat:—*v.t.* **1,** to brown or heat at a fire; as, to *toast* bread; **2,** to heat or warm thoroughly; as, *toast* your hands at the fire.—*n.* **toast′er.**

[2]toast (tōst), *n.* **1,** a short speech made before drinking in honour of someone; as, they called for a *toast* to the winner; **2,** the person or thing toasted; as, she was the *toast* of the evening:—*v.t.* to drink or propose a toast to.

to-bac-co (to-bak′ō), *n.* [*pl.* tobaccos], **1,** a large-leaved plant with pink or white trumpet-shaped flowers; **2,** the dried leaves of this plant treated in various ways and used for smoking and chewing, or as snuff.

to-bog-gan (to-bog′an), *n.* a kind of long, flat sled without runners, curving up at the front and often carrying four or more persons: used in winter sports:—*v.i.* to ride or coast on such a sled.—*n.* **to-bog′gan-er; to-bog′gan-ist.**

to-day (too-dā′), *adv.* **1,** on the present day; as, you must go *today;* **2,** in these times; as, *today* many people travel by airplane:—*n.* **1,** the present day; as, *today* is Tuesday; **2,** this present time or age; as, the fashions of *today* change fast.

tod-dler (tod′lėr), *v.i.* [tod-dled, tod-dling], a small child who is just learning to walk.—*v.i.* **tod′dle** [toddled, toddl-ing] (walk with small, uncertain steps).

to-do (too-dōō′), *n. Colloq.* a fuss; commotion; stir.

toe (tō), *n.* **1,** one of the five separate divisions or digits of the foot; **2,** the front of the foot, or of a stocking or other foot covering; as, the child tore the *toe* of its sock; **3,** anything resembling a toe:—*v.t.* [toed, toe-ing], to touch, reach, or strike with the toe; as, to *toe* the mark in a race.—*n.* **toe′nail′.**

tof-fee (tof′i), *n.* a hard, chewy taffy, made with molasses or brown sugar and butter.

to-fu (tō′fōō), *n.* a whitish curd made from soybean extract: it is used as a source of protein in much Asian and vegetarian cooking.

to-ga (tō′ga), *n.* a loose, outer garment, once worn by Roman citizens.

to-geth-er (too-ge*th*′ėr), *adv.* **1,** in company or association; as, to live *together*; **2,** mixed or in contact with; as, the ingredients were mixed *together*; **3,** at the same time; simultaneously; as, the firecrackers exploded *together*; **4,** in agreement; as, the council voted *together* to accept the proposal.

tog-gle (tog′l) *n.* in *computing*, a function that is activated or deactivated by the same key or command: the key or command is always activated in the same way, but each occasion it is used, it has the opposite effect:—*v.t.* and *v.i.* to switch something back and forth; as, in some programs, the Insert key *toggles* insert mode: the Insert key turns insert mode on, if it is off, and off, if it is on.

toil (toil), *v.i.* **1,** to work hard or long; labour; **2,** to move with difficulty; plod; trudge:—*n.* work or effort that exhausts the body or mind.

toi-let (toi′lit), *n.* a bathroom fixture that consists of a large bowl partly filled with water, a tank, a seat, a lid, and a flushing mechanism: it is used to flush body wastes into a sewer or septic system.

to-ken (tō′ken), *n.* **1,** something representing something else; a sign, symbol, or indication; as, the four-leaf clover is a *token* of good luck; **2,** a memento; keepsake; as, the old locket was a *token* from her sister; **3,** a piece of metal or plastic that looks like a coin and is used in place of money; as, you can use *tokens* on the transit system:—*adj.* done only to meet a requirement; slight or insignificant; as, a *token* effort.

told (tōld), *p.t.* and *p.p.* of *tell.*

tol-er-a-ble (tol′ėr-a-bl), *adj.* **1,** capable of being suffered or endured; **2,** passable; fairly good.—*adv.* **tol′er-a-bly.**

toler-ance (tol′ėr-ans), *n.* **1,** an attitude of allowing others to have ideas and beliefs that are different from one's own and accepting people who are from a different background; **2,** the ability or quality of being able to resist or endure something; as, that person has a low *tolerance* for stress.

tol-er-ant (tol′ėr-ant), *adj.* willing or inclined to put up with views or opinions which are different from one's own.—*adv.* **tol′er-ant-ly.**

tol-er-ate (tol′ėr-āt′), *v.t.* [tolerat-ed, tolerat-ing], **1,** to allow something that one does not agree with to be done; as, members of Parliament debate the issues, but they must *tolerate* laws once they are passed even if they don't agree with them; **2,** to be willing to accept or put up with; as, our teacher will not *tolerate* cheating.—*n.* **tol′er-a′tion.**

[1]**toll** (tōl), *n.* **1,** a fee paid for the right to use something; as, for using a bridge, highway, or canal; **2,** any serious loss or damage; as, the death *toll* from the recent floods.

[2]**toll** (tōl), *v.t.* **1,** to cause to sound with slow strokes spaced at regular intervals; as, the bell-ringer *tolls* the bell; **2,** to sound or strike; as, "the curfew *tolls* the knell of parting day":—*v.i.* to give forth a slow, regular, ringing sound, as a bell in announcing a death.—*n.* **tolls** (the slow, regular ringing of a bell).

tom (tom), *adj.* male, as in *tom*cat.

tom-a-hawk (tom′a-hôk), *n.* in *history*, a kind of hatchet or axe used as a tool and weapon by some Aboriginal peoples.

to-ma-to (to-mā′tō; to-mä′tō), *n.* [*pl.* tomatoes], a garden plant with yellow flowers, and a red or yellow fruit which is used for food; also, the fruit.

tomb (to͞om), *n.* a grave or vault for the dead.

tomb-stone (to͞om′stōn′), *n.* a stone marking a grave.

to-mor-row (too-mor′ō), *n.* **1,** the day after today; **2,** the future; as, the world of *tomorrow*:—*adv.* on the day after today.

ton (tun), *n.* a measure of weight formerly used in Canada and still in use in the United States, equal to 2000 pounds (about 907 kg.).

tone (tōn) *n.* **1,** the nature of a sound in terms of its pitch, loudness, length, etc.; as, the mellow *tones* of a cello; **2,** the quality of the voice in expressing feeling; as, she spoke in an imploring *tone*; **3,** the difference in higher or lower pitch between two musical notes on a scale; **4,** normal or healthy condition; as, good muscular *tone*; **5,** the quality and harmony of the colours of a painting; **6,** a hue, tint, or shade of colour; as, a grey *tone*; **7,** the general character or spirit; as, I did not like the *tone* of the letter.

ton-er (tōn′ėr) *n.* black powder used in photocopiers and laser printers to make the image on paper; made of tiny particles of plastic which melt easily.

tongs (tôngz), *n.pl.* a device with two arms joined by a hinge, used for grasping, lifting, etc.; as, barbecue *tongs*; fireplace *tongs*.

tongue (tung), *n.* **1,** the muscular organ in the mouth, used in tasting, chewing and swallowing food: in humans, also used for forming sounds in words; **2,** a language; as, their native *tongue*; **3,** manner of speaking; as, a sharp *tongue*; **4,** anything resembling a tongue in shape, position, or use; as, a *tongue* of flame; the vibrating reed in the mouthpiece of some musical instruments, etc.; **5,** the tongue of an animal used for food; as, ox *tongue*; **6,** the ability to speak; as, to find or lose one's *tongue*; **7,** the narrow, flat piece of leather located under the laces or buckle of a shoe.

tongue–tied (tung′–tīd′), *adj.* **1,** unable to speak because of fear, shyness, etc.

ton-ic (ton′ik), *adj.* **1,** tending to strengthen; bracing; as, the *tonic* effect of a high altitude; **2,** something that is meant to bring health or strength; **3,** in *music*, relating to the keynote:—*n.* **1,** a medicine that brings new strength; **2,** in *music,* the keynote of a scale or composition.

to-night (too-nīt′), *n.* the night of the present day:—*adv.* on, or during, the present or coming night.

tonne (tun) *n.* [*pl.* tonnes], a unit of measure for weight, equal to 1000 kilograms; formerly spelled *ton.*

ton-nage (tun′ij), *n.* **1,** the weight of goods carried in a ship; **2,** the carrying capacity of a vessel, stated in tons; **3,** the duty or toll on vessels, based on the burden carried; **4,** the entire shipping of any port or country, stated in tons.

ton-sil (ton′sil), *n.* one of two oval-shaped masses of tissue on the inside back part of the throat.

ton-sil-lec-to-my (ton′si-lek′to-mi), *n.* surgical removal of the tonsils.

ton-sil-li-tis (ton′si-lī′tis), *n.* inflammation of the tonsils (a form of sore throat).

too (to͞o), *adv.* **1,** also; likewise; as, he is going, *too;* **2,** more than enough; as, *too* long; **3,** so much more than enough as to be painful, intolerable, etc.; as, that is *too* annoying; **4,** exceedingly; very; as, I am *too* happy to see you.

took (took), *p.t.* of *take.*

tool (to͞ol), *n.* **1,** an instrument used in doing work, esp. one used with the hand; as a chisel, hammer, saw, etc.; **2,** a person or thing that is used for a certain purpose; as, computers are excellent research *tools:*—*v.t.* to shape with a tool; as, this leather was *tooled* by hand.—*n.* **tool′ mak′er.**

tool-box (to͞ol′bôks′), *n.* **1,** in *computing,* a group of icons that represent commands that are used frequently: can be displayed across the top or down the side of the screen or sometimes can be dragged to other locations with the mouse; **2,** a box for storing or carrying tools.

too-nie (to͞o′nē), *Colloq.* the Canadian two-dollar coin.

toot (to͞ot), *v.t.* to cause (a horn, whistle, etc.) to sound:—*v.i.* to make short, quick sounds:—*n.* a short blast on a horn.

tooth (to͞oth), *n.* [*pl.* teeth (tēth)], **1,** one of a set of hard, bony structures in the mouth used for biting and chewing: animals sometimes use teeth to protect themselves and to attack prey; **2,** any projection resembling a tooth, as on a gearwheel, a comb, a rake, or a saw.—*adj.* **toothed.**—*n.* **tooth′ache′; tooth′brush′; tooth′paste′.**

TOOTH: *A,* ENAMEL COVERING CROWN; *B,* PULP; *C,* DENTINE; *D,* CEMENT COVERING ROOTS

tooth-pick (to͞oth′pik), *n.* a small, thin piece of wood, plastic, or other material used to remove food from between the teeth.

[1]**top** (top), *n.* **1,** the highest part; summit; as, the *top* of a hill; also used in combinations such as mountain*top,* hill*top,* roof*top;* **2,** the upper surface, side, or part, as of a table, a shoe, or a page; **3,** head; upper end; as, the *top* of a street; **4,** the most important person, place, or rank; as, she is the *top* in her area of research; **5,** the crown of the head; **6,** something that goes on the higher or upper part; as, put the *top* on the jar; **7,** the very highest step or degree; as, he has reached the *top* of his ambition:—*v.t.* [topped, top-ping], **1,** to put a cover on; cap; as, to *top* a bottle; **2,** to be at the head of; as, she *tops* the list of graduates; **3,** to surpass; as, he *topped* his own record; **4,** to cut off the upper part of (a plant):—*adj.* **1,** the highest part; highest; as, the *top* shelf; **2,** highest in degree; greatest; as, at *top* speed.—*adj.* **top′flight′** (best); **top′-heav′y; top′-notch′.**—*n.* **top′ping** (on food; as, whipped cream).

[2]**top** (top), *n.* a child's cone-shaped toy with a point on which it can be made to spin rapidly by means of a spring or string.

to-paz (tō′paz), *n.* a mineral often used as a gem, varying in colour from yellow to brown.

top-ic (top′ik), *n.* the subject of conversation, argument, literary composition, etc.—*adj.* **top′i-cal.**

top-most (top′mōst), *adj.* highest; at the very top or summit.

to-pog-ra-phy (to-pog′ra-fi), *n.* [*pl.* topographies], **1,** the surface features of an area of land, including such physical characteristics as mountains, rivers, cities, communication routes, etc.; **2,** the science of showing these features on a map.—*adj.* **top′o-graph′i-cal.**

top-ple (top′l), *v.t.* [top-pled, top-pling], to overturn; to push over; as, they *toppled* the old wall:—*v.i.* to fall over; as, the flagpole *toppled* in the wind.

top-soil (top′soil′), *n.* a rich surface layer of soil that has most of the materials needed by plants to grow.

top-sy-tur-vy (top′si-tûr′vi), *adv.* and *adj.* **1,** upside down; **2,** in confusion:—*n.* a state of upset or confusion.

To-rah or **to-rah** (tôr′a), *n.* **1,** the first five books of the Jewish bible; **2,** the sacred writings and laws of the Jewish religion.

torch (tôrch), *n.* **1,** a light, made by burning wood, etc., carried at the end of a pole or handle; **2,** any of various devices which give out a flare or hot flame; as, a blow*torch.*—*n.* **torch′light′.**

tore (tōr), *p.t.* of *tear.*

tor-ment (tôr′ment), *n.* **1,** extreme mental or physical suffering; **2,** that which causes pain or anguish:—*v.t.* (tôr-ment′), **1,** to put to extreme pain of mind or body; torture; as, he was *tormented* with doubt and fear; **2,** to tease; annoy; as, she *tormented* her mother with questions.—*n.* **tor-ment′er; tor-men′tor.**

torn (tōrn), *p.p.* of *tear.*

tor-na-do (tôr-nā′dō), *n.* [*pl.* tornadoes], a violent storm of whirling, destructive wind, produced from a funnel-shaped cloud that travels rapidly along a narrow path: also called a *twister.*

tor-pe-do (tôr-pē′dō), *n.* [*pl.* torpedoes], **1,** a self-propelled weapon used to sink ships, made up of a long, tube-shaped metal shell filled with explosives: torpedoes are fired from submarines, ships, or planes and then travel under the water to the target; **2,** a marine ray (fish) that gives an electric shock:—*v.t.* to destroy or blow up with a torpedo; as, to *torpedo* a ship.

tor-pid (tôr′pid), *adj.* **1,** inactive, sluggish; as, a *torpid* liver; **2,** dormant; as, a snake is *torpid* in winter; **3,** dull; stupid; as, a *torpid* intellect.—*n.* **tor′por; tor-pid′i-ty.**

torque (tôrk), *n.* a force that tends to produce a rotating or twisting motion; as, the *torque* exerted on a shaft.

tor-rent (tor′ent), *n.* **1,** a violent, raging stream; **2,** any similar violent flow; as, a *torrent* of words; *torrents* of rain.—*adj.* **torren′tial** (to-ren′shal).

tor-rid (tor′id), *adj.* dried by the sun's heat; extremely hot; as, a *torrid* desert.

tor-sion (tôr′shun), *n.* **1,** a twisting force, applied esp. to one end of a body while the other is held fast; **2,** the force with which a twisted rod, wire, etc., tends to return to its previous position.

tor-so (tôr′sō), *n.* **1,** the part of the human body between the waist and the shoulders; the trunk; **2,** part of a statue, esp. one without head or limbs.

tort (tôrt), *n.* in *law,* any wrong, injury, or damage (not involving a breach of contract) for which a civil action can be brought.

tor-til-la (tôr-tē′ya), a flat, thin bread made of corn, usually stuffed with a meat, cheese, or vegetable filling, called a *fajita.*

tor-toise (tôr′tis), *n.* a turtle, esp. one that lives only on land.

tor-tu-ous (tôr′tū-us), *adj.* **1,** crooked; winding; as, a *tortuous* channel; **2,** not straightforward; as, *tortuous* business policies.—*adv.* **tor′tu-ous-ly.**

tor-ture (tôr′tūr), *n.* **1,** agony of mind or body; extreme pain; **2,** the inflicting of extreme pain or torment; as, they used *torture* to make the man confess:—*v.t.* [tortured, tortur-ing], to inflict extreme agony upon, as a punishment or as a means of persuasion.—*adj.* **tor′tur-ous** (causing torture).—*n.* **tor′tur-er.**

To-ry (tōr′i), a member of the *Progressive Conservative Party* in Canada: opposed to radical parties or policies:—**Tories,** the *Progressive Conservative Party.*

toss (tôs), *v.t.* **1,** to make a short or quick throw; pitch; as, to *toss* a ball; **2,** to lift or throw up quickly; as, to *toss* the head; **3,** to put into violent motion; cause to rise and fall; as, the waves *tossed* the vessel; the horse *tossed* its rider; **4,** to coat (food) with a dressing; as, to *toss* a salad:—*v.i.* **1,** to roll or tumble; throw oneself from side to side; be restless; as, he *tossed* on the bed in pain; **2,** to be made to rise and fall; as, the ship *tossed* on the waves:—*n.* **1,** a quick or short throw; pitch; as, a *toss* of the ball; **2,** a quick upward movement, as of the head:—**toss-up,** an even chance; as, it's a *toss-up* who will win the election.

to-tal (tō′tal), *adj.* **1,** whole; not divided; as, the *total* amount; **2,** complete; utter; as, *total* silence:—*n.* the whole sum or amount:—*v.t.* [totalled, total-ling], **1,** to find the sum of; add; as, to *total* figures; **2,** to amount to; as, the costs *total* $500; **3,** *Colloq.* to wreck completely; as, they *totalled* their car.—*adv.* **to′tal-ly.**—*n.* **to-tal′i-ty.**

to-tal-i-ta-ri-an (tō-tal′i-tâ′ri-an), *adj.* relating to a country in which one political group or party has complete control and allows no rival parties or loyalties: the government has complete power and control over the lives of its citizens.—*n.* **to-tal′i-tar′i-an-ism.**

tote (tōt), *v.t. Colloq.* **1,** to carry, esp. in person; as, to *tote* an armful of wood; **2,** to haul, as by wagon or sled.—*n.* **tote′bag′** (used for carrying personal items, etc.).

to-tem (tō′tem), *n.* **1,** in the beliefs of certain cultures, an animal, plant, or other natural object that is taken as the symbol for a family or tribe; **2,** a carved or painted representation of this animal or plant:—**totem pole,** a pole with carved and painted images of totems created by some Aboriginal tribes of the Pacific coast.

tot-ter (tot′ėr), *v.i.* **1,** to be unsteady on one's feet; stagger; **2,** to shake as if about to collapse; lose strength and firmness; as, the building *tottered.*

tou-can (tōō′kan; tōō′kän), *n.* a noisy, fruit-eating bird with a very large beak and bright plumage, found in Central and South America.

touch (tuch), *v.t.* **1,** to come into contact with; to put a hand, finger, or other part of the body against; as, she couldn't *touch* the bottom of the lake; **2,** to bring into contact with; as, he *touched* his hand to his cheek; **3,** to be in contact with; join; as, the two building lots *touch* each other; **4,** to strike lightly; play on; as, she *touched* the keys of the piano; **5,** to add a light stroke to; also, to improve; as, he *touched* up the drawing; **6,** to mark slightly with some aspect of colour; as, the sky was *touched* with rose and gold at sunset; **7,** to take a portion of; taste; as, they have not *touched* food for three days; **8,** to affect; injure or hurt; as, the books were not *touched* by the fire; this decision does not *touch* you; **9,** to affect mentally; derange; as, he has been *touched* by sorrow; **10,** to affect the senses or feelings of; as, her sorrow *touches* us deeply; **11,** to refer to; as, to *touch* a subject in conversation; **12,** to reach; as, to be *touched* by a scandal; **13,** to equal; compare with; as, your books can't *touch* mine:—*v.i.* **1,** to be in contact, as, the two carpets *touch*; **2,** to speak of a subject briefly; as, to *touch* on art:—*n.* **1,** the act or fact of touching; **2,** a slight tap; as, she attracted my attention by a *touch* on the arm; **3,** the sense or feeling by which objects are felt and known by the hands and other body parts; **4,** a distinctive manner of execution; as, the *touch* of a master in painting; **5,** the manner of action of the fingers or hand; as, she plays the piano with a light *touch*; **6,** a particular feeling sensed through the hands or other body parts; as, velvet has a silky, smooth *touch*; **7,** communication; as, she kept in *touch* with her family while she was away; **8,** a very slight amount; as, a *touch* of pepper; a light attack; as, a *touch* of influenza:—**touch football**, an informal game played chiefly in schools (without defensive equipment), the ball carrier being "downed" by a touch rather than a tackle:—**to touch up**, to make small changes or improvements.

touch-down (tuch′doun′), *n.* **1,** in *football*, a score (6 points), made by moving the ball, or otherwise legally possessing it, beyond the opponent's goal-line; **2,** the landing or moment of landing of a spacecraft or other aircraft.

tou-ché (tōō′shā′; tōō-shā′), *adj.* and *interj.* **1,** being scored against in an argument, or an acknowledgment of this; **2,** in *fencing*, touched by the opponent's weapon.

touch-ing (tuch′ing), *adj.* arousing sympathy; pathetic; as, a *touching* tale of a dog's devotion.

touch screen, in *computing*, a type of computer screen that the user can activate by touching with a finger or stylus to select options or enter data.

touch-stone (tuch′stōn′), *n.* any standard for testing quality; as, time is the *touchstone* of merit.

touch-y (tuch′i), *adj.* [touch-i-er, touch-i-est], irritable; very sensitive; easily offended.—*n.* **touch′i-ness.**

tough (tuf), *adj.* **1,** difficult to break, cut, tear, or chew; strong; as, *tough* wood or *tough* meat; **2,** able to endure hardship or strain; as, a *tough* body; **3,** hard to change; stubborn; as, he is *tough* to reason with; **4,** difficult; as, a *tough* problem; **5,** likely to fight; mean; rough; as, Lara is a *tough* but interesting character:—*n.* **tough′ness.**

tough-en (tuf′en), *v.t.* and *v.i.* **1,** to make or become hard to break or divide; **2,** to make or become strong, stubborn, etc.

tou-pee (tōō-pā′; -pē′), *n.* a small wig to cover a bald spot.

tour (tōōr), *n.* **1,** a journey, an excursion, or a trip; as, to make a *tour* of the Maritime provinces; to *tour* a museum; **2,** a period of time for fulfilling a required task or service; as, a tour of duty as a peacekeeper:—*v.i.* to make a journey:—*v.t.* to make a trip through; as, to *tour* the country.

tour-ist (tōōr′ist), *n.* one who travels, esp. for sight-seeing or pleasure.—*n.* **tour′ism.**

tour-na-ment (tōōr′na-ment; tûr′na-ment), *n.* **1,** in the Middle Ages, a contest with blunt lances or swords, by knights on horseback; also, a complete series of such contests occurring at one meeting; **2,** now, any meeting for a trial of skill, esp. a series of meetings to determine a championship, as in tennis.

tour-ni-quet (tōōr′ni-ket′), *n.* a device for compressing a blood vessel to control the flow of blood, consisting of a bandage twisted tight by a stick, an elastic rubber bandage, a pad that can be pressed tight by a screw, etc.

tou-sle (tou′zl). *v.t.* to dishevel; put into disorder; as, *tousled* hair, clothes, etc.

tow (tō), *v.t.* to pull or drag by a rope or line; as, to *tow* a boat; *tow* an automobile:—*n.* the act of pulling or the condition of being pulled; as, a boat in *tow*; they had to get a *tow*.—*n.* **tow′rope′.**

to-ward (tō′ėrd; tōrd; too-wôrd′) or **towards** (tō′ėrdz; tōrdz; too-wôrdz′,) *prep.* **1,** in the direction of; as, go *toward* the city; **2,** with respect to; regarding; as, her attitude *toward* free trade; **3,** near to; close upon; as, *toward* evening; **4,** with a view to; for; contributing to; as, take this money *toward* your charity drive.

tow-el (tou′el), *n.* a cloth or piece of absorbent paper for drying anything wet:—*v.t.* [towelled, towelling; also toweled, toweling], to wipe or dry; as, he *towelled* himself after his shower.—*n.* **tow′ell-ing.**

tow-er (tou′ėr), *n.* **1,** a high structure, rising above its surroundings, either standing alone or attached to a building; as, a bell *tower;* **2,** a citadel or fortress; **3,** anything resembling a tower in actual height or in being above other things or people in strength, endurance, etc.:—*v.i.* to rise to a height; to extend above other objects or persons; as, the giant *towered* above everyone.

tow-er-ing (tou′ėr-ing), *adj.* **1,** very high; lofty; as, a *towering* tree; **2,** intense; very great; outstanding; as, a *towering* fury or a *towering* figure in science.

town (toun), *n.* **1,** a collection of houses, buildings, etc., where people live and work: larger than a village but smaller than a city; **2,** the citizens of such a place; as, the *town* opposed the tax; **3,** the business or shopping centre area; as, let's drive into *town*; **4,** a unit of local government.—*n.* **town′hall′.**

town-ship (toun′ship), *n.* **1,** a district or unit of local government; **2,** in the Prairie Provinces, an area of land of about 93 square kilometres.

tox′ic (tok′sik), *adj.* having to do with or being a poison; as, *toxic* fumes:—**toxic waste,** the poisonous remains of industrial chemicals.

tox-in (tok′sin), *n.* any of various poisons produced by certain bacteria and viruses and causing diseases.

toy (toi), *n.* **1,** a child's plaything; **2,** something that is made to amuse or entertain; **3,** a dog that is much smaller than one of the regular breed; as, a *toy* poodle:—*v.i.* to play with something; handle or treat something idly; as, she *toyed* with her purse; to *toy* with the idea of going abroad:—*adj.* like, or made as, a plaything; as, a *toy* soldier.

trace (trās), *v.t.* [traced, trac-ing], **1,** to follow a route, trail, or course of someone or something; as, to *trace* the route of the pioneers; **2,** to copy by following the lines of, as with a pencil on transparent or tracing paper placed over the original; **3,** to follow up; study; as, to *trace* a family record:—*v.i.* to make one's way; follow a trail:—*n.* **1,** a mark, indication, or sign left by something that has passed by or disappeared; as, there were *traces* of deer tracks in the snow; **2,** a small quantity or portion of something; as, a *trace* of poison was found in the food.—*adj.* **trace′a-ble.**

tra-che-a (trā′kē-a; tra-kē′a), *n.* [*pl.* tracheae (trā′ki-ē; tra-kē′ē)], the windpipe; the air tube that runs between the throat and the lungs.

trac-ing (trā′sing), *n.* that which is copied, as a copy of a pattern or design made by marking on thin paper over the original.

track (trak), *n.* **1,** a mark or impression left by the foot, a wheel, etc.; a trace; **2,** a beaten path; road; as, a *track* has been worn through the woods; also, the path which something takes; as, the *track* of a storm; **3,** the state of maintaining contact with current events, people, etc.; as, he kept *track* of all the graduates of the school; **4,** a course laid out for a special purpose; as, a race *track* for horse-racing; **5,** a set of rails that a train runs on; **6,** the continuous metal belts that tanks and tractors move on; **7,** a music selection on a CD-ROM:—*v.t.* **1,** to seek or follow by means of traces or marks; to trail; as, to *track* a deer; **2,** to make footprints upon or with; as, to *track* a floor with dirt; to *track* dirt across a floor:—**keep (lose) track of,** to keep (fail to keep) informed about or in communication with; as, we had so much fun, we lost track of the time.

track and field, a group of sporting events that involve running, jumping, and throwing.

track meet, an event in which athletes come together to compete in track and field events.

track-ball (trak′bôl), *n.* in *computing,* a small ball in a holder that can be rotated to move a cursor on a screen: similar in function to a mouse.

track-ing (trak′ing), *n.* in *computing,* using a mouse to move a pointer or other device over a computer screen.

tract (trakt), *n.* **1,** a large area of land; as, my family owns a large *tract* of land by a lake; **2,** a system of parts or organs in the body that work together; as, the digestive *tract.*

trac-ta-ble (trak′ta-bl), *adj.* **1,** docile; easily led or managed; as, a *tractable* child; **2,** easily handled or worked; as, gold is a *tractable* metal.

trac-tion (trak′shun), *n.* **1,** the act of drawing or pulling, as by a tractor, etc., **2,** the power to grip the surface of the road or ground and not slip while in motion; as, *traction* is important on icy roads.

trac-tor (trak′tėr), *n.* anything that draws or hauls, esp. a heavy motor vehicle with large tires or continuous metal tracks for pulling farm machinery, trucks, etc.

trac-tor–trai-ler (trak′tėr–trā′lėr), *n.* a vehicle with two attached parts, such as a tractor and a trailer, used for hauling; a tandem (def. 4).

trade (trād), *n.* **1,** the act or business of buying and selling goods and services; as, Canada carries on *trade* with the United States and other countries; **2,** a particular way of working for a living, usually manual or mechanical, which a person learns and practices; as, he is a carpenter by *trade;* **3,** a particular type of business; as, the construction *trade;* **4,** all the persons engaged in a particular business; as, she deals with the clothing *trade*; **5,** the exchange of one thing for another:—*adj.* relating to business; as, a *trade* journal:—*v.i.* [trad-ed, trad-ing], **1,** to buy and sell goods; as, to *trade* in oil; **2,** to take unfair advantage; as, to *trade* on a person's sympathy:—*v.t.* to exchange; as, professional sports teams often trade players:—**to trade in,** to give something as part of the payment when buying a new item of the same kind; as, they want to *trade in* their old car and get a new one.

trade-mark (trād′–märk′), *n.* **1,** a word, logo, or design, used by a merchant or manufacturer to distinguish his or her products from the products made or sold by others; **2,** any distinctive feature that identifies a person or thing; as, former Prime Minister Trudeau's *trademark* was a flower in his lapel.

trad-er (trād′ėr), *n.* **1,** a person who takes part in trade; as, a fur *trader*; a person who trades in stocks; **2,** a ship used to carry on trade:—**trade route,** a sea or land route used to travel from one place to another for trade, especially in former times.

trade union, an association formed to protect and expand the rights of workers, esp. those working in one trade, and to bargain with employers for contracts.

trad-ing post (trād′ing pōst), *n.* a store in a frontier region where people could sell or exchange goods like furs for food and other supplies.

tra-di-tion (tra-dish′un), *n.* **1,** the handing down of information, opinions, doctrines, practices, etc., by word of mouth, from generation to generation; **2,** that which is so handed down; as, family *traditions*; **3,** an old custom so well established as to be almost as effective as a law.—*adj.* **tra-di′tion-al.**—*adv.* **tra-di′tion-al-ly.**

traf-fic (traf′ik), *n.* **1,** the business of buying and selling goods, esp. illegal goods; as, the drug *traffic*; **2,** the moving of cars, trucks, ships, planes, buses, or other vehicles along a certain route; as, the downtown *traffic* is getting worse every year:—*v.i.* [trafficked, traffick-ing], to buy, sell, or deal in goods, esp. stolen or illegal goods; as, to *traffic* in elephant ivory.—*n.* **traf′fick-er.**

trag-e-dy (traj′e-di), *n.* [*pl.* tragedies], **1,** a play in which the main character meets death or ruin through fate or because of some fault in his or her character; as, *Macbeth* is one of Shakespeare's most powerful *tragedies*; **2,** any story, poem, etc., that has a sad ending; **3,** a melancholy occurrence; a fatal event; a natural disaster.

trag-ic (traj′ik), *adj.* **1,** relating to tragedy; as, a *tragic* play; **2,** terrible; sad; as, a *tragic* accident.

trail (trāl), *v.t.* **1,** to draw or drag along behind; as, to *trail* oars in the water; **2,** to hunt or follow by tracking; as, the hunters *trailed* the bear:—*v.i.* **1,** to fall or hang down so as to sweep along the ground; as, her dress *trailed*; **2,** to grow to some length; as, the morning-glory *trails* along the wall; **3,** to follow the tracks or path of; also, to move in a long and straggling line; as, they *trailed* home one by one; **4,** to lag behind; be last; as, to *trail* in a race:—*n.* **1,** a track left by a person, an animal, or a moving object; as, the hurricane left a *trail* of ruin; **2,** a footpath or track through a wilderness; as, a hiking *trail*; **3,** the scent followed in hunting; as, the dogs lost the *trail* when they came to the river; a trace or clue; **4,** anything drawn out in the wake of something; as, a *trail* of dust followed the car:—**trail off,** to become weaker and fade away; as, the sound of the band became weaker and weaker.

trail-er (trāl′ėr), *n.* **1,** any vehicle drawn by a car, truck, tractor, etc.; as, they liked to go camping in their *trailer*; **2,** in *film*, a series of short excerpts showing scenes from a forthcoming feature picture.

train (trān), *n.* **1,** a connected line of railway cars pulled by an engine; **2,** that part of a formal dress or robe that trails on the ground behind the wearer; **3,** a group of vehicles, pack animals, or people traveling together; **4,** any series of connected ideas or events; as, a *train* of ideas:—*v.t.* **1,** to instruct by practice; to drill; discipline; educate; as, the hockey coach *trains* the players; **2,** to teach to perform certain motions, tricks, etc.; as, to *train* seals; *train* horses; **3,** to direct the growth of; as, to *train* a plant:—*v.i.* to prepare oneself for a contest of strength or skill; drill.—*n.* **train′er; train-ee′** (a person who is being trained).—*adj.* **trained.**

train-ing (trān′ing), *n.* **1,** education or instruction in how to do something; **2,** a program for good physical conditioning; as, you need to be in *training* for months before you run a marathon.

trait (trāt), *n.* a feature or characteristic; as, a *trait* of character.

trai-tor (trā′tėr), *n.* a person guilty of treason; one who betrays his or her country, cause, or friends.—*adj.* **trai′tor-ous.**

tra-jec-to-ry (tra-jek′to-ri), *n.* the curve described by a body moving through space, as the path of a bullet shot from a rifle.

tramp (tramp), *v.t.* and *i.* **1,** to step upon forcibly and repeatedly; as, to *tramp* the grass down; **2,** to travel by foot; to walk or hike; **3,** to walk with a heavy step:—*n.* **1,** a person who has no home or job and wanders from place to place; **2,** a walk or hike; **3,** the sound of heavy footsteps; **4,** a freight steamer that picks up a cargo wherever it can.

tram-ple (tram′pl), *v.t.* [tram-pled, tram-pling], to tread down under the feet; as, don't *trample* the grass:—*v.i.* to walk heavily; to inflict hurt or grief by unkind treatment; as, to *trample* on a person's feelings.

tram-po-line (tram′po-lin), *n.* a strong piece of canvas or other material tightly stretched on a frame: used by acrobats and gymnasts for feats of jumping, tumbling, etc.

trance (trȧns), *n.* **1,** a half-conscious or sleeplike state in which the mind and senses cannot be aroused: may be the result of hypnotism; **2,** a daze or stupor; **3,** a state of mind in which a person is completely absorbed by something and not aware of what is happening; as, Anna sat in a *trance* staring at the water.

tran-quil (trang′kwil; tran′kwil), *adj.* [tranquil-ler, tranquil-lest], calm; quiet; serene; as, a *tranquil* mind; a *tranquil* scene.—*adv.* **tran′quil-ly.**—*n.* **tran-quil′i-ty.**

tranquil-liz-er (trang′kwi-līz′ėr; tran′), *n.* a drug taken to reduce tension, anxiety, etc.:—*v.t.* **tran′quil-lize′.** Also, **tran′quil-ize′; tran′quil-iz′er.**

trans-act (tran-zakt′; trans-akt′), *v.t.* to conduct or manage, as business; also, to close; complete; as, to *transact* a deal.—*n.* **trans-ac′tion.**

trans-at-lan-tic (trans′at-lan′tik), *adj.* **1,** beyond the Atlantic; **2,** crossing the Atlantic; as, a *transatlantic* flight.

tran-scend (tran-send′), *v.t.* **1,** to rise above or go beyond; exceed; as, the need for justice should *transcend* the concern for money; **2,** to surpass; excel; as, his ability *transcends* mine.—*adj.* **tran-scend′ent; tran′scen-den′tal.**—*n.* **tran-scend′ence.**

trans-con-ti-nen-tal (trans′kon-ti-nen′tal; tranz′), *adj.* extending across a continent; as, a *transcontinental* road.

tran-scribe (tran-skrīb′), *v.t.* [transcribed, transcrib-ing], to make a written copy of something; as, the mediaeval monks *transcribed* many manuscripts.—*n.* **tran-scrip′tion.**

tran-script (tran′skript), *n.* a written or officially recorded copy: often a student's grades.

trans-fer (trans-fûr′), *v.t.* [transferred, transfer-ring], **1,** to move a person officially from one job, position, or location to another; as, her company *transferred* her from New Delhi to Vancouver; **2,** in *law*, to give over the possession or ownership of; as, to *transfer* a piece of land; **3,** to change or move from one place to another; as, Mario *transferred* a file from the hard drive to a disk:—*v.i.* to change from one streetcar, train, bus, etc., to another at a junction point:—*n.* (trans′fûr), **1,** the making over of a right, title, property, etc., from one person to another; **2,** the act or fact of transferring; a move from one place to another; as, computers speed up the *transfer* of information; **3,** a ticket permitting a person to change from one streetcar, bus, etc., to another.—*adj.* **trans-fer′a-ble** (trans-fûr′a-bl; trans′fėr-a-bl).—*n.* **trans′fer-ence** (trans′fėr-ens; trans-fûr′ens).

trans-fix (trans-fiks′), *v.t.* **1,** to make motionless; as, the sight *transfixed* me with horror.

trans-form (trans-fôrm′), *v.t.* **1,** to change the shape or appearance of; to change into something else; **2,** to change the nature of; convert; as, to *transform* a child by kindness; **3,** to change (an electric current) from higher to lower, or from lower to higher, voltage; **4,** to change (one form of energy) into another.—*n.* **trans′for-ma′tion; trans-form′er.**

trans-fu-sion (trans-fū′zhun), *n.* the transfer of blood from one person to another by medical means: usually after an accident or operation.

tran-sient (tran-zi-ent; tran′shent), *adj.* **1,** fleeting; brief; passing; as, *transient* hopes; **2,** coming and going; temporary; as, *transient* tenants:—*n.* a temporary tenant.

tran-sis-tor (tran-zis′tėr; -sis′), *n.* a tiny electronic device that is used to control the flow of electricity in computers, portable radios, televisions, satellites, etc.: in *computing,* transistors act as switches.

trans-it (tran′zit; tran′sit), *n.* the act of carrying or moving something; as, in a city, the system for moving people is usually called public *transit.*

tran-si-tion (tran-zish′un; tran-sizh′un; tran-sish′un), *n.* the passage from one place, period, state, subject, etc. to another; in *music,* an abrupt change from one key to another.—*adj.* **tran-si′tion-al.**

tran-si-tive (tran′si-tiv), *adj.* in *grammar,* requiring or taking a direct object to complete the meaning; as, "wrote" and "mailed" in the sentence "I wrote a card and mailed it" are *transitive* verbs:—*n.* a transitive verb. Compare *intransitive.*

tran-si-tory (tran′si-tėr-i), *adj.* brief; lasting but a short time; quickly passing; as, this *transitory* life.

trans-late (trans-lāt′), *v.t.* [translat-ed, trans-lat-ing], **1,** to change from one language into another; as, to *translate* a story from French into English; **2,** to explain or say in other words; as, her little "nap" *translated* into a five-hour sleep.—*n.* **trans-la′tor; trans-la′tion.**

trans-lu-cent (trans-lū′sent), *adj.* permitting light to go through, but not transparent; as, frosted glass is *translucent.*

trans-mis′sion (tranz-mish′un), *n.* **1,** the act of transmitting; sending or passing something from one place or body to another; as, some rodents can *transmit* diseases; **2,** the broadcasting or sending out of radio and television signals; **3,** the series of gears that transfer power from the engine to the wheels of a car, truck, or other vehicle; **4,** in *computing,* the transferring of signals between parts of a computer system:—**transmission speed**, in *computing,* the rate at which data can be received and sent: usually referred to as the *baud rate.*

trans-mit (tranz-mit′; trans-), *v.t.* [trans-mit-ted, transmit-ting], **1,** to send or pass on from one person or place to another; as, to *transmit* documents over the Internet; **2,** to conduct; as, iron *transmits* heat; **3,** to send out radio or television signals.

trans-mit-ter (tranz-mit′ėr; trans-), *n.* an electronic device for sending out radio or television signals.

trans-mute (tranz-mūt′; trans-), *v.t.* to change from one form, substance, or class to another; as, to *transmute* a base metal into gold; to *transmute* aimlessness into purpose.—*n.* **trans′mu-ta′tion.**

trans-o-ce-an-ic (tranz′ō-shi-an′ik; trans′), *adj.* across, or crossing, the ocean.

tran-som (tran′sum), *n.* a window over a door or other window, usually hinged to a crossbar.

trans-par-ent (trans-pâr′ent; trans-par′ent), *adj.* **1,** so clear or thin that one can see through it; as, *transparent* glass; *transparent* gauze; **2,** easily detected; as, a *transparent* lie; **3,** easily understood; evident; clear; as, some people want government policy-making to be more *transparent.*—*n.* **trans-par-en-cy.**—*adv.* **trans-par-ent-ly.**

tran-spire (tran-spīr′), *v.t.* to give off (vapour, moisture, etc.) through the skin or surface; as, in summer some plants *transpire* many times their weight of water:—*v.i.* to leak out; become public; as, it *transpired* that he had no qualifications for the job.—*n.* **tran′spi-ra′tion.**

trans-plant (trans-plant′), *v.t.* **1,** to dig up and move a plant from one place to another; **2,** to move from one place to another; as, she *transplanted* her family from Toronto to Halifax; **3,** to transfer an organ or body part from one person to another through surgery:—*n.* the act or fact of transplanting, as, a kidney *transplant.*

trans-port (trans-pōrt′), *v.t.* **1,** to carry from one place to another; as, to *transport* supplies or soldiers; **2,** to carry away emotionally; as, he was *transported* with delight; **3,** in *history,* to banish or deport (a criminal) from a country:—*n.* (trans′pōrt), **1,** the act of conveying or being conveyed; as, the *transport* of grain; **2,** a means of conveyance; esp. a vessel for transporting troops, stores, etc.; an airplane (for freight or passengers); a van or trailer (pulled by tractor); **3,** a strong burst of emotion; as, a *transport* of rage.

trans-por-ta-tion (trans′pōr-tā′shun), *n.* **1,** the fact of moving people or things from one place to another; **2,** the method of moving people or things; as, they used a hydrofoil for *transportation* from island to island; **3,** in *history,* the act of banishing, or sending away, a convicted criminal.

trans-pose (trans-pōz′), *v.t.* [transposed, transpos-ing], **1,** to change the place or order of; as, to *transpose* letters in a word; **2,** in *music,* to change the key of; **3,** in *algebra,* to change (a term) from one side of an equation to the other.—*n.* **trans′po-si′tion; trans-pos′er.**

trans-verse (trans-vûrs′; trans′vûrs), *adj.* lying across, or crosswise; as, *transverse* lines:—*n.* anything that lies crosswise.—*n.* and *adj.* **trans-ver′sal.**

trap (trap), *n.* **1,** a device for catching wild animals; as, a lobster *trap;* **2,** an ambush; a means of tricking people; also, a hazard on a golf course; **3,** a device, as an S-shaped or a U-shaped bend, for sealing a drain-pipe with water against the return of sewer-gas:—*v.t.* [trapped, trap-ping], **1,** to catch; as, to *trap* rabbits; **2,** to ambush (an enemy); to capture by trickery:—*v.i.* to set traps.

trap-door (trap′dōr′), *n.* a small door set in a floor, ceiling, or roof which slides or lifts up to open.

tra-peze (tra-pēz′), *n.* a swinging horizontal bar hung between two ropes; used by acrobats in circus acts.

trap-e-zoid (trap′i-zoid′), *n.* a flat, geometric figure with four sides, only two of which are parallel.

TRAPEZOID

trap-per (trap′ėr), *n.* a person who traps animals, esp. fur-bearing animals, for their skins.

trap-pings (trap′ingz), *n.pl.* ornaments, esp. adornments of dress; as, the *trappings* of royalty: originally used of horses.

trash (trash), *n.* anything that is thrown away; refuse; rubbish.—*adj.* **trash′y.**

trau-ma (trô′ma), *n.* **1,** bodily injury; a wound; **2,** shock.—*adj.* **trau-mat′ic** (being or causing a great injury or shock).

trav-el (trav′el), *v.i.* [travelled, travel-ling], **1,** to journey from place to place for pleasure, recreation, or adventure; **2,** to move from place to place in the course of business; as, she *travels* for a paint firm; **3,** to move on or proceed; as, the train *travels* from Toronto to Ottawa:—*v.t.* to journey over or through; as, to *travel* a hard road; he has *travelled* the North from end to end:—*n.* a journey; as, for them, *travel* is a passion; a record of one's *travels.*—*n.* **trav′el-ler.**

trav-e-logue or **trav-e-log** (trav′e-lôg′), *n.* **1,** a lecture on travels, illustrated by visuals; **2,** a film of travels.

trav-erse (trav′ėrs), *v.t.* [traversed, travers-ing], **1,** to cross in travelling; travel or pass over; as, to *traverse* a city; also, to move forward and backward over; cross and recross; as, the beams of a searchlight *traverse* the sky; **2,** to extend across; as, canals *traverse* the country:—*n.* something placed or lying across something else; a crosspiece:—*adj.* lying across.

trav-es-ty (trav′is-ti), *n.* **1,** an absurd or fantastic imitation of a serious literary work; **2,** any serious subject that has been ridiculed; as, a *travesty* of justice.

trawl (trôl), *n.* **1,** a dragnet used in sea fishing; also called *trawlnet;* **2,** a long fishing line to which many short lines are attached; a trawl line:—*v.i.* and *v.t.* to fish with a trawl, or trawl line.—*n.* **trawl′er** (a ship for trawling).

tray (trā), *n.* a flat, shallow receptacle of wood, metal, etc., with a raised rim, used for carrying or displaying things.

treach-er-ous (trech′ėr-us), *adj.* **1,** betraying a trust or pledge; **2,** not to be trusted in spite of appearances; as, a *treacherous* friend; not safe; as, a *treacherous* sea.—*adv.* **treach′er-ously.**—*n.* **treach′er-y.**

tread (tred), *v.i.* [*p.t.* trod (trod), *p.p.* trod-den (trod′n) or trod, *p.pr.* tread-ing], **1,** to step or walk; as, *tread* carefully on the carpet; **2,** to press something beneath the foot; trample; as, don't *tread* on my toes:—*v.t.* **1,** to walk on; **2,** to press or crush under the feet; as, to *tread* grapes:—*n.* **1,** the act or sound of walking or stepping; also, the manner or style of walking; as, a firm *tread;* **2,** in a flight of stairs, the horizontal surface of a step; **3,** the part of a wheel or tire that touches the road or rail; also, the mark or rut left by a wheel or tire on a road.

tread-mill (tred′mil′) *n.* **1,** a mill worked by persons or animals walking on a wheel or endless belt; also, a similar device used for exercise; as, a *treadmill* in a health club; **2,** any tiresome routine.

trea-son (trē′zn), *n.* the betrayal of one's country by aiding its enemies; an attempt to overthrow the government of one's country; as, the traitor was passing military information to the enemy.—*adj.* **trea′son-ous; trea′son-a-ble.**

treas-ure (trezh′ėr), *n.* **1,** an abundance of wealth such as gold, silver, money, or jewels; **2,** anything highly valued; a person dear to one:—*v.t.* [treasured, treasur-ing], **1,** to retain in the mind; as, to *treasure* up memories; **2,** to value highly; as, to *treasure* an heirloom:—**treasure–trove, 1,** treasure found hidden, the original owner being unknown; **2,** any valuable discovery.

treas-ur-er (trezh′ėr-ėr), *n.* a person who has charge of receiving and paying out money for a business, club, government, or other organization.

treas-ur-y (trezh′ėr-i), *n.* [*pl.* treasuries], a place where wealth is stored, esp., a place where public funds, or the funds of an organization, are kept and paid out; also, the funds:—**Treasury,** that department of a government that has charge of the public funds; the officials of such a department.

treat (trēt), *v.t.* **1,** to handle, deal with, or manage; as, the speaker *treated* his subject cleverly; **2,** to behave or act toward; as, to *treat* others kindly; **3,** to regard or consider; as, to *treat* a matter lightly; **4,** to expose to a chemical or physical process to improve or change the condition of something; as, to *treat* the wood with a preservative; **5,** to entertain; as, he *treated* his guests to music; also, to pay the cost of entertainment for (someone); **6,** to give medical care or treatment; as, a doctor *treats* his patients; to *treat* a cold:—*v.i.* **1,** to discuss or deal with; as, the book *treats* of Canadian economic policy; **2,** to negotiate; as, they were ready to *treat* with the smugglers:—*n.* **1,** the act of paying for entertainment, food, etc., for a friend; also, the entertainment or food given; **2,** something which gives great pleasure; as, the circus is a *treat.*

trea-tise (trē′tiz), *n.* a long, written discussion or essay on a particular subject.

treat-ment (trēt′ment), *n.* **1,** manner of dealing with a person, problem, etc.; as, a firm's generous *treatment* of employees; **2,** medical or surgical care of a person.

trea-ty (trē′ti), *n.* [*pl.* treaties], a formal agreement between two or more groups or nations, for settling differences, arranging commercial relations, or ending wars; as, the *Treaty* of Versailles in 1919 officially ended World War I.

tre-ble (treb′l), *adj.* **1,** threefold or triple; **2,** in *music,* relating to the highest vocal or instrumental part; of high pitch:—*n.* **1,** in *music,* the highest part; **2,** a soprano singer or instrument; also, a high-pitched voice or sound:—*v.t.* and *v.i.* [tre-bled, tre-bling], to make or become three times as great.—*adv.* **tre′bly.**

tree (trē), *n.* **1,** a tall, woody plant with a main trunk from which branches and leaves or needles grow; **2,** in *computing,* a visual representation showing the hierarchical structure of directories: subdirectories branch from directories that branch from a root directory, etc.:—**family tree,** an outline or diagram, sometimes shaped like a tree, showing family descent and relationships:—*v.t.* [treed, tree-ing], to drive up a tree; as, to *tree* an opossum.

trek (trek), *v.i.* **1,** in *history,* to travel or migrate, as by ox-wagon (esp. in South Africa); **2,** to make a long, difficult journey; to travel slowly or laboriously; as, they *trekked* across prairies, deserts, and mountains:—*n.* a long, difficult journey.

trel-lis (trel′is), *n.* a frame of wood or metal for plants to grow on; a latticework:—*v.t.* to provide with a lattice for vines; train (vines) on a lattice.

trem-ble (trem′bl), *v.i.* [trem-bled, trem-bling], **1,** to shake or shiver without control, as with fear or cold; shudder; **2,** to quaver, as a sound:—*n.* an involuntary shaking; a shiver; shudder.—*adj.* and *n.* **trem′bling.**—*adv.* **trem′bling-ly.**

tre-men-dous (tri-men′dus), *adj.* **1,** exciting fear or terror because of unusual size or violence; terrible; as, a *tremendous* crash; **2,** astonishing; extraordinary; as, a *tremendous* feat.—*adv.* **tre-men′dous-ly.**

trem-o-lo (trem′o-lō′), *n.* in *music,* a tremulous or vibrating effect, as made by a rapid or fluttering repetition of a tone or chord; **2,** a device in an organ for making such a tone.

trem-or (trem′ėr; trē′mėr), *n.* **1,** a trembling, quivering, or shaking; as, an earthquake *tremor;* **2,** a thrill or quiver of excitement.

trem-u-lous (trem′ū-lus), *adj.* **1,** trembling; quivering; shaking; **2,** showing fear or timidity; as, a *tremulous* voice; **3,** marked by unsteadiness; as, *tremulous* writing.—*adv.* **trem′u-lous-ly.**

trench (trench), *n.* **1,** a long, narrow ditch in the earth; an open ditch for draining; **2,** a deep ditch dug by soldiers in a zone of battle and held as a defensive position or as a base from which to attack; **3,** a long, narrow, depression in the ocean floor:—*v.t.* **1,** to cut a ditch in; to drain by ditches; **2,** to dig trenches for (an army):—**trench coat,** a short, lined, belted raincoat.

trench-ant (tren′chant), *adj.* **1,** sharp; keen; as, a *trenchant* sword; also, cutting or biting; as, *trenchant* satire; **2,** forceful and clear; as, a *trenchant* explanation.

trend (trend), *n.* the general direction taken by something; as, the northeasterly *trend* of the Gulf Stream; general tendency or drift; as, the *trend* of public opinion:—*v.i.* **1,** to take a particular direction or course; **2,** to have a general tendency; as, prices are *trending* upward.

trend-y (trend′i), *adj.* [-ier, -iest], *Colloq.* keeping up with or influenced by the latest styles, as a *trendy* haircut.

trep-i-da-tion (trep′i-dā′shun), *n.* **1,** a trembling or vibration; **2,** a state of nervous alarm; fear mingled with uncertainty.

tres-pass (tres′pas), *v.i.* **1,** to enter unlawfully upon the property of another; **2,** to make an unjustified claim on a person's time, presence, attention, etc.:—*n.* **1,** in *law*, the act of trespassing; **2,** an older word for a wrong act or sin.—*n.* **tres′pass-er.**

tres-tle (tres′l), *n.* the framework that supports a bridge or other structure.

tri- (trī), *prefix* meaning three; as, *tri*cycle; *tri*angle.

tri-ad (trī′ad), *n.* a group of three; as, a *triad* of virtues; in *music*, a common chord; in *chemistry*, an element, atom, or radical with the power of combining with three hydrogen atoms.

tri-al (trī′al), *n.* **1,** the act of testing or putting to a test; as, the *trial* of the new airplane proved it unsatisfactory; **2,** the state of being tested; a chance to make good; as, give this coffee a week's *trial;* **3,** hardship; as, a time of *trial* and suffering; **4,** a person or thing that puts faith, mercy, or patience to the test; as, he was a great *trial* to his family; **5,** the process of hearing and judging evidence in a court of law to determine a person's guilt or innocence.

tri-an-gle (trī′ang′gl), *n.* **1,** a figure with three sides and three angles; **2,** anything shaped like a triangle; **3,** a musical instrument used in orchestras, etc., consisting of a steel rod bent in the form of a triangle open at one corner, sounded with a light metal rod.—*adj.* **tri-an′gu-lar.**

tri-ath-lon (trī-ath′lon), *n.* a competition in which athletes take part in three different events, usually swimming, long-distance running, and cycling.—*n.* **tri-ath′lete.**

tribe (trīb), *n.* **1,** a group of people who live in the same area and share certain things in common like language, customs, and religious beliefs; **2,** a group of people sharing a common profession or hobby; as, a *tribe* of actors.—*adj.* **trib′al.**

trib-u-la-tion (trib′u-lā′shun), *n.* severe affliction or distress; deep sorrow; also, a cause of affliction or distress.

tri-bu-nal (trī-bū′nal; tri-bū′nal), *n.* a board, esp. one set up by a government to settle disputes of various types; as, a human rights *tribunal.*

trib-u-tar-y (trib′ū-tėr-i-), *n.* [*pl.* tributaries], a river or stream flowing into a larger river.

trib-ute (trib′ūt), *n.* **1,** a forced payment, esp. in *history,* when states paid *tribute* to the Roman Empire; **2,** an act done to show respect or to honour someone; as, the club paid *tribute* to their president for all her good work.

trice (trīs), *n.* an instant; as, in a *trice.*

trick (trik), *n.* **1,** a clever, crafty, or deceitful device or action, used in order to gain an advantage, to fool, or to cheat; **2,** an exhibition of skill and dexterity; as, a card *trick*; **3,** a mischievous, sometimes annoying, prank; **4,** a particular skill; knack; as, there is a *trick* to pole-vaulting; **5,** all the cards played in one round of a game; as, they took four *tricks*:—*v.t.* to cheat; fool; deceive; as, they *tricked* their parents into thinking they were at the library.—*n.* **trick′ster.**

trick-ery (trik′ėr-i), *n.* [*pl.* trickeries], deception; cheating; fraud.

trick-le (trik′l), *v.i.* [trick-led, trick-ling], to flow gently in a small stream; also, to drip; fall in drops; as, water *trickled* from the tap:—*n.* a small amount (of liquid) flowing gently or dripping; as, a *trickle* of visitors.

trick-y (trik′i), *adj.* [trick-i-er, trick-i-est], **1,** inclined to play tricks; also, deceptive; cunning; sly; as, a *tricky* horse; **2,** requiring careful handling or skill; as, steering a boat through the rocky channel can be very *tricky.*

tri-col-our (trī′kul′ėr), *n.* a flag of three colours arranged in equal stripes; esp., the national flag of France, of blue, white, and red vertical stripes.

tri-cy-cle (trī′sik-l), *n.* a light, three-wheeled vehicle, with a single seat, and usually operated by pedals.

tri-dent (trī′dent), *n.* a three-pronged fish-spear, as of Neptune or Britannia.

tried (trīd), *p.t.* and *p.p.* of *try.*

tri-fle (trī′fl), *n.* **1,** anything of little value

or importance; **2,** a small amount, as of money; as, the repairs cost only a *trifle;* **3,** a dessert made of cake, custard, and jam:—**a trifle,** rather; somewhat; as, a *trifle* disturbed:—*v.i.* [tri-fled, tri-fling], **1,** to act or talk without seriousness; **2,** to dally; toy; play; as, she *trifled* with her necklace as she talked:—*v.t.* to waste; as, to *trifle* away time.—*n.* **tri′fler.**—*adj.* and *n.* **tri′fling.**

trig-ger (trig′ėr), *n.* a lever which, when pulled by the finger, releases the hammer of a gun; also, a catch serving a similar purpose, as for springing a trap:—*v.t.* to cause or start something; as, to *trigger* a chain reaction.

trig-o-nom-e-try (trig′o-nom′e-tri), *n.* the branch of mathematics dealing with the ratios among the sides and angles of triangles, esp. the right triangle; the application of these ratios to surveying, navigating, engineering, etc.

trill (tril), *n.* **1,** a trembling or quavering on a musical tone; as, the *trill* of a bird; also, a vibration of the tongue, as in pronouncing *r,* or the sound produced by such vibration; **2,** in *music,* a quick alternation of two notes a step or a half step apart; also, the mark indicating this:—*v.t.* to utter with a vibration; as, to *trill* one's r's:—*v.i.* to make the voice vibrate.

tril-lion (tril′yun), *n.* a thousand billion: 1, 000,000,000,000.

tril-li-um (tril′i-um), *n.* a plant with three leaves surrounding a large, three-petalled flower; also, the flower:—**white trillium,** Ontario's floral emblem.

TRILLIUM

tri-lo-bite (trī′lo-bīt′), *n.* any of a group of marine arthropods with a segmented outside skeleton divided in three lobes: often found as fossils.

tril-o-gy (tril′o-ji), *n.* a series of three plays, or three musical, literary, or artistic compositions, closely related in spirit or theme, but each complete in itself, as Shakespeare's *Henry VI.*

trim (trim), *v.t.* [trimmed, trim-ming], **1,** to make tidy and neat; as, to *trim* the branches off a bush; to have one's hair *trimmed;* **2,** to decorate; as, to *trim* a dress with lace; **3,** to make smooth or ready for use; as, to *trim* lumber by planing it; **4,** to adjust or balance (a ship) by proper distribution of cargo; also, to arrange (the yards and sails) to take advantage of the wind:—*n.* **1,** the state of being in good physical shape or condition; **2,** something used to decorate or finish; as, she sewed a *trim* on the bottom of her skirt; **3,** the inside woodwork of a building around the windows, doors, etc.; **4,** of a vessel, fitness for sailing; also, its position in the water:—*adj.* [trim-mer, trim-mest], **1,** neat; tidy; as, a *trim* cabin; **2,** in good condition or shape.—*adv.* **trim′ly.**—*n.* **trim′mer.**

trim-ming (trim′ing), *n.* something used to decorate or ornament:—**trimmings, 1,** things that usually go along with something else; as, a turkey dinner with all the *trimmings;* **2,** cuttings from something that has been trimmed; as, *trimmings* from a rose bush.

tri-month-ly (trī-munth′li), *adj.* occurring every three months.

trin-ket (tring′kit), *n.* **1,** a small ornament or jewel; **2,** a trifle; toy.

tri-o (trē′ō), *n.* [*pl.* trios], **1,** a set of three; **2,** in *music,* a composition for three performers; also, a group of three musicians, either vocal or instrumental.

trip (trip), *n.* the act of traveling from one place to another, as in a car, train, plane, etc.:—*v.i.* [tripped, trip-ping], **1,** to catch the foot and lose one's balance; fall or almost fall; **2,** to run or walk lightly or nimbly; take short, quick steps; skip:—*v.t.* **1,** to cause to stumble or trip; as, the rug *tripped* me; **2,** to release or set free by pulling a catch, trigger, etc.:—**to trip up,** to cause to make a mistake; as, the last question *tripped* me *up.*

tripe (trīp), *n.* **1,** the walls of the stomach of cattle, used for food; **2,** *Colloq.* something bad or useless; as, we first thought his story was true, but now, we think it was just *tripe.*

triph-thong (trif′thong), *n.* the combining of three vowel sounds in a single syllable, as in *wye* (oo + ä + ē); three vowels used to represent one vowel sound, as in b*eau*ty (ū).

tri-ple (trip′l), *adj.* **1,** being in threes; threefold; as, a *triple* window; **2,** three times as much or as many; three times the size, strength, value, etc.; also, done three times; as, a *triple* knock:—*n.* **1,** a group or combination of three; **2,** in *baseball,* a three-base hit:—*v.t.* [tri-pled, tri-pling], to increase threefold; multiply by three; as, he *tripled* his efforts:—*v.i.* **1,** to increase to three times as much; **2,** in *baseball,* to make a three-base hit.

tri-plet (trip′lit), *n.* **1,** any group of three, such as three lines of poetry; **2,** one of three children born at one birth.

tri-plex (trī′pleks), *n.* and *adj.* threefold, or something triple; as, a *triplex* measure in music, a *triplex* building with three apartments, etc.

trip-li-cate (trip′li-kit; -kāt′), *adj.* and *n.* (made in) three identical copies:—*v.t.* to produce by threes.

tri-pod (trī′pod), *n.* **1,** a three-legged support or stand, used for holding steady a surveying instrument, camera, telescope, etc.; **2,** any article, such as a stool or vase, with three feet or legs.

tri-sect (trī-sekt′), *v.t.* in *geometry*, to cut into three equal parts, as a line, surface, or angle.—*n.* **tri-sec′tion.**

tri-syl-la-ble (trī-sil′a-bl; trī-), *n.* a word of three syllables, as *telephone*.

trite (trīt), *adj.* worn out; used far too much; commonplace; as, a *trite* reply.

tri-umph (trī′umf), *n.* **1,** a great victory; **2,** a marked success or achievement; as, the new singer scored a *triumph:—v.i.* **1,** to rejoice in success; **2,** to be successful or victorious.—*adj.* **tri-um′phal** (trī-um′fal).—*adj.* **tri-um′phant.**

tri-um-vi-rate (trī-um′vi-rit; rāt′), *n.* a government of three people ruling jointly; as, Caesar, Pompey, and Cassius (the First *Triumvirate*, B.C. 59).

triv-i-al (triv′i-al), *adj.* minor; insignificant; of little worth or importance.—*n.* **triv′i-al′i-ty.**

triv′i-a (triv′ē-a), *n.pl.* **1,** things that are not important; **2,** a quiz or game of short factual questions about history, the arts, entertainment, sports, etc.

trod (trod), *p.t.* and a *p.p.* of *tread.*

[1]**troll** (trōl), *v.t.* to fish by letting out a line and hook behind a slow-moving boat; as, she loved to *troll* for trout every summer.

[2]**troll** (trōl), in Scandinavian and other *folklore*, a giant or dwarf living in a cave, underground, or under a bridge.

trol-ley (trol′i), *n.* [*pl.* trolleys], **1,** a small wheel that moves along an overhead electrical wire to run a streetcar, train, or bus; **2,** an electric streetcar that gets its power from a trolley.

trom-bone (trom′bōn; trom-bōn′), *n.* a brass musical instrument made up of two long U-shaped tubes that are connected: the sound is changed by moving a sliding piece back and forth.

troop (tro͞op), *n.* **1,** a number of persons, or sometimes of animals, gathered together; a company; **2,** a unit of cavalry, under the command of a captain:—**troops,** armed forces:—*v.i.* to move in crowds; flock together; as, we all *trooped* into the hall:—*v.t.* to organize (persons) into a troop.

troop-er (tro͞op′ẽr), *n.* **1,** a member of a troop of mounted police or soldiers; **2,** a cavalry horse.

tro-phy (trō′fi), *n.* [*pl.* trophies], a small statue, cup, or other object awarded to someone for winning a contest or sports event.

trop-ic (trop′ik), *n.* **1,** either of the two imaginary circles on the earth's surface, parallel to the equator, at a distance of 23°30′ north and south of it, called *Tropic of Cancer* and *Tropic of Capricorn* respectively, marking the limits of the Torrid Zone:—**tropics,** the region of the earth lying between these two circles, on or near the equator; the Torrid Zone.

trop-i-cal (trop′i-käl), *adj.* having to do with or found in the tropics.

trot (trot), *n.* **1,** a jogging pace, as of a horse, faster than a walk, in which the right forefoot and left hind foot are lifted together, and then the left forefoot and right hind foot; **2,** any jogging gait:—*v.i.* [trot-ted, trot-ting], **1,** to move at a trot; **2,** to run in a jogging gait:—*v.t.* to cause (a horse) to trot.

trou-ba-dour (tro͞o′ba-door′, tro͞o′ba-dōr′), *n.* one of a class of poets and singers of love songs, who flourished in France and Italy during the 11th, 12th, and 13th centuries.

trou-ble (trub′l), *v.t.* [trou-bled, trou-bling], **1,** to distress, perturb, or worry; as, he was *troubled* by her silence; **2,** to cause inconvenience to; as, may I *trouble* you for a glass of water? **3,** to stir up or agitate; as to *trouble* the waters; **4,** to cause pain or illness; as, her injured knee keeps *troubling* her:—*v.i.* to take pains; put oneself out; as, don't *trouble* to apologize:—*n.* **1,** mental excitement, distress, or worry; **2,** the cause of such disturbance; as, an uncooperative child is a great *trouble* to his parents; **3,** extra effort or work; as, she went to much *trouble* to be present; **4,** illness; an ailment; as, heart *trouble.*—*adj.* **trou′ble-some.**

trou-ble-shoot (trubl′ sho͞ot) *v.t.* **1,** in *computing*, to look for the cause of a hardware or software problem and fix it; **2,** to find and fix problems in other kinds of machinery, equipment, systems, plans, etc.

trough (trôf), *n.* **1,** a long, shallow, uncovered container of wood, metal, or concrete, for watering or feeding livestock; **2,** any similar container, for kneading dough, washing ore, etc.; **3,** a long, narrow uncovered gutter or drain for carrying off water; as, a pump *trough*; an eaves*trough*; **4,** any long, natural hollow; as, a *trough* between waves or hills.

trounce (trouns), *v.t.* [trounced, trouncing], to beat soundly; flog; also, to overcome or get the better of (an opponent).

troupe (tro͞op), *n.* a company, as of actors.—*n.* **troup′er** (an actor of long experience).

trou-sers (trou′zẽrz), *n.pl.* a piece of clothing with two legs that covers the body from the waist to the ankles; pants; slacks.

trous-seau (tro͞o′sō′; tro͞o′sō), *n.* [*pl.* trousseaux (tro͞o′sō′) or trousseaus (tro͞o′sōz′; tro͞o′sōz)], clothes and household items that a bride collects before a wedding.

trout (trout), *n.* [*pl.* trout], any of several kinds of fish that live in cool, clear, fresh water, such as the brook *trout*, lake *trout*, or brown *trout*: often eaten as food and popular as a game fish.

trow-el (trou′el), *n.* **1,** a flat-bladed hand tool, used by bricklayers, masons, and plasterers, for spreading mortar, plaster, etc.; **2,** a scoop-shaped tool used by gardeners for moving small plants.

tru-ant (trōō′ant), *n.* **1,** a pupil who stays away from school without permission; **2,** a person who fails to do his work or duty:—*adj.* playing the truant; idle; wandering; as, a *truant* teenager:—*n.* **tru′an-cy.**

truce (trōōs), *n.* **1,** a temporary peace or interruption of war by mutual agreement; an armistice; **2,** a lull in a period of stress and strain.

truck (truk), *n.* **1,** a motor vehicle for carrying heavy or bulky loads, esp. a large, heavy, strongly built motor vehicle for this purpose: can vary from light pickup trucks to huge tractor-trailer trucks; **2,** a strong frame or platform on wheels with a handle at one end, used for moving heavy objects by hand: refrigerators, furniture, etc.; a hand truck:—*v.t.* to carry by truck:—*v.i.* **1,** to carry goods by truck; **2,** to drive a truck for a livelihood.—*n.* **truck′er.**

truc-u-lent (truk′ū-lent; trōō′), *adj.* **1,** quarrelsome; savagely threatening or bullying; **2,** fierce; cruel; **3,** rude; scathing, esp. in speech or writing.—*n.* **truc′u-lence.**

trudge (truj), *v.i.* [trudged, trudg-ing], to travel on foot, usually with effort or labour:—*n.* a long or fatiguing walk; as, a long *trudge* to the station.

true (trōō), *adj.* [tru-er, tru-est], **1,** in accord with fact or reality; as, hers was the only *true* account of the robbery; **2,** faithful and loyal; reliable; as, a *true* friend; **3,** genuine; not pretended; as, *true* love; **4,** rightful; legitimate; as, the *true* heir; **5,** corresponding to a standard; as, a *true* colour; the spider is not a *true* insect; **6,** correct; exact; as, a *true* copy:—*adv.* **1,** truthfully; **2,** accurately; as, the hunter aimed *true*:—*v.t.* [trued, tru-ing or true-ing], to make accurate; as, to *true* a window-frame:—**to come true,** to happen just as one has dreamed, hoped, expected, etc.—*n.* **tru′ism** (platitude).

true believer, 1, a person who genuinely believes in a treatment, cause, etc.; as, she is a *true believer* in the benefits of organic food; **2,** a person who strongly or fanatically supports a position, esp. a political or religious movement; a zealot; as, the *true believers* will not listen to any other arguments.

tru-ly (trōō′li), *adv.* **1,** in agreement with truth or fact; precisely; as, *truly* told; **2,** sincerely honestly; as, *truly* grateful; **3,** in fact; indeed; as, *truly*, I am sorry.

trump (trump), *n.* in *cards*, the suit which temporarily outranks the other suits; also, any card of this suit:—*v.t.* **1,** to play a trump when trump has not been led; as, to *trump* a trick; **2,** to think up or invent; as, to *trump* up an excuse:—*v.i.* to play trump when trump has not been led:—*adj.* **trumped′ up′** (invented, false).

trum-pet (trum′pit), *n.* **1,** a metal wind-instrument formed of a single curved tube with a bell-shaped mouth, regulating keys, valves, etc.; **2,** something shaped like a trumpet or that makes such a sound; as, the elephant's *trumpet* in the jungle:—*v.t.* to proclaim or annouce loudly; as, to *trumpet* her success:—*v.i.* to utter a sound like that of a trumpet.—*n.* **trum′pet-er.**

trun-cat-ed (trung′kā-tid), *adj.* having the top or apex cut off; as, a *truncated* cone or pyramid.

trun-dle (trun′dl), *v.t.* [trun-dled, trun-dling], to roll, as a hoop; to cause to move on wheels; as, to *trundle* a go-cart:—*v.i.* to roll along; move on, or as on, small wheels:—*n.* **1,** a small wheel; caster; **2,** a kind of low-wheeled truck; **3,** a kind of low bed on casters: also called *trundle-bed.*

trunk (trungk), *n.* **1,** the thick, main stem of a tree, from which the branches and roots grow; **2,** in humans and other animals, the body exclusive of the head and limbs; **3,** the chief part, or stem, of anything that branches; as, the *trunk* of a nerve; **4,** the elongated nose, or proboscis, of an elephant, used for drawing in water, food, and air and for grasping objects; **5,** a large box or chest to hold clothes and other personal belongings for a journey; **6,** an enclosed area in a car, usually at the rear, for carrying or storing things:— *adj.* pertaining to a main line; as, a *trunk* line on a railroad; a telephone *trunk* line:—**trunks,** shorts worn by swimmers, boxers, etc.; as, swimming *trunks.*

truss (trus), *n.* **1,** a brace or framework of timbers or bars supporting a roof or bridge; **2,** a bandage or support for a rupture; **3,** a weighed measure, or a bundle, of hay or straw:—*v.t.* **1,** to bind or fasten with skewers and string; as, to *truss* a turkey; **2,** to support with a brace, framework, etc.

trust (trust), *n.* **1,** confidence; faith; belief in someone's goodness; **2,** expectation or hope; as, she put no *trust* in the future; **3,** credit granted to a buyer or borrower, because of belief in his or her honesty; as, to sell goods on *trust*; **4,** something involving duties and responsibilities; as, he regarded his wealth as a public *trust*; **5,** property, an interest in property, or money, held and managed by one party (the trustee) for the benefit of another; as, the will created *trusts* for the children; also, the state of property so held; as, the estate was held in *trust* for him; **6,** an agreement by which a group of different businesses or companies combine to control how much of a product is available and how much it will cost: trusts of this type are often illegal because they eliminate competition and drive up prices:—*v.t.* **1,** to place confidence in; rely upon; as, to *trust* one's own judgment; **2,** to believe in; as, I *trust* his word; **3,** to entrust to someone's care; **4,** to sell to on credit; to hope with confidence; as, we *trust* that you will come again:—*v.i.* to have confidence; as, we *trust* in the future:—*adj.* held in charge for someone else; as, a *trust* fund.—*adj.* **trust′ed; trust′ful; trust′worth′y.**

trus-tee (trus-tē′), *n.* **1,** a person or firm to whom property, or the management of property, is entrusted; **2,** one of a group of people who manage the affairs of a school district, church, or other such organization.

trust-ing (trus′ting), *adj.* inclined to believe in others; unsuspicious.

trust-y (trus′ti), *adj.* [trust-i-er, trust-i-est], faithful; as, a *trusty* messenger; *Colloq.* reliable; as, a *trusty* vehicle.

truth (trōōth), *n.* **1,** something that agrees with facts; something that is true; as, a witness must swear to tell the *truth*; also, correctness; accuracy; **2,** sincerity of speech and action; as, there is no *truth* in him; **3,** a generally accepted or proved fact; as, the *truths* of science.

truth-ful (trōōth′fool), *adj.* **1,** according to the facts; true; as, a *truthful* statement; **2,** naturally given to telling the truth; as, a *truthful* nature.—*adv.* **truth′ful-ly.**—*n.* **truth′fulness.**

try (trī), *v.t.* [tried, try-ing], **1,** to put to a trial or experiment; test; as, to *try* a new dish in cooking; **2,** to use something in order to test its quality or effect; as, to *try* a new brand of tea; **3,** to subject to trouble, affliction, or annoyance; as, she *tries* her parents sorely; **4,** to test the strength or endurance of; as, he *tries* my patience; **5,** to work toward doing something; make an effort; as, she is *trying* to get better grades; **6,** to attempt; endeavour to use; as, I have *tried* argument in vain; **7,** in *law*, to examine the case of an accused person before a court; put a person on trial:—*v.i.* to make an effort; as, do *try* to come:—*n.* [*pl.* tries], an attempt; as, to succeed after several *tries*:—**to try on,** to put on clothing to see how it looks or fits.

try-ing (trī′ing), *adj.* annoying; hard to bear; distressing.

try-out (trī′out′), *n.* a test to see how well a person can do something; as, they had *tryouts* for the basketball team:—*v.i.* **to try out** [tried out, try-ing out], to test or attempt to see how well one can do, esp. in a competition; as, to *try out* for the play.

tryst (trist; trīst), *n.* **1,** an engagement to meet at a certain time and place, esp. between lovers; **2,** a meeting, or place of meeting, called a **tryst′ing place:**—*v.t.* and *v.i.* to arrange or agree to a time or place of meeting.

tsar (tsär), *n.* Same as **czar.**

tsa-ri-na (tsä-rē′na), *n.* Same as **czarina.**

tset-se fly or **tzet-ze fly** (tset′si flī; tsēt′), *n.* **1,** a small African fly which by its bite causes germs to enter the blood of domestic animals, producing a severe disease; **2,** another fly of this kind which in the same way produces in humans a disease called sleeping sickness.

T-shirt (tē′shûrt), *n.* a light casual shirt with short sleeves, often made of cotton or a knit fabric: has the form of a "T" when laid flat.

Tsim-shi-an (tsim′shē-an; tsim′shen; tsim′ shan′; chim′-), *n.* [*pl.* Tsimshian or Tsimshians] **1,** an Aboriginal people living on the western coast of British Columbia; **2,** the group of languages spoken by these people.

T-square (tē′–skwâr), *n.* ruler with a crossbar at one end, used in mechanical drawing.

tub (tub), *n.* **1,** an open circular vessel of wood or metal, used for washing, etc.; **2,** a large, deep, stationary receptacle in a laundry, kitchen, or bathroom, used for washing, bathing, etc.; **3,** a small wooden cask for lard, butter, etc.; **4,** the amount contained in a tub; as, a *tub* of water; **5,** *Colloq.*: **a,** a bath; as, a hot *tub;* **b,** a slow or clumsy boat:—*v.t.* and *Colloq. v.i.* [tubbed, tub-bing], to bathe in a tub.—*adj.* **tub′by** (*Colloq.* short and fat).

tu-ba (tū′ba), *n.* a very large brass wind instrument, very low in pitch, used in bands and orchestras.

tube (tūb), *n.* **1,** a hollow cylinder, much longer than it is wide, of glass, rubber, metal, etc., for holding or conveying liquids or gases; as, a test *tube*; also, any living structure of similar shape; as, the bronchial *tubes*; **2,** a container that is long and narrow and must be squeezed to get its contents out; as, a *tube* of toothpaste; **3,** an underground or underwater tunnel through which a train or subway runs.

tu-ber (tū′bėr), *n.* a thick, roundish part of an underground stem, bearing small buds or eyes, as the potato.—*adj.* **tu′ber-ous** or **tu′ber-ose′** (-ōs).

tu-ber-cu-lo-sis (tū-bûr′kū-lō′sis), *n.* a serious disease that affects the lungs or other parts of the body; also called *TB* (formerly, *consumption*):—*adj.* **tu-ber′cu-lous; tu-ber′cu-lar.**

tub-ing (tūb′ing), *n.* **1,** a piece of tube; **2,** cylindrical material for tubes; also, a set or series of tubes; **3,** *Colloq.* a water sport where a person rides on a large tube pulled behind a motorboat.

tu-bu-lar (tū′bū-lėr), *adj.* pertaining to, shaped like, or consisting of, one or more hollow cylinders, or tubes.

tuck (tuk), *v.t.* **1,** to roll or fold; as, to *tuck* up one's sleeves; also, to turn under the loose ends of; as, to *tuck* up one's hair; **2,** to cover snugly; as to *tuck* a child into bed; **3,** to stow away neatly or into a small space; as, to *tuck* bills into a purse:—*n.* a fold of cloth that is sewn into a piece of clothing as a decoration or to make it fit better.

tuck-ered (tuk′ėrd), *adj. Colloq.* tired;

exhausted: used with *out*; as, he was *tuckered out*.

Tues-day (tūz′di; dā), *n.* the day after Monday and before Wednesday.

tuft (tuft), *n.* **1,** a small, compact bunch of feathers, threads, etc., growing together or held together at the base; as, a *tuft* of grass; *tufts* in a mattress; **2,** a cluster or clump; as, a *tuft* of asters:—*v.t.* to provide with a tuft or tufts; specifically, to reinforce (mattresses, quilts, upholstery, etc.) with thread drawn through tightly at regular intervals, tied, and finished with cotton tufts or buttons.—*adj.* **tuft′ed.**

tug (tug), *v.t.* [tugged, tug-ging], **1,** to pull or haul with an effort; **2,** to tow with a tugboat:—*v.i.* to pull; as, the child *tugs* at her mother's skirt:—*n.* a strain or pull made with great effort; also, a struggle.

tug-boat or **tug** (tug′bōt; tug), *n.* a small but powerful boat that pushes or pulls larger boats or ships, or barges loaded with cargo.

tu-i-tion (tū-ish′un), *n.* the fee charged for study at a university, college or private school.

tu-lip (tū′lip), *n.* a plant of the lily family, bearing brilliantly coloured, cup-shaped flowers; also, its bulb or flower.

tul-li-bee (tul′i-bē′), *n.* a smaller, deep-bodied cisco or whitefish of the larger Canadian prairie lakes and Great Lakes: marketed fresh, frozen, or smoked.

tum-ble (tum′bl), *v.i.* [tumbled, tum-bling], **1,** to fall suddenly and hard; **2,** to roll in play; as, the baby *tumbled* about on the floor; **3,** to perform acrobatic feats, such as springs, somersaults, etc.; **4,** to move in a careless, blundering fashion; as, he *tumbled* wearily into the chair:—*v.t.* **1,** to fling down; **2,** to cause to roll over and over like a football; **3,** to rumple; disorder; as, to *tumble* a heap of clothes:—*n.* **1,** a fall; **2,** a state of confusion or disorder; also, a disordered heap.—*n.* **tum′ble-weed′.**

tum-bler (tum′blėr), *n.* **1,** a person who performs feats of leaping, somersaulting, etc.; an acrobat; **2,** a stemless drinking glass with straight sides; also, the amount it holds; as, a *tumbler* of milk; **3,** that part of a lock which must be put into a certain position, generally by a key, before the lock will open; **4,** a kind of pigeon which turns somersaults in the air: also called *tumbler pigeon*.

tu-mour (tū′mėr), *n.* an abnormal swelling or growth of tissue within or upon the body caused by excessive cell growth: can be benign (not harmful) or malignant (dangerous):—*adj.* **tu′mor-ous.**

tu-mult (tū′mult), *n.* **1,** much noise and confusion, esp. as caused by a crowd of excited people; **2,** violent agitation, as of the mind.—*adj.* **tu-mul′tu-ous.**

tu-na (tōō′na), *n.* [*pl.* tuna or tunas], any of several kinds of large ocean fish found in warm seas throughout the world; caught in large numbers for use as food.

tun-dra (tun′dra), *n.* flat, rolling, treeless plains in the Arctic, with permanently frozen subsoil called permafrost and mucky topsoil of mosses, lichens, dwarf herbs, and shrubs; as, broad expanses of *tundra* are found in the Canadian North and Siberia.

tune (tūn), *n.* **1,** a series of musical tones having rhythm and melody and forming a complete theme; an air or melody; **2,** a musical setting, as for a hymn or ballad; also, any easy, simple musical composition; as, I love an old *tune*; **3,** the state of giving forth tones of the proper pitch; **4,** proper adjustment in respect to musical sounds; as, the piano and the violin are in *tune*; **5,** state of harmonious adjustment; fitting mood; as, to be in *tune* with one's surroundings:—*v.t.* [tuned, tun-ing], **1,** to cause to produce the proper sounds; adjust (a voice or an instrument) to the correct musical pitch; **2,** to put into harmony with something; as, he was *tuned* to the mood of the party; **3,** to put into proper working condition; as, to *tune* or *tune up* a motor; **4,** to adjust a radio or television to get a clearer sound or picture or to bring in a certain station:—**in (out) of tune, 1,** at (not at) the correct musical pitch or key; **2,** in (not in) agreement or sympathy; as, he is *out of tune* with his generation.—*adj.* **tune′less.**

tune-ful (tūn′fool), *adj.* full of music or melody; harmonious; as, a *tuneful* voice.

tun-er (tūn′ėr), *n.* **1,** the part of a radio or television that receives signals and changes them into sound or pictures; **2,** a person who tunes a musical instrument to the proper pitch; as, a piano *tuner*.

tung-sten (tung′sten), *n.* a metal which in its impure form is hard, brittle, and grey: used as an alloy of steel and in electric lamp filaments.

tu-nic (tū′nik), *n.* **1,** a kind of shirt, often sleeveless and reaching to about the knees, worn by both men and women in ancient Greece and Rome; **2,** now, a woman's loose outer garment or overblouse reaching down to, or below, the hips; **3,** the close-fitting short coat of a soldier's or policeman's uniform.

tun-ing fork (tūn′ing fôrk), *n.* a U-shaped metal object that always sounds the same tone when struck: used as a guide in tuning a musical instrument.

tun-nel (tun′el), *n.* an underground passage cut through a hill or under a river; as, a railroad *tunnel*; also, an underground passage dug by a burrowing animal:—*v.i.* and *v.t.* [tunnelled, tunnel-ling], to make or dig a tunnel or something shaped like a tunnel.

tuque or **toque** (tūk; tūk) *n.* a close-fitting knitted hat or cap.

tur-ban (tûr′ban), *n.* a covering for the head made of a long scarf that is wound around and around: worn especially by Muslim and Sikh men; **2,** a simliar head covering worn by a woman.

tur-bid (tûr′bid), *adj.* **1,** having the sediment stirred up; hence, muddy; thick; as, *turbid* waters; **2,** unsettled; confused; as, a *turbid* state of mind.

tur-bine (tûr′bīn; tûr′bin), *n.* a machine with blades that are turned by the force of moving air, steam, water, etc.: used to power electric generators, water pumps, jet engines, and other devices.

tur-bo-jet (tûr′bō-jet′), *n.* a jet engine in which air from a turbine-driven compressor supplies a chamber equipped with a discharge nozzle that directs exhaust gases rearward for thrust.

tur-bo-prop (tûr′bō-prop′), *n.* a jet engine that operates a turbine, which in turn drives the propeller.

tur-bu-lent (tûr′bū-lent), *adj.* **1,** violent; not easily controlled; as, *turbulent* emotions; **2,** agitated; wild, as a stormy sea; **3,** riotous; creating disturbance; as, a *turbulent* crowd.—*n.* **tur′bu-lence.**

tu-reen (tu-rēn′), *n.* a deep, covered dish, as for soup.

turf (tûrf), *n.* **1,** the top layer of soil, containing plant debris, matted grass roots, etc., from which grasses and small plants grow; sod or a piece of sod; **2,** (also **the turf**) a grass course over which horses race, or the sport of horse racing itself; **3,** *Informal* an area controlled by a certain person or group; as, he claimed the basement as his *turf.*

tur-gid (tûr′jid), *adj.* **1,** swollen; inflated; bloated; as, *turgid* waters; **2,** bombastic; pompous; as, *turgid* prose.

tur-key (tûr′ki), *n.* [*pl.* turkeys], a large wild or domestic North American fowl; also, its flesh used as food.

turkey vulture or turkey buzzard, a large, carrion-eating, North American vulture with dark feathers and a bare red head.

tur-moil (tûr′moil), *n.* confusion and disturbance; upheaval; agitation; unrest.

turn (tûrn), *v.t.* **1,** to cause to revolve or go round; as, to *turn* a wheel; to revolve in the mind or ponder; as, to *turn* over a new idea; **2,** to do or perform by means of a revolving motion; as, to *turn* a handspring; **3,** to shape by revolving against a sharp edge, as in a lathe; **4,** to change the direction, attitude, or position of; as, to *turn* an automobile; **5,** to unsettle or upset (the stomach); **6,** to change (something) into something else; as, to *turn* failure into success; **7,** to cause to go; send; as, to *turn* a panhandler away; to *turn* an employee off; **8,** to move to the other side of; go around; as, to *turn* a corner; **9,** to move or set a dial or other such control; as, please *turn* up the volume; **10,** to spoil; sour; as, the hot weather *turned* the cream:—*v.i.* **1,** to have a circular motion; revolve; rotate; as, the earth *turns* on its axis; **2,** to depend; hinge; as, my action *turns* on yours; **3,** to change one's direction or position; as, he *turned* away; also, to change one's attitude; as, he *turned* against his friend; **4,** to seem to whirl or spin; reel; as, my head is *turning*; **5,** to change in condition; as, the cider *turned* to vinegar:—*n.* **1,** the act of revolving; a single revolution or twisting; as, the *turn* of a wheel; **2,** a change of direction; also, a bend or curve; as, a *turn* in the road; **3,** a short walk for exercise; **4,** a deed or act; as, you did me a good *turn*; **5,** the time for some act which one does in rotation with others; as, it's your *turn* now; **6,** a change in condition; as, her luck took a *turn* for the better; **7,** tendency; bent; particular cast of mind; as, she is of a mechanical *turn*; **8,** *Colloq.* a startling surprise or shock; as, the news gave me a *turn*:—**to turn out 1,** to gather for a meeting; **2,** to end up; to prove to be; as, this game *turned out* to be fun.—*n.* **turn′o′ver; turn′ -out′** (as, a big voter *turnout*).

turn-coat (tûrn′kōt′), *n.* a person who abandons his principles; one who goes over to the opposite camp; a deserter; renegade.

tur-nip (tûr′nip), *n.* **1,** the fleshy, rounded, edible root, white or yellow, of a certain plant, the leaves of which may also, when tender, be cooked and eaten; **2,** the plant.

turn-pike (tûrn′pīk′), *n.* **1,** a gate or bar to stop wagons, carriages, etc., until toll is paid; a tollgate; **2,** a road which now has or once had tollgates; **3,** loosely, a main highway: also called *turnpike road* or *pike.*

turn-stile (tûrn′stīl′), *n.* **1,** formerly, a gate at the entrance of a road, bridge, etc., made of four arms pivoted on the top of a post and turning to let persons through, one by one; **2,** now a similar but more complicated device, as at a doorway or subway entrance, to regulate or record the number of persons passing through.

tur-pen-tine (tûr′pen-tīn′), *n.* a strong-smelling, oily liquid distilled from the sap of certain pine trees: used mainly to thin paints or to remove paint stains.

tur-pi-tude (tûr′pi-tūd′), *n.* baseness; depravity; wickedness; as, the moral *turpitude* of the crime.

tur-quoise (tûr′koiz; tûr′kwoiz), *n.* **1,** an opaque, light-blue or greenish-blue stone, much used as a gem; **2,** the greenish-blue colour of this stone:—*adj.* as, he wore his *turquoise* shirt.

tur-ret (tur′it), *n.* **1,** a small tower, usually at the corner of a building, sometimes merely decorative; **2,** a low towerlike, rotating structure or platform, mounted on battleships, fortifications, or tanks, to house one or more guns.

tur-tle (tûr′tl), *n.* one of a group of reptiles that have a low, flat body covered by a hard, upper shell: the turtle can pull its head, tail, and limbs inside the shell for protection: turtles that live on land are usually called **tortoises.**

tur-tle-dove (tur′tl-duv′), *n.* any of several Old World doves, esp. a European dove, noted for its gentleness and its soft cooing.

tur-tle-neck (tur′tl-nek′), *n.* a sweater or shirt that has a high, turned-down collar that fits closely around the neck.

Tus-ca-ror-a (tus′ka-rôr′a), *n.* [*pl.* Tuscarora or Tuscaroras], **1,** an Aboriginal people who originally lived in North Carolina but now live in Ontario and New York; **2,** the Iroquoian language of these people.

tusk (tusk), *n.* **1,** one of the two outside pointed teeth which project from the mouth, when closed, of certain animals, such as the elephant and walrus; **2,** any abnormally large, projecting tooth.

WALRUS TUSKS

tus-sle (tus′l), *n.* a scuffle, as in sport:—*v.i.* [tus-sled, tus-sling], to scuffle or struggle.

tus-sock (tus′uk), *n.* a hummock of grass or twigs; also, a tuft of hair or feathers.

tut (tut), *interj.* hush! be quiet! expressing rebuke, impatience, etc.

tu-te-lage (tū′ti-lij), *n.* protection; the act of guarding or teaching; as, the *tutelage* of a patron saint.—*adj.* **tu′te-la-ry** (as, a *tutelary* deity).

tu-tor (tū′tėr), *n.* **1,** a person whose profession it is to teach or instruct, esp. a private teacher; **2,** a teacher or helper who gives special lessons to a particular student outside of regular class time:—*v.t.* to instruct or teach privately:—*v.i.* **1,** to do the work of a tutor; **2,** *Colloq.* to be taught privately; as, he had to be *tutored* in Latin.—*adj.* **tu-tor′i-al** (tū-tōr′i-al) (in *computing,* onscreen instruction in how to use a computer program).

tux-e-do (tuk-sē′dō), *n.* a man's dress dinner jacket, usually black or a dark colour: worn for formal occasions.

twad-dle (twod′l), *n.* and *v.i.* silly talk.

twang (twang), *n.* **1,** a sharp, quick, vibrating sound; **2,** a sharp nasal tone in speech; as, a Yankee *twang:*—*v.t.* to cause to sound with a twang:—*v.i.* to sound or speak with a twang.

tweak (twēk), *v.t.* to pinch or twist with a jerk:—*n.* a sudden, sharp pinch.

tweed (twēd), *n.* a rough fabric, usually woollen, showing two or more colours generally mixed in the yarn.

tweez-ers (twēz′ėrz), *n.pl.* a small instrument for taking hold of, or pulling out, something tiny, as a hair.

twelfth (twelfth), *adj.* next after the eleventh: the ordinal of twelve:—*n.* one of the 12 equal parts of anything.

twelve (twelv), *adj.* composed of one more than 11:—*n.* **1,** the number consisting of 11 plus one; a dozen; **2,** a sign representing twelve units, as 12 or XII.

twen-ti-eth (twen′ti-eth), *adj.* next after the nineteenth: the ordinal of twenty:—*n.* one of the 20 equal parts of anything.

twen-ty (twen′ti), *adj.* composed of one more than 19:—*n.* [*pl.* twenties], **1,** the number consisting of 19 plus one; a score; **2,** a sign representing twenty units, as 20 or XX.

twice (twīs), *adv.* **1,** two times; as I told him *twice*; **2,** doubly; as *twice* as old.

twid-dle (twid′l), *v.t.* [twid-dled, twid-dling], to twirl; as, to *twiddle* one's thumbs.

twig (twig), *n.* a small branch or shoot growing from a tree or other woody plant.

twi-light (twī′līt′), *n.* **1,** the faint light that prevails before sunrise and after sunset; **2,** a time when a period of success or glory begins to fade away, or a period of advancing age; as, the *twilight* of a career:—*adj.* **1,** pertaining to the time before sunrise or after sunset; **2,** dim; obscure.

twill (twil), *n.* **1,** a weave of cloth that shows diagonal lines or ribs on the surface; **2,** a fabric woven with such ribs, as serge:—*v.t.* to weave (cloth) so as to show diagonal lines or ribs.

twin (twin), *adj.* **1,** made of two separate, but equal, parts; double; as, *twin* towers; **2,** very like each other; **3,** born at the same birth; as, *twin* sisters:—*n.* **1,** one of two born at one birth; **2,** a person or thing very like another.

twine (twīn), *n.* **1,** a kind of strong thread or string; **2,** a twist or tangle:—*v.t.* [twined, twin-ing], **1,** to make by twisting; as, to *twine* a wreath of flowers, etc.; **2,** to encircle; as, to *twine* a pole with ribbons:—*v.i.* to wind; as, the vine *twines* over the porch.

twinge (twinj), *n.* a sudden, darting pain; as, to feel a *twinge:*—*v.i.* [twinged, twinging], to exert a sharp pain; as, my leg *twinged.*

twin-kle (twing′kl), *v.i.* [twin-kled, twin-kling], **1,** to shine with a gleam that grows alternately dimmer and brighter; flicker; as, a star *twinkles;* to sparkle, as the eyes; **2,** to flash in and out rapidly, as the feet in dancing:—*n.* **1,** a flash or flicker of light; **2,** a sparkle or gleam (of an eye); **3,** the time occupied by a very brief moment:—**in the twinkling of an eye,** in an instant.—*n.* **twin′kling.**

twirl (twûrl), *v.t.* **1,** to turn (something) around rapidly; whirl; as, to *twirl* a baton; **2,** to twist something round and round; as, she always *twirls* her hair while writing an essay; **3,** *Slang* in *baseball*, to pitch:—*v.i.* **1,** to rotate rapidly; **2,** *Slang* to pitch:—*n.* a quick, circular motion; a twist.

twist (twist), *v.t.* **1,** to wind (strands) together; also, to form (a rope or twine) by this means; **2,** to twine or wind something around; as, to *twist* a scarf around one's neck; **3,** to wrench or turn; as, to *twist* one's wrist; **4,** to change the meaning of; as, to *twist* someone's words to mean something else; **5,** to change from a normal shape or position; as, the girl *twisted* her mittens into little balls:—*v.i.* **1,** to become joined together by winding; also, to form knots; as, this silk *twists* badly; **2,** to become wrenched or turned; as, my ankle *twisted*; **3,** to take a winding course; as, the stream *twists* through the valley:—*n.* **1,** something having a curled or bending shape; **2,** something made by winding strands together, as certain kinds of silk or cotton thread; **3,** a wrench, as of a muscle; **4,** an unexpected change or development; as, our trip took a new *twist* when our flight was cancelled.

twist-er (twis′tėr), *n.* a tornado, cyclone, waterspout, dust whirl, etc.; **2,** a ball, thrown or batted, that curves or weaves, as in baseball or cricket.

twitch (twich), *v.i.* **1,** to pull at something with a sudden jerk; **2,** to move jerkily; as, her fingers *twitched*:—*n.* **1,** a sudden jerk or pull; **2,** a short, jerky contraction of a muscle.

twit-ter (twit′tėr), *v.i.* **1,** to chirp; make a series of small, sharp sounds, as does a bird; **2,** to feel a slight nervous excitement:—*v.t.* to utter in short, broken sounds:—*n.* **1,** a series of short, broken sounds; **2,** a nervous trembling.

two (to͞o), *adj.* one more than one:—*n.* [*pl.* twos], **1,** the sum of one and one; **2,** a sign representing two units, as 2 or II:—*adj.* **two′some** (a game for two, or two people who play it).

two-fold (to͞o′fōld′), *adj.* made of two parts; double; as, a *twofold* errand:—*adv.* (to͞o′fōld′), doubly.

ty-coon (tī-ko͞on′), *n.* a prominent financier, industrialist, business leader, etc.

ty-ing (tī′ing), *p.pr.* of *tie.*

tyke (tīk), *n. Colloq.* a lively or mischievous child: used affectionately.

tym-pa-num (tim′pa-num), *n.* [*pl.* tympanums or tympana (tim′pa-na)], **1,** the eardrum, or middle ear; **2,** the thin membrane dividing the outer from the middle ear: also called *tympanic membrane.*—*adj.* **tym-pan′ic** (tim-pan′ik).

type (tīp), *n.* **1,** a person or thing possessing the characteristic qualities of a group; as, that *type* of unambitious person always comes last; **2,** a particular class or kind; as, an analytical *type* of person; a juicy *type* of apple; **3,** a group of persons or things having common characteristics; as, women of an athletic *type*; also, in *biology*, a group or division of animals, plants, etc., having a common structure or form; as, an animal of the cat *type;* **4,** in *printing*, a piece of film, metal, wood, etc., with a letter, number, or design on it, for use in printing; as, this sentence is in italic *type*:—*v.t.* [typed, typ-ing], **1,** to write something using a keyboard; **2,** to find out what group a person or thing belongs to; consider to be a certain type.

type-face (tīp′fās) *n.* in printing, a particular style or design of type; as bold *typeface.*

type-set-ter (tīp′set′ėr), *n.* one who sets type or formats type.

type-writ-er (tīp′rīt′ėr), *n.* a machine with a set of keys that prints letters on paper: it has now been largely replaced by computers with keyboards, word processing programs, and printers.

ty-phoid or **ty-phoid fe-ver** (tī′foid; tī′foid fē′vėr), *n.* an infectious, often fatal, disease, traceable to bacteria-infected food, milk, or drinking water.

ty-phoon (tī-fo͞on′), *n.* a violent windstorm that begins over tropical waters in the western Pacific Ocean and the China Sea.

ty-phus (tī′fus), *n.* an infectious disease from the bite of lice, fleas, etc., marked by fever, mental disorder, and eruption of red spots on the skin.

typ-i-cal (tip′i-kl), *adj.* **1,** characteristic; like others of its class; as, my son is *typical* of all small boys; a *typical* country store; **2,** symbolic; representing a whole class.—*adv.* **typ′i-cal-ly.**

typ-i-fy (tip′i-fī′), *v.t.* [typified, typify-ing], **1,** to bear or show the striking characteristics of (a class or group); represent; **2,** to symbolize; as, the lamb *typifies* meekness.

ty-po-graph-i-cal (tī′po-graf′i-kl), *adj.* dealing with printing, esp. typesetting; as, a *typographical* error.—*n.* **ty-pog′ra-phy.**

ty-ran-no-saur-us (ti-ran′ō-sôr′us), *n.* a huge, flesh-eating dinosaur that walked erect on powerful hind limbs and lived in North America about 100 million years ago: fossil remains found esp. in western areas as Alberta, Montana, Utah, etc.

tyr-an-ny (tir′a-ni), *n.* [*pl.* tyrannies], **1,** a government in which one ruler has total power and control over all the laws and the citizens of the state; **2,** total or absolute power that is used cruelly and unjustly.—*adj.* **tyran′ni-cal; tyr′an-nous.**

ty-rant (tī′rant), *n.* **1,** a ruler who has absolute power over others and uses it in a cruel and unjust manner; a despot; **2,** any person who uses power cruelly or unfairly; as, her boss was a *tyrant* who would fire anyone who disagreed with him.

tzar (tsär), *n.* Same as **czar.**

U

U, u (ū), *n.* [*pl.* U's, u's], **1,** the 21st letter of the alphabet, following T; **2,** anything with the shape of a U.

u-biq-ui-tous (ū-bik′wi-tus), *adj.* being, or seeming to be, everywhere at the same time.—*n.* **u-biq′ui-ty.**

ud-der (ud′ėr), *n.* in certain animals, a baglike part of the female in which milk is produced.

ugh (ookh; oo; u; ukh), *interj.* an exclamation of aversion, disgust, or horror.

ug-ly (ug′li), *adj.* [ug-li-er, ug-li-est], **1,** displeasing to the eye; hideous; **2,** morally repulsive; evil; as, *ugly* deeds; **3,** threatening or dangerous; as, the clouds were dark and *ugly*; **3,** *Colloq.* **1,** suggesting trouble; as, an *ugly* rumour; **2,** quarrelsome; as, an *ugly* disposition.—*n.* **ug′li-ness.**

UI (ū′ī′), *abbrev.* in *computing,* short for *user interface.*

U-krain-i-an (ū-krā′nē-en), *n.* **1,** a person who inhabits or originates from Ukraine; **2,** the Slavic language spoken by these people:—*adj.* relating to the country, the people, the language, or the culture of Ukraine.

u-ku-le-le (ū′ku-lā′li), *n.* a small musical instrument shaped like a guitar and having four strings.

ul-cer (ul′sėr), *n.* **1,** an open sore that can be on the outside or inside of the body and may be very painful; **2,** a corrupt influence; a public evil; as, his actions were like an *ulcer* on political life in the city.—*adj.* **ul′cer-ous.**

ul-na (ul′na), *n.* the inner and larger of the two bones of the forearm: the other is the **radius.**

ul-te-ri-or (ul-tē′ri-ėr), *adj.* **1,** lying beyond; more distant; **2,** beyond what is expressed or admitted; as, an *ulterior* purpose.

ul-ti-mate (ul′ti-mit), *adj.* **1,** last; final; as, the *ultimate* decision; **2,** fundamental; basic; as, *ultimate* facts of nature; **3,** greatest or extreme; as, my *ultimate* challenge.—*adv.* **ul′ti-mate-ly.**

ul-ti-ma-tum (ul′ti-mā′tum), *n.* [*pl.* ultimatums or ultimata (ul′ti-mā′ta)], a final condition; one's last word on a matter; esp., the final terms stated by one nation to another, the rejection of which may be expected to lead to war.

ul-tra (ul′tra), *adj.* extreme; going to extremes; as, she is *ultra* quarrelsome.

ul-tra- (ul′tra-), *prefix* meaning **1,** *beyond, on the other side of*; as in *ultra*violet; **2,** *beyond the limit of*; as in *untra*sonic, *ultra*microscopic; **3,** *excessive*; as in *ultra*conservative, *ultra*fashionable.

ul-tra-vi-o-let (ul′tra-vī′ō-lit), *adj.* designating the rays of very short wave length that lie just beyond the violet end of the visible spectrum: these rays are one form of energy from the sun. Abbreviated as *UV*:—**ultraviolet (UV) rays,** invisible rays from the sun, now known to cause sunburn and skin cancer, to some degree related to the thinning of the ozone layer in the atmosphere.

u-lu (o͞o′lo͞o), *n.* a traditional knife used by the Inuit: it has a crescent blade and handle made of wood, ivory, or bone.

um-ber (um′bėr), *n.* **1,** a brown earth used as colouring matter; **2,** a rich, dark-brown colour:—*adj.* of or like umber; umber-coloured.

um-bil-i-cal (um-bil′i-kl′), *adj.* **1,** relating to the navel or umbilical cord; **2,** connecting someone or something to an essential source of supplies:—**umbilical cord, 1,** a flexible cordlike structure containing blood vessels through which the fetus of a mammal receives food and eliminates waste into the circulatory system of the mother; **2,** a supply cable; as, an *umbilical cord* kept the astronaut attached to the spacecraft.

um-bra (um′bra), *n.* the dark cone of shadow cast by a planet or satellite on the side opposite the sun.

um-brage (um′brij), *n.* resentful displeasure; offence; as, she took *umbrage* at my remark.

um-brel-la (um-brel′a), *n.* a circular piece of cloth or plastic stretched over a frame that can be folded up when not in use; it is held over the head by a long handle and used to give protection from the rain or sun.

u-mi-ak or **oo-mi-ak** (o͞o′mē-ak), *n.* a flat-bottomed boat made out of skins stretched over a wood frame, traditionally used by the Inuit in Canada for carrying goods and families.

um-laut (oom′lout), *n.* a diacritical or pronunciation mark [¨] placed over a vowel, esp. in German, to show that its sound is modified because of a vowel that follows.

um-pire (um′pīr), *n.* in *baseball* and other sports, a person who rules on plays:—*v.t.* and *v.i.* [umpired, umpir-ing], to act as an umpire.

un (un-), *prefix* meaning *not, no, lack of, opposite to*; as in *un*accented, *un*accounted; *un*adulterated, *un*aided, *un*alloyed (pure, as *unalloyed* bliss), *un*bridled (uncontrolled), *un*complaining, *un*compromising, *un*conventional, *un*deterred, *un*earned, *un*essential, *un*equivocal, *un*fathomable, *un*fathomed, *un*fettered, *un*forgettable, *un*friendliness, *un*friendly, *un*gracious, *un*grammatical, *un*guarded, *un*hurt, *un*interested, *un*knowable, *un*learn, *un*loved, *un*lovely, *un*manageable, *un*mentionable, *un*obtrusive, *un*orthodox, *un*pardonable, *un*parliamentary, *un*popular, *un*premeditated, *un*pretentious, *un*quenchable, *un*questioned, *un*ready, *un*readable, *un*ready, *un*real, *un*reality, *un*regenerate, *un*reliable, *un*repentant, *un*righteous, *un*sanitary, *un*satisfactory, *un*schooled, *un*searchable, *un*scientific, *un*serviceable, *un*shaven, *un*slaked, *un*sociable, *un*sparing, *un*spoken, *un*sterilized, *un*stressed, *un*studied, *un*succesful, *un*suitable, *un*sullied, *un*surpassed, *un*suspecting, *un*sympathetic, *un*taught, *un*tenable, *un*trammeled or *un*trammelled, *un*trustworthy, *un*uttered, *un*varying, *un*wanted, *un*wept, *un*wholesome, *un*worldly, *un*wrap, *un*yielding.

un-a-ble (un-ā′bl), *adj.* incapable; not able; lacking power or ability.

un-ac-cept-a-ble (un′ak-sept′a-bl), *adj.* something that will not be or should not be accepted; as, the raw meat was *unacceptable.*

un-ac-count-a-ble (un′a-koun′ta-bl), *adj.* **1,** not capable of explanation; as, an *unaccountable* delay; **2,** not responsible; irresponsible.—*adv.* **un′ac-count′a-bly.**

un-ac-cus-tomed (un′a-kus′tumd), *adj.* **1,** not usual or customary; as, *unaccustomed* speed; **2,** not familiar with or used to; as, she is *unaccustomed* to the work.

un-ad-vised (un′ad-vīzd′), *adj.* **1,** not discreet or prudent; rash; as, an *unadvised* act; **2,** without having received advice.—*adv.* **un′ad-vis′ed-ly.**

un-af-fect-ed (un′a-fek′tid), *adj.* **1,** without pretence; natural in manner; **2,** not influenced.—*adv.* **un′af-fect′ed-ly.**

u-nan-i-mous (ū-nan′i-mus), *adj.* **1,** united in a single opinion; agreeing; as, we were *unanimous* in our decision; **2,** showing that all agree; as, a *unanimous* vote.—*n.* **u′nanim′i-ty** (ū-na-nim′i-ti).

un-armed (un-ärmd′), *adj.* without weapons; defenceless.

un-as-sum-ing (un′a-sūm′ing), *adj.* modest; unaffected.

un-a-vail-ing (un′a-vāl′ing), *adj.* without effect; useless; as, *unavailing* efforts to rescue a person from drowning.

un-a-void-a-ble (un′a-void′a-bl), *adj.* not to be escaped; inevitable; as, an *unavoidable* accident.—*adv.* **un′a-void′a-bly.**

un-a-ware (un′a-wâr′), *adj.* not knowing; ignorant of; as, he was *unaware* of my presence.

un-a-wares (un′a-wârz′), *adv.* **1,** without previous planning; **2,** by surprise; as, they caught the enemy *unawares.*

un-bal-anced (un-bal′anst), *adj.* **1,** of unequal weight; out of equilibrium; as, *unbalanced* scales; **2,** mentally disordered; slightly insane.

un-bear-a-ble (un-bâr′a-bl), *adj.* something that cannot be endured; intolerable.—*adv.* **un-bear′a-bly.**

un-be-com-ing (un′bi-kum′ing), *adj.* **1,** not suitable or fit; improper; as, conduct *unbecoming* a child; **2,** not suited to one's appearance; as, an *unbecoming* suit.

un-be-lieve-a-ble (un′bi-lēv′a-bl), *adj.* **1,** something that cannot be believed; **2,** very hard to believe; very surprising or shocking.

un-bend (un-bend′), *v.t.* [unbent (unbent′), unbend-ing], **1,** to make straight; loosen; as, to *unbend* a bow; **2,** to free from strain; relax; as, to *unbend* the mind; **3,** to unfasten (a sail) from a spar:—*v.i.* **1,** to become straight; **2,** to become less severe or stiff; become gracious.

un-bend-ing (un-ben′ding), *adj.* **1,** stiff; rigid; **2,** unyielding; obstinate.

un-bi-ased or **un-bi-assed** (un-bī′ast), *adj.* impartial; without prejudice.

un-bind (un-bīnd′), *v.t.* [unbound (unbound′), unbind-ing], **1,** to make loose; untie; as, to *unbind* a bandage; **2,** to release; free (a person) from bonds.

un-blem-ished (un-blem′isht), *adj.* stainless; unmarred.

un-blush-ing (un-blush′ing), *adj.* shameless.

un-bolt (un-bōlt′), *v.t.* to draw back a bolt from; unfasten; as, to *unbolt* a gate.

un-born (un-bôrn′), *adj.* **1,** not yet born; **2,** yet to come; future.

un-bos-om (un-booz′um; b͞oo′), *v.t.* to unburden (oneself) of a secret:—*v.i.* to free one's mind by telling one's thoughts.

un-bound-ed (un-boun′did), *adj.* **1,** without limits; as, *unbounded* space; **2,** extreme; as, *unbounded* admiration.

un-bri-dled (un-brī′dld), *adj.* **1,** not fastened with a bridle; **2,** not restrained; as, an *unbridled* tongue.

un-bro-ken (un-brō′kn), *adj.* **1,** whole; intact; **2,** untamed; **3,** continuous; not interrupted; **4,** not broken.

un-buck-le (un-buk′l), *v.t.* [unbuckled, unbuck-ling], to undo the buckle or buckles of; as, to *unbuckle* a belt.

un-bun-dled (un-bun′dld), *adj.* in *computing,* relating to the availability for purchase of a software program that is also sold as part of package; as, you can purchase this draw/paint program *unbundled* from the desktop publishing software.

un-bur-den (un-bûr′dn), *v.t.* **1,** to relieve of a burden; as, to *unburden* oneself of a secret; **2,** to throw off (a burden).

un-but-ton (un-but′n), *v.t.* to unfasten the button or buttons of.

un-called–for (un-kôld′–fôr′), *adj.* not

needed; out of place; as, an *uncalled-for* comment.

un-can-ny (un-kăn′i), *adj.* not to be explained by reason; unearthly; seeming to be beyond normal powers; mysterious.

un-cer-e-mo-ni-ous (un′ser-e-mō′ni-us), *adj.* **1,** informal; familiar, as a visit; **2,** abrupt; discourteous.—*adv.* **un-cer′e-mo′ni-ous-ly.**

un-cer-tain (un-sûr′tin), *adj.* **1,** not sure; doubtful; as, the result is *uncertain*; **2,** indefinite as to quantity or quality; as, an *uncertain* number; an *uncertain* flavour; **3,** not positive; not decided; as, we are *uncertain* about going; **4,** not steady; as, the platform gave but *uncertain* support; **5,** changing; fluctuating; as, the *uncertain* tide.—*n.* **un-cer′tain-ty.**

un-chain (un-chān′), *v.t.* to unfasten the chains of; let loose; as, to *unchain* a dog.

un-changed (un-chānj′d), *adj.* not changed or changing.

un-char-i-ta-ble (un-char′i-ta-bl), *adj.* **1,** not generous toward the needy; **2,** unkind; harsh in judging others.

un-chris-tian (un-kris′chan), *adj.* not in keeping with Christian principles, esp. selfish or uncaring behaviour.

un-civ-il (un-siv′il), *adj.* rude; discourteous.

un-civ-i-lized (un-siv′i-līzd′), *adj.* savage; barbarous.

un-clasp (un-klåsp′), *v.t.* to release the clasp of; as, to *unclasp* a necklace; to unfasten; as, to *unclasp* one's fingers.

unc-le (ung′kl), *n.* **1,** the brother of one's father or mother; **2,** the husband of one's aunt.

un-clean (un-klēn′), *adj.* **1,** soiled; filthy; **2,** impure; obscene.

un-clean-ly (un-klen′li), *adj.* **1,** habitually dirty; foul; filthy; **2,** obscene.—*n.* **un-clean′li-ness.**

un-clear (un-klēr′), *adj.* [unclear-er, unclear-est], not easy to understand; not clear.

un-clothe (un-klō*th*′), *v.t.* [unclothed, uncloth-ing], to remove the clothes or covering from; undress.

un-coil (un-koil′), *v.t.* to unwind; as, to *uncoil* a spring:—*v.i.* to become loose or unwound; as, a snake *uncoils*.

un-com-fort-a-ble (un-kum′fėrt-a-bl), *adj.* **1,** not at ease physically or mentally; **2,** causing discomfort; as, an *uncomfortable* chair.—*adv.* **un-com′fort-a-bly.**

un-com-mon (un-kom′un), *adj.* out of the ordinary; rare; strange.—*adv.* **un-com′mon-ly.**

un-con-cern (un′kon-sûrn′), *n.* lack of interest or anxiety.

un-con-cerned (un′kon-sûrnd′), *adj.* **1,** not anxious; **2,** uninterested.

un-con-di-tion-al (un′kon-dish′un-al), *adj.* without any limitations; absolute; as, an *unconditional* promise.—*adv.* **un′con-di′tion-al-ly.**

un-con-scion-a-ble (un-kon′shun-a-bl), *adj.* **1,** unreasonable, immoderate, or excessive; as, an *unconscionable* delay; **2,** unscrupulous.—*adv.* **un-con′scion-a-bly.**

un-con-scious (un-kon′shus), *adj.* **1,** without consciousness; without apparent life; **2,** without realization or understanding; as, a person *unconscious* of ridicule; **3,** not deliberate; accidental; as, an *unconscious* omission.—*n.* **un-con′scious-ness.**—*adv.* **un-con′scious-ly.**

un-con-sti-tu-tion-al (un′kon-sti-tū′shun-al), *adj.* not in accord with the constitution or political principles of a country; as, some laws in Canada have been declared *unconstitutional* by the Supreme Court.—*n.* **un′con-sti-tu′tion-al′i-ty.**

un-con-ven-tion-al (un′kon-ven′shun-al), *adj.* out of the ordinary; not following the usual customs of society; as, her *unconventional* clothing made her seem very interesting.

un-cork (un-kôrk′), *v.t.* to pull out the cork of; as, to *uncork* a bottle of wine.

un-cou-ple (un-kup′l), *v.t.* [uncoupled, uncou-pling], to set free; to unleash; also, to unloose from a coupling; detach; as, to *uncouple* a locomotive.

un-couth (un-ko͞oth′), *adj.* **1,** awkward; ungainly; **2,** crude; boorish; not showing good manners.

un-cov-er (un-kuv′ėr), *v.t.* **1,** to remove a top or cover from; **2,** to take the hat or cap from; **3,** to make known; bring to light, as a plot; as, his uncle *uncovered* a plot against his neighbour.

unc-tion (ungk′shun), *n.* **1,** the act of putting oil or ointment on a person for medical or religious reasons; **2,** an ointment; anything soothing; **3,** excessive courtesy; a smooth, oily manner; insincerity; **4,** a fervent way of expressing oneself that reflects excessive emotion.

unc-tu-ous (ungk′tū-us), *adj.* **1,** oily; smooth; **2,** complacently agreeable; suave; bland; as, an *unctuous* speech.—*n.* **unc′tu-ous-ness.**

un-cul-ti-vat-ed (un-kul′ti-vāt′id), *adj.* **1,** untilled; as, *uncultivated* land; also, undeveloped; as, an *uncultivated* talent; **2,** uncivilized; unrefined.

un-curl (un-kûrl′), *v.t.* to cause to straighten out; as, to *uncurl* feathers:—*v.t.* to become straight.

un-daunt-ed (un-dônt′id), *adj.* not frightened or discouraged.

un-de-cid-ed (un′di-sīd′id), *adj.* **1,** doubtful; unsettled; as, an *undecided* issue; **2,** wavering; as, *undecided* what to do.

un-de-filed (un′di-fīld′), *adj.* not corrupted; pure.

un-de-ni-a-ble (un′di-nī′a-bl), *adj.* **1,** not to

be contradicted; unquestionable; as, he possesses *undeniable* skill; **2,** decidedly good; as, a person of *undeniable* character.—*adv.* **un′de-ni′a-bly.**

un-der (un′dėr), *prep.* **1,** below or beneath; as, *under* a ladder; *under* the skin; *under* the sea; also, lower than, in position, authority, excellence, or value; as, a captain is *under* a major; **2,** less than, in height, weight, age, or number; as, *under* six metres; *under* 10 years; *under* five dollars; **3,** subject to the action or effect of; as, *under* treatment; *under* a strain; *under* orders; **4,** because of; as, *under* the circumstances; **5,** in conformity with; as, *under* a rule of the firm; in a certain group or category; as, *under* this topic; **6,** during the rule of; as, England *under* the Tudors:—*adj.* **1,** lower in position; as, the *under*surface; **2,** lower in rank; as, an *under*study:—*adv.* in or to a lower place or subordinate position.—*n.* **un′der-clothes.**—*v.t.* **un′der-charge′; un′der-es′ti-mate′.**

un-der-brush (un′dėr-brush′), *n.* low bushes, shrubs, and small trees growing among larger trees in a woods or forest; undergrowth.

un-der-cov-er (un′dėr-cov′ėr), *adj.* in a secret or hidden way; as, she served as an *undercover* agent:—*adv.* in a secretive or hidden way; as, last month, she worked *undercover.*

un-der-cur-rent (un′dėr-kûr′ent), *n.* **1,** a current, as of air or water, below another current or below the surface; **2,** hence, a concealed tendency of thought or feeling.

un-der-de-vel-oped (un′dėr-di-vel′upt), *adj.* not completely or properly developed; as, poverty is a problem in *underdeveloped* countries.

un-der-dog (un′dėr-dôg), *n.* **1,** a person or team that is expected to lose a game or contest; as she likes to cheer for the *underdog;* **2,** a person or group treated in an unfair way by those in power.

un-der-foot (un-dėr-foot′), *adv.* **1,** under the feet; as, the floor *underfoot* was very uneven; **2,** in the way, as if under one's feet; as, their little dogs were always *underfoot.*

un-der-gar-ment (un′dėr-gär′ment), *n.* a garment worn under the outer clothing.

un-der-go (un′dėr-gō′), *v.t.* [*p.t.* underwent (-went′), *p.p.* undergone (-gôn′), *p.pr.* undergo-ing], to be subjected to; to experience something, esp. something difficult or unpleasant; as, to *undergo* an operation.

un-der-grad-u-ate (un′dėr-grad′ū-it), *n.* a college or university student who has not yet received a degree.

un-der-ground (un′dėr-ground′), *adj.* **1,** below the surface of the earth; as, an *underground* tunnel; **2,** acting in secret; as, an *underground* spy network; **3,** questioning or opposing the established order or ruling government; as, the *underground* press:—*adv.* (un′dėr-ground′), beneath the earth's surface:—*n.* (un′dėr-ground′), **1,** something below the surface of the earth; as, in London, England, the subway is called the *underground;* **2,** groups that work in secret to oppose a foreign ruling power or a dictatorship; as, in World War II, the *underground* was an important force in opposing Hitler's rule in Europe.

Underground Railway, a secret network of safe houses and transportation set up to assist slaves from the southern U.S. to escape to Canada or to the free northern U.S. before the American Civil War.

un-der-growth (un′dėr-grōth′), *n.* low shrubs and bushes in a forest; underbrush.

un-der-hand (un′dėr-hand′), *adj.*, **1,** acting secretly or deceitfully; also, characterized by deceit; as, *underhand* methods; **2,** of a ball, thrown with an upward swing of the arm, with the palm of the hand turned up:—*adv.* (un′dėr-hand′), **1,** secretly; **2,** unfairly.

un-der-hand-ed (un′dėr-han′did), *adj.* dishonest; not aboveboard; underhand.—*adv.* **un′der-hand′ed-ly.**

un-der-lie (un′dėr-lī′), *v.t.* [*p.t.* underlay (-lā′), *p.p.* underlain (-lān′), *p.pr.* underly-ing], **1,** to lie or be beneath; **2,** to be at the bottom of; serve as the basis of; as, what motives *underlie* his acts?

un-der-line (un′dėr-līn′; un′dėr-līn′), *v.t.* [underlined, underlin-ing], *v.t.* **1,** to draw a line beneath; underscore; as, to *underline* a word; **2,** to show the importance of; emphasize; as, the mayor's speech *underlined* the need for safer parks.

un-der-ling (un′dėr-ling), *n.* a person occupying a low position; a subordinate.

un-der-mine (un′dėr-mīn′), *v.t.* [undermined, undermin-ing], **1,** to dig beneath; form a tunnel under; **2,** to weaken; work against secretly; as, to *undermine* one's health; *undermine* one's influence.

un-der-neath (un′dėr-nēth′), *adv.* and *prep.* beneath; below.

un-der-pass (un′dėr-pås′), *n.* a road that goes under another road or a bridge.

un-der-pin-ning (un′dėr-pin′ing), *n.* **1,** a foundation, esp. beneath a wall; **2,** a support; **3,** *pl. Colloq.* the legs.

un-der-priv-i-leged (un′dėr-priv′i-lijd), *adj.* lacking fundamental social rights or security, through poverty, discrimination, etc.

un-der-rate (un′dėr-rāt′), *v.t.* [underrated, underrat-ing], to place too low a value or estimate upon.

un-der-score (un′dėr-skōr′), *v.t.* [underscored, underscor-ing], **1,** to draw a line under; underline; **2,** to make important; to stress; as, recent accidents *underscored* the need for more safety measures.

un-der-sell (un′dėr-sel′), *v.t.* [undersold (-sōld′), undersell-ing], to sell at a lower price than (another).

un-der-shirt (un′dėr-shûrt′), *n.* a garment

for the upper half of the body worn under other clothing, next to the skin.

un-der-side (un′dėr-sīd′), *n.* the side underneath; the bottom; as, the cat was all black except for a *white* underside.

un-der-skirt (un′dėr-skûrt′), *n.* a skirt worn under an outer garment; a petticoat.

un-der-stand (un′dėr-stand′), *v.t.* [under-stood (-stood′), understand-ing], **1,** to comprehend or grasp; as, she *understands* what you mean; **2,** to know a person's nature or character; be in sympathy with; as, to *understand* how a person feels; **3,** to see clearly; realize; as, you do not *understand* what the consequences will be; **4,** to accept as a fact without positive knowledge; believe; as, I *understand* he will come; **5,** to assume or accept as true; as, if a book is a "limited edition," it's *understood* that only a certain number of copies will be made:—*v.i.* to comprehend; as, say no more; I *understand.*—*adj.* **un′der-stan′da-ble.**—*adv.* **un′der-stan′da-bly.**

un-der-stand-ing (un′dėr-stan′ding), *adj.* intelligent; also, sympathetic:—*n.* **1,** knowledge; as, she has an *understanding* of algebra; **2,** ability to understand; intelligence; as, John is superior to him in *understanding;* **3,** the agreement of two minds; as, the perfect *understanding* between them; **4,** something assumed; a belief or opinion; as, her *understanding* is that this pass can only be used at certain times.

un-der-state (un′dėr-stāt′), *v.t.* [understat-ed, understat-ing], to tell less than the truth about; state (facts) too weakly.

un-der-stud-y (un′dėr-stud′i), *n.* and *v.t.* **1,** one who learns the role of another (actor) to be ready to substitute if necessary; **2,** one trained to take another's place.

un-der-take (un′dėr-tāk′), *v.t.* [*p.t.* under-took (-took′), *p.p.* undertak-en (-tāk′en), *p.pr.* undertak-ing], **1,** to take upon oneself; attempt; as, to *undertake* a task; **2,** to contract to do; promise; as, she *undertook* to finish the work by June.

un-der-tak-er (un′dėr-tāk′ėr), *n.* one who makes a business of preparing the dead for burial and of conducting funerals.

un-der-tak-ing (un′dėr-tāk′ing), *n.* **1,** the taking upon oneself of a task or responsibility; **2,** a task or enterprise; as, writing a dictionary is quite an *undertaking.*

un-der-tone (un′dėr-tōn′), *n.* **1,** a subdued tone of voice or sound (much lower than normal); as, she spoke in an *undertone;* **2,** any subordinate element, as a subdued shade of colour; **3,** a partly hidden feeling or thought; as, there was an *undertone* to her conversation that made me think she wasn't telling the truth.

un-der-tow (un′dėr-tō′), *n.* a current below the surface of water, moving in a direction opposite to the current of the surface; at the seashore, the outgoing current below the incoming breakers.

un-der-val-ue (un′dėr-val′ū), *v.t.* to rate below actual worth; as, to *undervalue* honour.

un-der-wa-ter (un′dėr-wô′tėr), *adj.* and *adv.* used, done, or lying below the surface of the water; as, an *underwater* camera; to swim *underwater.*

un-der-wear (un′dėr-wâr′), *n.* garments worn under the ordinary outer clothing.

un-der-world (un′dėr-wûrld′), *n.* **1,** people who engage in organized crime; **2,** in *myth,* the place of the dead under the earth.

un-der-write (un′dėr-rīt′), *v.t.* **1,** in *insurance,* to sign a policy (on behalf of a company) as a guarantee that a certain liability will be met in event of loss, damage, death, etc.; **2,** to sign one's name to:—*v.i.* to carry on the business of insurance.—*n.* **un′der-writ′er.**

un-de-sir-a-ble (un′di-zīr′a-bl), *adj.* objectionable; not pleasing or wanted; disagreeable.

un-de-vi-at-ing (un-dē′vi-āt′ing), *adj.* not turning aside, diverging, or erring (from a proper standard, etc.)

un-dis-ci-plined (un-dis′i-plind), *adj.* not trained in self-control, character, orderliness, efficiency, etc.

un-do (un-dōō′), *v.t.* [*p.t.* undid (-did′), *p.p.* undone (-dun′), *p.pr.* undo-ing], **1,** to do away with the result of; as, going out in the sun will *undo* the effect of the medicine; **2,** to destroy; ruin; as, evil company will *undo* him; **3,** to loosen; unfasten; as, to *undo* a knot; **4,** in *computing,* a command that allows the user to reverse the last action or series of actions, as in typing or formatting.—*adj.* **un-done** (not done; not finished; as, he left the cleaning *undone* while the hockey playoffs were on).

un-do-ing (un-dōō′ing), *n.* **1,** a setting aside, or reversal, of something that has been done; **2,** ruin; downfall; as, gambling was his *undoing.*

un-doubt-ed (un-dout′id), *adj.* certain; not to be doubted; as, an *undoubted* fact.—*adv.* **un-doubt′ed-ly** (without a doubt; certainly).

un-dress (un-dres′), *v.i.* to take off one's clothes; strip:—*v.t.* to take off the clothes or covering of; strip.

un-due (un-dū′; un′dū′), *adj.* **1,** wrong or illegal; as, an *undue* course of action; **2,** more than is proper or suitable; excessive; as, *undue* attention to trifles.

un-du-late (un′dū-lāt′), *v.i.* and *v.t.* [undu-lat-ed, undulat-ing], to move, or cause to move, with a wavy motion; as, a field of grain *undulates* in the wind.—*n.* **un′du-la′tion.**

un-du-ly (un-dū′li), *adv.* **1,** improperly; **2,** excessively.

un-dy-ing (un-dī′ing), *adj.* lasting; seeming to last forever; eternal.

un-earth (un-ûrth′), *v.t.* **1,** to take from the earth; dig from underground; uncover; **2,** to bring to light; discover; as, to *unearth* a crime.

un-earth-ly (un-ûrth′li), *adj.* **1,** not according to, or like, nature; supernatural; **2,** weird; uncanny; as, an *unearthly* light.

un-easy (un-ēz′i), *adj.* [uneas-i-er, uneas-i-est], **1,** not calm or relaxed; disturbed; anxious; as, his failure in school made him *uneasy*; **2,** awkward in manner; constrained.—*n.* **un-eas′i-ness.**—*adv.* **un-eas′i-ly.**

un-em-ployed (un′em-ploid′), *adj.* **1,** not being used; as, *unemployed* funds; **2,** out of work:—**the unemployed**, all the people out of work.—*n.* **un′em-ploy′ment.**—*adj.* **un′em-ploy′a-ble.**

un-e-qual (un-ē′kwal), *adj.* **1,** not of the same strength, amount, size, etc.; as, *unequal* triangles; **2,** not well balanced or matched; as, *unequal* teams; **3,** not sufficiently large, strong, or able; as, *unequal* to the job; **4,** irregular.—*adv.* **un-e′qual-ly.**

un-eth-i-cal (un-eth′i-kal), *adj.* dishonest; not following the rules of a profession or business; as, some business leaders were accused of *unethical* behaviour when they sold their shares.

un-e-ven (un-ē′ven), *adj.* **1,** not level; not smooth or flat; as, an *uneven* board; **2,** not uniform; as, *uneven* pressure; her performance on the cello was *uneven*; **3,** not even; odd; as, seven is an *uneven* number.

un-ex-celled (un′ek-seld′), *adj.* best of its kind; unsurpassed.

un-ex-cep-tion-al (un′ek-sep′shun-al), *adj.* **1,** usual; not out of the ordinary; as, *unexceptional* skills; **2,** not to be deviated from; as, *unexceptional* orders.

un-ex-pect-ed (un′eks-pek′tid), *adj.* not looked for; coming or happening without notice.—*n.* **un′ex-pect′ed-ness.**—*adv.* **un-ex-pect′ed-ly** (as, we found California to be *unexpectedly* cloudy).

un-fail-ing (un-fāl′ing), *adj.* **1,** not likely to fail; as, an *unfailing* water supply; **2,** reliable; as, an *unfailing* friend.

un-fair (un-fâr′), *adj.* not fair; not impartial.—*adv.* **un-fair′ly.**—*n.* **un-fair′ness.**

un-faith-ful (un-fāth′fool), *adj.* **1,** false; untrue; **2,** not exact; not reliable.—*adv.* **un-faith′ful-ly.**—*n.* **un-faith′ful-ness.**

un-fa-mil-iar (un′fa-mil′yėr), *adj.* **1,** strange; unknown; **2,** without knowledge; not acquainted; as, *unfamiliar* with the law.

un-fas-ten (un-fäs′n), *v.t.* to untie; loosen:—*v.i.* to become untied.

un-fa-vour-a-ble (un-fā′vėr-a-bl), *adj.* disapproving; adverse; as, an *unfavourable* opinion.—*adv.* **un-fa′vour-a-bly.**

un-feel-ing (un-fēl′ing), *adj.* **1,** cruel; brutal; **2,** without feeling or sensation.

un-feigned (un-fānd′), *adj.* real; sincere; without pretense; as, *unfeigned* liking.

un-fin-ished (un-fin′isht), *adj.* **1,** not complete; imperfect; **2,** not perfected; lacking artistic finish.

un-fit (un-fit′), *v.t.* [unfit-ted, unfit-ting], *adj.* **1,** not suitable; not qualified; **2,** not in good physical shape.—*n.* **un-fit′ness.**

un-flag-ging (un-flag′ing), *adj.* not drooping or languishing; as, *unflagging* zeal, courage, energy, etc.

un-fledged (un-flejd′), *adj.* **1,** without feathers, as a very young bird; **2,** undeveloped; immature.

un-flinch-ing (un-flinch′ing), *adj.* standing steadfast; resolute; firm; as, *unflinching* courage.

un-fold (un-fōld′), *v.t.* **1,** to spread open, as a pocket map; **2,** to reveal by degrees:—*v.i.* to open, as a flower.

un-for-get-ta-ble (un-fôr-get′a-bl), *adj.* impossible or difficult to forget; memorable.

un-for-tu-nate (un-fôr′tū-nit), *adj.* **1,** not lucky; not prosperous; **2,** badly chosen; regrettable; as, an *unfortunate* speech:—*n.* an unlucky or unsuccessful person.—*adv.* **un-for′tu-nate-ly.**

un-found-ed (un-foun′did), *adj.* **1,** without basis; not established; **2,** without basis of fact; as, an *unfounded* rumor.

un-friend-ly (un-frend′li), *adj.* [unfriend-li-er, unfriend-li-est], showing dislike or coldness toward others; not friendly.

un-furl (un-fûrl′), *v.t.* to loose from its fastenings and spread out, as a flag or sail:—*v.i.* to be spread out or unfolded.

un-gain-ly (un-gān′li), *adj.* clumsy; awkward; as, a tall, *ungainly* figure.

un-god-ly (un-god′li), *adj.* wicked; sinful; **2,** *Colloq.* outrageous; shocking; as, she went to bed at an *ungodly* hour.—*n.* **un-god′li-ness.**

un-gov-ern-a-ble (un-guv′ėr-na-bl), *adj.* uncontrollable; unruly; rebellious; as, an *ungovernable* temper.

un-grate-ful (un-grāt′fool), *adj.* not thankful; not appreciative.—*adv.* **un-grate′ful-ly.**—*n.* **un-grate′ful-ness.**

un-ground-ed (un-groun′did), *adj.* **1,** without reason; baseless; as, *ungrounded* fear; **2,** without instruction; untaught.

un-gu-late (ung′gū-lit), *adj.* hoofed:—*n.* a hoofed animal.

un-hal-lowed (un-hal′ōd), *adj.* **1,** not set apart as sacred; **2,** wicked; godless.

un-hand (un-hand′), *v.t.* to let go of; release from one's grasp.

un-hand-y (un-han′di), *adj.* [unhandi-er, unhand-i-est], clumsy; inconvenient.

un-happy (un-hap′i), *ads.* [unhap-pier, unhap-pi-est], **1,** sorrowful; wretched; as, an *unhappy* homeless person; **2,** unfortunate; unsuccessful; as, an *unhappy* venture; **3,** unsuitable; as, an *unhappy* choice.—*n.* **un-hap′pi-ness.**—*adv.* **un-hap′pi-ly.**

un-health-y (un-hel′thi), *adj.* [unhealth-i-er, un-health-i-est], **1,** not well; sickly; **2,** harmful to health; as, his *unhealthy* eating habits made him overweight.

un-heard (un-hûrd′), *adj.* **1,** not heard; as, an *unheard* cry; **2,** not given a hearing:—**unheard–of, 1,** not heard of before; not previously known or done; as, an *unheard-of* scientific experiment; **2,** not normally done; strange or unusual; as, *unheard-of* logic.

un-hinged (un-hinjd′), *adj.* unsettled; disordered (of a mind, person, opinions, etc.).

un-ho-ly (un-hō′li), *adj.* [unho-li-er, unho-li-est], not sacred; godless; wicked.—*adv.* **un-ho′li-ly.**—*n.* **un-ho′li-ness.**

uni- (ū′ni), *prefix* meaning *one*; as, *uni*colour, *uni*cycle.

u-ni-corn (ū′ni-kôrn′), *n.* an imaginary animal resembling a horse, with one straight horn projecting from its forehead: often found in art and stories of the Middle Ages.

u-ni-cy-cle (ū′ni-sī′kl), *n.* a vehicle like a bicycle but with only one wheel and a seat above it, used in circuses, on stages, etc.

u-ni-form (ū′ni-fôrm′), *adj.* **1,** not changing in form, degree, or character; unvarying; as, a *uniform* climate; **2,** like one another; as, the two cities have *uniform* traffic laws:—*n.* an official or regulation dress belonging to a particular class or profession:—*v.t.* to furnish with uniforms.—*adv.* **u′ni-form′ly.**—*n.* **u′ni-form′i-ty.**—*adj.* **u′ni-formed.**

u-ni-fy (ū′ni-fī′), *v.t.* [unified, unify-ing], **1,** to form into one; unite; **2,** to make alike in form.—*n.* **u′ni-fi-ca′tion.**

u-ni-lat-er-al (ū′ni-lat′ėr-al), *adj.* relating to, involving, or affecting one (side, party, nation, etc.) only; as, a *unilateral* declaration of peace; a *unilateral* contract (binding on one party; *unilateral* action (by one member of an associated group).

un-in-hab-i-ted (un′in-hab′i-ted), *adj.* not lived in; having no inhabitants.

un-in-tel-li-gi-ble (un′in-tel′i-ji-bl), *adj.* incapable of being understood.

un-in-ter-es-ted (un-in′tėr-es-tid; un-in′tris-tid), *adj.* not interested; as, Mika was completely *uninterested* in what her mother was saying.

un-ion (ūn′yun), **1,** *n.* the act of joining two or more things into one whole; the state of being so joined; **2,** that which is made one by the joining of parts; **3,** a league; confederation; **4,** a coupling for connecting pipes or rods; **5,** agreement; harmony; as, we work together in perfect *union*:—**labour union** or **trade union**, an association of workers that negotiates contracts with management, often trying to get higher wages and better working conditions for their workers.—*v.t.* **un′ion-ize′** [unionized, unioniz-ing].—*n.* **un′ion-ism; un′ion-ist.**

union jack, a jack, or small flag, emblematic of union:—**Union Jack,** the British flag.

THE UNION JACK

u-nique (ū-nēk′), *adj.* **1,** unlike anything else; without an equal; **2,** extremely unusual; striking; as, a *unique* design.—*adv.* **u-nique′ly.**—*n.* **u-nique′ness.**

u-ni-son (ū′ni-sun; ū′ni-zun), *n.* harmony; agreement; concord:—**in unison**, sounding the same notes, making the same sounds, or doing the same thing at the same time; as, all the performers sang the part *in unison.*

u-nit (ū′nit), *n.* **1,** one person or thing of a number constituting a group; as, each citizen is a *unit* in the national body; also, a single group in an association made up of groups; as, a patrol is one of the *units* of a scout troop; **2,** in *mathematics*, the smallest whole number; one; **3,** a fixed amount, quantity, distance, etc., taken as a standard of measurement; as, the kilogram is a *unit* of weight; **4,** a piece of equipment or furniture having a special purpose; as, an air-conditioning *unit.*

u-nite (ū-nīt′), *v.t.* [unit-ed, unit-ing], **1,** to join together; combine so as to make one; as, to *unite* states into a nation; **2,** to bring into close association; as, *united* in friendship:—*v.i.* **1,** to be joined together; **2,** to act together; as, let us *unite* to make this a success.—*adj.* **u′ni′ted.**

United Church of Canada, the Protestant church established in Canada in 1925 with the union of the Methodist and Congregationalist churches as well as many Presbyterians.

United Nations, an international organization for cooperation in the preservation of peace, formed after World War II on a charter drawn up in San Francisco in 1945. With over 180 member nations, it has three main bodies: a Security Council, General Assembly, and Secretariat, along with many specialized agencies. Its permanent headquarters are in New York City.

u-ni-ty (ū′ni-ti), *n.* [*pl.* unities], **1,** the state of being one; union of parts; **2,** harmony; agreement; as, to act in *unity.*

u-ni-ver-sal (ū′ni-vûr′sal), *adj.* **1,** relating to the entire universe; as, the *universal* law of gravitation; also, embracing or including the whole; prevailing everywhere; as, *universal* peace; **2,** entire; whole; **3,** of, for, or shared by everyone; as, her writing touched on *universal* themes:—**Universal Product Code,** in *computing*, the series of black bars and lines (bar code) appearing on food packages and other products to allow them to be automatically identified by a computer: used in retail sales and for inventory control.—*adv.* **u′ni-ver′sal-ly.**—*n.* **u′ni-ver-sal′i-ty.**

u-ni-verse (ū′ni-vûrs′), *n.* everything that exists: the earth, planets, stars, and all other things.

u-ni-ver-si-ty (ū′ni-vûr′si-ti), *n.* [*pl.* universities], an institution for instruction and study in the higher branches of learning, as in the arts, medicine, law, etc.

un-just (un-just′), *adj.* unfair; not just.—*adv.* **un-just′ly.**—*n.* **un-just′ness.**

un-kempt (un-kempt′), *adj.* **1,** not neat; dishevelled; **2,** slovenly.

un-kind (un-kīnd′), *adj.* not kind or sympathetic; harsh; as, *unkind* words.—*n.* **unkind′ness.**—*adv.* **un-kind′ly.**

un-known (un-nōn′), *adj.* not known or familiar; not recognized or discovered:—*n.* an unknown person or thing, esp. in *mathematics* the symbol for an unknown quantity.

un-lace (un-lās′), *v.t.* [unlaced, unlac-ing], to undo the lacing of; as, to *unlace* a shoe.

un-law-ful (un-lô-fool), *adj.* contrary to law; illegal.—*adv.* **un-law′ful-ly.**

un-less (un-les′), *conj.* if not; except when; as, we can't pass the exams *unless* we study.

un-like (un-līk′), *adj.* having no resemblance; different:—*prep.* **1,** different from; not like; as, *unlike* the others, she loved to go to the mountains; **2,** not typical of; as, *unlike* all the other stars, this one did not twinkle.—*n.* **un-like′ness.**

un-like-li-hood (un-līk′li-hood′) *n.* improbability.

un-like-ly (un-līk′li), *adj.* [unlike-li-er, unlike-li-est], **1,** not probable; not likely to happen; **2,** not giving promise of success; as, an *unlikely* plan.

un-lim-it-ed (un-lim′i-tid), *adj.* without boundaries; as, an *unlimited* area; also, without restriction; as, *unlimited* power or resources.

un-load (un-lōd′), *v.t.* **1,** to remove freight or a cargo from; as, to *unload* a train; **2,** to remove from a car, wagon, ship, etc.; as, to *unload* freight; **3,** to free or relieve from care or trouble:—*v.i.* to discharge freight.

un-lock (un-lok′), *v.t.* **1,** to unfasten; to release the catch on (a door, trunk, etc., that has been fastened with a lock); **2,** to make clear; reveal; as, to *unlock* a mystery.

un-loose (un-lo͞os′), *v.t.* [unloosed, unloos-ing], to unfasten; set at liberty.

un-luck-y (un-luk′i), *adj.* [unluck-i-er, unluck-i-est], **1,** not lucky or fortunate; as, an *unlucky* speculator; **2,** accompanied by, or tending to bring, bad luck; as, an *unlucky* day.—*adv.* **un-luck′i-ly.**

un-man-ner-ly (un-man′ėr-li), *adj.* rude; without courtesy; impolite.

un-mask (un-måsk′), *v.t.* to remove a disguise from; show the true nature of:—*v.i.* to lay aside a mask; also, to reveal one's true nature.

un-mean-ing (un-mēn′ing), *adj.* senseless; without significance.

un-mer-ci-ful (un-mûr′si-fool), *adj.* without kindness or pity; cruel.—*adv.* **un-mer′ci-ful-ly.**—*n.* **un-mer′ci-ful-ness.**

un-mis-tak-a-ble (un′mis-tāk′a-bl), *adj.* incapable of being mistaken or misunderstood; clear.—*adv.* **un′mis-tak′a-bly.**

un-mit-i-gat-ed (un-mit′i-gāt′id), *adj.* **1,** not lessened or softened; as, *unmitigated* suffering; **2,** absolute; as, an *unmitigated* liar.

un-moved (un-mo͞ovd′), *adj.* **1,** not affected by feelings of pity or sympathy; as, she was *unmoved* by the child's tears; **2,** not changed in position; not moved or disturbed; as, all the furniture in the house remained *unmoved* for a decade.

un-nat-u-ral (un-nat′ū-ral), *adj.* **1,** not natural or normal; artificial; strange; **2,** cruel; inhuman.

un-nec-es-sar-y (un-nes′e-sėr-i), *adj.* not needed.—*adv.* **un-nec′es-sar-i-ly.**

un-nerve (un-nûrv′), *v.t.* [unnerved, unnerv-ing], to deprive of control, strength, or courage; as, the accident *unnerved* him.

un-num-bered (un-num′bėrd), *adj.* **1,** not counted; **2,** not having numbers; **3,** countless; numerous.

un-of-fic-ial (un′o-fish′al), *adj.* not formal or official; as, the *unofficial* opening of the new subway line.—*adv.* **un-o-ffic′ially.**

un-or-tho-dox (un-ôr′tho-doks′), *adj.* not usual or typical; unconventional; as, an *unorthodox* method of pitching.

un-pack (un-pak′), *v.t.* **1,** to take out; as, to *unpack* books from a box; **2,** to remove the contents of; as, to *unpack* the box.

un-paid (un-pād′), *adj.* **1,** not yet paid or settled: as, an *unpaid* debt; **2,** without pay; as, she took an *unpaid* leave of absence.

un-par-al-leled (un-par′a-leld), *adj.* unrivalled; without an equal; having no parallel.

un-pin (un-pin′), *v.t.* [unpinned, unpin-ning], to unfasten by taking out pins.

un-pleas-ant (un-plez′ant), *adj.* disagreeable; distasteful.—*n.* **un-pleas′ant-ness.**—*adv.* **un-pleas′ant-ly.**

un-pop-u-lar (un-pop′ū-lėr), *adj.* not generally liked or approved.

un-prec-e-dent-ed (un-pres′i-den′tid), *adj.* without precedent; unusual; novel.

un-pre-dict-a-ble (un-pri-dikt′a-bl), *adj.* not possible to predict; not able to be known or judged in advance; as, his friends didn't like his *unpredictable* moods.

un-pre-pared (un′pri-pârd′), *adj.* not ready; not equipped; done without preparation.

un-prin-ci-pled (un-prin′si-pld), *adj.* lacking moral standards; unscrupulous.

un-qual-i-fied (un-kwol′i-fīd′; un-kwôl′i-fīd′), *adj.* **1,** lacking the proper qualifications; unfit; **2,** absolute; utter; as, *unqualified* disapproval.

un-ques-tion-a-ble (un-kwes′chun-a-bl), *adj.* not to be doubted or questioned; indisputable.—*adv.* **un-ques′tion-a-bly.**

un-rav-el (un-rav′el), *v.t.* [unravelled, unravel-ling], **1,** to untangle; pull out, as knitting; **2,** to solve, as a mystery:—*v.i.* to become untangled or solved.

un-re-al (un-rē′al), *adj.* not true or real; imaginary.—*n.* **un-re-al′i-ty.**

un-re-al-is-tic (un′rē-al-is′tik), *adj.* not realistic or practical; as, he was *unrealistic* about being a professional ballplayer.—*adv.* **un-real-is′tic-ally.**

un-rea-son-a-ble (un-rē′zn-a-bl), *adj.* **1,** not influenced or controlled by reason; **2,** demanding too much; exorbitant; as, *unreasonable* prices.—*adv.* **un-rea′son-a-bly.**

un-re-li-a-ble (un-ri-lī′a-bl), *adj.* not to be trusted or depended on; not reliable.

un-re-served (un′ri-zûrvd′), *adj.* **1,** not held in reserve; **2,** frank; outspoken.—*adv.* **un′re-serv′ed-ly.**

un-rest (un-rest′), *n.* **1,** social or political protest or disturbances; an uneasy or troubled state; as, we have been experiencing a lot of *unrest* around the world; **2,** lack of peace; restlessness.

un-ri-valled or **un-ri-valed** (un-rī′vald), *adj.* unequalled; without a rival; peerless.

un-roll (un-rōl′), *v.t.* **1,** to open out (something which is rolled); **2,** to display:—*v.i.* to unfold; develop.

un-ruf-fled (un-ruf′ld), *adj.* serene; calm; smooth; not agitated or disturbed: used of a person, water, etc.

un-rul-y (un-rōōl′i), *adj.* paying no attention to rules or commands; hard to manage or control; ungovernable; as, an *unruly* crowd.—*n.* **un-rul′i-ness.**

un-sa-vour-y (un-sā′vėr-i), *adj.* **1,** lacking taste or seasoning; **2,** disagreeable to taste or smell; **3,** not to be trusted or morally questionable; as, her *unsavoury* behaviour made everyone nervous.

un-scathed (un-skā*th*d′), *adj.* uninjured.

un-screw (un-skrōō′), *v.t.* to take the screws from; **2,** to take out or loosen by turning; as, to *unscrew* a nut.

un-scru-pu-lous (un-skrōō′pū-lus), *adj.* unprincipled; indifferent to right and wrong.—*n.* **un-scru′pu-lous-ness.**

un-seal (un-sēl′), *v.t.* to open by breaking or removing the seal.

un-sea-son-a-ble (un-sē′zn-a-bl), *adj.* **1,** coming at an ill-chosen time; untimely; as, an *unseasonable* request; **2,** out of season; as, the weather was *unseasonable.*

un-seat (un-sēt′), *v.t.* **1,** to remove from a seat; **2,** to depose; deprive of the right to sit as representative; as, to *unseat* a senator or member of Parliament.

un-seem-ly (un-sēm′li), *adj.* [unseem-li-er, unseem-li-est], improper; not fitting; not done with good manners or proper behaviour; not polite; as, your table manners are *unseemly*:—*adv.* in an unsuitable manner.

un-seen (un-sēn′), *adj.* **1,** not seen; beyond the range of vision; **2,** invisible.

un-self-ish (un-sel′fish), *adj.* not selfish; generous; thoughtful of others.

un-set-tle (un-set′l), *v.t.* [unset-tled, unset-tling], to change from a firm position or state; disturb; make uncertain.

un-set-tled (un-set′ld), *adj.* **1,** not determined; undecided; as, an *unsettled* question; **2,** not settled; uncertain; as, weather; **3,** unpaid; as, an *unsettled* bill; **4,** uninhabited by settlers; **5,** disturbed; disordered; as, *unsettled* times.—*adj.* **un-sett′ling** (uneasy or disturbing; as, we found his political opinions *unsettling*).

un-shak-a-ble (un-shāk′a-bl), *adj.* firm; determined; as, an *unshakable* belief.

un-sheathe (un-shē*th*′), *v.t.* [unsheathed, unsheath-ing], to take from its sheath, as a dagger or sword.

un-sight-ly (un-sīt′li), *adj.* not pleasant to see; ugly.

un-skilled (un-skild′), *adj.* not expert; untrained; not having learned a trade.

un-skill-ful or **un-skil-ful** (un-skill′fool), *adj.* not expert or skillful; awkward.

un-so-phis-ti-cat-ed (un′so-fis′ti-kāt′id), *adj.* **1,** lacking experience with social situations and interactions; not having much exposure to a broader world; **2,** basic; uncomplicated; naive.

un-sound (un-sound′), *adj.* **1,** not strong or solid; weak; as, the bridge was built on *unsound* foundations; **2,** not based on truth or clear thinking; as, *unsound* ideas.—*n.* **unsound′ness.**

un-speak-a-ble (un-spēk′a-bl), *adj.* **1,** not to be expressed or described in words; as, *unspeakable* happiness; **2,** inexpressibly bad; as, an *unspeakable* crime.—*adv.* **un-speak′a-bly.**

un-sta-ble (un-stā′bl), *adj.* **1,** not firm or stable; easily unbalanced; as, the table was too *unstable* to hold the heavy vase; **2,** not having a firm control of the mind or feelings; as, the boy became *unstable* after he suffered a terrible fright.

un-stead-y (un-sted′i), *adj.* [unstead-i-er, unste- ad-i-est], not steady; shaky; as, *unsteady* nerves; also, unreliable.

un-strung (un-strung′), *adj.* **1,** having the strings loosened or missing, as a harp, banjo, violin, etc.; **2,** nervously upset; unnerved.

un-sub-stan-tial (un′sub-stan′shal), *adj.* **1,**

not strong; not firmly put together; **2,** imaginary; not real.

un-suc-cess-ful (un-suk-ses′fool), *adj.* not having a good result; not successful.—*adv.* **un-suc-cess′ful-ly.**

un-sure (un-shoor′), *adj.* not sure; doubtful; as, she has just started snowboarding, and she's still *unsure* of herself on the hills.

un-tan-gle (un-tang′gl), *v.t.* [untangled, untan-gling], to take out knots or snarls from; as, to *untangle* yarn.

un-think-a-ble (un-thingk′a-bl), *adj.* not to be thought of or considered; not acceptable; as, cheating on a test is *unthinkable* to me.

un-ti-dy (un-tī′di), *adj.* [unti-di-er, unti-di-est], not neat; not in order; slovenly.—*adv.* **un-ti′di-ly.**—*n.* **un-ti′di-ness.**

un-tie (un-tī′), *v.t.* [untied, unty-ing], to unfasten by loosening (a knot); to unfasten (an object) by loosening the knot that holds it; as, to *untie* a tie; to *untie* a shoe; to loose or set free; as, to *untie* a dog:—*v.i.* to become unfastened.

un-til (un-til′), *prep.* to or up to; as, he played *until* noon:—*conj.* to the degree, time, or place that; as, she talked *until* she became hoarse; she studied *until* the moon was high.

un-time-ly (un-tīm′li), *adj.* not at the right moment or on the right occasion; happening too soon:—*adv.* inopportunely; too soon.

un-told (un-tōld′), *adj.* **1,** not expressed or revealed; **2,** too great to be counted; as, *untold* riches.

un-true (un-trōō′), *adj.* **1,** false; contrary to the truth; **2,** not faithful to one's duty; disloyal; **3,** varying from a standard; not straight, as lines, angles, etc.

un-truth (un-trōōth′), *n.* **1,** lack of adherence to fact; incorrectness; **2,** a falsehood or lie.

un-used (un-ūzd′), *adj.* **1,** not in use; not put to use; **2,** not used to; not accustomed; as, *unused* to luxury.

un-u-su-al (un-ū′zhoo-al), *adj.* uncommon; strange; remarkable.—*adv.* **un-u-su-al-ly.**

un-ut-ter-a-ble (un-ut′ėr-a-ble), *adj.* unspeakable; not to be expressed in words; as, *unutterable* grief.—*adv.* **un-ut′ter-a-bly.**

un-veil (un-vāl′), *v.t.* [unveil-ed, unveil-ing], to reveal by taking off a veil or covering; uncover, as; they *unveiled* the new monument at noon yesterday; to *unveil* the truth about the murder:—*v.i.* to take off one's veil.

un-want-ed (un-wônt′d), *adj.* not needed or wished for; not wanted.

un-war-y (un-wâr′i), *adj.* not cautious; careless; heedless.—*adv.* **un-war′i-ly.**

un-wel-come (un-wel′kum), *adj.* not well-received; not welcome; as, her arrival was an *unwelcome* surprise.

un-well (un-wel′), *adj.* not in good health.

un-wield-y (un-wēl′di), *adj.* difficult to move or manage because of size, shape, or weight; bulky; clumsy.—*n.* **un-wield′i-ness.**

un-will-ing (un-wil′ing), *adj.* reluctant; not willing; disinclined.—*adv.* **un-will′ing-ly.**—*n.* **un-will′ing-ness.**

un-wind (un-wīnd′), *v.t.* and *v.i.* [unwound (un-wound′), unwind-ing], **1,** to loosen or become loose by uncoiling; **2,** to become free from tension; relax; as, her partner likes to *unwind* by cooking dinner and listening to music.

un-wise (un-wīz′), *adj.* lacking good judgment; indiscreet.—*adv.* **un-wise′ly.**

un-wit-ting (un-wit′ing), *adj.* unaware; unconscious; not deliberate; as, he was the *unwitting* cause of all our trouble.—*adv.* **un-wit′ting-ly.**

un-wor-thy (un-wûr′*th*i), *adj.* [unwor-thi-er, unwor-thi-est], **1,** lacking merit; discreditable; as, an *unworthy* suggestion; **2,** not deserving; as, he is *unworthy* of our confidence; **3,** not suitable or becoming; as, such conduct is *unworthy* of you.—*n.* **un-wor′thi-ness.**

un-wrap (un-rap′), *v.t.* [un-wrapped, un-wrap-ping], to remove the wrapping from; open or uncover; as, to *unwrap* a package.

un-writ-ten (un-rit′n), *adj.* **1,** not expressed or recorded in writing; **2,** oral rather than written text; as, *unwritten* legends or folktales; **3,** blank; without writing; as, an *unwritten* page:—**unwritten law** or **unwritten rule,** something that doesn't have legal force but is accepted as common practice; as, she insisted there was an *unwritten law* against cutting down trees on personal property.

up (up), *adv.* **1,** from a lower to a higher position or degree; opposite of *down*; as, to go *up* in an elevator; come *up* from a mine; **2,** into notice or consideration; as, to bring *up* a question; **3,** at or to a higher scale, price, or volume; as, the prices are going *up*; to swell *up*; **4,** even with something in time, degree, space, amount, etc.; as, to catch *up* in a race; keep *up* with the news; **5,** on one's feet; out of bed; as, to be or get *up*; **6,** to a person, point, or place; as, he came *up* to us to ask directions; **7,** used with many verbs to give emphasis or to indicate that the action is finished; as, to tear *up* a report; to store *up* wealth; to finish *up* a job; to nail *up* a box; to be swallowed *up* in a crowd; the stream has dried *up*:—*prep.* **1,** from a lower to a higher place on or along; as, to walk *up* the hill; **2,** toward the source of; as, *up* the river; also, toward the interior of (a country or region); **3,** to, at, or near the top of; as, to climb *up* a rope:—*adj.* **1,** leading, moving, or sloping toward a higher place; upward; as, on the *up* grade; **2,** in *golf,* ahead of an opponent; as, two holes *up*; **3,** well-informed; abreast of the times; as, *up* on politics; **4,** exhausted; at an end; as, my stay is *up*; **5,** above the horizon; as, the sun is *up*; **6,** out of bed; as, the patient will be *up* tomorrow; **7,** in *computing,* in running or working order; as, we got the network *up* this morning after it crashed last evening:—**up to,** to a certain point; as, that school goes *up to* grade 10.

up-bring-ing (up′bring′ing), *n.* one's rearing from childhood; care and training of the young while growing up.

up-com-ing (up′kum-ing), *adj.* coming up; coming near; as, the school band is practising for an *upcoming* concert.

up-date (up-dāt), *v.t.* to bring up-to-date; make more modern or current; as, they needed to *update* this dictionary:—*n.* something that brings or is brought up-to-date; as, the report gave an *update* on the election results.

up-grade (up-grād′), *v.t.* and *v.i.* to improve the quality or level of; as, they *upgraded* the cafeteria to a fancy restaurant; the cafeteria *upgraded* to a fancy restaurant; to *upgrade* a computer:—*n.* (up′grād), something that is an improvement in quality or level; as, the airline gave him an *upgrade* from economy to business class.

up-heav-al (up-hēv′al), *n.* **1,** a lifting from below, esp., an elevation of some part of the earth's crust, as in an earthquake; **2,** a violent political or social disturbance, as a revolution.

up-hill (up′hil′), *adv.* to a higher level or point on a slope; upward; as, we climbed *uphill*:—*adj.* (up′hil′), **1,** sloping upward; ascending; **2,** tiresome; difficult; as, study is sometimes *uphill* work.

up-hold (up-hōld′), *v.t.* [upheld (-held′), uphold-ing], **1,** to support; hold up; keep erect; **2,** to encourage or aid; also, to defend; as, to *uphold* the right of free speech; **3,** to maintain or confirm; as, the umpire's decision was *upheld.*

up-hol-ster (up-hōl′stėr), *v.t.* to provide (furniture) with cushions, springs, and coverings.—*n.* **up-hol′ster-er; up-hol′ster-y.**

up-keep (up′kēp′), *n.* the maintaining of a house, automobile, etc., in good order and repair; also, the cost of maintenance.

up-land (up′land′; up′land), *n.* an elevated region, esp. in the interior of a country:—*adj.* pertaining to an elevated region or to a hilly land.

up-lift (up-lift′), *v.t.* **1,** to raise; elevate; **2,** to improve; to better the condition of, esp. morally, socially, or intellectually; **3,** to raise the spirits of; encourage good feeling; as, the lively music *uplifted* the crowd:—*n.* (up′lift′), **1,** an elevation; **2,** a tendency to move toward a higher standard; as, the economy was given an *uplift* by the discovery of diamonds; **3,** a positive or elevating influence; as, reading the novel gave her spirits an *uplift.*—*adj.* **up-lift′ing.**

up-link (up-lingk), *n.* in *computing,* **1,** a connection that allows signals to be sent to a satellite; **2,** a connection from one hub to another.

up-load (up-lōd′), *v.t.* in *computing,* to transfer a file to a central computer from a computer at another location or from a smaller computer:—*n.* this type of transfer.

up-on (u-pon′), *prep.* **1,** on; resting on the top or surface of; as, *upon* the shelf; **2,** against; as, *upon* the wall; **3,** at the moment of; as, *upon* arrival; **4,** so as to meet or find; as, to come *upon* a bargain.

up-per (up′ėr), *adj.* **1,** higher in place, position, rank, etc.; as, the *upper* storey of a house; the *upper* classes; **2,** farther inland; as, the *upper* St. Lawrence River:—**the upper hand,** a position of control; the advantage; as, to have the *upper hand* in a game.—*adj.* **up′per-case** (in printing, the capital letters; as, A, B, and C are *uppercase* letters).

up-per-most (up′ėr-mōst′), *adj.* highest in place, rank, or authority: opposite of *lowermost.*

up-right (up′rīt′; up-rīt′), *adj.* **1,** standing erect; in a vertical position; **2,** just; honest; honourable:—*adv.* in an erect position:—*n.* (up′rīt′), something set or standing straight up, as a timber supporting a beam:—*adv.* in a vertical or erect position; as, I put the shovel *upright* beside the house.

up-ris-ing (up-rīz′ing; up′rīz′ing), *n.* a rebellion against authority; revolt.

up-roar (up′rōr′), *n.* a loud disturbance; confusion.

up-root (up-ro͞ot′), *v.t.* **1,** to pull up by the roots; to remove; get rid of; **2,** to send or force away; remove; as, the family was *uprooted* by the tornado that destroyed their home.

up-set (up-set′), *v.t.* [upset, upset-ting], **1,** to knock over; overturn; as, to *upset* a chair; **2,** to disturb the normal order of things; to interfere with; as, losing her luggage *upset* her travel plans; **3,** to make worried, nervous, or unhappy; as, his friend's nasty remark *upset* him; **4,** to make slightly sick, esp. in the stomach; **5,** to win a game or contest that one had been expected to lose; as, the underdog team *upset* the favourite:—*v.i.* to overturn; as, the car *upset* at the corner:—*adj.* **1,** overturned; also, interfered with; **2,** worried, nervous, or unhappy; **3,** sick, as a stomach ailment:—*n.* (up′set′), **1,** the act of overturning or disturbing; **2,** the state of being overturned; **3,** mental or physical disturbance; **4,** a loss instead of a win; as, the hockey team's loss was a big *upset.*

up-shot (up′shot′), *n.* final result; conclusion; outcome.

up-side (up′sīd′), *n.* the upper part

up-side down (up′sīd′ doun), *adv.* **1,** with

the top part of something at the bottom; as, the opossum can hang *upside down* by its tail; **2,** in disorder or confusion; topsy–turvy.

up-stage (up′stāj′), *adv.* toward the rear of the stage:—*adj.* **1,** pertaining to the back of the stage; **2,** *Colloq.* haughtily aloof; conceited.

up-stairs (up′stârz′), *adv.* toward or on an upper floor:—*adj.* (up′stârz′), belonging to, or on, an upper floor; as, an *upstairs* room:—*n.* (up′stârz′), the part of a building above the first floor.

up-stand-ing (up-stan′ding), *adj.* **1,** of *persons*, erect and tall (with good posture); **2,** upright; honourable.

up-start (up′stärt′), *n.* a person who has suddenly risen from obscurity to wealth, power, or honour, esp. one who presumes on his or her success.

up-stream (up′strēm′), *adv.* against the current:—*adj.* situated, directed, or taking place upstream.

up-surge (up′sûrj′), *n.* a surge upward:—*v.i.* (up-sûrj′), to surge up.

up-swing (up′swing′), *n.* a trend upward; as, her career is on an *upswing.*

up-thrust (up′thrust′), *n.* **1,** a push upward; **2,** in *geology*, an upward lift (often violent) of part of the earth's crust.

up–to–date (up′–too–dāt′), *adj.* up to the minute in style, fads, information, etc.

up-town (up′town), *adv.* toward the upper part of a town or city, esp. the part away from the main business section.

up-turn (up-tûrn′), *v.t.* to turn upward or over; as, to *upturn* sod:—*n.* (up′tûrn′), a change for the better; as, there has been an *upturn* in business.

up-ward (up′wėrd), *adj.* moving toward a higher place or level; as, an *upward* march.

up-ward (up′wėrd) or **up-wards** (up′wėrdz), *adv.* **1,** in an ascending direction; from lower to higher; **2,** toward a higher rank or position; as, to climb *upward* in a profession; **3,** toward the source; as, the explorers followed the river *upward*; **4,** indefinitely more; as, children of three years and *upward.*

up-ward-ly com-pat-i-ble (up-wėrd′li kom-pat′i-bl), *adj.* in *computing,* relating to features, computers, and programs that can accommodate upgrades and newer features; as, that word processing program will be *upwardly compatible* with the newer computers.

u-ran-i-nite (ū-ran′i-nīt′), *n.* a black mineral containing uranium, radium, thorium, and lead: the massive variety, pitchblende: first mined by Eldorado Mining and Refining Ltd. at Port Radium, NWT, later north of Lake Athabasca in Saskatchewan, and by 1957 at Elliot Lake in Northern Ontario.

u-ra-ni-um (ū-rā′ni-um), *n.* a heavy, radioactive, metallic element: a natural component of pitchblende and other ores: capable of nuclear fission and used in research, nuclear weapons, and in the production of nuclear energy. Compare *uraninite.*

U-ra-nus (ū-rā′nus), *n.* **1,** the third largest planet in the solar system and the seventh-closest planet to the sun: Uranus has five moons circling it; **2,** in the religion of the ancient Greeks, the god of the sky and the father of a race of giants.

ur-ban (ûr′ban), *adj.* relating to a city or city life; as, *urban* residents.

ur-bane (ûr-bān′), *adj.* suavely courteous; polite; affable.—*adv.* **ur-bane′ly.**—*n.* **ur-ban′i-ty.**

ur-chin (ûr′chin), *n.* a small child, esp. a mischievous one.

u-re-thra (ū-rē′thra), *n.* the canal through which urine is discharged from the bladder.

urge (ûrj), *v.t.* [urged, urg-ing], **1,** to force onward; drive faster; as, he *urged* on his horse; **2,** to advocate strongly; as, to *urge* the necessity of help; **3,** to try to influence or persuade (a person) by arguments, entreaties, etc.; as, we *urged* him to accept the nomination:—*n.* a strong desire or wish.

ur-gen-cy (ûr′jen-si), *n.* the pressure of necessity; need for instant action; as, the *urgency* of the case is unquestioned.

ur-gent (ûr′jent), *adj.* **1,** calling for immediate attention; pressing; as, an *urgent* need; **2,** insistent; eager; as, an *urgent* plea.—*adv.* **ur′gent-ly.**

u-rine (ū′rin), *n.* the clear, yellow fluid secreted by the kidneys, and eliminated as body waste.—*n.* **u′ri-nal** (a place or fixture for urinating, used by men and boys).—*v.i.* **u′ri-nate** (to pass urine).—*n.* **u′ri-nal′y-sis** (analysis of the urine).—*adj.* **u′ri-na-ry.**

urn (ûrn), *n.* **1,** a kind of vase, usually with a rounded body and a base or pedestal; **2,** a closed vessel with a tap and a heating device, used for making and keeping hot such beverages as tea and coffee.

URN

us (us), *pron.* the pronoun "we" when used as an object; as, we needed to go home, so her mom gave *us* a ride.

us-a-ble (ūz′a-bl), *adj.* fit to be employed or used.

us-age (ūz′ij; ūs′ij), *n.* **1,** the way of using; treatment; as, the furniture shows rough *usage*; **2,** the way that words are used in speaking or writing; as, the word "thine" meaning "yours" is no longer found in common *usage.*

use (ūz), *v.t.* [used, us-ing], **1,** to make use of; employ; as, to *use* the best material; **2,** to put into action or service for a special purpose; as, Johan *used* a wooden match to light the stove; **3,** to treat, act, or take advantage of; as, she was using Ed and had him drive her to school; **4,** to finish or consume (often used with *up*); as, Anna *used up* all the hot water:—**used to, 1,** having the habit of; accustomed to; as, he was *used to* going away every summer; **2,** did at one time or did in the past; as, her grandmother *used to* tell her stories about her life:—*n.* (ūs), **1,** the act of employing; the application of anything to a particular purpose; as, the *use* of steel for rails; **2,** the condition of being used; as, this room is in *use*; **3,** the quality of being useful or helpful; as, it is no *use* looking for the dog as it has been missing for over two weeks; **4,** a need or purpose for which something is used; as, the Internet has many *uses*, such as research, paying bills, and buying products; **5,** practical worth; utility; as, an ornament of no *use*; **6,** reason for employing; as, we have no *use* for the goods; **7,** the power or right to use something; as, she had the *use* of her parents' car.—*adj.* **use′ful.**—*adv.* **use′ful-ly.**

used (ūzd), *adj.* having been used by someone else; not new; second-hand; as, she bought a *used* car.

use-ful (ūz′fool), *adj.* having a good use or purpose; helpful.—*n.* **use-ful-ness.**

use-less (ūs′lis), *adj.* **1,** having, or being of, no practical worth; as, the old television was *useless*; **2,** without results; as, *useless* efforts.

us-er (ūs′ėr), *n.* a person who uses some stated thing; as, there are many Internet *users* in the libraries now.

us-er–friend-ly (ūs′ėr-frend′li), *adj.* **1,** in *computing,* relating to programs, software, etc., that are easy to understand and operate for computer users who are not computer experts: it often includes clear onscreen instructions, prompts, and online help; **2,** *Colloq.* relating to anything that is easy to understand; easy to operate; as, our new stove is very user-friendly.

user interface, in *computing,* how a computer communicates with the user: generally, there are three types of interfaces: command languages, menus, and graphical environments, often those in which the user selects icons with a mouse. Abbreviated as *UI.*

ush-er (ush′ėr), *n.* **1,** a person who shows people to their seats in a theatre, stadium, etc.:—*v.t.* **1,** to act as an usher; escort someone; **2,** to cause something to come or go; lead the way; as, high winds often *usher* in the month of March.

u-su-al (ū′zhoo-al), *adj.* customary; regular; as, come at the *usual* time:—**as usual**, relating to a regular routine; as, she came at two o'clock *as usual.*

u-su-al-ly (ū′zhoo-al-li), *adv.* in a way that is usual; normally; as a rule.

u-su-rer (ū′zhoo-rėr), *n.* a person who lends money and demands an unlawfully high rate of interest.

u-surp (ū-zûrp′), *v.t.* to take possession of by force or unjust means; as, to *usurp* the power of the elected president.—*n.* **u-surp′er; u′sur-pa′tion** (ū′zûr-pā′shun).

u-su-ry (ū′zhoo-ri), *n.* **1,** the practice of lending money at a rate higher than the lawful rate; **2,** a very high rate of interest.

u-ten-sil (ū-ten′sl), *n.* an implement, tool, or small object that is useful and has a special purpose; as, she had to buy new kitchen *utensils* when she set up her new apartment.

u-ter-us (ū′tėr-us), *n.* [*pl.* uteri (-ī)], the womb, a hollow muscular organ in which the young are conceived, developed, and nourished till birth.

u-til-i-tar-i-an (ū′til-i-târ′i-an); *adj* characterized primarily by usefulness, rather than by beauty of appearance.—*n.* **u-til′i-tar′i-an-ism.**

u-til-i-ty (ū-til′i-ti), *n.* [*pl.* utilities], **1,** the quality of being useful; usefulness; **2,** a company that sells a basic service to the public: it can be publicly or privately owned; as, telephone, gas, and electric companies are *utilities*:—*adj.* in *computing,* a program designed to improve the performance or efficiency of a computer but not to do the main work of the machine; as, programs that compress data are *utility* programs, while word processing is an application program.

u-ti-lize (ū′ti-līz′), *v.t.* [utilized, utiliz-ing], to make profitable; make use of; as, surgery now *utilizes* laser technology.—*n.* **u′ti-li-za′tion.**

ut-most (ut′mōst), *adj.* **1,** greatest; of the highest degree; as, use the *utmost* care; **2,** most removed in space or time; farthest; as, satellites reach the *utmost* points of the globe:—*n.* **1,** the extreme limit; as, he can be trusted to the *utmost*; **2,** all that is possible; as, I will do my *utmost* to aid.

u-to-pi-a (ū-tō′pē-a), *n.* an impractical, idealistic scheme:—**Utopia**, an imaginary place offering a perfect life where complete happiness is enjoyed by all.

u-to-pi-an (ū-tō′pē-an), *adj.* visionary; ideal; impossibly perfect; as, *utopian* schemes, dreams, etc.:—*n.* an idealist or visionary.

[1]**ut-ter** (ut′tėr), *adj.* entire; absolute; complete; as, *utter* absurdity; *utter* gloom.—*adv.* **ut′ter-ly.**

[2]**ut-ter** (ut′ėr), *v.t.* to speak; sound.

ut-ter-ance (ut′ėr-ans), *n.* **1,** expression by the voice; speech; also, style of speaking; as, indistinct *utterance*; **2,** something, usually of importance, expressed in words.

ut-ter-most (ut′ėr-mōst′), *adj.* utmost; in the farthest, greatest, or highest degree:—*n.* the furthest extent or degree; as, he worked to the *uttermost* to finish the job.

UV (ū′vē′), *abbrev.* short for *ultraviolet.*

u-vu-la (ū′vū-la), *n.* the small, fleshy projection hanging from the soft palate above the back of the tongue.

V

V, v (vē), *n.* [*pl.* V's, v's], **1,** the 22nd letter of the alphabet, following U; **2,** anything shaped like the letter V; **3,** the Roman numeral for five.

va-can-cy (vā′kan-si), *n.* [*pl.* vacancies], **1,** the state of being empty; emptiness; **2,** a position open to applicants; **3,** a room or rooms offered for rent; **4,** an empty space; blank.

va-cant (vā′kant), *adj.* **1,** empty, as an unoccupied room; **2,** lacking thought or expression; as, a *vacant* look.

va-cate (va-kāt′), *v.t.* [vacat-ed, vacat-ing], to make empty; give up the possession of; as, to *vacate* a house:—*v.i.* to give up a house, office, etc.; move out.

va-ca-tion (va-kā′shun), *n.* **1,** a time away from school, work, or other regular activities; **2,** a time spent in travel or amusement; a pleasure trip:—*v.i.* to take a vacation.—*n.* **va-ca′tion-er; va-ca′tion-ist.**

vac-ci-nate (vak′si-nāt′), *v.t.* [vaccinat-ed, vaccinat-ing], to give a vaccine in order to protect a person from disease.—*n.* **vac′ci-na′tion.**

vac-cine (vak′sēn; vak′sin), *n.* a solution containing weakened or dead disease germs, injected into a person's bloodstream to help the person build up resistance against the actual disease.

vac-il-late (vas′i-lāt′), *v.i.* [vacillat-ed, vacillat-ing], to be changeable or uncertain in opinion, course of action, etc.—*n.* **vac′il-la′tion.**

va-cu-i-ty (va-kū′i-ti), *n.* [*pl.* vacuities], **1,** space not filled or occupied; **2,** mental inactivity or emptiness; **3,** lack of intelligence in facial expression.—*adj.* **vac′u-ous.**

vac-uum (vak′ū-m; vak′ū-um), *n.* **1,** a space entirely empty of matter, including air; **2,** an area or condition cut off from outside events and influences; as, he knows nothing about current events and he seems to live in a *vacuum*:—**vac′u-um clean′er,** an electrical appliance that cleans floors, carpets, furniture, etc., by suction:—*v.i.* and *v.t.* to clean with a vacuum cleaner.

vac-u-um–packed (vak′ūm–pakt′; vak′ū-um–pakt′), *adj.* relating to food or other items sealed in an airtight bag or container from which all or most of the air has been removed: this process preserves freshness.

vag-a-bond (vag′a-bond), *n.* a person who roams about from place to place with no permanent home; a vagrant or tramp:—*adj.* wandering about without a fixed dwelling place; roaming.

va-gar-y (va-gâr′i), *n.* [*pl.* vagaries], a wild or extravagant notion or act; eccentricity; freak of fancy; whim; as, *vagaries* of conduct; the *vagaries* of fortune.

va-gi-na (va-jī′na), *n.* the canal leading from the cervix of the uterus to the vulva in women and most female mammals.—*adj.* **vag′i-nal.**

va-grant (vā′grant), *adj.* wandering from place to place without purpose and without a settled home:—*n.* a tramp.—*n.* **va′gran-cy** (as, he was held on a charge of *vagrancy*).

vague (vāg), *adj.* [va-guer, va-guest], not clearly seen, stated, or understood; hazy; as, a *vague* answer.—*adv.* **vague′ly.**

vain (vān), *adj.* **1,** valueless; empty; idle; as, *vain* boasting; **2,** not successful; useless; as, *vain* efforts; **3,** having too much pride in one's appearance or ability; conceited:—**in vain,** as, she tried to help, but her efforts were *in vain.*—*adv.* **vain′ly.**

vain-glor-y (vān′glōr′i), *n.* excessive vanity or pride in oneself or one's accomplishments.—*adj.* **vain′glor′i-ous.**

val-ance (val′ans) *n.* a short curtain hung across the top of a window or around a bed, dresser, etc.

vale (vāl), *n.* in *poetry*, a valley.

val-e-dic-to-ry (val′e-dik′to-ri), *n.* and *adj.* a farewell speech, esp. one given at a school, university, or college commencement.—*n.* **val′e-dic-to′ri-an** (the person who gives the farewell address).

va-lence (vā′lens), *n.* **1,** in *chemistry*, the combining power of an element measured by the number of hydrogen atoms that one atom or one radical of the element will unite with: thus, oxygen has a *valence* of two since it combines with two atoms of hydrogen; **2,** in *biology*, the degree of power existing between chromosomes, serums, etc., to combine or produce a specific effect upon each other.

val-en-tine (val′en-tīn′), *n.* **1,** a greeting card or gift sent on Valentine's Day (February 14): named after Saint Valentine, a Christian saint who lived in Rome in the third century A.D.; **2,** a sweetheart chosen on that day.

va-le-ri-an (va-lē′ri-an). *n.* **1,** an herb with small pink or white flowers and a peculiarly pungent odour; **2,** a drug obtained from the dried root of this plant, with sedative properties.

val-et (val′it; val′ā), *n.* **1,** a servant (usually male) who personally attends a person, taking care of his or her apartment, clothes, etc.; **2,** a hotel employee who provides guests with various services including cleaning, parking cars, acquiring tickets, etc.:—*v.t.* to serve (someone) as a valet.

val-iant (val′yant), *adj.* brave; heroic; as, *valiant* warriors; *valiant* deeds.

val-id (val′id), *adj.* **1,** based on fact; sound; as, a *valid* argument; **2,** having force under the law; legally binding; as, a *valid* contract.—*adv.* **val′id-ly.**—*n.* **va-lid′it-y** (va-lid′i-ti).

val-i-date (val′i-dāt′), *v.t.* [validat-ed, vali-dat-ing], to ratify; confirm; make valid.

va-lise (va-lēs′), *n.* a small bag for travelling, usually of leather, for holding clothes and toilet articles.

val-ley (val′i), *n.* [*pl.* valleys], low land between hills or mountains, often with a river flowing through it.

val-our or **val-or** (val′ėr), *n.* fearlessness in facing danger; great courage or bravery, esp. in war.—*adj.* **val′or-ous.**

val-u-a-ble (val′ū-a-bl), *adj.* **1,** costly, or worth a good price as, a *valuable* jewel; **2,** of great importance or use; as, a *valuable* hint:—**valuables,** costly possessions, esp. small personal things, as jewellery.

val-u-a-tion (val′ū-ā′shun), *n.* **1,** the act of estimating the worth of something; **2,** an estimated worth or price.

val-ue (val′ū), *n.* **1,** worth; the quality that makes a thing worth possessing; as, this ring has sentimental *value*; **2,** a fair or adequate return; as, to receive *value* for money spent; **3,** worth in money; as, the *value* of the property increased; **4,** estimated worth; as, he gives his ability a high *value*:—**values,** the standards or beliefs that someone has about how to act or to conduct one's life:—*v.t.* [valued, valu-ing], **1,** to estimate the worth of; put a price on; as, to *value* a property; **2,** to esteem highly; hold dear; as, to *value* a friendship.

valve (valv), *n.* **1,** a mechanical device for opening and closing a pipe, and thus regulating or directing the movement through it of a gas, liquid, etc.; **2,** a device, as in a blood vessel, consisting often of two or more folds, or flaps, that open in the direction of the flow of the blood or other fluids and are closed by a reversal of the flow; **3,** either of the two pieces of the shell of a clam, oyster, etc.

vamp (vamp), *n.* **1,** the part of a shoe just above the sole, covering the toes and extending to the sides; **2,** anything patched up, esp. a literary work based on old material; **3,** *Slang* an unscrupulous female flirt:—*v.t.* to patch with new material.

vam-pire (vam′pīr), *n.* **1,** according to superstition, a ghost, or a corpse restored to life, supposed to suck the blood of sleeping persons; **2,** one who preys on others or makes a living at the expense of others; **3,** any of various bats, esp. in South America, that suck the blood of animals.

van (van), *n.* **1,** a large covered truck used to haul goods or animals; as, a moving *van*; **2,** a motor vehicle like a small bus having seats for passengers and extra room for cargo; as, after they had four children, the family decided to buy a *van*.

van-dal (van′d'l), *n.* a person who intentionally destroys, defaces, or damages someone else's property.—*n.* **van′dal-ism.**

vane (vān), *n.* **1,** a blade that is moved around a centrepoint by water or wind: fans, propellers, windmills, and wind turbines have vanes; **2,** the flat, spreading part of a feather:—**weather vane,** a revolving pointed object mounted on a high point, sometimes the chimney of a house, to show wind direction.

van-guard (van′gärd′), *n.* **1,** the first line or advance guard of an army; **2,** a place at the front of a movement or new activity; as, Canada could be in the *vanguard* of new technologies for generating electricity.

va-nilla (va-nil′a), *n.* **1,** a tropical climbing plant of the orchid family; **2,** the pod or bean of various species of this plant, used to make a flavouring extract; **3,** the flavouring: used to flavour ice cream and other foods.

van-ish (van′ish), *v.i.* **1,** to disappear; fade from sight; as, the ship *vanished* beyond the horizon; **2,** to pass out of existence; be lost; as, hopes *vanish*.

van-i-ty (van′i-ti), *n.* [*pl.* vanities], **1,** too much pride in one's appearance, abilities, or accomplishments; conceit; **2,** the quality of being worthless; futility; as, the *vanity* of human arrogance; **3,** a small dressing table or unit with a sink and cupboard beneath: often found in bathrooms.

van-quish (vang′kwish), *v.t.* to conquer; subdue; defeat; as, to *vanquish* an enemy.

van-tage (vån′tij), *n.* **1,** a superior position or opportunity; advantage; as, to gain a point of *vantage* in a game; **2,** in *tennis*, advantage; the first point scored following deuce.

vap-id (vap′id), *adj.* lacking life or spirit; flat; pointless; as, *vapid* talk.

va-por-ize (vā′pėr-īz′), *v.t.* and *v.i.* [vaporized, vaporiz-ing], to change, or be changed, into vapour.—*n.* **va′por-iz′er** (a device that adds moisture to the air by changing water to water vapour).

va-por-ware (vā′pėr-wār), *n.* in *computing*, software that is announced by a seller but is never actually put on the market.

va-pour or **va-por** (vā′pėr), *n.* **1,** the gaseous form of a liquid or solid; as, water *vapour*, or steam, is formed when water is boiled; **2,** tiny particles of a liquid or gas that can be seen or smelled floating in the air: clouds, steam, and gasoline fumes are kinds of vapour.—*adj.* **va′por-ous; va′pour-y.**

var-i-a-ble (vâr′i-a-bl), *adj.* changeable; inconstant; fitful; as, a *variable* wind:—*n.* that which is subject to change.—*n.* **var′i-a-bil′i-ty; var′i-a-ble-ness.**

var-i-ance (vâr′i-ans), *n.* **1,** the state of being changeable or different; change; difference; also, the degree of change; as, a *variance* of several dollars in price; **2,** a difference of opinion; discord; as, it is painful to be at *variance* with one's friends.

var-i-ant (vâr′i-ant), *adj.* differing from others in the same general class; showing variation; as, a *variant* form of a word:—*n.* something that varies; a different form; as, "color" is a *variant* of "colour."

var-i-a-tion (vâr′i-ā′shun), *n.* **1,** a modification or change; diversity; as, roses show great *variations* in colour; **2,** amount or extent of change or difference; as, there is little *variation* in the temperature; **3,** in *music*, the repetition of a single melody with changes and elaborations.

var-i-cose (var′i-kōs′; vâr′), *adj.* swollen or dilated; as, *varicose* veins.

var-ied (vâr′id), *adj.* **1,** of different sorts; diversified; as, a *varied* collection of pictures; **2,** variegated.

var-i-e-gate (vâr′i-e-gāt′; vâr′i-gāt′), *v.t.* [variegat-ed, variegat-ing], to change the appearance of by marking with different colours; streak; spot.—*n.* **var′i-e-ga′tion.**

va-ri-e-ty (va-rī′e-ti), *n.* [*pl.* varieties], **1,** the state of being different; diversity; change; as, we like the *variety* of city life; **2,** a collection of unlike objects; as, she received a *variety* of gifts; **3,** a plant or animal differing in some details from others of the same general class or kind; as, one *variety* of palm bears dates, another *variety* bears coconuts:—**variety store,** convenience store.

var-i-om-e-ter (vâr′i-om′e-tėr), *n.* an instrument for determining changes in magnetism, esp. in the earth's magnetic field.

var-i-ous (vâr′i-us), *adj.* **1,** different; diverse; of several sorts; as, the *various* colours of autumn leaves; **2,** several; as, she met the man on *various* occasions.—*adv.* **var′i-ous-ly.**

var-nish (vär′nish), *n.* **1,** a paintlike liquid spread on wood or another surface to give it a hard, shiny coating; **2,** the coating of gloss resulting from an application of varnish; **3,** superficial smoothness or polish; outside show:—*v.t.* **1,** to cover with varnish; give a gloss to; **2,** to cover up the defects of; gloss over; as, he tried to *varnish* over his bad behaviour.

var-si-ty (vär′si-ti), *n. Colloq.* university:—*adj.* relating to a college or university sports team; also the most advanced level of a high school team.

var-y (vâr′i), *v.t.* [varied, vary-ing], to alter in appearance, shape, substance, etc.; change; as, to *vary* the order of events:—*v.i.* to undergo a change; differ; as, the price *varies* daily.

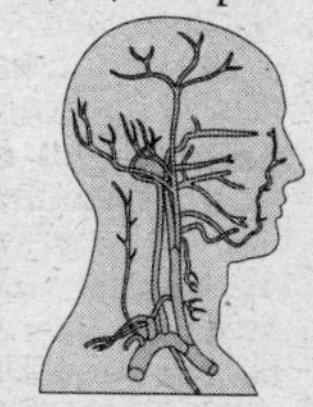
BLOOD VESSELS IN THE HEAD

vas-cu-lar (vas′kū-lėr), *adj.* pertaining to the vessels of an animal or vegetable body that carry or convey fluids, as blood vessels and lymph vessels in animals and sap ducts in plants:—**vascular bundle,** in stems, roots, and leaves of plants, the sheaf of tissues composed of the actively growing cells (cambium), the woody tissue (xylem), and the food-conducting tissue (phloem).

vas def-er-ens (vas def′ėr-ens), *n.* the main duct that carries sperm from the testicle to the urethra.

vase (vās; väz; vāz), *n.* a container of glass, pottery, etc., used for decoration or for holding flowers.

va-sec-to-my (va-sek′tō-mi), *n.* removal by surgery of all or part of the vas deferens, esp. as a method of contraception.

vas-sal (vas′al), *n.* **1,** formerly in the feudal system, a person who placed himself under the protection of a lord or master and in return offered loyalty and military service; one who held land under the feudal system; **2,** a servant.

vast (våst), *adj.* very great in size, extent, amount, etc.; as, a *vast* plain; a *vast* fortune.—*n.* **vast′ ness.**—*adv.* **vast′ly.**

vat (vat), *n.* a large tank, tub, or vessel, esp. one for holding liquors, dyes, etc., in the process of manufacture.

vaude-ville (vōd′vil; vô′di-vil), *n.* a kind of theatrical performance consisting of a series of songs, dances, acrobatic feats, short dramatic sketches, etc.

[1]**vault** (vôlt), *n.* a leap or jump made with the use of the hands or with the aid of a pole; as, a pole *vault*:—*v.i.* and *v.t.* to leap over; jump; as, to *vault* a fence.—*n.* **vault′er.**

[2]**vault** (vôlt), *n.* **1,** an arched roof or ceiling; also, any arched covering, esp. the arch of the sky; **2,** storage space, as in a cellar; **3,** a cavern; tomb; **4,** a room with strong walls and locks, as in a bank, in which valuables are kept:—*v.t.* to shape like a vault; provide with an arched ceiling.

vaunt (vônt; vänt), *v.i.* to brag:—*v.t.* to boast of; display boastfully; as, to *vaunt* one's courage:—*n.* a boast; brag; vain display.—*adj.* **vaunt′ing.**

VCR (vē′sē′är′), *abbrev.* short for *videocassette recorder.*

VDT (vē′dē′tē′), *abbrev.* short for *video display terminal* (or computer screen).

veal (vēl), *n.* the meat from a calf.

vec-tor (vek′tėr), *n.* and *adj.* **1,** in *biology*, an organism, as, an insect, that transmits a disease-producing microorganism; **2,** in *mathematics*, a quantity having direction as well as magnitude, denoted by a system of equal and parallel line segments.

Ve-da (vā′da), *n.* the oldest Hindu sacred writings: composed in Sanskrit and organized into four collections.

V-E Day (vē′ē′ dā′), *n. abbrev.* short for *Victory in Europe* Day; May 8, the day marking the surrender of German troops to the Allies in Europe, in 1945.

veer (vēr), *v.t.* and *v.i.* to change direction; shift; as, the car *veered* suddenly to the left.

Ve-ga (vē′ga), *n.* a blue-white star of the constellation Lyra, one of the brightest in the Northern Hemisphere.

ve-gan (vā′gan), *n.* a vegetarian who eats no animal products such as eggs or cheese: only plant products.

veg-e-ta-ble (vej′e-ta-bl), *n.* **1,** a plant, esp. one cultivated for food, as potatoes, corn, beans, etc.: usually refers to plants eaten as part of the main meal or in a salad, rather than sweet fruits eaten separately or for dessert; **2,** the edible portion of such a plant:—*adj.* **1,** pertaining to plants; **2,** derived from plants; as, *vegetable* fats.

veg-e-tar-i-an (vej′e-târ′i-an), *n.* a person who chooses not to eat meat or fish:—*adj.* **1,** pertaining to vegetarians; **2,** consisting of vegetables; as, a *vegetarian* diet.

veg-e-tate (vej′e-tāt′), *v.i.* [vegetat-ed, vegetat-ing], to lead an idle, unthinking existence.—*adj.* **veg′e-ta′tive.**

veg-e-ta-tion (vej′e-tā′shun), *n.* **1,** the act of growing or vegetating; **2,** plant life; plants in general; as, the dense *vegetation* of the rain forest.

ve-he-ment (vē′e-ment), *adj.* **1,** very violent; furious; as, a *vehement* wind; **2,** passionate; earnest; as, *vehement* words.—*adv.* **ve′he-ment-ly.**—*n.* **ve′he-mence.**

ve-hi-cle (vē′i-kl; vē′hi-kl), *n.* **1,** any conveyance used to move or carry people or goods on land, in or on the water, or in the air, such as trucks, trains, buses, cars, vans, boats, submersibles, spaceships, etc.; **2,** anything that may be used as a medium for communicating thought, feeling, knowledge, etc., as a newspaper, radio, etc.—*adj.* **ve-hic′u-lar** (vē-hik′ū-lėr).

veil (vāl), *n.* **1,** a very thin cloth or netting that a woman wears over her head or face as a covering or decoration; as, a bridal *veil*; **2,** a curtain or covering that conceals something; as, a *veil* of clouds over the mountains; **3,** anything that hides; as, a *veil* of mystery:—*v.t.* **1,** to cover with, or as if with, a veil or curtain; as, volcanic dust *veiled* the mountain; **2,** to hide; as, she *veiled* her past in mystery.

vein (vān), *n.* **1,** one of the tubelike vessels that carries blood back to the heart from all parts of the body; **2,** a tubelike structure that carries food and water in a leaf or provides support in the wing of an insect; **3,** a crack or seam in rock; also, ore, etc., filling a fissure in rock; as, a *vein* of coal; **4,** a long streak of a different colour, as in wood or marble; **6,** a certain style or mood; disposition; peculiarity of speech, etc.; as, he spoke in a solemn *vein*:—*v.t.* to cover, fill, or form with veins.—*adj.* **veined** (vānd); **vein′y.**

vel-lum (vel′um), *n.* **1,** a fine parchment, formerly made of calfskin, intended for binding books, writing upon, etc.; **2,** a kind of paper or cotton cloth made in imitation of this.

ve-loc-i-pede (ve-los′i-pēd′), *n.* **1,** a tricycle; **2,** an early form of the bicycle or tricycle; **3,** a railway hand- or gas-driven car.

ve-loc-i-ty (ve-los′i-ti), *n.* [*pl.* velocities], the rate of motion of a moving object; speed; swiftness; as, the *velocity* of a bullet.

ve-lour or **ve-lours** (ve-lo͝or′), *n.* [*pl.* velours], any of various woven fabrics having a pile, or nap, like that of velvet.

vel-vet (vel′vit), *n.* a closely woven material with a short, thick pile, or nap, of fine upright threads:—*adj.* **1,** made of velvet; **2,** very soft and smooth; as, a *velvet* voice.—*adj.* **vel′ve-ty.**

ve-nal (vē′nl), *adj.* **1,** that can be bribed; as, a *venal* judge; **2,** that can be bought; as, *venal* services; **3,** mercenary; corrupt; as, a *venal* bargain, arrangement, etc.—*n.* **ve-nal′i-ty.**

ve-na-tion (vē-nā′shun), *n.* the vein structure or arrangement, as in a plant leaf or an insect's wing.

vend (vend), *v.t.* to sell; offer for sale.

ven-det-ta (ven-det′a), *n.* **1,** a private feud in which those close to a murdered person seek revenge by bloodshed against the murderer or the murderer's family; **2,** any bitter, long-standing rivalry or quarrel.

vend-ing ma-chine (vend′ing ma-shēn′), *n.* a machine with a slot where money is deposited in order to get soft drinks, candy, stamps, and other such small items.

ven-dor or **vend-er** (ven′dėr), *n.* **1,** a person who sells something on the street or from door to door; **2,** anyone who sells something.

ve-neer (ve-nēr′), *v.t.* **1,** to glue or bond a thin sheet of fine wood to a material of lesser value; as, to *veneer* a pine table with walnut; **2,** to cover or conceal (something cheap or mean) with a surface polish; give a gloss to:—*n.* **1,** a thin surface of fine wood overlaying wood of a poorer quality; **2,** outside show; pretence; surface elegance; as, a *veneer* of charm.

ven-er-a-ble (ven′ėr-a-bl), *adj.* **1,** so old and wise as to be worthy of great respect; as, a *ven-*

erable historian; **2,** worthy of reverence by reason of associations of a religious or historic nature; as, a *venerable* cathedral.—*adv.* **ven′er-a-bly.**

ven-er-ate (ven′ėr-āt′), *v.t.* [venerat-ed, venerat-ing], to regard with the highest respect and honour; reverence.—*n.* **ven′er-a′tion.**

ve-ne-tian blind or **Ve-ne-tian blind** (vi-nē′shan), *n.* a window blind of horizontal, overlapping slats on cords, adjustable so as to admit or exclude light or air.

venge-ance (ven′jans), *n.* punishment inflicted for a wrong or injury; repayment for an offence; as, he swore *vengeance* on his adversary:—**with a vengeance,** with great force or violent energy.

venge-ful (venj′fool), *adj.* vindictive; desiring revenge.—*adv.* **venge′ful-ly.**

ve-ni-al (vē′ni-al), *adj.* **1,** not very serious; pardonable; **2,** excusable, as a fault, error, or slip.

ven-i-son (ven′zn; ven′i-zn), *n.* deer's flesh used for meat.

ven-om (ven′um), *n.* **1,** the poison secreted by certain snakes, spiders, etc., through their bites or stings: can by harmful and sometimes fatal; **2,** strong, bitter feelings; hatefulness.

ven-om-ous (ven′um-us), *adj.* **1,** full of poison; **2,** capable of giving a poisonous bite or sting; as, a *venomous* snake; **3,** spiteful; as, a *venomous* rumour.—*adv.* **ven′om-ous-ly.**

ve-nous (vē′nus), *adj.* pertaining to veins; as, *venous* blood (which has lost its oxygen, become charged with carbon dioxide, and is now dark red).

vent (vent), *n.* **1,** an opening that allows gas or liquid to escape or enter; as, a heating *vent;* **2,** an outlet; free play; utterance; as, to give *vent* to one's indignation:—*v.t.* **1,** to let out through a hole, as steam; **2,** to give an outlet to; relieve by speech or action; as, she *vented* her displeasure in words.

ven-ti-late (ven′ti-lāt′), *v.t.* [ventilat-ed, ventilat-ing], **1,** to provide with a proper circulation of air, by letting in fresh and driving out stale air, as through open windows, shafts, etc.; **2,** to purify by exposure to fresh air; **3,** to bring out (a subject) for public examination and discussion.—*n.* **ven′ti-la′tion.**

ven-ti-la-tor (ven′ti-lā′tėr), *n.* **1,** a device for admitting fresh air and letting out foul or stagnant air; **2,** in *medicine,* an apparatus that helps a person breathe.

ven-tral (ven′tral), *adj.* relating to, or situated on or near, the belly of an animal; as, the *ventral* fins of a fish.

ven-tri-cle (ven′tri-kl), *n.* either of the two lower chambers of the heart, from which blood is forced into the arteries.

ven-tril-o-quism (ven-tril′o-kwizm), *n.* the art of speaking in such a way that the voice appears to come from another person or place, often from a puppet.—*n.* **ven-tril′o-quist.**

ven-ture (ven′tūr), *n.* **1,** a dangerous or daring undertaking; **2,** an enterprise involving risk; as, a business *venture:*—*v.t.* [ventured, ventur-ing], **1,** to risk; expose to danger; as, she *ventured* her life in the attempt; also, to stake; as, she *ventured* all her money in the enterprise; **2,** to hazard; give; as, to *venture* a guess:—*v.i.* **1,** to dare; **2,** to take a chance; run a risk:—**venture capital,** money invested in businesses with substantial risk but with the chance of making great profits: often in new or expanding businesses in exchange for shares.

ven-ture-some (ven′tūr-sum), *adj.* **1,** daring; bold; as, a *venturesome* spirit; **2,** dangerous; as, a *venturesome* undertaking.

ven-tur-ous (ven′tūr-us), *adj.* **1,** fearless; venturesome; **2,** full of risks.

Ven-us (vē′nus), *n.* **1,** the second-closest planet to the sun and sixth-largest planet in the solar system: also the brightest natural object in the sky after the sun and moon; **2,** in *Roman myth,* the goddess of love and beauty, corresponding to the Greek goddess Aphrodite.

ve-rac-i-ty (ve-ras′i-ti), *n.* **1,** honesty; truthfulness; as, this politician is known for her *veracity;* **2,** truth; reliability; accuracy; as, her reports always have *veracity.*—*adj.* **ve-racious′.**

ve-ran-da or **ve-ran-dah** (ve-ran′da), *n.* a long open porch, usually roofed and attached to one or more sides of a house or building.

verb (vûrb), *n.* that part of speech which expresses action, state of being, or condition; a word that states something; as, in the sentence "Anton studied his lesson," the *verb* is "studied."

ver-bal (vûr′b'l), *adj.* **1,** relating to words; also, consisting merely of words; as, a speech can give a *verbal* analysis; **2,** spoken; not written; as, a *verbal* agreement; **3,** literal; word for word; as, a *verbal* translation from Italian; **4,** talkative; skilled with words:—*n.* in *grammar,* a verb form that can be a noun, adjective, or adverb: gerunds, infinitives, and participles are verbals.—*adv.* **ver′bal-ly.**

ver-ba-tim (vėr-bā′tim), *adv.* word for word; as, to report a speech *verbatim:*—*adj.* literal.

ver-bi-age (vûr′bi-ij), *n.* the use of many unnecessary words in speech or writing; wordiness; verbosity.

ver-bose (vėr-bōs′), *adj.* wordy, long-winded.—*n.* **ver-bos′i-ty** (-bos′).

ver-dant (vûr′dant), *adj.* **1,** covered with

fresh green grass or foliage; fresh; green; as, a *verdant* landscape; **2,** *Colloq.* fresh and untried in knowledge or judgment; inexperienced; as, a *verdant* intern.

ver-dict (vûr′dikt), *n.* **1,** the decision of a jury or judge on a case in court; as, the jury's *verdict* was for acquittal; **2,** any judgment or opinion.

ver-dure (vûr′dūr), *n.* **1,** greenness or freshness, esp. of grass and growing plants; **2,** green grass, growing plants, etc.—*adj.* **ver′dur-ous.**

[1]**verge** (vûrj), *n.* the point at which some action or condition is about to take place; as, the country was on the *verge* of revolution.

[2]**verge** (vûrj), *v.i.* [verged, verg-ing], **1,** to approach closely; be on the border; as, his actions *verge* on criminal; **2,** to tend; incline; as, a day *verging* toward its close.

ver-i-fy (ver′i-fī′), *v.t.* [verified, verify-ing], to check the truth or correctness of; as, to *verify* the answer to a physics problem; to prove or show to be true.—*n.* **ver′i-fi-ca′tion; ver′i-fi′er.**—*adj.* **ver′i-ta-bly.**

ver-i-ta-ble (ver′i-ta-bl), *adj.* actual; genuine; true; as, the rain was a *veritable* blessing.—*adv.* **ver′i-ta-bly.**

ver-i-ty (ver′i-ti), *n.* [*pl.* verities], the quality or state of being true; reality; also, that which is true; a truth; fact.

ver-mil-ion (vėr-mil′yun), *n.* and *adj.* a brilliant red pigment; a vivid red colour like this pigment.

ver-min (vûr′min), *n.* [*pl.* vermin], **1,** usually in *pl.*, harmful and offensive insects or small animals, such as flies, lice, rats, mice, etc.; as, garbage in the streets can attract *vermin*; **2,** undesirable or offensive person or persons; as, the characters in her play were portrayed as *vermin.*—*adj.* **ver′min-ous.**

ver-mouth (vûr-mo͞oth′), *n.* a fortified white wine flavoured with herbs, etc.: used esp. in cocktails.

ver-nac-u-lar (vėr-nak′ū-lėr), *n.* and *adj.* **1,** the language used in a country or area; **2,** informal speech or dialect of a particular country or place: often distinguished from the *literary*; **3,** the vocabulary peculiar to a business, profession, etc.; as, the legal *vernacular.*

ver-nal (vûr′nal), *adj.* **1,** pertaining to or appearing in the spring; as, *vernal* breezes; **2,** springlike; youthful.

ver-sa-tile (vûr′sa-tīl′; vûr′sa-til), *adj.* capable of dealing with many subjects, or of doing many things equally well; as, a *versatile* writer; a *versatile* worker.—*n.* **ver′sa-til′i-ty** (vûr′sa-til′i-ti).

verse (vûrs), *n.* **1,** words put together in a certain pattern of sounds, often with rhyme, as in poetry; **2,** a group of metrical lines within a poem or song; a stanza or section; as, they didn't know the second *verse* of "O Canada"; **3,** a form of literary composition possessing rhythm; a poem; **4,** any of the short divisions of a chapter in the Bible:—**free verse,** poetry written without rhyme, with lines of different lengths that don't have a regular rhythm.—*v.i.* **ver′si-fy′** [versi-fied, versi-fy-ing].—*n.* **ver′si-fi-ca′tion.**

versed (vûrst), *adj.* thoroughly trained; skilled; learned; as, *versed* in computer technology.

ver-sion (vûr′zhun; vûr′shun), *n.* **1,** a translation from one language into another; as, a revised *version* of the ancient myths; **2,** a report or description of an occurrence from an individual point of view; as, her *version* of the accident differs from mine; **3,** a form of a written work or other work of art; as, I haven't read the novel, but I have seen the movie *version.*

ver-sus (vûr′sus), *prep.* against; opposed to; as, Edmonton *versus* Montreal.

ver-te-bra (vûr′te-bra), *n.* [*pl.* vertebrae (vûr′te-brā′; vûr′te-brē′) or vertebras (vûr′te-braz)], one of the single bones, or segments, that are joined together to make the backbone of animals.

ver-te-brate (vûr′te-brāt′; -brit), *adj.* having a backbone, or spinal column:—*n.* an animal with a backbone: mammals, fish, birds, reptiles, and amphibians are vertebrates.

ver-tex (vûr′teks), *n.* [*pl.* vertexes (vûr′teksez) or vertices (vûr′ti-sēz′)], the highest point; top; apex; as, the *vertex* of a pyramid.

ver-ti-cal (vûr′ti-k′l), *adj.* upright; straight up and down, as in the direction in which a tree grows: opposite of *horizontal*; as, the flagpole in our schoolyard is *vertical.*—*adv.* **ver′ti-cal-ly.**

ver-ti-go (vûr′ti-gō′), *n.* in *medicine*, dizziness or giddiness.

verve (vûrv), *adj.* enthusiasm, vigour, or energy, esp. in literary or artistic work; as, his sculpture has life and *verve.*

ver-y (ver′i), *adj.* [ver-i-er, ver-i-est], **1,** absolute; complete; as, the *very* truth; **2,** identical; the same; as, that is the *very* dress; **3,** mere; as, the *very* thought of an accident frightens me:—*adv.* **1,** in a high degree; extremely; as, she does *very* good work; the book was *very* dull; **2,** totally or in the fullest; as, my *very* own apartment.

ves-sel (ves′l), *n.* **1,** a hollow container, usually for liquids, as a barrel, cup, etc.; **2,** a tube or canal in the body through which a fluid passes; as, a blood *vessel*; **3,** a ship; boat, esp. a large one.

vest (vest), *n.* **1,** a piece of clothing without sleeves or a collar, worn over a shirt or blouse and extending to or just below the waist; **2,** a woven or knitted undershirt; an undervest:—*v.t.* **1,** to dress in a garment;

as, they *vested* the choir in blue robes; **2,** to give authority, power, etc.; as, the council *vested* its members with certain powers; **3,** to put into the care of another; as, the management of the company is *vested* in its officials.

ves-tal (ves′tl), *adj.* and *n.* pure; chaste:—**vestal virgin**, in *Roman myth*, one of the six virgin priestesses who tended the sacred perpetual fire on the altar in the temple of Vesta in ancient Rome.

ves-ti-bule (ves′ti-būl′), *n.* a small, enclosed entry between the outer and inner doors of a house or other building; also, an enclosed entrance to a railway coach.

ves-tige (ves′tij), *n.* originally, a footprint or track; a visible sign or trace of something that is gone or has disappeared; as, not a *vestige* of the house remained.—*adj.* **ves-tig′i-al** (imperfectly developed or rudimentary).

vest-ment (vest′ment), *n.* a robe, esp. an official or ceremonial garment, or one worn by priests, ministers, choir, etc., during services.

ves-try (ves′tri), *n.* [*pl.* vestries], **1,** a room in a church where the clergy put on their vestments, or where the sacred vessels of the service are kept; **2,** in some Protestant churches, a room or building attached to a church, and used as a chapel or Sunday-school room; **3,** in the Anglican Church, a body of people who direct the affairs of a parish.—*n.* **ves′try-man.**

vet-er-an (vet′ėr-an), *adj.* possessing experience due to age; long trained or practised, esp. as a soldier:—*n.* **1,** a person who has served in the armed forces, especially during wartime; **2,** a person who has held a position for a long time or has a lot of experience; as, after 20 years, Ms. Wong is a *veteran* in the ESL classroom.

vet-er-i-nar-y (vet′ėr-i-nėr-i), *adj.* relating to the treatment of diseases and injuries of animals; as, a *veterinary* surgeon:—*n.* [*pl.* veterinaries], one who practises veterinary medicine or surgery.—*n.* **vet′er-i-nar′i-an.**

ve-to (vē′tō), *n.* [*pl.* vetoes], **1,** the legal right or power to prevent or forbid; as, in Canada, the Senate has the power of *veto* over most bills passed by the House of Commons; **2,** a similar power held by someone in authority:—*v.t.* to prohibit; refuse to approve; as, the teacher *vetoed* the idea of a class party; esp., to stop the passing of a law with a veto.—*n.* **ve′to-er.**

vex (veks), *v.t.* **1,** to irritate by small annoyances; harass; make angry; **2,** to agitate; disquiet; as, angry winds *vexed* the sea.—*adj.* **vex′ing.**

vex-a-tion (veks-ā′shun), *n.* annoyance; displeasure; irritation; as, she plainly showed her *vexation*; also, a source of annoyance; as, his sore finger was a *vexation*.—*adj.* **vex-a′tious.**

vi-a (vī′a), *prep.* by way of; through; as, she travelled *via* the St. Lawrence River.

vi-a-ble (vī′a-bl), *adj.* **1,** able to live, grow, or maintain a separate existence; as a *viable* infant (esp. one of premature birth); *viable* seeds; **2,** able to succeed or function; as, a *viable* idea for a fundraiser.—*n.* **vi′a-bil′i-ty.**

vi-a-duct (vī′a-dukt), *n.* a series of arches or other types of supports carrying a road or railway across a valley or ravine.

vi-al (vī′al), *n.* a small glass bottle with a stopper: in former times, for medicines.

vi-brant (vī′brant), *adj.* **1,** vigorous; full of life and feeling; **2,** resonant; resounding; having vibrations; vibrating; as, the *vibrant* tones of a violin.—*adv.* **vi′brant-ly.**

vi-brate (vī-brāt′), *v.i.* [vibrat-ed, vibrat-ing], **1,** to move back and forth with a regular motion; **2,** to quiver, as the voice; make a tremulous sound:—*v.t.* **1,** to cause to move back and forth; **2,** to cause to quiver.—*n.* **vi-bra′tor.**—*adj.* **vi′bra-to-ry.**

vi-bra-tion (vī-brā′shun), *n.* a quivering or trembling, as of the voice; also, regular motion to and fro or up and down; as, the *vibrations* caused by the truck made the windows rattle.

vi-ca-ri-ous (vi-kâr′i-us), *adj.* **1,** enjoyed or experienced second-hand as through the imagination; as, the movie offered them the *vicarious* experience of war; **2,** felt by sympathetic participation in another's experience; as, *vicarious* pleasure.

vice (vīs), *n.* **1,** a bad or evil habit or form of behaviour, as drunkenness, smoking, or excessive gambling; **2,** wickedness; corruption; **3,** vise.

vice– (vīs–), *prefix* meaning *in place of, deputy*; as, *vice*-chancellor, *vice*-regal.

vice pres-i-dent or **vice–pres-i-dent** (vīs′ prez′i-dent; vīs′–prez′i-dent), *n.* the officer next in rank below a president, who takes the place of the president during the latter's absence, disability, or death.

vice-roy (vīs′roi), *n.* in *history,* a ruler of a colony or province, representing, and ruling with the authority of a king or queen.—*adj.* **vice′re′gal.**

vi-ce ver-sa (vī′si vûr′sa), *adv.* in the opposite way; the other way around; as, Mia blamed Erik for the mistake, and *vice versa.*

vi-cin-i-ty (vi-sin′i-ti), *n.* [*pl.* vicinities], **1,** nearness; closeness; **2,** a region about or near; neighbourhood.

vi-cious (vi′shus), *adj.* **1,** having or showing hate or cruelty; spiteful; mean; as, *vicious* gossip; **2,** intense; severe; fierce; violent; as, a *vicious* beating; **3,** bad-tempered; likely or able to cause harm; dangerous; as, a *vicious* dog.—*adv.* **vi′cious-ly.**—*n.* **vi′cious-ness.**

vi-cis-si-tude (vi-sis′i-tūd′), *n.* a complete,

unexpected change of circumstances; as, the *vicissitudes* of war.

vic-tim (vik′tim), *n.* **1,** a person or animal injured or killed in some misfortune or calamity; **2,** a sufferer from mental or physical disease; **3,** a person who is cheated, fooled, or taken advantage of by another; as, a *victim* of an Internet scam.—*v.t.* **vic′tim-ize′.**—*adj.* **vic′ti-mized.**

vic-tor (vik′tėr), *n.* a person who is victorious; one who wins.

vic-tor-i-ous (vik-tōr′i-us), *adj.* **1,** having won a fight, struggle, or competition; triumphant; as, our swim team was *victorious*; **2,** marked by or ending in victory.

vic-to-ry (vik′to-ri), *n.* [*pl.* victories], **1,** the act of winning a battle, struggle, or contest.

vict-ual (vit′l), *v.t.* to supply or stock with food:—**victuals**, food for human beings; provisions.

vid-e-o (vid′ē-ō′), *n.* **1,** the act of recording, reproducing, and broadcasting visual images on magnetic tape; **2,** the visual part of most television broadcasts; **3,** a recording made on videotape, esp. one produced for sale or rent on videocassette:—*adj.* **1,** having to do with what is seen on a television or computer screen; **2,** having to do with television or the television industry; **3,** relating to, for, or of a video; as, a *video* camera:—*v.t.* to record in this manner.

video card, in *computing,* a plug-in circuit board that enables the display of graphics on a computer monitor (screen).

vid-e-o-cas-sette (vid′ē-ō-ka-set′), *n.* a plastic case containing a roll of videotape, which can be blank, have a commercially available product like movies, or be used to record from television.

videocassette recorder, a machine used to play or record on videotapes: abbreviated as *VCR*.

vid-e-o-con-fer-ence (vid′ē-ō-kon-fûr-ens), *n.* an arrangement where video cameras, television screens, and telephone lines are used to allow people in different locations to meet together through the use of transmitted visuals and sound.

video display terminal, in *computing,* a computer screen or monitor: abbreviated as *VDT*.

video game, an electronic game that is played by using a joystick to move images around a television screen, computer monitor, or the screen of a game in a video arcade.

video memory, in *computing,* the memory in which a computer keeps track of the present contents of the screen.

vid-e-o-tape (vid′ē-ō-tāp), *n.* **1,** a special type of magnetic tape that can be used to record television shows for later viewing; **2,** a prerecorded commercial production, usually for rent or purchase; as, they used to rent more than a dozen *videotapes* each weekend: often referred to as a *video*:—*v.t.* [videotaped, videotap-ing], to record something on videotape; as, they still *videotape* that show every week.

vie (vī), *v.i.* [vied, vying], to compete, as in games, schoolwork, etc.; contend for superiority.

Vi-et-nam-ese (vē-et′na-mēz′; vē-et′na-mēs′; vē-it′na-mēz′; vyet′na-mēz′), *n.* **1,** a person who inhabits or originates from Vietnam; **2,** the language spoken by these people:—*adj.* relating to the country, the people, the language, or the culture of Vietnam.

view (vū), *n.* **1,** the act of seeing; inspection; as, this is worth a closer *view*; **2,** that which is seen; scene; as, a splendid *view* of the river; **3,** a range of mental perception; as, to take a broad *view* of the matter; **4,** range of vision; as, the top of the hill is beyond our *view*; **5,** a picture of a scene, object, or person; **6,** a way of thinking; opinion; as, she held advanced *views*; **7,** purpose or aim; as, to make your plans with a *view* to success:—**in view of,** because of; considering; as, *in view of* your poor marks, we think you should study more:—*v.t.* **1,** to see; gaze at; look upon; **2,** to think about; form an opinion of.

view-er (vū′ėr), *n.* **1,** a person who watches something, esp. someone who watches television; **2,** a device to look through to see something, as on a camera.

view-point (vū′point′), *n.* the position or place from which one looks at something, esp. a way of looking at or judging things; as, a person of very narrow *viewpoint*.

vig-il (vij′il), *n.* **1,** the act of keeping awake during a time usually devoted to sleep; watchfulness; **2,** any such time of careful watching; as, she kept a silent *vigil* over her sick dog.

vig-i-lant (vij′i-lant), *adj.* keenly watchful; alert.—*n.* **vig′i-lance.**

vig-i-lan-te (vij′i-lan′ti) *n.* a person who takes or supports the taking of the law into one's own hands.

vi-gnette (vin-yet′), *n.* **1,** a short but memorable scene from a play, novel, film, etc.; **2,** an ornamental design (as of vine leaves, grapes, etc.) used on a title page, or as the headpiece or tailpiece of a chapter, etc.; **3,** a short literary composition marked by grace, delicacy, or subtlety.

vig-or-ous (vig′ėr-us), *adj.* **1,** full of energy; healthy and active; **2,** having force and strength; as, whitewater kayaking is a *vigorous* activity.—*adv.* **vig′or-ous-ly.**

vig-our or **vig-or** (vig′ėr), *n.* physical or mental strength; healthy energy; vitality.—*adj.* **vig′or-ous.**

Vi-king (vī′king), *n.* one of the group of seagoing Scandinavians who raided the coasts of Europe from the late 700s to about

1100: also, Viking explorers are known to have settled briefly at L'Anse aux Meadows on the northern tip of Newfoundland around 1000 A.D.

vile (vīl), *adj.* [vil-er, vil-est], **1,** mean; shameful; wicked; as, a *vile* person; **2,** foul or offensive; bad; as, *vile* odours.

vil-i-fy (vil′i-fī), *v.t.* to speak evil of; slander; defame; as, he *vilified* his mother-in-law.—*n.* **vil′i-fi-ca′tion.**

vil-la (vil′a), *n.* a large suburban or country residence, usually set in extensive grounds.

vil-lage (vil′ij), *n.* a small group of houses in a country district, smaller than a town; also, the people who live in a village.—*n.* **vil′lag-er.**

vil-lain (vil′in), *n.* **1,** a wicked person; scoundrel; **2,** in a play, novel, movie, or television show, the character who opposes the hero.

vil-lain-ous (vil′in-us), *adj.* evil; wicked; also, *Colloq.* bad; as, a rascal.

vil-lain-y (vil′in-i), *n.* [*pl.* villainies], **1,** wickedness; **2,** an act of wickedness; a crime.

vim (vim), *n.* energy; vitality.

vin-di-cate (vin′di-kāt′), *v.t.* [vindicat-ed, vindicat-ing], to defend successfully against unjust accusation; clear from suspicion of wrong or dishonour.—*n.* **vin′di-ca′tion.**

vin-dic-tive (vin-dik′tiv), *adj.* revengeful; inclined to hold a grudge.

vine (vīn), *n.* **1,** a climbing, woody-stemmed plant, esp. the grapevine; **2,** any climbing or trailing plant with a long, thin stem that crawls along or around something like a tree or fence and holds onto it for support.

vin-e-gar (vin′i-gėr), *n.* a sour liquid obtained by the fermentation of cider, wine, etc., and used to season or preserve food.—*adj.* **vin′e-gar-y.**

vine-yard (vin′yėrd), *n.* a place where grapevines are cultivated and the grapes are used to make wine.

vin-tage (vin′tij), *n.* **1,** the act of, or the season for, gathering grapes and making wine; **2,** the yearly produce of a vineyard, or of the vineyards of a country; **3,** the wine produced in a given season; as, the *vintage* of 1992:—*adj.* **1,** the crop or product of a certain time; as, she likes buying *vintage* clothing; **2,** outstanding; excellent; as, a *vintage* crop.

vi-nyl (vī′nil), *n.* any of several kinds of shiny, flexible plastic used to make floor and furniture covering, raincoats, and other products.

vi-o-la (vī-ō′la; vi-ō′la), *n.* a stringed instrument of the violin class, between the violin and cello in size and range.

vi-o-late (vī′ō-lāt′), *v.t.* [violat-ed, violat-ing], **1,** to treat roughly or severely; ill-use; **2,** to trespass upon; **3,** to treat irreverently; as, to *violate* a sacred burial ground; **4,** to break a rule or law; as, to *violate* the law; also, to disregard or break, as a promise.—*n.* **vi′o-lat-or.**

vi-o-la-tion (vī′ō-lā′shun), *n.* **1,** interruption; disturbance; as, *violation* of a person's privacy; **2,** irreverent treatment, as of sacred or venerable things; **3,** the act of breaking a promise, law, rule, etc.

vi-o-lence (vī′ō-lens), *n.* **1,** great force or strength; as, the *violence* of the wind; **2,** furious, vehement feeling or action; **3,** the use of strong physical force to cause injury or damage; **4,** injury to something that should be respected; as, to do *violence* to a shrine.

vi-o-lent (vī′ō-lent), *adj.* **1,** marked by, or acting with, great physical force; as, a *violent* storm; **2,** marked by, or due to, strong feeling; intense; as, a *violent* dislike; **3,** resulting from the use of force; as, a *violent* death; **4,** extreme; as, a *violent* shock.—*adv.* **vi′o-lent-ly.**

vi-o-let (vī′ō-lit), *n.* **1,** a colour made up of blue and a small amount of red; a bluish-purple colour; the colour of the common violet; **2,** a low-growing plant with violet, yellow, or white flowers; also, the flower:—*adj.* of a violet colour: the purple violet is New Brunswick's official floral emblem.

VIOLET

vi-o-lin (vī′ō-lin′), *n.* the smallest and highest-tuned of modern four-string musical instruments played with a bow.—*n.* **vi′o-lin′ist.**

vi-o-lon-cel-lo (vī′ō-lon-chel′ō; vē′ō-lon-chel′ ō), *n.* [*pl.* violoncellos], a large four-string instrument of the violin class, tuned below the viola: abbreviated as *cello* (chel′ō).—*n.* **vi′o-lon-cel′list.**

vi-per (vī′pėr), *n.* **1,** a poisonous snake with large, hinged fangs, usually with a broad head and a stout body; **2,** a malignant or evil person.

vir-gin (vûr′jin), *n.* a maid or unmarried woman; a person who has not yet had sexual intercourse:—*adj.* **1,** chaste; maidenly; **2,** not yet touched, used, or marked; pure; as, they hiked in a *virgin* wilderness that had not yet been explored or opened up.—*n.* **vir-gin′i-ty.**—*adj.* **vir′gin-al.**

Vir-go (vûr′gō), *n.* **1,** an equatorial constellation, the Virgin, due south of the handle of the Dipper: tradition says it represents a young woman or goddess associated with the harvest; **2,** the sixth sign of the zodiac (♍), which the sun enters about August 22.

vir-gule (vûr′gūl), *n.* a slanting stroke (/) between two words to show that either may be used in interpreting the sense; as, *and/or.*

vir-ile (vir′īl; vī′rīl), *adj.* **1,** masculine strength or energy; as, *virile* strength; **2,** forceful; powerful; as, his writing was elegant but *virile.*—*n.* **vi-ril′i-ty** (vi-ril′i-ti).

vir-tu-al (vûr′tū-al), *adj.* existing in essence or effect, though not in fact; as, his words amounted to a *virtual* confession of guilt.

vir-tu-al-ly (vûr′tū-al-i), *adv.* almost completely; practically; as, *virtually* every culture has stories about how the world began.

virtual reality, in *computing*, a computer-generated, simulated world that allows the viewer, using special equipment, to interact with the images.

vir-tue (vûr′tū), *n.* **1,** the right way of thinking and acting; goodness; good living; morality; **2,** a particular kind of goodness; as, patience is a *virtue*; **3,** excellence or merit; as, this room has the *virtue* of being cool in summer; **4,** efficacy or effectiveness; as, the *virtue* of physical exercise; **5,** a certain good quality of character; as, Tran tells me that my determination and willingness to work hard are my best *virtues*:—**by virtue of,** because of; as, he won *by virtue of* superior strength.

vir-tu-o-so (vûr′tū-ō′sō; chōō-), *n.* **1,** a person of great technical skill in a fine art, as singing or playing a piano, violin, etc.—*n.* **vir′tu-os′i-ty.**

vir-tu-ous (vûr′tū-us), *adj.* possessing or showing good moral behaviour.

vir-u-lent (vir′ū-lent; vir′oo-lent), *adj.* **1,** poisonous; deadly; as, a *virulent* disease; **2,** hostile; bitter; as, *virulent* abuse.—*n.* **vir′u-lence.**

vi-rus (vī′rus), *n.* **1,** a tiny, living thing that grows in the cells of other living things: it can cause diseases such as the common cold, influenza, etc.; **2,** poison that affects the mind or soul; **3,** in *computing,* an illegal program hidden in apparently normal software that can disrupt or destroy normal computer functioning: often acquired from downloaded software or through the Internet.

vi-sa (vē′za), *n.* an official document or mark placed on a person's passport to show that the person has permission to enter and travel within a particular country or region; as, she had to get a *visa* to travel to Pakistan.

vis-age (viz′ij), *n.* the face.

vis-count (vī′kount′), *n.* a title of nobility next below that of earl or count and next above that of baron.—*n.fem.* **vis′count′ess.**

vise (vīs), *n.* a device with two jaws that may be drawn together to hold objects firmly while work is being done on them.

vis-ible (viz′i-bl), *adj.* **1,** in sight; as, the ocean is *visible* from here; **2,** apparent; open; as, *visible* signs of grief.—*adv.* **vis′i-bly.**—*n.* **vis′i-bil′i-ty.**

vi-sion (vizh′un), *n.* **1,** the power to see; also, the act or faculty of seeing; sight; as, the accident impaired his *vision;* **2,** that which is seen in a dream or trance; as, the *visions* of a prophet; also, a phantom; **3,** a mental image; a picture created in the imagination; as, a boy's *visions* of glory; **4,** imagination; foresight; as, a leader must be a person of *vision;* **5,** a thing that is seen, esp. something of great beauty:—*v.t.* to see in, or as in, a vision; imagine.

vi-sion-ar-y (vizh′un-ėr-i), *adj.* **1,** dreamy; inclined to accept fancies as realities; **2,** not practical; as, a *visionary* undertaking; **3,** having vision or foresight:—*n.* [*pl.* visionaries], an impractical person; a person with foresight; a dreamer.

vis-it (viz′it), *v.t.* **1,** to go or come to see, as on pleasure, friendship, business, or courtesy; **2,** to afflict; as, the city was *visited* with an epidemic:—*v.i.* to be a guest:—*n.* **1,** a brief stay as a guest; **2,** an official or professional call; **3,** the act of going to see a person, place, or thing.—*n.* **vis′i-tor.**

vis-it-a-tion (viz′i-tā′shun), *n.* **1,** the act of visiting, or state of being visited; **2,** any unusual event causing pleasure or pain, esp. a severe affliction; **3,** after a divorce or separation, the rights of the parent to visit a child.

vi-sor or **vi-zor** (vī′zėr), *n.* **1,** the movable front piece of a helmet that protects the upper part of the face, made so that it can be pushed up; **2,** the brim of a cap that protects the eyes and face from the sun, as on a baseball cap; **3,** a wide flap inside a car that can be turned down over part of the windshield to block the sun.

VISOR

vis-ta (vis′ta), *n.* **1,** a long, narrow view, as between trees or buildings; also the trees, buildings, etc., forming such a view; **2,** a mental view of a series of events.

vis-u-al (vizh′ū-al), *adj.* **1,** concerned with, or used in, seeing; **2,** capable of being seen; visible; **3,** received through the sense of sight; as, *visual* impressions:—**visuals,** charts, pictures, slides, or other graphics used to illustrate a presentation or story, or for promotion.—*v.t.* **vis′u-al-ize′** [visualized, visualiz-ing], (form a mental picture).—*adj.* **vis′u-al-ly.**

vi-tal (vī′t'l), *adj.* **1,** relating to, or concerned with, life; as, *vital* functions; **2,** essential to life; as, air is a *vital* necessity; **3,** full of life and energy; lively; **4,** very important; as, a *vital* question:—**vital signs,** in *medicine,* the basic indications of a person's health, such as pulse rate and blood pressure.—*adv.* **vi′tal-ly.**

vi-tal-i-ty (vī-tal′i-ti), *n.* **1,** ability to sustain life; **2,** strength; energy.

vi-ta-min (vī′ta-min), *n.* **1,** any of a class of natural substances that are present in small quantities in foods in their natural state and that are necessary to the health and normal growth of people and animals: vitamins are identified by letters of the alphabet; as, *vitamin* C; **2,** one or more of these substances concentrated in the form of a pill or liquid, taken as an aid to health.

vi-ti-ate (vish′i-āt′), *v.t.* **1,** to corrupt morally; debase; pervert; as, these plays *vitiate* one's taste; **2,** to contaminate; pollute; as, bus fumes *vitiate* the air; **3,** to make legally ineffective; as, fraud *vitiates* a contract.

vit-re-ous (vit′ri-us), *adj.* transparent, brittle, and hard, like glass; as, *vitreous* rocks.

vit-ri-fy (vit′ri-fī′), *v.t.* to turn into glass or a glassy substance, or to give a smooth, hard surface (to) by heating and fusing.

vit-ri-ol (vit′ri-ul), *n.* **1,** sulphuric acid; **2,** any of several of the salts of this acid, as blue vitriol, or copper sulphate; **3,** cruel, abusive, or biting language; as, his mother hurt him with her *vitriol.*—*adj.* **vit′ri-ol′ic** (vit′ri-ol′ik).

vi-tu-per-a-tion (vi-tū′pėr-a′shun) *n.* wordy abuse; harsh criticism.—*v.t.* **vi-tu′per-ate′** [vituperated, vituperat-ing], (berate; revile).—*adj.* **vi-tu′per-a-tive** (abusive).

vi-va-cious (vi-vā′shus; vī-vā′shus), *adj.* lively; full of spirit.—*adv.* **vi-va′cious-ly.**—*n.* **vi-vac′i-ty** (vī-vas′i-ti; vi-vas′i-ti).

viv-id (viv′id), *adj.* **1,** brilliant; intense: said of light or colours; as, a *vivid* red; **2,** lifelike; giving a clear picture to the mind; as, a *vivid* description; **3,** full of life and energy; lively; active; as, a *vivid* imagination.—*adj.* **viv′id-ly.**—*n.* **viv′id-ness.**

viv-i-fy (viv′i-fī), *v.t.* to give life to; quicken; animate; as, the spring sun *vivifies* all nature.

viv-i-sec-tion (viv′i-sek′shun), *n.* dissecting, or experimenting with, live animals in order to gain scientific knowledge calculated to save human life.—*v.t.* **viv′i-sect′.**

vix-en (vik′sn), *n.* **1,** a female fox; **2,** a quarrelsome, ill-tempered woman.

vi-zier (vi-zēr′; viz′i-er; viz′yėr), *n.* a high official in some Muslim countries, esp. formerly in Turkey under the Ottoman Empire.

vi-zor (vī′zėr). *n.* Same as **visor.**

vo-cab-u-lar-y (vō-kab′ū-lėr-i), *n.* [*pl.* vocabularies], **1,** a list or collection of words arranged alphabetically and explained or translated; **2,** the stock of words employed by a language, class, or individual; **3,** the particular set of words used by a certain group of people; as, the *vocabulary* of medicine; **4,** all the words of a language.

vo-cal (vō′k'l), *adj.* **1,** having to do with, or uttered by, the voice; as, a *vocal* protest; **2,** expressing oneself by the voice; loud; vehement; as, she was *vocal* in her denial of guilt:—**vocal chords,** folds of the lining membrane found in the larynx, the voice being produced by the vibration as the air is passed up through them from the lungs.—*adv.* **vo′cal-ly.**—*n.* **vo′cal-ist.**—*v.t.* and *v.i.* **vo′cal-ize′** [vocalized, vocaliz-ing].

vo-ca-tion (vō-kā′shun), *n.* **1,** occupation; trade; profession; as, his *vocation* is the law; **2,** a strong desire to enter a certain type of work, esp. one of service; as, even as a small child, she felt her *vocation* was to be a doctor.—*adj.* **vo-ca′tion-al.**

vo-cif-er-ous (vō-sif′ėr-us), *adj.* making a loud outcry; clamorous; noisy.

vod-ka (vod′ka), *n.* a Russian alcoholic liquor distilled from corn, rye, wheat, or potatoes.

vogue (vōg), *n.* **1,** the fashion of the moment; as, long skirts are in *vogue;* **2,** popularity; as, his books were very much in *vogue.*

voice (vois), *n.* **1,** sound proceeding from the mouth, esp. human utterance; specifically, sound produced by the vibration of the vocal cords; **2,** the power or ability to produce sound; as, he lost his *voice;* **3,** anything resembling or likened to human speech or utterance; **4,** opinion, or an expression of opinion; as, the *voice* of the majority; **5,** the right to express a choice or opinion; as, in a democracy, everyone's *voice* should count; **6,** in *grammar,* the form of the verb showing whether the subject acts or is acted upon; as, active or passive *voice:*—*v.t.* [voiced, voic-ing], to give expression to; put into speech; as, he *voiced* his protest.—*adj.* **voice′less.**

voice mail, a system through which conventional telephone messages are received, recorded, and played back automatically when requested by the recipient: voice mail systems are computer controlled, and messages are stored in digital form.

voice recognition, in *computing,* the recognition of spoken words by a computer.

void (void), *adj.* **1,** empty; vacant; **2,** lacking; wanting; as, *void* of humour; **3,** without effect; having no power in law; not legally valid; as, a *void* contract:—*v.t.* **1,** to cause to be empty; **2,** to annul or cancel; as, to *void* a law:—*n.* an empty space.

vol-a-tile (vol′a-tīl; vol′a-til), *adj.* **1,** readily evaporating or changing into vapour; unstable; as, ether is a *volatile* liquid; **2,** changeable; fickle; unstable; **3,** in *computing,* not retaining information or data once the computer is turned off.

vol-ca-no (vol-kā′nō), *n.* [*pl.* volcanoes or volcanos], **1,** an opening in the earth's surface, generally surrounded by a mass of ejected material forming a hill or mountain, from which molten rock, hot gases, ashes, etc., are expelled; **2,** the mountain or hill formed by a volcano.—*adj.* **vol-can′ic** (vol-kan′ik).

vole (vōl), *n.* any of several small, burrowing, plant-eating, mouselike rodents.

vo-li-tion (vō-lish′un), *n.* **1,** the exercise or use of the will; choice; as, she came of her own *volition*; **2,** the power to will something.

vol-ley (vol′i), *n.* [*pl.* volleys], **1,** the throwing of many missiles, as arrows, bullets, etc., at the same time; also, the missiles so thrown; **2,** a sudden burst of any sort; as, a *volley* of words:—*v.t.* and *v.i.* to discharge, or be discharged, all at the same time.

vol-ley-ball (vol′i bôl′), *n.* **1,** a game between two teams in which a large, inflated ball is hit back and forth over a net with the fingers, fist, or forearm: the object is to keep the ball in the air; **2,** the ball used in this game.

volt (vōlt), *n.* a unit used for measuring the strength of electric current: a volt is the amount of force needed to cause a current of electricity to flow through a conductor against resistance.

volt-age (vōl′tij), *n.* the total number of volts in a particular electrical current, measuring its electrical power.

vol-tam-e-ter (vol-tam′e-tėr), *n.* an instrument for measuring the quantity of electricity passing through a conductor (by the amount of electrolysis it produces).

volt-me-ter (vōlt′mē′tėr), *n.* an instrument for measuring the pressure of electricity in volts.

vol-u-ble (vol′ū-bl), *adj.* smooth or ready in speech; talkative.—*n.* **vol′u-bly.**

vol-ume (vol′ūm), *n.* **1,** a number of printed sheets bound together; a book; **2,** one of the books within a series of books that form a complete work; as, the second *volume* of an encyclopedia; **3,** the amount of space occupied by a body, as measured by cubic units; as, the *volume* of water in a tank; **4,** a large quantity; **5,** the amount of sound; loudness; as, could you please turn up the *volume* of the radio.

vo-lu-mi-nous (vo-lū′mi-nus), *adj.* **1,** large; bulky; **2,** filling many volumes; as, a *voluminous* history.

vol-un-tary (vol′un-tėr-i), *adj.* **1,** done or made freely, not forced by another; as, a *voluntary* choice; **2,** acting of one's own free will; as, a *voluntary* worker; **3,** intentional; deliberate; as, *voluntary* manslaughter; **4,** controlled by the will; as, *voluntary* muscles.—*adv.* **vol′un-tar-i-ly** (vol′un-tėr-i-li).

vol-un-teer (vol′un-tēr′), *n.* **1,** one who enters into any service of his or her own free will, esp. one who volunteers for military service without being drafted; **2,** a person who willingly offers to do a job without pay; as, many services in a community depend on *volunteers*; **3,** a person who agrees to take on a difficult or unpleasant task; as, they asked for *volunteers* to clean the washrooms at the camp:—*v.i.* to offer one's services freely:—*v.t.* to offer freely of one's own accord; as, to *volunteer* information:—*adj.* pertaining to free services; voluntary.

vo-lup-tu-ous (vo-lup′tū-us), *adj.* **1,** giving delight to the senses; sensuous; **2,** devoted to luxurious pleasures; as, *voluptuous* living.—*n.* **vo-lup′tu-ous-ness.**

vom-it (vom′it), *v.i.* to throw up the contents of the stomach:—*v.t.* **1,** to throw up from the stomach; **2,** to discharge with violence; belch forth; as, the smokestack *vomits* clouds of black smoke:—*n.* matter thrown up by the stomach.

voo-doo (vōō′dōō), *n.* a religion followed in some areas of the West Indies that combines West African spiritual traditions with elements of Roman Catholicism: characterized by monism and a belief in spirits that communicate through dreams, trances, and ritual possessions:—*n.* **voo′doo-ism.**

vo-ra-cious (vō-rā′shus), *adj.* **1,** greedy in eating; as, their dog was a *voracious* animal; **2,** marked by greediness; as, a *voracious* appetite; **3,** extremely eager in any pursuit; as, a *voracious* reader.—*adv.* **vo-ra′cious-ly.**—*n.* **vo-rac′i-ty** (vō-ras′i-ti).

vor-tex (vôr′teks), *n.* [*pl.* vortexes (vôr′tek-sez) or vortices (vôr′ti-sēz′)], **1,** air or water with a rotary motion tending to suck bodies caught in it into a depression or vacuum at the centre; an eddy or whirlpool; **2,** anything similar to this, such an inescapable situation; as, she was drawn into a *vortex* of illegal activity.

vo-ta-ry (vō′ta-ri), *n.* [*pl.* votaries], a dedicated follower of a cause, occupation, person, or religion.

vote (vōt), *n.* **1,** the showing of an opinion or choice in an election; the choosing of one person or course of action; as, a member of Parliament is elected by the *vote* of the people; **2,** the means of expressing such choice; as, some wanted the *vote* by secret ballot, others by a show of hands; **3,** the right to express such a choice; as, women were not given the *vote* in Canada until the 20th century; **4,** the entire number of such expressions; as, the *vote* was 55 to 30; also, such expressions of a particular class or group taken as a whole; as, the student *vote*; **5,** a resolution resulting from the formal expression of the choice or will of a majority; as, a *vote* of thanks:—*v.t.* [vot-ed, vot-ing], **1,** to declare or authorize by a vote; as, to *vote* a reform; **2,** to grant; as, to *vote* money; **3,** *Colloq.* to pronounce, by general consent; as, we *voted* the meeting a failure:—*v.i.* **1,** to cast a ballot; **2,** to show an opinion or choice in an election; to choose one person or course of action.—*n.* **vot′er.**

vo-tive (vō′tiv), *adj.* given, offered, etc., in fulfillment of a vow; as, *votive* offerings.

vouch (vouch), *v.i.* **1,** to give evidence or assurance based on personal experience; as, I can *vouch* for the truth of his statement; **2,** to confirm the good character or identity of a person; as, she *vouched* for me at the airport after I lost my passport.

vouch-er (vouch′ėr), *n.* **1,** a paper, etc., that bears witness to something, specifically, a receipt for payment; **2,** a piece of paper, such as a gift certificate or coupon, entitling the bearer to receive something for free; as, a *voucher* for a free meal at the restaurant.

vow (vou), *n.* **1,** a serious promise or pledge that a person is determined to keep; as, a marriage *vow*:—*v.t.* to promise or assert solemnly; swear:—*v.i.* to make a solemn promise; to declare with emphasis.

vow-el (vou′el), *n.* **1,** a simple vocal sound made with the mouth and lips more or less open and the vocal cords vibrating, as opposed to a *consonant,* where the air is blocked in some way; **2,** a letter representing such a sound, as *a, e, i, o, u* and sometimes *y*: in English, every syllable has at least one vowel:—*adj.* pertaining to a vowel.

voy-age (voi′ij), *n.* a trip or journey, esp. a long trip over water:—*v.i.* [voyaged, voyaging], to travel on a voyage:—*v.t.* to sail, or travel, over; traverse.

voy-a-geur (vwå′yå′zhûr′), *n.* in *Canadian history,* a person, usually French-speaking or Métis, who worked the large freight canoes for the merchants in Montreal and transported goods and men to the trading posts in the interior of the country where the goods were exchanged for furs, etc.; **2,** any such person who travelled by canoe into the Canadian wilderness.

vul-can-ize (vul′kan-īz′), *v.t.* [vulcanized, vulcaniz-ing], to harden (rubber, etc.) by treating, esp. with sulphur, at a high temperature.—*n.* **vul′can-i-za′tion.**

vul-gar (vul′gėr), *adj.* **1,** showing poor taste or bad manners; crude or disgusting; **2,** unrefined.—*adv.* **vul′gar-ly.**—*n.* **vul-gar′i-ty; vul′gar-ism.**

vul-ner-a-ble (vul′nėr-a-bl), *adj.* **1,** capable of being wounded or hurt; **2,** open to injury or criticism; as, a *vulnerable* reputation.—*n.* **vul′ner-a-bil′i-ty.**

vul-ture (vul′tūr), *n.* **1,** a large bird of prey that feeds on carrion and is allied to the hawks and eagles; **2,** a cruel, greedy person who gains from the troubles of others.

vy-ing (vī′ing), *p.pr.* of *vie.*

W

W, w (dub′l-ū), *n.* [*p.t.* W's, w's], the 23th letter of the alphabet, following V.

wad (wod; wôd), *n.* **1,** a small mass or bundle of soft material; **2,** a soft bunch of cotton, wool, rope, etc., used to stop an opening; **3,** *Colloq.* a large roll of paper money:—*v.t.* [wad-ded, wad-ding], **1,** to form, as some soft material, into a compact mass or bunch; **2,** to insert a wad into; close, as an opening with a small compact mass; as, Luisa *wadded* up the hole in the bucket.

wad-dle (wod′l; wôd′l), *v.i.* [wad-dled, wad-dling], to sway from side to side in walking; walk with short, clumsy steps, as does an animal like a duck with short legs set wide apart:—*n.* **wad′dler.**

wade (wād), *v.i.* [wad-ed, wad-ing], **1,** to walk through water, mud, snow, or other substances that make movement difficult; **2,** to proceed with difficulty; as, to *wade* through a tiresome lesson; **3,** to go at something with great force; as, to *wade* into one's work:—*v.t.* to cross by walking through water, mud, etc.—*n.* **wad′er.**

wafer (wā′fėr), *n.* **1,** a thin cake or biscuit; **2,** a small, coloured disk of adhesive paper used for fastening letters and sealing official papers, esp. legal documents.

[1]**waf-fle** (wof′l; wôf′l), *n.* a flat, crisp cake made of batter and marked by a pattern of small squares from the waffle iron in which it is baked:—**waffle iron,** a device for baking waffles, consisting of a pair of iron plates, hinged so as to close over batter poured upon one of them.

[2]**waf-fle** (wof′l; wôf′l), *v.i.* [waffled, waffling], to avoid making a decision; as, she *waffled* when asked what she wanted to do.

waft (wåft), *v.i.* and *v.t.* to float along through the air or on the water; as, the current *wafted* the leaves downstream:—*n.* **1,** a waving or beckoning movement of the hand; **2,** a gust or puff, as of wind.

[1]**wag** (wag), *v.t.* [wagged, wag-ging], to move, or cause to swing, from side to side; as, to *wag* a finger:—*v.i.* to move from side to side:—*n.* a wagging movement.

[2]**wag** (wag), *n.* a practical joker; a wit.—*n.* **wag′ ger-y.**

wage (wāj), *v.t.* [waged, wag-ing], to engage in vigorously; carry on; as, to *wage* war:—*n.* payment for work done; as, a weekly *wage.*

wa-ger (wā′jėr), *n.* something risked on an uncertainty; a bet:—*v.t.* and *v.i.* to bet.

wag·es (wāj′iz), *n.pl.* money paid or received for labour, calculated by the hour, day, week, etc.

wag·gish (wag′ish), *adj.* **1,** given to playing good-natured jokes on others; **2,** done in good-humoured jesting; mischievous.

wag·gle (wag′l), *v.t.* to wag with short, quick motions; as, to *waggle* a finger; to *waggle* a golf club (above a ball in line of play).

wag·on (wag′un), *n.* **1,** a large, heavy four-wheeled vehicle, used for hauling freight, carrying heavy loads, etc.: often pulled by horses, oxen, mules, etc.; **2,** a low, small, open four-wheeled vehicle with a long handle, pulled by hand: used as a toy or for pulling small children, etc.

waif (wāf), *n.* a homeless or lost person or animal, esp. a lost or homeless child.

wail (wāl), *v.i.* to make a long, loud cry because of sadness or pain; to make a mournful sound; as, the ambulance siren *wailed* in the distance:—*n.* a mournful cry.

wain·scot·ing (wān′skot-ing; wān′skut-ing), *n.* wooden panelling, often lining the lower part of the walls of a room.

waist (wāst), *n.* **1,** the narrowest part of the human body, between the ribs and the hips; **2,** a piece of clothing that covers this area; as, those pants have an elastic *waist.*—*n.* **waist′band′; waist′line′.**

waist·coat (wāst′kōt′; wes′kut), *n.* a short, sleeveless garment, formerly ornamental, worn under the coat; a vest.

wait (wāt), *v.i.* **1,** to stay or remain in a place until something happens or someone comes; as, to *wait* for news; **2,** to delay or be delayed; as, let's *wait* until next weekend to paint the cottage:—**wait on** or **upon, 1,** to attend or serve, as in a store or restaurant; **2,** to call on formally; as, he *waited upon* the premier:—*v.t.* **1,** to expect or remain around for; as, to *wait* permission; **2,** *Colloq.* to delay; as, to *wait* supper:—*n.* **1,** the act of delaying or remaining in a place; as, we enjoyed the *wait* for the bus as there was lots to see; **2,** the length of time during which one lingers in expectation; delay; as, a *wait* of half an hour; **3,** ambush; hiding; as, to lie in *wait* for an enemy.

wait·er (wāt′ėr), *n.* **1,** a person who works in a restaurant serving tables; **2,** a serving tray for dishes.—*n.fem.* **wait′ress.**

waive (wāv), *v.t.* [waived, waiv-ing], to agree to give up a right or claim; as, to *waive* an inheritance.—*n.* **waiv′er** (the act or fact of waiving).

Wa·kash·an (wôk′a-shon; wo-kash′un), *n.* the group of languages spoken by the Nootka, Kwakiutl, and other Aboriginal groups in the Pacific Northwest.

[1]**wake** (wāk), *v.i.* [*p.t.* woke (wōk) or waked, *p.p.* waked, *p.pr.* wak-ing], **1,** to stop sleeping; as, to *wake* at 10 o'clock; also, to be roused from sleep; **2,** to be aroused, excited, or made aware; as, we *woke* to the danger of the high waves as the wind grew stronger; the principal *woke* to the situation:—**wake up, 1,** to stop sleeping; as, Tran *woke up* early this morning; **2,** to become active and aware; as, she *woke up* when the coach threatened to remove her from the team:—*v.t.* **1,** to rouse from sleep; to awake; as, he *woke* his father; **2,** to make active; arouse; as, music can *wake* the emotions:—*n.* **1,** a vigil, esp. a gathering to watch over the body of a dead person before burial and to pay last respects to the one who died; **2,** a gathering to remember and celebrate the life of a person who has died: usually with food and drink.

[2]**wake** (wāk), *n.* **1,** the trail left behind a ship, boat, or other object moving through water; **2,** any track, trail, or path left by something; as, the runner left many competitors in her *wake*:—**in the wake of,** following close behind; after; as, many fallen trees were left *in the wake of* the storm.

wake·board·ing (wāk′bōrd-ing), *n.* a water sport in which people ride on a short, wide board, towed behind a motor boat.

wake·ful (wāk′fool), *adj.* **1,** free from sleepiness; unable to sleep; **2,** watchful; vigilant; as, a *wakeful* guard.—*n.* **wake′ful-ness.**

wak·en (wāk′en), *v.t.* **1,** to rouse from sleep or inaction; **2,** to excite; move to action:—*v.i.* to become awake.

wake–rob·in (wāk′–rob′in), *n.* Same as **trillium.**

walk (wôk), *v.i.* **1,** to go by foot at a normal rate: distinguished from *run*; **2,** to take a stroll:—*v.t.* **1,** to pass over on foot; as, to *walk* a golf course; **2,** to cause to go on foot; as, she *walked* her dog everyday; also, to ride or drive at a slow pace; as, to *walk* a horse; **3,** in *baseball,* to allow a batter to go to first base by pitching four balls:—*n.* **1,** the act of walking, esp. for pleasure or exercise; also, a stroll or promenade; **2,** the distance or time to be walked; as, it's about a five-minute *walk* from here; **3,** a special place for walking, as a path around a lake; **4,** in *baseball,* the act of allowing a batter to go to first base by pitching four balls; **5,** one's circle or environment; as, he was from a humble *walk* of life.—*n.* **walk′way.**

walk′er (wôk′ėr), *n.* **1,** a person who walks; as, you're a fast *walker*; **2,** a device used to help a person walk, as a young child or a disabled person.

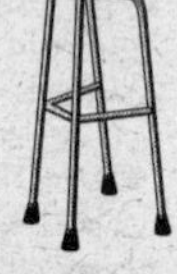
WALKER

walk·ing stick (wôk′ing stik′), *n.* **1,** a cane or wooden stick used as an aid in walking; **2,** an insect with a long, slender body resembling a twig or stick.

walk-out (wôk′out′), *n.* **1,** a labour strike by workers; **2,** a departure or exit from a workplace or organization by a group of people to protest some action or policy: often done suddenly and in anger.

wall (wôl), *n.* **1,** a solid structure, usually vertical, which forms any one of the sides of a building or the side of a room; **2,** a structure of stone, brick, etc., serving as an enclosure, defence, etc.; **3,** the side or inside surface of any cavity, vessel, or receptacle:—**walls,** fortifications:—*v.t.* **1,** to surround with, or as with, a structure for enclosure, security, or defence; **2,** to fill in or close up, as an opening.—*n.* **wall′board.**

wal-la-by (wäl′a-bi), *n.* in Australia, any of various marsupials related to kangaroos but smaller and often having a colourful coat.

wal-la-roo (wäl′a-roo͞′), *n.* in Australia, a species of large kangaroo with long narrow hind feet and reddish or grey fur.

wal-let (wol′it; wôl′it), *n.* a small, flat folding case used for holding money, cards, photographs, identifcation, etc.

wall-eye (wôl′ī′), *n.* a large freshwater fish in North America, characterized by large, prominent eyes: has value as a sport and food fish: sometimes called a pike or pickerel.

wal-lop (wol′up; wôl′up), *v.t.* **1,** *Colloq.* to beat; flog; **2,** to strike very hard; as, to *wallop* a ball:—*n. Colloq.* **1,** a very hard blow; **2,** the power to have a large impact; as, the movie delivered quite a *wallop.*

wal-low (wol′ō; wôl′ō), *v.i.* **1,** to roll about in, or as in, mud, as a hog does; **2,** to live in and enjoy; indulge; as, to *wallow* in luxury; *wallow* in self-pity:—*n.* the act of rolling or revelling in mud, vice, etc.

wall-pa-per (wôl′pā-pėr), *n.* **1,** paper that is used to cover and decorate the walls of a room: usually printed with colours and designs; **2,** in *computing,* in a Windows operating system, a picture or pattern chosen as background on a computer screen:—*v.t.* to put wallpaper on; as, to *wallpaper* a room.

wal-nut (wôl′nut), *n.* **1,** any of several trees bearing edible nuts, esp. the black walnut tree; **2,** the nut of such a tree; **3,** the hard, strong wood of the tree, valuable in making furniture.

wal-rus (wôl′rus; wol′rus), *n.* a large, amphibious, Arctic sea mammal related to the seal: it has a thick neck, two long tusks, and a thick wrinkled hide.

waltz (wôlts), *n.* **1,** a smooth, graceful dance in triple time; **2,** music for such a dance:—*v.i.* **1,** to dance a waltz; **2,** to move in an easy or confident way; as, Daniel *waltzed* into the room as if he was a star.—*n.* **waltz′er.**

wam-pum (wom′pum; wôm′pum), *n.* beads made of shells, strung into strands for necklaces, bracelets, or belts: once used as money by some Native peoples of eastern North America.

wan (won; wôn), *adj.* [wan-ner, wan-nest], pale; sickly; languid; as, a *wan* child; a *wan* smile.—*adv.* **wan′ly.**

WAN (wôn), *abbrev.* short for *wide-area network.*

wand (wond; wônd), *n.* a slender stick or rod, esp. one held or waved around by a magician during a magic act: as, a magic *wand.*

wan-der (won′dėr; wôn′dėr), *v.i.* **1,** to go or move around with no particular place to go; **2,** to stray or lose one's way; as, he *wandered* from the right path; **3,** to come slowly in a long, winding course; as, the sheep *wandered* back to the fold; **4,** to lose focus; as, my attention *wandered* from the movie:—*n.* the act of wandering.—*n.* **wan′der-er.**

wan-der-lust (wôn′dėr-lust′), *n.* eager desire or impulse to travel.

wane (wān), *v.i.* [waned, wan-ing], **1,** to grow smaller; decrease: applied esp. to the moon; **2,** to decline in power, importance, etc.:—*n.* **1,** the decrease in the visible bright part of the moon from full to new; also, the period of that decrease; **2,** decrease, as of power, importance, etc.

wan-gle (wang′gl), *v.t. Colloq.* to persuade or induce someone to acquire or do something by dubious or scheming methods; as, he *wangled* a pass to the game; she *wangled* her way into the show even though she didn't have a ticket:—*v.i.* to wriggle (out of some difficult situation).

want (wont; wônt), *n.* **1,** the fact of needing or lacking something; as, for *want* of a ticket, he couldn't get on the streetcar; **2,** something that is desired or needed; as, after the fire, the family had many *wants*:—*v.t.* **1,** to be without; lack; as, the soldier *wants* courage; **2,** to need; require; as, we *want* food when we are hungry; **3,** to wish to do or have a desire for; as, I *want* to take a trip to Europe:—*v.i.* to be in poverty.

want-ing (won′ting; wôn′ting), *adj.* **1,** short of; lacking; as, they are *wanting* in good nutrition; **2,** falling short of what is expected; as, *wanting* in courage; **3,** missing; as, one page was *wanting.*

wan-ton (won′tun; wôn′tun), *adj.* **1,** done without any reason or purpose; reckless; as, the town experienced acts of *wanton* destruction; **2,** unrestrained; unruly; as, *wanton* curls; **3,** heartless; outrageous; as, a *wanton* murder.—*adv.* **wan′ton-ly.**—*n.* **wan′ton-ness.**

wap-i-ti (wop′i-ti; wôp′i-ti), *n.* [*pl.* wapiti or wapitis], a large light-brown or grayish-brown North American deer with large branching antlers.

war (wôr), *n.* **1,** a conflict by force of arms

between nations, or parts of the same nation; also, the condition created by such a conflict; as, to be at *war*; **2,** the science or art of the profession of arms; as, skilled in *war*; **3,** any contest or contention; as, a *war* of words:—*v.i.* [warred, war-ring], **1,** to engage in an armed conflict; fight; **2,** to contend.—*n.* **war′path′; war′ship′; war′time′.**

[1]**war-ble** (wôr′bl), *v.i.* [war-bled, war-bling], to trill or make a similar sound, as a bird; to make a melodious sound, as a stream:—*v.t.* to sing with trills, runs, and other embellishments:—*n.* **1,** the act of warbling; **2,** a soft, sweet flow of sounds.

[2]**war-ble** (wôr′bl), *n.* **1,** a swelling on the back of cattle, horses, deer, etc., caused by larvae of the warble fly; **2,** a hard lump on a horse's back caused by the rubbing of the saddle:—**warble fly,** any of several flies, the larvae of which live under the skin of horses and cattle.

war-bler (wôr′blėr), *n.* any of several small songbirds, often brightly coloured.

war crime (wôr′ krīm′), *n.* a crime that goes against the international laws of war or, in the case of genocide, is a crime against humanity.

ward (wôrd), *v.t.* to turn aside; avert; as, to *ward* off an attack:—*n.* **1,** the act of guarding; protection; **2,** a person under the care or protection of a guardian or a court, esp. a person who, because of youth, mental illness, etc., is placed under protection; **3,** one of the sections into which a town or city is divided for election or other purposes; **4,** a section of a hospital or prison.—*n.* **ward′ship.**

ward-en (wôr′dn), *n.* **1,** a person who is in charge of a prison; **2,** an official who makes sure that certain laws are obeyed; as, a game *warden*.

ward-robe (wôrd′rōb′), *n.* **1,** a large piece of furniture or a closet for hanging and keeping clothes; **2,** a person's collection of clothing.

ward-room (wôrd′rōōm′), *n.* in a warship, the messroom for the use of commissioned officers.

ware (wâr), *n.* **1,** manufactured articles of a particular kind or for a specific use; as, silver*ware*, kitchen*ware*, hard*ware*, soft*ware*, etc.; **2,** articles for sale; as, the merchant peddled his *wares*.

ware-house (wâr′hous′), *n.* a building for storing goods, esp. one where goods are stored before being delivered to a store or to a customer.

war-fare (wôr′fâr′), *n.* open hostilities between enemies; armed conflict.

war-head (wôr′hed′), *n.* the front part of a torpedo, missile, etc., that carries the explosive charge.

war-i-ly (wâr′i-li), *adv.* cautiously; in a wary manner; as, the chipmunk ate *warily*, ready to run if we came too close.

war-like (wôr′līk′), *adj.* **1,** fit for, or fond of, military life or fighting; as, *warlike* peoples; **2,** of or for war; as, *warlike* preparations; **3,** ready for war; favouring or threatening war.

warm (wôrm), *adj.* **1,** moderately heated; not cold; as, *warm* water; *warm* weather; **2,** having little cold weather; as, a *warm* climate; **3,** giving out warmth; as, a *warm* fire; also, serving to keep heat near the body; as, *warm* fur; **4,** heated with passion, anger, excitement, etc.; as, a *warm* dispute; **5,** kindly; affectionate; as, a *warm* greeting; **6,** having tones that give a feeling of warmth, as red, yellow, or orange:—*v.t.* and *v.t.* **1,** to make or become warm; as, to *warm* milk; the milk is *warming* on the stove; **2,** to make or become eager, excited, etc.:—**warm up,** to get a person or object to operate; as, it's a good idea to let the engine *warm up*.—*adv.* **warm′ly.**

warm–blood-ed (worm′–blud′ed), *adj.* having blood that stays at about the same temperature, even when the temperature of the surrounding air or water changes: mammals and birds are warm–blooded.

warm boot, in *computing,* the act of restarting a computer system without turning it off, often done after the malfunction of a program or a piece of hardware that locks the system or causes erratic functioning: also called a *warm start*.

war-mon-ger (wôr′mung′gėr), *n.* one who advocates war or tries to bring it about.

warmth (wôrmth), *n.* **1,** the quality or state of having moderate heat; as, the *warmth* of the climate; **2,** earnestness; zeal; as, the *warmth* of an appeal.

warm–up or **warm-up** (wôrm–′up′; wôrm′ up′), *n.* **1,** the act of warming up; **2,** a workout or practice before a game, contest, race, etc.; as, a 10-minute *warm–up*:—*adj.* relating to, of, or for a warm–up; as, a *warm–up* suit.

warn (wôrn), *v.t.* **1,** to put on guard; make aware of possible danger; caution; as, we *warned* him not to go out in the storm; **2,** to notify; as, why didn't you *warn* us that you were coming?

warn-ing (wôr′ning), *n.* previous notice, esp. of danger; as, the black clouds gave *warning* of an approaching storm; also, that which notifies or cautions; as, this is a *warning* to you:—*adj.* relating to, of, or for a warning; as, a distant early *warning* system.

warp (wôrp), *n.* a twist, distortion, or bend, as in a board:—*v.t.* **1,** to turn or twist out of shape; as, dampness *warps* wood; **2,** to turn from what is right or healthy; his mind is *warped* by misfortune:—*v.i.* to become twisted or distorted.

war-rant (wor′ant; wôr′ant), *n.* **1,** an official paper giving authority to receive money, to make an arrest, etc.; also, authorization so given; **2,** that which vouches for or guarantees anything; as, his presence is a *warrant* of his sincerity; **3,** justification; as, he acted without *warrant*:—*v.t.* **1,** to guarantee; as, this silver is *warranted* sterling; **2,** to give (a person) authority to do something; also, to authorize (a course of action); **3,** to justify; give just grounds for or to; as, this state of affairs *warrants* action; **4,** to declare as certain; as, I *warrant* this will happen.

war-ran-ty (wor′an-ti), *n.* a written statement from the seller of a product guaranteeing that the product is being sold as it is described, and that for a certain period of time, the seller will repair or replace the item if it fails to work as promised.

war-ren (wor′en; wôr′en), *n.* **1,** a place for breeding rabbits or other small animals; also, a place where small animals abound; **2,** a crowded place.

war-ri-or (wor′i-ėr; wôr′i-ėr; wôr′yėr), *n.* **1,** a person experienced in fighting wars or battles; **2,** any person who takes part in a difficult struggle or conflict; as, she has been a *warrior* in the fight for human rights for over a decade.

war-ship (wôr′ship′), *n.* a ship built and equipped for combat and armed with weapons.

wart (wôrt), *n.* **1,** a small, usually hard, lump that grows on the skin: caused by a virus; **2,** a similar lump on a plant stem.—*adj.* **wart′y.**

wart hog or **wart-hog** (wôrt′ hog′), *n.* a wild hog of Africa, with warty growths on the face and with large tusks.

war-y (wâr′i), *adj.* [war-i-er, war-i-est], **1,** constantly on guard; as, a *wary* foe; **2,** marked by caution; as, *wary* speeches.

was (woz; wuz), *p.t.* 1st and 3rd person sing. of *be.*

wash (wosh; wôsh), *v.t.* **1,** to get rid of dirt or stains by using water or water and soap; as, to *wash* your hands; **2,** to cover with water; flow against; as, the breakers *wash* the shore; **3,** to take away, or remove, by the action of water; as, the flood *washed* the bridge away; **4,** to overlay with a thin coat of metal, colour, etc.:—*v.i.* **1,** to become clean by the use of water; **2,** to cleanse clothes, linen, etc., in water; as, he *washes* on Saturdays; **3,** to stand without injury the process of being cleaned in water; as, this material will *wash* well; **4,** to be removed or worn away by the action of water; as, the spot will *wash* out; the bank has *washed* away; **5,** to move with a flowing, lapping sound; to splash:—*n.* **1,** the act of washing or a place where this is done; as, a car *wash*; **2,** a collection of articles which are to be, or have been, washed; as, there are six sheets in the *wash*; **3,** the dash or sound of a body of water; **4,** material deposited by water, as wreckage on a beach; **5,** disturbed water behind the propellers, oars, etc., of a boat; also, disturbed air behind a moving airplane; **6,** liquid with which anything is tinted or washed; as, whitewash; eyewash.—*adj.* **wash′a-ble.**—*n.* **wash′board′; wash′ cloth′; wash′day′; wash′rag′; wash′tub′.**

wash-er (wosh′ėr; wôsh′ėr), *n.* **1,** one who washes; as, a window *washer*; **2,** a machine that washes, as a machine for washing dishes, clothes, etc.; **3,** a flat ring of metal, leather, etc., used to secure the tightness of a joint or screw.

wasp (wosp; wôsp), *n.* an insect with strong wings, a very slender body, and a powerful sting.—*adj.* **wasp′ish** (like a wasp; bad-tempered).

was-sail (wos′il; was′il), *n.* **1,** a festive occasion, marked by drinking and carousing, esp. in former times during Christmas; **2,** the wine, ale, etc., used in a drinking bout, often flavoured with spices, sugar, etc.

waste (wāst), *v.t.* [wast-ed, wast-ing], **1,** to lay in ruins; destroy; **2,** to wear away gradually the strength of; as, disease *wastes* the body; **3,** to spend recklessly, as, to *waste* money:—*v.i.* to lose vigour, substance, or strength gradually; as, she is *wasting* away with the disease:—*adj.* **1,** useless or unused, as unproductive land; **2,** desolate; dreary; **3,** discarded; no longer useful; as, *waste* products; **4,** used for carrying away or holding waste products; as, a *waste* pipe:—*n.* **1,** the act or fact of wasting; as, a *waste* of time; **2,** things of no use or value; refuse; **3,** material that is not digested for use as food and that is eliminated from the body.—*adj.* **waste′ful.**—*n.* **wast′age; waste′pa′per.**

waste-bas-ket (wāst′bås′kit), *n.* a basket or other container used to hold things to be thrown away: also called *wastepaper basket.*

waste-land (wāst′land), *n.* **1,** an area of land where there are very few plants and animals and where few people live, such as a desert or a polar region; **2,** an area without life or spirit, as an abandoned industrial area, or an area of rundown housing where few people want to live.

wast-rel (wās′trel) or **wast-er** (wās′tėr), *n.* a spendthrift; a person who wastes things, esp. money.

watch (woch; wôch), *n.* **1,** the act or fact of looking carefully; close attention; as, she kept a close *watch* over the sleeping child; **2,** one or more people ordered to stay awake and alert to guard or protect others, as on a ship at night; **3,** the period of time when people do this; as, they were on the night *watch*; **4,** a small device that tells the time, usually worn on the wrist:—*v.t.* **1,** to look carefully at some event or activity; as, to *watch* a sports event; **2,** to keep guard over; look at, so as to protect or care for; as, her mom asked her to *watch* her little sister:—*v.i.* **1,** to wait; as, to *watch* for an opening to speak; **2,** to look carefully; keep one's attention on; as, the enemy watched from the distant hills; **3,** to be careful or concerned about; as, the investors *watched* to see whether the market would go up or down.—*n.* **watch′er; watch′mak′er; watch′tow′er.**

watch-dog (woch′dôg), *n.* **1,** a dog that is kept to guard a house or property and to warn of intruders; **2,** a person or group that tries to guard against illegal pollution, crime, abuse, etc.; as, Amnesty International acts as a *watchdog* against human rights abuses.

watch-ful (woch′fool; wôch′fool), *adj.* vigilant; on the lookout; carefully watching; alert.—*adv.* **watch′ful-ly.**

watch-word (woch′wûrd′; wôch′wûrd′), *n.* **1,** a password; **2,** a rallying cry.

wa-ter (wô′tėr), *n.* **1,** a clear, colourless, odourless, tasteless liquid, H_2O, essential to the life of animals and plants; **2,** the liquid that forms lakes, rivers, etc., and that comes from the clouds as rain; **3,** the liquid used for cooking, washing, drinking, etc.; **4,** any clear liquid like or containing water, as tears; **5,** a body of water, as a sea, river, lake, etc.; as, to cross the *water* in a sailboat:—*v.t.* **1,** to supply with water; as, to *water* the lawn; **2,** to flow through; irrigate; as, the Fraser River *waters* a large valley; **3,** to give a drink to; as, to *water* the horses; **4,** to dilute with water; as, to *water* alcohol:—*v.i.* **1,** to obtain or take in water; also, to drink water: said usually of animals; **2,** to secrete or fill with liquid; as, his eyes *watered*:—*adj.* **1,** used for holding or conducting water; as, a *water* pipe; **2,** living, feeding, etc., in, on, or near water; as, a *water* plant:—**water down, 1,** to make a liquid weaker by adding water; **2,** to make weaker or less effective; as, the committee *watered down* the resolution.—*n.* **wa′ter-mark′; wa′ter-side′; wa′ter-works′.**

wa-ter-bed (wô′tėr-bed), *n.* a type of bed that uses a plastic bag filled with water instead of a regular mattress.

water buffalo, an Asian buffalo, with large swept-back horns, often domesticated for its milk and for pulling heavy loads, etc.

wa-ter-col-our or **wa-ter-col-or** (wô′tėr-kul′ėr), *n.* **1,** a paint moistened with water; **2,** a picture made with paints of this kind, as distinguished from one painted with oil paints; **3,** the art of painting with such colours.

wa-ter-course (wô′tėr-kôrs′), *n.* **1,** a stream of water; **2,** a channel for flowing water, either natural or artificial.

wa-ter-cress (wôt′ėr-kres), *n.* a type of plant that grows in water, with sharp-tasting leaves that can be used in salads and sandwiches.

wa-ter-fall (wô′tėr-fôl′), *n.* a stream of water that falls straight down from a high place, as over a cliff; as, Niagara Falls is a spectacular *waterfall.*

wa-ter-fowl (wô′tėr-foul′), *n.* [*pl.* waterfowl or waterfowls], a bird that lives on or close to a body of water, as ducks, geese, loons, cormorants, etc.; also, all such birds as a class.

wa-ter-front (wô′tėr-frunt), *n.* **1,** land that is at the edge of a body of water; **2,** the part of a city that is alongside a body of water, esp. where there is a port, docks, and/or tourist, entertainment, and recreation facilities.

water lily, a plant that grows in water (aquatic) with large, flat, floating leaves and fragrant, cup-shaped flowers; also, the flower itself.

wa-ter-logged (wô′tėr-logd′), *adj.* so soaked or filled with water as to be heavy and unmanageable.

wa-ter-mark (wô′tėr-märk′), *n.* **1,** a mark that shows the height or limit of the rise of water; **2,** a faintly visible marking or design in some kinds of paper, seen when the paper is held to the light.

wa-ter-mel-on (wô′tėr-mel′un), *n.* a large edible melon with a hard, green rind, red, sweet, juicy pulp, and many seeds that grows on a vine.

wa-ter-proof (wô′tėr-prōōf′), *adj.* not permitting water to come through; as, *waterproof* garments:—*v.t.* (wô′tėr-prōōf′), to make secure against water; as, to *waterproof* a fabric.

wa-ter-shed (wô′tėr-shed′), *n.* **1,** a height or ridge of land separating river systems that flow in different directions; **2,** the total land area drained by a single river or lake system; **3,** a crucial dividing point in the course of events; as, the debate was a *watershed* in the mayor's defeat.

wa-ter–ski (wô′tėr–skē), *v.i.* to glide over water on skis while holding on to a tow rope attached to a power boat.

wa-ter-spout (wô′tėr-spout′), *n.* **1,** a column of water drawn up by a whirlwind at sea to meet a descending funnel-shaped cloud; **2,** a spout for the discharge of water, esp. of rainwater.

wa-ter-tight (wô′tėr-tīt′), *adj.* **1,** so closely made or fastened as to permit no water to leak out or to enter; **2,** well reasoned; convincing; impossible to refute; as, she put forward a *watertight* case in court.

wa-ter-way (wô′tėr-wā′), *n.* a river, canal, or other such body of water on whch ships and boats travel.

water wheel, a wheel turned by the weight of water falling on it: used to produce power.

wa-ter-y (wô′tėr-i), *adj.* [wa-ter-i-er, wa-ter-i-est] **1,** relating to, or like, water; **2,** containing or discharging water; as, *watery* eyes; **3,** soggy; soft; as, *watery* potatoes.

watt (wot; wôt), *n.* the unit used to measure electric power; as, a 100-*watt* bulb.

wat-tle (wot′l; wôt′l), *n.* **1,** a twig; a rod easily bent; also, a framework of pliant rods; **2,** material made of pliant twigs twisted together and used for walls, fences, etc.; **3,** the folds of loose red flesh under the throat of certain birds or reptiles:—**wattles,** rods used in a roof to support thatch made of straw, etc.:—*v.t.* [wattled, wat-tling], **1,** to twist or interweave (twigs or rods) into a framework, fence, etc.; **2,** to cover or fence in with rods.—*adj.* **wat′tled.**

wave (wāv), *n.* **1,** a moving ridge or high point on the surface of a body of water; **2,** the wavelike motion by which sound, light, and the electromagnetic waves used in radio and television broadcasting, etc., are carried; **3,** anything like a wave, whether natural or artificial; as, *waves* in hair; **4,** a steady increase or sweeping advance of any feeling, condition, etc.; as, a *wave* of enthusiasm; a crime *wave*; a heat *wave*; new *wave*; **5,** an up-and-down motion, as with the hand; also, a signal made by motions of the hand or some object:—*v.i.* [waved, wav-ing], **1,** to move up and down or back and forth; as, the flag *waved* in the breeze; **2,** to signal by such a motion; as, he *waved* to us to stop; **3,** to form into ripples; as, her hair *waves* beautifully:—*v.t.* **1,** to cause to move back and forth; as, to *wave* a banner; **2,** to signal by such movement; as, to *wave* goodbye; **3,** to form into ripples; as, to *wave* the hair.

wave-length (wāv′length′), *n.* the distance from a certain point on one wave to the same point on the next wave, esp. from the top of one wave to the top of another: often used in the measurement of light or sound:—**on the same wavelength,** a certain way of thinking, in relation to how another or others think; as, Kate and I are on the same *wavelength* when it comes to music.

waver (wā′vėr), *v.i.* **1,** to tremble; sway; flicker, as a flame; **2,** to hesitate, as in forming an opinion; **3,** to begin to give way; as, the line of troops *wavered.*—*adj.* **wa′ver-ing.**

wav-y (wāv′i), *adj.* [wav-i-er, wav-i-est], **1,** moving to and fro in waves or swells; as, *wavy* grass; **2,** full of waves or curves; sinuous; wavering; as, *wavy* lines.—*n.* **wav′i-ness.**

[1]**wax** (waks), *v.i.* **1,** to increase in size, power, degree, etc.; grow: used of the moon in its first and second quarters; **2,** to pass gradually into a specified condition; become; as, the party *waxed* louder and louder; *wax* poetic.

[2]**wax** (waks), *n.* **1,** a sticky, yellowish substance, made by bees, from which the honeycomb is built; beeswax; **2,** any of various thick, fatty substances that come from plants or animals or are made artificially, usually a lipid or hydrocarbon: wax melts or softens when it is heated; as, ear*wax*; paraffin *wax*; **3,** any of various materials containing wax or a similar substance: used as a polish for floors and cars, to make candles, etc.:—*v.t.* **1,** to coat or polish with wax; as, to *wax* floors; **2,** to remove unwanted hair by coating the hair with wax and peeling off both hair and wax together.—*adj.* **wax′y** (made of or like wax; as, a *waxy* complexion).—*n.* **wax′i-ness.**

wax-en (wak′sen), *adj.* **1,** made of, or covered with, wax; as, a *waxen* image; **2,** resembling wax; as, *waxen* paleness.

way (wā), *n.* **1,** a road, street, path, or passage; as, a covered *way*; room for passing; as, make *way* for the procession; **2,** the route from one place to another; the direction or best route to go; as, please tell me the *way* to the post office; also, distance in space or time; as, it is a long *way* to China; summer is a long *way* off; **3,** progress; advance; headway; as, the ship gathers *way*; she made her *way* in business; **4,** manner; as, she has a winning *way*; also, methods or means; as, find a *way* to do it; **5,** a habitual or determined course of action or mode of life; as, she goes her *way* through life; he was set in his *ways*; have your own *way* about it; **6,** a point or item to be considered; as, in some *ways*, it proved a success; **7,** neighbourhood; as, out our *way*; **8,** condition; state; as, we're in a bad *way*:—*adv.* far; as, we are *way* off course.

way-bill (wā′bil′), *n.* a document issued with a freight shipment to show the precise nature of contents, route, charges, etc.

way-far-er (wā′fâr′ėr), *n.* a traveller, esp. one who goes on foot.

way-lay (wā′lā′; wā′lā′), *v.t.* [waylaid (-lād′; -lād′), waylay-ing], to lie in wait for with an intent to rob, kill, etc.; to seize or attack on the way.—*n.* **way′lay-er.**

way-side (wā′sīd′), *n.* the edge of a road or path:—*adj.* located or growing near the edge of the road; as, *wayside* flowers.

way-ward (wā′wėrd), *adj.* **1,** disobedient; as, a *wayward* child; **2,** freakish; unaccountable.

we (wē), *pron.* the first person plural of the personal pronoun *I*: **1,** the pronoun by which the writer or speaker denotes himself or herself and the group of which he or she is a part; **2,** the pronoun sometimes used by sovereigns and writers instead of the singular *I* in official proclamations, unsigned articles, editorials, etc.

weak (wēk), *adj.* **1,** lacking in strength of body or in endurance; as, he is *weak* from illness; also, not capable of supporting a heavy weight; as, a *weak* platform; **2,** easily overcome; as, *weak* objections; **3,** wanting in mental or moral strength; easily influenced; as, a *weak* will; **4,** faulty; below standard; as, a *weak* point in the plan; *weak* in math; **5,** faint in sound; feeble; as, a *weak* cry; also, diluted; thin; watery; as, *weak* tea; **6,** not skillful, experienced, etc.; as, a *weak* swimmer.—*adj.* and *adv.* **weak′ly.**—*adj.* **weak′–kneed′.**

weak-en (wēk′en), *v.t.* and *v.i.* to make or become less strong.

weak-ling (wēk′ling), *n.* a person lacking strength of body or character.

weak-ness (wēk′nis), *n.* **1,** the fact of being weak; a lack of strength; **2,** a weak point; a fault or flaw; as, his poor start was his *weakness* in the race; **3,** a special liking that is hard to resist; as, her *weakness* is chocolate.

wealth (welth), *n.* **1,** riches; large amounts of money, property, or valuable possessions; **2,** abundance of anything; as there is a *wealth* of detail in this story.—*adj.* **wealth′y.**

wean (wēn), *v.t.* **1,** to accustom (a baby or any young animal) to substitute other food for the mother's milk; **2,** to draw away the affections or interests of (a person or animal) from any object or habit; as, they *weaned* him from smoking.

weap-on (wep′un), *n.* **1,** any instrument for fighting or for defence; **2,** anything used for attack or defence; as, words can sometimes be a stronger *weapon* than force.

wear (wâr), *v.t.* [*p.t.* wore (wōr), *p.p.* worn (wōrn), *p.pr.* wear-ing], **1,** to have certain clothes on the body; as, to *wear* a coat; **2,** to have or show on the face or body; as, she *wore* a look of disbelief; **3,** to use up or consume, wholly or in part, esp. by personal use; as, he *wears* clothes out rapidly; **4,** to diminish or lessen the quality or value of, by rubbing, scraping, etc.; as, the steps were *worn* by the children's feet; to weaken; weary; fatigue; as, anxiety *wore* the woman out; **5,** to bring about by use, friction, etc.; as, to *wear* a hole in a rug:—*v.i.* **1,** to go through, or endure, the process of being used; as, these gloves *wear* like iron; **2,** to become used up; be diminished in value as a result of use; as, these shoes *wore* out too soon; **3,** to pass gradually; as, the night *wore* on:—*n.* **1,** the act of using or state of being used; use; as, suits for spring *wear*; **2,** things to be worn; clothing of a certain type; as, they deal in children's *wear*; also, sports*wear*; evening *wear*; **3,** damage caused by use; as, to show *wear*; **4,** lasting quality; service; as, these give good *wear*.—*adj.* **wear′a-ble.**

wea-ri-some (wē′ri-sum), *adj.* causing fatigue; tedious; as, *wearisome* work.

wea-ry (wē′ri), *adj.* [wea-ri-er, wea-ri-est], **1,** fatigued, tired; as *weary* in body and mind; **2,** exhausted, as in patience, by continuance of something tiresome; **3,** characteristic of, or showing, fatigue; as, a *weary* sigh; **4,** causing, or accompanied by, fatigue; as, to walk many *weary* miles:—*v.t.* [wearied, weary-ing], **1,** to wear out or make tired; **2,** harass or worry by something irksome:—*v.t.* to become weary.—*adv.* **wea′ri-ly.**—*n.* **wea′ri-ness.**

wea-sel (wē′zl), *n.* a small, active animal of the same family as the mink and the skunk, mostly reddish brown in colour, with a pointed face and a long, thin body: destructive to poultry, mice, etc.:—**weasel words,** remarks that are deliberately ambiguous.

weath-er (we*th*′ėr), *n.* the state of the air or atmosphere as to cold, heat, wetness, dryness, etc.; as, fair *weather*:—*v.t.* **1,** to expose to the air; season by exposure to the elements; also, to break down; as, wind and water *weather* rocks; **2,** to endure or resist; to pass through a difficult experience safely, as if going through a storm; withstand; as, to *weather* a problem:—*v.i.* to undergo action of the air, sun, rain, etc.—*n.* **weath′er-man′.**—*adj.* **weath′er–beat′en.**

weath-er-vane (we*th*′ėr-vān′), *n.* a device with an arrow or pointer that is moved by the wind: usually fastened to a spire, roof, or pole to show which way the wind blows.

weave (wēv), *v.t.* [*p.t.* wove (wōv), *p.p.* woven (wō′ven) or wove, *p.pr.* weav-ing], **1,** to pass threads or strips over and under each other to form cloth or other material, as on a loom; as, to *weave* a rug; **2,** of an insect, to spin a web or cocoon; as, the spider *weaves* a web; **3,** to compose or fabricate; as, to *weave* a story:—*v.i.* **1,** to make cloth on a loom; to spin a web; **2,** to become twisted together or interlaced; **3,** to move quickly in and out; go by twisting and turning, as through a crowd:—*n.* a particular pattern in weaving; as, cloth with a plain *weave*.—*n.* **weav′er.**

web (web), *n.* **1,** the pattern of fine threads that is spun by a spider to catch its prey: also called cob*web* or spider*web*; **2,** a piece of cloth that is being woven; **3,** anything of a complicated structure or arrangement; as, she wove a *web* of lies; **4,** the skin between the toes of many water birds and some water animals.—*adj.* **web′–toed′.**

Web (web), *abbrev.* short for *World Wide Web.*

Web address, in *computing,* a string of characters that identifies a file viewable on the World Wide Web, as, www.home.ca: it usually follows a transfer protocol like http.

webbed (webd), *adj.* **1,** having a web; **2,** having fingers or toes joined by webs; as, the *webbed* hind feet of beavers.

Web browser, in *computing,* a program used to find and access hypertext documents on the World Wide Web.

Web-cam (web′cam), *n.* in *computing,* a video or digital camera, the images from which are broadcast continuously over the Web: used to show traffic in cities, animals in game parks, etc.

Web-cast (web′kåst), *n.* in *computing,* an event intended to be viewed simultaneously by many people connecting to the same Web site at the same time: often used for celebrity events, interviews, etc.

web–foot-ed (web′–foot′id), *adj.* having toes that are joined by webs; as, swans are *web-footed.*

Web-mas-ter (web′mås′tėr), *n.* in *computing,* the person responsible for maintaining a Web site: responsibilities include keeping the information current, making sure the hyperlinks work, etc.

Web page, in *computing,* a file of information available on the World Wide Web: seen by the user as a page of information on the screen.

Web server, in *computing,* a computer connected to the Internet that contains Web pages (as HTML files) that can be accessed through a Web browser: all Web pages are located on a server somewhere, and the Web server has to be connected to the Internet continuously: Web servers accept requests from Web browsers and deliver the required documents to the user requesting them.

Web site, in *computing,* a group of Web pages (data files) linked by a common theme and/or related to a particular person, subject, or organization and accessed through one address on the World Wide Web: pages often contain hyperlinks to related documents and other Web sites.

wed (wed), *v.t.* [*p.t.* wed-ded, *p.p.* wed-ded or wed, *p.pr.* wed-ding], **1,** to marry; **2,** to join in marriage; **3,** to join or attach closely:—*v.i.* to marry.

wed-ding (wed′ing), *n.* **1,** a marriage; a marriage ceremony; a celebration that goes along with a marriage; **2,** a marriage anniversary; as, a golden *wedding.*

wedge (wej), *n.* **1,** a piece of wood or metal, thick at one end and thin at the other, used for splitting wood or rocks, raising heavy objects, etc.: the thin end is forced into a narrow opening, usually by pounding on the thick end; **2,** anything that has the triangular shape of a wedge; as, a *wedge* of land; **3,** any action used to create an opening or lead to further developments:—*v.t.* [wedged, wedg-ing], **1,** to split or force apart with a wedge; **2,** to fasten with a wedge, as a door or wheel; **3,** to force in (something) to serve as a wedge; to press or crowd in; as, to *wedge* packing into a crack; to *wedge* five people into a tiny booth.

Wednes-day (wenz′di; dā), *n.* the fourth day of the week; the day after Tuesday and before Thursday.

wee (wē), *adj.* [wee-er, wee-est], very little; tiny.

weed (wēd), *n.* a wild plant that grows in cultivated areas like fields and gardens where it is not wanted:—*v.t.* **1,** to take the weeds out; as, to *weed* a garden; **2,** to remove something not wanted; as, she *weeded* out all her worn-out clothing:—*v.i.* to take out weeds or anything obnoxious.—*adj.* **weed′y.**—*n.* **weed′er.**

week (wēk), *n.* **1,** a period of seven days in a row, esp. one starting with Sunday and ending with Saturday; **2,** the part of a seven-day period when a person works or goes to school; as, Friday is the end of the work *week*; **3,** the part of the week from Monday to Friday, as distinguished from the weekend; as, the museum is open during the *week.*—*n.* **week′end′.**

week-day (wēk′dā′), *n.* any day of the week except Saturday and Sunday.

week-end (wēk′end; wēk-end′), *n.* the time from the end of one work or school week to the beginning of the next, usually Saturday and Sunday.

week-ly (wēk′li), *adj.* **1,** of a week; for a week; as, a *weekly* visit; **2,** happening or coming every seven days; as, a *weekly* paper or report:—*adv.* once a week; every week:—*n.* [*pl.* weeklies], a paper or magazine issued once every seven days.

weep (wēp), *v.i.* [wept (wept), weep-ing], **1,** to shed tears or cry, as to express emotion; **2,** to show grief or sadness; **3,** give out moisture; as, the skies *weep*:—*v.t.* **1,** to shed, as tears; **2,** to shed tears for.—*n.* **weep′er; weep′ing** (as, a fit of *weeping*).

wee-vil (wē′vl; wē′vil), *n.* a small hard-shelled beetle having the head extended into a beak with the mouth parts at the end: destructive to grain, nuts, fruits, leaves, etc.

weigh (wā), *v.t.* **1,** to find out how heavy something or someone is by using a scale or balance or by lifting; as, I *weighed* the stone in my hand; **2,** to ponder; reflect on carefully; consider; as, to *weigh* the evidence; **3,** to distribute in definite quantities as by the use of scales; as, to *weigh* out sugar; **4,** to press heavily upon; as, care *weighs* her down; **5,** to raise: used only in to *weigh anchor*:—*v.i.* **1,** to have a certain weight; as, this book *weighs* less than a kilogram; **2,** to bear down heavily; **3,** to be considered important; as his testimony didn't *weigh* much with the jury.

weight (wāt) *n.* **1,** the relative heaviness of an object; how heavy a thing is; as, his weight is about 30 kilograms; **2,** in *physics,* the force with which an object is attracted to Earth, as in gravitational pull; **3,** a metal object that has a standard weight: in *sports,* used in weight lifting and fitness activities; also used for judging the weight of other objects on a balance scale; **4,** a heavy object used to hold something down; as, she put a paper*weight* on her papers; **5,** degree of heaviness; as, two boys of the same *weight*; **6,** something that bears down on a person like a heavy load; as, Dinah felt the *weight* of the world's problems on her shoulders; **7,** power; importance; value; as, your ideas carry a lot of *weight* in the community:—*v.t.* **1,** to put weight upon; load down; as, to *weight* a bag with heavy groceries; **2,** to oppress with a load; as, many cares *weighted* him down.

weight-less (wāt′lis), *adj.* **1,** having little or no weight; **2,** free from the pull of gravity, as objects are in a spacecraft in outer space.

weight-lift-ing (wāt′lift-ing), *n.* an exercise or competition in which a person lifts an iron bar with heavy weights attached to it.—*n.* **weight′lift-er.**

WEIGHTLIFTING

weight-y (wāt′i) *adj.* [weight-i-er, weight-i-est], **1,** heavy; as, a *weighty* body; burdensome; as, *weighty* cares; **2,** important; influential; as, *weighty* considerations; **3,** serious in looks; as, a *weighty* expression.

weir (wēr), *n.* **1,** a dam placed across a river or stream to divert or control the level or flow of the water; **2,** stakes and netting placed in water, often a stream or along a shore, to trap fish.

weird (wērd), *adj.* **1,** strange in a way that is frightening or disturbing; uncanny or unearthly; as, she had a *weird* feeling that something had happened to her son; **2,** *Colloq.* odd or unusual; as, the shirt has a *weird* pattern.

welch (welch), *v.* Same as *welsh.*

wel-come (wel′kum) *adj.* **1,** received with gladness or hospitality; as, a *welcome* guest; producing gladness; as, *welcome* gifts; **2,** free to have or use; as, you're *welcome* to stay:—*n.* a greeting; as, the dancers were given a tremendous *welcome*:—*v.t.* [welcomed, wel-com-ing], **1,** to greet with kindness; receive with hospitality; **2,** to be glad to accept; to get with pleasure; as, I *welcome* your ideas.

weld (weld), *v.t.* **1,** to join (pieces of metal) by heating to the melting point and pressing or hammering together or permitting to flow together: the work is called *welding*; **2,** to unite closely; as, he *welded* the states into a nation:—*v.i.* to become welded, or firmly joined together; as, iron *welds* easily:—*n.* **1,** the state of being welded; **2,** a welded joint.—*n.* **wel′der** (a person who welds).

wel-fare (wel′fâr′), *n.* **1,** the state or condition of having good health, prosperity, etc; as, the principal was concerned about the *welfare* of the students; **2,** a government program to provide a basic level of support, as in money, food, housing, etc., to people in need:—*adj.* pertaining to welfare.

[1]**well** (wel), *n.* **1,** a shaft sunk deep in the earth, for obtaining water, gas, oil, etc.; **2,** an enclosed or sunken space resembling such a shaft; **3,** a natural spring or fountain used as a source of water; **4,** a source of steady or continuous supply; as, she provided a *well* of support after the tragedy:—*v.i.* to flow, as from a spring; as, tears *welled* into her eyes.

[2]**well** (wel), *adv.* [*comp.* bet-ter, *superl.* best], **1,** in a good, proper, or favourable manner; as, the work was *well* done; **2,** satisfactorily or suitably; as, to dine *well*; **3,** with reason; justifiably; as, he may *well* question the verdict; **4,** fortunately; favourably; as, the store is *well* situated; **5,** to a considerable extent or degree; as, the woman was *well* over 50; **6,** intimately; as, we are *well* acquainted with him; **7,** definitely; clearly; as, they knew perfectly *well* the outcome:—*adj.* **1,** in good health; **2,** in a satisfactory state; as, all is *well*:—*interj.* **1,** an exclamation of wonder, relief, resignation, etc.; **2,** used to show surprise; as, *well*! I thought you were never coming home; **3,** used to begin a new remark or continue with one after a pause or interjection; as, *well*, I guess it's time to move to the next item on the agenda:—*n.* **well′do′ing.**—*adj.* **well′-groomed′; well′-in-ten′tioned; well′-made′; well′-man′ nered; well′ -read′.**

well-be-ing (wel′-bē′ing), *n.* the state of being healthy and happy; health and happiness.

well-bred (wel′-bred′), *adj.* refined in manners; cultivated; polite.

well-done (wel-dun′), *adj.* **1,** done well or properly; as, the mayor congratulated the volunteers on a *well-done* job; **2,** cooked for a long time; thoroughly cooked; as, they ordered their beef *well-done*, not rare.

well-known (wel′-nōn′), *adj.* familiar; famed; generally recognized; as, a *well-known* nursery tale; a *well-known* author.

well-mean-ing (wel-mēn′ing), *adj.* done with good intentions, though not always having the result wanted; as, he's *well-meaning*, but he doesn't always get the job done.

Welsh (welsh; welch), *n.* **1**, a person who inhabits or originates from Wales; **2,** the language of these people:—*adj.* relating to the country, the people, the language, or the culture of Wales.

welsh (welsh), *v.t.* and *v.i. Slang* to cheat, as by evading payment or other obligation.

welt (welt), *n.* a red, swollen mark raised on the skin by a blow from a rod or whip or from an allergic reaction.

wel-ter (wel′tėr), *n.* a confusion of things or people.

wench (wench), *n. Colloq.* **1,** a young girl or woman; **2,** formerly, a prostitute or mistress.

wend (wend), *v.i.* to go; journey:—*v.t.* to direct or continue; as, to *wend* one's way.

wen-di-go or **win-di-go** (wen′di-gō′), *n.*

in *Cree* and *Algonquian myth*, an evil spirit thought to eat humans or possess them and cause them to become cannibals.

went (went), *p.t.* of *go*.

wept (wept), *p.t.* and *p.p.* of *weep*.

were (wûr; wâr), **1,** past indicative *pl.* of *be*; **2,** past subjunctive *sing.* and *pl.* of *be*.

were-wolf or **wer-wolf** (wēr′woolf′; wer′ woolf′), *n.* in *folklore*, a person changed into a wolf by an evil spell or able at will to assume a wolf's shape.

west (west), *n.* **1,** the direction the sun goes in when it sets in the evening; one of the four points of the compass: opposite of *east*; **2,** any place or region in this direction:—**the West, 1,** Europe and the Americas, as distinguished from Asia; in *history*, the non-Communist countries of Europe and the Americas; **2,** in Canada, the territory lying between the western boundary of Ontario and the Pacific Ocean:—*adj.* **1,** coming from the west; as, a *west* wind; **2,** in the direction of the west; as, a *west* door:—*adv.* toward the west; as, facing *west*.

west-er-ly (wes′tėr-li), *adj.* **1,** toward the west; **2,** from the west, as a wind:—*adv.* in the direction of the west:—*n.* [*pl.* westerlies], a wind blowing from the west.

west-ern (wes′tėrn), *adj.* **1,** grown or produced in the west; as, *western* wheat; **2,** situated in the west; as, a *western* city; also, going toward, or coming from, the west; as, a *western* train:—**Western, 1,** relating to any district or region called the West; **2,** having to do with the western part of the world; as, countries in the *Western* world use much more energy per person than the rest of the world:—*n.* a book, movie, or television show about life in the North American West in the 1800s.—*n.* **West′ern-er** (a person born or living in the West).

west–north-west (west′–nôrth′west′), *adv., adj.,* and *n.* two points, or 22° 30′, north of due west.

west–south-west (west′–south′west′), *adv., adj.,* and *n.* two points, or 22° 30′, south of due west.

[1]**west-ward** (west′wėrd), *adj.* toward the west; as, steer a *westward* course.

[2]**west-ward** (west′wėrd) or **west-wards** (-wėrdz), *adv.* toward the west; as, to travel *westward*.—*adv.* **west′ward-ly.**

wet (wet), *v.t.* [wet or wet-ted, wet-ting], to moisten or soak with water or some other liquid; to cause to be wet:—*n.* water; moisture; also, rainy or misty weather; as, come in out of the *wet*:—*adj.* [wet-ter, wet-test], **1,** covered or soaked with water or some other liquid; as, *wet* streets; also, of paint, varnish, ink, etc., not dry; **2,** rainy or misty; as, *wet* weather; **3,** *Colloq.* favouring the manufacture and sale of alcoholic beverages.

wet-land (wet′land), *n.* a low-lying area that is partly covered with water and has very damp soil, such as a swamp or marsh: wetlands are very important as homes and breeding areas for animal and plant life.

whack (wak; hwak), *n. Colloq.* a sharp, resounding blow, or the sound of it; a smack:—*v.t.* and *v.i.* to slap or strike (a sharp, resounding blow).—*adj.* **whack′y; wack′y** (*Slang* erratic, irrational, or eccentric).

whale (wāl; hwāl), *n.* any of the large marine mammals that have the general shape of a fish, fins as forelimbs, tails with horizontal flukes, and breathing holes on top of their heads.

whal-ing (wāl′ing; hwāl′ing), *n.* the business of hunting whales for meat, bone, and fat called blubber: most countries now outlaw whaling because of the threat to the whale population.—*n.* **whal′er.**

whang (wang; hwang), *v.t. Colloq.* to strike with a sharp, ringing, resounding blow, as on metal:—*n.* such a sound.

wharf (wôrf; hwôrf), *n.* [*pl.* wharves (wôrvz) or wharfs], a structure of wood, steel, or stone built at the water's edge, at which ships may be tied up for loading and unloading; a pier or quay.

what (wot; wôt; hwot; hwôt), *pron.* **1,** in *questions*, which thing or things; as, *what* is wrong? *what* is your business? **2,** in *relative clauses*, that or those which; the thing or things that; as, *what* you have just said is wrong; also, anything that; everything that; all that; as, give her *what* she wants; I'll give *what* I can; **3,** in *exclamations*, what things; how much; as, *what* he has suffered!—*adj.* **1,** in *questions*, which; as, *what* job do you do? how much; as, *what* good will that do? **2,** in *relative clauses*, that or those which; which in particular; as, I want to know *what* car I should take; also, any; all; whatever; as, I'll contribute *what* flowers I have; as many as; as, take *what* pencils you please; as much as; as, take *what* drinks you need; what sort of; as, I wonder *what* magazines she likes; **3,** in *exclamations*, how great, strange, unusual, etc.; as, *what* recklessness!—*adv.* **1,** partly; in part; as, *what* with the cold and *what* with the darkness we could go no farther; **2,** in *questions*, how much; in what way; as, *what* does it profit a person? **3,** in *exclamations*, such; as, *what* bright colours!—*conj. Colloq.* that; as, I do not know but *what* it is true:—*interj.* an exclamation expressing surprise; as, *what!* the car stolen?

what-ev-er (wot-ev′ėr; wôt-; hwot-ev′ėr; hwôt-), *pron.* **1,** all that; anything that; as, give *whatever* you can; **2,** no matter what; as, we must have sugar, *whatever* its cost; **3,** used interrogatively, as an emphatic form of *what*, expressing surprise, wonder, etc.; as, *whatever* made you do it?—*adj.* **1,** of any kind; as, he owns no property *whatever*; **2,** any and all; as, *whatever* dinner is left over, we'll save for tomorrow's lunch.

what-not (wôt′not′; hwôt′not′), *n.* **1,** a miscellaneous article or object; **2,** a stand of shelves for ornaments, books, etc.

what-so-ev-er (wot′sō-ev′ėr; wôt′-; hwot′sō-ev′ėr; hwôt′-), *pron.* and *adj.* the formal or emphatic form of *whatever*; of any kind; at all; as, there's no reason *whatsoever* for you to be late for school.

wheat (wēt; hwēt), *n.* **1,** a tall, cultivated, grass plant that has long spikes of seeds: the most important of the cereal grains, important as a source of food; **2,** the seeds (kernels) of this grass that are ground up and used in the making of flour, cereals, breads, pastas, etc.

wheat germ, the centre or inner part of a kernel of wheat, which contains many vitamins and is often added to other foods.

whee-dle (wē′dl; hwē′dl) *v.t.* [whee-dled, whee-dling], **1,** to persuade by flattery; cajole; coax; as, she *wheedled* her father into consenting; **2,** to get by coaxing or flattery:—*v.i.* to coax.

wheel (wēl; hwēl), *n.* **1,** a circular frame or disk designed to turn on a central axis or axle that allows a car, bicycle, or other vehicle to move, or allows a machine to work; **2,** a vehicle or machine that uses a wheel, such as a spinning *wheel* or a water*wheel*:—**steering wheel,** the circular frame used to control the movement of a car or other such vehicle; as, her mother took the *wheel* so Janet could have a rest:—**wheels,** the inner workings of anything; as, the *wheels* of the federal government:—*v.t.* **1,** to roll or move (something) on wheels; as, he wheeled the baby carriage into town:—*v.i.* **1,** to turn on, or as if on, an axis; **2,** to move on wheels; as, the car *wheeled* away from the accident.—*adj.* **wheeled.**

wheel-bar-row (wēl′bar′ō; hwēl′bar′ō), *n.* a light vehicle with two handles and usually one wheel, used for moving small loads.

wheel-chair or **wheel chair** (wēl′châr; hwēl′ châr), *n.* a special chair mounted on wheels, used as a way of moving about by people who cannot use their legs or who are too ill to walk.

wheeze (wēz; hwēz), *v.i.* [wheezed, wheezing], **1,** to breathe noisily and with difficulty; **2,** to make a whistling or gasping sound; as, the pump *wheezes*:—*n.* a whistling or gasping breath, as in asthma, or any similar sound.—*adj.* **wheez′y.**

whelp (welp; hwelp), *n.* the young of a dog, lion, fox, etc.; a cub:—*v.t.* and *v.i.* of animals, to give birth to (young).

when (wen; hwen), *adv.* **1,** in *questions*, at or during what time; as, *when* are you coming? **2,** in *relative clauses*, at which time; as, she knew *when* she had to work:—*conj.* **1,** at or after the time; as, *when* he came, it was too late; on any occasion that; whenever; at whatever time; as, *when* I meet him, he does not speak; as soon as; as, *when* dinner is over, you may leave; **2,** whereas; while on the contrary; in spite of the fact that; as, she gave me ten dollars *when* she owed me only five; **3,** considering that; as, how can you eat that pizza *when* you've just had an upset stomach?—*pron.* what or which time; as, since *when* have you become an expert on computers?

whence (wens; hwens), *adv.* **1,** in *questions*, from what place, source, or origin; for what reason; **2,** in *relative clauses,* from which; as, the place *whence* (not "from" whence) I came.

when-ev-er (wen-ev′ėr; hwen-ev′ėr), *adv.* and *conj.* at whatever time; as often as; as, *whenever* a student has a problem, the counsellor will help.

where (wâr; hwâr), *adv.* **1,** in *questions*, at or in what place; as, *where* do they live?; in what part; in what respect; as, *where* am I wrong?; to what place; as, *where* are you going?; from what source or place; as, *where* did you get that? **2,** in *relative clauses*, in, at, or to which; as, the house *where* I lived:—*conj.* **1,** in, at, or to whatever place; wherever; as, stay *where* you are; **2,** whereas; as, he did much, *where* we expected little; **3,** in the situation or circumstances in which; as, Bryn is getting to the point *where* all she does is play computer games:—*pron.* the place at, in, or to which; as, that is *where* I made my mistake.

where-a-bouts (wâr′a-bouts′; hwâr′a-bouts′), *adv.* in or near what place; as, *whereabouts* did you last see my book?—*n.* the place where a person or thing is; as, her *whereabouts* are still unknown.

where-as (wâr-az′; hwâr-az′), *conj.* **1,** on the other hand; while; as, mammals give birth to live animals, *whereas* most reptiles and birds hatch their young from eggs; **2,** taking into consideration the fact that, esp. in legal preambles; as, *whereas* the government of Canada takes the position that, etc.

where-by (wâr-bī′; hwâr-bī′), *adv.* and *conj.* **1,** in *relative clauses,* by means of which; through which; as, education is the process *whereby* people learn new skills; **2,** in *questions*, by what means; how; as, *whereby* did you acquire that painting?

where-fore (wâr′fôr ; hwâr′fôr), *adv.* and *conj.* for what reason; why: used mainly in older writings; as, "O Romeo, Romeo! wherefore art thou Romeo?" (*Romeo and Juliet,* William Shakespeare).

where-in (wâr-in′; hwâr-in′), *adv.* and *conj.* **1,** in what way or manner; **2,** in which: used mainly in literary or formal writing.

where-of (wâr-ov′; hwâr-ov′), *adv.* **1,** in *relative clauses*, of which; of whom; as, the people *whereof* she speaks; **2,** in *questions*, of what; as, *whereof* do you speak?

where-up-on (wâr u-pon′; hwâr u-pon′), *conj.* at which time; as, *whereupon* the Queen knighted the boy and gave him the finest horse.

wher-ev-er (wâr-ev′ėr; hwâr-ev′ėr), *adv.* and *conj.* **1,** at, to, or in whatever place; as, the cat sleeps *wherever* it will get the sun and warmth; **2,** where; as, I don't swim every day; *wherever* did you get that idea?

where-with-al (wâr′*with*-ôl′; hwâr′*with*-ôl′), *n.* that with which a thing can be bought or done; as, she has the *wherewithal* to buy a house.

whet (wet; hwet), *v.t.* [whet-ted, whet-ting], **1,** to sharpen a knife or blade, as by rubbing it against a sharpening stone; as, to *whet* an axe; **2,** to make eager; stimulate; as, the rumour *whets* my curiosity; the aroma from the kitchen is *whetting* my appetite.

wheth-er (we*th*′ėr ; hwe*th*′ėr), *conj.* **1,** if one or the other; in either or any case; as, *whether* you go or *whether* you stay, I shall help you; *whether* he fails or not, it's worth trying; **2,** if it is likely that; as, I wonder *whether* they will come today.

whet-stone (wet′stōn′; hwet′stōn′), *n.* a fine-grained stone for sharpening edged tools.

whew (fū; hwū; hū), *interj.* an exclamation expressing relief, surprise, disgust, or dismay.

whey (wā; hwā), *n.* the thin, watery part of milk that may be separated from the curds, as in making cheese.

which (wich; hwich), *pron.* **1,** in *questions*, what one or ones (of several); as, *which* is your book? **2,** in *relative clauses*, that; as the books *which* (or "that") we have read; the one that; as, point out *which* is yours; also, any that; whichever; as, take *which* of these books you please:—*adj.* **1,** in *questions*, what one; as, *which* house is yours? **2,** in *relative clauses*, what; as, after a month, during *which* time he did nothing; point out *which* hat is yours.

which-ev-er (wich-ev′ėr; hwich-ev′ėr), *pron.* any one or ones that; as, take *whichever* you please:—*adj.* no matter which; any; whatever; as, *whichever* book you choose.

whiff (wif; hwif), *n.* **1,** a sudden breath or gust, as of air or smoke; a puff; **2,** a faint odour; a trace:—*v.t.* and *v.i.* to puff or blow out or away in sudden breaths; waft.

while (wīl; hwīl), *n.* **1,** a period of time; as, he stayed only a little *while*; **2,** time or effort required in doing something; as, it will be worth your *while* to go:—*conj.* **1,** as long as; during the time that; at the same time that; as, you might read *while* I am gone; **2,** on the other hand, although; as, *while* I like fruit, I dislike apples; **3,** whereas, but; as, this computer is easy to use, *while* that one is more up–to–date:—*v.t.* [whiled, whil-ing], to cause to pass; spend; as, to *while* away the time between planes.

whim (wim; hwim), *n.* a sudden desire or wish to do something, esp. something that is not serious; as, on a *whim*, they went to the beach.

whim-per (wim′pėr; hwim′pėr), *v.i.* to cry in a low, broken sound; as, a lost puppy *whimpers*:—*n.* a fretful whining.

whim-si-cal (wim′zi-k'l; hwim′zi-k'l), *adj.* **1,** full of humorous or lighthearted ideas; **2,** odd; quaint.

whim-sy or **whim-sey** (wim′zi; hwim′zi), *n.* [*pl.* -sies or -seys], **1,** a whim, caprice, or odd fancy; a sudden freakish idea; **2,** quaint or fanciful humour; as, a movie, television show, novel, poem, or play full of *whimsy*.

whine (wīn; hwīn), *v.i.* [whined, whin-ing], **1,** to complain in a childish way; as, Kira *whined* about missing the television show; **2,** to cry in a complaining way; as, the child *whined* all day because she was overtired:—*v.t.* to utter in a fretful or complaining way:—*n.* **1,** the sound or act of whining; **2,** a weak, fretful complaining.—*adj.* **whin′y.**—*n.* **whin′er.**

whin-ny (win′i; hwin′i), *v.i.* [whinnied, whinny-ing], to neigh:—*n.* [*pl.* whinnies], the low, gentle sound like that made by a horse or similar animal.

whip (wip; hwip), *v.t.* [whipped or whipt (wipt; hwipt), whip-ping], **1,** to hit with a whip, strap, or other such device; beat; **2,** to beat cream, eggs, or other food into a foam or froth; as, to *whip* cream; **3,** to move or take suddenly; snatch; jerk; as, Greg *whipped* the ball out of my hands; **4,** to make go suddenly; as, the wind *whipped* the sails, moving the boat quickly ahead; **5,** to defeat in a contest; as, just once, our team would like to *whip* the Cougars:—*v.i.* **1,** to thrash about, as a loose sail; **2,** to move quickly or nimbly; as, the fox *whipped* out of sight:—*n.* **1,** a device made up of a long cord or rope with a handle at one end: jockeys in horse races use whips to make their horses go faster; **2,** in *cooking,* a preparation, usually a dessert, that is made up largely of cream or the whites of eggs beaten stiff:—**party whip**, in *politics*, a member of each political party whose job is to make sure the members of his or her party are present for voting.—*n.* **whip′per.**—*adj.* **whipped** (as, *whipped* cream).

whip-lash (wip′lash; hwip′lash), *n.* an injury to the neck caused by the sudden forward and backward movement of the head, such as can happen in a car accident.

whip-per-snap-per (wip′ėr-snap′ėr; hwip′ėr-snap′ėr), *n. Colloq.* a young person who acts overconfident, brash, or impertinent; also, any presumptuous person.

whip-poor-will (wip′poor-wil′; hwip′ poor-wil′; hwip′poor-wil′), *n.* a small North American bird, mottled brown, black, and buff, with an unusual call that sounds like its name.

whir (wûr; hwûr), *v.i.* [whirred, whir-ring], to move, fly, or revolve with a buzzing or humming noise:—*n.* a buzzing or humming noise caused by rapid motion; as, the *whir* of an airplane propeller.

whirl (wûrl; hwûrl), *v.t.* **1,** to turn or cause to revolve rapidly; as, to *whirl* a top to entertain a child; **2,** to carry onward or away quickly, with a revolving motion:—*v.i.* **1,** to revolve with great speed; as, the earth *whirls* on its axis; **2,** to move along swiftly; as, the leaves *whirled* away in the wind; **3,** to seem to spin around; as, my brain *whirled*:—*n.* **1,** a rapid rotation or circular motion; **2,** something revolving rapidly; as, a *whirl* of dust; **3,** confused and bustling activity; as, the *whirl* of social life.

whirl-pool (wûrl′po͞ol′; hwûrl′po͞ol′), *n.* **1,** a swift-moving, circling eddy or current in a river or sea, with a central depression into which floating objects are drawn by suction; **2,** a turbulent, confused situation that is difficult to escape from; as, Tanya was drawn into the *whirlpool* of office politics.

whirl-wind (wûrl′wind′; hwûrl′wind′), *n.* a violent windstorm marked by a whirling, spiral motion of the air:—*adj.* relating to something rapid and forceful that moves ahead quickly; as, a *whirlwind* romance.

whisk (wisk; hwisk), *v.t.* **1,** to sweep or brush lightly and rapidly; **2,** to take or carry off with a quick, sweeping motion; as, the wind *whisked* away the scrap of paper; **3,** to beat (eggs, cream, etc.) into a froth:—*v.i.* to move rapidly and nimbly; as, the squirrel *whisked* up the tree:—*n.* **1,** the act of brushing with a quick motion; **2,** a quick, nimble movement; **3,** a small broom or brush with a short handle; **4,** a kitchen utensil for whipping eggs, cream, etc.

whisk-er (wis′kėr; hwis′kėr), *n.* **1,** (usually *whiskers*), the hair growing on a man's face; **2,** one of the long, bristly hairs growing near the mouth of a cat, dog, rabbit, rat, etc.—*adj.* **whisk′ ered.**

whis-ky or **whis-key** (wis′ki; hwis′ki), *n.* [*pl.* whiskies or whiskeys], a strong alcoholic liquor distilled from grains, as corn, barley, or rye.

whis-per (wis′pėr; hwis′pėr), *v.i.* **1,** to speak in a low voice or under the breath; **2,** to rustle; as, leaves *whispered* in the breeze:—*v.t.* to say under the breath; tell privately:—*n.* **1,** a low, hushed tone of voice; **2,** a hint or suggestion; rumour; as, a *whisper* of scandal; **3,** a soft, rustling sound.

whist (wist; hwist), *n.* a card game for four persons, from which the modern game of bridge has been developed.

whis-tle (wis′l; hwis′l), *v.i.* [whis-tled, whis-tling], **1,** to make a clear, sharp, or musical sound by forcing the breath between the teeth or puckered lips, or by forcing air, steam, etc., through a small opening, as in a valve; **2,** to make any similar shrill sound; as, the wind *whistles*; **3,** to go or pass swiftly with a sharp, shrill sound; as, arrows *whistled* past him:—*v.t.* **1,** to utter by whistling; as, to *whistle* a tune; **2,** to call or signal by whistling:—*n.* **1,** the shrill noise made by forcing air, steam, etc., through an opening; **2,** an instrument to produce such a sound.—*n.* **whis′tler.**

whit (wit; hwit), *n.* the smallest particle; as, there is not a *whit* of truth in the rumour.

white (wīt; hwīt), *adj.* [whit-er, whit-est], **1,** the lightest of all colours; as, the *white* snow; **2,** light in colour as compared to other things of the same kind; as, *white* rice:—**White,** belonging to any of the groups of people having light skin; Caucasian:—*n.* **1,** the colour of clean snow; **2,** the albumen of an egg; as, egg *whites*:—**White,** a member of any of the groups of people having light skin; a Caucasian.—*n.* **white′ness.**

white-board (wīt′bōrd′; hwīt′bōrd′), *n.* in *computing,* a simulated panel on which several people can write at the same time, with the results visible to all: used in conferencing on the Internet.

white-cap (wīt′kap′; hwīt′kap′), *n.* a wave crest whitened with foam.

white–col-lar (wīt′kol′ėr; hwīt′kol′ėr), *adj.* having to do with jobs that are done in offices or indoors and that do not involve heavy physical labour: the term comes from white dress shirts that were worn by early office workers; as, he left his *white-collar* job in the bank to work outdoors in forestry.

white-fish (wīt′fish′; hwīt′fish′), *n.* an edible, freshwater fish of the salmon family.

whit-en (wīt′n; hwīt′n), *v.t.* to bleach or make white:—*v.i.* to become white; to bleach or blanch; as, linen *whitens* in the sun.—*n.* **whit′en-ing; whit′en-er**

white noise, 1, noise that has almost identical intensities at all the frequencies of its range; **2,** in *computing,* sound, with equal amounts of energy at all frequencies, produced by a computer, the effect of which is a hissing sound: used often in computer sound effects.

white-out (wīt′out; hwīt′out), *n.* a weather condition in which blowing snow blankets and blinds the field of vision; as, during the *whiteout,* drivers couldn't see the cars ahead of them, and there were many accidents.

white-wash (wīt′wosh′; -wôsh′; hwīt′wosh′; -wôsh′), *n.* **1,** a white mixture of lime and water, for coating walls, fences, etc.; **2,** a coverup of a mistake, fraud, fault, etc., to protect a reputation, career, etc.; as, everyone said the investigation was a *whitewash* because no fault was ever found:—*v.t.* **1,** to cover with whitewash; **2,** to cover up a crime or mistake.—*n.* **white′wash′er.**

[1]**whit-ing** (wīt′ing; hwīt′ing), *n.* powdered or ground chalk used in making whitewash, metal polish, putty, etc.

[2]**whit-ing** (wīt′ing; hwīt′ing), *n.* a food fish of the cod family.

Whit-sun-day (wit′sen-dē; wut′sen-dā), *n.* Same as **Pentecost** (def. 1).

whit-tle (wit′l; hwit′l), *v.t.* [whit-tled, whit-tling], **1,** to cut, shape, or carve with a knife; as, to *whittle* a wooden toy; **2,** to reduce bit by bit by, or as if by, cutting away; as, to *whittle* down debts:—*v.i.* to shape a piece of wood slowly with a knife.

whiz or **whizz** (wiz; hwiz), *v.i.* [whizzed, whiz-zing], to move rapidly with a humming or hissing sound; as, the car *whizzed* past us:—*n.* **1,** a humming or hissing noise; **2,** *Colloq.* a person with a special skill; as, Jess was a *whiz* at computers.

who (ho͞o), *pron.* [*nominative* who, *possessive* whose (ho͞oz), *objective* whom (ho͞om)], **1,** in *questions,* what person or persons; as, *who* else was there with you? *whom* did you choose? also, what sort of person or persons; as, *who* am I to be so honoured? **2,** in *relative clauses,* that; as, the doctor, *who* lives near me; the one that; the person that; as, I know *who* was there; I don't know *who* you are; he, she, or they that; whoever; as, *who* betrays my friends betrays me.

whoa (wō; hwō), *interj.* Stop! (used esp. to horses).

who-ev-er (ho͞o-ev′ėr), *pron.* anyone or everyone who; whatever person or persons; as, *whoever* wishes, may come along.

whole (hōl), *adj.* **1,** in good health; uninjured; **2,** not defective or broken; intact; **3,** not divided into parts; not broken, cut up, or ground; as, *whole* cloves; undivided in devotion, allegiance, etc.; as, to work with one's *whole* heart and soul; **4,** complete; entire; containing all the parts or members; as, the *whole* school:—*n.* all the parts or members of something taken together; a total; as, the *whole* of a nation:—**on the whole** or **as a whole,** in general; as, a few people complained about the noise, but *on the whole,* the party was a success.—*n.* **whole′ness.**

whole-heart-ed (hōl′här′tid), *adj.* sincere; completely earnest; hearty; as, *wholehearted* co-operation.

whole number, *n.* a number that does not contain a fraction or decimal, such as 12 or 367, as opposed to 12.5 or 367 1/2.

whole-sale (hōl′sāl′), *n.* the selling of goods in large quantities, usually to store owners who then sell them to the public at a higher price: opposite of *retail:*—*adj.* **1,** buying or selling in large quantities; also, relating to such trade; as, *wholesale* prices; **2,** in too large an amount or quantity; as, in the late 1800s, hunters caused the *wholesale* slaughter of buffalo:—*v.t.* [wholesaled, wholesal-ing], to sell at wholesale.—*n.* **whole′sal′er.**

whole-some (hōl′sum), *adj.* [wholesom-er, wholesom-est], **1,** good for the health of body or mind; healthful; as, a *wholesome* meal; **2,** characteristic of, or suggesting, health; as, a *wholesome* appearance; **3,** good for the mind or character; as, *wholesome* family entertainment.

whole–wheat (hōl–wēt′; hōl–hwēt′), *adj.* of bread or flour, made from the entire grain of wheat: contains more nutrients than white bread or flour.

whol-ly (hōl′li; hōl′i), *adv.* completely; entirely; altogether; as, he was *wholly* satisfied with his purchase.

whom (ho͞om), *pron.* the objective case of *who*: used as the object of a verb or preposition; as, to *whom* are you speaking? Also, *relative* or *conj. pron.* **whom-ev′er** (objective case of *whoever*) and **whom′so-ev′er** (objective case of *whosoever*).

whoop (ho͞op), *v.i.* **1,** to utter a loud and prolonged cry; shout; **2,** to make the gasping sound that follows a fit of coughing in whooping cough:—*v.t.* to drive, call, or urge with loud cries or shouts:—*n.* **1,** a loud shout; **2,** a gasping sound following a fit of coughing.

whoo-pee (ho͞op′ē′; hwo͞o′pē′;), *interj.* expressing hilarious enjoyment.—*n.* merry and noisy hilarity:—**make whoopee, 1,** to have a very enjoyable time; **2,** *Colloq.* to make love.

whoop-ing cough (ho͞op′ing kôf′), *n.* an infectious disease to which children are particularly susceptible, characterized by violent coughing fits that end with a high-pitched whoop: in Canada, now mainly preventible through vaccination.

whoop-ing crane (ho͞op′ing krān), *n.* a tall North American bird with long legs, a white body, and wings with black tips, named for the loud cry it makes: now endangered.

whoosh (wo͞osh; hwo͞osh), *interj.* and *v.i.* to emit a sibilant or hissing sound, as of something rushing through the air; as, the transport *whooshed* past; it passed with a *whoosh.*

whop-per (wop′ėr; hwop′ėr), *n. Colloq.* **1,** something unusually large; **2,** a big lie.—*adj. Colloq.* **whop′ping.**

whore (hōr), *n. Colloq.* a prostitute.

whorl (wûrl; wôrl; hwûrl; hwôrl), *n.* **1,** the circular arrangement of leaves, petals, etc., at one level on a stem; **2,** one of the turns of a spiral shell.—*adj.* **whorled.**

WHORL

whose (ho͞oz), *pron. adj.* the possessive case of *who;* as, *whose* dirty dishes are those on the table?

who-so-ev-er (ho͞o′sō-ev′ėr), *pron.* any person who; whoever.

why (wī; hwī), *adv.* **1,** in *questions,* for what reason, with what motive or for what purpose; on what account; as, *why* did you leave? **2,** in *relative clauses,* on account of which; for which; as, I don't know the reason *why* she went; the reason for which; as, I do not understand *why* he is so angry:—*n.* [*pl.* whys (wīz; hwīz)], a cause or reason; motive; as, psychology explains the *why* of human conduct:—*interj.* expressing surprise; as, *why,* it's snowing!

Wic-ca (wi′ka), *n.* the cult of neopaganism that emphasizes the importance of nature, magic, etc.: it is often referred to as modern witchcraft, but its followers reject sorcery and other such aspects often associated with it.—*n.* and *adj.* **Wic′can.**

wick (wik), *n.* the cord or tape of twisted fibres in a candle or oil lamp, through which the melted tallow or oil is drawn to feed the flame.

wick-ed (wik′id), *adj.* [wick-ed-er, wick-ed-est], **1,** evil; bad; as, a *wicked* criminal; **2,** mischievous; roguish; as, a *wicked* look; **3,** harmful; dangerous; as, a *wicked* blow.—*n.* **wick′ed-ness.**—*adv.* **wick′ed-ly.**

wick-er (wik′ėr), *n.* **1,** flexible twigs or reeds woven together into baskets, furniture, etc.:—*adj.* made of wicker; as, a *wicker* table.—*n.* **wick′er-work′** (an object made of wicker).

wick-et (wik′it), *n.* **1,** a small door or gate, esp. one in a larger door or gate; **2,** a windowlike opening, esp. one with a grill or grate, as in a ticket office; **3,** in *cricket,* either of the two frames at which the ball is bowled; **4,** in *croquet,* one of the arches through which the ball must be driven.

wide (wīd), *adj.* [wid-er, wid-est], **1,** extending far from side to side; broad; as, a *wide* road; also, stretching for a specified distance from side to side; as, the room is three metres *wide;* **2,** vast; spacious; as, a *wide* expanse of land; **3,** inclusive of much; comprehensive; as, a person of *wide* experience; **4,** far from a point aimed at; as, *wide* of the mark; **5,** opened to the fullest extent; as, eyes *wide* with wonder:—*adv.* **1,** over a large area; widely; as, her fame spread far and *wide;* **2,** of a door, gate, window, etc., fully open; **3,** far from the point aimed at.—*adv.* **wide′ly.**—*n.* **wide′ness.**

wide–area network, *n.* in *computing,* a group of widely separated computers connected together; as, a worldwide airline reservation system is a *wide-area network*: abbreviated as *WAN.*

wid-en (wīd′n), *v.t.* and *v.i.* to make or become broader or larger; as, to *widen* a path.

wide-spread (wīd′spred′), *adj.* **1,** spread to the fullest extent; as, *widespread* publicity; **2,** widely distributed; as, English is a *widespread* language; **3,** happening over or affecting a large area; as, the Manitoba flooding caused *widespread* damage.

wid-ow (wid′ō), *n.* **1,** a woman whose husband is dead and who has not remarried; **2,** in *printing,* a short line of type, as one ending a paragraph, that was carried over to the top of the next page or column: type is often adjusted to avoid these; **3,** in *computing,* the first line of a paragraph when it appears by itself as the last line of a page: some word processors automatically adjust page breaks so that there are no widows.

wid-ow-er (wid′ō-ėr), *n.* a man whose wife is dead and who has not remarried.

wid-ow-hood (wid′ō-hood), *n.* the state or condition of being a widow.

width (width), *n.* the extent of a thing from side to side; breadth; as, this lot is 25 metres in *width.*

wield (wēld), *v.t.* **1,** to use with the hands; as, to *wield* an axe; **2,** to exercise (power, authority, etc.).—*n.* **wield′er.**

wie-ner (wē′nėr), *n.* a kind of smoked sausage made with beef, pork, chicken, etc.; a frankfurter.

wife (wīf), *n.* [*pl.* wives (wīvz)], a woman who is married.

wig (wig), *n.* a covering for the head made of artificial or real hair.

wig-gle (wig′l), *v.i.* and *v.t.* [wig-gled, wig-gling], to squirm; wriggle; move from side to side in quick, short motions.—*n.* **wig′gler** (esp. the larva of a mosquito).—*adj.* **wig′gly.**

wig-wag (wig′wag′), *v.t.* and *v.i.* [wig-wagged, wigwag-ging], **1,** to move back and forth; **2,** to signal with flags or lights, moved or flashed according to a code.

wig-wam (wig′wäm; wig′wôm), *n.* a type of living space made of a framework of poles, covered with bark or hide: used by certain Native peoples. Compare *teepee.*

wild (wīld), *adj.* **1,** living in the natural state; untamed; as, the lion is a *wild* animal; also, not cultivated; as *wild*flowers; **2,** not lived in or settled; as, the *wild* areas of the country are rapidly decreasing in size; **3,** of a region, uninhabited; like a wilderness; **4,** uncontrolled; as, *wild* anger; **5,** fantastic; unreasonable; as, a *wild* scheme; **6,** not having the proper aim or direction; as, he took a *wild* guess; **7,** *Colloq.* eager; as,

I am *wild* to go:—*adv.* without control; wildly:—**wilds,** *n.pl.* a desert or wilderness.—*n.* **wild′flow′er; wild′ life′; wild′ness.**—*adv.* **wild′ly.**

wild-cat (wīld′kat′), *n.* **1,** a name for various small, wild members of the cat family, such as bobcats or lynx; **2,** a violent or hot-tempered person; **3,** a sudden strike or work stoppage; **4,** an oil well at the exploration stage:—*adj.* **1,** having to do with a sudden and unofficial work stoppage by members of a union; as, a *wildcat* strike; **2,** having to do with the speculative exploration for oil; as, the oil prospectors drilled some *wildcat* wells.

wil-de-beest (wil′de-bēst′), *n.* [*pl.* wildebeests or wildebeest]. Same as **gnu.**

wil-der-ness (wil′dėr-nis), *n.* an area that is in its natural state, with wild animals and plants and few inhabitants; as, much of the Yukon is still *wilderness.*

wild-fire (wīld′fīr′), *n.* a fire that spreads quickly:—**like wildfire,** in a very fast, uncontrolled way; as, the news of the factory closing spread *like wildfire* around the town.

wild-life (wīld′līf), *n.* wild animals and plants that live in a natural, undomesticated state.

wild rose, any of many varieties with but one circle of petals in the flower: the floral emblem of Alberta.

wile (wīl), *n.* a subtle, crafty trick or subtle words, meant to lure or deceive:—*v.t.* [wiled, wil-ing], **1,** to obtain by trickery; **2,** to pass (time).

wil-ful (wil′fool), *adj.* Same as **willful.**

[1]will (wil), *n.* **1,** the power of the mind to decide upon and carry out a course of action; **2,** control exercised over impulse; self-control; as, *will*power; **3,** a deliberate choice, desire, intention, or determination directed toward a special end or purpose; as, the *will* to live helps a patient to recover; **4,** strong determination; enthusiasm; energy; as, she went to work with a *will;* **5,** the power to achieve one's goals, often by controlling others; as, the dictator imposed his *will* on the rest of the citizens; **6,** the power to act as one wishes or sees fit; as, he comes and goes at *will;* **7,** a legal paper in which a person directs how his or her property is to be disposed of after death; as, the last *will* and testament:—*v.t.* [willed, will-ing], **1,** to influence or compel by exercising the power of the mind; as, she *willed* him to turn around; **2,** to leave property; as, he *willed* half his estate to his cousin:—*v.i.* to decide, choose, or determine; as, if fate so *wills,* we'll win this struggle yet.

[2]will (wil), *v.* [*sing.* I will, you will, he or she will, *pl.* will; *p.t.* would (wood); no other parts], used with other verbs to show **1,** something expected to happen in the future; as, she *will* like this novel; they *will* be there; **2,** something that should be done; as, you *will* clean up your room now! **3,** something that is able to be done; as, this theatre *will* seat 150 people; **4,** something that is done by habit or custom; as, she *will* often find herself walking to her old house; she *would* sit and read for hours on end; **5,** the determination to do something in spite of opposition or bad conditions; as, I *will* do it whether you approve or not; she *will* go in spite of the weather; **6,** something that is destined to be; as, children *will* grow up; accidents *will* happen; **7,** something that a person is asked to do or agrees to do; as, *will* you stay for lunch? thank you, I *will.*

will-ful or **wil-ful** (wil′fo͝ol), *adj.* **1,** determined to get one's own way, even at the expense of others; stubborn; headstrong; as, a *willful* child; **2,** intentional; deliberate; as, *willful* murder.—*adv.* **will′ful-ly.**—*n.* **will′fulness.**

wil-lies (wil′iz), *n. Slang* a fit of nervousness; (the) jitters; as, it gives me the *willies.*

will-ing (wil′ing), *adj.* **1,** cheerfully ready; not lazy or slow; as, a *willing* worker; **2,** given or done freely or gladly; as, a *willing* service; **3,** favourably disposed; as, he is *willing* to buy it.—*adv.* **will′ing-ly.**—*n.* **will′ing-ness′.**

will-o'-the-wisp (wil′-o-*th*ė-wisp′), *n.* **1,** a light that is seen flitting above marshy ground at night; **2,** anything that misleads one or eludes one's grasp.

wil-low (wil′ō), *n.* a tree or shrub with slender flexible branches, usually growing near water; also, its wood, used in making baskets, furniture, etc.:—**weeping willow,** a species of willow with drooping branches.—*adj.* **wil′low-y.**

wil-ly-nil-ly (wil′i-nil′i), *adv.* willingly or un- willingly; without choice; as he must go, *willy-nilly:*—*adj.* loosely, irresolute; uncertain; as, a *willy-nilly* customer.

wilt (wilt), *v.i.* **1,** to wither or droop, as a flower; **2,** to lose strength; become faint or weak:—*v.t.* to cause to wither.

wil-y (wīl′i), *adj.* [wil-i-er, wil-i-est], cunning; crafty; as, the *wily* fox.—*n.* **wil′iness.**

win (win), *v.i.* [won (wun), win-ning], to gain a victory; prevail; as, to *win* in a battle:—*v.t.* **1,** to acquire by effort or perseverance; obtain; as, to *win* promotion; **2,** to gain in a contest; as, she *won* the prize; **3,** to be victorious in; as, to *win* a game; **4,** to persuade; induce; as, try to *win* him over to our side:—*n.* a victory or success; as, our team has had six *wins* this year.

wince (wins), *v.i.* [winced, winc-ing], to shrink or draw back suddenly, as from a blow; flinch:—*n.* the act of flinching.

winch (winch), *n.* a device used for lifting or pulling heavy objects, made up of a large drum or pulley with a rope and chain that wraps around it: it can be operated by machine or by hand.

[1]**wind** (wind), *n.* **1,** a natural current of air; breeze; **2,** breath; also, the ability to breathe without difficulty while engaged in exercise; as, a person out of good physical shape quickly loses his or her *wind;* **3,** scent; as, the hounds got *wind* of the escaped convict; **4,** gas formed in the digestive organs; **5,** brass and wooden wind instruments in an orchestra; as, the *winds* were tuning up:—*v.t.* and *v.i.* (wind), **1,** to be or to cause to be out of breath due to a punch, blow, etc., or to exertion; as, the punch to her stomach *winded* her; we were *winded* after the race; **2,** to allow to rest, so as to permit recovery of breath; as, we stopped after the race to *wind* the horses.—*n.* **wind′storm′.**

[2]**wind** (wīnd), *v.i.* [wound (wound), winding], **1,** to turn; move with changing direction; as, the stream *winds* through the valley; **2,** to twist or twine round and round; as, the ivy *winds* around the tree:—*v.t.* **1,** to twist or wrap string, thread, wire, etc., around itself or around something else; **2,** to cover with something wrapped around; as, to *wind* a tire with tape; **3,** to tighten the springs of, by turning; as, to *wind* a toy; **4,** to make or pursue (one's way); as, he *wound* his course across the hill:—**wind up, 1,** to bring to a close; as, it's time to *wind up* the meeting; **2,** of a pitcher in *baseball,* to move the arms and body before throwing the ball; **3,** the act of turning or twisting.

wind-break (wind′brāk′), *n.* a shelter or protection from the wind, as a wall or a grove of trees.

wind-break-er (wind′brāk′ėr), *n.* a short, light jacket with close-fitting elastic cuffs and waistband that protects against the wind.

wind chill, a way to measure how cold the air feels to the surface of the skin:—**wind-chill factor,** that which takes into consideration both the actual air temperature and the force of the wind; as, if the temperature is −10° C and there is a strong wind, the *wind-chill factor* might make it feel like −20° C.

wind-ed (win′did), *adj.* out of breath.

wind-fall (wind′fôl′), *n.* **1,** something blown down, as ripe fruit, etc.; **2,** an unexpected piece of good fortune; a lucky event.

win-di-go (win′di-go′), *n.* Same as **wendigo.**

wind-ing (wīnd′ing), *adj.* full of bends or turns; as, a *winding* mountain road.

wind instrument, a musical instrument, as the flute, oboe, trumpet, or clarinet, played by blowing air into it.

wind-mill (wind′mil′), *n.* a machine that uses large blades to capture the power of the wind and turn it into energy: windmills have been used for pumping water, but increasingly, are being used to generate emissions-free electrical energy.

win-dow (wĭn′dō), *n.* **1,** an opening in the wall of a building or vehicle, fitted with a frame and glass to let in light and that often can be opened to let in air; **2,** the framework and glass that fills such an opening; **3,** in *computing,* a separate rectangular viewing area on a computer screen, giving different information from the rest of the screen.—*n.* **win′dow-pane** (a sheet of glass used in a window).

wind-pipe (wind′pīp′), *n.* the trachea, or breathing tube, which connects the throat to the lungs, carrying air in and out.

wind-shield (wind′shēld′), *n.* the clear window at the front of a car or other vehicle:—**windshield wiper,** a device used to clear dirt, rain, snow, etc., from a windshield.

wind-up (wīnd′up′), *n.* **1,** conclusion; end; close; **2,** in *baseball,* a preliminary motion of the arm before pitching the ball:—*adj.* related to, of, or for a windup; as, a *windup* toy; *windup* pitch.

wind-ward (wind′wėrd), *n.* the direction from which the wind is blowing:—*adj.* on the side from which the wind blows:—*adv.* toward the wind.

wind-y (win′di), *adj.* [wind-i-er, wind-i-est], **1,** characterized by winds; breezy; as, March is a *windy* month; also, exposed to the wind; as, the *windy* side of the house; **2,** noisy, wordy, or boastful; as, a *windy* braggart.—*n.* **wind′i-ness.**

wine (wīn), *n.* **1,** the fermented juice of grapes, used as an alcoholic drink; **2,** the fermented juice of other fruits or plants used similarly:—*v.t.* [wined, win-ing], to furnish or entertain with wine, as a guest; as, to *wine* and dine our friends.

wing (wing), *n.* **1,** one of the broad, flat, movable organs or parts of birds, insects, and bats, by means of which they fly; **2,** a flat structure extending out from either side of an airplane that helps it stay in the air as it moves forward; **3,** a part of a building projecting from the main structure; as, the north *wing* of the school; **4,** in a theatre, the stage platform extended at either side, or one of the pieces of scenery for these sides; **5,** in *sports* such as soccer and hockey, a player whose position is near the side of the playing area:—**under one's wing,** under one's protection; in one's care:—*v.i.* **1,** to use the wings; fly; as, the geese were *winging* their way north; **2,** to wound slightly in the wing or arm; as, the bear had been *winged* by the bullet.—*adj.* **winged** (having wings; as, beetles and flies are *winged* insects).

wing-span (wing′span), *n.* the distance

between the tip of one extended wing and the other: used to measure the size of a bird or aircraft: also called *wingspread.*

wink (wingk), *v.i.* **1,** to close and open one eyelid quickly; **2,** to convey a hint or signal by a quick motion of one eyelid; **3,** to keep oneself from seeing something; as, to *wink* at slight errors; **4,** to twinkle; gleam at regular intervals, as the light of a lighthouse:—*v.t.* **1,** to remove by winking; as, to *wink* the tears away:—*n.* **1,** the act of winking, esp. the act of closing one eye for a moment as a signal; also, a hint or command given this way; **2,** the time required for a wink; an instant; as, I didn't sleep a *wink* last night.

win-ner (win′ėr), *n.* a person or thing that wins or is successful; anything exceptionally good.

win-ning (win′ing), *adj.* **1,** successful, as in a competition; as, the *winning* team; **2,** attractive; charming; as, a *winning* personality; *winning* smile:—*n.* the act of gaining or conquering:—**winnings,** something that is won, esp. money won in gambling.

win-some (win′sum), *adj.* attractive; charming.—*adv.* **win′some-ly.**

win-ter (win′tėr), *n.* **1,** the coldest season of the year; in any region, that one of the four seasons of the year when the sun shines least directly; in the Northern Hemisphere, the period from the winter solstice, about December 21, to the vernal equinox, about March 21; **2,** any time, as of gloom or sorrow, suggesting winter; also, figuratively, a year of life:—*adj.* pertaining to winter:—*v.i.* to pass the months of the cold season; as, snakes *winter* in the ground:—*v.t.* to keep during the cold season; as, to *winter* cattle:—**winter solstice,** in the Northern Hemisphere, the time when the sun reaches the Tropic of Capricorn (Dec. 21); in the Southern Hemisphere, when it reaches the Tropic of Cancer (June 21).—*adj.* **win′try.**—*n.* **win′ter-time′.**

win-ter-green (win′tėr-grēn′), *n.* **1,** a low-growing, woody, evergreen plant that bears white blossoms, pungent red berries, and leaves that yield an aromatic oil called *oil of winter-green*; **2,** this oil; also, its flavour.

win-ter-ize (win′tėr-īz′), *v.t.* to prepare for winter use, esp. an automobile or airplane, by employing antifreeze, lighter greasing, etc.

win-try (win′tri), *adj.* having to do with or like winter; as, it's still October, but it feels quite *wintry.*

wipe (wīp), *v.t.* [wiped, wip-ing], **1,** to dry or cleanse by rubbing with something soft; as, to *wipe* dishes; to *wipe* furniture; **2,** to remove by rubbing; as, to *wipe* away tears; *wipe* off dirt:—*n.* the act of cleansing or rubbing:—**wipe out,** to kill or destroy completely; as, the wolf was almost completely *wiped out* by overhunting.—*n.* **wip′er.**

wire (wīr), *n.* **1,** a long, thin, flexible piece of metal that has a standard thickness for its entire length: often used to join or fasten things; **2,** such a piece of metal used to carry electricity; **3,** a message sent by telegraph wire: a telegram:—*v.t.* [wired, wiring], **1,** to install wires for electricity; as, to *wire* a house for electricity; **2,** to repair; as, to *wire* a broken chair together; **3,** to send (a message), or send a message to (a person), by telegraph; as, *wire* the results of the game; *wire* him to come.—*n.* **wir′ing** (a system of wires used to carry electricity).

wire-less (wīr′lis), *adj.* without the use of wires; as, *wireless* communications systems:—*n.* a wireless telegraph or telephone system; as, to send news by *wireless*; also, a message transmitted this way.

wireless communication, 1, the transfer of electromagnetic signals from place to place without cables, usually using infrared light or radio waves; as, television remote controls use *wireless communication*; **2,** in *computing,* the linking of computers or peripherals, such as a mouse, to a computer using radio or infrared light rays instead of wires.

wiry (wīr′i), *adj.* [wir-i-er, wir-i-est], **1,** like wire; stiff; **2,** lean and slight, but sinewy; as, a *wiry* child.—*n.* **wir′i-ness.**

wis-dom (wiz′dum), *n.* **1,** good judgment as to what is true and right, gained through knowledge and experience; **2,** learning; knowledge:—**wisdom tooth,** the third molar, or extreme back tooth, on each side in each jaw: so called because the wisdom teeth come in later than the other teeth, when a person is older.

¹wise (wīz), *adj.* [wis-er, wis-est], **1,** having knowledge and the ability to use it; having good judgment; **2,** showing this ability to judge and decide; sensible; as, a *wise* decision; **3,** having great learning; erudite; **4,** suggesting wisdom; as, a *wise* smile.—*adv.* **wise′ly.**

²wise (-wīz), *suffix* **1,** used to form adjectives meaning *showing common sense, being careful*; as, a media*wise* politician; **2,** *Colloq.* used to form adverbs meaning *with regard to*; as, travel*wise*, business*wise.*

wise-a-cre (wīz′ā′kėr), *n.* **1,** *Slang* a foolish person who affects to possess wisdom; **2,** a wise or learned person, used ironically or contemptuously; a know-it-all.

wise-crack (wīz′krak′), *n.* and *v.i. Slang* a flippant, facetious, or sarcastic remark, esp. a quip, gibe, etc.

wish (wish), *v.i.* to have a strong desire; as, I *wish* to stay; we *wish* for peace:—*v.t.* **1,** to desire; as, what do you *wish*? also, to express (a desire); as, I *wish* I had a dog; **2,** to express (a hope, etc.) for, or against, someone; as, to *wish* a person good fortune; also, to express (a greeting); as, I *wish* you good morning:—*n.* **1,** a strong or eager desire; **2,** the object or thing desired; as, popularity in school was his only *wish;* **3,** a request.—*n.* **wish′er.**—*adj.* **wish′ful.**

wish-y–wash-y (wish′i–wosh′i), *adj. Colloq.* insipid; feeble; forceless; as, a *wishy-washy* speech.

wisp (wisp), *n.* **1,** a small bit or bunch, as of hair; **2,** a thin fragment or bit, as of smoke, cotton, etc.—*adj.* **wisp′y.**

wist-ful (wist′fool), *adj.* pensive; longing; wishful; as, a *wistful* expression.—*n.* **wist′ful-ness.**—*adv.* **wist′ful-ly.**

wit (wit), *n.* **1,** wisdom; intelligence; as, he hasn't the *wit* to meet an emergency; **2,** the ability quickly to perceive that which is odd or amusing in a situation or idea and to express it in an unexpected and amusing way; as, Oscar Wilde was an extraordinary *wit;* she possessed a great *wit;* **3,** a person noted for this ability; also, the clever or brilliant things he or she says or writes:—**wits,** mental faculty or power; as, keep your *wits* about you.—*adj.* **wit′less; wit′ty.**

witch (wich), *n.* **1,** a person, usually a woman, supposed to have supernatural powers given her by evil spirits; an enchantress: in *history,* a person believed to bring bad luck, illness, etc.; **2,** a person who follows the religious cult of modern witchcraft; a Wiccan.

witch-craft (wich′kråft′), *n.* dealings with evil spirits; sorcery; magic.

with (wi*th*; with), *prep.* **1,** by the side of; as, put the glove *with* its mate; in the employ, association, or company of; as, she has been *with* the firm for years; favourable to; as, we have the wind *with* us; **2,** between oneself and another; as, we trade *with* the United States; **3,** in the care, keeping, or possession of; as, leave the child *with* me; **4,** characterized by; as, a man *with* a sad expression; **5,** by means of; as, slain *with* a knife; **6,** in the state, condition, or manner of; as, she performed *with* ease; **7,** as a result of; as, to perish *with* hunger; **8,** in spite of; as, *with* all his learning, he was a fool; **9,** during; as, the river rose higher *with* every minute; at the same time as; as, she was up *with* the sun; **10,** from; as, we parted *with* our friends at noon; **11,** in opposition to; against; as, I played tennis *with* my brother; **12,** because of or concerning; as, I have a problem *with* my computer.

with-draw (wi*th*-drô′; with-drô′), *v.t.* [*p.t.* withdrew (-drōō′), *p.p.* withdrawn (-drôn′), *p.pr.* withdraw-ing], **1,** to remove; take away; as, the school *withdrew* its team from the tournament; **2,** to retract; take back; as, to *withdraw* a charge in court; **3,** to go away in order to be alone; to stay to oneself; as, Mara has *withdrawn* from her friends lately:—*v.i.* to leave; depart.

with-draw-al (wi*th*-drô-al; with-drô′al), *n.* **1,** a removal; also, a taking back; as, the *withdrawal* of a promise; a cash *withdrawal* from the bank; **2,** the process of breaking a drug or alcohol addiction.

with-drawn (wi*th*-drôn′), *adj.* appearing to want to be alone; not friendly; as, Frank was a very *withdrawn* person; he never spoke to anyone.

with-er (wi*th*′ėr), *v.t.* to cause to shrink, fade, droop, or decay:—*v.t.* to lose sap or juice; dry up or fade; languish.

with-hold (wi*th*-hōld′; with-hōld′), *v.t.* [withheld (wi*th*-held′; with-held′), with-hold-ing], **1,** to hold back, as from action; restrain; **2,** to keep back; refuse to give.

with-in (wi*th*-in′), *adv.* **1,** in the inner part; inside; **2,** inwardly; **3,** in the house; indoors:—*prep.* **1,** inside of; **2,** in the limits of; as, *within* an hour; I live *within* the city limits:—*n.* an inner position or place; as, she felt fear from *within.*

with-out (wi*th*-out′), *adv.* **1,** outside; **2,** outwardly; **3,** outdoors:—*prep.* **1,** outside of; **2,** beyond; as, *without* question; **3,** in the absence of; lacking in; as, *without* hope.

with-stand (wi*th*-stand′; with-stand′), *v.t.* [withstood (-stood′), withstand-ing], to oppose; resist; endure; as, to *withstand* cold weather.

wit-ness (wit′nis), *n.* **1,** testimony; evidence; as, his friends bore *witness* to his good character; **2,** a person or thing that gives evidence; as, a receipted bill is *witness* that the bill has been paid; **3,** a person who tells in court under oath what she knows of a fact or event; **4,** one who puts her signature to a document to show that she has seen it signed; **5,** one who from actual presence knows of an occurrence: also called *eyewitness:*—*v.t.* **1,** to give evidence of, as in court; **2,** to reveal; betray; as, her startling pallor *witnessed* her sudden fear; **3,** to sign (a document) to indicate knowledge of another's signing; **4,** to see or know personally; as, to *witness* a performance of a play:—*v.i.* to testify.

wit-ti-cism (wit′i-sizm), *n.* a witty remark; a clever saying.

wit-ting-ly (wit′ing-li), *adv.* with knowledge; intentionally; as, I would not *wittingly* hurt your feelings.

wit-ty (wit′i), *adj.* [wit-ti-er, wit-ti-est], **1,** having the faculty of arousing laughter by a clever and amusing way of expressing ideas; **2,** marked by wit.—*adv.* **wit′ti-ly.**

wiz-ard (wiz′ėrd), *n.* **1,** a magician; conjurer; **2,** *Colloq.* a very clever person; as, a financial *wizard*: abbreviated as *wiz;* **3,** in *computing,* a computer expert who is gifted in solving problems or who has acquired an enormous store of knowledge about computer hardware and software: abbreviated as *wiz;* as, she is a computer *wizard* and can fix any computer problems; **4,** in *computing,* a utility that can automate some tasks in application software, different from templates because they collect information specific to the user and create a unique document or template of use only to that user; as, after collecting information from the user about a company name and address, a word processor *wizard* can create a letterhead for the company.—*n.* **wiz′ard-ry.**

wiz-ened (wiz′nd), *adj.* dried up; shrivelled.—*v.t.* and *v.i.* **wiz′en.**

wob-ble (wob′l; wôb′l), *v.i.* [wob-bled, wob-bling], **1,** to move unsteadily from side to side; **2,** to be undecided in opinion or actions:—*v.t.* to cause to waver or totter:—*n.* a swaying motion.—*adj.* **wob′bly.**

woe (wō), *n.* deep sorrow; inconsolable grief; suffering, esp. in older writings: today, often used in a lighter sense; as, I'm ready to hear your tale of *woe.*

woe-be-gone (wō′bi-gôn′), *adj.* overwhelmed with sadness; showing great grief or misery; as, a *woebegone* appearance.

woe-ful (wō′fool), *adj.* **1,** sorrowful; miserable; **2,** mean; paltry; wretched.—*adv.* **woe′ful-ly.**

wok (wok), *n.* a wide, bowl-shaped pot, used especially in Asian cooking.

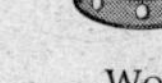

Wok

wolf (woolf), *n.* [*pl.* wolves (woolvz)], a large, powerful wild animal that is related to the dog and that bands together in packs to hunt larger animals like deer: wolves used to live over most of the northern half of the world, but through hunting and loss of habitat, they have been driven into a few remote areas of the world:—*v.t.* to eat quickly and hungrily; as, Josh *wolfed* down a huge plate of spaghetti.

wolf-hound (woolf′hound′), *n.* any of several breeds of tall, swift dogs, esp. Irish and Russian, formerly used for hunting wolves.

wol-ver-ine (wool′vėr-ēn′), *n.* an animal with a heavy, powerful body, thick fur, and a bushy tail, which feeds mainly on other animals and lives mostly in northern areas.

wom-an (woom′an), *n.* [*pl.* women (wim′in)], a full grown female person; a female who is no longer a girl.—*n.pl.* **wom′en** (adult females as a group).

womb (wōōm), *n.* the uterus; the organ in a female body where a baby is developed and nourished before being born.

won (wun), *p.t.* and *p.p.* of *win.*

won-der (wun′dėr), *n.* **1,** the feeling of surprise and admiration produced by anything new, strange, unexpected, or surprising; astonishment; as, the actor's amazing performance left me with a feeling of great *wonder;* **2,** a cause of surprise; marvel; miracle; as, the snowcapped mountains are only one of the many *wonders* of Banff National Park; **3,** something that is surprising or unusual; as, it was small *wonder* that I was able to find their secret hideout:—*v.i.* to feel surprise or amazement; be astonished; as, he *wondered* at the display of fireworks in the sky; **2,** to feel doubt or curiosity; speculate:—*v.t.* to be doubtful about; have a desire to know; as, I *wonder* what I ought to do.—*n.* **won′der-land′; won′der-ment.**

won-der-ful (wun′dėr-fool), *adj.* **1,** astonishing; strange; marvellous; **2,** very good; excellent; fine.—*adv.* **won′der-ful-ly.**

won-drous (wun′drus), *adj.* marvellous; remarkable.—*adv.* **won′drous-ly.**

woo (wōō), *v.t.* **1,** to court or seek favour or love of; **2,** to coax; entreat; **3,** to seek; try to gain; as, to *woo* success:—*v.i.* to go courting.—*n.* **woo′er.**

wood (wood), *n.* **1,** a large number of trees growing on an extensive tract of land; a grove or forest; **2,** the hard part of a tree under the bark; **3,** trees cut for firewood or trimmed ready for use in building; lumber; timber:—**woods,** used as *sing.* or *pl.,* a thick growth of trees; a forest.—*adj.* **wood′ed; wood′en; wood′y.** —*n.* **wood′shed′.**

wood-chuck (wood′chuk′), *n.* a coarse-furred, brownish rodent, about 30 to 40 centimetres long, with short legs and a short, hairy tail: burrows in the ground and hibernates in winter, found in Canada and the U.S.: also called *groundhog.*

wood-craft (wood′kråft′) *n.* **1,** knowledge of the woods and woodland life, together with skill in scouting, camping, etc.; **2,** skill in working with wood.

wood-cut (wood′kut′), *n.* an engraving cut on wood; a print from such an engraving: also called *wood engraving.*

wood-ed (wood′ed), *adj.* having trees; covered with many trees; as, acres of *wooded* land.

wood-en (wood′en), *adj.* **1,** made of wood; **2,** like wood; stiff and lifeless; as, he gave his speech with a *wooden* delivery.

wood-land (wood′land′; wood′land), *n.* land covered with trees; a forest:—*adj.* peculiar to, or dwelling in, the woods.

wood-peck-er (wood′pek′ėr), *n.* a bird with feet and tail feathers adapted for climbing and a long, strong, pointed bill for piercing the bark of trees for insects to eat.

woodwinds (wood′windz′), *n.* in an orchestra, the wind instruments (originally made of wood) collectively, including oboe, bassoon, clarinet, English horn, flute, and piccolo: the sound is produced by the passing of air across the mouthpiece or through the vibration of reeds in the mouthpiece.

wood-work (wood′wûrk′), *n.* objects, or parts of objects, made of wood, esp. the wooden finishings of a house, as staircases, doors, etc.—*n.* **wood′work′er.**

wood·work·ing (wood′wûrk′ing), *n.* the art or skill of making objects out of wood, esp. furniture.

wool (wool), *n.* **1,** the soft, curly coat of the sheep and some related animals, which is used to make clothing, rugs, blankets, etc.; **2,** anything like wool; **3,** yarn or cloth made of wool.—*adj.* **wool′len; wool′ly**

wool·gath·er·ing (wool′gath′ėr-ing), *n.* daydreaming; the state of being absent-minded.

word (wûrd), *n.* **1,** a sound or combination of sounds used in any language as a symbol of an idea, and forming a grammatical part of speech; **2,** the printed or written letters or other characters that represent the spoken word; **3,** a brief speech; saying; remark; as, a *word* of praise; **4,** information; message; report; as, she received *word* of their arrival; **5,** a password; **6,** a command; **7,** a promise; as, to keep one's *word*:—**words,** language used in anger; as, they had *words* yesterday:—*v.t.* to express in words; as, to *word* a message.

word·ing (wûrd′ing), *n.* the way of expressing something in words; as, the strong *wording* of this letter shows the anger of the person who wrote it.

word processing, in *computing,* the activity of producing written documents by means of a computer: word processing allows the writer to add to, edit, delete, reprint, etc., a document without retyping it.

word·y (wûrd′i), *adj.* using too many words or more words than necessary for the thought expressed; as, a *wordy* essay.

wore (wōr), *p.t.* of *wear.*

work (wûrk), *v.i.* [worked (wûrkt), working], **1,** to put forth physical or mental effort; labour; toil; **2,** to be occupied in business; be employed; as, she *works* in the steel mill; **3,** to act, operate, or run, esp. to act effectively; as, the laser printer *works* well; **4,** to progress slowly or laboriously; as, the nail *worked* loose; the rain *worked* through the roof; **5,** to cause to act in the proper way; as, the video showed us how to *work* the new computer:—*v.t.* **1,** to operate, manage, or set in motion; as, to *work* a mine; *work* a scheme; **2,** to prepare for use; manipulate; as, to *work* the soil; **3,** to bring or move gradually or laboriously; as, he *worked* the stone into place; **4,** to perform, produce, or cause; as, she *worked* marvellous cures; the storm works great ruin; **5,** to make or fashion; also, to embroider; as, the metal was beautifully *worked*; she *worked* the linen with fine stitches; **6,** to exact labour from; cause to labour, as horses; **7,** to solve; as, to *work*, or *work* out, a problem; **8,** to canvass in the interest of one's political party; as, the candidate *worked* the town; **9,** to network; as, she *worked* the room and handed out her business card:—*n.* **1,** physical or mental effort directed to some end or purpose; toil; labour; **2,** occupation; employment; job; **3,** a task; undertaking; **4,** a product of mental or physical effort; as, the *works* of Shakespeare; a *work* of art; **5,** manner or style of working; as, painstaking *work*:—**works 1,** the moving parts of any machinery; as, the *works* of a printer; **2,** structures connected with engineering projects such as bridges, docks, dams, embankments, etc.; **3,** often used as *sing.*, a manufacturing plant, etc., with its contents, outbuildings, etc.; as, a steel *works*; water *works*.—*n.* **work′book′; work′er; work′house′; work′ out′; work′shop′.**—*adj.* **work′a-day′** (prosaic; commonplace).

work·a·ble (wûrk′a-bl), *adj.* able to work; working well; as, a *workable* plan.

work·day (wûrk′dā′), *n.* a day for working, as distinguished from weekends, holidays, etc.; also, the length of such a day.

work·er (wûrk′ėr), *n.* **1,** a person who works; **2,** someone who works in a particular area; as, a social *worker*; a factory *worker*; a health services *worker*; **3,** a female bee, ant, or other insect that does most of the work in the hive or colony but is unable to produce young.

work·group (wûrk′ groo͞p), *n.* in *computing,* **1,** a group of people who use a computer network to share information and to work together on a single project; **2,** a group of computers treated as a small unit of a larger network.

work·man·ship (wûrk′man-ship′), *n.* **1,** the skill and methods of a worker; **2,** the finish or peculiar quality of anything made; as, a vase of exquisite *workmanship*.

work·out (wûrk′out), *n.* a period of using the body in an active way, as a form of exercise for health or physical training.

work·shop (wûrk′shop′), *n.* **1,** a room or building where work is being done by hand or with machines; **2,** a meeting of people to work on or study a specific subject; as, there will be a *workshop* on voting reform next week.

work·sta·tion (wûrk′stā′shun), *n.* in *computing,* **1,** a powerful microcomputer often used for scientific and engineering calculations; **2,** any personal computer (PC); **3,** any input device attached to a network, usually with a monitor screen, but without the ability to process independently.

world (wûrld), *n.* **1,** the planet on which human beings and all other living things live; the earth; **2,** any one of the planets or stars imagined as similar to the earth; as, are there other *worlds* than ours? **3,** some special branch of civilization; as, the Roman *world*; **4,** any separate system, state, or sphere of existence, viewed as a whole; as the literary *world*; the *world* of dreams; the plant *world*; **5,** all people; everyone; as, the whole *world* watched as the astronauts landed on the moon; **6,** a certain area or part of the earth; as, the developing *world*; **7,** a large amount; a great deal; as, non-governmental organizations have done a *world* of good for many people in need:—**World War I**, the war between 1914 and 1918 in which the Allies (Canada, United States, Great Britain, France, Italy, Russia, etc.) defeated Germany, Austria-Hungary, and others:—**World War II**, the war between 1939 and 1945 in which the Allies (Canada, United States, Great Britain, France, Poland, Soviet Union, etc.) defeated Germany, Japan, and Italy.—*n.* **world′li-ness.**—*adj.* **world′ -wide′.**

world-ly (wûrld′li), *adj.* [world-li-er, world-li-est], **1,** of or having to do with the world of human existence, rather than with gods or religion; **2,** knowing or caring about the affairs of the world; as, Emily was a *worldly* person who had travelled around much of the globe; **3,** experienced; sophisticated.

world-wide (wûrld-wīd), *adj.* and *adv.* all over the world; as, many companies now have *worldwide* operations.

World Wide Web, in *computing,* a loosely organized international network of computer sites that publish information, often incorporating multimedia and hypertext links for accessing and retrieving information: anyone can access the information through the Internet: abbreviated as *Web* or *WWW.*

worm (wûrm), *n.* **1,** any of various small creeping or burrowing animals with a long, thin body, which may be segmented into rings, and no limbs or backbone; as, an earth*worm*; **2,** in *computing,* a corruptive program that replicates and grows until it takes over the entire space on a hard drive or network:—**worms,** parasites that live in the intestines or other internal organs:—*v.t.* **1,** to get something by a special trick or effort; as, to *worm* her secret from her; he *wormed* himself into favour; **2,** to move by crawling or wriggling, as a worm does; as, she *wormed* her way along the bottom of the ditch.—*adj.* **worm′y.**—*n.* **worm′hole′.**

worn (wōrn), *p.p.* of *wear*:—*adj.* **1,** damaged or made thin by long, hard use; **2,** looking tired or week; as, her face was thin and *worn.*

worn–out (wōrn–out), *adj.* **1,** having had such long and hard wear that something is no longer useful; as, his shoes were *worn-out*; **2,** very tired or weak; exhausted.

wor-ry (wûr′i), *v.t.* [worried, worry-ing], **1,** to shake, tear, or mangle with the teeth; as, the cat *worried* the mouse; **2,** to trouble; tease; harass; as, she *worried* her father:—*v.i.* to be anxious; fret; to have a thought or feeling that something bad may happen; as, he *worried* about the safety of the children:—*n.* [*pl.* worries], **1,** the act or fact of worrying; a feeling of anxiety or being uncomfortable; as, the *worry* of looking after a sick child; **2,** something that causes this feeling; as, Nadia's big *worry* was that she would fail the exam.—*n.* **wor′ri-er.**—*adj.* **wor′ri-some.**

worse (wûrs), *adj.* [*comp.* of *bad* or *ill*], **1,** more extreme in degree; as, he's a *worse* liar than his brother; **2,** less well in health; sicker; as, the sick woman is *worse*:—*adv.* [*comp.* of *badly* or *ill*], **1,** in a more evil or extreme manner; less well; as, Antonio plays the piano *worse* than Peter; **2,** less; as, she is even *worse* suited to teaching than to office work:—*n.* a thing or state even more undesirable than another; as, the patient took a turn for the *worse.*

wors-en (wûrs′en), *v.t.* and *v.i.* to make or become worse.

wor-ship (wûr′ship), *n.* **1,** love and respect for a god, or an action showing this; **2,** religious services; **3,** excessive admiration; devotion; adoration; as, hero *worship*:—*v.t.* [worshipped, worship-ping], **1,** to admire excessively; idolize; **2,** to love and respect a god or gods of one's religion:—*v.i.* **1,** to show love and respect to a god, as by taking part in a religious service; **2,** feel excessive admiration.—*n.* **wor′ship-per.**

worst (wûrst), *adj.* [*superl.* of *bad* or *ill*], bad, evil, or ill in the highest degree; as, he had the *worst* grade in the class:—*adv.* [*superl.* of *badly* or *ill*], in the most bad or evil way; most extreme in degree; least well:—*n.* that which is most bad or evil; as, the *worst* has happened:—*v.t.* to defeat; as, our team *worsted* theirs.

worth (wûrth), *n.* **1,** excellence or desirable qualities; merit; as, a person of great *worth*; a gift of much *worth*; **2,** value as expressed in money; as, the *worth* of the chair is $30; **3,** personal wealth; as, their total *worth* is in the millions:—*adj.* **1,** deserving of; good enough; as, this movie is *worth* seeing; **2,** of the actual value of; as, *worth* the price; **3,** priced at; as, *worth* $10; **4,** possessed of.

worth-less (wûrth′lis), *adj.* having no worth; without value; useless; as, my cheap watch broke within a day; it was *worthless.*

worth-while (wûrth-hwīl′), *adj.* having value or importance; worth spending time or money on; as, it's not *worthwhile* to get this computer fixed; it would cost less to buy a new one.

wor-thy (wûr′*th*i), *adj.* [wor-thi-er, wor-thi-est], **1,** having value or excellence; as, a *worthy* person; **2,** deserving; having merit; as, a *worthy* cause.—*n.* **wor′thi-ness.**

would (wood), past tense of [2]*will,* used to express: **1,** intention; as, he said he *would* go; **2,** determination; as, you *would* play, although you were told not to; **3,** expectation; as, she said you *would* return soon; **4,** custom or habit; as, he *would* come to see us every day; **5,** used in polite requests or questions; as, *would* you like to see a movie with me?

[1]**wound** (wo͞ond), *n.* **1,** a hurt or injury caused by violence; a cut; stab; as, he had a *wound* in his foot; **2,** an injury to one's feelings or good name:—*v.i.* to hurt by violence; cut; slash; also, to hurt the feelings of.

[2]**wound** (wound), *p.t.* and *p.p.* of *wind.*

wove (wōv), *p.t.* and *p.p.* of *weave.*

wo-ven (wōv′en), *p.p.* of *weave.*

wraith (rāth), *n.* **1,** a ghost; a shadowy presence; **2,** the ghost of a person, supposed to be seen just before or just after death; a spectre.

wran-gle (rang′gl), *v.i.* [wran-gled, wran-gling], to dispute noisily:—*n.* a noisy, angry dispute:—*v.t.* to herd or round up livestock:—*n.* **wran′gler, 1,** one who argues or bickers; **2,** a cowboy.

wrap (rap), *v.t.* [wrapped, wrap-ping], **1,** to roll or fold around something; as, *wrap* the blanket around the child; **2,** to envelop; conceal by enveloping with something; as, the girl *wrapped* her doll in a towel; **3,** to do up securely; as, *wrap* the fish in paper:—*n.* an outer garment worn for warmth, such as a coat:—**wrapped up in,** completely or only interested in; as, Kira is so *wrapped up in* ballet, she does nothing else.

wrap-per (rap′ẽr), *n.* a covering, usually made of paper: used to wrap something; as, a candy *wrapper.*

wrap-ping (rap′ing), *n.* covering, as for a package, parcel, bundle, etc.

wrath (råth; räth), *n.* **1,** deep indignation; violent anger; fury; **2,** punishment; vengeance.—*adj.* **wrath′ful.**

wreak (rēk), *v.t.* **1,** to express; inflict; as, he *wreaked* his fury on the old machine by beating it with a club; **2,** to damage; as, the hurricane could *wreak* havoc on the community.

wreath (rēth), *n.* [*pl.* wreaths (rē*th*z)], a group of branches, leaves, or flowers woven together to form a ring; as, a Christmas *wreath.*

wreathe (rē*th*), *v.t.* [wreathed, wreath-ing], to encircle; adorn with something like a wreath; as, clouds *wreathed* the mountain.

wreck (rek), *n.* **1,** destruction by crash, collision, fire, storm, etc., esp. the destruction of a car or vessel afloat; shipwreck; **2,** the remains of anything that has been ruined or disabled in this way, as a ship, automobile, house, etc.; as, the *wreck* of the boat was left on the shore:—*v.t.* **1,** to ruin or disable by violence; as, the accident *wrecked* his health; **2,** to involve in destruction or ruin; **3,** to dismantle; as, to *wreck* a building.—*n.* **wreck′er.**

wreck-age (rek′ij), *n.* the remains of a destroyed car, ship, train, building, etc.

wren (ren), *n.* a very small, brown, song bird with a short, perky, erect tail.

wrench (rench), *n.* **1,** a violent turn; a sideways pull or twist; **2,** a sprain, as at a joint; **3,** a pang; a sudden distressed feeling; **4,** a tool for grasping and turning nuts, bolts, etc.:—*v.t.* **1,** to twist; wring or pull sideways with effort; as, to *wrench* the top off a box; **2,** to give a sudden sharp twist to; sprain; as, she *wrenched* her ankle.

wrest (rest), *v.t.* to turn or wrench, esp. from a normal state; pull or take away by force or violence; as, he *wrested* the football from my arms.

wres-tle (res′l), *v.i.* [wres-tled, wres-tling], **1,** to struggle with an opponent in an effort to force him or her to the ground; **2,** to struggle; strive earnestly, esp. with something difficult; as, to *wrestle* with arithmetic; **3,** to take part in the sport or contest of wrestling.—*n.* **wres′tler.**

wres-tling (res′ling), *n.* in *sports,* a competition in which two opponents try to force each other to the ground or hold each other in certain positions, in a test of strength.

wretch (rech), *n.* **1,** an unfortunate or miserable person; **2,** a mean, contemptible person.

wretch-ed (rech′id), *adj.* **1,** miserable; unhappy; unfortunate; suffering; **2,** causing unhappiness or suffering; as, this *wretched* headache is making me feel sick; **3,** of very poor quality; as, a *wretched* hovel; **4,** *Colloq.* used to express annoyance; as, this *wretched* printer is out of paper.—*n.* **wretch′ed-ness.**

wrig-gle (rig′l), *v.i.* [wrig-gled, wrig-gling], **1,** to move by twisting and turning; squirm; as, the students *wriggled* in their seats; **2,** to proceed by trickery or underhand means; as, to *wriggle* out of a lie:—*n.* the act of twisting or squirming; a squirming motion.—*n.* **wrig′gler.**

wring (ring), *v.t.* [wrung (rung), wring-ing], **1,** to twist and squeeze; as, to *wring* wet clothes; **2,** to force out by twisting or pressure; as, to *wring* water from clothes; **3,** to extort; to get by force or threat; as, to *wring* a confession; the workers tried to *wring* better conditions from their employer.—*n.* **wring′er.**

[1]**wrin-kle** (ring′kl), *n.* a slight ridge or crease on a smooth surface caused by folding, puckering, or rumpling:—*v.t.* [wrin-kled, wrin-kling], to form small ridges or creases in; pucker; as, the rain *wrinkled* his suit:—*v.i.* to become creased; as, my dress *wrinkles* easily.—*adj.* **wrin′kly.**

[2]**wrin-kle** (ring′kl), *n.* **1,** a clever trick, idea, or device; as, the latest *wrinkle;* **2,** *Colloq.* difficulty, challenge; snag; as, a *wrinkle* in our plans.

wrist (rist), *n.* the joint between the hand and forearm.—*n.* **wrist′band′.**

wrist-watch (rist′wach′), *n.* a type of watch that is held onto the wrist by a band made of metal, leather, plastic, or cloth.

writ (rit), *n.* **1,** a written document issued in the name of a ruler or a court that gives an order to a person or group of people to act or not to act in a certain manner in a specified situation; **2,** the document a government publishes to order an election.

write (rīt), *v.t.* [*p.t.* wrote (rōt), *p.p.* writ-ten (rit′n), *p.pr.* writ-ing], **1,** to put letters and words on a surface with an instrument, as a pen, pencil, etc., or on a computer, etc.; **2,** to express in words or characters on paper with a pen or pencil or on a computer, etc.; as, to *write* one's name; **3,** to produce as an author; compose; as, she *wrote* a book of adventure; **4,** to leave traces on; as, trouble is *written* on his face; **5,** to compose and send a letter to; as, I *wrote* my sister today:—*v.i.* **1,** to form letters, as with a pen; **2,** to compose; write books, etc.; **3,** to communicate by letter.

write–pro-tect (rīt′–prō-tekt′), *v.t.* in *computing,* to set a disk or tape so that a computer will not write, erase, or change data on it:—**write protect**, a feature of a computer program that stops overwriting a file or specified data in the file.

writ-er (rīt′ėr), *n.* **1,** one who writes; as, the *writer* of this e-mail is known to me; **2,** a person whose occupation in life is writing; as, Farley Mowat is a versatile *writer* who publishes books on many different subjects.

write–up (rīt′–up′), *n.* a written account; a review.

writhe (rī*th*), *v.i.* [writhed, writh-ing], **1,** to squirm or twist, as from acute pain or distress; **2,** to experience mental stress or embarrassment; as, to *writhe* at an insult.

writ-ing (rīt′ing), *n.* **1,** the act of forming letters with a pen, pencil, on a computer, etc.; **2,** something in the form of words on paper or on a computer, etc.; something written; as, your *writing* is impossible to read; **3,** the art of literary production as in writing a poem, play, novel, etc; the art of a writer; as, I am taking a creative *writing* course; **4,** writings, things written; literary work; as, his *writings* include romantic and mystery novels.

wrong (rông), *adj.* **1,** not morally right or just; not according to what is right or proper; as, it is *wrong* to cheat; **2,** not according to fact; incorrect; as, he gave me the *wrong* directions; **3,** amiss; out of order; as, the clock is *wrong*; **4,** contrary to law; illegal; as the judge ruled that it was *wrong* of her to speed; **5,** not suited to the purpose; as, David wore the *wrong* clothes and felt embarrassed:—*n.* that which is contrary to moral right, fact, principles, intention, purpose, etc.; evil; injury; crime: opposite of *right;* as, you are in the *wrong:*—*adv.* **1,** in a manner not right morally; as, to go *wrong;* **2,** incorrectly; as, to guess *wrong:*—*v.t.* to treat unjustly; harm.—*adv.* **wrong′ly.**—*n.* **wrong′do′er; wrong′do′ing.**

wrong-ful (rông′fool), *adj.* evil; injurious; unjust.—*adv.* **wrong′ful-ly.**

wrote (rōt), *p.t.* of *write.*

wroth (rôth), *adj.* wrathful; indignant.

wrung (rung), *p.t.* and *p.p.* of *wring.*

wry (rī), *adj.* [wri-er, wri-est], **1,** of a smile, remark, etc., showing dislike or lack of feeling; forced or twisted; **2,** humorous and slightly sarcastic; she often made *wry* comments that we found very amusing.—*adv.* **wry′ly.**

WWW (dub′l-ū-dub′l-ū-dub′l-ū), *abbrev.* short for *World Wide Web.*

Wy-an-dot or **Wy-an-dotte** (wī′en-dot), *n.* [*pl.* Wyandot or Wyandots; Wyandotte or Wy- andottes]. Same as **Petun.**

X, x (eks), *n.* [*pl.* X's, x's], **1,** the 24th letter of the English alphabet, following W; **2,** the Roman numeral for 10.

Xan-a-du (zan′a-dōō), *n.* a beautiful, perfect place: the word comes from the poem "Kubla Khan" by Samuel Taylor Coleridge.

xe-ni-a (zē′ni-a), *n.* in *cross-pollination,* the influence of foreign pollen upon the seed or fruit which is pollinated.

xe-no- (zēn′ō-), *prefix* meaning **1,** *stranger* or *foreigner;* as in *xeno*phobia (fear of strangers) and *xeno*philia (an attraction to that which is foreign, as foreign cultures, peoples, etc.); **2,** *strange* or *foreign;* as in *xeno*biotic (foreign to living organisms; used with reference to chemical compounds).

xe-non (zē′non), *n.* a heavy, colourless, gaseous element present in very small traces in the air (about 1 part in 170 million by volume), which has various technical uses.

xe-ro- (zēr′ō-), *prefix* meaning *dry,* as in *xero*phyte (a plant adapted to dry conditions).

xe-ro-gra-phy (zē-rô′grå-fiā), *n.* a dry copying process in which a black or coloured powder sticks to parts of a surface remaining electrically charged after the surface has been exposed to light from an image of the document being copied.

Xe-rox (zē′rôks), *n. trademark* a copy made by *xerography;* as, she made several *Xeroxes:*—*v.t.*

to copy; as they *Xeroxed* many pages. The correct and legal term is *photocopy*.

X-mas (eks′mas or kris′mas) *n. Colloq. abbrev.* the Christian celebration of Christmas: Xmas is an old word, going back to the 1500s: the letter "X" is an ancient symbol for Christ, and in Greek the word *Christ* begins with this letter.

X–ray or **x–ray** (eks′–rā′), **1,** a powerful form of energy made up of waves of very short length, which are capable of penetrating many substances, as the human body, which ordinary light rays cannot penetrate; **2,** a photographic film made with X–rays, used by doctors, etc., to study bones, fractures, the inside of the body, etc., and to aid in the diagnoses of medical problems.

xy-lem (zī′lem), *n. botany* the woody tissue, esp. of timber trees: it conveys water and minerals, gives mechanical support, and stores food in dormant periods.

xy-lo-phone (zī′lo-fōn′; zil′o-fōn′), *n.* a musical instrument of great antiquity, made of parallel wooden bars of graduated length, which are struck with two small, flexible, wooden mallets.—*n.* **xy-loph′o-nist.**

XYLOPHONE

Y

Y, y (wī), *n.* [*pl.* Y's, y's], the 25th letter of the alphabet, following X.

yacht (yot), *n.* a large, expensive boat used for pleasure cruising or for racing:—*v.i.* to sail in a yacht.—*n.* **yacht′ing.**

yak (yak), *n.* a wild or domesticated ox of the high mountains of central Asia, with a hump and with long hair hanging from its shoulders, sides, and tail: raised for meat and milk and used to pull heavy loads:—*v.i. Colloq.* to talk a lot in a trivial manner; chatter; as, the girls *yakked* all night at the sleepover.

yam (yam), *n.* **1,** a tropical trailing vine with a thick root that can be eaten; also, the root; **2,** a kind of sweet potato.

yam-mer (yam′ėr), *v.t.* and *n. Colloq.* **1,** to whimper; whine; complain; **2,** to make a loud outcry; wail.

yang (yang), *n.* **1,** in Taoism, the positive force in the cosmos: opposite of the *yin*; **2,** in Chinese dualistic philosophy, the active male principle of the universe: compare *yin*.

yank (yangk), *v.t.* to jerk or pull quickly; as, to *yank* a coat from a hook:—*n.* a hard, sudden pull.

Yan-kee or **Yank** (yang′kē; yank), *n.* a nickname for: **1,** a person from one of the six New England states of the northeastern U.S.; **2,** a person who fought on the side of the Union in the U.S. Civil War; **3,** any person from the U.S.

yap (yap), *v.i.* and *n.* **1,** to bark or yelp; **2,** *Slang* to jabber; chatter.

¹yard (yärd), *n.* **1,** nonmetric unit of linear measure, equal to about 90 centimetres: in Canada, now replaced by metric measures; **2,** a long, slender beam slung crosswise to a mast, used to support the top edge of sails.

²yard (yärd), *n.* **1,** a small piece of enclosed ground beside or around a building; as, a front *yard*; **2,** a space, often enclosed, where a specific kind of work is carried on; as, a railway *yard*.

yard sale (yärd′ sāl′), *n.* Same as **garage sale**.

yard-stick (yärd′stik′), *n.* **1,** a measuring stick one yard in length; **2,** any way of measuring or comparing something; as, scores on a standard test are one *yardstick* for judging math skills.

yar-mul-ke or **yar-mel-ke** (yär′mel-ka; yäm-el-ka), *n.* a skullcap worn by Jewish men and boys, esp. for prayer and ceremonial occasions.

yarn (yärn), *n.* **1,** a spun thread, esp. thread used for weaving, or heavy woollen thread used for knitting; **2,** an adventure story, esp. one that is told for entertainment.

yaw (yô), *v.i.* of a ship or an airplane, to fail to hold a steady course; also, of a pilot, to steer off the straight line of a course:—*n.* a temporary change from a straight course, as of a ship or an airplane.

yawn (yôn), *n.* an unintentional opening of the jaws, as from sleepiness:—*v.i.* **1,** to open the mouth wide, as from hunger, surprise, etc.; **2,** esp., to open the mouth unintentionally as wide as possible while inhaling deeply, as the result of sleepiness or boredom; **3,** to open wide; as, the mouth of a cave *yawned* before us:—*v.t.* to utter with a yawn.—*n.* **yawn′er.**

ye (yē), *pron.* an old word for "you" used in such writings as the Bible and Shakespeare.

yea (yā), *n.* a vote in favour of something; as, the *yeas* have won: opposite of *nay*:—*adv.* an old way of saying "yes."

year (yēr), *n.* **1,** the length of time it takes the earth to make one complete revolution around the sun, or 365 days, 5 hours, 48 minutes, and 46 seconds; **2,** a period of 12 months, consisting of 365 days (in the case of a leap year, 366 days), from January 1 to December 31; **3,** a period of time, usually less than a year, devoted to some particular activity; as, a school *year*; **4,** any period of 12 months.—*n.* **year′book′.**

year-ling (yēr′ling; yûr′ling), *n.* an animal between one and two years old, often used for racehorses, farm animals, or deer:—*adj.* one year old; of a year's duration.

year-ly (yēr′li; yûr′li), *adj.* **1,** occurring once a year or every year; as, a *yearly* visit; **2,** by the year; as, a *yearly* rent; **3,** for a year; as, a *yearly* lease:—*adv.* annually; as, to get a bonus *yearly*.

yearn (yûrn), *v.i.* to be filled with longing, compassion, or tenderness; as, to *yearn* for rest; to *yearn* over a child.

yeast (yēst), *n.* a growth of minute cells, causing fermentation in sugar solutions and starchy substances, used in making beer and in causing bread dough to rise: made of tiny cells of a certain fungus plant.—*adj.* **yeast′y.**

yell (yel), *n.* **1,** a sharp, loud cry, as of pain, rage, or terror; a shriek; **2,** a characteristic shout, as used in warfare or by a group of persons; as, a university *yell*:—*v.t.* to cry out loudly; as, to *yell* defiance:—*v.i.* to cry out, as with pain.

yel-low (yel′ō), *n.* **1,** the colour of butter, ripe lemons, etc.; **2,** something having this colour; **3,** the yolk of an egg:—*adj.* **1** having the colour yellow; **2,** of the colour between green and orange in the spectrum:—*v.i.* and *v.t.* to make or become yellow in colour; as, the papers *yellowed* over the years.

yellow fever, a tropical disease carried by the bite of certain female mosquitoes, which causes fever, chills, and sometimes death.

yel-low-ish (yel′ō-ish), *adj.* coloured somewhat like yellow; having a yellow tinge.

yellow jacket, any of several wasps with black and yellow markings, often called *hornet*: wasps live in colonies in paperlike nests in the ground.

Yel-low-knife (yel′ō-nīf), *n.* **1,** an Aboriginal people originally living in the southeast of the Northwest Territories; **2,** the Athapaskan language of these people; **3,** capital city of the Northwest Territories.

yelp (yelp), *v.i.* to utter a sharp bark, as a dog when hurt:—*n.* a sharp, quick bark.

[1]**yen** (yen), *n.* the unit of money used in Japan.

[2]**yen** (yen), *n. Colloq.* a longing; intense desire or urge.

yes (yes), *adv.* **1,** it is so: the affirmative answer to a question; opposite of *no*; **2,** furthermore; more than this; as, he is strong, *yes*, very strong:—*n.* **1,** the saying of the word *yes*; **2,** a confirmation or affirmation; as, I got a *yes* when I asked for her support; **3,** a vote in favour of a proposal or motion; as, the *yeses* outnumbered the noes.

yes-ter-day (yes′tėr-dā; yes′tėr-di′), *n.* **1,** the day before today; **2,** a recent day; as, it seems only *yesterday* that we came:—*adv.* on the day before today.

yet (yet), *adv.* **1,** up until now; as, she has not come *yet*; **2,** now as previously; still; as, I have your present *yet*; **3,** even; still; besides; as, more important *yet*; **4,** sooner or later; as, the day will *yet* come; **5,** even though this is so; as, *yet* I cannot understand it:—*conj.* **1,** nevertheless; however; **2,** although; though; as, he knew the bad news, *yet* he still couldn't believe it.

Yid-dish (yid′ish), *n.* a language that developed from German, spoken by Jews in Central and Eastern Europe, and by Jewish immigrants in other places.

yield (yēld), *v.t.* **1,** to bring forth; produce; as, that orchard *yields* thousands of apples each fall; **2,** to concede; as, I *yield* the point; **3,** to surrender; **4,** to afford; permit; as, to *yield* space; **5,** to give as return for labour, money invested, etc.:—*v.i.* **1,** to assent; comply; **2,** to give way; submit; **3,** to give a return; produce:—*n.* the return for labour put out or for capital invested.

yin (yin), *n.* **1,** in Taoism, the negative force in the cosmos: the counterpart to the *yang*; **2,** the passive female principle in cosmic Chinese dualistic philosophy: compare *yang*.

yo-del (yō′dl), *v.t.* and *v.i.* [yodelled, yodelling], to sing or call with sudden changes in the voice from chest tones to falsetto:—*n.* a call or song so sung.—*n.* **yo′del-ler.**

yo-ga or **Yo-ga** (yō′ga) *n.* **1,** in *Hinduism*, intense contemplation and ascetic discipline practised to establish identity of consciousness with the object of concentration, the universal spirit; **2,** a system of slow, rhythmic body movements, breathing exercises, and relaxation techniques: originally practised in the Hindu religion and now used in a nonreligious manner for physical, mental, and emotional health.

yo-gurt or **yo-ghurt** or **yo-ghourt** (yō′goort), *n.* a food prepared from milk that has been thickened by the addition and action of certain bacteria.

yoke (yōk), *n.* **1,** a wooden crosspiece that is fastened over the necks of two oxen or other animals so that they can move together to pull a plow, wagon, or other device; as, a *yoke* of oxen; **2,** a frame of wood fitted to a person's shoulders, for carrying buckets hung from each end; **3,** the upper part of a garment made to fit the neck and shoulders; **4,** that which binds; a bond or tie; **5,** bondage; as, the *yoke* of slavery:—*v.t.* [yoked, yok-ing], **1,**

to put a yoke on; as, to *yoke* oxen; **2,** to couple or link.

yo-kel (yō′kl), *n. Colloq.* a rustic; country bumpkin.

yolk (yōk), *n.* the yellow part of an egg, surrounded by the white.

Yom Kip-pur (yom kip′oor), a Jewish holiday that falls in September or October: it is a day of not eating and of praying for forgiveness for wrongdoings or sins: also called the *Day of Atonement*.

yon-der (yon′dėr), *adj.* mainly in older writings; **1,** situated at a distance, but in sight; over there; as, *yonder* hills; **2,** more distant; as, the *yonder* side of the valley:—*adv.* at that place; there; as, situated *yonder*.

yore (yōr), *n.* time long since past; as, days of *yore*.

you (ū), *pron.* the second person of the personal pronoun (*sing.* or *pl.*, but always taking a plural verb) [*nominative* you, *possessive* your, yours, *objective* you], **1,** the person or persons spoken to; as, how are *you*? **2,** one; anyone; a person; people; as, *you* must have your passport to enter most foreign countries.

young (yung), *adj.* **1,** being in the early part of life or growth; as, a father with his *young* son; **2,** vigorous; fresh; strong; as, old in body, but *young* in heart:—*n.* **1,** those who are young; as, *young* and old came to hear her; **2,** the offspring of animals; as, a wolf with its *young*.

young-ster (yung′stėr), *n.* a person in early years; a child or young person.

your (yoor), *adj.* a possessive form of the personal pronoun *you*: **1,** belonging to you; as, *your* coat; **2,** coming from, or relating to, you; as, *your* kindness; **3,** *Colloq.* any one; a, an, or the; as, my grandmother is not *your* average grandparent; she is travelling across Africa on foot!

yours (yoorz), a possessive form of the personal pronoun *you*: it is used alone; **1,** as an *adj.*, in the predicate: belonging or relating to you; as, whose is this glass? it is *yours*; **2,** as a *pron.*, a person or thing that belongs to you; as, which car shall we use? let's take *yours*.

your-self (yoor-self′), *pron.* [*pl.* yourselves (-selvz′)], **1,** a reflexive form of *you*; as, you fooled *yourself*; **2,** an emphatic form of *you*; as, you *yourself* must go; **3,** the one that you are; your own self; as, I knew I couldn't fix this; you should have done it *yourself*.

youth (ūth), *n.* [*pl.* youths (ūthz; ūths), or, collectively, youth], **1,** the state or quality of being young; **2,** the time of life between childhood and maturity; **3,** a young person; **4,** young people; as, the *youth* of a nation.

youth-ful (ūth′fool), *adj.* **1,** not old; as, a *youthful* person; **2,** pertaining or fitting to youth; as, *youthful* pleasures.

yowl (youl), *n.* and *v.i.* a howl; a long yell, esp. a mournful one.

yo–yo (yō′–yō′), *n.* a toy that is made of two disks connected at the centre by a piece that has a string wrapped around it: the toy goes up and down the string as the string winds and unwinds around the centre piece when dropped from a height, as from a child's hand.

yuc-ca (yuk′a), *n.* a plant of the lily family, having long, pointed leaves and white flowers; also, the flowers.

Yule (ūl), *n.* another term for the Christian celebration of Christmas or the Christmas feast:—**yule log,** a huge log brought indoors for an open fire on Christmas Eve.

Yule-tide (ūl′tīd′), *n.* Christmas time.

Z

Z, z (zed; zē), *n.* [*pl.* Z's, z's], the 26th letter of the alphabet, following Y.

Zam-bon-i (zam-bōn′i), *n. trademark* for a machine like a tractor that scrapes rough ice and sprays water to make a new, hard, smooth surface: used in hockey and skating arenas.

ZAMBONI

za-ny (zā′ni), *adj.* ridiculous in a comic or crazy manner; wild; comically foolish.

zeal (zēl), *n.* great interest or enthusiasm, esp. for a cause or goal; great earnestness; tireless work to achieve a goal.

zeal-ot (zel′ut), *n.* an enthusiast; a person of too great zeal; a fanatic.

zeal-ous (zel′us), *adj.* eager; enthusiastic.—*adv.* **zeal′ous-ly.**

ze-bra (zē′bra), *n.* an African wild animal belonging to the horse family, esp. one with dark stripes on a white or tawny body.

ze-nith (zē′nith; zen′ith), *n.* **1,** that part of the sky directly above the place where one stands: opposite of *nadir*; **2,** the most important point; the peak; as, at the *zenith* of power.

zeph-yr (zef′ėr), **1,** a mild, gentle breeze; **2,** the west wind.

zep-pe-lin or **Zep-pe-lin** (zep′i-lin), *n.* in *history,* a large, rigid, cigar-shaped airship or blimp, supported by gases inside: developed for military purposes in the early 20th century.

ze-ro (zē′rō), *n.* [*pl.* zeros or zeroes], **1,** the number that leaves any other number the same when added to it; 0; **2,** a point on a scale of measurement; as, on a Celsius scale, water freezes at *zero;* **3,** nothing; none at all; as, the score was three to *zero;* **4,** the lowest point; as, her courage sank to *zero:—adj.* of or at zero; as, during the snowstorm, there was *zero* visibility.

zest (zest), *n.* **1,** great vigour, energy, and enthusiasm; keen enjoyment; as, Zia always had a *zest* for life; **2,** an exciting or interesting quality; as, the yellow paint gave the room new *zest;* **3,** the outside coloured layer of a citrus fruit, which is often grated to add flavour to food.—*adj.* **zest′ful.**

Zeus (zūs), *n.* in *Greek mythology,* the son of Cronus, who overthrew his father and became the supreme god: identified with Roman *Jupiter.*

zig-zag (zig′zag′), *n.* **1,** one of a number of short, sharp angles or turns; **2,** something characterized by sharp turns, as a path:—*adj.* having short, sharp turns; as, a *zigzag* line:—*adv.* crookedly; with sharp turns; as, the path climbs *zigzag:—v.t.* and *v.i.* [zigzagged, zigzag-ging], to move or be in, or form, quick, sharp turns; as, to *zigzag* one's way; a path *zigzags* up the hill.

zinc (zingk), *n.* a greyish-white metal that is a chemical element.

zing (zing), *n.* a shrill, high-pitched humming sound.

zin-ni-a (zin′i-a), *n.* a plant bearing bright-coloured, showy flowers; also, a flower of this plant.

zip (zip), *n.* **1,** a sharp hissing sound as of a bullet in flight, or like the tearing of canvas, etc.; **2,** energy, vigour; as, there was a lot of *zip* in the way they played the game; **3,** *Colloq.* zest or high flavour; as, this salsa has a lot of *zip;* **4,** *Colloq.* nothing, zero; as, when they got home, there was *zip* in the fridge:—*v.i.* **1,** *Colloq.* to move with energy; vigour; as, I'll just *zip* over to the store quickly; **2,** to move with speed; as, the train *zipped* along through the countryside:—*v.t.* **1,** to fasten with a zipper.

Zip disk (zip′ disk), *n. trademark* in *computing,* a disk that can hold a great deal of data.

Zip drive (zip′ drīv), *n. trademark* in *computing,* a removable disk drive, which is often used in graphic arts to transfer data files too large for diskettes.

ZIP file (zip′ fīl), *n. trademark* in *computing,* a data file compressed by a specific program or software: several files can be stored in a single file with the extension *.zip*: used to save space and to keep a group of related files together.

zip-per (zip′ėr), *n.* a fastener made up of two rows of metal or plastic teeth that can be joined or separated by sliding a catch up or down: used on clothing, suitcases, etc.—*adj.* **zip-ped.**

zir-con (zûr′kon), *n.* a silicate of zirconium occurring in square prisms, etc., of brown, yellow, and red: when transparent used as gems.

zir-co-ni-um (zėr-kō′ni-um), *n.* a grey or black metallic element found in zircon, etc., used in alloys and as a heat and acid resistant.

zith-er (zith′ėr), *n.* a musical instrument with about 30 or 40 strings over a shallow sounding box, which is played by plucking the strings.

zo-di-ac (zō′di-ak), *n.* **1,** an imaginary belt in the sky along which the sun appears to travel: divided into 12 equal parts, called *signs:*—**signs of the zodiac,** the 12 divisions of the zodiac, each of which is named after a different group of stars, as Taurus, Libra, etc.—*adj.* **zo-di′a-cal.**

zom-bie or **zom-bi** (zom′bi), *n.* [*pl.* -bies or -bis], **1,** *Colloq.* a dull, lifeless, or extremely tired person; as, she acted like a *zombie* after staying up all night to finish her essay; **2,** a supernatural force that can reanimate a dead body, or a body that has been brought back to life in this manner; **3,** a drink of rum or brandy and fruit juices mixed.

zone (zōn), *n.* **1,** any area that has some special quality, condition, or use; as, a war *zone;* a volcanic *zone;* **2,** any of the five regions of the earth's surface divided accordingly to climate; as, near the North and South Poles are the two Frigid *Zones;* the area on either side of the equator with hot temperatures is the Torrid *Zone;* between these are the two Temperate *Zones* that have a more even climate; **3,** a certain part of a city or town, classified by what kind of buildings are permitted there; as, an industrial *zone:—v.t.* [zoned, zon-ing], **1,** to divide into areas or zones; as, the council *zoned* the city into five sections; **2,** to include within an area or zone:—*v.i.* [zoned, zon-ing], to be divided into zones.—*n.* **zon′ing** (the process of controlling land by dividing into zones).

zo-o- (zō′ō-), *prefix* meaning *animal;* as in *zoo*chemistry (chemistry of animal bodies), *zoo*geography (geographical distribution of animals), *zoo*phyte (an animal, as a sponge, coral, sea anemone, etc., with some of the characteristics of plants), and *zoo*spore (the spore of certain fungi and algae able to move by cilia).

zoo (zōō), *n.* a special park or other large enclosure in which living animals are kept for public exhibition, research, maintenance of threatened species, etc.

zo-o-log-i-cal (zō′ō-loj′i-kal), *adj.* relating to zoology, the science of animal life:—**zoological garden,** a park in which animals are kept for exhibition; a zoo.

zo-ol-o-gy (zō-ol′o-ji), *n.* [*pl.* zoologies], the branch of biology dealing with animals and animal life.—*n.* **zo-ol′o-gist.**

zoom (zo͞om), *v.i.* **1,** to move with a humming or buzzing sound; **2,** in *aviation,* to climb for a short time at a very steep angle; **3,** to move or go suddenly and quickly; as, we *zoomed* down the rough path on our mountain bikes; **4,** in *photography,* to move the lens closer to the object or person being photographed, thereby enlarging the image without distorting the focus:—*v.t.* to cause (an airplane) to zoom:—*adj.* relating to, of, or for zooming; as, a *zoom* camera lens.

zuc-chi-ni (zo͞o-kē′nē), *n.* a type of green-skinned squash that looks like a cucumber and that is eaten as a vegetable.

zy-go (zī′gō-), *prefix* meaning *yoke* or *pair;* as in *zygo*morphic (with identical or symmetrical halves), *zygo*phyte (a plant that reproduces by union of two similar cells, as with some algae and fungi), and *zygo*spore (a spore formed by the union of two similar sexual spores, called gametes).

zy-gote (zī′gōt), *n.* the cell that two gametes form when they join together, esp. a fertilized ovum before division.